DSM-IV	Diagnostic and Statistical Manual of Mental Disorders	HIV	Human immunodeficiency virus
DT	Delirium tremens	h/o	History of
DTR	Deep tendon reflex	H₂O₂	Hydrogen peroxide
D5W	Dextrose 5% in water	HPI	History of present illness
Dx	Diagnosis	HR	Heart rate
EBV	Epstein-Barr virus	HSV	Herpes simplex virus
ECF	Extended care facility; extracellular fluid	HT; HTN	Hypertension
		hx; Hx	History
ECG	Electrocardiogram, electrocardiograph	I & O	Intake and output
		IBW	Ideal body weight
ECHO	Echocardiography	ICP	Intracranial pressure
ECT	Electroconvulsive therapy	ICU	Intensive care unit
ED	Emergency department; effective dose	IDDM	Insulin-dependent diabetes mellitus
EDD	Estimated date of delivery	Ig	Immunoglobulin
EEG	Electroencephalogram, electroencephalograph	IM	Intramuscular
		IPPB	Intermittent positive-pressure breathing
EENT	Eye, ear, nose, and throat	IRV	Inspiratory reserve volume
ELISA	Enzyme-linked immuno-sorbent assay	IUD	Intrauterine device
		IV	Intravenous
EMG	Electromyogram	IVP	Intravenous pyelogram; intravenous push
EMS	Emergency medical service	K	Potassium
EMT	Emergency medical technician	KCl	Potassium chloride
		KUB	Kidney, ureter, and bladder
ENT	Ear, nose, and throat	KVO	Keep vein open
ER	Emergency room (hospital); external resistance	L	Left; liter; length; lumbar; lethal; pound
ERV	Expiratory reserve volume	lab	Laboratory
ESR	Erythrocyte sedimentation rate	L & D	Labor and delivery
		LDL	Low-density lipoprotein
ESRD	End-stage renal disease	LE	Lower extremity; lupus erythematosus
FBS	Fasting blood sugar		
Fe	Iron	LLE	Left lower extremity
FEV	Forced expiratory volume	LLL	Left lower lobe
FH, Fhx	Family history	LLQ	Left lower quadrant
FHR	Fetal heart rate	LMP	Last menstrual period
FTT	Failure to thrive	LOC	Level/loss of consciousness
FUO	Fever of unknown origin		
fx	Fracture	LP	Lumbar puncture
GB	Gallbladder	LR	Lactated Ringer's
GC	Gonococcus or gonorrheal	LUE	Left upper extremity
GI	Gastrointestinal	LUL	Left upper lobe
Grav I, II, etc.	Pregnancy one, two, three, etc. (Gravida)	LUQ	Left upper quadrant
		LV	Left ventricle
GSW	Gunshot wound	LVH	Left ventricular hypertrophy
gtt	Drops (guttae)		
GU	Genitourinary	MABP	Mean arterial blood pressure
Gyn	Gynecology		
H & P	History and physical	MCH	Mean corpuscular hemoglobin
HAV	Hepatitis A virus		
Hb	Hemoglobin	MCHC	Mean corpuscular hemo-globin concentration
HBV	Hepatitis B virus		
HCG	Human chorionic gonadotropin	MCV	Mean corpuscular volume
		MD	Muscular dystrophy
HCT	Hematocrit	MDI	Medium dose inhalant; metered dose inhaler
HDL	High-density lipoprotein		
HEENT	Head, eye, ear, nose, and throat	mEq	Milliequivalent
		MI	Myocardial infarction
Hg	Mercury	mm Hg	Millimeters of mercury

MOSBY'S POCKET

DICTIONARY

of Medicine, Nursing & Health Professions

7TH EDITION

MOSBY'S POCKET DICTIONARY

of Medicine, Nursing & Health Professions

7TH EDITION

Editor

Marie T. O'Toole, EdD, RN, FAAN
Associate Dean for Academic Affairs and Stratford
  Campus School of Nursing
University of Medicine and Dentistry of New Jersey

MOSBY
ELSEVIER

3251 Riverport Lane
St. Louis, MO 63043

MOSBY'S POCKET DICTIONARY OF MEDICINE,
NURSING & HEALTH PROFESSIONS   ISBN: 978-0-3230-8855-8

Copyright © 2014 by Mosby, an imprint of Elsevier Inc.
Copyright © 2010, 2006, 2002, 1998, 1994, 1990 by Mosby, Inc., an affiliate of Elsevier Inc.

Notices

Knowledge and best practice in this field are constantly changing. As new research
and experience broaden our understanding, changes in research methods, professional
practices, or medical treatment may become necessary.

Practitioners and researchers must always rely on their own experience and knowledge in evaluating and using any information, methods, compounds, or experiments
described herein. In using such information or methods they should be mindful of their
own safety and the safety of others, including parties for whom they have a professional
responsibility.

With respect to any drug or pharmaceutical products identified, readers are advised
to check the most current information provided (i) on procedures featured or (ii) by
the manufacturer of each product to be administered, to verify the recommended dose
or formula, the method and duration of administration, and contraindications. It is the
responsibility of practitioners, relying on their own experience and knowledge of their
patients, to make diagnoses, to determine dosages and the best treatment for each individual patient, and to take all appropriate safety precautions.

To the fullest extent of the law, neither the Publisher nor the authors, contributors,
or editors, assume any liability for any injury and/or damage to persons or property as a
matter of products liability, negligence or otherwise, or from any use or operation of any
methods, products, instructions, or ideas contained in the material herein.

Library of Congress Cataloging-in-Publication Data
Mosby's pocket dictionary of medicine, nursing & health professions. -- 7th ed.
    p. ; cm.
    Pocket dictionary of medicine, nursing & health professions
    Mosby's pocket dictionary of medicine, nursing and health professions
    ISBN 978-0-323-08855-8 (pbk. : alk. paper)
    I. Title: Pocket dictionary of medicine, nursing & health professions. II. Title: Mosby's
pocket dictionary of medicine, nursing and health professions.
    [DNLM: 1. Medicine--Dictionary--English. 2. Allied Health Occupations--Dictionary--
English. 3. Nursing--Dictionary--English. W 13]
    610.3--dc23   2012038325

Content Strategist: Nancy O'Brien
Associate Content Development Specialist: Jennifer Shropshire
Publishing Services Manager: Deborah L. Vogel
Project Manager: John W. Gabbert
Design Direction: Maggie Reid

CONTENTS

CONTENTS

ix

FOREWORD

The complexity and continuing evolution of health science vocabularies require that students and professionals alike have an affordable, compact, and thorough quick reference to the language of their fields. *Mosby's Pocket Dictionary of Medicine, Nursing & Health Professions* provides students and practitioners of the health sciences with a succinct and portable abridgement of *Mosby's Dictionary of Medicine, Nursing & Health Professions*, which has been used by hundreds of thousands of nurses, health professionals, and physicians in their education and practice. *Mosby's Pocket Dictionary of Medicine, Nursing & Health Professions* was the first pocket dictionary to address the broad spectrum of health science terminology in the medical, nursing, and health professions.

To reflect new developments in many facets of health care, all new and former entries were reviewed by experts from disciplines spanning the spectrum of health science today. This extensive review process resulted in a revision that accurately reflects current knowledge and practice.

To assist our readers in recognizing alternate spellings, selected British spellings have been added where appropriate. A popular appendix provides Spanish translations for key medical vocabulary to better enable health care providers working in a bilingual environment. Another appendix displays the basic signs for the alphabet and numbers one through ten from American Sign Language. Also, we have provided a list of abbreviations commonly used in health care on the inside of the front and back covers.

The extensive vocabulary of the larger dictionary has been retained by restructuring and condensing its many encyclopedic entries while retaining the essential content of the definitions. The pocket dictionary shares a tradition of excellence with the parent dictionary, *Mosby's Dictionary of Medicine, Nursing and Health Professions*, by providing a portable, usable reference for the clinical area. The user will continue to find many of the valuable features from our larger dictionary, including clear pronunciations and etymologies for thousands of terms.

Development of this seventh edition of *Mosby's Pocket Dictionary* has taken the effort of many people. I appreciatively acknowledge the work of all who have participated. The valuable contributions by all who were involved in the parent work and in particular the authors whose works were consulted are also gratefully acknowledged. I have been involved with several dictionaries published by Elsevier. The care that is taken with the vocabulary of health care is admirable. In particular, the team that worked on this dictionary, led by Nancy O'Brien, is exemplary. John Gabbert and Jennifer Shropshire are enthusiastic colleagues with excellent attention to detail. I am grateful for their expertise and commitment to excellence. My colleagues and students at the University of Medicine and Dentistry of New Jersey provide a rich and collaborative environment in which to explore vocabularies. The faculty and colleagues at Nazareth College in Rochester, New York, are also resources that can be consistently depended upon for consultation and advice. Over the years, students and colleagues who use the language of health care to better understand or improve practice have been generous with suggestions. Those suggestions are incorporated.

The extremely positive response to the first six editions leads me to believe that *Mosby's Pocket Dictionary of Medicine, Nursing & Health Professions* will remain an eminently useful and usable resource. I welcome your comments and suggestions for improving future editions.

—Marie O'Toole, Editor

GUIDE TO THE DICTIONARY

A. Alphabetic order

The entries are alphabetized in dictionary style; that is, letter by letter, disregarding spaces or hyphens between words:

anion
anion-exchange resin
anion gap
aniridia

The alphabetization is alphanumeric: words and numbers form a single list with numbers positioned as though they were spelled-out numerals: **Fourier transform imaging / 4 n / Four-poster orthosis.** (An example of the few exceptions to this rule is the sequence **17-hydroxycorticosteroid / 11-hydroxy-etiocholanolone / 5-hydroxyindoleacetic acid**, which can be found between the entries **hydroxychloroquine sulfate** and **hydroxyl**, not, as may be expected, 17-… in letter "S," 11-… in letter "E," and 5-… in letter "F.")

Small subscript and superscript numbers are disregarded in alphabetizing: **No / NO / N₂O / NOC.**

Compound headwords are given in their natural word order: **abdominal surgery**, not surgery, abdominal; **achondroplastic dwarf**, not dwarf, achondroplastic.

(NOTE: In this guide, the term "headword" is used to refer to any alphabetized and nonindented definiendum, be it a single-word term or a compound term.)

In some cases, there may be one or more terms that are synonymous with a headword or derived from a headword. If the synonym or derivation would immediately precede or follow the definition, it is not included as a separate entry. Therefore, if a term is not listed at the expected place, the reader might find it among the boldface terms of the immediately preceding or immediately following entry.

B. Etymology

ETYMOLOGY is shown for principal entries and in other instances where it contributes immediately to a better understanding of the meaning.

C. Pronunciation

All sounds, both English and non-English, are represented by letters or combinations of letters of the alphabet with few adaptations, and with the schwa (/ə/), the neutral vowel. Pronunciations are shown between slants. The following pronunciation key shows the symbols used:

Vowels

SYMBOLS	KEY WORDS
/a/	hat
/ä/	father
/ā/	fate
/è/	flesh
/ē/	she
/er/	air, ferry
/i/	sit
/ī/	eye
/ir/	ear
/o/	proper
/ō/	nose
/ô/	saw
/oi/	boy
/ōō/	move
/ŏŏ/	book
/ou/	out
/u/	cup, love
/ur/	fur, first
/ə/	the neutral vowel, always unstressed, as in ago, focus
/ər/	teacher, doctor
/œ/	as in (French) feu /fœ/; (German) schön /shœn/
/Y/	as in (French) tu /tY/; (German) grün /grYn/
/N/	This symbol does not represent a sound but indicates that the preceding vowel is a nasal, as in French bon /bôN/, or international /aNternäsyōnäl/.

Consonants

SYMBOLS	KEY WORDS
/b/	book
/ch/	chew
/d/	day
/f/	fast
/g/	good
/h/	happy
/j/	gem
/k/	keep
/l/	late
/m/	make
/n/	no
/ng/	sing, drink
/ng·g/	finger
/p/	pair
/r/	ring
/s/	set
/sh/	shoe, lotion
/t/	tone
/th/	thin
/th/	than
/v/	very
/w/	work

/y/	yes
/z/	zeal
/zh/	azure, vision
/kh/	as in (Scottish) loch /loch/; (German) Rorschach /rôr′shokh/
/nyə/	Occurring at the end of French words, this symbol is not truly a separate syllable but an /n/ with a slight /y/ (similar to the sound in "onion") plus a near-silent /ə/, as in Bois de Boulogne (bōō/lō′ nyə/)

ACCENTS: Pronunciation is shown with primary and secondary accents. A raised dot shows that two vowels (or occasionally, two consonants) are pronounced separately.

Many of the numerous *Latin* terms in this dictionary are not given with pronunciation, mainly because there are different ways (all of them understood) in which Latin is pronounced by the English speaker and may be pronounced by speakers elsewhere. However, guidance is given in many cases, often to reflect common usage.

LATIN AND GREEK PLURALS: The spelling of Latin and Greek plurals is shown in most instances. However, when the plural formation is regular according to Latin and Greek rules, the pronunciation is usually not included.

NOTE: Notwithstanding the listing of Latin and Greek plurals in this dictionary, and the rules of Latin and Greek pluralization, in most instances it is acceptable or even preferable to pluralize Latin and Greek words according to the rules of English words. (For certain kinds of entries, both the English and the foreign plurals are given in this dictionary, usually showing the English form first, as, for example, in nearly all-oma nouns: **hematoma,** *pl.* **hematomas, hematomata.**)

Å, symbol for **angstrom,** a unit for distance. $1 Å = 10^{-10}$ m.

a, symbol for **arterial blood,** as in Pao$_2$.

A68, symbol for a protein found in the brain tissue of Alzheimer's disease patients. It is also found in the developing normal brains of fetuses and infants but begins to disappear by the age of 2 years.

AA, 1. abbreviation for **achievement age. 2.** abbreviation for **Alcoholics Anonymous. 3.** abbreviation for **amplitude of accommodation. 4.** abbreviation for **anesthesiologist assistant. 5.** abbreviation for **amino acid. 6.** abbreviation for *anterior apical.* **7.** abbreviation for *aortic arch.* **8.** abbreviation for *arm-ankle (pulse rate).*

AAA, 1. abbreviation for *American Association of Anatomists.* **2.** abbreviation for *acquired aplastic anemia.* **3.** abbreviation for **abdominal aortic aneurysm.**

āa, aa, AA, (in prescriptions) abbreviation for *ana,* indicating an equal amount of each ingredient to be compounded.

AAAI, abbreviation for **American Academy of Allergy and Immunology.**

AACE, 1. abbreviation for *American Association of Clinical Endocrinologists.* **2.** abbreviation for *Association for the Advancement of Computing in Education.*

AACN, 1. abbreviation for **American Association of Colleges of Nursing. 2.** abbreviation for **American Association of Critical-Care Nurses.**

AAFP, abbreviation for *American Academy of Family Physicians.*

AAI, abbreviation for *ankle-arm index.*

AAIN, abbreviation for **American Association of Industrial Nurses.**

AAL, abbreviation for **anterior axillary line.**

AAMC, abbreviation for **American Association of Medical Colleges.**

AAMI, abbreviation for **Association for the Advancement of Medical Instrumentation.**

AAN, abbreviation for **American Academy of Nursing.**

AANA, abbreviation for **American Association of Nurse Anesthetists.**

AANN, 1. abbreviation for **American Association of Neuroscience Nurses. 2.** abbreviation for **American Association of Neurological Nurses.**

AAO–HNS, abbreviation for *American Academy of Otolaryngology–Head and Neck Surgery.*

AAOMS, abbreviation for *American Association of Oral and Maxillofacial Surgeons.*

AAPA, abbreviation for **American Academy of Physician Assistants.**

Aaron's sign [Charles D. Aaron, American physician, 1866–1951], a diagnostic sign in appendicitis indicated by pain or distress when pressure is applied over McBurney's point in the epigastric region.

AARP, abbreviation for **American Association of Retired Persons,** a voluntary U.S. organization of older persons, who may or may not be retired, with the goal of improving the welfare of persons over 50 years of age. The AARP advocates for older individuals on legislative, consumer, education, and legal issues.

Aarskog's syndrome /ärs′kog/ [Dagfinn Charles Aarskog, Norwegian pediatrician, b. 1928], an X-linked syndrome characterized by wide-set eyes, anteverted nostrils, broad upper lip, peculiar scrotal "shawl" above the penis, and small hands.

AART, abbreviation for **American Association for Respiratory Therapy.**

Aase's syndrome /äz/ [Jon Morton Aase, American pediatrician, b. 1936], a familial syndrome characterized by mild growth retardation, hypoplastic anemia, variable leukocytopenia, triphalangeal thumbs, narrow shoulders, and late closure of fontanels, and occasionally by cleft lip, cleft palate, retinopathy, and webbed neck. A recessive mode of inheritance has been suggested.

AAUP, abbreviation for **American Association of University Professors.**

AAV, abbreviation for **adenoassociated virus.**

Ab, abbreviation for **antibody.**

abacavir, an antiviral that is a nucleoside reverse transcriptase inhibitor.

abacterial /ab′aktēer′ē-əl/, any atmosphere or condition free of bacteria; literally, without bacteria.

abaissement /ä′bäsmäN′/ [Fr, a lowering], **1.** a falling or depressing. **2.** (in ophthalmology) the displacement of a lens.

abalienation /əbāl′yənā′shən/, a state of physical deterioration or mental decay. —**abalienate**, *v.,* **abalienated**, *adj.*

Ab amyloid, an abnormal peptide varying from 40 to 43 amino acids in length and found in aggregates in the cerebrovascular walls and the cores of the plaques in Alzheimer's disease. It is derived from a large transmembrane glycoprotein, amyloid precursor protein, and is postulated to be neurotoxic.

A band, in muscle tissue, the area between two I bands of a sarcomere, marked by partial overlapping of actin and myosin filaments and appearing dark.

abandonment of care /əban′dənment/, **1.** (in law) wrongful cessation of the provision of care to a patient, usually by a physician or a nurse. **2.** unilateral termination of care without the patient's consent or knowledge, or without adequate notice, while the patient is still in need.

abapical /abap′əkəl/, opposite the apex.

abarelix, a gonadotropin-releasing hormone antagonist used in the palliative treatment of prostate cancer.

abarognosis /aber′agnō′sis/ [Gk, *a,* not, *baros,* weight, *gnosis,* knowledge], an inability to judge or compare the weight of objects, particularly those held in the hand.

abarticular /ab′ärtik′yŏŏlər/. [L, *ab,* away from, *articulus,* joint], **1.** pertaining to a condition that does not affect a joint. **2.** pertaining to a site or structure remote from a joint.

abarticular gout, gout that affects structures other than joints, such as ligaments.

abarticulation /ab′ärtik′yəlā′shən/, **1.** dislocation of a joint. **2.** a synovial joint.

abasia /əbā′zhə/ [Gk, *a* +*basis,* not step], the inability to walk, caused by lack of motor coordination.—**abasic, abatic,** *adj.*

abatacept, an antirheumatic agent used to treat acute or chronic rheumatoid arthritis that has not responded to other disease-modifying agents.

abate /əbāt′/ [ME, *abaten,* to beat down], to decrease or reduce in severity or degree.

abatement /əbāt′mənt/, a decrease in severity of symptoms.—**abate,** *v.*

abatic, pertaining to an inability to walk.

abaxial /abak′sē-əl/ [L, *ab* +*axis,* from axle], **1.** pertaining to a position outside the axis of a body or structure. **2.** pertaining to a position at the opposite extremity of a structure.

Abbe-Estlander flap /ab′ē est′landər/ [Robert Abbe, American surgeon, 1851–1928; Jakob A. Estlander, Finnish surgeon, 1831–1881], a surgical procedure that transfers a full-thickness section of one oral lip to the other lip.

Abbe-Zeiss apparatus /äbā′ tsīs′/ [Ernst K. Abbe, German physicist, 1840–1905; Carl Zeiss, German optician, 1816–1885], an apparatus for calculating the number of blood cells in a measured amount of blood.

Abbokinase, a trademark for a plasminogen activator (urokinase).

Abbott pump, a trademark for a small portable pump that can be adjusted and finely calibrated to deliver precise amounts of medication in solution through an IV infusion set.

ABC, 1. abbreviation for *airway breathing circulation.* **2.** abbreviation for **aspiration biopsy cytology.**

abciximab /absik′simab/, a platelet aggregation inhibitor prescribed as an adjunct to percutaneous transluminal coronary angioplasty or atherectomy.

Abdellah, Faye Glenn [b. 1919], a nursing theorist who introduced a typology of 21 nursing problems in 1960 in *Patient-Centered Approaches to Nursing.* The concepts of nursing, nursing problems, and the problem-solving process are central to Abdellah's work. The typology provided a scientific body of knowledge unique to nursing, making it possible to move away from the medical model of educating nurses. The nursing diagnosis classification system may be considered an outgrowth of Abdellah's typology.

abdomen /ab′dəmən, abdō′mən/ [L, *abdominis,* belly], the portion of the body between the thorax and the pelvis. The abdominal cavity is lined by the peritoneum; contains the inferior portion of the esophagus, the stomach, the intestines, the liver, the spleen, the pancreas, and other organs; and is bounded by the diaphragm and the pelvis.—**abdominal** /abdom′inəl/, *adj.*

abdominal adhesion /abdom′inəl/, the binding together of tissue surfaces of abdominal organs, usually involving the intestines and causing obstruction. The condition may be a response to surgery or result from trauma or chronic inflammation. The patient experiences abdominal distention, pain, nausea, vomiting, and increased pulse rate. Surgery may be required.

abdominal aorta, the portion of the descending aorta that passes from the aortic hiatus of the diaphragm into the abdomen, descending ventral to the vertebral column and ending at the fourth lumbar vertebra, where it divides into the two common iliac arteries. It supplies blood to abdominal structures such as the testes, ovaries, kidneys, and stomach. Its branches are the celiac, superior mesenteric, inferior mesenteric, middle suprarenal, renal, testicular, ovarian, inferior phrenic, lumbar, middle sacral, and common iliac arteries.

abdominal aortic aneurysm (AAA), abnormal dilatation of the abdominal aorta, usually in an area of severe atherosclerosis.

abdominal aortography, a radiographic study of the abdominal aorta after the introduction of a radiopaque contrast medium through a catheter inserted in the aorta through the femoral artery.

abdominal aponeurosis, the conjoined sheetlike tendons of the oblique and transverse skeletal muscles of the abdomen.

abdominal arteries, the arteries that branch from the anterior surface of the abdominal aorta to supply the abdominal part of the GI tract, as well as the liver, pancreas, and gallbladder. The celiac artery supplies the foregut, the superior mesenteric artery supplies the midgut, and the inferior mesenteric artery supplies the hindgut.

abdominal bandage, a broad multilayered absorbent gauze or other material commonly used after abdominal surgery.

abdominal binder, a bandage or elasticized wrap that is applied around the lower part of the torso to support the abdominal musculature.

abdominal breathing, a pattern of inhalation and exhalation in which most of the ventilatory work is done with the abdominal muscles. The contractile force of the abdomen is used to elevate the diaphragm.

abdominal cavity, the space within the abdominal walls between the diaphragm and the pelvic area, containing the liver, stomach, intestines, spleen, gallbladder, kidneys, and associated tissues and blood and lymphatic vessels, surrounded by the abdominal fascia.

abdominal decompression, an obstetric technique to reduce pressure on the abdomen during the first stage of labor. The abdomen is enclosed in a chamber that permits surrounding pressure to be controlled. The technique is no longer used.

abdominal examination, the physical assessment of a patient's abdomen by visual inspection and the use of auscultation, percussion, and palpation. Visual inspection of the normally oval shape of the abdominal surface while the patient is supine may reveal abnormal surface features indicating effects of disease, surgery, or injury. Subsurface tumors, fluid accumulation, or hypertrophy of the liver or spleen may be observed as an abnormal surface feature. Auscultation may reveal

vascular sounds that provide information about arterial disorders such as aortic aneurysms and bowel sounds that indicate intestinal function. In pregnancy, auscultation can detect fetal heartbeat and blood circulation in the placenta. Percussion helps to detect the condition of internal organs. Palpation is used to detect areas of tenderness or rigidity, muscle tone and skin condition, and shapes and sizes of subsurface organs or masses.

abdominal fascia, an inclusive term for the fascia that forms part of the general layer lining the walls of the abdominal cavity and investing the abdominal organs.

abdominal fistula, an abnormal passage or tract leading from an abdominal organ to the external surface of the abdomen.

abdominal gestation, the implantation of a fertilized ovum outside the uterus but within the peritoneal cavity.

abdominalgia /abdom′onal′jə/ [L, *abdomen,* belly; Gk, *algos,* pain], a pain in the abdomen.

abdominal girth, the circumference of the abdomen, usually measured at the umbilicus.

abdominal hernia, a hernia in which a loop of bowel protrudes through the abdominal musculature, often through the site of an old surgical scar that has stretched and thinned.

abdominal hysterectomy, the removal of the uterus through an incision in the abdominal wall.

abdominal inguinal ring, an opening of the inguinal canal on the abdominal wall through which the male spermatic cord or the female round ligament pass.

abdominal nephrectomy [L, *abdominis,* belly; Gk, *nephr,* kidney, *ektomē,* cutting out], the surgical removal of a kidney through an abdominal incision.

abdominal nerves, the network of nerve fibers passing through the posterior abdominal region anterolateral to the lumbar vertebral bodies, including the sympathetic trunks and associated splanchnic nerves, the abdominal prevertebral plexus and ganglia, and the lumbar plexus.

abdominal pain, acute or chronic, localized or diffuse pain in the abdominal cavity. Abdominal pain is a significant symptom because its cause may require immediate surgical or medical intervention. The most common causes of severe abdominal pain are inflammation, perforation of an intraabdominal structure, circulatory obstruction, intestinal or ureteral obstruction, intestinal cramping, and rupture of an organ located within the abdomen. Specific conditions include appendicitis, perforated peptic ulcer, strangulated hernia, superior mesenteric arterial thrombosis, diverticulitis, and small and large bowel obstruction. Gynecologic causes that may require surgery include PID, ruptured ovarian cyst, and ectopic pregnancy. Abdominal pain associated with pregnancy may be caused by the weight of the enlarged uterus; rotation, stretching, or compression of the round ligament; or squeezing or displacement of the bowel. In addition, uterine contractions associated with preterm labor may produce severe abdominal pain. Chronic abdominal pain may be functional or may result from overeating or aerophagy. When symptoms are recurrent, an organic cause is considered. Organic sources include peptic ulcer, hiatal hernia, gastritis, chronic cholecystitis and cholelithiasis, chronic pancreatitis, pancreatic carcinoma, chronic diverticulitis, intermittent low-grade intestinal obstruction, and functional indigestion. Some systemic conditions may cause abdominal pain.

abdominal paracentesis [L, *abdominis,* belly; Gk, *para,* near, *kentesis,* puncturing], the surgical puncture of the abdominal cavity for the removal of fluid for diagnosis or treatment.

abdominal pregnancy, an extrauterine pregnancy in which the conceptus develops in the abdominal cavity after being extruded from the fimbriated end of the fallopian tube or through a defect in the tube or uterus. The placenta may implant on the abdominal or visceral peritoneum. Abdominal pregnancy may be suspected when the abdomen has enlarged but the uterus has remained small for the length of gestation. Abdominal pregnancies constitute approximately 2% of ectopic pregnancies and approximately 0.01% of all pregnancies. The condition results in perinatal death of the fetus in most cases and maternal death in approximately 6%. Because of its rarity, the condition may be unsuspected, and diagnosis is often delayed. Surgical removal of the placenta, sac, and embryo or fetus is necessary if attached to the posterior part of the tube, ovary, broad ligament, and uterus.

abdominal pressure, a sensation or application of pressure surrounding structures within the abdomen.

abdominal prevertebral plexus, the network of nerve fibers surrounding the abdominal aorta. It extends from the aortic hiatus of the diaphragm to the bifurcation of the aorta into the right and left common iliac arteries. Along its route, it is subdivided into the celiac plexus, the abdominal aortic plexus, and the superior hypogastric plexus.

abdominal pulse, the pulse of the abdominal aorta.

abdominal quadrant, any of four topographic areas of the abdomen divided by two imaginary lines, one vertical and one horizontal, intersecting at the umbilicus. The divisions are the left upper quadrant (LUQ), the left lower quadrant (LLQ), the right upper quadrant (RUQ), and the right lower quadrant (RLQ).

abdominal reflex, a superficial neurologic reflex obtained by firmly stroking the skin of the abdomen. It normally results in a brisk contraction of abdominal muscles in which the umbilicus moves toward the site of the stimulus. This reflex is lost in diseases of the pyramidal tract and can also be lost with age or abdominal surgery.

abdominal regions, the nine topographic subdivisions of the abdomen, determined by four imaginary lines imposed over the anterior surface in a tic-tac-toe pattern. The upper horizontal line passes along the level of the cartilages of the ninth rib, the lower along the iliac crests. The two vertical lines extend on each side of the body from the cartilage of the eighth rib to the center of the inguinal ligament. The lines divide the abdomen into three upper, three middle, and three lower zones: right hypochondriac, epigastric, and left hypochondriac regions (upper zones); right lateral (lumbar), umbilical, and left lateral (lumbar) regions (middle zones); right inguinal (iliac), pubic (hypogastric), and left inguinal (iliac) regions (lower zones).

abdominal salpingectomy, a salpingectomy done through an incision in the abdomen.

abdominal splinting, a rigid contraction of the abdominal wall muscles usually occurring as an involuntary reaction to the pain of a visceral disease or disorder or postoperative discomfort. Abdominal splinting, in turn, may result in hypoventilation and respiratory complications.

abdominal sponge, a special type of gauze pad used as an absorbent and sterile covering for the viscera.

abdominal surgery, any operation that involves an incision into the abdomen. In preparation for surgery, laboratory, radiographic, and cardiac tests and consultations may be done. Immediately before surgery, body hair is clipped and skin is cleansed from the nipples to the pubis. Food and fluids by mouth are withheld for up to 6 hours or more before surgery. After surgery the nurse ensures that the airway is patent and vital signs are stable, checks tubes and catheters, connects drainage tubes to collection containers, checks the dressing for excessive bleeding or drainage, and records fluid intake and output. The patient is turned and is helped to breathe deeply every hour and, if secretions are present, to cough.

abdominal testis, an undescended testis located in the abdominal cavity.

abdominal ultrasound test, an ultrasound test that provides accurate visualization of the abdominal aorta, liver, gallbladder, pancreas, biliary ducts, kidneys, ureters, and bladder. This test is used to diagnose and locate cysts, tumors, calculi, and malformations; to document the progression of various diseases; and to guide the insertion of instruments during surgical procedures.

abdominal viscera, the internal organs enclosed within the abdominal cavity, including the stomach, liver, intestines, spleen, pancreas, and parts of the urinary and reproductive tracts.

abdominal wall, the lining of the abdomen, consisting partly of fascia but mostly of muscle.

abdominal wound, a break in the continuity of the abdominal wall. A wound that exposes or penetrates the viscera raises the danger of infection or peritonitis.

abdominocardiac reflex /-kär′dē·ək/, an immediate, involuntary response of the heart to stimulation of the abdominal viscera. The reflex is mediated through the vagus nerve.

abdominogenital /-jen′itəl/, pertaining to the abdomen and reproductive system.

abdominohysterotomy /-his′tərot′əmē/, an incision in the uterus utilizing an abdominal approach.

abdominopelvic cavity /-pel′vik/, the space between the diaphragm and the groin. There is no structurally distinct separation between the abdomen and pelvic regions.

abdominoperineal /-per′inē′əl/, pertaining to the abdomen and the perineum, including the pelvic area, female vulva and anus, and male anus and scrotum.

abdominoplasty, a surgical procedure for tightening the abdominal muscles.

abdominoscopy /abdom′inos′kəpē/ [L, *abdomen*; Gk, *skopein,* to view], a procedure for examining the contents of the peritoneum in which an electrically illuminated tubular device is passed through a trocar into the abdominal cavity.

abdominoscrotal /-skrō′təl/, pertaining to the abdomen and scrotum.

abdominothoracic arch /-thôras′ik/, the boundary between the thorax and the abdomen.

abdominovaginal /-vaj′inəl/, pertaining to the abdomen and vagina.

abdominovesical /-ves′ikəl/, pertaining to the abdomen and bladder.

abducens muscle, the extraocular lateral rectus muscle that moves the eyeball outward.

abducens nerve [L, *abducere,* to take away], either of the paired sixth cranial nerves. It controls the lateral rectus muscle, turning the eye outward. It arises in the pons near the fourth ventricle, leaves the brainstem between the medulla oblongata and pons, and passes through the cavernous sinus and the superior orbital fissure. .

abducent /abdoo′sənt/ [L, drawing away], pertaining to a movement away from the median line of the body.

abduction [L, *abducere,* to take away], movement of a limb away from the midline or axis of the body.—**abduct,** *v.*

abduction boots, a pair of orthopedic casts for the lower extremities, available in both short-leg and long-leg configurations, with a bar incorporated at ankle level to provide hip abduction.

abductor /abduk′tər/ [L, *abducere*], a muscle that draws a body part away from the midline or axis, or one part from another.

abductor digiti minimi of the foot, a muscle on the lateral side of the foot that abducts the little toe at the metatarsophalangeal joint. It is innervated by the lateral plantar branch of the tibial nerve.

abductor digiti minimi of the hand, a muscle that is the principal abductor of the little finger.

abductor hallucis, a muscle that forms the medial margin of the foot and contributes to a soft tissue bulge on the medial side of the sole. It abducts and flexes the great toe at the metatarsophalangeal joint and is innervated by the medial plantar branch of the tibial nerve.

abductor pollicis brevis, one of the three thenar muscles. It abducts the thumb, principally at the metacarpophalangeal joints.

abductor pollicis longus, a muscle that originates from the proximal posterior surfaces of the radius and ulna and from the related interosseous membrane and forms a tendon that passes into the thumb and inserts on the lateral side of the base of the first metacarpal. Its major function is to abduct the thumb at the joint between the first metacarpal and trapezium bones.

abembryonic /ab′embrē·on′ik/, opposite the position of the embryo.

Abernethy's sarcoma /ab′ərnē′thēz/ [John Abernethy, British surgeon, 1764–1831], a malignant neoplasm of fat cells, usually occurring on the trunk.

aberrant goiter, an enlargement of a supernumerary or ectopic thyroid gland.

aberrant ventricular conduction (AVC), the temporary abnormal intraventricular conduction of a supraventricular impulse. It is usually associated with an increase in the duration of the QRS complex to more than 120 ms.

aberration /ab′ərā′shən/ [L, *aberrare,* to wander], **1.** any departure from the usual course or normal condition. **2.** abnormal growth or development. **3.** (in psychology) an illogical and unreasonable thought or belief, often leading to an unsound mental state. **4.** (in genetics) any change in the number or structure of the chromosomes. **5.** (in optics) any imperfect image formation or blurring caused by unequal refraction or focalization of light rays through a lens. **6.** (in botany and zoology) pertaining to an abnormal individual, such as certain atypical members of a species.—**aberrant,** *adj.*

abetalipoproteinemia /əbā′təlip′ōprō′tinē′mē-ə/ [Gk, *a* + *beta,* not beta, *lipos,* fat, *proteios,* first rank, *haima,* blood], a group of rare inherited disorders of fat metabolism, characterized by absence of apoprotein B-100 and manifested by acanthocytosis, low or absent serum betalipoproteins, and hypocholesterolemia. In severe cases, steatorrhea, ataxia, nystagmus, motor incoordination, and retinitis pigmentosa occur.

abeyance /əbā′əns/ [Fr], a temporary state of inaction or temporary interruption of function.

ABG, abbreviation for **arterial blood gas.**

ABI, abbreviation for **ankle-brachial index.**

abient /ab′ē-ənt/ [L, *abire,* to go away], characterized by a tendency to move away from stimuli.—**abience,** *n.*

ability /əbil′itē/, the capacity to act in a specified way because of the possession of appropriate skills and mental or physical fitness.

abiogenesis /ab′ē-ōjen′əsis/ [Gk, *a* + *bios,* not life, *genein,* to produce], spontaneous generation; the idea that life can originate from inorganic, inanimate matter.—**abiogenetic,** *adj.*

abiosis /ab′ē-ō′sis/ [Gk, *a* + *bios* not life], a nonviable condition or a situation that is incompatible with life.—**abiotic,** *adj.*

abiotrophy /ab′ē-ot′rəfē/ [Gk, *a* + *bios* + *trophe* nutrition, growth], degeneration or loss of function that is not due to any apparent injury.—**abiotrophic** /ab′ē-ətrō′fik/, *adj.*

ablastemic /ab′lastem′ik/, nongerminal or not germinating.

ablation /ablā′shən/ [L, *ab* + *latus,* carried away], **1.** an amputation, an excision of any part of the body, or a removal of a growth or harmful substance. **2.** reduction by melting.—**ablate,** *v.*

ABLB test, abbreviation for **alternate binaural loudness balance test.**

ablepharia /ab′ləfer′ē·ə/, a defect or congenital absence of the eyelids (partial or total).

ablepsia /əblep′sē·ə/ [Gk, *a* + *blepein,* not to see], the condition of being blind.

ABLS, abbreviation for **advanced burn life support.**

ablution /ablōō′shən/ [L, *abluere,* wash away], **1.** the act of washing or bathing. **2.** the act of cleaning the body.

ABMS, abbreviation for *American Board of Medical Specialties.*

abnerval current /abnur′vəl/ [L, *ab,* from; Gk, *neuron,* nerve], an electrical current that passes from a nerve to and through muscle.

abneural /abnŏŏr′əl/, away from the CNS or the neural axis.

abnormal behavior /abnôr′məl/ [L, *ab* + *norma,* away from rule], behavior that deviates from what is commonly accepted by a group or society.

abnormality /ab′nôrmal′itē/ [L, *ab* + *norma,* away from rule], a condition that differs from the usual cultural or scientifically accepted standards.

abnormal psychology, the study of any behavior that deviates from culturally accepted norms.

abnormal tooth mobility, excessive movement of a tooth within its alveolus (socket) as a result of injury or disease in the supporting peridontium.

ABO blood group, a system for classifying human blood on the basis of the antigenic components of RBCs and their corresponding antibodies. The ABO blood group is identified by the presence or absence of two different antigens, A and B, on the surface of the RBC. The four blood types in this grouping, A, B, AB, and O, are determined by and named for these antigens.

aboiement /ä′bô·ämäN′/, an involuntary making of abnormal, animal-like sounds such as barking. Aboiement may be a clinical sign of Gilles de la Tourette's syndrome.

abort /əbôrt′/ [L, *ab,* away from, *oriri,* to be born], **1.** to deliver a nonviable fetus; to miscarry. **2.** to terminate a pregnancy before the fetus has developed enough to live outside the uterus. **3.** to terminate in the early stages or to discontinue before completion, as to arrest the usual course of a disease, to stop growth and development, or to halt a project.

aborted systole, a contraction of the heart that is usually weak and is not associated with a radial pulse.

abortifacient /əbôr′tifā′shənt/, **1.** causing abortion. **2.** any agent that causes abortion.

abortion /əbor'shən/ [L, *ab* + *oriri*], the spontaneous or induced termination of pregnancy before the fetus has developed to the stage of viability.

abortionist, a person who performs abortions.

abortion on demand, the absence of restrictive legal statures giving a woman the right to terminate a pregnancy at her request. That right may be limited by time of gestation, or it may pertain to any period of gestation.

abortive infection /əbôr'tiv/, an infection in which some or all viral components have been synthesized but no infective virus is produced. The situation may result from an infection with defective viruses or because the host cell is nonpermissive and prohibits replication of the particular virus.

abortus /əbôr'təs/, any incompletely developed fetus that results from an abortion, particularly one weighing less than 500 g.

abortus fever, a form of brucellosis caused by *Brucella abortus,* an organism so named because it causes abortion in cows.

abouchement /ä'bŏōshmäN'/ [Fr, a tube connection], the junction of a small blood vessel with a large blood vessel.

above-elbow (AE) amputation, an amputation of the upper limb between the elbow and the shoulder. A short amputation (near the shoulder) results in the loss of shoulder rotation. After a long amputation (just above the elbow), the patient should retain good shoulder function.

ABP, abbreviation for **arterial blood pressure.**

ABR, abbreviation for **auditory brainstem response.**

abrachia /əbrā'kē·ə/ [Gk, *a* + *brachion*, without arm], the absence of arms. —**abrachial,** *adj.*

abrasion /əbrā'zhən/ [L, *abradere*, to scrape off], a scraping, or rubbing away of a surface, such as skin or teeth, by friction. Abrasion may be the result of trauma such as a skinned knee; of therapy, as in dermabrasion of the skin for removal of scar tissue; or of normal function, such as the wearing down of a tooth by mastication.—**abrade,** *v.,* **abrasive,** *adj.*

abrasion arthroplasty, reshaping of a joint by using a small tool or burr to grind down the surface inducing bleeding and fibrocartilaginous repair tissue to form a new articular surface.

abrasion layer, a protective covering of gelatin enclosing an emulsion on x-ray film.

abrasive, a substance used for grinding or polishing a surface.

abreaction /ab'rē·ak'shən/ [L, *ab,* from, *re,* again, *agere,* to act], an emotional release resulting from mentally reliving or bringing into consciousness, through the process of catharsis, a long-repressed, painful experience.—**abreact,** *v.*

abrosia /əbrō'zhə/ [Gk, fasting], a condition caused by fasting.

abruption [L, *ab,* away from, *rumpere,* to rupture], a sudden breaking off or tearing apart.

abruptio placentae [L, *ab,* away from, *rumpere,* to rupture], separation of the placenta implanted in normal position in a pregnancy of 20 weeks or more or during labor before delivery of the fetus. It occurs in approximately 1 in 200 births, and because it often results in severe hemorrhage, it is a significant cause of maternal and fetal mortality. Cesarean section must be performed immediately and rapidly. If the pregnancy is near term, labor may be permitted or induced by amniotomy. A premature pregnancy may be allowed to continue under close observation of the mother at bed rest.

abscess /ab'ses/ [L, *abscedere,* to go away], **1.** a cavity containing pus and surrounded by inflamed tissue, formed as a result of suppuration in a localized infection, characteristically caused by staphylococci but also caused by parasites and foreign substances. Healing usually occurs when the abscess drains or is incised. **2.** an abscess that develops anywhere along the root length of a tooth.

abscissa /absis'ə/ [L, *ab,* away, *scindere,* to cut], a point on a horizontal Cartesian coordinate plane measured from the *y*- (or vertical) axis running perpendicular to the plane, or *x*-axis.

abscission /absish'ən/ [L, *abscindere,* to cut away], the process of cutting away, as in corneal abscission, removal of the prominence of the cornea.

absconsio /abskon'shō/ [L, *ab,* away from, *condo,* hidden], a cavity or fossa.

abscopal /abskō'pəl/ [L, *ab,* away, *scopos*], pertaining to the effect of irradiated tissue on remote tissue not exposed to radiation.

absence seizure, an epileptic seizure characterized by a sudden, momentary LOC. Occasionally it is accompanied by minor myoclonus of the neck or upper extremities, frequent blinking, slight symmetric twitching of the face, or loss of muscle tone. The seizures usually occur many times a day without a warning aura and are most frequent in children and adolescents, especially at puberty. The patient experiencing a typical seizure has a vacant facial expression and ceases all voluntary motor activity; with the rapid return of consciousness, the patient may resume conversation at the point of interruption without realizing what occurred. During and between seizures, the patient's EEG shows 3-Hz spike-and-wave discharges.

absenteeism /ab'sŏnte͞e'izəm/, (for health or related reasons) absence from work. The most common causes of absenteeism include influenza and occupationally related skin diseases.

absent without leave (AWOL) /ā'wôl/ [L, *absentia*], a term used to describe a patient who departs from a psychiatric facility without authorization or from a medical facility against medical advice.

abs feb, abbreviation for *absente febre,* a Latin phrase meaning "in the absence of fever."

Absidia /absid'ē-ə/, a genus of fungi belonging to the class Phycomycetes of the order Mucorales, which currently contains 21 species, most of which are soil-borne. *A. corymbifera* is the only recognized pathogen of the *Absidia* species and causes zygomycosis (mucormycosis), but is relatively rare. *A. corymbifera* is found on decaying plants and baked goods.

absolute /ab'səlo͞ot/, unconditional, unrestricted, or independent of arbitrary standards.

absolute agraphia [L, *absolutus,* set loose; Gk, *a,* not, *graphein,* to write], a complete inability to write caused by a CNS lesion. The person is unable to write even the letters of the alphabet.

absolute alcohol, a clear, colorless, highly hygroscopic liquid with a burning taste, containing at least 99.5% ethyl alcohol by volume.

absolute (A) temperature, temperature that is measured from a base of absolute zero on the Kelvin scale or Rankine scale.

absolute discharge [L, *absolutus,* set free], a final and complete termination of the patient's relationship with a caregiving agency.

absolute glaucoma [L, *absolutus;* Gk, cataract], complete blindness in which a glaucoma-induced increase in intraocular pressure results in permanent vision loss. The optic disc is white and deeply excavated, and the pupil is usually widely dilated and immobile.

absolute growth, the total increase in size of an organism or a particular organ or part, such as the limbs, head, or trunk.

absolute humidity, the actual mass or content of water in a measured volume of air. It is usually expressed in grams per cubic meter or pounds per cubic foot or cubic yard.

absolute neutrophil count (ANC), the number of neutrophils in a milliliter of blood, having a reference value of approximately 1500-7700 per μL. The ANC is a measure of a person's immune status. Generally, if the count is above 1000, the person may safely mingle with other people or undergo chemotherapy, while a count below 500 indicates that the person is at high risk for infection and should be kept away from those with infectious diseases.

absolute threshold [L, *absolutus,* set loose; AS, *therscold*], **1.** the lowest point at which a stimulus can be perceived. **2.** pertaining to millivolts of electrical charge determined by ion fluctuations or movement across plasma membranes that result in nerve or muscle stimulation.

absolute zero, the temperature at which all molecular activity except vibration ceases. It is a theoretical value derived by calculations and projections from experiments with the behavior of gases at extremely low temperatures. Absolute zero is estimated to be equal to −273° C or −460° F.

absorbable cotton /əbsôr'bəbəl/, oxidized cellulose.

absorbable gauze /əbsôr'bəbəl/, a material produced from oxidized cellulose that can be absorbed. It is applied directly to tissue to stop bleeding. After a clot forms, the gauze turns into a gel.

absorbable surgical suture [L, *absorbere,* to suck up; Gk, *cheirourgos,* surgery; L, *sutura*], a suture made from material that can be completely digested (by enzyme activity) or hydrolyzed (by water).

absorbance /əbsôr'bəns/, the degree of absorption of light or other radiant energy by a medium exposed to the energy. Absorbance varies with factors such as wavelength, solution concentration, and path length.

absorbed dose, the energy imparted by ionizing radiation per unit mass of irradiated material at the place of interest. The SI unit of absorbed dose is the gray, which is 1 J/kg and equals 100 rad.

absorbefacient /absôr'bifā'shənt/ [L, *absorbere,* to suck up, *facere,* to make], **1.** any agent that promotes or enhances absorption. **2.** causing or enhancing absorption.

absorbent /absôr'bənt/ [L, *absorbere,* to suck up], **1.** capable of attracting and incorporating substances into itself. **2.** a product or substance that can absorb liquids or gases.

absorbent dressing, a clean or sterile covering applied to a wound or incision to suck secretions into itself. Kinds of absorbent dressing are Teflon-coated gauze squares, fluffed gauze, and abdominal bandages.

A

absorbent gauze, a fabric or pad with various forms, weights, and uses. It may be a rolled, single-layered fine fabric for spiral bandages, or it may be a thick, multi-layered pad for a sterile pressure dressing. There may also be an adhesive backing.

absorption /absôrp′shən/ [L, *absorptio*], **1.** the incorporation of matter by other matter through chemical, molecular, or physical action such as the dissolving of a gas in a liquid or the taking up of a liquid by a porous solid. **2.** (in physiology) the passage of substances across and into tissues such as the passage of digested food molecules into intestinal cells or the passage of liquids into kidney tubules. **3.** (in radiology) the process of absorbing radiant energy by living or nonliving matter with which the radiation interacts.— **absorb,** *v.*

absorption coefficient, the factor by which the intensity of electromagnetic energy decreases as it interacts with a unit thickness of an absorbing material. It is usually expressed per unit thickness.

absorption rate constant, a value describing how much drug is absorbed per unit of time.

absorption spectrum, a plot of percent transmittance, absorbance, logarithm of absorbance, or absorptivity of a compound as a function of wavelength, wave number, or frequency of radiation.

absorptivity /ab′sôrptiv′itē/, absorbance at a particular wavelength divided by the product of the concentration of a substance and the sample path length.

abstinence /ab′stinəns/, voluntarily avoiding a substance, such as food or alcohol, or refraining from the performance of an act, such as sexual intercourse.

abstract /ab′strakt, abstrakt′/ [L, *abstrahere,* to drag away], **1.** a condensed summary of a scientific article, literary piece, or address. **2.** to collect data such as from a medical record. **3.** a preparation containing the soluble principles of a medication concentration mixed with lactose. **4.** difficult to understand because of lack of practability.

abstraction /abstrak′shən/ [L, *abstrahere,* to drag away], a condition in which teeth or other maxillary and mandibular structures are inferior to their normal position, away from the occlusal plane.

abstract thinking, the final, most complex stage in the development of cognitive thinking, in which thought is characterized by adaptability, flexibility, and the use of concepts and generalizations. This type of thinking is developed by 12 to 15 years of age, usually after some degree of education. In psychiatry, many disorders are characterized by the inability to think abstractly.

abulia /əbōō′lyə/ [Gk, *a + boule,* without will], a loss of the ability or a reduced capacity to exhibit initiative or to make decisions.

abuse /abyōōs′/ [L, *abuti,* to waste, *abusus,* using up,], **1.** improper use of equipment, a substance, or a service, such as a drug or program, either intentionally or unintentionally. **2.** physical or verbal attack or injury.

abuse cessation, a nursing outcome from the Nursing Outcomes Classification (NOC) defined as evidence that the victim is no longer hurt or exploited.

abused person [Fr, *abuser,* to disuse; L, *persona,* a role played], an individual who has been harmed or maltreated emotionally, verbally, sexually, or physically by another person or by a situation.

abuse protection, a nursing outcome from the Nursing Outcomes Classification (NOC) defined as protection of self and/or dependent others from abuse.

abuse protection support, a nursing intervention from the Nursing Interventions Classification (NIC) defined as identification of high-risk dependent relationships and actions to prevent further infliction of physical or emotional harm.

abuse protection support: child, a nursing intervention from the Nursing Interventions Classification (NIC) defined as identification of high-risk, dependent child relationships and actions to prevent possible or further infliction of physical, sexual, or emotional harm or neglect of basic necessities of life.

abuse protection support: domestic partner, a nursing intervention from the Nursing Interventions Classification (NIC) defined as identification of high-risk, dependent domestic relationships and actions to prevent possible or further infliction of physical, sexual, or emotional harm, or exploitation of a domestic partner.

abuse protection support: elder, a nursing intervention from the Nursing Interventions Classification (NIC) defined as identification of high-risk, dependent elder relationships and actions to prevent possible or further infliction of physical, sexual, or emotional harm; neglect of basic necessities of life; or exploitation.

abuse protection support: religious, a nursing intervention from the Nursing Interventions Classification (NIC) defined as identification of high-risk, controlling, religious relationships and actions to prevent infliction of physical, sexual, or emotional harm and/or exploitation.

abuse recovery, a nursing outcome from the Nursing Outcomes Classification (NOC) defined as extent of healing following physical or psychological abuse that may include sexual or financial exploitation.

abuse recovery: emotional, a nursing outcome from the Nursing Outcomes Classification (NOC) defined as extent of healing of psychological injuries due to abuse.

abuse recovery: financial, a nursing outcome from the Nursing Outcomes Classification (NOC) defined as extent of control of monetary and legal matters following financial exploitation.

abuse recovery: physical, a nursing outcome from the Nursing Outcomes Classification (NOC) defined as extent of healing of physical injuries due to abuse.

abuse recovery: sexual, a nursing outcome from the Nursing Outcomes Classification (NOC) defined as extent of healing of physical and psychological injuries due to sexual abuse or exploitation.

abusive behavior self-restraint, a nursing outcome from the Nursing Outcomes Classification (NOC) defined as self-restraint of abusive and neglectful behaviors toward others.

abutment /əbut′mənt/ [Fr, *abouter* to place end to end], a tooth, root, or implant that supports and provides retention for a fixed or removable dental prosthesis.

abutment tooth, a tooth selected to support a prosthesis.

ABVD, an anticancer drug combination of DOXOrubicin, bleomycin, vinBLAS-Tine, and dacarbazine.

Ac, 1. symbol for the element **actinium.** 2. abbreviation for **acetyl CH₃CO.**

AC, 1. abbreviation for **alternating current.** 2. abbreviation for *accommodative convergence.*

a.c., (in prescriptions) abbreviation for *ante cibum,* a Latin phrase meaning "before meals."

A-C, abbreviation for *alveolar-capillary.*

acacia gum, a dried, gummy exudate of the acacia tree (*Acacia senegal*) used as a suspending or emulsifying agent in medicines.

academic ladder /ak′ədem′ik/ [Gk, *akademeia,* school], the hierarchy of faculty appointments in an academic setting (university, college, or community college) through which a faculty member advances from the rank of instructor to assistant professor to associate professor to professor.

acalculia /a′kalkoo̅′lyə/ [Gk, *a,* not; L, *calculare,* to reckon], the inability to perform simple mathematic calculations the patient previously knew. Commonly seen in neurologic disorders, it is assessed by having a patient count forward or backward or do mental addition or subtraction.

acamprosate, an antialcoholic agent used for the maintenance of abstinence from alcohol in alcohol dependence.

acampsia /əkamp′sē-ə/ [Gk, *a* + *kampsein,* not to bend], a condition in which a joint is rigid.

acantha /əkan′thə/ [Gk, *akantha,* thorn], a spine or a spinous projection. —**acanthoid,** *adj.*

acanthamebiasis /əkan′thəmēbī′əsis/, a potentially fatal meningoencephalitis infection caused by *Acanthamoeba castellani,* a free-living ameboflagellate. It is commonly acquired by swimming in water contaminated by the microorganism. Cleaning contact lenses in contaminated solution can also cause keratitis.

Acanthamoeba /əkan′thəmē′bə/, a genus of free-living ameboid protozoa typically found in moist soil and water. The organisms may enter the body through a break in the skin, causing a localized infection, or even through the nose or eyes, causing systemic infections of the lung, genitourinary system, brain, and CNS.

acanthesia /ak′anthē′zhə/, pin prick paresthesia; an abnormality of cutaneous sensory perception that causes a simple touch to be felt as a painful pin prick.

acanthiomeatal line /əkan′thē-ō′mē-ā′təl/, a hypothetical line extending from the external auditory meatus to the acanthion. In dentistry, a full maxillary denture is constructed so that its occlusal plane is parallel with this line.

acanthion, a craniometric point at the center of the base of the anterior nasal spine.

Acanthocheilonema perstans /akan′thōkī′lə nē′mə/, a long, thread like worm usually found in Africa. It commonly infects wild and domestic animals and occasionally invades the bloodstream of humans, causing a rash, muscle and joint pains, various neurologic disorders, and nodules in the subcutaneous tissue.

acanthocyte /əkan′thəsīt′/ [Gk, *akantha* + *kytos,* cell], an abnormal erythrocyte with spurlike projections. Large numbers are present in abetalipoproteinemia; fewer occur in cirrhosis and in certain malabsorption syndromes.

acanthocytosis /akan′thōsītō′sis/ [Gk, *akantha* + *kytos* + *osis,* condition], the presence of acanthocytes in the circulating blood.

acanthoid, resembling a spinous process.

acanthoma /ak′anthō′mə/ [Gk, *akantha* + *oma,* tumor], hypertrophy that arises from the stratum spinosum and is localized rather than diffuse. It may be benign or malignant.

acanthoma fissuration, the development of a fissure bordered by increased thickening at sites of friction of the stratum spinosum.

acanthoma fissuratum, a benign, firm, skin-colored or erythematous nodule, grossly resembling basal cell carcinoma, occurring on the bridge of the nose or behind the ear, resulting from constant minor mechanical trauma caused by poorly fitting glasses.

acanthorrhexis /əkan'thôrek'sis/, the rupture of intercellular bridges of the stratum spinosum, as in eczema or allergic contact dermatitis.

acanthosis /ak'ənthō'sis/ [Gk, *akantha* + *osis*, condition], an abnormal, diffuse hypertrophy of the stratum spinosum, as in eczema and psoriasis. —**acanthotic,** *adj.*

acanthosis nigricans /nē'grikanz'/, a skin disease characterized by hyperpigmented, velvety thickening of the skin, common in the neck, axilla, and groin.

acapnia /akap'nē·ə/, a deficiency of carbon dioxide in the blood.

AC/A ratio, (in ophthalmology) the proportion between accommodative convergence (AC) and accommodation (A), or the amount of convergence automatically resulting from the dioptric focusing of the eyes at a specified distance. The ratio of accommodative convergence to accommodation is usually expressed as the quotient of accommodative convergence in prism diopters divided by the accommodative response in diopters.

acarbia /akär'bē·ə/ [Gk, *a*, not; L, *carbo*, coal], a decrease in the bicarbonate level in the blood.

acarbose, an insulin-control drug, prescribed in the treatment of type 2 diabetes mellitus.

acardia /akär'dē·ə/ [Gk, *a* + *kardia*, without heart], a rare congenital anomaly in which the heart is absent. It is almost exclusively seen in a conjoined twin whose survival depends on the circulatory system of its twin. —**acardiac,** *adj.*

acardius acephalus, a fetus that lacks a head, heart, and most of the upper part of the body.

acardius acormus, a fetus that lacks a heart and has a grossly defective trunk.

acardius amorphus, an acardiac fetus with a rudimentary body that does not resemble the normal form.

acariasis /ak'ərī'əsis/ [Gk, *akari,* mite, *osis,* condition], a disease, usually of the skin, caused by an infestation with mites.

acarid /ak'ərid/, one of the many mites and ticks that are members of the order

Acarina, which includes a great number of parasitic and free-living organisms. Those associated with disease act as intermediate hosts of pathogenic agents, directly cause skin or tissue damage, and cause loss of blood or tissue fluids. Important as vectors of scrub typhus and other rickettsial agents are the six-legged larvae of mites from the family Trombiculidae, which are parasitic of humans, other mammals, and birds.

acarodermatitis /ak'ərōdur'məti'tis/ [Gk, *akari,* mite, *derma,* skin, *itis,* inflammation], a skin inflammation caused by mites or ticks.

acarophobia /-fō'bē·ə/, a morbid dread of tiny parasites or the delusion that tiny insects such as mites have invaded the skin.

acaudal /akô'dəl/ [Gk, *a,* without; L, *cauda,* tail], without a tail.

acc, Acc, abbreviation for **accommodation.**

ACC, abbreviation for *American College of Cardiology.*

accelerated idiojunctional rhythm, an automatic junctional rhythm whose rate is greater than 59 beats/min but less than 100 beats/min.

accelerated idioventricular rhythm (AIVR), an automatic ectopic ventricular rhythm, whose rate is greater than 49 beats per minute but less than 100 beats per minute without retrograde conduction to the atria. In acute MI an AIVR can be a sign of spontaneous reperfusion or a result of thrombolytic therapy.

accelerated junctional rhythm, an ectopic heart junctional rhythm whose rate exceeds the normal firing rate of junctional tissue, with or without retrograde atrial conduction.

accelerated respiration, an abnormally rapid rate of breathing, usually more than 25 breaths per minute.

acceleration /aksel'ərā'shən/ [L, *accelerare,* to quicken], an increase in the speed or velocity of an object or reaction.—**accelerate,** *v.*

acceleration-deceleration injury, injury resulting from a collision between a body part and another object or body part while both are in motion.

acceleration phase, the first period of active labor, stage I, characterized by an increased rate of dilation of the cervical canal as charted on a Friedman curve.

accelerator /aksel'ərātər/ [L, *accelerare,* to quicken], **1.** a nerve or muscle that increases the rate of performance of some function. **2.** an agent or apparatus used to increase the rate at which a substance acts or a function proceeds.

accentuation /aksen'chōō·ā'shən/ [L, *accentus,* accent], an increase in distinctness or loudness, as in heart sounds.

acceptable daily intake (ADI), the maximum amount of any substance that can be safely ingested by a human. Ingestion that exceeds this amount may cause toxic effects. This term is usually applied to additives, residues, or chemicals not normally found in foods.

acceptance: health status, a nursing outcome from the Nursing Outcomes Classification (NOC) defined as reconciliation to significant change in health circumstances.

acceptance of individuality, (in psychiatry) an index of family health in which differentiation or individuation is a valued goal.

acceptance of separation, an indicator of mental well-being in which a loss is mourned in a healthy manner. It indicates higher level of adaptability.

acceptor /aksep′tər/ [L, *accipere,* to receive], **1.** an organism that receives living tissue, such as transfused blood or a transplanted organ, from another organism. **2.** a substance or compound that combines with, or accepts, a part of another substance or compound, such as an atom, an electron, or an electron pair.

access /ak′ses/, a means of approach, such as the space needed for the manipulation of dental or surgical instruments.

access cavity [L, *accedere,* to approach], a coronal opening to the center (pulp chamber) of a tooth, required for effective cleaning, shaping, and obturation of the pulp canals and chamber during endodontic or root canal therapy.

accessory /akses′ərē/ [L, *accessonis,* appendage], **1.** a supplementary item, desirable but not necessary, used chiefly for convenience or for safety, such as the electric elevator mechanisms for hospital beds. **2.** a structure that serves one of the main anatomic systems, such as the accessory sex organs in men and women or the accessory organs of the skin, including the hair, the nails, and the skin glands. **3.** one who aids in perpetrating a crime.

accessory diaphragm, a rare congenital anomaly in which a second diaphragm or part of a diaphragm develops in the chest. It may be separated from the true diaphragm by a lobe of a lung.

accessory gland, glandular tissue that contributes in a secondary way to the function of a similar gland, which may be nearby or some distance away.

accessory ligament [L, *accessus,* extra, *ligare,* to bind], a ligament that helps strengthen a union between two bones, even though it is not part of a joint capsule.

accessory movement, a joint movement that is necessary for a full range of motion but is not under direct voluntary control. Examples include rotation and gliding.

accessory muscle, a relatively rare anatomic duplication of a muscle that may appear anywhere in the muscular system.

accessory muscle of respiration, any of the muscles of the neck, back, and abdomen that may assist the diaphragm and the internal and external intercostal muscles in respiration, especially in some breathing disorders or during exercise.

accessory nasal sinuses [L, *accessus,* extra, *nasus,* nose, *sinus,* hollow], the paranasal sinuses that occur as hollows within the skull but open into the nasal cavity and are lined with a mucous membrane continuous with the nasal mucous membrane.

accessory nerve, either of a pair of cranial nerves essential for speech, swallowing, and certain movements of the head and shoulders. Each nerve has a cranial and a spinal part, communicates with certain cervical nerves, and connects to the nucleus ambiguus of the brain.

accessory organ, an organ or other distinct collection of tissues that contributes to the function of another similar organ, such as the ocular muscles and eyelids, which contribute to the function of the eye.

accessory organs of the eye, the eyelids, eyelashes, eyebrows, conjunctival sac, lacrimal apparatus, and extrinsic muscles of the eye.

accessory pancreas [L, *accessus,* extra; Gk, *pan,* all, *kreas,* flesh], small clusters of pancreatic cells detached from the pancreas and sometimes found in the wall of the stomach or intestines.

accessory pancreatic duct, the small duct that branches from the pancreatic duct and open into the duodenum near the mouth of the common bile duct.

accessory pathway, an abnormal conduction path between an atrium and a ventricle. Ventricular activation via an accessory pathway slows initial ventricular contraction, producing preexcitation and the delta wave of Wolff-Parkinson-White syndrome. The delta wave shortens the PR interval, and broadens the QRS complex. The most common associated arrhythmias are paroxysmal supraventricular tachycardia and atrial fibrillation.

accessory phrenic nerve, the nerve that joins the phrenic nerve at the root of the neck or in the thorax, forming a loop around the subclavian vein.

accessory placenta [L, *accessionis,* a thing added, *placenta,* flat cake], a small placenta that may develop attached to the main placenta by umbilical blood vessels.

accessory root canal, an anatomic lateral branching of the pulp canal in a tooth, usually occurring in the apical third of the root.

accessory sign, a sign that is not typical or characteristic of a particular disease.

accessory spleen [L, *accessus,* extra; Gk, *splen*], small nodules of splenic tissue that may occur in the gastrosplenic ligament, greater omentum, or other visceral sites.

accessory thymus [L, *accessus,* extra; Gk, *thymos,* thymelike], a nodule of thymus tissue that is isolated from the gland.

accessory tooth, a supernumerary tooth that does not resemble a normal tooth in size, shape, or position.

accident /ak'sidənt/ [L, *accidere,* to happen], any unexpected or unplanned event that may result in death, injury, property damage, or a combination of serious effects.

accident-prone, describing a person who experiences accidents and accompanying injuries at a much greater than average rate.

acclimate /əklī'mit, ak'limāt/ [L, *ad,* toward; Gk, *klima,* region], to adjust physiologically to a different climate or environment or to changes in altitude or temperature.—**acclimation, acclimatization,** *n.*

acclimatization to heat [L, *ad,* toward; Gk, *klima,* region], a process whereby the body adapts to warmer environmental temperatures.

accommodation (A, acc, Acc) /əkom'ədā'shən/ [L, *accommodatio,* adjustment] **1.** the state or process of adapting or adjusting one thing or set of things to another. **2.** the continuous process or effort of the individual to adapt or adjust to surroundings to maintain a state of homeostasis, both physiologically and psychologically. **3.** the adjustment of the eye to variations in distance. **4.** (in sociology) the reciprocal reconciliation of conflicts between individuals or groups concerning habits and customs, usually through a process of compromise, arbitration, or negotiation.

accommodation reflex, an adjustment of the eyes for near vision, consisting of pupillary constriction, convergence of the eyes, and increased convexity of the lens.

accommodative strabismus /əkom'ədā'tiv/ [L, *accommodatio,* adjustment; Gk, *strabismos,* squint], **1.** strabismus resulting from abnormal demand on accommodation, such as esotropia resulting from uncorrected hyperopia or exotropia resulting from uncorrected myopia. **2.** strabismus resulting from the act of accommodation in association with a high AC/A ratio.

accomplishment quotient /əkom'plishmənt/, a numeric evaluation of a person's achievement age compared with mental age, expressed as a ratio multiplied by 100.

accountability /əkoun'təbil'itē/, accountability or responsibility for the moral and legal requirements of proper patient care.

accreditation /əkred'itā'shən/, a process whereby a professional association or nongovernmental agency grants recognition to a school or health care institution for demonstrated ability to meet predetermined criteria for established standards.

Accreditation Review Committee on Education in Surgical Technology (ARC-ST), a committee created in 1972 to establish, maintain, and promote standards of quality for educational programs in surgical technology and surgical assisting recognized through programmatic accreditation in cooperation with the Commission on Accreditation of Allied Health Education Programs (CAAHEP), the American College of Surgeons (ACS), and the Association of Surgical Technologists (AST).

accrementition /ak'rəmentish'ən/, a growth or increase in size by the addition of similar tissue or material, as in cell division, binary fission, budding, or gemmation.

accretio cordis /əkrē'shē·ō/ [L, *accrescere,* to increase, *cordis,* heart], an abnormal condition in which the pericardium adheres to the plurae, diaphragm, or chest wall.

accretion /əkrē'shən/ [L, *accrescere,* to increase], **1.** growth by the addition of material similar to that already present. **2.** the adherence or growing together of parts that are normally separated. **3.** an accumulation of foreign material, especially within a cavity.—**accrete,** *v.,* **accretive,** *adj.*

acculturation /əkul'chərā'shən/, **1.** the process of adopting the cultural traits or social patterns of a different population group. **2.** the modification of the culture of a group resulting from association with another group.

accumulated dose equivalent /əkyōō'm yəlā'tid/, an estimate of an individual's absorbed dose of radiation over a lifetime, expressed in rem. Occupationally exposed persons are allowed no more than 5 rem per year, or 1 rem times age at any time during the person's lifetime.

accuracy /ak'yərəsē'/, the extent to which a measurement is close to the true value.

accurate empathy /ak'yərit/, a communication technique used by a nurse to convey an understanding of the patient's feelings and experiences.

Accurbron, a trademark for a bronchodilator (theophylline).

Accutane, a trademark for an antiacne agent (isotretinoin).

ACDF, abbreviation for **anterior cervical decompression and fusion.**

ACE, abbreviation for **angiotensin-converting enzyme.**

Ace bandage, a trademark for a woven elastic bandage applied to the extremities for exsanguination, pressure dressing to prevent swelling, or holding traction set-ups.

acebutolol /as′əbōō′təlol/, a beta-adrenergic blocking agent prescribed in the treatment of hypertension, angina pectoris, ventricular arrhythmias, and other cardiovascular disorders.

acedia /əse̅′de̅·ə/ [Gk, *akedia,* apathy], a condition of listlessness and a form of melancholia, marked by indifference and sluggish mental processes.

acellular /āsel′yələr/, without cells.

acentric /āsen′trik/ [Gk, *a* + *kentron,* not center], **1.** having no center. **2.** (in genetics) describing a chromosome fragment that has no centromere.

ACEP, abbreviation for **American College of Emergency Physicians.**

acephalobrachia /asef′ələbrā′ke̅·ə/ [Gk, *a* without, *kephale,* head, *brachion,* arm], a congenital anomaly in which a fetus lacks both arms and the head.

acephalocardia /-kär′de̅·ə/ [Gk, *a,* without *kephale,* head, *cardia,* heart], the congenital absence of both the head and the heart.

acephalus /əsef′ələs/ [Gk, *a* + *kephale,* without head], a headless fetus.

acephaly /əsef′əle̅/ [Gk, *a* + *kephale,* without head], a congenital defect in which the head is absent or not properly developed.—**acephalic,** *adj.*

acerola /as′ərō′lə/, a small, cherrylike fruit of the genus *Malpighia* that grows in tropical climates. It is a richer source of vitamin C than any other known fruit.

acesulfame-K /as′əsul′fäm/, a synthetic, noncaloric sweetener marketed under the trademark Sunnette. It is approximately 200 times sweeter than is sucrose.

acet, abbreviation for an acetate carboxylate anion. Also abbreviated *OAc.*

acetabular /as′ətab′yələr/ [L, *acetabulum,* little saucer], pertaining to the acetabulum.

acetabular angle, the angle between the acetabular line and Hilgenreiner's line, normally between 27 and 30 degrees in the neonatal hip. It is used in the radiographic assessment of developmental dysplasia of the hip.

acetabular labrum, a fibrocartilaginous collar on the rim of the acetabulum that crosses the acetabular notch as the transverse acetabular ligament and converts the notch into a foramen.

acetabular line, a line following the slope of the acetabulum that is used in radiographic assessment of the hip joint. With Hilgenreiner's line it forms the acetabular angle.

acetabular notch, an indentation in the margin of the acetabulum.

acetabuloplasty /as′ətab′yəlōplas′te̅/, plastic surgery performed to reshape the acetabulum.

acetabulum /as′ətab′yələm/ *pl.* **acetabula** [L, vinegar cup], the large, cup-shaped cavity at the juncture and lateral surface of the ilium, the ischium, and the pubis, in which the ball-shaped head of the femur articulates.

acetal, **1.** /as′-ə-təl/ a colorless liquid, C_2H_4 $(OC_2H_5)_2$, sometimes used as a hypnotic. **2.** any compound with the general formula $R_2C(OR)_2$ or $RCH(OR)_2$, in which R indicates an alkyl or aryl group.

acetaldehyde (CH_3CHO) /as′ətəlde̅′hīd/, a colorless, volatile liquid aldehyde with a pungent odor produced by the oxidation of ethyl alcohol. In the human body, acetaldehyde is produced in the liver by the action of alcohol dehydrogenase and other enzymes. Exposure to high levels can result in headache, corneal injury, rhinitis, and respiratory disorders.

acetaminophen /əset′əmin′əfen/, an analgesic and antipyretic drug used in many nonprescription pain relievers. It has no antiinflammatory properties. It may be used in combination with other products that do not contain additional acetaminophen. It is often recommended for treatment of mild to moderate pain and fever.

acetaminophen poisoning, a toxic reaction to the ingestion of excessive doses of acetaminophen. Dosages exceeding 140 mg/kg can produce liver failure, and larger doses can be fatal.

acetate (CH_3CO_2-) /as′itāt/, an anion of formula $C_2H_3O_2$. It is the conjugate base of acetic acid.

acetate kinase, an enzyme that catalyzes the transfer of a phosphate group from adenosine triphosphate to acetate.

acetaZOLAMIDE /as′ətəzō′ləmīd/, a carbonic anhydrase inhibitor diuretic agent, prescribed for the treatment of glaucoma and edema and as an adjunctive agent for the treatment of refractory epilepsy and altitude sickness.

Acetest, a trademark for a product used to test for the presence of abnormal quantities of acetone in the urine of patients with diabetes mellitus or other metabolic disorders.

acetic /əse̅′tik, əset′ik/ [L, *acetum,* vinegar], pertaining to substances having the sour properties of vinegar or acetic acid;

also, chemical compounds possessing the radical CH₃CO−.

acetic acid (HC₂H₃O₂), a clear, colorless, pungent liquid that is miscible with water, alcohol, glycerin, and ether and that constitutes 3% to 5% of vinegar.

acetic fermentation, the production of acetic acid or vinegar from a weak alcoholic solution.

acetoacetic acid /as′ətō-əsē′tik, əsē′tō-/, a colorless, oily keto acid produced by the metabolism of lipids and pyruvates. It is excreted in trace amounts in normal urine and in elevated levels in DM, especially in ketoacidosis, and during starvation.

acetoHEXAMIDE /-hek′səmīd/, a sulfonylurea oral antidiabetic prescribed in the treatment of type 2 DM.

acetohydroxamic acid /as′e-to-hī′droks am′ik/, an inhibitor of bacterial urease used in the prophylaxis and treatment of struvite renal calculi, whose formation is favored by urease-producing bacteria, and as an adjunct in the treatment of URIs caused by urease-producing bacteria. It is administered orally.

acetol kinase, an enzyme that catalyzes the transfer of a phosphate group from adenosine triphosphate to hydroxyacetone.

acetone /as′ətōn/, a colorless, aromatic, volatile liquid ketone body found in small amounts in normal urine and in larger quantities in the urine of persons with diabetes who are experiencing ketoacidosis or starvation. Commercially prepared acetone is used to clean the skin before injections.

acetone in urine test, a test for the presence of dimethylketone in the urine of patients, used as a laboratory indication of ketosis and the severity of DM. Chemically treated test paper strips or sticks are exposed to urine. If acetone is present in the urine as the result of incomplete breakdown of fatty and amino acids in the body, the test strips change color. A similar test uses a compound added directly to a urine sample.

acetonide grouping, an acetone-based ketal or ketone-alcohol derivative present in some corticosteroid drugs.

acetonuria /as′ətōnŏŏr′ē-ə/, the presence of acetone and diacetic bodies in the urine.

acetyl (CH₃CO, Ac), a monovalent radical associated with derivatives of acetic acid.

acetylcholine (ACh) /as′ətilkō′lēn, əsē′til-/, a direct-acting cholinergic neurotransmitter agent widely distributed in body tissues, with a primary function of mediating synaptic activity of the nervous system and skeletal muscles. It is also a stimulant of the vagus nerve and parasympathetic nervous system and functions as a vasodilator and cardiac depressant.

acetylcholine receptor (AChR) antibody test, one of three blood tests for AChR to diagnose myasthenia gravis, the most sensitive of which is the AChR-modulating antibody test and the least sensitive of which is the AChR-blocking antibody test. The test used most often is the AChR-binding antibody test.

acetylcholinesterase (AChE) /-kō′lines′tərās/, an enzyme present at the endings of voluntary nerves and parasympathetic involuntary nerves and autonomic nerve ganglia. It inactivates and prevents accumulation of the neurotransmitter acetylcholine released during nerve impulse transmission by hydrolyzing the substance to choline and acetate. The action reduces or prevents excessive firing of neurons at neuromuscular junctions.

acetylcoenzyme A /əsē′tilkō·en′zīm, as′ətil-/, a biomolecule that carries an activated form of the 2-carbon acetyl unit that is found in the course of several important metabolic processes. The formation of acetylcoenzyme A is the critical intermediate step between anaerobic glycolysis and the citric acid cycle.

acetylcysteine /-sis′tēn/, a mucolytic and acetaminophen antidote prescribed in the treatment of chronic pulmonary disease, acute bronchopulmonary disease, atelectasis resulting from mucous obstruction, and acetaminophen poisoning.

acetylene /əset′əlēn/, a colorless, highly flammable gas that is the simplest of the alkynes.

acetylsalicylic acid poisoning /əsē′təlsal′ isil′ik, asətəl-/, the toxic effects of overdosage of the commonly used antipyretic and analgesic drug, aspirin. Early symptoms include dizziness, ringing in the ears, changes in body temperature, GI discomfort, and hyperventilation. Severe poisoning is marked by respiratory alkalosis, which may lead to metabolic acidosis. Children and the elderly are particularly vulnerable to the potential toxic effects of salicylates.

acetyltransferase /-trans′fərās/, any of several enzymes that transfer acetyl groups from one compound to another.

Ace wrap/dressing, a trademark for an elasticized wrap.

ACG, abbreviation for **apexcardiography.**

ACh, abbreviation for **acetylcholine.**

ACH, abbreviation for **adrenocortical hormone.**

achalasia /ak′ələ′zhə/ [Gk, *a + chalasis,* without relaxation], an abnormal condition characterized by the constriction of the lower portion of the esophagus because of the inability of a muscle to relax (cardiospasm), particularly the lower esophageal sphincter.

Achard-Thiers syndrome /ăsh′är tērz′/ [Emile C. Achard, French physician, 1860–1941; Joseph Thiers, French physician, b. 1885], a hormonal disorder seen in postmenopausal women with DM, characterized by the growth of body hair in a masculine distribution.

ache /āk/ [OE, *acan,* to hurt], **1.** a pain characterized by persistence, dullness, and usually moderate intensity. An ache may be localized or general. **2.** to suffer from a dull, persistent pain of moderate intensity.

AChE, abbreviation for **acetylcholinesterase.**

acheiria /əkī′rē·ə/ [Gk, *a,* not, *cheir,* hand], a congenital absence of one or both hands.

acheiropody /ak′īrop′ədē/ [Gk, *a,* not, *cheir,* hand, *pous,* foot], an absence of the hands and feet.

achievement age (AA) /əchēv′mənt/, the level of a person's educational development as measured by an achievement test and compared with the normal score for chronologic age.

achievement quotient (AQ), a numeric expression of a person's achievement age determined by various achievement tests, divided by the chronologic age and expressed as a multiple of 100.

achievement test, a standardized test for the measurement and comparison of knowledge or proficiency in various fields of vocational or academic study.

Achilles tendon /əkil′ēz/ [*Achilles,* Greek mythologic hero], the common distal tendon of the soleus and gastrocnemius muscles of the leg. It is the thickest and strongest tendon in the body and connects the triceps surae to the heel bone. In an adult it is about 15 cm long.

Achilles tendon reflex, a deep tendon reflex consisting of plantar flexion of the foot when a sharp tap is given directly to the tendon of the gastrocnemius muscle at the back of the ankle. This reflex is often absent in people with peripheral neuropathies or diabetes.

achiral, pertaining to the absence of chirality in a compound, as in stereochemical isomers.

achlorhydria /ā′klôrhī′drē·ə/ [Gk, *a* + *chloros,* not green, *hydor,* water], an abnormal condition characterized by the absence of hydrochloric acid in gastric secretions. Achlorhydria occurs most commonly in atrophy of the gastric mucosa, gastric carcinoma, and pernicious anemia. It is also found in severe iron deficiency anemia. Malignancy is expected when achloryhydria is seen in combination with peptic ulcers.—**achlorhydric,** *adj.*

achloropsia /ā′klôrop′sē·ə/ [Gk, *a,* not, *chloros,* green, *opsis,* vision], an inability to see green; green blindness.

acholia /akō′lē·ə/ [Gk, *a* + *chole,* without bile], **1.** the absence or decrease of bile secretion. **2.** any condition that suppresses the flow of bile into the small intestine. —**acholic,** *adj.*

acholuria /ak′əlŏŏr′ē·ə/ [Gk, *a* + *chole,* without bile, *ouron,* urine], the absence or lack of bile pigments in the urine. It occurs in some forms of jaundice.

achondrogenesis /ākon′drōjen′əsis/, the most severe form of chondrodysplasia, typically lethal before or soon after birth.

achondroplasia /ākon′drōplā′zhə/ [Gk,*a*+ *chondros,* without cartilage, *plassein,* to form], a disorder of the growth of cartilage in the epiphyses of the long bones and skull. It results in premature ossification, permanent limitation of skeletal development, and dwarfism typified by protruding forehead and short, thick arms and legs on a normal trunk.

achondroplastic dwarf /-plas′tik/, the most common type of dwarf, characterized by disproportionately short limbs, a normal-sized trunk, a large head with a depressed nasal bridge and a small face, stubby hands, and lordosis.

AChR, abbreviation for **acetylcholine receptor.**

achroma /akrō′mə/ [Gk, *a,* without, *chroma,* color], lack of color.

achromatic, **1.** free of color. **2.** color blind. **3.** a substance not colored by common staining agents.

achromatic lens /ak′rəmat′ik/ [Gk, *a,* without, *chroma,* color; L, *lens*], a lens in which the focal lengths for red and blue colors of the spectrum are the same, refracting light without decomposing it into its component colors.

achromia /akrō′mēə/ [Gk, *a* + *chroma,* without color], **1.** depigmentation. **2.** the absence or loss of natural pigmentation of the skin and iris. It may be congenital or acquired.

Achromobacter /akrō′mōbak′tər/, a genus of gram-negative, rod-shaped, flagellated bacteria that do not form pigment on agar. Most species in the genus are saprophytic, nonpathogenic organisms found in water, soil, or the human digestive tract, but they may cause infection in the compromised host.

achromocyte /akrō′məsīt/, a red cell artifact that stains more faintly than intact red cells.

Achromycin V, a trademark for an antibiotic (tetracycline hydrochloride).

achylia /ākī′lē·ə/ [Gk, *a* + *chylos,* not juice], an absence or severe deficiency of hydrochloric acid and pepsinogen (pepsin) in the stomach. This condition may also occur in the pancreas when the exocrine part of that gland fails to produce digestive enzymes.

achylous /əkīˈləs/, **1.** pertaining to a lack of gastric juice or other digestive secretions. **2.** pertaining to a lack of chyle.

acicular /əsikˈyələr/ [L, *aciculus,* little needle], needle-shaped, such as certain leaves and crystals.

acid /asˈid/ [L, *acidus,* sour], **1.** a compound that yields hydrogen ions when dissociated in aqueous solution (Arrhenius definition), acts as a hydrogen ion donor (Brønsted definition), or acts as an electron pair acceptor (Lewis definition). Acids turn blue litmus red, have a sour taste, and react with bases to form salts. Acids have chemical properties essentially opposite to those of bases. **2.** *slang.* lysergic acid diethylamide (LSD). **3.** sour or bitter to the taste.— **acidic,** *adj.,* **acidify,** *v.*

acidalbumin, a substance formed by the action of mild acid solutions on albumin.

acid-base balance, a condition existing when the net rate at which the body produces acids or bases equals the net rate at which acids or bases are excreted. The result of acid-base balance is a stable concentration of hydrogen ions in body fluids.

acid-base management, a nursing intervention from the Nursing Interventions Classification (NIC) defined as promotion of acid-base balance and prevention of complications resulting from acid-base imbalance.

acid-base management: metabolic acidosis, a nursing intervention from the Nursing Interventions Classification (NIC) defined as promotion of acid-base balance and prevention of complications resulting from serum HCO_3 levels lower than desired.

acid-base management: metabolic alkalosis, a nursing intervention from the Nursing Interventions Classification (NIC) defined as promotion of acid-base balance and prevention of complications resulting from serum HCO_3 levels higher than desired.

acid-base management: respiratory acidosis, a nursing intervention from the Nursing Interventions Classification (NIC) defined as promotion of acid-base balance and prevention of complications resulting from serum pCO_2 levels higher than desired.

acid-base management: respiratory alkalosis, a nursing intervention from the Nursing Interventions Classification (NIC) defined as promotion of acid-base balance and prevention of complications resulting from serum pCO_2 levels lower than desired.

acid-base metabolism, the metabolic processes that maintain the balance of acids and bases essential in regulating the composition of body fluids. Acids release hydrogen ions, and bases accept them; the concentration of hydrogen ions present in a solution governs whether it is acid, alkali, or neutral. Hydrogen ions in water are measured on a pH scale of 0.0 to 14.0, with a reading of 7.0 indicating neutral at 25° C. Above 7.0, the solution is alkaline; below 7.0, it is acid. Blood is slightly alkaline, ranging from 7.35 to 7.45. Metabolic buffer systems within the body maintain this ratio, and, when the ratio is upset, either acidosis or alkalosis results.

acid-base monitoring, a nursing intervention from the Nursing Interventions Classification (NIC) defined as collection and analysis of patient data to regulate acid-base balance.

acid burn, damage to tissue caused by exposure to an acid. The severity of the burn is determined by the strength of the acid and the duration and extent of exposure. Emergency treatment includes irrigating the affected area with large amounts of water.

acid dust, an accumulation of highly acidic particles of dust. Such substances accumulate in the atmosphere and account for much of the smog hanging over large metropolitan areas. Many respiratory illnesses, such as lung cancer and asthma, may be aggravated or caused by such dust.

acidemia /asˈidēˈmē·ə/, decreased pH status of the blood or abnormal acidity in the blood.

acid etching, etching of dental enamel with an acid to remove the smear layer and open enamel tubules, increase retention of resin sealant, and promote mechanical retention.

acid-fast bacillus (AFB), a type of bacillus that resists decolorizing by acid after accepting a stain. Examples include *Mycobacterium tuberculosis* and *M. leprae.*

acid-fast stain, a method of staining used in bacteriology in which a smear on a slide is treated with carbol-fuchsin stain or auramine-rhodamine stain, decolorized with acid alcohol, and counterstained with methylene blue or potassium permanganate to identify acid-fast bacteria. The stain is most commonly used in examining sputum for *Mycobacterium tuberculosis.*

acid flush, a runoff of precipitation with a high acid content, as may occur during thaws.

acidity /asidˈitē/ [L, *acidus,* sour], **1.** the degree of sourness, sharpness of taste, or ability of a chemical to yield hydrogen ions in an aqueous solution. 2. the degree of gastric acid in the stomach. The acidity varies during any 24-hour period, but the pH averages 0.9 to 1.5.

acid mist, mist containing a high concentration of acid or particles of any toxic chemical, such as carbon tetrachloride or silicon tetrachloride.

acid mucopolysaccharide, a major chemical constituent of ground substance in the dermis.

acidophil /as'idōfil, əsid'əfil/ [L, *acidus*; Gk, *philein*, to love], 1. a cell or cell constituent with an affinity for acid dyes. 2. an organism that thrives in an acid medium.—**acidophilic,** *adj.*

acidophilic adenoma, a tumor of the pituitary gland characterized by cells that can be stained red with an acid dye. Gigantism and acromegaly can result from the hypersecretion of growth hormone caused by an acidophilic adenoma.

acidophilus milk /as'idof'ələs/, milk inoculated with cultures of *Lactobacillus acidophilus,* used in various enteric disorders to change the bacterial flora of the GI tract.

acidosis /as'idō'sis/ [L, *acidus*; Gk, *osis*, condition], an abnormal increase in hydrogen ion concentration in the body, resulting from an accumulation of an acid or the loss of a base. It is indicated by a blood pH below the normal range (7.35 to 7.45).—**acidotic,** *adj.*

acidosis dialysis, a type of metabolic acidosis that may develop when contaminating bacteria alter the pH of the dialysis bath.

acid phosphatase, an enzyme found in the kidneys, serum, semen, and prostate gland. It is elevated in serum in prostate cancer and in trauma.

acid phosphatase test, a rarely used blood test used to diagnose end-stage prostatic carcinoma and to monitor the efficacy of treatment. It has mostly been replaced by the prostate-specific antigen test. It is also used to test for the presence of semen in suspected rape cases.

acid poisoning, a toxic condition caused by the ingestion of a toxic acid agent, such as hydrochloric, nitric, phosphoric, or sulfuric acid, some of which are ingredients in common household cleaning compounds.

acid rain, the precipitation of moisture, as rain, with high acidity caused by release into the atmosphere of pollutants from industry, motor vehicle exhaust, and other sources.

acid rebound, the hypersecretion of gastric acid that may occur after the initial buffering effect of an antacid. It occurs most noticeably when antacids containing calcium carbonate are used.

acid salt, a salt formed from an acid with two or more bases by only partial replacement of hydrogen ions from the related acid, leaving some degree of acidity.

acid therapy, a method for removing verrucae that uses plaster patches impregnated with acid, such as 40% salicylic acid, or with acid drops.

acidulous /əsid'yələs/, slightly acidic or sour.

aciduria [L, *acidus*; Gk, *ouron*, urine], the excretion of an acid in the urine. The condition may be caused by a diet rich in meat proteins or certain fruits, the introduction of a medication used to treat a urinary tract disorder, an inborn error of metabolism, or ketoacidosis.

acinar cell /as'inər/ [L, *acinus*, grape], a cell of the tiny lobules of a compound gland or similar saclike structure such as an alveolus.

Acinetobacter /as'inē'təbak'tər/, a genus of nonmotile, aerobic bacteria of the family Neisseriaceae that often occurs in clinical specimens. It is mainly found in water, and its disease activity is opportunistic. Most human disease is caused by *A. baumannii*.

acinic cell adenocarcinoma /asin'ik/ [L, *acinus*, grape], an uncommon low-grade malignant neoplasm that develops in the secreting cells of racemose glands, especially the salivary glands.

aciniform /asin'ifôrm/ [L, *acinus*, grape; *forma*, shape], shaped like a cluster of grapes. The term refers particularly to glandular tissue.

acinitis /as'inī'tis/, any inflammation of the tiny, grape-shaped parts of certain glands.

acinotubular gland /as'inōt(y)ŏŏb'yə lər/ [grape-shaped], a gland in which the acini are tube-shaped.

acinus /as'inəs/ *pl.* **acini** [L, grape], any small saclike structure, particularly one found in a gland.

acitretin /as'e-tret'in/, a second generation retinoid used in treatment of severe psoriasis. It is administered orally.

A.C. joint, abbreviation for *acromioclavicular joint.*

ACL, abbreviation for **anterior cruciate ligament.**

Aclovate, a trademark for a topical corticosteroid (alclometasone dipropionate).

ACLS, abbreviation for **advanced cardiac life support.**

acme /ak'mē/ [Gk, *akme*, point], the peak or highest point, such as the peak of intensity of a uterine contraction during labor.

acne /ak'nē/, a chronic disorder of the hair follicles and sebaceous glands characterized by pimple outbreaks, cysts, infected abscesses, and sometimes scarring. Characteristic lesions include open (blackhead) and closed (whitehead) comedones, inflammatory papules, pustules, and nodules.

acne atrophica /atrof'ikə/, a skin disorder characterized by small scars or pits left by an earlier occurrence of acne vulgaris.

acne cachecticorum, an eruption or irritation of the skin that may occur in patients who are very weak and debilitated. It is characterized by soft, mildly infiltrated pustular lesions.

acne conglobata /kon'glōbā'tə/, a severe form of acne with abscess, cyst, scar, and keloid formation.

acneform /ak'nifôrm/, resembling acne.

acneform drug eruption, any of various skin reactions to a drug characterized by papules and pustules resembling acne.

acne fulminans, severe scarring acne in teenage males, which may be accompanied by fever, polyarthralgia, crusted ulcerative lesions, weight loss, anemia, arthritis, and blood disorders.

acnegenic /ak'nijen'ik/ [Gk, akme + genein, to produce], causing or producing acne.

acne keloid [Gk, akme, point, kelis, spot, eidos, form], an acneform disorder in which secondary pyogenic infection in and around pilosebaceous structures results in keloidal scarring. It is manifested as persistent folliculitis of the back of the neck associated with occlusion of the follicular orifices.

acne medicamentosa, any type of acne resulting from a reaction to medication, such as to a steroid or the salt of a halogen.

acne necrotica miliaris, a rare, chronic type of pruritic, pustular folliculitis of the scalp, occurring mostly in adults and characterized by tiny pustules.

acne neonatorum, a skin condition of newborns caused by sebaceous gland hyperplasia and characterized by the localized formation of grouped comedones or papules on the nose, cheeks, and forehead.

acne papulosa, a common skin condition in which comedones develop moderately inflamed papules. It is considered a papular form of acne vulgaris.

acne pustulosa, a form of acne in which the predominant lesions are pustular and may result in scarring.

acne urticaria /ur'tiker'ē·ə/, a form of acne marked by papules that are predominantly edematous and wheal-like and that have been aggravated by scratching.

ACNM, abbreviation for American College of Nurse-Midwives.

ACOEM, abbreviation for **American College of Occupational and Environmental Medicine.**

ACOG, abbreviation for **American College of Obstetricians and Gynecologists.**

acognosia /ak'ognō'zhə/, a knowledge of remedies.

acorea /ā'kôrē'ə/ [Gk, a, without, kore, pupil], an absence of the pupil of the eye.

acoria /akôr'ē·ə/ [Gk, a, without, koros, satiety], a condition characterized by constant hunger and eating, even when the appetite is small.

acorn-tipped catheter, a flexible catheter with an acorn-shaped tip used in various diagnostic procedures, especially in urology.

acousma pl. **acousmas, acousmata** /əkooz'mə/ [Gk, akousma, something heard], a hallucinatory impression of strange sounds.

acoustic /əkoos'tik/ [Gk, akouein, to hear], pertaining to sound or hearing.

acoustic apparatus, the various components of the sense of hearing.

acoustic cavitation, a potential biologic effect of ultrasonography, marked by large-amplitude oscillations of microscopic gas bubbles.

acoustic center, the portion of the brain, in the temporal lobe of the cerebrum, in which the sense of hearing is located.

acoustic-immittance audiometry, audiologic testing used to evaluate the status of the external and middle ears and of the acoustic reflex arc. It includes tympanometry, static-compliance testing, and acoustic reflex measures.

acoustic impedance, interference with the passage of sound waves by objects in the path of those waves. It equals the velocity of sound in a medium multiplied by the density of the medium. Testing middle ear acoustic impedance is part of audiologic evaluation batteries used to detect middle ear problems.

acoustic meatus [Gk, akoustikos, hearing; L, meatus, a passage], the external or internal canal of the ear.

acoustic microscope, a microscope in which the object being viewed is scanned with sound waves and its image reconstructed with light waves.

acoustic neuroma, a benign unilateral or bilateral tumor that develops from the vestibulocochlear nerve and grows within the auditory canal. Depending on the location and size of the lesion, tinnitus, progressive hearing loss, headache, facial numbness, papilledema, dizziness, and an unsteady gait may result.

acoustic reflex, a contraction of the stapedius and tensor tympani muscles in the middle ear in response to a loud sound. The muscle contractions pull the stapes out of the oval window and thus protect the inner ear from damage caused by loud noise. Acoustic reflexes are usually elevated or absent in cases of conductive or neural hearing loss and present at normal or lower levels in the case of cochlear (inner ear) hearing loss.

acoustics /əkōōs′tiks/ [Gk, *akoustikos*, hearing], the science of sound.

acoustic shadow, in an ultrasound image, the absence of echoes produced by the presence of dense material, such as calculi, which impede the transmission of sound waves.

acoustic trauma, a sudden loss of hearing, partial or complete, caused by an extremely loud noise, a severe blow to the head, or other trauma. It may be temporary or permanent.

acoustooptics /əkōōs′tō·op′tiks/, a field of physics that studies the generation of light waves by ultra high-frequency sound waves.

ACP, 1. abbreviation for *American College of Pathologists*. **2.** abbreviation for **American College of Physicians. 3.** abbreviation for **American College of Prosthodontists.**

acquired /əkwī′ərd/ [L, *acquirere*, to obtain], pertaining to a characteristic, condition, or disease originating after birth, not caused by hereditary or developmental factors but by a reaction to environmental influences outside of the organism.

acquired cystic kidney disease, the development of cysts in a formerly noncystic kidney during end-stage renal disease.

acquired hypogammaglobulinemia [L, *acquirere,* to obtain; Gk, *hypo,* a deficiency, *gamma,* third letter of Greek alphabet; L, *globulus,* small globe; Gk, *haima,* blood], an acquired deficiency of the gamma globulin blood fraction.

acquired immunity, any form of immunity that is not innate and is obtained during life. It may be naturally or artificially acquired and actively or passively induced. Naturally acquired immunity is obtained by the development of antibodies resulting from an attack of infectious disease or by the transmission of antibodies from the mother through the placenta to the fetus or to the infant through colostrum and breast milk. Artificially acquired immunity is obtained by vaccination or by the injection of immune globulin.

acquired immunodeficiency syndrome (AIDS), a syndrome involving a defect in cell-mediated immunity that has a long incubation period, follows a protracted and debilitating course, is manifested by various opportunistic infections, and without treatment has a poor prognosis. The disorder originally was found in homosexual men and IV drug users but now occurs increasingly among heterosexual men and women and children of those with the disease.

acquired pellicle, an acellular film composed of salivary glycoproteins that closely and firmly adheres to the oral cavity. It is distinct from bacterial plaque, which is cellular and loosely adhered to the teeth until calcified into calculus.

acquired sterility [L, *acquirere,* to obtain, *sterilis,* barren], the failure to conceive after once bearing a child.

acquired trait [L, *acquirere,* to obtain, *trahere,* to draw], a physical characteristic that is not inherited but may be an effect of the environment or of a somatic mutation.

ACR, abbreviation for **American College of Radiology.**

acral /ak′rəl/ [Gk, *akron,* extremity], pertaining to an extremity or apex.

acral erythema, erythema localized to the palms and soles, as in hand-foot syndrome.

Acremonium /ak′rē-mo′ne-um/, a genus of Fungi imperfecti of the former class Hyphomycetes. Some species produce cephalosporin antibiotics. Formerly called *Cephalosporium.*

acrid /ak′rid/ [L, *acris,* sharp], sharp or pungent, bitter and unpleasant to the smell or taste.

acridine /ak′ridēn/, a dibenzopyridine compound used in the synthesis of dyes and drugs.

acrimony /ak′rəmō′nē/ [L, *acrimonia,* pungency], a quality of bitterness, harshness, or sharpness.

acrivastine /ak′rivas′tēn/, a nonsedating antihistamine used in the treatment of hay fever. It is administered orally.

acrocentric /ak′rōsen′trik/ [Gk, *akron,* extremity, *kentron,* center], pertaining to a chromosome in which the centromere is located near one of the ends so that the arms of the chromosome are extremely uneven in length.

acrocephalopolysyndactyly [*acrocephaly* + *polysyndactyly*], any of several inherited disorders characterized by a peaked cranium and webbed fingers and toes along with extra fingers or toes.

acrocephalosyndactyly /ak′rōsef′əlōsin dak′tilē/ [*acrocephaly* + *syndactyly*], any of a group of autosomal dominant disorders in which premature fusion of the cranium results in a conical deformity of the skull. Webbed fingers and toes are also present. The term is often used alone to denote **Apert's syndrome.**

acrochordon /ak′rōkôr′don/, a benign, pedunculated growth commonly occurring on the eyelids, neck, axilla, or groin.

acrodermatitis /-dur′mətī′tis/ [Gk, *akron* + *derma,* skin, *itis,* inflammation], inflammation of the skin of the hands and feet caused by a parasitic mite belonging to the order Acarina.

acrodermatitis enteropathica /en′tərōpath′ikə/, a rare, chronic disease of infants characterized by vesicles and bullae of the skin and mucous membranes, alopecia, diarrhea, and failure to thrive.

acrodynia /ak′rōdin′ē·ə/ [Gk, *akron* + *odyne,* pain], a disease occurring in infants and young children in which mercury poisoning is strongly implicated as the cause. Symptoms include edema, pruritus, generalized rash, pink coloration of the extremities, scarlet coloration of the cheeks and nose, swollen and painful extremities, cold and clammy skin, profuse sweating, digestive disturbances, photophobia, polyneuritis, extreme irritability alternating with periods of listlessness and apathy, and failure to thrive.

acroesthesia /ak′rō·esthē′zhə/ [Gk, *akron, aisthesis,* sensation], a condition of increased sensitivity or pain in the hands or feet.

acrokeratosis verruciformis /ak′rōker′ətō′sis/, a skin disorder characterized by the appearance of flat wartlike lesions on the dorsum of the hands and feet and occasionally on the wrists, forearms, and knees.

acrokinesis /-kīnē′sis/ [Gk, *akron,* extremity, *kinesis,* motion], a state in which the limbs possess an abnormally wide ROM.

acromegalic eunuchoidism /-məgal′ik/, a rare disorder characterized by genital atrophy and the development of female secondary sex characteristics, occurring in men with advanced acromegaly caused by a tumor in the anterior pituitary gland.

acromegaly /ak′rəmeg′əlē/ [Gk, *akron* + *megas,* great], a chronic metabolic condition in adults caused by oversecretion of growth hormones by the pituitary gland. It is characterized by gradual, marked soft tissue enlargement and widening and thickening of skeletal bones in the face, jaw, hands, and feet. Complications from increased growth hormone levels include atherosclerosis, peripheral neuropathy, hypertension, hyperglycemia, airway obstruction, cardiomyopathy, and visceromegaly involving the salivary glands, liver, spleen, and kidneys. Treatment normally includes radiation, pharmacologic agents, or surgery, often involving partial resection of the pituitary gland. —**acromegalic,** *adj.*

acromicria /ak′rəmik′rē·ə/, an anomaly characterized by abnormally small hands and feet. The person may also possess unusually small facial features.

acromioclavicular articulation /-mī′ōkla vik′yələr/, the gliding joint between the acromial end of the clavicle and the medial margin of the acromion of the scapula. It forms the highest part of the shoulder.

acromiocoracoid /-kôr′əkoid/, pertaining to the acromion and coracoid processes.

acromiohumeral /-hyōō′mərəl/, pertaining to the acromion and the humerus.

acromion /əkrō′mē·ən/ [Gk, *akron* + *omos,* shoulder], the lateral extension of the spine of the scapula, forming the highest point of the shoulder and connecting with the clavicle at a small oval surface in the middle of the spine. It gives attachment to the deltoideus and trapezius muscles.— **acromial,** *adj.*

acromioscapular /-skap′yələr/, pertaining to the acromion and the scapula.

acroosteolysis /ak′rō·os′tē·ol′isis/, destruction of the digit tips, including the bone, usually caused by vasospasm. It is characterized by Raynaud's phenomenon, loss of bone tissue in the hands, and sensitivity to cold temperatures.

acroparesthesia /ak′rōpar′isthē′zhə/ [Gk, *akron* + *para,* near, *aisthesis,* feeling], **1.** an extreme sensitivity at the tips of the extremities of the body, caused by nerve compression in the affected area or by polyneuritis. **2.** a disease characterized by tingling, numbness, and stiffness in the extremities, especially in the fingers, hands, and forearms.

acrophobia [Gk, *akron* + *phobos,* fear], a pathologic fear or dread of high places that results in extreme anxiety.

acrosomal reaction /ak′rəsō′məl/, the pattern of various chemical changes that occur in the anterior of the head of the spermatozoon in response to contact with the ovum and that lead to the sperm's penetration and fertilization of the ovum.

acrosome /ak′rəsōm′/ [Gk, *akron* + *soma,* body], the caplike structure surrounding the anterior end of the head of a spermatozoon.—**acrosomal,** *adj.*

acrotic /əkrot′ik/ [Gk, *a* + *krotos,* not beating], **1.** pertaining to the surface of the body or to the skin glands. **2.** pertaining to an absent or weak pulse.

acrylate, an anion, salt, ester, or conjugate base of acrylic acid.

acrylic acid (CH₂COOH) /əkril′ik/, a corrosive liquid used in the production of plastic materials used in medical and dental procedures.

acrylic resin base, a form made of acrylic resin molded to conform to tissues of the alveolar process, used to support teeth of a prosthesis.

acrylic resin dental cement, a cement for restoring or repairing damaged teeth.

ACS, 1. abbreviation for *American Cancer Society.* **2.** abbreviation for *American Chemical Society.* **3.** abbreviation for **American College of Surgeons. 4.** abbreviation for *anodal closing sound.* **5.** abbreviation for **acute confusional state. 6.** abbreviation for *Association of Clinical Scientists.* **7.** abbreviation for *abdominal compartment syndrome.*

ACSM, abbreviation for *American College of Sports Medicine.*

ACTH, abbreviation for **adrenocorticotropic hormone.**

Acthar, a trademark for adrenocorticotropic hormone injection (ACTH corticotropin).

Actifed, a trademark for a fixed-combination drug containing an adrenergic vasoconstrictor (pseudoephedrine hydrochloride) and an antihistamine (triprolidine hydrochloride).

actigraph /ak′tigraf/, any instrument that records changes in the activity of a substance or an organism and produces a graphic record of the process, such as an ECG.

actin, a protein forming the thin filaments in muscle fibers that are pulled on by myosin cross-bridges to cause a muscle contraction.

acting out, the expression of intrapsychic conflict or painful emotion through overt behavior that is usually pathologic, defensive, and unconscious and that may be destructive or dangerous.

actinic /aktin′ik/ [Gk, *aktis,* ray], pertaining to radiation, such as sunlight or x-rays.

actinic burn, a burn caused by exposure to sunlight or another source of ultraviolet radiation.

actinic conjunctivitis [Gk, *aktis,* ray; L, *conjunctivus,* connecting; Gk, *itis,* inflammation], an inflammation of the conjunctiva caused by exposure to the ultraviolet radiation of sunlight or other sources, such as acetylene torches, therapeutic lamps (sun lamps), and klieg lights.

actinic dermatitis, a skin inflammation or rash resulting from exposure to sunlight, x-ray, or atomic particle radiation. Chronic or recurrent actinic dermatitis can predispose to skin cancer.

actinic keratosis, a slowly developing, localized thickening and scaling of the outer layers of the skin as a result of chronic, prolonged exposure to the sun. Treatment of this premalignant lesion includes surgical excision, cryotherapy, and topical chemotherapy.

actinism, the ability of sunlight or similar forms of radiation to produce chemical changes.

actinium (Ac), a rare, radioactive metallic element. Its atomic number is 89; its atomic mass is 227. It occurs in some ores of uranium.

Actinobacillus /ak′tinōbasil′əs/, a genus of small, gram-negative bacillus, with members that are pathogenic for humans and other animals. The species *Actinobacillus actinomycetemcomitans* is the cause of actinomycosis in humans.

Actinomyces /ak′tinōmī′sēz/, *pl.* **actinomycetes** [Gk, *aktis,* ray, *mykes,* fungus], a genus of anaerobic or facultative anaerobic, gram-positive bacteria. Species that may cause disease in humans, such as *Actinomyces israelii,* are normally present in the mouth and throat.

actinomycin A, the first of a group of chromopeptide antibiotic agents derived from soil bacteria. Most are derivatives of phenoxazine and contain actinocin. They are generally active against gram-positive and gram-negative bacteria and some fungi. Because of their cytotoxic properties, they are effective for certain types of neoplasms.

actinomycin B, an antibiotic antineoplastic agent derived from *Actinomyces antibioticus.*

actinomycosis /ak′tinōmīkō′sis/, a chronic bacterial disease most frequently located in the jaw, thorax, or abdomen. It is characterized by deep, lumpy abscesses that extrude a thin, granular pus through multiple sinuses. The most common causative organism in humans is *Actinomyces israelii,* a normal inhabitant of the bowel and mouth. Disease occurs after tissue damage, usually in the presence of another infectious organism.

actinomyosin, the complex consisting of parallel threads of actin and myosin proteins that constitutes muscle fibers. It is responsible for the contraction and relaxation of muscle. When a muscle fiber contracts, the two proteins slide past each other, shortening the fiber while increasing its apparent thickness.

actinotherapy, the use of ultraviolet light, other parts of the spectrum of the sun's rays, or x-rays to treat various disorders, particularly skin diseases.

action, activity used to carry out a function or produce an effect.

action level, the level of concentration at which an undesirable or toxic component of a food is considered dangerous enough to public health to warrant government prohibition of the sale of that food. The U.S. Food and Drug Administration tests foods for action levels.

action potential, an electric impulse consisting of a self-propagating series of polarizations and depolarizations, transmitted across the plasma membranes of a nerve fiber during the transmission of a nerve impulse and across the plasma membranes of a muscle cell during contraction or another activity.

action tremor [L, *agere,* to do, *tremor,* shaking], a slight shaking that occurs or is evident during voluntary movements of the upper extremities.

Activase, a trademark for a commercial form of tissue plasminogen activator (alteplase recombinant).

activated charcoal, a general-purpose emergency antidote and a powerful pharmaceutic adsorbent prescribed in the treatment of acute poisoning and the control of flatulence.

activated clotting time (ACT) test, a blood test primarily used to measure the effect of heparin as an anticoagulant during cardiac angioplasty, hemodialysis, and cardiopulmonary bypass surgery (CPB). It can also be used to monitor the dose of protamine sulfate required to reverse the effect of heparin.

activated prothrombin complex concentrate (APCC), antiinhibitor coagulant complex.

activating enzyme, an enzyme that promotes or sustains an activity, such as catalyzing the combination of amino acids to form peptides or proteins.

activation /ak′tivā′shən/, **1.** the promotion or production of an activity, such as the generation of a catalyst, protein synthesis, or enzymatic function. **2.** the treatment of sewage using a combination of bacteria and air.

activation energy [L, *activus,* active], the energy required to convert reactants to transition-state species or an activated complex that will spontaneously proceed to products.

activator /ak′tivā′tər/, **1.** a substance, force, or device that stimulates activity in another substance or structure, especially a substance that activates an enzyme. **2.** a substance that stimulates the development of an anatomic structure in the embryo. **3.** an internal secretion of the pancreas. **4.** an apparatus for making substances radioactive, such as a cyclotron or neutron generator. **5.** (in dentistry) a removable orthodontic appliance that functions as a passive transmitter and stimulator of the perioral muscles.

active anaphylaxis [Gk, *ana,* up, *phylaxis,* protection], hypersensitivity caused by the reaction of the immune system to the injection of a foreign protein.

active assisted exercise [L, *activus*], the movement of the body or any of its parts primarily through the individual's own efforts but accompanied by the aid of a member of the health care team or some device such as an exercise machine.

active carrier [OFr, *carier*], a person without signs or symptoms of an infectious disease who carries the causal microorganisms and can transmit the disease to others.

active electrode [Gk, *elektron,* amber, *hodos,* way], an electrode that is applied at a specific point to produce stimulation in a concentrated area in electrotherapy or electrocautery.

active euthanasia, the ending of life by the deliberate administration of drugs.

active exercise, a repetitive movement of a part of the body as a result of voluntary contraction and relaxation of the controlling muscles.

active expiration [L, *expirare,* to breathe out], a forced exhalation, using the abdominal wall, internal intracostal muscles, and diaphragm.

active hyperemia [L, *activus;* Gk, *hyper,* excessive, *haima,* blood], the increased flow of blood into a particular body part, caused by an increase in vasoactive metabolites.

active immunity, a form of long-term, acquired immunity. It protects the body against a new infection as the result of antibodies that develop naturally after an initial infection or artificially after a vaccination.

active labor [L, *activus,* active, *labor,* work], the normal progress of the birth process, including uterine contractions, full dilation of the cervix, and descent of the fetus into the birth canal.

active listening[1], the act of alert intentional hearing, interpretation, and demonstration of an interest in what a person has to say through verbal signal, nonverbal gestures, and body language.

active listening[2], a nursing intervention from the Nursing Interventions Classification (NIC) defined as attending closely to and attaching significance to a patient's verbal and nonverbal messages.

active matrix array (AMA), a large-area integrated circuit that consists of millions of identical semiconductor elements and acts as the flat-panel image receptor in digital radiographic and fluoroscopic systems.

active movement, the movement of parts of the body as a result of voluntary effort.

active-passive, (in psychiatry) a concept that characterizes persons as either actively involved in shaping events or passively reacting to them.

active play, any activity from which one derives amusement, entertainment, enjoyment, or satisfaction by taking a participatory rather than a passive role.

active range of motion (AROM), the range of movement through which a patient can actively (without assistance) move a joint using the adjacent muscles.

active resistance exercise, the movement or exertion of the body or any of its parts performed totally through the individual's own efforts against a resisting force.

active resistance training (ART), a conditioning or rehabilitation program designed to enhance a patient's muscular strength, power, and endurance through progressive active resistance exercises and muscle overloading.

active sensitization [L, *agere,* to do, *sentire,* to feel], the condition that results when a specific antigen is injected into a person known to be susceptible to it.

active site, the place on the surface of an enzyme where its catalytic action occurs.

active specific immunotherapy, a therapy that attempts to stimulate specific antitumor responses with tumor-associated antigens as the immunizing materials.

active transport, the movement of materials across the membranes and epithelial layers of a cell by means of chemical activity that allows the cell to admit otherwise impermeable molecules against a concentration gradient. Expediting active transport are carrier molecules within the cell that bind and enclose themselves to incoming molecules. Active transport is the means by which the cell absorbs glucose and other substances needed to sustain life and health.

activities of daily living (ADL) /aktiv'itēz/, the activities usually performed in the course of a normal day in the person's life, such as eating, toileting, dressing, bathing, or brushing the teeth. The ability to perform ADL may be compromised by a variety of causes, including chronic illnesses and accidents. The limitation may be temporary or permanent; rehabilitation may involve relearning the skills or learning new ways to accomplish ADL.

activity, the action of an enzyme on an amount of substrate that is converted to product per unit of time under defined conditions.

activity coefficient, a proportionality constant, γ, relating activity, α, to concentration, expressed in the equation $\alpha = \gamma c$.

activity theory, a concept proposed by Robert J. Havighurst (1900–1990) that continuing activities from middle age promotes well-being and satisfaction in aging.

activity therapy, a nursing intervention from the Nursing Interventions Classification (NIC) defined as prescription of and assistance with specific physical, cognitive, social, and spiritual activities to increase the range, frequency, or duration of an individual's (or group's) activity.

activity tolerance[1], the type and amount of exercise a patient may be able to perform without undue exertion or possible injury.

activity tolerance[2], a nursing outcome from the Nursing Outcomes Classification (NOC) defined as physiologic response to energy-consuming movements with daily activities.

actual cautery /ak'chŏŏ-əl/ [L, *actus,* act], the application of heat, rather than a chemical substance, in the destruction of tissue.

actual charge, the amount actually charged or billed by a practitioner for a service. The actual charge usually is not the same as that paid for the service by an insurance plan.

actualization, 1. the fulfillment of a potential, as by a person who may develop capabilities through experience and education. **2.** to fulfill the highest level of human needs based on Maslow's hierarchy of needs.—**actualize,** *v.*

acuity /əkyōō'itē/ [L, *acuere,* to sharpen], the clearness or sharpness of perception.

acuminate /əkyōō'mināt/ [L, *acuminatus*], **1.** sharp-pointed. **2.** to sharpen something or to make it tapered.

acupressure[1] /ak'yəpresh'ər/ [L, *acus,* needle, *pressura,* pressure], a therapeutic technique of applying digital pressure in a specified way on designated points on the body to relieve pain, produce anesthesia, or regulate a body function.

acupressure[2], a nursing intervention from the Nursing Interventions Classification (NIC) defined as application of firm, sustained pressure to special points on the body to decrease pain, produce relaxation, and prevent or reduce nausea.

acupressure needle, 1. a slender pointed device used for insertion and manipulation at acupressure points to improve health and well-being. **2.** any of several needles inserted near a source of bleeding to help control blood loss. The needles exert pressure on tissues adjacent to the damaged vessel.

acupuncture /ak'yəpunk'chər/ [L, *acus* + *punctura,* puncture], a traditional Chinese method of producing analgesia or altering the function of a body system by inserting fine, wire-thin needles into the skin at specific sites on the body along a series of lines, or channels, called meridians. Acupuncture is highly effective in treating both acute and chronic pain associated with multiple causes.

acupuncture point, one of many discrete points on the skin along the several meridians, or chains of points of the body. Stimulation of any of the various points may induce an increase or a decrease in function or sensation in an area or a system of the body.

acus /ā′kəs/, any needle-like structure.

acute /əkyōōt′/ [L, *acutus,* sharp], **1.** (of a disease or disease symptoms) beginning abruptly with marked intensity or sharpness, then subsiding after a relatively short period. **2.** sharp or severe.

acute abdomen, an abnormal condition characterized by the acute onset of severe pain within the abdominal cavity. An acute abdomen requires immediate evaluation and diagnosis because it may indicate a condition that calls for surgical intervention. Information about the onset, duration, character, location, and symptoms associated with the pain is critical in making an accurate diagnosis.

acute abscess, a recently formed collection of pus with little or no fibrosis in the wall of the cavity. It is accompanied by localized inflammation, pain, pyrexia, and swelling.

acute air trapping, a condition of bronchiolar obstruction that results in early airway closure and trapping of air distal to the affected bronchiole. Air trapping can occur in persons with COPD or asthma.

acute alcoholism, intoxication resulting from excessive consumption of alcoholic beverages. The syndrome is temporary and is characterized by depression of the higher nerve centers, causing impaired motor control, stupor, lack of coordination, and often nausea, dehydration, headache, and other physical symptoms.

acute angle [L, *acutus + angulus*], any angle of less than 90 degrees.

acute anicteric hepatitis [Gk, *a,* without, *ikteros,* jaundice, *hēpar,* liver, *itis,* inflammation], an acute hepatitis not accompanied by jaundice.

acute ascending myelitis [L, *ascendere,* to go up; Gk, *myelos,* marrow, *itis,* inflammation], a severe inflammation of the spinal cord that extends progressively upward with corresponding interference in nerve functions.

acute ascending spinal paralysis, a severe progressive spinal paralysis that spreads upward toward the brain.

acute atrophic paralysis [Gk, *a +trophe,* without nourishment, *paralyein,* to be palsied], a severe poliomyelitis involving the anterior horns of the spinal cord. It results first in flaccid paralysis of involved muscle groups and later in atrophy of those muscles.

acute care, a pattern of health care in which a patient is treated for a brief but severe episode of illness, for the sequelae of an accident or other trauma, or during recovery from surgery. Acute care is usually given in a hospital by specialized personnel using complex and sophisticated technical equipment and materials, and it may involve intensive care, critical care, or emergency care.

acute catarrhal sinusitis [Gk, *kata + rhoia,* flow; L, *sinus,* hollow], an inflammation that involves the nose and sinuses.

acute childhood leukemia, a progressive, malignant disease of the blood-forming tissues. It is characterized by the uncontrolled proliferation of immature leukocytes and their precursors, particularly in the bone marrow, spleen, and lymph nodes. It is the most frequent cancer in children, with a peak onset occurring between 2 and 5 years of age. Acute leukemia is classified according to cell type: acute lymphoid leukemia (ALL) includes lymphatic, lymphocytic, lymphoblastic, and lymphoblastoid types; acute nonlymphoid leukemia (ANLL) includes granulocytic, myelocytic, monocytic, myelogenous, monoblastic, and monomyeloblastic types (the myelocytic and monocytic series are abbreviated AML). ALL is predominantly a disease of childhood, whereas AML and ANLL occur in all age groups.

acute circulatory failure /sur′kyələtôr′ē/, a drop in heart output resulting from cardiac or noncardiac causes and leading to tissue hypoxia. If not controlled immediately, the condition usually progresses to one of shock syndrome.

acute circumscribed edema [L, *circum,* around, *scribere,* to draw; Gk, *oidema,* swelling], a localized edema, often associated with an inflammatory lesion or process.

acute confusional state (ACS), a form of delirium caused by interference with the metabolic or other biochemical processes essential for normal brain functioning. Symptoms may include disturbances in cognition and levels of awareness, short-term memory deficit, retrograde and anterograde amnesia, and disturbances in orientation, accompanied by restlessness, apprehension, irritability, and apathy. The condition may be associated with an acute physiologic state, delirium, toxic psychosis, or acute brain syndrome.

acute confusion level, a nursing outcome from the Nursing Outcomes Classification (NOC) defined as severity of disturbance in consciousness and cognition that develops over a short period of time.

acute coronary syndrome, a classification encompassing clinical presentations ranging from unstable angina through MIs not characterized by alterations in Q waves. The classification sometimes also includes MIs characterized by altered Q waves.

acute delirium, an episode of acute organic reaction that is sudden, severe, and transient.

acute diarrhea [Gk, *dia + rhein,* to flow], a sudden severe attack of diarrhea.

acute diffuse peritonitis [L, *diffundere,* to pour out; Gk, *peri,* near, *tenein,* to stretch, *itis,* inflammation], an acute widespread attack of peritonitis affecting most of the peritoneum and usually caused by infection or by a perforation of an abdominal organ. It is also a complication of peritoneal dialysis.

acute disease, a disease characterized by a relatively sudden onset of symptoms that are usually severe. An episode of acute disease results in recovery to a state comparable to the patient's condition of health and activity before the disease, in passage into a chronic phase, or in death.

acute disseminated encephalomyelitis (ADEM), an acute disease of the brain and spinal cord with variable symptoms. It is thought to be an allergic reaction or immune attack on the myelin tissue after a viral infection, such as measles, or, less often, after vaccination for measles, mumps, or rubella. Early symptoms may include fever, headache, vomiting, and drowsiness and progress to seizures, coma, and paralysis. It is often misdiagnosed as a severe attack of MS. Frequently patients who recover experience neurologic disorders.

acute diverticulitis, a sudden severe, painful disorder of the intestinal tract, resulting from inflammation of one or more diverticula in the wall of the bowel.

acute epiglottitis, a severe, rapidly progressing bacterial infection of the upper respiratory tract that occurs in young children, primarily between 2 and 7 years of age. It is characterized by sore throat, croupy stridor, and inflamed epiglottis, which may cause sudden respiratory obstruction and possibly death. The infection is generally caused by *Haemophilus influenzae* type b, although streptococci may occasionally be the causative agents. Transmission occurs via infection with airborne particles or contact with infected secretions.

acute fatigue, a sudden onset of physical and mental exhaustion or weariness, particularly after a period of severe exertion. Physical factors usually include an accumulation of waste products of muscle contractions.

acute fibrinous pericarditis [L, *fibra,* fibrous; Gk, *peri,* near, *kardia,* heart, *itis,* inflammation], acute inflammation of the endothelial cells of the pericardium with fibers extending into the pericardial sac.

acute goiter [L, *guttur,* throat], a sudden enlargement of the thyroid gland.

acute hallucinatory paranoia, a form of psychosis in which hallucinations are combined with delusions of paranoia.

acute hemorrhagic conjunctivitis, a highly contagious eye disease usually caused by enterovirus type 70 but also by Coxsackievirus A24. Clinical features include sudden onset of severe ocular pain, blurred vision, photophobia, subconjunctival hemorrhage, chemosis, and profuse watery discharge from the eye. Spontaneous improvement occurs within 2 to 4 days and is complete by 7 to 10 days.

acute hemorrhagic pancreatitis [Gk, *haima,* blood, *rhegnynei,* to gush, *pan,* all, *kreas,* flesh], a potentially fatal inflammation of the pancreas characterized by bleeding, necrosis, and paralysis of the digestive tract.

acute hypoxia, a sudden or rapid depletion in available oxygen at the tissue level. The condition may result from asphyxia, airway obstruction, acute hemorrhage, blockage of the alveoli by edema or infectious exudate, or abrupt cardiorespiratory failure. Clinical signs may include hypoventilation or hyperventilation to the point of air hunger and neurologic deficits ranging from headache and confusion to LOC.

acute illness, any illness characterized by signs and symptoms that are of rapid onset and short duration. It may be severe and impair normal functioning of the patient.

acute infectious paralysis [L, *inficere,* to stain; Gk, *paralyein,* to be palsied], acute disease caused by a poliovirus. Symptoms of minor disease include fever, headache, vomiting, sore throat, and frequently stiff back and neck. Major disease includes CNS involvement, pleocytosis in spinal fluid, and paralysis.

acute intermittent porphyria (AIP), an autosomal-dominant, genetically transmitted metabolic hepatic disorder characterized by acute attacks of neurologic dysfunction that can be started by environmental or endogenous factors. Any part of the nervous system can be affected, and an initial common effect is mild to severe abdominal pain. Other effects can include tachycardia, hypertension, hyponatremia, peripheral neuropathy, and organic brain dysfunction marked by seizures, coma, hallucinations, and respiratory paralysis.

acute lobar pneumonia, a form of pneumonia characterized by lobar distribution of the consolidation of the serofibrous fluid exuded by the alveoli. The condition results from an infection by a virulent type of *Streptococcus pneumoniae.* The onset is sudden. Symptoms include pleuritic chest pain, dry cough, and rust-colored sputum.

acute lymphocytic leukemia (ALL), a hematologic, malignant disease characterized by large numbers of lymphoblasts in the bone marrow, circulating blood, lymph nodes, spleen, liver, and other organs. The number of normal blood cells is usually reduced. More than three fourths of the cases in the United States occur in children, with the greatest number diagnosed between 2 and 5 years of age. The disease has a sudden onset and rapid progression marked by fever, pallor, anorexia, fatigue, anemia, hemorrhage, bone pain, splenomegaly, and recurrent infection.

acute myelitis, a sudden, severe inflammation of the spinal cord.

acute myeloid leukemia (AML), a malignant neoplasm of blood-forming tissues characterized by the uncontrolled proliferation of immature granular leukocytes that usually have azurophilic Auer rods in their cytoplasm. Typical symptoms are spongy bleeding gums, anemia, fatigue, fever, dyspnea, moderate splenomegaly, joint and bone pains, and repeated infections. AML occurs most frequently in adolescents and young adults. The risk of the disease is increased among people who have been exposed to massive doses of radiation and who have certain blood dyscrasias.

acute myocardial infarction (AMI) [L, *acutus;* Gk, *mys,* muscle, *kardia,* heart; L, *infarcire,* to stuff], the early critical stage of necrosis of heart muscle tissue caused by blockage of a coronary artery. It is characterized by elevated S-T segments in the reflecting leads and elevated levels of cardiac enzymes.

acute necrotizing hemorrhagic encephalopathy, a degenerative brain disease, characterized by marked edema, numerous minute hemorrhages, necrosis of blood vessel walls, demyelination of nerve fibers, and infiltration of the meninges with neutrophils, lymphocytes, and histiocytes. Typical signs are severe headache, fever, and vomiting; seizures may occur, and the patient may rapidly lose consciousness.

acute nephritis, a sudden inflammation of the kidney, characterized by albuminuria and hematuria, but without edema or urine retention. It affects children most

commonly and usually involves only a few glomeruli.

acute nicotine poisoning [L, *Nicotiana, potio,* drink], a toxic effect produced by nicotine. Characteristics include burning sensation in the mouth, nausea and vomiting, diarrhea, palpitations, salivation, agitation, respiratory depression, and convulsions that may lead to death.

acute nongonorrheal vulvitis [L, *non,* not; Gk, *gone,* seed, *rhoia,* flow; L, *vulva,* wrapper; Gk, *itis,* inflammation], an inflammation of the vulva resulting from chafing of the lips of the vulva, accumulation of sebaceous material, atopic reactions, local infections, or other causes that are nonvenereal.

acute nonspecific pericarditis [Gk, *peri,* around, *kardia,* heart, *itis,* inflammation], inflammation of the pericardium, with or without effusion. It often is associated with myocarditis but usually resolves without complications.

acute pain, severe pain, as may follow surgery or trauma or accompany MI or other conditions and diseases. Acute pain occurring in the first 24 to 48 hours after surgery is often difficult to relieve, even with drugs. Acute pain in individuals with orthopedic problems originates from the periosteum, the joint surfaces, and the arterial walls. Muscle pain associated with bone surgery results from muscle ischemia rather than muscle tension.

acute pancreatitis [Gk, *pan,* all, *kreas,* flesh, *itis,* inflammation], a sudden inflammation of the pancreas caused by autodigestion and marked by symptoms of acute abdomen and escape of pancreatic enzymes into the pancreatic tissues. The condition is associated with biliary disease or alcoholism.

acute pleurisy, inflammation of the pleura, often as a result of lung disease. It is characterized by irritation without recognizable pleural effusion and is localized.

acute primary myocarditis, 1. an inflammation of the heart muscle, most commonly caused by a bacterial infection initiated locally or carried through the bloodstream. 2. a severe inflammation of the heart muscle associated with degeneration of the muscle fibers and release of leukocytes into the interstitial tissues.

acute promyelocytic leukemia (AProL), a malignancy of the blood-forming tissues, characterized by the proliferation of promyelocytes and blast cells with distinctive Auer rods. Symptoms include severe bleeding and bruises. The patient may also have a low fibrinogen level and platelet count.

acute psychosis, one of a group of disorders in which ego functioning is either impaired or inhibited. The ability to process reality-based information is diminished and disordered. The cause may be a known psychologic abnormality. In situations in which a physiologic abnormality is not recognized, the functional impairment is still clearly present.

acute pyogenic arthritis, an acute bacterial infection of one or more joints, caused by trauma or a penetrating wound and occurring most frequently in children. Typical signs are pain, redness, and swelling in the affected joint; muscular spasms in the area; chills; fever; sweating; and leukocytosis.

acute rejection [L, *rejicere,* to throw back], after organ transplantation, the rapid reaction against allograph or xenograph tissue that is incompatible. It often occurs over a week after treatment, during which the immune response increases in intensity.

acute renal failure (ARF), renal failure of sudden onset, such as from physical trauma, infection, inflammation, or toxicity. Symptoms include uremia and usually oliguria or anuria, with hyperkalemia and pulmonary edema. Three types are distinguished: prerenal, associated with poor systemic perfusion and decreased renal blood flow; intrarenal, associated with disease of the renal parenchyma; and postrenal, resulting from obstruction of urine flow out of the kidneys.

acute respiratory failure (ARF) [L, *acutus + respirare,* respiratory, *fallere,* to deceive], a sudden inability of the lungs to maintain normal respiratory function. The condition may be caused by an obstruction in the airways or by failure of the lungs to exchange gases in the alveoli.

acute rheumatic arthritis, joint inflammation that occurs during the acute phase of rheumatic fever.

acute schizophrenia, a disorder consisting of various degrees of psychosis, characterized by the sudden onset of personality disorganization. Symptoms include disturbances in thought, mood, and behavior. Positive symptoms include delusions, which may be bizarre in nature; hallucinations, especially auditory; disorganized speech; inappropriate affect; and disorganized behavior. Negative symptoms include flat affect, avolition, alogia, and anhedonia. Episodes appear suddenly in persons whose previous behavior has been relatively normal and are usually of short duration. Recurrent episodes are common, and in some instances a more chronic type of the disorder may develop.

acute secondary myocarditis, a sudden, severe inflammation of the heart muscle, resulting from a disease of the endocardium or pericardium or a generalized infection.

acute septic myocarditis [Gk, *septikos,* putrid, *mys,* muscle, *kardia,* heart, *itis,* inflammation], a severe inflammation of the myocardium associated with pus formation, necrosis, and abscess formation.

acute suppurative arthritis [L, *suppurare,* to form pus], a form of arthritis characterized by an invasion of the joint space by pyogenic organisms and the formation of pus in the joint cavity. It most commonly affects children from 5 to 10 years of age.

acute suppurative sinusitis [L, *acutus,* sharp, *suppurare,* to form pus, *sinus,* hollow; Gk, *itis,* inflammation], a purulent infection of the sinuses. Symptoms are pain over the inflamed area, headache, chills, and fever.

acute tonsillitis [L, *acutus,* sharp, *tonsilla;* Gk, *itis,* inflammation], an inflammation of one or both tonsils associated with a catarrhal exudate over the tonsil or the discharge of caseous or suppurative material from the tonsillar crypts.

acute toxicity, the harmful effect of a toxic agent that manifests itself in seconds, minutes, hours, or days after ingestion or exposure.

acute transverse myelitis, an inflammation of the entire thickness of the spinal cord, affecting both the sensory and motor nerves. It can develop rapidly and is accompanied by necrosis and neurologic deficit that commonly persist after recovery. Patients in whom spastic reflexes develop soon after the onset of this disease are more likely to recover. This disorder may result from a variety of causes, such as MS, measles, pneumonia, viral infections, and the ingestion of certain toxic agents.

acute tubular necrosis (ATN), acute renal failure with mild to severe damage or necrosis of tubule cells, usually as a result of either nephrotoxicity, ischemia after major surgery, trauma, severe hypovolemia, sepsis, or burns.

acute tubulointerstitial nephritis, an early stage of tubulointerstitial nephritis similar to acute pyelonephritis but with involvement farther into the renal medulla to involve the tubules.

acute urethral syndrome [Gk, *ourethra,* urethra, *syn,* together, *dromos,* course], a group of pelvic area symptoms experienced by women, including dysuria, urinary frequency, urinary tenesmus, lower back pain, and suprapubic aching and cramping. Clinical evidence of a pathogen or other factor to account for the symptoms may be absent.

acute vulvar ulcer, a nonvenereal, usually shallow lesion of the vulva, often associated with a febrile illness. Its cause is uncertain.

acyanotic /ā′sī·ənot′ik/ [Gk, *a*, not, *kyanos*, blue], lacking a blue appearance of the skin and mucous membranes.

acyanotic congenital defect, a heart defect present at birth that does not produce blue discoloration of the skin and mucous membranes under normal circumstances. However, the condition does increase the load on the pulmonary circulation and may lead to cyanosis, right ventricular failure, or other complications during physical exertion.

acyclovir /əsī′klōvir/, an antiviral agent with activity against herpesvirus types 1 and 2 and varicella zoster virus. It is prescribed topically in an ointment for the treatment of herpes simplex lesions (cold sores) and both orally and systemically (oral and IV) in other types of herpes infections.

acyesis /ā′sī·ē′sis/, **1.** the absence of pregnancy. **2.** sterility in women.

acyl /ā′sil/, an organic radical derived from an organic acid by removal of the hydroxyl group from the carboxyl group. It is represented as $R—CO—$.

acylation /as′ilā′shən/, the incorporation into a molecule of an organic compound of an acyl group.

AD, abbreviation for **Alzheimer's disease.**

a.d., abbreviation for *auris dextra.*

A/D, **1.** abbreviation for **analog-to-digital. 2.** abbreviation for *anodal duration.* **3.** abbreviation for *average deviation.*

ADA, **1.** abbreviation for *American Dental Association.* **2.** abbreviation for *American Diabetes Association.* **3.** abbreviation for *American Dietetic Association.* **4.** abbreviation for **adenosine deaminase.**

ADAA, abbreviation for *American Dental Assistants Association.*

adactyly /ādak′tilē/ [Gk, *a* + *daktylos*, not finger or toe], a congenital defect in which one or more digits of the hand or foot are missing.

Adair-Dighton syndrome [Charles Adair-Dighton, British physician, b. 1885]

Adalat, a trademark for a calcium channel blocker (NIFEdipine).

adalimumab, an antirheumatic immunomodulating agent used to treat patients older than 18 years of age with moderate to severe rheumatoid arthritis.

Adam, Evelyn (b. 1929), a Canadian nursing theorist who applied the structure of a conceptual model for nursing in her book, *Être Infirmière* in 1979 (*To Be a Nurse,* 1980). She describes the goal of nursing as maintaining or restoring the client's independence in the satisfaction of 14 fundamental needs. Each need has biologic, physiologic, and psychosocial aspects. The nurse complements and supplements the client's strength, knowledge, and will.

Adams-Stokes syndrome [Robert Adams, Irish surgeon, 1791–1875; William Stokes, Irish physician, 1804–1878], a condition characterized by sudden, recurrent episodes of loss of consciousness caused by incomplete heart block. Seizures may accompany the episodes.

adapalene /əhədap′ahəlēn/, a synthetic analog of retinoic acid used topically in the treatment of acne vulgaris.

adaptation /ad′aptā′shən/ [L, *adaptatio*, act of adapting], a change or response to stress of any kind, such as inflammation of the nasal mucosa in infectious rhinitis or increased crying in a frightened child. Adaptation may be normal, self-protective, and developmental.

adaptation model, (in nursing) a conceptual framework that focuses on the patient as an adaptive system, one in which nursing intervention is required when a deficit develops in the patient's ability to cope with the internal and external demands of the environment. These demands are classified into four groups: physiologic needs, the need for a positive self-concept, the need to perform social roles, and the need to balance dependence and independence. Nursing care is planned to promote adaptive responses to cope successfully with the current stress on the patient's well-being.

adaptation to physical disability, a nursing outcome from the Nursing Outcomes Classification (NOC) defined as adaptive response to a significant functional challenge due to a physical disability.

adapted clothing, clothing that has been modified to permit disabled persons to dress themselves with minimal difficulty.

adapter [L, *adaptatio*, the process of adjusting], a device for joining or connecting two or more parts of a system to enable it to function properly, usually with tubing.

adaptive device /adap′tiv/ [L, *adaptatio*, process of adapting; OFr, *devise*], any structure, design, instrument, contrivance, or equipment that enables a person with a disability to function independently.

adaptive hypertrophy [L, *adaptatio*, process of adapting; Gk, *hyper*, excessive, *trophe*, nourishment], a reactive increase in the amount of tissue that compensates for a loss of the same or similar tissue so that function is not impaired.

adaptive response, an appropriate reaction to an environmental demand.

ADA Seal of Acceptance, an approval given by the American Dental Association Council on Scientific Affairs to oral care products that are supported by adequate research evidence as to their safety and efficacy.

ADC, abbreviation for **AIDS-dementia complex.**

ADCC, abbreviation for **antibody-dependent cell-mediated cytotoxicity.**

ADC Van Disal /ā′dē′sē′ van dī′səl/, a term used as a mnemonic device for recalling the protocol of hospital admission orders. The letters stand for admission authorization, diagnosis, condition, vital signs, activity, drugs, instructions, special studies, allergies, laboratory tests.

ADD, abbreviation for **attention deficit disorder.**

Addams, Jane [1860–1935], an American social reformer. In Chicago in 1889 she founded Hull House, one of the first social settlements in the United States, where volunteers from many disciplines, including nursing, lived and worked in their professions. She was co-recipient of the Nobel peace prize in 1931.

adder, any of numerous venomous elapid and viperine snakes. The death adder is found in Australia and New Guinea, and the puff adder is found in Africa and Arabia.

addict /ad′ikt/ [L, addicere, to devote], a person who has become physiologically or psychologically dependent on a chemical such as alcohol or other drugs to the extent that normal social, occupational, and other responsible life functions are disrupted.

addiction /ədik′shən/, compulsive, uncontrollable dependence on a chemical substance, habit, or practice to such a degree that either the means of obtaining or ceasing use may cause severe emotional, mental, or physiologic reactions.

addictive personality /ədik′tiv/, a personality marked by traits of compulsive and habitual use of a substance or practice in an attempt to cope with psychic pain engendered by conflict and anxiety.

addisonism [Thomas Addison, London physician, 1793–1860], a condition characterized by the physical signs of Addison's disease, although loss of adrenocortical functions is not involved. The signs include an increase in bronze pigmentation of the skin and mucous membranes caused by increased levels of melanocyte-stimulating hormone, as well as general debility.

Addison's disease [Thomas Addison], a life-threatening condition caused by partial or complete failure of adrenocortical function, often resulting from autoimmune processes, infection (especially tubercular or fungal), neoplasm, or hemorrhage in the gland. All three general functions of the adrenal cortex (glucocorticoid, mineralocorticoid, and androgenic) are lost. The disease is characterized by increased bronze pigmentation of the skin and mucous membranes; weakness; decreased endurance; anorexia; dehydration; weight loss; GI disturbances; salt cravings; anxiety, depression, and other emotional distress; and decreased tolerance to physical and emotional stress. The onset is usually gradual, over a period of weeks or months. Laboratory tests reveal abnormally low blood concentrations of sodium and glucose, a greater than normal level of serum potassium, and a decreased urinary output of certain steroids.

addition [L, additio, something added], a chemical reaction in which two complete molecules combine to form a new product, usually by attachment to carbon atoms at a double or triple bond of one of the molecules.

additive /ad′itiv/, any substance added intentionally or indirectly that becomes a part of the food, pharmaceutical, or other product.

additive effect [L, additio, something added, effectus], the combined effect of drugs that, when used in combination, produce an effect that is greater than the sum of their separately measured individual effects.

adducent /ədoo′sənt/, an agent or other stimulus that causes a limb to be drawn toward the midline or axis of the body or causes the fingers or toes to move together.

adduction /əduk′shən/ [L, adducere, to bring to], the movement of a limb toward the midline or axis of the body.—**adduct,** v.

adductor /əduk′tər/, a muscle that draws a part toward the axis or midline of the body.

adductor brevis, a somewhat triangular muscle in the thigh and one of the five medial femoral muscles. It acts to adduct and rotate the thigh laterally and to flex the leg.

adductor canal, a triangular channel beneath the sartorius muscle and between the adductor longus and vastus medialis through which the femoral vessels and the saphenous nerve pass.

adductor hiatus, the opening in the tendon of insertion of the adductor magnus through which the femoral artery and vein pass into the popliteal space.

adductor longus, the most superficial of the three adductor muscles of the thigh and one of five medial femoral muscles. It functions to adduct and flex the thigh.

adductor magnus, the long, heavy triangular muscle of the medial aspect of the thigh. The adductor magnus acts to adduct the thigh. The proximal portion acts to rotate the thigh medially and to flex it on the hip; the distal portion acts to extend the thigh and rotate it laterally.

adductor pollicis, a large triangular muscle that is a powerful adductor of the thumb and opposes the thumb to the rest of the digits in gripping.

adefovir dipivoxil, an antiviral agent used to treat chronic hepatitis B.

ADEM, abbreviation for **acute disseminated encephalomyelitis.**

adenalgia /ad′ənal′jə/ [Gk, *aden,* gland, *algos,* pain], pain in any of the glands.

adenectomy /ad′ənek′təmē/ [Gk, *aden* + *ektomē,* excision], the surgical removal of any gland.

adenine /ad′ənin/, a purine base that is a component of DNA, RNA, adenosine monophosphate (AMP), cyclic AMP, adenosine diphosphate (ADP), and adenosine triphosphate (ATP).

adenitis /ad′əni′tis/, an inflammation of a lymph node. Acute adenitis of the cervical lymph nodes may accompany a sore throat and stiff neck, simulating mumps if severe. It is most often related to an oral, a pharyngeal, or an ear infection. Scarlet fever may cause an acute suppurative cervical adenitis. Swelling of the lymph nodes in the back of the neck is often the result of a scalp infection, insect bite, or infestation by head lice. Inflammation of the lymph nodes of the mesenteric part of the peritoneum often produces pain and other symptoms similar to those of appendicitis.

adenoacanthoma /ad′ənō·ak′anthō′mə/ [Gk, *aden* + *akantha,* thorn, *oma,* tumor], a neoplasm that may be malignant or benign, derived from glandular tissue with squamous differentiation shown by some of the cells.

adenoameloblastoma /ad′ənō·amel′ōblastō′mə/ *pl.* **adenoameloblastomas, adenoameloblastomata,** a benign tumor of the maxilla or mandible composed of ducts lined with columnar or cuboidal epithelial cells. It develops in tissue that normally gives rise to the teeth, and it most often occurs in young people.

adenoassociated virus (AAV) /ad′ənō-/, a defective virus, belonging to a group of DNA viruses of the Parvoviridae family that can reproduce only in the presence of adenoviruses. It is not yet known what role, if any, these organisms have in causing disease.

adenocarcinoma /ad′ənōkärsinō′mə/ *pl.* **adenocarcinomas, adenocarcinomata** [Gk, *aden* + *karkinos,* crab, *oma*], any one of a large group of malignant epithelial cell tumors of the glandular tissue. Specific tumors are diagnosed and named by cytologic identification of the tissue affected.— **adenocarcinomatous,** *adj.*

adenocarcinoma in situ, a localized growth of abnormal glandular tissue that may become malignant. It is most common in the endometrium and large intestine.

adenocarcinoma of the lung, a type of bronchogenic carcinoma made up of a discrete mass of cuboidal or columnar cells, generally at the lung periphery. Growth is slow, but there may be early invasion of blood and lymph vessels by metastases while the primary lesion is still asymptomatic.

adenocele /ad′ənōsēl′/, a cystic, glandular tumor.

adenochondroma /ad′ənōkondrō′mə/ *pl.* **adenochondromas, adenochondromata** [Gk, *aden* + *chondros,* cartilage, *oma,* tumor], a neoplasm of cells derived from glandular and cartilaginous tissues, as a mixed tumor of the salivary glands.

adenocyst /ad′ənōsist′/ [Gk, *aden* + *kytis,* bag], a benign tumor in which the cells form cysts.

adenocystic carcinoma, an uncommon malignant neoplasm composed of cords of uniform small epithelial cells arranged in a sievelike pattern around cystic spaces that often contain mucus. The tumor occurs most frequently in the salivary glands, breast, mucus glands of the upper and lower respiratory tract, and occasionally in vestibular glands of the vulva.

adenoepithelioma /ad′ənō·ep′ithē′lē·ō′mə/ *pl.* **adenoepitheliomas, adenoepitheliomata** [Gk, *aden* + *epi,* on, *thele* nipple, *oma*], a neoplasm consisting of glandular and epithelial components.

adenofibroma /ad′ənōfibrō′mə/ *pl.* **adenofibromas, adenofibromata** [Gk, *aden*; L, *fibra,* fiber; Gk, *oma*], a tumor of the connective tissues that contains glandular elements.

adenofibroma edematodes, a neoplasm consisting of glandular elements and connective tissue in which marked edema is present.

adenohypophysis /ad′ənō′hīpof′isis/ [Gk, *aden* + *hypo,* beneath, *phyein,* to grow], the anterior lobe of the pituitary gland. It secretes growth hormone, TSH, adrenocorticotropic hormone, melanocyte-stimulating hormone, follicle-stimulating hormone, luteinizing hormone, prolactin, beta lipotropin molecules, and endorphins. The release of hormones from the hypothalamus regulate secretions.

adenoid /ad′ənoid/ [Gk, *aden* + *eidos,* form], having a glandular appearance, particularly lymphoid.

adenoidal speech, an abnormal manner of speaking caused by hypertrophy of the adenoidal tissue that normally exists in the nasopharynx of children. It is often characterized by hyponasality.

adenoidectomy /ad′ənoidek′təmē/ [Gk, *aden* + *eidos,* form, *ektomē,* excision], the removal of the lymphoid tissue in the nasopharynx. The surgical procedure may be performed because the adenoids are enlarged, chronically infected, or causing obstruction.

adenoid facies, a long face and open-mouth posture, sometimes seen in children with hypertrophy of the pharyngeal tonsils ("adenoids").

adenoid hyperplasia, enlarged adenoid glands, especially in children. Enlarged adenoids, often in association with enlarged tonsils, are a frequent cause of recurrent otitis media, sinusitis, conductive hearing loss, and partial respiratory obstruction.

adenoid hypertrophy [Gk, *aden,* gland, *eidos,* form, *hyper,* excessive, *trophe,* nourishment], the unusual growth of the pharyngeal tonsil.

adenoiditis /ad′ənoidī′tis/, an inflammation of the adenoids.

adenoids, one of two masses of lymphoid tissue situated on the posterior wall of the nasopharynx behind the posterior nares.

adenoleiomyofibroma /ad′ənōlī′ōmī′ōfī′brō′mə/ *pl.* **adenoleiomyofibromas, adenoleiomyofibromata** [Gk, *aden* + *leios,* smooth, *mys,* muscle; L, *fibra,* fiber; Gk, *oma*], a glandular tumor with smooth muscle, connective tissue, and epithelial elements.

adenolipoma /ad′ənōlipō′mə/ *pl.* **adenolipomas, adenolipomata** [Gk, *aden* + *lipos,* fat, *oma*], a benign neoplasm consisting of elements of glandular and adipose tissue.

adenolipomatosis /ad′ənōlip′ōmətō′sis/, a condition characterized by the growth of adenolipomas in the groin, axilla, and neck.

adenoma /ad′ənō′mə/ *pl.* **adenomas, adenomata** [Gk, *aden* + *oma*], a benign tumor of glandular epithelium in which the cells of the tumor are arranged in a recognizable glandular structure. An adenoma may cause excess secretion by the affected gland.—**adenomatous,** *adj.*

adenoma sebaceum /sebā′sē·əm/, an abnormal skin condition consisting of multiple wartlike, yellowish red, waxy papules on the face that are not sebaceous. The lesions are composed chiefly of fibrovascular tissue and are usually benign.

adenomatosis /ad′ənōmətō′sis/, an abnormal condition in which hyperplasia or tumor development affects two or more glands, usually the thyroid, adrenals, or pituitary.

adenomatous goiter /ad′ənō′mətəs/, an enlargement of the thyroid gland caused by an adenoma or numerous colloid nodules.

adenomatous polyp [Gk, *aden,* gland, *oma,* tumor, *polys,* many, *pous,* foot], a tumor that develops in glandular tissue. It is characterized by benign neoplastic changes in the epithelium.

adenomatous polyposis coli (APC), a gene associated with familial adenomatous polyposis (FAP), an inherited disorder characterized by the development of myriad polyps in the colon, beginning in late adolescence or early adulthood. Untreated, the condition may lead to colon cancer.

adenomyofibroma /ad′ənōmī′ōfībrō′mə/ *pl.* **adenomyofibromas, adenomyofibromata** [Gk, *aden* + *mys,* muscle; L, *fibra,* fiber; Gk, *oma*], a fibrous tumor that contains glandular and muscular components.

adenomyoma /ad′ənōmī·ō′mə/, *pl.* **adenomyomas, adenomyomata** a tumor of the endometrium of the uterus characterized by a mass of smooth muscle containing endometrial tissue and glands.

adenomyomatosis /ad′ənōmī′ōmətō′sis/, an abnormal condition characterized by the formation of benign nodules resembling adenomyomas, found in the uterus or in parauterine tissue.

adenomyosis /ad′ənōmī·ō′sis/, **1.** a benign neoplastic condition characterized by tumors composed of glandular tissue and smooth muscle cells. **2.** a malignant neoplastic condition characterized by the invasive growth of uterine mucosa in the uterus, pelvis, colon, or oviducts.

adenopathy /ad′ənop′əthē/ [Gk, *aden* + *pathos,* suffering], an enlargement of any gland.—**adenopathic,** *adj.*

adenopharyngitis /ad′ənōfer′injī′tis/, an inflammation of the adenoids and the pharynx.

adenosarcoma /ad′ənōsärkō′mə/ *pl.* **adenosarcomas, adenosarcomata** [Gk, *aden* + *sarx,* flesh + *oma*], a mixed malignant glandular tumor of the soft tissues of the body. It contains both glandular and sarcomatous elements.

adenosarcorhabdomyoma /ad′ənōsär′kōrab′dōmī·ōō′mə/ *pl.* **adenosarcorhabdomyomas, adenosarcorhabdomyomata** a tumor composed of glandular and connective tissue and striated muscle elements.

adenosine /əden′əsin, -sēn/, a compound derived from nucleic acid, composed of

A

adenine and a sugar, D-ribose. Adenosine is the major molecular component of the nucleotides adenosine monophosphate, adenosine diphosphate, and adenosine triphosphate and of the nucleic acids DNA and RNA.

adenosine deaminase (ADA) /dē·am'inās/, an enzyme that catalyzes the conversion of adenosine to the nucleoside inosine through the removal of an amino group. A deficiency of ADA can lead to **severe combined immunodeficiency syndrome.**

adenosine diphosphate (ADP), a product of the hydrolysis of adenosine triphosphate.

adenosine hydrolase, an enzyme that catalyzes the conversion of adenosine into adenine and ribose.

adenosine kinase, an enzyme in the liver and kidney that catalyzes the transfer of a phosphate group from adenosine triphosphate to produce adenosine diphosphate.

adenosine monophosphate (AMP), an ester, composed of nucleoside adenosine and phosphoric acid, that participates in energy released by working muscle.

adenosine phosphate, a compound consisting of the nucleotide adenosine attached through its ribose group to one, two, or three phosphate units or phosphoric acid molecules.

adenosine triphosphatase (ATPase), an enzyme in skeletal muscle and other tissues that catalyzes the hydrolysis of adenosine triphosphate to adenosine diphosphate and inorganic phosphate. Among various enzymes in this group, mitochondrial ATPase is involved in obtaining energy for cellular metabolism, and myosin ATPase is involved in muscle contraction.

adenosine triphosphate (ATP), a compound consisting of the nucleotide adenosine (A) attached through its ribose group to three phosphoric acid molecules (P). Hydrolysis of adenosine triphosphate to adenosine diphosphate (D) releases energy.

adenosis /ad'ənō'sis/, **1.** any disease of the glands, especially a lymphatic gland. **2.** an abnormal development or enlargement of glandular tissue.

adenotomy /ad'ənot'əmē/ [Gk, *aden,* gland, *tomé,* a cutting], a dissection of or incision into a gland.

adenotonsillectomy /ad'ənōton'silek 'təmē/, the surgical removal of the adenoids and tonsils.

adenovirus /ad'ənōvī'rəs/ [Gk, *aden;* L, *virus,* poison], any one of the 49 medium-sized viruses of the Adenoviridae family, pathogenic to humans, that cause conjunctivitis, URI, cystitis, or GI infection.—**adenoviral,** *adj.*

adenylate /əden'ilāt/, a salt or ester of adenylic acid.

adenylate cyclase, an enzyme that initiates the conversion of adenosine triphosphate to cyclic adenosine monophosphate, a mediator of many physiologic activities.

adenylate kinase, an enzyme in skeletal muscle that makes possible the reaction ATP + AMP = 2ADP.

adequate and well-controlled studies, the clinical and laboratory studies that the sponsors of a new drug are required by law to conduct to demonstrate the truth of the claims made for its effectiveness.

adermia /ədur'mē·ə/ [Gk, *a* + *derma,* without skin], a congenital or acquired skin defect or the absence of skin.

ADH, abbreviation for **antidiuretic hormone.**

ADHA, abbreviation for the **American Dental Hygienists' Association.**

adherence /adhir'əns/, **1.** the quality of clinging or being closely attached. **2.** the process in which a person follows rules, guidelines, or standards, especially as a patient follows a prescription and recommendations for a regimen of care.— **adhere,** *v.,* **adherent,** *adj.*

adherence behavior, a nursing outcome from the Nursing Outcomes Classification (NOC) defined as self-initiated actions taken to promote optimal wellness, recovery, and rehabilitation.

adherence behavior: healthy diet, a nursing outcome from the Nursing Outcomes Classification (NOC) defined as personal actions to monitor and optimize a healthy and nutritional dietary regimen.

adherent placenta [L, *adhaerens,* sticking to, *placenta,* flat cake], a placenta that remains attached to the uterine wall beyond the normal time after birth of the fetus.

adhesin /adhē'sin/, a bacterial product that enables bacteria to adhere to and colonize a host. Adherence is often an essential step in pathogenesis.

adhesion /adhē'zhən/ [L, *adhaerens,* sticking to], a band of scar tissue that binds anatomic surfaces that normally are separate from each other. Adhesions most commonly form in the abdomen, after abdominal surgery, inflammation, or injury. A loop of intestine may adhere to unhealed areas. Scar tissue constricting the bowel's lumen may cause intestinal obstruction.

adhesiotomy /adhē'sē·ot'əmē/ [L, *adhaerens;* Gk, *temnein* to cut], the surgical division or separation of adhesions, usually performed to relieve an intestinal obstruction.

adhesive /adhē'siv/ [L, *adhaerens,* sticking to], the quality of a substance that enables it to become attached to another substance.

adhesive capsulitis, a shoulder condition characterized by stiffness, pain, and limited ROM. It most often occurs in midlife and may be associated with surgery or injury.

adhesive peritonitis, an inflammation of the peritoneum, characterized by a fibrinous exudate that mats together the intestines and various other organs.

adhesive pleurisy, an inflammation of the pleura with exudation. It causes obliteration of the pleural space through the fusion of the visceral pleura covering the lungs and the parietal pleura lining the walls of the thoracic cavity.

adhesive skin traction, a type of short-term skin traction in which the therapeutic pull of traction weights is applied with adhesive straps that stick to the skin over the body structure involved, especially a fractured bone.

adhesive tape, a strong fabric covered on one side with an adhesive. Often water-repellent, it may be used to hold bandages and dressings in place, to immobilize a part, or to exert pressure.

ADI, abbreviation for **acceptable daily intake.**

adiadochokinesia /ā′dē·ad′əkō′kinē′zhə, ədī′ədō′kō-/, an inability to perform rapidly alternating movements such as pronation and supination or flexion and extension.

adiaphoresis /ā′dē·əfôrē′sis/, an absence or deficiency of sweat.

adiastole /ā′dī·as′təlē/ [Gk, *a*, not, *dia*, across, *stellein*, to set], the absence or imperceptibility of the diastolic stage of the cardiac cycle.

adiathermance /a′dī·əthur′məns/ [Gk, *a* + *dia*, not across, *therme*, heat], the quality of being unaffected by radiated heat.

adient /ad′ē·ənt/ [L, *adire*, moving toward], characterized by a tendency to move toward rather than away from stimuli.—**adience,** *n.*

Adie's pupil /ā′dēz/ [William J. Adie, English physician, 1886–1935], an abnormal condition of the eyes marked by one pupil that reacts much more slowly to light changes or to accommodation or convergence than the pupil of the other eye.

Adie's syndrome [William J. Adie], Adie's pupil accompanied by depressed or absent tendon reflexes, particularly the Achilles tendon and patellar reflexes.

adipic /ədip′ik/ [L, *adeps*, fat], pertaining to fatty tissue.

adipocele /ad′ipōsēl′/ [L, *adeps*; Gk, *kele*, hernia], a hernia containing fat or fatty tissue.

adipocyte /ad′ipōsīt′/, a fat (adipose) cell, potentially containing a large fat vacuole consisting mainly of triglycerides.

adipofibroma /ad′ipōfibrō′mə/ *pl.* **adipofibromas, adipofibromata** [L, *adeps* + *fibra*, fiber; Gk, *oma*], a fibrous neoplasm of the connective tissue with fatty components.

adipokinesis /ad′ipō′kinē′sis/, the mobilization of fat or fatty acids in lipid metabolism.

adipokinin /ad′ipōkī′nin/, a hormone of the adenohypophysis that causes mobilization of fat from adipose tissues.

adipometer /ad′ipom′ətər/, an instrument for measuring the thickness of a skin area as a guide to calculating the amount of subcutaneous fat.

adiponecrosis /ad′ipōnikrō′sis/ [L, *adeps*; Gk, *nekros*, dead, *osis* condition], a rarely used term referring to necrosis of fatty tissue in the body. The condition may be associated with hemorrhagic pancreatitis.

adiponecrosis subcutanea neonatorum, an abnormal dermatologic condition of the newborn characterized by patchy areas of hardened subcutaneous fatty tissue and a bluish red discoloration of the overlying skin.

adipose /ad′ipōs/, tissue composed of fat-containing cells arranged in lobules.

adipose capsule [L, *adeps*, fat, *capsula*, little box], a capsule of fatty tissue surrounding the kidney.

adipose tissue [L, *adeps*, fat; OFr, *tissu*], a collection of fat cells.

adiposogenital dystrophy /ad′ipō′sōjen′itəl/ [L, *adeps* + *genitalis*, generation], a disorder occurring in males, characterized by genital hypoplasia and feminine secondary sex characteristics, including female distribution of fat. It is caused by hypothalamic malfunction or by a tumor in the anterior pituitary gland.

adipsia /ādip′sē·ə/ [Gk, *a* + *dipsa*, not thirst], absence of thirst.

aditus /ad′itəs/ [L, going to], an approach or an entry.

adjunct /ad′jungkt/ [L, *adjungere*, to join], (in health care) an additional substance, treatment, or procedure used for increasing the efficacy or safety of the primary substance, treatment, or procedure or for facilitating its performance.—**adjunctive,** *adj.*

adjunctive group /adjungk′tiv/, a group with specific activities and focuses, such as socialization, perceptual stimulation, sensory stimulation, or reality orientation.

adjunctive psychotherapy, a form of psychotherapy that concentrates on improving general mental and physical well-being without trying to resolve basic emotional problems.

adjunct to anesthesia, one of a number of drugs or techniques that are used to enhance anesthesia but are not classified as anesthetics. Adjuncts to anesthesia are used before an anesthetic is administered as premedications and during anesthesia to augment anesthetic effects or diminish undesirable side effects.

adjustable orthodontic band /adjus′təbəl/, a thin metal ring, usually made of stainless steel, equipped with an adjusting screw to allow alteration in size, that is fitted to a tooth and allows the attachment of orthodontic appliances.

adjustment, the changing of something to modify its relationship to something else.

adjustment disorder [L, *adjustare,* to bring together], a temporary disorder of varying severity that occurs as an acute reaction to overwhelming stress in persons of any age who have no apparent underlying mental disorders. Symptoms include anxiety, withdrawal, depression, brooding, impulsive outbursts, crying spells, attention-seeking behavior, enuresis, loss of appetite, aches, pains, and muscle spasms.

adjuvant /ad′jəvənt/ [L, *ad + juvare,* to help], **1.** a substance, especially a drug, added to a prescription to assist in the action of the main ingredient. **2.** (in immunology) a substance added to an antigen that enhances or modifies the antibody response to the antigen. **3.** an additional treatment or therapy.

adjuvant chemotherapy, the use of anticancer drugs after or in combination with another form of cancer treatment, as after apparently complete surgical removal of a cancer. The method is used when there is a significant risk that micrometastasis may still be present.

adjuvant radiotherapy, radiotherapy used in addition to surgical resection or chemotherapy in the treatment of cancer.

adjuvant therapy, the treatment of a disease with substances that enhance the action of drugs, especially drugs that promote the production of antibodies.

ADL, abbreviation for **activities of daily living.**

adlerian psychology [Alfred Adler, Viennese psychiatrist, 1870–1937], a branch of psychoanalysis that focuses on physical security, sexual satisfaction, and social integration.

ad lib, abbreviation of the Latin phrase *ad libitum,* meaning to be taken as desired.

ADME, an abbreviation for the time course of drug distribution, representing the terms *absorption, distribution, metabolism,* and *elimination.*

Administration on Aging (AOA), the principal U.S. agency designated to carry out the provisions of the Older Americans Act of 1965. The AOA advises the Secretary of the U.S. Department of Health

and Human Services and other federal departments and agencies on the characteristics and needs of older people and develops programs designed to promote their welfare.

admission, **1.** the act of being received into a place or class of things. **2.** a patient accepted for inpatient service in a hospital. **3.** a concession or acknowledgment.

admission care, a nursing intervention from the Nursing Interventions Classification (NIC) defined as facilitating entry of a patient into a health care facility.

ADN, abbreviation for **Associate Degree in Nursing.**

ad nauseam [L, *ad,* to; Gk, *nausia,* seasickness], to the extent of inducing nausea and vomiting.

adneural /adnŏŏr′əl/, **1.** located near or toward a nerve or nerve ending. **2.** pertaining to the stage of a nervous disorder in which the symptoms are apparent.

adnexa /adnek′sa/ *sing.* **adnexum** [L, *adnectere,* to tie together], tissue or structures in the body that are adjacent to or near another, related structure. The ovaries and the uterine tubes are adnexa of the uterus.—**adnexal,** *adj.*

adnexectomy /ad′neksek′təmē/ [Gk, *ektomē,* excision], the surgical removal of accessory structures.

adnexitis /ad′neksī′tis/, an inflammation of the adnexal organs of the uterus.

adnexopexy /adnek′sōpek′sē/, a surgical procedure in which the fallopian tubes and ovaries are elevated and sutured to the abdominal wall.

adolescence /ad′əles′əns/ [L, *adolescere,* to grow up], **1.** the period in development between the onset of puberty and adulthood. It usually begins between 11 and 13 years of age with the appearance of secondary sex characteristics and spans the teenage years, terminating at 18 to 20 years of age with the completion of the development of the adult form. **2.** the state or quality of being adolescent or youthful.

adolescent, **1.** pertaining to adolescence. **2.** one in the state or process of adolescence; a teenager.

adoption /ədop′shən/ [L, *adoptere,* to choose], a selection and inclusion in an established relationship or a choice of treatment protocol.

ADP, abbreviation for **adenosine diphosphate.**

ADPKD, abbreviation for *autosomal-dominant polycystic kidney disease.*

adrenal /ədrē′nəl/ [L, *ad,* to, *ren,* kidney], pertaining to the adrenal, or suprarenal glands, which are located on top of the kidneys.

adrenal cortex [L, *ad,* to, *ren,* kidney], the outer and greater portion of the adrenal gland, fused with the gland's medulla. In response to adrenocorticotropic hormone secreted by the adenohypophysis, it secretes cortisol and androgens. —**adrenocortical,** *adj.*

adrenal cortical carcinoma, a malignant neoplasm of the adrenal cortex that may cause adrenal virilism or Cushing syndrome. Such tumors vary in size and may occur at any age. Metastases frequently occur in the lungs, liver, and other organs.

adrenal crisis, an acute, life-threatening state of profound adrenocortical insufficiency in which immediate therapy is required. It is characterized by glucocorticoid deficiency, a drop in extracellular fluid volume, and hyperkalemia.

adrenalectomy /ədrē′nəlek′təmē/ [L, *ad* + *ren;* Gk, *ektomē,* excision], the total or partial surgical resection of one or both adrenal glands. It is performed to reduce the excessive secretion of adrenal hormones caused by an adrenal tumor or a malignancy of the breast or prostate. When both glands are removed, the maintenance dosage of steroids continues for life. Stress and fatigue must be avoided.

adrenal gland, either of two secretory organs perched atop of the kidneys and surrounded by the protective fat capsule of the kidneys. Each consists of two parts having independent functions: the cortex and the medulla.

Adrenalin, a trademark for an adrenergic (epINEPHrine).

adrenal insufficiency [L, *ad,* to, *ren,* kidney, *in,* not, *sufficere,* to suffice], a condition in which the adrenal gland is unable to produce adequate amounts of cortical hormones.

adrenalism /ah-dren′al-izm/, any disorder of adrenal function, whether of decreased or of heightened function.

adrenalize /ədrē′nəlīz/, to stimulate or excite.

adrenal medulla, the inner portion of the adrenal gland. Its cells secrete the catecholamines epinephrine and norepinephrine when stimulated by the sympathetic division of the autonomic nervous system.

adrenal virilism, a condition characterized by hypersecretion of adrenal androgens, resulting in somatic masculinization. Excessive production of the hormone may be caused by a virilizing adrenal tumor, congenital adrenal hyperplasia, or an inborn deficiency of enzymes required to transform endogenous androgenic steroids to glucocorticoids.

adrenarche /ad′rinär′kē/ [L, *ad* + *ren;* Gk, *arche,* beginning], the intensified activity in the adrenal cortex that occurs at about 8 years of age and increases the elaboration of various hormones, especially androgens.

adrenergic /ad′rinur′jik/ [L, *ad* + *ren;* Gk, *ergon,* work], pertaining to sympathetic nerve fibers of the autonomic nervous system that liberate norepinephrine at a synapse where a nerve impulse passes.

adrenergic bronchodilator, a drug that acts on the beta-2 sympathetic nervous system receptors to relax bronchial smooth muscle cells. Examples include drugs that contain epINEPHrine, epHEDrine, isoproterenol, or albuterol.

adrenergic fiber, nerve fibers of the autonomic nervous system that release the neurotransmitter norepinephrine and, in some areas, dopamine. Most postganglionic sympathetic nerve fibers are of this type.

adrenergic receptor [L, *ad* + *ren,* kidney; Gk, *ergon,* work; L, *recipere,* to receive], a site in a sympathetic effector cell that reacts to adrenergic stimulation. Two types of adrenergic receptors are recognized: **alpha-adrenergic** and **beta-adrenergic.** In general, stimulation of alpha receptors is excitatory of the function of the host organ or tissue, and stimulation of the beta receptors is inhibitory.

adrenocortical cytomegaly, an abnormal enlargement of cells in the outer layer of the adrenal cortex.

adrenocortical hormone (ACH) [L, *ad,* to, *ren,* kidney, *cortex,* bark; Gk, *hormaein,* to set in motion], any of the hormones secreted by the cortex of the adrenal gland, including the glucocorticoids, mineralocorticoids, and androgens.

adrenocorticotropic /ədrē′nōkôr′tikōtrop′ik/ [L, *ad* + *ren* + *cortex,* bark; Gk, *trope,* a turning], pertaining to stimulation of the adrenal cortex.

adrenocorticotropic hormone (ACTH), a hormone of the anterior pituitary gland that stimulates the growth of the adrenal gland cortex and the synthesis and secretion of corticosteroids. ACTH secretion, regulated by corticotropin releasing hormone (CRH) from the hypothalamus, increases in response to a low level of circulating cortisol and to stress, fever, acute hypoglycemia, and major surgery. Under normal conditions a diurnal rhythm occurs in ACTH secretion, with an increase beginning after the first few hours of sleep and reaching a peak at the time a person awakens and a low in the evening. ACTH may be used in the treatment of rheumatoid arthritis, MS, and myasthenia.

A

adrenocorticotropic hormone test, a blood test used to study the functioning of the adenohypophysis by measuring cortisol levels. The test is used to diagnose Cushing's syndrome and Addison's disease.

adrenocorticotropic hormone (ACTH) stimulation test with cosyntropin, a blood test performed on patients with adrenal insufficiency to indicate whether the adrenal gland is normal and capable of functioning if stimulated or if the patient has Addison's disease or Cushing's syndrome.

adrenocorticotropic hormone (ACTH) stimulation test with metyrapone, a blood or urine test similar to the ACTH stimulation test with cosyntropin. The test can confirm adrenal hyperplasia or adrenal adenoma or carcinoma. It can document that adrenal insufficiency exists as a result of pituitary disease rather than primary adrenal pathology. Metyrapone is associated with life-threatening adrenal crisis in patients with primary insufficiency and should not be used on such patients.

adrenocorticotropin /-trop′in/, the adrenocorticotropic hormone (**ACTH**) secreted by the adenohypophysis that stimulates secretion of corticosteroid hormones by the adrenal cortex.

adrenodoxin /ədrē′nōdok′sin/, a nonheme iron protein produced by the adrenal glands that participates in the transfer of electrons within animal cells.

adrenoleukodystrophy (ALD), a rare hereditary childhood metabolic disorder that is transmitted as a recessive sex-linked trait and affects mainly males. It is characterized by adrenal atrophy and widespread cerebral demyelination, producing progressive mental deterioration, aphasia, apraxia, eventual blindness, and tetraplegia. In the neonate form, prognosis is poor, with death occurring usually in 1 to 5 years. The childhood form may be chronic and treatable for a few years with a special diet.

adrenomegaly /-meg′əlē/ [L, *ad* + *ren;* Gk, *megaly,* large], an abnormal enlargement of one or both adrenal glands.

adrenomimetic /-mimet′ik/, mimicking the functions of the adrenal hormones.

adrenotropic /-trop′ik/, having a stimulating effect on the adrenal glands.

Adriamycin RDF, a trademark for an antibiotic antineoplastic agent (DOXOrubicin hydrochloride).

Adrucil, a trademark for an antineoplastic (fluorouracil).

ADRV, abbreviation for **adult rotavirus.**

ADS, abbreviation for *antidiuretic substance.*

Adson-Brown forceps [Alfred W. Adson, American neurosurgeon, 1887–1951; James B. Brown, American plastic surgeon, 1899–1971], a thumb forceps similar to the Adson forceps, having fine teeth at the tip, used for grasping delicate tissue.

Adson forceps [Alfred W. Adson], a small thumb forceps having a fine tip, with or without teeth.

Adson's maneuver [Alfred W. Adson], a test for the thoracic outlet syndrome. It is performed with the patient sitting with hands on the thighs. The examiner palpates both radial pulses as the patient takes a deep breath and holds it while extending the neck and turning the head toward the affected side. If the radial pulse on the affected side is significantly diminished or there is numbness or tingling in the hand, the result is regarded as positive.

adsorbent /adsôr′bənt/, a substance, such as activated charcoal, that takes up another by the process of adsorption, as by the attachment of one substance to the surface of the other.

adsorption /adsôrp′shən/ [L, *ad* + *sorbere,* to suck in], a natural process whereby molecules of a gas or liquid adhere to the surface of a solid. The phenomenon depends on an assortment of factors such as surface tension and electrical charges.

ADT, abbreviation for *Accepted Dental Therapeutics,* a journal published by the Council on Dental Therapeutics of the American Dental Association.

adult /ədult′, ad′ult/ [L, *adultus,* grown up], **1.** one who is fully developed and matured and who has attained the intellectual capacity and emotional and psychologic stability that are characteristic of maturity. **2.** a person who has reached full legal age. **3.** any fully grown and mature organism.

adult day-care center, a facility for the supervised care of older adults, providing such activities as meals and socialization one or more days a week during specified daytime hours.

adult ego state, (in psychiatry), a part of the self that analyzes and solves problems, using information received from the parent and child ego states.

adulteration /ədul′tərā′shən/ [L, *adulterare,* to defile], the debasement or dilution of the purity of any substance, process, or activity by the addition of extraneous material.

adulthood, the phase of development characterized by physical and mental maturity.

adult nurse practitioner, a registered nurse who has received additional education in the primary health care of adults. The additional education may be obtained through a master's degree program or a nondegree-granting continuing education certificate program.

adult respiratory distress syndrome (ARDS), severe pulmonary congestion characterized by diffuse injury to alveolar-capillary membranes. Fulminating sepsis, especially when gram-negative bacteria are involved, is the most common cause.

adult rotavirus (ADRV), a form of rotavirus that causes severe diarrhea in adults.

advanced burn life support (ABLS), assessment and management of burn patients provided by emergency care personnel from the scene of injury through the first 24 hours following injury. It includes evaluation of the patient, airway management and ventilatory support, fluid resuscitation, and determination of whether the patient should be transferred to a burn center.

advanced cardiac life support (ACLS), emergency medical procedures in which basic life support efforts of CPR are augmented by establishment of an IV fluid line, possible defibrillation, drug administration, control of cardiac arrhythmias, endotracheal intubation, and use of ventilation equipment.

advance directive [Fr, *avancer,* to move forward; L, *dirigere,* to direct], an advance declaration by a person of treatment preferences if he or she is unable to communicate his or her wishes.

advanced life support (ALS), a higher level of emergency medical care, usually provided by EMT-intermediates or paramedics. Typically, ALS includes invasive techniques such as IV therapy, intubation, and/or drug administration.

advanced practice nurse (APN), a registered nurse having education beyond the basic nursing education and certified by a nationally recognized professional organization in a nursing specialty, or meeting other criteria established by a Board of Nursing.

Advanced Trauma Life Support, An educational program developed by the American College of Surgeons emphasizing a standardized approach to the care of patients in emergency situations.

advancement /advans′/ [Fr, *avancer,* to move forward], a surgical technique in which a muscle or tendon is detached and then reattached at an advanced point.

adventitia /ad′ventish′ə/ [L, *adventitius,* coming from abroad], the outermost layer, composed of connective tissue with elastic and collagenous fibers, of an artery or other structure.

adventitious, 1. pertaining to an accidental condition or an arbitrary action. **2.** not hereditary. **3.** occurring at an inappropriate place, such as a coating on an artery.

adventitious bursa, an abnormal bursa that develops as a response to friction or pressure.

adventitious crisis, an accidental, uncommon, and unexpected tragedy that may affect an entire community or population, such as an earthquake, flood, or airplane crash.

adventitious cyst, pseudocyst.

adventitious sound, a breath sound that is not normally heard, such as a crackle, gurgle, rhonchus, or wheeze. It may be superimposed on normal breath sounds.

adverse drug effect /advurs′, ad′vers/, an unintended reaction to a drug administered at normal dosage.

adverse drug reaction, any unintended effect on the body as a result of the use of therapeutic drugs, drugs of abuse, or the interaction of two or more pharmacologically active agents.

adverse reaction, any harmful or unintended effect of a medication, diagnostic test, or therapeutic intervention.

advocacy /ad′vəkas′ē/, **1.** a process whereby a nurse provides a patient with the information to make certain decisions. **2.** a method by which patients, their families, attorneys, health professionals, and citizen groups can work together to develop programs that ensure the availability of high-quality health care for a community. **3.** pleading a cause on behalf of another, such as a nurse pleading for better care of a patient.

adynamia /ad′inā′mē·ə/ [Gk, *a + dynamis,* not strength], lack of physical strength resulting from a pathologic condition. —**adynamic,** *adj.*

adynamia episodica hereditaria, a condition seen in infancy, characterized by periodic muscle weakness and episodes of flaccid paralysis. It is inherited as an autosomal-dominant trait.

adynamic fever, a malignant or putrid fever accompanied by great muscular debility.

AECMN, abbreviation for **Association for the Education of Children with Medical Needs.**

AED, abbreviation for **automated external defibrillator.**

Aedes /ā·ē′dēz/ [Gk, *aedes,* unpleasant], a genus of mosquito prevalent in tropical and subtropical regions. Several species are capable of transmitting pathogenic organisms to humans, including dengue, equine encephalitis, St. Louis encephalitis, tularemia, and yellow fever.

aeration [Gk, *aer,* air], **1.** the exchange of carbon dioxide for oxygen by blood in the lungs. **2.** the process of exposing a tissue or fluid to air or artificially charging it with oxygen or another gas such as carbon dioxide.—**aerate,** *v.*

aerobe /er′ōb/ [Gk, *aer* + *bios,* life], a microorganism able to live, and grow, in the presence of free oxygen. An aerobe may be facultative or obligate. —**aerobic,** *adj.*

aerobic /erō′bik/, **1.** pertaining to the presence of air or oxygen. **2.** able to live and function in the presence of free oxygen. **3.** requiring oxygen for the maintenance of life. **4.** chemical requiring the presence of oxygen.

aerobic capacity, the maximum amount of physiologic work that an individual can do as measured by oxygen consumption. It is determined by combination of aging and cardiovascular conditioning and is associated with the efficiency of oxygen extraction in the tissue.

aerobic exercise, any physical exercise that requires additional effort by the heart and lungs to meet the skeletal muscles' increased demand for oxygen. Aerobic exercise increases the breathing rate and ultimately raises heart and lung efficiency. Prolonged aerobic exercises (at least 20 minutes five times per week) is recommended for the maintenance of a healthy cardiovascular system.

AeroBid, /ār′ōōbid′/, a trademark for an oral inhalation preparation of flunisolide.

aerodontalgia /er′ōdontal′jə/ [Gk, *aer* + *odous,* tooth, *algos,* pain], a painful sensation in the teeth caused by a change in atmospheric pressure, as may occur at high altitudes.

aerodynamics, the study of air or other gases in motion or of bodies moving in air.

aerodynamic size, pertaining to the behavior of various aerosol particle sizes and densities.

Aeromonas /er′ōmō′nəs/, a genus of pathogenic rod-shaped gram-negative bacteria (schizomycetes) found in fresh and salt water, soil, and sewage. Various species affect fish, reptiles, and animals as well as humans, causing wound infections and gastroenteritis.

aerophagy /erof′əjē/ [Gk, *aer* + *phagein,* to eat], the excessive swallowing of air, usually an unconscious process associated with anxiety, resulting in abdominal distension or belching, gastric distress, and flatulence.

aerosinusitis /er′ōsī′nəsī′tis/ [Gk, *aer*; L, *sinus,* curve; Gk. *itis*], inflammation, edema, or hemorrhage of the frontal sinuses, caused by an expansion of air within the sinuses when barometric pressure is decreased, as in aircraft at high altitudes.

aerosol /er′əsol′/ [Gk, *aer*; L, *solutus,* in dissolved], **1.** nebulized particles suspended in a gas or air. **2.** a pressurized gas containing a finely nebulized medication for inhalation therapy. **3.** a pressurized gas containing a nebulized chemical agent for sterilizing the air of a room.

aerosol bronchodilator therapy, the use of drugs that relax the respiratory tract smooth muscle tissue when administered as tiny droplets or a mist to be inhaled.

aerosol therapy, the use of an aerosol for respiratory care in the treatment of bronchopulmonary disease. Aerosol therapy allows the delivery of medications, humidity, or both to the mucosa of the respiratory tract and pulmonary alveoli. Agents delivered by aerosol therapy may relieve spasm of the bronchial muscles and reduce edema of the mucous membranes, liquify bronchial secretions so that they are more easily removed, humidify the respiratory tract, and administer antibiotics locally by depositing them in the respiratory tract.

aerospace medicine /er′ōspās/, a branch of medicine concerned with the physiologic and psychologic effects of living and working in an artificial environment beyond the atmospheric and gravitational forces of the earth. The stress of extraterrestrial travel requiring long periods of weightlessness is a major concern.

aerotherapy /er′ōther′əpē/, the use of air in treating disease, as in hyperbaric oxygenation.

aerotitis /er′ətī′tis/ [Gk, *aer* + *otikos,* ear, *itis*], an inflammation of the ear caused by changes in atmospheric pressure.

aerotitis media, inflammation or bleeding in the middle ear caused by a difference between the air pressure in the middle ear and that of the atmosphere, as occurs in sudden changes in altitude, in scuba diving, or in hyperbaric chambers. Symptoms are pain, tinnitus, diminished hearing, and vertigo.

Æsculapius /es′ky˘oolā′pē·əs/, the ancient Greek god of medicine. According to legend, Æsculapius, the son of Apollo, was trained by the centaur Chiron in the art of healing; he became so proficient that he not only cured sick patients but also restored the dead to life. Serpents were regarded as sacred by Æsculapius, and he is symbolized in modern medicine by a staff with a serpent entwined about it.

AF, 1. abbreviation for **atrial fibrillation. 2.** abbreviation for **atrial flutter.**

AFB, abbreviation for **acid-fast bacillus.**

afebrile /āfe′bril, afeb′ril/ [Gk, *a* + *febris,* not fever], without fever.

affect /əfekt'/ [L, *affectus,* influence], an outward, observable manifestation of a person's expressed feelings or emotions, such as flat, blunted, bland, or bright. —**affective,** *adj.*

affection /əfek'shən/ [L, *affectus,* influence], **1.** an emotional state expressed by a warm or caring feeling toward another individual. **2.** a disease process affecting all or a part of the human body.

affective intimacy, a measure of wellbeing in a family group that focuses on whether members feel close to one another, yet do not lose their individuality.

affective learning, the acquisition of behaviors involved in expressing feelings in attitudes, appreciation, and values.

affective psychosis, a psychologic reaction in which the ego's functioning is impaired and the primary clinical feature is a severe disorder of mood or emotions.

affect memory, a particular emotionally expressed feeling that recurs whenever a significant experience is recalled.

afferent /af'ərənt/ [L, *ad + ferre,* to carry], proceeding toward a center, as applied to arteries, veins, lymphatics, and nerves.

afferent nerve [L, *ad + ferre,* to bear, *nervus*], a nerve fiber that transmit impulses from the periphery toward the CNS.

afferent pathway [L, *ad + ferre,* to bear; AS, *paeth + weg*], the course or route taken, usually by a linkage of neurons, from the periphery of the body toward the CNS.

afferent tract [L, *ad + ferre,* to bear, *tractus*], a pathway for nerve impulses traveling inward or toward the brain, the center of an organ, or another body structure.

affidavit /af'idā'vit/ [L, he has pledged], a written statement that is sworn to before a notary public or an officer of the court.

affiliated hospital /əfil'ē·ā'ted/ [L, *ad + filius,* to son], a hospital that is associated to some degree with a medical school, a health profession, a health program, or another health care institution.

affinity /əfin'itē/ [L, *affinis,* related], the measure of the binding strength of the antibody-antigen reaction.

affirmation [L, *affirmare,* to make firm], (in psychology) autosuggestion, the point at which a tendency toward positive reaction or belief is observed by the therapist.

affirmative defense /əfur'mətiv/ [L, *affirmare,* to make firm], (in law) a denial of guilt or wrongdoing based on new evidence rather than on simple denial of a charge, as a plea of immunity according to Good Samaritan legislation. The defendant bears the burden of proof in an affirmative defense.

affusion /afyōō'zhən/ [L, *affundere,* to pour out], a culturally based form of therapy in which water is sprinkled or poured over the body or a particular body part. It is used for fever or other conditions.

afibrinogenemia /afī'brinō'jenē'mē·ə/ [Gk, *a,* not; L, *fibra,* fiber; Gk, *genein,* to produce, *haima,* blood], Congenital absence of fibrinogen from the plasma associated with moderate to severe bleeding. Also spelled **afibrinogenaemia.**

aflatoxins /af'lātok'sins/ [Gk, *a,* not; L, *flavus,* yellow; Gk, *toxikon,* poison], a group of carcinogenic and toxic factors produced by *Aspergillus flavus* food molds.

AFMC, abbreviation for **Association of Faculties of Medicine of Canada.**

AFO, abbreviation for **ankle-foot orthosis.**

AFP, abbreviation for **alpha-fetoprotein.**

African tick fever, a tickborne or spotted fever caused by *Rickettsia africae* that develops into a diffuse rash. Multiple eschars, lymphangitis, lymphadenopathy, and edema are common.

African tick typhus, 1. a rickettsial infection transmitted by ixodid ticks and characterized by fever, chills, maculopapular rash, headache, myalgia, arthralgias, and swollen lymph nodes. **2.** a tickborne rickettsial disease of the eastern hemisphere similar to Rocky Mountain spotted fever but less severe.

African trypanosomiasis, a disease caused by the parasite *Trypanosoma brucei gambiense* (West African or Gambian trypanosomiasis) or *T. brucei rhodesiense* (East African or Rhodesian trypanosomiasis), transmitted to humans by the bite of the tsetse fly.

Afrin, a trademark for an adrenergic vasoconstrictor (oxymetazoline hydrochloride).

afterbirth [AS, *aefter* + ME, *burth*], the placenta, the amnion, the chorion, and some amniotic fluid, blood, and blood clots expelled from the uterus after childbirth.

aftercare [AS, *aefter + caru*], health care offered a patient after discharge from a hospital or other health care facility.

afterdepolarization /-dēpō'lərizā'shən/, a membrane potential depolarization that follows an action potential. In cardiac muscles, it may be early (during phases 2 and 3 of the action potential) or delayed (during phase 4) and it is thought to cause atrial and ventricular tachycardia, especially in the setting of a long Q-T interval or digitalis poisoning.

aftereffect, a physical or psychologic effect that continues after the stimulus is removed.

afterimage, a visual sensation that continues after the stimulus ends. The image may appear in colors complementary to those of the stimulus.

afterload [AS, *aefter* + ME *lod*], the load, or resistance, against which the left ventricle must eject its volume of blood during contraction.

afterloading, a technique in which an unloaded applicator or needle is placed within a patient at the time of an operative procedure and subsequently loaded with a radioactive source. The loading is done under controlled conditions in which health care personnel are protected against radiation exposure.

aftermovement, an involuntary contraction of a muscle that causes a continued movement of a limb after a strong exertion against resistance has stopped.

afterpain [AS, *aefter*; Gk, *poine*, penalty], one of many contractions of the uterus common during the first days after childbirth. Afterpains tend to be strongest during breastfeeding, in multiparas, after the birth of large babies, and after overdistention of the uterus. They usually resolve spontaneously but may require analgesia.

afterperception, the apparent perception of a stimulus that continues after the stimulus is removed.

afterpotential wave /-pəten′shəl/, either of two smaller waves, positive or negative, that follow the main spike potential wave of a nerve impulse, as recorded on an oscillograph tracing an action potential that propagates along a nerve fiber.

Ag, symbol for the element silver.

AGA, abbreviation for **appropriate for gestational age.**

against medical advice (ama), a phrase pertaining to a client's decision to discontinue a therapy despite the advice of medical professionals.

agalactia /ā′gəlak′shə/ [Gk *a* + *gala*, not milk], the inability of the mother to secrete enough milk to breastfeed a neonate immediately after childbirth.

agalsidase beta, a miscellaneous agent used to treat Fabry disease.

agamete /āgam′ēt/ [Gk *a* + *gamos* not marriage], **1.** any of the unicellular organisms, such as bacteria and protozoa, that reproduce asexually by multiple fission instead of by the production of gametes. **2.** any asexual reproductive cell, such as a spore or merozoite, that forms a new organism without fusion with another gamete.—**agametic, agamous,** *adj.*

agamic /āgam′ik/, reproducing asexually, without the union of gametes; asexual.

agammaglobulinemia /āgam′əglob′yoolinē′mē·ə/ [Gk *a* + *gamma*, not gamma (third letter of Greek alphabet); L, *globulus*, small sphere; Gk, *haima*, blood], the absence of the serum immunoglobulin gamma globulin, associated with an increased susceptibility to infection. The condition may be transient, congenital, or acquired.

agamogenesis /əgam′ōjen′əsis/ [Gk, *a* + *gamos*, not marriage, *genein*, to produce], asexual reproduction, as by budding, simple fission of cells, or parthenogenesis.—**agamocytogenic, agamogenetic, agamogenic, agamogonic,** *adj.*

aganglionosis /əgang′lē·ənō′sis/ [Gk, *a*, not, *gagglion*, knot, *osis*, condition], an absence of parasympathetic ganglion cells in the myenteric plexus, a diagnostic sign of congenital megacolon.

agar-agar /a′gär a′gär/ [Malay], a dried hydrophilic, colloidal product obtained from certain species of red algae. Because it is unaffected by bacterial enzymes, it is widely used as the basic ingredient in solid culture media in bacteriology.

agarose /ag′ärōs/, an essentially neutral fraction of agar used as a medium in electrophoresis, particularly for separation of serum proteins, hemoglobin variants, and lipoprotein fractions.

agastria /əgas′trē·ə/ [Gk, *a* + *gaster*, without stomach], the absence of a stomach.—**agastric,** *adj.*

AGC, abbreviation for *absolute granulocyte count.* Also called the absolute neutrophil count (ANC).

age [L, *aetus*, lifetime], **1.** a stage of development at which the body has arrived, as measured by physical and laboratory standards, to what is normal for a male or age. **2.** to grow old.

age-associated mental impairment, progressive decline in cognitive function that occurs as the result of the normal aging process. It can be caused by a number of factors, including nutrient deficiencies, the damaging effect of free radicals, adverse effects of medication, altered hormone balance, and decreased oxygen supply to brain cells.

aged /ājd/, a state of having grown older or more mature than others of the population group.

ageism /ā′jizəm/ [L, *aetas*, lifetime], an attitude that discriminates, separates, stigmatizes, or otherwise disadvantages older adults on the basis of chronologic age.

agency [L, *agere*, to do], **1.** (in law) a relationship between two parties in which one authorizes the other to act on his or her behalf as an agent. **2.** the business of any power or firm empowered to act for another.

Agency for Healthcare Research and Quality (AHRQ), a governmental agency of the U.S. Department of Health and Human Services. Its mission is to support research "to improve the outcomes and quality of health care, reduce its costs, address patient safety and medical errors, and broaden access to effective service." The agency systematically develops statements and recommendations to help individuals, institutions, and agencies make better decisions about health care based on research that provides evidence-based information. It publishes scientific information for other agencies and organizations on which to base clinical guidelines, performance measures, and other quality-improvement tools through its evidence-based practice centers, outcomes research findings for clinicians, and technology reviews. It provides access to scientific evidence, recommendations on clinical preventive services, and information on how to implement recommended preventive services in clinical practice. Formerly called the Agency for Health Care Policy and Research.

Agency for Toxic Substances and Disease Registry (ATSDR), an agency of the U.S. Department of Health and Human Services, charged with performing specific functions concerning the effect on public health of hazardous substances in the environment. These functions include public health assessments of waste sites, health consultations concerning specific hazardous substances, health surveillance and registries, emergency responses to release of hazardous substances, applied research in support of public health assessments, information development and dissemination, and education and training concerning hazardous substances in the environment.

agenesia corticalis /ā′jenē′zhə/ [Gk, *a* + *genein*, not to produce; L, cortex], the failure of the cortical cells of the brain, especially the pyramidal cells, to develop in the embryo, resulting in infantile cerebral paralysis and severe mental retardation.

agenesis /ājen′əsis/ [Gk, *a* + *genein*, not to produce], **1.** a congenital absence of an organ or part, usually caused by a lack of primordial tissue and failure of development in the embryo. **2.** impotence or sterility. —**agenic,** *adj.*

agenetic fracture /ā′jenet′ik/, a spontaneous fracture caused by a defect or imperfection in bone development.

ageniocephaly /ājen′ē·ōsef′əlē/ [Gk, *a* + *genein*, not to produce, *kephale*, head], a form of otocephaly in which the brain, cranial vault, and sense organs are intact but the lower jaw is malformed. —**ageniocephalic, ageniocephalous,** *adj.*

agenitalism /ājen′itəliz′əm/, any condition caused by the lack of sex hormones and the absence or malfunction of the ovaries or testes.

agenosomia /əjen′əsō′mē·ə/, a congenital malformation characterized by the absence or defective formation of the genitals and protrusion of the intestines through an incompletely developed abdominal wall.

agenosomus /əjen′əsō′məs/ [Gk, *a* + *genein*, not to produce, *soma*, body], a fetus with agenosomia.

agent [L, *agere*, to do], (in law) a party authorized to act on behalf of another and to give the other an account of such actions.

Agent Orange, a U.S. military code name for a mixture of two herbicides, 2,4-D and 2,4,5-T, used as a defoliant during the Vietnam War between 1961 and 1971. The herbicides were unintentionally contaminated with the highly toxic chemical dioxin, believed to be a cause of cancer and birth defects in animals and established as a cause of chloracne and porphyria cutanea tarda in humans.

age of consent, (in medical jurisprudence) the age at which an individual is legally free to act as an adult, without parental permission for such activities as marrying, having sexual intercourse or giving permission for medical treatment or surgery. The specific age of consent varies from 13 to 21, according to local laws.

age of majority, the age at which a person is considered to be an adult in the eyes of the law. It varies by activity from state to state.

age-specific, a description of data in which the age of the individual is significant for epidemiologic or statistical purposes.

age 30 transition, (in psychiatry) a period between 28 and 33 years of age when an individual may reevaluate the choices made in his or her twenties.

ageusia /əgyoo′sē·ə/ [Gk, *a* + *geusis,* without taste], a loss or impairment of the sense of taste.

agger /ag′ər, aj′ər/, a small protuberance or eminence of tissue, such as the curved elevation above the atrium of the nose.

agglomeration [L, *agglomerare,* to gather into a ball], a mass or cluster of individual units. —**agglomerate,** *v.*

agglutinant /əgloo′tənənt/ [L, *agglutinare,* to glue], something that causes adhesion, such as a circulating antibody that is stimulated by the presence of an antigen to adhere to it.

agglutination /əgloo′tinā′shən/ [L, *agglutinare,* to glue], the clumping of cells or particulate antigens as a result of interaction and crosslinking with agglutinins. —**agglutinate,** *v.*

agglutination-inhibition test, a serologic technique useful in testing for certain unknown soluble antigens.

agglutination reaction, the formation of an aggregate after the mixing of a soluble antibody with particulate antigen molecules in an aqueous medium. The visible aggregates are formed when specific antibody cross-links the antigens.

agglutination titer, the highest dilution of a serum that will produce clumping of cells or particulate antigens. It is a measure of the concentration of specific antibodies in the serum.

agglutinin /əglōō'tinin/, an antibody that interacts with antigens, resulting in agglutination.

agglutinin absorption, the removal of an antibody from immune serum via treatment with homologous antigen. The antibody attaches to the antigen, followed by centrifugation and separation of the antigen-antibody complex from the serum.

agglutinogen /ag'lōōtin'əjen/ [L, *agglutinare* + Gk, *genein,* to produce], any antigenic substance that causes agglutination by the production of agglutinin.

aggregate /ag'rəgāt/ [L, *ad* + *gregare,* to gather together], the total of a group of substances or components making up a mass or complex.

aggregate anaphylaxis, an exaggerated immune reaction of immediate hypersensitivity induced by an antigen that forms a soluble antigen-antibody complex.

aggregation /ag'rəgā'shən/ [L, *ad* + *gregare,* to gather together], an accumulation of substances, objects, or individuals, as in the clumping of blood cells or the clustering of clients with the same disorder.

aggression /əgresh'ən/ [L, *aggressio,* to attack], a forceful behavior, action, or attitude that is expressed physically, verbally, or symbolically. It may arise from innate drives or occur as a defensive mechanism, often resulting from a threatened ego.

aggression self-control, a nursing outcome from the Nursing Outcomes Classification (NOC) defined as self-restraint of assaultive, combative, or destructive behaviors toward others.

aggressive infantile fibromatosis, an uncommon condition, present at birth or developing during infancy or childhood, characterized by fast-growing, firm, painless, single or multiple nodules involving subcutaneous tissue, muscle, fascia, and tendons and seen anywhere on the body. Tumors are locally invasive but do not metastasize and have a high tendency to recur after excision.

aggressive personality, a personality with behavior patterns characterized by irritability, impulsivity, destructiveness, or violence in response to frustration.

aggressive-radical therapy, (in psychiatry) a form of therapy that introduces the political and social viewpoints of the therapist into the therapeutic process.

aging [L, *aetas,* lifetime], the process of growing old. Biologic aging results in part from a failure of body cells to function normally or to produce new body cells to replace those that are dead or malfunctioning. Sociologic and psychologic theories of aging seek to explain the other influences on aging caused by the environment, engagement, personality, and nonbiologic influences.

agitated depression, a severe depressive disorder characterized by severe anxiety accompanied by continuous physical restlessness, and, frequently, somatic symptoms.

agitation, a state of chronic restlessness and increased psychomotor activity that is generally observed as an expression of emotional tension and characterized by purposeless, restless activity.—**agitate,** *v.*

agitation level, a nursing outcome from the Nursing Outcomes Classification (NOC) defined as severity of disruptive physiologic and behavioral manifestations of stress or biochemical triggers.

agitographia /aj'itōgraf'ē·ə/ [L, *agitare*; Gk, *graphein,* to write], a condition characterized by abnormally rapid writing in which words or parts of words are unconsciously omitted.

agitophasia /aj'itōfā'zhə/ [L, *agitare*; Gk, *phasis,* speech], a condition characterized by abnormally rapid speech in which words, sounds, or syllables are unconsciously omitted, slurred, or distorted. The condition is commonly associated with agitographia.

Agkistrodon /ag·kis'trōdon/, a genus of venomous pit vipers. *A. contortrix* is the copperhead and *A. piscivorus* is the water moccasin.

aglossia /əglos'ē·ə/ [Gk, *a* + *glossa,* without tongue], congenital absence of the tongue.

agnathia /ag·nath'ē·ə/ [Gk, *a*+ *gnathos,* without jaw], a developmental defect characterized by total or partial absence of the lower jaw.—**agnathous,** *adj.*

agnathocephalus /ag·nath'əsef'ələs/, a fetus with agnathocephaly.

agnathocephaly /ag·nath'əsef'əlē/ [Gk, *a*+ *gnathos* + *kephale,* head], a congenital malformation characterized by the absence of the lower jaw, defective formation of the mouth, and placement of the eyes low on the face with fusion or approximation of the zygomas and the ears.—**agnathocephalic, agnathocephalous,** *adj.*

agnathus /ag·nath'əs/ [Gk, *a* + *gnathos,* without jaw], a fetus with agnathia.

agnosia /ag·nō'zhə/ [Gk, *a* + *gnosis,* not knowledge], total or partial loss of the ability to recognize familiar objects or persons through sensory stimuli as a result of organic brain damage or dementia. The condition may affect any of the senses and is classified accordingly as auditory, visual, olfactory, gustatory, or tactile agnosia.

agonal /ag′ənəl/ [Gk, *agon,* struggle], pertaining to death and dying.

agonal thrombus, a mass of blood platelets, fibrin, clotting factors, and cellular elements that forms in the heart of a dying patient.

agonist /ag′ənist/ [Gk, *agon,* struggle], **1.** a contracting muscle whose contraction is opposed by another muscle (an antagonist). **2.** a drug or other substance having a specific cellular affinity that produces a predictable response.

agony /ag′ənē/ [Gk, *agon*], severe physical or emotional anguish or distress.

agoraphobia /ag′ōrə-/ [Gk, *agora,* marketplace, *phobos,* fear], an anxiety disorder characterized by a fear of being in an open, crowded, or public place, such as a field, tunnel, bridge, congested street, or busy department store, where escape is perceived as difficult or help not available in case of sudden incapacitation.

agranulocyte /āgran′yŏŏlōsīt′/ [Gk, *a,* not; L, *granulum,* small grain; Gk, *kytos,* cell], a type of leukocyte characterized by the lack of cytoplasmic granules. —**agranulocytic,** *adj.*

agranulocytosis /āgran′yŏŏlō′sītō′sis/, a severe reduction in the number of white blood cells (basophils, eosinophils, and neutrophils).

agraphia /āgraf′ē-ə/ [Gk, *a* + *graphein,* not to write], a loss of the ability to write, resulting from injury to the language center in the cerebral cortex.—**agraphic,** *adj.*

A:G ratio, the ratio of albumin to globulin in the blood serum. On the basis of differential solubility with a neutral salt solution, the normal values are 3.5 to 5 g/dL for albumin and 2.5 to 4 g/dL for globulin.

agrimony, a herb found in Asia, Europe, and the United States. It is used for mild diarrhea, gastroenteritis, intestinal secretion of mucus, inflammation of the mouth and throat, cuts and scrapes, and amenorrhea. There is insufficient reliable information to assess its effectiveness.

Agrobacterium, an environmental gramnegative bacillus. *A. tumefaciens* has been implicated in health care–associated UTIs, peritonitis, wound infections, prosthetic valve endocarditis, and sepsis.

agrypnocoma /agrip′nōkō′mə/ [Gk, *agrypnos,* sleepless], a coma in which there is some degree of wakefulness.

agrypnotic /ag′ripnot′ik/, **1.** an insomniac. **2.** a medication or other substance that prevents sleep. **3.** causing wakefulness.

AGS, 1. abbreviation for *American Geriatrics Society.* **2.** abbreviation for *adrenogenital syndrome.*

agyria /əjī′rē-ə/, a congenital lack or underdevelopment of the convolutionary pattern of the cerebral cortex. The cortical tissue is reduced, leading to severe mental retardation.

AHA, abbreviation for **American Hospital Association.**

"aha" reaction /ähä′/, (in psychology) a sudden realization or inspiration, experienced especially during creative thinking.

AHCPR, abbreviation for *Agency for Health Care Policy and Research.*

AHF, abbreviation for **antihemophilic factor.**

AHH, abbreviation for **aryl hydrocarbon hydroxylase.**

AHIMA, abbreviation for *American Health Information Management Association.*

AHRQ, abbreviation for **Agency for Healthcare Research and Quality.**

Ahumada-del Castillo syndrome /ä′hŏŏmä′dä del′kästē′yō/ [Juan Carlos Ahumada, b. 1890, Argentine gynecologist; Enrique B. del Castillo [1897–1969], Argentine physician and endocrinologist], a form of secondary amenorrhea that may be associated with a pituitary gland tumor.

AI, 1. abbreviation for **artificial intelligence. 2.** abbreviation for **artificial insemination.**

AICC, abbreviation for **antiinhibitor coagulant complex.**

AICD, abbreviation for **automatic implanted cardioverter defibrillator.**

aid, assistance given a person who is ill, injured, or otherwise unable to cope with the normal demands of life.

AID, abbreviation for **artificial insemination by donor.**

AIDS /ādz/, abbreviation for **acquired immunodeficiency syndrome.**

AIDS cholangiopathy, bile duct disease seen complicating AIDS. The most common effect is primary sclerosing cholangitis; some patients also have sphincter of Oddi dysfunction.

AIDS-dementia complex (ADC), a neurologic effect of encephalitis or brain inflammation experienced by nearly one third of all patients with AIDS. The condition is characterized by memory loss and by varying levels and forms of dementia. It may be caused by the destruction of brain neurons by the HIV virus, as autopsies indicate that the density of the neurons may be 40% lower in patients with AIDS than in healthy persons.

AIDS-related complex (ARC), a stage before AIDS, with symptoms such as swollen lymph glands, long-lasting night sweats, fevers, and unusual weight loss.

AIDS serology test (AIDS screen, HIV antibody test, Western blot test, ELISA), a test used to detect the antibody to HIV.

AIDS-wasting syndrome, a syndrome associated with AIDS. Signs and symptoms may include weight loss, fever, malaise, lethargy, oral thrush, and immunologic abnormalities characteristic of AIDS.

AIH, abbreviation for **artificial insemination—husband.**

AILD, abbreviation for **angioimmuno-blastic lymphadenopathy with dysproteinemia.**

ailment [OE, *eglan*], any disease, physical disorder, or complaint, generally of a chronic, acute, or mild nature.

air [Gk, *aer*], the colorless, odorless gaseous mixture constituting the earth's atmosphere. It consists of 78% nitrogen; 20% oxygen; almost 1% argon; small amounts of carbon dioxide, hydrogen, and ozone; traces of helium, krypton, neon, and xenon; and varying amounts of water vapor.

air abrasion, a type of microabrasion in which a jet of air blows tiny particles against the tooth or cavity surface.

air bath, the exposure of the naked body to warm air for therapeutic purposes.

airborne contaminant, a material in the atmosphere that can affect the health of persons in the same or nearby environments. Particularly vulnerable are tissues of the upper respiratory tract and lungs.

airborne precautions, guidelines recommended by the Centers for Disease Control and Prevention for reducing the risk of airborne transmission of infectious agents. Airborne transmission occurs by dissemination of either airborne droplet nuclei or dust particles containing the infectious agent. Special air handling and ventilation are required to prevent airborne transmission. Airborne precautions apply to patients known or suspected to be infected with epidemiologically important pathogens that can be transmitted by the airborne route.

air compressor, a mechanical device that compresses air for storage and is used in handpieces and other air-driven medical and dental tools.

air embolism, the abnormal presence of air in the cardiovascular system, resulting in obstruction of blood flow. Air embolism may occur if a large quantity of air is inadvertently introduced by injection, as during IV therapy or surgery, or by trauma, as a puncture wound.

air entrainment, the movement of room air into the chamber of a jet nebulizer used to treat respiratory diseases. Air entrainment increases the rate of nebulization and the amount of liquid administered per unit of time.

airflow pattern, the pattern of movement of respiratory gases through the respiratory tract. The pattern is affected by factors such as gas density and viscosity.

air fluidization, the process of blowing temperature-controlled air through a collection of microspheres to create a fluid-like movement. The technique is used in special mattresses designed to reduce pressure against a patient's skin.

air-fluidized bed, a bed with body support provided by thousands of tiny soda-lime glass beads suspended by pressurized temperature-controlled air. The bed is designed for use by patients with or at risk for posterior pressure ulcers or posterior grafts, burns, or donor areas.

air hunger, a form of respiratory distress characterized by gasping, labored breathing, or dyspnea.

airplane splint, a splint used to immobilize a shoulder during healing from injury or surgery. The splint holds the arm in an abducted position at or below shoulder level, with the elbow bent.

air pollution [L, *polluere*, to defile], contamination of the air by noxious fumes, aromas, or toxic chemicals.

air pump, a pump that forces air into or out of a cavity or chamber.

air sac, a small, terminal cavity in the lung, consisting of the alveoli connected to one terminal bronchiole.

air sickness, a form of kinesia caused by flying and, in some cases, by traveling on land at high elevations.

air spaces, the alveolar ducts, alveolar sacs, and alveoli of the respiratory tract.

air splint, a device for temporarily immobilizing fractured or otherwise injured extremities. It consists of an inflatable cylinder that can be closed at both ends and becomes rigid when filled with air under pressure.

air swallowing, the intake of air into the digestive system, usually involuntary and during eating, drinking, or chewing gum. Air swallowing may also be an effect of anxious behavior. The problem occurs commonly in infants as a result of faulty feeding methods.

air thermometer, a thermometer using air as its expansible medium.

airway [Gk, *aer*; AS, *weg*, way], **1.** a tubular passage for movement of air into and out of the lung. **2.** a respiratory anesthesia device. **3.** an oropharyngeal tube used for mouth-to-mouth resuscitation.

airway conductance (G_aw), the instantaneous rate of gas flow in the airway per unit of pressure difference between the mouth, nose, or other airway opening and the alveoli. It is the reciprocal of airway resistance.

airway division, one of the 18 segments of the bronchopulmonary system. The segments are usually numbered from 1 to 10 for the right lung, which has three lobes, and from 1 to 8 for the left lung, which has two lobes.

airway insertion and stabilization, a nursing intervention from the Nursing Interventions Classification (NIC) defined as insertion or assisting with insertion and stabilization of an artificial airway.

airway management, a nursing intervention from the Nursing Interventions Classification (NIC) defined as facilitation of patency of air passages.

airway obstruction, a mechanical impediment to the delivery of air to the lungs or to the absorption of oxygen in the lungs.

airway resistance (R_aw), a measure of the impedance to airflow through the bronchopulmonary system. It is the reciprocal of airway conductance.

airway suctioning, a nursing intervention from the Nursing Interventions Classification (NIC) defined as removal of airway secretions by inserting a suction catheter into the patient's oral airway and/or trachea.

AIUM, abbreviation for *American Institute of Ultrasound in Medicine.*

akaryocyte /ăker′ē·əsīt′/ [Gk, *a*, not, *karyon*, kernel], a cell without a nucleus, such as an erythrocyte.

akathisia /ak′əthē′zhə/ [Gk, *a* + *kathizein*, not to sit], a pathologic condition characterized by restlessness and agitation. **—akathisiac,** *adj.*

akeratosis /ăker′ətō′sis/, a skin condition in which there is a lack of horny tissue in the epidermis.

akinesia /ā′kinē′zhə, ā′kīnē′zhə/ [Gk, *a*, *kinesis*, without movement], an abnormal state of motor and psychic hypoactivity or muscular paralysis.—**akinetic,** *adj.*

akinesthesia /ăkin′esthē′zhə/, a loss of the sense of movement.

akinetic apraxia, the inability to perform a spontaneous movement.

akinetic mutism, a state of apparent alertness in which a person is unable or refuses to move or to make sounds, resulting from neurologic or psychologic disturbance.

akinetic seizure, a type of seizure disorder observed in children. It is a brief, generalized seizure in which the child suddenly falls to the ground.

Akineton, a trademark for a peripheral anticholinergic (biperiden hydrochloride).

Al, symbol for the element **aluminum.**

ala /ā′lə/ *pl.* **alae** [L, wing], **1.** any winglike structure. **2.** the axilla.

Ala, abbreviation for the amino acid **alanine.**

ALA, abbreviation for **aminolevulinic acid.**

ala cerebelli /ser′əbel′ī/, a winglike structure of the central lobule of the cerebellum.

ala cinerea /sinir′ē·ə/, the triangular area on the floor of the brain's fourth ventricle from which the autonomic fibers of the vagus nerve arise.

Alagille's syndrome /ä·läzhēl′/ [Daniel Alagille, French pediatrician, b. 1925], an autosomal-dominant syndrome of neonatal jaundice, cholestasis with peripheral pulmonary stenosis, and occasionally septal defects or patent ductus arteriosus, resulting from a low number or an absence of intrahepatic bile ducts. It is characterized by unusual facies and ocular, vertebral, and nervous system abnormalities.

ala nasi /nā′sī/, the outer flaring cartilaginous wall of the outer side of each nostril.

alanine (Ala or A) /al′ənin/, a nonessential amino acid found in many food protein sources as well as in the body. It is degraded in the liver to produce important biomolecules such as pyruvate and glutamate. Its carbon skeleton also can be used as an energy source.

alanine aminotransferase (ALT), an enzyme normally present in the serum and tissues of the body, especially the tissues of the liver. This enzyme catalyzes the transfer of an amino group from *l*-alanine to alpha-ketoglutarate, forming pyruvate and 1-glutamate.

alanine aminotransferase (ALT) test, a blood test that measures levels of alanine aminotransferase. Formerly called glutamate pyruvate transamininase test.

alanine transferase, an intracellular enzyme in amino acid and carbohydrate metabolism found in high concentration in brain, liver, and muscle. An increased level indicates necrosis or disease in these tissues.

Al-Anon, an international organization that offers guidance, counseling, and support for the relatives, friends, and associates of alcoholics.

ala of the ethmoid, a small projection on each side of the crista galli of the ethmoid bone. Each ala fits into a corresponding depression of the frontal bone.

ala of the ilium, the upper flaring part of the iliac bone.

ala of the sacrum, the flat extension of bone on each side of the sacrum.

ALARA, an abbreviation for *as low as reasonably achievable*. It refers to the principle that all radiation exposure, both to patients and to radiologic personnel, should be minimized in diagnostic imaging.

alar fold, 1. a fringed margin on either side of an infrapatellar fat pad in the knee joint formed by the synovial membrane. **2.** a fold extending from the nostril to the ventral nasal concha.

alar lamina [L, *ala,* wing, *lamina,* thin plate], the posterolateral area of the embryonic neural tube through which sensory nerves enter.

alar ligament, one of a pair of ligaments that connect the axis to the occipital bone and limit rotation of the cranium.

alarm reaction, the first stage of the general adaptation syndrome. It is characterized by the release of adrenocorticotropic hormone (ACTH) by the pituitary gland and of epinephrine by the adrena medulla, which cause increased blood glucose levels and a faster respiration rate, increasing the oxygen level of the blood. These actions provide the body with increased energy for dealing with a stressful situation.

alar process [L, *ala,* wing, *processus*], a projection of the cribriform plate of the ethmoid bone articulating with the frontal bone.

alaryngeal speech /ā′lärin′jē·əl spēch/ [Gk, *a,* without + *larynx*; ME, *speche*], methods of speech communication used after laryngectomy, including communication with an electrolarynx, a tracheoesophageal voice prosthesis and use of esophageal speech.

alastrim /al′əstrim/ [Port, *alastrar,* to spread], a mild form of smallpox, with little rash. It is thought to be caused by a weak strain of *Poxvirus variolae*.

Alateen, an international organization that offers guidance, counseling, and support for the children of alcoholics.

alatrofloxacin /ah-lat′ro-flok′sah-sin/, a broad-spectrum antibacterial that is the prodrug of trovafloxacin, to which it is rapidly converted after IV infusion; used in the form of the mesylate salt.

alatrofloxacin/trovafloxacin, a quinolone antibiotic used to treat nosocomial pneumonia, community-acquired pneumonia, chronic bronchitis, acute sinusitis, complicated intraabdominal infections, infections of the skin and skin structure, UTIs, chronic bacterial prostatitis, urethral gonorrhea in males, PID, and cervicitis caused by susceptible organisms.

ala vomeris /vō′məris/, an extension of bone on each side of the upper border of the unpaired facial bones of the skull.

alba /al′bə/, literally, "white," as in *linea alba*.

albedo /albē′dō/, *pl.* albedos [L, *albus,* white], a whiteness, as a surface reflection.

albendazole /alben′dahzōl/, a broad-spectrum anthelmintic used against many parasites, including those that cause echinococcosis and cysticercosis.

Albers-Schönberg disease /-shœn′burg, -shōn′-/ [Heinrich E. Albers-Schönberg, German radiologist and surgeon, 1865–1921], a form of osteopetrosis characterized by marble-like calcification of bones, causing spontaneous fractures.

Albert's disease [Eduard Albert, Austrian surgeon, 1841–1900], an inflammation of the calcaneal bursa that lies between the Achilles tendon and the calcaneus. It is most frequently caused by injury but may also result from the wearing of poorly fitted shoes, increased strain on the tendon, or rheumatoid arthritis.

albicans /al′bikənz/ [L, *albus,* white], white or whitish.

albinism /al′biniz′əm/, a rare inherited disorder characterized by a lack of melanin in the skin. Total albinos have pale skin that does not tan, white hair, pink eyes, nystagmus, astigmatism, and photophobia.

Albini's nodule /äl·be·nēz′/ [Giuseppe Albini, Italian physiologist, 1827–1911], a gray nodule the size of a small grain, sometimes seen on the free edges of the atrioventricular valves of infants. Albini's nodules are remains of fetal structures.

albino /albī′nō/ [L, *albus,* white], an individual with albinism.

albinuria /al′binŏŏr′ē·ə/, white or colorless urine.

Abl's ring, a calcified ring-shaped shadow of a cerebral aneurysm visible on a skull radiograph.

Albright's syndrome /ôl′brīts/ [Fuller Albright, American physician and endocrinologist, 1900–1969], a disorder characterized by fibrous dysplasia of bone, isolated brown macules on the skin, and endocrine dysfunction. It causes precocious puberty in girls but not in boys.

albumin /albyŏŏ′min/ [L, *albus,* white], a water-soluble, heat-coagulable protein. Various albumins are found in practically all animal tissues and in many plant tissues.

albumin A, a blood serum constituent that gathers in cancer cells and is deficient in circulation in cancer patients.

albuminaturia, urine that contains a high level of albumin salts and has a low specific gravity.

albumin/creatinine ratio, the ratio of albumin to creatinine in the urine, calculated as a measure of albuminuria.

albumin (human), a plasma-volume expander prescribed in the treatment of hypoproteinemia, hyperbilirubinemia, and hypovolemic shock.

albumin microsphere sonicated, a microbubble, mean size 2 to 4.5 mm, created by heat treatment and sonication of diluted human albumin in the presence of octafluoropropane gas. Sonicated albumin microspheres are injected intravenously as a diagnostic adjunct in echocardiography.

albumin test [L, *albus,* white], any of several tests for the presence of albumin in the urine. One type of albumin test depends on the change in color of a chemically treated strip of paper in the presence of albumin.

albuminuria, presence of albumin in the urine, a common sign of renal or chronic disease.

albuterol, a β-2 receptor adrenergic agent prescribed in the treatment of bronchospasm in patients with reversible obstructive airway disease, including asthma.

alcalase, an enzyme found in certain laundry detergents. It is a cause of enzymatic detergent asthma.

Alcaligenes, an environmental gram-negative bacillus that can be found in the GI tract of humans and that can cause nosocomial infections in the compromised host.

alclometasone /alklōōmet′asōn′/, a synthetic corticosteroid used topically in the dipropionate form for the relief of inflammation and pruritus.

alclometasone dipropionate, a topical corticosteroid prescribed for the relief of symptoms of inflammation and pruritus of corticosteroid-responsive dermatoses.

Alcock's canal [Benjamin Alcock, Irish anatomist, b. 1801], a canal formed by the obturator internus muscle and the obturator fascia through which the pudendal nerve and vessels pass.

alcohol /al′kəhôl/ [Ar *alkohl,* subtle essence], **1.** a preparation containing at least 92.3% and not more than 93.8% by weight of ethyl alcohol, used as a topical antiseptic and solvent. **2.** a clear, colorless, volatile liquid that is miscible with water, chloroform, or ether, obtained by the fermentation of carbohydrates with yeast. **3.** a compound derived from a hydrocarbon by replacing one or more hydrogen atoms with an equal number of hydroxyl groups.

alcohol abuse cessation behavior, a nursing outcome from the Nursing Outcomes Classification (NOC) defined as personal actions to eliminate alcohol use that poses a threat to health.

alcohol bath, an obsolete procedure for decreasing an elevated body temperature. It is no longer used because of the danger of inhaled fumes and absorption through the skin causing toxicity.

alcoholic, 1. pertaining to alcohol or its effects on other substances. **2.** a person who has developed a dependency on alcohol through abuse of the substance.

alcoholic ataxia [Ar, *alkohl,* essence; Gk, *ataxia,* disorder], a loss of coordination in performing voluntary movements associated with peripheral neuritis as a result of alcoholism. A similar form of ataxia may occur with neuritis resulting from other toxic agents.

alcoholic blackout, a form of amnesia in which a person has no memory of what occurred during a period of alcohol abuse.

alcoholic cardiomyopathy [Ar, *alkohl,* essence; Gk, *kardia,* heart, *mys,* muscle, *pathos,* disease], a cardiac disease associated with alcohol abuse and characterized by an enlarged heart and low cardiac output.

alcoholic coma [Ar, *alkohl;* Gk, *koma,* deep sleep], a state of unconsciousness that results from severe alcoholic intoxication.

alcoholic dementia [Ar, *alkohl;* L, *de,* away, *mens,* mind], a deterioration of normal cognitive and intellectual functions associated with long-term alcohol abuse.

alcoholic dyspepsia, a digestive disorder characterized by abdominal discomfort and provoked by the consumption of alcohol.

alcoholic fermentation, the conversion of carbohydrates to ethyl alcohol.

alcoholic hallucinosis, a form of alcoholic psychosis characterized primarily by auditory hallucinations occurring in a clear sensorium, abject fear, and persecutory delusions. The condition develops in acute alcoholism as withdrawal symptoms, shortly after stopping or reducing prolonged and heavy alcohol intake, usually within 48 hours.

alcoholic hepatitis, an acute toxic liver injury associated with excess ethanol consumption. It is characterized by necrosis, inflammation caused by the accumulation of polymorphonuclear leukocytes, and in many instances Mallory bodies.

alcoholic hepatopathy, a liver disease resulting from alcoholism, progressing in time to fibrosis and cirrhosis.

alcoholic ketoacidosis, the fall in blood pH (acidosis) sometimes seen in alcoholics and associated with a rise in the levels of serum ketone bodies.

alcoholic neuropathy, damaage affecting the peripheral nerves as a result of alcohol consumption.

alcoholic-nutritional cerebellar degeneration, a sudden, severe incoordination in the lower extremities characteristic of poorly nourished alcoholics. The patient walks, if at all, with an ataxic or a wide-based gait.

alcoholic psychosis, any of a group of severe mental disorders in which the ego's functioning is impaired, including pathologic intoxication, DT, Korsakoff's psychosis, and acute hallucinosis. It is characterized by brain damage or dysfunction that results from excessive alcohol use.

Alcoholics Anonymous (AA), an international nonprofit organization, founded in 1935, consisting of abstinent alcoholics whose purpose is to stay sober and help others recover from the disease of alcoholism through a 12-step program, including group support, shared experiences, and faith in a higher power.

alcoholic trance, a state of automatism resulting from ethanol intoxication.

alcoholism /al'kəhôliz'əm/, the extreme dependence on excessive amounts of alcohol, associated with a cumulative pattern of deviant behaviors. Alcoholism is a chronic illness with a slow, insidious onset, which may occur at any age. The most frequent medical consequences of alcoholism are CNS depression and cirrhosis of the liver.

alcohol poisoning, poisoning caused by the ingestion of any of several alcohols, of which ethyl, isopropyl, and methyl are the most common. Ethyl alcohol (ethanol) is found in beverages, hairspray, and mouthwashes. Ordinarily, it is lethal only if large quantities are ingested in a brief period. Isopropyl (rubbing) alcohol is more toxic. Methyl alcohol (methanol) is extremely poisonous: in addition to nausea, vomiting, and abdominal pain, it may cause blindness; death may follow the consumption of only 2 ounces.

alcohol withdrawal syndrome, the clinical symptoms associated with cessation of alcohol consumption. These may include tremor, hallucinations, autonomic nervous system dysfunction, and seizures.

ALD, abbreviation for **adrenoleukodystrophy.**

Aldactazide, a trademark for a fixed-combination drug containing a thiazide diuretic (hydrochlorothiazide) and a potassium-sparing diuretic (spironolactone).

Aldactone, a trademark for a potassium-sparing diuretic (spironolactone).

aldehyde /al'dəhīd'/ [Ar, alkohl; L, dehydrogenatum, dehydrogenated], any of a large category of organic compounds derived from oxidation of a corresponding primary alcohol, as in the conversion of ethyl alcohol to acetaldehyde.

aldesleukin, an antineoplastic agent used to treat metastatic renal cell carcinoma in adults and metastatic melanoma. It is also used as a phase II treatment in HIV in combination with zidovudine.

Aldoclor, a trademark for a fixed-combination antihypertensive drug containing a diuretic (chlorothiazide), and an antihypertensive (methyldopa).

aldolase /al'dəlās/, enzymes found in muscle tissue that catalyze the step in anaerobic glycolysis involving the breakdown of fructose 1,6-biphosphate to glyceraldehyde 3-phosphate (GAP).

aldolase test, a blood test that can be useful in indicating muscular or hepatic cellular injury or disease.

Aldomet, a trademark for an antihypertensive (methyldopa).

Aldoril, a trademark for a fixed-combination drug containing a thiazide diuretic (hydrochlorothiazide) and an antihypertensive (methyldopa).

aldose /al'dōs/, the chemical form of monosaccharides in which the carbonyl group is an aldehyde.

aldosterone /al'dōstərōn', aldos'tərōn/, a mineralocorticoid steroid hormone produced by the adrenal cortex with action in the renal tubule to retain sodium, conserve water by reabsorption, and increase urinary excretion of potassium.

aldosterone test, a blood or 24-hour urine test used to diagnose aldosteronism.

aldosteronism /al'dōstərō'nizəm, aldos'-/, a condition characterized by the hypersecretion of aldosterone, occurring as a primary disease of the adrenal cortex or, more often, as a secondary disorder in response to various extraadrenal pathologic processes. Primary aldosteronism may be caused by adrenal hyperplasia or by an aldosterone-secreting adenoma. Secondary aldosteronism is associated with increased plasma renin activity and may be induced by the nephrotic syndrome, cirrhosis, idiopathic edema, CHF, trauma, burns, or other kinds of stress.

aldosteronoma /al'dōstir'ənō'mə/, pl. **aldosteronomas, aldosteronomata** an aldosterone-secreting adenoma of the adrenal cortex that is usually small and occurs more frequently in the left than in the right adrenal gland. Aldosteronism with sodium retention, expansion of the extracellular fluid volume, and hypertension may occur.

Aldurazyme, a trademark for laronidase.

alefacept, an immunosuppressive agent used to treat adults with moderate to severe plaque psoriasis.

alemtuzumab /al'em-tuz͞uumab'/, a recombinant DNA–derived, humanized monoclonal antibody directed against the antigen

CD52. It is administered intravenously as an antineoplastic drug in the treatment of B-cell chronic lymphocytic leukemia.

alendronate, a bone-resorption inhibitor used to treat osteoporosis in postmenopausal women and Paget's disease.

alertness [Fr, *alerte*], a measure of being mentally quick, active, and keenly aware of the environment.

aleukemia, an acute form of leukemia characterized by a diminished total WBC content in the peripheral blood supply, accompanied by a loss of normal bone marrow function.

aleukemic leukemia /ā'lookē'mik/, a type of leukemia in which the total leukocyte count remains within normal limits and few abnormal forms appear in the peripheral blood.

aleukia /āloo'kē·ə/ [Gk, *a* + *leukos,* not white], a marked reduction in or complete absence of leukocytes or platelets.

aleukocytosis /āloo'kōsītō'sis/, absence of leukocytes from the blood.

Alexander's deafness [Gustav Alexander, Austrian otologist, 1873–1932]

Alexander's disease /al'egzan'dərz/ [W. Stewart Alexander, English pathologist, 20th century], an infantile form of leukodystrophy, characterized by collection of eosinophilic material at the surface of the brain and around its blood vessels, resulting in brain enlargement.

Alexander technique [Frederick Matthias Alexander, Australian actor, 1869–1955, who developed and taught the technique], a bodywork technique that uses psychophysical reeducation to correct dysfunctional habits of posture and movement. It is based on the principle that human movement is mostly fluid when the head leads and the spine follows to improve postural balance, coordination, and breathing; relieve stress and chronic pain; and improve general well-being.

alexandrite laser, a laser whose active medium is alexandrite doped with chromium, emitting light in the mid-infrared spectrum, tunable between 701 and 826 nm, and used usually at 755 nm. It is used for hair removal and other dermatologic procedures.

alexithymia /əlek'sithī'mē·ə, -thim'ē·ə/, an inability to experience and communicate feelings consciously.

alfacalcidol /al'fahəkal'sidol/, a synthetic analog of calcitriol, to which it is converted in the liver. It is used in the treatment of hypocalcemia, hypophosphatemia, rickets, and osteodystrophy associated with various medical conditions, including chronic renal failure and hypoparathyroidism.

alfalfa, a herb that is grown throughout the world. It is used for poor appetite, hay fever and asthma, and high cholesterol. It may also be used as a nutrient source.

alfuzosin, an antiadrenergic agent used to treat symptoms of benign prostatic hyperplasia.

ALG, abbreviation for *antilymphocyte globulin.*

alga *pl.* **algae** /al'gə/ [L, seaweed], any of a large group of mostly photosynthetic protists, found worldwide in fresh water, in salt water, and on land.—**algal,** *adj.*

algid /al'jid/ [L, *algere,* to be cold], chilly or cold.

algid malaria [L, *algere,* to be cold], a rare complication of tropical malaria (occurring in 0.37% of cases) caused by the protozoan *Plasmodium falciparum.* It is characterized by cold skin, profound weakness, and severe diarrhea.

alginate /al'jināt/, a salt of alginic acid, extracted from marine kelp. The calcium, sodium, and ammonium alginates have been used in foam, cloth, and gauze for absorbent surgical dressings. Soluble alginates, such as those of sodium, potassium, or magnesium, form a viscous sol that can be changed into a gel by a chemical reaction with compounds such as calcium sulfate; this makes them useful as materials for taking dental impressions.

algodystrophy /al'gōdis'trəfē/, a painful wasting of the muscles of the hands, often accompanied by tenderness and a loss of bone calcium.

algolagnia /al'gōlag'nē·ə/ [Gk, *algos,* pain, *lagneia,* lust], a form of sexual perversion characterized by sadism or masochism.

algologist /algol'əjist/, **1.** a person who specializes in the study of or the treatment of pain. **2.** a person who specializes in the study of algae.

algology, 1. the branch of medicine that is concerned with the study of pain. **2.** the branch of science that is concerned with algae.

algophobia [Gk, *algos,* pain, *phobos,* fear], an anxiety disorder characterized by an abnormal, pervasive fear of experiencing pain or of witnessing pain in others.

algor [L, cold], the sensation of cold or a chill, such as in the first stage of a fever.

algorithm /al'gərith'əm/, an explicit protocol with well-defined rules to be followed in solving a health care problem.

algor mortis, the reduction in body temperature and accompanying loss of skin elasticity that occur after death.

algospasm /al'gōspaz'əm/, an acute, painful spasm of the muscles.

aliasing, an artifact that is caused by undersampling of signal data in diagnostic imaging.

Alice in Wonderland syndrome, perceptual distortions of space and size, as experienced by the character Alice in the Lewis Carroll story. Similar hallucinogenic experiences have been reported by individuals using drugs of abuse and by patients with certain neurologic diseases.

alienation /āl′yənā′shən/ [L, *alienare,* to estrange], the act or state of being estranged or isolated.—**alien,** *adj.,* **alienate,** *v.*

alignment /əlīn′mənt/ [Fr, *aligner,* to put in a straight line], **1.** the arrangement of a group of points or objects along a line. **2.** the placing or maintaining of body structures in their proper anatomic positions, such as straightening of the teeth or repair of a fractured bone.

aliment [L, *alimentum,* to nourish], something that nourishes or feeds.—**alimentary,** *adj.*

alimentation, nourishment.

Alimta, a trademark for pemetrexed.

aliphatic /al′ifat′ik/ [Gk, *aleiphar,* oil], pertaining to fat or oil, specifically hydrocarbon compounds that are open chains of carbon atoms, such as the fatty acids, rather than aromatic ring structures.

aliphatic acid, an acid containing a hydrocarbon fragment derived from a non-aromatic hydrocarbon.

aliphatic alcohol, an alcohol containing a hydrocarbon fragment derived from a fatty, nonaromatic hydrocarbon.

aliskiren, an antihypertensive.

alitretinoin, a second-generation retinoid used to treat the cutaneous lesions of Kaposi's sarcoma.

alkalemia [Ar, *al + galiy,* wood ash; Gk, *haima,* blood], increased pH of the blood, above the normal range of 7.35 to 7.45.

alkali /al′kəlī/ [Ar, *al + galiy,* wood ash], a compound with the chemical characteristics of a base. Usually used with reference to hydroxides of Group I metals and ammonium, alkalis combine with fatty acids to form soaps, turn red litmus blue, and enter into reactions with carbon dioxide that form water-soluble carbonates.—**alkaline,** *adj.,* **alkalinity,** *n.*

alkali burn, damage to tissue caused by exposure to an alkaline compound such as lye.

alkaline ash /al′kəlīn/, residue in urine having a pH higher than 7.0.

alkaline ash–producing foods, foods that may be ingested to produce an alkaline pH in the urine, thereby reducing the incidence of acidic urinary calculi, or that may be avoided to reduce the incidence of alkaline calculi. Some foods that result in alkaline ash are milk, cream, and buttermilk.

alkaline bath, a bath taken in water containing sodium bicarbonate, used especially for skin disorders.

alkaline phosphatase, an enzyme present in all tissues and in high concentration in bone, kidneys, intestines, biliary ducts, plasma, and teeth. It may be elevated in the serum in some diseases of the bone and liver and in some other illnesses.

alkaline phosphatase test (ALP), a blood test used to determine a variety of liver and bone disorders, such as extrahepatic and intrahepatic obstructive biliary disease, cirrhosis, hepatic tumors, hepatotoxic drugs, hepatitis, osteoblastic metastatic tumors, Paget's disease, rheumatoid arthritis, and hyperparathyroidism.

alkaline reflux gastritis, chronic gastritis caused by reflux of alkaline intestinal contents after partial gastrectomy.

alkaline reserve, the additional amount of sodium bicarbonate that the body produces to maintain a normal arterial pH (7.35 to 7.45) when the carbon dioxide level increases as a result of hypoventilation. The alkaline reserve is maintained by the kidneys, which control the excretion of bicarbonate ions in urine.

alkalinity /al′kəlin′itē/, the acid-base relationship of any solution that has a lower concentration of hydrogen ions or a higher concentration of hydroxide ions than pure water, which is an arbitrarily neutral standard with a pH of 7.0 at 25° C.

alkalinization /al′kəliniəzāshən/, **1.** the act of making a substance alkaline, as through the addition of a base. **2.** the state of becoming alkaline.—**alkalinize,** *v.*

alkali poisoning, a toxic condition caused by the ingestion of an alkaline agent such as liquid ammonia, lye, and some detergent powders.

alkali reserves [Ar, *al + galiy,* wood ash; L, *reservare,* to save], the volume of carbon dioxide or carbonates at standard temperature and pressure in 100 mL of blood plasma. The principal buffer in blood is bicarbonate, which represents most of the alkali reserve. Hemoglobin phosphates and additional bases also act as buffers. If the alkali reserve is low, acidosis exists. If the alkali reserve is high, alkalosis exists.

alkaloid /al′kəloid/ [Ar, *al + galiy;* Gk, *eidos,* form], any of a large group of nitrogen-containing organic compounds produced by plants, including many pharmacologically active substances, such as atropine, caffeine, cocaine, morphine, nicotine, and quinine.

alkalosis /al′kəlō′sis/ [Ar, *al + galiy;* Gk, *osis,* condition], an abnormal condition of body fluids, characterized by a tendency toward a blood pH level greater than 7.45, caused by an excess of alkaline bicarbonate or a deficiency of acid.

alkane, a saturated aliphatic hydrocarbon containing no double or triple bonds in the carbon chain, such as propane.

alkaptonuria /alkap'tōnŏŏr'ē·ə/ [Ar, *al* + *galiy*; Gk, *haptein* to possess, *ouron* urine], a rare inherited disorder marked by the excretion of large amounts of homogentistic acid in the urine, which is the result of the incomplete metabolism of the amino acids tyrosine and phenylalanine. The presence of the acid is indicated by darkening of urine when exposed to air or brown or blue discoloration of the ears or eyes. —**alkaptonuric,** *adj.*

alkene /al'kēn/, an unsaturated aliphatic hydrocarbon containing one double bond in the carbon chain, such as ethylene.

Alkeran, a trademark for an alkylating antineoplastic agent (melphalan).

alkyl /al'kil/, a hydrocarbon fragment derived from an alkane by the removal of one of the hydrogen atoms.

alkylamine /al'kiləmīn'/, an amine in which an alkyl group replaces one to three of the hydrogen atoms that are attached to the nitrogen atom of ammonia, such as methylamine (amino-methane).

alkylating agent /al'kilā'ting/, any substance that contains an alkyl radical and is capable of replacing a free hydrogen atom in an organic compound, or one that acts by a similar mechanism. This type of chemical reaction results in interference with DNA synthesis and RNA transcription, which in turn results in interference with mitosis and cell division, especially in rapidly proliferating tissue. The agents are useful in the treatment of cancer and are a common class of chemotherapy agents.

alkylation, a chemical reaction in which an alkyl group is transferred from an alkylating agent.

alkyne /al'kīn/, an unsaturated aliphatic hydrocarbon containing at least one triple bond in the carbon chain, such as acetylene.

ALL, abbreviation for **acute lymphocytic leukemia.**

allachesthesia /al'əkesthē'zhə/ [Gk, *allache,* elsewhere], an abnormality of touch sensation in which a stimulus is perceived to be at a point distant from where it is actually applied.

allantoidoangiopagus /al'əntoi'dō·an'jē·op'əgəs/ [Gk, *allantoeides,* sausage-like, *angeion,* vessel, *pagos,* fixed], conjoined monozygotic twin fetuses of unequal size that are united by the vessels of the umbilical cord. —**allantoidoangiopagous,** *adj.*

allantoin /əlan'tō·in/, a chemical compound (5-ureidohydantoin), $C_4H_6N_4O_3$,

that occurs as a white crystallizable substance found in many plants and in the allantoic and amniotic fluids and fetal urine of primates.

allantois /əlan'tois/ [Gk, *allas,* sausage, *eidos,* form], a tubular extension of the endoderm of the yolk sac that extends with the allantoic vessels into the body stalk of the embryo. In human embryos, allantoic vessels become the umbilical vessels and the chorionic villi. —**allantoic,** *adj.*

allele /əlēl'/, **1.** one of two or more alternative forms of a gene that occupy corresponding loci on homologous chromosomes. **2.** one of two or more contrasting characteristics transmitted by alternative forms of a gene. —**allelic,** *adj.*

Allen-Doisy test [Edgar Allen, U.S. endocrinologist, 1892–1943; Edward Doisy, U.S. biochemist and Nobel laureate, 1893–1986], a bioassay test for estrogen and gonadotropins in which ovariectomized mice or rats are injected with an estrogenic substance. The appearance of cornified cells on vaginal smears and the disappearance of leukocytes constitute a positive reaction.

Allen's test [Edgar Van Nuys Allen, American physician, 1893–1986], a test for the patency of the radial artery after insertion of an indwelling monitoring catheter.

allergen /al'ərjen/ [Gk, *allos,* other, *ergein,* to work, *genein,* to produce], an environmental substance that can produce a hypersensitive allergic reaction in the body but may not be intrinsically harmful. Methods to identify specific allergens affecting individuals include the patch test, the scratch test, the radioallergosorbent test (RAST), and the Prausnitz-Küstner (PK) test. —**allergenic,** *adj.*

allergenic /al'ərjen'ik/, provoking allergic reactions.

allergenic extract, a protein-containing extract purified from a substance to which a person may be sensitive. The extract may be used for diagnosis or for hyposensitization therapy.

allergic arthritis, appearance of symptoms of arthritis such as swollen joints after the ingestion of allergenic foods or medications.

allergic asthma, a form of asthma caused by exposure of the bronchial mucosa to an inhaled airborne antigen. The antigen causes the production of antibodies that bind to mast cells in the bronchial tree. The mast cells then release histamine, which stimulates contraction of bronchial smooth muscle and causes mucosal edema.

allergic bronchopulmonary aspergillosis, a form of aspergillosis that occurs in asthmatics when the fungus *Aspergillus* *fumigatus,* growing within the bronchial lumen, causes a type I or type III hypersensitivity reaction. The characteristics of the condition are similar to those of asthma, including dyspnea and wheezing.

allergic conjunctivitis, inflammation of the conjunctiva caused by an allergy.

allergic coryza, acute rhinitis caused by exposure to any allergen to which the person is hypersensitive.

allergic dermatitis [Ger, *allergie,* reaction; Gk, *derma,* skin, *itis,* inflammation], a delayed type IV allergic reaction of the skin resulting from cutaneous contact with a specific allergen, with varying degrees of erythema, edema, and vesiculation.

allergic interstitial nephritis, acute interstitial nephritis that is part of an allergic reaction, such as to medication.

allergic proctitis, in children, allergic gastroenteropathy having its focus in the rectum; in adults, rectal irritation possibly caused by chemicals in the rectum, such as after medical procedures or anal intercourse.

allergic purpura [Gk, *allos,* other, *ergein,* to work; L, *purpura,* purple], a chronic disorder of the skin associated with urticaria, erythema, asthma, and rheumatic joint swellings. Unlike in other forms of purpura, platelet count, bleeding time, and blood coagulation are normal.

allergic reaction, an unfavorable physiologic response to an allergen to which a person has previously been exposed and to which the person has developed antibodies. The response may be characterized by a variety of symptoms, including urticaria, eczema, dyspnea, bronchospasm, diarrhea, rhinitis, sinusitis, laryngospasm, and anaphylaxis. Allergic reactions may be immediate or delayed.

allergic response: localized, a nursing outcome from the Nursing Outcomes Classification (NOC) defined as severity of localized hypersensitive immune response to a specific environmental (exogenous) antigen.

allergic response: systemic, a nursing outcome from the Nursing Outcomes Classification (NOC) defined as severity of systemic hypersensitive immune response to a specific environmental (exogenous) antigen.

allergic rhinitis, inflammation of the nasal passages, usually associated with watery nasal discharge and itching of the nose and eyes, caused by a localized sensitivity reaction to an allergen such as house dust, animal dander, or pollen. ♦

allergic vasculitis, an inflammatory condition of the blood vessels that is induced by allergens such as iodides, penicillin, sulfonamides, and thioureas. It is

characterized by itching, malaise, and a slight fever and by the presence of papules, vesicles, urticarial wheals, or small ulcers on the skin.

allergist /al'ərjist/, a physician who specializes in the diagnosis and treatment of allergic disorders.

allergy /al'ərjē/ [Gk, *allos,* other, *ergein,* to work], a hypersensitive reaction to common, often intrinsically harmless substances, most of which are environmental. More than 20 million Americans have allergic reactions to airborne or inhaled allergens such as cigarette smoke, house dust, and pollens. Severe allergic reactions, such as anaphylaxis and angioneurotic edema of the glottis, can cause systemic shock and death and commonly require immediate therapy with subcutaneous epINEPHrine or IV steroids.

allergy blood test, a blood test used to measure serum IgE, which is an effective method of diagnosing allergy and of specifically identifying the allergen. This test can be helpful when results of an allergy skin test are questionable, when the allergen is not available in a form for dermal injection, when the allergen may incite an anaphylactic reaction if injected into the patient, or when skin testing is particularly difficult.

allergy management, a nursing intervention from the Nursing Interventions Classification (NIC) defined as identification, treatment, and prevention of allergic responses to food, medications, insect bites, contrast material, blood, and other substances.

allergy skin test, a skin test used to detect allergic reactions. Properly performed, it is considered the most convenient and least expensive test for detecting such reactions. The test involves injecting or topically scratching an allergen into the skin and then evaluating the wheal (swelling) and flare (redness) responses that follow.

allergy testing, any one of the various procedures used in identifying the specific allergens that afflict a patient. Such tests are helpful in prescribing treatment to prevent allergic reactions or to reduce their severity.

allesthesia /al'esthē'zha/, a referred pain or other sensation that is perceived at a remote site on the same or opposite side of the body stimulated.

all fours position, the sixth stage in the Rood system of ontogenetic motor patterns. In this stage, the lower trunk and lower extremities are brought into a co-contraction pattern while stretching of the trunk and limb girdles develops co-contractions of the trunk flexors and extensors.

allicin /al′i·sin/ [*Allium,* the genus of garlic], an oily substance extracted from garlic, having antibacterial activity.

alligator forceps, 1. a forceps with heavy teeth and a double clamp, used in orthopedic surgery and in ear, nose, and throat procedures. **2.** a forceps with long, thin, angular handles and interlocking teeth.

Allis forceps, a curved forceps with serrated edges, used for grasping tissues.

allodiploid /al′ōdip′loid/ [Gk, *allos,* other, *diploos,* double, *eidos,* form], **1.** an individual, organism, strain, or cell that has two genetically distinct sets of chromosomes derived from different ancestral species, as occurs in hybridization. **2.** pertaining to such an individual, organism, strain, or cell.

allogenic /al′ōjen′ik/ [Gk, *allos* + *genein,* to produce], **1.** (in genetics) denoting an individual or cell type that is from the same species but genetically distinct. **2.** (in transplantation biology) denoting tissues, particularly stem cells from either bone marrow or peripheral blood, that are from the same species but antigenically distinct; homologous.

allograft /al′əgraft/ [Gk, *allos,* other + *graphion,* stylus], surgical transplantation of tissue between two genetically dissimilar individuals of the same species, such as between two humans who are not monozygotic twins. Tissues commonly used for allografts include cornea, cartilage, bone, artery, and cadaver skin stored in a skin-tissue bank.

allokeratoplasty /al′ōker′ətoplas′tē/, the repair of a cornea with synthetic transparent material.

allometric growth, the increase in size of different organs or parts of an organism at various rates.

allometron /əlom′itron/, a quantitative change in the proportional relationship of the parts of an organism as a result of evolution.

allometry /əlom′itrē/ [Gk, *allos* + *metron,* measure], the measurement and study of the changes in proportions of the various parts of an organism in relation to the growth of the whole or of such changes within a series of related organisms. —**allometric,** *adj.*

allomorphism /al′ōmôr′fizəm/ [Gk, *allos,* other, *morphe,* form], **1.** a change in crystalline form without a change in chemical composition. **2.** a change in the shape of a group of cells caused by pressure or other physical factors.

allopathic physician /al′ōpath′ik/, a physician who practices allopathy. Almost all practicing physicians in the United States are allopathic.

allopathy /əlop′əthē/ [Gk, *allos* + *pathos,* suffering], a system of medical therapy in which a disease or an abnormal condition is treated by creating an environment that is antagonistic to the disease or condition.

alloplast /al′ōplast/ [Gk, *allos,* other, *plassein,* to mold], a graft made of plastic, metal, or other material foreign to the human body.—**alloplastic,** *adj.*

alloplastic maneuver [Gk, *allos* + *plassein,* to mold], (in psychology) a process that is part of adaptation, involving an adjustment or change in the external environment.

alloplasty /al′ōplas′tē/ [Gk, *allos,* other, *plassein,* to mold], plastic surgery in which materials foreign to the human body are implanted.—**alloplastic,** *adj.*

allopolyploid /al′əpol′iploid/ [Gk, *allos* + *polyplous,* many times, *eidos* form], **1.** an individual, organism, strain, or cell that has more than two genetically distinct sets of chromosomes derived from two or more different ancestral species, as occurs in hybridization. **2.** pertaining to such an individual, organism, strain, or cell.

allopurinol /al′əpyŏŏr′ənôl/, a xanthine oxidase inhibitor uricosuric agent prescribed in the treatment of gout and other hyperuricemic conditions.

allorhythmia /al′ōrith′mē′ə/, an irregular heart rhythm that occurs repeatedly.

all-or-none law, 1. the principle in neurophysiology stating that a stimulus must be strong enough to reach threshold to trigger a nerve impulse. Once threshold is achieved, the entire impulse is discharged. A weak stimulus will not produce a weak reaction. **2.** the principle that the heart muscle, under any stimulus above a threshold level, will respond either with a maximal strength contraction or not at all.

allostatic load, a term coined as a more precise alternative to the term *stress,* used to refer to environmental challenges that cause an organism to begin efforts to maintain stability (allostasis).

allosteric sites /al′ōster′ik/ [Gk, *allos* + *stereos,* solid], the sites, other than the active site or sites, of an enzyme that bind regulatory molecules.

allotransplantation, the transplantation of an allograft.

allotriodontia /əlot′rē·ōdon′shə/, **1.** the development of a tooth in an abnormal location, such as in a dermoid tumor. **2.** the transplantation of teeth from one individual to another.

allotropic, 1. pertaining to a substance that is changed by digestion to retain some of its nutritive value. **2.** pertaining to an element that may exist in two or more forms at the atomic level, such as carbon in the diamond, graphite, and buckminsterfullerene forms.

allowable charge /əlou′əbəl/, the maximum amount that a third party, usually an insurance company, will reimburse a provider for a specific service.

allowable costs, charges for health care services and/or supplies for which insurance benefits are available. In general, costs of services not considered to be reasonable or necessary to the proper provision of health services are excluded from allowable costs. Allowable costs vary across insurance companies.

allowable error, the amount of error that can be tolerated without invalidating the medical usefulness of the analytic result. Allowable error has a 95% limit of analytic error; only 1 sample in 20 can have an error greater than this limit.

alloxan /əlok′san/, an oxidation product of uric acid that is found in the human intestine in diarrhea. Alloxan has been used to produce diabetes in experimental animals by destroying the insulin-secreting islet cells of the pancreas.

alloy /al′oi/ [Fr, aloyer, to combine metals], a mixture of two or more metals or of substances with metallic properties. A number of alloys have medical applications, such as those used for prostheses and in dental amalgams.

almond oil, an oil expressed from the kernels of the fruit of the sweet almond tree, Prunus amygdalus. The fixed oil is a demulcent and a mild laxative. Bitter almond oil is a volatile oil that contains lethal prussic acid.

almotriptan /al′mo-trip′tan/, an antimigraine agent used for the acute treatment of migraine with or without aura.

aloe, a succulent found throughout the world, used externally for minor burns, skin irritations, minor wounds, frostbite, and radiation-caused injuries. Internally, it is used to heal intestinal inflammation and ulcers and to stimulate bile secretion as a digestive aid.

alopecia /al′əpē′shə/ [Gk, alopex, fox mange], partial or complete lack of hair resulting from normal aging, endocrine disorder, drug reaction, anticancer medication, or skin disease.

alopecia areata /er′ē-ā′tə/, a disease of unknown cause in which sudden well-defined bald patches occur. The bald areas are usually round or oval and located on the head and other hairy parts of the body. The condition is usually self-limited and often clears completely within 6 to 12 months without treatment. Recurrences are common. Anxiety and stress are common precipitating factors.

alopecia congenitalis, congenital baldness in which there may be partial or complete absence of hair at birth.

alopecia neurotica, loss of hair, usually occurring at one site, after a disease or injury involving the nervous system.

alopecia prematura, baldness that occurs early in life, beginning as early as late adolescence.

alopecia senilis, natural hair loss that affects older persons.

alopecia totalis, an uncommon condition characterized by the loss of all the hair on the scalp. The cause is unknown, and the baldness is usually permanent.

alopecia toxica, a form of hair loss attributed to a febrile illness.

alopecia universalis, a total loss of hair on all parts of the body. The condition is occasionally an extension of alopecia areata.

Aloxi, a trademark for palonosetron.

alpha /al′fə/ [Gk, alpha, first letter of the Greek alphabet; L, cella, storeroom], A, α, the first letter of the Greek alphabet. It is commonly used as a scientific notation, denoting the position of an atom in a molecule, identifying a nuclear particle, or designating a particular physiologic rhythm. It is used in chemical nomenclature to distinguish one variation in a chemical compound from others.

alpha alcoholism, a mild form of alcoholism in which the dependence is psychologic rather than physical.

alpha₁-antitrypsin [Gk, anti, against, trypsin], a plasma protein produced in the liver that inhibits the action of proteolytic enzymes such as trypsin. Deficiencies are associated with liver disease in children and panacinar emphysema in adults. In the latter, the basic lesion is believed to result from effects of proteolytic enzymes on the walls of the alveoli.

alpha₁-antitrypsin test, a blood test useful for individuals with a family history of emphysema because a familial tendency to have a deficiency of alpha₁-antitrypsin antienzyme exists. A similar deficiency also exists in children with liver disease.

alpha biofeedback, a procedure in which a person is presented with continuous information, usually auditory, on the state of his or her brain-wave pattern, with the intent of increasing the percentage of alpha activity. This is done with the expectation that it will be associated with a state of relaxation and peaceful wakefulness.

alpha cell, one of a class of cells located in the adenohypophysis or in the pancreatic islets. Alpha cells in the pancreas produce glucagon.

alpha-fetoprotein (AFP), a protein that is normally synthesized by the liver, yolk sac, and GI tract of a human fetus, but may also be found at an elevated level in the sera of adults having certain malignancies. AFP measurements in amniotic fluid are used for early diagnosis of fetal neural tube defects such as spina bifida and anencephaly.

alpha-fetoprotein (AFP) test, a blood test used to assist in diagnosing certain neoplastic conditions such as hepatoma, some tumors and teratomas, Hodgkin's disease, lymphoma, and renal cell carcinoma. Increased AFP concentrations also may indicate cirrhosis, chronic active hepatitis, and neural tube defects in the fetus.

alpha-galactosidase, an enzyme that catalyzes the conversion of alpha-D-galactoside to D-galactose.

alpha-globulins, one of a group of serum proteins classified as alpha, beta, or gamma on the basis of their electrophoretic mobility. Alpha-globulins have the greatest negative charge.

alpha-glucosidase inhibitor, any of a group of oral antihyperglycemic agents that act by competitive inhibition of α-glucosidase, delaying intestinal carbohydrate absorption and lessening postprandial increases in glucose levels.

alpha hemolysis, the development of a greenish zone around a bacterial colony growing on blood agar, characteristic of pneumococci and certain streptococci and caused by the partial decomposition of hemoglobin.

alpha$_2$-interferon /in'tərfir'on/, a protein molecule effective in controlling the spread of common colds caused by rhinoviruses. It is administered as a nasal spray.

alpha-L-fucosidase, a lysosomal enzyme that catalyzes the hydrolysis of fucosides. A deficiency of this enzyme is a cause of fucosidosis.

alpha particle, a particle emitted from an atom during one kind of radioactive decay. It consists of two protons and two neutrons, the equivalent of a helium nucleus.

alpha receptor, any of the postulated adrenergic components of receptor tissues that respond to norepinephrine and to various blocking agents. The activation of the alpha receptors causes physiologic responses such as increased peripheral vascular resistance, pupil dilation, and contraction of arrector muscles.

alpha redistribution phase, a period after IV administration of a drug when the blood level begins to fall from its peak.

alpha state, a condition of relaxed, peaceful wakefulness devoid of concentration and sensory stimulation. It is characterized by alpha waves at a frequency of 8 to 13 Hz as recorded by an EEG and is accompanied by feelings of tranquility and a lack of tension and anxiety.

Alpha Tau Delta /al'fə tou' del'tə/, a national fraternity of professional nurses.

alpha-thalassemia [Gk, *thalassa,* sea + *haema,* blood], an anemia caused by decreased rate of synthesis of the alpha chains of hemoglobin. The homozygous form is incompatible with life, the stillborn infant displaying severe hydrops fetalis; the heterozygous form may be asymptomatic or marked by mild anemia.

alphavirus /al'favī'rəs/, any of a group of very small Toga viruses consisting of a single molecule of single-stranded RNA within a lipoprotein capsule.

alpha wave, one of several types of brain waves, characterized by a relatively high voltage or amplitude and a frequency of 8 to 13 Hz. Alpha waves are the "relaxed waves" of the brain.

Alport's syndrome [A.C. Alport, South African physician, 1880–1959], a form of hereditary nephritis with symptoms of glomerulonephritis, hematuria, progressive sensorineural hearing loss, and occasional ocular disorders.

alprazolam /alpraz'əlam/, a benzodiazepine antianxiety agent.

alprostadil, a proprietary form of prostaglandin E$_1$ used to treat impotence and (temporarily) to maintain the patency of the ductus arteriosus in certain neonates. It is recommended as palliative therapy for neonates awaiting surgery to correct congenital heart defects, such as tetralogy of Fallot and tricuspid atresia.

ALS, 1. abbreviation for **advanced life support. 2.** abbreviation for **amyotrophic lateral sclerosis.**

Alström's syndrome [Carl Henry Alström, Swedish geneticist, 1907–1993], an inherited disease characterized by multiple system resistance to hormones. Clinical features include retinal degeneration leading to childhood blindness, type 2 DM, infantile obesity, nerve deafness, baldness, hyperuricemia, and hypertriglyceridemia. Males may also have high plasma gonadotropin levels and hypogonadism.

ALT, abbreviation for **alanine aminotransferase.**

alteplase, a tissue plasminogen activator used for lysis of obstructing thrombi associated with acute myocardial infarction and for other ischemic conditions requiring thrombolysis.

alteration, change.

altered state of consciousness (ASC) [L, *alter,* other], any state of awareness that differs from the normal awareness of a conscious person. Altered states of consciousness have been achieved, especially in Eastern cultures, by many individuals using various techniques, such as prolonged fasting, deep breathing, whirling, and chanting.

alteregoism /ôl'tərē'gō·iz'əm/, an altruistic feeling for an individual who is similar to or in a similar situation as oneself.

alternate binaural loudness balance (ABLB) test, comparison of the intensity levels at which a given pure tone sounds equally loud to the normal ear and the ear with hearing loss. It is done to determine recruitment with unilateral sensorineural loss.

alternate generation /ôl'tərnit/ [L, *alter,* other of two], a type of reproduction in which a sexual generation alternates with one or more asexual generations, as in many plants and simple animals.

alternating current (AC) /ôl'tərnā'ting/, an electric current that reverses direction according to a consistent sinusoidal pattern.

alternating mydriasis, a visual disorder in which there is abnormal dilation of the pupils that affects the left and right eyes alternately.

alternation, the recurrent, successive occurrence of two functions or phases, such as when a nerve fiber responds to every other stimulus or when a heart produces an irregular beat with every other cardiac cycle.

alternation rules, (in psychology) the sociolinguistic rules that establish options available to a person when he or she is speaking to someone else.

alternative inheritance /ôltur'nətiv/, the acquisition of all genetic traits and conditions from one parent, as in self-pollinating plants and self-fertilizing animals.

alternative medicine, any of the systems of medical diagnosis and treatment differing in technique from that of the allopathic practitioner's use of drugs and surgery to treat disease and injury. Examples are faith healing, homeopathy, Indian Ayurvedic medicine, acupuncture, aroma therapy, and therapeutic touch.

alternative pathway of complement activation, a process of antigen-antibody interaction in which activation of the C3 step occurs without prior activation of C1, C4, and C2.

alternator, a device for generating an electric current that changes polarity a specified number of times per second.

alternobaric vertigo, a condition of dysequilibrium caused by unequalized pressure differences in the middle ear, as may be experienced by divers during ascent.

alt hor, (in prescriptions) abbreviation for the Latin phrase *alternis horis,* meaning "every other hour."

altitude /al'titood/ [L, *altitudo,* height], level of elevation of any location on earth with reference to a fixed surface point, which is usually sea level. High-altitude cardiac intolerance is usually worse in people with blood or pulmonary disorders.

altitude anoxia [L, *altus,* high; Gk, *a,* without, *oxys,* sharp, *genein,* to produce], oxygen deprivation in a high-altitude atmosphere.

altitude sickness, a syndrome associated with the relatively lower amount of oxygen in the atmosphere at altitudes encountered during mountain climbing or travel in unpressurized aircraft. Symptoms of mild altitude illness include headache, difficulty sleeping, loss of appetite, nausea and vomiting, fatigue, dizziness, rapid heart rate, and shortness of breath, especially on exertion. In severe cases, high-altitude pulmonary or cerebral edema may result.

altretamine, an antineoplastic agent used for the palliative treatment of recurrent, persistent ovarian cancer.

altruism /al'trōō·iz'əm/, a sense of unconditional concern for the welfare of others. It may be expressed at the level of the individual, group, or the larger social system.—**altruistic,** *adj.*

alum /al'əm/ [L, *alumen*], a topical astringent, used primarily in lotions and douches.

aluminum (Al) /əlōō'minəm/ [L, *alumen,* alum], a widely used metallic element and the third most abundant of all the elements. Its atomic number is 13; its atomic mass is 26.97. Its compounds are components of many antacids, antiseptics, and astringents. Aluminum hydroxychloride is the most commonly used agent in antiperspirants.

aluminum attenuator, an aluminum filter used to control the hardness of an x-ray beam. The attenuator removes low-energy x-ray photons before they can reach the patient and be absorbed.

aluminum hydroxide [L, *alumen,* alum; Gk, *hydor,* water, *oxys,* sharp; L, *gelare,* to congeal], an antacid that works by chemical neutralization and also by adsorption of hydrochloric acid, gases, and toxins.

aluminum oxide, Al_2O_3, a compound occurring naturally as various minerals. It is used in the production of abrasives, refractories, ceramics, and catalysts and in chromatography. It is also used to strengthen dental ceramics.

Alupent, a trademark for a beta-adrenergic bronchodilator (metaproterenol sulfate).

Alu sequences, a family of repeated DNA sequences found in large numbers in the human genome.

alveobronchitis [L, *alveolus,* little hollow; Gk, *brongchos,* windpipe, *itis,* inflammation], inflammation of the alveoli and bronchioles.

alveolar /alvē´ələr/ [L, *alveolus,* little hollow], pertaining to an alveolus.

alveolar air, the respiratory gases in an alveolus of the lung.

alveolar air equation, a mathematical expression relating the approximate alveolar oxygen tension to the arterial partial pressure of carbon dioxide ($PaCO_2$), the fractional inspired oxygen, and the ratio of carbon dioxide production to oxygen consumption.

alveolar arch, the arch of the upper or lower jaw from which the teeth project, formed by the alveolar processes.

alveolar-arterial end-capillary gas pressure difference, the gas pressure difference between the partial pressure of a gas, such as CO_2, in alveolar air and that in pulmonary capillary blood as the blood leaves the alveoli. It is measured in torr or mm Hg.

alveolar-arterial gas pressure difference, the difference between the partial pressure of a gas, such as CO_2, in the alveoli and that in systemic arterial blood. The difference may indicate ventilation-perfusion mismatching. It is measured in torr or mm Hg.

alveolar artery, one of two arteries, the posterior and the anterior, that supply the upper teeth.

alveolar canal, any of the canals of the maxilla through which the posterosuperior alveolar blood vessels and the nerves to the upper teeth pass.

alveolar-capillary membrane, a lung tissue structure, varying in thickness from 0.4 to 2 μm, through which diffusion of oxygen and carbon dioxide molecules occurs during respiration.

alveolar cleft, a break in the continuity of the alveolar process, usually congenital. It typically occurs with a cleft lip and/or a cleft palate.

alveolar crestal fiber, any of the many white, collagenous fibers of the periodontal ligament that extend from the alveolar process to the intermediate plexus, where their terminations mix with those of the cemental fibers.

alveolar cyst, an air-filled cavity in a lung or visceral tissues caused by rupture of an alveolus.

alveolar distending pressure, the pressure difference between the alveoli and the intrapleural space.

alveolar duct, any of the air passages in the lung that branch out from the bronchioles. The alveolar sacs arise from the alveolar ducts.

alveolar edema, an accumulation of fluid within the alveoli.

alveolar gas volume (V_A), the aggregate volume of gas in the alveoli of the lungs.

alveolar macrophage, a cell of the reticuloendothelial system in the lungs that engulfs and digests foreign substances inhaled into the alveoli.

alveolar microlithiasis, a disease characterized by the presence of calcium phosphate deposits in the alveoli and other parts of the bronchopulmonary system. The fine, sandlike deposits may cause the entire lung to appear radiopaque. The disease is familial in about half of cases.

alveolar period, the period or phase in lung development beginning in utero after the terminal saccular period (about 32 to 36 weeks) and lasting until about 8 years of age. The terminal alveolar saccules subdivide several more times and mature alveoli form.

alveolar periosteum [L, *alveolus,* little hollow; Gk, *peri,* near, *osteon,* bone], a dense layer of connective tissue that lines the alveolar cavities of the upper and lower jaws, joining the bones to the horizontal fibers on the cementum of the teeth.

alveolar pressure (PA), the pressure in the alveoli of the lungs.

alveolar process, the portion of the maxilla or the mandible that forms the dental arch and serves as a bony investment for the teeth.

alveolar proteinosis, a very rare disease marked by the accumulation of plasma proteins, lipoproteins, and other blood components in the alveoli of the lungs, impairing the ability of the lungs to exchange oxygen and carbon dioxide.

alveolar ridge, the bony ridge of the maxilla or the mandible that contains the alveoli of the teeth.

alveolar sac [L, *alveolus,* little hollow; Gk, *sakkos*], an air sac at one of the terminal cavities of lung tissue.

alveolar socket [L, *alveolus,* little hollow; OFr, *soket*], the space in the alveolar process of the maxilla and mandible that accommodates a tooth.

alveolar soft part sarcoma, a tumor in subcutaneous or fibromuscular tissue, consisting of numerous large round or polygonal cells in a netlike matrix of connective tissue.

alveolar ventilation, the volume of air that ventilates all the perfused alveoli, equal to total ventilation minus dead space ventilation. The normal average is between 4 and 5 L/minute.

alveolectomy /al´vē-əlek´təmē/ [L, *alveolus,* little hollow; Gk, *ektomē,* excision], the excision of a portion of the alveolar process performed to aid the extraction of a tooth or teeth, modify the alveolar contour after tooth extraction, or prepare the mouth for dentures.

alveolitis /al′vē·əlī′tis/, an inflammation of the alveoli of the lungs caused by the inhalation of an allergen. It is characterized by acute episodes of dyspnea, cough, sweating, fever, weakness, and pain in the joints and muscles lasting from 12 to 18 hours. X-ray films of the lungs may show cellular thickening of alveolar septa and ill-defined generalized infiltrates.

alveoloplasty /alvē′əlōplas′tē/, reconstruction by plastic surgery of the alveolar process or dental ridge.

alveolotomy /al′vē·əlot′əmē/, an incision of a dental alveolus performed to drain pus from a dental infection.

alveolus /alvē′ələs/ pl. **alveoli** [L, *alveolus*, little hollow], **1.** a small outpouching along the walls of the alveolar space through which gas exchange between alveolar air and pulmonary capillary blood takes place. **2.** a tooth socket. —**alveolar**, *adj*.

alymphocytosis /alim′fōsītō′sis/ [Gk, *a*, not; L, *lympha*, water; Gk, *kytos*, cell, *osis*, condition], absence of lymphocytes from the blood.

Alzheimer's disease (AD) /ôl′zīmərz/ [Alois Alzheimer, German neurologist, 1864–1915], a condition characterized by progressive mental deterioration, often with confusion, memory failure, disorientation, restlessness, agnosia, speech disturbances, inability to carry out purposeful movement, and hallucinosis. The patient may become hypomanic, refuse food, and lose sphincter control without focal impairment. The disease sometimes begins in middle life with slight defects in behavior and memory, usually an inability to incorporate new knowledge with old knowledge, but the symptoms can worsen dramatically after the age of 70.

Alzheimer's sclerosis [Alois Alzheimer; Gk, *sklerosis*, hardening], the degeneration of small cerebral blood vessels, resulting in mental changes.

Am, symbol for the element **americium.**

AMA, 1. abbreviation for **American Medical Association. 2.** abbreviation for **antimitochondrial antibody. 3.** abbreviation for **active matrix array. 4.** abbreviation for **antimyocardial antibody.**

ama, abbreviation for **against medical advice.**

amalgam /əmal′gəm/ [Gk, *malagma*, soft mass], **1.** a mixture or combination. **2.** an alloy of mercury, silver, and other metals commonly used as a dental filling.

amalgam carver, a dental instrument for shaping silver amalgam while in a plastic state, used in some tooth cavity fillings or restorations.

amalgam condenser, a dental instrument used for compacting silver amalgam while in a plastic state, used for restoring teeth to a natural contour.

amalgam core, a rigid base for retaining a cast crown restoration, used in the replacement of a damaged tooth crown.

amalgam tattoo, a discoloration of the gingiva or buccal membrane caused by particles of silver amalgam that migrate from an amalgam filling and become embedded under the tissue surface.

Amanita [Gk, *amanitai*, fungus], a genus of mushrooms. Some species, such as *Amanita phalloides*, are poisonous, causing hallucinations, GI upset, and pain that may be followed by liver, kidney, and CNS damage.

amantadine hydrochloride /əman′tədēn/, an antiviral and antiparkinsonian agent prescribed in the prophylaxis and early treatment of influenza virus A and in the treatment of parkinsonian symptoms and drug-induced extrapyramidal reactions.

amastia /əmas′tē·ə/ [Gk, *a* + *mastos*, not breast], the absence of the breasts in women caused by a congenital defect, an endocrine disorder resulting in faulty development, a lack of development of secondary sex characteristics, or a bilateral mastectomy.

amaurosis /am′ôrō′sis/ [Gk, *amaurorein*, to darken], blindness, especially lack of vision resulting from a systemic cause such as disease of the optic nerve or brain, diabetes, renal disease, acute gastritis, or systemic poisoning produced by excessive use of alcohol or tobacco, rather than from damage to the eye itself.—**amaurotic,** *adj*.

amaurosis fugax /foo′gaks/, a transient episodic blindness caused by decreased blood flow to the retina.

amaurosis partialis fugax, a transitory partial blindness, usually caused by vascular insufficiency of the retina or optic nerve as a result of carotid artery disease.

amber [Ar, *anbar*], a hard fossilized resin derived from pine trees. An oil of amber, *Oleum succini,* has been used in some pharmaceutical preparations.

amber mutation [Ar, *anbar*, ambergris], a genetic alteration that causes the synthesis of a polypeptide chain to terminate prematurely because the triplet of nucleotides that normally codes for the next amino

A

acid in the chain becomes uracil-adenine-guanine, the sequence that signals the end of the chain.

ambidextrous /am′bēdek′strəs/ [L, *ambo,* both, *dexter,* right], able to use either the left or right hand to perform a task and write.

ambient /am′bē·ənt/ [L, *ambire,* on both sides], pertaining to the surrounding area or atmosphere.

ambient air standard, the maximum tolerable concentration of any outdoor air pollutant as set by the Environmental Protection Agency (EPA) to protect public health and the environment. The EPA considers lead, the nitrogen oxides, particulate matter, sulfur dioxide, carbon monoxide, and ozone "criteria" pollutants.

ambient noise [L, *ambiens,* around; ME, *clamor*], the total noise in a given environment.

ambient pressure, the atmospheric pressure, or pressure in the environment or surrounding area. It is given a reference value of zero (0) cm H_2O.

ambient temperature [L, *ambi,* around, *temperatura*], the temperature of the environment.

ambiguous /ambig′yŏŏ·əs/ [L, *ambiguus,* to wander], having more than one direction, development, or interpretation or meaning.

ambiguous genitalia [L, *ambigere,* to go around], external genitalia that are not normal and morphologically typical of either sex, as occurs in pseudohermaphroditism.

ambilateral, pertaining to or affecting both the right and the left side.

ambivalence /ambiv′ələns/ [L, *ambo,* both, *valentia,* strength], 1. a state in which a person concomitantly experiences conflicting feelings, attitudes, drives, desires, or emotions, such as love and hate, tenderness and cruelty, or pleasure and pain toward the same person, place, object, or situation. 2. uncertainty and fluctuation caused by an inability to make a choice between opposites. 3. a continuous oscillation or fluctuation.—**ambivalent,** *adj.*

ambivert /am′bivurt′/ [L, *ambo,* both, *vertere,* to turn], a person who possesses characteristics of both introversion and extroversion.

amblyopia /am′blē·ō′pē·ə/ [Gk, *amblys,* dull, *ops,* eye], reduced vision in an eye not correctable by a manifest refraction and with no obvious pathologic or structural cause.

ambrisentan, an antihypertensive used to treat pulmonary arterial hypertension, alone or in combination with antihypertensives.

Ambu bag, a trademark for a resuscitator bag used to assist ventilation.

ambulance /am′byələns/, a vehicle designed to transport ill or injured patients. It may be used under emergency or nonemergency conditions and is equipped with supplies and personnel to provide patient care en route.

ambulation, a nursing outcome from the Nursing Outcomes Classification (NOC) defined as ability to walk from place to place independently with or without assistive device.

ambulation: wheelchair, a nursing outcome from the Nursing Outcomes Classification (NOC) defined as ability to move from place to place in a wheelchair.

ambulatory /am′byələtôr′ē/ [L, *ambulare,* to walk about], 1. able to walk. 2. pertaining to a patient who is not confined to bed. 3. pertaining to a health service for people who are not hospitalized.

ambulatory anesthesia, the administration of anesthesia when the intent is to admit and discharge the patient on the day of the surgical procedure.

ambulatory automatism, aimless wandering or moving about or performance of mechanical acts without conscious awareness of the behavior.

ambulatory blood pressure monitoring (ABPM), the recording of a patient's BP at regular intervals under normal living and working conditions.

ambulatory care, health services provided on an outpatient basis to those who visit a hospital or other health care facility and depart after treatment on the same day.

ambulatory schizophrenia, a mild form of psychosis, characterized mainly by a tendency to respond to questions with vague and irrelevant answers. The person also may seem somewhat eccentric and wander aimlessly.

ambulatory surgery center, a medical facility designed and equipped to handle surgery, pain management, and certain diagnostic procedures that do not require overnight hospitalization.

Ambu simulator, a trademark for a manikin used to teach CPR.

AM care /ā·em′/, routine hygienic care that is given before breakfast or early in the morning.

amcinonide /amsin′ōnīd/, a topical corticosteroid used to treat inflammatory skin conditions.

amdinocillin pivoxil, an ester of amdinocillin, administered orally in the treatment of UTIs. The form used can be the ester or the hydrochloride salt of the ester.

ameba /əmē′bə/ *pl.* **amebae, amebas** [Gk, *amoibe,* change], a microscopic, single-celled, parasitic organism. Several species may be parasitic in humans.—**amebic,** *adj.*

amebiasis /am̕ēbī̕əsis/, an infection of the intestine or liver by pathogenic amebae, particularly *Entamoeba histolytica,* acquired by ingesting fecally contaminated food or water. Infected carriers can be asymptomatic (luminal ambiasis); they may develop invasive intestinal disease with dysentery, colitis, or appendicitis or invasive extraintestinal disease with peritonitis and liver or lung abscess.

amebic abscess /əmē̕bik/, a collection of pus formed by disintegrated tissue in a cavity, usually in the liver, caused by *Entamoeba histolytica.*

amebic carrier state, a condition in which a patient may be a carrier of amebae without showing signs or symptoms of an amebic infection.

amebic dysentery, an inflammation of the intestine caused by infestation with *Entamoeba histolytica.* It is characterized by frequent, loose stools flecked with blood and mucus.

amebic hepatitis, an inflammation of the liver caused by an infection with any of the various amebae, usually after an attack of amebic dysentery.

amebicide /əmē̕bəsīd/, a drug or another agent that is destructive to amebae.

amebic liver abscess, the abscess formed in hepatic amebiasis, resulting from liquefaction necrosis caused by entrance of *Entamoeba histolytica* into the portal circulation.

ameboid movement /əmē̕boid/ [Gk, *amoibe,* ameba, *eidos,* form; L, *movere,* to move], the ameba-like movement of certain types of body cells that can migrate through tissues, such as leukocytes. The movement generally consists of extension of a portion of the plasma membrane, probably caused by internal rearrangement or movement of the cytoskeleton.

amelanotic /am̕ilənot̕ik/ [Gk, *a* + *melas,* not black], pertaining to tissue that is unpigmented because it lacks melanin.

amelanotic melanoma, a melanoma that lacks melanin.

amelia /əmē̕lyə/ [Gk, *a* + *melos,* not limb], **1.** a congenital anomaly, marked by the absence of one or more limbs. **2.** a psychologic trait of apathy or indifference associated with certain forms of psychosis.

amelification /əmel̕ifikā̕shən/ [OFr, *amel,* enamel; L, *facere,* to make], the differentiation of ameloblasts into the enamel of the teeth.

amelioration [L, *ad,* to, *melior,* better], an improvement in conditions.

ameloblast /am̕əlōblast̕/ [OFr, *amel;* Gk, *blastos,* germ], an epithelial cell from which tooth enamel is formed. **—ameloblastic** /-blas̕tik/, *adj.*

ameloblastic fibroma, an odontogenic neoplasm in which simultaneous proliferation of mesenchymal and epithelial tissues occurs without the formation of dentin or enamel.

ameloblastic fibro-odontoma, a tumor of the jaw that forms dentin and enamel.

ameloblastic hemangioma, a highly vascular tumor of cells covering the dental papilla.

ameloblastic sarcoma, a malignant odontogenic tumor, characterized by the proliferation of epithelial and mesenchymal tissue without the formation of dentin or enamel.

ameloblastoma /am̕əlōblastō̕mə/ [OFr, *amel;* Gk, *blastos,* germ, *oma*], a rare, highly destructive, benign, rapidly growing tumor of the jaw.

amelodentinal /am̕əlōden̕tinəl/ [OFr, *amel;* L, *dens,* tooth], pertaining to both the enamel and the dentin of the teeth.

amelogenesis /am̕əlōjen̕əsis/ [OFr, *amel;* Gk, *genein,* to produce], the formation of the enamel of the teeth.—**amelogenic,** *adj.*

amelogenesis imperfecta, a condition characterized by brown or white chalky discoloration of the teeth and resulting from either severe enamel hypocalcification or enamel hypoplasia. It is inherited as an autosomal dominant trait.

amenorrhea /ā̕menərē̕ə/ [Gk, *a,* without, *men,* month, *rhoia,* to flow], the absence of menstruation. Amenorrhea is normal before sexual maturity, during pregnancy, after menopause, and during the intermenstrual phase of the monthly hormonal cycle; it is otherwise caused by dysfunction of the hypothalamus, pituitary gland, ovary, or uterus; by the congenital absence or surgical removal of both ovaries or the uterus; or by medication.—**amenorrheic,** *adj.*

amentia /āmen̕shə/ [Gk, *a,* not; L, *mens,* mind]

American Academy of Allergy and Immunology (AAAI), a national organization of physicians specializing in the diagnosis and treatment of allergies and immune system disorders.

American Academy of Audiology, a professional association for audiologists.

American Academy of Nursing (AAN), the honorary organization of the American Nurses Association, created to recognize superior achievement in nursing in order to promote advances and excellence in nursing practice, education, and research. A person elected to membership is given the title of Fellow of the American Academy of Nursing and may use the abbreviation FAAN as an honorific.

American Academy of Physical Medicine and Rehabilitation (AAPMR), a national association of professional health care workers concerned with the diagnosis of physical impairment and the development of therapies and devices to improve physical function.

American Academy of Physician Assistants (AAPA), a national organization of physician assistants or associates.

American Association for Respiratory Therapy (AART), a national organization of respiratory therapists and other health care workers involved in improving the ventilatory function of the respiratory tract.

American Association of Colleges of Nursing (AACN), a national organization of baccalaureate and higher degree programs in nursing that was established to address issues in nursing education.

American Association of Critical-Care Nurses (AACN), a national organization of nurses working in critical care units.

American Association of Industrial Nurses (AAIN), a national professional association of nurses working in industry and concerned with issues in occupational health.

American Association of Medical Colleges (AAMC), a national organization of faculty members and deans of medical schools and colleges that was established to address issues in medical education.

American Association of Neurological Nurses (AANN), a national organization of nurses working in the field of neurology.

American Association of Neuroscience Nurses (AANN), a national organization of nurses working with neurologically impaired patients. The organization is affiliated with the American Association of Neurological Surgeons.

American Association of Nurse Anesthetists (AANA), a professional association of certified registered nurse anesthetists.

American Association of University Professors (AAUP), a national organization of faculty members of institutions of higher learning.

American College of Emergency Physicians (ACEP), a national professional organization of physicians specializing in emergency medicine.

American College of Obstetricians and Gynecologists (ACOG), the national organization of obstetricians and gynecologists.

American College of Occupational and Environmental Medicine (ACOEM), a professional organization whose members are concerned with the identification, prevention, diagnosis, and treatment of disorders associated with technology and industry.

American College of Physicians (ACP), a national professional organization of physicians.

American College of Prosthodontists (ACP), an organization of dentists who specialize in the restoration of dental prostheses and in the diagnosis and treatment of TMJ and maxillofacial disorders.

American College of Radiology (ACR), a national professional organization of physicians, medical oncologists, and clinical medical physicists who specialize in radiology.

American College of Surgeons (ACS), a national professional organization of physicians who specialize in surgery.

American Dental Hygienists' Association (ADHA), the largest organization of dental hygienists in the United States.

American Hospital Association (AHA), a national organization that represents and serves individuals, institutions, and organizations that work to improve health services for all people.

American Joint Committee on Cancer (AJCC), a nonprofit organization that creates and publishes systems of classification for cancer staging, such as the TNM staging system and Collaborative Stage Data collection systems.

American Journal of Nursing, a professional journal containing articles of general and specialized clinical interest to nurses.

American leishmaniasis, a group of infections caused by various species of the parasitic protozoa *Leishmania* of Central and South America, characterized by cutaneous lesions at the site of the sandfly bite and transmitting infection and causing disfiguring ulcerative lesions of the nose, mouth, and throat or visceral disease.

American Medical Association (AMA), a professional association whose membership is made up of the largest group of physicians and medical students in the United States, including practitioners in all recognized medical specialties, as well as general primary care physicians. The AMA is governed by a board of trustees and house of delegates who represent various state and local medical associations and U.S. government agencies. The AMA maintains directories of all qualified physicians (including nonmembers) in the United States, including graduates of foreign medical colleges; researches prescription and nonprescription drugs; advises congressional and state legislators regarding proposed health care laws; and publishes a variety of journals.

American National Standards Institute (ANSI), a private nonprofit organization that coordinates developments of standards for medical and other devices, services, and personnel in the

United States and represents the United States in matters related to international standardization.

American Nephrology Nurses' Association (ANNA), an organization of nurses and technicians working in the fields of dialysis and renal diseases.

American Nurses Association (ANA), the national professional association of registered nurses in the United States. It was founded in 1896 to improve standards of health and the availability of health care. ANA advances the nursing profession by fostering high standards for nursing, promoting the rights of nurses in the workplace, projecting a positive and realistic view of nursing, and lobbying Congress and regulatory agencies on health care issues affecting nurses and the public. ANA publications include *American Nurse, Publications List, American Nurse Today,* and *Online Journal of Nursing.*

American Nurses Association—Political Action Committee (ANA-PAC), an organization that raises funds for political contributions to candidates for public office at the state and national levels.

American Occupational Therapy Association (AOTA), a national professional association of occupational therapists, occupational therapy assistants, and students of occupational therapy.

American Psychiatric Association (APA), a national professional association for physicians who specialize in psychiatry. It is concerned with the development of standards for psychiatric facilities, the formulation of mental health programs, the dissemination of data, and the promotion of psychiatric education and research. It publishes the *Diagnostic and Statistical Manual of Mental Disorders (DSM).*

American Red Cross, one of more than 120 national organizations that seek to reduce human suffering through various health, safety, and disaster relief programs in affiliation with the International Red Cross and Red Crescent Societies. It is not a government agency. The American Red Cross has more than 1.2 million members throughout the United States. Some 97% of Red Cross staff is volunteer. The American Red Cross blood program collects and distributes more blood than any other single U.S. agency and coordinates distribution of blood and blood products to the U.S. Defense Department on request or during national emergencies. American Red Cross nursing and health programs include courses in the home on parenthood, prenatal and postnatal care, hygiene, and venereal disease. Nursing students may enroll for service in American Red Cross community programs and during disasters. The symbol of the American Red Cross, like that of most other Red Cross societies throughout the world, is a red cross on a field of white.

American Registry of Radiologic Technologists (ARRT), a national certifying body for radiologic technologists in the disciplines of radiation therapy, nuclear medicine, radiotherapy, mammography, computed tomography, magnetic resonance imaging, quality management, sonography, bone densitometry, vascular sonography, breast sonography, vascular-interventional radiography, cardiovascular-interventional radiography, and radiologist assistant.

American Sign Language (Ameslan, ASL), a method of manual communication used by some deaf persons. Messages are conveyed by manipulation of the hands and fingers. ASL is a distinct language, with its own grammar and syntax.

American Society for Investigative Pathology (ASIP), a national professional organization of specialists in pathology and bacteriology.

American Society of Parenteral and Enteral Nutrition (ASPEN), an organization that provides education, support, and accreditation to persons who specialize in nutrition that is provided through IV, enteral, or related types of feeding.

American Speech, Language, and Hearing Association (ASHA), a professional association that certifies audiologists and speech-language pathologists.

American Standard Safety System, a system of specifications for threaded high-pressure connections between compressed gas cylinders and their attachments.

Americans With Disabilities Act, legislation approved by the U.S. Congress in July 1990 that would bar discrimination against persons with physical or mental disabilities in the areas of employment, state and local government services, public accommodations, transportation, and telecommunication. The Act defines disability as a condition that "substantially limits" such activities as walking, seeing, caring for oneself, hearing, speaking, breathing, learning, and working. It applies to persons with AIDS, as well as to persons with diabetes, cancer, alcoholics, and substance abusers undergoing treatment. The law requires employers to make "reasonable accommodations" for workers who are otherwise qualified to carry out their job duties.

American Type Culture Collection (ATCC), a global nonprofit, nongovernmental organization that provides biologic products and technical and educational services to research centers and laboratories in the academic, scientific, and medical communities.

americium (Am) /am′ərish′ē·əm/, a synthetic radioactive element of the actinide group. Its atomic number is 95; its atomic mass is 243.

Ameslan /aməslan/, abbreviation for **American Sign Language.**

Ames test /āmz/ [Bruce Nathan Ames, American molecular geneticist, b. 1928], a method of testing substances for possible carcinogenicity by exposing a strain of *Salmonella* to a sample of the substance.

ametropia /amətrō′pē·ə/ [Gk, *ametros,* irregular, *opsis,* sight], a condition characterized by an optic defect involving an error of refraction, such as astigmatism, hyperopia, or myopia.—**ametropic,** *adj.*

Amevive, a trademark for alefacept.

AMI, abbreviation for **acute myocardial infarction.**

Amicar, a trademark for a hemostatic (aminocaproic acid).

amicrobic /am′īkrob′ik/, not caused by or related to microbes.

amidase /am′i·dās/, **1.** an enzyme that catalyzes the formation of a monocarboxylic acid and ammonia by hydrolytic cleavage of the C—N bond of a monocarboxylic acid amide. **2.** a term used in the recommended and trivial names of some hydrolases acting on amides, particularly those acting on linear amides.

amide, **1.** a chemical compound formed from an organic acid by the substitution of an amino (NH_2, NHR, or NR_2) group for the hydroxyl of a carboxyl (COOH) group. **2.** a chemical compound formed by the deprotonation of ammonia (NH_3) or a primary (RNH_2) or secondary (R_2NH) amine.

amide local anesthetic, any of the numerous compounds containing an amide chemical group that block nerve transmission. Amides are metabolized by microsomal P-450 enzymes in the liver.

amifostine, a cytoprotective agent for cisplatin that is used to reduce renal toxicity when cisplatin is given to treat ovarian cancer. It also reduces xerostomia in radiotherapy for head and neck cancer.

Amigo, a trademark for a battery-operated, scooter-like vehicle that gives mobility to some patients who cannot walk.

amikacin sulfate /am′ikā′sin/, an aminoglycoside antibiotic prescribed in the treatment of various severe infections caused by susceptible strains of gram-negative bacteria.

Amikin, a trademark for an aminoglycoside antibiotic (amikacin sulfate).

amiloride hydrochloride /am′ilôr′īd/, a potassium-sparing diuretic with antihypertensive activity prescribed as an adjunct in the treatment of CHF or hypertension. It is often given with a thiazide medication.

amiloxate /am′il-ok′sāt/, an absorber of ultraviolet B radiation, used topically as a sunscreen.

amine /am′in, əmēn′/ [L, *ammonia*], (in chemistry) an organic derivative of ammonia in which one or more hydrogen atoms are replaced by alkyl or aryl groups.

amine pump *informal.* an active transport system in the presynaptic nerve endings that takes up released amine neurotransmitters.

amino acid (AA) /əmē′nō/, an organic chemical compound composed of one or more basic amino groups and one or more acidic carboxyl groups. Twenty of the more than 100 amino acids that occur in nature are the building blocks of proteins. Peptide linkages between them form polypeptides or proteins (for example, the structural components of muscle). The eight essential amino acids are isoleucine (Ile), leucine (Leu), lysine (Lys), methionine (Met), phenylalanine (Phe), threonine (Thr), tryptophan (Trp), and valine (Val). Arginine (Arg) and histidine (His) are essential in infants. Cysteine (Cys) and tyrosine (Tyr) are semiessential because they may be synthesized from methionine (Met) and phenylalanine (Phe), respectively. The main nonessential amino acids are alanine (Ala), asparagine (Asn), aspartic acid (Asp), glutamine (Glm), glutamic acid (Glu), glycine (Gly), proline (Pro), and serine (Ser).

amino acid group, a category of organic chemicals containing an amino group (NH_2), a carboxylic acid group (COOH), and a variable R group on the carbon separating the amino and carboxyl groups (often referred to as the alpha carbon). The R group may be comprised of nonpolar, polar, acidic, or basic side chains. The presence of the R group creates defined three-dimensionality which is conserved in all naturally occurring amino acids.

aminoacidopathy /əmē′nō·as′idop′əthē/, any of various disorders caused by a defect in an enzymatic step in the metabolic pathway of one or more amino acids or in a protein mediator necessary for transport of an amino acid into or out of a cell.

amino acid profiles, a blood or urine test to diagnose defects in amino acid metabolism, most of which are genetic.

amino acid residue, an amino acid molecule that has lost a water molecule by becoming joined to a molecule of another amino acid.

aminoaciduria /əmē′nō·as′idoͦor′ē·ə/, the abnormal presence of amino acids in the urine that usually indicates an inborn metabolic defect, as in cystinuria.

p-**aminobenzoate** /amē'noben'zo·āt/, any salt or ester of paraaminobenzoic acid. The potassium salt is administered orally as an antifibrotic in some dermatologic disorders; various substituted esters, such as padimate O, are used as topical sunscreens.

aminobenzoic acid /-benzō'ik/, a metabolic product of the catabolism of the amino acid tryptophan.

aminocaproic acid /amē'nōkəprō'ik, am'inō-/, a hemostatic prescribed to stop excessive bleeding that results from hyperfibrinolysis.

aminolevulinic acid (ALA)[1] /am'inōlev'ōōlin'ik/, the aliphatic precursor of heme. It may be detected in the urine of some patients with porphyria, liver disease, and lead poisoning.

aminolevulinic acid[2], a photochemotherapeutic agent used to treat nonhyperkeratotic actinic keratosis of the face and scalp.

aminolevulinic acid hydrochloride, the hydrochloride salt of aminolevulinic acid, applied topically in the treatment of nonhyperkeratotic actinic keratoses of the face and scalp.

aminophylline /am'nōfil'in, əmē'nō-/, a bronchodilator prescribed in the treatment of bronchospasm associated with asthma, emphysema, and bronchitis.

aminophylline poisoning, an adverse reaction to an excessive intake of a methylxanthine drug such as caffeine or theophylline. Symptoms may include nausea, diarrhea, vomiting, abdominal pain, GI bleeding, headache, tinnitus, thirst, delirium, seizures, tachycardia, cardiac arrhythmias, and BP changes.

aminopyrine /-pī'rin/, a white chemical compound with analgesic and antipyretic effects. Its continued or excessive use may lead to agranulocytosis.

5-aminosalicylic acid /ah-mē'nōsal'əsil'ik/, mesalamine.

aminotransferase /-trans'fərās/, enzymes that catalyze the transfer of an amino group from an amino acid to an alpha-keto acid, with pyridoxal phosphate and pyridoxamine phosphate acting as coenzymes. Aspartate aminotransferase (AST), normally present in serum and various tissues, especially in the heart and liver, is released by damaged cells, and, as a result, a high serum level of AST may be diagnostic in MI or hepatic disease. Alanine aminotransferase, a normal constituent of serum and especially in the liver, is released by injured tissue and may be present in high concentrations in the sera of patients with acute liver disease.

amiodarone hydrochloride, an oral antiarrhythmic drug prescribed for the treatment of life-threatening recurrent ventricular fibrillation and recurrent, hemodynamically unstable ventricular tachycardia refractory to other drugs. It is not considered first-line therapy due to toxicities.

Amipaque, a trademark for an intrathecal and intravascular diagnostic drug (metrizamide).

Amitiza, a trademark for lubiprostone.

amitosis /am'ətō'sis/ [Gr, *a* + *mitos,* not thread], cell division in which there is binary fission of the nucleus and cytoplasm (as in bacteria) without the complex stages of chromosome separation that occur in mitosis.—**amitotic,** *adj.*

amitriptyline /am'itrip'tilin/, a tricyclic antidepressant prescribed in the treatment of depression. It also has unlabeled uses for treating neuropathic pain and headaches.

AML, abbreviation for **acute myeloid leukemia.**

amlexanox /amlek'sanoks/, a topical antiulcerative agent used in the treatment of recurrent aphthous stomatitis.

amlodipine /amlō'dipēn/, a calcium channel blocker administered orally in the form of the besylate salt in the treatment of hypertension and chronic stable and vasospastic angina.

ammonia (NH₃) /amō'nē·a/ [Gk, *ammoniakos,* salt of Ammon, Egyptian god], a colorless pungent gas produced by the decomposition of nitrogenous organic matter. Some of its many uses are as a fertilizer, an aromatic stimulant, a detergent, and an emulsifier.

ammoniacal fermentation /am'ənī'əkəl/, the production of ammonia and carbon dioxide from urea by the enzyme urease.

ammonia exposure, an adverse reaction to ammonia, which is formed as a product of amino acid and nucleic acid catabolism. In liver diseases such as cirrhosis, ammonia may accumulate in the blood, resulting in neurologic damage. Preventive measures include administering antibiotics that restrict the growth of ammonia-producing bacteria and limiting the amount of protein in the diet.

ammonia level test, a blood test used to help diagnose severe liver diseases such as fulminant hepatitis, cirrhosis, and hepatic encephalopathy.

ammonium (NH₄⁺), an ion formed by the reaction of ammonia (NH_3) with a hydrogen ion (H⁺).

ammonuria /am'ōnōōr'ē·ə/, urine that contains an excessive amount of ammonia.

amnesia /amnē'zhə/ [Gk, *a* + *mnasthai,* to forget], a loss of memory caused by brain damage or by severe emotional trauma.

amnesiac /amnē′sēak/, a person with a loss of memory caused by brain damage or severe emotional trauma.

amnesic aphasia [Gk, *a* + *mnasthai* + *a* + *phasis*, without speech], an inability to remember spoken words or to use words for names of objects, circumstances, or characteristics.

amnestic apraxia /amnes′tik/, the inability to carry out a movement in response to a request because of a lack of ability to remember the request.

amniocentesis /am′nē·ōsentē′sis/ [Gk, *amnos*, lamb's caul, *kentesis*, pricking], an obstetric procedure in which a small amount of amniotic fluid is removed for laboratory analysis. It is usually performed between the sixteenth and twentieth weeks of gestation to aid in the diagnosis of fetal abnormalities, especially genetic disorders.

amniography /am′nē·og′rəfē/, a seldom-used procedure to detect placement of the placenta by x-ray examination.

amnioinfusion, a nursing intervention from the Nursing Interventions Classification (NIC) defined as infusion of fluid into the uterus during labor to relieve umbilical cord compression or to dilute meconium-stained fluid.

amnion /am′nē·on/ [Gk, *amnos*, lamb's caul], a membrane, continuous with and covering the fetal side of the placenta, that forms the outer surface of the umbilical cord.—**amniotic,** *adj.*

amnionitis /am′nē·ōnī′tis/, an inflammation of the amnion. The condition may develop as a result of infection after early rupture of the fetal membranes.

amnioscopy /am′nē·os′kəpē/, a direct visual examination of the fetus and amniotic fluid with an endoscope that is inserted into the amniotic cavity through the uterine cervix or an incision in the abdominal wall.

amniotic band disruption sequence syndrome, an abnormal condition of fetal development characterized by the development of fibrous bands within the uterus that entangle the fetus, leading to deformities in structure and function.

amniotic cavity [Gk, *amnion*, fetal membrane; L, *cavum*], the fluid-filled cavity of the amniotic sac surrounding the fetus.

amniotic fluid, a liquid produced by the fetal membranes and the fetus. It surrounds the fetus throughout pregnancy, protecting it from trauma and temperature variations, providing freedom of fetal movements, and helping to maintain the fetal oxygen supply. The volume totals about 1000 mL at term. In addition to providing the fetus with physical protection, the amniotic fluid is a medium of active chemical exchange.

amniotic fluid embolism [Gk, *amnion*; L, *fluere,* to flow; Gk, *embolos,* plug], a quantity of amniotic fluid that enters the maternal blood system during labor and/or delivery and becomes lodged in a vessel. It is usually fatal to the mother if it is a pulmonary embolism.

amniotic fold, an embryonic growth feature observed in many vertebrates, particularly birds and reptiles. It consists of flaps of ectoderm and mesoderm that grow over the back of an embryo, fuse, and subsequently separate to form the amnion.

amniotic sac, a thin-walled bag that contains the fetus and amniotic fluid during pregnancy. It has a capacity of 4 to 5 L at term. The wall of the sac extends from the margin of the placenta. The amnion, chorion, and decidua that make up the wall are each a few cell layers thick. The intact sac and its fluid provide for the equilibration of hydrostatic pressure within the uterus. During labor the sac effects the uniform transmission of the force of uterine contractions to the cervix for dilation.

amniotomy /am′nē·ot′əmē/, the artificial rupture of the fetal membranes, usually performed to stimulate or accelerate the onset of labor.

amobarbital /am′ōbär′bətal/, a barbiturate sedative-hypnotic prescribed as an anticonvulsant and a preanesthetic and for short-term treatment of insomnia.

A-mode, amplitude modulation in diagnostic ultrasonography. It represents the time required for the ultrasound beam to strike a tissue interface and return its signal to the transducer.

A-mode ultrasound [L, *ultra,* beyond, *sonus,* sound], a display of ultrasonic echoes in which the horizontal axis of the cathode ray tube display represents the time required for the return of the echo and the vertical axis represents the strength of the echo. The mode is used in echoencephalography.

amok [Malay, *amoq,* furious], a psychotic frenzy with a desire to kill anybody encountered. The murderous episodes may follow periods of severe depression.

amoric /ah-mo′rik/, without particles.

amorph /ā′môrf, əmôrf′/ [Gk, *a* + *morphe,* not shape], **1.** a mutant allele that has little or no effect on the expression of a trait.—**amorphic,** *adj.* **2.** abbreviation for *amorphous.*

amorphous /əmôr′fəs/ [Gk, *a,* not, *morphe,* form], **1.** describing an object that lacks definite visible shape or form. **2.** (in chemistry) a substance that is not crystalline.

amorphous crystal, a shapeless, ill-defined crystal, usually a phosphate.

amoxapine /əmok'sepin/, a tricyclic antidepressant (secondary amine subclass) prescribed in the treatment of mental depression.

amoxicillin /əmok'səsil'in/, a beta-lactam semisynthetic oral penicillin antibiotic prescribed in the treatment of infections caused by susceptible gram-negative or gram-positive bacteria.

Amoxil, a trademark for a beta-lactam antibiotic (amoxicillin).

AMP, abbreviation for **adenosine monophosphate.**

ampere (A) /am'pēr/ [André-Marie Ampère, French physicist, 1775–1836], a unit of measurement of the amount of electric current. An ampere, according to the meter-kilogram-second (MKS) system, is the amount of current passed through a resistance of 1 ohm by an electric potential of 1 volt; in the International System (SI) of Units, an ampere is a unit of electric current that carries a charge of 1 coulomb through a conductor in 1 second. The standard international ampere is the amount of current that deposits 0.001118 g of silver per second when passed, according to certain specifications, through a silver nitrate solution.

amperometry /am'parom'ətrē/, the measurement of current at a single applied potential.

amphetamine poisoning, the toxic effects of overdosage of amphetamines. Symptoms usually include excitement, tremors, tachycardia, hallucinations, delirium, convulsions, and circulatory collapse.

amphetamines /amfet'əmēnz/, a group of nervous system stimulants, including amphetamine and its chemical congeners dextroamphetamine and methamphetamine, that are subject to abuse because of their ability to produce wakefulness, euphoria, and weight loss.

amphetamine sulfate, a colorless water-soluble salt of amphetamine that stimulates the CNS. It has been used to treat certain respiratory complaints, fatigue, narcolepsy, and effect weight loss. It formerly was used to treat obesity.

amphidiarthrodial joint /am'fēdī'ärthrō'dē ·əl/ [Gk, amphi, both kinds], a type of joint that combines amphiarthrosis with diarthrosis, permitting movement in more than one direction, such as that of the lower jaw.

amphigenetic /am'fijənet'ik/ [Gk, genein, to produce], **1.** produced by the union of gametes from both sexes. **2.** bisexual; having both testicular and ovarian tissue.

amphigenous inheritance /amfij'ənəs/, the acquisition of genetic traits and conditions from both parents.

amphigonadism /am'figō'nədiz'əm/, true hermaphroditism; the presence of both testicular and ovarian tissue.—**amphigonadic,** adj.

amphigony /amfig'ənē/ [Gk, amphi + gonos, generation], sexual reproduction. —**amphigonic** /am'figon'ik/, adj.

amphikaryon /am'fiker'ē·on/ [Gk, amphi + karyon, nucleus], a nucleus containing the diploid number of chromosomes. —**amphikaryotic,** adj.

amphimixis /am'fimik'sis/ [Gk, amphi + mixis, mingling], **1.** the union of germ cells in sexual reproduction. **2.** the union and integration of oral, anal, and genital libidinal impulses in the development of heterosexuality.

amphipathic /-path'ik/ [Gk, amphi both + pathos suffering], pertaining to a molecule having two sides with characteristically different properties, such as a detergent, which has both a polar (hydrophilic) end and a nonpolar (hydrophobic) end but is long enough that each end demonstrates its own solubility characteristics.

Amphojel, a trademark for aluminum hydroxide gel.

amphoric breath sound /amfôr'ik/ [Gk, amphoreus, jug], an abnormal, resonant, hollow, blowing sound heard with a stethoscope over the thorax. It indicates a cavity opening into a bronchus or a pneumothorax.

amphotericin B /am'fəter'isin/, an antifungal medication prescribed for topical or systemic use in the treatment of fungal infections.

amphotericin B cholesteryl complex, amphotericin B complexed with cholesteryl sulfate in a 1:1 ratio; administered by IV infusion in the treatment of disseminated aspergillosis in patients refractory to or intolerant of conventional amphotericin B therapy.

amphotericin B liposomal complex, amphotericin B intercalated into a single bilayer liposome. It is administered by IV infusion in the treatment of severe systemic fungal infections and kala-azars in patients refractory to or intolerant of conventional amphotericin B therapy.

amphoterism /-ter'izəm/ [Gk, amphoteros, pertaining to both], a quality of a chemical compound that permits it to act as an acid or a base.—**amphoteric,** adj., n.

ampicillin /am'pəsil'in/, a semisynthetic aminopenicillin prescribed in the treatment of infections caused by a broad spectrum of sensitive gram-negative and gram-positive organisms.

ampicillin sodium, the sodium salt of ampicillin, prescribed as an antibiotic to treat gram-positive organisms and some gram-negative organisms.

amplification /am'plifikā'shən/ [L, *amplificare*, to make wider], **1.** a genetic engineering process in which the amount of plasmid DNA increases in proportion to the amount of bacterial DNA via treatment with certain substances, including chloramphenicol. **2.** the replication in bulk of an entire DNA library. **—amplify,** *v.*

amplifier, a device that controls power from a mechanical, electrical, hydraulic, or other source so that the output is greater than the input.

amplifier T cells, a T cell of the CD8 cell type that modifies a developing immune response by releasing nonspecific signals to which other T cells (either effector or suppressor cells) respond.

amplitude /am'plityōod/ [L, *amplus*, wide], the width or breadth of range or extent.

amplitude of accommodation (AA), the total accommodative power of the eye, determined by the difference between the refractive power for farthest vision and that for nearest vision.

amplitude of convergence, the difference in the power needed to turn the eyes from their far point to their near point of convergence.

amprenavir, an antiviral (protease inhibitor) used to treat HIV in combination with other antiretroviral agents.

ampule /am'pyōol/ [Fr, *ampoule*, phial], a small, sterile glass or plastic container that usually contains a single dose of a solution.

ampulla /ampōol'ə/ *pl.* **ampullae** [L, flasklike bottle], a rounded, saclike dilation of a duct, canal, or any tubular structure, such as the lacrimal duct, semicircular canal, uterine tube, rectum, or vas deferens.

ampulla of the rectum, a flask-shaped dilation near the end of the rectum.

ampullar crest, the most prominent part of a localized thickening of the membrane that lines the ampullae of the semicircular ducts, covered with neuroepithelium containing endings of the vestibular nerve.

ampullary tubal pregnancy /ampōol'lərē, am'pələr'ē/, a tubal pregnancy in which implantation occurs in the ampulla of one of the fallopian tubes.

ampullula /ampōol'yələ/, a minute ampulla, such as a lymph or blood vessel.

amputation /am'pyōotā'shən/ [L, *amputare*, to excise], the surgical removal of a part of the body, a limb, or part of a limb to treat recurrent infections or gangrene in peripheral vascular disease, to remove malignant tumors, and to treat severe trauma.

amputation care, a nursing intervention from the Nursing Interventions Classification (NIC) defined as promotion of physical and psychological healing after amputation of a body part.

amputation flap, a flap of skin used to cover the end of an amputation stump.

amputation neuroma, a form of traumatic neuroma that may develop at the proximal end of a severed or injured nerve.

amputation-stump bandage, an elastic figure-eight bandage applied to cover the stump after an amputation. It helps to control edema and shape the remaining portion of the limb.

amputee /am'pyōotē'/, a person who has had one or more extremities traumatically or surgically removed.

AMRA, abbreviation for *American Medical Records Association*.

Amsler grid [Marc Amsler, Swiss ophthalmologist, 1891–1968], a checkerboard grid of intersecting dark horizontal and vertical lines with one dark spot in the middle. To discover a visual field defect, the person simply covers or closes one eye and looks at the spot with the other. A visual field defect is perceived as a defect, distortion, blank, or other fault in the grid. It is used in testing for macular degeneration.

AMT, abbreviation for *American Medical Technologists*.

amu, abbreviation for **atomic mass unit.**

amusia /ə·myōo'zē-ə/ [Gk, *amousia*, want of harmony], inability to recognize the significance of sounds manifests as loss of the ability to recognize or produce music.

amyelia /amī·ēl'yə/ [Gk, *a* + *myelos*, without marrow], the absence of a spinal cord.

amyelinic neuroma /amī'əlinik/ [Gk, *a* + *myelos*, without marrow, *neuron*, nerve, *oma*], a tumor that contains only nonmyelinated nerve fibers.

amygdaloid /-dəloid/, resembling a tonsil.

amygdaloid fossa [Gk, *amylon* + *eidos*, starchlike; L, *fossa*, ditch], a space in the wall of the oropharynx, between the pillars of the fauces, that is occupied by the palatine tonsil.

amygdaloid nucleus [Gk, *amygdale*, almond, *eidos*, form; L, *nucleus*, nut], one of the basal nuclei, found near the inferior horn of the lateral ventricle in the medial temporal lobe. It is considered part of the limbic system and is involved in memory and emotion.

amyl alcohol /am'il/ [Gk, *amylon*, starch], a colorless, oily liquid with the formula $C_5H_{11}OH$ that is only slightly soluble in water but can be mixed with ethyl alcohol, chloroform, or ether.

amylase /am′ilās/ [Gk, *amylon*, starch], an enzyme that catalyzes the hydrolysis of starch into smaller carbohydrate molecules. Alphaamylase, found in saliva, pancreatic juice, malt, certain bacteria, and molds, catalyzes the hydrolysis of starches to dextrins, maltose, and maltotriose. Beta-amylase, found in grains, vegetables, malt, and bacteria, is involved in the hydrolysis of starch to maltose. Normal blood findings are 56 to 190 IU/L.

amylase test, a rapidly performed blood or urine test that is most specific for pancreatitis and other pancreatic disorders. Increased amylase activity may also indicate nonpancreatic disorders such as bowel perforation, penetrating peptic ulcer, duodenal obstruction, and other conditions.

amylene hydrate /am′ilēn/, a clear, colorless liquid, $(CH_3)_2C(OH)CH_2CH_3$, with a camphorlike odor, miscible with alcohol, chloroform, ether, or glycerin and used as a solvent and a hypnotic.

amylic fermentation /əmil′ik/, the formation of amyl alcohol from sugar.

amyl nitrite, a vasodilator prescribed to relieve the angiospasm of angina pectoris and as an adjunct in the treatment of cyanide poisoning.

amyloid /am′iloid/ [Gk, *amylon,* starch, *eidos,* form], **1.** pertaining to or resembling starch. **2.** a starchlike proteincarbohydrate complex deposited abnormally in some tissues during certain chronic disease states, such as amyloidosis, rheumatoid arthritis, TB, and Alzheimer's disease.

amyloid degeneration, degeneration of tissue resulting from deposition of amyloid complexes.

amyloid liver [Gk, *amylon,* starch, *eidos,* form; AS, *lifer*], a liver in which the cells have been infiltrated with amyloid deposits.

amyloidosis /am′iloidō′sis/ [Gk, *amylon* + *eidos,* form, *osis,* condition], a disease in which a waxy, starchlike glycoprotein (amyloid) accumulates in tissues and organs, impairing their function. Primary amyloidosis refers to light chain amyloidosis seen in multiple myeloma. Patients with secondary amyloidosis usually suffer from another chronic infectious or inflammatory disease such as TB, osteomyelitis, rheumatoid arthritis, or Crohn's disease. Almost all organs can be affected, most often the heart, lungs, tongue, and intestines in primary amyloidosis and the kidneys, liver, and spleen in the secondary type.

amyloid osteopathy, local osteoarticular lytic lesions often found in patients with hemodialysis-associated amyloidosis.

amyloid precursor protein (APP), a large transmembrane glycoprotein expressed on the cell surface and of uncertain function. It may be cleaved on the cell surface to a soluble form. Alternatively, cleavage may follow endocytosis, and in some cases then yields abnormal 40 to 43 amino acid peptides, which aggregate to form Ab amyloid, associated with Alzheimer's disease.

amylolysis /am′ēlol′isis/ [Gk, *amylon,* starch, *lysis,* loosening], the digestive process whereby starch is converted into sugars and dextrins by hydrolysis or enzymatic activity.

amylophagia /am′əlo-f′jah/, the habit of eating starch, such as laundry starch, a form of pica.

amylopsin, pancreatic amylase.

amylose, a lesser constituent of starch consisting of a chain of glucose residues. It stains blue with iodine.

amyotonia /ā′mī-ōtō′nē-ə/ [Gk, *a,* without, *mys,* muscle, *tonos,* tone], an abnormal condition of skeletal muscle, characterized by a lack of tonus, weakness, and wasting, usually the result of motor neuron disease. —**amyotonic,** *adj.*

amyotrophic lateral sclerosis (ALS) /ā′mī-ōtrof′ik/ [Gk, *a* + *mys* + *trophe,* nourishment], a degenerative disease characterized by loss of the motor neurons, with progressive weakness and atrophy of the muscles of the hands, forearms, and legs, spreading to involve most of the body and face. It results from degeneration of the motor neurons of the anterior horns and corticospinal tracts, beginning in middle age and progressing rapidly, causing death within 2 to 5 years.

Amytal Sodium, a trademark for a barbiturate (sodium amobarbital).

ANA, 1. abbreviation for **American Nurses Association. 2.** abbreviation for **antinuclear antibody.**

anabolic steroid /an′əbol′ik/ [Gk, *anaballein,* to build up], any of several compounds derived from testosterone or prepared synthetically to promote general body growth, to oppose the effects of endogenous estrogen, or to promote masculinizing effects. All such compounds cause a mixed androgenic-anabolic effect. Anabolic steroids are prescribed in the treatment of aplastic anemia, red-cell aplasia, and hemolytic anemia and in anemias associated with renal failure, myeloid metaplasia, and leukemia.

anabolism /ənab′əliz′əm/ [Gk, *anaballein,* to build up], the constructive phase of metabolism characterized by the conversion of simple substances into the more complex compounds of living matter. —**anabolic,** *adj.*

anabolite /ənab′ōlīt/ [Gk, *anaballein,* to build up], a product of the process of anabolism.

anacatadidymus /an′əkat′ədid′iməs/ [Gk, *ana,* up, *kata,* down, *didymos,* twin], conjoined twins that are fused in the middle but separated above and below.

anaclisis /an′əklī′sis/ [Gk, *ana* + *klisis,* leaning], **1.** a condition, normal in childhood but pathologic in adulthood, in which a person is emotionally dependent on other people. **2.** a condition in which a person consciously or unconsciously chooses a love object because of a resemblance to the mother, father, or another person who was an important source of comfort and protection in infancy.—**anaclitic** *adj.*

anaclitic depression /an′əklit′ik/, a syndrome occurring in infants, usually after sudden separation from the mothering person. Symptoms include apprehension, withdrawal, detachment, incessant crying, refusal to eat, sleep disturbances, and eventually stupor leading to severe impairment of the infant's physical, social, and intellectual development.

anacrotic pulse [Gk, *ana* + *krotos,* stroke], a pulse characterized by a transient drop in amplitude of the primary elevation on a sphygmographic tracing. It is seen in valvular aortic stenosis.

anacrotism /ənak′rətiz′əm/ [Gk, *ana* + *krotos,* stroke], a condition characterized by two arterial expansions per heartbeat and observed as a notch on the ascending limb of an arterial pulse pressure tracing.—**anacrotic,** *adj.*

anacusis /an′əkōō′sis/ [Gk, *a* + *akouein,* not to hear], a total loss of hearing.

anadicrotic pulse /an′ədīkrot′ik/ [Gk, *ana* + *dis,* twice, *krotos,* stroke], (on a sphygmographic tracing) a pulse characterized by two transient drops in amplitude on the curve of primary elevation.

anadidymus /an′ədid′iməs/ [Gk, *ana* + *didymos,* twin], conjoined twins that are united at the pelvis and lower extremities but separated in the upper half.

anadipsia /an′ədip′sē·ə/ [Gk, *ana* + *dipsa,* thirst], extreme thirst, often occurring in the manic phase of bipolar mood disorder. The condition is the result of dehydration caused by the excessive perspiration, electrolyte imbalance, continuous urination, and relentless physical activity produced by the intense excitement characteristic of the manic phase.

Anadrol-50, a trademark for an anabolic steroid (oxymetholone).

anaerobe /aner′ōb/ [Gk, *a* + *aer,* not air, *bios,* life], a microorganism that grows and lives in the complete or almost complete absence of oxygen. An example is *Clostridium botulinum.* Anaerobes are widely distributed in nature and in the body.

anaerobic /an′ərō′bik/, pertaining to the absence of air or oxygen.

anaerobic catabolism, the breakdown of complex chemical substances into simpler compounds, with the release of energy, in the absence of oxygen.

anaerobic exercise, any short-duration exercise that is powered primarily by metabolic pathways that do not use oxygen. Such pathways produce lactic acid, resulting in metabolic acidosis. Examples of anaerobic exercise include sprinting and weight lifting.

anaerobic infection, an infection caused by an anaerobic organism, usually occurring in deep puncture wounds that exclude air or in tissue that has diminished oxygen-reduction potential as a result of trauma, necrosis, or overgrowth of bacteria.

anagen, the first phase of the hair cycle, during which synthesis of the hair takes place.

anagrelide, an antiplatelet agent prescribed for essential thrombocythemia.

anakinra, an antirheumatic agent and immunomodulator used to reduce the signs and symptoms of moderate to severe active rheumatoid arthritis in adults.

Ana-Kit, a trademark for an emergency kit for insect sting treatment. It contains chlorpheniramine epINEPHrine in a sterile 1-mL syringe.

anal canal, the final portion of the digestive tract, about 4 cm long, between the rectum and the anus.

anal character, (in psychoanalysis) a type of personality exhibiting patterns of behavior originating in the anal phase of childhood. It is characterized by extreme orderliness, obstinacy, perfectionism, cleanliness, punctuality, and miserliness, or their extreme opposites.

anal column, the highly vascular longitudinal folds of the anal canal, in which are found the hemorrhoidal blood vessels.

anal crypt, the depression between rectal columns that encloses networks of veins that, when inflamed, are called hemorrhoids.

anal cryptitis, an inflammation of the mucous membrane of the anal crypts.

anal eroticism, (in psychoanalysis) a libidinal fixation at or regression to the anal stage of psychosexual development, often reflected as an anal character.

anal fissure, a painful linear ulceration or laceration of the skin at the margin of the anus.

anal fistula, an abnormal opening on the cutaneous surface near the anus, usually resulting from a local abscess of the crypt and common in Crohn's disease. A perianal fistula may or may not communicate with the rectum.

anal fold, a slight elevation flanking the cloacal membrane and derived from a cloacal fold. Anal folds form the margin of the anus.

analgesia /an′əljē′zē·ə/ [Gk, *a + algos,* without pain], a decreased or absent sensation of pain.

analgesic /an′əljē′zik/, **1.** relieving pain. **2.** a drug that relieves pain. The opioid analgesics act on the CNS and alter the patient's perception; they are more often used for severe pain. The nonopioid analgesics act primarily at the periphery, do not produce tolerance or dependence, and do not alter the patient's perception; they are used for mild-to-moderate pain.

analgesic administration, a nursing intervention from the Nursing Interventions Classification (NIC) defined as use of pharmacologic agents to reduce or eliminate pain.

analgesic administration: intraspinal, a nursing intervention from the Nursing Interventions Classification (NIC) defined as administration of pharmacologic agents into the epidural or intrathecal space to reduce or eliminate pain.

analgesic nephropathy [Gk, *a + algos,* without pain, *nephros,* kidney, *pathos,* disease], toxic damage to one or both kidneys resulting from the consumption of excessive amounts of NSAIDs or similar analgesic medications.

analgia [Gk, *ana,* without, *algos,* pain], an absence of pain.

anal incontinence [L, *anus + incontinentia,* an inability to retain], the lack of voluntary control over fecal discharge.

analog /an′ɔlog/ [Gk, *analogos,* proportionate], **1.** a substance, tissue, or organ that is similar in appearance or function to another but differs in origin or development, such as the eye of a fly and the eye of a human. **2.** a drug or other chemical compound that resembles another in structure or constituents but has different effects. —**analogous,** *adj.*

analogous /ənal′əgəs/ [Gk, *analogos*], something that is similar to a degree in function or form but different in structure or origin.

analog signal, a continuous electric signal representing a specific condition such as temperature, ECG waveforms, telephones, or computer modems.

analog-to-digital (A/D) converter, a device for converting analog information, such as temperature or ECG waveforms, into digital form for processing by a digital computer.

anal orifice [L, *orificium,* an opening], **1.** the external opening at the end of the anal canal. **2.** the anus, surrounded by the anal sphincter muscle.

anal pecten, the corrugated epithelium within the anal transitional zone between the pectinate line and the anocutaneous line.

anal plug, a mass of epithelial cells that temporarily occludes the anal canal in the embryo.

anal reflex, a superficial neurologic reflex obtained by stroking the skin or mucosa of the region around the anus, which normally results in a contraction of the external anal sphincter.

anal region, the part of the perineal region that surrounds the anus.

anal sadism, (in psychoanalysis) a sadistic form of anal eroticism, manifested by such behavior as aggressiveness and selfishness.

anal sphincter, either of two sphincters (the internal and external anal sphincters) that open and close to control the evacuation of feces from the anus.

anal stage, (in psychoanalysis) the period in psychosexual development, occurring between 1 and 3 years of age, when preoccupation with the function of the bowel and the sensations associated with the anus are the predominant source of pleasurable stimulation. It is regarded as an important determinant of ultimate personality type.

anal verge [L, *anus + vergere,* to bend], the area between the anal canal and the perianal skin.

analysand /ənal′isand′/, a person undergoing psychoanalysis.

analysis /ənal′əsis/ [Gk, *ana + lyein,* to loosen], the separation of substances into their constituent parts and the determination of the nature, properties, and composition of compounds. —**analytic,** *adj.* **analyze,** *v.*

analysis of variance (ANOVA), a series of statistical procedures for comparing differences among three or more groups, rather than testing each pair of means separately, to determine if differences are due to chance. It is accomplished by examining the differences within the groups as well.

analyst /an′əlist/, **1.** a psychoanalyst. **2.** a person who analyzes the chemical, physical, or other properties of a substance or product.

analyte /an′əlīt/, any substance that is measured. The term is usually applied to a component of blood or another body fluid.

analytic chemistry, a branch of chemistry that deals with identifying (qualitative chemistry) and measuring (quantitative chemistry) the components of chemical compounds or mixtures of compounds.

analytic psychology /anʹəlitʹik/, **1.** the system in which phenomena such as sensations and feelings are analyzed and classified by introspective rather than experimental methods. **2.** a system of analyzing the psyche according to the concepts developed by Carl Gustav Jung. It differs from the psychoanalysis of Sigmund Freud in stressing a collective unconsciousand a mystic, religious factor in the development of the personal unconscious while minimizing the role of sexual influence on early emotional and psychologic development.

analyzing /anʹəlīʹzing/, (in five-step nursing process) a category of nursing behavior in which the health care needs of the client are identified and the goals of care are defined. The nurse interprets data; identifies problems (nursing diagnoses) involving the patient, the patient's family, and significant others; defines goals and establishes priorities; integrates the information; and projects the expected outcomes of nursing activities.

anamnesis /anʹamnēʹsis/ [Gk, *anamimneskein,* to recall], **1.** remembrance of the past. **2.** the accumulated data concerning a medical or psychiatric patient and the patient's background, including family, previous environment, experiences, and particularly recollections, for use in analyzing his or her condition.

anamnestic /anʹamnesʹtik/, **1.** pertaining to amnesia or memory. **2.** pertaining to the immunologic memory and the immune response to an antigen to which immunocompetent cells have been exposed. **3.** pertaining to the current or previous medical history of a patient.

ANA-PAC, abbreviation for **American Nurses Association–Political Action Committee.**

anaphase /anʹəfāz/ [Gk, *ana + phainein,* to appear], the third of four stages of division of the nucleus in mitosis and in each of the two divisions of meiosis. In anaphase of mitosis and of the second meiotic division, the centromeres divide, and the two chromatids, which are arranged along the equatorial plane of the spindle, separate and move to the opposite poles of the cell, forming daughter chromosomes. In anaphase of the first meiotic division, the pairs of homologous chromosomes separate from each other and move intact to the opposite poles of the cell.

anaphia /ənāʹfē·ə/, an inability to perceive tactile stimuli.

anaphoresis, (in electrophoresis) the movement of anions in a solution or suspension toward the anode.

anaphylactic hypersensitivity /anʹəfilakʹtik/ [Gk, *ana,* up, *phylaxis,* protection], an immediate, systemic hypersensitivity reaction to an exogenous antigen mediated by IgE. It can be triggered by many substances, including drugs, especially penicillin and other antibiotics; foreign proteins used as therapeutic agents such as insulin, vaccines, allergen extracts, and muscle relaxants; insect venom, especially from bees, wasps, hornets, and fire ants; and certain foods such as shellfish, berries, chocolate, eggs, and nuts.

anaphylactic reaction [Gk, *ana, phylaxis,* protection; L, *re, agere,* to act], an acute allergic response involving IgE–mediated, antigen-stimulated mast cell activation resulting in histamine release. Exposure to the antigen may result in dyspnea, airway obstruction, shock, urticaria, and in some cases death.

anaphylactic shock, a severe and sometimes fatal systemic allergic reaction to an allergen, such as a drug, vaccine, specific food, serum, allergen extract, insect venom, or chemical. This condition may occur within seconds to minutes from the time of exposure to the sensitizing factor (allergen) and is commonly marked by respiratory distress and vascular collapse. The first symptoms are intense anxiety, weakness, and a feeling of impending doom. Sweating and dyspnea may occur. These are often followed, usually quickly, by pruritus and urticaria. Other symptoms include hypotension, shock, arrhythmia, respiratory congestion, edema of the glottis, nausea, and diarrhea.

anaphylatoxin /anʹəfīʹlətokʹsin/, a fragment (C3a, C4a, or C5a) that is produced during the pathways of the complement system. Along with other mechanisms, it mediates changes in mast cells leading to the release of histamine and other immunoreactive or inflammatory reactive substances. If the degranulation of mast cells is too strong, it can cause allergic reactions.

anaphylaxis /anʹəfilakʹsis/ [Gk, *ana + phylaxis,* protection], an exaggerated, life-threatening hypersensitivity reaction to a previously encountered antigen. It is mediated by antibodies of the E or G class of immunoglobulins and results in the release of chemical mediators from mast cells. The reaction may consist of a localized wheal-and-flare reaction of generalized itching, hyperemia, angioedema, and in severe cases vascular collapse, bronchospasm, and shock. The severity of symptoms depends on the original sensitizing dose of the antigen, the number and distribution of antibodies, and the route of entry and dose of subsequently encountered antigen. Penicillin injection is the most common cause of anaphylactic shock. **—anaphylactic,** *adj.*

anaphylaxis management, a nursing intervention from the Nursing Interventions Classification (NIC) defined as promotion of adequate ventilation and tissue perfusion for an individual with a severe allergic (antigen-antibody) reaction.

anaplasia /an′əplā′zhə/ [Gk, *ana* + *plassein*, to shape], a change in the structure and orientation of cells, characterized by a loss of differentiation and reversion to a more primitive form. Anaplasia is characteristic of malignancy.**—anaplastic** /an′əplas′tik/, *adj.*

anapnea /anap′nē·ə/ [Gk, *ana* + *pnoia*, breath], restoration of breathing after a period of halted respiration.

anapophysis /an′əpof′isis/ [Gk, *an*, not, without + *apophysis*, a growing away], an accessory vertebral process, especially one on a thoracic or lumbar vertebra.

Anaprox, a trademark for an NSAID (naproxen sodium).

anarthria /anär′thrē·ə/ [Gk, *a* + *arthron*, not joint], a loss of control of the muscles of speech, resulting in the inability to articulate words. The condition is usually caused by damage to a central or peripheral motor nerve.

anasarca /an′əsär′kə/ [Gk, *ana* + *sarx*, flesh], severe generalized, massive edema. Anasarca often occurs in severe cardiovascular renal disease.**—anasarcous,** *adj.*

anastomosis /ənas′tōmō′sis/ *pl.* **anastomoses** [Gk, *anastomoien*, to provide a mouth], **1.** a connection between two vessels. **2.** a surgical joining of two ducts, blood vessels, or bowel segments to allow flow from one to the other. A vascular anastomosis may be performed to bypass an aneurysm or a vascular or arterial occlusion. **—anastomose,** *v.,* **—anastomotic,** *adj.*

anastomosis at elbow joint, a convergence of blood vessels at the elbow joint, consisting of various veins and portions of the brachial and deep brachial arteries and their branches.

anastrozole, a nonsteroidal aromatase inhibitor prescribed in the treatment of advanced breast cancer for postmenopausal women whose disease has not responded to treatment with tamoxifen.

anatomic age, the estimated age of an individual based on the stage of development or deterioration of the body as compared with that of other persons of the same chronologic age.

anatomic crown, the portion of the dentin of a tooth that is covered by enamel.

anatomic curve, the curvature of the different segments of the vertebral column. In the lateral contour of the back, the cervical and lumbar curves appear concave, and the thoracic and sacral curves appear convex.

anatomic height of contour, an imaginary line that encircles a tooth at the level of greatest circumference.

anatomic incontinence, urinary incontinence associated with instability or excessive mobility of the bladder neck and adjacent urethra.

anatomic neck of the humerus [Gk, *ana*, up, *temnein*, to cut; AS, *hnecca*; L, *humerus*, shoulder], the portion of the humerus where there is a slight constriction adjoining the head.

anatomic pathology [Gk, *ana*, up, *temnein*, to cut, *pathos*, disease, *logos*, science], the study of the effects of disease on the structure of the body.

anatomic position, a standard position of the body: standing erect, facing directly forward, feet pointed forward and slightly apart, and arms hanging down at the sides with palms facing forward. This position is used as a reference to describe sites or motions of various parts of the body.

anatomic snuffbox, a small, cuplike depression on the back of the hand near the wrist formed by the three tendons reaching toward the thumb and index finger as the thumb is abducted and extended.

anatomic topography [Gk, *ana* + *temnein*, to cut, *topos*, place, *graphein*, to write], a system of identification of a body part in terms of the region in which it is located and its nearby structures.

anatomic zero joint position, the beginning point of a joint ROM.

anatomy /ənat′əmē/ [Gk, *ana* + *temnein*, to cut], **1.** the study, classification, and description of structures and organs of the body. **2.** the structure of an organism. **—anatomic,** *adj.*

anatripsis /an′ətrip′sis/, a therapy that involves rubbing or friction with or without a simultaneous application of a medicine.

ANC, **1.** abbreviation for **absolute neutrophil count.** **2.** abbreviation for **Army Nurse Corps.**

ANCA, abbreviation for **antineutrophil cytoplasmic antibody.**

Ancef, a trademark for a semisynthetic cephalosporin antibiotic (cefazolin sodium).

ancestor [L, *antecessorem*], one from whom a person is descended, through the mother or the father. The term assumes a direct line of descent, excluding collateral family members of previous generations.

anchorage [Gk, *agkyra*, anchor], surgical fixation of a movable body part.

ancillary /an'səler'ē/ [L, *ancillaris,* handmaid], pertaining to something that is subordinate, auxiliary, or supplementary.

Ancobon, a trademark for an antifungal (flucytosine).

anconeus /angkō'nē·əs/ [Gk, *agkon,* elbow], one of seven superficial muscles of the posterior forearm. A small triangular muscle, it originates on the dorsal surface of the lateral condyle of the humerus and inserts in the olecranon. It functions to extend the forearm and abduct the ulna in pronation.

ancrod /ang'krod/, the venom of the Malayan pit viper, used to remove fibrinogen from the circulation to prevent clotting of the blood.

Ancylostoma /ang'kilos'təmə/ [Gk, *angkylos,* crooked, *stoma,* mouth], a genus of nematode that is an intestinal parasite and causes hookworm disease.

ancylostomiasis /an'səlos'təmī'əsis/, hookworm disease, more specifically that caused by *Ancylostoma duodenale, A. braziliense,* or *A. caninum.* Larvae enter the host via the skin; the adult worm lives in the intestine. The adult worms abrade the intestinal wall, eventually causing severe anemia and debilitation. Clinical manifestations and treatment are similar for all types of hookworms. Infection may be prevented by eliminating fecal pollution of soil and by wearing shoes.

Andersen's disease [Dorothy Hansine Andersen, American pediatrician and pathologist, 1901–1963], a rare glycogen storage disease characterized by a genetic deficiency of branching enzyme (alpha-1:4, alpha 1:6 transglucosidase), causing the deposition in tissues of abnormal glycogen with long inner and outer chains. Infants with the disease are normal at birth but fail to thrive and soon show hepatomegaly, splenomegaly, and hypotonia of muscle associated with the progressive development of cirrhosis or heart failure of unknown mechanisms. Diagnosis is by enzyme assays of leukocytes and fibroblasts. There is no specific therapy for the disease, which is usually fatal in the first few years of life.

Andersen's syndrome, Andersen's triad, bronchiectasis, CF, and vitamin A deficiency.

androgamone /an'drōgam'ōn/ [Gk, *andros,* man, *gamos,* marriage], a chemical secreted by male gametes that is believed to attract female gametes.

androgen /an'drəjin/ [Gk, *andros* + *genein,* to produce], any steroid hormone that increases male characteristics. **—androgenic,** *adj.*

androgenetic alopecia, a progressive, diffuse, symmetric loss of scalp hair. In men it begins in the 20s or early 30s with hair loss from the crown and the frontal and temple regions, ultimately leaving only a sparse peripheral rim of scalp hair. In females it begins later, with less severe hair loss in the front area of the scalp. The cause is unknown but is believed to be a combination of genetic factors and increased response of hair follicles to androgens.

androgynous /androj'inəs/, **1.** (of a man or woman) having some characteristics of both sexes. Social role, behavior, personality, and appearance are reflections of individuality and are not determined by gender. **2.** hermaphroditic.**—androgyny** /-droj'ənē/, *n.*

android [Gk, *andros* + *eidos,* form], pertaining to something that is typically masculine, or manlike, such as an android pelvis.

android obesity, obesity in which fat is localized around the waist and in the upper body, most frequently seen in men and having a poorer prognosis for morbidity and mortality than the gynoid type.

android pelvis, a type of pelvis with a structure characteristic of the male. It is also common in women. The bones are thick and heavy, and the pelvic inlet is heart-shaped.

andrology /androl'əjē/ [Gk, *andros,* man, *logos,* science], the study of the health of males.

andropause /an'drəpôs/, a change of life for males that may be expressed in terms of a career change, divorce, or reordering of life. It is associated with a decline in androgen levels that occurs in men during their late 40s or early 50s.

androstenedione test, a blood test used to identify the presence of androstenedione, a precursor of testosterone, which may be used orally by some athletes to enhance performance or increase body bulk.

androsterone /andros'tərōn/ [Gk, *andros* + *stereos,* solid], a male sex hormone, originally believed to be the principal male sex hormone. It is used less frequently in therapy since the discovery of testosterone.

anecdotal /an'əkdot'əl/ [Gk, *anekdotos,* unpublished], pertaining to knowledge based on isolated observations and not yet verified by controlled scientific studies.

anecdotal record, a medical finding usually based on one or a few observed episodes of patient care, as distinguished from results compiled in a large-scale scientific or systematic study.

anechoic /an'ekō'ik/, (in ultrasonography) free of echoes.

Anectine, a trademark for a depolarizing neuromuscular blocking agent (succinylcholine chloride).

anejaculation, a failure of ejaculation of semen from the urinary meatus during coitus.

anemia /ənē′mē·ə/ [Gk, *a + haima,* without blood], a decrease in quality hemoglobin in the blood to levels below the normal range of 12 to 16 g/dL for women and 13.5 to 18 g/dL for men or in circulating RBCs. Anemia may be caused by a decrease in erythrocyte production, an increase in erythrocyte destruction, or a loss of blood. Any one of three tests (hemoglobin, hematocrit, or RBC count) can be used to diagnose anemia.—**anemic,** *adj.*

anemia of chronic disease, a decrease in the number of circulating erythrocytes as a result of a chronic inflammatory state.

anemia of pregnancy, a condition of pregnancy characterized by a reduction in the concentration of hemoglobin in the blood. It may be physiologic or pathologic. In physiologic anemia of pregnancy, the reduction in concentration results from dilution because the plasma volume expands more than the RBC volume. In pathologic anemia of pregnancy, the oxygen-carrying capacity of the blood is deficient because of disordered erythrocyte production or excessive loss of erythrocytes through destruction or bleeding.

anemic anoxia, a condition characterized by an oxygen deficiency in body tissues, resulting from a decrease in the number of erythrocytes or in the amount of hemoglobin in the blood.

anencephalus /an′ənsef′ələs/, an infant with anencephaly.

anencephaly /an′ensef′əlē/ [Gk, *a + encephalos,* without brain], a neural tube defect in which absence of major portions of the brain and malformation of the brainstem occur. The cranium does not close and the vertebral canal remains a groove. It is thought to be caused by a combination of genetic and environmental factors. Anencephaly is not compatible with life. It can be detected early in gestation by amniocentesis and analysis or by ultrasonography.—**anencephalous,** *adj.*

anephric /ā·nef′rik/ [Gk, *a + nephros* without kidney], without kidneys.

anephrogenesis /anef′rōjen′əsis/ [Gk, *a,* without, *nephros,* kidney, *genein,* to produce], the condition of being born without kidneys.

anergia /ənur′jə/, **1.** a condition of lethargy or lack of physical activity. **2.** a diminished or absent sensitivity to commonly used test antigens.

aneroid /an′əroid/, not containing a liquid. The term is used especially to describe a device that does not contain liquid but performs the same function as a similar device containing liquid.

aneroid barometer, a device consisting of a flexible spring in a sealed, evacuated metal box that is used to measure atmospheric pressure. It is less accurate than a mercury barometer and is generally used for nonscientific work.

Anestacon, a trademark for a local anesthetic jelly (2% lidocaine hydrochloride) used for endourethral and endotracheal procedures.

anesthesia (A) /an′esthē′zhə/ [Gk, *anaisthesia,* lack of feeling], the absence of all sensation, especially sensitivity to pain, as induced by an anesthetic substance or by hypnosis or as occurs with traumatic or pathophysiologic damage to nerve tissue. Anesthesia induced for medical or surgical purposes may be topical, local, regional, or general and is named for the anesthetic technique or method.—**anesthetize,** *v.*

anesthesia administration, a nursing intervention from the Nursing Interventions Classification (NIC) defined as preparation for and administration of anesthetic agents and monitoring of patient responsiveness during administration.

anesthesia machine, an apparatus for administering inhalation anesthetic gases and vapors that is capable of controlling ventilation.

anesthesia patients, classification of, a system developed by the American Society of Anesthesiologists used to classify patients within six categories defined by health status, regardless of whether the health problems are related to the condition requiring anesthesia. Class I includes patients who are healthy and who are without organic, physiologic, biochemical, or psychiatric problems. Class II includes patients who have mild to moderate systemic disease that does not limit activity, such as anemia, mild controlled diabetes, moderate controlled hypertension, or obesity. Class III includes patients who have significant systemic disturbances or disease that limits their activity. Class IV includes patients who have severe systemic disease that is a constant threat to life. Class V includes moribund patient who is not expected to survive more than 24 hours with or without surgical intervention, such as a person in shock with a ruptured abdominal aneurysm or a massive pulmonary embolus. Class VI includes brain-dead patients who are undergoing organ harvest for donation. The letter E is added to the Roman numeral to indicate an emergency procedure that may preclude typical anesthesia preparation, such as nothing-by-mouth status, or an emergent medical condition requiring immediate surgical intervention.

anesthesia screen, a metal frame on upright poles, or a drape attached to IV poles on the right and left sides of the surgical table, that is used to suspend a sterile barrier separating the surgical field from the anesthetist's access to the patient.

anesthesiologist /ˌanˈəsthēˈzē·olˈəjist/, a physician who completes an accredited residency program in anesthesiology. Anesthesiologists may administer anesthesia directly or as part of an anesthesia team consisting of nurse anesthetists or anesthesiologist's assistants.

anesthesiologist assistant (AA), an allied health professional who, under the supervision of a licensed anesthesiologist, assists in developing and implementing the anesthesia care plan. Duties may include collecting preoperative data, performing various preoperative tasks, managing the airway and administering drugs for induction and maintenance of anesthesia, administering supportive therapy, providing recovery room care, and performing other functions and tasks relating to care in an intensive care unit or pain clinic, providing anesthesia monitoring services, and performing administrative and educational functions and tasks.

anesthesiology /-olˈəjē/, the branch of medicine that is concerned with the study and practice of anesthesia. It is a specialty requiring competency in general medicine, a broad understanding of surgical procedures, and a comprehensive knowledge of clinical obstetrics, chest medicine, neurology, pediatrics, pharmacology, biochemistry, cardiology, and cardiac and respiratory physiology.

anesthetist /ənesˈthətist/, a general term used to describe a health care professional trained to administer anesthesia.

anetoderma /anˈətōdurˈmə/ [Gk, *anetos,* relaxed, *derma,* skin], an idiopathic clinical change produced by focal damage to elastin fibers that results in looseness of skin.

aneuploid /anˈyo͞oploid/ [Gk, *a + eu,* not good, *ploos,* fold, *eidos,* form], **1.** an individual, organism, strain, or cell that has a chromosome number that is not an exact multiple of the haploid number characteristic of the species. **2.** pertaining to such an individual, organism, strain, or cell.

aneuploidy /anˈyo͞oploiˈdē/, any variation in chromosome number that involves individual chromosomes rather than entire sets of chromosomes. Individuals with aneuploidy have various abnormal physiologic and morphologic traits.

aneurysm /anˈyo͞orizˈəm/ [Gk, *aneurysma,* widening], a localized dilation of the wall of a blood vessel. It may be caused by atherosclerosis and hypertension, or less frequently by trauma, infection, or a congenital weakness in the vessel wall. Aneurysms are common in the aorta but also occur in peripheral vessels, especially in the popliteal arteries of older people. A sign of large arterial aneurysm is a pulsating swelling that produces a blowing murmur on auscultation. An aneurysm may rupture, causing hemorrhage, or thrombi may form in the dilation and give rise to emboli that may obstruct smaller vessels. —**aneurysmal,** *adj.*

aneurysmal bone cyst, a cystic lesion that tends to develop in the metaphyseal region of long bones but may occur in any bone, including the vertebrae. It may produce pain and swelling.

aneurysmal thrill, a vibration that can be felt over an aneurysm. In arterial aneurysms the vibration is felt only in systole, but in arteriovenous aneurysms it is felt during both systole and diastole.

aneurysmal varix [Gk, *aneurysma,* a widening; L, *varix,* a dilated vein], a varicose vein in which the enlargement is due to an acquired communication with an adjacent artery.

aneurysmectomy, the surgical removal of an aneurysm.

aneurysm needle, a needle equipped with a handle, used to ligate aneurysms.

ANF, 1. abbreviation for *American Nurses Foundation.* **2.** abbreviation for *Australian Nursing Federation.*

angelica, a herb that belongs to the parsley family, grown in Iceland and several northern areas. It is used in the treatment of heartburn, colic, poor blood flow to the extremities, bronchitis, poor appetite, psoriasis, and vitiligo. It is also used as an antiseptic.

Angelman's syndrome /änˈjəlmənz/, an autosomal-recessive syndrome characterized by jerky puppet-like movements, frequent laughter, mental and motor retardation, a peculiar open-mouthed facial expression, and seizures. It can be caused by a deletion on chromosome 15 inherited from the mother.

anger [L, *angere,* to hurt], an emotional reaction characterized by extreme displeasure, rage, indignation, or hostility. It is considered to be of pathologic origin when such a response does not realistically reflect a person's actual circumstances.

anger control assistance, a nursing intervention from the Nursing Interventions Classification (NIC) defined as facilitation of the expression of anger in an adaptive, nonviolent manner.

angiitis /anˈjē·rˈtis/ [Gk, *angeion,* vessel, *itis*], an inflammation of a vessel, chiefly a blood or lymph vessel.

angina /anjī′nə, an′jinə/ [L, *angor,* quinsy (strangling)], **1.** a spasmodic, cramplike choking feeling resulting from insufficient oxygen supply to the myocardium, commonly caused by coronary artery disease. **2.** characterized by a feeling of choking, suffocation, or crushing pressure and pain. —**anginal,** *adj.*

angina pectoris, a paroxysmal thoracic pain caused most often by myocardial anoxia as a result of atherosclerosis or spasm of the coronary arteries. The pain usually radiates along the neck, jaw, and shoulder and down the inner aspect of the left arm. It is frequently accompanied by a feeling of suffocation and impending death.

angina sine dolore /sē′nə dolôr′ə, sī′nē/, a painless episode of coronary insufficiency.

angioblast /an′jēōblast′/ [Gk, *angeion,* vessel, *blastos,* germ], **1.** the mesenchymal tissue of the embryo from which the blood cells and blood vessels differentiate. **2.** an individual vessel-forming cell.

angioblastic cord /an′jē-ōblas′tik/, any of the cordlike masses of splanchnic mesenchymal cells ventral to the primordial coelom. Angioblastic cords arrange themselves side by side to form the primordia of the endocardial tubes.

angioblastic meningioma, a tumor of the blood vessels of the meninges covering the spinal cord or the brain.

angioblastoma /an′jē-ōblastō′mə/ pl. **angioblastomas, angioblastomata** [Gk, *angeion,* vessel, *blastos,* germ, *oma*], a tumor of blood vessels in the brain.

angiocardiogram /an′jē-ōkär′dē-ōgram′/, a series of radiographic images produced by angiocardiography.

angiocardiography /-kär′dē-og′rəfē/ [Gk, *angeion* + *kardia,* heart, *graphein,* to record], the process of producing a radiograph of the heart and its great vessels. A radiopaque contrast medium is injected directly into the heart by a catheter introduced through the antecubital or femoral veins. X-ray images are taken as the contrast medium passes through the heart and great vessels.

angiocardiopathy /-kär′dē-op′əthē/ [Gk, *angeion,* vessel, *kardia,* heart, *pathos,* disease], a disease of the blood vessels of the heart.

angiocarditis /-kärdī′tis/, an inflammation of the heart and large blood vessels.

angiocatheter /an′jē-ōkath′ətər/, a hollow, flexible tube inserted into a blood vessel to withdraw or instill fluids.

angiochondroma /an′jē-ōkondrō′mə/ pl. **angiochondromas, angiochondromata** [Gk, *angeion* + *chondros,* cartilage, *oma*], a cartilaginous tumor characterized by an excessive formation of blood vessels.

angioedema /an′jē-ō′idē′mə/, a dermal, subcutaneous, or submucosal swelling that is acute, painless, and of short duration. It may involve the face, neck, lips, larynx, hands, feet, genitalia, or viscera. Angioedema may be hereditary or the result of food or drug allergy, infection, emotional stress, or a reaction to blood products.

angiofibroma /an′jē-ōfībrō′mə/ pl. **angiofibromas, angiofibromata** [Gk, *angeion;* L, *fibra,* fiber; Gk, *oma*], an angioma containing fibrous tissue.

angiogenesis /an′jē-ōjen′əsis/ [Gk, *angeion* + *genesis,* origin], the formation of new blood vessels, a process controlled by chemicals produced in the body that stimulate blood vessels or form new ones. Angiogenesis plays an important role in the growth and spread of cancer. Angiogenesis also occurs in the healthy body for healing of wounds and restoring blood flow to tissues after injury.

angiogenesis inhibitor, one of a group of drugs that prevent the growth of new blood vessels into a solid tumor.

angiogenin /an′jē-ōjen′in/, a protein that mediates the formation of blood vessels. Angiogenin is used experimentally to stimulate the development of new blood vessels in wound healing, CVA, or coronary artery disease.

angioglioma, pl. **angiogliomas, angiogliomata** /an′jē-ōglē-ō′mə/ [Gk, *angeion* + *glia,* glue, *oma,* tumor], a highly vascular tumor composed of neuroglia.

angiogram /an′jē-əgram/ [Gk, *angeion,* vessel, *gramma,* writing], a radiographic image of a blood vessel after injection of a radiopaque contrast medium.

angiograph /an′jē-əgraf/ [Gk, *angeion,* vessel, *graphein,* to record], an instrument that records the patterns of pulse waves inside blood vessels.

angiography /an′jē-og′rəfē/ [Gk, *angeion* + *graphein,* to record], the x-ray visualization of the internal anatomy of the heart and blood vessels after the intravascular introduction of radiopaque contrast medium.—**angiographic,** *adj.*

angioimmunoblastic lymphadenopathy with dysproteinemia (AILD), a systemic disorder resembling lymphoma, characterized by fever, night sweats, weight loss, and generalized lymphadenopathy. There are cellular infiltrate of lymphocytes, immunoblasts, and plasma cells; change or effacement of lymph node architecture; hepatosplenomegaly; maculopapular rash; polyclonal hypergammaglobulinemia; and Coombs′-positive hemolytic anemia. It is considered to be a nonmalignant hyperimmune reaction to chronic antigenic stimulation.

angiokeratoma /an′jē-ōker′ətō′mə/ pl. **angiokeratomas, angiokeratomata** [Gk, *angeion* + *keras,* horn, *oma*], a vascular, horny neoplasm on the skin, characterized by clumps of dilated blood vessels, clusters of verrucae, and thickening of the epidermis, especially the scrotum and the dorsal aspect of the fingers and toes.

angiokeratoma circumscriptum, a rare skin disorder characterized by discrete papules and nodules in small patches on the legs or on the trunk.

angiokeratoma corporis diffusum, an uncommon familial disease in which glycolipids are stored in many parts of the body, especially in the venal and cardiovascular systems, causing vasomotor, urinary, and cutaneous disorders and, in some cases, muscular abnormalities. Characteristic signs of the disease are dilation of blood vessels in the "bathing suit" areas, edema; hypertension; cardiomegaly, especially enlargement of the left ventricle; diffuse nodularity of the skin; albumin, erythrocytes, leukocytes, and casts in the urine; and vacuoles in muscle bundles.

angiolipoma /an'jē·ōlipō'mə/ *pl.* **angiolipomas, angiolipomata** [Gk, *angeion* + *lipos,* fat, *oma*], a benign neoplasm containing blood vessels and tissue.

angioma /an'jē·ō'mə/ *pl.* **angiomas, angiomata** [Gk, *angeion,* vessel + *oma,* tumor], any benign tumor with blood vessels (hemangioma) or lymph vessels (lymphangioma). Most angiomas are congenital; some, such as cavernous hemangiomas, may disappear spontaneously.

angioma arteriale racemosum /ärtir'ē·ā'lē ras'əmō'səm/ [Gk, *angeion* + *oma;* L, *arteria,* airpipe, *racemus,* grape], a vascular neoplasm characterized by the intertwining of many small, newly formed, dilated blood vessels.

angioma cutis, a nevus composed of a network of dilated blood vessels.

angioma serpiginosum /sərpij'inō'səm/ [Gk, *angeion* + *oma;* L, *serpere,* to creep], a cutaneous disease characterized by rings of tiny vascular points appearing as red dots.

angiomatosis /an'jē·ōmatō'sis/, a condition characterized by numerous vascular tumors.

angiomyoma /-mī·ō'mə/ *pl.* **angiomyomas, angiomyomata** [Gk, *angeion* + *mys,* muscle, *oma*], a tumor composed of vascular and muscular tissue elements.

angiomyosarcoma /mī'ōsärkō'mə/ *pl.* **angiomyosarcomas, angiomyosarcomata** [Gk, *angeion* + *mys,* muscle, *sarx,* flesh, *oma*], a tumor containing vascular, muscular, and connective tissue elements.

angioneurotic anuria /-n‿oorot'ik əny‿oor'ē·ə/ [Gk, *angeion* + *neuron,* nerve, *a* + *ouron,* not urine], an abnormal condition characterized by an almost complete absence of urination caused by destruction of tissue in the renal cortex.

angioneurotic gangrene [Gk, *angeion* + *neuron,* nerve, *gaggraina*], the death and putrefaction of tissue caused by an interruption of the blood supply resulting from thrombotic arteries or veins.

angiopathy /an'jē·op'əthē/ [Gk, *angeion,* vessel, *pathos,* disease], a disease of the blood vessels.

angioplasty /an'jēōplas'tē/ [Gk, *angeion,* vessel, *plassein,* to mold], the reconstruction of blood vessels damaged by disease or injury.

angiopoiesis /-poi·ē'sis/ [Gk, *angeion,* vessel, *poien,* to make], the process of blood vessel formation.

angiorrhaphy /an'jē·ôr'əfē/ [Gk, *angeion,* vessel, *rhaphe,* suture], the repair by suture of any blood vessel.

angiosarcoma /-särkō'mə/, a rare, malignant tumor consisting of endothelial and fibroblastic tissue that proliferates and eventually surrounds vascular channels.

angiosclerosis /-sklerō'sis/ [Gk, *angeion,* vessel, *skleros,* hard, *osis,* condition], a thickening and hardening of the walls of the blood vessels.

angioscope /an'jē·əskōp'/, a type of microscope that permits inspection of the capillaries.

angiospasm /an'jē·ōspaz'əm/, a sudden, transient constriction of a blood vessel.

angiostrongyliasis /an'jē·ō·stron'ji·lī'ə·sis/, infection by a species of *Angiostrongylus.* Infection comes after eating contaminated raw or insufficiently cooked hosts such as snails, slugs, prawns, or crabs. *A. cantonensis* larvae migrate to the CNS and cause eosinophilic meningitis.

Angiostrongylus [Gk, *angeion,* vessel, *strongylos,* round], a genus of parasitic nematodes. Species *A. cantonensis* and *A. costaricensis* normally infect other animals but can cause angiostrongyliasis in humans.

angiotensin /-ten'sin/ [Gk, *angeion;* L, *tendere,* to stretch], a polypeptide in the blood that causes vasoconstriction, increased BP, and the release of aldosterone from the adrenal cortex. Angiotensin is formed by the action of renin on angiotensinogen, an alpha-2-glycoprotein that is produced in the liver and constantly circulates in the blood.

angiotensin-converting enzyme (ACE), a glycoprotein (dipeptidyl carboxypeptidase) that catalyzes the conversion of angiotensin I to angiotensin II by splitting two terminal amino acids. ACE-inhibiting agents are used for controlling hypertension and for protecting the kidneys in DM.

angiotensin-converting enzyme (ACE) inhibitor, a protease inhibitor found in serum that promotes vasodilation by blocking the formation of angiotensin II and slowing the degradation of bradykinin and other kinins. It decreases sodium retention, water retention, BP, and heart size and increases cardiac output.

angiotensin-converting enzyme (ACE) test, a blood test used to detect the level of enzyme that converts angiotensinogen into angiotensin.

angiotensinogen /-tensin'əjən/, a serum glycoprotein produced in the liver that is the precursor of angiotensin.

angiotensin sensitivity test (AST), a test for sensitivity to angiotensin II by infusion of angiotensin II amide into the right cubital vein.

angle /ang'gəl/ [L, *angulus*], **1.** the space or the shape formed at the intersection of two lines, planes, or borders. The divergence of the lines, planes, or borders may be measured in degrees of a circle. **2.** (in anatomy and physiology) the geometric relationships between the surfaces of body structures and the positions affected by movement.

angle board, a device used in dentistry to establish reproducible angular relationships between a patient's head, the x-ray beam, the image receptor, and the x-ray film during dental imaging radiography.

angle former, a hoe-shaped, paired dental instrument whose cutting edges are at an oblique angle to the axis of the blade. It is used to accent angles in class III dental cavity preparations.

angle of convergence, an angle formed between the visual axis of an eye focused on an object and a median line.

angle of incidence, the angle at which an ultrasound beam hits the interface between two different types of tissues, such as the facing surfaces of bone and muscle.

angle of iris, the angle formed between the cornea and the iris at the periphery of the anterior chamber of the eye. The aqueous fluid normally drains through this angle, which may be blocked in glaucoma.

angle of Louis [Pierre Charles Alexandre Louis, French physician, 1787–1872], the sternal angle between the manubrium and the body of the sternum.

angle of mandible, the measure in degrees of the relationship between the body and the ramus of the mandible. It is used in cephalometric measurements of skull radiographs.

angle of refraction [L, *refringere*, to break apart], the angle that a refracted ray of light makes with a line perpendicular to the refracting surface at the point of refraction.

angle of Treitz /trīts/ [Wenzel Treitz, Czech physician, 1819–1872], a sharp curve or flexure at the junction of the duodenum and jejunum.

Angle's classification of malocclusion (modified) [Edward Hartley Angle, American orthodontist, 1855–1930], a classification of the various types of malocclusion, or abnormal contact between the teeth of the maxilla and those of the mandible. The classification is based on where the buccal groove of the mandibular first molar contacts the mesiobuccal cusp of the maxillary first molar: on the cusp (Class I, neutroclusion, or normal occlusion); distal to the cusp by at least the width of a premolar (Class II, distocclusion); or mesial to the cusp (Class III, mesiocclusion).

angor /ang'gôr/, a condition of extreme distress, usually occurring in intestinal or pectoral angina or during a sudden attack of blindness.

angstrom (Å) /ang'strəm/ [Anders Jonas Ångström, Swedish physicist, 1814–1874], a unit of measure of length equal to 0.1 nanometer (1/10,000,000,000 meter), or 10^{-10} meter.

angular artery /ang'gu·lər är'tə·re/, a branch of the facial artery to the medial angle of the eye that supplies the lacrimal sac, lower eyelid, and nose.

angular gyrus /ang'gyələr/ [L, *angulus*; Gk, *gyros*], a folded convolution in the inferior parietal lobe where it unites with the temporal lobe of the cerebral cortex.

angular movement [L, *angularis*, sharply bent], one of the four basic movements allowed by the various joints of the skeleton. It is a movement in which the angle between two adjoining bones is decreased, as in flexion, or increased, as in extension.

angular spinal curvature [L, *angulus* + *spina*, backbone, *curvatura*, bend], a sharp bending or sloping of the vertebral column.

angular vein, one of a pair of veins of the face, formed by the junction of the frontal and the supraorbital veins.

angulated fracture /ang'gyəlā'ted/, a fracture in which the fragments of bone are at angles to one another.

angulation [L, *angulatus*, bent], **1.** an angular shape or formation. **2.** the discipline of precisely measuring angles, as in mechanical drafting and surveying. **3.** (in radiography) the direction of the primary beam of radiation in relation to the object being radiographed and the film used to record its image.

anhedonia /an'hēdō'nē·ə/ [Gk, *a* + *hedone*, not pleasure], the inability to feel pleasure or happiness in response to experiences that are ordinarily pleasurable. It is often a characteristic of major depression and schizophrenia.—**anhedonic,** *adj.*

anhidrosis /an'hidrō'sis, an'hī-/ [Gk, *a* + *hidros*, without sweat], an abnormal condition characterized by inadequate perspiration.

anhidrotic /an'hidrot'ik, an'hī-/, **1.** pertaining to anhidrosis. **2.** an agent that reduces or suppresses perspiration.

anhidrotic ectodermal dysplasia, a congenital X-linked disorder fully expressed in males, or rarely an autosomal-recessive trait with full expression in both sexes, characterized by ectodermal dysplasia associated with aplasia or hypoplasia of the sudiferous glands, hypothermia, alopecia, anodontia, conical teeth, and typical facies with frontal bossing, midfacial hypoplasia, saddle nose, large chin, and thick lips.

anhydrase /anhī'drās/ [Gk, *a*, without, *hydor*, water], an enzyme that catalyzes the elimination of water molecules from certain compounds, as carbonic anhydrase dehydrates carbonic acid, thereby controlling the amount of carbon dioxide in the blood and lungs.

anhydride /anhī'drīd/ [Gk, *a* + *hydor*, without water], a chemical compound derived by the removal of water from one or more substances, especially an acid.

anhydrous /anhī'drəs/ [Gk, *a* + *hydor*, without water], an absence of water.

anicteric /an'ikter'ik/ [Gk, *a* + *icterus*, not jaundice], pertaining to the absence of jaundice.

anicteric hepatitis, a mild form of hepatitis in which there is no jaundice (icterus). Symptoms include anorexia, GI disturbances, and slight fever. Levels of aspartate aminotransferase and alanine aminotransferase are elevated. The infection may be mistaken for flu or be undetected.

anideus /anid'ē·əs/, an anomalous, rudimentary embryo consisting of a simple rounded mass with little indication of the body parts.—**anidean, anidian, anidous,** *adj.*

anidulafungin, a systemic, antifungal agent used to treat *Candida albicans*, *C. glabrata*, *C. parapsilosis*, and *C. tropicalis*.

anileridine hydrochloride, the hydrochloride salt of anileridine. It is administered orally in the treatment of moderate to severe pain.

aniline ($C_6H_5NH_2$) /an'ilēn/ [Ar, *alnil*, indigo], an oily, colorless poisonous liquid with a strong odor and burning taste, formerly extracted from the indigo plant and now made synthetically from nitrobenzene and used in the manufacture of aniline dyes. Industrial workers exposed to aniline are at risk for developing methemoglobinemia and bone marrow depression.

anilingus /ā'niling'gəs/, sexual stimulation of the anus by the tongue or lips.

anilism [Ar, *alnil*, indigo; Gk, *ismos*, state], a condition of poisoning resulting from exposure to aniline compounds. Symptoms generally include cyanosis, weakness, cold sweats, irregular pulse, breathing difficulty, coma, seizures, and possible sudden heart failure.

anima /an'imə/ [L, soul], **1.** the soul or life. **2.** the active ingredient in a drug. **3.** (in analytic psychology) a person's true inner unconscious being or personality. **4.** (in analytic psychology) the female component of the male personality.

animal, a multicellular organism that subsists on the breakdown of organic substances taken into the body, usually by ingestion. Most animals are capable of movement as a result of the actions of nervous tissue and muscle tissue, which are unique to animals.

animal-assisted therapy, a nursing intervention from the Nursing Interventions Classification (NIC) defined as purposeful use of animals to provide affection, attention, diversion, and relaxation.

animal pole [L, *anima*], the active, formative part of an ovum. It contains the nucleus and the bulk of the cytoplasm and is the site where the polar bodies form. In mammals, the animal pole is also the site where the inner cell mass develops and gives rise to germ layers.

animation, 1. the state of being alive. **2.** an ability to put into action a vivid appearance of life.

animus /an'iməs/ [L, spirit], **1.** the active or rational soul; the animating principle of life. **2.** (in analytic psychology) the male component of the female personality. **3.** (in psychiatry) a deep-seated antagonism that is usually controlled but may erupt with virulence under stress.

anion /an'ī·ən/ [Gk, *ana* + *ion*, backward going], a negatively charged ion that is attracted to the positive electrode (anode) in electrolysis.—**anionic,** *adj.*

anion-exchange resin, any one of the simple organic polymers with high molecular weights that exchange the resin anions with other anions in solution.

anion gap, the difference between the concentrations of serum cations and anions, determined by measuring the concentrations of sodium cations and chloride and bicarbonate anions. It is helpful in the diagnosis and treatment of acidosis.

anion gap test, a calculation used to help identify the causes of metabolic acidosis, most of which are associated with an increased anion gap.

aniridia /an'irid'ē·ə/ [Gk, *a*, without + *iris*], an absence of the iris, a usually bilateral, hereditary anomaly. Often a rudimentary stump is visible through a gonioscope.

anisakiasis /an'isəkī'əsis/, infection of humans or other animals with a nematode of the family Anisakidae, usually *Anisakis marina*. Human infection is usually caused by third-stage larvae eaten in undercooked infected marine fish such as herring.

Anisakis /an'isa'kis/ [Gk, *an-*, not, without + *isos*, equal + *akis*, point], a genus of nematodes of the family Anisakidae. Species *A. marina* is the usual cause of human anisakiasis.

anise /an'is/, the fruit of the *Pimpinella anisum* plant. Extract of anise is used in the preparation of carminatives and expectorants.

aniseikonia /an'īsīkō'nē·ə/ [Gk, *anisos*, unequal, *eikon*, image], an abnormal ocular condition in which each eye perceives the same image as being of a different form and size.

anismus /ānis'məs/, an extreme contraction of the external anal sphincter.

anisocoria /-kôr'ē·ə/ [Gk, *anisos*, unequal, *kore*, pupil], an inequality of the diameter of the pupils of the two eyes.

anisocytosis /anī'sōsītō'sis/ [Gk, *anisos* + *kytos*, cell], an abnormal condition of the blood characterized by excessive erythrocytes of variable and abnormal size.

anisogamete /-gam'ēt/ [Gk, *anisos* + *gamos*, marriage], a gamete that differs considerably in size and structure from the one with which it unites, such as the macrogamete and microgamete of certain sporozoa.—**anisogametic,** *adj.*

anisogamy /an'īsog'əmē/, sexual conjugation of gametes of unequal size and structure, as in certain thallophytes and sporozoa.—**anisogamous,** *adj.*

anisognathous /an'īsōnath'əs/ [Gk, *anisos* + *gnathos*, jaw], an abnormal condition in which the maxillary and mandibular arches or jaws are of significantly different sizes.—**anisognathic,** *adj.*

anisokaryosis /anī'sōker'ē·ō'sis/, a significant variation in nuclear size among cells of the same general type.—**anisokaryotic,** *adj.*

anisomastia /anī'sōmas'tē·ə/, a condition in which one female breast is much larger than the other.

anisometropia /anī'sōmetrō'pē·ə/ [Gk, *anisos* + *metron*, measure, *ops*, eye], an abnormal ocular condition characterized by a difference in the refractive powers of the eyes.

anisopia /an'īsō'pē·ə/, a condition in which the visual power of one eye is greater than that of the other.

anisopiesis /anī'sōpī·ē'sis/ [Gk, *anisos*, unequal, *piesis*, pressure], a condition of unequal arterial BP on the left and right sides of the body.

anistreplase, a plasminogen activator used in acute MI for lysis of coronary artery thrombi.

ankle [AS, *ancleow*], **1.** the joint of the tibia and fibula of the leg with the talus of the foot. **2.** the part of the leg where this joint is located.

ankle bandage, a figure-eight bandage looped under the sole of the foot and around the ankle. The heel may be covered or left exposed, although covering is preferable because it prevents "window edema."

ankle-brachial index (ABI), the ratio of ankle systolic pressure to the arm systolic pressure, used in assessing the status of lower extremity arteries. It is calculated by dividing the higher of the left and right ankle pressures by the higher of the two brachial artery pressures.

ankle clonus, an involuntary tendon reflex that causes repeated flexion and extension of the foot.

ankle-foot orthosis (AFO), any of a variety of protective external devices that can be applied to the ankle area to prevent injury in a high-risk athletic activity, to protect a previous injury such as a sprain, or to assist patients with chronic joint instability with walking.

ankle joint [AS, *ancleow*; L, *jungere*, to join], a synovial hinge joint between the leg and the foot. The rounded malleolar prominences on each side of the joint form a mortise for the upper surface of the talus.

ankyloblepharon /ang'kəlōblef'əron/ [Gk, *agkylos*, crooked, *blepharon*, eyelid], the adhesion of the ciliary edges of the eyelid to each other.

ankyloglossia /ang'kilōglos'ē·ə/ [Gk, *agkylos*, crooked, *glossa*, tongue], a severe restriction of tongue movement as a result of fusion or adherence of the tongue to the floor of the mouth. Partial ankyloglossia (tongue-tie) is caused by a lingual frenum that is abnormally short or is attached too close to the tip of the tongue; this condition may be surgically corrected by a simple excision. Complete ankyloglossia requires extensive surgical reconstruction of the tongue and the floor of the mouth.

ankylosed /ang'kilōst/, pertaining to the immobility of a joint resulting from pathologic changes in it or in adjacent tissues.

ankylosing spondylitis /ang'kilō'sing/, a chronic inflammatory disease associated with human leukocyte antigen B27, first affecting the spine and adjacent structures and commonly progressing to eventual fusion of the involved joints. In extreme cases a forward flexion of the spine, called a "poker spine" or "bamboo spine," develops. The disease primarily affects males under 30 years of age and generally follows a course of 20 years. There is a strong hereditary tendency. In addition to the spine, the joints of the hip, shoulder, neck, ribs, and jaw are often involved.

ankylosis /ang'kilō'sis/ [Gk, *ankylosis*, bent condition], **1.** the fusion of a joint, often in an abnormal position, usually resulting from destruction of articular cartilage and subchondral bone, as occurs in rheumatoid arthritis. It may also occur in immobilized patients when active or passive ROM is not provided. **2.** the surgically induced fixation of a joint to relieve pain or provide support.—**ankylosed,** *adj.*

ANLL, abbreviation for *acute nonlymphocytic leukemia.*

ANNA, abbreviation for **American Nephrology Nurses' Association.**

anneal [AS, *aelan,* to burn], **1.** to temper metals, glass, or other materials by controlled heating and cooling to make them more malleable and ductile. **2.** to cause the interaction of two separate strands of nucleic acid to form a duplex molecule, often by using a related technique of controlled heating and cooling.

annihilation /əni'əlā'shən/, the total transformation of matter into energy, as when an antimatter positron collides with an electron.

anode, the electrode at which oxidation occurs.—**anodal,** *adj.*

anodic stripping voltammetry /ənō'dik, anod'ik/, a process of electroanalytic chemistry used to detect trace metals.

anodontia /an'ōdon'tē·ə/ [Gk, *a,* not, *odous,* tooth], a congenital anomaly in which some or all of the teeth are missing. The term is generally applied to cases in which most teeth are missing and no tooth follicles are present.

anodyne /an'ədīn/ [Gk *a* + *odyne,* not pain], a drug that relieves or lessens pain.

anomaly /ənom'əlē/ [Gk, *anomalos,* irregular], **1.** deviation from what is regarded as normal. **2.** a congenital

malformation, such as the absence of a limb or the presence of an extra finger.—**anomalous,** *adj.*

anomia /ənō'mē·ə/ [Gk, *a* + *onoma,* without name], a form of aphasia characterized by the inability to name objects. Comprehension and repetition are unaffected.

anomie /an'əmē/, a state of apathy, alienation, anxiety, personal disorientation, and distress resulting from the loss of social norms and goals previously valued.

anonychia /an'ō·nik'e·ə/ [Gk, *a* + *onyx* without nail], an absence of a nail or nails.

anoopsia /an'ō·op'sē·ə/ [Gk, *ana,* up, *ops,* eye], a strabismus in which one or both eyes are deviated upward.

Anopheles /ənof'əlēz/ [Gk, *anopheles,* harmful], a genus of mosquito containing over 90 species, many of which are vectors of malaria.

anopia /ənō'pē·ə/ [Gk, *a* + *ops,* not eye], a blindness resulting from a defect in or the absence of one or both eyes.

anoplasty /an'ōplas'tē/ [L, *anus;* Gk, *plassein,* to shape], a restorative operation on the anus.

anorchia /anôr'kē·ə/ [Gk, *a* + *orchis,* not testis], the congenital absence of one or both testes.

anorectal /ān'ōrek'təl, ā'nō-/ [L, *anus* + *rectus,* straight], pertaining to the anal and rectal parts of the large intestine.

anorectal abscess [L, *anus* + *rectus,* straight, *abscedere,* to go away], an abscess in the area of the anus and rectum.

anorectal stricture [L, *anus* + *rectus,* straight, *strictura,* compression], a narrowing of the anorectal canal. It is sometimes congenital but also may result from surgery to correct a fissure or to remove hemorrhoids.

anorectic /an'ōrek'tik/, **1.** pertaining to anorexia. **2.** causing a loss of appetite, as an anorexiant drug.

anorectoperineal muscle, any of the bands of smooth muscle fibers extending from the perineal flexure of the rectum to the membranous urethra in the male.

anorexia /an'ōrek'sē·ə/ [Gk, *a* + *orexis,* not appetite], a lack or loss of appetite, resulting in the inability to eat.

anorexia nervosa, a disorder characterized by a prolonged refusal to eat, resulting in emaciation, amenorrhea, emotional disturbance concerning body image, and fear of becoming obese.

anorexiant /an'ôrek'sē·ənt/, a drug or other agent that suppresses the appetite, such as amphetamine.

anorgasmy /an'ôrgaz'mē/, inability to experience orgasm during coitus or masturbation.

anorthopia /an′ôrthō′pē·ə/, a visual disorder in which straight lines appear to be curved or angular.

anosmia /anoz′mē·ə/ [Gk, *a* + *osme*, without smell], a loss or an impairment of the sense of smell. It can occur as a temporary condition when a person has a head cold or respiratory infection or when intranasal swelling or other obstruction prevents odors from reaching the olfactory region. It becomes permanent when the olfactory neuroepithelium or any part of the olfactory nerve is destroyed as a result of intracranial trauma, neoplasms, or disease, such as atrophic rhinitis or the chronic rhinitis associated with the granulomatous diseases. In some instances, the condition may be caused by psychologic factors, such as a phobia or fear associated with a particular smell.—**anosmatic, anosmic,** *adj.*

anosmia gustatoria, the inability to smell foods.

anosognosia /an′əsog·nō′zhə/ [Gk, *a* + *nosos,* not disease, *gnosis,* knowing], lack of awareness or denial of a neurologic defect or illness in general, especially paralysis, on one side of the body. It may be attributable to a lesion in the right parietal lobe.

anotia /anō′tē·ə/ [Gk, *a* + *ous,* without ear], a congenital absence of one or both ears.

ANOVA, abbreviation for **analysis of variance.**

anovaginal /ā′nōvaj′inəl/ [L, *anus* + *vagina,* sheath], pertaining to the perineal region of the anus and vagina.

anovarism /anō′vərizəm/ [Gk, *a,* without; L, *ovum,* egg], an absence of the ovaries.

anovesical /-ves′ikəl/ [L, *anus* + *vesicula,* small bladder], pertaining to the anus and bladder.

anovular menstruation [Gk, *a* + *ovulum,* not egg], menstruation not associated with the production or release of an ovum. The ovum either remains within the ovarian follicle and undergoes degeneration or in rare cases becomes impregnated, resulting in an ovarian pregnancy.

anovulation /an′ovyəlā′shən/, a failure of the ovaries to produce, mature, or release eggs. The condition may result from ovarian immaturity or postmaturity; altered ovarian function, as in pregnancy and lactation; primary ovarian dysfunction, as in ovarian dysgenesis; or disturbed interaction of the hypothalamus, pituitary gland, and ovary caused by stress or disease. —**anovulatory** /anov′yələtôr′ē/, *adj.*

anoxemia /an′okse′mē·ə/, a deficiency of oxygen in the blood.

anoxia /anok′sē·ə/ [Gk, *a* + *oxys,* not sharp], an abnormal condition characterized by a local or systemic lack of oxygen in body tissues. It may result from an inadequate supply of oxygen to the respiratory system, an inability of the blood to carry oxygen to the tissues, or a failure of the tissues to absorb the oxygen from the blood. —**anoxic,** *adj.*

ansa /an′sə/, *pl.* **ansae** [L, handle], (in anatomy) a looplike structure resembling a curved handle of a vase.

ansa cervicalis, one of three loops of nerves in the cervical plexus, branches of which innervate the infrahyoid muscles.

ANSER system, a pattern of questionnaires for studying development, behavior, and health in children ages 3 to 12.

ANSI, abbreviation for **American National Standards Institute.**

Antabuse, a trademark for an alcohol-use deterrent (disulfiram).

antacid /antas′id/ [Gk, *anti,* against, *acidus,* sour], **1.** opposing acidity. **2.** a drug or dietary substance that buffers, neutralizes, or absorbs hydrochloric acid in the stomach.

antagonism /antag′oniz′əm/ [Gk, *antagonisma,* struggle], **1.** an inhibiting action between physiologic processes, such as muscle actions. **2.** the opposing actions of drugs.

antagonist /antagə′nist/ [Gk, *antagonisma,* struggle], **1.** one who contends with or is opposed to another. **2.** (in physiology) any agent, such as a drug or muscle, that exerts an opposite action to that of another or competes for the same receptor sites. **3.** (in dentistry) a tooth in the upper jaw that articulates during mastication or occlusion with a tooth in the lower jaw. —**antagonistic,** *adj.,* **antagonize,** *v.*

antagonistic reflexes [Gk, *antagonisma,* L, *reflectere,* to bend back], two or more reflexes initiated at the same time that produce opposite effects. An example is the opposition between the biceps and the triceps; the biceps flexes the arm while the triceps extends it.

antazoline /antaz′o-lēn/, a derivative of ethylenediamine, used as an antihistamine. The phosphate salt is applied topically to the eyes in treatment of allergic conjunctivitis.

antebrachial region /an′tə·brā′kē·əl/ [L. *ante,* before, *brachium,* arm], an anatomic term denoting the forearm.

antecedent /an′tise′dənt/ [L, *antecedentem*], a thing or period that precedes others in time or order.

antecubital /-kyōō′bitəl/ [L, *ante,* before, *cubitum,* elbow], in front of the elbow; at the bend of the elbow.

antecubital fossa [L, *ante,* before, *cubitum,* elbow, *fossa,* ditch], a depression at the bend of the elbow.

antecurvature /-kur′vəchər/, a slight degree of anteflexion or forward curvature.

anteflexion /-flek′shən/ [L, *ante* + *flectare,* bend], an abnormal position in which an organ is tilted acutely forward, folded over on itself.

antegonial notch /-gō′nē·əl/ [L, *ante* + *gonia,* angle], a depression or concavity commonly present on the lower edge of the mandible on each side, immediately in front of the angle, or corner of the jaw.

antegrade /an′təgrād/ [L, *ante,* before, *gredi,* to go], moving forward, or proceeding toward the front.

antegrade colonic enema, the creation of a continent stoma in the right colon through which an irrigation fluid may be infused. It is used in the management of chronic evacuation disorders.

ante mortem [L, *ante,* before, *mors,* death], before death.

antepartal /an′təpär′təl/ [L, *ante* + *parturire,* to have labor pains], pertaining to the period spanning conception and labor.

antepartal care, the care of a pregnant woman during the time in the maternity cycle that begins with conception and ends with the onset of labor.

antepartum hemorrhage [L, *ante,* before, *parturire,* to have labor pains; Gk, *haima,* blood, *rhegnynai,* to burst forth], bleeding from the uterus during a pregnancy in which the placenta appears to be normally situated, particularly after the 28th week.

antepyretic /-pīret′ik/ [L, *ante,* before; Gk, *pyretos,* fever], before the onset of fever.

anterior (A) /antir′ē·ər/ [L, *ante* + *prior,* foremost], **1.** the front of a structure. **2.** pertaining to a surface or part situated toward the front or facing forward.

anterior atlantoaxial ligament /atlan′tō·a k′sē·əl/, one of five ligaments connecting the atlas to the axis. It is fixed to the inferior border of the anterior arch of the atlas and to the ventral surface of the body of the axis.

anterior atlantooccipital membrane, one of two broad, densely woven fibrous sheets that form part of the atlantooccipital joint between the atlas and the occipital bone.

anterior axillary line (AAL), an imaginary vertical line on the body wall continuing the line of the anterior axillary fold with the upper arm.

anterior cardiac vein, one of several small vessels that return deoxygenated blood from the ventral part of the myocardium of the right ventricle to the right atrium.

anterior cerebral commissure [L, *ante* + *prior,* foremost, *cerebrum,* brain, *commissura,* ajoining], a bundle of fibers in the anterior wall of the prosencephalon connecting the olfactory bulb and olfactory cortex on one side with the similar structures on the other side.

anterior cervical decompression and fusion (ACDF), a surgical procedure to treat cervical disk herniation or degeneration in the spine.

anterior chamber [L, *ante* + *prior,* foremost; Gk, *kamara,* an arched cover], the part of the anterior cavity of the eye in front of the iris. It contains the aqueous humor.

anterior corticospinal tract, a group of nerve fibers in the anterior funiculus of the spinal cord, originating in the cerebral cortex.

anterior cruciate ligament (ACL), a strong band that arises from the posterior middle part of the lateral condyle of the femur, passes anteriorly and inferiorly between the condyles, and is attached to the depression in front of the intercondylar eminence of the tibia.

anterior cutaneous nerve, one of a pair of cutaneous branches of the cervical plexus. It arises from the second and third cervical nerves and divides into the ascending and descending branches.

anterior determinants of cusp, the characteristics of the anterior teeth that determine the cusp elevations and the fossae in restoration of the postcanine teeth. Such determinants include occlusion, alignment overlaps, and the capacity to disocclude conjointly with condylar trajectories.

anterior drawer sign or test, a test for rupture of the anterior cruciate ligament. The result is positive if there is increased anterior glide of the tibia when the knee is flexed at a 90-degree angle.

anterior ethmoidal artery, an artery that supplies the nasal septum and lateral wall and ends as the dorsal nasal artery.

anterior ethmoidal nerve, a nerve that innervates the anterior cranial fossa, the nasal cavity, and the skin of the lower half of the nose.

anterior fontanel, **1.** a diamond-shaped unossified area between the frontal and two parietal bones just above an infant's forehead at the junction of the coronal and sagittal sutures. **2.** informal. soft spot.

anterior guide, the portion of an articulator that is contacted by the incisal guide pin to maintain the selected separation of the upper and lower members of the articulator. The anterior guide influences the changing relationships of mounted casts in eccentric movements.

anterior horn [L, *ante* + *prior,* foremost, *cornu,* horn, *spina,* spine; Gk, *chorde,* string], one of the hornlike projections of gray matter into the white matter of the spinal cord. The anterior horn contains efferent fibers innervating skeletal muscle tissue.

anterior horn cell, motor neuron in the anterior horn.

anterior longitudinal ligament, the broad, strong ligament attached to the ventral surfaces of the vertebral bodies. It extends from the occipital bone and the anterior tubercle of the atlas to the sacrum.

anterior malleolar artery, one of two arteries, the medial and the lateral, that arise from the anterior tibial artery and connect with vessels from the posterior tibial and fibular arteries to form an anastomotic network around the ankle.

anterior mediastinal node, a node in one of the three groups of thoracic visceral nodes of the lymphatic system that drains lymph from the nodes of the thymus, pericardium, and sternum.

anterior mediastinum, a caudal part of the mediastinum in the middle of the thorax, bounded ventrally by the body of the sternum and parts of the fourth through the seventh ribs and dorsally by the parietal pericardium, extending downward as far as the diaphragm.

anterior nares, the ends of the nostrils that open anteriorly into the nasal cavity and allow the inhalation and exhalation of air. The anterior nares connect with the nasal fossae.

anterior nasal spine, the sharp anterosuperior projection at the anterior extremity of the line of union of the two maxillae.

anterior neuropore, the opening of the embryonic neural tube in the anterior part of the forebrain.

anterior ramus, a branch of each spinal nerve as it exits the vertebral canal. The anterior rami form the major somatic plexuses of the body.

anterior rhizotomy [L, *ante* + *prior,* foremost; Gk, *rhiza,* root, *temnein,* to cut], the surgical cutting of the ventral root of a spinal nerve, usually to relieve persistent spasm, involuntary movement, or intractable pain.

anterior spinal artery, an artery that originates within the cranial cavity and passes inferiorly along the surface of the spinal cord. It is reinforced along its length by 8 to 10 segmental medullary arteries, the largest of which is the artery of Adamkiewicz.

anterior temporal artery, the anterior temporal branch of the middle cerebral artery. Its origin is the middle cerebral artery, and it supplies blood to the cortex of the anterior temporal lobe.

anterior tibial artery, one of the two divisions of the popliteal artery, arising in the back of the knee, dividing into six branches, and supplying various muscles of the leg and foot.

anterior tibial node, one of the small lymph glands of the lower limb, lying on the interosseous membrane of the leg near the proximal portion of the anterior tibial vessels.

anterior tooth, any of the central incisors, lateral incisors, or canines of the maxillary or mandibular teeth.

anterior triangle of the neck, a triangular area bounded by the median line of the neck in front, the lower border of the mandible, and a line extending back to the sternocleidomastoid muscle.

anterocclusion /an'tərōklōō'shən/ [L, *ante* + *occludere,* to shut], a malocclusion in which the mandibular teeth are anterior to their normal position relative to the maxillary teeth.

anterograde amnesia [L, *ante* + *prior,* foremost, *gredi,* to go], **1.** the inability to form new memories. **2.** the inability to recall events that occur after the onset of amnesia, usually with an inability to form new memories.

anterograde memory, the ability to recall past events but not recent occurrences.

anteroinferior /an'tərō·infir′ē-ər/, situated in front of but at a lower level.

anterolateral /-lat′ərəl/, in front and on each side of another structure or object.

anterolateral thoracotomy, a surgical technique in which entry to the chest is made with an incision below the breast but above the costal margins. The incision involves the pectoralis, serratus anterior, and intercostal muscles.

anteromedial /an'tər-ō·mē'dē-əl/, located anteriorly and to the medial side.

anteromedial central artery, any of the branches of the anterior communicating artery that supply the corpus callosum, septum pellucidum, lentiform nucleus, and caudate nucleus.

anteroposterior (AP) /an'tərōpostir′ē-ər/ [L, *ante* + *prior,* foremost, *posterus,* coming after], from the front to the back of the body.

anteroposterior diameter of the pelvic outlet, the distance between the middle of the pubic symphysis and the upper border of the third sacral vertebra.

anteroposterior vaginal repair, a surgical procedure in which the upper and lower walls of the vagina are reconstructed to correct relaxed tissue.

anterosuperior, situated in front of but at a higher level.

anteversion /-vur′shən/ [L, *ante* + *versio,* turning], **1.** an abnormal position of an organ in which it is tilted or bent forward on its axis, away from the midline. **2.** (in dentistry) the tipping or the tilting of teeth or other mandibular structures more anteriorly than normal. **3.** the angulation created in the transverse plane between the neck and shaft of the femur.—**anteverted,** *adj.*

anthelmintic /ant′helmin′tik/ [Gk, *anti* + *helmins,* against worms], **1.** pertaining to a substance that destroys or prevents the development of parasitic worms. **2.** an anthelmintic drug. An anthelmintic may interfere with the parasites' carbohydrate metabolism, inhibit their respiratory enzymes, block their neuromuscular action, or render them susceptible to destruction by the host's macrophages.

anthracosis /an′thrəkō′sis/ [Gk, *anthrax,* coal, *osis,* condition], a chronic lung disease characterized by the deposit of coal dust in the lungs and by the formation of black nodules on the bronchioles, resulting in focal emphysema.

anthralin /an′thrəlin/, a topical antipsoriatic prescribed in the treatment of psoriasis and chronic dermatitis.

anthrax /an′thraks/ [Gk, *anthrax,* coal, carbuncle], an acute infectious disease caused by the spore-forming bacterium *Bacillus anthracis* and occurring most frequently in herbivores (cattle, goats, sheep). Humans can become infected through skin contact, ingestion, or inspiration of spores from infected animals or animal products. Inhalation causes the most serious form of anthrax in humans, but it is most often acquired when a break in the skin has direct contact with infected animals and their hides. Anthrax is an important potential bioterrorism agent.

anthrax vaccine, a cell-free protein extract of cultures of *Bacillus anthracis,* used for immunization against anthrax.

anthropoid /an′thrəpoid/ [Gk, *anthropos,* human, *eidos,* form], resembling a man or human.

anthropoid pelvis [Gk, *anthropos,* human, *eidos,* form], a type of pelvis in which the inlet is oval, and the anteroposterior diameter is much greater than the transverse. The posterior portion of the space in the true pelvis is much greater than the anterior portion.

anthropology [Gk, *anthropos,* human, *logos,* science], the science of human beings, from animal-like characteristics to social and environmental aspects.

anthropometry /an′thrəpom′ətrē/ [Gk, *anthropos* + *metron,* measure], the science of measuring the human body as to height, weight, and size of component parts, including skinfold thickness, to study and compare the relative proportions under normal and abnormal conditions.—**anthropometric,** *adj.*

anthropomorphism /an′thrəpōmôr′fizəm/ [Gk, *anthropos,* human, *morphe,* form], the assignment of human shapes and qualities to other animals.

antiadrenergic /an′ti·ad′rənur′jik, an′tī-/ [Gk, *anti;* L, *ad* + *ren,* to kidney], **1.** pertaining to the blocking of the effects of impulses transmitted by the adrenergic postganglionic fibers of the sympathetic nervous system. **2.** an antiadrenergic agent. These drugs block the response to norepinephrine bound to alpha receptors and reduce the tonus of smooth muscle in peripheral blood vessels, causing increased peripheral circulation and decreased BP. Alpha$_1$-blocking agents include ergotamine derivatives, phenoxybenzamine, phentolamine, and tolazoline hydrochloride; they are used to treat conditions such as migraines, Raynaud's disease, pheochromocytoma, diabetic gangrene, and spastic vascular disease. Beta$_1$-blocking agents decrease the rate and force of heart contractions and are administered for hypertension, angina, and arrhythmias; propranolol hydrochloride and its congeners are examples.

antiagglutinin /-əgloo′tinin/ [Gk, *anti,* against; L, *agglutinare,* to glue], a specific antibody that counteracts the effects of an agglutinin.

antiamebic /an′ti·əmē′bik/, pertaining to a medication that treats amebic infections.

antianabolic /-an′əbol′ik/, pertaining to drugs or other agents that inhibit or retard anabolic processes, such as cell division and the creation of new tissue by protein synthesis.

antianaphylaxis /-an′əfilak′sis/ [Gk, *anti,* against, *ana,* back, *phylaxis,* protection], a procedure to prevent anaphylactic reactions by injecting a patient with small desensitizing doses of the antigen.

antianemic /-ənē′mik/ [Gk, *anti* + *a* + *haima,* without blood], **1.** pertaining to a substance or procedure that counteracts or prevents a deficiency of erythrocytes. **2.** an agent used to treat or to prevent anemia.

antianginal /-anji′nəl/, **1.** pertaining to the reduction of myocardial oxygen consumption or the increase of oxygen supply to the myocardium to prevent symptoms of angina pectoris. **2.** an antianginal agent.

antiantibody /an′ti·an′tibod′ē/ [Gk, *anti* + *anti;* AS, *bodig*], an immunoglobulin formed as the result of the administration of an antibody that acts as an immunogen. The antiantibody then interacts with the antibody.

antiantitoxin /-tok′sin/ [Gk, *anti* + *anti* + *toxikon,* poison], an antiantibody that may form in the body during immunization, inhibiting or counteracting the effect of the antitoxin administered.

antianxiety agent, a drug that reduces anxiety. The group includes the benzodiazepine derivatives and a few less widely used nonbenzodiazepines such as meprobamate and hydroxyzine hydrochloride.

antiarrhythmic /-ərith′mik/ [Gk, *anti* + *rhythmos,* rhythm], **1.** pertaining to a procedure or substance that prevents, alleviates, or corrects an abnormal cardiac rhythm. **2.** an agent used to treat a cardiac arrhythmia. Two types of antiarrhythmic devices are defibrillators and pacemakers. Antiarrhythmic drugs include lidocaine hydrochloride; a combination of disopyramide, procainamide hydrochloride, and quinidine; propranolol hydrochloride; isoproterenol hydrochloride; atropine; and calcium channel blockers.

antiarthritic /-ärthrit′ik/ [Gk, *anti* + *arthron,* joint, *itis,* inflammation], **1.** pertaining to a therapy that relieves symptoms of arthritis. **2.** an antiarthritic agent.

antibacterial /-baktir′ē-əl/ [Gk, *anti* + *bakterion,* small staff], **1.** pertaining to a substance that kills bacteria or inhibits their growth or replication. **2.** an antibacterial agent. Antibiotics synthesized chemically or derived from various microorganisms exert their bactericidal or bacteriostatic effect by interfering with the production of the bacterial cell wall; by interfering with protein synthesis, nucleic acid synthesis, or cell membrane integrity; or by inhibiting critical biosynthetic pathways in the bacteria.

antibiotic /-bī-ot′ik/ [Gk, *anti* + *bios,* life], **1.** pertaining to the ability to destroy or interfere with the development of a living organism. **2.** an antimicrobial agent, derived from cultures of a microorganism or produced semisynthetically, used to treat infections. Classes of antibiotics include penicillins, aminoglycosides, macrolide antibiotics, polypeptide antibiotics, tetracyclines, and cephalosporins.

antibiotic anticancer agent, a drug that blocks mammalian cell proliferation in addition to microbial proliferation, making it too dangerous for treating bacterial infections but useful for treating cancer. Examples include bleomycin sulfate, dactinomycin, DAUNOrubicin citrate liposomal, and mitomycin.

antibiotic resistant, pertaining to strains of microorganisms that either developed a resistance to antibiotics or were never sensitive to them.

antibiotic sensitivity test, a laboratory method for determining the susceptibility of organisms to therapy with antibiotics. After the infecting organism has been recovered from a clinical specimen, it is cultured and tested against a panel of antibiotic drugs to determine whether or not a drug inhibits the growth of the organism.

antibody (Ab) /an′tibod′ē/ [Gk, *anti;* AS, *bodig*], an immunoglobulin produced by B-lymphocytes in response to bacteria, viruses, or other antigenic substances. An antibody is specific to an antigen.

antibody absorption, the process of removing or tying up undesired antibodies in an antiserum reagent by allowing them to react with their antigens.

antibody-instructive model, a hypothetic explanation for antibody formation. It postulates that each antigenic contact in the life of an individual causes a new antibody to develop. This model is not supported by experimental evidence.

antibody-specific model, a proposed explanation for antibody formation that states that precommitted clones of lymphoid cells produced in the fetus are capable of interacting with a limited number of antigenic determinants with which they may have contact. Any such cells that encounter their specific antigenic determinant in utero are destroyed or suppressed. This action removes cells programmed to produce endogenous autoantibodies and prevents the development of autoimmune diseases, leaving intact those cells capable of reacting with exogenous antigens.

antibody therapy, the administration of parenteral immunoglobulins as a treatment for patients with immunodeficiency diseases.

antibody titer, the concentration of antibodies circulating in the bloodstream of an individual. A rising titer usually indicates the body's response to antigens associated with an active infection.

anticancer diet /-kan′sər/, a diet, based on recommendations of the American Cancer Society, National Cancer Institute, and National Academy of Sciences, to reduce cancer risk factors associated with eating habits.

anticarcinogenic /-kär′sinəjen′ik/ [Gk, *anti,* against, *karkinos,* crab, *oma,* tumor, *genein,* to produce], pertaining to a substance or device that neutralizes the effects of a cancer-causing substance.

anticardiolipin antibodies test, a blood test used to diagnose SLE. Elevated levels can also indicate thrombosis, thrombocytopenia, syphilis, and acute infection.

anticentromere antibody test, a blood test used to diagnose CREST syndrome.

anticholinergic /-kō'linur'jik/ [Gk, *anti* + *chole*, bile, *ergein*, to work], **1.** pertaining to a blockade of acetylcholine receptors that results in the inhibition of the transmission of parasympathetic nerve impulses. **2.** an anticholinergic agent that functions by competing with the neurotransmitter acetylcholine for its receptor sites at synaptic junctions. Anticholinergic drugs are used to treat spastic disorders of the GI tract, to reduce salivary and bronchial secretions before surgery, or to dilate the pupil. Some anticholinergic agents reduce parkinsonian symptoms but are never considered primary agents for therapy.

anticholinergic poisoning, poisoning caused by overdosing with an anticholinergic agent or by ingesting plants such as jimsonweed that contain belladonna alkaloids. It is characterized by dry mouth; hot, dry, flushed skin; fixed, dilated pupils; sinus tachycardia; urinary retention; disorientation; agitation; impairment of short-term memory; slurred speech; hallucinations; respiratory depression; seizures; and coma.

anticholinesterase /an'tikol'ənes'tərās/, a drug that inhibits or inactivates the action of acetylcholinesterase. Drugs of this class cause acetylcholine to accumulate at the junctions of various cholinergic nerve fibers and their effector sites or organs, allowing potentially continuous stimulation of cholinergic fibers throughout the central and peripheral nervous systems.

anticipation /antis'ipā'shən/, an appearance before the expected time of a periodic sign or symptom. Examples are a malarial paroxysm and a hereditary disorder.

anticipatory adaptation /antis'əpətôr'ē/ [L, *anticipare*, to receive before], the act of adapting to a potentially distressing situation before actually confronting the problem.

anticipatory grief, feelings of grief that develop before, rather than after, a loss.

anticipatory guidance[1], the psychologic preparation of a person to help relieve fear and anxiety of an event expected to be stressful. It is also used to prepare parents for normal growth and development.

anticipatory guidance[2], a nursing intervention from the Nursing Interventions Classification (NIC) defined as preparation of patient for an anticipated developmental and/or situational crisis.

anticipatory nausea and vomiting, vomiting occurring before a new cycle of chemotherapy in response to conditioned stimuli, such as the smells, sights, and sound of the treatment room. It usually occurs after the person has experienced acute nausea and vomiting.

anticoagulant /-kō·ag'yələnt/ [Gk, *anti* + *coagulare*, curdle], **1.** pertaining to a substance that prevents or delays coagulation of the blood. **2.** an anticoagulant drug, such as heparin.

anticoagulant citrate phosphate dextrose adenine solution, citrate phosphate dextrose adenine.

anticoagulant citrate phosphate dextrose solution, citrate phosphate dextrose.

anticoagulant therapy [Gk, *anti*; L, *coagulare*, to curdle; Gk, *therapeia*], the use of drugs that suppress blood clot formation (thrombosis) and propagation. In patients who have experienced thrombotic events, anticoagulant therapy is used to prevent secondary coronary thrombosis, peripheral artery disease, cerebrovascular occlusion, thrombophlebitis, deep venous thrombosis, and pulmonary embolism. Anticoagulants are administered prophylactically subsequent to orthopedic surgery and in atrial fibrillation.

anticodon /an'tikō'don/ [Gk, *anti* + *caudex*, book], a sequence of three nucleotides found in transfer RNA. Each anticodon pairs complementarily with a specific codon of messenger RNA during protein synthesis and specifies a particular amino acid in the protein.

anticomplement, a substance other than an antigen-antibody complex that activates serum complement, resulting in complement fixation.

anticonvulsant /-kənvul'sənt// [Gk, *anti*; L, *convellere*, to shake], **1.** pertaining to a substance or procedure that prevents or reduces the severity of epileptic or other convulsive seizures. **2.** an anticonvulsant drug. Among the drugs in this category are hydantoin derivatives, succinic acid derivatives, valproic acid, and barbiturates. Some benzodiazepines are also useful as anticonvulsants.

anticyclic citrullinated peptide antibody test, a blood test used to diagnose rheumatoid arthritis in its early stages.

antideformity positioning and splinting /-dəfôr'mitē/, the use of splints, braces, or similar devices to prevent or control contractures or other musculoskeletal deformities that may result from disuse, burns, or other injuries.

antideoxyribonuclease-B titer test, a blood test used to diagnose acute rheumatic fever and poststreptococcal glomerulonephritis. Its results are variable and for accuracy should be done in conjunction with the antistreptolysin O titer test.

antidepressant /-dəpres'ənt/, **1.** pertaining to a substance or a measure that prevents or relieves depression. **2.** an antidepressant drug.

antidiabetic /-dī'əbet'ik/, pertaining to an agent that prevents or relieves symptoms of diabetes.

antidiarrheal /-dī'ərē'əl/, a drug or dietary fiber–forming agent that relieves the symptoms of diarrhea. The most effective antidiarrheal drugs are opioid derivatives, which slow intestinal motility to permit greater time for the absorption of water and electrolytes. Dietary fiber–forming agents improve stool consistency but may not decrease fluid and electrolyte loss.

antidiuretic /-dī'əret'ik/ [Gk, *anti* + *dia*, through, *ourein*, to urinate], **1.** pertaining to the suppression of urine formation. **2.** an antidiuretic hormone, produced in hypothalamic nuclei and stored in the posterior lobe of the pituitary gland, that suppresses urine formation by permitting the resorption of water collecting ducts in the kidneys.—**antidiuresis**, *n.*

antidiuretic hormone (ADH), a hormone that decreases the production of urine by increasing the reabsorption of water by the renal tubules. It is secreted by cells of the hypothalamus and stored in the neurohypophysis. ADH is released in response to a decrease in blood volume, an increased concentration of sodium or other substances in plasma, pain, stress, or the action of certain drugs. Synthetic ADH is used in the treatment of diabetes insipidus. Normal values are 1 to 5 pg/mL or less than 1.5 ng/L.

antidiuretic hormone (ADH) test, a blood test that may be used to diagnose diabetes insipidus (both the neurogenic and nephrogenic forms) and the syndrome of inappropriate ADH secretion (SIADH), which is associated with tumors, pulmonary diseases, infection, trauma, Addison's disease, and myxedema.

anti-DNA antibody test, a blood test that is useful for the diagnosis and follow-up of SLE. High titers characterize SLE, and low to moderate levels may indicate other rheumatic diseases as well as chronic hepatitis, infectious mononucleosis, and biliary cirrhosis.

antidote /an'tidōt/ [Gk, *anti* + *dotos*, that which is given], a drug or other substance that opposes the action of a poison.

antidromic conduction /an'tidrom'ik/ [Gk, *anti* + *dromos*, course], the conduction of a neural impulse backward from a receptor in the midpart of an axon. It is an unnatural phenomenon and may be produced experimentally. Because synaptic junctions allow conduction in one direction only, backward, antidromic impulses fail to pass the synapse, dying at that point.

antidyskinetic /an'te-, an'ti-dis'ki-net'ik/, **1.** pertaining to the relief or prevention of dyskinesia. **2.** an antidyskinetic agent.

antiembolism (AE) hose /-em'bəliz'əm/ [Gk, *anti* + *embolos*, plug], elasticized stockings worn to prevent the formation of emboli and thrombi, especially in patients who have had surgery or who have been restricted to bed. Return flow of the venous circulation is promoted, preventing venous stasis and dilation of the veins, conditions that predispose individuals to varicosities and thromboembolic disorders.

antiemetic /-imet'ik/ [Gk, *anti* + *emesis*, vomiting], **1.** pertaining to a substance or procedure that prevents or alleviates nausea and vomiting. **2.** an antiemetic drug or agent.

antiestrogen /-es'trəjən/, a hormone-based product used predominantly in cancer chemotherapy. They are used mainly in treating estrogen-dependent tumors, such as breast cancer.

antiextractable nuclear antigens test, a blood test used to help diagnose SLE and mixed connective tissue disease and to rule out other rheumatoid diseases.

antifibrillatory /-fibril'ətôr'ē/, pertaining to a medication or other agent that suppresses atrial or ventricular fibrillation.

antifilarial, **1.** pertaining to a substance or agent destructive to filariae. **2.** an antifilarial agent.

antiflux /an'ti·fluks/ [Gk, *anti*, against; L, *fluere*, to flow], a substance that prevents the attachment of solder.

antifungal /-fung'gəl/, **1.** pertaining to a substance that kills fungi or inhibits their growth or reproduction. **2.** an antifungal, antibiotic drug.

antigalactic /-gəlak'tik/, pertaining to a drug or other agent that prevents or reduces milk secretion in some mothers of newborns.

anti-GBM disease, a rare autoimmune disease; a kidney or pulmonary disorder in which the glomerular basement membrane is damaged by an antigen-antibody reaction. The kidney itself may serve as the antigenic target in the reaction.

antigen /an'tijən/ [Gk, *anti* + *genein*, to produce], a substance, usually a protein, that the body recognizes as foreign and that can evoke an immune response. —**antigenic**, *adj.*

antigen-antibody reaction, a process of the immune system in which immunoglobulin-coated B cells recognize a specific antigen and stimulate antibody production. T cells also play an essential role in the reaction. An antigen-antibody reaction begins with the binding of antigens to antibodies to form antigen-antibody complexes. These complexes may render toxic antigens harmless, agglutinize antigens on the surface of microorganisms, or activate the complement system by exposing the complement-binding sites on antibodies. Certain complement proteins immediately bind to these sites and trigger the activity of the other complement proteins, which cause antigen-bearing cells to lyse. Antigen-antibody reactions may start immediately with antigen contact or as much as 48 hours later. They normally produce immunity but may also be responsible for allergy, autoimmunity, and fetomaternal hematologic incompatibility.

antigenic determinant, a site on an antigen molecule to which an antibody molecule binds.

antigenic drift [Gk, *anti*, against, *genein*, to produce; AS, *drifan*, drift], a gradual relatively minor change in the antigenicity of a virus, periodically producing a mutant antigen requiring new antibodies and vaccines to combat its effects.

antigenicity /an′tijənis′ətē/, the ability to cause the production of antibodies. The degree of antigenicity of a substance depends on the kind and amount of that substance and on the degree to which the host is sensitive to it and able to produce antibodies.

antigenic shift, a sudden, major change in the antigenicity of a virus, seen especially in influenza viruses, resulting from the recombination of the genomes of two different strains. It is associated with pandemics, because hosts do not have immunity to the new strain.

antigen presentation, presentation of ingested antigens on the surface of macrophages, dendritic cells, and B cells. The antigens are taken up by endocytosis, broken into pieces in the lysosome, and displayed on the surface of the cell within the class II major histocompatibility molecule.

antigen-presenting cell, a cell that can break down protein antigens into peptides and present the peptides, in conjunction with major histocompatibility complex class II molecules, on the cell surface, where they can interact with T-cell receptors.

antigen processing, the steps that occur in an immune response after a protein is recognized as foreign.

antigen unit, the smallest amount of antigen required to fix one unit of complement.

antigenuria /an′tijenu′re-ah/, the presence of a specific antigen in the urine.

antiglaucoma /an′te-glaw-ko′mah, -glou-ko′mah/, **1.** preventing or alleviating glaucoma. **2.** an antiglaucoma agent.

antiglobulin /an′tiglob′yŏŏlin/ [Gk, *anti*; L, *globulus,* small globe], an antibody that occurs naturally or is prepared in laboratory animals to be used against human globulin. Specific antiglobulins are used in the detection of specific antibodies, as in blood typing.

antiglobulin test, a test for the presence of antibodies that coat and damage erythrocytes as a result of any of several diseases or conditions. The test can detect Rh antibodies in maternal blood and is used to anticipate hemolytic disease of the newborn. It is also used to diagnose and screen for autoimmune hemolytic anemias and to determine the compatibility of blood types.

antiglomerular basement membrane antibodies test, a blood or tissue test used to diagnose Goodpasture's syndrome, which is associated with the presence of circulating glomerular basement membrane antibodies.

antigravity muscle /-grav′itē/, any of the muscle groups involved in stabilization of joints or other body parts by opposing the effects of gravity.

antihelix, a small curved rim parallel and interior to the auricular helix.

antihemophilic factor (recombinant), a sterile, purified, coagulation factor VIII concentrate produced by recombinant technology that possesses biologic activity comparable with that of human plasma-derived coagulation factor VIII. It is used to prevent or stop hemorrhage during surgery or other procedures in patients with hemophilia A. It is administered intravenously.

antihemophilic factor VII concentrate (AHF) /-hē′mōfil′ik/, plasma derivative used to treat bleeding in hemophilia A patients. May be prepared by fractionation of human plasma or affinity column purification. A recombinant DNA product is also available.

antihemorrhagic /-hē′môraj′ik/, any drug or agent used to prevent or control bleeding.

antihistamine /-his′təmin/ [Gk, *anti* + *histos,* tissue, amine (ammonia compound)], any substance capable of reducing the physiologic and pharmacologic effects of histamine, including a wide variety of drugs that block histamine receptors. Antihistamines can both stimulate and depress the CNS.—**antihistaminic,** *adj.*

antihistamine poisoning, an adverse reaction to an excessive intake of antihistamines. Symptoms include fatigue, lethargy, delirium, hallucinations, loss of striated muscle control, hyperreflexia, tachycardia, dilated pupils, and in severe cases coma.

anti-Hu antibody, any of the polyclonal IgG autoantibodies directed against the proteins of the Hu antigen family. They are associated with paraneoplastic sensory neuronopathy and encephalomyelitis in small cell lung carcinoma and, more rarely, sarcoma and neuroblastoma.

antihypercholesterolemic /-hī′pərkō′les′tər ōlē′mik/, a drug that prevents or controls an increase of cholesterol in the blood.

antihyperglycemic /an′te-, an′tihī′perglīise′ mik/, **1.** pertaining to a substance or therapy that counteracts high levels of glucose in the blood. **2.** an antihyperglycemic agent.

antihyperkalemic /an′te-, an′tihī′pərkahl ēē′mik/, **1.** pertaining to a substance or procedure effective in decreasing or preventing hyperkalemia. **2.** an antihyperkalemic agent.

antihyperlipidemic /an′te-, an′tihī′pərlipi′ dēē′mik/, **1.** pertaining to a substance or procedure that promotes a reduction of lipid levels in the blood. **2.** an antihyperlipidemic agent.

antihypertensive /-hī′pərten′siv/, **1.** pertaining to a substance or procedure that reduces high BP. **2.** an antihypertensive agent.

antihypoglycemic /an′te-, an′tihī′poōglīis ēē′mik/, pertaining to a substance or therapy that counteracts low blood sugar.

antihypotensive /-hī′pōten′siv/, **1.** pertaining to a substance or other agent that tends to increase BP. **2.** an antihypotensive drug.

antiimmune /an′ti·imyoōn′/ [Gk, anti; L, immunis, free from], pertaining to the prevention or inhibition of immunity.

antiinfective /-infek′tiv/ [Gk, anti; L, inficere, to stain], **1.** pertaining to an agent that prevents or treats infection. **2.** an antiinfective drug.

antiinflammatory /-inflam′ətor′ē/ [Gk, anti; L, inflammare, to set afire], **1.** pertaining to a substance or procedure that counteracts or reduces inflammation. **2.** an antiinflammatory drug.

antiinhibitor coagulant complex (AICC), a concentrated fraction from pooled human plasma, which includes vitamin K–dependent coagulation factors (factors II, VII, IX, and X), factors of the kinin-generating system, and factor VIII coagulant antigen. It is administered intravenously as an antihemorrhagic in hemophilic patients with factor VIII inhibitors.

antiinitiator /-inish′ē·ātər/, a substance that is a potential cocarcinogen but that may protect cells against cancer development if given before exposure to an initiator.

antileprotic /-leprot′ik/, **1.** a substance or other agent that is effective in treating leprosy. **2.** an antileprotic drug.

antilipidemic /an′tilip′idē′mik/ [Gk, anti + lipos, fat, haima, blood], **1.** pertaining to a regimen, diet, or agent that reduces the amount of lipids in the serum. Anti-lipide-mic diets and drugs are prescribed to reduce the risk of atherosclerotic cardiovascular disease for two reasons: atheromatous plaques contain free cholesterol, and lower serum cholesterol levels and a lower incidence of coronary heart disease are found in populations consuming a low-fat diet than in those on a high-fat diet. **2.** an antilipidemic drug.

Antilirium, a trademark for an acetylcholinesterase inhibitor (physostigmine salicylate).

antimalarial /-məler′ē·əl/, **1.** pertaining to a substance that destroys or suppresses the development of malaria plasmodia or to a procedure that exterminates the mosquito vectors of the disease, such as spraying insecticides or draining swamps. **2.** an antimalarial drug.

antimessage, a strand of viral RNA that cannot act as messenger RNA because of its negative coding sequence. It must be converted to a positive-strand sequence by a viral transcriptase before its message can be translated in a host cell.

antimetabolite /-mətab′əlīt/ [Gk, anti + metabole, change], a drug or other substance that is an antagonist to or resembles a normal human metabolite and interferes with its function in the body, usually by competing for its receptors or enzymes. Many antineoplastic agents are antimetabolites.

antimicrobial /-mīkrō′bē·əl/ [Gk, anti + mikros, small, bios, life], **1.** pertaining to a substance that kills microorganisms or inhibits their growth or replication. **2.** an antimicrobial agent.

Antiminth, a trademark for an anthelmintic (pyrantel pamoate).

antimitochondrial antibody (AMA) /-mī′t ōkon′drē·əl/, an antibody that acts specifically against mitochondria. These antibodies are not normally present in the blood of healthy people.

antimitochondrial antibody (AMA) test, a blood test that is used to determine the presence of antimicrobial antibody in the blood. Low titers may occur in chronic hepatitis, drug-induced hepatotoxicity, and various other diseases. High titers are often diagnostic of primary biliary cirrhosis. Patients with autoimmune hepatitis, extrahepatic obstruction, or acute infection may also test positive for AMA.

antimitotic /-mītot′ik/, inhibiting cell division.

antimony (Sb) /an′təmō′nē/ [L, antimonium], a bluish, crystalline metallic element occurring in nature. Various antimony compounds are used in the treatment of filariasis, leishmaniasis, lymphogranuloma, schistosomiasis, and trypanosomiasis. They are also used as emetics.

antimony poisoning, a toxic effect caused by the ingestion or inhalation of antimony or antimony compounds. It is characterized by vomiting, diaphoresis, diarrhea, and a metallic taste in the mouth. Irritation of the skin or mucous membranes may result from external exposure. Severe poisoning resembles arsenic poisoning.

antimorph /an'təmôrf/ [Gk, *anti* + *morphe*, form], a mutant allele that inhibits or antagonizes the influence of the normal allele in the expression of a trait.

antimuscarinic /-mus'kərin'ik/ [Gk, *anti*; L, *musca*, fly], effective against the poisonous activity of muscarine.

antimutagen /-myo͞o'təjən/ [Gk, *anti*; L, *mutare*, to change; Gk, *genein*, to produce], **1.** any substance that reduces the rate of spontaneous mutations or counteracts or reverses the action of a mutagen. **2.** any technique that protects cells against the effects of mutagens.—**antimutagenic,** *adj.*

antimyasthenic /an'te-, an'timii'asthen'ik/, **1.** counteracting or relieving muscular weakness in myasthenia gravis. **2.** an antimyasthenic agent.

antimyocardial antibody (AMA) test, a blood test used to detect an autoimmune source of myocardial injury and disease, such as rheumatic heart disease, cardiomyopathy, postthoracotomy syndrome, and post-MI. This test may also be used to monitor the effect of treatment on these conditions.

antineoplastic /-nē'ōplas'tik/ [Gk, *anti* + *neos*, new, *plasma*, something formed], **1.** pertaining to a substance, procedure, or measure that prevents the proliferation of cells. **2.** a chemotherapeutic agent that controls or kills cancer cells. Drugs used in the treatment of cancer are cytotoxic but are generally more damaging to dividing cells than to resting cells. Most anticancer drugs prevent the proliferation of cells by inhibiting the synthesis of DNA by various mechanisms. Cytotoxic chemotherapeutic agents may be administered via the oral or IV route or by infusion. All have untoward and unpleasant side effects and are potentially immunosuppressive and dangerous.

antineoplastic antibiotic, a chemical substance derived from a microorganism or a synthetic analog of the substance, used in cancer chemotherapy. Antineoplastic antibiotics cause bone marrow depression and usually cause nausea and vomiting; several cause alopecia.

antineoplastic hormone, a chemically synthesized or a synthetic analog of the naturally occurring compound used to control certain disseminated cancers. Hormonal therapy is designed to counteract the effect of an endogenous hormone required for tumor growth.

antineoplaston, a naturally occurring peptide, amino acid derivative, or carboxylic acid proposed to control neoplastic cell growth using the patient's own biochemical defense system, which works jointly with the immune system.

antineutrophil cytoplasmic antibody (ANCA) test, a blood test used to diagnose Wegener's granulomatosis. It is also used to follow the course of the disease, monitor its response to therapy, and detect early relapse.

antinuclear antibody (ANA) /-no͞o'klē·ər/, an autoantibody directed against nuclear antigens. Antinuclear antibodies are found in the blood serum of patients with rheumatoid arthritis, SLE, Sjögren's syndrome, polymyositis, scleroderma, Raynaud's disease, mixed connective tissue disease, and a number of nonrheumatic disorders.

antinuclear antibody (ANA) test, a blood test used to detect antinuclear antibodies.

antioncogene /an'ti·on'kəjēn/, a tumor-suppressing gene that may act by controlling cellular growth. When an antioncogene is inactivated, tumor cellular proliferation begins, and tumor activity accelerates.

antioxidant /-ok'sidənt/, a chemical or other agent that inhibits or retards oxidation of a substance to which it is added. Examples are butylated hydroxyanisole and butylated hydroxytoluene, which are added to foods or the packaging of foods containing fats or oils to prevent oxygen from combining with the fatty molecules, thereby causing them to become rancid.

antioxidation /-ok'sidā'shən/, the prevention of oxidation.

antiparallel /-per'ələl/ [Gk, *anti* + *parallelos*, side-by-side], pertaining to molecules, such as strands of DNA, that are parallel but are oriented in opposite directions.

antiparasitic /-per'əsit'ik/ [Gk, *anti* + *parasitos*, guest], **1.** pertaining to a substance or procedure that kills parasites or inhibits their growth or reproduction. **2.** an antiparasitic drug such as an amebicide, an anthelmintic, an antimalarial, a schistosomicide, a trichomonacide, or a trypanosomicide.

antiparietal cell antibody (APCA) test, a blood test used to measure the level of APCA, the presence of which indicates pernicious anemia, atrophic gastritis,

Hashimoto's thyroiditis, myxedema, juvenile diabetes, or Addison's disease.

antiparkinsonian /-pär′kənsōnē-ən/, pertaining to a substance or procedure used to treat parkinsonism. Drugs for this neurologic disorder are of two kinds: those that compensate for the lack of DOPamine in the corpus striatum of parkinsonism patients, and anticholinergic agents that counteract the activity of the abundant acetylcholine in the corpus striatum.

antipathy /antip′əthē/ [Gk, *anti* + *pathos*, suffering], a strong feeling of aversion or antagonism to particular objects, situations, or individuals.—**antipathic**, *adj*.

antiperistalsis /-per′əstal′sis/, a wave of contractions in the digestive tract that moves toward the oral end of the tract. In the duodenum, stomach, or esophagus it results in regurgitation.

antiperistaltic /-per′əstal′tik/ [Gk, *anti* + *peristellein*, to wrap around], **1.** pertaining to a substance that inhibits or diminishes peristalsis. **2.** an antiperistaltic agent.

antiplatelet agent /-plat′lit/, any agent that destroys platelets or inhibits their function.

antipode /an′tipōd/, something that is diametrically opposite.

antipraxia /-prak′sē-ə/, a condition in which functions or symptoms appear to oppose each other.

antiprogestin /-prōjes′tin/, a substance that interferes with the production, uptake, or effects of progesterone.

antiprotease, a substance that can prevent the digestion of proteins.

antiprothrombin /-prōthrom′bin/, a substance that inhibits the conversion of prothrombin to thrombin.

antiprotoplasmatic /-prō′təplasmat′ik/, pertaining to an agent that damages the protoplasm of cells.

antiprotozoal /an′te-, an′tiprōōtōōzō′.əl/, **1.** destroying protozoa or checking their growth or reproduction. **2.** an antiprotozoal agent.

antipruritic /-prōōrit′ik/ [Gk, *anti*; L, *prurire*, to itch], **1.** pertaining to a substance or procedure that tends to relieve or prevent itching. **2.** an antipruritic drug.

antipsoriatic /an′tisôr̄ē-at′ik/ [Gk, *anti*; *psora*, itch], pertaining to an agent that relieves the symptoms of psoriasis.

antipsychotic /-sīkot′ik/ [Gk, *anti* + *psyche*, mind, *osis*, condition], **1.** pertaining to a substance or procedure that counteracts or diminishes symptoms of a psychosis. **2.** an antipsychotic drug.

antipyresis /-pīrē′sis/ [Gk, *anti* + *pyretos*, fever], the condition or state of being free from fever.

antipyretic /-pīret′ik/ [Gk, *anti* + *pyretos*, fever], **1.** pertaining to a substance or procedure that reduces fever.—**antipyresis,** *n.* **2.** an antipyretic agent. Such drugs usually lower the thermodetection set point of the hypothalamic heat regulatory center, with resulting vasodilation and sweating.

antipyretic bath, a bath in which tepid water is used to reduce body temperature.

antipyrotic /-pīrot′ik/ [Gk, *anti* + *pyr*, fire], pertaining to the treatment of burns or scalds.

antirabies serum, antiserum obtained from the blood serum or plasma of animals immunized with rabies vaccine. It is used for postexposure prophylaxis against rabies if rabies immune globulin is unavailable.

antirachitic /-rəkit′ik/, pertaining to an agent used to treat rickets.

antiretroviral /an′te-, an′tiret′rōōvī′rəl/, **1.** effective against retroviruses. **2.** a substance or drug that stops or suppresses the activity of retroviruses such as HIV.

anti-Rh agglutinin, an antibody to the Rh antigen on Rh^+ erythrocytes that causes these cells to agglutinate in Rh^- persons after exposure to Rh^+ erythrocytes, as when an Rh^- mother is pregnant with an Rh^+ fetus.

antirheumatic /-rōōmat′ik/ [Gk, *anti* + *rheumatismos*, that which flows], pertaining to the relief of symptoms of any painful or immobilizing disorder of the musculoskeletal system.

anti-Ri antibody, an autoantibody having neuronal binding characteristics similar to those of anti-Hu antibody but directed against a different RNA-binding site. It is associated with paraneoplastic opsoclonus-myoclonus in small cell lung carcinoma, cancer of the breast and fallopian tube.

antiscleroderma antibody test, a blood test to assist in the diagnosis of scleroderma.

antiseborrheic /-seb′ərē′ik/, pertaining to a drug or agent applied to the skin to control seborrhea or seborrheic dermatitis.

antisense /an′tēsens/, pertaining to an RNA molecule that is complementary to the messenger RNA (mRNA) produced by transcription of a given gene. Antisense RNA synthesized in the laboratory will hybridize with the complementary mRNA molecules, thereby blocking the synthesis of specific proteins.

antisense strand, the strand of a double-stranded nucleic acid that is complementary to the sense strand, in DNA being the template strand on which the mRNA is synthesized.

antisepsis /-sep'sis/ [Gk, *anti + sepein,* putrefaction], processes, procedures, or chemical treatments that kill or inhibit microorganisms to prevent infection.

antiseptic /-sep'tik/, **1.** tending to inhibit the growth and reproduction of microorganisms. **2.** a substance that tends to inhibit the growth and reproduction of microorganisms when applied to living tissue.

antiseptic dressing, a fabric, gauze, or pad treated with an antiseptic, a germicide, or a bacteriostatic solution and applied to a wound or an incision to prevent or treat infection.

antiserum /an'tisir'əm/ *pl.* **antisera, antiserums** [Gk, *anti*; L, whey], the serum of an animal or human containing antibodies against a specific disease, used to confer passive immunity to that disease. Antisera do not provoke the production of antibodies. Antibiotic drugs have largely replaced antimicrobial antisera. Caution is always to be used in administration of antiserum of any kind, because hepatitis or hypersensitivity reactions can result.

antiserum anaphylaxis, exaggerated hypersensitivity in a normal person after the injection of serum from a sensitized individual.

antisialogog /-sī·al'əgōg'/ [Gk, *anti + sialon,* saliva, *agogos,* leading], a drug that reduces saliva secretion.

anti–smooth muscle antibody test, a blood test used primarily to help diagnose active autoimmune chronic hepatitis, although a low-level positive result may be associated with viral infections, malignancy, MS, primary biliary cirrhosis, and *Mycoplasma* infections.

antisocial personality /-sō'shəl/ [Gk, *anti*; L, *socius,* companion], a person who exhibits attitudes and overt behavior contrary to the customs, standards, and moral principles accepted by society.

antisocial personality disorder, a condition characterized by repetitive behavioral patterns that are contrary to usual moral and ethical standards and cause a person to experience continuous conflict with society.

antispasmodic /-spazmod'ik/, a drug or other agent that prevents smooth muscle spasms, as in the uterus, digestive system, or urinary tract.

antispastic /an'te-, an'tispas'tik/, an antispasmodic with specific reference to skeletal muscle.

antisperm antibody (ASA), any of the various surface-bound antibodies found on spermatozoa after infection, trauma to the testes, or vasectomy; they interfere with the fertilization process or result in nonviable zygotes.

antispermatozoal antibody test, a fluid analysis or blood test used as a screening test for infertility. The test may be performed on men and women to detect the presence of sperm antibodies that may diminish fertility.

anti-SS-A (ro), anti-SS-B (La), and anti-SS-C antibody test, a blood test to measure the presence of antinuclear antibodies, which indicates Sjögren's syndrome.

antistreptolysin-O test (ASOT, ASO, ASLT) /an'tistrep'təli'sinō'/, a streptococcal antibody test for finding and measuring serum antibodies to streptolysin-O, an exotoxin produced by most group A and some group C and G streptococci. The test is often used as an aid in the diagnosis of rheumatic fever and glomerulonephritis.

antithrombin /-throm'bin/, a substance that inhibits the action of thrombin.

antithrombin III (ATT-III) test, a blood test used to confirm hypercoagulability and to help identify the cause of heparin resistance in patients receiving heparin therapy.

antithrombotic /-thrombot'ik/, preventing or interfering with the formation of a thrombus or blood coagulation.

antithymocyte globulin (ATG) /an'tithī'məsīt/, the gamma globulin fraction of antiserum derived from animals that have been immunized against human thymocytes.

antithymocyte globulin (rabbit), a purified gamma globulin obtained from rabbits immunized with human thymocytes. It is administered intravenously in the treatment of acute rejection occurring after renal transplantation.

antithyroglobulin antibody test, a blood test used primarily in the differential diagnosis of thyroid diseases such as Hashimoto's disease. This test is usually performed in conjunction with the antithyroid microsomal antibody test.

antithyroid drug /-thī'roid/, a preparation that inhibits the synthesis of thyroid hormones and is commonly used in the treatment of hyperthyroidism. The major antithyroid drugs are thioamides. Such substances interfere with the incorporation of iodine into the tyrosyl residues of thyroglobulin required for the production of the hormones thyroxine and triiodothyronine.

antithyroid microsomal antibody test, a blood test used primarily in the differential diagnosis of thyroid diseases such as Hashimoto's disease. This test is usually performed in conjunction with the antithyroglobulin antibody test.

antithyroid peroxidase antibody (anti-TPO) test, a blood test used in the differential diagnosis of thyroid diseases, such as Hashimoto's disease or chronic lymphocytic thyroiditis.

antitoxin /-tok'sin/ [Gk, *anti* + *toxikon*, poison], a subgroup of antisera usually prepared from the serum of horses immunized against a particular toxin-producing organism, such as botulism antitoxin given therapeutically in botulism and tetanus and diphtheria antitoxins given prophylactically to prevent those infections.

anti-TPO, abbreviation for **antithyroid peroxidase antibody.**

antitragus, an elevation of the auricle of the ear opposite the tragus and above the fleshy lobule.

antitrismus /-tris'məs/, a tonic muscular spasm that forces the mouth to open.

antitrust /-trust'/, (in law) against the operation, establishment, or maintenance of a monopoly in the manufacture, production, or sale of a commodity, provision of a service, or practice of a profession.

antitubercular /-tōōbur'kyələr/, any agent or group of drugs used to treat tuberculosis (TB). At least two drugs, and usually three, are required in various combinations in pulmonary TB therapy.

antitumor antibodies, natural products that interfere with DNA in such a way as to prevent its further replication and the transcription of RNA.

antitussive /an'titus'iv/ [Gk, *anti*; L, *tussive*, cough], **1.** against a cough. **2.** any of a large group of opioid and nonopioid drugs that act on the central and peripheral nervous systems to suppress the cough reflex. Because the cough reflex is necessary for clearing the upper respiratory tract of obstructive secretions, antitussives should not be used with a productive cough. Antitussives are administered orally, usually in a syrup with a mucolytic or expectorant and alcohol, or, sometimes, in a capsule with an antihistaminic and a mild analgesic.

antiurolithic /an'ti.yōō'rōō-lith'ik/, **1.** preventing the formation of urinary calculi. **2.** an antiurolithic agent.

antivenin /an'tiven'in/ [Gk, *anti*; L, *venenum*, poison], a suspension of venom-neutralizing antibodies prepared from the serum of immunized horses. Antivenin confers passive immunity and is given as a part of emergency first aid for various snake and insect bites.

Antivert, a trademark for an antihistaminic antivertigo agent (meclizine hydrochloride).

antiviral, destructive to viruses.

antivitamin factor [Gk, *anti* + L, *vita*, life, amine], a substance that inactivates a vitamin.

anti-Yo antibody, polyclonal IgG autoantibody directed against Purkinje's cells and associated with paraneoplastic cerebellar degeneration in oat cell carcinoma

of the lung and cancer of the breast or ovary.

Anton's syndrome [Gabriel Anton, German neuropsychiatrist, 1858–1933], a form of anosognosia in which a person with partial or total blindness denies being visually impaired, despite medical evidence to the contrary.

Antopol-Goldman lesion, a subepithelial hematoma of renal pelvis.

antral gastritis [Gk, *antron*, cave], an abnormal narrowing of the antrum of the stomach. The narrowing is not a true gastritis but a radiographic finding that may represent a peptic ulcer or tumor.

antrectomy /antrek'təmē/, the surgical excision of the pylorus.

antrum *pl.* **antra** [Gk, *antron*, cave], a cavity or chamber that is nearly closed and usually surrounded by bone.

Anturane, a trademark for a uricosuric drug (sulfinpyrazone).

anular /an'yələr/ [L, *annulus*, ring], describing a ring-shaped lesion surrounding a clear, normal, unaffected disk of skin.

anular ligament, a ligament that encircles the head of the radius and holds it in the radial notch of the ulna. Distal to the notch, the anular ligament forms a complete fibrous ring.

anulus /an'yələs/, a ring of circular tissue, such as the whitish tympanic anulus around the perimeter of the tympanic membrane.—**annular, anular,** *adj.*

anulus fibrosus, an outer ring of collagen in an intervertebral disk arranged in a lamellar configuration that surrounds a wider zone of fibrocartilage.

anuria /ənōōr'ē.ə/ [Gk, *a* + *ouron*, not urine], the absence of urine production or a urinary output of less than 100 mL per day. Anuria may be caused by kidney failure or dysfunction, a decline in BP below that required to maintain filtration pressure in the kidney, or an obstruction in the urinary passages. A rapid decline in urinary output, leading ultimately to anuria and uremia, occurs in acute renal failure. —**anuretic, anuric,** *adj.*

anus /ā'nəs/, the outlet at the terminal end of the anal canal lying in the fold between the buttocks.—**anal,** *adj.*

anxietas /angzī'ətas/ [L, anxiety], a state of anxiety, nervous restlessness, or apprehension, often accompanied by a feeling of oppression in the epigastrium.

anxietas presenilis [L, *anxietas* + *prae*, before, *senex*, aged], a state of extreme anxiety associated with the climacteric.

anxiety /angzī'ətē/ [L, *anxietas*], anticipation of impending danger and dread accompanied by restlessness, tension, tachycardia, and breathing difficulty not necessarily associated with an apparent stimulus.

anxiety attack, an acute, psychobiologic reaction manifested by intense anxiety and panic. Symptoms include palpitations, shortness of breath, dizziness, faintness, profuse diaphoresis, pallor of the face and extremities, GI discomfort, and a vague feeling of imminent doom or death. Attacks usually occur suddenly, last from a few seconds to an hour or longer, and vary in frequency.

anxiety disorder, a disorder in which anxiety is the most prominent feature. The symptoms range from mild, chronic tenseness, with feelings of timidity, fatigue, apprehension, and indecisiveness, to more intense states of restlessness and irritability that may lead to aggressive acts, persistent helplessness, or withdrawal. In extreme cases, the overwhelming emotional discomfort is accompanied by physical responses, including tremor, sustained muscle tension, tachycardia, dyspnea, hypertension, increased respiration, and profuse perspiration. Other physical signs include changes in skin color, nausea, vomiting, diarrhea, restlessness, immobilization, insomnia, and changes in appetite, all occurring without identification of a known underlying organic cause.

anxiety dream, a dream that is accompanied by restlessness and a gradual increase in pulse rate.

anxiety level, a nursing outcome from the Nursing Outcomes Classification (NOC) defined as severity of manifested apprehension, tension, or uneasiness arising from an unidentifiable source.

anxiety reaction [L, *anxietas + re + agere,* to act], a clinical characteristic in which anxiety is the predominant feature or is experienced by a person facing a dreaded situation to the extent that his or her functioning is impaired. The reaction may be expressed as a panic disorder, a phobia, or a compulsion.

anxiety reduction, a nursing intervention from the Nursing Interventions Classification (NIC) defined as minimizing apprehension, dread, foreboding, or uneasiness related to an unidentified source of anticipated danger.

anxiety self-control, a nursing outcome from the Nursing Outcomes Classification (NOC) defined as personal actions to eliminate or reduce feelings of apprehension, tension, or uneasiness from an unidentifiable source.

anxiety state [L, *anxietas + state*], a mental or emotional reaction characterized by apprehension, uncertainty, and irrational fear. Anxiety states may be accompanied by physiologic changes such as diaphoresis, tremors, rapid heartbeat, dilated pupils, and xerostomia.

AOA, abbreviation for **Administration on Aging.**

AORN, abbreviation for **Association of Operating Room Nurses.**

aorta /ā·ôr′tə/ [Gk, *aerein,* to raise], the main trunk of the systemic arterial circulation, comprising four parts: the ascending aorta, the arch of the aorta, the thoracic portion of the descending aorta, and the abdominal portion of the descending aorta. It starts at the aortic opening of the left ventricle, rises a short distance, bends over the root of the left lung, descends within the thorax on the left side of the vertebral column, and passes through the aortic hiatus of the diaphragm into the abdominal cavity.—**aortic,** *adj.*

aortic aneurysm, a localized dilation of the wall of the aorta caused by atherosclerosis, hypertension, connective tissue disease such as Marfan's syndrome, or, less frequently, syphilis. The lesion may be a saccular distension, a fusiform or cylindrical swelling of a length of the vessel. The more common atherosclerotic aneurysms are usually in the abdominal aorta below the renal arteries and above the bifurcation of the aorta.

aortic arch syndrome, any of a group of occlusive conditions of the aortic arch producing a variety of symptoms related to obstruction of the large branch arteries, including the brachiocephalic, left common carotid, and left subclavian. It may be caused by atherosclerosis, Takayasu's arteritis, syphilis, and other conditions. Symptoms include syncope, temporary blindness, hemiplegia, aphasia, and memory loss.

aortic atresia [Gk, *aerein + a + tresis,* a boring], a congenital anomaly in which the left side of the heart is defective and there is an imperforation of the aortic valve.

aortic body, one of several small structures on the arch of the aorta that contain neural tissue sensitive to the chemical composition of arterial blood. The aortic bodies respond primarily to large reductions in blood oxygen content and trigger an increase in respiratory rate.

aortic-body reflex, a neural reflex in which a decrease in the oxygen content of arterial blood is sensed by the aortic bodies, which signal the medullary respiratory center to increase respiratory rate.

aortic hiatus, an opening in the diaphragm for the aorta and thoracic duct.

aortic notch [Gk, *aerein,* to raise; OFr, *enochier*], the dicrotic notch on the descending limb of an arterial pulse sphygmogram. It marks the closure of the aortic valve.

aortic obstruction [L, *obstruere,* to build against], a blockage or impediment that interrupts the flow of blood in the aorta.

aorticopulmonary septum, a septum, formed by fusion of the bulbar ridges, that divides the bulbus cordis into aortic and pulmonary trunks.

aortic reconstruction, restoration of function to a damaged or atretic aorta as by bypass or aortoplasty.

aortic regurgitant murmur [Gk, *aeirein,* to raise; L, *re,* again, *gurgitare,* to flow, *murmur,* humming], a high-pitched, soft, blowing, decrescendo, early diastolic heart murmur that is a sign of aortic regurgitation.

aortic regurgitation, the flow of blood from the aorta back into the left ventricle during diastole, resulting from a failure of the aortic valve to close completely.

aortic sinus [Gk, *aeirein,* to raise; L, *sinus,* little hollow], any of three dilations, one anterior and two posterior, between the aortic wall and the semilunar cusps of the aortic valve.

aortic stenosis (AS) [Gk, *aeirein* + *stenos,* narrow, *osis,* condition], a narrowing or stricture of the aortic valve. Common causes include calcification of the valve because of age, congenital malformations such as bicuspid or unicuspid valves, or direct damage to the valve from rheumatic fever, which leads to fusion of the cusps. Aortic stenosis obstructs the flow of blood from the left ventricle into the aorta, causing decreased cardiac output and pulmonary vascular congestion. It may lead to congestive heart failure.

aortic thrill [Gk, *aeirein,* to raise; AS, *thyrlian*], a palpable chest vibration caused by aortic stenosis or an aortic aneurysm. It is usually felt in systole by placing the flat of the hand or the fingertips on the second intercostal space to the right of the sternum.

aortic valve, a valve in the heart between the left ventricle and the aorta. It is composed of three semilunar cusps that close in diastole to prevent blood from flowing back into the left ventricle from the aorta.

aortitis /ā·ôrtī′tis/, an inflammation of the aorta. It occurs most frequently in tertiary syphilis and occasionally in rheumatic fever.

aortocoronary /ā·ôr′tōkôr′əner′ē/ [Gk, *aeirein*; L, *corona,* crown], pertaining to the aorta and coronary arteries.

aortocoronary bypass [AS, *bi,* alongside; Fr, *passer*], a surgical procedure for treatment of angina pectoris or coronary vessel disease, in which a saphenous vein,

mammary artery, or other blood vessel or a synthetic graft is used to build a shunt from the aorta to one of the coronary arteries to bypass a circulatory obstruction.

aortogram /ā·ôr′təgram/ [Gk, *aerein* + *gramma,* record], a radiographic image of the aorta made after the injection of a radiopaque contrast medium in the blood.

aortography /ā·ôrtog′rəfē/ [Gk, *aerein* + *graphein,* to record], a radiographic process in which the aorta and its branches are injected with any of various contrast media for visualization.—**aortographic,** *adj.*

aortopulmonary fenestration /ā·ôr′tōpul′m əner′ē/ [Gk, *aerein*; L, *pulmoneus,* lung, *fenestra,* window], a congenital anomaly characterized by an abnormal fenestration in the ascending aorta and the pulmonary artery cephalad to the semilunar valve, allowing oxygenated and unoxygenated blood to mix, resulting in a decrease in the oxygen available in the peripheral circulation.

AOTA, abbreviation for **American Occupational Therapy Association.**

AOTF, abbreviation for *American Occupational Therapy Foundation.*

AP, abbreviation for **anteroposterior.**

APA, 1. abbreviation for **American Psychiatric Association. 2.** abbreviation for *American Psychological Association.*

APACHE /əpach′ē/, abbreviation for *Acute Physiology and Chronic Health Evaluation,* a system of classifying severity of illnesses in patients in the ICU.

apareunia /ā′pəroo͞′nē·ə/, an inability to perform coitus caused by a physical or psychologic sexual dysfunction.

apathetic hyperthyroidism /ap′əthet′ik/, a form of Graves' disease that tends to affect mainly older adults who have stereotyped "senile" physical features and whose behavior is apathetic and inactive rather than hyperkinetic.

apathy /ap′əthē/ [Gk, *a, pathos,* not suffering], an absence or suppression of emotion, feeling, concern, or passion; an indifference to stimuli found generally to be exciting or moving.—**apathetic,** *adj.*

apatite /ap′ətīt/ [Gk, *apate,* deceit], an inorganic mineral composed of calcium and phosphate that is found in the bones and teeth.

APC, 1. abbreviation for **atrial premature complex. 2.** abbreviation for **adenomatous polyposis coli.**

APCA, 1. abbreviation for **antiparietal cell antibody. 2.** abbreviation for **anti-Purkinje cell antibody.**

APCC, abbreviation for **activated prothrombin complex concentrate.**

APD, abbreviation for *adult polycystic disease.*

apepsia /āpep′sē·ə/ [Gk, *a*, without, *pepsis*, digestion], a condition involving a failure of the digestive functions.

aperient /əpir′ē·ənt/ [L, *aperire*, to open], a mild laxative.

aperistalsis /āper′istal′sis/ [Gk, *a*, without, *peristellein*, to clasp], a failure of the normal waves of contraction and relaxation that move contents through the digestive tract.

aperitive /əper′itiv/ [L, *aperere*, to open], a stimulant of the appetite.

Apert's syndrome /äperz′/ [Eugène Charles Apert, French pediatrician, 1868–1940], a rare genetic condition characterized by an abnormal craniofacial appearance in combination with partial or complete fusion (webbing) of the fingers and toes. A characteristic feature is the premature joining of cranial bones, with resultant growth disturbances.

aperture /ap′ərchər/ [L, *apertura*, an opening], an opening or hole in an object or anatomic structure.

aperture of the frontal sinus, an external opening of the frontal sinus into the nasal cavity.

aperture of the glottis, an opening between the true vocal cords and the arytenoid cartilages.

aperture of the larynx, an opening between the pharynx and larynx.

aperture of the sphenoid sinus, a round opening between the sphenoid sinus and nasal cavity, situated just above the superior nasal concha.

apex /ā′peks/ *pl.* **apices** [L, tip], the top, the end, the summit, or the extremity of a structure.—**apical,** *adj.*

apex beat, a pulsation of the left ventricle of the heart, palpable and sometimes visible at the fifth intercostal space.

apexcardiogram (ACG) /-kär′dē·əgram′/, a graphic representation of the pulsations of the chest over the heart in the region of the cardiac apex. The purpose is to provide additional information regarding the diagnosis of ventricular abnormalities.

apexcardiography (ACG) /-kär′dē·og′rəfē/, the recording of heart pulsations obtained from the cardiac apex.

apex cordis [L, *apex + cordis,* of the heart], the pointed lower border of the heart. It is directed downward, forward, and to the left and is usually located at the level of the fifth intercostal space.

apexification /-if′ikā′shən/ [L, *apex + facere,* to make], a process of promoting apical closure of the root in an endodontically treated tooth by placement of calcium hydroxide paste or other tissue-tolerant material in the root canal after an apicoectomy.

apexigraph /āpek′sigraf′/, a device used for determining the position of the apex of a tooth root.

apex murmur [L, *apex,* summit, *murmur,* humming], a heart sound heard best at the apex of the heart, which in most individuals is at the level of the fifth intercostal space.

apex of the heart, the lowest superficial part of the heart, formed by the inferolateral part of the left ventricle.

apex of the urinary bladder, the superior area of the urinary bladder, opposite the fundus. It is at the junction of the superior and inferolateral surfaces of the bladder, and from it the middle umbilical ligament (urachus) extends to the umbilicus.

apex pneumonia [L, *apex,* summit; Gk, *pnemon,* lung], pneumonia in which consolidation is limited to the upper lobe of one lung.

apex pulmonis /pəlmō′nis/ [L, *apex + pulmoneus,* lung], the rounded upper border of each lung, projecting above the clavicle.

APF, acidulated phosphate fluoride, a preparation of sodium fluoride acidulated with phosphoric acid for topical application to the teeth in the prevention of dental caries.

Apgar score /ap′gär/ [Virginia Apgar, American anesthesiologist, 1909–1974], an evaluation of a newborn's physical condition, usually performed 1 minute and again 5 minutes after birth, based on a rating of five factors that reflect the infant's ability to adjust to extrauterine life. The system rapidly identifies infants requiring immediate intervention or transfer to an NICU.

APHA, abbreviation for *American Public Health Association.*

aphagia /əfā′jē·ə/ [Gk, *a + phagein,* not to eat], a condition characterized by the loss of the ability to swallow as a result of organic or psychologic causes.

aphagia algera, a condition characterized by refusal to eat or swallow because doing so causes pain.

aphakia /əfā′kē·ə/ [Gk, *a + phakos,* not lens], (in ophthalmology) a condition in which the crystalline lens of the eye is absent, usually because it has been surgically removed, as in the treatment of cataracts.—**aphacic, aphakic,** *adj.*

aphasia /əfā′zhə/ [Gk, *a + phasis,* not speech], an abnormal neurologic condition in which language function is disordered or absent because of an injury to certain areas of the cerebral cortex. Aphasia may be complete or partial, affecting specific language functions. Most commonly, the condition is a mixture of incomplete sensory and motor aphasia. It may occur after severe head trauma, prolonged hypoxia, or CVA. It is sometimes transient, as when the swelling in the brain that follows aphrasia or injury subsides and language returns.—**aphasic,** *adj.*

aphemia /əfē′mē·ə/, a loss of the ability to speak. The term is applied to emotional disorders, as well as neurologic causes.—**aphemic,** *adj.*

apheresis /əfer′əsis, af′ərē′sis/ [Gk, *aphairesis,* removal], a procedure in which blood is temporarily withdrawn, one or more components are selectively removed, and the rest of the blood is reinfused into the donor. The process is used in treating various disease conditions in the donor, for obtaining blood elements for treatment of other patients or for research purposes.

aphonia /āfō′nē·ə/ [Gk, *a* + *phone,* without voice], a condition characterized by loss of the ability to produce normal speech sounds that results from overuse of the vocal cords, organic disease, or psychologic causes such as anxiety.—**aphonic, aphonous,** *adj.*

aphonia paralytica /par′əlit′ikə/, a condition characterized by a loss of the voice caused by paralysis or disease of the laryngeal nerves.

aphonic pectoriloquy /āfon′ik ′pek-tə-′ril-ə-kwē/, the abnormal transmission of voice sounds through a cavity or a serous pleural effusion detected during auscultation of a lung.

aphonic speech, abnormal speech in which vocalizations are whispered.

aphoria /əfôr′ē·ə/, a condition in which physical weakness is not lessened as a result of exercise.

aphrasia /əfrā′zhə/, a form of aphasia in which a person may be able to speak or understand single words but is not able to communicate with words that are arranged in meaningful phrases or sentences.

aphronia /əfrō′nē·ə/ [Gk, *a* + *phronein,* not to understand], (in psychiatry) a condition characterized by an impaired ability to make common-sense decisions. —**aphronic,** *adj.*

aphtha /af′thē/ *pl.* **aphthae** [Gk, *aphtha,* eruption], a small, shallow, painful ulceration that usually affects the oral mucosa but not underlying bone. Aphthae occasionally may affect other body tissues, including those of the GI tract and the external genitals. They do not appear to be infectious, contagious, or sexually transmitted.—**aphthous,** *adj.*

aphthous stomatitis /af′thəs/ [Gk, *aphtha,* eruption, *stoma,* mouth, *itis,* inflammation], a recurring condition characterized by the eruption of painful ulcers (commonly called canker sores) on the mucous membranes of the mouth.

APIC, abbreviation for **Association for Professionals in Infection Control and Epidemiology.**

apical curettage [L, *apex;* Fr, scraping], debridement of the apical surface of a tooth and removal of diseased soft tissues in the surrounding bony crypt.

apical fiber, one of the many fibers of the periodontal ligament. These fibers radiate around the apex of the tooth at approximately right angles to their cementum attachment, extending into the bone at the bottom of the alveolus. Apical fibers resist forces that tend to lift the tooth from the socket and, with the other fibers of the periodontal ligament, stabilize the tooth against tilting movements.

apical lordotic view /lôrdot′ik/, a radiograph made with the patient leaning backward at an angle of approximately 45 degrees, allowing visualization of the apices of the lung under the clavicle.

apical membrane, the layer of plasma membrane on the apical side (the side toward the lumen) of the epithelial cells in a body tube or cavity, separated from the basolateral membrane by the zonula occludens.

apical odontoid ligament /ōdon′toid/, a ligament connecting the axis to the occipital bone. It extends from the odontoid process of the axis (dens) to the anterior margin of the foramen magnum.

apical perforation, a mechanically induced channel running from the pulp canal into the periodontal space at or near the apex of the root.

apical periodontitis [L, *apex,* summit; Gk, *peri,* near, *odous,* tooth, *itis,* inflammation], an inflammation of the tissues around the apex of a tooth root.

apical pulse, the heartbeat as heard with a stethoscope placed on the chest wall adjacent to the apex cordi.

apicitis /ap′isī′tis/, an inflammation of the apex of a body structure.

apicoectomy /ap′ikō.ek′təmē/ [L, *apex;* Gk, *ektomē* excision], the surgical removal of the apex or the apical portion of an infected or damaged tooth root, usually in conjunction with apical curettage or root canal therapy.

apicotomy /ā′pikot′əmē/, a surgical incision into the apex of a body structure.

apituitarism /ā′pityōō′itəriz′əm/ [Gk, *a,* without; L, *pituita,* phlegm; Gk, *ismos,* a state], an absence or loss of function of the pituitary gland.

aplasia /əplā′zhə/ [Gk, *a* + *plassein,* not to form], **1.** a developmental failure resulting in the absence of an organ or tissue. **2.** (in hematology) a failure of the normal process of cell generation and development.—**aplastic,** *adj.*

aplasia cutis congenita [Gk, *a + plassein;* L, *cutis,* skin, *congenitus* born with], the congenital absence of a localized area of skin. It is usually covered by a thin, translucent membrane or scar tissue, or it may be raw and ulcerated.

aplastic anemia, a deficiency of all of the formed elements of blood (specifically erythrocytes, leukocytes, and platelets), representing a failure of the cell-generating capacity of bone marrow. Aplastic anemia is often of unknown origin and may involve destruction of bone marrow by exposure to toxic chemicals, ionizing radiation, or some antibiotics.

Apley's scratch test, a method for assessing the ROM of the shoulders. The patient is asked to scratch his or her back while reaching over the head with one hand and behind the back with the other hand. The test requires abduction and lateral rotation of one shoulder and adduction and medial rotation of the other shoulder.

Aplisol, a trademark for a tuberculin purified protein derivative used for tuberculin tests.

APMA, abbreviation for *American Podiatric Medical Society.*

APN, abbreviation for **advanced practice nurse.**

apnea /apnē′ə, ap′nē-ə/ [Gk, *a + pnein,* not to breathe], an absence of spontaneous respiration.—**apneic,** *adj.*

apnea monitor [Gk, *a + pnein,* not to breathe], a device designed to sound an alarm if an individual stops breathing for a given period of time. It may be a bed pad (alarm mattress) or a nasal flow sensor.

apnea monitoring, the act of closely observing the respiration of individuals, particularly infants. The procedure may involve the use of electronic devices that detect changes in thoracic or abdominal movements and in heart rate. Such devices may include an alarm that sounds if breathing stops.

apneumia /ap·nōō′mē-ə/ [Gk, *a + pneumon,* without lung], a congenital absence of the lungs.

apneustic breathing /apnōō′stik/ [Gk, *a + pneusis,* not breathing], a pattern of breathing characterized by a prolonged inspiratory phase followed by expiration apnea. This breathing pattern is often associated with head injury.

apneustic center, an area in the lower portion of the pons that controls the inspiratory phase of respiration.

apocrine gland /ap′əkrīn, -krin/ [Gk, *apo + krinein;* L, *secernere,* to separate], a gland whose secretion contains part of the secreting cell.

apocrine sweat gland [Gk, *apo,* from, *krinein,* to separate], one of the large dermal sudiferous glands located in the axillary, anal, genital, and mammary areas of the body. Apocrine glands become functional only after puberty. They secrete perspiration containing nutrients consumed by skin bacteria.

apodal /ə·pō′dəl/ [Gk, *a + pous,* without foot], having no feet.

apoenzyme /ap′ō-en′zīm/ [Gk, *apo + en,* into, *zyme,* ferment], the protein part of a holoenzyme. The nonprotein part is the prosthetic group, which is usually permanently attached to the apoenzyme.

apogee /ap′əjē/ [Gk, *apo + ge,* earth], the climax of a disease or the period of greatest severity of signs and symptoms, usually followed by a crisis.

Apokyn, a trademark for apomorphine.

apolipoprotein /ap′ōlip′ōprō′tēn/ [Gk, *apo + lipos,* fat, *protos,* first], the protein component of lipoprotein complexes.

apolipoprotein A-I, a protein component of lipoprotein complexes found in high-density lipoprotein (HDL) and chylomicrons.

apolipoprotein A-II, a protein component of lipoprotein complexes found in high-density lipoprotein and chlyomicrons, which activates hepatic lipase.

apolipoprotein A-III, a protein component of high-density lipoproteins.

apolipoprotein B-100, a protein component of lipoprotein involved in the hepatic transport of lipid as very-low-density lipoprotein and low-density lipoprotein.

apolipoprotein C-I, a protein component of lipid that activates lecithin-cholesterol acyltransferase.

apolipoprotein C-II, a protein component of chylomicrons and very-low-density lipoprotein that activates lipoprotein lipase.

apolipoprotein E, a protein component of lipoprotein complexes found in very low-density lipoprotein (VLDL), high-density lipoprotein (HDL), chylomicrons, and chylomicron remnants. It facilitates hepatic uptake of chylomicron and VLDL remnants and is elevated in patients with type III hyperlipoproteinemia.

apolipoprotein test, a blood test used to evaluate the risks of atherogenic disease of the heart and peripheral arteries. Specific levels of certain apolipoproteins are also associated with conditions such as Alzheimer's disease, low-density lipoprotein receptor disorder, some types of renal failure, nephrotic syndrome, and estrogen depletion in women over the age of 50.

apomorphine, an antiparkinsonian agent used for acute, intermittent treatment of hypomobility episodes in advanced parkinsonism.

aponeurosis /ap'ŏnŏŏrō'sis/ *pl.* **aponeuroses** [Gk, *apo* + *neuron,* nerve, sinew], a strong flat sheet of fibrous connective tissue that serves as a tendon to attach muscles to bone or as fascia to bind muscles together or to other tissues at their origin or insertion.—**aponeurotic,** *adj.*

aponeurosis of the external abdominal oblique, the strong membrane that covers the entire ventral surface of the abdomen and lies superficial to the rectus abdominis muscles. Fibers from both sides of the aponeurosis interlace in the midline to form the linea alba.

aponeurotic fascia /-nŏŏrot'ik/ [Gk, *apo,* from, *neuron,* tendon], a thickened layer of connective tissue that provides attachment to a muscle.

aponeurotic fibroma, a recurrent benign tumor seen mainly in persons under 20 years of age, most often on the hand, occurring as a firm, fixed nodule composed of fibroblastic tissue with finely stippled calcifications, not attached to the overlying skin and infiltrating into surrounding soft tissue.

Aponomma hydrosauri, a tick that infests reptiles. It is the arthropod reservoir for *Rickettsia honei* on Flinders Island, Australia, and transmits Flinders Island spotted fever.

apophyseal fracture, a fracture that separates the growth plate (apophysis) of a bone from the main osseous tissue at a point of strong tendinous or ligamentous attachment.

apophysis /əpof'isis/ [Gk, a growing away], any small projection, process, or outgrowth, usually on a bone without an independent center of ossification.— **apophyseal, apophysial,** *adj.*

apophysitis /əpof'əsī'tis/, an inflammation of an outgrowth, projection, or swelling, especially a bony outgrowth that is still attached to the rest of the bone.

apoprotein /ap'ōprō'tēn/, a polypeptide chain not yet complexed to its specific prosthetic group.

apoprotein B-48, a protein component of lipoprotein found in chylomicrons. It is involved in the intestinal absorption of lipids.

apoptosis /ā'pōtō'sis, ā'poptō'sis/ [Gk, *apo,* away, *ptosis,* falling], necrosis of keratinocytes in which the nuclei of the necrotic cells dissolve and the cytoplasm

shrinks, rounds up, and is subsequently phagocytized. The term generally refers to "programmed" cell death.

aposia /āpō'shə/ [Gk, *a,* not, *posis,* thirst], a complete lack of thirst.

apothecaries' measure /əpoth'əker'ēz/ [Gk, *apotheke,* store], a system of graduated liquid volumes originally based on the minim, formerly equal to 1 drop of water but now standardized to 0.06 mL; 60 minims equal 1 fluid dram, 8 fluid drams equal 1 fluid ounce, 16 fluid ounces equal 1 pint, 2 pints equal 1 quart, 4 quarts equal 1 gallon.

apothecaries' weight, a system of graduated amounts arranged in order of heaviness and based on the grain, formerly equal to the weight of a plump grain of wheat but now standardized to 65 mg; 20 grains equal 1 scruple, 3 scruples equal 1 dram, 8 drams equal 1 ounce, 16 ounces equal 1 pound.

apothecary /əpoth'əker'ē/ [Gk, *apotheke,* store], a pharmacist.

apparatus /ap'ərat'əs/ [L, *ad,* toward, *parare,* to make ready], a device or a system composed of different parts that act together to perform some special function.

apparent leukonychia, a white discoloration of the nail that fades when pressure is applied, with maintenance of transparency of the nail plate.

appendectomy /ap'əndek'təmē/ [L, *appendere;* Gk, *ektomē,* excision], the surgical removal of the vermiform appendix. This procedure can be performed via laparoscope or open laparotomy.

appendical reflex /əpen'dikəl/, extreme tenderness at McBurney's point on the abdomen, a diagnostic finding in appendicitis.

appendicectomy /əpendisek'təmē/, the surgical removal of an appendage.

appendicitis /əpen'disī'tis/ [L, *appendere;* Gk, *itis*], an inflammation of the vermiform appendix, usually acute, that, if undiagnosed, leads rapidly to perforation and peritonitis. The inflammation is caused by an obstruction such as a hard mass of feces or a foreign body in the lumen of the appendix, fibrous disease of the bowel wall, an adhesion, or a parasitic infestation.

appendicitis pain [L, *appendere,* to hang upon, *poena,* penalty], severe general abdominal pain that develops rapidly and usually becomes localized in the lower right abdominal quadrant. It is accompanied by extreme tenderness over the right rectus abdominis muscle with rebound pain at McBurney's point. Occasionally the pain is on the left side.

appendicular abscess, 1. an abscess on a limb. 2. an abscess of the vermiform appendix.

appendicular artery, one of the four branches of the ileocolic artery, supplying the mesoappendix and the appendix.

appendicular skeleton, the bones of the limbs and their girdles, attached to the axial skeleton.

appendix /əpen′diks/ *pl.* **appendices, appendixes,** an accessory part attached to a main structure.—**appendical, appendiceal, appendicial, appendicular,** *adj.*

appendix dyspepsia [L, *appendere*; Gk, *dys,* difficult, *peptein,* to digest], an abnormal condition characterized by impaired digestive function associated with chronic appendicitis.

apperception /ap′ərsep′shən/ [L, *ad,* toward, *percipere,* to perceive], **1.** mental perception or recognition. **2.** (in psychology) a conscious process of understanding or perceiving in terms of a person's previous knowledge, experiences, emotions, and memories.—**apperceptive,** *adj.*

appestat /ap′əstat/, the center in the hypothalamus of the brain that controls the appetite.

appetite[1] /ap′ətīt/ [L, *appetere,* to long for], a natural or instinctive desire, such as for food.

appetite[2], a nursing outcome from the Nursing Outcomes Classification (NOC) defined as desire to eat when ill or receiving treatment.

apple picker's disease, an allergic reaction with respiratory complaints, associated with the handling of apples that have been treated with a fungicide.

apple sorter's disease, a form of contact dermatitis caused by chemicals used in washing apples.

appliance /əplī′əns/ [L, *applicare,* to apply], **1.** a device used to perform a specific medical function or to have a specific therapeutic effect. **2.** (in dentistry) generally a device to correct a malocclusion, to correct an oral habit, or to stabilize an occlusion.

applicator /ap′likā′tər/, a rodlike instrument with a piece of cotton on the end, used for the local application of medication or probing of wound pockets/crevices.

applied anatomy /əplīd′/, the study of the structure of the organs of the body as it relates to the diagnosis and treatment of disease.

applied chemistry, the application of the study of chemical elements and compounds to industry and the arts.

applied kinesiology, a form of treatment using nutrition, physical manipulation, vitamins, diets, and exercise for the purpose of restoring and energizing the body.

Weak muscles are proposed to be a source of dysfunctional health.

applied psychology, **1.** the interpretation of historical, literary, medical, or other data according to psychologic principles. **2.** any branch of psychology that emphasizes practical rather than theoretic approaches and objectives.

AP portable chest radiograph, a radiographic examination of the chest performed with a portable x-ray machine in the room of an immobilized patient. The film holder is placed behind the patient and the x-ray tube in front. The patient is positioned as upright as possible to allow for visualization of fluid levels in the lungs.

apposition /ap′əsish′ən/ [L, *apponere,* to put to], the placing of objects in proximity, as in the layering of tissue cells or juxtaposition of facing surfaces side-by-side.

appositional growth, an increase in size by the addition of new tissue or similar material at the periphery of a particular part or structure, as in the addition of new layers in bone and tooth formation.

apposition suture, a suture that holds the margins of an incision close together.

approach, the steps in a particular surgical procedure, from division of the most superficial parts of the anatomy through exposure of the operation site.

approach-approach conflict [L, *ad + propiare,* to draw near], a conflict resulting from the simultaneous presence of two or more incompatible impulses, desires, or goals, each of which is desirable.

approach-avoidance conflict, a conflict resulting from the presence of a single goal or desire that is both desirable and undesirable.

appropriate for gestational age (AGA) infant /əprō′prē·it/ [L, *ad,* toward, *prorius,* ownership], a newborn whose size, growth, and maturation are normal for gestational age, whether delivered prematurely, at term, or later than term.

approximal /əprok′siməl/ [L, *approximare,* to approach], close, or very near.

approximate /əprok′simət/ [L, *ad + proximare,* to come near], **1.** to draw two tissue surfaces close together as in the repair of a wound or to draw the bones of a joint together as in physical therapy. **2.** almost correct.

approximator /əprok′səmā′tər/, a medical instrument used to draw together the edges of divided tissues, as in closing a wound or repairing a fractured rib.

apraxia /əprak′sē·ə/ [Gk, *a + pressein,* not to act], an impairment in the ability to perform purposeful acts or to manipulate objects without any loss of strength, sensation, or coordination.—**apraxic,** *adj.*

aprepitant, an antiemetic agent used to prevent nausea and vomiting associated with cancer chemotherapy.

Apresoline, a trademark for a nonnitrate arteriolar vasodilator antihypertensive (hydralazine hydrochloride).

aprosody /āpros'odē/ [Gk, *a* + *prosodia,* not modulated voice], a speech disorder characterized by the absence of the normal variations in pitch, loudness, intonation, and rhythm of word formation.

aprosopia /ā'prəsō'pē·ə/ [Gk, *aprosopos,* faceless], a congenital absence of part or all of the facial structures. The condition is usually associated with other malformations.

aprotinin /ap'ro-ti'nin/, an inhibitor of proteolytic enzymes, used as an antihemorrhagic to reduce perioperative blood loss in patients undergoing cardiopulmonary bypass during CABG.

APTA, abbreviation for *American Physical Therapy Association.*

aptitude /ap'tətyōōd/ [L, *aptitudo,* ability], a natural ability, tendency, talent, or capability to learn, understand, or acquire a particular skill; mental alertness.

aptitude test, any of a variety of standardized tests for measuring an individual's ability to learn certain skills.

Aptivus, a trademark for tipranavir.

Apt test, a test for blood in the stool of a newborn. The test differentiates between maternal and newborn blood. The presence of newborn blood indicates active GI bleeding or necrotizing enterocolitis.

apyrexia /ā'pīrek'sē·ə/ [Gk, *a* + *pyrexis,* without fever], an absence or remission of fever.

AQ, abbreviation for **achievement quotient.**

aqua (aq) /ā'kwə/, the Latin word for water.

AquaMEPHYTON, a trademark for a vitamin K compound (phytonadione).

aquaphobia /ä'kwəfō'bē·ə/ [L, *aqua,* water; Gk, *phobos,* fear], an irrational fear of water.

aquaporin /ak'wah-po'rin/, any of a family of proteins found in plasma membranes and forming a functional component of water channels.

aquapuncture /-pungk'chər/ [L, *aqua,* water, *punctura,* puncture], the injection of water under the skin or spraying of a fine jet of water onto the skin surface to relieve a mild irritation.

aquathermia pad /-thur'mē·ə/, a waterproof plastic or rubber pad that can be applied to areas of muscle sprain, edema, or mild inflammation. The pad contains channels through which heated or cooled water flows. The device is connected by hoses to a bedside control unit that contains a temperature regulator, a motor for circulating the water, and a reservoir of distilled water.

aqueduct /-dukt/ [L, *aqua,* water, *ductus,* act of leading], any canal, channel, or passage through or between body parts.

aqueous /ā'kwē·əs, ak'wē·əs/ [L, *aqua*], **1.** watery or water-like. **2.** a medication prepared with water. **3.** a solution containing water.

aqueous chamber [L, *aqua,* water; Gk, *kamara,* something with an arched cover], either the anterior and posterior chambers of the eye. The aqueous chambers contain the aqueous humor.

aqueous extract, a water-based preparation of a plant or an animal substance containing the biologically active part without the cellular residue.

aqueous humor, the clear, watery fluid circulating in the anterior and posterior chambers of the eye. It is produced by the ciliary body and is reabsorbed into the venous system primarily at the iridocorneal angle by means of the canal of Schlemm.

aqueous phase, a fluid stage of a substance that is based on water in a liquid state, such as a solution of a substance in water.

aqueous solution [L, *aqua,* water, *solutus,* dissolved], a homogenous liquid preparation of any substance dissolved in water.

Ar, 1. symbol for the element **argon. 2.** abbreviation for an aromatic group such as phenyl.

AR, abbreviation for *assisted respiration.*

arachidonic acid /ar'əkidon'ik/ [L, *arachos,* a legume], a long-chain polyunsaturated fatty acid that is a component of lecithin and serves as a starting material in the biosynthesis of prostaglandins and leukotrienes. In mammals, arachidonic acid is synthesized from linoleic acid.

arachnid [Gk, *arachne,* spider], a member of the phylum Arthropoda, class Arachnida, which includes spiders, scorpions, mites, and ticks.

arachnitis /ar'əknī'tis/, an inflammation of the arachnoid membrane.

arachnodactyly /ərak'nōdak'tilē/ [Gk, *arachne,* spider, *dactylos,* finger], a congenital anomaly in which the fingers and toes are long, thin, and spider-like. It is seen in Marfan's syndrome.

arachnoid /ərak'noid/ [Gk, *arachne,* spider, *eidos,* form], resembling a cobweb or spiderweb, such as the arachnoid membrane.—**arachnoidal,** *adj.*

arachnoid cyst, a fluid-filled cyst between the layers of the leptomeninges, lined with arachnoid membrane, most commonly occurring in the sylvian fissure.

arachnoid granulations, clumps of arachnoid villi that project into the superior sagittal sinus.

arachnoidism /ərak'noidiz'əm/ [Gk, *arachne,* spider, *eidos,* form], the condition produced by the bite of a venomous spider.

arachnoid membrane, a thin, delicate membrane enclosing the brain and the spinal cord, interposed between the pia mater and the dura mater.

arachnoid trabeculae, fine filaments that pass from the arachnoid to the pia mater. They are embryologic remnants.

arachnoid villi U.S., *pl.* [Gk, *arachne,* spider, *villus,* shaggy hair], one of the many projections of fibrous tissue from the arachnoid membrane.

arachnophobia /ərak'nōfō'bē·ə/, a morbid fear of spiders.

Aramine, a trademark for a mixed-adrenergic agonist (metaraminol bitartrate).

Aran-Duchenne muscular atrophy /aran' dooshen'/ [François A. Aran, French physician, 1817–1861; Guillaume B.A. Duchenne, French neurologist, 1806–1875], a form of amyotrophic lateral sclerosis affecting the hands, arms, shoulders, and legs at the onset before becoming more generalized.

arbitrary inference /är'bitrer'ē in'fərəns/, a form of cognitive distortion in which a judgement based on insufficient evidence leads to an erroneous conclusion.

arbitrator /är'bətrā'tər/ [L, *arbiter,* umpire], an impartial person appointed to resolve a dispute between parties. —**arbitration,** *n.*

arbovirus /är'bōvī'rəs/, any one of more than 300 viruses transmitted by the saliva of insects. Vertebrate infection occurs when a contaminated arthropod takes a blood meal. Vaccines have been developed to prevent infection from some arboviruses. —**arboviral,** *adj.*

arbutamine /ahr-bu'tah-mēn'/, a synthetic catecholamine used as a diagnostic aid in cardiac stress testing in patients unable to exercise sufficiently for the test. It is administered as the hydrochloride salt.

arc [L, *arcus,* bow], a part of the circumference of a circle.

ARC, abbreviation for **AIDS-related complex.**

arcade [L, *arcus,* bow], an arch or series of arches.

arch, any anatomic structure that is curved or has a bowlike appearance.

arch bar, any one of various types of wires, bars, or splints that conform to the arch of the teeth and are used in the treatment of fractures of the jaws and their supporting structures and in the stabilization of injured teeth.

archenteron /arken'təron/ *pl.* **archentera** [Gk, *arche,* beginning, *enteron,* intestine], the primitive digestive cavity formed by the invagination into the gastrula, which is lined with entoderm during the embryonic development of many animals. —**archenteric,** *adj.*

arches of the foot [L, *arcus,* bow; AS, *fot*], the bony curves of the instep, including the longitudinal (anteroposterior) and the transverse arches.

archetype /är'kətīp'/ [Gk, *arche* + *typos,* type], **1.** an original model or pattern from which a thing or group of things is made or evolves. **2.** (in analytic psychology) an inherited primordial idea or mode of thought derived from the experiences of the human race and present in the subconscious of the individual in the form of drives, moods, and concepts. —**archetypal, archetypic,** *adj.*

archiblastoma /är'kiblastō'mə/ *pl.* **archiblastomas, archiblastomata** [Gk, *arche* + *blastos,* germ, *oma*], a tumor composed of cells derived from the layer of tissue surrounding the germinal vesicle.

architectural barrier /är'kətek'chərəl/, any architectural feature of a home or a public building that limit access and mobility of disabled persons.

architecture /är'kitek'chər/ [Gk, *architekton,* master builder]

architis /ärkī'tis/ [Gk, *archos,* anus, *itis,* inflammation], an inflammation of the anus.

arch length /ärch/, the distance from the distal point of the most posterior tooth on one side of the upper or lower jaw to the same point on the other side, usually measured through the points of contact between adjoining teeth.

arch length deficiency, the difference in any dental arch between the length required to accommodate all the natural teeth and the actual length.

arch of the aorta, the proximal one of the four portions of the aorta, giving rise to three arterial branches called the innominate (brachiocephalic), left common carotid, and left subclavian arteries.

arch width, the distance between the left and right opposite in the upper or lower jaw, usually expressed in millimeters. The intercanine, interpremolar, or intermolar distance may be cited as the arch width.

arch wire, an orthodontic wire fastened to two or more teeth through fixed attachments, used to cause or guide tooth movement.

arcing spring contraceptive diaphragm /är′king/, a kind of contraceptive diaphragm in which the flexible metal spring that forms the rim is a combination of a flexible coil spring and a flat band spring made of stainless steel. This kind of diaphragm is prescribed for a woman whose vaginal musculature is relaxed and does not afford strong support, as in first-degree cystocele, rectocele, or uterine prolapse.

ARC-ST, abbreviation for **Accreditation Review Committee on Education in Surgical Technology.**

arcuate /är′kyoo-at/ [L, *arcuatus,* bowed], an arch or bow shape.

arcuate artery of the foot, a branch of the dorsalis pedis artery.

arcuate ligament of the diaphragm, one of the three arc-shaped ligaments of the diaphragm that attach to the vertebral column.

arcuate scotoma [L, *arcuatus,* bowed; Gk, *skotoma,* darkness], an arc-shaped blind area that may develop in the field of vision of a person with glaucoma. It is caused by damage to nerve fibers in the retina.

arcus senilis /senē′lis/ [L, bow, aged], an opaque ring, gray to white in color, that surrounds the periphery of the cornea. It is caused by deposits of cholesterol in the cornea or hyaline degeneration and occurs primarily in older persons.

ardeparin, an anticoagulant used to prevent deep vein thrombosis after knee replacement surgery.

ARDS, abbreviation for **adult respiratory distress syndrome.**

area /er′ē-ə/ [L, space], (in anatomy) a limited anatomic space that contains a specific structure of the body or within which certain physiologic functions predominate, such as the aortic area and the association areas of the cerebral cortex.

area restriction, a nursing intervention from the Nursing Interventions Classification (NIC) defined as use of least restrictive limitation of patient mobility to a specified area for purposes of safety or behavior management.

areata /erē-ā′tə/, occurring in patches or circumscribed areas, such as hair loss in alopecia areata.

area under the concentration curve (AUC), a method of measurement of the bioavailability of a drug based on a plot of blood concentrations sampled at frequent intervals. It is directly proportional to the total amount of unaltered drug in the patient's blood.

areflexia /ā′rēflek′sē-ə/, the absence of the reflexes.

Arenavirus /er′inəvi′rəs/, a genus of viruses usually transmitted to humans by contact with or inhalation of aerosolized excreta of wild rodents. Individual arenaviruses are identified with specific geographic areas. Arenavirus infections are characterized by slow onset, fever, muscle pain, rash, petechiae, hemorrhage, delirium, hypotension, and ulcers of the mouth.

areola pl. **areolae** /erē′ōlə/, **1.** a small space or a cavity within a tissue. **2.** a circular area of a different color surrounding a central feature, such as the discoloration about a pustule or vesicle. **3.** the part of the iris around the pupil.

areola of breast, the pigmented, circular area surrounding the nipple of each breast.

areolar /erē′ələr/ [L, *areola,* little space], pertaining to an areola.

areolar gland, one of the large modified sebaceous glands in the areolae encircling the nipples of the breasts of women. The areolar glands secrete a lipoid fluid that lubricates and protects the nipple during nursing and contain smooth muscle bundles that cause the nipples to become erect when stimulated.

areolar tissue, a kind of connective tissue having little tensile strength and consisting of loosely woven fibers and areolae. It occupies the interspaces of the body.

areolitis /er′ē-əli′tis/, an inflammation of the areolae of the breasts.

ARF, **1.** abbreviation for **acute respiratory failure.** **2.** abbreviation for **acute renal failure.**

arformoterol, a long-acting adrenergic beta₂-agonist, sympathomimetic, and bronchodilator used to treat COPD, including chronic bronchitis and emphysema.

Arg, abbreviation for the amino acid **arginine.**

argatroban /ahr-gat′ro-ban′/, an anticoagulant that binds to the thrombin active site and inhibits various thrombin-catalyzed reactions. It is used in the prophylaxis and treatment of thrombocytopenia resulting from treatment with heparin.

argentaffin cell /är′jentaf′in/ [L, *argentum,* gleaming, *affinitas,* affinity], a cell containing granules that stain readily with silver and chromium. Such cells occur in most regions of the GI tract and are especially abundant in the crypts of Lieberkühn.

argentaffinoma pl. **argentaffinomas, argentaffinomata** /är′jentaf′inō′mə/, a tumor that secretes large amounts of the hormone serotonin. It usually arises in the GI tract anywhere between the stomach and rectum and can metastasize to the liver.

Argentine hemorrhagic fever, an acute febrile viral illness caused by an arenavirus transmitted to humans by contact with or inhalation of aerosolized excreta of infected rodents. Initially, it is characterized by chills, fever, headache, myalgia, anorexia, nausea, vomiting, and a general feeling of malaise. As the disease progresses, the victim may develop a high fever, dehydration, hypotension, flushed skin, abnormally slow heartbeat, bleeding from the gums and internal tissues, hematuria, and hematemesis. There may be involvement of the CNS, shock, and pulmonary edema.

arginase /är′jinās/, an enzyme that catalyzes the hydrolysis of arginine during the urea cycle, producing urea and ornithine.

arginase deficiency, an autosomal-recessive aminoacidopathy involving the biosynthesis of urea. Clinical signs include psychomotor retardation, hepatomegaly, and scalp discoloration.

arginine (Arg) /är′jinin/, an amino acid formed during the urea cycle by the transfer of a nitrogen atom from aspartate to citrulline.

argininemia /är′jininē′mē·ə/, arginase deficiency.

arginine vasopressin, vasopressin containing arginine, as that from humans and most other mammals.

argininosuccinic acidemia /ärjin′ino′suksin ′ik/, an inherited amino acid metabolism disorder in which the lack of an enzyme, argininosuccinase, results in an excess of argininosuccinic acid in the blood. The condition is characterized by seizures and mental retardation.

argon (Ar) /är′gon/ [Gk, argos, inactive], a colorless, odorless, chemically inactive gas, making up approximately 1% of the atmosphere. Its atomic mass is 39.95; its atomic number is 18. It forms no known compounds.

Argyll Robertson pupil [Douglas M.C.L. Argyll Robertson, Scottish ophthalmologist, 1837–1909], a pupil that constricts on accommodation but not in response to light. It is most often seen with miosis and in advanced neurosyphilis.

argyria /ärjī′rē·ə/ [Gk, argyros, silver], a permanent dull blue or gray to bronze discoloration of the skin, conjunctiva, and internal organs caused by excessive oral intake of silver salts.

argyrophil /ärjī′rəfil/ [Gk, argyros, silver, philein, to love], a cell or other object that is easily stained or impregnated with silver.

ariboflavinosis /ārī′bōflā′vinō′sis/ [Gk, a, not, ribose; L, flavus, yellow; Gk, osis], a condition caused by deficiency of riboflavin (vitamin B_2) in the diet. It is characterized by bilateral lesions at the corners of the mouth, on the lips, and around the nose and eyes; by seborrheic dermatitis; and by various visual disorders.

Arica therapy, an alternative mental health treatment introduced by Oscar Ichazo that focuses on altered states of consciousness with a goal of increasing the powers of the mind.

aril, a botanical term used to denote an accessory seed coating that may form a fleshy, cuplike structure around the immature seed (ovule), as in yew and nutmeg. The aril is often brightly colored and edible.

Arimidex, a trademark for an aromatase inhibitor (anastrozole) used for treating estrogen-receptor-positive breast cancer, primarily in postmenopausal women.

aripiprazole, an antipsychotic agent used to treat schizophrenia.

Aristocort, a trademark for a glucocorticoid (triamcinolone).

Arkansas stone /är′kənsô/, a fine-grained stone of novaculite used to sharpen surgical instruments.

Arlidin, a trademark for a beta-adrenergic agonist peripheral vasodilator (nylidrin hydrochloride).

arm [L, armus], **1.** the portion of the upper limb of the body between the shoulder and the elbow. **2.** nontechnical. the arm and the forearm.

ARM, abbreviation for artificial rupture of (fetal) membranes.

armamentarium /är′məmenter′ē·əm/ [L, armamentum, implement], the total therapeutic assets of a physician or medical facility, including medicines and equipment.

arm board, 1. a board used to position the affected arm of a person with hemiplegia and of others with arm disabilities. It fastens to the armrest of a wheelchair, supporting the flaccid arm in the correct position to prevent or decrease subluxation of the shoulder joint, and to prevent edema. **2.** a board used to keep the arm still to permit the drawing of blood or starting of an IV needle.

arm cylinder cast, an orthopedic device of plaster of paris or fiberglass, used for immobilizing the upper limb from the wrist to the upper arm.

Army Nurse Corps (ANC), a branch of the U.S. Army, founded February 2, 1901, with headquarters in Falls Church, Virginia.

Arneth's classification of neutrophils
[Joseph Arneth, German physician, 1873–1953], a system for classifying neutrophils no longer used in the United States.

Arnold-Chiari malformation /är'nəld kē·är'ē/ [Julius Arnold, German pathologist, 1835–1915; Hans Chiari, French pathologist, 1851–1916], a congenital herniation of the brainstem and lower cerebellum through the foramen magnum into the cervical vertebral canal.

Arnold, Friedrich [German anatomist, 1803–1890], an investigator of structures and functions of the brain and nervous system, including the nerve center of the cough reflex.

-arol,

AROM, 1. abbreviation for **active range of motion.** 2. abbreviation for *artificial rupture of (fetal) membranes.*

aroma [Gk, spice], any agreeable odor or pleasing fragrance, especially of food, drink, spices, or medication.

aromatase /ah-ro'mah-tās/, an enzyme activity occurring in the endoplasmic reticulum and catalyzing the conversion of testosterone to the aromatic compound estradiol.

aromatase inhibitors, a class of drugs that inhibit aromatase activity and thus block production of estrogens. They are used to treat breast cancer and endometriosis.

aromatherapy[1], a form of herbal medicine that uses various oils from plants. The route of administration can be absorption through the skin or through inhalation.

aromatherapy[2], a nursing intervention from the Nursing Interventions Classification (NIC) defined as administration of essential oils through massage, topical ointments or lotions, baths, inhalation, douches, or compresses (hot or cold) to calm and soothe, provide pain relief, or enhance relaxation and comfort.

aromatic /er'ōmat'ik/ [Gk, *aroma,* spice], 1. pertaining to a strong but agreeable odor such as a pleasant spicy odor. 2. a stimulant or spicy medicine. 3. pertaining to organic chemical structures including 6-carbon rings such as benzol.

aromatic alcohol, a fatty alcohol in which one or more of the hydrogen atoms of the hydrocarbon portion of the alcohol is replaced by an aromatic ring.

aromatic ammonia spirit [Gk, *aroma,* Ammon temple, ancient source of ammonium chloride salt, *spiritus,* breath], a strongly fragrant solution of ammonium carbonate in dilute liquid ammonia, oils, alcohol, and water. It is used as a reflex stimulus, an antacid, and a carminative to relieve flatulence.

aromatic bath, a medicated bath in which aromatic substances or essential oils are added to the water.

aromatic compounds, organic compounds that contain a benzene, naphthalene, or analogous ring. Many of these compounds have agreeable odors.

aromatic elixir [Gk, *aroma*; Ar, *al-iksir,* philosophers' stone], a pleasant-smelling flavor agent added to some medications.

aromatic hydrocarbon [Gk, *aroma,* spice; *hydor,* water; L, *carbo,* coal], an organic compound that has a benzene or other aromatic ring, as distinguished from an open-chain aliphatic compound.

arousal, a state of responsiveness to sensory stimulation.

arousal level, the state of sensory stimulation needed to induce active wakefulness in a sleeping infant. Arousal levels range from deep sleep to a drowsy state.

ARPKD, autosomal-recessive polycystic kidney disease.

Arranon, a trademark for nelarabine.

array [ME, *aray,* preparation], an arrangement or order of components or other objects, usually according to a predetermined system or plan.

arrector pili *pl.* **arrectores pilorum** /ä·rek'tor pīʹlī/ [L, raisers of the hair], minute smooth muscles of the skin, attached to the connective tissue sheath of the hair follicles. When they contract, they cause the hair to stand erect.

arrest [L, *ad + restare,* to withstand], to inhibit, restrain, or stop, as to arrest the course of a disease.

arrested dental caries, tooth decay in which the area of decay has stopped progressing and infection is not present but in which the demineralized area in the tooth remains as a cavity.

arrested development, the cessation of one or more phases of the developmental process in utero before normal completion, resulting in congenital anomalies.

arrested labor [L, *ad + restare,* to withstand, *labor,* work], an interruption in the labor process that is associated with uterine contractions.

arrhenoblastoma /erē'nōblastō'mə/ [Gk, *arrhen,* male, *blastos,* germ, *oma,* tumor], an ovarian neoplasm whose cells mimic those in testicular tubules and secrete male sex hormone, causing virilization in females

arrhenogenic /erē'nōjen'ik/, producing only male offspring.

arrhenokaryon /erē'nōker'ē·on/ [Gk, *arrhen,* male, *karyon,* nucleus], an organism that is produced from an egg that has only paternal chromosomes.

arrhythmia /ərith′mē·ə/ [Gk, *a* + *rhythmos*, without rhythm], any deviation from the normal pattern of the heartbeat. —**arrhythmic, arrhythmical,** *adj.*

arrhythmic [Gk, *a* + *rhythmos,* without rhythm], pertaining to an absence or irregularity of normal rhythm in the heart's beating.

ARRT, abbreviation for **American Registry of Radiologic Technologists.**

arsenic (As) /är′sənik/ [Gk, *arsen,* strong], an element that occurs throughout the earth's crust in metal arsenides, arsenious sulfides, and arsenious oxides. Its atomic number is 33; its atomic mass is 74.92. This element has been used for centuries as a therapeutic agent and as a poison and continues to have limited use in some trypanosomicidal drugs such as melarsoprol and tryparsamide. Most arsenics are slowly excreted in the urine and feces, which accounts for the toxicity of the element.—**arsenic** /ärsen′ik/, *adj.*

arsenic poisoning, toxic effect caused by the ingestion or inhalation of arsenic or a substance containing arsenic, an ingredient in some pesticides, herbicides, dyes, and medicinal solutions. Small amounts absorbed over a period of time may result in chronic poisoning, producing nausea, headache, coloration and scaling of the skin, hyperkeratoses, anorexia, and white lines across the fingernails. Ingestion of large amounts of arsenic results in severe GI pain, diarrhea, vomiting, and swelling of the extremities.

arsenic stomatitis [Gk, *arsen,* strong; *stoma,* mouth, *itis,* inflammation], an abnormal oral condition associated with arsenic poisoning, characterized by dry, red, painful oral mucosa; ulceration; bleeding beneath the mucosa; and mobility of teeth.

arsenic trioxide, an oxidized form of arsenic, used in weed killers and rodenticides. It is also administered intravenously as an antineoplastic in the treatment of acute promyelocytic leukemia.

arsenism /ahr′sĕ-nizm/, chronic arsenic poisoning.

arsine /ahr′sēn/, any of several colorless, volatile arsenical bases that are highly toxic and carcinogenic. Some of these compounds have been used in warfare, and a major industrial use is in the production of microelectronic components. Inhalation leads to massive RBC hemolysis with secondary renal failure and jaundice.

ART, abbreviation for **active resistance training.**

Artane, a trademark for an anticholinergic (trihexyphenidyl hydrochloride).

arterectomy /är′tərek′təmē/, the surgical removal of a segment of an artery.

arterial (A) /ärtir′ē·əl/ [Gk, *arteria,* airpipe], pertaining to an artery.

arterial blood gas (ABG), the oxygen and carbon dioxide content of arterial blood, measured by various methods to assess the adequacy of ventilation and oxygenation and the acid-base status of the body.

arterial blood gases (ABG) test, blood test used to provide information that helps assess and manage a patient's respiratory (ventilation) and metabolic (renal) acid-base and electrolyte homeostasis, and to assess adequacy of oxygenation.

arterial blood pressure (ABP), the pressure of the blood in the arterial system, which depends on the heart's pumping pressure, the resistance of the arterial walls, elasticity of vessels, the blood volume, and its viscosity.

arterial capillaries, microscopic blood vessels (capillaries) extending beyond the terminal ends of arterioles.

arterial catheter [Gk, *arteria,* airpipe, *katheter,* a thing lowered into], a tubular instrument that can be inserted into an artery either to draw blood or to measure BP directly.

arterial circulation [Gk, *arteria*; L, *circulare,* to go around], the movement of blood through the arteries directed away from the heart to the tissues, as opposed to venous circulation away from the tissues to the heart.

arterial hemorrhage, the loss of blood from an artery, often associated with vessel trauma or the removal of a large-bore arterial catheter.

arterial insufficiency, inadequate blood flow in arteries. It may be caused by occlusive atherosclerotic plaques or emboli; damaged, diseased, or intrinsically weak vessels; arteriovenous fistulas; aneurysms; hypercoagulability states; or heavy use of tobacco.

arterial insufficiency of lower extremities, a condition characterized by hardening, thickening, and loss of elasticity of the walls of arteries in the legs. It causes decreased circulation, sensation, and function. Symptoms include sharp, cramping pain during exercise or rest at night; numbness; skin changes ranging from pallor to ulceration; thickened toenails; and loss of hair on the legs. Dorsalis pedis, posterior tibial, and popliteal pulses may be diminished or absent.

arterialized flap, a flap whose blood supply in the new site is maintained by a vein that is grafted to an artery.

arterial ligament, a small, nonfunctional ligament attached to the superior surface of the pulmonary trunk and the inferior surface of the aortic arch. It is a vestige of the ductus arteriosus.

arterial line (A-line, Art-line), an arterial blood monitoring system consisting of a catheter inserted into an artery and connected to pressure tubing, a transducer, and a monitor. The device permits continuous direct BP readings as well as access to the arterial blood supply when samples are needed for analysis.

arterial murmur, a sound produced by blood moving through a narrowed artery.

arterial nephrosclerosis [Gk, *arteria*, airpipe, *nephros*, kidney, *sklera*, hard, *osis*, condition], patchy atrophic scarring of the kidneys caused by arteriosclerotic narrowing of the lumens of the large branches of the renal artery, occurring in elderly or hypertensive persons and occasionally causing hypertension.

arterial network [Gk, *arteria*; L, *rete*, net], an anastomotic network of small arteries at a point before they branch into arterioles and capillaries.

arterial palpitation [Gk, *arteria*, airpipe; L, *palpitare*, to flutter], a pulsation felt in an artery.

arterial pH, the hydrogen ion concentration of arterial blood. Normal range is 7.35 to 7.45.

arterial plethysmography, a manometric test that is usually performed to rule out occlusive disease of the lower extremities. It can also be used to identify arteriosclerotic disease in the upper extremity.

arterial port, the opening at the arterial end of a synthetic arteriovenous access device.

arterial pressure, the stress exerted by circulating blood on the artery walls. It is the product of the cardiac output and the systemic vascular resistance. Arterial pressure is commonly measured with a sphygmomanometer and a stethoscope. Stress, hypervolemia, hypovolemia, and various drugs may alter the arterial pressure.

arterial rete /rē′tē/ [Gk, *arteria*, airpipe; L, *rete*, net], a network of arteries and arterioles.

arterial sclerosis [Gk, *arteria*, airpipe, *sklerosis*, hardening], a thickening and hardening of the arteries caused by fibrosis or calcium deposition.

arterial thrill, a vibration that can be felt over an artery. It is usually associated with turbulent blood flow within the artery.

arterial wall, the fibrous and muscular wall of vessels that carry oxygenated blood from the heart to structures throughout the body, and of the pulmonary arteries that carry deoxygenated blood from the heart to the lungs.

arteria radicularis magna, artery of Adamkiewicz.

arteriectomy /ärtir′ē·ek′təmē/ [Gk, *arteria* + *ektomē*, excision], the surgical removal of a portion of an artery.

arteriocapillary /ärtir′ē·ōkap′ilar′ē/ [Gk, *arteria*; L, *capillaris*, hairlike], pertaining to the arteries and the capillaries.

arteriofibrosis /ärtir′ē·ōfībrō′sis/, an inflammatory, fibrous thickening of the walls of the arteries and arterioles, resulting in a narrowing of the lumen of the vessels.

arteriogenic impotence, vasculogenic impotence caused by a disorder in the arteries supplying the penis, such as atherosclerosis or stenosis.

arteriogram /ärtir′ē·əgram′/, an x-ray film of an artery injected with a radiopaque medium.

arteriography /ärtir′ē·og′rəfē/ [Gk, *arteria*, airpipe, *graphein*, to record], a method of radiologic visualization of arteries performed after a radiopaque contrast medium is introduced into the bloodstream or into a specific vessel by injection or through a catheter.—**arteriographic,** *adj.*

arteriole /ärtir′ē·ōl/ [L, *arteriola*, little artery], the smallest of the arteries. Blood flowing from the heart is pumped through the arteries, to the arterioles, to the capillaries, into the veins, and returned to the heart. The muscular walls of the arterioles constrict and dilate in response to both local factors and neurochemical stimuli; thus arterioles play a significant role in peripheral vascular resistance and in regulation of BP.—**arteriolar,** *adj.*

arteriolosclerosis /ärtir′ē·ō′ləskləro′sis/, pathologic thickening, hardening, and loss of elasticity of arteriolar walls.

arteriopathy /ärtir′ē·op′əthē/ [Gk, *arteria* + *pathos*, suffering], a disease of an artery.

arterioplasty /ärtir′ē·əplas′tē/ [Gk, *arteria* + *plassein*, to mold], surgical repair or reconstruction of an artery.

arteriosclerosis /ärtir′ē·ō′sklərō′sis/ [Gk, *arteria* + *sklerosis*, hardening], a common disorder characterized by thickening, loss of elasticity, and calcification of arterial walls. It results in a decreased blood supply, especially to the cerebrum and lower extremities.—**arteriosclerotic,** *adj.*

arteriosclerosis obliterans [Gk, *arteria* + *skleros* + L, *obliterare*, efface], a gradual narrowing of the arteries with thrombosis and degeneration of the intima. The condition may lead to complete occlusion of an artery and subsequent gangrene.

arteriosclerotic /-sklərot′ik/ [Gk, *arteria* + *skleros*, hard], pertaining to a thickening, hardening, and calcification of the arterial wall.

arteriosclerotic aneurysm, an aneurysm arising in a large artery, most commonly the abdominal aorta, as a result of weakening of the wall in severe atherosclerosis.

arteriosclerotic heart disease (ASHD), a thickening and hardening of the walls of the coronary arteries.

arteriosclerotic retinopathy [Gk, *arteria,* + airpipe, *sklerosis,* hardening; L, *rete,* net; Gk, *pathos,* disease], a disorder of the retina associated with hardening and thickening of the arteries supplying that part of the eye. It often accompanies hypertension.

arteriospasm /ärtir′ē·ōspaz′əm/ [Gk, *arteria* + *spasmos,* spasm], a spasm of an artery.

arteriostenosis /-stənō′sis/, a narrowing of an artery.

arteriotomy /ärtir′ē·ot′əmē/, a surgical incision in an artery.

arteriovenous (AV) /-vē′nəs/ [Gk, *arteria;* L, *vena,* vein], pertaining to arteries and veins.

arteriovenous anastomosis [Gk, *arteria;* L, *vena;* Gk, *anastomoein,* to form a mouth], a communication between an artery and a vein, either as a congenital anomaly or as a surgically produced link between vessels.

arteriovenous aneurysm, a dilation affecting both an artery and a vein, often as an abnormal linkage of the two.

arteriovenous angioma of the brain, a congenital tumor consisting of a tangle of coiled, usually dilated arteries and veins, islets of sclerosed brain tissue, and occasionally cartilaginous cells.

arteriovenous fistula, an abnormal communication between an artery and vein. It may occur congenitally or result from trauma, infection, arterial aneurysm, or a malignancy.

arteriovenous oxygen (a-vO2) difference, the arterial oxygen content minus the central venous oxygen content.

arteriovenous shunt (AV shunt), a passageway, artificial or natural, that allows blood to flow from an artery to a vein without going through a capillary network.

arteritis /är′tərī′tis/ [Gk, *arteria* + *itis*], inflammation of the inner layers or the outer coat of one or more arteries. It may occur as a clinical entity or accompany another disorder.

arteritis umbilicalis, septic inflammation of the umbilical artery in newborns, usually caused by the bacterium *Clostridium tetani.*

artery /är′tərē/ [Gk, *arteria,* airpipe], one of the large blood vessels carrying blood in a direction away from the heart.

artery forceps, any forceps used for grasping, compressing, and holding the end of an artery during ligation. Generally self-locking, its handles are scissorlike.

arthralgia /ärthral′jə/ [Gk, *arthron,* joint, *algos,* pain], joint pain.—**arthralgic,** *adj.*

arthritis /ärthrī′tis/ [Gk, *arthron,* joint, *itis*], any inflammatory condition of the joints, characterized by pain, swelling, heat, redness, and limitation of movement.

arthrocentesis /är′thrōsintē′sis/ [Gk, *arthron* + *kentesis,* pricking], the puncture of a joint with a needle and the withdrawal of fluid, performed to obtain samples of synovial fluid for diagnostic purposes. It may also be used to instill medications and to remove fluid from joints to simply relieve pain.

arthrogram /är′thrəgram/, **1.** a radiographic record after introduction of opaque contrast material into a joint. **2.** a nuclear medicine study used to detect the loosening of a prosthetic device.

arthrography [Gk, *arthron,* joint, *graphein,* to record], a method of radiographically visualizing the inside of a joint by using a radiolucent or radiopaque contrast medium.

arthrogryposis multiplex congenita [Gk, *arthron* + *gryposis,* joint curve; L, *multus,* many, *plica,* fold, *congenitus,* born with], fibrous stiffness of one or more joints, present at birth. It is often associated with incomplete development of the muscles that move the involved joints and degenerative changes of the motor neurons that innervate those muscles.

arthrokinematic /är′thrəkin′əmat′ik/, pertaining to the movement of bone surfaces within a joint.

arthron /är′thron/ [Gk], a joint or articulation, including its various components of bones, cartilaginous inserts, all soft tissue structures intervening between the rigid skeletal parts, and the adjacent muscular elements.

arthropathy /ärthrop′əthē/ [Gk, *arthron* + *pathos,* suffering], any disease or abnormal condition affecting a joint.—**arthropathic,** *adj.*

arthroplasty /är′thrəplast′ē/ [Gk, *arthron* + *plassein,* to mold], the surgical reconstruction or replacement of a painful, degenerated joint, to restore mobility in osteoarthritis or rheumatoid arthritis or to correct a congenital deformity.

arthropod /är′thrəpod′/ [Gk, *arthron* + *pous,* foot], a member of the Arthropoda, a large phylum of animal life that includes crabs and lobsters as well as mites, ticks, spiders, and insects.

arthroscope /-skōp'/ [Gk, *arthron* + *skopein,* to watch], a type of endoscope used to examine joints.

arthroscopic anterior cruciate ligament reconstruction, reconstruction of the anterior cruciate ligament, performed on individuals whose activities are compromised by instability of the knee and who have failed to respond to nonsurgical treatment options.

arthroscopy /ärthros'kəpē/ [Gk, *arthron* + *skopein,* to watch], the examination of the interior of a joint performed by inserting a specially designed endoscope through a small incision. The procedure, used chiefly in knee problems, permits biopsy of cartilage or synovium, diagnosis of a torn meniscus, and, in some instances, removal of loose bodies in the joint space. —**arthroscopic,** *adj.*

arthrous /är'thrəs/ [Gk, *arthron*], **1.** pertaining to joints or the articulation of bones. **2.** pertaining to a disease of a joint.

Arthus reaction /ärtoōs'/ [Nicholas M. Arthus, French physiologist, 1862–1945], a rare, severe, immediate nonatopic hypersensitivity reaction to the injection of a foreign substance, that usually is not irritating but in certain individuals is antigenic. The reaction is thought to involve the formation of an antigen-antibody complex that activates complement.

articular capsule [L, *articulare,* to divide into joints], an envelope of tissue that surrounds a freely moving joint, composed of an external layer of white fibrous tissue and an internal synovial membrane.

articular cartilage [L, *articulare* + *cartilago*], a type of hyaline connective tissue that covers the articulating surfaces of bones within synovial joints.

articular disk, 1. a small oval plate between the condyle of the mandible and the mandibular fossa. **2.** the platelike cartilaginous end of certain bones in movable joints, sometimes closely associated with surrounding muscles or with cartilage.

articular fracture, a fracture involving the articulating surfaces of a joint.

articular head, a projection on a bone that forms a joint with another bone.

articular muscle, a muscle that is attached to the capsule of a joint.

articular process of vertebra, a bony outgrowth on a vertebra that forms a joint with an adjoining vertebra.

articulate /ärtik'yəlāt/ [L, *articulare,* to divide into joints], **1.** to form a joint. **2.** to configure the supraglottal airway to produce consonants and vowels, resulting in speech that is distinct and connected.— **articular,** *adj,* **articulation,** *n.*

articulated /ärtik'yəlā'ted/, united by a movable joint.

articulation, the process by which the supraglottal airway is shaped to form consonants and vowels into meaningful, understandable speech.

articulation of the pelvis /ärtik'yə-lā'shən/, any one of the connections between the bones of the pelvis, involving four groups of ligaments. The first group connects the sacrum and the ilium; the second, the sacrum and the ischium; the third, the sacrum and the coccyx; and the fourth, the two pubic bones.

articulator /ärtik'yəlā'tər/ [L, *articulare,* to divide into joints], a mechanical device used in the fabrication and testing of dental prostheses. It stimulates the TMJs and jaw members to which maxillary and mandibular casts may be attached.

artifact /är'təfakt/ [L, *ars,* skill, *facere,* to make], anything artificially made. It may be extraneous, irrelevant, or unwanted, such as a substance, structure, or piece of data or information. In radiologic imaging, spurious electronic signals may appear as an artifact in an image, thereby confusing the radiologist and the results of any examination.

artifactual modification /är'təfak'choo ·əl/, a change in protein structure caused by in vitro manipulation.

artificial /är'tifish'əl/ [L, *artificium,* not natural], **1.** made by human work as a substitute for something that is natural. **2.** simulated, resulting from art in imitation of nature.

artificial abortion, an abortion that is produced deliberately.

artificial airway [L, *artificiosum,* skillfully made], a plastic or rubber device that can be inserted into the upper or lower respiratory tract to facilitate ventilation or the removal of secretions.

artificial airway management, a nursing intervention from the Nursing Interventions Classification (NIC) defined as maintenance of endotracheal and tracheostomy tubes and prevention of complications associated with their use.

artificial ankylosis, a surgical procedure in which two or more parts of a joint are fixed so that the joint becomes immovable.

artificial anus, a surgical opening into the bowel, as in a colostomy.

artificial assists, any prosthetic devices or contrivances that may enable a physically challenged person to function. Examples include heart pacemakers, crutches, and artificial limbs.

artificial crown, a dental prosthesis that restores part or all of the crown of a natural tooth.

artificial eye, a prosthetic device resembling the anterior surface of a normal eyeball. It is fitted under the upper and lower eyelids of an eye that has been removed.

artificial genitourinary sphincter, an implantable prosthetic device for treating urinary incontinence caused by an incompetent or absent sphincter. An artificial sphincter is created with an inflatable cuff around the bladder neck or bulbar urethra.

artificial heart, a mechanical device of molded polyurethane, consisting of two ventricles implanted in the body and powered by an air compressor located outside the body.

artificial insemination (AI), the introduction of semen into the vagina or uterus by mechanical or instrumental means rather than by sexual intercourse. The procedure is planned to coincide with the expected time of ovulation so that fertilization can occur.

artificial insemination—donor (AID), artificial insemination in which the semen specimen is provided by an anonymous donor. The procedure is used primarily in cases where the husband is sterile.

artificial insemination—husband (AIH), artificial insemination in which the semen specimen is provided by the husband. The procedure is used primarily in cases of impotency, low sperm count, or a vaginal disorder or when the husband is incapable of sexual intercourse because of some physical disability.

artificial intelligence (AI), a system that makes it possible for a machine to perform functions similar to those performed by human intelligence, such as learning, reasoning, self-correcting, and adapting.

artificial kidney, a device used to remove the body waste, commonly excreted in urine, from circulating blood. It usually consists of a set of tubes or catheters that pass the blood through a dialysate solution where wastes are removed by osmosis and diffusion.

artificial labor [L, *artificiosum,* artificial, *labor,* work], induced labor, as when started with drugs or mechanical devices.

artificial menopause [L, *artificiosus,* artificial, *men,* month; Gk, *pauein,* to cease], the termination of menstrual periods by surgery, radiation, or other methods.

artificial saliva [L, *artificiosum,* artifice, *saliva,* spittle], a mixture of carboxymethylcellulose, sorbitol, sodium, and potassium chloride in an aqueous solution. It is available in a spray container for the treatment of xerostomia.

artificial selection, the process by which the genotypes of successive plant and animal generations are determined through controlled breeding.

artificial tears, a pharmaceutical preparation of various polymers that can be instilled in the eyes of patients suffering from dry eye or keratoconjunctivitis sicca.

artificial ventilation, the process of supporting respiration by manual or mechanical means when normal breathing is inefficient or has stopped. If artificial ventilation is unsuccessful, the patient is repositioned and the airway is tested for the presence of an obstruction.

art therapist, a human service professional who uses art media and images, the creative process, and client responses to artwork in order to assess, treat, and rehabilitate patients with mental, emotional, physical, or developmental disorders.

art therapy[1], the use of art media to reconcile emotional conflicts, foster self-awareness, and express unspoken and frequently unconscious concerns. Art therapy is often used when traditional forms of verbal psychotherapy have failed or been rejected by an individual and when individuals have difficulty expressing feelings or use verbalization as a defense mechanism.

art therapy[2], a nursing intervention from the Nursing Interventions Classification (NIC) defined as facilitation of communication through drawings or other art forms.

aryepiglottic fold /er′ē·ep′iglot′ik/, a mucosal fold on each of the lateral borders of the larynx. Together the folds enclose the superior margins of the quadrangular membranes and adjacent soft tissues. They function as a sphincter during swallowing.

aryl hydrocarbon hydroxylase (AHH), an enzyme that converts carcinogenic chemicals in tobacco smoke and in polluted air into active carcinogens within the lungs.

arytenoid cartilage /ärit′ənoid kär′tiləj/ [Gk, *arytaina,* ladle + *eidos,* form; L, *cartilago*], one of the paired, pitcher-shaped cartilages of the back of the larynx at the upper border of the cricoid cartilage with attachments to the vocal chords.

As, symbol for the element **arsenic.**

AS, abbreviation for **aortic stenosis.**

a.s., abbreviation for **auris sinistra.**

5-ASA, 5-aminosalicylic acid.

ASA, 1. abbreviation for *American Society of Anesthesiologists.* **2.** abbreviation for **aspirin** (acetylsalicylic acid). **3.** abbreviation for **antisperm antibody.**

ASAHP, 1. abbreviation for *American Society of Allied Health Professionals.*

2. abbreviation for *Association of Schools of Allied Health Professionals.*

ASAP, abbreviation for *as soon as possible.*

asbestos /asbes′təs/ [Gk, *asbestos,* unquenchable], a group of fibrous impure magnesium silicate minerals. Inhalation of the fibers can lead to pulmonary fibrosis if the fibers accumulate in terminal bronchioles. Continued exposure to asbestos fibers can result in lung cancer.

asbestos body, a structure found in the lungs of patients with asbestosis, consisting of an asbestos fiber engulfed by a macrophage or of a mass of asbestos spicules coated with calcium, iron salts, and other substances.

asbestosis [Gk, *asbestos,* inextinguishable, *osis,* condition], a chronic lung disease caused by the inhalation of asbestos fibers that results in the development of alveolar, interstitial, and pleural fibrosis.

ASC, abbreviation for **altered state of consciousness.**

ascariasis /as′kərī′əsis/ [Gk, *askaris,* intestinal worm, *osis,* condition], the most common parasitic infection in the world, caused by a parasitic worm, *Ascaris lumbricoides,* that migrates through the lungs in its larval stage. The eggs are passed in human feces, contaminating the soil and allowing transmission to the mouths of others through hands, water, or food. After hatching in the small intestine, the larvae travel through the wall of the intestine and are carried by the lymphatics and blood to the lungs. Early respiratory symptoms of coughing, wheezing, hemoptysis, and fever are caused by the passage through the respiratory tract. The larvae are swallowed; they mature in the jejunum, where they release eggs; and the cycle is repeated. Intestinal infection may result in abdominal cramps and obstruction.

Ascaris /as′kəris/, a genus of nematode worms; large parasitic intestinal roundworms found throughout temperate and tropic regions.

ascaris, a nematode of the genus *Ascaris.*

ascending aorta /asen′ding/ [L, *ascendere,* to climb], one of the four main sections of the aorta, branching into the right and left coronary arteries.

ascending colon, the segment of the colon that extends up the cecum in the lower right side of the colic fissure to the abdomen to the transverse colon at the hepatic flexure on the right side.

ascending neuritis [L, *ascendere,* to rise; Gk, *neuron,* nerve, *itis,* inflammation], a nerve inflammation that begins on the periphery and moves upward along a nerve trunk.

ascending neuropathy, a disease of the nervous system that begins at a lower place in the body and spreads upward.

ascending paralysis, a condition in which there is successive flaccid paralysis of the legs, then the trunk and arms, and finally the muscles of respiration. Causes include poliomyelitis, Guillain-Barré syndrome, and exposure to toxic chemicals.

ascending pharyngeal artery, one of the smallest arteries that branch from the external carotid artery, deep in the neck. It supplies various organs and muscles of the head.

ascending poliomyelitis [L, *ascendere,* to rise; Gk, *polios,* gray, *myelos,* marrow, *itis,* inflammation], poliomyelitis that begins in the legs and spreads upward to involve the trunk and respiratory muscles.

ascending pyelonephritis, pyelonephritis caused by a UTI that has spread up the ureter into the kidney.

ascending testis, a previously documented scrotal testicle that later ascends into an extrascrotal position.

asceticism /aset′isiz′əm/ [Gk, *askein,* to exercise], (in psychiatry) a defense mechanism that involves repudiation of all instinctual impulses.

Ascher's syndrome /äsh′ərz/ [Karl Wolfgang Ascher, Czech-born American ophthalmologist, 1887–1971], relaxation of the skin of the eyelid and redundancy of the mucous membrane and submucous tissue of the upper lip in goiter.

Aschoff bodies [Karl A.L. Aschoff, German pathologist, 1866–1942; AS, *bodig*], tiny rounded or spindle-shaped nodules containing multinucleated giant cells, fibroblasts, and basophilic cells. They are found in joints, tendons, the pleura, and the cardiovascular system of rheumatic fever patients.

ascites /əsī′tēz/ [Gk, *askos,* bag], an abnormal intraperitoneal accumulation of a fluid containing large amounts of protein and electrolytes. The condition may be accompanied by general abdominal swelling, hemodilution, edema, or a decrease in urinary output. Ascites is a complication of cirrhosis, CHF, nephrosis, malignant neoplastic disease, peritonitis, or various fungal and parasitic diseases.—**ascitic,** *adj.*

ascites praecox /prē′koks/ [Gk, *askos*; L, premature], an abnormal accumulation of fluid within the peritoneal cavity before the generalized edema associated with pericarditis.

ascitic fluid /əsit′ik/ [Gk, *askos,* bag], a watery fluid containing albumin, glucose, and electrolytes that accumulates in the peritoneal cavity in association with certain diseases, such as liver disease or CHF. The fluid occurs as leakage from the veins and lymphatics into extravascular spaces.

ASCO, abbreviation for *American Society of Clinical Oncology.*

ascorbemia /as'kôrbē'mē·ə/ [Gk, *a,* not; AS, *scurf,* scurvy; Gk, *haima,* blood], the presence of ascorbic acid in the blood in amounts greater than normal, usually reflecting only an excess of ascorbic acid (vitamin C) intake.

ascorbic acid /əskôr'bik/ [Gk, *a,* not; AS, *scurf,* scurvy], a water-soluble, white crystalline vitamin present in citrus fruits, tomatoes, berries, potatoes, and fresh green and leafy vegetables. It is essential for the formation of collagen and fibrous tissue for normal intercellular matrices in teeth, bone, cartilage, connective tissue, and skin, and for the structural integrity of capillary walls. It also aids in fighting bacterial infections and interacts with other nutrients.

ascorburia /as'kôrbyŏŏr'ē·ə/ [Gk, *a,* not; AS, *scurf,* scurvy; Gk, *ouron,* urine], the presence of ascorbic acid in the urine in amounts greater than normal. It usually reflects only an excess ascorbic acid intake.

ascribed role /əskrībd'/, an assigned role in society, based on age, sex, or other factors about which the individual has no choice.

ASD, abbreviation for **atrial septal defect.**

Asendin, a trademark for a tricyclic antidepressant (amoxapine).

asepsis /āsep'sis/ [Gk, *a* + *sepsis,* not decay], **1.** the absence of germs. **2.** medical asepsis, procedures used to reduce the number of microorganisms and prevent their spread. **3.** surgical asepsis, procedures used to eliminate any microorganisms; sterile technique.—**aseptic,** *adj.*

aseptic-antiseptic, both aseptic and antiseptic.

aseptic body image, an awareness by OR personnel of body, hair, makeup, clothing, jewelry, and placement with regard for maintenance of a sterile environment. The body image also includes an awareness of changing proximities between sterile and contaminated areas as a field becomes progressively contaminated.

aseptic bone necrosis, a type of bone and joint damage that may occur in people who repeatedly breathe compressed air, as in diving or tunneling occupations. It may also occur in patients taking corticosteroids or be associated with an injury to a joint. The condition may be asymptomatic or, if joint surfaces are involved, marked by severe pain and joint collapse.

aseptic fever, a fever not associated with infection. Mechanical trauma, as in a crushing injury, can cause fever even when no pathogenic microorganism is present.

aseptic gauze, any gauze that is free of microorganisms.

aseptic meningitis, an inflammation of the meninges that is caused by one of a number of viruses or that may be drug induced, such as with high-dose IV immunoglobulin.

aseptic necrosis [Gk, *a* + *sepsis,* without decay, *nekros,* dead, *osis,* condition], **1.** cystic and sclerotic degenerative changes in tissues, as may follow an injury in the absence of infection. **2.** a condition in which poor blood supply to an area of bone leads to bone death.

aseptic peritonitis [Gk, *a* + *sepsis,* without decay, *peri,* near, *teinein,* to stretch, *itis,* inflammation], peritonitis in which inflammation of the peritoneum is caused by chemicals, radiation, or injury, rather than by an infectious agent.

aseptic surgery [Gk, *a* + *sepsis,* without decay, *cheirourgos,* surgeon], the prevention of contamination during surgical procedures.

aseptic technique, any health care procedure in which added precautions, such as use of sterile gloves and instruments, are used to prevent contamination of a person, object, or area by microorganisms.

Asepto syringe, a trademark for a large bulb-fitted, blunt-tipped syringe used primarily for irrigating wounds.

asexual /āsek'shŏŏ·əl/ [Gk, *a,* not; L, *sexus,* male or female], **1.** not sexual. **2.** pertaining to an organism that has no sexual organs. **3.** pertaining to a process that is not sexual.—**asexuality,** *n.*

asexual dwarf, an adult dwarf whose genital organs are underdeveloped.

asexualization /āsek'shŏŏ·əlizā'shən/, the process of making one incapable of reproduction; sterilization of an individual or animal by castration, vasectomy, removal of the ovaries, or use of chemicals.

asexual reproduction, any type of reproduction that occurs without the union of male and female gametes, such as fission, budding, sporulation, or parthenogenesis.

ASHA, abbreviation for **American Speech, Language, and Hearing Association.**

ASHD, abbreviation for **arteriosclerotic heart disease.**

Asherman's syndrome, secondary amenorrhea in a hormonally normal woman, caused by obliteration of the endometrial cavity by adhesions that form as a result of curettage, infection, or uterine ablation.

asiderosis /ā'sidərō'sis/, an iron deficiency and a cause of anemia.

ASIP, abbreviation for **American Society for Investigative Pathology.**

Ask-Upmark kidney, a hypoplastic kidney with fewer lobules than usual and fissures on its surface; most affected persons have severe hypertension, sometimes with hypertensive encephalopathy and retinopathy.

ASL, abbreviation for **American Sign Language.**

ASLT, abbreviation for **antistreptolysin-O test.**

ASMT, abbreviation for *American Society for Medical Technology.*

Asn, abbreviation for the amino acid **asparagine.**

ASO, abbreviation for **antistreptolysin-O test.**

asocial /āsō'shəl/ [Gk, *a,* without; L, *socius,* companion], withdrawn or disengaged from normal contacts with other individuals.

asoma /āsō'mə/ [Gk, *a,* not, *soma,* body], a fetus with an incomplete trunk and head.

ASOT, abbreviation for **antistreptolysin-O test.**

ASPAN, abbreviation for *American Society of PeriAnesthesia Nurses.*

asparaginase /aspar'əjinās/ [Gk, *asparagos,* asparagus], an enzyme that catalyzes the hydrolysis of asparagine to asparaginic acid and ammonia. Asparaginase is used as a chemotherapeutic agent in the treatment of acute lymphoblastic leukemia and lymphosarcoma.

asparagine (Asn) /aspar'əjin/, a nonessential amino acid found in many food and body proteins.

aspartame /aspär'tām, as'pərtām/, a white, almost odorless crystalline powder that is used as an artificial sweetener. It is approximately 180 times as sweet as the same amount of sucrose. Excessive use of this nonnutritive sweetener should be avoided by patients with phenylketonuria (PKU) because the substance hydrolyzes to form aspartate and phenylalanine.

aspartate aminotransferase (AST) /aspär'tāt/, an enzyme normally present in body serum and in certain body tissues. This enzyme affects the intermolecular transfer of an amino group from aspartic acid to alpha-ketoglutaric acid, forming glutamic acid and oxaloacetic acid.

aspartate aminotransferase (AST) test, a blood test used in the evaluation of suspected coronary occlusive heart disease or hepatocellular diseases.

aspartate kinase, an enzyme that catalyzes the transfer of a phosphate group

from adenosine triphosphate to aspartate to produce phosphoaspartate.

aspartic acid (Asp) /aspär'tik/, a nonessential amino acid present in sugar cane, beet molasses, and breakdown products of many proteins. Aspartic acid is used in culture media, dietary supplements, detergents, fungicides, and germicides.

aspastic /āspas'tik/, not characterized by spasms.

aspect [L, *aspectus,* a look], the appearance, look, facing, or fronting of a person or object.

Asperger's syndrome /äs'pər·gərz/ [Hans Asperger, Austrian psychiatrist, 20th century], a pervasive developmental disorder similar to autistic disorder, characterized by severe impairment of social interactions and by restricted interests and behaviors, but lacking the delays in development of language, cognitive function, and self-help skills that additionally define autistic disorder.

aspergillic acid /as'pərjil'ik/, an antibiotic substance derived from *Aspergillus flavus,* an aflatoxin-producing mold found on corn, grain, and peanuts.

aspergillosis /as'pərjilō'sis/ [L, *aspergere,* to sprinkle; Gk, *osis,* condition], a relatively uncommon infection caused by inhalation of a fungus of the genus *Aspergillus* that can cause inflammatory, granulomatous lesions on or in any organ.

Aspergillus /as'pərjil'əs/ [L, *aspergere,* to sprinkle], a genus of fungi that is a common contaminant in the laboratory and a cause of nosocomial infection.

aspermatic /ā'spurmat'ik/, unable to secrete or ejaculate semen.

aspermatogenesis /āspur'mətōjen'əsis/, failure of the testes to produce spermatozoa.

aspermia /āspur'mē·ə/ [Gk, *a* + *sperma,* without seed], lack of formation or ejaculation of semen.

asphyxia /asfik'sē·ə/ [Gk, *a* + *sphyxis,* without pulse], severe hypoxia leading to hypoxemia and hypercapnia. Loss of consciousness, and, if not corrected, death. —**asphyxiate,** *v.,* **asphyxiated,** *adj.*

asphyxia livida /liv'idə/, an abnormal condition in which a newborn's skin is cyanotic, the pulse is weak and slow, and the reflexes are slow or absent.

asphyxia neonatorum, a condition in which a newborn does not breathe spontaneously. The asphyxia may develop before or during labor or immediately after delivery.

asphyxia pallida /pal'ədə/, an abnormal condition in which a newborn appears pale and limp, shows signs of apnea, and suffers from bradycardia as marked by a heartbeat of 80 beats/min or less.

asphyxiate /asfik′sē·āt/ [Gk, *a* + *sphyxis,* without pulse], to induce an inability to breathe. Causes may include circulatory congestion, chemical poisoning, electrical shock, or physical suffocation.

asphyxiation [Gk, *a* + *sphyxis,* without pulse], a state of asphyxia or inability to breathe.

aspirant /as′pirənt/, the fluid, gas, or solid particles that are withdrawn from the body by aspiration methods.

aspirant maneuver, a procedure used in making x-ray films of the laryngopharyngeal area. The patient exhales completely, then slowly inhales while making a harsh, high-pitched sound.

aspirate /-rāt/ [L, *aspirare,* to breathe upon], 1. to withdraw fluid or air from a cavity. The process is usually aided by use of a syringe or a suction device. 2. when all or part of a food/liquid bolus enters the airway. 3. (in phonetics) a release of air.

aspirating needle /-rā′ting/, a long hollow needle used to remove fluid from a cavity, vessel, or structure of the body.

aspirating syringe, a hypodermic syringe used to inject local anesthetics, especially in dentistry.

aspiration /as′pirā′shən/, 1. drawing in or out by suction. 2. the act of withdrawing a fluid, such as mucus or serum, from the body by a suction device.—**aspirate,** *n.*

aspiration biopsy, the removal of living tissue for microscopic examination by suction through a fine needle attached to a syringe. The procedure is used primarily to obtain cells from a lesion containing fluid or when fluid is formed in a serous cavity.

aspiration biopsy cytology (ABC), a microscopic examination of cells obtained directly from living body tissue by aspiration through a fine needle.

aspiration drug abuse, the inhalation of a liquid, solid, or gaseous chemical into the respiratory system for nontherapeutic purposes.

aspiration of vomitus, the inhalation of regurgitated gastric contents into the pulmonary system.

aspiration pneumonia, an inflammatory condition of the lungs and bronchi caused by inhaling foreign material or acidic vomitus.

aspiration precautions, a nursing intervention from the Nursing Interventions Classification (NIC) defined as prevention or minimization of risk factors in the patient at risk for aspiration.

aspiration prevention, a nursing outcome from the Nursing Outcomes Classification (NOC) defined as personal actions to prevent the passage of fluid and solid particles into the lung.

aspirator /as′pirā′tər/ [L, *aspirare,* to breathe upon], any instrument that removes a substance from a body cavity by suction, such as a bulb syringe, piston pump, or hypodermic syringe.

aspirin (ASA) /as′pirin/, an analgesic, antipyretic, and antiinflammatory prescribed to reduce fever and relieve pain and inflammation.

asplenia /āsplē′nē·ə/ [Gk, *a,* without, *spleen*], absence of a spleen. The condition may be congenital or result from surgical removal.

ASRT, abbreviation for *American Society of Radiologic Technologists.*

assault /əsôlt′/ [L, *assilirere,* to leap upon], 1. an unlawful act that places another person, without that person's consent, in fear of immediate bodily harm or battery. 2. the act of committing an assault. 3. to threaten a person with bodily harm or injury.

assay /asā′, as′ā/ [Fr, *essayer,* to try], the analysis of the purity, effectiveness, or concentration of drugs and other biologic substances, including laboratory and clinical observations.

assertiveness /əsur′tivnes/, behavior directed toward claiming one's rights without denying those of others.

assertiveness training, a nursing intervention from the Nursing Interventions Classification (NIC) defined as assistance with the effective expression of feelings, needs, and ideas while respecting the rights of others.

assertive training /əsur′tiv/ [L, *asserere,* to join to oneself], a therapeutic technique to help individuals become more self-assertive and self-confident in interpersonal relationships. It focuses on the direct, honest statement of feelings and beliefs, both positive and negative.

assessing /əses′ing/ [L, *assidere,* to sit beside], (in five-step nursing process) a category of nursing behavior that includes the gathering, verifying, and communicating of information related to the client. The nurse collects information from verbal interactions with the patient, the patient's family, and significant others; examines standard data sources for information; systematically checks for symptoms and signs; determines the patient's ability to perform self-care activities; assesses the patient's environment; and identifies reactions of the staff (including the nurse who is performing the assessment) to the patient and to the patient's family and significant others.

assessment /əses′mənt/ [L, *assidere,* to sit beside], 1. an evaluation or appraisal of a condition. **2.** the process of making such an evaluation. **3.** (in a problem-oriented medical record) an examiner's evaluation of the disease or condition based on the patient's subjective report of the symptoms and course of the illness or condition and the examiner's objective findings, including data obtained through laboratory tests, physical examination, medical history, and information reported by family members and other health care team members. —**assess**, *v.*

assessment of the aging patient, an evaluation of the changes characteristic of advancing years exhibited by an elderly person. A thorough physical assessment distinguishes the effects of pathologic disorders from those of aging and elucidates the care needed by the patient.

assimilate /əsim′əlāt/ [L, *assimilare,* to make alike], to absorb nutritive substances from the digestive tract to the circulatory system and convert them into living tissues.

assimilation [L, *assimulare,* to make alike], **1.** the process of incorporating nutritive material into living tissue; the end stage of the nutrition process, after digestion and absorption or simultaneous with absorption. **2.** (in psychology) the incorporation of new experiences into a person's pattern of consciousness. **3.** (in sociology) the process in which a person or a group of people of a different ethnic background become absorbed into a new culture.—**assimilate**, *v.*

assist-control mode, a system of mechanical ventilation in which the patient is allowed to initiate breathing, although the ventilator delivers a set volume with each breath. The ventilator can also be programmed to initiate breathing if the patient's breathing slows beyond a certain point or stops altogether.

assisted breech [L, *assistere,* to stand by], an obstetric operation in which a baby being born feet or buttocks first is permitted to deliver spontaneously as far as its umbilicus and is then extracted.

assisted circulation [L, *assistere,* to stand, *circulare,* to go around], a method of treating patients with severe circulatory deficiencies by introducing a mechanical pumping system to aid the blood flow.

assisted death, a form of euthanasia in which an individual expressing a wish to die prematurely is helped to accomplish that goal by another person, either by counseling and/or by providing a poison or other lethal instrument. The assisted death may be regarded as a homicide or suicide by local authorities, and the person giving

assistance may be held responsible for the death.

assisted embryo hatching/embryo hatching, a micromanipulation technique.

assisted reproductive technology, the manipulation of egg and sperm in treating infertility. The processes include the administration of drugs to induce ovulation, fertilization, gamete intrafallopian transfer, zygote intrafallopian transfer, and cryopreservation of gametes.

assisted respiration, the use of mechanical devices to facilitate a normal breathing pattern.

assisted suicide, a form of euthanasia in which a person wishes to commit suicide but feels unable to perform the act alone because of a physical disability or lack of knowledge about the most effective means. An individual who assists a suicide victim in accomplishing that goal may or may not be held responsible for the death, depending on local laws.

assisted ventilation, the use of mechanical or other devices to help maintain respiration, usually by delivering air or oxygen under positive pressure.

assistive listening device (ALD), a device other than a hearing aid that provides auditory assistance to those with hearing impairment or a central auditory processing disorder.

associated antagonist, one of a pair of muscles or group of muscles that pull in opposite directions but whose combined action results in moving a part in one direction.

Associate Degree in Nursing (ADN) /əsō′shē·āt/ [L, *associare,* to unite], an academic degree awarded on satisfactory completion of a 2-year course of study, usually at a community or junior college. The recipient is eligible to take the national licensing examination to become a registered nurse. An associate degree in nursing is not available in Canada.

associated movement, a movement of parts that act together, as of the eyes.

associate nurse, (in primary nursing, United States) a nurse who is responsible for implementing a primary nurse's care plans.

association /əsō′shē·ā′shən/ [L, *associare,* to unite], **1.** a connection, union, joining, or combination of things. **2.** (in psychology) the connection of remembered feelings, emotions, sensations, thoughts, or perceptions with particular persons, things, or ideas.

association area, any part of the cerebral cortex involved in the integration of sensory information.

Association for Professionals in Infection Control and Epidemiology (APIC), a multidisciplinary, international professional organization of health care professionals working in the field of infection control.

Association for the Advancement of Medical Instrumentation (AAMI), a nonprofit organization involved in education and standards relating to biomedical engineering.

Association for the Education of Children with Medical Needs (AECMN), an interdisciplinary organization that provides professional support to individuals involved in the education of children with chronic illnesses and medical challenges.

associationist model of learning /əsōˈshēā′shənist/, a theory that defines learning as behavioral change that is a result of reinforced practice.

Association of Faculties of Medicine of Canada (AFMC), a Canadian organization of the deans and faculty members of the nation's 17 medical schools.

association of ideas, a mental connection established between similar or simultaneously occurring ideas, feelings, or perceptions.

Association of periOperative Registered Nurses (AORN), the professional organization of perioperative nurses, which supports registered nurses in achieving optimal outcomes for patients undergoing operative or other invasive procedures.

Association of Surgical Technologists (AST), the national professional organization for surgical technologists and surgical assistants.

Association of Women's Health, Obstetric, and Neonatal Nurses (AWHONN), an organization of nurses working in obstetrics and gynecology in the United States.

association paralysis, a motor neuron disease in which atrophy, weakness, and fasciculation of the tongue, facial muscles, pharynx, and larynx occur.

association test, a technique used in psychiatric diagnosis and in educational and psychologic evaluation in which a person is asked to respond to a stimulus word with the first word that comes to mind.

associative play, a form of play in which a group of children participate in similar or identical activities without formal organization, group direction, group interaction, or a definite goal.

assortive mating, the matching of males and females for reproduction in a manner that eliminates random selection.

assumed role /əso͞omd′/, a role in life that an individual usually selects or achieves by choice, such as one's role in marriage or employment.

AST, 1. abbreviation for **aspartate aminotransferase.** 2. abbreviation for **angiotensin sensitivity test.** 3. abbreviation for **Association of Surgical Technologists.**

astasia /astā′zhə/ [Gk, *a* + *stasis,* not stand, *a* + *basis,* not step], a lack of motor coordination marked by an inability to stand or sit without assistance.

astasia-abasia, a form of ataxia in which the patient is unable to stand or walk because of lack of motor coordination but able to carry out natural leg movements when sitting or lying down.

astatine (At) [Gk, *astasis,* unsteady], a very unstable, radioactive element that occurs naturally in tiny amounts. Its atomic number is 85; the atomic mass of its longest-lived isotope is 210.

asteatosis /as′tē-ətō′sis/ [Gk, *a,* + *stear,* without tallow, *osis,* condition], a dry skin condition caused by a deficiency of sebaceous gland secretions. Scales and fissures may result from the dryness.

astereognosis /əstir′ē-ognō′sis/ [Gk, *a* + *stereos,* not solid, *gnosis,* knowledge], an inability to identify objects or shapes by touch.

asterixis /as′tərik′sis/ [Gk, *a* + *steririxis,* not fixed position], a hand-flapping tremor, often accompanying metabolic disorders.

asteroid body [Gk, *aster,* star, *eidos,* form], an irregular star-shaped structure that develops in the giant cells in certain diseases, including sarcoidosis, actinomycosis, and nocardiosis.

asthenia /asthē′nē-ə/ [Gk, *a* + *sthenos,* without strength], 1. the lack or loss of strength or energy; weakness; debility. 2. (in psychiatry) lack of dynamic force in the personality.—**asthenic,** *adj.*

asthenic /asthen′ik/ [Gk, *a* + *sthenos,* without strength]

asthenic habitus [Gk, *a* + *sthenos,* without strength; L, *habere,* to have], a body structure characterized by a slender build with long limbs, an angular profile, and prominent muscles or bones.

asthenic personality, a personality characterized by low energy, lack of enthusiasm, depressed emotions, and oversensitivity to physical and emotional strain.

asthenopia /as′thənō′pē-ə/ [Gk, *a* + *sthenos* + *ops,* eye], a condition in which the eyes tire easily because of weakness of the ocular or ciliary muscles.

asthma /az′mə/ [Gk, panting], a respiratory disorder characterized by recurring episodes of paroxysmal dyspnea, wheezing on expiration and/or inspiration caused by constriction of the bronchi, coughing, and viscous mucoid bronchial secretions.

The episodes may be precipitated by inhalation of allergens or pollutants, infection, cold air, vigorous exercise, or emotional stress.

asthma in children, a chronic inflammatory disorder of the airways in which many cells, including mast cells and eosinophils, play a part. The inflammation causes symptoms associated with obstructive airflow and characterized by recurring attacks of paroxysmal dyspnea, wheezing, prolonged expiration, and an irritative cough that is a common, chronic illness in childhood. It is a complex disorder involving biochemical, immunologic, infectious, endocrinologic, and psychologic factors.

asthma management, a nursing intervention from the Nursing Interventions Classification (NIC) defined as identification, treatment, and prevention of reactions to inflammation/constriction in the airway passages.

asthma self-management, a nursing outcome from the Nursing Outcomes Classification (NOC) defined as personal actions to prevent or reverse an inflammatory condition resulting in bronchial constriction of the airways.

asthmatic breathing /azmat'ik/ [Gk, *asthma,* panting; AS, *braeth*], breathing marked by prolonged wheezing on exhalation caused by spasmodic contractions of the bronchi.

asthmatic bronchitis, inflammation and swelling of the mucous membrane of the bronchi in a patient with asthma.

asthmatic cough [Gk, *asthma;* AS, *cohhetan*], a wheezing cough accompanied by signs of breathing difficulty.

asthmatic eosinophilia, a form of eosinophilic pneumonia, characterized by allergic bronchospasm, cough, fever, and expectoration of bronchial casts containing eosinophils and fungal mycelia. It is a result of hypersensitivity to the fungus *Aspergillus fumigatus* or *Candida albicans.* Untreated, it may result in pleural effusion, pericarditis, ascites, encephalitis, hepatomegaly, and respiratory failure.

astigmatic /as'tigmat'ik/ [Gk, *a* + *stigma,* without point], pertaining to astigmatism, or an error of refraction in which a ray of light is not sharply focused on the retinal tissue but is spread over a more diffuse area. Astigmatism is due to differences in curvature in the various meridians of the cornea and lens of the eye.

astigmatic keratotomy, an operation in which the cornea is relaxed by a series of transverse incisions to flatten the meridian in which the incisions are made and increase the curvature in the meridian 90

degrees away. It is done for the correction of astigmatism.

astigmatism /əstig'mətiz'əm/ [Gk, *a* + *stigma,* without point], an abnormal condition of the eye in which the light rays cannot be focused clearly in a point on the retina because the spheric curve of the cornea or lens is not equal in all meridians. Vision is typically blurred; the person cannot accommodate to correct the problem. The condition usually may be corrected with contact lenses or with eyeglasses ground to neutralize the condition.

Aston-Patterning, a bodywork technique to accommodate asymmetry and individual uniqueness of the human body to match human function to the environment. Appropriate alignment of the body provides the human structure with its most optimal support and adds the dynamic quality that facilitates motion.

astragalus, a herb used as an immune stimulant; for viral infections, HIV/AIDS, cancer, and vascular disorders; to improve circulation; and to lower BP. In most instances, there is insufficient reliable information regarding its effectiveness.

astringent /əstrin'jənt/ [Gk, *astringere,* to tighten], **1.** a substance that causes contraction of tissues on application, usually used locally. **2.** having the quality of an astringent.—**astringency,** *n.*

astringent bath, a bath in which alum, tannic acid, or another astringent is added to the water. An astringent contracts body tissue and, therefore, stops capillary bleeding or loosens secretions.

astringent douche, a cleansing stream containing substances such as alum that cause the mucous membrane of the vagina to constrict.

astroblastoma *pl.* **astroblastomas, astroblastomata** /as'trōblastō'mə/ [Gk, *aster,* star, *blastos,* germ, *oma,* tumor], a malignant neoplasm of the brain and spinal cord.

astrocyte /as'trōsīt'/ [Gk, *aster* + *kytos,* cell], a large, star-shaped neuroglial cell with many branches, found in certain tissues of the nervous system.

astrocytoma *pl.* **astrocytomas, astrocytomata** /as'trōsītō'mə/ [Gk, *aster* + *kytos* + *oma*], a primary tumor of the brain composed of astrocytes and characterized by slow growth, cyst formation, invasion of surrounding structures, and often development of a highly malignant glioblastoma within the tumor mass.

astrocytosis /as'trōsītō'sis/ [Gk, *aster* + *kytos* + *osis,* condition], an increase in the number of neuroglial cells with fibrous or protoplasmic processes frequently observed in an irregular area adjacent to degenerative lesions, such as abscesses, certain brain neoplasms, and encephalomalacia.

asymmetric /ā'simet'rik, as'imet'rik/ [Gk, *a* + *symmetria*, without proportion], 1. (of the body or parts of the body) unequal in size or shape. 2. different in placement or arrangement about an axis.—**asymmetry** /āsim'itrē/, *n*.

asymphytous /ə·sim'fə·təs/ [Gk, *a* + *symphysis*, not a growing together], separate or distinct; not grown together.

asymptomatic /āsimp'təmat'ik/ [Gk, *a*, without, *symptoma*, that which happens], without symptoms.

asymptomatic neurosyphilis [Gk, *a*, without, *symptoma* + *neuron*, nerve; Fr, *syphilide*], a form of neurosyphilis characterized by pathologic changes in the CSF, although there are no symptoms of nervous system damage. Asymptomatic neurosyphilis may occur many years before actual nervous system damage is noticeable.

asynchronous /āsing'krənəs/ [Gk, *a* + *synchronos*, not simultaneous]

asynclitism /āsing'klitiz'əm/ [Gk, *a* + *syn*, not together, *kleisis*, to lean], presentation of a parietal aspect of the fetal head to the maternal pelvic inlet in labor. The sagittal suture is parallel to the transverse diameter of the pelvis but anterior or posterior to it. In normal labor, the fetal head usually engages with some degree of asynclitism.

asyndesis /əsin'dəsis/, a mental disorder marked by an inability to assemble related ideas or thoughts into one coherent concept.

asynergy /āsin'ərjē/ [Gk, *a* + *syn* + *ergein*, to work], 1. a condition characterized by faulty coordination among groups of organs or muscles that normally function harmoniously. 2. the state of muscle antagonism found in cerebellar disease.

asyntaxia /ā'sintak'sē·ə/ [Gk, *a* + *syn* + *taxis*, arrangement], any interference with the orderly sequence of growth and differentiation of the fetus during embryonic development, resulting in one or more congenital anomalies.

asyntaxia dorsalis, failure of the neural tube to close during embryonic development.

asystole /āsis'təlē/ [Gk, *a* + *systole*, not contraction], a life-threatening cardiac condition characterized by the absence of electrical and mechanical activity in the heart. Clinical signs include apnea and lack of pulse.—**asystolic**, *adj*.

asystolic cardiac rhythm /ā'sistol'ik/, an ECG recording that appears as a flat line, indicating cardiac arrest.

At, symbol for the element **astatine**.

atabrine stomatitis, an abnormal oral condition characterized by skin changes that resemble those of lichen planus. It may be associated with the use of atabrine hydrochloride.

ataractic /at'ərak'tik/ [Gk, *ataraktos*, quiet], pertaining to a drug or other agent that has a tranquilizing or sedating effect.

Atarax, a trademark for an antianxiety, antiemetic, and anticholinergic (hydroxyzine hydrochloride).

ataraxia /at'ərak'sē'ə/ [Gk, *a*, not, *tarakos*, disturbed], a vague state of mental tranquility.

atavism /at'əviz'əm/ [L, *atavus*, ancestor], the appearance in an individual of traits or characteristics more like those of a grandparent or earlier ancestor than of the parents. Atavistic data may offer clues to an examining physician of genetic or familial health factors.—**atavistic**, *adj*.

atavistic [L, *atavus*, ancestor], pertaining to the tendency for a genetic trait of a remote ancestor to be expressed in an individual as a result of a chance recombination of genes.

ataxia /ətak'sē·ə/ [Gk, without order], an impaired ability to coordinate movement, often characterized by a staggering gait and postural imbalance.—**ataxial, ataxic**, *adj*.

ataxiaphasia /-fā'zhə/ [Gk, *ataxia*, without order], a state in which a person is unable to connect words properly as needed to form a sentence.

ataxia-telangiectasia syndrome /təlan'jē·ektā'zhə/ [Gk, *ataxia* + *telos*, end, *angeion*, vessel, *ektasis*, expansion], a rare genetic disorder involving deficits in immunoglobulin metabolism that is transmitted as an autosomal-recessive trait. It usually begins in infancy with impaired motor control (ataxia) and progresses slowly with increasing cerebellar degeneration to severe disability. Intellectual ability seems to stop at the level of 10 years of age in many cases.

ataxic breathing, a type of breathing associated with a lesion in the medullary respiratory center and characterized by a series of inspirations and expirations.

ataxic dysarthria, abnormal speech characterized by faulty formation of sounds because of neuromuscular dysfunction of the cerebellum.

atazanavir, an antiretroviral agent used to treat HIV-1 infection.

ATCC, abbreviation for **American Type Culture Collection**.

atelectasis /at'ilek'təsis/ [Gk, *ateles*, incomplete, *ektasis*, expansion], an abnormal condition characterized by the collapse of alveoli, preventing the respiratory exchange of carbon dioxide and oxygen in a part of the lungs. Symptoms may include diminished breath sounds, or aspiratory crackles, a mediastinal shift toward the side of the collapse, fever, and increasing dyspnea.

ateliosis /ətē'lē·ō'sis/ [Gk, *ateles,* incomplete, *osis,* condition], a form of dwarfism caused by the absence or destruction of eosinophil cells of the adenohypophysis. The person may appear childlike and have poorly developed muscles.

ateliotic dwarf /at'əlē·ot'ik/, a dwarf whose skeleton is incompletely formed as a result of the nonunion of the epiphyses and diaphyses during bone development.

atelorachidia /at'əlôr'əkid'ē·ə/ [Gk,*ateles,* incomplete, *rhachis,* spine], a defective, incomplete formation of the spinal column.

atenolol /aten'əlôl/, a β_1 selective blocker prescribed for the treatment of hypertension.

ATG, abbreviation for **antithymocyte globulin.**

athelia /āthē'lē·ə/ [Gk, *a,* not, *thele,* nipple], an absence of nipples.

atherectomy /ath'ərek'təmē/, surgical removal of an atheroma in a major artery.

atherectomy catheter, a specially designed catheter for cutting away atheromatous plaque from the lining of an artery. The catheter is positioned and monitored by fluoroscopy.

atheroembolic renal disease /ath'ərō·em bol'ik/, a condition of gradual or rapid kidney failure resulting from obstruction of the renal arteries by atheromas and emboli.

atheroembolism /ath'ərō·em'bəliz'əm/, obstruction of a blood vessel by an atherosclerotic embolism originating from an atheroma in a major artery.

atherogenesis [Gk, *athere,* porridge, *oma,* tumor, *genein,* to produce], the formation of subintimal plaques in the lining of arteries.—**atherogenic,** *adj.*

atheroma *pl.* **atheromas, atheromata** /ath'ərō'mə/ [Gk, *athere,* meal, *oma,* tumor], an abnormal mass of fat or lipids, as in a sebaceous cyst or in deposits in an arterial wall.—**atheromatous,** *adj.*

atheromatosis /ath'ərōmətō'sis/, the development of many atheromas.

atheromatous [Gk,*athere,* meal, *oma,* tumor]

atheromatous plaque, a yellowish raised area on the lining of an artery formed by fatty deposits indicative of atherosclerosis.

atherosclerosis /ath'ərō'sklərō'sis/ [Gk, *athere,* meal, *sklerosis,* hardening], a common disorder characterized by yellowish plaques of cholesterol, other lipids, and cellular debris in the inner layers of the walls of arteries. It usually occurs with aging and is often associated with tobacco use, obesity, hypertension, elevated low-density lipoprotein and depressed high-density lipoprotein levels, and DM. The plaque eventually creates a risk for thrombosis and is one of the major causes of coronary heart disease, angina pectoris, MI, and other cardiac disorders.

atherosclerotic aneurysm /-ot'ik/ [Gk, *athere* + *skleros,* hard, *aneurysma,* an arterial widening], a dilation that results from atherosclerotic weakening of the arterial wall.

atherothrombosis /ath'ərō'thrombō'sis/, a condition in which a thrombus originates in an atheromatous blood vessel.

athetoid /ath'ətoid/, pertaining to athetosis, as in the involuntary, purposeless weaving motions of the body or its extremities.

athetosis /ath'ətō'sis/ [Gk, *athetos,* not fixed], slow, writhing, continuous, and involuntary movement of the extremities, as seen in some forms of cerebral palsy and in motor disorders resulting from lesions in the basal ganglia, tabes dorsalis, or other conditions.

athiaminosis /əthī'əminō'sis/, a condition resulting from lack of thiamine in the diet.

athlete's heart /ath'lēts/, an enlarged but otherwise normal heart of an athlete trained for endurance. It is characterized by a low heart rate, an increased pumping capacity, and a greater ability to deliver oxygen to skeletal muscles.

athletic habitus /athlet'ik/, a physique characterized by a well-proportioned muscular body with broad shoulders, thick neck, deep chest, and flat abdomen.

athletic trainer, an allied health professional who, with the consultation and supervision of attending physicians, is an integral part of the health care system associated with sports. The athletic trainer provides a variety of services, including injury prevention and recognition and immediate care, treatment, and rehabilitation of athletic trauma.

Ativan, a trademark for a benzodiazepine antianxiety agent (lorazepam).

atlantoaxial /ətlan'tō·ak'sē·əl/ [Gk, *atlas,* to bear,*axis,* pivot], pertaining to the first two cervical vertebrae.

atlantooccipital joint /-oksip'itəl/ [Gk, *atlas,* to bear; L, *ob,* against, *caput,* head], one of a pair of condyloid joints formed by the articulation of the atlas of the vertebral column with the occipital bone of the skull.

atlas [Gk, *atlas,* to bear, a mythical giant, compelled to uphold the world], the first cervical vertebra, articulating with the occipital bone and the axis.—**atlantal,** *adj.*

ATLS, abbreviation for *advanced trauma life support.*

atm, 1. abbreviation for **atmosphere.**
2. abbreviation for **atmospheric.**

atman /ät′män/, (in psychiatry) a concept derived from Eastern Indian philosophy that the highest value is knowledge of one's true self.

atmosphere (atm) /at′məsfir/ [Gk, *atmos,* vapor, *sphaira,* sphere], 1. the natural body of air covers the surface of the earth. It is composed of approximately 20% oxygen, 78% nitrogen, and 1% argon and other gases, including small amounts of carbon dioxide hydrogen, and ozone as well as traces of helium, krypton, neon, and xenon and varying amounts of water vapor. 2. an envelope of gas, which may or may not duplicate the natural atmosphere in chemical components. 3. a unit of gas pressure that is usually defined as being equivalent to the average pressure of the earth's atmosphere at sea level, or about 14.7 pounds per square inch or 760 mm Hg.—**atmospheric,** *adj.*

atmospheric pressure /-fer′ik/, the pressure exerted by the weight of the atmosphere.

ATN, abbreviation for **acute tubular necrosis.**

atom /at′əm/ [Gk, *atmos,* indivisible], 1. (in chemistry and physics) the smallest division of an element that exhibits all the properties and characteristics of the element. It comprises neutrons, electrons, and protons. The number of protons in the nucleus of every atom of any given element is the same and is called its atomic number. 2. nontechnical. the amount of any substance that is so small that further division is not possible. —**atomic,** *adj.*

atomic mass (A), the average mass, relative to an atom of carbon, of an atom of an element based on the natural isotopic mix of that element.

atomic mass unit (amu) /ətom′ik/, the mass of a neutral atom of an element, expressed as $^1/_{12}$ of the mass of the isotope carbon-12, which has a value of exactly 12. The energy equivalent of 1 amu is 931.2 MeV. The mass equivalent of 1 amu is 1.66 (10^{-24} g).

atomic number, the number of protons in the nucleus of an atom of a particular element. In a neutral atom, the atomic number equals the number of electrons.

atomic theory [Gk, *atmos,* indivisible, *theoria,* speculation], the concept that all matter is composed of submicroscopic atoms that are in turn composed of protons, electrons, and neutrons. A chemical element is identified by the number of protons in its atoms.

atomizer /at′əmī′zər/, a device used to reduce a liquid and eject it as a fine spray or vapor.

atomoxetine, a nonstimulant psychotherapeutic agent used to treat attention deficit hyperactivity disorder.

atonia /ātō′nē·ə/ [Gk, *a + tonos,* without tone], decreased or absent muscle tone.

atonic /əton′ik/, 1. weak. 2. lacking normal tone, as in the case of a muscle that is flaccid. 3. lacking vigor, such as an atonic ulcer, which heals slowly.—**atony** /at′onē/, *n.*

atonic constipation, constipation caused by failure of the colon to respond to the normal stimuli for evacuation, caused by loss of muscle tone. It may occur in elderly or bedridden patients or after prolonged dependence on laxatives.

atopic /ātop′ik/ [Gk, *a + topos,* not place], pertaining to a hereditary tendency to experience immediate allergic reactions such as asthma or vasomotor rhinitis because of the presence of an antibody (atopic reagin) in the skin and sometimes the bloodstream.—**atopy** /at′opē/, *n.*

atopic allergy [Gk, *a + topos,* not place], a form of allergy that afflicts persons with a genetic predisposition to hypersensitivity to certain allergens.

atopic dermatitis, an intensely pruritic, often excoriated inflammation commonly found on the face and antecubital and popliteal areas of allergy-prone (atopic) individuals.

atopic reagin, an antibody associated with atopy; a substance present in senin and cerebrospinal fluid that induces frocculation in complement fluation and similar tests.

atopognosia /ātop′əgnō′zhə/ [Gk, *a + topos,* not place, *gnosis,* knowledge], a form of agnosia in which a person is unable to locate a tactile sensation correctly.

atorvastatin, an antihyperlipidemic used to lower the levels of both cholesterol and triglycerides in the plasma.

atovaquone /ah-to′vah-kwōn/, an antibiotic used in treatment of mild to moderate *Pneumocystis carinii* pneumonia and the prevention and treatment of falciparum malaria. It is administered orally.

ATP, abbreviation for **adenosine triphosphate.**

ATPase, abbreviation for **adenosine triphosphatase.**

ATPD, abbreviation for *ambient temperature, ambient pressure.*

ATPS, abbreviation for *ambient temperature, ambient pressure.*

atransferrinemic anemia /ā'transfer'inē'mik/, an iron-transport deficiency disease characterized by a failure of iron to move from the liver or other storage sites to tissues in which erythrocytes develop.

atraumatic /ā'trômat'ik/ [Gk, a, without, trauma], pertaining to therapies or therapeutic instruments and devices that are unlikely to cause tissue damage.

atresia /ɔtrē'zhɔ/ [Gk, a + tresis, not perforation], the absence of a normal body opening, duct, or canal, such as of the anus, vagina, or external ear canal.—**atresic, atretic,** adj.

atresic teratism /ɔtrē'sik/ [Gk, a + tresis + tera, monster], a congenital anomaly in which any of the normal openings of the body fails to form.

atrial complex, the P wave of the ECG, representing electrical activity of the atria.

atrial fibrillation (AF) /ā'trē-əl/, a cardiac arrhythmia characterized by disorganized electrical activity in the atria accompanied by an irregular ventricular response that is usually rapid. The atria quiver instead of pumping in an organized fashion, resulting in compromised ventricular filling and reduced stroke volume.

atrial flutter (AF), a type of atrial tachycardia characterized by contraction rates between 230/min and 380/min. Two kinds, typical and atypical, have been identified and are distinguished from each other by their rates and ECG patterns. During typical atrial flutter the atrial rate is between 290/min and 310/min and produces "fence post" or "sawtooth" ECG waves. During atypical atrial flutter the atrial rate is higher, and the ECG waves lack the sawtooth appearance and are often sinusoidal.

atrial myxoma, a benign, pedunculated, gelatinous tumor that originates in the interatrial septum of the heart. The tumor is characterized by palpitations, disseminated neuritis, nausea, weight loss, fatigue, dyspnea, fever, and occasional sudden loss of consciousness.

atrial natriuretic peptide (ANP), a hormone involved in natriuresis and the regulation of renal and cardiovascular homeostasis. It causes natriuresis, diuresis, and renal vasodilation; reduces circulating concentrations of renin, aldosterone, and antidiuretic hormone; and thereby normalizes circulating BP and volume.

atrial septal defect (ASD), a congenital cardiac anomaly characterized by an abnormal opening between the atria. The severity of the condition depends on the size and location of the opening. ASDs increase the flow of oxygenated blood into the right side of the heart, which is usually well tolerated because the blood is delivered under much lower pressure than in ventricular septal defect. Clinical manifestations include a characteristic harsh, scratchy systolic murmur and a fixed splitting of the second heart sound, which does not vary with respiration.

atrial septum [L, atrium, hall, saeptum, fence], a partition between the left and right atria of the heart.

atrial standstill, a condition of complete failure of the atria to contract. P waves are absent in all ECG surface leads, and A waves are absent in the jugular venous pulse and right atrial pressure tracings. Generally a junctional escape pacemaker maintains ventricular activity during atrial standstill.

atrial systole, the contraction of the atria of the heart, which precedes ventricular contraction by a fraction of a second.

atrial tachycardia [L, atrium, hall; Gk, tachys, quick, kardia, heart], rapid beating of the atria caused by abnormal automaticity, triggered activity, or intraatrial reentry. The atrial rate is usually less than 200/min; however, in cases of digitalis excess, the rate increases gradually to 130/min to 250/min as the digitalis is continued. Atrial tachycardia may be either nonparoxysmal (common) or paroxysmal (uncommon). Vagal maneuvers have no effect on atrial tachycardia, although they do cause atrioventricular block.

atrichia /ātrik'ē-ə/ [Gk, a, not, thrix, hair], **1.** pertaining to a group of bacteria that lack flagella. **2.** the congenital or acquired absence of hair.

atrichosis /ā'trikō'sis/ [Gk, a + trichia without hair, osis, condition], a congenital or acquired absence of hair.

atrioventricular (AV) /ā'trē-ōventrik'yə lər/ [L, atrium, hall, ventriculus], pertaining to a connecting conduction event or anatomic structure between the atria and ventricles.

atrioventricular block (AVB) [L, atrium + ventriculus, little belly], a disorder of cardiac impulse transmission that reflects prolonged, intermittent, or absent conduction of impulses between the atria and ventricles. It commonly occurs at the AV node or within the bundle branch system.

atrioventricular (AV) bundle, a band of atypical cardiac muscle fibers with few contractile units. It arises from the distal part of the AV node and extends across the AV groove to the top of the intraventricular septum, where it divides into the bundle branches.

atrioventricular (AV) dissociation, a breakdown in the normal conduction of excitation through the heart, allowing the atria and ventricles to beat independently under the control of their own pacemakers.

atrioventricular (AV) junction [L, *jungere*, to join], the region of the heart that separates the atria from the ventricles. It includes the AV bundle (bundle of His) and surrounds the AV node.

atrioventricular (AV) node, an area of specialized cardiac muscle that receives the cardiac impulse from the sinoatrial node and conducts it to the AV bundle and then to the Purkinje fibers and walls of the ventricles. The AV node is located in the septal wall between the left and right atria.

atrioventricular (AV) septum, a small part of membrane that separates the atria from the ventricles of the heart.

atrioventricular (AV) valve, a valve in the heart through which blood flows from the atria to the ventricles. The valve between the left atrium and left ventricle is the mitral (bicuspid) valve; the right AV valve is the tricuspid valve.

at risk, the state of an individual or population being vulnerable to a particular disease or event. The factors determining risk may be environmental, psychosocial, psychologic, or physiologic.

atrium *pl.* **atria** /ā′trē·əm/ [L, hall], a chamber or cavity, such as the right and left atria of the heart or the nasal cavity.

atrium of the ear, the external part of the ear, including the auricle and the tubular part of the external auditory meatus.

atrium of the heart, one of the two upper chambers of the heart. The right atrium receives deoxygenated blood from the superior vena cava, the inferior vena cava, and the coronary sinus. The left atrium receives oxygenated blood from the pulmonary veins.

atrium proper, the space anterior to the crista terminalis of the right atrium of the heart.

Atromid-S, a trademark for an antilipemic (clofibrate) used to lower plasma triglyceride (VLDL) levels.

atrophic /ătrof′ik/ [Gk, *a*, without, *trophe*, nourishment], characterized by a wasting of tissues, usually associated with general malnutrition or a specific disease state.

atrophic acne, acne vulgaris in which, after the disappearance of small papular lesions, a stippling of tiny atrophic pits and scars remains.

atrophic catarrh [Gk, *a + trophe*, without nourishment, *kata*, down, *rhoia*, flow], an abnormal condition characterized by inflammation and discharge from the mucous membranes of the nose, accompanied by the loss of mucosal and submucosal tissue.

atrophic cirrhosis [Gk, *a + trophe*, without nourishment, *kirrhos*, yellow-orange], a form of advanced portal cirrhosis with massive shrinking of the liver.

atrophic fracture, a spontaneous fracture caused by bone atrophy, as in the bones of a person with osteoporosis.

atrophic gastritis, a chronic inflammation of the stomach, associated with degeneration of the gastric mucosa. Seen in elderly patients and in persons with pernicious anemia, it rarely causes epigastric pain.

atrophic glossitis, a pathologic condition in which the various papillae are lost from the dorsum of the tongue, resulting in a very sore and highly sensitive surface that makes eating difficult.

atrophic rhinitis [Gk, *a + trophe*, without nourishment, *rhis*, nose, *itis*, inflammation], a nasal condition, a form of chronic rhinitis, in which there is atrophy of the mucous membrane of the nose, resulting in failure of the ciliary function and drying and crusting of the lining of the nasal passages.

atrophic vaginitis [Gk, *a + trophe*, without nourishment; L, *vagina*, sheath; Gk, *itis*, inflammation], degeneration of the vaginal mucous membrane after menopause due to decreased estrogen level, thinning, and dryness.

atrophied /at′rōfīd/ [Gk, *a + trophe*, without nourishment], decreased in size because of disuse or disease, as an organ, tissue, or body part.

atrophoderma /at′rōfədur′mə/ [Gk, *a + trophe + derma*, skin], the wasting away or decrease in thickness of the skin. The atrophy may affect the entire body surface or only localized areas.

atrophy /at′rəfē/ [Gk, *a + trophe*, without nourishment], a wasting or decrease in size or physiologic activity of a part of the body because of disease or other influences. —**atrophic,** *adj.,* **atrophy,** *v.*

atrophy of aging, senile atrophy.

atrophy of disuse [Gk, *a + trophe*; L, *dis*, opposite of, *usus*], a shrinkage of tissues resulting from immobility or lack of exercise.

atropine /at′rōpin/ [Gk, *Atropos*, one of the three Fates], an alkaloid from *Atropa belladonna* and *Datura stramonium* plants.

atropine sulfate, an antispasmodic and anticholinergic prescribed in the treatment of GI hypermotility to decrease the tone of the detrusor muscle of the urinary bladder in urinary tract disorders, of cycloplegic refraction and dilation of the pupil in inflammation of the iris or the uvea, of cardiac arrhythmias, of certain kinds of poisoning, and as an adjunct to anesthesia.

atropine sulfate poisoning [Gk, *Atropos*, fate; L, *sulphur* + *potio*, drink], toxic effects of an overdose of a drug sometimes used as an adjunct to general anesthesia and to treat bradycardia. Symptoms include tachycardia, hot and dry flushed skin, dry mouth with thirst, restlessness and excitement, urinary retention, constipation, and a burning pain in the throat.

attached gingiva, gum tissue that covers and is firmly attached to the alveolar process in the maxilla and mandible.

attachment [Fr, *attachement*], **1.** the state or quality of being affixed or attached. **2.** (in psychiatry) a mode of behavior in which one individual relates in an affiliative or dependent manner to another; a feeling of affection or loyalty that binds one person to another. **3.** (in dentistry) any device, such as a retainer or artificial crown, used to secure a partial denture to a natural tooth in the mouth. **4.** (in periodontology) the fixation of periodontal tissues to alveolar bone and tooth structure.

attachment apparatus, the various tissues that surround and support the teeth, including the cementum, the periodontal ligament, and the alveolar process.

attachment promotion, a nursing intervention from the Nursing Interventions Classification (NIC) defined as facilitation of the development of the parent-infant relationship.

attack, an episode in the course of an illness, usually characterized by acute and distressing symptoms.

attapulgite /atʹah-pulʹjīt/, a clay mineral that contains aluminum silicate and is the main ingredient of fuller's earth; *activated attapulgite* is a heat-treated form that is administered orally in the treatment of diarrhea.

attending [L, *attendo*, to notice], (in psychology) pertaining to an aroused readiness to perceive, with an adjustment of the brain and sense organs to focus on a situation.

attending physician [L, *attendere*, to stretch], the physician who is responsible for a particular patient. In a university hospital setting, an attending physician often also has teaching responsibilities, holds a faculty appointment, and supervises residents and medical students.

attention [L, *attendere*, to stretch], the element of cognitive functioning in which the mental focus is maintained on a specific issue, object, or activity.

attention deficit disorder (ADD), a syndrome characterized by short attention span, hyperactivity, and poor concentration. The symptoms may be mild or severe and are associated with functional deviations of the CNS without signs of major neurologic or psychiatric disturbance. The people affected are usually of normal or above average intelligence.

attention deficit hyperactivity disorder (ADHD), a childhood mental disorder with onset before 7 years of age and involving impaired or diminished attention, impulsivity, and hyperactivity.

attenuated /ətenʹyōō·āʹted/ [L, *attenuare*, to make thin], pertaining to the dilution of a solution or the reduction in virulence or toxicity of a microorganism or a drug by weakening it.

attenuated virus [L, *attenuare*, to make thin, *virus*, poison], a strain of virus whose virulence has been lowered by physical or chemical processes, or by repeated passage through the cells of another species. Vaccines made by attenuated strains are used to prevent smallpox, measles, mumps, rubella, polio, yellow fever, and other viruses.

attenuation /ətenʹyōō·āʹshən/ [L, *attenuare*, to make thin], the process of reduction, such as attenuation of an x-ray beam by reducing its intensity, weakening of the degree of virulence of a disease organism, or culturing under unfavorable conditions.

attenuation coefficient, in radiography or ultrasound, the difference between the energy that enters a body part and the energy that is not detected. The difference is caused by the absorption and scattering of energy within the body tissues.

attenuator /ətenʹyōō·āʹtər/ [L, *attenuare*, to make thin], an agent that weakens the toxicity of a poisonous substance or the virulence of a microorganism.

Attenuvax, a trademark for an active immunizing agent (live measles virus vaccine).

ATT-III, abbreviation for **antithrombin III.**

attitude /atʹətyōōd, -tōōd/ [L, *aptitude*, fitness], **1.** a body position or posture, particularly the fetal position in the uterus, as determined by the degree of flexion of the head and extremities. **2.** (in psychiatry) any of the major integrative forces in the development of personality that gives consistency to an individual's behavior.

attitudinal isolation /atʹətyōōʹdinəl/ [L, *attitudo*, posture], a type of social isolation that results from a person's own cultural or personal values.

attitudinal reflex, any reflex initiated by a change in position of the head or by a change in position of the head with respect to the position of the body.

attraction [L, *attrahere*, to draw to], a tendency of the teeth or other maxillary or mandibular structures to become elevated above their normal position.

ATTR amyloidosis, the most common form of familial amyloidosis, in which any of numerous mutations of the gene encoding transthyretin cause systemic autosomal-dominant disorders characterized by polyneuropathies, cardiomyopathies, and variable organ involvement.

attrition /ətrish′ən/ [L, *atterere,* to wear away], **1.** the process of wearing away or wearing down by friction. **2.** the physiologic wearing away of the teeth such as from normal mastication, grinding, bruxism, premature contacts, or abnormal tooth structures. See abrasion, abfraction, erosion. **3.** individuals who withdraw or are dismissed from a study or program of study.

at. wt., abbreviation for **atomic weight.**

atypia /ātip′ē·ə/ [Gk, *a* + *typos,* without type], a condition of being irregular or nonstandard.

atypical /ātip′əkəl/ [Gk, *a* + *typos,* without type], a condition or object that is not of a usual or standard type.

atypical measles syndrome (AMS), a form of measles (rubeola) reported in persons immunized with a killed measles vaccine used in the United States from 1962 to 1967 and in Canada until 1970. Symptoms differ from those of typical measles, beginning with a sudden high fever, headache, abdominal pain, and coughing.

atypical *Mycobacterium* [Gk, *a* + *typos,* without type, *mykes,* fungus, *bakterion,* small staff], a group of mycobacteria, including pathogenic and nonpathogenic forms, that are classified according to their ability to produce pigments, growth characteristics, and reactions to chemical tests. Mycobacteria, non-TB (atypical) does not require isolation precautions.

atypical pneumonia [Gk, *a* + *typos,* without type, *pneumon,* lung, *ia,* condition], a group of relatively mild symptoms of chills, headache, muscular pains, moderate fever, and coughing, but without evidence of a bacterial infection. Chest x-ray film may show mottling at the bases of the lungs. Eaton agent, or *Mycoplasma pneumoniae,* may be the cause of the symptoms.

atypical polypoid adenomyoma, a rare and benign tumor that may be clinically and histologically mistaken for malignancy.

atypical somatoform disorder, an abnormal condition marked by physical symptoms and complaints that appear related to a preoccupation with an imagined defect in one's personal appearance or ability.

Au, symbol for the element **gold.**

audible /ô′dibəl/ [L, *audire,* to hear], capable of being heard.

audioanalgesia /ô′dē·ō·an′əljē′sē·ə/ [L, *audire,* to hear; Gk, *a* + *algos,* not

pain], the use of music to enhance relaxation and to distract a patient's mind from pain.

audiogram /ô′dē·əgram′/ [Gk, *audire* + *gramma,* record], a chart showing the faintest level at which an individual is able to detect sounds of various frequencies, usually in octaves from 125 Hz to 8000 Hz.

audiologist, a health professional with graduate education in normal hearing processes and hearing loss, who detects and evaluates hearing loss and who determines how a client can best make use of remaining hearing. If a client can benefit from assistive listening devices such as hearing aids, the audiologist assists with the selection, fitting, and training in their use.

audiology /-ol′əjē/ [L, *audire;* Gk, *logos,* science], a field of research and clinical practice devoted to the study of hearing disorders, assessment of hearing, hearing conservation, and aural rehabilitation. —**audiologic,** *adj.*

audiometer /ô′dē·om′ətər/ [L, *audire;* Gk, *metron,* measure], an electronic device for testing hearing.

audiometrist /ô′dē·om′ətrist/, a technician who has received special training in the use of pure-tone audiometry equipment. An audiometrist conducts the hearing tests selected and interpreted by an audiologist, who supervises the process.

audiometry /ô′dē·om′ətrē/, the testing of the sensitivity of the sense of hearing. Various audiometric tests determine the lowest intensity of sound at which an individual can perceive auditory stimuli (hearing threshold) and distinguish different speech sounds. —**audiometric,** *adj.*

audiovisual /ô′dē·ōvizh′əl/, pertaining to communication that uses both sight and sound messages.

audit /ô′dit/, **1.** a final statement of account. **2.** a review and evaluation of health care procedures and documentation.

auditory /ô′dətôr′ē/ [L, *auditorius,* hearing], pertaining to the sense of hearing and the hearing organs involved.

auditory amnesia [L, *auditorius,* hearing; Gk, *amnesia,* forgetfulness], a loss of memory for the meaning of sounds.

auditory area [L, *auditorium,* hearing], the sound perception area of the cerebral cortex. It is located in the floor of the lateral fissure and on the dorsal surface of the superior temporal gyrus.

auditory brainstem response (ABR), an electrophysiologic test used to measure hearing sensitivity and evaluate the integrity of ear structures from the auditory nerve through the brainstem. It is also used to screen hearing of newborns.

auditory epilepsy, a reflex form of epilepsy provoked by sounds.

auditory hair [L, *audire,* to hear; AS, *haer*], one of the cells with hairlike processes in the spiral organ of Corti. The hairs, or cilia, function as sensory receptors.

auditory hallucination [L, *audire,* to hear, *alucinari,* a wandering mind], a subjective experience of hearing voices or other sounds despite the absence of an actual reality-based external stimulus to account for the phenomenon. It is commonly seen in schizophrenia.

auditory meatus [L, *audire,* to hear, *meatus,* passage], **1.** the external auditory meatus, a tubelike channel of the external ear extending from the auricle to the tympanum of the middle ear. **2.** the internal auditory meatus, a short channel extending from the petrous part of the temporal bone to the fundus near the vestibule. It contains the eighth cranial nerve.

auditory ossicles [L, *audire + ossiculum,* little bone], the malleus, the incus, and the stapes, three small bones in the middle ear that articulate with each other. As the tympanic membrane vibrates, it transmits sound waves through the ossicles to the cochlea.

auditory system assessment, an evaluation of the patient's ears and hearing and an investigation of present and past diseases or conditions that may be responsible for an auditory impairment.

auditory threshold [L, *audire,* to hear; AS, *threscold*], the lowest intensity at which a sound may be heard.

auditory vertigo [L, *audire,* to hear, *vertigo,* dizziness], vertigo associated with ear disease. It is characterized by sensations of gyration and, when severe, with prostration and vomiting.

Auerbach's plexus [Leopold Auerbach, German anatomist, 1828–1897; L, *plexus,* plaited], the myenteric plexus, a group of autonomic nerve fibers and ganglia located in the muscle tissue of the intestinal tract.

Auer rod /ou′ər/ [John Auer, American physiologist, 1875–1948], an abnormal, needle-shaped or round, pink-staining inclusion in the cytoplasm of myeloblasts and promyelocytes in acute myelogenous, promyelocytic, or myelomonocytic leukemia. The finding of Auer rods in stained blood smears helps to differentiate acute myelogenous leukemia from acute lymphoblastic leukemia.

augmentation /ôg′məntā′shən/ [L, *augmentare,* to increase], **1.** stimulation of an increased rate of biologic activity, such as faster cell division or heartbeat. **2.** breast enlargement through mammoplasty.

augmentation mammoplasty, a surgical procedure to enlarge the breasts.

aura /ôr′ə/ [L,breath], **1.** *pl.***aurae** /ôr′ē/ a sensation, as of light or warmth, or emotion (such as fear) that may precede an attack of migraine or an epileptic seizure. **2.** *pl.* **auras,** an emanation of light or color surrounding a person as seen in Kirlian photography and studied in current nursing research in healing techniques.

aural[1] /ôr′əl/, pertaining to the ear or hearing. —**aurally,** *adv.*

aural[2], pertaining to an aura.

aural forceps, a dressing forceps with fine, bent tips used in surgery.

aural rehabilitation, a form of therapy in which hearing-impaired individuals are taught to improve their ability to communicate. Methods taught include, but are not limited to, speech-reading, auditory training, use of hearing aids, and use of assistive listening devices such as telephone amplifiers.

auramine /ôr′əmēn/, a yellow aniline dye used in the manufacture of paints, textiles, and rubber products. The experimental carcinogen in animals has been identified as a cause of bladder cancer in humans.

auramine O, a fluorescent, yellow aniline dye used as a stain for the tubercle bacillus and for DNA.

auramine-rhodamine stain, a fluorescent dye consisting of auramine O, rhodamine B, and phenol that is used in the fluorochrome acid-fast staining method. The dye binds to mycolic acids in the cell wall of bacteria and resists decolorization with acid alcohol.

auranofin /ôr′ənof′in/, an oral gold disease-modifying antirheumatoid drug. It can be prescribed for the treatment of rheumatoid arthritis but is generally not first-line therapy.

aurantiasis cutis /ôr′əntī′əsis/ [L, *aurantium,* orange; Gk, *osis,* condition; L, *cutis,* skin], a yellowish skin pigmentation that results from eating excessive amounts of foods containing carotene, such as carrots.

auricle /ôr′ikəl/ [L, *auricula,* little ear], **1.** the external ear. **2.** the left or right cardiac atrium, so named because of its earlike shape.

auricular /ôrik′yələr/, **1.** pertaining to the auricle of the ear. **2.** otic.

auricular acupuncture, acupuncture performed using points on the ear that have been mapped to specific anatomic areas of the body.

auricularis anterior, one of three extrinsic muscles of the ear. It functions to move the auricula forward and upward.

auricularis posterior, one of three extrinsic muscles of the ear. It serves to draw the auricula backward.

auricularis superior, a thin, fan-shaped muscle that is one of three extrinsic muscles of the ear. It acts to draw the auricula upward.

auricular line, a hypothetical line passing through the external auditory meatuses and perpendicular to the Frankfort horizontal plane.

auricular point, the center of the external auditory meatus.

auricular tubercle, a small projection sometimes found on the edge of the helix of the ear.

auriculin /ôrik′yəlin/, a hormone-like substance with diuretic activity produced in the atria of the heart.

auriculocranial /-krā′nē-əl/, pertaining to the auricle of the ear and the cranium.

auriculotemporal /-tem′pərəl/, pertaining to the auricle of the ear and the temporal area of the skull.

auriculoventriculostomy /ôrik′yəlōventrik′yəlos′təmē/ [L, *auricula + ventriculus*, little belly; Gk, *stoma*, opening], a surgical procedure that directs CSF into the general circulation in the treatment of hydrocephalus, usually in the newborn. A polyethylene tube is passed from the lateral ventricle through a burr hole in the parietal skull area under the scalp and into the jugular vein or abdomen for the discharge of CSF.

auris dextra (a.d.), the Latin term for right ear.

auris sinistra (a.s.), the Latin term for left ear.

aurothioglucose /ôr′ōthī′ōglōō′kōs/, an organic gold compound used as a disease-modifying antirheumatoid drug. It is prescribed for adjunctive treatment of adult and juvenile rheumatoid arthritis, but generally is no longer considered first-line therapy.

auscultation /ôs′kəltā′shən/ [L, *auscultare,* to listen], the act of listening for sounds within the body to evaluate the condition of the heart, blood vessels, lungs, pleura, intestines, or other organs or to detect the fetal heart sound. Auscultation may be performed directly with the unaided ear, but most commonly a stethoscope is used to determine the frequency, intensity, duration, and quality of the sounds. —**auscultate,** *v.,* **auscultatory** /ôskul′tətôr′ē/, *adj.*

auscultatory gap, time in which sound is not heard in the auscultatory method of measuring BP with a sphygmomanometer, occurring particularly in hypertension and in aortic stenosis.

Austin Flint murmur [Austin Flint, American physiologist, 1812–1886], a low-pitched sound characteristic of severe aortic regurgitation without mitral valve disease. It is typically heard during ventricular middiastole at the mitral valve area.

Australia antigen, an envelope antigen found in acute or chronic hepatitis B.

Australian lift, a type of shoulder lift used to move a patient who is unable to assume a sitting position on a bed or other surface.

Australian Q fever, a variety of Q fever occurring in Australia. It is enzootic in Australian animals, especially bandicoots (large rats).

autacoid /ô′təkoid/, any one of the substances produced locally by one group of cells that exerts effects on other types of cells in the same region.

authenticity /ô′thəntis′itē/, (in psychiatry) emotional and behavioral openness; a quality of being genuine and trustworthy.

authoritarian personality, a group of behavioral traits characteristic of one who advocates obedience and strict adherence to rules.

authority /ôthôr′itē/, a relationship between two or more persons or groups characterized by the influence one may exercise over the other through ideas, commands, suggestions, or instructions.

authority figure, a person who by virtue of status, strength, knowledge, or other recognized superiority exerts influence over others.

autism spectrum disorders, a group of disorders characterized by impairment of development in multiple areas, including the acquisition of reciprocal social interaction, verbal and nonverbal communication skills, and imaginative activity, and by stereotyped interests and behaviors. It includes autistic disorder, Rett syndrome, childhood disintegrative disorder, and Asperger syndrome.

autistic disorder /ôtis′tik/ [Gk, *autos,* self], a pervasive developmental disorder with onset in infancy or childhood, characterized by impaired social interaction, impaired communication, and a restricted repertoire of activities and interests. —**autistic,** *adj.*

autistic phase, a period of preoedipal development, according to Mahler's system of personality stages. It lasts from birth to around 1 month and is considered normal.

autistic thought, a form of thinking that is internally stimulated in which the ideas have a private meaning to the individual. Autistic thinking is a symptom in patients with schizophrenia. Fantasy life may be interpreted as reality.

autoactivation /-ak'tivā'shən/ [Gk, *autos,* self, *activus,* active], self-activation, as when a gland is stimulated by its own secretions.

autoagglutination /-əgloo'tinā'shən/ [Gk, *autos,* self; L, *agglutinare,* to glue], **1.** the clumping of RBCs caused by an individual's own serum. **2.** the clumping of certain antigens or antigen-bearing cells such as bacteria.

autoamputation /-amp'yooōtā'shən/, the spontaneous detachment of a body part, usually the fourth or fifth toe, as occurs among the males of some African peoples. The condition is usually painless and has no other symptoms.

autoantibody/ô'tō·an'tibod'ē/ [Gk, *autos* + *anti,* against; AS, *bodig,* body], an immunoglobulin produced by a person that recognizes an antigen on that person's own tissues.

autoantigen /ô'tō·an'tijen/ [Gk, *autos* + *anti,* against; *genein,* to produce], an endogenous body constituent that stimulates the production of autoantibodies and an autoimmune reaction.

autoantitoxin /-an'titok'sin/, an antibody produced as protection against a toxin resulting from infection in the same individual, such as *Escherichia coli* endotoxin.

autoaugmentation /-ôg'məntā'shən/, a surgical procedure in which the detrusor muscle of the bladder is removed, leaving the bladder epithelium otherwise intact.

autoblast /ô'təblast/, **1.** a free-living unicellular microorganism. **2.** an independent cell.

autocatheterization /kath'ətur'īzā'shən/, the insertion of a catheter by the patient.

autochthonous /ôtok'thənəs/ [Gk, *autos,* self, *chthon,* earth], relating to a disease or other condition that appears to have originated in the part of the body in which it was discovered.

autochthonous idea [Gk, *autos* + *chthon,* earth], an idea that originates in the unconscious and arises spontaneously in the mind, independent of the conscious train of thought.

autoclassis /ôtok'ləsis/ [Gk, *autos,* self, *klassis,* breaking], the rupturing or breaking of a part of the body caused by a force or agent arising from within the body itself.

autoclave /ô'təklāv/, an appliance used to sterilize medical instruments or other objects with steam under pressure.

autocrine /ô'təkrin/, denoting the effect of a hormone on cells that produce it.

autodigestion, a condition in which gastric juices in the pancreas or stomach digest the organ's own tissues.

autodiploid /ô'tōdip'loid/ [Gk, *autos* + *diploos,* double, *eidos,* form], **1.** an individual, organism, strain, or cell containing two genetically identical or nearly identical chromosome sets that are derived from the same ancestral species and result from the duplication of the haploid set. **2.** pertaining to such an individual, organism, strain, or cell.—**autodiploidy,** *n.*

autoeroticism /-irot'əsiz'əm/ [Gk, *autos* + *eros,* love], **1.** sensual, sexual gratification of the self, usually obtained through the stimulus of one's own body without the participation of another person. **2.** sexual feeling or desire occurring without any external stimulus. **3.** (in Freudian psychoanalytic theory) an early phase of psychosexual development, occurring in the oral and the anal stages.—**autoerotic,** *adj.*

autoerythrocyte sensitization /ô'tō·ərith'rəsīt/ [Gk, *autos* + *erythros,* red, *kytos,* cell], hypersensitivity to one's own RBCs. It results in the spontaneous appearance of painful, hemorrhagic spots on the anterior aspects of the arms and legs.

autogenesis /-ô'tōjen'əsis/ [Gk, *autos* + *genein,* to produce], **1.** abiogenesis. **2.** a self-produced condition; a condition originating from within the organism.—**autogenetic, autogenic,** *adj.*

autogenic therapy /-jen'ik/, a mental health therapy introduced by Wolfgang Luthe. It is based on the concept that natural forces in the brain are able to remove disturbing influences so that functional harmony can be restored in the mind and body.

autogenic training, a nursing intervention from the Nursing Interventions Classification (NIC) defined as assisting with self-suggestions about feelings of heaviness and warmth for the purpose of inducing relaxation.

autogenous /ôtoj'ənəs/, **1.** self-generating. **2.** originating from within the organism.

autogenous graft [Gk, *autos,* self, *genein,* to produce, *graphion,* stylus], a skin graft transplanted from one site to another in the same individual.

autogenous vaccine [Gk, *autos,* self, *genein,* to produce; L, *vacca,* cow], a vaccine prepared from cultures of an infectious agent taken from the patient to be treated.

autograft /ô'təgraft'/ [Gk, *autos* + *graphion,* stylus], surgical transplantation of any tissue from one part of the body to another location in the same individual. Autografts are used in several kinds of plastic surgery, most commonly to replace skin lost in severe burns.

autographism, a skin condition characterized by wheals that develop from tracing on the skin with the fingernail or a blunted instrument.

autohemolysis /-hēmol′isis/ [Gk, *autos*, self, *haima*, blood, *lysein*, to loosen], the destruction of erythrocytes by hemolytic agents found in an individual's own blood.

autohypnosis [Gk, *autos* + *hypnos*, sleep], the self-induction of hypnosis by an individual who concentrates on one subject to attain an altered state of consciousness. It may also occur in a person who has become habituated to the process by undergoing hypnosis a number of times.

autoimmune /-imyōōn′/ [Gk, *autos*; L, *immunus*, exempt], pertaining to an immune response to one's own tissues.

autoimmune disease, one of a large group of diseases characterized by altered function of the immune system of the body, resulting in the production of antibodies against the body's own cells. These reactions can affect almost any cell or tissue and cause a variety of diseases. Some autoimmune disorders are tissue specific, whereas others affect multiple organs and systems. Many autoimmune diseases are characterized by periods of crisis interrupted by periods of remission.

autoimmune hypothesis, a concept that defects occur in the body's immune system as one ages. As a result of the defects, a person's antibody-producing cells can no longer distinguish between "self" and "nonself" tissues. The body's own cells are then misidentified as foreign and are attacked by antibodies. However, circumstantial evidence links autoimmune diseases to preceding infections.

autoimmune theory of aging, a programmed theory of aging that ascribes aging and cell death to preprogrammed decline in T-cell function with age, which causes decreased self/nonself recognition and increased development of infections, tumors, and autoimmune disorders.

autoimmune thrombocytopenic purpura (ITP), abnormally low platelet count associated with mucocutaneous bleeding. Acute ITP is a disease of children that may follow a viral infection, lasts a few weeks to a few months, and usually has no residual effects. Chronic ITP appears in adolescents and adults, especially women of childbearing age, with insidious onset, and is usually lifelong.

autoimmunity /-imyōō′nitē/, an abnormal condition in which the body reacts against constituents of its own tissues.

autoimmunization /-im′yonizā′shən/, the process whereby a person's immune system develops antibodies against one or more of the person's own tissues.

autoinfection, 1. an infection by disease organisms already present in the body but developing in a different body part. 2. a reinfection by microbes or parasitic organisms.

autoinfusion /-infyōō′zhən/, a technique for forcing blood from the extremities to the body core by applying bandages. It may be used to control bleeding and, in surgery, to create a relatively bloodless surgical field.

autoinoculation /-inok′yəla′shən/ [Gk, *autos*; L, *inoculare*, to graft], a secondary infection originating from a focus of infection already present in the body.

autointoxication /-intok′sikā′shən/ [Gk, *autos*; L, *in*; Gk, *toxikon*, poison], a condition of poisoning by substances generated by one's own body, as by toxins resulting from a metabolic disorder.

autokeratoplasty /-ker′ətōplas′tē/, the surgical transfer of corneal tissue from one eye of a patient to repair the cornea of the other.

autokinesia /-kinē′zhə/, voluntary movement.

autolesion /-lē′zhən/, a self-inflicted injury.

Autolet /ô′tōlet/, a trademark for a small, sharp instrument, as a lancet, that is used to obtain a capillary blood specimen.

autologous graft [Gk, *autos* + *logos* + *graphion*, stylus], the transfer of tissue from one site to another on the same body.

autologous stem cell transplantation (ASCT), a treatment for advanced or refractory solid tumors, such as neuroblastomas, lymphomas, and Ewing's sarcoma. Stem cells from the bone marrow or blood are withdrawn before high-dose irradiation or chemotherapy that destroys many of the remaining cells. The removed cells are later reinfused to form a new population of blood cells.

autologous transfusion, a procedure in which blood is removed from a donor and stored for a variable period before it is returned to the donor's circulation.

autolysis /ôtol′isis/, the spontaneous destruction of tissues by intracellular enzymes. It generally occurs in the body after death.

automated external defibrillator (AED), a portable apparatus used to restart a heart that has stopped. It is programmed to analyze cardiac rhythms automatically and indicate to a health professional when to deliver a defibrillating shock after the health professional has determined that no one is in contact with the patient.

automated reagin test (ART), a modification of the rapid plasma reagin (RPR) test for use with automated analyzers. It is used in clinical chemistry.

automatic external defibrillator (AED), a portable defibrillator designed to be automated such that it can be used by persons without substantial medical training who are responding to a cardiac emergency.

automatic implanted cardioverter defib-rill-ator (AICD), a surgically implanted device that automatically detects and corrects potentially fatal arrhythmias.

automatic infiltration detector /ô'təmat'ik/ [Gk, *automatismos,* self-action], a temperature-sensitive device that activates an alarm and automatically stops an IV infusion when the IV fluid passes into tissue.

automaticity /ô'tōmətis'itē/, a property of specialized excitable tissue that allows self-activation through spontaneous development of an action potential, as in the pacemaker cells of the heart.

automatic speech, speech composed of or containing words or phrases, such as numbers, the alphabet, or greetings, that are overlearned and spoken rotely.

automation /ô'təmā'shən/, use of a machine designed to follow a predetermined sequence of individual operations repeatedly and automatically.

automatism /ôtom'ətiz'əm/ [Gk, *automatismos,* self-action], **1.** (in physiology) involuntary function of an organ system independent of apparent external stimuli, such as the beating of the heart, or dependent on external stimuli but not consciously controlled, such as the dilation of the pupil of the eye. **2.** (in philosophy) the theory that the body acts as a machine and that the mind, whose processes depend solely on brain activity, is a noncontrolling adjunct of the body. **3.** (in psychology) mechanical, repetitive, and undirected behavior that is not consciously controlled, as seen in psychomotor epilepsy, hysteric states, and such acts as sleepwalking.

automnesia /ô'tōmnē'zhə/, the recollection of a previous experience.

autonomic /ô'tənom'ik/ [Gk, *autos* + *nomos,* law], **1.** having the ability to function independently without outside influence. **2.** pertaining to the autonomic nervous system.

autonomic bronchodilators, a category of drugs with actions that dilate bronchiolar smooth muscle tissue by acting on the autonomic nervous system. Examples are adrenergic drugs and anticholinergic products.

autonomic drug, any of a large group of drugs that mimic or modify the function of the autonomic nervous system.

autonomic dysreflexia, a syndrome affecting persons with a spinal cord lesion above the midthoracic level (tetraplegics and some paraplegics) that is characterized by hypertension, bradycardia, severe headaches, pallor below and flushing above the cord lesions, and convulsions. It is the result of impaired function of the autonomic nervous system caused by simultaneous sympathetic and parasympathetic activity.

autonomic ganglion [Gk, *autos,* self, *nomos,* law, *ganglion,* knot], a physical grouping of autonomic neuron cell bodies.

autonomic hyperreflexia, a neurologic disorder characterized by a discharge of sympathetic nervous system impulses as a result of stimulation of the bladder, large intestine, or other visceral organs. It occurs in persons with certain spinal cord injuries.

autonomic imbalance [Gk, *autos,* self, *nomos,* law; L, *in,* not, *bilanx,* having two scales], a disruption of a segment of the autonomic nervous system, as in autonomic ataxia.

autonomic nerve [Gk, *autos,* self, *nomos,* law, *neuron,* nerve], a nerve of the autonomic nervous system. It possesses the ability to function independently and spontaneously as needed to maintain optimal status of body activities.

autonomic nervous system, the part of the nervous system that regulates involuntary body functions, including the activity of the cardiac muscle, smooth muscles, and glands. It has two divisions: The sympathetic nervous system accelerates heart rate, constricts blood vessels, and raises BP; the parasympathetic nervous system slows heart rate, increases intestinal peristalsis and gland activity, and relaxes sphincters.

autonomic reflex, any of a large number of normal reflexes governing and regulating the functions of the viscera. Autonomic reflexes control such activities of the body as BP, heart rate, peristalsis, sweating, and urination.

autonomy /ôton'əmē/ [Gk, *autos* + *nomos,* law], the quality of having the ability or tendency to function independently.—**autonomous,** *adj.*

autonomy drive, a behavioral trait characterized by the attempt of an individual to master the environment and to impose his or her purposes on it.

auto-PEEP /aw'to-pēp'/, intrinsic positive end-expiratory pressure.

autophagia /-fā'jə/, **1.** a mental disorder characterized by the biting or eating of one's own flesh, as may occur in Lesch-Nyan syndrome. **2.** the automatic consumption of one's own tissues by fasting or dieting. **3.** the metabolic action of catabolism.

autoplastic maneuver /-plas'tik/, (in psychology) a process that is part of adaptation, involving an adjustment within the self.

autoplasty /ô'təplas'tē/ [Gk, *autos* + *plassein,* to mold], a plastic surgery procedure in which autografts are used to replace or repair body areas damaged by disease or injury.

autoploid /ô'təploid/, having homologous chromosome sets, or two or more copies of a single haploid set.

autopodium /-pō'dē·əm/, the distal major subdivision of a hand or foot.

autopolyploid /ô'tōpol'iploid/ [Gk, *autos* + *polyploos,* many times, *eidos* form], **1.** an individual, organism, strain, or cell that has more than two genetically identical or nearly identical sets of chromosomes that are derived from the same ancestral species. **—autopolyploidy,** *n.* **2.** pertaining to such an individual, organism, strain, or cell.

autopsy /ô'topsē/ [Gk, *autos* + *opsis,* view], a postmortem examination performed to confirm or determine the cause of death.**—autopsic, autopsical,** *adj.,* **autopsist,** *n.*

autopsy pathology, the study of disease by the examination of the body after death by a pathologist.

autoregulation [Gk, *autos,* self; L, *regula,* rule], an intrinsic capacity of organs to regulate their own blood flow or metabolic activity. The former process results from the contraction or relaxation of selfexcitable smooth muscle, which causes the constriction or dilation of vessels. It allows organs to maintain constant blood flow and meet their metabolic needs despite variations in systemic arterial pressure.

autosensitization /-sen'sətīzā'shən/ [Gk, *autos,* self; L, *sentire,* to feel], the sensitization of an individual by humoral antibodies or by a delayed cellular reaction to substances in his or her own body tissues.

autosepticemia /-sep'tisē'mē·ə/, a systemic infection in which pathogens are present in the circulating bloodstream, developing from an infection within the body.

autoserous treatment /ô'təsir'əs/ [Gk, *autos;* L, *serum,* whey], therapy of an infectious disease by inoculating the patient with the patient's own serum.

autosite /ô'təsīt/ [Gk, *autos* + *sitos,* food], the larger, more normally formed member of unequal or asymmetric conjoined twins on whom the other smaller fetus depends for various physiologic functions and for nutrition and growth. **—autositic,** *adj.*

autosmia /ôtoz'mē·ə/ [Gk, *autos,* self, *osme,* smell], awareness of one's own body odor.

autosomal /ô'təsō'məl/ [Gk, *autos* + *soma,* body], **1.** pertaining to or characteristic of an autosome. **2.** pertaining to any condition transmitted by an autosome.

autosomal-dominant inheritance, a pattern of inheritance in which the transmission of a dominant allele on an autosome causes a trait to be expressed.

autosomal inheritance, a pattern of inheritance in which the transmission of traits depends on the presence or absence of certain alleles on the autosomes. The pattern may be dominant or recessive, and males and females are usually affected with equal frequency. The majority of hereditary disorders are the result of a defective gene on an autosome.

autosomal-recessive inheritance, a pattern of inheritance resulting from the transmission of a recessive allele on an autosome.

autosomatognosis /-sō'mətognō'sis/, a phantom sensation that an amputated part of the body is still attached.

autosome /ô'təsōm/, any chromosome that is not a sex chromosome and that appears as a homologous pair in a somatic cell. Humans have 22 pairs of autosomes, which transmit all genetic traits and conditions other than those that are sex-linked. **—autosomal,** *adj.*

autosplenectomy /ô'tōsplinek'təmē/ [Gk, *autos* + *splen,* spleen, *ektomē,* excision], a progressive shrinking of the spleen that may occur in sickle cell anemia. The spleen is replaced by fibrous tissue and becomes nonfunctional.

autosuggestion [Gk, *autos;* L, *suggerere,* to suggest], an idea, thought, attitude, or belief suggested to oneself, often as a formula or incantation, as a means of controlling one's behavior.

autotopagnosia /ô'tōtop'əgnō'zhə/ [Gk, *autos* + *topos,* place, *a* + *gnosis,* without knowledge], the inability to recognize or localize the various body parts because of organic brain damage.

autotoxemia /-toksē'mē·ə/, a form of poisoning caused by substances generated within the body as a result of the pathologic alteration of the person's own tissues.

autotoxic, pertaining to autotoxins.

autotransfusion¹ /-transfyoo'zhən/, the collection, anticoagulation, filtration, and reinfusion of blood from an active bleeding site. It may be used in cases of major trauma or in major surgery when blood can be collected from a sterile site.

autotransfusion², a Nursing Interventions Classification (NIC) defined as collecting and reinfusing blood that has been lost intraoperatively or postoperatively from clean wounds.

autovaccination, a second vaccination in which a virus from the first vaccine sore is used.

autozygous /-zī'gəs/, pertaining to genes in a homozygote that are copies of the same ancestral gene as a result of a mating between related individuals.

auxanology /ôks'ənol'əjē/ [Gk, *auxein,* to grow, *logos,* science], the scientific study of growth and development.—**auxanologic,** *adj.*

auxcardia [Gk, *auxein,* increase, *kardia,* heart], an enlarged heart.

auxesis, growth from increase in cell size without cell division.

auxiliary /ôksil'yərē/ [L, *auxilium,* aid], an individual or group serving in assistive, supporting, or complementary tasks in a clinical setting.

auxiliary enzyme [L, *auxilium,* assist], an enzyme that links the enzyme being measured with an indicator enzyme. It is a component of the coupled assay system.

auxotonic /ôk'sōton'ik/, pertaining to muscle contractions that increase in force as the muscle shortens.

auxotox [Gk, *auxein,* increase, *toxikon,* poison], a chemical with a particular atomic grouping that, if added to a relatively benign substance, increases the toxic characteristics of the mixture.

AV, 1. abbreviation for **arteriovenous. 2.** abbreviation for **arterioventricular.**

available arch length /əvā'ləbəl/ [ME, *availen,* to be of use], the length or space in a dental arch that is available for all the natural teeth of an individual.

avalvular /āvalv'yələr/ [Gk, *a,* without; L, *valva,* valve], pertaining to an absence of one or more valves.

Avandia, a trademark for an oral antidiabetic (rosiglitazone).

avascular /āvas'kyələr/ [Gk, *a,* without; L, *vasculum,* vessel], **1.** pertaining to a tissue area that is not receiving a sufficient supply of blood. **2.** pertaining to a kind of tissue that does not have blood vessels.

avascular graft [Gk, *a,* without; L, *vasculum,* vessel; Gk, *graphion,* stylus], a tissue graft in which there is no infiltration of blood vessels.

avascularization [Gk, *a,* without; L, *vasculum,* vessel], a diversion of blood flow away from tissues.

Avastin, a trademark for bevacizumab.

AVB, abbreviation for **atrioventricular block.**

average, (in mathematics) a value established by dividing the sum of a series by the number of its units.

aversion therapy /əvur'zhən/ [L, *aversus,* a turning away], a form of behavior therapy in which punishment or unpleasant or painful stimuli, such as electric shock or drugs that induce nausea, are used to suppress undesirable behavior.

aversive stimulus /əvur'siv/, an undesirable stimulus that causes psychic or physical pain.

avian influenza /ā've·ən/, a highly contagious viral disease of birds caused by an influenza A virus. It may be transmitted to humans through contact with bird droppings or surfaces contaminated by them or through intermediate hosts such as pigs. Person-to-person transmission appears to be rare.

avian tuberculosis, a strain of TB in birds, caused by *Mycobacterium avium.* The organism is also pathogenic in humans and is especially problematic in the immunocompromised.

aviation medicine /āv'ē·ā'shən/, a branch of medicine that is concerned with the health effects of travel by aircraft, including such aspects as jetlag, restricted body movement for long periods, and reaction to violent aircraft movement in turbulent weather.

aviation physiology, a branch of physiology that is concerned with the effects on humans and animals exposed for long periods to pressurized cabins; radiation hazards at high altitudes; weightlessness; and disturbances of biologic rhythms, acceleration, and mental functions under stressful flying conditions.

avidin, a glycoprotein in raw egg white that interacts with biotin to make it unavailable to the body. Cooking destroys avidin.

avidity /avid'itē/ [L, *avidus,* eager], an inexact measure of the binding strength of antibodies to multiple antigenic determinants on natural antigens.

A-V interval [L, *intervallum,* space between ramparts], the time between an atrial polarization and the next ventricular polarization in ECGs.

avirulent /āvir'yələnt/ [Gk, *a,* not; L, *virus,* poison], not virulent; not pathogenic.

avitaminosis /āvī'təminō'sis/ [Gk, *a,* not; L, *vita,* life, amine, *osis,* condition], a condition resulting from a deficiency of or lack of absorption or use of one or more dietary vitamins.

AV nicking, a vascular abnormality in the retina of the eye in which a vein is compressed by an arteriovenous crossing. The vein appears "nicked" as a result of constriction or spasm. It is a sign of hypertension, arteriosclerosis, or other vascular conditions.

avobenzone /av′o-ben′zōn/, a sunscreen that absorbs light in the UVA range.

Avogadro's law, a law in physics stating that equal volumes of all gases at a given temperature and pressure contain the identical number of particles.

Avogadro's number (NA), the number of atoms in exactly 12 g of the isotope of carbon ^{12}C, or 6.02×10^{23}. One mole of any monoatomic element contains this number of atoms and one mole of any polyatomic element or molecule contains this number of molecules.

avoidance [ME, *avoiden,* to empty], (in psychiatry) a conscious or unconscious defense mechanism, physical or psychologic, by which an individual tries to avoid or escape from unpleasant stimuli, conflicts, or feelings, such as anxiety, fear, pain, or danger.

avoidance-avoidance conflict, a conflict resulting from the confrontation of two or more alternative goals or desires that are equally aversive and undesirable.

avoidance conditioning, the establishment of certain patterns of behavior to avoid unpleasant or painful stimuli.

avoidant personality, a personality disorder characterized by hypersensitivity to rejection and a reluctance to start a relationship because of a fear of not being accepted uncritically.

avoirdupois weight /av′ərdəpoiz′/ [OF, *avoir de pois,* to have weight], the English system of weights in which there are 7000 grains, 256 drams, or 16 ounces to 1 pound. One ounce in this system equals 28.35 g, and 1 pound equals 453.59 g.

Avonex, a trademark for an antiviral and immune system regulator (interferon beta-1a) useful for treating MS.

avulsed tooth /əvulst/ [L, *avulsio,* a pulling away], a tooth that has been forcibly displaced from its normal position.

avulsion /əvul′shən/ [L, *avulsio,* a pulling away], the separation, by tearing, of any part of the body from the whole. —**avulse,** *v.*

avulsion fracture, a fracture caused by the tearing away of a fragment of bone where a strong ligamentous or tendinous attachment forcibly pulls the fragment away from osseous tissue.

awake anesthesia [ME, *awakenen*], an anesthetic procedure in which analgesia and anesthesia are accomplished without LOC.

AWHONN, abbreviation for **Association of Women's Health, Obstetric, and Neonatal Nurses.**

AWOL /ā′wôl/, abbreviation for **absent without leave.**

axenic culture, a pure culture of microorganisms, i.e., one free from contaminating microorganisms or, in the case of parasites, without the presence of the host.

axetil, contraction for *L-acetoxyethyl.*

axial (A) /ak′sē·əl/ [Gk, *axon,* axle], **1.** pertaining to or situated on the axis of a body structure or part. **2.** (in dentistry) relating to the long axis of a tooth.

axial current, the central part of the blood current.

axial gradient, 1. the variation in metabolic rate in different parts of the body. **2.** the development toward the body axis or its parts in relation to the metabolic rate in the various parts.

axial illumination, light transmitted along the axis of a microscope.

axial resolution, the ability of an ultrasound system to separate two objects lying along the axis of an ultrasound beam.

axial skeleton [L, *axis,* axle; Gk, *skeletos,* dried up], the bones forming the axis of the skeleton, including the skull, vertebrae, ribs, and sternum.

axial spillway, a groove that crosses a cusp ridge or a marginal ridge and extends onto a long surface of a tooth.

Axid, a trademark for an antiulcerative H_2-receptor agent (nizatidine).

axifugal /aksif′yəgəl/ [L, *axis,* axle, *fugere,* to flee], extending away from an axis or axion.

axilla *pl.* **axillae** /aksil′ə/ [L, wing], a pyramid-shaped space forming the underside of the shoulder between the upper arm and the side of the chest. —**axillary,** *adj.*

axillary abscess [L, *axilla,* wing, *abscedere,* to go away], an abscess in the armpit.

axillary artery [L, *axilla,* wing], one of a pair of continuations of the subclavian arteries that starts at the outer border of the first rib and ends at the distal border of the teres major, where it becomes the brachial artery.

axillary line, an imaginary vertical line on the body wall, passing through a point midway between the anterior and posterior folds of the axilla.

axillary nerve, one of the last two branches of the posterior cord of the brachial plexus before the posterior cord becomes the radial nerve.

axillary node, one of the lymph glands of the axilla that help fight infections in the chest, armpit, neck, and arm and drain lymph from those areas.

axillary node dissection, surgical removal of axillary nodes, through an incision in the axilla or as part of modified radical mastectomy.

axillary region, the area of the upper chest surrounding the axilla, lateral to the pectoral region.

axillary temperature [L, *axilla,* wing, *temperatura*], the body temperature as recorded by a thermometer placed in the armpit. The reading is generally 0.5° to 1° less than the oral temperature.

axillary vein, one of a pair of veins of the upper limb that becomes the subclavian vein at the outer border of the first rib.

axillary walls, the four walls of the axilla. The anterior wall is formed by the lateral part of the pectoralis major muscle, the pectoralis minor and subclavius muscles, and the clavipectoral fascia. The medial wall is formed by the upper thoracic wall and the serratus anterior muscle. The lateral wall is formed entirely by the intertubercular sulcus of the humerus. The posterior wall is formed by the costal surface of the scapula, the subscapularis muscle, the distal parts of the latissimus dorsi and teres major muscles, and the proximal part of the long head of the triceps brachii muscle.

axillofemoral bypass graft /ak′silō fem′ərəl/, a synthetic artery that is surgically anastomosed to the axillary and common femoral arteries in cases of peripheral arterial insufficiency. The graft shunts blood between those arteries, increasing blood flow to the lower extremities.

axion /ak′sē·on/, **1.** the brain and spinal cord. **2.** the cerebrospinal axis.

axis *pl.* **axes** /ak′sēz/ [Gk, *axon,* axle], **1.** (in anatomy) a line that passes through the center of the body, or a part of the body, such as the frontal axis, binauricular axis, and basifacial axis. **2.** the second cervical vertebra, about which the atlas rotates, allowing the head to be turned, extended, and flexed.

axis artery, one of a pair of extensions of the subclavian arteries, running into and supplying the upper limb, continuing into the forearm as the palmar interosseous artery.

axis deviation, an ECG trace in which the QRS axis of the heart in the frontal plane lies outside the usual range of −30 to 110 degrees. It represents an abnormal direction of ventricular depolarization.

axis traction, 1. the process of pulling a baby's head with obstetric forceps in a direction in line with the path of least resistance, following the curve of Carus through the mother's birth canal. **2.** informal. any mechanical device attached to obstetric forceps to facilitate pulling in the proper direction.

axoaxonic synapse /ak′sō·akson′ik/ [Gk, *axon,* axle (to) *axon,* axle], a synapse in which the axon of one neuron comes in contact with the axon of another neuron.

axodendritic synapse /-dendrit′ik/ [Gk, *axon + dendron,* tree], a synapse in which the axon of one neuron comes in contact with the dendrites of another neuron.

axodendrosomatic synapse /-den′drōsōmat′ ik/, a synapse in which the axon of one neuron comes in contact with both the dendrites and the cell body of another neuron.

axolysis /aksol′isis/, the degeneration of the axon of a nerve cell.

axon /ak′son/ [Gk, axle], an extension, usually long and slender, of a neuron capable of conducting action potentials or self-propagating nervous impulses.

axon flare, vasodilation, reddening, and increased sensitivity of the skin surrounding an injured area, caused by an axon reflex. It is considered part of a triple response in which injury or stroking of the skin results in local reddening, the release of histamine or a histamine-like substance, a surrounding flare, and wheal formation.

axonography /ak′sənog′rəfē/, the recording of electrical activity in the axon of a nerve cell.

axonotmesis /ak′sənotmē′sis/ [Gk, *axon + temnein,* to cut], an interruption of the axon from nerve injury, with subsequent wallerian degeneration of the distal nerve segment.

axon reflex [Gk, *axon,* axle], a neuron reflex in which an afferent impulse travels along a nerve fiber away from the cell body until it reaches a branching, where it is diverted to an end organ without entering the cell body. It does not involve a complete reflex arc, and therefore it is not a true reflex.

axon sheath [Gk, *axon;* AS, *scaeth*], a laminated myelin sheath that is interrupted at intervals by nodes of Ranvier.

axoplasm /ak′sōplaz′əm/, cytoplasm of an axon that encloses the neurofibrils.

axoplasmic flow /ak′sōplaz′mik/ [Gk, *axon + plassein,* to shape], the continuous pulsing, undulating movement of the cytoplasm between the cell body of a neuron, where protein synthesis occurs, and the axon fiber to supply it with the substances vital for the maintenance of activity and for repair.

axosomatic synapse /ak´sōsōmat´ik/ [Gk, *axon* + *soma*, body], a synapse in which the axon of one neuron comes in contact with the cell body of another neuron.

axotomy /ak´sot´əmē/, surgical transection of an axon.

Aygestin, a trademark for an oral progestin (norethindrone acetate).

ayurveda, a major health care system that emphasizes a preventive approach to health, focusing on an inner state of harmony and spiritual realization for self-healing. It includes special types of diets, herbs, and mineral parts and changes based on a system of constitutional categories in lifestyle. Enemas and purgation are used to cleanse the body of excess toxins.

azacitidine, an antineoplastic hormone used to treat myelodysplastic syndrome.

azatadine maleate /azat´ədēn/, an antihistamine with antiserotonin, anticholinergic, and sedative effects. It is used to treat allergic rhinitis and chronic urticaria.

azathioprine /az´əthī´ōprēn/, an immunosuppressive prescribed to prevent organ rejection after transplantation and to treat lupus erythematosus and other systemic inflammatory diseases, such as rheumatoid arthritis, that are unresponsive to other agents.

azelaic acid /az´ē-la´ik/, a dicarboxylic acid occurring in whole grains and animal products that has antibacterial effects on both aerobic and anaerobic organisms, particularly *Propionibacterium acnes* and *Staphylococcus epidermidis.* It normalizes keratinization and has a cytotoxic effect on malignant or hyperactive melanocytes. It is applied topically in the treatment of acne vulgaris.

azelastine, an H1-selective antihistamine that also inhibits leukotriene and platelet activating factor (PAF) synthesis and release. It is used to treat seasonal allergic rhinitis and seasonal allergic conjunctivitis.

Azelex /az´ē-leks/, a trademark for a preparation of azelaic acid used for treating acne.

Azilect, a trademark for rasagiline.

azithromycin, a macrolide antibiotic that suppresses the formation of protein by bacteria, retards bacterial growth, or causes death of the microorganisms. It does not suppress hepatic metabolism of other drugs and has a very long half-life, which makes it an appealing therapy against susceptible microorganisms. It is prescribed in the treatment of mild to moderate infections by certain bacteria in adults, including respiratory tract infections, skin disorders, and STDs.

azlocillin sodium /az´lōsil´in/, a semisynthetic penicillin antibiotic prescribed for lower respiratory tract, urinary tract, skin, bone, and joint infections and bacterial septicemia caused by susceptible strains of microorganisms, mainly *Pseudomonas aeruginosa.*

azo compounds /ā´zō/ [Fr, *azote,* nitrogen], one of many organic aromatic compounds containing the divalent chromophore, $-N=N-$. They are produced by the alkaline reduction of nitro compounds among other methods.

azo dye, a type of nitrogen-containing compound used in commercial coloring materials. Some forms of the chemical are potential carcinogens.

azoic /āzō´ik/ [Gk, *a,* not, *zoe,* life], devoid of life.

azole antifungal, any of a group of antifungals characterized by the presence of an azole ring structure, which includes the triazoles and the imidazoles. They are usually fungistatic but can be fungicidal at higher concentrations.

azoospermia /āzō´əspur´mē·ə/ [Gk, *a,* without, *zoon,* animal, *sperma* seed], lack of spermatozoa in the semen. It is associated with infertility, but not impotence.

azoprotein /ā´zōprō´tēn/, a protein coupled to another substance through a diazo $(-N=N-)$ linkage. Azoproteins are often used in immunochemical procedures.

azotemia /az´ōtē´mē·ə/ [Fr, *azote,* nitrogen; Gk, *haima,* blood], retention of excessive amounts of nitrogenous compounds in the blood. This toxic condition is caused by failure of the kidneys to remove urea from the blood and is characteristic of uremia.—**azotemic,** *adj.*

azoturia /az´ōtoor´ē·ə/ [Fr, *azote,* nitrogen; Gk, *ouron,* urine], an excess of nitrogenous compounds, including urea in the urine.

AZT, a trademark for an HIV inhibitor (zidovudine).

Azulfidine, a trademark for a sulfonamide antibacterial (sulfasalazine) used to treat ulcerative colitis and rheumatoid arthritis.

azure /āz´hər/, one of a group of basic blue methylthionine or phenothiazine dyes used in staining blood and cell nuclei.

azurophil, a substance that stains readily with an azure blue aniline dye.—**azurophilic,** *adj.*

azurophilia /āzh´oorəfil´yə/, a condition in which the blood contains some cells that have granules that stain readily with azure (blue) dye.

azygography /az´īgog´rəfē/, the radiographic imaging of the azygous venous system after injection of a radiopaque contrast medium.

azygospore /az'igəspôr/ [Gk, *a* + *zygon*, not yoke, *sporos*, seed], a spore that is produced directly from a gamete that has not undergone conjugation, as in certain algae and fungi.

azygous /az'igəs/ [Gk, *a* + *zygon*, not yoke], occurring as a single entity or part, such as any unpaired anatomic structure; not part of a pair. —**azygos** /az'əgos'/, *n.*

azygous lobe, a congenital anomaly of the lung caused by a fold of pleural tissue carried by the azygous vein during descent into the thorax during embryonic development. It produces an extra lobe in the right upper lung.

azygous vein, one of the seven veins of the thorax. In cases of obstruction to the inferior vena cava it is the principal vein that returns blood to the heart.

B

B, symbol for the element **boron**.

B6 bronchus sign, an artifact in a lung radiograph in which an air bronchogram appears in the lower lobe as a result of consolidation of atelectasis.

B19 virus, a strain of human parvovirus associated with a number of diseases, including hemolytic anemia, erythema infectiosum, fifth disease, and symptoms of arthritis and arthralgia.

Ba, symbol for the element **barium**.

BA, **1.** abbreviation for *Bachelor of Arts*. **2.** abbreviation for *blood alcohol*.

babbling, a stage in speech development characterized by the production of strings of speech sounds in vocal play, such as "ba-ba-ba."

Babcock's operation [William W. Babcock, American surgeon, 1872–1963], the removal of a varicosed saphenous vein by insertion of an acorn-tipped sound, tying the vein to the sound, and drawing it out.

babesiosis /bəbē′sē-ō′sis/ [Victor Babés, Romanian bacteriologist, 1854–1926], a potentially severe and sometimes fatal disease caused by infection with protozoa of the genus *Babesia*.

Babinski's reflex /bəbin′skēz/ [Joseph Babinski, French neurologist, 1857–1932], dorsiflexion of the big toe with extension and fanning of the other toes elicited by firmly stroking the lateral aspect of the sole of the foot. The reflex is normal in newborns and abnormal in children and adults.

Babinski's sign [Joseph Babinski], a series of partial responses that are pathognomonic of different degrees of upper motor neuron disease, including (1) absence of an ankle jerk in sciatica; (2) an extensor plantar response, with an extension of the great toe and adduction of the other toes; (3) a more pronounced concentration of platysma on the unaffected side during blowing or whistling; (4) pronation that occurs when an arm affected by paralysis is placed in supination; and (5) when a patient in a supine position with arms crossed over the chest attempts to assume a sitting position, the thigh on the affected side is flexed and the heel is raised, whereas the leg on the unaffected side remains flat.

baby [ME, *babe*], **1.** an infant or young child, especially one who is not yet able to walk or talk. **2.** to treat gently or with special care.

baby bottle tooth decay, a dental condition that occurs in children between 12 months and 3 years of age as a result of being given a bottle at bedtime, resulting in prolonged exposure of the teeth to milk or juice.

Baby-Friendly Hospital, an international initiative launched by WHO and UNICEF in 1991 designed to support practices that protect, promote, and support breastfeeding in hospitals.

Baby Jane Doe regulations, rules established in 1984 by the U.S. Department of Health and Human Services requiring state governments to investigate complaints about parental decisions involving the treatment of handicapped infants. The controversial regulations have been found illegal by a federal court.

baby talk, **1.** the speech patterns and sounds of young children learning to talk, characterized by mispronunciation, imperfect syntax, repetition, and phonetic modifications such as lisping or stuttering. **2.** the intentionally oversimplified manner of speech, imitative of young children learning to talk, used by adults in addressing children or pets. **3.** the speech patterns characteristic of regressive stages of various mental disorders, especially schizophrenia.

BAC, abbreviation for **bronchoalveolar carcinoma**.

bacampicillin hydrochloride, a semisynthetic penicillin prescribed in the treatment of respiratory tract, urinary tract, skin, and gonococcal infections.

Bachelor of Science in Nursing (BSN) /bach′ələr/, an academic degree awarded on satisfactory completion of a course of study in a college or university. The recipient is eligible to take the national certifying examination to become a registered nurse.

Bach remedies, a set of 38 flower essences, formulated to enhance mental or emotional well-being.

Bacillaceae /bas′əlā′si·ē/ [L, *bacillum*, small rod], a family of Bacilli of the order Bacillales, consisting of grampositive, rod-shaped cells that can produce cylindric, ellipsoid, or spheric endospores situated terminally, subterminally, or centrally. These cells are chemoheterotrophic and mostly saprophytic, commonly appearing in soil. Some are parasitic on insects and animals and are pathogenic. The family includes the genus *Bacillus,* which is aerobic, and the genus *Clostridium,* which is facultatively anaerobic.

bacillary angiomatosis /bas′əler′ē/, a condition of multiple angiomata caused by an infection of *Bartonella.* The infectious agent is associated with contact with young cats infected with fleas and is also the cause of cat-scratch fever. It is manifested in persons with cellular immunodeficiency as small hemangioma-like lesions of the skin but may also involve the lymph nodes and viscera. The skin lesions are often mistaken for Kaposi's sarcoma.

bacillary white diarrhea, pullorum disease.

bacille Calmette-Guérin (BCG)/kalmet′ gāran′/ [Léon C.A. Calmette, French bacteriologist, 1863–1933; Camille Guérin, French bacteriologist, 1872–1961], an attenuated strain of the *Mycobacterium bovis* bacillus that is given as a live bacterial vaccine to prevent the development of TB. It is most often administered intradermally, with a multiple-puncture disk. When administered to infants in high-prevalence areas, there is some evidence that it prevents the more serious forms of TB. It may have some efficacy against leprosy. BCG is also instilled into the bladder as a treatment for bladder cancer to stimulate the immune response in people who have certain kinds of malignancy.

bacille Calmette-Guérin vaccine, an active immunizing agent prepared from an attenuated bacille Calmette-Guérin strain of *Mycobacterium bovis.* It is prescribed most commonly for immunization against TB. It is instilled intravesically to treat carcinoma in situ of the urinary bladder in certain situations. It is seldom administered in the United States as an immunizing agent but is often given in many countries to infants, caregivers, and others who are at high risk for intimate and prolonged exposure to people with active TB.

bacillemia /bas′əlē′mē·ə/, a condition in which bacilli are circulating in the blood.

bacilli /bəsil′ī/ *sing.* **bacillum** [L, *bacillum,* small rod], any rod-shaped bacteria.

bacilliform /bəsil′ifôrm/, rod-shaped, like a bacillus.

bacillosis /bas′əlō′sis/, a condition in which bacilli have invaded tissues, inducing symptoms of an infection.

bacilluria /bas′əlŏŏr′ē·ə/ [L, *bacillum;* Gk, *ouron,* urine], the presence of bacilli in the urine.

Bacillus /bəsil′əs/, a genus of aerobic, gram-positive spore-producing bacteria in the family Bacillaceae, order Eubacteriales. The genus includes 34 species, 3 of which are pathogenic and the rest saprophytic soil forms; 25 species are considered medically important.

Bacillus anthracis, a species of gram-positive, facultative anaerobe that causes anthrax.

Bacillus cereus, a species of bacilli found in the soil. It causes food poisoning (an emetic type and a diarrheal type) by the formation of an enterotoxin in contaminated foods. It can also cause infections such as ocular infections.

bacitracin /bas′itrā′sin/ [L, *bacillum* + *Tracy,* surname of patient in whom toxin-producing bacillus species was isolated], an antibacterial that is a common component of topical antibiotic ointments used for treating skin infections.

back [AS, *baec*], the posterior or dorsal part of the trunk of the body between the neck and pelvis. The back is divided by a middle furrow that lies over the tips of the spinous processes of the vertebrae. The skeletal part of the back includes the thoracic and lumbar vertebrae and both scapulae. The nerves that innervate the various muscles of the back arise from the segmental spinal nerves.

backache /bak′āk/ [AS, *baec;* ME, *aken*], a pain in the lumbar, lumbosacral, or cervical region of the back, varying in sharpness and intensity. Causes may include muscle strain or other muscular disorders or pressure on the root of a nerve, such as the sciatic nerve, caused in turn by a variety of factors, including a herniated vertebral disk.

back-action condenser, an instrument for compacting dental amalgams that has a U-shaped shank, which develops the condensing force from a pulling motion rather than from the more common pushing motions.

backboard, a long, flat, rigid piece of wood or other material that is placed under an accident victim with possible spinal injury. It is used to transport the patient to a hospital or as a firm surface for CPR.

backcross [AS, *baec* + *cruc,* cross], **1.** a mating (cross) between a heterozygote and a homozygote. **2.** an organism or strain produced by such a cross.

background level, the usual intensity of a chemical or other stimulus in the environment.

background radiation [AS, *baec;* OE, *grund,* ground], naturally occurring radiation emitted by soil, groundwater, building materials, radioactive substances in the body (especially potassium 40), and cosmic rays from outer space. Each year the average person is exposed to 44 millirads (mrad) of external terrestrial radiation, 18 mrad of naturally occurring internal radioactive, and 44 mrad of cosmic radiation.

backing /bak′ing/ [AS, *baec*], in dentistry, the piece of metal that supports a porcelain or resin facing on a fixed or removable partial denture.

back pressure [AS, *baec*; L, *premere*, to press], pressure that builds in a vessel or a cavity as fluid accumulates.

baclofen, an antispastic agent prescribed to reduce the spasticity associated with MS, cerebral palsy, and spinal cord injury. It is not effective against spasticity caused by stroke.

bacteremia /bak′tirē′mē·ə/ [Gk, *bakterion*, small staff, *haima*, blood], the presence of bacteria in the blood.—**bacteremic,** *adj.*

bacteremic shock, septic shock caused by the release of toxins by bacteria, usually gram-negative bacteria, in the blood.

bacteria /baktir′ē·ə/ *sing.* **bacterium** [Gk, *bakterion*, small staff], a domain of life existing as small unicellular microorganisms. The genera vary morphologically, being spheric (cocci), rod-shaped (bacilli), spiral (spirochetes), or comma-shaped (vibrios). The nature, severity, and outcome of any infection caused by a bacterium are characteristic of that species.

bacterial adherence /baktir′ē.əl/, the process whereby bacteria attach themselves to cells or other surfaces before proliferating.

bacterial aneurysm, a localized dilation in the wall of a blood vessel caused by the growth of bacteria. It often follows septicemia or bacteremia and usually occurs in peripheral vessels.

bacterial cholangitis, the most common type of cholangitis, caused by bacterial infection. If bacteria invade the liver they can enter the bloodstream and cause septicemia that can be fatal.

bacterial endocarditis, an acute or subacute bacterial infection of the endocardium or the heart valves or both. The condition is characterized by heart murmur, prolonged fever, bacteremia, splenomegaly, and embolic phenomena.

bacterial enteritis, enteritis caused by bacterial infection. The most common types in humans are *Campylobacter* enteritis, *Salmonella* enteritis, *Shigella* enteritis, and *Yersinia* enteritis.

bacterial enzyme, an enzyme produced by a bacterium.

bacterial food poisoning, a toxic condition resulting from the ingestion of food contaminated by certain bacteria. Acute infectious gastroenteritis caused by various species of *Salmonella* is characterized by fever, chills, nausea, vomiting, diarrhea, and general discomfort beginning 8 to 48 hours after ingestion and continuing for several days. Similar symptoms caused by *Staphylococcus,* usually *S. aureus,* appear much sooner and rarely last more than a few hours. Food poisoning caused by the neurotoxin of *Clostridium botulinum* is characterized by GI symptoms, disturbances of vision, weakness or paralysis of muscles, and, in severe cases, respiratory failure.

bacterial inflammation [L, *bacterium* + *inflammare*, to set afire], any inflammation that is part of a body's response to a bacterial infection.

bacterial kinase, **1.** a kinase of bacterial origin. **2.** a bacterial enzyme that activates plasminogen, the precursor of plasmin.

bacterial laryngitis, a form of laryngitis caused by a bacterial infection and usually associated with rhinosinusitis or laryngotracheal bronchitis. Signs of a bacterial infection are a cough and purulent rhinorrhea.

bacterial plaque, a dense, nonmineralized complex composed primarily of colonies of bacteria embedded in a gelatinous matrix. It contains amino acids, carbohydrates, proteins, lipids, and salts from saliva and gingival fluid; soluble food substances; shed leukocytes and epithelial cells; and products of bacterial metabolism. Plaque is the major causative factor in most dental diseases.

bacterial pneumonia, pneumonia caused by bacteria, such as *Klebsiella pneumoniae, Mycoplasma pneumoniae, Staphylococcus aureus, Streptococcus pneumoniae,* and *Streptococcus pyogenes.*

bacterial prostatitis, a bacterial infection of the prostate. Acute bacterial infections usually involve gram-negative bacilli such as *Escherichia coli.* Abscesses may be associated with anaerobic bacteria. Chronic bacterial prostatitis is usually caused by gram-negative bacilli.

bacterial protein, a protein produced by a bacterium.

bacterial resistance, the ability of certain strains of bacteria to develop a tolerance toward specific antibiotics.

bacterial toxin [Gk, *bakterion*, small staff, *toxikon*, poison], any poisonous substance produced by a bacterium.

bacterial vaccine, a saline solution suspension of a strain of attenuated or killed bacteria prepared for injection into a patient to stimulate development of active immunity to that strain and to similar bacteria.

bacterial vaginosis [Gk, *bakterion*, small staff; L, *vagina*, sheath; Gk, *osis*, condition], a chronic inflammation of the vagina caused by bacterial imbalance.

bacterial virus, a virus with the ability to infect and/or destroy bacteria.

bactericidal antibiotic [Gk, *bakterion*; L, *caedere,* to kill; Gk, *anti,* against, *bios,* life], an antibiotic drug that kills bacteria.

bactericide /baktir′əsīd/ [GK, *bakterion*; L, *caedere,* to kill], any drug or other agent that kills bacteria.—**bactericidal,** *adj.*

bactericidin [Gk, *bakterion*; L, *caedere,* to kill], an antibody that kills bacteria in the presence of complement.

bacteriocin /baktir′ē·əsin/, protein produced by certain species of bacteria that are toxic to related strains of those bacteria.

bacteriocinogenic /baktir′ē·əsin′əjen′ik/, pertaining to an organism capable of producing bacteriocins.

bacteriogenic /baktir′ē·əjen′ik/, **1.** capable of producing bacteria. **2.** derived from or originating in bacteria. **3.** caused by bacteria.

bacteriologic /baktir′ē·ol′əj′ik′ [Gk, *bakterion*], pertaining to **bacteriology.**

bacteriologic sputum examination, a laboratory procedure to determine the presence or absence of bacteria in a sputum specimen. Part of the specimen is stained and examined microscopically on a glass slide, and part is inoculated on culture medium and allowed to incubate for more specific examination later.

bacteriologist /baktir′ē·ol′əjist/, a specialist in the scientific study of bacteria.

bacteriology /-ol′əjē/ [Gk, *bakterion* + *logos,* science], the scientific study of bacteria.

bacteriolysin /baktir′ē·əlī′sin/ [Gk, *bakterion* + *lyein,* to loosen], an antibody that causes the breakdown of a particular species of bacterial cell.

bacteriolysis /baktir′ē·ol′əsis/, the intracellular or extracellular breakdown of bacteria.—**bacteriolytic,** *adj.*

bacteriophage /baktir′ē·əfāj′/ [Gk, *bakterion* + *phagein,* to eat], any virus that infects host bacteria, including the bluegreen algae. Bacteriophages resemble other viruses in that each is composed of either RNA or DNA.—**bacteriophagic,** *adj.,* **bacteriophagy** /-of′əjē/, *n.*

bacteriophage typing, the process of identifying a species of bacterium according to the type of virus that attacks it.

bacteriospermia /baktir′ē·əspur′mē·ə/, the presence of bacteria in semen or ejaculate.

bacteriostasis /baktir′ē·os′təsis/ [Gk, *bakterion* + *stasis,* standing still], a state of suspended growth and/or reproduction of bacteria.—**bacteriostatic,** *adj.*

bacteriuria /baktir′ēyŏŏr′ē·ə/, the presence of bacteria in the urine.

bacteroid /bak′təroid/, **1.** pertaining to or resembling bacteria. **2.** a structure that resembles a bacterium.—**bacteroidal, bacterioidal,** *adj.*

Bacteroides /bak′təroi′dēz/ [Gk, *bakterion,* small staff, *eidos,* form], a genus of obligate anaerobic bacilli normally found in the colon, mouth, genital tract, and upper respiratory system. Severe infection may result from the invasion of the bacillus through a break in the mucous membrane into venous circulation.

Bactrim, a trademark for a fixed-combination drug containing two antibiotics (sulfamethoxazole and trimethoprim) commonly prescribed to treat UTI.

BAER, abbreviation for **brainstem auditory evoked response.**

baffling, the process of removing large water particles from suspension in a jet nebulizer so that the particles entering the patient's airways are of a uniform therapeutic size.

bag [AS, *baelg*], a flexible or dilatable sac or pouch designed to contain gas, fluid, or semisolid material such as crushed ice. Several types of bags are used in medical or surgical procedures to dilate the anus, vagina, or other body openings.

bagasse /bəgas′/ [Fr, cane trash], the crushed fibers or the residue of sugarcane, a source of the thermophilic actinomycetes antigen that is a cause of bagassosis hypersensitivity pneumonitis.

bagassosis /bag′əsō′sis/, a self-limited lung disease caused by an allergic response to bagasse, the fungi-laden, dusty debris left after the syrup has been extracted from sugarcane.

bagging *informal.* the artificial ventilation performed with a ventilator or respirator bag. The bag is squeezed to deliver air to the patient's lungs through a mask or an endotracheal tube.

bag-valve-mask resuscitator, a device consisting of a manually compressible container with a plastic bag of oxygen at one end and at the other a one-way valve and mask that fit over the mouth and nose of the person to be resuscitated.

Bainbridge reflex [Francis A. Bainbridge, English physiologist, 1874–1921], a cardiac reflex in which stimulation of stretch receptors in the wall of the left atrium causes an increased pulse rate.

Baker's cyst [William M. Baker, British surgeon, 1839–1896], a synovial cyst that forms at the back of the knee. It is often associated with rheumatoid arthritis and may appear only when the leg is straightened.

baker's itch [AS, *giccan,* to bake], a rash that may develop on the hands and forearms of bakery workers, probably as an allergic reaction to flours or other ingredients in bakery products.

BAL, 1. abbreviation for *British antilewisite.* 2. abbreviation for **bronchoalveolar lavage.**

balance[1] [L, *bilanx,* having two scales], 1. an instrument for weighing. 2. a normal state of physiologic equilibrium. 3. a state of mental or emotional equilibrium. 4. to bring into equilibrium.

balance[2], a nursing outcome from the Nursing Outcomes Classification (NOC) defined as ability to maintain body equilibrium.

balanced anesthesia, a highly variable technique of general anesthesia using narcotic analgesics, muscle relaxation, and minimal inhalation agent and nitrous oxide to render the patient unconscious.

balanced articulation, simultaneous contact between the upper and lower teeth as they glide over each other when the mandible is moved laterally.

balanced diet, a diet containing adequate energy and all of the essential nutrients that cannot be synthesized in adequate quantities by the body, in amounts adequate for growth, energy needs, nitrogen equilibrium, repair, and maintenance of normal health.

balanced occlusion, simultaneous contact between the upper and lower teeth on both sides and in the anterior and posterior occlusal areas of the jaws. This term is primarily associated with intraoral assessment of occlusal harmony but may also be used in the process of pretesting the occlusion while the dentures are mounted on casts attached to an anatomic articulator.

balanced polymorphism, in a population, the occurrence of a certain proportion of homozygotes and heterozygotes for specific genetic traits, which is maintained from generation to generation by the forces of natural selection.

balanced suspension, a system of splints, ropes, slings, pulleys, and weights for suspending the lower extremities of the body, used as an aid to realignment and healing from fractures or from surgical intervention.

balanced traction, a system of balanced suspension that supplements traction in the treatment of fractures of the lower extremities or after various operations affecting the lower parts of the body.

balanced translocation, the transfer of segments between nonhomologous chromosomes in such a way that the configuration and total number of chromosomes change but each cell contains the normal amount of diploid or haploid genetic material. A person with a balanced translocation is phenotypically normal but may produce children with trisomies.

balancing side, the side of the mouth opposite the working side of dentition or a denture.

balanic /bəlan′ik/ [Gk, *balanos,* acorn], pertaining to the glans penis or the glans clitoritis.

balanitis /bal′ənī′tis/ [Gk, *balanos* + *itis*], inflammation of the glans penis.

balanitis diabetica, an inflammation of the glans penis or glans clitoritis caused by the sugar content of the urine and commonly seen in persons with diabetes.

balanitis xerotica obliterans /zirot′ikə oblit′ərans/ [Gk, *balanos* + *itis* + *xeros,* dry, *tokos,* labor; L, *obliterare,* to efface], a chronic skin disease *(lichen sclerosis et atrophicus)* of the penis, characterized by a white indurated area surrounding the meatus, that may result in urethral stenosis.

balanoplasty /bal′ənōplas′tē/ [Gk, *balanos* + *plassein,* to mold], an operation involving plastic surgery of the glans penis to correct a congenital defect or to serve an aesthetic purpose.

balanoposthitis /bal′ənōposthī′tis/ [Gk, *balanos* + *posthe,* penis, foreskin + *itis*], a generalized inflammation of the glans penis and prepuce in uncircumcized males, usually caused by poorly retractile foreskin and poor hygiene. It is characterized by soreness, irritation, and discharge, which occur as a complication of bacterial or fungal infection.

balanopreputial /bal′ənōpripyo͞o′shəl/ [Gk, *balanos;* L, *praeputium,* foreskin], pertaining to the glans penis and the prepuce.

balanorrhagia /bal′ənōrā′jē·ə/ [Gk, *balanos* + *rhegnynai,* to burst forth], balanitis in which pus is discharged copiously from the penis.

balantidiasis /bal′əntidī′əsis/, an infection caused by ingestion of cysts of the protozoan *Balantidium coli,* which usually causes diarrhea. Infrequently the infection progresses, and the protozoal invades the intestinal wall and produces ulcers or abscesses, which may cause dysentery and death.

Balantidium coli /bal′əntid′ē·əm/ [Gk, *balantidion,* little bag, *kolon,* colon], the largest and the only ciliated protozoal species that is pathogenic to humans, causing balantidiasis.

baldness [ME, *balled*], absence of hair, especially from the scalp.

BAL in Oil, a trademark for a heavy metal antagonist (dimercaprol).

Balint's syndrome [Rudolph Balint, Hungarian neurologist, 1874–1929], a group of visual symptoms characterized by simultaneous anagnosia and optic ataxia. The patient experiences nystagmus, or loss of control of eye movements, and the inability to perceive all parts of a scene simultaneously. The patient may begin to follow a moving object but lose it. The cause is bilateral disease of the parietotemporal areas of the brain.

Balkan traction frame, an overhead, rectangular frame attached to the bed and used for attaching splints, suspending or changing the position of immobilized limbs, or providing continuous traction with weights and pulleys.

Balkan tubulointerstitial nephritis /tōō′byəlō·in′tərstish′əl/, a chronic kidney disorder marked by renal insufficiency, proteinuria, tubulointerstitial nephritis, and anemia. The disease is endemic in the Balkans but is not hereditary.

ball [ME, *bal*], a spherical object, such as one of the collagen balls embedded in hyaline cartilage.

Ballance's sign [Charles A. Ballance, English surgeon, 1856–1936], a dull percussion resonance sound heard on the right flank of a patient lying in the left decubitus position, an indication of a ruptured spleen. The sound is caused by an accumulation of liquid blood on the right side and coagulated blood on the left.

ball-and-socket joint, a synovial or multiaxial joint in which the globular (ball-shaped) head of an articulating bone is received into a cuplike cavity, allowing the distal bone to move around an indefinite number of axes with a common center, such as in hip and shoulder joints.

ball-catcher position, a position of the hands for making a radiograph to diagnose rheumatoid arthritis. The hands are held with the palms upward and the fingers cupped, as if to catch a ball.

Baller-Gerold syndrome /bä′lər ga′rōlt/ [Friedrich Baller, German physician, 20th century; M. Gerold, German physician, 20th century], an autosomal-recessive syndrome characterized by craniosynostosis and absence of the partial or complete absence of the radius.

ballismus /bôl′iz′məs/ [Gk, *ballismo*, dancing], an abnormal neuromuscular condition characterized by uncoordinated swinging of the limbs and jerky movements, associated with extrapyramidal disorders such as Sydenham's chorea.

ballistic movement /bəlis′tik/, a high-velocity musculoskeletal movement, such as a tennis serve or boxing punch, requiring reciprocal coordination of agonistic and antagonistic muscles.

ballistics /bəlis′tiks/ [Gk, *ballein*, to throw], the study of the motion, trajectory, and impact of projectiles, including bullets and rockets.

ballistocardiograph [Gk, *ballein*, to throw, *kardia,* heart, *graphein,* to record], an apparatus for recording body movements caused by the thrust of the heart during systolic ejection of the blood into the aorta and the pulmonary arteries.

ballistocardiography /balis′tōkär′dē·og′rəfē/, the recording of body movements in reaction to the beating of the heart and the circulation of the blood.

ball of the foot, the part of the foot composed of the distal heads of the metatarsals and their surrounding fatty fibrous tissue pad.

balloon angioplasty /bəlōōn′/, a method of dilating or opening an obstructed blood vessel by threading a small, balloon-tipped catheter into the vessel. The balloon is inflated to compress arteriosclerotic lesions against the walls of the vessel, leaving a larger lumen, through which blood can pass.

balloon compression, a percutaneous therapy for trigeminal neuralgia. A balloon is inflated to compress the gasserian ganglion and produce trigeminal injury.

balloon tamponade [Fr, *tamponnade*], a procedure in which a device consisting of a flexible tube and two balloons is inserted into a passageway and the balloons are expanded to restrict the flow of blood or to force open a stenosis.

balloon-tip catheter, a catheter bearing a nonporous inflatable sac around its far end. After insertion of the catheter, the sac can be inflated with air or sterile water introduced via injection into a special port at the near end of the catheter.

ballottable /bəlot′əbəl/ [Fr, *balloter,* a shaking about], pertaining to a use of palpation to detect movement of objects suspended in fluid, such as a fetus in amniotic fluid, or the patella bumping against the femur.

ballottable head [Fr, *ballotage*, shaking up], a floating fetal head; a fetal head that has not descended and has not become fixed in the maternal bony pelvis.

ballottement /bä′lôtmäN′, bəlot′ment/ [Fr, *tossing*], a technique of palpating an organ or floating structure by bouncing it gently and feeling it rebound.

ball thrombus, a relatively round, coagulated mass of blood, containing platelets, fibrin, and cellular fragments, that may obstruct a blood vessel or an orifice, usually the mitral valve of the heart.

ball-valve action, the intermittent opening and closing of an orifice by a buoyant, ball-shaped mass, which acts as a valve. Some kinds of objects that may act in this manner are kidney stones, gallstones, and blood clots.

B

balm /bäm/ [Gk, *balsamon*, balsam], **1.** a healing or a soothing substance such as any of various medicinal ointments. **2.** an aromatic plant of the genus *Melissa* that relieves pain.

balneology /bal′nē·ol′əjē/ [L, *balneum*, bath; Gk, *logos*, science], a field of medicine that deals with the chemical compositions of various mineral waters and their healing characteristics, especially in baths. —**balneologic,** *adj.*

balneotherapy /bal′nē·ōther′əpē/ [L, *balneum*; Gk, *therapeia*, treatment], use of baths in the treatment of many diseases and conditions.

balsalazide /balsal′ahəzīd/, a gastrointestinal antiinflammatory agent used to treat active ulcerative colitis.

balsam /bôl′səm/ [Gk, *balsamon*], any of a variety of resinous saps, generally from evergreens, usually containing benzoic or cinnamic acid. Balsam is sometimes used in rectal suppositories and dermatologic agents as a counterirritant.

Baltimore Longitudinal Study of Aging (BLSA), a long-range examination of interrelations between multiple correlates of aging. Although men of varied backgrounds were selected for the original study (1955) to explore uncontrolled factors that might lead to new knowledge regarding aging, the BLSA now includes both men and women.

Bamberger's sign [Heinrich Bamberger, Austrian physician, 1822–1888], **1.** a neural disorder characterized by the feeling of a tactile stimulation at a corresponding point on the opposite side of the body. **2.** pericardial effusion signs at the level of the scapula that disappear when the patient leans forward.

bamboo spine /bamboo′/ [Malay, *bambu*], (in radiology) the appearance of the thoracic or lumbar spine with rigid characteristic of advanced ankylosing spondylitis.

band [ME, *bande*, strip], **1.** (in anatomy) a bundle of fibers, as seen in striated muscle, that encircles a structure or binds one part of the body to another. **2.** (in dentistry) a strip of metal that fits around a tooth and serves as an attachment for orthodontic components. **3.** *informal.* the immature form of a segmented neutrophil characterized by a sausage-shaped nucleus.

band adapter, an instrument for aiding in the fitting of a circumferential orthodontic band to a tooth.

bandage /ban′dij/ [ME, *bande*, strip], **1.** a strip or roll of cloth or other material that may be wound around a part of the body in a variety of ways to secure a dressing, maintain pressure over a compress, or immobilize a limb or other part of the body. **2.** to apply a bandage.

bandage shears, a sturdy pair of scissors used to cut through bandages. The blades of most bandage shears are angled to the shaft of the instrument, and the lower blade is rounded and blunt to facilitate insertion under the bandage without harming the patient's skin.

band cell, a developing granular (immature) leukocyte in circulating blood, characterized by a curved or indented nucleus.

band heterotopia, an anomaly of the cerebral cortex in which a heterotopic band of gray matter is found between the lateral ventricles and the cortex. Affected patients may have mental retardation or epilepsy.

banding [ME, *bande*, strip], any of several techniques of staining chromosomes with fluorescent stains or chemical dyes that produce a series of transverse light and dark areas whose intensity and position are characteristic of each chromosome.

bandpass, (in radiology) a measure of the number of times per second an electron beam can be modulated, expressed as hertz (Hz). It is a factor that influences horizontal resolution on a cathode-ray tube. The higher the bandpass, the greater the horizontal resolution.

band pusher, an instrument used for seating metal circumferential orthodontic bands into correct position on a tooth.

band remover, an instrument used to help take circumferential orthodontic bands off teeth.

bandwidth, the range of frequencies that can be satisfactorily transmitted or processed by a system.

bank blood [It, *banca*, bench; AS, *blod*], anticoagulated preserved blood collected from donors, usually in units of 500 mL, and stored in CPDA-1 anticoagulant for a maximum of 35 days.

Banting, Sir Frederick G. [Canadian physician, 1891–1941], co-winner, with John J. Macleod, of the 1923 Nobel prize for medicine and physiology for their research, with the Canadian physiologist Charles H. Best, showing the link between the pancreas and insulin in the control of diabetes.

Banti's syndrome /ban′tēz/ [Guido Banti, Italian pathologist, 1852–1925], a chronic, progressive disorder involving several organ systems, characterized by portal hypertension, splenomegaly, anemia, leukopenia, GI tract bleeding, and cirrhosis of the liver.

BAO, abbreviation for **basal acid output.**

bar, (in physical science) a measure of air pressure. It is equal to 1000 millibars, or 10^6 dyne/cm², or approximately 1 standard atmosphere (1 atm).

Baraclude, a trademark for entecavir.

baralyme /ber′əlīm/ [Gk, *barys*, heavy; AS, *lim*, lime], a mixture of calcium and barium compounds used to absorb exhaled carbon dioxide in an anesthesia rebreathing system.

barbiturate /bärbich′ŏŏrāt, -ərit/ [Saint Barbara, drug discovered on day of the saint, 1864], a derivative of barbituric acid that acts as a sedative or hypnotic. These derivatives act by depressing the respiratory rate, BP, temperature, and CNS. They have great addiction potential.

barbiturate coma [Ger, Saint Barbara's Day; Gk, *koma,* deep sleep], an effect of barbituric acid or its derivatives, which may be rapid-acting sedatives, hypnotics, and respiratory depressants. Barbiturate coma may be intentionally induced for the treatment of some neurologic conditions.

barbiturism /bärbich′əriz′əm/, **1.** acute or chronic poisoning by any of the derivatives of barbituric acid. **2.** addiction to a barbiturate.

bar clasp arm, (in prosthetic dentistry) a clasp arm that originates from a denture base and serves as an extracoronal retainer to an abutment tooth.

Bard-Pic syndrome /bärd pik′/ [Louis Bard, French anatomist, 1857–1930; Adrian Pic, French physician, b. 1863], a condition characterized by progressive jaundice, enlarged gallbladder, and cachexia, associated with advanced pancreatic cancer.

Bard's sign [Louis Bard], the increased oscillations of the eyeball in organic nystagmus when the patient tries to visually follow a target moved from side to side across the line of sight.

bare lymphocyte syndrome, an immune deficiency condition caused by defective beta-2 microglobulin, one of the major histocompatibility antigens on cell surfaces. It is inherited as an autosomal-recessive trait.

baresthesia /bär′esthē′zhə/, sensitivity to weight or pressure.

bar graph [OF, *barre*], a graph in which frequencies are represented by bars extending from the ordinate or the abscissa, allowing the distribution of the entire sample to be seen at once.

bariatrics /ber′ē·at′riks/ [Gk, *baros,* weight, *iatros,* physician], the field of medicine that focuses on the treatment and control of obesity and diseases associated with obesity.

bariatric surgery, surgery on part of the GI tract as a treatment for morbid obesity.

baritosis /ber′ətō′sis/, a benign form of pneumoconiosis caused by an accumulation of barium dust in the lungs, most likely to affect persons involved in the mining and processing of barite.

barium **(Ba)** /ber′ē·əm/ [Gk, *barys,* heavy], a pale yellow, metallic element classified with the alkaline earths. Its atomic number is 56; its atomic mass is 137.36.

barium enema, a rectal infusion of barium sulfate, a radiopaque contrast medium, which is retained in the lower intestinal tract during roentgenographic studies for diagnosis of obstruction, tumors, or other abnormalities.

barium meal, the ingestion of barium sulfate, a radiopaque contrast medium, for the radiographic examination of the esophagus, stomach, and intestinal tract in the diagnosis of such conditions as dysphagia, peptic ulcer, and fistulas.

barium poisoning, a condition characterized by a severe, rapid decrease in plasma potassium levels and a shift of potassium into cells caused by the ingestion of soluble barium salts. The patient may experience nausea, vomiting, abdominal cramps, bloody diarrhea, dizziness, arrhythmias, ringing in the ears, cardiac arrest, and respiratory failure.

barium sulfate, a radiopaque medium used as a diagnostic aid in radiology. It is prescribed for x-ray examination of the GI tract.

barium swallow [Gk, *barys,* heavy; AS, *swelgan,* to swallow], the oral administration of a radiopaque barium sulfate suspension given to radiographically demonstrate possible defects in the esophagus and abnormal borders of the posterior aspects of the heart.

Barker, Phil, a nursing theorist who developed the Tidal Model of Health Recovery for psychiatric and mental health nursing. The life stories, or experiences, of psychiatric patients must be carefully evaluated to determine what resources they have for recovery and what kind of support is needed from and for the nurses who are caring for the patients.

Barlow's syndrome [John B. Barlow, South African cardiologist, 1924–2008], an abnormal cardiac condition characterized by an apical systolic murmur, a systolic click, and an ECG indicating inferior ischemia. These signs are associated with mitral regurgitation caused by prolapse of the mitral valve.

Barnard, Kathryn E. [b. 1938], a nursing theorist who developed the Child Health Assessment Interaction Model. Her model and theory were the outcome of the Nursing Child Assessment Project (1976–1979). Barnard believes that the parent-infant system is influenced by individual characteristics of each member. Those characteristics are modified to meet the needs of the system by adaptive behavior. A major issue in Barnard's theoretic assertions is that the nurse gives support to the mother's sensitivity and response to her infant's cues rather than trying to change her characteristics or mothering style.

barognosis /ber´ognō´sis/ *pl.* **barognoses** [Gk, *baros,* weight, *gnosis,* knowledge], the ability to perceive and evaluate weight, especially that held in the hand.

barograph /ber´ograf´/ [Gk, *baros + graphein,* to record], an instrument that continually monitors barometric pressure and records pressure changes on paper.

barometer /bərom´ətər/ [Gk, *baros + metron,* measure], an instrument for measuring atmospheric pressure, commonly consisting of a slender tube filled with mercury, sealed at one end, and inverted into a reservoir of mercury. At sea level the normal height of mercury in the tube is 760 mm.—**barometric,** *adj.*

baroreceptor /ber´ōrisep´tər/ [Gk, *baros+* L, *recipere,* to receive], one of the pressure-sensitive nerve endings in the walls of the atria of the heart, the aortic arch, and the carotid sinuses. Baroreceptors stimulate central reflex mechanisms that allow physiologic adjustment and adaptation to changes in BP via changes in heart rate, vasodilation, or vasoconstriction.

Barosperse, a trademark for a radiopaque medium (barium sulfate).

barotrauma /ber´ōtrô´mə, -trou´mə/ [Gk, *baros + trauma,* wound], physical injury sustained as a result of exposure to changing air pressure or rupture of the tympanic membranes, as may occur among scuba divers or caisson workers or anyone near nuclear or atomic blasts.

barrel chest, a large, rounded thorax, as in the inspiratory phase, considered normal in some stocky individuals and certain others who live in high-altitude areas and consequently have increased vital capacity. Barrel chest may also be a sign of pulmonary emphysema.

barrel distortion, outward bowing of gridded straight lines in an image, resulting from lens distortion such that the lateral magnification at the center of the image is greater than that at the edges.

Barré's pyramidal sign /bäräz´/ [Jean A. Barré, French neurologist, 1880–1971], a diagnostic sign indicating a disease of the pyramidal tracts. The patient lies face down and the legs are flexed at the knee. The patient is unable to maintain this position.

Barrett's esophagus [Norman R. Barrett, English surgeon, 1903–1979], a disorder of the lower esophagus marked by a benign ulcerlike lesion in columnar epithelium, resulting most often from chronic irritation of the esophagus by gastric reflux of acidic digestive juices. The lesion is considered premalignant.

Barrett's syndrome [Norman R. Barrett, English surgeon, 1903–1979]

barrier /ber´ē-ər/ [ME, *barrere*], **1.** a wall or other obstacle that can restrain or block the passage of substances. **2.** something nonphysical that obstructs or separates such as barriers to communication or compliance. **3.** (in radiography) any device that intercepts beams of x-rays.

barrier creams, ointments, lotions, and similar preparations applied to exposed areas of the skin to protect skin cells from exposure to various allergens, irritants, and carcinogens, including sunlight.

barrier-free design [AS, *freo,* barreres; L, *designare,* to mark out], the design of homes, workplaces, and public buildings that allows physically challenged individuals to make regular use of such structures.

barrier methods, contraceptive methods, such as condoms and diaphragms, in which a plastic or rubber barrier blocks passage of spermatozoa through the vagina or cervix.

Barsony-Koppenstein method, a procedure for making radiographic images of the cervical intervertebral foramina.

Barthel Index (BI) [D.W. Barthel, twentieth century American psychiatrist], a disability profile scale developed to evaluate a patient's self-care abilities in 10 areas, including bowel and bladder control. The patient is scored from 0 to 15 points in various categories, depending on his or her need for help.

bartholinitis /bär´təlini´tis/ [Caspar T. Bartholin, Danish anatomist, 1655–1738; Gk, *itis*], an inflammatory condition of one or both Bartholin's glands, caused by bacterial infection. The condition is characterized by swelling of one or both glands, pain, and development of an abscess in the infected gland.

Bartholin's abscess /bär´təlinz/ [Caspar T. Bartholin; L, *abscedere,* to go away], an abscess of the greater vestibular gland of the vagina.

Bartholin's cyst [Caspar T. Bartholin], a cyst that arises from one of the vestibular glands or from its ducts and fills with clear fluid that replaces the suppurative exudate characteristic of chronic inflammation.

Bartholin's duct [Caspar T. Bartholin], the major duct of the sublingual salivary gland.

Bartholin's gland [Caspar T. Bartholin], one of two small mucus-secreting glands located on the posterior and lateral aspect of the vestibule of the vagina.

Bartholin's gland carcinoma [Caspar T. Bartholin], a rare malignancy that occurs deep in the labia majora.

Barton, Clara, (1821–1912), an American philanthropist, humanitarian, and founder of the American National Red Cross. During the U.S. Civil War, she was a volunteer nurse, and at its end she organized a bureau of records to help in the search for missing men. When the Franco-Prussian War erupted, she assisted in the organization of military hospitals in Europe in association with the International Red Cross. This led to her advocacy of the establishment of an American Red Cross organization, of which she became the first president.

Bartonella /bär'tənel'ə/ [Alberto Barton, Peruvian bacteriologist, 1871–1950], a genus of small gram-negative flagellated pleomorphic coccobacilli. Members of the genus infect RBCs and the epithelial cells of the lymph nodes, liver, and spleen. They are transmitted at night by the bite of a sandfly of the genus *Phlebotomus.* Three species are considered important in human disease: *B. bacilliformis, B. henselae,* and *B. quintana,* which causes trench fever and may cause peliosis of the liver.

Bartonella henselae, the etiologic agent of cat-scratch fever.

bartonellosis /bär'tənəlō'sis/, an acute infection caused by *Bartonella bacilliformis,* transmitted by the bite of a sandfly. It is characterized by fever, severe anemia, bone pain, and, several weeks after the first symptoms are observed, multiple nodular or verrucous skin lesions.

Barton's fracture [John R. Barton, American surgeon, 1794–1871], a break in the distal articular surface of the radius, which may be accompanied by the dorsal dislocation of the carpus on the radius.

Bartter's syndrome /bär'tərz/ [Frederick C. Bartter, American physiologist, 1914–1983], a rare hereditary disorder, characterized by hyperplasia of the juxtaglomerular area and secondary hyperaldosteronism.

basal /bā'səl/ [Gk, *basis,* foundation], pertaining to the fundamental or the basic, as basal anesthesia and the basal metabolic rate.

basal acid output (BAO), the minimum volume of gastric fluid produced by an individual in a given period. Normal adult volume is 2 to 5 mEq/hr. It is used infrequently in the diagnosis of various diseases of the stomach and intestines.

basal body temperature method of family planning, a natural method of family planning that relies on identification of the fertile period of the menstrual cycle by noting the rise in basal body temperature that occurs with ovulation. Abstinence is required to avoid pregnancy from 6 days before the earliest day that ovulation was noted to occur during the preceding 6 months until the third day after the rise in temperature in the current cycle. The basal body temperature method is more effective when used with the ovulation method than when either method is used alone.

basal body temperature (BBT), the temperature of the body under conditions of absolute rest, taken orally or rectally, after sleep and before the patient does anything, including getting out of bed, smoking a cigarette, moving around, talking, eating, or drinking.

basal bone, 1. (in prosthodontics) the osseous tissue of the mandible and the maxilla, except for the rami and the processes, which provides support for artificial dentures. **2.** (in orthodontics) the fixed osseous structure that limits the movement of teeth in the creation of a stable occlusion.

basal cell, any one of the cells in the deepest layer of stratified epithelium.

basal cell carcinoma [Gk, *basis*; L, *cella,* storeroom; Gk, *karkinos,* crab, *oma,* tumor], a malignant epithelial cell tumor that begins as a pearly-appearing papule and enlarges peripherally, developing a central crater that erodes, crusts, and bleeds. It occurs most frequently in sun-exposed areas of the body.

basal ganglia [Gk, *basis* + *ganglion,* knot], the islands of gray matter, largely composed of cell bodies, within each cerebral hemisphere. The most important are the caudate nucleus, the putamen, and the pallidum.

Basaljel, a trademark for an antacid (aluminum carbonate gel).

basal lamina [Gk, *basis*; L, *lamina,* plate], a thin, noncellular layer of ground substance lying just under epithelial surfaces.

basal layer of endometrium, the deepest layer of the endometrium, which contains the blind ends of the uterine glands.

basal membrane, a sheet of tissue that forms the outer layer of the choroid and lies just under the pigmented layer of the retina.

basal metabolic rate (BMR), the amount of energy used in a unit of time by a fasting, resting subject to maintain vital functions. The rate, determined by the amount of oxygen used, is expressed in calories consumed per hour per square meter of body surface area or per kilogram of body weight.

basal metabolism [Gk, *basis* + *metabole,* change], the amount of energy needed to maintain essential body functions, such as respiration, circulation, temperature, peristalsis, and muscle tone. Basal metabolism is measured when the subject is awake and at complete rest, has not eaten for 14 to 18 hours, and is in a comfortable, warm environment.

basal narcosis [Gk, *basis,* foundation, *narkosis,* a benumbing], a narcosis induced with sedatives in a surgical patient before general anesthetic is administered. It is less profound than that of general anesthesia. The patient is unresponsive to verbal stimuli but may respond to noxious stimuli.

basaloid carcinoma /bā'səloid/ [Gk, *basis* + *eidos,* form, *karkinos,* crab, *oma,* tumor], a rare transitional malignant neoplasm of the anal canal containing areas that resemble basal cell carcinoma of the skin.

basal seat, (in dentistry) the oral structures that support a denture.

basal seat outline, a profile on the oral mucous membrane or on a cast of the entire oral area to be covered by a denture.

basal temperature chart [Gk, *basis,* foundation; L, *temperatura* + *charta,* paper], a daily temperature chart, usually including the temperature on awakening. A basal temperature chart is sometimes used by women to establish a date of ovulation, when the temperature may show a sudden increase.

basal tidal volume, the amount of air inhaled and exhaled by a healthy person at complete rest, with all bodily functions at a minimal level of activity, adjusted for age, weight, and sex.

base [Gk, *basis,* foundation], **1.** a chemical compound that increases the concentration of hydroxide ions in aqueous solution. **2.** a molecule or radical that takes up or accepts hydrogen ions. **3.** an electron pair donor. **4.** the major ingredient of a compounded material, particularly one that is used as a medication. **5.** (in radiology) the rigid but flexible foundation of a sheet of x-ray film.

base analog [Gk, *basis* + *analogos,* proportionate], a chemical analog of one of the purine or pyrimidine bases normally found in RNA or DNA.

Basedow's goiter /bä'sədōz/ [Karl A. von Basedow, German physician, 1799–1854], a name for colloid goiter, an enlargement of the thyroid gland characterized by the hypersecretion of thyroid hormone after iodine therapy. The condition causes increased basal metabolic rate, insomnia, and fine motor tremor.

base excess, a measure of metabolic alkalosis or metabolic acidosis (negative value of base excess).

base-forming food, a food that increases the pH of the urine. Base-forming foods mainly are fruits, vegetables, and dairy products, which are sources of sodium and potassium.

baseline /bās'līn/ [Gk, *basis*; L, *linea*], **1.** a known value or quantity with which an unknown is compared when measured or assessed. **2.** the patient's initial information at diagnosis or assessment against which later tests will be compared. **3.** (in radiology) any of several basic anatomic planes or locations used for positioning purposes.

baseline behavior, a specified frequency and form of a particular behavior during preexperimental or pretherapeutic conditions.

baseline condition, an environmental condition during which a particular behavior reflects a stable rate of response before the introduction of experimental or therapeutic conditions.

baseline fetal heart rate, the fetal heart rate pattern between uterine contractions.

baseline pain, the average intensity of pain experienced for 12 or more hours in a 24-hour period.

Basel Nomina Anatomica **(BNA),** an international system of anatomic terminology adopted at Basel, Switzerland.

basement membrane [Fr, *soubassement,* under base], the fragile noncellular layer that secures the overlying epithelium to the underlying tissue. It is the deepest layer and may contain reticular fibers.

base of gastric gland, the main part of a gastric gland interior to the neck.

base of renal pyramid, the part of a renal pyramid that is directed away from the renal sinus.

base of the heart, the portion of the heart opposite the apex. It forms the upper border of the heart, lies just below the second rib, and primarily involves the left atrium, part of the right atrium, and the proximal portions of the great vessels.

base of the skull, the floor of the skull, containing the anterior, middle, and posterior cranial fossae and numerous foramina.

base pair, a pair of nucleotides in the complementary strands of a DNA molecule that interact through hydrogen bonding across the axis of the helix. One of the nucleotides in each pair is a purine (either adenine or guanine), and the other is a pyrimidine (either thymine or cytosine). Because of distinct hydrogen bonding capacity, adenine always pairs with thymine, and guanine always pairs with cytosine.

base pairing, the formation of base pairs in DNA.

baseplate [Gk, *basis*; ME, *plate*], a temporary prosthetic structure that represents the base of a denture, used for making records of maxillomandibular relationships, for evaluating lip line and lip fullness, for arranging artificial denture teeth, or for ensuring a precise fit of a denture by trial placement in the mouth.

baseplate wax, a dental wax containing about 75% paraffin or ceresin with additions of beeswax and other waxes and resins; used chiefly to establish the initial arch form in making trial plates for the arrangement of artificial denture teeth, and for the construction of complete dentures.

base plus fog, the optical density of a processed film in the absence of any radiation exposure.

base ratio, the ratio of the molar quantities of purine and pyrimidine bases in DNA and RNA.

bas-fond /bäfôN'/ [Fr, bottom], the bottom or fundus of any structure, especially the fundus of the urinary bladder.

basic aluminum carbonate gel, an aluminum hydroxide aluminum carbonate gel. It is used as an antacid, for treatment of hyperphosphatemia in renal insufficiency, and to prevent phosphate urinary calculi.

basic amino acid, an amino acid that has a positive electric charge in solution at a pH of 7.0. The basic amino acids are arginine, histidine, and lysine.

Basic Cardiac Life Support, Emergency procedures implemented to maintain viability of heart tissue until advanced support is available. It includes cardiopulmonary resuscitation and automated external defibrilator use.

basic group identity, (in psychiatry) the shared social characteristics, such as world view, language, values, and ideologic system, that evolve from membership in an ethnic group.

basic health services, the minimum degree of health care considered to be necessary to maintain adequate health and protection from disease.

basic human needs, the elements required for survival and normal mental and physical health, such as food, water, shelter, protection from environmental threats, and love.

basic life support (BLS) [Gk, basis, foundation; AS, lif; L, supportare, to bring up to], emergency treatment of a victim of cardiac or respiratory arrest through CPR and emergency cardiac care.

basic salt, a salt that contains an unreplaced hydroxide ion from the base generating it, such as Ca(OH)Cl.

Basidiobolus /bəsid'ē·ob'ələs/ [Gk, basis, foundation, bolos, a throw], a mainly saprobic genus of fungi of the family Basidiobolaceae. The species B. ranarum causes entomophthoromycosis in humans and horses.

basifacial /bā'sifā'shəl/ [Gk, basis; L, facies, face], pertaining to the lower part of the face.

basilar /bas'ilər/ [Gk, basis, foundation], pertaining to a base or a basal area.

basilar artery, the single posterior arterial trunk formed by the junction of the two vertebral arteries at the base of the skull. It extends from the inferior to the superior border of the pons before dividing into the left and right posterior cerebral arteries.

basilar artery insufficiency syndrome, the composite of clinical indicators associated with insufficient blood flow through the basilar artery, a condition that may be caused by arterial occlusion.

basilar artery occlusion, an obstruction of the basilar artery, resulting in dysfunction involving cranial nerves III through XII, cerebellar dysfunction, hemiplegia or quadriplegia, and loss of proprioception.

basilar membrane, the cellular structure that forms the floor of the cochlear duct and is supported by bony and fibrous projections from the cochlear wall.

basilar plexus [Gk, basis; L, braided], the venous network interlaced between the layers of the dura mater over the basilar portion of the occipital bone.

basilar sulcus [Gk, basis; L, furrow], the sulcus that cradles the basilar artery in the midline of the pons.

basilar vertebra, the lowest or last of the lumbar vertebrae.

basilic vein /bəsil'ik/, one of the four superficial veins of the arm, beginning in the ulnar part of the dorsal venous network and running proximally on the posterior surface of the ulnar side of the forearm.

basiliximab, a monoclonal antibody used for immunosuppression. This drug is used in combination with cyclosporine and corticosteroids to treat acute allograft rejection in renal transplant patients.

basiloma terebrans /ter'əbranz/ [Gk, basis + oma; L, terebare, to bore], an invasive basal cell epithelioma.

basin, 1. a receptacle for collecting or holding fluids. 2. term used to describe the shape of the pelvis.

basioccipital /bā'si·oksip'ətəl/ [Gk, basis; L, occiput, back of the head], pertaining to the basilar process of the occipital bone.

basion /bā'sē·on/ [Gk, basis, foundation], the midpoint on the anterior margin of the foramen magnum of the occipital bone.

basis, the lower part, designating the base of an organ or other structure, such as the base of the cerebrum.

basket /bas·ket/, a container made of material woven together, or something resembling such a container.

basket cell [L, bascauda, dishpan], 1. deep stellate cells (neurons) of the cerebral cortex with a horizontal axon that sends out branches. Each axon branch or collateral breaks up into a basket-like mesh that surrounds a Purkinje cell. 2. myoepithelial cells of mammary glands stimulated by oxytocin.

basolateral membrane, the layer of plasma membrane of epithelial cells that is adjacent to the basement membrane and separated from the apical membrane by the zonula occludens.

basophil /bā'sǒfil/ [Gk, *basis* + *philein,* to love], a granulocytic WBC characterized by cytoplasmic granules that stain blue when exposed to a basic dye. Basophils represent 1% or less of the total WBC count.

basophilic adenoma [Gk, *basis* + *philein,* to love, *aden,* gland, *oma*], a tumor of the pituitary gland composed of cells that can be stained with basic dyes.

basophilic erythrocyte,

basophilic leukemia [Gk, *basis* + *philein,* to love, *leukos,* white, *haima,* blood], an acute or chronic malignant neoplasm of blood-forming tissues, characterized by large numbers of immature basophilic granulocytes in peripheral circulation and in tissues.

basophilic stippling [Gk, *basis* + *philein,* to love; D, *stippen,* to prick], the presence of punctate blue nucleic acid remnants in red blood cells, observed under the microscope on a Wright-Giemsa-stained blood film. Stippling is characteristic of lead poisoning.

basosquamous cell carcinoma /bā'sŏskwā'məs/ [Gk, *basis*; L, *squamosus,* scaly], a malignant epidermal tumor composed of basal and squamous cells.

bath [AS, *baeth*], (in the hospital) a cleansing procedure performed by or for patients, as needed for hygienic or therapeutic purposes, to help prevent infection, preserve the unbroken condition of the skin, stimulate circulation, promote oxygen intake, maintain muscle tone and joint mobility, and provide comfort.

bath blanket, a thin, lightweight cloth used to cover a patient during a bath.

bathesthesia /bath'əsthē'zhə/ [Gk, *bathys,* deep, *aisthesia,* feeling], sensitivity to deep structures in the body.

bathing, a nursing intervention from the Nursing Interventions Classification (NIC) defined as cleaning of the body for the purposes of relaxation, cleanliness, and healing.

bathyanesthesia /bath'ēan'esthē'zhə/ [Gk, *bathys,* deep, *anaisthesia,* loss of feeling], a loss of deep feeling, such as that associated with organs or structures beneath the body surface or with muscles and joints; a loss of sensitivity to deep structures in the body.

bathycardia /bath'ēkär'dē·ə/ [Gk, *bathys,* deep, *kardia,* heart], a condition in which the heart is located at an abnormally low site in the thorax.

Batten disease /bat'en/, any or all of the group of disorders constituting neuronal ceroid lipofuscinosis

Batten's disease [Frederick E. Batten, English ophthalmologist neurologist, 1865–1918], a progressive childhood encephalopathy characterized by disturbed metabolism of polyunsaturated fatty acids. It occurs in children between 5 and 10 years of age. The child experiences sudden blindness and progressive mental deterioration. Also called Vogt-Spielmeyer disease.

battered woman syndrome (BWS), repeated episodes of physical assault on a woman by the person with whom she lives or with whom she has a relationship, often resulting in serious physical and psychologic damage to the woman. Such violence tends to follow a predictable pattern, starting with verbal abuse, progressing to acute, violent activity, and followed by apologies, remorse, and promises of change. Over time, the violent episodes escalate in frequency and severity.

battery [Fr, *batterie*], **1.** a device of two or more electrolytic cells connected to form a single source providing direct current or voltage. **2.** a series or a combination of tests to determine the cause of a particular illness or the degree of proficiency in a particular skill or discipline. **3.** the unlawful use of force on a person.

Battey bacillus /bat'ē/ [Battey Hospital, in Rome, Georgia, where bacteria strain was first isolated], a bacillus, later renamed *Mycobacterium intracellulare,* that causes a chronic pulmonary disease resembling TB. It is considered an opportunistic pathogen and does not commonly infect healthy individuals.

battledore placenta /bat'əldôr'/ [ME, *batyldoure,* a beating instrument; L, *placenta,* flat cake], a condition in which the umbilical cord is attached at the margin of the placenta.

Battle's sign [William H. Battle, English surgeon, 1855–1936], a palpable bogginess of area behind the ear. It may indicate a fracture of a bone of the lower skull.

batyl alcohol /bat'əl/, an alcohol found in fish liver oil that is used to treat bracken poisoning in cattle.

bay, an anatomic depression or recess, usually containing fluid, such as the lacrimal bay of the eye.

Bayes' theorem /bāz'/ [Thomas Bayes, British mathematician, 1702–1761], a mathematic statement of the relationships of test sensitivity, specificity, and the predictive value of a positive test result. The predictive value of the test is the number that is useful to the clinician. A positive result demonstrates the conditional probability of the presence of a disease.

Bayetta, a trademark for exenatide.

Bayley Scales of Infant Development [Nancy Bayley, American psychologist, 1899–1994], a three-part scale for assessing the development of children between the ages of 2 months and 2½ years. Infants are tested for perception, memory, and vocalization on the mental scale; sitting, stair climbing, and manual manipulation on the motor scale; and attention span, social behavior, and persistence on the behavioral scale.

Baylisascaris /bā'lisas'käris/, a genus of nematodes found in the intestines of mammals. Fecal contamination from raccoons and rodents can spread to domestic animals and humans, resulting in larva migrans or eosinophilic encephalitis.

bayonet condenser [Fr, *baionette*], an instrument used in dentistry for compacting restorative material, used primarily for varying the line of force in the compaction of gold.

BBB, **1.** abbreviation for **bundle branch block.** **2.** abbreviation for **blood-brain barrier.**

BBT, abbreviation for **basal body temperature.**

BCAA, abbreviation for **branched-chain amino acids.**

B cell, a category of lymphocyte that originates in the bone marrow and produces antibodies. A precursor of the plasma cell, it is one of the two lymphocytes that play a major role in the body's immune response.

B cell–growth/differentiation factor, one of several substances, such as interleukins IL-4, IL-5, and IL-6, that are derived from T-cell cultures and are necessary for the differentiation, growth, and maturation of plasma cells and B memory cells.

B-cell lymphoma, any in a large group of non-Hodgkin's lymphomas characterized by malignant transformation of the B lymphocytes.

B cell–mediated immunity, the ability to produce an immune response induced by B lymphocytes. Contact with a foreign antigen stimulates B cells to differentiate into plasma cells, which release antibodies. Plasma cells also generate memory cells, which provide a rapid response if the same antigen is encountered again.

BCG, abbreviation for **bacille Calmette-Guérin.**

BCG solution, an aqueous suspension of bacille Calmette-Guérin for instillation into the bladder to activate the immune system in treatment of superficial bladder cancers. It reduces the risk of a subsequent

bladder cancer developing, although the exact mechanism of action is unknown.

BCHC diet, abbreviation for **Bristol Cancer Help Center diet.**

BCLS, abbreviation for *basic cardiac life support.*

B complex vitamins, a large group of water-soluble nutrients that includes thiamine (vitamin B_1), cyanocobalamin (vitamin B_{12}), niacin (vitamin B_3), pyridoxine (vitamin B_6), riboflavin (vitamin B_2), biotin, folic acid, and pantothenic acid. The B complex vitamins are essential, for example, for the conversion of simple carbohydrates like glucose and the carbon skeletons of amino acids into energy, and for the metabolism of fats and proteins.

BDI, abbreviation for **Beck's depression inventory.**

B-DNA, a long, thin form of DNA in which the helix is right-handed.

Be, symbol for the element **beryllium.**

beaded /bē'ded/ [ME, *bede*], **1.** having a resemblance to a row of beads. **2.** pertaining to bacterial colonies that develop along the inoculation line in various stab cultures. **3.** pertaining to stained bacteria that develop more deeply stained beadlike granules.

beak, **1.** any pointed anatomic structure, such as the beak of the sphenoid bone. **2.** a pair of dental pincers used in shaping prostheses. **3.** a radiographic image of a bony protuberance adjacent to a degenerative intervertebral disk.

beak sign, the appearance of abnormal structures on radiographic images of the GI tract: a distal esophagus in achalasia and a proximal pyloric canal in pyloric stenosis.

Beals' syndrome /bēlz/ [Rodney Kenneth Beals, American orthopedic surgeon, b. 1931], An autosomal-dominant syndrome characterized by long, thin extremities with abnormally long fingers and toes, multiple joint contractures, kyphoscoliosis, and malformed auricles of the ears; it is a form of hereditary bone dysplasia.

beam [ME, *beem,* tree], **1.** a bedframe fitting for pulleys and weights, used in the treatment of patients requiring weight traction. **2.** (in radiology) the primary beam of radiation emitted from the x-ray tube.

BEAM /bēm, bē'ē'ā'em'/, abbreviation for **brain electrical activity map.**

beam alignment, in radiography, the process of positioning the radiographic tube head so that it is aligned properly with the x-ray film.

beam collimation, the restriction of x-radiation to the area being examined or treated by confining the beam with metal diaphragms or shutters with high radiation-absorption power.

beam hardening, the process of increasing the average energy level of an x-ray beam by filtering out the low-energy photons.

BE amputation, abbreviation for **below-elbow amputation.**

beam quality, the energy of an x-ray beam.

beam restrictor, a device that reduces the size of the beam of radiation from x-ray equipment.

beam splitter, a device that reflects light from the output phosphor of an image intensifier to a photographic recording.

beam-splitting mirror, a device that allows a radiologist to view a fluoroscopic examination of a patient while the same view is being recorded on film.

bean [ME, *bene*], the pod-enclosed flattened seed of numerous leguminous plants. Beans used in pharmacologic preparations are alphabetized by specific name.

bearing down /ber'ing/ [OE, *beran*, to bear, *adune*, down], a voluntary effort by a woman in the second stage of labor to aid in the expulsion of a fetus. By applying the Valsalva maneuver, the mother increases intraabdominal pressure.

bearing down pains [OE, *beran*, to bear, *adune*, down; L, *poena*, penalty], the pains experienced by a woman during the second stage of labor while performing the Valsalva maneuver to help expel the fetus.

beat, the mechanical contraction or electric activity of the heart muscle, which may be detected and recorded as the pulse or on the ECG, respectively.

Beau's lines /bōz'/ [Joseph H.S. Beau, French physician, 1806–1865], transverse depressions that appear as white lines across the fingernails as a sign of an acute severe illness such as malnutrition, a systemic disease, thyroid dysfunction, or coronary occlusion.

becaplermin /bĕkap'lermin/, a recombinant platelet-derived growth factor used in treatment of chronic severe dermal ulcers of the lower limbs in diabetes mellitus.

Beck, Cheryl Tatano, a nursing theorist whose Postpartum Depression Theory asserts that postpartum depression results from a combination of physiologic, psychologic, and environmental stressors and that symptoms are varied and likely to be multiple.

Becker's muscular dystrophy [Peter E. Becker, German geneticist, b. 1908], a chronic degenerative disease of the muscles, characterized by progressive weakness. It occurs in childhood between 8 and 20 years of age. It occurs less frequently, progresses more slowly, and has a better prognosis than the more common pseudohypertrophic form of muscular dystrophy.

The pathophysiologic characteristics of the disease are not understood; it is transmitted genetically as an autosomal-recessive trait.

Beck's depression inventory (BDI) [Aaron T. Beck, American psychiatrist, b. 1921], a system of classifying a total of 18 criteria of depressive illness. The BDI is similar to the 21-criteria DSM-IV diagnostic system of the 1980s except that the DSM-IV scale includes loss of interest, restlessness, and sulkiness, which are missing from the BDI; the Beck inventory lists somatic complaints and loneliness, which are criteria not included in the DSM-III inventory.

Beck's triad [Claude Schaeffer Beck, American surgeon, 1894–1971], a combination of three symptoms that characterize cardiac tamponade: high central venous pressure, low arterial pressure, and a small, quiet heart.

Beckwith's syndrome [John B. Beckwith, American pathologist, b. 1933], a hereditary disorder of unknown cause associated with neonatal hypoglycemia and hyperinsulinism. Clinical manifestations include gigantism, macroglossia, omphalocele or umbilical hernia, visceromegaly, and other abnormalities.

beclomethasone dipropionate, a glucocorticoid prescribed in a metered-dose inhaler in the maintenance treatment of bronchial asthma as prophylactic therapy and as an aerosol for inhalation to treat chronic rhinitis.

becquerel (Bq) /bekrel', bek'ərel'/ [Antoine H. Becquerel, French physicist, 1852–1908], the SI unit of radioactivity, equal to one radioactive decay per second.

bed [AS, *bedd*], (in anatomy) a supporting matrix of tissue, such as the nailbeds of modified epidermis over which the fingernails and the toenails move as they grow.

bed board, a board that is placed under a mattress to give added support to a patient with back problems.

bedbug [AS, *bedd*; ME, *bugge,* hobgoblin], a blood-sucking arthropod of the species *Cimex lectularius* or the species *C. hemipterus* that feeds on humans and other animals. The bite causes itching, pain, and redness.

bed cradle, a frame placed over a bed to prevent sheets or blankets from touching the patient.

Bedford finger stall, a removable finger splint that holds the injured and an adjacent finger in a brace or cast.

Bednar's aphthae /bed'närz/ [Alois Bednar, Austrian pediatrician, 1816–1888], the small, yellowish, slightly elevated ulcerated patches that occur on the posterior portion of the hard palate of

B

infants who place infected objects in their mouths.

bed pan, a vessel, made of metal or plastic, used to collect feces and urine of bedridden patients.

bed rest, the restriction of a patient to bed for therapeutic reasons for a prescribed period.

bed rest care, a nursing intervention from the Nursing Interventions Classification (NIC) defined as promotion of comfort and safety and prevention of complications for a patient unable to get out of bed.

bedridden, describing a person who is unable or unwilling to leave the bed because of illness or injury.

bedside laboratory testing, a nursing intervention from the Nursing Interventions Classification (NIC) defined as performance of laboratory tests at the bedside or point of care.

bedside manner, the behavior of a nurse or doctor as perceived by a patient or peers.

BEE, abbreviation for *basal energy expenditure.*

beef tapeworm infection [OF, *buef,* cow; AS, *taeppe* + *wyrm*], an infection caused by the tapeworm *Taenia saginata,* transmitted to humans when they eat contaminated beef. The infection is rarely found when beef is carefully inspected and thoroughly cooked before eating.

bee sting [AS, *beo* + *stingan*], an injury caused by the venom of bees, usually accompanied by pain and swelling.

beet sugar, sucrose from sugar beets.

behavior /bihā′vyər/ [ME, *behaven*], **1.** the manner in which a person acts or performs. **2.** any or all of the activities of a person, including physical actions, that are observed directly, and mental activity, which is inferred and interpreted.

behavioral isolation /behā′vyərəl/, social isolation that results from a person's socially unacceptable behavior.

behavioral marital therapy, a form of marital therapy using principles and techniques from behavior therapy. It attempts to alleviate marital distress by increasing positive, pleasant interactions between the couple.

behavioral medicine, a segment of psychosomatic medicine focused on psychologic means of influencing physical symptoms, such as biofeedback or relaxation.

behavioral objective, a goal in therapy or research that concerns an act or a specific behavior or pattern of behavior.

behavioral science, any of the various interrelated disciplines, such as psychiatry, psychology, sociology, and anthropology, that observe and study human activity, including psychologic and emotional development, interpersonal relationships, values, and mores.

behavioral systems model, a conceptual framework describing factors that may affect the stability of a person's behavior. The model examines systems of behavior, not the behavior of an individual at any particular time.

behavior disorder, any of a group of antisocial behavior patterns occurring primarily in children and adolescents, such as overaggressiveness, overactivity, destructiveness, cruelty, truancy, lying, disobedience, perverse sexual activity, criminality, alcoholism, and drug addiction.

behaviorism, a school of psychology founded by John B. Watson that studies and interprets behavior by observing measurable responses to stimuli without reference to consciousness, mental states, or subjective phenomena, such as ideas and emotions.

behaviorist, an advocate of the school of behaviorism.

behavior management, a nursing intervention from the Nursing Interventions Classification (NIC) defined as helping a patient to manage negative behavior.

behavior management: overactivity/inattention, a nursing intervention from the Nursing Interventions Classification (NIC) defined as provision of a therapeutic milieu that safely accommodates the patient's attention deficit and/or overactivity while promoting optimal function.

behavior management: self-harm, a nursing intervention from the Nursing Interventions Classification (NIC) defined as assisting the patient to decrease or eliminate self-mutilating or self-abusive behaviors.

behavior management: sexual, a nursing intervention from the Nursing Interventions Classification (NIC) defined as delineation and prevention of socially unacceptable sexual behaviors.

behavior modification, a nursing intervention from the Nursing Interventions Classification (NIC) defined as promotion of a behavior change.

behavior modification: social skills, a nursing intervention from the Nursing Interventions Classification (NIC) defined as assisting the patient to develop or improve interpersonal social skills.

behavior therapy, a kind of psychotherapy that attempts to modify observable maladjusted patterns of behavior by substituting a new response or set of responses to a given stimulus.

Behçet's disease /bä′sets/ [Hulusi Behçet, Turkish dermatologist, 1889–1948], a rare, severe, chronic, multisystem inflammatory illness of unknown cause, mostly affecting young males and characterized by severe uveitis and retinal vasculitis. Some other signs are optic atrophy and aphthous lesions of the mouth and the genitals, indicating diffuse vasculitis.

BEI, abbreviation for *butanol-extractable iodine*.

bejel /bej'əl/ [Ar, *bajal*], a nonvenereal form of endemic syphilis prevalent among children in the Middle East and North Africa, caused by the spirochete *Treponema pallidum* subspecies *endemicum*. It is transmitted by person-to-person contact and by the sharing of drinking and eating utensils.

Békésy audiometry /bek'əse/ [George von Békésy, Hungarian-American physicist and Nobel laureate, 1899–1972], a type of hearing test in which the subject controls the intensity of the stimulus by pressing a button while listening to a pure tone whose frequency slowly moves through the entire audible range.

bel [Alexander G. Bell, Canadian inventor, 1847–1922], a unit that expresses intensity of sound. It is the logarithm (to the base 10) of the ratio of the power of any specific sound to the power of a reference sound. The most common reference sound has a power of 10^{-16} watt per square centimeter, or the approximate minimum intensity of sound at 1000 cycles per second that is perceptible to the human ear.

belladonna /bel'ədon'ə, belädôn'ä/ [It, fair lady], the dried leaves, roots, and flowering or fruiting tops of *Atropa belladonna*, a common perennial called deadly nightshade, containing the alkaloids hyoscine and hyoscyamine. Hyoscyamine has anticholinergic and antispasmodic properties.

belladonna alkaloids, a group of anticholinergic alkaloids occurring in belladonna.

belladonna and atropine poisons [It, *belladonna*, fair lady; Gk, *Atropos*, one of three Fates; L, *potio*, drink], two powerful poisons obtained from solanaceous plants. Atropine, derived from *Atropa belladonna*, blocks the effects of acetylcholine in effector organs supplied by postganglionic cholinergic nerves.

bellows murmur /bel'ooz/ [AS, *belg*, bag; L, humming], a blowing sound, such as that of air moving in and out of a bellows.

bellows ventilator, a respiratory care device in which oxygen and other gases are mixed in a mechanism that contracts and expands. The system pressure is increased or decreased in the chamber surrounding the bellows.

bell-shaped curve, the curve of the probability density function of the normal distribution.

Bell's law [Charles Bell, Scottish surgeon, 1774–1842], an axiom stating that the anterior spinal nerves are only motor and the posterior spinal roots are sensory.

Bell's palsy [Charles Bell, Scottish surgeon, 1774-1842], a unilateral paralysis of the facial nerve, thought to result from trauma to the nerve, compression of the nerve, or infection, of which HSV is thought to be the most common. Any or all branches of the nerve may be affected. The person may not be able to close an eye or control salivation on the affected side. It usually resolves over weeks but can leave some permanent damage.

Bell's phenomenon [Charles Bell], a sign of peripheral facial paralysis, manifested by the upward and outward rolling of the eyeball when the affected individual tries to close the eyelid.

Bell's spasm [Charles Bell], a convulsive facial tic.

belly [AS, *beig*, bag], **1.** the fleshy central bulging portion of a muscle. **2.** informal term for **abdomen.**

belonephobia /bel'ənəfo'be·ə/ [Gk, *belone*, needle, *phobos*, fear], a morbid fear of objects with sharp points, especially needles and pins.

below-elbow (BE) amputation, an amputation of the arm below the elbow.

belt restraint, a device used around the waist to secure a patient on a stretcher or in a chair.

Benadryl, a trademark for a first-generation antihistamine (diphenhydramine hydrochloride).

Benassi method /bənas'e/, a positioning procedure for producing x-ray images of the liver.

Bence Jones protein /bens/ [Henry Bence Jones, English physician, 1814–1873], a protein found almost exclusively in the urine of patients with multiple myeloma.

Bence Jones protein test, a urine test whose positive result most commonly indicates multiple myeloma. The test is used to detect and monitor the treatment and clinical course of multiple myeloma and similar diseases.

bench research informal, (in medicine) any research done in a controlled laboratory setting using nonhuman subjects.

Bender's Visual Motor Gestalt test [Lauretta Bender, American psychiatrist, 1897–1987; L, *visus*, vision, *movere*, to move; Ger, *Gestalt*, form; L, *testum*, crucible], a standard psychologic test in which the subject copies a series of patterns.

bending fracture, 1. a fracture indirectly caused by the bending of an extremity, such as the foot or the big toe. **2.** a deformity of a long bone caused by multiple small fractures.

B

bendroflumethiazide /ben'drōflōō'məthī'ə-zīd/, a diuretic and antihypertensive prescribed in the treatment of hypertension and edema.

Benedict's qualitative test [Stanley R. Benedict, American biochemist, 1884–1936], a test for sugar in the urine based on the reduction by glucose of cupric ions. Formation of an orange or red precipitate indicates more than 2% sugar (called 4+), yellow indicates 1% to 2% sugar (called 3+), olive green indicates 0.5% to 1% sugar (called 2+), and green indicates less than 0.5% sugar (called 1+). It is not in common use.

Benedict's solution [Stanley R. Benedict], a term referring to two reagents (a qualitative and a quantitative) used in the examination of urine specimens. When the solution is heated, the color of the resulting mixture depends on the concentration of glucose in the urine.

beneficiary /ben'əfish'ərē/, a person or group designated to receive certain profits, benefits, or advantages, as the recipient of a will or insurance policy.

Benemid, a trademark for a uricosuric (probenecid).

benign /benīn'/ [L, benignus, kind], (of a tumor) noncancerous and therefore not a direct threat to life, even though treatment eventually may be required for health or cosmetic reasons.

benign congenital hypotonia, a condition marked by signs of weakness and floppiness in babies, resulting from nonprogressive weakness of skeletal muscles from birth.

benign cystic nephroma, multilocular cyst of kidney.

benign familial chronic pemphigus [L, benedicere, to bless, familia, household; Gk, pemphix, bubble], a hereditary condition of the skin characterized in the early stages by blisters that break, leaving red, eroded areas followed by crusts.

benign familial hematuria, a rare, usually benign disorder characterized by abnormally thin basement membranes of the glomerular capillaries and persistent hematuria. Autosomal-dominant inheritance is suspected.

benign forgetfulness, a temporary memory block in which some fact from the recent or remote past is forgotten but later recalled.

benign hypertension, a misnomer implying a harmless elevation of BP. Because any sustained elevation of BP may adversely affect health, it is incorrect to refer to the condition as "benign."

benign juvenile melanoma, a noncancerous pink or fuchsia raised papule with a scaly surface, usually on a cheek. Occurring most commonly in children between 9 and 13 years of age, it may be mistaken for a malignant melanoma.

benign mesenchymoma [L, benignare; Gk, meso, middle, egchyma, infusion, oma, tumor], a benign neoplasm that has two or more definitely recognizable mesenchymal elements in addition to fibrous tissue.

benign neoplasm [L, benignare; Gk, neos, new, plasma, formation], a localized tumor that has a fibrous capsule, limited potential for growth, a regular shape, and cells that are well differentiated. A benign neoplasm does not invade surrounding tissue or metastasize to distant sites.

benign nephrosclerosis, a renal disorder marked by arteriosclerotic lesions in the kidney. It is associated with hypertension.

benign paroxysmal positional vertigo, recurrent vertigo and nystagmus occurring when the head is placed in certain positions.

benign prostatic hyperplasia (BPH), a histologic diagnosis associated with non-malignant, noninflammatory enlargement of the prostate, most common among men over 50 years of age. BPH diagnosis can only be made after biopsy or resection; otherwise the diagnosis is benign prostatic enlargement.

benign stupor, a state of apathy or lethargy, such as occurs in severe depression.

Benner, Patricia, a nursing theorist who confirmed the levels of skill acquisition in nursing practice in From Novice to Expert: Excellence and Power in Clinical Nursing Practice (1984). Benner used systematic descriptions of five stages: novice, advanced beginner, competent, proficient, and expert. Benner's work describes nursing practice in the context of what nursing actually is and does rather than from context-free descriptions.

Bennett angle [Norman G. Bennett, English dentist, 1870–1947], the angle formed by the sagittal plane and the path of the advancing condyle during lateral mandibular movement, as viewed in the horizontal plane.

Bennett hand tool test, a test used in occupational therapy and prevocational testing to measure hand function and coordination and speed in performance.

Bennett's fracture [Edward H. Bennett, Irish surgeon, 1837–1907], a fracture that runs obliquely through the base of the first metacarpal bone and into the carpometacarpal joint, detaching the greater part of the articular facet.

Benoquin, a trademark for a depigmenting agent (monobenzone).

benserazide /benser′azīd/, an inhibitor of the decarboxylation of peripheral levodopa to dopamine, having actions similar to those of carbidopa. It is used orally in conjunction with levodopa as an antiparkinsonian agent.

bentiromide test, a test for pancreatic function. Bentiromide is administered orally, and its cleavage into benzoyl-tyrosyl and *p*-aminobenzoic acid is monitored as a measure of pancreatic production of chymotrypsin.

bentonite [Fort Benton, Montana], colloidal, hydrated aluminum silicate used as a bulk laxative and as a base for skin care preparations.

bentonite test, a flocculation test for the presence of rheumatoid factor in patient blood samples. After sensitized bentonite particles are added to the serum, the test result is considered positive for rheumatoid arthritis if adsorption has occurred with 50% of the particles.

bentoquatam /ben′to-kwah′tam/, a topical skin protectant used to prevent or reduce allergic contact dermatitis from contact with poison ivy, oak, and sumac.

Bentyl, a trademark for an anticholinergic antispasmodic (dicyclomine hydrochloride).

benz, abbreviation for a *benzoate carboxylate anion*.

benzalkonium chloride, a disinfectant and fungicide prepared in an aqueous solution in various strengths.

benzene /ben′zēn/, a colorless, highly flammable liquid hydrocarbon (C_6H_6) originally derived by fractional distillation of coal tar. It is now derived by catalytic reforming during petroleum refining. The prototypical aromatic compound, it is used in the production of various organic compounds, including pharmaceuticals.

benzene poisoning, a toxic condition caused by ingestion of benzene, inhalation of benzene fumes, or exposure to benzene-related products, such as toluene or xylene, characterized by blurred vision, nausea, headache, dizziness, and incoordination.

benzethonium chloride /ben′zəthō′nē·əm/, a topical antiinfective used for disinfecting the skin and for treating some infections of the eye, nose, and throat. It is also used as a preservative in some pharmaceutical preparations.

benzo[a]pyrene dihydrodiol epoxide (BPDE-I), a carcinogenic derivative of benzo(a)pyrene associated with tobacco smoke.

benzocaine /ben′zəkān/, an ester-type, local anesthetic agent derived from aminobenzoic acid that is most useful when applied topically. It is used in many OTC compounds for pruritus and pain.

benzodiazepine derivative /ben′zōdī·az′əpin/, one of a group of psychotropic agents, including the tranquilizers chlordiazepoxide, diazepam, oxazepam, lorazepam, and chlorazepate, prescribed to alleviate anxiety. The hypnotics flurazepam and triazolam are prescribed in the treatment of insomnia.

benzoic acid /benzō′ik/, a keratolytic agent, usually used with salicylic acid as an ointment in the treatment of athlete's foot and ringworm of the scalp.

benzonatate /benzō′nətāt/, a nonopiate antitussive prescribed to suppress the cough reflex.

benzoyl peroxide /benzō′il/, an antibacterial, keratolytic drying agent prescribed in the treatment of acne.

benzquinamide /benzkwin′əmīd/, an antiemetic prescribed in the treatment of postoperative nausea and vomiting.

benzthiazide /benzthī′əzid/, a diuretic and antihypertensive prescribed in the treatment of hypertension and edema.

benztropine mesylate /benztrō′pēn/, an anticholinergic and antihistaminic agent that may be prescribed as adjunctive therapy in the treatment of drug-induced extrapyramidal symptoms and all forms of parkinsonism.

benzyl alcohol /ben′zil/, a clear, colorless, oily liquid, derived from certain balsams, used as a topical anesthetic and as a bacteriostatic agent in solutions for injection.

benzyl benzoate /benzō′āt/, a clear, oily liquid with a pleasant, pervasive aroma. It is used as an agent to destroy lice and scabies, as a solvent, and as a flavor for gum.

bepridil /bep′ridil/, a calcium channel blocking agent used orally as the hydrochloride salt in treatment of chronic angina pectoris.

beractant /berak′tant/, a substance obtained from bovine lungs containing mostly phospholipids. It mimics the action of human pulmonary surfactant and is used in prevention and treatment of respiratory distress syndrome of the newborn. It is administered by endotracheal intubation.

Berdon's syndrome, megacystis-microcolon-intestinal hypoperistalsis.

bereavement /bərēv′mənt/ [ME, *bereven*, to rob], a form of grief with anxiety symptoms that is a common reaction to the loss of a loved one. It may be accompanied by insomnia, hyperactivity, and other effects.

Berger's disease [Jean Berger, French nephrologist, 1930–2011], a kidney disorder characterized by recurrent episodes of macroscopic hematuria, proteinuria, and a granular deposition of IgA from the glomerular mesangium. The onset of disease is usually in childhood or early adulthood, and males are affected twice as often as females.

Berger's paresthesia [Oskar Berger, nineteenth century German neurologist; Gk, *para,* near, *aisthesia,* sensation], a condition of tingling, prickliness, or weakness and a loss of feeling in the legs without evidence of organic disease. The condition affects young people.

Bergonié-Tribondeau law /ber'gônē' tribôdō'/ [Jean A. Bergonié, French radiologist, 1857–1925; Louis F.A. Tribondeau, French physician, 1872–1918], a rule stating that the radiosensitivity of a tissue depends on the number of undifferentiated cells in the tissue, their mitotic activity, and the length of time they are actively proliferating.

beriberi /ber'ēber'ē/ [Sinhalese, *beri,* weakness], a disease of the peripheral nerves caused by a deficiency of or an inability to assimilate thiamine. It frequently results from a diet limited to polished white rice. Symptoms are fatigue, diarrhea, appetite and weight loss, disturbed nerve function causing paralysis and wasting of limbs, edema, and heart failure.

berkelium (Bk) /burk'lē-əm/ [Berkeley, California], an artificial radioactive transuranic element. Its atomic number is 97; the atomic mass of its longest-lived isotope is 247.

berlock dermatitis [Fr, *breloque,* bracelet charm], a temporary skin condition characterized by hyperpigmentation and skin lesions. It is caused by a unique reaction to psoralen-type photosynthesizers commonly used in perfumes, colognes, and pomades, such as oil of bergamot.

Bernard-Soulier syndrome /bernär' sōōlyā'/ [Jean A. Bernard, French hematologist, 1907–2006; Jean-Pierre Soulier, French hematologist, 1915–2003], an autosomal-recessive bleeding disorder characterized by an absence of or a deficiency in the ability of the platelets to adhere to von Willebrand factor because of the relative lack of membrane glycoprotein Ib/V/IX.

Bernoulli's principle /bərnōō'lēz/ [Daniel Bernoulli, Swiss scientist, 1700–1782], (in physics) the principle stating that the sum of the velocity and the kinetic energy of a fluid flowing through a tube is constant. The greater the velocity, the less the lateral pressure on the wall of the tube. Thus, if an artery is narrowed by an atherosclerotic plaque, the flow of blood through the constriction increases in velocity and decreases in lateral pressure.

Bernoulli theorem /bərnōō'lē/, in an experiment involving probability, the larger the number of trials, the closer the observed probability of an event approaches its theoretical probability.

berry aneurysm [ME, *berye*; Gk, *aneurysma,* widening], a small, saccular dilation of the wall of a cerebral artery. It occurs most frequently at the junctures of vessels in the circle of Willis. Smoking and hypertension increase the likelihood of rupture.

Bertel method /bur'təl/, a positioning procedure for producing x-ray images of the inferior orbital fissures.

Bertin's column hypertrophy, congenital enlargement of renal columns (columns of Bertin), a benign condition sometimes mistaken for a renal tumor.

berylliosis /bəril'ē-ō'sis/, poisoning that results from the inhalation of dusts or vapors containing beryllium or beryllium compounds. It is characterized by granulomas throughout the body and by diffuse pulmonary fibrosis, resulting in a dry cough, shortness of breath, and chest pain.

beryllium (Be), a steel-gray, lightweight metallic element. Its atomic number is 4; its atomic mass is 9.012. Beryllium occurs naturally as beryl and is used in metallic alloys and in fluorescent powders.

bestiality /bes'chē-al'itē/ [L, *bestia,* beast], **1.** a brutal or animal-like character or nature. **2.** conduct or behavior characterized by beastlike appetites or instincts. **3.** sexual relations between a human being and an animal. **4.** sodomy.

beta /bē'tə, bā'tə/, B, β, the second letter of the Greek alphabet, used in scientific notation to denote position of a carbon atom in a molecule, a type of protein configuration, or identification of a type of activity, as beta blocker, beta particle, or beta rhythm. It is used in statistics to define an error in the interpretation of study results.

beta-alaninemia /-al'ɔninē'mē-ə/, an inherited metabolic disorder marked by a deficiency of an enzyme, beta-alanine-alpha-ketoglutarate aminotransferase. The clinical signs include seizures, drowsiness, and, if uncorrected, death.

beta blocker, a popular term for a beta-adrenergic blocking (or beta receptor antagonist) agent.

beta-carotene [Gk, beta; L, *carota,* carrot], a vitamin A precursor and ultraviolet screening agent prescribed to ameliorate photosensitivity in patients with erythropoietic protoporphyria.

beta cells, 1. insulin-producing cells situated in the islets of Langerhans. Their insulin-producing function tends to accelerate the movement of glucose, amino acids, and fatty acids out of the blood and into the cellular cytoplasm. **2.** the basophilic cells of the anterior lobe of the pituitary gland.

beta decay, a type of radioactivity that results in the emission of beta particles, either electrons or positrons.

Betadine, a trademark for a topical antiinfective (povidone-iodine).

beta-fetoprotein, a protein found in fetal liver and in some adults with liver disease. It is now known to be identical with normal liver ferritin.

Betagan, a trademark for a topical glaucoma drug (levobunolol hydrochloride). The same brand name is also used for povidone-iodine germicidal solutions.

beta hemolysis, the development of a clear zone around a bacterial colony growing on blood agar medium, characteristic of certain pathogenic bacteria.

beta-hemolytic streptococci, the pyogenic streptococci of groups A, B, C, E, F, G, H, K, L, M, and O that cause hemolysis of RBCs in blood agar in the laboratory. These organisms cause most of the acute streptococcal infections seen in humans.

betahistine /ba'tah-his'tēn/, a histamine analog used as the hydrochloride salt and as a vasodilator to reduce the frequency of attacks of vertigo in Ménière's disease.

beta-hydroxyisovaleric aciduria, an inherited metabolic disease caused by a deficiency of an enzyme needed to metabolize the amino acid leucine. The condition results in an accumulation of leucine in the tissues, causing maple sugar odor in the urine, ketoacidosis, retardation, and muscle atrophy.

beta-lactam antibiotic, any of a group of antibiotics, including the cephalosporins and the penicillins, whose chemical structure contains a beta-lactam ring.

beta-lactamase /-lak'təmāz/ [*lactam,* a cyclic amide, *ase,* enzyme], a bacterial enzyme that catalyzes the hydrolysis of the beta-lactam ring of some penicillins and cephalosporins, producing penicilloic acid and rendering the antibiotic ineffective.

beta-lactamase-resistant antibiotics, antibiotics that are resistant to the enzymatic effects of **beta-lactamase.**

betamethasone, a glucocorticoid prescribed for topical corticosteroid-responsive dermatoses and injected directly into lesions (bursitis, rheumatoid arthritis, etc.) to help control pain and inflammation.

beta2-microglobulin (B₂M) test, a test that analyzes blood, urine, or fluid for increased levels of B_2M, a protein found on the surface of all cells. Increased levels in the urine indicate renal tubule disease; drug-induced renal toxicity; heavy metal–induced renal disease; lymphomas, leukemia, or myeloma; or AIDS. Increased serum levels indicate lymphomas, leukemia, or myeloma; glomerular renal disease; renal transplant rejection; viral infections, especially HIV and cytomegalovirus; or chronic inflammatory processes.

beta-naphthylamine /-nafthil'əmēn/, an aromatic amine used in aniline dyes and linked to the development of bladder cancer in humans.

beta-oxidation, a catabolic process in which fatty acids are used by the body as a source of energy.

Betapar, a trademark for a glucocorticoid (meprednisone).

beta particle, an electron emitted from the nucleus of an atom during radioactive decay of the atom. Beta particles have a range of 10 m in air and 1 mm in soft tissue.

Betapen-VK, a trademark for an antibiotic (penicillin V potassium).

beta phase, the period immediately following the alpha, or redistribution, phase of drug administration. During the beta phase the blood level of the drug falls more slowly as it is metabolized and excreted from the body.

beta rays, a stream of beta particles, as emitted from atoms of disintegrating radioactive elements.

beta receptor, any one of the postulated adrenergic (sympathetic fibers of autonomic nervous system) components of receptor tissues that respond to epinephrine and such blocking agents as propranolol. Activation of beta receptors causes various physiologic reactions such as relaxation of the bronchial muscles and an increase in the rate and force of cardiac contraction.

beta-thalassemia, an anemia that is caused by diminished synthesis of beta chains of hemoglobin. The homozygous form is known as thalassemia major and the heterozygous form is known as thalassemia minor.

betatron /bā'tətron/, a cyclic accelerator that produces high-energy electrons for radiotherapy.

beta wave, one of several types of brain waves, characterized by relatively low voltage and a frequency of more than 13 Hz. Beta waves are the "busy waves" of the brain, recorded by EEG from the frontal and central areas of the cerebrum when the patient is awake and alert with eyes open.

betaxolol hydrochloride /betak'səlol/, a topical drug for open-angle glaucoma prescribed for the relief of ocular hypertension and chronic open-angle glaucoma, and an oral preparation is prescribed for the management of hypertension.

bethanechol chloride /bethan'əkol/, a cholinergic prescribed in the treatment of fecal and urinary retention and neurogenic atony of the bladder.

Betopic, a trademark for a topical glaucoma medication (betaxolol hydrochloride).

Betz cells [Vladimir A. Betz, Russian anatomist, 1834–1894; L, *cella,* storeroom], **1.** large pyramidal neurons of the motor cortex with axons that form part of the pyramidal tract associated with voluntary movements. **2.** upper motor neurons.

bevacizumab, a DNA-derived monoclonal antibody that selectively binds to and inhibits activity of human vascular endothelial growth factor to reduce microvascular growth and inhibition of metastatic disease progression. This drug is used to treat metastatic carcinoma of the colon or rectum in combination with 5-FU IV. It is also being investigated for use as an adjunctive in breast and renal cancer.

bevel /bev′əl/ [OFr, *baif,* open mouth angle], **1.** any angle, other than a right angle, between two planes or surfaces. **2.** (in dentistry) any angle other than 90 degrees between a tooth cut and a cavity wall in the preparation of a tooth cavity.

bexarotene, a second-generation retinoid prescribed for cutaneous T-cell lymphoma. Investigational uses include treatment of breast cancer.

bezoar /bē′zôr/ [Ar, *bazahr,* protection against poison], a hard ball of hair or vegetable fiber that may develop within the stomach of humans. More often it is found in the stomachs of ruminants.

Bg (Bennett-Goodspeed) antigens, HLA class I antigens that may be expressed on red cells: HLA-B7 (Bga), HLA-B17 (B57 or B58) (Bgb), and HLA-A28 (A68 or A69) (Bgc).

Bh, symbol for the element **bohrium.**

bhang /bang/ [Hindi, *bag*], an Asian Indian hallucinogenic, composed of dried leaves and the young stems of uncultivated *Cannabis sativa.* It is usually ingested as a boiled mixture with milk, sugar, or water. It also may be smoked or chewed.

BHC, abbreviation for *benzene hexachloride.*

Bi, symbol for the element **bismuth.**

BIA, abbreviation for **bioelectric impedance analysis.**

bias /bī′əs/ [MFr, *biais*], **1.** an oblique or a diagonal line. **2.** a prejudiced or subjective attitude. **3.** (in statistics) the distortion of statistical findings from the true value. **4.** (in electronics) a voltage applied to an electronic device, such as a vacuum tube or a transistor, to control operating limits.

biased sample /bī′əst/ [OFr, *biais,* slant; L, *exemplum,* sample], (in research) a sample of a group in which all factors or participants are not equally balanced or objectively represented.

biasing /bī′əsing/, a method of treating neuromuscular dysfunction by contracting a muscle against resistance, causing the muscle spindles to readjust to the shorter length and the muscle tissue to be more responsive and sensitive to stretching.

biauricular /bī′awrik′yōolər/ [L, *bis,* twice + *auriculus,* little ear], pertaining to the two auricles of the ears.

Biavax, a trademark for a rubella and mumps vaccine.

bibliotherapy¹, a type of group therapy in which books, poems, and newspaper articles are read in the group to help stimulate thinking about events in the real world and to foster relations among group members.

bibliotherapy², a nursing intervention from the Nursing Interventions Classification (NIC) defined as therapeutic use of literature to enhance expression of feelings, active problem solving, coping, or insight.

bicalutamide, an anticancer chemotherapy agent prescribed in the treatment of metastatic prostate cancer.

bicameral /bīkam′ər·əl/ [L, *bis,* twice, *camera,* vaulted chamber], having two chambers.

bicameral abscess /bīkam′ərəl/, an abscess with two separate cavities or chambers.

bicapsular /bī·kap′syōo′lər/ [L, *bis,* twice, *capsula,* little box], having two capsules, as an articular capsule.

bicarbonate (HCO₃⁻) /bīkär′bənāt/ [L, *bis,* twice, *carbo,* coal], an anion of carbonic acid in which only one of the hydrogen atoms has been removed, as in sodium bicarbonate ($NaHCO_3{}^-$).

bicarbonate precursor, an injection of sodium lactate used in the treatment of metabolic acidosis. It is metabolized in the body to sodium bicarbonate.

bicarbonate therapy, a procedure to increase a patient's stores of bicarbonate when there are signs of severe acidosis.

bicarbonate transport, the route by which most of the carbon dioxide is carried in the bloodstream. Once dissolved in the blood plasma, carbon dioxide combines with water to form carbonic acid, which immediately ionizes into hydrogen and bicarbonate ions.

bicellular /bī·sel′yōo·lər/ [L, *bis,* twice, *cella,* storeroom], made up of two cells, or having two cells.

biceps brachii /bī′seps brā′kē·ī/ [L, *bis,* twice, *caput,* head, *brachium,* arm], the long fusiform muscle of the upper arm on the anterior surface of the humerus, arising in two heads from the scapula. It flexes the arm and the forearm and supinates the hand.

biceps femoris [L, *bis,* twice, *caput,* head, *femoris,* thigh], one of the posterior femoral muscles. It has two heads at its origin. The biceps femoris flexes the leg and rotates it laterally and extends the thigh, rotating it laterally. It is one muscle of the hamstring muscle group.

biceps reflex, a contraction of a biceps muscle produced when the tendon is tapped with a percussor in testing deep tendon reflexes.

Bichat's membrane /bishäz/ [Marie F.X. Bichat, French anatomist, 1771–1802], an elastic lining beneath the endothelium of an arterial wall.

bichromatic analysis /-krōmat'ik/ [Gk, *bios* + *chroma*, color], the spectrophotometric monitoring of a reaction at two wavelengths. It is used to correct for background color.

Bicillin C-R /bi-sil'in/, a trademark for combination preparations of the antibiotics penicillin G benzathine and penicillin G procaine.

bicipital aponeurosis, a flat sheet of connective tissue that fans out from the medial side of the tendon to blend with deep fascia covering the anterior compartment of the forearm.

bicipital groove /bīsip'ətəl/ [L, *bis,* twice, *caput,* head; D, *groeve*], a groove between the greater and lesser tubercles of the humerus for passage of the tendon of the long head of the biceps muscle.

Bickerdyke, Mary Ann /bik'ərdīk/, (1817–1901), an American nurse who, after taking a short course in homeopathy, cared for the sick and wounded on battlefields during the U.S. Civil War. She insisted on cleanliness, good food, and the best of medical care for her patients.

biclor /bī'klôr/, abbreviation for *two chloride anions* in a salt.

biconcave /bīkon'kāv/ [L, *bis,* twice, *concavare,* to make hollow], concave on both sides, especially as applied to a lens. **—biconcavity,** *n.*

biconvex /bīkon'veks/ [L, *bis* + *convexus,* vaulted], convex on both sides, especially as applied to a lens. **—biconvexity,** *n.*

bicornate /bīkôr'nāt/ [L, *bis* + *cornu,* horn], having two horns or processes.

bicornate uterus, an abnormal uterus that may be either a single or a double organ with two horns or branches.

bicuspid /bīkus'pid/ [L, *bis* + *cuspis,* point], having two cusps or points.

bicycle ergometer [L, *bis,* twice; Gk, *kyklos,* circle, *ergon,* work, *metron,* measure], a stationary bicycle dynamometer that measures the strength of an individual's muscle contraction.

b.i.d., (in prescriptions) abbreviation for *bis in die* /dē'ä/, a Latin phrase meaning "twice a day."

bidactyly /bīdak'tilē/ [L, *bis*; Gk, *daktylos,* finger], an abnormal condition in which the second, third, and fourth digits on a hand are missing and only the first and fifth are present. **—bidactylous,** *adj.*

bidermoma /bī'dərmō'mə/ *pl.* **bidermomas, bidermomata** [L, *bis*; Gk, *derma,* skin, *oma,* tumor], a teratoid neoplasm composed of cells and tissues originating in two germ layers.

bidet /bidā'/ [Fr, pony], a fixture resembling a toilet bowl, with a rim to sit on and usually equipped with plumbing implements for cleaning the genital and rectal areas.

biduotertian fever /bī'dōō·ətur'shən/ [L, *bis* + *dies,* day, *tertius,* three], a form of malaria characterized by overlapping paroxysms of chills, fever, and other symptoms. It is caused by infection with two strains of *Plasmodium,* each having its own cycle of symptoms, such as in quartan and tertian malaria.

Bier block /bēr blok/ [August Karl Gustav Bier, German surgeon, 1861–1949], regional anesthesia accomplished after IV injection of a dilute local anesthetic such as lidocaine. It is limited to procedures of short duration (less than 1 hour).

bifid /bī'fid/ [L, *bis* + *findere,* to cleave], cleft, or split into two parts.

bifid scrotum, separation of the two halves of the scrotum, as in penoscrotal transposition.

bifid tongue [L, *bis* + *findere,* to cleave; AS, *tunge*], a tongue divided by a longitudinal furrow.

bifid ureter, one in which proximal segments come from two different collecting systems but join to form one ureter before reaching the bladder.

bifid uvula, bifurcation of the uvula, an incomplete form of cleft palate.

bifocal /bīfō'kəl/ [L, *bis* + *focus,* hearth], **1.** pertaining to the characteristic of having two foci. **2.** (of a lens) having two areas of different focal lengths.

bifocal contact lens, a contact lens that contains corrections for both near and far vision.

bifocal glasses [L, *bis,* twice, *focus,* hearth; AS, *glaes*], eyeglasses in which each lens is made up of two segments of different refractive powers or strength. Generally, the upper part of the lens is used for ordinary or distant vision, and the smaller, lower section for near vision for close work.

biforate /bīfôr'āt/ [L, *bis* + *forare,* to pierce twice], having two perforations or foramina.

bifrontal suture /bīfron'təl/ [L, *bis* + *frons,* front + *sutura*], the interlocking lines of fusion between the frontal and parietal bones of the skull.

bifurcate /bīfur'kāt/ [L, *bis,* twice, *furca,* fork], pertaining to the division or

B

branching of an object into two branches, such as the branching of blood vessels or bronchi.—**bifurcated,** *adj.*

bifurcate ligament, a V-shaped ligament in the foot that connects the anterior process of the calcaneus to the cuboid and navicular bones.

bifurcation /bī'fərkā'shən/ [L, *bis* + *furca,* fork], a splitting into two branches, such as the trachea, which branches into the two bronchi.

Bigelow's lithotrite /big'əlōz/ [Henry J. Bigelow, American surgeon, 1818–1890; Gk, *lithos,* stone; L, *terere,* to rub], a long-jawed instrument, passed through the urethra, for crushing a calculus in the bladder.

bigeminal /bījem'inəl/ [L, *bis,* twice, *geminus,* twin], pertaining to pairs, twins, or dual events.

bigeminal pregnancy, a twin pregnancy.

bigeminal pulse, an abnormal pulse in which two beats in close succession are followed by a pause during which no pulse is felt.

bigeminal rhythm [L, *bis* + *geminus,* twin; Gk, *rhythmos*], an abnormal heartbeat in which ectopic ventricular or atrial beats alternate with and are precisely coupled to sinus beats, or in which ventricular ectopic beats occur in pairs, as in ventricular tachycardia with 3:2 exit block.

bigeminy /bījem'inē/ [L, *bis* + *geminus,* twin], an association in pairs.—**bigeminal,** *adj.*

bilabe /bī'lāb/ [L, *bis* + *labium,* lip], a narrow forceps used to remove small calculi from the bladder by way of the urethra.

bilabial /bīlā'bē-əl/, a consonantal speech sound produced using the two lips, such as *b, p,* or *m.*

bilaminar /bīlam'ənər/ [L, *bis* + *lamina,* plate], pertaining to or having two layers.

bilaminar blastoderm, the stage of embryonic development before mesoderm formation in which only the ectoderm and endoderm primary germ layers have formed.

bilateral /bilat'ərəl/ [L, *bis* + *lateralis,* side], **1.** having two sides. **2.** occurring or appearing on two sides. A patient with bilateral hearing loss may have partial or total hearing loss in both ears. **3.** having two layers.

bilateral carotid artery [L, *bis,* twice, *latus,* side; Gk, *karos,* heavy sleep], a main artery to the head and neck that divides into left and right branches and again into external and internal branches.

bilateral lithotomy [L, *bis,* twice, *latus,* side; Gk, *lithos,* stone, *temnein,* to cut], a surgical procedure for removing urinary tract stones from the bladder by making an incision across the peritoneum.

bilateral long-leg spica cast, an orthopedic device of plaster of paris, fiberglass, or other casting material that encases and immobilizes the trunk cranially as far as the nipple line and both legs caudally as far as the toes. It is used to aid the healing of fractures of the hip, the femur, the acetabulum, and the pelvis and to correct hip deformities.

bilateral strabismus [L, *bis* + *latus,* side; Gk, *strabismos*], an eye disorder, characterized by bilateral squint, which is caused by a failure of ocular accommodation.

bilateral symmetry [L, *bis* + *latus,* side; Gk, *syn,* together, *metron,* measure], similar structure of the halves of an organism.

Bilbao tube /bilbō'ə/, a long, thin, flexible tube that is used to inject barium into the small intestine. The tube is guided with a stiff wire from the mouth to the end of the duodenum under fluoroscopic control.

bilberry, a herb found in the central, Northern, and Southeastern regions of Europe. This herb is used for diabetic retinopathy, macular degeneration, glaucoma, cataract, capillary fragility, varicose veins, hemorrhoids, and mild diarrhea. It is possibly effective for some indications, but controlled clinical trials do not support its use for improving vision.

bile /bil/ [L, *bilis*], a bitter, yellowgreen, viscid alkaline fluid secreted by the liver. Stored in the gallbladder, bile receives its color from the presence of bile pigments such as bilirubin. Bile emulsifies fats (breaks them into smaller particles and lowers the surface tension), preparing them for further digestion and absorption in the small intestine.—**biliary,** *adj.*

bile acid, a steroid acid of the bile produced during the metabolism of cholesterol. On hydrolysis, bile acid yields glycine and choleic acid.

bile acid breath test, a breath test for overgrowth of bacteria in the intestine. The patient is given a dose of a conjugated bile acid labeled with carbon 14, and the amount of radioactively labeled carbon dioxide in the breath is measured at hourly intervals. Excessive labeled carbon dioxide in the breath indicates excessive bacteria in the intestine breaking down the bile acids.

bile acid therapy, administration of bile acids for treatment of hyperliposis.

bile duct abscess, a cavity containing pus and surrounded by inflamed tissue in the bile duct.

bile pigments, a group of substances that contribute to the colors of bile, which may range from a yellowish green to brown. A common bile pigment is bilirubin.

bile salts [L, *bilis,* bile; AS, *sealt*], a mixture of sodium salts of the bile acids and cholic and chenodeoxycholic acids synthesized in the liver as a derivative of cholesterol. Their low surface tension contributes to the emulsification of fats in the intestine and their absorption from the GI tract.

bile solubility test, a bacteriologic test used in the differential diagnosis of pneumococcal and streptococcal infections.

biliary /bil′ē·er·ē/, pertaining to bile or to the gallbladder and bile ducts, which transport bile.

biliary abscess, an abscess of the gallbladder or liver.

biliary atresia, congenital absence or underdevelopment of one or more of the biliary structures, causing jaundice and early liver damage.

biliary calculus [L, *bilis,* bile, *calculus,* pebble], a stone formed in the biliary tract, consisting of cholesterol or bile pigments and calcium salts. Biliary calculi may cause jaundice, right upper quadrant pain, obstruction, and inflammation of the gallbladder.

biliary cirrhosis [L, *bilis:* Gr, *kirrhos,* yellow-orange, *osis,* condition], an inflammatory condition in which the flow of bile through the ductules of the liver is obstructed. Primary biliary cirrhosis is characterized by itching, jaundice, steatorrhea, and enlargement of the liver and spleen. The disease is slowly progressive. Secondary biliary cirrhosis caused by obstruction of the biliary structures outside the liver can be treated more successfully.

biliary colic [L, *bilis;* Gr, *kolikos,* colon pain], a type of smooth muscle or visceral pain specifically associated with the passing of stones through the bile ducts.

biliary duct, one of the muscular ducts through which bile passes from the liver and gallbladder to the duodenum.

biliary dyskinesia, pain or discomfort in the epigastric region resulting from spasm, especially of the sphincter of Oddi, following cholecystectomy. It interferes with bile drainage.

biliary dyspepsia, a digestive upset caused by an inadequate flow of bile into the duodenum.

biliary fistula, an abnormal passage from the gallbladder, a bile duct, or the liver to an internal organ or the surface of the body.

biliary glands,

biliary obstruction, blockage of the common or cystic bile duct, usually caused by one or more gallstones. It impedes bile drainage and produces an inflammatory reaction. Biliary obstruction is characterized by severe epigastric pain, often radiating to the back and shoulder, nausea, vomiting, and profuse diaphoresis.

biliary pseudolithiasis, pain in the bile ducts with symptoms resembling those of cholelithiasis but in the absence of gallstones.

biliary tract [L, *bilis,* bile, *tractus*], the pathway for bile flow from the canaliculi in the liver to the opening of the bile duct into the duodenum.

biliary tract cancer, a rare adenocarcinoma in a bile duct often causing jaundice, pruritus, and weight loss. The lesion may be papillary or flat and ulcerated. The tumor is often unresectable at diagnosis.

biligenesis /bil′ijen′əsis/, the process by which bile is produced.

bilingulate /bīling′gyəlit/ [L, *bis,* twice, *lingula,* little tongue], having two tongues or two tonguelike structures.

biliopancreatic diversion, a surgical treatment for morbid obesity consisting of resection of the distal two thirds of the stomach and attachment of the ileum to a stoma so that the entire duodenum and jejunum are bypassed. The duodenum and jejunum empty their secretions into the distal ileum through a new stoma.

bilious /bil′yəs/ [L, *bilis,* bile], **1.** pertaining to bile. **2.** characterized or affected by disordered liver function and especially excessive secretion of bile.

bilious vomiting, the vomiting of bile.

bilirubin /bil′iroo′bin/ [L, *bilis* + *ruber,* red], the orange-yellow pigment of bile, formed principally by the breakdown of hemoglobin in RBCs after termination of their normal lifespan. In a healthy person, about 250 mg of bilirubin is produced daily. The majority of bilirubin is excreted in the stool. The characteristic yellow pallor of jaundice is caused by the accumulation of bilirubin in the blood and in the tissues of the skin.

bilirubin blood test, a blood test performed in cases of jaundice to help determine whether the jaundice is caused by hepatocellular dysfunction (as in hepatitis) or extrahepatic obstruction of the bile ducts (as with gallstones or tumor blocking the bile ducts). Total serum bilirubin is made up of conjugated (direct) and unconjugated (indirect) bilirubin, with varying ratios of each characterizing different diseases.

bilirubin cast, a cast containing bilirubin, giving it a yellow-brown color, as seen with obstructive jaundice.

bilirubin diglucuronide, a conjugated water-soluble form of bilirubin, formed in the liver by esterification of two molecules of glucuronide to the bilirubin molecule. It is the usual form in which bilirubin is found in the bile.

bilirubinemia /-ē′mē·ə/ [L, *bilis,* bile, *ruber,* red; Gk, *haima,* blood], the presence of bilirubin in the blood.

bilirubinuria /-ŏŏr′ē·ə/, the presence of bilirubin in urine.

biliuria /bil′iyŏŏr′ē·ə/ [L, *bilis;* Gk, *ouron,* urine], the presence of bile pigments in the urine.

biliverdin /bil′ivur′din/ [L, *bilis;* + *virdis,* green], a greenish bile pigment formed in the breakdown of hemoglobin and converted to bilirubin.

Billings method, a way of estimating ovulation time by changes in the cervical mucus that occur during the menstrual cycle.

Billroth's operation I [Christian A. Billroth, Austrian surgeon, 1829–1894], the surgical removal of the pylorus in the treatment of gastric cancer or peptic ulcer. The proximal end of the duodenum is anastomosed to the stomach.

Billroth's operation II [Christian A. Billroth], the surgical removal of the pylorus and duodenum. The cut end of the stomach is anastomosed to the jejunum, which is pulled through the transverse mesocolon from the lower abdomen. The remaining duodenum carrying biliary and pancreatic secretions drains into the ileum through a new anastomosis in the lower abdomen.

Bill's maneuver [Arthur H. Bill, American obstetrician, 1877–1961], an obstetric procedure in which a forceps is used to rotate the fetal head at midpelvis before extraction of the head during birth.

bilobate /bīlō′bāt/ [L, *bis,* twice, *lobus,* lobe], having two lobes.

bilobate placenta [L, *bis,* twice, *lobus,* lobe, *placenta,* flat cake], a placenta with two connected lobes.

bilobulate /bīlob′yəlāt/, having two lobules.

bilocular /bīlok′yələr/ [L, *bis* + *loculus,* compartment], **1.** divided into two cells. **2.** containing two cells.

Biltricide, a trademark for an anthelmintic (praziquantel).

bimanual /bīman′yŏŏ·əl/ [L, *bis* + *manus,* hand], with both hands.

bimanual examination [L, *bis* + *manos,* hand], an examination that requires the use of both of the examiner's hands.

bimanual palpation, the examination of a woman's pelvic organs in which the examiner places one hand on the abdomen and one or two fingers of the other hand in the vagina. The size, shape, and consistency of the cervix, uterus, and adnexa are then assessed and noted.

bimanual percussion [L, *bis,* twice, *manus,* hand, *percutere,* to strike through], a diagnostic technique of producing sound vibrations in body cavities by the use of two hands, one serving as the plexor, or "hammer," and the other as the pleximeter, or "striking plate."

bimastoid /bīmas′toid/, pertaining to the two mastoid processes of the temporal bone.

bimatoprost /bi-mat′o-prost/, a synthetic prostaglandin analogue that acts as an ocular hypotensive. It is applied topically to the conjunctiva in the treatment of open-angle glaucoma and ocular hypertension.

bimaxillary /bīmak′siler′ē/ [L, *bis* + *maxilla,* jawbone], pertaining to both the upper and lower jaws.

bimodal distribution /bīmo′dəl/ [L, *bis* + *modus,* measure], the distribution of quantitative data into two clusters. It is suggestive of two separate, normally distributed populations from which the data are drawn.

bimolecular reaction (E^2, S_N2) /bī′molek′yələr/, a reaction in which more than one molecule is involved in the slow step.

binangle /bin′ang·gəl/ [L, *bini,* twofold, *angulus,* angle], a double-ended surgical or operative instrument that has a shank with two offsetting angles to keep the cutting edge of the instrument within 3 mm of the shaft axis.

binary fission /bī′nərē/ [L, *bini,* twofold, *fissio,* splitting], the division of a cell or nucleus into two equal parts. It is the common form of asexual reproduction among bacteria, protozoa, and other unicellular organisms.

binary number, a number in base 2 represented by 0s and 1s.

binaural /bīnaw′rol/ [L, *bis,* twice + *auris,* ear], pertaining to both ears.

bind [AS, *binden*], **1.** to bandage or wrap in a band. **2.** to join together with a band or with a ligature. **3.** (in chemistry) to combine or unite molecules by using reactive groups within the molecules or by using a binding chemical.

binder, a bandage made of a large piece of material to fit and support a specific body part.

binding energy, 1. the amount of energy required to separate a nucleus into its individual nucleons. **2.** the energy released as the nucleus forms from nucleons.

binding site [ME, *binden;* L, *situs*], the location on the surface of a cell or a molecule where other cell fragments or molecules attach to initiate a chemical or physiologic action.

binding sites, 1. concave features on antibody molecules that serve as locations for binding antigens. Because of possible variations in antibody amino acid sequences and molecule configurations, each kind of antibody can provide combining sites for a specific antigen. **2.** locations on protein molecules where drugs or other substances may become bound by electrochemical attraction.

Binet age /bina′/ [Alfred Binet, French psychologist, 1857–1911], the mental age of an individual, especially a child, as determined by the Binet-Simon tests, which are evaluated on the basis of tested intelligence of the "normal" individual at any given age. The Binet age corresponding to "profoundly retarded" is 1 to 2 years; to "severely retarded," 3 to 7 years; and to "mildly retarded," 8 to 12 years.

binocular /bīnok′yələr, bin-/ [L, *bini* + *oculus*, eye], **1.** pertaining to both eyes, especially regarding vision. **2.** a microscope, telescope, or field glass that can accommodate viewing by both eyes.

binocular fixation, the process of having both eyes directed at the same object at the same time, which is essential for good depth perception.

binocular ophthalmoscope, an ophthalmoscope having two eyepieces used for stereoscopic examination of the eye.

binocular parallax /per′əlaks/ [L, *bini* + *oculus*; Gk, *parallax*, in turn], the difference in the angles formed by the sight lines to two objects situated at different distances from the eyes. Binocular parallax is a major factor in depth perception.

binocular perception, the visual ability to judge depth or distance by virtue of having two eyes.

binocular vision, the simultaneous use of both eyes so that the images perceived by each eye are combined to appear as a single image.

binomial /bīnō′mē·əl/, **1.** containing two names or terms. **2.** the unique, two-part scientific name used to identify a plant. The first name is the genus; the second, the species.

binomial nomenclature [L, *bis*, twice; Gk, *nomos*, law; L, *nomenclatio*, calling by name], a system of classification of animals, plants, and other life forms (developed by Carl Linné) that assigns a two-part Latinized name referring respectively to the organism's genus and species, such as *Homo sapiens* for humans.

binovular /bīnov′yələr/ [L, *bini* + *ovum*, egg], developing from two distinct ova, as in dizygotic twins.

Binswanger's disease /bin′swängərz/ [Otto Binswanger, German neurologist, 1852–1929], a degenerative dementia of presenile onset caused by thinning of the subcortical white matter of the brain. It is associated with multiple subcortical strokes.

binuclear /bīnoo′klē·ər/ [L, *bis*, twice, *nucleus*, nut kernel], having two nuclei, as in the example of a heterokaryon or binucleate hybrid cell.

bioactive [Gk, *bios*, life; L, *activus*, with energy], having an effect on or causing a reaction in living tissue.

bioactivity /-aktiv′itē/, any response from or reaction in living tissue.—**bioactive,** *adj*.

bioassay /bī′ō·as′ā, -asā′/ [Gk, *bios*; Fr, *assayer*, to try], the laboratory determination of the concentration of a drug or other substance in a specimen by comparing its effect on an organism, an animal, or an isolated tissue with that of a standard preparation.

bioastronautics /-as′trōnôt′iks/, the science dealing with the biologic aspects of space travel.

bioavailability /-əvā′libil′itē/ [Gk, *bios*; ME, *availen*, to serve], the degree of activity or amount of an administered drug or other substance that becomes available for activity in the target tissue.

biocenosis /-sənō′sis/ [Gk, *bios*, life, *koinos*, common], an ecologic community.

biochemical marker /-kem′ikəl/ [Gk, *bios* + *chemeia*, alchemy], any hormone, enzyme, antibody, or other substance that is detected in the urine or other body fluids or tissues that may serve as a sign of a disease or other abnormality.

biochemistry /-kem′istrē/, the chemistry of organisms and life processes.—**biochemical,** *adj*.

biochemorphics /-kemôr′fiks/, the study of the relationship between chemical structure and biologic function.

bioclimatology /-klī′mətol′əjē/, the study of the relationship and interactions between climate and organisms.

biocybernetics /-sī′bərnet′iks/, the science of communication and control within and among organisms and of the interaction between organisms and mechanical or electronic systems.

biodegradable /-digrā′dəbəl/ [Gk, *bios*, life; L, *de*, away, *gradus*, step], the natural ability of a chemical substance to be broken down into less complex compounds or compounds having fewer carbon atoms by bacteria or other microorganisms.

biodynamics /-dīnam′iks/, the study of the effects of dynamic processes, such as radiation, on organisms.

bioelectric impedance analysis (BIA) /-ilek′trik/, a method of measuring the fat composition of the body, compared with other tissues, by its resistance to electricity. Fat tissue does not conduct electricity. Muscle and bone are poor conductors.

bioelectricity /-ilektris′itē/ [Gk, *bios* + *elektron*, amber], electrical current that is generated by living tissues such as nerves and muscles.

bioenergetics /-en′ərjet′iks/ [Gk, *bios* + *energein*, to be active], a system of exercises based on the concept that natural healing will be enhanced by bringing the patient's body rhythms and the natural environment into harmony.

bioequivalent /brī′ōikwiv′ələnt/ [Gk, *bios*; L, *aequus*, equal, *valere*, to be strong], **1.** (in pharmacology) pertaining to a drug that has the same effect on the body as another drug, usually one nearly identical in its chemical formulation but possibly requiring different amount to see the same effect. **2.** going in and out of the body at the same rate.—**bioequivalence**, *n.*

bioethics /brī′ō·eth′iks/ [Gk, *bios*, life + *ethos*, the habits of humans or animals], obligations of a moral nature relating to biologic research and its applications.

biofeedback[1] /-fēd′bak/ [Gk, *bios*; AS, *faedan*, food, *baec*, back], a process providing a person with visual or auditory information about the autonomic physiologic functions of his or her body, such as BP, muscle tension, and brain wave activity. By trial and error, the person learns consciously to control these processes, which were previously regarded as involuntary.

biofeedback[2], a nursing intervention from the Nursing Interventions Classification (NIC) defined as assisting the patient to gain voluntary control over physiological responses using feedback from electronic equipment that monitor physiologic processes.

biofilm /bī′ōōfilm′/, a thin layer of microorganisms adhering to the surface of a structure, which may be organic or inorganic, together with the polymers that they secrete.

bioflavonoid /brī′ōflā′vənoid/ [Gk, *bios*; L, *flavus*, yellow; Gk, *eidos*, form], a generic term for any of a group of colored flavones found in many fruits. Bioflavonoids are now considered nonessential nutrients.

biogenesis /brī′ōjen′əsis/ [Gk, *bios* + *genein*, to produce], **1.** the doctrine that living material can originate only from preexisting life and not from inanimate matter. **2.** the origin of life; ontogeny and phylogeny.—**biogenetic**, *adj.*

biogenic /brī′ōjen′ik/, **1.** produced by the action of a living organism, such as fermentation. **2.** essential to life and the maintenance of health, such as food, water, and proper rest.

biogenic amine, one of a large group of naturally occurring biologically active compounds, most of which act as neurotransmitters. The most dominant is norepinephrine. These substances are active in regulating BP, elimination, body temperature, and many other centrally mediated body functions.

biogenous /brī′oj′ənəs/, **1.** biogenetic. **2.** biogenic.

biogravics /-grav′iks/, the study of the effects of gravity, including reduced and increased gravitational forces, on organisms.

biohazard /-haz′ərd/ [Gk, *bios*, life; OFr, *hasard*], anything that is a risk to organisms, such as ionizing radiation or harmful bacteria or viruses.

bioimpedance analysis, a method for analyzing the water content of the body through variations in bioimpedance between different types of tissue.

bioinstrument, a sensor or other device implanted into or attached to a living organism for the purpose of recording physiologic data, such as brain activity or heart function.

biokinetics /-kinet′iks/ [Gk, *bios*, life, *kinetikos*, moving], the study of the movements within developing organisms.

biological /-loj′ik/ [Gk, *bios* + *logos*, science], **1.** Pertaining to organisms and their products. **2.** any preparation made from organisms or their products and used as a diagnostic, preventive, or therapeutic agent such as antigens, antitoxins, sera, and vaccines.

biological activity, the inherent capacity of a substance, such as a drug or toxin, to alter one or more chemical or physiologic functions of a cell, tissue, organ, or organism.

biological half-life, the time required for the body to eliminate half of an administered dose of any substance by regular physiologic processes.

biological monitoring, **1.** a process of measuring the levels of various physiologic substances, drugs, or metabolites within a patient during diagnosis or therapy. **2.** the measurement of toxic substances in the environment and the identification of health risks to the population.

biological plausibility, a method of reasoning used to establish a cause-and-effect relationship between a biological factor and a particular disease.

biological rhythm [Gk, *bios*, life, *logos*, science, *rhythmos*], the periodic recurrence of a biological phenomenon such as the respiratory cycle, the sleep cycle, or the menstrual cycle.

biologic armature, the connective tissue–rich aggregate of larger ducts, vessels, and autonomic nerves that in many mammalian exocrine glands serve as an internal framework whose function of support, and often anchorage, resembles that of the armature within a clay sculpture.

biologic death, death attributed to natural causes. In CPR terms, biologic death refers to permanent cellular damage, resulting from lack of oxygen, that is not reversible.

biologic dressing, a dressing for burn injuries that is made from pigskin or synthetic materials with characteristics like those of human skin. The dressing is most effective in treating burns that are of uniform depth and of superficial partial thickness. It should be applied as soon as possible after the injury and should adhere to the wound during healing. Once adherence is established, the wound can be left open, and the patient can bathe and wear clothing over it.

biologic psychiatry, a school of psychiatric thought that stresses the physical, chemical, and neurologic causes of and treatments for mental and emotional disorders.

biologist /bī·ol'əjist/ [Gk, *bios,* life, *logos,* science], a person who studies life sciences.

biology /bī·ol'əje/, the scientific study of life.

biolysis /bī·ol'isis/ [Gk, *bios,* life, *lysis,* loosening], the disintegration or dissolution of organic matter resulting from the activity of organisms, such as bacterial action on living tissue.

biome /bī'ōm/ [Gk, *bios* + *oma,* tumor, mass], the collection of all biologic communities existing in and characteristic of a broad geographic region such as desert, tropical forest, or savanna.

biomechanic adaptation, a process in which a patient with a physical disability adjusts to the use of an orthotic device. Adaptation requires the CNS input received during therapeutic exercises with the orthotic appliance.

biomechanics [Gk, *bios* + *mechane,* machine], the study of mechanical laws and their application to living organisms, especially the human body and its locomotor system.—**biomechanic, biomechanical,** *adj.*

biomedical, pertaining to the biologic aspects of medicine.

biomedical engineering /-med'ikəl/ [Gk, *bios;* L, *medicare,* to heal], a system of scientific techniques that are applied to biologic processes to solve practical medical problems or answer questions in biomedical research.

biometry /bī·om'ətrē/, the application of statistical methods in analyzing data obtained in biologic or anthropologic research.

biomicroscopy /-mīkros'kəpē/, **1.** microscopic examination of living tissue in the body. **2.** ophthalmic examination of the eye by use of a slit lamp and a magnifying lens.

bionics /bī·on'iks/, the science of applying electronic principles and devices, such as computers and solid-state miniaturized circuitry, to medical problems, such as the

development of artificial pacemakers to correct abnormal heart rhythms.—**bionic,** *adj.*

biopharmaceutics /-fär'məsōō'tiks/, the study of the chemical and physical properties of drugs, their components, and their activities in living organisms.

biophore /bī'əfôr/ [Gk, *bios* + *phora,* bearer], according to the German biologist A.F.L. Weismann (1834–1914), the basic hereditary unit contained in the germ plasm from which all living cells develop and all inherited characteristics are transmitted.

biophysics, the application of physical laws and science to life processes of organisms.

biopotentials /-pəten'shəls/, a voltage produced by a tissue of the body, particularly muscle tissue during a contraction.

biopsy /bī'opsē/ [Gk, *bios* + *opsis,* view], **1.** the removal of a small piece of living tissue from an organ or other part of the body for microscopic examination to confirm or establish a diagnosis, estimate prognosis, or follow the course of a disease. **2.** the tissue excised for examination. **3.** informal. to excise tissue for examination.—**bioptic** /bī·op'tik/, *adj.*

biopsychic /bī'ōsī'kik/ [Gk, *bios* + *psyche,* mind], pertaining to mental factors as they relate to living organisms.

biopsychosocial /bī'ōsī'kōsō'shəl/ [Gk, *bios* + *psyche,* mind; L, *socius,* companion], pertaining to the complex of biologic, psychologic, and social aspects of life.

biopsychosocial diagnosis, a holistic approach to diagnosis that takes into consideration the medical, developmental, psychologic, spiritual, and social conditions and symptoms that are present, and how they interact to produce a particular patient's condition.

bioptome tip catheter /bī·op'tōm/, a catheter with a special end designed for obtaining endomyocardial biopsy samples. The bioptome tip device is used to monitor heart transplantation patients for early signs of tissue rejection.

biosafety, a system for the safe handling of toxic and dangerous biologic and chemical substances. Guidance in biosafety is offered by the U.S. Centers for Disease Control and Prevention, Occupational Safety and Health Administration, and National Institute for Occupational Safety and Health.

biostatistics /-stətis'tiks/, numeric data on births, deaths, diseases, injuries, and other factors affecting the general health and condition of human populations.

biosynthesis /-sin'thəsis/ [Gk, *bios* + *synthesis,* putting together], any one of thousands of chemical processes continually occurring throughout the body in which less complex molecules form more complex biomolecules, especially the carbohydrates, lipids, proteins, nucleotides, and nucleic acids.—**biosynthetic,** *adj.*

biosystem, any organism or complex system of organisms.

biotaxis /bī′ōtak′sis/ [Gk, *bios* + *taxis,* arrangement], the ability of cells to develop into certain forms and arrangements.—**biotactic,** *adj.*

biotaxy /bī′ōtak′sē/, **1.** biotaxis. **2.** the systematic classification of organisms according to their phenotypic characteristics; taxonomy.

biotechnology /-teknol′əjē/ [Gk, *bios* + *techne,* art, *logos,* science], **1.** the study of the relationships between humans or other living organisms and machinery, such as the health effects of computer equipment on office workers. **2.** the industrial application of the results of biologic research, particularly in fields such as recombinant DNA or gene splicing.

biotelemetry /-təlem′ətrē/, the transmission of physiologic data such as ECG and EEG recordings, heart rate, and body temperature by radio or telephone systems.

bioterrorism, the calculated use, or threatened use, of biologic agents against civilian populations in order to attain political or ideologic goals by intimidation or coercion.

bioterrorism infected agents testing, testing for infectious agents used in bioterrorism. Testing may include blood tests, urine tests, stool tests, tissue culture, sputum culture, lymph node biopsy, and skin tests.

bioterrorism preparedness, a nursing intervention from the Nursing Interventions Classification (NIC) defined as preparing for an effective response to bioterrorism events or disaster.

biotherapy, a type of cancer therapy that uses agents to stimulate the body's own immune system to kill cancer. Examples are interleukins, interferons, and hematopoietic growth factors.

biotic factor /bī′ot′ik/, an environmental influence on living things, as distinguished from climatic or geologic factors.

biotic potential, the possible growth rate of a population of organisms under ideal conditions, which include an absence of predators and an unlimited availability of nutrients and space for expansion.

biotin /bī′ətin/ [Gk, *bios,* life], a colorless, crystalline, water-soluble B complex vitamin that acts as a coenzyme in fatty acid production and in the oxidation of fatty acids and carbohydrates. It also aids in the use of protein, folic acid, pantothenic acid, and vitamin B_{12}.

biotin deficiency syndrome, an abnormal condition caused by a deficiency of biotin. It is characterized by dermatitis, hyperesthesia, muscle pain, anorexia, slight anemia, and changes in ECG activity of the heart.

biotope /bī′ətōp/ [Gk, *bios* + *topos,* place], a specific biologic habitat or site.

biotoxin /bī′ətoks′in/, poison produced by and derived from plants and animals. Biotoxins can be absorbed by ingesting or inhaling the toxin. Inhalation of ricin or abrin causes severe respiratory distress, and ingestion of these agents causes nausea and vomiting. Multisystem organ failure and death may occur. Strychnine attacks communication between the nerves and muscles and may lead to death from respiratory failure as the respiratory muscles tire.

biotransformation /-trans′fôrmā′shən/ [Gk, *bios;* L, *trans,* across, *formare,* to form], the chemical changes a substance undergoes in the body, such as by the action of enzymes.

Biot's respiration /bē·ōz′/ [Camille Biot, French physician, 1878–1918], an abnormal respiratory pattern, characterized by short episodes of rapid, uniformly deep inspirations followed by 10 to 30 seconds of apnea.

bipalatinoid /bī′palat′inoid, -pal′-/, describing a two-compartment capsule with different medications in each side. It is designed so that the two substances become mixed and activated as the gelatin capsule dissolves.

bipara /bip′ərə/, a woman who has given birth twice in separate pregnancies.

biparietal /bīpərī′ətəl/ [L, *bis,* twice, *paries,* wall], pertaining to the two parietal bones of the head.

biparietal diameter (BPD), the transverse distance between the protuberances of the two parietal bones of the skull.

biparietal suture [L, *bis* + *paries,* wall, *sutura*], the interlocking lines of fusion between the two parietal bones of the skull.

biparous /bip′ərəs/ [L, *bis,* twice, *parere,* to produce], pertaining to the birth of two infants in separate pregnancies.

bipartite /bīpär′tīt/, having two parts.

biped /bī′ped/, **1.** having two feet. **2.** any animal with only two feet.

bipedal /bīpē′dəl, -ped′əl/ [L, *bis,* twice, *pes,* foot], capable of locomotion on two feet.

bipenniform /bīpen′ifôrm/ [L, *bis* + *penna,* feather, *forma,* form], (of body structure) having the bilateral symmetry of a feather, such as the pattern formed by the fasciculi that converge on both sides of a muscle tendon in the rectus femoris.

B

biperforate /bī'pər'fərāt/ [L, *bis*, twice + *perforatus*, bored through], having two perforations.

biperiden hydrochloride /bīper'idən/, a synthetic anticholinergic agent prescribed in the treatment of Parkinson's disease and drug-induced extrapyramidal disorders.

biphasic /bīfā'zik/ [L, *bis*; Gk, *phasis*, appearance], having two phases, parts, aspects, or stages.

bipolar /bīpō'lər/ [L, *bis* + *polus*, pole], **1.** having two poles, such as in certain electrotherapeutic treatments using two poles or in certain types of bacterial staining that affect only the two poles of the microorganism under study. **2.** (of a nerve cell) having an afferent and an efferent process.

bipolar cell, a cell, such as a retinal neuron, with two main processes arising from the cell body.

bipolar disorder, a major mental disorder characterized by episodes of mania, depression, or mixed mood. One or the other phase may be predominant at any given time, one phase may appear alternately with the other, or elements of both phases may be present simultaneously. Characteristics of the manic phase are excessive emotional displays, such as excitement, elation, euphoria, or in some cases irritability accompanied by hyperactivity, boisterousness, impaired ability to concentrate, decreased need for sleep, and seemingly unbounded energy. In the depressive phase, marked apathy and underactivity are accompanied by feelings of profound sadness, loneliness, guilt, and lowered self-esteem.

bipolar electrocautery, an electrocautery in which both active and return electrodes are incorporated into a single handheld instrument, so that the current passes between the tips of the two electrodes and affects only a small amount of tissue.

bipolar lead /lēd/, **1.** an ECG conductor having two electrodes placed on different body regions, with each electrode contributing to the record. **2.** informal. a tracing produced by such a lead on an ECG.

bipolar version, a method for changing the position of a fetus in which one hand is placed on the abdomen of the mother and two fingers of the other hand are inserted into the uterus.

bipotentiality /bī'pəten'shē·al'itē/ [L, *bis* + *potentia*, power], the characteristic of acting or reacting according to either of two possible states.

birth [ME, *burth*], **1.** the event of being born, the entry of a new person out of its mother into the world. **2.** the childbearing event, the bringing forth by a mother of a

baby. **3.** a medical event, the delivery of a fetus by an obstetric attendant.

birth canal informal. the passage that extends from the inlet of the true pelvis to the vaginal orifice through which an infant passes during vaginal birth.

birth center, a health facility with services limited to maternity care for women judged to be at minimum risk for obstetric complications that would require hospitalization.

birth certificate, a legal document recording information about a birth, including, among other details, the date, time, and location of the event; identity of the mother and father; and identity of the attending physician or licensed midwife.

birthing, a nursing intervention from the Nursing Interventions Classification (NIC) defined as delivery of a baby.

birthing chair, a special seat used in labor and delivery to promote the comfort of the mother and facilitate the birthing process. The newer birthing chairs allow women to sit straight up or to recline.

birth injury, trauma suffered by a baby while being born.

birth mother, the biologic mother or woman who bears a child. The child may have been conceived in a surrogate mother with sperm of the biologic father.

birth palsy [ME, *burth*; Gk, *paralyein*, to be palsied], a loss of motor or sensory nerve function in some body part caused by a nerve injury during the birth process.

birth parent, one of an individual's two biologic parents.

birth rate, the proportion of the number of live births in a specific area during a given period to the total population of that area, usually expressed as the number of births per 1000 of population.

birth trauma, **1.** any physical injury suffered by an infant during the process of delivery. **2.** the supposed psychic shock, according to some psychiatric theories, that an infant suffers during delivery.

birth weight, the measured heaviness of a baby when born, usually about 3500 g (7.5 pounds).

bisacodyl /bisak'ōdil/, a cathartic prescribed in the treatment of acute or chronic constipation or for emptying of the bowel before or after surgery or before diagnostic radiographic procedures.

bisacromial /bīsəkrō'mē·əl/, pertaining to both acromions, the triangular, flat, bony plates at the end of the scapula.

bisalbuminemia /bis'albyōōm'inē'mē·ə/, a condition in which two types of albumin exist in an individual. The two types are expressed by heterozygous alleles of the albumin gene and are detected by differences in the mobility of the types on electrophoretic gels.

bisect /bīsekt'/ [L, *bis* + *secare,* to cut], to divide into two equal lengths or parts.

bisexual /bīsek'shoo̅·əl/ [L, *bis* + *sexus,* male or female], **1.** hermaphroditic; having gonads of both sexes. **2.** possessing physical or psychologic characteristics of both sexes. **3.** engaging in both heterosexual and homosexual activity. **4.** desiring sexual contact with persons of both sexes.

bisexual libido, (in psychoanalysis) the tendency in a person to seek sexual gratification with people of either sex.

bisferious pulse /bisfer'ē·əs/ [L, *bis* + *ferire,* to beat], an arterial pulse that has two palpable peaks, the second of which is slightly weaker than the first. It may be detected in cases of aortic regurgitation and obstructive cardiomyopathy.

bis in die (b.i.d.) /dē'ā/, a Latin phrase, used in prescriptions, meaning "twice a day." It is more commonly used in its abbreviated form.

bismuth (Bi) /biz'məth, bis'-/ [Ger, *wismut,* white mass], a reddish, crystalline, trivalent metallic element. Its atomic number is 83; its atomic mass is 208.98.

bismuth gingivitis, a dark bluish line along the gingival margin caused by bismuth administered in the treatment of systemic disease.

bismuth stomatitis, an abnormal oral condition caused by the systemic use of bismuth compounds over prolonged periods. It is characterized by a blue-black line on the inner aspect of the gingival sulcus or dark pigmentation of the buccal mucosa, sore tongue, metallic taste, and burning sensation in the mouth.

bismuth subsalicylate, a bismuth salt of salicylic acid, administered orally in the treatment of diarrhea and gastric distress, including nausea, indigestion, and heartburn.

bisoprolol /bis'o-pro'lol/, a synthetic beta-adrenergic blocking agent, used as the fumarate salt. It is administered orally as an antihypertensive agent.

bitart, abbreviation for a **bitartrate carboxylate anion.**

bitartrate /bītär'trāt/, the monoanion of tartaric acid, $C_4H_5O_6^-$.

bitartrate carboxylate anion, an ionotropic agent used in the treatment of cardiovascular patients.

bite [AS, *bitan*], **1.** the act of cutting, tearing, holding, or gripping with the teeth. **2.** the lingual portion of an artificial tooth between its shoulder and its incisal edge. **3.** an occlusal record or relationship between the upper and lower teeth or jaws.

bitegauge /bīt'gāj'/ [AS, *bitan*; OFr, *gauge,* measure], a prosthetic dental device that helps attain proper occlusion of the upper and lower teeth.

biteguard [AS, *bitan*; OFr, *garder,* to defend], a resin appliance that covers the occlusal and incisal surfaces of the teeth. It is used to stabilize the teeth, to provide a platform for the excursive glides of the mandible, and to eliminate the effects of nocturnal grinding of the teeth.

biteguard splint, a device, usually made of resin, for covering the occlusal and incisal surfaces of the teeth and for protecting them from traumatic occlusal forces during immobilization and stabilization processes.

bitelock /bīt'lok'/, a dental device for retaining occlusion rims in the same relation outside and inside the mouth.

bitemporal /bītem'pərəl/ [L, *bis,* twice, *tempora,* temples], pertaining to both temples or both temporal bones.

bitemporal hemianopia [L, *bis,* twice, *tempora,* temples; Gk, *hemi,* half, *opsis,* vision], a loss of the temporal half of the vision in each eye, usually resulting from a lesion in the chiasmal area such as a pituitary tumor.

biteplane /bīt'plān/, **1.** a metal sheet laid across the biting surfaces of the upper or lower teeth to determine the relationship of the teeth to the occlusal plane. **2.** an orthodontic appliance of acrylic resin worn over the maxillary occlusal surfaces and used to treat pain of the TMJ and adjacent muscles.

biteplate /bīt'plāt/, a device used in dentistry as a diagnostic or therapeutic aid for prosthodontics or orthodontics. It is made of wire and plastic and worn in the palate. It may also be used in the correction of TMJ problems or as a splint in restoring the full mouth.

bite reflex, a swift, involuntary biting action that may be triggered by stimulation of the oral cavity.

bite wing film image [AS, *bitan*; ME, *winge*], a dental radiographic film on which a tab is placed so the teeth can hold the film in position during exposure, used to view the interproximal area of posterior teeth.

bite wing radiograph, a dental radiograph that reveals the coronal portions of maxillary and mandibular teeth and portions of the interdental septa on the same film.

Bithynia /bəthin'ē·ə/, a genus of snails, species of which act as intermediate hosts to *Opisthorchis.*

biting in childhood, a natural behavior trait and reflex action in infants, acquired at about 5 to 6 months of age in response to the introduction of solid foods in the diet and the beginning of the teething process. The activity represents a significant modality in the psychosocial development of the child, because it is the first aggressive action the infant learns, and through it the infant learns to control the environment.

bitolterol /bitol′terol/, a beta-adrenergic receptor agonist that is used as a bronchodilator. It is administered by inhalation as the mesylate salt.

biitolterol mesylate /bitol′tərol mes′ilāt/, an orally inhaled bronchodilator used in the treatment of bronchial asthma and reversible bronchospasm.

Bitot's spots /bitōz′/ [Pierre Bitot, French surgeon, 1822–1888], white or gray triangular deposits on the bulbar conjunctiva adjacent to the lateral margin of the cornea, a clinical sign of vitamin A deficiency.

bitrochanteric lipodystrophy /bī′trōkən ter′ik/ [L, bis; Gk, trochanter, runner, lipos, fat, dys, bad, trophe, nourishment], an abnormal and excessive deposition of fat on the buttocks and the outer aspect of the upper thighs, occurring most commonly in women.

biuret test /bī′yŏŏret/ [L, bis; Gk, ouron, urine], a method for detecting proteins in serum. In alkaline solution, copper sulfate ions react with the peptide bonds of proteins to produce a pink to purple color, called the biuret reaction. The amount of serum protein in a sample solution is estimated by comparing its color with that of a standard solution whose protein concentration is known.

bivalent /bīvā′lənt/ [L, bis + valere, to be powerful], (in genetics) a pair of synapsed homologous chromosomes that are attached to each other by chiasmata during the early first meiotic prophase of gametogenesis. The structure serves as the basis for the tetrads from which gametes are produced during the two meiotic divisions. —**bivalence,** n.

bivalent antibody, an antibody that has two or more binding sites that can crosslink one antigen to another.

bivalent chromosome, a pair of synapsed homologous chromosomes during the early stages of gametogenesis.

bivalirudin /bi-val′roo-din/, an inhibitor of the clot-promoting activity of thrombin, used in conjunction with aspirin as an anticoagulant in patients with unstable angina pectoris who are undergoing percutaneous transluminal coronary angioplasty.

bivalved cast [L, bis + valva, valve], a cast that is cut in half to detect or relieve pressure underneath, especially when a patient has decreased or no sensation in the portion of the body surrounded by the cast.

bivalve speculum, a speculum with two blades that are adjustable.

biventricular pacing, that in which a lead is used to deliver current directly to the left ventricle, in addition to those used to deliver current to the right atrium and ventricle, so that the ventricles can be induced to pump in synchrony.

Björnstad's syndrome /byôrn′städz/ [R. Björnstad, Swedish dermatologist, 20th century], an autosomal-recessive disorder characterized by congenital sensorineural deafness and kinky hair.

Bk, symbol for the element **berkelium.**

BK amputation, abbreviation for below-knee amputation.

black cohosh, a perennial herb that grows throughout the United States and in parts of Canada. It is used to treat the symptoms of menopause (hot flashes and nervous conditions) and dysmenorrhea (menstrual cramps, pain, inflammation). It is generally considered to be effective against mild symptoms but is not a substitute for estrogen-containing prescriptions needed to control more severe vasomotor symptoms.

Black Creek Canal virus, a virus of the genus Hantavirus that causes hantavirus pulmonary syndrome.

Blackett-Healy method, a positioning procedure for producing x-ray images of the subscapularis area. The patient is supine with the affected shoulder joint centered on the midline of the film, the arm abducted, and the elbow flexed. The opposite shoulder is raised about 15 degrees and supported with a sandbag.

black eye, contusion around the eye with bruising, discoloration, and swelling.

black haw, a herb used for dysmenorrhea, menstrual cramps and pain, menopausal metrorrhagia, hysteria, asthma, and heart palpitations. It is also used to lower BP. It is possibly effective at relieving uterine spasms, but effectiveness in other instances has not been verified.

black measles [AS, blac; OHG, masala], an acute tickborne illness caused by the bacterium Rickettsia rickettsii. The disease is characterized by a sudden onset of headache, chills, and fever, which can persist for 2 to 3 weeks. A characteristic rash appears on the extremities and trunk about the fourth day of illness.

blackout, informal. a temporary loss of vision or consciousness.

black spots film fault, a defect in a radiograph, seen as dark spots throughout the image area.

blackwater fever, a serious complication of chronic falciparum malaria, characterized by jaundice, hemoglobinuria, acute renal failure, and passage of bloody dark red or black urine caused by massive intra-vascular hemolysis.

Blackwell, Elizabeth [1821–1910], a British-born American physician, the first woman to be awarded a medical degree. She established the New York Infirmary, a 40-bed hospital staffed entirely by women. Her influence helped establish nursing schools to improve patient care.

black widow spider [AS, *blac* + *widewe;* ME, *spithre*], *Latrodectus mactans*, a spe-cies of spider found in the United States, whose bite causes pain and sometimes death.

black widow spider antivenin, a passive immunizing agent prescribed in the treat-ment of black widow spider bite.

black widow spider bite [AS, *blac* + *widewe;* ME, *spithre;* AS, *bitan*], the bite of the spider species *Latrodectus mactans*. The bite is perceived as a sharp pinprick pain, followed by a dull pain in the area of the bite; restlessness; anxiety; sweating; weakness; and drooping eyelids. Muscular rigidity starts at the location of the bite and moves in peripherally to the chest.

bladder [AS, *blaedre*], **1.** a membranous sac serving as a receptacle for secretions, such as the gallbladder. **2.** the urinary bladder.

bladder augmentation, augmentation cystoplasty, often achieved with the addi-tion of a flap of bowel or stomach to the bladder to increase bladder volume.

bladder cancer, the most common malig-nancy of the urinary tract, characterized by multiple growths that tend to recur in a more aggressive form. Bladder cancer occurs 2.3 times more often in men than in women and is more prevalent in urban than in rural areas. The risk of bladder cancer increases with cigarette smoking and exposure to ani-line dyes, beta-naphthylamine, mixtures of aromatic hydrocarbons, or benzidine and its salts. Symptoms of bladder cancer include hematuria, frequent urination, dysuria, and cystitis. Urinalysis, excretory urography, cystoscopy, or transurethral biopsy is per-formed for diagnosis. A majority of bladder malignancies are transitional cell carcino-mas; a small percentage are squamous cell carcinomas or adenocarcinomas.

bladder cancer markers test, a urine test used to diagnose recurrent bladder cancer.

bladder flap informal. the vesicouterine fold of peritoneum incised during low cer-vical cesarean section so that the bladder can be separated from the uterus to expose the lower uterine segment for incision.

bladder hernia, a protrusion of the bladder through an opening in the abdominal wall.

bladder irrigation[1] [AS, *blaedre;* L, *irrig-are,* to conduct water], the washing out of the bladder by a continuous or intermit-tent flow of saline or a medicated solution. The bladder also may be irrigated by an oral intake of fluid.

bladder irrigation[2], a nursing interven-tion from the Nursing Interventions Clas-sification (NIC) defined as instillation of a solution into the bladder to provide cleans-ing or medication.

bladder neck dyssynergia, incomplete opening of the bladder neck during urina-tion resulting in partial obstruction of uri-nary flow.

bladder neck incision, surgical incision of the bladder neck, an operation similar to but less extensive than bladder neck resection.

bladder neck resection, surgical removal of tissue from the bladder neck to treat obstruction.

bladder neck suspension, any of various methods of surgical fixation of the urethro-vesical junction area and the bladder neck to restore the neck to a high retropubic position for relief of stress incontinence.

bladder outlet obstruction (BOO), obstruction of the outflow of urine from the bladder resulting from various etiologies.

bladder retraining [AS, *blaedre;* L, *tra-here,* to draw], a system of therapy for urinary incontinence in which a patient practices withholding urine while main-taining a normal intake of fluid.

bladder sphincter [AS, *blaedre;* Gk, *sphingein,* to bind], a circular muscle surrounding the opening of the urinary bladder into the urethra.

bladder wall, the surrounding structure of the urinary bladder, consisting of the serous coat, subserous layer, muscular coat, submucous layer, and mucus coat.

Blalock-Taussig procedure /blā'lok tô'sig/ [Alfred Blalock, American surgeon, 1899–1964; Helen B. Taussig, American physician, 1898–1986], surgical con-struction of a shunt between the right subclavian artery and the right pulmonary artery as a temporary measure to over-come congenital heart malformations in which there is insufficient pulmonary blood flow.

blame placing, the process of placing responsibility for one's behavior on others.

blanch /blanch, blänch/ [Fr, *blanchir,* to become white], **1.** to cause to become pale, as a nailbed may be blanched by using digital pressure. **2.** to press blood away and wait for return, such as blanch-ing of fingernails and return of blood. **3.** to become white or pale, as from vasocon-striction accompanying fear or anger.

blanch test [Fr, *blanchir,* to become white; L, *testum,* crucible], a test of blood circulation in the fingers or toes. Pressure is applied to a fingernail or toenail until normal color is lost. The pressure is then removed, and if the circulation is normal, color should return almost immediately, within about 2 seconds.

bland [L, *blandus*], mild or having a soothing effect.

bland aerosols, aerosols that consist of water, saline solutions, or similar substances that do not have important pharmacologic action. They are primarily used for humidification and liquefaction of secretions.

bland diet, a diet that is mechanically, chemically, physiologically, and sometimes thermally nonirritating to the GI tract. The clinical value of the traditional bland diet has never been proven.

blank, a solution containing all of the reagents needed for analysis of a substance except the substance tested.

blanket bath [OFr, *blanchet,* a white garment], the procedure of wrapping the patient in a wet pack and then in blankets.

blast, 1. a primitive cell, such as an embryonic germ cell. 2. a cell capable of building tissue, such as an osteoblast in growing bone.

blast cell [Gk, *blastos,* germ], any immature cell, such as an erythroblast, lymphoblast, or neuroblast.

blastema /blastĕ′mə/ *pl.* **blastemas, blastemata** [Gk, bud], 1. any mass of cells capable of growth and differentiation, specifically the primordial, undifferentiated cellular material from which a particular organ or tissue develops. 2. in certain animals, a group of cells capable of regenerating a lost or damaged part or creating a complete organism in asexual reproduction. 3. the budding or sprouting area of a plant. —**blastemal, blastematic, blastemic,** *adj.*

blastic transformation, a late stage in the progress of chronic granulocytic leukemia. Signs of anemia and blood platelet deficiency are present, and half of the blood cells in the bone marrow are immature forms. Blastic transformation indicates that resistance to therapy has developed in the patient who has entered a terminal stage of leukemia.

blastid /blas′tid/ [Gk, *blastos,* germ], the site in the fertilized ovum where the pronuclei fuse and the nucleus forms.

blastin /blas′tin/ [Gk, *blastanein,* to grow], any substance that provides nourishment for or stimulates the growth or proliferation of cells, such as allantoin.

blastocoele /blas′təsēl′/ [Gk, *blastos,* germ, *koilos,* hollow], the fluid-filled cavity of the blastocyst in mammals and the blastula or discoblastula of lower animals. The cavity increases the surface area

of the developing embryo to allow better absorption of nutrients and oxygen.

blastocyst /blas′təsist/ [Gk, *blastos* + *kystis,* bag], the embryonic form that follows the morula in human development. Implantation in the wall of the uterus usually occurs at this stage, approximately 8 to 13 days after fertilization.

blastocyst cavity, the fluid-filled cavity developing in the morula as it becomes a blastocyst.

blastocyte /blas′təsīt/ [Gk, *blastos* + *kytos,* cell], an undifferentiated embryonic cell that precedes germ layer formation.— **blastocytic,** *adj.*

blastoderm /blas′tədurm′/ [Gk, *blastos* + *derma,* skin], the layer of cells forming the wall of the blastocyst in mammals and the blastula in lower animals during the early stages of embryonic development. It is produced by the cleavage of the fertilized ovum and gives rise to the primary germ layers, the ectoderm, mesoderm, and endoderm, from which the embryo and all of its membranes are derived.—**blastodermal, blastodermic,** *adj.*

blastodisk /blas′tədisk/, the disklike, yolk-free area of cytoplasm surrounding the animal pole in a yolk-rich ovum such as that of birds and reptiles. It is the site where cleavage occurs after fertilization.

blastogenesis /blas′tōjen′əsis/ [Gk, *blastos* + *genein,* to produce], 1. asexual reproduction by budding. 2. the transmission of hereditary characteristics by the germ plasm. 3. the early development of an embryo during cleavage and formation of the germ layers. 4. the process of transforming small lymphocytes in tissue culture into large, blastlike cells by exposure to phytohemagglutinin or other substances, often for the purpose of inducing mitosis.—**blastogenetic,** *adj.*

blastogenic /-jen′ik/, 1. originating in the germ plasm. 2. initiating tissue proliferation. 3. relating to or characterized by blastogenesis.

blastogenic factor, lymphocyte-transforming factor.

blastogeny /blastoj′ənē/, the early stages in ontogeny. The germ plasm history of an organism or species, which traces the history of inherited characteristics.

blastokinin /blas′təkī′nin/ [Gk, *blastos* + *kinein,* to move], a globulin, secreted by the uterus in many mammals, that may stimulate and regulate the implantation process of the blastocyst in the uterine wall.

blastolysis /blastol′isis/ [Gk, *blastos* + *lysis,* loosening], destruction of a germ cell or blastoderm.—**blastolytic,** *adj.*

blastoma /blastō′mə/ *pl.* **blastomas, blastomata** [Gk, *blastos* + *oma,* tumor], a

B

neoplasm of embryonic tissue that develops from the blastema of an organ or tissue. A blastoma derived from a number of scattered cells is pluricentric; one arising from a single cell or group of cells is unicentric. —**blastomatous** /blastom'ətəs/, *adj.*

blastomatosis /blast″ōmətō′sis/ [Gk, *blastos* + *oma,* tumor, *osis,* condition], the development of many tumors from embryonic tissue.

blastomere /blas′təmēr/ [Gk, *blastos* + *meros,* part], any of the cells formed from the first mitotic division of a fertilized ovum (zygote). The blastomeres further divide and subdivide to form a multicellular morula in the first several days of pregnancy.—**blastomeric,** *adj.*

blastomere biopsy, a technique for preimplantation genetic diagnosis, in which a blastomere is removed from a 6- or 8-cell embryo and tested for genetic abnormalities.

blastomerotomy /-merot′əmē/ [Gk, *blastos* + *meros,* part, *tome,* cut], destruction of blastomeres.—**blastomerotomic,** *adj.*

Blastomyces /blas′tōmī′sēz/ [Gk, *blastos* + *mykes,* fungus], a genus of yeastlike fungi, usually including the species *Blastomyces dermatitidis,* which causes North American blastomycosis, and *Paracoccidioides brasiliensis,* which causes South American blastomycosis.

blastomycosis /blas′tōmīkō′sis/ [Gk, *blastos* + *mykes,* fungus, *osis,* condition], an infectious disease caused by a yeastlike fungus, *Blastomyces dermatitidis.* It usually affects only the skin but may cause acute pneumonitis or disseminated disease and may invade the lungs, kidneys, CNS, and bones.

blastopore /blas′təpôr/ [Gk, *blastos* + *poros,* opening], (in embryology) the opening into the archenteron made by invagination of the blastula.

blastula /blas′tyələ/ [Gk, *blastos,* germ], an early stage of the process through which a zygote develops into an embryo, characterized by a fluid-filled sphere formed by a single layer of cells.

blastulation, the transformation of the morula into a blastocyst or blastula by the development of a central cavity, the blastocoele.

BLB mask, abbreviation for **Boothby-Lovelace-Bulbulian mask.**

bleaching /blēch′ing/ [ME, *blechen*], the act or process of removing stains or color by chemical means.

bleaching agents, medications and OTC preparations used to depigment the skin. The products may be used by persons whose skin has become hyperpigmented

through exposure to sunlight and particularly for melasma associated with pregnancy, the use of oral contraceptives, or hormone replacement therapy.

bleach poisoning, an adverse reaction to ingestion of hypochlorite salts commonly found in household and commercial bleaches. Symptoms include pain and inflammation of the mouth, throat, and esophagus; vomiting; shock; and circulatory collapse.

bleb /bleb/ [ME, blob], an accumulation of fluid under the skin.

bleed [AS, *blod,* blood], **1.** to lose blood from the blood vessels of the body. **2.** to cause blood to flow from a vein or an artery.

bleeder, informal **1.** a person who has hemophilia or any other vascular or hematologic condition associated with a tendency to hemorrhage. **2.** a blood vessel that bleeds, especially one cut during a surgical procedure.

bleeding, the release of blood from the vascular system as a result of damage to a blood vessel.

bleeding diathesis, a predisposition to abnormal blood clotting.

bleeding precautions, a nursing intervention from the Nursing Interventions Classification (NIC) defined as reduction of stimuli that may induce bleeding or hemorrhage in at-risk patients.

bleeding reduction, a nursing intervention from the Nursing Interventions Classification (NIC) defined as limitation of the loss of blood volume during an episode of bleeding.

bleeding reduction: antepartum uterus, a nursing intervention from the Nursing Interventions Classification (NIC) defined as limitation of the amount of blood loss from the pregnant uterus during the third trimester of pregnancy.

bleeding reduction: gastrointestinal, a nursing intervention from the Nursing Interventions Classification (NIC) defined as limitation of the amount of blood loss from the upper and lower gastrointestinal tract and related complications.

bleeding reduction: nasal, a nursing intervention from the Nursing Interventions Classification (NIC) defined as limitation of the amount of blood loss from the nasal cavity.

bleeding reduction: postpartum uterus, a nursing intervention from the Nursing Interventions Classification (NIC) defined as limitation of the amount of blood loss from the postpartum uterus.

bleeding reduction: wound, a nursing intervention from the Nursing Interventions Classification (NIC) defined as limitation of the blood loss from a wound that may be a result of trauma, incisions, or placement of a tube or catheter.

bleeding time, the time required for blood to stop flowing from a tiny wound.

bleeding time test, a blood test used to evaluate the vascular and platelet factors associated with hemostasis. This test is occasionally performed preoperatively to ensure adequate hemostasis.

blemish [OFr, *bleme*, to deface], a skin stain, alteration, defect, or flaw.

blended family [ME, *blenden*, to mix], a family formed when parents bring together children from previous marriages.

blending inheritance, the apparent fusion in offspring of distinct, dissimilar characteristics of the parents. Blended characteristics are usually of a quantitative nature, such as height, and fail to segregate in successive generations.

blennorrhea /blen'ərē'ə/ [Gk, *blennos*, mucus, *rhoia*, flow], excessive discharge of mucus.

Blenoxane, a trademark for an antineoplastic (bleomycin sulfate).

bleomycin sulfate /blē·əmī'sin/, an antineoplastic antibiotic prescribed in the treatment of a variety of neoplasms.

blepharal /blef'ərəl/ [Gk, *blepharon*, eyelid], pertaining to the eyelids.

blepharedema /blef'əridē'mə/, a fluid accumulation in the eyelid, causing a swollen appearance.

blepharitis /blef'ərī'tis/ [Gk, *blepharon + itis*], an inflammatory condition of the lash follicles and meibomian glands of the eyelids, characterized by swelling, redness, and crusts of dried mucus on the lids.

blepharoadenoma /-ad'inō'mə/, *pl.* **blepharoadenomas, blepharoadenomata,** a glandular epithelial tumor of the eyelid.

blepharoatheroma /-ath'ərō'mə/, *pl.* **blepharoatheromas,** a tumor of the eyelid.

blepharochalasis /blef'ərōkal'əsis/ [Gk, *blepharon*, eyelid, *chalasis*, relaxation], relaxation of the skin of the eyelid because of atrophy of the intercellular tissue.

blepharoclonus /blef'ərok'lōnəs/, a condition characterized by muscle spasms of the eyelid, appearing as increased winking.

blepharoncus /blef'əron'kəs/ [Gk, *blepharon + onkos*, swelling], a tumor of the eyelid.

blepharophimosis /blef'ərōfimō'sis/ [Gk, *blepharon*, eyelid, *phimōsis*, a muzzling], abnormal narrowness of the palpebral fissure in the horizontal direction, caused by lateral displacement of the medial canthus.

blepharoplasty /blef'əroplas'tē/ [Gk, *blepharon*, eyelid, *plassein*, to mold], the use of plastic surgery to restore or repair the eyelid and eyebrow.

blepharoplegia /-plē'jē·ə/ [Gk, *blepharon + plege*, stroke], paralysis of muscles of the eyelid.

blepharospasm /blef'ərōspaz'əm/ [Gk, *blepharon*, eyelid, *spasmos*, spasm], the involuntary contraction of eyelid muscles.

blessed thistle, an annual herb found in Europe and Asia, used for loss of appetite, indigestion, and intestinal gas. It is probably safe when used as recommended, but evidence of effectiveness is lacking.

Bleuler, Eugen /bloi'lər/ [Swiss psychiatrist, 1857–1939], a pioneer investigator in the fields of autism and schizophrenia. Bleuler introduced the term *schizophrenia* to replace *dementia praecox* and identified four primary symptoms of schizophrenia, known as Bleuler's "4 As": ambivalence, associative disturbance, autistic thinking, and affective incongruity.

blighted ovum /blī'tid/, a fertilized ovum that fails to develop.

blind fistula [AS, *blind*; L, pipe], an abnormal passage with only one open end; the opening may be on the body surface or on or within an internal organ or structure.

blind loop [AS, *blind*; ME, *loupe*], a redundant segment of intestine. Blind loops may be created inadvertently by surgical procedures such as side-to-side ileotransverse colostomy.

blindness [AS, *blind*], the absence of sight. The term may indicate a total loss of vision or may be applied in a modified manner to describe certain visual limitations, as in yellow color blindness (tritanopia) or word blindness (dyslexia). Legal blindness is defined as best corrected visual acuity less than 20/200 in the better eye.

blind spot, 1. a normal gap in the visual field occurring when an image is focused on the space in the retina occupied by the optic disc. **2.** an abnormal gap in the visual field caused by a lesion on the retina or in the optic pathways or resulting from hemorrhage or choroiditis, often perceived as light spots or flashes.

blink reflex [ME, *blenken*; L, *reflectere*, to bend back], the automatic closure of the eyelid when an object is perceived to be rapidly approaching the eye.

blister, a vesicle or bulla of the skin, containing watery matter or serum.

blister agents/vesicants, chemicals that cause blistering of the skin or mucous membranes on contact.

bloat [ME, *blout*], a swelling or filling with gas such as distension of the abdomen that results from swallowed air or from intestinal gas.

Blocadren, a trademark for a beta-adrenergic receptor blocking agent (timolol maleate).

block [OFr, *bloc*], **1.** a disruption in the conduction of a nerve impulse. The term may apply to stoppage of nerve conduction as produced by local anesthetics, inhibition of beta receptors by beta-blocker drugs, or prevention of neuromuscular transmission by blockade of nicotinic receptors by muscle-relaxant drugs. **2.** a device to maintain separation of the teeth, such as a bite block.

blockade /blokād´/, an agent that interferes with or prevents a specific action in an organ or tissue, such as a cholinergic blockade that inhibits transmission of acetylcholine-stimulated nerve impulses along fibers of the autonomic nervous system.

blocked communication, a situation in which communication with a patient is made difficult because of incongruent verbal and nonverbal messages and messages that contain discrepancies and inconsistencies.

blocking [ME, *blok*], **1.** preventing the transmission of an impulse, such as by an antiadrenergic agent or by the injection of an anesthetic. **2.** interrupting an intracellular biosynthetic process, such as by the injection of actinomycin D or the action of an antivitamin. **3.** an interruption in the spontaneous flow of speech or thought. **4.** repressing an idea or emotion to prevent it from obtruding into the consciousness.

blocking agent, an agent that inhibits a biologic action, such as movement of an ion across the cell membrane, passage of a neural impulse, or interaction with a specific receptor.

blocking antibody, an antibody that reacts with an antigen but fails to cross-link with other antigens and cause agglutination.

blockout /blok´out/ [OFr, *bloc*; AS, *ūt*], in dentistry, elimination in a cast of undesirable undercut areas by filling them in with a suitable material.

blood [AS, *blod*], the liquid pumped by the heart through all the arteries, veins, and capillaries. The blood is composed of a clear yellow fluid, called plasma, and the formed elements, which are red cells, white cells, and platelets. The major functions of the blood are to transport oxygen and nutrients to the cells and to remove carbon dioxide and other waste products.

blood agar, a culture medium consisting of blood (usually sheep's blood) and nutrient agar, used in bacteriology to cultivate certain microorganisms, including *Staphylococcus epidermidis, Streptococcus pneumoniae,* and *Clostridium perfringens.*

blood agents, poisons that affect the body by being absorbed into the blood. Blood agents include arsine and cyanide.

blood albumin [AS, *blod*; L, *albus*], the plasma protein circulating in blood serum.

blood and urine cortisol, a blood or urine test that assists in the evaluation of adrenal activity. Adrenal hyperfunction may indicate Cushing's disease, adrenal adenoma or carcinoma, ectopic adrenocorticotropic hormone (ACTH)-producing tumors, or hyperthyroidism, whereas hypofunction may indicate congenital adrenal hyperplasia, Addison's disease, hypopituitarism, hypothyroidism, or liver disease.

blood and urine uric acid, a blood or urine test that detects levels of uric acid to determine the presence of hyperuricemia (elevated uric acid in the blood) and uricosuria (elevated uric acid in the urine).

blood bank, an organizational unit responsible for collecting, processing, and storing blood and components for transfusion and other purposes. The blood bank is usually a subdivision of a laboratory in a hospital and is often charged with the responsibility for pretransfusion compatibility testing and other serologic tests.

blood bank technology specialist, a medical laboratory scientist with a specialty certification in immunohematology and transfusion medicine, SBB(ASCP). SBBs are responsible for the operations of blood banks and transfusion services, from routine testing to the most advanced procedures. Most are technical supervisors and laboratory managers and oversee reference laboratories, but they may also work in other areas such as education and research.

blood bilirubin test, a blood test performed in cases of jaundice to help determine whether the jaundice is caused by prehepatic causes (as with hemolytic anemia), hepatocellular dysfunction (as in hepatitis), or extrahepatic obstruction of the bile ducts (as with gallstones or tumors blocking the bile ducts).

blood blister, a blister containing blood. It may be caused by a pinch, a bruise, or persistent friction.

blood-borne pathogens, pathogenic microorganisms that are transmitted via human blood and cause disease in humans. They include, but are not limited to, HBV and HIV.

blood-brain barrier (BBB) [AS, *blod + bragen;* ME, *barrere*], an anatomicphysiologic feature of the brain thought to consist of walls of capillaries in the central nervous system and surrounding astrocytic glial membranes. The barrier prevents or slows the passage of some drugs and other chemical compounds, radioactive ions, and disease-causing organisms into the CNS.

blood buffers [AS, *blod;* ME, *buffe,* to cushion], whole blood, carbon dioxide, and bicarbonate ions that maintain the proper pH.

blood capillaries [AS, *blod;* L, *capillaris,* hairlike], the tiny vessels that convey blood between the arterioles and the venules and allow for internal respiration and nourishment of tissues.

blood cell, any of the formed elements of the blood, including erythrocytes, leukocytes, and thrombocytes. Blood cells constitute about 50% of the total volume of the blood.

blood cell casts [AS, *blod;* L, *cella,* storeroom; ONorse, *kasta*], urinary sediment containing blood cells, typically red or white blood cells.

blood chloride test, a blood test performed as part of a panel of electrolyte testing. It is performed along with other electrolyte tests to indicate the patient's acid-base balance and hydration status.

blood circulation [AS, *blod;* L, *circulare,* to go around], the circuit of blood through the body, from the heart through the arteries, arterioles, capillaries, venules, and veins and back to the heart.

blood clot [AS, *blod* + *clott,* lump], a semisolid, gelatinous mass, the final result of the clotting process in blood. Red cells, white cells, and platelets are enmeshed in an insoluble fibrin network of the blood clot.

blood clotting, the conversion of blood from a free-flowing liquid to a semisolid gel. Although clotting can occur within an intact blood vessel, the process usually starts with tissue damage. Within seconds of injury to the vessel wall, platelets clump at the site. If normal amounts of calcium, platelets, and tissue factors are present, prothrombin is converted to thrombin. Thrombin acts as a catalyst for the conversion of fibrinogen to a mesh of insoluble fibrin, in which all the formed elements are immobilized.

blood coagulation, a nursing outcome from the Nursing Outcomes Classification (NOC) defined as the extent to which blood clots within a normal period of time.

blood component therapy, transfusion of one or more of the components of whole blood to treat a specific deficiency.

blood corpuscle [AS, *blod* + L, *corpusculum,* little body]

blood creatinine test, a blood test that measures the amount of creatinine in the blood, to diagnose impaired renal function.

blood crossmatching, the direct matching of donor and recipient blood to prevent the transfusion of incompatible blood types. Crossmatching tests for agglutination of (1) donor RBCs by recipient serum and (2) recipient RBCs by donor serum.

blood culture and sensitivity test, a blood culture obtained to detect the presence of bacteria in the blood (bacteremia). Bacteria present are identified and tested for resistance to antibiotics.

blood culture medium, a liquid enrichment medium for the growth of bacteria in the diagnosis of blood infections (bacteremia and septicemia). It contains a suspension of brain tissue in meat broth with dextrose, peptone, and citrate and has a pH of 7.4.

blood donor, an individual who gives blood or blood components.

blood doping, the administration of blood, RBCs, or related blood products to an athlete to enhance performance. It is often preceded by the withdrawal of blood so that training continues in a blood-depleted state.

blood dyscrasia [AS, *blod;* Gk, *dys,* bad, *krasis,* mingling], a pathologic condition in which any of the constituents of the blood are abnormal in structure, function, or quality, as in leukemia or hemophilia.

blood fluke, a parasitic flatworm of the class Trematoda, genus *Schistosoma,* including the species *S. haematobium, S. japonicum,* and *S. mansoni.*

blood gas, 1. gas dissolved in the liquid part of the blood. Blood gases include oxygen, carbon dioxide, and nitrogen. 2. a laboratory test to determine oxygen, carbon dioxide, bicarbonate, and hydrogen ion (pH) concentrations in whole blood.

blood gas analysis, the determination of oxygen and carbon dioxide concentrations and pressures with the pH of the blood by laboratory tests. Measurements may include PO_2, partial pressure of oxygen in arterial blood; PCO_2, partial pressure of carbon dioxide in arterial blood; SO_2, percent saturation of hemoglobin with oxygen in arterial blood; the total CO_2 content of (venous) plasma; and the pH.

blood gas determination, an analysis of the pH of the blood and the concentration and pressure of oxygen and carbon dioxide in the blood. Blood gas determination is often important in the evaluation of cardiac failure, hemorrhage, kidney failure, drug overdose, shock, uncontrolled DM, or any other condition of severe stress.

blood gas tension, the partial pressure of a gas in the blood.

blood glucose [AS, *blod;* OFr, *livel;* Gk, *glykys,* sweet], the concentration of glucose in the blood, represented in milligrams of glucose per deciliter of blood.

blood glucose level, a nursing outcome from the Nursing Outcomes Classification (NOC) defined as the extent to which glucose levels in plasma and urine are maintained in normal range.

blood glucose test, a blood test used to detect hyperglycemia or hypoglycemia.

This test must be performed frequently in patients with newly diagnosed DM, in order to assist in monitoring and adjusting the insulin dose.

blood group, the classification of blood based on the presence or absence of genetically determined antigens on the surface of the red cell. Many blood group systems have been described, including ABO, Rh, MNS, P, Kell, Duffy, Kidd, Lutheran, Kx, H, Xg , and others, as well as collections of high- and low-frequency antigens.

blood island, one of the clusters of mesodermal cells that proliferates on the outer surface of the embryonic yolk sac and gives it a lumpy appearance.

blood lactate, lactic acid that appears in the blood as a result of anaerobic metabolism when oxygen delivery to the tissues is insufficient to support normal metabolic demands.

blood lavage [AS, *blod;* L, *lavere,* to wash], the removal of toxic elements from the blood by the injection of serum into the veins.

bloodless, 1. any organ or body part that lacks blood or appears to lack blood. **2.** a surgical field in which the normal local blood supply has been shunted to other areas.

bloodless phlebotomy [AS, *blod;* ME, *les;* Gk, *phleps,* vein, *tomos,* cutting], a technique of trapping blood in a body region by the application of tourniquet pressure that is less than the pressure needed to interrupt arterial blood flow.

bloodletting, the therapeutic opening of an artery or vein to withdraw blood from a particular area. It is sometimes performed to treat polycythemia and CHF.

blood level, the concentration of a drug or other substance in a measured amount of plasma, serum, or whole blood.

blood loss severity, a nursing outcome from the Nursing Outcomes Classification (NOC) defined as the severity of internal or external bleeding/hemorrhage.

blood osmolality [AS, *blod;* Gk, *ōsmos,* impulsion], the osmotic pressure of blood. The normal values in serum are 280 to 295 mOsm/L.

blood osmolality test, a blood test that measures the concentration of dissolved particles in the blood. It is useful in evaluating patients with fluid and electrolyte imbalance, seizures, coma, and ascites and in monitoring and evaluating hydration status, acid-base balance, and suspected antidiuretic hormone (ADH) abnormalities.

blood pH, the hydrogen ion concentration of the blood, a measure of blood acidity or alkalinity. The normal pH values for arterial whole blood are 7.35 to 7.454; for venous whole blood, 7.36 to 7.41; for venous serum or plasma, 7.35 to 7.45.

blood plasma [AS, *blod;* Gk, *plassein,* to mold], the liquid part of the blood, free of its formed elements and particles. Plasma represents approximately 50% of the total volume of blood and contains glucose, proteins, amino acids, and other nutritive materials; urea and other excretory products; and hormones, enzymes, vitamins, and minerals.

blood potassium (K+) test, a blood test that detects the serum concentration of potassium, the major cation within cells.

blood pressure (BP) [AS, *blod;* L, *premere,* to press], the pressure exerted by the circulating volume of blood on the walls of the arteries and veins and on the chambers of the heart. BP is regulated by the homeostatic mechanisms of the body by the volume of the blood, the lumen of the arteries and arterioles, and the force of cardiac contraction. In the aorta and large arteries of a healthy young adult, BP is approximately 120 mm Hg during systole and 70 mm Hg during diastole.

blood pressure monitor [AS, *blod;* L, *premere,* to press, *monere,* to warn], a device that automatically measures BP and records the information continuously. Automatic monitoring of BP is often used in surgery or in an ICU.

blood products administration, a nursing intervention from the Nursing Interventions Classification (NIC) defined as administration of blood or blood products and monitoring of patient's response.

blood protein [AS, *blod;* Gk, *proteios,* of first rank], any of the large variety of proteins normally found in the blood, such as albumin, globulin, and hemoglobin, and proteins bound to hormones or other compounds.

blood protein test (blood albumin), a blood test that measures levels of albumin, a protein that makes up approximately 60% of the total protein and whose major effect is to maintain colloidal osmotic pressure.

blood pump, 1. a device for regulating the flow of blood into a blood vessel during transfusion. **2.** a component of a heart-lung machine that pumps the blood through the machine for oxygenation and then through the peripheral circulatory system of the body.

blood relative, a related person who shares some of the same genetic material through a common ancestry.

bloodshot, a redness of the conjunctiva or sclera of the eye caused by dilation of blood vessels in the tissues.

blood smear, a blood test used to provide information concerning drugs and diseases that affect the morphology of RBCs and WBCs and to help diagnose certain congenital and acquired diseases.

blood sodium test (Na⁺), a blood test used to determine the presence of hyponatremia or hypernatremia by measuring levels of sodium, the major cation in the extracellular space.

bloodstream, the blood that flows freely through the circulatory system.

blood substitute, a substance used for a replacement or volume expansion for circulating blood. Plasma, human serum albumin, packed red cells, platelets, leukocytes, and concentrates of clotting factors are often administered in place of whole blood transfusions in the treatment of various disorders. Substances that are sometimes used to expand blood volume include dextran, hetastarch, albumin solutions, and plasma protein fraction.

blood sugar, one of a group of closely related substances, such as glucose, fructose, and galactose, that are normal constituents of the blood and essential for cellular metabolism.

blood test, any test that yields information about the characteristics or properties of the blood.

blood transfusion [AS, *blod*; L, *transfundere,* to pour through], the administration of whole blood or a component, such as packed red cells, to replace blood lost through trauma, surgery, or disease.

blood transfusion reaction, a nursing outcome from the Nursing Outcomes Classification (NOC) defined as the severity of complications with blood transfusion reaction.

blood typing, the determination of the character of the blood of prospective blood donors and of expectant mothers and newborns on the basis of agglutinogens in the erythrocytes.

blood urea nitrogen (BUN) [AS, *blod*; Gk, *ouron,* urine, *nitron,* soda, *genein,* to produce], a measure of the amount of urea in the blood. The BUN, determined by a blood test, is directly related to the metabolic function of the liver and the excretory function of the kidney. A critical value of 100 mg/dL indicates serious impairment of renal function.

blood vessel, any one of the network of muscular tubes that carry blood.

blood warming coil, a device constructed of coiled plastic tubing used for the warming of reserve blood before massive transfusions such as those often required for patients who experience extensive bleeding. Administration of cold blood in such

transfusions may cause the patient to go into a state of shock.

bloody sputum [AS, *blod*; L, *sputum,* spittle], blood-tinged material expelled from the respiratory passages. The amount and color of blood in sputum expelled by coughing or clearing the throat may indicate the cause and location of the bleeding.

blooming, an increase in x-ray focal spot size due to electrostatic repulsion.

Bloom's syndrome [David Bloom, American physician, b. 1892], a rare genetic disease occurring mainly in Ashkenazi Jews. It is transmitted as an autosomal-recessive trait and is characterized by growth retardation, dilated capillaries of the face and arms, sensitivity to sunlight, and an increased risk of malignancy.

blot, 1. a technique for transferring electrophoretically separated components from a gel onto a nitrocellulose membrane, chemically treated paper, or filter for analysis. **2.** the substrate containing the transferred material.

blotch, a skin discoloration that may vary in severity from an area of pigmentation to large pustules or blisters.

blow-out fracture, a break in the floor of the orbit caused by a blow that suddenly increases the intraocular pressure.

blowpipe /blō′pīp/ [AS, *blāwan* + *pīpe*], a tube through which a current of air or other gas is forced on a flame to concentrate and intensify the heat.

BLS, abbreviation for **basic life support.**

blue baby [OFr, *blou*; ME, *babe*], an infant born with cyanosis caused by a congenital heart lesion, most commonly tetralogy of Fallot.

blue cohosh, a perennial herb found in the midwest and eastern regions of the United States. It is used to treat menopausal symptoms and uterine and ovarian pain, to improve the flow of menstrual blood, and as an antiinflammatory and antirheumatic. It is also a popular remedy in African American ethnic medicine.

Blue Cross, an independent nonprofit U.S. corporation that functions as a health insurance agency, providing protection for an enrolled patient by covering all or part of the person's hospital expenses. Blue Cross programs vary in different communities because of state laws regulating them.

blue diaper syndrome [OFr, *blou*; ME, *diapre,* patterned fabric], a defect of tryptophan absorption in which, because of intestinal bacterial action on the tryptophan, the urine contains abnormal indoles, giving it a blue color.

blue dome cyst, a spheric dilation of a mammary duct in which bleeding has occurred.

B

blue dot sign, a tender blue or black spot beneath the skin of the testis or epididymis, a sign of testicular torsion of the appendix testis or, less commonly, appendix epididymis.

blue fever informal. Rocky Mountain spotted fever, so named for the dark cyanotic discoloration of the skin after the initial rickettsial infection.

blue-green algae, misnomer formerly applied to the group now called the cyanobacteria.

blue line, a bluish discoloration sometimes observed on the gingival side of the mouth in cases of gingivitis. It is a sign of chronic lead or bismuth poisoning.

blue nevus [OFr, *blou;* L, *naevus,* mole], a sharply circumscribed, usually benign, steel blue skin nodule. It is found on the face and upper extremities, grows very slowly, and persists throughout life. The dark color is caused by large, densely packed melanocytes deep in the dermis of the nevus. Any sudden change in the size of such a lesion demands surgical attention and biopsy.

blue phlebitis, a severe form of thrombosis of a deep vein, usually the femoral vein. The condition is acute and fulminating and is usually accompanied by vast edema and cyanosis of the limb distal to the occluding thrombus.

blue rubber bleb nevus [OFR, *blou,* blue; ME, *rubben,* to scrape, *bleb,* blob; L, *naevus,* mole], a type of congenital nevus characterized by blue hemangiomas with soft elevated nipple-like centers, found on the skin surface, in the GI tract, and sometimes on mucous membranes. It may be accompanied by pain, regional hyperhidrosis, or GI bleeding.

blues informal. a designation for **Blue Cross** and **Blue Shield.**

Blue Shield, an independent nonprofit U.S. corporation that offers patient protection for costs of surgery and other medical services. Although Blue Cross and Blue Shield are technically separate organizations, they generally coordinate their functions in providing benefits covering both hospital costs and physician fees.

blue spot, **1.** one of a number of small, grayish-blue spots that may appear near the armpits or around the groins of individuals infested with lice. **2.** one of a number of dark blue round or oval spots that may appear as a congenital condition in the sacral regions of certain children less than 4 or 5 years of age. They usually disappear spontaneously as the affected individual matures.

blunt dissection [ME, *blunt;* L, *dissecare,* to cut apart], a dissection performed by separating tissues along natural lines of cleavage without cutting.

blunt-ended DNA, a segment of DNA in which the ends of both strands are even with each other.

blunthook /blunt'hŏŏk/ [ME, *blunt;* AS, *hoc*], **1.** a sturdy hook-shaped bar used in obstetrics for traction between the abdomen and the thigh in cases of difficult breech deliveries. **2.** a hook-shaped device with a blunt end used in embryotomy.

blunting, a decrease in the intensity of emotional expression from the level one would normally expect as a reaction to a specific situation.

blurred film fault /blurd'/, a defect in a photograph or radiograph that appears as an indistinct or blurred image.

blush [ME, *blusshen,* to redden], a brief, diffuse erythema of the face and neck, commonly the result of dilation of superficial small blood vessels in response to heat or sudden emotion.

BLV-HTLV retroviruses, a genus similar in morphology and replication to the type C retroviruses. Organisms have a long latency and cause B- and T-cell leukemia and lymphoma and neurologic disease.

B/M, abbreviation for *black male,* often used in the initial identifying statement in a patient record.

B₂M, abbreviation for **beta₂-microglobulin.**

BMA, abbreviation for **British Medical Association.**

BMD, abbreviation for **Bureau of Medical Devices.**

BMI, abbreviation for **body mass index.**

B-mode, brightness modulation in diagnostic ultrasonography. Bright dots on an oscilloscope screen represent echoes, and the intensity of the brightness indicates the strength of the echo.

BMR, abbreviation for **basal metabolic rate.**

BNA, abbreviation for *Basel Nomina Anatomica.*

BNP, abbreviation for **brain natriuretic peptide.**

BOA, abbreviation for **born out of asepsis.**

board,

board and care, nonmedical, community-based residential care for individuals who can care for themselves. Meals and supervision are provided.

board certification, a process by which physicians are certified in a given medical specialty or subspecialty. Certification is awarded by the 23-member boards of the American Board of Medical Specialties on completion of accredited training and examinations and fulfillment of individual requirements of the board.

board certified, denoting a physician who has completed the certification requirements established by a medical specialty board and has been certified as a specialist in a particular field of medicine.

board eligible, denoting a physician who has completed all of the requirements for admission to a medical specialty board.

boarder baby, 1. an infant abandoned to a hospital because the mother is unable to care for him or her. **2.** in some hospitals, any infant still in the nursery after the mother's discharge for any reason (even if only temporarily).

board of health, an administrative body acting on a municipal, county, state, provincial, or national level. Among the tasks of most boards of health are disease prevention, health education, and implementation of laws pertaining to health.

bobbing, the act of moving up and down, usually with a jerking motion.

Bochdalek's hernia, a hernia through the defect in the left posterior pleuroperitoneal canal of the diaphragm.

Bodansky unit /bōdăn'skē/ [Aaron Bodansky, American biochemist, 1887–1961], the quantity of alkaline phosphatase that liberates 1 mg of phosphate ion from glycerol 2-phosphate in 1 hour at 37° C and under other standardized conditions.

body [AS, *bodig*], **1.** the whole structure of an individual with all the organs. **2.** a cadaver (corpse). **3.** the largest or main part of any structure, such as the body of the stomach.

body burden, 1. the state of activity of a radioactive chemical in the body at a specified time after administration. **2.** chemicals stored in the body that may be detected by analysis.

body cast [AS, *bodig*, body; ONorse, *kasta*], a molded cast that may extend from the chest to the groin to immobilize the spine.

body cavity, any of the spaces in the human body that contain organs.

body composition, the relative proportions of protein, fat, water, and mineral components in the body. It varies among individuals as a result of differences in body density and degree of obesity.

body fluid [AS, *bodig*; L, *fluere*, to flow], fluid contained in the three fluid compartments of the body: the plasma of the circulating blood, the interstitial fluid between the cells, and the cell fluid within the cells.

body image[1] [AS, *bodig*; L, *imago*, likeness], a person's concept of his or her physical appearance. The mental representation, which may be realistic or unrealistic, is constructed from self-observation, the reactions of others, and a complex interaction of attitudes, emotions, memories, fantasies, and experiences, both conscious and unconscious.

body image[2], a nursing outcome from the Nursing Outcomes Classification (NOC) defined as the perception of one's own appearance and body functions.

body image enhancement, a nursing intervention from the Nursing Interventions Classification (NIC) defined as improving a patient's conscious and unconscious perceptions and attitudes toward his/her body.

body jacket, an orthopedic cast that encases the trunk of the body but does not extend over the cervical area; it may be equipped with shoulder straps. The cast is used to help position and immobilize the trunk for the healing of spinal injuries and scoliosis and after spinal surgery.

body language [AS, *bodig*; L, *lingua*, tongue], a set of nonverbal signals, including body movements, postures, gestures, spatial positions, facial expressions, and body adornment, that give expression to various physical, mental, and emotional states.

body mass index (BMI), a formula for determining obesity. It is calculated by dividing a person's weight in kilograms by the square of the person's height in meters. A BMI of 30 or greater indicates obesity.

body mechanics, the field of physiology that studies muscular actions and the function of muscles in maintaining body posture.

body mechanics performance, a nursing outcome from the Nursing Outcomes Classification (NOC) defined as personal actions to maintain proper body alignment and to prevent muscular skeletal strain.

body mechanics promotion, a nursing intervention from the Nursing Interventions Classification (NIC) defined as facilitating the use of posture and movement in daily activities to prevent fatigue and musculoskeletal strain or injury.

body movement, motion of all or part of the body, especially at a joint or joints.

body odor, a fetid smell associated with stale perspiration. Common body odor usually can be eliminated by bathing with soap and water. Body odors can also be the result of discharges from a variety of skin conditions, including cancer, fungus, hemorrhoids, leukemia, and ulcers.

body of Retzius /ret'sē-əs/ [Magnus G. Retzius, Swedish anatomist, 1842–1919], any one of the masses of protoplasm containing pigment granules at the lower end of a hair cell of the organ of Corti in the internal ear.

body plethysmograph [AS, *bodig*; Gk, *plethynein*, to increase, *graphein*, to record], a device for studying alveolar pressures, lung volumes, and airway resistance. The patient sits or reclines in an airtight compartment and breathes normally. The pressure changes in the alveoli are reciprocated in the compartment and are recorded automatically.

body position, attitude or posture of the body.

body positioning: self-initiated, a nursing outcome from the Nursing Outcomes Classification (NOC) defined as the ability to change one's own body position independently with or without assistive devices.

body scheme, a piagetian term for a cognitive structure that develops in infants in the sensorimotor period during the first 2 years of life as they learn to differentiate between themselves and the world around them.

body-section radiography, a radiographic technique in which the film and x-ray tube are moved in opposite directions to produce a more distinct image of a selected body plane.

body stalk, the elongated part of the embryo that is connected to the chorion.

body systems model, (in nursing education) a conceptual framework in which illness is studied in relation to the functional systems of the body such as the circulatory, nervous, GI, and reproductive. In this model, nursing care is directed to manipulating the patient's environment in such a way that the signs and symptoms of the health problem are alleviated.

body temperature, the level of heat produced and sustained by the body processes. Variations and changes in body temperature are major indicators of disease and other abnormalities. Normal adult body temperature, as measured orally, is 98.6° F (37° C). Oral temperatures ranging from 96.5° F to 99° F are consistent with good health, depending on the person's physical activity, the environmental temperature, and that person's usual body temperature. Axillary temperature is usually from 0.5° F to 1° F lower than the oral temperature. Rectal temperatures may be 0.5° F to 1° F higher than oral readings. Body temperature appears to vary 1° F to 2° F throughout the day, with lows recorded early in the morning and peaks between 6 PM and 10 PM.

body type, the general physical appearance of an individual human body. Three commonly used terms for body types are **ectomorph, endomorph,** and **mesomorph.**

body-weight ratio, a relation expressed by dividing the body weight in grams by the height in centimeters.

Boerhaave's syndrome /bôr′hävz/ [Hermann Boerhaave, Dutch physician, 1668–1738], a condition marked by spontaneous rupture of the esophagus, leading to mediastinitis and pleural effusion. Clinical manifestations are violent retching or vomiting.

Bohr effect [Christian Bohr, Danish physiologist, 1855–1911], the effect of CO_2 and H^+ on the affinity of hemoglobin for molecular O_2. Increasing PCO_2 and H^+ decrease oxyhemoglobin saturation, whereas decreasing concentrations have the opposite effect.

boil [AS, *byle,* sore], a skin abscess. A tender, swollen area that forms around a hair follicle.

boiling point [ME, *boilen,* to make bubbles; L, *pungere,* to prick], **1.** the temperature at which a substance passes from the liquid to the gaseous state at a particular atmospheric pressure. **2.** the temperature at which the vapor pressure of a liquid equals the external pressure.

bole /bōl/, any of a variety of soft, friable clays of various colors, although usually red from iron oxide. They consist of hydrous silicate of aluminum, are used as pigments, and were once commonly used as absorbents and astringents.

Bolivian hemorrhagic fever /bəliv′ē·ən/, an infectious disease caused by an arenavirus, generally transmitted by contact with or inhalation of aerosolized rodent urine. After an incubation period of 1 to 2 weeks, the patient experiences chills, fever, headache, muscle ache, anorexia, nausea, and vomiting. The mortality rate may reach 30%.

bolus /bō′ləs/ [Gk, *bolos,* lump], **1.** a round mass, specifically a masticated lump of food ready to be swallowed. **2.** a large round preparation of medicinal material for oral ingestion, usually soft and not prepackaged. **3.** a dose of a medication or a contrast material, radioactive isotope, or other pharmaceutic preparation injected all at once intravenously. **4.** (in radiotherapy) material used to fill in irregular body surfaces to improve dose distribution for hyperthermia or to increase the dose to the skin when high-energy photon beams are used. **5.** a clumping in the stomach of ingested foreign material, often the result of habitual behavior.

bolus dose, an amount of IV medication administered rapidly to decrease the response time or to be used as a loading dose prior to an infusion.

bombard /bombärd′/, to shower a drug or tissue sample with radioactive particles from a nuclear isotope source.

Bombay phenotype /bombā′/ [Bombay (now Mumbai), India, where first reported], a rare genetic trait in which there is no expression of the A, B, or H antigens on the red blood cells.

bombesin /bom'bəsin/, a neurohormone and pressor substance found in small amounts in brain and intestinal tissue under normal conditions and in increased amounts in certain pulmonary and thyroid tumors. It is a potent mitogen, and its effects on gastrin and other hormones are attributed to increased cell numbers.

bond, a strong coulombic force between atoms in a substance due to attraction of ions of opposite charge for each other or of the nuclei for shared electrons.

bonding [ME, *band,* to bind], **1.** (in dentistry) a technique of joining orthodontic brackets or other attachments directly to the enamel surface of a tooth, using orthodontic adhesives. **2.** the reciprocal attachment process that occurs between an infant and the parents, especially the mother. Bonding is significant in the formation of affectionate ties that later influence both the physical and psychologic development of the child.

bond specificity, the nature of enzyme action that causes the disruption of only certain bonds between atoms.

bone [AS, *ban*], **1.** the dense, hard, and somewhat flexible connective tissue constituting the bones of the human skeleton. It is composed of compact osseous tissue surrounding spongy cancellous tissue permeated by many blood vessels and nerves and enclosed in membranous periosteum. **2.** any single element of the skeleton such as a rib, the sternum, or the femur.

bone age [AS, *ban*; L, *aetas*], the stage of development or decline of the skeleton or its segments, as seen in radiographic examination, when compared with x-ray views of the bone structures of other individuals of the same chronologic age.

bone-anchored hearing aid, a hearing aid that allows direct bone conduction of sound to the cochlea by means of a sound processing device attached to an osseointegrated titanium fixture implanted posterior to the ear.

bone cancer [AS, *ban*; Gk, *karkinos,* crab], a skeletal malignancy occurring as a sarcoma or a myeloma in an area of rapid growth or as metastasis from cancer elsewhere in the body. Primary bone tumors are rare. The incidence peaks during adolescence, decreases, and then rises slowly after 35 years of age. In adults, bone cancer is linked to exposure to ionizing radiation. Paget's disease, hyperparathyroidism, chronic osteomyelitis, old bone infarcts, and fracture callosities increase the risk of many bone tumors. Bone cancers progress rapidly but are often difficult to detect.

bone cell [AS, *ban*; L, *cella,* storeroom], an osteocyte, osteoblast, or osteoclast, a cell with myriad spidery processes embedded in the matrix of bone.

bone-cutting forceps, a type of forceps that has long handles, single or double joints, and heavy blades for cutting bone.

bone cyst [AS, *ban*; Gk, *kytis,* cyst], **1.** a dilation in the wall of a blood vessel in a bone, usually eccentrically placed. **2.** a sac in bone tissue in the parathyroid disorder osteitis fibrosa.

bone densitometry, any of several methods of determining bone mass by measuring radiation absorption by the skeleton. Common techniques include single-photon absorptiometry (SPA) of the forearm and heel, dual-photon absorptiometry (DPA) and dual-energy x-ray absorptiometry (DXA) of the spine and hip, quantitative computed tomography (QCT) of the spine and forearm, radiographic absorptiometry (RA) of the hand, and quantitative ultrasound (QU).

bone graft, the transplantation of a piece of bone from one part of the body to another to repair a skeletal defect.

bone healing, a nursing outcome from the Nursing Outcomes Classification (NOC) defined as the extent of regeneration of cells and tissues following bone injury.

bone lamella [AS, *ban,* bone, *lamella,* plate], a thin plate of bone matrix, a basic structural unit of mature bone.

bone marrow [AS, *ban*; ME, *marowe*], the soft, organic, spongelike material in the cavities of bones. It is a network of blood vessels and special connective tissue fibers that hold together a composite of fat and blood-producing cells. Its chief function is to manufacture erythrocytes, leukocytes, and platelets. These blood cells normally do not enter the bloodstream until they are fully developed so that the marrow contains cells in all stages of growth. **Red marrow** is found in many bones of infants and children and in the spongy (cancellous) bone of the proximal epiphyses of the humerus and femur and the sternum, ribs, and vertebral bodies of adults. Fatty **yellow marrow** is found in the medullary cavity of most adult long bones.

bone marrow aspiration, Removal of bone marrow fluid via a needle to diagnose a number of conditions including leukemia, lymphoma, and multiple myeloma.

bone marrow biopsy, a microscopic tissue examination used to help evaluate patients with hematologic diseases.

bone marrow failure, failure of the hematopoietic function of the bone marrow.

bone marrow infusion, a method of injecting a fluid substance through an aspiration needle directly into the marrow cavity of a long bone. The substance is absorbed into the general circulation almost immediately.

bone marrow reserve, a storage pool of mature neutrophils in the bone marrow, which can be released as necessary.

bone marrow suppression, suppression of bone marrow activity, resulting in reduction in the number of platelets, red cells, and white cells, such as in aplastic anemia.

bone marrow transplantation, the transplantation of bone marrow from a healthy donor to stimulate production of normal blood cells. The bone marrow is removed from the donor by aspiration and infused intravenously into the recipient.

bone plate [AS, *ban,* bone; OFr, *plate*], a metal plate used to reconstruct a bone that has been fractured. The plate is designed to hold bone fragments in apposition.

bone recession [AS, *ban*; L, *recedere,* to recede], apical progression of the level of the alveolar crest, resulting in decreased bone support for the teeth.

bone scan, the injection of a radioactive substance to enable visualization of a bone via the image produced by emission of radioactive particles.

bone tissue [AS, *ban*; OFr, *tissu*], a hard form of connective tissue composed of osteocytes and a calcified collagenous intercellular substance arranged in thin plates.

bone turnover biochemical markers test, a blood or urine test to identify small changes in bone metabolism. This test is used primarily to determine the effectiveness of treatment for osteoporosis, Paget's disease, hyperparathyroidism, and bone tumors.

bone x-ray, radiographic studies to detect abnormalities of the bones or joints.

Bonine, a trademark for an antiemetic (meclizine hydrochloride).

Bonnie Pruden myotherapy, a method of applying manual pressure on muscles with the fingers, knuckles, and elbows to defuse trigger points and relax muscle spasm, improve circulation, and alleviate pain.

Bonwill's triangle [William G.A. Bonwill, American dentist, 1833–1899], an equilateral triangle formed by lines from the contact points of the lower central incisors (or the median line of the residual ridge of the mandible) to the mandibular condyle on each side and from one condyle to the other.

bony labyrinth, a series of bony cavities in the inner ear.

bony landmark [AS, *ban;* AS, *land, mearc*], a groove or prominence on a bone that serves as a guide to the location of other body structures.

bony thorax [AS, *ban*; Gk, *thorax,* chest], the skeletal part of the chest,

including the thoracic vertebrae, ribs, and sternum.

book retinoscopy, a measure of accommodation in which retinoscopy is performed while the patient focuses on reading a book. It is commonly used with children.

booster injection, the administration of an additional dose of antigen within a defined period of time, such as a vaccine or toxoid, usually in a smaller amount than the original immunization. It is given to maintain the immune response at an appropriate level.

booster phenomenon /bōō′s′ter/, on a tuberculin test, an initial false-negative result caused by a diminished amnestic response that becomes positive on subsequent testing.

boot, 1. a shoelike prosthetic device for holding a leg or arm during treatment. **2.** a basketweave bandage that covers the foot and lower leg. **3.** an airtight device in which the arm or leg can be inserted and the air pumped out, creating a partial vacuum to divert blood flow from the surrounding area.

Boothby-Lovelace-Bulbulian (BLB) mask, an apparatus for the administration of oxygen consisting of a mask fitted with an inspiratory-expiratory valve and a rebreathing bag.

borage, an annual herb used as an antiinflammatory for PMS, rheumatoid arthritis, Raynaud's disease, and other inflammatory conditions. It is also used to treat atopic dermatitis, infant cradle cap, CF, high BP, and diabetes; however, effectiveness is not proven.

borage oil, the oil extracted from the seeds of borage (*Borago officinalis*). It is used for the treatment of neurodermatitis and as a food supplement.

borate /bôr′āt/, any salt of boric acid. Borate salts and boric acid, although formerly used as mild antiseptic irrigant solutions, especially for ophthalmic conditions, are highly poisonous when taken internally or absorbed through a cut, abrasion, or other wound in the skin. Because of the potential for fatal poisoning, such solutions are rarely used now.

borax bath [Ar, *bauraq*; AS, *baeth*], a medicated bath in which borax and glycerin are added to the water.

borborygmos /bôr′bərig′məs/ *pl.* **borborygmi** [Gk, *borborygmos,* bowel rumbling], an audible abdominal sound produced by hyperactive intestinal peristalsis. Borborygmi are very loud rumbling, gurgling, and tinkling noises heard in auscultation.

border [OFr, *bordure*], an edge or boundary of a body structure.

borderline [OFr, *bordure*; L, *linea*], pertaining to a state of health in which the patient has some of the signs and symptoms of a disease but not enough to justify a definite diagnosis.

borderline personality [OFr, *bordure;* L, *linea + personalis*], a personality in which there is a pervasive pattern of instability of self-image, interpersonal relationships, and mood.

Bordetella /bôr′ditel′ə/ [Jules J.B.V. Bordet, Belgian bacteriologist, 1870–1961], a genus of gram-negative coccobacilli, some species of which are pathogens of the respiratory tract of humans, including *B. bronchiseptica, B. parapertussis,* and *B. pertussis.*

boric acid /bôr′ik/, a white, odorless powder or crystalline substance used as a buffer and formerly used as a topical antiseptic and eyewash.

boric acid poisoning, an adverse reaction to the ingestion or absorption through the skin of boric acid, a mild but potentially lethal antiseptic. Symptoms include nausea, vomiting, diarrhea, convulsions, and shock. Absorption of boric acid from diapers is a threat to infants.

born out of asepsis (BOA), (in a hospital) denoting a newborn who was not delivered in the usual place in an obstetric unit. Depending on the policy of the institution, a BOA-designated infant may have been born on the way to the hospital or in the hospital, on the way to the delivery suite, or in a labor room.

boron (B) /bôr′on/, a nonmetallic element, whose atomic number is 5; its atomic mass is 10.81. Elemental boron occurs in the form of dark crystals and as a greenish yellow amorphous mass. It is the characteristic element of boric acid, which is used chiefly as a dusting powder and ointment for minor skin disorders.

Borrelia /bərel′ē·ə/ [Amédée Borrel, French bacteriologist, 1867–1936], a genus of coarse, unevenly coiled helical spirochetes, several species of which cause tickborne and louseborne relapsing fever. Many animals serve as reservoirs and hosts for *Borrelia.*

Borrelia burgdorferi /burg′dôrfer′ī/, the causative agent in Lyme disease. The organism is transmitted to humans by tick vectors, primarily *Ixodes dammini.*

bortezomib, a miscellaneous antineoplastic used to treat multiple myeloma when at least two other treatments have failed.

bosentan, a vasodilator used to treat pulmonary arterial hypertension.

boss [ME, *boce*], a swelling, eminence, or protuberance on an organ, such as a tumor or overgrowth on a bone surface or a tooth.

Boston exanthema [Boston; Gk, *ex,* out, *anthema,* blossoming], an epidemic disease characterized by scattered, pale red maculopapules on the face, chest, and back, occasionally accompanied by small ulcerations on the tonsils and soft palate. It is caused by echovirus 16 and requires no treatment.

Botox, a trademark for a preparation of botulinum toxin, type A.

bottle feeding[1] [OFr, *bouteille;* AS, *faeden*], feeding an infant or young child from a bottle with a rubber nipple on the end as a substitute for or supplement to breastfeeding.

bottle feeding[2], a nursing intervention from the Nursing Interventions Classification (NIC) defined as preparation and administration of fluids to an infant via a bottle.

botulinum toxin /boch′əlī′nəm/ [L, *botulus,* sausage; Gk, *toxikon,* poison], any of a group of potent bacterial toxins produced by different strains of *Clostridium botulinum.* It may be used therapeutically for blepharospasm or cosmetically to relax facial wrinkles.

botulism /boch′əliz′əm/ [L, *botulus,* sausage], an often fatal form of food poisoning caused by an endotoxin produced by the bacillus *Clostridium botulinum.* Symptoms usually appear 18 hours up to 1 week after ingestion of a contaminated food substance. Severity of symptoms is related to the quantity of the botulinum toxin that was ingested and include dry mouth, diplopia, loss of pupillary light reflex; nausea, vomiting, cramps, and diarrhea, which precede dysphagia, dysarthria, and progressive descending muscular paralysis.

Bouchard's node /booshärz′/ [Charles J. Bouchard, French physician, 1837–1915], an abnormal cartilaginous or bony enlargement of a proximal interphalangeal joint of a finger, usually occurring in diseases of the joints, such as rheumatoid arthritis.

Bouchut's tubes /booshoo′z/ [Jean E.W. Bouchut, French physician, 1818–1891], a set of short cylindric devices used for intubation of the larynx.

bougie /boo′zhē, boo′zhē′/ [Fr, candle], a thin cylindric instrument made of rubber, waxed silk, or other flexible material for insertion into canals of the body in order to dilate, examine, or measure them.

boundary /boun′dərē/, (in psychology) an aspect of family health in which the generations are clearly defined and issues are dealt with by the appropriate generation. This term can also apply to the roles of patient and therapist in psychotherapy.

boundary lubrication, a coating of a thin layer of molecules on each weight-bearing surface of a joint to facilitate a sliding action by the opposing bone surfaces.

boundary maintenance mechanisms, (in psychology) behavior and practices that exclude members of some groups from the customs and values of another group.

bound carbon dioxide, carbon dioxide that is transported in the bloodstream as part of a sodium bicarbonate molecule, as distinguished from dissolved carbon dioxide or bicarbonate ion.

bounding pulse [OFr, *bondir,* to leap; L, *pulsare,* to beat], a pulse that feels full and springlike on palpation as a result of an increased thrust of cardiac contraction or an increased volume of circulating blood within the elastic structures of the vascular system.

bound water, water in the tissue of the body bound to macromolecules or organelles.

Bourdon regulator, a commonly used adjustable device with an attached pressure gauge for controlling the flow of oxygen or other gases from cylinders in medical applications.

bouton /boootôN′, boo′ton/ [Fr, button], **1.** a button, pustule, or knoblike swelling, such as the expanded end of an axon at a synapse (terminaux), which comes into contact with cell bodies of other neurons. **2.** a lesion associated with cutaneous leishmaniasis. **3.** a small abscess of the intestinal mucosa in amebic dysentery.

boutonneuse fever /boo′tǝnooz′/ [Fr, *bouton,* button; L, *febris*], a febrile disease of the Mediterranean area, the Crimea, Africa, and India caused by infection with *Rickettsia conorii,* transmitted to humans through the bite of a tick. The onset of the disease is characterized by a lesion called a *tache noire,* or black spot, at the site of the infection; fever lasting from a few days to 2 weeks; and a papular erythematous rash that spreads over the body to include the skin of the palms and soles.

boutonnière deformity /boo′tônyer′/ [Fr, buttonhole], an abnormality of a finger marked by fixed flexion of the proximal interphalangeal joint and hyperextension of the distal interphalangeal joint. The condition occurs in rheumatoid arthritis and can occur following trauma to a finger.

bovine spongiform encephalopathy (BSE), an infection of cattle characterized by degenerative, clumsy, apprehensive behavior and death. The BSE brain tissue is perforated and spongy in appearance. It has been associated with other spongiform encephalopathies. In European "mad cow" disease, it was believed the disease was transmitted to cattle through livestock feed that contained remains of scrapie-infected sheep. The disease was then transmitted to humans who ate BSE-infected beef.

bovine tuberculosis /bo′vīn/ [L, *bos,* ox, *tuber,* swelling; Gk, *osis,* condition], a form of TB caused by *Mycobacterium tuberculosis* that primarily affects cattle but is occasionally found in deer. Mastitis and pulmonary symptoms can occur.

bowel bypass syndrome, a series of adverse effects that may follow bowel bypass surgery, which include chills, fever, joint pain, and skin inflammation on the arms, legs, and thorax.

bowel continence, a nursing outcome from the Nursing Outcomes Classification (NOC) defined as control of passage of stool from the bowel.

bowel elimination, a nursing outcome from the Nursing Outcomes Classification (NOC) defined as the formation and evacuation of stool.

bowel incontinence care, a nursing intervention from the Nursing Interventions Classification (NIC) defined as promotion of bowel continence and maintenance of perianal skin integrity.

bowel incontinence care: encopresis, a nursing intervention from the Nursing Interventions Classification (NIC) defined as promotion of bowel continence in children.

bowel irrigation, a nursing intervention from the Nursing Interventions Classification (NIC) defined as the instillation of a substance into the lower gastrointestinal tract.

bowel management, a nursing intervention from the Nursing Interventions Classification (NIC) defined as establishment and maintenance of a regular pattern of bowel elimination.

bowel resection, an excision of a diseased or injured section of the small or large intestine through a laparoscope or an abdominal incision to treat obstruction, inflammatory bowel disease, cancer, ruptured diverticulum, ischemia, or traumatic injury. After excision, the bowel is reanastomosed.

bowel training[1] [OFr, *boel*], a method of establishing regular evacuation by reflex conditioning used in the treatment of fecal incontinence, impaction, chronic diarrhea, and autonomic hyperreflexia. The patient is instructed to recognize and respond promptly to signals indicating a full bowel, such as goose pimples, perspiration, and piloerection on arms or legs, and to develop cues to stimulate the urge to defecate such as drinking coffee or massaging the abdomen. Fluids to 3000 mL daily are encouraged; exercise is increased as able, and the importance of eating well-balanced meals that include bulk and roughage or of avoiding constipating or gas-producing foods, such as bananas, beans, and cabbage, is discussed.

bowel training², a nursing intervention from the Nursing Interventions Classification (NIC) defined as assisting the patient to train the bowel to evacuate at specific intervals.

bowel urgency, the sudden, almost uncontrollable, need to defecate.

Bowen's disease [John T. Bowen, American dermatologist, 1857–1941], a form of intraepidermal carcinoma (squamous cell). It is characterized by red-brown scaly or crusted lesions that resemble a patch of psoriasis or dermatitis.

Bowen technique, a system of gentle but powerful soft tissue mobilizations using the thumbs and fingers over muscles, tendons, nerves, and fascia to restore the self-healing mechanism of the body. This technique has been used for conditions affecting the musculoskeletal system, including back, neck, hip, and shoulder pain.

Bowman's capsule /bō′manz/ [William Bowman, English anatomist, 1816–1892], the cup-shaped end of a renal tubule or nephron enclosing a glomerulus. With the glomerulus, it is the site of filtration in the kidney.

Bowman's glands [William Bowman; L, *glans,* acorn], branched tubuloalveolar glands in the mucous membranes of the mouth. They keep the mouth surfaces moist.

Bowman's lamina [William Bowman; L, *lamina,* plate], a tough membrane beneath the corneal epithelium.

bowtie filter /bō′tī/, a filter shaped like a bowtie that may be used in CT to compensate for the shape of the patient's head or body.

boxer's fracture [Dan, *bask,* a blow; L, *fractura,* break], a break in one or more metacarpal bones, usually the fourth or the fifth, caused by punching a hard object. Such a fracture is often distal, angulated, and impacted.

boxing, the forming of vertical walls, most commonly made of wax, to produce the desired shape and size of the base of a dental cast.

boxing wax [L, *buxis,* box; AS, *weax*], (in dentistry) a thin sheet of flexible wax used for boxing.

Boyd's amputation, amputation at the ankle with removal of the talus and fusion of the tibia and calcaneus.

Boykin, Anne, a nursing theorist who, with Savina O. Schoenhofer, wrote *Nursing as Caring: A Model for Transforming Practice,* which postulates that caring is the end, not the means, of nursing.

Boyle's law /boilz/ [Robert Boyle, English scientist, 1627–1691], (in physics) the law stating that the product of the volume and pressure of a gas contained at a constant temperature remains constant.

BP, abbreviation for **blood pressure.**

BPD, 1. abbreviation for **biparietal diameter. 2.** abbreviation for **bronchopulmonary dysplasia.**

BPDE-I, abbreviation for **benzopyrene dihydrodiol epoxide.**

BPH, abbreviation for **benign prostatic hypertrophy.**

bpm, abbreviation for *beats per minute.*

BPRS, abbreviation for **Brief Psychiatric Rating Scale.**

Br, symbol for the element **bromine.**

brace [OFr, *bracier,* to embrace], an orthotic device, sometimes jointed, used to support and hold any part of the body in the correct position to allow function and healing such as a leg brace that permits walking and standing.

brachial /brā′kē·əl/ [Gk, *brachion,* arm], pertaining to the arm.

brachial artery, the principal artery of the upper arm that is the continuation of the axillary artery. It has three branches and terminates at the bifurcation of its main trunk into the radial artery and the ulnar artery.

brachialgia /-al′jē·ə/ [L, *brachium,* arm; Gk, *algos,* pain], a severe pain in the arm, often related to a disorder involving the brachial plexus.

brachialis /brā′kē·al′is/ [Gk, *brachion,* arm], a muscle of the upper arm, covering the distal half of the humerus and the anterior part of the elbow joint. It functions to flex the forearm.

brachial paralysis [L, *brachium,* arm; Gk, *paralyein,* to be palsied], paralysis of an arm or a hand as a result of a lesion of the brachial plexus.

brachial plexus [Gk, *brachion;* L, braided], the plexus that innervates the upper limb, formed by the anterior rami of cervical spinal nerves C5 to C8 and T1. It is initially formed in the neck and continues through the axillary inlet into the axilla.

brachial plexus anesthesia, an anesthetic block of the upper extremity, performed by injecting local anesthetic near the plexus formed by the last four cervical and first two thoracic spinal nerves.

brachial pulse [Gk, *brachion;* L, *pulsare,* to beat], the pulse of the brachial artery, palpated in the antecubital space.

brachial region, an anatomic term used to refer to the arm (shoulder to elbow), divided into anterior and posterior brachial regions.

brachial vein, a vein in the arm that accompanies the brachial artery and drains into the axillary vein.

brachiocephalic, relating to the arm and head.

brachiocephalic artery, first branch of the aortic arch.

brachiocephalic vein, the vein feeding the superior vena cava, collecting blood from the subclavian and jugular veins.

brachiocubital /-kyōō′bitəl/ [Gk, *brachion;* L, *cubitus,* elbow], pertaining to the arm and forearm.

brachioplasty, a surgical procedure to lift and tighten skin of the upper arm.

brachioradialis /-rā′dē-al′is/, the most superficial muscle on the radial side of the forearm. It functions to flex the forearm.

brachioradialis reflex [Gk, *brachion;* L, *radial* + *reflectare,* to bend backward], a deep tendon reflex elicited by striking the lateral surface of the forearm proximal to the distal head of the radius, characterized by normal slight elbow flexion and forearm supination.

brachybasia /-bā′zhə/, abnormally slow walking, with a short, shuffling gait. The condition is associated with cerebral hemorrhage or pyramidal tract disease, or Parkinson's disease.

brachycephaly /-sef′əlē/ [Gk, *brachys,* short, *kephale,* head], a congenital malformation of the skull in which premature closure of the coronal suture results in excessive lateral growth of the head, giving it a short, broad appearance.—**brachycephalic** /-səfal′ik/, **brachycephalous** /-sef′ələs/, *adj.*

brachydactyly /-dak′təlē/, a condition in which fingers or toes are abnormally short.

brachytherapy [Gk, *brachys,* short, *therapeia,* treatment], the placement of radioactive sources in contact with or implanted into the tumor tissues to be treated for a specific period.

bracket /brak′ət/ [Fr, *braguette,* codpiece], a support projecting from the main structure. An orthodontic bracket is a small metal attachment soldered or welded to an orthodontic band or cemented directly to the teeth, serving to fasten the arch wire to the band or tooth.

Bradford frame [Edward H. Bradford, American surgeon, 1848–1926], a rectangular orthopedic frame made of pipes to which heavy movable straps of canvas are attached. The straps run from side to side to support a patient in a prone or supine position. They can be removed to permit the patient to urinate or defecate while remaining immobile.

Bradford solid frame, a rectangular metal orthopedic device that provides support for the entire body and is especially appropriate for patients who are younger than 5 years of age, hyperactive, or mentally challenged. The main purpose of the device is to assist in maintaining proper immobilization, positioning, and alignment by controlling movement.

Bradford split frame, a rectangular metal orthopedic device covered with two separate pieces of canvas fastened at both ends of the frame. Used especially in pediatrics to aid in the immobilization of children in traction, it is divided in the middle by a large opening designed to accommodate the excretory functions of an incontinent patient in a hip spica cast. The division also allows the upper and lower extremities of the patient to be elevated separately and the cast to be kept clean and dry.

Bradley method [Robert Bradley, twentieth century American physician], a method of psychophysical preparation for childbirth, comprising education about the physiologic characteristics of childbirth, exercise and nutrition during pregnancy, and techniques of breathing and relaxation for control and comfort during labor and delivery. The father is extensively involved in the classes and acts as the mother's "coach" during labor. Among the advantages of the method are its simplicity, the father's involvement, and the realistic approach to the efforts and discomfort of labor.

bradyarrhythmia /-ərith′mē·ə/ [Gk, *bradys,* slow, *a* + *rhythmos,* without rhythm], any disturbance of cardiac rhythm in which the heart rate is less than 60 beats/min.

bradycardia /-kär′dē·ə/ [Gk, *bradys,* slow, *kardia,* heart], a condition in which the heart rate is less than 60 beats/min. Bradycardia takes the form of sinus bradycardia, sinus arrhythmia, and second- or third-degree atrioventricular block.

bradycardia-tachycardia syndrome [Gk, *bradys* + *kardia* + *tachys,* fast, *kardia* + *syn,* together, *dromos,* course], a disorder characterized by a heart rate that alternates between being abnormally low (less than 60 beats/min) and abnormally high (greater than 100 beats/min).

bradyesthesia /-esthē′zhə/ [Gk, *bradys,* slow, *aisthesis,* feeling], a slowness in perception.

bradykinesia /-kinē′zhə, -kīnē′zhə/ [Gk, *bradys* + *kinesis,* motion], an abnormal condition characterized by slowness of all voluntary movement and speech, such as caused by parkinsonism, other extrapyramidal disorders, and certain tranquilizers.

bradykinin /-kī′nin/ [Gk, *bradys* + *kinein*, to move], a peptide containing nine amino acid residues produced from alpha₂-globulin by the enzyme kallikrein. Bradykinin is a potent vasodilator.

bradyphagia /-fā′jə/, a habit of eating very slowly.

bradyphasia /-fā′zhə/, an abnormally slow manner of speech, often associated with mental illness.

bradypnea /-pnē′ə/ [Gk, *bradys* + *pnein*, to breath], an abnormally low rate of breathing (lower than 12 breaths/min).

bradyspermatism /-spur′mətiz′əm/, ejaculation that lacks normal force so that semen trickles slowly from the penis.

bradyuria /brad′ēyŏŏr′ē-ə/, slow urination.

Bragg curve [William H. Bragg, English physicist, 1862–1942], the path followed by ionizing particles used in a radiation treatment. Because certain particles reach a peak of potential near the end of their path, the Bragg curve can be used to direct the radiation to deep-seated tumors while significantly sparing normal overlying tissues.

Braille /brāl, brä′yə/ [Louis Braille, French teacher of the blind, 1809–1852], a system of printing for the blind consisting of raised dots or points that can be read by touch.

brain [AS, *bragen*], the portion of the CNS contained within the cranium. It consists principally of the cerebrum, thalamus, hypothalamus, cerebellum, midbrain, pons, and medulla.

brain abscess [AS, *bragen*; L, *abscedere*, to go away], a pocket of infection in a part of the brain. It is usually a result of the spread of an infection from another source, such as the skull, sinuses, or other structures in the head. The infection also may be secondary to a disease in the bones, the nervous system outside the brain, or the heart.

brain attack, term signifying that a stroke is in progress and an emergency situation exists.

brain concussion [AS, *bragen*; L, *concussus*, a shaking], a bruising to cerebral tissues caused by a violent jarring or shaking or other blunt, nonpenetrating injury to the brain, resulting in a sudden change in momentum of the head. After a mild concussion, there may be a transient LOC followed, on awakening, by a headache. Severe concussion may cause prolonged unconsciousness and disruption of certain vital functions of the brainstem, such as respiration and vasomotor stability.

brain death [AS, *bragen* + *death*], an irreversible form of unconsciousness characterized by a complete loss of brain function while the heart continues to beat. The legal definition of this condition varies from state to state. The usual clinical criteria for brain death include the absence of reflex activity, movements, and spontaneous respiration requiring mechanical ventilation or life support to continue any cardiac function. The pupils are dilated and fixed. Because hypothermia, anesthesia, poisoning, or drug intoxication may cause deep physiologic depression that resembles brain death, these parameters must be within normal limits prior to testing. Diagnosis of brain death may require evaluating and demonstrating that electrical activity of the brain is absent on two EEGs performed 12 to 24 hours apart.

brain electric activity map (BEAM), a topographic map of the brain created by a computer that is able to respond to the electric potentials evoked in the brain by a flash of light. Potentials recorded at 4-msec intervals are converted into a many-colored map of the brain, showing them to be positive or negative.

brain fever, any inflammation of the brain or meninges.

brain natriuretic peptide (BNP), a hormone, originally isolated from porcine brain tissue, having biologic effects similar to those of atrial natriuretic peptide and stored mainly in the myocardium of the cardiac ventricles. Blood levels of BNP are elevated in hypervolemic states, such as CHF and hypertension.

brain scan [AS, *bragen*; L, *scandere*, to climb], a diagnostic procedure used to image the brain. Common modalities include CT, MRI, and PET. Imaging can be done with a radioisotope used to localize and identify intracranial masses, lesions, tumors, or infarcts. Intravenously injected radioisotopes accumulate in abnormal brain tissue and are traced and photographed by a scintillator or scanner.

Brain's reflex [Walter R. Brain, English physician, 1895–1966; L, *reflectere*, to bend back], the reflexive extension of the flexed paralyzed arm of a hemiplegia patient when assuming a quadrupedal posture.

brainstem [AS, *bragen* + *stemm*], the part of the brain comprising the medulla oblongata, the pons, and the mesencephalon. It performs motor, sensory, and reflex functions and contains the corticospinal and reticulospinal tracts. The 12 pairs of cranial nerves from the brain arise mostly from the brainstem.

brainstem auditory evoked response (BAER), the electric activity that may be recorded from the brainstem in the first

10 msec after presentation of an auditory stimulus. A delayed, normally shaped waveform may indicate a hearing loss caused by a middle or inner ear disorder; one or more missing peaks may indicate a neural disorder.

brain syndrome, a group of symptoms resulting from impaired function of the brain. It may be acute and reversible, or chronic and irreversible.

brain tumor, an invasive neoplasm of the intracranial portion of the CNS. In adults 20% to 40% of malignancies in the brain are metastatic lesions from cancers in the breast, lung, GI tract, or kidney or a malignant melanoma. Gliomas, chiefly astrocytomas, are the most common malignancies. Medulloblastomas occur often in children. Symptoms of a brain tumor are often those of ICP, such as headache, nausea, vomiting, papilledema, lethargy, and disorientation.

brainwashing, intensive indoctrination, usually of a political or religious nature, applied to individuals to develop in their minds a specific belief and motivation.

brain wave [AS, *bragen* + *wafian*], any of a number of patterns of rhythmic electric impulses produced in different parts of the brain. Most patterns, identified by the Greek letters alpha, beta, delta, gamma, kappa, and theta, are similar for all normal persons and are relatively stable for each individual. Brain waves help in the diagnosis of certain neurologic disorders such as epilepsy or brain tumors.

bran, a coarse outer covering or coat (seed husk) of cereal grain such as wheat or rye.

bran bath [OFr, *bren;* AS, *baeth*], a bath in which bran has been boiled in the water. It is used for the relief of skin irritation.

branch, (in anatomy) an offshoot arising from the main trunk of a nerve or blood vessel.

branched-chain amino acids (BCAA), leucine, isoleucine, and valine. They are incorporated into proteins or catabolized for energy.

branched tubular gland [OFr, *branche*], one of the many multicellular glands with one excretory duct from two or more tube-shaped secretory branches, such as some of the gastric glands.

branchial /brang′kē·əl/ [Gk, *branchia*, gills], pertaining to body structures of the face, neck, and throat area, particularly the muscles.

branchial arches [Gk, *branchia*, gills; L, *arcus*, bow], arched structures in the embryonic pharynx.

branchial cleft [Gk, *branchia*, gills; ME, *clift*], a linear depression in the pharynx of the early embryo opposite a branchial or pharyngeal pouch.

branchial cyst [Gk, *branchia*, gills, *kystis*, bag], a cyst derived from a branchial remnant in the neck.

branchial fistula, a congenital abnormal passage from the pharynx to the external surface of the neck, resulting from the failure of a branchial cleft to close during fetal development.

branchiogenic /brang′kē·ō·jen′ik/ [Gk, *branchia*, gills, *genein*, to produce], pertaining to any tissues originating in the branchial cleft or arch.—**branchiogenous,** adj.

branchio-oto-renal syndrome /brang′kē·ō·ō′tō·rē′nol/ [Gk, *branchia*, gills, *ous*, ear; L, *ren*, kidney], branchial arch anomalies (preauricular pits, branchial fistulas or pits) associated with congenital deafness resulting from dysgenesis of the organ of Corti, and with renal dysplasia. It is inherited as an autosomal-dominant trait with high penetrance and variable expression.

Brandt-Andrews maneuver [Thure Brandt, Swedish obstetrician, 1819–1895; Henry R. Andrews, English obstetrician, 1871–1942], a method of expressing the placenta from the uterus in the third stage of labor. One hand grasps the umbilical cord while the other is placed on the mother's abdomen with the fingers over the anterior surface of the uterus. While the hand on the abdomen is pressed backward and slightly upward, the other applies gentle traction on the cord.

Braschi valve, a one-way valve put into the inspiratory limb of a ventilator circuit to measure the intrinsic PEEP.

brassy cough [AS, *brase*, brassy, *cohhetan*, to cough], a high-pitched cough caused by irritation of the recurrent pharyngeal nerve or by pressure on the trachea.

brawny arm, a swollen arm caused by lymphedema, usually after a mastectomy.

Braxton Hicks version /brak′stən hiks′/ [John Braxton Hicks, English physician, 1823–1897], one of several types of maneuvers sometimes used to turn the fetus from an undesirable position to one that is more likely to facilitate delivery.

BRCA1, symbol for a breast cancer gene. A healthy BRCA1 gene produces a protein that protects against unwanted cell growth. The protein is packaged by the cell's Golgi apparatus into secretory vesicles, which release their contents on the cell's surface. The protein circulates in the intracellular space, attaching itself to neighboring cell receptors. The receptors signal the cell nuclei to stop growing. When the gene is defective, it produces

B

a faulty protein that is unable to prevent proliferation of abnormal cells as they evolve into potentially deadly breast cancer. BRCA1 may also normally inhibit ovarian cancer.

BRCA2, symbol for a breast cancer gene with activity similar to that of BRCA1.

BRCA3, symbol for a breast cancer gene.

breach of contract, the failure to perform as promised or agreed in a contract.

breach of duty, 1. the failure to perform an act required by law. **2.** the performance of an act in an unlawful way.

break test, a test of a person's muscle strength by application of resistance after the person has reached the end of an ROM. Resistance is applied gradually in a direction opposite to the line of pull of the muscle or muscle group being tested.

breakthrough, (in psychiatry) a sudden new insight into a problem and its solution after a period of little or no progress.

breakthrough analgesia, analgesia administered for the relief of breakthrough pain.

breakthrough bleeding, the escape of uterine blood between menstrual periods, a possible side effect of fibroids or oral contraceptive use.

breakthrough dose, the dose of an analgesic required for the relief of breakthrough pain.

breakthrough pain, a transient increase in pain intensity that occurs in patients with stable, baseline persistent pain.

breast [AS, *breast*], **1.** the anterior aspect of the surface of the chest. **2.** a mammary gland.

breast abscess, an abscess of a mammary gland, usually during lactation or weaning.

breast cancer, a malignant neoplastic disease of breast tissue, a common malignancy in women in the United States. The incidence increases with age from the third to the fifth decade and reaches a second peak at age 65. Risk factors include certain genetic abnormalities, a family history of breast cancer, nulliparity, exposure to ionizing radiation, early menarche, late menopause, obesity, diabetes, hypertension, chronic cystic disease of the breast, and, possibly, postmenopausal estrogen therapy. Initial symptoms, detected in most cases by self-examination, include a small painless lump, thick or dimpled skin, or nipple retraction. As the lesion progresses, there may be nipple discharge, pain, ulceration, and enlarged axillary glands. The diagnosis may be established by a careful physical examination, mammography, and cytologic examination of tumor cells obtained by biopsy.

breast cancer genetic screening test (BRCA genetic testing), a blood test used to detect the presence of breast cancer genes, which indicates an increased susceptibility for development of breast cancer. One breast cancer gene also confers an increased susceptibility for ovarian cancer.

breast cancer tumor analysis, a microscopic examination of breast cancer tissue to predict the probability of cancer recurrence.

breast ductal lavage, a fluid analysis of exfoliated cells from breast ducts to assess breast cancer risk. There is no statistical support for the accuracy of this test.

breast examination¹, a process in which the breasts and their accessory structures are observed and palpated in assessing the presence of changes or abnormalities that could indicate malignant disease.

breast examination², a nursing intervention from the Nursing Interventions Classification (NIC) defined as inspection and palpation of the breasts and related areas.

breastfeeding [AS, *braest;* ME, *feden*], **1.** suckling or nursing, giving a baby milk from the breast. Breastfeeding encourages postpartum uterine involution and slows the natural return of the menses. **2.** taking milk from the breast.

breastfeeding assistance, a nursing intervention from the Nursing Interventions Classification (NIC) defined as preparing a new mother to breastfeed her infant.

breastfeeding establishment: infant, a nursing outcome from the Nursing Outcomes Classification (NOC) defined as infant attachment to and sucking from the mother's breast for nourishment during the first 3 weeks of breastfeeding.

breastfeeding establishment: maternal, a nursing outcome from the Nursing Outcomes Classification (NOC) defined as maternal establishment of proper attachment of an infant to and sucking from the breast for nourishment during the first 3 weeks of breastfeeding.

breastfeeding maintenance, a nursing outcome from the Nursing Outcomes Classification (NOC) defined as continuation of breastfeeding from establishment to weaning for nourishment of an infant/toddler.

breastfeeding weaning, a nursing outcome from the Nursing Outcomes Classification (NOC) defined as progressive discontinuation of breastfeeding of an infant/toddler.

breast implant, the surgical placement of prosthetic material in a breast, either to increase the breast's size or for reconstruction after a mastectomy.

breast milk [AS, *braest + meoluc*], human milk. It is easily digested, clean, and warm and confers some immunities (bronchiolitis and gastroenteritis are rare in breastfed babies). Infants fed breast milk are less likely to become obese and to have dental malocclusion.

breast milk jaundice, jaundice and hyperbilirubinemia in breastfed infants that occur in the first weeks of life as a result of a metabolite in the mother's milk that inhibits the infant's ability to conjugate bilirubin to glucuronide for excretion.

breast pump, a mechanical or electronic device for withdrawing milk from the breast.

breast scintigraphy, a nuclear scan used to identify breast cancer in patients whose dense breast tissue precludes accurate evaluation by conventional mammography. It is also used as a second-line imaging modality in patients with an indeterminate mammogram and in women with lumpy breasts.

breast shadows, artifacts caused by breast tissue that appear on chest radiographs of women. The shadows accentuate the underlying tissue and may cause the appearance of an interstitial disease process.

breast sonogram, an ultrasound test that is used primarily to determine if a mammographic abnormality or a palpable lump is a cyst (fluid-filled) or a solid tumor (benign or malignant). It is also used to examine symptomatic women who should not be exposed to mammographic radiation, such as pregnant women and women under the age of 25.

breast transillumination [AS, *braest;* L *trans,* through, *illuminare,* to light up], a method of examining the inner structures of the breast by directing light through the outer wall.

breath, the air inhaled and exhaled during ventilation of the lungs.

Breathalyzer /breth'əlī'zər/, a trademark for a device that analyzes exhaled air. It is commonly used to test for blood alcohol levels; the test is based on the relationship between alcohol in the breath and alcohol in the blood circulating through the lungs.

breath-holding /breth-/ [AS, *braeth;* ME, *holden*], a form of voluntary apnea that is usually but not necessarily performed with a closed glottis. Although breath-holding may be prolonged for several minutes, it is invariably terminated either voluntarily or when the person or child loses consciousness.

breathing biofeedback, the monitoring of breathing rate, volume, rhythm, and location by sensors placed on the chest and abdomen, used in the treatment of asthma, hyperventilation, and anxiety. The feedback is displayed to the patient visually and is used by the patient to learn to

breathe more slowly, deeply, and rhythmically using the abdominal muscles.

breathing cycle /brē'thing/, a ventilatory cycle consisting of an inspiration followed by the expiration of a volume of gas called the tidal volume. The duration or total cycle time of a breathing cycle is the breathing or ventilatory period.

breathing nomogram [AS, *braeth;* Gk, *nomos,* law, *gramma,* a record], a chart that presents scales of data for body weight, breathing frequency, and predicted basal tidal volume arranged so that one can find an unknown value on one scale by drawing a line that connects known values on the other two scales.

breathing-related sleep disorder, any of several disorders characterized by sleep disruption caused by some sleep-related breathing problem, resulting in excessive sleepiness or insomnia. Included are central sleep apnea, obstructive sleep apnea, and primary alveolar hypoventilation (Ondine's curse).

breathing work, the energy required for breathing movements. It is the cumulative product of the instantaneous pressure developed by the respiratory muscles and the volume of air moved during a breathing cycle.

breath odor, an odor usually produced by substances or diseases in the lungs or mouth. Certain specific odors are associated with some diseases such as diabetes, liver failure, uremia, or a lung abscess.

breath sound [AS, *braeth;* L, *sonus*], the sound of air passing in and out of the lungs, as heard with a stethoscope. Decreased breath sounds may indicate an obstruction of an airway, collapse of a portion or all of a lung, thickening of the pleurae of the lungs, emphysema, or other COPD. They also occur with frail clients who are not physically able to breathe deeply.

breath test, any of various tests in which a person's breath is analyzed for presence of something abnormal.

breath tests, diagnostic tests for intestinal disorders such as bacterial overgrowth, ileal disease, lactase deficiency, and steatorrhea.

Breckinridge, Mary [1881–1965], the American nurse who founded the Frontier Nursing Service in Kentucky to improve the obstetric care of women living in remote mountainous areas. The service began training midwives and stimulated the establishment of other midwifery schools.

breech birth [ME, *brech + burth*], parturition in which the infant emerges feet, knees, or buttocks first. Breech birth is often hazardous: The body may deliver easily, but the aftercoming head may become trapped by an incompletely dilated cervix, because infants' heads are usually larger than their bodies.

breech extraction [ME, *brech;* L, *ex,* out, *trahere,* to pull], an obstetric operation in which an infant being born feet or buttocks first is grasped before any part of the trunk is born and delivered by traction.

breech presentation [ME, *brech;* L, *praesentare,* to show], intrauterine position of the fetus in which the buttocks or feet present. It occurs in approximately 3% of labors.

bregma /breg'mə/ [Gk, front of the head], the junction of the coronal and sagittal sutures on the top of the skull. —**bregmatic,** *adj.*

bregmacardiac reflex /breg'məkär'dē·ək/ [Gk, *bregma,* front of the head], a phenomenon in which pressure on the anterior fontanel of an infant's skull causes the heart to slow.

bremsstrahlung radiation /brems'shträ'lŏŏng/ [Ger, braking radiation], a type of radiation produced by the interaction between projectile electrons and the nuclei of target atoms.

Brenner tumor [Fritz Brenner, German pathologist, 1877–1969], an uncommon benign ovarian neoplasm consisting of nests or cords of epithelial cells containing glycogen that are enclosed in fibrous connective tissue. The tumor may be solid or cystic.

Brethine, a trademark for a beta$_2$ receptor agonist agent (terbutaline sulfate).

bretylium tosylate /britil'ē·əm/, an antiarrhythmic agent prescribed in the treatment of selected life-threatening ventricular arrhythmias when other measures have not been effective.

Brevicon, a trademark for a norethindrone-ethinyl estradiol oral contraceptive.

Brevital Sodium, a trademark for a barbiturate (methohexital sodium).

brewer's yeast /brŏŏ'ərz/ [ME, *brewen,* to boil, *yest,* foam], a preparation containing the dried pulverized cells of a yeast, such as *Saccharomyces cerevisiae,* that is used as a leavening agent and as a dietary supplement. It is one of the best sources of the B complex vitamins and a rich source of many minerals and a high grade of protein.

Bricanyl, a trademark for a beta$_2$ receptor agonist agent (terbutaline sulfate).

brick dust urine, a reddish discoloration signaling precipitated urates in acidic urine.

bridgework, a fixed partial denture that is cemented permanently to abutment teeth.

bridging [AS, *brycg*], **1.** a nursing technique of positioning a patient so that bony prominences are free of pressure on the mattress by using pads, bolsters of foam rubber, or pillows to distribute body weight over a larger surface. **2.** a nursing technique for supporting a part of the body, such as the testicles in treating orchitis, using a Bellevue bridge made of a towel or other material. **3.** a physical rehabilitation technique that strengthens abdominal and leg muscles. Reclining with knees bent, the patient plants the feet on a firm surface and lifts the buttocks off the surface.

Brief Psychiatric Rating Scale (BPRS), a rating scale for assessing psychopathology on the basis of a small number of items, usually 16 to 24, encompassing psychosis, depression, and anxiety symptoms.

brief psychotherapy, (in psychiatry) treatment directed to the active resolution of personality or behavioral problems rather than to the speculative analysis of the unconscious.

brief psychotic disorder, an episode of psychotic symptoms (incoherence, loosening of associations, delusions, hallucinations, disorganized or catatonic behavior) with sudden onset, lasting less than 1 month.

brief reactive psychosis, a short episode, usually less than 2 weeks, of psychotic behavior that occurs in response to a significant psychosocial stressor.

brightness gain /brīt'nes/, the increase in illumination level of a radiograph produced by an image intensifier.

Brill-Zinsser disease /bril' zin'sər/ [Nathan E. Brill, American physician, 1860–1925; Hans Zinsser, American bacteriologist, 1878–1940], a mild form of epidemic typhus that recurs in a person who appears to have completely recovered from a severe case of the disease years earlier. Some rickettsiae remain in the body after the symptoms of the disease abate, causing the recurrence of symptoms.

brim, 1. edge or margin. **2.** the edge of the upper border of the true pelvis, or the pelvic inlet.

brimonidine /brimō'nidēn/, an alphaadrenergic receptor agonist used as the tartrate salt in treatment of open-angle glaucoma and ocular hypertension. It is administered topically to the conjunctiva.

Brinnell hardness test [Johann A. Brinnell, Swedish engineer, 1849–1925], a means of determining the surface hardness of a material by measuring the resistance the material offers to the impact of a steel ball. The Brinnell hardness test is commonly used to measure abrasion resistance in materials used in dental restorations, such as amalgams, cements, and porcelains.

brinzolamide /brinzō'lahmīd/, a carbonic anhydrase inhibitor used in treatment of open-angle glaucoma and ocular hypertension.

Brissaud's dwarf /brisōz'/ [Edouard Brissaud, French physician, 1852–1909], a person affected with infantile myxedema in which short stature is associated with hypothyroidism.

Bristol Cancer Help Center (BCHC) diet, a stringent diet of raw and partly cooked vegetables with proteins from soy. It is claimed to enhance the quality of life and attitude toward illness in cancer patients.

British Medical Association (BMA), a voluntary professional organization of physicians and medical students in the United Kingdom.

British Pharmacopoeia **(BP),** the official British reference work setting forth standards of strength and purity of medications and containing directions for their preparation, to ensure that the same prescription written by different doctors and filled by different pharmacists will contain exactly the same ingredients in the same proportions.

British thermal unit (BTU), a unit of heat energy; the amount of thermal energy that must be absorbed by 1 lb of water to raise its temperature by 1° F at 39.2° F. It is also equivalent to 1055 joules or 252 Calories.

brittle diabetes, poorly controlled DM in which blood glucose levels are unstable.

broach, an elongated, tapering dental instrument used in removing pulpal material.

broad beta disease, type III familial hyperlipoproteinemia in which a lipoprotein, high in cholesterol and triglycerides, accumulates in the blood. It is characterized by yellowish nodules (xanthomas) on the elbows and knees, peripheral vascular disease, and elevated serum cholesterol levels. Persons with this disease are at risk for development of early coronary disease.

broad ligament [ME, *brood;* L, *ligare,* to tie], a folded sheet of peritoneum draped over the uterine tubes, the uterus, and the ovaries.

broad ligament of the liver [ME, *brod;* L, *ligare,* to bind; AS, *lifer*], a crescent-shaped fold of peritoneum attached to the lower surface of the diaphragm, connecting with the liver and the anterior abdominal wall.

broad-spectrum antibiotic, an antibiotic that is effective against a wide range of infectious microorganisms.

Broca's aphasia /brō'kəz/ [Pierre P. Broca, French neurologist, 1824–1880], a type of aphasia consisting of nonfluent speech,

with a laconic and hesitant, telegraphic quality caused by a large dominant hemisphere frontal lesion extending to the central sulcus. The patient's agrammatic speech is characterized by abundant nouns and verbs but few articles and prepositions; the resulting speech is economic but lacking in syntax.

Broca's area [Pierre P. Broca], an area involved in speech production situated on the inferior frontal gyrus of the brain.

Broca's fissure [Pierre P. Broca], a cleft or groove encircling Broca's area in the left frontal area of the brain.

Broca's plane [Pierre P. Broca], a plane that includes the tip of the interalveolar septum between the upper central incisors and the lowest point of the left and right occipital condyles.

Brödel's bloodless line, a longitudinal light-colored zone on the anterior surface of the kidney near the convex border, considered to be less vascularized than other areas because it is the border between two areas of arterial distribution.

Brodie's abscess [Benjamin Brodie, English surgeon, 1783–1862], a subacute form of osteomyelitis consisting of an indolent staphylococcal infection of bone, usually in the metaphysis of a long bone of a child, characterized by a necrotic cavity surrounded by dense granulation tissue.

Brodmann's areas /brod'manz, brōt'mons/ [Korbinian Brodmann, German anatomist, 1868–1918], the 47 different areas of the cerebral cortex that are associated with specific neurologic functions and distinguished by different cellular components.

brom, abbreviation for a *bromide anion*.

bromazepam /brōōmaz'əpam/, a benzodiazepine used as an antianxiety agent and as a sedative and hypnotic. It is administered orally.

bromelain /brō'məlān/, any of several enzymes that catalyze cleavage of proteins on the carboxyl side of alanine, glycine, lysine, and tyrosine bonds. The enzyme is administered orally as an anti-inflammatory agent (especially to relieve swelling in the nasal and paranasal sinuses) and is also used in immunology to render red cells agglutinable by incomplete antibody.

Bromfed, a trademark for a fixed-combination decongestant containing brompheniramine maleate and pseudoephedrine maleate.

bromhidrosis /brō'midrō'sis/ [Gk, *bromos,* stench, *hidros,* sweat], an abnormal condition in which the apocrine sweat has an unpleasant odor.

bromide /brō'mīd/ [Gk, *bromos,* stench], an anion of bromine. Bromide salts, once widely prescribed as sedatives, are now seldom used for that purpose because they may cause serious mental disturbances as side effects.

bromide poisoning, an adverse reaction to ingested bromide. Symptoms include nausea, vomiting, an acnelike rash, slurred speech, ataxia, psychotic behavior, and coma.

bromine (Br) /brō'mēn/, a corrosive, toxic red-brown liquid element of the halogen group. Its atomic number is 35; its atomic mass is 79.904. Bromine gives off a red vapor that is extremely irritating to the eyes and the respiratory tract. Liquid bromine causes serious skin burns. Compounds of bromine have been used as sedatives, hypnotics, and analgesics and are still used in some nonprescription, OTC preparations. Prolonged use of these products may cause brominism, a toxic condition characterized by acneform eruptions, headache, loss of libido, drowsiness, and fatigue.

bromocriptine mesylate /brō'mōkrip'tēn/, a dopamine receptor agonist. It is prescribed for the treatment of amenorrhea and galactorrhea associated with hyperprolactinemia, female infertility, and Parkinson's disease.

bromoderma /brō'mōdur'mə/ [Gk, *bromos*, stench, *derma* skin], an acneform, bullous, or nodular skin rash occurring as a hypersensitivity reaction to ingested bromides.

brompheniramine maleate /brom'fənir'əmin/, an antihistamine prescribed in the treatment of allergic reactions, including rhinitis, skin reactions, and itching.

Brompton's cocktail, an analgesic solution containing alcohol, morphine, or heroin, and, in some cases, a phenothiazine. It is administered to control pain in the terminally ill patient. Given frequently at the lowest effective dose, it may relieve pain for many months.

bronchial /brong'kē·əl/ [Gk, *bronchos*, windpipe], pertaining to the bronchi or bronchioles.

bronchial artery, the nutritive vasular system of the pulmonary tissues, originating from the thoracic aorta or one of its branches. The bronchial arteries interconnect within the lung with branches of the pulmonary arteries and veins.

bronchial atresia, occlusion or obstruction of a lobar or segmental bronchus, usually in the left upper lobe; the affected lung segment is often hyperinflated because of leakage of air through the alveolar pores.

bronchial breath sound [Gk, *bronchos*, windpipe], a normal sound heard with a stethoscope over the main airways of the lungs, especially the trachea. Expiration and inspiration produce noise of equal loudness and duration, sounding like blowing through a hollow tube.

bronchial cast, a cylindric solid or semisolid plug that blocks a bronchus and is sometimes expectorated.

bronchial challenge, bronchial challenge test, a challenge test in which a nonspecific agent such as histamine or methacholine is applied to the bronchi and they are assessed for a bronchoconstriction reaction.

bronchial cough, a cough associated with bronchiectasis and heard in early stages as hacking and irritating, becoming looser in later stages.

bronchial fremitus, a vibration that can be palpated on the chest wall (usually the posterior thorax) over a bronchus. It results from congestion by secretions that rattle as air passes during respiration.

bronchial hyperreactivity [Gk, *bronchos* + *hyper*, excess; L, *re*, again, *agere*, to act], an abnormal respiratory condition characterized by reflex bronchospasm in response to histamine or a cholinergic drug such as methacholine. It is a universal feature of asthma and is used in the differential diagnosis for asthma and heart disease.

bronchial murmur, a murmur heard as a blowing sound, caused by air flowing in and out of the bronchial tubes.

bronchial secretion, a substance produced in the bronchial tree that consists of mucus secreted by the goblet cells and mucous glands of the bronchi, protein salts released from disintegrating cells, plasma fluid, and proteins, including fibrinogen, that have escaped from pulmonary capillaries.

bronchial toilet, special care that is given to patients with tracheostomies and respiratory disorders, including stimulation of coughing, deep breathing, and suctioning of the respiratory tract.

bronchial tree, an anatomic complex of the trachea and bronchi. The bronchi branch from the trachea.

bronchial washing [Gk, *bronchos,* windpipe; ME, *wasshen,* to wash], irrigation of the bronchi and bronchioles performed during bronchoscopy to cleanse the tubes and to collect specimens for laboratory examination.

bronchiectasis /brong'kē·ek'tasis/ [Gk, *bronchos* + *ektasis,* stretching], an abnormal condition of the bronchial tree characterized by irreversible dilation and destruction of the bronchial walls. Symptoms include a constant cough producing copious purulent sputum; hemoptysis; chronic sinusitis; clubbing of fingers; and persistent moist, coarse crackles.

bronchiolar collapse /brong'kyəlar/ [L, *bronchiolus,* little windpipe, *conlabi,* to fall], a condition in which bronchioles, which are pliable and lack cartilaginous support, become compressed by surrounding structures in the absence of inflowing air needed to keep them inflated. The condition occurs in disorders such as emphysema, CF, and bronchiectasis.

bronchiole /brong'kē·ōl/ [L, *bronchiolus,* little windpipe], a small airway of the respiratory system extending from the bronchi into the lobes of the lung. There are two divisions of bronchioles: terminal bronchioles and respiratory bronchioles. —**bronchiolar** /brongkē'ələr/, *adj.*

bronchiolitis /brong'kē·ōlī'tis/ [L, *bronchiolus,* little windpipe; Gk, *itis,* inflammation], an acute viral infection of the lower respiratory tract that occurs primarily in infants younger than 18 months of age. It is characterized by expiratory wheezing, respiratory distress, inflammation, and obstruction at the level of the bronchioles. The most common causative agents are the respiratory syncytial viruses and the parainfluenza viruses. *Mycoplasma pneumoniae,* rhinoviruses, enteroviruses, and measles virus are less common causative agents. Transmission occurs by infection with airborne particles or by contact with infected secretions.

bronchiolitis obliterans, a form of bronchiolitis in which the exudate is not expectorated but becomes organized and obliterates the bronchial tubes, causing collapse of the affected part of the lungs.

bronchioloalveolar carcinoma /brong'kē·ō'lō·alvē'ələr/, a less common variant of the two types of adenocarcinoma of the lung, with columnar to cuboidal epithelial cells lining the alveolar septa and projecting into alveolar spaces in branching papillary formations.

bronchitis /brongkī'tis/ [Gk, *bronchos,* windpipe, *itis,* inflammation], acute or chronic inflammation of the mucous membranes of the tracheobronchial tree.

bronchoalveolar /-alvē'ələr/ [Gk, *bronchos,* windpipe; L, *alveolus,* little hollow], pertaining to the terminal air sacs at the ends of the bronchioles.

bronchoalveolar lavage (BAL), a diagnostic procedure in which small amounts of physiologic solution are injected through a fiberoptic bronchoscope into a specific area of the lung while the rest of the lung is sequestered by an inflated balloon. The fluid is then aspirated and inspected for pathogens, malignant cells, and mineral bodies.

bronchoaortic constriction, thoracic constriction of the esophagus.

bronchoconstriction [Gk, *bronchos,* windpipe; L, *constringere,* to draw tight], a narrowing of the lumen of the bronchi, restricting airflow to and from the lungs.

bronchodilation /-di'lā'shən/ [Gk, *bronchos,* windpipe; L, *dilatare,* to widen], a widening of the lumen of the bronchi, allowing increased airflow to and from the lungs.

bronchodilator /-dilā'tər/, a substance, especially a drug, that relaxes contractions of the smooth muscle of the bronchioles to improve ventilation to the lungs. Pharmacologic bronchodilators are prescribed to improve aeration in asthma, bronchiectasis, bronchitis, and emphysema.

bronchofibroscopy, the visual examination of the tracheobronchial tree through a fiberoptic bronchoscope. It is also used for diagnosing/treating hemoptysis.

bronchogenic /-jen'ik/ [Gk, *bronchos* + *genein,* to produce], originating in the bronchi.

bronchogenic adenocarcinoma, the more common type of adenocarcinoma of the lung.

bronchogenic carcinoma, one of the more than 90% of malignant lung tumors that originate in bronchi. Lesions, usually resulting from cigarette smoking, may cause coughing and wheezing, fatigue, chest tightness, and aching joints. In the late stages, bloody sputum, clubbing of the fingers, weight loss, and pleural effusion may be present.

bronchogenic cyst, a cyst that develops in the lungs or mediastinum. It may be asymptomatic or cause cough, stridor, wheezing, or dyspnea. It may also become infected or malignant, requiring surgical removal.

bronchogram /brong'kōgram/ [Gk, *bronchos,* windpipe, *gramma,* something drawn or written], the radiogram obtained by bronchography.

bronchography /brongkog'rəfē/, an x-ray examination of the bronchi after they have been coated with a radiopaque substance.

broncholithiasis /-lithī'əsis/, inflammation of the bronchi caused by an accumulation of hard concretions or stones on their lining.

bronchomediastinal trunk, one of the two lymphatic vessels, right and left, that drain the lung and bronchi, mediastinal structures, and thoracic wall.

bronchomotor tone, the state of contraction or relaxation of the smooth muscle in the bronchial walls that regulates the caliber of the airways.

bronchophony /brongkof'ənē/ [Gk, *bronchos* + *phone,* voice], an increase in the intensity and clarity of **vocal resonance** that may result from an increase in lung tissue density, such as in the consolidation of pneumonia. It is assessed by having the patient repeat a phrase such as 99 during auscultation.

bronchopleural fistula /-plŏŏr′əl/, an abnormal passageway between a bronchus and the pleural cavity.

bronchopneumonia [Gk, *bronchos* + *pneumon*, lung], an acute inflammation of the lungs and bronchioles, characterized by chills, fever, high pulse and respiratory rates, bronchial breathing, cough with purulent bloody sputum, severe chest pain, and abdominal distention. The disease is usually a result of the spread of infection from the upper to the lower respiratory tract, most commonly caused by the bacterium *Mycoplasma pneumoniae*, *Staphylococcus pyogenes*, or *Streptococcus pneumoniae*.

bronchoprovocation inhalation test, a pulmonary function test performed on patients with a history of asthma who have normal pulmonary function at rest. In a specific test, the patient inhales a particular antigen while the forced expiratory volume (FEV) is measured. In a nonspecific test, the patient inhales a substance such as histamine periodically at increasing concentrations while the FEV is measured.

bronchopulmonary /-pul′mŏner′ē/ [Gk, *bronchos*; L, *pulmonis*, lung], pertaining to the bronchi and the lungs.

bronchopulmonary dysplasia (BPD) /-pŏŏl′məner′ē/, a chronic respiratory disorder characterized by scarring of lung tissue, thickened pulmonary arterial walls, and mismatch between lung ventilation and perfusion.

bronchopulmonary hygiene, the care and cleanliness of the respiratory tract and of ventilatory/respiratory therapy. Hygienic care may include providing assistance with postural drainage and controlled coughing techniques, percussion, vibration, and rib shaking.

bronchopulmonary lavage [Gk, *bronchos,* windpipe; L, *pulmonis,* lung; Fr, *lavage,* washing out], the irrigation or washing out of the bronchi and bronchioles to remove pulmonary secretions.

bronchopulmonary segment, the area of lung supplied by a segmental bronchus and its accompanying pulmonary artery branch. Each segment is shaped like an irregular cone with the apex at the origin of the segmental bronchus and the base projected peripherally onto the surface of the lung.

bronchoscope /brong′kəskōp′/, a curved, flexible tube for visual examination of the bronchi. It contains fibers that carry light down the tube and project an enlarged image up the tube to the viewer.—**bronchoscopic,** *adj.*

bronchoscopy /brongkos′kəpē/, the visual examination of the tracheobronchial tree, using a bronchoscope. The procedure also may be used for suctioning; for obtaining a biopsy specimen and fluid for examination; for removing foreign bodies; for diagnosing such conditions as localized atelectasis, bronchial obstruction, and lung abscess; and for tracheal extubation.

bronchospasm /-spaz′əm/, an excessive and prolonged contraction of the smooth muscle of the bronchi and bronchioles, resulting in an acute narrowing and obstruction of the respiratory airway. Bronchospasm is a chief characteristic of asthma.

bronchospirometry /-spīrom′ətrē/, a technique for the study of the ventilation and gas exchange of each lung separately by the introduction of a catheter into either the left or right mainstem bronchus.

bronchotomogram /-tom′əgram/, an image of the respiratory system from the trachea to the lower bronchi produced by tomography. The procedure is used to detect tumors or other causes of obstruction of the respiratory tract.

bronchovesicular /-vesik′yələr/, pertaining to the bronchi, bronchioles, and alveoli.

bronchovesicular sounds [Gk, *bronchos,* windpipe; L, *vesicula,* small bladder, *sonus,* sound], one of three normal breath sounds that occur between the sounds of the bronchial tubes and those of the alveoli, or a combination of the two sounds.

bronchus /brong′kəs/ *pl.* **bronchi** /-kī/ [L; Gk, *bronchos,* windpipe], any one of several large air passages in the lungs through which pass inhaled and exhaled air. Each bronchus has a wall consisting of three layers. The outermost is made of dense fibrous tissue reinforced with cartilage. The middle layer is a network of smooth muscle. The innermost layer consists of ciliated mucous membrane. —**bronchial,** *adj.*

Bronkodyl, a trademark for a smooth muscle relaxant (theophylline).

Bronkosol, a trademark for a bronchodilator (isoetharine hydrochloride).

Brønsted acid [Johannes N. Brønsted, Danish physical chemist, 1879–1947], a molecule or an ion that acts as a hydrogen ion donor.

Brønsted base [Johannes N. Brønsted], a molecule or an ion that acts as a hydrogen ion acceptor.

broth, **1.** a fluid culture medium, such as a solution of lactose or thioglycollate, used to support the growth of bacteria for laboratory analysis. **2.** a beverage or other clear fluid made with meat extract and water.

Brovana, a trademark for arformoterol.

brow, the forehead, particularly the eyebrow or ridge above the eye.

brow lift, the removal or alteration of muscles and tissues of forehead to raise the eyebrows and minimize frown lines.

Brown-Adson forceps [James B. Brown, American plastic surgeon, 1899–1971; Alfred W. Adson, American neurosurgeon, 1887–1951]

brown fat [ME, *broun;* AS, *faett,* filled], a type of fat present in newborns and rarely found in adults. Brown fat is a unique source of heat energy for the infant because it has greater thermogenic activity than ordinary fat.

Brownian motion /brou′nyən/ [Robert Brown, Scottish botanist, 1773–1858], a random movement of microscopic particles suspended in a liquid or gas. The movement is produced by the natural kinetic activity of molecules of the fluid that strike the foreign particles.

brown recluse spider, a small poisonous arachnid, *Loxosceles reclusa*. The bite produces a characteristic necrotic lesion. The venom usually creates a blister surrounded by concentric white and red circles. There is little or no initial pain, but localized pain develops in about an hour. The patient may experience systemic symptoms; nausea, fever, and chills are common, but the reaction is usually self-limited.

Brown-Séquard's syndrome /broun′sākärz/ [Charles E. Brown-Séquard, French physiologist, 1817–1894], a traumatic neurologic disorder resulting from compression or transaction of one side of the spinal cord, above the tenth thoracic vertebra, characterized by spastic paralysis and loss of postural sense (proprioception) on the body's injured side, and loss of the senses of pain and heat on the other side of the body.

brow presentation, an obstetric situation in which the brow, or forehead, of the fetus is the first part of the body to enter the birth canal. Because the diameter of the fetal head at this angle may be greater than that of the mother's pelvic outlet, a cesarean section may be recommended. However, the fetus usually converts to a vertex presentation.

brucellosis /broo′səlo′sis/ [David Bruce, English pathologist, 1855–1931], a disease caused by any of several species of the gram-negative coccobacillus *Brucella*. Brucellosis is most prevalent in rural areas among farmers, veterinarians, meat packers, slaughterhouse workers, and livestock producers. Laboratory workers are also at risk. It is primarily a disease of animals (including cattle, pigs, sheep, camels, goats, and dogs); humans usually acquire it by ingestion of contaminated milk or milk products or raw meat or marrow, through a

break in the skin, through contact with an infected animal, or through inhalation of dust from contaminated soil. It is characterized by fever, chills, sweating, malaise, and weakness. The fever often occurs in waves, rising in the evening and subsiding during the day, at intervals separated by periods of remission.

Brudzinski's sign /broodzin′skēz/ [Josef Brudzinski, Polish physician, 1874–1917], an involuntary flexion of the hip, and knee when the neck is passively flexed. It occurs in patients with meningitis.

Brugia /bruj′ə/ [S.L. Brug, Dutch parasitologist in Indonesia, 1879–1946], a genus of nematodes of the superfamily Filarioidea that parasitize humans and other mammals.

bruit /broo′ē/ [Fr, noise], an abnormal blowing or swishing sound or murmur heard while auscultating a carotid artery, organ, or gland, resulting from blood flowing through a narrow or partially occluded artery. The specific character of the bruit, its location, and the time of its occurrence in a cycle of other sounds are all of diagnostic importance.

Brunnstrom hemiplegia classification, an evaluation procedure that assesses muscle tone and voluntary control of movement patterns in a stroke patient. Results indicate the patient's progress through stages of recovery.

brush biopsy, the use of a catheter with bristles that is inserted into the body to collect cells from tissues.

brush border, microvilli on the free surfaces of certain epithelial cells, particularly the absorptive surfaces of the intestine and the proximal convoluted tubules of the kidney.

Brushfield's spots [Thomas Brushfield, English physician, 1858–1937; ME, *spotte,* stain], pinpoint white or light yellow spots on the iris of a child with Down syndrome. Occasionally, they are seen in normal infants.

Bruton's agammaglobulinemia [Ogden C. Bruton, American physician, 1908–2003], a sex-linked, inherited condition characterized by the absence of gamma globulin in the blood. Those (usually children) affected by the syndrome are deficient in antibodies and susceptible to repeated infections.

bruxism /bruk′sizəm/ [Gk, *brychein,* to gnash the teeth], the compulsive, unconscious grinding or clenching of the teeth, especially during sleep or as a mechanism for releasing tension during periods of extreme stress in the waking hours.

Bryant's traction [Thomas Bryant, English physician, 1828–1914; L, *trahere,* to pull]], an orthopedic mechanism used to immobilize both lower extremities in the treatment of a fractured femur or in the correction of a congenital hip dislocation. The mechanism consists of a traction frame supporting weights, which are connected by ropes that run through pulleys to traction foot plates.

BSA, 1. abbreviation for *body surface area.* 2. abbreviation for *bovine serum albumin.*

BSE, 1. abbreviation for *breast self-examination.* See **self-breast examination.** 2. abbreviation for **bovine spongiform encephalopathy.**

BSN, abbreviation for **Bachelor of Science in Nursing.**

BSP, abbreviation for **Bromsulphalein.**

BT, abbreviation for **bleeding time.**

BTPD, abbreviation for **body temperature, ambient pressure, dry.**

BTPS, abbreviation for **body temperature, ambient pressure, saturated** (with water vapor).

BTU, abbreviation for **British thermal unit.**

bubble-diffusion humidifier, a device that provides humidified oxygen or other therapeutic gases by allowing the gas to bubble through a reservoir of water.

bubble goniometer, a device used for measuring joint angles, consisting of a spirit level and a pendulum.

bubble oxygenator, a heart-lung device that oxygenates the blood while it is diverted outside the patient's body.

bubo /byoō′bō/ *pl.* **buboes** [Gk, *boubon,* groin], a greatly enlarged, tender, inflamed lymph node, usually in the groin, that is associated with diseases such as chancroid, lymphogranuloma venereum, and syphilis.

bubonic plague /byoōbon′ik/ [Gk, *boubon,* groin; L, *plaga,* stroke], the most common form of plague. It is characterized by painful buboes in the axilla, groin, or neck; fever often rising to 106° F (41.11° C); prostration with a rapid, thready pulse; hypotension; delirium; and bleeding into the skin from the superficial blood vessels. The symptoms are caused by an endotoxin released by a bacillus, *Yersinia pestis,* usually introduced into the body by the bite of a rat flea that has bitten an infected rat. Inoculation with plague vaccine confers partial immunity; infection provides lifetime immunity.

bucardia /boōkär′dē·ə/, extreme enlargement of the heart.

buccal /buk′əl/ [L, *bucca,* cheek], pertaining to the inside of the cheek, the surface of a tooth, or the gum beside the cheek.

buccal administration of medication, oral administration of a drug, usually in the form of a tablet, by placing it between the cheek and the teeth or gum until it dissolves.

buccal artery, a branch of the maxillary artery that supplies the buccinator muscle, the skin, and mucous membrane of the cheek.

buccal bar, a portion of an orthodontic appliance consisting of a rigid metal wire that extends anteriorly from the buccal side of a molar band.

buccal cavity, the vestibule of the mouth, specifically the area lying between the teeth and cheeks.

buccal contour [L, *bucca* + *cum,* together with, *tornare,* to turn], the shape of the buccal side of a posterior tooth. It is usually characterized by a slight occlusocervical convexity that has its largest prominence at the gingival third of the clinical buccal surface.

buccal fat pad, a fat pad in the cheek under the subcutaneous layer of the skin, over the buccinator. It is particularly prominent in infants.

buccal fentanyl, an opioid analgesic used to treat breakthrough pain in cancer patients who are taking regularly scheduled doses of another opiate pain medication and who are tolerant to opiates.

buccal flange [L, *bucca;* OFr, *flanche,* flank], the part of a denture base that occupies the cheek side of the mouth and extends distally from the buccal notch.

buccal frenum, a fold or band of mucous membrane connecting the alveolar ridge to the cheek and separating the labial vestibule from the buccal vestibule.

buccal glands [L, *bucca,* cheek, *glans,* acorn], small salivary glands located between the buccinator muscle and the mucus membranes in the vestibule of the mouth.

buccal mucosa, the mucus membranes lining the inside of the mouth.

buccal nerve, a branch of the anterior trunk of the mandibular nerve that supplies general sensory nerves to the skin of the cheek, oral mucosa, and buccal gingivae of the lower molars. It may also carry the motor innervations to the lateral pterygoid muscle and to part of the temporalis muscle.

buccal notch, a depression in a denture flange that accommodates the buccal frenum.

buccal smear, a sample of cells removed from the buccal mucosa for purposes of obtaining a karyotype to determine the genetic sex of an individual.

buccal splint, material, usually plaster, that is placed on the buccal surfaces of fixed partial denture units to hold the units in position for assembly.

B

buccal vestibule, that portion of the vestibule of the mouth that lies between the cheeks and the teeth and gingivae or residual alveolar ridges.

buccinator /buk′sinā′tər/ [L, *buccina,* trumpet], the main muscle of the cheek, one of the 12 muscles of the mouth. The buccinator, innervated by buccal branches of the facial nerve, compresses the cheek, acting as an important accessory muscle of mastication by holding food under the teeth.

buccocclusion /buk′əklōō′zhən/ [L, *bucca,* cheek, *occludere,* to close up], a malocclusion in which the dental arch or the quadrant of a dental arch or group of teeth is positioned closer to the cheek than normal.

buccogingival /buk′ōjinjī′vəl/, pertaining to the internal mouth structures, particularly the cheeks and gums.

buccolinguomasticatory triad /buk′ōling′w ōmas′təkətôr′e/ [L, *bucca,* cheek, *lingua,* tongue, *masticare,* to gnash the teeth], a complex of involuntary lip, tongue, jaw, and head movements seen in tardive dyskinesia.

buccopharyngeal /buk′ōfərin′jē·əl/, pertaining to the cheek and pharynx or to the mouth and pharynx.

buccopharyngeal fascia, a thin layer of fascia that coats the outside of the muscular part of the pharyngeal wall.

buccula /buk′yələ/ [L, *bucca,* cheek], a fold of fatty tissue; literally, a "little cheek" beneath the chin.

bucket handle fracture [OFr, *buket,* tub; ME, *handel,* part grasped; L, *fractura,* break], a fracture of the wider end of a long bone along the growth plate forming an arc along the proximal margin. New bone formation leads to a thickened appearance and simulates the appearance of a handle; usually indicative of child abuse related injury.

bucking informal. **1.** gagging, coughing. **2.** involuntarily resisting positive pressure ventilation in a patient with an endotracheal tube in place.

buck knife, a periodontal surgical knife with a spear-shaped cutting point, used to make an interdental incision associated with a gingivectomy.

Buck's fascia [Gurdon Buck, American surgeon, 1807–1877], the deep fascia encasing the erectile tissue of the penis.

Buck's skin traction [Gurdon Buck], an orthopedic procedure that applies traction to the lower extremity with the hips and the knees extended. It is used in the treatment of hip and knee contractures, in postoperative positioning and immobilization, and in disease processes of the hip and knee. It is also used to maintain alignment of the hip and leg in patients with hip fractures until reduction of the hip can be performed.

Buck's traction [Gurdon Buck; L, *trahere,* to pull], one of the most common orthopedic mechanisms by which pull is exerted on the lower extremity with a system of ropes, weights, and pulleys. Buck's traction is used to immobilize, position, and align the lower extremity in the treatment of contractures and diseases of the hip and knee.

buckwheat allergy, an allergic reaction to buckwheat, *Fagopyrum esculentum.* It is characterized primarily by photosensitivity.

Bucky diaphragm [Gustav P. Bucky, American radiologist, 1880–1963; Gk, *diaphragma,* partition], a moving grid that limits the amount of scattered radiation reaching a radiographic film, thereby increasing the film contrast.

buclizine hydrochloride /bōō′kləzēn/, an antiemetic/antivertigo drug derived from piperazine that has anticholinergic and antihistaminic properties. It is used to treat nausea, vomiting, and dizziness of motion sickness.

bud [ME, *budde*], any small outgrowth that is the beginning stage of a living structure, as a limb bud from which an arm or leg develops.

Budd-Chiari syndrome /bud kē·är′ē/ [George Budd, English physician, 1808–1882; Hans Chiari, Czech-French pathologist, 1851–1916], a disorder of hepatic circulation, marked by occlusion of the hepatic veins, that leads to liver enlargement, ascites, extensive development of collateral vessels, and severe portal hypertension.

budding [ME, *budde*], a type of asexual reproduction in which an organism produces a budlike projection containing chromatin that eventually detaches and develops into an independent organism. It is common in simple organisms, such as sponges, yeasts, and molds.

buddy splint, a splinting technique commonly used after a finger or toe injury requiring immobilization. The injured and an adjacent digit are typically taped together to limit the ROM of the affected digit.

budesonide, a nasal corticosteroid antiinflammatory agent. It is prescribed in the management of symptoms of seasonal or perennial allergic rhinitis or perennial nonallergic rhinitis. Neubulizer solutions are used for the treatment of asthma in children.

Buerger's postural exercises [Leo Buerger, American physician, 1879–1943; L, *ponere,* to place, *exercere,* to continue working], exercises designed to maintain circulation in a limb.

buffalo hump, an accumulation of fat on the back of the neck associated with the prolonged use of large doses of glucocorticoids or the hypersecretion of cortisol caused by Cushing's syndrome.

buffer [ME, *buffe,* to cushion], a substance or group of substances that tends to control the hydrogen ion concentration in a solution by reacting with hydrogen ions of an acid added to the system and releasing hydrogen ions to a base added to the system. Buffers minimize significant changes of pH in a chemical system. Among the functions carried out by buffer systems in the body is maintenance of the acid-base balance of the blood and of the proper pH in kidney tubules.

buffer anions, the negatively charged bicarbonate, protein, and phosphate ions that comprise the buffer systems of the body.

buffer cations, the positively charged ions associated with the buffering anions of the body's electrolytes, including sodium, potassium, and magnesium.

buffered insulin human, human insulin buffered with phosphate.

buffer solution [ME, *buffet;* L, *solutus,* dissolved], a solution that will minimize changes in pH value despite dilution or addition of a small amount of base or acid.

buffy coat [ME, *buffet;* Fr, *cote*], a grayish-white layer of WBCs and platelets that accumulates on the surface of sedimented erythrocytes when blood plasma is allowed to stand or is centrifuged.

buffy coat transfusion, light stratum of a blood clot seen when the blood is centrifuged or allowed to stand in a test tube.

bulb [L, *bulbus,* swollen root], any rounded structure, such as the eyeball, hair roots, and certain sensory nerve endings.

bulbar /bul′bər/ [L, *bulbus*], **1.** pertaining to a bulb. **2.** pertaining to the medulla oblongata of the brain and the cranial nerves.

bulbar ataxia [L, *bulbus,* swollen root; Gk, *ataxia,* without order], a loss of motor coordination caused by a lesion in the medulla oblongata or pons.

bulbar myelitis [L, *bulbus,* swollen root; Gk, *myelos,* marrow, *itis,* inflammation], an inflammation of the CNS involving the medulla oblongata.

bulbar palsy [L, *bulbus,* swollen root; Gk, *paralyein,* to be palsied], a form of paralysis resulting from a defect in the motor centers of the medulla oblongata.

bulbar paralysis, a degenerative neurologic condition characterized by progressive paralysis of cranial nerves and involving the lips, tongue, mouth, pharynx, and larynx.

bulbar poliomyelitis [L, *bulbus,* swollen root; Gk, *polios,* gray, *myelos,* marrow, *itis,* inflammation], a form of poliomyelitis that involves the medulla oblongata and gradually progresses to bulbar paralysis, with respiratory and circulatory failure.

bulbiform /bul′bifôrm/, shaped like a bulb.

bulbocavernosus /bul′bōkav′ərnō′səs/ [L, *bulbus,* swollen root, *cavernosum,* full of hollows]

bulbocavernosus reflex, bulbospongiosus reflex, the contraction of the bulbospongiosus muscle when the dorsum of the penis is tapped or the glans penis is compressed.

bulbospongiosus, a muscle that covers the bulb of the penis in the male and the bulbus vestibuli in the female.

bulbourethral gland /-yŏŏrē′thrəl/, one of two small glands located on each side of the prostate, draining to the wall of the urethra. Bulbourethral glands secrete a fluid component of the seminal fluid.

bulbous [L, *bulbus,* swollen root], pertaining to a structure that resembles a bulb or that originates in a bulb.

bulb syringe, a device with a flexible bulb that replaces the plunger for instillation or aspiration. Bulb syringes can be used to irrigate an external orifice, such as the auditory canal.

bulimia /bŏŏlim′ē-ə/ [Gk, *bous,* ox, *limos,* hunger], a disorder characterized by an insatiable craving for food, often resulting in episodes of continuous eating and often followed by purging, depression, and self-deprivation.

bulimic /bŏŏlim′ik/, pertaining to bulimia.

bulk cathartic [ME, *bulke,* heap; Gk, *kathartikos,* evacuation of bowels], a cathartic (laxative) that acts by softening and increasing the mass of fecal material in the bowel. Bulk cathartics contain a hydrophilic agent such as methylcellulose or psyllium seed.

bulla /bŏŏl′ə, bul′ə/ *pl.* **bullae** [L, bubble], a thin-walled blister of the skin or mucous membranes greater than 1 cm in diameter containing clear, serous fluid. **—bullous,** *adj.*

bulldog forceps, short spring forceps for clamping an artery or vein for hemostasis. The jaws may be padded to avoid injury to vascular tissue.

bullet forceps, a kind of forceps that has thin, curved, serrated blades that are designed for extracting a foreign object, such as a bullet, from the base of a puncture wound.

bullous disease /bŏŏl'əs/, any disease marked by eruptions of blisters, or bullae, filled with fluid, on the skin or mucous membranes.

bullous emphysema, single or multiple large cystic alveolar dilations of lung tissue.

bullous impetigo, a form of impetigo in which the skin lesions are bullae instead of vesicles. The crusts are thin and greenish yellow.

bullous myringitis [L, *bulla* + *myringa,* eardrum], an inflammatory condition of the eardrum, characterized by painful fluid-filled vesicles on the tympanic membrane and the sudden onset of severe pain in the ear.

bullous pemphigoid [L, *bulla,* bubble; Gk, *pemphix,* bubble, *eidos,* form], a rare, relatively benign subepidermal autoimmune blistering disease of the elderly. It is of unknown origin.

bumetanide /boomet'ənīd/, a loop (high ceiling) diuretic related to furosemide. It is prescribed for edema caused by cardiac, hepatic, or renal disease.

Bumex, a trademark for a diuretic (bumetanide).

Buminate, a trademark for a blood volume expander (human albumin).

BUN, abbreviation for **blood urea nitrogen.**

bundle, a group of nerve fibers or other threadlike structures running in the same direction.

bundle branch [Dan, *bondel;* Fr, *branche*], a segment of the network of specialized conducting fibers that transmits electrical impulses within the ventricles of the heart. Bundle branches are a continuation of the atrioventricular (AV) bundle.

bundle branch block (BBB), an inability of cardiac impulses to be conducted down the bundle branches, causing a broad and abnormally shaped QRS complex. BBB is commonly seen in high-risk, acute, anterior wall MI.

bunion /bun'yən/ [Gk, *bounion,* turnip], an abnormal medial enlargement of the joint at the base of the great toe. It is caused by inflammation of the bursa and is characterized by soreness, swelling, thickening of the skin, and lateral displacement of the great toe.

bunionectomy /bun'yənek'təmē/, excision of a bunion.

bunionette /bun'yənet'/, an abnormal enlargement and inflammation of the joint at the base of the small toe.

Bunnell block, a trademark for a small wooden block used in exercise of the fingers after surgery.

Bunsen burner /boon'sən, bun'sən/ [Robert E.W. Bunsen, German chemist,

1811–1899], a standard laboratory gas burner designed to produce nearly complete combustion in a smokeless flame.

Bunyamwera virus infection /bun'yəm wir'ə/ [Bunyamwera, town in Uganda where the type species was isolated], one of a group of arthropod-borne viruses of the genus *Bunyavirus* that infect humans and are carried by mosquitoes from rodent hosts. Related viruses cause California encephalitis, Rift Valley fever, and other diseases characterized by headache, weakness, low-grade fever, myalgia, and a rash.

buoyant density, the thickness or compactness of a substance that allows it to float in a standard fluid.

bupivacaine hydrochloride /byoopiv'əkān/, a local anesthetic prescribed for caudal, epidural, peripheral, or sympathetic anesthetic block.

Buprenex, a trademark for a parenteral analgesic (buprenorphine hydrochloride).

buprenorphine /bu'prenor'fēn/, a synthetic opioid agonist-antagonist derived from thebaine, used in the form of the hydrochloride salt as an analgesic for moderate to severe pain and as an anesthesia adjunct. It is administered sublingually or by IM or IV injection.

buPROPion /booprō'pē·on/, a heterocyclic mood-elevating drug used to treat some types of depression and also to promote smoking cessation.

Burch procedure /berch/, a type of bladder neck suspension for stress incontinence, consisting of fixation of the lateral vaginal fornices to the iliopectineal ligaments.

burden, 1. load. 2. a heavy, oppressive load, as a disabling clinical load.

burdock root, a perennial herb found in the United States, China, and Europe. This herb is used for skin diseases, inflammation, rashes, colds and fever, cancer, gout, and arthritis. However, there are insufficient data available to know if it is effective.

buret /byooret'/ [Fr, small jug], a laboratory utensil used to deliver a wide range of volumes accurately.

buried suture [L, *sutura*], a suture, often absorbable, that is inserted to draw together soft tissues between the viscus and the skin.

Burke, Mary Lermann, a nursing theorist who, with Georgene Gaskill Eakes and Margaret A. Hainsworth, developed the Theory of Chronic Sorrow to describe the ongoing feelings of loss that arise from illness, debilitation, or death.

Burkholderia /bərk'holdēr'ēə/, a genus of gram-negative, aerobic, rod-shaped bacteria that includes several species formerly classified in the genus *Pseudomonas,* including the agents of glanders and melioidosis. The bacteria are both human and plant pathogens. Their role in the biodegradation of polychlorinated biphenols also makes them important environmental bacteria.

Burkholderia cepacia, a group of bacteria that is often resistant to common antibiotics. Immunocompromised persons or those with chronic lung disease, especially CF, are susceptible to infection.

Burkholderia mallei, a nonmotile species that causes glanders. It is pathogenic chiefly for horses, but may also infect humans and other animals.

Burkholderia pickettii, a group of bacteria responsible for epidemics of bloodstream infections associated with contaminated distilled or sterile water.

Burkholderia pseudomallei, a species that inhabits water and soil and causes melioidosis. Infection is spread via contact with a contaminated source and is a predominant disease of tropical climates.

Burkitt's lymphoma /bur'kits/ [Denis P. Burkitt, English surgeon in Africa, b. 1911], a malignant neoplasm composed of undifferentiated lymphoreticular cells that form a large osteolytic lesion in the jaw or, in children, an abdominal mass.

burn [AS, *baernan*], any injury to tissues of the body caused by hot objects or flames, electricity, chemicals, radiation, or gases, in which the extent of the injury is determined by the nature of the agent, length of time exposed, body part involved, and depth of burn. Burns are sometimes classified as first, second, third, or fourth degree, depending on depth of tissue damage.

burn center, a health care facility that is designed to care for patients who have been severely burned.

burner syndrome, a condition of burning pain, especially in the upper extremities, and sometimes accompanied by shoulder girdle weakness. It may be experienced during contact sports, such as football, as a result of a blow to the head or shoulder. It is attributed to an upper trunk neuropathy of the brachial plexus.

burn healing, a nursing outcome from the Nursing Outcomes Classification (NOC) defined as the extent of healing of a burn site.

burning drops sign, a sensation of hot liquid dripping into the abdominal cavity caused by a perforated stomach ulcer.

burning feet syndrome, a neurologic disorder characterized by symptoms of a burning sensation in the sole of the foot. The burning tends to be more intense at

night and may also involve the hands. Possible causes include causalgia from injury to the sciatic nerve, degeneration of the spinal cord, and polyneuropathy.

burning mouth syndrome, a burning sensation in the mouth that is often associated with menopause.

burning pain [AS, *baernan,* to burn; L, *poena,* penalty], the pain experienced as a result of a thermal burn. The term is sometimes used to describe heartburn or myocardial pain.

burnisher /bur'nishər/ [ME, *burnischen,* to make brown], a dental instrument shaped with rounded smooth edges of the nib, used to closely adapt, polish, or work-harden a metallic material to an underlying object, usually the margin of a gold restoration.

burnishing /bur'nish·ing/ [ME, *burnischen,* to make brown], **1.** (in dentistry) the process of adapting, polishing, and/or work-hardening a metal restoration under the sliding pressure of a smooth hard instrument, as in finishing the surface of a gold filling. **2.** (in dentistry) smoothing and adapting the margins of a thin, annealed sheet of platinum to form a band about a tooth as a matrix for a porcelain restoration.

burnout, a popular term for mental or physical energy depletion after a period of chronic, unrelieved job-related stress, characterized sometimes by physical illness.

burn recovery, a nursing outcome from the Nursing Outcomes Classification (NOC) defined as the extent of overall physical and psychological healing following major burn injury.

burn therapy, the management of a patient burned by flames, hot liquids, explosives, chemicals, or electric current. During the acute stage of a burn, the patient's BP, pulse, respiration, and cerebrovascular pressure are checked every 30 to 60 minutes, and the rectal temperature every 2 to 4 hours. Oral hygiene and assistance in turning, coughing, and deep breathing are provided every 2 hours, and the patient's sensorium is evaluated hourly. If oral fluids are ordered, juices and carbonated drinks are offered, but plain water and ice chips are avoided. Fluid intake and output are measured hourly. Blood transfusions, steroid therapy, and antipyretics may be ordered; aspirin is contraindicated. Local treatment of the burn may use the closed method or the more frequently used open method, in which the injured area is cleansed and exposed to air and the patient is kept warm by a blanket or linen over a bed cradle or by a heater or lamp. In the closed method, a germicidal

B

or bacteriostatic cream, ointment, or solution is applied to the burn, and the wound is covered with a dressing. A porcine heterograft may be used to cover the wound temporarily; this technique prevents fluid loss and reduces the risk of infection, but the graft dries in 1 or 2 days and may pull and cause pain. Newly developed artificial skin holds great promise for treating severe burns.

Burow's solution /byŏŏr'ōz/ [Karl A. Burow, German physician, 1809–1874], a liquid preparation containing aluminum sulfate, acetic acid, precipitated calcium carbonate, and water used as a topical astringent, antiseptic, and antipyretic for a wide variety of skin disorders.

burp informal. **1.** to belch, or eructate; to expel gas from the stomach through the mouth. **2.** a belch, or eructation.

burr, a rotary instrument fitted into a handpiece and used to cut teeth or bone.

burr cell [ME, *burre;* L, *cella,* store-room], a form of mature erythrocyte in which the cells or cell fragments have spicules, or tiny projections, on the surface.

burr holes, holes drilled in the skull during surgery to drain and irrigate an abscess.

bursa /bur'sə/ *pl.* **bursae** [Gk, *byrsa,* wine-skin], **1.** a fibrous sac between certain tendons and the bones beneath them. Lined with a synovial membrane that secretes synovial fluid, the bursa acts as a small cushion that allows the tendon to move over the bone as it contracts and relaxes. **2.** a sac or closed cavity.

bursa-equivalent tissue, bursal equivalent tissue, a hypothesized lymphoid tissue in nonavian vertebrates, equivalent to the bursa of Fabricius in birds: the site of B lymphocyte maturation. It now appears that B lymphocyte maturation occurs primarily in the bone marrow.

bursal abscess /bur'səl/, a collection of pus in the cavity of a bursa.

bursa of Achilles, bursa separating the tendon of Achilles and the calcaneus.

bursectomy /bərsek'təmē/ [Gk, *byrsa,* wineskin, *ektomē,* cutting out], the excision of a bursa.

bursitis /bərsī'tis/, inflammation of the bursa. Bursitis may be precipitated by arthritis, infection, injury, or excessive or traumatic exercise or effort. The chief symptom is severe pain of the affected joint, particularly on movement.

burst, to break suddenly while under tension or expansion.

burst fracture [ME, *bersten;* L, *fractura,* break], any fracture that disperses multiple bone fragments, usually at or near the end of a bone. It frequently occurs in a vertebra.

Burton's line [Henry Burton, English physician, 1799–1849], a dark blue stippled line along the gingival margin, which is a sign of lead poisoning.

Buruli ulcer /bŏŏr'əle/ [Buruli, district in Uganda], an ulcer of the skin with widespread necrosis of subcutaneous fat, caused by a species of *Mycobacterium ulcerans,* manifested by a small, firm, painless, movable subcutaneous nodule that enlarges and ulcerates.

bushy chorion, the region of the chorion that bears villi.

BuSpar, a trademark for an oral antianxiety drug (busPIRone hydrochloride).

busPIRone hydrochloride /bŏŏspir'ōn/, an oral antianxiety drug that, unlike benzodiazepines, does cause sedation, has low abuse potential, takes several days to weeks to exert its effect, and does not intensify the effects of other CNS depressants. It is prescribed for generalized anxiety disorders.

busulfan /bŏŏsul'fən/, an alkylating agent prescribed in the treatment of chronic myelocytic leukemia.

butabarbital sodium /byŏŏ'təbär'bitôl/, a sedative; intermediate-acting barbiturate. It is prescribed for the relief of anxiety, nervous tension, and insomnia.

butamben picrate /byŏŏtam'bən pik'rāt/, a topical local anesthetic for the temporary relief of pain from minor burns.

butane (C_4H_{10}), a colorless petroleum-based gas. It is the fourth member of the paraffin series of hydrocarbons.

Butazolidin, a trademark for an antirheumatic (phenylbutazone).

butenafine /bu-ten'əfēn/, a topical antifungal agent used as the hydrochloride salt in the treatment of athlete's foot, jock itch, and ringworm.

Butisol Sodium, a trademark for a sedative (butabarbital sodium).

Butler-Albright syndrome, a type of distal renal tubular acidosis occurring later than infancy and having autosomal-dominant inheritance.

butoconazole nitrate /byŏŏ'təkŏ'nəzōl/, an intravaginal antifungal cream prescribed for the treatment of vulvovaginal fungal infections caused by *Candida* species.

butorphanol tartrate /byŏŏtôr'fənôl/, an agonist/antagonist opioid of the phenanthrene family. It is administered parenterally for surgical premedication, as an analgesic component of balanced anesthesia, for prompt relief of moderate to severe pain associated with surgical procedures, and as a nasal spray for the relief of migraine pain.

butt, 1. to place two flat surfaces together to form a joint. **2.** (in dentistry) to place directly against the tissues covering the residual alveolar ridge.

butter, a soft, solid substance, such as the oily mass produced by churning cream.

butterfly bandage [AS, *buttorfleoge*], a narrow adhesive strip with broader wing-like ends used to approximate the edges of a superficial wound and to hold the edges together as they heal. It is used in place of a suture in certain cases.

butterfly fracture, a bone break in which the center fragment contained by two cracks forms a triangle.

butterfly needle, a short needle attached to plastic stabilizers at 90 degrees. It is used for IV access of small veins of adults and children. Usual gauge is 25 with a length of 22.

butterfly rash, an erythematous eruption of both cheeks joined by a narrow band of rash across the nose. It may be seen in lupus erythematosus, rosacea, and seborrheic dermatitis.

buttermilk [Gk, *boutyron,* butter; AS, *meoluc*], **1.** the slightly sour-tasting liquid residue remaining after the solids in cream have been churned into butter. It is nearly fat free and is nutritionally comparable to whole milk. **2.** cultured milk made by the addition of certain organisms to fat-free milk.

butter stools, a fatty fecal discharge from the bowels, as may occur in steatorrhea.

buttock augmentation, a reconstructive procedure in cosmetic surgery for reshaping the buttocks.

buttocks, the fleshy hillocks at the lower posterior part of the torso comprising fat and the gluteal muscles.

button /but′ən/ [OFr, *boton*], **1.** a knob-like elevation or structure. **2.** a small appliance shaped like a spool or disk, used in surgery for construction of an intestinal anastomosis.

buttonhole [OFr, *boton;* AS, *hol*], a small slitlike hole in the wall of a structure or a cavity of the body.

buttonhole fracture, a fracture caused by a straight perforation of a bone, such as by a bullet.

buttonhole stenosis, an extreme narrowing of a vessel. The term usually refers to the mitral valve, in which the valve cusps are contracted to form an opening shaped like a buttonhole.

buttonhook, an adaptive device designed to help patients with limited finger ROM, dexterity, or weakness with fastening buttons on clothing.

button suture, a technique in suturing in which the ends of the suture material are passed through buttons on the surface of the skin and tied. It is used to prevent the suture from cutting through the skin.

buttressing, a phenomenon of osteoarthritis in which osteophytes at the hip joint extend across the femoral neck inferior to the femoral head and combine, with a proliferation along the medial aspect of the femoral neck.

buttress plate, a thin, flat metal plate used to provide support in the surgical repair of a fracture.

butyl /byo͞o′til/ [Gk, *butyron,* butter, *hyle,* matter], a hydrocarbon radical (C_4H_9), most compounds of which are obtained from petroleum. Butyl compounds, some of which are toxic and irritating, are used in a variety of industrial and medical applications, including anesthesia.

butyl alcohol (C_4H_9OH), a clear, toxic liquid used as an organic solvent.

butyric acid (C_4H_7OOH) /byo͞otir′ik/, a clear, colorless liquid with an odor of rancid butter or vomit that is miscible with water, alcohol, glycerin, and ether. Butyric acid is obtained commercially from 1-butanol by oxidation and can be obtained from carbohydrates by butyric fermentation. It is used in the production of artificial flavors.

butyric fermentation, the conversion of carbohydrates to butyric acid.

butyrophenone /byo͞o′tərōfē′nōn/, one of a small group of major tranquilizers. They are used in treating psychosis, to decrease the choreic symptoms of Huntington's disease and the tics and coprolalia of Gilles de la Tourette's syndrome, and are used as adjunct in neuroleptanesthesia.

Buzzard's maneuver [Thomas Buzzard, English neurologist, 1831–1919], a modified patellar reflex in which the patient's toes are firmly pressed on the floor while the quadriceps muscle is tapped.

BWS, abbreviation for **battered woman syndrome.**

Byler's disease, progressive familial intrahepatic cholestasis; an autosomal-recessive disorder caused by an error in conjugated bile salt metabolism, with early onset of loose, foul-smelling stools; jaundice; hepatosplenomegaly; and dwarfism.

bypass [AS, *bi,* alongside; Fr, *passer*], **1.** any one of various surgical procedures to divert or shunt the flow of blood or other natural fluids from normal anatomic courses. A bypass may be temporary or permanent. Bypass surgery is commonly performed in the treatment of cardiac and GI disorders. **2.** a term used by some hospitals to signal that its ED lacks the personnel and equipment to handle additional patients, thereby advising that ambulances transporting new patients be diverted to other hospitals.

by-product material, 1. the radioactive waste of nuclear reactors. 2. something produced in the making of something else.

byssinosis /bis′inō′sis/ [Gk, *byssos,* flax, *osis,* condition], an occupational respiratory disease characterized by shortness of breath, cough, and wheezing. The condition is an allergic reaction to dust or fungi in cotton, flax, and hemp fibers.

The symptoms are reversible in the early stages, but prolonged exposure results in chronic airway obstruction, bronchitis, and emphysema with fibrosis, leading to respiratory failure, pulmonary hypertension, and cor pulmonale.

Byzantine arch palate /biz′əntēn/, a congenital anomaly of the roof of the mouth marked by incomplete fusion of the palatal process and the nasal spine.

B

C, 1. symbol for **capacitance. 2.** symbol for **clearance** (subscripts denote the substance; e.g., C_I or C_{In} denotes inulin clearance). **3.** symbol for *heat capacity*.

c, 1. symbol for **small calorie. 2.** symbol for *centi-*. **3.** symbol for *capillary blood*.

C, 1. symbol for **canine (tooth). 2.** symbol for **carbon** (molecular carbon atoms are frequently designated C1, C2, C3, etc., or α-C, β-C, etc., beginning from one end or other standard reference point). **3.** symbol for *large calorie*. **4.** symbol for **compliance** (subscripts denote the structure; e.g., C_L denotes lung compliance). **5.** symbol for **cathode. 6.** symbol for **Celsius** (scale). **7.** symbol for **clonus. 8.** symbol for **complement** (C1 through C9). **9.** symbol for **contraction. 10.** symbol for **coulomb. 11.** abbreviation for **cytosine. 12.** abbreviation for **cervical vertebra** (C1 through C7).

C1, C2, ..., 1. symbols for cervical nerves. **2.** symbols for cervical vertebrae.

C1 INH, abbreviation for *C1 inhibitor*.

C1q nephropathy, a type of immune complex glomerulonephritis with deposits of complement component C1q. Symptoms include loss of protein and/or blood in the urine resulting from damage to the kidneys. It may ultimately cause kidney failure.

C3 NeF, abbreviation for **C3 nephritic factor.**

C3 nephritic factor (C3 Nef), a complement protein that may be deposited in glomerular capillary walls and mesangial tissues, precipitating or contributing to local inflammation and kidney damage.

Ca, symbol for the element **calcium.**

CA 125, abbreviation for *cancer cell surface antigen 125,* blood tumor marker for ovarian or other glandular cell carcinomas. Increasing levels of the antigen mean continuing tumor growth, which may indicate a poor prognosis.

CA 19-9, abbreviation for cancer antigen 19-9 antigen, a blood tumor marker for pancreatic, hepatobiliary and colorectal cancer. This tumor marker is used in diagnosis, evaluation of a patient's response to treatment, and surveillance of the disease.

CA 15-3 tumor marker test, a blood test used to determine the presence of the CA 15-3 tumor-associated serum marker, a marker used for staging breast cancer and monitoring its treatment.

CA 27.29, abbreviation for cancer antigen CA 27.29, a blood tumor marker used for staging breast cancer and monitoring its treatment.

CA 125 tumor marker test, a blood test used to determine the presence of CA 125 serum tumor marker, which has a high degree of sensitivity and specificity for ovarian cancer. It is also used to determine a patient's response to therapy, to predict the outcome of second-look laparotomies, and for posttreatment surveillance.

cabergoline /cabur'gōlēn/, a dopamine receptor agonist used in treatment of hyperprolactinemia, administered orally.

CABG, abbreviation for **coronary artery bypass graft.**

Cabot rings /kab'ot/ [Richard C. Cabot, American physician, 1868–1939], thread-like figures, often appearing as loops or rings, in RBCs of patients with severe anemia.

Cabot's splint [Arthur T. Cabot, American surgeon, 1852–1912], a metal splint worn behind the thigh and leg for support.

CaC₂, the formula for **calcium carbide.**

CaC₂O₄, the formula for **calcium oxalate.**

cacao /kəkā'ō/, **1.** cocoa. **2.** the substance *Theobroma cacao*. **3.** the seeds of *Theobroma cacao*.

cachectic /kəkek'tik/ [Gk, *kakos,* bad, *hexis,* state], pertaining to a state of generally poor health, malnutrition, and weight loss.

cachet /käshā'/ [Fr, tablet], any lenticular edible capsule that encloses a dose of medicine.

cachexia /kəkek'sē·ə/ [Gk, *kakos,* bad, *hexis,* state], general ill health and malnutrition, marked by weakness and emaciation, usually associated with severe disease, such as TB or cancer.—**cachectic,** *adj.*

cachinnation /kak'ənā'shən/ [L, *cachinnare,* to laugh aloud], excessive laughter with no apparent cause, often part of the behavioral pattern in schizophrenia. —**cachinnate,** *v.*

cacodemonomania /kak′ōdē′mənōmā′nē-ə/ [Gk, kakos + daimon, spirit, mania, madness], an abnormal mental condition in which the patient claims to be possessed by an evil spirit.

cacophony /kəkof′ənē/ pl. **cacophonies** [Gk, kakos + phone, voice], a harsh or discordant sound or a mixture of confused, different sounds.—**cacophonic, cacophonous,** adj.

cacoplastic /kak′əplas′tik/, 1. pertaining to a low or inferior grade of structure or organization. 2. pertaining to a state of morbid growth.

cacosmia /kakoz′mē-ə/ [Gk, kakos + osme, odor], the perception of foul odor or stench when none exists. In most instances the condition results from psychologic factors, as in olfactory hallucinations.

CAD, 1. abbreviation for **coronary artery disease.** 2. abbreviation for *computer-assisted design.*

cadaver /kədä′vər/ [L, dead body], a corpse used for dissection and study.

cadaver graft, the transfer of tissue from the body of a dead individual to repair a defect in a living person.

cadaveric /kad′äver′ik/, pertaining to or resembling a cadaver or dead body.

cadaveric donor, an organ or tissue donor who has already died.

cadaveric donor transplantation, allogeneic transplantation of an organ or tissue from a cadaver.

cadaveric renal transplant (CRT), a kidney transplant from a dead donor.

cadence /kā′dəns/ [L, cadere, to fall], a rhythm as in voice, music, or movement.

cadmium (Cd) /kad′mē-əm/, [Gk, kadmeia, zinc ore], a metallic bluish white element that resembles tin. Its atomic number is 48; its atomic mass is 112.40.

cadmium nephropathy, chronic tubulointerstitial nephritis caused by prolonged low-level cadmium poisoning.

cadmium poisoning, poisoning resulting from the inhalation of cadmium in fumes created by welding, smelting, or other industrial processes involving solder. Cadmium bromide, used in engraving, lithography, and photography, can cause severe GI symptoms if swallowed. Cadmium may also cause poisoning by the ingestion of acidic foods prepared and stored in cadmium-lined containers, as lemonade in certain metal cans. The effects may include vomiting, dyspnea, headache, prostration, pulmonary edema, and, possibly, years later, cancer.

caduceus /kədoo′sē-əs/ [L; Gk, karykeion, herald], the wand of the god Hermes or Mercury, used as the symbol for the U.S. Army Medical Corps. It is represented as a staff with two serpents coiled around it and is often confused with the staff of Æsculapius, a rod with one snake entwined about it.

café-au-lait spot /kaf′ā-ōlā′/ [Fr, coffee with milk], a pale tan macule, the color of coffee with milk. Simultaneous development of several café-au-lait spots is associated with neurofibromatosis, but occasional café-au-lait spots occur normally.

café coronary /kəfā′/, a collapse of a person who is eating, caused by asphyxiation that results from obstruction of the glottis by a food bolus. Because the signs are similar to those of a heart attack, such episodes are frequently mistaken for coronary occlusions.

Cafergot, a trademark for a fixed-combination drug containing caffeine and ergotamine, commonly administered in the treatment of migraine headaches.

caffeine /kafēn′, kaf′ē-in/ [Ar, qahwah, coffee], a CNS stimulant prescribed to counteract migraine, drowsiness, and mental fatigue.

caffeine breath test, a breath test for liver function in which the patient is given a dose of caffeine labeled with carbon 13. Excessively low levels of labeled carbon dioxide in the patient's breath indicate inadequate metabolism of it by the liver.

caffeine poisoning [Ar, qahwah, coffee; L, potio, drink], a toxic condition caused by the chronic ingestion of excessive amounts of caffeine, which is found in coffee, tea, cola beverages, and certain stimulant drugs. Symptoms include restlessness, anxiety, general depression, tachycardia, arrhythmias (premature atrial contractions), tremors, nausea, diuresis, and insomnia.

Caffey's syndrome [John Caffey, American pediatrician, 1895–1978], the battered baby syndrome, first described by John Caffey in 1946.

CAGE /kāj/, a mnemonic abbreviation formed by the first letters of four questions designed to screen alcoholic patients: Cut down, Annoyed by criticism, Guilt about drinking, and Eye-opener drinks.

CAH, 1. abbreviation for **chronic active hepatitis.** 2. abbreviation for **congenital adrenal hyperplasia.**

CAHEA, abbreviation for *Committee on Allied Health Education and Accreditation.*

caked /kākt/ [ONorse, kaka], formed into a compact mass or crust, as the scab of coagulated blood on a healing wound.

caked breast, an accumulation of milk in the secreting ducts of the breast after childbirth, causing all or a part of the breast to become hardened and the tissues to become engorged.

cal, abbreviation for **calorie.** 4.184 cal = 1 Joule.

Cal, abbreviation for **Calorie.** Cal is used to describe the calorie content of food. 1000 cal = 1 Cal.

Calabar swelling /kal′əbär/ [Calabar, a Nigerian seaport], a localized angioedema and erythema usually on the extremities, characterized by fugitive, swollen lumps of subcutaneous tissue, caused by a parasitic filarial worm endemic to Central and West Africa. The swollen areas migrate with the worm through the body at a speed of about 1 cm per minute and may become as large as a small egg.

Caladryl, a trademark for a topical fixed-combination drug containing a skin-protective substance (calamine) and an antihistaminic (diphenhydraMINE hydrochloride).

calamine /kal′əmīn/ [Gk, kadmeia, zinc ore], a pink odorless powder used as a protectant or as an astringent and sometimes prepared as a lotion. It is composed of zinc oxide with 0.5% ferric oxide.

Calan, a trademark for a calcium channel blocker (verapamil hydrochloride).

calcaneal, toward the heel.

calcaneal epiphysitis, a painful disorder involving the calcaneus at its epiphysis. The condition tends to affect mainly children who are physically active and whose heel bones are still divided by a layer of cartilage.

calcaneal spur, abnormal, often painful bony outgrowth on the lower surface of the calcaneus, resulting from chronic traumatic pressure on the heel.

calcaneal tuberosity, a transverse elevation on the plantar surface of the calcaneus to which are attached the abductor digiti minimi, the long plantar ligament, and various other muscles.

calcaneodynia /kalkā′nē-ōdin′ē-ə/ [L, calcaneum; Gk, odyne, pain], a painful condition of the heel.

calcaneum, calcaneus /kalkā′nē-əs/ [L, calcaneum, heel], the heel bone. The largest of the tarsal bones, it articulates proximally with the talus and distally with the cuboid. —**calcaneal, calcanean,** adj.

calcar /kal′kär/ pl. **calcaria,** a spur or a structure that resembles a spur.

calcar avis /ā′vis/ [L, calcar, spur, avis, bird], a projection on the medial wall of the posterior horn of the lateral ventricle of the brain. It is associated with the lateral extension of the calcarine fissure.

calcareous /kalker′ē-əs/ [L, calcar, spur], pertaining to calcium or lime.

calcar femorale /kal′kär fem′ə·rā′lē/ [L], the plate of strong tissue that strengthens the neck of the femur.

calcarine /kal′kərīn/, **1.** having the shape of a spur. **2.** pertaining to the calcar.

calcarine fissure, a groove between the cuneus and the lingual gyrus on the medial surface of the occipital lobe of the brain.

calcereous metastasis, the deposition of calcium salts in visceral organs as a result of hyperparathyroidism, an absorptive disease of the bone, or any cause of hypercalcemia, particularly when associated with hyperphosphatemia.

calcergy /kal′sərjē/, local calcification of soft tissues at the site of injection of certain types of chemicals.

calcifediol /kal′sifē′dē·ol/, a major transport form of vitamin D prescribed in the treatment of metabolic bone disease associated with chronic renal failure.

calciferol /kalsif′ərol/ [L, calx, lime, ferre, to bear], a fat-soluble, crystalline unsaturated alcohol produced by ultraviolet irradiation of ergosterol in plants. It is used as a dietary supplement in the prophylaxis and treatment of rickets, osteomalacia, and other hypocalcemic disorders.

calcific aortic disease [L, calx, lime], an abnormal condition characterized by small deposits of calcium in the aorta.

calcification [L, calx + facere, to make], the accumulation of calcium salts in tissues. Normally, about 99% of all the calcium entering the human body is deposited in the bones and teeth; the remaining 1% is dissolved in body fluids such as blood.

calcific tendinitis [L, calx, lime, facere, to make, tendo, tendon; Gk, itis, inflammation], a chronic inflammation of a tendon resulting from an accumulation of calcium deposits in the tissue.

Calcimar, a trademark for calcitonin.

calcination /kal′sinā′shən/ [L, calcinare, to burn lime], the heating of inorganic materials to drive off water. It is used in dentistry to manufacture plaster and stone from gypsum.

calcinosis /kal′sənō′sis/, a condition characterized by abnormal deposits of calcium salts in various tissues. The deposits appear as nodules or plaques. Usually the nodules occur secondary to dermatomyositis or to a preexisting inflammatory degenerative or neoplastic dermatosis, primarily scleroderma.

calcipenia /kal′sipē′nē·ə/, a deficiency of calcium in the body tissues and fluids.

calcipotriene /kal′sipōōtrī′ēn/, a synthetic derivative of cholecalciferol (vitamin D₃), applied to the skin to treat psoriasis.

calcitonin /kal′sitō′nin/ [L, calx; Gk, tonos, tone], a hormone produced in parafollicular cells of the thyroid that participates in regulating the blood level of calcium and stimulates bone mineralization. A synthetic preparation of the hormone is used in the treatment of certain bone disorders.

calcitonin test, a blood test used to evaluate patients who have or are suspected to have medullary carcinoma of the thyroid. It is also used to monitor response to therapy, to predict recurrence of the cancer, and to screen those with a family history of the disease.

calcitriol /kalsit′rē-ôl/, the active form of vitamin D, a regulator of calcium metabolism prescribed in the management of hypocalcemia in patients undergoing chronic renal dialysis and in patients with hypoparathyroidism.

calcium (Ca) /kal′sē-əm/ [L, calx, lime], an alkaline earth metal element. Its atomic number is 20; its atomic mass is 40.08. Its metallic form is a white flammable solid, brittle and somewhat harder than lead. Calcium is the fifth most abundant element in the human body and is mainly present in the bone. The body requires calcium ions for the transmission of nerve impulses, muscle contraction, blood coagulation, cardiac functions, and other processes. The average daily human intake of calcium varies, from 200 to 2500 mg. The daily dietary allowances recommended by the Food and Nutrition Board vary from 360 mg for infants to 1200 mg for women 15 to 18 years of age. Vitamin D, calcitonin, and parathyroid hormone are essential in the metabolism of calcium. Abnormally high levels of ionized calcium in the extracellular fluid can produce muscle weakness, lethargy, and coma. A relatively small decrease from the normal level of this element can produce tetanic seizures. Normal adult blood levels of calcium are 9 to 10.5 mg/dL or 2.25 to 2.75 nmol/L.

calcium carbide (CaC$_2$), a gray or black crystalline compound produced from lime and coke. When mixed with water, it yields acetylene gas (C$_2$H$_2$), which has been used as an anesthetic.

calcium carbonate (CaCO$_2$), precipitated chalk; a white powder sometimes used in antacids.

calcium channel blocker, a drug that inhibits the flow of calcium ions across the membranes of smooth muscle cells. By reduction of the calcium flow, smooth muscle tone is relaxed and the risk of muscle spasms is diminished. Calcium channel blockers are used primarily in the treatment of heart diseases marked by coronary artery spasms (e.g., variant angina).

calcium channel, a slow voltage-gated channel very permeable to calcium ions and slightly permeable to sodium ions, existing in three subtypes designated L, M, and N and located throughout the body. Calcium channels are the main cause of action potentials in certain smooth muscles, and the N channels regulate neurotransmitter release.

calcium chloride (CaCl$_2$), a white granular chemical with an unpleasant taste. It is used in a concentrated solution of the chloride salt of calcium to replenish calcium in the blood and also has uses in cardiac resuscitation. It is prescribed for the treatment of hypocalcemic tetany and as an antidote for lead or magnesium poisoning or magnesium sulfate overdose.

calcium citrate, a salt used as a calcium replenisher. It is also used in the treatment of hyperphosphatemia in renal osteodystrophy.

calcium gluconate (C$_{12}$H$_{22}$CaO$_{14}$), an odorless, tasteless white powder or granules administered orally or intravenously to replenish the body's calcium stores, as after a transfusion.

calcium glycerophosphate, a calcium salt administered intramuscularly or intravenously in conjunction with calcium lactate in the treatment and prophylaxis of hypocalcemia.

calcium hydroxide (Ca[OH]$_2$), a bitter-tasting white powder that may be used in the preparation of treatments for infant diarrhea or in apexification.

calcium hydroxide solution, a clear, colorless liquid sometimes used as an alkali and antidote.

calcium infusion test, a test for hyperglycinemia in which calcium gluconate is administered to the fasting patient for 180 minutes. Serum samples are obtained 30 minutes before infusion, at its initiation, and every 30 minutes for 2 hours afterwards. The patient with a gastrinoma will show a sharp rise in production of gastrin.

calcium oxalate (CaC$_2$O$_4$), a small, colorless crystal that may be present in urine or may be a component of renal calculi.

calcium oxide (CaO), a compound formed by the calcination of chalk or marble and sometimes used in the preparation of caustic pastes.

calcium phosphate (Ca$_3$[PO$_4$]$_2$), an odorless, tasteless white powder used as a calcium supplement, laxative, and antacid.

calcium pump, a theorized energy-requiring mechanism for transmitting calcium ions across a plasma membrane from a region of low calcium ion concentration to one of higher concentration.

calcium sulfate (CaSO₄), a moisture-absorbing white powder used for making plaster casts.

calcium (Ca) test, a blood or urine test used to evaluate parathyroid function and calcium metabolism by directly measuring the total amount of calcium in the blood. It is used to monitor patients with renal failure, renal transplantation, hyperparathyroidism, and various malignancies, as well as to monitor calcium levels during and after large-volume blood transfusions.

calcium urate, the calcium salt of uric acid; a less common type of renal calculus.

calciuria /kal'sĭŏŏr'ē·ə/ [L, *calx*, lime; Gk, *ouron*, urine], the presence of calcium in the urine.

calcofluor white stain, a nonspecific fluorochrome stain that binds to cellulose and chitin in cell walls of fungi, *Pneumocystis jirovecii* cysts, and parasites. It is used to detect these organisms in clinical specimens.

calcospherite /kal'kəsfir'īt/, a spheric mass of calcium salts and organic matter found in an area of calcification.

calculogenesis /kal'kyəlōjen'əsis/, the formation of calculi.

calculous /kal'kyələs/, **1.** describing a substance that has the hardness of stone. **2.** pertaining to calculus.

calculous pyelonephritis, infection of the kidney in association with urinary calculi, which may be obstructive.

calculous pyonephrosis, pus and calculi in the kidney.

calculus /kal'kyələs/ *pl.* **calculi** [L, little stone], **1.** an abnormal stone formed in body tissues by an accumulation of mineral salts. Calculi are usually found in biliary and urinary tracts. **2.** (in dentistry) a deposit of calcium phosphate, calcium carbonate, and organic matter that accumulates on the teeth or a dental prosthesis.

Calderol, a trademark for a transport form of vitamin D (calcifediol).

Caldwell-Moloy pelvic classification /kôl'dwel məloi'/ [William E. Caldwell, American obstetrician, 1880–1943; Howard C. Moloy, American gynecologist, 1903–1953], a system for classifying the structure of the bony pelvis of the female. The types in this system are android, anthropoid, gynecoid, and platypelloid. The sacrum, coccyx, sidewalls, sacrosciatic notch, ischial spines, pubic arch, and ischial tuberosities are the anatomic points of reference used to determine pelvic type.

calefacient /kal'əfā'shənt/ [L, *calare*, to be warm, *facere*, to make], **1.** making or tending to make anything warm or hot. **2.** an agent that imparts a sense of warmth when applied, such as a hot-water bottle or a hot compress.

calf *pl.* **calves** [ONorse, *kalfi*], the fleshy mass at the back of the leg below the knee, composed chiefly of the gastrocnemius muscle.

calfactant, a natural lung surfactant extract used in the prevention and treatment (rescue) of respiratory distress syndrome in premature infants.

calf muscle pump, an action of the calf (soleus) muscles in which the muscles contract and squeeze the popliteal and tibial veins, forcing the blood in those veins to move upward toward the heart.

caliber /kal'ibər/ [Fr, *calibre,* the bore of a gun], **1.** the inside diameter of a tube or a canal, as any of the blood vessels. **2.** measure of quality.

calibration /kal'ibrā'shən/ [Fr, *calibre,* the bore of a gun], the process of measuring or calibrating against an established standard, such as a deciliter or kilogram.

calibrator, **1.** an instrument used to measure the size of an opening. **2.** an instrument used to increase the diameter of an opening, as a dilator of a urethral stricture.

Caliciviridae /kalis'ivir'idē/, a family of plus-stranded RNA viruses that have a nonenveloped virion 35 to 40 nm in diameter. It is associated with episodes of gastroenteritis in humans and animals.

caliculus /kalik'yələs/, a cup-shaped structure.

California encephalitis, arthropod-borne encephalitis or encephalomeningitis, induced by an arbovirus. Infection usually is caused by a mosquito bite. The infection generally follows one of two clinical courses: The mild form is characterized by headache, malaise, GI symptoms, and a fever that may reach 104° F. The more severe form may be marked by a sudden onset of fever, vomiting, headaches, lethargy, and signs of neurologic involvement such as loss of reflexes, disorientation, seizure, LOC, and flaccid paralysis. Recovery usually begins in 1 week. Mortality rate is very low, but a significant number of patients have neurologic sequelae for 1 year or more.

californium (Cf) [state of California], an artificial element in the actinide group. Its atomic number is 98; the atomic mass of its longest-lived isotope is 251. Californium-252 is a potent source of neutrons.

caliorraphy /kal'ə·ôr'əfē/, surgical repair of the calyces of the kidney, usually performed to improve urinary drainage into the ureters.

calipers /kal'ipərz/ [Fr, *calibre,* the bore of a gun], an instrument with two hinged, adjustable, curved legs, used to measure the thickness or the diameter of a convex or solid body. It is also used to measure space on a graph and in measuring ECG patterns.

caliper splint, a leg splint consisting of two metal rods running from the back of a band around the thigh or from a cushioned ring around the lower portion of the pelvis to a metal plate under the shoe below the arch of the foot.

calisthenics /kal'isthen'iks/, a system of exercise in which emphasis is on movements of muscle groups rather than power and effort. An objective is usually to elevate the heart rate for prolonged periods of time.

Calliphoridae /kal'əfôr'ədē/ [Gk, *kallos,* beauty, *pherein,* to bear], a family of medium-sized to large flies that belong to the order Diptera, serve as pathogenic vectors, and may cause intestinal or nasopharyngeal myiasis in humans.

callomania /kal'ōmā'nē·ə/ [Gk, *kallos,* beauty, *mania,* madness], an abnormal psychologic condition characterized by delusions of personal beauty.

callosal /kəlō'səl/ [L, *callosus,* hard], pertaining to the corpus callosum.

callosal agenesis, defect of the callosal structures of the brain; congenital absence of corpus callosum.

callosal fissure /kəlōs'əl/ [L, *callosus,* hard, *fissura,* cleft], a groove following the convex aspect of the corpus callosum.

callosomarginal fissure /kəlō'sōmär'jənəl/, a long, irregular groove on the medial surface of a cerebral hemisphere. It divides the cingulate gyrus from the medial frontal gyrus and from the paracentral lobule.

callous ulcer /kal'əs/ [L, *callosus,* hard, *ulcus,* ulcer], an ulcer with a hard indurated base and thick inelastic margins. It lacks a blood supply and is frequently associated with edema of the legs.

callus /kal'əs/ [L, hard skin], **1.** a common, usually painless thickening of the stratum corneum at locations of external pressure or friction. **2.** bony deposit formed between and around the broken ends of a fractured bone during healing. —**callous,** *adj.*

calmative /kä'mətiv/, having a calming or quieting effect.

calming technique, a nursing intervention from the Nursing Interventions Classification (NIC) defined as reducing anxiety in a patient experiencing acute distress.

calmodulin /kalmod'yəlin/, a calcium-binding protein that mediates a variety of biochemical and physiologic processes, including the contraction of smooth muscles and the release of norepinephrine.

calor /kal'ôr/ [L, warmth], heat, as that generated by inflammation of tissues or from the body's normal metabolic processes.

caloric /kalôr'ik/, pertaining to heat or calories.

caloric test, a procedure in which the ear canal is alternately irrigated with warm water or air and cold water or air. The warm irrigation produces a rotatory nystagmus toward the irrigated side. Cold irrigation produces a rotatory nystagmus away from the irrigated side. If the vestibular part of the ear is normal, all irrigations will produce nystagmus that is approximately equal in intensity. If the vestibular part of the ear is diseased, irrigation may produce less nystagmus than the normal ear.

calorie (cal) /kal'ôrē/ [L, *calor,* warmth], the amount of heat required to raise the temperature of 1 g of water 1° C at atmospheric pressure. —**caloric,** *adj.*

Calorie (Cal, kcal), 1. the amount of heat (energy) needed to raise the temperature of 1 kilogram of water 1° C. **2.** a unit, equal to the large calorie, used to denote the heat expenditure of an organism and the fuel and energy value of food.

calorific /kal'ərif'ik/, pertaining to the production of heat.

calorigenic /kalôr'ijen'ik/ [L, *calor,* warmth; Gk, *genein,* to produce], pertaining to a substance or process that produces heat or energy or increases the consumption of oxygen.

calorimeter /kal'ərim'ətər/, a device used for measuring quantities of heat generated by friction, chemical reaction, or the human body. —**calorimetric,** *adj.*

calorimetry /kal'ərim'ətrē/ [L, *calor,* warmth; Gk, *metron,* measure], the measurement of the amounts of heat radiated and the amounts of heat absorbed. —**calorimetric,** *adj.*

calvaria /kalver'ē·ə/, the skullcap or superior part of the skull, which varies greatly in shape from individual to individual.

calvities /kalvish'i·ēz/ [L, *calvus,* without hair], baldness. —**calvous,** *adj.*

calyceal fornix, the inner border of a renal calyx where it touches a papilla or papillae.

calyx /kā'liks/ *pl.* **calyces** /kal'isēz/, **calyxes** [Gk, *kalyx,* shell], **1.** a cup-shaped structure within an organ. **2.** a renal calyx. **3.** the wall of an ovarian follicle after expulsion of the ovum at ovulation.

CAM, abbreviation for **complementary and alternative medicine.**

cambium layer [L, *cambire,* to exchange], **1.** the loose inner cellular layer of the periosteum that develops during ossification. **2.** a cellular layer of formative tissue that lies between the wood and the bark in plants.

camera /kam'ərə/ [L, vaulted chamber], (in anatomy) any compartment, cavity, or chamber, as those of the eye, tooth, or heart.

Cameron ulcer, a peptic ulcer within a sliding hiatal hernia. It may be accompanied by chronic bleeding or be clinically silent.

Camey neobladder, a formerly widely used type of ileal neobladder made from a U-shaped section of ileum after a cystectomy.

cAMP, abbreviation for **cyclic adenosine monophosphate.**

Camper's fascia, the superficial fatty layer of the superficial fascia of the abdominal wall.

camphor /kam'fər/ [L, *camphora*], a colorless or white crystalline substance with a penetrating odor and pungent taste, occurring naturally in certain plants, especially *Cinnamomum camphora*.

camphorated oil /kam'fərā'tid/ [Malay, *kapur*, chalk; L, *oleum*, oil], a colorless-to-yellowish liquid with the penetrating, pungent odor of camphor. It is derived from a combination of a dozen organic chemicals, including terpenes, safrole, and acetaldehyde obtained from the camphor laurel plant. It is used mainly as a liniment, counterirritant, and rubefacient.

camphor bath, an air bath in which the air is filled with camphor vapor.

camphor liniment, a pharmaceutic preparation of 12.5% camphor, with alcohol, lavender oil, and ammonia, used as a rubefacient in the relief of rheumatic symptoms.

camphor poisoning, a severe toxic condition resulting from the accidental ingestion of camphorated oils. Symptoms may include headache, hallucinations, nausea, vomiting, diarrhea, convulsions, and kidney failure.

camphor salicylate, a crystalline substance formed by the fusion of 84 parts of camphor and 65 parts of salicylic acid, previously used in skin ointments and administered internally for diarrhea.

campimeter /kampim'ətər/, (in ophthalmology) an instrument for determining the integrity of the central field of vision.

Campral, a trademark for **acamprosate.**

camptocormia /kamp'tōkôr'mē-ə/, a condition in which the back is habitually tilted forward although the spinal column remains flexible. It is frequently diagnosed as a psychologic conversion, and there is often a history of trauma.

camptodactyly /kamp'tədaktəlē/ [Gk, *kamptos*, bent, *daktylos*, finger], the permanent flexion of one or more fingers. **—camptodactylic,** *adj.*

camptomelia /kamp'təmē'lyə/ [Gk, *kamptos*, bent, *melos*, arm], a congenital anomaly characterized by bending of one or more limbs, causing permanent bowing or curving of the affected area.—**camptomelic,** *adj.*

Campylobacter [Gk, *campylos*, curved, *bakterion*, small staff], a genus of bacteria found in the family Spirillaceae. The organisms consist of gram-negative, nonspore-forming, spirally curved motile rods that have a single polar flagellum at either or both ends of the cell. They move in a characteristic coil-like motion. The organisms are facultative aerobes requiring little or no oxygen for growth. The type species is *C. fetus*, which consists of several subspecies that cause human infections, as well as abortion and infertility in cattle.

Campylobacter enteritis, intestinal infection of humans or other mammals by a species of *Campylobacter*, characterized by diarrhea that may be bloody, abdominal pain with cramps, and fever. The cause is usually ingestion of contaminated food or water.

Campylobacter gastroenteritis, bacterial gastroenteritis in humans or other mammals, caused by infection with *Campylobacter jejuni*, most commonly acquired from contact with infected individuals; from consumption of contaminated food, water, or other beverages; or from exposure to contaminated objects or environmental surfaces. Infection is usually characterized by diarrhea that may be bloody, abdominal pain with cramps, and fever.

campylobacteriosis /kam'pəlōbaktēr'ē-ō'sis/,infection with organisms of the genus *Campylobacter*.

camsylate, shortened word form for *camphorsulfonate*.

Camurati-Engelmann disease [Mario Camurati, Italian physician, 1896–1948; Guido Engelmann, twentieth-century Czechoslovakian surgeon], an inherited disorder of bone development marked by onset of symptoms of muscular pain, weakness, and wasting, mainly in the legs, during childhood. The symptoms vary individually from mild to disabling. In some cases, compression of nerve tissue may occur. The symptoms usually subside during early adulthood.

CAN, abbreviation for **Center for American Nurses.**

Canadian Association of Occupational Therapists (CAOT), Canadian professional association for occupational therapists.

Canadian Association of University Schools of Nursing (CAUSN), a national Canadian organization of baccalaureate and higher degree programs in nursing in Canada.

Canadian Association of University Teachers (CAUT), a Canadian national organization representing the interests of all who teach in the universities of the provinces and territories of Canada. The official languages of the CAUT are English and French.

Canadian crutch, a wooden or metal device that helps a patient with impaired mobility to stand or walk. It consists of two uprights with a crosspiece to accommodate the hand and a concave crosspiece that fits the upper arm for support.

Canadian Journal of Public Health **(CJPH),** the official publication of the Canadian Public Health Association.

Canadian Medical Association Journal **(CMAJ),** the official publication of the Canadian Medical Association.

Canadian Nurses Association (CNA), the official national organization for the professional registered nurses of Canada who are members of the nine provincial nurses' associations, the Northwest Territories Registered Nurses Association, and the Yukon Registered Nurses Association. The chief objective of the CNA is to promote high standards of nursing practice, education, research, and administration to achieve high quality of nursing care in the interest of the people of Canada.

Canadian Nurses Association Testing Service (CNATS), the organizational affiliate of the Canadian Nurses Association concerned with testing graduates of approved schools of nursing to qualify them as registered nurses.

Canadian Nurses Foundation (CNF), a national Canadian foundation organized to support scholarship in nursing.

Canadian Nurses Respiratory Society (CNRS), an organization of nurses working with or interested in alleviating the problems of respiratory disease.

Canadian Orthopedic Nurses Association (CONA), a national Canadian organization concerned with the nursing care of orthopedic patients and the continuing education of nurses working in orthopedics.

Canadian Public Health Association (CPHA), a national Canadian organization concerned with issues in public health and epidemiology.

canal /kənal′/ [L,*canalis*,channel], **1.** (in anatomy) a narrow tube or channel. **2.** (in dentistry) one of the accessory root canals and collateral pulp canals in the teeth.

canalicular /kan′əlik′yələr/, pertaining to a small canal.

canalicular period, the period or phase of prenatal lung development lasting in different parts of the lungs from the sixteenth or seventeenth week to the twenty-sixth week or later and followed by the terminal saccular period. Basic structures of the gas-exchanging parts of the lungs form and become vascular, and primordial alveoli called the terminal saccules begin to form, enabling respiration to begin.

canalicular testis, an undescended testis located between the internal and external inguinal rings.

canaliculus /kan′əlik′yələs/ *pl.* **canaliculi** [L, little channel], a very small tube or channel, such as the microscopic haversian canaliculi throughout bone tissue.

canaliculus of chorda tympani, a small canal that opens off the facial canal just before its termination, transmitting the chorda tympani nerve into the tympanic cavity.

canalization /kan′əlizā′shən/, the formation of canals or passages through any tissue.

canal obturation, in root canal therapy, the filling of the pulp, or root, canal completely and densely with a nonirritating hermetic sealing agent.

canal of Corti [Alfonso Corti, Italian anatomist, 1822–1888], a space between the inner and outer rods and the basilar membrane of the cochlea in the organ of Corti.

canal of Schlemm /shlem/ [Friedrich Schlemm, German anatomist, 1795–1858], a tiny vein at the angle of the anterior chamber of the eye that connects with the pectinate villi, draining the aqueous humor and funneling it into the bloodstream.

canavanine /kan′əvan′in/, an amino acid antagonist present in alfalfa sprouts that can displace arginine in cellular proteins, thereby rendering them inactive.

cancellous /kan′siləs/ [L, *cancellus,* lattice], (of tissue) lattice-like, porous, spongy. Cancellous tissue is normally present in the interior of many bones, where the spaces are usually filled with marrow.

cancellous bone, a reticular lattice-like arrangement of bony plates and trabeculae occurring at the ends of the long bones.

cancer /kan′sər/ [L, crab], **1.** a neoplasm characterized by the uncontrolled growth of anaplastic cells that tend to invade surrounding tissue and to metastasize to distant body sites. **2.** any of a large group of malignant neoplastic diseases characterized by the presence of malignant cells. Each cancer is distinguished by the nature, site, or clinical course of the lesion. The basis of cancer is believed to reside in alterations in DNA (genes), usually at several loci, but many potential causes are recognized. Cancer is second only to heart disease as a cause of mortality in the United States and is a leading cause of death in children between 3 and 14 years of age.

cancericidal /kan'sərisĭ'dəl/ [L, *cancer,* crab, *caedere,* to kill], pertaining to a substance or procedure capable of destroying cancer cells.

cancer of the small intestine, a neoplastic disease of the duodenum, jejunum, or ileum. Its characteristics vary, depending on the kind of tumor and the site, but may include abdominal pain, vomiting, weight loss, diarrhea, intermittent bowel obstruction, GI bleeding, or a mass in the right abdomen. Adenocarcinomas, the most common tumors, occur more frequently in the duodenum or upper jejunum and form polypoid or constricting napkin-ring growths. Lymphomas, found most often in the lower small intestine, may impair bowel motility by invading nerves and in some cases are associated with a malabsorption syndrome.

cancerous /kan'sərəs/ [L, *cancer,* crab, *oma,* tumor], pertaining to or resembling a cancer.

cancer staging, a system for describing the size and extent of spread of a malignant tumor, used to plan treatment and predict prognosis. Staging may involve a physical examination, diagnostic procedures, surgical exploration, and histologic examination. The system developed by the American Joint Committee for Cancer Staging and End Results Reporting uses the letter *T* to represent the tumor, *N* for the regional lymph node involvement, *M* for distant metastases, and numeric subscripts in each category to indicate the degree of dissemination.

cancriform /kang'krifôrm'/ [L, *cancer,* crab, *forma,* form], pertaining to a lesion resembling a cancer.

cancroid [L, *cancer,* crab; Gk, *eidos,* form], **1.** pertaining to a lesion resembling a cancer. **2.** a moderately malignant skin cancer.

cancrum /kang'krəm/, a gangrenous, ulcerative, inflammatory condition.

candesartan, an antihypertensive in the angiotensin II receptor antagonist class. It is used to treat hypertension, either alone or in combination with other drugs.

Candida /kan'didə/ [L, *candidus,* white], a genus of yeast.

Candida albicans /al'bəkanz/, a common budding yeast; a microscopic fungal organism normally present in the mucous membranes of the mouth, intestinal tract, and vagina of healthy people. Under certain circumstances, it may cause superficial infections of the skin, mouth, or vagina. Infection of the esophagus and severe invasive systemic infections may occur in persons with HIV.

Candida endocarditis, mycotic endocarditis caused by a species of *Candida.*

Candida guilliermondii, a species that sometimes causes cutaneous candidiasis, onychomycosis, meningitis, and endocarditis.

Candida kefyr, an opportunistic species that occasionally causes human disease and has been isolated from nails and pulmonary specimens.

Candida krusei, an extremely rare non-albicans species of *Candida* occasionally associated with candidiasis, esophagitis, endocarditis, and vaginitis.

Candida lusitaniae, an extremely rare species that causes opportunistic infections in humans. This species often demonstrates resistance to amphotericin B, the major antifungal antimicrobial used to treat invasive infections and mycoses.

Candida peritonitis, peritonitis caused by a species of *Candida,* usually as a complication of peritoneal dialysis, with symptoms that include abdominal pain with or without mild fever, nausea, and vomiting.

Candida stellatoidea, a species that sometimes causes *Candida* vaginitis or endocarditis. It is closely related to *Candida albicans.*

candidiasis /kan'didĭ'əsis/ [L, *candidus*; Gk, *osis,* condition], any infection caused by a species of *Candida,* usually *Candida albicans.* The nails, rectum, and skinfolds are sites of infection. Diaper rash, intertrigo, vaginitis, conjunctivitis, and thrush are common topical manifestations of candidiasis.

candiru fever /kan'dĭroo'/, an arbovirus infection transmitted to humans by the bite of a sandfly, characterized by an acute fever, headache, and muscle aches.

candle [L, *candela,* light], (in optics) the basic unit of measurement for luminous intensity, equal to 1/60 of the luminous intensity of a square centimeter of a black body heated to 1773.51°/4° C or the solidification temperature of platinum, adopted in 1948 as the international standard of luminous intensity.

candy-striper *informal.* a hospital volunteer, named for the striped pink and white uniforms formerly worn by the young women who originally performed this service.

cane [Ar, *qanah,* reed], a sturdy wooden or metal shaft or walking stick used to give support and mobility during walking to a person with impaired mobility.

cane sugar, sucrose from sugar cane.

canine fossa /kā'nīn/ [L, *canis,* dog + ditch], (in dentistry) either of the wide depressions on the external surface of each maxilla, superolateral to the canine tooth socket.

canine tooth, any of the four teeth, one on each side of the upper and lower jaws, situated between the lateral incisor and the first premolar. The canine teeth are larger and stronger than the incisors and have characteristics of both anterior and posterior teeth. They project beyond the occlusal level of the other teeth in both arches. Their roots sink deeply into the bones, causing marked prominences on the alveolar arch. The deciduous canines erupt about 16 to 20 months after birth, whereas the permanent canines erupt during the eleventh or twelfth year of life.

canities /kanish′i-ēz/, loss of pigment, as in the graying of hair or the appearance of white streaks in the nails.

canker /kang′kər/ [L, *cancer*, crab], an ulcer or sore in the mouth or genitals.

canker sore, an ulcerous lesion of the mouth, characteristic of aphthous stomatitis. It is hereditary and not contagious.

cannabis /kan′əbis/ [Gk, *kannabis*, hemp], a psychoactive herb (marijuana) derived from the flowering tops of hemp plants. It has limited clinical use in the United States (where it is marketed as marinol) as an antiemetic in some cancer patients to counter the nausea and vomiting associated with chemotherapy. Cannabis is controlled under Schedule I of the Controlled Substances Act of 1970. All parts of the plant contain psychoactive substances. Tetrahydrocannabinol is believed to cause the most characteristic psychologic effects, which include alterations of mood, memory, motor coordination, cognitive ability, and self-perception.

cannon A wave [L, *cane*, tube; AS, *wafian*], a powerful atrial wave in the jugular venous pulse, caused by the contraction of the right atrium against a closed tricuspid valve. Rapid, regular cannon A waves are diagnostic of paroxysmal supraventricular tachycardia. Irregular cannon A waves are seen in atrioventricular dissociation and are therefore especially helpful in the diagnosis of ventricular tachycardia.

cannula /kan′yələ/ *pl.* **cannulas, cannulae** [L, small tube], a flexible tube that may be inserted into a duct or cavity to deliver medication or drain fluid. —**cannular, cannulate,** *adj.*

cannulation /kan′yəlā′shən/, the insertion of a cannula into a body duct or cavity, as into the trachea, bladder, or a blood vessel. —**cannulate, cannulize,** *v.*

cantering rhythm [Gk, *rhythmos*, beat], a pattern of three heart sounds in each cardiac cycle, resembling the canter of a horse.

cantharis /kan′thäris/ *pl.* **cantharides** [Gk, *kantharis*, beetle], the dried insect *Cantharis vesicatoria*, which contains cantharidin, formerly used as a topical vesicant to remove warts.

canthoplasty /kan′thōplas′tē/, a form of plastic surgery used to lengthen the palpebral fissure through the lateral canthus or to restore a defective canthus.

canthorraphy /kanthôr′əfē/, surgery to suture the eyelids at either canthus.

canthus /kan′thəs/ *pl.* **canthi** [Gk, *kanthus*, corner of the eye], the angle at the medial and lateral margins of the eyelids. —**canthic,** *adj.*

Cantil, a trademark for an anticholinergic antispasmodic (mepenzolate bromide).

Cantor tube [Meyer O. Cantor, American physician, b. 1907], a long, single-lumen nasoenteric tube with a small, sealed, mercury-filled rubber bag at the distal end, used to relieve obstructions in the small intestine. The tube also contains drainage holes to allow for aspiration of intestinal contents.

CaO, chemical formula for calcium oxide.

Ca(OH)$_2$, chemical formula for calcium hydroxide.

CAOT, abbreviation for **Canadian Association of Occupational Therapists.**

cap, abbreviation for Latin *capiat,* "let him or her take," used in prescriptions.

CAP, 1. abbreviation for **College of American Pathologists. 2.** (in molecular genetics) abbreviation for *catabolic activator protein.*

capacitance *(C)* /kəpas′itəns/, a measure of electrostatic capacity or the amount of stored electric charge per unit of electric potential.

capacitance vessels [L, *capacitas,* capacity], **1.** the blood vessels that hold the major part of the intravascular blood volume. **2.** the veins.

capacitation /kəpas′itā′shən/, the process in which the spermatozoon, after it reaches the ampulla of the fallopian tube, undergoes a series of changes that lead to its ability to fertilize an ovum.

capacity /kəpas′i-tē/ [L, *capacitas*], **1.** power or ability to hold, retain, or contain, or the ability to absorb. **2.** mental ability to receive, accomplish, endure, or understand. **3.** the volume or potential volume of material (solid, liquid, or gas) that can be held or contained.

capacity factor /kəpas′itē/ [L, *capacitas* + *factum,* to make], the ratio of the elution volume of a substance to the void volume in the column.

Capastat, a trademark for an antibiotic (capreomycin).

CAPD, abbreviation for **continuous ambulatory peritoneal dialysis.**

capecitabine, an antineoplastic and antimetabolite used to treat metastatic colorectal and breast cancers.

capeline bandage /kap′əlin/ [Fr, hooded cape], a covering applied like a cap. It is used for protecting the head, the shoulder, or a stump.

Capgras' syndrome /käpgrä′/ [Jean Marie Joseph Capgras, French psychiatrist, 1873–1950], a form of delusional misidentification in which the patient believes that other persons in the environment are not their real selves but doubles.

Capillaria /kap′ilarē′ə/ [L, *capillaris*, hairlike], a genus of nematodes of the family Trichuridae. *C. philippinensis* is a parasite of the human intestine in the Philippines.

capillariasis /kap′ilərī′əsis/, infection with nematodes of the genus *Capillaria*. Human infection is usually by *C. philippinensis*, which infests the intestines and causes severe diarrhea, malabsorption, and often death. More rarely, infection with *C. hepatica* can cause human hepatic capillariasis, and *C. aerophila* can cause human pulmonary capillariasis.

capillaritis /kap′ilərī′tis/ [L, *capillaris*, hairlike; Gk, *itis*, inflammation], inflammation of a capillary or capillaries characterized by a progressive pigmentary disorder of the skin and capillaries. It does not involve any systemic problems and runs a benign self-limiting course.

capillary /kap′ilerē/ [L, *capillaris*, hairlike], one of the microscopic blood vessels (about 0.008 mm in diameter) joining arterioles and venules. The wall consists of a single layer of endothelial cells, which are specialized squamous epithelial cells. Blood and tissue fluids exchange various substances across these walls.

capillary action, the process involving molecular adhesion by which the surface of a liquid in a tube is either elevated or depressed, depending on the cohesiveness of the liquid molecules.

capillary bed, a capillary network.

capillary blood sample, a nursing intervention from the Nursing Interventions Classification (NIC) defined as obtaining an arteriovenous sample from a peripheral body site, such as the heel, finger, or other transcutaneous site.

capillary fracture, any thin, hairlike break in a bone.

capillary fragility, a condition in which weakened capillaries rupture easily when stressed, observed as bleeding under the skin.

capillary hemangioma, a blood-filled birthmark or benign tumor consisting of closely packed small blood vessels. Commonly found during infancy, it first grows, then may spontaneously disappear in early childhood without treatment.

capillary hemorrhage, an oozing of blood from the capillaries.

capillary permeability [L, *capillaris*, hairlike, *permeare*, to pass through], a condition of the capillary wall structure that allows blood elements and waste products to pass through the capillary wall to tissue spaces.

capillary pressure [L, *capillaris*, hairlike, *premere*, to press], the BP within a capillary.

capillary refilling, the process whereby blood returns to a portion of the capillary system after its blood supply has been interrupted briefly. A capillary refill time of more than 3 seconds is considered a sign of sluggish digital circulation, and a time of 5 seconds is regarded as abnormal.

capillary tufting, an abnormal condition in which pulmonary capillaries project as tufts, or small masses, into the alveoli.

capillus /kəpil′əs/ pl. **capilli** [L, filament], one of the hairs of the body, especially one of the hairs of the scalp.

capital /kap′itəl/ [L, *caput*, head], 1. of the highest importance; involving danger to life. 2. of or pertaining to the head of the femur.

capitate /kap′itāt/, having the shape of a head.

capitate bone [L, *caput*, head; AS, *ban*], one of the largest carpal bones, located at the center of the wrist and having a rounded head that fits the concavity of the scaphoid and the lunate bones.

capitation, a payment method for health care services. The physician, hospital, or other health care provider is paid a contracted rate for each member assigned, referred to as "per-member-per-month" rate, regardless of the number or nature of services provided. The contractual rates are usually adjusted for age, gender, illness, and regional differences.

capitulum /kəpich′ələm/ pl. **capitula** [L, small head], 1. a small, rounded prominence on a bone where it articulates with another bone. 2. the lateral humeral condyle.

capitulum of the humerus, a rounded eminence at the distal end of the humerus that articulates with the radius.

Caplan's syndrome [Anthony Caplan, English physician, 1907–1976], a condition of pneumoconiosis with symptoms of rheumatoid arthritis and radiographic evidence of intrapulmonary nodules. It is caused by inhalation of coal dust and results in inflammation and scarring of the lungs.

capnograph /kap′nəgraf′/ [Gk, *kapnos*, smoke, *graphein*, to record], an instrument used in anesthesia, intensive care, and respiratory therapy to produce a capnogram, a tracing that shows the proportion of carbon dioxide in exhaled air.

capnometry /kapnom′ətrē/, the measurement of carbon dioxide in a volume of gas. The most common monitoring units are based on the selective absorption of infrared light by carbon dioxide and water vapor.

capotement /käpōtmäN′, kəpōt′mənt/, a splashing sound made by fluid movements in a dilated stomach that contains air and fluid.

Capoten, a trademark for an angiotensin-converting enzyme inhibitor (captopril).

capping, a process by which cell-surface molecules aggregate on a plasma membrane.

cap polyposis, a rare type of polyposis coli in which inflammatory polyps have elongated crypts and caps of purulent, fibrinous exudate.

capreomycin /kap′rē·ōmī′sin/, an antibiotic and antitubercular agent prescribed in the treatment of pulmonary infections caused by capreomycin-susceptible strains of *Mycobacterium tuberculosis* when the primary agents are ineffective or cannot be used.

capric acid (CH$_3$(CH$_2$)$_8$COOH) /kap′rik/ [L, *caper,* goat], a white crystalline carboxylic acid with a rancid odor, occurring as a glyceride in natural oils. Capric acid is used in the production of perfumes, flavors, wetting agents, and food additives.

caprizant /kap′rizant/, describing an irregular leaping or bounding pulse.

caproic acid (CH$_3$(CH$_2$)$_4$COOH) /kaprō′ik/, a carboxylic acid present in milk fat and some plant oils. It is used in the production of artificial flavors.

capsaicin /kapsā′isin/, an alkaloid irritating to the skin and mucous membranes, the pungent active principle in capsicum. It is used in a cream that is a counterirritant and topical analgesic, and also in pepper spray.

capsicum, a herbal product derived from peppers native to tropical areas of the Americas. It is used for muscle spasms, the pain of inflammation, neuromas, psoriasis, and dry mouth. It is also used as a food antioxidant and as a food seasoning.

capsid /kap′sid/ [L, *capsa,* box], the layer of protein enveloping the genome of a virion.

capsomere /kap′səmir/, one of the building blocks of a viral capsid. It consists of groups of identical protein molecules and is visible in an electron microscope.

capsular /kap′sələr/ [L, *capsula,* little box], pertaining to or resembling a small container.

capsular pattern, a series of limitations of joint movement when the joint capsule is a limiting structure. It occurs only in synovial joints that are controlled by muscles and not in joints that depend primarily on ligamentous stability, such as the sacroiliac.

capsular swelling test, the swelling of capsules of bacteria when they are mixed with their specific antigen.

capsular vascular plexus, a plexus somewhere around or within the renal capsule.

capsulation /kap′syoō·lā′shən/ [L, *capsula,* little box], the enclosure of a medicine in a capsule.

capsule /kap′syəl, kap′səl/ *pl.* capsuli [L, *capsula,* little box], 1. a small soluble container, usually made of gelatin, used for enclosing a dose of medication for swallowing. 2. a membranous shell surrounding certain microorganisms, such as the pneumococcus bacterium. 3. a well-defined anatomic structure that encloses an organ or part, such as the capsule of the adrenal gland.

capsulectomy /kap′səlek′təmē/, the surgical excision of a capsule, usually the capsule of a joint or of the lens of the eye.

capsule of the kidney, the fibrous connective enclosure of the kidney.

capsulitis /-ī′tis/ [L, *capsula,* little box; Gk, *itis,* inflammation], inflammation of an anatomic capsule.

capsuloma /kap′səlō′mə/ *pl.* capsulomas, capsulomata [L, *capsula*; Gk, *oma,* tumor], a neoplasm of the capsule or the subcapsular area of the kidney.

capsuloplasty /kap′səlōplas′tē/, plastic surgery performed on the capsule of a joint.

capsulorraphy /kap′səlôr′əfē/, surgical repair of a tear in the capsule of a joint.

capsulorrhexis /kap′səlōrek′sis/, a surgical technique in which a continuous circular tear in the anterior capsule is made in the crystalline lens to allow phacoemulsification of the lens nucleus during cataract surgery.

capsulotomy /kap′səlot′əmē/ [L, *capsula*; Gk, *temnein,* to cut], an incision into a capsule, such as in an operation to remove a cataract.

captain-of-the-ship doctrine, the historical medicolegal principle that the physician is ultimately responsible for all patient-care activities and that he or she thus may be held accountable and may be sued for negligence or malpractice when the act at issue is performed by an employee or other person under the physician's control, even if not ordered by the physician.

captive reinsurance company, a reinsurance company organized to serve only one client.

captopril /kap'tōpril/, an angiotensin-converting enzyme inhibitor prescribed for the treatment of hypertension and CHF.

capture /kap'chər/, **1.** the catching and holding of a nuclear particle, as an electron, or an electric impulse originating elsewhere. **2.** (in cardiology) the capture of control of the atria or ventricles after a period of independent beating caused by ectopic beats or an atrioventricular block. **3.** (in cardiology) the ability of a pacemaker to electrically stimulate a cardiac chamber.

capture beat, the return of atrial control over ventricular contraction, following a period of atrioventricular dissociation.

capture-recapture method, a plan for epidemiologic studies of health problems such as AIDS, substance abuse, or prostitution. The method provides for comparative analysis of data from various independent sources and adjusting for missing cases.

caput /kā'pət, kap'ət/ pl. **capita** [L, head], **1.** the head. **2.** the enlarged or prominent extremity of an organ or part.

caput femoris /fem'əris/, the head of the femur. It articulates with the acetabulum.

caput fibulae /fib'yəlē/, the head of the fibula. It articulates with the lateral condyle of the tibia.

caput humeri /hyoo'mərī/, the head of the humerus. It articulates with the glenoid cavity of the scapula.

caput mallei /mal'ē·ī/, the head of the malleus. It articulates with the incus.

caput mandibulae /mandib'yəlē/, the articular process of the ramus of the mandible.

caput medusae /mədoo'sē/ [L, head of Medusa (a mythical snake-haired Gorgon)], a pattern of dilated cutaneous veins radiating from the umbilical area of a newborn. The feature is also observed in adults with cirrhosis of the liver with portal hypertension.

caput ossis metacarpalis, the metacarpal head. It articulates with the proximal phalanx of the same digit.

caput phalangis /falan'jis/, the articular head at the distal end of the proximal and middle phalanges.

caput radii /rā'dē·ī/, the head of the radius. It articulates with the capitulum of the humerus.

caput stapedis /stapē'dis/, the head of the stapes.

caput succedaneum /suk'sədənē'əm/ [L, caput, head, succeder, to replace], a localized pitting edema in the scalp of a fetus that may overlie sutures of the skull. It is usually formed during labor as a result of the circular pressure of the cervix on the fetal occiput.

Carabelli's cusp [Georg Carabelli, Austrian dentist, 1787–1842], an accessory cusp usually found on the mesiolingual cusp of a maxillary permanent first molar. It may be unilateral or bilateral and varies in size.

Carafate, a trademark for an antiulcer drug that forms a protective layer over the ulcer site (sucralfate).

caramiphen /käram'ifen/, an anticholinergic agent with actions similar to but weaker than those of atropine. The edisylate ester is administered orally as an antitussive, and the hydrochloride ester is administered orally in the treatment of Parkinson's disease.

carapace /kar'əpās/ [Sp, carapacho, hard shell], a horny shield or shell covering the dorsal surface of an animal such as a turtle.

carb, abbreviation for **carbonate.**

carbam, abbreviation for a carbamate carboxylate anion.

carbamate /kär'bəmāt/, any of a group of anticholinesterase enzymes that cause reversible inhibition of cholinesterase. They are used in certain medications and insecticides. Some carbamates are toxic and may cause convulsions and death through ingestion or skin contact. Atropine is a commonly recommended antidote.

carbamate kinase, a liver enzyme that catalyzes the transfer of a phosphate group from adenosine triphosphate, associated with ammonia and carbon dioxide, to form adenosine diphosphate and carbamoylphosphate.

carbamazepine /kär'bəmaz'əpin/, an anticonvulsant and specific analgesic. It is often a drug of choice for treating partial seizures, generalized tonic-clonic seizures, and other mixed seizures. It is prescribed in the treatment of trigeminal and glossopharyngeal neuralgia and has unlabeled uses for certain affective disorders (e.g., bipolar disorder).

carbamide peroxide /kär'bəmīd/, a topical antiinfective prescribed to treat canker sores and other minor inflammatory conditions of the gums and mouth and to soften impacted earwax.

carbamino compound /kärbam'inō/, a chemical compound formed by the binding of carbon dioxide molecules to plasma proteins.

carbaminohemoglobin, a chemical complex formed by carbon dioxide and hemoglobin after the release of oxygen by the hemoglobin to a tissue cell. The action is similar to that of the formation of a carbamino compound. It accounts for nearly 25% of the carbon dioxide released in the lung.

carbenicillin disodium /kär'bənəsil'in/, a semisynthetic penicillin antibiotic with an extended spectrum that includes *Pseudomonas aeruginosa*. It is prescribed in the treatment of certain infections caused by sensitive gram-negative aerobic bacilli.

carbetapentane /kärbä'täpen'tān/, an antitussive agent with mild atropine-like antisecretory activity used as the tannate salt in treatment of cough associated with upper respiratory infections.

carbide, a binary compound of carbon. The various compounds range in stability from explosive copper or silver carbides to hard abrasive compounds, such as silicon carbide.

carbidopa /kär'bidō'pə/, a dopa decarboxylase inhibitor that cannot cross the blood-brain barrier. It is prescribed in combination with levodopa in the treatment of idiopathic Parkinson's disease.

carbinoxamine maleate /kär'bənok'səmēn/, an antihistamine found in some fixed-combination cold and allergy medications. It is prescribed in the treatment of allergic reactions, including rhinitis, skin reactions, and itching.

Carbocaine hydrochloride, a trademark for a local anesthetic (mepivacaine hydrochloride).

carbohydrate /kär'bōhī'drāt/ [L, *carbo,* coal; Gk, *hydor,* water], any of a group of organic compounds, the most important of which are the saccharides, starch, cellulose, and glycogen. Carbohydrates constitute the main source of energy for all body functions, particularly brain functions, and are necessary for the metabolism of other nutrients. They are synthesized by all green plants and in the body are either absorbed immediately or stored in the form of glycogen. Current dietary goals of the United States recommend that carbohydrates provide 55% to 60% of total calories. Cereals, vegetables, fruits, rice, potatoes, legumes, and flour products are the major sources of carbohydrates.

carbohydrate intolerance, inability to properly metabolize one or more carbohydrates, as in fructose intolerance and glucose intolerance.

carbohydrate loading, a dietary practice of some endurance athletes, such as marathon runners, intended to increase glycogen stores in the muscle tissue. The current approach advocates that athletes routinely consume the high-carbohydrate diet recommended for the general population (55% to 60% of total calories) and eat extra carbohydrates (70%) for 3 days before an event. The practice is controversial and is not universally accepted.

carbohydrate metabolism, the sum of the anabolic and catabolic processes of the body involved in the synthesis and breakdown of carbohydrates, principally glucose, fructose, and galactose. Some of the processes are glycogenesis and glycolysis. Energy-rich phosphate bonds are produced in many metabolic reactions requiring carbohydrates.

carbohydrate utilization test, any of several tests for identification of yeasts and certain other organisms according to a profile of carbohydrate assimilation.

carbolated camphor /kär'bōlā'tid/ [L, *carbo,* coal, *camphora*], a mixture of 1.5 parts camphor with 1 part each of alcohol and phenol, sometimes used as an antiseptic dressing for wounds.

carbol-fuchsin solution /kär'bolfŏŏk'sin/ [L, *carbo,* coal; Leonard Fuchs, German botanist, 1501–1566], a preparation used in the treatment of superficial fungal infections. It contains boric acid, phenol, resorcinol, fuchsin, acetone, and alcohol in water.

carbol-fuchsin stain [L, *carbo,* coal; Leonard Fuchs], a solution of dilute phenol and basic fuchsin used on microorganisms and cell nuclei for microscopic examination.

carbolic acid (C_6H_5OH) /kärbol'ik/ [L, *carbo,* coal, *acidus,* sour], a poisonous, colorless to pale pink crystalline compound obtained from coal tar distillation or oxidation of cumene, and converted to a clear liquid with a strong odor and burning taste by the addition of 10% water.

carbolism /kär'bōliz'əm/, poisoning by phenol, also known as carbolic acid.

carbon (C) /kär'bən/ [L, *carbo,* coal], a nonmetallic, almost always tetravalent element. Its atomic number is 6; its atomic mass is 12.011. Carbon occurs in pure form in diamonds, graphite, and fullerenes and is a component of all living tissue. The study of organic chemistry focuses on the vast number of carbon compounds. Carbon is essential to the chemical mechanisms of the body, participating in many metabolic processes and acting as a component of carbohydrates, amino acids, triglycerides, DNA and RNA, and many other compounds.

carbon-11 (^{11}C), a radioisotope of carbon with a half-life of 20 minutes. It is produced by a cyclotron and emits positrons.

carbon-13 (^{13}C), a naturally occurring isotope of carbon, with an atomic mass of 13, occurring 1.11% of the time. It is used as a tracer in liver function tests and a few metabolic tests.

carbon-14 (^{14}C), a beta-emitter with a half-life of about 5700 years. It occurs naturally, arising from cosmic rays, and is used as a tracer in studying various aspects of metabolism and in dating relics that contain natural carbonaceous materials.

carbon arc lamp, an electric lamp producing a strong white light of adjustable intensity from an arc of current between carbon electrodes.

carbonate (CO$_3^{2-}$) /kär′bənāt/, a CO$_3^{2-}$ anion. Carbonates are in equilibrium with bicarbonates in water and frequently occur in compounds as insoluble salts, such as calcium carbonate.

carbon cycle, the steps by which carbon in the form of carbon dioxide is extracted from and returned to the atmosphere by living organisms. The process starts with the photosynthetic production of carbohydrates by plants, progresses through the consumption of carbohydrates by animals and human beings, and ends with the exhalation of carbon dioxide by those same animals and human beings and with the release of carbon dioxide during the decomposition of dead plants and animals.

carbon dioxide (CO$_2$) [L, *carbo*; Gk, *dis*, twice, *oxys*, sharp], a colorless, odorless gas produced by the oxidation of carbon. Carbon dioxide, as a product of cell respiration, is carried by the blood to the lungs and is exhaled. The acid-base balance of body fluids and tissues is affected by the level of carbon dioxide and its carbonate compounds. Solid carbon dioxide (dry ice) is used in the treatment of some skin conditions.

carbon dioxide bath, a bath taken in water that is saturated with carbon dioxide.

carbon dioxide content (CO$_2$ content) test, a blood test used to measure CO$_2$ content in the blood. It is used to assist in evaluating the patient's pH status and electrolytes.

carbon dioxide inhalation, a procedure in which high concentrations of carbon dioxide gas are administered to stimulate breathing in a patient, sometimes as a part of resuscitation efforts.

carbon dioxide (CO$_2$) narcosis, a condition of confusion, tremors, convulsions, and possible coma that may occur if blood levels of carbon dioxide increase to 70 mm Hg or higher. Individuals with COPD can have CO$_2$ narcosis without these symptoms because they develop a tolerance to elevated CO$_2$. When ventilation is sufficient to maintain a normal oxygen partial pressure in the arteries, the carbon dioxide partial pressure is generally near 40 mm Hg.

carbon dioxide poisoning, a condition of toxic effects caused by inhaling excessive amounts of carbon dioxide. High concentrations of 10% or greater can cause unconsciousness and death from ventilatory failure. Particularly vulnerable are persons who work in confined spaces with poor air circulation. Faulty home furnaces also have been implicated in many deaths.

carbon dioxide response, the ventilatory reaction to increased concentrations of carbon dioxide in inhaled air. The respiration rate increases linearly up to a concentration of 8% to 10%, rises more gradually up to a concentration of about 20%, and decreases at higher concentrations. At concentrations of around 25%, the person is conscious but unable to perform simple tasks. At concentrations of 30%, carbon dioxide is an anesthetic.

carbon dioxide retention, any increased body stores of carbon dioxide resulting from impaired carbon dioxide elimination in conditions such as alveolar hypoventilation, strangulation, apnea, and ventilation-perfusion abnormalities. Respiratory acidosis may result from carbon dioxide retention.

carbon dioxide slush, solid carbon dioxide combined with a solvent, such as acetone, and sometimes also alcohol, used as an escharotic to treat skin lesions, such as warts and moles, and as a peeling agent in chemabrasion.

carbon dioxide stores, the amount of carbon dioxide contained in the body as a gas and in the form of carbonic acid, carbonate, bicarbonate, and carbaminohemoglobin. During a steady state of ventilation and aerobic respiration, the rate at which carbon dioxide leaves the body equals the rate at which it is produced, and carbon dioxide stores remain constant.

carbon dioxide tension (PCO$_2$), the partial pressure of carbon dioxide, a measure of the relative concentration of the gas in air or in a fluid, such as plasma. It is expressed quantitatively in millimeters of mercury (mm Hg). Alveolar PCO$_2$ directly reflects pulmonary gas exchange in relation to blood flow: alveolar PCO$_2$ usually decreases as the respiration rate increases. Normal values for arterial and alveolar PCO$_2$ are between 35 and 45 mm Hg.

carbon dioxide therapy, the therapeutic inhalation of a low concentration of carbon dioxide gas. Such therapy may be used to dilate the blood vessels, stimulate the cardiovascular brain centers and CNS, overcome hyperventilation, assist in developing a productive cough needed to remove mucous secretions, and control hiccups.

carbon dioxide titration curve, a line plotted on a graph showing the blood pH and total carbon dioxide concentration changes that result from the addition or removal of carbon dioxide.

carbonemia /kär″bənē′mē·ə/, excessive carbonic acid in the blood.

carbon fiber, a material consisting of graphite fibers in a plastic matrix. It is used in radiologic devices to reduce patient exposure to x-rays.

carbonic acid (H_2CO_3) /kärbon′ik/ [L, *carbo,* coal, *acidus,* acid], an unstable acid formed by dissolving carbon dioxide in water. It is the basis of carbonated beverages and is related to the carbonate group of compounds. Its production in the body is catalyzed by carbonic anhydrase.

carbonic anhydrase /anhī′drās/, a zinc-containing enzyme in RBCs that assists in the hydration of carbon dioxide to carbonic acid in the RBC so that it can be transported from the tissue cell to the lungs.

carbonic anhydrase inhibitor, a substance that decreases the rate of carbonic acid and H^+ production in the kidney, thereby increasing the excretion of solutes and the rate of urinary output.

carbon monoxide (CO) [L, *carbo;* Gk, *monos,* single, *oxys,* sharp], a colorless, odorless, poisonous gas produced by the combustion of carbon or organic fuels in a limited oxygen supply, as in the cylinders of an internal combustion engine or an improperly set oil or gas furnace. CO combines irreversibly with hemoglobin, preventing the formation of oxyhemoglobin and reducing the oxygen supply to the tissues. Prolonged exposure to high levels of carbon monoxide results in asphyxiation.

carbon monoxide poisoning, a toxic condition in which carbon monoxide gas has been inhaled and binds to hemoglobin molecules, thus displacing oxygen from the RBCs and decreasing the capacity of the blood to carry oxygen to the cells of the body. Characteristically, headache, dyspnea, drowsiness, confusion, cherry-pink skin, unconsciousness, and apnea occur in sequence as the level of carbon monoxide in the blood increases. Cherry-red skin is a late sign most commonly noted in fatalities.

carbon tetrachloride (CCl_4) [L, *carbo;* Gk, *tetra,* four, *chloros,* greenish], a colorless, volatile toxic liquid used as a solvent.

carbon tetrachloride poisoning [L, *carbo,* coal; Gk, *tetra,* four, *chloros,* greenish; L, *potio,* drink], toxic effects of exposure to carbon tetrachloride. It may attack both liver and kidneys. Symptoms include persistent headache, nausea, vomiting, diarrhea, uremia, lethargy, confusion resulting from CNS depression, and degeneration of the liver and kidneys. In poisoning by inhalation, ventilatory assistance and oxygen may be necessary.

carboplatin /kär′bōplat′in/, one of a series of platinum analog drugs used in cancer therapy. It is commonly administered intravenously for the treatment of ovarian cancer.

carboprost, a synthetic analog of dinoprost used as an oxytocic for termination of pregnancy and missed abortion, administered intramuscularly.

carboxyfluoroquinolone /kärbok′sēflōō′ər ōkwī′nəlōn/, any of a group of oral quinolone antibiotics that are generally effective against Enterobacteriaceae and show varying activity against *Pseudomonas* and other species.

carboxyhemoglobin /kärbok′sēhē′məglō′ bin, -hem′-/ [L, *carbo;* Gk, *oxys,* sharp, *haima,* blood; L, *globus,* ball], a hemoglobin variant produced by the exposure of hemoglobin to carbon monoxide.

carboxyhemoglobin test, a blood test for carbon monoxide poisoning.

carboxyl /kärbok′sil/, a monovalent radical characteristic of organic acids. The hydrogen of the radical can be replaced by metals to form salts.

carboxylase /kärbok′səlās/, an enzyme that catalyzes the addition of a molecule of carbon dioxide to another compound to form a carboxyl group.

carboxylation /-lā′shən/, a chemical process in which a carboxyl group (COOH) replaces a hydrogen atom.

carboxylic acid /kär′bok·sil′ik as′id/, any of a group of organic acids containing the carboxyl radical M—COOH, including amino acids and fatty acids.

carboxymethylcellulose /kärbok′semeth′il sel′ulōs/, a substituted cellulose polymer of variable size. The sodium or calcium salt is used as a pharmaceutical suspending agent, tablet excipient, and viscosity-increasing agent. The sodium salt is also used as a laxative.

carboxymethylcellulose calcium, the calcium salt of carboxymethylcellulose, used as a tablet disintegrant in pharmaceutical preparations.

carbuncle /kär′bungkəl/ [L, *carbunculus,* little coal], a large site of staphylococcal infection containing purulent matter in deep, interconnecting subcutaneous pockets. Pus eventually discharges to the skin surface through openings. Common sites for carbuncles are the back of the neck and the buttocks.

carbunculosis /karbung′kyəlō′sis/, an abnormal condition characterized by a cluster of deep painful abscesses that drain through multiple openings onto the skin surface, usually around hair follicles. Carbunculosis is a form of folliculitis, most commonly caused by the coagulase-positive *Staphylococcus aureus*. The lesions caused by this condition may cause fever and malaise.

carcinoembryonic antigen (CEA) /kär′sə nō·em′brē·on′ik/ [Gk, *karkinos*, crab, *en*, into, *bryein*, to grow, *anti*, against, *genein*, to produce], an antigen present in very small quantities in adult tissue. Changes in CEA values are used to monitor tumor response to treatment.

carcinogen /kärsin′əjin/ [Gk, *karkinos* + *genein*, to produce], a substance or agent that causes the development or increases the incidence of cancer.—**carcinogenic,** *adj.*

carcinogenesis /kär′sinəjen′əsis/, the process of initiating and promoting cancer.

carcinogenic /kär′sinəjen′ik/, pertaining to the ability to cause the development of a cancer.—**carcinogenicity,** *n.*

carcinoid /kär′sinoid/ [Gk, *karkinos* + *eidos*, form], a small yellow tumor derived from argentaffin cells in the GI mucosa that secrete serotonin and other catecholamines.

carcinoid syndrome, the systemic effects of serotonin-secreting carcinoid tumors, which include flushing, diarrhea, cramps, skin lesions resembling pellagra, labored breathing, palpitations, and valvular heart disease, especially of the tricuspid and pulmonary valve.

carcinolysis /kär′sinol′isis/ [Gk, *karkinos* + *lysis,* loosening], the destruction of cancer cells.—**carcinolytic,** *adj.*

carcinoma /kär′sinō′mə/ *pl.* **carcinomas, carcinomata** [Gk, *karkinos* + *oma*, tumor], a malignant epithelial neoplasm that tends to invade surrounding tissue and to metastasize to distant regions of the body. Carcinomas develop most frequently in the skin, large intestine, lungs, stomach, prostate, cervix, or breast. The tumor is firm, irregular, and nodular, with a well-defined border.—**carcinomatous,** *adj.*

carcinoma en cuirasse /äN kēräs′/ [Gk, *karkinos* + *oma*; Fr, breastplate], a rare manifestation of advanced breast cancer characterized by progressive extensive fibrosis and rigidity of the skin of the chest, neck, back, and abdomen.

carcinoma in situ /in sit′ōō, in sī′tōō/ [Gk, *karkinos* + *oma*; L, in position], a premalignant neoplasm that has not invaded the basement membrane but shows cytologic characteristics of cancer. Such neoplastic changes in stratified squamous or glandular epithelium frequently occur on the uterine cervix and in the anus, bronchi, buccal mucosa, esophagus, eye, lip, penis, uterine endometrium, and vagina.

carcinoma lenticulare /len′tikōōlär′ə/ [Gk, *karkinos* + *oma*; L, lens], a form of carcinoma tuberosum or scirrhous skin

cancer characterized by the development of many small, flat nodules that coalesce to form larger areas resembling a fungus infection.

carcinoma scroti /skrō′tī/, an epithelial cell carcinoma of the scrotum.

carcinoma spongiosum /spon′jē·ō′səm/, a soft and spongy carcinoma with small and large cavities.

carcinoma telangiectaticum /telan′jē·ektat′ikəm/ [Gk, *karkinos* + *oma* + *telos*, end, *angeion*, vessel, *ektasis*, dilation], a neoplasm of the capillaries of the skin causing dilation of the vessels and red spots on the skin that blanch with pressure.

carcinomatoid /kär′sinō′mətoid/, resembling a carcinoma.

carcinomatous /-om′ətəs/, pertaining to carcinoma.

carcinophilia /kär′sinō·fil′yə/ [Gk, *karkinos* + *philein*, to love], the property in which there is an affinity for carcinomatous tissue. —**carcinophilic,** *adj.*

carcinosarcoma /kär′sinōsärkō′mə/ *pl.* **carcinosarcomas, carcinosarcomata** [Gk, *karkinos* + *sarx*, flesh, *oma*, tumor], a malignant neoplasm composed of carcinomatous and sarcomatous cells. Tumors of this type may occur in the esophagus, thyroid gland, and uterus.

carcinosis /kär′sinō′sis/ *pl.* **carcinoses,** a condition characterized by the development of many carcinomas throughout the body.

carcinosis pleurae /plōō′rē/, a secondary malignancy of the pleura in which nodules develop throughout the membranes.

carcinostatic /kär′sinōstat′ik/ [Gk, *karkinos* + *statikos*, causing to stand], pertaining to the tendency to slow or halt the growth of a carcinoma.

Cardarelli's sign [Antonio Cardarelli, Italian physician, 1831–1927], a lateral pulsation of the trachea in aneurysm, particularly in dilation of the aortic arch.

cardia /kär′dē·ə/ [Gk, *kardia*, heart], **1.** the opening between the esophagus and the cardiac part of the stomach. **2.** the part of the stomach surrounding the esophagogastric connection, characterized by the absence of acid cells. —**cardiac,** *adj.*

cardiac /kär′dē·ak/ [Gk, *kardia*, heart], **1.** pertaining to the heart. **2.** pertaining to a person with heart disease. **3.** pertaining to the part of the stomach closest to the esophagus.

cardiac action potential, the transmembrane potential in the heart, consisting of five phases: 0, the upstroke or rapid depolarization, which initiates the heartbeat; 1, early rapid repolarization; 2, plateau; 3, final rapid repolarization; and 4, resting membrane potential and diastolic depolarization. Abnormalities of the heart or its conduction system that alter the cardiac action potential lead to the development of cardiac arrhythmias.

cardiac apnea [Gk, *kardia* + a, not, *pnein,* to breathe], an abnormal, temporary absence of respiration, such as occurs in Cheyne-Stokes respiration.

cardiac arrest [Gk, *kardia*; L, *ad* + *restare,* to withstand], a sudden cessation of cardiac output and effective circulation. It is usually precipitated by ventricular fibrillation or ventricular asystole. Delivery of oxygen and removal of carbon dioxide stop, tissue cell metabolism becomes anaerobic, and metabolic and respiratory acidosis ensue.

cardiac arrhythmia [Gk, *kardia* + a, without, *rhythmos,* rhythm], an abnormal cardiac rate or rhythm. The condition is caused by a failure of the sinus node to maintain its pacemaker function or by a defect in the electrical conduction system.

cardiac asthma, the wheezing that can occur in patients with left heart failure. Cardiac asthma is not true asthma. The wheezing is due to a decrease in airway diameter caused by pulmonary congestion, not bronchoconstriction.

cardiac atrophy, a wasting of heart muscle usually caused by cachexia, aging, or a mediastinal tumor.

cardiac care, a nursing intervention from the Nursing Interventions Classification (NIC) defined as limitation of complications resulting from an imbalance between myocardial oxygen supply and demand for a patient with symptoms of impaired cardiac function.

cardiac care: acute, a nursing intervention from the Nursing Interventions Classification (NIC) defined as limitation of complications for a patient recently experiencing an episode of an imbalance between myocardial oxygen supply and demand resulting in impaired cardiac function.

cardiac care: rehabilitative, a nursing intervention from the Nursing Interventions Classification (NIC) defined as promotion of maximum functional activity level for a patient who has experienced an episode of impaired cardiac function that resulted from an imbalance between myocardial oxygen supply and demand.

cardiac catheter, a long, fine catheter designed to be passed into the heart through a blood vessel.

cardiac catheterization, a diagnostic procedure in which a catheter is introduced through an incision into a large vein, usually of an arm or a leg, and threaded through the circulatory system to the heart.

The course of the catheter is followed with fluoroscopy, and radiographs may be taken. Many conditions may be accurately identified and assessed, including congenital heart disease, tricuspid stenosis, and valvular incompetence.

cardiac cirrhosis [Gk, *kardia,* heart, *kirrhos,* yellow-orange, *osis,* condition], an increase of fibrous tissue in the liver resulting from CHF, chronic myocarditis, or cardiac fibrosis.

cardiac conduction defect, any impairment of the electrical pathways and specialized muscular fibers that conduct impulses through the heart and result in atrial and ventricular contraction.

cardiac cycle [Gk, *kardia* + *kyklos,* circle], the cycle of events in the heart during which an electrical impulse is conducted from the sinus node to the atrioventricular (AV) node, to the AV bundle, to the bundle branches, and to the Purkinje fibers, causing depolarization of the atria followed by depolarization of the ventricles. Depolarization leads to contraction. The contractions of the left and the right atria are nearly simultaneous; they precede the nearly simultaneous contractions of the ventricles.

cardiac decompensation, a condition of CHF in which the heart is unable to ensure adequate cellular perfusion in all parts of the body without assistance. Causes may include MI, increased workload, infection, toxins, or defective heart valves.

cardiac depressant [L, *deprimere,* to press down], an agent that decreases heart rate and contractility.

cardiac disease self-management, a nursing outcome from the Nursing Outcomes Classification (NOC) defined as personal actions to manage heart disease, its treatment, and prevent disease progression.

cardiac dyspepsia, a digestive disorder associated with heart disease.

cardiac dyspnea [Gk, *dys,* difficult, *pnoia,* breath], breathing distress caused by heart disease. It is most commonly the result of pulmonary venous congestion.

cardiac edema [Gk, *oidema,* swelling], an accumulation of serum fluid from blood plasma in the interstitial tissues as a result of CHF. In severe cases the fluid may also accumulate in serous cavities.

cardiac electric axis, the main direction of electrical current flow in the heart. It may be calculated in the frontal plane limb leads or the horizontal plane by using precordial leads.

cardiac exercise stress test, a noninvasive electrodiagnostic and/or nuclear test used to evaluate chest pain in patients with suspected coronary disease, to determine the safe limits of exercise during a cardiac rehabilitation program, to detect labile or exercise-related hypertension, to detect intermittent claudication, to evaluate the effectiveness of antianginal or antiarrhythmic drugs, and to evaluate the effectiveness of cardiac surgical intervention.

cardiac hypertrophy, an abnormal enlargement of the heart muscle. It frequently accompanies long-standing hypertension and CHF.

cardiac impulse [Gk, *kardia* + L, *impellere,* to set in motion], **1.** the mechanical movement of the thorax caused by the beating of the heart. **2.** the electric stimulus generated by the heart for pacing purposes.

cardiac index, a measure of the cardiac output of a patient per square meter of body surface area. Its normal range in a healthy adult is 2.8 to 4.2 L/min/m^2.

cardiac insufficiency, the inability of the heart to pump efficiently.

cardiac massage, repeated, rhythmic compression of the heart applied directly, during surgery, or through the intact chest wall in an effort to maintain circulation after cardiac arrest or ventricular fibrillation.

cardiac monitor, a device for the continuous observation of cardiac function.

cardiac monitoring, a continuous check on the functioning of the heart with an electronic instrument that provides an ECG reading on an oscilloscope.

cardiac murmur, an abnormal sound heard during auscultation of the heart, caused by altered blood flow into a chamber or through a valve. A murmur is classified by its time of occurrence during the cardiac cycle, its duration, and its intensity. In certain age groups, many systolic murmurs are benign and of no significance, whereas others signal a cardiac disorder. Diastolic murmurs are always pathologic.

cardiac muscle, a special striated muscle of the myocardium, containing dark intercalated disks at the junctions of abutting fibers. Cardiac muscle is an exception among involuntary muscles, which are characteristically smooth. Its contractile fibers resemble those of skeletal muscle but are only one third as large in diameter, are richer in sarcoplasm, and contain centrally located instead of peripheral nuclei.

cardiac nerves, the three autonomic nerves that supply the heart, including the inferior, superior, and middle (or great) cardiac nerves.

cardiac nuclear scanning, a nuclear scan used to detect myocardial ischemia, infarction, wall dysfunction, and decreased ejection fraction. It is commonly used as the imaging method portion of cardiac stress testing.

cardiac output (CO), the volume of blood expelled by the ventricles of the heart with each beat (the stroke volume) multiplied by the heart rate. A normal, resting adult has a cardiac output of 4 to 8 L per minute.

cardiac plexus [Gk, *kardia;* L, pleated], one of several nerve networks situated close to the arch of the aorta. The cardiac plexuses contain sympathetic and parasympathetic nerve fibers that follow the right and left coronary arteries into the heart.

cardiac precautions, a nursing intervention from the Nursing Interventions Classification (NIC) defined as prevention of an acute episode of impaired cardiac function by minimizing myocardial oxygen consumption or increasing myocardial oxygen supply.

cardiac pump effectiveness, a nursing outcome from the Nursing Outcomes Classification (NOC) defined as adequacy of blood volume ejected from the left ventricle to support systemic perfusion pressure.

cardiac radionuclide imaging [Gk, *kardia;* L, *radiare,* to shine, *nucleus,* nut kernel, *imago,* image], the noninvasive examination of the heart, using a radiopharmaceutical, such as thallium-201, and a detection device, such as a gamma camera, positron camera, or rectilinear scanner.

cardiac reflex [L, *reflectere,* to bend back], a neural mechanism that automatically increases or reduces the heart rate. Stimulation of stretch receptors in the right side of the heart by increased venous return increases the heart rate, whereas increased arterial BP stimulates nerve endings in the carotid sinus and aortic arch to the heart rate.

cardiac regurgitation [Gk, *kardia,* heart; L, *re* + *gurgitare,* to flow], a backward flow of blood through one or more defective heart valves.

cardiac rehabilitation [Gk, *kardia,* heart; L, *re* + *habilitas,* ability], a supervised program of progressive exercise, psychologic support, education, and training to enable a patient to resume ADL on an independent basis following an MI.

cardiac reserve, the potential capacity of the heart to function well beyond its basal level, in response to alterations in physiologic demands.

cardiac rhythm [Gk, *kardia,* heart, *rhythmos*], the recurring beat of the heart.

cardiac souffle /soo′fəl/ [Gk, *kardia,* heart; Fr, puff], a heart murmur having a soft, blowing sound.

cardiac sphincter [Gk, *kardia* + *sphingein,* to bind], a sphincter between the esophagus and the stomach, opening at the approach of food that can then be swept into the stomach by rhythmic peristaltic waves.

cardiac standstill, the complete cessation of ventricular contractions and ejection of blood by the heart.

cardiac stenosis [Gk, *kardia,* heart, *stenos,* narrow, *osis,* condition], a nonvalvular obstruction of blood flow through any heart chamber. The cause may be a thrombosis or tumor.

cardiac stimulant, a pharmacologic agent that increases the action of the heart. Cardiac glycosides increase the force of myocardial contractions and decrease the heart rate and conduction velocity. They are used in the treatment of CHF, atrial flutter and fibrillation, paroxysmal atrial tachycardia, and cardiogenic shock. Epinephrine, a potent vasopressor and cardiac stimulant, is sometimes used to restore heart rhythm in cardiac arrest but is not used in treating heart failure or cardiogenic shock. Isoproterenol hydrochloride, which is related to epinephrine, may be used in treating heart block. Amrinone, dobutamine hydrochloride, and dopamine are used in the short-term treatment of cardiac decompensation resulting from depressed contractility.

cardiac syncope /sing′kəpē/ [Gk, *kardia,* heart, *syncope,* fainting], a temporary LOC caused by inadequate cerebral blood flow resulting from a sudden failure in cardiac output for any reason.

cardiac tamponade /tam′pənäd′/, compression of the heart produced by the accumulation of blood or other fluid in the pericardial sac.

cardiac thrombosis [Gk, *kardia,* heart, *thrombos,* lump, *osis,* condition], a blood clot located at a heart valve or in one of the heart chambers. A left ventricular thrombosis may follow a large MI.

cardial notch, the superior angle created when the esophagus enters the stomach.

cardiasthenia /kar′dē·asthē′nē·ə/ [Gk, *kardia,* heart, *a,* without, *sthenos,* strength], a form of neurasthenia in which cardiovascular symptoms are prominent.

cardiectomy /kär′dē·ek′təmē/, **1.** removal of the heart. **2.** removal of the cardiac part of the stomach.

cardiectopia /kär′dē·ektō′pē·ə/, abnormal positioning of the heart in the thoracic cavity.

cardinal /kär′dənal/ [L, *cardo,* hinge], pertaining to something so fundamental that other things hinge on it, such as a cardinal trait that influences one's total behavior.

cardinal frontal plane [L, *cardo,* hinge, *frons,* forehead, *planum,* level ground], the plane that divides the body into front and back parts.

cardinal ligament [L, *cardo,* hinge, *ligare,* to bind], a sheet of subserous fascia extending across the female pelvic floor as a continuation of the broad ligament.

cardinal movements of labor, the typical sequence of positions assumed by the fetus as it descends through the pelvis during labor and delivery. The positions are usually designated as engagement, flexion, descent, internal rotation, extension, and external rotation or restitution, and expulsion.

cardinal position of gaze, (in ophthalmology) one of six positions to which the normal eye may be turned. This test evaluates the functioning of the six extraocular muscles and cranial nerves III, IV, and VI. The positions and the corresponding muscles and nerves are as follows: (1) straight nasal: medial rectus and the third cranial nerve; (2) up nasal: inferior oblique and the third cranial nerve; (3) down nasal: superior oblique and the fourth cranial nerve; (4) straight temporal: lateral rectus and the sixth cranial nerve; (5) up temporal: superior rectus and the third cranial nerve; and (6) down temporal: inferior rectus and the third cranial nerve.

Cardiobacterium, a gram-negative genus of facultative anaerobic rod-shaped bacteria that is part of the normal flora of the human nasopharynx region. It is associated with endocarditis.

cardiocele /kär′dē·ōsēl′/, protrusion of the heart through an opening in the diaphragm or the abdominal wall.

cardiocirculatory /kär′dē·ōsur′kyo͝olətôr′ē/ [Gk, *kardia* heart; L, *circulare,* to go around], pertaining to the heart and the circulation.

cardioesophageal reflux /-əsof′əjē′əl/ [Gk, *kardia,* heart, *oisophagos,* gullet; L, *refluere,* to flow back], a backward flow or regurgitation of stomach contents into the esophagus.

cardiogenic /-jen′ik/, originating in the heart muscle.

cardiogenic mesoderm, the splanchnic mesoderm in the cardiogenic region where the embryonic heart develops that gives rise to the paired endocardial tubes.

cardiogenic shock [Gk, *kardia + genein,* to produce; Fr, *choc*], an abnormal condition often but not always characterized by a low cardiac output associated with acute MI and CHF.

cardiohepatomegaly /-hep′ətōmeg′əlē/, enlargement of the heart and liver.

cardioinhibitory /kär′dē·ō′inhib′itôr′ē/, slowing or inhibiting the rate or strength of ventricular contractions.

cardiokinetic /kä'rdē·ōki·net'ik/ [Gk, *kardia,* heart + *kinesis,* motion], **1.** stimulating the action of the heart. **2.** an agent that stimulates action of the heart.

cardiologist /-ol'əjist/, a physician who specializes in the diagnosis and treatment of disorders of the heart.

cardiology /-ol'əjē/ [Gk, *kardia* + *logos,* science], the study of the anatomy, normal functions, and disorders of the heart.

cardiomegaly /kär'dē·ōmeg'əlē/ [Gk, *kardia* + *megas,* large], enlargement of the heart.

cardiomyopathy, any disease of the myocardium causing enlargement.

cardiomyopexy /kär'dē·omī'əpek'sē/ [Gk, *kardia* + *mys,* muscle, *pexis,* fixation], a surgical procedure in which the blood supply from the nearby pectoral muscles of the chest is diverted directly to the coronary arteries of the heart.

cardiopathy /kär'dē·op'əthē/ [Gk, *kardia,* heart, *pathos,* disease], a disease of the heart.

cardiopericarditis /-per'ikärdī'tis/, inflammation of the heart and the pericardium.

cardioplasty /kär'dē·ōplas'tē/, a surgical procedure to correct a defect in the cardiac sphincter of the esophagus that frequently leads to cardiospasm.

cardioplegia /-plē'jə/ [Gk, *kardia* + *plege,* stroke], **1.** paralysis of the heart. **2.** the arrest of myocardial contractions by hypothermia, electrical stimuli, or injection of chemicals for the purpose of performing surgery on the heart.

cardioprotectant /kär'dē·ōprōtek'tant/, **1.** counteracting cardiotoxic effects. **2.** an agent that so acts.

cardiopulmonary /-pul'mənər'ē/ [Gk, *kardia* + L, *pulmo,* lung], pertaining to the heart and lungs.

cardiopulmonary bypass, a procedure used in heart surgery in which the blood is diverted from the right atrium or vena cava by means of a pump oxygenator and returned directly to the aorta.

cardiopulmonary murmur [Gk, *kardia,* heart; L, *pulmo,* lung, *murmur,* humming], a sound heard over the heart during breathing and during the heartbeat caused by vibrations that result when the heart strikes the lung tissue with every beat.

cardiopulmonary resuscitation (CPR), a basic emergency procedure for life support, consisting of artificial respiration and manual external cardiac massage. It is used in cases of cardiac arrest to establish effective circulation and ventilation to prevent irreversible cerebral damage resulting from anoxia. External cardiac massage compresses the heart between the lower sternum and the thoracic vertebral column. During compressions, blood is forced into systemic and pulmonary circulation, and venous blood refills the heart when the compression is released. Mouth-to-mouth breathing or a mechanical form of ventilation is used concomitantly with CPR to oxygenate the blood being pumped through the circulatory system.

cardiopulmonary status, a nursing outcome from the Nursing Outcomes Classification (NOC) defined as adequacy of blood volume ejected from the ventricles and exchange of carbon dioxide and oxygen at the alveolar level.

cardiorrhaphy /kär'dē·ôr'əfē/ [Gk, *kardia* + *rhaphe,* suture], an operation in which the heart muscle is sutured.

cardioselectivity /-sel'əktiv'itē/, selectivity of a drug, such as a beta-blocker, for heart tissue over other tissues of the body.

cardiospasm /kär'dē·əspaz'əm/ [Gk, *kardia* + *spasmos,* pull], a form of achalasia characterized by a failure of the cardiac sphincter at the distal end of the esophagus to relax. It causes dysphagia and regurgitation and sometimes requires surgical division of the muscle.

cardiotachometer /kär'dē·ō'təkom'ətər/ [Gk, *kardia* + *tachos,* speed, *metron,* measure], an instrument that continually monitors and records the heartbeat.

cardiotherapy, treatment of heart disease.

cardiothoracic ratio /-thôras'ik/, the ratio of the diameter of the heart at its widest point to the maximum width of the thoracic cavity, assessed by examining a chest x-ray. The normal ratio is 1:2.

cardiotomy /kär'dē·ot'əmē/ [Gk, *kardia* + *temnein,* to cut], **1.** an operation in which the heart is incised. **2.** an operation in which the cardiac end of the stomach or cardiac orifice is incised.

cardiotomy reservoir, in cardiopulmonary bypass, a collection chamber for blood suctioned from the heart chambers and pericardium.

cardiotonic /kär'dē·ōton'ik/ [Gk, *kardia* + *tonos,* tone], **1.** pertaining to a substance that tends to increase the efficiency of contractions of the heart muscle. **2.** a pharmacologic agent that increases the force of myocardial contractions.

cardiotoxic /-tok'sik/ [Gk, *kardia* + *toxikon,* poison], having a toxic or injurious effect on the heart.

cardiovascular /kär'dē·ōvas'kyələr/ [Gk, *kardia* + L, *vasculum,* small vessel], pertaining to the heart and blood vessels.

cardiovascular assessment, an evaluation of the condition, function, and abnormalities of the heart and circulatory system.

cardiovascular disease, any abnormal condition characterized by dysfunction of the heart and blood vessels. In the United States, cardiovascular disease is the leading cause of death.

cardiovascular reflex, a reflex in which heart and circulatory functions are altered in response to changes in heart rate, vascular tone, blood volume, or other variables.

cardiovascular shunt [Gk, *kardia,* heart; L, *vasculum,* small vessel; ME, *shunten*], any abnormal passage between chambers of the heart or between the systemic and pulmonary circulatory systems.

cardiovascular system, the network of anatomic structures, including the heart and blood vessels, that circulate blood throughout the body. The system includes thousands of kilometers of vessels that deliver nutrients and other essential materials to the fluids surrounding the cells and that remove waste products and convey them to excretory organs.

cardiovascular technologist, an allied health professional who performs diagnostic examinations at the request or direction of a physician in invasive cardiology, noninvasive cardiology, and/or peripheral vascular study.

cardioversion /-vur′zhən/ [Gk, *kardia*; L, *vertere,* to turn], the restoration of the heart's normal sinus rhythm through an electric shock delivered by a defibrillator. Cardioversion is used to slow the heart or to restore the heart's normal sinus rhythm when drug therapy is ineffective at doing so.

cardioverter /-vur′tər/, a defibrillator or other instrument used to convert abnormal heart rhythms into normal rhythms.

carditis /kärdī′tis/, inflammation of the heart muscle, usually resulting from infection. In most cases more than one layer of muscle is involved. Chest pain, cardiac arrhythmia, circulatory failure, and damage to the structures of the heart may occur.

Cardizem, a trademark for a calcium channel blocker (diltiazem).

career ladder, 1. (in nursing education) a pathway for upward mobility that begins with a course of study in practical nursing or a program that grants an **Associate Degree in Nursing.** The candidate may continue up the ladder, to earn a **Bachelor of Science in Nursing,** and then to the graduate level to earn a master's degree and a doctoral degree in nursing. **2.** a pathway for advancement in the professional nursing role in an institution.

caregiver, one who contributes the benefits of medical, social, economic, or environmental resources to a dependent or partially dependent individual, such as a critically ill person.

caregiver adaptation to patient institutionalization, a nursing outcome from the Nursing Outcomes Classification (NOC) defined as adaptive response of family caregiver when the care recipient is moved to an institution.

caregiver emotional health, a nursing outcome from the Nursing Outcomes Classification (NOC) defined as emotional well-being of a family care provider while caring for a family member.

caregiver home care readiness, a nursing outcome from the Nursing Outcomes Classification (NOC) defined as preparedness of a caregiver to assume responsibility for the health care of a family member in the home.

caregiver lifestyle disruption, a nursing outcome from the Nursing Outcomes Classification (NOC) defined as severity of disturbances in the lifestyle of a family member due to caregiving.

caregiver-patient relationship, a nursing outcome from the Nursing Outcomes Classification (NOC) defined as positive interactions and connections between the caregiver and care recipient.

caregiver performance: direct care, a nursing outcome from the Nursing Outcomes Classification (NOC) defined as provision by family care provider of appropriate personal and health care for a family member.

caregiver performance: indirect care, a nursing outcome from the Nursing Outcomes Classification (NOC) defined as arrangement and oversight by family care provider of appropriate care for a family member.

caregiver physical health, a nursing outcome from the Nursing Outcomes Classification (NOC) defined as physical well-being of a family care provider while caring for a family member.

caregiver role endurance, a nursing outcome from the Nursing Outcomes Classification (NOC) defined as factors that promote a family care provider's capacity to sustain caregiving over an extended period of time.

caregiver stressors, a nursing outcome from the Nursing Outcomes Classification (NOC) defined as severity of biopsychosocial pressure on a family care provider caring for another over an extended period of time.

caregiver support, a nursing intervention from the Nursing Interventions Classification (NIC) defined as provision of the necessary information, advocacy, and support to facilitate primary patient care by someone other than a health care professional.

caregiver well-being, a nursing outcome from the Nursing Outcomes Classification (NOC) defined as extent of positive perception of primary care provider's health status.

care of the chronically ill, medical and nursing services that focus on long-term care of people with chronic diseases or conditions, either at home or in a medical facility.

care of the sick, (in public health nursing) the care of ill patients in their homes, as distinguished from health supervision. Public health nursing agencies are reimbursed for the nursing services rendered by the nurses according to the kind of service rendered, such as a sick visit or a health supervision visit.

CARF, abbreviation for *Commission on Accreditation of Rehabilitation Facilities.*

carina /kərē′nə/ *pl.* **carinae** [L, keel], any structure shaped like a ridge, cleft, or keel, such as the carina of the trachea, which projects from the lowest tracheal cartilage.

caring behaviors, actions characteristic of concern for the well-being of a patient, such as sensitivity, comfort, attentive listening, honesty, and nonjudgmental acceptance.

cariocas /kär′ē-ō′kəs/, a form of lateral movement in a gait cycle in which the side-stepping leg is moved successively behind and then in front of the stance leg.

cariogenic /ker′ē-ōjen′ik/, tending to produce dental caries.

carisoprodol /ker′isōprō′dol/, a skeletal muscle relaxant prescribed for the relief of muscle spasm.

c-arm, an imaging scanner intensifier, so named because of its configuration. C-arms have radiographic capabilities, though they are used primarily for fluoroscopic imaging during surgical, orthopedic, critical care, and emergency care procedures.

carminative /kärmin′ətiv/ [L, *carminare,* to cleanse], **1.** pertaining to a substance that relieves flatulence and abdominal distension. **2.** an agent that relieves gaseous distension and painful spasms, especially after meals.

carmine dye /kär′min/ [AR, *qirmize*; AS, *deag*], a red coloring substance, produced by the addition of alum to an extract of cochineal, that is used for staining histologic specimens.

carmustine /kärmus′tin/, a lipid-soluble nitrosourea, 1,3-bis(2-chloroethyl)-1-nitrosourea, used as a single antineoplastic agent or with other approved chemotherapeutic agents in the treatment of brain tumors, multiple myeloma, Hodgkin's disease, and non-Hodgkin's lymphomas.

carnal /kär′nəl/ [L, *caro,* flesh], pertaining to the flesh or body, or worldly things as distinguished from spiritual.

carneous /kär′nē·əs/, having the quality of flesh.

carnitine /kär′nitin/, a substance found in skeletal and cardiac muscle and certain other tissues that functions as a carrier of fatty acids across the membranes of the mitochondria. It is used therapeutically in treating angina and certain deficiency diseases and as an antithyroid agent. It has actions that closely resemble those of amino acids and B vitamins.

carnitine palmitoyltransferase /kär′nitēn päl′mitō′əltrans′fərās/, an enzyme that catalyzes the transfer between coenzyme A and carnitine of long chain fatty acids. Deficiency is a cause of defective fatty acid oxidation.

carnitine palmityltransferase deficiency /kär′nitēn päl′mitiltrans′fərās dēfish′ənsē/, an autosomal-recessive disorder of lipid metabolism, seen more often in men, in which the altered enzyme is abnormally regulated, resulting in muscle aches, fatigability, and myoglobinuria (but without lipid accumulation), occurring after prolonged exercise, particularly in the cold or after fasting.

Carnitor, a trademark for an amino acid derivative (levocarnitine).

carnivore /kär′nivôr/ [L, *caro,* flesh, *vorare,* to devour], an animal belonging to the order Carnivora, classified as a flesh eater, with appropriate teeth and a characteristically simple stomach and a short intestine for such a diet.—**carnivorous** /kärniv′ərəs/, *adj.*

carnosine /kär′nōsēn/ [L, *caro*], a dipeptide composed of alanine and histidine, in humans found in skeletal muscle and in the brain, particularly in the primary olfactory pathways. It may play a role as a neurotransmitter.

carnosinemia /kär′nōsinē′mē·ə/, accumulation of carnosine in the blood.

carob /kar′əb/ [Ar. *al kharrubah*], *Ceratonia siliqua,* a tree native to the Mediterranean basin.

carob bean, the fruit of the carob tree, whose seed is leguminous. The finely pulverized meal of the dried ripe fruit contains albuminous proteins, carbohydrates, and small amounts of fat and crude fiber, and has been used for centuries in pharmaceutic formulations as an adsorbent and demulcent in treatment of diarrhea. It is generally regarded as safe, but its effectiveness in treating diarrhea has not been rigorously assessed.

carotene /kar′ətin/ [L, *carota,* carrot], a red or orange organic compound found in carrots, sweet potatoes, egg yolk, and leafy vegetables, such as beet greens, spinach, and broccoli. Beta-carotene is a provitamin and in the body is converted to vitamin A.

carotenemia /kar'ətinē'mē·ə/, the presence of high levels of carotene in the blood, which result in an abnormal yellow appearance of the plasma and skin. It differs from jaundice in that the conjunctivae are not discolored.

carotenoid /kərot'ənoid/, any of a group of red, yellow, or orange highly unsaturated pigments that are found in foods such as carrots, sweet potatoes, and leafy green vegetables. Many of these substances, such as carotene, are used in the formation of vitamin A in the body, whereas others show no vitamin A activity.

caroticotympanic canaliculi, tiny passages in the temporal bone interconnecting the carotid canal and the tympanic cavity that carry communicating twigs between the internal carotid and tympanic plexuses.

caroticotympanic nerves, the plexus of nerves surrounding the internal carotid artery.

carotid /kərot'id/ [Gk, karos, heavy sleep], pertaining to the arteries that supply the head and neck.

carotid arch [Gk, karos, heavy sleep; L, arcus, bow], the third arch of the aorta, the source of the common carotid arteries.

carotid artery duplex scanning, a noninvasive ultrasound test for occlusive disease of the extracranial carotid artery.

carotid body [Gk, karos; AS, bodig], a small structure containing neural tissue at the bifurcation of the carotid arteries. It monitors the pressure and oxygen content of the blood and therefore assists in regulating respiration.

carotid-body reflex [Gk, karos; AS, bodig; L, reflectere, to bend back], a normal chemical reflex initiated by a decrease in oxygen concentration in the blood and, to a lesser degree, by increased carbon dioxide and hydrogen ion concentrations that act on chemoreceptors at the bifurcation of the common carotid arteries. The resulting nerve impulses cause the respiratory center in the medulla to increase respiratory activity.

carotid-body tumor, a benign round, firm growth that develops at the bifurcation of the common carotid artery. The tumor may cause dizziness, nausea, and vomiting if it impedes the flow of blood and pressure is increased in the vascular system.

carotid bruit, a murmur heard over the carotid artery in the neck, suggesting arterial narrowing. It is usually secondary to atherosclerosis. Stroke is likely if the narrowing is severe and the condition is untreated.

carotid duplex scanning, a noninvasive ultrasound test used on the extracranial carotid artery to detect occlusive disease directly. It is recommended for patients with headaches and with neurologic symptoms such as TIAs, hemiparesis, paresthesia, and acute speech or visual defects.

carotid endarterectomy (CEA), surgical excision of atheromatous segments of the endothelium and tunica media of the carotid artery, leaving a smooth tissue lining and facilitating blood flow through the vessel. The surgery is done to decrease the risk of stroke.

carotid plexus [Gk, karos; L, pleated], any one of three nerve plexuses associated with the carotid arteries.

carotid pulse, the pulse of the carotid artery, palpated by gently pressing a finger in the area between the larynx and the sternocleidomastoid muscle in the neck.

carotid sheath, the fibrous tissue enclosing the carotid artery, jugular vein, and vagus nerve on each side of the neck.

carotid sinus [Gk, karos; L, curve], a dilation of the arterial wall at the bifurcation of the common carotid artery. It contains sensory nerve endings from the glossopharyngeal nerve that respond to changes in BP.

carotid sinus massage, firm rubbing at the bifurcation of the carotid artery at the angle of the jaw. It creates an elevation of BP in the carotid sinus that results in reflex slowing of atrioventricular conduction and sinus rate.

carotid sinus reflex, a neural mechanism in which an increase in BP in the carotid artery at the level of its bifurcation trigger a decrease in heart rate.

carotid sinus syndrome, a temporary LOC that sometimes results in provoked convulsive seizures as a result of the intensity of the carotid sinus reflex when pressure builds in one or both carotid sinuses.

carotidynia /kərot'idin'ē·ə/ [Gk, karos + odyne, pain], a pain along the length of the common carotid artery caused by pressure.

carpal /kär'pəl/ [Gk, karpos, wrist], pertaining to the carpus, or wrist.

carpal arch, the arch formed by the carpal bones; the sides and roof of the carpal tunnel.

carpal bones, the eight bones of the wrist, which are arranged in two rows, a proximal and a distal row, each consisting of four bones. The proximal row consists of the scaphoid (navicular), the lunate, the triquetrum, and the pisiform bones. The distal row consists of the trapezium (greater multiangular), the trapezoid (lesser multiangular), the capitate, and the hamate bones.

carpal ligaments, four ligaments of the hand: the dorsal ligament, a thick band of white fibrous tissue on the dorsum of the wrist, attached to the lower end of the radius and to the styloid process of the ulna; the radiate ligament of the wrist, which projects from the head of the capitate bone to the volar aspects of other carpal bones; the broad, flat transverse ligament, which is attached to the tubercle of the scaphoid and the crest of the trapezium; and the volar ligament, a superficial part of the flexor retinaculum.

carpal spasm, a sudden, powerful, involuntary contraction observed as a tetanic flexion of the hands and wrists.

carpal tunnel [Gk, *karpos;* Fr, *tonnel*], a tunnel formed by the carpal bones and the flexor retinaculum through which pass the median nerve and the tendons of the flexor digitorum profundus, the flexor digitorum superificialis, and the flexor pollicis longus.

carpal tunnel release, a surgical procedure for treating carpal tunnel syndrome in which the flexor retinaculum of the wrist is cut to release compression of the median nerve.

carpal tunnel syndrome, a common painful disorder of the wrist and hand, caused by compression on the median nerve between the inelastic carpal ligament and other structures within the carpal tunnel. It is often seen in cumulative trauma to the wrist.

Carpenter's syndrome /kär′pəntərz/ [George Carpenter, British physician, 1859–1910], an autosomal-recessive form of acrocephalopolysyndactyly characterized also by mental retardation and shortened digits.

carpometacarpal(CMC)joint/-met′əkär′pəl/ [Gk, *karpos,* wrist, *meta,* next, *karpos*], any of the joints formed by the distal row of carpal bones and the bases of the metacarpals.

carpopedal /-ped′əl/ [Gk, *karpos,* wrist; L, *pes,* foot], pertaining to the wrist and foot.

carpopedal spasm [Gk, *karpos;* L, *pes,* foot], a spasm of the hand, thumbs, foot, or toes that sometimes accompanies tetany.

carrier /ker′ē·ər/ [OFr, *carier*], **1.** a person or animal who harbors and spreads an organism that causes disease in others but does not become ill. **2.** one whose chromosomes carry a recessive gene. **3.** an immunogenic molecule or part of a molecule that is recognized by T cells in an antibody response.

carrier-free, 1. relating to a radioisotope in pure form, free of dilution by stable isotope carriers. **2.** describing a substance in which every molecule is marked by a radioactive tracer or other tag.

Carroll Quantitative Test of Upper Extremity Function, a six-part test of a person's ability to grasp and lift objects of different shapes and sizes. It is designed to measure the ability to perform general arm and hand movements required for the ADL.

carrying angle, the angle at which the humerus and radius articulate.

carry-over [L, *carrus,* wagon; AS *ofer*], contamination of a specimen by the previous one.

car sickness [L, *carrus,* wagon; AS, *seoc*], a form of kinesia caused by the motion of a vehicle.

carteolol /kär′te·älol/, a beta-adrenergic blocking agent with intrinsic sympathetic activity, administered orally as an antihypertensive and applied topically to the conjunctiva in the treatment of glaucoma and ocular hypertension.

cartilage /kär′tilij/ [L, *cartilago*], a nonvascular dense supporting connective tissue composed of chondrocytes and various fibers or ground substance. It is found chiefly in the joints, the thorax, and various rigid tubes such as the larynx, trachea, nose, and ear. Temporary cartilage, such as sesamoid bones (knee) and those that compose most of the fetal skeleton at an early stage, are later replaced by bone. Permanent cartilage remains unossified, except in certain diseases and, sometimes, in advanced age. **—cartilaginous,** *adj.*

cartilage graft, the transplantation of cartilage to correct congenital ear and nose defects in children and to treat severe injuries in adults.

cartilage-hair hypoplasia [L, *cartilago;* AS, *haer;* Gk, *hypo,* under, *plasis,* forming], a genetic disorder characterized by dwarfism caused by hypoplasia of the cartilage; multiple skeletal abnormalities; and excessively sparse, short, fine, brittle hair that is usually light colored.

cartilage of auditory tube, the cartilage on the inferomedial surface of the temporal bone that supports the walls of the cartilaginous portion of the auditory tube.

cartilaginous bone, bone that develops by endochondral ossification in a preexisting cartilage.

cartilaginous joint [L, *cartilago* + *jungere,* to join], a slightly movable joint in which cartilage unites bony surfaces. Two types of articulation involving cartilaginous joints are synchondrosis and symphysis.

cartilaginous septum of nose, the plate of cartilage forming the anterior part of the nasal septum.

cartilaginous skeleton [L, *cartilago*; Gk, *skeletos,* dried up], the parts of the skeleton that are formed by cartilage.

Cartrol, a trademark for an antihypertensive agent (carteolol hydrochloride).

caruncle /kär′ungkəl/ [L, *caruncula,* small piece of flesh], a small, fleshy projection, such as one of the lacrimal caruncles at the inner canthus of the eye or the hymenal caruncles.

carunculae hymenales [L, *caruncula*; Gk, *hymen,* membrane], remnants of a ruptured hymen that appear as irregular projections of normal skin around the introitus to the vagina.

carvedilol, an alpha-/beta-adrenergic blocker used to treat CHF and essential hypertension, either alone or in combination with other antihypertensives.

carve-out, a service not covered in a health insurance contract. It is usually reimbursed according to a different arrangement or rate formula than those services specified under the contract umbrella.

CAS, abbreviation for *coronary artery scan.*

CASA, abbreviation for **computer-aided semen analysis.**

cascade /kaskād′/ [L, *cadere,* to fall], any process that develops in stages, with each stage dependent on the preceding one, often producing a cumulative effect.

cascade humidifier, a bubbling respiratory care device in which gases travel down a tower and pass through a grid into a chamber of heated water.

cascara sagrada, a herbal product taken from the bark of a tree native to parts of the coast in the Pacific Northwest. It is used for chronic constipation, hepatitis, and gallstones.

case [L, *causus,* a happening], 1. an episode of illness or injury. 2. a container.

caseation /kā′sē·ā′shən/ [L, *caseus,* cheese], a form of tissue necrosis in which cellular outline is lost and the appearance is that of crumbly or liquified cheese. It is typical of TB. —**caseate,** *v.*

case-control study, an investigation using an epidemiologic approach in which previous cases of the condition are used. A group of patients with a particular disease or disorder is compared with a control group of persons who have not had that medical problem.

case fatality rate [L, *causus,* a happening, *fatum,* fate, *(pro) rata*], the number of registered deaths caused by any specific disease, expressed as a percentage of the total number of reported cases of a specific disease.

case finding, the act of locating individuals with a disease.

case history [L, *causus* + *historia*], a patient's complete medical record before a current illness or injury. The history includes any infectious diseases experienced by the person; all immunizations, hospitalizations, and therapies; information relating to deaths or illnesses of parents and other close family members; allergies; and congenital or acquired physical defects.

casein, a white powder protein that occurs naturally in milk. It contains phosphorus and sulfur and is regarded as a "complete protein" because it contains all essential amino acids. Casein is precipitated when milk turns sour.

case management[1], 1. a problem-solving process through which appropriate services to individuals and families are assured. 2. a method of structuring acute care for all patients in three dimensions: work design, clinical management roles, and concurrent monitoring and feedback. 3. a patient-centered, goal-oriented process of assessing the need of an individual for particular services and obtaining those services and monitoring care.

case management[2], a nursing intervention from the Nursing Interventions Classification (NIC) defined as coordinating care and advocating for specified individuals and patient populations across settings to reduce cost, reduce resource use, improve quality of health care, and achieve desired outcomes.

case method, a type of nursing care delivery system.

case nursing [L, *casus,* a happening, *nutrix,* nourish], an organizational mode for allocation of nursing staff in which one nurse is assigned to provide total nursing care to one or more patients.

caseous /kā′sē·əs/, 1. cottage cheese-like; describing the mixture of fat and protein that appears in some body tissues undergoing necrosis. 2. pertaining to cheesy covering on fetuses that protects them from prolonged presence in amniotic fluid.

caseous fermentation [L, *caseus,* cheese, *fermentum,* yeast], the coagulation of soluble casein to form insoluble calcium paracaseinate through the action of rennin.

caseous necrosis, necrosis that transforms tissue into a dry cheeselike mass. It occurs primarily in TB.

case rate, a pricing method in which a flat amount, often a per diem rate, covers a defined group of procedures and services. It is often used in services such as obstetrics and cardiovascular surgery for exceptions to a relative value scale or resource-based relative value scale.

case study, a detailed analysis of a person or group with a particular disease or condition, noting characteristics of the disease or condition. Case studies are often used to call attention to new diseases or to diseases entering new populations.

CaSO₄, the formula for **calcium sulfate.**

Casodex, a trademark for an anticancer chemotherapy agent (bicalutamide).

cassette /kaset′/ [Fr, little box], a device used in radiography for holding a sheet of x-ray film and one or two screens. It may also have a grid to absorb scattered radiation.

cast [ONorse, kasta], **1.** a stiff, solid dressing formed with plaster of paris or other material around a limb or other body part to immobilize it during healing. **2.** a mold of a part or all of a patient's teeth and internal jaw area for fitting prostheses or dentures. **3.** a tiny structure formed by deposits of mineral or other substances on the walls of renal tubules, bronchioles, or other organs. Casts often appear in samples of urine or blood collected for laboratory examination. **4.** the deviation of an eye from the normal parallel lines of vision, such as in strabismus.

cast brace, a combination of a brace within a cast at a joint.

cast care: maintenance, a nursing intervention from the Nursing Interventions Classification (NIC) defined as care of a cast after the drying period.

cast care: wet, a nursing intervention from the Nursing Interventions Classification (NIC) defined as care of a new cast during the drying period.

cast core [ONorse, *kasta*; L, *cor,* heart], a metal casting, shaped like a stump of a tooth and incorporating a post in the root canal for the retention of an artificial tooth crown.

casting, 1. the act of encasing a body part in a cast. **2.** (in dentistry) the process by which crowns, inlays, and other metallic restorations are produced.

casting tape, an adhesive or resin-impregnated mesh used for shaping lightweight casts.

Castleman's disease /kas′əlmənz/ [Benjamin Castleman, American pathologist, 1906–1982], a condition resembling lymphoma but without recognizable malignant cells, characterized by isolated masses of lymphoid tissue and lymph node hyperplasia, usually in the abdominal or mediastinal area. The disease may be either benign or premalignant and overlap with autoimmune diseases.

castor oil /kas′tər/ [L, beaver, *oleum,* olive oil], an oil derived from *Ricinus communis,* used as a stimulant cathartic. It is prescribed as a cleansing preparation of the bowel or colon before examination and, rarely, for constipation.

castration /kastrā′shən/ [L, *castrare,* to castrate], the surgical excision of one or both testicles or ovaries, performed most frequently to reduce the production and secretion of certain hormones that may stimulate the proliferation of malignant cells in women with breast cancer or in men with prostate cancer.

castration anxiety, 1. the fantasized fear of injury or loss of the genital organs, often as the reaction to a repressed feeling of punishment for forbidden sexual desires. **2.** a general threat to the masculinity or femininity of a person or an unrealistic fear of bodily injury or loss of power.

cast saw, a tool used to cut through a cast.

cast shoe, a shoe worn over a foot that is encased in a cast.

cast stabilization, the use of rods, pins, wooden shafts, or other devices to lend stability to a cast.

casualty /kazh′əltē/ [L, *casus,* chance], **1.** a serious or fatal accident. **2.** the victim of a serious or fatal accident. **3.** a person, killed, wounded, or otherwise disabled in war.

casuistics /kazh′əwis′tiks/ [L, *casus,* a happening], the recording and study of the cases of any disease.

CAT /kat/, abbreviation for *computerized axial tomography.*

catabasis /kətab′əsis/ *pl.* **catabases** [Gk, *kata,* down, *bainein,* to go], the phase in which a disease declines.—**catabatic** /kat′əbat′ik/, *adj.*

catabiosis /kat′əbī·ō′sis/, the normal aging of cells.—**catabiotic,** *adj.*

catabolic illness /kat′əbol′ik/, a disorder characterized by weight loss and diminished muscle mass and body fat. Underlying causes include infection, injury, organ system failure, chemotherapy, and uncontrolled DM, particularly type 1.

catabolism /kətab′əliz′əm/ [Gk, *kata* + *ballein,* to throw], a metabolic process in which complex substances are broken down by living cells into simple compounds.—**catabolic,** *adj.*

catachronobiology /kat′əkrō′nōbī·ol′əjē/, the study of the harmful effects of time on living systems.

catacrotism /kətak′rətiz′əm/ [Gk, *kata* + *krotein,* to strike], an anomaly of the pulse, characterized by one or more small additional waves in the descending limb of the pulse tracing.—**catacrotic,** *adj.*

catagen, the brief portion of the hair cycle in which growth of the hair (anagen) stops and resting (telogen) begins.

catagenesis /kat′əjen′əsis/ [Gk, *kata,* down, *genein,* to produce], a form of evolution that is retrogressive.

catalase /kat′əlās/ [Gk, *katalein,* to dissolve], a heme enzyme, found in almost all biologic cells, that catalyzes the decomposition of hydrogen peroxide to water and oxygen.

catalepsy /kat′əlep′sē/ [Gk, *kata* + *lambanein,* to seize], an abnormal state characterized by a trancelike LOC and postural rigidity. It occurs in hypnosis and in certain organic and psychologic disorders such as schizophrenia, epilepsy, and hysteria.— **cataleptic,** *adj.*

catalysis /kətal′əsis/ [Gk, *katalein,* to dissolve], an increase in the rate of a chemical reaction that is caused by a substance that is neither permanently altered nor consumed by the reaction.— **catalytic,** *adj.*

catalyst /kat′əlist/ [Gk, *katalein,* to dissolve], a substance that influences the rate of a chemical reaction without being permanently altered or consumed by the process. Most catalysts, including enzymes in living organisms, accelerate chemical reactions; negative catalysts retard such reactions.

catamnesis /kat′amnē′sis/ [Gk, *kata* + *men,* month], the medical history of a patient from the onset of an illness.

cataphoria /kat′əfôr′ē·ə/, a tendency of the visual axes of both eyes to assume a low plane after the visual fusional stimuli have been eliminated.

cataphylaxis /kat′əfəlak′sis/ [Gk, *kata* + *phylax,* guard], **1.** the migration of leukocytes and antibodies to the site of an infection. **2.** the deterioration of the natural defense system of the body.— **cataphylactic,** *adj.*

cataplexy /kat′əplek′sē/ [Gk, *kata* + *plexis,* stroke], a condition characterized by sudden loss of muscle tone, usually resulting in a fall, caused by strong emotions such as anger, fear, or surprise, often associated with narcolepsy.— **cataplectic,** *adj.*

Catapres, a trademark for an antihypertensive (clonidine hydrochloride).

cataract /kat′ərakt/ [Gk, *katarrhakies,* waterfall], an abnormal progressive condition of the lens of the eye, characterized by loss of transparency. A gray-white opacity can be observed within the lens, behind the pupil. Most cataracts are caused by degenerative changes, often occurring after 50 years of age. The tendency to develop cataracts is inherited. Trauma, such as a puncture wound, may result in cataract formation. Less often, exposure to such poisons as dinitrophenol or naphthalene causes them.

cataractogenic /kat′ərak′tōjen′ik/, pertaining to agents that may cause cataracts.

cataract removal, removal of a cloudy lens from the interior of the eye. The most common method of removal is extracapsular, in which the lens cortex and nucleus are expressed from the eye after the anterior portion of the capsule is removed, leaving the posterior capsule behind. An intraocular lens is usually implanted after lens removal for visual correction. In recent years, sutureless cataract techniques have increased in popularity because of the rapidity of rehabilitation. Clear cornea microincisions allow the use of topical anesthesia in place of retrobulbar anesthesia.

catarrh /kətär′/ [Gk, *kata* + *rhoia,* flow], inflammation of the mucous membranes with discharge, especially inflammation of the air passages of the nose and the trachea.— **catarrhal, catarrhous,** *adj.*

catarrhal conjunctivitis [Gk, *kata* + *rhoia*; L, *conjunctivus,* connecting; Gk, *itis,* inflammation], a simple form of inflammation of the conjunctiva, usually associated with an infection such as a cold, allergy, exposure to pollution, or physical irritation, as by an eyelash in the eye. It is accompanied by discharge and can be acute or chronic.

catarrhal croup [Gk, *kata* + *rhoia*; Scot, to croak], severe laryngitis accompanied by a croupy cough.

catarrhalophthalmia [Gk, *kata* + *rhoia* + *ophthalmos,* eye], a catarrhal inflammation of the conjunctiva with a discharge.

catastrophic care /kat′əstrof′ik/ [Gk, *katastrophe,* sudden downturn; L, *garrire,* to babble], a pattern of medical and nursing care that involves intensive, highly specialized life-support care of an acutely ill or severely traumatized patient.

catastrophic health insurance, health insurance that awards benefits to pay for the cost of severe or lengthy disability or illness. Most policies have a limit in total benefits paid, and payment for certain kinds of services may be precluded or limited to a maximum indemnity.

catastrophic illness, any illness that requires lengthy hospitalization, extremely expensive therapies, or other care that would deplete a family's financial resources, unless covered by special medical insurance policies. In Canada, catastrophic illness is covered by Medicare.

catastrophic reaction [Gk, *katastrophe,* sudden downturn; L, *re,* again, *agere,* to act], the uncoordinated response to a drastic shock or a sudden threatening condition, as often occurs in the victims of car crashes and disasters.

catatonia /kat′ətō′nē·ə/ [Gk, *kata* + *tonos,* tension], a state of psychologically induced immobility with muscular rigidity at times interrupted by agitation.—**catatonic,** *adj.*

catatonic excitement /kat′əton′ik/, a state of extreme agitation that may occur when a patient is unable to maintain catatonic immobility.

catatonic schizophrenia [Gk, *kata* + *tonos* + *schizein,* to split, *phren,* mind], a form of schizophrenia characterized by alternating periods of extreme withdrawal and extreme excitement. During the withdrawal stage, stupor, waxy flexibility, muscular rigidity, mutism, blocking, negativism, and catalepsy (cerea flexibilitas) may be seen. During the period of excitement, purposeless and impulsive activity may range from mild agitation to violence.

catatonic stupor, a form of catatonia characterized by a marked decrease in response to the environment with a reduction in spontaneous movement.

CAT-CAM, abbreviation for **contoured adducted trochanteric controlled alignment method.**

catchment /kach′ment/, the catching or collecting of water.

catchment area [L, *capere,* to take, *area,* space], the specific geographic area for which a particular institution, especially a mental health center, is responsible.

catch-up growth [L, *capere*; As, *uf* + *gruowan*], an acceleration of the growth rate following a period of growth retardation caused by a secondary deficiency such as acute malnutrition or severe illness. The phenomenon, which routinely occurs in premature infants, involves rapid increase in weight, length, and head circumference and continues until the normal individual growth pattern is resumed.

cat-cry syndrome [L, *catta,* cat, *quiritare,* to cry out; Gk, *syndromos,* course], a rare, congenital disorder recognized at birth by a kitten-like cry caused by a laryngeal anomaly. The condition is associated with a defect in chromosome 5. Other characteristics include low birth weight, microcephaly, "moon face," wide-set eyes, strabismus, and low-set misshapen ears. Infants are hypotonic; heart defects and mental and physical retardation are common.

catecholamine /kat′əkəlam′in/, any one of a group of sympathomimetic compounds composed of a catechol (1,2-dihydroxyphenyl) moiety carrying an alkyl side chain with an amine group on the side chain. Some catecholamines are produced naturally by the body and function as key neurologic chemicals.

catechol-*O*-methyl transferase (COMT) /kat′əkol′ōmeth′il/, an enzyme that deactivates the catecholamines dopa, dopamine, epinephrine, and norepinephrine.

categoric data /kat′əgôr′ik/ [Gk, *kategorikos,* affirmation; L, *datus,* giving], (in research) any data that are classified by name rather than by number, such as race, religion, ethnicity, or marital status.

categoric variable, one of the variables that are not continuous but instead put data into categories.

Category A Diseases/Agents, bioterrorism diseases or agents that can be easily disseminated or transmitted from person to person, result in high mortality rates and have the potential for major public health impact, might cause public panic and social disruption, and require special action for public health preparedness.

Category B Diseases/Agents, bioterrorism diseases or agents that are moderately easy to disseminate, result in moderate morbidity rates and low mortality rates, and require specific enhancements of CDC's diagnostic capacity and enhanced disease surveillance.

Category C Diseases/Agents, emerging pathogens that could be engineered for mass dissemination in the future because of availability, ease of production and dissemination, and potential for high morbidity and mortality rates and major health impact.

cat-eye syndrome [L, *catta*; AS, *eage*; Gk, *syndromos,* course], a rare congenital autosomal anomaly, marked by the presence of an extra, small chromosome 22 and pupils that resemble the vertical pupils of a cat.

catgut [L, *catta*; AS, *guttas*], an absorbable suture material, prepared from the intestines of mammals, used to close surgical wounds. It can be treated with chronic salts to delay absorption and enhance strength.

catharsis /kəthär′sis/, **1.** a cleansing or purging. **2.** the therapeutic release of pent-up feelings and emotions by open discussion of ideas and thoughts. **3.** the process of drawing repressed ideas and feelings into the consciousness by the technique of free association, often in conjunction with hypnosis and the use of hypnotic drugs.

cathartic /kəthär′tik/ [Gk, *katharsis,* cleansing], **1.** pertaining to a substance that causes evacuation of the bowel. **2.** an agent that promotes bowel evacuation by stimulating peristalsis, increasing the fluidity or bulk of intestinal contents, softening the feces, or lubricating the intestinal wall.

catheter /kath′ətər/ [Gk, *katheter,* something lowered], a hollow flexible tube that can be inserted into a vessel or cavity of the body to withdraw or instill fluids, directly monitor various types of information, and visualize a vessel or cavity.

catheter hub, a threaded plastic connection at the end of an IV catheter.

catheterization /kath′ətur′īzā′shən/, the introduction of a catheter into a body cavity or organ to inject or remove a fluid. —**catheterize** /kath′ətərīz/, *v.*

cathexis /kəthek′sis/ [Gk, *kathexis,* retention], the conscious or unconscious attachment of emotional feeling and importance to a specific idea, person, or object. —**cathectic,** *adj.*

cathode (C) /kath′ōd/ [Gk, *kata,* down, *hodos,* way], **1.** the electrode at which reduction occurs. **2.** the negative side of the x-ray tube, which consists of the focusing cup and the filament.

cathode ray, a stream of electrons emitted by a negative electrode when it is bombarded by positive ions, in a gaseous discharge device called a cathode ray tube. The ray is focused and deflected by electromagnets that control the position at which it strikes a screen coated with a phosphor, creating a visible pattern.

cathode ray oscilloscope [Gk, *kata* + *hodos;* L, *radius* + *ocillare,* to swing; Gk, *skopein,* to view], an instrument that produces a visual representation of electrical variations by means of the fluorescent screen of a cathode ray tube. Oscilloscopes have many applications in medicine and in nursing, such as the displaying of patients' brain waves and heartbeats for monitoring and diagnostic purposes.

cathode ray tube (CRT), a vacuum tube that focuses a beam of electrons onto a spot on a screen coated with a phosphor, creating a visible image of information on the face of the tube.

cation /kat′ī·on/ [Gk, *kata,* down, *ion,* going], a positively charged ion.

cation-exchange resin, any one of various insoluble organic polymers with high molecular weights that exchange their cations for other ions in solution.

catling, a long, sharp, double-edged knife used in amputation.

catoptric /kətop′trik/ [Gk, *katoptron,* mirror], pertaining to a reflected image or reflected light, such as from a mirror.

cat's claw, a herb that belongs to the madder family, found in South America and Southeast Asia. It is used for cancer, herpes, arthritis, gastritis, gout, wounds, and gastric ulcers. There may be short-termed benefits when used for osteoarthritis, but effectiveness for other indications has not been proven.

cat-scratch fever, a disease that results from the scratch or bite of a healthy cat. It is caused by the bacterium *Bartonella.* Inflammation and pustules are found on the scratched skin and lymph nodes in the neck, head, groin, or axilla swell later. Fever, headache, and malaise may occur, and symptoms can persist for months.

cat's eye amaurosis [L, *catta;* AS, *aege;* Gk, *amauroin,* to darken], a monocular blindness, with a bright reflection from the pupil caused by a white mass in the vitreous humor resulting from inflammation or a malignant lesion.

Caucasian, pertaining to a person whose ancestors were believed to have in ancient times inhabited the geographic region of the Caucasus in southeastern Europe or whose ancestors were members of the hypothetical Indo-European cultures identified with the Caucasus.

caudad /kô′dad/ [L, *cauda,* tail], toward the tail or end of the body, away from the head.

cauda equina [L, *cauda* + *equus,* horse], the lower end of the spinal cord at the first lumbar vertebra and the bundle of lumbar, sacral, and coccygeal nerve roots that emerge from the spinal cord and descend through the spinal canal of the sacrum and coccyx.

caudal /kô′dəl/, toward the distal end of the body or an inferior position.

caudal anesthesia, the injection of a local anesthetic agent into the caudal portion of the epidural space through the sacral hiatus to anesthetize sacral and lower lumbar nerve roots. It is now rarely performed except in pediatric anesthesia.

caudal eminence, a tail-like eminence produced by a proliferating mass of mesodermal cells at the caudal end of the early vertebrate embryo. It is the remnant of the primitive node and the precursor of hindgut, adjacent notochord and somites, and the caudal part of the spinal cord.

caudal ligaments, bands of fibrous tissue attaching the skin to the coccyx. Remnants of the embryonic notochord, they form a small cup-shaped depression.

caudal regression syndrome, failure of formation of part or all of the coccygeal, sacral, and occasionally lumbar vertebral units and the corresponding segments of the caudal spinal cord, with resulting neurogenic dysfunction of bowel and bladder.

caudate /kô′dāt/, having a tail.

caudate lobe of the liver [L, *cauda,* tail; Gk, *lobos,* lobe; AS, *lifer*], a part of the right lobe of the liver that lies near the vena cava.

caudate nucleus [L, *cauda*, tail, *nucleus*, nut kernel], a crescent-shaped mass of gray matter lateral to the thalamus in the floor of the anterior horn and body of the lateral ventricle.

caudate process [L, *cauda* + *processus*, projection], a small elevation of tissue that extends obliquely from the lower extremity of the caudate lobe of the liver to the visceral surface of the right lobe.

caudocephalad /kô'dōsef'əlad/ [L, *cauda*, tail; Gk, *kephale*, head; L, *ad*, toward], movement from the tail toward the head.

caul /kôl/ [ME, *cawel*, basket], the intact amniotic sac surrounding the fetus at birth. The sac usually ruptures or is ruptured during the course of labor or delivery. When it remains intact, it must be torn or cut to allow the baby to breathe.

cauliflower ear [L, *caulis*, cabbage, *fiore*, flower; AS, *eare*], a thickened, deformed pinna and external ear caused by repeated trauma, such as that suffered by boxers.

caumesthesia /kô'məsthē'zhə/ [Gk, *kauma*, heat, *aisthesis*, feeling], an abnormal condition in which a patient has a low temperature but experiences a sense of intense heat. —**caumesthetic**, *adj.*

causalgia /kôzal'jə/ [Gk, *kausis*, burning, *algos*, pain], a severe sensation of burning pain, often in an extremity, sometimes accompanied by local erythema of the skin caused by peripheral nerve injury.

causal hypothesis /kô'səl/ [L, *causa*, cause; Gk, *hypotithenia*, foundation], (in research) a hypothesis that predicts a cause-and-effect relationship among the variables to be studied.

causal hypothesis testing study, (in nursing research) an experimental design used in testing a hypothesis that predicts a cause-and-effect relationship within the data to be studied.

causality /kôsal'itē/, (in research) a relationship between one phenomenon or event (A) and another (B) in which A precedes and causes B. The direction of influence and the nature of the effect are predictable and reproducible and may be empirically observed.

causation /kôsā'shən/ [L, *causa*], (in law) the existence of a reasonable connection between the misfeasance, malfeasance, or nonfeasance of the defendant and the injury or damage suffered by the plaintiff.

cause [L, *causa*], any process, substance, or organism that produces an effect or condition.

CAUSN, abbreviation for **Canadian Association of University Schools of Nursing.**

caustic /kôs'tik/ [Gk, *kaustikos*, burning], **1.** any substance that is destructive to living tissue such as silver nitrate, nitric acid, or sulfuric acid. **2.** exerting a burning or corrosive effect.

caustic poisoning, the accidental ingestion of strong acids or alkalis, resulting in burns and tissue damage to the mouth, esophagus, and stomach.

caustics, strong alkaline chemicals, such as hydrofluoric acid, that destroy soft body tissues, resulting in deep penetrating burns and corrosion of the skin, eyes, and mucous membranes on contact. Exposure may be by inhalation or ingestion.

CAUT, abbreviation for **Canadian Association of University Teachers.**

cauterization /kô'tərīzā'shən/ [Gk, *kauterion*, branding iron], the process of burning a part of the body by cautery.

cauterize /kô'tərīz/ [Gk, *kauterion*, branding iron], **1.** to burn tissues by thermal heat, including steam, hot metal, or solar radiation; electricity; or another agent, such as laser or dry ice, usually with the objective of destroying damaged or diseased tissues, preventing infections, or coagulating blood vessels. **2.** to apply a cautery; to perform cauterization.

cautery /kô'tərē/ [Gk, *kauterion*, branding iron], **1.** a device or agent used in the coagulation of tissue by heat or caustic substances. **2.** a destructive effect produced by a cauterizing agent.

cautery knife, a surgical knife that cuts tissue and seals it to prevent bleeding. The knife is connected to an electric source that generates the heat necessary for cauterization.

Cavell, Edith /kəvel'/, an English nurse. Trained at London Hospital, she was named head of a nurses' training school in Brussels in 1907, with the task of raising nursing standards to match those of Britain. After the Germans occupied Belgium in World War I, she nursed or sheltered more than 200 fleeing soldiers and helped them reach Holland. For this, she was arrested by the Germans, tried, and shot on October 12, 1915. Her execution, which she met with courage and fortitude, brought her widespread fame.

caveola *pl.* **caveolae,** a small pit, depression, or invagination, such as any of the minute pits or incuppings of the cell membrane formed during pinocytosis, which close and then pinch off to form small, free, fluid-filled vesicles in the cytoplasm.

Caverject, a trademark for an injectable prostaglandin-derived drug for the treatment of male impotence (alprostadil).

cavernous /kav'ərnəs/ [L, *caverna*, hollow place], containing cavities or hollow spaces.

cavernous hemangioma [L, *caverna*, hollow place; Gk, *haima*, blood, *oma*, tumor], a benign, congenital red or purple tumor consisting of enlarged red vessels. The scalp, face, and neck are the most common sites.

cavernous nerve, one of the terminal branches of the inferior hypogastric plexuses that innervate the erectile tissues of the penis.

cavernous sinus [L, *caverna* + *sinus*, curve], one of a pair of irregularly shaped bilateral venous channels between the sphenoid bone of the skull and the dura mater. It is one of the five anterior inferior venous sinuses that drain the blood from the dura mater into the internal jugular vein.

cavernous sinus syndrome, an abnormal condition characterized by edema of the conjunctiva, the upper eyelid, and the root of the nose and by paralysis of the third, fourth, and sixth cranial nerves. It is caused by a thrombosis of the cavernous sinus.

cavernous sinus thrombosis, a syndrome, usually secondary to infections near the eye or nose, characterized by orbital edema, venous congestion of the eye, and palsy of the nerves supplying the extraocular muscles. The infection may spread to involve the CSF and meninges.

CAVH, abbreviation for *continuous arteriovenous hemofiltration.*

cavitary /kav'iter'ē/ [L, *cavus*, hollow], **1.** denoting the presence of one or more cavities. **2.** any entozoon having a body cavity or an alimentary canal.

cavitate /kav'itāt/ [L, *cavus*, hollow], to rapidly form and collapse vapor pockets or bubbles in a flowing fluid with low-pressure areas, often causing damage to surrounding structures.

cavitation, 1. the formation of cavities within the body, such as those formed in the lung by TB. **2.** any cavity within the body, such as the pleural cavities.

cavity /kav'itē/ [L, *cavus*], **1.** a hollow space within a larger structure, such as the peritoneal or oral cavity. **2.** *nontechnical*. a space in a tooth formed by dental caries.

cavity classification, a method for describing dental caries based on the tooth surfaces on which they occur (labial, buccal, lingual, incisal, occlusal, or root), the type of surface on which they occur (pit and fissure or smooth), their frequency of occurrence, and their numeric designation according to the **classification of caries.**

cavity preparation, a procedure for the removal of diseased hard tissues of a tooth and the shaping of the surgical site to an acceptable form necessary to receive and retain a restoration.

cavogram /kav'əgram'/ [L, *cavus*; Gk, *gramma*, record], an angiogram of the inferior or superior vena cava.

cavosurface /kāv'ōsur'fəs/ [L, *cavus*, cavity + *superficies*, surface], the surface of a cavity, as of a tooth.

cavosurface angle /kāv'ōsur'fəs/, the angle formed by the junction of the wall of a prepared tooth cavity with the external surface of the tooth.

cavosurface bevel [L, *cavus* + *superficies*, surface; OFr, *baif*, open mouth], the incline of the cavosurface angle of a prepared tooth cavity wall relative to the enamel wall.

cavum /kā'vəm/ *pl.* **cava, 1.** any hollow or cavity. **2.** the inferior or superior vena cava.

cavus /kā'vəs/ [L, *cavus*, cavity], an abnormally high or exaggerated arch of the foot.

CBA, abbreviation for **cost-benefit analysis.**

CBC, abbreviation for **complete blood count.**

CBF, abbreviation for **cerebral blood flow.**

CBI, abbreviation for **continuous bladder irrigation.**

cc, abbreviation for **cubic centimeter.**

CC, 1. abbreviation for **chief complaint. 2.** abbreviation for *Commission Certified.*

CCD, abbreviation for **charge-coupled device.**

CCK test, abbreviation for **cholecystokinin.**

CCNE, abbreviation for **Commission on Collegiate Nursing Education.**

CCP, abbreviation for **complement control protein.**

CCPD, abbreviation for **continuous cycling peritoneal dialysis.**

CCRN, 1. abbreviation for *Certified Critical Care Registered Nurse.* **2.** a trademark of **American Association of Critical-Care Nurses Certified Corporation.**

CCU, 1. abbreviation for **coronary care unit. 2.** abbreviation for **critical care unit.**

Cd, symbol for the element **cadmium.**

CD4, (cluster designation 4) symbol for a glycoprotein expressed on the surface of helper T lymphocytes and other immune cells. CD4 serves as a receptor for HIV envelope glycoprotein gp120. Binding of the viral glycoprotein gp120 to CD4 is the first step in viral entry, leading to the fusion of viral and cell membranes.

CD4/CD8 count, the ratio of the number of helper T lymphocytes to the number of suppressor and cytotoxic T lymphocytes. The cells are counted with the use of monoclonal antibodies to the surface glycoproteins CD4 on helper T cells and CD8 on suppressor and cytotoxic T cells.

In healthy individuals the ratio ranges from 1.6 to 2.2. The ratio is important in monitoring the function of the immune system in patients who have viral infections or who have undergone tissue transplantation.

CD4 cell, CD4+ cell, a major classification of T lymphocytes, referring to those that carry the CD4 antigen. Most are helper cells.

CD4+ cell count, a measure of the number of helper T cells that carry the CD4 glycoprotein on their cell surface and that help B cells produce certain antibodies. HIV binds to CD4 and kills T cells bearing this glycoprotein. Thus the CD4+ cell count is an indicator of the progress of an HIV infection and helps measure the effectiveness of anti-HIV drugs.

CD8 cell, a T lymphocyte that secretes large amounts of gamma-interferon, a lymphokine involved in the body's defense against viruses. CD8 cells prevent the unnecessary formation of antibodies.

CD8 cell, CD8+ cell, a major classification of T lymphocytes, referring to those that carry the CD8 antigen; the major subtypes are the cytotoxic T lymphocytes and the suppressor cells.

CD8 T lymphocytes, CD8+ T lymphocytes,

CDA, abbreviation for **certified dental assistant.**

CD antigen, any of a number of cell-surface markers expressed by leukocytes and used to distinguish cell lineages, developmental stages, and functional subsets. Such markers can be identified by specific monoclonal antibodies and are numbered by their cluster of differentiation, as in CD1, CD2, etc.

cdc, abbreviation for **cell division cycle.**

CDC, abbreviation for **Centers for Disease Control and Prevention.**

CDE, **1.** the major symbols used in one system for the nomenclature of the Rh system, in which D is the same as Rh0, the major determining factor of Rh positivity. **2.** abbreviation for **common duct exploration.** **3.** abbreviation for *Certified Diabetes Educator.*

CDH, abbreviation for **congenital dislocation of the hip.**

CDK, abbreviation for **cyclin-dependent kinase.**

CDR, abbreviation for **computed dental radiography.**

Ce, symbol for the element **cerium.**

CEA, **1.** abbreviation for **carcinoembryonic antigen.** **2.** abbreviation for **carotid endarterectomy.**

ceasmic /sē-az′mik/ [Gk, *keazein,* to split], pertaining to or characterized by a persistent embryonic fissure or abnormal cleavage of parts.

ceasmic teratism [Gk, *keazein + teras,* monster], a congenital anomaly, caused by developmental arrest, in which body parts that should be fused remain in their fissured embryonic state, such as in cleft palate.

cecal /sē′kəl/ [L, *caecus,* blind, blind gut], **1.** pertaining to the cecum. **2.** pertaining to the optic disc or the blind spot in the retina.

cecal artery, one of the branches of the ileocolic artery that supply the cecum.

cecal volvulus, a type of colonic volvulus consisting of twisting or displacement and anomalous rotation of the cecum, such as in volvulus neonatorum or Ladd's syndrome.

cecitis /sē-sī′tis/ [L, *caecus,* blind, blind gut], inflammation of the cecum.

Ceclor, a trademark for a cephalosporin antibiotic (cefaclor).

cecocolostomy /sē′kōkələos′təmē/ [L, *caecus,* blind, blind gut; Gk, *kolon,* colon, *stoma,* mouth], **1.** a surgical operation that creates an anastomosis between the cecum and the colon. **2.** the anastomosis produced by this operation.

cecoileostomy /-il′ē-os′təmē/ [L, *caecus + ilia,* intestine, *stoma,* mouth], a surgical operation that connects the ileum with the cecum.

cecopexy /sē′kōpek′sē/ [L, *caecus;* Gk, *pexis,* fix], a surgical operation that fixes or suspends the cecum to correct its excessive mobility.

cecostomy /sēkos′təmē/ [L, *caecus;* Gk, *stoma,* mouth], the surgical construction of an opening into the cecum, performed as a temporary measure to relieve intestinal obstruction in a patient who cannot tolerate major surgery.

cecum /sē′kəm/ [L,*caecus,*blind,blindgut], a pouchlike structure or cul-de-sac constituting the first part of the large intestine.

Cedax, a trademark for an oral cephalosporin (ceftibuten).

CeeNU, a trademark for an antineoplastic (lomustine).

cefaclor /sē′fəklôr/, a cephalosporin antibiotic prescribed in the treatment of selected infections caused by susceptible strains of bacteria.

cefadroxil monohydrate /sē′fədrok′sil/, a cephalosporin antibiotic prescribed in the treatment of selected bacterial infections.

Cefadyl, a trademark for an antibiotic (cephapirin).

cefamandole nafate /sēfəman′dōl naf′āt/, a cephalosporin antibiotic prescribed in the treatment of infections caused by susceptible bacterial strains.

cefazolin sodium /sēfaz′ōlin/, a cephalosporin antibiotic prescribed in the treatment of infections caused by susceptible bacterial strains.

cefdinir, a broad-spectrum cephalosporin (third generation) antibiotic used to treat *Haemophilus influenzae, H. parainfluenzae, Morganella catarrhalis, Streptococcus pneumoniae, Staphylococcus pyogenes,* and *S. aureus.*

cefditoren pivoxil, an antiinfective agent used to treat acute bacterial exacerbation of chronic bronchitis, pharyngitis/tonsillitis, uncomplicated skin, and skin structure infections.

cefepime, a fourth-generation cephalosporin used to treat infections caused by gram-negative bacilli, including *Escherichia coli, Proteus,* and *Klebsiella;* gram-positive organisms, including *Streptococcus pneumoniae, S. pyogenes,* and *Staphylococcus aureus;* and infections of the lower respiratory tract, urinary tract, skin, and bone.

cefepime hydrochloride, the hydrochloride salt of cefepime, used in treatment of infections of the skin and soft tissue and of the respiratory and urinary tracts.

Cefizox, a trademark for a cephalosporin antibiotic (ceftizoxime).

Cefobid, a trademark for a cephalosporin antibiotic (cefoperazone).

cefonicid sodium /sĕfon′isid/, a parenteral cephalosporin-type antibiotic prescribed for bacterial infections of the lower respiratory or urinary tract, skin, bones and joints; septicemia; and surgical prophylaxis.

cefoperazone sodium /sē′fōper′əzōn/, a third-generation cephalosporin antibiotic prescribed in the treatment of respiratory tract, bone joint, skin, and female genital tract infections and of bacterial septicemia.

Cefotan, a trademark for a cephalosporin antibiotic (cefotetan disodium).

cefotaxime sodium /sēfōtak′zēm/, a third-generation cephalosporin antibiotic prescribed for lower respiratory tract, genitourinary, gynecologic, skin, bone and joint, and CNS infections and for bacterial septicemia caused by strains of susceptible microorganisms.

cefotetan disodium /sē′fōtet′ən/, a parenteral second-generation cephalosporin antibiotic with greater activity against anaerobes and gram negative bacilli than first-generation cephalosporins. It is prescribed for bacterial infections of the lower respiratory tract, urinary tract, skin, abdomen, bones or joints, or reproductive organs and for surgical prophylaxis.

cefoxitin sodium /sēfok′sitin/, a parenteral second-generation cephalosporin antibiotic with greater activity against anaerobes and gram-negative bacilli than first-generation cephalosporins. It is prescribed for bacterial infections of the lower respiratory tract, urinary tract, skin, abdomen, bones or joints, or reproductive organs and for surgical prophylaxis.

ceftazidime /seftaz′idēm/, a parenteral third-generation cephalosporin-type antibiotic prescribed for treatment of documented *Pseudomonas aeruginosa* infection and other bacterial infections of the lower respiratory tract, urinary tract, skin, abdomen, blood, bones and joints, and CNS.

ceftibuten, an oral third-generation cephalosporin prescribed in the treatment of chronic bronchitis, acute bacterial otitis media, pharyngitis, and tonsillitis.

ceftizoxime sodium /sef′tizok′zēm/, a third-generation cephalosporin antibiotic. It is prescribed in the treatment of infections caused by susceptible bacterial strains (does not include *Pseudomonas aeruginosa*), primarily in the respiratory system, genitourinary system, bone, joints, and skin.

ceftriaxone sodium /sef′trī-ak′sōn/, a parenteral third-generation cephalosporin antibiotic prescribed for infections of the lower respiratory tract, urinary tract, skin, abdomen, bones, and joints. It is also used to treat gonorrhea, septicemia, and meningitis and in surgical prophylaxis, particularly in coronary bypass operations.

cefuroxime sodium /sef′o͞orok′zēm/, a cephalosporin antibiotic prescribed in the treatment of lower respiratory tract, urinary tract, skin, and gonococcal infections; bacterial septicemia; and meningitis and for the prevention of postoperative infections.

celecoxib /sel′ekok′sib/, an NSAID of the COX-2 inhibitors group, administered orally for symptomatic treatment of arthritis.

Celestone, a trademark for a glucocorticoid (betamethasone).

Celexa /sĕ-lek′sə/, a trademark for a preparation of citalopram hydrobromide, an antidepressant.

celiac /sē′lē-ak/ [Gk, *koilia,* belly], pertaining to the abdominal cavity.

celiac artery [Gk, *koilia,* belly, *arteria,* airpipe], a thick visceral branch of the abdominal aorta, arising caudal to the diaphragm, usually dividing into the left gastric, common hepatic, and splenic arteries.

celiac disease [Gk, *koilia;* L, *dis,* opposite of; Fr, *aise,* ease], an inborn error of metabolism characterized by the inability to hydrolyze peptides contained in gluten. The disease affects adults and young children who suffer from abdominal distension, vomiting, diarrhea, muscle wasting, and extreme lethargy. A characteristic sign is a pale, foul-smelling stool that floats on water because of its high fat content.

celiac ganglion, a group of nerve cells located on each side of the crura of the diaphragm. The cells are connected to the celiac plexus.

celiacoduodenal part of suspensory muscle of duodenum, a band of smooth muscle that passes from the terminal duodenum to join the phrenicocoeliac part (pars phrenicocoeliaca) and end in connective tissue that attaches to the celiac trunk.

celiac rickets [Gk, *koilia* + *rhachis,* spine, *itis,* inflammation], arrested growth and osseous deformities resulting from malabsorption of fat and calcium.

celiocolpotomy /sē′lē·ōkəlpot′əmē/ [Gk, *koilia* + *kolpos,* vagina, *temnein,* to cut], an incision into the abdomen through the vagina.

cell [L, *cella,* storeroom], the fundamental unit of all living tissue. **Eukaryotic cells** consist of a nucleus, cytoplasm, and organelles surrounded by a plasma membrane. Within the nucleus are the nucleolus (containing RNA) and the chromatin (containing protein and DNA), which form chromosomes, wherein are located the determinants of inherited characteristics. Organelles within the cytoplasm include the endoplasmic reticulum, ribosomes, Golgi apparatus, mitochondria, lysosomes, and centrosome. **Prokaryotic cells** are much smaller and simpler than eukaryocytic cells, even lacking a nucleus. The specialized nature of body tissue reflects the specialized structure and function of its constituent cells.

cella /sel′ə/ *pl.* **cellae** [L, storeroom], an enclosed space.

cell bank, a storage facility for frozen tissue samples held for research purposes and for surgical reconstruction of damaged body structures.

cell body [L, *cella;* AS, *bodig*], the part of a cell that contains the nucleus and surrounding cytoplasm exclusive of any projections or processes, such as the axon and dendrites of a neuron or the tail of a spermatozoon.

cell culture [L, *cella,* storeroom, *colere,* to cultivate], living cells that are maintained in vitro in artificial media of serum and nutrients for the study and growth of certain strains of microorganisms or for experiments in controlling diseases, such as cancer. They are routinely used to culture viruses that infect patients.

cell death, **1.** terminal failure of a cell to maintain essential life functions. **2.** the point in the process of dying at which vital functions have ceased at the cellular level. **3.** programmed cell death.

cell determination, the process by which an undifferentiated embryonic cell becomes committed to develop into a specific type of cell. Cell determination appears to involve the selective activation of certain sets of genes and the inactivation of others.

cell division, the continuous process by which a cell alternates between a long interphase period and mitosis. Cell division does not occur in discrete steps: each phase is part of a continuous process that may require hours for its completion. During the interphase period, new DNA, RNA, and protein molecules are synthesized before the start of the next prophase.

cell division cycle (cdc), the sequence of events that occur during the growth and division of cells.

CELLector, a trademark for a device that modifies human blood cells by circulating them through a box containing a number of polystyrene plates.

cell inclusion [L, *cella,* storeroom, *in* + *claudere,* to shut], any foreign matter or residual elements of the cytoplasm that are enclosed within a cell.

cell line [L, *cella* + *linea*], a colony of animal cells derived and developed as a subculture from a primary cell culture.

cell-mediated cytotoxicity, cytolysis of a target cell by effector lymphocytes, such as cytotoxic T lymphocytes or natural killer cells. It may be antibody-dependent *(antibody-dependent cell-mediated cytotoxicity)* or independent, as in certain type IV hypersensitivity reactions.

cell-mediated hypersensitivity, hypersensitivity initiated by antigen-specific T lymphocytes. Unlike forms of hypersensitivity mediated by antibodies, it takes one or more days to develop and can be transferred by lymphocytes but not by serum.

cell-mediated immune response, a delayed reaction of the immune system, mediated primarily by sensitized T lymphocytes rather than antibodies. Cellmediated immune response reactions are responsible for defense against certain bacterial, fungal, and viral pathogens; malignant cells; and other foreign proteins and tissues.

cell organelle [L, *cella,* storeroom; Gk, *organon,* instrument], any of a number of membrane-bound structures within a cell that have specific functions, such as reproduction or metabolism.

cell receptor, a protein located either on a cell's surface, in its cytoplasm, or in its nucleus that binds to a specific ligand, initiating signal transduction and a change in cellular activity.

cells of Paneth /pä′nət, pan′əth/ [Josef Paneth, Austrian physiologist, 1857–1890], large granular epithelial cells found in intestinal glands. They secrete digestive enzymes and bactericidal lysozyme.

cell-surface marker, an antigenic determinant found on the surface of a specific type of cell.

cell theory, the proposition that cells are the basic units of all living tissues or organisms and that cellular function is the essential process of living things.

cellular /sel′yələr/ [L, *cella,* storeroom], pertaining to or consisting of cells.

cellular immunity [L, *cellula,* little cell, *immunis,* exempt], the mechanism of acquired immunity characterized by the dominant role of T-cell lymphocytes. Cellular immunity is involved in resistance to infectious diseases caused by viruses and some bacteria and in delayed hypersensitivity reactions, some aspects of resistance to cancer, certain autoimmune diseases, graft rejection, and certain allergies.

cellular infiltration, the migration and grouping of cells, especially blood cells, within tissues throughout the body.

cellulite /sel′yəlīt/, a nonmedical term for fat and fibrous tissue deposits that result in dimpling of the skin.

cellulitis /sel′yəlī′tis/ [L, *cellula,* little cell; Gk, *itis,* inflammation], a diffuse, acute bacterial infection of the skin and subcutaneous tissue characterized most commonly by local heat, redness, pain, and swelling and occasionally by fever, malaise, chills, and headache. Abscess and tissue destruction usually follow if antibiotics are not taken.

cellulose /sel′yŏŏlōs/ [L, *cellula,* little cell], a colorless, insoluble, indigestible, transparent, solid polysaccharide that is the primary constituent of the cell walls of plants. In the diet, it provides the bulk necessary for proper digestive tract functioning.

cellulose sodium phosphate, an insoluble, nonabsorbable cation exchange resin prepared from cellulose. It binds calcium and is used to prevent formation of calcium-containing kidney stones.

cell wall, the structure that covers and protects the plasma membrane in some kinds of cells, such as certain bacteria and all fungi and plant cells.

Celontin, a trademark for an anticonvulsant (methsuximide).

celosomia /sē′ləsō′mē·ə/ [Gk, *kele,* hernia, *soma,* body], a congenital malformation characterized by a fissure or absence of the sternum and ribs and protrusion of the viscera.

celosomus /sē′ləsō′məs/, a fetus with celosomia.

Celsius (°C) /sel′sē·əs/ [Anders Celsius, Swedish scientist, 1701–1744], temperature scale on which 0° is the freezing point of water and 100° is the boiling point of water at sea level.

cement /siment′/ [L, *caementum,* rough stone], **1.** a sticky or mucilaginous substance that hardens into a firm mass and helps neighboring tissue cells stick together. **2.** any of a variety of dental materials used to fill cavities or to hold bridgework or other dental prostheses in place. **3.** a material used in the fixation of a prosthetic joint in adjacent bone, such as methyl methacrylate.

cemental fiber /simen′təl/ [L, *caementum,* rough stone, *fibra*], any one of the many fibers of the periodontal membrane that extend from the cementum to the intermediate plexus.

cementation /sē′məntā′shən/ [L, *caementum,* rough stone], the attachment of anything with cement, such as restorative material to a natural tooth or an orthodontic band.

cement base, a layer of dental cement material, sometimes medicated, that is pressed into the bottom of a prepared tooth cavity to protect the pulp, reduce the bulk of metallic restoration, or eliminate undercuts in a tapered preparation.

cementifying fibroma /-ifī′ing/ [L, *caementum* + *facere,* to make, *fibra,* fiber; Gk, *oma,* tumor], **1.** an intraosseous lesion composed of fibrous connective tissue enclosing foci of calcified material resembling cementum. **2.** a rare odontogenic tumor composed of varying amounts of fibrous connective tissue resembling cementum. **3.** central jaw lesion.

cementoblast /simen′təblast′/, (in dentistry) one of the large cuboidal cells that are responsible for the formation of cementum on the root dentin of developing teeth.

cementoblastoma /simen′tōblastō′mə/ *pl.* **cementoblastomas, cementoblastomata** [L, *caementum*; Gk, *blastos,* germ, *oma,* tumor], an odontogenic fibrous tumor consisting of cells developing into cementoblasts but containing only a small amount of calcified tissue.

cementocyte /simen′təsīt/, a cell found in the cementum of teeth.

cementoenamel junction, the junction of the coronal border of the cementum and the apical border of the enamel.

cementoma /sē′mentō′mə/ *pl.* **cementomas, cementomata** [L, *caementum*; Gk, *oma,* tumor], any benign, dysplastic cementum-producing tumor associated with the apices of teeth.

cementum /simen'təm/, the bonelike connective tissue that covers the roots of the teeth and helps to support them by providing a place of attachment for the periodontal ligament fibers and overlying dentin.

cen, abbreviation for **centromere.**

CEN, abbreviation for **certified emergency nurse.**

cenesthesia /sē'nesthē'zhə/ [Gk, *kenos,* empty, *aisthesis,* feeling], the general sense of existing, derived as the aggregate of all the various stimuli and reactions throughout the body at any specific moment to produce a feeling of health or illness.

cenogenesis /sē'nōjen'əsis/ [Gk, *kenos,* empty, *genein,* to produce], the development of structural characteristics that are absent in earlier forms of a species, as an adaptive response to environmental conditions.—**caenogenetic, cenogenetic, coenogenetic,** adj.

censor [L, *censere,* to assess], **1.** a person who monitors or evaluates books, newspapers, plays, works of art, speech, or other means of expression to suppress certain kinds of information. **2.** (in psychoanalysis) a psychic suppression that allows unconscious thoughts to rise to consciousness only if they are heavily disguised.

census [L, *censere,* to assess], **1.** an enumeration of the population, usually conducted periodically as a function of an official agency. In addition to counting heads, the census often collects information about members of a household, sources of income, types of dwellings, and matters relating to the health of the community. **2.** in the hospital setting, the number of patients in the hospital.

center [Gk, *kentron*], **1.** the middle point of the body or geometric entity, equidistant from points on the periphery. **2.** a group of neurons with a common function, such as the accelerating center in the brain that controls the heartbeat.

center-edge angle of Wiberg, the angle formed by a line drawn perpendicular to a baseline that passes through the center of the femoral heads and a line connecting the center of the femoral head and the superior border of the acetabulum, used in radiographic evaluation of the hip joint. It is less than 20 degrees in developmental dysplasia of the hip.

Center for American Nurses (CAN), a unit of the American Nurses Association whose activities concern the creation of a healthy work environment.

Center for Devices and Radiological Health (CDRH), an agency of the U.S. Food and Drug Administration organized in 1982 with the responsibility of providing standards for and regulation of the manufacture and uses of medical devices.

Center for Devices and Radiological Health (CDRH), an agency of the U.S. Food and Drug Administration organized in 1982 with the responsibility of providing standards for and regulation of the manufacture and uses of medical devices.

center of excellence, a tertiary or quaternary health care provider that is identified as the most expert and cost-efficient and produces the best outcomes. The term often refers to organ transplantation centers.

center of gravity, the midpoint or center of the weight of a body or object. In the standing adult human, the center of gravity is in the midpelvic cavity, between the symphysis pubis and the umbilicus.

Centers for Disease Control and Prevention (CDC), a federal agency of the U.S. government that provides facilities and services for the investigation, identification, prevention, and control of disease. It is concerned with all of the epidemiologic aspects and the laboratory diagnosis of disease. Immunization programs, quarantine regulations and programs, laboratory standards, and community surveillance for disease are among the activities of the CDC, which is located in Atlanta.

centesis /sentē'sis/ [Gk, *kentesis,* pricking], a perforation or a puncture of a cavity, such as paracentesis or thoracocentesis.

centigram (cg), a mass equal to one hundredth of a gram, or 10 milligrams.

centigray (cGy) /sen'tigrā̄ā/, a unit of absorbed radiation dose equal to one hundredth (10^{-2}) of a gray, or 1 rad.

centiliter (cL), a volume equal to one hundredth of a liter, or 10 milliliters.

centimeter (cm) /sen'timē'tər/ [L, *centum,* hundred; Gk, *metron,* measure], the metric unit of measurement equal to one hundredth of a meter, or 0.3937 inch.

centimeter-gram-second system (cgs, CGS), the internationally accepted scientific system of expressing length, mass, and time in basic units of centimeters, grams, and seconds. The CGS system is gradually being replaced by the SI unit, based on the meter, kilogram, and second.

centipede bite /sen'təpēd/ [L, *centum,* hundred, *pes,* foot], a wound produced by the poison claws and the first body segment of a centipede, an elongate arthropod with many pairs of legs. The bite of a few species, including *Scolopendra morsitans* in the southern United States, may cause painful local inflammation, fever, headache, vomiting, and dizziness.

centipoise /sen'təpois/ [Jean L.M. Poiseuille, French physiologist, 1797–1869], a measure of the viscosity of a liquid, equal to one hundredth of a poise.

centrad [L, *centum,* hundred], **1.** pertaining to a central direction, toward the center. **2.** a unit of measure equal to one hundredth part of a radian. **3.** a measure of the refractive strength of a prism.

central [Gk, *kentron,* center], pertaining to or situated at a center.

central amaurosis [Gk, *kentron + amauroein,* to darken], blindness caused by a disease of the CNS.

central anesthesia, a loss of feeling or sensation as a result of a lesion in the CNS.

central auditory processing disorder (CAPD), difficulty in processing and interpreting auditory stimuli in the absence of a peripheral hearing loss, usually resulting from a problem in the brainstem or cerebral cortex.

central biasing /bī'əsing/, a theory of pain modulation in which higher centers such as the cerebral cortex influence the perception of and response to pain.

central canal of spinal cord [Gk, *kentron;* L, *canalis,* channel], the conduit that runs the entire length of the spinal cord and contains most of the 140 mL of CSF in the body of the average individual. The central canal of the spinal cord lies in the center of the cord between the ventral and the dorsal gray commissures and extends toward the cranium into the medulla oblongata, where it opens into the fourth ventricle of the brain.

central catheter [Gk, *kentron,* central, *katheter,* a thing lowered into], a catheter inserted into either a central artery or a central vein for diagnostic or therapeutic procedures.

central chemoreceptor, any of the sensory nerve cells or chemical receptors that are located in the medulla of the brain.

central chondrosarcoma [Gk, *kentron + chondros,* cartilage, *sarx,* flesh, *oma,* tumor], a malignant cartilaginous tumor that forms inside a bone.

central core disease, an autosomal-dominant muscle disorder characterized by dense, amorphous hyaline changes in the central portion of the myofibrils, which lack organelles. Onset is in infancy and causes delayed motor development, especially in the lower limbs.

central electrode, a key part of a radiation detection instrument. It consists of a positively charged rigid wire in the center of a gas-filled cylinder.

central facilitation, (in chiropractic) a model based on neurophysiologic findings that explains the symptoms of subluxogenic pain and discomfort that arise from nonspinal sites.

central incisor, one of the two teeth located closest to the sagittal plane in the upper and lower jaws.

central line, IV tubing inserted for continuous access to a central vein for administering fluids and medicines and for obtaining diagnostic information. Keeping the central line in place ensures accessibility to the venous system in case the peripheral veins collapse.

central lobe, one of the lobes constituting each of the cerebral hemispheres, lying hidden in the depths of the lateral sulcus. The central lobe can be seen only if the lips of the sulcus are parted or cut away.

central necrosis [Gk, *kentron,* central, *nekros,* dead, *osis,* condition], death of the central part of a tissue or organ.

central nervous system (CNS) [Gk, *kentron;* L, *nervus,* nerve; Gk, *systema*], one of the two main divisions of the nervous system, consisting of the brain and the spinal cord. The CNS processes information to and from the peripheral nervous system and is the main network of coordination and control for the entire body.

central nervous system depressant, any drug that decreases the function of the CNS, such as alcohol, tranquilizers, barbiturates, and hypnotics. These substances depress excitable tissue throughout the CNS by stabilizing neuronal membranes, decreasing the amount of transmitter released by the nerve impulse, and generally depressing postsynaptic responsiveness and ion movement.

central nervous system stimulant, a substance that quickens the activity of the CNS by increasing the rate of neuronal discharge or by blocking an inhibitory neurotransmitter. Many natural and synthetic compounds stimulate the CNS, but only a few are used therapeutically.

central nervous system (CNS) syndrome, a constellation of neurologic and emotional signs and symptoms that results from a massive whole-body dosage of radiation. It includes hysteria and disorientation, which increase during the last 24 to 48 hours before death.

central nervous system tumor, a neoplasm of the brain or spinal cord that characteristically does not spread beyond the cerebrospinal axis, although it may be highly invasive locally and have widespread effects on body functions. Intracranial neoplasms are about four times more common than those arising in the spinal cord. From 20% to 40% of brain tumors are metastatic lesions from primary cancer elsewhere.

central neurogenic hyperventilation (CNHV) [Gk, *kentron + neuron,* nerve, *genein,* to produce], a pattern of breathing during coma marked by rapid, regular ventilations at a rate of about 25 per minute. Increasing regularity rather than rate indicates an increasing depth of coma.

central neuronal plasticity, (in chiropractic) the tendency for the neuronal responses to noxious stimuli to spread to other central pathways, producing the symptoms of referred pain.

central pain [Gk, *kentron;* L, *poena,* penalty], pain caused by a lesion in the CNS.

central paralysis [Gk, *kentron* + *paralyein*, to be palsied], paralysis caused by a lesion in the CNS.

central pathway, a nerve tract in the brain or spinal cord.

central placenta previa [Gk, *kentron*; L, *placenta*, flat cake, *praevius*, preceding], placenta previa in which the placenta is implanted in the lower segment of the uterus and completely covers the internal os of the uterine cervix. In labor, as the cervix dilates, the placenta is gradually separated from the underlying blood vessels in the uterine lining, causing bleeding that usually begins slowly, is painless, and progresses to hemorrhage that is life-threatening to the mother and baby.

central ray (CR), the portion of an x-ray beam that is directed toward the center of the film or of the object being radiographed.

central scotoma [Gk, *kentron* + *skotos*, darkness, *oma*, tumor], an area of blindness or site of depressed vision involving the macula of the retina.

central sensitization, (in chiropractic) a state in which neurons activated by noxious mechanical and chemical stimuli are sensitized by such stimuli and become hyperresponsive to all subsequent stimuli delivered to the neurons' receptive fields.

central sleep apnea, a form of sleep apnea resulting from decreased respiratory center output. It may involve primary brainstem medullary depression.

central slip, the part of the extensor tendon of a finger that inserts into the middle phalanx.

central sulcus [Gk, *kentron*; L, furrow], a cleft separating the frontal from the parietal lobes of the brain.

central tendon, a broad connective tissue sheet that forms the diaphragm. It is composed of interlacing fibers that arise from the lumbar vertebrae, the costal margin, and the xiphoid process of the sternum.

central venous blood pressure, the BP in the superior vena cava, measured by inserting a catheter attached to a manometer directly outside the right atrium.

central venous catheter, a catheter that is threaded through the internal jugular, antecubital, or subclavian vein, usually with the tip resting in the superior vena cava or the right atrium of the heart.

central venous oxygen saturation (CVSO₂), the oxygen saturation in the vena cava. The $CVSO_2$ is measured through a central venous catheter and is useful in measuring cardiac output.

central venous pressure (CVP), the BP in the large veins of the body, as distinguished from peripheral venous pressure in an extremity. It is measured with a water manometer that may be attached to the head of a patient's bed and to a central venous catheter inserted into the vena cava.

central venous pressure monitor (CVP monitor), a device for measuring and recording the venous BP by means of an indwelling venous catheter and a pressure manometer. It is used to evaluate the right ventricular function, the right atrial filling pressure, and the circulating blood volume.

central venous return, the blood from the venous system that flows into the right atrium through the vena cava.

central vertigo [Gk, *kentron*; L, *vertigo*, dizziness], vertigo that is caused by a CNS disorder.

central vision, vision that results from images falling on the macula of the retina.

central zone, a cone-shaped area of the prostate composed mainly of stromal cells, found deep to the peripheral zone and extending from there to the base of the prostate.

Centrax, a trademark for a benzodiazepine antianxiety agent (prazepam).

centrencephalic /sen'trensifal'ik/ [Gk, *kentron* + *enkephalos*, brain], pertaining to the center of the encephalon.

centriacinar emphysema /sentrē-əsin'ər/, one of the types of emphysema, characterized by enlargement of air spaces in the proximal part of the acinus, primarily at the level of the respiratory bronchioles.

centric /sen'trik/, (in dentistry) a shorthand term referring to centric relation or centric occlusion.

centriciput /sentris'ipŏot/, the central part of the head, between the occiput and the sinciput.

centrifugal /sentrif'yəgəl/, **1.** denoting a force that is directed outward, away from a central point or axis. The force does not actually exist but is a manifestation of **inertia. 2.** pertaining to a direction away from the head.

centrifugal current, an electrical current in the body with the positive pole near the nerve center and the negative pole at the periphery.

centrifugal force, an inertial force in a rotating system, directed outward from the axis of rotation and inversely proportional to the distance from the axis of rotation. The force is the product of the mass of an object and its radial acceleration; thus in centrifugation the heavier components of a mixture are separated from the other components by being thrown to the periphery of the orbit.

centrifuge /sen'trifyo͞oj'/ [Gk, *kentron*; L, *fugere*, to flee], a device for separating components of different densities contained in liquid by spinning them at high speeds. —**centrifugal**, *adj.*, **centrifuge**, *v.*

centrilobular /sen'trəlob'yələr/ [Gk, *kentron*; L, *lobulus*, small lobe], pertaining to the center of a lobule.

centriole /sen'trē-ōl'/ [Gk, *kentron*], an intracellular organelle, usually as a component of the centrosome. Often occurring in pairs, centrioles are associated with cell division. They appear to aid in the formation of the spindle that develops during mitosis.

centripetal /sentrip'ətəl/ [Gk, *kentron*; L, *petere*, to seek], 1. denoting an afferent direction, such as that of a sensory nerve impulse traveling toward the brain. 2. denoting the direction of a force pulling an object toward an axis of rotation or constraining an object to a specific curved path (centrifugal).

centripetal current, an electric current passing through the body from a peripheral positive electrode to a negative pole near the nerve center.

centripetal force, the force, directed toward the axis of rotation, required to keep an object moving in a circular path.

centromere (cen) /sen'trəmir/ [Gk, *kentron* + *meros*, part], the constricted region of a chromosome that joins the two chromatids to each other and attaches to spindle fibers in mitosis and meiosis. During cell division, the centromeres split longitudinally, half going to each of the new daughter chromosomes. —**centromeric**, *adj.*

centrosome [Gk, *kentron* + *soma*, body], a self-propagating cytoplasmic organelle present in animal cells and in those of some lower plants. The structure, which consists of the centrosphere and the centrioles, is located near the nucleus of the cell center or attraction sphere and functions as the dynamic center of the cell, especially during mitosis.

centrosphere [Gk, *kentron* + *sphaira*, ball], the condensed area of cytoplasm surrounding the centrioles in the centrosome of a cell.

centrostaltic /sen'trōstôl'tik/, pertaining to the center of movement.

centrum *pl.* **centra** [Gk, *kentron*], any kind of center, especially one related to a body structure, as the centrum semiovale of a cerebral hemisphere.

CEO, C.E.O., abbreviation for **chief executive officer.**

CEP, abbreviation for **congenital erythropoietic porphyria.**

cephalad /sef'əlad/ [Gk, *kephale*, head], toward the head, away from the end or tail.

cephalalgia /sef'əlal'jə/ [Gk, *kephale*, head, *algos*, pain], headache, often combined with another word to indicate a specific type of headache, such as histamine cephalalgia.

cephalea agitata, cephalea attonita /sef'əlē'ə/, a violent headache that is frequently an early symptom of an infection.

cephaledema /sef'əlidē'mə/, a swelling of the brain caused by fluid accumulation.

cephalexin /sef'əlek'sin/, an oral first-generation cephalosporin antibiotic prescribed for oral treatment of selected infections caused by susceptible bacterial strains, especially lower respiratory tract, urinary tract, skin and soft tissue, and bone and joint infections. It is also used as a prophylaxis against bacterial endocarditis in high-risk patients undergoing surgical or dental procedures.

cephalhematoma /sef'əlhē'mətō'mə, -hem'ətō'mə/, swelling of the head caused by subcutaneous bleeding and accumulation of blood.

cephalic /sifal'ik/, pertaining to the head.

cephalic index [Gk, *kephale*, head, *index*, pointer], a ratio between the breadth and length of the head.

cephalic presentation, a classification of fetal position in which the head of the fetus is at the uterine cervix. Cephalic presentation is usually further qualified by an indication of the part of the head presenting, such as the occiput, brow, or chin.

cephalic vein, one of the four superficial veins of the upper limb. It receives deoxygenated blood from the dorsal and palmar surfaces of the forearm.

cephalocaudal /sef'əlōkô'dəl/ [Gk, *kephale*; L, *cauda*, tail], pertaining to the long axis of the body, or the relationship between the head and the base of the spine.

cephalocele /sef'əlōsēl'/, the protrusion of a part of the brain through an opening in the skull.

cephalocentesis /-sentē'sis/, the puncture of the skull with a hollow needle, performed to allow drainage of fluid or an abscess.

cephalomelus /sef'əlom'ələs/ [Gk, *kephale* + *melos*, limb], a deformed individual who has a structure resembling an arm or a leg protruding from the head.

cephalometric radiograph projection /sef'əlōmet'rik rā'dē-ōgraf/, a radiograph of the head, including the mandible, in full lateral view, used for making cranial measurements.

cephalometric tracing, a line drawing of structural outlines of craniofacial landmarks and facial bones made directly from a cephalometric radiograph.

cephalometry /-ətrē/, scientific measurement of the head, such as that performed in dentistry to determine appropriate orthodontic procedures for correcting malocclusions and other abnormal conditions. —**cephalometric,** adj.

cephalomotor /sef′əlōmō′tər/ [Gk, kephale, head; L, motare, to move about], moving the head; pertaining to motions of the head.

cephalopelvic /-pel′vik/, pertaining to a relationship between the fetal head and the maternal pelvis.

cephalopelvic disproportion (CPD) [Gk, kephale; L, pelvis, basin, dis, opposite of, proportio, similarity], an obstetric condition in which a baby's head is too large or a mother's birth canal too small to permit normal labor or birth.

cephalopelvimetry /-pelvim′ətrē/, radiographic measurement of the fetal head in utero.

cephalophlebitis, an inflammation of the vena cava.

cephalothin sodium /sef′əlō′thin/, a parenteral first-generation cephalosporin antibiotic. It is prescribed in the treatment of infections caused by susceptible bacterial strains causing respiratory, genitourinary, GI, skin and soft tissue, and bone and joint infections or septicemia. It is effective against many gram-positive bacilli and cocci (other than enterococcus) and some gram-negative bacilli.

cephapirin /sef′əprin/, a parenteral first-generation cephalosporin antibiotic. It is prescribed in the treatment of bacterial infections caused by cephapirin-susceptible strains of a wide variety of microorganisms that cause septicemia, endocarditis, osteomyelitis, and bacterial infections of the respiratory tract, urinary tract, and skin.

cephradine /sef′rədēn/, an oral first-generation cephalosporin antibiotic. It is prescribed in the treatment of certain infections caused by susceptible bacterial strains causing respiratory, genitourinary, GI, skin and soft tissue, and bone and joint infections, or septicemia. It is effective against may gram-positive bacilli and cocci (other than enterococci) and some gram-negative bacilli.

cera, wax. Ordinary yellow beeswax is sometimes identified as cera flava; white beeswax, bleached by exposure to air and sunlight, is known as cera alba.

ceramics /səram′iks/, (in dentistry) the process of making dental restorations from fused porcelain and other glasses.

ceramidase /səram′idās/, an enzyme of the hydrolase class that catalyzes the cleavage of a ceramide to form sphingosine and

a fatty acid anion, a step in the degradation of sphingolipids.

ceramide /ser′əmīd/, the basic unit of the sphingolipids, consisting of sphingosine or a related base attached by means of its amino group to a long-chain fatty acyl group.

cercaria /sərker′ē-ə/ pl. **cercariae** [Gk, kerkos, tail], a minute, wormlike early developmental form of trematode. It develops in a freshwater snail and is released into the water. Cercariae enter the body of the next host by ingestion, by direct invasion through the skin, or through a cut or other break in the skin. They encyst and complete their development in various organs of the body. Each species tends to migrate to one organ, such as Fasciola hepatica, which grows to become a liver fluke.

cerclage /serkläzh′/ [Fr, cask hooping], **1.** an orthopedic procedure in which the ends of an oblique bone fracture or the chips of a broken patella are bound together with a wire loop or a metal band to hold them in position until healed. **2.** a procedure in which a taut silicone band is applied around the sclera to restore contact between the retina and the choroid when the retina is detached. **3.** an obstetric procedure in which a nonabsorbable suture is used for holding the cervix closed to prevent spontaneous abortion in a woman who has an incompetent cervix.

cerea flexibilitas /sirē′ə flek′sibil′itas/ [L, waxlike flexibility], a cataleptic state, frequently observed in catatonic schizophrenia, in which the limbs maintain the positions in which they are placed for an indefinite period.

cerebellar /ser′əbel′ər/ [L, cerebellum, small brain], pertaining to the cerebellum.

cerebellar angioblastoma [L, cerebellum; Gk, angeion, vessel, blastos, germ, oma], a cystic tumor in the cerebellum composed of a mass of blood vessels. It is frequently associated with von Hippel-Lindau disease.

cerebellar artery, one of the three major arteries (superior, posterior inferior, and anterior inferior) on each side that supply the cerebellum.

cerebellar artery occlusion, an obstruction of one of the arteries supplying the cerebellum. It can result in ipsilateral ataxia, facial analgesia, contralateral hemiparesis, and loss of temperature and pain sensations.

cerebellar ataxia [L, cerebellum, small brain; Gk, ataxia, without order], a loss of muscle coordination caused by a lesion in the cerebellum.

cerebellar atrophy [L, *cerebellum*; Gk, *a* + *trophe*, without nourishment], deterioration and wasting of tissues of the cerebellum.

cerebellar cortex, the superficial gray matter of the cerebellum covering the white substance in the medullary core. It consists of two layers, an external molecular layer and an internal granule cell layer.

cerebellar cyst, a cyst that develops in the white matter of the cerebellum and is often associated with an astrocytoma.

cerebellar falx, a small sickle-shaped process of the dura mater attached to the occipital bone above and projecting into the posterior cerebellar notch between the two cerebellar hemispheres.

cerebellar gait [L, *cerebellum*, small brain; ONorse, *geta*, a way], a staggering gait in which the person walks with a wide base and has difficulty turning. The feet are thrown outward, and the person puts his or her weight first on the heel and then on the toes. The condition is caused by a lesion in the cerebellum or cerebellar pathways.

cerebellar hemangioblastoma, hemangioblastoma of the cerebellum, often cystic. An autosomal-dominant form is associated with von Hippel-Lindau disease.

cerebellar inferior peduncle [L, *cerebellum*, small brain, *inferior*, lower, *pes*, foot], a band of nerve fibers that forms the lateral boundary of the bottom part of the fourth ventricle and carries afferent fibers into the cerebellum.

cerebellar middle peduncle [L, *cerebellum*, small brain, *medius* + *pes*, foot], a lateral extension of the transverse nerve fibers of the pons. It consists mainly of fibers from the pontine nuclei to the neocerebellum.

cerebellar notch, **1.** anteriorly, a broad depression that lies dorsal to the midbrain and separates the cerebellar hemispheres rostral to the vermis. **2.** posteriorly, a deep depression adjacent to the falx cerebelli.

cerebellar rigidity, a stiffness of the trunk muscles caused by a midline lesion in the cerebellum. In some cases, the limbs may also be rigid and the neck and back arched, as in opisthotonos.

cerebellar speech [L, *cerebellum*; AS, *spaec*], abnormal speech caused by diseases of the cerebellum, characterized by slow, jerky, and slurred articulation that may be intermittent and explosive or monotonous and unvaried in pitch.

cerebellar superior peduncle [L, *cerebellum*, small brain, *superior* + *pes*, foot], a band of nerve fibers that passes from the cerebellum on either side of the superior medullary velum. It includes nerve tracts linking the dentate nucleus to the red nucleus of the midbrain and to the thalamus.

cerebellar tentorium, a horizontal projection of the meningeal dura mater that covers and separates the cerebellum in the posterior cranial fossa from the posterior parts of the cerebral hemispheres. It is attached posteriorly to the occipital bone and laterally to the superior border of the petrous part of the temporal bone. The anterior and medial borders of the tentorium cerebelli are free, forming an oval opening into the midline through which the midbrain passes.

cerebellar tremor [L, *cerebellum*, small brain, *tremor*, shaking], an intention tremor or trembling during voluntary movements, caused by lesions in the cerebellum.

cerebellopontine /ser′əbel′ōpon′tīn/ [L, *cerebellum* + *pons*, bridge], leading from the cerebellum to the pons varolii.

cerebellospinal /ser′əbel′ōspī′nəl/ [L, *cerebellum* + *spina*, backbone], leading from the cerebellum to the spinal cord.

cerebellum /ser′əbel′əm/ *pl.* **cerebellums,** **cerebella** [L, small brain], the part of the brain located in the posterior cranial fossa behind the brainstem. It consists of two lateral cerebellar hemispheres, or lobes, and a middle section called the vermis. Three pairs of peduncles link it with the brainstem. Its functions are concerned primarily with coordinating voluntary muscular activity.

cerebral /ser′əbrəl, sərē′brəl/, pertaining to the cerebrum.

cerebral amyloid angiopathy, vascular amyloidosis affecting small- and medium-size arteries of the leptomeninges and cerebral cortex, resulting in microinfarcts or in hemorrhage. It may be asymptomatic or may result in hemorrhagic stroke or dementia.

cerebral aneurysm [L, *cerebrum*, brain; Gk, *aneurysma*, a widening], an abnormal, localized dilation of a cerebral artery. It is most commonly the result of congenital weakness of the tunica media or muscle layer of the arterial wall. Cerebral aneurysms may also be caused by infection and by neoplasms, arteriosclerosis, and trauma. The most frequent sites are the middle cerebral, internal carotid, basilar, and anterior cerebral arteries, especially at bifurcations of vessels.

cerebral angiography [L, *cerebrum*, brain; Gk, *angeion*, vessel, *graphein*, to record], a radiographic procedure used to visualize the vascular system of the brain after injection of a radiopaque contrast medium.

cerebral anoxia, a condition in which oxygen is deficient in brain tissue. This state, which is caused by circulatory failure, can exist for no more than 4 to 6 minutes before the onset of irreversible brain damage.

cerebral aqueduct [L, *cerebrum* + *aqueductus,* water canal], the narrow conduit, between the third and the fourth ventricles in the midbrain, that conveys the CSF.

cerebral artery, one of the arteries that supply the brain.

cerebral blood flow, 1. the blood supply to the brain in a given period of time. **2.** the circulation of blood through the vascular system of the brain.

cerebral compression [L, *cerebrum,* brain, *comprimere,* to press together], any abnormal condition resulting from hemorrhage, abscess, or tumor that increases ICP.

cerebral cortex [L, *cerebrum* + *cortex,* bark], a layer of neurons and synapses (gray matter) on the surface of the cerebral hemispheres, folded into gyri with about two thirds of its area buried in fissures. It integrates higher mental functions, general movement, visceral functions, perception, and behavioral reactions.

cerebral depressant [L, *cerebrum,* brain, *deprimere,* to press down], a drug or other agent that has a sedating effect on the brain, reducing activity and alertness and, in some instances, causing LOC.

cerebral dominance, the specialization of each of the two cerebral hemispheres in the integration and control of different functions. In 90% of the population, the left cerebral hemisphere specializes in or dominates language functions. The areas that control these activities are situated in the frontal, parietal, and temporal lobes of the left hemisphere. In the other 10% of the population, either the right hemisphere or both hemispheres dominate the language functions. The right cerebral hemisphere dominates the integration of certain sounds other than those associated with language. The right cerebral hemisphere perceives tactile stimuli and visual spatial relationships better than the left cerebral hemisphere.

cerebral edema [L, *cerebrum;* Gk, *oidema,* swelling], an accumulation of fluid in the brain tissues. Causes include infection, tumor, trauma, and exposure to certain toxins. Early symptoms are changes in LOC: sluggishness, then dilation of pupils, and a gradual LOC.

cerebral edema management, a nursing intervention from the Nursing Interventions Classification (NIC) defined as limitation of secondary cerebral injury resulting from swelling of brain tissue.

cerebral embolism [L, *cerebrum;* Gk, *embolos,* plug], a condition in which an embolus blocks blood flow through the vessels of the cerebrum, resulting in tissue ischemia distal to the occlusion.

cerebral falx, a sickle-shaped fold of dura mater membrane extending into and following along the longitudinal fissure and separating the two hemispheres of the cerebrum.

cerebral fossa, the stem of the lateral sulcus of the cerebrum, which forms a furrow separating the orbital surface of the frontal lobe from the temporal lobe.

cerebral gigantism [L, *cerebrum;* Gk, *gigas,* giant], an abnormal condition characterized by excessive weight and size at birth, accelerated growth during the first 4 or 5 years after birth without any increase in the level of growth hormone, and then reversion to normal growth. Some typical signs of this condition are prognathism, antimongoloid slant, dolichocephalic skull, moderate mental retardation, and impaired coordination.

cerebral hemiplegia [L, *cerebrum;* Gk, *hemi,* half, *plege,* stroke], paralysis of one side of the body caused by a brain lesion.

cerebral hemisphere [L, *cerebrum;* Gk, *hemi,* half, *sphaira,* ball], one of the halves of the cerebrum. The two cerebral hemispheres are divided by a deep longitudinal fissure and are connected medially at the bottom of the fissure by the corpus callosum. Prominent grooves subdivide each hemisphere into four major lobes. Each hemisphere also has a fifth major lobe deep in the brain. The hemispheres consist of an external gray layer and an internal white substance that surrounds islands of gray matter called nuclei.

cerebral hemorrhage [L, *cerebrum;* Gk, *haima,* blood, *rhegnynei,* to burst forth], a hemorrhage from a blood vessel in the brain. Three criteria used to classify cerebral hemorrhages are location (subarachnoid, extradural, subdural), kind of vessel involved (arterial, venous, capillary), and origin (traumatic, degenerative). Each kind of cerebral hemorrhage has distinctive clinical characteristics. Most cerebral hemorrhages occur in the region of the basal ganglia and are caused by the rupture of a sclerotic artery as a result of hypertension. Other causes of rupture include congenital aneurysm, cerebrovascular thrombosis, and head trauma.

cerebral lobes, the well defined areas of the cerebral cortex, demarcated by fissures, sulci, and arbitrary lines, which include the frontal, temporal, parietal, and occipital lobes.

cerebral localization, 1. the determination of various areas in the cerebral cortex associated with specific functions. 2. the diagnosis of a cerebral condition by analyzing the signs manifested by the patient to determine the area of the brain affected.

cerebral palsy (CP) [L, *cerebrum*; Gk, *para*, beyond, *lysis*, loosening], a motor function disorder caused by a permanent, nonprogressive brain defect or lesion present at birth or shortly thereafter. The neurologic deficit may result in spastic hemiplegia, monoplegia, diplegia, or quadriplegia; athetosis or ataxia; seizures; paresthesia; varying degrees of mental retardation; and impaired speech, vision, and hearing. The disorder is usually associated with premature or abnormal birth and intrapartum asphyxia, causing damage to the nervous system. Abnormalities in breathing, sucking, swallowing, and responsiveness are usually apparent soon after birth, but the characteristic stiff, awkward movements of the infant's limbs may be overlooked for several months. Beginning to walk is usually delayed, and when it is attempted, the child manifests a typical scissors gait. The arms may be affected only slightly, but the fingers are often spastic. Deep-tendon reflexes are exaggerated, and there may be slurred speech, delay in development of sphincter control, and athetotic movements of the face and hands.

cerebral peduncle [L, *cerebrum*, brain, *pes*, foot], a pair of ovoid masses of nerve fibers at the upper border of the pons that disappear into the left and right hemispheres of the cerebrum. It includes corticopontine and pyramidal-tract fibers and helps constitute the central portion of the midbrain.

cerebral perfusion pressure (CPP), a parameter that is related to the amount of blood flow to the brain. It is calculated by subtracting the ICP from the mean systemic arterial BP.

cerebral perfusion promotion, a nursing intervention from the Nursing Interventions Classification (NIC) defined as promotion of adequate perfusion and limitation of complications for a patient experiencing or at risk for inadequate cerebral perfusion.

cerebral sulci, the furrows on the surface of the brain between the gyri.

cerebral thrombosis [L, *cerebrum*; Gk, *thrombos*, lump, *osis*, condition], an abnormal condition in which a blood clot forms in a cerebral blood vessel.

cerebral vertigo [L, *cerebrum*, brain, *vertigo*, dizziness], vertigo that is caused by organic brain disease.

cerebral vomiting, vomiting caused by a disorder of the CNS, especially stimulation of the vomiting center, usually without preceding nausea.

cerebrocerebellar atrophy /ser′əbrōser′ə bel′ər/ [L, *cerebrum*, brain, *cerebellum*, small brain; Gk, *a* + *trophe*, without nourishment], a deterioration of the cerebellum caused by certain abiotrophic diseases.

cerebrocostomandibular syndrome /ser′ə brōkos′tō·mandib′yoolar/ [L, *cerebrum*, brain + *costa*, rib, *mandibula*, mandible], an autosomal-recessive syndrome of severe micrognathia and costovertebral abnormalities, including small bell-shaped thorax, incompletely ossified aberrant rib structure, and abnormal rib attachment to vertebrae. There are also palatal defects, glossoptosis, prenatal and postnatal growth deficiencies, and mental retardation, the last perhaps because of neonatal respiratory distress.

cerebrohepatorenal syndrome /ser′əbrō hep′ətō·rē′nəl/, an autosomal-recessive disorder characterized by craniofacial abnormalities, hypotonia, hepatomegaly, polycystic kidneys, jaundice, and death in early infancy, and associated with absence of peroxisomes in the liver and kidneys.

cerebroid /ser′əbroid/ [L, *cerebrum*; Gk, *eidos*, form], resembling the substance of the brain.

cerebroma /ser′əbrō′mə/ *pl*. **cerebromas, cerebromata,** any unusual mass of brain tissue.

cerebroside /ser′əbrōsīd′/, any of a group of glycolipids found in the brain and other tissues of the nervous system, especially the myelin sheath.

cerebroside sulfatase [L, *cerebrum*, brain, *sulfur*, brimstone, *ase*, enzyme], an enzyme of the hydrolase class that catalyzes the reaction of cerebroside 3-sulfate + H_2O. A deficiency of the enzyme, which is transmitted through an autosomal-recessive gene, causes metachromatic leukodystrophy.

cerebrospinal /ser′əbrōspī′nəl, sərē′brō-/, pertaining to or involving the brain and spinal cord.

cerebrospinal axis [L, *cerebrum*, brain, *spina*, spine, *axle*], a line formed by the brain and spinal cord about which the body turns.

cerebrospinal fluid (CSF), the fluid that flows through and protects the four ventricles of the brain, the subarachnoid spaces, and the spinal canal. It is composed mainly of secretions of the choroid plexi in the lateral ventricles and in the third and fourth ventricles of the brain and is clear and colorless.

cerebrospinal ganglion, a cluster of sensory ganglia neurons on roots of cranial and spinal nerve. The neurons lack dendrites and have no synapses on their cell bodies.

cerebrospinal nerves, the 12 pairs of cranial nerves and 31 pairs of spinal nerves that originate in the brain and spinal cord.

cerebrospinal otorrhea, a discharge of CSF from the ear.

cerebrospinal pressure [L, *cerebrum* + *spina* + *premere,* to press], the pressure of CSF in the CNS, usually between 100 and 150 mm of H_2O. Measurement is accomplished using a manometer attached to the end of a needle after it has been inserted into the subarachnoid space via lumbar puncture (most commonly).

cerebrospinal rhinorrhea [L, *cerebrum,* brain, *spina,* spine; Gk, *rhis,* nose, *rhoia,* flow], a discharge of CSF from the nose.

cerebrovascular /ser'əbrōvas'kyələr,sərē'brō-/ [L, *cerebrum* + *vasculum,* little vessel], pertaining to the vascular system and blood supply of the brain.

cerebrovascular accident (CVA), an abnormal condition of the brain characterized by occlusion by an embolus, thrombus, or cerebrovascular hemorrhage or vasospasm, resulting in ischemia of the brain tissues normally perfused by the damaged vessels. The sequelae of a cerebrovascular insult depend on the location and extent of ischemia. Paralysis, weakness, sensory change, speech defect, aphasia, or death may occur.

cerebrum /ser'əbrəm, sərē'brəm/ *pl.* **cerebrums, cerebra** [L, brain], the largest and uppermost section of the brain, divided by a longitudinal fissure into the left and right cerebral hemispheres. The internal structures of the hemispheres merge with those of the diencephalon and further communicate with the brainstem through the cerebral peduncles. The cerebrum performs sensory functions, motor functions, and less easily defined integration functions associated with various mental activities.—**cerebral,** *adj.*

Cerezyme, a trademark for an analog of the human enzyme beta-glucocerebrosidase (imiglucerase) used for long-term therapy of Type 1 Gaucher's disease.

cerium (Ce) /sir'ē-əm/ [L, *Ceres,* Roman goddess of agriculture], a ductile gray rare earth element. Its atomic number is 58; its atomic mass is 140.13. A compound of cerium, cerium oxalate, is used as a sedative, an antiemetic, and an antitussive.

cerium nitrate, a topical antiseptic used in the treatment of burns to control bacterial and fungal infections.

cerivastatin, an HMG-CoA reductase inhibitor (Baycol) withdrawn from the market in August 2001 after several cases of fatal rhabdomyolysis.

ceroid /sir'oid/ [L, *cera,* wax; Gk, *eidos,* form], a golden, waxy pigment appearing in the cirrhotic livers of some individuals, in the GI tract, in the nervous system, and in the muscles.

ceroma /sirō'mə/ *pl.* **ceromas, ceromata** [L, *cera,* wax; Gk, *oma,* tumor], a neoplasm that has undergone waxy degeneration.

certifiable /sur'tifī'əbəl/ [L, *certus,* certain, *facere,* to make], **1.** a term pertaining to a patient with a mental illness who has been found incompetent and requires care by a guardian or in a hospital. **2.** pertaining to infectious diseases or dangerous conditions that must be reported to local health authorities.

certificate-of-necessity, certificate-of-need (CON), a statement or certificate issued by a governmental agency for proposed construction or modification of a health facility that ensures that the facility will be needed at the time of its completion.

certification [L, *certus,* certain, *facere,* to make], **1.** a process in which an individual, an institution, or an educational program is evaluated and recognized as meeting certain predetermined standards. Certification is usually made by a nongovernmental agency. **2.** (in nursing) a process in which the professional organization or association verifies that a person who is licensed has met the standards for specialty practice specified by the profession.

certification for excellence, (in nursing) certification that recognizes professional achievement, advanced education, and superior performance in a specialty or subspecialty field of practice.

certification in nursing, one of two processes, certification in nursing and entry-level certification, in which a professional organization formally recognizes the competence of a nurse to practice a subspecialty of nursing.

certified dental assistant (CDA) /sur'tifīd/, a person who has successfully completed the education, training, and testing of the Dental Assisting National Examination or of the American Dental Assistants' Association. A dental assistant may also become certified without receiving a formal education by working for 2 years as a full-time chairside dental assistant before taking the certification examination.

certified emergency nurse (CEN), a nurse who has had training in emergency nursing and successfully completed an examination given by the Board of Certification of Emergency Nursing.

Certified First Assistant (CFA), 1. credential offered by the National Board of Surgical Technology and Surgical Assisting. **2.** individual who has earned the credential of CFA and performs the roles and duties of a surgical assistant.

certified milk, raw milk that is obtained, handled, and marketed in compliance with state health laws. The milk must be produced by disease-free cows that are regularly inspected by a veterinarian and milked by sterilized equipment in hygienic surroundings. It must contain less than a specified low bacterial count and must be delivered within 36 hours.

certified nurse administrator (CNA), a nurse who supervises nursing staff, establishes work schedules and budgets, maintains medical supply inventories, and manages resources to ensure high-quality patient care. To apply for certification, a nurse must have an active RN license; hold a baccalaureate degree in nursing (or higher); have held an administrative position as a nurse manager or nurse executive, a faculty position teaching graduate students nursing administration, or a nursing management or executive consultation position,for at least 24 months full-time equivalent in the previous 5 years; have completed 30 hours of continuing education in nursing administration within the previous 3 years; and pass the credentialing examination by the American Nurses Credentialing Center.

certified nurse-midwife (CNM), (according to the American College of Nurse-Midwives) "an individual educated in the two disciplines of nursing and midwifery, who possesses evidence of certification according to the requirements of the American College of Nurse-Midwives."

certified occupational therapy assistant (COTA), an allied health paraprofessional who, under the direction of an occupational therapist, directs an individual's participation in selected tasks to restore, reinforce, and enhance performance; facilitates learning of skills and functions essential for adaptation and productivity; diminishes or corrects disorders; and promotes and maintains health.

Certified Registered Nurse Anesthetist, an advanced practice nurse who provide anesthetics to patients in practice settings for all types of surgeries and procedures. The certified registered nurse anesthetist (CRNA) has completed postgraduate education and passed a national certification examination.

certified respiratory therapist (CRT), a health care professional who performs routine care, management, and treatment of patients with respiratory disorders. Certification requires completion of an approved training course and passing of an examination by the National Board for Respiratory Care.

Certified Surgical Technologist (CST), 1. credential offered by the National Board of Surgical Technology and Surgical Assisting. **2.** an allied health professional who as a member of the surgical team is responsible for providing an optimal surgical environment by performing perioperative duties.

certify /sur′tifī/, **1.** to guarantee formally that certain requirements based on expert knowledge of significant, pertinent facts have been met. **2.** to attest, by a legal process, that someone is insane. **3.** to attest to the fact of someone's death in writing, usually on a form required by a local authority. **4.** to declare that a person has satisfied certain requirements for membership or acceptance into a professional or other group.—**certifiable,** *adj,* **certification,** *n.*

Cerubidine, a trademark for an antineoplastic (DAUNOrubicin hydrochloride).

cerulean /sirŏŏ′lē-ən/ [L, *caelum,* sky], sky-blue in color.

ceruloplasmin /sirŏŏ′lōplaz′min/ [L, *caelum,* sky; Gk, *plassein,* to shape], a blue glycoprotein in plasma that transports 96% of the plasma copper.

cerumen /sirŏŏ′mən/ [L, *cera,* wax], a yellowish or brownish waxy secretion produced by vestigial apocrine sweat glands in the external ear canal.

ceruminolytic agent [L, *cera,* wax; Gk, *lysis,* a loosening; L, *agere,* to do], a medication that dissolves or loosens cerumen to allow for its removal.

ceruminoma /serŏŏ′minō′mə/, an adenocarcinoma in the external auditory meatus.

ceruminosis /sirŏŏ′minō′sis/, excessive buildup of cerumen in the external auditory canal.

ceruminous /sirŏŏ′minəs/, pertaining to earwax.

ceruminous gland, one of a number of tiny structures in the external ear canal, believed to be modified sweat glands. They secrete a waxy cerumen instead of watery sweat.

cervical /sur′vikəl/ [L, *cervix,* neck], **1.** pertaining to the neck or the region of the neck. **2.** pertaining to the constricted area of a necklike structure, such as the neck of a tooth or the cervix of the uterus.

cervical abortion [L, *cervix* + *ab,* away from, *oriri,* to be born], spontaneous expulsion of a cervical pregnancy.

cervical adenitis [L, *cervix;* Gk, *aden,* gland, *itis,* inflammation], an abnormal condition characterized by enlarged, tender lymph nodes of the neck.

cervical amputation, the removal of the cervix.

cervical artery, an artery that supplies the muscles of the neck.

cervical biopsy, the removal of cervical tissue for microscopic examination to diagnose chronic cervical infection or cervical cancer.

cervical canal, the canal within the uterine cervix, which protrudes into the vagina. The uterine end of the canal is closed at the internal os and, in the nullipara, at the distal end by the external os. The canal is a passageway through which the menstrual flow escapes and, vastly dilated and effaced by labor, through which the infant must pass to be delivered vaginally. Sperm must travel upward through the canal to reach the uterus and fallopian tubes.

cervical cancer, a neoplasm of the uterine cervix that can be detected in the early, curable stage by the Papanicolaou (Pap) test. Factors that may be associated with the development of cervical cancer are coitus at an early age, relations with many sexual partners, genital herpesvirus infections, multiparity, and poor obstetric and gynecologic care. About 90% of cervical tumors are squamous cell carcinomas, less than 10% are adenocarcinomas, and others are mixtures of these kinds, or, in rare cases, sarcomas.

cervical cap, a contraceptive device similar to the diaphragm but much smaller, consisting of a cup that fits directly over the cervix to prevent spermatozoa from entering the cervical canal. It is only 60% effective for women who have already given birth.

cervical cauterization, the destruction, usually by heat or electrical current or by freezing, of abnormal superficial tissues of the cervix.

cervical conization, the excision of a cone-shaped tissue section from the endocervix, performed to obtain a tissue sample to establish a precise diagnosis.

cervical cyst [L, *cervix,* neck; Gk, *kystis,* bag], a mucous cyst of the uterine cervix caused by closure of the ducts of nabothian glands in the uterine cervix. It results from the healing of an erosion.

cervical dilation /dil'ā'shən/ [L, *dilatare,* to widen], the diameter of the opening of the cervix in labor as measured on vaginal examination. It is expressed in centimeters or finger breadths; one finger breadth is approximately 2 cm. At full dilatation the diameter of the cervical opening is 10 cm.

cervical disk syndrome, an abnormal condition characterized by compression or irritation of the cervical nerve roots in or near the intervertebral foramina before the roots divide into the anterior and posterior rami. When it is caused by ruptured intervertebral disks, degenerative cervical disk disease, or cervical injuries, it may produce varying degrees of malalignment, causing nerve root compression. Most cervical disk syndromes are caused by injuries that involve hyperextension. Edema usually occurs. Pain, the most common symptom, usually emanates from the cervical area but may radiate down the arm to the fingers and increase with cervical motion. Other signs and symptoms may be paresthesia, headache, blurred vision, decreased skeletal function, and weakened hand grip. Physical examination may reveal varying degrees of muscular atrophy, sensory abnormalities, muscular weakness, and decreased reflexes.

cervical dysplasia, abnormal tissue development of the uterine cervix, with atypical epithelium that may slowly progress to carcinoma.

cervical erosion [L, *cervix* + *erodere,* to consume], a condition in which the squamous epithelium of the cervix is abraded as a result of irritation caused by infection or trauma and replaced by columnar epithelium.

cervical fistula, an abnormal passage from the cervix to the vagina or bladder. It may be caused by a malignant lesion, radiotherapy, surgical trauma, or injury during childbirth. A cervical fistula communicating with the bladder permits leakage of urine, causing irritation, odor, and embarrassment.

cervical infertility, female factor infertility caused by abnormal interaction between the sperm and the cervical mucus.

cervical intraepithelial neoplasia (CIN) /in'trə·ep'ithē'lē·əl/, abnormal changes in the basal layers of the squamous epithelial tissues of the uterus. The disorder is graded according to its pathologic progress, from CIN1 to CIN3; CIN3 represents carcinoma of the cervix. The disorder is associated with human papillomaviruses.

cervical lordosis, the dorsally concave curvature of the cervical spinal column when seen from the side.

cervical mucus, a secretion of the columnar epithelium lining the upper part of the cervical canal of the uterus.

cervical mucus method of family planning, a type of natural family planning.

cervical nerves [L, *cervix,* neck, *nervus,* nerve], the eight pairs of spinal nerves that arise from the cervical segments of the spinal cord, from above the atlas to below the seventh vertebra. The first four supply the head and neck; the other four mainly innervate the upper limbs, scalp, and back.

cervical pleura, the dome-shaped layer of parietal pleura lining the cervical extension of the pleural cavity.

cervical plexus, the network of nerves formed by the ventral primary divisions of the first four cervical nerves. The plexus is located opposite the cranial aspect of the first four cervical vertebrae. It communicates with certain cranial nerves and numerous muscular and cutaneous branches.

cervical plexus block, anesthetic nerve block at any point below the mastoid process from the second cervical vertebra to the sixth cervical vertebra. This method is used for operations on the area between the jaw and clavicle.

cervical polyp [L, *cervix*; Gk, *polys*, mean, *pous*, foot], an outgrowth of columnar epithelial tissue of the endocervical canal. It is usually attached to the canal wall by a slender pedicle.

cervical radiculopathy, disease of the cervical nerve roots, often manifesting as neck or shoulder pain.

cervical regions, the various anatomic regions of the neck, including anterior, lateral, and posterior cervical regions and the region over the sternocleidomastoid muscle.

cervical rib, a supernumerary rib that articulates with a cervical vertebra, usually the seventh, but does not reach the sternum.

cervical smear [L, *cervix*; AS, *smero*, grease], a small amount of the secretions and superficial cells of the cervix, secured from the external os of the cervix with a sterile applicator or special small wooden or plastic spatula. For a Papanicolaou (Pap) smear, it is obtained from the squamocolumnar junction of the uterine cervix and from the vaginal vault and endocervical canal.

cervical spinal fusion, surgery to relieve severe pain in the neck, shoulders, arms, and hands caused by abnormal movement or adjustment of adjacent vertebrae, a pinched nerve, or spinal compression. The adjacent vertebrae are joined with metal devices and/or a bone graft made from human bone or a ceramic material.

cervical spine (C-spine), that portion of the spine comprising the cervical vertebrae.

cervical spondylosis [L, *cervix*; Gk, *spondylos*, vertebra, *osis*, condition], a form of degenerative joint and disk disease affecting the cervical vertebrae and resulting in compression of the associated nerve roots. Symptoms include pain or loss of feeling in the affected arm and shoulder and stiffness of the cervical spine.

cervical stenosis [L, *cervix*; Gk, *stenos*, narrow, *osis*, condition], a narrowing or complete closure of the canal between the body of the uterus and the cervical os.

cervical traction, a system of traction applied to the cervical spine by applying a force to lift the head.

cervical triangle, one of two triangular areas formed in the neck by the oblique course of the sternocleidomastoideus. The anterior triangle is bounded by the midline of the throat anteriorly, the sternocleidomastoideus laterally, and the body of the mandible superiorly. The posterior triangle is bounded by the clavicle inferiorly and by the borders of the sternocleidomastoideus and the trapezius superiorly.

cervical vertebra (C), one of the first seven segments of the vertebral column. They differ from the thoracic and lumbar vertebrae through the presence of a vertical foramen in each transverse process.

cervicitis /sur'vis'ī'tis/, acute or chronic inflammation of the uterine cervix. Acute cervicitis is infection of the cervix marked by redness, edema, and bleeding on contact. Chronic cervicitis is a persistent inflammation of the cervix that usually occurs among women in their reproductive years. Symptoms include a thick, irritating, malodorous discharge that may in severe cases be accompanied by significant pelvic pain. The cervix looks congested and enlarged, nabothian cysts are often present, and there are signs of eversion of the cervix and often old lacerations from childbirth.

cervicodynia /sur'vikōdin'ē·ə/, pain in the neck.

cervicogenic dorsalgia, back pain caused by a cervical spine disorder.

cervicogenic headache, (in chiropractic) a condition in which headaches, particularly those classified as muscle tension headaches involving referred pain, are the result of cervical subluxations.

cervicogenicity dysfunction /-jenis'itē/, (in chiropractic) a syndrome of hypomobility, tender points in soft tissues, reduced regional ranges of cervical motion, and static misalignment.

cervicogenic sympathetic syndrome, (in chiropractic) any of a large group of bodily disorders involving the cervical spine and the associated sympathetic trunk of nerve fibers. The effects usually include causalgia and reflex sympathetic dystrophy.

cervicolabial /sur'vikōlā'bē·əl/ [L, *cervix* + *labium*, lip], pertaining to or situated on the lip side of the neck of an incisor or a canine tooth.

cervicoplasty /sur'vikōplas'tē/, plastic surgery performed on either the uterine cervix or the neck.

cervicothoracic /-thōras'ik/, pertaining to the neck and thorax.

cervicotomy /sur'vikot'əmē/, **1.** incision of the neck. **2.** incision of the uterine cervix.

cervicouterine /sur'vikōyoo̅'tərin/, pertaining to or situated at the cervix of the uterus.

cervicovaginitis /-vaj'inītis/, an inflammation of the cervix and vagina.

cervicovesical /sur'vikōves'ikəl/ [L, *cervix* + *vesica*, bladder], pertaining to the cervix of the uterus and the bladder.

cervix /sur'viks/ *pl.* **cervices** /sur'visēz/, **cervixes,** the part of the uterus that protrudes into the cavity of the vagina. The cervix is divided into the supravaginal portion and the vaginal portion. The supravaginal portion is separated ventrally from the bladder by the parametrium. The vaginal portion of the cervix projects into the cavity of the vagina and contains the cervical canal and the internal and external os of the canal.

ceryl alcohol /sē'ril/ [L, *cera*, wax; Ar, *alkohl*, essence], a fatty alcohol present in many waxes.

Cesamet, a trademark for nabilone.

cesarean hysterectomy /sizer'ē-ən/ [L, *Caesar lex,* Caesar's law; Gk, *hystera,* womb; *ektomē,* excision], a surgical operation in which the uterus is removed at the time of cesarean section. It is performed most often for complications of cesarean section, usually intractable hemorrhage.

cesarean postmortem section [L, *Caesar lex + post,* after, *mors,* death, *sectio*], the surgical removal of the fetus immediately after the mother's death.

cesarean section (CS) [L, *Caesar lex + sectio*], a surgical procedure in which the abdomen and uterus are incised and a baby is delivered transabdominally. It is performed when abnormal maternal or fetal conditions make vaginal delivery hazardous. Maternal indications for the operation include placenta previa or abruptio placentae and dysfunctional labor. Prior delivery by cesarean section is no longer considered an absolute indication for repeating it in future deliveries. Fetal indications for the operation include fetal distress, cephalopelvic disproportion, and abnormal presentation, such as breech and transverse lie.

cesarean section care, a nursing intervention from the Nursing Interventions Classification (NIC) defined as preparation and support of the patient delivering a baby by cesarean section.

cesium (Cs) /sē'zē-əm/ [L, *caesius,* sky blue], an alkali metal element. Its atomic number is 55; its atomic mass is 132.9.

cesium-137 (^{137}Cs), a radioactive material with a half-life of 30.2 years that is used in radiotherapy as a sealed source of gamma rays intended for application to various malignancies that are treated by brachytherapy.

cestoid /ses'toid/ [Gk, *kestos,* girdle, *eidos,* form], **1.** cestodelike, or resembling a tapeworm. **2.** a class of platyhelminth flatworms of the Cestoda subclass, usually found in the small intestine.

CET, abbreviation for *certified enterostomal therapist.*

Cetacaine, a trademark for a fixed-combination, anesthetic spray, containing several local anesthetics (benzocaine, butyl aminobenzoate, tetracaine), applied to mucous membranes.

cetirizine, an H_1-histamine antagonist used to treat allergy symptoms and rhinitis.

cetrorelix /set'rorel'iks/, a gonadotropin-releasing hormone antagonist used to inhibit premature luteinizing hormone surges in women undergoing controlled ovarian stimulation during infertility treatment, administered subcutaneously.

cetuximab, a miscellaneous antineoplastic, monoclonal antibody that inhibits epidermal growth factor receptors.

cetyl alcohol ($C_{16}H_{33}OH$) /sē'til/ [L, *cetus,* whale; Ar, *alkohl,* essence], a fatty alcohol, derived from spermaceti, used as an emulsifier and stiffening agent in creams and ointments.

cetyl palmitate, esters of cetyl alcohol and saturated high-molecular-weight fatty acids, principally palmitic acid, used as an emulsifying and stiffening agent.

cetylpyridinium chloride /sē'təlpī'ridin'ē ·əm/, an antiinfective used as a preservative in pharmaceutic preparations and as a topical cleanser and local anesthetic (Cepacol). It is prescribed prophylactically to prevent infection of the skin or mucous membranes.

CEU, abbreviation for **continuing education unit.**

cevimeline /sevim'älēn/, a cholinergic agonist used as the hydrochloride salt in the treatment of xerostomia associated with Sjögren's syndrome.

Cf, symbol for the element **californium.**

CFA, abbreviation for **Certified First Assistant.**

cg, abbreviation for **centigram.**

CGC, abbreviation for *certified gastrointestinal clinician.*

CGD, abbreviation for **chronic granulomatous disease.**

cGMP, abbreviation for **cyclic guanosine monophosphate.**

cgs, CGS, abbreviation for **centimeter-gram-second system.**

cGy, abbreviation for **centigray.**

C_2H_2, chemical formula for **acetylene** (ethyne).

C_2H_4, chemical formula for **ethylene.**

C_6H_6, chemical formula for **benzene.**

Ch1, symbol for **Christchurch chromosome.**

Chaddock reflex [Charles G. Chaddock, American neurologist, 1861–1936], an abnormal reflex, induced by firmly stroking the ulnar surface of the forearm, characterized by flexion of the wrist and extension of the fingers in fanlike position. It is seen on the affected side in hemiplegia.

Chaddock's sign [Charles G. Chaddock], a variation of Babinski's reflex, elicited by firmly stroking the side of the foot just distal to the lateral malleolus, characterized by extension of the great toe and fanning of the other toes. It is seen in pyramidal tract disease.

Chadwick's sign /chad′wiks/ [James R. Chadwick, American gynecologist, 1844–1905], a sign of pregnancy that develops after the sixth week and consists of a dark bluish or purplish-red color of the vaginal or cervical mucosa as a result of increased blood supply to the area.

chafe [L, *calefacere*, to make warm], to irritate the skin by friction, such as when rough material rubs against an unprotected area of the body.

chafing, superficial irritation of the skin by friction.

Chagas' disease /chag′əs/ [Carlos Chagas, Brazilian physician, 1879–1934], a protozoal infection caused by *Trypanosoma cruzi*, transmitted to humans by bloodsucking reduviid (triatomine) bugs. The most recognized sign of acute infection, which is common in children and rare in adults, is a swelling of the eyelids on the side of the face near the insect bite, known as Romaña's sign. The acute form is also marked by a lesion at the site of the bite, fever, weakness, enlarged spleen and lymph nodes, edema of the face and legs, and tachycardia. This form resolves within 4 months unless complications, such as encephalitis, develop. The chronic form may be manifested by cardiomyopathy or by dilation of the esophagus or colon.

Chagres fever /chag′ris/ [Chagres River, Panama; L, *febris*], a phlebotomus arbovirus infection transmitted to humans through the bite of a sandfly. The disease is characterized by fever, headache, and muscle pains of the chest or abdomen.

chain [L, *catena*], **1.** a length of several units linked together in a linear pattern, such as a polypeptide chain of amino acids or a chain of atoms forming a chemical molecule. **2.** a group of individual bacteria linked together, such as streptococci formed by a chain of cocci. **3.** the serial relationship of certain structures essential to function, such as the chain of ossicles in the middle ear. **4.** a connected series, such as a chain of events.

chaining, a system of learning behaviors in which each response is a stimulus for the next response.

chain ligature [L, *catena* + *ligare*, to bind], an interlocking ligature that ties off a pedicle at several places by passing a long thread through the pedicle at different points.

chain reaction, **1.** (in chemistry) a reaction that proceeds through one or more reactive intermediates; one of the required reactive intermediates (usually free radicals) is formed in each step of the reaction. **2.** (in physics) a reaction that perpetuates itself by the proliferating fission of nuclei and the release of atomic particles that cause more nuclear fissions.

chain reflex, a series of reflexes, each stimulated by the preceding one.

chain-stitch suture, a continuous surgical stitch in which each loop of the suture is secured by the next loop.

chalasia /kəlā′zhə/ [Gk, *chalasis*, relaxation], abnormal relaxation or incompetence of the cardiac sphincter of the stomach, resulting in reflux of the gastric contents into the esophagus with subsequent regurgitation.

chalazion /kəlā′zion/ [Gk, hailstone], a small, nonmalignant localized swelling of the eyelid resulting from obstruction and retained secretions of the meibomian glands.

chalicosis /kal′ikō′sis/, a type of fibrosis that results from the inhalation of impure calcium dusts. Respiratory impairment is generally caused by the presence of free silica in the calcium dust.

chalkitis /kalkī′tis/ [Gk, *chalkos*, brass, *itis*, inflammation], deposits of copper in the ocular tissue that cause inflammation of the eyes and result from rubbing the eyes with the hands after touching or handling brass.

challenge, **1.** a method of testing the sensitivity of an individual to a hormone, allergen, or other substance by administering a sample. **2.** a term used to describe the rapid or concentrated infusion of a substance such as potassium or magnesium in the face of a life-threatening deficiency or a rapid infusion of IV fluid to differentiate between fluid deficit or renal failure as the cause of severely decreased urine output.

chalone /kā′lōn/ [Gk, *chalan*, to relax], any one of numerous polypeptide inhibitors that are elaborated by a tissue and function like hormones on specific target organs.

chamaeprosopy /kam′əpros′əpē/ [Gk, *chamai*, low, *prosopon*, face], a facial appearance characterized by a low brow and a broad face.—**chamaeprosopic**, *adj.*

chamber [Gk, *kamara*, vaulted enclosure], **1.** a hollow but not necessarily empty space or cavity in an organ, as in the anterior and posterior chambers of the eye or the atrial and ventricular chambers of the heart. **2.** a room or closed space used for research or therapeutic purposes, such as a decompression chamber or hyperbaric oxygen chamber.

Chamberlain's line [W.E. Chamberlain, American radiologist, 1891–1947], a line that extends from the posterior of the hard palate to the dorsum of the foramen magnum.

Chamberlen forceps [Peter Chamberlen, English obstetrician, 1560–1631], one of the earliest kinds of obstetric forceps, introduced in the seventeenth century.

chamfer /cham′fər/, the finish line on an extracoronal cavity preparation for a crown restoration in which the junction between the crown and the remaining tooth structure is formed to create a sloping shoulder at the apical terminus of the restoration.

chamomile /kam′əmēl/, a herb with both annual and perennial forms. It is used externally as an antiseptic and soothing agent for inflamed skin and minor wounds. Internally it is used as an antispasmodic, gas-relieving, and antiinflammatory agent for the treatment of digestive problems; as a light sleep aid and sedative for adults and children; and as a possible anticancer agent. It is likely safe when used in medicinal amounts for a short term.

CHAMPUS, abbreviation for **Civilian Health and Medical Programs for Uniformed Services.**

chancre /shang′kər/ [Fr, canker], **1.** a skin lesion, usually of primary syphilis, that begins at the infection site as a papule and develops into a red, bloodless, painless ulcer with a scooped-out appearance. The chancre teems with *Treponema pallidum* spirochetes and is highly contagious. **2.** a papular lesion or ulcerated area of the skin that marks the point of infection of a nonsyphilitic disease, such as TB.

chancroid /shang′kroid/ [Fr, *chancre,* canker; Gk, *eidos,* form], a highly contagious STD caused by infection with the bacillus *Haemophilus ducreyi.* It characteristically begins as a papule, usually on the skin of the external genitalia; it then grows and ulcerates; other papules form, and if untreated, the bacillus spreads, causing buboes in the groin.

chancrous /shang′krəs/, describing a condition of chancres or lesions resembling chancres.

change agent, **1.** a role in which communication skills, education, and other resources are applied to help a client adjust to changes caused by illness or disability. **2.** a role to help members of an organization adapt to organizational change or to create organizational change.

channel [L, *canalis,* pipe], **1.** a passageway or groove that conveys fluid, such as the central channels that connect the arterioles with the venules. **2.** membrane-bound globular proteins that allow diffusion of specific ions and molecules across a cell membrane.

channeling, referral of increased numbers of patients in exchange for discounted prices.

channel ulcer [L, *canalis,* pipe, *ulcus,* sore], a rare type of peptic ulcer found in the pyloric canal between the stomach and the duodenum.

Chantix, a trademark for varenicline.

chaos /kā′əs/, total disorganization with no causal relationships operating.

chaparral, a herbal product that is potentially toxic to the liver and kidneys.

Chapman lymphatic reflexes, (in chiropractic) a method of using body wall reflexes to influence the motion of fluids. After a surface locus has been contacted by the tip of the examiner's finger, a firm gentle contact is maintained, and a rotary motion is imparted to the finger to express the fluid content of the locus into the surrounding tissues.

chapped /chapt/ [ME, *chappen,* cracked], pertaining to skin that is roughened, cracked, or reddened by exposure to cold or excessive moisture evaporation. Stinging or burning sensations often accompany the disorder.—**chap,** *v.*

character [Gk, *charassein,* to engrave], the integrated composite of traits and behavioral tendencies that enable a person to react in a relatively consistent way to the customs and mores of society.

character analysis, a systematic investigation of the personality of an individual, with special attention to psychologic defenses and motivations, usually undertaken to improve behavior.

character disorder, a chronic, habitual maladaptive and socially unacceptable pattern of behavior and emotional response.

characteristic /kar′əktəris′tik/ [Gk, *charassein,* to engrave], **1.** typical of an individual or other entity. **2.** a trait that distinguishes an individual or entity.

characteristic curve /ker′əktəris′tik/, a graphic relationship between the density (blackness) of an x-ray film and the exposure.

characteristic radiation, radiation produced when a projectile electron interacts with and displaces an inner-shell electron of a target atom. It is a key process in x-ray production.

Charcot-Bouchard aneurysm /shärkō' booshär'/ [Jean M. Charcot, French neurologist, 1825–1893; Charles J. Bouchard, French physician, 1837–1886], a small, round dilation of a small artery in the cerebral cortex or basal ganglia. Charcot-Bouchard aneurysms often occur in individuals with very high BP.

Charcot-Leyden crystal /shärkō' lī'dən/ [Jean M. Charcot; Ernst V. von Leyden, German physician, 1832–1910], any of the proteinaceous crystalline structures shaped like narrow, double pyramids found in the sputum of persons suffering from asthma and in the feces of dysentery patients.

Charcot-Marie-Tooth disease /shärkō' mərē' tooth'/ [Jean M. Charcot; Pierre Marie, French neurologist, 1853–1940; Howard H. Tooth, English neurologist, 1856–1925], a progressive hereditary disorder characterized by degeneration of the peroneal muscles of the fibula, resulting in clubfoot, footdrop, and ataxia. Progressive arm weakness can also be present as distal muscles atrophy.

Charcot's fever /shärkōz'/ [Jean M. Charcot], a syndrome characterized by recurrent chills and fever, jaundice, and abdominal pain in the right upper quadrant that occurs with inflammation of the bile ducts.

Charcot's foot /shär·kōz'/ [Jean M. Charcot], a deformity of the foot associated with neuropathies.

Charcot's triad [Jean M. Charcot; Gk, *trias,* three], a set of three signs of brainstem involvement in MS: intention tremor, nystagmus, and scanning speech.

CHARGE association, a syndrome of associated defects, including *c*oloboma of the eye, *h*eart anomaly, choanal *a*tresia, *r*etardation, and *g*enital and *e*ar anomalies.

charge-coupled device (CCD), an array of semiconductors so arranged that the output of each serves as the input of the next. CCDs are often used to convert light patterns into electrical signals.

charge-coupled image sensor, two-dimensional electronic array for converting light patterns into electrical signals.

charge nurse, the nurse assigned to manage the operations of the patient care area for the shift. Responsibilities may include staffing, admissions and discharge, and coordination of activities in the patient care area.

charlatan /shär'lətən/ [Fr, imposter], a totally unqualified individual posing as an expert, especially an individual pretending to be a physician.—**charlatanic,** *adj.*

charley horse /chär'lē hôrs'/, a sudden painful condition of the quadriceps or hamstring muscles characterized by soreness and stiffness. It is the result of a strain, tear, or bruise of the muscle.

chart /chärt/ [L, *charta,* paper], **1.** informal. a patient record of data in tabular or graphic form. **2.** to note data in a patient record, usually at prescribed intervals.

charta /kär'tə/ *pl.* **chartae** [L, paper], a piece of paper, especially one treated with medicine, as for external application, or with a chemical for a special purpose, such as litmus paper.

charting, the act of compiling data on clinical records or charts. The charts are updated regularly to keep physicians and other health care workers advised of changes in the patient's condition. The data usually include fluctuations in temperature, pulse, respiration, other variable factors, and much more.

chauffeur's fracture /shō'fərz/ [Fr, stoker; L, *fractura,* break], any fracture of the radial styloid, produced by a twisting or a snapping type of injury.

Chaussier's areola /shôsyäz'/ [François Chaussier, French anatomist, 1746–1828; L, little space], an areola of indurated tissue surrounding a malignant pustule.

CHB, abbreviation for **complete heart block.**

CHC, abbreviation for *community health center.*

CHD, 1. abbreviation for **coronary heart disease. 2.** abbreviation for **congenital heart disease.**

checkup [Fr, *eschec,* acquire; AS, *uf*], a thorough study or examination of the health of an individual.

Chédiak-Higashi syndrome /ched'ē·ak higä'shē/ [Moises Chédiak, twentieth-century Cuban physician; Ototaka Higashi, twentieth-century Japanese physician], a congenital, autosomal-recessive disorder, characterized by partial albinism, photophobia, pale optic fundi, massive leukocytic inclusions, psychomotor abnormalities, recurrent infections, and early death.

cheek [AS, *ceace*], a fleshy prominence, especially the fleshy protuberances on both sides of the face between the eye and the jaw and the ear and the nose and mouth.

cheesy abscess [AS, *cese*; L, *abscedere,* to go away], an abscess that contains a yellowish semisolid, cheeselike material, such as a tuberculous abscess.

cheesy necrosis, tissue death in which the structures have degenerated into a white, cheesy mass.

cheilectomy /kīlek'təmē/, surgical removal of irregular surfaces in the lining of a joint.

cheilitis /kīlī′tis/ [Gk, *cheilos*, lip, *itis*, inflammation], an abnormal condition of the lips characterized by inflammation and cracking of the skin.

cheilocarcinoma /kī′lōkär′sinō′mə/ *pl*. **cheilocarcinomas, cheilocarcinomata**, a malignant epithelial tumor of the lip.

cheiloplasty /kī′ləplas′tē/ [Gk, *cheilos*, lip, *plassein*, to mold], surgical correction of a defect of the lip.

cheilorrhaphy /kīlôr′əfē/ [Gk, *cheilos*, lip, *raphe*, suture], a surgical procedure that sutures the lip, such as in the repair of a congenitally cleft lip or a lacerated lip.

cheilosis /kīlō′sis/, a noninflammatory disorder of the lips and mouth characterized by bilateral scales and fissures, resulting from a deficiency of riboflavin in the diet.

cheiralgia /kīral′jə/ [Gk, *cheir* + *algos*, pain], a pain in the hand, especially that associated with arthritis.—**cheiralgic,** *adj*.

cheirognostic /kī′ragnos′tik/ [Gk, *cheir*, hand, *gnostikos*, knowing], pertaining to the ability to distinguish between the left and right hands and sides of the body.

cheiromegaly /kī′rōmeg′əlē/ [Gk, *cheir* + *megas*, large], an abnormal condition characterized by excessively large hands. —**cheiromegalic,** *adj*.

cheiroplasty /kī′rōplas′tē/, a surgical procedure to restore an injured or congenitally deformed hand to normal use.—**cheiroplastic,** *adj*.

chelate /kē′lāt/ [Gk, *chele*, claw], 1. to form a bond, thus creating a ringlike complex. 2. (in medicine) any coordination compound composed of a central metal ion and an organic molecule with multiple bonds arranged in ring formations, used especially in chemotherapeutic treatments for metal poisoning. 3. pertaining to chelation.

chelating agent /kē′lāting/, a substance that promotes chelation. Chelating agents are used in the treatment of metal poisoning.

chelation /kēlā′shən/, a chemical reaction in which there is a combination with a metal to form a ring-shaped molecular complex in which the metal is firmly bound and isolated.

chelation therapy, the use of a chelating agent to remove toxic metals from the body, the treatment of heavy metal poisoning. In complementary medicine, it is also used for the treatment of atherosclerosis and other disorders.

chemabrasion /kem′əbrā′zhən/ [Gk, *chemeia*, alchemy; L, *ab* + *radere*, to scrape off], a method of treating scars, chromatosis, or other skin disorders by applying chemicals that remove the surface layers of skin cells.

chemical /kem′əkəl/ [Gk, *chemeia*, alchemy], 1. a substance composed of chemical elements or a substance produced by or used in chemical processes. 2. pertaining to chemistry.

chemical action, any process in which elements and/or compounds react with each other to produce a chemical change. For example, hydrogen and oxygen combine to produce water.

chemical affinity [Gk, *chemeia*, alchemy; L, *affinis*, related], 1. an attraction that results in the formation of molecules from atoms. 2. an attraction between chemicals caused by polarity, as used in affinity chromatography.

chemical agent, any chemical power, active principle, or substance that can produce an effect in the body by interacting with various body substances, such as aspirin, which produces an analgesic effect.

chemical antidote [Gk, *chemeia* + *anti*, against, *dotos*, that which is given], any substance that reacts chemically with a poison to form a compound that is harmless.

chemical burn, tissue damage caused by exposure to a strong acid or alkali.

chemical carcinogen [Gk, *chemeia*, alchemy, *karkinos*, crab, *oma*, tumor, *genein*, to produce], any chemical agent that can induce the development of cancer in living tissue.

chemical cauterization [Gk, *chemeia* + *kauterion*, branding iron], the corroding or burning of living tissue by a caustic chemical substance, such as potassium hydroxide.

chemical cystitis, allergic cystitis occurring in reaction to a chemical substance in the body.

chemical disaster, the accidental release of a quantity of toxic chemicals into the environment, resulting in death or injury to workers or members of nearby communities.

chemical equivalent, a drug or chemical containing similar amounts of the same ingredients as another drug or chemical.

chemical fog, a curtain effect on x-ray film that causes the loss of image quality. It appears as a dull gray discoloration and is usually caused by chemical contamination of the developer.

chemical gastritis, inflammation of the stomach caused by the ingestion of a chemical compound.

chemical indicator, 1. a commercially prepared device that monitors all or part of the physical conditions of the sterilization cycle. 2. a compound added to a reaction system to show, typically by a change in color, when the process is complete, as in an acid-base titration.

chemical mediator, a neurotransmitter chemical such as acetylcholine.

chemical name, the exact designation of the chemical structure of a drug as determined by the rules of accepted systems of chemical nomenclature.

chemical peel, a therapy to reduce or improve wrinkles, blemishes, pigment spots, and sun-damaged areas of the skin. Using a chemical solution of phenol, trichloroacetic acid (TCA), or alpha hydroxy fruit acid, the top skin layers are peeled away, allowing new, smoother skin with tighter cells to occupy the surface. Immediately after the peel, there may be considerable swelling, which subsides after 7 to 10 days as new skin begins to form.

chemical peritonitis [Gk, *chemeia,* alchemy, L, *peri,* near, *teinein,* to stretch, *itis,* inflammation], an inflammation of the peritoneum resulting from chemicals, including digestive substances, in the peritoneum.

chemical restraint[1] [Gk, *chemeia,* alchemy; L, *restringere,* to confine], the use of psychotropics, hypnotics, or anxiolytics to control a potentially violent patient.

chemical restraint[2], a nursing intervention from the Nursing Interventions Classification (NIC) defined as the administration, monitoring, and discontinuation of psychotropic agents used to control an individual's extreme behavior.

chemical shift, (in nuclear magnetic resonance spectrometry) the position of a resonance in the substance of interest relative to the position of the resonance of a standard.

chemical shift artifacts, artifacts in magnetic resonance caused by small differences in resonance frequencies of different chemical compounds (e.g., water and fat).

chemical sympathectomy, the removal of a sympathetic nerve tract or ganglion by injection of a corrosive chemical such as phenol.

chemical warfare, the waging of war with poisonous chemicals and gases.

cheminosis /kem'ənō'sis/ [Gk, *chemeia* + *osis,* condition], any disease caused by a chemical substance.

chemist, 1. a person with special education and training in the structures, characteristics, and actions of chemicals. 2. In Great Britain, Australia, and New Zealand, a pharmacist.

chemistry /kem'istrē/ [Gk, *chemeia,* alchemy], the science dealing with the elements, their compounds, and the molecular structure and interactions of matter.

chemistry, normal values, the amounts of various substances in the normal human body, determined by testing a large sample of people presumed to be healthy. Normal values are expressed in ranges of numbers, and ranges vary for different age groups and from laboratory to laboratory.

chemoattractant /kē'mō·ətrak'tənt/ [Gk, *chemeia,* alchemy; L, *attrahere,* to draw to], a chemotactic factor that induces positive chemotaxis.

chemodifferentiation /-dif'ərən'shē·ā'shən/, a stage in embryonic development that precedes and controls specialization and differentiation of the cells into rudimentary organs.

chemokine /kē'mōkīn/ [Gk, *chemeia,* alchemy, *kinēsis,* movement], any of a group of low-molecular-weight cytokines, such as interleukin-8, identified on the basis of their ability to induce chemotaxis or chemokinesis in leukocytes (or in particular populations of leukocytes) in inflammation. They function as regulators of the immune system and may also play roles in the circulatory system and CNS.

chemokinesis /kē'mōkinē'sis/ [Gk, *chemeia,* alchemy, *kinesis* movement], increased nondirectional activity of cells caused by the presence of a chemical substance.

chemonucleolysis /-noo'klē·ol'isis/ [Gk, *chemeia;* L, *nucleus,* nut kernel; Gk, *lysein,* to loosen], a method of dissolving the nucleus pulposus of an intervertebral disk by the injection of a chemolytic agent such as the enzyme chymopapain.

chemoprophylaxis /-prō'filak'sis/ [Gk, *chemeia* + *prophylax,* advance guard], administration of a medicine or chemical agent with the purpose of disease prevention, such as the use of antimicrobial drugs to prevent the acquisition of pathogens in an endemic area or to prevent their spread from one body area to another.

chemoprotectant, 1. providing protection against the toxic effects of chemotherapy agents. 2. an agent that so acts.

chemoradiotherapy, combined modality therapy using chemotherapy and radiotherapy, designed to reduce the need for surgery by maximizing the interaction between the radiation and the therapeutic agent or agents.

chemoreceptor /-risep'tər/ [Gk, *chemeia;* L, *recipere,* to receive], a sensory nerve cell activated by chemical stimuli. For example, chemoreceptors in the carotid artery are sensitive to the partial pressure of carbon dioxide in the blood; they signal the respiratory center in the brain to increase or decrease the rate of breathing.

chemoreflex /-rē'fleks/, any reflex initiated by the stimulation of chemical receptors, such as the carotid and aortic bodies, which respond to changes in carbon dioxide, hydrogen ion, and oxygen concentrations in the blood.

chemoresistance, 1. a specific resistance by components of a cell to chemical substances. **2.** the resistance of bacteria or a cancer cell to a chemical designed to treat the disorder.

chemosis /kimō′sis/ [Gk, *cheme,* cockle, *osis,* condition], an abnormal edematous swelling of the mucous membrane covering the eyeball and lining the eyelids. Usually the result of local trauma or infection, chemosis may also occur in acute conjunctivitis.

chemostat /kē′məstat′/, a device that assures a steady rate of cell division in bacterial populations by maintaining a constant environment.

chemosurgery /-sur′jərē/ [Gk, *chemeia* + *cheirourgos,* surgeon], the destruction of malignant, infected, or gangrenous tissue by the application of chemicals. The technique is used successfully to remove skin cancers.

chemotaxis /-tak′sis/ [Gk, *chemeia* + *taxis,* arrangement], movement toward or away from a chemical stimulus. Chemotaxis is a cellular function, particularly of neutrophils and monocytes.—**chemotactic,** *adj.*

chemotherapeutic agent /-ther′əpyo͞o′tik/, any chemical used to treat cancer. It is usually used to refer to antineoplastic drugs.

chemotherapeutic index, a system for judging the safety and effectiveness of a drug as a ratio between the dose that is lethal to 50% of animals (LD_{50}) and the median effective (ED_{50}) or minimal curative dose.

chemotherapy /-ther′əpē/, the treatment of cancer, infections, and other diseases with chemical agents. The cytotoxic agents used in cancer treatments generally do not kill the cancer cells directly but instead impair their ability to replicate by interfering with DNA and RNA activities associated with cell division. Chemotherapeutic agents are often used in combination with radiation treatments for their synergistic effect.

chemotherapy-induced nausea and vomiting (CINV), nausea and vomiting occurring as a reaction to chemotherapeutic agents.

chemotherapy management, a nursing intervention from the Nursing Interventions Classification (NIC) defined as assisting the patient and family to understand the action and minimize side effects of antineoplastic agents.

chemotherapy (unsealed radioactive), the oral or parenteral administration of a radioisotope such as iodine 131 (^{131}I) for the treatment of hyperthyroidism or thyroid cancer or phosphorus 32 (^{32}P) for leukemia, polycythemia vera, or peritoneal ascites resulting from widely disseminated carcinoma.

chenodeoxycholic acid /kē′nōdē·ok′sikō′lik/, a secondary bile acid. It is used in vivo to dissolve cholesterol gallstones, particularly in the elderly and poor-risk patients.

cherophobia /kē′rō′fō′bē·ə/, a morbid aversion to cheerfulness.

cherry angioma [L, *cerasus;* Gk, *angeion,* vessel, *oma,* tumor], a small, bright red, clearly circumscribed vascular tumor on the skin. It occurs most often on the trunk but may appear anywhere on the body. The lesion is common.

cherry red spot, an abnormal red circular area of the choroid, visible through the fovea centralis of the eye and surrounded by a contrasting white edema. It is associated with cases of infantile cerebral sphingolipidosis and sometimes appears in the late infantile form of amaurotic familial idiocy.

cherubism /cher′əbiz′əm/ [Heb, *kerubh*], an abnormal hereditary condition characterized by progressive bilateral swelling at the angle of the mandible, especially in children.

chest [AS, *box*], the outside front part of the basic thoracic structure.

chest bandage, any of several types of fabric dressings for chest injuries, including a three-cornered open chest wrapping, a figure-eight roller bandage spica, or a scultetus pattern of narrow strips that can be overlapped and pinned.

chest binder, a broad bandage or girdle, with or without shoulder straps, that encircles the chest and aids in supplying heat or other therapies. A chest binder also may be used to support the breasts.

chest drainage, the withdrawal of air, blood, or fluids from the chest cavity through a tube commonly inserted into the pleural space. The tube may be connected to a suction device that helps reinflate a collapsed lung.

chest lead /lēd/, **1.** an ECG conductor in which the exploring positive electrode is placed on the chest or precordium. The indifferent electrode is placed on the patient's back for a chest back lead, on the front of the chest for a chest front lead, on the left arm for a chest left lead, and on the right arm for a chest right lead. **2.** informal. the tracing produced by such a lead on an ECG.

chest pain [AS, *cest*, box; L, *poena*, punishment], a physical complaint that requires immediate diagnosis and evaluation.

chest physiotherapy, a nursing intervention from the Nursing Interventions Classification (NIC) defined as assisting the patient to move airway secretions from peripheral airways to more central airways for expectoration and/or suctioning.

chest prominences and depressions, any unnatural surface features of the chest that may be caused by congenital defects, diseases such as emphysema, enlarged organs, tumors, traumas, or occupational hazards.

chest regions, the topographic parts or subdivisions of the chest: presternal, mammary, inframammary, and axillary.

chest thump [AS, *cest*, box], a sharp blow delivered to the chest in the precordial area to restore a normal heartbeat after cardiac arrest.

chest tube, a catheter inserted through the rib space of the thorax into the pleural space to remove air and/or fluid, thereby restoring negative pressure in the pleural space, commonly used after chest surgery and lung collapse.

chest x-ray, radiographic assessment of the pulmonary and cardiac systems.

chewing reflex, a pathologic sign in brain-damaged adults, characterized by repetitive chewing motions when the mouth is stimulated.

Cheyne's nystagmus /shānz/ [John Cheyne, Scottish physician, 1777–1836], an involuntary eyeball movement with a rhythm that resembles that of Cheyne-Stokes respiration.

Cheyne-Stokes respiration (CSR) [John Cheyne; William Stokes, Irish physician, 1804–1878; L, *respirare* to breathe], an abnormal pattern of respiration, characterized by alternating periods of apnea and deep, rapid breathing. The respiratory cycle begins with slow, shallow breaths that gradually become abnormally rapid and deep. Breathing gradually becomes slower and shallower and is followed by 10 to 20 seconds of apnea before the cycle is repeated. Each episode may last from 45 seconds to 3 minutes.

CHF, abbreviation for **congestive heart failure.**

chi /kī/, X, χ, the 22nd letter of the Greek alphabet, sometimes used in scientific notation to designate the 22nd in a series.

ch'i, a Chinese concept of a fundamental life energy that flows in orderly ways along meridians, or channels, in the body. The energy can be either positive or negative.

CHI, abbreviation for **creatinine height index.**

Chiari-Frommel syndrome /kē·är´ēfrom'əl/ [Johann B. Chiari, German obstetrician, 1817–1854; Richard Frommel, German gynecologist, 1854–1912], a hormonal disorder that occurs after pregnancy in which weaning does not spontaneously end lactation.

Chiari's malformation /kē·ä´rēz/ [Hans Chiari, Austrian pathologist, 1851–1916], a congenital anomaly in which the cerebellum and medulla oblongata, which is elongated and flattened, protrude into the spinal canal through the foramen magnum. It may be accompanied by hydrocephalus, spina bifida, syringomyelia, and mental defects.

chiasm /kī´azəm/ [Gk, *chiasma*, lines that cross], **1.** the crossing of two lines or tracts, as of the optic nerves at the optic chiasm. **2.** (in genetics) the crossing of two chromatids in the prophase of meiosis. —**chiasmal, chiasmic,** *adj.*

chiasma /kī·az´mə/ *pl.* **chiasmata** [Gk, lines that cross], a visible connection between homologous chromosomes during the first meiotic division in gametogenesis. Chiasmata appear as X-shaped configurations during the late prophase stage and provide the means by which homologous chromosomes exchange genetic material. —**chiasmatic, chiasmic,** *adj.*

chiasmapexy /kī·az´mǝpek´sē/, surgery involving the optic chiasm.

chickenpox /chik´ǝnpoks´/ [AS, *cicen*; ME, *pokke*], an acute, highly contagious viral disease caused by a herpesvirus, varicella zoster virus (VZV). It occurs primarily in young children and is characterized by crops of pruritic vesicular eruptions on the skin. The disease is transmitted by direct contact with skin lesions or, more commonly, by droplets spread from the respiratory tract of infected persons, usually in the prodromal period or the early stages of the rash. The vesicular fluid and the scabs are infectious until entirely dry.

chiclero ulcer /chikler´ō/ [Mex, *tzictli*, chicle; L, *ulcus*], a kind of American leishmaniasis caused by *Leishmania mexicana.* It is endemic among the workers in the Yucatan and Central America who harvest chicle from the forest. The disease is characterized by cutaneous ulcers on the head that usually heal spontaneously by 6 months, except for those on the pinna of the ear, which may last for years and cause scarring and deformities.

chicory, a perennial herb used as a coffee substitute, as a source of fructo-oligosaccharides, as a mild laxative for children, and as a treatment for gout, rheumatism, loss of appetite, and digestive distress. It is generally recognized as safe in foods and

Chido-Rodgers blood group /chē′dō roj′ərz/, a blood group consisting of nine antigens that are fragments of the C4 component of complement that attaches to the red cell from plasma.

chief cell [Fr, *chef;* L, *cella,* storeroom], **1.** any one of the columnar or cuboidal epithelial cells that line the gastric glands and secrete pepsinogen and intrinsic factor, which are needed for the absorption of vitamin B_{12} and the normal development of RBCs. Pernicious anemia may be caused by the absence of intrinsic factor. **2.** any one of the epithelioid cells with pale-staining cytoplasm and a large nucleus containing a prominent nucleolus. Cords of such cells form the main substance of the pineal body. **3.** any one of the polyhedral epithelial cells, within the parathyroid glands, which contain pale, clear cytoplasm and a vesicular nucleus.

chief complaint (CC), a subjective statement made by a patient describing his or her most significant or serious symptoms or signs of illness or dysfunction.

chief executive officer (CEO, C.E.O.), the most senior official of an organization or institution.

chief resident, a senior resident physician who acts temporarily as the clinical and administrative director of the house staff in a department of the hospital.

chief surgeon, a surgeon appointed or elected head of the surgeons on the staff of a health care facility.

chigger /chig′ər/ [Fr, *chique*], the larva of *Trombicula* mites found in tall grass and weeds. It sticks to the skin and causes irritation and severe itching.

chigoe /chig′ō/, a flea, *Tunga penetrans,* found in tropical and subtropical America and Africa. The pregnant female flea burrows into the skin of the feet, causing an inflammatory condition that may lead to spontaneous amputation of a toe.

chikungunya /chik′ungun′yə/ [Swahili, that which bends up], a self-limited disease resembling dengue, seen mainly in Africa and Southeast Asia, caused by an alphavirus transmitted chiefly by mosquitoes of the genus *Aedes.* Its most prominent symptoms are musculoskeletal and it has occasionally been associated with hemorrhagic fever.

chikungunya encephalitis /chik′əngun′yə/ [Swahili, that which bends up; Gk, *enkephalos,* brain, *itis,* inflammation], a togavirus infection characterized by a high fever that begins abruptly, muscle aches, a rash, and pain in the joints. It is transmitted by the bite of a mosquito. The fever may last for a week, then rise again after a remission of several days. Pain in the joints may continue after other symptoms have ceased.

chilblain /chil′blān/ [AS, *cele,* cold, *bleyn,* blister], redness and swelling of the skin caused by excessive exposure to cold. Burning, itching, blistering, and ulceration similar to those characteristic of a thermal burn may occur.

chilblain lupus erythematosus, a form of discoid lupus erythematosus aggravated by cold, initially resembling chilblains, in which the lesions consist of small, hardened, reddened nodular areas on the exposed areas of the body, especially the finger knuckles.

child [AS, *cild*], **1.** a person of either sex between the time of birth and adolescence. **2.** an unborn or recently born human being; fetus; neonate; infant. **3.** an offspring or descendant; a son or daughter or a member of a particular tribe or clan. **4.** one who is like a child or immature.

child abuse, the physical, sexual, or emotional maltreatment of a child. Parents at high risk for abuse are characterized as having unsatisfied needs, difficulty in forming adequate interpersonal relationships, unrealistic expectations of the child, and a lack of nurturing experience, often involving neglect or abuse in their own childhoods.

child adaptation to hospitalization, a nursing outcome from the Nursing Outcomes Classification (NOC) defined as the adaptive response of a child from 3 years through 17 years of age to hospitalization.

childbearing period [AS, *cild + beran,* to bear; Gk, *peri,* around, *hodos,* way], the reproductive period in a woman's life, from puberty to menopause. It is the time during which she is physiologically able to conceive children.

childbirth center, a health facility where prenatal care and delivery services are made available to low-risk pregnant women by a team of nurse-midwives, obstetricians, pediatricians, and ancillary health professionals.

childbirth preparation, a nursing intervention from the Nursing Interventions Classification (NIC) defined as providing information and support to facilitate childbirth and to enhance the ability of an individual to develop and perform the parental role.

child development, the various stages of physical, social, and psychologic growth that occur from birth through young adulthood.

child development: 1 month, a nursing outcome from the Nursing Outcomes Classification (NOC) defined as milestones of

C

physical, cognitive, and psychosocial progression by 1 month of age.

child development: 2 months, a nursing outcome from the Nursing Outcomes Classification (NOC) defined as milestones of physical, cognitive, and psychosocial progression by 2 months of age.

child development: 4 months, a nursing outcome from the Nursing Outcomes Classification (NOC) defined as milestones of physical, cognitive, and psychosocial progression by 4 months of age.

child development: 6 months, a nursing outcome from the Nursing Outcomes Classification (NOC) defined as milestones of physical, cognitive, and psychosocial progression by 6 months of age.

child development: 12 months, a nursing outcome from the Nursing Outcomes Classification (NOC) defined as milestones of physical, cognitive, and psychosocial progression by 12 months of age.

child development: 2 years, a nursing outcome from the Nursing Outcomes Classification (NOC) defined as milestones of physical, cognitive, and psychosocial progression by 2 years of age.

child development: 3 years, a nursing outcome from the Nursing Outcomes Classification (NOC) defined as milestones of physical, cognitive, and psychosocial progression by 3 years of age.

child development: 4 years, a nursing outcome from the Nursing Outcomes Classification (NOC) defined as milestones of physical, cognitive, and psychosocial progression by 4 years of age.

child development: 5 years, a nursing outcome from the Nursing Outcomes Classification (NOC) defined as milestones of physical, cognitive, and psychosocial progression by 5 years of age.

child development: middle childhood, a nursing outcome from the Nursing Outcomes Classification (NOC) defined as milestones of physical, cognitive, and psychosocial progression from 6 years through 11 years of age.

child development: adolescence, a nursing outcome from the Nursing Outcomes Classification (NOC) defined as milestones of physical, cognitive, and psychosocial progression from 12 years through 17 years of age.

childhood, 1. the period in human development that extends from birth until the onset of puberty. **2.** the state or quality of being a child.

childhood aphasia, an inability to process language that is caused by a brain dysfunction in childhood.

childhood disintegrative disorder, pervasive developmental disorder characterized by marked regression in a variety of skills, including language, social skills or adaptive behavior, play, bowel or bladder control, and motor skills, after at least 2 but less than 10 years of apparently normal development.

childhood myxedema [AS, *cildhad*; Gk, *myxa*, mucus, *oidema*, swelling], a juvenile form of hypothyroidism characterized by atrophy of the thyroid gland after a severe infection of the gland.

childhood-onset pervasive developmental disorders, disturbances in thought, affect, social relatedness, and behavior that emerge usually between the ages of 30 months and 12 years of age. An example is autism.

childhood triad, three types of behavior—fire setting, bedwetting, and cruelty to animals—that may predict emerging sociopathy when they occur consistently and in combination.

child life specialist, a professional who specializes in the use of use of developmental, educational, and therapeutic interventions that help children and their families cope with challenging life events and experiences, such as those related to health care and hospitalization.

child neglect, the failure by parents or guardians to provide for the basic human needs of a child by physical or emotional deprivation that interferes with normal growth and development or that places the child in jeopardy.

child psychology, the study of the mental, emotional, and behavioral development of infants and children.

Child-Pugh classification, a classification of severity of cirrhosis with five different parameters assigned scores of 1 to 3, with 3 being the most negative or severe finding, that are then added together. The parameters are hepatic encephalopathy, ascites, total bilirubin, serum albumin, and prothrombin time.

child welfare, a service agency sponsored by the community or special organizations that provide for the physical, social, or psychologic care of children.

chill [AS, *cele*], **1.** the sensation of cold caused by exposure to a cold environment. **2.** an attack of shivering with pallor and a feeling of coldness, often occurring at the beginning of an infection and accompanied by a rapid rise in temperature.

Chilomastix /kī'lōmas'tiks/, a genus of flagellate protozoa, such as *Chilomastix mesnili,* a nonpathogenic intestinal parasite of humans. Infection with this organism may be the occasional cause of diarrhea in children.

chimera /kimir'ə, kīmir'ə/ [Gk, *khimaros,* fire-breathing monster], an organism carrying cell populations derived from two or more different zygotes of the same or different species. Chimeras include recipients of tissue grafts from other individuals.

chimerism /kimir′izəm/, a state in bone marrow transplantation in which bone marrow and host cells exist compatibly without signs of graft-versus-host rejection disease.

chin, the raised triangular part of the mandible below the lower lip. It is formed by the mental protuberance.

Chinese herbal medicine, a highly complex system of diagnosis and treatment using medicinal herbs, one of the branches of traditional Chinese medicine. Herbs used range from the nontoxic and rejuvenating, such as ginseng, which are used to support the body's healing system, to highly toxic ones, such as aconite, used in the treatment of disease.

Chinese restaurant syndrome, a group of transient symptoms consisting of tingling and burning sensations of the skin, facial pressure, headache, and chest pain that occur immediately after eating food containing monosodium glutamate, frequently used in Chinese cooking. It is a pharmacologic reaction and not an allergic reaction.

chip [AS, *kippen*, to slice], **1.** a relatively small piece of a bone or tooth. **2.** to break off or cut away a small piece. **3.** n, a semiconductor in which an integrated circuit is embedded.

chip fracture, any small fragmental fracture, usually one involving a bony process near a joint.

chip graft, a transplant consisting of small pieces of cartilage or bone that are packed into defective bone structures.

chiral, (in physical science) describing a compound that cannot be superimposed on its mirror image.

chiralgia /kəral′jə/, a pain in the hand, particularly one that does not result from a nerve injury or disease.

chiropractic /kī′rōprak′tik/ [Gk, *cheir*, hand, *practikos*, efficient], a system of therapy based on the theory that the state of a person's health is determined in general by the condition of his or her nervous system. In most cases, treatment provided by chiropractors involves the mechanical manipulation of the spinal column. Some practitioners employ radiology for diagnosis and use physiotherapy and diet in addition to spinal manipulation. Chiropractic does not use drugs or surgery. A chiropractor is awarded the degree of Doctor of Chiropractic, or D.C., after completing at least 2 years of premedical studies followed by 4 years of training in an approved chiropractic school.

chiropractor /-prak′tər/, a practitioner of **chiropractic.**

chisel fracture, any fracture in which there is oblique detachment of a bone fragment from the head of the radius.

chi square (χ^2) /kī/, (in statistics) a statistic test for an association between observed data and expected data represented by frequencies. The test yields a statement of the probability of the obtained distribution having occurred by chance alone.

chi square distribution /kī skwar/, a theoretic probability distribution of the sum of the squares of a number *(k)* of normally distributed variables whose mean is 0 and standard deviation is 1. The parameter *k* is the number of degrees of freedom.

Chlamydia /kləmid′ē·ə/ [Gk, *chlamys*, cloak], **1.** a microorganism of the genus *Chlamydia.* **2.** a genus of microorganisms that live as intracellular parasites, have a number of properties in common with gram-negative bacteria, and are currently classified as specialized bacteria. *C. trachomatis* is responsible for inclusion conjunctivitis, lymphogranuloma venereum, PID, and trachoma. *C. psittaci* causes a type of pneumonia in humans. *C. pneumoniae* is the causative organism of Taiwan acute respiratory disease, which is responsible for both upper and lower respiratory tract infections and commonly causes community acquired pneumonias.—**chlamydial,** *adj.*

chlamydial perihepatitis, perihepatitis caused by extension of a chlamydial infection.

Chlamydia pneumoniae **pneumonia** /kləmid′ē·ə nōōmō′nē·ē/, a mild form of primary atypical pneumonia caused by infection with *Chlamydia pneumoniae,* characterized by fever, rales, and infiltration of a middle or lower lobe.

Chlamydia **test,** a microscopic examination or blood test used to determine the presence of the many *Chlamydia* species that cause human diseases.

Chlamydia trachomatis **pneumonia** /kləmid′ē·ə trəkom′ətis/, a mild type of bacterial pneumonia, usually seen in infants whose mothers are infected with *Chlamydia trachomatis.* Characteristics include coughing, tachypnea, and eosinophilia.

chloasma /klō·az′mə/ [Gk, *chloazein,* to be green], tan or brown pigmentation, particularly of the forehead, cheeks, and nose, commonly associated with pregnancy, the use of oral contraceptives, or hormone replacement therapy.

chloasma traumaticum, a pigmentary discoloration that results from friction on the skin.

chloasma uterinum, a skin discoloration on the face that occurs in pregnant women or in women who take progestin-based oral contraceptives.

chloracne /klôrak′nē/ [Gk, *chloros,* green, *akme,* point], a skin condition characterized by small, black follicular plugs and papules on exposed surfaces, especially on the arms, face, and neck, of workers in contact with chlorinated compounds such as cutting oils, paints, varnishes, and lacquers.

chloral camphor /klôr′əl/, a mixture of equal parts of camphor and chloral hydrate used externally as a sedative.

chloral hydrate, a sedative and hypnotic prescribed for the short-term (less than 2 weeks) relief of insomnia, anxiety, or tension and for diagnostic procedures.

chloral hydrate poisoning, an adverse reaction to ingestion of trichloroethylidine glycol, also known as chloral hydrate. Symptoms include irritation of the digestive tract, vomiting, depressed breathing, shock, confusion, and injury to the liver and kidneys.

chlorambucil /klôr′amboo′sil/, an alkylating agent prescribed in the treatment of a variety of malignant neoplastic diseases, including chronic lymphocytic leukemia and Hodgkin's disease.

chloramphenicol /-amfĕ′nikol/, an antibacterial and anti-rickettsial used for the treatment of serious infections when the microorganism is resistant to less toxic antibiotics, and also when its ability to penetrate to the site of the infection is superior to less toxic alternative antibiotics.

chlordiazepoxide /klôr′dī-az′əpok′sīd/, an antianxiety drug of the benzodiazepine type prescribed in the treatment of anxiety, nervous tension, and alcohol withdrawal symptoms.

chlorhexidine /-hek′sidēn/, an antimicrobial agent used as a surgical scrub, hand rinse, and topical antiseptic. It is effective against gram-positive organisms, gram-negative organisms, aerobes, facultative anaerobes, and yeast.

chloride /klôr′īd/ [Gk, *chloros,* green], an anion of chlorine. Metal chlorides are salts of hydrochloric acid; the most common is sodium chloride (table salt).

chloride blood test, a blood test performed as part of multiphasic testing of electrolytes. It is performed along with other electrolyte tests to indicate the patient's acid-base balance and hydrational status.

chloride shift, an exchange of chloride ions in RBCs in peripheral tissues in response to PCO_2 of blood. The shift reverses in the lungs.

chloridometer /klôr′idom′ətər/, an instrument for measuring the level of chlorides in body fluids.

chloriduria, an excessive level of chlorides in the urine.

chlorinated /klôr′ənā′tid/ [Gk, *chloros,* greenish], pertaining to material that contains or has been treated with chlorine.

chlorinated organic insecticide poisoning, poisoning resulting from the inhalation, ingestion, or absorption of chlorophenothane (DDT) or other insecticides containing chlorophenothane such as heptachlor, dieldrin, and chlordane. It is characterized by vomiting, weakness, malaise, convulsions, tremors, ventricular fibrillation, respiratory failure, and pulmonary edema.

chlorination [Gk, *chloros,* green], the disinfection or treatment of water or other substances with free chlorine.

chlorine (Cl) /klôr′ēn/, a yellowish-green gaseous element of the halogen group. Its atomic number is 17; its atomic weight (mass) is 35.453. It has a strong, distinctive odor; is irritating to the respiratory tract; and is poisonous if ingested or inhaled. It occurs in nature chiefly as a component of sodium chloride in sea water and in salt deposits. It is used as a bleach and as a disinfectant to purify water for drinking or for use in swimming pools.

chloroacetophenone (CN) /klo′ro·as′etofe′nōn/, a commonly used tear gas.

chloroform /klôr′əfôrm/ [Gk, *chloros*; L, *formica,* ant], a nonflammable volatile liquid that was the first inhalation anesthetic to be discovered. Chloroform has a low margin of safety and significant toxicity. The drug is not used in the United States.

chloroleukemia /klôr′olookĕ′mē-ə/ [Gk, *chloros,* green, *leukos,* white, *haima,* blood], a kind of myelogenous leukemia in which specific tumor masses are not seen at autopsy but body fluids and organs are green.

chlorolymphosarcoma /-lim′fōsärkō′mə/ *pl.* **chlorolymphosarcomas, chlorolymphosarcomata** [Gk, *chloros* + L, *lympha,* water; Gk, *sarx,* flesh, *oma,* tumor], a greenish neoplasm of myeloid tissue occurring in patients with myelogenous leukemia. The mononuclear cells in the peripheral blood are believed to be lymphocytes rather than myeloblasts, such as found with chloroma.

chloroma /klôrō′mə/ *pl.* **chloromas, chloromata,** a malignant greenish neoplasm of myeloid tissue that occurs anywhere in the body of patients who have myelogenous leukemia.

Chloromycetin, a trademark for an antibacterial and antirickettsial (chloramphenicol).

C

chlorophyll /klôr′əfil/ [Gk, *chloros* + *phyllon*, leaf], one of several pigments that absorb light energy and participate in the production of carbohydrates in photosynthetic organisms.

chloroprocaine /-prō′kān/, a local anesthetic with a chemical structure similar to that of procaine.

chloroquine /klôr′əkwīn′/, an antimalarial prescribed in the treatment of malaria, extraintestinal amebiasis, rheumatoid arthritis, discoid lupus erythematosus, scleroderma, pemphigus, and photoallergic reactions.

chlorosis /klôrō′sis/, obsolete.an iron deficiency anemia of young women characterized by hypochromic, microcytic erythrocytes and a small reduction in the total number of erythrocytes.

chlorothiazide /-thī′əzīd/, a thiazide diuretic chemically related to sulfonamides. It is an antihypertensive prescribed in the treatment of hypertension and edema.

chlorpheniramine maleate /-fenir′əmēn/, an antihistamine prescribed in the treatment of a variety of hypersensitivity reactions, including rhinitis, skin rash, and pruritus.

chlorpheniramine polistirex, sulfonated styrene-divinylbenzene copolymer complex with chlorpheniramine, having the same actions as the base, used in cough and cold preparations.

chlorpheniramine tannate, the tannate salt of chlorpheniramine, having the same actions as the base, used in cough and cold preparations.

chlorproMAZINE /-prō′məzēn/, a phenothiazine drug used as an antipsychotic and antiemetic. It is prescribed in the treatment of psychotic disorders (mania, schizophrenia), severe nausea and vomiting, and intractable hiccups.

chlorproPAMIDE /-prō′pəmīd/, an oral antidiabetic prescribed in the treatment of non-insulin-dependent DM.

chlortetracycline hydrochloride /-tet′rəsī′klēn/, a tetracycline antibiotic used as a topical antiinfective, prescribed in the treatment of bacterial infections.

chlorthalidone /-thal′idōn/, a diuretic and antihypertensive; a sulfonamide derivative. It is prescribed in the treatment of high BP and edema.

Chlor-Trimeton, a trademark for an antihistamine (chlorpheniramine maleate).

chlorzoxazone /-zok′səzōn/, a skeletal muscle relaxant prescribed for the relief of muscle spasm.

CHN, abbreviation for *certified hemodialysis nurse.*

choana /kō′ənə/ *pl.* **choanae,** a funnel-shaped channel.

choanal atresia /kō′ənəl/ [Gk, *choane,* funnel, *a* + *tresis,* not hole], a congenital anomaly in which a bony or membranous occlusion blocks the passageway between the nose and pharynx.

chocolate cyst [Mex, *chocolatl*; Gk, *kystis,* bag], a darkly pigmented cyst sometimes found on the ovaries as a result of endometriosis. It results from an accumulation of extrauterine endometrial tissue.

choke [ME, *choken*], to interrupt breathing by compression or obstruction of the larynx or trachea.

chokes, a respiratory condition, occurring in decompression sickness, characterized by shortness of breath, substernal pain, and a nonproductive paroxysmal cough caused by bubbles of gas in the blood vessels of the lungs.

choke-saver, a curved forceps that can be inserted into the throat of a person who is choking on a food bolus or similar swallowed object. The tweezers-like device can grasp and retrieve the object.

choking, the condition in which a respiratory passage is blocked by constriction of the neck, an obstruction in the trachea, or swelling of the larynx. It is characterized by decreased movement of air through the airways or sudden coughing and a red face that rapidly becomes cyanotic.

choking/lung/pulmonary agents, chemicals that cause severe irritation or swelling of the respiratory tract. Agents include ammonia, bromine, chlorine, osmium tetraoxide, phosgene, phosphine, and phosphorus. When inhaled, they cause damage to the lungs, either by their corrosive effects or by cytotoxicity, leading to respiratory distress and death from respiratory failure.

cholagogue /kō′ləgog/ [Gk, *chole,* bile, *agogein,* to draw forth], a drug that stimulates the flow of bile.

cholangiectasis /kōlan′jē·ek′təsis/, dilation of the bile ducts.

cholangiocarcinoma /kōlan′jē·ōkär′sinō′mə/, a cancer of the biliary epithelium. Risk factors include ulcerative colitis and infestation of liver flukes.

cholangiogram /kōlan′jē·əgram′/, an x-ray film of the bile ducts produced after injection of a radiopaque contrast medium.

cholangiography /kōlan′jē·og′rəfē/, a special roentgenographic test procedure for outlining the major bile ducts by the IV injection or direct instillation of a radiopaque contrast material.

cholangiohepatitis /kōlan′jē·ōhep′ətī′tis/ [Gk, *chole,* bile, *angeion,* vessel + *hepar,* liver, *-itis,* inflammation], severe inflammation of the bile passages, often associated with liver fluke infestation that causes obstruction of the bile ducts.

cholangiohepatoma /kōlan'jē·ōhep'ətō'mə/ *pl.* **cholangiohepatomas, cholangiohepatomata,** a primary carcinoma of the liver that develops in the bile ducts in which an abnormal mixture of liver cord cells and bile ducts exists.

cholangiolitis /-lī'tis/, an abnormal condition characterized by inflammation of the fine tubules of the bile duct system, which may cause cholangiolitic cirrhosis.—**cholangiolitic,** *adj.*

cholangioma /kōlan'jē·ō'mə/ *pl.* **cholangiomas, cholangiomata,** a neoplasm of the bile ducts.

cholangioscopy /kōlan'jē·os'kəpē/, direct examination of the bile ducts with a fiberoptic endoscope.

cholangiostomy /kōlan'jē·os'təmē/ [Gk, *chole,* bile, *angeion,* vessel, *stoma,* mouth], a surgical operation performed to form an opening in a bile duct.

cholangitis /kō'lanjī'tis/, inflammation of the bile ducts, caused either by bacterial invasion or by obstruction of the ducts by calculi or a tumor. The condition is characterized by severe right upper quadrant pain, jaundice (if an obstruction is present), and intermittent fever.

cholate, any salt or ester of cholic acid; an anion of cholic acid.

cholecystagogue /kō'ləsis'təgog'/, a drug that stimulates emptying of the gallbladder.

cholecystectomy /kō'lisistek'təmē/ [Gk, *chole* + *kystis,* bag, *ektomē,* excision], the surgical removal of the gallbladder, performed to treat cholelithiasis, cholecystitis, and gallbladder cancer.

cholecystic /kō'lisis'tik/, pertaining to the gallbladder.

cholecystitis /kō'lisistī'tis/ [Gk, *chole* + *kystis,* bag, *itis,* inflammation], acute or chronic inflammation of the gallbladder. Acute cholecystitis is usually caused by a gallstone that cannot pass through the cystic duct. Chronic cholecystitis, the more common type, has an insidious onset.

cholecystoduodenostomy /kō'lēsis'tōdōō'ō dənos'təmē/ [Gk, *chole* + *kystis;* L, *duodeni,* twelve fingers], surgical anastomosis of the gallbladder and the duodenum.

cholecystogram /kō'lisis'təgram'/, an x-ray film of the gallbladder, made after the ingestion or injection of a radiopaque substance, usually a contrast material containing iodine.

cholecystography /kō'lisistog'rəfē/, an x-ray examination of the gallbladder. At least 12 hours before the study, the patient has a fat-free meal and ingests a contrast material containing iodine. The iodine,

which is opaque to x-rays, is excreted by the liver into the bile in the gallbladder. After the procedure, the patient consumes a fatty meal or cholecystokinin, which stimulates the gallbladder to contract, expelling bile and contrast material into the bile duct.

cholecystoileostomy /kō'lisis'tō·il'ē·os' təmē/ [Gk, *chole,* bile, *kystis,* bag, *eilein,* to twist, *stoma,* mouth], a surgical procedure performed to connect the gallbladder to the ileum.

cholecystojejunostomy /kō'lē·sis'tōjəjōōnos' təmē/ [Gk, *chole* + *kystis;* L, *jejunus,* empty], surgical anastomosis of the gallbladder and the jejunum.

cholecystokinin /-kī'nin/ [Gk, *chole* + *kystis,* bag, *kinein,* to move], a hormone produced by the mucosa of the upper intestine that stimulates contraction of the gallbladder and secretion of pancreatic enzymes.

cholecystokinin test (CCK test), a test to assess gallbladder function. After IV administration of cholecystokinin, the resultant pancreatic secretion of amylase, trypsin, and lipase is measured by collection through a tube in the duodenum. This test is often combined with the secretin test and called the **secretin-cholecystokinin test.**

cholecystolithiasis /kō'lisis'tōlithī'əsis/, the presence of gallstones in the gallbladder.

cholecystolithotomy /ko'lisis'tōlithot' āmē/, incision of the gallbladder for removal of gallstones.

cholecystolithotripsy /kō'lisis'tōlith'ətripsē/, a procedure for crushing gallstones in the gallbladder or common bile duct with a lithotrite.

cholecystosonography /kō'lisis'tōsōno g'rəfē/, a method of examining the gallbladder using ultrasound.

choledochal /-dok'əl/ [Gk, *chole,* bile, *dochus,* containing], pertaining to the common bile duct.

choledochojejunostomy /kōled'ədok'ōjē' jōōnos'təmē/ [Gk, *chole,* bile, *dochus,* containing; L, *jejunus,* empty; Gk, *stoma,* mouth], a surgical procedure in which the bile duct is connected to the jejunum.

choledocholith /kōled'ə'kōlith'/, a gallstone in the common bile duct.

choledocholithotomy /-lithot'əmē/ [Gk, *chole* + *dochus,* containing, *lithos,* stone, *temnein,* to cut], a surgical operation to make an incision in the common bile duct to remove a gallstone.

choledocholithotripsy /-lith'ətrip'sē/, a procedure for crushing gallstones in the common bile duct with a lithotrite.

choledocholitis, an inflammation of the common bile duct.

Choledyl, a trademark for a theophylline derivative (oxtriphylline).

choleic /kōlē′ik/, pertaining to bile.

cholelithiasis /-lithī′əsis/ [Gk, *chole* + *lithos,* stone, *osis,* condition], the presence of gallstones in the gallbladder. The condition affects about 20% of the population above 40 years of age and is more prevalent in women and in persons with cirrhosis of the liver. Many patients complain of unlocalized abdominal discomfort, eructation, and intolerance to certain foods.

cholelithic dyspepsia /kō′lilith′ik/ [Gk, *chole* + *lithos,* stone, *dys,* bad, *peptein,* to digest], an abnormal condition characterized by sudden attacks of indigestion associated with dysfunction of the gallbladder.

cholelithotomy /-lithot′əmē/, a surgical operation to remove gallstones through an incision in the gallbladder.

cholera /kol′ərə/ [Gk, *chole* + *rhein,* to flow], an acute bacterial infection of the small intestine, characterized by severe diarrhea, vomiting, muscular cramps, dehydration, and depletion of electrolytes. The disease is spread by water and food that have been contaminated by feces of persons previously infected.

choleragen /kol′ərəjin/, an exotoxin, produced by the cholera vibrio, that stimulates the secretion of electrolytes and water into the small intestine in Asiatic cholera.

cholera sicca, an old term for a malignant form of cholera, seen during epidemics, in which the patient experiences a massive outpouring of fluid and electrolytes into the digestive system and dies of toxemia before the usual symptoms of vomiting and diarrhea develop.

cholera vaccine, an active immunizing agent against cholera.

choleresis /kō′lərē′sis/, the secretion of bile by the liver.

choleretic /kō′ləret′ik/ [Gk, *chole* + *eresis,* removal], **1.** stimulating the production of bile in the liver either by cholepoiesis or by hydrocholeresis. **2.** a choleretic agent.

choleric /kol′ərik, kəler′ik/, having a hot temper or an irritable nature.

choleriform /kōler′ifôrm/, resembling cholera.

cholescintigraphy /kō′ləsintig′rəfē/, examination of the gallbladder and bile ducts by scanning with radionuclides.

cholestasis /-stā′sis/ [Gk, *chole* + *stasis,* standing still], interruption in the flow of bile through any part of the biliary system, from liver to duodenum. It is essential for the physician to discover whether the cause is within the liver (intrahepatic) or outside it (extrahepatic). Symptoms of both types of cholestasis include jaundice, pale and fatty stools, dark urine, and intense itching over the skin.—**cholestatic,** *adj.*

cholestatic hepatitis, jaundice with bile stasis in inflamed intrahepatic bile ducts, usually caused by the toxic effects of a drug. Signs are persistent jaundice, itching, and elevated alkaline phosphatase levels.

cholestatic jaundice /-stat′ik/, a yellowing of the skin caused by thickening of bile, obstruction of hepatic ducts, or changes in liver cell function.

cholesteatoma /kōles′tē-ətō′mə/ [Gk, *chole* + *stear,* fat, *oma,* tumor], a cystic mass composed of epithelial cells and cholesterol that is found in the middle ear and occurs as a congenital defect or as a serious complication of chronic otitis media. The mass may occlude the middle ear, or enzymes produced by it may destroy the adjacent bones, including the ossicles.

cholesterase /kəles′tərās′/ [Gk, *chole* + *aither,* air; Ger, *saure,* acid; *ase,* enzyme suffix], an enzyme in the blood and other tissues that forms cholesterol and fatty acids by hydrolyzing cholesterol esters.

cholesterol /kəles′tərôl/ [Gk, *chole* + *steros,* solid], a waxy lipid soluble compound found only in animal tissues. It is an integral component of every cell in the body. It facilitates the absorption and transport of fatty acids. Cholesterol acts as the precursor for the synthesis of various steroid hormones, including cortisol, cortisone, and aldosterone in the adrenal glands; and of the sex hormones progesterone, estrogen, and testosterone. It sometimes precipitates along with other compounds in the gallbladder to form gallstones. Increased levels of low-density lipoprotein cholesterol may be associated with the pathogenesis of atherosclerosis, whereas higher levels of high-density lipoprotein cholesterol appear to lower the person's risk for heart disease. Normal adult levels of blood cholesterol are 150 to 200 mg/dL or 3.9 to 5.2 mmol/L (SI units).

cholesterol embolism, an embolism resulting from fracture of a plaque of atherosclerosis.

cholesterolemia /-ē′mē-ə/, **1.** the presence of excessive amounts of cholesterol in the blood. **2.** the abnormal condition of the presence of excessive amounts of cholesterol in the blood.

cholesteroleresis /kəles′tərōler′isis, -erē′sis/ [Gk, *chole* + *steros* + *eresis,* removal], the increased elimination of cholesterol in the bile.

cholesterol metabolism, the sum of the anabolic and catabolic processes in the synthesis and degradation of cholesterol in the body. Serum cholesterol level is increased when it is ingested and is quickly absorbed. Cholesterol is also synthesized in the liver and can be synthesized by most other body tissues. Cholesterol is removed from the body by degradation in the liver and excretion in the bile.

cholesterolopoiesis /kəles′tərō′lōpō-ē′sis/ [Gk, *chole* + *steros* + *poiesis*, producing], the elaboration of cholesterol by the liver.

cholesterolosis /kəles′tərəlō′sis/, an abnormal condition, found in about 5% of patients with chronic cholecystitis, in which deposits of cholesterol occur within large macrophages in the submucosa of the gallbladder.

cholesterol test, a blood test used to identify patients who are at risk for arteriosclerotic heart disease. Because cholesterol alone is not a totally accurate predictor of heart disease, this test is usually done as a part of lipid profile testing.

cholesteryl ester storage disease /kōles′təril/, an inherited disorder in which there is an accumulation of neutral lipids, such as cholesterol esters and glycerides, in body tissues.

cholesteryl ester transfer protein (CETP), a plasma glycoprotein that plays a role in the movement of cholesterol from the peripheral tissue to the liver by mediating the transfer of cholesteryl esters from HDL cholesterol to apolipoprotein B–containing proteins, which are then metabolized to lipoproteins that are removed from the circulation by receptors in the liver.

cholestyramine /-tir′əmēn/, a drug used to treat hypercholesterolemia that acts on the liver's bile acids. It binds to bile acids and causes increased fecal elimination, which causes increased oxidation of cholesterol to bile acids, thereby lowering blood cholesterol levels.

cholestyramine resin, an ion-exchange resin and antihyperlipemic agent prescribed to increase bile acid excretion in the stool, for the treatment of hyperlipoproteinemia, and for pruritus resulting from partial biliary obstruction.

cholic acid, a bile acid synthesized in the liver from cholesterol. Cholan-24-oic acid is stored in the liver bound to coenzyme A and converted to glycine and taurine bile salts before secretion into bile.

choline /kō′lēn/ [Gk, *chole*, bile], a lipotropic substance that can be synthesized by the body. Found in most animal tissues, choline is a primary component of acetylcholine and functions with inositol as a basic constituent of lecithin. It prevents fat deposits in the liver and facilitates the movement of fats into the cells.

choline bitartrate, the bitartrate salt of choline, used as a dietary supplement.

choline chloride, the chloride salt of choline, used as a dietary supplement.

choline esters, a group of cholinergic drugs that act at sites or organs where acetylcholine is the neurotransmitter.

choline magnesium trisalicylate, a combination of choline and magnesium salicylates, used as an analgesic, antipyretic, antiinflammatory, and antirheumatic.

cholinergic /-ur′jik/ [Gk, *chole* + *ergon*, to work], **1.** pertaining to nerve fibers that liberate acetylcholine at the myoneural junctions. **2.** the tendency to transmit or to be stimulated by or to stimulate the elaboration of acetylcholine.

cholinergic blocking agent, any agent that blocks the action of acetylcholine and substances similar to acetylcholine. Such agents, in effect, block the action of cholinergic nerves that transmit impulses by the release of acetylcholine at their synapses.

cholinergic crisis, a pronounced muscular weakness and respiratory paralysis caused by excessive acetylcholine, often apparent in patients suffering from myasthenia gravis as a result of overmedication with anticholinesterase drugs.

cholinergic fiber [Gr, *chole*, bile, *ergon*, work; L, *fibra*], a nerve fiber of the autonomic nervous system that releases the neurotransmitter acetylcholine. Cholinergic fibers include all preganglionic fibers, all postganglionic sympathetic fibers to sweat glands, and efferent fibers innervating skeletal muscle.

cholinergic nerve, a nerve that releases the neurotransmitter acetylcholine at its synapse. The cholinergic nerves include all the preganglionic sympathetic and preganglionic parasympathetic nerves, the postganglionic parasympathetic nerves, the somatic motor nerves to skeletal muscles, and some nerves to sweat glands and to certain blood vessels.

cholinergic receptor [Gk, *chole*, bile, *ergein*, to work; L, *recipere*, to receive], a specialized sensory nerve ending that responds to the stimulation of acetylcholine.

cholinergic urticaria [Gk, *chole* + *ergon*, to work; L, *urtica*, nettle], an abnormal and usually temporary vascular reaction of the skin, often associated with sweating in susceptible individuals subjected to stress, strong exertion, or hot weather. The condition is characterized by small, pale, itchy papules surrounded by reddish areas.

choline salicylate, the choline salt of salicylic acid, used as an analgesic, antipyretic, antiinflammatory, and antirheumatic.

cholinesterase /kō'lines'tərās/, an enzyme that acts as a catalyst in the hydrolysis of acetylcholine to choline and acetate. It provides the off mechanism during cholinergic neurotransmission.

cholinesterase test, a blood test done to identify patients with pseudocholinesterase deficiency before anesthesia or to identify patients who may have been exposed to phosphate poisoning.

choliopancreatography /kō'lē·ōpan'krē·āátog'rəfē/ [Gk, chole + pan, all, kreas, flesh, graphein, to record], the radiographic examination of the bile and pancreatic ducts.

Cholografin, a trade name of a diagnostic contrast medium used in radiology (iodipamide).

Choloxin, a trademark for an antihyperlipoproteinemic (dextrothyroxine sodium).

cholyltaurine, a bile salt, the taurine conjugate of cholic acid.

chondral /kon'drəl/, pertaining to cartilage.

chondralgia /kondral'jə/, pain that appears to originate in cartilage.

chondrectomy /kondrek'təmē/, the surgical excision of a cartilage.

chondrial bone [Gk, chondros, cartilage; AS, ban, bone], bone that forms under the periosteal membrane.

chondriocont /kon'drē·ōkont'/, a threadlike or rod-shaped mitochondrion.

chondriome /kon'drē·ōm/ [Gk, chondros, cartilage], the total mitochondrial content of a cell, taken as a unit.

chondriomite /kon'drē·ōmīt'/ [Gk, chondros + mitos, thread], a single, granular mitochondrion or a group of such mitochondria that appear in a chain formation.

chondritis /kondrī'tis/, any inflammatory condition affecting the cartilage.

chondroangioma /kon'drō·an'jē·ō'mə/ pl. **chondroangiomas, chondroangiomata** [Gk, chondros + angeion, vessel, oma, tumor], a benign mesenchymal tumor containing vascular and cartilaginous elements.

chondroblast /kon'drōblast/ [Gk, chondros + blastos, germ], any one of the cells that develop from the mesenchyma and form cartilage. Chondroblasts play an important role in endochondrial ossification and especially in longitudinal bone growth.

chondroblastoma /kon'drōblastō'mə/ pl. **chondroblastomas, chondroblastomata,** a benign tumor, derived from precursors of cartilage cells, that develops most frequently in epiphyses of the femur and humerus.

chondrocalcinosis /kon'drōkal'sinō'sis/ [Gk, chondros; L, calyx, lime; Gk, osis, condition], an arthritic disease in which calcium deposits are present in the peripheral joints. It resembles gout and often occurs in patients over 50 years of age who have osteoarthritis or DM.

chondrocarcinoma /kon'drōkär'sinō'mə/ pl. **chondrocarcinomas, chondrocarcinomata** [Gk, chondros + karkinos, crab, oma, tumor], a malignant epithelial tumor in which cartilaginous metaplasia is present.

chondroclast /kon'drōklast'/ [Gk, chondros + klasis, breaking], a giant multinucleated cell associated with the resorption of cartilage.—**chondroclastic,** adj.

chondrocostal /kon'drōkos'təl/ [Gk, chondros; L, costa, rib], pertaining to the ribs and costal cartilages.

chondrocyte /kon'drəsīt/ [Gk, chondros + kytos, cell], any one of the polymorphic cells that form the cartilage of the body. —**chondrocytic,** adj.

chondrodysplasia /kon'drōdisplā'zhə/ [Gk, chondros + dys, bad, plassein, to form], an inherited disease characterized by abnormal growth at the ends of bones, particularly the long bones of the arms and legs.

chondrodysplasia punctata, an inherited form of dwarfism characterized by skin lesions, radiographic evidence of epiphyseal stippling, and a pug nose. There are two types of the anomaly: a benign Conradi-Hünermann form marked by mild asymmetric limb shortening and a lethal rhizomelic form.

chondrodystrophia calcificans congenita /-distrō'fē·ə/ [Gk, chondros + dys, bad, trophe, nourishment; L, calyx, lime, congenitus, born with], an inherited defect characterized by many small opacities in the epiphyses of the long bones. Dwarfism, contractures, cataracts, mental retardation, and short stubby fingers develop as the infant grows into childhood.

chondrodystrophy /kon'drōdis'trəfē/ [Gk, chondros + dys, bad, trophe, nourishment], a group of disorders in which there is abnormal conversion of cartilage to bone, particularly in the epiphyses of the long bones. Patients are dwarfed, with normal trunks and shortened extremities.

chondroectodermal dysplasia /kon'drō·ek'tədur'məl/, an inherited form of dwarfism marked by distal limb shortening, postaxial polydactyly, and cardiovascular abnormalities.

chondroendothelioma /kon'drō·en'dōthē'lē·ō'mə/ pl. **chondroendotheliomas, chondroendotheliomata** [Gk, chondros + endon, within, thele, nipple, oma, tumor], a benign mesenchymal tumor containing cartilaginous and endothelial components.

chondrofibroma /kon′drōfĭbrō′mə/ *pl.* **chondrofibromas, chondrofibromata,** a fibrous tumor that contains cartilaginous components.

chondrogenesis /kon′drōjen′əsis/, the development of cartilage. —**chondrogenetic,** *adj.*

chondroid /kon′droid/, resembling cartilage.

chondroid lipoma, an uncommon benign fatty neoplasm occurring as a well-circumscribed, yellow, sometimes encapsulated, slowly growing mass, most often involving the limb girdles or proximal extremities.

chondrolipoma /kon′drōlipō′mə/ *pl.* **chondrolipomas, chondrolipomata,** a benign mesenchymal tumor containing fatty and cartilaginous components.

chondroma /kondrō′mə/ *pl.* **chondromas, chondromata** a benign, fairly common tumor of cartilage cells that grows slowly within cartilage (enchondroma) or on the surface (ecchondroma). —**chondromatous,** *adj.*

chondromalacia /kon′drōməlā′shə/ [Gk, *chondros* + *malakia,* softness], a softening of cartilage. Chondromalacia fetalis is a lethal congenital form of the condition in which a stillborn infant has soft and pliable limbs. Chondromalacia patellae occurs in young adults after knee injury and is characterized by swelling, pain, and degenerative changes, which are revealed on x-ray examination.

chondromatosis /kon′drōmətō′sis/, a condition characterized by the presence of many cartilaginous tumors.

chondromere /kon′drōmir/ [Gk, *chondros* + *meros,* part], a cartilaginous embryonic vertebra and its costal component.

chondromyoma /kon′drōmī·ō′mə/ *pl.* **chondromyomas, chondromyomata** [Gk, *chondros* + *mys,* muscle, *oma,* tumor], a benign mesenchymal tumor containing myomatous and cartilaginous tissue.

chondromyxofibroma /kon′drōmik′sōfĭbrō′mə/ [Gk, *chondros* + *myxa,* mucus; L, *fibra,* fiber, *oma,* tumor], a benign tumor that develops from cartilage-forming connective tissue. The lesion, typically a firm, grayish-white mass, tends to occur in the knee and small bones of the foot.

chondromyxoid /kon′drōmik′soid/ [Gk, *chondros* + *myxa,* mucus, *eidos,* form], composed of cartilaginous and myxoid elements.

chondrophyte /kon′drōfīt′/ [Gk, *chondros* + *phyton,* growth], an abnormal mass of cartilage. —**chondrophytic,** *adj.*

chondroplasia /-plā′zhə/ [Gk, *chondros,* cartilage, *plassein,* to form], the formation of cartilage.

chondroplasty /kon′drōplas′tē/ [Gk, *chondros* + *plassein,* to mold], the surgical repair of cartilage.

chondrosarcoma /kon′drōsärkō′mə/ *pl.* **chondrosarcomas, chondrosarcomata** [Gk, *chondros* + *sarx,* flesh, *oma,* tumor], a malignant neoplasm of cartilaginous cells or their precursors that occurs most frequently in long bones, the pelvic girdle, and the scapula. —**chondrosarcomatous,** *adj.*

chondrosarcomatosis /kon′drōsär′kōmətō′sis/, a condition characterized by multiple malignant cartilaginous tumors.

chondrosis /kondrō′sis/, **1.** the development of the cartilage of the body. **2.** a cartilaginous tumor.

chondrotomy /kondrot′əmē/, a surgical procedure for dividing a cartilage.

CHOP /chop/, abbreviation for an anticancer drug combination that includes cyclophosphamide, DOXOrubicin hydrochloride, vincristine (Oncovin), and prednisone.

chopping, a therapeutic exercise to improve the strength and coordination of upper trunk nerves and muscles by lifting the arms overhead and lowering them in a chopping or slashing movement.

chorda /kôr′də/, a string filament such as a nerve or tendon.

chorda tympani, a branch of the facial nerve that carries taste from the anterior two thirds of the tongue and parasympathetic innervation to all salivary glands below the level of the oral fissure.

chordee /kôr′dē, kôr′dā/ [Gk, *chorde,* cord], a congenital defect of the genitourinary tract resulting in a ventral curvature of the penis, caused by presence of a fibrous band of tissue instead of normal skin along the corpus spongiosum.

chordencephalon /kôrd′ensef′əlon/ [Gk, *chorde* + *enkephalos,* brain], the portion of the CNS that develops in the early weeks of pregnancy from the neural tube and includes the mesencephalon, the rhombencephalon, and the spinal cord. —**chordencephalic,** *adj.*

chorditis /kôrdī′tis/, **1.** inflammation of a spermatic cord. **2.** inflammation of the vocal cords or of the vocal folds.

chorditis nodosa, the formation of small white nodules on one or both vocal cords in persons who use their voices excessively.

chordoid /kôr′doid/ [Gk, *chorde* + *eidos,* form], resembling the notocord or notochordal tissue.

chordoma /kôrdō′mə/ *pl.* **chordomas, chordomata,** a rare tumor that develops from the fetal notochord.

chordotomy /kôrdot′əmē/ [Gk, *chorde* + *temnein,* to cut], surgery in which the anterolateral tracts of the spinal cord are surgically divided to relieve pain.

chorea /kôrē′ə/ [Gk, *choreia,* dance], a condition characterized by involuntary purposeless, rapid motions, as flexing and extending of the fingers, raising and lowering of the shoulders, or grimacing.—**choreic** /kôrā′ik/, *adj.*

chorea gravidarum /kôr′ē·əgrav′idär′əm/, Sydenham's chorea that occurs during the early months of pregnancy with or without a previous history of rheumatic disease. Similar symptoms may develop in a woman who is taking oral contraceptives.

choreic ataxia /kôrē′ik/ [Gk, *choreia,* dance, *ataxia,* without order], a form of ataxia in which patients lack muscular coordination and movements are marked by involuntary twitching and abrupt jerking.

choreiform /kərē′əfôrm′/, resembling the rapid jerky movements associated with chorea.

choreiform spasm [Gk, *choreia,* dance; L, *forma;* Gk, *spasmos*], a condition of involuntary muscle contractions that result in dancing motions.

choreoathetoid cerebral palsy /kôr′ē·ō·ath′ətoid/, a form of CP characterized by choreiform and athetoid movements.

choreoathetosis /kôr′ē·ō·ath′ətō′sis/ [Gk, *choreia,* dance, *athetos,* not fixed], irregular involuntary movements that may involve the face, neck, trunk, extremities, or respiratory muscles, giving an appearance of restlessness. The writhing movements may vary from subtle to wild and ballistic and are commonly associated with administration of levodopa and parkinsonism.

chorioadenoma /kərē′ō·ad′inō′mə/ *pl.* **chorioadenomas, chorioadenomata** [Gk, *chorion,* skin, *aden,* gland, *oma,* tumor], an epithelial cell tumor of the outermost fetal membrane that is intermediate in the malignant development of a hydatid mole to invasive choriocarcinoma.

chorioadenoma destruens /-des′trŏŏ· əns/ [Gk, *chorion* + *aden* + *oma;* L, *destruere,* to pull down], an invasive hydatidiform mole in which the chorionic villi of the mole penetrate into the myometrium and parametrium of the uterus and metastasize to distant parts of the body.

chorioamnionic /-am′nē·ot′ik/, pertaining to the chorion and the amnion.

chorioamnionitis /-am′nē·ōnī′tis/ [Gk, *chorion* + *amnion,* fetal membrane, *itis,* inflammation], an inflammatory reaction in the amniotic membranes caused by bacteria or viruses in the amniotic fluid.

choriocarcinoma /kôr′ē·ōkär′sinō′mə/ *pl.* **choriocarcinomas, choriocarcinomata,**

an epithelial malignancy of fetal origin that develops from the chorionic part of the products of conception. The primary tumor usually appears in the uterus as a soft, dark red, crumbling mass; may invade and destroy the uterine wall; and may metastasize through lymph or blood vessels.

choriocele /kôr′ē·əsēl′/ [Gk, *chorion* + *kele,* hernia], a hernia or protrusion of the tissue of the choroid layer of the eye.

choriogenesis /kôr′ē·ōjen′əsis/, the development of the chorion, which is first evident in the first month of pregnancy. —**choriogenetic,** *adj.*

choriogonadotropin alfa, HCG produced by recombinant technology, used to induce ovulation and pregnancy in certain infertile, anovulatory women, and to increase the numbers of oocytes for patients attempting conception using assisted reproductive technologies.

chorion /kôr′ē·on/ [Gk, *chorion,* skin], the outermost extraembryonic membrane composed of trophoblast lined with mesoderm. It develops villi about 2 weeks after fertilization and is vascularized by allantoic vessels 1 week later. It gives rise to the placenta and persists until birth as the outer of the two layers of membrane containing the amniotic fluid and the fetus.

chorionic cavity, extraembryonic coelom.

chorionic gonadotropin (CG) /kôr′ē·on′ik/ [Gk, *chorion* + *gone,* seed, *trophe,* nutrition], a chemical component of the urine of pregnant women and pregnant mares. This glycoprotein hormone is secreted by the placental trophoblastic cells. It is composed of two subunits, alpha and beta, and helps maintain the corpus luteum during pregnancy. Chorionic gonadotropin is also administered in the treatment of some cases of cryptorchidism and male hypogonadism and in the induction of ovulation in some infertile women.

chorionic plate [Gk, *chorion* + *platys,* flat], the part of the fetal placenta that gives rise to chorionic villi, which attach to the uterus during the early stage of formation of the placenta.

chorionic sac [Gk, *chorion,* skin, *sakkos,* sack], the saclike membrane that develops from the blastocyst wall to envelop the embryo.

chorionic villus [Gk, *chorion;* L, *villus,* shaggy hair], any of the tiny vascular fibrils on the surface of the chorion that infiltrate the maternal blood sinuses of the endometrium and help form the placenta.

chorionic villus sampling (CVS) [Gk, L, shaggy hair, *exemplum*], the sampling of placental tissues for prenatal diagnosis of potential genetic defects. The sample is obtained through a catheter inserted into the cervix. It can be done earlier in pregnancy than amniocentesis.

chorioretinitis /kôr'ē-ōret'ini'tis/, an inflammatory condition of the choroid and retina of the eye, usually as a result of parasitic or bacterial infection. It is characterized by blurred vision, photophobia, and distorted images.

chorioretinopathy /kôr'ē-ōret'inop'əthē/ [Gk, *chorion*; L, *rete*, net; Gk, *pathos*, disease], a noninflammatory process caused by disease that involves the choroid and the retina.

choroid /kôr'oid/ [Gk, *chorion* + *eidos*, form], a vascular layer of the eye between the retina and sclera of the eye that supplies blood to the outer retina.

choroidal malignant melanoma /kôroi'dəl/ [Gk, *chorion* + *eidos*; L, *malignus*, ill-disposed; Gk, *melas*, black, *oma*, tumor], a tumor of the choroid coat of the eye that grows into the vitreous humor, causing detachment and degeneration of the overlying retina.

choroideremia /kôr'oidərē'mē-ə/ [Gk, *chorion*, skin + *eidos*, form; *erēmia*, destitution], hereditary primary degeneration of the choroid, transmitted as an X-linked trait and beginning in the first decade of life. In males, the earliest symptom is usually night blindness, followed by constricted visual field and eventual blindness. In females, it is nonprogressive; usually there is normal vision and often an atypical pigmentary retinopathy.

choroiditis /kôr'oidi'tis/, an inflammatory condition of the choroid membrane of the eye.

choroid membrane, a vascular layer of tissue between the retina and the sclera of the eye.

choroidocyclitis /kôroi'dōsikli'tis/ [Gk, *chorion* + *eidos* + *kyklos*, circle, *itis*, inflammation], an abnormal condition characterized by inflammation of the choroid and the ciliary processes.

choroidopathy /kôr'oidop'əthē/, noninflammatory degeneration of the choroid.

choroid plexectomy /pleksek'təmē/ [Gk, *chorion* + *eidos*; L, *plexus*, pleated; Gk, *ektome*, excision], a surgical procedure for the reduction of CSF production in the ventricles of the brain in hydrocephalus, usually in the newborn.

choroid plexus [Gk, *chorion* + *eidos*; L, pleated], any one of the tangled masses of tiny blood vessels contained within the lateral, the third, and the fourth ventricles of the brain, responsible for producing CSF.

Christchurch chromosome (Ch1) [Christchurch, city in New Zealand], an abnormally small, acrocentric chromosome (either chromosome 21 or chromosome 22), in which the short arm is missing or partially deleted. The aberration is associated with chronic lymphocytic leukemia.

Christian Science, a religious system founded in 1879 with health practices by Mary Baker Eddy [1821–1910], based on the metaphysical teachings of Phineas P. Quimby. It holds that healing should be achieved through spiritual means, that sickness and death are illusions resulting from a false sense of separation from God.

Christian-Weber disease [Henry A. Christian, American physician, 1876–1951; Frederick Parkes Weber, English physician, 1863–1962], a rare form of panniculitis characterized by nodular formations in the subcutaneous tissues and prolonged intermittent relapsing fever.

chromaffin /krō'məfin/ [Gk, *chroma*, color; L, *affin*, affinity], having an affinity for strong staining with chromium salts.

chromaffin cell, any one of the special cells that compose the paraganglia and are connected to the ganglia of the celiac, renal, suprarenal, aortic, and hypogastric plexuses. The chromaffin cells of the adrenal medulla secrete two catecholamines, epinephrine and norepinephrine.

chromate (CrO_4^{2-}), any salt of chromic acid.

chromatic /krōmat'ik/ [Gk, *chroma*, color], **1.** pertaining to color. **2.** stainable by a dye. **3.** pertaining to chromatin.

chromatic dispersion [Gk, *chroma*; L, *dis*, apart, *spargere*, to scatter], the splitting of light into its various component wavelengths or frequencies, such as with a prism.

chromatid /krō'mətid/ [Gk, *chroma*, color], one of the two identical, threadlike filaments of a chromosome. During anaphase of mitosis and meiosis II, the chromatids separate to become daughter chromosomes.

chromatid deletion, the breakage of a chromatid. If the breakage occurs before DNA synthesis, subsequent replication will produce two sister chromatids with material missing and two acentromeric fragments called isochromatids.

chromatin /krō'mətin/ [Gk, *chroma*, color], the material within a cell nucleus from which the chromosomes are formed. It consists of fine, threadlike strands of DNA attached to proteins called histones. —**chromatinic,** *adj.*

chromatin-negative, lacking sex chromatin. The term applies to the nuclei of cells in normal males as well as those in individuals with certain chromosomal abnormalities.

chromatin-positive, containing sex chromatin. The term applies to the nuclei of cells in normal females as well as those in individuals with certain chromosomal abnormalities.

chromatism /krō′mətiz′əm/ [Gk, *chroma,* color, *ismos,* condition], **1.** an abnormal condition characterized by hallucinations in which the affected individual sees colored lights. **2.** abnormal pigmentation or aberration.

chromatogram /krōmat′əgram′/, **1.** the record produced by the separation of gaseous substances or dissolved chemical substances moving through a column of absorbent material that filters out the various absorbates in different layers. **2.** any graphic record produced by any chromatographic method.

chromatography /krō′mətog′rəfē/, any one of several processes for separating and analyzing various gaseous or dissolved chemical materials.—**chromatographic,** *adj.*

chromatopsia /krō′mətop′sē·ə/ [Gk, *chroma* + *opsis,* vision], **1.** an abnormal visual condition that makes colorless objects appear tinged with color. **2.** a form of color blindness characterized by the imperfect perception of various colors. It may be caused by a deficiency in one or more of the retinal cones or by defective nerve circuits that convey color-associated impulses to the cerebral cortex. The most common defect in color sense is the inability to distinguish red from green.

chromatosis /-ō′sis/, condition of abnormal skin pigmentation in any part of the body.

chromaturia /-ŏŏr′ē·ə/ [Gk, *chroma,* color, *ouron,* urine], the production of urine that has an abnormal color.

chromesthesia /krō′misthē′zhə/ [Gk, *chroma* + *aisthesis,* feeling], **1.** the color sense that depends on the mixture of wavelengths in the light that enters the eye and the response of the different types of retinal cones associated with color vision. **2.** an abnormal condition characterized by the confusion of other senses such as taste and smell with imagined sensations of color.

chromhidrosis /krō′midrō′sis/ [Gk, *chroma* + *hidros,* sweat], a rare, functional disorder in which apocrine sweat glands secrete colored sweat.

chromic catgut /krō′mik/ [Gk, *chroma,* color; L, *catta;* AS, *guttas*], surgical catgut that has been treated with chromium trioxide to strengthen it. It is an absorbable suture.

chromic myopia, a kind of color blindness characterized by the ability to distinguish colors only of those objects that are close to the eye.

chromium (Cr) /krō′mē·əm/ [Gk, *chroma,* color], a hard, brittle metallic element. Its atomic number is 24; its atomic mass is 51.99. It does not occur naturally in pure form but exists in combination with iron and oxygen in chromite. Traces of chromium occur in plants and animals, and there is evidence this element may be important in human nutrition, especially in carbohydrate metabolism. Workers in chromite mines are susceptible to pneumoconiosis caused by the inhalation of chromite dust particles that lodge in the lung. Chromate salts have been identified as potential carcinogens.

chromium alum, a chemical commonly used to fix, or harden, the emulsion of an x-ray film during manual processing.

chromium Cr 51 edetate, a complex of chromium 51 with edetic acid, used in the measurement of the glomerular filtration rate.

chromobacteriosis /krō′məbaktir′ē·ō′sis/, an extremely rare, usually fatal systemic infection caused by a gram-negative bacillus, *Chromobacterium violaceum.* It is found in fresh water in tropic and subtropic regions and enters the body through a break in the skin.

chromoblastomycosis /krō′mōblas′tōmī kō′sis/ [Gk, *chroma* + *blastos,* germ, *mykes,* fungus, *osis,* condition], a chronic infectious skin disease caused by any multiple species to two genera of fungi, *Cladosporium* and *Phialophora,* found in the soil. Infection is characterized by the appearance of pruritic, warty nodules that develop in a cut or other break in the skin, occurring typically on the leg or foot.

chromogen /krō′mōjən/, a substance that absorbs light, producing color.

chromomere /krō′məmir/ [Gk, *chroma* + *meros,* part], any of the series of beadlike structures that lie along the chromonema of a chromosome during the early stages of cell division.

chromonema /krō′mənē′mə/ *pl.* **chromonemata** [Gk, *chroma* + *nema,* thread], the part of a chromosome along which the chromomeres lie during cell division.—**chromonemal, chromonematic, chromonemic,** *adj.*

chromophilic /krō′məfil′ik/ [Gk, *chroma* + *philein,* to love], denoting a cell, tissue, or microorganism that is easily stained, particularly certain leukocytes.

chromophobia /krō′məfō′bē·ə/ [Gk, *chroma* + *phobos,* fear], **1.** the resistance of certain cells and tissues to stains. **2.** a morbid aversion to colors.—**chromophobe,** *n.*

chromophobic /krō′məfō′bik/, denoting a cell, tissue, or microorganism that is not easily stained, particularly certain cells of the anterior lobe of the pituitary gland.

chromophobic adenoma, a tumor of the pituitary gland composed of cells that do not stain with acid or basic dyes.

chromosensitive, descriptive of a substance that is affected by and responds to changes in chemical composition.

chromosomal aberration /-sō′məl/ [Gk, *chroma* + *soma*, body; L, *aberrare*, to wander], any change in the structure or number of any of the chromosomes of a given species. In humans, a number of physical disabilities and disorders are directly associated with aberrations of both the autosomes and the sex chromosomes.

chromosomal nomenclature, a standard nomenclature system for identifying chromosomes in an individual, as well as any deletions or additions of specific chromosomes or parts of chromosomes.

chromosomal sex [Gk, *chroma*, color, *soma*, body; L, *sexus*, male or female], the sex of an individual as determined, in mammals, by the presence or absence of a Y chromosome.

chromosome /krō′məsōm/ [Gk, *chroma* + *soma*, body], any of the threadlike structures in the nucleus of a cell that function in the transmission of genetic information. Each consists of a double strand of DNA attached to proteins called histones. The genes, which contain the genetic material that controls the inheritance of traits, are arranged in a linear pattern along the length of each DNA strand. Each species has a characteristic number of chromosomes in each somatic cell. In humans, there are 46 chromosomes, including 22 homologous pairs of autosomes and 1 pair of sex chromosomes.—**chromosomal,** *adj.*

chromosome analysis, a laboratory procedure that isolates the chromosome pairs so that they may be visualized.

chromosome coil, the spiral formed by the coiling of two or more chromonemata in a chromosome.

chromosome complement, the normal number of chromosomes found in the somatic cells of a given species.

chromosome karyotype test, a blood test used to study an individual's chromosome makeup to determine chromosomal defects associated with disease or the risk of developing disease. It is useful in evaluating congenital anomalies, mental retardation, and delayed puberty, as well as in the prenatal diagnosis of serious congenital diseases.

chromosome puff, a band of accumulated chromatin located at a specific site on a giant chromosome. It is indicative of gene activity, specifically DNA and RNA synthesis at that site.

chromosome walking, a molecular genetic technique by which overlapping molecular clones that span large chromosomal intervals are isolated.

chromotherapy /krō′məther′əpē/, a system of treating disease with colored lights chosen from specific regions of the spectrum.

chromotrope /krō′mətrōp/ [Gk, *chroma* + *trepein*, to turn], **1.** a component of tissue that stains metachromatically with metachromatic dyes. **2.** any one of several dyes differentiated by numeric suffixes. —**chromotropic,** *adj.*

chronaxy /krō′naksē/ [Gk, *chronos*, time, *axia*, value], (in electroneuromyography) a measure of the shortest duration of an electric stimulus needed to excite nerve or muscle tissue.

chronic /kron′ik/ [Gk, *chronos*, time], (of a disease or disorder) persisting for a long period, often for the remainder of a person's lifetime.

chronic active hepatitis (CAH), a potentially fatal form of hepatitis complicated by portal inflammation and extending into the parenchyma. There may be progressive destruction of the liver lobule with necrosis and fibrosis leading to scarring and cirrhosis. Possible causes include viral infections, drugs, and autoimmune reactions.

chronic airway obstruction, a type of pulmonary disorder, such as ephysema and chronic bronchitis, in which the upper or lower airway is chronically obstructed. The patient, when at rest, breathes at a normal rate and may have prolongation of the expiratory phase with pursed-lip breathing. The patient may be barrel-chested and have large supraclavicular fossae. During inspiration, the intercostal spaces retract, and accessory muscles are used.

chronic alcoholism, a pathologic condition resulting from the habitual use of alcohol in excessive amounts. The syndrome usually impairs an individual's health and ability to function normally in society. Symptoms of the disease include anorexia, diarrhea, weight loss, neurologic and psychiatric disturbances (most notably depression), and fatty deterioration of the liver, sometimes leading to cirrhosis.

chronic anterior poliomyelitis, an inflammation of the gray matter in the spinal cord, resulting in atrophy of muscles of the upper extremities and neck, with long periods of remission of symptoms.

chronic appendicitis, a type of appendicitis characterized by thickening or scarring of the vermiform appendix, caused by previous inflammation.

chronic bronchitis, a very common, debilitating pulmonary disease, characterized by greatly increased production of mucus by the glands of the trachea and bronchi and resulting in a cough with expectoration for at least 3 months of the year for more than 2 consecutive years. The condition has a strong association with smoking.

chronic calcific pancreatitis, pancreatitis with calcification in the ducts, usually associated with exocrine insufficiency and DM.

chronic carrier, an individual who acts as host to pathogenic organisms for an extended period without displaying any signs of disease.

chronic delirium [Gk, *chronos,* time; L, *delirare,* to rave], a form of delirium in which the patient shows signs of an altered state of awareness but is afebrile. The condition is sometimes associated with exhaustion, malnutrition, and wasting.

chronic dieting syndrome, the extreme practice of following fad diets, often leading to harmful physical and psychologic effects.

chronic disease, a disease that persists over a long period. The symptoms of chronic disease are sometimes less severe than those of the acute phase of the same disease.

chronic endoarteritis [Gk, *chronos,* time, *endon,* within, *arteria,* airpipe, *itis,* inflammation], persistent inflammation of the tunica intima of an arterial wall. It may be accompanied by fatty degeneration of arterial tissue and calcium deposits.

chronic endocarditis [Gk, *chronos,* time, *endon,* within, *kardia,* heart, *itis,* inflammation], persistent inflammation of the endocardium that usually follows an attack of acute endocarditis, syphilis, or an atheroma. It frequently involves the cardiac valves, making them incompetent.

chronic fatigue syndrome (CFS), a condition characterized by disabling fatigue, accompanied by a constellation of symptoms, including muscle pain, multijoint pain without swelling, painful cervical or axillary adenopathy, sore throat, headache, impaired memory or concentration, unrefreshing sleep, and postexertional malaise.

chronic glomerulonephritis, a noninfectious disease of the glomeruli of the kidney characterized by proteinuria, hematuria, edema, and decreased production of urine. It progresses to kidney failure.

chronic gout [Gk, *chronos,* time; L, *gutta,* drop], a persistent disorder of purine metabolism, characterized by abnormally high levels of serum uric acid and attacks of arthritis, with deposits of urates in the joints. The disorder may be familial and if untreated can lead to renal failure.

chronic granulomatous disease, sex-linked recessive disorder in which myeloperoxidase is diminished in the primary granules of neutrophils, causing delayed intracellular killing of fungi and bacteria by neutrophils.

chronic hepatitis [Gk, *chronos,* time, *hēpar,* liver, *itis,* inflammation], a state in which symptoms of hepatitis continue for several months and may increase in severity. In some cases of hepatitis B, the patient may become a lifelong carrier of the antigen and may show prolonged evidence of the infection.

chronic hyperplastic rhinitis [Gk, *chronos,* time, *hyper,* excess, *plassein,* to form, *rhis,* nose, *itis,* inflammation], chronic inflammation of the mucous membranes of the nose, with polyp formation.

chronic hyperplastic sinusitis [Gk, *chronos,* time, *hyper,* excess, *plassein,* to form; L, *sinus,* hollow; Gk, *itis,* inflammation], chronic sinus inflammation, with polyp formation in the nose and sinuses.

chronic hypertrophic rhinitis [Gk, *chronos,* time, *hyper,* excess, *trophe,* nourishment, *rhis,* nose, *itis,* inflammation], a condition of chronic inflammation of the nasal mucosa associated with enlargement of the mucous membrane.

chronic hypoxia, a usually slow, insidious reduction in tissue oxygenation resulting from gradually destructive or fibrotic lung diseases, congenital or acquired heart disorders, or chronic blood loss. The patient experiences persistent mental and physical fatigue, shows sluggish mental responses, and complains of a loss of ability to perform physical tasks.

chronic illness, any disorder that persists over a long period and affects physical, emotional, intellectual, vocational, social, or spiritual functioning.

chronic inflammatory demyelinating polyneuropathy (CIDP), a slowly progressive autoimmune neurologic disorder with demyelination of the peripheral nerves and nerve roots, characterized by progressive weakness and impaired sensory function in the limbs and enlargement of the peripheral nerves and usually by elevated protein in the CSF. Presenting symptoms often include tingling or numbness of the digits, weakness of the limbs, hyporeflexia or areflexia, fatigue, and abnormal sensations.

chronic inflammatory demyelinating polyradiculoneuropathy, a rare form of symmetrical motor neuron paralysis similar to Guillain-Barré syndrome but progressing more slowly or in a fluctuating pattern.

chronic intractable pain [Gk, *chronos,* time; L, *intractabilis + poena,* penalty], persistent pain that fails to respond to nonnarcotic analgesics and other treatment measures.

chronicity /krōnis′itē/, a state of being chronic.

chronic leg ulcer [Gk, *chronos,* time; ONorse, *leggr;* L, *ulcus,* ulcer], a slow-healing ulcer of the leg (usually the lower leg), typically associated with varicose veins, deep venous insufficiency, or a similar circulatory obstacle.

chronic lingual papillitis [Gk, *chronos;* L, *lingua,* tongue, *papilla,* nipple; Gk, *itis*], an inflammatory disorder of the tongue, sometimes extending to the buccal mucosa and palate. It is characterized by irregularly scattered red patches, thinning of the lingual papillae, severe burning pain, and shedding of epidermal tissue.

chronic low blood pressure, a condition in which systolic and diastolic BPs are consistently below normal values (approximately 120 and 70 mm Hg, respectively, in a young adult).

chronic lymphocytic leukemia (CLL) [Gk, *chronos;* L, *lympha,* water; Gk, *kytos,* cell, *leukos,* white, *haima,* blood], a neoplasm of blood-forming tissues characterized by a proliferation of small, long-lived lymphocytes, chiefly B cells, in bone marrow, blood, liver, and lymphoid organs. The disease has an insidious onset and progresses to cause malaise, ready fatigability, anorexia, weight loss, nocturnal sweating, lymphadenopathy, and hepatosplenomegaly.

chronic mountain sickness [Gk, *chronos,* time; L, *montana;* AS, *soec*], a form of altitude sickness in which the increased production of red cells results in polycythemia. Some symptoms, such as headache, weakness, and limb aches, occasionally develop in indigenous mountain dwellers as well as in persons who had become acclimatized to the higher altitudes.

chronic mucocutaneous candidiasis, a heterogeneous group of disorders, unified by impaired cell-mediated immunity against *Candida* species; a rare form of candidiasis characterized by candidal infection lesions of the skin, mucous membranes, GI tract, and respiratory tract. The humoral immune system functions normally in this disease. The onset of infections associated with the disease may precede endocrinopathy.

chronic myelocytic leukemia (CML), a malignant neoplasm of blood-forming tissues, characterized by a proliferation of granular leukocytes and often of megakaryocytes. Its progress is marked by malaise, fatigue, heat intolerance, bleeding gums, purpura, skin lesions, weight loss, hyperuricemia, abdominal discomfort, and massive splenomegaly.

chronic myelogenous leukemia /mī′əlōsit′ik/, Myeloproliferative neoplasm characterized by the unregulated and excessive production of cells of the myelocytic maturation series and presence of the BCR/ABL1 mutation.

chronic myocarditis [Gk, *chronos,* time, *mys,* muscle, *kardia,* heart, *itis,* inflammation], inflammation of the myocardium that persists after an acute bacterial infection. Chronic myocarditis is characterized by degeneration of muscle tissue and fibrosis or infiltration of interstitial tissues.

chronic nephritis [Gk, *chronos,* time, *nephros,* kidney, *itis,* inflammation], a form of kidney inflammation usually secondary to another disease, such as chronic pyelonephritis. In chronic interstitial nephritis, the kidney becomes small and granular with thickening of arteries and arterioles and proliferation of interstitial tissue. There may be functional abnormalities, such as urea retention, hematuria, and casts.

chronic nephropathy, a kidney disorder characterized by generalized or local damage to the tubulointerstitial areas of the kidney. The condition frequently results from more than a single cause. Symptoms include polyuria, renal acidosis, edema, proteinuria, and blood in the urine.

chronic nonerosive gastritis, any type of chronic gastritis that does not involve deep penetration of the gastric mucosa.

chronic obstructive pancreatitis, pancreatitis caused by dilatation of one of the major ducts proximal to an obstruction, usually from a tumor or scarring.

chronic obstructive pulmonary disease (COPD), a progressive and irreversible condition characterized by diminished inspiratory and expiratory capacity of the lungs. The condition is aggravated by cigarette smoking and air pollution. COPDs include asthma, chronic bronchiectasis, chronic bronchitis, and emphysema.

chronic pain, pain that continues or recurs over a prolonged period, caused by various diseases or abnormal conditions. Chronic pain may be less intense than acute pain. The person with chronic pain does not usually display increased pulse and rapid respiration because these autonomic reactions to pain cannot be sustained for long periods.

chronic pancreatitis [Gk, *chronos,* time, *peri,* near, *teinein*-all, *kreas,* flesh, *itis,* inflammation], chronic inflammation of the pancreas with fibrosis and calcification of the gland. It may follow repeated acute attacks and can lead to diabetes.

chronic peritonitis [Gk, *chronos,* time, *peri,* near, *tenein,* to stretch, *itis,* inflammation], a form of peritonitis in which the peritoneum thickens and ascites develops. The condition is usually associated with another disorder, such as pericarditis or polyserositis.

chronic pigmented purpura, any of a group of benign dermatoses of unknown cause, not associated with underlying systemic disease, consisting of minimal inflammation with tiny hemorrhages from capillaries in the upper dermis. Included are lichen aureus, pigmented purpuric lichenoid dermatitis, purpura annularis telangiectodes, and Schamberg disease.

chronic progressive myelopathy, gradually progressive spastic paraparesis associated with infection by human T-lymphotropic virus 1, characterized by progressive difficulty in walking and weakness of the lower extremity, sensory disturbances, and urinary incontinence, with no evidence of spinal compression or motor neuron involvement.

chronic rejection, immune rejection of transplanted tissue that may continue for several months.

chronic renal failure (CRF), gradual loss of kidney function, with progressively more severe renal insufficiency until the stage called chronic irreversible kidney failure or end-stage renal disease. Symptoms may include polyuria, anorexia or nausea, dehydration, and neurologic symptoms.

chronic rheumatism [Gk, *chronos,* time, *rheumatismos,* that which flows], a persistent, nonspecific, painful condition of the musculoskeletal tissues, including nonarticular forms of arthritis.

chronic synovitis [Gk, *chronos,* time, *syn,* together; L, *ovum,* egg; Gk, *itis,* inflammation], chronic inflammation of the synovial membrane of a joint.

chronic tetanus [Gk, *chronos,* time, *tetanos,* convulsive tension], **1.** a form of tetanus with a delayed onset, slow progression of the disease, and milder than usual symptoms. **2.** a reactivated tetanus infection in a healed wound.

chronic thromboembolic pulmonary hypertension, persistent pulmonary hypertension caused by obstruction of a major pulmonary artery by an unresolved embolus or multiple small pulmonary emboli.

chronic tuberculous mastitis, a rare infection of the breast resulting from extension of TB of underlying ribs.

chronic tubulointerstitial nephritis, tubulointerstitial nephritis that has progressed to the point where there is interstitial fibrosis with shrunken kidneys, a lowered glomerular filtration rate, and danger of renal failure.

chronic undifferentiated schizophrenia, a condition marked by the symptoms of more than one of the classic types of schizophrenia—simple, paranoid, or catatonic.

chronobiologist /krä-nō-bī′olǝjist/, a specialist in chronobiology.

chronobiology, the study of the effects of time on living sytems.

chronograph /kron′ǝgraf/ [Gk, *chronos* + *graphein,* to record], a device that records small intervals of time, such as a stopwatch.—**chronographic,** *adj.*

chronologic /kron′ǝloj′ik/ [Gk, *chronos* + *logos,* reason], **1.** arranged in time sequence. **2.** pertaining to chronology.

chronologic age, the age of an individual expressed as time that has elapsed since birth. The age of an infant is expressed in hours, days, or months. The age of children and adults is expressed in years.

chronopsychophysiology /kron′ōsī′kofis′ē-ol′ǝjē/, the science of physiologic cyclic processes in the body.

chronotherapeutics /kron′ōther′ǝpyōō′tiks/, a branch of medicine concerned with effects of circadian rhythms in human health, such as the hour of the day when asthma symptoms or heart attacks are most likely to occur and the best time of day for treating certain complaints.

chronotropism /krǝnot′rǝpiz′ǝm/ [Gk, *chronos* + *trepein,* to turn], the act or process of affecting the regularity of a periodic function, especially interference with the rate of the heartbeat.—**chronotropic,** *adj.*

Chrysanthemum /krisan′thǝmǝm/, a genus of perennial flowering herbs of the family Compositae. They are a common cause of contact dermatitis, and their powdered flowers are insecticidal and scabicidal and a source of pyrethrins.

chrysarobin /kris′ǝrō′bin/, a substance obtained from the wood of araboa trees and used as an irritant in the treatment of parasitic skin diseases and psoriasis.

chrysiasis /krǝsī′ǝsis/ [Gk, *chrysos,* gold, *osis,* condition], an abnormal condition that may develop after gold therapy, characterized by the deposition of gold in body tissues.

chrysotherapy /kris′ōther′ǝpē/ [Gk, *chrysos* + *therapeia,* treatment], the treatment of any disease with gold salts.—**chrysotherapeutic,** *adj.*

Chua K'a, a holistic counseling system of muscle tension release that emphasizes clarification and cleansing of the mind and emotions.

Churg-Strauss syndrome /churg′ strous′/ [Jacob Churg, twentieth-century American pathologist; Lotte Strauss, twentieth-century American pathologist], a form of systemic necrotizing vasculitis in which there is prominent lung involvement with severe asthma, eosinophilia, and granulomatous reactions. If present, skin lesions consist of tender subcutaneous nodules and bruiselike spots.

Chvostek's sign, Chvostek-Weiss sign /khvôsh′teks/ [Franz Chvostek, Austrian surgeon, 1835–1884], an abnormal spasm of the facial muscles elicited by light taps on the cheek to stimulate the facial nerve in patients who are hypocalcemic. It is a sign of tetany.

chyle /kīl/ [Gk, *chylos,* juice], the cloudy or turbid, white or pale yellow liquid products of digestion taken up by the small intestine. Consisting mainly of emulsified fats, chyle passes through finger-like projections in the small intestine and into the lymphatic system for transport to the venous circulation at the thoracic duct in the neck.—**chylous,** *adj.*

chyle cistern, a dilatation at the beginning of the thoracic duct, situated ventrally to the body of the second lumbar vertebra, on the right side and dorsally to the aorta. It receives the two lumbar lymphatic trunks and the intestinal lymphatic trunk.

chylemia /kīlē′mē·ə/, a condition in which chyle appears in the blood.

chylocele /kī′ləsēl/, a cystic lesion caused by an effusion of chylous fluid into the tunica vaginalis of the testes.

chyloid /kī′loid/, resembling the chyle that fills the lacteals of the small intestine during the digestion of fatty foods.

chylomediastinum /kī′lōmē′dē·astī′nəm/ [Gk, *chylos,* juice; L, *mediastinus,* midway], the presence of chyle in the mediastinum.

chylomicron /kī′lōmī′kron/ [Gk, *chylos* + *mikros,* small], minute lipoproteins measuring less than 0.5 μm in diameter. Chylomicrons consist of about 90 triglycerides with small amounts of cholesterol, phospholipids, fat-soluble vitamins, and protein. They are synthesized in the GI tract and carry dietary fat from the intestinal mucosa via the thoracic lymphatic duct into the plasma and ultimately to the liver and tissues.

chylothorax /kī′lōthôr′aks/ [Gk, *chylos* + *thorax,* chest], a condition marked by the effusion of chyle from the thoracic duct into the pleural space.

chylous /kī′ləs/ [Gk, *chylos,* juice], pertaining to or resembling chyle.

chylous ascites, an abnormal condition characterized by an accumulation of chyle in the peritoneal cavity.

chyluria /kīlŏŏr′ē·ə/ [Gk, *chylos* + *ouron,* urine], a milky appearance of the urine caused by the presence of chyle.

chymase /kī′mās/, a serine proteinase present in human mast cells, most prominent in skin and connective tissue, where it can cleave angiotensin and stimulate mucous glands.

chyme /kīm/ [Gk, *chymos,* juice], the viscous, semifluid contents of the stomach present during digestion of a meal.

chymopapain /kī′mōpəpā′ēn/ [Gk, *chymos*; Sp, *papaya*], a proteolytic enzyme isolated from the fruit of *Carica papaya* and related to papain. It is used in the treatment of prolapsed intervertebral or herniated disks.

chymotrypsin /kī′mōtrip′sin/ [Gk, *chymos* + *tryein,* to rub, *pepsin,* digestion], **1.** a proteolytic enzyme produced by the pancreas that catalyzes the hydrolysis of casein and gelatin. **2.** a yellow crystalline powder prepared from an extract of ox pancreas that is used in treating digestive disorders in which the enzyme is present in less than normal amounts or is totally lacking.

chymotrypsinogen /kī′mōtripsin′əjən/, a substance, produced in the pancreas, that is the zymogen precursor to the enzyme chymotrypsin. It is converted to chymotrypsin by trypsin.

Ci, abbreviation for **curie.**

CI, 1. abbreviation for *Colour Index.* **2.** abbreviation for *convergence insufficiency.*

Cialis, a trademark for tadalafil.

cibophobia /sē′bə-/ [L, *cibus,* food; Gk, *phobos,* fear], an abnormal or morbid aversion to food or to eating.

CIC, abbreviation for *Certified Infection Control.*

cicatricial alopecia /sisətrish′əl/, a form of baldness produced by scar formation in dermatoses such as lupus erythematosus, usually progressing to permanent baldness.

cicatricial pemphigoid [L, *cicatrix,* scar; Gk, *pemphix,* blister or bubble, *eidos,* form], a benign, chronic, usually bilateral, subepidermal blistering disease chiefly involving the mucous membranes, especially those of the mouth and eye. It heals by scarring and may lead to slow shrinkage of the affected tissues, and to blindness if untreated.

cicatricial scar [L, *cicatrix,* scar; Gk, *eschara,* scab], a fibrous scar that remains after a wound has healed.

cicatricial stenosis [L, *cicatrix*, scar; Gk, *stenos*, narrow, *osis*, condition], the narrowing of a duct or tube caused by the formation of scar tissue.

cicatrix /sik′ətriks, sikā′triks/ *pl.* **cicatrices** [L, scar], scar tissue that is avascular, pale, contracted, and firm after the earlier phase of skin healing characterized by redness and softness.—**cicatricial** /sik′ətrish′əl/, *adj.,* **cicatrize,** *v.*

cicatrize /sik′ətrīz/ [L, *cicatrix,* scar], to heal so as to form a scar.

ciclopirox /sī′kləpī′roks/, a topical antifungal agent prescribed in the treatment of tinea and candidiasis.

cicutism /sik′yŏŏtiz′əm/ [L, *Cicuta,* hemlock; Gk, *ismos,* process], poisoning caused by water hemlock, resulting in cyanosis, dilated pupils, convulsions, and coma.

CID, abbreviation for **cytomegalic inclusion disease.**

cidofovir, an antiviral used to treat cytomegalovirus retinitis in patients with AIDS.

cigarette smoking, the inhalation of the gases and hydrocarbon vapors generated by slowly burning tobacco in cigarettes. In addition to nicotine, nearly 1000 other chemicals have been identified in cigarette smoke, including carcinogenic polycyclic aromatic alcohols, cocarcinogenic phenols and fatty acids, carbon monoxide, hydrogen sulfide, hydrocyanic acid, nitrogen oxides, and various irritants that suppress protease inhibition and impair alveolar macrophage function. Cigarette smoke is addictive and is considered more dangerous than pipe or cigar smoke because it is less irritating and therefore more likely to be inhaled.

ciguatera /sē′gwôter′ə/, a form of fish poisoning, marked by GI and neurologic symptoms, caused by ingestion of tropical or subtropical marine fish, such as barracuda, grouper, or snapper, that have accumulated ciguatoxin in their tissues. Ciguatoxin is heat-resistant and is not detoxified by cooking.

ciguatera poisoning /sē′gwôter′ə/, [Sp, *cigua,* sea snail; L, *potio,* drink], a nonbacterial food poisoning that results from eating fish contaminated with the ciguatoxin. Many of the over 300 varieties of fish from the Caribbean or South Pacific have been implicated; barracuda is a common source. The toxin is believed to block acetylcholinesterase activity. Characteristics of ciguatera poisoning are vomiting, diarrhea, tingling or numbness of extremities and the skin around the mouth, itching, muscle weakness, pain, and respiratory paralysis. Cold liquids feel hot to the surfaces of the mouth and throat.

ciguatoxin /se′gwätok′sin/, a heat-stable toxin originating in a dinoflagellate as a pretoxin and concentrating in active form in the tissue of certain marine fish.

cilia /sil′ē-ə/ *sing.* **cilium** [L, eyelids or eyelashes], **1.** the eyelids or eyelashes. **2.** small, hairlike processes projecting from epithelial cells on the outer surfaces of some cells, aiding metabolism by producing motion, eddies, or current in a fluid.

ciliary /sil′ē-er′ē/ [L, *cilia*], pertaining to the eyelashes or eyelids.

ciliary artery, any of the branches of the ophthalmic artery that, along with the retinal artery, supply the eye.

ciliary body [L, *cilia*], the thickened part of the vascular tunic of the eye that joins the iris with the anterior portion of the choroid.

ciliary canal, the spaces of the iridocorneal angle.

ciliary disc, the thin part of the ciliary body extending between its crown and the ora serrata retinae.

ciliary ganglion, a small parasympathetic ganglion in the orbit of the eye, which controls pupillary and accommodative reflexes.

ciliary gland, one of the numerous tiny, modified sweat glands arranged in several rows near the free margins of the eyelids.

ciliary margin, the peripheral border of the iris, continuous with the ciliary body.

ciliary movement, the upward waving motion of the hairlike processes projecting from the epithelium of the respiratory tract and from certain microorganisms.

ciliary mucus transport, the movement of mucus-trapped particles from the upper respiratory tract to the lower pharynx, propelled by the motion of microscopic cilia lining the tract.

ciliary muscle, a semitransparent circular band of smooth muscle fibers attached to the choroid of the eye. It draws the ciliary process centripetally, allowing the lens to become more convex.

ciliary process, any one of about 80 tiny fleshy projections on the posterior surface of the iris. They secrete nutrient fluids to nourish the lens, cornea, and vitreous body.

ciliary ring, a small grooved band of tissue, about 4 mm wide, that forms the posterior part of the ciliary body of the eye. It extends from the ora serrata of the retina to the ciliary processes.

ciliary zone, an outer circular area on the anterior surface of the iris, separated from the inner circular area by the angular line. The ciliary zone contains the stroma of the iris.

Ciliata /sil′ē-ā′tə/, a class of protozoa of the subphylum Ciliophora, characterized by cilia throughout the life cycle. The only significant ciliate affecting humans is the intestinal parasite *Balantidium coli,* which causes dysentery.

ciliate /sil′ē·it/, of or having cilia, as certain epithelial cells of the body or protozoa of the class Ciliata.

ciliated epithelium /sil′ē·ā′ted/ [L, *cilia;* Gk, *epi,* upon, *thele,* nipple], any epithelial tissue that projects cilia from its surface, such as portions of the epithelium in the respiratory tract.

Ciliophora, a phylum of protozoa whose members, called ciliates, use cilia for locomotion and feeding.

ciliospinal /sil′ē·ōspī′nəl/, pertaining to a relationship between the ciliary body and the eye and the spinal cord.

ciliospinal reflex [L, *cilia* + *spina,* backbone, *reflectere,* to bend back], a normal brainstem reflex initiated by scratching or pinching the skin of the neck or face, causing dilation of the pupil.

cilostazol, a platelet aggregation inhibitor used to treat intermittent claudication.

cimbia /sim′bē·ə/, a girdlelike band of white fibers that extends across the surface of the cerebral peduncle.

cimetidine /simet′idēn/, an H₂-receptor antagonist prescribed to inhibit the production and secretion of acid in the stomach in the treatment of gastroesophageal reflux disease, pancreatitis, duodenal ulcers, and hypersecretory conditions. It is also used in the treatment of warts.

CIN, abbreviation for **cervical intraepithelial neoplasia.**

cinacalcet, a calcium receptor agonist that directly lowers parathyroid hormone levels by increasing sensitivity of calcium-sensing receptors to extracellular calcium. This drug is used to treat hypercalcemia in parathyroid carcinoma and secondary hyperparathyroidism in chronic kidney disease requiring dialysis.

cinchona /singkō′nə, chinchō′nə/ [countess of Chinchon, Peru], the dried bark of the stem or root of species of *Cinchona,* containing the alkaloids quinine and quinidine.

cinchonine, an alkaloid of cinchona used as an antimalarial agent, chiefly in the form of the sulfate salt.

cinchonism /sin′kōniz′əm/, a condition resulting from excessive ingestion of cinchona bark or its alkaloid derivatives. Cinchonism is characterized by hearing loss, headache, tinnitus, and signs of cerebral congestion.

cineangiocardiogram /sin′ē·an′jē·ōkär′dē·əgram′/, a radiograph produced by cineangiocardiography.

cineangiocardiography /sin′ē·an′jē·ōkär′dē·og′rəfē/ [Gk, *kinesis,* movement, *angeion,* vessel, *kardia,* heart, *graphein,* to record], the production of images of the cardiovascular system by a combination of fluoroscopic, radiographic, and motion-picture techniques.

cineangiogram /sin′ē·an′jē·əgram′/, a motion-picture recording of a blood vessel or of a portion of the cardiovascular system obtained after injecting the patient with a nontoxic radiopaque medium.

cineangiograph /sin′ē·an′jē·əgraf′/, a movie camera used for recording fluorescent images of the cardiovascular system.

cine film /sin′ē/, a type of motion picture film used in cineradiography, usually in cardiac catheterization or GI studies.

cineradiography /sin′irā′dē·og′rəfē/ [Gk, *kinesis,* movement; L, *radiere,* to shine; Gk, *graphein,* to record], the filming with a movie camera of the images that appear on a fluorescent screen, especially images of body structures following injection of a nontoxic radiopaque medium.

cingulate /sing′gyəlit/ [L, *cingulum,* girdle], 1. having a zone or girdle, usually with transverse markings. 2. pertaining to a cingulum.

cingulectomy /sing′gyo͞olek′təmē/ [L, *cingulum;* Gk, *ektomē,* excision], the surgical excision of a portion of the cingulate gyrus in the frontal lobe of the brain and the immediately surrounding tissue.

cingulotomy /sing′gyo͞olot′əmē/ [L, *cingulum;* Gk, *temnein,* to cut], a procedure in brain surgery to alleviate intractable pain by producing lesions in the tissue of the cingulate gyrus of the frontal lobe.

cinnamon /sin′əmən/ [Gk, *kinnamomon*], the aromatic inner bark of several species of thr tree *Cinnamomum.* Saigon cinnamon is commonly used as a carminative, an aromatic stimulant, and a spice.—**cinnamic,** *adj.*

CINV, abbreviation for **chemotherapy-induced nausea and vomiting.**

CIPM, abbreviation for **Comité International des Poids et Mesures (International Committee for Weights and Measures).**

circa [L, about], approximate, as an approximate date or number.

circadian dysrhythmia /sərkā′dē·ən, sur′kədē′ən/ [L, *circa,* about, *dies,* day; Gk, *dys,* bad, *rhythmos,* rhythm], the biologic and psychologic stress effects of jet lag, or rapid travel through several time zones. In addition to a shift in normal eating and sleeping patterns, disruption of medication schedules and other therapies may occur.

C

circadian rhythm [L, *circa,* about, *dies,* day; Gk, *rhythmos,* rhythm], a pattern based on a 24-hour cycle, especially the repetition of certain physiologic phenomena, such as sleeping and eating.

circinate /sur′sināt/ [L, *circinare,* to make round], having a ring-shaped outline or formation; annular.

circle [L, *circulus*], (in anatomy) a circular or nearly circular structure of the body, as the circle of Willis and circle of Zinn. —**circular,** *adj.*

circle of least confusion, 1. (in optics) a disc representing the image of a theoretic point made by a spherocylindrical lens. 2. smallest cross section of the blur circle between two focal lines formed by an astigmatic lens.

circle of Willis [Thomas Willis, English physician, 1621–1675], a vascular network at the base of the brain formed by the interconnection of the middle cerebral, anterior cerebral, posterior cerebral, basilar, anterior communicating, and posterior communicating arteries.

CircOlectric (COL) bed, a trademark for an electronically controlled bed that can be vertically rotated 210 degrees and allows a patient to move vertically from the prone to the supine position. It is used especially in orthopedics and in the treatment of patients with severe burns and decubitus ulcers.

circuit /sur′kit/ [L, *circuitus,* going around], a course or pathway, particularly one through which an electric current passes. Current passes through a closed or continuous circuit and stops if the circuit is open, interrupted, or broken.

circuit training, a method of physical exercise in which activities are arranged in sets and the participant moves quickly from one activity to another with a minimum of rest between activities.

circular bandage /sur′kyələr/ [L, *circularis,* round], a bandage wrapped around an injured part, usually a limb or a digit.

circular fiber, any one of the many fibers in the free gingiva that encircle the teeth.

circular fold, one of the numerous annular projections in the small intestine. They vary in size and frequency and are formed by mucous and submucous tissue.

circulation /sur′kyəlā′shən/ [L, *circulatio,* to go around], movement of an object or substance through a circular course so that it returns to its starting point, such as the circulation of blood through the circuitous network of arteries and veins.

circulation rate [L, *circulatio,* to go around, *ratum,* calculation], the rate of blood flow, usually expressed as the amount of blood pumped through the heart per minute.

circulation status, a nursing outcome from the Nursing Outcomes Classification (NOC) defined as unobstructed, unidirectional blood flow at an appropriate pressure through large vessels of the systemic and pulmonary circuits.

circulation time, the time required for blood to flow from one part of the body to another. Timing a particle of blood involves injecting a traceable dye or radioisotope into a vein and timing its reappearance in an artery at the point of injection. The resulting time helps determine problems with heart failure and decreased cardiac output.

circulatory care: arterial insufficiency, a nursing intervention from the Nursing Interventions Classification (NIC) defined as promotion of arterial circulation.

circulatory care: mechanical assist device, a nursing intervention from the Nursing Interventions Classification (NIC) defined as temporary support of the circulation through the use of mechanical devices or pumps.

circulatory care: venous insufficiency, a nursing intervention from the Nursing Interventions Classification (NIC) defined as promotion of venous circulation.

circulatory failure [L, *circulatio + fallere,* to deceive], inability of the cardiovascular system to supply the cells of the body with enough oxygenated blood to meet their metabolic demands.

circulatory overload [L, *circulatio,* to go around; AS, *ofer*; ME, *lod*], an elevation in BP caused by an increased blood volume, as by transfusion. The condition can lead to heart failure or pulmonary edema.

circulatory precautions, a nursing intervention from the Nursing Interventions Classification (NIC) defined as protection of a localized area with limited perfusion.

circulatory system, the network of channels through which the nutrient fluids (blood) of the body circulate.

circumanal /sur′kəmā′nəl/ [L, *circum,* around + *anus*], pertaining to the area surrounding the anus.

circumcision /-sizh′ən/ [L, *circum,* around, *cadere,* to cut], a surgical procedure in which the prepuce of the penis or the prepuce of the clitoris is excised.

circumcision care, a nursing intervention from the Nursing Interventions Classification (NIC) defined as preprocedural and postprocedural support to males undergoing circumcision.

circumcorneal /-kôr′nē·əl/, pertaining to the area of the eye surrounding the cornea.

circumduction /sur′kəmduk′shən/ [L, *circum + ducere,* to lead], 1. one of the four basic movements allowed by the various joints of the skeleton. It is a combination of abduction, adduction, extension, and flexion. An example is the motion of a bone whose head articulates with a cavity, such as the femur with the acetabulum. The motion of the bone circumscribes a cone, the apex of which is in the cavity and the base of which is described by the distal end of the bone. **2.** the circular movement of a limb or of the eye.

circumference /surkum'fərens/ [L, *circum,* around, *ferre,* to bear], **1.** the perimeter or periphery of a circle. **2.** a circular plane surface of a joint.

circumferential /sərkum'fəren'shəl/, encircling; pertaining to a circumference or perimeter.

circumferential fibrocartilage [L, *circum + ferre,* to bring, *fibra,* fiber, *cartilago*], a structure made of fibrocartilage, in which fibrocartilaginous rims surround the margins of various articular cavities, deepening such cavities and protecting their edges.

circumflex /sur'kəmfleks/ [L, *circum,* around, *flexcere,* to bend], winding around; pertaining to blood vessels or nerves that wind around other body structures.

circumlocution /-lōkoō'shən/, the subconscious use of pantomime or nonverbal communication or word substitution by a patient because a word is difficult to retrieve or has been forgotten.

circummarginate placenta, a placenta with a thinner ring of membranous tissue on the fetal surface than that of a circumvallate placenta.

circumoral /sur'kəmôr'əl/ [L, *circum + os,* mouth], pertaining to the area of the face around the mouth.

circumoral pallor [L, *circum,* around, *os,* mouth, *pallor,* paleness], paleness of the skin area around the mouth, a possible sign of scarlet fever.

circumscribed /-skrībd'/ [L, *circum,* around, *scribere,* to draw], within a well-defined area, or in one with definite boundaries or limits.

circumscribed abscess [L, *circum,* around, *scribere,* to draw, *abscedere,* to go away], an abscess separated from surrounding tissues by a wall of fibroblasts.

circumscribed scleroderma, localized scleroderma.

circum-speech [L, *circum;* AS, *spaec*], (in psychiatry) behavioral characteristics associated with conversation. The characteristics include body language, maintenance of personal space between individuals, hand sweeps, head nods, and task-oriented activities such as walking or knitting while carrying on a conversation.

circumstantiality /-stan'shē·al'itē/ [L, *circum + stare,* to stand], (in psychiatry) a speech pattern in which a patient has difficulty separating relevant from irrelevant information while describing an event.

circus movement, 1. an unusual and involuntary rolling or somersaulting caused by injured neural structures that control body posture such as the cerebral pedicles or the vestibular apparatus. **2.** an unusual circular gait caused by injury to the brain or spinal cord. **3.** a mechanism associated with the excitatory wave of the atrium of the heart and atrial flutter or fibrillation.

cirrhosis /sirō'sis/ [Gk, *kirrhos,* yellow-orange, *osis,* condition], a chronic degenerative disease of the liver in which the lobes are covered with fibrous tissue, the parenchyma degenerates, and the lobules are infiltrated with fat. Gluconeogenesis, detoxification of drugs and alcohol, bilirubin metabolism, vitamin absorption, GI function, hormonal metabolism, and other functions of the liver deteriorate. Cirrhosis is most commonly the result of chronic alcohol abuse; other causes include nutritional deprivation, hepatitis, and cardiac problems.

cisatracurium, a nondepolarizing neuromuscular blocker used to facilitate endotracheal intubation and skeletal muscle relaxation during mechanical ventilation, surgery, or general anesthesia.

cis configuration /sis/, **1.** the presence of the dominant alleles of two or more pairs of genes on one chromosome and the recessive alleles on the homologous chromosome. **2.** the presence of the mutant genes of a pair of pseudoalleles on one chromosome and the wild-type genes on the homologous chromosome. **3.** (in chemistry) a form of isomerism in which two substituent groups are on the same side of a double bond or aliphatic ring.

cisplatin /sisplat'in/, an antineoplastic prescribed in combination with vinBLAStine and bleomycin in the treatment of neoplasms, such as metastatic testicular, prostatic, ovarian tumors, and Hodgkin's lymphoma.

cistern /sis'tərn/ [L, *cisterna,* vessel], a storage reservoir for fluids.

cisterna /sistur'nə/ *pl.* **cisternae** [L, vessel], a cavity that serves as a reservoir for lymph or other body fluids.

cisternal puncture /sistur'nəl/ [L, vessel, *punctura,* a piercing], the insertion of a needle into the cerebellomedullary cistern to withdraw CSF for examination. The puncture is made between the atlas and the occipital bone.

cistron /sis'tron/ [L, *cis,* this side, *trans,* across], a fragment or portion of DNA that codes for a specific polypeptide. It is the smallest unit functioning as a transmitter of genetic information. In modern molecular genetics, the cistron is essentially synonymous with the gene. —**cistronic,** *adj.*

cisvestitism /sisves'titiz'əm/ [L, *cis,* this side, *vestis,* garment], the practice of wearing attire appropriate to the sex of the individual involved but not suitable to the age, occupation, or status of the wearer.

cit, abbreviation for *citrate anion.*

citalopram, an antidepressant in the selective serotonin-reuptake inhibitor class. It is used to treat major depressive disorder.

Citanest Hydrochloride, a trademark for a local anesthetic (prilocaine hydrochloride).

citicoline /sit'ikō'lin/, a natural substance that is a component of cell membranes. A pharmaceutic version is used to help stroke victims by inducing injured membranes to repair themselves, limiting cell death.

citrate /sit'rāt, sī'trāt/ [L, *kitron,* citron], **1.** an anion of citric acid. **2.** the act of treating with a citrate or citric acid. —**citration,** *n.*

citrated plasma, plasma from blood collected and mixed with sodium citrate, which prevents clotting. Citrated plasma is most often used for coagulation testing.

citric acid /sit'rik/ [Gk, *kitron,* citron; L, *acidus,* sour], a white, crystalline organic acid soluble in water and alcohol. It is extracted from citrus fruits, especially lemons and limes, or obtained by fermentation of sugars and is used as an acidulating agent, an antioxidant, and a flavoring agent in foods, carbonated beverages, and certain pharmaceutic products, especially laxatives.

citric acid cycle [Gk, *kitron,* citron; L, *acidus,* sour; Gk, *kyklos,* circle], a sequence of enzymatic reactions involving the metabolism of carbon chains of sugars, fatty acids, and amino acids to yield carbon dioxide, water, and high-energy phosphate bonds. The cycle is initiated when pyruvate combines with coenzyme A (CoA) to form a two-carbon unit, acetyl-CoA, which enters the cycle by combining with four-carbon oxaloacetic acid to form six-carbon citric acid. In subsequent steps, isocitric acid, produced from citric acid, is oxidized to oxalosuccinic acid, which loses carbon dioxide to form alpha-ketoglutaric acid. Succinic acid, resulting from the oxidative decarboxylation of alpha-ketoglutaric acid, is oxidized to fumaric acid, and its oxidation regenerates oxaloacetic acid, which condenses with acetyl-CoA, closing the cycle. The citric acid cycle provides

a major source of adenosine triphosphate energy and also produces intermediate molecules that are starting points for a number of vital metabolic pathways including amino acid synthesis.

citrin /sit'rin/ [Gk, *kitron,* citron], a crystalline flavonoid concentrate that is used as a source of bioflavonoid.

citrulline /sitrul'ēn/ [L, *Citrullus,* watermelon], an amino acid produced from ornithine during the urea cycle. It is subsequently transformed to arginine by the transfer of a nitrogen atom from aspartate.

citrullinemia /-ē'mē-ə/, a disorder of amino acid metabolism caused by a deficiency of an enzyme, argininosuccinic acid synthetase. The clinical features include vomiting, convulsions, and coma.

CJPH, abbreviation for *Canadian Journal of Public Health.*

C/kg, a unit of radiation exposure in the SI system, coulombs per kilogram of air. 1 roentgen = 2.58×10^{-4} C/kg.

CK isoenzyme fraction, one of several blood-borne enzymes that are released after myocardial necrosis. The isoenzyme of creatine kinase (CK) is identified as MB isomer, or MB-CK and is a diagnostic clue to heart damage.

cL, abbreviation for **centiliter.**

Cl, symbol for the element **chlorine.**

clade /klād/, a grouping of genetic variants within a single species.

Claforan, a trademark for an antibiotic (cefotaxime sodium).

claim, an itemized statement of services and costs from a health care provider or facility submitted to the insurer for payment.

claims-made policy [L, *clamere,* to cry out; ME, *maken*; L, *politicus,* the state], a professional liability insurance policy that covers the holder for the period in which a claim of malpractice is made. The alleged act of malpractice may have occurred at some previous time, but the policy insures the holder when the claim is made.

clairvoyance /klervoi'əns/, the alleged power or ability to perceive or to be aware of objects or events without the use of the physical senses.

clamp [AS, *clam,* to hold together], an instrument with serrated jaws and locking handles, used for gripping, holding, joining, supporting, or compressing an organ, vessel, or tissue.

clang association /klang/ [L, *clangere,* to resound, *associare,* to unite], the mental connection between dissociated ideas made because of similarity in the sounds of the words used to describe the ideas. The phenomenon occurs frequently in schizophrenia.

clapping [AS, *cloeppan*, to beat], (in massage) the procedure of making percussive movements on the patient's body, usually on the chest wall or back, by lowering the cupped palms alternately in a series of rapid, stimulating blows.

Clapton's line [Edward Clapton, English physician, 1830–1909], a greenish line at the base of the teeth, indicative of copper poisoning.

clarification /klerʹifikāʹshən/ [L, *clarus*, clear, *facere*, to make], (in psychology) an intervention technique designed to guide the patient in focusing on and recognizing gaps and inconsistencies in his or her statements.

clarify /klerʹəfī/, (in chemistry) to clear a turbid liquid by allowing any suspended matter to settle, by adding a substance that precipitates any suspended matter, or by heating.—**clarification,** *n.*

Clark's rule [Cecil Clark, twentieth century British physician; L, *regula*, model], a method of calculating the approximate pediatric dosage of a drug for a child by using this formula: weight in pounds/150 × adult dose. It is now considered obsolete.

clasp [ME, *clippen*, to embrace], **1.** (in dentistry) a sleevelike fitting that is fastened over a tooth to hold a partial denture in place. **2.** (in surgery) any device for holding together tissues, especially bones.

clasp arm, an extension, usually from a minor connector, of the clasp of a removable partial denture, that provides retention, reciprocation, or stabilization to an abutment tooth.

clasp-knife reflex, an abnormal sign in which a spastic limb resists passive motion and then suddenly gives way, similar to the motion of the blade of a jackknife.

clasp-knife spasticity, clasp-knife rigidity.

clasp torsion, the twisting of a retentive clasp arm on a removable partial denture.

classical conditioning, a form of learning in which a previously neutral stimulus begins to elicit a given response through associative training.

classical Western massage, methods of massage based on European concepts of anatomy and physiology and using five basic techniques: effleurage, pétrissage, friction, tapotement, and vibration.

classic cesarean section [L, *classicus*, first-class, Caesar, *sectio*, a cutting], a method for surgically delivering a baby through a vertical midline incision of the upper segment of the uterus.

classic tomography [L, *classicus* + Gk, *tome*, section, *graphein*, to record], a method that moves the x-ray source and the x-ray plate during an exposure to produce an image in which all but a particular plane is blurred out.

classic visceral leishmaniasis, a form of leishmaniasis caused by *Leishmania donovani*, transmitted by the sandfly *Phlebotomus argentipes*, usually affecting older children or young adults. Humans are the only reservoir hosts.

classification /klasʹifikāʹshən/ [L, *classis*, collection, *facere*, to make], (in research) a process in data analysis in which data are grouped according to previously determined characteristics.—**classify,** *v.*

classification of caries [L, *classis*, collection, *facere*, to make, *caries*, decay], a system for dividing dental caries into several classes based on the part of the tooth they affect. Class I caries are pits and fissures in the occlusal surfaces of posterior teeth or the lingual surfaces of maxillary incisors. Class II caries affect the proximal surfaces of premolars and molars but have not broken through to the occlusal surfaces. Class III caries affect the proximal surfaces of incisors and canines, excluding the incisal angles. Class IV caries affect the proximal surfaces of incisors and canines, including the incisal angles. Class V pertains to caries that affect the gingival third of the labial, buccal, and lingual surfaces.

classification schemes, systems of organizing data or information, usually involving categories of items with similar characteristics.

class II biologic safety cabinet, a container that recirculates air through a high-efficiency filter. It is usually located in a hospital pharmacy and is used to prepare chemotherapeutic agents in an environment that protects personnel from exposure.

claudication /klôʹdikāʹshən/ [L, *claudicatio*, a limping], cramplike pains in the calves caused by poor circulation of the blood to the leg muscles. The condition is commonly associated with atherosclerosis.

claustrophobia /klôsʹtrə-/ [L, *claustrum*, a closing; Gk, *phobos*, fear], a morbid fear of being in or becoming trapped in enclosed or narrow places.

claustrum /klôsʹtrəm/ *pl.* **claustra** [L, a closing], **1.** a barrier, as a membrane that partially closes an aperture. **2.** a thin sheet of gray matter, composed chiefly of spindle cells, situated lateral to the external capsule of the brain and separating the internal capsule from white matter of the insula.

clavicle /klavʹikəl/ [L, *clavicula*, little key], a long curved, horizontal bone directly above the first rib, forming the ventral portion of the shoulder girdle. It articulates medially with the sternum and laterally with the acromion of the scapula and accommodates the attachment of numerous muscles.

clavicle strap, strapping applied to immobilize the clavicle during fracture healing.

clavicular /kləvik′yələr/, pertaining to the clavicle (collarbone).

clavicular notch [L, *clavicula*; OFr, *enochier*], one of a pair of oval depressions at the superior end of the sternum.

clavipectoral fascia, a thick sheet of connective tissue that connects the clavicle to the floor of the axilla.

clavipectoral triangle, an anatomic triangle formed by the clavicle, the deltoid, and the pectoralis major. It contains the cephalic vein.

clawfoot, a deformity of the foot characterized by an excessively high arch with hyperextension of the toes at the metatarsophalangeal joints, flexion at the interphalangeal joints, and shortening of the Achilles tendon. The condition may be present at birth or appear later as a result of contractures or an imbalance of the muscles of the foot, as in neuromuscular diseases.

clawhand [AS, *clawu* + hand], an abnormal condition of the hand characterized by extreme flexion of the middle and distal phalanges and hyperextension of the metacarpophalangeal joints.

claw-type traction frame, an orthopedic apparatus that holds various pieces of traction equipment. It consists of two metal uprights, one at the head of the bed and the other at the foot. Both uprights are secured to the bed by clawlike attachments and support an overhead metal bar secured to the uprights by metal clamps.

clean-catch specimen, a urine specimen that is as free of bacterial contamination as possible without the use of a catheter.

cleansing enema, an enema, usually composed of soapsuds, administered to remove all formed fecal material from the colon.

clearance (*C*) /klir′əns/ [L, *clarus,* clear], the removal of a substance from the blood via the kidneys.

clear cell [L, *clarus* + *cella*, storeroom], **1.** a type of cell found in the parathyroid gland that does not take on a color with the ordinary tissue stains used for microscopic examination. **2.** the principal cell of most renal cell carcinomas and occasionally of ovarian and parathyroid tumors. **3.** a specific type of epidermal cell, probably of neural origin, that has a dark-staining nucleus but clear cytoplasm with hematoxylin and eosin stain.

clear cell carcinoma, 1. a malignant tumor of the tubular epithelium of the kidney. Characteristically the malignant cells contain abundant clear cytoplasm. **2.** an uncommon ovarian neoplasm characterized by cells with clear cytoplasm.

clearing agent, a chemical, such as ammonium thiosulfate, used in the processing of exposed x-ray film to remove unexposed and undeveloped silver halides from the emulsion.

clearing test, an ROM test that moves the joint to its limits, stretching the capsule and other soft tissues in an attempt to reproduce symptoms. If the ROM is normal and no symptoms are produced, the joint is cleared as a cause of a musculoskeletal disorder.

clear-liquid diet [L, *clarus* + *liquere,* to flow], a diet that supplies fluids and provides minimal fiber primarily to relieve thirst and maintain water balance. It consists primarily of dissolved sugar and flavored liquids. The diet is nutritionally inadequate and should not be used for more than two days.

cleavage /klē′vij/ [AS, *cleofan,* to split], **1.** the series of repeated mitotic cell divisions that occur in an ovum immediately after fertilization. It transforms the single-celled zygote into a multicellular embryo capable of growth and differentiation. During cleavage, the embryo remains uniform in size as its cells become smaller with each division. **2.** the act or process of splitting, primarily a complex molecule into two or more simpler molecules.— **cleave,** *v.*

cleavage fracture, any fracture that splits cartilage with the avulsion of a small piece of bone from the distal portion of the lateral condyle of the humerus.

cleavage line, any one of a number of linear striations in the skin that delineate the general structural pattern, direction, and tension of the subcutaneous fibrous tissue. They are present in all areas of the body but are visible only in certain sites, as the palms of the hands and soles of the feet.

cleavage plane, 1. the area in a fertilized ovum where cleavage takes place; the axis along which any cell division occurs. **2.** any plane within the body where organs or structures can be separated with minimal damage to surrounding tissue.

cleft [ME, *clift*], **1.** division. **2.** a fissure, especially one that originates in the embryo, as the branchial cleft or the facial cleft.

cleft cheek, a transverse facial cleft, appearing as an abnormally large mouth. It is caused by the failure of the maxillary and mandibular processes to fuse during embryonic facial development.

cleft foot, an abnormal condition in which the division between the third and fourth toes extends into the metatarsus of the foot.

cleft hand, a hand that develops in two parts because of the failure of a digit and metacarpal to form normally during embryonic development.

cleft jaw, an abnormal jaw resulting from failure of the left and right mandibles to fuse properly during embryonic development.

cleft lip, a congenital anomaly consisting of one or more clefts in the upper lip that result from the failure in the embryo of the maxillary and median nasal processes to close.

cleft-lip repair, the surgical correction of a unilateral or bilateral congenital interruption of the upper lip.

cleft palate, a congenital defect characterized by a fissure in the midline of the palate, resulting from the failure of the two sides to fuse during embryonic development. The fissure may be complete, extending through both the hard and soft palates into the nasal cavities, or it may show any degree of incomplete or partial cleft.

cleft-palate repair, the surgical correction of a congenital fissure in the midline of the partition separating the oral and nasal cavities. A cleft lip often accompanies a cleft palate. Repair of a cleft palate is usually undertaken when a child is at least 6 months old. Depending on the extent and nature of a cleft palate, it may be repaired in one or in several operations. Some experts believe that early repair of a defect in the bony palate can lead to structural malrelations and advise delaying the operation until the child is between 5 and 7 years of age and has achieved more bone growth.

cleft-palate speech, faulty speech due to a cleft palate, often characterized by hypernasality; difficulty with pressure consonants, voice, and articulation; and other problems resulting from the velopharyngeal insufficiency.

cleft sternum, a fissure in the sternum caused by a failure in embryonic development.

cleft tongue [ME, *clift*; AS, *tunge*], a tongue divided by a longitudinal fissure.

cleft uvula, an abnormal congenital condition in which the uvula is split into halves as a result of the failure of the posterior palatine folds to unite.

cleidocranial dysostosis /klī′dōkrā′nē-əl/ [Gk, *kleis*, key, *kranion*, skull, *dys*, bad, *osteon*, bone], a rare abnormal hereditary condition characterized by defective ossification of the cranial bones and by the complete or partial absence of the clavicles. The defective ossification of the cranial bones delays the closing of the cranial sutures and produces large fontanels. This condition also involves dental and vertebral anomalies.

clemastine /klemas′tēn/, an antihistamine prescribed in the treatment of symptoms of allergic rhinitis, pruritus, or conjunctivitis.

clenching /klench′ing/ [ME, *clenchen*], the clamping and pressing of the jaws and teeth together in centric occlusion, frequently associated with acute nervous tension or physical effort.

Cleocin, a trademark for an antibacterial (clindamycin).

cleoid /klē′oid/ [ME, *cle*, claw; Gk, *eidos*, form], a carving instrument with a blade shaped like a pointed spade or claw, with cutting edges on both sides.

clergyman's sore throat, loss of the voice from overuse, as by clergymen.

click [Fr, *cliquer*, to clash], an extra heart sound that occurs during systole.

clicking /klik′ing/ [Fr, *cliquer*, to clash], a series of sounds, such as the snapping, cracking, or crepitant noise evident on excursions of the mandibular condyle. The sound is associated with TMJ dysfunction.

client /klī′ənt/ [L, *clinare*, to lean], **1.** a person who is the recipient of a professional service. **2.** a recipient of health care regardless of the state of health. **3.** a patient.

client-centered therapy, a nondirective method of group or individual psychotherapy, originated by Carl Rogers, in which the therapist's role is to listen to and then reflect or restate without judgment or interpretation the words of the client.

client satisfaction, a nursing outcome from the Nursing Outcomes Classification (NOC) defined as the extent of positive perception of care provided by nursing staff.

client satisfaction: access to care resources, a nursing outcome from the Nursing Outcomes Classification (NOC) defined as the extent of positive perception of access to nursing staff, supplies, and equipment needed for care.

client satisfaction: caring, a nursing outcome from the Nursing Outcomes Classification (NOC) defined as the extent of positive perception of nursing staff's concern for the client.

client satisfaction: case management, a nursing outcome from the Nursing Outcomes Classification (NOC) defined as the extent of positive perception of case management services.

client satisfaction: communication, a nursing outcome from the Nursing Outcomes Classification (NOC) defined as the extent of positive perception of information exchanged between client and nursing staff.

client satisfaction: continuity of care, a nursing outcome from the Nursing Outcomes Classification (NOC) defined as the extent of positive perception of coordination of care as the client moves from one care setting to another.

client satisfaction: cultural needs fulfillment, a nursing outcome from the Nursing Outcomes Classification (NOC) defined as the extent of positive perception of integration of cultural beliefs, values, and social structures into nursing care.

client satisfaction: functional assistance, a nursing outcome from the Nursing Outcomes Classification (NOC) defined as the extent of positive perception of nursing assistance to achieve mobility and self-care.

client satisfaction: pain management, a nursing outcome from the Nursing Outcomes Classification (NOC) defined as the extent of positive perception of nursing care to relieve pain.

client satisfaction: physical care, a nursing outcome from the Nursing Outcomes Classification (NOC) defined as the extent of positive perception of nursing care to maintain body functions and cleanliness.

client satisfaction: physical environment, a nursing outcome from the Nursing Outcomes Classification (NOC) defined as the extent of positive perception of living environment, treatment environment, and equipment and supplies in acute or long-term care settings.

client satisfaction: protection of rights, a nursing outcome from the Nursing Outcomes Classification (NOC) defined as the extent of positive perception of protection of a client's legal and moral rights provided by nursing staff.

client satisfaction: psychological care, a nursing outcome from the Nursing Outcomes Classification (NOC) defined as the extent of positive perception of nursing assistance to cope with emotional issues and perform mental activities.

client satisfaction: safety, a nursing outcome from the Nursing Outcomes Classification (NOC) defined as the extent of positive perception of procedures, information, and nursing care to prevent harm or injury.

client satisfaction: symptom control, a nursing outcome from the Nursing Outcomes Classification (NOC) defined as the extent of positive perception of nursing care to relieve symptoms of illness.

client satisfaction: teaching, a nursing outcome from the Nursing Outcomes Classification (NOC) defined as the extent of

positive perception of instruction provided by nursing staff to improve knowledge, understanding, and participation in care.

client satisfaction: technical aspects of care, a nursing outcome from the Nursing Outcomes Classification (NOC) defined as the extent of positive perception of nursing staff's knowledge and expertise used in providing care.

climate /klī′mit/ [Gk, *klima,* inclination], **1.** a composite of the prevailing weather conditions that characterize any particular geographic region. Because these factors affect health, they must be considered in the diagnosis and treatment of certain illnesses, especially those affecting respiration. **2.** the general condition surrounding something, as in a climate of goodwill.—**climatic,** *adj.*

climax /klī′maks/ [Gk, *klimax,* ladder], a peak of intensity, such as a sexual orgasm or the high point of a fever.

climbing fiber [ME, *climben;* L, *fibra*], a type of nerve fiber that carries impulses to the Purkinje cells of the cerebellar cortex.

clindamycin hydrochloride /klin′dəmī′sin/, an antibacterial prescribed in the treatment of certain serious bacterial infections (including anaerobic and some gram-positive organisms).

clinic [Gk, *kline,* bed], **1.** an ambulatory caresite where persons who do not require hospitalization receive medical care. **2.** a group practice of doctors, such as the Mayo Clinic. **3.** a meeting place for doctors, nurses, and medical students where instruction can be given at the bedside of a patient or in a similar setting. **4.** a seminar or other scientific medical meeting. **5.** a detailed published report of the diagnosis and treatment of a health care problem.

clinical /klin′ikəl/ [Gk, *kline,* bed], **1.** pertaining to a clinic. **2.** pertaining to direct bedside medical or nursing care. **3.** pertaining to materials or equipment used in the care of a sick person. **4.** pertaining to experience of students in an educational program or experience.

clinical analysis, the use of laboratory data, including blood tests, urinalysis, and microscopic tissue studies, in determining a diagnosis and treatment regimen.

clinical assessment, an evaluation of a patient's physical condition and prognosis based on information gathered from physical and laboratory examinations and the patient's medical history.

clinical assistant, a person who follows standard operating procedures to collect and prepare specimens and who performs appropriate laboratory tests.

clinical crown, that portion of enamel visibly present in the oral cavity; the visible portion of the tooth that is occlusal to the deepest part of the gingival crevice.

clinical-crown/clinical-root ratio, the length of the part of a tooth that is coronal to the junctional epithelium divided by the length of the tooth's root that is apical to the junctional epithelium. The ratio is useful in the diagnosis and prognosis of periodontal disease.

clinical cytogenetics, the branch of genetics that studies the relationship between chromosomal aberrations and pathologic conditions.

clinical diagnosis, a diagnosis made on the basis of knowledge obtained by medical history and physical examination alone, without benefit of laboratory tests or x-ray films.

clinical disease, a stage in the history of a pathologic condition that begins with anatomic or physiologic changes that are sufficient to produce recognizable signs and symptoms of a disease.

clinical epidemiology, the application of the science of epidemiology in a clinical setting. Emphasis is on a medically defined population, as opposed to statistically formulated disease trends derived from examination of larger population categories.

clinical genetics, a branch of genetics that studies inherited disorders and investigates the possible factors that may influence the occurrence of pathologic conditions.

clinical horizon, the imaginary line above which detectable signs and symptoms of a disease first begin to appear.

clinical humidity therapy, respiratory therapy in which water vapor is added to the therapeutic gases to make breathing them more comfortable.

clinical judgment, the application of information based on actual observation of a patient combined with subjective and objective data that lead to a conclusion.

clinical laboratory, a laboratory in which tests directly related to the care of patients are performed.

clinical laboratory scientist/medical technologist (CLS/MT), an allied health professional who, in conjunction with pathologists or other physicians or medical scientists, performs specialized chemical, microscopic, and bacteriologic tests of blood, tissue, and fluids. Clinical laboratory scientists/medical technologists perform complex analyses, fine-line discrimination, and error correction. They have knowledge of physiologic conditions affecting test results so they can develop data that may be used by a physician in determining the presence, extent, and as far as possible, cause of a disease. They are held accountable for accurate results, establish and monitor quality assurance programs, and modify procedures as necessary. Preparation includes a baccalaureate degree and at least 1 year of professional/clinical education.

clinical laboratory technician/medical laboratory technician — associate degree, an allied health professional who, under the supervision of a pathologist or other physician, clinical laboratory scientist/medical technologist, or other medical scientist, performs specialized chemical, microscopic, and bacteriologic tests of blood, tissue, and fluids. The technician can demonstrate discrimination between similar items and correction of errors by the use of preset strategies, is able to recognize factors that directly affect procedures and results, and monitors quality assurance procedures. Preparation is usually 2 academic years, with the graduate receiving an associate's degree.

clinical laboratory technician/medical laboratory technician — certificate, an allied health professional who, under the supervision of a pathologist or other physician, clinical laboratory scientist/medical technologist, or other medical scientist, performs routine, uncomplicated laboratory tests of blood, tissue, and fluids. Clinical education is usually 12 months, with the graduate receiving a certificate. This certificate is no longer being offered for new students.

clinical medicine, a system of health maintenance based on direct observation of and communication with a patient.

clinical nurse specialist (CNS), an advanced practice registered nurse who holds a master's degree in nursing and who has acquired advanced knowledge and clinical skills in a specific area of nursing practice. Historically, CNS has included research involvement.

clinical-pathologic conference, a teaching conference in which a case is presented to a clinician, who then demonstrates the process of reasoning that leads to his or her diagnosis. A pathologist then presents an anatomic diagnosis, based on the study of tissue removed at surgery or obtained in autopsy. The pathologist's diagnosis is usually the definitive one.

clinical pathology, the laboratory study of disease by a pathologist using techniques appropriate to the specimen being studied.

clinical pathway, a description of practices likely to result in favorable outcomes for patients with a particular diagnosis that uses prospectively defined resources to minimize cost. It may be based on research, literature, or common practice.

clinical pearl, a short, straightforward piece of clinical advice.

clinical pelvimetry, a process used to assess the size of the birth canal by means of the systematic vaginal palpation of specific bony landmarks in the pelvis and an estimation of the distances between them. Findings are commonly recorded in terms such as adequate, borderline, or inadequate, rather than in centimeters or inches.

clinical practice guideline, systematically developed statements to assist practitioner and patient decisions about appropriate health care in specific clinical circumstances.

clinical psychology, the branch of psychology concerned with the diagnosis, treatment, and prevention of a wide range of personality and behavioral disorders.

clinical reasoning, higher-order thinking in which the health care provider, guided by best evidence or theory, observes and relates concepts and phenomena to develop an understanding of their significance.

clinical research center, an organization, often associated with a medical school or a teaching hospital, that studies, analyzes, correlates, and describes medical cases. Such centers usually have extensive laboratory facilities and specialized staffs of physicians and medical technicians.

clinical specialist, a physician or nurse who has advanced training in a particular field of practice.

clinical thermometer [Gk, *kline,* bed, *thermē,* heat, *metron,* measure], an electronic thermometer with disposable sheaths, designed for measuring body temperature.

clinical thermometry, a method for determining temperature in heated tissue.

clinical trial exemption (CTX), authorization to administer an investigational agent to patients or volunteer subjects under specified conditions of a particular research study in a clinical setting.

clinical trials, organized studies to provide large bodies of clinical data for statistically valid evaluation of treatment to determine safety and efficacy.

clinician /klinish′ən/, a health professional whose practice is based on direct observation and treatment of a patient, as distinguished from other types of health workers.

clinic without walls, a health care system formed by the merger of selected functions, such as administrative, billing and collections, purchasing, personnel, and payroll, of various physician groups, without the merger of any physical facilities.

Clinitest, a trademark for reagent tablets used to test for the presence of reducing sugars, such as glucose, in the urine. It is rarely used in current practice.

clinocephaly /klī′nōsef′əlē/ [Gk, *klinein,* to bend, *kephale,* head], a congenital anomaly of the head in which the upper surface of the skull is saddle shaped or concave.—**clinocephalic, clinocephalous,** *adj.*

clinodactyly /klī′nōdak′təlē/ [Gk, *klinein* + *daktylos,* finger], a congenital anomaly characterized by abnormal lateral or medial bending of one or more fingers or toes.—**clinodactylic, clinodactylous,** *adj.*

clinoid processes /klī′noid/ [Gk, *kline,* bed, *eidos,* form; L, *processus*], the anterior, middle, and posterior processes of the sphenoid bone at the base of the skull.

clinometer /klīnom′ətər/, an instrument used to measure angular convergence of the eyes or the degree of paralysis of extraocular muscles.

Clinoril, a trademark for an NSAID (sulindac).

clip [AS, *clyppan,* to embrace], a surgical device used for grasping the skin to align the edges of a wound and to stop bleeding, especially of the smaller blood vessels. It is also used in radiography for localization.

clitoridectomy /klit′əridek′təmē/, the excising of all or part of the clitoris, and sometimes part of the labia, a form of ritual mutilation performed on over 100 million girls and women in more than 40 countries. It is usually performed at 4 to 12 years of age, without anesthesia, with crude cutting tools, and with few or no precautions against infection. As of June 1996, the U.S. Board of Immigration Appeals recognized genital mutilation as a form of persecution and a basis for asylum for girls and women.

clitoridotomy, 1. an incision into the clitoris. **2.** removal or splitting of the clitoral hood, comparable to male circumcision, with associated risks of infection and scarring. It is done culturally by lay providers.

clitoris /klit′əris/ [Gk, *kleitoris*], the vaginal erectile structure of the female homologous to the corpora cavernosa of the penis. It consists of two corpora cavernosa within a dense layer of fibrous membrane, joined along their inner surfaces by an incomplete fibrous septum.—**clitoral,** *adj.*

clitoritis /klit′ōrī′tis/, inflammation of the clitoris.

clivus /klī′vəs/ [L, slope], an inclined surface, as on the sphenoid bone.

CLL, abbreviation for **chronic lymphocytic leukemia.**

cloaca /klō-ā′kə/ *pl.* **cloacae** [L, sewer], **1.** (in embryology) the end of the hindgut before the developmental division into the rectum, the bladder, and the primitive genital structures. **2.** (in pathology) an opening into the sheath of tissue around a necrotic bone.

cloacal fold, a slight elevation located just lateral to the cloacal membrane early in the fifth week of embryonic development, later dividing into urogenital folds and anal folds.

cloacal membrane /klō-ā′kəl/, a thin sheath that separates the internal and external parts of the cloaca in the developing embryo.

cloacal sphincter, the developing muscle surrounding the caudal end of the cloaca in the embryo. Its posterior part will become the external anal sphincter and its anterior part will become the superficial transverse perineal, bulbospongiosus, and ischiocavernosus muscles.

clobetasol   propionate /klōbet′əsol prō′pyōnāt/, a topical corticosteroid antiinflammatory prescribed for the short-term treatment of inflammation and pruritus associated with certain moderate to severe types of dermatitis.

clocortolone   pivalate /klōkôr′təlōn piv′əlāt/, a topical corticosteroid antiinflammatory prescribed for the short-term treatment of inflammation and pruritus associated with certain moderate to severe types of dermatitis.

clofibrate /klō′fəbrāt/, an antihyperlipidemic prescribed in the treatment of high blood levels triglycerides occurring alone or in combination with high cholesterol levels.

Clomid, a trademark for a nonsteroidal fertility drug (clomiPHENE citrate).

clomiPHENE citrate /klō′məfēn/, a nonsteroidal drug that acts to stimulate ovulation by interacting with estrogen receptors in the hypothalamus in a manner that leads to the release of pituitary gonadotropins. It is prescribed primarily for the treatment of anovulation and oligoovulation in women desiring pregnancy.

clomiPHENE stimulation test, a test used to evaluate gonadal function in males who show signs of abnormal pubertal development. ClomiPHENE, a nonsteroidal analog of estrogen, stimulates the hypothalamic-pituitary system to raise follicle-stimulating hormone and luteinizing hormone levels of the blood. Failure to respond to clomiPHENE indicates hypothalamic-pituitary disease, possibly a pituitary tumor.

clomiPRAMINE /klōmip′rämēn/, **1.** a tricyclic antidepressant of the dibenzazepine class, used in the form of the hydrochloride salt, also used as an antianxiety agent and

investigationally to relieve symptoms of obsessive-compulsive disorder. **2.** a tricyclic antidepressant with anxiolytic activity, also used in treatment of obsessive-compulsive disorder, panic disorder, bulimia nervosa, cataplexy associated with narcolepsy, and chronic, severe pain.

clonal /klō′nəl/, pertaining to a clone.

clonal marker, a defective or functionally unidentified DNA sequence in a clone of cancer cells. Such sequences are used to monitor the growth of cancer cells after chemical or other treatments.

clonazepam /klōnaz′əpam/, a benzodiazepine anticonvulsant prescribed in the treatment of absence seizures in patients unresponsive to succimides, of atonic and myolonic seizures, and of panic disorder.

clone [Gk, *klon*, a plant cutting], a group of genetically identical cells or organisms derived from a single common cell or organism through mitosis.—**clonal,** *adj.*

clonic /klon′ik/ [Gk, *klonos*, tumult], pertaining to increased reflex activity, as in upper motor neuron lesions when repetitive muscular contractions and relaxations in rapid succession are induced by stretching.

clonic convulsion [Gk, *klonos*, tumult; L, *convulsio*, cramp], a form of seizure characterized by rhythmic alternate involuntary contraction and relaxation of muscle groups.

clonicity /klōnis′itē/, a state of clonus.

clonic spasm [Gk, *klonos*, tumult, *spasmos*], involuntary alternating contractions and relaxations of muscles.

clonidine hydrochloride /klō′nədēn/, an alpha$_2$-agonist used as an antihypertensive. It stimulates alpha$_2$-adrenergic receptors in the brainstem to decrease sympathetic nervous system outflow. It is prescribed alone or in combination for the reduction of high BP and is an adjunct for the treatment of cancer pain when pain persists during intraspinal opiate treatments.

cloning /klō′ning/, a procedure for producing multiple copies of genetically identical organisms or cells or of individual genes. Organisms may be cloned by transplanting blastocysts from one embryo into an empty zona pellucida, or nuclei from the cells of one individual into enucleated oocytes. Cells may be cloned by growing them in culture under conditions that promote cell reproduction. Genes may be cloned by isolating them from the genome of one organism and incorporating them into the genome of an asexually reproducing organism, such as a bacterium or a yeast.

clonogenic cell /klō′nōjen′ik/, a cell that can proliferate into a colony of genetically identical cells.

clonorchiasis /klŏ′nôrkī′əsis/, an infestation of the Chinese liver fluke, *Clonorchis sinensis*.

Clonorchis sinensis /klōnôr′kis sinen′sis/, The Chinese or Oriental liver fluke, a trematode that is acquired by humans who eat raw, imperfectly cooked pickled, salted, or smoked fish that is the intermediate host of the parasite. In human hosts the liver fluke lives in the bile ducts and gallbladder, causing chronic liver disease with enlargement of the liver, diarrhea, edema, and, eventually, death. Cholangitis, cholelithiasis, pancreatitis, and cholangiosarcoma are common complications and may be fatal.

clonus (C) /klō′nəs/ [Gk, *klonos*, tumult], an abnormal pattern of neuromuscular activity, characterized by rapidly alternating involuntary contraction and relaxation of skeletal muscle.—**clonic,** *adj.*

C-loop, a surgically formed loop of bowel with a C-shape.

clopidogrel, a platelet aggregation inhibitor used to reduce the risk of stroke and MI in high-risk patients.

clor, abbreviation for a *chloride anion*.

clorazepate dipotassium /klôraz′əpāt dī′pətas′ē·əm/, a benzodiazepine antianxiety drug prescribed in the treatment of anxiety, nervous tension, and alcohol withdrawal.

closed amputation [L, *claudere*, to shut, *amputare*, to cut away], a kind of amputation in which one or two broad flaps of muscular and cutaneous tissue are retained to form a cover over the end of the bone. It is performed only when no infection is present.

closed bite [L, *claudere*; AS, *bitan*], an abnormal overbite; a decrease in the occlusal vertical dimension produced by various factors, such as tooth abrasion and insufficient eruption of supportive posterior teeth.

closed-cavity tympanomastoidectomy, tympanomastoidectomy with tympanoplasty and maintenance of an intact posterior wall of the ear canal.

closed-chain, (in organic chemistry) pertaining to a compound in which the carbon atoms are bonded to form a closed ring.

closed-chain exercise, exercise in which the distal aspect of the extremity is in contact with a support surface such as the floor or a balance board.

closed-circuit breathing, rebreathing of a contained gas mixture, either directly or after recirculation of the gas through a water-absorbing or carbon dioxide–absorbing unit.

closed-circuit helium dilution, a technique for measuring residual lung volume

and functional residual capacity in which a patient breathes through a spirometer containing a known concentration of helium.

closed dislocation [L, *claudere,* to shut, *dis,* apart, *locare,* to place], a joint dislocation not accompanied by a break in the skin.

closed fracture [L, *claudere,* to shut, *fractura*], an uncomplicated fracture in which the bone does not break the skin.

closed group, (in psychotherapy) a group in which all members are admitted at the same time and vacancies that occur in the membership are not filled.

closed loop, a biologic feedback system in which a substance produced in the body affects the mechanism that causes its own production.

closed-panel HMO, (in the United States) a health maintenance organization (HMO) in which physicians are either employees of the HMO or belong to a group of physicians that contracts with it.

closed physician-hospital organization (PHO), (in the United States) an organization of selected physicians on a hospital medical staff who have proved to be high-quality, cost-effective practitioners.

closed reduction of fractures [L, *claudere,* to shut, *reducere,* to lead back, *fractura*], the manual correction of fractures without incision.

closed system, a system that does not interact with its environment.

closed-system helium dilution method, a technique for measuring functional residual capacity and residual volume.

closed-wound suction, any one of several techniques for draining potentially harmful fluids, such as blood, pus, serosanguineous fluid, and tissue secretions, from surgical wounds. Such fluids interfere with wound healing and often promote infection. Closed-wound suction may be accomplished with a variety of reliable devices that create a gentle negative pressure to drain away undesirable exudates. It is generally used whenever the wound drainage is greater than 100 mL in 24 hours. Closed-wound suction devices usually consist of disposable transparent containers attached to suction tubes and portable suction pumps.

closing capacity (CC), a measure of lung volume equal to the sum of closing volume and residual volume.

closing volume (CV), the volume of gas remaining in the lungs when the small airways begin to close during a controlled maximum exhalation.

clostridial /klostrid′ē·əl/ [Gk, *kloster*, spindle], pertaining to anaerobic spore-forming bacteria of the genus *Clostridium*.

clostridial toxin assay, a stool test to diagnose *Clostridium difficile* bacterial infection of the intestine.

Clostridium /-ē·əm/ [Gk, *kloster,* spindle], a genus of spore-forming anaerobic bacteria of the Bacillaceae family: *Clostridium novyi, C. septicum,* and *C. bifermentans* are involved in gas gangrene; *C. botulinum* causes botulism and produces the toxin Botox used in some cosmetic procedures; *C. perfringens* causes food poisoning, cellulitis, and wound infections; *C. tetani* is the cause of tetanus.

Clostridium botulinum [Gk, *kloster,* spindle], a species of anaerobic bacteria that causes botulism in humans and botulism-like diseases in other animals. Botulinum food poisoning results from ingesting food containing preformed toxins produced by the species. It is a proteolytic pathogen commonly present in soil, where its endospores can survive for years. Their resistance to heat makes them an important source of poisoning in improperly cooked or canned foods.

Clostridium difficile /difis'ilē/, a pathogenic species of anaerobic bacteria that cause pseudomembranous colitis and diarrhea, particularly after the patient has received antibiotic therapy, and that are a frequent cause of nosocomial diarrhea.

Clostridium perfringens [Gk, *kloster,* spindle], a species of anaerobic gram-positive bacteria capable of causing gas gangrene and food poisoning in humans and various digestive and urinary tract diseases in livestock.

closure /klō'zhər/ [L, *claudere,* to shut], **1.** the surgical closing of a wound by suture or staple. **2.** a visual phenomenon in which the mind sees an entire figure when only a portion is actually visible. **3.** the ending of something, as in closure of the grieving process.

closylate /klos'ilāt/, a contraction for *p-chlorobenzene sulfonate.*

clot retraction, the shrinking of a semisolid mass formed by the coagulation of blood, lymph, or other fluid. A normal standing blood clot is completely retracted in about 24 hours, although the time depends on such factors as the number of platelets in the clot.

clot retraction test, a blood test used to evaluate bleeding disorders such as thrombocytopenia and Glanzmann's thrombasthenia. It measures the time required for blood in a test tube to form a clot and for the clot's edges to retract from the sides of the glass tube.

clotrimazole /klōtrim'əzōl/, a broad-spectrum antifungal agent of the imidazole group used in topical applications to treat fungal and yeast infections. Oral troches

are used for prophylaxis against fungal infections in neutropenic patients.

clotting time [AS, *clott*], the time required for blood to form a clot, tested by collecting 4 mL of blood in a glass tube and examining it for clot formation.

cloud baby [AS, *clud* + *babe*], a newborn who appears well and healthy but is a carrier of infectious bacterial or viral organisms. The infant may contaminate the surrounding environment as airborne droplets from the respiratory tract form clouds of the organisms.

clouding of consciousness, a mental state in which a patient is confused about or is not fully aware of the immediate surroundings.

clove /klōv/ [L, *clavus,* nail], the dried flower bud of *Eugenia caryophyllata.* It contains the lactone caryophyllin and a volatile oil used as a dental analgesic, a germicide, and a salve.

clove-hitch sling, a bandage that begins with a clove-hitch knot at the center. The loop made is fitted to the hand. The two loose ends are extended over and behind the shoulders and tied beside the neck.

cloverleaf nail /klō'vərlēf'/ [AS, *clafre* + *leaf* + *nagel*], a surgical nail shaped in cross section like a cloverleaf, used especially in the repair of fractures of the femur.

cloverleaf skull deformity, a congenital defect characterized by a trilobed skull resulting from the premature closure of multiple cranial sutures during embryonic development.

cloxacillin sodium /klok'səsil'in/, a penicillinase-resistant penicillin prescribed in the treatment of serious bacterial infections, primarily those caused by penicillase-producing strains of staphylococci.

CLS/MT, abbreviation for **clinical laboratory scientist/medical technologist.**

CLT/MLT, abbreviation for **clinical laboratory technician/medical laboratory technician.**

clubbed penis [ME, *clubbe*; L, *penis*], a penis that is curved or twisted or both.

clubbing [ME, *clubbe*], an abnormal enlargement of the distal phalanges with a flattening of the curvature of the nail margin at the cuticle. It usually is associated with cyanotic heart disease or advanced chronic pulmonary disease but sometimes occurs with biliary cirrhosis, colitis, chronic dysentery, thyrotoxicosis, and sickle cell anemia. Clubbing occurs in all the digits but is most easily seen in the fingers.

clubfoot [ME, *clubbe*; AS, *fot*], a congenital deformity of the foot, sometimes resulting from intrauterine constriction and characterized by unilateral or bilateral deviation of the metatarsal bones of the forefoot. Ninety-five percent of clubfoot deformities are equinovarus, characterized by medial deviation and plantar flexion of the forefoot, but a few are calcaneovalgus, or calcaneovarus, characterized by lateral deviation and dorsiflexion either outward from or inward toward the midline of the body.

club hair, a hair in the resting or final stage of the growth cycle.

cluster analysis [AS, *clyster,* growing together; Gk, *analyein,* to loosen], (in statistics) a complex technique of data analysis of numeric scale scores that produces clusters of variables related to one another. The technique is performed with computer software or statistics programs.

cluster breathing, a breathing pattern in which a closely grouped series of respirations is followed by apnea. The activity is associated with a lesion in the lower pontine region of the brainstem.

cluster headache, a condition characterized by attacks of intense unilateral pain, occurring most often over the eye and forehead. It is accompanied by flushing and watering of the eyes and nose. The attacks occur in groups with a duration of several hours.

clusterin /klus'terin/, a multifunctional glycoprotein with roles in the metabolism and transport of lipids and membrane fragments, secretion of hormones, reproductive biology, inhibition of assembly of the membrane attack complex of complement activation, programmed cell death, and modulation of intercell interactions. Its expression is enhanced in tissue injury and remodeling, and in degenerative diseases such as Alzheimer's disease.

cluster-of-differentiation (CD) antigen, one of a group of cell-surface molecules that are used to classify leukocytes into subsets.

cluttering [ME, *clotter*], a speech disorder characterized by a rapid delivery with uneven rhythmic patterns and omission or transposition of various speech sounds or syllables. The condition is commonly associated with other learning disabilities.

clysis /klī'sis/ [Gk, *klyster,* washout], the nonoral insertion or injection of a fluid into tissue spaces, such as the administration of an enema.

cm, abbreviation for **centimeter.**

Cm, symbol for the element **curium.**

cm², abbreviation for **square centimeter.**

cm³, abbreviation for **cubic centimeter.**

CMA, abbreviation for *Canadian Medical Association.*

CMAJ, abbreviation for **Canadian Medical Association Journal.**

CMC, abbreviation for **carpometacarpal.**

CMF, an anticancer drug combination of cyclophosphamide, methotrexate, and fluorouracil.

CMHC, abbreviation for **community mental health center.**

CML, abbreviation for **chronic myelogenous leukemia.**

cmm, abbreviation for **cubic millimeter.**

CMRNG, abbreviation for *chromosomally mediated resistant Neisseria gonorrhoeae.*

CMS, abbreviation for *Centers for Medicare & Medicaid Services,* an agency of the U.S. Department of Health and Human Services.

CMT, abbreviation for *certified medical transcriptionist.*

CMV, abbreviation for **cytomegalovirus.**

CN, abbreviation for **chloroacetophenone.**

CNA, 1. abbreviation for **Canadian Nurses Association.** 2. abbreviation for **certified nurse administrator.** 3. abbreviation for *certified nursing assistant.*

CNAA, abbreviation for *certified nurse administrator, advanced.*

CNATS, abbreviation for **Canadian Nurses Association Testing Service.**

-cnemia.

CNF, abbreviation for **Canadian Nurses Foundation.**

CNHV, abbreviation for **central neurogenic hyperventilation.**

Cnidaria, a phylum of invertebrate animals that includes jellyfish, sea anemones, hydroids, and corals.

CNM, abbreviation for **certified nurse-midwife.**

CNNT, abbreviation for *Council of Nephrology Nurses and Technicians.*

CNOR, abbreviation for *certified nurse, operating room.*

CNP, 1. abbreviation for **community nurse practitioner.** 2. abbreviation for *certified nurse practitioner.*

CNRN, abbreviation for *certified neuroscience registered nurse.*

CNRS, abbreviation for **Canadian Nurses Respiratory Society.**

CNS, 1. abbreviation for **central nervous system.** 2. abbreviation for **clinical nurse specialist.**

CNSN, abbreviation for *certified nutrition support nurse.*

CNS sympathomimetic, a drug, such as cocaine or an amphetamine, whose effects mimic those of sympathomimetic nervous system stimulation.

Co, symbol for the element **cobalt.**

CO, 1. formula for **carbon monoxide.** 2. abbreviation for **cardiac output.**

CO₂, formula for **carbon dioxide.**

CoA, abbreviation for **coenzyme A.**

coagglutination /kō′əglōō′tənā′shən/ [L, *cum + agglutinare,* to glue], a clumping of RBCs by mixtures of protein antigens and their antisera.

coagulability /kō·ag′yələbil′itē/ [L, *coagulare,* to curdle], the state of being able to coagulate or form blood clots.

coagulant /kō·ag′yələnt/ [L, *coagulare,* to curdle], an agent that causes a coagulum, or blood clot, to form.

coagulase /kō·ag′yəlās/ [L, *coagulare,* to curdle], an enzyme produced by bacteria, particularly *Staphylococcus aureus,* that promotes the formation of fibrin from fibrinogen to form thrombi.

coagulate /kō·ag′yəlāt/, to undergo or cause to undergo the chemical process whereby a fluid becomes curdled or clotted.

coagulated /kō·ag′yəlā′ted/, curdled; changed to a clotted state.

coagulation /kō·ag′yəlā′shən/ [L, *coagulare,* to curdle], 1. the process of transforming a liquid into a solid, especially of the blood. 2. (in clinical chemistry) the transforming of the liquid dispersion medium into a gelatinous mass. 3. the hardening of tissue by some physical means, as by electrocoagulation or photocoagulation.—**coagulable,** *adj.*

coagulation cascade, the series of steps beginning with activation of the intrinsic or extrinsic pathways of coagulation and proceeding through the common pathway of coagulation to the formation of the fibrin clot. Each step involves activation of a proenzyme (zymogen), the activated form catalyzing activation of the following step.

coagulation current, an electric current delivered by a needle ball or variously shaped points to bind tissues together.

coagulation factor, one of 13 factors in the blood, the interactions of which are responsible for the process of blood clotting.

coagulation factor IX (human), a purified, sterile, dried concentrate of factor IX derived from pooled human plasma, used in the prophylaxis and treatment of bleeding in patients with hemophilia B.

coagulation factor IX (recombinant), a sterile, dried concentrate of factor IX prepared by recombinant means, used in the prophylaxis and treatment of bleeding in patients with hemophilia B.

coagulation factors concentration test, a set of blood tests used to measure the quantity of a number of specific factors suspected to be responsible for suspected defects in hemostasis, and to help the clinician determine the appropriate treatment.

coagulation factor VIIa, recombinant, an antihemophilic prescribed to prevent the bleeding associated with hemophilia A or B when inhibitors to factor VIII or IX are present.

coagulation necrosis, necrosis in which tissue becomes a dry, opaque, eosinophilic mass containing outlines of anucleated cells. It results from the denaturation of proteins after hypoxic injury such as that caused by ischemia in infarction.

coagulative /kō·ag′yəlā′tiv/, 1. causing blood clot formation. 2. an agent that assists in the formation of blood clots.

coagulopathy /kō·ag′yəlop′əthē/, a pathologic condition that reduces the ability of the blood to coagulate, resulting in uncontrolled bleeding.

coalesce /kō′əles′/ [L, *coalescere,* to grow together], 1. to grow together. 2. to unite.

coal tar, a topical drug for treating eczema. It is prescribed in the treatment of chronic skin conditions, such as dandruff, seborrheal dermatitis, and psoriasis.

coal tar creosote, creosote obtained by high temperature carbonization of bituminous coal. It is a brown-to-black, oily liquid, a mixture of aromatic hydrocarbons, tar acids, and tar bases, mainly used as a wood preservative. It is toxic to humans and other animals by contact, ingestion, or inhalation, and coal tar is a human carcinogen.

Coanda effect, a phenomenon of fluid movement similar to the Bernoulli effect, in which passage of a stream of gas next to a wall results in a pocket of turbulence between the wall and the gas flow. The turbulence forms a low-pressure bubble that makes the gas stream adhere to the wall. The principle is used in fluidic ventilators.

coaptation splint /kō′aptā′shən/ [L, *coaptare,* to fit together; ME *splinte*], a small splint fitted to a fractured limb to prevent overriding of the fragments of bone during adjustment of the fracture.

coarct /kō·ärkt′/ [L, *coarctare,* to press together], the act of narrowing or constricting, especially the lumen of a blood vessel.

coarctate retina /kō·ärk′tāt/ [L, *coarctare,* to press together, *rete,* net], a funnel-shaped retina caused by a leakage of fluid between the retina and the choroid.

coarctation /kō′ärktā′shən/, a compression, shriveling, or stricture of the walls of a vessel, such as the aorta.

coarctation of the aorta, a congenital cardiac anomaly characterized by a localized narrowing of the aorta. It results in increased pressure proximal to the defect and decreased pressure distal to it.

coarse /kôrs/ [ME, *cors,* common], (in physiology) involving a wide range of movements, such as those associated with tremors and other involuntary motions of the skeletal muscle.

coarse crackle [ME, *cors,* common, *krakelen*], an abnormal breathing sound inspiratory caused by air moving through an excessive amount of fluid in an airway, as in pulmonary edema.

coarse fremitus, a rough, loud, tremulous vibration of the chest wall noted on palpation of the chest during a physical examination as the person inhales and exhales.

coarse tremor [ME, *cors,* common; L, *tremor,* shaking], a tremor in which the movements are relatively slow and may involve larger muscle groups.

coat [ME, *cote*], **1.** a membrane that covers the outside of an organ or part. **2.** one of the layers of a wall of an organ or part, especially a canal or vessel.

coated tablet [ME, *cote*; Fr, *tablette*], a solid disc of one or more pharmaceutical agents that is (1) coated with sugar or a flavoring to mask the taste or (2) entericcoated, meaning that it is coated with a substance that resists dissolution in the stomach but allows release of the medication in the intestine.

coated tongue [ME, *cote*; AS, *tunge*], a tongue with a white, yellow, or brown furred surface, representing a possible accumulation of mycelia, bacteria, food debris, or desquamated epithelial cells.

cobalamin /kōbôl′əmin/ [Ger, *kobold,* mine goblin], a generic term for a chemical portion of the vitamin B_{12} molecule.

cobalt (Co) /kō′bôlt/ [Ger, *kobold,* mine goblin], a metallic element that occurs in the minerals cobaltite, smaltite, and linnaeite. Its atomic number is 27; its atomic mass is 58.93. Cobalt is a component of vitamin B_{12}, is found in most common foods, and is readily absorbed by the GI tract. Some amounts of cobalt stimulate the production of erythropoietin, but large doses depress erythrocyte production.

cobalt-60 (^{60}Co), a radioactive isotope of the element cobalt with a mass of 60 and a half-life of 5.2 years. ^{60}Co emits highenergy gamma rays and is the most frequently used radioisotope in radiotherapy.

cobalt poisoning, poisoning from longterm excessive exposure to cobalt, seen in those who work with it. Symptoms include nausea, vomiting, tinnitus, nerve deafness, and cardiomyopathy.

Coban, a trademark for an elastic pressure wrap applied to reduce edema. It adheres to itself and may be used as a secondary dressing for patients allergic to tape.

Cobb collar, congenital stenosis of the bulbar urethra.

cobra /kō′brä/, any of numerous extremely poisonous elapid snakes commonly found in Africa, Asia, and India. They are capable of expanding the neck region to form a hood and have two comparatively short, erect, deep grooved fangs. A serum obtained from animals inoculated with cobra venom is used in counteracting the effects of the venom.

COBRA /kō′brə/, abbreviation for **Consolidated Omnibus Reconciliation Act.**

Cobra head deformity, the appearance of a ureterocele in excretory urography, with the distal ureter slightly dilated and projecting into the bladder and an area of lesser density visible around it.

cobra venom solution [L, *colubra,* snake, *venenum,* venom, *solutus,* dissolved], a sterile physiologic salt solution containing minute amounts of cobralysin, the hemolytic substance in cobra venom.

coca, a species of South American shrubs. It is a natural source of cocaine.

cocaine baby /kōkān′/, an infant with birth defects caused by exposure to cocaine in utero.

cocaine hydrochloride, a white crystalline powder used as a local anesthetic. It was originally derived from coca leaves but can also be prepared synthetically. Cocaine is a Schedule I drug under the Controlled Substances Act of 1970. In solution, the drug is sometimes used as a topical anesthetic applied to mucous membranes.

cocaine hydrochloride poisoning [Sp, *coca*; L, *potio,* drink], toxic effects of exposure to the colorless crystalline alkaloid derived from coca leaves. Although used as a local analgesic for a century, cocaine is highly toxic, with moderate vasoconstrictor activity and serious psychotropic effects. Symptoms include nervous excitement, restlessness, incoherent speech, fever, hypertension, stroke, and cardiac arrhythmias, leading to convulsions, collapse, respiratory arrest, and death. The euphoric effect of cocaine lasts about 30 minutes.

cocarcinogen /kōkär′sənəjən/ [L, *cum,* together with; Gk, *karkinos,* crab, *genein,* to produce], an agent that alone does not transform a normal cell into a cancerous state but in concert with another agent can effect the transformation.

Coccidia, a subclass of parasitic protozoa found in humans, other vertebrates, and some invertebrates.

coccidian, **1.** pertaining to Coccidia. **2.** a protozoan in the subclass Coccidia.

Coccidioides /kok·sid′ē·oi′dēz/, a pathogenic dimorphic genus of Fungi Imperfecti of the form-class Euascomycetes, form-family Onygenaceae. In soil, it grows as a mycelium with infectious units called arthrospores; in tissue as a spherule with endospores.

coccidioidomycosis /koksid´ē·oi´dōmīkō´sis/ [Gk, *kokkos,* berry, *eidos,* form, *mykes,* fungus, *osis,* condition], an infectious fungal disease caused by the inhalation of spores of the protozoan *Coccidioides immitis* or *C. posadasii,* which is carried on wind-borne dust particles. The disease is endemic in hot, dry regions of the southwestern United States and Central and South America and is an opportunistic disease associated with HIV infection and leukemia. Primary infection is characterized by symptoms resembling those of the common cold or pulmonary infection. Secondary infection, occurring after a period of remission and lasting from weeks to years, is marked by low-grade fever, anorexia and weight loss, cyanosis, dyspnea, hemoptysis, focal skin lesions resembling erythema nodosum, and arthritic pain in the bones and joints.

coccidiosis /kok´sidē·ō´sis/ [Gk, *kokkos* + *osis,* condition], a parasitic disease of tropical and subtropical regions caused by the ingestion of oocysts of the protozoan *Isospora belli* or *I. hominis.* Symptoms include fever, malaise, abdominal discomfort, and watery diarrhea.

coccoid /kok´oid/ [Gk, *kokkos,* berry, *eidos,* form], having a spherical shape; resembling a micrococcus.

coccus /kok´əs/ *pl.* **cocci** [Gk, *kokkos,* berry], a bacterium that is round, spheric, or oval, such as streptococcus. —**coccal,** *adj.*

coccyalgia /kok´si·al´jə/, a pain in or near the coccyx.

coccygeal vertebra, one of the four segments of the vertebral column that fuse to form the adult coccyx. They are considered rudimentary vertebrae and have no pedicles, laminae, or spinous processes.

coccygeus /koksij´ē·əs/ [Gk, *kokkyx,* cuckoo's beak], one of two muscles in the pelvic diaphragm. Stretching across the pelvic cavity like a hammock, it is a triangular sheet of muscle and tendinous fibers. It acts to draw the coccyx ventrally, helping to support the pelvic floor.

coccygodynia /kok´sigōdin´ē·ə/, a pain in the coccygeal area.

coccyx /kok´siks/ *pl.* **coccyges** [Gk, *kokkyx,* cuckoo's beak], the beaklike bone joined to the sacrum by a disk of fibrocartilage at the base of the vertebral column. It is formed by the union of three to five probably vestigial rudimentary vertebrae. —**coccygeal** /koksij´ē·əl/, *adj.*

cochineal /koch´inēl´/ [L, *coccineus,* bright red], a red dye prepared from the dried female insects and young larvae of the species *Dactylopius coccus cacti*

cochlea /kok´lē·ə/ [L, snail shell], the auditory portion of the inner ear. It is a spiral tunnel about 30 mm long with two full and three quarter-turns, resembling a tiny snail shell and containing the sense organ for hearing. —**cochlear,** *adj.*

cochlear canal /kok´lē·ər/ [L *cochlea* + *canalis* channel], a bony spiral tunnel within the cochlea of the internal ear. It contains one opening that communicates with the tympanic cavity, a second that connects with the vestibule, and a third that leads to a tiny canal opening on the inferior surface of the temporal bone.

cochlear hearing loss, sensorineural hearing loss resulting from a defect in the receptor or transducing mechanisms of the cochlea.

cochlear implant, an electronic device that is surgically implanted into the cochlea of a deaf individual. The patient receives electrical pulses that are translated into sound vibrations that can be distinguished as neural sensations. Although the implant does not transmit speech as clearly as it would be perceived by a person with normal hearing, it allows the individual to perceive and distinguish sounds that would not otherwise be audible to him or her and to use those sounds along with other environmental cues to improve communication.

cochlear nerve [L, *cochlea,* snail shell, *nervus,* nerve], one of the main divisions of the eighth cranial nerve, with fibers that arise in spiral ganglion cells of the spiral organ and terminate in the dorsal and ventral cochlear nuclei of the brainstem.

cochlear toxicity, poisonous effects of drugs that may result in hearing disorders, such as sensorineural hearing loss and tinnitus.

cochleovestibular /kok´lē·ō´vestib´yələr/, pertaining to the cochlea and vestibule of the ear.

Cockayne's syndrome /kok·ānz´/ [Edward Alfred Cockayne, English physician, 1880–1956], an autosomal-recessive syndrome of dwarfism with retinal atrophy and deafness, associated with progeria, prognathism, mental retardation, and photosensitivity.

cockroach, the common name of members of the Blattidae family of insects that infest homes, workplaces, and other areas inhabited by humans. Cockroaches transmit a number of disease agents, including bacteria, protozoa, and eggs of parasitic worms.

cockscomb papilloma /kok'skōm/ [AS, *cocc* + *camb*; L, *papilla*, nipple; Gk, *oma*, tumor], a benign small red lesion that may project from the uterine cervix during pregnancy; it regresses after delivery.

cocktail [AS, *cocc* + *toegel*], an unofficial mixture of drugs, usually in solution, combined to achieve a specific purpose. This term is frequently used in combining medications to treat patients who are HIV positive.

cockup splint, a splint used to immobilize the wrist and leave the fingers free.

coconsciousness /kōkon'shəsnəs/, (in psychiatry) conscious states of which the patient is not aware because they are not in the focus of attention but on the fringe of the content of consciousness.

cocontraction /kō'kəntrak'shən/, the simultaneous contraction of agonist and antagonist muscles around a joint.

COD, abbreviation for *cause of death*.

code [L, *caudex*, book], **1.** (in law) a published body of statutes, such as a civil code. **2.** a collection of standards and rules of behavior, such as a dress code. **3.** a symbolic means of representing information for communication or transfer, such as a genetic code. **4.** a system of notation that allows information to be transmitted rapidly, such as Morse code, or in secrecy, such as a cryptographic code. **5.** informal. a discreet signal used to summon a special team to resuscitate a patient, as in "Code zero, 3 west" announced over a public address system to summon the team to the west wing of the third floor without alarming patients or visitors. "To code" means to cease respirations and/or heart function.

Code for Nurses, a set of guidelines for carrying out nursing responsibilities adopted by the American Nurses Association in 1985. In 1994, the American Nurses Association determined that these guidelines were non negotiable and determined that each nurse had an obligation to adhere to the Code, and in 2001 a completely revised version of the Code of Ethics for Nurses was accepted by the ANA.

codeine phosphate, an opioid analgesic and antitussive prescribed to suppress cough and to relieve mild to moderate pain.

codeine sulfate, a water-soluble salt of monomethylmorphine, an alkaloid derived from opium. It is used as a mild hypnotic, an analgesic, and a cough reflex suppressant.

code management, a nursing intervention from the Nursing Interventions Classification (NIC) defined as coordination of emergency measures to sustain life.

code of ethics, a statement encompassing the set of rules based on values, and standards of conduct to which practitioners of a profession are expected to conform.

codependent, a state of close association with a person who is dependent on or addicted to a potentially destructive behavior, such as substance abuse, gambling, or smoking. The codependent person facilitates the behavior of the dependent one.

code team, a specially trained and equipped team of physicians, nurses, and technicians that is available to provide ACLS when summoned by an emergency code set by the institution.

coding [L, *caudex*, book], the process of organizing information into categories, which are assigned codes for the purposes of sorting, storing, and retrieving the data.

cod-liver oil, a pale-yellow fatty oil extracted from the fresh livers of the cod. It is a rich source of fat-soluble vitamins A and D, useful in the treatment of nutritional deficiency of those vitamins.

Codman's exercise [Ernest A. Codman, American surgeon, 1869–1940; L, *exercere*, to keep at work], mild exercises for restoring ROM and function in the arms or shoulders after injury and immobilization of the limbs.

codominance /kōdom'ənənts/ [L, *cum*, together with, *dominare*, to rule], the equal degree of dominance of two alleles or traits fully expressed in a phenotype, as when a person inherits both the I^A and I^B genes of the ABO blood group and has type AB blood.—**codominant,** *adj.*

codominant inheritance, the transmission of a trait or condition in which both alleles of a pair are given full expression in a heterozygote, as in the alleles for the AB or MNS blood group antigens and the leukocyte antigens.

codon /kō'don/, a unit of three adjacent nucleotides along a DNA or messenger RNA molecule that designates a specific amino acid to be incorporated into a polypeptide.

coefficient /kō'efish'ənt/ [L, *cum*, together with, *efficere*, to effect], a mathematic relationship between factors that can be used to measure or evaluate a characteristic under specified conditions.

coelenteron /sēlen'təron/ *pl.* **coelentera** [Gk, *koilos*, hollow, *enteron*, intestine], the digestive cavity of animals in the phylum Cnidaria, such as the hydra and the jellyfish.

coelom /sē'ləm/ [Gk, *koilos*, hollow], the body cavity of the developing embryo.—**celomic, coelomic,** *adj.*

coelosomy /sē'ləsō'mē/ [Gk, *koilos* + *soma*, body], a congenital anomaly characterized by protrusion of the viscera from the body cavity.

coenzyme /kō·en′zīm/ [L, *cum,* together with, *en,* in, *zyme,* ferment], a nonprotein substance that combines with an apoenzyme to form a complete enzyme or holoenzyme. Coenzymes include some of the vitamins, such as B_1 and B_2, and have smaller molecules than enzymes.

coenzyme A (CoA) [L, *cum + en,* into, *zyme,* ferment], an important metabolite in the citric acid cycle. Although not a true enzyme, it plays a significant role in the transfer of acetyl groups and the metabolism of acids and amino acids.

coenzyme Q, any of several quinines that function as electron-carrying coenzymes.

coffee [Ar, *qahwah*], the dried and roasted ripe seeds of *Coffea arabica, C. liberica,* and *C. robusta* trees. Coffee contains the alkaloid caffeine and is the basis for a stimulating drink that has been used in treating the common headache, chronic asthma, and narcotic poisoning.

coffee-ground vomitus, dark brown vomitus the color and consistency of coffee grounds, composed of gastric juices and old blood and indicative of slow upper GI bleeding.

Coffin-Lowry syndrome /kof′in lou′rē/ [Grange S. Coffin, American pediatrician, b. 1923; R. Brian Lowry, Irish-born Canadian physician, twentieth century], a condition with onset in the postnatal period characterized by incapability of speech; severe mental deficiency; and muscle, ligament, and skeletal abnormalities. It is transmitted with X-linked intermediate inheritance.

Coffin-Siris syndrome /kof′in sir′is/ [G.S. Coffin; Evelyn Siris, American radiologist, 1914–1987], hypoplasia or absence of the fifth fingers and toenails associated with growth and mental deficiencies; coarse facies; mild microcephaly; hypotonia; lax joints; mild hirsutism; and occasionally cardiac, vertebral, or GI anomalies.

Cogan's oculomotor apraxia /ko′gənz/ [David Glendenning Cogan, American ophthalmologist, 1908–1993], an absence or defect of horizontal eye movements, so that when the patient tries to look at an object off to one side, the head must turn to bring the eyes into line with the object and the eyes exhibit nystagmus. The cause is probably a brain lesion.

Cogentin, a trademark for an antiparkinson drug (benztropine mesylate).

Cognex, a trademark for a cognition enhancer and analeptic (tacrine). It is a reversible cholinesterase inhibitor and may have a role in early Alzheimer's disease to improve some cognitive functions. It does not affect the prognosis of the disease.

cognition[1] /kognish′ən/ [L, *cognoscere,* to know], the mental process characterized by knowing, thinking, learning, understanding, and judging.—**cognitive,** *adj.*

cognition[2], a nursing outcome from the Nursing Outcomes Classification (NOC) defined as the ability to execute complex mental processes.

cognitive /kog′nitiv/, pertaining to the mental processes of comprehension, judgment, memory, and reasoning, as contrasted with emotional and volitional processes.

cognitive development, the developmental process by which an infant becomes an intelligent person, acquiring knowledge with growth and improving his or her ability to think, learn, reason, and abstract.

cognitive dissonance [L, *cognoscere,* to know, *dis,* opposite of, *sonare,* to sound], a state of tension resulting from a discrepancy in a person's emotional and intellectual frame of reference for interpreting and coping with his or her environment.

cognitive distortion, errors in thinking that continue even when there is obvious contradictory evidence.

cognitive function, an intellectual process by which one becomes aware of, perceives, or comprehends ideas.

cognitive learning, 1. learning that is concerned with acquisition of problem-solving abilities and with intelligence and conscious thought. **2.** a theory that defines learning as a behavioral change based on the acquisition of information about the environment.

cognitive orientation, a nursing outcome from the Nursing Outcomes Classification (NOC) defined as the ability to identify person, place, and time accurately.

cognitive psychology, the study of the development of thought, language, and intelligence in humans.

cognitive restoration, an intervention technique designed to restore cognitive functioning.

cognitive restructuring[1], a change in attitudes, values, or beliefs that alters a person's self-expression; it occurs as a result of insight or behavioral achievement.

cognitive restructuring[2], a nursing intervention from the Nursing Interventions Classification (NIC) defined as challenging a patient to alter distorted thought patterns and view self and the world more realistically.

cognitive stimulation, a nursing intervention from the Nursing Interventions Classification (NIC) defined as promotion of awareness and comprehension of surroundings by utilization of planned stimuli.

cognitive structuring, the process of reviewing with a patient the changes that have occurred in his or her thinking in order to instill a sense of those changes, and of his or her role in bringing about those changes.

cognitive therapy, any of the various methods of treating mental and emotional disorders that help a person change attitudes, perceptions, and patterns of thinking.

cogwheel respiration, a breathing pattern characterized by a repeated series of brief interruptions of inhalation and exhalation.

cogwheel rigidity [ME, *cugge*, tooth on a gear; AS, *hweol*; L, *rigiditas*, unbending], an abnormal rigor in muscle tissue, characterized by jerky movements when the muscle is passively stretched. The condition is often found in cases of Parkinson's disease.

cohabitate /kōhab′itāt/, to live together in a relationship when not married.

Cohen technique, a type of ureteroneocystostomy in which the ureter is excised from its attachment to the bladder and reimplanted in a new submucosal tunnel that is directed laterally across the trigone (transtrigonal) toward the contralateral side.

cohere /kōhir′/ [L, *cohaerere*, to cling together], to stick together, as similar molecules of a common substance.

coherence /kōhir′əns/, 1. the property of sticking together. 2. (in psychology) the logical pattern of expression and thought evident in the speech of a normal, stable individual.—**coherent,** *adj.*

cohesive bandage /kōhē′siv/, a dressing material that will adhere to itself but not to other surfaces.

cohesiveness /kōhē′sivnəs/ [L, *cohaerere*, to cling together], 1. (in psychiatry) a force that attracts members to a group and causes them to remain in it. 2. (in dentistry) a property of annealed pure gold that allows it to fuse together under pressure and to closely adapt to the walls of a tooth preparation.

cohesive terminus, a single-stranded end projecting from a double-stranded DNA segment that can be joined by molecular genetics techniques to an introduced DNA fragment.

COHN, abbreviation for *certified occupational health nurse.*

cohort /kō′hôrt/ [L, *cohors* large group], (in statistics) a collection or sampling of individuals who share a common characteristic, such as members of the same age or sex.

cohort study, (in research) a study concerning a specific subpopulation, such as the children born between December and May in 1975.

coiled tubular gland [L, *colligere*, to gather together, *tubulus*, small tube, *glans*, acorn], one of the many multicellular glands that contain a coiled, tube-shaped secretory portion, such as the sweat glands.

coil spring contraceptive diaphragm, a kind of contraceptive diaphragm in which the flexible metal ring that forms the rim is a coiled, circular spring.

coincidence counting /kō·in′sidəns/ [L, *coincidere*, to occur together], the detection of two photons that arrive at separate counters simultaneously as the result of annihilation of a positron (created during a radioactive decay) and an electron. Coincidence counting greatly reduces the significance of any background radiation in radiography.

coinfection /kōō′infek′shun/, simultaneous infection by separate pathogens, as by hepatitis B and hepatitis D viruses.

coital headache /kō′itəl/, an uncommon type of headache, mainly affecting men, that begins during or immediately after coitus.

coitus /kō′itəs/ [L, *coire*, to come together], the sexual union of two people of opposite sex in which the penis is introduced into the vagina, typically resulting in mutual excitation and usually orgasm. —**coital,** *adj.*

COL, abbreviation for *CircOlectric.*

Colace, a trademark for a stool softener (docusate sodium sulfosuccinate).

colation /kōlā′shən/ [L, *colare*, to strain], the act of filtering or straining, as urine is often strained for medical examination.

ColBENEMID, a trademark for an antigout medication (probenecid-colchicine combination product).

colchicine /kol′chəsēn/ [Gk, *kolchikon*], a gout suppressant that suppresses leukocyte mobility and phagocytosis in joints. It may be prescribed in the treatment of acute gout and prophylaxis of recurrent gouty arthritis.

cold [AS, *kald*], 1. the absence of heat. 2. a contagious viral infection of the upper respiratory tract, usually caused by a strain of rhinovirus. It is characterized by rhinitis, tearing, low-grade fever, and malaise. 3. a distant method of relating; not friendly.

COLD /kōld/, abbreviation for *chronic obstructive lung disease.*

cold abscess, an abscess that does not show common signs of heat, redness, and swelling.

cold agglutinin, a nonspecific antibody, found on the surface of RBCs in certain diseases, that may cause clumping of the cells at temperatures below 36° C and may cause hemolysis. The phenomenon does not occur at body temperature. *Mycoplasma* pneumonia, infectious mononucleosis, and many lymphoproliferative disorders are associated with cold agglutinins.

cold agglutinin disease [AS, *kald*; L, *agglutinare*, to glue, *dis*, without; Fr, *aise*, ease], a disorder characterized by autoantibodies that agglutinate red blood cells at below normal body temperatures. They occur in the sera of patients with mycoplasmal pneumonia.

cold bath, a bath in which the water temperature is approximately 50° F (10° C) to 65° F (18° C), used primarily to reduce body temperature.

cold-blooded, unable to regulate body heat, as fishes, reptiles, and amphibians, which have internal temperatures that are close to the temperatures of the environments in which they live.

cold caloric irrigation, a procedure for testing the integrity of brainstem function. It is carried out by irrigating the external auditory canal of the patient with a cold saline solution while the head is flexed at approximately 30 degrees, after checking the patency of the ear canal. The stimulus results in nystagmus in a normal patient. Absence of the reaction may be a sign of a lesion at the pontine level of the brainstem.

cold compress [AS, *kald*; L, *comprimere*, to press together], a pad of damp, thickly folded, soft absorbent cloth, dipped into cold water, wrung out, and applied to a body part for the relief of pain or reduction of inflammation or as a comfort measure.

cold environment, a human environment arbitrarily designated as one in which the temperature is 10° C (50° F). The human body generally begins to experience some functional impairment when unprotected in temperatures below 10° C (50° F).

cold injury, any of several abnormal and often serious physical conditions caused by exposure to cold temperatures.

cold pack [AS, *kald*; ME, *pakke*], a method of lowering body temperature by wrapping the patient in a blanket or sheet that has been dipped into cold water and wrung out. It is generally no longer done.

cold-pressor test, a test for the tendency to develop essential hypertension. One hand of the individual is immersed in ice water for about 60 seconds. An excessive rise in BP or an unusual delay in the return of normal BP when the hand is removed from the water is believed to indicate that the individual is at risk for hypertension.

cold-sensitive mutation, a genetic alteration resulting in a gene that functions only at high temperature.

cold ulcer, a small gangrenous ulceration on an extremity caused by poor circulation.

cold urticaria [AS, *kald*; L, *urtica*, nettle], wheals caused by exposure to cold temperatures.

cold-wet-sheet pack, a seldom-used form of somatic therapy for agitated patients. The patient is swathed in cold, wet sheets, which are then warmed by body heat. The warmth and immobilization are reported to be soothing to very agitated patients.

colectomy /kəlek'təmē/ [Gk, *kolon*, colon, *ektomē*, excision], surgical excision of part or all of the colon, performed to treat cancer of the colon, diverticulitis, or severe chronic ulcerative colitis.

coleotomy /kō'lē-ot'əmē/, a surgical incision into the pericardium or vagina.

colesevelam /ko'lesev'elam/, a polymer that binds bile acids in the intestine and prevents them from being reabsorbed, resulting in decreased serum levels of total cholesterol, low-density lipoprotein cholesterol, and apolipoprotein B and increased levels of high-density lipoprotein cholesterol.

Colestid, a trademark for an antihyperlipidemic (colestipol hydrochloride).

colestipol hydrochloride /kōles'tipol/, an antihyperlipidemic that acts by sequestering bile acids in the intestine for excretion, thus reducing plasma levels of cholesterol when the liver removes cholesterol to synthesize new bile. It is prescribed in the treatment of hypercholesterolemia and xanthoma.

colfosceril /kolfos'eril/, a synthetic pulmonary surfactant used as the palmitate ester in combination with tyloxapol and as an alcohol in prophylaxis and treatment of neonatal respiratory distress syndrome. It is instilled into the endotracheal tube for intratracheal administration.

colic /kol'ik/ [Gk, *kolikos*, colon pain], **1.** sharp visceral pain resulting from torsion, obstruction, or smooth muscle spasm of a hollow or tubular organ, such as a ureter or the intestines. **2.** pertaining to the colon. —**colicky,** *adj.*

colicinogen /kol'isin'əjən/ [(*E.*) *coli* + L, *caedere*, to kill; Gk, *genein*, to produce], an extrachromosomal segment of DNA in some strains of *Escherichia coli* that induces secretion of a colicin, a protein lethal to other strains of the bacterium.

coliform /kol'ifôrm/ [(*E.*) *coli* + L, *forma*, form], **1.** pertaining to the colon-aerogenes group, or the *Escherichia coli* species of microorganisms, which comprises most of the intestinal flora in humans and other animals. Presence of coliforms is used as a standard indication of water pollution with fecal matter. **2.** having the characteristic of a sieve or cribriform structure, such as some of the porous bones of the skull.

colistimethate sodium /kō′listim′əthāt/, an antibiotic prescribed in the treatment of GI infections caused by certain gram-negative microorganisms and as a topical medication.

colistin sulfate /kōlis′tin/, an antibacterial and steroid agent prescribed topically in the treatment of infections of the outer ear and systemically for the treatment of serious gram-negative infections and gastroenteritis caused by *Escherichia coli.*

colitis /kōlī′tis/, an inflammatory condition of the large intestine characterized by severe diarrhea, bleeding, and ulceration of the mucosa of the intestine. Weight loss and pain are significant.—**colitic,** *adj.*

collaborative power structure /kəlab′ərə tiv′/, an arrangement whereby adult members of a functional family make major decisions and are in agreement about power distribution.

collagen /kol′əjən/ [Gk, *kolla,* glue, *genein,* to produce], a fibrous insoluble protein consisting of bundles of tiny reticular fibrils that combine to form the white glistening inelastic fibers of the tendons, the ligaments, and the fascia.—**collagenous** /kəlaj′ənəs/, *adj.*

collagenase /kəlaj′ənās/, a medication applied as an ointment for debridement of decubitus ulcers, burns, and other epidermal lesions. It is also injected into the penis for treatment of Peyronie's disease and into the wrist, ankle, etc. for the treatment of Dupuytren's disease (restricted movement due to thickening of the fascia). It is an enzyme preparation derived from the fermentation of *Clostridium histolyticum.*

collagen disease, an abnormal condition characterized by extensive disruption of the connective tissue, often involving inflammation and fibrinoid degeneration.

collagen injection, a reconstructive technique in cosmetic surgery to enhance the lips or fatten sunken facial skin.

collagenoblast /kəlaj′ənōblast′/ [Gk, *kolla + genein + blastos,* germ], a cell that differentiates from a fibroblast and functions in the formation of collagen. It can also transform into cartilage and bone tissue by metaplasia.

collagenous colitis /kəlaaˈjənəs kolī′tis/, a type of colitis of unknown cause, characterized by deposits of collagenous material beneath the epithelium of the colon, with crampy abdominal pain; marked reduction in fluid and electrolyte absorption, leading to watery diarrhea; and no mucosal ulceration.

collagenous fiber /kəlaj′ənəs/, any one of the tough, white protein fibers that constitute much of the intercellular substance and the connective tissue of the body.

collagen shield, a material derived from porcine scleral tissue, used in promotion of corneal healing. The shield enhances the penetration and effective time of subconjunctival antibiotics and corticosteroids. The collagen shield is designed to dissolve within 12 hours.

collagen vascular disease, any of a group of acquired disorders that have in common diffuse immunologic and inflammatory changes in small blood vessels and connective tissue. Common features include arthritis, skin lesions, iritis and episcleritis, pericarditis, pleuritis, subcutaneous nodules, myocarditis, vasculitis, and nephritis.

collapse /kəlaps′/ [L, *collabi,* to fall together], **1.** nontechnical, a state of extreme depression or a condition of complete exhaustion caused by physical or psychosomatic problems. **2.** an abnormal condition characterized by shock. **3.** the abnormal sagging of an organ or the obliteration of its cavity.

collapse of the lung [L, *collabi,* to fall together; AS, *lungen*], a reduction in the volume of a lung. The condition results from increased intrapleural pressure caused by accumulation of air or fluid in the pleural cavity or from a loss of internal pressure and elastic recoil of the lung.

collar [L, *collum,* neck], any structure that encircles another, usually around its neck, such as the periosteal bone collars that form around the diaphyses of young bones.

collateral /kōlat′ərəl/ [L, *cum,* together with, *lateralis,* side], **1.** secondary or accessory. **2.** (in anatomy) a small branch, such as any one of the arterioles or venules in the body, as in collateral circulation.

collateral circulation [L, *cum + latus,* side, *circulare,* to go around], an accessory blood pathway developed through enlargement of secondary vessels after obstruction of a main channel.

collateral fissure, a fissure separating the subcalcarine and subcollateral gyri of the cerebral hemisphere.

collateral innervation, reinnervation of denervated neurons caused by sprouting of uninjured axons in the vicinity.

collateral ligaments of interphalangeal joints of foot, fibrous bands, one on either side of each of the interphalangeal joints of the toes.

collateral ligaments of interphalangeal joints of hand, massive fibrous bands on each side of the interphalangeal joints of the fingers. They are placed diagonally, the proximal ends being near the dorsal, and the distal ends near the palmar margins of the digits.

collateral ligaments of the metacarpophalangeal joints, massive, strong fibrous bands on either side of each metacarpophalangeal joint, holding the two bones involved in each joint firmly together.

collateral ligaments of the metatarsophalangeal joints, strong fibrous bands on either side of each metatarsophalangeal joint, holding the two bones involved in each joint firmly together.

collateral pulp canal, a branch of a tooth's pulp canal that emerges from the root at a place other than the apex.

collateral ventilation, the ventilation of alveoli in the lungs through indirect pathways, such as Kohn's pores in alveolar septa or anastomosing bronchioles.

collateral vessel [L, *cum* + *latus,* side, *vascellum,* small vase], a branch of an artery or vein used as an accessory to the blood vessel from which it arises.

collecting system, a group of renal calices and its pelvis considered as a unit.

collecting tubule [L, *colligere,* to gather, *tubulus,* small tube], any one of the many relatively straight tubules of the kidney that funnel urine into papillary ducts in the renal pelvis. The small collecting tubules play an important role in maintaining the fluid balance of the body by allowing water to osmose through their membranes into the interstitial fluid in the renal medulla.

collective bargaining /kəlekʹtiv/, the use of collective action by employees in negotiating working conditions and economic issues with their employer.

collective unconscious [L, *colligere,* to gather; AS, *un,* not; L, *conscious,* aware], (in analytic psychology) that portion of the unconscious common to all humans.

collector, (in medicine) a device with various modifications, used for gathering secretions from the bronchi and esophagus for bacteriologic and cytologic examination.

college [L, *collegium,* society], **1.** an institution of higher learning. **2.** an organization of individuals with common professional training and interests, such as the American College of Nurse-Midwives.

College of American Pathologists (CAP), a national professional organization of physicians who specialize in pathology.

Colles' fascia /kolʹēz/ [Abraham Colles, Irish surgeon, 1773–1843; L, band], the deep inner layer of the subcutaneous, superficial fascia of the perineum, constituting a distinctive structure in the urogenital region of the body.

Colles' fracture [Abraham Colles], a break in or near the distal radius within 1 inch of the joint of the wrist, which causes

displacement of the hand to a dorsal and lateral position.

colligative /kolʹigăʹtiv/ [L, *colligere,* to gather], (in physical chemistry) pertaining to those properties of matter (especially solutions) that depend on the numbers of particles, such as molecules and ions, rather than the chemical properties of any substance. Colligative properties of solutions include boiling point, freezing point, vapor, pressure, and osmotic pressure.

collimate [L, *collineare,* to align], to make parallel.

collimator /kolʹimāʹtər/ [L, *collinare,* to bring into alignment], a device for limiting the size and shape of a radiation beam.

colliquation /kolʹikwāʹshən/ [L, *cum,* together with, *liquifacere,* to make liquid], **1.** the degeneration of a body tissue to a liquid state, usually associated with necrotic tissue. **2.** abnormal discharge of a body fluid.

colliquative /kolʹikwāʹtiv/, characterized by a profuse fluid discharge, as in suppurating wounds and body structures that are infected.

collision tumor /kəlizhʹən/ [L, *cum,* together with, *laedere,* to strike], a tumor formed when two separate growths, developing close to each other, join.

collodion /kəlōʹdē-ən/ [Gk, *kolla,* glue, *eidos,* form], a clear or slightly opaque, highly inflammable liquid composed of pyroxylin, ether, and alcohol. It dries to a strong, transparent film that is used as a surgical dressing.

collodion baby, an infant whose skin at birth is covered with a scaly, parchment-like membrane.

colloid /kolʹoid/ [Gk, *kolla,* glue, *eidos,* form], a state or division of matter in which large molecules or aggregates of molecules (1 to 100 nm in size) do not precipitate and are dispersed in another medium.

colloidal solution /koloiʹdəl/ [Gk, *kolla,* glue, *eidos,* form; L, *solutus,* dissolved], a solution in which small particles, such as large polymeric molecules, are homogenously dispersed through a liquid medium.

colloidal sulfur, a form of very finely divided sulfur that is used in the treatment of acne and other skin disorders.

colloid bath, a bath taken in water that contains such substances as bran, gelatin, and starch, used to relieve irritation and inflammation.

colloid chemistry, the science dealing with the composition and nature of chemical colloids.

colloid corpuscle, a starchlike body found in the nervous tissue, prostate, and pulmonary alveoli.

colloid cyst [Gk, *kolla,* glue, *eidos,* form, *kystis,* bag], **1.** a thyroid gland follicle distended with thyroid secretion. **2.** a cyst in the third ventricle, leading to hydrocephalus. **3.** a cyst with gelatinous contents.

colloid substance, a jelly-like substance formed in the deterioration of the protoplasm of tissues.

colloid suspension [Gk, *kolla,* glue, *eidos,* form; L, *suspendere,* to hang], a system of solids dispersed in a liquid medium, with particles generally smaller than 100 nm.

collum /kol′əm/, the anatomic necklike structure between the head and shoulders.

collyrium /kolir′ē·əm/, an eyewash, or an ophthalmic liquid containing medications to be instilled into the eye.

coloboma /kol′əbō′mə/ *pl.* **colobomas, colobomata** [Gk, *koloboma,* defect], a congenital or pathologic defect in the ocular tissue of the body, usually affecting the iris, ciliary body, or choroid by forming a cleft that extends inferiorly. Colobomas are usually the result of failure of part of the fetal fissure to close.—**colobomatous,** *adj.*

colon /kō′lən/ [Gk, *kolon*], the portion of the large intestine extending from the cecum to the rectum. It has four segments: the ascending colon, transverse colon, descending colon, and sigmoid colon. —**colonic** /kəlon′ik/, *adj.*

colon hydrotherapy, an extended and more complete form of an enema as well as a method of removing waste from the large intestine without using drugs. Colon hydrotherapy is used to treat constipation or impaction, as preparation for diagnostic studies of the large intestine, and as preparation for or after surgery. The procedure is also used for bowel training for paraplegics or tetraplegics, those with arthritis, and patients who have suspected autointoxication or intestinal toxemia.

colonic fistula [Gk, *kolon*; L, *pipe*], an abnormal passage from the colon to the surface of the body or an internal organ or structure.

colonic intussusception, intussusception involving two segments of the colon; telescoping of the colon.

colonic irrigation, a procedure for washing the inner wall of the colon by filling it with water and then draining it. It is not considered an enema but rather a technique for removing any material that may be present high in the colon.

colonic volvulus, volvulus involving any portion of the colon. The most common types are cecal volvulus, sigmoid volvulus, and transverse colon volvulus.

colonization /kol′ənīzā′shən/, **1.** the invasion of a new habitat by a new species.

2. the presence and multiplication of microorganisms without tissue invasion or damage.

colonography /ko′lonog′rāfē/, imaging of the colon, as by CT or MRI.

colonoscope /kō′lənōskōp′/ [Gk, *kolon* + *skopein,* to watch], a long, flexible endoscope, usually fiberoptic, that permits examination of the interior of the entire colon.

colonoscopy /kō′lənos′kəpē/, the examination of the mucosal lining of the colon by using a colonoscope, an elongated endoscope.

colony /kol′ənē/ [L, *colonia*], **1.** (in bacteriology) a mass of microorganisms in a culture that originates from a single cell. Some kinds of colonies, according to different configurations, are smooth colonies, rough colonies, and dwarf colonies. **2.** (in cell biology) a mass of cells in a culture or in certain experimental tissues, such as a spleen colony.

colony counter, a device used for counting colonies of bacteria growing in a culture. It usually consists of an illuminated, transparent plate divided into sections of known area.

colony-stimulating factor (CSF), a growth factor that allows cells to pass a restriction point in their reproductive cycle. It is no longer needed after cells have entered the DNA synthesis phase.

coloproctectomy /kō′ləproktek′təmē/, surgical removal of the colon and rectum.

coloproctitis /kō′ləproktī′tis/, an inflammation of both the colon and rectum.

coloptosis /kō′lōptō′sis/ [Gk, *kolon* + *ptosis,* fall], the prolapse or downward displacement of the colon, especially of the transverse portion.

Colorado tick fever, a relatively mild, self-limited arbovirus infection transmitted to humans by the bite of the wood tick *Dermacentor andersoni.* Symptoms occur in two phases separated by a period of remission and include chills, fever, and headache; pain in the eyes, legs, and back; and sensitivity to light.

color blindness [L, color; AS, *blint*], an abnormal condition characterized by an inability to distinguish colors of the spectrum clearly. In most cases it is not a blindness but a weakness in perceiving colors distinctly. There are two forms of color blindness: **Daltonism,** the more common form, is characterized by an inability to distinguish reds from greens. It is an inherited, sex-linked disorder. **Total color blindness,** or **achromatic vision,** or **achromatic,** is characterized by an inability to perceive any color at all. Only white, gray, and black are seen. It may be the result of a defect in or absence of the cones in the retina.

color dysnomia /disnō'mē·ə/ [L, color; Gk, *dys,* difficult, *onoma,* name], an inability to name colors despite an ability to match and distinguish them. It may be caused by expressive dysphasia.

colorectal /kō'lōrek'təl/ [Gk, *kolon,* colon; L, *rectus,* straight], pertaining to or affecting the colon and rectum.

colorectal cancer /kō'lərek'təl/ [Gk, *kolon,* colon; L, *rectus,* straight], a malignant neoplastic disease of the large intestine, characterized by a change in bowel habits; the passing of blood (melena), which may be occult initially; and anemias.

colorimetry /kol'ərim'ətrē/, measurement of the intensity of color in a fluid or substance as compared with that in a standard solution.

color therapy, the therapeutic use of light of specific colors. It encompasses a number of methods used in complementary medicine and is often employed as a complementary treatment for seasonal affective disorder, depression, and stress.

color vision, a recognition of color as the result of changes in the pigments of the cones in the retina that react to varying intensities of red, green, and blue light.

colosigmoidoscopy /kō'ləsig'moidos'kəpē/ [Gk, *kolon* + *sigma,* S-shaped, *eidos,* form, *skopein,* to look], the direct examination of the sigmoid part of the colon with a sigmoidoscope.

colostomate /kəlos'təmāt/ [Gk, *kolon* + *stoma,* mouth; L, *atum,* one acted upon], a person who has undergone a colostomy.

colostomy /kəlos'təmē/ [Gk, *kolon* + *stoma,* mouth], surgical creation of an artificial anus on the abdominal wall by incising the colon and drawing it out to the surface, performed for cancer of the colon, benign obstructive tumors, and severe abdominal wounds. A colostomy may be single-barreled, with one opening, or double-barreled, with distal and proximal loops opening onto the abdomen.

colostomy irrigation, a procedure used by colostomates to clear the bowel of fecal matter and to help establish an evacuation schedule. A flexible catheter, lubricated with water-soluble lubricant, is gently inserted into the stoma to a depth of no more than 3 inches. An irrigating bag containing 500 to 1000 mL of warm solution is held 12 to 18 inches above the stoma, and the fluid is allowed to flow slowly into the colon. The fluid is retained for several minutes and then drained through outlet tubing into a basin or

commode. The character and amount of the return flow are noted. The peristomal skin is cleaned, rinsed, and dried well.

colostrum /kəlos'trəm/ [L, first milk after birth], the fluid secreted by the breast during pregnancy and the first days after delivery before lactation begins. It consists of immunologically active substances (maternal antibodies) and WBCs, water, protein, fat, minerals, vitamins, and carbohydrate in a thin, yellow serous fluid. Compare **breast milk.**

colotomy /kōlot'əmē/, a surgical incision into the colon, usually performed through the abdominal wall.

Colour Index **(CI),** a publication of dyers, colorists, and textile chemists that specifies all the standard industrial pigments and stains according to five-digit numbers associated with chemical coloring materials.

colovaginal /kō'lōvaj'inəl/ [Gk, *kolon,* colon; L, *vagina,* sheath], pertaining to the colon and vagina, or to a communication between the two structures.

colovesical fistula, a fistula connecting the colon and the urinary bladder.

colpalgia /kolpal'jə/, a pain in the vagina.

colpectomy /kolpek'təmē/, the surgical excision of the vagina.

colpitis /kolpī'tis/, an inflammation of the vagina.

colpocystitis /kol'pōsistī'tis/, an inflammation of the vagina and urinary bladder.

colpocystocele /kol'pəsis'təsēl/, the prolapse of the urinary bladder into the vagina, usually through the anterior vaginal wall.

colpohysterectomy /-his'tərek'təmē/ [Gk, *kolpos,* vagina, *hystera,* womb, *ektomē,* excision], vaginal hysterectomy.

colporrhaphy /kolpôr'əfē/ [Gk, *kolpos* + *raphe,* suture], a surgical procedure in which the vagina is sutured to narrow it.

colposcope /kol'pəskōp/, a lighted instrument with lenses for direct examination of the surfaces of the vagina and cervix.

colposcopy /kolpos'kəpē/ [Gk, *kolpos* + *skopein,* to watch], an examination of the vagina and cervix with an optical magnifying instrument (colposcope).

colposuspension /kol'pəsuspen'shun/, bladder neck suspension.

colpotomy /kolpot'əmē/ [Gk, *kolpos* + *temnein,* to cut], any surgical incision into the wall of the vagina.

columella, **1.** a small column. **2.** the fleshy terminal part of the nasal septum.

column, any elongated, cylindric anatomic structure, usually oriented vertically.

columnar cell /kəlum'nər/ [L, *columna,* column, *cella,* storeroom], an epithelial cell that appears long and narrow when sectioned along its long axis.

columnar epithelium [L, *columna,* column; Gk, *epi,* upon, *thele,* nipple], a type of epithelial cell that resembles a hexagonal prism.

column chromatography [L, *columna;* Gk, *chroma,* color, *graphein,* to record], the process of separating and analyzing a group of substances according to the differences in their absorption affinities for a given absorbent as evidenced by pigments deposited during filtration through the same absorbent contained in a glass cylinder or tube. The substances are dissolved in a liquid that is passed through the absorbent. The absorbates move down the column at different rates and leave behind a band of pigments that is subsequently washed with a pure solvent to develop discrete pigmented bands that constitute a chromatograph.

Coly-Mycin M, a trademark for a parenteral antibacterial (colistimethate sodium).

Coly-Mycin S, a trademark for an otic steroid and antibiotic combination containing hydrocortisone, neomycin, and colistin.

coma /kō′mə/ [Gk, *koma,* deep sleep], a state of profound unconsciousness, characterized by the absence of spontaneous eye openings, response to painful stimuli, and vocalization. The person cannot be aroused.

comatose /kō′mətōs/, pertaining to a state of coma, or abnormally deep sleep, caused by illness or injury.

combat fatigue [L, *com,* together, *battuere,* to beat, *fatigare,* to tire], any of a variety of psychoneurotic disorders, usually temporary but sometimes permanent, resulting from exhaustion, the stress of combat, or the cumulative emotions and psychologic strain of warfare or other traumatic situations. It is characterized by anxiety, depression, irritability, memory and sleep disorders, and various related symptoms.

combination chemotherapy /kom′binā′shən/, the simultaneous use of two or more anticancer drugs.

combined carbon dioxide [L, *com,* together, *bini,* twofold], the part of the total carbon dioxide that is contained in blood carbonate, calculated as the difference between the total and dissolved carbon dioxide.

combined cycling ventilator, a mechanical ventilator that has more than one mechanism to recycle gases, such as equipment that may have time cycling or pressure cycling as a backup to a volume cycling control device.

combined oral contraceptive, an oral contraceptive that includes both an estrogen and a progestogen, which may be administered in either two or three different phases during each menstrual cycle.

combined oxygen, the oxygen that is physically bound to hemoglobin as oxyhemoglobin (HbO_2). One gram-molecular weight of oxygen can combine with 16,700 g of hemoglobin, and each gram of hemoglobin can bind with and carry 1.34 mL of oxygen.

combined patterns, a method of evaluating a patient's neuromuscular functions through tests that reveal the degree of coordination between movement patterns of the trunk and the extremities.

combined system disease, a disorder of the nervous system caused by a deficiency of vitamin B_{12} that results in pernicious anemia and degeneration of the spinal cord and peripheral nerves, marked by increased difficulty in walking, spasticity in lower extremities, a feeling of vibration in the legs, and a loss of sense of position.

Combitube /kom′bit(y)ōōb′/, a trademark for a double-lumen tube with inflatable balloon cuffs that seal off the hypopharynx from the oropharynx and esophagus, used for airway management. It is inserted blindly, entering either the esophagus or the trachea. If it enters the esophagus, one lumen, which has a blind distal end and side holes, functions as an esophageal obturator airway. If it enters the trachea, the other lumen, which has an open distal end, functions as a standard cuffed endotracheal tube.

Combivir /kom′bivir/, a trademark for a combination preparation of the nucleoside analogs zidovudine and lamivudine, used in treatment of HIV infection and AIDS.

combustion /kəmbus′chən/, the process of burning or oxidation, which may be accompanied by light and heat. Oxygen itself does not burn, but it supports combustion. The rate of combustion is influenced by both oxygen concentration and its partial pressure.

comedo /kom′idō/ *pl.* **comedones** [L, *comedere,* to consume], blackhead (open comedo) or whitehead (closed comedo), the basic lesion of acne vulgaris, caused by an accumulation of keratin and sebum within the opening of a hair follicle.

comedocarcinoma /kom′idōkär′sinō′mə/ *pl.* **comedocarcinomas, comedocarcinomata** [L, *comedere,* to consume; Gk, *karkinos,* crab, *oma,* tumor], a malignant intraductal neoplasm of the breast, in which the central cells degenerate and may be easily expressed from the cut surface of the tumor.

comedogenicity /kom′idōjənis′itē/, the ability of certain drugs or agents, such as anabolic steroids, to produce acne comedones.

comedomastitis, mammary duct ectasia.

comfortable death, a nursing outcome from the Nursing Outcomes Classification (NOC) defined as physical, psychospiritual, sociocultural, and environmental ease with the impending end of life.

comfort measure [L, *com,* together, *fortis,* strong], any action taken to promote the soothing of a patient such as a back rub, a change in position, the prewarming of a stethoscope or bedpan, or administration of selected medications or treatments.

comfort status, a nursing outcome from the Nursing Outcomes Classification (NOC) defined as the overall physical, psychospiritual, sociocultural, and environmental ease and safety of an individual.

comfort status: environment, a nursing outcome from the Nursing Outcomes Classification (NOC) defined as the environmental ease, comfort, and safety of surroundings.

comfort status: physical, a nursing outcome from the Nursing Outcomes Classification (NOC) defined as the physical ease related to bodily sensations and homeostatic mechanisms.

comfort status: psychospiritual, a nursing outcome from the Nursing Outcomes Classification (NOC) defined as the psychospiritual ease related to self-concept, emotional well-being, source of inspiration, and meaning and purpose in one's life.

comfort status: sociocultural, a nursing outcome from the Nursing Outcomes Classification (NOC) defined as the social ease related to interpersonal, family, and societal relationships within a cultural context.

comfort zone [ME, *comforten*; Gk, *zone,* belt], **1.** the boundaries of temperature, humidity, wind velocity, and solar radiation within which a person dressed in a specified manner can perform certain tasks without discomfort. **2.** the psychologic feeling of belonging or being comfortable in a specific area and/or role.

comfrey, a perennial herb used for bruises, sprains, broken bones, acne, and boils. It is considered safe and possibly effective when used topically.

Comité International des Poids et Mesures (CIPM) /kômitä′ aNternäsyō nä1′ dä pô·ä ämesYr′/, a group of scientists who meet periodically to define the international (SI) units of physical quantities, as the volume of a liter, the length of a meter, or the precise amount of time in a minute.

command automatism, a condition characterized by an abnormal mechanical responsiveness to commands, usually followed without critical judgment, such as may be seen in hypnosis and certain psychotic states.

command hallucination, a condition in which individuals hear and sometimes obey voices that command them to perform certain acts.

commensal /kəmen′səl/ [L, *com,* together, *imensa,* table], (two different species) living together in an arrangement that is not harmful to either and that may be beneficial to both.

commensalism /kəmen′səliz′əm/, a symbiosis in which one species benefits but the other species is neither helped nor harmed.

comminuted /kom′inyo͞o′tid/ [L, *comminuere,* to break into pieces], crushed or broken into a number of pieces.

comminuted fracture, a fracture in which the bone is broken in several places or is shattered, creating numerous fragments.

Commission E, a German interdisciplinary regulatory committee, whose function is to review herbal drugs and preparations from medicinal plants and evaluate and approve their safety and efficacy.

Commission on Collegiate Nursing Education (CCNE), an autonomous accrediting agency whose mission includes the assessment and identification of nursing programs that engage in effective educational practices, having a scope of the institutions of higher education in the United States.

commissure /kom′iso͞or, -syo͞or/, **1.** a band of nerve fiber or other tissue that crosses from one side of the body to the other, usually connecting two structures or masses of tissue. **2.** a site of union of two anatomic parts, as the corner of the eye, lips, or labia.

commissurotomy /kom′isho͞orot′əme/ [L, *commissura,* a connection; Gk, *temnein,* to cut], the surgical division of a fibrous band or other ring connecting corresponding parts of a body structure.

commitment [L, *committere,* to entrust], **1.** the placement or confinement of an individual in a specialized hospital or other institutional facility. **2.** the legal procedure of admitting a mentally ill person to an institution for psychiatric treatment. **3.** a pledge or contract to fulfill some obligation or agreement, used especially in some forms of psychotherapy or marriage counseling.

common baldness, androgenetic alopecia.

common bile duct [L, *communis,* common, *bilis,* bile, *ducere,* to lead], the duct formed by the juncture of the cystic and hepatic ducts.

common carotid artery [L, *communis*; Gk, *karos,* heavy sleep; L, *arteria,* airpipe], one of the major arteries supplying blood to the head and neck. Each divides into an external common carotid and an internal common carotid. Branches of the external carotid supply the face, scalp, and most of the neck and throat tissues. The internal carotids supply the brain and other tissues generally accessible from within the skull, as the eyes.

common carotid plexus, a network of nerves on the common carotid artery, supplying sympathetic fibers to the head and the neck, with branches that accompany the cranial blood vessels.

common fibular nerve, a nerve originating from the sciatic nerve that gives origin to two cutaneous branches: the sural communicating nerve, which contributes to the innervation of the skin over the lower posterolateral side of the leg, and the lateral sural cutaneous nerve, which innervates the skin over the upper lateral leg. It then continues around the neck of the fibula and enters the lateral compartment, where it divides into the superficial fibular nerve and the deep fibular nerve. The superficial fibular nerve innervates the fibularis longus and brevis and some of the dorsal areas of the foot and toes. The deep fibular nerve innervates the anterior compartment of the leg.

common hepatic artery, the visceral branch of the celiac trunk of the abdominal aorta, passing posterior to the pylorus and dividing into five branches.

common iliac artery, a division of the abdominal aorta, starting to the left of the fourth lumbar vertebra and dividing into external and internal iliac arteries.

common iliac node, a node in one of the seven groups of parietal lymph nodes serving the abdomen and the pelvis. They drain the internal and external iliac nodes and pass their materials to the lateral aortic nodes.

common iliac vein, one of the two veins that are the sources of the inferior vena cava, formed by the union of the internal and external iliac veins.

common pathway of coagulation, the pathway common to both intrinsic and extrinsic coagulation pathways. Once activated, factor X forms a complex with its cofactor, factor V, to convert prothrombin to thrombin. Thrombin splits peptides from fibrinogen to produce a fibrin clot.

common tendinous ring, the thickening of the periorbita around the optic canal and the central part of the superior orbital fissure in the posterior part of the bony orbit. It is the point of origin of the four rectus muscles.

common variable immunodeficiency (CVID), a heterogeneous group of disorders characterized by hypogammaglobulinemia, decreased antibody production

in response to antigenic challenge, and recurrent pyogenic infections, and often associated with hematologic and autoimmune disorders. Most patients have normal numbers of circulating B cells that can identify antigens and proliferate, but they lack plasma cells and may have an intrinsic defect of B-cell differentiation.

commotio cordis, damage to the heart, frequently fatal, resulting from a sharp nonpenetrating blow to the adjacent body surface.

commune /kom′yōōn/, a small community of people who share certain social and economic objectives. Members may also share property ownership and control local political leadership and are committed to the concept of holistic medicine.

communicability period /kəmyōō′nəkə bil′itē/, the time during which an infectious agent may be transferred directly or indirectly from an infected person to another person, from an infected animal to humans, or from an infected person to animals, including arthropods.

communicable /kəmyōō′nəkəbəl/ [L, *communis,* common], transmissible by direct or indirect means.

communicable disease, any disease transmitted from one person or animal to another directly, by contact with excreta or other discharges from the body; indirectly, by means of substances or inanimate objects such as contaminated drinking glasses, toys, or water; or by means of vectors such as flies, mosquitoes, ticks, or other insects. Many communicable diseases, by law, must be reported to the local health department.

communicable disease management, a nursing intervention from the Nursing Interventions Classification (NIC) defined as working with a community to decrease and manage the incidence and prevalence of contagious diseases in a specific population.

communicating hydrocephalus /kəmyōō′ nikā′ting/ [L, *communicans;* Gk, *hydor,* water, *kephale,* head], a form of hydrocephalus in which there is an increase in CSF that involves the entire ventricular system and the subarachnoid space. It is caused by an abnormality in the ability to absorb fluid in the subarachnoid space. No obstruction exists in the ventricular pathways.

communication¹ /kəmyōō′nikā′shən/ [L, *communis,* common], any process in which a message containing information is transferred, especially from one person to another, by any of a number of media.

communication², a nursing outcome from the Nursing Outcomes Classification

(NOC) defined as the reception, interpretation, and expression of spoken, written, and nonverbal messages.

communication channels, (in communication theory) any gesture, action, sound, written word, or visual image used in transmitting messages.

communication disorders, a *DSM-IV* classification defined as mental disorders involving difficulties in speech or language, severe enough to be a problem academically, occupationally, or socially.

communication enhancement: hearing deficit, a nursing intervention from the Nursing Interventions Classification (NIC) defined as assistance in accepting and learning alternate methods for living with diminished hearing.

communication enhancement: speech deficit, a nursing intervention from the Nursing Interventions Classification (NIC) defined as assistance in accepting and learning alternate methods for living with impaired speech.

communication enhancement: visual deficit, a nursing intervention from the Nursing Interventions Classification (NIC) defined as assistance in accepting and learning alternate methods for living with diminished vision.

communication: expressive, a nursing outcome from the Nursing Outcomes Classification (NOC) defined as the expression of meaningful verbal and/or nonverbal messages.

communication: receptive, a nursing outcome from the Nursing Outcomes Classification (NOC) defined as the reception and interpretation of verbal and/or nonverbal messages.

communication theme, (in psychiatry) a recurrent concept or idea that ties together components of communication.

communication theory, a hypothesis that describes a model for information transfer consisting of a source of information (the sender), a transmitter, a communication channel, a source of noise (interference), a receiver, and a purpose for the message.

community /kəmyo͞o'nitē/ [L, *communis,* common], **1.** a group of species who reside in a designated geographic area and who share common interests or bonds. **2.** A person's natural environment, that is where the person works, plays, and performs other daily activities.

community-acquired infection, an infection contracted outside of a health care setting or an infection present on admission. Community-acquired respiratory infections commonly involve strains of *Haemophilus influenzae* or *Streptococcus pneumoniae* and are usually more antibiotic-sensitive than are nosocomial infections.

community competence, a nursing outcome from the Nursing Outcomes Classification (NOC) defined as the capacity of a community to collectively problem solve to achieve community goals.

community disaster preparedness, a nursing intervention from the Nursing Interventions Classification (NIC) defined as preparing for an effective response to a large-scale disaster.

community disaster readiness, a nursing outcome from the Nursing Outcomes Classification (NOC) defined as community preparedness to respond to a natural or man-made calamitous event.

community disaster response, a nursing outcome from the Nursing Outcomes Classification (NOC) defined as the community response following a natural or man-made calamitous event.

community health development, a nursing intervention from the Nursing Interventions Classification (NIC) defined as assisting members of a community to identify a community's health concerns, mobilize resources, and implement solutions.

community health nursing, a field of nursing that blends primary health care and nursing practice with public health nursing, based on the belief that care directed to the individual, the family, and the group contributes to the health care of the population as a whole.

community health status, a nursing outcome from the Nursing Outcomes Classification (NOC) defined as the general state of well-being of a community or population.

community health status: immunity, a nursing outcome from the Nursing Outcomes Classification (NOC) defined as the resistance of community members to the invasion and spread of an infectious agent that could threaten public health.

community medicine, a branch of medicine that is concerned with the health of the members of a community, municipality, or region. The emphasis is on the early diagnosis of disease, the recognition of environmental and occupational hazards to good health, and the prevention of disease in the community.

community mental health, a treatment philosophy based on the social model of psychiatric care that advocates that a comprehensive range of mental health services be readily accessible to all members of the community.

community mental health center (CMHC), a community-based center that provides comprehensive mental health services, including ambulatory and inpatient care. The specific services to be provided are defined in an act of the U.S. Congress, the Community Mental Health Centers Act.

community nurse practitioner (CNP), a nurse who has completed a postbaccalaureate program in community nursing.

community psychiatry, the branch of psychiatry concerned with the development of an adequate and coordinated program of mental health care for residents of specified catchment areas.

community rating system, a program of health maintenance organizations (HMOs) that uses revenues and membership targets to determine health insurance premium rates. The HMO uses its own history in the calculation of rates.

community reintegration, the return and acceptance of a disabled person as a participating member of the community.

community risk control: chronic disease, a nursing outcome from the Nursing Outcomes Classification (NOC) defined as community actions to reduce the risk of chronic diseases and related complications.

community risk control: communicable disease, a nursing outcome from the Nursing Outcomes Classification (NOC) defined as community actions to eliminate or reduce the spread of infectious agents that threaten public health.

community risk control: lead exposure, a nursing outcome from the Nursing Outcomes Classification (NOC) defined as community actions to reduce lead exposure and poisoning.

community risk control: violence, a nursing outcome from the Nursing Outcomes Classification (NOC) defined as community actions to eliminate or reduce intentional violent acts resulting in serious physical or psychological harm.

community violence level, a nursing outcome from the Nursing Outcomes Classification (NOC) defined as the incidence of violent acts compared with local, state, or national values.

Comolli's sign /kōmō'lēs/ [Antonio Comolli, Italian pathologist, 1879–1975], a triangular swelling corresponding to the shape of the scapula after a fracture of that bone.

comorbidity, two or more coexisting medical conditions or disease processes that are additional to an initial diagnosis.

compact bone /kom'pakt, kompakt'/ [L, *compingere,* to put together], hard, dense bone that is usually found at the periphery of skeletal structures, as distinguished from spongy cancellous bone.

companion animal, a dog, cat, or other pet that provides health benefits to a person. Companion animals may help relieve stress or serve a more active role, as do guide dogs for blind persons and dogs trained to detect telephone or doorbell sounds for deaf persons.

companionship /kampan'yanship'/ [L, *com,* together, *panis,* food], (in psychiatric nursing) the assignment of a staff member to stay with a disturbed patient to provide support and to protect the patient from self-harm or harm to others.

comparative anatomy /kamper'ativ/ [L, *com + par,* equal], the study of the morphologic characteristics of all living animals.

comparative embryology, the study of the similarities and differences among various organisms during the embryologic period of development.

comparative genomic hybridization, a cytogenetic technique in which reference DNA and the DNA to be studied, as from a tumor or an embryo, are labeled with green- and red-fluorescing fluorochromes, respectively. Genetic abnormalities are detected by changes in the green-to-red ratio.

comparative method, the analytic method to which the test method is compared in the comparison-of-methods experiment.

comparative physiology, the study of the similarities and differences of the vital processes found in various species of living organisms to determine fundamental physiologic relationships.

comparative psychology, 1. the study of human behavior as it relates to, or differs from, animal behavior. **2.** the study of the psychologic and behavioral differences among various peoples.

compartment model /kampärt'mant/, a mathematic representation of the body or an area of the body created to study physiologic or pharmacologic kinetic characteristics. A compartment model can simulate all of the biologic processes involved in the kinetic behavior of a drug after it has been introduced into the body, leading to a better understanding of its pharmacodynamic effects.

compartment syndrome [L, *com + partiri,* to share], a pathologic condition caused by elevation of tissue pressure within a closed space, resulting in the progressive development of compression and consequent reduction of blood supply. The compression may result from swelling within an overly restrictive dressing or cast or from nonexpansive muscle fascia. Clinical manifestations include swelling, restriction of movement, brown urine, myoglobinuria, vascular compromise, and severe pain or lack of sensation.

compatibility /kəmpat′əbil′itē/ [L, *compatibilis,* agreeable], **1.** the quality or state of existing together in harmony; congruity. **2.** the orderly, efficient integration of the elements of one system with those of another. **3.** the formation of a stable chemical or biochemical system, specifically in medication, so that two or more drugs can be administered at the same time without producing undesired side effects or without canceling or affecting the therapeutic effects of the others. **4.** (in immunology) the degree to which the body's defense system tolerates the presence of foreign material, such as transfused blood, grafted tissue, or transplanted organs, without an immune reaction. **5.** (in blood grouping or crossmatching) the lack of reaction between blood groups so that there is no agglutination when the RBCs of one sample are mixed with the serum of another sample; no reaction from transfused blood. —**compatible,** *adj.*

compatible, 1. capable of harmonious coexistence, said of two or more medications that are suitable for simultaneous administration without nullification or aggravation of their effects. **2.** denoting a donor and recipient of a blood transfusion in which there is no transfusion reaction. **3.** histocompatible.

Compazine, a trademark for a phenothiazine (prochlorperazine).

compendium /kəmpen′dē-əm/ *pl.* **compendia** [L, *compendere,* to weigh], a collected body of information on the standards of strength, purity, and quality of drugs. The official compendia in the United States are the *United States Pharmacopoeia* and the *Homeopathic Pharmacopoeia of the United States* and their supplements.

compensated acidosis /kom′pənsā′ted/ [L, *compensare,* to balance, *acidus,* sour; Gk, *osis,* condition], a condition in which the pH of the blood is maintained within normal limits (adult/child: 7.35 to 7.45) although the blood bicarbonate level is below normal or the PCO_2 is above normal. This compensation is accomplished by the lungs and kidneys altering their functions.

compensated alkalosis, a condition in which the blood bicarbonate is increased or the PCO_2 is decreased but compensation by the lung and kidneys keeps the blood pH within the normal range.

compensated flowmeter [L, *compensare,* to balance], a gas therapy device with a scale that is calibrated against a constant pressure of 50 psi instead of the atmosphere.

compensated gluteal gait, one of the more common abnormal gaits associated with a weakness of the gluteus medius. It involves the dropping of the pelvis on the unaffected side of the body during the walking cycle between the moment of heel strike on the affected side and before the moment of heel strike on the unaffected side. This gait is also characterized by the dropping of the entire trunk downward and sideways over the affected hip and a short step on the unaffected side. The trunk is forcibly thrown laterally during the weight-bearing or stance phase in the movement of the affected lower limb.

compensated heart failure, an abnormal cardiac condition in which heart failure is compensated for by such mechanisms as increased sympathetic stimulation of the heart, fluid retention with increased venous return, increased end-diastolic ventricular volume and fiber length, and ventricular hypertrophy.

compensating current /kom′pənsā′ting/, an electric current that neutralizes the intensity of a muscle current.

compensating curve, the curvature of alignment of the occlusal surfaces of the teeth, developed to compensate for the paths of the condyles as the mandible moves from centric to eccentric positions.

compensating filter, a device, such as a wedge of aluminum, clay, or plastic, that is placed over a body area during radiography to compensate for differences in radiopacity.

compensation /kom′pənsā′shən/ [L, *compensare,* to balance], **1.** the process of counterbalancing any defect in body structure or function. **2.** the process of maintaining an adequate blood flow through such cardiac and circulatory mechanisms as tachycardia, fluid retention with increased venous return, and ventricular hypertrophy. Lack of compensation indicates a diseased heart muscle. **3.** a complex defense mechanism that allows one to avoid the unpleasant or painful emotional stimuli that result from a feeling of inferiority or inadequacy. **4.** changes in structural relationships that accommodate foundation disturbances and maintain balance.

compensator /kom′pənsā′tər/, a device used in radiotherapy to correct for irregularities in body surfaces by providing a differential attenuation of the x-ray beam before it reaches the patient.

compensatory hypertrophy /kəmpen′sətôr′ē/ [L, *compensare,* to balance], an increase in the size or function of an organ or part to counteract a structural or functional defect.

compensatory pause, a pause noted on an ECG after a premature complex. It precedes the next normal complex.

competence /kom'pətəns/ [L, *competentia,* capable], **1.** (in embryology) the total capacity of an embryonic cell to react to determinative stimuli with various types of differentiation. **2.** the ability of bacteria to take up donor DNA molecules.

competent community /kom'pətənt/, a population that is aware of resources and alternatives, can make reasoned decisions about issues facing the group, and can cope adaptively with problems.

competitive antagonist, a substance that interferes with usual metabolic activity by competing for binding sites on a substrate or on an enzyme that ordinarily attacks the substrate. The antagonist is usually an analog of the substrate.

competitive-binding assay /kompet'itiv/ [L, *competere,* to come together], an analytic procedure based on the reversible binding of a ligand to a binding protein.

competitive displacement, the tendency of one drug to displace another at nonspecific protein-binding sites (e.g., plasma albumin) when both drugs are taken at the same time. Only the free drug is able to bind to its specific target proteins.

competitive identification, the unconscious modeling of one's personality on that of another as a means of outdoing or bettering the other person.

competitive inhibitor, an inhibitor of an enzyme reaction that competes with the substrate by binding at the active site.

complaint [L, *complangere,* to beat the breast], **1.** (in law) a pleading by a plaintiff made under oath to initiate a suit. It is a statement of the formal charge and the cause for action against the defendant. **2.** informal. any ailment, problem, or symptom identified by the client, patient, member of the person's family, or other knowledgeable person.

complement (C) /kom'pləmənt/ [L, *complementum,* that which completes], a system of at least 20 complex enzymatic serum proteins. In an antigen-antibody reaction, activation of complement causes cell lysis. Complement is also involved in other physiologic reactions, including inflammation, anaphylaxis, and phagocytosis.

complement abnormality, an unusual condition characterized by deficiencies or by dysfunctions of any of the 11 serum proteins known as complement and designated C1 to C11. Patients with complement abnormalities may be more

susceptible to infections and to collagen vascular diseases.

complemental inheritance /kom'pləmen'təl/, the expression of a trait as a result of the presence of two independent pairs of nonallelic genes. Both of the genes must be present for the trait to appear in the phenotype.

complementary and alternative medicine (CAM), a large and diverse set of systems of diagnosis, treatment, and prevention based on philosophies and techniques other than those used in conventional Western medicine. Such practices may be described as *alternative,* that is, existing as a body separate from and as a replacement for conventional Western medicine, or *complementary,* that is, used in addition to conventional Western practice. CAM is characterized by its focus on the whole person as a unique individual, on the energy of the body and its influence on health and disease, on the healing power of nature and the mobilization of the body's own resources to heal itself, and on the treatment of the underlying causes, rather than symptoms, of disease. Some of the techniques used are the subject of controversy and are now being validated.

complementary feeding /kom'pləmen'tərē/ [L, *complementum,* that which completes], a supplemental feeding given to an infant who is still hungry after breastfeeding.

complementary gene, either member of two or more nonallelic gene pairs that interact to produce an effect not expressed in the absence of any of the pairs.

complement assay, a blood test used primarily to measure serum complement in an effort to diagnose angioedema and to monitor the activity of disease in patients with SLE nephritis, membranoproliferative nephritis, or poststreptococcal nephritis.

complement cascade, a biochemical process involving the C1 to C9 complement proteins in which one protein interacts with another in a specific sequence called a complement pathway. C5b with C6, C7, C8, and C9 form the membrane attack complex that initiates cell lysis. Other molecules, such as C3a and C5a, act as cytokines, leading to inflammation.

complement control protein (CCP), any of a large family of proteins involved in complement regulation, encoded in a closely linked gene cluster, and having one or more stretches of a common short repeated sequence.

complement fixation, an immunologic reaction in which an antigen combines with an antibody and its complement, causing the complement factor to become inactive or fixed.

complement-fixation test, any serologic test in which complement fixation is detected, indicating the presence of a particular antigen. They are rarely used in clinical practice today.

complement inactivation [L, *in* + *activus, complere,* to complete], the loss of activity of complement proteins in blood, achieved by heating the serum to about 133° F (56° C).

complement protein molecule [L, *complementum* + *proteios,* first rank], any of the protein molecules that are chief humoral mediators of antigen-antibody reactions in the immune system. Nine are involved in the "classical pathway" cascade that results in the lysis of antibody-coated bacteria.

complete abortion [L, *complere,* to fill up], termination of pregnancy in which the conceptus is expelled or removed in its entirety.

complete bed bath, a bath in which the entire body of a patient is washed while he or she is in bed.

complete blood count (CBC), a determination of the number of RBCs and WBCs per cubic millimeter of blood. A CBC is one of the most routinely performed tests in a clinical laboratory and one of the most valuable screening and diagnostic techniques. The RBC count in adult males is 4.7 to 6.1 million/mm³. In adult females, the normal RBC is 4.2 to 5.4 million/mm³. The normal adult WBC count is 5000 to 10,000/mm³.

complete breech, a fetal presentation in which the buttocks present with the legs folded on the thighs and the thighs on the abdomen. The position of the fetus is the same as in a normal vertex presentation but upside down.

complete color blindness, monochromatic vision.

complete dislocation [L, *complere,* to fill up, *dis,* apart, *locare,* to place], a dislocation in which the articular surfaces of the joint are completely separated.

complete fistula, an abnormal passage from an internal organ or structure to the surface of the body or to another internal organ or structure.

complete fracture, a bone break that completely disrupts the continuity of a bone across its entire width.

complete health history, a health history that includes a history of the chief complaint, present illness, past and present health history, social history, occupational history, sexual history, and family health history.

complete heart block (CHB) [L, *complere,* to fill up; Gk, *kardia,* heart; OFr, *bloc*], total failure of impulses to be conducted from the atria to the ventricles. It causes the atria and ventricles to beat independently.

complete hernia [L, *complere,* to fill up, *hernia,* rupture], a hernia characterized by protrusion of the hernial sac and abdominal contents through the abdominal wall.

complete paralysis [L, *complere,* to fill up; Gk, *paralyein,* to be palsied], paralysis characterized by a complete loss of motor function.

complete protein, a protein that contains all the essential amino acids in appropriate amounts to allow normal growth and tissue maintenance when adequate energy is provided in the diet.

complete rachischisis, a rare congenital fissure of the entire vertebral column and spinal cord, resulting from failure of the embryonic neural tube to close.

complete response (CR), (in oncology) the total disappearance of a tumor.

complex /kom′pleks, kəmpleks′/ [L, *complexus,* an embrace], **1.** a group of items, as chemical molecules, that are related in structure or function, as are the iron and protein portions of hemoglobin or the cobalt and protein portions of vitamin B_{12}. **2.** a combination of signs and symptoms of disease that forms a syndrome. **3.** (in psychology) a group of associated ideas with strong emotional overtones that affect a person's attitudes toward a specific subject.

complex carbohydrate, a polysaccharide, such as a carbohydrate, that is composed of a large number of glucose molecules, so called to distinguish it from a simple sugar.

complex cavity, a cavity that involves more than one surface of a tooth.

complex fracture, a closed fracture in which the soft tissue surrounding the bone is severely damaged.

complex protein, a protein that contains a simple protein and at least one molecule of another substance, as a glycoprotein, lipoprotein, nucleoprotein, or hemoglobin.

complex relationship building, a nursing intervention from the Nursing Interventions Classification (NIC) defined as establishing a therapeutic relationship with a patient to promote insight and behavioral change.

complex spatial relations, the perceptual relationship of one figure or part of a figure to another.

complex sugars, sugar molecules that can be hydrolyzed or digested to yield two molecules of the same or different simple sugars, such as sucrose, lactose, and maltose.

compliance (C) /kəmplī′əns/ [L, *complere,* to complete], **1.** fulfillment by a patient of a caregiver's prescribed course of treatment. **2.** (in respiratory physiology) a measure of distensibility of the lung volume produced by a unit pressure change.

compliance behavior, a nursing outcome from the Nursing Outcomes Classification (NOC) defined as personal actions to promote wellness, recovery, and rehabilitation recommended by a health professional.

compliance behavior: prescribed diet, a nursing outcome from the Nursing Outcomes Classification (NOC) defined as personal actions to follow food and fluid intake recommended by a health professional for a specific health condition.

compliance behavior: prescribed medication, a nursing outcome from the Nursing Outcomes Classification (NOC) defined as personal actions to administer medication safely to meet therapeutic goals as recommended by a health professional.

compliance factor, a measure of the expansion of the flexible tubing in a mechanical ventilating system when pressure is applied.

complicated dislocation [L, *complicare,* to fold together, *dis,* apart, *locare,* place], a joint dislocation accompanied by damage to other tissues.

complicated fracture, a fracture accompanied by injury to neighboring soft tissues such as nerves and blood vessels.

complicated labor [L, *complicare,* to fold together, *labor,* work], any labor that is made more difficult or complex by a deviation from the normal procedure.

complication [L, *complicare,* to fold together], **1.** a disease or injury that develops during the treatment of a preexisting disorder, frequently altering the prognosis. **2.** a problem that arises during labor that puts the neonate, mother, or both at risk.

component /kəmpōʹnənt/ [L, *componere,* to assemble], a significant part of a larger unit.

component drip set, a device used for delivering IV fluids, especially whole blood. It includes plastic tubing and a combination drip-chamber and filter.

component syringe set, a device used for delivering IV fluids. It includes plastic tubing, two slide clamps, a Y-connector, and a syringe.

component therapy, transfusion of an individual blood component rather than whole blood, to treat a specific deficiency, avoid volume overload, and prevent reactions to unneeded blood products.

composite core /kəmposʹit/ [L, *componere,* to assemble], a buildup of composite resin designed and placed in the pulp chamber and root canal of an endodontically treated tooth to allow the tooth to be used as a foundation for a crown or bridge.

composite graft, a transplantation that involves more than one type of tissue such as skin and cartilage. The term may also refer to an artificial vessel graft, an aortic valve prosthesis used to replace the ascending aorta valve.

composite odontoma, a tumor arising in the tooth or tooth tissue consisting of both enamel and dentin.

compos mentis /komʹpōs menʹtis/, having a sound mind.

compound [L, *componere,* to assemble], /komʹpound/, **1.** (in chemistry) a substance composed of two or more different elements, chemically combined in definite proportions, that cannot be separated by physical means. **2.** any substance composed of two or more different ingredients. **3.** denoting an injury characterized by multiple factors, such as a compound fracture. **4.** to make a substance by combining ingredients, such as a pharmaceutic.

compound aneurysm, a localized dilatation of an arterial wall in which some of the layers of the wall are distended and others are ruptured or dissected.

compound fracture, a fracture in which the broken end or ends of the bone have torn through the skin.

compound joint [L, *componere,* to assemble, *jungere,* to join], a joint that involves more than two bones. The elbow and knee joints are two examples.

compound microscope [L, *componere,* to assemble; Gk, *mikros,* small, *skopein,* to view], a microscope with two or more simple or complex lens systems.

compound tubuloalveolar gland /tooʹbyə lōʹalvēʹələr/, one of the many multicellular glands with more than one secretory duct that contains both tube-shaped and sac-shaped portions, such as the salivary glands.

Comprehensive Health Manpower Training Act of 1971, legislation passed by the U.S. Congress to provide educational funding for nurse-practitioner and physician-assistant programs.

Comprehensive Health Planning (CHP) and Public Health Services Amendments, legislation passed by the U.S. Congress in 1966 that emphasized regional planning and introduced the concept that each person has a "right to health care."

comprehensive medical care, a health care program that provides for preventive medical care and rehabilitative services in addition to traditional chronic and acute illness services.

compress /komʹpres/ [L, *comprimere,* to press together], a soft pad, usually made of cloth, used to apply heat, cold, or medication to the surface of a body area. A compress also may be applied over a wound to help control bleeding.

compressibility factor /kəmpres′ibil′itē/, a measure of the amount of tidal volume that may be trapped in a mechanical ventilator system in relation to the water pressure applied. It is expressed in milliliters of gas per centimeter of water pressure.

compressible volume /kəmpres′əbəl/, a part of the tidal volume of gas produced by a mechanical ventilator that is prevented from reaching a patient by compression of the gas and expansion of the flexible tubing in the equipment.

compression /kəmpresh′ən/ [L, *comprimere,* to press together], **1.** the act of pressing, squeezing, or otherwise applying pressure to an organ, tissue, or body area. **2.** the pressing or squeezing of substances together so that they occupy a smaller volume of space (e.g., compressing gas into a pressurized aerosol can).

compression fracture, a bone break, especially in a short bone, that disrupts osseous tissue and collapses the affected bone.

compression neuropathy, any of several disorders involving damage to sensory nerve roots or peripheral nerves, caused by mechanical pressure or localized trauma. It is characterized by paresthesia, weakness, or paralysis. The carpal, peroneal, radial, and ulnar nerves are most commonly involved.

compression paralysis [L, *comprimere,* to press together; Gk, *paralyein,* to be palsied], a paralysis that is caused by sustained pressure on a peripheral nerve. The condition may be temporary or permanent, depending on the duration and intensity of pressure.

compressions, (in physical science) regions of high molecular density, such as a great amount of ultrasound energy, within a longitudinal wave.

compressive atelectasis /kəmpres′iv/, a condition in which a region of the lung cannot be ventilated as a result of intrathoracic pressures that compress the alveoli in that region. The condition may result from a pulmonary embolism.

compressor naris /kompres′ôr när′is/, the transverse part of the nasalis muscle that serves to depress the cartilage of the nose and to draw the ala toward the septum.

compromise /kom′prəmīs/ [L, *com,* together, *promittere,* to promise], **1.** an action that may involve a change in a person's behavior, as in substituting goals or delaying satisfaction of needs in one area to reduce stress in another. **2.** an illness or condition that can affect another part of the body.

compromise body image, a new body image acquired by a patient as part of his or her adjustment to a physical dysfunction. A compromise body image incorporates and modifies unacceptable features of the condition through psychologic defense mechanisms such as denial, sublimation, repression, and overcompensation.

compromised host, a person who is less than normally able to resist infection because of immunosuppressive therapy, immunologic defect, severe anemia, or concurrent disease or condition, including HIV infection, metastatic malignancy, cachexia, or severe malnutrition.

Compton scatter [Arthur H. Compton, American physicist, 1892–1962], the principal interaction process of photons with tissue in the diagnostic and therapeutic radiology energy range.

compulsion [L, *compellere,* to urge], an irresistible, repetitive irrational impulse to perform an act that is usually contrary to one's ordinary judgments or standards yet results in overt anxiety if it is not completed.—**compulsive,** *adj.*

compulsion need [L, *compellere,* to urge; Gk, *neuron,* nerve, *osis,* condition], an irresistible, irrational urge to perform certain acts repeatedly in spite of conscious recognition that doing so is abnormal behavior.

compulsive eating, an eating disorder characterized by continuous or frequent excessive eating over which the individual does not feel he or she has control, and which usually leads to weight gain and obesity. Eating is not connected to hunger, and food intake may be rapid or secret.

compulsive idea [L, *compellere,* to urge], a recurring irrational idea that persists in the mind, usually generating an irresistible urge to perform an inappropriate act.

compulsive personality, a type of character structure with a pattern of chronic and obsessive adherence to rigid standards of conduct. The person is usually excessively conscientious and inhibited, is extremely inflexible, has an extraordinary capacity for work, and lacks a normal ability to relax and to relate to other people.

compulsive personality disorder, a condition in which an irrational preoccupation with order, rules, ritual, and detail interferes with everyday functioning and normal behavior.

compulsive polydipsia, a compelling urge to drink excessive amounts of liquid. The condition is not caused by any organic dysfunction or physical deprivation. Extreme cases can result in death from water intoxication and electrolyte imbalance.

compulsive ritual, a series of acts a person feels must be carried out even though he or she recognizes that the behavior is useless and inappropriate, commonly seen in obsessive-compulsive disorder.

computed dental radiography (CDR), a computer-assisted method for projecting digital radiographic images of the teeth and jaws on a video monitor. CDR may expose a patient to less radiation than conventional dental radiography.

computed radiography (CR), digital radiography that records radiographic images on photostimulable phosphor plates instead of film/screen image receptors. The acquired image data are converted to electronic signals and digitized so they can be stored and manipulated by a computer and displayed on a high-resolution monitor or recorded on film using a laser printer.

computed tomography (CT) /kəmpyōō'tid/, a radiographic technique that produces an image of a detailed cross section of tissue. The procedure is painless and noninvasive and requires no special preparation. It is 100 times more sensitive than conventional radiography. CT uses a narrowly collimated beam of x-rays that rotates in a full arc around the patient to image the body in cross-sectional slices. The image is created by a computer that uses multiple attenuation readings taken around the periphery of the body part. The computer calculates tissue absorption and produces a representation of the tissues that demonstrates the densities of the various structures. Tumor masses, infractions, bone displacement, and accumulations of fluid may be detected.

computed tomography angiography, the use of CT to visualize the blood vessels of the heart.

computed tomography of the abdomen, a noninvasive radiographic procedure performed with contrast dye to diagnose pathologic conditions of the abdominal and retroperitoneal organs.

computed tomography of the brain, a radiographic procedure performed with contrast dye to diagnose pathologic conditions of the brain. It can also identify MS and other degenerative abnormalities.

computed tomography of the chest, a noninvasive radiographic procedure performed with contrast dye to diagnose and evaluate pathologic conditions of the chest. Fractures can also be seen.

computed tomography portogram, an x-ray test with contrast dye used to identify tumors of the liver smaller than 2 cm. The contrast medium is injected through a catheter in the splenic artery, rather than through a peripheral vein as in a routine CT scan.

computed tomography scanogram, a CT technique used especially to measure discrepancies in limb length. CT scout images of the joints of the upper or lower extremity are taken followed by placement of the CT cursors over the joints to obtain measurements. The CT scanogram is more consistently reproduced and radiation doses are lower than in the conventional imaging technique (orthoroentgenography).

computer-aided semen analysis (CASA), any of various methods of automated, objective, standardized evaluation of sperm concentration and movement in a semen sample, assessing the individual's potential fertility or infertility. Most techniques use video recordings showing movements of multiple spermatozoa.

COMT, abbreviation for **catechol-o-methyl transferase.**

CON, abbreviation for **certificate-of-need.**

CONA, abbreviation for **Canadian Orthopedic Nurses Association.**

conation /kōnā'shən/ [L, *conari*, to attempt], the mental process characterized by desire, impulse, volition, and striving.—**conative,** *adj.*

concanavalin A /kon'kənav'əlin/, a protein isolated from the jack bean that reacts with polyglucosans in the blood of mammals and causes blood cells to agglutinate. It has been used in immunology to stimulate T-cell production.

concatenates /kənkat'ənāts/, long molecules formed by continuous repeating of the same molecular subunit.

concave [L, *concavare,* to make hollow], curved like the interior of an arched circle.

concave-convex joint relationship /kon'kāv, konkāv'/, a relationship in which one of a joint's articulating surfaces is concave and the other is convex.

concave spherical lens [L, *concavare,* to make hollow; Gk, *sphaira,* ball; L, *lentil*], a lens with curved, depressed surfaces that cause light rays to diverge. It is used for the management of myopia.

concavity /kənkav'itē/, a deep depression or inward curving surface of an organ or body structure.

concealed accessory pathway /kənsēld/ [L, *con,* together, *celare,* to hide], a connection between the atria and ventricles that is capable of retrograde conduction only. The patient is prone to paroxysmal supraventricular tachycardia caused by orthodromic circus movement tachycardia.

concealed hemorrhage, the escape of blood from a ruptured vessel into internal organs or cavities.

concealed junctional extrasystole, an impulse that arises in and discharges the atrioventricular (AV) node or the AV bundle but fails to reach either the atria or the ventricles.

concealed penis, a small penis concealed beneath a fat pad or the skin of the scrotum, abdomen, or thigh.

conceive /kənsēv'/ [L, *concipere,* to take together], to become pregnant.

concentrate /kon'səntrāt/ [L, *con* + *centrum,* center], **1.** to decrease the bulk of a liquid mixture and increase the quantity of dissolved substances per unit of volume by the removal of solvent through evaporation or other means. **2.** a substance, particularly a liquid, that has been strengthened and reduced in volume through such means.

concentration[1] /kon'səntrā'shən/ [L, *concentratio*], **1.** an increase in strength by evaporation. **2.** the ratio of the mass or volume of a solute to the mass or volume of the solution or solvent.

concentration[2], a nursing outcome from the Nursing Outcomes Classification (NOC) defined as ability to focus on a specific stimulus.

concentration gradient, a difference in the concentration of a substance on two sides of a permeable barrier.

concentric /kənsen'trik/ [L, *con* + *centrum,* center], describing two or more circles that have a common center.

concentric contraction, a common form of muscle contraction that occurs in rhythmic activities when the muscle fibers shorten as tension develops.

concentric fibroma, a fibrous tumor surrounding the uterine cavity.

concentric hypertrophy [L, *con* + *centrum,* center; Gk, *hyper,* excessive, *trophe,* nourishment], a type of tissue overgrowth in which the walls of an organ continue to increase but the exterior size remains the same and the internal size diminishes.

concept [L, *concipere,* to take together], a construct or abstract idea or thought that originates and remains within the mind. —**conceptual,** *adj.*

conception /kənsep'shən/ [L, *concipere,* to take together], **1.** the beginning of pregnancy, usually taken to be the instant that a spermatozoon enters an ovum and forms a viable zygote. **2.** the act or process of fertilization. **3.** the act or process of creating an idea or notion. **4.** the idea or notion created; a general impression resulting from the interpretation of a symbol or set of symbols.

conceptional age, in fetal development, the number of weeks since conception. It is assumed to be 2 weeks less than gestational age.

conceptive /kənsep'tiv/ [L, *concipere,* to take together], **1.** able to become pregnant. **2.** pertaining to or characteristic of the mental process of forming ideas or impressions.

concept mapping, a method of visualizing relationships among various concepts. A branching, hierarchical diagram of concepts shows how they are connected.

conceptual disorder /kənsep'choō-əl/ [L, *concipere,* to take together], a disturbance in thought processes, cognitive activities, or ability to formulate concepts.

conceptual framework, a group of concepts that are broadly defined and systematically organized to provide a focus, a rationale, and a tool for the integration and interpretation of information.

conceptus /kənsep'təs/ [L, *concipere,* to take together], the product of conception; the fertilized ovum and its enclosing membranes at all stages of intrauterine development, from implantation to birth.

concha /kong'kə/, a body structure that is shell-shaped, as the cavity in the external ear that surrounds the external auditory canal meatus.

conchitis /kongkī'tis/, an inflammation of a concha of the ear or nose.

concoction /kənkok'shən/ [L, *con* + *coquere,* to cook], a remedy prepared from a mixture of two or more drugs or substances that have been heated.

concomitant /konkom'itənt/ [L, *con* + *comitari,* to accompany], designating one or more of two or more things, occurring simultaneously, that may or may not be interrelated; accompanying.

concomitant strabismus, a condition of crossed eyes in which the angle of squint is the same in all directions of gaze.

concomitant symptom, any symptom that accompanies a primary symptom.

concordance /kənkôr'dəns/ [L, *concordare,* to agree], the expression of one or more specific traits in both members of a pair of twins.—**concordant,** *adj.*

concrescence /kənkres'əns/ [L, *concrescere* to be formed], **1.** a growing together; a union of parts originally separate. **2.** (in embryology) the flowing together and piling up of cells. **3.** (in dentistry) the union of the roots of two adjacent teeth by a deposit of excess cementum.

concreteness /kənkrēt'nes/ [L, *concrescere,* to be formed], communication in the here and now; simplicity; lack of abstraction.

concrete operation /kon'krēt, konkrēt'/, a thought process based on tangible rather than abstract points of reference.

concrete thinking, a stage in the development of the cognitive thought processes in the child. During this phase, thought becomes increasingly logical and coherent so that the child is able to classify, sort, order, and organize facts while still being incapable of generalizing or dealing in abstractions.

concurrent infection [L, *concurrere*, to run together, *inficere*, to stain], a condition during which a person has two or more simultaneous infections.

concurrent review, part of a utilization management program in which inpatient or home health care is reviewed as it is provided. Reviewers, usually nurses, monitor appropriateness of the care, the setting, and the progress of discharge plans.

concurrent sterilization, a method of preparing an infant-feeding formula in which all ingredients and equipment are sterilized before mixing.

concurrent validity, validity of a test or a measurement tool that is established by simultaneously applying a previously validated tool or test to the same phenomenon, or data base, and comparing the results.

concussion /konkush'ən/ [L, *concutere*, to shake violently], damage to the brain caused by a violent jarring or shaking, such as a blow or an explosion.

condensation /kon'dənsā'shən/ [L, *condensare*, to make thick], **1.** a reduction to a denser form, such as from water vapor to a liquid. **2.** (in psychology) a process often present in dreams in which two or more concepts are fused so that a single symbol represents the multiple components.

condensation nuclei, neutral particles, such as dust, in the atmosphere that are able to absorb or adsorb water and grow. At relatively high humidities they form fogs or hazes. Condensation nuclei consisting of sulfuric or nitric acid vapors or nitrogen oxides may be a source of respiratory irritants.

condensed milk, a thick liquid prepared by the evaporation of half of the water content of cow's milk.

condenser, an instrument for compacting restorative material into a prepared tooth cavity. It has a working end, or nib, with a flat or serrated face.

condition /kəndish'ən/ [L, *condicere*, to make arrangements], **1.** a state of being, specifically in reference to physical and mental health or well-being. **2.** anything that is essential to or restricts or modifies the appearance or occurrence of something else. **3.** to train a person or an animal, usually through specific exercises and repeated exposure to a particular state or thing. **4.** (in psychology) to subject a person or an animal to conditioning or associative learning so that a specific stimulus always elicits a particular response.

conditional discharge /kəndish'ənəl/, a specified leave of absence or liberty from a psychiatric hospital in which certain behaviors are expected from the patient and the original commitment order remains in effect.

conditionally essential nutrients, those that must be supplied to the body only under special conditions, such as stress, illness, or aging.

conditioned avoidance response, a learned reaction that is performed either consciously or unconsciously to avoid an unpleasant or painful stimulus.

conditioned escape response, a learned reaction that is performed either consciously or unconsciously to stop or escape from an aversive stimulus.

conditioned orientation response (COR), the response, in a child under the age of 2 years, of turning his or her head toward the source of a sound. When the child responds appropriately by turning toward the sound, he or she is rewarded by seeing a toy move or light up.

conditioned reflex, a reflex developed gradually by training in association with a specific repeated external stimulus.

conditioned response, an automatic reaction to a stimulus that does not normally elicit such response but has been learned through training. Such responses can be physical or psychologic and are produced by repeated association of some physiologic function or behavioral pattern with an unrelated stimulus or event.

conditioned stimulus [L, *conditio* + *stimulus*, goad], any stimulus to which a reflex response has been conditioned by previous training or experience.

conditioning /kəndish'əning/ [L, *condicere*, to make arrangements], a form of learning based on the development of a response or set of responses to a stimulus or series of stimuli.

condom /kon'dəm/, a soft, flexible sheath made of plastic, rubber, or skin that covers the penis. Condoms prevent the exchange of body fluids during sexual activity, thereby preventing infection and conception.

condom catheter, an external urinary collection device that fits over the penis like a condom. It is used in the management of urinary incontinence.

conduct disorder /kon'dukt/, (in psychiatry) an enduring set of behaviors that evolves over time, characterized by aggression and violations of the rights of others.

conduction /kənduk'shən/ [L, *conducere,* to lead], **1.** (in physics) a process in which heat is transferred from one substance to another because of a difference in temperature; a process in which energy is transmitted through a conductor. **2.** (in physiology) the process by which a nerve impulse is transmitted.—**conductive,** *adj.*

conduction anesthesia, a loss of sensation, especially pain, in a region of the body, produced by injecting a local anesthetic along the course of a nerve or nerves to inhibit the conduction of impulses to and from the area supplied by that nerve or nerves.

conduction aphasia, a dissociative speech phenomenon in which a patient has no difficulty in comprehending words seen or heard and no dysarthria, yet has problems in self-expression. The patient may substitute words similar in sound or meaning for the correct ones but is unable to repeat from dictation, to spell, or to read aloud.

conduction pathway, the route followed by nerve impulses propagated along synaptically connected neurons.

conduction system, specialized tissue that carries electric impulses, such as bundle branches and Purkinje fibers in the heart.

conduction system of the heart, the network of highly specialized muscle tissue that transmits the electrical impulses needed for a heartbeat. It includes the sinus and atrioventricular (AV) nodes, the conducting fibers between the nodes, the AV bundle, the left and right bundle branches, and the Purkinje fibers.

conduction velocity, the speed with which an electrical impulse can be transmitted through excitable tissue, as in the movement of an action potential through His-Purkinje fibers of the heart.

conductive hearing loss /kənduk'tiv/ [L, *conducere,* to lead], a form of hearing loss in which sound is inadequately conducted through the external or middle ear to the sensorineural apparatus of the inner ear. Sensitivity to sound is diminished, but clarity (interpretation of the sound) is not changed as long as the sound is sufficiently loud.

conductivity, the ability of an electrical or other system to transmit sound, heat, light, or electromagnetic energy.

conductor, **1.** any substance through which electrons flow readily. **2.** (in psychiatry) a family therapist who uses his or her own personality to give direction to patients in therapy.

conduit /kon'dit, kon'doo·it/, **1.** an artificial channel or passage that connects two organs or different parts of the same organ. **2.** a tube or other device for conveying water or other fluids from one region to another.

condylar fracture /kon'dilər/ [Gk, *kondylos,* knuckle], any break in a condyle, a rounded projection on a bone at a hinge joint. Such fractures usually occur at the distal end of the humerus or the femur and frequently detach a bone fragment that includes the condyle.

condylar guide, a mechanical device on a dental articulator, designed to guide articular movement similar to that produced by the condyles in the TMJs.

condyle /kon'dīl/ [Gk, *kondylos,* knuckle], a rounded projection at the end of a bone that anchors muscle ligaments and articulates with adjacent bones.— **condylar,** *adj.*

condyloid /kon'diloid/ [Gk, *kondylos,* knuckle], resembling a knuckle.

condyloma latum, a flat, moist papular growth that appears in secondary syphilis in the coronal sulcus of the perineum or on the glans penis.

condyloma acuminatum, a warty growth in the uterine cervix as a result of a human papillomavirus infection.

cone /kōn/ [Gk, *konos,* cone], **1.** a photoreceptor cell in the retina of the eye that enables a person to visualize colors. There are three kinds of retinal cones, one each for the colors blue, green, and red; other colors are seen by stimulation of more than one type of cone. **2.** a cone-shaped device attached to radiologic equipment to focus x-rays on a small target of tissue.—**conic** /kon'ik/, *adj.*

cone biopsy, surgical removal of a cone-shaped segment of the cervix, including both epithelial and endocervical tissue.

cone cutting, interference with an x-ray beam by a radiographic cone caused by misalignment of the tube, cone, and film.

confabulation /kənfab'yəlā'shən/ [L, *con* + *fabulari,* to speak], the fabrication of experiences or situations, often recounted in a detailed and plausible way, to fill in and cover up cognitive impairment or memory loss.

confession /kənfesh'ən/, an act of seeking expiation through another from guilt for a real or imagined transgression.

confidence coefficient [L, *confidere,* to rely on + *coefficiens*], the probability that a confidence interval will contain the true value of the population parameter. For example, if the confidence coefficient is 0.95, 95% of the confidence intervals so calculated for each of a large number of random samples would contain the parameter.

confidence interval [L, *confidere,* to rely on, *intervallum,* area within ramparts], a type of statistic interval estimate for an unknown parameter: a range of values believed to contain the parameter, with a predetermined degree of confidence.

confidence limits [L, *confidere,* to rely on, *limes,* limit], the endpoints or boundaries of a confidence interval, delineating the minimum and maximum values of the range expected to contain the parameter.

confidentiality /kon′fiden′shē·al′itē/, 1. the nondisclosure of information except to another authorized person. 2. (in research) protection of study participants such that an individual participant's identity cannot be linked to the information provided to the researcher and is never publicly divulged.

confinement /kənfīn′mənt/ [L, *confinis,* common boundary], 1. a state of being held or restrained within a specific place to hinder or minimize activity. 2. the final phase of pregnancy, during which labor and childbirth occur.

confinement deprivation, an emotional disorder that may result when an individual is separated from familiar surroundings or denied contact with familiar persons or objects. It may occur when one is confined to a single room.

conflict /kon′flikt/ [L, *conflictere,* to strike together], 1. a mental struggle, either conscious or unconscious, resulting from the simultaneous presence of opposing or incompatible thoughts, ideas, goals, or emotional forces, such as impulses, desires, or drives. 2. a painful state of consciousness caused by the arousal of such opposing forces and the inability to resolve them. 3. (in psychoanalysis) the unconscious emotional struggle between the demands of the id and those of the ego and superego or between the demands of the ego and the restrictions imposed by society.

conflict mediation, a nursing intervention from the Nursing Interventions Classification (NIC) defined as facilitation of constructive dialogue between opposing parties with a goal of resolving disputes in a mutually acceptable manner.

confluence of the sinuses /kon′floo·əns/ [L, *confluere,* to flow together], the wide union of the superior sagittal, the straight, and the occipital sinuses with the two large transverse sinuses of the dura mater.

confluent /kon′floo·ənt/ [L, *confluere,* to flow together], running together, such as the sinuses of the dura mater or some skin eruptions.

conformational disease, a general term for a number of disorders, such as Alzheimer's disease and Pick's disease, caused by a mutation in the structure of specific proteins, leading to the aggregation and deposition of abnormal proteins.

confounding /konfoun′ding/, 1. interference by a third variable so as to distort the association being studied between two other variables, because of a strong relationship with both of the other variables. 2. a relationship between two causal factors such that their individual contributions cannot be separated.

confrontational visual field testing /kon′frəntā′shənəl/ [L, *con* + *frons,* forehead], a method of assessing a patient's visual field by moving an object into the periphery of each of the visual quadrants. The test is conducted while one eye is covered and the vision of the other is fixed on a point straight ahead. The patient reports when the moving object is first detected at the edge of the visual field.

confusion /kənfyoo′shən/ [L, *confundere,* to mingle], a mental state characterized by disorientation regarding time, place, person, or situation. It causes bewilderment, perplexity, lack of orderly thought, and inability to choose or act decisively and perform ADL.—**confusional,** *adj.*

confusional state, a mild form of delirium. The confusion may be characterized by failure to perform ADL, memory deficits, disruptive behavior, and inappropriate speech.

congener /kon′jənər/ [L, *con* + *genus,* origin], one of two or more things that are similar or closely related in structure, function, or origin. An example of congeners is muscles that function identically.—**congenerous** /kənjen′ərəs/, *adj.*

congenital /kənjen′itəl/ [L, *congenitus,* born with], present at birth, as a congenital anomaly or defect.

congenital absence of sacrum and lumbar vertebrae, an abnormal condition present at birth and characterized by varying degrees of deformity, ranging from the absence of the lower segment of the coccyx to the absence of the entire sacrum and all lumbar vertebrae.

congenital adrenal hyperplasia (CAH), a group of disorders that have in common an enzyme defect resulting in low levels of cortisol and increased secretion of adrenocorticotropic hormone. During intrauterine life the disorder leads to pseudohermaphroditism in female infants and macrogenitosomia in male infants.

congenital amputation, the absence of a fetal limb or part at birth. The condition previously was attributed to amputation by constricting bands in utero but now is regarded as a developmental defect.

congenital anomaly, any abnormality present at birth, particularly a structural one, which may be inherited genetically, acquired during gestation, or inflicted during parturition.

congenital cardiac anomaly, any structural or functional abnormality or defect of the heart or great vessels present at birth. Congenital heart anomalies are classified broadly cyanotic, in which unoxygenated blood mixes with oxygenated blood in the systemic circulation, and acyanotic, in which such mixing does not occur. The general physical symptoms of these pathophysiologic alterations are growth retardation, decreased exercise tolerance, recurrent respiratory infections, dyspnea, tachypnea, tachycardia, cyanosis, tissue hypoxia, and murmurs, all of which vary in severity, depending on the type and degree of the defect.

congenital cyanosis [L, *congenitus,* born with; Gk, *kyanos,* blue, *osis,* condition], cyanosis present at birth caused by a congenital heart disease or atelectasis of the lungs.

congenital cyst [L, *congenitus,* born with; Gk, *kystis,* bag], a cyst present at birth, as a dermoid cyst resulting from an embryonic defect in the skin or midline structures.

congenital dermal sinus, a channel present at birth, extending from the surface of the body and passing between the bodies of two adjacent lumbar vertebrae to the spinal canal.

congenital dislocation of the hip (CDH), an orthopedic defect, present at birth, in which the head of the femur does not articulate with the acetabulum as a result of an abnormal shallowness of the acetabulum.

congenital erythropoietic porphyria (CEP) [L, *congenitus,* born with; Gk, *erythros,* red, *poein,* to make, *porphyros,* purple], a rare autosomal-recessive trait caused by a defect in hemoglobin synthesis in erythrocytes and release of porphyrin from normoblasts in the bone marrow. Symptoms may include mutilating lesions, hemolytic anemia, splenomegaly, excessive urinary excretion of uroporphyrin and coproporphyrin, and invariably erythrodontia and hypertrichosis.

congenital generalized fibromatosis, the presence of small, hard, round fibromas of the subcutaneous and muscle tissues, the viscera, and the osseous systems, usually at birth. Visceral involvement may cause symptoms such as intestinal obstruction, diarrhea, and respiratory disturbances. Death is usually during the first few months of life.

congenital glaucoma, a rare form of glaucoma affecting infants and young children, which results from a congenital closure of the iridocorneal angle by a membrane that obstructs the flow of aqueous humor and increases the intraorbital pressure. The condition is progressive, is usually bilateral, and may damage the optic nerve.

congenital goiter, an enlargement of the thyroid gland at birth. It may be caused by a deficiency of enzymes or iodine required for the production of thyroxine.

congenital hernia [L, *congenitus,* born with, *hernia,* rupture], a hernia caused by a defect present at birth.

congenital hypogammaglobulinemia [L, *congenitus,* born with; Gk, *hypo,* deficiency, *gamma,* third letter of Greek alphabet; L, *globus,* small globe, *haima,* blood], a genetic disease characterized by a deficiency of gamma globulin and antibody in the serum. The cause may be a genetic defect leading to a failure of development of a normal beta-lymphocyte system and immune responses.

congenital immunity [L, *congenitus,* born with, *immunis,* free from], the immunity one has at birth that is acquired from the mother's antibodies as they pass through the placenta.

congenital jaundice [L, *congenitus,* born with; Fr, *jaune,* yellow], jaundice present at birth or during the first 24 hours of life. It is usually caused by poorly developed bile ducts.

congenital laryngeal stridor [L, *congenitus,* born with; Gk, *larynx;* L, *stridens,* a grating noise], a harsh respiratory sound that some infants make the first weeks after birth.

congenital lobar emphysema [L, *congenitus,* born with; Gk, *lobos,* lobe, *en,* in, *physema,* a blowing], a condition characterized by overinflation, commonly affecting one of the upper lobes and causing respiratory distress in early life.

congenital nonspherocytic hemolytic anemia, a group of blood disorders made up of a number of similar inherited diseases, each with a deficiency of one of the enzymes of red cell glycolysis. Most are associated with varying degrees of hemolysis, but all are less severe than the more serious disorder associated with spherocytosis.

congenital pouch colon, a developmental anomaly of the colon in which part or all of it is replaced by a dilated pouch, accompanied by anorectal malformation and a fistula between the colon and the genitourinary tract.

congenital pulmonary arteriovenous fistula, a direct connection between the arterial and venous systems of the lung present at birth that results in a right-to-left shunt and permits unoxygenated blood to enter the systemic circulation. The fistula may be single or multiple and may occur in any part of the lung.

congenital rubella syndrome, a collection of birth defects caused by transmission of the rubella virus from an infected mother to a fetus during the first trimester of pregnancy.

congenital scoliosis, an abnormal condition present at birth, characterized by a lateral curvature of the spine. It results from specific congenital rib and vertebral anomalies. The degree of obvious deformity caused by congenital scoliosis depends on the cause of the disease. The deformity increases with growth and age, usually progressing slowly during periods of slow growth of the trunk of the body.

congenital short neck syndrome, a rare congenital malformation of the cervical spine in which the cervical vertebrae are fused, usually in pairs, into one mass of bone, causing decreased neck motion and decreased cervical length, sometimes with neurologic involvement. When the deformity involves nerve-root compression, symptoms of peripheral nerve involvement, such as pain or a burning sensation, may be evident, accompanied by paralysis, hyperesthesia, or paresthesia.

congenital syphilis [L, *congenitus,* born with; Gk, *syn,* together, *philein,* to love], a form of syphilis acquired in utero, caused by the spirochete *Treponema pallidum.* It is generally characterized by osteitis, rashes, coryza, and wasting in the first months of life. Later childhood signs of the infection include interstitial keratitis, deafness, and notches in the incisor teeth. Some infected infants may appear disease-free at birth, but typical signs of the disease develop in adolescence.

congested /kənjes'tid/, having an excessive accumulation of a substance such as blood.

congestion /kənjes'chən/ [L, *congerere,* to accumulate], an abnormal accumulation of fluid in an organ or body area. The fluid is often mucus, but it may be bile or blood.

congestive /kənjes'tiv/, pertaining to congestion.

congestive cardiomyopathy [L, *congerere,* to accumulate; Gk, *kardia,* heart, *mys,* muscle, *pathos,* disease], a heart muscle disease characterized by heart failure and enlargement.

congestive dysmenorrhea [L, *congerere,* to accumulate; Gk, *dys,* difficult, *men,* month, *rhein,* to flow], a form of secondary dysmenorrhea caused by pelvic congestion, which arises from an increased blood supply in the area caused by a pelvic disease.

congestive heart failure (CHF), an abnormal condition that reflects impaired cardiac pumping. Its causes include MI, ischemic heart disease, and cardiomyopathy. Failure of the ventricles to eject blood efficiently results in volume overload, ventricular dilation, and elevated intracardiac pressure. Increased pressure in the left side of the heart causes pulmonary congestion. Increased pressure in the right side causes systemic venous congestion and peripheral edema.

congestive splenomegalia [L, *congerere,* to accumulate; Gk, *splen + megas,* large], an enlarged spleen associated with gastric hemorrhage, anemia, portal hypertension, and cirrhosis of the liver.

conglomerate silicosis /kənglom'ərit/ [L, *con + glomerare,* to wind into a ball], a severe form of silicosis marked by conglomerate masses of mineral dust in the lungs, causing acute shortness of breath, coughing, and production of sputum. Cor pulmonale usually develops.

congruent communication /kong'grōō·ənt/, a communication pattern in which the person sends the same message on both verbal and nonverbal levels.

Conidiobolus /konid'e·ob'olus/, a genus of perfect fungi. *C. coronatus* is usually a saprobe but sometimes causes entomophthoromycosis in humans and horses.

coning, the squeezing of the brain and brainstem through the foramen magnum as a result of swelling. It may lead to a loss of basic cardiorespiratory function.

conivaptan, a vasopressin receptor antagonist used to treat hyponatremia in those hospitalized.

conization /kon'īzā'shən/, the removal of a cone-shaped sample of tissue.

conjoined manipulation /kənjoind'/ [L, *con + jungere,* to yoke together], the use of both hands in obstetric and gynecologic procedures, with one positioned in the vagina and the other on the abdomen.

conjoined twins, two fetuses developed from the same ovum who are physically united at birth. Conjoined twins result when separation of the blastomeres in early embryonic development does not occur until a late cleavage phase and is incomplete, causing the fused condition.

conjoint family therapy /kənjoint'/, a form of psychotherapy in which a therapist sees a single nuclear family and addresses the issues and problems raised by family members.

conjugata /kon'jəgā'tə/ [L, *conjugere,* to yoke together], pertaining to the combined diameters of the pelvis, measured from the center of the promontory of sacrum to the back of the symphysis pubis.

conjugate /kon′jəgit/ [L, *con* + *jungere,* to yoke together], (in pelvimetry) the measurement of the female pelvis to determine whether the presenting part of a fetus can enter the birth canal.

conjugated estrogen /kon′jəgā′tid/, a mixture of sodium salts of estrogen sulfates, chiefly those of estrone, equilin, and 17-alpha-dihydroequilin. Conjugated estrogens may be prescribed to relieve postmenopausal vasomotor symptoms, such as hot flushes; to treat atrophic vaginitis, female hypogonadism, or primary ovarian failure; and to provide palliation in advanced prostatic carcinoma and metastatic breast cancer. The drug is also used to treat and prevent osteoporosis.

conjugate deviation [L, *conjugere,* to yoke together, *deviare,* to turn aside], pertaining to movements of the two eyes in which their visual axes function in parallel. The cause is a dysfunction of the ocular muscles, chiefly those of the ocular muscles, which allows the eyes to diverge to the same side when at rest.

conjugated hyperbilirubinemia, hyperbilirubinemia caused by defective excretion of conjugated bilirubin by the liver cells or by anatomic obstruction to bile flow within the liver or in the extrahepatic bile duct system.

conjugated protein, a compound that contains a protein molecule united to a nonprotein substance.

conjugate paralysis [L, *conjugere,* to yoke together; Gk, *paralyein,* to be palsied], a condition of paralysis of the conjugate movements of the two eyes, up or down or to the right or left. There is no diplopia. The cause is a cranial nerve lesion.

conjugation /kon′jəgā′shən/, an exchange or transfer of genetic information between two individuals in certain types of unicellular organisms, including bacteria and some protozoa. The exchanged material is incorporated and passed on to progeny after replication.

conjugon /kon′jŏŏgon/, an extrachromosomal segment of DNA that induces bacterial conjugation.

conjunctiva /kon′jungktī′və/ [L, *conjunctivus,* connecting], the mucous membrane lining the inner surfaces of the eyelids and anterior part of the sclera.—**conjunctival,** *adj.*

conjunctival burn /-ī′vəl/, chemical burn of the conjunctiva.

conjunctival reflex, a protective mechanism of the eye in which the eyelids close whenever the conjunctiva is touched.

conjunctival ring, a narrow ring at the junction of the conjunctiva and the periphery of the cornea.

conjunctival sac [L, *conjunctivus,* connecting; Gk, *sakkos*], the potential space enclosed by the conjunctiva and the eyelids.

conjunctival test, a procedure used to identify offending allergens by instilling the eye with a dilute solution of the allergenic extract.

conjunctivitis /kənjungk′tivī′tis/, inflammation of the conjunctiva, caused by bacterial or viral infection, allergy, or environmental factors. Red eyes, thick discharge, sticky eyelids in the morning, and inflammation without pain are characteristic.

conjunctivitis of newborn [L, *conjunctivus,* connecting; *itis,* inflammation; ME, *newe* + *borne*], a condition characterized by a purulent discharge from the eyes of an infant during the first 3 weeks of life. Frequent causes include gonococcal and chlamydial infections, which may lead to blindness if untreated.

connecting fibrocartilage [L, *con* + *nectere,* to bind], a disk of fibrocartilage found between many joints, especially those with limited mobility, such as the spinal vertebrae. Each disk is composed of concentric rings of fibrous tissue separated by cartilaginous laminae.

connective /kənek′tiv/ [L, *cum,* together with, *nectere,* to bind], pertaining to a binding or connection.

connective tissue, tissue that supports and binds other body tissue and parts. It derives from the mesoderm of the embryo and is dense, containing large numbers of cells and large amounts of intercellular material. The intercellular material is composed of fibers in a matrix or ground substance, which may be liquid, gelatinous, or solid such as in bone and cartilage. Connective tissue fibers may be collagenous or elastic.

connector /kə·nek′tər/ [L, *con* + *nectere,* to bind], **1.** anything serving as a link between two separate objects or units. **2.** (in dentistry) the part of a fixed partial denture that unites the retainer and the pontic; it may be rigid or nonrigid.

connexin 26, a protein found on the GJB2 gene. Autosomal-recessive mutation of the gene encoding it is the most common cause of congenital sensorineuronal hearing loss.

connexon /kənek′son/ [L, *con* + *nectere,* to bind], the functional unit of a gap junction; the hexagonal array of membrane-spanning proteins around a central channel that connects with its counterpart in an adjacent cell to form the intercellular pore of the gap junction.

Conn's syndrome [Jerome W. Conn, American physician, 1907–1891; Gk, *syn,* together, *dromos,* course], primary aldosteronism, characterized by excessive secretion of aldosterone with symptoms of headache, fatigue, nocturia, and polyuria. The patient may also experience hypertension, hypokalemic alkalosis, potassium depletion, and hypervolemia.

conoid tubercle, a tubercle on the inferior surface of the lateral third of the clavicle that gives attachment to the coracoclavicular ligament.

Conradi-Hünermann syndrome /kon·rä′dē hu′nər·män/ [Erich Conradi, German physician, 20th century; Carl Hünermann, German physician, 20th century], an autosomal-dominant form of chondrodysplasia punctata, characterized by asymmetric shortening of the limbs and scoliosis, with normal intelligence and life expectancy. The syndrome is also associated with maternal use of warfarin sodium during pregnancy.

consanguinity /kon′sang·gwin′itē/ [L, *con* + *sanguis*, blood], a hereditary or "blood" relationship between persons that results from a common parent or ancestor.

conscience [L, *conscientia*, to be privy to information], **1.** the moral, self-critical sense of what is right and wrong. **2.** (in psychoanalysis) the part of the superego system that monitors thoughts, feelings, and actions and measures them against internalized values and standards.

conscientiousness /kon′she·en′shusnes/, **1.** a principled commitment to do something, such as to provide health care. **2.** acting in a way that is considered right or proper.

conscious /kon′shəs/ [L, *conscire*, to be aware], **1.** (in neurology) capable of responding to sensory stimuli; awake, alert; aware of one's external environment. **2.** (in psychiatry) that part of the psyche or mental functioning in which thoughts, ideas, emotions, and other mental content are in complete awareness.

consciousness /kon′shəsnes/, a clear state of awareness of self and the environment in which attention is focused on immediate matters.

conscious proprioception, the conscious awareness of body position and movement of body segments. It is regulated by the lemniscal system through pathways that begin in joint receptors and end in the parietal lobe of the cerebral cortex; it enables the cortex to refine voluntary movements.

conscious sedation[1], See **moderate sedation.**

conscious sedation[2], a nursing intervention from the Nursing Interventions Classification (NIC) defined as administration of sedatives, monitoring of the patient's response, and provision of necessary physiologic support during a diagnostic or therapeutic procedure.

consensual /konsen′shoo·əl/ [L, *con* + *sentire*, to feel], pertaining to a reflex action in which stimulation of one body part results in a response in another.

consensual light reflex, a normally present crossed reflex in which light directed at one eye causes the opposite pupil to contract.

consensually validated symbols, symbols that are accepted by enough people that they have an agreed-upon meaning.

consensual reaction, contraction of the pupil of one eye when the contralateral retina is stimulated. It is a normal reflex.

consensual reflex /konsen′shoo·əl/ [L, *con* + *sentire*, to feel], pertaining to a reflex action in which stimulation of one body part results in a response in another.

consensual validation, 1. a mutual agreement by two or more persons about a particular meaning that is to be attributed to verbal or nonverbal behavior. **2.** the determination that a measuring tool (e.g., a test) measures what it is supposed to measure.

consensus sequence /kənsen′səs/, a sequence of nucleotides or amino acids similar or identical between regions of homology in different but related DNA, RNA, or protein sequence.

consensus statement, a document developed by an independent panel of experts, usually multidisciplinary, convened to review the research literature for the purpose of advancing the understanding of an issue, procedure, or method.

consent /kənsent′/ [L, *consentire*, to agree], to give approval, assent, or permission. A person must be of sufficient mental capacity and of the age at which he or she is legally recognized as competent to give consent.

consenting adult, an adult who willingly agrees to participate in an activity with one or more other adults. The term is usually applied to sexual activity.

consequences /kon′səkwen′səs/, stimulus events that follow a behavior that strengthen or weaken it. They may be either reinforcers or punishers, positive or negative.

conservation of energy /kon′sərvā′shən/ [L, *conservare*, to preserve], (in physics) a law stating that in any closed system the total amount of energy is constant.

conservation of matter, (in physics) a law stating that matter can be neither created nor destroyed and that the amount of matter in the universe is finite.

conservation principles of nursing, a conceptual framework for nursing that is directed to maintaining the wholeness or integrity of the patient when the normal ability to cope is disturbed or exceeded by stress. Nursing intervention is determined by the patient's need to conserve energy and to maintain structural, personal, and social integrity.

Consolidated Omnibus Budget Reconciliation Act (COBRA), legislation that provides for limited continuation of health coverage for individuals and families at the individual's own expense when the individual terminates employment from an organization that provides health insurance.

consolidation /kənsol′idā′shən/ [L, *consolidare,* to make solid], **1.** the combining of separate parts into a single whole. **2.** a state of solidification. **3.** (in medicine) the process of becoming solid, as when the lungs become firm and inelastic in pneumonia.

consolidation of individuality and emotional constancy, (in psychiatry) the fourth and final subphase in Mahler's system of the separation-individuation phase of preoedipal development. It begins toward the end of the second year. A degree of object constancy is accomplished, and separation of self and object representations is established.

constancy /kon′stənsē/, an absence of variation in quality of distinctive features despite location, rotation, size, or color of an object.

constant /kon′stant/, a fact or principle that is not subject to change.

constant pressure generator, a machine that provides or generates a constant gas pressure throughout the inspiratory cycle of breathing. The pressure may range from a low value, such as 12 cm H_2O, to a high value of as much as 3500 cm H_2O, as required.

constant region, the part of an immunoglobulin in which the amino acid sequence is relatively constant in all molecules of that class of immunoglobulin.

constant touch, a technique to diagnose the sensitivity of an injured body part by pressing the eraser end of a pencil or another object in various areas to determine the person's ability to detect the pressure.

constipation /kon′stipā′shən/ [L, *constipare,* to crowd together], difficulty in passing stools or incomplete or infrequent passage of hard stools. There are many causes, both organic and functional. Among the organic causes are intestinal obstruction, diverticulitis, and tumors. Complications include fecal impaction and perforation of the colon. Chronic

constipation can lead to diverticulosis and mucosal ulcers of the rectum, particularly in older adults.

constipation/impaction management, a nursing intervention from the Nursing Interventions Classification (NIC) defined as prevention and alleviation of constipation/impaction.

constitution, the general bodily health of an individual, expressed by the person's physical and mental abilities to function adequately in adverse circumstances.

constitutional delay /kon′stityoo′shənəl/ [L, *constituere,* to establish], a period in a child's development during which growth may be interrupted.

constitutional disease [L, *constituere,* to set up; Gk, *dis,* without; Fr, *aise,* ease], any disease associated with the inborn physical condition of the client, such as a hereditary susceptibility.

constitutional psychology, the study of the relationship of individual psychologic makeup to body morphologic characteristics and organic functioning.

constitutional symptom, a symptom that affects the general well-being or general status of a patient.

constitutive resistance /kənstich′ootiv/, the bacterial resistance to antibiotics that is contained in the DNA molecules of the organism. The trait can be passed on to daughter cells through cell division, but it cannot be transmitted to other species of bacteria.

constriction /kənstrik′shən/ [L, *constringere,* to draw tight], an abnormal closing or reduction in the size of an opening or passage of the body, as in vasoconstriction of a blood vessel.

constriction ring, a band of contracted uterine muscle that forms a stricture around part of the fetus during labor, usually after premature rupture of the membranes and sometimes impeding labor.

constrictive cardiomyopathy /kənstrik′tiv kär′dē·omī·op′əthe/ [L, *constringere,* to draw tight; Gk, *kardia,* heart, *mys,* muscle, *pathos,* disease], a heart disorder characterized by decreased diastolic compliance of the ventricles, imitating constrictive pericarditis.

constrictive pericarditis, a fibrous thickening of the pericardium caused by gradual scarring or fibrosis. The pericardium may undergo calcification and gradually becomes rigid, resisting the normal dilatation of the heart chambers during the blood-filling phases of the cardiac cycle.

constrictor /kənstrik′tər/, a muscle that binds or restricts an opening, such as the ciliary body fibers that control the size of the pupil.

constructional apraxia /kənstruk′shənəl/ [L, *construere,* to build], a form of apraxia characterized by the inability to copy drawings or to manipulate objects to form patterns or designs. It is caused by a right hemisphere lesion.

constructive aggression /kənstruk′tiv/, an act of self-assertiveness in response to a threatening action for purposes of self-protection and preservation.

constructive interference, (in ultrasonography) an increase in amplitude of sound waves that results when multiple waves of equal frequency are transmitted precisely in phase.

construct validity /kon′strəkt/, validity of a test or measurement tool that is established by demonstrating its ability to identify or measure the variables or constructs that it proposes to identify or measure.

consultant /kənsul′tənt/ [L, *consultare,* to deliberate], a person who by training and experience has acquired a special knowledge in a subject area that has been recognized by a peer group.

consultation¹ /kon′səltā′shən/ [L, *consultare,* to deliberate], a process in which the help of a specialist is sought to identify ways to correct problems in patient management or in planning and implementation of health care programs.

consultation², a nursing intervention from the Nursing Interventions Classification (NIC) defined as using expert knowledge to work with those who seek help in problem solving to enable individuals, families, groups, or agencies to achieve identified goals.

consultee-centered communication /kon′sultē′/, expert advice or guidance that is given to a consultee (health care worker) to improve the consultee's capacity to function more effectively in working with patients.

contact [L, *contingere,* to touch], **1.** the touching or drawing together of two surfaces, as those of upper and lower teeth. **2.** the moving together, either directly or indirectly, of two individuals so as to allow the transmission of an infectious organism from one to the other. **3.** a person who has been exposed to an infectious disease.

contact allergy, hypersensitivity to a substance that produced a reaction in a previous contact or that is structurally similar to another substance that produced such a reaction.

contact dermatitis, skin rash resulting from exposure to a primary irritant or to a sensitizing antigen. In the nonallergic type, a primary irritant such as an alkaline detergent or an acid causes a lesion similar to a thermal burn. In the allergic type, sensitizing antigens cause an immunologic change in certain lymphocytes. Subsequent exposure to the antigen causes the lymphocytes to release irritating chemicals, leading to inflammation, edema, and vesiculation.

contact hour, a 50-minute "hour" used to measure time for continuing education programs.

contact lens, a small, curved lens, primarily plastic in composition, shaped to fit the person's eye either to correct refractive error or to enhance appearance. The two primary forms of contact lenses are (1) rigid gas-permeable lenses and (2) soft lenses.

contact lens care, a nursing intervention from the Nursing Interventions Classification (NIC) defined as the prevention of eye injury and lens damage by proper use of contact lenses.

contactor /kəntak′tər/, a switching device that is part of the timer for the control of voltage across an x-ray tube.

contact precautions, guidelines recommended by the Centers for Disease Control and Prevention for reducing the risk of transmission of epidemiologically important microorganisms by direct or indirect contact. Direct-contact transmission involves skin-to-skin contact and physical transfer of microorganisms to a susceptible host from an infected or colonized person. Indirect-contact transmission involves contact of a susceptible host with a contaminated intermediate object, usually inanimate, in the patient's environment. Contact precautions apply to specified patients known or suspected to be infected or colonized with epidemiologically important microorganisms that can be transmitted by direct or indirect contact.

contact shield, a protective device constructed of lead or other material that is positioned directly over the eyes or gonads of a patient to be exposed to an x-ray beam.

contagion /kəntā′jən/ [L, *contingere,* to touch], the transmission of an infection by direct contact, droplet spread, or contact with contaminated fomites, such as clothing, bedding, dishes, or other objects the infected person has used.

contagious /kəntā′jəs/ [L, *contingere,* to touch], infectious; transmitted from person to person by direct or indirect contact. **—contagion,** *n.*

contagious pustular dermatitis [L, *contingere,* to touch, *pustula,* pustule; Gk, *derma,* skin, *itis,* inflammation], a skin disease normally affecting sheep but transmitted to humans who handle infected animals. It is caused by a poxvirus and results in lesions on the hands and occasionally on the face.

containment, the keeping of something within limits.

contaminant /kəntam′inənt/ [L, *contaminare,* to bring in contact], an agent that causes contamination, pollution, or spoilage, such as a mold spore that makes food unsafe to eat.

contaminated culture /kəntam′inātid/, a bacterial culture that has acquired unwanted foreign microorganisms.

contamination /-ā′shən/ [L, *contaminare,* to pollute], a condition of being soiled, stained, touched, or otherwise exposed to harmful agents, making an object potentially unsafe for use as intended or without barrier techniques.

content validity, validity of a test or measurement as a result of the use of previously tested items or concepts within the tool.

context [L, *contextus,* to weave together], (in communications theory) the setting, meaning, and language of a message.

continence /kon′tinəns/ [L, *continere,* to contain], **1.** the ability to control bladder or bowel function. **2.** the use of self-restraint, particularly in regard to sexual intercourse.

continent ileal reservoir, an intraabdominal pouch having a volume of at least 500 mL and a valve created from a portion of the ileum, pulled through the stoma, and lying flat against the abdominal wall. It maintains continence of feces and is emptied by a catheter when full.

continent ileostomy /kon′tinənt/, an ileostomy that drains into a surgically created pouch or reservoir in the abdomen. Involuntary discharge of intestinal contents is prevented by a nipple valve created from the ileum. This method eliminates the need for the patient to wear an external pouch over the stoma.

contingency contracting /kəntin′jənsē/ [L, *contingere,* to touch], a formal agreement between a psychotherapist and a patient undergoing behavior therapy regarding the consequences of certain actions by both parties.

contingency management, any of a group of techniques used in behavior therapy that attempts to modify a behavioral response by controlling the consequences of that response.

continuing care nurse /kəntin′yoo·ing/ [L, *continuare,* to unite], a nurse who specializes in coordination of the overall needs of the patient with the potential health care resources of the community. Continuing care nursing responsibilities and discharge planning ideally begin at the time a patient is admitted to a hospital.

continuing education, formal educational programs designed to promote knowledge, skills, and professional attitudes. The programs are usually short-term and specific. A certificate may be awarded for completion of a course, and a number of continuing education units or contact hours may be conferred. Continuing education is required for relicensure in many states.

continuing education unit (CEU), a point awarded to a professional person by a professional organization for having attended an educational program relevant to the goals of the organization.

continuity theory /kon′tinyoo′itē/, a concept that an individual's personality does not change as the person ages, with the result that his or her behavior becomes more predictable.

continuous ambulatory peritoneal dialysis (CAPD) /kəntin′yoo·əs/ [L, *continuare,* to unite, *ambulare,* to walk about; Gk, *peri,* near, *tenein,* to stretch, *dia,* through, *lysis,* loosening], a maintenance system of peritoneal dialysis in which an indwelling catheter permits fluid to drain into and out of the peritoneal cavity by gravity.

continuous bladder irrigation (CBI), a continuous infusion of a sterile solution into the bladder, usually by using a three-way irrigation closed system with a triple-lumen catheter. One lumen is used to drain urine; another is used to inflate the catheter balloon; and the final lumen carries the irrigation solution. CBI is primarily used following genitourinary surgery to keep the bladder clear and free of blood clots or sediment.

continuous cycling peritoneal dialysis (CCPD), a type of dialysis in which the patient is attached to an automatic cycler for short exchanges while sleeping at night. During waking hours the patient receives long dialysis exchanges but has ambulatory freedom.

continuous fever, a fever that persists steadily for a prolonged period.

continuous murmur [L, *continuare,* to unite, *murmur,* humming], an uninterrupted heart murmur or cervical venous hum that characteristically begins in systole and persists through diastole.

continuous negative chest wall pressure, a pressure below ambient pressure that is applied to the chest wall during the entire respiratory cycle, thus increasing transpulmonary pressure.

continuous passive motion (CPM), a technique for maintaining or increasing the amount of movement in a joint, using a mechanical device that applies force to produce joint motion without normal muscle function.

continuous phase [L, *continuare,* to unite; Gk, *phasis,* appearance], the phase of a colloidal solution corresponding to that of the solvent of a true solution.

continuous positive airway pressure (CPAP), a method of noninvasive or invasive ventilation assisted by a flow of air delivered at a constant pressure throughout the respiratory cycle. It is performed for patients who can initiate their own respirations but who are not able to maintain adequate arterial oxygen levels without assistance. CPAP may be given through a ventilator and endotracheal tube, through a nasal cannula, or into a hood over the patient's head.

continuous positive pressure ventilation (CPPV), a pressure above ambient pressure maintained in the upper airway throughout the breathing cycle. The term is usually applied to positive-end-expiratory pressure and mechanical ventilation.

continuous quality improvement (CQI), a system that seeks to improve the provision of services with an emphasis on future results. Once a process that needs improvement is identified, a team of knowledgeable individuals is gathered to research and document each step of that process. Once specific expectations and the means to measure them are established, implementation aims at preventing future failures and involves the setting of goals, education, and the measurement of results.

continuous regional anesthesia [L, *continuare,* to unite], a method for maintaining regional nerve block. A local anesthetic solution is infused at intervals or at a slow rate to infiltrate epidural or spinal spaces, usually via an indwelling catheter.

continuous reinforcement, a schedule of strengthening or rewarding behavior in which omission of a response is followed by a reinforcing event or behavior.

continuous tremor, fine, rhythmic, purposeless movements that persist during rest but sometimes disappear briefly during voluntary movements.

continuous tub bath, a therapeutic bath, usually prescribed in the treatment of some dermatologic conditions, in which the patient lies supported in a medicated solution of tepid water.

continuous wave (CW), **1.** an uninterrupted flow of energy such as a beam of laser light. **2.** sound intensity that remains constant while ultrasound is being produced.

continuum /kəntin'yoo·əm/ *pl.* **continua, 1.** a continuous series or whole. **2.** (in mathematics) a system of real numbers.

contour /kon'toor/ [Fr], **1.** the normal outline or configuration of the body or of a part. **2.** to shape a solid along certain desired lines.

contoured adducted trochanteric controlled alignment method (CAT-CAM) /kon'toord/, a design for an artificial lower limb for persons who have undergone above-the-knee amputations.

contouring /kon'tooring/, the process of forming a contour.

contra-angle /kon'trə·ang'gəl/ [L, *contra,* against, *angulus,* angle], an angulation by which the working point of a surgical instrument is brought close to the long axis of its shaft. It may involve two, three, or four bends, or angles, in its shank.

contra-angle handpiece, a handpiece (dental drill) in which two or more angles or bends are used to set the shaft at a desired angle to access hard-to-reach areas of the oral cavity.

contra bevel [L, *contra,* against; OFr, *baif,* open mouth], **1.** the angle between a dental cutting blade and the base of the periodontal pocket when the blade is held so that it separates the sulcular epithelium from the external epithelium of the gingiva. **2.** an external bevel of a tooth preparation extending onto a buccal or lingual cusp from an intracoronal restoration.

contraception /kon'trəsep'shən/ [L, *contra* + *concipere,* to take in], a process or technique for preventing pregnancy by means of a medication, device, or method that blocks or alters one or more of the processes of reproduction in such a way that sexual union can occur without impregnation.

contraceptive /kon'trəsep'tiv/ [L, *contra* + *concipere,* to take in], any device or technique that prevents conception.

contraceptive diaphragm, a contraceptive device consisting of a hemisphere of thin rubber bonded to a flexible ring, inserted into the vagina together with spermicidal jelly or cream to prevent conception.

contraceptive diaphragm fitting, a procedure, performed in an office or clinic, in which a contraceptive diaphragm is selected according to the clinical assessment of anatomic factors specific to the woman being fitted, including size of the vagina, position of the uterus, depth of the arch behind the symphysis pubis, and degree of support afforded by the muscles surrounding the vagina.

contraceptive effectiveness, the success of a method of contraception in preventing pregnancy. It is sometimes represented as a percentage but more accurately as the number of pregnancies per 100 woman-years. A contraceptive method that results in a pregnancy rate of fewer than 10 pregnancies per 100 woman-years is considered highly effective.

contraceptive jelly [L, *contra*, opposed, *concipere*, to take in, *gelare*, to congeal], a gelatinous preparation containing a spermicide to be introduced into the vagina to prevent conception.

contraceptive method, any act, device, or medication for avoiding conception or a viable pregnancy.

contract [L, *con*, with, *trahere*, to draw], **1.** an agreement or a promise that meets certain legal requirements, including competence of both or all parties to the contract, proper lawful subject matter, mutuality of agreement, mutuality of obligation, and consideration (the exchange of something of value in payment for the obligation undertaken). **2.** to make such an agreement or promise.—**contractual,** *adj.*

contracted kidney, a kidney that is greatly reduced in size and function as a result of an overgrowth of fibrous tissue and a diminished blood supply. The condition occurs in arteriolar nephrosclerosis and glomerulonephritis.

contractile /kəntrak′til/ [L, *con*, with, *trahere*, to draw], capable of becoming reduced in size or length or of being drawn together in response to some stimulus.

contractile ring dysphagia [L, *con* + *trahere*, to draw; AS, *hring*], an abnormal condition characterized by difficulty in swallowing caused by an overreactive interior esophageal sphincteric mechanism that induces painful sticking sensations under the lower sternum.

contractility /kon′traktil′itē/, the ability of muscle tissue to contract when its thick (myosin) and thin (actin) filaments slide past each other.

contraction /kəntrak′shən/ [L, *con* + *trahere*, to draw], **1.** a reduction in size, especially of muscle fibers. **2.** an abnormal shrinkage. **3.** (in labor) a rhythmic tightening of the musculature of the upper uterine segment that begins as mild tightening and becomes very strong late in labor, occurring as frequently as every 2 minutes and lasting over 1 minute. **4.** abnormal smallness of the birth canal or part of it, a cause of dystocia.

contractions stress test (CST), ultrasound monitoring of the fetal heart rate during uterine contractions induced by oxytocin administration or nipple stimulation.

contract-model HMO, a model in which the health maintenance organization (HMO) contracts with individual physicians rather than groups of providers for services not provided directly by the HMO.

contract suicide, assisted suicide for remuneration.

contracture /kəntrak′chər/ [L, *contractura*, a pulling together], an abnormal,

usually permanent condition of a joint characterized by flexion and fixation. It may be caused by atrophy and shortening of muscle fibers, resulting from immobilization, or by loss of the normal elasticity of connective tissues or the skin, such as from the formation of extensive scar tissue over a joint.

contraindicate /kon′trə·in′dikāt/ [L, *contra*, against, *indicare*, to make known], to report the presence of a disease or physical condition that makes it impossible or undesirable to treat a particular client in the usual manner or to prescribe medicines that might otherwise be suitable.

contraindication /-in′dikā′shən/ [L, *contra*, against, *indicare*, to make known], a factor that prohibits the administration of a drug or the performance of an act or procedure in the care of a specific patient.

contralateral /-lat′ərəl/ [L, *contra* + *lateralis*, side], affecting or originating in the opposite side of a point or reference, such as a point on a body.

contralateral reflexes [L, *contra*, against, *latus*, side, *reflectere*, to bend back], an overflow phenomenon of the nervous system in which a reflex is elicited on one side of the body by a stimulus to the opposite side.

contrast /kon′trast/ [L, *contra*, against, *stare*, to stand], a measure of the difference in optic density, radiation transmission, or other parameters between two adjacent areas in a radiographic image. Contrast plays an important role in the ability of a radiologist to perceive image detail.

contrast bath, a bath in which the patient alternately immerses a part of the body, usually the hands or feet, in hot and cold water for a specified period. The procedure is used to increase the blood flow to a particular area.

contrast examination, the use of radiopaque materials to make internal organs visible on x-ray film.

contrast medium, a substance that is injected into the body, introduced via catheter, or swallowed to facilitate radiographic imaging of internal structures that otherwise are difficult to visualize on x-ray films.

contrast nephropathy, kidney damage caused by a contrast medium, usually seen in patients already weakened by some other condition, such as DM. There is usually a sharp decline in the glomerular filtration rate after administration of the agent, sometimes with acute renal failure, followed in a few days by return to the patient's previous level of function.

contrasuppressor cell /kon′trəsəpres′ər/, one of a group of T cells that inhibit the function of suppressor T cells.

contrecoup injury /kôtrekoo′/ [L, *contra,* against; Fr, *coup,* blow; L, *injuria*], an injury, usually involving the brain, in which the tissue damage is on the side opposite the trauma site, as when a blow to the left side of the head results in brain damage on the right side.

contributory negligence /kəntrib′yətôr′ē/, a legal term describing a situation in which both the plaintiff and the defendant share in the negligence that caused injury to the plaintiff.

control [Fr, *controler,* to register], **1.** to exercise restraint or maintain influence over a situation. **2.** a standard against which conclusions may be measured, as in a "control group."

control cable, a stainless steel wire, usually contained in a flexible stainless steel housing, used to move or lock a prosthesis into place.

control gene, a gene, such as an operator or a regulator, that controls the transcription of a structural gene by either inducing or repressing RNA synthesis.

control group, a set of items or people that serves as a standard or reference for comparison with an experimental group. A control group is similar to the experimental group in number and is identical in specified characteristics but does not receive the experimental treatment or intervention.

controlled area, a part of a hospital or other health facility that is occupied primarily by personnel who work with radioactive materials. It is designed with barrier shielding to confine the radiation.

controlled association, 1. a direct connection of relevant ideas that results from a specific stimulus. **2.** a process of drawing repressed ideas into the consciousness in response to words spoken by a psychoanalyst.

controlled ovarian hyperstimulation, a method of assisted reproductive technology consisting of carefully monitored administration of agents designed to induce ovulation by a greater number of ovarian follicles and thus increase the probability of an oocyte's being fertilized.

controlled oxygen therapy, the administration of oxygen to a patient on a dose-response basis in which oxygen is regarded as a drug and only the smallest amount of it is used to obtain a desired therapeutic effect.

controlled substance [Fr, *controle,* to register; L, *substantia,* essence], any drug defined in the five categories of the federal **Controlled Substances Act** of 1970. The categories, or schedules, cover opium and its derivatives, hallucinogens, depressants, and stimulants. Schedule I drugs have a high abuse potential and no approved medical uses. Drugs in Schedules II to V all have approved medical indications, with decreasing abuse and dependence liabilities as the schedule number increases.

controlled substance checking, a nursing intervention from the Nursing Interventions Classification (NIC) defined as promoting appropriate use and maintaining security of controlled substances.

Controlled Substances Act, a U.S. law enacted in 1970 that regulates the prescribing and dispensing of psychoactive drugs. The act lists five categories of restricted drugs, organized by their medical acceptance, abuse potential, and ability to produce dependence.

controlled ventilation, the use of an intermittent positive pressure breathing unit or other respirator that has an automatic cycling device that replaces spontaneous respiration.

control of hemorrhage, the limitation of the flow of blood from a break in the wall of a blood vessel. Some of the methods for controlling hemorrhage are direct pressure, use of a tourniquet, and application of pressure on pressure points proximal to the wound.

control process, a system of establishing standards, objectives, and methods and measuring actual performance, comparing results, reinforcing strengths, and taking necessary corrective action.

contuse /kontooz′/, to injure a body part without breaking the skin.

contusion /kənt(y)oo′zhən/ [L, *contundere,* to bruise], an injury that does not disrupt the integrity of the skin, caused by a blow to the body and characterized by swelling, discoloration, and pain. The immediate application of cold may limit the development of a contusion.

convalescence /kon′vəles′əns/ [L, *convalescere,* to grow strong], the period of recovery after an illness, injury, or surgery.

convalescent carrier, a person who has recovered from the symptoms of an infectious disease but is still capable of transmitting pathogens to others.

convection /kənvek′shən/ [L, *convehere,* to bring together], (in physics) the transfer of heat through a gas or liquid by the circulation of heated particles.

convergence /kənvur′jəns/ [L, *convergere,* to bend together], the movement of two objects toward a common point, such as the turning of the eyes inward to see an object close to the face.

convergent evolution, the evolution of nonhomologous organs in distantly related species in response to similar environmental conditions.

convergent nystagmus, an intermittent spasmodic movement of the eyes in which they move rhythmically toward each other and slowly return to the original position. It is usually caused by a tumor of the anterior aqueduct of Silvius, third ventricle, or midbrain.

conversion /kənvur′zhən/ [L, *convertere,* to turn around], **1.** changing from one form to another, transmutation. **2.** (in obstetrics) the correction of a fetal position during labor. **3.** (in psychiatry) an unconscious defense mechanism by which emotional conflicts that ordinarily cause anxiety are repressed and transformed into symbolic physical symptoms that have no organic basis.

conversion disorder, an abnormality in which repressed emotional conflicts are changed into sensory, motor, or visceral symptoms with no underlying organic cause, such as blindness. Causal factors include a conscious or unconscious desire to escape from or avoid some unpleasant situation or responsibility or to obtain sympathy or some other secondary gain.

conversion dysphonia, an inability to produce vocal sounds, usually psychogenic in nature.

conversion factor, a dollar value multiplied by a procedure's unit value, from the **Current Procedural Terminology (CPT)** codes or a relative value scale, used to calculate the payment for contracted services or to set a price for a service.

conversion reaction, an ego defense mechanism whereby intrapsychic conflict is expressed symbolically through physical symptoms.

convex [L, *convextus,* vaulted], having a surface that curves outward.

convex spherical lens [L, *convehere,* to bring together; Gk, *sphaira,* ball; L, lentil], a lens that has sides that curve outward and that brings light to a focus. It is used in the treatment of hyperopia (farsightedness).

convoluted /kon′vəloo̅′tid/ [L, *convolutus,* rolled together], twisted, rolled together, with one part over another in a scroll.

convoluted kidney tubules [L, *convolutus,* rolled together; ME, *kidenei;* L, *tubulus*], pertaining to the proximal convoluted tubule of the nephron that leads from the glomerulus to the connecting ducts and between Bowman's capsule and the loop of Henle. The proximal and distal sections are convoluted, whereas the ascending and descending limbs of Henle's loop are relatively straight.

convoluted seminiferous tubules, the long threadlike tubes in the areolar tissue of the testes. The testes also contain straight segments of seminiferous tubules.

convolution /kon′vəloo̅′shən/ [L, *convolutus,* rolled together], a tortuous irregularity or elevation caused by a structure being infolded on itself, such as the gyri of the cerebrum.

convulsive seizure /kənvul′siv/ [L, *convulsio,* cramp; OFr, *seisir*], a sudden onset of a disease characterized by convulsions, palpitations, and other symptoms. The term is sometimes applied to an attack of an epileptic disorder.

convulsive tic, a disorder of the facial nerve, causing involuntary spasmodic contractions of the facial muscles supplied by that nerve.

Cook catheter, a flexible catheter sometimes used in place of the Tenckhoff catheter in peritoneal dialysis.

Coolidge tube [William D. Coolidge, American physician, 1873–1977], a basic type of hot-cathode x-ray tube that, with modern refinements, has been used by radiologists since it was invented in 1913.

cooling [AS, *colian,* cool], reducing body temperature by the application of a hypothermia blanket, cold moist dressings, ice packs, or an alcohol bath.

cooling rate, the rate at which temperature decreases with time (°C/min) immediately after the completion of hyperthermia treatment.

Coombs' positive hemolytic anemia /koomz/ [Robin R.A. Coombs, British immunologist, 1921–2006], a form of anemia that results from premature destruction of circulating RBCs.

cooperative play /kō·op′erətiv′/, any organized recreation among a group of children in which activities are planned for the purpose of achieving some goal.

coordinated movement, a nursing outcome from the Nursing Outcomes Classification (NOC) defined as the ability of muscles to work together voluntarily for purposeful movement.

coordinated reflex /kō·ôr′dinā′tid/ [L, *coordinare,* to arrange], a sequence of muscular actions that occur in a purposeful, orderly progression, such as the act of swallowing.

CO-oximeter, a device that uses spectrophotometry to measure relative blood concentrations of oxyhemoglobin, carboxyhemoglobin, methemoglobin, and reduced hemoglobin.

copayment /kō′pāmənt/, (in the United States) an amount paid by a health insurance plan enrollee for each office or ED visit or purchase of prescription drugs in addition to the amount paid by the insurance company.

COPD, abbreviation for **chronic obstructive pulmonary disease.**

Cope loop catheter, a type of nephrostomy catheter with a loop at the end to hold it in place.

coping[1] [Gk, *kolaphos*, buffet], a process by which a person deals with stress, solves problems, and makes decisions. The process has two components, cognitive and noncognitive. The cognitive component includes the thought and learning necessary to identify the source of the stress. The noncognitive components are automatic and focus on relieving the discomfort.

coping[2], a nursing outcome from the Nursing Outcomes Classification (NOC) defined as personal actions to manage stressors that tax an individual's resources.

coping enhancement, a nursing intervention from the Nursing Interventions Classification (NIC) defined as assisting a patient to adapt to perceived stressors, changes, or threats that interfere with meeting life demands and roles.

coping mechanism, any effort directed to stress management, including task-oriented and ego defense mechanisms, the factors that enable an individual to regain emotional equilibrium after a stressful experience.

coping resources, the characteristics of a person, group, or environment that are helpful in assisting individuals in adapting to stress.

coping style, the cognitive, affective, or behavioral responses of a person to problematic or traumatic life events.

copolymer /kōpol′əmər/ [L, *co-,* together or with; Gk, *polys,* many, *meros,* parts], a polymer containing monomers of more than one kind.

COPP, an anticancer drug combination of cyclophosphamide, procarbazine, predniSONE, and vinCRIStine.

copper (Cu) [L, *cuprum*], a malleable, reddish-brown metallic element. Its atomic number is 29. Its atomic mass is 63.55. Copper occurs in a pure state in nature and in many ores. It is a component of several important enzymes in the body and is essential to good health. Copper deficiency is rare because only 2 to 5 mg daily, easily obtained from a variety of foods, is sufficient for a proper balance. Copper accumulates in individuals with Wilson's disease, primary biliary cirrhosis, and, occasionally, chronic extrahepatic biliary tract obstruction.

copper gluconate, a salt of copper used in the prophylaxis and treatment of copper deficiency.

copperhead /kop′ərhed/ [L, *cuprum*; ME, *hed*], a poisonous pit viper (*Agkistrodon contortrix*) found mainly in the southeastern United States. The reddish brown, darkly banded snake is responsible for nearly 40% of the snake bites in the United States. Few bites are fatal. Pain, swelling, fang marks, and a bruise are usually present.

Copper T, a trademark for a T-shaped plastic IUD.

coprolalia /kop′rōlā′lyə/ [Gk, *kopros,* dung, *lalein,* to babble], the excessive use of obscene language.

coprolith /kop′rōlith/, a hard mass of feces in the intestinal tract, usually caused by excessive absorption of water from the large intestine.

coproporphyria /kop′rōpôrfir′ē·ə/ [Gk, *kopros* + *porphyros,* purple], a rare autosomal-dominant hereditary metabolic disorder in which large quantities of nitrogenous substances, called porphyrins, are excreted in the feces. Attacks, with varying GI and neurologic symptoms, may be precipitated by certain drugs.

coproporphyrin /kop′rōpôr′firin/ [Gk, *kopros* + *porphyros,* purple], **1.** any of the nitrogenous organic substances normally excreted in the feces that are products of the breakdown of bilirubin from hemoglobin decomposition. **2.** a test used for RBC porphyrin levels.

copula /kop′ōōlə/ [L], **1.** any connecting part or structure. **2.** a median ventral elevation on the embryonic tongue, formed by union of the second pharyngeal arches, that represents the future root of the tongue.

CoQ, abbreviation for **coenzyme Q.**

cor /kôr/, **1.** the heart. **2.** relating to the heart.

coracoacromial /kôr′əkō·əkrō′mē·əl/, pertaining to the coracoid process and the acromion of the scapula.

coracobrachialis /kôr′əkōbrā′kē·al′is/, a muscle with its origin on the scapula and its insertion on the inner side of the humerus. It functions to adduct and flex the arm.

coracoid process /kôr′əkoid/ [Gk, *korax,* crow, *eidos,* form; L, *processus*], the thick, curved extension of the superior border of the scapula, to which the pectoralis minor is attached.

coral snake, a poisonous snake with transverse red, yellow, and black bands that is native to the southern United States. Bites are rare. Pain does not always result, but neuromuscular and respiratory effects may be severe.

cord [Gk, *chorde,* string], any long, rounded, flexible structure. The body contains many different cords, such as the spermatic, vocal, spinal, neural, umbilical, and hepatic cords. —**cordal,** *adj.*

cordal, pertaining to a cord, such as the umbilical cord.

Cordarone, a trademark for an oral antiarrhythmic (amiodarone hydrochloride).

cord blood, blood taken from the umbilical cord vein or artery of the fetus. Like bone marrow, cord blood is rich in stem cells. It can be frozen and stored for later transfusion.

cord blood transplantation, the removal of blood from the umbilical cord of a fetus or its placenta for the treatment of blood diseases.

cordiform /kor'diform/, heart-shaped.

corditis /kôrdī'tis/ [Gk, *chorde* + *itis,* inflammation], an inflammation of the spermatic cord, accompanied by pain in the testis, often caused by an infection originating in the urethra or by a tumor, hydrocele, or varicocele.

Cordran, a trademark for a topical glucocorticoid (flurandrenolide).

core [L, *cor,* heart], **1.** (in dentistry) a section of a mold, usually of plaster, made over assembled parts of a dental restoration to record and maintain their relationships so that the parts can be reassembled in their original position. **2.** the center of a structure, as in core temperature of the body.

core temperature [L, *cor,* heart + *temperatura*], the temperature of deep structures of the body such as the liver, as compared with that of peripheral tissues.

Corgard, a trademark for a nonselective beta-adrenergic blocking agent (nadolol).

Cori cycle [Carl F. Cori, American physician, 1896–1984; Gerty T. Cori, American biochemist, 1896–1957; co-Nobel laureates in 1947], a physiologic mechanism whereby lactate, produced by glycolysis of glucose in contracting muscle, is converted back to glucose in the liver and returned via the circulation to the muscles.

Cori's disease /kôr'ēz/ [Carl F. Cori; Gerty T. Cori], a rare type of glycogen storage disease, in which the lack of an enzyme results in abnormally large deposits of glycogen in the liver, skeletal muscles, and heart. Signs are an enlarged liver, hypoglycemia, acidosis, and, occasionally, stunted growth.

corkscrew esophagus /kôrk'skrōō/ [ME *cork,* bark; L, *scrofa,* sow; Gk, *oisophagos,* gullet], a neurogenic disorder in which normal peristaltic contractions of the esophagus are replaced by spastic movements that occur spontaneously or with swallowing or gastric acid reflux.

cork worker's lung, hypersensitivity pneumonitis seen in cork handlers, caused by inhalation of moldy cork dust containing spores of various species of *Penicillium.*

corn [L, *cornu,* horn], a horny mass of condensed epithelial cells overlying a bony prominence. Corns result from chronic friction and pressure.

cornea /kôr'nē·ə/ [L, *corneus,* horny], the convex, transparent anterior part of the eye, comprising one sixth of the outermost tunic of the eye bulb. It is a fibrous structure with five layers: the anterior corneal epithelium, continuous with that of the conjunctiva; the anterior limiting layer: the substantia propria; the posterior limiting layer; and the endothelium of the anterior chamber (keratoderma). It is dense, uniform in thickness, and nonvascular.

corneal abrasion /kôr'nē·əl/ [L, *corneus,* horny, *abrasio,* scraping], the rubbing off of the outer layers of the cornea.

corneal corpuscle, one of the fixed flattened connective tissue cells between the lamellae of the cornea.

corneal grafting, transplantation of corneal tissue from one human eye to another, performed to improve vision in corneal scarring or distortion or to remove a perforating ulcer.

corneal loupe, (in ophthalmology) a magnifying lens designed especially for examining the cornea.

corneal reflex, a protective mechanism for the eye in which the eyelids close when the cornea is touched.

Cornelia de Lange's syndrome /kôr·nā·lē·ä dä läng'əz/ [Cornelia de Lange, Dutch pediatrician, 1871–1950], a congenital syndrome of severe mental retardation with many other abnormalities, such as dwarfism, brachycephaly, low-set ears, webbed neck, carp mouth, peculiar shape of the nose, bushy eyebrows meeting at the midline, unruly coarse hair on the forehead and neck, and flat spadelike hands with short tapering fingers.

cornification /kôr'nifikā'shən/, the conversion of cells into the horny layer of the skin. —**cornify,** *v.*

corn oil, a refined fixed oil obtained from the corn plant, *Zea mays;* used as a solvent and vehicle for medicinal agents and as a vehicle for injections. It has also been promoted as a source of polyunsaturated fatty acids in special diets.

corn pad, a device that helps relieve the pressure and pain of a corn on the toes by transferring the pressure to surrounding unaffected areas.

cornua /kôr'nōō·ə/, an anatomic structure that resembles a horn.

cornual pregnancy /kôr′nyoo·əl/ [L, *cornu*, horn, *praegnans*, childbearing], an ectopic pregnancy in one of the straight or curved extensions of the body of the uterus. The signs include a uterus that is asymmetric and tender, as well as cramping the pregnancy. The cornu of the uterus usually ruptures between 12 and 16 weeks of the pregnancy unless the condition is treated surgically.

corona /kərō′nə/ [L, crown], **1.** a crown. **2.** a crownlike projection or encircling structure, such as a process extending from a bone.—**coronal, coronoid,** *adj.*

coronal section [L, *corona*, crown + *sectio*], a section of the body cut in the plane of the coronal suture, or parallel to it.

coronal suture, the serrated transverse suture between the frontal bone and the parietal bone on each side of the skull.

coronary /kôr′əner′ē/ [L, *corona*, crown], **1.** pertaining to encircling structures such as the coronary arteries. **2.** pertaining to the heart. **3.** nontechnical, an MI or occlusion.

coronary arteriovenous fistula, an unusual congenital abnormality characterized by a direct communication between a coronary artery, usually the right, and the right atrium or ventricle, the coronary sinus, or the vena cava. A large shunt may result in growth failure, limited exercise tolerance, dyspnea, and anginal pain.

coronary artery, one of a pair of arteries that branch from the aorta, including the left and right coronary arteries. Because these vessels and their branches supply the heart, any dysfunction or disease that affects them can cause serious, sometimes fatal complications. The branches of the coronary arteries are affected by many different disorders such as embolic, neoplastic, inflammatory, and noninflammatory diseases.

coronary artery bypass graft (CABG), open heart surgery in which a prosthesis or a section of a vein or internal mammary artery is grafted from the aorta onto one of the coronary arteries, bypassing a narrowing or blockage in the coronary artery. The operation is performed in coronary artery disease to improve the blood supply to the heart muscle and to relieve anginal pain. Usually double or triple grafts are done for multiple areas of blockage.

coronary artery disease (CAD), any abnormal condition that may affect the heart's arteries and produce various pathologic effects, especially the reduced flow of oxygen and nutrients to the myocardium. The most common kind of coronary artery disease is coronary atherosclerosis. Angina pectoris, the classic symptom of

coronary artery disease, results from myocardial ischemia.

coronary artery fistula, a congenital anomaly characterized by an abnormal connection between a coronary artery and the right side of the heart or pulmonary artery.

coronary artery scan (CAS), a noninvasive method for the early detection of coronary atherosclerosis, using electron beam CT to detect and measure calcium, which is the marker for atherosclerosis, in the coronary arteries.

coronary care nursing, the nursing care provided in a hospital in a coronary care unit. Nursing in this setting requires technical knowledge, judgment, and skills, as well as ability to give emotional support to patients and their families during the acute stage of cardiac dysfunction.

coronary care unit (CCU), a critical care unit used for the treatment and monitoring of patients experiencing acute cardiac episodes.

coronary collateralization, the spontaneous development of new blood vessels in or around areas of restricted blood flow to the heart muscle.

coronary ligament, one of the ligaments that connects the liver to the diaphragm.

coronary occlusion, an obstruction of an artery that supplies the heart muscle. When complete, it causes MI; when incomplete, it may cause angina. The underlying pathophysiologic characteristic is atherosclerotic plaque, which usually develops slowly by buildup of lipid and macrophage complexes.

coronary plexus [L, *corona*, crown, *plexus*, plaited], a network of autonomic nerve fibers located near the base of the heart.

coronary sinus, the wide venous channel, about 2.25 cm long, situated in the coronary sulcus and covered by muscular fibers from the left atrium. It drains five coronary veins: the great cardiac vein, the small cardiac vein, the middle cardiac vein, the posterior vein of the left ventricle, and the oblique vein of the left atrium.

coronary sulcus, a surface groove encircling the heart that separates the atria from the ventricles. It contains the right coronary artery, the small cardiac vein, the coronary sinus, and the circumflex branch of the left coronary artery.

coronary thrombosis, development of a thrombus that blocks a coronary artery, often causing MMI and death. Coronary thromboses commonly develop in segments of arteries with atherosclerotic lesions.

coronary valve [L, *corona*, crown, *valva,* folding door], a semicircular fold of endocardium that prevents backflow of blood from the right atrium into the coronary sinus.

coronary vein, one of the veins of the heart that drain blood from the capillary beds of the myocardium through the coronary sinus into the right atrium.

Coronaviridae /kôr′ənəvir′idē/, a family of four antigenic groups of single-stranded RNA viruses. Some strains of the organism are associated with URIs in humans.

coronavirus /kôr′ənəvī′rəs/ [L, *corona* + *virus,* poison], a member of Coronaviridae, a family of viruses that includes several types capable of causing acute respiratory illnesses, including SARS. Along with rhinoviruses, coronaviruses are considered the primary causes of the common cold. Reinfection with the same genotype can occur. Other diseases caused by coronaviruses include hepatitis, neurologic disease, infectious peritonitis, nephritis, and pancreatitis.

coroner /kôr′ənər/ [L, *corona,* crown], a public official who investigates the causes and circumstances of deaths that occur within a specific legal jurisdiction or territory, especially those that may have resulted from unnatural causes.

coronoid fossa /kô′rənoid/ [L, *corona;* Gk, *eidos,* form; L, *fossa,* ditch], a small depression in the distal dorsal surface of the humerus that receives the coronoid process of the ulna when the forearm is flexed.

coronoid process of the mandible, a prominence on the anterior surface of the ramus of the mandible to which each temporal muscle attaches.

coronoid process of the ulna, a wide, flaring projection of the proximal end of the ulna. The proximal surface of the process forms the lower part of the trochlear notch.

corpectomy, the removal of a vertebral body.

corporate practice of medicine, (in the United States) the role of nonpracticing physicians or nonprofessional corporations in employment relationships with physicians engaged in providing health care. Laws governing corporate practice of medicine vary among different states, but generally may require practitioner control over diagnosis and treatment, practitioner setting of fees, a reasonable relationship between services provided by laypersons or corporations and amounts charged to the practitioner, and an unaltered practitioner-patient relationship.

corpse /kôrps/ [L, *corpus,* body], the body of a dead human being.

cor pulmonale /kôr pŏŏl′mənal′ē/ [L, heart + *pulmoneus,* lungs], enlargement of the heart's right ventricle caused by primary lung disease. Cor pulmonale eventually results in failure of the right ventricle, which cannot accommodate an increase in pressure as easily as the left ventricle.

corpus albicans /kôr′pəs/, a pale white spot on the surface of the ovary that arises from the corpus luteum if conception does not occur.

corpus callosum /kôr′pəs kalō′səm/, **1.** a transverse band of nerve fibers joining the cerebral hemispheres. It is located at the bottom of the longitudinal fissure between the two hemispheres and is covered by the cingulate gyrus. **2.** the largest commissure of the brain, connecting the cerebral hemispheres.

corpus cavernosum [L, body + *caverna,* hollow place], a type of spongy erectile tissue within the penis or clitoris. The tissue becomes engorged with blood during sexual excitement.

corpuscle /kôr′pəsəl/ [L, *corpusculum,* little body], **1.** any cell of the body. **2.** an RBC or WBC.—**corpuscular,** *adj.*

corpuscular radiation /kôrpus′kyələr/ [L, *corpusculum* + *radiare,* to emit rays], the radiation associated with subatomic particles, such as electrons, protons, neutrons, or alpha particles, which travel in streams at various velocities.

corpus femoris, body of femur; the main part or shaft of the femur.

corpus luteum /kôr′pəs lōō′tē·əm/ *pl.* **corpora lutea** [L, *corpus,* body, *luteus,* yellow], an anatomic structure on the ovary's surface, consisting of a spheroid of yellowish tissue 1 to 2 cm in diameter that grows within the ruptured ovarian follicle after ovulation. During a woman's reproductive years, a corpus luteum forms after every ovulation. It acts as a short-lived endocrine organ that secretes progesterone, which serves to maintain the decidual layer of the uterine endometrium in the richly vascular state necessary for implantation and pregnancy. If conception occurs, the corpus luteum grows and secretes increasing amounts of progesterone.

corpus spongiosum /spon′jē·ō′səm/, one of the cylinders of spongy tissue, erectile tissue, with the corpora cavernosa, on the dorsum of the penis from bulb to glans. It contains the urethra and erectile tissue within the labia minora.

corpus uteri, that part of the uterus above the isthmus and below the orifices of the fallopian tubes.

corrected pressure [L, *corrigere,* to make straight], a method of applying Boyle's law of gas pressures to adjust simultaneously for changes in both pressure and humidity.

corrective emotional experience /kərek′tiv/, a process by which a patient gives up old behavior patterns and learns or relearns new patterns by reexperiencing early unresolved feelings and needs.

correlation /kôr′ələ′shən/ [L, *com* + *relatio*, a carrying back], (in statistics) a relationship between variables that may be negative (inverse), positive, or curvilinear.

correlative differentiation /kərel′ətiv/, (in embryology) specialization or diversification of cells or tissues caused by an inductor or other external factor.

correspondence, (in ophthalmology) the relationship between corresponding points on each retina. The simultaneous stimulation of the points results in the sensation of viewing a single object.

Corrigan's pulse [Dominic J. Corrigan, Irish physician, 1802–1880], a bounding pulse in which a great surge is felt, followed by a sudden and complete absence of force or fullness in the artery. This kind of pulse is associated with aortic regurgitation and occurs in excited emotional states; in various abnormal cardiac conditions, including patent ductus arteriosus; and as a result of systemic arteriosclerosis.

corrosion /kərō′zhen/, a result of an oxidation-reduction reaction, or deterioration of a substance by a destructive agent.

corrosion of surgical instruments [L, *corrodere*, to gnaw away], the rusting of surgical instruments or the gradual wearing away of their polished surfaces caused by oxidation and the action of contaminants. It usually results from inadequate cleaning and drying of surgical instruments after use, sterilization with solutions that eat into the surface, overexposure to such solutions, or a faulty autoclave. Cleanliness is the single most important factor in preventing corrosion. Most corrosion of surgical instruments is superficial and may be removed by soaking in a solution of ammonia and alcohol or by repolishing by the manufacturer.

corrosive /kərō′siv/ [L, *corrodere*, to gnaw away], **1.** eating away of a substance or tissue, especially by chemical action. **2.** an agent or substance that eats away a substance or tissue.—**corrode**, *v.*, **corrosion**, *n.*

corrosive gastritis, an acute inflammatory condition of the stomach caused by the ingestion of an acid, alkali, or other corrosive chemical in which the lining of the stomach is eaten away by the corrosive substance.

corrugator supercilii /kôr′əgā′tər soo͞o′pər sil′ē-ī/ [L, *corrugare*, to wrinkle, *super*, above, *cilium*, eyelash], one of the three muscles of the eyelid. It functions to draw the eyebrow downward and inward, as if to frown.

cortex *pl.* **cortices** /kôr′tisēz/ [L, bark], the outer layer of a body organ or other structure, as distinguished from the internal substance.—**cortical**, *adj.*

cortex corticis, part of the renal cortex, consisting of a narrow peripheral zone where the renal columns do not have visible renal corpuscules.

cortex of the lens, the softer, external part of the lens of the eye.

cortical blindness /kôr′tikəl/ [L, *cortex*; AS, *blind*], loss of vision that results from a lesion in the visual center of the cerebral cortex of the brain.

cortical bone, bone that is 70% to 90% mineralized.

cortical evoked potential, an evoked potential recorded from the cerebral cortex.

cortical fracture [L, *cortex* + *fractura*, break], a fracture that involves the cortex of a bone.

cortical labyrinth, a network of tubules and blood vessels in the renal cortex.

cortical radiate arteries, arteries originating from the arcuate arteries of the kidney and distributed to the renal glomeruli.

cortical rim sign, in CT of the kidney, a thin rim of peripheral cortex that is perfused and visible when other parts of the cortex are not, because of capsular collateral arteries. It indicates cortical necrosis, renal vein thrombosis, or infarction of the nonperfused parts.

corticomedullary border, the area where the renal medulla and cortex come together.

corticopontocerebellar fibers, the corticopontine fibers and pontocerebellar fibers considered together.

corticospinal tract, two groups of nerve fibers that originate in the cerebral cortex and run through the spinal cord.

corticosteroid /kôr′tikōstir′oid/ [L, *cortex* + *steros*, solid], any one of hormones elaborated by the adrenal cortex (excluding the sex hormones of adrenal origin) that influence or control key processes of the body. These processes include carbohydrate and protein metabolism, maintenance of serum glucose levels, electrolyte and water balance, and functions of the cardiovascular system, the skeletal muscle, the kidneys, and other organs. The corticosteroids synthesized by the adrenal glands include the glucocorticoids and the mineralocorticoids. The principal glucocorticoids are cortisol and corticosterone. The only physiologically important mineralocorticoid in humans is aldosterone.

corticotroph /kor′tikōtrof/, a small, irregularly stellate, acidophilic cell of the adenohypophysis, having small, sparsely distributed secretory granules and secreting adrenocorticotropic hormone and beta-endorphin.

corticotropinoma /kor′ti·kō·trō′pi·nō′mə/, a pituitary adenoma made up predominantly of corticotrophs. Excessive adrenocorticotropic hormone (corticotropin) secretion may cause Cushing's disease or Nelson's syndrome.

corticotropin-releasing hormone (CRH) /kôr′tikōtrop′in/, a polypeptide hormone secreted by the hypothalamus into the pituitary portal system, where it triggers the release of adrenocorticotropic hormone from the pituitary gland.

cortisol /kôr′təsôl/, a steroid hormone produced naturally by the adrenal gland, identical to chemically synthesized hydrocortisone. It is prescribed for adrenocortical insufficiency, topically for inflammation, and as an adjunct for the treatment of ulcerative colitis.

cortisone /kôr′təsōn/, a synthetic glucocorticoid. It is prescribed for adrenocortical insufficiency inflammation.

Cortisporin, a trademark for several topical fixed-combination drugs that contain a glucocorticoid (hydrocortisone) and 2-3 antibacterials (neomycin sulfate, polymyxin B sulfate, and/or bacitracin zinc).

cor triatriatum /kôr trī·ā′trē·ā′tum/, a congenital anomaly caused by failure of resorption of the embryonic common pulmonary vein, resulting in division of the left atrium by a fibromuscular diaphragm, the posterosuperior chamber receiving the pulmonary venous return and the anteroinferior chamber communicating with the left atrial appendage and mitral orifice. The orifice between the two compartments may be reduced or absent, producing pulmonary venous obstruction.

Corvert, a trademark for a drug that controls atrial fibrillation and atrial flutter (ibutilide).

Corynebacterium /kôr′inē′baktir′ē·əm/ [Gk, *koryne,* club, *bakterion,* small staff], a common genus of aerobic and facultative, anaerobic, gram-positive, nonmotile, rod-shaped curved bacilli that includes many species. The most common pathogenic species are *C. acnes,* commonly found in acne lesions, and *C. diphtheriae,* the cause of diphtheria.

Corzide, a trademark for a combination antihypertensive medication (nadolol and bendroflumethiazide).

cosine law /kō′sīn/, a rule that optimal irradiation occurs when the source of radiation is at right angles to the center of the area being irradiated.

Cosmegen, a trademark for an antineoplastic (dactinomycin).

cosmesis /kosmē′sis/, the use of cosmetics or surgery for preserving or enhancing self-image.

cosmetic acne, a type of contact acne, usually of a low grade, seen on the chin and cheeks of persons habitually using facial cosmetics. The usual lesions are closed comedones or papular pustules.

cosmetic dermatitis /kosmet′ik/ [Gk, *kosmesis,* adornment], a form of irritant or allergic contact dermatitis caused by ingredients in cosmetic products. The meaning is commonly broadened to include soaps, shampoos, deodorants, and depilatories in addition to perfumes, coloring agents, and toiletries.

cosmetic surgery, reconstruction of cutaneous or underlying tissues, performed to improve and correct a structural defect or to remove a scar, birthmark, or normal evidence of aging.

cosmic radiation /kos′mik/, high-energy particles with great penetrating power that originate in outer space and reach the earth as normal background radiation. The particles include high-energy atomic nuclei.

costa /kos′tə/ pl. **costae** /kos′tē/, a rib.

costal /kos′təl/ [L, *costa,* rib], **1.** pertaining to a rib. **2.** situated near a rib or on a side close to a rib.

costal arch [L, *costa + arcus,* bow], an arch formed by the shafts of the ribs.

costal cartilage, the cartilage at the anterior end of each rib.

costal facet, one of three sites on each side of a typical thoracic vertebra for articulation with ribs.

costalgia /kostal′jə·ə/ [L, *costa,* rib; Gk, *algos,* pain], a pain in the ribs.

costal groove, a groove along the inferior margin of the superior rib that accommodates the intercostal nerves and associated major arteries and veins.

costal notch, an indentation beside a costal cartilage on the side of the sternum.

cost analysis [L, *costare,* to stand firm; Gk, *ana,* again, *lyein,* to loosen], an analysis of the disbursements of an activity, agency, department, or program.

COSTAR /kō′stär/, abbreviation for *COmputer STored Ambulatory Record* system, a system that creates and stores electronic patient records.

cost-based value, a relative value scale used to determine the total units of services provided by a medical practice. The total cost of running the practice and the total units of service are then used to calculate the costs for each service provided.

cost-benefit analysis (CBA), a type of economic evaluation of medical care expense. It compares the monetary benefit derived from different health interventions with the expected cost of providing each of the interventions to determine the best or most profitable option.

cost-benefit ratio, a mathematic representation of the relationship of the cost of an activity to the benefit of its outcome or product.

cost cap *informal.* a limit on the amount of money that an agency, department, or institution may spend.

cost center, a department, division, or other subunit of an institution established within its accounting system so that the income and expenses of the subunit can be separated from the income or expenses of other centers and monitored for cost and benefit.

cost containment, a nursing intervention from the Nursing Interventions Classification (NIC) defined as management and facilitation of efficient and effective use of resources.

cost control, the process of monitoring and regulating the expenditure of funds by an agency or institution. Budgets, reports, and cost-accounting procedures are performed to achieve cost control.

costectomy /kostek′tamē/, surgical removal of a rib or resection of rib.

cost-effectiveness, the extent to which an activity is thought to be as valuable as it is expensive. A public assistance program that issues vouchers for nutritious foods in pregnancy might be considered cost-effective if it lowers the costly incidence of perinatal morbidity.

cost-effectiveness analysis (CEA), a type of economic evaluation used to determine the best use of money available for medical care. It compares different kinds of interventions with similar but not identical effects on the basis of cost per unit achieved.

cost model, (in the United States) a managed care system in which all components of patient care are defined as costs as opposed to sources of revenue.

costocervical /kos′tōsur′vikal/ [L, *costa,* rib, *cervix,* neck], pertaining to or involving the ribs and the neck.

costochondral /kos′takon′dral/ [L, *costa;* Gk, *chondros,* cartilage], pertaining to a rib and its cartilage.

costochondritis /kos′takondrī′tis/, an inflammation of the costal cartilage of the anterior chest wall, characterized by pain and tenderness.

costoclavicular /-klavik′yalar/ [L, *costa* + *clavicula,* little key], pertaining to or involving the ribs and the clavicle.

costoclavicular line, an imaginary vertical line between the sternal and midclavicular lines.

costophrenic (CP) angle /-fren′ik/ [L, *costa* + *phrenicus,* diaphragm], the angle between the diaphragm and the chest wall at the bottom of the lung.

costosternal /-stur′nal/, pertaining to or involving the ribs and the sternum.

costotransverse articulation /-transvurs′/ [L, *costa* + *transversus,* a cross direction], any of the 20 gliding joints between the ribs and articulating vertebrae, except the eleventh and twelfth ribs.

costovertebral /-vur′tabral/, of or relating to a rib and the vertebral column.

costovertebral angle (CVA), one of two angles that outline a space over the kidneys. The angle is formed by the lateral and downward curve of the lowest rib and the vertical column of the spine itself.

cost-sharing program, (in the United States) a financial risk-management strategy often used by insurance companies and self-insured employers in which employees share the cost of health services, such as through deductibles and coinsurance.

cost shifting, (in the United States) a mechanism for reducing inpatient costs by providing services in an outpatient setting. The inpatient cost per case is reduced, but the overall cost to the organization does not change.

cost-utility analysis (CUA), a type of economic evaluation of different approaches to managed health care costs. It compares the degree to which quality of life is improved per dollar spent. A quality-of-life index is used to compare interventions, including quality-adjusted life years.

cosyntropin /kō′sintrop′in/, a synthetic form of adrenocorticotropic hormone that is used in the diagnosis and treatment of adrenal hypofunction disorders such as Addison's disease to determine if the disorder is primary (adrenal dysfunction) or secondary (hypothalamic-pituitary axis dysfunction).

COTA, abbreviation for **Certified Occupational Therapy Assistant.**

Cotazym, a trademark for an enzyme (pancrelipase).

cotton /kot′n/, **1.** a plant of the genus *Gossypium.* **2.** a textile material derived from the seeds of this plant.

cottonmouth, a poisonous pit viper commonly found near water and swamps of the southeastern part of the United States. The symptoms of the bite of a cottonmouth are rapid swelling, severe pain, skin discoloration at bite marks, and weakness.

Cotton's fracture, a fracture involving the medial, lateral, and posterior malleoli of the ankle.

cotton-wool exudate [Ar, *qutun*; AS, *wull*; ME, *spot*], a white, fluffy-appearing lesion, an infarction of the nerve fiber layer, observed on the retina of patients with certain systemic conditions, such as diabetes, AIDS, hypertension, and lupus. It can also be observed in retinal infections.

cotyledon /kot'ilē'don/ [Gk, *kotyledon,* cup-shaped], one of the visible segments on the maternal surface of the placenta. A typical placenta may have 15 to 28 cotyledons, each consisting of fetal vessels, chorionic villi, and intervillous space.

cotyloid /kot'iloid/, cup-shaped, as the acetabulum.

coudé catheter /kōōdā'/ [Fr, *coude,* elbow], an elbowed catheter with an olive tip for a strictured urethra.

cough /kôf/ [AS, *cohhetan*], a sudden audible expulsion of air from the lungs. Coughing is preceded by inspiration, the glottis is partially closed, and the accessory muscles of expiration contract to expel the air forcibly from the respiratory passages. Coughing is an essential protective response that serves to clear the lungs, bronchi, and trachea of irritants and secretions or to prevent aspiration of foreign material into the lungs. It is a common symptom of diseases of the chest and larynx.

cough enhancement, a nursing intervention from the Nursing Interventions Classification (NIC) defined as promotion of deep inhalation by the patient with subsequent generation of high intrathoracic pressures and compression of underlying lung parenchyma for the forceful expulsion of air.

cough fracture, a break in a rib, usually the fourth to eighth rib, caused by violent coughing.

cough syncope [AS, *cohhetan*; Gk, *syncope,* fainting], a temporary LOC during coughing. The coughing increases the intrathoracic pressure enough to impede venous return, thereby interfering with normal blood flow to the brain.

cough variant asthma, asthma characterized by minimal wheezing and a nonproductive, often severe cough lasting from a few hours to days.

coulomb (C) /kōō'lôm/ [Charles A. de Coulomb, French physicist, 1736–1806], the SI unit of electricity equal to the quantity of charge transferred in 1 second across a conductor in which there is a constant current of 1 ampere, or 1 ampere-second.

Coulomb's law [Charles A. de Coulomb], (in physics) a law stating that the force of attraction or repulsion between two electrically charged bodies is directly proportional to the strength of the electrical charges and inversely proportional to the square of the distance between them.

coulometry /kōōlom'ətrē/, a type of electroanalytic chemistry in which a reagent generated at the surface of an electrode reacts with a substance to be measured. The substance, usually a metal ion, is measured in terms of the coulombs required for the reaction.

Coulter counter /kōl'tər/ [W.H. Coulter, twentieth century American engineer], a trademark for an electric device that rapidly identifies and counts RBCs and WBCs present in a small specimen of human blood.

Coumadin, a trademark for an anticoagulant (warfarin sodium).

coumarin /kōō'mərin/, a class of orally active anticoagulant agents with warfarin as its prototype, prescribed for prophylaxis and treatment of thrombosis and embolism.

counseling¹ [L, *consulere,* to consult], the act of providing advice and guidance to a patient or his or her family. It is a therapeutic technique that helps the patient recognize and manage stress and that facilitates interpersonal relationships.

counseling², a nursing intervention from the Nursing Interventions Classification (NIC) defined as use of an interactive helping process focusing on the needs, problems, or feelings of the patient and significant others to enhance or support coping, problem-solving, and interpersonal relationships.

counselor, a human services professional who deals with human development concerns through support, therapeutic approaches, consultation, evaluation, teaching, and research.

count [L, *computere,* to calculate], a computation of the number of objects or elements present per unit of measurement.

counterclaim [L, *contra,* against, *clamere,* to cry out], (in law) a claim made by a defendant establishing a cause for action in his or her favor against a plaintiff. The purpose of a counterclaim is to oppose or detract from a plaintiff's claim or complaint.

counterconditioning, a process used in behavioral therapy in which a learned response is replaced by an alternative response that is less disruptive.

countercurrent, a change in the direction of flow of a fluid. An example is the countercurrent in the ascending branch of a kidney tubule where osmolality undergoes a reversal after a gradual change in sodium chloride concentrations.

countercurrent multiplication, the mechanism in the loops of Henle of the renal tubules by which urine is concentrated. It is dependent on unique solute transport processes at different parts of the loops of Henle and the vasa recta.

counterinjunction /-injungk'shən/, (in transactional analysis) an overt message from the parent ego state of the mother or father that may be difficult to follow if it conflicts with earlier parental instructions.

counterirritant, an agent used to produce an irritation in one part of the body intended to relieve irritation in some other part.

counterphobic behavior /-fō'bik/, an expression of reaction to a phobia by a patient who actively seeks exposure to the type of situation that precipitates phobic symptoms.

counterpulsation /-pulsā'shən/ [L, *contra* + *pulsare,* to beat], **1.** the action of a circulatory-assist pumping device that is synchronized with cardiac systole and diastole to decrease the work of the heart. **2.** the process of increasing the intraaortic pressure in diastole by inflation of an intraaortic balloon and deflation of the balloon immediately before the next systole.

counterregulatory hormones, glucagons, epinephrine, growth hormones, and core tissue that work to increase blood glucose levels by stimulating glucose production and liver output and decreasing movement of glucose into cells.

countershock [L, *contra*; Fr, *choc*], a high-intensity, short-duration electric shock applied to an area of the heart, resulting in total cardiac depolarization.

counterstain, a second stain added to a previously stained tissue sample to make cellular details more distinct.

countertraction /-trak'shən/ [L, *contraz* + *trahere,* to pull], a force that counteracts the pull of traction, such as the force of body weight resulting from the pull of gravity.

countertransference /-transfur'əns/, the conscious or unconscious emotional response of a psychotherapist or psychoanalyst to a patient. The response may be positive or negative but can provide useful data in the therapy.

countertransport /-trans'pôrt/ [L, *contra* + *trans,* across, *portare,* carry], the simultaneous transport of two different substances across the same membrane, each in the opposite direction.

counting cell hemocytometer [OFr, *conter* + L, *cella,* storeroom; Gk, *haima,* blood, *metron,* measure], a device for counting the number of cells in a volume of blood or other fluid. It consists of a microscope slide with a counting chamber. The chamber has a known volume, and the slide has a ruled area to help count the cells.

counts per minute (cpm), a measure of the rate of ionizing emissions by radioactive substances.

coup /ko͞o/ [Fr, blow], **1.** any blow or stroke or the effects of such a blow to the body, usually used with a French word identifying a type of stroke. **2.** *coup de sabre* /ko͞odəsäb'r(ə)/, a wound resembling a sword cut. **3. coup sur coup** /ko͞o sYr ko͞o'/, administration of a drug in small amounts over a short period, rather than in a single larger dose. **4. contrecoup** /kôNtrəko͞o'/, an injury most often associated with a blow to the skull in which the force of the impact is transmitted through the skull bones to the opposite side of the head, where the bruise, fracture, or other sign of injury appears.

couples' therapy, psychotherapy in which couples, who may be married or unmarried but living together, undergo therapy together.

coupling /kup'ling/ [L, *copula,* bonding], **1.** the act of coming together, joining, or pairing. **2.** (in genetics) the situation in linked inheritance in which the nonalleles of two or more mutant genes are located on the same chromosome and are close enough that they are likely to be inherited together. **3.** (in radiation therapy) the efficiency of transfer of power from an applicator to the treatment site. **4.** (in cardiology) the regular occurrence of a premature beat.

coupling interval, the interval between the dominant heartbeat and a linked ectopic beat.

Courvoisier's law /ko͞orvô·äzē·āz'/ [Ludwig Courvoisier, Swiss surgeon, 1843–1918], a statement that the gallbladder is smaller than usual if a gallstone blocks the common bile duct but is dilated if the common bile duct is blocked by something other than a gallstone, such as pancreatic cancer.

couvade /ko͞oväd'/, a custom in some non-Western cultures whereby the husband goes through mock labor while his wife is giving birth.

Couvelaire uterus /ko͞ovəler'/ [Alexandre Couvelaire, French obstetrician, 1873–1948], a hemorrhagic process in uterine musculature that may accompany severe abruptio placentae. Extravasated blood effuses between the muscle fibrils and under the uterine peritoneum. The uterus takes on a purplish color and does not contract well.

covalent bond, a chemical bond that forms by the sharing of two electrons between atoms. A double bond is formed when four electrons are shared between two atoms; a triple bond is formed when six electrons are shared between two atoms.

coverage /kuv′ərij/, the extent to which services rendered by a health care program cover the potential need for them.

covered benefit, a health service included in the premium of a policy paid by or on behalf of the enrolled patient.

Cowden's disease [Cowden, family name of the first recorded case], an autosomal-dominant disorder characterized by hypertrichosis, gingival fibromatosis, facial papules, hemangiomas, and postpubertal fibroadenomatous breast enlargement.

Cowper's gland /kou′pərz/ [William Cowper, English surgeon, 1666–1709], either of two round, pea-sized tubular glands embedded in the urethral sphincter of the male, beneath the bulb of the urethra, that empties mucus into the urethra.

Cowper's syringocele, a cystlike swelling of a Cowper's gland or one of its ducts, seen in infant boys or occasionally in older males. Those in the duct are caused by obstruction of its orifice.

cowpox /kou′poks/ [AS, *cu*; ME, *pokkes*], a mild infectious disease characterized by a pustular rash, caused by the vaccinia virus, usually transmitted by domesticated cats. Cowpox infection usually confers immunity to smallpox because of the similarity of the variola and vaccinia viruses.

COX-2 inhibitors, cyclooxygenase-2 inhibitors, a group of NSAIDs that act by inhibiting cyclooxygenase-2 activity. They have fewer GI side effects than other NSAIDs.

coxa /kok′sə/ *pl.* **coxae** [L, hip], the hip joint; the head of the femur and the acetabulum of the innominate bone.

coxal articulation /kok′səl/ [L, *coxa* + *articularis*, relating to the joints], the ball-and-socket joint of the hip, formed by the articulation of the head of the femur into the cup-shaped cavity of the acetabulum.

coxa magna, an abnormal widening of the head and neck of the femur.

coxa valga, a hip deformity in which the angle normally formed by the axis of the head and neck of the femur and the axis of its shaft is significantly increased.

coxa vara, a hip deformity in which the angle formed by the axis of the head and neck of the femur and the axis of its shaft is decreased.

coxa vara luxans, a fissure or crack in the neck of the femur with dislocation of the head, caused by coxa vara.

Coxiella burnetii, a gram-negative bacterium that grows preferentially in the vacuoles of the host cell and causes **Q fever.**

coxsackie virus /koksak′ē-/ [Coxsackie, New York; L, *virus,* poison], any of 30 serologically different small RNA enteroviruses associated with a variety of symptoms and primarily affecting children during warm weather. Coxsackie viruses can be divided into two groups. Group A is the milder form, causing herpangina and hand-foot-and-mouth disease. Group B causes epidemic pleurodynia.

CP, 1. abbreviation for *candlepower.* 2. abbreviation for **cerebral palsy.** 3. abbreviation for *chemically pure.*

CPAN, abbreviation for *certified postanesthesia nurse.*

CPAP, abbreviation for **continuous positive airway pressure.**

CPD, 1. abbreviation for **cephalopelvic disproportion.** 2. abbreviation for **childhood polycystic disease.** 3. abbreviation for **congenital polycystic disease.**

CPDA-1, abbreviation for *citrate phosphate dextrose adenine.*

C peptide, a biologically inactive residue of insulin formation in the beta cells of the pancreas.

C-peptide test, a blood test used to evaluate levels of C-peptide. Direct measurement of C-peptide measures the capacity of the pancreatic beta cells to secrete insulin. It is used to evaluate patients with suspected insulinoma, renal failure, pancreas transplant, factitious hypoglycemia, radical pancreatectomy, and DM.

CPHA, abbreviation for **Canadian Public Health Association.**

CPK, abbreviation for **creatine phosphokinase.**

CPM, abbreviation for **continuous passive motion**

cpm, abbreviation for **counts per minute.**

CPNP/A, abbreviation for *certified pediatric nurse practitioner/associate.*

CPPB, abbreviation for *continuous positive pressure breathing.* See **continuous positive airway pressure.**

CPPD, abbreviation for *calcium pyrophosphate dihydrate.*

CPPV, abbreviation for **continuous positive pressure ventilation.**

CPR, abbreviation for **cardiopulmonary resuscitation.**

CPRAM, abbreviation for *controlled partial rebreathing anesthesia method.*

cps, abbreviation for *cycle per second.*

CPT™ codes, a coding system, defined in the publication *Current Procedural Terminology,* for medical procedures that allows for comparability in pricing, billing, and utilization review.

CQI, abbreviation for **continuous quality improvement.**

CR, 1. abbreviation for **computed radiography.** 2. abbreviation for *controlled respiration.*

Cr, symbol for the element **chromium.**

crab louse [AS, *crabba* + *lus*], a species of louse, *Pthirus pubis,* that infests the hairs of the genital area. It is often transmitted between persons by sexual contact but can also be spread by shared bedding.

crack [ME, *craken*], a street drug made by chemically converting cocaine hydrochloride to a form that can be smoked.

crack baby, an infant who was exposed to effects of cocaine in utero by a mother who used the "crack" form of the drug while pregnant.

cracked-pot sound [ME, *craken* + *pott;* L, *sonus,* sound], a sound sometimes heard on percussion over a cavity with an opening to a bronchus.

cracked tooth syndrome [ME, *craken;* AS, *toth*], a group of symptoms caused by the presence of a cracked tooth, including pain on pressure or application of cold, with pulpitis if untreated.

crackle, a common, abnormal respiratory sound consisting of discontinuous bubbling noises heard on auscultation of the chest during inspiration.

cradle cap [AS, *cradel* + *caeppe*], a common seborrheic dermatitis of infants, which consists of thick, yellow greasy or waxy scales on the scalp.

cramp [AS, *crammian,* to fill], **1.** a spasmodic and often painful contraction of one or more muscles. **2.** a pain resembling a muscular cramp.

cranberry, a herbal product whose berries are harvested from a small shrub. It is used for UTIs and works by decreasing bacterial adherence to the walls of the bladder, urethra, etc.

cranial bones /krā′nē·əl/ [Gk, *kranion,* cranium; AS, *ban*], the bones of the skull, particularly the part of the cranium that encloses the brain.

cranial cavity, the cavity of the skull containing the brain and other tissues.

cranial fibrous joints, the sutures and ligaments connecting the bones of the skull to each other and the syndesmoses holding the teeth in their sockets.

cranial nerves [Gk, *kranion,* skull; L, *nervus*], the 12 pairs of nerves emerging from the cranial cavity through various openings in the skull. Beginning with the most anterior, they are designated by Roman numerals and named (I) olfactory, (II) optic, (III) oculomotor, (IV) trochlear, (V) trigeminal, (VI) abducens, (VII) facial, (VIII) vestibulocochlear (acoustic), (IX) glossopharyngeal, (X) vagal, (XI) accessory, and (XII) hypoglossal. The cranial nerves originate in the base of the brain and carry impulses for such functions as smell, vision, ocular movement, pupil contraction, muscular sensibility, general sensibility, mastication, facial expression, glandular secretion, taste, cutaneous sensibility, hearing, equilibrium, swallowing, phonation, tongue movement, head movement, and shoulder movement.

cranial sensory ganglion, the ganglion found on the root of each cranial nerve, containing the cell bodies of afferent (sensory) neurons.

cranial sutures, the interlocking lines of fusion of the bones forming the skull. The lines gradually become less prominent as a person matures.

cranial synchondroses, the cartilaginous junctions between the bones of the cranium.

craniectomy /krā′nē·ek′təmē/ [Gk, *kranion,* cranium, *ektomē,* excision], the surgical removal of a portion of the cranium.

craniocervical /krā′nē·ōsur′vikəl/ [Gk, *kranion* + L, *cervix,* neck], pertaining to the junction of the skull and neck, particularly the area of the foramen magnum.

craniodidymus /krā′nē·ōdid′iməs/ [Gk, *kranion*; *didymos,* twin], a two-headed fetus in which the bodies are fused.

craniofacial /-fā′shəl/ [Gk, *kranion,* cranium; L, *facies,* face], pertaining to the cranium and the face.

craniofacial dysostosis [Gk, *kranion*; L, *facies,* face; Gk, *dys,* bad, *osteon,* bone], an abnormal hereditary condition characterized by acrocephaly, exophthalmos, hypertelorism, strabismus, parrot-beaked nose, and hypoplastic maxilla with relative mandibular prognathism.

craniohypophyseal xanthoma /krā′nē·ōhī′pōfiz′ē·əl/ [Gk, *kranion* + *hypo,* deficient, *phyein,* to grow, *xanthos,* yellow, *oma,* tumor], a condition in which cholesterol deposits are formed around the hypophyses of the bones, as in Hand-Schüller-Christian disease.

craniology /krā′nē·ol′əjē./, the study of the shape, size, proportions, and other features of the human skull. It is usually associated with anthropologic research.

craniometaphyseal dysplasia /-met′əfiz′ē·əl/, an inherited bone disorder characterized by paranasal overgrowth, thickening of the skull and jaw, and entrapment of cranial nerves. The patient may experience nasorespiratory infections, associated with bone overgrowth at the sinuses, and malocclusion of the jaws.

craniopagus /krā′nē·op′əgəs/ [Gk, *kranion* + *pagos,* fixed], conjoined twins united at the heads. Fusion can occur at the frontal, occipital, or parietal region.

craniopharyngeal /krā′nē·ōfərin′jē·əl/ [Gk, *kranion* + *pharynx,* throat], pertaining to the cranium and pharynx.

craniopharyngioma /krā'nē·ōfərin'jē·ō'mə/ pl. **craniopharyngiomas, craniopharyngiomata,** a congenital pituitary tumor, appearing most often in children and adolescents, that arises in cells derived from Rathke's pouch or the hypophyseal stalk. The tumor may interfere with pituitary function, damage the optic chiasm, disrupt hypothalamic control of the autonomic nervous system, and cause hydrocephalus.

cranioplasty /krā'nē·ōplas'tē/, plastic surgery performed on the skull.

craniosacral therapy, a form of gentle manual manipulation used for diagnosis and for making corrections in a system made up of CSF, cranial and dural membranes, cranial bones, and sacrum. Through touch and pressure, tension is supposed to be reduced and cranial rhythms normalized, leading to improvement in health.

craniospinal /krā'nē·ōspī'nəl/ [Gk, kranion, skull; L, spina, backbone or spine], pertaining to the cranium and the vertebral column.

craniostenosis /krā'nē·ō'stənō'sis/ [Gk, kranion + stenos, narrow, osis, condition], a congenital deformity of the skull that results from premature closure of the sutures between the cranial bones.—**craniostenotic,** adj.

craniostosis /krā'nē·ostō'sis/ [Gk, kranion + osteon, bone, osis, condition], premature ossification of the sutures of the skull, often associated with other skeletal defects. Without surgical correction the growth of the skull is inhibited, the head is deformed, and the eyes and brain are often damaged.

craniotabes /krā'nē·ōtā'bēz/ [Gk, kranion; L, tabes, wasting], benign congenital thinness of the top and back of the skull of a newborn. The condition is common because the rate of brain growth exceeds the rate of calcification of the skull during the last month of gestation.

craniotomy /krā'nē·ot'əmē/ [Gk, kranion, cranium, temnein, to cut], any surgical opening into the skull, performed to relieve ICP, to control bleeding, or to remove a tumor.

craniotubular /-tŏŏb'yələr/, pertaining to a bossing, or overgrowth, of bone that produces an abnormal contour and increased bone density.

cranium /krā'nē·əm/ [Gk, kranion, skull], the bony skull that holds the brain. It is composed of eight bones: the frontal, occipital, sphenoid, ethmoid, and paired temporal and parietal bones.—**cranial,** adj.

crankcase-spool catheter /krangk'kās/, a special elastic catheter stored within a plastic spool to facilitate its insertion, especially for hyperalimentation. When fully inserted, the crankcase-spool catheter is usually lodged in the subclavian vein. The catheter is highly flexible, and each revolution of the spool feeds about 5 inches of the catheter into the vein involved.

crash cart, a cart carrying emergency equipment and supplies. Hospital EDs and ICUs usually have several crash carts equipped according to prescribed specifications.

crater, a pitlike depression, such as where an ulcer has been surgically removed.

cravat bandage /krəvat'/ [Fr, cravate, scarf, bande, strip], a triangular bandage, folded lengthwise. It may be used as a circular, figure-eight, or spiral bandage to control bleeding or to tie splints in place.

cravat bandage for clenched fist, a pressure dressing made by folding the points of a triangular bandage to form a band about the fist.

cravat bandage for fracture of the clavicle, a sling dressing that includes a 2- to 4-inch soft pad in the armpit. The triangular bandage is placed with the center point on the affected shoulder. The hand and wrist are laid against it. The opposite ends are lifted to cover and support the arm. The bandage ends are drawn together and tied at the back.

cravat elbow bandage, a triangular dressing that holds the elbow at a 45-degree angle, beginning with the center over the point of the elbow. The bandage is completed with one end around the forearm and the other around the upper arm.

cravat sling bandage, a support for a fractured arm prepared by laying the wrist on the center of the triangular bandage while the forearm is at a right angle. The two ends of the bandage are carried around the neck and tied.

C-reactive protein (CRP) /-rē·ak'tiv/, a protein not normally detected in the serum but present in many acute inflammatory conditions and with necrosis.

C-reactive protein (CRP) test, a blood test used to detect and diagnose bacterial infectious disease, postsurgical wound infection, and inflammatory disorders such as acute rheumatic fever and rheumatoid arthritis. In addition, it is used as an adjunct in detecting acute bacterial meningitis in an acutely febrile child and as a cardiovascular risk assessment marker when high-sensitivity assays are used.

cream [Gk, chrisma, oil], **1.** the part of milk rich in butterfat. **2.** any fluid mixture of thick consistency, often used as a method of applying medication to the surface of the body.

crease [ME, *creste*, crest], an indentation or margin formed by a doubling back of tissue such as the folds on the palm of the hand and sole of the foot.

creatinase /krē·at'inās/ [Gk, *kreas*, flesh], an enzyme that catalyzes the conversion of creatine to sarcosine and urea.

creatine /krē'ətēn, -tin/ [Gk, *kreas*, flesh], an important nitrogenous compound produced by metabolic processes in the body. Combined with phosphorus, it forms high-energy phosphate.

creatine kinase (CK), an enzyme of the transferase class in muscle, brain, and other tissues. It catalyzes the transfer of a phosphate group from adenosine triphosphate to creatine, producing adenosine diphosphate and phosphocreatine.

creatine kinase (CK) test, a blood test used to detect damage to the heart muscle, skeletal muscles, and brain. Serum CK levels are elevated whenever such damage occurs.

creatine phosphate (CP) [Gk, *kreas*, flesh; Du, *potasschen*], an enzyme that increases in blood levels when muscle damage has occurred, as in pseudohypertrophic muscular dystrophy.

creatinine /krē·at'inēn, -nin/, a substance formed from the metabolism of creatine, commonly found in blood, urine, and muscle tissue.

creatinine clearance test, a diagnostic test for kidney function. It measures the rate at which creatinine is cleared from the blood by the kidney.

creatinine height index (CHI), a measurement of a 24-hour urinary excretion of creatinine, which is generally related to the patient's muscle mass and is an indicator of malnutrition, particularly in young males.

creatinuria /krēē'ətinŏŏr'ē·ə/, increased concentration of creatine in the urine.

creatorrhea, the presence of undigested muscle fibers in the feces.

credentialing /kriden'shəling/, examination and review of the credentials of individuals meeting a set of educational or occupational criteria and therefore being licensed in their field.

credentials /kriden'shelz/, a predetermined set of standards, such as licensure or certification, establishing that a person or institution has achieved professional recognition in a specific field of health care.

Credé's maneuver /kredā'z/ [Karl S. Credé, German physician, 1819–1892], a technique for aiding the expulsion of the placenta. The uterus is pushed toward the birth canal by pressure exerted by the thumb of one hand on the posterior surface of the abdomen and the other hand on the anterior surface.

Credé's method /kredā'z/ [Karl S. Credé], a technique for promoting the expulsion of urine by manual compression of the bladder through external pressure on the lower abdominal wall.

Credé's prophylaxis /kredāz'/ [Karl S. Credé], the instillation of a 1% silver nitrate solution into the conjunctiva of newborns to prevent ophthalmia neonatorum.

creep, a rheologic effect of metals and other solid materials that may become elongated or deformed as a result of a load being applied for a long period. For example, creep can occur in silver amalgam fillings that have been in place for some time.

cremaster /krimas'tər/ [Gk, *kremastos*, hanging], a thin muscular layer that spreads out over the spermatic cord in a series of loops. It is a continuation of the obliquus internus. It functions to draw the testis up toward the superficial inguinal ring in response to cold or to stimulation of the nerve.

cremasteric arteries, the arteries that originate from the external iliac artery and accompany the spermatic cord into the scrotum in men or follow the round ligament of the uterus through the inguinal canal in women.

cremasteric fascia, a layer contributed by the internal oblique muscle to the coverings of the structures traversing the inguinal canal. This layer contains the cremasteric muscle.

cremasteric reflex /krē'məster'ik/, a superficial neural reflex elicited by stroking the skin of the upper inner thigh in a male. This action normally results in a brisk retraction of the testis on the side of the stimulus.

crematorium /krē'mətôrē·əm/, a facility for the disposal of dead bodies by burning.

crenation /krinā'shən/ [L, *crena*, notch], the formation of notches or leaflike scalloped edges on an object. RBCs exposed to a hypertonic saline solution acquire a notched, shriveled surface as a result of the osmotic effect of the solution. They are then called crenated RBCs.—**crenate, crenated,** *adj.*

creosol /krē'əsol/, an oily liquid that is one of the active constituents (phenol) of creosote. It should not be confused with **cresol.**

creosote /krē'əsōt/, a flammable oily liquid with a smoky odor that is used primarily as a wood preservative. It can cause a wide variety of health problems, ranging from cancer and corneal damage to convulsions.

crepitant /krep'itənt/ [L, *crepitans*, crackling], pertaining to the feel or sound of crackling or rattling, or of rough surfaces being rubbed together.

crepitant crackle [L, *crepitans*, crackling], an abnormal breathing sound produced at the end of inspiration and caused by air entering collapsed alveoli or just collapsed alveoli and atelectasis that contain fibrous exudate. It occurs in pneumonia, TB, and pulmonary edema.

crepitus /krep′itəs/ [L, crackling], **1.** flatulence or the noisy discharge of fetid gas from the intestine through the anus. **2.** a sound or feel that resembles the crackling noise heard when rubbing hair between the fingers or throwing salt on an open fire. Crepitus is associated with gas gangrene, rubbing of bone fragments, air in superficial tissues, or crackles of a consolidated area of the lung in pneumonia. **3.** a clicking sound often heard in movement of joints, for example, in TMJ resulting from joint irregularities.

crescendo angina /krishen′dō/ [L, *crescere*, to increase], a form of angina pectoris associated with ischemic ECG changes and marked by increased frequency, provocation, intensity, or character.

crescendo murmur [L, *crescere*, to increase, *murmur*, humming], a murmur of steadily increasing intensity to a sudden termination.

crescent /kres′ənt/ [L, *crescere*, to increase], **1.** shaped like a new moon. **2.** a structure that has this shape.

crescent bodies /kres′ənt/, **1.** (in a blood smear) large, pale, crescent-shaped cells produced from fragile erythrocytes as the blood film preparation is made. **2.** large, round bodies with pink crescent-like margins found in the blood of some anemia patients.

cresol /krē′sol/, a mixture of three isomers of an organic acid in a liquid with a phenolic odor, derived from coal tar and used in synthetic resins and disinfectants. Cresol is a potentially lethal poison that can be absorbed through the skin. Symptoms of chronic poisoning include skin eruptions, digestive disorders, uremia, jaundice, nervous disorders, vertigo, and mental changes. Acute poisoning by oral intake of 8 g or more can cause circulatory collapse and death.

crest, a narrow elongated elevation, as the iliac crest.

Crestor, a trademark for rosuvastin.

CREST syndrome /krest/, abbreviation for *c*alcinosis, *R*aynaud's phenomenon, *e*sophageal dysfunction, *s*clerodactyly, and *t*elangiectasis. CREST syndrome is a disease of skin and blood vessels and, in severe cases, the lungs, digestive tract, or heart. It is often associated with scleroderma.

cretin dwarf /krē′tən/, a person in whom short stature is caused by infantile hypothyroidism and severe deficiency of thyroid hormone.

cretinism /krē′təniz′əm/ [Fr, *cretin*, idiot], a congenital condition characterized by severe hypothyroidism and often associated with other endocrine abnormalities. Typical signs of cretinism include dwarfism, mental deficiency, puffy facial features, dry skin, large tongue, umbilical hernia, and muscular incoordination. The disorder occurs usually in areas where the diet is deficient in iodine and where goiter is common. —**cretin**, *n*. **cretinoid, cretinous,** *adj.*

Creutzfeldt-Jakob disease /kroits′felt yä′kôp/ [Hans G. Creutzfeldt, German neurologist, 1885–1964; Alfons M. Jakob, German neurologist, 1884–1931], a rare fatal encephalopathy caused by infectious prion particles. Symptoms are progressive dementia, dysarthria, muscle wasting, and various involuntary movements such as myoclonus and athetosis.

crevice /krev′is/, a cleft or fissure, like that between the gum and the neck of a tooth.

CRH, abbreviation for **corticotropin-releasing hormone.**

crib /krib/ [L, *cribrum*, sieve], **1.** any racklike structure. **2.** a removable anchorage from an orthodontic appliance. **3.** a habit-breaking orthodontic appliance.

cribriform /krib′rifôrm′/ [L, *cribrum*, sieve], describing a structure with many perforations or punctures.

cribriform plate of the ethmoid bone, a sieve like structure that allows small olfactory nerve fibers to pass through its foramina from the nasal mucosa to the olfactory bulb.

cricoarytenoid muscles, muscles that open and close the rima glottidis, innervated by the laryngeal branches of the vagus nerves.

cricoid /krī′koid/ [Gk, *krikos*, ring, *eidos*, form], having a ring shape.

cricoid cartilage, a ring-shaped cartilage of the larynx, consisting of a narrow anterior arch and a posterior wide quadrilateral lamina.

cricoidectomy /-ek′təmē/ [Gk, *krikos* + *eidos* + *ektomē*, excision], a surgical procedure for removing the cricoid cartilage.

cricoid pressure, a technique to reduce the risk of the aspiration of stomach contents during induction of general anesthesia. The cricoid cartilage is pushed against the body of the sixth cervical vertebra, compressing the esophagus to prevent passive regurgitation.

cricopharyngeal /krī′kōfərin′jē-əl/ [Gk, *krikos* + *pharynx*, throat], pertaining to the cricoid cartilage and the pharynx.

cricopharyngeal incoordination, a defect in the normal swallowing reflex. The cricopharyngeus muscle ordinarily serves as a sphincter to keep the top of the esophagus closed except when the person is swallowing, vomiting, or belching. The trachea remains open for breathing, but air normally does not enter the esophagus during respiration. When the series of neuromuscular actions is not properly coordinated as a result of disease or injury, the patient may choke, swallow air, regurgitate fluid into the nose, or experience discomfort in swallowing food.

cricothyroid membrane /-thī′roid/, a fibroelastic membrane, including the cricothyroid ligament that connects the cricoid and thyroid cartilages.

cricothyrotomy /krī′kōthīrot′əmē/ [Gk, *krikos* + *thyreos,* shield, *eidos,* form, *temnein,* to cut], an emergency incision into the larynx performed to open the airway in a person who is choking. Also called **cricothyroidotomy.**

cricotracheal ligament, the ligament that runs from the lower border of the cricoid cartilage to the adjacent upper border of the first tracheal cartilage.

Crigler-Najjar syndrome /krig′lər naj′är/ [John F. Crigler, Jr., American pediatrician, b. 1919; Victor A. Najjar, Lebanese-born American microbiologist, b. 1914], a congenital familial autosomal anomaly, in which glucuronyl transferase, an enzyme, is deficient or absent. The condition is characterized by nonhemolytic jaundice, an accumulation of unconjugated bilirubin in the blood, and severe disorders of the CNS.

crime [L, *crimen*], any act that violates a law and may have criminal intent.

Crimean-Congo hemorrhagic fever /krīmē′ən/, an arbovirus infection caused by the virus *Nairovirus* of the family Bunyaviridae, transmitted to humans through the bite of a tick, characterized by fever, dizziness, muscle ache, vomiting, headache, and other neurologic symptoms.

criminal psychology, the study of the mental processes, motivational patterns, and behavior of criminals.

crisis /krī′sis/ [Gk, *krisis,* turning point], **1.** a transition for better or worse in the course of a disease, usually indicated by a marked change in the intensity of signs and symptoms. **2.** a turning point in events affecting the emotional state of a person such as death or divorce. **3.** a characteristically self-limiting period of from 4 to 6 weeks that constitutes a transitional phase, representing both the danger of increased psychologic vulnerability and an opportunity for personal growth.

crisis intervention¹, (in psychiatry) a short-term intense therapy that emphasizes identification of the event that triggered the emotional trauma. Focus is on neutralizing the trauma and mobilizing coping skills.

crisis intervention², a nursing intervention from the Nursing Interventions Classification (NIC) defined as use of short-term counseling to help the patient cope with a crisis and resume a state of functioning comparable to or better than the precrisis state.

crisis-intervention unit, a group trained in emergency medical treatment and in various methods for rendering psychiatric therapeutic assistance to a person or group of persons during a period of crisis, especially instances involving suicide attempts or drug abuse.

crisis resolution, (in psychiatry) the development of effective adaptive and coping devices to resolve a crisis.

crisis theory, a conceptual framework for defining and explaining the phenomena that occur when a person faces a problem that appears to be insoluble.

crisscross inheritance [*Christ cross;* L, *in* + *hereditas,* in heredity], the inheritance of characteristics or conditions from the parent of the opposite sex.

crista ampullaris /kris′tə am′pəlar′is/ [L], the most prominent part of a localized thickening of the membrane that lines the ampullae of the semicircular ducts, covered with neuroepithelium containing endings of the vestibular nerve.

crista galli, a prominent wedge of bone projecting superiorly from the ethmoid.

crista obliqua, an elevated crest of variable prominence, consisting jointly of the triangular ridge of the distobuccal cusp and the distal ridge of the mesiolingual cusp. It courses obliquely across the occlusal surface of the maxillary molars to link the apices of the distobuccal and the mesiolingual cusps.

criterion /krītir′ē·ən/ *pl.* **criteria** [Gk, *kriterion,* a means for judging], a standard or rule by which something may be judged, such as a health condition, or a diagnosis established.

critical care unit (CCU), a specially equipped hospital area designed for the treatment of patients with sudden, life-threatening conditions. CCUs contain resuscitation and monitoring equipment and are staffed by personnel specially trained and skilled in recognizing and immediately responding to cardiac and other emergencies.

critical organs /krit′ikəl/ [Gk, *krisis,* turning point, *organon,* instrument], tissues that are the most sensitive to irradiation, such as the gonads, lymphoid organs, and intestine. The skin, cornea, oral cavity, esophagus, vagina, cervix, and optic lens are the next-most sensitive organs to irradiation.

critical path development, a nursing intervention from the Nursing Interventions Classification (NIC) defined as constructing and using a timed sequence of patient care activities to enhance desired patient outcomes in a cost-efficient manner.

critical period [Gk, *kritikos,* critical, *peri,* near, *hodos,* way], a period during a developmental or rehabilitation crisis.

critical period of development, 1. a specific time during which the environment has its greatest impact on an individual's development. **2.** the time during gestation when critical organ systems are formed.

critical point, the temperature and pressure at which, in a sealed system, the density of the liquid form of a substance is equal to the density of its gas form, and the two are not visibly separated, becoming a single fluid phase instead.

critical pressure, the pressure exerted by a fluid in a closed system at the critical temperature.

critical temperature, the highest temperature at which a substance can exist as a liquid.

Crixivan, a trademark for an antiretroviral protease inhibitor (indinavir).

CRNA, abbreviation for **certified registered nurse anesthetist.**

CRNI, abbreviation for *certified registered nurse, intravenous.*

crocodile shagreen /shagrēn′/, a rare degenerative disorder involving either of two membranes of the cornea in which the cornea exhibits opacities separated by clear zones.

Crohn's disease /krōnz/ [Burrill B. Crohn, American physician, 1884–1983], a chronic inflammatory bowel disease of unknown origin, usually affecting the ileum, the colon, or another part of the GI tract. Diseased segments may be separated by normal bowel segments, which give it the characteristic "skip lesions."

Cromer blood group /krō′mər/, a blood group consisting of 12 red cell antigens located on the complement regulatory glycoprotein, decay-accelerating factor (DAF of CD55).

cromolyn sodium /krom′əlin/, a drug that blocks mast cell degranulation in response to antigen, which leads to decreased release of histamine, leukotrienes, and other inflammatory mast cell products. It is prophylactically prescribed to prevent bronchial asthma.

Cronkhite-Canada syndrome /krong′kīt/ [Leonard W. Cronkhite, American physician, 1919–1947; Wilma J. Canada, twentieth-century American radiologist], an abnormal familial condition characterized by GI polyposis accompanied by ectodermal defects such as nail atrophy, alopecia, and excessive skin pigmentation. In some individuals, it is also accompanied by protein-losing enteropathy, malabsorption, and deficiency of blood calcium, potassium, and magnesium.

cross [L, *crux*], **1.** (in genetics) a mating between individuals with different phenotypes. **2.** any individual, organism, or strain produced from such a mating.

cross-bite [L, *crux*; AS, *bitan*], occlusion of the mandibular teeth anterior and/or buccal to the maxillary teeth.

crossbreeding [L, *crux*; AS, *bredan*], the production of offspring by the mating of individuals of different varieties, strains, or species; hybridization;—**crossbred,** *adj.*

crossed amblyopia [L, *crux,* cross; Gk, *amblys,* dull, *ops,* eyes], a visual disorder in which the patient is unable to see on one side of the visual field, associated with hemianesthesia of the opposite side of the body.

crossed extension reflex, one of the spinally mediated reflexes normally present in the first 2 months of life. It is demonstrated by the adduction and extension of one leg when the foot of the other leg is stimulated.

crossed fused ectopic kidney, one with crossed renal ectopia.

crossed grid, an assembly of two parallel x-ray grids that are oriented at right angles to each other to eliminate scattered radiation from more than one direction during radiography.

crossed leg palsy, palsy of the fibular nerve, caused by sitting with one leg crossed over the other.

crossed reflex, any neural reflex in which stimulation of one side of the body results in a response on the other, such as the consensual light reflex.

cross-fertilization, 1. the union of gametes from different species or varieties to form hybrids. **2.** the fertilization of the flower of one plant by the pollen of a different plant.

cross infection [L, *crux,* cross, *inficere,* to stain], the transmittal of an infection from one patient in a hospital or health care setting to another patient with different pathogenic microorganisms in the same environment. It is often seen in autoimmune diseases.

crossing over, the exchange of sections of chromatids between homologous pairs of chromosomes during the prophase stage of the first meiotic division.

cross-link /kros'link'/, a bond formed between polymer chains, either between different chains or between different parts of the same chain.

crossmatching [L, *crux*; AS, *gemaecca*, matching], a procedure in blood transfusions and organ transplantation. The recipient's erythrocytes or leukocytes are incubated with the donor's serum and vice versa. Various testing procedures are then performed to ensure that the donor and the recipient have blood group compatibility or histocompatibility.

crossover /kros'ovər/ [L, *crux*; AS, *ofer*], the result of the recombination of genes on homologous pairs of chromosomes during meiosis.

cross-reacting antibody [L, *crux*, cross, *re* + *agere*, to act; Gk, *anti*; AS, *bodig*, body], an antibody that reacts with antigens that are similar to but different from the specific antigens with which it originally reacted.

cross-resistance, resistance to a particular antibiotic that often results in resistance to other antibiotics, usually from a similar chemical class, to which the bacteria may not have been exposed.

cross section, 1. a transverse section cut through a structure. 2. (in nuclear physics) of a specific atom or particle at a specific radiation, the area perpendicular to the direction of the radiation that one attributes to the atom or particle.

cross-sectional [L, *crux* + *secare*, to cut], (in statistics) pertaining to the sampling of a defined population at one point in time, performed in a nonexperimental research design.

cross-sectional anatomy, the study of the relationship of the structures of the body by the examination of cross-sections of the tissue or organ.

cross-sensitivity, a sensitivity to one substance that predisposes an individual to sensitivity to other substances that are related in chemical structure.

cross-sequential /-sikwen'shəl/ [L, *crux* + *sequi*, to follow], (in statistics) pertaining to data that compare several cohorts at different points in time.

cross-species transplant, a tissue or organ from an animal of one species that has been implanted into an animal of another species.

cross-tolerance, a tolerance to other drugs that develops after exposure to a different agent.

crotalid /krot'älid/, pit viper.

Crotalus /krot'älus/, a large genus of venomous rattlesnakes with numerous species in North America and others in Central and South America.

crotamiton /krōtam'iton/, a scabicide prescribed in the treatment of scabies and other pruritic skin diseases.

croup /krōōp/ [Scot, to croak], an acute viral infection of the upper and lower respiratory tracts that occurs primarily in infants and young children 3 months to 3 years of age after an upper respiratory tract infection. It is characterized by hoarseness; irritability; fever; a distinctive harsh, brassy cough; persistent stridor during inspiration; and dyspnea and tachypnea resulting from obstruction of the larynx. The most common causative agents are the parainfluenza viruses, especially type 1, followed by the respiratory syncytial viruses (RSVs) and influenza A and B viruses.—**croupous, croupy,** *adj.*

Croupette /krōōpet'/, a trademark for a device that provides cool humidification with the administration of oxygen or of compressed air. This device is most often used with pediatric patients to relieve hypoxia and liquefy secretions.

Crouzon's disease /krōōzonz'/ [Octave Crouzon, French neurologist, 1874–1938; L, *dis*; Fr, *aise*, ease], a familial disease characterized by a malformed skull and various ocular disorders, including exophthalmos, divergent squint, and optic atrophy.

crowding /kroud'ing/ [ME, *crowden*], the condition in which the teeth are too close together and have abnormal positions such as overlapping, displacement in various directions, or torsion.

crown [L, *corona*], 1. the upper part of an organ or structure, such as the top of the head. 2. the portion of a human tooth that is covered by enamel.

crown-heel length [L, *corona*; AS, *hela* + *lengthu*], the length of an embryo, fetus, or newborn as measured from the crown of the head to the heel.

crowning [L, *corona*], (in obstetrics) the phase at the end of labor in which the fetal head is seen at the introitus of the vagina. The labia are stretched in a crown around the head just before birth.

crown-rump length, the length of an embryo, fetus, or newborn as measured from the crown of the head to the prominence of the buttocks.

crown static, an x-ray film artifact caused by a buildup and discharge of electrons in the film emulsion. It is most likely to appear during periods of low environmental humidity.

CRP, abbreviation for **C-reactive protein.**

CRRN, abbreviation for *certified rehabilitation registered nurse.*

CRT, 1. abbreviation for **cadaveric renal transplant.** 2. abbreviation for cathode-ray tube. 3. abbreviation for certified respiratory therapist.

crucial /krōō'shəl/ [L. *crucialis*], severe and decisive.

cruciate /krōō'shē·āt/ [L, *crux,* cross], shaped like a cross.

cruciate anastomosis /krōō'shē·āt/ [L, *crux,* cross; Gk, *anastomoein,* to provide a mouth], an anastomosis in the upper part of the thigh, formed between the first perforating branch of the profunda femoris artery, the inferior gluteal artery, and the lateral and medial circumflex arteries.

cruciate ligament of the atlas [L, *crux,* cross, *ligare,* to bind], a crosslike ligament attaching the atlas to the base of the occipital bone above and the posterior surface of the body of the axis below.

crucible /krōō'səbəl/, a cone-shaped vessel made of a refractory material, used in chemistry to melt or calcine materials at temperatures too high for other laboratory equipment to tolerate.

cruciform /krōō'sifôrm/ [L, *crux,* cross], in the shape of a cross.

cruciform ligament, any cross-shaped band of white fibrous tissue connecting bones and forming a joint capsule.

crude birth rate [L, *crudus,* raw; ME, *burth;* L, *reri,* to reckon], the number of births per 1000 people in a population during 1 year.

crude herb, the raw plant, before it is processed or dried.

cruor /krōō'ôr/ [L, blood], a blood clot containing erythrocytes.

crural /krōō'rəl/, pertaining to the leg, between the knee and ankle.

crural hernia [L, *crus,* leg, *hernia,* rupture], **1.** a hernia that protrudes behind the posterior layer of the femoral sheath. **2.** a common type of groin hernia that occurs most often in obese females.

crura of anthelix, the two ridges on the external ear marking the superior termination of the anthelix and bounding the triangular fossa.

crus /krus/ *pl.* **crura** [L, leg], **1.** the leg, from knee to foot. **2.** a structure resembling a leg, such as the crura of anthelix.

crus cerebri /ser'əbrī, -brē/ [L, *crus* + *cerebrum,* brain], either of the two cerebral peduncles, composed of the descending fiber tracts passing from the cerebral cortex to form the longitudinal fascicles of the pons.

crushing wound /krush'ing/ [ME, *crushen;* AS, *wund*], a break in the external surface of the body caused by a severe force applied against the tissues. The body structures may be crushed without signs of external bleeding.

crush syndrome [ME, *crushen*], a severe, life-threatening condition caused by extensive crushing trauma, characterized by destruction of muscle and bone tissue, hemorrhage, and fluid loss resulting in hypovolemic shock, hematuria, renal failure, and coma.

crust [L, *crusta,* shell], a solidified, hard outer layer formed by the drying of a body exudate, common in dermatologic conditions such as eczema, impetigo, seborrhea, and favus and during the healing of burns and lesions; a scab.

crutch [AS, *cryce*], a wooden or metal staff that aids a person in walking.

Crutchfield tongs [William G. Crutchfield, American neurosurgeon, 1900–1972; ME, *tonges*], an instrument that is attached to the skull to hyperextend the head and neck of patients with fractured cervical vertebrae for the purpose of immobilizing and aligning the vertebrae.

crutch gait, a gait achieved by a person using crutches. The gait selected and learned is determined by the physical and functional abilities of the patient and the diagnosis.

crutch palsy, the temporary or permanent loss of sensation or muscle control resulting from pressure on the radial nerve by a crutch.

Cruveilhier-Baumgarten syndrome /krYvä yä' boum'gärtən/ [Jean Cruveilhier, French pathologist, 1791–1874; Paul Baumgarten, German pathologist, 1848–1928], recanalization of the paraumbilical veins with cirrhosis of the liver, portal hypertension, and splenomegaly.

crux /kruks, krŏŏks/ [L], **1.** cross. **2.** a difficult problem. **3.** a vital, basic, or decisive point.

cry [OFr, *crier*], **1.** a sudden, loud voluntary or automatic vocalization in response to pain, fear, or a startle reflex. **2.** weeping, as a reaction to pain or an emotional response to depression or grief.

crying vital capacity (CVC), a measurement of the tidal volume while an infant is crying. The CVC may be valuable in monitoring infants with lung diseases that cause changes in functional residual capacity.

cryoanesthesia /krī'ō·an'isthē'zhə/ [Gk, *kryos,* cold, *aisthesis,* feeling], local anesthesia produced by applying a tourniquet and chilling a body part to near freezing temperature. It is used to diminish neural sensitivity to pain during brief minor surgical procedures.

cryocautery /krī'ōkô'tərē/ [Gk, *kryos* + *kauterion,* branding iron], the application of any substance, such as solid carbon dioxide, that destroys tissue by freezing.

cryogen /krī'əjən/ [Gk, *kryos* + *genein,* to produce], **1.** a chemical that induces freezing, used to destroy diseased tissue without injury to adjacent structures. Cell death is caused by dehydration after cell membranes rupture. **2.** (in MRI) a chemical used to cool the MRI electromagnet so that the magnet remains superconducting and higher magnified strengths can be achieved.—**cryogenic,** *adj.*

cryoglobulin /krī'ōglob'yōōlin/ [Gk, *kryos*; L, *globulus,* small sphere], an abnormal plasma protein that precipitates and coalesces at low temperatures and dissolves and disperses at body temperature.

cryoglobulinemia /krī'ōglob'yōōlinē'mē·ə/ [Gk, *kryos*; L, *globulus,* small sphere; Gk, *haima,* blood], the presence of cryoglobulins in the blood.

cryoglobulin test, a blood test to assess the presence of cryoglobulin, which is associated with lymphoid malignancies, connective tissue disease, acute and chronic infections, and liver disease.

cryonics /krī·on'iks/ [Gk, *kryos,* cold], the techniques in which cold is applied for a variety of therapeutic goals, including brief local anesthesia, destruction of superficial skin lesions, and preservation of cells, tissue, organs, or the entire body. —**cryonic,** *adj.*

cryoprecipitate /-prisip'itāt/, **1.** any precipitate formed on cooling of a solution. **2.** a preparation rich in factor VIII needed to restore normal coagulation in hemophilia. It is collected from fresh human plasma that has been frozen and thawed.

cryopreservation /krī'ōpres'ərvā'shən/, a method of preserving tissues and organs in a viable state at extremely low temperatures.

cryostat /krī'ōstat/ [Gk, *kryos* + *statos,* standing], a device used in surgical treatment of pathologic disorders that consists of a special microtome used for freezing and slicing sections of tissue for study by a surgical pathologist.

cryosurgery /-sur'jərē/ [Gk, *kryos* + *cheirourgos*], use of subfreezing temperature to destroy tissue. Cryosurgery is performed to destroy the ganglion of nerve cells in the thalamus in the treatment of Parkinson's disease, to destroy the pituitary gland to halt the progress of some kinds of metastatic cancer, and to treat various cancers and lesions of the skin. The process is also used in ophthalmology to cause the edges of a detached retina to heal and to remove cataracts. The coolant is circulated through a metal probe, chilling it to as low as −160° C (−256° F).

cryotherapy /krī'ōther'əpē/ [Gk, *kryos* + *therapeia*], a treatment using cold as a destructive medium. Cutaneous tags, warts, condyloma acuminatum, and actinic keratosis are some of the common skin disorders responsive to cryotherapy. Solid carbon dioxide or liquid nitrogen is applied briefly with a sterile cotton-tipped applicator or cryospray instrument. Blistering, followed by necrosis, results.

crypt /kript/ [Gk, *kryptos,* hidden], a blind pit or tube on a free surface.

cryptic /krip'tik/ [Gk, *kryptos,* hidden], pertaining to something concealed.

cryptocephalus /krip'tōsef'ələs/ [Gk, *kryptos* + *kephale,* head], a malformed fetus that has a small, underdeveloped head. —**cryptocephalic, cryptocephalous,** *adj.,* **cryptocephaly,** *n.*

cryptococcosis /krip'tōkokō'sis/, an infectious disease caused by the fungus *Cryptococcus neoformans,* which after inhalation, spreads from the lungs to the brain and CNS, skin, skeletal system, and urinary tract. It is characterized by the development of nodules or tumors filled with a gelatinous material in visceral and subcutaneous tissues. Initial symptoms may include coughing or other respiratory effects because the lungs are a primary site of infection. After the fungus spreads to the meninges, neurologic symptoms, including headache, blurred vision, and difficulty in speaking, may develop.

Cryptococcus /-kok'əs/, a genus of yeast-like fungi that reproduce by budding rather than producing spores. Many nonpathogenic species are commonly found in the soil and on the skin and mucous membranes of people who are well.

Cryptococcus neoformans, a species of yeastlike fungus that causes cryptococcosis.

cryptodidymus /krip'tōdid'əməs/ [Gk, *kryptos* + *didymos,* twin], conjoined twins one of which fetus is a small, underdeveloped fetus concealed within the body of the other, more fully formed autosite.

crypt of iris, any one of the small pits in the iris along its free margin encircled by the circulus arteriosus minor.

cryptogenic /-jen'ik/ [Gk, *kryptos,* hidden, *genein,* to produce], **1.** pertaining to a disease of unknown cause. **2.** a parasitic organism living within another organism.

cryptogenic infection, a disease caused by pathogenic microorganisms of obscure or unknown origin.

cryptogenic septicemia, a systemic infection in which pathogens are present in the bloodstream but no primary focus of infection can be identified.

cryptomenorrhea /krip'tōmenôrē'ə/ [Gk, *kryptos*; L, *mens,* month; Gk, *rhoia,* flow], an abnormal condition in which the products of menstruation are retained within the vagina because of an imperforate hymen or, less often, within the uterus because of an occlusion of the cervical canal. — **cryptomenorrheal**, *adj.*

cryptophthalmos /krip′tǝfthal′mǝs/ [Gk, *kryptos* + *ophthalmos*, eye], a developmental anomaly characterized by complete fusion of the eyelids, usually with defective formation of, or lack of, eyes.

cryptorchidism /kriptôr′kidiz′ǝm/ [Gk, *kryptos*, hidden, *orchis*, testis], a developmental defect in which one or both testicles fail to descend into the scrotum and are retained in the abdomen or inguinal canal.

cryptosporidiosis, an opportunistic infection caused by the intestinal parasites *Cryptosporidium parvum,* a very common parasite in animals, and *C. hominis.* Sources of infection include contaminated water, raw or undercooked foods contaminated with *Cryptosporidium* oocysts, and direct contact with infected humans or animals. Symptoms of watery diarrhea, abdominal cramps, nausea, vomiting, and low-grade fever may appear 2 to 10 days after infection. They may lead to dehydration and weight loss.

cry reflex, a normal infantile reaction to pain, hunger, or need for attention. The reflex may be absent in an infant born prematurely or in poor health.

crystal /kris′tǝl/ [Gk, *krystallos*], a solid substance, either organic or inorganic, the atoms or molecules of which are arranged in a regular, repeating three-dimensional pattern, which determines the shape of a crystal. — **crystalline,** *adj.*

crystalline, describing material with a regular geometric shape. Crystalline substances have a very narrow melting point range.

crystalline lens /kris′tǝlin, -līn/ [Gk, *krystallos*; L, *lentil*], a transparent structure of the eye, enclosed in a capsule, situated between the iris and the vitreous humor, and slightly overlapped at its margin by the ciliary processes. It refracts light to focus images on the retina. The lens is a transparent biconvex structure with the posterior surface more convex than the anterior. It is composed of a soft cortical material, a firm nucleus, and concentric laminae.

crystallization /kris′tǝlīzā′shǝn/ [Gk, *krystallos*, rock crystal], the production of crystals, either by cooling a liquid or gas to a solid state or by cooling a solution until the solute precipitates as a crystalline deposit. — **crystallize,** *v.*

crystalloid /kris′tǝloid/ [Gk, *krystallos* + *eidos,* form], a substance in a solution

that can diffuse through a semipermeable membrane.

crystalluria /kris′tǝlo͝or′ē-ǝ/, the presence of crystals in the urine. The condition may be a source of urinary tract irritation; adequate intake of alkali can prevent it. However, crystals are commonly found in urine and are usually insignificant.

Crystodigin, a trademark for a cardiac glycoside (digitoxin).

Cs, symbol for the element **cesium.**

CS, abbreviation for **cesarean section.**

CSF, 1. abbreviation for **cerebrospinal fluid. 2.** abbreviation for **colony-stimulating factor.**

CSN, abbreviation for *certified school nurse.*

C-spine, abbreviation for **cervical spine.**

CSR, abbreviation for **Cheyne-Stokes respiration.**

c-src, a tyrosine kinase that participates in signal transduction pathways that regulate growth of cells. It hybridizes with oncogenes of the highly virulent Rous sarcoma virus.

CST, 1. abbreviation for **contraction stress test. 2.** abbreviation for **Certified Surgical Technologist.**

CT, abbreviation for **computed tomography.**

CTX, abbreviation for **clinical trial exemption.**

Cu, symbol for the element **copper.**

CUA, abbreviation for **cost-utility analysis.**

cubic centimeter (cc, cu cm, cm³) [Gk, *kybos;* L, *centum,* hundred; Gk, *metron,* measure], a theoretic cube or its equivalent, each edge of which is 1 centimeter long. One cubic centimeter is equivalent to 1 mL.

Cubicin, a trademark for daptomycin.

cubic millimeter (cu mm, mm³), a unit of volume equal to one millionth of a liter. One cubic millimeter is equivalent to 1 microliter.

cubital /kyo͞o′bitǝl/, pertaining to the elbow or the forearm.

cubital fossa, a depression in the front of the elbow, immediately lateral to the tendon of the biceps brachii muscle.

cubitus /kyo͞o′bitǝs/, **1.** the elbow. **2.** the forearm.

cuboidal epithelium /kyo͞oboi′dǝl/ [Gk, *kybos,* cube, *eidos,* form, *epi,* above, *thele,* nipple], simple epithelial cells that are generally cube-shaped and one layer thick.

cuboid bone /kyo͞o′boid/ [Gk, *kybos,* cube, *eidos,* form], the outer cuboidal tarsal bone on the lateral side of the foot, proximal to the fourth and fifth metatarsal bones.

cu cm, abbreviation for **cubic centimeter.**

cue /kyo͞o/, a stimulus that determines or may prompt the nature of a person's response.

cuff, an inflatable elastic tube that is placed around a limb and inflated with air to restrict arterial circulation during BP examination.

cuffed endotracheal tube, an endotracheal tube with a balloon at one end that may be inflated to tighten the fit in the lumen of the airway. The balloon forms a cuff that prevents gastric contents from passing into the lungs and gas from leaking back from the lungs.

cuffing, a pathologic condition in which cufflike borders of leukocytes form around small blood vessels, as in certain infections.

cuirass /kwiras'/ [Fr, *cuirasse,* breastplate], **1.** a negative-pressure full-body respirator. An electrically driven pump is adjusted to match the timing of the patient's spontaneous breathing. **2.** a tightly fitted chest bandage.

cul-de-sac /kul'dəsak, kYdesok'/ *pl.* **culs-de-sac, cul-de-sacs** [Fr, bottom of the bag], a blind pouch or cecum, such as the conjunctival cul-de-sac and the dural cul-de-sacs.

cul-de-sac of Douglas [James Douglas, Scottish anatomist, 1675–1742], a pouch formed by the caudal part of the parietal peritoneum.

culdocentesis /kul'dōsentē'sis/, the use of needle puncture or incision through the vagina to remove intraperitoneal fluid, including purulent material.

culdoplasty /kul'dōplas'tē/ [Fr, *cul-de-sac,* bottom of the bag; Gk, *plassein,* to mold], plastic surgery to correct a defect in the posterior fornix of the vagina.

culdoscope /kul'dəskōp'/, an endoscope with an attached light that can be inserted through the posterior wall of the vagina for examination of the pelvic viscera.

culdotomy /kuldot'əmē/, incision or needle puncture of the cul-de-sac of Douglas by way of the vagina.

Culex /ko͞o'leks/, a genus of humpbacked mosquitoes. It includes species that transmit viral encephalitis and filariasis.

Cullen's sign [Thomas S. Cullen, American gynecologist, 1868–1953], the appearance of faint, irregularly formed hemorrhagic patches on the skin around the umbilicus. The discolored skin is usually blue-black and becomes greenish brown or yellow. Cullen's sign may appear 1 to 2 days after the onset of anorexia and the severe, poorly localized abdominal pains that are characteristic of acute pancreatitis.

Culp-De Weerd pyeloplasty, pyeloplasty in which a spiral flap is turned down and incorporated into the adjacent ureter.

cult, a specific complex of beliefs, rites, and ceremonies associated with some particular person or object, which is maintained by a social group. A cult is often considered as having magical significance.

cultural assimilation /kul'chərəl/, a process by which members of an ethnic minority group lose cultural characteristics that distinguish them from the dominant cultural group or take on the cultural characteristics of another group.

cultural event, a communication of meaning that takes place each time one member of a society interacts with another member.

cultural healer, a member of an ethnic or cultural group who uses traditional methods of healing rather than modern scientific methods to provide health care for other members of the group or members of another ethnic minority group.

culturally relativistic perspective, an ability to understand the behavior of transcultural patients (those who move from one culture to another) within the context of their own culture.

cultural relativism, a concept that health and normality emerge within a social context and that the content and form of mental health will greatly vary from one culture to another.

culture /kul'chər/ [L, *colere,* to cultivate], **1.** (in microbiology) a laboratory test involving the cultivation of microorganisms or cells in a special growth medium. **2.** (in psychology) a set of learned values, beliefs, customs, and behavior that is shared by a group of interacting individuals.

culture-bound, pertaining to a health condition that is specific to a particular culture, such as a belief in the effects of certain kinds of prayer or the "evil eye."

culture brokerage, a nursing intervention from the Nursing Interventions Classification (NIC) defined as the deliberate use of culturally competent strategies to bridge or mediate between the patient's culture and the biomedical health care system.

culture procedure, (in bacteriology) any of several techniques for growing colonies of microorganisms to identify a pathogen and to determine its sensitivity to various antibiotics.

culture shock, the psychologic effect of a drastic change in the cultural environment of an individual. The person may exhibit feelings of helplessness, discomfort, and disorientation in attempting to adapt to a different cultural group with dissimilar practices, values, and beliefs.

cum /ko͞om/ [L], together with.

cu mm, abbreviation for **cubic millimeter.**

C

cumulative /kyo͞o′myələ′tiv/ [L, *cumulare,* to pile on], increasing by incremental steps with an eventual total that may exceed the expected result.

cumulative action, 1. the increased activity of a therapeutic measure or agent when administered repeatedly. **2.** the increased activity demonstrated by a drug when repeated doses accumulate in the body and exert a greater biologic effect than the initial dose.

cumulative dose, the total dosage that accumulates as a result of repeated exposure to radiation or a radiopharmaceutic product.

cumulus /kyo͞o′myo͞o′ləs/ *pl.* **cumuli** [L], a little mound, usually formed by a collection of cells.

cuneate /kyo͞o′nē-āt/ [L, *cuneus,* wedge], (of tissue) wedge-shaped; especially in relation to cells of the nervous system.

cuneiform /kyo͞onē′əfôrm′/ [L, *cuneus,* wedge + *forma*], **1.** (of bone and cartilage) wedge-shaped. **2.** bone of the foot between the navicular and metatarsals.

cuneiform cartilage [L, *cuneus,* wedge, *forma* + *cartilago*], one of two small pieces of yellow elongated elastic laryngeal cartilage at the edge of the aryepiglottic fold, above and anterior to the corniculate cartilage.

cuneus /kyo͞o′nē-əs/, a wedge-shaped region of the cerebral cortex lying between the parietooccipital and postcalcarine sulci on the mesial surface of the occipital lobe.

cunnilingus /kun′əling′gəs/, the oral stimulation of the female genitalia.

cup arthroplasty of the hip joint [L, *cupa,* cask; Gk, *arthron,* joint, *plassein,* to mold], surgical replacement of the head of the femur by a metal or plastic mold to relieve pain and increase motion in arthritis or to correct a deformity. The damaged or diseased bone is removed, and the acetabulum and the head of the femur are reshaped. A cup is inserted between the two and becomes the articulating surface of the femur.

cup/disc ratio, (in ophthalmology) the mathematic relationship between the horizontal or vertical diameter of the optic nerve cup and the diameter of the optic disc.

cupping, a counterirritant technique of applying a suction device to the skin to draw blood to the surface of the body.

cupping and vibrating, a technique for dislodging and removing mucus and fluid from the lungs. Cupping consists of the rhythmic percussion of the affected segments of the lungs or bronchi by the practitioner's cupped hands. It is begun

gently and increased in forcefulness as the patient's tolerance increases. To perform vibrating, the practitioner places his or her hands over the affected area and alternately tenses and contracts the muscles of the hand, arm, and shoulder. The vibratory movements are transmitted to the patient's chest, increasing the turbulence and velocity of exhaled air in the small bronchi.

cupric /kyo͞o′prik/ [L, *cuprum,* copper], pertaining to copper in its divalent form, as cupric sulfate.

cupric sulfate, a crystalline salt of copper used as an emetic, astringent, and fungicide, as an oral antidote to phosphorus poisoning, as a topical treatment of cutaneous phosphorus burns, and as a catalyst in iron deficiency anemia.

Cuprimine, a trademark for a chelating agent used in treating poisoning by heavy metals (D-penicillamine).

cupula /kyo͞o′pələ/, any cup- or dome-shaped structure, such as the top of a lymphatic nodule in the small intestine.

cupular caecum of cochlear duct, the closed blind apical end of the cochlear duct.

cupulolithiasis /kyo͞o′pyo͞olōlithī′əsis/ [L, *cupula,* little cup; Gk, *lithos,* stone], a severe, long-lasting vertigo brought on by movement of the head to certain positions. In addition to extreme dizziness, signs are nausea, vomiting, and ataxia.

curare /kyo͞orä′rē/ [S. Am. Indian, *ourari*], a potent neuromuscular blocker that acts by preventing transmission of neural impulses across the myoneural junctions. A large dosage can cause complete paralysis, but action is usually reversible with acetylcholinesterase inhibitors (cholinergic agonists). Pharmacologic preparations of curare are used as adjuncts to general anesthesia. The use of curare or other neuromuscular blocking agents requires respiratory and ventilatory assistance by a qualified anesthetist or anesthesiologist.

curariform /kyo͞orä′rifôrm′/ [*curare*; L, *forma*], **1.** chemically similar to curare. **2.** having the effect of curare.

cure /kyo͞or/ [L, *cura*], **1.** restoration to health of a person afflicted with a disease or other disorder. **2.** the favorable outcome of the treatment of a disease or other disorder. **3.** a course of therapy, a medication, a therapeutic measure, or another remedy used in treatment of a medical problem, as faith healing, fasting, rest cure, or work cure.

curet /kyo͞oret′/ [Fr, *curette,* scoop], **1.** a surgical instrument shaped like a spoon or scoop used for scraping and removing material or tissue from an organ, cavity, or surface.

2. to remove tissue or debris with such a device.

curettage /kyŏŏr′ətäzh′/ [Fr, *curette*, scoop], scraping of material from the wall of a cavity or other surface, performed to remove tumors or other abnormal tissue or to obtain tissue for microscopic examination. Curettage also refers to clearing unwanted material from fistulas and areas of chronic infection.

curie (Ci) /kyŏŏr′ē/ [Marie Skladowska Curie, Polish-born chemist and physicist, 1867–1934; Pierre Curie, French chemist and physicist, 1859–1906; both Nobel laureates], a unit of radioactivity used before adoption of the becquerel (Bq) as the SI unit. It is equal to 3.70×10^{10} Bq.

curing /kyŏŏr′ing/ [L, *curare*, to take care of or heal], (in dentistry) a method for promoting and accelerating hardening processes by using dampness, heat, cold, chemical agents, electromagnetic radiation, or other agents.

curium (Cm) /kyŏŏr′ē·əm/ [Marie S. Curie; Pierre Curie], a radioactive metallic element. Its atomic number is 96. Its atomic mass is 247. Curium is an artificial element produced by bombarding plutonium with helium ions in a cyclotron.

Curling's ulcer [Thomas B. Curling, English surgeon, 1811–1888], a duodenal ulcer that develops in people who have suffered severe stress.

CURN, abbreviation for *Certified Urological Registered Nurse.*

currant jelly clot /kur′ənt/ [ME, *corauns*; L, *gelare*, to congeal; AS, *clott*], a red, jelly-like blood clot that is rich in hemoglobin from erythrocytes in the clot.

current /kur′ənt/ [L, *currere*, to run], **1.** a flowing or streaming movement. **2.** a flow of electrons along a conductor in a closed circuit; an electric current. **3.** certain physiologic electrical activity and characteristics of blood circulation.

Current Procedural Terminology (CPT™), a system developed by the American Medical Association for standardizing the terminology and coding used to describe medical services and procedures.

curriculum vitae (CV) /kərik′ələm wē′tī, -vē′tē/ *pl.* **curricula vitae** [L, *curriculum*, course, *vita*, life], a summary of educational and professional experiences, including activities and honors, to be used in applications for employment, for biographic citations on professional meeting programs, or for related purposes.

Curschmann's spiral /kŏŏrsh′monz/ [Heinrich Curschmann, German physician, 1846–1910; Gk, *speira*, coil], coiled fibril of mucus occasionally found in the sputum of persons with bronchial asthma.

curtain effect /kur′tən/, an artifact produced when chemical processing stains are not properly squeezed from an x-ray film during development of a radiograph.

curvature /kur′vəchər/, a bending or curving of a line from the course of a straight line.

curvature myopia, a type of nearsightedness caused by refractive errors associated with an excessive curvature of the cornea.

curve [L, *curvare*, to bend], (in statistics) a straight or curved line used as a graphic method of demonstrating the distribution of data collected in a study or survey.

curve of Carus [Karl G. Carus, German anatomist, 1789–1869], the normal axis of the pelvic outlet.

curve of occlusion, 1. an imaginary curved surface that is described by the incisal and occlusal surfaces of the teeth. **2.** the curve of dentition on which lies the occlusal surfaces of the teeth.

curve of Spee /shpā, spē/ [Ferdinand Graf von Spee, German embryologist, 1855–1937], the anatomic curvature of the occlusal alignment of the teeth. It begins at the tip of the lower canine, follows the buccal cusps of the natural premolars and molars, and continues to the anterior border of the mandibular ramus.

curve of Wilson /wil′sən/, the curvature of the cusps of the teeth as projected on the frontal plane. That of the mandibular dental arch is concave, and that of the maxillary dental arch is convex.

curvilinear /cur′vilin′ē·ər/ [L, *curvus*, bent, *linea*, line], pertaining to a curved line.

curvilinear trend [L, *curvus*, bent, *linea*, line; AS, *trendan*, to turn], (in statistics) a trend in which a graphic representation of the data yields a curved line.

Curvularia /ker′vular′eə/, a genus of imperfect fungi commonly found in soil and elsewhere. *C. lunata* is found in human mycetomas.

cushingoid /kŏŏsh′ingoid/ [Harvey W. Cushing, American surgeon, 1869–1939; Gk, *eidos*, form], having the habitus and facies characteristic of Cushing's disease.

Cushing's disease /kŏŏsh′ingz/ [Harvey W. Cushing], a metabolic disorder characterized by abnormally increased secretion of adrenocortical steroids, particularly cortisol, caused by increased amounts of adrenocorticotropic hormone secreted by the pituitary gland. Excess adrenocortical hormones result in accumulations of fat on the abdomen, chest, upper back, and face and occurrence of edema, hyperglycemia, increased gluconeogenesis, muscle weakness, purplish striae on the skin, decreased immunity to infection, osteoporosis with susceptibility to bone fractures, acne, and facial hair growth in women.

Cushing's syndrome [Harvey W. Cushing], a metabolic disorder resulting from the chronic and excessive production of cortisol by the adrenal cortex or by the administration of glucocorticoids in large doses for several weeks or longer. When occurring spontaneously, the syndrome represents a failure in the body's ability to regulate the secretion of cortisol or adrenocorticotropic hormone (ACTH). The most common cause of the syndrome is a pituitary tumor that increases secretion of ACTH.

cushion [OFr, *coissin*], any anatomic structure that resembles a pad or pillow.

cusp [L, *cuspis,* point], **1.** a sharp projection or a rounded eminence that rises from the chewing surface of a tooth, such as the two pyramidal cusps that arise from the premolars. **2.** any one of the small flaps on the valves of the heart, as the ventral, dorsal, and medial cusps of the right atrioventricular valve.

cuspid /kus′pid/ [L, *cuspis,* point], a tooth with one cusp, or point; a canine tooth.

cuspless tooth /kusp′les/, a tooth without cusps, or prominences, on its occlusal surface, possibly as a result of attrition.

custodial care /kəstō′dē·əl/ [L, *custodia,* guarding, *garrire,* to chatter], services and care of a nonmedical nature provided on a long-term basis, usually for convalescent and chronically ill individuals.

customary and reasonable charge, (in the United States) a fee usually established by health insurance or government agencies that is considered to be the "usual" cost of a specific medical service. The fee is commonly based on the amount the company or agency will pay for that service and may vary with geographic area.

cut, a split in both strands of a DNA molecule.

cutaneous /kyŏŏtā′nē·əs/ [L, *cutis,* skin], pertaining to the skin.

cutaneous absorption, the taking up of substances through the skin.

cutaneous anaphylaxis, a localized hypersensitivity reaction in the form of a wheal and flare. It occurs in sensitized individuals when an antigen is injected into the skin of a sensitized individual as a test of sensitivity to various allergens.

cutaneous horn, a protruding kerotic growth of the skin, the base of which may show changes of actinic keratosis or carcinoma.

cutaneous immunofluorescence biopsy, a microscopic examination of skin tissue for evaluation and diagnosis of immunologic-mediated dermatitis.

cutaneous larva migrans, a skin condition caused by a hookworm, *Ancylostoma braziliense,* a parasite of cats and dogs. Its ova are deposited in the ground with the feces of infected animals, develop into larvae, and invade the skin of people, particularly bare feet, although any skin may be involved. As they migrate through the epidermis, a trail of inflammation follows the burrow, causing severe pruritus. Secondary infections often occur if the skin has been broken by scratching.

cutaneous leishmaniasis, a dermatologic disease caused by the parasite *Leishmania tropica,* transmitted to humans by the bite of the sand fly and characterized by ulcerative lesions.

cutaneous lupus erythematosus, one of the two main types of lupus erythematosus. It may involve only the skin or may precede involvement of other body systems. It may be chronic (discoid lupus erythematosus); subacute (SLE); or acute (characterized by an acute edematous, erythematous eruption, often with systemic exacerbations).

cutaneous nerve, any mixed peripheral nerve that supplies a region of the skin.

cutaneous nevus [L, *cutis,* skin, *naevus,* birthmark], a congenital discoloration of a skin area, such as a strawberry birthmark.

cutaneous papilloma, a small brown or flesh-colored outgrowth of skin, occurring most frequently on the neck of an older person.

cutaneous sensation [L, *cutis,* skin, *sentire,* to feel], a sensation experienced in or arising from receptors of the skin.

cutaneous stimulation, a nursing intervention from the Nursing Interventions Classification (NIC) defined as stimulation of the skin and underlying tissues for the purpose of decreasing undesirable signs and symptoms such as pain, muscle spasm, or inflammation.

cutdown [ME, *cutten* + *doun*], a dissection to access a vein for puncture that is not accessible by venipuncture.

cuticle /kyŏŏ′təkəl/ [L, *cuticula,* little skin], **1.** the sheath of a hair follicle. **2.** the thin edge of cornified epithelium at the base of a nail.

cuticula /kyŏŏtik′yələ/, the cuticle, a narrow region of epidermis that covers the proximal surface of a fingernail or toenail.

cutis laxa /kyŏŏ′təs/ [L, skin, *laxus,* loose], abnormally loose, relaxed skin resulting from an absence of elastic fibers in the skin, usually a hereditary condition.

cutis marmorata, skin that has a "marbled" appearance caused by conspicuous dilatation of small vessels.

cutting oil dermatitis, a skin disorder that affects machinists and others who use cutting oils as coolants and lubricants. Exposure to the oil obstructs hair follicles, sweat ducts, and sebaceous glands, leading to development of comedones and folliculitis.

cuvette /kyōōvet′/ [Fr, *cuva,* tub], a small, transparent tube or container with specific optical properties. It is used in laboratory research and analyses, such as photometric evaluations, colorimetric determinations, and turbidity studies.

CV, 1. abbreviation for **closing volume. 2.** abbreviation for **curriculum vita.**

CVA, 1. abbreviation for **cerebrovascular accident. 2.** abbreviation for **costovertebral angle.**

CVB, abbreviation for *chorionic villus biopsy.*

CVC, abbreviation for **crying vital capacity.**

CVID, abbreviation for **common variable immunodeficiency.**

CVP, 1. abbreviation for **central venous pressure. 2.** an anticancer drug combination of cyclophosphamide, vinCRIStine, and predniSONE.

CVP monitor, abbreviation for **central venous pressure monitor.**

CW, abbreviation for **continuous wave.**

cyanide poisoning /sī′ənid, -nīd/ [Gk, *kyanos,* blue], poisoning resulting from the ingestion or inhalation of cyanide from such substances as bitter almond oil, wild cherry syrup, prussic acid, hydrocyanic acid, or potassium or sodium cyanide. Characterized by tachycardia, drowsiness, seizures, headache, apnea, and cardiac arrest, it may cause death within 1 to 15 minutes.

cyanobacteria /sī′ənōbaktir′ē·ə/ [Gk, *kyanos,* blue, *bacterion,* small staff], the blue-green bacteria, unicellular or filamentous organisms that fix both carbon dioxide (in the presence of light) and nitrogen. Several species are common causes of water pollution and cause cyanobacteria poisoning.

cyanobacteria poisoning, poisoning by cyanobacteria, usually as a result of drinking contaminated water. In most cases, it is a subacute condition characterized by liver damage with jaundice and sometimes bloody diarrhea and photosensitization. Drinking heavily contaminated water may cause acute symptoms including muscle tremors, ataxia, dyspnea, cyanosis, and hyperesthesia.

cyanocobalamin /sī′ənōkōbal′əmin/ [Gk, *kyanos;* Ger, *kobald,* mine goblin], a red crystalline, water-soluble substance that is the common pharmaceutic form of vitamin

B_{12}. It is involved in the metabolism of protein, fats, and carbohydrates; normal blood formation; and neural function. Rich dietary sources are liver, kidney, meats, fish, and dairy products. Deficiency can be caused by the absence of intrinsic factor (produced in the stomach), which is necessary for the absorption of cyanocobalamin from the GI tract. Deficiency can also occur in persons whose diet is strictly vegetarian. Symptoms of deficiency include nervousness, neuritis, numbness and tingling in the hands and feet, poor muscular coordination, and menstrual disturbances.

cyanomethemoglobin /sī′ənō′methē′mə glō′bin/ [Gk, *kyanos* + *meta,* together with, *haima,* blood; L, *globus,* ball], product of an in vitro reaction in which hemoglobin from whole blood is reduced to methemoglobin and converted to a stable red pigment using potassium ferricyanide and potassium cyanide. Cyanmethemoglobin has absorption peaks at 416 and 541 nm.

cyanopsia /sī′ənop′sē·ə/, a visual condition in which everything appears to have a blue tint.

cyanosed /sī′ənōst/, having a bluish discoloration of the skin, fingernails, and mucous membranes caused by a deficiency of oxygen in the blood.

cyanosis /sī′ənō′sis/ [Gk, *kyanos,* blue, *osis,* condition], bluish discoloration of the skin and mucous membranes caused by an excess of deoxygenated hemoglobin in the blood or a structural defect in the hemoglobin molecule, such as in methemoglobin.—**cyanotic,** *adj.*

cyanotic congenital heart defect /sī′ənot′ik/, an inborn heart defect that allows the mixing of unsaturated (venous) blood with saturated (arterial) blood to produce cyanosis.

cyberknife /sī′bərnīf/, a robotic radiosurgery system that delivers multiple beams of radiation, used to treat benign tumors and cancers and other medical conditions located anywhere in the body. It consists of a linear accelerator and a robotic arm.

cybernetics /sī′bərnet′iks/, the science of control and communication in living and nonliving systems, as in comparative study of electronic computers and the living brain.

cyclamate /sī′kləmāt/, an artificial nonnutritive sweetener formerly used in the form of calcium or sodium salt.

cyclandelate /sīklan′dəlāt/, a peripheral vasodilator prescribed in the treatment of muscular ischemia and peripheral vascular obstruction or spasm.

cyclarthrosis /sī′klärthrō′sis, sik′-/, a pivot joint, capable of rotation.

cycle [Gk, *kyklos,* circle], a series of events that recurs at specified intervals.

cyclencephaly /sīk′lənsef′əlē/ [Gk, *kyklos,* circle, *enkephalos,* brain], a developmental anomaly characterized by the fusion of the two cerebral hemispheres. —**cyclencephalic, cyclencephalous,** *adj.,* **cyclencephalus,** *n.*

cyclic /sik′lik, sī′klik/ [Gk, *kyklos,* circle], pertaining to or occurring in a cycle or cycles, such as a chemical compound that contains a ring of atoms in the nucleus.

cyclic adenosine monophosphate (cAMP) /sik′lik, sī′klik/, a cyclic nucleotide formed from adenosine triphosphate by the action of adenyl cyclase. This cyclic compound, known as the "second messenger," participates in the action of catecholamines, vasopressin, adrenocorticotropic hormone, and many other hormones.

cyclic guanosine monophosphate (cGMP), a substance that mediates the action of certain hormones in a manner similar to that of cyclic adenosine monophosphate. In response to the stimulation of cholinergic receptors in a parasympathetic nerve, guanylate cyclase triggers the conversion of guanosine triphosphate to cGMP with the release of various enzymes.

cyclic neutropenia /sik′lik no̅o̅′trōpē′nē·ə/, a chronic type of neutropenia that abates and recurs, accompanied by malaise, fever, stomatitis, and various types of infections.

cyclic vomiting, periodic episodes of vomiting associated with migraine.

cyclin /sī′klin/, one of a class of intracellular proteins that appear during the eukaryotic cell cycle. The cyclin concentration increases during the cycle until halfway to the mitosis stage, when it drops to zero.

cyclin-dependent kinase (CDK), a protein kinase that is activated by cyclin.

cycling /si′kling/, the ending of an inspiratory phase of mechanical ventilation.

cyclitis /siklī′tis/ [Gk, *kyklos* + *itis*], inflammation of the ciliary body that causes redness of the sclera adjacent to the cornea of the eye.

cyclizine hydrochloride /sī′klizēn/, an antihistamine and antiemetic/antivertigo agent prescribed in the treatment or prevention of motion sickness or vertigo.

cyclobenzaprine hydrochloride /sī′klōben′zəprēn/, a muscle relaxant prescribed in the short-term treatment of muscle spasm.

Cyclocort, a trademark for a glucocorticoid (amcinonide).

cyclodestruction /sī′klədistruk′shən/, (in ophthalmology) a procedure to damage the ciliary body in order to diminish the production of aqueous fluid in the treatment of glaucoma, usually done by cryotherapy.

cyclodialysis /-dī·al′isis/, **1.** a surgical procedure performed on patients with glaucoma. A pathway is opened between the anterior chamber of the eye and the suprachoroidal space, allowing excess fluid to drain and reducing intraocular pressure. **2.** separation of the ciliary body from the sclera, usually as a result of trauma, causing decreased intraocular pressure, or hypotony.

cycloduction /-duk′shən/, (in ophthalmology) the range of rotation of an eye around its visual axis, which allows binocular single vision to be maintained when the head is tilted.

cyclooxygenase /sī′klō·ok′səjenās/, an activity of the enzyme prostaglandin endoperoxide synthase.

cyclophosphamide /-fos′fəmīd/, an alkylating agent prescribed in the treatment of neoplasms and as an immunosuppressant in organ transplantation.

cyclopia /sīklō′pē·ə/ [Gk, *Cyclops,* mythic one-eyed giant], a developmental anomaly characterized by fusion of the orbits into a single cavity containing one eye. —**cyclops,** *n.*

cycloplegia /sī′kləplē′jə/ [Gk, *kyklos* + *plege,* stroke], paralysis of accommodation, as induced by certain ophthalmic drugs to allow examination of the eye.

cycloplegic /sī′kləplē′jik/, **1.** pertaining to a drug or treatment that causes paralysis of the ciliary muscles of the eye. **2.** one of a group of anticholinergic drugs used to paralyze the ciliary muscles of the eye for ophthalmologic examination or surgery.

cycloplegic refraction, a type of static refraction, measured after lens accommodation is paralyzed by administration of cycloplegic eyedrops.

cyclopropane /sī′klōprō′pān/, an explosive anesthetic gas no longer used in the United States.

cycloSERINE /sī′klōser′ēn/, an antibiotic prescribed in the treatment of active pulmonary and extrapulmonary TB.

Cyclospora cayetanensis, a pathogenic protozoan that causes diarrhea, cramps, and fever in humans.

cycloSPORIN[1] /-spôr′ēn/, an alternative term for cyclosporin A, an immunosuppressive medication often administered after organ transplants.

cyclosporin[2] /-spôr′in/, any of a group of biologically active metabolites of *Tolypocladium inflatum Gams* and certain other fungi. The major forms are cyclic oligopeptides with immunosuppressive, antifungal, and antipyretic effects. As immunosuppressants, cyclosporines primarily affect T lymphocytes. They are widely used in organ transplantation to suppress rejection.

cyclothymic disorder /-thīm′ik/ [Gk, *kyklos* + *thymos,* mind], a disorder of mood wherein the essential feature is a chronic mood disturbance of at least 2 years' duration, involving numerous periods of depression and hypomania, but not of sufficient severity and duration to meet the criteria for a major depressive or manic episode.

cyclothymic personality, a personality characterized by swings in mood from elation to depression.

cyclotomy /sīklot′əmē/, a surgical procedure for the correction of a defect in the ciliary muscle of the eye.

cyclotron /sī′klətron/ [Gk, *kyklos* + *electron,* amber], a device used to accelerate charged particles or ions. The particles bombard targets, where they create radioactive species, which can be used as radiopharmaceuticals or to make neutrons for radiotherapy.

cyclotropia /sī′klōtrō′pe·ə/, (in ophthalmology) a condition in which the ocular position of one eye is rotated around its axis with respect to the other eye.

cylinder, a solid body having a circular transverse section.

cylindrical grasp /silin′drikəl/, the normal position of the hand and fingers when holding cylindrical objects. The fingers and thumb close and flex around the object, which is stabilized against the palm of the hand. It occurs as a reflex action in infants and later develops into a voluntary gross grasp.

cylindrical lens, one with at least one nonspherical surface, used to correct astigmatism.

cylindroma /sil′indrō′mə/ *pl.* **cylindromas, cylindromata** [Gk, *kylindros,* cylinder], a tumor that appears to have cylinders of stroma surrounded by epithelial cells.

cyma line /sī′mə/, an S-shaped line seen on radiographs at the articulation of the talonavicular and calcaneocuboid bones of the foot.

Cymbalta, a trademark for duloxetine.

cyproheptadine hydrochloride /sī′prōhep′tədēn/, an antihistamine prescribed in the treatment of hypersensitivity reactions, including rhinitis, skin rash, and pruritus.

Cys, abbreviation for the amino acid **cysteine.**

cyst /sist/ [Gk, *kystis,* bag], a closed sac in or under the skin lined with epithelium and containing fluid or semisolid material. It may or may not be infected.—**cystic,** *adj.*

cystadenocarcinoma /sis′tədē′nəkär′sinō′mə/, a type of pancreatic tumor that evolves from a mucus cystadenoma.

Clinical features include epigastric pain and a palpable abdominal mass.

cystadenoma /sis′tədinō′mə/ *pl.* **cystadenomas, cystadenomata** [Gk, *kystis* + *aden,* gland, *oma,* tumor], **1.** an adenoma associated with a cystoma. **2.** an adenoma containing multiple cystic structures. The cysts may be serous, containing serum; or pseudomucinous, containing clear serous fluid or thick, viscid fluid.

Cystagon, a trademark for a product used in the treatment of nephropathic cystinosis (cysteamine bitartrate).

cystathioninemia /sis′təthī′oninē′mē·ə/, an inherited metabolic disorder caused by a deficiency of the enzyme cystathionase, that causes an excess of the amino acid methionine. Some patients may be asymptomatic, whereas others show signs of mental retardation as well as thrombocytopenia and acidosis.

cysteamine /siste′ämēn′/, a sulfhydryl amine that is part of coenzyme A. It reduces intracellular cystine levels and is used in treatment of nephropathic cystinosis.

cysteamine bitartrate, an anticysteine that reacts with cystine in the cell lysosomes to convert it to cysteine and a mixed disulfide—compounds that can then exit the lysosome in patients with a metabolic defect causing cystinosis. It is prescribed in the treatment of an inherited amino acid metabolic disease in which cysteine accumulates in the cells and can lead to the formation of crystals that can damage various organs, especially the kidneys.

cystectomy /sistek′təmē/ [Gk, *kystis* + *ektomē,* excision], a surgical procedure in which all or part of the urinary bladder is removed, as may be required in treating bladder cancer.

cysteine (Cys) /sis′tēn/, an amino acid found in many proteins in the body, including keratin. It is a metabolic precursor of cystine and an important source of sulfur for various body functions.

cystic /sis′tik/ [Gk, *kystis,* bag], **1.** pertaining to a cyst. **2.** pertaining to a fluid-filled sac, such as the gallbladder or urinary bladder.

cystic bile, concentrated bile stored in the gallbladder.

cystic carcinoma, a malignant neoplasm containing closed cavities or saclike spaces. These tumors may occur in the breast and ovary.

cystic diverticulum, a ventral outgrowth at the base of the hepatic diverticulum in the embryo. It gives rise to the gallbladder and cystic duct.

cystic duct, the duct through which bile from the gallbladder passes into the common bile duct.

cysticercosis /sis′tisərkō′sis/ [Gk, *kystis* + *kerkos*, tail, *osis*, condition], an infection and infestation by the larval stage of the pork tapeworm *Taenia solium* or the beef tapeworm *T. saginata*. The invasive, early phase of the infection is characterized by fever, malaise, muscle pain, and eosinophilia. Years later seizures and personality change may appear if the brain is affected, and calcification and destruction of local structures are apparent in other infested areas of the body.

cysticercus /sis′tisur′kəs/, a larval form of tapeworm. It consists of a single scolex enclosed in a bladder-like cyst.

cystic fibroma, a fibrous tumor in which cystic degeneration has occurred.

cystic fibrosis (CF), an inherited autosomal-recessive disorder of the exocrine glands, causing those glands to produce abnormally thick secretions of mucus, elevation of sweat electrolytes, increased organic and enzymatic constituents of saliva, and overactivity of the autonomic nervous system. The glands most affected are those in the pancreas and respiratory system and the sweat glands. CF is usually recognized in infancy or early childhood. The earliest manifestation is meconium ileus, an obstruction of the small bowel by viscid stool. Other early signs are a chronic cough; frequent, foul-smelling stools; and persistent URIs. The most reliable diagnostic tool is the sweat test, which shows elevations of levels of both sodium and chloride.

cystic fibrosis transmembrane conductance regulator, a regular of secretion in many exocrine tissues. Abnormalities in the gene cause CF, leading to abnormal chloride channels in cell membranes of the respiratory epithelium, pancreas, salivary glands, sweat glands, intestines, and reproductive tract.

cystic goiter, an enlargement of the thyroid gland, containing cysts resulting from mucoid or colloid degeneration, or liquefaction.

cystic kidney [Gk, *kystis*, bag; ME, *kidenei*], pertaining to any of several kidney disorders in which cysts form, including congenital polycystic disease, solitary renal cysts, or cortical cysts associated with nephrosclerosis.

cystic lymphangioma, a cystic growth formed by lymph vessels, usually congenital and occurring most frequently in the neck, axilla, or groin of children.

cystic mastitis, a form of mammary dysplasia with inflammation and the formation of nodular cysts in the breast tissue. The cysts contain a turbid fluid. Symptoms may vary with individual breast changes that occur during the menstrual cycle.

cystic myxoma, a tumor of connective tissue that has undergone cystic degeneration.

cystic nephroblastoma, multilocular cyst of the kidney.

cystic neuroma, a neoplasm of nerve tissue that has degenerated and become cystic.

cystic pyelitis, pyelitis with formation of submucosal cysts.

cystic pyeloureteritis, a type of ureteral inflammation in which there are subendothelial cysts projecting into the lumen of the ureter and renal pelvis.

cystic renal dysplasia, renal or kidney developmental abnormality in which there are cysts.

cystic tumor, a tumor with cavities or sacs containing a semisolid or a liquid material.

cystine /sis′tin/, a compound consisting of of two cysteine residues joined by a disulfide (S-S) linkage.

cystinosis /sis′tinō′sis/ [*cystine* + Gk, *osis*, condition], a congenital disease characterized by glucosuria; proteinuria; cystine deposits in the liver, spleen, bone marrow, and cornea; rickets; excessive amounts of phosphates in the urine; and retardation of growth.

cystinuria /sis′tinŏŏr′ē·ə/ [*cystine* + Gk, *ouron,* urine], **1.** abnormal presence of the amino acid cystine in the urine collected in a 24-hour specimen. **2.** an inherited defect of the renal tubules, characterized by excessive urinary excretion of cystine and several other amino acids.

cystitis /sistī′tis/ [Gk, *kystis* + *itis*, inflammation], an inflammatory condition of the urinary bladder and ureters, characterized by pain, urgency and frequency of urination, and hematuria. It may be caused by a bacterial infection, calculus, or tumor.

cystitis colli, inflammation of the bladder and bladder neck.

cystitis cystica, cystitis with formation of multiple submucosal cysts in the bladder wall.

cystocele /sis′təsēl′/ [Gk, *kystis* + *kele*, hernia], a herniation or protrusion of the urinary bladder through the wall of the vagina.

cystochromoscopy /sis′təkrōmos′kəpē/, examination of the bladder after administration of a colored dye, performed as an investigation of renal function and urinary system condition.

cystofibroma /-fībrō′mə/, a fibrous benign tumor that contains or is covered with cysts.

cystogram /sis′təgram′/ [Gk, *kystis* + *gramma,* record], a radiograph produced by cystography.

cystography /sistog′rəfē/, the radiographic examination of the urinary bladder after introduction of a radiopaque contrast medium.

cystoid /sis′toid/ [Gk, *kystis*, bag + *eidos*, form], pertaining to or resembling a cyst or bladder.

cystoid macular edema, thickening of the macula with cystic changes, increased fluid within the sensory retina of the macula, and disruption of the blood-retinal barrier and consequent leakage on fluorescein angiography, with leaking capillaries in the posterior pole and around the optic disc. It is often a result of cataract surgery.

cystojejunostomy /-ji′jōōnos′təmē/, drainage of a cyst, such as a pancreatic pseudocyst, into the jejunum.

cystolithalopaxy /-lith′əlōpek′sē/, removal of a kidney stone from the urinary bladder by crushing, followed by extraction of the particles via irrigation.

cystolithotomy /-lithot′əmē/, removal of a bladder stone from the urinary bladder following surgical opening of the bladder.

cystoma /sistō′mə/ *pl.* **cystomas, cystomata** [Gk, *kystis* + *oma,* tumor], any tumor or growth containing cysts, especially one in or near the ovary.

cystometer /sistom′ətər/, an instrument that measures bladder capacity in relation to changing urine pressure.

cystometrogram /sis′tōmet′rəgram′/, the graphic results of the measurements made during cystometrography.

cystometrography (CMG) /sis′tōmətrog′rəfē/, a urologic procedure that measures the amount of pressure exerted on the bladder at various bladder volumes. The test helps determine bladder capacity, bladder wall compliance, detrusor stability, and sensations of filling.

cystometry /sistom′ətrē/ [Gk, *kystis* + *metron*, measure], the study of bladder function by use of a cystometer.

cystoparesis /sis′tōpäre′sis/, paralysis of the urinary bladder.

cystoprostatectomy /-pros′tətek′təmē/, surgical removal of the bladder, prostate gland, and seminal vesicle.

cystosarcoma phyllodes /sis′tōsärkō′mə filō′dēs/, a malignant stromal breast tumor that grows rapidly and tends to recur if not adequately excised.

cystoscope /sis′təskōp′/ [Gk, *kystis* + *skopein,* to look], an instrument for examining and treating lesions of the urethra or bladder. There are both rigid and flexible types. The rigid instrument consists of an obturator for introduction, an outer sheath, a lighting system, a viewing lens, and ports for catheters and operative devices. The flexible cystoscope is a self-contained endoscope with ports for instrumentation and irrigation. Flexible cystoscopes are more commonly used today and incorporate fiberoptics.

cystoscopy /sistos′kəpē/, insertion of a rigid or flexible cystoscope into the urethra for visualization and instrumentation of the lower urinary tract. The procedure is often performed in urologic offices with local anesthesia. The bladder is distended with water while the patient is supine or in the lithotomy position.— **cystoscopic,** *adj.*

Cystospaz, a trademark for an anticholinergic/antispasmodic (L-hyoscyamine).

cystostomy /sistos′təmē/, an opening made in the bladder for drainage, usually through a catheter inserted through the abdominal skin.

cystotomy /sistot′əmē/, incision of the urinary bladder, often performed for removal of a calculus.

cystoureterography /sis′təyōōr′ətərog′rəfē/, the radiographic examination of the bladder and ureters after introduction of a radiopaque contrast medium.

cystourethrogram /sis′təyōōrē′thrəgram′/, a radiograph produced by cystourethrography.

cystourethrography /sis′təyōōr′ēthrog′rəfē/, the radiographic examination of the urethra and urinary bladder after introduction of a radiopaque contrast medium.

cysts of liver, small single, simple watery cysts, usually secondary to another disorder such as cystic kidney disease.

Cytadren, a trademark for an inhibitor of adrenocorticosteroid biosynthesis (aminoglutethimide).

cytapheresis /sī′tōfer′əsis/ [Gk, *kytos* + *aphairesis,* withdrawal], selective removal of a cellular component of blood by apheresis. Red cells, granulocytes, or platelets may be harvested. Cytapheresis is used to collect specific components from blood donors, or, in the case of therapeutic cytapheresis, to remove excess cellular components from patients with blood disorders.

cytarabine /siter′əbēn/, an antineoplastic agent prescribed in the treatment of acute and chronic myelocytic leukemia, acute lymphocytic leukemia, and erythroleukemia.

cytoanalyzer /sī′tō·an′əlī′zər/, an electronic device that screens samples of smears of suspected malignancies.

cytoarchitectonic /sī′tō·är′kitekton′ik/ [Gk, *kytos,* cell; L, *architectura,* architecture], pertaining to the cellular arrangement within a tissue or structure.

cytoarchitecture /-är′kitek′chər/, the typical pattern of cellular arrangement within a particular tissue or organ, as in the cerebral cortex. —**cytoarchitectural,** *adj.*

cytochemism /sī'tōkem'izəm/ [Gk, *kytos* + *chemeia*, alchemy], the chemical activity within the living cell, specifically the various reactions to and affinity for chemical substances.

cytochemistry /-kem'istrē/, the study of the various chemicals within a living cell and their actions and functions.

cytochrome /si'tōkrōm/ [Gk, *kytos,* cell, *chroma,* color], **1.** a class of hemoproteins whose function is electron transport. These proteins have the ability to change the valence of the heme iron, alternating between ferrous and ferric states. **2.** proteins involved in mitochondrial electron transport systems associated with adenosine triphosphate (ATP) production.

cytochrome-*c* oxidase, an enzyme complex of the inner mitochondrial membrane that catalyzes the transfer of electrons from cytochrome *c* to oxygen, oxidizing cytochrome and reducing oxygen in the final step of the electron transport chain by which oxygen is used for fuel combustion.

cytochrome-*c* oxidase deficiency, a hereditary defect in the cytochrome-*c* oxidase complex that prevents the transfer of electrons from cytochrome *c* to molecular oxygen, ultimately halting adenosine triphosphate production. Manifestations are extremely variable and include myopathies, encephalopathies, ocular and cardiac defects, sensorineural deafness, Fanconi syndrome, DM, and short stature.

cytochrome P-450 [Gk, *kytos,* cell, *chroma,* color], a protein involved with extramitochondrial electron transport in the liver and during drug detoxification.

cytocide [Gk, *kytos*; L, *caedere,* to kill], any substance that is destructive to cells. —**cytocidal,** *adj.*

cytoclesis /sī'tōklē'sis/ [Gk, *kytos* + *klesis,* calling for], the influence exerted by one cell on the action of other cells; the vital principle of all living tissue. —**cytobiotactic, cytocletic,** *adj.*

cytoctony /sītok'tənē/ [Gk, *kytos* + *ktonos,* killing], the destruction of cells in culture by viruses.

cytode /sī'tōd/ [Gk, *kytos* + *eidos,* form], the simplest type of cell, consisting of a protoplasmic mass without a nucleus, such as a bacterium.

cytodiagnosis /-dī'əgnō'sis/, diagnosis of a suspected pathologic tissue by a microscopic examination of the cells in the sample.

cytodieresis /sī'tōdī·er'isis/ *pl.* **cytodiereses** [Gk, *kytos* + *diairesis,* separation], cell division, especially the phenomena involving the division of the cytoplasm. —**cytodieretic,** *adj.*

cytodifferentiation /-dif'ərən'shē·ā'shən/ [Gk, *kytos*; L, *differentia,* difference], **1.** a process by which embryonic cells acquire biochemical and morphologic properties essential for specialization and diversification. **2.** the total and gradual transformation from an undifferentiated to a fully differentiated state.

cytofluorograph /-flôr'əgraf/, a diagnostic instrument used to measure the level of CD4 T lymphocytes in HIV-positive patients. The lymphocytes are stained with specific monoclonal antibodies.

cytogene /sī'təjēn/ [Gk, *kytos* + *genein,* to produce], a self-replicating particle within the cytoplasm of a cell that is derived from genes in the nucleus and is capable of transmitting hereditary information.

cytogenesis /sī'tōjen'əsis/ [Gk, *kytos* + *genein,* to produce], the origin, development, and differentiation of cells. —**cytogenetic, cytogenic,** *adj.*

cytogeneticist /sī'tōjənet'isist/, a scientist who specializes in cytogenetics.

cytogenetics /sī'tōjənet'iks/, the branch of genetics that studies the cellular constituents concerned with heredity, primarily the structure, function, and origin of the chromosomes. —**cytogenetic,** *adj.*

cytogenetic technologist, an allied health professional who studies chromosomes. The cytogenetic technologist determines how specimens will be collected, transported, and handled for cytogenetic analysis.

cytogenic /-jen'ik/, pertaining to the formation of cells.

cytogenic gland, a glandular organ that secretes living cells, specifically the testes and ovary.

cytogenic reproduction, the formation of a new organism from a germ cell, either sexually through the fusion of gametes to form a zygote or asexually by means of spores.

cytogeny /sītoj'ənē/, the origin and development of cells. —**cytogenic, cytogenous,** *adj.*

cytohistogenesis /sī'tōhis'tōjen'əsis/ [Gk, *kytos* + *histos,* tissue, *genein,* to produce], the structural development and formation of cells. —**cytohistogenetic,** *adj.*

cytoid /sī'toid/ [Gk, *kytos* + *eidos,* form], like a cell.

cytoid body, a small white spot on the retina of each eye seen by using an ophthalmoscope to examine the eyes, often noted in patients affected with SLE.

cytokerastic /sī'tōkəras'tik/ [Gk, *kytos* + *kerastos,* mixed], pertaining to or characteristic of cellular development from a simple to a more complex arrangement.

cytokine /sī'təkīn/, one of a large group of low-molecular-weight proteins secreted by various cell types and involved in cell-to-cell communication, coordinating antibody and T-cell immune interactions, and amplifying immune reactivity. Cytokines include colony-stimulating factors, interferons, interleukins, and lymphokines, which are secreted by lymphocytes.

cytokine assay, a blood test to detect interleukins, used predominantly for research.

cytokine network, a group of cytokines that modulate and regulate signaling between cells during immune responses. According to the immune network model, T cells and B cells mutually interact, responding to cytokines as well as antigens. This interaction allows the cytokines to direct T cells to antiviral or antitumor functions or to promote allergic reactions.

cytokinesis /sī′tōkĭne′sis, -kīne′sis/ [Gk, *kytos* + *kinesis,* movement], the division of the cytoplasm, exclusive of nuclear division, that occurs during the final stages of mitosis and meiosis to form daughter cells. —**cytokinetic,** *adj.*

cytologic map [Gk, *kytos* + *logos,* science; L, *mappa,* table napkin], a graphic representation of the location of genes on a chromosome, based on correlating the genetic recombination results of testcrosses with the structural analysis of chromosomes that have undergone changes, such as deletions or translocations, as detected by banding techniques.

cytologic sputum examination, a microscopic examination of a specimen of bronchial secretions, including a search for cells that may be cancerous or otherwise abnormal.

cytologist /sītol′əjist/, a biologist who specializes in the study of cells, especially one who uses cytologic techniques in the differential diagnosis of neoplasms.

cytology /sītol′əjē/ [Gk, *kytos* + *logos,* science], the study of cells, including their formation, origin, structure, function, biochemical activities, and pathologic characteristics. —**cytologic,** *adj.*

cytolysin /sītol′isin/ [Gk, *kytos* + *lyein,* to loosen], an antibody that dissolves antigenic cells.

cytolysis /sītol′isis/ *pl.* **cytolyses** [Gk, *kytos* + *lyein,* to loosen], the destruction or breakdown of cells, primarily by the disintegration of the plasma membrane. —**cytolytic,** *adj.*

cytomegalic /sī′tōmegal′ik/, describing a condition characterized by abnormally large cells.

cytomegalic inclusion disease (CID) [Gk, *kytos* + *megas,* large; L, *in, claudere,* in enclosure], a viral infection caused by the *cytomegalovirus* (CMV), a member of the herpesviruses family. It is characterized by malaise, fever, lymphadenopathy, pneumonia, hepatosplenomegaly, and superinfection with various bacteria and fungi as a result of depression of the immune response characteristic of herpesviruses. It is primarily a congenitally acquired disease of newborns, transmitted in utero. Results may range from spontaneous abortion or fatal neonatal illness to birth of a normal infant.

cytomegalovirus (CMV) /sī′tōmeg′əlōvī′rəs/ [Gk, *kytos* + *megas,* large; L, *virus,* poison], a member of a group of large species-specific herpes-type viruses with a wide variety of disease effects. It causes serious illness in persons with HIV, in newborns, and in people being treated with immunosuppressive drugs and therapy, especially after organ transplantation.

cytomegalovirus (CMV) test, a blood test for CMV infection.

cytomegalovirus immune globulin, a purified immunoglobulin derived from pooled adult human plasma selected for high titers of antibody against cytomegalovirus. It is administered intravenously for treatment and prophylaxis of cytomegalovirus disease in transplant recipients.

cytomegaly /sī′tōmeg′älē/, abnormal enlargement of a cell or group of cells.

Cytomel, a trademark for a thyroid hormone (liothyronine sodium).

cytometer /sītom′ətər/ [Gk, *kytos* + *metron,* measure], a device for counting and measuring the number of cells within a specified amount of CSF.

cytometry /sītom′ətrē/, the counting and measuring of cells, specifically blood cells. —**cytometric,** *adj.*

cytomitome /sī′təmī′tōm/ [Gk, *kytos* + *mitos,* thread], the fibrillary network within the cytoplasm of a cell, as contrasted with that inside the nucleus.

cytomorphology /-môrfol′əjē/ [Gk, *kytos* + *morphe,* shape, *logos,* science], the study of the various forms of cells and the structures contained within cells. —**cytomorphologic,** *adj.,* **cytomorphologist,** *n.*

cytomorphosis /sī′tōmôr′fəsis/ *pl.* **cytomorphoses** [Gk, *kytos* + *morphosis,* shaping], the various changes that occur within a cell during the entire course of its life cycle.

cytopathic /-path′ik/, pertaining to the effect of disease or another disorder on a cell, such as damage from a virus or nuclear radiation.

cytopathogenic effect /-path′əjen′ik/, the morphologic changes in a cultured cell caused by cytopathic damage.

cytopathology /-pathol′əjē/, the study of changes at the cellular level caused by disease.

cytopenia /-pē′nē-ə/ [Gk, *kytos* + *penes,* poor], a deficiency in numbers of the blood cell elements.

cytophagy /sītof′əjē/, cell destruction by phagocytes.

cytophotometer /sī'tōfətom'ətər/ [Gk, *kytos* + *phos,* light, *metron,* measure], an instrument for measuring light density through stained parts of cytoplasm, used for locating and identifying chemical substances within cells.

cytophotometry /sī'tōfətom'ətrē/, the identification of chemical substances within cells, using a cytophotometer. —**cytophotometric,** *adj.*

cytophysiology /-fis'ē·ol'əjē/ [Gk, *kytos* + *physis,* nature, *logos,* science], the study of the biochemical processes involved in the functioning of individual cells. —**cytophysiologic,** *adj.,* **cytophysiologist,** *n.*

cytoplasm /sī'təplaz'əm/ [Gk, *kytos* + *plassein,* to mold], all of the substance of a cell other than the nucleus and the cell wall.

cytoplasmic inheritance /sī'tōplaz'mik/, the acquisition of traits or conditions controlled by self-replicating substances within the cytoplasm, such as mitochondria or chloroplasts, rather than by genes on the chromosomes. The phenomenon occurs in plants and some animals but has not been demonstrated in humans.

Cytosar-U, a trademark for an antineoplastic (cytarabine).

cytoscopy /sītos'kəpē/ [Gk, *kytos* + *skopein,* to watch], the diagnostic study of cells obtained from patient specimens with the aid of microscopes and other laboratory equipment.

cytosine (C) /sī'təsin/, a pyrimidine base that is a component of DNA and RNA. In free or uncombined form, it occurs in trace amounts in most cells, usually as a product of the enzymatic hydrolysis of nucleic acids and nucleotides.

cytosis /sītō'sis/, a condition in which there is a greater than normal number of cells in a tissue or organ.

cytoskeleton /-skel'ətən/ [Gk, *kytos* + *skeletos,* dried body], the cytoplasmic elements, including the tonofibrils, keratin, and other microfibrils, that function as a supportive system within a cell, especially an epithelial cell.

cytosol /sī'təsôl/, the liquid medium of the cytoplasm, i.e., cytoplasm minus organelles and nonmembranous insoluble components.

cytosome /sī'təsōm/, a multilayered, membrane-bound, lamellar body found in type II pneumocytes. It is a precursor of pulmonary surfactant.

cytotechnologist, an allied health professional who works with a pathologist to detect changes in body cells that may be important in early diagnosis of cancer and other diseases. The cytotechnologist prepares cellular samples and examines them under a microscope to evaluate for abnormalities in structure.

cytotoxic anaphylaxis [Gk, *kytos* + *toxikon,* poison, *hyper,* above], complement-dependent, hypersensitivity to foreign cells or to alterations of cell-surface antigens that is mediated by IgG or IgM. It causes immediate destruction of cells, as seen in hemolytic disease of the newborn and in severe transfusion reactions.

cytotoxic drug, any pharmacologic compound that inhibits the proliferation of cells within the body. Such compounds as the alkylating agents and the antimetabolites designed to destroy cells (with a high growth fraction) are commonly used in chemotherapy. Cytotoxic agents have a potential for producing teratogenesis, mutagenesis, and carcinogenesis.

cytotoxic killer T cell, a type of T lymphocyte that has the ability to cause lysis of specific target cells, such as those containing viral antigens.

cytotoxin /sī'tōtok'sin/ [Gk, *kytos* + *toxikon,* poison], a substance that has a toxic effect on certain cells. An antibody may act as a cytotoxin.—**cytotoxic,** *adj.*

cytotrophoblast /sī'tōtrof'əblast'/ [Gk, *kytos* + *trophe,* nutrition, *blastos,* germ], the inner layer of cells of the trophoblast of the early mammalian embryo that gives rise to the outer surface and villi of the chorion.—**cytotrophoblastic,** *adj.*

cytotropism /sī'tōtrop'izm/, a characteristic of some cells and agents that enables them to approach other cells or selectively bind them.

Cytovene, a trademark for an antiviral (ganciclovir).

Cytoxan, a trademark for an antineoplastic (cyclophosphamide).

cytoxic T lymphocytes [L, *natura* + ME, *kullen,* to kill, *cella,* storeroom], a lymphocyte that is capable of binding to and killing virus-infected cells and some tumor cells by releasing cytotoxins. It is found in the bone marrow and spleen.

CYVADIC, an anticancer drug combination of cyclophosphamide, vinCRIStine, DOXOrubicin, and dacarbazine.

D

d, symbol for one tenth.

D, 1. symbol for *dead space gas.* 2. symbol for **diffusing capacity.** 3. abbreviation for **diopter.** 4. abbreviation for **dexter.** 5. abbreviation for **vitamin D.** 6. symbol for **density.** 7. symbol for **diameter.**

d4T, symbol for *dideoxythymidine.*

DA, abbreviation for **developmental age.**

daboia /dəboi′ə/ [Hind, *dabna,* to lurk], a local name for Russell's viper, a large, very poisonous snake indigenous to India and Southeast Asia. Its venom is used in some laboratories to test the coagulation pathway.

dacarbazine /dekär′bəzēn/, an alkylating agent used as an antineoplastic, prescribed primarily in the treatment of malignant melanoma and Hodgkin's disease.

daclizumab, an immunosuppressant prescribed to help prevent acute allograft rejection in renal transplant patients.

Dacogen, a trademark for decitabine.

dacrocystorhinotomy (DCR), the establishment of a new lacrimal duct for direct drainage into the nasal cavity to treat dacryocystitis resistant to antibiotic treatment.

Dacron cuff, a sheath of Dacron surrounding an atrial or a venous catheter to prevent accidental displacement.

dacryoadenitis /dak′rē·ō·ad′ənī′tis/, an inflammation of the lacrimal gland.

dacryocyst /dak′rē·ōsist′/ [Gk, *dakryon,* tear, *kytis,* bag], a lacrimal sac at the medial angle of the eye.

dacryocystectomy /dak′rē·ōsistek′təmē/ [Gk, *dakryon* + *kytis,* bag, *ektomē,* excision], partial or total excision of the lacrimal sac.

dacryocystitis /dak′rē·ōsistī′tis/, an infection of the lacrimal sac caused by obstruction of the nasolacrimal duct. It is characterized by tearing and discharge from the eye.

dacryocystorhinostomy /dak′rē·ōsis′ tôrīnos′təmē/ [Gk, *dakryon* + *kytis,* bag, *rhis,* nose, *stoma,* mouth], a surgical procedure for restoring drainage into the nose from the lacrimal sac when the nasolacrimal duct is obstructed.

dacryostenosis /dak′rē·ōstinō′sis/ [Gk, *dakryon* + *stenos,* narrow, *osis,* condition], an abnormal stricture of the nasolacrimal duct, occurring either as a congenital condition or as a result of infection or trauma.

dactinomycin /dak′tinōmī′sin/, an antibiotic used as an antineoplastic agent, prescribed in the treatment of a variety of malignant neoplastic diseases, including testicular cancer, melanoma, Wilms' tumor, and rhabdomyosarcoma.

dactyl /dak′til/ [Gk, *daktylos,* finger], a digit (finger or toe).—**dactylic** /daktil′ik/, *adj.*

dactyledema /dak′tilidē′mə/, edema of the fingers or toes.

dactylion /daktil′ē·on/, a condition of complete or partial webbing of fingers.

dactylitis /dak′tilī′tis/, 1. a painful inflammation of the fingers or toes, usually associated with sickle cell anemia or certain infectious diseases, particularly syphilis or TB. 2. a sausage-shaped digit associated with psoriatic arthritis.

DAF, abbreviation for *decay accelerating factor.*

DAI, abbreviation for **diffuse axonal injury.**

daily adjusted progressive resistance exercise (DAPRE), a program of isotonic exercises that allows for individual differences in the rate at which a patient regains strength in an injured or diseased body part.

Daily Reference Values (DRVs), a set of dietary standards for eight nutrients and food compartments: total fat, saturated fat, cholesterol, total carbohydrates, dietary fiber, protein, potassium, and sodium. They are part of the U.S. Food and Drug Administration Daily Value label reference.

dairy food substitute, a group of foods that includes imitation cream, coffee whitener, cheese, and ice cream. Some substitutes may contain milk components despite nondairy claims.

Dakin's solution [Henry D. Dakin, American biochemist, 1880–1952; L, *solutus,* dissolved], an antiseptic solution containing boric acid and 0.4% to 0.5% of sodium hypochlorite, used for wound irrigation and treatment of athlete's foot.

dalfopristin /dalfo′pristin/, a semisynthetic antibacterial effective against a variety of gram-positive organisms. It is used in conjunction with quinupristin in the treatment of serious bacteremia caused by vancomycin-resistant *Enterococcus faecium* and complicated skin and skin structure infections caused by *Strepto-coccus pyogenes* or methicillin-sensitive *Staphylococcus aureus*.

Dalmane, a trademark for a benzodi-azepine sedative-hypnotic (flurazepam hydrochloride).

dalteparin sodium, a low-molecular-weight heparin prescribed to prevent deep vein thrombosis in adults undergo-ing abdominal surgery who are at risk for clotting. It is also used for the treatment of unstable angina and non–Q-wave MI to prevent ischemic complications in patients with concurrent aspirin therapy.

dalton [John Dalton, English chemist and mathematician, 1766–1844], **1.** an unof-ficial unit of atomic mass, based on $^1/_{16}$ of the gram mass of oxygen, now based on $^1/_{12}$ the mass of carbon-12. **2.** in biochemistry, unit (kilodaltons) that expresses the molecular weight (mass) of proteins and nucleic acids.

daltonism /dôl'təniz'əm/ [John Dal-ton], *informal.* a form of red-green color blindness. It is genetically transmitted as a sex-linked autosomal-recessive trait.

Dalton's law of partial pressures /dôl'tənz/ [John Dalton], in physics, a law stating that the total pressure exerted by a mixture of gases is equal to the sum of the pres-sures that could be exerted by the gases if they were present alone in the container in the same quantity.

dam, a barrier to the flow of fluid, as a dam placed around a tooth to protect it from saliva during restoration.

damages /dam'ijəs/ [L, *damnum,* loss], in law, a sum of money awarded to a plaintiff by a court as compensation for any loss, detriment, or injury to the plain-tiff's person, property, or rights caused by the malfeasance or negligence of the defendant. Actual damages are awarded to reimburse the plaintiff for the loss or injury sustained. Nominal damages are awarded to show that a legal wrong has been committed, although no recoverable loss can be determined. Punitive damages exceed the actual cost of injury or damage and are awarded when the defendant has acted with malice or reckless disregard of the plaintiff's rights.

damp [AS, vapor], a potentially lethal atmosphere in caves and mines. Black damp or choke damp is caused by absorp-tion of the available oxygen by coal seams. Fire damp is composed of methane and other explosive hydrocarbon gases. White damp is another name for carbon monoxide.

damping [AS, vapor], a gradual decrease in the amplitude of a series of waves or oscillations, such as an arterial pressure waveform.

danaparoid, an anticoagulant used to pre-vent vein thrombosis in hemodialysis, stroke, elective surgery for malignancy or total hip replacement, and hip fracture surgery.

danazol /dan'əzol/, a synthetic androgen that acts to suppress the output of gonado-tropins from the pituitary, suppress ovarian hormone production, and directly block ovarian hormone receptors. It is prescribed in the treatment of endometriosis, fibro-cystic breast disease, and hereditary angio-edema when alternative hormonal therapy is ineffective, contraindicated, or intolerable.

dance/movement therapy, a movement-based therapeutic technique that aids in release of expressions or feelings and aids in promoting feeling and awareness.

dance reflex [ME, *dauncen*; L, *reflectere,* to bend back], a normal response in the neonate to simulate walking by a recipro-cal flexion and extension of the legs when held in an erect position and inclined forward, with the soles touching a hard surface.

dander, dry scales shed from the scalp.

dandruff /dan'druf/, an excessive amount of scaly material composed of dead, kera-tinized epithelium shed from the scalp that may be a mild form of seborrheic dermati-tis or psoriasis.

Dandy-Walker cyst [Walter E. Dandy, American neurosurgeon, 1886–1946; Arthur E. Walker, American surgeon, b. 1907], a cystic malformation of the fourth ventricle of the brain, resulting from hydrocephalus.

Danocrine, a trademark for an anterior pituitary suppressant (danazol).

danthron /dan'thron/, a stimulant laxa-tive. Products containing danthron are no longer available in the U.S. since it was found to be carcinogenic in animal models.

Dantrium, a trademark for a skeletal muscle relaxant used in the treatment of malignant hyperthermia or hyperpyrexia (dantrolene sodium).

dantrolene sodium /dan'trəlēn/, a skel-etal muscle relaxant that acts directly on the skeletal muscle to prevent the release of calcium from the sarcoplasmic reticu-lum that is needed for muscle contraction. It is prescribed in the treatment of muscle spasticity resulting from injury to the spinal cord or cerebrum when the person is immobile and flaccid limbs are prefer-able to spastic limbs. It is used intrave-nously for the management of malignant hyperthermia.

DAP, 1. abbreviation for **Draw-A-Person Test. 2.** abbreviation for **dose area product.**

dapiprazole /däpip'räzōl/, an alpha-adre-nergic blocking agent applied topically to the conjunctiva as the hydrochloride salt to reverse pharmacologically induced mydriasis.

DAPRE, abbreviation for **daily adjusted progressive resistance exercise.**

dapsone (DDS) /dap'sōn/, a bacteriostatic and bactericidal sulfone derivative. It is prescribed in the treatment of leprosy and dermatitis herpetiformis, and for prophylaxis against toxoplasmosis and *Pneumocystis carinii* in immunocompromised patients.

daptomycin, a miscellaneous antiinfective used to treat complicated skin and skin structure infections caused by *Staphylococcus aureus* (including methicillin-resistant strains), *S. agalactiae, S. dysgalactiae,* and *Enterococcus faecalis* (vancomycin-susceptible strains only).

Daraprim, a trademark for an antimalarial (pyrimethamine).

darbepoetin alfa, a hematopoietic agent used to treat anemia associated with chronic renal failure or anemia in nonmyeloid malignancies.

Darbid, a trademark for an anticholinergic (isopropamide iodide).

Darier's sign /däryāz'/ [Jean F. Darier, French dermatologist, 1856–1938], a burning or itching sensation induced by stroking skin lesions in cases of urticaria pigmentosa.

dark adaptation, a normal increase in sensitivity of the retinal rod cells of the eye to detect any light that may be available for vision in a dimly lighted environment. The process is accompanied by an adjustment of the pupils to allow more light to enter the eyes.

darkfield microscopy [AS, *deorc,* hidden, *feld,* field; Gk, *mikros,* small, *skopein,* to look], examination of a microscopic specimen illuminated by a peripheral light source. The illumination causes the specimen to appear to glow against a dark background. In laboratory diagnosis, the technique is used primarily to identify the syphilis spirochete.

dark-film fault [AS, *deorc,* hidden, *filmen,* skin; L, *fallere,* to disappoint], a defect in a photograph or radiograph that appears as an excessively darkened image or image area.

darkroom, a room in a hospital or similar facility for the storage and processing of light-sensitive materials such as x-ray film.

dartoic tissue, tissue that resembles the tunica dartos, as in a tumor with muscular elements.

dartos fascia, the thin layer of subcutaneous tissue underlying the skin of the scrotum, consisting mainly of nonstriated muscle fibers (the dartos muscle).

darunavir, an antiretroviral used to inhibit HIV-1 protease by preventing maturation of the virus.

Darvocet-N, a trademark for a fixed-combination drug containing an analgesic-antipyretic (acetaminophen) and an opioid analgesic (propoxyphene napsylate).

Darvon, a trademark for an opioid analgesic (propoxyphene hydrochloride).

Darvon Compound, a trademark for a fixed-combination drug containing an opioid analgesic (propoxyphene hydrochloride) and aspirin.

Darvon-N, a trademark for an opioid analgesic (propoxyphene napsylate).

darwinian ear /därwin'ē-ən/ [Charles R. Darwin, English naturalist, 1809–1882], an external ear with an upper border that projects upward in a flat, sharp edge.

darwinian theory [Charles R. Darwin], the theory of Charles Darwin that organic evolution results from the natural selection of those variants of organisms that are best suited to survive in their environment.—**darwinian,** *adj., n.*

dasatinib, a miscellaneous antineoplastic used to treat chronic myelogenous leukemia, accelerated blast crisis, and chronic phase and acute lymphoblastic leukemia.

DASE, abbreviation for **Denver Articulation Screening Examination.**

DASH (Dietary Approach to Stop Hypertension) diet, a diet high in fruits, vegetables, and low-fat dairy products; low in saturated and total fats; low in cholesterol; and high in fiber. Research studies support the hypothesis that this diet reduces BP and may play a role in prevention of high BP.

data /dā'tə, dat'ə, dä'tə/ *sing.* **datum** [L, *datum,* giving], pieces of information, especially those that are part of a collection to be used in an analysis of a problem.

data acquisition system (DAS), a radiation detection system that measures the amount of radiation passing through a patient.

data analysis, in research, the phase of a study that includes classifying, coding, and tabulating information needed to perform quantitative or qualitative analyses according to the research design and appropriate to the data.

data clustering, the grouping of related information from a patient's health history, physical examination, and laboratory results as part of the process of making a diagnosis.

data collection, in research, the phase of a study that includes the gathering of information and identification of sampling units as directed by the research design.

data retrieval, the recovery of information from an organized filing system, such as a computer database, an index card file, or color-coded record folders.

data source, the origin of information relevant to a patient's level of wellness and health patterns.

data validation, the process of determining whether information gathered during the process of data collection is complete and accurate.

date/acquaintance rape, a sexual assault or rape by a person known to the victim, such as a date, employer, friend, or casual acquaintance.

daughter cell [ME, *doughter*, female, child; L, *cella*, storeroom], one of the cells produced by the division of a parent cell.

daughter chromosome [ME, *doughter*, female, child; Gk, *chroma*, color, *soma*, body], either of the paired chromatids that separate and migrate to the opposite ends of the cell during the anaphase stage of mitosis. Each contains the complete genetic information of the original chromosome.

daughter cyst, a small secondary parasitic cyst, usually a derivative of a hydatid cyst.

daughter element, an element that results from the radioactive decay of another element.

DAUNOrubicin citrate liposomal /dô′nō rōō′bisin/, an anthracycline antibiotic antineoplastic agent prescribed in the treatment of advanced Kaposi's sarcoma in HIV patients.

da Vinci surgical system /də vin′chē/, a proprietary robotic platform for minimally invasive surgery, consisting of a console, a patient-side cart to which a set of up to four electromechanical arms is attached, and a 3-D video display system. Instruments mounted on the robotic arms are introduced into the patient's body through minute incisions. The system translates the hand motions of the surgeon seated at the console into movements of the instruments inside the patient. The surgeon views the operative field through a 3-D camera attached to one of the arms.

Davis ureterotomy, an open procedure combining a ureteral incision with intubation, usually for long or multiple strictures below the ureteropelvic junction.

DAWN /dôn/, abbreviation for **Drug Abuse Warning Network.**

dawn phenomenon [ME, *daunen*; Gk, *phainomenon*, anything seen], a tendency for persons with type 1 DM to experience hyperglycemia upon awakening in the morning because of increased cortisol and growth hormone secretion in the predawn hours.

day care [OE, *daeg* + *cearu*], a specialized program or facility that provides care for preschool children, usually within a group framework, either as a substitute for or an extension of home care.

daydream, a usually nonpathologic reverie that occurs while a person is awake. The content is usually the imagined fulfillment of wishes that are not disguised.

day health care services, the provision of hospitals, nursing homes, or other facilities for health-related services to adult patients who are ambulatory or can be transported and who regularly use such services for a certain number of daytime hours but do not require continuous inpatient care.

day hospital [OE, *daeg*; L, *hospes*, guest], a psychiatric facility that offers a therapeutic program during daytime hours for patients.

dB, abbreviation for **decibel.**

Db, symbol for the element **dubnium.**

D&C, abbreviation for **dilation and curettage.**

DC, abbreviation for **direct current.**

d/c, 1. abbreviation for *discontinue.* **2.** abbreviation for *diarrhea and constipation.* **3.** abbreviation for **discharge.**

DCC gene, (*d*eleted in *c*olorectal *c*arcinoma) a gene normally expressed in the mucosa of the colon but reduced or absent in a small proportion of patients with colorectal cancer.

DCR, abbreviation for **dacrocystorhinotomy.**

DD, abbreviation for **developmental disability.**

DDAVP, a trademark for an antidiuretic (desmopressin acetate).

ddC, abbreviation for 2′,3′-dideoxycytidine, an antiretroviral drug used in the treatment of AIDS.

DDD pacing, a specific type of electrical heart pacemaker. The letters indicate *D*ual pacing for both chambers, *D*ual chamber activity sensing, and *D*ual response (triggering and inhibition).

ddI, 1. abbreviation for 2′,3′-dideoxyinosine, an antiretroviral medication. **2.** abbreviation for **dideoxyinosine.**

D-dimer test, a simple and confirmatory test for disseminated intravascular coagulation that can also indicate when a clot is lysed by thrombolytic therapy.

D.D.S., abbreviation for *Doctor of Dental Surgery.*

DDST, abbreviation for **Denver Developmental Screening Test.**

DDT (dichlorodiphenyltrichloroethane), a non-biodegradable water-insoluble chlorinated hydrocarbon once used worldwide as a major insecticide, especially in agriculture. In recent years, knowledge of its adverse impact on the environment has led to restrictions in its use. Its use was banned in the United States by the FDA in 1971 and it has been largely replaced by organophosphate insecticides.

D&E, abbreviation for **dilation and evacuation.**

DE, abbreviation for **dose equivalent.**

DEA, abbreviation for *Drug Enforcement Agency.*

deactivation /dē·ak′tivā′shən/ [L, *de,* from, *activus,* active], the process of becoming or making something inactive or inoperable.

dead, pertaining to the absence of all vital functions in a previously living organism.

dead-end host [AS, *dead* + *ende*; L, *hospes,* guest], **1.** a host from which infectious agents are not transmitted to other susceptible hosts. **2.** any host organism from which a parasite cannot escape to continue its life cycle.

dead fetus syndrome, a condition in which the fetus has died but has remained in the uterus for some time. The condition leads to a blood coagulation disorder, and the eventual delivery is usually accompanied by massive bleeding.

dead space [AS, dead; L, *spatium*], **1.** a cavity that remains after the incomplete closure of a surgical or traumatic wound, leaving an area in which blood can collect and delay healing. **2.** the amount of lung in contact with ventilating gases but not with pulmonary blood flow. Alveolar dead space is characterized by alveoli that are ventilated by the pulmonary circulation but are not perfused. Anatomic dead space is an area in the trachea, bronchi, and air passages containing air that does not reach the alveoli during respiration. *Physiologic dead space* is an area in the respiratory system that includes the anatomic dead space together with the space in the alveoli occupied by air that does not contribute to the oxygen–carbon dioxide exchange.

dead space effect, any of several potential adverse effects, including hypoxemia and hypercapnia, produced by dead space in the lungs, particularly alveolar dead space.

deaf [AS], **1.** unable to hear; hard of hearing. **2.** people who are unable to hear or who have hearing impairment.—**deafness,** *n.*

deafferentation /dē·af′ərəntā′shən/ [L, *de,* from, *ad* + *ferre,* to bear], the elimination or interruption of afferent nerve impulses.

deaf-mute, a person who is unable to hear or to speak.

deaf-mutism [AS, *deaf,* L, *mutus*], a state of being both unable to hear and unable to speak.

deafness, a condition characterized by a loss of hearing that makes it impossible for an individual to understand speech through hearing alone.

deaminase /dēam′inās/ [L, *de,* away, *amine,* ammonia; Fr, *diastase,* enzyme], one of the subclasses of enzymes that catalyze the hydrolysis of the NH_2 bond in amino compounds.

deamination /dē′aminā′shən/, the removal, usually by hydrolysis, of the NH_2 radical from an amino compound.

dean [L, *decanus,* chief of ten], chief executive and educational officer of a unit of a university, school, or college.

dean's tax, a portion of physician practice plan income in an academic medical center that is allocated for the support of the medical school.

dearterialization /dē′ärtir′ē·əlīzā′shən/, **1.** conversion of oxygenated arterial blood into venous blood. **2.** interruption of the supply of arterial blood to an organ or body part.

death [AS], **1.** apparent death; the cessation of life as indicated by the absence of all vital functions. **2.** legal death; the total absence of activity in the brain and CNS, the cardiovascular system, and the respiratory system as observed and declared by a qualified professional.

death instinct, instinctive behavior that tends to be self-destructive.

death mask [AS, *death*; Fr, *masque*], an image or cast made from clay, wax, plaster of paris, or other moldable material of the face after death.

death rate, the number of deaths occurring within a specified population during a particular period, usually expressed in terms of deaths per 1000 persons per year.

death rattle, a sound produced by air moving through mucus that has accumulated in the throat of a dying person who has lost the cough reflex.

death trance, a state in which a person appears to be dead.

"death with dignity" [AS, *death* + L, *dignus,* worthy], the philosophic concept that a terminally ill client should be allowed to die naturally and comfortably, rather than experience a comatose, vegetative life prolonged by mechanical support systems.

DeBakey forceps, atraumatic tissue forceps used to grasp fine tissue.

debility /dibil′itē/, feebleness, weakness, or loss of strength.—**debilitating,** *adj.*

debridement /debrēdmäN′/ [Fr, *debrider,* to remove], the removal of dirt, foreign objects, damaged tissue, and cellular debris from a wound or a burn to prevent infection and to promote healing. In treating a wound, debridement is the first step in cleansing.—**debride,** *v.*

debris /dəbrē′/, the dead, diseased, or damaged tissue and any foreign material that is to be removed from a wound or other area being treated.

Debrox, a trademark for a topical antiinfective (carbamide peroxide).

debt /det/ [L, *debere,* to owe], something owed.

Decaderm, a trademark for a synthetic analog of cortisol (dexamethasone).

Decadron, a trademark for a glucocorticoid (dexamethasone).

Deca-Durabolin, a trademark for an androgen (nandrolone decanoate).

decalcification /dēkal′sifikā′shən/ [L, *de* + *calyx,* lime, *facere,* to make], loss of calcium salts from the teeth and bones caused by malnutrition, malabsorption, or other dietary or physiologic factors, such as immobility.

decannulation /dēkan′yəlā′shən/ [L, *de,* from, *cannula,* small reed], the removal of a cannula or tube that may have been inserted during a surgical procedure.

decant, the process of separating fluid from a solid sediment by pouring off the top liquid layer.

decapitation /dēkap′itā′shən/, literally, cutting off the head, as the head of a bone or the head of a fetus when delivery is not possible otherwise. This is no longer used in clinical practice.

decay /dikā′/, **1.** a gradual deterioration that accompanies the end of life. **2.** a gradual deterioration, usually caused by bacteria and other decomposers, of the body of an organism after death. **3.** the process of disintegration of a radioactive substance.

decay product [L, *de* + *cadere,* to fall, *producere,* to produce], a stable or radioactive nuclide formed by the disintegration of a radionuclide, either directly or as a result of successive transformation in a radioactive series.

decay time, the period required for a wavelength to go from peak amplitude to 0 volt.

deceleration /dēsel′ərā′shən/ [L, *de* + *accelerare,* to hasten], a decrease in the speed or velocity of an object or reaction.

deceleration injury, an injury resulting from a collision between a rapidly moving body part and a stationary object.

deceleration phase, in obstetrics, the latter part of active labor, characterized by a decreased rate of dilation of the cervical os on a Friedman curve.

decerebrate /dēser′əbrāt/, **1.** lacking a cerebrum. **2.** lacking neural communication between the cerebrum and lower portions of the CNS.

decerebrate posture [L, *de* + *cerebrum,* brain, *ponere,* to place], the position of a patient who is usually comatose, in which the arms are extended and internally rotated and the legs are extended with the feet in forced plantar flexion. It is usually observed in patients afflicted by compression of the brainstem at a low level.

decerebration /-brā′shən/ [L, *de,* from + *cerebrum*], the process of removing the brain or cutting the brainstem above the level of the red nucleus, thus eliminating cerebral function.

decibel (dB) /des′əbəl/ [L, *decimus,* one tenth; *bel,* Alexander G. Bell, Canadian inventor, 1847–1922], a unit of measure of the intensity of sound. A decibel is one tenth of 1 bel (B); an increase of 1 B is perceived as a 10-fold increase in loudness, based on a sound-pressure reference level of 0.0002 dyne/cm^2, or 20 micropascals.

decidua /disij$\overline{oo}$·ə/ [L, *decidere,* to fall off], the epithelial tissue of the endometrium lining the uterus. It envelops the conceptus during gestation and is shed in the puerperium. It is also shed periodically with menstruation.

decidua basalis, the decidua of the endometrium in the uterus that lies beneath the implanted ovum.

decidua capsularis, the decidua of the endometrium of the uterus covering the implanted ovum.

decidual endometritis /disij$\overline{oo}$·əl/, an inflammation or infection of any part of the decidua during pregnancy.

decidua menstrualis, the endometrial mucosa shed during menstruation.

decidua vera, the decidua of the endometrium lining the uterus, except for those areas beneath and above the implanted and developing ovum.

deciduoma /disij$\overline{oo}$·ō′mə/, a benign or malignant tumor of endometrial tissue. It may be detected on a Papanicolaou (Pap) smear.

deciduous /dəsid′y$\overline{oo}$·əs/ [L, *decidere,* to fall off], falling off or shed at maturity.

decigram (dg), a unit of mass in the metric system equal to 100 milligrams or one tenth of a gram.

deciliter (dL), a unit of volume in the metric system equal to 100 milliliters or one tenth of a liter.

decimeter (dm), a unit of length in the metric system equal to 10 centimeters or one tenth of a meter.

decision making, the process of evaluating available information and reaching a judgment or conclusion based on that information.

decision-making, a nursing outcome from the Nursing Outcomes Classification (NOC) defined as the ability to make judgments and choose between two or more alternatives.

decision-making support, a nursing intervention from the Nursing Interventions Classification (NIC) defined as providing information and support for a patient who is making a decision regarding health care.

decision tree, a systematic method of managing a problem by graphically organizing the probabilities of outcomes of alternative treatments. At each decision node or branch a possible alternative is matched with its relative worth, quality of life, freedom from disability, and other factors on which a prognosis may be based.

decitabine, an agent that prevents DNA methylation, halting growth of rapid proliferation blasts, used to treat naive and experienced myelodysplastic syndrome.

declarative memory /dĕkler′ətiv/, the mental registration, retention, and recall of past experiences, sensations, ideas, knowledge, and thoughts.

Declomycin, a trademark for an antibacterial (demeclocycline hydrochloride).

decoction /dikok′shən/ [L, *de + coquere*, to cook], a liquid medicine made from an extract of water-soluble substances, usually with the aid of boiling water. Herbal remedies are usually decoctions.

decode /dikōd′/, to interpret coded information into a form usable by a receiver.

decoded message, in communication theory, a message as translated by a receiver.

decoloration, the natural loss or removal of color, as by bleaching.

decompensation /dē′kəmpənsā′shən/ [L, *de + compensare*, to balance], **1.** the failure of a system, as cardiac decompensation in heart failure. **2.** in psychology, the failure of a defense mechanism.

decomposition /dē′kəmpəsish′ən/ [L, *de + componere*, to put together], the breakdown of a substance into simpler chemical forms.—**decompose,** *v.*

decompression /dē′kəmpresh′ən/ [L, *de + comprimere*, to press together], **1.** a technique used to readapt an individual to normal atmospheric pressure after exposure to higher pressures, as in scuba diving. **2.** the removal of pressure caused by gas or fluid in a body cavity, such as the stomach or intestinal tract.

decompression sickness, a painful, sometimes fatal syndrome caused by the formation of nitrogen bubbles in the tissues of divers, caisson workers, and aviators who move too rapidly from environments of higher to those of lower atmospheric pressures. Nitrogen breathed in air under pressure dissolves in tissue fluids. When ambient pressure is reduced too rapidly, nitrogen goes out of solution faster than it can be circulated to the lungs for expiration. Gaseous nitrogen then accumulates in the joint spaces and peripheral circulation, impairing tissue oxygenation. Disorientation, severe pain, and syncope follow.

decongestant [L, *de + congerere*, to pile up], **1.** pertaining to a substance or procedure that eliminates or reduces congestion or swelling. **2.** a decongestant drug. Adrenergic drugs (α-1 stimulants), such as ephedrine and pseudoephedrine, that cause vasoconstriction of nasal mucosa, are used as decongestants.

decontamination /dā′kəntam′inā′shən/, the process of removing foreign material such as blood, body fluids, or radioactivity. It does not eliminate microorganisms but is a necessary step preceding disinfection or sterilization.

decorticate posture /dēkôr′tikāt/ [L, *de + cortex,* bark, *ponere,* to place], the position of a comatose patient in which the upper extremities are rigidly flexed at the elbows and at the wrists. The legs also may be flexed. The decorticate posture indicates a lesion in a mesencephalic region of the brain.

decortication /dēkôr′tikā′shən/ [L, *de + cortex,* bark], in medicine, the removal of portions of the cortex or surface layer of an organ or structure, such as the kidney, brain, and lung.—**decorticate,** *v., adj.*

decrement /dek′rəmənt/ [L, *de + crescere,* to grow], a decrease or stage of decline, as of a uterine contraction.

decremental conduction /dek′rəmen′təl/, transmission of an electric impulse in which the amplitude of the impulse decreases with distance.

decrepitate percussion /dēkrep′itit/, a crackling noise produced by tapping the thoracic or abdominal wall of a patient with a respiratory disorder.

decrudescence /dē′krōōdes′əns/ [L, *de,* from, *crudescere,* to become bad], a decrease in the severity of symptoms.

decubital /dikyōō′bitəl/ [L, *decumbere,* to lie down], pertaining to bedsores.

decubitus /dikyōō′bitəs/ [L, *decumbere,* to lie down], a recumbent or horizontal position, such as lateral decubitus, lying on one side.

decubitus angina, a condition characterized by periodic attacks of cardiac pain that occur when a person is lying down.

decubitus position, a position used in producing a radiograph of the chest or abdomen of a patient who is lying down, with the central ray horizontal. The patient may be prone (ventral decubitus), supine (dorsal decubitus), or lying on his or her left or right side (left or right lateral decubitus).

decubitus posture, the position assumed by a bedridden patient to rest on his or her side to relieve the pressure of body weight on the sacrum, heels, or other areas vulnerable to pressure (decubitus) ulcers.

decussate /dəkus′āt/ [L, *decussis,* intersection], to cross in the form of an "X,"as certain nerve fibers from the retina cross at the optic chiasm.

decussation /di′kusā′shən/ [L, *decussare,* to make a cross], a crossing of CNS fibers in the brain, as some fibers on the left side cross to the right side and vice versa.

decussation of pyramids [L, *decussare,* to make a cross; Gk, *pyramis*], the crossing of nerve fibers of the corticospinal motor tract at the ventral side on the lower part of the medulla oblongata.

deductible /dēduk′tibəl/, an amount paid each year by a health insurance plan enrollee before benefits begin. It is not synonymous with copayment.

deduction [L, *deducere,* to lead], a system of reasoning that leads from a known principle to an unknown, or from the general to the specific. Deductive reasoning is used to test diagnostic hypotheses.

deemed status /dēmd/ [AS, *deman,* to judge; L, *status,* a standing], a status conferred on a hospital or other organization by a professional standards review organization in formal recognition that the organization's review, continued-stay review, and medical care evaluation programs meet certain effectiveness criteria.

deep artery of the thigh, the largest branch of the femoral artery and the major source of blood supply to the thigh.

deep auricular artery, a small branch of the maxillary artery that contributes to the blood supply of the external acoustic meatus.

deep brachial artery [As, *dyppan,* to dip; Gk, *brachion,* arm, *arteria,* airpipe], a branch of each of the brachial arteries, arising at the distal border of the teres major and supplying the humerus and muscles of the upper arm.

deep brain stimulation (DBS), patient-controlled, continuous, high-frequency electrical stimulation of a specific area of the brain by means of an implanted electrode, which is controlled by a battery implanted just below the clavicle. The electrical signals block those signals from the brain causing tremors and some other related problems.

deep breathing and coughing exercises, movements used to improve pulmonary gas exchange or to maintain respiratory function, especially after prolonged inactivity or general anesthesia. Incisional pain after surgery in the chest or abdomen often inhibits normal respiratory movements. The patient is assisted to a comfortable position, supine or sitting up. An analgesic may be given before the exercises if pain is present. Inhalation through the nose and exhalation through the mouth are encouraged. With the incision supported, the patient is asked to cough after a deep inhalation. If pain prevents the patient

from producing a deep, effective cough, a series of short barklike coughs (also known as machine gun or huf-huf coughs) may be encouraged.

deep circumflex iliac artery, a branch of the external iliac artery that, with the interior epigastric artery, supplies the inferior part of the abdominal wall.

deep dorsal vein, the vein that drains the erectile tissues of the clitoris and penis.

deep fascia, the most extensive of three kinds of fascia comprising an intricate series of connective sheets and bands that hold the muscles and other structures in place throughout the body, wrapping the muscles in gray, feltlike membranes.

deep heat, the application of heat in the treatment of deep body tissues, particularly muscles and tendons. The thermal effects may be produced with shortwave therapy, phonophoresis, or ultrasound.

deep lamellar endothelial keratoplasty (DLEK), a procedure in which a small incision is used to remove only the diseased tissue without transplanting the entire cornea. Only the inside layer of the cornea is replaced. This technique avoids the astigmatism that often occurs with penetrating keratoplasty and greatly reduces the risk of infection.

deep massage, massage techniques whose purpose is to reach structures beneath the superficial tissue, using effleurage, direct pressure, or friction applied perpendicular to the fibers of the affected tissue.

deep palmar arch, the termination of the radial artery, joining the deep palmar branch of the ulnar artery in the palm of the hand.

deep perineal pouch, a thin space superior to the perineal membrane that contains a layer of skeletal muscle and various neurovascular elements.

deep petrosal nerve, a nerve formed in the internal carotid plexus that leaves the plexus in the middle cranial fossa and joins the greater petrosal branch of the facial nerve. It carries postganglionic sympathetic fibers destined mainly for blood vessels.

deep reflexes [ME, *dep,* hollow; L, *reflectere,* to bend back], any reflexes caused by stimulation of a deep body structure such as a tendon reflex.

deep sensation, the awareness or perception of pain, pressure, or tension in the deep layers of the skin, muscles, tendons, or joints.

deep structure, in linguistics and neurolinguistics, the deeper experience and meaning to which surface structures in a communication may refer.

deep temporal artery, one of the branches of the maxillary artery on each side of the head. It branches into the anterior portion and the posterior portion.

deep tendon reflex (DTR), a brisk contraction of a muscle in response to a sudden stretch induced by a sharp tap by a finger or rubber hammer on the tendon of insertion of the muscle.

deep transverse metatarsal ligaments, the ligaments that link together the distal heads of the metatarsals at the metatarsophalangeal joints.

deep transverse perineal muscle, a muscle on each side of the perineal membrane thought to stabilize the position of the perineal body, a midline structure along the posterior edge of the perineal membrane.

deep vein, one of the many systemic veins that accompany the arteries, usually enclosed in a sheath that wraps both the vein and the associated artery.

deep vein thrombosis (DVT), a disorder involving a thrombus in one of the deep veins of the body, most commonly the iliac or femoral vein. Symptoms include tenderness, pain, swelling, warmth, and discoloration of the skin.

deep x-ray therapy, the treatment of internal neoplasms with ionizing radiation from an external source. Deep x-ray therapy frequently causes nausea, malaise, diarrhea, and skin reactions such as blanching, erythema, itching, burning, oozing, or desquamation, but with modern techniques the ray is beamed directly to the site, and the skin can be spared.

DEET, abbreviation for *diethyltoluamide,* an insect repellant.

defamation /def′əmā′shən/ [L, *diffamare,* to discredit], any communication, written or spoken, that is untrue and that injures the good name or reputation of another or in any way brings that person into disrepute.

default judgment /difôlt′/ [L, *defallere,* to lack, *judicare,* to decide], in law, a judgment rendered against a defendant as a result of the defendant's failure to appear in court or to answer the plaintiff's claim within the proper time.

defecation /def′ikā′shən/ [L, *defaecare,* to clean], the elimination of feces from the digestive tract through the rectum. —**defecate** /def′ikāt/, *v.*

defecography /def′əkog′rəfē/, the radiographic examination of the rectum and anal canal of patients with defecative dysfunction. A barium sulfate paste is instilled directly into the rectum, and the patient is seated on a radiolucent commode in front of a fluoroscope. Lateral projections of the rectum and anal canal are recorded during defecation.

defective /difek′tiv/ [L, *defectus,* a failing], pertaining to something that is imperfect, or, as in an outdated term, to an individual who may be suffering from any disorder.

defendant /difen′dənt/, in law, the party named in a plaintiff's complaint and against whom the plaintiff's allegations are made. The defendant must respond to the allegations.

defense /də·fens′/ [L, *defendere,* to ward off], the practice of, or measures taken to ensure, self-protection.

defense mechanism [L, *defendere,* to repulse, *mechanicus,* machine], an unconscious intrapsychic reaction that offers protection to the self from stress or a threat. Defense mechanisms are of two types: those that diminish anxiety and are used by an individual to integrate more fully into society and those that do not reduce anxiety but simply postpone the effects of feeling it.

defense reflex, an autonomic defensive response by an animal when threatened. The response may consist of dilated pupils, baring of claws, or raising of feathers or hair.

defensin /difen′sin/, a peptide with natural antibiotic activity found within human neutrophils. Three types of defensins have been identified, each consisting of a chain of about 30 amino acids.

defensive radical therapy /difen′siv/, in psychology, a view of the therapeutic process in which the therapist begins at the patient's present state and encourages the patient to avoid self-defeating behavior as as survival tactic.

deferasirox, a rarely used heavy metal–chelating agent used to treat chronic iron overload.

deferens /def′ərenz/ [L], carrying away.

deferoxamine mesylate /dē′fərok′səmēn/, a chelating agent with specific affinity for ferric iron and low affinity for calcium, prescribed in the treatment of acute iron intoxication and chronic iron overload.

defervescence /di′fərves′əns/ [L, *defervescere,* to reduce heat], the diminishing or disappearance of a fever.—**defervescent,** *adj.*

defibrillation /difī′brilā′shən/, the termination of ventricular fibrillation or pulseless ventricular tachycardia (inefficient, asynchronous contraction) by delivery of an electric shock to the patient's precordium. It is a common emergency measure generally performed by a physician or specially trained nurse or paramedic. —**defibrillate,** *v.*

defibrillator /difī′brilā′tər, difib′-/, a device that delivers an electrical shock at a preset voltage to the myocardium. It is used for restoring the normal cardiac rhythm and rate when the heart has stopped beating or is fibrillating.

defibrillator management: external, a nursing intervention from the Nursing Interventions Classification (NIC) defined as care of the patient receiving defibrillation for termination of life-threatening cardiac rhythm disturbances.

defibrillator management: internal, a nursing intervention from the Nursing Interventions Classification (NIC) defined as care of the patient receiving permanent detection and termination of life-threatening cardiac rhythm disturbances through the insertion and use of an internal cardiac defibrillator.

defibrination, the in-vitro removal of fibrin from blood to prevent clotting.

deficiency /difish'ənsē/, a lack or shortage of something.

deficiency disease [L, *de* + *facere*, to make, *dis,* opposite of; Fr, *aise,* ease], a condition resulting from the lack of one or more essential nutrients in the diet; from metabolic dysfunction; or from impaired digestion or absorption, excessive excretion, or increased biologic requirements.

deficiency of sweating [AS, *swaetan*], a failure of the sweat glands to secrete perspiration in normal amounts. The condition may be the result of a congenital defect, a blockage of the sweat ducts as a sequel to prickly heat, excessive heat, autonomic neuropathy, or conditions such as hemorrhage or diarrhea that cause body fluid loss.

deficit /def'isit/, any deficiency or difference from that which is normal, such as an oxygen deficit, a cause of hypoxia.

defined formula diet, nutritional support provided by simple elemental nutritive components that require no further digestive breakdown and thus are readily absorbed.

definitive /difin'ətiv/ [L, *definitivus*, a limiting], **1.** final; clearly established without doubt or question. **2.** in embryology, fully formed in the final differentiation of a tissue, structure, or organ. **3.** in parasitology, pertaining to the host in which the parasite undergoes the sexual phase of its reproductive cycle.

definitive host, any host organism in which a parasite reproduces sexually.

definitive prosthesis, a permanent prosthetic device that replaces an immediate-fit appliance such as a pylon.

definitive treatment, any therapy generally accepted as a specific cure of a disease.

defloration /def'lôrā'shən/ [L, *de* + *flos,* flower, *-atio,* process], the rupture of the vaginal hymen.

deformity /difôr'mitē/ [L, *deformis,* misshapen], distortion, disfigurement, flaw, malformation, or misshape that affects the body in general or any part of it.

deg, 1. abbreviation for **degeneration.** **2.** abbreviation for **degree.**

degenerate [L, *degenerare*], **1.** to change from a higher to a lower type or form. **2.** characterized by degeneration.

degeneration (deg) /dijen'ərā'shən/ [L, *degenerare,* to become unlike others], the gradual deterioration of normal cells and body functions.

degenerative /dijen'ərətiv/ [L, *degenerare,* to become unlike others], pertaining to or involving degeneration or change to a lower or dysfunctional form.

degenerative disease, any disease in which deterioration of structure or function of tissue occurs.

degenerative lesion [L, *degenerare,* to become unlike others, *laesio,* hurting], an injury or disease state that results in loss of function.

degenerative neuralgia [L, *degenerare,* to become unlike others; Gk, *neuron,* nerve, *algos,* pain], a form of neuralgia caused by degenerative changes in nervous tissue, which usually affects older people.

degenerative neuritis [L, *degenerare,* to become unlike others; Gk, *neuron,* nerve, *itis,* inflammation], an inflammation caused by degenerative changes in nervous tissue.

degloving /dēglov'ing/ [L, *de*; AS, *glof*], **1.** an injury to an extremity—finger, hand, arm, leg, or foot—in which the soft tissue down to the bone, including neurovascular bundles and sometimes tendons, is peeled off. **2.** in dentistry, the exposure of the bony mandibular anterior or posterior regions by oral surgery or trauma. **3.** removal of latex or vinyl hand coverings.

deglutition /di'glo͞otish'ən/ [L, *deglutire,* to swallow], swallowing.

deglutition apnea, the normal absence of respiration during swallowing.

degradation /di'grədā'shən/ [L, *de* + *gradu,* step], the conversion of a chemical compound to a less complex compound, usually by splitting off one or more groups or subgroups of atoms, as in deamination.—**degrade,** *v.*

degranulation /dēgran'yəlā'shən/, the release of granules from cells such as mast cells and basophils.

degree (deg) [Fr, *degre*], one of the divisions or intervals marked on a scale of units of measurement.

degrees of freedom (df), a statistic measure of the number of independent observations or choices among members in a sample. It is used in determining the statistic significance of findings during data analysis.

degustation /dē'gəstā'shən/ [L, *degustare,* to taste], the act of tasting.

dehiscence /dihis'əns/ [L, *dehiscere,* to gape], the separation of a surgical incision or rupture of a wound closure.

dehumanization /dihyoo'mənīzā'shən/ [L, *de,* from, *humanitas,* human nature], the process of losing altruistic or individual qualities, as may occur in some psychotic states or in environments that produce emotional trauma (prisoner-of-war).

dehumidifier /dē'yoomid'ifī'ər/, an apparatus to remove moisture in the atmosphere.

dehydrate /dihī'drāt/ [L, *de;* Gk, *hydor,* water], 1. to remove or lose water from a substance. 2. to lose excessive water from the body.

dehydrated alcohol, a clear, colorless, highly hygroscopic liquid with a burning taste, containing at least 99.5% ethyl alcohol by volume.

dehydration /di'hīdrā'shən/, 1. excessive loss of water from body tissues. Dehydration is accompanied by a disturbance in the balance of essential electrolytes, particularly sodium, potassium, and chloride. Signs of dehydration include poor skin turgor (not a reliable sign in the elderly), flushed dry skin, coated tongue, dry mucous membranes, oliguria, irritability, and confusion. 2. rendering a substance free from water.

dehydration fever, a fever that frequently occurs in newborns, thought to be caused by dehydration.

dehydration of gingivae, the drying of gum tissue, often the result of mouth breathing. Dehydration lowers the resistance of the gingivae to infection.

dehydrogenate, to remove hydrogen atoms, as in the oxidation processes.

deinstitutionalization /dē·in'stityoo'shən al'īzā'shən/ [L, *de* + *instituere,* to put in place], a change in the location and focus of mental health care from an institutional to a community setting.

Deiters' nucleus /dī'tərz, dē'terz/ [Otto F.C. Deiters, German anatomist, 1834–1863], one of the vestibular nuclei located in the brainstem.

DEJ, abbreviation for **dentinoenamel junction.**

déjà vu /däzhä vY', -vē', -voo'/ [Fr, previously seen], the sensation or illusion that one is encountering a set of circumstances or a place that was previously experienced.

Déjérine-Sottas disease /dezh'ərin sot'əz, -sotäz'/ [Joseph J. Déjérine, French neurologist, 1849–1917; Jules Sottas, French neurologist, 1866–1943], a rare congenital spinocerebellar disorder characterized by the development of palpable thickenings along peripheral nerves, degeneration of the peripheral nervous system, pain, paresthesia, ataxia, and diminished sensation and deep tendon reflexes.

del, abbreviation for **deletion.**

Delaney clause, a 1960 amendment to the 1938 Federal Food, Drug, and Cosmetic Act regulating food additives. It prohibits the use of any food substance found to be carcinogenic in humans or animals. Food products not previously found to be carcinogenic were classified historically as "Generally Regarded As Safe," or GRAS.

Delano, Jane A, an American nurse who organized the American Red Cross Nursing Service, an association formed to supply nurses to the military forces.

delavirdine, a nonnucleoside reverse transcriptase inhibitor prescribed to treat HIV-1 in combination with zidovudine or didanosine.

delayed echolalia [Fr, *delai,* time extension; Gk, *echo,* sound, *lalein,* to babble], a phenomenon, commonly seen in schizophrenia, involving the meaningless automatic repetition of overheard words and phrases. It occurs hours, days, or even weeks after the original stimulus.

delayed graft [ME, *delaein,* to leave; Gk, *graphein,* stylus], a type of skin graft that is partially elevated and reinserted later in the same place.

delayed hypersensitivity, the type of hypersensitivity that takes 24 to 72 hours to develop and is mediated by T lymphocytes rather than by antibodies.

delayed hypersensitivity reaction, a reaction of cellular immunity, named in contrast to immediate hypersensitivity reactions because its onset is 24 to 72 hours after the antigenic challenge. The term is usually used to denote the subset of type IV hypersensitivity reactions involving cytokine release and macrophage activation, as opposed to direct cytolysis, but can be used more broadly, sometimes even as a synonym for type IV hypersensitivity reaction. The classic delayed hypersensitivity reaction is the tuberculin reaction observed in skin testing.

delayed language, failure of language to develop at the expected age.

delayed onset muscle soreness, muscle weakness, restricted ROM, and tenderness on palpation, occurring 24 to 48 hours after intense or prolonged muscular activity.

delayed postpartum hemorrhage, hemorrhage occurring later than 24 hours after giving birth. It is most often caused by retained fragments of the placenta, a laceration of the cervix or vagina that was not discovered or was not completely sutured, or subinvolution of the placental site within the uterus.

delayed sensation, a feeling or impression that is not experienced immediately after a stimulus.

delayed symptom [Fr, *delai*; Gk, *symptoma*, that which happens], a symptom such as shock that may not appear until after the precipitating cause.

delayed treatment seeker, in psychology, a person who delays seeking treatment for a problematic life event such as a sexual assault until months or years after the event, usually after a precipitating event such as an anniversary reaction.

delayed-type hypersensitivity (DTH), a delayed hypersensitivity.

delayed vomiting, vomiting occurring much later than its stimulus, such as several hours after a meal or several days after a course of chemotherapy.

Delecato-Doman theory, a therapeutic concept that full neurologic organization of a disabled or mentally retarded child requires that the child pass through developmental patterns covering progressively higher anatomic levels of the nervous system.

delegation, a nursing intervention from the Nursing Interventions Classification (NIC) defined as transfer of responsibility for the performance of patient care while retaining accountability for the outcome.

deleterious /del'itir'ē-əs/ [Gk, *deleterios*, destroyer], harmful or dangerous.

deletion (del) /dilē'shən/ [L, *deletio*, destruction], the loss of a piece of a chromosome.

deletion syndrome, any of a group of congenital autosomal anomalies that result from the loss of part of a chromosome as a result of breakage of a chromatid during meiosis. An example is cat-cry syndrome, which results from the absence of the short arm of chromosome 5.

deliberate biologic programming /dilib'ərit/ [L, *deliberare*, to weigh carefully], the Hayflick theory of aging, based on studies showing that human cells contain biologic clocks that predetermine death after undergoing mitosis a finite number of times.

deliberate hypotension, a technique in general anesthesia in which a short-acting hypotensive agent is given to reduce BP and thus bleeding during surgery. The procedure facilitates surgery by making vessels and tissues more visible and reducing blood loss.

delinquency /diling'kwənsē/ [L, *delinquere*, to fail], 1. negligence or failure to fulfill a duty or obligation. 2. an offense, fault, misdemeanor, or misdeed; a tendency to commit such acts.

delinquent /diling'kwənt/, 1. characterized by neglect of duty or violation of law. 2. one whose behavior is characterized by persistent antisocial, illegal, violent, or criminal acts.

délire de toucher /dālir' də tōōshā'/ [Fr], an abnormal desire or irresistible urge to touch objects.

delirious mania /dilir'ē-əs/, an extreme form of the manic state in which activity is so frenzied, confused, and incoherent that it is difficult to discern any link between affect and behavior.

delirium /dilir'ē-əm/ [L, *delirare*, to rave], 1. a state of frenzied excitement or wild enthusiasm. 2. an acute organic mental disorder characterized by confusion, disorientation, restlessness, clouding of the consciousness, incoherence, fear, anxiety, excitement, and, often, illusions; hallucinations, usually of visual origin; and, at times, delusions. The condition is caused by disturbances in cerebral functions that may result from a wide range of disorders. Delirium places medically ill individuals at greater risk for medical complications (pneumonia and decubiti) and is associated with functional decline and institutional placement. Delirium may lead to dementia. —**delirious,** *adj.*

delirium constantium, in psychiatry, a patient's reiteration of a fixed idea.

delirium management, a nursing intervention from the Nursing Interventions Classification (NIC) defined as provision of a safe and therapeutic environment for the patient who is experiencing an acute confusional state.

delirium of persecution [L, *delirare*, to rave, *persecutor*, to pursue], a state of clouded consciousness or decreased sensorium in which the person believes others are threatening or conspiring against him or her.

delirium tremens (DTs), an acute and sometimes fatal psychotic reaction caused by cessation of excessive intake of alcoholic beverages over a long period. Initial symptoms include loss of appetite, insomnia, and general restlessness, which are followed by agitation; excitement; disorientation; mental confusion; vivid and often frightening hallucinations; acute fear and anxiety; illusions and delusions; coarse tremors of the hands, feet, legs, and tongue; fever; increased heart rate; extreme perspiration; GI distress; and precordial pain.

delivery /diliv'ərē/ [L, *de* + *liberare*, to free], in obstetrics, the birth of a child.

delivery room, a unit of a hospital used for childbirth and infant resuscitation.

DeLorme technique, a method of exercise with weights for the purpose of strengthening muscles in which sets of repetitions are repeated with rests between sets. The technique involves isotonic exercise and determination of the maximum level of resistance.

delousing /dēlou′sing/ [L, *de,* from; AS, *lus*], to rid a person or object of an infestation of lice.

delta /del′tə/, Δ, δ, fourth letter of the Greek alphabet.

delta-9-tetrahydrocannabinol (THC), a pharmacologically active ingredient of cannabis that has been used in treating some cases of nausea and vomiting associated with cancer chemotherapy.

delta agent, a defective viral agent that occurs only in association with hepatitis B infection. It causes chronic hepatitis and progressive liver damage.

delta-aminolevulinic acid test, a urine test to diagnose porphyria. It can also be used to diagnose lead intoxication, chronic alcoholic disorders, and diabetic ketoacidosis.

delta optical density analysis [Gk, *delta,* fourth letter of Greek alphabet, *optikos,* of sight; L, *densus,* thick; Gk, a loosening], a technique used to diagnose anemia in a fetus by measuring the proportion of bilirubin decomposition products in the amniotic fluid.

Deltavirus /del′təvī′rəs/ [hepatitis *delta* + *virus*], a genus of satellite viruses that require a helper HBV for their replication. It contains a single species, hepatitis D virus.

delta wave, 1. the slowest of the four types of brain waves, characterized by a frequency of 4 Hz and a relatively high voltage. Delta waves are "deep-sleep waves" associated with a dreamless state. **2.** in cardiology, a slurring of the QRS portion of an ECG tracing caused by preexcitation in Wolff-Parkinson-White syndrome.

deltoid /del′toid/ [Gk, *delta,* triangular, *eidos,* form], **1.** triangular. **2.** pertaining to the deltoid muscle that covers the shoulder.

deltoid ligament [Gk, *delta;* L, *ligamentum*], the medial ligament of the ankle joint.

deltoid muscle, a large, thick triangular muscle that covers the shoulder joint. It is the prime mover of arm abduction. It is also a synergist of arm flexion, extension, and medial and lateral rotation.

delusion /dilo͞o′zhən/ [L, *deludere,* to deceive], a persistent aberrant belief or perception held inviolable by a person despite evidence that refutes it.

delusion management, a nursing intervention from the Nursing Interventions Classification (NIC) defined as promoting the comfort, safety, and reality orientation of a patient experiencing false, fixed beliefs that have little or no basis in reality.

delusion of being controlled, the false belief that one's feelings, beliefs, thoughts, and acts are governed by some external force, as experienced in various forms of schizophrenia.

delusion of grandeur /grän′dyo͞or/, the gross exaggeration of one's importance, wealth, power, or talents, as manifested in such disorders as megalomania, general paresis, and paranoid schizophrenia.

delusion of persecution, a morbid belief that one is being mistreated, harassed, or conspired against, as seen in paranoia and paranoid schizophrenia.

delusion of poverty, in psychology, a false belief of a person that he or she is impoverished or will be deprived of material possessions.

demand pacemaker [L, *demandere,* to give in charge, *passus,* step; ME, *maken*], a device used to stimulate the heart electrically when the heart's own impulses are not sufficient. The device measures the interval between the heart's native beats and delivers a stimulating pulse whenever that interval exceeds a set value.

demarcation /dē′märkā′shən/ [L, *de,* from, *marcare,* to mark], the process of setting limits or boundaries.

demarcation current [L, *de* + *marcare,* to mark], an electrical current that flows from an uninjured to an injured end of a muscle.

deme /dēm/ [Gk, *demos,* common population], a small, local, closely related, interbreeding population of organisms, usually occupying a circumscribed area.

demecarium bromide /dē′məker′ē-əm/, an ophthalmic anticholinesterase agent prescribed in the treatment of open-angle glaucoma.

demeclocycline hydrochloride /dēmek′lōsī′klēn/, a tetracycline antibiotic prescribed in the treatment of various gram-positive and gram-negative bacterial infections, including those in which use of penicillin is contraindicated.

demented /dimen′tid/ [L, *de,* away from, *mens,* mind], pertaining to a form of mental disorder in which cognitive functions are affected.

dementia /dimen′shə/ [L, *de* + *mens,* mind], a progressive organic mental disorder characterized by chronic personality disintegration, confusion, disorientation, stupor, deterioration of intellectual capacity and function, and impairment of control of memory, judgment, and impulses. Alzheimer's disease, Pick's disease, and other organic forms of dementia are generally considered irreversible, progressive, and incurable. However, conditions that cause the decline may be treatable or partially reversible.

dementia management, a nursing intervention from the Nursing Interventions Classification (NIC) defined as provision of a modified environment for the patient who is experiencing a chronic confusional state.

dementia management: bathing, a nursing intervention from the Nursing Interventions Classification (NIC) defined as the reduction of aggressive behavior during cleaning of the body.

dementia of the Alzheimer type, dementia occurring in Alzheimer disease, being of insidious onset and gradually progressive course, with histopathologic changes characteristic of Alzheimer disease that are not due to other CNS, systemic, or substance-induced conditions known to cause dementia.

dementia syndrome of depression, reversible dementia occurring in association with depression in the elderly, the cognitive deficits resolving with treatment of the depression.

Demerol, a trademark for an opioid analgesic (meperidine hydrochloride).

Demerol Hydrochloride, a trademark for an opioid analgesic (meperidine hydrochloride).

demigauntlet bandage /dem'igônt'lit/ [L, _demidus,_ half; Fr, _gant,_ glove], a glovelike bandage over the hand that leaves the fingers free.

demineralization /dēmin'əral'ĪZā'shən/ [L, _de + minera,_ mine], a decrease in the amount of minerals or inorganic salts in tissues, as occurs in certain diseases.

demise /dimīz'/ [OFr, _demettre,_ to put away], death, destruction, or end of existence.

democratic style /dem'okrat'ik/, people-centered leadership in which the group participates openly in decision making for group goals.

demography /dəmog'rəfē/ [Gk, _demos,_ people, _graphein,_ to record], the study of human populations, particularly the size, distribution, and characteristics of members of population groups. Demography is applied in studies of health problems involving ethnic groups; populations of a specific geographic region; religious groups with special dietary restrictions; and members of population groups that may represent a typical cross section of the entire nation.

demonstrative /dimon'strətiv/, pertaining to a concept or an action that accompanies and illustrates speech.

Demser, a trademark for an antihypertensive (metyrosine).

demulcent /dimul'sənt/ [L, _demulcere,_ to stroke down], **1.** any of several oily substances used for soothing and reducing irritation of surfaces that have been abraded or irritated, especially mucosal surfaces. **2.** soothing, as a counterirritant or balm.

Demulen, a trademark for an oral contraceptive containing an estrogen (ethinyl estradiol) and a progestin (ethynodiol diacetate).

demyelinate /dēmī'əlināt'/, to remove or destroy the myelin surrounding the axons of nerve cells.

demyelination /dimī'əlinā'shən/ [L, _de;_ Gk, _myelos,_ marrow], the process of destruction or removal of the myelin sheath from a nerve or nerve fiber.

denaturation /dēnā'chərā'shən/ [L, _de + natura,_ natural], **1.** the alteration of the basic nature or structure of a substance. **2.** the process of making a potential food or beverage substance unfit for human consumption although it may still be used for other purposes, such as a solvent.

denatured alcohol /dēnā'chərd/, ethyl alcohol made unfit for ingestion by the addition of acetone or methanol, used as a solvent and in chemical processes.

denatured protein [L, _de,_ from, _natura, proteios,_ first rank], a protein that has undergone change that causes its original properties to be lost. A protein can be denatured by radiation, heat, strong acids, or alcohol.

dendrite /den'drīt/ [Gk, _dendron,_ tree], a slender branching process that extends from the cell body of a neuron and that is capable of being stimulated by a neurotransmitter. Each neuron usually possesses several dendrites, which receive synapses where chemical transmission occurs from axons to dendrites (or an axon, in the case of unipolar neurons). The number of dendrites varies with the functions of a neuron.

dendritic /dendrit'ik/, **1.** treelike, with branches that spread toward or into neighboring tissues, as dendritic keratitis. **2.** pertaining to a dendrite.

dendritic calculus [Gk, _dendron,_ tree, _calculus,_ pebble], a large calculus lodged in the pelvis of the kidney and shaped to fit the branches of the calyx.

dendritic cell, a cell that captures antigens and migrates to the lymph nodes and spleen, where it presents the processed antigens to T cells.

dendritic keratitis, inflammation of the cornea and conjunctiva caused by herpesvirus type 1. It is characterized by an ulceration of the surface of the cornea resembling a tree with knobs at the ends of the branches. Photophobia, the sensation of a foreign body in the eye, pain, and conjunctivitis are usual.

dendrodendritic synapse /den'drōden-drit'ik/ [Gk, _dendron + dendron + synaptein,_ to join], a type of synapse in which a dendrite of one neuron comes in contact with that of another neuron.

denervated /dēnur'vātid/ [L, _de + nervus,_ nerve], having a nerve impulse route interrupted, as by excision or administration of a drug that blocks the pathway. The result is decreased or no transmission of impulses through this pathway.

dengue fever /deng'gē, den'gā/ [Sp, influenza; L, *febris*, fever], an acute *Flavivirus* infection caused by one of four antigenically distinct serotypes, which determine the severity of infection. It is transmitted to humans by the bite of an infected *Aedes aegypti* mosquito. The disease usually produces a triad of symptoms: fever; rash; and severe head, back, and muscle pain.

dengue hemorrhagic fever shock syndrome (DHFSS), a grave form of dengue fever characterized by shock with collapse or prostration; cold, clammy extremities; a weak, thready pulse; respiratory distress; and all of the symptoms of dengue fever. Hemorrhages, bruises, small reddish spots indicating bleeding from skin capillaries, and bloody vomit, urine, and feces may be experienced and may precede circulatory collapse.

denial /dinī'əl/ [L, *denegare*, to negate], **1.** refusal or restriction of something requested, claimed, or needed, often causing physical or emotional deficiency. **2.** an unconscious defense mechanism in which emotional conflict and anxiety are avoided by refusal to acknowledge the thoughts, feelings, desires, impulses, or facts that are consciously intolerable.

denileukin diftitox, a miscellaneous antineoplastic prescribed to treat cutaneous T-cell lymphoma that expresses the CD25 component of the IL-2 receptor.

Denis Browne splint [Denis J.W. Browne, twentieth-century Australian surgeon], a splint for the correction of clubfoot, composed of a curved bar attached to the soles of a pair of high-topped shoes.

denitrogenation /dēnī'trōjənā'shən/, the elimination of nitrogen from the lungs and body tissues during a period of breathing pure oxygen.

Denman's spontaneous evolution [Thomas Denman, English physician, 1733–1815; L, *sponte*, voluntarily, *evolvere*, to roll forth], a natural, unassisted turning of the fetus from the transverse presentation. The head rotates back, and, as the breech descends, the shoulder ascends in the pelvis. The back of the fetus is generally posterior.

dens *pl.* **dentes** /den'tēz/ [L, tooth], **1.** a tooth or toothlike structure or process. The term is sometimes modified to identify a particular tooth, such as dens caninus. **2.** the cone-shaped odontoid process of the axis, or second cervical vertebra.

dense connective tissue, connective tissue characterized by dense groups of fibers.

dense fibrous tissue [L, *densus*, thick], a fibrous connective tissue consisting of compact, strong, inelastic bundles of mostly parallel collagenous fibers that are

glistening white. Dense regular fibrous tissue comprises the tendons, the aponeuroses, and the ligaments; dense irregular fibrous tissue comprises the fascial membranes, the dermis of the skin, the periosteum, and the capsules of organs.

dens in dente /den'tə/, an anomaly of the teeth, found chiefly in the maxillary lateral incisors and characterized by invagination of the enamel. The condition causes a radiographic image suggestive of a tooth within a tooth.

densitometer /den'sitom'ətər/ [L, *densus*; Gk, *metron*, measure], a device that uses a photoelectric cell to detect differences in the intensity of light transmitted through a substance such as x-ray film.

density (D) /den'sitē/ [L, *densus,* thick], **1.** the amount of mass of a substance in a given volume. The greater the mass in a given volume, the greater the density. **2.** in radiology, the degree of x-ray film blackening.

density gradient, a variation in the density of a solution caused by a change in concentration of a solute in a confined solution.

dental [L, *dens*, tooth], pertaining to a tooth or the teeth.

dental alveolus /alvē'ələs/, a tooth socket in the mandible or maxilla.

dental amalgam, an alloy of silver, tin, and mercury with small amounts of zinc and sometimes copper, used for restoring tooth surfaces affected by dental caries or trauma.

dental anesthesia, any of several methods to reduce or block pain and discomfort during dental procedures.

dental ankylosis, solid fixation of a tooth resulting from fusion of the cementum and alveolar bone, with obliteration of at least a portion of the periodontal ligament.

dental anomaly, an aberration in which one or more teeth deviate from the normal in form, function, or position.

dental appliance, any device placed in or on a patient by a dentist as part of a treatment protocol. Dental appliances include orthodontic, prosthetic, retaining, and habit-modification devices.

dental arch, the curving shape formed by the arrangement of a normal set of teeth in each jaw.

dental assistant, a person who aids a dentist in the performance of generalized tasks, including chairside aid, clerical work, reception, and some radiography and dental laboratory work.

dental biomechanics, the study and use of mechanical devices and physical forces to effect desirable changes in oral structures.

dental bur, a rotary drill bit made of steel or diamond impregnated material attached to a steel shank, available in varying degrees of sharpness, lengths, shapes, and sizes, used in the preparation of teeth to receive a dental restoration.

dental calculus, a salivary deposit of calcium phosphate and calcium carbonate with organic matter on the teeth or a dental prosthesis.

dental caries, a tooth disease caused by the complex interaction of food, especially starches and sugars, with saliva and the bacteria that form dental plaque. The term also refers to the tooth cavities that result from the disease. —**carious,** *adj.*

dental chart, a simplified graphic representation of the teeth on which clinical, radiologic, and forensic information may be recorded.

dental crypt, the space in the alveolar process occupied by a developing tooth.

dental emergency, an acute disorder of oral health that requires medical attention, including broken, loose, or evulsed teeth caused by traumas; infections and inflammations of the soft tissues of the mouth; and complications of oral surgery, such as dry tooth socket.

dental engine, an apparatus consisting of a hand instrument to which various rotating drills or other tools can be fitted.

dental erosion, the chemical or mechanochemical destruction of tooth material that causes variously shaped depressions, generally at the cementoenamel junctions of teeth. The surfaces of these depressions, unlike those of dental caries, are hard and smooth.

dental ethics [L, *dens,* tooth; Gk, *ethos,* ethics], a system of moral principles governing the professional conduct of dental and dental hygienic practices.

dental examination, an inspection of the teeth and surrounding soft tissues of the oral cavity.

dental extracting forceps, a hand instrument used for grasping teeth during their removal from the socket.

dental film, an x-ray film of the teeth, exposed either intraorally or extraorally. Intraoral films are small, double-emulsion films without screens but with a lead foil backing to reduce patient dose, enclosed in a moisture-resistant envelope. Extraoral films are large, single-emulsion, screen films.

dental fistula, an abnormal passage from the apical periodontal area of a tooth to the surface of the oral mucous membrane, permitting the discharge of inflammatory or suppurative material.

dental floss, a thread used to clean interproximal tooth surfaces and spaces between the teeth.

dental granuloma, a pathologic mass of granulation tissue that is attached to the apex of a tooth and is surrounded by a fibrous capsule.

dental handpiece, a dental instrument that holds various disks, cups, or burs, used to prepare a tooth to receive a restoration or to contour, clean, or polish a tooth or restoration.

dental history, a record of a patient's oral health, general health, and medical care, including surgeries and medication use, allergies, childhood diseases, radiographic history, and personal dental care.

dental hygienist, an oral health care professional authorized to provide clinical and therapeutic services under the supervision of a licensed dentist, including dental prophylaxis, radiography, administration of medications, and dental education at chairside and in the community. In some states, a dental hygienist with additional education may perform additional duties.

dental identification [L, *dens,* tooth, *idem,* the same, *facere,* to make], the process of establishing the unique characteristics of the teeth and dental work of an individual, thereby permitting the identification of the individual by comparison with his or her dental charts, records, plaster casts, radiographs or dental images, bite marks, and records.

dental impaction, the blocking of a tooth by a physical barrier, usually other teeth, so that it cannot erupt.

dental implant, a plastic or metal anchor that is inserted into a jawbone to provide permanent support for a crown, fixed bridge, or denture when the bone itself would provide insufficient support.

dental jurisprudence [L, *dens,* tooth, *juris prudentia,* knowledge of the law], the application of the principles of law to the practice of dentistry, dental therapy, and of dental hygiene and the relations of dentists, dental therapists, and dental hygienists to patients, society, and each other.

dental laboratory technician, a person who makes dental prostheses and orthodontic appliances as prescribed by a dentist, either in a private laboratory or on the premises of a dentist.

dental laser, a device utilizing laser light of a certain frequency to remove pathological dental tissue and prepare the tooth to accept a dental restoration. Also a device used to remove or recontour oral soft tissue.

dental operculum [L, *dens,* tooth, *operculum,* a covering structure], a hood or flap of gingival tissue overlying the crown of an erupting tooth. This tissue is usually chewed away as the tooth erupts.

dental papilla [L, *dens,* tooth, *papilla,* nipple], a small mass of mesenchymal tissue in the enamel organ that differentiates into dentin and dental pulp during tooth development. The innermost layer consists of a cell-free zone of reticular fibers that form the basement membrane.

dental pathology, the branch of pathology that deals with dental changes that occur in disease.

dental plate [L, *dens,* tooth; OFr, *plate,* flat structure], a dental prosthesis made to the shape of the maxilla or mandible jaw to support artificial teeth.

dental porcelain, a type of porcelain used in dental restorations, either jacket crowns or inlays, artificial teeth, or metal-ceramic crowns. It is essentially a mixture of particles of feldspar and quartz.

dental prosthesis [L, *dens,* tooth; Gk, *prosthesis,* an addition], a fixed or removable appliance used to replace one or more lost or missing natural teeth.

dental public health, a recognized specialty that is the science and art of preventing and controlling dental diseases and promoting dental health through organized community efforts.

dental pulp, a small mass of connective tissue, blood vessels, and nerves located in a chamber within the dentin layer of a tooth. The pulp chamber is found in the crown and root of a tooth.

dental radiograph [L, *dens,* tooth, *radire,* to shine; Gk, *graphein,* to record], an intraoral and extraoral x-ray film of teeth and the bone surrounding them.

dental sealant /sē′lənt/, a plastic film coating that is applied to and adheres to the caries-free chewing surfaces of teeth to seal pits and fissures where plaque, food, and bacteria usually become trapped. Dental sealants are reported to reduce the incidence of caries in children's teeth by 50%.

dental stone, a calcined gypsum derivative similar to but stronger than plaster of paris, used for making dental casts and dies.

dental surgeon [L, *dens,* tooth; Gk, *cheirourgos,* surgeon], a dentist who is able to diagnose pathology and disease, and performs surgical procedures involving the teeth and surrounding oral tissues. There are nine recognized dental specialties. See **dentist** and **dentistry.**

dental trephination, surgical creation of a fistula by puncturing the soft tissue and bone overlying the root apex to provide drainage.

dental tubules, minute channels in dentin, extending from the pulp cavity to the cementum and enamel.

dentate fracture /den′tāt/ [L, *dens*], any fracture that causes serrated bone ends that fit together like the teeth of gears.

dentate nucleus, a deep cerebellar nucleus. It receives fibers from the lateral zone of the cerebellar cortex and appears to act as a trigger for the motor cortex, governing intentional movements as well as properties of ongoing movements.

dentibuccal /den′tibuk′əl/ [L, *dens,* tooth, *bucca,* cheek], pertaining to the teeth and cheek.

denticle /den′tikəl/, a calcified body in the pulp chamber of a tooth. If it is composed of irregular dentin, it is known as a true denticle.

denticulate /dentik′yəlit/ [L, *denticulus,* little tooth], having very small teeth or toothlike projections.

dentifrice /den′tifris/ [L, *dens + fricare,* to rub], a pharmaceutic compound used with a toothbrush for cleaning and polishing the teeth.

dentigerous cyst /dentij′ərəs/ [L, *dens + gerere,* to bear], one of three kinds of follicular cyst, consisting of an epithelium-lined sac filled with fluid or viscous material that surrounds the crown of an unerupted tooth or odontoma.

dentin /den′tin/ [L, *dens*], the chief material of teeth, surrounding the pulp and situated inside the enamel and cementum. Harder and denser than bone, it consists of solid organic substratum infiltrated with lime salts.

dentin eburnation /ē′burnā′shən/, a change in carious teeth in which softened and decalcified dentin develops a hard, brown, polished appearance.

dentin globule, a small spheric body in peripheral dentin, created by early calcification.

dentinoenamel /den′tinō-inam′əl/ [L, *dens*; OFr, *enesmail,* enamel], pertaining to both the dentin and the enamel of the teeth.

dentinoenamel junction (DEJ), the interface of the enamel and the dentin of a tooth crown, generally conforming to the shape of the crown.

dentinogenesis /den′tinōjen′əsis/ [L, *dens*; Gk, *genein,* to produce], the formation of the dentin of the teeth.—**dentinogenic,** *adj.*

dentinogenesis imperfecta, 1. a genetic disturbance of the dentin, characterized by early calcification of the pulp chambers, marked attrition, and an opalescent hue of the teeth. **2.** a localized form of mesodermal dysplasia affecting the dentin of the teeth. **3.** a genetic condition that produces defective dentin but normal tooth enamel.

dentist [L, *dens*], a person who is qualified by training and licensed by a state or region to diagnose and treat abnormalities of the teeth, gums, and underlying bone, including conditions caused by disease, trauma, and heredity.

dentistry /den′tistrē/ [L, *dens*], the art and science of practicing the diagnosis,

D

prevention, and treatment of diseases and disorders of the teeth and surrounding structures of the oral cavity. Responsibilities include the repair and restoration of teeth, the replacement of missing teeth, and the detection of diseases, such as blood dyscrasias and tumors, that would require treatment by a dental specialist or physician. In addition to the general practice of dentistry, there are nine recognized specialties, each requiring additional training after graduation from a dental college: dental public health, endodontics, oral and maxillofacial pathology, oral and maxillofacial surgery, orthodontics and dentofacial orthopedics, pediatric dentistry, periodontics, and prosthodontics.

dentition /dentish′ən/ [L, *dentire*, to cut teeth], **1.** the development and eruption of the teeth. **2.** the arrangement, number, and kind of teeth as they appear in the dental arches of the mouth. **3.** the teeth of an individual or species as determined by their form and arrangement.

dentoalveolar abscess /den′tō-alvē′ələr/ [L, *dens + alveolus*, little hollow, *abscedere*, to go away], the formation and accumulation of pus in a tooth socket or the jawbone around the base of a tooth.

dentofacial /-fā′shəl/, pertaining to the mouth or the jaw.

dentofacial anomaly, a condition in which a mouth or jaw structure deviates from the normal in form, function, or position.

dentogingival fiber /-jinjī′vəl/ [L, *dens + gingiva*, gum], any of the many peridental connective tissue fibers that emerge from the supraalveolar part of the cementum of a tooth, spread like a fan, and terminate in the free gingiva.

dentogingival junction, the interface between the junctional epithelium and the surface of the teeth.

dentoperiosteal fiber /den′tōper′ē·os′te·əl/ [L, *dens*; Gk, *peri*, around, *osteon*, bone], any of the many peridental connective tissue fibers that emerge from the supraalveolar part of the cementum of a tooth and extend apically beyond the alveolar crest into the mucoperiosteum of the attached gingiva.

dentulous /den′tyələs/ [L, *dens*, tooth, *-ulosus*, characterized by], possessing one or more natural teeth.

dentulous dental arch, a dental arch that contains one or more natural teeth.

denture /den′chər/ [L, *dens*, tooth], an artificial tooth or a set of artificial teeth not permanently fixed or implanted.

denture base, the part of a denture that covers the soft tissue of the mouth. It is commonly made of resin or a combination of resins and metal.

denture flask, a sectional metal case in which plaster of paris or artificial stone is molded and in which dentures or other resin restorations are processed.

denture packing, the laboratory procedure of filling and compressing a denture-base material into a mold in a denture flask.

denturist /den′chərist/, a person other than a dentist who engages in the practice of dentistry, usually only to the extent of providing complete or partial dentures. Most states in the United States have laws restricting such activity.

denucleated /dēnyoo′klē·ā′tid/ [L, *de*, from, *nucleus*, nut kernel], pertaining to a condition in which the nucleus has been removed.

denudation /den′oodā′shən/ [L, *denudare*, to make bare], **1.** the process of stripping bare. **2.** a condition of losing an outside layer such as an epithelium.

Denver Articulation Screening Examination (DASE), a test for evaluating the clarity of pronunciation in children 2½ to 6 years of age. Each child's performance may be compared with a standardized norm for the age.

Denver classification, a system for identifying and classifying human chromosomes according to their size and the position of the centromere as determined during mitotic metaphase. The chromosomes are divided into seven major groups, designated A through G, which are arranged according to decreasing length.

Denver Developmental Screening Test (DDST), a test for evaluating development in children from 1 month to 6 years of age. The developmental level of motor, social, and language skills is expressed as a ratio in which the child's age is the denominator and the age at which the norm possesses skills equal to those of the child being tested is the numerator.

deodorant /dē·ō′dərənt/ [L, *de + odor*, smell], **1.** destroying or masking odors. **2.** a substance that destroys or masks odors.

deodorized alcohol /dē·ō′dərīzd/, a liquid, free of organic impurities, containing 92.5% absolute alcohol.

deodorizing douche, a stream of air or liquid that masks or absorbs foul odors, applied at moderate pressure into a body cavity or onto a body surface.

deontologism /dē′ontol′əgiz′əm/ [Gk, *deon*, obligation, *logos*, science], a doctrine of ethics that states that moral duty or obligation is binding even though a moral action may be difficult or result in painful consequences.

deossification /dē·os′ifikā′shən/, the loss of mineral matter from bones.

deoxidizer, an agent that removes oxygen.

deoxygenation /dē·ŏk´sijənā´shən/ [L, *de,* from; Gk, *oxys,* sharp, *genein,* to produce], the removal of oxygen from a chemical compound.

deoxyribonucleic acid (DNA) /dē·ŏk´sirī´bōnōōklē´ik/, a large, double-stranded, helical molecule that is the carrier of genetic information. In eukaryotic cells, it is found principally in the chromosomes of the nucleus. DNA is composed of four kinds of serially repeating nucleotide bases: adenine, cytosine, guanine, and thymine. Genetic information is coded in the sequence of the nucleotides.

deoxyribose /dē·ŏk´sē·rī´bōs/, ribose that has been transformed into a deoxy sugar, found in DNA.

deoxy sugar /dē·ŏk´sē shŏŏg´ər/, a sugar in which one or more carbon atoms have been reduced, thus losing their hydroxyl groups.

Depakene, a trademark for an anticonvulsant (divalproex sodium).

Depakote, a trademark for an anticonvulsant drug (divalproex sodium).

Department of Health and Human Services (DHHS), a cabinet-level department of the U.S. government with responsibility for the functions of various federal social welfare and health delivery agencies such as the Food and Drug Administration (FDA). It also directs the U.S. Office of Consumer Affairs, Office of Civil Rights, Administration on Aging, Public Health Service, Indian Health Service, Social Security Administration, and National Institutes of Health.

Department of Transportation (DOT), a cabinet-level department of the U.S. government responsible for national transportation policies, including maritime, aviation, railroad, and highway safety and regulation of the transport of hazardous materials, such as medical gases.

dependence /dipen´dəns/ [L, *de* + *pendere,* to hang upon], **1.** the state of being dependent. **2.** the total psychophysical state of one addicted to drugs or alcohol, who must receive an increasing amount of the substance to prevent the onset of withdrawal symptoms.

dependency needs /dipen´dənsē/, the sum of the physical and emotional requirements of an infant for survival, including parenting, love, affection, shelter, protection, food, and warmth. Reliance on others to satisfy these needs decreases with age and maturity.

dependent, pertaining to a condition of being reliant on someone or something else for help, support, favor, and other needs, as a child is dependent on a parent, a narcotics addict is dependent on a drug, or one variable is dependent on another. **—depend,** *v.*

dependent care, health care provided for persons, particularly children and handicapped or elderly individuals, who are dependent on others for part or all of ADL.

dependent edema [L, *de,* from, *pendere,* to hand; Gk, *oidema,* swelling], a fluid accumulation in the tissues that is influenced by gravity. It is usually greater in the lower part of the body than in the part above the level of the heart.

dependent intervention, a therapeutic action based on the written or verbal orders of another health professional.

dependent personality, behavior characterized by excessive or compulsive needs for attention, acceptance, and approval from other people to maintain security and self-esteem.

dependent personality disorder, a persistent mental state characterized by a lack of self-confidence and an inability to function independently.

dependent variable, in research, a factor that is measured to learn the effect of one or more independent variables.

depersonalization /dēpur´sənəlīzā´shən/ [L, *de* + *persona,* mask], a feeling of strangeness or unreality concerning oneself or the environment, often resulting from anxiety or fatigue.

depersonalization disorder, an emotional disturbance characterized by depersonalization feelings in which a dreamlike atmosphere pervades the consciousness. The body may not feel like one's own, and dramatic and important events may be watched with equanimity.

depilation /dep´ilā´shən/ [L, *de* + *pilum,* hair], the removal or extraction of hair from the body, either temporarily by mechanical or chemical means or permanently by electrolysis, which destroys the hair follicle.**—depilate,** *v.*

depilatory /dipil´ətōrē/, **1.** pertaining to a substance or procedure that removes hair. **2.** a depilatory agent.

depilatory techniques [L, *depilare,* to deprive of hair; Gk, *technikos,* skillful], methods of removing unwanted body hair, such as plucking, external application of chemicals, electrolysis, application of melted wax, or laser treatments.

deplete /də·plēt´/ [L, *deplere,* to empty], to empty or unload; to cause depletion.

depletion /də·plē´shən/ [L, *deplere,* to empty], **1.** the act or process of emptying or removing such as of fluid from a body compartment. **2.** an exhausted state resulting from excessive loss of blood.

depolarization /dēpō´lərīzā´shən/, the reduction of a membrane potential to a less negative value.

D

deposit /dəpoz'it/ [L, *de,* from + *ponere* to place], **1.** sediment or dregs. **2.** extraneous inorganic matter collected in the tissues or in a viscus or cavity. **3.** hard or soft material laid down on a tooth surface, such as dental calculus or plaque.

deposition /dep'əzish'ən/ [L, *deponere,* to lay down], in law, sworn pretrial testimony given by a witness in response to oral or written questions and cross-examination.

deposition/testimony, a nursing intervention from the Nursing Interventions Classification (NIC) defined as the provision of recorded sworn testimony for legal proceedings based upon knowledge of the case.

depot /dē'pō, dep'ō/ [Fr, depository], **1.** any area of the body in which drugs or other substances such as fat are stored and from which they can be distributed. **2.** of a drug, injected or implanted to be slowly absorbed into the circulation.

depot injection, an IM injection of a drug in an oil suspension that results in a gradual release of the medication over several days.

depressant /dipres'ənt/ [L, *deprimere,* to press down], **1.** of a drug, tending to decrease the function or activity of a system of the body. **2.** such a drug.

depressed [L, *deprimere,* to press down], **1.** pertaining to a body structure that has been forced below the surface of surrounding parts, as in a skull fracture. **2.** pertaining to a condition in which general body activity is diminished, as in depressed urine output during dehydration. **3.** pertaining to an emotional condition, characterized by emotional dejection, loss of initiative, listlessness, loss of appetite, and concentration difficulty.

depressed fracture, a break in the skull in which bone fragments are pushed below the normal surface of the skull.

depression /dipresh'ən/ [L, *deprimere,* to press down], **1.** a depressed area, hollow, or fossa. **2.** downward or inward displacement. **3.** a decrease of vital functional activity. **4.** a mood disturbance characterized by feelings of sadness, despair, and discouragement resulting from and normally proportionate to some personal loss or tragedy. **5.** an abnormal emotional state characterized by exaggerated feelings of sadness, melancholy, dejection, worthlessness, emptiness, and hopelessness that are inappropriate and out of proportion to reality.—**depressive,** *adj.*

depression level, a nursing outcome from the Nursing Outcomes Classification (NOC) defined as severity of melancholic mood and loss of interest in life events.

depression self-control, a nursing outcome from the Nursing Outcomes Classification (NOC) defined as personal actions to minimize melancholy and maintain interest in life events.

depression with psychotic features [L, *deprimere,* to press down; Gk, *psyche,* mind, *osis,* condition], a type of depressive disorder or mood disorder in which there are psychotic features, usually of a paranoid or somatic nature.

depressive personality disorder, a *DSM-IV* psychiatric disorder characterized by a persistent and pervasive pattern of depressive cognitions and behaviors such as chronic unhappiness, low self-esteem, pessimism, critical and derogatory attitudes toward oneself and others, feelings of guilt or remorse, and an inability to relax or feel enjoyment.

depressive pseudodementia, a term whose use is discouraged as technically incorrect because the cognitive deficits are now believed to be real, if reversible.

depressive reaction, a condition of depressive emotional response to an external situation.

depressor /dipres'ər/ [L, *deprimere,* to press down], any agent that reduces activity when applied to nerves and muscles.

depressor anguli oris, a muscle that is active during frowning, depressing the corner of the mouth.

depressor labii inferioris, a muscle that depresses the lower lip and moves it laterally.

depressor reflex [L, *deprimere,* to press down, *reflectere,* to bend back], a neural mechanism that produces an involuntary vasodilation and fall in arterial BP in response to mechanical stimulation of the carotid sinus.

depressor septi /sep'tī/, one of the three muscles of the nose. It lies between the mucous membrane and the muscular structure of the lip and serves to draw down the ala, constricting the nostril.

deprivation /dep'rivā'shən/ [L, *deprivare,* to deprive], the loss of something considered valuable or necessary by taking it away or denying access to it.

deprivation of sleep effects [L, *deprivare,* to deprive; ME, *slep*; L, *efficere,* to accomplish], the result of interference with a basic physiologic urge to sleep, which appears to be governed by sleep centers in the hypothalamus and reticular activating system. Sleep deprivation results in progressive mental aberrations after 30 to 60 continuous hours. After this point, boring tasks become intolerable, speech begins to be slurred, and performance becomes increasingly poor. After a week of sleep deprivation, symptoms of psychosis may appear.

depth dose [AS, *diop*; Gk, *dosis*, giving], in radiotherapy, the relationship between the dose at any depth from a beam of radiation and the dose at the entrance from that beam.

depth perception, the ability to judge depth or the relative distance of objects in space and to orient one's position in relation to them. Binocular vision is essential to this ability.

depth psychology, any approach to psychology that emphasizes the study of personality and behavior in relation to unconscious motivation.

de Quervain's fracture /dəkərvānz'/ [Fritz de Quervain, Swiss surgeon, 1868–1940], a break in the navicular bone of the hand, with dislocation of the lunate bone.

de Quervain's thyroiditis [Fritz de Quervain; Gk, *thyreos*, shield, *itis*, inflammation], an acute inflammatory condition of the thyroid. It is characterized by swelling and tenderness of the gland; low-grade fever; dysphagia; fatigue; and severe pain in the neck, ears, and jaw. The disorder often occurs after a viral infection of the upper respiratory tract. It tends to remit spontaneously and to recur several times. Treatment may include antiinflammatory medication, such as aspirin or NSAIDs, if the condition continues for more than a few days. Corticosteroids are prescribed for prolonged or severe cases.

der, abbreviation for **derivative chromosome.**

derailment /dirāl'mənt/, a pattern of speech in which incomprehensible, disconnected, and unrelated ideas replace logical and orderly thought.

Dercum's disease /dur'kəmz/ [Francis X. Dercum, U.S. neurologist, 1856–1931], a potentially fatal disorder characterized by painful localized fatty swellings and nerve lesions. The disease mainly affects menopausal women.

dereflection /dē'rəflek'shən/ [L, *de* + *reflectere*, to bend back], a technique of logotherapeutic psychology that is directed to taking a person's mind off a certain goal through a positive redirection to another goal, with emphasis on assets and abilities rather than the problems at hand.

dereistic thought /dē'rē·is'tik/ [L, *de* + *res*, thing], a type of mental activity in which fantasy is not modified by logic, experience, or reality.

derivative /dəriv'ətiv/ [L, *derivare*, to turn away], anything that originates in another substance or object.

derivative chromosome (der), a chromosomal aberration caused by translocation.

derived protein /dirīvd'/, a small protein obtained by enzymatic or chemical hydrolysis of a larger protein source.

derived quantity, any secondary quantity such as volume that is derived from a combination of base quantities such as mass, length, and time.

dermabrasion /dur'məbrā'zhən/ [Gk, *derma*, skin; L, *abradere*, to scrape], a treatment for the removal of superficial scars on the skin by the use of revolving wire brushes or sandpaper. It may be performed to reduce facial scars of severe acne.

Dermacentor /dur'məsen'tər/, a genus of ticks. It includes species that transmit Rocky Mountain spotted fever, tularemia, and brucellosis.

dermal graft [Gk, *derma*, skin, *graphion*, stylus], the transplantation of any living skin tissue that contains dermis and thus is capable of regenerating and secreting sweat and sebum and generating new hair growth.

dermal neurofibroma, a neurofibroma arising within the skin as a small, fleshy nodule that may become pedunculated, overlying a palpable subcutaneous lesion.

dermal papilla [Gk, *derma*, skin; L, *papilla*, nipple], any small elevation in the dermis, such as the elongated alpine papilla seen in psoriasis.

dermatitis /dur'mətī'tis/ [Gk, *derma* + *itis*, inflammation], an inflammatory condition of the skin. Various cutaneous eruptions occur and may be unique to a particular allergen, disease, or infection.

dermatitis herpetiformis, a chronic, severely pruritic skin disease with symmetrically located groups of red papulovesicular, vesicular, bullous, or urticarial lesions.

dermatocellulitis /dur'mətōsel'yəlī'tis/, an inflammation of the skin and subcutaneous connective tissue.

dermatocyst /dur'mətōsist'/, a cystic tumor of cutaneous tissues.

dermatofibroma /dur'mətōfībrō'mə/ *pl.* **dermatofibromas, dermatofibromata** [Gk, *derma*; L, *fibra*, fiber, *oma*, tumor], a cutaneous nodule that is painless, round, firm, gray or red, elevated, and commonly found on the extremities.

dermatofibrosarcoma /-fī'brōsärkō'mə/ [Gk, *derma*, skin; L, *fibra*, fiber; Gk, *sarx*, flesh, *oma*, tumor], a specific type of fibrous tumor of the skin.

dermatoglyphics /dur'mətōglif'iks/ [Gk, *derma* + *glyphe*, a carving], the study of the skin ridge patterns on fingers, toes, palms of hands, and soles of feet. The patterns are used as a basis of identification and also have diagnostic value because of associations between certain patterns and chromosomal anomalies.

dermatologic agent /dur'mətoloj'ik/, a drug used to treat reactions or disorders of the skin.

dermatologist /dur′mətol′əjist/, a physician specializing in the skin and its properties of health and disease.

dermatology /-ol′əjē/ [Gk, *derma* + *logos,* science], the study of the skin, including its anatomic, physiologic, and pathologic characteristics and the diagnosis and treatment of skin disorders.

dermatoma /dur′mətō′mə/, **1.** a skin tumor. **2.** a patch of abnormally thick skin.

dermatome /dur′mətōm/ [Gk, *derma* + *temnein,* to cut], **1.** in embryology, the mesodermal layer in the early developing embryo that gives rise to the dermal layers of the skin. **2.** in surgery, an instrument used to cut thin slices of skin for grafting. **3.** an area on the surface of a body innervated by afferent fibers from one spinal root.

dermatomycosis /dur′mətō′mīkō′sis/ [Gk, *derma* + *mykes,* fungus, *osis,* condition], a superficial fungal infection of the skin, characteristically found on parts that are moist and protected by clothing such as the groin or feet. It is caused by a dermatophyte.—**dermatomycotic,** *adj.*

dermatomyositis /dur′mətōmī′ōsī′tis/ [Gk, *derma* + *mys,* muscle, *itis,* inflammation], a disease of the connective tissues, characterized by pruritic or eczematous inflammation of the skin and tenderness and weakness of the muscles. Muscle tissue is destroyed, and loss is often so severe that the person may become unable to walk or to perform simple tasks. Swelling of the eyelids and face and loss of weight are common manifestations.

dermatopathy /dur′mətop′əthē/, any disorder of the skin.

Dermatophagoides /-fagoi′dēz/ [Gk, *derma* + *phagein,* to eat, *eidos,* form], a genus of household dust mite responsible for allergic reactions in sensitive individuals.

dermatophyte /dur′mətōfīt′, dərmat′əfīt/, any of several fungi that cause parasitic skin disease in humans.

dermatophytid /dur′mətōf′itid, dur′mətōfī′tid/ [Gk, *derma* + *phyton,* plant], an allergic skin reaction characterized by small vesicles and associated with dermatomycosis.

dermatophytosis /dur′mətō′fītō′sis/ [Gk, *derma* + *phyton,* plant, *osis,* condition], a superficial fungus infection of the skin caused by *Microsporum, Epidermophyton,* or *Trichophyton* species of dermatophyte. On the trunk and upper extremities it is commonly called "ringworm" infection and is characterized by round or oval scaly patches with slightly raised borders and clearing centers. On the feet small vesicles, cracking, itching, scaling, and often secondary bacterial infections occur and are commonly called "athlete's foot."

dermatoplasty /dur′mətōplas′tē/, a surgical procedure in which skin tissue is transplanted to a body surface damaged by disease or injury.

dermatosclerosis /-sklərō′sis/ [Gk, *derma* + *sklerosis,* hardening], a skin disease characterized by fibrous thickening of the skin.

dermatosis /dur′mətō′sis/ [Gk, *derma* + *osis,* condition], any disorder of the skin, especially those not associated with inflammation.

dermatosis papulosa nigra, a common condition in individuals with darkly pigmented skin. It consists of multiple tiny, benign skin-colored or hyperpigmented papules on the face, neck, and cheeks.

dermis, the layer of the skin just below the epidermis, consisting of papillary and reticular layers and containing blood and lymphatic vessels, nerves and nerve endings, glands, and hair follicles.

dermoid /dur′moid/ [Gk, *derma* + *eidos,* form], pertaining to the skin.

dermoid cyst, a tumor, derived from embryonal tissues, consisting of a fibrous wall lined with epithelium and a cavity containing fatty material, hair, teeth, bits of bone, and cartilage.

derotation brace /dē′rōtā′shən/, a customized orthosis that provides stability at the knee joint. It consists of a single-joint hinged bar on one side and a rotating dial pad on the opposite side.

DES, abbreviation for **diethylstilbestrol.**

desalination /dēsal′inā′shən/ [L, *de,* from, *sal,* salt], the process of removing salt from water or other substances.

desaturation /dēsach′ərā′shən/ [L, *de,* from, *saturare,* to fill], the formation of an unsaturated chemical compound from a saturated one.

Descemet's membrane /desemāz′/ [Jean Descemet, French physician, 1732–1810], a deep layer of the cornea, between the substantia propria externally and the endothelium internally.

descendens /disen′dənz/, **1.** the descending branch of the hypoglossal nerve. **2.** the cervicalis nerve formed by branches of the second and third cervical nerves.

descending aorta /disen′ding/ [L, *descendere,* to descend; Gk, *aerein,* to raise], the main portion of the aorta, consisting of the thoracic aorta and the abdominal aorta, which continues from the aortic arch into the trunk of the body. It supplies many structures, including the esophagus, lymph glands, ribs, stomach, liver, spleen intestines, kidneys, reproductive organs, and, eventually, the lower limbs.

descending colon, the segment of the colon that extends from the end of the transverse colon at the splenic flexure on the left side of the abdomen down to the beginning of the sigmoid colon in the pelvis.

descending myelitis [L, *descendere,* to descend; Gk, *myelos,* marrow, *itis,* inflammation], a form of myelitis in which the pathologic changes spread downward along the spinal cord.

descending neuritis [L, *descendere,* to descend; Gk, *neuron,* nerve, *itis,* inflammation], a form of neuritis that spreads downward from the upper part of the nervous system.

descending neuropathy [L, *descendere,* to descend; Gk, *neuron,* nerve, *pathos,* disease], a disease of the peripheral nervous system that spreads downward from the upper part of the body.

descending tract [L, *descendere,* to descend + *tractus*], a nerve tract in the spinal cord that carries impulses away from the brain axis of the body or body part.

descensus /disen′səs/, the process of falling or descending.

descriptive anatomy /diskrip′tiv/ [L, *describere,* to write], the study of the morphologic characteristics of the body by systems, such as the vascular system and the nervous system.

descriptive embryology, the study of the changes that occur in cells, tissues, and organs during the progressive stages of prenatal development.

descriptive epidemiology, the first stage of epidemiologic investigation. It focuses on describing disease distribution by characteristics relating to time, place, and person.

descriptive psychiatry, the study of external, readily observable behavior.

descriptive statistics, statistics that measure and describe characteristics of groups without drawing inferences about the population in general.

DES daughters, a group of women with increased susceptibility to cancer of the vagina and other reproductive organs because their mothers were given an estrogen medication, diethylstilbestrol (DES), from the 1940s through the 1960s to prevent miscarriage. Several other abnormalities have been reported. Sons of women who took DES have an increased risk of undescended testes or other genital disorders.

Desenex, a trademark for various over-the-counter products containing antifungal agents.

desensitize /dēsen′sitīz/ [L, *de* + *sentire,* to feel], 1. in immunology, to render an individual insensitive or less sensitive to any of the various antigens. 2. in psychiatry, to relieve an emotionally disturbed person of the stress of phobias and neuroses by encouraging discussion of the anxieties

and the stressful experiences that cause the emotional problems involved. 3. in dentistry, to remove or reduce the painful response of vital exposed dentin to irritating substances and temperature changes.

Desferal Mesylate, a trademark for an iron-chelating agent (deferoxamine mesylate).

desiccant /des′ikənt/ [L, *desiccare,* to dry thoroughly], any agent or procedure that promotes drying or causes a substance to dry up.

desiccate /des′ikāt/, 1. to dry thoroughly. 2. to preserve by drying, especially food.

designer drugs [L, *de* + *signare,* to mark], synthetic organic compounds that are designed as analogs of illicit drugs, with the same opioid or other dangerous effects. Because designer drugs are generally not listed as controlled substances by the U.S. Drug Enforcement Agency, prosecution of manufacturers, distributors, or users is frequently difficult.

desipramine hydrochloride /desip′rəmēn/, a tricyclic antidepressant prescribed in the treatment of mental depression and as adjunctive therapy for the treatment of chronic pain.

desirudin, an anticoagulant agent used as prophylaxis for deep vein thrombosis in those undergoing hip replacement.

desloratadine /des′lärat′ädēn/, a nonsedating antihistamine (H_1 receptor antagonist) used for treatment of allergic rhinitis and chronic idiopathic urticaria.

desmoid tumor /dez′moid/ [Gk, *desmos,* band, *eidos,* form], a fibrous neoplasm that may occur in the head, neck, upper arm, abdomen, or lower extremities. The tumor is usually a firm, rubbery mass.

desmopressin acetate /dez′mōpres′in/, a synthetic antidiuretic analog of arginine vasopressin, the naturally occurring human antidiuretic hormone. It is prescribed as an antidiuretic in the treatment of diabetes insipidus and primary nocturnal enuresis and is used to control bleeding in hemophilia A and mild von Willebrand's disease.

desmosis /dezmō′sis/, any disease of the connective tissue.

desmosome /dez′məsōm/ [Gk, *desmos,* band, *soma,* body], a small, circular, dense area within the intercellular bridge that forms the site of adhesion between certain epithelial cells, especially the stratified epithelium of the epidermis.

desogestrel /des′ojes′trel/, a progestational agent having little androgenic activity. It is used in combination with an estrogen component as an oral contraceptive.

Desonate, a trademark for desonide.

desonide, a rarely used topical antiinflammatory used to treat atopic dermatitis.

desoximetasone /desok'simet'əsōn/, a topical corticosteroid prescribed for the treatment of skin inflammation.

Desoxyn, a trademark for a CNS stimulant (methamphetamine hydrochloride).

despair, a feeling of hopelessness.

desquamation /des'kwəmā'shən/ [L, *desquamare,* to take off scales], a normal process in which the cornified layer of the epidermis is sloughed in fine scales.—**desquamate,** *v.,* **desquamative** /deskwam'ətiv/, *adj.*

desquamative gingivitis /deskwam'ətiv/, a gingival inflammation characterized by peeling of the epithelium. In its chronic state, it is most frequently associated with the hormonal changes of menopause.

desquamative interstitial pneumonia (DIP), a respiratory disease characterized by an accumulation of cellular matter in the alveoli and bronchial tubes. It leads to a fibrotic condition with symptoms of coughing, chest pain, weight loss, and dyspnea.

destructive aggression /distruk'tiv/ [L, *destruere,* to destroy, *aggressio,* an attack], an act of hostility unnecessary for self-protection or self-preservation that is directed at an external object or person.

destructive interference, a phenomenon that results when propagated waves are out of phase, so that maximum molecular compression for one wave occurs at the same point as maximum rarefaction for the second wave, causing the two waves to cancel each other out.

destructive lesion [L, *destruere,* to destroy, *laesio,* a hurting], a disorder that leads to the damage or necrosis of an organ or tissue.

desudation /des'ōōdā'shən/, profuse sweating. It is sometimes followed by a skin rash.

desynchrony, a condition in which the environmental cues and patterns, such as sleeping and eating, conflict with an individual's existing pattern, as in jet lag.

Desyrel, a trademark for an antidepressant (trazodone).

detection bias /ditek'shən/, a potential artifact in epidemiologic data caused by the use of a particular diagnostic technique or type of equipment.

detector /ditek'ter/, a device by which an object or condition can be discovered.

detergent /ditur'jənt/ [L, *detergere,* to cleanse], **1.** a cleansing agent. **2.** in respiratory therapy, a wetting agent that is administered to mediate the removal of respiratory tract secretions from airway walls.

deterioration /ditir'ē·ərā'shən/ [L, *deterior,* worse], a condition that is gradually worsening.

determinant evolution /ditur'minənt/ [L, *determinare,* to limit], the idea that evolution progresses according to a predetermined course.

determinant of occlusion, one of the classifiable factors that influence proper closure of the teeth. Common fixed factors are intercondylar distance, anatomic characteristics, mandibular centricity, and the relationship of the jaws. The common changeable factors are tooth shape, tooth position, and vertical dimensions of occlusion, cusp height, and fossa depth.

determinate cleavage /ditur'minit/, mitotic division of the fertilized ovum into blastomeres that are each destined to form a specific part of the embryo. Damage to or destruction of any of these cells results in malformation of an organism.

detoxification /dētok'sifikā'shən/ [L, *de from*; Gk, *toxikon,* poison; L, *facere,* to make], the removal of a poison or its effects from a patient.

detoxification service, a hospital service providing treatment to diminish or remove from a patient's body the toxic effects of chemical substances, such as alcohol or drugs, usually as an initial step in the treatment of a chemical-dependent person. The service may also be used to remove poisonous substances to which a person may have been exposed.

detoxification therapy, cleansing of the body through nutritional action, centering on GI function. It is used to assist in the transition from an unhealthy life-style to a healthier one by an improved selection of nutrients and elimination of some modern-day abuses, such as nicotine.

detoxify /dētok'sifī/ [L, *de,* from; Gk, *toxikon,* poison], to make a poisonous substance harmless or to overcome the effects of a poison.

detrition /dətrish'ən/ [L, *de,* from, *terere* to wear], a wearing away, as of the teeth, by friction.

detrusor areflexia, failure of the detrusor muscle to respond to stimuli, usually owing to a lesion of a lower motoneuron, resulting in failure to empty the bladder completely on urination.

detrusor leak point pressure, the level of pressure at which leakage of urine through the urethra occurs as the bladder fills without an increase in abdominal pressure. It is a measure of both strength of the urethral sphincters and compliance of the detrusor urinae muscle.

detrusor muscle of bladder, the bundles of smooth muscle fibers forming the muscular coat of the urinary bladder, which are arranged in a longitudinal and a circular layer and, on contraction, serve to expel urine.

detrusor overactivity, involuntary contractions of the detrusor urinae muscle from any cause.

detrusor pressure, the pressure exerted inwards by the detrusor urinae muscles of the bladder wall, one of the components of the total intravesical pressure.

detrusor-sphincter dyssynergia, contraction of the sphincter muscle of the urethra at the same time the detrusor muscle of the bladder is contracting, resulting in obstruction of normal urinary outflow.

detrusor urinae muscle /ditrōō′zər/ [L, *detruder,* to thrust; Gk, *ouron,* urine; L, *musculus*], a complex of longitudinal fibers that form the external layer of the muscular coat of the bladder.

deuteranomaly /dōō′terănom′ālē/, a type of anomalous trichromatic vision in which the second, or green-sensitive, cones have decreased sensitivity. It is the most common color vision deficiency.

deuteranopsia /dōō′terănop′se·ă/, a dichromacy characterized by retention of the sensory mechanism for 2 hues only (blue and yellow).

deuterium (²H) /dyōōtir′ē·əm/ [Gk, *deuteros,* second], a stable isotope of the hydrogen atom, used as a kinetic tracer.

deutoplasm /dōō′təplaz′əm/ [Gk, *deuteros + plasma,* something formed], the inactive elements of the cytoplasm, primarily the stored nutritive material contained in yolk.

DEV, abbreviation for *duck embryo vaccine.*

devascularization /dēvas′kyələr̄īzā′shən/ [L, *de,* from, *vasculum,* small vessel], the drawing away of blood from a body part or the stoppage of blood flow to it or the traumatic disruption of vascular supply to an organ.

developer fog, a defect in a radiographic image characterized by insufficient contrast. Causes include incorrect developer temperature, concentration, and immersion time.

development [Fr, *developper,* to unfold], **1.** the gradual process of change and differentiation from a simple to a more advanced level of complexity. **2.** in biology, the series of events that occur within an organism from the time of fertilization of the ovum to the adult stage.—**developmental,** *adj.*

developmental age (DA) /divel′əpmen′təl/, an expression of a child's maturational progress stated in age and determined by standardized measurements, as of body size and dimensions; by social and psychologic functioning; by motor skills; and by mental and aptitude tests.

developmental agraphia, a deficiency in a child's ability to learn to form letters and write. Other learning is normal, and the child usually has no musculoskeletal or neurologic problems.

developmental anatomy, the study of the differentiation and growth of an organism from one cell to birth.

developmental anomaly, any congenital defect that results from interference with the normal growth and differentiation of the fetus.

developmental apraxia [L, *developper,* development; Gk, *a,* not, *prassein,* to do], a condition of ineffective motor planning and execution in children caused by immaturity of their CNS.

developmental care, a nursing intervention from the Nursing Interventions Classification (NIC) defined as structuring the environment and providing care in response to the behavioral cues and states of the preterm infant.

developmental crisis, severe, usually transient stress that occurs when a person is unable to complete the tasks of a psychosocial stage of development and is therefore unable to move on to the next stage.

developmental disability (DD), a pathologic condition that starts developing before 18 years of age.

developmental disorder, a form of mental retardation that develops in some children after they have progressed normally for the first 3 or 4 years of life.

developmental dysplasia of the hip (DDH), instability of the hip joint leading to dislocation in the neonatal period. Usually there is laxity of the hip ligaments. Although it may be associated with various neuromuscular disorders, such as myelodysplasia, or occur in utero, it most commonly occurs in neurologically normal infants and is multifactorial in origin.

developmental dyspraxia, a disorder of sensory integration characterized by an impaired ability to plan skilled, nonhabitual coordinated movements.

developmental enhancement: adolescent, a nursing intervention from the Nursing Interventions Classification (NIC) defined as facilitating optimal physical, cognitive, social, and emotional growth of individuals during the transition from childhood to adulthood.

developmental enhancement: child, a nursing intervention from the Nursing Interventions Classification (NIC) defined as facilitating or teaching parents/caregivers to facilitate the optimal gross motor, fine motor, language, cognitive, social, and emotional growth of preschool and school-aged children.

developmental groove, a fine, recessed line in the enamel of a tooth that marks the union of the lobes of the crown in its development.

developmental guidance, comprehensive orthopedic control over the growth of the

D

jaws and the eruption of the teeth. Guidance may be needed at various developmental stages throughout the entire growth and maturation of the face, beginning at the earliest detection of a developing malformation.

developmental horizon, any of 25 stages in the development of the human embryo from the one-cell stage at conception to the morphologically and physiologically complex organism at the end of the seventh week of gestation.

developmental model, 1. a conceptual framework devised to be used as a guide in making a diagnosis, understanding a developmental process, and forming a prognosis for continued development. **2.** in nursing, a conceptual framework describing four stages, or processes, of development in the patient during therapy. In the first stage, called *orientation,* the patient begins a relationship with the nurse or other therapist and begins to clarify the problem with his or her help. In the second stage, called *identification,* the patient develops a sense of closeness and attachment to the therapist. In the third stage, called *exploitation,* the patient makes full use of the nursing services offered, begins to assume some control of the interactions, and becomes more independent. During the last stage, called *resolution,* the therapeutic relationship is terminated; the patient is independent and no longer needs the nurse or therapist.

developmental physiology, the study of the physiologic processes as they relate to embryonic development.

developmental quotient (DQ), the numeric expression of a child's developmental level as measured by dividing the developmental age by the chronologic age and multiplying by 100.

developmental sequence [Fr, *developper;* L, *sequi,* to follow], the order in which structure and function change during the process of growth and development of an organism.

developmental task, a physical or cognitive skill that a person must accomplish during a particular age period to continue development. An example is walking, which precedes the development of a sense of autonomy in the toddler period.

developmental theories of aging, concepts based on the identification of traits and characteristics that may be developed early in life or may change emphasis at different stages of development.

development: late adulthood, a nursing outcome from the Nursing Outcomes Classification (NOC) defined as the cognitive, psychosocial, and moral progression from 65 years of age and older.

development: middle adulthood, a nursing outcome from the Nursing Outcomes Classification (NOC) defined as the cognitive, psychosocial, and moral progression from 40 through 64 years of age.

development: young adulthood, a nursing outcome from the Nursing Outcomes Classification (NOC) defined as the cognitive, psychosocial, and moral progression from 18 through 39 years of age.

deviance /dē'vē-əns/ [L, *deviare,* to turn aside], behavior that is contrary to the accepted standards of a community or culture.

deviant /dē'vē-ənt/ [L, *deviare,* to turn aside], pertaining to a person or object that departs from what is considered normal or standard.

deviant behavior, actions that exceed the usual limits of accepted behavior and involve failure to comply with the social norm of the group.

deviate /dē'vē-it/ [L, *deviare,* to turn aside], **1.** a person or an act that varies from that which is considered standard or that which is within a statistic norm. **2.** to vary from that which is considered standard or within a statistic norm.—**deviant,** *adj.,* **deviation,** *n.*

deviated septum, a shifted medial partition of the nasal cavity, a condition affecting many adults. The nasal septum more commonly shifts to the left during normal growth, but severe deflection of the septum may significantly obstruct the nasal passages and result in infection, sinusitis, shortness of breath, headache, or recurring nosebleeds.

deviation from normal, a quality, characteristic, symptom, or clinical finding that is different from what is commonly regarded as normal, such as an elevated temperature, multiple gestation, or an extra digit.

deviation of tongue [L, *deviare,* to turn aside; AS, *tunge*], a tendency of the tongue to turn away from the midline when extended or protruded. The condition is associated with a hypoglossal nerve defect, and the tongue deviates to the side of the injured nerve.

device /divīs'/ [OFr, *deviser,* to divide], an item other than a drug that has application in the healing arts. Devices include orthopedic appliances, crutches, artificial heart valves, pacemakers, prostheses, wheelchairs, cervical collars, hearing aids, and eyeglasses.

Devic's disease /dəvēks'/ [Eugène Devic, French physician, 1869–1930], combined, but not usually clinically simultaneous, demyelination of the optic nerve and the spinal cord, marked by diminution of vision and sometimes blindness, flaccid paralysis of the extremities, and sensory and genitourinary disturbances.

devil's claw, a perennial herb, *Harpagophytum procumbens*. Its dried tubular secondary roots and lateral tubers are used for dyspepsia, loss of appetite, and rheumatism. It is also used in homeopathy for rheumatism and in folk medicine for a wide variety of disorders.

devitalized /dēvī′təlīzd/, pertaining to tissues with a reduced oxygen supply and blood flow.

dewar /dyōō′ər/, a double chamber used to maintain the temperature of superconducting magnet coils near absolute zero. The outer chamber is filled with liquid nitrogen at a temperature of about −196° C (−321° F), and the inner chamber is filled with liquid helium at a temperature of −270° C (−454° F). A dewar is part of MRI equipment.

dew point /dyōō/, the temperature at which air becomes saturated with water vapor and the water vapor condenses to liquid. In aerosol therapy, water may condense on containers, tubing, and other surfaces when the dew point is reached.

DEXA, abbreviation for **dual-energy x-ray absorptiometry.**

dexamethasone /dek′səmeth′əsōn/, a long-acting synthetic adrenocorticoid with intense antiinflammatory activity and mineralocorticoid activity, prescribed topically and systemically in the treatment of inflammatory conditions.

dexamethasone suppression test (DST), a test of the blood or urine after administration of dexamethasone, a synthetic steroid similar to cortisol, that is used to diagnose Cushing's syndrome.

dexchlorpheniramine maleate /deks′klôr fənir′əmēn mal′ē·it/, an antihistamine prescribed in the treatment of hypersensitivity reactions, including rhinitis, skin rash, and pruritus.

Dexedrine, a trademark for a CNS stimulant with indications for narcolepsy and ADD with hyperactivity (dextroamphetamine sulfate).

dexmedetomidine, an alpha-2-adrenoceptor agonist sedative prescribed to sedate mechanically ventilated and intubated patients in the ICU.

dexmethylphenidate, a CNS stimulant used to treat attention deficit hyperactivity disorder.

dexrazoxane, a cardioprotective agent prescribed in the protection of women from heart problems caused by doxorubicin treatment of breast cancer.

dexter (D) /deks′tər/ [L, *dexter,* right], right side, right.

dexterity /dekster′itē/ [L, *dexteritas*], skillfulness in the use of one's hands or body.

dextrad /deks′trad/ [L, *dexter,* right], toward the right side.

dextrad writing /deks′trad/ [L, *dexter,* right; ME, *writen*], writing that moves from left to right.

dextran fermentation /dek′strən/ [L, *dexter,* right; *fermentare,* to cause to rise], the conversion of dextrose to dextran by the action of *Leuconostoc mesenteroides* dextran (LMD) bacteria.

dextran preparation, any of a group of solutions containing polysaccharides, water, and, in some preparations, electrolytes. These solutions are used as plasma volume extenders in cases of hypovolemia from hemorrhage, dehydration, or another cause.

dextrin, a glucose polymer formed by the hydrolysis of starch. It is a tasteless, colorless, gummy substance, soluble in water. Dextrin is an intermediate during the conversion of starch into monosaccharides, such as glucose.

dextroamphetamine sulfate /deks′trō·am fet′əmēn/, a CNS stimulant prescribed in the treatment of narcolepsy, hyperkinetic disorders, and ADD in children and as an anorexiant in treating exogenous obesity.

dextrocardia /-kär′dē·ə/, the location of the heart in the right hemithorax, either as a result of displacement by disease or as a congenital defect.

dextrocardiogram /-kär′dē·ōgram′/ [L, *dexter,* right; Gk, *kardia,* heart, *gramma,* record], an ECG made from a unipolar electrode facing the right ventricle, producing a small R wave and a large S wave.

dextromethorphanhydrobromide/-methôr′ fən/, an antitussive derived from morphine but lacking opioid effects, prescribed for the suppression of nonproductive cough.

dextrose /dek′strōs/ [L, *dexter,* right], glucose available in various solutions for IV administration. It is prescribed for the treatment of calorie deficit, for hypoglycemia, and in solution for fluid deficit.

dextrose and sodium chloride injection, a fluid, nutrient, and electrolyte replenisher. It is available for parenteral use in a variety of concentrations.

df, abbreviation for **degrees of freedom.**

DFA-TP test, abbreviation for *direct fluorescent antibody*–Treponema pallidum test.

dg, abbreviation for **decigram.**

D gene, one of a set of genes lying between the V and J genes, which code for the D region of heavy chain or for the beta or delta chain of the T-cell receptor.

D.H.E. 45, a trademark for a vasconstrictor that works primarily by stimulating alpha-adrenergic receptors (dihydroergotamine mesylate).

DHFSS, abbreviation for **dengue hemorrhagic fever shock syndrome.**

DHHS, abbreviation for **Department of Health and Human Services.**

dhobie itch /dō′bē/ [Hindi, *dhobie,* laundryman; AS, *giccan*], a fungal infection, such as jock itch or athlete's foot, that attacks moist parts of the body.

DHT, abbreviation for **dihydrotestosterone.**

DiaBeta, a trademark for an oral antidiabetic drug (glyBURIDE).

diabetes /dī′ǝbē′tēz/ [Gk, *diabainein,* to pass through], a clinical condition characterized by the excessive excretion of urine. The excess may be caused by a deficiency of antidiuretic hormone as in diabetes insipidus, or it may be the polyuria resulting from the hyperglycemia that occurs in DM.

diabetes insipidus /insip′idǝs/, a metabolic disorder caused by injury of the neurohypophyseal system. It is characterized by copious excretion of urine and excessive thirst, caused by deficient production or secretion of the antidiuretic hormone (ADH) or inability of the kidney tubules to respond to ADH. Rarely the symptoms are self-induced by an excessive water intake.

diabetes mellitus (DM) /mǝlī′tǝs/, a complex disorder of carbohydrate, fat, and protein metabolism that is primarily a result of a deficiency or complete lack of insulin secretion by the beta cells of the pancreas or resistance to insulin. Type 1 DM includes patients with diabetes caused by an autoimmune process, dependent on insulin to prevent ketosis. This group was previously called type I, insulin-dependent DM (IDDM), juvenile-onset diabetes, brittle diabetes, or ketosis-prone diabetes. Patients with type 2 DM are those previously designated as having type II, non-insulin-dependent DM (NIDDM), maturity-onset diabetes, adult-onset diabetes, ketosis-resistant diabetes, or stable diabetes. The onset of type 1 DM is sudden in children. Type 2 diabetes often begins insidiously. Those with gestational DM are women in whom glucose intolerance develops during pregnancy. Other types of diabetes are associated with a pancreatic disease, hormonal changes, adverse effects of drugs, or genetic or other anomalies. A fourth subclass, the impaired glucose tolerance group, also called prediabetes, includes persons whose blood glucose levels are abnormal although not sufficiently above the normal range to be diagnosed as having diabetes. Contributing factors to the development of diabetes are heredity, obesity, sedentary life style, high-fat low-fiber diets, hypertension, and aging.

diabetes mellitus autoantibody panel, a blood test to screen for diabetes in relatives of insulin-dependent DM patients.

diabetes self-management, a nursing outcome from the Nursing Outcomes Classification (NOC) defined as personal actions to manage diabetes mellitus, its treatment, and prevent disease progression.

diabetic /dī′ǝbet′ik/, **1.** pertaining to diabetes. **2.** affected with diabetes. **3.** a person who has diabetes mellitus.

diabetic acidosis [Gk, *diabainein,* to pass through; L, *acidus,* acid; Gk, *osis,* condition], a type of acidosis that may occur in DM as a result of excessive production of ketone bodies during oxidation of fatty acids.

diabetic amaurosis [Gk, *diabainein,* to pass through, *amaurorein,* to darken], blindness associated with DM, caused by a proliferative hemorrhagic form of retinopathy that is characterized by capillary microaneurysms and hard or waxy exudates. Cataracts are also common in type 2 diabetes; in type 1 diabetes, snowflake cataracts may progress until the entire lens is milky white.

diabetic coma, a life-threatening condition occurring in persons with DM. It is caused by undiagnosed diabetes; inadequate treatment; failure to take prescribed insulin; excessive food intake; or, most frequently, infection, surgery, trauma, or other stressors that increase the body's need for insulin. Without insulin to metabolize glucose, fats are used for energy, resulting in ketone waste accumulation and metabolic acidosis. The body's effort to counteract acidosis depletes the alkali reserve; causes a loss of sodium, chloride, potassium, and water; increases respiratory exhalation of carbon dioxide (Kussmaul breathing) and urinary excretion; and leads to dehydration and generalized hypoxia. Warning signs of diabetic coma include a dull headache, fatigue, inordinate thirst, epigastric pain, nausea, vomiting, parched lips, flushed face, and sunken eyes. The temperature usually rises and then falls. The systolic BP drops, and circulatory collapse may occur.

diabetic diet, a diet prescribed in the treatment of type 2 DM. It usually contains limited amounts of simple sugars or readily digestible carbohydrates and amounts of proteins, complex carbohydrates, and unsaturated fats similar to those recommended for the general public. Dietary regulation depends on the severity of the disease and on the type and extent of insulin therapy.

diabetic foot and leg care, the special attention given to prevent the circulatory disorders and infections that frequently occur in the lower extremities of diabetic patients. The patient's legs and feet are examined daily for signs of dry, scaly, red, itching, or cracked skin; blisters; corns; calluses; abrasions; infection; blueness and swelling around varicosities; and thickened, discolored nails. The feet are bathed daily in tepid water with mild or superfatted soap and are dried gently but thoroughly with a soft towel. A lanolin-based lotion is then applied.

diabetic gangrene [Gk, *diabainein,* to pass through, *gaggraina*], gangrene, usually involving the lower extremities, that develops secondary to sensory peripheral neuropathy and peripheral vascular disease complications related to the diabetic disease process.

diabetic glycosuria [Gk, *diabainein,* to pass through; *glykys,* sweet, *ouron,* urine], excessive excretion of glucose into the urine as an effect of poorly controlled DM.

diabetic ketoacidosis (DKA), an acute, life-threatening complication of uncontrolled DM. In this condition urinary loss of water, potassium, ammonium, and sodium results in hypovolemia, electrolyte imbalance, extremely high blood glucose levels, and breakdown of free fatty acids, causing acidosis, often with coma.

diabetic neuropathy, a noninflammatory disease process associated with DM and characterized by sensory and/or motor disturbances in the peripheral nervous system. Patients commonly experience degeneration of sensory nerves and pathways. Early symptoms, which include pain and loss of reflexes in the legs, may occur in patients with only mild hyperglycemia. Diabetes is associated with a wide range of neuropathies, including mononeuritis multiplex, compression and entrapment mononeuropathies, cranial neuropathies, and autonomic and small fiber neuropathies. Differential diagnosis is difficult because not all sensorimotor neuropathies are caused by diabetes.

diabetic polyneuritis, an inflammation involving many nerves. It usually occurs as a complication in long-term cases of DM.

diabetic polyneuropathy, a long-term complication of DM in which a number of nerves are involved at the same time. CNS, autonomic, and peripheral nerves may be affected. Neuropathic ulcers commonly develop on the feet.

diabetic retinopathy, a disorder of retinal blood vessels. It is characterized by capillary microaneurysms, hemorrhage, exudates, and the formation of highly permeable new vessels. The disorder occurs most frequently in patients with long-standing poorly controlled DM.

diabetic tabes, a wasting condition associated with diabetic peripheral neuropathy. It may be accompanied by sharp pain, muscle weakness, atrophy of intrinsic foot muscles, and weakness of the toes' extensors and flexors. It may lead to footdrop because of ankle weakness.

diabetic treatment, management of DM by means of a controlled carbohydrate low-fat meal plan, insulin injections, exercise/activity, blood glucose level monitoring, and oral agents such as insulin secretagogues, alpha-glucosiderase inhibitors, meglitinides, biguanides, and insulin sensitizers (for patients with type 2 DM).

diabetic vulvovaginitis [Gk, *diabainein,* to pass through; L, *vulva,* wrapper, *vagina,* sheath; Gk, *itis,* inflammation], a form of mycotic inflammation of the vulva and vagina that is associated with diabetes.

diabetic xanthoma, an eruption of yellow papules or plaques on the skin in uncontrolled DM. The lesion disappears as the metabolic functions are stabilized and the disease is controlled.

diabetogenic state /dī′əbet′ōjen′ik/, a health condition manifested by signs and symptoms of diabetes.

Diabinese, a trademark for an oral antidiabetic (chlorproPAMIDE).

diacet, abbreviation for a *diacetate anion.*

diacondylar fracture /dī′əkon′dilər/ [Gk, *dia,* through, *kondylos,* knuckle; L, *fracturà,* break], any fracture that runs across the line of a condyle.

diadochokinesia /dī′ad′ōkōkīnē′zhə/ [Gk, *diadochos,* successor, *kinesis,* motion], the normal ability of the muscles to move a limb alternately in opposite directions by flexion and extension.

diagnose /dī′agnōs/, to determine the type and cause of a health condition on the basis of signs and symptoms of the patient; data obtained from laboratory analysis of fluid, tissue specimens, and other tests; and family and occupational background information, such as recent injuries or exposure to toxic substances.

diagnosis /dī′agnō′sis/ *pl.* **diagnoses** [Gk, *dia* + *gnosis,* knowledge], **1.** identification of a disease or condition by a scientific evaluation of physical signs, symptoms, history, laboratory test results, and procedures. **2.** the art of naming a disease or condition.—**diagnostic,** *adj.,* **diagnose,** *v.*

diagnosis by exclusion [Gk, *dia,* through, *gnosis,* knowledge; L, *excludere,* to shut out], diagnosis made by eliminating other possible causes of disease symptoms.

diagnosis-related group (DRG), a group of patients classified for measuring a medical facility's delivery of care. The classifications, used to determine Medicare payments for inpatient care, are based on primary and secondary diagnosis, primary and secondary procedures, age, and length of hospitalization.

diagnostic /dī′agnos′tik/, pertaining to a diagnosis.

Diagnostic and Statistical Manual of Mental Disorders (DSM), a manual, published by the American Psychiatric Association, listing the official diagnostic classifications of mental disorders. The *DSM* recommends the use of a multiaxial evaluation system as a holistic diagnostic approach. It consists of five axes, each of which refers to a different class of information, including mental and physical data. Axes I and II include all of the mental disorders, classified broadly as clinical syndromes and personality disorders; axis III contains physical disorders and conditions; and axes IV and V provide a coded outline of supplemental information that may be useful for planning individual treatment and predicting its outcome. Each of the classifications of the mental disorders contains a code that provides a reference to the WHO *International Classification of Diseases (ICD).*

diagnostic anesthesia, a procedure in which analgesia is induced to a depth adequate to permit comfortable performance of moderately painful diagnostic procedures of short duration.

diagnostician /dī′agnostish′ən/, a person skilled and trained in making diagnoses.

diagnostic medical sonographer, an allied health professional who provides patient services, using diagnostic ultrasound under the supervision of a doctor of medicine or osteopathy responsible for the use and interpretation of ultrasound procedures. The sonographer assists the physician in gathering sonographic data necessary to reach diagnostic decisions.

diagnostic molecular scientist, an allied health professional who performs diagnostic tests on various specimen types after determining how the specimens will be handled.

diagnostic peritoneal lavage (DPL), a procedure used to detect intraabdominal bleeding or viscus perforation after abdominal trauma. The open or operative approach allows direct visual examination of the peritoneum when the catheter is inserted. Gastric and bladder decompression must precede performance of DPL.

diagnostic process, the act of determining a patient's health status and evaluating the factors influencing that status.

diagnostic radiology, medical imaging using external sources of radiation.

diagnostic radiopharmaceutical, a radioactive drug administered to a patient as a diagnostic tracer to differentiate normal from abnormal anatomic structures or biochemical or physiologic functions.

diagnostic sensitivity, the conditional probability that a person having a disease will be correctly identified by a clinical test, i.e., the number of true positive results divided by the total number with the disease (which is the sum of the numbers of true positive plus false negative results).

diagnostic services, activities related to the diagnosis made by a physician or nurse practitioner, which may also be performed by nurses or other health professionals.

diagnostic specificity, the conditional probability that a person not having a disease will be correctly identified by a clinical test, i.e., the number of true negative results divided by the total number of those without the disease (which is the sum of the numbers of true negative plus false positive results).

diagonal artery, an inconstant artery, occasionally duplicated, arising from the trunk of the left anterior descending coronary artery and crossing the anterior aspect of the left ventricle diagonally, toward the left margin.

diagonal conjugate /dī′ag′ənəl/, a radiographic measurement of the distance from the inferior border of the symphysis pubis to the sacral promontory.

diakinesis /dī′əkinē′sis, dī′əkī-/ [Gk, *dia + kinesis,* motion], the final stage in the first meiotic prophase in gametogenesis, in which the chromosomes achieve their maximum thickness.

dial, a circular diagram with black lines radiating outward across a white background from the center, as is used in tests of astigmatism.

dialect /dī′əlekt/, a variation of spoken language different from other forms of the same language in pronunciation, syntax, and word meanings.

Dialose, a trademark for a fixed-combination GI drug containing a stool softener (docusate) and a laxative (sodium carboxymethylcellulose).

dialysate, the material that passes through the membrane in dialysis.

dialysis /dī′al′isis/ [Gk *dia + lysis,* a loosening], **1.** the process of separating colloids and crystalline substances in solution by the difference in their rate of diffusion through a semipermeable membrane. **2.** a medical procedure for the removal of certain elements from the blood or lymph by virtue of the difference in their rates of diffusion through an external semipermeable membrane or, in the case of peritoneal dialysis, through the peritoneum.

dialysis access maintenance, a nursing intervention from the Nursing Interventions Classification (NIC) defined as the preservation of vascular (arterial-venous) access sites.

dialysis dementia, a neurologic disorder that occurs in some patients undergoing dialysis. The precise cause is unknown, but the effect is believed to be related to chemicals in the dialyzing fluid, drugs administered to the dialysis patient, or both.

dialysis disequilibrium syndrome, a disorder caused by a rapid change in extracellular fluid composition during dialysis. It may be marked by cerebral or neurologic disturbances, cardiac arrhythmias, and pulmonary edema.

dialysis shunt [Gk, *dia,* through, *lysis,* loosening; ME, *shunten*], an external artificial link between a peripheral artery and a vein in an arm or leg for use in hemodialysis.

dialysis technician [Gk, *dia,* through, *lysis,* loosening, *technikos,* skillful], an allied health professional who operates and maintains dialysis equipment for patients with kidney diseases.

dialyzer /dī′əlī′zər/ [Gk, *dia* + *lysis,* loosening], **1.** a machine used in dialysis. **2.** a semipermeable membrane or porous diaphragm in a dialysis machine.

diameter (D) /dī·am′ətər/ [Gk, *diametros*], **1.** the length of a straight line passing through the center of a circle and connecting opposite points on its circumference. **2.** the distance between two specified opposite points on the periphery of a structure such as the cranium or pelvis.

Diameter-Index Safety System (DISS), a system of standardized connections between cylinders of medical gases and flowmeters or pressure regulators. Each gas has connections of a specific size to prevent accidental hookup of the wrong gas.

diameter of fetal skull [Gk, *diametros*; L, *fetus*; AS, *skulle,* bowl], the average distances between certain landmarks of the fetal skull as measured at term. These measurements include the following: biparietal, the fetal head between the two parietal eminences, 9.25 cm; occipitofrontal, from the external occipital protuberance to the most prominent point of the frontal midline, 11 cm; occipitomental, from the external occipital protuberance to the midpoint of the chin, 13 cm; and suboccipitobregmatic, from the lowest posterior point of the occipital bone to the center of the anterior fontanel, 9.5 cm.

Diamond-Blackfan syndrome, a rare congenital disorder evident in the first 3 months of life, characterized by severe anemia and very low reticulocyte count but normal numbers of platelets and white cells. It is caused by a deficiency of erythrocyte precursors.

diamond bur /dī′(ə)mənd/, a rotary device that contains diamond particles and is used as an abrasive in dentistry.

Diamox, a trademark for a carbonic anhydrase inhibitor (acetaZOLAMIDE), a diuretic.

diapedesis /dī′əpidē′sis/ [Gk, *dia* + *pedesis,* an oozing], the passage of white blood cells through the walls of the blood vessels without damage to the vessels.

diaper rash [ME, *diapre,* patterned fabric], an erythematous, papular, or scaly eruption in the diaper area of infants, caused by irritation from feces, moisture, heat, or ammonia produced by the bacterial decomposition of urine. Secondary infection by *Candida albicans* is common.

diaper restraint, a therapeutic device used for countertraction with lower extremity traction when other methods of countertraction are not effective. One device is used in treating children with orthopedic diseases and abnormalities. It is designed to fit over the pelvic area like diapers, with rings at each of four corners. A webbing strap is threaded through the rings and attached to the top side of the bedspring frame.

diaphanography /dī·af′ənog′rəfē/ [Gk, *diaphanes,* shining through, *graphein,* to record], a type of transillumination used to examine the breast that uses selected wavelengths of light and special imaging equipment.

diaphanoscope /dī·af′ənəskōp′/, an instrument that transilluminates body tissues. It is sometimes used in the diagnosis of breast tumors.

diaphoresis /dī′əfərē′sis/ [Gk, *dia* + *pherein,* to carry], the secretion of sweat, especially the profuse secretion associated with an elevated body temperature, physical exertion, exposure to heat, and mental or emotional stress.

diaphragm /dī′əfram/ [Gk, *diaphragma,* partition], **1.** in anatomy, a dome-shaped musculofibrous partition that separates the thoracic and abdominal cavities. The convex cranial surface of the diaphragm forms the floor of the thoracic cavity; the concave surface forms the roof of the abdominal cavity. The diaphragm aids respiration by moving up and down. During inspiration it moves down and increases the volume of the thoracic cavity. During expiration it moves up, decreasing the volume. **3.** in optics, an opening that controls the amount of light passing through an optical network. **4.** a thin, membranous partition, as that used in dialysis. **5.** in radiography, a metal plate with a small opening that limits the diameter of the radiographic beam. **—diaphragmatic,** *adj.*

D

diaphragmatic breathing /dī·əfragmat′ik/ [Gk, *diaphragma,* partition], a pattern of exhalation and inhalation in which most of the ventilatory work is done with the diaphragm. The technique is taught to patients with COPD to facilitate respiration.

diaphragmatic constriction, the narrowing in the esophagus where it crosses the diaphragm at the esophageal hiatus.

diaphragmatic flutter, rapid, rhythmic contractions of the diaphragm. The condition may simulate atrial flutter.

diaphragmatic hernia [Gk, *diaphragma,* partition; L, *rupture*], the protrusion of part of the stomach through an opening in the diaphragm, most commonly an abnormally enlarged esophageal hiatus. In some cases, the intestines may also herniate into the chest.

diaphragmatic node, a node in one of three groups of thoracic parietal lymph nodes, situated on the thoracic side of the diaphragm and consisting of the anterior set, the middle set, and the posterior set.

diaphragmatic peritonitis, an inflammation of the lower surface of the diaphragm.

diaphragmatic pleurisy, inflammation of the pleural covering of the diaphragm, which produces severe pain in the epigastric and hypochondrial regions and, occasionally, referred pain via the phrenic nerve to the shoulder.

diaphragm stethoscope, an instrument for auscultation of bodily sounds. It consists of a vibrating disk, or diaphragm, which transmits sound waves through tubing to two earpieces.

diaphyseal aclasis /dī′əfiz′ē·əl ak′ləsis/ [Gk, *dia* + *phyein,* to grow, *a* + *klasis,* not breaking], a relatively rare abnormal condition that affects the skeletal system. Characterized by multiple exostoses or bony protrusions, it is inherited as a dominant trait.

diaphyseal-epiphyseal fusion, a surgical procedure to eliminate the epiphyseal line and unite the epiphyseal and diaphyseal bones.

diaphysis /dī·af′isis/ [Gk, *dia* + *phyein,* to grow], the shaft of a long bone, consisting of a tube of compact bone enclosing the medullary cavity.

diarrhea /dī′ərē′ə/ [Gk, *dia* + *rhein,* to flow], the frequent passage of loose, watery stools. The stool may also contain mucus, pus, blood, or excessive amounts of fat. Diarrhea is usually a symptom of some underlying disorder. Conditions in which diarrhea is an important symptom are dysenteric disorders, malabsorption syndrome, lactose intolerance, irritable bowel syndrome, GI tumors, and inflammatory bowel disease. In addition to stool frequency, patients may complain of abdominal cramps and generalized weakness.—**diarrheal, diarrheic,** *adj.*

diarrhea management, a nursing intervention from the Nursing Interventions Classification (NIC) defined as management and alleviation of diarrhea.

diarticular /dī′artik′yələr/ [Gk, *di,* twice; L, *articulare,* to divide into joints], having two joints.

Diasone Sodium Enterab, a trademark for a leprostatic antibacterial (sulfoxone sodium).

diastalsis /dī′əstal′sis/, a wave of alternating relaxation and contraction of the smooth muscles lining the walls of the small intestine in response to distension of the intestine.

diastasis /dī·as′təsis/ [Gk, separation], the forcible separation of two parts that are normally joined, such as parts of a bone at an epiphysis, two bones that lack a synovial joint, or two muscles.

diastasis recti abdominis, the separation of the two rectus muscles along the median line of the abdominal wall. In a newborn, the condition is the result of incomplete development.

diastatic fermentation /dī′əstat′ik/ [Gk, *diastasis,* separation; L, *fermentare,* to cause to rise], the conversion of starch to glucose by the enzyme ptyalin.

diastema /dī′əstē′mə/ [Gk, interval], a space between two teeth in the same dental arch not caused by the loss of a tooth between them. It occurs most commonly between the maxillary central incisors in adults.

diastole /dī·as′təlē/ [Gk, *dia* + *stellein,* to set], the period between contractions of the atria or the ventricles during which blood enters the relaxed chambers from the systemic circulation and the lungs. Ventricular diastole begins with the onset of the second heart sound and ends with the first heart sound.

diastolic /dī′əstol′ik/, pertaining to diastole, or the BP at the instant of maximum cardiac relaxation.

diastolic augmentation, an increase in arterial diastolic BP produced by a counterpulsation device such as an intraaortic balloon pump.

diastolic blood pressure, the minimum level of BP measured between contractions of the heart. It may vary with age, gender, body weight, emotional state, and other factors.

diastolic filling pressure, the BP in a ventricle during diastole, resulting from venous return.

diastolic murmur [Gk, *dia,* between, *stellein,* to set; L, *murmur,* humming], a noise caused by turbulence of blood flow during ventricular relaxation. With few exceptions, diastolic murmurs are caused by organic heart disease.

diastolic thrill, a vibration felt over the heart during ventricular diastole. It may be caused by mitral valve stenosis, a patent ductus arteriosus, or severe aortic insufficiency.

diastrophic /dī'əstrof'ik/ [Gk, *diastrephein,* to distort], pertaining to a bent or curved condition of bones or distortion of other structures.

diastrophic dwarf, a person in whom short stature is caused by osteochondrodysplasia and is associated with various deformities of the bones and joints, including scoliosis, clubfoot, micromelia, hand defects, multiple joint contractures and subluxations, ear deformities, and cleft palate.

diataxia /dī'ətak'sē-ə/, ataxia affecting both sides of the body.

diathermal /dī'əthur'məl/, pertaining to the use of elevated local temperature in the treatment of a disorder. The raised temperature may be produced by high-frequency electric current, ultrasound, or microwave radiation.

diathermy /dī'əthur'mē/ [Gk, *dia + therme,* heat], the production of heat in body tissues for therapeutic purposes by high-frequency currents that are insufficiently intense to destroy tissues or to impair their vitality.

diathesis /dī-əthē'sis/ *pl.* **diatheses** [Gk, arrangement], an inherited physical constitution predisposing to certain diseases or conditions, many of which are believed associated with the Y chromosome because males appear to be more susceptible than females.

diazepam /dī-az'əpam/, a benzodiazepine sedative and antianxiety agent prescribed in the treatment of anxiety, nervous tension, and muscle spasm and as an anticonvulsant.

diazoxide /dī'əzok'sīd/, a vasodilator used as an antihypertensive. It also inhibits insulin release from the pancreas. It is prescribed parenterally for emergency reduction of BP in malignant hypertension and orally in some cases of hypoglycemia.

dibasic potassium phosphate, the dipotassium salt, K_2HPO_4, used alone or in combination with other phosphate compounds as an electrolyte replenisher.

dibasic sodium phosphate, a salt of phosphoric acid. Used alone or in combination with other phosphate compounds, it is given intravenously as an electrolyte replenisher, orally or rectally as a laxative, and orally as a urinary acidifier and for prevention of kidney stones.

dibenzazepine /di'benzaz'epēn/, any of a group of structurally related drugs including the tricyclic antidepressants clomiPRAMINE, desipramine, imipramine, and trimipramine.

Dibenzyline, a trademark for an alpha-1 receptor blocker (phenoxybenzamine hydrochloride).

dibucaine /dī'bəkān/, a topical anesthetic ointment often used to treat pain and itch of hemorrhoids.

dic, abbreviation for *dicentric.*

DIC, abbreviation for **disseminated intravascular coagulation.**

dicalcium phosphate and calcium gluconate with vitamin D /dīkal'sē·əm/, a source of calcium and phosphorus prescribed for hypocalcemia, especially in pregnancy and lactation.

dicarboxylic acid /dī'kär·bok·sil'ik as'id/, any of various organic acids that contain two carboxyl (COOH) groups, such as oxalic acid and tartaric acid.

dicentric (dic) /desen'trik/ [Gk, *di,* twice, *kentron,* center], in genetics, pertaining to a structurally abnormal chromosome with two centromeres.

dicephalus, fetus with two heads.

dicephaly /dīsef'əlē/ [Gk, *di,* twice, *kephale,* head], a developmental anomaly in which a fetus has two heads.—**dicephalic, dicephalous,** *adj.,* **dicephalus,** *n.*

dichlorphenamide /dī'klôrfen'əmīd/, a carbonic anhydrase inhibitor prescribed in the treatment of chronic open-angle glaucoma and before surgery for angle-closure glaucoma.

dichotomy /dīkot'əmē/ [Gk, *dicha,* in two, *temnein,* to cut], a division or separation into two equal parts.

dichroic stain /dīkrō'ik/, a radiographic film artifact caused by a colored chemical stain. The color may range from yellow to purple and is usually the result of improper processing.

dichromatic vision /dī'krōmat'ik/ [Gk, *di,* twice, *chroma,* color; L, *visio*], a form of color vision in which only two of the three primary colors are perceived.

dichromic /di-krō'mik/, having, or pertaining to, two colors.

Dick test [George F. Dick, 1881–1967; Gladys R.H. Dick, 1881–1963; American physicians], a skin test formerly used for determining sensitivity to an erythrotoxin produced by the group A streptococci that cause scarlet fever. A skin test dose of the toxin is injected intradermally. An area of inflammation 3 to 5 cm in diameter indicates that the person is not immune, has no antitoxin, and therefore is susceptible to the toxin.

diclofenac /diklo'fenak/, an NSAID used systemically as the potassium or sodium salt in the treatment of rheumatic and nonrheumatic inflammatory conditions and as the potassium salt to relieve pain and dysmenorrhea. It is also applied topically to the conjunctiva as a sodium salt to reduce ocular inflammation or photophobia after certain kinds of surgery and to the skin to treat actinic keratoses.

diclofenac potassium, the potassium salt of diclofenac, administered orally in the treatment of rheumatoid arthritis, osteoarthritis, ankylosing spondylitis, a variety of nonrheumatic inflammatory conditions, pain, and dysmenorrhea.

dicloxacillin sodium /dī'kloksəsil'in/, a penicillinase-resistant penicillin prescribed in the treatment of bacterial infections, especially those caused by penicillinase-producing strains of staphylococci.

DICOM, abbreviation for *digital imaging and communications in medicine,* the standard used for the electronic transferring of digital image data.

Dicor, a trademark for a castable ceramic dental material.

dicrotic /dīkrot'ik/ [Gk, *dikrotos* double beating], pertaining to a waveform that has two separate peaks.

dicrotic notch /dīkrot'ik/, a small, downward deflection observed on the downstroke of an arterial pressure waveform. It represents closure of the aortic or pulmonic valve at the onset of ventricular diastole.

dicrotic pulse, a pulse with two separate peaks, the second usually weaker than the first.

dicrotic wave, in an arterial pulse recording, the portion of the descending limb after the aortic notch, including a second, smaller peak attributed to the reflected impulse of closure of the aortic valve.

dicumarol /dīkyoo'mərol/, an anticoagulant coumarin derivative prescribed for the prophylaxis and treatment of thrombosis and embolism.

dicyclomine hydrochloride /dīsī'kləmīn/, an anticholinergic/antispasmodic prescribed as an adjunct to ulcer therapy and as a treatment for functional/irritable bowel syndrome.

didactic /dīdak'tik/ [Gr, *didaskein,* to teach], pertaining to classroom teaching or instruction.

dideoxycytidine /dī'dē·ok'sēsī'tidēn/, an antiretroviral drug that prevents HIV from multiplying. It is chemically related to dideoxyinosine (ddI).

dideoxyinosine (ddI) /dī'dē·okse·in'ōsēn/, an antiretroviral drug used in the treatment of HIV infections. ddI inhibits the enzyme reverse transcriptase, thereby restricting viral replication activity.

DIDMOAD syndrome, abbreviation for **diabetes insipidus, diabetes mellitus, optic atrophy, deafness syndrome.**

Didrex, a trademark for an anorexiant (benzphetamine hydrochloride).

Didronel, a trademark for a calcium regulator (etidronate disodium).

didymus /did'iməs/, a testis.

die[1], to cease living.

die[2], a model of a prepared tooth made from a hard substance, usually dental stone.

diecious /dī·ē'shəs/ [Gk, *di* + *oikos,* house], pertaining to an organism that has either male or female reproductive organs.

dieldrin /dīel'drin/, a highly toxic pesticide that is also poisonous to humans and animals if ingested, inhaled, or absorbed through the skin. It causes dysfunction of the CNS and may be a carcinogen.

dielectric /di'elek'trik/, **1.** transmitting electric effects by induction, but not by conduction. The term is applied to an insulating substance through or across which electric force is acting or may act by induction without conduction. **2.** an insulating substance that transmits through or across which electric force is acting or may act by induction without conduction.

diencephalic syndrome /dis'ensəfal'ik/, failure to thrive and emaciation, sometimes with wartlike nevi.

diencephalon /dī'ənsef'əlon/ [Gk, *di* + *enkephalon,* brain], the portion of the brain between the cerebrum and the mesencephalon. It consists of the hypothalamus, thalamus, metathalamus, and the epithalamus and includes most of the third ventricle.

diener /dē'nər/ [Ger, man servant], an individual who maintains the hospital laboratory or equipment and facilities. The morgue diener may also assist the pathologist in performing autopsies.

dieresis /dī·er'əsis/, separation of a structure's parts by surgery or other means.

diet /dī'it/ [Gk, *diaita,* way of living], **1.** food and drink considered with regard to their nutritional qualities, composition, and effects on health. **2.** nutrients prescribed, regulated, or restricted as to kind and amount for therapeutic or other purposes. **3.** the customary allowance of food and drink regularly provided or consumed. —**dietetic,** *adj.*

dietary /dī'əter'ē/, pertaining to diet.

dietary amenorrhea [Gk, *diaita,* way of living, *a,* absence, *men,* month, *rhoia,* to flow], an interruption of menstruation caused by malnutrition, starvation, or excessive voluntary dieting.

Dietary Approach to Stop Hypertension (DASH) diet, a diet high in fruits, vegetables, and low-fat dairy products; low in saturated and total fats; low in cholesterol; and high in fiber. Research studies support the hypothesis that this diet reduces BP and may play a role in prevention of high BP.

dietary fiber, a generic term for nondigestible carbohydrate substances found in plant cell walls and surrounding cellular material, each with a different effect on various GI functions. Dietary fiber may be water-soluble or insoluble. The risk of development of constipation, hemorrhoids, diverticular disease, and colon cancer may be decreased by regular consumption of sufficient amounts of fiber. Most experts recommend intake of 20 to 30 g per day.

dietetic food, 1. a specially prepared low-calorie food, often containing natural or artificial sweeteners. **2.** a food prepared for any specific dietary need or restriction, such as salt-free or vegetarian food.

dietetics /dī'itet'iks/, the science of applying nutritional principles to the planning and preparation of foods and regulation of the diet in relation to both health and disease.

dietetic technician, a person trained in food and nutrition who may work independently or in a team with a registered dietitian. Dietetic technicians often screen patients to identify nutrition problems, provide patient education and counseling, develop menus and recipes, supervise food service personnel, purchase food, and monitor inventory and food quality.

diethylpropion hydrochloride /dī'eth'ilprō'pē·on/, an appetite suppressant; a CNS stimulant. It is prescribed as a short-term adjunct in the treatment of exogenous obesity.

diethylstilbestrol (DES) /-stilbes'trol/, a synthetic hormone with estrogenic properties. This agent was used extensively from 1948 to 1971 to decrease miscarriages, but it is now contraindicated because it is known to increase the risk of vaginal clear cell carcinoma in the women exposed to it in utero.

Dietl's crisis /dē'təlz/ [Joseph Dietl, Polish physician, 1804–1878; Gk, krisis, turning point], a sudden excruciating pain in the kidney, caused by distention of the renal pelvis, rapid ingestion of very large amounts of liquid, or kinking of a ureter that produces temporary occlusion of the flow of urine from the kidney.

diet staging, a nursing intervention from the Nursing Interventions Classification (NIC) defined as instituting required diet restrictions with subsequent progression of diet as tolerated.

diet therapy, the branch of dietetics concerned with the use of foods for therapeutic purposes.

difenoxin /dī'fēnok'sin/, an agent used as the hydrochloride salt for its antiperistaltic action in treatment of diarrhea.

differential /dif'əren'shəl/, pertaining to or creating a difference.

differential absorption [L, differentia, difference], the difference in absorption of x-rays by different body tissues. In a radiograph of a body part, such as an arm, the image of the bone is produced because more x-rays are absorbed by bone than by the surrounding soft tissue.

differential diagnosis, the distinguishing between two or more diseases with similar symptoms by systematically comparing their signs and symptoms.

differential growth, a difference in the size or rate of growth of dissimilar organisms, tissues, or structures.

differential threshold, the lowest limit at which two stimuli can be differentiated or distinguished.

differential white blood cell count, enumeration and classification of the leukocytes in a Wright-stained blood film. The different categories of white blood cells are counted and reported as percentages of the total examined.

differentiating agent, a substance, such as a retinoid, that induces a cell to stop dividing and to differentiate.

differentiation /dif'əren'shē·ā'shən/ [L, differentia, difference], **1.** in embryology, a process in development in which unspecialized cells or tissues are systemically modified and altered to achieve specific and characteristic physical forms, physiologic functions, and chemical properties. **2.** progressive diversification leading to complexity. **3.** acquisition of functions and forms different from those of the original. **4.** distinguishing of one thing or disease from another, as in differential diagnosis. **5.** (in psychology) mental autonomy or separation of intellect and emotions so that one is not dominated by reactive anxiety of a family or group emotional system. **6.** the first subphase of the separation-individuation phase in Mahler's system of preoedipal development.—**differentiate,** v.

differentiation therapy, a cancer therapy technique in which the malignant cell is regarded as having escaped the normal controls of cell growth and differentiation. The cancer cell is regarded as pathologically arrested at an early stage of differentiation, retaining the ability to proliferate. It is treated with agents that remove this block and allow the cells to differentiate along more normal lines until they eventually lose their ability to divide and replicate.

diffraction /difrak'shən/ [L, dis, opposite of, frangere, to break], the bending and scattering of wavelengths of light or other radiation as the radiation passes around obstacles or through narrow slits. X-ray diffraction is used in the study of the internal structure of cells.

diffuse /difyōōz'/ [L, *diffundere,* to spread out], becoming widely spread, such as through a membrane or fluid.

diffuse abscess, an abscess that spreads into neighboring tissues beyond fibrous walls.

diffuse axonal injury (DAI), a type of brain injury caused by shearing forces that occur between different parts of the brain as a result of rotational acceleration. DAI most commonly occurs in motor vehicle crashes when the vehicle suddenly stops.

diffused light, light in which the precise source cannot be seen while the apparent area of the source is increased.

diffuse erythema, skin redness or inflammation that is spread over a large body surface.

diffuse esophageal spasm, abnormal contractions of the esophagus leading to difficult or painful swallowing and chest pain.

diffuse goiter, an enlargement of all parts of the thyroid gland. Symptoms are those of hyperthyroidism.

diffuse hypersensitivity pneumonia, an immunologically mediated inflammatory reaction in the lungs induced by exposure to an allergen or a drug. The disorder is characterized by cough, fever, dyspnea, malaise, pulmonary edema, and infiltration of the alveoli with eosinophils and large mononuclear cells.

diffuse idiopathic skeletal hyperostosis, a form of degenerative joint disease in which the ligaments along the spinal column become calcified and lose their flexibility.

diffuse myocardial fibrosis, a type of heart disease characterized by a generalized distribution of fibrous tissue that replaces normal heart muscle cells.

diffuse peritonitis [L, *diffundere,* to spread out; Gk, *peri,* near, *teinein,* to stretch, *itis,* inflammation], widespread peritonitis affecting most of the peritoneum, usually caused by a ruptured stomach or appendix.

diffuse sclerosis [L, *diffundere,* to spread out; Gk, *sklerosis,* hardening], a form of sclerosis that extends through much of the CNS.

diffusing capacity (D) /difyōō'sing/, the rate of gas transfer through a unit area of a permeable membrane per unit of gas pressure difference across it. It is affected by specific chemical reactions that may occur in the blood.

diffusing capacity of lungs (D$_L$), the volume of a gas that diffuses from the lung across the alveolar-capillary membrane into the bloodstream per minute per mm Hg difference in pressure across the membrane.

diffusion /difyōō'zhən/ [L, *diffundere,* to spread out], the process in which particles in a fluid move from an area of higher concentration to an area of lower concentration, resulting in an even distribution of the particles in the fluid.

diffusion constant, a mathematical constant relating to the ability of a substance to spread widely.

diffusion defect, any impairment in the diffusion of oxygen across the alveolar-capillary membrane caused by pathologic changes in any of the structures of the membrane.

diffusion deposition, the absorption of an aerosol particle on the surface of an alveolar membrane or other airway structure.

diffusion of gases, a natural process, essential in respiration, in which molecules of a gas pass from an area of high concentration to one of lower concentration.

diflorasone diacetate /dīflôr'əsōn dī·as'ətāt/, a topical corticosteroid with high potency prescribed for the treatment of skin inflammation.

Diflucan, a trademark for a broad-spectrum antifungal agent (fluconazole).

diflucortolone /diflōōkor'tählōn/, a synthetic corticosteroid used as the valerate salt and applied topically in treatment of inflammation and pruritus of dermatoses.

diflunisal /dīflōō'nisal/, a nonsteroidal antiinflammatory drug prescribed for the treatment of mild to moderate pain and inflammation in osteoarthritis and other musculoskeletal disorders.

digastricus /dīgas'trikəs/ [Gk, *di,* twice, *gaster,* stomach], one of four suprahyoid muscles having two parts, an anterior belly and a posterior belly. The anterior belly acts to open the jaw and draw the hyoid bone forward. The posterior belly acts to draw back and raise the hyoid bone.

DiGeorge's syndrome /dijôrj'əz/ [Angelo M. DiGeorge, American physician, 1921–2009], a congenital disorder characterized by severe immunodeficiency and structural abnormalities, including hypertelorism; notched, low-set ears; small mouth; downward-slanting eyes; cardiovascular defects; and absence of the thymus and parathyroid glands.

digest /dijest', dijest', dī'jəst/ [L, *digerere,* to break down], **1.** to soften by heat and moisture. **2.** to break into smaller parts and simpler compounds by mastication, hydrolysis, and action of intestinal secretions and enzymes. **3.** any material that results from digestion or hydrolysis.

digestant /dijes'tənt/, a substance, such as pepsin, that is added to the diet as an aid to the digestion of food.

digestible /dijes'tibəl/, capable of being digested.

digestion /dijes'chən/ [L, *digerere*, to break down], the conversion of food into absorbable substances in the GI tract. Digestion is accomplished through the mechanical and chemical breakdown of food into smaller and smaller molecules, with the help of glands located both inside and outside the gut.—**digestive,** *adj.*

digestive enzyme /dijes'tiv/ [L, *digerere*, to break down; Gk, *en* + *zyme*, ferment], any digestive system enzyme that hydrolyzes fats, proteins, or carbohydrates for absorption.

digestive fever, a slight rise in body temperature that normally accompanies the digestive process.

digestive gland, any one of the many structures that secrete agents involved in the breaking down of food into the constituent absorbable substances needed for metabolism. Some kinds of digestive glands are the salivary glands, gastric glands, intestinal glands, liver, and pancreas.

digestive juice, thin, colorless secretion of the glands of the human stomach, composed mainly of hydrochloric acid, chymosin, pepsinogen, intrinsic factor, and mucus.

digestive system, the organs, structures, and accessory glands of the digestive tube of the body through which food passes from the mouth to the esophagus, stomach, and intestines.

digestive tract, a musculomembranous tube, about 9 m long, extending from the mouth to the anus and lined with mucous membrane. Its various parts are the mouth, pharynx, esophagus, stomach, small intestine, and large intestine. The tube, which is part of the digestive system, includes numerous accessory organs.

Digibind, a trademark for the antibody used in the treatment of digoxin toxicity (digoxin immune Fab, ovine).

digit /dij'it/ [L, *digitus*], a finger or toe.

digital[1] /dij'itəl/ [L, *digitus,* finger], **1.** pertaining to a digit, that is, a finger or toe. **2.** resembling a finger or toe. **3.** an electronic device that gives its reading/values in numbers, e.g., digital clock.

digital[2], **1.** the characterization or measurement of a signal in terms of a series of numbers rather than some continuously varying value. **2.** use of the binary system in computer technology, or computerized communications, such as digital telephone, pagers, and cellular telephones.

digital angiography, a technique of producing computer-enhanced radiographic images of the heart and great vessels.

digital compression [L, *digitus,* finger, *comprimere,* to press together], the act of pressing with the fingers, as when arresting the blood flow from a wound.

digital fluoroscopy, the projection of a radiographic image on an image-intensifying fluorescent screen coupled to a digital video image processor.

digital image, a depiction recorded electronically to allow viewing or transmission on a computer.

digitalis /dij'ital'is/ [L, *digitus,* finger or toe], a general term for cardiac glycoside, prescribed in the treatment of CHF and certain cardiac arrhythmias.

digitalis poisoning [L, *digitalis,* of the fingers, *potio,* drink], the toxic effects of digitalis medications. Toxicity may result from the cumulative effect of the drug or from hypokalemia. Symptoms include vomiting, headache, heartbeat abnormalities, disorientation, and visual color distortions.

digitalis therapy, the administration of a digitalis preparation to a person with a heart disorder to increase the force of myocardial contractions; produce a slower, more regular apical rate; and slow the transmission of impulses through the conduction system.

digitalization /dij'ətal'īzā'shən/, the administration of digitalis in doses sufficient to achieve maximum pharmacologic effects without producing toxic symptoms.

digitalized /dij'ətəlīzd'/, having a therapeutic total body level of digitalis, a cardiac glycoside.

digitalizing dose, the amount of digitalis needed to achieve a desired therapeutic effect.

digital radiography (DR) /dij'itəl/, any method of radiographic image formation that uses a computer to store and manipulate data.

digital reflex, 1. a finger-jerk reaction produced by tapping the palmar aspect of the terminal phalanges of the fingers when they are slightly flexed. **2.** sudden flexion of the terminal phalanx of the thumb produced by tapping the terminal phalanx of the middle finger.

digital subtraction angiography (DSA), a method in which radiographic images of blood vessels filled with contrast material are digitized and then subtracted from images obtained before administration of the material. The method increases the contrast between the vessels and the background.

digital-to-analog converter, a device for translating digital information into a continuous form, as from an ohmmeter or thermometer.

digital tomosynthesis, a system of tomography, using a computer and a digital fluoroscopy unit, that can synthesize any tomographic plane from a single tomographic pass. As only one tomographic pass is required, patient radiation exposure and time in examination are reduced.

digitate /dij′itāt/ [L, *digitatus,* having fingers], having fingers or finger-like projections.

digitate wart, a fingerlike horny projection that arises from a pea-shaped base. It is a benign viral infection of the skin and the adjacent mucous membrane.

digitoxin /dij′itok′sin/, a cardiac glycoside obtained from leaves of *Digitalis purpurea* prescribed in the treatment of CHF and certain cardiac arrhythmias.

digit span test, an examination of the ability of a child to recall a sequence of numbers just spoken.

diglyceride /dīglis′ərīd/, a chemical compound, an ester of glycerol in which the hydrogen in two of the hydroxyl groups is replaced by an acyl radical.

dignathus /dīnath′əs, dignā′thəs/, **1.** a fetus with a double lower jaw. **2.** a person with a cleft of the mandible.

dignified life closure, a nursing outcome from the Nursing Outcomes Classification (NOC) defined as personal actions to maintain control during approaching end of life.

digoxin /digok′sin/, a cardiac glycoside obtained from leaves of *Digitalis lanata* prescribed in the treatment of CHF and certain cardiac arrhythmias.

digoxin immune FAB, ovine, a preparation of antigen-binding fragments derived from specific antidigoxin antibodies produced in sheep that have been immunized with digoxin coupled as a hapten to human serum albumin. It is prescribed for the treatment of life-threatening digoxin or digitoxin toxicity.

dihybrid /dī′hī′brid/ [Gk, *di,* twice; L, *hybrida,* mongrel offspring], pertaining to an individual, an organism, or a strain that is heterozygous for two specific traits.

dihybrid cross, the mating of two individuals, organisms, or strains that have different gene pairs that determine two specific traits or that have two particular characteristics or gene loci being followed.

dihydric alcohol /dīhī′drik/, an alcohol containing two hydroxyl groups.

dihydroergotamine mesylate /dīhī′drō-ərgot′əmēn me′silāt/, an ergot alkaloid causing vasoconstriction through stimulation of several types of receptors, including alpha-adrenergic receptors and serotonin receptors. It is prescribed for the treatment of migraine and vascular headache.

dihydrotachysterol /dīhī′drōtəkis′tə rol/, a rapid-acting form of vitamin D prescribed in the treatment of hypocalcemia resulting from hypoparathyroidism and pseudohypoparathyroidism.

dihydrotestosterone (DHT) /di-hi′drōtestos′ terōn/, an androgenic hormone formed in peripheral tissue from testosterone. It is thought to be the androgen responsible for development of the male primary sex characters during embryogenesis and of male secondary sex characters at puberty, and for adult male sexual function.

dilaceration /dī·las′ərā′shən/ [L, *di-,* apart or through, *lacerare,* to tear], **1.** a tearing apart, as of a cataract. **2.** in dentistry, a condition resulting from injury to a tooth during its developmental period, with a crease or band at the junction of the crown and root, or with tortuous roots having abnormal curvatures.

Dilantin, a trademark for an anticonvulsant used to control tonic-clonic and psychomotor seizures (phenytoin).

dilatancy /dīlā′tənsē/ [L, *dilatare,* to widen], an unusual behavior observed in cytoplasm (and in some physical systems) during which its viscosity and applied force both increase.

dilatant, one exhibiting dilatancy.

dilate /dī′lāt/, to cause a physiologic increase in the diameter of a body opening, blood vessel, or tube.

dilation /dīlā′shən/ [L, *dilatare,* to widen], **1.** the condition of being dilated or stretched. **2.** the process of causing a physiologic increase in the diameter of a body opening, blood vessel, or tube.

dilation and curettage (D&C), widening of the uterine cervix and scraping of the endometrium of the uterus. It is done to diagnose disease of the uterus, to correct heavy or prolonged vaginal bleeding, or to empty the uterus of the products of conception. It is also performed to remove tumors, to rule out carcinoma of the uterus, and to remove retained placental fragments after delivery or after an incomplete abortion.

dilation and evacuation (D&E) [L, *dilatare,* to widen, *evacuare,* to empty], the removal of the products of conception, using suction curettage and forceps, during the second trimester of pregnancy; a type of abortion.

dilation of the heart [L, *dilatare,* to widen; AS, *heorte*], an enlargement of the heart caused by stretching of a weakened myocardium. The condition is associated with acute pulmonary embolism and heart failure.

dilator /dī′lātər/ [L, *dilatare,* to widen], a device for expanding a body opening or cavity.

dilator naris, the alar part of the nasalis muscle that dilates the nostril.

dilator pupillae, a muscle that contracts the iris of the eye and dilates the pupil.

Dilaudid, a trademark for an opioid analgesic (hydromorphone hydrochloride).

Dilor, a trademark for a bronchodilator (dyphylline).

diltiazem /diltī′əzam/, a calcium channel blocker or calcium antagonist prescribed for the treatment of vasospastic and effort-associated angina, in addition to hypertension.

diluent /dil′ōō·ənt, dil′yōō·ənt/ [L, *diluere,* to wash], a substance, generally a fluid, that makes a solution or mixture less concentrated, less viscous, or more liquid.

dilute /dilōōt′, dī′lōōt/ [L, *diluere,* to wash], **1.** pertaining to a solution that contains a relatively small amount of solute in proportion to solvent. **2.** to make a more concentrated solution less concentrated.

diluting agent /dilōō′ting/, a substance used to reduce the viscosity of respiratory tract secretions so they can be removed easily.

dimenhyDRINATE /dim′ənhī′drināt/, an antiemetic prescribed in the treatment of nausea and motion sickness.

dimension, a measure of the width, length, or height of a space, usually described in units of a linear scale.

dimensional stability /dimen′shənəl/, the resistance of radiographic film to image distortion from warping or changing size or shape during processing.

dimer /dī′mər/ [Gk, *di,* twice, *meros,* parts], a compound formed by the union of two radicals or two molecules of a single simpler compound.

dimercaprol /dī′mərkap′rol/, a heavy-metal antagonist prescribed in the treatment of Wilson's disease and acute arsenic, mercury, or gold poisoning, as from an overdosage with mercurial diuretics, arsenics, or gold salts.

Dimetane, a trademark for an antihistamine (brompheniramine maleate).

Dimetapp, a trademark for a fixed-combination drug containing a decongestant (pseudoephedrine) and an antihistamine (brompheniramine maleate). It may also contain the antitussive dextromethorphan.

dimethoxymethylamphetamine (DOM) /dī′məthok′səmeth′iləmfet′əmēn/, a psychoactive or hallucinogenic agent.

dimethylamine [(CH₃)₂NH], a secondary amine found in guano and decomposing fish.

dimethyl sulfoxide (DMSO) /dīmeth′il/, an organic solvent used as an antiinflammatory agent. It is instilled into the bladder for the treatment of interstitial cystitis.

dimorphous /dīmôr′fəs/ [Gk, *di,* twice, *morphe,* form], pertaining to an organism or substance that exists in two distinct forms.

dimple, 1. a slight natural indentation or depression on a body surface, such as on the cheek. **2.** a depression on a body surface resulting from contracting scar tissue or trauma.

dimpled sign, a physical diagnostic test to differentiate between a benign dermatofibroma lesion and a nodular melanoma. On pressure of the examiner's thumb and index finger, benign tumors dimple, but malignant growths do not.

dimpling [ME, *dympull*], small, abnormal indentations or depressions on the surface of a body or organ.

dinitrochlorobenzene (DNCB) /dīnī′trōklô r′ōben′zēn/, a substance applied topically as a test for delayed hypersensitivity reactions. The compound has also been used as an immunotherapeutic agent to treat skin tumors.

2,4-dinitrophenol (DNP), 1. a dye used in biochemical research into oxidative processes. **2.** a hapten commonly used to induce immune response.

dinucleotide, a compound containing two nucleotides.

diode /dī′od/, **1.** an electron tube or x-ray tube having a cathode and an anode. **2.** an electrical device that has a higher conductance for current flowing in one direction than for current flowing in the opposite direction.

diode laser, a solid-state semiconductor used as a lasering medium.

diolamine /dī·ol′əmēn/, abbreviated form for *diethanolamine.*

Dionysian /dē·onis′ē·ən/ [Gk, *Dionysos,* Greek god of wine], the personal attitude of one who is uninhibited, mystic, sensual, emotional, and irrational and who may seek to escape from the boundaries imposed by the limits of the senses.

diopter (D) /dī·op′tər/ [Gk, *dioptra,* optical measuring instrument], a metric measure of the refractive power of a lens. It is equal to the reciprocal of the focal length of the lens in meters.

dioptric power /dī·op′trik/, the refractive power of an optic lens as measured in diopters.

diovulatory /dī·ov′yələtôr′ē/ [Gk, *di,* twice; L, *ovum,* egg], routinely releasing two ova during each ovarian cycle.

dioxide /dī·ok′sīd/ [Gk, *di,* twice, *oxys,* sharp, *genein,* to produce], an oxide that contains two oxygen atoms.

dioxin /dī·ok′sin/, a contaminant of the herbicide 2,4,5-trichlorophenoxyacetic acid (2,4,5-T), widely used throughout the world. Exposure to dioxin is associated with chloracne and porphyria cutanea tarda. Dioxin was a contaminant of the jungle defoliant Agent Orange.

DIP, abbreviation for **desquamative interstitial pneumonia.**

dipeptidases /dīpep'tidāzəs/, the final enzymes in the protein-splitting system of digestion. They complete the task of breaking two-amino-acid dipeptides into single amino acids.

dipeptide, an organic compound formed by the union of two amino acids, with the link provided by the carboxyl group of one molecule and the amine group of the other.

diphallus, a rare congenital anomaly that occurs when two genital tubercles develop. The penis is partly or completely duplicated and may or may not be symmetric. It is often associated urogenital or other anomalies.

diphasic /dīfā'zik/ [Gk, *di,* twice, *phasis,* appearance], pertaining to something that occurs in two stages or phases.

diphenhydrAMINE hydrochloride, an antihistamine prescribed in the treatment of hypersensitivity reactions, including rhinitis, skin rash, and pruritus, and in the treatment of motion sickness and insomnia.

diphenoxylate hydrochloride /dī'fənok'silāt/, an opioid antidiarrheal that contains subclinical amounts of atropine sulfate to limit abuse. It is prescribed in the treatment of noninfectious diarrhea and intestinal cramping.

2,3-diphosphoglycerate test, a blood test used in the evaluation of nonspherocytic anemia.

2,3-diphosphoglyceric acid (DPG) /dīfos 'fōgliser'ik/, a substance in the erythrocyte that affects the affinity of hemoglobin for oxygen. It is a chief end product of glucose metabolism and a link in the biochemical feedback control system that regulates the release of oxygen to the tissues.

diphosphonate /difos'fonāt/, any of a group of related phosphorus-containing compounds that are structurally similar to pyrophosphate but have enhanced stability to enzymatic and chemical hydrolysis and have affinity for sites of osteoid mineralization. They are used as sodium salts to inhibit bone resorption and are complexed with technetium Tc 99m for bone imaging.

diphtheria /difthir'ē-ə, dipthir'ē-ə/ [Gk, *diphthera,* leather membrane], an acute contagious disease caused by the bacterium *Corynebacterium diphtheriae.* It is characterized by the production of a systemic toxin and an adherent false membrane lining of the mucous membrane of the throat. The toxin is particularly damaging to the tissues of the heart and CNS, and the dense pseudomembrane in the throat may interfere with eating, drinking, and breathing.

diphtheria and tetanus toxoids (DT), an active immunizing agent prescribed for immunization against diphtheria and tetanus when pertussis vaccination is contraindicated.

diphtheria and tetanus toxoids and pertussis vaccine (DPT), an active immunizing agent prescribed for the routine immunization of children less than 6 years of age against diphtheria, tetanus, and pertussis.

diphtheria and tetanus toxoids and pertussis vaccine adsorbed and *Haemophilus* b conjugate vaccine, a combination of diphtheria toxoid, tetanus toxoid, pertussis vaccine, and *Haemophilus* b conjugate vaccine, administered intramuscularly to children 18 months to 5 years of age for simultaneous immunization against diphtheria, tetanus, whooping cough, and infection by *H. influenzae* type b.

diphtheria antitoxin [Gk, *diphtheria,* leather membrane, *anti,* against, *toxikon,* poison], an antitoxin prepared by immunizing horses with diphtheria toxoid and extracting the serum.

diphtherial cough /difthir'ē-əl/, a brassy, noisy, crouplike cough accompanied by stridor, observed mainly in children with laryngeal diphtheria.

diphtheria toxin [Gk, *diphtheria* + *toxikon,* poison], the filtrate of a broth culture used to prepare an intradermal injectable form of toxin for Schick tests.

diphtheritic croup /dif'thirit'ik/ [Gk, *diphtheria;* Scot, *croak,* to speak hoarsely], a diphtheritic inflammation of the larynx.

diphtheritic laryngitis [Gk, *diphtheria* + *larynx* + *itis,* inflammation], inflammation of the larynx caused by the bacterium *Corynebacterium diphtheriae.* A serious complication is the formation of a false membrane.

diphtheritic membrane, a membrane of coagulated fiber with bacteria and leukocytes. It is usually white or grayish yellow with well-defined margins.

diphtheritic pharyngitis [Gk, *diphtheria* + *pharynx,* throat, *itis,* inflammation], an inflammation of the pharynx caused by the bacterium *Corynebacterium diphtheriae* and associated with the formation of a false membrane.

diphtheritic sore throat, an inflammation of the pharynx or larynx caused by an infection of *Corynebacterium diphtheriae.*

diphtheritic stomatitis, an inflammation of the mucous membrane of the mouth, caused by *Corynebacterium diphtheriae.*

diphtheroid /dif'thəroid/ [Gk, *diphthera,* leather membrane, *eidos,* form], **1.** pertaining to diphtheria. **2.** resembling the bacillus *Corynebacterium diphtheriae.*

Diphyllobothrium /dəfil'ōboth'rē-əm/ [Gk, *di,* twice, *phyllon,* leaf, *bothrion,* pit], a genus of large parasitic intestinal flatworms having a scolex with two slitlike grooves. The species that most often infects humans is *Diphyllobothrium latum.*

dipivefrin /dī′pivef′rin/, an ophthalmic sympathomimetic agent prescribed in the treatment of open-angle glaucoma.

diplegia /dīple′je̅-ə/ [Gk, *di,* twice, *plege,* stroke], paralysis of both sides of any body part or of like parts on the opposite sides of the body.—**diplegic,** *adj.*

diplococcus /dip′lōkok′əs/ *pl.* diplococci [Gk, *diploos,* double, *kokkos,* berry], **1.** a member of the Coccaceae family that occurs in pairs. Diplococci are often found as parasites or saprophytes. **2.** describing bacteria of the Coccaceae family, which occur as pairs of cocci.

diploë /dip′lō-e̅/, the loose tissue filled with red bone marrow between the two layers of the cranial bones.

diploid (2n) /dip′loid/ [Gk, *diploos* + *eidos,* form], having two complete sets of homologous chromosomes.—**diploidy,** *n.*

diploid nucleus, a nucleus having two sets of chromosomes, as normally found in the somatic cells of higher organisms.

diploidy /dip′loide̅/, the state or condition of having two complete sets of homologous chromosomes.

diplokaryon /dip′lōker′e̅-on/ [Gk, *diploos* + *karyon,* nut], a nucleus that contains twice the diploid number of chromosomes.

diploma program in nursing, a basic educational program that is designed to prepare nursing students for entry into practice, usually in 2 or 3 years. The recipient of a diploma is eligible to take the national certifying registration examination to become a registered nurse.

diplomate /dip′ləmāt/, an individual who has earned a diploma or certificate, especially a physician who has been certified by a specialty board.

diplonema /dip′ləne̅′mə/ [Gk, *diploos* + *nema,* thread], the looplike formation of the chromosomes in the diplotene stage of the first meiotic prophase in gametogenesis.

diplopagus /diplop′əgəs/ [Gk, *diploos* + *pagos,* something fixed], conjoined twins who are more or less equally developed, although one or several internal organs may be shared.

diplopia /diplō′pe̅-ə/ [Gk, *diploos* + *opsis,* vision], double vision caused by defective function of the extraocular muscles or a disorder of the nerves that innervate the muscles.

diplornavirus /dī′plôrnəvī′rəs/, a double-stranded RNA virus that is the cause of Colorado tick fever. It is related to the reoviruses that are associated with various respiratory infections.

diplosomatia /dip′lōsōmā′shə/ [Gk, *diploos* + *soma,* body], a congenital anomaly in which fully formed twins are joined at one or more areas of their bodies.

diplotene /dip′lətēn/ [Gk, *diploos* + *tainia,* ribbon], the fourth stage in the first meiotic prophase in gametogenesis, in which chiasmata form between the chromatids of paired homologous chromosomes and crossing over occurs.

dipodial symmelia /dīpō′de̅-əl/ [Gk, *di,* twice, *pous,* foot, *syn,* together, *melosi* limb], a developmental anomaly characterized by the fusion of the limbs and the presence of two feet.

dipole /dī′pōl/, **1.** a molecule whose ends carry opposite partial charges. **2.** a molecule with areas of opposing electrical charges, as hydrogen chloride, which has a predominance of electrons and a partial negative charge about the chloride portion and a partial positive charge on the hydrogen side.

diprop, abbreviation for a *dipropionate* anion.

diprosopus /dīpros′əpəs, dī′prəsō′pəs/ [Gk, *di,* twice, *pro-sopon,* face], a malformed fetus that has a double face showing varying degrees of development.

dipsesis /dipsē′sis/, extreme thirst.

dipsomania /dip′sōmā′ne̅-ə/ [Gk, *dipsa,* thirst, *mania,* madness], an uncontrollable, often periodic craving for and indulgence in alcoholic beverages.

dipstick, a chemically treated strip of paper used in the analysis of urine or other fluids.

dipus /dī′pəs/, conjoined twins that have only two feet.

dipygus /dīpī′gəs, dip′əgəs/ [Gk, *di,* twice, *pyge,* rump], a malformed fetus that has a double pelvis, one of which is usually not fully developed.

dipyridamole /dī′pirid′əmōl/, an antiplatelet agent. When used in combination with coumarin anticoagulants, it is used to prevent postoperative thromboembolic complications of cardiac valve replacement.

direct agglutination test, a test for the presence of antibodies to a specific antigen in which a dilute antiserum is mixed with the antigen in question.

direct amplification test, a method used to rapidly identify pathogenic organisms found in patient specimens. The RNA of an organism is copied (amplified) and then detected using a nucleic acid probe. A small number of viruses and bacteria can be identified in a few hours in comparison to days or weeks needed for culturing.

direct antagonist [L, *diregere,* to direct; Gk, *antagonisma,* struggle], one of a pair or a group of muscles that pull in opposite directions, whose combined action prevents the part from moving.

direct blood donation, the donation of a unit of blood for transfusion into a specific individual.

direct bone conduction, the conduction of sound to the inner ear from a hearing aid implanted into the skull.

direct calorimetry, the measurement of the amount of heat directly generated by reaction.

direct causal association, a cause-and-effect relationship between a causative factor and a disease with no other factors intervening in the process.

direct contact, mutual touching of two individuals or organisms. Many communicable diseases may be spread by direct contact between an infected and a healthy person.

direct Coombs' test, a blood test performed to identify hemolysis or to investigate hemolytic transfusion reactions. This test demonstrates whether the patient's RBCs have been attacked by antibodies in the patient's own bloodstream.

direct costs, in managed care, the costs of labor, supplies, and equipment to provide direct patient care services.

direct current (DC), an electric current that flows in one direction only and is substantially constant in value.

directed donation donor, Specific donor who makes a blood donation designated for transfusion to a specific recipient. The directed donor blood must meet the same criteria and undergo the same tests as any volunteer allogenic blood donor.

direct-exposure film, a type of radiograph film that is directly exposed by x-rays. It is used most often in dental radiography.

direct fluorescent antibody–*Treponema pallidum* **test (DFA-TP test),** a treponemal antibody test for syphilis using direct immunofluorescence to detect antibodies against *T. pallidum* in the serum.

direct fracture, any fracture occurring at a specific point of injury that is a direct result of that injury.

direct gold, any form of pure gold that may be compacted or condensed directly into a prepared tooth cavity to form a restoration.

direct intervention, hands-on therapy to increase the potential for new motor learning when there are deficits in movement and postural control.

direct intraperitoneal insemination (DIPI), a method of assisted reproductive technology in which semen is injected into the pouch of Douglas.

directional atherectomy, atherectomy done with a directional atherectomy catheter.

directional atherectomy catheter, a type of atherectomy catheter whose direction can be shifted to shave off additional plaque.

directive therapy [L, *diregere*, to direct, *therapeia*, treatment], a psychotherapeutic approach in which the psychotherapist

directs the course of therapy by intervening to ask questions and offer interpretations.

direct laryngoscopy [L, *diregere*, to direct; Gk, *larynx* + *skopein*, to watch], an examination of the larynx by means of a lighted instrument inserted through the mouth.

direct lead /lēd/, **1.** an ECG conductor in which the exploring electrode is placed directly onto the surface of the exposed heart. **2.** *informal.* a tracing produced by such a lead on an ECG.

direct light reflex, the constriction of a pupil receiving increased illumination, as by a light source inserted during an ophthalmologic examination.

direct measurement of blood pressure [L, *diregere*, to direct, *mensura*, to measure; ME, *blod*; L, *premere*, to press], measurement of BP by means of a catheter inserted into an artery.

direct nursing care functions, liaison nursing activities that are focused on a particular patient, a patient's family, or a group for whom the nurse is directly responsible and accountable.

direct patient care, in nursing, care of a patient provided personally by a staff member.

direct provider reimbursement, a method of direct payment for health care services, as fee-for-service.

direct-question interview, an inquiry that usually requires simple one- or two-word responses.

direct reflex, a response that occurs on the same side of the body as the stimulus.

direct retainer, a clasp, attachment, or assembly fastened to an abutment tooth for the purpose of maintaining a removable restoration in its planned position in relation to oral structures.

direct self-destructive behavior (DSDB), any form of suicidal activity such as suicide threats, attempts, or gestures and the act of suicide itself. The person is aware that death is the desired outcome.

direct transfusion [L, *dirigere*, to direct, *transfundere*, to pour through], the transfer of whole blood directly from a vein of the donor to a vein of the recipient.

dirithromycin, an antiinfective prescribed to treat infections of the respiratory tract caused by *Moraxella catarrhalis, Streptococcus* spp. (*S. pneumoniae, S. agalactiae, S. viridans*), *Legionella pneumophila, Mycoplasma pneumoniae, Streptococcus pyogenes, Staphylococcus aureus, Bordetella pertussis,* and *Propionibacterium acnes.*

dirofilariasis /dīˈrōfilˈərīˈəsis/, a human infestation of the dog heartworm, *Dirofilaria immitis,* and the closely related *D. (Nochtiella) repens,* both of which may be transmitted through the bite of any of several species of mosquitoes. The filaria migrate through the bloodstream to the lung, producing pulmonary nodules and causing chest pain, coughing, and hemoptysis. The disease is rare among humans.

dirty bomb, an explosive device that disperses radioactive material over a wide area, contaminating land, buildings, and people. Its purpose is to cause fear and to make an area unusable for a long time.

disability /dis′əbil′itē/ [L, *dis*, opposite of, *habilis*, fit], the loss, absence, or impairment of physical or mental fitness.

disablement model /disā′bəlmənt/, an evaluation and treatment model based on specific impairment, functional loss, and attainable quality of life rather than a medical diagnosis.

disaccharidase /disak′əridās′/, in humans, the enzyme that hydrolyzes disaccharides. The disaccharidases are located in the brush border membrane of the small intestine and hydrolyze the oligosaccharides and disaccharides produced after luminal digestion of starches and other carbohydrates.

disaccharide /dīsak′ərīd/ [Gk, *di* + *sakcharon*, sugar], a general term for simple carbohydrates formed by the union of two monosaccharide molecules.

disaccharide intolerance, the inability to properly metabolize one or more disaccharides, usually resulting from deficiency of the corresponding disaccharidases. After ingestion of the disaccharide, there may be abdominal symptoms such as diarrhea, flatulence, borborygmus, distension, and pain.

disadvantaged /dis′ədvan′tijd/ [L, *dis* + *abante*, superior position], **1.** any group of people who lack money, education, literacy, or another status advantage. **2.** a euphemism for "poor."

disarticulation /dis′ärtik′yəlā′shən/ [L, *dis* + *articulare*, to divide into joints], separation of a joint without cutting through a bone.

disaster [L, *dis*, apart, *astrum*, a star], any mishap or misfortune that is ruinous, distressing, or calamitous.

disaster-preparedness plan [L, *dis* + *astrum*, favorable stars, *praeparare*, to prepare], a formal plan of action, usually prepared in written form, for coordinating the response of a hospital staff in the event of a disaster within the hospital or the surrounding community.

discernment, insight related to a patient problem or dilemma; the ability to analyze and understand a patient situation.

discharge (d/c) /dis′chärj/ [OFr, *deschargier*, to expel], **1.** to release a substance or object. **2.** to release a patient from a hospital. **3.** to release an electrical charge, which may be manifested by a spark or surge of electricity. **4.** to release a burst of energy from or through a neuron. **5.** in psychology, a release of emotions, often accompanied by a wide range of voluntary and involuntary reflexes, weeping, rage, or other emotional displays. **6.** a substance or object discharged. **7.** the flow of a secretion or an excretion.

discharge abstract, items of information compiled from medical records of patients discharged from a hospital, organized and recorded in a uniform format to provide data for statistical studies, reports, or research.

discharge coordinator, an individual who arranges with community agencies and institutions for the continuing care of patients after their discharge from a hospital or another health care facility.

discharge planning[1], the activities that facilitate a patient's movement from one health care setting to another, or to home. It is a multidisciplinary process involving physicians, nurses, social workers, and possibly other health professionals; its goal is to enhance continuity of care.

discharge planning[2], a nursing intervention from the Nursing Interventions Classification (NIC) defined as preparation for moving a patient from one level of care to another within or outside the current health care agency.

discharge readiness: independent living, a nursing outcome from the Nursing Outcomes Classification (NOC) defined as the readiness of a patient to relocate from a health care institution to living independently.

discharge readiness: supported living, a nursing outcome from the Nursing Outcomes Classification (NOC) defined as the readiness of a patient to relocate from a health care institution to a lower level of supported living.

discharge summary, a clinical report prepared by a physician or other health professional at the conclusion of a hospital stay or series of treatments. It outlines the patient's chief complaint, the diagnostic findings, the therapy administered and the patient's response to it, and recommendations on discharge.

discharging lesion [OFr, *deschargier*; L, *laesio*, hurting], an injury or infection of the CNS that causes sudden abnormal episodes of discharging nerve impulses.

dischronation /dis′krōnā′shən/, a disorder of time awareness.

disciform keratitis /dis′ifôrm/ [Gk, *diskos*, flat plate; L, *forma*, form; Gk, *keras*, horn, *itis*, inflammation], an inflammatory condition of the eye that often follows an attack of dendritic keratitis, believed to be an immunologic response to an ocular herpes simplex infection. The condition is characterized by disclike opacities in the cornea, usually with inflammation of the iris.

disclosing solution [L, *dis* + *claudere*, to close, *solutus*, dissolved], a topically applied dye solution used to stain and reveal plaque and other deposits on teeth.

discoblastula /dis'kōblas'tyələ/ [Gk, *diskos*, flat plate, *blastos*, germ], a blastula formed from the partial cleavage that occurs in a fertilized ovum containing a large amount of yolk.

discocyte /dis'kəsīt/ [Gk, *diskos* + *kytos*, cell], a mature normal erythrocyte in the form of a biconcave disk without a nucleus.

discoid /dis'koid/ [Gk, *diskos*, flat plate, *eidos*, form], having a flat, round shape.

discoid lupus erythematosus (DLE) [Gk, *diskos* + *eidos*, form; L, *lupus*, wolf; Gk, *erythema*, redness, *osis*, condition], a chronic, recurrent disease, primarily of the skin, characterized by lesions that are covered with scales and extend into follicles. The lesions are typically distributed on the face but may also be present on other parts of the body. On healing, the lesions often leave atrophic, hyperpigmented, or hypopigmented scars. If hairy areas are involved, alopecia may result.

discoid meniscus, an abnormal condition characterized by a discoid rather than a semilunar shape of the cartilaginous meniscus of the knee. It is a developmental anomaly that is asymptomatic in infants and young children; it appears most often between 6 and 8 years of age. Common complaints are that the knee joint clicks or gives way, often but not always associated with an injury to the knee.

discoid placenta [Gk, *diskos*, quoit, *eidos*, form; L, *placenta*, flat cake], a round placenta.

discomfort level, a nursing outcome from the Nursing Outcomes Classification (NOC) defined as the severity of observed or reported mental or physical discomfort.

disconfirmation /diskon'fərmā'shən/, a dysfunctional communication that negates, discounts, or ignores information received from another person.

discordance /diskôr'dəns/ [L, *discordare*, to disagree], the expression of one or more specific traits in only one member of a pair of twins. —**discordant**, *adj.*

discordant twins, twins showing a marked difference in size (greater than 10% in weight) at birth.

discovery /diskov'ərē/ [L, *dis* + *coopiere*, to cover], (in law) a pretrial procedure that allows one party to examine vital witnesses and documents held exclusively by the adverse party.

discrete /diskrēt'/ [L, *discretus*, separated], **1.** individually distinct. **2.** composed of distinct parts.

discrimination /diskrim'inā'shən/ [L, *discrimen*, division], the act of distinguishing or differentiating.

discriminator /diskrim'inā'tər/, an electronic device capable of accepting or rejecting a pulse of energy on the basis of the pulse's amplitude. It is used to separate low-energy from high-energy radionuclides.

disease [L, *dis*; Fr, *aise*, ease], **1.** a condition of abnormal vital function involving any structure, part, or system of an organism. **2.** a specific illness or disorder characterized by a recognizable set of signs and symptoms, attributable to heredity, infection, diet, or environment.

disease-modifying antirheumatic drug (DMARD), a classification of antirheumatic agents referring to their ability to modify the course of disease, as opposed to simply treating symptoms. Agents in this group include auranofin, azathioprine, cycloSPORINE, gold salts, hydroxychloroquine, leflunomide, methotrexate, D-penicillamine, and sulfasalazine.

disease prevention, activities designed to protect patients or other members of the public from actual or potential health threats and their harmful consequences.

disengagement /dis'engāj'mənt/ [Fr, *disengager*, to release from engagement], **1.** an obstetric manipulation in which the presenting part of the baby is dislodged from the maternal pelvis as part of an operative delivery. **2.** the release or detachment of oneself from other persons or responsibilities. **3.** in transactional family therapy, a role assumed by a nurse or other therapist in observing and restructuring intervention without becoming actively and directly involved in the problem.

disengagement theory, the psychosocial concept that normally aging individuals and society mutually withdraw from normal interaction.

disequilibrium /dise'kwilib'rē-əm/ [L, *dis*, apart + *aequilibrium*], the loss of balance or adjustment, particularly mental or psychologic balance.

dishpan fracture [AS, *disc*, plate; L, *patina*, dish; *fractura*, break], a fracture that depresses the skull.

disinfect /dis'infekt'/ [L, *dis*, apart, *inficere*, to infect], to eliminate many or all pathogenic microorganisms with the exception of bacterial spores.

disinfectant /dis'infek'tənt/, a liquid chemical that can be applied to objects to eliminate many or all pathogenic microorganisms with the exception of bacterial spores.

disinfection /dis'infek'shən/, the process of killing pathogenic organisms or rendering them inert.

disinfestation /dis'infestā'shən/ [L, *dis*, apart, *infestare*, to infest], elimination of a threat of infestation by vermin, rodents, lice, or other noxious organisms.

disinhibition /dis'inhibish'ən/ [L, *dis,* apart, *inhibere,* to restrain], the removal of inhibition.

disintegrative psychosis /disin'təgrā'tiv/, a mental disorder of childhood that usually has an onset after 3 years of age and after normal development of speech, social behavior, and other traits. The child becomes irritable and undergoes mental deterioration, eventually reaching a stage of severe mental retardation.

disjunction /disjungk'shən/ [L, *disjungere,* to disjoint], the separation of paired homologous chromosomes during anaphase of the first meiotic division, or the separation of the chromatids of a chromosome during anaphase of mitosis and the second meiotic division.

disk [Gk, *diskos,* flat plate], **1.** chiefly in ophthalmology, a flat, circular platelike structure, as an articular disk or an optic disc. **2.** *informal.* an intervertebral disk. **3.** media used to store data in a computerized format.

diskectomy /dis·kek'tə·me/ [Gk, *diskos,* flat plate, *ektome,* incision], excision of an intervertebral disk.

diskography /diskog'rəfē/, the radiographic examination of individual intervertebral disks after introduction of a radiopaque contrast medium into the center of the disk. It has largely been replaced by MRI and CT myelography.

dislocation /dis'lōkā'shən/ [L, *dis* + *locare,* to place], the displacement of any part of the body from its normal position, particularly a bone from its normal articulation with a joint.—**dislocate,** *v.*

dislocation fracture, a fracture of the bony components of a joint associated with a displacement of a bone from its normal articulation with the joint.

dislocation of the clavicle [L, *dis,* apart, *locare,* to place, *clavicula,* little key], displacement of the collarbone. It may occur either at the sternal end or at the acromial or scapular extremity.

dislocation of the finger [L, *dis,* apart, *locare,* to place; AS, *finger*], displacement of a finger at a joint, as a result of trauma. In the absence of an accompanying fracture the dislocated finger can usually be reduced by steadying the hand at the wrist and maneuvering the dislocated bone back into place.

dislocation of the hip [L, *dis,* apart, *locare,* to place; AS, *hype*], displacement of the femoral head out of the hip joint, usually accompanied by pain, edema, rigidity, shortening of the leg, and loss of function. It may be congenital or acquired.

dislocation of the jaw [L, *dis,* apart, *locare,* to place; ME, *jowe*], unilateral or bilateral displacement of the mandible, typically as a result of a blow, a fall, or yawning. The mandible is fixed in an open position.

dislocation of the knee [L, *dis,* apart, *locare,* to place; AS, *cneow*], displacement of one of the bones of the knee joint.

dislocation of the shoulder [L, *dis* + *locare*; AS, *sculder*], any of several kinds of displacement of the bones of the shoulder joint, including acromial joint disruption and separation and dislocation of the glenohumeral joint with the humeral head displaced anteriorly and inferiorly.

dislocation of the toe, displacement of a metatarsal bone at a joint.

dismembered pyeloplasty, a pyeloplasty procedure for redundancy of the renal pelvis, consisting of excision of the ureteropelvic junction and part of the pelvis and reattachment of the spatulated end of the ureter to the remaining pelvis.

dismiss [L, *dis* + *mittere,* to send], in law, to discharge or dispose of an action, suit, or motion trial.—**dismissal,** *n.*

disopyramide phosphate /dī'sōpir'əmīd/, a cardiac antiarrhythmic prescribed in the treatment of artrial fibrillation, atrial flutter, ventricular premature complexes, and coupled ventricular tachycardias.

disorder [L, *dis,* apart, *ordo,* rank], a disruption of or interference with normal functions or established systems, as a mental or nutritional disorder.

disordered metabolism, changes in metabolism that result from disease and medications administered to control diseases.

disorder of movement [L, *dis,* apart, *ordo,* rank, *movere,* to move], any perverse or abnormal function of muscular action that may result from infection, injury, or congenital disability, such as ataxia, involuntary grimacing, and chorea.

disorder of sleep [L, *dis* + *ordo*; AS, *slaep*], any condition that interferes with normal sleep patterns, such as sleep apnea, phase shift, use of alcohol and certain drugs, excessive sleepiness, sleep walking, nightmares, sleep paralysis, restless leg syndrome, and narcolepsy.

disorder of written expression, a learning disorder in which the affected skill is written communication, characterized by errors in spelling, grammar, or punctuation; by poor paragraph organization; or by poor story composition or thematic development.

disorganized schizophrenia /disôr'gənīzd/ [L, *dis*; Gk, *organon,* organ], a subtype of schizophrenia characterized by an earlier age of onset, usually at puberty, and a more severe disintegration of the personality than occurs in other forms of the disease. The essential features include incoherence, loose associations, gross disorganization of behavior, and flat or inappropriate affect.

disorient /disôr′ē·ənt/, to cause to lose awareness or perception of space, time, or personal identity and relationships.

disorientation /-ā′shən/ [L, *dis + orienter,* to proceed from], a state of mental confusion characterized by inadequate or incorrect perceptions of place, time, or identity.

disparate twins /dis′pərāt, disper′it/, twins who are distinctly different from each other in weight and other features.

dispense /dispens′/ [L, *dis,* apart, *pensare,* to weigh], to prepare and issue drugs or drug mixtures from a pharmaceutical outlet or department.

disperse /dispərs′/ [L, *dis + spargere* to scatter], to scatter the component parts, as of a tumor or of the fine particles in a colloid system; also the particles so scattered.

dispersing agent /dispur′sing/ [L, *dis + spargere,* to scatter, *agere,* to do], a chemical additive used in pharmaceutics to cause the even distribution of the ingredients throughout the product, such as in dermatologic emulsions containing both oil and water.

dispersion /dispur′shən/, the scattering or dissipation of finely divided material, as when particles of a substance are scattered throughout the volume of a fluid.

displaced fracture /displāst′/ [Fr, *deplacement,* to remove], a traumatic bone break in which two ends of a fractured bone are separated and out of their normal positions.

displaced testis [Fr, *deplacement;* L, *testis,* testicle], a testis that is located in the pelvis, inguinal canal, or elsewhere after it normally would have descended into the scrotum.

displacement /displās′mənt/ [Fr, *deplacement,* to remove], **1.** the state of being displaced or the act of displacing. **2.** in chemistry, a reaction in which an atom, molecule, or radical is removed from combination and replaced by another. **3.** (in physics) the displacing in space of one mass by another, as when the weight or volume of a fluid is displaced by a floating or submerged body. **4.** in psychiatry, an unconscious defense mechanism for avoiding emotional conflict and anxiety by transferring emotions, ideas, or wishes from one object to a substitute that is less anxiety-producing.

DISS, abbreviation for **Diameter-Index Safety System.**

dissect /disekt′/ [L, *dissecare,* to cut apart], **1.** to cut apart tissues for visual or microscopic study using a scalpel, a probe, or scissors. **2.** to tear away the intima of

an artery, creating a false lumen that allows blood to flow into the wall of the artery. Branching vessels can be obstructed. —**dissection,** *n.*

dissecting aneurysm [L, *dissecare,* to cut apart; Gk, *aneurysma,* a widening], a localized dilation of an artery, most commonly the aorta, characterized by a longitudinal separation of the outer and middle layers of the vascular wall. Blood entering a tear in the intimal lining of the vessel causes a separation of weakened elastic and fibromuscular elements in the medial layer and leads to the formation of cystic spaces filled with matrix. Rupture of a dissecting aneurysm may be fatal in less than 1 hour.

disseminated /disem′inā′tid/, dispersed or spread throughout, as in an organ or the whole body.

disseminated intravascular coagulation (DIC) [L, *dis + seminare,* to sow, *intra,* within, *vasculum,* little vessel, *coagulare,* to curdle], a grave coagulopathy resulting from the activation of clotting and anticlotting processes in response to disease or injury, such as septicemia, acute shock, poisonous snakebites, neoplasms, obstetric emergencies, severe trauma, extensive surgery, and hemorrhage. The primary disorder initiates generalized intravascular clotting, which in turn activates fibrinolytic mechanisms. As a result, the initial hypercoagulability is succeeded by a deficiency in clotting factors with coagulopathy and hemorrhaging.

disseminated myelitis, an inflammation of the spinal cord.

disseminated neuritis, inflammation of peripheral nerves, with pain, tenderness, and loss of function. Lesions may affect the parenchyma of peripheral sensory and motor tracts.

dissent /disent′/ [L, *dis + sentire,* to feel], **1.** to differ in belief or opinion; disagree. **2.** in law, a statement written by a judge who disagrees with the decision of the majority of the court, stating explicit reasons for the contrary opinion.—**dissenting,** *adj.*

dissociation /disō′shē·ā′shən/ [L, *dis + sociare,* to unite], **1.** the act of separating into parts or sections. **2.** an unconscious defense mechanism by which an idea, thought, emotion, or other mental process is separated from the consciousness and thereby loses emotional significance. —**dissociative** /disō′shē·ətiv/, *adj.*

dissociation syndrome, a loss of the ability to sense painful and thermal stimuli, while retaining the sense of touch, tactile discrimination, and position sense.

dissociative anesthesia /disō′shē·ətiv/, a unique anesthesia characterized by analgesia and amnesia without loss of respiratory function. The patient does not appear to be anesthetized and can swallow and open eyes but does not process information. This form of anesthesia may be used to provide analgesia during brief, superficial operative procedures or diagnostic processes. Emergence may be accompanied by delirium, excitement, disorientation, and confusion.

dissociative disorder, a category of *DSM-IV* disorder in which emotional conflicts are so repressed that a separation or split in the personality occurs, resulting in an altered state of consciousness or a confusion in identity. Symptoms may include amnesia, somnambulism, fugue, dream state, and dissociative identity disorder.

dissociative identity disorder, a psychiatric disorder characterized by the existence of two or more distinct, clearly differentiated personality structures within the same individual, any of which may dominate at a particular time. Each personality is a complex unit with separate well-developed emotional and thought processes, behavior patterns, and social relationships.

dissolution /dis'əloo'shən/ [L, *dis* + *solvere,* to loosen], **1.** the separation of a complex chemical compound into simpler molecules. **2.** the dissolving of chemical substances into a homogenous solution. **3.** the loss of mental powers.

dissolve, to disperse the molecules or ions of one substance throughout the bulk of another substance.

dissolved gas /disolvd'/ [L, *dis* + *solvere,* to loosen], gas in a simple physical solution, as distinguished from gas that has reacted chemically with a solvent or other solutes and is chemically combined.

dissonance, the interference between sound waves of different pitches.

distal /dis'təl/ [L, *distare,* to be distant], **1.** away from or the farthest from a point of origin or attachment. **2.** away from or the farthest from the midline or a central point, as a distal phalanx.

distal acinar emphysema, one of the principal types of emphysema, limited to the distal ends of the alveoli along the interlobular septa and beneath the pleura, forming bullae.

distal latency, in electroneuromyography, the interval between the stimulation of a compound muscle and the observed response.

distal muscular dystrophy, a rare form of muscular dystrophy that usually affects adults. It is characterized by moderate weakness and by wasting that begins in the arms and legs and then extends gradually to the proximal and facial muscles.

distal myopathy, an autosomal-dominant form of muscular dystrophy, appearing in

two types. The first has onset in infancy, does not progress past adolescence, and is not incapacitating. The second has onset in adulthood.

distal part of prostatic urethra, the segment of the urethra that extends through the penis from the end of the membranous urethra to the navicular fossa.

distal phalanx, any one of the small distal bones in the third row of phalanges of the hand or the foot (second phalanx in the thumb and great toe).

distal radioulnar articulation, the pivotlike articulation of the head of the ulna and the ulnar notch on the lower end of the radius, involving two ligaments.

distal renal tubular acidosis (RTA), an abnormal condition characterized by excessive acid accumulation and bicarbonate excretion. It is caused by the inability of the kidney's distal tubules to secrete hydrogen ions, thus decreasing the excretion of titratable acids and ammonium and increasing the urinary loss of potassium and bicarbonate. Primary distal RTA occurs mostly in females, adolescents, older children, and young adults. It may occur sporadically or result from hereditary defects. Secondary distal RTA is associated with numerous disorders such as cirrhosis of the liver, malnutrition, starvation, and various genetic abnormalities.

distal sparing, a condition in which the spinal cord remains intact below a lesion. The reflex arc remains but is not modified by supraspinal influences. As a result, spastic movements may occur distal to the level of the lesion.

distal tubule, the part of the nephron lying between Henle's loop and the collecting duct in the kidney.

distance regulation [L, *distantia* + *regula,* rule], behavior that is related to the control of personal space. Most humans establish a quantum of space between themselves and others that offers security from either psychologic or physical threat while not creating a feeling of isolation.

distance vision, the ability to see objects clearly from a distance, usually from 20 feet, 6 m, or more.

distemper /distem'pər/ [L, *dis,* apart, *temperare,* to regulate], **1.** any mental or physical disorder or indisposition. **2.** a potentially fatal viral disease of animals characterized by rhinitis, fever, and a loss of appetite.

distend /distend'/ [L, *distendere,* to stretch], to enlarge or dilate something.

distensibility /disten'sibil'itē/ [L, *distendere,* to stretch], the ability of something to become stretched, dilated, or enlarged.

distension /disten´shən/, the state of being distended or swollen.

distillate /distil´it/ [L, *distillare,* to drop down], the liquid vaporized, condensed, and collected in a distillation.

distillation /dis´tilā´shən/ [L, *distillare,* to drop down], the process of vaporization followed by condensation in another part of the system.

distilled water /distild´/ [L, *distillare,* to drop down; AS, *waeter*], water that has been purified by being heated to a vapor form and then condensed into another container as liquid water free of nonvolatile solutes.

distocclusion /dis´tə-klōō´zhən/ [L, *distare,* to be distant, *occludere,* to close up], malocclusion in which the mandibular arch is in a posterior position in relation to the maxillary arch, generally considered identical with Class II in Angle's classification of malocclusion.

distogingival /dis´tōjinjī´vəl/, pertaining to the surfaces of a tooth nearest the gum and back of the mouth.

distolabial /dis´tōlā´bē-əl/, pertaining to the surfaces of a tooth nearest the lips and back of the mouth.

distorted thought self-control, a nursing outcome from the Nursing Outcomes Classification (NOC) defined as self-restraint of disruption in perception, thought processes, and thought content.

distortion /distôr´shən/ [L, *dis* + *torquere,* to twist], **1.** in psychology, the process of shifting experience in one's perceptions. Distortions represent personal constructs of truth, validity, and right and wrong. **2.** in radiology, radiographic image artifacts that may be caused by variations in the size and shape or position of the object.

distoversion /dis´tō-vər´zhən/ [L, *distare,* to be distant; *vertere,* to turn], the position of a tooth that is farther than normal from the median line of the face along the dental arch.

distractibility /distrak´tibil´itē/ [L, *dis* + *trahere,* to draw apart], a mental state in which attention does not remain fixed on any one subject but wavers or wanders.

distraction¹ /distrak´shən/ [L, *dis* + *trahere,* to draw apart], **1.** a procedure that prevents or lessens the perception of pain by focusing attention on sensations unrelated to pain. **2.** a method of straightening a spinal column by the forces of axial tension pulling on the joint surfaces.

distraction², a nursing intervention from the Nursing Interventions Classification (NIC) defined as purposeful focusing of attention away from undesirable sensations.

distraught /distrôt´/ [OFr, *destrait,* inattentive], a mental state of confusion, distraction, or absentmindedness.

distress /distres´/ [ME, *distressen,* to cause sorrow], an emotional or physical state of pain, sorrow, misery, suffering, or discomfort.

distributing artery, an artery with a tunica media composed of circularly arranged smooth muscle. It receives blood from conducting arteries and distributes the blood to organs and tissues.

distribution, the location of medications in various organs and tissues after administration. As body fat increases, drugs that are distributed primarily in body fat have a more prolonged effect.

distributive analysis and synthesis /distrib´yətiv/, the system of psychotherapy used by the psychobiologic school of psychiatry. It involves an extensive and systematic investigation and analysis of a person's total past experiences.

distributive care, a pattern of health care that is concerned with environment, heredity, living conditions, life style, and early detection of pathologic effects. The system is usually directed to continuous care of persons not confined to hospitals or other health care facilities.

district [L, *distringere,* to compel], **1.** in hospital nursing, a group of patients in an area of the unit, usually a subdivision of a ward, for whom a nurse manager or primary nurse is responsible. **2.** the area of a city or town assigned to a public health nurse.

disulfiram /dīsul´firam/, an alcohol-use deterrent prescribed in the treatment of chronic alcoholism. It causes severe intestinal cramping, diaphoresis, and nausea and vomiting if alcohol is ingested. It requires that the patient explicitly know that, when combined with alcohol intake, death may occur.

disuse phenomena /disyōōs´/ [L, *dis* + *usus,* to make use of; Gk, *phainein,* to show], the physical and psychologic changes, usually degenerative, that result from the lack of use of a body part or system. Disuse phenomena are associated with confinement and immobility, especially in orthopedics.

Ditropan, a trademark for an antispasmodic (oxybutynin chloride).

Diucardin, a trademark for a diuretic (hydroflumethiazide).

Diupres, a trademark for a fixed-combination drug containing a diuretic (chlorothiazide) and an antihypertensive (reserpine).

diurese /dī´yŏŏrēs/, the act of effecting diuresis.

diuresis /dī´yŏŏrē´sis/ [Gk, *dia,* through, *ouron,* urine], increased formation and secretion of urine. Diuresis occurs in conditions such as DM, diabetes insipidus, and acute renal failure.

diuresis renography, a diagnostic procedure in which a well-hydrated patient with an empty bladder is administered a radiopharmaceutical agent and 20 minutes later a diuretic, such as furosemide. The pattern of washout of the radiopharmaceutical is monitored to assess first the functioning of the collecting system and then the transport capacity of the upper urinary tract.

diuretic /dī'yŏōret'ik/, **1.** of a drug or other substance, tending to promote the formation and excretion of urine. **2.** a drug that promotes the formation and excretion of urine. Diuretic drugs are classified by chemical structure and pharmacologic activity into groups: carbonic anhydrase inhibitors, loop diuretics, mercurials, osmotics, potassium-sparing diuretics, and thiazides. Diuretics are prescribed to reduce the volume of extracellular fluid in the treatment of many disorders, including hypertension, CHF, and edema. Several adverse reactions, including hypovolemia and electrolyte imbalance, are common to all diuretics.

diuretic ceiling effect, the effect of possible increased drug toxicity without additional clinical benefit with the administration of more than a certain amount of diuretic drugs in a 24-hour period.

Diuril, a trademark for a thiazide diuretic (chlorothiazide).

diurnal /dīyŏōr'nəl/ [L, *diurnalis*, of a day], happening daily, as sleeping and eating.

diurnal enuresis [L, *diurnalis*, of a day; Gk, *enourein*, to urinate], involuntary voiding of urine during daylight hours.

diurnal mood variation, a change in mood that is related to the time of day.

diurnal rhythm [L, *diurnalis*, of a day; Gk, *rhythmos*], patterns of activity or behavior that follow day-night cycles, such as breakfast-lunch-dinner schedules.

diurnal variation, **1.** the variability of output or excretion of a substance during the day versus the night or over a 12-hour interval. **2.** expected high and low levels of a substance during a 24-hour period.

divalent, (in chemistry) an atom with two additional or two missing electrons producing a dianion (e.g., O^{2-}) or a dication (Ca^{2+}), respectively.

divalproex sodium, an anticonvulsant drug used to treat epilepsy and seizures, controlling simple and complex absence seizures alone or in combination with other anticonvulsant drugs. It is also approved for the treatment of migraines.

divergence /divur'jəns/ [L, *di* + *vergere*, to incline], a separation or movement of objects away from each other, as in the simultaneous turning of the eyes outward as a result of an extraocular muscle defect.

divergent dislocation /divur'jənt/, the temporary displacement of two bones, such as the radius and ulna.

diverticular hernia /dī'vurtik'yŏōlər/, the protrusion of a congenital intestinal diverticulum through an opening in the abdominal cavity.

diverticulectomy /dī'vurtik'yŏōlek'təmē/, surgical removal of a diverticulum.

diverticulitis /dī'vurtik'yŏōlī'tis/ [L, *diverticulare*, to turn aside; Gk, *itis*, inflammation], inflammation of one or more diverticula. The penetration of fecal matter through the thin-walled diverticula causes inflammation and abscess formation in the tissues surrounding the colon. With repeated inflammation the lumen of the colon narrows and may become obstructed. During periods of inflammation the patient experiences crampy pain, particularly over the sigmoid colon, fever, and leukocytosis.

diverticulosis /dī'vurtik'yŏōlō'sis/ [L, *diverticulare*, to turn aside; Gk, *osis*, condition], the presence of pouchlike herniations through the muscular layer of the colon, particularly the sigmoid colon. Most patients with this condition have few symptoms except occasional bleeding from the rectum. Diverticulosis may lead to diverticulitis.

diverticulum /dī'vurtik'yŏōləm/ *pl.* **diverticula** [L, *diverticulare*, to turn aside], a pouchlike herniation through the muscular wall of a tubular organ. A diverticulum may be present in the stomach, the small intestine, or, most commonly, the colon. —**diverticular,** *adj.*

divided dose, a measured fraction of a full dose of a medication given at short intervals so that the full dose is eventually taken within a specified period.

diving, the act of work or recreation in an underwater environment. The main health effects are related to the increased pressure to which the person is subjected.

diving goiter [AS, *dyypan*, to dip; L, *guttur*, throat], a large movable thyroid goiter located at times above the sternal notch and at other times below the notch.

diving reflex, a neural mechanism that produces an automatic change in the cardiovascular system when the face and nose are immersed in cold water. The heart rate decreases and the BP remains stable or increases slightly while blood flow to all parts of the body except the brain is reduced, thereby helping the body to conserve oxygen.

division [L, *dividere*, to divide], **1.** an administrative subunit in a hospital, such as a division of medical or surgical nursing. **2.** in public health nursing, an area that encompasses several geographic districts. **3.** the separation of something into two or more parts or sections.

divorce therapy, a type of counseling that attempts to help divorced couples disengage from their former relationship and malicious behavior toward each other or their children.

Dix, Dorothea Lynde [1802–1887], an American humanitarian who achieved fame as a social reformer, primarily for her work in improving prison conditions and care of the mentally ill. During her lifetime she helped to establish mental institutions in 30 states and Canada. During the U.S. Civil War she was appointed superintendent of army nurses for government hospitals.

Dix-Hallpike test /hôl′pīk/, a method for evaluating the function of the vestibule of the ear in patients with vertigo or hearing loss. The patient's position is quickly changed from sitting to lying down with the neck hyperextended, and then returned to sitting. Nystagmus can then be evaluated, and specific disorders of the vestibule may be diagnosed.

dizygotic /dī′zīgot′ik/ [Gk, *di,* twice, *zygotos,* yolked together], pertaining to twins from two fertilized ova.

dizygotic twins, two offspring born of the same pregnancy and developed from two ova that were released from the ovary simultaneously and fertilized at the same time. They may be of the same or opposite sex, differ both physically and genetically, and have two separate and distinct placentas and membranes, both amnion and chorion.

dizziness [AS, *dysig,* stupid], a sensation of faintness and whirling or an inability to maintain normal balance in a standing or seated position, sometimes associated with giddiness, mental confusion, nausea, and weakness.

DKA, abbreviation for **diabetic keto-acidosis.**

dL, abbreviation for **deciliter.**

DLE, abbreviation for **discoid lupus erythematosus.**

DLEK, abbreviation for **deep lamellar endothelial keratoplasty.**

DM, abbreviation for **diabetes mellitus.**

DMARD, abbreviation for **disease-modifying antirheumatic drug.**

D.M.D., abbreviation for *Doctor of Dental Medicine.* It is equivalent to a **D.D.S.** degree.

DMSO, abbreviation for **dimethyl sulfoxide.**

DNA, abbreviation for **deoxyribonucleic acid.**

DNA amplification, artificial increase in the number of copies of a particular DNA fragment into millions of copies through replication of the segment into which it has been cloned, a type of nucleic acid amplification.

DNA blotting, the transfer of separated DNA fragments from an electrophoretic gel to a nitrocellulose.

DNA chimera /kīmē′rə/, a recombinant molecule of DNA composed of segments from more than one source.

DNA-DNA hybridization, the formation of double-helical DNA from two complementary single strands. It is used to compare genome relationships between different species.

DNA fingerprint, the highly specific hybridization pattern generated by tandem repeats and other patterns of the DNA in an individual's genome.

DNA fingerprinting, a technique for comparing the nucleotide sequences of fragments of DNA from different sources. The fragments are obtained by treating the DNA with various endonucleases, enzymes that break DNA strands at specific sites. There is a chance of 1 in 30 billion that two persons who are not monozygotic twins would have identical DNA fingerprints. The specificity of the probe makes it applicable to questions of forensic science.

DNA gyrase, an enzyme that nicks and seals the DNA and relieves supercoiling.

DNA helicase, an enzyme that catalyzes the energy-dependent unwinding of the DNA double helix during DNA replication.

DNA library, a collection of DNA fragments of one organism, each carried by a plasmid or virus and cloned in an appropriate host. A DNA probe is used to locate a specific DNA sequence in the library.

DNA ligase, an enzyme that can repair breaks in a strand of DNA by synthesizing a bond between adjoining nucleotides. Under some circumstances the enzyme can join together loose ends of DNA strands, and in some cases it can repair breaks in RNA.

DNA polymerase, in molecular genetics, an enzyme that catalyzes the assembly of deoxyribonucleoside triphosphates into DNA, with single-stranded DNA serving as the template.

DNA probe, a labeled segment of DNA or RNA used to find a specific sequence of nucleotides in a DNA molecule. Probes may be synthesized in the laboratory, with a sequence complementary to the target DNA sequence.

DNAR, abbreviation for **do not attempt resuscitation.**

DNCB, abbreviation for **2,4-dinitrochlorobenzene.**

DNP, abbreviation for **2,4-dinitrophenol** or *2, 4-dinitrophenyl.*

DNR, abbreviation for **do not resuscitate.**

D.O., abbreviation for *Doctor of Osteopathy.*

DOA, abbreviation for *dead on arrival.*

Dobie's globule /dō'bēz/ [William M. Dobie, English physician, 1828–1915], a very small stainable body in the transparent disk of a striated muscle fiber.

DOBUTamine hydrochloride /dōbyoo'tə mēn/, a beta-adrenergic stimulating agent, acting primarily on beta-1 receptors. It is prescribed to increase cardiac output in severe chronic CHF and to provide adjunct in cardiac surgery.

Dobutrex, a trademark for a synthetic catecholamine (DOBUTamine hydrochloride), which stimulates beta-adrenergic receptors.

Dock, Lavinia Lloyd [1858–1956], an American public health nurse. She started a visiting nurse service in Norwalk, Connecticut, then joined the New York City Mission before becoming an assistant to Isabel Hampton Robb at Johns Hopkins Hospital in Baltimore. She returned to public health nursing when she joined the Henry Street Settlement in New York. She advocated an international public health movement and the improvement of education for nurses. With M. Adelaide Nutting, she wrote *History of Nursing,* a classic in nursing literature.

docosanol /doko'sänol/, an antiviral agent effective against activity viruses with a lipid envelope, including HSV. It is administered topically in the treatment of recurrent herpes labialis.

doctoral program in nursing, an educational program that offers preparation for a doctoral degree in the field of nursing designed to prepare nurses for advanced practice, academia, and research. On satisfactory completion of the course of study, the Ph.D. with a major in nursing, D.N.Sc. (Doctor of Nursing Science), or D.S.N. (Doctor of Science in Nursing) degree is awarded.

documentation, a nursing intervention from the Nursing Interventions Classification (NIC) defined as recording of pertinent patient data in a clinical record.

docusate /dok'yoōsāt/, a stool softener prescribed in the treatment of constipation.

Dodd, Marylin J., a nursing theorist who, with Carolyn L. Wiener, developed the Theory of Illness Trajectory, which involves not only the patient but the family and caregivers. The theory helps elucidate how patients and families tolerate the states of uncertainty caused by the illness and manage the illness.

Döderlein's bacillus /dā'dərlīnz, dō'dərlēnz/ [Albert S. Döderlein, German physician,

1860–1941], a gram-positive bacterium present in normal vaginal secretions.

dofetilide, a class III antidysrhythmic prescribed to treat atrial fibrillation and flutter.

doff /dôf/ [ME, contraction of *do off,* take off], to take off (clothing).

Döhle's inclusion bodies /dā'les, dōls/ [Karl G.P. Döhle, German pathologist, 1855–1928], blue inclusions in the cytoplasm of some leukocytes in May-Hegglin anomaly and in blood smears from patients with acute viral infections.

dolasetron, an antiemetic used to prevent the nausea and vomiting associated with cancer chemotherapy and radiotherapy and to prevent postoperative nausea and vomiting.

Dolene, a trademark for an analgesic (propoxyphene hydrochloride).

doll's eye reflex, a normal response in newborns to keep the eyes stationary as the head is moved to the right or left. The reflex disappears as ocular fixation develops.

doll's head maneuver, a test for CNS brainstem damage in a comatose patient. The head is quickly rotated from side to side. Normally the eyes deviate to the opposite direction. Failure of the eyes to make the movement is an indication of severe brainstem damage.

Dolobid, a trademark for a nonsteroidal antiinflammatory agent (diflunisal).

Dolophine Hydrochloride, a trademark for an opioid agonist analgesic (methadone hydrochloride).

dolor /dō'lôr/ [L, pain], any condition of physical pain, mental anguish, or suffering from heat. It is one of the four signs of inflammation. The others are calor (heat), rubor (redness), and tumor (swelling).

DOM, abbreviation for **dimethoxymethylamphetamine.**

domain, a region of a protein or polypeptide whose three-dimensional configuration enables it to interact specifically with particular receptors, enzymes, or other proteins.

dome fracture [L, *domus,* house, *fractura,* break], a break in the acetabulum, specifically one involving a weight-bearing surface.

domestic abuse, abuse or violence commonly describing spouse or partner abuse, including physical and/or sexual violence (use of physical force) or threats of such violence or psychologic and/or emotional abuse and/or coercive tactics.

dominance /dom'inəns/ [L, *dominari,* to rule], the property of an allele in which the allele is fully expressed in the phenotype, even when only one copy of the allele is present.—**dominant,** *adj.*

dominant /dom'inənt/ [L, *dominari,* to rule], **1.** exerting a ruling or controlling influence. **2.** in genetics, capable of expression when carried by only one of a pair of homologous chromosomes. **3.** in coronary artery anatomy, supplying the posterior diaphragmatic part of the interventricular septum and the diaphragmatic surface of the left ventricle; said of the right and left coronary arteries.

dominant allele /L, *dominari,* to rule; Gk, *genein* to produce], one of two or more alternative forms of a gene that is fully expressed in a heterozygote.

dominant eye /dom′inənt/, the eye that is customarily used for monocular tasks. It may or may not be related to hand preference.

dominant group, a social group that controls the value system and rewards in a particular society.

dominant idiotype, a segment of an immunoglobulin molecule that is present on a large proportion of the immunoglobulins generated in response to a particular antigen.

dominant trait, an inherited characteristic that is determined by a dominant allele.

don /don/ [ME, contraction of *do on,* put on], to put on (clothing).

Donath-Landsteiner syndrome /dō′not land′stīnər/ [Julius Donath, Austrian physician, 1870–1960; Karl Landsteiner, Austrian-American pathologist, 1868–1943], a rare blood disorder marked by hemolysis minutes or hours after exposure to cold. Systemic symptoms include the passage of dark urine, severe pain in the back and legs, headache, vomiting, diarrhea, and moderate reticulocytosis.

donation /dōna′shun/, **1.** a gift. **2.** the act of giving.

Done nomogram, a graph on which a number of variables are plotted so that the value of a dependent variable can be read on the appropriate line when the values of the other variables are given.

donepezil, a reversible cholinesterase used to treat mild to moderate dementia in Alzheimer's disease.

dong quai, a perennial herb used to restore vitality in tired women; for a variety of gynecologic, menstrual, and menopausal symptoms; and to treat cirrhosis of the liver. Current research suggests dong quai is ineffective for treating menopausal symptoms, and there are insufficient data to gauge its effectiveness for other indications.

Don Juan, a legendary Spanish libertine cited in many works of literature as a seductive and sexually promiscuous man.

Donnatal, a trademark for a GI fixed-combination drug containing a sedative (phenobarbital) and three anticholinergics (hyoscyamine sulfate, atropine sulfate, and hyoscine hydrobromide), used to decrease the motility of the GI tract.

donor /dō′nər/ [L, *donare,* to give], **1.** a human or other organism that gives living tissue to be used in another body, for example, blood for transfusion or a kidney for transplantation. **2.** a substance or compound that gives part of itself to another substance.

donor card [L, *donare,* to give + *charta*], a document in which a person offers to make an anatomic gift of body parts, at the time of death, for transplantation to recipients needing replacement of vital organs or tissues. The information can also be found on a state driver's license. Consent for organ donation generally requires consent from family of the organ donor.

do not attempt resuscitation (DNAR), an advisory that resuscitation of a patient should not even be attempted. The order is more strictly defined than the **DNR** *(do not resuscitate),* which may be interpreted as authorizing an attempt at resuscitation.

Donovan bodies /don′əvan/ [Charles Donovan, Irish physician, 1863–1951], encapsulated gram-negative rods of the species *Calymmatobacterium granulomatis,* present in the cytoplasm of mononuclear phagocytes obtained from the lesions of granuloma inguinale.

donut pad /dō′nut/, a pad designed to protect an injured joint. Cut to fit over the site of the injury, it causes the force on the body part to be transferred to surrounding areas.

DOOR syndrome, a rare syndrome of congenital *d*eafness, *o*nycho-*o*steodystrophy, and mental *r*etardation, existing in autosomal-dominant and autosomal-recessive forms.

dopa /dō′pə/, an amino acid, produced by oxidation of tyrosine, that occurs naturally in plants and animals. It is a precursor of dopamine, epINEPHrine, norepinephrine, and melanin.

dopamine /dō′pəmin/, a naturally occurring sympathetic nervous system neurotransmitter that is the precursor of norepinephrine. It is produced in the substantia nigra and transmitted to the putamen and caudate nucleus. It has an inhibitory effect on movement. A depletion of dopamine produces the symptoms of rigidity, tremors, and bradykinesia that are characteristic of Parkinson's disease.

DOPamine hydrochloride, a sympathomimetic catecholamine; lower doses preferentially stimulate peripheral dopamine receptors to cause primarily renal mesenteric vasodilation, while higher doses also stimulate beta-1 and alpha adrenergic receptors and act to increase BP. It is prescribed in the treatment of shock, hypotension, and low cardiac output to reduce the risk of renal failure.

dopaminergic /dō'pəminur'jik/, having the effect of dopamine.

dopaminergic receptor, a protein on the surfaces of certain cells that binds specifically to the neurotransmitter dopamine. Such receptors on vascular epithelial cells, when stimulated by dopamine, cause the renal mesenteric, coronary, and cerebral arteries to dilate and the flow of blood to increase.

dopant /do'pant/, an impurity purposely added, as to a laser crystal or a semiconductor, during manufacturing to create a desired characteristic.

dope [AS, *dyppan*, to dip], *slang.* morphine, heroin, or another opioid; marijuana; or another substance illicitly bought or sold and often self-administered for sedative, hypnotic, euphoric, or other mood-altering purposes.

doped /dōpt/, having impurities (dopants) added purposely during manufacturing.

Doppler color flow /dop'lər/ [Christian J. Doppler, Austrian physicist and mathematician, 1803–1853], an ultrasonic technique for detecting anatomic details by color coding of velocity shifts. In cardiography blood flowing in one direction appears red, and blood flowing in the opposite direction appears blue. The technique can also indicate the velocity of red blood corpuscles moving through the circulatory system. In laparoscopy, Doppler color flow allows for rapid identification and differentiation of ducts and valves in the viscera, particularly in detection and diagnosis of pancreatic and liver tumors and colorectal liver metastases.

Doppler echocardiography [Christian J. Doppler], a technique in which Doppler ultrasonography is used to evaluate the direction and pattern of blood flow within the heart.

Doppler effect [Christian J. Doppler; L, *effectus*], the apparent change in frequency of sound or light waves emitted by a source as it moves away from or toward an observer. The frequency increases as the source moves toward the observer and decreases as it moves away.

Doppler-guided injection [Christian J. Doppler], the use of a handheld ultrasound detector in sclerotherapy to guide a needle or syringe for injecting sclerosing fluid.

Doppler probe [Christian J. Doppler], a handheld diagnostic device that emits ultrasonic waves into the body. Reflection of the waves by a moving structure causes a change in their frequency.

Doppler ultrasonography [Christian J. Doppler], a technique used in ultrasound imaging to monitor moving substances or structures. The frequency of ultrasonic waves reflected by a moving surface is slightly different from that of the incident waves. The detected frequency shift yields information about the moving surface. The technique can be used to locate vessel obstructions, observe fetal heart sounds, localize the placenta, and image heart functions.

Doribax, a trademark for doripenem.

doripenem, a miscellaneous antiinfective used to treat serious infections caused by *Acinetobacter baumannii, Bacteroides caccae, B. fragilis, B. thetaiotaomicron, B. uniformis, B. vulgates, Escherichia coli, Klebsiella pneumonia, Peptostreptococcus micros, Proteus mirabilis, Pseudomonas aeruginosa, Streptococcus contellatus,* and *S. intermedius;* complicated UTIs; pyelonephritis; and complicated intraabdominal infections.

Dormia basket, a tiny apparatus consisting of four wires that can be advanced through an endoscope into a body cavity or tube, manipulated to trap a calculus or other object, and withdrawn.

dornase alfa /dôr'nās/, a natural enzyme that depolymerizes DNA molecules. Because as much as 70% of the solid matter of purulent material consists of viscous DNA derived from the nuclei of nutrophils, dornase is used in respiratory therapy of diseases such as CF to help break down purulent secretions in the airways.

dorsal /dôr'səl/ [L, *dorsum*, the back], pertaining to the back or posterior.—**dorsum,** *n.*

dorsal digital expansion, a triangular aponeurotic extension of the digital extensor tendon on the dorsum of the proximal phalanx of each digit, to which the tendons of the lumbrical and interosseous muscles are also attached. It forms a movable hood around the metacarpophalangeal joint.

dorsal digital vein, one of the communicating veins along the sides of the fingers.

dorsal flexure [L, *dorsalis*, back, *flectere*, to bend], the dorsal convexity of the thoracic region of the spine.

dorsal impaction syndrome, dorsal wrist pain after weight-bearing activities involving hyperextension, as may occur in weight lifting and gymnastics.

dorsal inertia posture, a tendency of a debilitated or weak person to slip downward in bed when the head of the bed is raised.

dorsal interossei of the foot, the most superior muscles in the sole of the foot that abduct the second to fourth toes. These four muscles also act through the dorsal expansions to resist extension of the metatarsophalangeal joints and flexion of the interphalangeal joints.

dorsal interossei of the hand, four muscles between and attached to the shafts of the metacarpals.

dorsal interventricular artery, the arterial branch of the right coronary artery, branching to supply both ventricles.

dorsalis pedis artery, the continuation of the anterior tibial artery, starting at the ankle joint, dividing into five branches, and supplying various muscles of the foot and toes.

dorsalis pedis pulse, the pulse of the dorsalis pedis artery, palpable at the prominent arch of the top of the foot between the first and second metatarsal bones.

dorsal lip, the marginal fold of the blastopore during gastrulation in the early stages of embryonic development of many animals.

dorsal nasal artery, a terminal branch of the ophthalmic artery that exits the orbit in the medial corner and supplies the dorsum of the nose.

dorsal recumbent [L, *dorsalis,* back; *recumbere,* to lie down], lying on the back, as in a supine position.

dorsal recumbent position [L, *dorsalis,* back + *positio*], the supine position with the person lying on the back, head, and shoulders.

dorsal rigid posture, a position in which a patient lying in bed holds one or both legs drawn up to the chest. It often involves only the right leg and is intended to relieve the pain of appendicitis, peritonitis, kidney stones, or pelvic inflammation.

dorsal root [L, *dorsalis,* back; AS, *rot*], the sensory component or posterior root of a spinal nerve, attached centrally to the spinal cord.

dorsal root ganglion [L, *dorsalis*; AS, *rot*; Gk, *ganglion,* knot], a swelling consisting of sensory neuron cell bodies whose axons constitute the dorsal root of a spinal nerve.

dorsal scapular nerve, one of a pair of supraclavicular branches from the roots of the brachial plexus. It supplies the rhomboideus major and the rhomboideus minor and sends a branch to the levator scapulae.

dorsiflect /dôr'siflekt/ [L, *dorsum* + *flectere,* to bend], to bend or flex backward, as in the upward bending of the fingers, wrist, foot, or toes.

dorsiflexion /dôr'siflek'shən/, upward or backward flexion of a part of the body.

dorsiflexor /dôr'siflek'sər/, a muscle causing backward flexion of a part of the body, as the hand or foot.

dorsiflexor gait, an abnormal gait caused by the weakness of the dorsiflexors of the ankle. It is characterized by footdrop during the entire gait cycle and excessive knee and hip flexion to allow clearance of the involved extremity during the swing phase.

dorsodynia /dôr'sōdin'ē·ə/, back pain, particularly in the muscles of the upper back area.

dorsolateral /dôr'sōlat'ərəl/, pertaining to the back of the body and to the side.

dorsolumbar /dôr'sōlum'bər/, pertaining to the back of the body and the lumbar region.

dorsosacral /dôr'sōsā'krəl/, pertaining to the back of the body and the sacrum.

dorsoventral /dôr'sōven'trəl/ [L, *dorsum,* back, *venter,* belly], pertaining to the axis that passes through the back of the body and the abdomen.

dorsum /dôr'səm/ [L, *dorsum,* back], the back of the body or the posterior or upper surface of a body part.

dorsum sellae /sel'ē/, the posterior boundary of the sella turcica of the sphenoid bone. It bears the posterior clinoid process and is an anatomic marker for the location of the pituitary gland at the base of the skull.

dorzolamide hydrochloride /dorzo'lämīd/, a carbonic acid anhydrase inhibitor, used in treatment of open-angle glaucoma and ocular hypertension. It is administered topically to the conjunctiva as the hydrochloride salt.

dosage /dō'sij/ [Gk, *didonai,* to give], the regimen governing the size, amount, frequency, and number of doses of a therapeutic agent to be administered to a patient.

dosage compensation, a mechanism by which the expression of X-linked traits is equalized in males, which have one X chromosome, and females, which have two. In mammals, it is accomplished by the inactivation of one of the X chromosomes in the somatic cells of females.

dose /dōs/ [Gk, *didonai,* to give], the amount of a drug or other substance to be administered at one time.

dose area product (DAP), the product of the entrance skin dose and the cross-sectional area of the x-ray beam.

dose calculations, formulas for adjusting drug dosages for children, elderly adults, or other patients who may lack mechanisms for metabolizing and excreting average adult levels of medications.

dose calibrator, an ionization chamber used in nuclear medicine to measure the amount of radioactivity of a radionuclide before injection into a patient.

dose equivalent (DE), a quantity used in radiation-safety work that expresses the amount of radiation dose and the physical damage that it may produce. It is the product of the dose (in rad or gray) and a quality factor specific to the type and energy of the radiation delivering that dose. The unit of dose equivalent is the sievert (Sv) or the rem.

dose-limiting recommendations, the absorbed dose equivalent limit of radiation exposure, which may vary for different body or organ exposures. For example, the absorbed dose equivalent limit for the skin or forearms of a radiation worker is much higher than the whole-body exposure.

dose-limiting side effects, drug effects that prevent a drug from being administered in higher doses.

dose rate, the amount of delivered radiation absorbed per unit time.

dose ratemeter /rāt′mētər/, an instrument for measuring the dose rate of radiation.

dose response, a range of doses over which response occurs. Doses lower than the threshold produce no response while those in excess of the threshold exert no additional response.

dose-response relationship, a mathematic relationship between the dose of a drug or radiation and the body's reaction to it. In a linear dose-response relationship, the response is proportional to the dose. In a linear nonthreshold relationship, any dose, regardless of size, can theoretically cause a response.

dose threshold, the minimum amount of a drug or absorbed radiation that produces a detectable effect.

dose to skin, the amount of absorbed radiation at the center of the irradiation field on the skin. It is the sum of the dose in the air and the scatter from body parts.

dosimeter /dōsim′ətər/ [L, *dosis*; Gk, *metron,* measure], an instrument used to detect and measure accumulated radiation exposure. It consists of a pencil-sized ionization chamber with a self-reading electrometer.

dosimetry /dōsim′ətrē/ [Gk, *dosis,* giving, *metron,* measure], **1.** the determination of the amount, rate, and distribution of radiation or radioactivity from a source of ionizing radiation. **2.** the accurate determination of medicinal doses based on body size, sex, age, and other factors.

DOT, 1. abbreviation for **Department of Transportation. 2.** abbreviation for *direct observation therapy.*

double [L, *duplus*], twice as much in strength, size, or amount.

double bind /bīnd/ [L, *duplus,* double; AS, *bindan,* to bind], a "no win" situation resulting from two conflicting messages from a person who is crucial to one's survival, such as a verbal message that differs from a nonverbal message.

double-blind study, an experiment designed to test the effect of a treatment or substance by using groups of experimental and control subjects in which neither the subjects nor the investigators know which treatment or substance is being administered to which group.

double-channel catheter [L, *duplus,* double; ME, *chanel;* Gk, *katheter,* a thing lowered into], a catheter with two lumens (channels) used to irrigate an internal cavity, with fluid entering one lumen and draining through the other.

double collecting system, a collecting system involving a double ureter. There may be either a duplex kidney or an ectopic kidney.

double-contrast arthrography, a method of making a radiographic image of a joint by injecting two contrast agents, usually a gaseous medium and a water-soluble iodinated agent, into the capsular space. The technique is most commonly used in radiography of the knee.

double-contrast barium enema [L, *duplus,* double, *contra,* against, *stare,* to stand; Gk, *barys,* heavy, *enienai,* to inject], an enema of radiopaque barium followed by evacuation and injection of air. The purpose is to detail radiographically the mucosal lining of the large intestine.

double-emulsion film, x-ray film that is coated with emulsion on both sides.

double-flap amputation [L, *duplus,* double; ME, *flappe,* flap; L, *amputare*], an amputation in which two flaps are made from the soft tissues to cover an area that has lost its integument from surgery or accident.

double fracture, a fracture consisting of breaks or cracks in two places in a bone, producing more than two bone segments.

double innervation, innervation of effector organs by fibers of the sympathetic and parasympathetic divisions of the autonomic nervous system. The pelvic viscera, bronchioles, heart, eyes, and digestive system are all doubly innervated.

double-lumen drain, a drain, such as a sump drain, consisting of two tubes, one inside the other.

double-needle entry, a technique for injecting a contrast medium or other agent with two needles, one with a larger bore. In diskography a 20-gauge needle is used to perform a spinal puncture and reach the anulus fibrosus of the disk, after which a longer, 26-gauge needle is passed through the guide needle to the injection target area.

double personality [L, *duplus,* double, *personalis,* of a person], a state of dissociation in which the individual presents personas to others at different times as two different persons, each with a different name and different personality traits. The two personalities are generally independent, contrasting, and unaware of the existence of the other.

double pneumonia, acute lobar pneumonia affecting both lungs.

double quartan fever, a form of malaria in which paroxysms of fever occur in a repeating pattern of 2 consecutive days followed by 1 day of remission. The pattern is usually the result of concurrent infections by two species of the genus *Plasmodium*, one causing paroxysms every 72 hours and the other every 48 hours.

double setup, a nursing procedure in which an obstetric OR is prepared for both vaginal delivery and cesarean section. The circulating and scrub nurses lay out the equipment required for both procedures.

double system ureterocele, a ureterocele involving a double collecting system; seen most often in girls in an ectopic ureter.

double ureter, existence of a second ureter on one side. It may be a complete connection from the kidney to the bladder or a partial tube forming a blind pouch. Most are asymptomatic, but some are accompanied by ectopic ureterocele.

double-void, a urinalysis procedure in which the first specimen is discarded and a second, obtained 30 to 45 minutes later, is tested. This method gives a more accurate measure of the amount of glucose in the urine at that particular time.

doubling dose, that dose of radiation expected to double the number of genetic mutations in a generation.

douche /do͞osh/ [Fr, shower-bath], **1.** a procedure in which a liter or more of a solution of a medication or cleansing agent in warm water is introduced into the vagina under low pressure. The woman often performs the procedure herself. Douching may be recommended in the treatment of various pelvic and vaginal infections. **2.** to perform a douche.

Douglas's cul-de-sac [James Douglas, Scottish anatomist, 1675–1742; Fr, bottom of the bag], a rectouterine pouch or recess formed by a fold of peritoneum that extends between the rectum and the uterus.

dowager's hump /dow′ijorz/, an abnormal backward curvature of the cervical spine, the result of compression fractures of osteoporosis.

dowel /dow′əl/ [ME, *doule*, part of a wheel], a small rod or pin, usually metal, fitted into a prepared hole within the root canal and cemented in place, serving to retain a dental restoration such as a crown.

dowel graft, a cylindrical plug of bone used to immobilize adjacent vertebrae in anterior spinal fusion.

Downey cells [Hal Downey, American hematologist, 1877–1959], lymphocytes identified in one system of classification of the blood cells of patients with infectious mononucleosis and hepatitis. The cells are designated as Downey I, II, or III lymphocytes.

down-regulation /doun reg-u-la′shun/, a decrease in the number of receptors for a chemical or drug on cell surfaces in a given area, usually caused by long-term exposure to the agent.

Down syndrome [John L. Down, English physician, 1828–1896], a congenital condition characterized by varying degrees of mental retardation and multiple defects. It is caused by the presence of an extra chromosome 21 in the G group or, in a small percentage of cases, by the translocation of chromosome 14 or 15 in the D group and chromosome 21 or 22. It is associated with advanced maternal age, particularly over 35 years of age. Infants with the syndrome are small and hypotonic, with characteristic microcephaly, brachycephaly, a flattened occiput, and typical facies with a mongoloid slant to the eyes, depressed nasal bridge, low-set ears, and a large, protruding tongue that is furrowed and lacks a central fissure. The hands are short and broad with a transverse palmar or simian crease; the fingers are stubby and show clinodactyly, primarily of the fifth finger. The feet are broad and stubby with a wide space between the first and second toes and a prominent plantar crease. Other anomalies associated with the disorder are bowel defects, congenital heart disease (primarily septal defects), chronic respiratory infections, visual problems, abnormalities in tooth development, and susceptibility to acute leukemia. The most significant feature of the syndrome is mental retardation, which varies considerably. The average intelligence quotient (IQ) is in the range of 50 to 60, so that the child is generally trainable and in most instances can be reared at home. The mortality rate is high within the first few years, especially in children with cardiac anomalies.

doxacurium, a nondepolarizing neuromuscular blocker used to facilitate endotracheal intubation and skeletal muscle relaxation during mechanical ventilation, surgery, or general anesthesia.

doxapram hydrochloride /dok′sopram/, a respiratory stimulant prescribed to improve respiratory function after anesthesia, in drug-induced CNS depression, and for chronic pulmonary disease associated with acute hypercapnia.

doxepin hydrochloride /dok′sopin/, a tricyclic antidepressant prescribed in the treatment of depression. A topical preparation is also available for treating atopic dermatitis, and unlabeled uses include the treatment of neuropathic pain.

doxercalciferol, a parathyroid agent (calcium regulator) used to lower high parathyroid hormone levels in patients undergoing chronic kidney dialysis.

DOXOrubicin hydrochloride /dok′sərōō′bisin/, an anthracycline antibiotic prescribed in the treatment of a wide variety of malignant neoplastic diseases including leukemias, lymphomas, sarcomas, germ cell turmors and carcinomas (e.g., lung, breast, prostate, ovary).

doxycycline /dok′sisī′klēn/, a tetracycline antibiotic prescribed in the treatment of infections caused by susceptible bacterial strains, especially *Chlamydia, Rickettsia,* and *Mycoplasma.*

doxylamine succinate /dok′silam′ēn/, an antihistamine prescribed for the treatment of acute allergic symptoms produced by the release of histamine.

dP/dt, the rate of change of pressure with respect to time.

DPG, abbreviation for **2,3-diphosphoglyceric acid.**

D.P.H., abbreviation for *Diploma in Public Health.*

DPL, abbreviation for **diagnostic peritoneal lavage.**

D.P.M., abbreviation for *Doctor of Podiatric Medicine.*

DPT vaccine, abbreviation for **diphtheria and tetanus toxoids and pertussis vaccine.**

DQ, abbreviation for **developmental quotient.**

dr., 1. abbreviation for *drachm.* 2. abbreviation for **dram.**

Dr., abbreviation for *doctor.*

dracunculiasis /drakun′kyōōlī′əsis/ [Gk, *drakontion,* little dragon, *osis,* condition], a parasitic infection caused by infestation by the nematode *Dracunculus medinensis.* It is characterized by ulcerative skin lesions on the legs and feet that are produced by the emergence of gravid female worms. People are infected by drinking contaminated water or eating contaminated shellfish.

Dracunculus medinensis /drakun′kyōōləs/, a parasitic nematode that causes dracunculiasis.

drag-to gait [ME, *dragen* + *gate,* path], a method of walking with crutches in which the feet are dragged rather than lifted with each step.

drain, a tube or other device used to remove air or a fluid from a body cavity or wound. The drain may be a closed system, designed to provide complete protection against contamination, or an open system in which there is a continual exchange of material.

drainage /drā′nij/ [AS, *drachen,* teardrop], the removal of fluids from a body cavity, wound, or other source of discharge by one or more methods. Closed drainage is a system of tubing and other apparatus attached to the body to remove fluid in an airtight circuit that prevents environmental contaminants from entering the wound or cavity. Continuous bladder irrigation is drainage in which a body area is washed out by alternately flooding and then emptying it with the aid of gravity, a technique that may be used in treating a urinary bladder disorder. Open drainage is drainage in which discharge passes through an open-ended tube into a receptacle. Suction drainage uses a pump or other mechanical device to assist in extracting a fluid.

drainage tube, a heavy-gauge catheter used for the evacuation of air or a fluid from a cavity or wound in the body.

draining sinus [AS, *drachen,* teardrop; L, *sinus,* hollow], an abnormal channel or fistula permitting the escape of exudate to the outside of the body.

Draize test /drāz/, a controversial method of testing the toxicity of pharmaceutic and other products to be used by humans by placing a small amount of the substance in the eyes of rabbits. The eye-irritancy potential of a substance is considered a measure of the possible effect of the product on similar human tissues.

dram (dr.) /dram/ [Gk, *drachme,* weight of the same value], a unit of mass equivalent to an apothecary's measure of 60 grains or ⅛ ounce and to $^1/_{16}$ ounce or 27.34 grains avoirdupois.

Dramamine, a trademark now used for two different antiemetics, dimenhyDRINATE, and more recently meclizine (causes less sedation).

dramatic play [Gk, *drama,* deed; AS, *plegan,* game], an imitative activity in which a child fantasizes and acts out various domestic and social roles and situations, as rocking a doll, pretending to be a doctor or nurse, or teaching school.

drape [ME, *drap,* cloth], a sheet of fabric or paper, usually the size of a small bed sheet, for covering all or a part of a person's body during a physical examination or treatment. —**drape,** *v.*

Drash's syndrome /drashəs/ [Allan Lee Drash, American pediatrician, 1931–2009], a syndrome of male pseudohermaphroditism, nephropathy leading to renal failure, and, in most cases, Wilms' tumor, caused by a genetic abnormality in chromosome 11.

Draw-a-Person (DAP) Test [AS, *dragan*; L, *personalis* + *testum,* crucible], a test based on the interpretation of drawings of human figures of both sexes. Interpretation depends on the subject's verbalizations, self-image, anxiety, and sexual conflicts and other factors.

drawer sign [AS, *dragan,* to drag], a diagnostic sign of a ruptured or torn anterior cruciate or posterior cruciate knee ligament. Testing involves having the patient flex the knee at a right angle while the lower leg is grasped just below the knee and moved first toward, then away from the examiner. The test result is positive for the knee injury if the head of the tibia can be moved more than a half inch from the joint.

drawing, a vague sensation of muscle tension.

drawsheet, a sheet that is smaller than a bottom or top sheet of a bed and is usually placed over the middle of the bottom sheet to keep the mattress and bottom linens dry. The drawsheet can also be used to turn or move a patient in bed.

dream [ME, *dreem,* joyful noise], **1.** a sequence of ideas, thoughts, emotions, or images that pass through the mind during the rapid-eye-movement stage of sleep. **2.** the sleeping state in which this process occurs. **3.** a visionary creation of the imagination experienced during wakefulness. **4.** in psychoanalysis, the expression of thoughts, emotions, memories, or impulses repressed from the consciousness. **5.** in analytic psychology, the wishes, emotions, and impulses that reflect the personal unconscious and the archetypes that originate in the collective unconscious.

dream analysis, a process of gaining access to the unconscious mind by means of examining the content of dreams, usually through the method of free association.

dream association, a relationship of thoughts or emotions discovered or experienced when a dream is remembered and analyzed.

dream state, a condition of altered consciousness in which a person does not recognize the environment and reacts in a manner opposed to his or her usual behavior, as by flight or an act of violence.

dress code [OFr, *dresser,* to arrange; L, *codex,* book], the standards set by an institution for the appropriate attire of its members.

dressing[1] [OFr, *dresser,* to arrange], a clean or sterile covering applied directly to wounded or diseased tissue to absorb secretions, protect from trauma, administer medications, maintain wound cleanliness, or stop bleeding.

dressing[2], a nursing intervention from the Nursing Interventions Classification (NIC) defined as choosing, putting on, and removing clothes for a person who cannot do this for self.

dressing forceps, a kind of forceps that has narrow blades and blunt or notched teeth designed for dressing wounds, removing drainage tubes, or extracting fragments of necrotic tissue.

Dressler's syndrome /dres′lərz/ [William Dressler, American physician, 1890–1969], an autoimmune disorder that may occur several days to several months after acute coronary infarction, characterized by fever, pericarditis, pleurisy, pleural effusions, and joint pain. It results from the body's immunologic response to a damaged myocardium and pericardium.

DRG, abbreviation for **diagnosis-related group.**

DRI, abbreviation for *Dietary Reference Intake.*

drift [AS, *drifan,* to move forward], a gradual movement away from the original position.

drifting tooth, a tooth that migrates from its normal position.

drill /dril/ [Dutch, *drillen,* to bore], a rotating cutting instrument for making holes in hard substances, such as bones or teeth.

Drinker respirator [Philip Drinker, American engineer, 1894–1972], an airtight respirator consisting of a metal tank that encloses the entire body, except the head. Used for long-term therapy, it alternates positive and negative air pressure within the tank, providing artificial respiration by contracting and expanding the walls of the chest.

drip [AS, *dryppan,* to fall in drops], **1.** the process in which a liquid or moisture forms and falls in drops. **2.** the slow but continuous infusion of a liquid into the body, as into the stomach peritoneum or a vein. **3.** to infuse a liquid continuously into the body.

drip gavage, a method of feeding a liquid formula diet through a tube inserted through the nostrils to the stomach.

drip system, in IV therapy, an apparatus for delivering specific volumes of IV solutions within predetermined periods and at a specific flow rate.

drive [AS, *drifan,* to move forward], a basic, compelling urge. Primary drive refers to one that is innate and in close contact with physiologic processes. A secondary drive is one that evolves during the process of growth and that incites and directs behavior.

Drixoral, a trademark for a fixed-combination drug containing an antihistamine (dexbrompheniramine maleate) and a vasoconstrictor (pseudoephedrine sulfate), used for the relief of congestion of the upper respiratory tract.

dromedary hump, a bulge on the lateral surface of a kidney (usually the left), resembling the hump of a dromedary camel, seen in persons whose spleen or liver presses down.

dromostanolone propionate /drō'mostan'əlōn/, a synthetic androgen prescribed for the treatment of female breast cancer.

dromotropic, an agent that influences the conduction of electrical impulses. A positive dromotropic agent enhances the conduction of electrical impulses to the heart.

dronabinol /drōnab'inol/, an oral antiemetic that is a synthetic derivative of THC, the principal psychotropic constituent of marijuana. It is prescribed for the treatment of refractory nausea and vomiting caused by cancer chemotherapy.

drooping lily sign, a deformity seen on IV urography of a duplex kidney, with the forcing of the lower collecting system and ureter outward and downward to resemble the shape of a drooping lily. It is caused by obstruction and dilation of the upper collecting system.

drop (gtt) [AS, *dropa*], a small spherical mass of liquid. It may vary in size with differences in temperature, viscosity, and other factors. For therapeutic purpose, a drop is regarded as having a volume of 0.06 to 0.1 mL, or 1 to 1.5 minims; 1.5 drops = 1 mL.

drop arm test, a diagnostic test for a tear in the supraspinatus tendon. The result is positive if the patient is unable to lower the affected arm slowly and smoothly from a position of 90 degrees of abduction.

drop attack, a form of TIA in which a brief interruption of cerebral blood flow causes a person to fall to the floor without losing consciousness. The fall may be caused by a disrupted sense of balance or decreased leg muscle tone.

droperidol /drōper'ədol/, an antipsychotic, sedative drug of the butyrophenone group, used most commonly with an opioid analgesic (fentanyl) in neuroleptanesthesia.

droplet infection [AS, *dropa*; L, *inficere,* to infect], an infection acquired by the inhalation of pathogenic microorganisms suspended in particles of liquid exhaled, sneezed, or coughed by another infected person or animal.

Droplet Precautions, safeguards designed to reduce the risk of droplet transmission of infectious agents. Droplet transmission involves contact of the conjunctivae or the mucous membranes of the nose or mouth of a susceptible person with large-particle droplets (larger than 5 μm in size) containing microorganisms generated from a person who has a clinical disease or is a carrier

of the disease. Droplets are generated from the source person primarily during coughing, sneezing, talking, and performance of certain procedures such as suctioning and bronchoscopy. Large-particle droplet transmission requires close contact between source and recipient persons, because droplets do not remain suspended in the air and generally travel only short distances (usually 3 feet or less).

dropper, a glass or plastic tube narrowed at one end with a rubber bulb at the other end to dispense a liquid medication one drop at a time.

Drosophila /drōsof'ilə/ [Gk, *drosos,* dew, *philein,* to love], a genus of fly, which includes *Drosophila melanogaster,* the Mediterranean fruit fly. It is useful in genetic experiments because of the large chromosomes found in its salivary glands and its sensitivity to environmental effects, as exposure to radiation.

drospirenone /drospi'rēnōn/, a spironolactone analog that acts as a progestational, used in combination with an estrogen component as an oral contraceptive.

drotrecogin alfa, a thrombolytic agent used to treat severe sepsis associated with organ dysfunction.

drowning [ME, *drounen*], asphyxiation caused by submersion in a liquid.

drowsiness, a decreased LOC characterized by sleepiness and difficulty in remaining alert but easy arousal by stimuli. It may be caused by a lack of sleep, medications, substance abuse, or a cerebral disorder.

drox, abbreviation for a *hydroxide anion.*

DrPH, abbreviation for *Doctor of Public Health.*

DRS, abbreviation for **Dementia Rating Scale.**

DRSP, abbreviation for **drug-resistant** *Streptococcus pneumoniae.*

drug [Fr, *drogue*], **1.** any substance taken by mouth; injected into a muscle, the skin, a blood vessel, or a cavity of the body; or applied topically to treat or prevent a disease or condition. **2.** *informal.* any substance that can be abused for its stimulant, depressant, euphoric, or hallucinogenic effects.

drug absorption, the process whereby a drug moves from the muscle, digestive tract, or other site of entry into the body toward the circulatory system.

drug abuse, the use of a drug for a nontherapeutic effect. Some of the most commonly abused drugs are alcohol; nicotine; marijuana; amphetamines; barbiturates; cocaine; methaqualone; opium alkaloids; synthetic opioids; benzodiazepines, including flunitrazepam (Rohypnol), gamma-hydroxybutyrate (GHB); 3,4-methylenedioxymethamphetamine (MDMA, ecstasy); phencyclidine;

ketamine; and anabolic steroids. Drug abuse may lead to organ damage, addiction, and disturbed patterns of behavior.

drug abuse cessation behavior, a nursing outcome from the Nursing Outcomes Classification (NOC) defined as personal actions to eliminate drug use that poses a threat to health.

Drug Abuse Warning Network (DAWN), a system of collecting information about admissions to emergency treatment facilities for drug abuse.

drug action, the means by which a drug exerts a desired effect.

drug addiction, a condition characterized by an overwhelming desire to continue taking a drug to which one has become habituated through repeated consumption because it produces a particular effect, usually an alteration of mental status. Addiction is usually accompanied by a compulsion to obtain the drug, a tendency to increase the dose, a psychologic or physical dependence, and detrimental consequences for the individual and society.

drug agonist, a drug that is capable of binding to a neurotransmitter or hormone receptor and causing a response similar to the endogenous hormone or neurotransmitter.

drug allergy, hypersensitivity to a pharmacologic agent. Manifestations range from a mild rash to anaphylactic shock, depending on the dose, the allergen, and the sensitivity of the individual.

drug clearance, the elimination of a drug from the body. Drugs and their metabolites are excreted primarily by the kidneys into the urine, but other routes for elimination include bile, sweat, saliva, breast milk, and expired air. The rate of clearance helps determine the size and frequency of a dosage of a particular medication.

drug compliance, the reliability of the patient in using a prescribed medication exactly as ordered by the physician. Noncompliance occurs when a patient forgets or neglects to take the prescribed dosages at the recommended times or decides to discontinue the drug without consulting the physician.

drug concentration, the amount of drug in a given volume of plasma (e.g., number of micrograms per milliliter). Toxic drug levels may be observed when the body's normal mechanisms for metabolizing and excreting drugs are impaired, as commonly occurs in patients with liver or kidney disorders and in infants with immature organs.

drug dependence, a psychologic craving for, habituation to, abuse of, or physiologic reliance on a chemical substance.

drug dispensing, the preparation, packaging, labeling, record keeping, and transfer of a prescription drug to a patient or an intermediary, who is responsible for administration of the drug.

drug disposition, general term for the absorption, distribution, metabolism, and excretion of a drug that has been administered.

drug distribution, the pattern of distribution of drug molecules by various tissues after the chemical enters the circulatory system. Because of differences in pH, lipid content, cell membrane functions, and other individual tissue factors, most drugs are not distributed equally in all parts of the body.

drug-drug interaction, a modification of the effect of a drug when administered with another drug. The effect may be an increase or a decrease in the action of either substance, or it may be an adverse effect that is not normally associated with either drug.

Drug Enforcement Agency (DEA), an agency of the Drug Enforcement Administration of the federal government, empowered to enforce regulations that control the import or export of narcotic drugs and certain other substances or the traffic of these substances across state lines.

drug fever, a fever caused by the pharmacologic action of a medication, its thermoregulatory action, a local complication of parenteral administration, or, most commonly, an immunologic reaction mediated by drug-induced antibodies. The onset of fever occurs usually between 7 and 10 days after the medication is begun; a return to normal is ordinarily seen within 2 or 3 days of discontinuance of the drug.

drug-food interaction, the effect produced when some drugs and certain foods or beverages are taken at the same time. For example, grapefruit juice blocks the metabolism of some drugs in the GI tract, an action that can cause normal dosages of a drug to reach toxic levels in the plasma.

drug holiday, a period of drug withdrawal to reverse ineffectiveness of a drug resulting from receptor desensitization or adverse effects that may result from chronic treatment.

drug-induced cystitis, allergic cystitis occurring in reaction to a medication.

drug-induced hepatopathy, toxic hepatopathy in which the hepatotoxin is a drug.

drug-induced parkinsonism, a reversible syndrome with the clinical features of Parkinson's disease but caused by the acetylcholine-dopamine imbalance of antipsychotic drugs.

drug-induced teratogenesis, congenital anomalies that reflect toxic effects of drugs on the developing fetus.

drug interaction, alteration of the effects of a drug by reaction with another drug or drugs, with foods or beverages, or with a preexisting medical condition.

drug metabolism, the transformation of a drug by the body tissues, primarily those of the liver, into a more water-soluble metabolite that can be eliminated.

drug monograph, a statement that specifies the kinds and amounts of ingredients a drug or class of drugs may contain, the directions for the drug's use, the conditions in which it may be used, and the contraindications to its use.

drug overdose (OD) [Fr, *drogue,* drug; AS, *ofer;* Gk, *dosis,* giving], an accidental or purposeful dose of a drug large enough to cause severe adverse reactions.

drug potency, the amount of drug required to produce a given percentage of its maximal effect, irrespective of the size of maximal effect. A drug can have high potency but poor efficacy, meaning that response is seen at very low doses and remains small even at high doses.

drug profile, an outline or summary of the characteristics of a drug or drug family, listing dosage types, pregnancy category, prescription or OTC forms, generics if available, contraindications, and classification if covered by controlled-substance laws.

drug psychosis [Fr, *drogue,* drug; Gk, *psyche,* mind, *osis,* condition], a psychotic state induced by excessive dosage of certain therapeutic drugs as well as drugs of abuse.

drug rash, a skin eruption, usually an allergic reaction, that is caused by a particular drug. A drug rash that is a sensitivity reaction does not occur the first time the drug is taken. The effect is observed with subsequent uses.

drug receptor, any part of a cell, usually a large protein molecule, on the cell surface or in the cytoplasm with which a drug molecule interacts to trigger a response or effect.

drug rehabilitation center, an agency that provides treatment for a person with a chemical or drug dependency.

drug resistance, the ability of disease organisms to resist effects of drugs that previously were toxic to them. Bacterial resistance to an antibiotic can result from mutation of a strain that has been exposed to an antibiotic or similar agent. Such acquired resistance may result from a chromosomal disruption or acquisition of a stray bit of DNA on a resistant plasmid. It can also be caused by extrachromosomal pieces of DNA that carry codes for antibiotic-resistant genes from a transposon, a DNA segment capable of insertion into a bacterial chromosome-resistant plasmid, or both. Decreased permeability to an antimicrobial is a common form of intrinsic resistance. Alteration or inactivation of the antibiotic is perhaps the most common mechanism of drug resistance. Acquired resistance to beta-lactam antibiotics is determined by the production of enzymes that inactivate the antibiotic. Drug resistance may also result from a change in the target site on which it acts.

drug-resistant *Streptococcus pneumoniae* **(DRSP),** a widespread strain of respiratory pathogen that is drug resistant. Until the 1960s, *S. pneumoniae* was almost uniformly susceptible to penicillin alone. In 1967, resistance to penicillin and other microbial drugs was first reported in Australia. It has since spread worldwide.

drug-seeking behavior (DSB), a pattern of seeking narcotic pain medication or tranquilizers with forged prescriptions, false identification, repeated requests for replacement of "lost" drugs or prescriptions, complaints of severe pain without an organic basis, and abusive or threatening behavior manifested when denied drugs.

drug sequestration, the process by which certain drugs are stored in the body tissues. Examples are tetracycline, which may be stored in bone tissue, and chloroquine, which is stored in the liver.

drug tolerance, a condition of cellular adaptation to a pharmacologically active substance so that increasingly larger doses are required to produce the same physiologic or psychologic effect obtained earlier with smaller doses.

drug trial, the process of determining an adequate and effective therapeutic dose or duration of treatment of a specific drug for a particular disease state.

drum cartridge catheter technique, a method used in central vein cannulation. The vein is cannulated with an introducer cannula. The needle is removed and replaced by the drum cartridge catheter, which is left in place.

drum electrode, an induction electrode that produces a strong magnetic field, used primarily with pulsed short-wave diathermy.

drusen /drŌŌ′zən/ [Ger, *Drüse,* stony granule], small yellowish hyaline deposits that develop beneath the retinal pigment epithelium, sometimes appearing as nodules within the optic nerve head. They are commonly associated with age-related macular degeneration.

DRVs, abbreviation for **Daily Reference Values.**

dry abscess, 1. a collection of pus that disperses without reaching a point of bursting. **2.** the remains of an abscess after the pus is absorbed.

dry catarrh [AS, *dryge*; Gk, *kata,* down, *rhoia,* flow], a dry cough that occurs in severe coughing spells. It is associated with asthma and emphysema in older people.

dry cough, a cough that does not produce sputum.

dry crackle, an abnormal chest sound produced by air passing through fibrotic alveolar sacs.

dry dressing, a plain dressing containing no medication, applied directly to an incision or a wound to prevent contamination or trauma or to absorb secretions.

dry eye syndrome, a dryness of the cornea and conjunctiva caused by a deficiency in tear production or altered tear film composition. It results in a sensation of a foreign body in the eye, burning eyes, keratitis, and erosion of the epithelial layers of the cornea and conjunctiva.

dry gas (D), a gas that contains no water vapor.

dry heat, a thermal effect produced by adding dry air or reducing the humidity of the environment.

dry heat sterilization [AS, *dryge* + *haetu*; L, *sterilis*], a method of sterilization that uses heated dry air at a temperature of 320° F to 356° F (160° C to 180° C) for 90 minutes to 3 hours.

dry heaves, retching.

dry ice, solid carbon dioxide, with a temperature of about −140° F (−78° C). It is used in cryotherapy of various skin disorders, such as the removal of warts.

dry labor, *informal.* labor in which amniotic fluid has already escaped. As amniotic fluid is continually produced, no labor is really dry.

dry pleurisy [AS, *dryge,* dry; Gk, *pleuritis*], inflammation of the pleura without effusion of serum. The cause may be a localized injury. Dry pleurisy may also be an early sign of TB.

dry rale, a fine sound associated with any of various interstitial lung diseases, such as idiopathic pulmonary fibrosis.

Drysdale's corpuscle /drīz′dālz/ [Thomas M. Drysdale, American gynecologist, 1831–1904], one of a number of transparent cells in the fluid of some ovarian cysts.

dry skin, epidermis that lacks moisture or sebum, often characterized by a pattern of fine lines, scaling, and itching.

dry socket, an inflamed condition of a tooth socket (alveolus) after a tooth extraction. The socket is not actually dry but is filled with a degenerating, infective blood clot. Normally a blood clot forms over the alveolar bone at the base of the socket after an extraction. If the clot fails to form properly or becomes dislodged, the bone tissue is exposed to the oral environment and can become infected, a usually painful condition.

dry vomiting [AS, *dryge*; L, *vomere,* to vomit], nausea with retching that does not produce vomitus.

DSA, abbreviation for **digital subtraction angiography.**

DSB, abbreviation for **drug-seeking behavior.**

DSDB, abbreviation for **direct self-destructive behavior.**

DSM, abbreviation for *Diagnostic and Statistical Manual of Mental Disorders.*

DSM-IV-TR, a text revision of the *DSM-IV* published in 2000, incorporating changes in diagnostic criteria for Tourette's syndrome, Alzheimer-type dementia, dementia caused by other medical conditions, personality change as a result of a general medical condition, exhibitionism, frotteurism, pedophilia, sexual sadism, and voyeurism.

DSN, abbreviation for *Doctor of Science in Nursing.*

DSR, abbreviation for **dynamic spatial reconstructor.**

DST, abbreviation for **dexamethasone.**

DT, abbreviation for **diphtheria and tetanus toxoids.**

DTaP, abbreviation for *diphtheria and tetanus toxoids and pertussis vaccine* in which the pertussis vaccine component is in the acellular rather than whole-cell form.

dTc, abbreviation for the muscle relaxant drug *d-tubocurarine.*

DTH, abbreviation for **delayed-type hypersensitivity.**

DTIC-Dome, a trademark for an antineoplastic (dacarbazine).

DTP vaccine, a combination of diphtheria and tetanus toxoids and acellular pertussis that is administered intramuscularly for active immunization against these diseases.

DTR, abbreviation for **deep tendon reflex.**

DTs, abbreviation for **delirium tremens.**

dual-energy absorptiometry (DEXA), an imaging technique that uses two low-dose x-ray beams with different levels of energy to produce a detailed image of body components, used primarily to measure bone mineral density.

dual-energy imaging /dyo͞o′əl/, a radiographic imaging technique in which two radiographs using two different kilovoltages are taken of the same target area. Because the radiographic image of soft tissue and bone varies with the kilovoltage, one radiograph isolates bone contrast and the other isolates soft tissue contrast. The combined x-ray films can facilitate a more precise identification of an abnormality.

dual-focus tube, an x-ray tube used for diagnostic imaging. It has one large and one small focal spot. The large focal spot is used when techniques that produce high heat are required; the small focal spot is used to produce fine, detailed images.

duality of central nervous system control /dyōō·al'itē/, a theory that the normal CNS is regulated by a check-and-balance feedback program. The theory is based on studies of posture-movement, mobility-stability, flexion-extension synergies, and similar action-reaction examples related to laws of basic physics.

Duane's syndrome /dwānz/ [Alexander Duane, American ophthalmologist, 1858–1926], an autosomal-dominant syndrome in which the affected eye shows limitation or absence of abduction, restriction of adduction, retraction of the globe on adduction, narrowing of the palpebral fissure on adduction and widening on abduction, and deficient convergence.

DUB, 1. abbreviation for **dysfunctional uterine bleeding. 2.** a genetically determined human blood factor that is associated with immunity to certain diseases.

Dubin-Johnson syndrome /dōō'bin jon'sən/ [Isadore N. Dubin, American pathologist, 1913–1980; Frank B. Johnson, American pathologist, b. 1919], a rare chronic hereditary hyperbilirubinemia, characterized by nonhemolytic jaundice, abnormal liver pigmentation, and abnormal function of the gallbladder.

dubnium (Db) [Joint Institute for Nuclear Research at Dubna, Russia], a transuranic element. Its atomic number is 105; the mass of its best-known isotope is 260. It is produced by an induced nuclear reaction.

DuBois formula /dōōboiz'/, a logarithmic method of calculating the number of square meters of body surface area of an individual from the height in centimeters, the weight in kilograms, and a constant, 0.007184.

Dubowitz assessment [Victor Dubowitz, South African–English pediatrician, b. 1931], a system of estimating the gestational age of a newborn according to such factors as posture, ankle dorsiflexion, and arm and leg recoil.

Duchenne-Aran disease /dōōshen' äräN'/ [Guillaume B.A. Duchenne, French neurologist, 1806–1875; François A. Aran,

French physician, 1817–1861], muscular atrophy caused by degeneration of the anterior horn cells of the spinal cord and primarily affecting the upper extremities. Chronic muscle wasting and weakness first appear in the hands and advance progressively to the arms and shoulders, eventually affecting the legs and other body areas.

Duchenne's disease /dōōshenz'/ [Guillaume B.A. Duchenne, French neurologist, 1806–1875], a series of three different neurologic conditions: **spinal muscular atrophy, bulbar paralysis,** and **tabes dorsalis.**

Duchenne's muscular dystrophy [Guillaume B.A. Duchenne], an abnormal congenital condition characterized by progressive symmetric wasting of the leg and pelvic muscles. It is an X-linked recessive disease that appears insidiously between 3 and 5 years of age and spreads from the leg and pelvic muscles to the involuntary muscles. Associated muscle weakness produces a waddling gait and pronounced lordosis. Muscles rapidly deteriorate, and calf muscles become firm and enlarged as a result of fatty deposits. Affected children experience contractures, have difficulty climbing stairs, often stumble and fall, and display wing scapulae when they raise their arms. Such persons are usually confined to a wheelchair by 12 years of age, and progressive weakening of cardiac muscle causes tachycardia and pulmonary problems.

Duchenne's paralysis [Guillaume B.A. Duchenne; Gk, *paralyein,* to be palsied], a form of motor neuron disease characterized by wasting and weakness in the laryngeal, pharyngeal, tongue, and facial muscles, leading to dysarthria and dysphagia. There may also be pyramidal tract involvement.

duct [L, *ducere,* to lead], a narrow tubular structure, especially one through which material is secreted or excreted.

duct carcinoma, a neoplasm of the epithelium of ducts, especially in the breast or pancreas.

duct ectasia, an abnormal dilation of a duct by lipids and cellular debris.

ductile, having the property of allowing metals to be drawn into the thinness of a wire.

ductility /duktil'itē/, the property of a material of having a large elastic range and tending to deform before failing from stress.

duction /duk'shən/, the movement of an individual eyeball from the primary to secondary or tertiary position of gaze.

ductless gland /dukt'les/, a gland lacking an excretory duct, such as an endocrine gland, that secretes hormones directly into blood or lymph.

duct of Rivinus /rivē′nəs/ [Augustus Q. Rivinus, German anatomist, 1652–1723; L, *ducere,* to lead], one of the minor sublingual ducts.

ductoscopy, endoscopy that assesses early changes in the breast ducts in women.

ductus /duk′təs/ *pl.* **ductus** /duk′tōōs/, the Latin term for **duct.**

ductus arteriosus, a vascular channel in the fetus that joins the pulmonary artery directly to the descending aorta.

ductus epididymidis, a tube into which the efferent ductules of the testes empty.

ductus venosus, the vascular channel in the fetus passing through the liver and joining the umbilical vein with the inferior vena cava. Before birth it carries highly oxygenated blood from the placenta to the fetal circulation.

due diligence, efforts made by responsible persons to prevent causing harm to others or their property or organization.

Duke longitudinal study, long-range in-depth research into the normal aging process of middle-aged and older men and women conducted at Duke University Medical Center, Durham, NC. The Duke studies led to development of the "longevity quotient" (LQ) used to evaluate an individual's rate of aging. It is calculated by the number of years a person survives beyond a given time divided by the expected number of years derived from actuarial tables.

Dukes' classification, a staging system for colorectal tumors, from A to D, according to the degree of tissue invasion and metastasis. A Dukes' A tumor is one that is confined to the mucosa and submucosa. A B tumor is one that has invaded the musculature but has not involved the lymphatic system. C tumors have invaded the musculature with metastatic involvement of the regional lymph nodes. D tumors are those that have metastasized to distant organ tissues.

Dulcolax, a trademark for a stimulant laxative (bisacodyl).

dull, 1. blunt. **2.** sluggish. **3.** not sharp, vivid, or intense.

dull pain [ME, *dul,* not sharp; L, *poena,* penalty], a mildly throbbing acute or chronic pain.

duloxetine, a miscellaneous antidepressant used to treat major depressive disorder and neuropathic pain associated with diabetic neuropathy.

dumping syndrome [ME, *dumpen,* to throw down], the combination of profuse sweating, nausea, dizziness, and weakness experienced by patients who have had a subtotal gastrectomy. Symptoms are felt soon after eating, when the contents of

the stomach empty too rapidly into the duodenum.

Duncan's mechanism [James M. Duncan, English obstetrician, 1826–1890; Gk, *mechane,* machine], a technique for delivery of the placenta with the maternal surface rather than the fetal surface presenting.

Dunlop skeletal traction, an orthopedic mechanism that helps immobilize the upper limb in the treatment of contracture or supracondylar fracture of the elbow. The mechanism uses a system of traction weights, pulleys, and ropes and may be accompanied by skin traction.

Dunlop skin traction, an orthopedic mechanism consisting of adhesive or nonadhesive skin traction that helps immobilize the upper limb in the treatment of contracture or supracondylar fracture of the elbow. The mechanism uses a system of traction weights, pulleys, and ropes, usually applied unilaterally but sometimes bilaterally.

duodenal /dōō′ədē′nəl/ [L, *duodeni,* 12 fingers], pertaining to the duodenum.

duodenal atresia, congenital absence or occlusion of a portion of the duodenum, characterized by vomiting a few hours after birth, cessation of bowel movements after 1 to 3 days, and usually distension of the epigastrium.

duodenal bulb, the first part of the superior portion of the duodenum, which has a bulblike appearance on radiographic views of the small intestine.

duodenal digestion [L, *duodeni,* 12 fingers, *digere,* to separate], digestion that occurs in the first intestinal segment beyond the pylorus, where secretions of the liver and pancreas are received and mixed with the partially digested food from the stomach. Chyle is formed, fats are emulsified, starch is hydrolyzed, and proteolytic enzymes begin to break down proteins.

duodenal switch, a surgical treatment for morbid obesity consisting of resection of the greater curvature of the stomach, leaving in place the pylorus and a little of the duodenum, which are anastomosed to the ileum. The rest of the duodenum and jejunum simply empty their secretions into the distal ileum through a new anastomosis.

duodenal ulcer, an ulcer in the duodenum, the most common type of peptic ulcer.

duodenectomy /dōō′ədēnek′təmē/ [L, *duodeni,* 12 fingers; Gk, *ektomē,* excision], the total or partial excision of the duodenum.

duodenitis /dōō′ədēnī′tis/ [L, *duodeni,* 12 fingers; Gk, *itis,* inflammation], a condition of inflammation of the duodenum.

duodenogastric reflux /dōō′ədē′nōgas′trik/ [L, *duodeni,* 12 fingers; Gk, *gaster,* stomach; L, *refluere,* to flow back], reflux of the contents of the duodenum into the stomach, which may occur normally, especially during fasting.

duodenography /doo'ədənog'rəfē/ [L, *duodeni*, 12 fingers; Gk, *graphein*, to record], the radiographic examination of the duodenum and pancreas.

duodenoscope /doo'ədē'nəskōp'/, an endoscopic instrument, usually fiberoptic, inserted via the mouth for the visual examination of the duodenum.

duodenoscopy /doo'ədənos'kəpē/, the visual examination of the duodenum by means of an endoscope.

duodenostomy /doo'ədēnos'təmē/ [L, *duodeni*, 12 fingers; Gk, *stoma*, mouth], the surgical creation of a direct opening to the duodenum through the abdominal wall.

duodenum /doo'ədē'nəm, doo·od'inəm/ *pl.* **duodena, duodenums** [L, *duodeni*, 12 fingers], the shortest, widest, and most fixed part of the small intestine, taking an almost circular course from the pyloric valve of the stomach so that its termination is close to its starting point. It is about 25 cm long and is divided into superior, descending, horizontal, and ascending portions.

dup, in cytogenetics, abbreviation for *duplication*.

duplex kidney /doo'pleks/, a kidney that has two separate collecting systems, with either a duplex ureter or a single ureter.

duplex scanner /doo'pleks/, an ultrasound machine that generally combines a 7.5- or 10-MHz imaging probe with a 3-MHz pulsed Doppler to allow visualization of a portion of the venous system. The scanner can determine the direction of blood flow within the veins.

duplex transmission [L, *duplex,* twofold], the passage of a neural impulse in both directions along a nerve fiber.

duplex ultrasonography, a combination of real-time and Doppler ultrasonography.

duplicating film /doo'plikā'ting/, a single-emulsion film used to copy an existing radiographic image by exposing it to ultraviolet light.

dupp /dup/, a syllable used to represent the second heart sound in auscultation. It is shorter and higher-pitched than the first heart sound.

Dupuytren's contracture /dYpY·itraNs', dēpē·itranz'/ [Guillaume Dupuytren, French surgeon, 1777–1835; L, *contractura*, drawing together], a progressive painless thickening and tightening of subcutaneous tissue of the palm, causing the fourth and fifth fingers to bend into the palm and resist extension. Tendons and nerves are not involved.

durable power of attorney for health care /dyoor'əbəl/, a document that designates an agent or proxy to make health care decisions if the patient is no longer able to make them. The document directs the surrogate person to function as "attorney-in-fact" and make decisions regarding all treatment, including the final decision about cessation of treatment.

Durabolin, a trademark for an anabolic steroid (nandrolone phenpropionate).

dural sac /dyoor'əl/, the blind pouch formed by the lower end of the dura mater, at the level of the second sacral segment.

dural sheath, an extension of the dura mater covering the optic nerve and spinal nerve roots.

dural venous sinuses, endothelial-lined spaces between the outer periosteal and inner meningeal layers of the dura mater into which empty the cerebral veins, the cerebellar veins, and the veins draining the brainstem and that lead to the internal jugular veins.

dura mater /doo'rə mā'tər, dyoo'rə/ [L, *durus,* hard, *mater,* mother], the outermost and most fibrous of the three membranes surrounding the brain and spinal cord. The dura mater encephali covers the brain, and the dura mater spinalis covers the cord.

Duranest, a trademark for a local anesthetic (etidocaine hydrochloride).

duration, the length of time a current is flowing.

duress /dyoores'/ [L, *durus,* hard], in law, an action compelling another person to do what he or she would not do voluntarily. A consent form signed under duress is not valid.

Durham-Humphrey Amendment, a 1952 modification of the 1938 U.S. Food, Drug, and Cosmetic Act. It differentiates between prescription and OTC medications and specifies medications that can or cannot be refilled without a new prescription. It also identifies which original prescriptions and refills can be authorized over the telephone.

Duroziez' murmur /dY'rōzyäs, dir'-, doo'r-/ [Paul L. Duroziez, French physician, 1826–1897; L, *murmur*], a systolic murmur heard over the femoral or another large artery when the artery is compressed. The phenomenon is associated with high arterial pulse pressure or aortic insufficiency. A diastolic murmur may also be heard when pressure on the artery is increased distal to the stethoscope.

dust [AS], any fine, particulate, dry matter.

dustborne infection, a disease in which the pathogenic organism is airborne in dust particles, as in coccidioidomycosis.

dutasteride, a sex hormone 5 alpha-reductase inhibitor used to treat benign prostatic hyperplasia in men with an enlarged prostate gland.

Dutton's relapsing fever [Joseph E. Dutton, English pathologist, 1877–1905], an infection caused by a spirochete, *Borrelia duttonii,* which is transmitted by a soft tick, *Ornithodoros moubata,* found in human dwellings in tropical Africa. The spirochete enters the lesion through a tick bite, characteristically producing a high fever, chills, rapid heartbeat, headache, joint and muscle pain, vomiting, and neurologic disorders.

duty [ME, *duete,* conduct], in law, an obligation owed by one party to another. Duty may be established by statute or other legal process, as by contract or oath supported by statute, or it may be voluntarily undertaken.

duty cycle, the percentage of time that ultrasound is being generated (pulse duration) over one pulse period.

Duverney's fracture /doo'vərnāz'/ [Joseph G. Duverney, French anatomist, 1648–1730], a break in the ilium just below the anterior superior spine.

Duvoid, a trademark for a cholinergic receptor agonist (bethanechol chloride).

dV/dt, the rate of change of voltage with respect to time.

DVM, abbreviation for *Doctor of Veterinary Medicine.*

DVT, abbreviation for **deep vein thrombosis.**

DVWR, abbreviation for **ventilatory weaning process, dysfunctional.**

dwarf /dwôrf/ [AS, *dweorge*], **1.** an abnormally short, undersized person, especially one whose body parts are not proportional. **2.** to prevent or retard, for example, normal growth.

dwarfism /dwôrf'izəm/, the abnormal underdevelopment of the body, characterized predominantly by extreme shortness of stature. Dwarfism has multiple causes, including genetic defects; endocrine dysfunction involving either the pituitary or the thyroid gland; and chronic diseases such as rickets, renal failure, intestinal malabsorption defects, and psychosocial stress, as in the maternal deprivation syndrome.

dwarf tapeworm infection, a type of intestinal parasitic disease caused by an infestation of *Hymenolepis nana.* It usually affects children who ingest eggs by placing contaminated materials into the mouth.

Dwayne-Hunt law /dwān' hunt'/, the principle that x-ray energy is inversely proportional to the photon wavelength. Thus, as the photon wavelength increases, photon energy decreases, and vice versa.

dwell time, the time that something therapeutic or diagnostic remains inside a patient's body. In peritoneal dialysis, the time needed for the dialysis solution to remain in the body for equilibration to be reached on the two sides of the membrane.

dwindles, a condition of physical deterioration involving several body systems, usually in an elderly person.

Dwyer instrumentation /dwī'ər/, one method for correcting the spinal curvature associated with scoliosis, involving a cable that is inserted to assist in maintaining the corrected curvature while the fusion heals. It is not usually removed unless there is postoperative indication of displacement or a pattern of associated symptoms. Dwyer cable instrumentation involves surgical intervention through the pulmonary cavity and the rib cage and is accompanied by a relatively greater surgical risk than a posterior approach. It is often inadequate to correct the spinal curvature involved and must frequently be followed several weeks later by a posterior spinal fusion.

D-xylose absorption test, a blood or urine test whose results reflect intestinal absorption, of the monosaccharide D-xylose, which is not metabolized by the body. In patients with malabsorption, intestinal D-xylose absorption is diminished, and as a result, blood levels and urine excretion are reduced. The test is used to separate patients with diarrhea caused by maldigestion (pancreatic/biliary dysfunction) from those with diarrhea caused by malabsorption (sprue, Whipple's disease, Crohn's disease).

D-xylose breath test, a breath test for bacterial overgrowth in the intestine. The fasting patient is administered a dose of D-xylose labeled with carbon 14, and the amount of radiolabeled carbon dioxide in the breath is measured at regular time intervals. Excessive levels of carbon dioxide mean that there are high levels of anaerobic bacteria in the intestines breaking down the xylose.

Dy, symbol for the element **dysprosium.**

dyad /dī'ad/ [Gk, *dyas,* two], one of the paired homologous chromosomes, consisting of two chromatids, which result from the division of a tetrad in the first meiotic division of gametogenesis.—**dyadic,** *adj.*

dyadic interpersonal communication /dī·ad'ik/, a process in which two people interact face to face as senders and receivers, as in a conversation.

Dyazide, a trademark for a fixed-combination drug containing two diuretic agents (potassium-sparing triamterene and potassium-losing hydrochlorothiazide).

dyclonine hydrochloride /dī'klənīn/, a local anesthetic, with bactericidal and fungicidal properties, for oral pain, pruritus, insect bites, and minor skin burns and injuries.

dye /dī/ [AS, *deag*], 1. to apply coloring to a substance. 2. a chemical compound capable of imparting color to a substance to which it is applied. Various dyes are used in medicine as stains for tissues, test reagents, therapeutic agents, and coloring agents in pharmaceutic preparations.

dye laser, a system of highly selective laser destruction of skin blemishes using various dyes at wavelengths at the longer oxygenated hemoglobin absorption peaks to overcome interference from overlying melanin.

dying care, a nursing intervention from the Nursing Interventions Classification (NIC) defined as the promotion of physical comfort and psychological peace in the final phase of life.

Dymelor, a trademark for an antidiabetic (acetoHEXAMIDE).

dynamic /dīnam′ik/ [Gk, *dynamis*, force], 1. tending to change or to encourage change, such as a dynamic nurse-patient relationship. 2. in respiratory therapy, a condition of changing volume.

dynamic cardiac work, the energy transfer that occurs during the ventricular ejection of blood.

dynamic compliance, the distensibility of the lungs, as measured by plethysmography during the breathing cycle.

dynamic equilibrium, the ability of a person to adjust to displacements of the body's center of gravity by changing its base of support.

dynamic ileus, an intestinal obstruction with associated recurrent and continuous muscle spasms.

dynamic imaging, the ultrasonographic imaging of an object in motion at a frame rate that does not cause significant blurring of images and at a repetition rate sufficient to represent the movement pattern adequately.

dynamic nurse-patient relationship, a conceptual framework in which the interpersonal aspects of the nurse-patient relationship are analyzed. Many factors affect the relationship. Elements in the process include the behavior of the patient, the reaction of the nurse, and the actions of the nurse that are intended to aid the patient.

dynamic psychiatry, the study of motivational, emotional, and biologic factors as determinants of human behavior.

dynamic range, 1. in radiology, the range of voltage or input signals that result in a digital output. 2. the range of sound intensity from the faintest sound a person can hear to the level that causes pain.

dynamic response, the accuracy with which a physiologic monitoring system such as an ECG simulates the actual event being recorded.

dynamic retinoscopy, a type of retinoscopy in which the patient fixes the gaze on a target at a near distance. Accommodation is active.

dynamic spatial reconstructor (DSR), a radiographic device that allows moving, three-dimensional images of organs to be examined from any direction. It is used in research.

dynamic splint [Gk, *dynamis*, force; D, *splinte*], any splint that incorporates springs, elastic bands, or other materials that produce a constant active force to counteract deforming forces of a splint.

dynamometer /dī′nəmom′ətər/ [Gk, *dynamis*, force, *metron*, measure], a device for measuring the degree of force used in the contraction of a group of muscles.

Dynapen, a trademark for an antibiotic (dicloxacillin sodium).

dyne /dīn/, a unit of force, specifically the force required to accelerate a free mass of 1 g at 1 cm/sec. One dyne equals 10^{-5} newton.

dynode /dī′nōd/, one of a series of plate-like elements that amplify electron pulses in a photomultiplier tube. Each electron that strikes a dynode causes several secondary electrons to be emitted. The dynode gain is the ratio of the number of secondary electrons to the number of incident electrons.

dynorphin /dīnôr′fən/, an endogenous opioid derived from the prohormone pro-dynorphin. It is a neuroactive peptide with potent analgesic effects.

dyphylline /dīfil′in/, a methylxanthine bronchodilator. It can be prescribed in the treatment of bronchospasm in acute bronchial asthma, bronchitis, and emphysema, but is no longer widely used.

Dyrenium, a trademark for a potassium-sparing diuretic (triamterene).

dysacusis /dis′əkōō′sis/ [Gk, *dys*, difficult, *akouein*, to hear], 1. any impairment of hearing involving difficulty processing details of sound as opposed to any loss of sensitivity to sound. 2. pain or discomfort in the ear from exposure to sound.

dysadrenia /dis′adrē′nē·ə/ [Gk, *dys*, bad; L, *ad*, to, *ren*, kidney], abnormal adrenal function characterized by decreased hormone production, as in hypoadrenalism or hypoadrenocorticism, or by increased secretion of the products of the gland, as in hyperadrenalism or hyperadrenocorticism.

dysarthria /disär′thrē·ə/ [Gk, *dys* + *arthroun*, to articulate], difficult, poorly articulated speech, resulting from interference in the control and execution over the muscles of speech, usually caused by damage to a central or peripheral motor nerve.

dysarthrosis /dis′ärthrō′sis/ [Gk, *dys,* difficult, *arthron,* joint], any disorder of a joint, including disease, dislocation, or deformity, that makes movement of the joint difficult.

dysautonomia /disô′tonō′mē·ə/ [Gk, *dys* + *autonomia,* self-government], an autosomal-recessive disease of childhood characterized by defective lacrimation, skin blotching, emotional instability, motor incoordination, total absence of pain sensation, and hyporeflexia, seen almost exclusively in Ashkenazi Jews.

dysbarism /dis′bäriz′əm/, a reaction to a sudden change in environmental pressure, such as rapid exposure to the lower atmospheric pressures of high altitudes. It is marked by symptoms similar to those of decompression sickness.

dysbasia /disbā′zhə/, difficulty in walking caused by a nerve lesion or lameness associated with atherosclerosis.

dyscholia /diskō′lē·ə/ [Gk, *dys* + *chole,* bile], any abnormal condition of the bile, related to either the quantity secreted or the condition of the constituents.

dyschroic film fault /diskrō′ik/, a defect in a photograph or radiograph that appears as a pinkish coloration when the film is viewed by transmitted light and as a green coloration when the film is viewed by reflected light.

dyscrasia /diskrā′zhə/ [Gk, *dys* + *krasis,* mingling], pertaining to an abnormal condition of the blood or bone marrow, such as leukemia, aplastic anemia, or prenatal Rh incompatibility.

dyscrastic fracture /diskras′tik/, any fracture caused by the weakening of a specific bone as a result of a debilitating disease.

dysdiadochokinesia /dis′dī·ədō′kōkinē′zhə/ [Gk, *dys* + *diadochos,* working in turn, *kinesis,* movement], an inability to perform rapidly alternating movements, such as rhythmically tapping the fingers on the knee. The cause is a cerebellar lesion and is related to dysmetria.

dyseidetic /dis′idet′ik/, dyslexic regarding the sight or recognition of whole words.

dysenteric /dis′enter′ik/ [Gk, *dys* + *enteron,* intestine], pertaining to or resembling dysentery.

dysentery /dis′inter′ē/ [Gk, *dys* + *enteron,* intestine], an inflammation of the intestine, especially of the colon. The most common causes are bacterial (*Shigella* infection) and amebic (*Entamoeba histolytica* infection), although it can also be caused by chemical irritants. It is characterized by frequent and bloody stools, abdominal pain, and tenesmus.

dysentery toxin, an exotoxin produced by *Shigella dysenteriae.*

dysergia /disur′jē·ə/ [Gk, *dys* + *ergon,* work], a condition characterized by lack of muscle coordination caused by a defect of efferent nerve impulses.

dyserythropoiesis, defective development of erythrocytes.

dysesthesia /dis′esthē′zhə/, a common effect of spinal cord injury characterized by sensations of numbness, tingling, burning, or pain felt below the level of the lesion.

dysfibrogenemia /disfi′brojĕne′mīə/, the presence in the blood of abnormal fibrinogen.

dysfluency /disflōō′ənsē/ [Gk, *dys-,* difficult; L, *fluere,* to flow], difficulty of proceeding, said of speech disorders such as stuttering.—**dysfluent,** *adj.*

dysfunctional /disfungk′shənəl/ [Gk, *dys;* L, *functio,* performance], of a body organ or system, unable to function normally.—**dysfunction,** *n.*

dysfunctional communication, a communication that results from inaccurate perceptions, faulty internal filters (personal interpretations of information), and social isolation.

dysfunctional stereotype, a stereotype in which structural or impaired aspects of a culture are emphasized.

dysfunctional uterine bleeding (DUB), abnormal uterine bleeding that is not caused by a tumor, inflammation, or pregnancy. It may be characterized by painless, irregular heavy bleeding or intermenstrual spotting or periods of amenorrhea. The condition is associated with anovulation and unopposed estrogen stimulation.

dysgammaglobulinemia /disgam′əglob′yə linē′mē·ə/, an inherited immunodeficiency disease. Affected individuals do not produce adequate numbers of immunoglobulins, including antibodies, and therefore are susceptible to infection, cancer, and other diseases.

dysgenesis /disjen′əsis/ [Gk, *dys* + *genein,* to produce], **1.** defective or abnormal formation of an organ or part, primarily during embryonic development. **2.** impairment or loss of ability to procreate.—**dysgenic,** *adj.*

dysgenics /disjen′iks/, the study of factors or situations that are genetically detrimental to the future of a race or species.

dysgenitalism /disjen′itəliz′əm/ [Gk, *dys;* L, *genitalis,* belonging to birth], any condition involving the abnormal development of the genital organs.

dysgerminoma /dis′jərminō′mə/ *pl.* **dysgerminomas, dysgerminomata** [Gk, *dys;* L, *germen,* germ; Gk, *oma,* tumor], a rare malignant tumor of the ovary that occurs in young women and is believed to arise from the undifferentiated germ cells of the embryonic gonad.

dysgeusia /disgoo′zhə/ [Gk, *dys* + *geusis,* taste], an abnormal or impaired sense of taste.

dysglandular /disglan′dyələr/, caused by or related to excessive or inadequate secretion by a gland.

dysgnathic anomaly /disnath′ik/ [Gk, *dys* + *gnathos,* jaw], an abnormality that affects one or both jaws.

dysgraphia /disgraf′ē·ə/ [Gk, *dys* + *graphein,* to write], an impairment of the ability to write.

dyshidrosis /dishīdrō′sis/ [Gk, *dys,* difficult, *hidros,* sweat], any disorder of the eccrine sweat glands.

dyskeratosis /dis′kerətō′sis/ [Gk, *dys* + *keras,* horn, *osis,* condition], an abnormal or premature keratinization of epithelial cells.

dyskeratosis congenita, an X-linked syndrome with onset in childhood, characterized by nail dystrophy, reticular cutaneous hyperpigmentation, mucosal leukokeratosis, and pancytopenia resembling that of Fanconi's syndrome.

dyskinesia /dis′kinē′zhə/ [Gk, *dys* + *kinesis,* movement], an impairment of the ability to execute voluntary movements. —**dyskinetic** /-et′ik/, *adj.*

dyskinesia intermittens, a condition of intermittent limping caused by circulatory impairment.

dyskinetic syndrome /dis′kinet′ik/, a form of CP involving a basal ganglion disorder. Clinical features include athetoid movements of the extremities and sometimes the trunk. There may also be choreiform movements that tend to increase with emotional tension and diminish during sleep.

dyslexia /dislek′sē·ə/ [Gk, *dys* + *lexis,* word], an impairment of the ability to read, as a result of a variety of pathologic conditions, some of which are associated with the CNS. Dyslexic persons often reverse letters and words, cannot adequately distinguish the letter sequences in written words, and have difficulty determining left from right.—**dyslexic,** *adj.*

dyslipidemia /dislip′id·ē′mē·ə/ [Gk, *dys,* difficult + *lipid* + Gk, *haima,* blood], abnormality in, or abnormal amounts of, lipids and lipoproteins in the blood.

dysmaturity /dis′machōōr′itē/ [Gk, *dys*; L, *maturare,* to make ripe], **1.** the failure of an organism to develop, ripen, or otherwise achieve maturity in structure or function. **2.** the condition of a fetus or newborn that is abnormally small or large for its age of gestation.—**dysmature,** *adj.*

dysmegalopsia /dis′megəlop′sē·ə/ [Gk, *dys* + *megas,* large, *opsis,* appearance], an inability to judge the size or measure of an object accurately.

dysmelia /dismē′lyə/ [Gk, *dys* + *melos,* limb], an abnormal congenital condition characterized by missing or shortened extremities of the body and associated with abnormalities of the spine in some individuals. It is caused by abnormal metabolism during the embryonic development of the limbs.

dysmenorrhea /dis′menərē′ə/ [Gk, *dys* + *men,* month, *rhein,* to flow], pain associated with menstruation. Primary dysmenorrhea is menstrual pain that results from factors intrinsic to the uterus and the process of menstruation. It is extremely common, occurring at least occasionally in almost all women. In approximately 10% of women, dysmenorrhea is sufficiently severe to cause episodes of partial or total disability. Pain occurs typically in the lower abdomen or back and is crampy, occurring in successive waves—apparently in conjunction with intense uterine contractions and slight cervical dilation. Pain usually begins just before, or at the onset of, menstrual flow and lasts from a few hours to 1 day or more. Pain is frequently associated with nausea, vomiting, and frequent bowel movements with intestinal cramping. Dizziness, fainting, pallor, and obvious distress may also be observed.

dysmetria /dismē′trē·ə/ [Gk, *dys* + *metron,* measure], an abnormal condition that prevents the affected individual from properly measuring distances associated with muscular acts and from controlling muscular action. It is associated with cerebellar lesions and typically characterized by overestimating or underestimating the ROM needed to place the limbs correctly during voluntary movement.

dysmnesic syndrome /disnē′sik/, a memory disorder characterized by an inability to learn simple new skills, although the person can still perform highly complex skills learned before the onset of the condition. The cause is a disease or injury that affects only certain brain tissues associated with memory.

dysmorphogenesis /dis′môrfōjen′əsis/, the development of ill-shaped or otherwise malformed body structures.

dysmorphophobia /-fō′bē·ə/ [Gk, *dys* + *morphe,* form, *phobos,* fear], **1.** a fundamental delusion of body image. **2.** the morbid fear of deformity.

dysmyelination /dismī′ē-lina′shun/, breakdown or defective formation of a myelin sheath, usually involving biochemical abnormalities.

dysorexia /dis'ŏrek'sē·ə/, **1.** an eating disorder associated with emotional or psychologic impairment. **2.** a diminished, disordered, or unnatural appetite.

dysostosis /dis'ostŏ'sis/ [Gk, *dys* + *osteon*, bone, *osis*], an abnormal condition characterized by defective ossification, especially defects in the normal ossification of fetal cartilages.

dyspareunia /dis'pərŏŏ'nē·ə/, an abnormal pain during sexual intercourse due to a spasm. It may result from abnormal conditions of the genitalia, dysfunctional psychophysiologic reaction to sexual union, forcible coition, or incomplete sexual arousal. Dyspareunia is also associated with hormonal changes of menopause and lactation that result in drying of the vaginal tissues as well as with endometriosis.

dyspepsia /dispep'sē·ə/ [Gk, *dys* + *peptein*, to digest], a vague feeling of epigastric discomfort after eating. There is an uncomfortable feeling of fullness, heartburn, bloating, and nausea. Dyspepsia is not a distinct condition, but it may be a sign of an underlying intestinal disorder. —**dyspeptic,** *adj.*

dysphagia /disfā'jē·ə/ [Gk, *dys* + *phagein*, to swallow], difficulty in swallowing commonly associated with obstructive or motor disorders of the oropharynx, hypopharynx, or esophagus. Patients with obstructive disorders, such as esophageal tumor or lower esophageal ring, are unable to swallow solids but can tolerate liquids. Persons with motor disorders such as achalasia are unable to swallow solids or liquids.

dysphagia lusoria, an abnormal condition, characterized by difficulty in swallowing, caused by the compression of the esophagus from an anomalous right subclavian artery that arises from the descending aorta and courses behind or in front of the esophagus.

dysphonia /disfō'nē·ə/ [Gk, *dys* + *phone*, voice], any abnormality in the speaking voice such as hoarseness. Dysphonia puberum refers to the voice changes that occur in adolescent boys.

dysphoria /disfôr'ē·ə/, a disorder of affect characterized by depression and anguish.

dysphylaxia /dis'filek'sē·ə/, a sudden awakening from deep sleep or a condition marked by too early awakening.

dyspigmentation /dispig'məntā'shən/, any abnormal increase or decrease in the production or distribution of skin pigment.

dysplasia /displā'zhə/ [Gk, *dys* + *plassein*, to form], any abnormal development of tissues or organs.

dysplasia epiphysealis hemimelica, a rare condition characterized by swellings in the extremities, usually on the inner and outer aspects of the ankles and knees, consisting of bone covered with epiphyseal cartilage, leading to limitation of motion of the joints.

dysplastic nevus, an acquired atypical nevus with an irregular border, indistinct margin, and mixed coloration, often occurring in large numbers and often a precursor of malignant melanoma.

dysplastic nevus syndrome, an inherited genetic syndrome that causes the individual to have a large number of nevi (moles), often 100 or more.

dyspnea /dispnē'ə/ [Gk, *dys* + *pnoia*, breathing], a distressful subjective sensation of uncomfortable breathing that may be caused by many disorders, including certain heart and respiratory conditions, strenuous exercise, and anxiety.—**dyspneal, dyspneic,** *adj.*

dyspraxia /disprak'sē·ə/ [Gk, *dys* + *prassein*, to do], a partial loss of the ability to perform skilled, coordinated movements in the absence of any associated defect in motor or sensory functions.

dysprosium (Dy) /disprŏ'sē·əm/ [Gk, *dys* + *prositos*, to approach], a rare-earth metallic element. Its atomic number is 66; its atomic mass is 162.50. Radioactive isotopes of dysprosium are used in radioisotope scanning, particularly in studies of the bones and joints.

dysproteinemia /disprŏ'tēnē'mē·ə/ [Gk, *dys* + *protos*, first, *haima*, blood], an abnormality of the protein content of the blood, usually involving the immunoglobulins.

dysraphia /disrā'fē·ə/ [Gk, *dys* + *raphe*, seam], failure of a raphe (an atomic seam) to fuse completely, as in incomplete closure of the neural tube.

dysraphic syndrome /disraf'ik/, a developmental disorder, usually involving the spinal cord, such as encephalocele or myelomeningocele.

dysreflexia management, a nursing intervention from the Nursing Interventions Classification (NIC) defined as prevention and elimination of stimuli that cause hyperactive reflexes and inappropriate autonomic responses in a patient with a cervical or high thoracic cord lesion.

dysregulation hypothesis /disreg'yələ'shən/, the view that depression and affective disorders do not simply reflect decreased or increased catecholamine activity but that they are failures of the regulation of these systems.

dysrhythmia /disrith'mē·ə/, any disturbance or abnormality in a normal rhythmic pattern, specifically, irregularity in the brain waves or cadence of speech.

dysrhythmia management, a nursing intervention from the Nursing Interventions Classification (NIC) defined as preventing, recognizing, and facilitating treatment of abnormal cardiac rhythms.

dyssebacea /disibā′shē·ə/ [Gk, *dys*; L, *sebum,* suet], a skin condition characterized by red, scaly, greasy patches on the nose, eyelids, scrotum, and labia. It results from a deficiency of vitamin B_2.

dyssynergia /dis′inur′jē·ə/ [Gk, *dys* + *syn,* together, *ergein,* work], any disturbance in muscular coordination, as in cases of ataxia.

dystaxia /distak′sē·ə/ [Gk, *dys* + *taxis,* order], partial ataxia, such as dystaxia agitans, in which a spinal cord irritation causes a tremor but no paralysis.

dysthymia /disthim′ē·ə/ [Gk, *dys* + *thymos,* mind], a form of chronic unipolar depression that tends to occur in elderly persons with debilitating physical disorders, multiple interpersonal losses, and chronic marital difficulties. Several depressive episodes may merge into a low-grade chronic depressive state.

dysthymic disorder /disthim′ik/ [Gk, *dys* + *thymos,* mind], a disorder of mood in which the essential feature is a chronic disturbance of mood of at least 2 years' duration. It involves either depressed mood or loss of interest or pleasure in all or almost all usual activities and pastimes, and associated symptoms but not of sufficient severity and duration to meet the criteria for a major depressive episode.

dysthyroid orbitopathy /disthī′roid or′bitop′əthē/ [Gk, *dys-,* difficult + *thyreos,* shield + *eidos,* form; L, *orbita,* wheel track; Gk, *pathos,* disease], the inflammatory changes of the eye orbit associated with thyroid dysfunction, usually in Graves' disease.

dystocia /distō′shə/ [Gk, *dys* + *tokos,* birth], pathologic or difficult labor that may be caused by an obstruction or constriction of the birth passage or abnormal size, shape, position, or condition of the fetus.

dystonia /distō′nē·ə/ [Gk, *dys* + *tonos,* tone], any impairment of muscle tone. The condition commonly involves the head, neck, and tongue and often occurs as an adverse effect of a medication.

dystonia musculorum deformans, a rare abnormal condition characterized by intense, irregular torsion muscle spasms that contort the body. The muscles of the trunk, shoulder, and pelvis are commonly involved.

dystonic /diston′ik/, referring to impairments of muscle tone, often excessive increase in tone when the muscle is in action and to hypotonia when it is at rest, often resulting in postural abnormalities.

dystrophic /distrof′ik/ [Gk, *dys* + *trophe,* nourishment], pertaining to a usually congenital disorder of structure or function of an organ or tissue that is aggravated by defective nutrition, such as accumulation of calcium salts in the cornea.

dystrophic calcification [Gk, *dys* + *trophe,* nourishment; L, *calx,* lime, *facere,* to make], the pathologic accumulation of calcium salts in necrotic or degenerated tissues.

dystrophin /distrof′in/, a protein that is missing or defective in Duchenne muscular dystrophy, which is localized to the sarcolemma of the muscle cell membrane. Its absence results in abnormal cell permeability, which may lead to cell destruction.

dystrophin-glycoprotein complex (DGC), a large oligomeric complex of proteins and glycoproteins of the sarcolemma that are critical to the stability of muscle fiber membranes and to the linking of the actin cytoskeleton to the extracellular matrix. Abnormalities of the plasma membrane of the muscle fiber that destroy this complex have been associated with several types of muscular dystrophy and with cardiomyopathy.

dystrophy /dis′trəfē/ [Gk, *dys* + *trophe,* nourishment], any abnormal condition caused by defective nutrition. It often entails a developmental change in muscles that does not involve the nervous system, such as fatty degeneration associated with increased size but decreased strength.

dysuria /disyŏŏr′ē·ə/ [Gk, *dys* + *ouron,* urine], painful, burning urination, usually caused by a bacterial infection, inflammation, or obstruction of the urinary tract. Laboratory examination of the urine may reveal the presence of blood, bacteria, or WBCs.

E

E, symbol for **expired gas.**

E, **1.** symbol for *elastance*. **2.** symbol for *energy*. **3.** symbol for *illumination*.

E₁, symbol for **monomolecular elimination reaction.**

E₂, symbol for **bimolecular reaction.**

ea, abbreviation for *each*.

Eakes, Georgene Gaskill, a nursing theorist who, with Mary Lermann Burke and Margaret A. Hainsworth, developed the Theory of Chronic Sorrow to describe the ongoing feelings of loss that arise from illness, debilitation, or death.

Eales' disease /ēlz/ [Henry Eales, British physician, 1852–1913], a condition marked by recurrent hemorrhages into the retina and vitreous, affecting mainly males in the second and third decades of life.

E and GW, abbreviation for **Economic and General Welfare.**

ear [AS, *eare*], one of two organs of hearing and balance, consisting of the external, middle, and internal ear. The external ear includes the skin-covered cartilaginous auricle visible on either side of the head and the part of the external auditory canal outside the skull. The middle ear contains three small bones, the malleus, incus, and stapes, which transmit vibrations caused by sound waves reaching the tympanic membrane to the oval window of the inner ear. The inner ear contains two separate organs: the vestibular apparatus, which provides the sense of balance, and the cochlea, with the organ of Corti, which receives vibrations from the middle ear and translates them into nerve impulses, which are interpreted by brain cells as specific sounds.

earache /ir'āk/ [AS, *eare* + *acan,* to hurt], a pain in the ear, sensed as sharp, dull, burning, intermittent, or constant. The cause is not necessarily a disease of the ear, because infections and other disorders of the nose, oral cavity, larynx, and TMJ can produce referred pain in the ear.

ear care, a nursing intervention from the Nursing Interventions Classification (NIC) defined as prevention or minimization of threats to ear or hearing.

eardrop instillation, the instillation of a medicated solution into the external auditory canal of the ear. The patient is asked to turn the head to the side so that the ear being treated faces upward. The orifice is exposed, and the drops of medicine are directed toward the internal wall of the canal. The tragus is then pushed against the ear canal to ensure that the drops stay in the canal.

eardrops [AS, *eare* + *dropa*], a topical, liquid form of medication for the local treatment of various conditions of the ear, such as inflammation or infection of the lining of the external auditory canal or impacted cerumen.

Early and Periodic Screening Diagnosis and Treatment (EPSDT), a section of the Medicaid program that requires all states to maintain a program to determine the physical and mental defects of persons who are covered by the program and to provide short- and long-range treatment.

ear oximeter [AS, *eare*; Gk, *oxys,* sharp, *genein,* to produce, *metron,* measure], a device placed over the earlobe that transmits a beam of light through the ear lobe tissue to a receiver. It is a noninvasive method of measuring the level of saturated hemoglobin in the blood.

ear speculum [AS, *eare*; L, *speculum,* mirror], a short, funnel-shaped tube attached to an otoscope for examining the ear canal.

ear thermometry, the measurement of the temperature of the tympanic membrane by detection of infrared radiation from the eardrum.

eating disorders, a group of behaviors often fueled by unresolved emotional conflicts symptomized by altered food consumption. Disorders include anorexia nervosa, bulimia nervosa, and binge eating.

eating disorders management, a nursing intervention from the Nursing Interventions Classification (NIC) defined as prevention and treatment of severe diet restriction and overexercising or bingeing and purging of food and fluids.

Eaton-Lambert syndrome [Lee M. Eaton, American neurologist; Edward H. Lambert, twentieth-century American physiologist], a form of myasthenia that tends to be associated with lung cancer.

Ebner's glands [Victor von Ebner, Austrian histologist, 1842–1925], serous glands of the tongue, opening at the bottom of the trough surrounding the circumvallate papillae.

Ebola virus disease /ēbōʹlə/ [Ebola River District, Congo], an infection caused by a species of RNA viruses of the *Filovirus* genus that is characterized by hemorrhage and fever. Initial symptoms include high fever, headache, chills, myalgia, sore throat, red itchy eyes, and malaise. Later symptoms include severe abdominal pain, chest pain, bleeding, shock, vomiting, and diarrhea. Maculopapular rash may occur in some patients.

EBP, abbreviation for **epidural blood patch.**

Ebstein's anomaly [Wilhelm Ebstein, German physician, 1836–1912; Gk, *anomalia,* irregularity], a congenital heart defect in which the tricuspid valve is displaced downward into the right ventricle. The abnormality is often associated with right-to-left atrial shunting and Wolff-Parkinson-White syndrome.

EBV, abbreviation for **Epstein-Barr virus.**

ECC, 1. abbreviation for **emergency cardiac care. 2.** abbreviation for *external cardiac compression.*

eccentric /eksenʹtrik/ [Gk, *ek,* out, *centre,* center], **1.** pertaining to an object or activity that departs from the usual course or practice. **2.** pertaining to behavior that may appear to be odd or unconventional but does not necessarily reflect a disorder.

eccentric contraction, a type of muscle contraction that occurs as the muscle fibers lengthen, such as when a weight is lowered through an ROM.

eccentric exercise, a voluntary muscle activity in which there is an overall lengthening of the muscle in response to external resistance.

eccentric implantation [Gk, *ek,* out, *centre,* center], in embryology, the embedding of the blastocyst within a fold or recess of the uterine wall, which then closes off from the main cavity.

eccentricity /ekʹsentrisʹitē/, behavior that is regarded as odd or peculiar for a particular culture or community, although not unusual enough to be considered pathologic.

eccentric jaw relation, any jaw relation other than centric relation at closure.

eccentric occlusion [Gk, *ek* + *centre*; L, *occludere,* to close up], a closed position of the teeth that does not coincide with centric relation, resulting in premature tooth contacts.

ecchondroma /ekʹəndrōʹmə/ [Gk, *ek* + *chondros,* cartilage, *oma,* tumor], a benign tumor that develops on the surface of a cartilage or under the periosteum of bone.

ecchymoma /ekʹimōʹmə/, a swelling caused by accumulation of blood on the site of a bruise.

ecchymosis /ekʹimōʹsis/ *pl.* **ecchymoses** [Gk, *ek, chymos,* juice], bluish discoloration of an area of skin or mucous membrane caused by the extravasation of blood into the subcutaneous tissues as a result of trauma to the underlying blood vessels or fragility of the vessel walls.

ecchymotic /ekʹimotʹik/ [Gk, *ek,* out, *chymos,* juice], pertaining to a discolored area on the skin or membrane caused by blood seeping into the tissue as a result of a contusion.

ecchymotic mask [Gk, *ek* + *chymos*; Fr, *masque*], a cyanotic or bluish discoloration of the face of a victim of traumatic asphyxia, as in strangulation or choking. The color is the result of petechial hemorrhages.

ecchymotic rash [Gk, *ek* + *chymos,* juice; OFr, *rasche,* scurf], a skin eruption characterized by black-blue spots caused by extravasation of blood into the tissues, usually as a result of a contusion.

eccrine /ekʹrin/ [Gk, *ekkrinein,* to secrete], pertaining to a sweat gland that secretes outwardly through a duct to the surface of the skin.

eccrine gland, one of the sudoriferous glands located in the dermis. Such glands are unbranched, coiled, and tubular. They promote cooling by evaporation of their secretion, which is clear, has a faint odor, and contains water, sodium chloride, and traces of albumin, urea, and other compounds.

ECF, 1. abbreviation for **extended care facility. 2.** abbreviation for **extracellular fluid.**

ECG, 1. abbreviation for **electrocardiogram. 2.** abbreviation for **electrocardiograph. 3.** abbreviation for **electrocardiography.**

echinacea, a perennial herb used for those with low immune status, for hard-to-heal superficial wounds, and as a sun protectant. It is most commonly used to treat the common cold and URIs. It has no apparent protective effects but may decrease the duration and symptoms of the infection if started when symptoms are first noticed. There are insufficient reliable data for other indications.

echinococcosis /ekīʹnōkokōʹsis/ [Gk, *echinos,* prickly husk, *kokkos,* berry, *osis,* condition], an infestation, usually of the liver, caused by the larval stage of a tapeworm of the genus *Echinococcus.* Dogs are the principal hosts of the adult worm. Humans, especially children, can become infested with larvae by ingesting eggs shed in the stool of infected dogs and cats or by petting or handling household dogs or cats. Fluid-filled cysts form in affected organs such as the liver, lungs, brain, bones, or heart. Clinical manifestations and prognosis vary, depending on the tissue invaded and the extent of infestation.

Echinococcus /ikī'nōkok'əs/ [Gk, *echinos*, prickly husk, *kokkos*, berry], a genus of small tapeworms that primarily infect canines.

echo /ek'ō/, **1.** the reflection of an ultrasound wave back to the transducer from a structure in the plane of the sound beam. **2.** *informal.* echoradiography.

echocardiogram /ek'ōkär'dē·əgram'/ [Gk, *echo*, sound, *kardia*, heart, *gramma*, record], a graphic outline of the movements of heart structures produced by ultrasonography.

echocardiography /ek'ōkär'dē·og'rəfē/ [Gk, *echo* + *kardia*, heart, *graphein*, to record], a diagnostic, noninvasive procedure for studying the structure and motion of the heart. Ultrasonic waves directed through the heart are reflected backward, or echoed, when they pass from one type of tissue to another.

echoencephalogram (EEG) /ek'ōensef'ələgram'/ [Gk, *echo* + *enkephalos*, brain, *gramma*, record], a recording produced by an echoencephalograph.

echoencephalography /ek'ō·ensef'əlog'rəfē/, the use of ultrasound to study the intracranial structures of the brain. —**echoencephalographic,** *adj.*

echogram /ek'ōgram/ [Gk, *echo*, sound, *gramma*, record], a recording of ultrasound echo patterns of a body structure, such as a gravid uterus.

echo home, an independent housing facility for an older person in or near the family home.

echolalia /ek'ōlā'lyə/ [Gk, *echo* + *lalein*, to babble], **1.** in psychiatry, the automatic and meaningless repetition of another's words or phrases, especially as seen in schizophrenia. **2.** in pediatrics, a baby's imitation or repetition of sounds or words produced by others. It occurs normally in early childhood development.—**echolalic,** *adj.*

echo planar imaging (EPI), a fast MRI mode.

echopraxia /ek'ōprak'sē·ə/ [Gk, *echo* + *prassein*, to practice], imitation or repetition of the body movements of another person, sometimes practiced by schizophrenic patients.

echoradiography /ek'ōrā'dē·og'rəfē/ [Gk, *echo*; L, *radius*, ray; Gk, *graphein*, to record], a diagnostic procedure using ultrasonography and various devices for the visualization of internal structures of the body.

echo sign, a repeated sound heard on percussion of a hydatid cyst.

echothiophate iodide /-thī'ōfāt/, an anticholinesterase used for ophthalmic purposes. It is prescribed for the treatment of chronic open-angle glaucoma and accommodative esotropia.

echovirus /ek'ō vī'rəs/ [enteric *c*ytopathogenic *h*uman *o*rphan; L, *virus*, poison], a picornavirus associated with many clinical syndromes but not identified as the causative organism of any specific disease. ECHO stands for *e*nteric, *c*ytopathic, *h*uman, *o*rphan. There are many ECHO viruses. Bacterial or viral disease may be complicated by ECHO virus infection, as aseptic meningitis accompanying some severe bacterial and viral infections.

Eck's fistula [Nikoli V. Eck, Russian physiologist, 1849–1917], an artificial passage between the end of the hepatic portal vein and the side of the inferior vena cava. It is used to treat esophageal varices in portal hypertension.

eclampsia /iklamp'sē·ə/ [Gk, *ek*, out, *lampein*, to flash], the gravest form of pregnancy-induced hypertension. It is characterized by grand mal seizure, coma, hypertension, proteinuria, and edema. The symptoms of impending seizure often include body temperature of up to 104°F, anxiety, epigastric pain, severe headache, and blurred vision.

eclectic /iklek'tik/ [Gk, *eklektikos*, selecting], pertaining to a therapy that selects, combines, and incorporates diverse techniques from several systems or theories into an integrated approach.

eclipse scotoma /iklips'/ [Gk, *ekleipsis*, abandoning, *skotos*, darkness, *oma*, tumor], a small central area of depressed or lost vision caused by looking directly at the sun without adequate protection.

ECM, abbreviation for *erythema chronicum migrans.*

ECMO, abbreviation for **extracorporeal membrane oxygenator.**

ecologic chemistry /ikaloj'ik/, the study of chemical compounds synthesized by plants that influence ecologic characteristics through chemical communication or toxic effects.

ecologic fallacy, a false assumption that the presence of a pathogenic factor and a disease in a population can be accepted as proof that a particular individual is the cause of the disease.

ecology /ikol'əjē/ [Gk, *oekos*, house, *logos*, science], the study of the interaction between organisms and their environment.

econazole /ikon'əzōl/, a topical antifungal agent prescribed in the treatment of tinea pedis, tinea cruris, tinea corporis, tinea versicolor, and candidiasis.

Economic and General Welfare (E and GW), a structural unit of the American Nurses Association and state nurses' associations whose major goal is to upgrade the salaries, benefits, and working conditions of nurses.

ecosystem /ek′ōsis′təm/, the total of all living things within a particular area and the nonliving things with which they interact.

EC space, abbreviation for *extracellular space.*

ecstasy /ek′stəsē/ [Gk, *ekstasis,* derangement], **1.** an emotional state characterized by exultation, rapturous delight, or frenzy. **2.** *informal.* popular name for 3,4-methylenedioxymethamphetamine, a hallucinogenic drug of abuse.

ECT, 1. abbreviation for **electroconvulsive therapy. 2.** abbreviation for **emission computed tomography.**

ecthyma /ek′thīmə/ [Gk, *ek,* out, *thyein,* to rush], an ulcerative pyoderma characterized by large pustules, crusts, and ulcerations surrounded by erythema. It is caused by a streptococcal infection after a minor trauma. The skin on the legs is most frequently affected.

ectocytic /ek′təsit′ik/ [Gk, *ektos,* outside, *kytos,* cell], outside a cell and not part of its organization.

ectoderm /ek′tədurm/ [Gk, *ektos,* outside, *derma,* skin], the outermost of the three primary cell layers of an embryo. The ectoderm gives rise to the nervous system; the organs of special sense, such as the eyes and ears; the epidermis and epidermal tissue, such as fingernails, hair, and skin glands; and the mucous membranes of the mouth and anus.—**ectodermal, ectodermic,** *adj.*

ectodermal cloaca /ek′tədur′məl/, a part of the cloaca in the developing embryo that lies external to the cloacal membrane and eventually gives rise to the anus and anal canal.

ectodermal dysplasia, any of a group of hereditary disorders involving tissues and structures derived from the embryonic ectoderm. Ectodermal dysplasia is a component of various syndromes, including anhidrotic ectodermal dysplasia and EEC syndrome.

ectodermoidal /ek′tədərmoi′dəl/ [Gk, *ektos,* outside, *derma,* skin, *eidos,* form], resembling or having the characteristics of ectoderm.

ectomorph /ek′təmôrf′/ [Gk, *ektos* + *morphe,* form], a person whose physique is characterized by slenderness, fragility, and a predominance of structures derived from the ectoderm.

ectoparasite /ek′tōper′əsīt/ [Gk, *ektos* + *parasitos,* guest], in medical parasitology, an organism that lives on the outside of the body of the host, such as a louse.

ectopic /ektop′ik/ [Gk, *ek* + *topos,* place], **1.** (of an object or organ) situated in an unusual place, away from its normal location. **2.** (of an event) occurring at the wrong time, as a premature heartbeat or premature ventricular contraction.

ectopic beat [Gk, *ek,* out, *topos,* place; AS, *beatan*], an impulse that originates in the heart at a site other than the sinus node.

ectopic focus, an area in the heart that initiates abnormal beats. Ectopic foci may occur in both healthy and diseased hearts and are usually associated with irritation of a small area of myocardial tissue.

ectopic kidney, one not in the usual position. The most common types are abdominal, lumbar, pelvic, thoracic, and crossed fused ectopic kidneys.

ectopic pregnancy, an abnormal pregnancy in which the conceptus implants outside the uterine cavity.

ectopic rhythm [Gk, *ek* + *topos,* place, *rhythmos,* beat], an abnormal heart rhythm caused by the formation of impulses in a focus outside the sinus node. Such a rhythm may be protective in cases of failure of the sinus node or excessive slowing of its rhythm, or it may indicate an active abnormal focus.

ectopic tachycardia [Gk, *ek* + *topos,* place, *tachys,* swift, *kardia,* heart], an abnormally rapid heartbeat caused by excitation arising from a focus outside the sinus node.

ectopic teratism, a congenital anomaly in which one or more parts are misplaced, such as dextrocardia, palatine teeth, and transposition of the great vessels.

ectopic testis, a testis that has descended from the abdominal cavity and settled in the suprapubic area, the thigh, or the perineum instead of the scrotum.

ectopic ureter, a ureter that opens in a place other than the bladder wall.

ectoplasm, the compact, peripheral part of the cytoplasm of a cell.

ectopy /ek′təpē/ [Gk, *ek,* out, *topos,* place], a condition in which an organ or substance is not in its natural or proper place.

ectrodactyly /ek′trōdak′təlē/ [Gk, *ektrosis,* miscarriage, *daktylos,* finger], a congenital anomaly characterized by the absence of part or all of one or more of the fingers or toes.

ectrogenic teratism /-jen′ik/ [Gk, *ektrosis* + *genein,* to produce, *teras,* monster], a congenital anomaly caused by developmental failure in which one or more parts or organs are missing.

ectrogeny /ektroj′ənē/ [Gk, *ektrosis* + *genein,* to produce], the congenital absence or defect of any organ or part of the body.—**ectrogenic,** *adj.*

ectromelia /ek′trōmē′lyə/ [Gk, *ektrosis* + *melos,* limb], the congenital absence or incomplete development of the long bones of one or more of the limbs.—**ectromelic,** *adj.,* **ectromelus,** *n.*

ectropic /ektrop′ik/, inside-out.

ectropion /ektro͞′pē·on/ [Gk, *ek* + *trepein,* to turn], eversion, most commonly of the eyelid, exposing the conjunctival membrane lining the eyelid and part of the eyeball.

ectrosyndactyly /ek′trōsindak′təlē/ [Gk, *ektrosis* + *syn,* together, *daktylos,* finger], a congenital anomaly characterized by the absence of some but not all of the digits, with those that are formed webbed so as to appear fused.

eculizumab, a monoclonal antibody used to treat proximal nocturnal hemoglobinuria, a rare, genetic form of hemolytic anemia.

eczema /ek′simə/ [Gk, *ekzein,* to boil over], a general superficial dermatitis of unknown cause. In the early stage it may be pruritic, erythematous, papulovesicular, edematous, and weeping. Later it becomes crusted, scaly, thickened, or lichenified. Exacerbating factors include sudden temperature changes, humidity, psychologic stress, illness, allergies, fibers, detergents, and perfumes.—**eczematous,** *adj.*

eczema herpeticum, a generalized vesiculopustular rash caused by HSV or vaccinia virus infection of a preexisting rash such as atopic dermatitis.

eczematous conjunctivitis /eksem′ətəs/, conjunctival and corneal inflammation associated with multiple tiny ulcerated vesicles.

eczopiclone, a sedative/hypnotic used to treat insomnia.

ED, **1.** abbreviation for **effective dose.** **2.** abbreviation for **emergency department.**

ED₅₀, symbol for **median effective dose.**

ED₉₀, the dose of a therapeutic agent that eradicates 90% of the target pathogen.

edaphon /ed′əfon/, the composite of organisms that live in the soil.—**edaphic,** *adj.*

EDB, **1.** abbreviation for **ethylene dibromide.** **2.** abbreviation for *expected date of birth.*

EDC, abbreviation for *expected date of confinement.*

EDD, abbreviation for **expected date of delivery.**

eddy currents, small circular electric fields induced when a magnetic field is created. They result in intramolecular oscillation or vibration of tissue contents, causing generation of heat.

Edecrin Sodium, a trademark for a loop diuretic (ethacrynate sodium).

EDE limit, abbreviation for **effective dose equivalent limit.**

edema /idē′mə/ [Gk, *oidema,* swelling], the abnormal accumulation of fluid in interstitial spaces of tissues such as in the pericardial sac, intrapleural space, peritoneal cavity, or joint capsules.

edema of glottis [Gk, *oidema,* swelling, *glossa,* tongue], a swelling caused by fluid accumulation in the soft tissues of the larynx. Symptoms include stridor, hoarseness, and dyspnea. The condition, usually inflammatory, may result from infection, injury, or inhalation of toxic gases.

edematogenic /edem′ətōjen′ik/, causing edema.

edentulism /eden′tulizem/, the condition of being without teeth.

edentulous /ēden′chələs/, lacking natural teeth.

edetate calcium disodium (EDTA) /ed′ətāt/, a chelating agent used to treat lead poisoning. It is not the same as edetate disodium.

edetate disodium, a parenteral chelating agent used to lower plasma calcium levels. It should be prescribed only when clinical conditions such as hypercalcemic crisis or ventricular arrhythmia and heart block resulting from digitalis toxicity mandate aggressive therapy.

edetic acid (EDTA) /idet′ik/, a chelating agent.

EDG, abbreviation for **electrodynograph.**

edge /ej/ [ME, *egge*], **1.** a thin side or border. **2.** the end of a surface, e.g., the edge of a cliff.

edge enhancement, the enhancement of structure margins (edges) using digital processing techniques.

edge response function (ERF), the ability of a CT system to produce a sharp image of a high-contrast edge, such as the edge of the heart.

edgewise appliance, a fixed orthodontic appliance whose attachment brackets have a rectangular slot that engages a round or rectangular arch wire. The most widely prescribed orthodontic appliance, it is used to correct or improve malocclusion.

edible, pertaining to a substance that can be eaten.

EDRF, abbreviation for **endothelial-derived relaxing factor.**

edrophonium chloride /ed′rōfo͞′nē·əm/, a cholinesterase inhibitor that acts as an antidote to curare and other nondepolarizing neuromuscular blockers and is an aid in the diagnosis of myasthenia gravis. It is prescribed to reverse neuromuscular blockade, to treat curare toxicity, and to aid in the diagnosis of suspected myasthenia gravis.

edrophonium test, a test for myasthenia gravis in which an IV solution of edrophonium chloride is injected into a patient. A brief improvement in muscle activity is regarded as a positive result. Edrophonium

E

chloride is also used to distinguish between myasthenia gravis and a cholinergic crisis.

Edsall's disease [David L. Edsall, American physician, 1869–1945], a cramping condition that is the result of excessive exposure to heat.

EDTA, 1. abbreviation for *ethylenediamineteraacetic acid* (edetic acid). 2. abbreviation for **edetate calcium disodium.**

educational psychology /ej'əkā'shənəl/ [L, *educatus,* to rear; Gk, *psyche,* mind, *logos,* science], the application of psychologic principles, techniques, and tests to educational problems.

EEC syndrome, an autosomal-dominant syndrome involving both ectodermal and mesodermal tissues, with ectodermal dysplasia associated with hypopigmentation of skin and hair, scanty hair and eyebrows, absence of lashes, nail dystrophy, small or missing teeth, missing digits, and cleft lip and palate.

EEE, abbreviation for *eastern equine encephalitis.*

EEG, 1. abbreviation for **electroencephalogram.** 2. abbreviation for **electroencephalograph.** 3. abbreviation for **electroencephalography.**

eelworm /ēl'werm/, a nematode, especially any of various small, free-living or plant parasitic roundworms.

EENT, abbreviation for *eyes, ears, nose, and throat.*

EEOC, abbreviation for **Equal Employment Opportunity Commission.**

EFA, abbreviation for **essential fatty acid.**

efalizumab, a rarely used immunosuppressant used in adults 18 years of age and older to treat moderate to severe plaque psoriasis.

efavirenz, an antiviral used to treat HIV-1 in combination with other antiretroviral agents.

effacement /ifās'mənt/ [Fr, *effacer,* to erase], the shortening of the vaginal part of the cervix and thinning of its walls as it is stretched and dilated by the fetus during labor.

effect, the result of an agent or cause.

effective atomic number, the average atomic number obtained from a weighted summation of the atomic constituents of a compound.

effective compliance /ifek'tiv/ [L, *effectus,* performance], the ratio of tidal volume to peak airway pressure.

effective dose (ED), 1. on a graded dose-response curve in the laboratory, the dosage of a drug that may be expected to cause a response of the desired magnitude. 2. in a clinical setting, the dose needed to cause the desired response in a percentage of the people to whom it is given (e.g.,

an ED_{50} dosage of a drug is expected to produce a response in 50% of the patients receiving it).

effective dose equivalent limit (EDE limit), the largest amount of ionizing radiation a person may receive according to radiation protection guidelines. It combines both internal and external dose and has replaced the concept of maximum permissible dose for occupational exposures. The EDE limit is prescribed for various organs as well as whole body and for various working conditions.

effective half-life (ehl), the time required for a radioactive element in an animal body to be diminished by 50% as a result of radioactive decay and biologic elimination.

effective osmotic pressure, the part of total osmotic pressure of a solution that determines the tendency of the solvent to pass through a boundary, such as a semipermeable membrane.

effective radiating area, the total area of the surface of the transducer that actually produces the sound wave.

effector /ifek'tər/ [L, *efficere,* to accomplish], 1. an organ that produces an effect, such as glandular secretion, as a result of nerve stimulation. 2. a molecule, such as an enzyme, that can start or stop a chemical reaction.

effector cell, 1. a terminally differentiated leukocyte that performs more than one specific function. 2. a muscle cell or gland cell.

effeminate /ifem'init/ [L, *effeminare,* to make womanish], womanly or female in physical and mental characteristics, regardless of biologic sex.

efferent /ef'ərənt/ [L, *effere,* to carry out], directed away from a center such as certain arteries, veins, nerves, kidney, and lymphatics.

efferent duct, any duct through which a gland releases its secretions.

efferent nerve, a nerve that transmits impulses away or outward from a nerve center, such as the brain or spinal cord, usually causing a muscle contraction or release of a glandular secretion.

efferent pathway [L, *effere,* to carry out; ME, *paeth + weg*], 1. the route of nerve fibers carrying impulses away from a nerve center. 2. the system of blood vessels that convey blood away from a body part.

effervesce [Gk, *effervescere,* to foam up], to produce small bubbles or foam on the release of gas from a fluid.

effervescence /ef'ərves'əns/ [L, *effervescere,* to foam up], the production of small bubbles or foam associated with the escape of gas from a fluid.

effervescent /ef′ərves′ənt/, producing and releasing gas bubbles.

efficacy /ef′əkəsē/ [L, *effectus,* performance], (of a drug or treatment) the ability of a drug or treatment to produce a specific result, regardless of dosage.

efficiency /ifish′ənsē/, **1.** the production of desired results with the minimum waste of time and effort. **2.** the amount of achievement compared with the effort expended. **3.** in radioassay, the counts perceived by a beta or gamma counter relative to the known disintegration rate of a comparable standard radioactive source.

effleurage /ef′ləräzh/ [Fr, skimming the surface], a technique in massage in which long, light, or firm strokes are used, usually over the spine and back.

effluent /ef′lo͞o·ənt/, a liquid, solid, or gaseous emission, such as the discharge or outflow from a machine or an industrial process.

effluvium /iflo͞o′vē·əm/ [L, *effluvium,* a flowing out], an outflow of gas or vapor, usually malodorous or toxic.

effort syndrome [Fr, exertion; Gk, *syn,* together, *dromos,* course], an abnormal condition characterized by chest pain; dizziness; fatigue; palpitations; cold, moist hands; and sighing respiration. The pain often mimics angina pectoris but is more closely connected to anxiety states and occurs after rather than during exercise.

effort thrombosis, an abnormal condition in which a clot develops within the subclavian or axillary vein after strenuous exercise. The condition is accompanied by pain, edema, and skin discoloration in the shoulder and upper arm.

effraction /ifrak′shən/, a breaking open or weakening.

effusion /ifyo͞o′zhən/ [L, *effundere,* to pour out], **1.** the escape of fluid, for example, from blood vessels as a result of rupture or seepage, usually into a body cavity. The condition is usually associated with a circulatory or renal disorder and is often an early sign of congestive heart disease. **2.** the outward spread of a bacterial growth.

eflornithine hydrochloride /eflôr′nithēn/, an inhibitor of the enzyme ornithine decarboxylase, applied in creams by females over age 12 to limit unwanted facial hair growth and administered by injection to treat the meningoencephalitic stage of a protozoal infection caused by *Trypanosoma brucei.*

EFM, abbreviation for **electronic fetal monitor.**

Efudex, a trademark for an antineoplastic (fluorouracil).

EGD, abbreviation for **esophagogastroduodenoscopy.**

egest /ijest′/ [L, *egerere,* to expel], to discharge or evacuate a substance from the body, especially to evacuate unabsorbed residue of foods from the intestines. —**egesta,** *n. pl.,* **egestive,** *adj.*

EGF, abbreviation for **epidermal growth factor.**

egg /eg/ [ONorse], a female reproductive cell at any stage before fertilization.

eglandulous /ēglan′dyələs/, describing an absence of glands.

ego /ē′gō, eg′ō/ [Gk, I or self], **1.** the conscious sense of the self; those elements of a person, such as thinking, feeling, and willing, that distinguish him or her as an individual. **2.** in psychoanalysis, the part of the psyche that experiences and maintains conscious contact with reality and tempers the primitive drives of the id and the demands of the superego with the social and physical needs of society.

ego analysis, in psychoanalysis, the intensive study of the ego, especially the defense mechanisms.

ego boundary, in psychiatry, a sense or awareness that there is a distinction between the real and unreal.

egocentric /ē′gōsen′trik/ [Gk, *ego* + *kentron,* center], **1.** regarding the self as the center, object, and norm of all experience and having little regard for the needs, interests, ideas, and attitudes of others. **2.** a person possessing these characteristics.

ego-dystonic /ē′gōdiston′ik/, describing elements of a person's behavior, thoughts, impulses, drives, and attitudes that are unacceptable to him or her and cause anxiety.

ego-dystonic homosexuality, a psychosexual disorder characterized by discomfort with one's sexuality and a persistent desire to change sexual orientation to heterosexuality.

ego ideal, the image of the self to which a person aspires both consciously and unconsciously and against which he measures himself or herself and judges personal performance.

ego-integrity, an acceptance of self, both successes and failure. It implies a healthy psychologic state.

egoism /ē′gō·iz′əm, eg′-/, **1.** selfishness, an overvaluation of the importance of the self, expressed as a willingness to gain an advantage at the expense of others. **2.** the belief that individual self-interest is, or ought to be, the basic motive for all conscious behavior.

egoist /ē′gō·ist, eg′-/, **1.** a selfish person, one who seeks to satisfy his or her own interests at the expense of others. **2.** a person who believes in or acts in accordance with the concept that all conscious action is justifiably motivated by self-interest. —**egoistic,** *adj.*

ego libido, in psychoanalysis, concentration of the libido on the self; self-love.

egomania /ē'gōmā'nē·ə/ [Gk, *ego,* I, *mania,* madness], a pathologic preoccupation with the self and an exaggerated sense of one's own importance.

egophony /ēgof'ənē/, a change in the voice sound of a patient with pleural effusion as heard on auscultation, particularly over an area of consolidated or compressed lung above the effusion.

ego strength, in psychotherapy, the ability to maintain the ego by a cluster of traits that together contribute to good mental health.

ego-syntonic /ē'gō sinton'ik/, describing those elements of a person's behavior, thoughts, impulses, drives, and attitudes that are acceptable to him or her and are consistent with the total personality.

egotism /ē'gotiz'əm, eg'-/, vanity, conceit, or overvaluation of the importance of the self and undervaluation or contempt of others.—**egotistic,** *adj.*

egotist /ē'gətist, eg'-/, one who is vain or conceited or who places too much importance on the self and is boastful, egocentric, and arrogant.

egress /ē'gres/, the act of emerging or moving forward.

EHD, abbreviation for **electrohemodynamics.**

EHEC, abbreviation for **enterohemorrhagic** *Escherichia coli.*

ehl, abbreviation for **effective half-life.**

Ehlers-Danlos syndrome /ā'lərz dan'los/ [Edward Ehlers, Danish physician, 1863–1937; Henri A. Danlos, French physician, 1844–1912], a hereditary disorder of connective tissue, marked by hyperplasticity of skin, tissue fragility, and hypermotility of joints.

Ehrlichia, a genus of small spherical to ellipsoidal, nonmotile gram-negative bacteria. They occur singly or in compact inclusions in circulating mammalian leukocytes. Two human tickborne diseases have been associated with *Ehrlichia* species: human monocytic ehrlichiosis caused by *E. chaffeensis* and human granulocytic ehrlichiosis caused by *E. equi.*

ehrlichiosis, a sometimes fatal tickborne infection with symptoms similar to those of Lyme disease. The disease usually begins about 10 days after the bite of an infected tick, although some cases have begun abruptly, within hours, with influenza-like symptoms, including painful muscle aches, headaches, fever, chills, loss of appetite, and depressed blood cell counts.

eicosanoic acid /ī'kōsənō'ik/ [Gk, *eikosa,* twenty], a saturated fatty acid containing 20 carbon atoms in a straight chain, found in peanut oil, butter, and other fats.

eicosapentaenoic acid /ī·kō'sə·pen'tə·ē·nō'ik/, a 20-carbon fatty acid found almost exclusively in fish and marine animal oils.

EID, abbreviation for **electronic infusion device.**

eidetic /īdet'ik/ [Gk, *eidos,* a form or shape seen], **1.** pertaining to or characterized by the ability to visualize and reproduce accurately the image of objects or events previously seen or imagined. **2.** a person possessing such ability.

eidetic image, an unusually vivid, elaborate, and apparently exact mental image resulting from a visual experience and occurring as a fantasy, dream, or memory.

einsteinium (Es) /īnstī'nē·əm/ [Albert Einstein, German-born physicist and Nobel laureate, 1879–1955], a synthetic transuranic metallic element. Its atomic number is 99; the mass of its longest-lived, best-known isotope is 254. It decays rapidly into berkelium.

Einthoven's formula /īnt'hōvənz/ [Willem Einthoven, Dutch physiologist, scientist, and Nobel laureate, 1860–1927; L, *forma,* pattern], a mathematic expression relating the voltages measured by ECG leads. The formula states that the sum of the voltages from lead I plus those from lead III minus those from lead II equals zero $(I + III - II = 0)$. This formula is based on the principle that the sum of the voltages in any closed path equals zero.

Einthoven's triangle [Willem Einthoven], an equilateral triangle whose vertices lie at the left and right shoulders and the pubic region and whose center corresponds to the vector sum of all electric activity occurring in the heart at any given moment.

Eisenmenger's complex /ī'sənmeng'ərz/ [Victor Eisenmenger, German physician, 1864–1932; L, *complexus,* encirclement], a congenital heart disease characterized by a defect of the ventricular septum, a malpositioned aortic root that overrides the interventricular septum, and a dilated pulmonary artery.

Eisenmenger's syndrome /ī'sənmeng'ərz/ [Victor Eisenmenger, German physician, 1864–1932], ventricular septal defect with pulmonary hypertension and cyanosis resulting from right-to-left (reversed) shunt of blood. It is sometimes defined as pulmonary hypertension and cyanosis with the shunt being at the atrial, ventricular, or great vessel area.

ejaculate /ijak'yəlit/, the semen discharged in a single emission.—**ejaculate** /ijak'yəlāt/, *v.*

ejaculation /-ā'shən/ [L, *ejaculari,* to hurl out], the sudden emission of semen from the male urethra, usually during copulation, masturbation, or nocturnal emission. —**ejaculatory,** *adj.*

ejaculatory duct /ijak'yələtôr'ē/ [L, *ejicere,* to cast out], the passage formed by the junction of the duct of the seminal vesicles and ductus deferens through which semen enters the urethra.

ejection /ijek'shən/ [L, *ejicere,* to cast out], forceful expulsion, as of blood from a ventricle of the heart.

ejection click, a sharp, clicking sound arising from near the heart. It may be caused by sudden swelling of a pulmonary artery, abrupt dilation of the aorta, or forceful opening of the aortic cusps.

ejection fraction (EF), the fraction of the total ventricular filling volume that is ejected during each ventricular contraction. The normal EF of the left ventricle is 65%.

ejection period, the second phase of ventricular systole, when the semilunar valves are open and blood is being discharged into the aortic and pulmonary arteries.

ejection sound, a sharp, clicking sound heard early in systole, coinciding with the onset of either right or left ventricular ejection. Aortic ejection sounds are commonly heard in aortic valvular stenosis, aortic insufficiency, coarctation of the aorta, and hypertension with aortic dilation. Pulmonary ejection sounds are heard in mild to moderate pulmonary stenosis, pulmonary hypertension, and dilation of the pulmonary artery.

EKC, abbreviation for **epidemic keratoconjunctivitis.**

EKG, abbreviation for **electrocardiogram.**

elaboration /ilab'ərāshən/ [L, *elaborare,* to work out], (in endocrinology) a process by which a gland synthesizes a complex substance from simpler substances and secretes it, usually under the stimulation of a tropic hormone from the pituitary gland.—**elaborate,** *adj.*

elapid /el'əpid/, **1.** pertaining to the members of a family of pit vipers that includes the genera *Micruroides* and *Micrurus.* **2.** any of the members of this group.

Elaprase, a trademark for **idursulfase.**

Elase, a trademark for a topical fixed-combination drug containing enzymes (fibrinolysin and desoxyribonuclease).

Elase with Chloromycetin, a trademark for a topical fixed-combination drug containing two lytic enzymes (fibrinolysin and desoxyribonuclease) and an antibacterial (chloramphenicol).

elastance /ilas'təns/ [Gk, *elaunein,* to drive], **1.** the quality of recoiling or returning to an original form after the removal of pressure. **2.** the degree to which an air- or fluid-filled organ, such as a lung, bladder, or blood vessel, can return to its original dimensions when a distending or compressing force is removed.

3. the measurement of the unit volume of change in such an organ per unit of decreased pressure change. **4.** the reciprocal of compliance.

elastase, an enzyme that cleaves bonds adjacent to neutral amino acids in elastin.

elastic bandage /ilas'tik/ [Gk, *elaunein,* to drive; Fr, *bande,* strip], a bandage of stretchable fabric that provides support and allows movement.

elastic-band fixation, a method of treatment of fractures of the jaw using rubber bands to connect metal splints or wires that are attached to the maxilla and mandible. Rubber bands are safer than rigid wires in the event of vomiting.

elastic bougie, a flexible bougie that can be passed through angular or winding channels.

elastic cartilage, the most pliant of the three kinds of cartilage, consisting of elastic fibers in a flexible fibrous matrix. It is yellow and is located in various parts of the body, such as the external ear, the auditory tube, and the epiglottis.

elasticity /i'lastis'itē/, the ability of tissue to regain its original shape and size after being stretched, squeezed, or otherwise deformed.

elastic recoil /rē'koil/, the difference between intrapleural pressure and alveolar pressure at a given lung volume under static conditions.

elastic stocking, a type of hosiery that applies gradient pressure to the legs to prevent excessive blood accumulation in the lower extremities caused by faulty vein valves. The stockings are commonly prescribed for patients with varicose veins.

elastic tissue [Gk, *elaunein,* to drive; OFr, *tissu*], a type of connective tissue containing elastic fibers. It is found in ligaments of the spinal column, in the cartilage of the external ear, and in the walls of some large blood vessels.

elastic traction [Gk, *elaunein,* L, *trahere,* to draw], any therapeutic apparatus that uses an elastic device to pull on a limb.

elastin /ilas'tin/ [Gk, *elaunein,* to drive], a protein that forms the principal substance of yellow elastic tissue fibers.

elastofibroma /ilas'tōfībrō'mə/, a benign nonencapsulated mass of collagenous, fibrous, and elastic tissue that develops in subscapular fatty tissue in older persons.

elastomer /ilas'tōmər/ [Gk, *elaunein,* to drive + *meros,* part], a synthetic rubber; any of various soft, elastic, rubberlike polymers used in dentistry as an impression material and for maxillofacial extraoral prostheses.—**elastomeric,** *adj.*

elation /ilā'shən/ [L, *elatus,* a lifting up], an emotional reaction characterized by euphoria, excitement, extreme joyfulness, optimism, and self-satisfaction. It is considered to be of pathologic origin when such a response does not realistically reflect a person's actual circumstances.

Elavil, a trademark for a tricyclic antidepressant (amitriptyline hydrochloride).

elbow [AS, *elboga*], the bend of the arm at the joint that connects the upper arm and the forearm.

elbow joint, the hinged articulation of the humerus, the ulna, and the radius. The elbow joint allows flexion and extension of the forearm and accommodates the radioulnar articulation.

elder, an herb found in the United States and Europe as a tall shrub. This berry or flower may be useful for limiting the duration of symptoms from colds and flu; the flower is also used as a mouthwash and applied topically as an astringent for nasal and chest congestion, earache associated with chronic congestion, and hay fever.

elder abuse, a reportable offense of physical, psychologic, or material abuse, as well as violation of the rights of safety, security, and adequate health care of older adults.

elderly primigravida, a woman who becomes pregnant for the first time after the age of 34.

Eldopaque, a trademark for a dermatologic bleaching agent (hydroquinone).

elective /ilek'tiv/ [L, *eligere,* to choose], pertaining to a procedure that is performed by choice and is not essential, such as elective surgery.

elective abortion, induced termination of a pregnancy, usually before the fetus has developed enough to live if born, deemed necessary by the woman carrying it and performed at her request.

Electra complex /ilek'trə/, in psychiatry, the libidinous desire of a daughter for her father.

electret /ilek'trət/, an insulator carrying a permanent charge similar to a permanent magnet.

electrically stimulated osteogenesis /ilek'triklē/ [Gk, *elektron,* amber; L, *stimulare,* to incite; Gk, *osteon,* bone, *genein,* to produce], a bone regeneration process induced by surgically implanted electrodes conveying electric current, especially at nonunion fracture sites. The process is effective because of the different electric potentials within bone tissue. Electric stimulation of fractures can accelerate osteogenesis, forming bone more quickly in the area of a surgically inserted negative electrode.

electrical silence, in electroencephalography and electromyography, absence of measurable electrical activity in tissue.

electric blood warmer, a device for heating blood before infusions, especially massive transfusions in which cold blood may cause a state of shock.

electric burn, the tissue damage resulting from heat of up to 5000° C generated by an electric current. The points of entrance and exit on the skin are burned, along with the muscle and subcutaneous tissues through which the current passes. Fatal cardiac arrhythmia may result.

electric circuit, the path of the electron flow from a generating source through various components and back to the generating source.

electric current, the net movement of electrons along a conducting medium.

electric field, the lines of force exerted on charged ions in the tissues by the electrodes that cause charged particles to move from one pole to another.

electric impedance, an opposition to electron flow in a conducting material.

electricity /i'lektris'itē/ [Gk, *elektron,* amber], a form of energy expressed by the activity of electrons and other subatomic particles in motion as in dynamic electricity or at rest as in static electricity. Electricity can be produced by heat; generated by a voltaic cell; or produced by induction, rubbing of nonconductors with dry materials, or chemical activity. Electricity may be negative, when there is a surplus of electrons, or positive, when there is a surplus of protons or a deficiency of electrons.

electric muscle stimulator (EMS), a therapeutic electric current used to stimulate muscle directly, such as when the muscle is denervated and peripheral nerves are not functioning.

electric potential, the potential difference between charged particles.

electric shock, a traumatic physical state caused by the passage of electric current through the body. It usually involves accidental contact with exposed parts of electric circuits in home appliances and domestic power supplies but may also result from lightning or contact with high-voltage wires. The resultant damage depends on the intensity of the electric current, the type of current, and the duration and the frequency of current flow. Severe electric shock commonly causes unconsciousness, respiratory paralysis, muscle contractions, bone fractures, and cardiac disorders.

electric spinal orthosis (ESO), an electric device that helps control curvature of the spine by stimulating back muscles. The portable battery-powered machine does not correct scoliosis, but prevents it from worsening.

electroacupuncture after Voll (EAV), a system of diagnosis and treatment based on the measurement of the electrical characteristics of acupoints, the results being used to determine a specific remedy.

electroanalgesia /ilek′trō·an′əljē′sē·ə/, the use of an electric current to relieve pain.

electroanalytic chemistry /-an′əlit′ik/ [Gk, *elektron* + *analysis,* a loosening, *chemeia,* alchemy], the branch of chemistry concerned with the analysis of compounds by use of electric properties to produce characteristic observable change in the substance being studied.

electroanesthesia /-an′esthē′zhə/, the use of an electric current to produce local anesthesia.

electrocardiogram (ECG, EKG) /-kär′dē·ə gram′/ [Gk, *elektron* + *kardia,* heart, *gramma,* record], a graphic record produced by an electrocardiograph.

electrocardiograph (ECG) /-kär′dē·əgraf′/, a device used for recording the electrical activity of the myocardium to detect transmission of the cardiac impulse through the conductive tissues of the muscle. Electrocardiography allows diagnosis of specific cardiac abnormalities.—**electrocardiographic,** *adj.*

electrocardiographic technician /-kär′dē·ō graf′ik/, an allied health worker with special training and experience in operating and maintaining ECG equipment and providing recorded data for diagnostic review by a physician.

electrocardiograph lead /lēd/, **1.** an electrode placed on part of the body and connected to an ECG. **2.** a record, made by the ECG, that varies with the site of the electrode. Electrocardiography is generally performed with the use of six limb leads and six leads placed on the precordium. The peripheral or extremity leads are designated I, II, III, AVR, AVL, and AVF. The chest leads are designated V_1, V_2, V_3, V_4, V_5, and V_6 to indicate the points on the precordium on which the electrodes are placed.

electrocardiography (ECG) /-kär′dē·og′rəfē/ [Gk, *elektron* + *kardia,* heart, *graphein,* to record], the study of records of electric activity generated by the heart muscle.

electrocatalysis, the chemical decomposition of tissues caused by the application of electric current to the body.

electrocautery /ilek′trōkô′tərē/ [Gk, *elektron* + *kauterion,* branding iron], the application of a needle or snare heated by electric current for the destruction of tissue, such as for removing warts or polyps and cauterizing small blood vessels to limit blood loss during surgery.

electrochemistry, the study of the electrical effects that accompany chemical action and the chemical activity produced by electrical influence.

electrocoagulation /-kō·ag′yəlā′shən/ [Gk, *elektron*; L, *coagulare,* to curdle], a therapeutic destructive form of electrosurgery in which tissue is hardened by the passage of high-frequency current from an electric cautery device.

electroconvulsive therapy (ECT) /-kənvul′ siv/, the induction of a brief convulsion by passing an electric current through the brain for the treatment of affective disorders, especially in patients resistant to psychoactive-drug therapy. ECT is primarily used when rapid definitive response is required for either medical or psychiatric reasons, such as for a patient who is extremely suicidal and when the risks of other treatments outweigh the risk of ECT. A secondary use of ECT is treatment failure of other choices.

electroconvulsive therapy (ECT) management, a nursing intervention from the Nursing Interventions Classification (NIC) defined as assisting with the safe and efficient provision of electroconvulsive therapy in the treatment of psychiatric illness.

electrocution /-kyoō′shən/, death caused by the passage of electric current through the body.

electrode /ilek′trōd/ [Gk, *elektron* + *hodos,* way], **1.** a contact for the induction or detection of electrical activity. **2.** a medium for conducting an electrical current from the body to physiologic monitoring equipment.

electrodermal /-dur′məl/, pertaining to electrical properties of the skin, particularly altered resistance.

electrodermal activity therapy, a type of biofeedback therapy in which sensors attached to the palm or the palmar aspect of the fingers are used to monitor sweat output in response to stress. It is used in the treatment of stress, anxiety disorders, chronic pain, and hyperhidrosis.

electrodermal audiometry [Gk, *elektron* + *derma,* skin; L, *audire,* to hear; Gk, *metron,* measure], a method to determine hearing thresholds in which a harmless electric shock is used to condition the subject to a pure tone, which thereafter, coupled with the anticipation of a shock, elicits a brief electrodermal response. It is a very old procedure and rarely used today.

electrodesiccation /-des′ikā′shən/ [Gk, *elektron* + *desiccare,* to dry up], a technique in electrosurgery in which tissue is destroyed by burning with an electric spark. It is used primarily for eliminating small superficial growths but may also be used with curettage for eradicating

E

abnormal tissue deeper in the skin or to stop bleeding.

electrodiagnosis /-dī′agnō′sis/ [Gk, *elektron* + *dia*, twice, *gnosis*, knowledge], the diagnosis of disease or injury by electric stimulation of various nerves and muscles.

electrodynamics /-dīnam′iks/, the study of electrostatic charges in motion, such as the flow of electrons in an electric current.

electrodynograph (EDG) /-din′əgraf′/ [Gk, *elektron* + *dynamis*, force, *graphein*, to record], an electronic device used to measure pressures exerted in biologic activity, such as those exerted by the human foot in walking, running, jogging, or climbing stairs.

electroencephalogram (EEG) /ilek′trō·en sef′ələgram′/ [Gk, *elektron* + *enkephalos*, brain, *gramma*, record], a graphic chart on which is traced the electric potential produced by the brain cells, as detected by electrodes placed on the scalp. Variations in brain wave activity are correlated with neurologic conditions, psychologic states, and LOC.

electroencephalograph (EEG) /ilek′trō·en sef′ələgraf′/, an instrument for receiving and recording the electric potential produced by the brain cells.

electroencephalographic technologist /ilek′trō·ensef′ələgraf′ik/, a person trained in the management of an EEG laboratory. The technologist may supervise EEG technicians, who are generally responsible for the operation and maintenance of the equipment.

electroencephalography (EEG) /ilek′trō· ensef′əlog′rəfē/, the process of recording brain wave activity.

electrogram /ilek′trōgram/ [Gk, *elektron* + *gramma*, record], a unipolar or bipolar record of the electric activity of the heart as recorded by electrodes within the cardiac chambers or on the epicardium.

electrohemodynamics (EHD) /ilek′trōhē′ mōdīnam′iks/ [Gk, *elektron* + *haima*, blood, *dynamis*, force], a technique for noninvasively measuring the mechanical properties and hemodynamic characteristics of the vascular system, including arterial BP, electric impedance, blood flow, and resistance to blood flow.

electrolarynx /i·lek′troler′ingks/ [Gr, *elektron*, amber + *larynx*], an electromechanical device that enables a laryngectomized person to speak. When it is placed against the region of the laryngectomy a buzzing sound is produced, which is converted into simulated speech by movements of the organs of articulation (lips, tongue, glottis).

electrolysis /il′ektrol′isis/ [Gk, *elektron* + *lysis*, loosening], a process in which electric energy causes a chemical change in a conducting medium, usually a solution or a molten substance, or the decomposition of a substance such as hair follicles. —**electrolytic,** *adj.*

electrolyte /ilek′trōlīt/ [Gk, *elektron* + *lytos,* soluble], an element or compound that, when melted or dissolved in water or another solvent, dissociates into ions and is able to conduct an electric current. Electrolytes differ in their concentrations in blood plasma, interstitial fluid, and cell fluid and affect the movement of substances between those compartments. Proper quantities of principal electrolytes and balance among them are critical to normal metabolism and function. —**electrolytic,** *adj.*

electrolyte & acid/base balance, a nursing outcome from the Nursing Outcomes Classification (NOC) defined as the balance of electrolytes and nonelectrolytes in the intracellular and extracellular compartments of the body.

electrolyte balance, the equilibrium between electrolytes in the body.

electrolyte imbalance, serum concentrations of an electrolyte that are either higher or lower than normal.

electrolyte management, a nursing intervention from the Nursing Interventions Classification (NIC) defined as promotion of electrolyte balance and prevention of complications resulting from abnormal or undesired serum electrolyte levels.

electrolyte management: hypercalcemia, a nursing intervention from the Nursing Interventions Classification (NIC) defined as the promotion of calcium balance and prevention of complications resulting from serum calcium levels higher than desired.

electrolyte management: hyperkalemia, a nursing intervention from the Nursing Interventions Classification (NIC) defined as the promotion of potassium balance and prevention of complications resulting from serum potassium levels higher than desired.

electrolyte management: hypermagnesemia, a nursing intervention from the Nursing Interventions Classification (NIC) defined as promotion of magnesium balance and prevention of complications resulting from serum magnesium levels higher than desired.

electrolyte management: hypernatremia, a nursing intervention from the Nursing Interventions Classification (NIC) defined as the promotion of sodium balance and prevention of complications resulting from serum sodium levels higher than desired.

electrolyte management: hyperphosphatemia, a nursing intervention from the Nursing Interventions Classification (NIC) defined as the promotion of phosphate balance and prevention of complications resulting from serum phosphate levels higher than desired.

electrolyte management: hypocalcemia, a nursing intervention from the Nursing Interventions Classification (NIC) defined as the promotion of calcium balance and prevention of complications resulting from serum calcium levels lower than desired.

electrolyte management: hypokalemia, a nursing intervention from the Nursing Interventions Classification (NIC) defined as the promotion of potassium balance and prevention of complications resulting from serum potassium levels lower than desired.

electrolyte management: hypomagnesemia, a nursing intervention from the Nursing Interventions Classification (NIC) defined as the promotion of magnesium balance and prevention of complications resulting from serum magnesium levels lower than desired.

electrolyte management: hyponatremia, a nursing intervention from the Nursing Interventions Classification (NIC) defined as the promotion of sodium balance and prevention of complications resulting from serum sodium levels lower than desired.

electrolyte management: hypophosphatemia, a nursing intervention from the Nursing Interventions Classification (NIC) defined as the promotion of phosphate balance and prevention of complications resulting from serum phosphate levels lower than desired.

electrolyte monitoring, a nursing intervention from the Nursing Interventions Classification (NIC) defined as collection and analysis of patient data to regulate electrolyte balance.

electrolyte solution, any solution containing electrolytes prepared for oral, parenteral, or rectal administration for the replacement or supplementation of ions necessary for homeostasis. Electrolyte solutions containing combinations of sodium, potassium, calcium, magnesium, chloride, bicarbonate, phosphate, and/or lactate may be given to treat acid-base disturbance, as seen in chronic renal dysfunction, diabetic ketoacidosis, or imbalances caused by vomiting, by diarrhea, or by the action of certain medications. The solutions are available in a wide range of balanced formulas for replacement or maintenance, and most include various trace minerals.

electromagnetic /-magnet′ik/ [Gk, *elektron, Magnesia,* ancient source of lodestone], **1.** pertaining to magnetism that is induced by an electric current. **2.** pertaining to radiation such as light, microwaves, x-rays, gamma rays, or radio waves.

electromagnetic induction [Gk, *elektron* + *magnes,* lodestone; L, *inducere,* to bring in], the production of electric current in a circuit when it is passed through a changing magnetic field.

electromagnetic radiation, radiation that is produced with a combination of magnetic and electric forces. It exists as a continuous spectrum of radiation, from that with the highest energy level and shortest wavelength (gamma rays) to that with the lowest energy and longest wavelength (long radio waves).

electromagnetic spectrum, the range of frequencies and wavelengths associated with radiant energy.

electromallet condenser /-mal′ət/ [Gk, *elektron*; OFr, *mail,* maul; L, *condensare,* to make dense], an electromechanical device formerly used for compacting direct-filling gold, such as gold foil restorations in prepared tooth cavities.

electromotive force (EMF) /-mō′tiv/, the electrical potential, or ability of electrical energy to perform work. EMF is usually measured in joules per coulomb, or volts. The higher the voltage, the greater the potential of electric energy.

electromyogram (EMG) /ilek′trōmī′ə gram′/, a record of the intrinsic electric activity in a skeletal muscle. Such data aid the diagnosis of neuromuscular problems and are obtained by applying surface electrodes or by inserting a needle electrode into the muscle and observing electric activity.

electromyographic biofeedback /-mī′ə graf′ik/, a therapeutic procedure that uses electronic or electromechanical instruments to measure, process, and feed back reinforcing information with auditory and visual signals accurately. It is used to provide information about muscle activity during ambulation.

electromyographic technician /-mī′əgraf′ik/, a health care provider with special training and experience to assist the physician in recording and analyzing muscle action potentials with the use of various electronic devices.

electromyography (EMG) /-mī·og′rəfē/, the electric recording of muscle action potentials.

electromyography of pelvic floor sphincter, an electrodiagnostic test performed to evaluate the neuromuscular function of the urinary or anal sphincter. It is done most often in patients with urinary or fecal incontinence.

electron /ilek′tron/ [Gk, *elektron,* amber], **1.** a negatively charged elementary particle that has a specific charge, mass, and spin. The number of electrons associated with the nucleus of an atom is equal to the atomic number of the substance. **2.** a negative beta particle emitted from a radioactive substance.

electronarcosis /ilek′trŏnärkō′sis/ [Gk, *elektron + narkosis*, numbness], anesthesia produced by passing an electric current through the brain.

electron beam computed tomography (EBCT), ultrafast CT done with a scanner in which the patient is surrounded by a large circular anode that emits x-rays as the electron beam is guided around it.

electron capture, a radioactive decay process in which an atomic nucleus with an excess of protons draws an electron into itself, creating a neutron out of a proton and decreasing the atomic number by 1.

electroneurodiagnostic technologist, an allied health professional who, in collaboration with an electroencephalographer, obtains interpretable recordings of patients' nervous system function. The electrodiagnostic technologist takes a patient history; applies adequate recording electrodes and uses optimal EEG, evoked potential (EP), and polysomnography (PSG) techniques; and documents the clinical condition of patients.

electroneurography, an electrodiagnostic test that assists in detecting and locating peripheral nerve injury or disease. This study is usually done in conjunction with electromyography.

electroneuromyography /ilek′trŏnōō′rōmī′og′rəfē/ [Gk, *elektron + neuron*, nerve, *mys*, muscle, *graphein*, to record], a procedure for testing and recording neuromuscular activity by electric stimulation of nerves. Needle electrodes are inserted into any skeletal muscle being studied, electric current is applied to the electrodes, and neuromuscular functions are observed and recorded.

electronic fetal monitor (EFM) [Gk, *elektron*; L, *fetus + monere*, to warn], a device that allows observation of the fetal heart rate and the maternal uterine contractions. It may be applied externally or internally. With an external monitor, the fetal heart is detected by an ultrasound transducer positioned on the abdomen. Internal monitoring of the fetal heart rate is accomplished via an electrode clipped to the fetal scalp.

electronic fetal monitoring: antepartum, a nursing intervention from the Nursing Interventions Classification (NIC) defined as electronic evaluation of fetal heart rate response to movement, external stimuli, or uterine contractions during antepartal testing.

electronic fetal monitoring: intrapartum, a nursing intervention from the Nursing Interventions Classification (NIC) defined as electronic evaluation of fetal heart rate response to uterine contractions during intrapartal care.

electronic infusion device (EID), an automated system of introducing a fluid other than blood into a vein. The device may have programmable settings that control the amount of fluid to be infused, rate, low-volume notification level, and a keep-vein-open rate. Some EIDs have titration modes that allow a change in the delivery rate without interrupting fluid flow.

electronic stethoscope, a stethoscope designed and equipped to detect and amplify body sounds.

electronic thermometer, a battery-powered thermometer that registers temperature by electronic means.

electron microscope, an electronic instrument that scans cell and tissue sections with a beam of electrons, instead of visible light.

electron microscopy, a technique using an electron microscope in which a beam of electrons is focused by an electromagnetic lens and directed onto an extremely thin specimen.

electron transfer flavoprotein (ETF), a component of a side chain of redox reactions by which electrons are funneled to ubiquinone and thus the electron transport chain. Electrons from acyl coenzyme A (CoA) thioesters and choline are transferred via the flavin of acyl CoA dehydrogenases, dimethylglycine dehydrogenase, and sarcosine dehydrogenase to the flavin adenine dinucleotide prosthetic group of ETF, which is then oxidized via reduction of electron transfer flavoprotein ubiquinone oxidoreductase. Deficiency of ETF results in glutaric aciduria, type II.

electron volt (eV), a unit of energy equal to the energy acquired by an electron falling through a potential difference of 1 volt. One eV equals 1.6×10^{-12} erg or 1.6×10^{-19} J.

electronystagmography /ilek′trŏnis′tagmog′rəfē/ [Gk, *elektron + nystagmos*, nodding, *graphein*, to record], a method of assessing and recording eye movements by measuring the electric activity of the extraocular muscles.

electropalatography, a technique for recording the timing and location of tongue contact with the hard palate during speech, using an artificial palate that fits against the roof of the mouth and has electrodes embedded in the surface that faces the tongue. A computer records and displays the pattern of the pulses generated by contact of the tongue with the electrodes.

electrophoresis /ilek′trōfərē′sis/ [Gk, *elektron + pherein*, to bear], the movement of charged suspended particles through a liquid medium in response to changes in an electric field. The pattern of migration can be recorded in bands on an electrophoretogram. The technique is widely used to separate and identify serum proteins and other substances. —**electrophoretic,** *adj.*

electrophysiologic study (EPS), an invasive electrodiagnostic or manometric procedure that uses electrode catheters to pace the heart and potentially induce arrhythmias. The test identifies defects in the heart conduction system and arrhythmias that are otherwise inapparent. It also is used to assess the effectiveness of antiarrhythmic drugs.

electrophysiology /-fis′ē-ol′əjē/ [Gk, *elektron* + *physis*, nature, *logos*, science], a branch of biology concerned with the relationship between electric phenomena and biologic function.

electroplating /i·lek′trōplāt′ing/ [Gk, *electron*, amber; Fr, *plat*, flat dish], plating or coating of an object with a layer of metal through the use of electrolytic processes.

electroporation /-pôrā′shən/, a type of osmotic transfection in which an electrical current is used to produce temporary holes in cell membranes, allowing the entry of nucleic acids or macromolecules (a way of introducing new DNA into the cell).

electroresection /-risek′shən/ [Gk, *elektron*; L, *re*, again, *secare* to cut], a technique for the removal of bladder tumors or prostate tissue by electrocautery. A wire is guided to the site through the urethra and electricity is passed through the wire when the wire is properly located in the tissue to be destroyed.

electroshock [Gk, *elektron*; Fr, *choc*], a condition of shock caused by accidental contact with an electrical current. The symptoms are similar to those of shock produced by thermal burns, trauma, or coronary thrombosis.

electrosleep therapy [Gk, *elektron*; AS, *slaep*; Gk, *therapeia*, treatment], a technique designed to induce sleep, especially in psychiatric patients, by administering a low-amplitude pulsating current to the brain. The cathode is placed supraorbitally, and the anode is placed over the mastoid process. The current, which is discharged for 15 to 20 minutes, produces a tingling sensation but does not always induce sleep.

electrostatic imaging /-stat′ik/ [Gk, *elektron* + *stasis*, standing still; L, *imago*, image], a radiographic technique in which the ionic charge liberated during the irradiation process is converted into a visible image.

electrostimulation /-stim′yəlā′shən/, the application of electric current to stimulate bone or muscle tissue for therapeutic purposes, such as facilitation of muscle activation and muscle strengthening.

electrosurgery /-sur′jərē/ [Gk, *elektron* + *cheiourgos*, surgeon], surgery performed with various electrical instruments that operate on high-frequency electrical current.

electrotherapeutic current, any of three types of electric current, which, when introduced into biologic tissue, is capable of producing specific physiologic changes. The three types are direct monophasic, alternating biphasic, and pulsed polyphasic electric current.

electrotherapist /-ther′əpist/, a health care provider who has specific training and experience in the therapeutic uses of electricity.

electrotonic current [Gk, *elektron* + *tonos*, tension], a current induced in a nerve sheath without the generation of new current by an action potential.

electrotonic synapse, a gap junction that transmits electrical impulses in electrically excitable tissue.

electrovalence, the valence of an ion, equal to the absolute value of its charge.

eleidin /əlē′ədin/ [Gk, *elaia*, olive tree], a transparent, proteinaceous substance resembling keratin, found in the outer stratum lucidum of the epidermis.

element [L, *elementum*, first principle], one of more than 100 primary, simple substances that cannot be broken down by chemical means into any other substance. Each atom of any element contains a specific number of protons in the nucleus and an equal number of electrons outside the nucleus. In most elements, the nucleus may contain a variable number (high or low) of neutrons.

elementary particle, in physics, a subatomic particle such as an electron, neutron, or proton.

eleoma /ē′lē-ō′mə/, a lipogranuloma, or swelling, usually caused by subcutaneous injection of oil.

elephantiasis /el′əfəntī′əsis/ [Gk, *elephas*, elephant, *osis*, condition], the end-stage lesion of filariasis, characterized by extensive swelling, usually of the external genitalia and the legs, resulting from obstruction of the lymphatics by filariae. The overlying skin becomes dark, thick, and coarse.

elephantine psoriasis /el′əfan′tīn/, a rare form of psoriasis that is characterized by thick, scaly plaques on the hips, thighs, and back.

eletriptan, an antimigraine agent used for the acute treatment of migraine with or without aura.

elevation /el′əva′shən/ [L, *elevare*, to lift], a raised area, or point of greater height.

elevator /el′əvā′tər/ [L, *elevare*, to lift], an instrument for lifting tissues, removing bony fragments, or removing roots of teeth.

eligibility /el'əjəbil'itē/, entitlement of an individual to receive services based on that individual's enrollment in a health care plan.

Eligibility Guarantee Payment, a contract provision for guaranteeing payment from the health maintenance organization to the provider for services already delivered to enrollees whose coverage is terminated retroactively. Not applicable in Canada.

elimination /i·lim'i·nā'shən/ [L, *ex,* out, *limen,* threshold], **1.** the act of expulsion or of extrusion, especially of expulsion from the body. **2.** omission or exclusion, as in an elimination diet.

elimination diet /ilim'inā'shən/ [L, *eliminare,* to expel; Gk, *diata,* way of living], a procedure for identifying a food or foods to which a person is allergic by successively omitting from the diet certain foods in order to detect those responsible for the symptoms.

ELISA /əlī'zə/, abbreviation for **enzyme-linked immunosorbent assay,** a technology used to measure a variety of proteins and antigens.

elixir /ilik'sər/ [Ar, *il-iksir,* seen as the philosopher's stone], a clear liquid containing water, alcohol, sweeteners, or flavors, used primarily as a vehicle for the oral administration of a drug.

Elixophyllin, a trademark for a bronchodilator (theophylline) used as a bronchodilator.

ellipsis /ilip'sis/, in psychiatry, the omission by a patient of meaningful thoughts and ideas while undergoing therapy.

ellipsoidal, describing an object that has the shape of a spindle or an ellipse.

ellipsoid joint, a synovial joint in which a condyle is received into an elliptic cavity, as the wrist joint. A condyloid joint permits no axial rotation but allows flexion, extension, adduction, abduction, and circumduction.

elliptical trainer, exercise equipment designed to simulate motions such as stairclimbing and running by using pedals that move back and forth in an oval (elliptical) pattern to minimize the impact on the hips, back and knees.

elliptocyte /ilip'təsīt/ [Gk, *elleipsis,* ellipse, *kytos,* cell], an oval RBC.

elliptocytic anemia, hereditary elliptocytosis.

elliptocytosis /ilip'tōsītō'sis/ [Gk, *elleipsis* + *kytos* + *osis,* condition], an abnormal condition of the blood characterized by increased numbers of elliptocytes or oval erythrocytes.

elongation /i'longā'shən/ [L, *elongatio,* a prolonging], a state of being lengthened or extended.

elope /ilōp'/ [ME, *gantlopp,* to run away], informal.to leave a locked or secured

psychiatric institution without notice or permission.

elopement occurrence, a nursing outcome from the Nursing Outcomes Classification (NOC) defined as the number of times in the past 24 hours/1 week/1 month (select one) that an individual with a cognitive impairment escapes a secure area.

elopement precautions, a nursing intervention from the Nursing Interventions Classification (NIC) defined as minimizing the risk of a patient leaving a treatment setting without authorization when departure presents a threat to the safety of patient or others.

elopement propensity risk, a nursing outcome from the Nursing Outcomes Classification (NOC) defined as the propensity of an individual with cognitive impairment to escape a secure area.

Elspar, a trademark for an antineoplastic (asparaginase).

eluate /el'yoo·āt/ [L, *eluere,* to wash out], a solution or substance that results from an elution process.

eluent /el'yoo·ənt/, a solvent or solution used in an elution process, such as column chromatography.

elution /eloo'shən/, the removal of an absorbed substance from a porous bed or chromatographic column by means of a stream of liquid or gas or the application of heat. The term is also applied to the removal of antibodies or radioactive tracers from erythrocytes.

em, abbreviation for **extrinsic muscle.**

EM, abbreviation for **erythema multiforme.**

emaciation /imā'shi·ā'shən/ [L, *emaciare,* to make lean], **1.** excessive leanness caused by disease or lack of nutrition. **2.** characterized by an extreme loss of subcutaneous fat that results in an abnormally lean body, such as with starvation.— **emaciated,** *adj.*

emancipated minor /iman'sipā'tid/ [L, *emancipare,* to set free], a person who is not legally an adult but who, because he or she is married, in the military, or otherwise no longer dependent on his or her parents, may not require parental permission for medical or surgical care. State and national laws vary in specific interpretations of the rule.

emasculation /imas'kyəlā'shən/, a loss of the testes or penis or both.

embalming /embä'ming/, the practice of applying antiseptics and preservatives to a corpse to retard the natural decomposition of tissues.

Embden-Meyerhof defects /emb'den mī'ərhof/ [Gustav G. Embden, German biochemist, 1874–1933; Otto F. Meyerhof, German biochemist, 1884–1951], a group of hereditary hemolytic anemias caused by enzyme deficiencies.

embedded tooth, an unerupted tooth, usually completely covered with bone.

embolectomy /em′bəlek′təmē/ [Gk, *embolos,* plug, *ektomē,* excision], a surgical incision into an artery for the removal of an embolus or clot, performed as emergency treatment for arterial embolism.

embolic gangrene [Gk, *embolos* + *gaggraina*], the death and decay of body tissues caused by an embolus blocking the blood supply to that part.

embolic necrosis, death of a portion of tissue that results from an infarction caused by an embolus.

embolic thrombosis [Gk, *embolos,* plug, *thrombos,* lump, *osis,* condition], a clot that develops at the site of an impacted embolus (foreign body) in a blood vessel.

emboliform nucleus, a small cerebellar nucleus lying between the dentate nucleus and the globose nucleus and contributing to the superior cerebellar peduncles.

embolism /em′bəliz′əm/, an abnormal condition in which an embolus travels through the bloodstream and becomes lodged in a blood vessel. Symptoms vary with the character of the embolus, the degree of occlusion that results, and the size, nature, and location of the occluded vessel.—**embolic,** *adj.*

embolization agent, a substance used to occlude or drastically reduce blood flow within a vessel.

embolized atheroma, a fat particle lodged in a blood vessel.

embolotherapy /em′bəlōther′əpē/, a technique of blocking a blood vessel with a balloon catheter. It is used for treating bleeding ulcers and blood vessel defects and for stopping blood flow to a tumor during surgery.

embolus /em′bələs/ *pl.* **emboli** [Gk, *embolos,* plug], a foreign object, quantity of air or gas, bit of tissue or tumor, or piece of a thrombus that circulates in the bloodstream until it becomes lodged in a vessel. —**embolic, emboloid,** *adj.*

embolus care: peripheral, a nursing intervention from the Nursing Interventions Classification (NIC) defined as limitation of complications for a patient experiencing, or at risk for, occlusion of peripheral circulation.

embolus care: pulmonary, a nursing intervention from the Nursing Interventions Classification (NIC) defined as limitation of complications for a patient experiencing, or at risk for, occlusion of pulmonary circulation.

embolus precautions, a nursing intervention from the Nursing Interventions

Classification (NIC) defined as reduction of the risk of an embolus in a patient with thrombi or at risk for thrombus formation.

embolysis /embol′isis/, the dissolution of an embolus, especially one caused by a blood clot.

embrasure /embrā′zhər/, a normally occurring space between adjacent teeth resulting from variations in the positions and contours of teeth. Embrasures provide a spillway for the escape of food during mastication.

embryectomy /em′brē·ek′təmē/ [Gk, *en,* in, *bryein,* to grow, *ektomē,* excision], the surgical removal of an embryo, most commonly in an ectopic pregnancy.

embryo /em′brē·ō/ [Gk, *en,* in, *bryein,* to grow], **1.** any organism in the earliest stages of development. **2.** in humans, the stage of prenatal development from the time of fertilization of the ovum until the end of the eighth week.

embryocidal /em′brē·əsī′dəl/, pertaining to the killing of an embryo.

embryoctony /em′brē·ok′tənē/ [Gk, *en* + *bryein* + *kteinein,* to kill], the intentional destruction of a living embryo or fetus in utero.

embryogenesis /em′brē·ōjen′əsis/ [Gk, *en* + *bryein* + *genein,* to produce], the process in sexual reproduction by which an embryo forms from the fertilization of an ovum.—**embryogenetic, embryogenic,** *adj.*

embryologic development /-loj′ik/, the various intrauterine stages and processes involved in the growth and differentiation of the conceptus from the time of fertilization of the ovum until the eighth week of gestation. The stages are related to the biologic status of the unborn child and involve the differentiation of the various cells, tissues, and organ systems and the development of the main external features of the embryo. It occurs from approximately the end of the second week to the eighth week of intrauterine life. The fetal stage follows these stages, beginning at about the ninth week of gestation.

embryologist /em′brē·ol′əjist/, one who specializes in embryology.

embryology /em′brē·ol′əjē/ [Gk, *en, bryein* + *logos,* science], the study of the origin, growth, development, and function of an organism from fertilization to birth. —**embryologic,** *adj.*

embryoma /em′brē·ō′mə/ *pl.* **embryomas, embryomata** [Gk, *en* + *bryein* + *oma,* tumor], a tumor that arises from embryonic cells or tissues.

embryomorph /embrē′əmôrf′/ [Gk, *en* + *bryein* + *morphe,* form], any structure that resembles an embryo, especially a mass of tissue that may represent an aborted conceptus.—**embryomorphous,** *adj.*

embryonal carcinoma /em′brē-ənəl/, a malignant neoplasm derived from germinal cells that usually develops in gonads, especially the testes. Bodies resembling a 1- or 2-week-old embryo are occasionally seen in these tumors.

embryonate /em′brē-ənāt′/ [Gk, *en* + *bryein;* L, *atus,* shaped like], **1.** impregnate. **2.** pertaining to or resembling an embryo. **3.** containing an embryo.

embryonic abortion, 1. termination of pregnancy before the twentieth week of gestation. **2.** products of conception expelled before the twentieth week.

embryonic anideus [Gk, *en* + *bryein* + *an,* not, *eidos,* form], a blastoderm in which the axial elongation of the primitive streak and primitive groove fail to develop.

embryonic blastoderm, the area of the blastoderm that gives rise to the primitive streak from which the embryonic body develops.

embryonic competence, the ability of an embryonic cell to react normally to the stimulation of an inductor, allowing continued normal growth or differentiation of the embryo.

embryonic disk, the thickened plate from which the embryo develops in the second week of pregnancy.

embryonic layer, one of the three layers of cells in the embryo: endoderm, mesoderm, and ectoderm. From these layers of cells arise all of the structures and organs and parts of the body.

embryonic period, the earliest period or phase of lung development in utero, lasting from the third week after conception to the sixth week. During this period, a ventral respiratory diverticulum (lung bud) arises from the caudal end of the laryngotracheal groove and grows into bronchial buds and the primordial trachea.

embryonic pole, the area of the blastocyst where the embryoblast and the trophoblast are in contact. The embryoblast attaches to the endometrial epithelium at this pole.

embryonic rest, a portion of embryonic tissue that remains in the adult organism.

embryonic stage, in embryology, the interval of time from fertilization to the eighth week.

embryonic tissue [Gk, *en* + *bryein,* to grow; OFr, *tissu*], **1.** a loose, gelatinous mass of connective tissue cells. The gelatinous matrix is caused by the presence of mucopolysaccharides. **2.** pertaining to tissue of an embryo.

embryoniform /em′brē-on′ifôrm′/ [Gk, *en* + *bryein;* L, *forma,* form], resembling an embryo.

embryopathy /em′brē-op′əthē/ [Gk, *en* + *bryein* + *pathos,* disease], any anomaly occurring in the embryo or fetus as a result of interference with normal intrauterine development.

embryoplastic /em′brē-ōplas′tik/ [Gk, *en* + *bryein* + *plassein,* to mold], pertaining to the formation of an embryo, usually with reference to cells.

embryoscopy /em′brē-os′kəpē/, the direct examination of an embryo by insertion of a lighted instrument through the mother's abdominal wall and uterus.

embryotome /em′brē-ətōm′/ [Gk, *en* + *bryein* + *temnein,* to cut], a cutting instrument for the removal of a fetus when normal birth is not possible.

embryotomy /em′brē-ot′əmē/ [Gk, *en* + *bryein* + *temnein,* to cut], **1.** the dismemberment or mutilation of a fetus for removal from the uterus when normal delivery is not possible. **2.** the dissection of an embryo for examination and analysis.

embryo transfer, a process of implanting a fertilized ovum in a uterus.

embryotroph /em′brē-ətrof′/ [Gk, *en* + *bryein* + *trophe,* nourishment], the liquefied uterine nutritive material, composed of glandular secretions and degenerative tissue, that nourishes the mammalian embryo until placental circulation is established.

embryotrophy /em′brē-ot′trəfē/, the nourishment of the embryo.—**embryotrophic,** *adj.*

embryulcia /em′brē-ul′sē-ə/ [Gk, *en* + *bryein* + *elkein,* to draw], the surgical extraction of the embryo or fetus from the uterus.

Emcyt, a trademark for an antineoplastic agent (estramustine phosphate sodium).

emedastine /em′ĕdas′tēn/, an antihistamine applied topically to the conjunctiva as *emedastine difumarate* in treatment of allergic conjunctivitis.

Emend, a trademark for aprepitant.

emergence /imur′jəns/ [L, *emergere,* to come forth], the point in the process of recovery from general anesthesia at which a return of spontaneous respiration, airway reflexes, and consciousness occurs.

emergency /imur′jənsē/ [L, *emergere,* to come forth], a perilous situation that arises suddenly and threatens the life or welfare of a person or a group of people, as a natural disaster, medical crisis, or trauma situation.

emergency cardiac care (ECC) [L, *emergeere,* to come forth; Gk, *kardia;* ME, *caru,* sorrow], the concentration of personnel and facilities organized to sustain the cardiovascular and pulmonary systems when an MI or cardiac arrest occurs. The interventions assure prompt availability of basic life support, monitoring and treatment facilities, prevention of complications, emergency care

453

emetic

and psychologic reassurance. If cardiac arrest occurs outside a hospital, efforts are devoted to stabilizing the patient's cardiovascular and pulmonary systems before removing the individual to a hospital.

emergency care, a nursing intervention from the Nursing Interventions Classification (NIC) defined as providing life-saving measures in life-threatening situations.

emergency cart checking, a nursing intervention from the Nursing Interventions Classification (NIC) defined as the systematic review and maintenance of the contents of an emergency cart at established time intervals.

emergency childbirth, a birth that occurs accidentally or precipitously in or out of the hospital, without standard obstetric preparations and procedures.

emergency department (ED), in a health care facility, a section of an institution that is staffed and equipped to provide rapid and varied emergency care, especially for those who are stricken with sudden and acute illness or who are the victims of severe trauma.

emergency doctrine, in law, a doctrine that assumes a person's consent to medical treatment when he or she is in imminent danger and unable to give informed consent to treatment. Emergency doctrine assumes that the person would consent if able to do so.

emergency medical service (EMS), a network of services coordinated to provide aid and medical assistance from primary response to definitive care, involving personnel trained in the rescue, stabilization, transportation, and advanced treatment of traumatic or medical emergencies.

emergency medical technician (EMT), a person trained in and responsible for the administration of specialized emergency care and the transportation of victims of acute illness or injury to a medical facility in compliance with national standards developed by the U.S. Department of Transportation. EMTs receive ongoing training in new procedures and must qualify for national recertification every 2 years.

emergency medical technician-advanced life support (EMT-ALS), a third-level EMT. The EMT-ALS is locally certified in all the skills of the basic-level EMT and EMT-IV. The EMT-ALS may also administer certain medications after the protocols or orders of the hospital physician, with whom radio contact is maintained. An EMT-ALS is also trained in the use of advanced life support systems, including electric defibrillation equipment.

emergency medical technician-intermediate (EMT-I), a second-level emergency medical technician nationally certified as both an EMT-ALS and an EMT-IV.

emergency medical technician-intravenous (EMT-IV), a second-level emergency medical technician. The EMT-IV is trained and locally certified in IV therapy, endotracheal intubation, and use of other antishock techniques.

emergency medical technician-paramedic (EMT-P), an advanced-level emergency medical technician who works in prehospital care settings under the direction of a physician, often through radio contact. The EMT-P is nationally certified in all the skills of EMTs of other levels and has additional training in pharmacology and administration of emergency drugs.

emergency medicine, a branch of medicine concerned with the diagnosis and treatment of conditions resulting from trauma or sudden illness.

Emergency Nurses' Association (ENA), a national professional organization of ED nurses that defines and promotes emergency nursing practice.

emergency nursing, nursing care provided to prevent imminent severe damage or death or to avert serious injury. Activities that exemplify emergency nursing are basic life support, CPR, and control of hemorrhage.

emergency readiness, a state of having made advance plans for coping with an unexpected natural disaster, civil disturbance, or military attack that may threaten death and injury to a local population.

emergent /imur'jənt/ [L, *emergens*, emerging], arising, often unexpectedly, or improving or modifying an existing thing.

emergent evolution, the theory that evolution occurs in a series of major changes at certain critical stages and results from the total rearrangement of existing elements so that completely new and unpredictable characteristics appear within the species.

Emery-Dreifuss syndrome /em'ərē drī'fəs/ [Alan E.H. Emery, British geneticist, b. 1928; Fritz E. Dreifuss, twentieth-century British physician, 1926–1997], an X-linked recessive form of muscular dystrophy that begins in early childhood and is characterized by joint contractures and cardiac conduction disorders.

emesis basin /em'əsis, əmē'sis/ [Gk, *emesis*, vomiting; Fr, *bassin*, hollow vessel], a kidney-shaped bowl or pan that fits against the neck to collect vomitus.

emesis gravidarum, vomiting associated with pregnancy.

Emete-con, a trademark for an antiemetic (benzquinamide hydrochloride).

emetic /imet'ik/, **1.** pertaining to a substance that causes vomiting. **2.** an emetic agent, such as apomorphine hydrochloride or syrup of ipecac.

Emetrol, a trademark for a fixed-combination drug containing fructose, glucose, and orthophosphoric acid, used to treat nausea and vomiting.

EMG, 1. abbreviation for **electromyogram.** 2. abbreviation for **electromyography.**

EMG syndrome, a hereditary disorder transmitted as an autosomal-recessive trait, characterized by umbilical hernia (exomphalos), macroglossia, and gigantism, often accompanied by visceromegaly, dysplasia of the renal medulla, and enlargement of the cells of the adrenal cortex.

emissary veins /em′əser′ē/ [L, *emittere,* to send forth], the small vessels in the skull that connect the sinuses of the dura mater with the veins on the exterior of the skull through a series of anastomoses.

emission /imish′ən/ [L, *emittere,* to send out], a discharge or release of something, as a fluid from the body, electronic signals from a radio transmitter, or an alpha or beta particle from an atomic nucleus during radioactive decay.

emission computed tomography (ECT) [L, *emittere,* to send forth, *computare,* to count; Gk, *tome,* section, *graphein,* to record], a form of tomography in which the emitted decay products, as positrons or gamma rays, from an ingested radioactive pharmaceutical are recorded in detectors outside the body.

emit [L, *emittere,* to send out], to give or send out something, such as energy, sound, heat, or radiation.

emmetropia /em′ətrō′pē-ə/ [Gk, *emmetros,* proportioned, *opsis,* vision], a state of normal vision characterized by the proper relationship between the refractive system of the eyeball and its axial length. This correlation ensures that light rays entering the eye parallel to the optic axis are focused exactly on the retina. —**emmetropic,** *adj.*

Emmet's operation, a surgical procedure for repair of a lacerated perineum or ruptured uterine cervix.

emollient /imol′yənt/ [L, *emolliere,* to soften], a substance that softens tissue, particularly the skin and mucous membranes.

emollient bath, a bath taken in water containing an emollient, such as bran, to relieve irritation and inflammation.

emotion /imō′shən/ [L, *emovere,* to disturb], 1. the outward expression or display of mood or feeling states. 2. the affective aspect of consciousness as compared with volition and cognition.

emotional abuse /imō′shənəl/, the debasement of a person's feelings that causes the individual to perceive himself or herself as inept, not cared for, and worthless.

emotional age [L, *emovere,* to disturb, *aetas,* age], the age of an individual as determined by the stage of emotional development reached.

emotional amalgam, an unconscious effort to deny or counteract anxiety.

emotional amenorrhea, a suppression of menstrual discharge from the uterus caused by psychologic factors.

emotional care of the dying patient, the compassionate, consistent support offered to help the terminally ill patient and the family cope with impending death.

emotional deprivation [L, *emovere,* to disturb, *deprivare,* to deprive], a lack of adequate warmth, affection, and interest, especially of a parent or significant nurturer. It is a relatively common problem among institutionalized persons or children from broken homes.

emotional diarrhea, the frequent passage of liquid stools caused by extreme emotional stress.

emotional glycosuria, a temporary increase in the level of sugar excretion in the urine resulting from extreme emotional disturbances.

emotional hyperhidrosis, an autosomal-dominant disorder of the eccrine sweat glands, most often of the palms, soles, and axillae, in which emotional stimuli and sometimes mental or sensory stimuli elicit volar or axillary sweating.

emotional lability, a condition of excessive emotional reactions and frequent mood changes.

emotional need, a psychologic or mental requirement of intrapsychic origin. It usually centers on such basic feelings as love, fear, anger, sorrow, anxiety, frustration, and depression and involves the understanding, empathy, and support of one person for another. Such needs normally occur in everyone but usually increase during periods of excessive stress or physical and mental illness and during various stages of life. If these needs are not routinely met by appropriate, socially accepted means, they can precipitate psychopathologic conditions.

emotional response, a reaction to a particular intrapsychic feeling or feelings, accompanied by physiologic changes that may or may not be outwardly manifested but that motivate or precipitate some action or behavioral response.

emotional support[1], the sensitive, and understanding approach that helps patients accept and deal with their illnesses; communicate their anxieties and fears; derive comfort from a gentle, sympathetic, caring person; and increase their ability to care for themselves.

emotional support², a nursing intervention from the Nursing Interventions Classification (NIC) defined as provision of reassurance, acceptance, and encouragement during times of stress.

empathic /empath′ik/ [Gk, *en,* into, *pathos,* feeling], pertaining to or involving the entering of one person into the emotional state of another while remaining objective and distinctly separate.

empathy /em′pəthē/ [Gk, *en,* in, *pathos,* feeling], the ability to recognize and to some extent share the emotions and states of mind of another and to understand the meaning and significance of that person's behavior. It is an essential quality for effective psychotherapy.—**empathic,** *adj.,* **empathize,** *v.*

emphysema /em′fəsē′mə/ [Gk, *en* + *physema,* a blowing], an abnormal condition of the pulmonary system, characterized by overinflation and destructive changes in alveolar walls. It results in a loss of lung elasticity and decreased gas exchange. There are 3 primary types: centriacinar emphysema, distal acinar emphysema, and panacinar emphysema. The patient may have dyspnea on exertion or at rest, cough, orthopnea, unequal chest expansion, tachypnea, tachycardia, and an elevated temperature and breath sounds if there is an infection. Anxiety, increased $PaCO_2$, restlessness, confusion, weakness, anorexia, hypoxemia, and respiratory failure are common in advanced cases. — **emphysematous,** *adj.*

emphysematous abscess, an abscess in which air or gas is present.

emphysematous gastritis, infectious gastritis in which the infectious agents are gas-producing bacteria. Radiologically it resembles gastric emphysema but is much more serious, even life threatening.

emphysematous pyelitis, pyelitis with air or gas only in the collecting system.

empiric /empir′ik/ [Gk, *empeirikos,* experimental], pertaining to a method of treating disease based on observations and experience without an understanding of the cause or mechanism of the disorder or the way the therapeutic agent or procedure used affects improvement or cure.

empirical formula, a chemical formula that shows the smallest whole number ratio of atoms of different elements in a molecule. It does not indicate structural linkage.

empiricism /empir′isiz′əm/, a form of therapy based on the therapist's personal experience and that of other practitioners. —**empiricist,** *n.*

Employment Retirement Income Security Act (ERISA), a federal law, enacted in 1974, regulating employee welfare benefit plans, including group health plans.

emprosthotonos /em′prosthot′ənəs/ [Gk, *emprosthen,* forward, *tenein,* to cut], a position of the body characterized by forward, rigid flexure at the waist. The position is the result of a prolonged involuntary muscle spasm that is most commonly associated with tetanus infection or strychnine poisoning.

empty follicle syndrome, a condition in which oocytes are absent from stimulated follicles.

empty sella syndrome [AS, *oemettig,* unoccupied; L, *sella,* saddle], an abnormal enlargement of the sella turcica filled with CSF. The pituitary gland may be smaller than normal and flattened, or it may be absent. Signs and symptoms of hormonal imbalance (for example, hypopituitarism) may be present, as may headache, but some patients are asymptomatic.

empyema /em′pī-ē′mə, em′pē-ē′mə/ [Gk, *en* + *ipyon,* pus], an accumulation of pus in the pleural space, as a result of bacterial infection, such as pleurisy or TB.

EMS, 1. abbreviation for **electrical muscle stimulator. 2.** abbreviation for **emergency medical service. 3.** abbreviation for **eosinophilia-myalgia syndrome.**

EMS standing orders, routine medical procedures approved in advance for EMS crews to perform before consulting a physician.

EMT, abbreviation for **emergency medical technician.**

EMT-A, abbreviation for *emergency medical technician–ambulance,* a member of an emergency medical services crew.

EMT-ALS, abbreviation for **emergency medical technician–advanced life support.**

EMT-B, abbreviation for *emergency medical technician–basic,* an entry-level emergency medical technician who is trained in basic emergency care skills such as defibrillation, airway maintenance, CPR, spinal immobilization, bleeding control, and fracture management.

EMT-D, abbreviation for *emergency medical technician–defibrillator,* a member of an emergency medical services crew with special training in the use of cardiac defibrillating equipment.

EMT-I, abbreviation for **emergency medical technician–intermediate.**

EMT-IV, abbreviation for **emergency medical technician–intravenous.**

EMT-P, abbreviation for **emergency medical technician–paramedic.**

E

emtricitabine, an antiretroviral agent used with other retrovirals to treat HIV infection.

Emtriva, a trademark for **emtricitabine.**

emulsification /imul'sifikā'shən/, the breakdown of large fat globules into smaller, uniformly distributed particles. Emulsification is the first preparation of fat for chemical digestion by specific enzymes.

emulsifier /imul'sifī'ər/ [L, *emulgere,* to milk out, *facere,* to make], a substance such as egg yolk or gum arabic that can cause oil to be suspended in water.

emulsify [L, *emulgere,* to milk out, *facere,* to make], to disperse a liquid into another liquid with which it is immiscible, making a colloidal suspension. Soaps and detergents emulsify by surrounding small globules of fat, preventing them from settling out. Bile acts as an emulsifying agent in the digestive tract by dispersing ingested fats into small globules. —**emulsification,** *n.*

emulsion /imul'shən/ [L, *emulgere,* to milk out], **1.** a system consisting of two immiscible liquids, one of which is dispersed in the other in the form of small droplets. **2.** in photography, a composition sensitive to actinic rays of light, consisting of one or more silver halides suspended in gelatin applied in a thin layer to film.

ENA, abbreviation for **Emergency Nurses' Association.**

enabler /enā'blər/, a significant other of a substance abuser who provides either implicit or explicit support of substance-abusing or dysfunctional behavior.

enalapril maleate /enal'əpril/, an angiotensin-converting enzyme inhibitor used as an oral antihypertensive drug. It is prescribed in the treatment of hypertension or heart failure or as a preventive for MI, stroke, or cardiovascular death.

enamel /inam'əl/ [OFr, *esmail*], the hard, white crystalline substance of the minerals hydroxyapatite and/or fluorapatite that forms the outermost covering of the clinical and anatomic crown of a tooth. It contains no nerves or blood vessels and is the hardest bony substance in the body. It is produced by epithelial cells called ameloblasts.

enamel hypocalcification, a defect in which the enamel of the teeth is soft and undercalcified and opaque in appearance but normal in quantity. The teeth are chalky in consistency, their surfaces wear down rapidly, and a yellowish-brown stain appears on the teeth as the underlying dentin is exposed.

enamel hypoplasia, a defect in which the enamel of the teeth is hard but thin and deficient in amount as a result of defective enamel matrix formation with a shortage of the cementing substance. It is characterized by lack of contact between teeth, rapid breakdown of occlusal surfaces, and a yellowish-brown stain that appears where the dentin is exposed.

enamel niche, either of two depressions on a tooth, located between the lateral dental lamina and the developing dental germ.

enamel organ, a complex epithelial structure on the dental papilla. It produces enamel for the developing tooth.

enanthema /en'anthē'mə/ [Gk, *en* + *anthema,* blossoming], a sudden eruptive lesion of the surface of a mucous membrane.

enantiomer, in physical science, one of the two nonsuperimposable mirror image forms of a chiral compound.

en bloc /enblok', äNblôk'/ [Fr, in a block], all together, or as a whole.

encapsulated /enkaps'yəlā'tid/ [Gk, *en*; L, *capsula,* little box], (of arteries, muscles, nerves, and other body parts) enclosed in fibrous or membranous sheaths.

encephalalgia /ənsef'əlal'jə/, headache.

encephalitis /ensef'əlī'tis/, *pl.* **encephalitides** [Gk, *enkephalos,* brain, *itis,* inflammation], an inflammatory condition of the brain. The cause is usually an arbovirus infection transmitted by the bite of an infected mosquito, but it may be the result of lead or other poisoning or of hemorrhage. Postinfectious encephalitis occurs as a complication of another infection such as chickenpox, influenza, or measles or after smallpox vaccination. The condition is characterized by headache, neck pain, fever, nausea, and vomiting. Neurologic disturbances, including seizures, personality change, irritability, lethargy, paralysis, weakness, and coma, may occur. Usually the inflammation involves the spinal cord and brain; hence in most cases a more accurate term is **encephalomyelitis.**

encephalocele /ensef'ələsēl'/ [Gk, *enkephalos* + *koilia,* cavity], **1.** protrusion of the brain through a congenital defect in the skull. **2.** hernia of the brain.

encephalodysplasia, any congenital anomaly of the brain.

encephalogram /ensef'ələgram'/ [Gk, *enkephalos* + *gramma,* record], a radiograph of the brain made during encephalography.

encephalography /ensef'əlog'rəfē/, radiographic delineation of the structures of the brain. CSF is withdrawn and replaced by a gas, such as air, helium, or oxygen. The procedure is used mainly for indicating the site of CSF obstruction in hydrocephalus or structural abnormalities of the posterior fossa. —**encephalographic,** *adj.*

encephalomeningitis /-men'injī'tis/ [Gk, *enkephalos*, brain, *meninx*, membrane, *itis*, inflammation], an inflammation of the brain and meninges.

encephalomyelitis /ensef'əlōmī'əlī'tis/ [Gk, *enkephalos* + *myelos*, marrow + *itis*], an inflammatory condition of the brain and spinal cord that damages myelin, characterized by fever, headache, stiff neck, back pain, and vomiting. Depending on the cause, the age and condition of the person, and the extent of the inflammation and irritation to the CNS, seizures, paralysis, personality changes, a decreased LOC, coma, or death may occur.

encephalomyocarditis /ensef'əlōmī'ōkärdī'tis/ [Gk, *enkephalos* + *mys*, muscle, *kardia*, heart, *itis*, inflammation], an infectious disease of the CNS and heart tissue caused by a group of small RNA picornaviruses. Symptoms are generally similar to those of poliomyelitis. Most victims recover promptly without sequelae.

encephalon [Gk, *enkephalos*, brain], **1.** the cerebrum and its related structures of cerebellum, pons, and medulla oblongata. **2.** the contents of the cranium.

encephalopathy /ensef'əlop'əthē/ [Gk, *enkephalos* + *pathos*, disease], any abnormal condition of the structure or function of brain tissues, especially chronic, destructive, or degenerative conditions.

enchondroma /en'kəndrō'mə/, *pl.* **enchondromas, enchondromata** [Gk, *en* + *chondros*, cartilage, *oma*, tumor], a benign, slowly growing tumor of cartilage cells that arises in the extremity of the shaft of tubular bones in the hands or feet.

enchondromatosis /en'kəndrō'mətō'sis/ [Gk, *en* + *chondros*, cartilage, *oma*, tumor, *osis*, condition], a congenital disorder characterized by the proliferation of cartilage within the extremity of the shafts of bones, causing thinning of the cortex and distortion in length.

enchondromatous myxoma /en'kondrō'mətəs/, a tumor of the connective tissue, characterized by the presence of cartilage between the cells of connective tissue.

enclave /en'klāv, enklāv'/, a detached mass of tissue enclosed in an organ or in a different kind of tissue.

encoded message, in communication theory, a message as transmitted by a sender to a receiver.

encopresis /en'kōprē'sis/, fecal holding with constipation and fecal soiling. —**encopretic,** *adj.*

encounter [Gk, en; L, *contra,* against], in psychotherapy, the interaction between a patient and a psychotherapist, such as occurs in existential therapy or among several members of a small group, such as encounter or sensitivity training groups. In an encounter, emotional change and personal growth are affected by participants' expression of strong feelings.

encounter data, information showing use of provider services by health plan enrollees that is used to develop cost profiles of a particular group of enrollees and then to guide decisions about or provide justification for the maintenance or adjustment of premiums.

encounter group, in psychology, a small group of people who meet to increase self-awareness, promote personal growth, and improve interpersonal communication.

enculturation /enkul'chərā'shən/ [Gk, *en*; L, *cultura,* cultivation], the process of learning the concepts, values, and behavioral standards of a particular culture.

encyst /ensist'/, to form a cyst or capsule. —**encysted,** *adj.*

encysted pleurisy, a form of pleurisy with adhesions that surround the effused material.

end, abbreviation for **endoreduplication.**

Endameba, any ameba of the genus Endamoeba.

Endamoeba, a genus of amebic parasites in invertebrates, originally described from cockroaches.

endarterectomy /en'därtərek'təmē/ [Gk, *endon,* within, *arteria,* airpipe, *ektomē,* excision], the surgical removal of the intimal lining of an artery. The procedure is done to clear a major artery that may be blocked by plaque accumulation.

endarteritis /en'därtərī'tis/ [Gk, *endon* + *arteria* + *itis,* inflammation], inflammation of the inner layer of one or more arteries, which may become partially or completely occluded.

endarteritis obliterans, an inflammatory condition of the lining of the arterial walls in which the intima proliferates, narrowing the lumen of the vessels and occluding the smaller vessels.

end artery, a blood vessel that does not join with any other vessel.

end bud [AS, *ende*; Gk, *bolbos,* onion], a mass of undifferentiated cells produced from the remnants of the primitive node and the primitive streak at the caudal end of the developing embryo after formation of the somites is completed.

end-diastolic pressure /-dī'əstol'ik/ [AS, *ende*; Gk, *dia* + *stellein,* to set; L, *premere,* to press], the pressure of the blood in the ventricles at the end of diastole.

endemic /endem'ik/ [Gk, *endemos,* native], (of a disease or microorganism) the expected or "normal" incidence indigenous to a geographic area or population.

E

endemic disease, a physical or mental disorder caused by health conditions constantly present within a community. It usually describes an infection that is transmitted directly or indirectly between humans and is occurring at the usual expected rate.

endemic goiter, an enlargement of the thyroid gland caused by the intake of inadequate amounts of dietary iodine. Iodine deprivation leads to diminished production and secretion of thyroid hormone by the gland. The goiter may grow during the winter months and shrink during the summer months when the person eats more iodine-containing fresh vegetables. Initially the goiter is diffuse; later it becomes multinodular. Endemic goiter occurs occasionally in adolescents at puberty and widely in population groups in geographic areas in which limited amounts of iodine are present in soil, water, and food.

endemic syphilis, a chronic infectious skin disease that is closely related to *Treponema pallidum* infection and is frequently contracted in childhood without venereal contact.

end-feel, the sensation imparted to the examiner's hands at the end point of the available ROM. It varies according to the limiting structure or tissue. Types of end-feel include capsular, bone-on-bone, spasm, and springy block.

endobronchitis /en′dōbrongkī′tis/, inflammation of the smaller bronchi, often caused by a bronchial mucosal infection.

endocardial, pertaining to the **endocardium.**

endocardial cushion defect /en′dōkär′dē·əl/, any cardiac defect resulting from the failure of the endocardial cushions in the embryonic heart to fuse and form the atrial septum.

endocardial cushions, a pair of thickened tissue sections in the embryonic atrial canal. During embryonic development they meet and fuse to form a septum, dividing the canal into two channels that eventually become the atrioventricular orifices.

endocardial fibroelastosis /fī′brō·ē′lastō′sis/ [Gk, *endon* + *kardia,* heart; L, *fibra,* fiber; Gk, *elaunein,* to drive, *osis,* condition], an abnormal condition characterized by the development of a thick, fibroelastic endocardium that can cause failure of the heart to pump blood.

endocardial murmur, a continuous, soft sound made by an abnormality within the heart.

endocardial tubes, paired, longitudinal, endothelial-lined channels formed from the cardiogenic mesoderm in embryonic development that fuse to form the primordial heart tube.

endocarditis /en′dōkärdī′tis/ [Gk, *endon* + *kardia,* heart, *itis,* inflammation], inflammation of the endocardium and heart valves. The condition is characterized by lesions caused by a variety of diseases.

endocardium /en′dōkär′dē·əm/, *pl.* **endocardia,** the lining of the heart chambers, containing small blood vessels and a few bundles of smooth muscle. It is continuous with the endothelium of the great blood vessels.

endocervical /-sur′fikəl/ [Gk, *endon;* L, *cervix,* neck], pertaining to the interior of the cervix.

endocervicitis /en′dōsur′visī′tis/, an abnormal condition characterized by inflammation of the epithelium and glands of the canal of the uterine cervix.

endocervix /en′dōsur′viks/, **1.** the membrane lining the canal of the uterine cervix. **2.** the opening of the cervix into the uterine cavity.

endochondral /-kon′drəl/ [Gk, *endon,* within, *chondros,* cartilage], pertaining to something within the cartilage.

endocrinasthenia /-krin′asthē′nē·ə/, a neural deficit caused by an alteration of the endocrine system.

endocrine /en′dəkrēn, -krīn/ [Gk, *endon* + *krinein,* to secrete], pertaining to a process in which a group of cells secretes into the blood or lymph circulation a substance (for example, hormone) that has a specific effect on the tissues in another part of the body.

endocrine diabetes mellitus [Gk, *endon,* within, *krinein,* to secrete, *diabainein,* to pass through, *mellitus,* honeyed], a form of diabetes associated with diseases of other glands, such as the adrenals, pituitary, or thyroid, classified under other specific types in the American Diabetes Association Classification.

endocrine fracture /-krēn/, any fracture that results from weakness of a specific bone caused by an endocrine disorder such as hyperparathyroidism, in which calcium loss from bone is accelerated.

endocrine gland, a ductless gland that produces and secretes hormones into the blood or lymph nodes, affecting metabolism and other body processes. The endocrine glands include the pituitary, pineal, hypothalamus, thymus, thyroid, parathyroid, adrenal cortex, medulla, pancreatic islands of Langerhans, and gonads. Cells in other structures, such as the GI mucosa, kidneys, heart, and placenta, also have endocrine functions.

endocrine system [Gk, *endon* + *krinein,* to secrete; *systema*], the network of ductless glands and other structures that elaborate and secrete hormones directly into the bloodstream, affecting various processes throughout the body such as metabolism, growth, and secretions from other organs. Glands of the endocrine system include the thyroid, the parathyroid, the anterior pituitary, the posterior pituitary, the pancreas, the suprarenal glands, and the gonads. The pineal gland is also considered an endocrine gland because it is ductless.

endocrinologist /en'dōkrinol'əjist/, a physician who specializes in the endocrine system and its disorders.

endocrinology /-krinol'əjē/ [Gk, *endon* + *krinein,* to secrete, *logos,* science], the study of the anatomic, physiologic, and pathologic characteristics of the endocrine system and of the treatment of endocrine problems.

endocrinopathy /-krinop'əthē/ [Gk, *endon,* within, *krinein,* to secrete, *pathos,* disease], a disease involving an endocrine gland or a dysfunction that decreases the quality or quantity of its secretion or response to a hormone.

endocytosis /en'dōsītō'sis/ [Gk, *endon,* within, *kytos,* cell], uptake by a cell of material from the environment by invagination of its plasma membrane, which may be either phagocytosis or pinocytosis.

endoderm /en'dədurm/ [Gk, *endon* + *derma,* skin], in embryology, the innermost of the cell layers that develop from the embryonic disk of the inner cell mass of the blastocyst. From the endoderm arises the epithelium of the trachea, bronchi, lungs, GI tract, liver, pancreas, urinary bladder and canal, pharynx, thyroid, tympanic cavity, tonsils, and parathyroid glands.

endodermal /-dur'məl/ [Gk, *endon,* within, *derma,* skin], pertaining to the inner of the three layers of the embryo, the epithelial lining of the respiratory system, the digestive tract, and other tissues.

endodermal cloaca, a part of the cloaca in the developing embryo that lies internal to the cloacal membrane and gives rise to the bladder and urogenital ducts.

endodermal sinus tumor, yolk sac tumor.

endodontics [Gk, *endon,* within, *odous,* tooth], As defined by the ADA, the branch of dentistry which is concerned with the morphology, physiology and pathology of the human dental pulp and periradicular tissues. Its study and practice encompass the basic and clinical sciences including biology of the normal pulp, the etiology, diagnosis, prevention and treatment of diseases and injuries of the pulp and associated periradicular conditions.

endodontist /-don'tist/ [Gk, *endon,* within, *odous,* tooth], a dentist who specializes in endodontics.

endogenous /endoj'ənəs/ [Gk, *endon* + *genein,* to produce], **1.** growing within the body. **2.** originating from within the

body or produced from internal causes, such as a disease caused by the structural or functional failure of an organ or system. —**endogenic,** *adj.*

endogenous carbon dioxide, carbon dioxide produced within the body by metabolic processes.

endogenous infection, an infection caused by the reactivation of previously dormant organisms, as in coccidioidomycosis, histoplasmosis, and TB.

endogenous obesity, obesity resulting from dysfunction of the endocrine or metabolic system.

endogenous opioid, an opiate-like substance, such as an endorphin, produced by the body.

endogenous uric acid [Gk, *endon,* within, *genein,* to produce, *ouron,* urine; L, *acidus*], uric acid produced by the metabolism of purines in the body's own nucleoproteins, as distinguished from metabolism of purine products in foods.

endointoxication /en'dō·intok'sikā'shən/, poisoning caused by a toxin produced within the body, such as from dead and infected tissue in gangrene.

endolymph /en'dəlimf/ [Gk, *endon* + *lympha,* water], the pale fluid in the membranous labyrinth (cochlear duct) of the internal ear.

endolymphatic appendage, an outgrowth of the otic vesicle that forms the endolymphatic duct and sac during embryonic development.

endolymphatic duct /-limfat'ik/, a labyrinthine passage joining an endolymphatic sac with the utricle and saccule.

endolymphatic sac, the blind end of an endolymphatic duct.

endomastoiditis /-mas'toidī'tis/, an inflammation within the mastoid cavity and cells.

endometrial /en'dōmē'trē·əl/ [Gk, *endon* + *metra,* womb], **1.** pertaining to endometrium. **2.** pertaining to the uterine cavity.

endometrial biopsy, a microscopic examination of a sample of endometrial tissue to assess corpus luteum function.

endometrial cancer, an adenocarcinoma of the endometrium of the uterus. It is the most prevalent gynecologic malignancy, most often occurring in the fifth or sixth decade of life. Although the cause of endometrial cancer is not clear, some of the risk factors associated with an increased incidence of the disease are a medical history of infertility; anovulation, late menopause (>52 years); administration of exogenous estrogen; uterine polyps; and a combination of diabetes, hypertension, and obesity. Abnormal vaginal bleeding, especially in a postmenopausal woman, is the cardinal symptom. Lower abdominal and low back pain may also be present; a large, boggy uterus is often a sign of advanced disease.

endometrial cyst [Gk, *endon*, within, *metra*, womb, *kystis*, bag], **1.** an endometrial tumor. **2.** an ovarian cyst that develops as a distension of an endometrial gland.

endometrial hyperplasia, an abnormal condition characterized by overgrowth of the endometrium resulting from sustained stimulation by estrogen (of endogenous or exogenous origin) that is not opposed by progesterone. Estrogen acts as a growth hormone for the endometrium. Endometrial hyperplasia often results in abnormal uterine bleeding. Such bleeding, particularly in older women, constitutes an indication for biopsy or curettage of the endometrium to establish histopathologic diagnosis and to rule out malignancy.

endometrial polyp, a pedunculated overgrowth of endometrium, usually benign. Polyps are a common cause of vaginal bleeding in perimenopausal women and are often associated with other uterine abnormalities, such as endometrial hyperplasia or fibroids.

endometriosis /en'dōmē'trē·ō'sis/ [Gk, *endon metra*, womb, *osis*, condition], an abnormal gynecologic condition characterized by ectopic growth and function of endometrial tissue. The tissue is microscopically similar to or identical with endometrium, having glands or glandlike structures, stroma, and areas of hemorrhage. Fragments may be found in the wall of the uterus or on its surface; in or on the tubes, ovaries, rectosigmoid, or pelvic peritoneum; or occasionally in remote extrapelvic areas.

endometritis /en'dōmitrī'tis/ [Gk, *endon*, within, *metra*, womb, *itis*, inflammation], an inflammatory condition of the endometrium or decidua, with extension into the myometrium and parametrial tissues. It is usually caused by bacterial infection, commonly by gonococci or hemolytic streptococci. The condition is characterized by fever, abdominal pain, tachycardia, malodorous discharge, tenderness, and enlargement of the uterus. It occurs most frequently after childbirth or abortion and is associated with the use of an IUD.

endometrium /en'dōmē'trē·əm/ [Gk, *endon* + *metra*, womb], the mucous membrane lining of the uterus, consisting of the stratum compactum, the stratum spongiosum, and the stratum basale. The endometrium changes in thickness and structure with the menstrual cycle.

endomorph /en'dəmôrf'/ [Gk, *endon* + *morphe*, form], a person whose body build is characterized by a soft, round physique with a large trunk and thighs, tapering extremities, an accumulation of fat

throughout the body, and a predominance of structures derived from the endoderm.

endomyocardial fibrosis [Gk, *endon*, within, *mys*, muscle, *kardia*, heart; L, *fibra*, fiber, *osis*, condition], idiopathic myocardiopathy occurring endemically in various parts of Africa and rarely in other areas, characterized by cardiomegaly; marked thickening of the endocardium with dense, white fibrous tissue that frequently extends to involve the inner third or half of the myocardium; and CHF.

endomyocarditis /-mī'ōkärdī'tis/ [Gk, *endon*, within, *mys*, muscle, *kardia*, heart, *itis*, inflammation], an inflammation of the lining of the heart.

endonuclease, an enzyme that cleaves or hydrolyzes phosphodiester bonds within a polynucleotide chain.

endoparasite /en'dōper'əsīt/ [Gk, *endon* + *parasitos*, guest], in medical parasitology, an organism that lives within the internal organs or tissues of the host, such as a tapeworm.

endopathy /endop'əthē/, any disease originating within the person.

endopeptidase /en'dōpep'ti·dās/ [Gk, *endon*, within, *peptein*, to digest, *ase*, enzyme suffix], any peptidase that catalyzes the cleavage of internal peptide bonds in a polypeptide or protein.

endophthalmitis /endof'thalmī'tis/ [Gk, *endon* + *ophthalmos*, eye, *itis*], an infectious condition of the internal eye in which the primary signs are decreased vision, vitritis, and development of a hypopyon. Patients usually complain of pain. Other symptoms include erythema and edema.

endophytic /en'dōfit'ik/ [Gk, *endon* + *phyton*, plant], pertaining to the tendency to grow inward, such as a tumor that grows into the wall of a hollow organ.

endoplasm /en'dōplaz'əm/ [Gk, *endon*, within, *plasma*, plasm], the inner portion of cytoplasm.

endoplasmic reticulum /-plaz'mik/ [Gk, *endon* + *plassein*, to mold], an extensive network of membrane-enclosed tubules in the cytoplasm of cells. The structure functions in the synthesis of proteins and lipids and in the transport of these metabolites within the cell.

endoprosthesis /-prosthē'sis, -pros'thəsis/ [Gk, *endon* + *prosthesis*, addition], a prosthetic device installed within the body such as an internal cardiac pacemaker.

endopyelotomy /en'dōpi'ēlot'əme/, an incision procedure to correct a stenosed ureteropelvic junction by cutting from within using an instrument inserted through an endoscope.

endoreduplication (end) /en'dōridoo'plikā'shən/ [Gr, *endon;* L, *re-*, again, *duplicare*, to duplicate], replication of the chromosomes without subsequent cell division.

end-organ [AS, *ende;* Gk, *organon,* instrument], a nerve ending in which the terminal nerve filaments are encapsulated.

endorphin /endôr′fin/ [Gk, *endon* + *morphe,* shape], one of the three groups of endogenous opioid peptides composed of many amino acids, elaborated by the pituitary gland and other brain areas, and acting on the central and the peripheral nervous systems to reduce pain. There are three known, designated alpha, beta, and gamma. Beta-endorphin has been isolated in the brain and in the GI tract and seems to be the most potent of the endorphins. Behavioral tests indicate that beta-endorphin is a powerful analgesic in humans and animals.

endorsement /endôrs′mənt/ [Gk, *en;* L, *dorsum,* the back], a statement of recognition of the license of a health practitioner in one state by another state.

endoscope /en′dəskōp′/ [Gk, *endon* + *skopein,* to look], an illuminated optic instrument for the visualization of the interior of a body cavity or organ. Although it is generally introduced through a natural opening in the body, it may also be inserted through an incision. Instruments for viewing specific areas of the body include the bronchoscope, cystoscope, gastroscope, laparoscope, otoscope, and vaginoscope. —**endoscopic,** *adj.*

endoscopic retrograde cholangiopancreatography (ERCP), an endoscopic test that provides radiographic visualization of the bile and pancreatic ducts. A flexible fiberoptic duodenoscope is placed into the common bile duct, a radiopaque substance is instilled, and serial x-ray films are taken.

endoscopy /endos′kəpē/, the visualization of the interior of organs and cavities of the body with an endoscope.

endoskeletal prosthesis /-skel′ətəl/ [Gk, *endon* + *skeletos,* dried up, *prosthesis,* addition], a lower-limb support consisting of an internal pylon usually covered with a lightweight material such as plastic foam.

endoskeleton, the internal network of bones, to which muscles are attached. Compare **exoskeleton.**

endosteal hyperostosis /endos′tē·əl/, an inherited bone disorder characterized by an overgrowth of the mandible and brow areas. The excessive bone growth can lead to entrapment of cranial nerves, causing facial palsy and loss of hearing.

endosteal implant [Gk, *endon,* within, *osteon,* bone], a dental implant consisting of a blade, screw, pin, or vent, inserted into the jaw bone through the alveolar or basal bone, with a post protruding through the mucoperiosteum into the oral cavity to serve as an abutment for dentures or orthodontic appliances, or to serve in fracture fixation.

endothelial /en′dōthē′lē·əl/ [Gk, *endon,* within, *thele,* nipple], pertaining to endothelium.

endothelial cell [Gk, *endon,* within, *thele,* nipple; L, *cella,* storeroom], a lining cell of a body cavity or of the cardiovascular system. It is usually seen as a flat, nucleated cell.

endothelium-derived relaxing factor (EDRF), nitric oxide or related substances produced by the endothelial cells lining blood vessels. Its vasodilatory effect on neighboring vascular smooth muscle cells is an important regulator of local blood flow.

endothelin (ET) /-thē′lin/, any of a group of vasoconstrictive peptides produced by endothelial cells. Three known endothelins, designated ET-1, ET-2, and ET-3, are chemically related to asp venom. ET-1 is the most potent vasoconstrictor yet discovered, being 10 times stronger than the second-most potent vasoconstrictor known, angiotensin II.

endothelium /en′dōthē′lē·əm/ [Gk, *endon* + *thele,* nipple], the layer of simple squamous epithelial cells that lines the heart, the blood and lymph vessels, and the serous cavities of the body.

endothoracic fascia /-thōras′ik/, a sheet of connective tissue within the thorax. The outer boundary of the thoracic cavity. It separates the parietal pleura from the chest wall and the diaphragm. A thickened portion also attaches to the medial border of the first rib.

endotoxin /en′dōtok′sin/ [Gk, *endon* + *toxikon,* poison], a toxin contained in the cell walls of some microorganisms, especially gram-negative bacteria, that is released when the bacterium dies and is broken down in the body.

endotoxin shock [Gk, *endon,* within, *toxikon,* poison; Fr, *choc*], a septic shock in response to the release of endotoxins produced by gram-negative bacteria. The toxin is released on the death of the bacterial cell.

endotracheal /en′dōtrā′kē·əl/ [Gk, *endon, tracheia, arteria,* airpipe], within or through the trachea.

endotracheal anesthesia, anesthesia that is achieved by the inhalation of an anesthetic gas or mixture of gases through an endotracheal tube into the lungs, where it is absorbed into the bloodstream.

endotracheal extubation, a nursing intervention from the Nursing Interventions Classification (NIC) defined as purposeful removal of the endotracheal tube from the nasopharyngeal or oropharyngeal airway.

endotracheal intubation, the management of the patient with an airway catheter inserted through the mouth or nose into the trachea. An endotracheal tube may be used to maintain a patent airway, to prevent aspiration of material from the digestive tract in the unconscious or paralyzed patient, to permit suctioning of tracheobronchial secretions, or to administer positive-pressure ventilation that cannot be given effectively by a mask.

endotracheal tube, a large-bore catheter inserted through the mouth or nose and into the trachea to a point above the bifurcation of the trachea. It is used for delivering oxygen under pressure when ventilation must be totally controlled and in general anesthetic procedures.

endovasculitis /-vas'kyəlī'tis/, inflammation of the tunica intima of a blood vessel.

endoxin /endok'sin/, an endogenous analog of digoxin that occurs naturally in humans. It is a hormone that may regulate the excretion of salt.

end plate [AS, *ende*; ME, *plat*], the motor end plate in the nervous system, located at the terminal membrane of an axon and the postjunctional membrane of the adjoining muscle tissue.

end point, 1. in chemistry, the point at which the condition of equivalence is reached during a titration. **2.** the point or time at which an activity is finished. **3.** the point at which a chemical indicator changes color.

end-positional nystagmus, a horizontal rhythmic oscillation of the eyes on extreme lateral gaze. It occurs in normal eyes when the fixation point is outside the binocular field.

end product /endprod'əkt/, the chemical compound resulting from completion of a sequence of metabolic reactions.

end-stage disease [AS, *ende*; OFr, *estage*; L, *dis*; Fr, *aise*, ease], a disease condition that is essentially terminal because of irreversible damage to vital tissues or organs.

end-tidal capnography /end'tīdəl/, the process of continuously recording the level of carbon dioxide in expired air. The percentage of carbon dioxide at the end of expiration can be estimated and gives a close approximation of the alveolar carbon dioxide concentration. The process is used to monitor critically ill patients and in pulmonary function testing.

end-tidal CO_2 determination, the concentration of carbon dioxide in a patient's end-tidal breath, assumed to reflect arterial carbon dioxide tension.

end-to-side anastomosis, an anastomosis connecting the end of one vessel with the side of another one.

endurance[1] /endyŏŏr'əns/, the ability to continue an activity despite increasing physical or psychologic stress. Although endurance and strength are different qualities, weaker muscles tend to have less endurance than do strong muscles.

endurance[2], a nursing outcome from the Nursing Outcomes Classification (NOC) defined as the capacity to sustain activity.

Enduron, a trademark for a thiazide diuretic (methyclothiazide) used to treat hypertension.

Enduronyl, a trademark for a fixed-combination cardiovascular drug containing a diuretic (methyclothiazide) and an antihypertensive (deserpidine).

enema /en'əmə/ [Gk, *enienai*, to send in], the introduction of a solution into the rectum for cleansing or therapeutic purposes.

energy /en'ərjē/ [Gk, *energia*], the capacity to do work or to perform vigorous activity. Energy may occur in the form of heat, light, movement, sound, or radiation. Human energy is usually expressed as muscle contractions and heat production. Chemical energy is that released as a result of a chemical reaction, as in the metabolism of food.—**energetic,** *adj.*

energy conservation[1], a principle that energy cannot be created or destroyed although it can be changed from one form into another, as when heat energy is converted to light energy.

energy conservation[2], a nursing outcome from the Nursing Outcomes Classification (NOC) defined as personal actions to manage energy for initiating and sustaining activity.

energy cost of activities, the metabolic cost in calories or kilojoules of various forms of physical activity. For example, the average metabolic (MET) equivalent of walking at a rate of 3 km/hr is 2 METs per minute, and the energy cost of walking at a speed of 6 km/hour is 5 METs per minute.

energy field, the flow of energy surrounding a person.

energy management, a nursing intervention from the Nursing Interventions Classification (NIC) defined as regulating energy use to treat or prevent fatigue and optimize function.

energy output, the amount of energy expended by work or activity by the body per specified period.

energy subtraction, a radiographic technique in which two different x-ray beams are used alternately to provide a subtraction image resulting from differences in photoelectric interaction.

enervation /en'ərvā'shən/ [L, *enervare,* to weaken], **1.** reduction or lack of nervous energy; weakness; lassitude; languor. **2.** removal of a complete nerve or a section of nerve.

en face /äNfäs′, enfäs′/, "face-to-face"; a position in which the mother's face and the infant's face are approximately 8 inches apart and on the same plane, as when the mother holds the infant up in front of her face or when she nurses the child.

enflurane /en′flŏŏrān/, a nonflammable anesthetic gas of the ether family. Its use has almost entirely been supplanted by newer, shorter-acting agents. It is used for maintenance of general anesthesia.

enfuvirtide, an antiretroviral agent used in combination with other antiretrovirals to treat HIV-1 infection.

engagement /engāj′mənt/ [Fr, a bonding], **1.** fixation of the presenting part of the fetus in the maternal true pelvis. The largest diameter of the presenting part is at or below the level of the ischial spines. **2.** fixation of the fetal head in the maternal midpelvis with the biparietal diameter of the head level with the ischial spines.

engorged /in·gôrjd′/ [Fr, *engorger,* to fill up], distended or swollen with fluids.

engorgement /engôrj′mənt/ [Fr, *engorger,* to fill up], distension or vascular congestion of body tissues, such as the swelling of breast tissue caused by an increased flow of blood and lymph before true lactation.

engram /en′gram/, **1.** a hypothetical neurophysiologic storage unit in the cerebrum that is the source of a particular memory. **2.** an interneuronal circuit involving specific neurons and muscle fibers that can be coordinated to perform specific motor activity patterns. **3.** the permanent trace left by a stimulus in nerve tissue.

enhancement /enhas′mənt/ [ME, *enhauncen,* to raise], the act of improving, heightening, or augmenting.

enkephalin /enkef′əlin/ [Gk, *enkepalos,* brain, *in,* within], one of two pain-relieving pentapeptides produced in the body, located in the pituitary gland, brain, and GI tract. Enkephalins function as neurotransmitters or neuro-modulators and inhibit neurotransmitters in the pathway for pain perception, thereby reducing the emotional as well as the physical impact of pain. Methionine-enkephalin and isoleucine-enkephalin can depress neurons throughout the CNS. The enkephalins are natural painkillers and may be involved, with other neuropeptides, in the development of psychopathologic behavior in some cases.

enkephalinergic neuron /enkef′əlinur′jik/, a nerve cell that releases the peptide neurotransmitter enkephalin.

enol /ē′nol/, an organic compound with an alcohol or hydroxyl group directly attached (bonded) to a double bond.

enophthalmos /en′əfthal′məs/ [Gk, *en,* in, *ophthalmos,* eye], backward displacement of the eye in the bony socket, caused by traumatic injury or developmental defect.—**enophthalmic,** *adj.*

enoxacin /ĕ-nok′säsin/, an antibacterial effective against many gram-positive and gram-negative bacteria, administered orally in the treatment of gonorrhea and UTIs.

enoxaparin /e-nok′säpar′in/, a low-molecular-weight heparin used as the sodium salt to prevent pulmonary embolism and deep venous thrombosis after hip or knee replacement or high-risk abdominal surgery. It is also used together with warfarin in the treatment of deep venous thrombosis and together with aspirin in the prevention of coronary thrombosis associated with unstable angina or certain kinds of MI.

enoximone /enok′sīmōn/, a vasodilator similar to inamrinone, used as a cardiotonic in the short-term management of CHF.

enriched, 1. in nutrition, pertaining to foods to which vitamins or minerals have been added within limits specified by the U.S. Food and Drug Administration, usually to replace nutrients lost during processing. **2.** in chemistry, pertaining to a substance containing a proportion of isotope greater than that found in the naturally occurring form of the same element. **3.** in chemistry, pertaining to a compound containing a greater proportion of one of two possible forms.

enrollee, an individual who has signed up to receive health care under a particular type of plan. Not applicable in Canada.

ensulizole /ensul′īzōl/, a water-soluble absorber of ultraviolet B radiation, used topically as a sunscreen.

Ensure, a trademark for a lactose-free nutritional supplement containing protein, carbohydrates, fat, vitamins, and minerals.

ENT, abbreviation for *ear, nose, and throat.*

entacapone, an antiparkinson agent used to treat parkinsonism in patients who are experiencing end-of-dose decreased effect.

ental /en′tal/ [Gk, *entos,* within], central or inner; interior or inside.

Entamoeba /en′təmē′bə/ [Gk, *entos,* within, *amoibe,* change], a genus of intestinal amebic parasites of which several species are pathogenic to humans.

Entamoeba coli, a common nonpathogenic amebic parasite found in the intestines of humans and other mammals. It is similar to and sometimes confused with *E. histolytica,* the causal agent of amebic dysentery.

Entamoeba gingivalis, a temperature-resistant species of ameba found in the mouth of humans and other mammals. As a causal agent of gingivitis, it is associated with poor dental hygiene.

Entamoeba histolytica /his'təlit'ikə/, a pathogenic species of ameba that causes amebic dysentery and hepatic ameabiasis in humans.

entecavir, an antiviral used to treat chronic hepatitis B.

enteral /en'tərəl, enter'əl/ [Gk, *enteron,* bowel], within the small intestine, or via the small intestine.

enteral feeding, a mode of feeding that uses the GI tract, such as oral or tube feeding.

enteral nutrition, the provision of nutrients through the GI tract when the client cannot ingest, chew, or swallow food but can digest and absorb nutrients.

enteral tube feeding[1] [Gk, *enteron,* bowel; L, *tubus;* AS, *faedan*], the introduction of nutrients directly into the GI tract by feeding tube.

enteral tube feeding[2], a nursing intervention from the Nursing Interventions Classification (NIC) defined as delivering nutrients and water through a GI tube.

enterectomy /en'tərek'təmē/ [Gk, *enteron,* intestine, *ektomē,* excision], the surgical removal of a portion of intestine.

enteric /enter'ik/ [Gk, *enteron,* bowel], pertaining to the intestinal tract.

enteric coating, a layer added to oral medications that allows the medication to pass through the stomach and be absorbed in the intestinal tract. The coating protects against the effects of stomach juices, which can interact with, destroy, or degrade these drugs.

enteric infection, a disease of the intestine caused by any infection. Among bacteria commonly involved in enteric infections are *Escherichia coli, Vibrio cholerae,* and several species of *Salmonella, Shigella,* and anaerobic streptococci. Enteric infections are characterized by diarrhea, abdominal discomfort, nausea and vomiting, and anorexia. A significant loss of fluid and electrolytes may result from severe vomiting and diarrhea.

enteric intussusception, intussusception involving two segments of the small intestine.

entericoid fever /enter'ikoid/ [Gk, *enteron* + *eidos,* form], a typhoidlike febrile disease characterized by intestinal inflammation and dysfunction.

enteric orphan virus [Gk, *enteron,* bowel, *orphanos,* bereft; L, *virus,* poison], an enterovirus isolated from humans and other animals that was not originally associated with the disease.

enteritis /en'tərī'tis/, inflammation of the mucosal lining of the small intestine, resulting from a variety of causes—bacterial, viral, functional, and inflammatory.

Enterobacter cloacae /en'tirōbak'tər klō·ā'kē, klō·ā'sē/ [Gk, *enteron* + *bakterion,* small staff; L, *cloaca,* sewer], a common species of gram-negative rod-shaped bacteria found in human and animal feces, dairy products, sewage, soil, and water. *E. cloacae* and *E. aerogenes* are important nosocomial pathogens responsible for a number of infections such as bacteremia, lower respiratory tract infections, UTIs, and septic arthtitis.

Enterobacteriaceae /en'tirōbaktir'ē·ā'si·ē/ [Gk, *enteron* + *bakterion,* small staff], a family of aerobic and anaerobic bacteria that includes both normal and pathogenic enteric microorganisms. Among the significant genera of the family are *Escherichia, Klebsiella, Proteus,* and *Salmonella.*

enterobacterial /-baktir'ē·əl/ [Gk, *enteron* + *bakterion,* small staff], pertaining to a species of bacteria found in the digestive tract.

enterobiasis /en'tirōbī'əsis/ [Gk, *enteron* + *bios,* life, *osis,* condition], a parasitic infestation with *Enterobius vermicularis,* the common pinworm. The nematodes infect the large intestine, and the females deposit eggs in the perianal area, causing pruritus and disturbed sleep.

Enterobius vermicularis /en'tərō'bē·əs/ [Gk, *enteron* + *bios,* life; L, *vermiculus,* small worm], a common parasitic nematode that resembles a white thread between 0.5 and 1 cm long.

enterocele /en'tirōsēl'/, **1.** a hernia of the intestine. **2.** posterior vaginal hernia.

enteroclysis /en'tərok'lisis/, a radiographic procedure in which a contrast medium is injected into the duodenum to permit examination of the small intestine.

enterococcemia /en'terokokse'meä/, blood infection by enterococci.

Enterococcus /en'terokok'us/ *pl.* **enterococci** [Gk, *enteron* + *kokkos,* berry], a genus of gram-positive, facultatively anaerobic bacteria of the family Streptococcaceae, formerly classified in the genus *Streptococcus. E. faecalis* and *E. faecium* are normal inhabitants of the human intestinal tract that occasionally cause UTIs, infective endocarditis, bacteremia, and life-threatening nosocomial infections; *E. avium* is found primarily in the feces of chickens and may be associated with appendicitis, otitis, and brain abscesses in humans.

enterocoele, the abdominal cavity.

enterocolitis /-kōlī'tis/ [Gk, *enteron* + *kolon,* bowel + *itis*], an inflammation involving both the large and small intestines.

enterocutaneous fistula, a cutaneous fistula connecting the body surface and some part of the intestine.

enterocystoplasty /en'terosis'toplas'te/, the most common type of augmentation cystoplasty, using a portion of intestine for the graft. Common types include ileocystoplasty, ileocecocystoplasty, and sigmoid cystoplasty.

enterodynia /-din′ē-ə/, intestinal pain.

enteroenterostomy /en′tərō-en′təros′təmē/, the surgical creation of an artificial connection between two segments of the intestine.

enteroglucagon /-glōō′kəgon/, any of a group of glucagon-like hyperglycemic peptides, released by cells in the mucosa in the upper intestine in response to the ingestion of carbohydrates and fat and stimulating intestinal epithelial cell preparation and renewal.

enterohemorrhagic Escherichia coli (EHEC) /-hem′ôraj′ik/, a strain of *E. coli* that causes hemorrhage in the intestines. The organism produces a toxin that damages bowel tissue, causing intestinal ischemia and colonic necrosis. Spread by contaminated beef, unpasteurized milk and juice, sprouts, lettuce, and salami, as well as contaminated water, the infection can be serious although there may be no fever.

enterohepatic circulation /en′tərōhəpat′ik/, a route by which part of the bile produced by the liver enters the intestine, is resorbed by the liver, and then is recycled into the intestine. The remainder of the bile is excreted in feces.

enterokinase /en′tirōkī′nās/ [Gk, *enteron* + *kinesis*, movement, *ase*, enzyme], an intestinal juice enzyme that activates the proteolytic enzymes in pancreatic juice as they enter the duodenum.

enterolith /en′tərōlith′/ [Gk, *enteron* + *lithos*, stone], a stone consisting of ingested material found within the intestine.

enterolithiasis /en′tərōlithī′əsis/, the presence of enteroliths in the intestine.

enteropathic Escherichia coli (EPEC) /path′ik/, a strain of *E. coli* that is the cause of epidemic infantile diarrhea.

enteropathy /en′tərop′əthē/, a disease or other disorder of the intestines.

enterostomal therapist /-stō′məl/, a registered nurse who is qualified by education in an accredited program in enterostomal therapy to provide care for persons with stomas, draining wounds, fistulae, incontinence, and actual or potential alterations in tissue integrity.

enterostomy /en′təros′təmē/ [Gk, *enteron* + *stoma*, mouth], a surgical procedure that produces an artificial anus or fistula in the intestine through an incision in the abdominal wall.

enterotoxigenic /-tok′sijen′ik/, producing an enterotoxin.

enterotoxigenic Escherichia coli (ETEC), a strain of *E. coli* that is a frequent cause of diarrhea in travelers.

enterotoxin /-tok′sin/, a toxic substance that causes an adverse reaction by cells of the intestinal mucosa. Most enterotoxins are produced by certain species of bacteria, such as *Staphylococcus*.

enterovesical fistula, a fistula connecting some part of the intestine with the urinary bladder.

Enterovirus /-vī′rəs/ [Gk, *enteron*; L, *virus*, poison], a genus of Picornaviridae that preferentially replicates in the mammalian intestinal tract. Kinds of *Enteroviruses* are **coxsackievirus, ECHO virus,** and **poliovirus.—enteroviral,** *adj.*

enthesitis /en′thəsī′tis/, an inflammation of the insertion of a muscle with a strong tendency toward fibrosis and calcification. It is usually only painful when the involved muscle is activated.

enthesopathy /en′thəsop′əthē/, an arthritic condition affecting tendons and ligaments rather than joint membranes.

entomophthoromycosis basidiobolae, a chronic infection caused by *Basidiobolus ranarum*, a filamentous fungus, in which gradually enlarging granulomas form in the subcutaneous tissues of the arms, chest, and trunk. Multiple purulent ulcers may develop. The infection is seen in children and adolescents in tropical areas of Indonesia, India, and Africa.

entopic /entop′ik/, occurring in the proper place.

entopic phenomena, sensations perceived for mechanical reasons within the eye, such as floaters or flashes caused by retinal changes.

entrainment /entrān′mənt/ [Fr, *entrainer,* to drag along], a phenomenon observed in the microanalysis of sound films in which the speaker moves several parts of the body and the listener responds by moving in ways that are coordinated with the rhythm of the sounds. Entrainment is thought to be an essential factor in the process of maternal-infant bonding.

entrance block [Fr, *entrer,* to enter; AS, *blok*], a theoretic zone that surrounds a pacemaker focus and protects it from discharge by an extraneous impulse that might trigger ectopic ventricular contractions.

entrance exposure, the skin dose of radiation as the beam enters the patient. It may be expressed in milliroentgens or C/kg.

entrapment neuropathy /entrap′mənt/ [OFr, *entraper,* to catch in a trap; Gk, *neuron,* nerve, *pathos,* disease], injury or inflammation of single nerves caused by pressure from surrounding tissues, such as ligaments and fascia.

entropion /entrō′pē-on/ [Gk, *en + tropos,* a turning], turning inward or turning toward, usually a condition in which the eyelid turns inward toward the eye. In either the upper or lower eyelid, cicatricial entropion can result from scar tissue formation. Spastic entropion results from an inflammation or other factor that affects tissue tone. An inflammation of the eyelid may be the result of an infectious disease or irritation from an inverted eyelash.

entropy /en'trəpē/ [Gk, *en* + *tropos*, a turning], the tendency of a system to change from a state of order to a state of disorder, expressed in physics as a measure of the part of the energy in a thermodynamic system that is not available to perform work.

enucleation /inoo′klē·ā′shən/ [L, *e*, without, *nucleus*, nut], **1.** removal of an organ or tumor in one piece. **2.** removal of the entire eyeball, performed for malignancy, severe infection, extensive trauma, or control of pain in glaucoma.

enucleator /inoo′klē·ā′tər/ [L, *e*, without, *nucleus*, nut], a procedure or device for removing a nucleus from a cell.

enuresis /en′yŏŏrē′sis/ [Gk, *enourein*, to urinate], incontinence of urine, especially nocturnal bed-wetting.

envenomation /enven′əmā′shən/, the injection of snake, arachnid, or insect venom into the body.

environment [Gk, *en*, in; L, *viron*, circle], all of the many factors, as physical and psychologic, that influence or affect the life and survival of a person.—**environmental**, *adj*.

environmental carcinogen /envī′rənmen′təl/, any of the natural or synthetic substances that can cause cancer. Such agents may be divided into chemical agents, physical agents, hormones, and viruses.

environmental control unit (ECU), an apparatus for disabled persons that controls devices such as lamps, television, radio, telephone, and alarm systems. Similar to television remote control devices, they are typically switches manipulated by the lips, chin, or other body movements.

environmental health, the total of various aspects of substances, forces, and conditions in and about a community that affect the health and well-being of the population.

environmental health technician, a health care professional who performs technical assistance under professional supervision in monitoring environmental health hazards such as radioactive contamination, air and water pollution, and disposal of chemical wastes of industry.

environmental management, a nursing intervention from the Nursing Interventions Classification (NIC) defined as the manipulation of the patient's surroundings for therapeutic benefit, sensory appeal, and psychologic well-being.

environmental management: attachment process, a nursing intervention from the Nursing Interventions Classification (NIC) defined as manipulation of the patient's surroundings to facilitate the development of the parent-infant relationship.

environmental management: comfort, a nursing intervention from the Nursing Interventions Classification (NIC) defined as manipulation of the patient's surroundings for promotion of optimal comfort.

environmental management: community, a nursing intervention from the Nursing Interventions Classification (NIC) defined as monitoring and influencing of the physical, social, cultural, economic, and political conditions that affect the health of groups and communities.

environmental management: home preparation, a nursing intervention from the Nursing Interventions Classification (NIC) defined as preparing the home for safe and effective delivery of care.

environmental management: safety, a nursing intervention from the Nursing Interventions Classification (NIC) defined as monitoring and manipulation of the physical environment to promote safety.

environmental management: violence prevention, a nursing intervention from the Nursing Interventions Classification (NIC) defined as monitoring and manipulation of the physical environment to decrease the potential for violent behavior directed toward self, others, or environment.

environmental management: worker safety, a nursing intervention from the Nursing Interventions Classification (NIC) defined as monitoring and manipulation of the worksite environment to promote safety and health of workers.

environmental medicine, a practice of medicine in which the major focus is on cause-and-effect relationships in health. Evaluations are made of such factors as eating and living habits and types of air breathed. Testing in the patient's own environment is performed to determine what precipitators are present that may be related to disease or other health problems.

environmental risk protection, a nursing intervention from the Nursing Interventions Classification (NIC) defined as preventing and detecting disease and injury in populations at risk from environmental hazards.

environmental services, a functional unit of a health care facility. It has the responsibility for laundry, liquid and solid waste control, safe disposal of materials contaminated by radiation or pathogenic organisms, and general maintenance of safety and housekeeping.

enzacamene /en′zah-kam′ēn/, an absorber of ultraviolet radiation, used topically as a sunscreen.

enzymatic debridement /en′zīmat′ik/, the use of nonirritating, nontoxic vegetable enzymes to remove dead tissue from a wound without destroying normal tissue.

enzymatic detergent asthma, an allergic reaction experienced by persons who have become sensitized to alcalase, an enzyme contained in some laundry detergents.

enzyme /en′zīm/ [Gk, *en,* in, *zyme,* ferment], a complex produced by living cells that catalyzes chemical reactions in organic matter. Most enzymes are produced in tiny quantities and catalyze reactions that take place within the cells. Digestive enzymes, however, are produced in relatively large quantities and act outside the cells in the lumen of the digestive tract.

Enzyme Commission (EC), the International Commission on Enzymes, a committee established in 1956 by the International Union of Biochemistry to standardize enzyme classification and nomenclature.

enzyme deficiency anemia, a deficiency of enzymes in the pathways that metabolize glucose and adenosine triphosphate, which frequently leads to premature RBC destruction.

enzyme induction [Gk, *en + zyme,* ferment; L, *inducere,* to lead in], the increase in the rate of a specific enzyme synthesis from basal to maximum level caused by the presence of a substrate or substrate analog that acts as an inducer. The inducer may be a substance that inactivates a repressor chemical in the cell.

enzyme-linked immunosorbent assay (ELISA), a laboratory technique for detecting specific antigens or antibodies by using enzyme-labeled immunoreactants and a solid-phase binding support, such as a test tube. A number of different enzymes can be used. Products of the reaction may be detected by fluorometry or photometry. ELISA is nearly as sensitive as radioimmunoassay and more sensitive than complement fixation, agglutination, and other techniques.

enzyme therapy, in complementary medicine, the oral administration of proteolytic enzymes for the purpose of improving immune system function, used for a wide variety of disorders, including trauma, inflammation, autoimmune diseases, and viral infection, and as adjunctive therapy in cancer treatment.

enzymology /en′zīmol′əjē/, the study of enzymes and their actions.

enzymolysis /en′zīmol′isis/ [Gk, *en,* in, *zyme,* ferment, *lysis,* loosening], destruction or change of a substance caused by means of enzymatic action.

enzymopenia /en′zīmōpē′nē-ə/, the deficiency of an enzyme.

enzymuria /en′zīmŏŏr′ē-ə/, the presence of enzymes in urine.

EOA, abbreviation for **esophageal obturator airway.**

EOMs, 1. abbreviation for **extraocular muscles. 2.** abbreviation for **extraocular movements.**

eosin /ē′əsin/, a group of red acidic xanthine dyes often used in combination with a blue-purple basic dye such as hematoxylin to stain tissue slides in the laboratory.

eosinopenia /ē′əsinəpē′nē-ə/, an abnormally low number of eosinophil leukocytes in the blood.

eosinophil /ē′əsin′əfil/ [Gk, *eos,* dawn, *philein,* to love], a granulocytic bilobed leukocyte characterized by large numbers of regular refractile cytoplasmic granules that stain bright orange with the acid dye eosin.—**eosinophilic,** *adj.*

eosinophilia /ē′əsin′ōfil′yə/, abnormal increase in blood film eosinophils, accompanying an allergic response or parasitic infestation.

eosinophilia-myalgia syndrome, tryptophan-induced, a potentially fatal disorder resulting from ingestion of tryptophan. It is characterized by a symptom complex of severe muscle pain, tenosynovitis, muscle edema, and skin rash lasting several weeks.

eosinophilic /ē′əsin′əfil′ik/, **1.** the tendency of a cell, tissue, or organism to be readily stained by the dye eosin. **2.** pertaining to an eosinophilic leukocyte.

eosinophilic cholangitis, a rare type of cholangitis resulting from eosinophilic infiltration and characterized by multiple strictures in the bile ducts.

eosinophilic enteropathy, a rare form of food allergy that is characterized by nausea, crampy abdominal pain, diarrhea, urticaria, an elevated eosinophil count in the blood, and eosinophilic infiltrates in the intestine.

eosinophilic fasciitis, inflammation of fasciae of the limbs, associated with eosinophilia, edema, and swelling. The cause is unknown, but the condition often occurs after strenuous exercise.

eosinophilic gastroenteritis, a disorder marked by infiltration of the mucosa of the small intestine by eosinophils, with edema but without vasculitis, and by eosinophilia of the peripheral blood. Symptoms, including abdominal pain, diarrhea, nausea, fever, and malabsorption, depend on the site and extent of the disorder.

eosinophilic granuloma, a simple or multiple growth in the bone or lung characterized by numerous eosinophils and histiocytes. Eosinophilic granulomas occur most frequently in children and adolescents.

E

eosinophilic leukemia, a malignant neoplasm of the blood-forming tissues in which eosinophils are the predominant cells.

eosinophilic meningitis, meningitis with an increase in lymphocytes and a high percentage of eosinophils in the CSF. It usually results from infection with *Angiostrongylus cantonensis.*

eosinophilic myeloencephalitis, a complex of neurologic symptoms produced by invasion of the CNS by *Gnathostoma spinigerum,* including severe nerve root pain, followed by paralysis of extremities and sudden sensorial impairment, accompanied by increased number of eosinophils in the CSF, which is often bloody or yellowish.

eosinophilic pneumonia, inflammation of the lungs, characterized by infiltration of the alveoli with eosinophils and large mononuclear cells, pulmonary edema, fever, night sweats, cough, dyspnea, and weight loss.

EP, abbreviation for **evoked potential.**

EPA, abbreviation for *Environmental Protection Agency.*

epaxial muscles, the intrinsic muscles of the back.

EPEC, abbreviation for **enteropathic** *Escherichia coli.*

ependyma /ipen'dimə/ [Gk, an upper garment], a layer of ciliated epithelial membrane that lines the central canal of the spinal cord and the ventricles of the brain. —**ependymal** /ipen'diməl/, *adj.*

ependymal glioma, a large, vascular, fairly solid tumor in the fourth ventricle, composed of malignant glial cells.

ependymitis /ipen'dimī'tis/, an inflammation of the ependymal tissue.

ependymoblastoma /ipen'dimōblastō'mə/, a malignant neoplasm composed of primitive cells of the ependyma.

ependymoma /ipen'dimō'mə/ [Gk, *ependyma,* an upper garment, *oma,* tumor], a neoplasm composed of differentiated cells of the ependyma.

ephapse /ef'aps/ [Gk, *ephasis,* a touching], a point of lateral contact between nerve fibers across which impulses may be transmitted directly through the cell membranes rather than across a synapse. —**ephaptic,** *adj.*

ephaptic transmission /ifap'tik/, the passage of a neural impulse from one nerve fiber, axon, or dendrite to another through the membranes.

ephebiatrics /ēfeb'ē·at'riks/ [Gk, *ephebos,* puberty, *iatros,* physician], a branch of medicine that specializes in the health of adolescents.

ephedra, an evergreen herb that was used for seasonal and chronic asthma, nasal congestion, and cough. The sale of ephedra

was banned in the U.S. by the FDA in 2003 because of safety concerns, making it the first OTC nutritional supplement to be banned.

epHEDrine /ef'ədrēn/, an alpha- and beta-adrenergic agonist that also promotes the release of norepinephrine from sympathetic nerve terminals. It is prescribed in the treatment of asthma and bronchitis and is used topically as a nasal decongestant. The drug is historically important, but its use is now limited because of the availability of more selective beta-2 agonists for treating asthma.

ephemeral /ifem'ərəl/ [Gk, *epi,* above, *hemera,* day], pertaining to a short-lived condition such as a fever.

ephemeral fever, an infection of cattle caused by the bovine ephemeral fever virus.

EPI, abbreviation for **echo planar imaging.**

epiblast /ep'iblast'/ [Gk, *epi,* upon, *blastos,* germ], the primordial outer layer of the blastocyst or blastula, before differentiation of the germ layers, that gives rise to the ectoderm and contains cells capable of forming the endoderm and mesoderm. —**epiblastic,** *adj.*

epicanthus /ep'ikan'thəs/ [Gk, *epi + kanthos,* lip of a vessel], a vertical fold of skin over the angle of the inner canthus of the eye. It is a hereditary trait in Asian people and is of no clinical significance. —**epicanthal, epicanthic,** *adj.*

epicardia /-kär'dē·ə/ [Gk, *epi,* above, *kardia,* heart], the part of the esophagus that lies between the cardiac orifice of the stomach and the esophageal opening of the diaphragm.

epicardium /ep'ikär'dē·əm/ [Gk, *epi + kardia,* heart], the outermost of the three layers of tissue that form the heart wall. The epicardium is the visceral portion of the serous pericardium and folds back on itself to form the parietal portion of the serous pericardium. —**epicardial,** *adj.*

epicondylar fracture /-kon'dilər/, any fracture that involves the medial or lateral epicondyle of a specific bone, such as the humerus.

epicondyle /ep'ikon'dəl/ [Gk, *epi + kondylos,* knuckle], a projection on the surface of a bone above its condyle. —**epicondylar,** *adj.*

epicondylitis /ep'ikon'dilī'tis/, a painful and sometimes disabling inflammation of the muscle and surrounding tissues of the elbow, caused by repeated strain on the forearm near the medial or lateral epicondyle of the humerus. The strain may result from violent extension or supination of the wrist against a resisting force.

epicranial aponeurosis /-krā'nē·əl/ [Gk, *epi + kranion,* skull, *apo,* away, *neuron,* tendon], a fibrous membrane that covers the cranium between the occipital and frontal muscles of the scalp.

epicranium /-krā′nē-əm/ [Gk, *epi* + *kranion*, skull], the complete scalp, including the integument, the muscular sheets, and the aponeuroses.—**epicranial,** *adj.*

epicranius [Gk, *epi* + *kranion*, skull], the broad muscular and tendinous layer of tissue covering the top and sides of the skull from the occipital bone to the eyebrows.

epicritic /-krit′ik/, pertaining to the somatic sensations of fine discriminative touch, vibration, two-point discrimination, stereognosis, and conscious and unconscious proprioception.

epidemic /-dem′ik/ [Gk, *epi* + *demos*, people], **1.** affecting a significantly large number of people at the same time. **2.** a disease that spreads rapidly through a demographic segment of the human population, such as everyone in a given geographic area. **3.** a disease or event whose incidence is beyond what is expected.

epidemic diarrhea in newborns [Gk, *epi*, above, *demos*, the people, *dia*, through, *rhein*, flow; ME, *newe* + *beren*], any severe gastroenteritis epidemic among a community of newborns, as may occur in a hospital nursery.

epidemic encephalitis, any diffuse inflammation of the brain occurring in epidemic form.

epidemic hemorrhagic conjunctivitis [Gk, *epi*, above, *demos*, the people, *haima*, blood, *rhegnynei*, to gush; L, *conjunctivus*, connecting; Gk, *itis*, inflammation], a highly contagious infection, commonly involving an enterovirus, that begins with eye pain accompanied by swollen eyelids and hyperemia of the conjunctiva. It is a self-limiting disorder that has no specific remedy.

epidemic hemorrhagic fever, a severe viral infection marked by fever and bleeding. The disorder develops rapidly and is characterized initially by fever and muscle ache, possibly followed by hemorrhage, peripheral vascular collapse, hypovolemic shock, and acute kidney failure. The arbovirus or other pathogen is believed transmitted by mosquitoes, ticks, mites, or rodents.

epidemic keratoconjunctivitis (EKC) [Gk, *epi*, above, *demos*, the people, *keras*, horn; L, *conjunctivus*; Gk, *itis*, inflammation], an adenovirus infection consisting of an acute, severely painful conjunctivitis followed by a keratitis. EKC is quite contagious and prone to epidemics which may be quite large.

epidemic myalgia, a disease caused by *Coxsackie* B virus. It is characterized by sudden acute chest or epigastric pain and fever lasting 3 to 14 days, followed by complete spontaneous recovery.

epidemic pleurodynia, an acute infectious disease caused by strains of enterovirus *Coxsackie,* type B, mainly affecting children. It is characterized by severe intermittent pain in the abdomen or lower chest, fever, headache, sore throat, malaise, and extreme myalgia. The symptoms may continue for weeks or subside after a few days and recur for a period of weeks. Transmission is through the fecal-oral route.

epidemic typhus, an acute severe rickettsial infection characterized by prolonged high fever, headache, and a dark maculopapular rash that covers most of the body. The causative organism, *Rickettsia prowazekii,* is transmitted indirectly as a result of the bite of the human body louse or squirrel flea or louse; the pathogen is contained in feces of the louse and enters the body tissues as the bite is scratched. Disease is manifested by the abrupt onset of an intense headache and a fever reaching 40° C (104° F) beginning after an incubation period of 1 week. The rash follows on the fifth day of onset.

epidemic vomiting, an episode of sudden vomiting by members of a group of people in close contact. The vomiting, caused by RNA Norwalk virus infection, usually begins without previous signs or symptoms of illness and may continue for several hours, ending abruptly. The vomiting may be accompanied by headache, abdominal pain, and diarrhea.

epidemiologist /-dē′mē-ol′əjist/, a physician or medical scientist who studies the incidence, prevalence, spread, prevention, and control of disease in a community or a specific group of individuals.

epidemiologist nurse, a registered nurse with special education and experience in the control of infections in the health care facility and community.

epidemiology /-dē′mē-ol′əjē/ [Gk, *epi* + *demos*, people, *logos*, science], the study of the determinants of disease events in populations.—**epidemiologic,** *adj.*

epidermal growth factor (EGF) /ep′idur′məl/, a mitogenic polypeptide produced by many cell types and made in large amounts by some tumors. It promotes growth and differentiation, is essential in embryogenesis, and is also important in wound healing.

epidermal nevus /-dur′məl/ [Gk, *epi* + *derma*, skin; L, *naevus*, birthmark], a discrete discolored congenital lesion caused by an overgrowth of epidermis. It may be seen in newborns.

epidermis /ep′idur′mis/ [Gk, *epi* + *derma*, skin], the superficial avascular layers of the skin, made up of an outer dead, cornified part and a deeper living, cellular part. —**epidermal, epidermoid,** *adj.*

epidermitis /ep′idurmī′tis/, an inflammation of the epidermis, the outer layer of the skin.

epidermoid carcinoma /-dur′moid/ [Gk, *epi + derma + eidos,* form], a malignant neoplasm in which the tumor cells tend to differentiate in the manner of epidermal cells, then form horny cells called prickle cells.

epidermoid cyst, a common benign cavity lined by keratinizing epithelium and filled with a cheesy material composed of sebum and epithelial debris. The cyst is in the skin, connected to the surface by a pore.

epidermolysis bullosa /ep′idərmol′isis/ [Gk, *epi + derma + lysis,* loosening], a group of rare hereditary skin diseases in which vesicles and bullae develop, usually at sites of trauma. Severe forms may also involve mucous membranes and may leave scars and contractures on healing.

epidermolytic hyperkeratosis [Gk, *epi + derma,* skin, *lysis,* loosening; Gk, *hyper,* excess + *keras,* horn, *osis,* condition], a rare autosomal-dominant form of ichthyosis with a high frequency of spontaneous mutations. Present at birth, it is characterized by generalized erythroderma and severe hyperkeratosis with small wartlike scales over the entire body, especially in body folds, and sometimes on the palms and soles. There are also recurrent bullae on the lower limbs.

epidermophytosis /ep′idur′mōfītō′sis/, a superficial fungus infection of the skin.

epididymal appendix, a cystic structure sometimes found on the head of the epididymis. It represents a remnant of the mesonephros.

epididymis /ep′idid′imis/ *pl.* **epididymides** [Gk, *epi + didymos,* pair], one of a pair of long, tightly coiled ducts that carry sperm from the seminiferous tubules of the testes to the vas deferens.

epididymitis /ep′idid′imī′tis/ [Gk, *epi + didymos + itis,* inflammation], acute or chronic inflammation of the epididymis. It may result from venereal disease, UTI, prostatitis, prostatectomy, or prolonged use of indwelling catheters. Symptoms include fever and chills; pain in the groin; and tender, swollen epididymides.

epididymoorchitis /ep′idid′imō′ôrkī′tis/ [Gk, *epi +, didymos + orchis,* testis, *itis*], inflammation of the epididymis and of the testis.

epididymovesiculography /ep′idid′imōves′ikyəlog′rəfē/, the radiographic examination of the seminal ducts. It is usually performed in cases of sterility, cysts, tumors, abscesses, or inflammation.

epidural /ep′idoor′əl/ [Gk, *epi + dura,* hard], outside or above the dura mater.

epidural abscess, a disorder characterized by inflammation and a collection of pus between the dura mater of the brain and skull, or between the dura mater of the spinal cord and the vertebral canal. The infection is usually caused by a bacterium such as *Staphylococcus,* but it can also be secondary to a chronic ear or sinus infection, a penetrating head injury, or mastoiditis. Fever, headache, and neurologic symptoms are common.

epidural anesthesia/analgesia, a type of anesthesia block in which a local anesthetic is injected into the epidural space surrounding the spinal cord. Epidurals are most commonly performed in the lumbar area by an injection of medication through a catheter placed in the epidural space. Epidural anesthesia or analgesia can be tailored to affect an area of the body from the lower extremities up to the upper abdomen.

epidural blood patch (EBP), a treatment for postdural puncture headache in which 15 to 20 mL of a patient's autologous blood is injected into the epidural space at or near the location of a dural puncture. The volume injected displaces CSF from the lumbar CSF space into the area surrounding the brain, often yielding immediate relief.

epidural hematoma, accumulation of blood in the epidural space, caused by damage to and leakage of blood from the middle meningeal artery, producing compression of the dura mater and thus of the brain.

epidural hemorrhage, a hemorrhage that produces a collection of blood outside the dura mater of the brain or spinal cord. It usually results from tearing of the middle meningeal artery and may be rapidly life threatening.

epidural space, the space immediately above and surrounding the dura mater of the brain or spinal cord, beneath the endosteum of the cranium and the spinal column.

epifascial /ep′ifash′ē-əl/ [Gk, *epi*; L, *fascia,* band], on a fascia.

epifolliculitis /ep′ifolik′yəlī′tis/, an inflammation of the hair follicles of the head.

epigastric /-gas′trik/ [Gk, *epi,* above, *gaster,* stomach], pertaining to the epigastrium, the area above the stomach.

epigastric arteries, the arteries (superficial, superior, and inferior) that supply the medial abdominal wall.

epigastric hernia, the protrusion of an internal organ through the linea alba.

epigastric node [Gk, *epi + gaster,* stomach; L, *nodus,* knot], a node in one of the seven groups of parietal lymph nodes serving the abdomen and pelvis, comprising about four nodes along the caudal part of the inferior epigastric vessels.

epigastric pain [Gk, *epi,* above, *gaster,* stomach; L, *poena,* penalty], pain in the upper middle part of the abdomen.

epigastric reflex [Gk, *epi,* above, *gaster,* stomach; L, *reflectere,* to bend back], a contraction of the rectus abdominis muscle that occurs when the skin surface in the upper and middle abdominal region is stimulated. The reflex also may be induced by stimulation of the axillary region of the fifth and sixth dorsal nerves.

epigastric region, the part of the abdomen in the upper zone between the right and left hypochondriac regions.

epigastric sensation, a weak, sinking feeling of undefined nature that is usually localized in the pit of the stomach but may occur throughout the abdominal region.

epigenesis /ep′ijen′əsis/ [Gk, *epi* + *genein,* to produce], in embryology, a theory of development in which the organism grows from a simple to a more complex form through the progressive differentiation of an undifferentiated cellular unit.—**epigenesist,** *n.,* **epigenetic,** *adj.*

epiglottic vallecula, a depression between the lateral and median glossoepiglottic folds on each side.

epiglottis /ep′iglot′is/ [Gk, *epi* + *glossa,* tongue], the thin, leaf-shaped cartilaginous structure that overhangs the larynx like a lid and prevents food from entering the larynx and the trachea while swallowing.

epiglottitis /ep′iglotī′tis/ [Gk, *epi* + *glossa,* tongue, *itis,* inflammation], an inflammation of the epiglottis. Acute epiglottitis is a severe form of the condition, which primarily affected children 2 to 7 years of age before a significant decrease in the occurrence of the disease resulting from the introduction of the *Haemophilus influenzae* B vaccine in 1985. It is characterized by fever; sore throat; drooling; stridor; croupy cough; and an erythematous, swollen epiglottis. The patient may become cyanotic and require an emergency tracheostomy to maintain respiration.

epilating forceps /ep′ilā′ting/ [L, *e* + *pilus,* without hair], a kind of small spring forceps, used for removing unwanted hair.

epilepsy /ep′ilep′sē/ [Gk, *epilepsia,* seizure], a group of neurologic disorders characterized by recurrent episodes of convulsive seizures, sensory disturbances, abnormal behavior, LOC, or all of these. Common to all types of epilepsy is an uncontrolled electric discharge from the nerve cells of the cerebral cortex. The frequency of attacks may range from many times a day to intervals of several years.

Most epileptic attacks are brief.—**epileptic,** *adj., n.*

epileptic cry /ep′ilep′tik/, a loud vocalization by a person with epilepsy, often immediately before onset of a seizure.

epileptic dementia [Gk, *epilepsia,* seizure; L, *de* + *mens,* mind], a loss of cognitive and intellectual functions that develops in some cases of incompletely controlled epilepsy. Symptoms include slowness and circumstantiality of speech and narrowed attention span.

epileptic stupor, the state of unawareness and unresponsiveness that follows an epileptic seizure or post-epileptical state.

epileptic vertigo [Gk, *epilepsia,* seizure; L, *vertigo,* dizziness], an aura of dizziness that may precede, accompany, or follow an epileptic seizure.

epileptogenic /ep′ilep′tōjen′ik/, causing epileptic seizures.

epimysium /ep′imiz′ē·əm/ [Gk, *epi* + *mys,* muscle], the outermost fibrous sheath that covers a muscle, continuous with the perimysium.

epINEPHrine /ep′ənef′rin/ [Gk, *epi* + *nephros,* kidney], an endogenous adrenal hormone and synthetic adrenergic agent. It acts as an agonist at alpha-1, alpha-2, beta-1, and beta-2 receptors. It is prescribed to treat anaphylaxis, acute bronchial spasm, and nasal congestion and to increase the effectiveness of a local anesthetic.

epiotic /ep′ē·ot′ik/, **1.** pertaining to the portion of the temporal bone that is the ossification center for the mastoid. **2.** above the ear.

epipastic /ep′ipas′tik/ [Gk, *epipassein,* to sprinkle about], dusting powder.

epiphyseal /ep′ifiz′ē·əl, ipif′əsē′əl/ [Gk, *epi,* above, *phyein,* to grow], pertaining to or resembling the epiphysis.

epiphyseal fracture [Gk, *epi* + *phyein,* to grow, *fractura,* break], a fracture involving the epiphyseal plate of a long bone, which causes separation or fragmentation of the plate.

epiphyseal plate [Gk, *epi,* above, *phyein,* to grow, *platys,* flat], a thin layer of cartilage between the epiphysis, a secondary bone-forming center, and the bone shaft. The new bone forms along the plate. Epiphyseal plates remain open until late adolescence.

epiphysis /epif′isis/, *pl.* **epiphyses** [Gk, *epi* + *phyein,* to grow], the enlarged proximal and distal ends of a long bone.—**epiphyseal** /ipif′əsē′əl/, *adj.*

epiphysitis /ipif′isī′tis/, an inflammation of the epiphysis, usually of a long bone, such as the femur or humerus.

epipial /ep′i·pi′əl/ [Gk, *epi* + L, *pia,* soft or tender], situated on the pia mater.

E

epiploic /ep'iploʻik/, pertaining to the omentum.

epiploic appendix, one of the fat pads, 2 to 10 cm long, scattered through the peritoneum along the colon and the upper part of the rectum, especially along the transverse and the sigmoid colon.

epiploic foramen [Gk, *epiploon,* caul; L, *foramen,* a hole], an opening between the greater and lesser omentum. It is lined with peritoneum and is approximately 3 cm in diameter.

epiretinal /ep'iret'inal/, overlying the retina.

epiretinal membrane, a pathologic membrane partially covering the surface of the retina, probably originating from the retinal pigment epithelial and glial cells. Membranes peripheral to the macula are generally asymptomatic, but those involving the macula or adjacent to it may cause reduction in vision, visual distortion, and diplopia.

epirubicin, an antibiotic antineoplastic used as an adjuvant therapy to treat breast cancer with axillary node involvement following resection.

episcleritis /ep'isklərī'tis/, inflammation of the outermost layers of the sclera and the tissues overlying its posterior parts.

episcope, a skin surface microscope that uses the technology of epiluminescence microscopy (the application of oil to produce translucence of the epidermis on a skin lesion). The episcope is placed gently over the lesion to observe its general appearance, surface, pigment pattern, border, and depigmentation.

episiotomy /epē'zē·ot'əmē/ [Gk, *episeion,* pubic region, *temnein,* to cut], a surgical procedure in which an incision is made in a woman's perineum to enlarge her vaginal opening for delivery. It is performed most often electively to prevent tearing of the perineum, to hasten or facilitate birth of the baby, or to prevent stretching of perineal muscles and connective tissue.

episode /ep'isōd/ [Gk, *episodion,* coming in besides], an incident or event that stands out from the continuity of everyday life, such as an episode of illness or a traumatic event in the course of a child's development.—**episodic,** *adj.*

episode of hospital care, the services provided by a hospital in the continuous course of care of a patient with a health condition.

episodic care /-sod'ik/, a pattern of medical and nursing care in which services are provided to a person for a particular problem, without an ongoing relationship being established between the person and health care professionals. EDs provide episodic care.

episome /ep'isōm/ [Gk, *epi* + *soma,* body], an extrachromosomal replicating unit that exists autonomously or functions with a chromosome.

epispadias /ep'ispă'dē·əs/ [Gk, *epi* + *spadon,* a rent], a congenital defect in which the urethra opens on the dorsum of the penis at any point below the internal sphincter. Other pelvic abnormalities may be present.

epistasis /epis'təsis/ [Gk, a standing still], **1.** suppression of a secretion or excretion, as of blood, menses, or lochia. **2.** an interaction between genes at different loci in which one gene masks or suppresses the expression of the other.—**epistatic,** *adj.*

epistaxis /ep'istak'sis/ [Gk, a dropping], bleeding from the nose caused by local irritation of mucous membranes, violent sneezing, fragility of the mucous membrane or of the arterial walls, chronic infection, trauma, hypertension, leukemia, vitamin K deficiency, or, most often, picking the nose.

episternal /ep'istur'nəl/, situated on or over the sternum.

epithalamus /ep'ithal'əməs/ [Gk, *epi* + *thalamos,* chamber], the uppermost portion of the diencephalon. It includes the trigonum habenulae, the pineal body, and the posterior commissure, and the medullary layers of thalamus.—**epithalamic,** *adj.*

epithelial /-thē'lē·əl/ [Gk, *epi,* above, *thele,* nipple], pertaining to or involving the outer layer of the skin.

epithelial cancer [Gk, *epi,* above, *thele,* nipple; L, *cancer,* crab], a carcinoma that develops from epithelium or related tissues in the skin, hollow viscera, and other organs.

epithelial cell, any one of several cells arranged in one or more layers that form part of a covering or lining of a body surface. The cells usually adhere to one another along their edges and surfaces.

epithelial cyst, **1.** any cyst lined by keratinizing stratified squamous epithelium, found most often in the skin. **2.** epidermal cyst.

epithelial debridement [Gk, *epi,* above, *thele,* nipple; Fr, *débridement,* incision], the removal of the entire inner lining and the attachment from the gingival or periodontal pocket in gingival curettage.

epithelialization /-thē'lē·al'izā'shən/ [Gk, *epi,* above, *thele,* nipple; L, *-ization,* process], the regrowth of skin over a wound.

epithelial peg [Gk, *epi* + *thele,* nipple], any of the papillary projections of the epithelium that penetrate the underlying stroma of connecting tissue and normally develop in mucous membranes and dermal tissues.

epithelial tissue [Gk, *epi,* above, *thele,* nipple; OFr, *tissu*], a closely packed single or stratified layer of cells covering the body and lining its cavities, with the exception of the blood and lymph vessels.

epithelioblastoma /ep′ithē′lē·ō′blastō′mə/, a tumor composed of epithelial cells.

epithelioid leiomyoma/ep′ithē′lē·oid/ [Gk, *epi + thele + eidos*, form], an uncommon neoplasm of smooth muscle in which the cells are polygonal in shape. It usually develops in the stomach.

epithelioma/-thē′lē·ō′mə/ [Gk, *epi*+*thele*+ *oma*, tumor], a neoplasm derived from the epithelium.

epithelium /-thē′lē·əm/ [Gk, *epi + thele*, nipple], the covering of the internal and external organs of the body and the lining of vessels, body cavities, glands, and organs. It consists of cells bound together by connective material and varies in the number of layers and the kinds of cells. —**epithelial**, *adj.*

epitympanic recess /-timpan′ik/ [Gk, *epi + tympanon*, drum], the area of the tympanic cavity cranial to the tympanic membrane. It contains the upper half of the malleus and greater part of the incus.

epizootic /ep′izō·ot′ik/, a disease or condition that occurs at about the same time in many individuals of the same species in a geographic area.

eplerenone, an antihypertensive agent.

EPO, 1. abbreviation for **erythropoietin.** 2. abbreviation for **Exclusive Provider Organization.**

eponym /ep′ənim/ [Gk, *epi*, above, *onyma*, name], a name for a disease, organ, procedure, or body function that is derived from the name of a person, usually a physician or scientist who first identified the condition or devised the object bearing the name. Examples include fallopian tube, Parkinson's disease, and Billing's method.

epoophoron /ep′ō·of′əron/ [Gk, *epi + oophoron*, ovary], a rudimentary structure that is situated in the mesosalpinx between the ovary and the uterine tube. The epoophoron is a persistent portion of the embryonic mesonephric duct.

epoprostenol /e′popros′tēnol/, name for prostacyclin when used pharmaceutically. It is used in the form of the sodium salt as an inhibitor of platelet aggregation for blood contacting nonbiologic systems, as in renal dialysis, as a pulmonary antihypertensive, and as a vasodilator.

epoxy, an organic chemical substructure consisting of a three-membered ring derived from the union of an oxygen atom and two carbon atoms. Epoxy resins are used as bonding agents.

eprosartan /ep′rosar′tan/, an angiotensin II antagonist that causes vasodilatation and decreases the effects of aldosterone, used as an antihypertensive.

EPSDT, abbreviation for **Early and Periodic Screening Diagnosis and Treatment.**

epsilon /ep′silon/, E, ε, the fifth letter of the Greek alphabet.

EPSP, abbreviation for *excitatory postsynaptic potential.*

Epstein-Barr virus (EBV) /ep′stīn bär′/ [Michael A. Epstein, b. 1921, English pathologist; Yvonne M. Barr, twentieth-century English virologist; L, *virus*, poison], the herpesvirus that causes infectious mononucleosis and is associated with nasopharyngeal sarcoma, Hodgkin's disease, B cell lymphoma, leukoplakia, CNS lymphoma in AIDS, and Burkitt's lymphoma, especially in immunodeficient patients such as posttransplant patients on immunosuppressive therapy. It is also thought to cause oral hairy leukoplakia.

Epstein-Barr virus (EBV) titer, a blood test to indicate chronic EBV infection and associated illnesses.

Epstein's pearls [Alois Epstein, Czechoslovakian physician, 1849–1918; L, *perla*, a mussel], small, white pearl-like epithelial cysts that occur on both sides of the midline of the hard palate of the newborn.

e.p.t., a trademark for a human pregnancy test kit that uses monoclonal antibody technology to detect the presence of HCG in urine.

EP test, abbreviation for *erythrocyte protoporphyrin* test.

eptifibatide, an antiplatelet agent used to treat acute coronary syndrome, including patients with percutaneous coronary intervention.

epulis /epyoo′lis/ *pl.* **epulides** [Gk, *epi + oulon*, gum], any tumor or growth on the gingiva.

epulosis /ep′yəlō′sis/, a healing process by scar formation, resulting in the production of a cicatrix.

Equagesic, a trademark for a fixed-combination CNS drug that contains an analgesic (aspirin) and a sedative (meprobamate).

equal cleavage /ē′kwəl/ [L, *aequare*, to make alike; AS, *cleofan*], mitotic division of the fertilized ovum into blastomeres of identical size, as occurs in humans and most other mammals.

equal distribution, a capitation method in which income is distributed equally among providers. It is used when the patient population is geographically and clinically homogeneous. Not applicable in Canada.

Equal Employment Opportunity Commission (EEOC), a body appointed by the president of the United States to administer the Civil Rights Act of 1964, particularly to investigate complaints of discrimination in employment in businesses engaged in interstate commerce.

Discrimination based on race, color, creed, or national origin is forbidden, but certain kinds of employers and certain conditions of employment allow exceptions to the act.

Equanil, a trademark for a sedative (meprobamate).

equation [L, *aequare,* to make equal], an expression in symbols of equality or equivalence.

equator /ē·kwā′tər/ [L, *aequator,* equalizer], an imaginary line encircling a globe, equidistant from the poles, used in anatomic nomenclature to designate such a line on a spherical organ, dividing the surface into two approximately equal parts.

equatorial plane /ēk′wətōr′ē·əl/ [L, *aequare,* to make alike; Fr, *flat* + *vessel*], the plane at the center of the spindle in which the chromosomes are arranged during metaphase of mitosis and meiosis.

equianalgesic dose /ē′kwē·an′əljē′sik/, a dose of one analgesic that is equivalent in pain-relieving effects to that of another analgesic. This equivalence permits substitution of medications to prevent possible adverse effects of one of the drugs. The term is also applied to equivalent alternative dose sizes and routes of administration.

equilibration /ē′kwilibrā′shən/ [L, *aequus,* equal, *libra,* balance], the balancing and integrating of new experiences with those of the past in the psychologic development of an individual.

equilibrium /ē′kwilib′rē·əm/ [L, *aequilibrium*], **1.** a state of balance or rest resulting from the equal action of opposing forces such as calcium and phosphorus in the body. **2.** in psychiatry, a state of mental or emotional balance. **3.** in radiotherapy, a point at which the rate of production of a daughter element is equal to the rate of decay of the parent element and the activities of parent and daughter are identical.

equilibrium reaction, any of several reflexes that enable the body to recover balance.

equilin /ek′wəlin/, an estrogen isolated from the urine of pregnant horses.

equine antitoxin, an antitoxin derived from the blood of healthy horses immunized against a specific bacterial toxin.

equine encephalitis /ē′kwīn, ek′win/ [L, *equus,* horse; Gk, *enkephalon,* brain, *itis,* inflammation], an arbovirus infection with a member of the Togaviridae family, Alphavirus, characterized by inflammation of the nerve tissues of the brain and spinal cord. Other characteristics include high fever, headache, nausea, vomiting, myalgia, and neurologic symptoms, such as visual disturbances, tremor, lethargy, and disorientation. The virus is transmitted by the bite of an infected mosquito.

Eastern equine encephalitis is a severe form of the infection. It occurs primarily along the eastern seaboard of the United States and lasts longer and causes more deaths and residual morbidity than **western equine encephalitis (WEE),** which produces a mild, brief illness, as does **Venezuelan equine encephalitis (VEE).**

equine gait [L, *equus,* horse; ONorse, *gate,* a way], a manner of walking characterized by footdrop. The condition is the result of damage to the peroneal nerve, which causes the foot to hang in a toes-downward position.

equinus /ēkwī′nəs/ [L, horse], a condition characterized by tiptoe walking on one or both feet. It is usually associated with clubfoot.

equipotential, 1. in physics, indicating bodies that have the same electrical potential. **2.** pertaining to lines of force that have the same electrical potential.

equity model /ek′witē/, an organizational model for medical providers that offers the provider equity in the company instead of cash payments. Not applicable in Canada.

equivalence /ikwiv′ələns/, a state of being equal in value.

equivalent weight [L, *a* + *aequus, valere,* equal value; AS, *gewiht*], **1.** the weight of an element in any given unit (such as grams) that will displace a unit weight of hydrogen from a compound or combine with or replace a unit weight of hydrogen. **2.** the weight of an acid or base that will produce or react with 1.008 grams of hydrogen ion. **3.** the weight of an oxidizing or reducing agent that will produce or accept one electron in a chemical reaction.

equivocal symptom [L, *aequus,* equal, *vocare,* to call; Gk, *symptoma,* that which happens], a symptom that may be attributed to more than one cause or that may occur in several diseases.

Er, symbol for the element **erbium.**

ER, E.R., abbreviation for **emergency room.**

eradication /irad′ikā′shən/, the process of completely removing or destroying something.

Eraxis, a trademark for **anidulafungin.**

Erbitux, a trademark for **cetuximab.**

erbium (Er) /ur′bē·əm/ [Ytterby, Sweden], a metallic rare earth element. Its atomic number is 68; its atomic mass is 167.26.

Erb's muscular dystrophy [Wilhelm H. Erb, German neurologist, 1840– 1921], a form of muscular dystrophy that first affects the shoulder girdle and later often involves the pelvic girdle. It is a progressively crippling disease.

Erb's palsy, a kind of paralysis caused by traumatic injury to the upper brachial plexus. It occurs most commonly as a result of forcible traction during childbirth, with injury to one or more cervical nerve roots. Signs include loss of sensation in the arm and paralysis and atrophy of the deltoid, the biceps, and the brachialis muscles.

Erb's point [Wilhelm H. Erb], a landmark of the brachial plexus on the upper trunk, located about 1 inch (2.5 cm) above the clavicle at about the level of the sixth cervical vertebra.

erectile /irek′til, -til/ [L, *erigere,* to erect], capable of being erected or raised to an erect position. The term is usually used to describe spongy tissue of the penis or clitoris that becomes turgid and erectile when filled with blood.

erectile dysfunction, failure by a male to attain or maintain erection until completion of sexual relations on an ongoing basis. The cause may be physical or psychologic in nature.

erectile myxoma, an angioma that contains areas of myxomatous tissue.

erection /irek′shən/ [L, *erigere,* to erect], the condition of hardness, swelling, and elevation observed in the penis and to a lesser degree in the clitoris, usually caused by sexual arousal but also occurring during sleep or after physical stimulation. Erection enables the penis to enter the vagina and to emit semen.

erector spinae reflex [L, *erigere,* to erect, *spina,* spine, *reflectere,* to bend back], a reflex characterized by contraction of the sacrospinalis and other back muscles when the overlying skin is stimulated.

erg /urg, erg/, a unit of energy in the centimeter-gram-second system equal to the work done by a force of 1 dyne through a distance of 1 cm. 1 erg = 10^{-7} J.

ergastoplasm /ərgas′təplaz′əm/ [Gk, *ergaster,* worker, *plassein,* to mold], a network of cytoplasmic structures that show basophilic staining properties; granular endoplasmic reticulum.

ergogenic /ur′gōjen′ik/, a tendency to increase work output.

ergogenic aid, a substance, such as a steroid, used by athletes with the expectation that it will provide a competitive edge.

ergoloid mesylate /ur′gōloid/, an ergot alkaloid preparation with psychotropic actions but lacking significant vasoconstrictor or vasodilator effects. It is occasionally prescribed in the treatment of symptomatic age-related decline in mental capacity with an unknown cause, as in senile dementia, but its efficacy is not well established.

Ergomar, a trademark for an ergot alkaloid (ergotamine tartrate).

ergometry /ərgom′ətrē/, the study of physical work activity, including that performed by specific muscles or muscle groups. The studies may involve testing with equipment such as stationary bicycles, treadmills, or rowing machines.

ergonomics /ur′gōnom′iks/ [Gk, *ergon,* work, *nomos,* law], a scientific discipline devoted to the study and analysis of human work, especially as it is affected by individual anatomic, psychologic, and other human characteristics.—**ergonomic,** *adj.*

ergonovine maleate /ur′gōnō′vēn/, an oxytocic ergot alkaloid. It is prescribed to contract the uterus in the treatment or prevention of postpartum or postabortion hemorrhage caused by uterine atony.

ergot /ur′gət/ [L, *ergota,* a grain fungus], a fungus structure that replaces the seed of rye and other cereal grasses infested with the parasitic fungus *Claviceps purpurea.*

ergot alkaloid, one of a large group of alkaloids derived from a common fungus, *Claviceps purpurea.* The alkaloids comprise three groups: the amino acid alkaloids typified by ergotamine, the dihydrogenated amino acid alkaloids such as dihydroergotamine, and the amine alkaloids such as ergonovine. Ergonovine, given orally or intravenously, is currently used in obstetrics to treat or prevent postpartum uterine atony and to complete an incomplete or missed abortion. Ergotamine is prescribed to relieve migraine headache.

ergotamine tartrate /ərgot′əmēn/, a vasoconstrictor, it binds to several receptor populations (e.g., alpha-adrenergic, DOPamine, serotonin) and, depending upon the receptor, can be an agonist or an antagonist. It is prescribed to abort or prevent vascular headaches such as migraines.

ergotherapy /ur′gōther′əpē/ [Gk, *ergon,* work, *therapeia,* treatment], the use of physical activity and exercise in the treatment of disease. By extension the therapy includes any procedure that increases the blood supply to a diseased or injured part, such as massage or various types of hot baths.—**ergotherapeutic,** *adj.*

ergotism /ur′gətiz′əm/ [L, *argota,* a grain fungus], **1.** an acute or chronic disease caused by excessive dosages of medications containing ergot. Symptoms may include cerebrospinal manifestations such as spasms, cramps, and dry gangrene. **2.** a chronic disease caused by ingestion of cereal products made with rye flour contaminated by ergot fungus.

ergot poisoning [L, *ergota,* a grain fungus, *potio,* drink], the toxic effects of ingesting food or medications containing ergot alkaloids, particularly ergotamine.

ergotropic /ur′gōtrop′ik/, **1.** pertaining to an activity or work state involving somatic muscle, sympathetic nervous system, and cortical alpha rhythm activity. **2.** pertaining to the administration of medications or other therapies to energize the power of the body's blood and other tissues to resist infections.

Erikson, Erik, a psychologist who described the development of identity of the self and the ego through successive stages that naturally unfold throughout the lifespan. The eight stages are trust vs. mistrust (infancy); autonomy vs. shame and doubt (toddlerhood); initiative vs. guilt (preschool); industry vs. inferiority (middle childhood); identity vs. role confusion (adolescence); intimacy vs. isolation (young adulthood); generativity vs. stagnation (middle adulthood); and ego integrity vs. despair (older adulthood).

Eriksson, Katie, a nursing theorist who developed the Theory of Caritative Care, which distinguishes between caring ethics, the practical relation between the patient and the nurse, and nursing ethics, the ethical principles and rules that guide decision-making. Caritative caring consists of love and charity, or caritas, and respect and reverence for human holiness and dignity. Suffering related to lack of caritative care violates human dignity.

ERISA, abbreviation for **Employment Retirement Income Security Act.**

erlotinib, a miscellaneous antineoplastic used in the treatment of non–small cell lung cancer.

erogenous /iroj′ənəs/ [Gk, *eros,* love, *genein,* to produce], pertaining to the production of erotic sensations or sexual excitement.

erogenous zones, areas of the body in which sexual tension tends to become concentrated and can be relieved by manipulation of the region. The areas include the mouth, anus, nipples, and genitals.

Eros /ir′os, er′os/ [Gk, mythic love-inciting son of Aphrodite], a Freudian term for the drive or instinct for survival, including self-preservation and continuation of the species through reproduction.

erosion /irō′zhən/ [L, *erodere,* to consume], the wearing away or gradual destruction of a surface. For example, a mucosal or epidermal surface may erode as a result of inflammation, injury, or other causes.

erosive gastritis /irō′siv/, an inflammatory condition characterized by multiple erosions of the mucous membrane lining the stomach. Nausea, anorexia, pain, and gastric hemorrhage may occur.

eroticism /irot′isiz′əm/ [Gk, *erotikos,* sexual love], **1.** sexual impulse or desire. **2.** the

arousal or attempt to arouse the sexual instinct through suggestive or symbolic means. **3.** the expression of sexual instinct or desire. **4.** an abnormally persistent sexual drive.

erratic /irat′ik/ [L, *erraticus,* wandering], deviating from the normal but with no apparent fixed course or purpose.

error [L, *errare,* to wander], in research, a defect in the design of a study, in the development of measurements or instruments, or in the interpretation of findings.

error theory of aging, a stochastic theory of aging that ascribes aging to the accumulation of errors in the process of information flow from genes to proteins. The errors create faulty proteins that do not function normally, resulting in impaired cell function and death.

ERT, abbreviation for **external radiation therapy.**

ertapenem, an antiinfective agent used to treat adults with moderate to severe infections, complicated skin and skin structure infections, and complicated UTIs.

erucic acid /erōō′sik/, a fatty acid that has been associated with heart disease. It is present in rapeseed oil.

eructation /ē′ruktā′shən/ [L, *eructare,* to belch], the act of drawing up air from the stomach with a characteristic sound through the mouth.

eruption /irup′shən/ [L, *eruptio,* bursting forth], the appearance of rapidly forming skin lesions, especially of a viral exanthem, or of a rash that commonly accompanies a drug reaction.

eruptive fever /irup′tiv/ [L, *eruptio,* bursting forth; *febris*], a febrile disease caused by infection with *Rickettsia conorii.*

eruptive gingivitis, inflammation of the gums that may occur when the secondary teeth break through.

eruptive xanthoma, a skin disorder associated with elevated triglyceride levels in the blood. Numerous erythematous or pale, raised papules suddenly appear on the trunk, legs, arms, and buttocks.

ERV, abbreviation for **expiratory reserve volume.**

erysipelas /er′isip′ələs/ [Gk, *erythros,* red, *pella,* skin], an infectious skin disease characterized by redness, swelling, vesicles, bullae, fever, pain, and lymphadenopathy. It is caused by a strain of group A beta-hemolytic streptococci.

erysipeloid /er′isip′əloid/ [Gk, *erythros* + *pella* + *eidos,* form], an infection of the hands characterized by blue-red patches and occasionally by erythema. It is acquired by handling meat or fish infected with *Erysipelothrix rhusiopathiae.*

erythema /er′ithē′mə/ [Gk, *erythros,* red], redness or inflammation of the skin or mucous membranes that is the result of dilation and congestion of superficial capillaries. Examples of erythema are nervous blushes and mild sunburn.—**erythematous,** *adj.*

erythema infectiosum, 1. an acute benign infectious disease, mainly of childhood. It is characterized by fever and an erythematous rash that begins on the cheeks and later appears on the arms, thighs, buttocks, and trunk. As the rash progresses, earlier lesions fade. Sunlight aggravates the eruption, which usually lasts about 10 days. For a period the rash may reappear whenever the skin is irritated. It is caused by parvovirus B$_{19}$. 2. a virus that lives only in humans.

erythema marginatum, a skin disorder seen in acute rheumatic fever characterized by temporary disk-shaped nonpruritic reddened macules that fade in the center, leaving raised margins.

erythema migrans (EM), a disease that begins as small papules that spread peripherally, characterized by a raised, red margin and clearing in the center. It may mark the site of a tick bite and is a diagnostic sign of **Lyme disease.**

erythema multiforme (EM) /mul'tifôr'mē, mo͞ol'tēfôr'mä/, any of three major clinical syndromes characterized by lymphocytic infiltrates in the skin that cause keratinocyte necrosis. The patient may experience polymorphous eruption of skin and mucous membranes. Macules, papules, nodules, vesicles or bullae, and target (bullseye-shaped) lesions are seen. EM minor is an acute form of the disease, characterized by three-ring target lesions on the extremities. EM major is characterized by the presence of target lesions, blistering, and detachment of the skin and mucous membranes. The condition is associated with detachment of large sheets of skin.

erythema neonatorum, a common skin condition of neonates characterized by a pink papular rash frequently superimposed with vesicles or pustules. The rash appears within 24 to 48 hours after birth and disappears spontaneously after several days.

erythema nodosum, a hypersensitivity reaction characterized by reddened, tender subcutaneous nodules on the extensor aspects of the extremities such as the shins. The nodules last for several days or weeks, never ulcerate, and are often associated with mild fever, malaise, and pain in muscles and joints.

erythema perstans, a persistent local redness of the skin, characteristically annular.

erythematous pemphigus [Gk, *erythros*, red, *pemphix*, bubble], a skin disorder characterized by bullous eruptions on the trunk and a facial eruption that resembles that of lupus erythematosus. The

condition may be accompanied by seborrheic dermatitis.

erythemogenic /er'ithe'mojen'ik/, producing or causing erythema.

erythralgia /er'ithral'jə/ [Gk, *erythros*, red, *algos*, pain], a skin disorder characterized by a painful burning sensation, raised skin temperature, and redness, generally of the lower limbs.

erythrasma /er'ithraz'mə/ [Gk, *erythros*, red], a bacterial skin infection common in the axillary or inguinal region, characterized by irregular reddish-brown areas.

erythremia /er'ithrē'mē-ə/ [Gk, *erythros* + *haima*, blood], an abnormal increase in the number of RBCs.

erythroblast /erith'rəblast'/, an immature form of an RBC. It is normally found only in bone marrow and contains hemoglobin.

erythroblastoma /-blastō'mə/ [Gk, *erythros*, red, *blastos*, germ, *oma*, tumor], a myeloma tumor (osteolytic neoplasm) in which the cells resemble erythroblasts.

erythroblastosis /-blastō'sis/, the presence of abnormally large numbers of erythroblasts in the peripheral blood.

erythroblastosis fetalis /-blastō'sis/ [Gk, *erythros* + *blastos*, germ, *osis*, condition; L, *fetus*, bringing forth], a type of hemolytic anemia in newborns that results from maternal-fetal blood group incompatibility, specifically involving the Rh factor and the ABO blood groups. The condition is caused by an antigen-antibody reaction in the bloodstream of the infant resulting from placental transmission of maternally formed antibodies against the incompatible antigens of the fetal blood. In Rh factor incompatibility, the hemolytic reaction occurs only when the mother is Rh negative and the infant is Rh positive. The isoimmunization process rarely occurs in the first pregnancy, but there is increased risk with each succeeding pregnancy.

erythrochromia /-krō'mē-ə/, 1. a red coloration or stain. 2. red pigmentation in spinal fluid caused by the presence of blood.

Erythrocin, a trademark for an antibiotic (erythromycin).

erythrocyanosis /-sī'ənō'sis/, a condition characterized by bluish-red discoloration of skin, accompanied by swelling, burning, and itching.

erythrocyte /erith'rəsīt'/ [Gk, *erythros* + *kytos*, cell], a mature RBC.

erythrocyte reinfusion, the process of injecting into an individual's bloodstream RBCs previously taken from that individual and preserved temporarily by freezing.

erythrocyte sedimentation rate (ESR), the rate at which RBCs settle out in a tube of unclotted blood, expressed in millimeters per hour. Elevated sedimentation rates

E

are not specific for any disorder but most commonly indicate the presence of inflammation. Serial evaluations of erythrocyte sedimentation rate are useful in monitoring the course of inflammatory activity in rheumatic diseases and, when performed with a WBC count, can indicate infection. Certain noninflammatory conditions, such as pregnancy, are also characterized by high sedimentation rates. Other diseases that alter blood proteins can also cause abnormal ESRs.

erythrocythemia /erith'rōsīthē'mē·ə/ [Gk, *erythros + kytos + haima,* blood], an increase in the number of erythrocytes circulating in the blood.

erythrocytopenia /-sī'təpē'nē·ə/ [Gk, *erythros,* red, *kytos,* cell, *penes,* poor], a condition characterized by a deficiency or decrease in number of erythrocytes.

erythrocytosis /erith'rōsītō'sis/ [Gk, *erythros + kytos + osis,* condition], an abnormal increase in the number of circulating red cells.

erythroderma /erith'rōdur'mə/ [Gk, *erythros + derma,* skin], an abnormal redness of the skin.

erythrogenesis, the creation of RBCs.

erythroid /erith'roid/, **1.** reddish in color. **2.** pertaining to erythrocytes.

erythroleukemia /-lookē'mē·ə/ [Gk, *erythros + leukos,* white, *haima,* blood], a malignant blood disorder characterized by a proliferation of erythropoietic elements in bone marrow, erythroblasts with bizarre lobulated nuclei, and abnormal myeloblasts in peripheral blood. The disease may have an acute or chronic course.

erythroleukosis, an abnormal increase in numbers of granulocytes and RBCs.

erythromelalgia /erith'rōmilal'jə/ [Gk, *erythros + melos,* limb, *algos,* pain], a rare disorder characterized by a paroxysmal dilation of the peripheral blood vessels.—**erythromelalgic,** *adj.*

erythromycin /erith'rōmī'sin/, an antibiotic (of the macrolide type) prescribed in the treatment of many bacterial and mycoplasmic infections, particularly those that cannot be treated by penicillin.

erythron /erith'ron/, the total mass of circulating RBCs and the RBC-forming tissues from which they are derived.

erythropathy /er'ithrop'əthē/, any disease involving the RBCs (erythrocytes).

erythrophage /erith'rəfāj/, a phagocyte that ingests RBCs or blood pigment.

erythrophobia /-fō'bē·ə/ [Gk, *erythros + phobos,* fear], **1.** an anxiety disorder characterized by an irrational fear of blushing or of displaying embarrassment. **2.** a symptom manifested by blushing at the slightest provocation. **3.** a morbid fear

of or aversion to the color red.—**erythrophobic,** *adj.*

erythrophthisis /erith'rōtī'sis/, grave damage to the restorative power of red corpuscles.

erythroplasia of Queyrat /erith'rōplā'zhə/ [Gk, *erythros + plasis,* forming]. Louis A. Queyrat, French dematologist, 1856–1933], a premalignant lesion on the glans or corona of the penis. It is a shiny, velvety, well-circumscribed reddish patch on the skin.

erythropoiesis /erith'rōpō·ē'sis/ [Gk, *erythros + poiein,* to make], the process of erythrocyte production in the bone marrow involving the maturation of a nucleated precursor into a hemoglobin-filled, nucleus-free erythrocyte that is regulated by erythropoietin, a hormone produced by the kidney. —**erythropoietic,** *adj.*

erythropoietic protoporphyria (EPP), an autosomal-dominant disorder, a form of erythropoietic porphyria, characterized by increased levels of protoporphyrin in the erythrocytes, plasma, liver, and feces and a wide variety of photosensitive skin changes, ranging from a burning or pruritic sensation to erythema, plaquelike edema, and wheals.

erythropoietin (EPO) /erith'rōpō·ē'tin/ [Gk, *erythros + poiein,* to make], a glycoprotein hormone synthesized mainly in the kidneys and released into the bloodstream in response to anoxia.

erythropoietin (EPO) test, a blood test measuring the hormone erythropoietin, used in the diagnosis of anemia and polycythemia.

Erythrovirus /erith'rōvi'rus/, a genus of parvoviruses containing viruses that infect erythrocyte progenitor cells. It includes the species B19 virus.

Es, symbol for the element **einsteinium.**

ESADDI, abbreviation for **Estimated Safe and Adequate Daily Dietary Intake.**

escape beat [ME, *escapen,* to flee; *beten,* to beat], an automatic beat of the heart that occurs after an interval equal to or longer than the duration of its normal cycle. Escape beats function as safety mechanisms, and anything that produces a long pause in the prevailing heart cycle may allow an escape to occur. Pauses in which escape beats occur may be caused by sinoatrial block, atrioventricular (AV) block, or sinus bradycardia.

escape rhythm [OFr, *escaper*; Gk, *rhythmos,* beat], a sustained heartbeat that occurs when the sinus or atrioventricular (AV) node is depressed or blocked. Under such conditions, the heart rate is controlled by the AV junction or the His-Purkinje system.

eschar /es'kär/ [Gk, *eschara,* scab], a scab or dry crust that results from trauma, such as a thermal or chemical burn, infection, or excoriating skin disease.—**escharotic,** *adj.*

escharotomy /es'kärot'əmē/, a surgical incision into necrotic tissue resulting from a severe burn. The procedure is sometimes necessary to prevent edema from generating sufficient interstitial pressure to impair capillary filling, causing ischemia.

Escherichia coli (E. coli) /eshirī'kē·ə kō'lī/ [Theodor Escherich, German physician, 1857–1911; Gk, *kolon,* colon], a species of coliform bacteria of the family Enterobacteriaceae, normally present in the intestines and common in water, milk, and soil. *E. coli* is the most frequent cause of UTI and is a serious gram-negative pathogen in wounds.

escitalopram, an antidepressant, selective serotonin reuptake inhibitor used to treat major depressive disorders.

escutcheon /eskuch'ən/ [L, *scutum,* shield], the pattern of distribution of coarse, adult pubic hair, rhomboid in the male and triangular in the female.

Eskalith, a trademark for a medication used to treat bipolar affective disorders (lithium carbonate).

Esmarch's bandage /es'märks/ [Johann F. A. von Esmarch, German surgeon, 1823–1908], a broad, flat elastic bandage wrapped around an elevated limb to force blood out of the limb. It is used before certain surgical procedures to create a blood-free field.

esomeprazole /es'omep'räzōl/, a proton pump inhibitor administered orally as the magnesium salt in the treatment of gastroesophageal reflux disease and in the treatment of duodenal ulcer associated with *Helicobacter pylori* infection.

esophageal atresia /əsof'əjē'əl, es'ofā'jē·əl/ [Gk, *oisophagos,* gullet], an abnormal esophagus that ends in a blind pouch or narrows to a thin cord and thus does not provide a continuous passage to the stomach.

esophageal cancer, a rare malignant neoplastic disease of the esophagus. Risk factors associated with the disease are heavy consumption of alcohol, tobacco smoking, betel-nut chewing, Plummer-Vinson syndrome, Barrett's esophagus, and achalasia.

esophageal dilator, a bougie or similar instrument for dilation of an esophageal stricture or the lower esophageal sphincter.

esophageal dysfunction, any disturbance, impairment, or abnormality that interferes with the normal functioning of the esophagus, such as dysphagia, esophagitis, or sphincter incompetence. The condition is one of the primary symptoms of scleroderma.

esophageal function studies, manometric tests used to assess esophageal function. These include tests for acid reflux, acid clearing, and acid perfusion.

esophageal lead /lēd/, **1.** an ECG conductor in which the exploring electrode is placed within the lumen of the esophagus. It is used in identifying cardiac arrhythmias. **2.** *informal.* a tracing produced by such a lead on an ECG.

esophageal obturator airway (EOA), an emergency device that consists of a large tube that is inserted into the mouth through an airtight face mask. The esophagus is blocked by inflating a balloon at the end of the tube. Because of the design, air passes only into the trachea.

esophageal peristalsis, strong, uncoordinated nonpropulsive contractions of the esophagus evoked by swallowing, especially in the elderly.

esophageal varices, a complex of longitudinal tortuous veins at the lower end of the esophagus, enlarged and swollen as the result of portal hypertension.

esophageal web, a thin membrane that may develop across the lumen of the esophagus, usually near the level of the cricoid cartilage. The abnormal condition is generally associated with iron deficiency anemia.

esophagectomy /esof'əjek'təmē/ [Gk, *oisophagos + ektomē,* excision], a surgical procedure in which all or part of the esophagus is removed, as may be required to treat severe recurrent bleeding, esophageal varices, or esophageal cancer.

esophagitis /esof'əjī'tis/ [Gk, *oisophagos + itis*], inflammation of the mucosal lining of the esophagus, caused by infection, irritation from a nasogastric tube, or, most commonly, backflow of gastric juice from the stomach.

esophagocele /esof'əgōsēl'/, a hernia of the mucous membrane through a weakened area in the wall of the esophagus.

esophagogastroduodenoscopy (EGD) /əsof'əgōgas'trōdoo'odənos'kəpe/, an endoscopic test that permits direct visualization of the upper GI tract.

esophagogastronomy /esof'əgō'gastron'əmē/ [Gk, *oisophagos,* gullet, *gaster,* stomach, *stoma,* mouth], the surgical creation of a passage between the esophagus and the stomach.

esophagogastroscopy /-gastros'kəpē/ [Gk, *oisophagos,* gullet, *gaster,* stomach, *skopein,* to watch], the examination with an endoscope of the esophagus and stomach.

esophagogastrostomy /-gastros'təmē/, an artificial anastomosis of the esophagus to the stomach.

esophagojejunostomy /-jij'ōōnos'təmē/ [Gk, *oisophagos*, gullet; L, *jejunum*, empty, *stoma*, mouth], the surgical creation of a direct passage from the esophagus to the jejunum, bypassing the stomach. The procedure is used after total gastrectomy.

esophagomyotomy /-mī'ot'əmē/, a longitudinal incision in the lower part of the esophageal muscle made to treat esophageal achalasia, an obstruction to the passage of food.

esophagoscopy /esof'əgos'kəpē/ [Gk, *oisophagos* + *skopein*, to look], examination of the esophagus with an endoscope.

esophagospasm /esof'əgōspaz'əm/ [Gk, *oisophagos*, gullet + *spasmos*], spasmodic contractions of the walls of the esophagus.

esophagostomy /esof'əgos'təmē/, a surgical opening into the esophagus for enteral tube feeding.

esophagus /esof'əgəs/ [Gk, *oisophagos*], the musculomembranous canal, about 24 cm long, extending from the pharynx to the stomach. It is composed of a fibrous coat, a muscular coat, and a submucous coat and is lined with mucous membrane. —**esophageal**, *adj.*

esophoria /es'əfôr'ē·ə/ [Gk, *eso*, inward, *pherein*, to bear], the latent medial deviation of the visual axis of one eye in the absence of visual stimuli for fusion.—**esophoric**, *adj.*

esotropia /es'ətrō'pē·ə/ [Gk, *eso* + *tropos*, turning], a medical deviation of one eye relative to the other fixating eye.—**esotropic**, *adj.*

ESP, abbreviation for **extrasensory perception.**

espundia /espun'dē·ə/ [Sp, cancerous ulcer], a cutaneous form of American leishmaniasis most common in Brazil, caused by *Leishmania brasiliensis*. The primary lesion often disappears spontaneously, followed by mucocutaneous lesions that destroy the mucosal surface of the nose, pharynx, and larynx. If the condition is untreated, potentially fatal secondary bacterial infections and disfigurement may occur.

ESR, abbreviation for **erythrocyte sedimentation rate.**

essential /esen'shəl/, a necessary part of a thing without which it could not exist.

essential amino acid [L, *essentia*, quality], an organic compound not synthesized in the body that is essential for protein synthesis in adults and optimal growth in infants and children. Adults require isoleucine, leucine, lysine, methionine, phenylalanine, threonine, tryptophan, and valine. Infants need these amino acids plus arginine and histidine. Cysteine and tyrosine are derived from methionine and phenylalanine, respectively, and are considered semiessential.

essential convulsion, central convulsion.

essential fatty acid (EFA), a polyunsaturated acid essential in the diet for proper growth, maintenance, and functioning of the body. EFAs are prostaglandin precursors that play important roles in metabolism. They are also necessary for the normal functioning of the reproductive and endocrine systems and the breaking up of cholesterol deposits on arterial walls. Although rare, a deficiency of EFAs causes changes in cell structure and enzyme function, resulting in decreased growth and other disorders.

essential fever, fever occurring in the absence of a known infectious disease.

essential hypertension, an elevated systemic arterial pressure for which no cause can be found. It is often the only significant clinical finding.

essential mixed cryoglobulinemia, a rare condition characterized by deposition of type II cryoglobulins without a detectable cause, inducing cutaneous vasculitis, synovitis, and glomerulonephritis.

essential nutrients, the carbohydrates, proteins, fats, minerals, vitamins, and water necessary for growth, normal function, and body maintenance.

essential oils, a class of generally aromatic volatile oils; the essences extracted from plants for use in flavoring foods, perfumes, and medicines.

essential pruritus [L, *essentia*, quality, *prurire*, to itch], localized or general pruritus that begins without a preexisting skin disorder.

essential tremor, an involuntary fine shaking of the hand, the head, and the face, especially during routine body movements. It is a familial disorder inherited as an autosomal-dominant trait and appears during adolescence or in middle age. Essential tremor is aggravated by activity and emotion.

essential vertigo [L, *essentia*, quality, *vertigo*, dizziness], a form of vertigo for which no organic cause has been found.

EST, 1. abbreviation for *electric shock therapy*. **2.** abbreviation for *electroshock therapy*.

established name, the name assigned to a drug by the U.S. Adopted Names Council. The established name, generally shorter than the chemical name, is the name by which the drug is known to health practitioners.

Estar, a trademark for a coal tar preparation used to treat eczema and psoriasis.

estazolam /estaz'olam/, a benzodiazepine used as a sedative and hypnotic in the treatment of insomnia.

ester /es′tər/ [Ger, *Essigäther,* acetic ether], a class of chemical compounds formed by the bonding of an alcohol and one or more organic acids, with the loss of a water molecule for each ester group formed. Fats are esters, produced by the bonding of fatty acids with the alcohol glycerol.

esterase /es′tərās/, any enzyme that splits esters.

esterification, the process of combining an organic acid (RCOOH) with an alcohol (ROH) to form an ester (RCOOR) and water.

esterified estrogen /ester′ifīd/, an ester of natural estrogen prescribed for menstrual irregularities, contraception, and menopausal symptoms.

esterify, to convert into an ester.

ester local anesthetic, a class of local anesthetics with an ester chemical group that differentiates it from the amide group of local anesthetics.

esthesia /esthē′zhə/, **1.** capacity for perception. **2.** sensitivity or feeling. **3.** any disorder of the nervous system that affects perception or sensitivity.

esthesiophysiology /esthē′zē-ōfiz′ē-ol′əjē/, the study of sense organ function.

esthetics /esthet′iks/ [Gk, *aisthetikos,* sensitivity], the branch of philosophy dealing with the forms and psychologic effects of beauty. In medicine, esthetics may be applied to dental reconstruction and plastic surgery.

estimated hepatic blood flow (EHBF), an estimate of the rate of blood flow through the liver in a liver function test, such as by calculating indocyanine green clearance.

Estimated Safe and Adequate Daily Dietary Intake (ESADDI), nutrient intake recommendations, made by the National Academy of Sciences' Food and Nutrition Board, that give what is considered a safe range of intake for some nutrients because not enough information is available to set recommended dietary allowance values for them.

Estinyl, a trademark for an estrogen (ethinyl estradiol).

Estrace, a trademark for an estrogen (estradiol).

estradiol /es′trədī′ôl/, the most potent naturally occurring human estrogen.

estramustine /es′trämus′tēn/, an antineoplastic agent containing estradiol joined to mechlorethamine, administered orally for palliative treatment of metastatic or progressive carcinoma of the prostate.

estramustine phosphate sodium /es′trəmus′tēn/, an antineoplastic agent. It is prescribed for palliative treatment of metastatic or progressive carcinoma of the prostate.

estrangement /estränj′mənt/ [L, *extraneus,* not belonging], **1.** a psychologic effect of the separation of a mother from her newborn required when the infant is ill or premature or has a congenital defect, thereby diverting the mother from establishing a normal relationship with her child. **2.** the feeling that external objects have a strange, unfamiliar, or unreal quality, caused by a failure of cathexis of the external ego boundary, one of whose functions is to identify external objects as real and familiar.

Estratab, a trademark for esterified estrogens.

estriol /es′trē-ôl/, a relatively weak naturally occurring human estrogen found in high concentrations in urine.

estrogen /es′trojən/ [Gk, *oistros,* gadfly, *genein,* to produce], one of a group of hormonal steroid compounds that promote the development of female secondary sex characteristics. Human estrogen level is elaborated in the ovaries, adrenal cortices, testes, and fetoplacental unit. During the menstrual cycle, estrogen renders the female genital tract suitable for fertilization, implantation, and nutrition of the early embryo.

estrogen fractions test, a 24-hour urine or blood test that measures levels of the three major estrogens. Test results aid in the evaluation of menopausal status, sexual maturity, gynecomastia or feminization syndromes, certain ovarian tumors, and placental function and fetal normality in high-risk pregnancies.

estrogen receptor assay, a microscopic examination of breast tumor tissue used to determine the probable response of a tumor to endocrine therapy.

estrogen replacement therapy, administration of an estrogen to treat estrogen deficiency, such as that occurring after menopause. Indications for use include the prevention of postmenopausal osteoporosis and coronary artery disease, and the prevention and treatment of vasomotor symptoms, such as hot flashes, and of thinning of the skin and vaginal epithelium, atrophic vaginitis, and vulvar atrophy. In women with a uterus, a progestational agent is usually included to prevent endometrial hyperplasia.

estrone /es′trōn/, a relatively potent endogenous estrogen.

estropipate /es′trəpip′āt/, an estrogen prescribed in the treatment of vasomotor symptoms of menopause, atrophic vaginitis, kraurosis vulvae, female hypogonadism, female castration, and primary ovarian failure.

estrus /es′trəs/, the cyclic period of sexual receptivity in mammals other than primates, marked by intense sexual urge and

E

coinciding with the time that fertilization can take place.

estrus cycle [Gk, *oistros*, gadfly, *kyklos*, circle], the periodic changes in the female body that occur under the influence of sex hormones.

ESWL, abbreviation for **extracorporeal shock-wave lithotripsy.**

eta /ē′tə, ā′tə/, H, η, the seventh letter of the Greek alphabet.

etanercept, a biologic agent used to treat acute, chronic rheumatoid arthritis that has not responded to other treatments.

état criblé /ätä′ krēblä′/ [Fr, sievelike state], a condition or state of multiple sievelike perforations in swollen lymphatic nodules in the intestine. It is a frequently fatal complication of untreated typhoid fever.

etching /ech′ing/, the cutting of a hard surface, such as metal or glass, by a corrosive chemical, usually an acid, to create a design.

ETEC, abbreviation for **enterotoxigenic *Escherichia coli.***

ethacrynic acid /eth′əkrin′ik/, a loop diuretic prescribed as a treatment for severe edema, such as nephrotic syndrome, hepatic cirrhoses, and ascites of malignancy.

ethambutol /etham′butol/, an antibacterial agent specifically effective against *Mycobacterium tuberculosis.*

ethambutol hydrochloride /eth′əmbyōō′təl/, a tuberculostatic antibiotic prescribed in the treatment of pulmonary TB in combination with other drugs.

ethanol /eth′ənol/, ethyl alcohol.

ethanolamine, an amino alcohol formed by the decarboxylation of serine. It is a component of certain cephalins and phospholipids and is used as a surfactant in pharmaceutical products.

ethanol test, a blood, urine, gastric, or breath test usually performed to evaluate alcohol-impaired drivers or those with alcohol overdose.

ethaverine hydrochloride /eth′əver′ēn/, a smooth muscle relaxant prescribed to relieve spasm of the GI or genitourinary tract, arterial vasospasm, cerebral insufficiency, and peripheral and cerebrovascular insufficiency.

ether /ē′thər/ [Gk, *aither*, air], **1.** any of a class of organic compounds in which two hydrocarbon groups are linked by an oxygen atom. **2.** a nonhalogenated volatile liquid no longer used in clinical practice as a general anesthetic.

ethereal /ithir′ē·əl/ [Gk, *aither*, air], pertaining to or resembling ether.

ethics /eth′iks/ [Gk, *ethikos*, moral duty], the science or study of moral values

or principles, including ideals of autonomy, beneficence, and justice.—**ethical,** *adj.*

Ethics in Patient Referrals Act, a federal law, the Stark Law, enacted in 1989, that prohibits referrals by a physician to a clinical laboratory in which the physician has a financial interest. A 1994 amendment includes other services and equipment such as physical and occupational therapy; radiology and other diagnostic services; radiation therapy; parenteral and enteral nutrients, equipment, and supplies; and home health services.

ethinyl estradiol /eth′inil/, an estrogen prescribed in the treatment of postmenopausal breast cancer, menstrual cycle irregularities, prostatic cancer, and hypogonadism and for contraception and relief of menopausal vasomotor symptoms.

ethionamide /eth′ē·ənam′īd/, a tuberculostatic antibacterial prescribed for the treatment of TB in conjunction with other drugs when frontline therapy has failed.

ethmocarditis /eth′mōkärdī′tis/, a chronic inflammation of the cardiac connective tissue.

ethmoid /eth′moid/ [Gk, *ethmos,* sieve, *eidos,* form], **1.** pertaining to the ethmoid bone. **2.** having a large number of sievelike openings.

ethmoidal air cell /ethmoi′dəl/ [Gk, *ethmos,* sieve, *eidos,* form], one of the numerous small thin-walled cavities in the ethmoid bone of the skull. The cavities are lined with mucous membrane continuous with that of the nasal cavity and lie between the upper part of the nasal cavities and the orbits.

ethmoidal process, an outgrowth on the superior border of the inferior concha that articulates with the uncinate process of the ethmoid.

ethmoid bone, the very light, sievelike, and spongy bone at the base of the cranium, also forming the roof and most of the walls of the superior part of the nasal cavity.

ethmoidofrontal suture /ethmoi′dōfron′təl/, a line in the skull between the cribriform plate of the ethmoid and the orbital plate and posterior margin of the nasal process.

ethmoidolacrimal suture /-lak′riməl/, a line in the skull between the orbital plate of the ethmoid and the posterior margin of the lacrimal bone.

ethmosphenoid suture /eth′mōsfē′noid/, a line in the skull between the crest of the sphenoid bone and the perpendicular and cribriform plates of the ethmoid.

ethnic group /eth′nik/, a population of individuals organized on the basis of an assumed common cultural origin.

ethnocentrism /eth′nōsen′trizm/ [Gk, *ethnos,* nation, *kentron,* center], **1.** a belief in the inherent superiority of the "race" or group to which one belongs. **2.** a proclivity to consider other ethnic groups in terms of one's own racial origins.

ethnography /ethnog′rəfē/ [Gk, *ethnos,* nation, *graphein,* to record], a branch of anthropology that is concerned with the history of nations and ethnic populations.

ethoheptazine /eth′o-hep′tah-zēn/, an analgesic, used as the citrate salt to control mild to moderate pain.

ethology /ethol′əjē/ [Gk, *ethos,* character, *logos,* science], **1.** in zoology, the scientific study of the behavioral patterns of animals, specifically in their native habitat. **2.** in psychology, the empiric study of human behavior, primarily social customs, manners, and mores.—**ethologic,** *adj.,* **ethologist,** *n.*

ethosuximide /eth′ōsuk′simīd/, an anticonvulsant prescribed in the treatment of absence seizures.

ethotoin /eth′ōtō′in/, an anticonvulsant prescribed in the treatment of generalized tonic-clonic and complex-partial seizures.

Ethrane, a trademark for an inhalational general anesthetic (enflurane).

ethyl chloride /eth′il/, a topical anesthetic used in short operations. It is prescribed in the treatment of skin irritations and in minor skin surgery.

ethylene /eth′əlēn/ [Gk, *aither,* air, *hyle,* stuff], a colorless flammable gas that is lighter than air and has a slightly sweet odor and taste. It was previously used as a general anesthetic.

ethylenediamine /eth′əlēndi·am′ēn/, a clear thick liquid having the odor of ammonia. It is used as a solvent, an emulsifier, and a stabilizer with aminophylline injections.

ethylene dibromide (EDB), a volatile liquid used as an insecticide and gasoline additive. Because it has been found to be a cause of cancer in animals, the Environmental Protection Agency has restricted the use of EDB to control insect pests in grains and fruits intended for human use.

ethylene dichloride poisoning, the toxic effects of exposure to ethylene dichloride, a hydrocarbon solvent, diluent, and fumigant, which is one of the most abundant of all chlorinated organic chemicals. It is an eye, ear, nose, throat, and skin irritant. Inhalation or ingestion can lead to serious illness or death.

ethylene glycol poisoning, the toxic reaction to ingestion of ethylene glycol or diethylene glycol, chemicals used in automobile antifreeze preparations. Symptoms in mild cases may resemble those of alcohol intoxication but without the breath odor produced by alcoholic beverages.

Vomiting, carpopedal spasm, lumbar pain, renal failure, respiratory distress, convulsions, and coma may also occur.

ethylene oxide (CH₂CH₂O), a highly flammable gas used to sterilize surgical instruments and other supplies.

ethylestrenol, an anabolic steroid.

ethynodiol diacetate and ethinyl estradiol, an oral estrogen-progestin combination contraceptive. It is prescribed for prevention of pregnancy.

etidocaine, an amide local anesthetic that has fallen out of use because it is more likely to block motor nerves than sensory nerves.

etidronate disodium /etid′rənāt/, a regulator of calcium metabolism prescribed in the treatment of Paget's disease and heterotopic ossification caused by injury to the spinal cord and after total hip replacement.

etiology /ē′tē·ol′əjē/ [Gk, *aitia,* cause, *logos,* science], **1.** the study of all factors that may be involved in the development of a disease, including the susceptibility of the patient, the nature of the disease agent, and the way in which the patient's body is invaded by the agent. **2.** the cause of a disease.—**etiologic,** *adj.*

etodolac /etodo′lak/, an NSAID used as an analgesic and antiinflammatory agent, especially to treat arthritis.

etomidate /etom′idāt/, a short-acting and hypnotic nonbarbiturate IV agent for induction of general anesthesia. It has minimal adverse cardiovascular and respiratory effects, thus providing a *greater margin of safety in patients at risk because of heart disease.*

etoposide, an antineoplastic or chemotherapeutic agent and mitotic inhibitor prescribed in the treatment of several forms of cancer, including lymphomas, cancer of the testicles, prostate, and small cell lung cancer, to prevent tumor cells from dividing and spreading.

etoposide phosphate, the phosphate salt of etoposide, having the same actions and uses as the base.

Etrafon, a trademark for a CNS fixed-combination drug containing an antipsychotic (perphenazine) and an antidepressant (amitriptyline hydrochloride).

etretinate /etret′ināt/, a synthetic derivative of vitamin A prescribed for severe recalcitrant psoriasis, including generalized pustular and erythrodermic psoriasis.

etymology [Gk, *etymos,* base; L, *logos,* words], the study of the origin and development of words.

etymon (*pl.* **etyma**) an earlier form of a word.

Eu, symbol for the element **europium.**

Eubacterium /yoo'baktir'ē·əm/, a large genus of nonsporulating gram-positive anaerobic rod-shaped bacteria normally found in soil and water. The organisms are also found in the skin and cavities of humans and other mammals, where they may cause soft-tissue infections. *Eubacterium* is susceptible to penicillin, cliridamycin, and metronidazole.

eubiotics /yoo'bī·ot'iks/ [Gk, *eu,* well, *bios,* life], the science of healthy living.

eucalyptol /yoo'kəlip'tol/, a substance with an aromatic odor obtained from the volatile oil of *Eucalyptus* and used in nasal emollients.

eucholia /yookō'lyə/ [Gk, *eu,* well, *chole,* bile], the normal state of the bile as to the quantity secreted and the condition of the constituents.

euchromatin /yookrō'mətin/ [Gk, *eu + chroma,* color], the part of a chromosome that is active in gene expression. It stains most deeply during mitosis. —**euchromatic,** *adj.*

eugamy /yoo'gəmē/ [Gk, *eu + gamos,* marriage], the union of gametes that contain the same haploid number of chromosomes.—**eugamic,** *adj.*

eugenics /yoojen'iks/ [Gk, *eu + genein,* to produce], the study of methods for controlling the characteristics of future populations through selective breeding.

euglobulin /yooglob'yəlin/ [Gk, *eu;* L, *globulus,* small sphere], that fraction of serum globulin that is insoluble in distilled water but soluble in saline solutions. This is one of a number of different properties used to classify proteins.

euglobulin lysis time test, a blood test used to identify primary and secondary systemic fibrinolysis and to monitor streptokinase or urokinase therapy in patients with acute MI.

eugnathia /yoona'thē·ə/ [Gk, *eu,* well + *gnathos,* jaw], an abnormality of the oral cavity that is limited to the teeth and their immediate alveolar supports and does not include the jaws.

eugnathic anomaly /yoonath'ik/ [Gk, *eu + gnathos,* jaw; *anomalia,* irregularity], an abnormality of the teeth and their alveolar supports.

eukaryocyte /yooker'ē·ōsīt'/ [Gk, *eu + karyon,* nut, *kytos,* cell], a cell that has a true nucleus, found in all organisms except bacteria.

eukaryon /yooker'ē·on/ [Gk, *eu,* good, *karyon,* nut], a cell nucleus that is highly complex and organized and is surrounded by a double membrane.

eukaryosis /yooker'i·ō'sis/ [Gk, *eu + karyon,* nut, *osis,* condition], the state of having a eukaryon.

eukaryote /yooker'ē·ot/ [Gk, *eu + karyon,* nut], an organism whose cells contain a true nucleus. All organisms except bacteria are eukaryotes.—**eucaryotic, eukaryotic,** *adj.*

eukaryotic cell, a cell with a true nucleus.

Eulexin, a trademark for an antiandrogen antineoplastic agent (flutamide).

eunuch /yoo'nək/ [Gk, *eune,* couch, *echein,* to guard], a male whose testicles have been destroyed or removed. If this occurs before puberty, secondary sex characteristics fail to develop.

eunuchism /yoo'nəkiz'əm/, the condition of being a eunuch.

eunuchoidism /yoo'nəkoidiz'əm/, a condition resulting from a deficiency in the production or effectiveness of male hormones. The deficiency leads to sterility, abnormal tallness, small testes, and impaired development of secondary sexual characteristics, libido, and sexual potency.

euphoretic /yoo'faret'ik/ [Gk, *eu + pherein,* to bear], **1.** (of a substance or event) tending to produce a condition of well-being or elation. **2.** a substance tending to produce a feeling of well-being or elation, such as marijuana and hallucinogenic drugs.

euphoria /yoofôr'ē·ə/ [Gk, *eu + pherein,* to bear], **1.** a feeling or state of well-being or elation. **2.** an exaggerated or abnormal sense of physical and emotional well-being not based on reality or truth, disproportionate to its cause, and inappropriate to the situation.

euploid /yoo'ploid/ [Gk, *eu + ploos,* multiple], **1.** an individual, organism, strain, or cell whose chromosome number is an integral multiple of the normal haploid number characteristic of the species. Euploids may be as diploid, triploid, tetraploid, or polyploid. **2.** pertaining to such an individual, organism, strain, or cell. —**euploidy,** *n.*

euploidy /yoo'ploidē/, the state or condition of having a variation in chromosome number that is an exact multiple of the characteristic haploid number.

eupnea /yoop·nē'ə/ [Gk, *eu,* well, *pnein,* to breathe], normal, quiet breathing at a rate of 12 to 20 breaths per minute in adults.

Eurax, a trademark for a scabicide (crotamiton).

europium (Eu) /yoorō'pē·əm/ [Europe], a metallic rare earth element. Its atomic number is 63; its atomic mass is 151.96.

eustachian salpingitis, an inflammation of the eustachian tube.

eustachian tube /yoostā'shən/ [Bartolomeo Eustachio, Italian anatomist, 1524–1574; L, *tubus*], a tube lined with mucous membrane that joins the nasopharynx and the middle ear cavity. It is normally closed but opens during yawning, chewing, and swallowing to allow equalization of the air pressure in the middle ear with atmospheric pressure.

eustress /yōō'stres/, **1.** a positive form of stress. **2.** a balance between selfishness and altruism through which an individual develops the drive and energy to care for others.

euthanasia /yōō'thənā"zhə/ [Gk, *eu,* good; *thanatos,* death], **1.** the deliberate causing of the death of a person who is suffering from an incurable disease or condition. It may be active, such as by administration of a lethal drug, or passive, such as by withholding of treatment. **2.** an easy, quiet, painless death.

euthenics /yōōthen'iks/ [Gk, *eu + tithenai,* to place], the science that deals with improvement of the human species through the control of environmental factors, such as pollution, malnutrition, disease, and drug abuse.

euthymia, 1. a pleasant, relaxed state of tranquility. **2.** stable mood.

euthymic, pertaining to a normal mood in which the range of emotions is neither depressed nor highly elevated.

euthymism /yōōthī'mizəm/ [Gk, *eu + thymos,* thyme flowers], the characteristic of normal mood responses.

euthyroid /yōōthī'roid/ [Gk, *eu,* well, *thyreos,* oblong shield], pertaining to a normal thyroid gland and normal thyroid gland function.

evacuant /ivak'yōō·ənt/ [L, *evacuare,* to empty], any medicine or other agent that causes an organ to discharge its contents, as an emetic or laxative.

evacuate /ivak'yōō·āt/ [L, *evacuare,* to empty], **1.** to discharge or to remove a substance from a cavity, space, organ, or tract of the body. **2.** a substance discharged or removed from the body, such as evacuation of stool.—**evacuation,** *n.*

evacuator /ivak'yōō·ā'tər/, an instrument for emptying a cavity, such as removing a calculus from the urinary bladder.

evagination /ēvaj'inā'shən/, the turning inside out or protrusion of a body part or organ.

evaluating /ival'yōō·ā'ting/ [L, *ex,* away, *valare,* to be strong], in five-step nursing process, a category of nursing behavior in which the extent to which the established goals of care have been met is determined and recorded. To make this judgment, the nurse estimates the degree of success in meeting the goals, evaluates the implementation of nursing measures, investigates the patient's compliance with therapy, and records the patient's response to therapy. The nurse evaluates effects of the measures used, the need for change in

goals of care, the accuracy of the implementation of nursing measures, and the need for change in the patient's environment or in the equipment or procedures used. The impact of the care or treatment on the patient, the patient's family, and the staff is evaluated; the accuracy of tests and measurements is checked; and the patient's and family's understanding of the information given them is evaluated.

Evans blue [Herbert Evans, American anatomist, 1882–1971], a nontoxic blue-green dye used to determine blood and plasma volumes.

evaporated milk /ivap'ərā'tid/, homogenized whole milk from which 50% to 60% of the water content has been evaporated. It is fortified with vitamin D, canned, and sterilized.

evaporation /ivap'ərā'shən/ [L, *ex + vapor,* steam], the change of a substance from a liquid state to a gaseous state. The process of evaporation is hastened by an increase in temperature and a decrease in atmospheric pressure.—**evaporate,** *v.*

evening primrose oil, an oil produced by cold extraction from the ripe seeds of *Oenothera biennis,* the evening primrose, used internally in the treatment of mastalgia, PMS, and atopic eczema.

eventration /ē'vəntrā'shən/, the protrusion of the intestines from the abdomen.

event-related potential (ERP) [L, *evenire,* to happen, *relatus,* carry back, *potentia,* power], a type of brain wave that is associated with a response to a specific stimulus, such as a particular wave pattern observed when a patient hears a clicking sound.

evergreen contract, a health care contract that is automatically renewed for the term of the contract unless it is renegotiated. Not applicable in Canada.

eversion /ivur'zhən/, a turning outward or inside-out, such as a turning of the foot outward at the ankle.

evidence-based dentistry, a systematic practice of dentistry in which the dentist finds, assesses, and implements methods of diagnosis and treatment on the basis of the best available current research, the dentist's clinical expertise, and the needs and preferences of the patient.

evidence-based medicine, the practice of medicine in which the physician finds, assesses, and implements methods of diagnosis and treatment on the basis of the best available current research, the physician's clinical expertise, and the needs and preferences of the patient.

evidence-based nursing, the practice of nursing in which the nurse makes clinical decisions on the basis of the best available current research evidence, his or her own clinical expertise, and the needs and preferences of the patient.

evidence-based pharmacy, the practice of pharmacy in which the pharmacist makes decisions by taking into account the best available current research evidence, his or her own expertise, and the needs and preferences of the patient.

evidence-based practice, the practice of health care in which the practitioner systematically finds, appraises, and uses the most current and valid research findings as the basis for clinical decisions.

evisceration /ivis′ərā′shən/ [L, *ex* + *viscera*, entrails], **1.** the removal of the viscera from the abdominal cavity; disembowelment. **2.** the removal of the contents from an organ or an organ from its cavity. **3.** the protrusion of an internal organ through a wound or surgical incision, especially in the abdominal wall.—**eviscerate,** *v.*

evocation /ev′ōkā′shən/ [L, *evocare,* to call forth], a specific morphogenetic change within a developing embryo that results from the action of a single hormone or other chemical.

evocator /ev′ōkā′tər/ [L, *evocare,* to call forth], a specific chemical substance or hormone that is emitted from the organizer part of the embryonic tissue and acts as a morphogenetic stimulus in the developing embryo.

evoked potential (EP) /ivōkt′/ [L, *evocare,* to call forth, *potentia,* power], an electrical response in the brainstem or cerebral cortex that is elicited by a specific stimulus. The stimulus may affect the visual, auditory, or somatosensory pathway, producing a characteristic brain wave pattern. It may be monitored during surgery to allow the surgeon to prevent damage to the nerves. Evoked potentials are also used to diagnose MS and various disorders of hearing and of sight.

evoked potential (EP) studies, an electrodiagnostic test indicated for patients with suspected sensory deficit who are unable to indicate or unreliable in indicating stimulus recognition. Evoked potential studies are used to evaluate areas of the cortex that receive incoming stimulus from the eyes, ears, and lower/upper extremity sensory nerves; to monitor natural progression or treatment of deteriorating neurologic diseases; and to identify histrionic or malingering patients with sensory deficit complaints.

evoked response audiometry, a method of testing hearing ability at the level of the brainstem and auditory cortex. Evoked response audiometry is useful in diagnosing possible defects in the vestibulocochlear nerve and brainstem auditory pathways.

evolution /ev′əloo′shən/ [L, *evolvere,* to roll forth], **1.** a gradual, orderly, and continuous process of change and development from one condition or state to another. **2.** a change in the genetic composition of a population of organisms over time. **3.** the appearance over long periods of time of new taxonomic groups of organisms from preexisting groups.—**evolutionist,** *n.*

evolution of infarction, the normal healing process after a MI, as demonstrated on successive ECGs.

Ewing's sarcoma /yoo′ingz/ [James Ewing, American pathologist, 1866–1943], a malignant tumor that develops from bone marrow, usually in long bones or the pelvis. It is characterized by pain, swelling, fever, and leukocytosis.

exacerbation /igzas′ərbā′shən/ [L, *exacerbare,* to provoke], an increase in the seriousness of a disease or disorder as marked by greater intensity in the signs or symptoms of the patient being treated.

examination, a critical inspection and investigation, usually following a particular method, performed for diagnostic or investigational purposes.

examination assistance, a nursing intervention from the Nursing Interventions Classification (NIC) defined as providing assistance to the patient and another health care provider during a procedure or exam.

exanthem /ig′zan′thəm/ [Gk, eruption], a rapidly erupting rash that may have specific diagnostic features of an infectious disease. Chickenpox, measles, roseola infantum, and rubella are usually characterized by a particular type of exanthem.—**exanthematous,** *adj.*

exanthematous /ig′zənthem′ətəs/ [Gk, *ex,* out, *anthema,* blossoming], pertaining to an eruptive disease or the skin rash that accompanies it.

excavator /eks′kəvāt′ər/ [L, *ex,* out + *cavus,* hollow], **1.** an instrument for hollowing out something by removing the center or inner part, or for making a hole or cavity such as the removal of caries or granulation tissue. **2.** a scoop, spoon, or gouge for surgical use.

excess /ek′ses/, an amount more than is normal or necessary.

excessive sweat /ikses′iv/ [L, *excedere,* to go out; AS, *swaeaten*], perspiration greater than normal for the ambient environment. It is usually a sign of septic fever, pulmonary TB, hyperthyroidism, chronic renal disease, or malaria. Abnormal sweating of the hands and feet is often a sign of nervous irritability or other emotional stress.

excess mortality /ikses′/ [L, *excedere,* to go out, *mortalis,* mortal], a premature death, or one that occurs before the average life expectancy for a person of a particular demographic category.

Exchange Lists for Meal Planning, a grouping of foods in which the carbohydrates, fats, proteins, and calories are similar for the serving sizes listed. The lists, published by the American Dietetic Association and the American Diabetes Association, are used in meal planning for various diseases as well as for weight reduction. The carbohydrate group is subdivided into lists of starch, fruit, milk, other carbohydrates, and vegetables.

exchange transfusion, the removal of all or most of a patient's diseased blood and its simultaneous replacement with an equal volume of normal blood.

exchange transfusion in the newborn /iks·chāng′/ [L, *ex + cambire,* to change], the introduction of whole blood in exchange for 75% to 85% of an infant's circulating blood that is repeatedly withdrawn in small amounts and replaced with equal amounts of donor blood. The procedure is performed to improve the oxygen-carrying capacity of the blood in the treatment of erythroblastosis fetalis by removing Rh and ABO antibodies, sensitized erythrocytes that produce hemolysis, and accumulated bilirubin.

eximer laser /ek′simər/, one of a class of lasers with output in the ultraviolet range of the electromagnetic spectrum. The name is derived from the symbol formed by the combination of xenon atoms (Xe) and halogen atoms (X) to yield xenon-halide compounds to be XEX eximer. Also spelled *excimer*.

excision /iksish′ən/ [L, *ex + caedere,* to cut], **1.** the process of excising or amputating. **2.** in molecular genetics, the process by which a genetic element is removed from a strand of DNA.—**excise,**v.

excitability /iksī′təbil′itē/ [L, *excitare,* to arouse], the property of a cell that enables it to react to irritation or stimulation.

excitant /eksī′tənt/, a drug or other agent that arouses the CNS or other body system in a particular manner.

excitation /ek′sitā′shən/ [L, *excitare,* to arouse], nerve or muscle action as a result of impulse propagation; a state of mental or physical excitement.

excitatory amino acids /eksī′tətôr′ē/, one of a group of amino acids that affects the CNS by acting as neurotransmitters and, in some cases, as neurotoxins. Examples include glutamate and aspartate.

excitatory impulse, a sudden force that stimulates activity.

excited state /eksī′tid/ [L, *excitare,* to rouse, *status*], in chemistry and physics,

an energy level of a system that is higher than the ground state. The system decays to the ground state and emits the energy difference, usually in the form of photons.

excitement /eksīt′mənt/, in psychiatry, a pathologic state marked by emotional intensity, impulsive behavior, anticipation, and arousal. Excitement in schizophrenic inpatients tends to result from blocked communications and hostile feelings between the patients and the hospital staff.

exciting eye, in sympathetic ophthalmia, the eye that sustains a penetrating injury and causes an inflammatory reaction in the fellow eye.

exclusion from base price, a health care contract provision in which high-cost variable items beyond the control of the provider, such as organ procurement costs, are excluded from the base price. Not applicable in Canada.

Exclusive Provider Organization (EPO), a type of managed health care organization in which no coverage is typically provided for services received outside the EPO.

excoriation /ekskôr′ē·ā′shən/ [L, *excoriare,* to flay], an injury to a surface of the body caused by trauma, such as scratching, abrasion, or a chemical or thermal burn.

excrement /eks′krəment/, any waste matter, particularly feces, discharged from the body.

excreta /ekskrē′tə/ [L, *excernere,* to separate], any waste matter discharged from the body.

excrete /ekskrēt′/ [L, *excernere,* to separate], to evacuate a waste substance from the body, often via a normal secretion, for example, a drug that may be excreted in breast milk.

excretion /ekskrē′shən/, the process of eliminating, shedding, or getting rid of substances by body organs or tissues, as part of a natural metabolic activity. Excretion usually begins at the cellular level.

excretory /eks′krətôr′ē/ [L, *excernere,* to separate], relating to the process of excretion, often used in combination with a term to identify an object or procedure associated with excretion.

excretory duct, a duct that is conductive but not secretory.

excretory organ, an organ that is concerned primarily with the production and discharge of body wastes.

excretory urography [L, *excernere,* to separate; Gk, *ouron,* urine, *graphein,* to record], the radiographic examination of the urinary tract. It is accomplished with the use of contrast medium that is injected into the blood, filtered by the kidneys, and passed through the tract.

E

excursion /ikskur′zhən/ [L, *ex*, out, *currere*, to run], a departure or deviation from a direct or normal course.

execute /ek′səkyo͞ot/, of a computer, to follow a set of instructions to complete a program or specified function.

executive physical /iksek′yətiv/, a physical examination that includes extensive laboratory, radiographic, and other tests that may be provided periodically to management level personnel at employer expense.

exemestane, an antineoplastic used to treat advanced breast cancer in postmenopausal patients whose cancer is unresponsive to other therapies.

exenatide, an antidiabetic drug given in combination with metformin or a sulfonylurea to treat type 2 DM.

exencephaly /ek′sənsef′əlē/ [L, *ex*, out; Gk, *enkephalos*, brain], a developmental anomaly characterized by lack of all or part of the skull, so that the brain is exposed.

exenteration /eksen′tera′shun/, **1.** surgical removal of the inner organs; evisceration. **2.** in ophthalmology, removal of the entire contents of the orbit.

exercise /ek′sərsiz/ [L, *exercere*, to exercise], **1.** the performance of any physical activity for the purpose of conditioning the body, improving health, or maintaining fitness or as a means of therapy for correcting a deformity or restoring the organs and body functions to a state of health. **2.** any action, skill, or maneuver that causes muscle exertion and is performed repeatedly to develop or strengthen the body or any of its parts. **3.** to use a muscle or part of the body in a repetitive way to maintain or develop its strength.

exercise amenorrhea, a suppression of ovulation and thus menstruation that affects some women who participate in high-intensity athletics.

exercise electrocardiogram (ECG), a record of the electrical activity of the heart taken during graded increases in the rate of exercise. It is important in the diagnosis of coronary artery disease. Abnormal changes in cardiac function that are absent during rest may occur with exercise.

exercise-induced anaphylaxis, a severe allergic reaction brought on by strenuous exercise.

exercise-induced asthma /-indyo͞ost′/, a form of asthma that produces symptoms after strenuous exercise. The effect may be acute but is reversible.

exercise prescription [L, *exercere* + *prae* + *scribere*, to write], an individualized schedule for physical fitness exercises.

exercise promotion, a nursing intervention from the Nursing Interventions Classification (NIC) defined as the facilitation of regular physical activity to maintain or advance to a higher level of fitness and health.

exercise promotion: strength training, a nursing intervention from the Nursing Interventions Classification (NIC) defined as facilitation of regular resistive muscle training to maintain or increase muscle strength.

exercise promotion: stretching, a nursing intervention from the Nursing Interventions Classification (NIC) defined as facilitation of systematic slow-stretchhold muscle exercises to induce relaxation, to prepare muscles/joints for more vigorous exercise, or to increase or maintain body flexibility.

exercise therapy: ambulation, a nursing intervention from the Nursing Interventions Classification (NIC) defined as promotion and assistance with walking to maintain or restore autonomic and voluntary body functions during treatment and recovery from illness or injury.

exercise therapy: balance, a nursing intervention from the Nursing Interventions Classification (NIC) defined as the use of specific activities, postures, and movements to maintain, enhance, or restore balance.

exercise therapy: joint mobility, a nursing intervention from the Nursing Interventions Classification (NIC) defined as use of active or passive body movement to maintain or restore joint flexibility.

exercise therapy: muscle control, a nursing intervention from the Nursing Interventions Classification (NIC) defined as use of specific activity or exercise protocols to enhance or restore controlled body movement.

exercise tolerance, the level of physical exertion an individual may be able to achieve before reaching a state of exhaustion. Exercise tolerance tests are commonly performed on a treadmill under the supervision of a health professional who can stop the test if signs of distress are observed.

exeresis /ekser′əsis/ [Gk, *ex* + *eresis*, removal], the surgical removal of a part, organ, or body structure.

exertional headache /igzur′shənəl/ [L, *exserere*, to stretch out; AS, *heafod* + *acan*, headache], an acute headache that occurs during strenuous exercise. It usually recedes when the level of effort is reduced, when an analgesic medication is taken, or both.

exfoliation /eksfō′lē·ā′shən/ [L, *ex* + *folium*, leaf], peeling and sloughing off of tissue cells. This is a normal process that may be exaggerated in certain skin diseases or after a severe sunburn or may be done deliberately, such as with **microdermabrasion.**—**exfoliative,** *adj.*

exfoliative cytology /eksfō′lē·ətiv/, the microscopic examination of desquamated cells for diagnostic purposes. The cells are obtained from lesions, sputum, secretions, urine, and other material by aspiration, scraping, a smear, or washings of the tissue.

exfoliative dermatitis, any inflammatory skin disorder characterized by excessive peeling or shedding of skin.

exhaustion /igzôs′chən/ [L, *exhaurire,* to drain away], a state of extreme loss of physical or mental abilities caused by fatigue or illness.

exhaustion delirium, a delirium that may result from prolonged physical or emotional stress, fatigue, or shock associated with severe metabolic or nutritional problems.

exhaustion psychosis [L, *exhaurire,* to drain out; Gk, *psyche,* mind, *osis,* condition], an abnormal mental condition attributed to physical exhaustion. The main symptom, a delirious state, may develop in some explorers, mountain climbers, persons lost in the wilderness, and terminally ill patients.

exhibitionism /ek′sibish′əniz′əm/ [L, *exhibere,* to exhibit], **1.** the flaunting of oneself or one's abilities to attract attention. **2.** in psychiatry, a psychosexual disorder that occurs primarily in men in which the repetitive act of exposing the genitals in socially unacceptable situations is the preferred means of achieving sexual excitement and gratification.—**exhibitionist,** *n.*

eximer laser /ek′simir/, a small laser designed to break up organic molecules, such as cholesterol deposits, without producing intense heat excimer. Also spelled *excimer.*

existential psychiatry /eg′zisten′shəl/ [L, *existere,* to spring forth; Gk, *psyche,* mind, *iatreia,* medical care], a school of psychiatry based on the philosophy of existentialism that emphasizes an analytic, holistic approach in which mental disorders are viewed as deviations within the total structure of an individual's existence rather than as results of any biologically or culturally related factors.

existential therapy, a kind of psychotherapy that emphasizes the development of a sense of self-direction through choice, awareness, and acceptance of individual responsibility.

exit block [L, *exire,* to depart; Fr, *bloc*], the failure of an expected impulse to emerge from its focus of origin and cause depolarization of cardiac muscle.

exit dose, the amount of radiation at the surface of the body opposite that to which the radiation is directed.

Exjade, a trademark for deferasirox.

exocrine /ek′səkrin/ [Gk, *exo,* outside, *krinein,* to secrete], pertaining to the process of secreting outwardly through a duct to the surface of an organ or tissue or into a vessel.

exocrine gland, a gland that discharges its secretions through ducts opening on internal or external surfaces of the body.

exocytosis /ek′sōsītō′sis/ [Gk, *exos,* outside, *kytos,* a hollow vessel], discharge from a cell of particles that are too large to diffuse through the wall.

exoenzyme /ek′sō·en′zīm/, an enzyme that does not function within the cells from which it is secreted.

exogenous /igzoj′ənəs/ [Gk, *exo* + *genein,* to produce], **1.** outside the body. **2.** originating outside the body or an organ of the body or produced from external causes, such as a disease caused by a bacterial or viral agent foreign to the body.—**exogenic,** *adj.*

exogenous infection [Gk, *exo,* outside, *genein,* to produce; L, *inficere,* to infect], an infection that develops from bacteria normally outside the body that have gained access to the body.

exogenous obesity, obesity caused by a caloric intake greater than needed to meet the metabolic needs of the body.

exogenous uric acid [Gk, *exo,* outside, *genein,* to produce, *ouron,* urine; L, *acidus*], the accumulation of uric acid in the body produced by the metabolism of purine-rich foods.

exon /ek′son/ [Gk, *exo* + *genein,* to produce], the part of a DNA molecule that contains the code for the final messenger RNA.

exonuclease /ek′sōnoo′klē·ās/ [Gk, *exo;* L, *nucleus,* nut; *ase,* enzyme], an enzyme that digests DNA or RNA from the ends of the strands.

Exophiala /ek′sofī′ə·lə/, a widespread genus of saprobic Fungi Imperfecti. *E. jeanselmei* is commonly found in soil and sewage and causes mycetoma and opportunistic infections in humans. *Hortae werneckii* (formerly classified as *E. werneckii*) is the cause of tinea nigra. Because it is so variable, some authorities have proposed dividing it into more than one species.

exophoria /ek′səfôr′ē·ə/ [Gk, *exo* + *pherein,* to bear], the latent lateral deviation of the visual axis of one eye outward. It occurs in the absence of visual stimuli for fusion.—**exophoric,** *adj.*

exophthalmia /ek′softhal′mē·ə/ [Gk, *exo* + *ophthalmos,* eye], an abnormal condition characterized by a marked protrusion of the eyeballs, usually resulting from the increased volume of the orbital contents caused by a tumor; swelling associated with cerebral, intraocular, or intraorbital edema or hemorrhage; paralysis of or trauma to the extraocular muscles; or cavernous sinus thrombosis. It may also be caused by endocrine disorders such as hyperthyroidism and Graves' disease, varicose veins within the orbit, or injury to orbital bones. Visual acuity may be impaired in exophthalmia; keratitis, ulceration, infection, and blindness may also occur. —**exophthalmic,** *adj.*

exophthalmic goiter /ek′softhal′mik/, exophthalmos that occurs in association with goiter, as in Graves' disease.

exophthalmometer /ek′softhalmom′ətər/ [Gk, *exo* + *ophthalmos,* eye, *metron,* measure], an instrument used for measuring the degree of forward displacement of the eye in exophthalmos.

exophytic /ek′səfit′ik/ [Gk, *exo* + *phyton,* plant], pertaining to the tendency to grow outward, such as a tumor that grows into the lumen of a hollow organ rather than into the wall.

exophytic carcinoma, a malignant epithelial neoplasm that resembles a papilloma or wart.

exoskeletal prosthesis /ek′səskel′ətəl/ [Gk, *exo* + *skeletos,* dried up, *prosthesis,* addition], a prosthetic device in which support is provided by an outside structure (not an implant), such as an artificial limb.

exoskeleton /ek′səskel′ətən/ [Gk, *exo,* outside, *skeletos,* dried up], the hard outer covering of many invertebrates, such as crustaceans, which lack the bony internal skeleton of vertebrates.

exostosis /ek′sostō′sis/ [Gk, *exo* + *osteon,* bone], an abnormal benign growth on the surface of a bone.—**exostosed, exostotic,** *adj.*

exostosis cartilaginea [Gk, *ex,* out, *osteon,* bone; L, *cartilago,* cartilage], an outgrowth of cartilage at the ends of long bones.

exoteric /ek′sətər′ik/ [Gk, *exoterikos,* external], lying outside an organism.

exothermic, indicating a chemical process accompanied by the release of heat, such as the loss of body surface heat.

exotoxin /ek′sətok′sin/ [Gk, *exo* + *toxikon,* poison], a toxin that is secreted or excreted by a living microorganism.

exotropia /eksotrō′fēə/, a deviation of the lines of sight between the two eyes in which the nonfixating eye is pointed outward. The eye has defective vision.

expanded function dental assistant, a dental assistant with training beyond basic dental assisting, who has passed a competency examination, and who has state-granted permission to perform certain dental procedures other than the removal, altering, or shaping of human tissue. Examples of some expanded functions are placement of post-extraction and sedative dressings; placing periodontal dressings; sizing stainless steel crowns; placing and condensing amalgam for Class I, V, and VI restorations; carving amalgam; placing composite for Class I, V, and VI restorations; polishing the coronal surfaces of teeth; minor palliative care of dental emergencies (placing sedative filling); preliminary bending of archwire; removal of orthodontic bands and bonds; final cementation of any permanent appliance or prosthesis; minor palliative care of orthodontic emergencies (bend/clip wire, remove broken appliance); making impressions for the fabrication of removable prosthesis; placement of temporary soft liners in a removable prosthesis; place retraction cord in preparation for fixed prosthodontic impressions; making impressions for the fabrication of fixed prosthesis; extra-oral adjustment of fixed prosthesis; extra-oral adjustment of removable prosthesis during and after insertion; and placement and cementation of orthodontic brackets and/or bands.

expanded role [L, *expandere,* to spread out; OFr, *rolle,* an assumed character], the functions of a nurse that are not specified in the traditional limits of nursing practice legislation. Common roles are primary nurse and nurse practitioner.

expansion /ekspan′shən/ [L, *expandere,* to spread out], **1.** the process or state of being increased in extent, surface, or bulk. **2.** a region or area of increased bulk or surface.

expectant treatment /ekspek′tənt/ [L, *exspectare,* to wait for; Fr, *traitment*], application of therapeutic measures to relieve symptoms as they arise in the course of a disease, rather than treatment of the cause of illness.

expectation /eks′pektā′shən/ [L, *exspectare,* to wait for], **1.** in nursing, anticipation by the staff of a patient's behavior that is based on a knowledge and understanding of the person's abilities and problems. **2.** anticipation of the performance of the nursing staff in defined roles, as role expectation.

expected date of delivery (EDD), the predicted date of a pregnant woman's delivery. Pregnancy lasts approximately 266 days, or 38 weeks from the day of fertilization, but is considered clinically to last 280 days, or 40 weeks, or 10 lunar months, or $9^{1}/_{3}$ calendar months from the first day of the last menstrual period (LMP).

expectorant /ikspek′tərənt/ [Gk, *ex,* out, *pectus,* breast], **1.** pertaining to a substance that promotes the ejection of mucus or other exudates from the lung, bronchi, and trachea. **2.** an agent that promotes expectoration by reducing the viscosity of pulmonary secretions or by decreasing the tenacity with which exudates adhere to the lower respiratory tract. Expectorant drugs include acetylcysteine, guaifenesin, and terpin hydrate.—**expectorate,** *v.*

expectoration /ikspek'tərā'shən/, the ejection of mucus, sputum, or fluids from the trachea and lungs by coughing or spitting.

experience rating /ikspir'ē·əns/ [L, *experientia,* testing, *rata,* proportion], a system used by insurance companies in the United States to set the premium to be paid by the insured on the basis of the risk to the company of providing the insurance.

experiment, an investigation in which one or more variables may be altered under controlled circumstances to study the effects of altering variables.

experimental design /eksper'imen'təl/ [L, *experimentum + designare,* to mark out], in research, a study design used to test cause-and-effect relationships between variables. The classic experimental design specifies an experimental group and a control group. The independent variable is administered to the experimental group and not to the control group, and both groups are measured on the same dependent variable. True experiments must have control, randomization, and manipulation.

experimental embryology, the study and analysis through experimental techniques of the factors, mechanisms, and relationships that determine and influence prenatal development.

experimental epidemiology, a type of epidemiologic investigation that uses an experimental model for studies to confirm a causal relationship suggested by observational studies.

experimental group, a set of items or people under study to determine the effect of an event, a substance, or a technique.

experimental medicine, a branch of the practice of medicine in which new drugs or treatments are evaluated for safety and efficacy in a clinical laboratory setting by using animals or, in certain cases, human subjects.

experimental pathology, the study of diseases deliberately induced in laboratory animals.

experimental physiology, a branch of the study of physiology in which the functions of various body systems are evaluated in a clinical laboratory setting by using animals or, in some cases, human subjects.

experimental psychology, the study of mental processes and phenomena by observation in a controlled environment using various tests, manipulations, and experiments.

expertise /eks'pərtēz'/ [L, *experiri,* to try], special skills or knowledge acquired by a person through education, training, or experience.

expert witness /ikspurt', ek'spərt/ [L, *experiri,* to try; AS, *witnes,* knowledge], a person who has special knowledge of a subject about which a court requests testimony.

expiration /ik'spirā'shən/ [L, *expirare,* to breathe out], **1.** breathing out, normally a passive process, depending on the elastic qualities of lung tissue and the thorax. **2.** termination or death.—**expiratory,** *adj.*

expiratory center /ik'spirə, *expirare,* to breathe out; Gk, *kentron,* center], one of several regions of the medulla, responsible for control of respiration. It is a subregion specifically involved in carrying out the activity of expiration.

expiratory phase, the part of the respiratory cycle that involves exhalation, or moving air out of the lungs. In a ventilated patient, the expiratory phase may be passive.

expiratory reserve volume (ERV), the maximum volume of gas that can be exhaled after a resting volume exhalation.

expiratory retard, in respiratory care, a mode of mechanical ventilation that mimics the prolonged expiratory phase and pursed-lip breathing of emphysema. The method adds some resistance to expiration.

expire /ikspī'ər/ [L, *expirare,* to breathe out], **1.** to breathe out. **2.** to die.

expired gas (E), any gas exhaled from the lungs.

explantation /ex-plan-ta'shun/, the removal of an implant.

exploratory /iksplôr'ətôr'ē/ [L, *explorare,* to search out], pertaining to investigation, as in exploratory surgery.

exploratory operation [L, *explorare,* to search out, *operari,* to work], surgical intervention to find the cause of a disorder by opening a body cavity or organ and examining the interior.

explosion, 1. a sudden and violent decomposition of a chemical compound. **2.** a sudden radical breakout.

explosive personality /iksplō'siv/ [L, *ex,* out, *plaudere,* to clap], behavior characterized by episodes of uncontrolled rage and physical abusiveness in reaction to relatively minor stressors.

explosive speech, abnormal speech characterized by slow, jerky articulation interspersed with sudden loud enunciation of words, often seen in brain disorders. The term is less often used by speech-language pathologists.

exponent /ikspō'nənt/, a superscript on a number that indicates how many times a

E

number is to be multiplied by itself (for example, $3^4 = 3 \times 3 \times 3 \times 3 = 81$). In medical or scientific reports powers of 10 are commonly used to indicate very large or very small numbers, such as in the examples 10^6 representing 1,000,000 and 10^{-6} representing $^1/_{1,000,000}$. Exponents also are indicated by prefixes such as mega- for 10^6 and micro- for 10^{-6}.

exposed pulp [L, *exponere,* to lay out, *pulpa,* flesh], dental pulp that becomes exposed to the oral environment and potential bacterial infection. Causes include fracture of the crown through trauma and loss of a tooth crown or penetration of the dentin during restorative preparation or caries excavation.

exposure /ikspō'zhər/ [L, *exponere,* to lay out], **1.** a measure of the ionization of air produced by a beam of radiation. It is expressed as coulombs per kilogram of air. **2.** a state of being in the presence of or subjected to a force or influence (e.g., viral exposure, heat exposure).

exposure angle, the angle of the arc described by the movement of a radiographic tube and film during a tomographic exposure. The exposure angle influences the thickness of the tomographic section: smaller angles produce thicker sections.

exposure switch, in radiology, a control device designed to interrupt the power automatically when pressure by the operator's hand or foot is released. The purpose is to prevent accidental continuing exposure of the patient to radiation.

exposure unit, any of the conventional or SI units used to measure radiation exposure: roentgen (R), rad, rem, curie, gray, sievert, and becquerel (Bq).

expression /ikspresh'ən/ [L, *exprimere,* to express], **1.** the indication of a physical or emotional state through facial appearance or vocal intonation. **2.** the act of pressing or squeezing to expel something, such as milk from the breast when lactating or the fetus from the uterus by exertion of pressure on the abdominal wall. **3.** in genetics, the detectable effect or appearance in the phenotype of a particular trait or condition.—**express,** *v.*

expressive language disorder, a communication disorder characterized by problems with expression of language, either oral or signed. It includes difficulties such as limited speech or vocabulary, vocabulary errors, difficulty or hesitation in word selection, oversimplification of grammatical or sentence structure, omission of parts of sentences, unusual word order, and slowed acquisition of language skills.

expressivity /eks'presiv'itē/ [L, *exprimere,* to make clear], the variability with

which basic patterns of inheritance are modified, both in degree and in variety, by the effect of a given gene in people of the same genotype.

expulsive stage of labor /ikspul'siv/ [L, *expellere,* to drive out, *stare,* stand, *labor,* work], the second stage of labor, during which the mother's uterine contractions are accompanied by a bearing-down reflex. It begins after full dilation of the cervix and continues to the complete birth of the infant.

exsanguinate /eksang'gwināt/ [L, + *sanguis,* blood], to drain away or deprive an organ of blood.

exsanguination /eksang'gwinā'shən/, a massive loss of blood.

exstrophy /ek'strōfē/ [Gk, *ekstrephein,* to turn inside-out], a congenital malformation in which a hollow organ has its wall turned inside-out, establishing a communication with the exterior.

exstrophy-epispadias complex, a group of congenital defects of the anterior abdominal wall, including exstrophy of the bladder, exstrophy of cloaca, and epispadias, under the theory that they are all expressions of the same developmental anomaly.

exstrophy of the bladder, a developmental anomaly marked by absence of part of the lower abdominal wall and the anterior wall of the urinary bladder, with eversion of the posterior wall of the bladder through the defect, as well as an open pubic arch and widely separated ischia connected by a fibrous band.

extended care facility (ECF) [L, *extendere,* to stretch], an institution devoted to providing medical, nursing, or custodial care for an individual over a prolonged period, such as during the course of a chronic disease or the rehabilitation phase after an acute illness.

extended family, a family group consisting of the biologic or adoptive parents, their children, the grandparents, and other family members. The extended family is the basic family group in many societies.

extended insulin-zinc suspension, a long-acting insulin that is slowly absorbed and slow to act.

extended-wear contact lens, a refractive index device that fits over the cornea, designed to permit air permeation. Oxygen may pass between the lens and the cornea, thereby reducing the risk of corneal irritation.

extender, something that causes an increase in time or size, such as a substance added to a medication to stretch the time required for the drug to be absorbed.

Extendryl, a trademark for a fixed-combination nasal decongestant drug containing an adrenergic (phenylephrine hydrochloride), an antihistaminic (chlorpheniramine maleate), and an anticholinergic (methscopolamine nitrate).

extension /iksten'shən/ [L, *extendere,* to stretch], a "straightening" movement allowed by certain joints of the skeleton that increases the angle between two adjoining bones, such as extending the leg, which increases the posterior angle between the femur and the tibia.

extensor /iksten'sər/ [L, *extendere,* to stretch out], any muscle that extends a body part.

extensor carpi radialis brevis [L, *extendere*; Gk, *karpos,* wrist; L, *radius,* ray, *brevis,* short], one of the muscles of the posterior forearm. It functions to extend the hand and forearm.

extensor carpi radialis longus, one of the seven superficial muscles of the posterior forearm. It serves to extend the hand and flex the forearm.

extensor carpi ulnaris, one of the muscles of the lateral forearm. It functions to extend and adduct the hand.

extensor digiti minimi, an extensor muscle of the posterior forearm. It functions to extend the little finger and hand.

extensor digitorum, a muscle of the posterior forearm. It divides distally into four tendons that pass under the extensor retinaculum and diverge on the back of the hand. It functions to extend the phalanges and, by continued action, the wrist.

extensor digitorum brevis, a muscle that flexes the three middle toes and the proximal metatarsophalangeal joint of the great toe.

extensor digitorum longus, a penniform muscle located at the lateral part of the anterior leg. It extends the proximal phalanges of the four small toes and dorsiflexes the foot.

extensor hallucis longus, a muscle that extends the great toe and dorsiflexes the foot at the ankle joint.

extensor lag, the amount of drooping at a weakened joint that can extend only passively, no longer actively.

extensor pollicis brevis, a muscle that extends the metacarpophalangeal and carpometacarpal joints of the thumb.

extensor pollicis longus, a muscle that extends all the joints of the thumb.

extensor retinaculum of the ankle, either of two thick layers of fascia holding dorsiflexor tendons in place in the ankle.

extensor retinaculum of the hand, the thick band of antebrachial fascia that wraps tendons of the extensor muscles of the forearm at the distal ends of the radius and the ulna.

extensor thrust, a spinal-level reflex present in a human in the first 2 months of life. It is an exaggeration of the positive support reflex and consists of an uncontrolled extension of a flexed leg when the sole of the foot is stimulated.

extern /eks'turn/ [L, *externus,* outward], a medical or dental student who lives outside the institution but provides medical or dental care to patients as an extracurricular activity under the professional supervision of hospital staff members. Compare **intern.**

external /ikstur'nəl/ [L, *externus,* outward], **1.** being on the outside or exterior of the body or an organ. **2.** acting from the outside, such as an external influence or exogenous factor. **3.** pertaining to the outward or visible appearance.

external abdominal oblique muscle, one of a pair of muscles that are the largest and the most superficial of the five anterolateral muscles of the abdomen. It is a broad, thin four-sided muscle that acts to compress the contents of the abdomen and assists in micturition, defecation, emesis, parturition, and forced expiration. Both sides acting together serve to flex the vertebral column, drawing the pubis toward the xiphoid process. One side alone functions to bend the vertebral column laterally and to rotate it, drawing the shoulder of the same side forward.

external absorption, the taking up of substances through the mucous membranes or the skin.

external acoustic meatus, the canal of the external ear, composed of bone and cartilage, extending from the auricle to the tympanic membrane.

external aperture of aqueduct of vestibule, an external opening for the small canal extending from the vestibule of the inner ear, located on the internal surface of the petrous part of the temporal bone lateral to the opening for the internal acoustic passage.

external aperture of canaliculus of cochlea, an external opening of the cochlear channel on the margin of the jugular opening in the temporal bone.

external aperture of tympanic canaliculus, the lower opening of the tympanic channel on the inferior surface of the petrous part of the temporal bone.

external beam radiotherapy, treatment by radiation emitted from a source located at a distance from the body.

external carotid artery, one of a pair of arteries with eight major temporal or maxillary branches, rising from the common carotid arteries. It supplies various parts and tissues of the head and neck.

external carotid plexus, a network of nerves around the external carotid artery, formed by the external carotid nerves from

E

the superior cervical ganglion. It supplies sympathetic fibers associated with branches of the external carotid artery.

external cervical os, an external opening of the uterus that leads into the cavity of the cervix.

external conjugate, the distance measured with obstetric calipers from the depression below the lowest lumbar vertebra posteriorly to the upper border of the symphysis anteriorly (usually about 21 cm).

external counterpulsation, a noninvasive technique for providing counterpulsation (assisted heart pumping). In one technique the limbs are placed in inflatable trousers. Inflation and deflation are synchronized with the cardiac cycle, generating augmented blood flow during diastole and assisted ejection during systole.

external ear, the outer structure of the ear, consisting of the auricle and the external acoustic meatus.

external fertilization, the union of male and female gametes outside the bodies from which they originated, such as occurs in frogs and most fish.

external fistula, an abnormal passage between an internal organ or structure and the cutaneous surface of the body.

external fixation, a method of holding together the fragments of a fractured bone by using transfixing metal pins through the fragments and a compression device attached to the pins outside the skin surface.

external iliac artery, the larger, more superficial division of the common iliac artery, which descends into the thigh and becomes the femoral artery. The external iliac supplies the lower limb.

external iliac node, a node in one of the seven groups of parietal nodes serving the lymphatic system in the abdomen and the pelvis.

external iliac vein, one of a pair of veins in the lower body that join the internal iliac vein to form the two common iliac veins.

external jugular vein, the more superficial and lateral of a pair of large vessels on each side of the neck that receive most of the blood from the exterior of the cranium and the deep tissues of the face.

external malleolus /male'ōlas/ [L, *externus,* outward, *malleolus,* little hammer], a rounded bony prominence on either side of the ankle joint.

external occipital crest, a ridge extending downward from the external occipital protuberance.

external occipital protuberance, a midline projection of the occipital bone with curved lines extending laterally from it.

external pacemaker [L, *externus,* outward, *passus,* step; ME, *maken,* to make], **1.** a device used to stimulate the heartbeat electrically by means of impulses conducted through the chest wall, as used in emergency care of significant bradyarrhythmias. **2.** a similar device in which the impulse generator is outside the chest but is connected with the heart by wires that pass under the skin. The wires are placed during open-heart surgery and are removed after surgery, when the risk of bradycardia has diminished.

external pin fixation, a method of holding together the fragments of a fractured bone by means of pins that are attached to the bone and that protrude from the skin.

external pterygoid muscle, one of the four short, thick, somewhat conical muscles of mastication that function to open the jaws, protrude the mandible, and move the mandible from side to side.

external radiation therapy (ERT), the therapeutic application of ionizing radiation from an external beam of a kilovoltage radiographic machine; a megavoltage cobalt 60 machine; or a supervoltage linear accelerator, cyclotron, or betatron.

external respiration, the part of the respiratory process that involves the exchange of gases in the alveoli of the lungs.

external rotation, turning outwardly or away from the midline of the body, such as when a leg is externally rotated with the toes turned outward or away from the body's midline.

external shunt, a device for the passage of body fluid from one compartment to another. It consists of a tube or catheter (or a series of such containers) that passes from one compartment or cavity to another over the body surface rather than inside the body.

external sphincter of female urethra, a sphincter that compresses the central part of the urethra. It originates in the ramus of the pubis and is innervated by the perineal nerves.

external sphincter of male urethra, a sphincter that compresses the membranous part of the urethra. It originates in the ramus of the pubis and is innervated by the perineal nerves.

external ventricular drain, a ventricular catheter connected to a drainage system and a closed collection bag. It allows the clinician to control fluid flow and, to some extent, pressure in the cranial vault.

external version, an obstetric procedure in which a fetus is turned, usually from a breech to a vertex presentation, by external manipulation through the abdominal wall.

exteroceptive /ek'starōsep'tiv/ [L, *externus,* outside, *recipere,* to receive], pertaining to stimuli that originate from outside the body or to the sensory receptors that they activate.

exteroceptor /ek´stərōsep´tər/ [L, *externus*, outside, *recipere*, to receive], any sensory nerve ending that responds to stimuli originating outside the body, such as touch, pressure, or sound.

extinction /iksting´shən/, a state of being lost or destroyed.

extirpation /ek´stərpā´shən/ [L, *extirpare*, to root out], the total removal of a diseased organ or body part.

extraarticular /ek´strə-ärtik´yələr/ [L, *extra*, outside, *articulare*, to divide into joints], pertaining to the area outside a joint or within the joint.

extra beat [L, *extra*, outside; AS, *beatan*], an extra heart contraction. It is indicated by a premature atrial, junctional, or ventricular complex on an ECG.

extracapsular /-kaps´yələr/ [L, *extra*, outside, *capsula*, little box], pertaining to something outside a capsule.

extracapsular dendrite [L, *extra* + *capsula*; Gk, *dendron*, tree], pertaining to dendrites of some autonomic nerves that penetrate the capsule boundary and extend some distance from the cell body.

extracapsular fracture [L, *extra* + *capsula*, little box], any fracture that occurs near a joint but does not directly involve the joint capsule. This type of fracture is extremely common in the hip.

extracellular /-sel´yələr/ [L, *extra* + *cella*, storeroom], occurring outside a cell or cell tissue or in cavities or spaces between cell layers or groups of cells.

extracellular fluid (ECF), the part of the body fluid comprising the interstitial fluid and blood plasma. The adult body contains about 11.2 L of interstitial fluid, constituting about 16% of body weight, and about 2.8 L of plasma, constituting about 4% of body weight.

extracellular matrix, a substance containing collagen, elastin, proteoglycans, glycosaminoglycans, and fluid, produced by cells and in which the cells are embedded.

extrachromosomal /-krō´məsō´məl/, occurring without direct involvement of the chromosomes.

extracoronal /eks´trəkor´ənəl/ [L, *extra* + *corona*, crown], outside the crown of a tooth.

extracoronal retainer /-kôr´ənəl/ [L, *extra* + *corona*, crown, *retinere*, to hold], **1.** a dental anchor that incorporates a cast restoration lying largely external to the coronal portion of a tooth and complements the contour of the tooth crown. **2.** a direct clasp-type retainer that engages an abutment tooth on its external surface, used to retain and stabilize a

removable partial denture. **3.** a manufactured direct retainer, the protruding portion of which is attached to the external surface of a cast crown on an abutment tooth.

extracorporeal /ek´strakôr´pôr´ē-əl/ [L, *extra* + *corpus*, body], something that is outside the body such as extracorporeal circulation in which venous blood is diverted outside the body to a heart-lung machine and returned to the body through a femoral or other artery.

extracorporeal membrane oxygenator (ECMO), a device that oxygenates a patient's blood outside the body and returns the blood to the patient's circulatory system. The technique may be used to support an impaired respiratory system.

extracorporeal oxygenation, the use of an artificial membrane outside the body to provide for oxygenation of the blood in a patient with severe lung disease.

extracorporeal photochemotherapy, a procedure for treating pemphigus vulgaris by treating the patient's blood outside the body. Certain drugs are first administered to the patient. Some of the patient's blood is then removed temporarily for exposure to ultraviolet light outside the body. The blood, after treatment, is returned to the patient.

extracorporeal shock-wave lithotripsy (ESWL) [L, *extra*, outside, *corpus*, body; Fr, *choc*; AS, *wafian*; Gk, *lithos*, stone, *tribein*, to wear away], use of vibrations of powerful sound waves to break up calculi in the urinary tract or gallbladder.

extracranial /-krā´nē-əl/ [L, *extra*, outside; Gk, *kranion*, skull], pertaining to something outside or unconnected with the skull.

extract [L, *ex*, out, *trahere*, to draw], **1.** a substance, usually a biologically active ingredient of a plant or animal tissue, prepared by the use of solvents or evaporation to separate the substance from the original material. **2.** a concentrated form of an herb that is derived when the crude herb is mixed with water, alcohol, or another solvent and distilled or evaporated. Extracts may be either fluid or solid. **3.** to remove a tooth from the oral cavity by means of elevators or forceps or both.—**extraction,** *n.*

extractor /ikstrak´tər/, a medical instrument, such as a forceps, used to remove a foreign body, tissue sample, or medical device placed in a body cavity.

extradural /ek´trədōōr´əl/ [L, *extra* + *dura*, hard], outside the dura mater.

extradural anesthesia, anesthetic nerve block achieved by the injection of a local anesthetic solution into the space in the spinal canal outside the dura mater of the spinal cord.

extradural space, the space between the cranial cavity and the outer layer of dura mater.

extraembryonic blastoderm /-em′brē·on′ik/ [L, *extra*; Gk, *en,* in, *bryein,* to grow], the area of the blastoderm outside the embryo that gives rise to the membranes that surround the embryo during gestation.

extraembryonic coelom, a cavity external to the developing embryo that forms between the mesoderm of the chorion and that covers the amniotic cavity and yolk sac.

extraembryonic mesoderm [L, *extra,* outside; Gk, *en + bryein,* to grow, *mesos,* middle, *derma,* skin], any mesoderm in the uterus that is not involved with the embryo itself. Included are mesoderms in the amnion, chorion, yolk sac, and connecting stalk.

extrahepatic cholestasis, cholestasis occurring outside the liver, caused by blockage of a bile duct or ducts. It may be caused by a tumor or stricture, a gallstone or other damage in the duct, pancreatitis, or other causes.

extramammary Paget's disease /-mam′ərē/ [L, *extra,* outside, *mamma,* breast; James Paget, English surgeon, 1814–1899; L, *dis*; Fr, *aise,* ease], a gradually spreading red, scaly and crusted lesion resembling that of Paget's disease, but not occurring on the breast. A common area is the vulva. The lesions give rise to carcinoma in approximately 50% of the cases.

extramarital /-mer′itəl/, happening outside a marriage.

extramedullary /-med′yəler′ē/ [L, *extra + medulla,* marrow], pertaining to something outside or unrelated to any medulla.

extramedullary myeloma [L, *extra + medulla,* marrow], a plasma cell tumor that occurs outside the bone marrow, usually affecting the visceral organs or the nasopharyngeal and oral mucosa.

extramedullary myelopoiesis, the formation and development of myeloid tissue outside the bone marrow.

extraneous /exstrā′nē·əs/ [L, strange], originating or entering from outside the organism.

extraocular /-ok′yōōlər/ [L, *extra + oculus,* eye], outside the eye.

extraocular muscle palsy, an abnormal condition characterized by paralysis of the extrinsic muscles of the eye.

extraocular muscles (EOMs), the six sets of muscles that control movements of the eyeball. They are the superior rectus and inferior rectus, which move the eye up and down; the medial rectus and the lateral rectus, which move the eye to either side; and the superior oblique and inferior oblique, which move the eye downward and inward, and upward and inward, respectively.

extraoral anchorage /-ôr′əl/ [L, *extra + oralis,* mouth, *ancora,* hook], an orthodontic holding device outside the mouth, typically linking dental attachments to a wire bow or to hooks extending between the lips and attached by elastic to a cap, neck strap, or other device outside the mouth.

extraperitoneal /-per′itənē′əl/ [L, *extra*; Gk, *peri,* near, around, *teinein,* to stretch], occurring or located outside the peritoneal cavity.

extraperitoneal cesarean section, a method for surgically delivering a baby through an incision in the lower uterine segment without entering the peritoneal cavity. The uterus is approached through the paravesical space.

extrapleural /-plŏŏr′əl/, outside the pleural cavity.

extrapleural pneumothorax, a condition in which a pocket of air or gas forms between the endothoracic fascia-pleura layer and the adjacent chest wall.

extrapsychic conflict /-sī′kik/ [L, *extra*; Gk, *psyche,* mind; L, *confligere,* to strike together], an emotional conflict that usually occurs when one's inner needs and desires do not coincide with the restrictions of the environment or society.

extrapulmonary /-pul′mɒnər′ē/, outside of or unrelated to the lungs.

extrapulmonary small cell carcinoma, a primary small cell cancer with a histologic diagnosis of small cell carcinoma but located in body areas outside the lungs. It occurs most frequently around the head and neck; in the pancreas, colon, and rectum; and in the genitourinary tract.

extrapyramidal /ek′strəpiram′ədəl/ [L, *extra*; Gk, *pyramis,* pyramid], **1.** pertaining to the tissues and structures outside the cerebrospinal pyramidal tracts of the brain that are associated with movement of the body, excluding motor neurons, the motor cortex, and the corticospinal and corticobulbar tracts. **2.** pertaining to the function of these tissues and structures.

extrapyramidal disease, any of a large group of conditions affecting the extrapyramidal tracts and characterized by involuntary movement, changes in muscle tone, and abnormal posture. Examples include tardive dyskinesia, chorea, athetosis, and Parkinson's disease.

extrapyramidal side effects, side effects that mimic extrapyramidal disease and are caused by drugs that block dopamine receptor sites in the extrapyramidal system tract.

extrapyramidal system, the part of the nervous system that includes the basal nuclei (substantia nigra, subthalamic nucleus, etc.), part of the midbrain, and the motor neurons of the spine.

extrapyramidal tracts, the uncrossed tracts of motor nerves from the brain to the anterior horns of the spinal cord, except the crossed fibers of the pyramidal tracts. Within the brain extrapyramidal pathways comprise various relays of motoneurons between motor areas of the cerebral cortex, the basal nuclei, the thalamus, the cerebellum, and the brainstem. The extrapyramidal pathways are functional rather than anatomic units.

extrasensory /-sen′sərē/ [L, *extra + sentire,* to feel], pertaining to alleged awareness of events that cannot be observed by any of the five basic senses. It includes telepathy, clairvoyance, and psychokinesis.

extrasensory perception (ESP) [L, *extra + sentire,* to feel, *percipere,* to perceive], alleged awareness or knowledge acquired without using the physical senses.

extrauterine /-yōō′tərin/ [L, *extra + uterus,* womb], occurring or located outside the uterus, as an ectopic pregnancy.

extravasation /ikstrav′əsā′shən/ [L,*extra+ vas,* vessel], **1.** a passage or escape into the tissues, usually of blood, serum, lymph or infusion. **2.** passage or escape into tissue of antineoplastic chemotherapeutic drugs. Signs and symptoms may be sudden onset of localized pain at an injection site, sudden redness or extreme pallor at an injection site, or loss of blood return in an IV needle. Tissue slough and necrosis may occur if the condition is severe. —**extravasate,** *v.*

extravascular fluid /-vas′kyələr/ [L, *extra,* outside, *vasculum,* small vessel, *fluere,* to flow], fluid in the body that is outside the blood vessels. Examples are lymph and CSF.

extremity /ikstrem′itē/ [L, *extremitas*], an arm or a leg. The arm may be identified as an upper extremity and the leg as a lower extremity.

extrinsic /ikstrin′sik/ [L, *extrinsecus,* on the outside], pertaining to anything external or originating outside a structure or organism, including parts of an organ that are not wholly contained within it, as an extrinsic muscle.

extrinsic muscle (em) [L, *extrinsecus,* on the outside], **1.** a muscle that is outside the organ it controls, as the extraocular muscles that control eye movements. **2.** a muscle that links a limb to the trunk of the body.

extrinsic pathway of coagulation, the mechanism that produces fibrin after tissue injury, beginning with formation of an activated complex between tissue factor and activated factor VII and leading to activation of factor X, which induces the reactions of the common pathway of coagulation.

extroversion /-vur′zhən/ [L, *extra + vertere,* to turn], **1.** the tendency to direct one's interests and energies toward external values or things outside the self. **2.** the state of being totally or primarily concerned with what is outside the self.

extrovert /ik′strəvurt′/, **1.** a person whose interests are directed away from the self and concerned primarily with external reality and the physical environment rather than with inner feelings and thoughts. **2.** a person characterized by extroversion.

extroverted personality /-vur′tid/ [L, *extra,* outside, *vertere,* to turn, *personalis,* of a person], a persona that is directed to a greater degree toward the outer world of people and events rather than the subjective inner world experience.

extrude /ekstrōōd′/ [L, *extrudere,* to push out], to thrust out from a surface or from alignment.

extrusion /ek·strōō′zhən/ [L, *extrudere,* to push out], **1.** thrusting or pushing out; expulsion by force. **2.** the overeruption or movement of a tooth beyond its normal occlusal plane in the absence of opposing occlusal force. **3.** an orthodontic technique for the elongation or elevation of a tooth.

extrusion reflex /ekstrōō′zhən/ [L, *extrudere,* to push out, *reflectere,* to bend back], a normal response in infants to force the tongue outward when touched or depressed. The reflex begins to disappear by about 3 or 4 months of age.

extubation /iks′t(y)ōōbā′shən/ [L, *ex,* out, *tuba,* tube], the process of withdrawing a tube from an orifice or cavity of the body. —**extubate,** *v.*

exudate /eks′yŏŏdāt/ [L, *exsudare,* to sweat out], fluid, cells, or other substances that have been slowly exuded, or discharged, from cells or blood vessels through small pores or breaks in cell membranes.

exudation /eks′yədā′shən/ [L, *exudare*], the oozing of fluid, pus, or serum. The exudate may or may not contain fibrous or coagulated material.

exudative /igzōō′dətiv/, relating to the oozing of fluid and other materials from cells and tissues, usually as a result of inflammation or injury.

exudative enteropathy, diarrhea that occurs in diseases characterized by inflammation or destruction of intestinal mucosa.

exudative inflammation [L, *exudare,* to sweat out, *inflammare,* to set afire], an inflammation of a serous or raw cavity in which fluid is released from the inflamed surface.

exudative retinopathy, a condition marked by masses of white or yellowish exudate in the posterior part of the fundus oculi, with deposit of cholesterin and blood debris from retinal hemorrhage, that leads to destruction of the macula and blindness.

eye [AS, *eage*], one of a pair of organs of sight, contained in a bony orbit at the front of the skull, with retrobulbar fat, and innervated by four cranial nerves: optic, oculomotor, trochlear, and abducens. Associated with the eye are certain accessory structures, such as the muscles, the fasciae, the eyebrow, the eyelids, the conjunctiva, and the lacrimal gland. The bulb of the eye is composed of segments of two spheres with nearly parallel axes that constitute the outside tunic and one of three fibrous layers enclosing two internal cavities separated by the crystalline lens. The smaller cavity anterior to the lens is divided by the iris into two chambers, both filled with aqueous humor. The posterior cavity is larger than the anterior cavity and contains the jellylike vitreous body that is divided by the hyaloid canal. The outside tunic of the bulb consists of the transparent cornea anteriorly and the opaque sclera posteriorly. The intermediate vascular, pigmented tunic consists of the choroid, the ciliary body, and the iris. The internal tunic of nervous tissue is the retina. Light waves passing through the lens strike a layer of rods and cones in the retina, creating impulses that are transmitted by the optic nerve to the brain. Eye movement is controlled by six muscles: the superior and inferior oblique muscles and the superior, inferior, medial, and lateral rectus muscles.

eye bank [AS, *eage*; It, *banca*, bench], a facility for collecting and storing corneas and other ocular tissues for transplantation to recipients.

eyebrow [AS, *eage* + *bru*], **1.** the supraorbital arch of the frontal bone that separates the orbit of the eye from the forehead. **2.** the arch of hairs growing along the ridge formed by the supraorbital arch of the frontal bone.

eye care, a nursing intervention from the Nursing Interventions Classification (NIC) defined as prevention or minimization of threats to eye or visual integrity.

eyecup, a small vessel or cup that is shaped to fit over the eyeball and used to bathe the exposed surface of the eye.

eye deviation [AS, *eage*; L, *deviare,* to turn aside], **1.** a movement of one or both eyes, singly or jointly, from the median line or from the original direction of fixation. Manifest deviation is the number of degrees by which the visual axis of one eye deviates from that of the other in cases of squint, when both eyes are open. **2.** in strabismus, the departure of the foveal line of sight of one eye from the point of fixation.

eye dominance, an unconscious preference to use one eye rather than the other for certain purposes, such as looking through a telescope.

eyedrops, a liquid medicine that is administered by allowing it to fall in drops onto the conjunctival surface.

eye glasses, transparent lenses held in metal or plastic frames in front of the eyes to correct refractive errors or to protect the eyes from harmful electromagnetic waves or flying objects.

eyeground, the fundus of the eye as revealed by ophthalmoscopic examination.

eyelash [AS, *eage*; ME, *lasche*], one of many stiff hairs like cilia growing in double or triple rows along the border of the eyelids in front of a row of ciliary glands that are in front of a row of meibomian glands.

eyelid [AS, *eage* + *hlid*], one of two movable folds of protective thin skin over the eye, with eyelashes and ciliary and meibomian glands along its margin. The orbicularis oculi muscle and the oculomotor nerve control the opening and closing of the eyelid.

eye patching, 1. placement of a soft patch over a closed eye to restrict lid movement during corneal reepithelialization or a similar healing procedure in progress. **2.** occlusion of the better eye by patch placement in young patients with strabismic amblyopia to force greater use of the amblyopic eye. **3.** patching used in cases of diplopia (double vision).

eye reanimation, microsurgical restoration of function of a paralyzed eye sphincter.

eye shielding, protection of an injured eye by securing a metal or plastic eye shield or a disposable cup to prevent further injury.

eye wash, an apparatus for irrigating the eyes after exposure to dust or other debris or chemical contamination. The shower directs one or two streams of water so that they flush over the eyes and lids.

ezetimibe, an antilipemic agent used to treat hypercholesterolemia, homozygous low-density lipoprotein receptor disorder, and homozygous sitosterolemia.

F

f, **1.** symbol for *breaths per unit time.* **2.** symbol for *respiratory frequency.*

F, **1.** abbreviation for **Fahrenheit.** **2.** abbreviation for **farad. 3.** symbol for **fluorine. 4.** abbreviation for **frequency.**

F₁, symbol for **first filial generation.**

F₂, symbol for **second filial generation.**

F_{ab}, the fragment of an antibody molecule that contains the antigen-binding site, consisting of a light chain and part of a heavy chain.

F_c, a part of a molecule of an antibody that has been split by a proteolytic enzyme. It represents the relatively constant region, as distinguished from the F_{ab} portion, that contains the binding sites. F_c portion is sometimes identified as the crystallizable fragment.

FA, **1.** abbreviation for **fatty acid. 2.** abbreviation for **femoral artery. 3.** abbreviation for **folic acid.**

FAAN, abbreviation for **Fellow of the American Academy of Nursing.**

Fab [*f*ragment, *a*ntigen-*b*inding], originally, either of two identical fragments, each containing an antigen-combining site, obtained by papain cleavage of the IgG molecule. It is now generally used as an adjective in terms such as Fab *fragment* or *region,* referring to an "arm" of any immunoglobulin monomer, i.e., one light chain and the adjoining heavy chain V_H and C_H1 domains. Also written F_{ab}.

FAB classification, (*French-American-British*) a classification of acute leukemia produced by a three-nation joint collaboration. Acute lymphoblastic leukemia is subdivided into three types and acute myelogenous leukemia is subdivided into eight types.

fabere, abbreviation for *f*lexion, *ab*duction, *e*xternal *r*otation, then *e*xtension.

Fabrazyme, a trademark for agalsidase beta.

fabrication /fab′rikā′shən/, a psychologic reaction in which false statements are contrived to mask memory defects. It is a clinical feature of Korsakoff's syndrome and other disorders.

FAC, an anticancer drug combination of fluorouracil, DOXOrubicin, and cyclophosphamide.

FACCP, abbreviation for *Fellow of the American College of Chest Physicians.*

FACD, abbreviation for *Fellow of the American College of Dentists.*

face [L, *facies*], **1.** the front of the head from the chin to the brow, including the skin and muscles and structures of the forehead, eyes, nose, mouth, cheeks, and jaw. **2.** the visage or countenance. **3.** to direct the face toward something.— **facial,** *adj.*

face-bow [L, *facies;* AS, *boga*], a device resembling a caliper for measuring the relationship of the maxilla to the TMJs. The measurement is used in the fabrication of denture casts and major restorative procedures involving natural teeth.

face lift, a plastic surgery procedure in which wrinkles and other signs of aging skin are eliminated.

face presentation [L, *facies,* face, *praesentare,* to show], an obstetric presentation in which the chin of the fetus is the point of direction.

facet /fas′it/ [Fr, *facette,* little face], **1.** in dentistry, a flattened, highly polished wear pattern on a tooth. **2.** a small, smooth-surfaced process for articulation.

facetectomy /fas′itek′təmē/, surgical removal of a facet, particularly the articular facet of a vertebra.

facet joint, synovial joint between articular processes (zygapophytes) of the vertebrae.

facial angle /fā′shəl/ [L, *facies* + *angulus,* a corner], the degree of protrusion of the lower face, assessed by measuring the inclination of the facial plane relative to the horizontal reference plane.

facial artery, one of a pair of tortuous arteries that arise from the external carotid arteries, divide into four cervical and five facial branches, and supply various organs and tissues in the head.

facial bones, the 14 bones that form the face of the skull. They include two each of the nasal, palatine, inferior nasal concha, maxilla, lacrimal, and zygomatic bones, plus the mandible and vomer.

facial diplegia, a rare neuromuscular condition characterized by bilateral paralysis of various muscles of the face.

facial hemiplegia, paralysis of the muscles of one side of the face.

facial muscle, one of numerous muscles of the face that seldom remains distinct over its entire length because of a tendency to merge with a neighboring muscle at its termination or its attachment. The five groups of facial muscles are the muscles of the scalp, the extrinsic muscles of the ear, the muscles of the nose, the muscles of the eyelid, and the muscles of the mouth.

facial nerve, either of a pair of mixed sensory and motor cranial nerves that arise from the brainstem at the base of the pons and divide immediately in front of the ear into six branches, innervating the scalp, forehead, eyelids, muscles of facial expression, cheeks, and jaw.

facial nerve paralysis, a loss of voluntary control of the muscles of the face, usually on one side.

facial neuralgia, the occurrence of pain in the middle ear and auditory canal caused by inflammation of the otic ganglion.

facial palsy [L, *facies,* face; Gk, *paralyein,* to be palsied], a loss of motor nerve function in the muscles of the face.

facial paralysis, an abnormal condition characterized by the partial or total loss of the functions of the facial muscles or the loss of sensation in the face. It may be caused by disease or by trauma.

facial perception, the ability to judge the distance and direction of objects through the sensation felt in the skin of the face. The phenomenon is commonly experienced by those who are blind.

facial reanimation, the use of surgical procedures to improve facial appearance and motion in facial paralysis.

facial tic [L, *facies,* face; Fr, *tic,* twitching], any repetitive, spasmodic, and involuntary contraction of groups of facial muscles.

facial vein, one of a pair of superficial veins that drain deoxygenated blood from the superficial structures of the face.

facies /fā′shē-ēs/ *pl.* **facies** [L, face], **1.** the face. **2.** the surface of any body structure, part, or organ. **3.** facial expression or appearance.

facilitation /fəsil′itā′shən/ [L, *facilitas,* easiness], **1.** the enhancement or reinforcement of any action or function so that it can be performed more easily. **2.** in neurology, the phenomenon whereby two or more afferent impulses that individually are not strong enough to elicit a response in a neuron can collectively produce a reflex discharge greater than the sum of the separate responses.

facilitory casting /fəsil′itôr′ē/, a method of making prosthetic casts with materials that increase muscle tone in a specific group while increasing or decreasing ROM.

faciolingual /fā′shōling′gwəl/, pertaining to the face and tongue.

FACOG, abbreviation for *Fellow of the American College of Obstetricians and Gynecologists.*

FACP, abbreviation for *Fellow of the American College of Physicians.*

FACS, abbreviation for *Fellow of the American College of Surgeons.*

facsimile (fax), a method of transmitting images or printed matter by electronic means. Images are scanned, converted into electronic signals, and sent over telephone lines to a fax receiver, which reconverts the electronic data into a duplicate of the original image.

FACSM, abbreviation for *Fellow of the American College of Sports Medicine.*

factitial /fakti′shəl/ [L, *facticius,* artificial], artificial or self-induced.

factitial dermatitis, self-induced skin lesions resulting from habitual rubbing, scratching, hair pulling, malingering, or mental disturbance.

factitious diarrhea, that caused by something the patient is doing to his or her own body, usually surreptitious laxative abuse.

factitious disorder /faktish′əs/, a *DSM-IV* diagnosis marked by disease symptoms caused by deliberate efforts of a person to gain attention. Such actions may be repeated, even when the individual is aware of the hazards involved.

Factive, a trademark for **gemifloxacin.**

factor, 1. one of a number of elements contributing to a whole. **2.** a number by which another number is exactly divisible. **3.** one of a number of elements that affect a specific result.

factor III, obsolete designation for a membrane protein found normally in subendothelial tissue. When exposed to blood, it forms a complex with factor VIIa to activate extrinsic coagulation.

factor IV, a designation for calcium that is involved in the process of blood coagulation.

factor V, coagulation cofactor to factor Xa; forms complex that converts prothrombin rapidly to thrombin.

factor VII, a serine protease procoagulant present in the plasma and synthesized in the liver in the presence of vitamin K.

factor VIII, a coagulation factor present in normal plasma but deficient in the blood of persons with hemophilia A and von Willebrand disease.

factor IX, a serine protease coagulation factor present in normal plasma but deficient from the blood of persons with hemophilia B

factor IX complex, a hemostatic containing factors II, VII, IX, and X. It is prescribed in the treatment of hemophilia B. It is a vitamin K–dependent protein synthesized in the liver.

factor X, a serine protease coagulation factor in normal plasma that forms a complex with its cofactor, factor V, to convert prothrombin to thrombin.

factor XI, a serine protease coagulation factor present in normal plasma that activates factor IX. Deficiency results in Rosenthal disease.

factor XII, a serine protease coagulation factor present in normal plasma that activates factor XI in the presence of prekallikrein and high-molecular-weight kininogen.

factor XIII, a transamidase coagulation factor present in normal plasma that cross-links fibrin polymer to produce a stable fibrin clot.

factor-searching study, in nursing research, a study design that produces a qualitative narrative description that includes categories or classifications of phenomena.

factor V–Leiden (FVL) test, a blood test for FVL, a genetic mutation of factor V, used to diagnose the risk of venous thrombosis.

factor Xa, a serine endopeptidase that catalyzes the conversion of prothrombin to active thrombin.

facultative /fak′əltā′tiv/ [L, *facultas,* capability], not obligatory; having the ability to adapt to more than one condition, such as a facultative anaerobe.

facultative aerobe, an organism able to grow under anaerobic conditions but that develops most rapidly in an aerobic environment.

facultative anaerobe, an organism able to grow under aerobic conditions but that develops most rapidly in an anaerobic environment.

faculty /fak′əltē/ [L, *facultas,* capability], **1.** any normal physiologic function or natural ability of a living organism, such as the digestive faculty or the ability to perceive and distinguish sensory stimuli. **2.** an ability to do something specific, such as learn languages or remember names. **3.** any mental ability or power, such as memory or thought. **4.** a department in an institution of learning or the people who teach in a department of such an institution.

FAD, abbreviation for *fetal activity determination.*

fading time, the time required for a constant stimulus applied to a fixed area of the peripheral visual field to stop.

Faget's sign /fazhāz′/ [Jean C. Faget, French physician, 1818–1884], a falling pulse rate associated with a constant temperature, or a constant pulse associated with a rising temperature. It is an unusual sign found in yellow fever.

fagicladosporic acid /faj′iklad′ōspôr ′ik/, a toxin produced by *Cladosporium epiphyllum,* a member of a genus of fungi that cause "black spot" in stored meat, tinea nigra, and black degeneration of the brain.

Fahrenheit (F) /fer′ənhīt/ [Daniel G. Fahrenheit, German physicist, 1686–1736], a scale for the measurement of temperature in which the boiling point of water is 212° F and the freezing point of water is 32° F at sea level.

failed forceps, an attempted mid-forceps operation that is abandoned because there is a greater degree of resistance to rotation or traction than anticipated.

failure to thrive (FTT) /fāl′yər/ [L, *fallere,* to deceive; ME, *thriven,* to grasp], the abnormal retardation of growth and development of an infant resulting from conditions that interfere with normal metabolism, appetite, and activity.

faint [OFr, *faindre,* to feign], *nontechnical.* **1.** to lose consciousness, as in a syncopal attack. **2.** a syncopal attack.

faith healing [L, *fidere,* to trust; AS, *hoelen,* to make whole], alleged healing through the power to cause a cure or recovery from an illness or injury without the aid of conventional medical treatment. The healer is believed to have been given that power by a supernatural force.

falciform ligament /fal′sifôrm/, a triangular or sickle-shaped ligament of the body.

falcine herniation, a herniation of the brain beneath the falx cerebri, caused by focal cerebral edema.

falciparum malaria /falsip′ərəm/ [L, *falx,* sickle, *forma,* form; It, *mal,* bad, *aria,* air], the most severe form of malaria, caused by the protozoon *Plasmodium falciparum.* The condition is characterized by extremely grave systemic symptoms, mild jaundice, mental confusion, enlarged spleen and liver, increased respiratory rate, edema, GI symptoms, and anemia.

fall /fawl/, a coming down freely, usually under the influence of gravity.

fallen arch, a flattened foot arch, which often results in a flat deformity or splay-foot. The condition may involve the longitudinal arch, the transverse arch, or both.

fallopian canal [Gabriello Fallopio, Italian anatomist, 1523–1562; L, *canalis*], a passageway for the facial nerve through the petrous bone.

fallopian tube /fəlō′pē·ən/ [Gabriello Fallopio], one of a pair of ducts opening at one end into the uterus and at the other end into the peritoneal cavity, over the ovary. Each tube serves as the passage through which an ovum is carried to the uterus and through which spermatozoa move out toward the ovary.

fallout [AS, *feallan,* to fall + *ut*], the deposition of radioactive debris after a nuclear explosion.

fall prevention, a nursing intervention from the Nursing Interventions Classification (NIC) defined as instituting special precautions with patient at risk for injury from falling.

fall prevention behavior, a nursing outcome from the Nursing Outcomes Classification (NOC) defined as personal or family caregiver actions to minimize risk factors that might precipitate falls in the personal environment.

falls occurrence, a nursing outcome from the Nursing Outcomes Classification (NOC) defined as the number of times an individual falls.

false ankylosis [L, *fallere,* to deceive; Gk, *agkylosis,* joint stiffness], a type of joint immobility that results from abnormal inflexibility of body parts outside the joint.

false diverticulum [L, *fallere,* to deceive, *diverticulare,* to turn aside], a protrusion of mucous membrane through a muscular coat defect of a hollow organ.

false glottis, the triangular opening between the two adjacent vestibular folds at the entrance to the middle chamber of the laryngeal cavity.

false imprisonment [L, *falsus,* deceptive; ME, *imprisonen*], in law, an intentional tort; the intentional unjustified, nonconsensual detention or confinement of a person within fixed boundaries for any length of time.

false joint [L, *fallere,* to deceive, *jungere,* to join], a joint that develops at the site of a former fracture.

false negative, an incorrect result of a diagnostic test or procedure that falsely indicates the absence of a finding, condition, or disease.

false-negative rate [L, *fallere,* to deceive, *negare,* to deny, *ratum,* calculate], the rate of occurrence of negative test results in subjects known to have the disease or behavior for which an individual is being tested.

false neuroma, a neoplasm that does not contain nerve elements.

false pelvis, the part of the pelvis superior to a plane passing through the linea terminalis.

false personification, in psychiatry, the labeling and prejudgment of others without validating evidence.

false positive, a test result that wrongly indicates the presence of a disease or other condition the test is designed to reveal.

false-positive rate [L, *fallere,* to deceive, *positivus + ratum,* calculate], the rate of occurrence of positive test results in subjects known to be free of a disease or disorder for which an individual is being tested.

false suture, an immovable fibrous joint in which rough articulating surfaces form the connection between certain bones of the skull.

false transactions, in transactional analysis, transactions in which communication is stopped or distorted when one individual relates from a different ego state than what is expected.

false vertebra, one of the vertebral segments that form the sacrum and the coccyx.

false vocal cord, either of two thick folds of mucous membrane in the larynx separating the ventricle from the vestibule.

falx /falks, fôlks/ *pl.* **falces** [L, sickle]. **1.** a sickle-shaped structure. **2.** sickle-shaped.

falx ligamentosa, the broad ligament of the liver.

FAM, an anticancer drug combination of fluorouracil, DOXOrubicin (Adriamycin), and mitomycin.

famciclovir, an antiviral drug prescribed in the treatment of acute herpes zoster and recurrent genital herpes.

familial /fəmil′yəl/ [L, *familia,* household], pertaining to a characteristic, condition, or disease that is present in some families and not others or that occurs in more family members than would be expected by chance.

familial adenomatous polyposis (FAD), an inherited disorder characterized by the development of myriad polyps in the colon, beginning in late adolescence or early adulthood. Untreated, the condition nearly always leads to colon cancer.

familial cretinism, a rare genetic disorder caused by an inborn error of metabolism resulting from an enzyme deficiency that interferes with thyroid hormone biosynthesis. Clinical manifestations include lethargy, stunted growth, and mental retardation.

familial hemophagocytic lymphohistiocytosis an autosomal-recessive disease characterized by anemia, granulocytopenia, and thrombocytopenia. Phagocytosis of blood cells and infiltration of bone marrow by macrophages commonly cause death in childhood.

familial Hibernian fever, a periodic syndrome associated with a mutation in a receptor for tumor necrosis factor. This defect causes recurrent high fevers, rash, and abdominal pain.

familial Mediterranean fever, an autosomal-recessive intestinal disorder characterized by short recurrent attacks of fever with pain in the abdomen, chest, or joints and erythema resembling that seen in erysipelas. It is sometimes complicated by secondary amyloidosis.

familial periodic fever, a rare autosomal-dominant syndrome that includes an abnormality on the cell receptor for tumor necrosis factor, characterized by periodic fever with any of various skin disorders lasting for 4 days to 3 weeks and mild systemic manifestations, such as abdominal pain, headache, and chest pain.

familial periodic paralysis [L, *familia,* household; Gk, *peri,* near, *hodos,* way, *paralysein,* to be palsied], a rare inherited disorder in which clients suffer attacks of general flaccid paralysis after attacks of hypokalemia. The episodes may follow administration of glucose and are relieved by administration of potassium chloride.

familial polyposis, an abnormal condition characterized by multiple polyps in the colon and rectum. The disease has high malignancy potential and is inherited.

familial visceral amyloidosis, a rare autosomal-dominant type of amyloidosis characterized by nephropathy, arterial hypertension, hepatosplenomegaly, albuminuria, hematuria, and pitting edema. Affected patients usually die within 10 years of onset of clinical manifestations.

family [L, *familia,* household], a group of people related by heredity, such as parents, children, and siblings. The term sometimes is broadened to include persons related by marriage or those living in the same household who are emotionally attached, interact regularly, and share concerns for the growth and development of the group and its individual members.

family Apgar, a family therapy rating system in which the name Apgar contains the first letters of five words—*a*daptability, *part*nership, *growth,* *affection,* and *resolve*—that represent the questionnaire categories. Each family member indicates a degree of satisfaction in each of the five categories on a scale of 0 to 2. The system is used most frequently in studies of families with a geriatric member.

family care leave, absence from a job that is permitted for an employee to care for a family member who is ill, disabled, or pregnant. The U.S. Family and Medical Leave Act of 1993 provides 12 weeks of unpaid leave per year from a job for the birth or adoption of a child; for the care of a seriously ill child, spouse, or parent; or for a serious illness affecting the employee. The law applies only to companies with 50 or more employees. Employers must guarantee that a worker can return to the same or a comparable job.

family-centered care, primary health care that includes an assessment of the health of an entire family, identification of actual or potential factors that might influence the health of its members, and implementation of interventions needed to maintain or improve the health of the unit and its members.

family-centered maternity care, a system for the delivery of safe, high-quality health care adapted to the physical and psychosocial needs of the patient, the patient's entire family, and the newly born offspring.

family-centered nursing care, nursing care directed to improving the potential health of a family or any of its members.

family coping, a nursing outcome from the Nursing Outcomes Classification (NOC) defined as family actions to manage stressors that tax family resources.

family counseling, a program of providing information and professional guidance to members of a family concerning specific health matters, such as the care of a severely retarded child or the risk of transmitting a known genetic defect.

family disorganization, a breakdown of a family system. It may be associated with parental overburdening or loss of significant others who served as role models for children or support systems for family members. Family disorganization can contribute to the loss of social controls that families usually impose on their members.

family dynamics, the forces at work within the family that produce particular behaviors or symptoms.

family functioning, a nursing outcome from the Nursing Outcomes Classification (NOC) defined as the capacity of the family system to meet the needs of its members through developmental transitions.

family functions, processes by which the family operates as a whole, including communication and manipulation of the environment for problem solving.

family health status, a nursing outcome from the Nursing Outcomes Classification (NOC) defined as overall health and social competence of family unit.

family history, an essential part of a patient's medical history in which he or she is asked about the health of members of the immediate family in a series of specific questions to discover any disorders to which the patient may be particularly vulnerable.

family integrity, a nursing outcome from the Nursing Outcomes Classification (NOC) defined as family members' behaviors that collectively demonstrate cohesion, strength, and emotional bonding.

family integrity promotion, a nursing intervention from the Nursing Interventions Classification (NIC) defined as promotion of family cohesion and unity.

family integrity promotion: childbearing family, a nursing intervention from the Nursing Interventions Classification (NIC) defined as facilitation of the growth of individuals or families who are adding an infant to the family unit.

family involvement promotion, a nursing intervention from the Nursing Interventions Classification (NIC) defined as facilitating participation of family members in the emotional and physical care of the patient.

family medicine, the branch of medicine that is concerned with the diagnosis and treatment of health problems in people of either sex and any age. Practitioners of family medicine often act as the primary health care providers.

family mobilization, a nursing intervention from the Nursing Interventions Classification (NIC) defined as utilization of family strengths to influence patient's health in a positive direction.

family myths, myths that are constructed to deny the reality of family situations.

family normalization, a nursing outcome from the Nursing Outcomes Classification (NOC) defined as capacity of the family system to develop strategies for optimal functioning when a member has a chronic illness or disability.

family nurse practitioner (FNP), a nurse practitioner possessing skills necessary for the detection and management of acute self-limiting conditions and management of chronic stable conditions. An FNP provides primary ambulatory care for families in collaboration with primary care physicians.

family of origin, the family into which a person is born.

family of procreation, the family a person forms through marriage and/or childbearing.

family participation in professional care, a nursing outcome from the Nursing Outcomes Classification (NOC) defined as family involvement in decision-making, delivery, and evaluation of care provided by health care personnel.

family physician, a medical practitioner of the specialty of family medicine.

family planning: contraception, a nursing intervention from the Nursing Interventions Classification (NIC) defined as facilitation of pregnancy prevention by providing information about the physi-

ology of reproduction and methods to control conception.

family planning: infertility, a nursing intervention from the Nursing Interventions Classification (NIC) defined as management, education, and support of the patient and significant other undergoing evaluation and treatment for infertility.

family planning, natural, methods of preventing conception without the use of artificial contraceptive means.

family planning: unplanned pregnancy, a nursing intervention from the Nursing Interventions Classification (NIC) defined as facilitation of decision-making regarding pregnancy outcome.

family practice [L, *familia,* household; Gk, *praktikos,* ready for action], a medical specialty that encompasses several branches of medicine, including internal medicine, preventive medicine, pediatrics, surgery, psychiatry, and obstetrics and gynecology. It includes client management, counseling, problem solving, and coordination of total health care delivery to all members of a family, regardless of sex or age.

family practice physician, a practitioner of family medicine, usually one who has completed a residency program in the specialty.

family presence facilitation, a nursing intervention from the Nursing Interventions Classification (NIC) defined as facilitation of the family's presence in support of an individual undergoing resuscitation and/or invasive procedures.

family processes, the psychosocial, physiologic, and spiritual functions and relationships within the family unit.

family process maintenance, a nursing intervention from the Nursing Interventions Classification (NIC) defined as minimization of family process disruption effects.

family resiliency, a nursing outcome from the Nursing Outcomes Classification (NOC) defined as positive adaptation and function of the family system following significant adversity or crisis.

family social climate, a nursing outcome from the Nursing Outcomes Classification (NOC) defined as supportive milieu as characterized by family member relationships and goals.

family structure, the composition and membership of the family and the organization and patterning of relationships among individual family members.

family support, a nursing intervention from the Nursing Interventions Classification (NIC) defined as promotion of family values, interests, and goals.

family support during treatment, a nursing outcome from the Nursing Outcomes Classification (NOC) defined as family presence and emotional support for an individual undergoing treatment.

family therapy[1], in psychiatry, a therapy modality that focuses treatment on the process between family members that supports and perpetuates symptoms; a way of conceptualizing human relationship problems that focuses on the context in which an emotional problem is generated.

family therapy[2], a nursing intervention from the Nursing Interventions Classification (NIC) defined as assisting family members to move their family toward a more productive way of living.

famotidine /famot′idēn/, an oral and parenteral antiulcer drug; an H_2-receptor antagonist. It is prescribed in treatment of duodenal ulcer and pathologic hypersecretory conditions and for stress-ulcer prophylaxis.

Famvir, a trademark for an antiviral drug (famciclovir).

fan beam, a geometric pattern produced by collimating a spatially extended x-ray beam with a long, narrow slit.

FANCAP, a mnemonic device for helping student nurses learn to assess, provide, and evaluate direct patient care. It stands for *f*luids, *a*eration, *n*utrition, *c*ommunication, *a*ctivity, and *p*ain.

Fanconi's anemia /fankō′nēs/ [Guido Fanconi, Swiss pediatrician, 1892–1979], a rare, usually congenital disorder transmitted as an autosomal-recessive trait, characterized by aplastic anemia in childhood or early adult life, bone abnormalities, chromatin breaks, and developmental anomalies.

Fanconi's syndrome [Guido Fanconi], a group of disorders that includes pancytopenia, renal tubular dysfunction, glycosuria, phosphaturia, and bicarbonate wasting. The condition is often marked by osteomalacia, acidosis, rickets, and hypokalemia. Two main types of the syndrome have been differentiated. Idiopathic Fanconi's syndrome is inherited and usually accompanies other genetic disorders. Acquired Fanconi's syndrome is usually the result of toxicity from various sources, including ingestion of outdated tetracycline, heavy metal poisoning, or vitamin D deficiency.

fango /fän′gō/ [It, mud], mud taken from thermal springs at Battaglia, Italy, and used to treat gout and other rheumatic diseases.

fan lateral projection, a technique for making a radiographic image of the hand without superimposition of the phalanges. The patient places the fingers around a sponge wedge shaped so that each finger appears separately, in a fanlike pattern, on the x-ray film.

Fansidar, a trademark for a fixed-combination antimalarial agent (pyrimethamine and sulfadoxine).

fantasy /fan′təsē/ [Gk, *phantasia,* imagination], **1.** the unrestrained free play of the imagination. **2.** a mental image, usually distorted or grotesque, that is often the result of the action of drugs or a disease of the CNS. **3.** the mental process of transforming undesirable experiences into imagined events.

FAOTA, abbreviation for *Fellow of the American Occupational Therapy Association.*

FAP, abbreviation for *familial adenomatous polyposis.*

FAPTA, abbreviation for *Fellow of the American Physical Therapy Association.*

farad (F) /fer′əd/ [Michael Faraday, English scientist, 1791–1871], a unit of capacitance that increases the potential difference between the plates of a capacitor by 1 volt with a charge of 1 coulomb.

Faraday cage /fer′ədā/, a wire-mesh cage that surrounds a magnetic resonance (MR) scanner and shields it from stray radiofrequency waves that would otherwise distort the results of MR imaging.

Farber's disease, Farber's lipogranulomatosis /fär′bərz/ [Sidney Farber, American pediatrician, 1903–1973], a lysosomal storage disease of ceramide metabolism resulting from defective ceramidase, marked by hoarseness; aphonia; a brownish desquamating dermatitis that begins at about 3 months of age; foam cell infiltration of bones and joints that causes deformations; granulomatous reaction in lymph nodes, heart, lungs, and kidneys; and psychomotor retardation.

Farber test, a microscopic examination of newborn meconium for lanugo and squamous cells. The absence of hair or skin cells is suggestive of intestinal obstruction or atresia and requires further evaluation.

Far Eastern hemorrhagic fever, a form of epidemic hemorrhagic fever, indigenous to Asia, that is transmitted by a virus carried by Asian rodents and causes hemorrhagic fever with renal syndrome. The infection is characterized by four phases: febrile phase, hypotensive phase, oliguric phase, and polyuric phase.

farmer's lung [L, *firmare,* to make firm], a respiratory disorder caused by the inhalation of actinomycetes or other microbes in dusts from moldy hay. It is a form of hypersensitivity pneumonitis and is characterized by coughing, dyspnea, cyanosis, tachycardia, nausea, chills, and fever.

far point [ME, *farr*; L, *punctus*, pricked], **1.** the farthest distance from the eye at which an object can be seen clearly when the eye is at rest and accommodation is fully relaxed. **2.** the point at which the visual axes of the two eyes meet when at rest.

F²ARV, abbreviation for *Fear/Frustration* (F²), *Anger, Rage,* and *Violence,* a highly volatile emotional reaction that escalates from fear or frustration and proceeds sequentially through anger and rage to violence.

FAS, abbreviation for **fetal alcohol syndrome.**

fascia /fash′ē-ə/ *pl.* **fasciae** [L, band], the fibrous connective membrane of the body that may be separated from other specifically organized structures, such as the tendons, the aponeuroses, and the ligaments, and that covers, supports, and separates muscles. It varies in thickness and density and in the amounts of fat, collagenous fiber, elastic fiber, and tissue fluid it contains.—**fascial,** *adj.*

fascia lata, deep fascia in the thigh and gluteal region.

fascial cleft /fash′ē-əl/ [L, *fascia*; ME, *clift*], a place of cleavage between two contiguous fascial surfaces, such as the deep fasciae and the subcutaneous fasciae.

fascial compartment, a part of the body that is walled off by fascial membranes, usually containing a muscle or group of muscles or an organ.

fascial membrane lamination, a pad of connective tissue that contains fat and an occasional blood vessel or lymph node. It is found where a fascial membrane splits into two sheets.

fascia of piriform muscle, an extension of the parietal pelvic fascia that surrounds the piriform muscle.

fascicular /fəsik′yələr/ [L, *fasciculus,* little bundle], pertaining to something arranged as a bundle of rods, such as groups of nerve or muscle fibers.

fascicular neuroma, a neoplasm composed of myelinated nerve fibers.

fasciculation /fasik′yŏŏlā′shən/ [L, *fasciculus,* little bundle, *atio,* process], a localized uncoordinated, uncontrollable twitching of a single muscle group innervated by a single motor nerve fiber or filament that may be palpated and seen under the skin. In anesthesia it refers to muscle twitches that occur with administration of the depolarizing muscle relaxant succinylcholine. It also may be symptomatic of a number of disorders. Fasciculation of the heart muscle is known as fibrillation.—**fascicular,** *adj.,* **fasciculate,** *v.*

fasciculus /fəsik′yələs/ *pl.* **fasciculi** [L, little bundle], a small bundle of muscle, tendon, or nerve fibers wrapped by a layer of connective tissue called the perimysium (muscle) or

perineurium (nerve fiber). The arrangement of fasciculi in a muscle is correlated with the power of the muscle and its ROM.—**fascicular,** *adj.*

fasciitis /fas′ē-ī′tis/, **1.** an inflammation of the connective tissue that may be caused by streptococcal or other types of infection, an injury, or an autoimmune reaction. **2.** an abnormal benign growth (pseudosarcomatous fasciitis) resembling a tumor that develops in the subcutaneous oral tissues, usually in the cheek.

fasciodesis /fā′sē-ōde′sis/, a surgical procedure in which a fascia is attached to another fascia or to a tendon.

fascioliasis /fas′ē-ōlī′əsis/ [L, *fasciola,* little bug; Gk, *osis,* condition], infection by a river fluke of the species *Fasciola hepatica* or *F. gigantica.* It is characterized by epigastric pain, fever, hepatomegaly, jaundice, eosinophilia, urticaria, and diarrhea. Fibrosis of the liver is a consequence of prolonged infection.

fasciolopsiasis /fas′ē-ōlopsī′əsis/ [L, *fasciola,* little band; Gk, *opsis,* appearance, *osis,* condition], an intestinal infection of humans and pigs characterized by abdominal pain, diarrhea, constipation, eosinophilia, ascites, and sometimes edema. It is caused by the fluke *Fasciolopsis buski.*

Fasciolopsis buski /fas′ē-əlop′sis bus′kē/, a species of fluke that is an important intestinal parasite endemic in Asia and the tropics. In the United States and other countries, it is occasionally found in imported food products.

fascioscapulohumeral muscular dystrophy /fas′ē-ō- skap′yəlōhyōo′mərəl/ [L, *fasciculus,* little bundle, *scapula,* shoulderblade, *humerus,* shoulder], an abnormal congenital condition that is one of the main types of muscular dystrophy. It is characterized by progressive symmetric wasting of the skeletal muscles, especially the muscles of the face, the shoulders, and the upper arms, without any associated neural or sensory disorders.

fasciotomy /fas′ē-ot′əmē/, a surgical incision into an area of fascia.

FASRT, abbreviation for *Fellow of the American Society of Radiologic Technologists.*

fast, 1. resistant to change, especially to the action of a specific medication or chemical, as a staining agent. **2.** abstinence from all or certain foods. **3.** occurring quickly and in a short span of time.

fast brushing, the use of a battery-powered brush to stimulate C fibers (group IV afferent neurons), which send many collaterals to the reticular activating system.

fast channel, a protein channel, such as a sodium channel, that becomes activated relatively quickly; a fast voltage-gated channel has a much lower activation potential than does the slow type.

fastigial nucleus /fastij'ē-əl/, one of a group of deep cerebellar nuclei that receive input from the medial zone of the cerebellum. It is involved in the control of posture and equilibrium.

fastigium /fastij'ē-əm/ [L, ridge], **1.** the highest point in the course of a fever, or the most symptomatic point in the course of an illness. **2.** the angle at the top of the roof of the fourth ventricle in the brain. **3.** the highest point.

fasting [AS, *foestan,* to observe], **1.** the act of abstaining from food for a specific period, usually for therapeutic or religious purposes. **2.** the elimination of foods with the addition of fluids such as mineral water, herbal and fruit teas, broth, and fruit juices for a limited period of time. This therapy requires the supervision of a health professional experienced in this form of therapy.

fasting blood sugar, a colloquial term for the determination of plasma glucose levels after fasting.

fasting plasma glucose (FPG), a measurement of the concentration of glucose in the plasma after the patient has not eaten for at least 8 hours.

fasting serum gastrin, measurement of the levels of gastrin in blood serum after the patient has fasted for 12 hours. It is markedly increased in conditions such as Zollinger-Ellison syndrome and G-cell hyperplasia.

fast neutron therapy, a radiotherapeutic technique used in the treatment of certain soft tissue sarcomas.

fast pain, a localized sensation of discomfort felt immediately after a noxious stimulus is delivered.

fast smear, a cytologic sample of tissue scrapings from the vaginal-cervical area, smeared on a microscope slide and fixed immediately for routine screening.

fast spin-echo (FSE), an MRI technique that uses multiple spin-echoes to reduce imaging times in comparison to spin-echo imaging.

fast-twitch (FT) fiber, a muscle fiber that can develop high tension rapidly. FT fibers are used in such activities as sprinting, jumping, and weight lifting.

fat [AS, *faett*], **1.** a substance composed of lipids or fatty acids and occurring in various forms or consistencies ranging from oil to tallow. **2.** a type of body tissue composed of cells containing stored fat (depot fat). Stored fat is usually identified as white fat, which is found in large cellular vesicles, or brown fat, which consists of lipid droplets. Stored fat contains more than twice as many calories per gram as sugars and serves as a source of body energy. In addition, stored fat helps cushion and insulate vital organs.

fatal /fā'təl/ [L, *fatum,* what has been spoken], causing death.

fatality /fātal'itē/ [L, *fatalis,* preordained], **1.** an individual case of death. **2.** a condition, disease, or disaster resulting in death.

fatality rate, the death rate observed in a specified group of people involved in a simultaneous event.

fat embolism, a circulatory condition characterized by the blocking of an artery by a plug of fat. The plug enters the circulatory system after the fracture of a long bone or, less commonly, after traumatic injury to adipose tissue or to a fatty liver. Fat embolism usually occurs suddenly 12 to 36 hours after an injury and is characterized by symptoms related to the site occluded, such as severe chest pain, pallor, dyspnea, tachycardia, delirium, prostration, and, in some cases, coma. Classic signs of systemic fat embolism are petechial hemorrhages on the neck, shoulders, axillae, and conjunctivae that appear 2 or 3 days after the injury.

FA test, abbreviation for **fluorescent antibody test.**

father complex [L, *pater* + *complecti,* to embrace], *non-technical.* a repressed desire for an incestuous relationship with one's father.

father fixation, an arrest in psychosexual development characterized by an abnormally persistent, close, and often paralyzing emotional attachment to one's father.

fatigability /fat'igobil'itē/, a tendency to become tired or exhausted quickly or easily. It may occur in certain types of cells that undergo periods of excessive activity.

fatigue /fatēg'/ [L, *fatigare,* to tire], **1.** a state of exhaustion or a loss of strength or endurance, such as may follow strenuous physical activity. **2.** loss of ability of tissues to respond to stimuli that normally evoke muscular contraction or other activity. **3.** an emotional state associated with extreme or extended exposure to psychic pressure, as in battle or combat fatigue.

fatigue fever, a benign episode of fever and muscle pain after overexertion. The symptoms are caused by an accumulation of the metabolic waste products of muscle contractions.

fatigue fracture, any fracture that results from excessive physical activity and not from any specific injury, as commonly occurs in the metatarsal bones of runners.

fatigue level, a nursing outcome from the Nursing Outcomes Classification (NOC) defined as the severity of observed or reported prolonged generalized fatigue.

F

fatigue state [L, *fatigare,* to tire, *status,* condition], the state of lowest energy of a system.

fat injection, transplantation of a patient's own fat to other areas on the body, as to the face to minimize wrinkles or to the lips or penis to augment size.

fat metabolism, the biochemical process by which fats are broken down, incorporated, and used by the cells of the body. Fats provide more food energy (9 kcal/g) than carbohydrates (4.1 kcal/g). The body synthesizes fats from fatty acids and glycerol or from compounds derived from excess glucose or from amino acids. The body can synthesize only saturated fatty acids. Essential unsaturated fatty acids can be supplied only by diet. Fat metabolism is controlled by hormones such as insulin, growth hormone, adrenocorticotropic hormone, and glucocorticoids.

fat necrosis [AS, *faett*; Gk, *nekros,* dead, *osis,* condition], a condition caused by trauma or infection in which neutral tissue fats are broken down into fatty acids and glycerol. Fat necrosis occurs most commonly in the breasts and subcutaneous areas. It also may develop in the abdominal cavity after an episode of pancreatitis causes a release of enzymes from the pancreas.

fat overload syndrome, a condition of hepatosplenomegaly, anemia, GI disturbances, and very high triglyceride levels resulting from IV administration of fat emulsion.

fat pad, a mass of closely packed fat cells surrounded by fibrous tissue septa. Fat pads may be generously supplied with capillaries and nerve endings. Intraarticular fat pads are also covered by a layer of synovial cells.

fatty acid (FA) [AS, *faett*; L, *acidus,* sour], any of several organic acids produced by the hydrolysis of neutral fats and consisting of a long hydrocarbon chain ending in a carboxyl group. Essential fatty acids are unsaturated molecules that cannot be produced by the body and must therefore be included in the diet.

fatty alcohol, a hydroxy derivative of a hydrocarbon from the paraffin series.

fatty cirrhosis [AS, *faett*; Gk, *kirrhos,* yellow-orange, *osis,* condition], a form of cirrhosis that develops over a long period of poor nutrition resulting in fatty infiltration of the liver.

fatty degeneration [AS, *faett*; L, *degenerare,* to deviate], the abnormal deposition of fat within cells or the invasion of organs by fatty tissue.

fatty diarrhea, the excretion of fatty, foul-smelling stools that float on water. The condition is associated with chronic pancreatic disease and other malabsorption disorders.

fatty infiltration, a normal phase of breast development characterized by accumulation of increased amounts of fat around the parenchymal breast tissue.

fatty infiltration of heart [AS, *faett*; L, *in* + *filtrare*; AS, *heorte*], an accumulation of large amounts of fat within the cells of the heart. The heart muscle may be marked by irregular, pale streaks representing areas of fatty infiltration. The condition is sometimes associated with severe and prolonged anemia.

fatty liver, an accumulation of triglycerides in the liver. The causes include obesity, diabetes, excessive consumption of alcohol, IV administration of drugs such as tetracycline and corticosteroids, and exposure to toxic substances such as carbon tetrachloride and yellow phosphorus. The symptoms are anorexia, hepatomegaly, and abdominal discomfort.

fatty stool [AS, *faett* + *stol,* seat], feces containing an abnormally large amount of fat, as indicated by their floating on water.

fatty tissue [AS, *faett*; OFr, *tissu*], loose connective tissue with many cells that contain fat vacuoles.

faucial isthmus /fô'shəl/, the aperture of the mouth into the pharynx. The anterior pillars of the fauces form the glossopalatine arch; the posterior pillars form the pharyngopalatine arch.

faulty restoration /fôl'tē/ [L, *fallere,* to deceive, *restaurare,* to renew], any dental filling or fabrication that contains flaws such as overhanging or incomplete fillings, voids, and incorrect anatomic characteristics of occlusal and marginal ridge areas.

favism /fā'vizəm/ [It, *fava,* bean], an acute hemolytic anemia caused by ingestion of the beans or inhalation of the pollen from the *Vicia faba* (fava) plant. Symptoms include dizziness, headache, vomiting, fever, jaundice, eosinophilia, and often diarrhea.

favus /fā'vəs/ [L, honeycomb], a fungal infection of the scalp, skin, or nails, more common in children than in adults. It is caused by *Trichophyton* fungi. Favus is characterized by thick yellow crusts with suppuration, a honeycomb appearance, a distinct "mousy" odor, permanent scars, and alopecia.

fax, abbreviation for **facsimile.**

FBS, abbreviation for *fasting blood sugar.*

FCAP, abbreviation for *Fellow of the College of American Pathologists.*

FCC, abbreviation for **Federal Communications Commission.**

FDA, abbreviation for **Food and Drug Administration.**

FDI numbering system [Fr, Fédération Dentaire Internationale], an internationally used two-digit system for identifying and referring to teeth, established through the FDI, headquartered in Paris, France.

Fe, symbol for the element **iron.**

fear level, a nursing outcome from the Nursing Outcomes Classification (NOC) defined as the severity of manifested apprehension, tension, or uneasiness arising from an identifiable source.

fear level: child, a nursing outcome from the Nursing Outcomes Classification (NOC) defined as the severity of manifested apprehension, tension, or uneasiness arising from an identifiable source in a child from 1 year through 17 years of age.

fear self-control, a nursing outcome from the Nursing Outcomes Classification (NOC) defined as personal actions to eliminate or reduce disabling feelings of apprehension, tension, or uneasiness from an identifiable source.

fear-tension-pain syndrome, a concept formulated by Grantly Dick-Read, M.D., to explain the pain commonly expected and reported in childbirth. The concept proposes that attitudes induce anxiety before labor and cause fear in labor. This fear causes muscular and psychologic tension that interferes with the natural processes of dilation and delivery, resulting in pain. He advocated education, exercise, and warm emotional and physical support in labor to counteract the syndrome and coined the term *natural childbirth* for a labor or delivery in which the woman joyfully, comfortably, and with a calm, cooperative attitude participates in a natural experience.

febrifacient /feb′rifā′shənt/, an agent that induces a fever.

febrile /fē′bril, feb′ril/ [L, *febris,* fever], pertaining to or characterized by an elevated body temperature, such as a febrile reaction to an infectious agent. A body temperature above 100° F (37.8° C), or 99.6° F (37.6° C) rectally, is commonly regarded as febrile.—**febrility,** *n.*

febrile/cold agglutinins test, blood tests used to diagnose infectious diseases and some neoplastic diseases. The febrile agglutinins serologic studies are used to diagnose salmonellosis, rickettsial diseases, brucellosis, tularemia, and some leukemias and lymphomas, while cold agglutinins are found in patients infected by *Mycoplasma pneumoniae,* influenza, mononucleosis, rheumatoid arthritis, and lymphomas.

febrile delirium [L, *febris,* fever, *delirare,* to rave], a symptom of disordered CNS function, with excitement, restlessness, and disorientation, accompanying some acute fevers.

febrile seizure, a seizure associated with a febrile illness. Generalized recurrent febrile seizures in children may be treated as grand mal epilepsy.

febrile state [L, *febris,* fever, *status,* condition], a significant increase in body temperature accompanied by increased pulse and respiration rates, anorexia, constipation, insomnia, headache, pains, and irritability.

febrile urine, a deep orange-colored, strong-smelling urine of a patient with a fever, usually caused by concentration of the urine as a result of dehydration.

fecal fat test, a stool test performed to confirm the diagnosis of steatorrhea.

fecal fistula [L, *faex,* waste matter, *fistula,* pipe], an abnormal passage from the colon to the external surface of the body, for discharging feces.

fecal impaction, an accumulation of hardened or inspissated feces in the rectum or sigmoid colon that the individual is unable to move. Diarrhea may be a sign of fecal impaction, because only liquid material is able to pass the obstruction. Persons who are dehydrated, nutritionally depleted, on long periods of bed rest, receiving constipating medications, or undergoing barium radiographic studies are at risk for developing fecal impaction.

fecalith /fē′kəlith/ [L, *faex;* Gk, *lithos,* stone], a hard, impacted mass of feces in the colon.

fecal softener, a drug that lowers the surface tension of the fecal mass, allowing the intestinal fluids to penetrate and soften the stool.

feces /fē′sēz/ *sing.* **faex** [L, *faex,* waste matter], waste or excrement from the digestive tract that is formed in the intestine and expelled through the rectum. Feces consist of water, food residue, bacteria, and secretions of the intestines and liver.—**fecal,** *adj.*

fecundation /fē′kəndā′shən, fek′-/ [L, *fecundare,* to make fruitful], impregnation or fertilization; the act of fertilizing. — **fecundate,** *v.*

fecundity /fikun′ditē/, the ability to produce offspring, especially in large numbers and rapidly; fertility.—**fecund** /fek′ənd, fē′kənd/, *adj.*

Federal Communications Commission (FCC), a federal agency of the United States that regulates interstate and international communications by radio, television, wire, satellite, cable, and 911.

Federal Register, a document published by the U.S. government each working day to inform the public of executive regulations,

F

presidential orders, hearings and meeting schedules of various federal agencies, and related matters. The *Federal Register* contains announcements of the Food and Drug Administration, the Environmental Protection Agency, and other government bureaus that regulate matters of health and safety.

Federal Tort Claims Act, a statute passed in 1946 that allows the federal government of the United States to be sued for the wrongful action or negligence of its employees.

Federal Trade Commission (FTC), an agency in the executive branch of the federal government of the United States created to promote trade and to prevent practices that restrain free enterprise and competition, including the area of health care.

feedback [AS, *faedan* + *baec*], in communication theory, **1.** information produced by a receiver and perceived by a sender that informs the sender of the receiver's reaction to the message. **2.** the return of some of the output so as to exert some control in the process.

feedback loop, the circular path seen in a system that has feedback, such that the output of the system participates in the control of the system.

feedforward control, an anticipatory correction in motor behavior. During movement, various brain centers depend on feedback from receptors to control motor behavior. If the actual and intended motor behaviors do not match, an error signal is generated, and alterations are made.

feeding[1] [AS, *faedan*], the act or process of taking or giving food or nourishment.

feeding[2], a nursing intervention from the Nursing Interventions Classification (NIC) defined as providing nutritional intake for patient who is unable to feed self.

feeding tube, a tube for introducing fluids of high caloric value into the stomach.

fee-for-service [AS, *feoh*, property; L, *servitum*, slavery], **1.** a charge made for a professional activity, such as a physical examination, the fitting of a contraceptive diaphragm, or the monitoring of a person's BP. **2.** a system for the payment of professional services in which the practitioner is paid for the particular service rendered, rather than receiving a salary.

fee-for-service equivalent, in U.S. managed care, a specialty capitation method in which a fee schedule is developed for service and providers are paid a percentage of the fee schedule.

feeling, **1.** a quality of mood. **2.** a subjective experience caused by stimulation of a sensory nerve.

FEES, service mark for **fiberoptic endoscopic evaluation of swallowing.**

fee schedule, in U.S. managed care, the specific dollar amount to be charged for each service offered.

fee screen system, a method of establishing payment for physician services that is based on the usual, customary, or reasonable charge according to a regional evaluation.

FEF, abbreviation for **forced expiratory flow.**

Fehling's solution /fā'lingz/ [Hermann C. von Fehling, German chemist, 1812–1885], a solution containing cupric sulfate with sodium hydroxide and potassium sodium tartrate, used for testing for the presence of glucose and other reducing substances in the urine.

Feingold diet /fīn'gōld/ [Benjamin Feingold, American pediatrician, 1900–1982], a diet developed to treat hyperactive children. The diet excludes foods manufactured with synthetic colorings, flavorings, and preservatives and limits the intake of fruits and vegetables that contain salicylates. Studies have shown the Feingold diet to be ineffective.

felbamate /fel'bämāt/, an anticonvulsant used in treatment of epilepsy.

Feldene, a trademark for an antiinflammatory agent (piroxicam).

Feldenkrais Method /fel'dənkrīs/, **1.** in psychiatry, a proprietary system that uses an exploratory technique to enable patients to relearn dysfunctional movement patterns. **2.** a bodywork technique that integrates principles of physics, judo, and yoga to treat physical impairments through the learning of new movement patterns.

feldspar /feld'spär/ [Ger, *feld*, field, *spath*, spar], a crystalline mineral of aluminum silicate with potassium, sodium, barium, and calcium. It is an important component of dental porcelain.

fellatio /fəlā'shē·ō/, oral stimulation of the male genitalia.

fellow [AS, *feolaga*, friendly association], **1.** a member of a learned society. **2.** a graduate student who holds a position in a university or college. **3.** a peer, associate, or person of the same class or rank.

Fellow of the American Academy of Nursing (FAAN), a member of the American Academy of Nursing.

fellowship /fel'ōship/ [As, *feolaga*, friendly association], a grant given to a person to pay for study or training or to allow payment for work on a special project.

felon /fel'ən/ [L, *fel*, venom], a suppurative abscess on the distal phalanx of a finger.

felony /fel'ənē/, in criminal law, a crime declared by statute to be more serious than a misdemeanor and deserving of a more severe penalty. In many states there is current, pending, or new legislation that essentially bars applicants from taking examinations in health care disciplines if certain felonies exist in their history.

Felty's syndrome /fel'tēz/ [Augustus R. Felty, American physician, 1895–1963], a group of pathologic changes that occurs with adult rheumatoid arthritis, characterized by splenomegaly, leukopenia, frequent infections, and sometimes thrombocytopenia and anemia.

female [L, *femella,* young woman], **1.** pertaining to the sex that has the ability to become pregnant and bear children; feminine. **2.** a female person.

female catheterization, a procedure for removing urine by means of a urinary catheter introduced through the urinary meatus and urethra into the bladder. The procedure is performed for relief of distension if voluntary micturition is not possible (such as after trauma or surgery), as a preparation for and during anesthesia, or if a specimen of urine from the bladder is required or medication is to be instilled into the bladder.

female circumcision, the surgical excision of the prepuce of the clitoris.

female condom, a sheath worn inside the vagina, also extending outward to cover the vulva. It is used to prevent pregnancy or transmission of infection.

female factor infertility, infertility of a couple because of a problem in the female's reproductive system. Types include cervical factor infertility and tubal factor infertility.

female genital mutilation, the ritual practice in some cultures of excising the entire clitoris without anesthetic, sometimes as part of a maturity initiation rite.

female pseudohermaphroditism, a form of the congenital gonadal disorder in which ovaries are present, irrespective of the condition of the external genitals.

female reproductive system assessment, an evaluation of a patient's genital tract and breasts with an investigation of past and present disorders that may be factors in the individual's current gynecologic condition.

female sexual dysfunction, impaired or inadequate ability of a woman to engage in or enjoy satisfactory sexual intercourse and orgasm. Causes may include anxiety, fear, negative emotions associated with sexual arousal and intercourse, and interpersonal problems. Neurologic dysfunction may also be present.

female sterility [L, *femella,* young woman, *sterilis,* barren], a condition of being an infertile woman. The inability to reproduce may result from congenital defects in the reproductive system or disease, injury, or corrective surgery that affects functioning of the ovaries, fallopian tubes, uterus, cervix, or vagina.

female urethra, a canal about 3.7 cm long, extending from the neck of the bladder above the anterior vaginal wall to the urinary meatus.

feminist therapy, an alternative therapy that is both a philosophic approach to the conduct of therapy and a specific type of therapy. The focus of both types is a consciousness raising that focuses on the presence of sexism and sex role stereotyping in society.

feminization /fem'inīzā'shən/ [L, *femina,* woman], **1.** the normal development or induction of female secondary sex characteristics. **2.** the induction of female sex characteristics in a genotypic male. Testicular feminization may be caused by the inability of target tissues to respond to endogenous or administered androgen. Some cases seem related to an absent or inadequate conversion of testosterone to dihydrotestosterone.

feminizing adrenal tumor /fem'inī'zing/, a rare neoplasm of the adrenal cortex, characterized in males by gynecomastia, hypertension, diffuse pigmentation, a high level of estrogen in urine, and loss of potency. Testicular atrophy frequently occurs. In women these tumors, which are extremely rare, are associated with precocious puberty.

femoral /fem'ərəl/ [L, *femur,* thigh], pertaining to the femur or the thigh.

femoral anteversion, inward twisting of the femur so that the knees and feet turn inward, usually seen in children or in persons with osteoarthritis of the hip.

femoral artery (FA), an extension of the external iliac artery into the lower limb, starting immediately distal to the inguinal ligament and ending at the junction of the middle and lower thirds of the thigh.

femoral catheter, a central venous catheter inserted through the femoral vein.

femoral condyle, one of a pair of large flared prominences on the distal end of the femur. They articulate with the patella and the tibia at the knee joint.

femoral epiphysis, a secondary bone-forming center of the femur, separated from the main part of the bone by cartilage during the period of bone immaturity.

femoral hernia, a hernia in which a loop of intestine descends through the femoral canal into the groin.

femoral nerve, the largest of the seven nerves stemming from the lumbar plexus and the main nerve of the anterior part of the thigh.

femoral pulse, the pulse of the femoral artery, palpated in the groin.

femoral reflex [L, *femur,* thigh, *reflectere,* to bend back], an extension of the knee

F

and a plantar flexion of the toes of the foot that occurs when the skin on the upper anterior third of the thigh is stimulated.

femoral stem, in arthroplasty of the hip or knee, the part of the prosthesis that inserts into the end of the trimmed and prepared femur.

femoral-to-popliteal artery bypass, grafting with a saphenous vein or straight synthetic graft to bypass an occluded section of the femoral artery and restore blood flow to the leg.

femoral torsion, an extreme lateral or medial twisting rotation of the femur on its longitudinal axis, which may be caused by the action of the gluteal or other muscles.

femoral triangle, a wedge-shaped depression formed by the muscles in the upper thigh at the junction between the anterior abdominal wall and the lower limb through which the femoral nerve, artery, and vein and lymphatic vessels pass.

femoral vein, a large vein in the thigh that is a continuation of the popliteal vein and that accompanies the femoral artery in the proximal two thirds of the thigh. Its distal portion lies lateral to the artery, and its proximal portion lies deeper to the artery. Near its termination, it is joined by the great saphenous vein.

Femstat, a trademark for an antifungal drug (butoconazole nitrate).

femur /fē'mər/ *pl.* **femora, femurs** [L, thigh], the thigh bone, which extends from the pelvis to the knee. It is largely cylindric and is the longest and strongest bone in the body.

fenestra /fines'trə/ *pl.* **fenestrae** [L, window], **1.** an aperture, as in a bandage or cast, that is cut out to relieve pressure or to administer regular skin care. **2.** a microscopic opening in certain capillaries specialized in filtration.

fenestrated drape, a drape with a round or slitlike opening in the center.

fenestration /fen'əstrā'shən/ [L, *fenestra,* window], **1.** a surgical procedure in which an opening is created to gain access to the cavity within an organ or a bone. **2.** an opening created surgically in a bone or organ of the body. **3.** in dentistry, a procedure to expose a root tip of a tooth to permit drainage of exudate. —**fenestrate,** *v.*

fenofibrate /fen'ofi'brāt/, an agent chemically related to clofibrate, used to treat hyperlipidemia.

fenoldopam, an antihypertensive used to treat hypertensive crisis when an urgent decrease of pressure is required, including malignant hypertension.

fenoprofen calcium /fē'nəprō'fen/, a nonsteroidal antiinflammatory agent and

analgesic prescribed in the treatment of arthritis and other painful inflammatory conditions.

fenoterol /fen'ōter'ol/, a beta-2-adrenergic receptor agonist used as a bronchodilator for the treatment and prophylaxis of reversible bronchospasm.

fentanyl citrate, a general anesthetic prescribed as an adjunct to general anesthesia, as a preoperative and postoperative analgesic, and as a component in neuroleptanesthesia and analgesia.

fenugreek, an annual herb found in Europe and Asia. This herb is used for loss of appetite, skin inflammation, water retention, cancer, constipation, diarrhea, high cholesterol, high blood glucose, and calcium oxalate stones. It may be effective at lowering blood glucose (slow intestinal absorption) and as a poultice for local inflammation, but there are insufficient reliable data on its efficacy for other uses.

Feosol, a trademark for a ferrous sulfate, an iron supplement prescribed to help increase hemoglobin production.

Fergon, a trademark for ferrous gluconate, an iron supplement prescribed to help increase hemoglobin production.

Ferguson's reflex, a contraction of the uterus after the cervix is stimulated. The reflex is an important function of labor.

fermentation /fur'məntā'shən/ [L, *fermentare,* to cause to rise], a chemical change that is brought about in a substance by the action of an enzyme or microorganism, especially the anaerobic conversion of foodstuffs to certain products.

fermentative dyspepsia /fərmen'tətiv/, an abnormal condition characterized by impaired digestion associated with the fermentation of digested food.

fermium (Fm) /fur'mē-əm/ [Enrico Fermi, Italian physicist, 1901–1954], a synthetic transuranic metallic element. Its atomic number is 100; the mass of its longest-lived, best-known isotope is 257.

ferning test /fur'ning/ [AS, *faern,* fern; L, *testum,* crucible], a technique used to determine the presence of estrogen in the uterine cervical mucus. It is often used to test for ovulation. High levels of estrogen cause the cervical mucus to dry in a fernlike pattern on a slide.

ferredoxin, a nonheme protein containing equal amounts of iron and sulfur. Ferredoxins are involved in electron transport in photosynthesis and nitrogen fixation.

ferric /fer'ik/, pertaining to a cation of iron in which the metal is trivalent, as in ferric chloride and ferric hydroxide.

ferritin /fer'itin/ [L, *ferrum,* iron], an iron compound formed in the intestine and stored in the liver, spleen, and bone marrow for eventual incorporation into hemoglobin.

ferritin test, a blood test used to determine available iron stores in the body. It is used to diagnose iron deficiency anemia, and when combined with the serum iron level and total iron-binding capacity tests, can differentiate and classify various kinds of anemias.

ferrokinetics /fer′ōkinet′iks/, the study of iron metabolism.

ferromagnetic /fer′ōmagnet′ik/, pertaining to substances such as iron, nickel, and cobalt that are strongly affected by magnetism.

ferrotherapy /fer′ōther′əpē/, the use of iron and iron compounds in the treatment of illness.

ferrous /fer′əs/, pertaining to a compound of iron in which the metal is divalent, such as ferrous ammonium sulfate.

ferrous sulfate, an antianemia (hematinic) agent prescribed in the treatment of iron deficiency anemia.

fertile /fur′təl/ [L, *fertilis,* fruitful], **1.** capable of reproducing or bearing offspring. **2.** of a gamete, capable of inducing fertilization or being fertilized. **3.** prolific; fruitful; not sterile.—**fertility,** *n.,* **fertilize,** *v.*

fertile eunuch syndrome, a hypogonadotropic hormonal disorder of males in which the levels of testosterone and follicle-stimulating hormone are inadequate to induce spermatogenesis and the development of secondary sexual characteristics.

fertile period, the time in the menstrual cycle during which fertilization may occur. Spermatozoa can survive for 5 days; the ovum lives for 24 hours. Thus the fertile period begins up to 6 days before ovulation and lasts for 1 day afterward.

fertility /fərtil′itē/, the ability to reproduce.

fertility preservation, a nursing intervention from the Nursing Interventions Classification (NIC) defined as providing information, counseling, and treatment that facilitate reproductive health and the ability to conceive.

fertility rate, the number of live births divided by the number of females aged 15 through 44 years of age. It is usually expressed as the number per 1000 women.

fertilization /fur′tilīzā′shən/ [L, *fertilis,* fruitful], the union of male and female gametes to form a zygote from which the embryo develops. The process usually takes place in the outer one third of the fallopian tube of the female when a spermatozoon, carried in the seminal fluid discharged during coitus, comes in contact with and penetrates the ovum.

fertilization membrane, a viscous membrane surrounding a fertilized ovum that prevents penetration of additional spermatozoa.

fertilizin /fərtil′izin/, a glycoprotein found on the plasma membrane of the ovum in various species.

Festal, a trademark for a fixed-combination GI drug that contains a group of digestive enzymes and bile constituents.

fester, **1.** to become superficially inflamed and pus-producing. **2.** to become increasingly virulent.

festinant /fes′tinənt/, pertaining to a gait pattern that accelerates involuntarily as a result of a nervous system disorder.

festinating gait /fes′tinā′ting/ [L, *festinare,* to hasten], a manner of walking in which a person's speed increases in an unconscious effort to "catch up" with a displaced center of gravity. It is a common characteristic of Parkinson's disease.

festoon [Fr, *feston,* scallop], a carving in the base material of a denture that simulates the contours of the natural gingival tissues.

FET, abbreviation for **forced expiratory time.**

fetal /fē′təl/ [L, *fetus,* fruitful], pertaining to the final stage of development of a prenatal mammal. In humans the fetal period extends from the first day of the ninth week of intrauterine life until birth.

fetal abortion [L, *fetus*], termination of pregnancy after the twentieth week of gestation but before the fetus has developed enough to live outside the uterus.

fetal advocate, a person who regards the health and well-being of the fetus as a matter of top priority.

fetal age, the age of the conceptus computed from the time elapsed since fertilization.

fetal alcohol syndrome (FAS) [L, *fetus;* Ar, *alkohl,* essence; Gk, *syn,* together, *dromos,* course], a set of congenital psychologic, behavioral, and physical abnormalities that tend to appear in infants whose mothers consumed alcohol during pregnancy. It is characterized by typical craniofacial and limb defects, cardiovascular defects, intrauterine growth retardation, and retarded development. The most serious cases have involved infants born to mothers who were chronic alcoholics and drank heavily during pregnancy, but it is not known whether there is a lower limit to alcohol consumption during pregnancy or a particular period in embryonic life when the offspring is most vulnerable to effects of alcohol.

fetal alveoli, the terminal pulmonary sacs of a fetus, which are filled with fluid before birth.

fetal asphyxia, a condition of hypoxemia, hypercapnia, and respiratory and metabolic acidosis that may occur in the uterus.

fetal attitude, the relationship of the fetal parts to each other. An example is the "military" attitude, in which the fetal head is not flexed and the chin is not on the chest as usual but is held straight up.

fetal biophysical profile, an ultrasound method of evaluating fetal status during the antepartal period based on five variables originating within the fetus: fetal heart rate, breathing movement, gross movements, muscle tone, and amniotic fluid volume.

fetal bradycardia, an abnormally slow fetal heart rate, usually below 100 beats/min.

fetal circulation, the pathway of blood circulation in the fetus. Oxygenated blood from the placenta travels through the umbilical vein to the heart. The blood enters the right atrium at a pressure sufficient to direct most of the flow across the atrium and through the foramen ovale into the left atrium; thus oxygenated blood is available for circulation through the left ventricle to the head and upper extremities. The blood returning from the head and arms enters the right atrium via the superior vena cava. It flows through the atrium at a relatively low pressure. Passing the tricuspid valve, it falls into the right ventricle, from which most of it is pumped through the pulmonary artery and the ductus arteriosus into the descending aorta for circulation to the lower parts of the body. A small amount of blood in the pulmonary artery is not shunted through the ductus and is carried to the lungs. The blood is returned to the placenta through the umbilical arteries.

fetal death, the intrauterine death of a fetus, or the death of a fetus weighing at least 500 g or after 20 or more weeks of gestation.

fetal distress, a compromised condition of the fetus, usually discovered during labor, characterized by a markedly abnormal rate or rhythm of myocardial contraction.

fetal dose, the estimated amount of radiation received by a fetus during a radiographic examination of a pregnant woman.

fetal fibronectin test, an analysis of vaginal secretions of a pregnant woman to determine the risk of preterm delivery.

fetal heart rate (FHR), the number of heartbeats in the fetus that occur in a given unit of time. The FHR varies in cycles of fetal rest and activity and is affected by many factors, including maternal fever, uterine contractions, maternal-fetal hypotension, and many drugs. The normal FHR is between 110 beats/min and 160 beats/min.

fetal heart sound [L, *fetus,* fruitful; AS, *heorte;* L, *sonus,* sound], a sound produced by the heart of a fetus, as detected by auscultation or by electronic fetal monitoring. The heart begins beating at about 14 days of intrauterine life.

fetal hemoglobin, hemoglobin F, the major hemoglobin present in the blood of a fetus and neonate.

fetal hemoglobin test, a test of maternal blood to detect leakage of fetal cells into the maternal circulation, an indication of fetal-maternal hemorrhage.

fetal hydantoin syndrome (FHS), a complex of birth defects associated with prenatal maternal ingestion of hydantoin derivatives. Symptoms of FHS include microcephaly, hypoplasia or absence of nails on the fingers or toes, abnormal facies, mental and physical retardation, and cardiac defects.

fetal lie, the relationship of the long axis of the fetus to the long axis of the mother.

fetal membranes, the structures that protect, support, and nourish the embryo and fetus, including the yolk sac, allantois, amnion, chorion, placenta, and umbilical cord.

fetal microchimerism, persistence in the mother's circulation of a low number of fetal cells. It may play a role in some autoimmune disorders.

fetal mortality rate, the number of fetal deaths per 1000 births, or per live births.

fetal movements [L, *fetus + movere,* to move], muscular motions produced by the fetus in utero beginning around the fifth month of life. The early fetal movements can be felt by the mother.

fetal nonstress test, an electrodiagnostic test to evaluate the viability of a fetus. It documents the function of the placenta in its ability to supply adequate blood to the fetus.

fetal placenta [L, *fetus + placenta,* flat cake], the portion of the placenta that is formed from the shaggy chorion frondosum, the villi of which invade the decidua basalis.

fetal position, the relationship of the part of the fetus that presents in the pelvis to four quadrants of the maternal pelvis, identified by initial L (left), R (right), A (anterior), and P (posterior). The presenting part is also identified by initial O (occiput), M (mentum), and S (sacrum). If a fetus presents with the occiput directed to the posterior aspect of the mother's right side, the fetal position is right occiput posterior (ROP).

fetal presentation, the part of the fetus that lies closest to or has entered the true pelvis. Cephalic presentations are vertex, brow, face, and chin. Breech presentations include frank breech, complete breech, incomplete breech, and single or double footling breech. Shoulder presentations are rare.

fetal respiration, the exchange of gases between the blood of the mother and that of the fetus through the placenta.

fetal rotation [L, *fetus* + *rotare,* to rotate], the turning of the head of the fetus as it begins the descent through the birth canal. The fetal head may be rotated by hand or with forceps if needed to guide the body in a proper position for delivery.

fetal scalp blood pH test, a measurement of fetal scalp blood pH used to diagnose fetal distress.

fetal stage, in embryology, the interval from the end of the embryonic stage, at the end of the seventh or eighth week of gestation, to birth, 38 to 42 weeks after the first day of the last menstrual period.

fetal status: antepartum, a nursing outcome from the Nursing Outcomes Classification (NOC) defined as the extent to which fetal signs are within normal limits from conception to the onset of labor.

fetal status: intrapartum, a nursing outcome from the Nursing Outcomes Classification (NOC) defined as the extent to which fetal signs are within normal limits from onset of labor to delivery.

fetal tachycardia, a fetal heart rate that continues at 160 beats/min or more for more than 10 minutes.

fetid /fet′id, fē′tid/ [L, *fetere,* to stink], pertaining to something that has a foul or putrid odor.

fetish [Fr, *fetiche,* artificial], **1.** any object or idea given unreasonable or excessive attention or reverence. **2.** in psychology, any inanimate object or any body part not of a sexual nature that arouses erotic feelings or fixation.—**fetishism,** *n.*

fetishist /fet′ishist/, a person who believes in or receives erotic gratification from fetishes.

fetochorionic /fē′tōkôr′ē·on′ik/ [L, *fetus,* fruitful; Gk, *chorion,* skin], pertaining to the fetus and the chorion.

fetoglobulins /fē′tōglob′yəlinz/, proteins found in fetal blood and normally in small amounts in adult blood.

fetography /fētog′rəfē/ [L, *fetus;* Gk, *graphein,* to record], roentgenography of the fetus in utero.

fetology /fētol′əjē/ [L, *fetus;* Gk, *logos,* science], the branch of medicine that is concerned with the fetus in utero, including the diagnosis of congenital anomalies, the prevention of teratogenic influences, and the treatment of certain disorders.

fetometry /fētom′ətrē/ [L, *fetus;* Gk, *metron,* measure], the measurement of the size of the fetus, especially the diameter of the head and circumference of the trunk.

fetoplacental /-pləsen′təl/ [L, *fetus* + *placenta,* flat cake], pertaining to the fetus and the placenta.

fetoprotein /-prō′tēn/ [L, *fetus;* Gk, *proteios,* first rank], an antigen that occurs naturally in fetuses and occasionally in adults as the result of certain diseases. An increased amount of alpha-fetoprotein in the fetus is diagnostic for neural tube defects. The presence of beta-fetoprotein in the blood of adults is associated with leukemia, hepatoma, sarcoma, and other neoplasms.

fetor hepaticus [L, stench, *hēpar,* liver], foul-smelling breath associated with severe liver disease.

fetoscope /fē′təskōp′/ [L, *fetus;* Gk, *skopein,* to look], a stethoscope for monitoring the fetal heartbeat through the mother's abdomen.

fetoscopy /fētos′kəpē/, a procedure in which a fetus may be directly observed in utero, using a fetoscope introduced through a small incision in the abdomen under local anesthesia.

fetotoxic /-tok′sik/ [L, *fetus;* Gk, *toxikon,* poison], pertaining to anything that is poisonous to a fetus.

fetus /fē′təs/ [L, fruitful], the unborn offspring of any viviparous animal after it has attained the particular form of the species; more specifically, the human being in utero after the embryonic period and the beginning of the development of the major structural features, from the ninth week after fertilization until birth.—**fetal, foetal,** *adj.*

fetus amorphus, a shapeless conceptus that has no formed or recognizable parts.

fetus in fetu /in fē′tōō/, a fetal anomaly in which a small, imperfectly formed twin, incapable of independent existence, is contained within the body of the normal twin, the autosite.

fetus papyraceus, a twin fetus that has died in utero early in development and has been pressed flat against the uterine wall by the living fetus.

fetus sanguinolentis /sang′gwinələn′tis/, a darkly colored, partly macerated fetus that has died in utero.

FEV, abbreviation for **forced expiratory volume.**

FEVC, abbreviation for **forced expiratory vital capacity.**

fever [L, *febris*], an elevation of body temperature above the normal circadian range as a result of an increase in the body's core temperature. Fever is a temperature above 37.2° C (98.9° F) in the morning or above 37.7° C (99.9° F) in the evening. Fever results from an imbalance between the elimination and the production of heat.

fever blister, a cold sore caused by herpesvirus I or II. It generally appears around the mouth or nasal mucous membranes following a febrile episode or cold.

feverfew, a perennial herb used for migraines, cluster headaches, fever, psoriasis, and inflammation. It is probably safe and effective when used over short terms at recommended levels of migraine prophylaxis and possibly safe for long-term use, but it does not abort migraine attacks. There are insufficient reliable data for other uses.

fever of unknown origin (FUO), a febrile illness of at least 3 weeks' duration with a temperature of at least 38.3° C on at least three occasions and failure to establish a diagnosis in spite of intensive inpatient or outpatient evaluation (three outpatient visits or 3 days' hospitalization).

fever treatment[1], the care and management of a person who has an elevated temperature. Treatment may include the administration of antibiotic, antipyretic, and sedative drugs. If the temperature is extremely high, a cooling tub bath, cold wet sheet, ice packs, or hypothermia blanket may be ordered.

fever treatment[2], a nursing intervention from the Nursing Interventions Classification (NIC) defined as management of a patient with hyperpyrexia caused by nonenvironmental factors.

fexofenadine, an antihistamine used to treat rhinitis and allergy symptoms.

FFA, abbreviation for **free fatty acid.**

F factor, an extrachromosomal segment of DNA that is present in conjugating male bacteria but absent in females.

^{18}F-FDG, symbol for [^{18}F]-2-fluoro-2-deoxy-D-glucose, a sugar analog used in PET to determine the local cerebral metabolic rate of glucose as a measure of neural activity in the brain.

FG syndrome [FG, initials of family names of patients in whom it was first observed], an X-linked recessive syndrome of mental retardation, megalencephaly, imperforate anus and other GI defects, delayed motor development, congenital hypotonia, characteristic facies and personality, short stature, skeletal anomalies, and congenital cardiac defects.

FGT cytologic smear, abbreviation for *female genital tract cytologic smear,* any sample of tissues from the female reproductive tract smeared on a microscope slide for examination.

FHR, abbreviation for **fetal heart rate.**

FHS, abbreviation for **fetal hydantoin syndrome.**

fiber /fī′bər/, **1.** a long, filmlike, thread-like, acellular structure found in plant and animal tissues. Plant fibers usually consist of structural carbohydrates such as cellulose in cell walls. Cellulose cannot be digested by enzymes in the human intestine. Animal fibers are composed mainly of the protein collagen, which forms elastic threads of loose connective tissue in skin and other organs. **2.** a skeletal muscle cell. **3.** the axon of a nerve cell.

fiberglass dermatitis, a pruritic papular skin disease produced by mechanical irritation from glass fibers.

fiber modified diet, a diet that contains more or less fiber than a normal diet.

fiberoptic bronchoscopy /-op′tik/ [L, *fibra*; Gk, *optikos,* sight], the visual examination of the tracheobronchial tree through a fiberoptic bronchoscope.

fiberoptic colonoscope, a colonoscope that uses fiberoptic technology.

fiberoptic duodenoscope, an instrument for visualizing the interior of the duodenum, consisting of an eyepiece, a flexible tube incorporating bundles of coated glass or plastic fibers with special optic properties, and a terminal light.

fiberoptic endoscopic evaluation of swallowing (FEES), diagnosis and treatment of swallowing disorders by means of a flexible fiberoptic endoscope introduced transnasally into the hypopharynx.

fiberoptics /-op′tiks/, the technical process by which an internal organ or cavity can be viewed, using glass or plastic fibers to transmit light through a specially designed tube and reflect a magnified image.—**fiberoptic,** *adj.*

fiberscope /fī′bərskōp/ [L, *fibra*; Gk, *skopein,* to look], a flexible fiberoptic instrument designed for the examination of particular organs and cavities of the body and used in bronchoscopy, endoscopy, and gastroscopy.

fibrates /fi′brāts/, a general term for fibric acid derivatives, such as gemfibrozil.

fibril /fī′bril/ [L, *fibrilla,* small fiber], a small filamentous fiber that often is a component of a cell, as in a mitotic spindle or a myofibril.—**fibrillary,** *adj.*

fibrillation /fī′brilā′shən/ [L, *fibrilla,* small fiber, *atio,* process], involuntary recurrent contraction of a single muscle fiber or of an isolated bundle of nerve fibers. Fibrillation is usually described by the part that is contracting abnormally, such as atrial fibrillation or ventricular fibrillation.

fibrillin /fibri′lin/ [L, *fibrilla,* small fiber], a major component of elastin-associated microfibrils. It is linked to Marfan syndrome by findings of immunohistochemical studies and is associated with arachnodactyly.

fibrin /fī′brin/ [L, *fibra,* fiber], a stringy insoluble protein produced by the action of thrombin on fibrinogen in the clotting process. Fibrin is responsible for the semisolid character of a blood clot.

fibrinocellular /fī′brinōsel′yələr/, composed of fibrin and cells, as occurs in some exudates that result from inflammation.

fibrinogen /fībrin′əjən/ [L, *fibra,* fiber; Gk, *genein,* to produce], a plasma protein that is converted into fibrin by thrombin in the presence of calcium ions.

fibrinogenopenia /fī′brinōjen′ōpē′nē·ə/ [L, *fibra;* Gk, *genein,* to produce, *penia,* poverty], a deficiency of fibrinogen in the blood.

fibrinogenous /fī′brinoj′ənəs/ [L, *fibra,* fiber; Gk, *genein,* to produce], pertaining to the characteristics or properties of fibrinogen or the production of fibrin.

fibrinogen test, a blood test that evaluates the blood clotting mechanism. Increased concentrations of fibrinogen may indicate tissue inflammation or necrosis and may predict increased risk of coronary artery or cerebrovascular disease. Low levels are seen with liver disease, malnutrition, and consumptive coagulopathy.

fibrinokinase /fī′brinōkī′nās/ [L, *fibra;* Gk, *kinesis,* motion], a non–water-soluble enzyme in animal tissue that activates plasminogen.

fibrinolysin /fī′brinol′isin/ [L, *fibra;* Gk, *lysein,* to loosen], a proteolytic enzyme that dissolves fibrin. It is formed from plasminogen in the blood plasma.

fibrinolysis /fī′brinol′isis/, the continual process of fibrin decomposition by fibrinolysin that is the normal mechanism for the removal of small fibrin clots.—**fibrinolytic,** *adj.*

fibrinopeptide /fī′brinōpep′tīd/ [L, *fibra;* Gk, *peptein,* to digest], a product of the action of thrombin on fibrinogen.

fibrinous pericarditis [L, *fibra,* fiber; Gk, *peri,* near, *kardia,* heart, *itis,* inflammation], a condition in which a lymphoid exudate accumulates on the pericardium and coagulates. The coagulated exudate may acquire a thick, buttery appearance.

fibroadenoma /fī′brō·ad′inō′mə/ *pl.* **fibroadenomas, fibroadenomata** [L, *fibra;* Gk, *aden,* gland, *oma*], a benign tumor composed of dense epithelial and fibroblastic tissue.

fibroblast /fī′brəblast/ [L, *fibra;* Gk, *blastos,* germ], a flat, elongated undifferentiated cell in the connective tissue that gives rise to various precursor cells such as the chondroblast, collagenoblast, and osteoblast, which form the fibrous, binding, and supporting tissue of the body.—**fibroblastic,** *adj.*

fibroblastoma /-blastōma/ *pl.* **fibroblastomas, fibroblastomata** [L, *fibra;* Gk, *blastos,* germ, *oma*], a tumor derived from a fibroblast, now differentiated as a fibroma or a fibrosarcoma.

fibrocartilage /-kär′tilij/ [L, *fibra* + *cartilago*], cartilage that consists of a dense matrix of white collagenous fibers. Of the three kinds of cartilage in the body, fibrocartilage has the greatest tensile strength.—**fibrocartilaginous,** *adj.*

fibrochondritis /-kondrī′tis/, an inflammation of fibrocartilage.

fibrochondroma /-kondrō′mə/, a tumor composed of mixed fibrous and cartilaginous tissues.

fibrocyst /fī′brəsist/, **1.** any cystic lesion within a fibrous connective tissue. **2.** a cystic fibroma.

fibrocystic /-sis′tik/, pertaining to a fibrocyst or cystic fibroma.

fibrocystic disease of the breast /-sis′tik/ [L, *fibra;* Gk, *kystis,* bag], the presence of single or multiple cysts that are palpable in the breasts. The cysts are benign and fairly common, yet must be considered potentially malignant and observed carefully for growth or change. Only about 5% of fibrocystic conditions could be considered a risk factor for development of cancer later in life.

fibroelastic membrane of larynx, a membrane linking the laryngeal cartilages that is composed of a lower cricothyroid ligament and an upper quadrangular ligament.

fibroepithelial papilloma /-ep′ithē′lē·əl/ [L, *fibra;* Gk, *epi,* above, *thele,* nipple; L, *papilla,* nipple; Gk, *oma,* tumor], a benign epithelial tumor containing extensive fibrous tissue.

fibroepithelioma /fī′brō·ep′ithē′lē·ō′mə/ *pl.* **fibroepitheliomas, fibroepitheliomata** [L, *fibra;* Gk, *epi,* above, *thele,* nipple, *oma,* tumor], a neoplasm consisting of fibrous and epithelial components.

fibrofolliculoma /-folik′yəlō′mə/, a benign tumor derived from the dermal part of a hair follicle.

fibrogliosis /-glī·ō′sis/, the formation of scar tissue in the brain in reaction to a penetrating injury. The scar is produced by fibroblasts and astrocytes.

fibroid /fī′broid/ [L, *fibra;* Gk, *eidos,* form], **1.** having fibers. **2.** *informal.* a fibroma or myoma, particularly of the uterus.

fibroidectomy /fī′broidek′təmē/ [L, *fibra,* fiber; Gk, *eidos,* form, *ektomē,* excision], the surgical removal of a fibrous tumor such as a uterine fibromyoma.

fibrolipoma /fī′brōlipō′mə/, a fibrous tumor that also contains fatty material.

fibroma /fī′brō′mə/ *pl.* **fibromas, fibromata** [L, *fibra;* Gk, *oma,* tumor], a benign neoplasm consisting largely of fibrous or fully developed connective tissue.

fibroma cavernosum, a tumor that contains large vascular spaces, an excessive amount of fibrous tissue, and blood or lymph vessels.

fibroma cutis, a fibrous tumor of the skin.

fibroma mucinosum, a fibrous tumor in which degenerating mucoid material is present.

fibroma of the breast [L, *fibra,* fiber; Gk, *oma,* tumor; AS, *braest*], a connective tissue tumor of the breast. It is usually benign and painless.

fibroma pendulum, a pendulous fibrous tumor of the skin.

fibromatosis /-mətō′sis/ [L, *fibra*; Gk, *oma,* tumor, *osis,* condition], a gingival enlargement believed to be hereditary, manifested in the secondary dentition. It is characterized by a firm hyperplastic tissue that covers the surfaces of the teeth.

fibromuscular dysplasia (FMD) /-mus′kyələr/, an arterial disorder sometimes associated with strokes or TIAs. The condition is characterized by intraluminal folds of fibrous endothelial tissue, which become the originating site of platelet adherence aggregation and thrombus formation. The condition commonly involves the renal arteries and is associated with hypertension.

fibromyalgia, a form of nonarticular rheumatism characterized by musculoskeletal pain, spasms, stiffness, fatigue, and severe sleep disturbance. Common sites of pain or stiffness include the lower back, neck, shoulder region, arms, hands, knees, hips, thighs, legs, and feet.

fibromyomectomy /fī′brōmī′ōmek′təmē/, a surgical procedure for removing a uterine fibroma or other type of fibromyoma.

fibromyositis /fī′brōmī′əsī′tis/ [L, *fibra*; Gk, *mys,* muscle, *itis,* inflammation], any one of a large number of disorders characterized by stiffness and joint or muscle pain, accompanied by localized inflammation of muscle and fibrous connective tissues.

fibroplasia /-plā′zhə/, the formation of a scar during the fibroblastic repair phase of healing.

fibrosarcoma /-särkō′mə/ *pl.* **fibrosarcomas, fibrosarcomata** [L, *fibra*; Gk, *sarx,* flesh, *oma,* tumor], a sarcoma that contains fibrous connective tissue.

fibrosing alveolitis /fī′brōsing/ [L, *fibra* + *alviolus,* small hollow; Gk, *itis,* inflammation], a severe form of alveolitis characterized by dyspnea and hypoxia. It occurs in advanced rheumatoid arthritis and other autoimmune diseases.

fibrosis /fībrō′sis/ [L, *fibra*; Gk, *osis,* condition], 1. a proliferation of fibrous connective tissue. 2. an abnormal condition in which fibrous connective tissue spreads over or replaces normal smooth muscle or other normal organ tissue. Fibrosis is most common in the heart, lung, peritoneum, and kidney.

fibrosis of the lungs [L, *fibra*; Gk, *osis,* condition; AS, *lungen*], the formation of scar tissue in the connective tissue of the lungs as a sequel to any inflammation or irritation caused by TB, bronchopneumonia, or a pneumoconiosis. Localized fibrosis may be complicated by infarction, abscess, or bronchiectasis.

fibrothorax /-thôr′aks/, fibrosis of the pleural membranes.

fibrous /fī′brəs/ [L, *fibra,* fiber], consisting mainly of fibers or fiber-containing materials.

fibrous astrocyte, a glial cell with long, fibrous processes found in the white matter of the brain and spinal cord.

fibrous capsule, 1. the external layer of an articular capsule. It surrounds the articulation of two adjoining bones. **2.** the external, tough membranous envelope surrounding some visceral organs, such as the liver.

fibrous dysplasia, an abnormal condition characterized by the fibrous displacement of the osseous tissue within the bones affected. The onset is usually during childhood. The initial signs may be a limp, a pain, or a fracture on the affected side. Radiographic examination usually reveals a well-circumscribed lesion occupying all or a portion of the shaft of the long bone involved.

fibrous goiter, an enlargement of the thyroid gland, characterized by hyperplasia of the capsule and connective tissue.

fibrous hamartoma of infancy, a benign, nonencapsulated tumor, sometimes present at birth but usually appearing during the first year of life, most frequently in the shoulder, axilla, or upper arm. It is a firm, painless, skin-colored nodule composed of well-defined fibrous trabeculae, immature mesenchymal tissue, and mature adipose cells.

fibrous joint, any one of many immovable joints, such as those of the skull segments, in which a fibrous tissue or sometimes a form of cartilage connects the bones.

fibrous thyroiditis, a rare disorder characterized by slowly progressive fibrosis of an enlarged thyroid, with replacement of normal thyroid tissue by dense fibrous tissue. The gland eventually becomes fixed to the adjacent muscles, nerves, blood vessels, and trachea by means of this fibrous tissue. Obstructive symptoms are uncommon but can include a choking sensation, dyspnea, and dysphagia. Hypothyroidism may occur, but in most patients the gland functions normally.

fibrous tissue, the connective tissue of the body, consisting of closely woven elastic fibers and fluid-filled areolae.

fibrous trigone, a thickened area of tissue between the aortic ring and the atrioventricular ring.

fibrovascular proliferation /-vas′kyələr/, the growth of new blood vessels and fibrous tissues on the surface of the retina and optic nerve in diabetic retinopathy.

fibula /fib′yələ/ [L, buckle], one of the two bones of the lower leg, lateral to and smaller in diameter than the tibia.

fibular /fib′yələr/ [L, *fibula,* clasp], pertaining to the fibula.

fibular collum, neck of fibula: the portion of the fibula between the head and shaft.

fibularis brevis, a muscle that assists in eversion of the foot.

fibularis longus, a muscle that everts and plantarflexes the foot and helps to support the arches of the foot, mainly the lateral and transverse arches.

fibularis tertius, a part of the extensor digitorum longus that assists in dorsiflexion and possibly eversion of the foot.

fibular notch, a depression on the lateral surface of the lower end of the tibia, which articulates with the lower end of the fibula.

Fick's law [Adolf E. Fick, German physiologist, 1829–1901], **1.** in chemistry and physics, an observed law stating that the rate at which one substance diffuses through another is directly proportional to the concentration gradient of the diffusing substance. **2.** in medicine, an observed law stating that the rate of diffusion across a membrane is directly proportional to the concentration gradient of the substance on the two sides of the membrane and inversely related to the thickness of the membrane.

Fick's principle, a method for making indirect measurements, based on the law of conservation of mass. It is used specifically to determine cardiac output, in which the amount of oxygen uptake of each unit of blood as it passes through the lungs is equal to the oxygen concentration difference between arterial and mixed venous blood.

FICS, abbreviation for *Fellow of the International College of Surgeons.*

fictive kin /fik′tiv/, people who are regarded as being part of a family even though they are not related.

FID, abbreviation for **free-induction decay.**

field [AS, *feld*], a defined space, area, or distance. The field of vision represents the total area that can be seen with one fixed eye. The binocular field is the area that can be seen with both eyes.

field fever, a form of leptospirosis caused by *Leptospira grippotyphosa,* which primarily affects agricultural workers. It is characterized by fever, abdominal pain, diarrhea, vomiting, stupor, and conjunctivitis.

field of vision [AS *feld*; L, *visio,* seeing], the area of space in which objects are visible at the same time when the eye is fixed and the face is turned so as to exclude the limiting effects of the orbital margins and nose.

FIGLU, abbreviation for **formiminoglutamic acid.**

FIGO staging system, a classification system for cancers of the uterine cervix established by the French Fédération Internationale de Gynécologie et d'Obstétrique. Tumors are classified by Roman numerals from I to IV, representing a range from precancerous or in situ to highly malignant. Classification subdivisions are represented by letters and numbers.

figure-eight bandage, a bandage with successive laps crossing over and around each other to resemble the numeric figure eight.

figure-eight suture [L, *sutura*], a suture that begins at the deepest layer on each side of a wound, then crosses over to pass through the superficial layers on the opposite side before being tied.

figure-ground relationship /fig′(y)ər/ [L, *figura,* form; AS, *grund*; L, *relatus,* carry back], a perceptual field that is divided into a figure, which is the object of focus, and a diffuse background.

filament /fil′əmənt/ [L, *filare,* to spin], a fine threadlike fiber. Filaments are found in most tissues and cells of the body and serve various morphologic or physiologic functions.

filamentous /fil′əmen′təs/ [L, *filare,* to spin], pertaining to something that is threadlike or capable of being drawn out into a threadlike structure.

Filaria /filärē′ə/ pl. *filariae* [L, *filum,* thread], a genus of slender nematodes of the superfamily Filarioidea.

filariasis /fil′ərī′əsis/ [L, *filum,* thread; Gk, *osis,* condition], a disease caused by the presence of filariae or microfilariae in body tissues. Filarial worms are round, long, and threadlike and tend to infest the lymph nodes, lymphatics, subcutaneous tissues, and skin after entering the body as microscopic larvae through the bite of various insects. The infection is characterized by occlusion of the lymphatic vessels, with swelling and pain of the limb distal to the blockage.

filariform /filer′ifôrm/, pertaining to a structure or organism that is threadlike.

Filarioidea /filar′ē-oi′dē-ə/ [L, *filum,* thread; Gk, *eidos,* form], the filariae, a superfamily or order of nematode parasites, the adults being threadlike worms that invade the tissues and body cavities where the female deposits embryonated eggs (prelarvae) known as microfilariae. Genera infecting humans include *Brugia, Loa, Mansonella, Onchocerca,* and *Wuchereria.*

file, 1. in dentistry, a tool for scaling or removing plaque and calcified deposits from the teeth, or in the preparation of the root canal during endodontic therapy. **2.** a collection of related data or information, assembled for a specified purpose and stored as a unit.

filial generation /fil'ē·əl/ [L, *filius,* son, *generare,* to beget], the offspring produced from a given mating or cross.

filiform bougie /fil'ifôrm/ [L, *filum,* thread, *forma,* form; Fr, *bougie,* candle], an extremely thin device for passage through a narrow pathway, such as a sinus tract.

filiform catheter, a catheter with a slender, threadlike tip that allows the wider portion of the instrument to be passed through canals that are constricted or irregular.

filling, a dental restoration consisting of a silver amalgam, composite, glass ionomer, or other material that is inserted into a prepared tooth cavity to repair a carious lesion.

filling factor [AS, *fyllan,* filling; L, *factor,* a maker], a measure of the geometric relationship between an MRI coil and the body.

film [AS, *filmen,* membrane], **1.** a thin sheet or layer of any material, such as a coating of oil on a metal part. **2.** in photography and radiography, a thin, flexible transparent sheet of cellulose acetate or polyester plastic material coated with a light-sensitive emulsion, used to record images.

film badge dosimeter, a photographic film packet, sensitive to ionizing radiation, used for estimating the exposure of personnel working with x-rays and other radioactive sources.

film development, the processing of photographic or x-ray films to manifest the latent image resulting from exposure to the chemically treated emulsion to electromagnetic radiation.

film fault, a defect in a photograph or radiograph, usually caused by a chemical, physical, or electric error in its production.

film on teeth, a collection of mucinous deposits that adhere to the teeth by means of acquired pellicle. The film contains microorganisms, desquamated tissue elements, blood cellular elements, and other debris.

film screen mammography, a breast radiographic technique in which a special single-emulsion film and high-detail intensifying screens are used.

filopressure, the temporary compression of a blood vessel by a ligature. The ligature is removed when the blood flow has stopped.

Filovirus, a genus of single-stranded negative-sense RNA viruses in the Filoviridae family that targets primates and causes hemorrhagic fevers.

filter [Fr, *filtrer,* to strain], **1.** a device or material through which a gas or liquid is passed to separate out unwanted matter. **2.** in radiology, a device added to radiographic equipment that selectively removes low-energy x-rays that have no chance of reaching the film.

filtered back projection, a mathematic technique used in MRI and CT to create images from a set of multiple projection profiles.

filtration /filtrā'shən/ [Fr, *filtrer,* to strain], the addition of sheets of metal to a beam of x-rays, for the purpose of altering the energy spectrum and thus the imaging characteristics and penetrating ability of the radiation.

filum /fī'ləm/, a threadlike structure.

fimbria /fim'brē·ə/ [L, fringe], any structure that forms a border or edge or that resembles a fringe.

fimbriae of uterine tube, the branched fingerlike projections at the distal end of each of the fallopian tubes.

fimbria hippocampi, a band of efferent fibers formed by the alveus hippocampi that is continuous with the posterior pillar of the fornix.

fimbrial tubal pregnancy /fim'brē·əl/, a kind of tubal pregnancy in which implantation occurs in the fimbriated distal end of one of the fallopian tubes.

fimbria ovarica, the longest of the fimbriae tubae. It extends from the infundibulum to the ovary.

fimbriated /fim'brē·ā'tid/ [L, *fimbria,* a fringe], having fimbria.

fimbriated fold, a rough fold lateral to the lingual vein on either side of the frenulum of tongue.

financial resource assistance, a nursing intervention from the Nursing Interventions Classification (NIC) defined as assisting an individual/family to secure and manage finances to meet health care needs.

finasteride /fin'əstərīd, finas'tərīd/, a drug used to treat benign prostatic hyperplasia by blocking the production of dihydrotestosterone, a major hormone stimulating prostate growth.

finding, 1. an observation made about a particular disease state, usually in relation to physical examination and laboratory tests. **2.** a conclusion drawn from an examination, study, or experiment.

fine motor skills [Fr, *fin,* thin; L, *movere;* ONor, *skilja,* to cut apart], the use of precise coordinated movements in such activities as writing, buttoning, cutting, tracing, or visual tracking.

fine-needle aspiration, a diagnostic technique that uses a very thin needle and gentle suction to obtain tissue samples. The needle is thinner than that used for venipuncture, and the procedure is less painful than drawing of blood.

fineness /fīn′nes/ [Fr, *fin,* thin], a means of grading alloys in relation to their gold content. The fineness of an alloy is designated in parts per thousand of pure gold.

fine tremor [Fr, *fin,* thin; L, *tremor,* to tremble], a vibration that occurs after a voluntary movement or one that results from fatigue in the corresponding muscle group.

finger [AS, *fingar*], any of the digits of the hand. The fingers are composed of three bony phalanges. Some anatomists regard the thumb as a finger.

finger agnosia, a neurologic disorder in which a patient is unable to distinguish between stimuli applied to two different fingers without visual clues, to recognize his or her own digits, or to recognize or identify another person's fingers.

finger goniometer [AS, *finger;* Gk, *gonia,* angle, *metron,* meter], an instrument for measuring the angle of a finger joint.

finger-nose test [AS, *finger* + *nosu;* L, *testum,* crucible], a test of the coordination of the arms. The patient is asked to draw the tip of the index finger quickly to the nose, then to touch the examiner's finger, and then to go back and forth quickly. An inability to perform the test accurately may be an indication of cerebellar disease.

finger phenomenon, a diagnostic test for organic hemiplegia. With the patient's elbow on the table, the examiner grasps the patient's wrist and uses the thumb to put pressure on the radial side of the patient's pisiform bone. If the hemiplegia is organic, the patient's fingers spread fanwise.

fingerprint, an image left on a smooth surface by the pattern of the pad of a distal phalanx. The distinctive pattern of loops and whorls represents the fine ridges marking the skin. Because each individual's fingerprints are unique, a classification system of the patterns is useful in identifying individuals.

finger pulse therapy, a form of biofeedback therapy in which a sensor attached to the finger monitors cardiac activity, used in the treatment of anxiety, hypertension, and some cardiac arrhythmias.

finger stick, the act of puncturing the tip of the finger to obtain a small sample of capillary blood.

finger sweep, a technique used when attempting to clear a visible mechanical obstruction from the upper airway of an unconscious patient.

FiO₂, abbreviation for **fraction of inspired oxygen.**

Fiorinal, a trademark for a group of fixed-combination drugs containing a sedative-hypnotic (butalbital); an analgesic, antipyretic, and antiinflammatory (aspirin); and a CNS stimulant (caffeine).

fire ant sting, a potentially lethal venomous injection of piperidine alkaloids by a fire ant. The ant attaches itself to the skin with its mandibles and injects venom through a stinger in the posterior part of its abdomen. The ant injects repeatedly as it rotates its body around the attachment site.

fire-setting precautions, a nursing intervention from the Nursing Interventions Classification (NIC) defined as prevention of fire-setting behaviors.

first aid¹ [AS, *fyrst;* Fr, *aider,* to help], the immediate care that is given to an injured or ill person before treatment by medically trained personnel. Attention is directed first to the most critical problems: evaluation of the patency of the airway, the presence of bleeding, and the adequacy of cardiac function.

first aid², a nursing intervention from the Nursing Interventions Classification (NIC) defined as providing initial care for a minor injury.

first-degree burn, a burn that affects the epidermis only, causing erythema and, in some cases, mild edema, without vesiculation.

first-dollar coverage, an insurance plan under which the third-party payer assumes liability for covered services as soon as the first dollar of expense for such services is incurred, without requiring the insured to pay a deductible.

first filial generation (F₁), the heterozygous offspring produced by the crossing of a homozygous dominant strain with a homozygous recessive strain.

first-generation scanner, an early type of CT device that used a finely collimated (pencil) x-ray beam and a single detector moving in a translate-rotate mode.

first metacarpal bone, the metacarpal bone of the thumb.

first-order change, a change within a system that itself remains unchanged.

first-order kinetics, a chemical reaction in which the rate of decrease in the number of molecules of a substrate is proportional to the concentration of substrate molecules remaining. In first-order reactions involving two substances, only one of the concentrations affects the rate. The rate of metabolism of most drugs follows the rule of first-order kinetics and is independent of the dose.

first responder, the first emergency person to arrive at the scene of a traumatic or medical situation.

first rib, the highest rib of the thoracic cage. It moves about the axis of its neck, raising and lowering the sternum.

first stage of labor [ME, *fyrst*; OFr, *estage*; L, *labor*, work], a period of 8 to 12 hours marked by the onset of regular contractions of the uterus with full dilation of the cervix and the appearance of a small amount of blood-tinged mucus. Danger signs of the first stage include abnormal bleeding, abnormal fetal heart rate, and abnormal fetal presentation and position.

fiscal resource management, a nursing intervention from the Nursing Interventions Classification (NIC) defined as procuring and directing the use of financial resources to assure the development and continuation of programs and services.

FISH, abbreviation for **fluorescence in situ hybridization.**

Fishberg concentration test /fish′berg/, a test for renal function. The patient is given supper with not more than 200 mL of fluid and nothing thereafter. Urine voided during the night is discarded. The morning urine is saved, the patient is kept in bed, and the urine of 1 hour later and of 2 hours later is saved. If the specific gravity of any of these three specimens is less than 1.024, there is impairment of renal concentration.

fish poisoning, poisoning caused by ingestion of poisonous fish. It is marked by various GI and neurologic disturbances that sometimes can be fatal.

fish tapeworm infection [AS, *fisc*, fish], an infection caused by the tapeworm *Diphyllobothrium latum* that is transmitted to humans when they eat contaminated raw or undercooked freshwater fish.

fission /fish′ən/ [L, *fissio*, splitting], **1.** the act or process of splitting or breaking up into two or more parts. **2.** a type of asexual reproduction common in bacteria, protozoa, and other simpler forms of life in which the cell divides into two or more equal components, each of which eventually develops into a complete organism. **3.** in physics, the splitting of the nucleus of an atom and subsequent release of energy.

fissiparous /fisip′ərəs/, reproduced by fission.

fissural angioma /fish′ərəl/ [L, *fissura*, cleft], a tumor composed of a cluster of dilated blood vessels found on the lip, face, or neck in an embryonal fissure.

fissure /fish′ər/ [L, *fissura*, cleft], **1.** a cleft or groove on the surface of an organ, often marking its division into parts, such as the lobes of the lung. **2.** a cracklike lesion of the skin, such as an anal fissure. **3.** a lineal fault on a bony surface that occurs during the development of a part, such as a fissure in the enamel of a tooth.— **fissured,** *adj.*

fissured tongue /fish′ərd/ [L, *fissura*, cleft; AS, *tunge*], a tongue with deep surface furrows that may radiate outward. It may be inherited as an autosomal-dominant trait.

fissure fracture, any fracture in which a crack extends into the cortex of the bone but not through the entire bone.

fistula /fis′chŏŏlə, -chələ/ *pl.* **fistulae, fistulas** [L, pipe], an abnormal passage from an internal organ to the body surface or between two internal organs.— **fistular, fistulate, fistulous,** *adj.*

fistulectomy /fis′chəlek′təmē/ [L, *fistula*, pipe; Gk, *ektomē*, excision], the surgical removal of a fistula.

fit, 1. *nontechnical.* a paroxysm or seizure. **2.** the sudden onset of an episode of symptoms, such as a fit of coughing. **3.** the manner in which one surface is aligned to another, such as the alignment of a denture with the gingiva and jaw.

fitness, a measure of the ability of a person to perform certain tasks.

Fitzgerald factor, a high-molecular-weight kininogen that may be required for the interaction of factors XI and XII in the coagulation process.

Fitz-Hugh–Curtis syndrome /fitz′-hyōō kər′tis/ [Thomas Fitz-Hugh, Jr., American physician, 1894–1963; Arthur H. Curtis, American gynecologist, 1881–1955], perihepatitis occurring as a complication of gonorrhea or chlamydial infection in women, marked by fever, upper quadrant pain, tenderness and spasm of the abdominal wall, and occasionally friction rub over the liver. This syndrome is characterized by adhesions between the liver and other sites in the peritoneum.

Fitzpatrick, Joyce J., a nursing theorist who derived her Life Perspective Rhythm Model from Martha Rogers' conceptualization of unitary man. Fitzpatrick proposes that the process of human development is characterized by rhythms that occur within the context of continuous person-environment interaction. Nursing activity focuses on enhancing the developmental process toward health.

five elements, in Ayurvedic tradition, the basic entities (earth, air, fire, water, and space) whose interaction gives rise to material existence.

five phases, in traditional Chinese medicine, a set of dynamic relations (designated earth, metal, water, wood, and fire) that can be used to categorize relationships among phenomena.

five-step nursing process, a nursing process comprising five broad categories of nursing behaviors: assessing, analyzing, planning, implementing, and evaluating.

fixating eye /fik′sāting/ [L, *figere,* to fasten; AS, *eage*], in strabismus, the eye that is directed to a given object to position that object on the fovea.

fixation /fiksā′shən/ [L, *figere,* to fasten, *atio,* process], in psychoanalysis, an arrest at a particular stage of psychosexual development, such as anal fixation.—**fixate,** *v.,* **fixated,** *adj.*

fixational ocular movements /fiksā′shənəl/, rotation of the eyes during voluntary fixation on an object.

fixation muscle, a muscle that acts to hold a part of the body in appropriate position.

fixative /fik′sətiv/ [L, *figere,* to fasten], **1.** any substance used to bind, glue, or stabilize. **2.** any substance used to preserve gross or histologic specimens of tissue for later examination.

fixator, a device composed of rods and pins designed to provide stabilization of a body part. The external skeletal apparatus may be attached directly to the bone.

fixed anions /fikst′/, anions that are not part of the body's buffer anions.

fixed bridgework, a dental device to replace missing teeth that incorporates artificial teeth permanently attached to natural teeth or implants in the jaw.

fixed cations, cations that are not part of the body's metabolic buffering system.

fixed-combination drug [L, *figere,* to fasten, *combinare,* to combine; Fr, *drogue*], any of a group of multiple-ingredient preparations that provide concomitant administration of specific amounts of two or more medications.

fixed coupling, the occurrence of a normal and an ectopic heartbeat with a constant interval between the two each time the ectopic beat occurs.

fixed delusion [L, *figere,* to fasten, *deludere,* to deceive], a delusion that is consistent, unaltered, and difficult to interrupt.

fixed dressing, a dressing usually made of gauze impregnated with a hardening agent, such as plaster of paris, sodium silicate, starch, or dextrin, applied to support or immobilize a part of the body.

fixed drug eruption, well-defined red to purple lesions that appear at the same sites on the skin and mucous membranes each time a particular drug is used.

fixed fulcrum, a tomographic fulcrum that remains at a fixed height.

fixed idea, 1. a persistent, obsessional thought or notion. **2.** in certain mental disorders, especially obsessive-compulsive disorder, an idea that dominates mental activity and persists despite contrary evidence or rational refutation.

fixed interval (FI) reinforcement, in psychiatry, reinforcement given after a specific amount of time has elapsed.

fixed macrophage [L, *figere,* to fasten; Gk, *makros,* large, *phagein,* to eat], a nonmotile mononuclear phagocyte found in connective tissue, liver sinuses, spleen, lymph glands, and bone marrow.

fixed orthodontic appliance, a mechanical device cemented to the teeth or attached by adhesive material, for changing the relative positions of the teeth.

fixed partial denture, a partial denture permanently held in position by attachments to adjacent prepared natural teeth, roots, or implants.

fixed pupil [L, *figere,* to fasten, *pupilla,* little girl], an abnormal condition in which the pupils fail to dilate or contract when stimulated. The cause is commonly adhesions binding the iris to the lens capsule or acute glaucoma causing interference with the nerve supply of the iris.

fixed rate pacemaker [L, *figere,* to fasten, *ratum,* calculate, *passus,* step; ME, *maken*], an electronic cardiac stimulator that delivers impulses to the cardiac muscle at a preset rate regardless of the heart's independent activity.

fixed ratio (FR) reinforcement, in psychiatry, reinforcement given after a specific number of responses have occurred.

fixed torticollis [L, *figere,* to fasten, *tortus,* twisted, *collum,* neck], a condition in which neck muscles on one side are so short that the head is held continuously in the same position.

fixer, a chemical used in processing photographic or x-ray film. Applied after the developing phase, it neutralizes any developer remaining on the film, removes undeveloped silver halides, and hardens the emulsion.

flaccid /flak′sid/ [L, *flaccus,* flabby], weak, soft, and flabby; lacking normal muscle tone, such as flaccid muscles.—**flaccidity, flaccidness,** *n.*

flaccid bladder, a bladder that is unable to contract sufficiently to empty. It may be secondary to neural deficiencies or chronic obstruction.

flaccid paralysis, an abnormal condition characterized by the weakening or the loss of muscle tone.

flagellant /flaj′ələnt/, a person who receives sexual gratification from the practice of flagellation.

flagellate /flaj′əlāt′, -lit/ [L, *flagellum,* whip], a protozoon or alga that propels itself with flagella.

F

flagellation /flaj′əlā′shən/, **1.** the act of whipping, beating, or flogging. **2.** a type of massage administered by tapping the body with the fingers. **3.** a type of sexual deviation in which a person is erotically gratified by being whipped or by whipping another. **4.** the arrangement of flagella on an organism; exflagellation.

flagellum /flajel′əm/ *pl.* **flagella** [L, whip], a long, hairlike projection that extends from some unicellular organisms and from the sperm of animals, algae, and some plants. Flagellar motion is a complex, whiplike undulation that propels cells through a fluid environment.

Flagyl, a trademark for an antibiotic and antiprotozoal (metronidazole).

flail chest /flāl/ [ME, *fleyl,* whip; AS, *cest,* box], a thorax in which there are two fractures on at least two adjacent ribs causing instability in part of the chest wall and paradoxic breathing, with the lung underlying the injured area contracting on inspiration and bulging on expiration. Flail chest is characterized by sharp pain; uneven chest expansion; shallow, rapid respirations; and decreased breath sounds. Tachycardia and cyanosis may be present. Potential complications include atelectasis, pneumothorax, hemothorax, cardiac tamponade, shock, and respiratory arrest.

flame photometry [L,*flagrare,* to burn; Gk, *phos,* light, *metron,* measure], measurement of the wavelength of light rays emitted by excited metallic electrons exposed to the heat energy of a flame, used to identify characteristics in clinical specimens of body fluids.

flammable, the property of igniting and burning easily and rapidly.

flange /flanj/, **1.** the part of a denture base that extends from the cervical ends of the teeth to the border of the denture. **2.** a prosthesis with a lateral vertical extension designed to direct a resected mandible into centric occlusion.

flank, the posterior portion of the body between the ribs and the ilium.

flap, a layer of skin or other tissue surgically separated from deeper structures for transplantation, coverage of an area that has been injured, or examination of deeper tissues.

flap reconstruction, an alternative to skin expansion as a method of breast reconstruction after mastectomy. It involves creation of a skin flap using tissue from another part of the body, such as the back or abdomen. The flap is attached to the chest to create a pocket for implantation or to build a breast mound.

flap surgery, a type of breast reconstruction that is performed in a single stage, in some cases at the same time as a mastectomy.

flare /fler/, **1.** a red blush on the skin at the periphery of an urticarial lesion seen in immediate hypersensitivity reactions. **2.** an expanding skin flush, spreading from an infective lesion or extending from the principal site of a reaction to an irritant. **3.** the sudden intensification of a disease.

flaring of nostrils, nasal widening during inspiration, a sign of air hunger or respiratory distress.

flash, a sudden or intermittent brief burst of intense heat or light.

flashback, a phenomenon experienced by persons who have taken a hallucinogenic drug or had psychologic trauma and unexpectedly reexperience its effects.

flash burn, a lesion caused by exposure to an extremely intense source of radiant energy or heat.

flashover phenomenon, an effect of a lightning strike or other intense electric discharge in which the electric current passes over the body instead of through it. The result is a red, feather-like branching pattern on the skin.

flask, 1. a narrow-neck glass vessel used for heating liquids, distilling chemicals, or culturing fluid media. **2.** a small glass receptacle for holding liquids or powders.

flask closure [L, *vasculum,* small vessel, *claudere,* to close], the joining of two halves of a flask that encloses and forms a mold for a denture base.

flasking /flask′ing/ [L, *vasculum,* small vessel], **1.** the act of investing in a flask. **2.** the process of investing the cast and a wax denture in a flask preparatory to molding the denture base material into the form of the denture.

flat affect, the absence or near absence of emotional response to a situation that normally elicits emotion. It is observed in schizophrenia and some depressive disorders.

flat bone [AS, *flet,* floor], any of the bones that provide structural contours of the skeleton. Examples are ribs and bones of the cranium.

flat electroencephalogram, a graphic chart on which no tracings are recorded during EEG, indicating a lack of brain wave activity.

flatfoot, an abnormal but relatively common condition characterized by the flattening out of the arch of the foot.

flat spring contraceptive diaphragm, a kind of contraceptive diaphragm in which the flexible metal spring that forms the rim is a thin, light, flat band made of stainless steel.

flatulence /flach′ələns/ [L, *flatus,* a blowing], the presence of an excessive amount of air or gas in the stomach and intestinal tract, causing distension of the organs and in some cases mild to moderate pain.

flatulence reduction, a nursing intervention from the Nursing Interventions Classification (NIC) defined as prevention of flatus formation and facilitation of passage of excessive gas.

flatulent /flach′ələnt/ [L, *flatus,* a blowing], pertaining to gas or air in the digestive tract.

flatus /flā′təs/ [L, a blowing], air or gas in the intestine that is passed through the rectum.

flaval ligaments [L, *ligare + flavus,* yellow], the bands of yellow elastic tissue connecting the laminae of adjacent vertebrae from the axis to the first segment of the sacrum. They help hold the body erect.

Flavivirus, a genus of a family of Flaviviridae single-stranded positive-sense RNA viruses. Most are arboviruses transmitted by mosquitoes or ticks.

flavocoxid, an oral nutritional supplement used for dietary management of osteoarthritis.

flavone /flā′vōn/ [L, *flavus,* yellow], a colorless crystalline flavonoid derivative and component of bioflavonoid.

flavoprotein, a group of conjugated proteins that make yellow enzymes essential for cellular respiration. They also are involved in liberation of hydrogen from oxidation of fatty acids and function as electron acceptors in oxidative phosphorylation.

flavoxate hydrochloride /flavok′sāt/, a smooth muscle relaxant prescribed for spastic conditions of the urinary tract.

flax, a flowering annual herb found in the United States, Canada, and Europe. The seeds are used for constipation and as a source of omega-3 fatty acids.

fl. dr., abbreviation for **fluid dram.**

flea [AS], a wingless, bloodsucking insect of the order Siphonaptera, some species of which transmit arboviruses to humans by acting as host or vector to the organism.

flea bite, a small puncture wound produced by a bloodsucking flea. Certain species of fleas transmit plague, murine typhus, and probably tularemia.

flecainide /flēka′nīd/, a sodium channel blocking agent that decreases the rate of cardiac conduction and increases the ventricular refractory period, used as the acetate salt in treatment of life-threatening arrhythmias.

flecainide acetate /flēkā′nīd/, an oral antiarrhythmic drug prescribed for the treatment of ventricular arrhythmias (e.g.,

sustained ventricular tachycardia) and for treating supraventricular tachycardia in the absence of conduction defects when other drugs have failed.

Fleet Enema, a trademark for a manufactured enema formula containing 16 g sodium biphosphate and 6 g sodium phosphate per 100 mL solution.

Fleischner method /flīsh′nər/ [Felix Fleischner, American radiologist, 1893–1969], a technique for producing lordotic x-ray projections of the lungs. The patient leans backward from the waist to a nearly 45-degree posterior inclination with his or her back against the x-ray film.

flesh, the soft, muscular tissues of the body.

Fletcher factor, a prekallikrein blood coagulation substance that interacts with both factor XII and Fitzgerald factor, activating both and accelerating thrombin formation.

Flexeril, a trademark for a muscle relaxant (cyclobenzaprine hydrochloride).

Flex-Foot, a trademark for a stored-energy foot prosthesis containing a J-shaped plastic beam that acts like a spring when the wearer walks or runs.

flexibility /flek′sibil′i-tē/ [L, *flectere,* to bend], the quality of being readily bent without breaking.

flexion /flek′shən/ [L, *flectere,* to bend], **1.** a movement allowed by certain joints of the skeleton that decreases the angle between two adjoining bones such as bending the elbow. **2.** a resistance to the descent of the fetus through the birth canal that causes the neck to flex so the chin approaches the chest.

flexion jacket, a corset designed to provide spinal immobility.

flexor /flek′sər/ [L, bender], a muscle that flexes a joint.

flexor carpi radialis [L, *flexor,* bender], a slender, superficial muscle of the forearm that lies on the ulnar side of the pronator teres. It functions to flex and to help abduct the hand.

flexor carpi ulnaris, a superficial muscle lying along the ulnar side of the forearm. It functions to flex and adduct the hand.

flexor digiti minimi brevis, 1. a short flexor muscle of the little finger; a muscle that inserts on the medial side of the proximal phalanx of the finger to flex it. **2.** a short flexor muscle of the little toe; a muscle that inserts on the lateral surface of the base of the proximal phalanx of the toe to flex it.

flexor digitorum brevis, a short flexor muscle of toes; a muscle that inserts on the middle phalanges of the four lateral toes and flexes them.

flexor digitorum longus, the muscle that flexes the lateral four toes. It is involved with gripping the ground during walking and propelling the body forward off the toes at the end of the stance phase of gait.

flexor digitorum profundus, one of two deep flexor muscles of the fingers; a muscle that inserts on the distal phalanges of the fingers and flexes them.

flexor digitorum superficialis, the largest superficial muscle of the forearm, lying on the ulnar side under the palmaris longus. The muscle flexes the second phalanx of each finger and, by continued action, the hand.

flexor hallucis brevis, a short flexor muscle of the great toe; a muscle that inserts in the base of the proximal phalanx of the great toe and flexes it.

flexor hallucis longus, the muscle that flexes the great toe.

flexor pollicis brevis, a thenar muscle that flexes the thumb.

flexor pollicis longus, the muscle that flexes the metacarpophalangeal joint of the thumb.

flexor retinaculum of ankle [L, *flexor,* bender, *retinaculum,* halter; AS, *ancleow*], **1.** a strong band of fascia from the medial malleolus to the calcaneum, passing over the long flexor tendons and blood vessels and nerves of the posterior leg. **2.** the roof of the tarsal tunnel.

flexor retinaculum of wrist [L, *flexor,* bender, *retinaculum,* halter; AS, *wrist*], a strong ligament across the front of the hollow of the carpus and over the flexor tendons of the fingers and median nerve.

flexor withdrawal reflex, a common cutaneous reflex consisting of a widespread contraction of physiologic flexor muscles and relaxation of physiologic extensor muscles. It is characterized by abrupt withdrawal of a body part in response to painful or injurious stimuli.

flextime /fleks′tīm/ [L, *flectere,* to bend; AS, *tima*], a system of staffing that allows the individualization of work schedules.

flexure /flek′shər/, a normal bend or curve in a body part, such as the colic flexure of the colon or the dorsal flexure of the spine.

flicks, rapid fixation involuntary movements of the eye.

flight into health [AS, *fleogan,* to fly], **1.** an abnormal but common reaction to an unpleasant physical sensation or symptom in which the person denies the feeling or observation, insisting that there is nothing wrong. **2.** voluntary and temporary suppression of mental or physical symptoms to prevent further analysis of the patient's emotional state.

flight of ideas, in psychiatry, a continuous stream of talk in which the patient switches rapidly from one topic to another and each subject is incoherent and unrelated to the preceding one or is stimulated by some environmental circumstance.

flight-or-fight reaction [AS, *fleogan,* to fly, *feohtan,* to fight; L, *reagere,* to act again], **1.** in physiology, the reaction of the body to stress, in which the sympathetic nervous system and the adrenal medulla act to increase the cardiac output, dilate the pupils of the eyes, increase the rate of the heartbeat, constrict the blood vessels of the skin, increase the levels of glucose and fatty acids in the circulation, and induce an alert, aroused mental state. **2.** in psychiatry, a person's reaction to stress by either fleeing from a situation or remaining and attempting to deal with it.

flight to illness, the effort of the patient to convince the therapist that he or she is too ill to terminate therapy and that continued support is needed.

flip angle, in MRI, the degree of rotation of the macroscopic magnetization vector produced by a radiofrequency pulse with respect to the direction of the static magnetic field.

floater [AS, *flotian,* to float], a spot that appears to drift in front of the eye, caused by a shadow cast on the retina by vitreous debris. Most floaters are benign and represent remnants of a network of blood vessels that existed prenatally in the vitreous cavity. The sudden onset of several floaters may indicate serious disease.

floating head [AS, *flotian,* to float + *heafod*], unengaged fetal head.

floating kidney, a kidney that is not securely fixed in the normal anatomic location because of congenital malplacement or traumatic injury.

floating patella [AS, *flotian*; L, *patella,* small pan], a patella that has been forced away from the femoral condyle by an effusion into the knee joint.

floating spleen, a spleen displaced and abnormally movable.

float nurse, a nurse who is available for assignment to duty on an ad hoc basis, usually to assist in times of unusually heavy workloads or to assume the duties of absent nursing personnel.

flocculant /flok′yōōlənt/, an agent or substance that causes flocculation.

flocculation test /flok′yōōlā′shən/ [L, *floccus,* flock of wool], a serologic test in which a positive result depends on the degree of flocculent precipitation produced in the material being tested.

flocculent /flok′yōōlənt/ [L, *floccus,* flock of wool], clumped or tufted, such as a cloud, or covered with a woolly, fuzzy surface.— **flocculate,** *v.,* **flocculation, flocculate,** *n.*

flooding [AS, *flod*], **1.** profuse bleeding from the uterus, especially after childbirth or prolonged menses. **2.** a technique used in behavior therapy for the reduction of anxiety associated with various phobias. Exposure to a stimulus that usually provokes anxiety desensitizes a person to that stimulus, thereby reducing fear and anxiety.

floor, the lower inner surface of any cavity or organ.

flora /flôr′ə/, microorganisms that live on or within a body to compete with disease-producing microorganisms and provide a natural immunity against certain infections.

florid /flôr′id/ [L, *floridus,* flowery], in human skin complexion or wound appearance, a bright red color.

Florone, a trademark for a topical corticosteroid (diflorasone diacetate).

Floropryl, a trademark for an inhibitor of cholinesterase (isoflurophate), used ophthalmically.

flossing, the mechanical cleansing of proximal tooth surfaces, subgingivally and supragingivally, by dental tape or waxed or unwaxed dental floss.

flotation device /flōtā′shən/ [Fr, *flotter,* to float], a foam mattress with a gel-like pad located in its center, designed to protect bony prominences and distribute pressure evenly against the skin's surface.

flotation therapy, a state of semiweightlessness produced by various types of hospital equipment and used in the treatment and prevention of pressure ulcers.

flow, 1. the movement of a liquid or gas. **2.** copious menstruation but less profuse than flooding.

flow cycling, the delivery of gas under positive pressure during inspiration until flow drops to a specified terminal level.

flow cytometry, a technique in which cells suspended in a fluid flow one at a time through a focus of exciting light, which is scattered in patterns characteristic to the cells and their components. The cells are often labeled with fluorescent markers so that light is first absorbed and then emitted at altered frequencies. A sensor detecting the scattered or emitted light measures the size and molecular characteristics of individual cells.

flower essences, aqueous extracts of the fresh flowers of various plants chosen for their effects on specific mental or emotional symptoms, combined with brandy as a preservative. They are used to address spiritual, mental, and emotional as well as physical problems.

flowmeter, a device that regulates and measures the flow of a fluid or gas. In an anesthetic gas machine it is the flowmeter that measures gases by speed of flow, according to their viscosity and density.

flow sheet, in a patient record, a graphic summary of several changing factors, especially the patient's vital signs or weight and the treatments and medications given. In labor, the flow sheet displays the progress of labor.

flow transducer, a measuring device that calculates volume by dividing flow by time.

flow trigger, a trigger for initiating assisted ventilation, consisting of a mechanism for measuring the patient's inspiratory effort and starting assisted ventilation when flow reaches a given level.

flow-volume curve, a graphic of the instantaneous rate of airflow during a forced expiration. It is plotted as a function of the volume. It may be a maximum expiratory flow-volume curve or a partial expiratory flow-volume curve.

flow-volume dysequilibrium, the lower than normal solute content of blood that has just gone through dialysis, which tends to draw solutes out of other fluid-containing body compartments, such as cells.

flow-volume loop, a graph of the rate of airflow as a function of lung volume during a complete respiratory cycle consisting of a forced inspiration followed by a forced expiration. The plotted curve appears as a loop and is used in assessing pulmonary function.

floxuridine /floksyŏŏr′ədēn/, an antineoplastic agent prescribed in the treatment of metastases to the liver from GI cancers.

fl. oz., abbreviation for **fluid ounce.**

flu /flōō/, *informal.* **1.** influenza. **2.** any viral infection, especially of the respiratory or intestinal system.

fluctuant /fluk′chōō·ənt/, pertaining to a wavelike motion that is detected when a structure containing a liquid is palpated.

fluctuation /fluk·chōō·ā′shən/ [L, *fluctuare,* to wave], **1.** a wavelike motion of fluid in a body cavity that follows a shaking motion. **2.** a variation in a fixed value or mass.

flucytosine /flōōsī′təsēn/, an antifungal prescribed as an adjunct in the treatment of certain serious fungal infections, usually *Candida* or *Cryptococcus.*

Fludara, a trademark for an antineoplastic (fludarabine).

fludarabine, an antimetabolite prescribed in the treatment of patients with B-cell chronic lymphocytic leukemia and as salvage therapy for non-Hodgkin's lymphoma and acute leukemias.

fludeoxyglucose F 18 /flōō′de·ok′segloo′kōs/, radiolabeled 2-deoxy-D-glucose, used in PET in the diagnosis of brain disorders, cardiac disease, and tumors of various organs.

fluent /flōō′ənt/ [L. *fluens,* flowing], flowing effortlessly. It is said of speech.

fluent aphasia /flōō′ənt/ [L, *fluere,* to flow; Gk, *a,* not, *phasis,* speech], a form of aphasia in which the patient articulates words easily, although the message may be unintelligible or may not be related to a particular stimulus.

fluid /floo'id/ [L, *fluere,* to flow], **1.** a substance, such as a liquid or gas, that is able to flow and to adjust its shape to that of a container because it is composed of molecules that are able to change positions with respect to each other without separating from the total mass. **2.** a body fluid, either intracellular or extracellular, involved in the transport of electrolytes and other vital chemicals to, through, and from tissue cells.

fluid balance[1], a state of equilibrium in which the amount of fluid consumed equals the amount lost in urine, feces, perspiration, and exhaled water vapor.

fluid balance[2], a nursing outcome from the Nursing Outcomes Classification (NOC) defined as water balance in the intracellular and extracellular compartments of the body.

fluid dram (fl. dr.), **(fl. dr.** or **dram),** a unit of liquid measure equal to 3.696 mL, 60 minims, or $1/8$ fluid ounce.

fluid/electrolyte management, a nursing intervention from the Nursing Interventions Classification (NIC) defined as regulation and prevention of complications from altered fluid and/or electrolyte levels.

fluidic ventilator /floo·id'ik/, a device used in respiratory therapy that applies the Coanda effect to the movement of the flow of air or gases.

fluidized air bed, a bed that minimizes pressure and distributes weight evenly over the support surface. A gentle flow of temperature-controlled air is projected upward through numerous tiny openings called ceramic microspheres.

fluid management, a nursing intervention from the Nursing Interventions Classification (NIC) defined as promotion of fluid balance and prevention of complications resulting from abnormal or undesired fluid levels.

fluid monitoring, a nursing intervention from the Nursing Interventions Classification (NIC) defined as collection and analysis of patient data to regulate fluid balance.

fluidotherapy /floo'idother'əpē/, a modality of dry heat that uses a suspended air stream with the properties of a liquid. It simultaneously performs the functions of applied heat, massage, sensory stimulation, levitation, and pressure oscillations.

fluid ounce (fl. oz.), a measure of liquid volume in the apothecaries' system, which is equal to 8 fluid drams or 29 mL, 480 minims, $1/20$ imperial pint, or the volume occupied by 437.5 grains of distilled water at a temperature of 16.7° C.

fluid overload, an excessive accumulation of fluid in the body caused by excessive parenteral infusion or deficiencies in cardiovascular or renal fluid volume regulation.

fluid overload severity, a nursing outcome from the Nursing Outcomes Classification (NOC) defined as the severity of excess fluids in the intracellular and extracellular compartments of the body.

fluid resuscitation, a nursing intervention from the Nursing Interventions Classification (NIC) defined as administering prescribed intravenous fluids rapidly.

fluid retention, a failure to excrete excess fluid from the body. Causes may include renal, cardiovascular, or metabolic disorders.

fluid therapy, the regulation of water balance in patients with impaired renal, cardiovascular, or metabolic function by careful measurement of fluid intake against daily losses.

fluid volume, the volume of the body fluids, including both intracellular fluid and extracellular fluid.

fluid volume imbalance, abnormally decreased or increased fluid volume or rapid shift from one compartment of body fluid to another.

fluke /flook/, a parasitic flatworm of the class Trematoda, including the genus *Schistosoma.*

flunisolide, an intranasal and oral inhalation steroid antiinflammatory agent. It is prescribed in the treatment of seasonal or continuing allergic rhinitis that involves inflammation of the mucous membranes of the nasal passages, and for the treatment of asthma.

fluocinolone acetonide /floo·ōsin'əlōn/, a topical glucocorticoid prescribed for severe dermatoses.

fluocinonide /floo·ōsin'ənīd/, a topical corticosteroid prescribed to reduce skin inflammation and the associated pruritus.

fluorescein dilaurate, an ester of fluorescein with two molecules of laurate, used in the pancreolauryl test of pancreatic function.

fluorescence /floores'əns/ [L, *flux,* a discharge], the emission of light of one wavelength by a substance when it is exposed to electromagnetic radiation of a shorter wavelength.—**fluoresce.**

fluorescence in situ hybridization (FISH), a genetic mapping technique using fluorescent tags for analysis of chromosomal aberrations and genetic abnormalities.

fluorescent antibody test (FA test) /floores'ənt/, a test in which a fluorescent dye is used to stain an antibody for identification of clinical specimens. The dyed organisms glow visibly when examined under a fluorescent microscope. The fluorescent antibody technique can be used in identification of *Mycobacterium* *tuberculosis* and in the most common serologic screening test for syphilis.

fluorescent microscopy, examination with a fluorescent microscope equipped with a source of ultraviolet light rays, used to study specimens that have been stained with fluorescent dye.

fluorescent treponemal antibody absorption test (FTA-ABS test), the standard treponemal antigen test for syphilis.

fluoridation /floor'idā'shən/ [L, *fluere*, to flow], the process of adding fluoride, especially to a public water supply, to reduce tooth decay.

fluoride /floor'īd/, an anion of fluorine. Fluoride compounds are introduced into drinking water or applied directly to the teeth to prevent tooth decay.

fluoride application, fluoride dental treatment [L, *fluere*, to flow, *dens*, tooth; Fr, *traitment*], the direct oral application of fluoride compounds to reduce the incidence of dental caries.

fluoride poisoning [L, *fluere*, to flow, *potio*, drink], the toxic effects of contact with compounds of fluorine, an intensely poisonous pale yellow gas.

fluorination /floor'inā'shən/, the addition of fluorine to a compound, such as those commonly found in topical corticosteroids.

fluorine (F) /floor'ēn, floo'ərēn/ [L, *fluere*, to flow], an element of the halogen family and the most reactive of the nonmetals. Its atomic number is 9, and its atomic mass is 19.00. In its pure form is a pale yellow toxic gas 1.6 times heavier than air. As a component of fluorides, it is widely distributed throughout the soils of the earth, enters plants, is ingested by humans, and is absorbed from the GI tract.

fluoroacetic acid (FCH2COOH) /floor'ō·asē'tik, -aset'ik/, a colorless water-soluble, highly toxic compound that blocks the citric acid cycle, causing convulsions and ventricular fibrillation. It is derived from a South African tree and is used in some potent pesticides.

fluorocarbons /floor'ōkär'bəns/ [L, *fluere*, to flow, *carbo*, coal], hydrocarbons where some or all of the hydrogens are replaced by fluorine. The compounds can produce mild upper respiratory tract irritation, and excessive exposure has been cited as a cause of CNS depression.

fluorochrome stain, a fluorescent dye used to stain the cell walls of fungi and bacteria. The organisms then fluoresce when exposed to UV light rays. It is commonly used to visualize acid-fast bacilli in specimens.

fluorodopa F 18 /floor'odo'pə/, a radiolabeled compound of fluorine and levodopa, used for PET of the cerebrum.

fluorometry /floorom'ətrē/ [L, *fluere*; Gk, *metron,* measure], measurement of fluorescence emitted by compounds when exposed to ultraviolet or other intense radiant energy. The atoms of certain substances produce fluorescence of a characteristic color and wavelength, allowing identification and quantification of several clinically significant compounds in biologic specimens.—**fluorometric,** *adj.*

Fluoroplex, a trademark for a topical preparation of the antineoplastic drug fluorouracil.

fluoroquinolone /floo'ōkwin'ōlōn/, any of a subgroup of quinolones that have a broader spectrum of activity than quinolones, such as **nalidixic acid.**

fluoroscope /floor'əskōp'/ [L, *fluere*; Gk, *skopein,* to look], a device used to project a radiographic image on a fluorescent screen for visual examination.—**fluoroscopic,** *adj.*

fluoroscopic compression device /floor'əskop'ik/, any of several objects that can be placed on a specific area of a patient's abdomen to compress the abdomen and separate loops of bowel during fluoroscopy of the digestive tract.

fluoroscopy /flooros'kəpē/, the visual examination of a part of the body or the function of an organ with a fluoroscope.

fluorosis /floorō'sis/ [L, *fluere*; Gk, *osis,* condition], the condition that results from excessive prolonged ingestion of fluorine. Severe chronic fluorine poisoning leads to osteosclerosis and other pathologic bone and joint changes in adults.

fluorouracil /floor'ōyōōr'əsil/, an antimetabolite antineoplastic prescribed in the treatment of malignant neoplastic disease of the skin, breast, and internal organs.

Fluothane, a trademark for an inhalational general anesthetic (halothane).

fluoxetine hydrochloride /floo·ok'sətēn/, an oral antidepressant that acts by selectively preventing serotonin reuptake. It is prescribed for major depressive disorder, obsessive-compulsive disorder, and bulimia nervosa.

fluoxymesterone /floo·ok'simes'tərōn/, an androgenic and anabolic steroid prescribed in the treatment of testosterone deficiency, breast cancer in females, and delayed puberty in males.

flupenthixol decanoate, a long-acting ester of flupenthixol, administered intramuscularly as a depot injection.

flupenthixol hydrochloride, the hydrochloride salt of flupenthixol.

fluphenazine hydrochloride /floo fen'əzēn/, a phenothiazine antipsychotic drug prescribed in the treatment of schizophrenia and other psychotic disorders.

flurandrenolide /flŏŏ'rəndren'əlīd/, a topical glucocorticoid prescribed for the treatment of skin inflammation.

flurazepam hydrochloride /flŏŏraz'əpam/, a benzodiazepine sedative-hypnotic agent prescribed in the short-term treatment of insomnia.

flurbiprofen /flˉoorbi'profen/, an NSAID administered orally in the treatment of arthritis, ankylosing spondylitis, bursitis, tendinitis, soft tissue injuries, and dysmenorrhea.

flurbiprofen sodium, the sodium salt of flurbiprofen, applied topically to the conjunctiva to inhibit miosis during, and as an antiinflammatory following, ophthalmic surgery.

flush [ME, *fluschen*], **1.** a blush or sudden reddening of the face and neck. **2.** a sudden subjective feeling of heat. **3.** a prolonged reddening of the face such as may be seen with fever, use of certain drugs, or hyperthyroidism. **4.** a sudden rapid flow of water or other liquid.

flush device, an apparatus in a hemodynamic monitoring system used to infuse normal saline to clear blood and assure line patency.

flutamide, a hormonal (antiandrogen) antineoplastic agent prescribed along with leuprolide in the treatment of metastatic prostate cancer and other cancers stimulated by male hormones. It is sometimes used to treat female hirsutism.

fluticasone /flŏŏtik'äsōn'/, a steroid antiinflammatory agent, used topically as the propionate salt in treatment of itching or inflammation, intranasally in the treatment of allergic rhinitis and other inflammatory nasal conditions and of nasal polyps, and by inhalation in treatment of asthma.

flutter, a rapid vibration or pulsation that may interfere with normal function.

flutter-fibrillation [AS, *fleotan*, to move quickly; L, *fibrilla*, small fiber], a type of atrial fibrillation (involuntary recurrent contraction) in which the irregular fibrillatory line resembles atrial flutter mixed with atrial fibrillatory waves.

fluvastatin, an antilipidemic used as an adjunct treatment in primary hypercholesterolemia (types Ia and Ib) and in coronary atherosclerosis associated with coronary artery disease.

fluvoxamine /flŏŏvok'sämēn/, a selective serotonin reuptake inhibitor.

fluvoxamine maleate, an antidepressant drug with selective inhibitory action on neuronal serotonin reuptake. It is prescribed in the treatment of obsessive-compulsive disorder in adult patients and has unlabeled uses for treating depression and panic attacks in adults and anxiety in children.

flux /fluks/ [L, *fluere*, to flow], **1.** an excessive flow or discharge. **2.** a substance that maintains the cleanliness of metals to be united and facilitates the easy flow and attachment of solder.

flux gain /fluks/, the ratio of the number of light photons at the output phosphor of a radiographic image intensifier tube to the number at the input phosphor.

fly [AS, *flyge*], a two-winged insect of the order Diptera, some species of which transmit arboviruses to humans.

fly bites, bites that may be caused by species of deerflies, horseflies, blackflies, or sand flies. Such bites produce a small painful wound with swelling caused by substances in the insect's saliva that are injected beneath the surface of the skin.

Fm, symbol for the element **fermium.**

FMD, abbreviation for **fibromuscular dysplasia.**

FMET, abbreviation for **formylmethionine.**

FMG, abbreviation for **foreign medical graduate.**

FML, a trademark for an ophthalmic glucocorticoid agent (fluorometholone).

FMR1, the symbol for a gene associated with a mental retardation disorder of the **fragile X syndrome.** The normal function of the gene has not been determined.

fMRI, abbreviation for **functional magnetic resonance imaging.**

FNP, abbreviation for **family nurse practitioner.**

foam /fōm/, **1.** a dispersion of gas in a liquid or solid, such as pumice or whipped cream. **2.** frothy saliva, produced particularly on exertion or pathologically. **3.** to produce or cause production of such a substance.

foam bath [AS, *fam* + *baeth*], a bath taken in water containing a saporin substance that covers the surface of the liquid and through which air or oxygen is blown to form the foam.

focal /fō'kəl/ [L, *focus*, hearth], pertaining to a focus.

focal dermal hypoplasia, an autosomal-dominant X-linked disorder found exclusively in females, characterized by linear areas of dermal hypoplasia with herniation of underlying tissue through the defects. There are also telangiectasias, areas of discoloration, localized fatty deposits, papillomas of mucous membranes around orifices, and limb anomalies such as syndactyly, adactyly, and oligodactyly.

focal emphysema, centriacinar emphysema associated with inhalation of environmental dusts, producing dilation of the terminal and respiratory bronchioles.

focal glomerular sclerosis, focal sclerosing lesions of renal glomeruli with proteinuria, hematuria, hypertension, and the nephrotic syndrome. Exacerbations and remissions may occur, most often in children; progression to renal failure occurs at a variable and unpredictable rate.

focal lesion [L, *focus* hearth, *laesio,* hurting], an infection, tumor, or injury that develops at a restricted or circumscribed area of tissue.

focal plane, the plane of tissue that is in focus on a tomogram.

focal point [L, *focus* + *punctus,* pricked], a point at which rays of light meet when deflected, either by reflection or refraction.

focal seizure [L, *focus,* hearth; OFr, *seisir*], a transitory disturbance in motor, sensory, or autonomic function that results from abnormal neuronal discharges in a localized part of the brain, most frequently motor or sensory areas adjacent to the central sulcus. Focal motor seizures commonly begin as spasmodic movements in the hand, face, or foot. Abnormal electric activity in the sensory strip of the cortex may be evident initially as a numb, prickling, tingling, or crawling feeling, and the neuronal discharge may spread to motor areas. Focal seizures may be caused by localized anoxia or a small brain lesion.

focal spot, the area on the anode of an x-ray tube or the target of an accelerator that is struck by electrons and from which the resulting x-rays are emitted. The shape and size of a focal spot influence the resolution of a radiographic image.

focal symptom [L, *focus,* hearth; Gk, *symptoma,* that which happens], a body function disturbance centered on a specific body system or part.

focal zone, in ultrasonography, the distance along the beam axis of a focused transducer assembly, from the point where the beam area first becomes equal to four times the focal area to the point beyond the focal surface where the beam area again becomes equal to four times the focal area.

focus /fō´kəs/ [L, hearth], **1.** a specific location, as the site of an infection or the point at which an electrochemical impulse originates. **2.** the point at which light rays converge after passing through a lens.

focused activity /fō´kəst/, a therapeutic technique of actively leading the patient to adaptive coping skills and away from maladaptive ones.

focused grid, an x-ray grid that has lead foils placed at an angle so that they all point to a focus at a specific distance.

Fogarty catheter, a type of balloon-tip catheter used to remove thrombi and emboli from blood vessels.

fogged film fault /fogd/ [Dan, *spray*; AS, *filmen,* membrane; L, *fallere,* to

deceive], a defect in a photograph or radiograph that appears as a foggy area.

fogging [ME, *fogge*], an optical method of determining refractive error, by placing excessively convex lenses in front of the eyes. The patient is made artificially hyperopic by means of the spheres in order to relax all accommodation.

fog nebulizer /neb´yəli´zer/, in respiratory care, a device that humidifies by producing large volumes of particles.

foil pellet, a loosely rolled piece of gold foil, used for making various dental restorations.

folate /fō´lāt/, **1.** a salt of folic acid. **2.** any of a group of substances found in some foods and in mammalian cells that act as coenzymes and promote the chemical transfer of single carbon units from one molecule to another.

folate deficiency, a deficiency of folic acid.

folded cravat sling, a bandage suspended from the neck, usually for supporting a forearm. It is prepared by placing a broad fold of cloth on the chest vertically with one end over the shoulder of the affected arm. The other end hangs in front of the chest, and the lower end is moved up and over the shoulder and tied.

Foley catheter /fō´lē/ [Frederick E.B. Foley, American physician, 1891–1966], a rubber catheter with a balloon tip to be filled with a sterile liquid after it has been placed in the bladder. This kind of catheter is used when continuous drainage of the bladder is desired, such as in surgery, or when repeated urinary catheterization would be necessary if an indwelling catheter were not used.

Foley Y-V pyeloplasty, pyeloplasty for repair of an obstructed and high ureteropelvic junction. A V-shaped flap is made from part of the renal pelvis and inserted into a Y-shaped incision whose angle is at the junction.

foliate papillae /fō´lē·āt/, a series of nipple-like processes that occur in folds along the lateral margins and in the front of the palatoglossus muscle of the tongue.

folic acid (FA) /fō´lik, fol´ik/, a yellow crystalline water-soluble vitamin essential for cell growth and reproduction. It functions as a coenzyme with vitamins B_{12} and C in the metabolism and use of proteins and in the formation of nucleic acids and heme for hemoglobin. Deficiency results in poor growth, graying of hair, glossitis, stomatitis, GI lesions, and diarrhea, and it may lead to megaloblastic anemia. Need for folic acid increases in pregnancy, infancy, and periods of stress. Rich dietary sources include spinach and other green leafy vegetables, liver, kidney, asparagus, lima beans, nuts, orange juice, and whole-grain cereals.

folic acid deficiency anemia, a form of megaloblastic (macrocytic) anemia caused by a lack of folic acid in the diet.

folic acid test (folate), a blood test performed to evaluate hemolytic disorders and to detect anemia caused by folic acid deficiency.

folie /fōlē'/ [Fr, madness], a psychiatric condition in a person who has previously been in good mental health.

folie du doute /dY dŏŏt'/ [Fr, madness of doubts], an extreme obsessive-compulsive reaction characterized by persistent doubting, vacillation, repetition of a particular act or behavior, and pathologic indecisiveness.

folie du pourquoi /dY pŏŏrkwô·ä'/ [Fr, madness of why], a psychopathologic condition characterized by the persistent tendency to ask questions, usually concerning unrelated topics.

folie gemellaire /zhemeler'/ [Fr, madness in twins], a psychotic condition that occurs simultaneously in twins, sometimes in those not living together or closely associated at the time.

folie musculaire /mYskYler'/, severe chorea.

folie raisonnante /rezônäNt'/ [Fr, deliberating reason], a delusional form of any psychosis marked by a thought process that seems logical but lacks common sense.

folinic acid /fōlin'ik/, an active form of folic acid used to treat megaloblastic anemias that are not caused by vitamin B_{12} deficiency and to counteract the toxic effects of antineoplastic folic acid antagonists.

folk illnesses /fōk/, health disorders that are attributed to nonscientific causes.

follicle /fol'ikal/ [L, *folliculus,* small bag], **1.** a small, secretory sac such as the dental follicles that enclose the teeth before eruption or the hair follicles within the epidermis. **2.** a fluid- or colloid-filled ball of cells in some glands such as the thyroid and the ovaries.—**follicular,** *adj.*

follicle recruitment, the process by which certain primordial ovarian follicles begin growing in a given menstrual cycle.

follicle-stimulating hormone (FSH), a gonadotropin that stimulates the growth and maturation of graafian follicles in the ovary and promotes spermatogenesis in the male. It is secreted by the anterior pituitary gland.

follicle-stimulating hormone–releasing factor (FSH-RF) [L, *folliculus,* small bag, *stimulare,* to incite; Gk, *horaein,* to set in motion], a hormone from the hypothalamus that stimulates the synthesis and release of FSH and luteinizing hormone from the anterior pituitary.

follicle-stimulating hormone surge, a sharp increase in serum levels of follicle-stimulating hormone seen around the middle of the menstrual cycle about 1 to 2 days before ovulation.

follicular /fōlik'yōōlər/ [L, *folliculus,* small bag], of or pertaining to a follicle or follicles.

follicular adenocarcinoma /fōlik'yəlɑr/, a neoplasm characterized by a follicular arrangement of cells often seen in the thyroid gland. The follicular thyroid carcinoma has a tendency to metastasize distantly to the lungs and bones.

follicular antrum, a cavity filled with follicular fluid on one side of a vesicular ovarian follicle in its later stages of growth just before ovulation.

follicular cyst, a tooth-forming sac that arises from the epithelium of a tooth bud and dental lamina. The kinds of follicular cysts are dentigerous, multilocular, and primordial.

follicular goiter, an enlargement of the thyroid gland characterized by proliferation of the follicles and epithelial tissue.

follicular phase, the long phase constituting the first half of the human menstrual cycle. The endometrium is stimulated by increasing levels of estrogen and increases in thickness to prepare for possible reproduction. At the end of this phase the luteinizing hormone surge and follicle-stimulating hormone surge begin, signaling the start of the ovulatory phase.

follicular stigma, a spot on the surface of an ovary where the vesicular ovarian follicle will rupture and permit passage of the ovum during ovulation.

follicular tonsillitis [L, *folliculus,* a small bag + *tonsilla*; Gk, *itis,* inflammation], inflammation of the tonsils accompanied by a purulent infection of the tonsillar crypts.

follicular vulvitis [L, *folliculus,* a small bag, *vulva,* a wrap per; Gk, *itis,* inflammation], an inflammation of the skin follicles of the vulva.

folliculitis /fōlik'yōōlī'tis/, inflammation of hair follicles, caused by an infection.

folliculogenesis /fōlik'yəlōjen'əsis/, **1.** the stimulation of follicle development in the ovary by hormones or drugs. **2.** the development of follicles in the ovary, normally under the influence of the follicle stimulating hormone secreted by the anterior pituitary gland.

folliculosis /fōlik'yōōlōsis/, a condition characterized by the development of a large number of lymph follicles, which may or may not be associated with an infection.

follitropin /folitro'pin/, a follicle-stimulating hormone.

follitropin alfa/follitropin beta, an ovulation stimulant used to induce ovulation during assisted reproductive technologies such as in vitro fertilization.

follow-up, 1. an act of renewing contact with sources of information and reviewing data needed to reinforce or evaluate a previous action or report. **2.** some further action taken after a procedure is finished, such as contact by a health care agency days or weeks after a patient has undergone treatment.

fomentation /fō'mentā'shən/ [L, *fomentare*, to apply a poultice], **1.** a topical treatment for pain or inflammation that uses a warm, moist application. **2.** a substance or poultice that is used as a warm, moist application.

fomite /fō'mīt/ [L, *fomes*, tinder], nonliving material such as bed linen that may transmit microorganisms.

fomivirsen /fomiv'ersin/, an antiviral agent administered by intravitreal injection in the treatment of cytomegalovirus retinitis associated with AIDS.

fondaparinux, an anticoagulant, antithrombotic agent used for the prevention of deep vein thrombosis and pulmonary emboli in hip and knee replacement and hip fracture surgery.

Fones' method /fōnz/ [Alfred C. Fones, American dentist,1869–1938], a toothbrushing technique that uses large, sweeping, scrubbing circles over occluded teeth, with the toothbrush held at right angles to the tooth surfaces.

Fonsecaea /fon'sese'ə/, a genus of imperfect fungi. *F. compactum* and *F. pedrosoi* are causal agents of chromoblastomycosis.

fontanel /fon'tənel'/ [Fr, *fontaine*, fountain], a space covered by tough membranes between the bones of an infant's cranium.

food [AS, *foda*], **1.** any substance, usually of plant or animal origin, consisting of carbohydrates, proteins, fats, and such supplementary elements as minerals and vitamins, that is ingested or otherwise taken into the body and assimilated to provide energy and to promote the growth, repair, and maintenance essential for sustaining life. **2.** nourishment in solid form, as contrasted with liquid form. **3.** a particular kind of solid nourishment, such as breakfast food or snack food.

food additive, a large variety of substances that are added to foods to prevent spoilage, improve appearance, enhance flavor or texture, or increase nutritional value. Most food additives must be approved by the U.S. Food and Drug Administration to determine whether they can cause cancer, birth defects, or other health problems.

food allergy, a hypersensitive state that results from the ingestion, inhalation, or other contact with a specific food antigen.

Food allergens are protein in nature and elicit an immunoglobulin response.

Food and Drug Administration (FDA), a U.S. federal agency responsible for the enforcement of regulations on the manufacture and distribution of food, drugs, and cosmetics. The regulations are intended to prevent the sale of impure or dangerous substances.

food and drug interactions, adverse health effects of certain combinations of foods and medications. Examples include reduced activity of drug-metabolizing enzymes and interference with the absorption of the drug.

food chain [AS, *foda* + *chaine*], an ecologic sequence in which the various organisms within a community subsist on organisms lower in the sequence, as the human eats the fish that eats the worm, and so on. Each level within the chain has a fundamental role, and destruction of any one member affects the rest of the chain negatively.

food challenge, a challenge test for determining food allergens. A small amount of a lyophilized preparation of the suspected allergen is administered orally and the patient is monitored for reactions such as rash, rhinorrhea, or diarrhea.

food contaminants /kəntam'inənts/, substances that make food unfit for human consumption. Examples include bacteria, toxic chemicals, carcinogens, teratogens, and radioactive materials. Basically harmless substances, such as water, that may be added to food to increase its weight are also regarded as contaminants.

food poisoning, any of a large group of toxic processes that result from the ingestion of a food contaminated by toxic substances or by bacteria that contain toxins.

food pyramid, a diagrammatic proportional representation of human nutritional needs updated in 2005 by the U.S. Department of Agriculture to replace the previous food pyramid created in 1992. Replaced in 2011 with the "My Plate" icon.

food sensitivity/hypersensitivity reaction, sensitivity to food items that is not a food allergy and does not involve the immune system.

food service administrator, a member of a hospital staff who is responsible for the planning and management of the food service system of the facility.

food service department, the section of a hospital or similar health facility that is responsible for food preparation and services to patients and personnel. It also provides nutritional care to patients.

foot [AS, *fot*], the distal extremity of the leg, consisting of the tarsus, the metatarsus, and the phalanges.

foot-and-mouth disease, an acute extremely contagious rhabdovirus, specifically vesicular stomatitis virus infection, primarily of cloven-hooved animals. It is characterized by the development of ulcers on the skin around the mouth, on the mucous membrane in the mouth, and on the udders. The virus is transmitted to humans by direct contact with infected animals or their secretions or with contaminated milk, although this is rare. Symptoms and signs in humans include headache, fever, malaise, and vesicles on the tongue, oral mucous membranes, hands, and feet.

footboard, a board, device, or open box placed at the end of a patient's bed and at a level above the top of the mattress to prevent the weight of the top sheet and blankets from resting on the feet. It is situated so that the soles of the feet are positioned firmly against the board with the legs at right angles to it. Its purposes are to help the bedridden patient retain normal posture and prevent footdrop.

foot-candle /foot′kandəl/ [AS, *fot;* L, *candela,* light], a unit of illumination being 1 lumen per square foot or equivalent to 1.0764 milliphots.

foot care, a nursing intervention from the Nursing Interventions Classification (NIC) defined as cleansing and inspecting the feet for the purposes of relaxation, cleanliness, and healthy skin.

footdrop /foot′drop/ [AS, *fot* + *dropa*], an abnormal neuromuscular condition of the lower leg and foot characterized by an inability to dorsiflex, or evert, the foot caused by damage to the common peroneal nerve.

footling breech [AS, *fot;* ME, *brech*], an intrauterine position of the fetus in which one or both feet are folded under the buttocks at the inlet of the maternal pelvis; one foot presents in a single footling breech, both in a double footling breech.

foot-pound, a unit for the measurement of work or energy. One foot-pound is the amount of work required to move 1 pound a distance of 1 foot in the same direction as that of the applied force.

footprinting, a method for determining the location of binding between a protein and a DNA molecule. The technique involves nuclease digestion of the unbound and therefore unprotected sequences of DNA. The protected DNA fragment that remains can be identified electrophoretically.

foramen /fôrā′mən/ *pl.* **foramina** [L, hole], an opening or aperture in a membranous structure or bone.

foramen caecum, a foramen immediately posterior to the frontal crest that may transmit emissary veins connecting the nasal cavity with the superior sagittal sinus.

foramen lacerum, an irregular opening in the temporal bone that is filled in life with cartilage.

foramen of Monro /monrō′/, a passage between the lateral and third ventricles of the brain.

foramenotomy, surgical removal of small pieces of bone around an intervertebral foramen, allowing more room for the spinal nerve. The procedure usually accompanies a laminectomy.

foramen spinosum, a small opening near the posterior angle of the greater wing of the sphenoid bone. It is the smallest of three pairs of sphenoidal foramina that transmit nerves and blood vessels.

foramina transversaria, openings in the transverse processes of the vertebrae that together form a longitudinal passage on each side of the cervical spine for the vertebral artery and veins.

Forbes-Albright syndrome /fôrbs ôl′brīt/ [Anne P. Forbes, American physician, 1911–1992; Fuller Albright, American physician, 1900–1969], an endocrine disease characterized by amenorrhea, prolactinemia, and galactorrhea, caused by an adenoma of the anterior pituitary.

forbidden clone hypothesis [AS, *forbeodan;* Gk, *klon,* a cutting, *theoria,* speculation], a proposed explanation for autoimmunity that postulates that clones of cells that can react against the body persist after birth and can be activated by a viral infection or by some metabolic change.

force [L, *fortis,* strong], **1.** energy applied so that it initiates motion, changes the speed or direction of motion, or alters the size or shape of an object. **2.** a push or pull defined as mass times acceleration.

forced expiratory flow (FEF), the average volumetric flow rate during any stated volume interval while a forced expired vital capacity test is performed. It is usually expressed as a percentage of vital capacity.

forced expiratory time (FET), the time required to exhale a given volume of air.

forced expiratory vital capacity (FEVC), the maximum volume of gas that can be forcibly and rapidly exhaled after a full inspiration.

forced expiratory volume (FEV), the volume of air that can be forcibly expelled in a fixed period after full inspiration.

forced-inhalation abdominal breathing, a respiratory therapy technique in which the patient inhales through the nose with an effort forceful enough to lift small sandbag weights placed on the abdomen.

forceps *pl.* **forceps** [L, pair of tongs], a pair of any of a large variety and number of surgical instruments, all of which have two handles or sides, each attached to a dull blade. The handles may be joined at one end, such as a pair of tweezers, or the two sides may be separate to be drawn together in use, such as obstetric forceps. Forceps are used to grasp, handle, compress, pull, or join tissue, equipment, or supplies.

forceps delivery, an obstetric operation in which instruments are used to deliver a baby. It is performed to overcome dystocia, to quickly deliver a baby experiencing fetal distress, or, most often, to shorten normal labor. Prerequisites to forceps delivery include full dilation of the cervix, engagement of the fetal head, certain knowledge of the position of the head, and ruptured membranes. Because cesarean section is performed more often now than formerly, traumatic forceps deliveries are uncommon.

forceps rotation, an obstetric operation in which forceps are used to turn a baby's head that is arrested in transverse or posterior position in the birth canal.

forcible inspiration [L, *fortis,* strong + *inspirare*], breathing that is assisted by a mechanical ventilator that forces air into the lungs during inhalation but allows the patient to exhale passively.

Fordyce-Fox disease /fôr′dis foks/ [G.H. Fox, American dermatologist, 1846–1937; John A. Fordyce, American dermatologist, 1858–1925], an apocrine gland disorder that produces symptoms similar to those of miliaria.

Fordyce's disease [John A. Fordyce], the presence of enlarged oil glands in the mucosal membranes of the lips, cheeks, gums, and genitalia. It is a common condition and may be symptomless.

forearm, the portion of the upper extremity between the elbow and the wrist. It contains two long bones, the radius and ulna.

forefinger, the first, or index, finger.

forefoot, the portion of the foot that includes the metatarsus and toes.

foregut /fôr′gut/ [AS,*fore,*in front+ *guttas*], the cephalic portion of the embryonic alimentary canal. It gives rise to the pharynx, esophagus, stomach, liver, pancreas, most of the small intestine, and respiratory ducts.

forehead /fôr′hed/ [AS,*fore,* in front, *heafod,* head], the region of the face superior to the eyes.

foreign body /fôr′in/ [Fr, *forain,* alien; AS, *bodig*], any object or substance found in an organ or tissue in which it does not belong under normal circumstances.

foreign body granuloma [OFr, *forain;* AS, *bodig;* L, *granulum,* little grain; Gk, *oma,* tumor], a chronic inflammatory mass of tissue that accumulates around foreign bodies such as gravel, splinters, or bits of sutures.

foreign body in airway, anything found in the airway that is not normally present. Examples are food, coins, small pieces of toys, and bones. It is crucial to determine the extent of airway obstruction. The patient may be asymptomatic or may exhibit dyspnea or changes in breathing pattern or color (cyanosis). Removal of the foreign body is generally performed with a fiberoptic laryngoscope and forceps or via bronchoscopy.

foreign body in ear [OFr,*forain;* AS, *bodig* + *eare*], any object found in the ear canal that is not normally part of it, such as a bean, insect, or pebble.

foreign body in esophagus [OFr, *forain;* AS, *bodig;* Gk, *oisophagos,* gullet], anything found in the esophagus that is not normally a part of the tissue.

foreign body in eye [OFr, *forain;* AS, *bodig* + *eage*], anything found in the eye that is not a normal part of the tissue. Foreign bodies may be superficially embedded in the tissue surfaces or may penetrate the globe.

foreign body in throat [OFr, *forain;* AS, *bodig* + *throte*], anything found in the throat that is not normally present. A common foreign body in the throat is a posteriorly displaced tongue.

foreign body obstruction, a disturbance in normal function or a pathologic condition caused by an object lodged in a body orifice, passage, or organ. Most cases occur in children who suddenly inhale or swallow a foreign object or insert it into a body opening.

foreign medical graduate (FMG), a physician trained in and graduated from a medical school outside the United States and Canada. U.S. citizens graduated from medical schools outside the United States and Canada are also classified as FMGs.

forensic /fôren′sik/ [L, *forum,* public place], **1.** pertaining to courts of law. **2.** relating to or dealing with the application of scientific knowledge to legal problems.

forensic data collection, a nursing intervention from the Nursing Interventions Classification (NIC) defined as the collection and recording of pertinent patient data for a forensic report.

forensic dentistry, the branch of dentistry that deals with the legal aspects of professional dental practices and treatment, with particular emphasis on the use of dental records to identify victims of crimes or accidents.

forensic medicine [L, *forum,* public place, *medicinus,* physician], a branch of medicine that deals with the legal aspects of health care.

forensic nursing, a nursing specialty involving provision of care to victims of crime, as well as collecting evidence, performing certain types of death investigations, and working with prison inmates.

forensic psychiatry [L, *forum,* public place; Gk, *psyche,* mind, *iatreia,* treament], a branch of psychiatry concerned with the application of psychiatry to law, including criminal responsibility, guardianship, and competence to stand trial.

foreplay /fôr'plā/, sexual activities, such as kissing and fondling, that precede coitus.

foreskin /fôr'skin/ [AS, *fore* + *skinn*], a loose fold of skin that covers the end of the penis or clitoris. Its removal constitutes circumcision.

Forestier's disease /fō'rest ē·äz'/ [Jacques Forestier, French neurologist, 20th century], hyperostosis of the anterolateral part of the vertebral column, especially in the thoracic region.

forestomach, a constricted passage from the esophagus to the stomach, lying just inside the opening formed by the cardiac sphincter.

forest yaws /fôr'ist/ [L, *foris,* outside; Afr, *yaw,* strawberry], a cutaneous form of American leishmaniasis, common in South and Central America, caused by *Leishmania guyanensis.* The disease is chronic, with multiple deep skin ulcers that occasionally spread to the nasal mucosa.

forewaters /fôr'wôtərs/ [AS, *fore* + *waeter*], the part of the amniotic sac that pouches into the cervix in front of the presenting part of the fetus.

forgiveness facilitation, a nursing intervention from the Nursing Interventions Classification (NIC) defined as assisting an individual's willingness to replace feelings of anger and resentment toward another, self, or higher power, with beneficence, empathy, and humility.

fork /fôrk/ [L, *furca*], **1.** an instrument with prongs. **2.** something resembling such an instrument.

formaldehyde (HCHO) /fərmal'dəhīd/, a toxic, colorless foul-smelling gas that is soluble in water and used in that form as a disinfectant, fixative, or preservative.

formalin /fôr'məlin/, a clear solution of formaldehyde in water. A 37% solution is used for fixing and preserving biologic specimens for pathologic and histologic examination.

formal operations, a form of thinking after the stage of concrete operations and representing the final, most mature state of thinking. It usually occurs after age 11 and is characterized by true logical thought, capability for deductive reasoning, abstract thinking, formulation and testing of hypotheses, appreciation for multiple perspectives

on an issue, and the manipulation of ideas and concepts.

formation /fôrmā'shən/, **1.** a cluster of people who occupy and therefore define a quantum of space. **2.** a structure, shape, or figure.

formative evaluation /fôr'mətiv/, **1.** judgments made about effectiveness of nursing interventions as they are implemented. **2.** in nursing education, periodic evaluation of a student during a course, usually a clinical practicum.

formboard, equipment used in tactile performance testing. It consists of a board with cutouts of various shapes and sizes and blocks of corresponding geometric characteristics. Subjects are tested on their ability to fit the blocks into the proper cutout spaces.

forme fruste /fôrm' frYst', fôrm' fro͞ost'/ *pl.* **formes frustes** [Fr, rough form], **1.** an incomplete or atypical form of a disease or a disease that is spontaneously arrested before it has run its usual course. **2.** in genetics, an inherited disorder in which there is minimal expression of an abnormal trait.

formic acid (HCOOH) /fôr'mik/, a colorless pungent liquid found in nature in nettles, in ants, and in other insects. It is prepared commercially from oxalic acid and glycerin and from the oxidation of formaldehyde. It currently has no therapeutic applications.

formiminoglutamic acid (FIGLU) /fôr mim'inōglo͞otam'ik/, a compound formed in the metabolism of histidine, present in urine in elevated levels in folic acid deficiency. Increased excretion of FIGLU may indicate folic acid deficiency.

formoterol fumarate, a beta-adrenergic agonist used to treat chronic obstructive pulmonary disorder, maintain and treat asthma, and prevent exercise-induced bronchospasm.

formula /fôr'm(y)ələ/ [L, *forma,* pattern], a simplified statement, generally using numerals and other symbols, expressing the constituents of a chemical compound, a method for preparing a substance, or a procedure for achieving a desired value or result.—**formulaic,** *adj.*

formulary /fôr'myələ'rē/ [L, *forma,* pattern], a listing of drugs intended to include a large enough range of medications and sufficient information about them to enable health practitioners to prescribe treatment that is medically appropriate. Hospitals maintain formularies that list all drugs commonly stocked in their pharmacy. Third-party organizations such as insurance companies usually maintain formularies that list drugs that the company will cover under plan benefits.

formulation /fôr'myəlā'shən/ [L, *forma*, pattern], **1.** a pharmacologic substance prepared according to a formula. **2.** a systematic and precise statement of a problem, a theory, or a method of analysis in research.

formylmethionine (FMET) /fôr'milməthī'ənēn/, in molecular genetics, the first amino acid in a protein sequence.

fornication /fôr'nikā'shən/ [L, *fornix*, arch], in law, sexual intercourse between two people who are not married to each other. The specific legal definition varies from jurisdiction to jurisdiction.

fornix /fôr'niks/ *pl.* **fornices** [L, arch], an archlike structure or space.

fornix cerebri /ser'əbrī/, an archlike body of nerve fibers that lies beneath the corpus callosum of the cranium and serves as the efferent pathway from the hippocampus.

forskolin (FSK), an activator of adenylate cyclase. FSK interacts directly with ion channels, increasing glutamate responses and amplitude and decay time of spontaneous excitatory postsynaptic currents.

Fortaz, a trademark for a cephalosporin antibiotic (ceftazidime).

fortified milk [L, *fortis*, strong; AS, *milc*], pasteurized milk enriched with one or more nutrients, usually vitamins A and D, that has been standardized at 400 International Units per quart.

forward chaining, a method of measuring rehabilitation performance. The patient performs the first step independently, and the therapist helps the patient perform the rest of the steps. The routine is then repeated with the patient performing the first two steps independently, then the first three steps, and so on.

forward-leaning posture, a respiratory therapy technique intended to reduce or eliminate the involvement of the accessory muscles of respiration in ambulatory patients with breathing difficulty. It involves walking while bent forward in a slightly stooped posture.

fosamprenavir, an antiretroviral agent used in combination with other antiretrovirals to treat HIV-1 infection.

Foscavir, a trademark for an antiviral drug (foscarnet) used in the treatment of cytomegalovirus retinitis in conjunction with ganciclovir and for the treatment of herpes simplex infections when acyclovir fails.

fosfomycin, a urinary antiinfective used to treat infections of the urinary tract caused by *Enterococcus faecalis* and *Escherichia coli.*

fosinopril, an angiotensin-converting enzyme inhibitor. It inhibits the formation of the hormone angiotensin II, which is a powerful vasoconstrictor that also stimulates the release of the sodium-retaining hormone aldosterone. It is prescribed alone or in combination for the treatment of high BP, CHF, and left ventricular dysfunction following MI.

fosphenytoin, an anticonvulsant used to treat generalized tonic-clonic seizures and status epilepticus.

Fosrenol, a trademark for lanthanum.

fossa /fos'ə/ *pl.* **fossae** [L, ditch], a hollow or depression, especially on the surface of the end of a bone.

Foster bed, a trademark for a special bed used in the care and treatment of severely injured patients, especially those with spinal injuries. It consists of two Bradford frames mounted on a castered base. The assembly is attached to a rotary bearing mechanism, permitting horizontal turning of the patient without moving the spine.

Foster Kennedy's syndrome /fos'tər ken'ə·dē/ [Robert Foster Kennedy, American neurologist, 1884–1952], a syndrome characterized by retrobulbar neuritis, central scotoma, optic disc atrophy on the side of the lesion, and papilledema on the opposite side, occurring in tumors of the frontal lobe of the brain which press downward.

fo-ti, a climbing perennial herb found in China. It is used for tiredness, constipation, cancer, and elevated cholesterol. It appears to be safe and effective as a laxative, but proof of efficacy for other indications is lacking.

foundation [L, *fundamentum*], in dentistry, any device or material added to a remaining tooth structure to enhance the stability and retention of an overlying cast restoration.

foundation model, a health maintenance organization or other health system that is legally established as a tax-exempt, not-for-profit corporation organized to operate as a charitable institution.

fourchette /fŏŏrshet'/ [Fr, fork], a tense band of mucous membranes at the posterior angle of the vagina that connects the posterior ends of the labia minora.

four-handed dentistry, a technique in which a dental assistant or dental hygienist works directly with the dentist on the procedures being done in the mouth of a patient. The technique reduces fatigue and improves the effectiveness of dental procedures.

Fourier transform (FT) /fŏŏryā'/ [Jean B.J. Fourier, French mathematician, 1768–1830; L, *transformare*, to change form], a mathematic procedure that separates out the frequency components of a signal from its amplitudes as a function of time, or vice versa.

Fourier transform imaging [Jean B.J. Fourier], in medical physics, nuclear magnetic resonance (NMR) imaging

F

techniques in which at least one dimension is phase encoded by applying variable gradient pulses along that dimension before "reading out" the NMR signal with a gradient magnetic field perpendicular to the variable gradient. The Fourier transform is then used to reconstruct an image from the set of encoded NMR signals.

Fournier's gangrene /fŏŏrnyāz'/ [Jean A. Fournier, French syphilographer, 1832–1914], an infective gangrene of the scrotum or vulva caused by an anaerobic hemolytic strain of streptococci. It is associated with diabetes. Infective agents are *Bacteroides fragilis* and aerobic *Escherichia coli*.

four-poster orthosis, an orthosis to immobilize the cervical vertebrae. It contains four vertical posts or poles on the anterior and posterior lateral sides of the head and is placed over the shoulders. The head is supported under the chin and occiput, and the posts prevent movement.

four-tailed bandage, a narrow piece of cloth with two ties on each end for wrapping a joint, such as an elbow or knee, or a prominence, such as the nose or chin.

fourth-degree burn, a burn that extends deeply into the subcutaneous tissue, completely destroying the skin, subcutaneous fat, and underlying tendons, and sometimes involving muscle, fascia, or bone.

fourth-generation cephalosporin, a broad-spectrum cephalosporin having the greatest activity against gram-negative organisms of any of the cephalosporins.

fourth-generation scanner, a CT machine in which the x-ray source rotates but the detector assembly does not.

fourth stage of labor [ME, *feower,* four; OFr, *estage;* L, *labor,* work], a postpartum period of about 4 hours after the third stage, or delivery of the placenta. Some complications, especially hemorrhage, occur at this time, necessitating careful observation of the mother.

fourth ventricle [ME, *feower,* four; L, *ventriculus,* little belly], a cavity with a diamond-shaped floor in the hindbrain, communicating below with the central canal of the spinal cord and above with the cerebral aqueduct of the midbrain. At the bottom of the ventricle are surfaces of the pons and medulla.

fovea capitis /fō'vē-ə/ [L, *fovea,* pit], 1. a depression on the proximal surface of the head of the radius where it meets the capitulum of the humerus. 2. a fovea on the head of the femur, where the ligamentum teres is attached.

fovea centralis, an area at the center of the retina where cone cells are concentrated and there are no rod cells.

Fowler's position /fou'lərz/ [George R. Fowler, American surgeon, 1848–1906],

the posture assumed by the patient when the head of the bed is raised 45 to 60 degrees and his or her knees are elevated slightly.

Fox-Fordyce disease /foks fôr'dīs/ [G.H. Fox, American dermatologist, 1846–1937; John Addison Fordyce, American dermatologist, 1858–1925], a chronic skin disease characterized by small papular eruptions and other skin changes of apocrine gland-bearing areas, especially the axillae and pubes, caused by obstruction and rupture of the intraepidermal part of the ducts of the glands.

foxglove /foks'glov/, the common name for *Digitalis purpura,* the plant that is a source of digitalis.

FPG, abbreviation for **fasting plasma glucose.**

Fr, symbol for the element **francium.**

fractional dilation and curettage /frak'shənəl/, a diagnostic technique in which each section of the uterus is examined and curetted to obtain specimens of the endometrium from all parts of the organ. It is often performed in the diagnosis of endometrial cancer.

fractional excretion of sodium (FE$_{Na}$), an assessment of acute renal failure comparing the sodium clearance with the creatinine clearance.

fractionation /frak'shonā'shon/ [L, *frangere,* to break], 1. in neurology, a mechanism within the neural arch of the vertebrae whereby only a portion of the efferent nerves innervating a muscle reacts to a stimulus, even when the reflex requirement is maximal, so that a reserve of neurons remains to respond to additional stimuli. 2. in chemistry, the separation of a substance into its basic constituents by using such procedures as fractional distillation or crystallization. 3. in bacteriology, the process of isolating a pure culture by successive culturing of a small portion of a colony of bacteria. 4. in histology, the process of isolating the different components of living cells by centrifugation. 5. in radiology, the process of administering a dose of radiation in smaller units over time to minimize tissue damage rather than in a single large dose.

fraction of inspired oxygen (FiO$_2$) [L, *frangere,* to break, *inspirare,* to breathe in; Gk, *oxys,* sharp, *genein,* to produce], the proportion of oxygen in the air that is inspired.

fracture /frak'chər/ [L, *frangere,* to break], a traumatic injury to a bone in which the continuity of the bone tissue is broken. A fracture is classified by the bone involved, the part of that bone, and the nature of the break, such as a comminuted fracture of the head of the tibia.

fracture-dislocation, a break in the bony structures of any joint, with associated dislocation of the same joint.

fracture of clavicle [L, *frangere* + *clavicula,* little key], a break in the long bone of the shoulder girdle. It is typically accompanied by pain, swelling, and a protuberance and depression over the site of the injury.

fracture of olecranon [L, *frangere*; Gk, *olekranon,* point of the elbow], a break in the bony prominence of the ulna at the elbow joint. Different types of olecranon fractures may occur, depending on the articular surfaces involved. The triceps, which normally extends the elbow, may become spastic as a result of the injury.

fracture of patella [L, *frangere* + *patella,* small pan], a break in the sesamoid knee cap. The damage is complicated by reflex bracing of the quadriceps femoris muscle, which pulls the fragments apart.

fracture of radius [L, *frangere* + *ray*], a break in the radius, usually with backward and radial displacement of the wrist and hand.

fracture of skull [L, *frangere*; AS, *skulle,* bowl], a break in one or more of the cranial bones. A fracture in the vault of the skull is usually a compound fracture and is complicated by possible damage to brain tissue, particularly if shards of bone are driven into the brain by the force of the trauma.

fracture threshold, a measure of bone density used in predicting osteoporosis risk factors.

fragile X syndrome /fraj'əl/, a reproductive disorder characterized by a nearly broken X chromosome, which has a tip hanging by a flimsy thread. It is the most common inherited cause of mental retardation. Some healthy individuals may possess fragile X chromosomes without exhibiting symptoms and may transmit the condition to children or grandchildren.

fragment /frag'mənt/ [L, *frangere,* to break], one of the small pieces into which a larger entity has been broken.

Fragmin, a trademark for a low-molecular-weight heparin (dalteparin sodium).

frail elder, an older person (usually above 85 years of age) who has multiple physical or mental disabilities that may interfere with the ability to perform ADL independently.

fraise /frāz/ [Fr, strawberry], a smooth hemispheric or conic bur with cutting edges. It is used for enlarging trephine openings or cutting osteopathic flaps.

Fraley's syndrome, nephralgia with dilation of the upper pole renal calyces around the kidney caused by compression of the adjacent infundibulum, usually caused by

pressure from vessels serving that part of the kidney.

frame /frām/, a structure, usually rigid, designed for giving support to or for immobilizing a part.

frame of reference [AS, *framian,* to help; L, *referre,* to carry back], the personal guidelines of an individual, taken as a whole. An individual frame of reference reflects the person's social status, cultural norms, and concepts.

Franceschetti's syndrome /fran'chesket'ēz/ [Adolphe Franceschetti, Swiss ophthalmologist, 1896–1968], a complete form of mandibulofacial dysostosis.

franchise dentistry /fran'chīz/ [Fr, exemption; L, *dens,* tooth], the practice of dentistry under a trade name purchased from another dentist or dental practice.

Francisella, a genus of nonmotile non–spore-forming gram-negative aerobic bacteria that is a facultative intracellular pathogen of macrophages. The organism causes tularemia in humans.

francium (Fr) /fran'sē-əm/ [France], a metallic element of the alkali metal group. Its atomic number is 87. The mass of its longest-lived isotope is 223. All of its 20 isotopes are radioactive and short-lived.

frank [L, *francus,* forthright], obvious or clinically evident, such as the unequivocal presence of a condition or a disease.

Frank biopsy guide, a trademark for a device consisting of a long needle containing a hooked wire used to obtain biopsy samples of breast tissue.

frank breech [L, *francus*; ME, *brec*], an intrauterine position of the fetus in which the buttocks present at the maternal pelvic inlet, the legs are straight up in front of the body, and the feet are at the shoulders.

Frankfurt horizontal plane [Frankfurt-am-Main (anthropologic) Agreement, 1882], in dentistry, a craniometric surface determined by the inferior borders of the bony orbits and the upper margin of the auditory meatus. It passes through the two orbitales and the two tragions and is commonly used as a reference surface in orthodontic diagnosis and treatment planning.

Frankfurt-mandibular incisor angle (FMIA), in dentistry, the precumbency of the mandibular incisor to the Frankfort horizontal plane.

Frank-Starling relationship [Otto Frank, German physiologist, 1865–1944; Ernest H. Starling, English physiologist, 1866–1927], a mathematic expression stating that stroke volume increases with diastolic volume. The relationship is based on the principle that the force exerted by the myocardial fibers during contraction is directly proportional to their length or degree of stretch at the start of contraction.

Fraser's syndrome /frā′zer/ [George Robert Fraser, Czechoslovakian-born American geneticist, b. 1932], an autosomal-recessive abnormality, characterized by absence of an opening in the eyelids, disorganization of one or both ocular globes, malformed ears, cleft palate, laryngeal stenosis, syndactyly, meningoencephalocele, imperforate anus, cardiac defects, and maldeveloped kidneys.

F-**ratio** [Sir Ronald Aylmer *Fisher,* British statistician, 1890–1962], **1.** the variance between the means of several groups relative to the variance within the groups, used in the *F*-test in the analysis of variance. **2.** the variance between or within treatments.

fraud /frôd/ [L, *fraudare,* to cheat], in law, the act of intentionally misleading or deceiving another person by any means so as to cause him or her legal injury, usually the loss of something valuable or the surrender of a legal right.

Fraunhofer's lines, absorption bands or lines seen in a spectrum, caused by the absorption of groups of light rays in their passage through solids, liquids, or gases.

Fraunhofer zone /froun′hōfər/ [Joseph von Fraunhofer, German optician, 1787–1826], the zone farthest from the face of an ultrasound transducer.

FRC, abbreviation for **functional residual capacity.**

FRCP, abbreviation for *Fellow of the Royal College of Physicians.*

FRCS, abbreviation for *Fellow of the Royal College of Surgeons.*

freckle [ME, *freken*], a brown or tan macule on the skin that results from exposure to sunlight. Freckles are harmless, but people who freckle easily should avoid excessive sun exposure or use protective sunscreens because they have a tendency toward development of more serious actinic skin changes.

free-air chamber [AS, *freo,* free; Gk, *aer,* air; L, *camera,* vault], a device used throughout the world as a primary standard for calibrating x-ray exposure.

free association, 1. spontaneous consciously unrestricted association of ideas, feelings, or mental images. **2.** spontaneous verbalization of thoughts and emotions that enter the consciousness during psychoanalysis.

freebasing, a chemical process used to increase the stimulating effect of illicit drugs, such as cocaine, by converting the salt of the drug into its noncharged base form that can more readily enter the brain. The resulting product is smoked.

free clinic, a clinic or health program, usually located in a neighborhood setting, that provides health care for ambulatory patients at nominal or no cost.

free fatty acid (FFA) [AS, *freo* + *faett*; L, *acidus,* sour], a nonesterified fatty acid, released by the hydrolysis of triglycerides within adipose tissue. Free fatty acids can be used as an immediate source of energy by many organs and can be converted by the liver into ketone bodies.

free-floating anxiety, a generalized, persistent, pervasive fear that is not attributable to any specific object, event, or source.

free-form foot orthosis, an orthosis that is molded directly to a patient's foot.

free gingiva, the unattached portion of the gum tissue located coronal to the junctional epithelium.

free gingival groove, a shallow line or depression on the gum surface at the junction of the free and attached gingivae.

free graft [AS, *freo*; Gk, *graphein,* stylus], a graft completely removed from its original site and replaced at a new site in a single one-stage operation.

free-induction decay (FID), a signal emitted by the atomic nuclei in a tissue after a radiofrequency pulse has excited the nuclear spins at resonance. The decaying oscillation of the nuclei back to their original state causes them to emit photons, which provide the signal from which an MRI is made.

free macrophage [AS, *freo*; Gk, *makros,* large, *phagein,* to eat], a motile macrophage derived from a monocyte. It responds to chemotactic stimuli and migrates from blood vessels to tissue spaces.

Freeman-Sheldon syndrome /frē′mən shel′dən/ [Ernest Arthur Freeman, British orthopedic surgeon, 1900–1975; Joseph Harold Sheldon, British physician, 1920–1964], a congenital anomaly transmitted as an autosomal-dominant trait, consisting of characteristic flattened, masklike facies; small mouth, the lips protruding as in whistling; deep-set eyes with hypertelorism; camptodactyly with ulnar deviation of the fingers; and clubfoot.

free nerve ending, a receptor nerve ending that is not enclosed in a capsule.

free radical, a species with at least one unpaired electron. Oxygen is a stable diradical, but most other free radicals are unstable and react readily with other molecules.

free-radical theory of aging, a concept of aging based on the premise that the main causative factor is an imbalance between the production and elimination in the body tissues of free chemical radicals from oxygen metabolism.

free-standing tax-exempt clinic, in U.S. managed care, an organization that may employ physicians or make arrangements with physicians as independent contractors. It is usually organized as a not-for-profit, tax-exempt corporation. It is the direct provider of health care and holds preferred provider organization and health maintenance organization contracts, bills and collects in its own name, and owns the accounts receivable department.

free thyroxine, the amount of the unbound, active thyroid hormone thyroxine circulating in the blood, measured by specific laboratory procedures.

free thyroxine index, the amount of unbound, physiologically active thyroxine in serum. This amount is determined by direct assay or, more frequently, calculated on the basis of an in vitro uptake test.

free thyroxine (FT₄) test, a blood test used to determine thyroid function, especially when the patient has concurrent clinical situations that may alter protein blood levels.

free water, that portion of the water in body tissue that is not bound by macromolecules or organelles.

free-water clearance, the calculated volume of water that must be added to a given volume of urine to make it isotonic to the plasma.

freeway space [AS, *freo* + *wegan*; L, *spatiaum*], the separation between the occlusal surfaces of the teeth when the mandible is in its rest position.

freezing, a sudden inability to initiate or continue repetitive motor activity of patients with Parkinson's disease. The patient may be unable to take the first step in walking or, if walking, may find a real or imagined obstacle that causes the feet to remain in one spot.

freezing point [ME, *fresen,* to be cold; L, *punctus,* pricked], the temperature at which a substance changes from a liquid to a solid state. The freezing point for water is 32° on the **Fahrenheit** scale and 0° on the **Celsius** scale.

Freiberg's infraction [Albert H. Freiberg, American surgeon, 1868–1940; L, *infarcire,* to stuff], an abnormal orthopedic condition characterized by osteochondritis or aseptic necrosis of bone tissue, most commonly affecting the head of the second metatarsal.

Frei's test /frī/ [William S. Frei, German dermatologist, 1885–1943], a test performed to confirm a diagnosis of lymphogranuloma venereum. Killed antigen is injected intradermally in one forearm. If a red, thickened papule develops at the injection site, the test result is positive.

Frejka splint /frā′kə/, a corrective device used to maintain abduction and articulation of the head of the femur with the

acetabulum in a baby born with dislocated hips. It consists of a pillow that is belted between the legs.

fremitus /frem′itəs/ [L, a growling], a tremulous vibration of the chest wall caused by vocalization that is primarily palpated during physical examination.

French scale (Fr), a method of sizing catheters, tubules, and sounds in which each Fr unit is equivalent to 1.3 mm.

frenectomy /frənek′təmē/ [L, *frenum,* bridle; Gk, *ektomē,* excision], a surgical procedure for excising a frenum or frenulum such as the excision of the lingual frenum from its attachment into the mucoperiosteal covering of the alveolar process to correct ankyloglossia.

Frenkel's exercises [Heinrich S. Frenkel, Swiss neurologist, 1860–1931], a system of slow repetitious exercises of increasing difficulty developed to treat ataxia in MS and similar disorders.

frenotomy /frənot′əmē/ [L, *frenum;* Gk, *temnein,* to cut], a surgical procedure for repairing a defective frenum, such as the cutting or lengthening of the lingual frenum to correct ankyloglossia.

frenulum of labia minora, the small transverse fold formed by the union of the labia minora posterior to the vestibule.

frenulum of the ileal orifice, a fold formed by the joined extremities of the ileal orifice, extending partly around the lumen of the colon.

frenulum of the lips /fren′yələm/, a fold of movement-limiting mucous membrane running from the gums to the lips or tongue.

frenulum of the tongue [L, *frenum,* bridle; AS, *tunge*], a longitudinal fold of mucous membrane connecting the floor of the mouth to the underside of the tongue in midline.

frenum /frē′nəm/ *pl.* **frenums, frena** [L, *frenum,* bridle], a restraining portion or structure, a fold of mucous membrane that connects two parts, one more or less movable.

frequency (F) /frē′kwənsē/ [L, *frequens,* frequent], **1.** the number of repetitions of any phenomenon within a fixed period, such as the number of heartbeats per minute. **2.** in biometry, the proportion of the number of persons having a discrete characteristic to the total number of persons being studied. **3.** in electronics, the number of cycles of a periodic quantity, such as alternating current, that occur in a period of 1 second. Electromagnetic frequencies are expressed in hertz (Hz).

freshening, a step in the process of wound repair in which fibrin, granulation, and early scar tissue are removed in preparation for secondary closure.

fresh frozen plasma [ME, *fresen*, to be cold; Gk, *plassein*, to mold], plasma separated from whole blood and frozen within 8 hours of collection. FFP has a shelf life of 12 months when stored at 18° C or below. Contains normal levels of all the coagulation proteins, including the labile factors V and VIII.

Fresnel zone /freznel'/ [Augustine J. Fresnel, French physicist, 1788–1827], the region nearest the face of an ultrasound transducer.

freudian /froi'dē-ən/ [Sigmund Freud], 1. pertaining to Sigmund Freud; his theories and doctrines, which stress the formative years of childhood as the basis for later psychoneurotic disorders, primarily through the unconscious repression of instinctual drives and sexual desires; and his system of psychoanalysis, based on free association and dream analysis, for treating such disturbances. 2. pertaining to anything that is easily interpreted according to the theories of Freud or in psychoanalytic terms. 3. pertaining to the school of psychiatry based on Freud's teachings. 4. one who adheres to Freud's school of psychiatry.

freudian fixation [Sigmund Freud], an arrest in psychosexual development characterized by a firm emotional attachment to another person or object.

freudianism /froi'dē-əniz'əm/, the school of psychiatry based on the psychoanalytic theories and psychotherapeutic methods of treating disorders developed by Sigmund Freud and his followers.

freudian slip, in freudian psychology, a behavioral error in speech or action that is believed to reveal a hidden motive in the unconscious thoughts or feelings of the perpetrator.

Freud, Sigmund /froid/ [Austrian neurologist, 1856–1939], founder of a complex integrated theory of psychologic causes of mental disorders, some, such as hysteria, with physical symptoms. Among tenets of freudian theory are that human beings are motivated by a pleasure principle; receive internal stimulation from a sex instinct and a death instinct; have personality structures that can be divided into ego, superego, and id; and have unconscious, preconscious, and conscious levels of mental activity.

friable /frī'əbəl/ [L, *friare*, to crumble], easily shattered, crumbled, or pulverized, such as tissues of the liver.

fricative /frik'ətiv/, a consonant speech sound such as an /f/ or /s/, made by forcing an air stream through a constricted opening.

Fricke dosimeter, a meter that quantifies radiation dose by measuring the change in the concentration of ferric ions in a solution subject to irradiation.

friction /frik'shən/ [L, *fricare*, to rub], 1. the act of rubbing one object against another. 2. a type of massage in which deeper tissues are stroked or rubbed, usually through strong circular movements of the hand.

frictional force /frik'shənəl/, the force component parallel to the surfaces at the point of contact between two objects. It may be increased or decreased by such factors as moisture on a surface.

friction burn, tissue injury caused by abrasion of the skin.

friction rub, a dry, grating sound heard with a stethoscope during auscultation. A friction rub auscultated over the pericardial area is suggestive of pericarditis; a rub over the pleural area may be a sign of lung disease.

Friedländer's pneumonia [Carl Friedländer; Gk, *pneumon,* lung], a form of bronchopneumonia with a high mortality rate, particularly among older patients, caused by the bacterium *Klebsiella pneumoniae.* The pneumonic patches tend to become confluent, and persons who survive may experience pulmonary abscesses and necrosis.

Friedman curve /frēd'mən/ [Emanuel A. Friedman, American obstetrician, b. 1926], a graph depicting the progress of labor, prepared by labor attendants to facilitate detection of dysfunctional labor. Observations of cervical dilation and fetal descent are plotted on the vertical axis against time on the horizontal axis.

Friedman's test [Maurice H. Friedman, American physiologist, 1903–1991], a modification of the Aschheim-Zondek test. A sample of urine from a woman is injected into a mature unmated female rabbit. If, days later, the rabbit ovaries contain fresh corpora lutea or hemorrhaging corpora, the result is positive, indicating that the woman is pregnant.

Friedreich's ataxia /frēd'rīshs/ [Nikolaus Friedreich, German physician, 1825–1882], a condition characterized by muscular weakness, loss of muscular control, weakness of the lower extremities, and an abnormal gait. The primary pathologic feature is pronounced sclerosis of the posterior columns of the spinal cord with possible involvement of the spinocerebellar tracts and the corticospinal tracts.

Friedreich's sign [Nikolaus Friedreich; L, *signum,* sign], the diastolic collapse of the jugular veins in adherent pericardium.

Fried's rule, a method of estimating the dose of medicine for a child by multiplying the adult dose by the child's age in months and dividing the product by 150.

frigid /frij'id/ [L, *frigidus,* cold], 1. lacking warmth of feeling; unemotional; unimaginative; without passion or ardor and stiff or formal in manner. **2.** of a woman, unresponsive to sexual advances or stimuli, abnormally indifferent or averse to sexual intercourse, or unable to have an orgasm during sexual intercourse.—**frigidity,** *n.*

fringe field /frinj/, in MRI, the part of the magnetic field that extends away from the confines of the magnet and cannot be used for imaging.

frit /frit, frē/ [Fr, fried], a partially or wholly fused porcelain that is cracked by plunging into water while hot. It is used to make dental porcelain powders.

frôle ment /frôlmäN′/ [Fr, brushing], **1.** the rustling type of sound often heard on auscultating the chest in diseases of the pericardium. **2.** a kind of massage that uses a light brushing stroke with the hand.

frontal bone /fron′təl/ [L, *frons,* forehead], a single cranial bone that forms the front of the skull, from above the orbits, posteriorly to a junction with the parietal bones at the coronal suture and sagittal suture.

frontal crest, a midline ridge of bone extending from the surface of the frontal bone. It is a point of attachment for the falx cerebri.

frontal lobe, the largest of five lobes constituting each of the two cerebral hemispheres. It lies beneath the frontal bone; occupies part of the lateral, the medial, and the inferior surfaces of each hemisphere; and extends posteriorly to the central sulcus and inferiorly to the lateral fissure. It is responsible for voluntary control over most skeletal muscles. It significantly influences personality and is associated with the higher mental activities, such as planning, judgment, and conceptualization.

frontal lobe dementia, any of various dementias caused by frontal lobe lesions.

frontal lobe syndrome, behavioral and personality changes usually observed after a neoplastic or traumatic frontal lobe lesion.

frontal nerve, the largest branch of the ophthalmic nerve. Its two terminal branches are the supratrochlear nerve and the supraorbital nerve.

frontal plane, any of the vertical planes passing through the body from the head to the feet, perpendicular to the sagittal planes; the plane parallel to the long axis of the body and at right angles to the median sagittal plane, dividing the body into front and back portions.

frontal pole [L, *frons,* forehead + *polus*], the anterior extremity of the frontal lobe of the cerebrum.

frontal section [L, *frons,* forehead, *sectio,* a cutting], a section of the head or other body part cut into anterior and posterior portions.

frontal sinus, one of a pair of small cavities in the frontal bone of the skull that communicates with the nasal cavity and lies above the orbits. Each sinus opens into the anterior part of the middle meatus through the frontonasal duct.

frontal-temporal dementia, any of several degenerative conditions of the frontal and anterior temporal lobes that cause personality and behavioral changes sometimes mistaken for those of Alzheimer's disease and may eventually progress to immobility and loss of speech.

frontal vein, one of a pair of superficial veins of the face, arising in the plexus of the forehead.

frontonasal dysplasia, a hereditary form of defective midline development of the head and face, including ocular hypertelorism, occult cleft nose and maxilla, and sometimes mental retardation or other defects.

front-tap reflex, in spinal irritability, contraction of the gastrocnemius muscle caused by a tap on the skin muscles of the extended leg.

frostbite [AS, *frost* + *bitan*], a traumatic effect of extreme cold on skin and subcutaneous tissues that is first recognized by distinct pallor of exposed skin surfaces, particularly the nose, ears, fingers, and toes. Vasoconstriction and damage to blood vessels impair local circulation and cause anoxia, edema, vesiculation, and necrosis. Manifestations for superficial frostbite present as a white, waxy, soft, and numb appearance of the injured area while it is still cold. As thawing occurs, the area becomes flushed, edematous, and painful, and may become mottled and purple. Within 24 hours, large blisters form and remain for about 2 weeks before turning into a hardened eschar, which separates in about a month, leaving painful, sensitive new skin that often sweats excessively. In deep frostbite, the injured part remains hard, cold, mottled, and blue-gray after thawing. Edema forms in entire limb and may remain for months. After several weeks, dead tissue blackens and sloughs off. Loss of digits, ears, nose, and extremities is possible, as is secondary infection and long-term residual symptoms, such as neuropathic pain, sensory deficits, hyperhidrosis, hair and nail deformities, and arthritis.

frottage /frôtäzh′/ [Fr, rubbing], **1.** sexual gratification obtained by rubbing (especially the genital area) against the clothing of another person, as can occur in a crowd. **2.** a massage technique using rubbing.

frotteur /frôtœr′/ [Fr], a person who obtains sexual gratification by the practice of frottage.

frovatriptan, an antimigraine agent used for the acute treatment of migraine with or without aura.

frozen red blood cells, red cells cryopreserved with glycerol and stored frozen at -65°C, for up to 10 years. Also called glycerolized red cells.

frozen section [ME, *fresen*; L, *sectio*], a histologic section of tissue that has been frozen by exposure to dry ice.

frozen section method [AS, *freosan*, to freeze; L, *sectio*, a cutting; Gk *meta*, order, *hodos* path], in surgical pathology, a method used in preparing a selected portion of tissue for pathologic examination. The tissue is moistened and, fixed or unfixed, is rapidly frozen and cut by a microtome in a cryostat.

FRSC, abbreviation for *Fellow of the Royal Society of Canada.*

fructokinase /fruk′tōkī′nās/, an enzyme that catalyzes the transfer of a high-energy phosphate group from adenosine triphosphate to D-fructose.

fructosamine test /frŏŏktōs′əmēn/, determination of the glycated albumin level by measuring the reduction of nitroblue tetrazolium to purple under alkaline conditions, used as an index of the average glycemic state over the preceding 2 to 3 weeks. It is not widely used; however, it is useful when glycosylated hemoglobin (hemoglobin A_{1C}) cannot be reliably measured.

fructose /fruk′tōs, frŏŏk′-/, a yellowish-to-white, crystalline, water-soluble levorotatory ketose monosaccharide that is sweeter than sucrose. It is found in honey and several fruits and combines with glucose to form the disaccharide sucrose.

fructose intolerance [L, *fructus*, fruit, *in* + *tolerare*, to bear], an inherited disorder marked by an absence of enzymes needed to metabolize fructose. Symptoms include sweating, tremors, confusion, digestive distress with vomiting, and failure of infants to grow.

fructosemia /frŏŏk′tōsē′mē·ə/ [L, *fructus*, fruit; Gk, *haima*, blood], the presence of fructose in the blood.

fructose test, a laboratory fertility examination of the semen of azoospermic men. Fructose comes primarily from the seminal vesicles. The purpose of the test is to rule out possible ejaculatory duct obstruction or agenesis of seminal vesicles.

fructosuria /frŏŏk′tōsŏŏr′ē·ə/, presence of the sugar fructose in the urine.

frustration /frustrā′shən/, a feeling that results from interference with one's ability to attain a desired goal or satisfaction.

FSE, abbreviation for **fast spin-echo.**

FSF, abbreviation for **fibrin-stabilizing factor.**

FSH, abbreviation for **follicle-stimulating hormone.**

FSH-RF, abbreviation for **follicle-stimulating hormone–releasing factor.**

FSK, abbreviation for **forskolin.**

FT, abbreviation for *fast-twitch.*

FTA-ABS test, abbreviation for **fluorescent treponemal antibody absorption test.**

FTC, abbreviation for **Federal Trade Commission.**

F-test [Sir Ronald Aylmer *Fisher,* British statistician, 1890–1962], a statistic test comparing the means of more than two groups simultaneously by comparing two different measures of variance of the observations. One statistic measures the variations between the means of the groups (the between-groups variation), the other the variations within the groups (the within-group variation). The test is the first step in the analysis of variance.

FTT, abbreviation for **failure to thrive.**

Fuchs method, a technique for a radiographic examination of the odontoid process projected through the foramen magnum. It is used when it is difficult to visualize the tip of the process on an image obtained by using the conventional open mouth method.

fucosidosis /fyŏŏ′kōsidō′sis/, a hereditary lysosomal storage disorder that results from the absence of the enzyme required to metabolize fucoside moieties. It causes mental retardation, neurologic deterioration, coarse facial features, thickened skin, and hepatosplenomegaly.

FUDR, a trademark for an antiviral and antineoplastic (floxuridine).

fugue /fyŏŏg/ [L, *fuga,* running away], a state of dissociative reaction characterized by amnesia and physical flight from an intolerable situation. During the episode the person appears normal and seems consciously aware of what may be very complex activities and behavior, but afterward he or she has no recollection of the actions or behavior.

Fukuyama type congenital muscular dystrophy /fŏŏ′kŏŏya′ma/ [Yukio Fukuyama, Japanese physician, 20th century], an autosomal-recessive type of muscular dystrophy evident in infancy. Muscle abnormalities resemble those of Duchenne's muscular dystrophy, and patients are mentally retarded with microgyria and other cerebral abnormalities.

fulcrum /fŏŏl′krəm, ful′-/ [L, *fulcire,* to support], **1.** the stable point or the position on which a lever, such as the ulna or the femur, turns. Numerous common body movements, such as raising the arm and walking, are combinations of lever actions involving fulcrums. **2.** in radiology, an imaginary pivot point about which the x-ray tube and film move.

fulfillment [AS, *fullfyllan*, to make full], a perception of harmony in life that results when an individual has found meaning and acts purposefully.

fulgurate /ful'gyərāt/ [L, *fulgur*, lightning], **1.** pertaining to sudden, intense, sharp pain. **2.** the use of a movable electrode to destroy superficial tissue.

full-arch wire, a wire that is attached to the teeth and extends from the molar region of one side, across the front of the mouth, to the molar region on the other side. It is used to cause or guide orthodontic tooth movement.

full bath [AS, *fol + baeth*], a bath in which the patient's body is immersed in water up to the neck.

full denture [AS, *fol*; L, *dens*, tooth], a removable dental prosthesis that replaces all of the natural teeth in the maxillary or mandibular dental arch. The denture is completely supported by the mouth tissues.

full-liquid diet, a diet consisting of only liquids and foods that liquefy at body temperature. The diet is prescribed after surgery, in some acute infections of short duration, in the treatment of acute GI disorders, and for patients too ill to chew.

full-lung tomography, a technique for producing general tomographic surveys of both lungs for the purpose of detecting possible occult nodules of metastases that usually cannot be visualized with conventional radiologic methods.

full pulse [AS, *fol + pulsare*, to beat], a large-volume pulse with a low pulse pressure.

full-risk HMO, in U.S. managed care, a health maintenance organization in which the hospital receives capitation (money paid) for all facility and hospital-based physician services. The physician group receives capitation and shares the deficit or surplus of the hospital risk pool.

full term [AS, *fol*, Gk, *terma*, limit], pertaining to the normal period of human gestation, between 38 and 41 weeks.

full-thickness graft, a tissue transplant that includes the full thickness of the skin and subcutaneous layers.

full weight-bearing (FWB) [AS, *fol + gewiht*; ME, *beren*], relating to a view in radiology that shows the response to stresses of a natural posture. Full weight-bearing views of the foot are useful in studying flatfoot and clawfoot.

full-width half maximum (FWHM), a measure of resolution equal to the width of an image line source at points where the intensity is reduced to half the maximum.

fulminant hepatitis, a rare and frequently fatal form of acute hepatitis B in which the patient's condition rapidly deteriorates, with hepatic encephalopathy, necrosis of the hepatic parenchyma, coagulopathy, renal failure, and coma.

fulminating /ful'minā'ting/ [L, *fulminare*, lightning flash], of a disease or condition, rapid, sudden, severe, such as an infection, fever, or hemorrhage.—**fulminate,** *v.*

fulvestrant, an antineoplastic agent used to treat advanced breast carcinoma in estrogen receptor–positive patients.

Fulvicin, a trademark for an antifungal (griseofulvin).

fumigate /fyoo'migāt/, to disinfect by exposing an area or object to pesticidal smoke or fumes.

fuming, producing a visible vapor.

function /fungk'shən/ [L, *functio*, performance], **1.** an act, process, or series of processes that serve a purpose. **2.** to perform an activity or to work properly and normally.

functional /fungk'shənəl/ [L, *functio*, performance], **1.** pertaining to a function. **2.** affecting the functions but not the structure of an organism or organ system.

functional age, a combination of the chronologic, physiologic, mental, and emotional ages.

functional analysis, in psychiatry, a type of therapy that traces the sequence of events involved in producing and maintaining undesirable behavior.

functional antagonism, in pharmacology, a situation in which two agonists interact with different receptors and produce opposing effects.

functional differentiation, in embryology, the specialization or diversification that results from the particular function of a cell or tissue.

functional disease, **1.** a disease that affects function or performance. **2.** a condition marked by signs or symptoms of an organic disease or disorder although careful examination fails to reveal any evidence of structural or physiologic abnormalities. Headache, impotence, certain heart murmurs, and constipation may be symptoms of functional disease.

functional dyspepsia, a condition characterized by impaired digestion caused by an atonic or a neurologic problem.

functional foods, foods and food supplements marketed for presumed health benefits, such as vitamin supplements and certain herbs.

functional hearing loss, hearing loss that lacks any organic lesion.

functional illness, a physical disorder with no known structural explanation for the symptoms.

functional imaging, a diagnostic procedure in which a sequence of radiographic or scintillation camera images of the distribution of an administered radioactive tracer delineates one or more physiologic processes in the body.

functional magnetic resonance imaging (fMRI), a radiographic technique for imaging brain activity in which a rapid succession of scans, designed to detect increases in oxygen consumption in various regions of the brain, reflects small changes in blood flow and increased activity in certain cells.

functional method, a type of nursing care delivery system.

functional murmur [L, *functio,* performance], a heart murmur caused by an alteration of function without structural heart disease or damage, as in a murmur related to anemia.

functional nursing, an organizational mode for assigning nursing personnel that is task- and activity-oriented, using auxiliary health workers trained in a variety of skills.

functional overlay, an emotional aspect of an organic disease. It is characterized by symptoms that continue long after clinical signs of the disease have ended.

functional pathology [L, *functio,* performance; Gk, *pathos,* disease, *logos,* science], a study of the functional changes that result from structural alterations in tissues.

functional position of the hand, a position for splinting the hand, including the wrist and fingers. The thumb is abducted and in opposition and alignment with the pads of the fingers.

functional progression, a rehabilitative sequence for a musculoskeletal or similar injury. The program usually progresses from immobilization for primary healing through protection of ROM to endurance and strengthening activities.

functional psychosis, a severe emotional disorder characterized by personality derangement and loss of ability to function in reality, but without evidence that the disorder is related to the physical processes of the brain.

functional residual capacity (FRC), the volume of gas in the lungs at the end of a normal tidal volume exhalation. The functional residual capacity is equal to the residual volume plus the expiratory reserve volume.

functional splint [L, *functio,* performance; ME, *splent*], an orthopedic device that allows or assists a patient's movements.

functional visual skills, various normal eye activities, such as depth perception, eye aiming and alignment, oculomotility,

convergence and divergence, and accomodative ability.

functional vomiting, vomiting whose physiologic cause is unknown.

fundal height /fun′dəl/ [L, *fundus,* bottom; AS, *heightho*], the height of the fundus, measured in centimeters from the top of the symphysis pubis to the highest point in the midline at the top of the uterus.

fundal placenta [L, *fundus,* bottom, *placenta,* flat cake], a placenta that is attached to the fundus of the uterus.

fundamentals of nursing /fun′dəmen′təls/, the basic principles and practices of nursing as taught in educational programs for nurses. A fundamentals of nursing course emphasizes the importance of the fundamental needs of humans, as well as competence in basic skills, as prerequisites to providing comprehensive nursing care.

fundic gastritis, gastritis whose focus is in the gastric fundus.

fundiform ligament of the penis /fun′difôrm/, a band of fibrous and elastic fibers blending with the fascia surrounding the penis. It extends from the linea alba above the pubic symphysis.

fundoplication /fun′dəplikā′shən/ [L, *fundus,* bottom, *plicare,* to fold], a surgical procedure involving making tucks (plication) in the fundus of the stomach around the lower end of the esophagus.

fundus /fun′dəs/ *pl.* **fundi** [L, bottom], the base or the deepest part of an organ; the portion farthest from the mouth of an organ such as the fundus of the uterus or the fundus of an eye.

fundus microscopy, examination of the interior of the eye using an instrument that combines an ophthalmoscope and a lens with high magnifying power for observing minute structures on the retina.

fundus of the gallbladder, the closed end of the gallbladder, adjacent to the inferior border of the liver.

fundus of the stomach, a cul-de-sac of the stomach that lies above the level of the cardiac orifice, where the esophagus joins the stomach.

fundus of the urinary bladder, the bottom of the bladder, formed by the convex posterior wall.

fungal abscess, a collection of pus produced by a fungal infection.

fungal antibody tests, a relatively unreliable blood test to detect fungal infections.

fungal infection [L, *fungus,* mushroom, *inficere,* to stain], any inflammatory condition caused by a fungus. Most fungal infections are superficial and mild, though persistent and difficult to eradicate.

fungal infection of nail, an infection of the horny cutaneous plates on the dorsal tips of the fingers and toes. The infection is commonly caused by *Trichophyton* organisms.

fungal pneumonia, pneumonia caused by inhaled fungi, usually *Blastomyces dermatitidis, Coccidioides immitis,* or *Histoplasma capsulatum.* Numerous other fungi, such as *Aspergillus* and *Candida,* infect immunocompromised patients.

fungal septicemia [L, *fungus;* Gk, *septikos,* putrid, *haima,* blood], a form of septicemia in which the causative agent is a fungus.

fungemia /funjē′mē·ə/ [L, *fungus;* Gk, *haima,* blood], the presence of fungi in the blood.

Fungi /fun′ji/, in the classification of living organisms, one of the kingdoms of eukaryotic organisms.

fungicide /fun′jisīd/, a drug that kills fungi.—**fungicidal,** *adj.*

fungiform /fun′jifôrm/ [L, *funis + forma*], shaped like a mushroom.

fungistatic /fun′jēstat′ik/, having an inhibiting effect on the growth of fungi.

Fungizone, a trademark for an antifungal (amphotericin B).

fungus /fun′gəs/ *pl.* **fungi** [L, *fungus,* mushroom], a eukaryotic, thallus-forming organism that feeds by absorbing organic molecules from its surroundings. Fungi lack chlorophyll and therefore are not capable of photosynthesis. They may be saprophytes or parasites. Unicellular fungi (yeasts) reproduce by budding; multicellular fungi, such as molds, reproduce by spore formation. Fungi may invade living organisms, including humans, as well as nonliving organic substances.—**fungal, fungous,** *adj.*

funic presentation /fyoo′nik/ [L, *funis + praesentare,* to show], in obstetrics, the appearance of the umbilical cord before the main presenting part of the fetus.

funic souffle /fyoo′nik soo′fəl/ [L, *funis,* cord; Fr, *souffle,* breath], a soft, muffled blowing sound produced by blood rushing through the umbilical vessels and synchronous with the fetal heart sound.

funicular hernia, an indirect inguinal hernia that includes part of the umbilical cord or spermatic cord.

funicular part of ductus deferens, a middle part of the ductus deferens, where it is within the spermatic cord.

funiculitis /fənik′yəlī′tis/, any abnormal inflammatory condition of a cordlike structure of the body, such as the spinal cord or spermatic cord.

funiculopexy /fənik′yəlōpek′sē/, a surgical procedure for correcting an undescended testicle, in which the spermatic cord is sutured to surrounding tissue.

funiculus /fənik′yələs/ [L, little cord], a division of the white matter of the spinal cord, consisting of fasciculi or fiber tracts.

funis /fyoo′nis, foo′nis/, a cordlike structure.

funnel chest [L, *fundere,* to pour], a skeletal abnormality of the chest characterized by a depressed sternum. The deformity may not interfere with breathing, but surgical correction is often recommended for cosmetic reasons.

funnel feeding, a technique in which liquids may be given orally to a patient who cannot move the lips or masticate, such as after surgery at the mouth or lips. A rubber tube attached to a funnel is placed in the mouth, usually at one corner, and a liquid is poured slowly through the funnel and tube into the mouth near the back of the tongue.

funny bone, a popular name for a point at the lower end of the humerus where the ulnar nerve crosses the elbow joint near the surface and, if subjected to external pressure, produces a tingling sensation.

FUO, abbreviation for **fever of unknown origin.**

Furadantin, a trademark for an antibacterial (nitrofurantoin).

furazolidone /foo′rəzol′idōn/, an antibiotic with antibacterial and antiprotozoal activity prescribed for the treatment of diarrhea caused by susceptible bacterial or protozoal infections (e.g., *Giardiasis, Vibrio*) of the GI tract.

furcation /fərka′shən/ [L, *furca,* fork], the region of division of tooth root.

furfuraceous desquamation /fur′fərə′sē·əs/ [L, *furfur,* bran, *desquamare,* to scale off], the shedding of epidermis in large scales.

furosemide /fooro′səmīd/, a loop diuretic prescribed in the treatment of edema caused by CHF, renal failure, or liver failure and alone or in combination for the treatment of hypertension.

Furoxone, a trademark for an antibacterial antiprotozoal drug (furazolidone).

furrow /fur′ō/ [AS, *furh*], a groove, such as the atrioventricular furrow that separates the atria from the ventricles of the heart.

furuncle /fyoor′ungkəl/ [L, *furunculus,* petty thief], a localized suppurative staphylococcal skin infection originating in a gland or hair follicle and characterized by pain, redness, and swelling.

furunculosis /fyoorung′kyoolō′sis/, an acute skin disease characterized by boils or successive crops of boils that are caused by staphylococci or streptococci.

fused teeth /fyoozd/ [L, *fundere,* to melt], partial or complete fusion of two or more individual teeth caused by union of two adjacent tooth buds by either enamel or cementum.

fusiform /fyoo′sifôrm/ [L, *fusus,* spindle, *forma,* form], a structure that is tapered at both ends.

fusiform aneurysm, a localized dilation of an artery in which the entire circumference of the vessel is distended.

fusiform gyrus [L, *fusus,* spindle, *forma,* form; Gk, *gyros,* turn], a convolution of the cerebral hemispheres that lies below the collateral fissures and joins the occipital and temporal lobes.

fusiform megalourethra, a huge diverticulum of the anterior urethra, owing to absence of an entire section of the corpus spongiosum.

fusimotor /fyoo′zimō′tər/ [L, *fusus* + *motare,* to move about], pertaining to the gamma efferent fibers that innervate the intrafusal fibers of the muscle spindle.

fusion /fyoo′zhən/ [L, *fusio,* outpouring], **1.** the joining into a single entity, as in optic fusion. **2.** the surgical joining of two or more vertebrae, performed to stabilize a segment of the spinal column after severe trauma, herniation of a disk, or degenerative disease. **3.** in psychiatry, the tendency of two people who are experiencing an intense emotion to unite.

fusional movement /fyoo′zhənəl/, a reflex that moves the visual axes to the point of fixation, producing stereoscopic vision.

fusion beat, in an ECG, a P wave or QRS complex resulting from the concurrent activation of the atria or the ventricles by two stimuli in the same chamber.

fusion imaging, a combination of two images from different modalities, such as CT and PET.

Fusobacterium, a large cigar-shaped anaerobic bacillus genus, only some of which are pathogenic to humans. *F. fusiforme* is sometimes associated with Vincent's angina. *F. nucleatum* is associated with pleuropulmonary infection and disease and also is one of the causes of gingivitis.

fusospirochetal disease /fyoo′zōspī′rōkē′təl/ [L, *fusus,* spindle; Gk, *speira,* coil, *chaite,* hair], any infection characterized by ulcerative lesions in which both a fusiform bacillus and a spirochete are found, such as trench mouth or Vincent's angina.

Fuzeon, a trademark for **enfuvirtide.**

factor VIII, a large glycoprotein containing more than 2300 amino acids, 24 cysteine residues, and 25 potential glycosylation sites. The factor is used to treat blood-clotting disorders.

FVL, abbreviation for *factor V–Leiden.*

F wave, a waveform recorded in electroneuromyographic and nerve conduction tests. It appears on supramaximal stimulation of a motor nerve and is caused by antidromic transmission of a stimulus. The F wave is used in studies of motor nerve function in the arms and legs.

f waves, in an ECG, wavy deflections at a rate of 400 or more per minute that represent atrial fibrillation.

FWB, abbreviation for **full weight-bearing.**

FWHM, abbreviation for **full-width half maximum.**

G

g, abbreviation for **gram.**

G1, a phase in the cell cycle during which the cell's future can be influenced by various positive and negative signals, such as growth factors. The signals determine whether the cell will advance beyond a certain checkpoint, past which the cell is committed to replicating its DNA in preparation for mitosis.

G2, a phase in the cell cycle that follows DNA replication. During G2, the cell checks the accuracy of DNA replication and prepares for mitosis.

G6PD deficiency, abbreviation for **glucose-6-phosphate dehydrogenase deficiency.**

Ga, symbol for the element **gallium.**

GA, abbreviation for **general anesthesia.**

GABA, abbreviation for *gamma-aminobutyric acid.*

gabapentin /gab′äpen′tin/, an anticonvulsant chemically related to alpha-aminobutyric acid, used in the treatment of partial seizures.

GABHS, abbreviation for *group A beta-hemolytic streptococcal skin disease.*

GAD, abbreviation for **generalized anxiety disorder.**

gadolinium (Gd) /gad′əlin′ē·əm/ [Johan Gadolin, Finnish chemist, 1760–1852], **1.** a rare earth metallic element. Its atomic number is 64, and its atomic mass is 157.25. It is now widely used in MRI as a contrast agent. **2.** in radiology, a phosphor used to intensify screens.

GAF, abbreviation for **Global Assessment of Functioning.**

gag [ME, *gaggen,* to strangle], **1.** a dental device for holding the jaws open during oral surgery or dental restoration. **2.** to retch or attempt to vomit.

gag reflex [ME, *gaggen,* to strangle; L, *reflectere,* to bend back], a normal neural reflex elicited by touching the soft palate or posterior pharynx, in which the responses are symmetric elevation of the palate, retraction of the tongue, and contraction of the pharyngeal muscles.

Gail model, a collection of epidemiologic and risk factor data used to calculate the risk of breast cancer.

gait [ONorse, *geta,* a way], the manner or style of walking, including rhythm, cadence, and speed.

Gait Assessment Rating Scale (GARS), a standardized test or inventory of 16 abnormal aspects of gait observed by an examiner as a patient walks at a self-selected pace. Each aspect is graded on a scale of 0-1-2-3, with lower numbers indicating less abnormality.

gait determinant, one of a number of the kinetic anatomic factors that govern an individual's locomotion in the process of walking. Some authorities have defined pelvic rotation, pelvic tilt, knee and hip flexion, knee and ankle interaction, and lateral pelvic displacement as the main determinants of gait.

gait disorder, an abnormality in the manner or style of walking, which usually results from neuromuscular, arthritic, or other body changes.

galactocele /gəlak′təsēl′/, a cyst or hydrocele caused by blockage of a mammary gland milk duct.

galactokinase /gəlak′tōkī′nās/ [Gk, *gala,* milk, *kinesis,* movement; Fr, *diastase,* enzyme], an enzyme that functions in the metabolism of glycogen.

galactokinase deficiency, an inherited disorder of carbohydrate metabolism in which the enzyme galactokinase is deficient or absent. As a result, dietary galactose is not metabolized, galactose accumulates in the blood, and cataracts may develop rapidly.

galactophorous duct /-fôr′əs/ [Gk, *gala* + *pherein,* to bear; L, *ducere,* to lead], a passage for milk in the lobes of the breast.

galactopoiesis, the maintenance of milk production.

galactorrhea /gəlak′tərē′ə/ [Gk, *gala* + *rhoia,* flowing], **1.** a spontaneous flow of milk from the nipple. **2.** lactation not associated with childbirth or nursing. The condition is sometimes a symptom of a pituitary gland tumor.

galactosamine, galactose that contains an amine group on the second group.

galactose /gəlak′tōs/ [Gk, *gala* + *glykys,* sweet], a simple sugar found in the dextrorotatory form in lactose (milk sugar), nerve cell membranes, sugar beets, gums, and seaweed and in the levorotatory form in flaxseed mucilage.

galactose breath test, a breath test of liver function, in which the fasting subject is administered a dose of galactose labeled with carbon-13 and levels of labeled carbon dioxide in the breath are measured at specific time intervals. Low levels of carbon dioxide indicate that the galactose is not being metabolized properly, indicating either an enzyme deficiency or liver dysfunction.

galactosemia /gəlak'tōsē'mē·ə/ [Gk, *gala* + *glykys*, sweet, *haima*, blood], a group of inherited autosomal recessive disorders of galactose metabolism. It is characterized by a deficiency of an enzyme involved in galactose metabolism, galactose-1-phosphate uridyl transferase. Shortly after birth an intolerance to milk occurs. It is evidenced by anorexia, nausea, vomiting, and diarrhea and causes failure to thrive. Hepatosplenomegaly, cataracts, and mental retardation develop.

galactose tolerance test, a test of the ability of the liver to remove galactose from the blood and convert it to glycogen. The test, which is used to estimate impaired liver function, measures the rate of galactose excretion after ingestion or injection of a measured amount of galactose.

galactoside /gəlak'tō'sīd/, a glycoside containing galactose.

galactoside permease, an enzyme that catalyzes the transport of lactose into the cell.

galactosidose, an enzyme that catalyzes the metabolism of galactosides.

galactosis /gal'əktōsis/, lactation; the formation of milk by the lacteal glands.

galactosuria /-sōōr'ē·ə/, the presence of galactose in the urine.

galactosyl ceramide lipidosis /gəlak'təsil/ [Gk, *gala* + *glykys*, sweet; L, *cera*, wax, *lipos*, fat, *osis*, condition], a rare, fatal inherited disorder of lipid metabolism, present at birth. Infants become paralyzed, blind, deaf, and increasingly retarded; eventually, they die of bulbar paralysis.

galactosyl transferase, an enzyme in the head of sperm that is required for sperm to bind to eggs.

galactozymase /-zī'māz/, an enzyme in milk that is able to hydrolyze starch.

galacturia /gal'əktōōr'ē·ə/ [Gk, *gala*, milk, *ouron*, urine], a condition in which the urine has a milky color caused by the abnormal presence of galactose in the urine.

galanin /galan'in, gal'ənin/, a neuropeptide in the small intestine and central and peripheral nervous systems that has a role in bowel motility, pancreas activity, and prolactin and growth hormone release.

galantamine /gälan'tämēn/, a reversible competitive inhibitor of acetylcholinesterase used as the hydrobromide salt in the treatment of mild to moderate Alzheimer's disease.

Galant reflex /gəlant'/, a normal response in the neonate when held in ventral suspension to move the hips toward the stimulated side when the back is stroked along the spinal cord.

Galeazzi's fracture /gal'ē·at'sēz/ [Riccardo Galeazzi, Italian surgeon, 1866–1952], a break in the distal radius accompanied by dislocation of the radioulnar joint.

Galen's vein /gā'lənz/ [Claudius Galen, Greek physician, circa CE 130–200], the large vein formed by the union of the two terminal cerebral veins. It curves around the splenium of the corpus callosum and continues as the straight sinus of the brain.

gall, a lump or ball that forms most often on the stems, leaves, or roots of plants at the site of injuries caused by insects, fungi, bacteria, or other organisms.

gallamine triethiodide /gal'ämēn trī'ē thi'odīd/, a quaternary ammonium compound, the triethiodide salt used as a skeletal muscle relaxant during surgery and other procedures, such as endoscopy or intubation.

gallbladder (GB) /gôl'blad'ər/ [ME, *gal*; AS, *blaedre*], a pear-shaped excretory sac lodged in a fossa on the visceral surface of the right lobe of the liver. It stores and concentrates bile, which it receives from the liver via the hepatic duct. In an adult, it holds about 32 mL of bile. During digestion of fats, the gallbladder contracts, ejecting bile through the common bile duct into the duodenum.

gallbladder carcinoma, a malignant neoplasm of the bile reservoir, characterized by anorexia, nausea, vomiting, weight loss, progressively worsening right upper quadrant pain, and eventually jaundice. Tumors of the gallbladder are predominantly adenocarcinomas and are often associated with biliary calculi and chronic cholecystitis.

gallbladder nuclear scanning, a nuclear scan used to evaluate the biliary tract. This test may also be used to evaluate the gallbladder for obstruction of the cystic duct, cholecystitis, and common bile duct obstruction.

gallium (Ga) /gal'ē·əm/ [L, *Gallia*, Gaul], a metallic element. Its atomic number is 31, and its atomic mass is 69.72. The melting point of gallium is 29.8° C (85.6° F); it will melt if held in the hand. Because of its high boiling point (1983° C [3601.4° F]), it is used in high-temperature thermometers. Radioisotopes of gallium are used in total body scanning procedures.

gallium scan, a nuclear scan of the total body performed after an IV injection of radioactive gallium, a radionuclide that concentrates in areas of inflammation and infection, abscess, and benign and malignant tumor. It is useful in detecting metastatic tumor, especially lymphoma.

gallop /gal'əp/ [Fr, *galop*], a third or fourth heart sound, which at certain heart rates sometimes sounds like the gait of a horse.

gallstone pancreatitis, acute pancreatitis accompanied by presence of gallstones, one of the most common types.

galoche chin /gəlosh/ [Fr, galosh; AS, cin], a narrow protruding or thrusting chin. It is a congenital condition.

galsulfase, a rarely used miscellaneous drug used to treat mucopolysaccharidosis VI and Maroteaux-Lamy syndrome.

galvanic /galvan'ik/ [Luigi Galvani, Italian physician, 1737–1798], pertaining to or involving electricity.

galvanic electric stimulation [Luigi Galvani], the use of a high-voltage electric stimulator to treat muscle spasms, edema of acute injury, myofascial pain, and certain other disorders.

galvanic skin response (GSR) [Luigi Galvani; AS, scinn; L, respondere, to reply], a reaction to certain stimuli as indicated by a change in the electrical resistance of the skin. The effect is related to subconscious activity of the sweat glands and may result from pleasant as well as unpleasant stimuli. The GSR is used in some polygraph examinations.

galvanometer /gal'vənom'ətər/ [Luigi Galvani], an instrument used to measure the strength and direction of flow of an electric current. Its action depends on the deflection of a magnetic needle in the field produced by current passing through a coil. Galvanometers are used in certain diagnostic instruments, such as ECGs.

Galveston Orientation and Amnesia Test (GOAT), a series of 10 questions asked of a patient to help evaluate posttraumatic amnesia. The test is repeated on a weekly basis and is scored on a scale of 0 to 100.

Gambian trypanosomiasis /gam'bē-ən/, a usually chronic form of African trypanosomiasis, caused by the parasite Trypanosoma brucei gambiense.

game knee [ME, gamen; AS, cneow], an informal term for any injury or condition that interferes with normal function of the knee joint.

gamete /gam'ēt/ [Gk, marriage partner], **1.** a mature male or female germ cell that is capable of functioning in fertilization or conjugation and contains the haploid number of chromosomes of the organism. **2.** an ovum or a spermatozoon. —**gametic,** adj.

gamete intrafallopian transfer (GIFT), a human fertilization technique in which male and female gametes are injected through a laparoscope into the fimbriated ends of the fallopian tubes.

gametic /gəmat'ik/, pertaining to a reproductive cell such as a spermatozoon or ovum.

gametic chromosome, any of the chromosomes contained in a haploid cell, specifically a spermatozoon or an ovum, as contrasted with those in a diploid, or somatic, cell.

gametocide /gəmē'tōsīd/ [Gk, gamete; L, caedere, to kill], any agent that is destructive to gametes or gametocytes. The term most commonly refers to agents specific for gametocytes of the protozoan Plasmodium, which causes malaria. —**gametocidal,** adj.

gametocyte /gəmē'tōsīt/ [Gk, gamete + kytos, cell], any cell capable of dividing into or in the process of developing into a gamete.

gametogenesis /gam'itōjen'əsis/ [Gk, gamete + genein, to produce], the origin and maturation of gametes, which occurs through meiosis. —**gametogenic, gametogenous,** adj.

gametophyte /gəmē'tōfīt/ [Gk, gamete + phyton, plant], a cell in the reproductive stage when the nuclei are in a haploid condition.

gamma /gam'ə/, Γ, γ, the third letter of the Greek alphabet. It is a symbol for photon, heavy-chain immunoglobulins, or the third component in a series of certain chemical groups.

gamma-aminobutyric acid (GABA), an amino acid that functions as an inhibitory neurotransmitter in the brain and spinal cord. It is also found in the heart, lungs, and kidneys and in certain plants.

gamma camera [Gk, gamma, third letter of Greek alphabet; L, camera, vault], a device that uses the emission of light from a crystal struck by gamma rays to produce an image of the distribution of radioactive material in a body organ. The gamma camera is a workhorse of nuclear medicine departments, where it is used to produce scans of patients who have been injected with small amounts of radioactive materials.

gamma efferent fiber [Gk, gamma; L, efferre, to carry out, fibra, fiber], any of the motor nerve fibers that transmit impulses from the CNS to the intrafusal fibers of the muscle spindle. They function in regulating the sensitivity of the spindle and the total tension of the muscle.

gamma-glutamyl transferase (GGT), an enzyme that appears in the serum of patients with several types of liver or gallbladder disorders, including drug hepatotoxicity, biliary tract obstruction, alcohol-induced liver disease, and liver carcinoma.

gamma-glutamyl transferase (GGT) test, a blood test that measures GGT and is used to detect liver cell dysfunction. It accurately indicates cholestasis, biliary obstruction, cholangitis, or cholecystitis. It can also detect chronic alcohol ingestion. Levels of GGT are also elevated after acute MI.

Gamma Knife, an apparatus that uses precisely aimed intersecting beams of gamma rays to deliver radiation therapies as treatment for intracranial lesions.

Gamma Knife stereotaxic radiosurgery, a method for destroying deep-seated brain tumors with a focused beam of gamma radiation.

gamma radiation [Gk, *gamma*; L, *radiare*, to emit rays], a very-high-frequency form of electromagnetic radiation consisting of photons emitted by radioactive elements in the course of nuclear transition. The wavelength of gamma radiation is characteristic of the radioactive elements involved and ranges from about 4×10^{-10} to 5×10^{-13} m. Gamma radiation can penetrate thousands of meters of air and several centimeters of soft tissue and bone. It is more penetrating than alpha radiation and beta radiation but has less ionizing power and is not deflected in electric or magnetic fields. Controlled application of gamma radiation is important in the diagnosis and treatment of various conditions, including skin cancer and malignancies deep within the body.

gammopathy /gamop′əthē/, an abnormal condition characterized by the presence of markedly increased levels of gamma globulin in the blood.

gamogenesis /gam′ōjen′əsis/ [Gk, *gamos*, marriage, *genein*, to produce], sexual reproduction through the fusion of gametes.—**gamogenetic,** *adj.*

gamone /gam′ōn/ [Gk, *gamos*, marriage], a chemical substance secreted by ova and spermatozoa that is believed to attract the gametes of the opposite sex to and facilitate union.

ganciclovir /gansik′lōvir/, an antiviral drug structurally related to acyclovir, used to prevent cytomegalovirus disease after transplantation and to treat or prevent cytomegalovirus retinitis in persons with AIDS.

gangliocytoma /gang′glē·ō·sītō′mə/, a benign tumor involving ganglion cells. These tumors are frequently found in the pituitary gland.

ganglion /gang′glē·on/ *pl.* **ganglia** [Gk, knot], **1.** a knot or knotlike mass of nervous tissue. **2.** one of the nerve cell bodies, chiefly collected in groups outside the CNS. The two types of ganglia in the body are the sensory ganglia on the dorsal roots of spinal nerves and on the sensory roots of the trigeminal, facial, glossopharyngeal, and vagus nerves and the autonomic ganglia of the sympathetic and parasympathetic systems.

ganglionar neuroma /gang·glē′ənər/ [Gk, *ganglion* + *neuron*, nerve, *oma*, tumor], a tumor composed of a solid mass of ganglia and nerve fibers, usually found in abdominal tissues and occurring most commonly in children.

ganglionated, having ganglia.

ganglionated nerve, a nerve of the sympathetic nervous system.

ganglionic blockade /gang′glē·on′ik/, the blocking of nerve impulses at synapses of autonomic ganglia, usually by the administration of ganglionic blocking agents.

ganglionic blocking agent, any one of a group of drugs prescribed to produce controlled hypotension, as required in certain surgical procedures or in emergency management of hypertensive crisis. The drugs act by occupying receptor sites (nicotinic neuronal receptors) on sympathetic and parasympathetic autonomic ganglia, preventing a response of these nerves to the action of acetylcholine liberated by the presynaptic nerve endings. These drugs are used with great caution in treating patients who are affected with coronary, cerebrovascular, or renal insufficiency or who have a history of severe allergy.

ganglionic cyst, a swollen area of the synovial sheath of a tendon that is common at the back of the wrist.

ganglionic glioma [Gk, *ganglion* + *glia*, glue, *oma*, tumor], a tumor composed of glial cells and nearly mature ganglion cells.

ganglion impar, the union of the two sympathetic trunks anterior to the coccyx.

ganglionitis /gang′glē·ənī′tis/, an inflammation of a nerve or lymph ganglion.

ganglioside /gang′glē·əsīd′/, a glycosphingolipid found in the brain and other nervous system tissues. Accumulation of gangliosides caused by an inborn error of metabolism results in gangliosidosis or Tay-Sachs disease.

gang rape, sexual intercourse against the will of the victim by a group of assailants.

gangrene /gang′grēn/ [Gk, *gangraina*, a gnawing sore], necrosis or death of tissue, usually the result of ischemia (loss of blood supply), bacterial invasion, and subsequent putrefaction. The extremities are most often affected. Dry gangrene is a late complication of DM that is already complicated by arteriosclerosis, in which the affected extremity becomes cold, dry, and shriveled and eventually turns black. Moist gangrene may follow a crushing injury or an obstruction of blood flow by an embolism, tight bandages, or a tourniquet.—**gangrenous,** *adj.*

gangrenous appendicitis /gang′grənəs/ [Gk, *gaggraina*, a gnawing sore; L, *appendere*, to hang upon; Gk, *itis*, inflammation], a condition in which the appendix becomes gangrenous because obstruction of its lumen blocks the flow of blood to that body part.

gangrenous vulvitis [Gk, *gaggraina*; L, *vulva*, wrapper; Gk, *itis*, inflammation], the death of tissues in the area of the vulva that results when an inadequate blood supply causes sloughing of cells.

ganirelix, a gonadotropin-releasing hormone antagonist used to inhibit premature luteinizing hormone surges in women undergoing controlled ovarian hyperstimulation.

Gantanol, a trademark for a sulfa antibiotic (sulfamethoxazole).

Gantrisin, a trademark for a sulfa antibiotic (sulfiSOXAZOLE).

gantry assembly /gan'trē/, a subsystem of the CT apparatus consisting of the x-ray tube, the detector array, the high-voltage generator, the patient support and positioning couch, and the mechanical support for each.

gap [OE, *gapa,* a hole], a short, missing segment in one strand of a DNA molecule.

gap junction, a type of junction between cells, consisting of a narrowed portion of the intercellular space that contains channels or pores composed of hexagonal arrays of membrane-spanning proteins around a central lumen (connexon), through which pass ions and small molecules.

gap phenomenon, a situation in which a premature cardiac stimulus encounters a block where an earlier or later stimulus could be conducted.

Garamycin, a trademark for an aminoglycoside antibacterial (gentamicin sulfate).

Gardner-Diamond syndrome [Frank H. Gardner, American physician, b. 1919; Louis K. Diamond, American physician, 1902–1999], a condition resulting from autoerythrocyte sensitization, marked by large, painful transient skin discolorations that appear without apparent cause but often accompany emotional upsets, various collagen disorders, and abnormalities of protein metabolism.

Gardnerella vaginalis /gärd'nərel'ə/ [Herman L. Gardner, twentieth-century American bacteriologist; L, *vagina,* sheath], a genus of rod-shaped gram-negative bacteria normally found in the female genital tract. The bacteria may also be a marker for bacterial vaginosis.

Gardnerella vaginalis **vaginitis** [Herman L. Gardner, L, *vagina,* sheath; Gk, *itis,* inflammation], a chronic inflammation of the vagina caused by a bacterium, *Gardnerella vaginalis.*

Gardner, Mary Sewell, an American public health nurse who wrote the classic *Public Health Nurse.* She was instrumental in the development of the National Organization for Public Health Nursing and of public health nursing in the American Red Cross.

Gardner's syndrome [Eldon J. Gardner, American geneticist, 1909–1989], familial polyposis of the large bowel, with fibrous dysplasia of the skull, extra teeth, osteomas, fibromas, and epidermal cysts.

Gardner-Wells tongs, pins that are attached to the skull of patients immobilized with cervical injuries. The pins are used to apply traction to reduce a fracture or dislocation while the patient is in a bed with a traction setup.

gargle /gär'gəl/ [Fr, *gargouille,* drainpipe], **1.** to hold and agitate a liquid at the back of the throat by tilting the head backward and forcing air through the solution. **2.** a solution used to rinse the mouth and oropharynx.

garlic, a herbal product used for vascular disease, elevated LDL, elevated triglycerides, low HDL, high BP, poor circulation, risk of cancer, inflammatory disorders, childhood ear infection, and yeast infection. The allicin of fresh garlic may cause a small decrease in LDL cholesterol and slight decrease in BP and may have some antibacterial properties, but garlic is not nearly as effective as prescribed drugs for these purposes. Its influence on cancer risk and efficacy for other uses has not been adequately documented.

GARS, abbreviation for **Gait Assessment Rating Scale.**

Garth method, a positioning method for producing x-ray images of the scapulohumeral joint and identifying shoulder dislocations, scapular fractures and bony defects involving the humeral head. The patient faces the x-ray tube with the affected shoulder joint centered to the midline of the image receptor (IR). The affected elbow is flexed and the forearm is placed across the patient's chest. The opposite shoulder is angled 45 degrees away from the IR. The central ray is directed at a 45-degree angle toward the patient's feet and passes through the affected shoulder joint.

Gartner's duct, one of two vestigial closed ducts, each parallel to a uterine tube.

gas [Gk, *chaos*], an aeriform fluid that possesses complete molecular mobility and the property of indefinite expansion. A gas has no definite shape, and its volume is determined by its container and by temperature and pressure.—**gaseous,** *adj.*

gas bacillus [Gk, *chaos;* L, *bacillum,* small rod], any of several species of bacillus that produce a gas as a by-product of their metabolism. Examples include *Escherichia coli,* which ferments lactose and glucose, and the clostridial species that produce gas gangrene.

gas chromatography, the separation and analysis of different substances according to their different affinities for a standard absorbent. In the process, a gaseous mixture of the substances is passed through a glass cylinder containing the absorbent, which may be dampened with a nonvolatile liquid solvent for one or more of the gaseous components. As the mixture passes through the absorbent, each substance is absorbed to a different extent and leaves a characteristic pigment.

gas embolism, an occlusion of one or more small blood vessels, especially in the muscles, tendons, and joints, caused by expanding gas bubbles. Gas emboli can rupture tissue and blood vessels, causing decompression sickness and death. They are most dangerous in the CNS because of associated neurologic changes, such as syncope, paralysis, and aphasia.

gas gangrene, necrosis accompanied by gas bubbles in soft tissue after surgery or trauma. It is caused by anaerobic organisms, such as various species of *Clostridium,* particularly *C. perfringens.* Symptoms include pain, swelling, and tenderness of the wound area; moderate fever; tachycardia; and hypotension. A characteristic finding is toxic delirium.

gas-scavenging system, the equipment used to prevent waste anesthetic gases from escaping into the atmosphere of the OR.

gas sterilization [Gk, *chaos,* gas; L, *sterilis,* barren], the use of a gas such as ethylene oxide, C_2H_4O, to sterilize medical equipment.

gas therapy, the use of medical gases in respiratory therapy.

gastrectasia /gas'trektā'zhə/ [Gk, *gaster,* stomach, *ektasis,* stretching], an abnormal dilation of the stomach. It may be accompanied by pain, vomiting, rapid pulse, and falling body temperature. Causes can include overeating, obstruction of the pyloric valve, or a hernia.

gastrectomy /gastrek'təmē/, surgical excision of all or, more commonly, part of the stomach, performed to remove a chronic peptic ulcer, to stop hemorrhage in a perforating ulcer, or to remove a malignancy.

gastric /gas'trik/ [Gk, *gaster,* stomach], pertaining to the stomach.

gastric analysis, examination of the contents of the stomach, primarily to determine the quantity of acid present and incidentally to ascertain the presence of blood, bile, bacteria, and abnormal cells. This procedure is rarely performed.

gastric antral vascular ectasia, a rare vascular anomaly of the gastric antrum, consisting of dilated and thrombosed capillaries and veins that form lines in the antrum that radiate toward the pylorus. It may result in chronic blood loss and anemia.

gastric areas, small patches of gastric mucosa, 1 to 5 mm in diameter, separated by the plicae villosae and containing the gastric pits.

gastric banding, a surgical treatment for morbid obesity consisting of creation of a gastric pouch by application to the proximal stomach of a silicone band, sometimes with an accompanying reservoir that can be filled with saline to adjust the size of the pouch's stoma.

gastric bypass, bariatric surgery performed to reduce stomach capacity and allow food to bypass part of the small intestine.

gastric cancer, a malignancy of the stomach. Approximately 97% of stomach tumors are adenocarcinomas. Lymphomas and leiomyosarcomas account for less than 3%. Symptoms of gastric cancer are vague epigastric discomfort, dysphagia, anorexia, weight loss, back pain, and unexplained iron deficiency anemia; however, many cases are asymptomatic in the early stages, and metastases may cause the first symptoms.

gastric digestion [Gk, *gaster,* stomach; L, *digere,* to separate], digestion by gastric juice in the stomach.

gastric dumping, excessively rapid movement of partially digested food from the stomach into the jejunum, occurring most often in patients who have had partial gastrectomy with gastrojejunostomy.

gastric dyspepsia, pain or discomfort localized in the stomach.

gastric emesis [Gk, *gaster,* stomach, *emesis,* vomiting], vomiting associated with a stomach disorder such as stomach cancer, stomach ulcer, or severe gastritis.

gastric fistula, an abnormal passage into the stomach, communicating most frequently with an opening on the external surface of the abdomen. A gastric fistula may be created surgically to provide tube feeding for patients with severe esophageal disorders.

gastric fundus, that part of the stomach to the left and above the level of the entrance of the esophagus.

gastric glands, the secreting glands of the stomach, including the fundic, cardiac, and pyloric glands.

gastric inhibitory polypeptide (GIP), a GI hormone found in the mucosa of the small intestine. Release of the hormone, mediated by the presence of glucose or fatty acids in the duodenum, results in the release of insulin by the pancreas and inhibition of gastric mobility acid secretion.

gastric intubation, a procedure in which a Levin tube or other small-caliber catheter is passed through the nose into the esophagus and stomach. It may be used for the introduction into the stomach of liquid formulas to provide nutrition for unconscious patients or for premature or sick newborns. Medication or a contrast medium may be instilled for treatment or for radiologic examination.

gastric juice, digestive secretions of the gastric glands in the stomach, consisting chiefly of pepsin, hydrochloric acid, rennin, and mucin. The pH is strongly acid (0.9 to 1.5).

gastric lavage, the washing out of the stomach with sterile water or a saline solution.

gastric motility, the spontaneous peristaltic movements of the stomach that aid in digestion, moving food through the stomach and out through the pyloric sphincter into the duodenum.

gastric mucin [Gk, *gaster,* stomach; L, *mucus*], a viscous secretion of glycoproteins produced from the mucous membrane lining of swine stomachs and formerly used in the treatment of peptic ulcers.

gastric node, a node in one of three groups of lymph glands associated with the abdominal and pelvic viscera supplied by branches of the celiac artery.

gastric resection [Gk, *gaster,* stomach; L, *re + secare,* to cut], the surgical removal of part or all of the stomach, usually performed in the treatment of stomach cancer or intractable peptic ulcer.

gastric restriction, any of various surgical treatments for morbid obesity in which part of the stomach is closed off from the flow of nutrients through the alimentary canal.

gastrin /gas′trin/ [Gk, *gaster,* stomach], a polypeptide hormone, secreted by the pylorus, that stimulates the flow of gastric juice and contributes to the stimulus for bile and pancreatic enzyme secretion.

gastrinoma /gas′trinŏ′mə/, a tumor found in the pancreas and duodenum associated with the presence of peptic ulcers.

gastrin-releasing peptide, a 27-amino acid linear neuropeptide, structurally and functionally related to bombesin, that mediates neural release of antral gastrin, causes bronchoconstriction and respiratory tract vasodilation, stimulates growth and mitogenesis of cells in culture, and may act as an excitatory neurotransmitter of enteric interneurons.

gastrin test, a blood test used to help identify patients with Zollinger-Ellison syndrome and G cell hyperplasia, who typically have high serum gastrin levels. Gastrin is a hormone that is secreted by cells of the stomach and causes secretion of hydrochloric acid.

gastritis /gastrī′tis/, an inflammation of the lining of the stomach that occurs in two forms. Acute gastritis may be caused by severe burns; major surgery; aspirin or other antiinflammatory agents (NSAIDs); corticosteroids; drugs; food allergens; or viral, bacterial, or chemical toxins. Symptoms include anorexia, nausea, vomiting, and discomfort after eating. Chronic gastritis is usually a sign of underlying disease

such as peptic ulcer, stomach cancer, Zollinger-Ellison syndrome, or pernicious anemia.

gastrocamera /gas′trōkam′ərə/, a small camera that can be lowered into the stomach through the esophagus and retrieved after recording images of the stomach lining.

gastrocnemius /gas′trŏnē′me·us/ [Gk, *gastroknemia,* calf of the leg], the most superficial calf muscle in the posterior part of the leg. It flexes the leg and plantarflexes the foot.

gastrocnemius gait, an abnormal gait associated with a weakness of the gastrocnemius, characterized by the dropping of the pelvis on the affected side at the last moment of the stance phase in the walking cycle, accompanied by lagging or slowness in forward pelvic movement.

gastrocnemius test, a test of the function of the gastrocnemius muscle by ankle plantar flexion while the patient is in a prone position. The examiner places fingers for palpation on the posterior of the calf while the patient pulls the heel upward. Flexion of the toes and forefoot before movement of the heel is evidence of muscle substitution.

gastrocolic reflex /-kol′ik/ [Gk, *gaster + kolon,* colon; L, *reflectere,* to bend backward], a mass peristaltic movement of the colon that often occurs 15 to 20 minutes after food enters the stomach.

gastrocystoplasty /gas′trosis′toplas′te/, augmentation cystoplasty using a portion of the stomach for the graft.

gastrodidymus /-did′iməs/ [Gk, *gaster + didymos,* twin], conjoined, equally developed twins united at the abdominal region.

gastrodisciasis /gas′trōdiskī′əsis/ [Gk, *gaster + diskos,* disk, *eidos,* form, *osis,* condition], an infection of trematodes of the genus *Gastrodiscoides,* which are digestive tract parasites.

gastroduodenal /-dōō′ədĕ′nəl/ [Gk, *gaster;* L, *duodeni,* 12 fingers], pertaining to the stomach and duodenum.

gastroduodenitis /-dōō′ədenī′tis/ [Gk, *gaster,* stomach; L, *duodeni,* 12 fingers; Gk, *itis,* inflammation], inflammation of the stomach and duodenum.

gastroduodenoscopy /-dōō′ədenos′kəpē/, inspection of the stomach and duodenum by means of a gastroscope passed through the oral cavity and esophagus.

gastroduodenostomy /-dōō′ədenos′təmē/, surgical establishment of a passageway between the stomach and the duodenum.

gastroenteritis /gas′trō·en′tərī′tis/ [Gk, *gaster + enteron,* intestine, *itis,* inflammation], inflammation of the stomach and intestines accompanying numerous GI disorders. Symptoms are anorexia, nausea, vomiting, fever (depending on causative factor), abdominal discomfort, and diarrhea. The condition may be attributed to bacterial enterotoxins, bacterial or viral invasion, chemical toxins, or miscellaneous conditions, such as lactose intolerance.

gastroenterologist /gas′trō·en′tərol′əjist/, a physician who specializes in diseases affecting the GI tract.

gastroenterology /gas′trō·en′tərol′əjē/ [Gk, *gaster* + *enteron,* intestine, *logos,* science], the study of diseases affecting the GI tract, including the stomach, intestines, gallbladder, and bile duct.

gastroenterostomy /gas′trō·en′təros′təmē/ [Gk, *gaster* + *enteron,* intestine, *stoma,* mouth], surgical formation of an artificial opening between the stomach and the small intestine, usually at the jejunum. The operation is performed with a gastrectomy to route food from the remainder of the stomach into the small intestine or alone to treat a perforating ulcer of the duodenum.

gastroesophageal /gas′trō·isof′əjē′əl/ [Gk, *gaster* + *oisophagos,* gullet], pertaining to the stomach and esophagus.

gastroesophageal reflux, a backflow of contents of the stomach into the esophagus that is often the result of incompetence of the lower esophageal sphincter. Gastric juices are acid and therefore produce burning pain in the esophagus.

gastroesophageal reflux scan, a nuclear scan that is used to evaluate patients with symptoms of heartburn, regurgitation, vomiting, and dysphagia, and to evaluate the medical or surgical treatment of patients with gastroesophageal reflux.

gastroesophagitis /gas′trō·isof′əjī′tis/, inflammation of the stomach and esophagus.

gastrofiberscope /-fī′bərskōp/, a flexible fiber endoscope for examination of the stomach.

gastrointestinal (GI) /gas′trō·intes′tinəl/ [Gk, *gaster*; L, *intestinum,* intestine], pertaining to the organs of the GI tract, from mouth to anus.

gastrointestinal allergy, an immediate reaction of hypersensitivity of the digestive system after the ingestion of certain foods or drugs. Characteristic symptoms include itching and swelling of the mouth and oral passages, nausea, vomiting, diarrhea (sometimes containing blood), severe abdominal pain, and, in severe cases, anaphylactic shock.

gastrointestinal bleeding, any bleeding from the GI tract. The most common underlying conditions are peptic ulcer, Mallory-Weiss syndrome, esophageal varices, diverticulosis, ulcerative colitis, and carcinoma of the stomach and colon.

Vomiting of bright red blood or passage of coffee ground vomitus indicates upper GI bleeding, usually from the esophagus, stomach, or upper duodenum. Tarry black stools indicate a bleeding source in the upper GI tract. Bright red blood from the rectum usually indicates bleeding in the distal colon.

gastrointestinal bleeding scan, a nuclear scan that is used to localize the site of bleeding in patients who are having active GI hemorrhage.

gastrointestinal function, a nursing outcome from the Nursing Outcomes Classification (NOC) defined as the extent to which foods (ingested or tube-fed) are moved from ingestion to excretion.

gastrointestinal infection, any infection of the digestive tract caused by bacteria, viruses, or parasites. All may have common clinical features of nausea, vomiting, diarrhea, and anorexia.

gastrointestinal intubation, a nursing intervention from the Nursing Interventions Classification (NIC) defined as insertion of a tube into the gastrointestinal tract.

gastrointestinal obstruction, any obstruction of the passage of intestinal contents, caused by mechanical blockage or failure of motility.

gastrointestinal series, an examination of the upper GI tract using barium as the contrast medium for a series of x-ray films.

gastrointestinal system assessment, an evaluation of the patient's digestive system and symptoms. The patient is asked about pain or tenderness in the oral cavity, gums, tongue, lips, abdomen, or rectum, and whether there have been instances of dysphagia, belching, heartburn, anorexia, nausea, vomiting, constipation, diarrhea, or painful defecation. Information is elicited about changes in eating; bowel habits; the color, character, and frequency of stools and urine; the use of laxatives or enemas; and the occurrence of fatigue, hemorrhoids, and edema of the extremities. The family history, especially of GI disease, carcinoma, and DM, is an important aspect of the evaluation. The patient's general appearance, weight, and temperature are noted; the BP, pulse, and respirations are checked, and the urinary output and color are determined. The abdomen is examined for distension, rigidity, ascites, symmetry, organomegaly, keloid tissue, visible peristalsis, bowel sounds, masses, and the presence of an ostomy. Diagnostic aids include a CBC, stool examination, prothrombin time, and determinations of levels of alkaline phosphatase, serum and urine bilirubin, aspartate aminotransferase, alanine aminotransferase, lactic acid dehydrogenase, BUN, serum lipase, cholinesterase, calcium, albumin, and glucose. Additional procedures may be required for the diagnosis.

gastrokinetic drugs /-kinet′ik/, chemicals that stimulate salivation, increase lower esophageal sphincter (LES) pressure, and improve esophageal clearance in the supine but not in the upright position. Metoclopramide, an agent in this category, has side effects that make it undesirable, and its efficacy is questionable in comparison to the now widely used proton pump inhibitors.

gastromalacia /-məlā′shə/ [Gk, *gaster*, stomach, *malakia*, softness], an abnormal softening of the walls of the stomach.

gastromegaly /-meg′ələ/ [Gk, *gaster* + *megas*, large], an abnormal enlargement of the stomach or abdomen.

gastroparesis /-pərē′sis/, **1.** paralysis of the stomach. **2.** failure of the stomach to empty caused by decreased gastric motility.

gastropericardial fistula, a fistula connecting the stomach with the pericardium, usually a complication after gastroesophageal surgery.

gastroplasty /gas′troplas′tē/ [Gk, *gaster* + *plassein*, to mold], any surgery performed to reshape or repair any stomach defect or deformity.

gastroschisis /gastros′kəsis/ [Gk, *gaster* + *schisis*, division], a congenital defect characterized by incomplete closure of the abdominal wall with protrusion of the viscera.

gastroscope /gas′trōskōp′/ [Gk, *gaster* + *skopein*, to look], a fiberoptic instrument for examining the interior of the stomach. —**gastroscopic,** *adj.*

gastroscopy /gastros′kəpē/, the visual inspection of the interior of the stomach by means of a gastroscope inserted through the esophagus. —**gastroscopic,** *adj.*

gastrostomy /gastros′təmē/ [Gk, *gaster* + *stoma,* mouth], surgical creation of an artificial opening into the stomach through the abdominal wall. It is performed to prevent malnutrition and starvation in patients who have esophageal cancer or tracheoesophageal fistula, who may be unconscious for a prolonged period, or who are unable to swallow as a result of a CVA, Alzheimer's disease, or another disorder.

gastrostomy feeding, the introduction of a nutrient solution through a tube that has been surgically inserted into the stomach through the abdominal wall.

gastrothoracopagus /gas′trōthôr′əkop′ə gəs/ [Gk, *gaster* + *thorax,* chest, *pagos,* fixture], conjoined twins who are united at the thorax and abdomen.

gastrula /gas′trŏŏlə/ [Gk, *gaster,* stomach], the early embryonic stage formed by the invagination of the blastula. The cup-shaped gastrula consists of an outer layer of ectoderm and an inner layer of mesentoderm that subsequently differentiate into the mesoderm and endoderm.

gastrulation /gas′trəlā′shən/ [Gk, *gaster,* stomach], the development of the gastrula in lower animals and the formation of the three germ layers in the embryo of humans and higher animals.

Gatch bed /gach/ [William D. Gatch, American surgeon, 1878–1961; AS, *bedd*], a bed that has an adjustable joint, allowing the knees to be flexed and the legs supported.

gate /gāt/, **1.** an electronic circuit that passes a pulse only when a signal (the gate pulse) is present at a second input. **2.** a mechanism for opening or closing a protein channel in a cell membrane, regulated by a signal such as increased concentration of a neurotransmitter, change in electrical potential, or physical binding of a ligand molecule to the protein to cause a conformational change in the protein molecule. **3.** to open and close selectively and function as a gate.

gatekeeper, a health care professional, usually a primary care physician or a physician extender, who is the patient's first contact with the health care system and triages the patient's further access to the system.

gatekeeper effect, a contraction of the endothelium mediated by IgG. It permits components of the blood to gain access to the extravascular space as a result of the increased vascular permeability.

gateway drugs, minor substances of abuse, such as inhalants, used in general by children or young people before they experiment with marijuana or hard drugs; entry drugs.

gatifloxacin, a broad-spectrum antiinfective used to treat acute bacterial exacerbation of chronic bronchitis, acute sinusitis, community-acquired pneumonia, gonorrhea, and infections caused by susceptible *Escherichia coli, Staphylococcus aureus, Haemophilus influenzae, H. parainfluenzae, Klebsiella pneumoniae, Moraxella catarrhalis, Neisseria gonorrhoeae, Proteus mirabilis, Chlamydia pneumoniae, Legionella pneumophila,* and *Mycoplasma pneumoniae.*

gating, the organizing of image data so that information used to construct an image originates in the same point in the cycle of a repeating movement, such as a heartbeat.

gating mechanism, 1. the increasing duration of an action potential from the atrioventricular node to a point in the distal Purkinje system, beyond which it decreases. **2.** a process that controls the opening and closing of cell-membrane ion channels.

Gaucher's disease /gôshāz'/ [Phillipe
C.E. Gaucher, French physician, 1854–
1918], a rare autosomal-recessive familial disorder of fat metabolism caused by
an enzyme deficiency, characterized by
widespread reticulum cell hyperplasia in
the liver, spleen, lymph nodes, and bone
marrow.

gauge /gāj/ [ME], an instrument for
determining physical properties of anything,
including caliber, dimensions, or pressure.

gauntlet bandage /gônt'lit/ [Fr, gantlet,
small glove, bande, strip], a glovelike
bandage covering the hand and fingers.

gauss /gôs, gous/ [J.K.F. Gauss, German
physicist, 1777–1855], a unit of mag-
netic field strength. It is equal to 10^{-5} tesla.

gauze /gôz/ [Fr, gaze], a transparent
fabric of open weave and differing degrees
of fineness, most often cotton muslin, used
in surgical procedures and for bandages
and dressings. It may be sterilized and permeated by an antiseptic or lotion.

gauze sponge [Fr, gaze; Gk, spoggia], a
piece of folded gauze used during surgery
to wipe up bleeding surfaces and thereby
help locate any sources of blood loss.

gavage /gäväzh'/ [Fr, gaver, to gorge],
the process of feeding a patient by a nasogastric tube.

gavage feeding of the newborn, a procedure in which a tube passed through the
nose or mouth into the stomach is used to
feed a newborn with weak sucking, uncoordinated sucking and swallowing, respiratory distress, tachypnea, or repeated apneic
spells.

gay [Fr, gai, merry], **1.** any person who
is homosexual. **2.** pertaining to
homosexuality.

Gay-Lussac's law /gā ləsaks'/ [Joseph L.
Gay-Lussac, French scientist, 1778–1850;
L, legu, a rule], in physics, a law stating
that the volume of a specific mass of a gas
increases as the temperature increases if
the pressure remains constant.

Gay Nurses' Alliance (GNA), a national
organization of homosexual and lesbian
nurses.

gaze /gāz/ [ME, gazen, to stare], a state
of looking in one direction. A person with
normal vision has six basic positions of
gaze, each determined by control of different combinations of contractions of extraocular muscles.

gaze paresis, a disturbance of eye conjugate movement in which gaze tends to be
tonically deviated in the direction of normal gaze.

gaze test, a test of ocular and vestibular
functioning. Movements of the eye are
recorded with the patient gazing straight at
an object and at positions off to different

sides of it, then with eyes closed for 20 seconds. The eyes normally should assume a
center gaze while they are closed.

GB, abbreviation for **gallbladder.**

GBIA, abbreviation for **Guthrie's bacterial inhibition assay.**

g.c., informal. abbreviation for **gonococcus.**

G cell hyperplasia, increased numbers
of G cells in the gastric mucosa, causing
marked hypergastrinemia resembling that
seen in the Zollinger-Ellison syndrome.

G-CSF, abbreviation for **granulocyte
colony–stimulating factor.**

Gd, symbol for the element **gadolinium.**

GDM, abbreviation for **gestational diabetes mellitus.**

GDNF, abbreviation for **glial cell line–
derived neurotrophic factor.**

Ge, symbol for the element **germanium.**

gefitinib, an antineoplastic used to treat
non–small cell lung cancer.

gegenhalten /gā'gənhäl'tən/ [Ger, coun-
terpressure], the involuntary resistance
to passive movement of the extremities.
The effect may be psychogenic in origin
or may be a sign of dementia or cerebral
deterioration.

Geiger-Müller (GM) counter /gī'gər
mil'ər/ [Hans Geiger, German physicist,
1882–1945; Walther Müller, twentieth-
century German physicist; Fr, conter, to
tell], an electronic device that indicates
the level of radioactivity of a substance by
counting the number of ionizing subatomic
particles emitted by the substance.

gel /jel/ [L, gelare, to congeal], a colloid that is firm although it contains a large
amount of liquid, used in many medicines
as a demulcent, a vehicle for other drugs,
an antacid, or an astringent, depending on
the drug from which it is derived.

gelatin buildup /jel'ətən/ an x-ray film
artifact that may appear as a sharp area of
either increased or reduced density.

gelatin film, absorbable, a hemostatic
used to attain hemostasis during surgery,
particularly neurologic, thoracic, and ophthalmic procedures.

gelatinous /jəlat'ənəs/ [L, gelare, to con-
geal], pertaining to or resembling a viscous, jellylike substance.

gelatin sponge, an absorbable local
hemostatic prescribed to control surgical
bleeding and treat pressure ulcers.

gel filtration, a method of separating molecules by size. A solution containing molecules of various sizes is passed through a filter
consisting of a polyacrylamide or polysaccharide. The larger molecules are excluded
from the interior of the filter and thus emerge
from it earlier than the smaller molecules.

Gelfoam, a trademark for an absorbable
hemostatic gelatin sponge.

Gell and Coombs classification /jel; ko̅o̅mz/, a classification of immune mechanisms of tissue injury, comprising four types of hypersensitivity reactions: *type I*, immediate (anaphylactic) hypersensitivity reactions, *type II*, antibody-mediated hypersensitivity reactions, *type III*, mediated (immune complex) hypersensitivity reactions, and *type IV*, delayed (cell-mediated) hypersensitivity reactions.

gemcitabine, a miscellaneous antineoplastic used to treat adenocarcinoma of the pancreas (nonresectable Stages II and III or metastatic Stage IV) and non–small cell lung cancer (Stages IIIA or IIIB and IV). It is also used in combination with cisplatin to treat inoperable, advanced, or metastatic non–small cell lung cancer.

gemellary /jem′əler′ē/   [L, *gemellus*, twin], pertaining to twins.

gemellipara /jem′əlip′ərə/   [L, *gemellus* + *parare*, to give birth],   a woman who has given birth to twins.

gemellology /jem′əlol′əjē/   [L, *gemellus*; Gk, *logos*, science],   the study of twins and the phenomenon of twinning.

gemellus /jəmel′əs/,   either of a pair of small muscles arising from the ischium. They rotate the thigh laterally.

gemellus test,   a test of the function of the gemellus superior and gemellus inferior muscles in hip external rotation while the patient is seated with the knees flexed. The examiner places one hand on the lateral aspect of the knee to prevent flexion or abduction of the hip while the patient rotates the thigh outward by moving the foot medially.

gemfibrozil /jemfī′brəzil/,   an antihyperlipidemic agent prescribed for the treatment of hyperlipidemia, specifically high levels of plasma triglycerides.

gemifloxacin,   an antiinfective agent that inhibits DNA gyrase. It is used to treat acute bacterial exacerbation of chronic bronchitis caused by *Streptococcus pneumoniae*, *Haemophilus influenzae*, *H. parainfluenzae*, and *Moraxella catarrhalis* and community-acquired pneumonia caused by *S. pneumoniae* (including multidrug-resistant strains), *H. influenzae*, *M. catarrhalis*, *Mycoplasma pneumoniae*, *Chlamydia pneumoniae*, and *Klebsiella pneumoniae*.

gemination,   in dentistry, the "twinning" of a single tooth bud. Geminated teeth usually have a single common root, a common pulp canal, and visible partial cleavage of the enamel crown. The normal quantity of teeth are present in the dental arch.

gemistocyte /gemis′təsīt/,   an astrocyte with an eccentric nucleus and swollen cytoplasm, as seen in areas of nervous tissue affected by edema, demyelination, or infarction.

gemma /jem′ə/ *pl.* **gemmae** [L, bud],   **1.** a budlike projection produced by some organisms during budding, a type of asexual reproduction. **2.** any budlike or bulb-like structure such as a taste bud or end bulb. —**gemmaceous,** *adj.*

gemmate /jem′āt/   [L, *gemma* + *atus*, function],   **1.** having buds or gemmae. **2.** to reproduce by budding.

gemmation /jemā′shən/   [L, *gemmare*, to produce buds],   the process of reproduction by budding.

gemmiferous /jemif′ərəs/   [L, *gemma* + *fer*, bearing],   having buds or gemmae; gemmiparous.

gemmiform /jem′ifôrm′/,   resembling a bud or gemma.

gemmipara /jemip′ərə/   [L, *gemma* + *parare*, to give birth],   an animal that produces gemmae or reproduces by budding, such as a hydra. —**gemmiparous,** *adj.*

gemtuzumab ozogamicin /gemto̅o̅′zo̅o̅mab′ o′zo-gah-mi′sin/,   a recombinant DNA-derived monoclonal antibody conjugated with a cytotoxic antitumor antibiotic used as an antineoplastic in the treatment of relapsed acute myelogenous leukemia.

gender /jen′dər/   [L, *genus*, kind],   **1.** the classification of the sex of a person into male, female, or ambivalent. **2.** the specific sex of a person.

gender identity,   the inner sense of maleness or femaleness.

gender identity disorder,   a condition characterized by a persistent feeling of discomfort or inappropriateness concerning one's anatomic sex.

gender role,   the expression of a person's gender identity; the image that a person presents to both himself or herself and others, demonstrating maleness or femaleness.

gender testing   [L, *genus*, kind, *testum*, crucible],   a procedure for validating the sex of an individual by examining a tissue sample, usually obtained from oral mucous membrane cells, for the presence of a Y chromosome.

gene /jēn/   [Gk, *genein*, to produce],   the biologic unit of inheritance, consisting of a particular nucleotide sequence within a DNA sequence that occupies a precise locus on a chromosome and codes for a specific polypeptide chain.

gene amplification   [Gk, *genein*, to produce; L, *amplus*, large],   a process in which a specific gene or set of genes is duplicated many times in certain cells in response to defined signals or environmental stresses.

gene amplification technique,   a term sometimes used to denote a nucleic acid amplification technique, although the segment of DNA or RNA undergoing amplification does not necessarily correspond to a single, entire gene.

gene expression, the flow of genetic information from gene to protein; the process, or the regulation of the process, by which the effects of a gene are manifested; the manifestation of a heritable trait in an individual carrying the gene or genes that determine it.

gene pool [Gk, *genein,* to produce; AS, *pol*], the total number of genes in a population.

gene probe, a device used in molecular biology for locating a particular gene on a chromosome. It involves pairing a short known segment of DNA or RNA with a matching sequence of bases on a chromosome.

general adaptation syndrome (GAS) [L, *genus,* kind *adaptare,* to fit; Gk, *syn,* together, *dromos,* course], the defense response of the body or the psyche to injury or prolonged stress. It consists of an initial stage of shock or alarm reaction, followed by a phase of increasing resistance or adaptation in which the various defense mechanisms of the body or mind are used, and culminates in a state of adjustment and healing or of exhaustion and disintegration.

general anesthesia (GA), the absence of sensation and consciousness as induced by various anesthetic medications, given by inhalation or IV injection.

generalization /jen'(ə)rəlīzā'shən/ [L, *genus,* kind; Gk, *izein,* to cause], **1.** the reasoning by which a basic conclusion is reached, with application to different items that have a common factor. **2.** the process of reducing or subsuming under a general rule or statement, such as classifying items in general categories. **3.** a principle with general application. **4.** in occupational therapy, the ability of a patient to apply knowledge and skills learned in therapy to a variety of similar but new situations.

generalized anaphylaxis /jen'(ə)rəlīzd'/, a severe reaction to an allergen characterized by itching, edema, wheezing respirations, apprehension, cyanosis, dyspnea, pupillary dilation, falling BP, and rapid, weak pulse that may quickly produce shock and death.

generalized anxiety disorder (GAD), an anxiety reaction characterized by persistent apprehension. The symptoms range from mild, chronic tenseness, with feelings of timidity, fatigue, apprehension, and indecisiveness, to more intense states of restlessness and irritability that may lead to aggressive acts. In extreme cases, the overwhelming emotional discomfort is accompanied by physical reactions.

generalized peritonitis [L, *genus,* kind; Gk, *peri,* near, *teinein,* to stretch, *itis,* inflammation], a bacterial infection of the peritoneum secondary to an infection in another organ, as when an appendix ruptures. The symptoms are usually acute and severe.

generally recognized as effective (GRAE), one of the statutory criteria that must be met by a drug before it can be approved as a new drug. Meeting these criteria relieves the manufacturer of the necessity of obtaining premarket approval as required by the Federal Food, Drug, and Cosmetic Act. To be recognized as effective, the drug must be, according to the act, considered safe and effective by "experts qualified by scientific training and experience."

generally recognized as safe (GRAS), a 1958 rule established by the U.S. Food and Drug Administration to identify foods regarded as safe to use because of lack of evidence that they may be harmful.

general paresis [L, *genus,* kind; Gk, paralysis], a neurologic disorder that results from chronic syphilitic infection. It is characterized by degeneration of the cortical neurons; progressive dementia, tremor, and speech disturbances; muscular weakness; and ultimately generalized paralysis. It is often accompanied by periods of exultation and delusions of grandeur.

general practice, old term for comprehensive medical care regardless of age of the patient or presence of a condition that may require the services of a specialist. This term has now largely been replaced by the term **family practice.**

general practitioner (GP) [L, *genus,* kind; Gk, *praktikos,* practical], a family practice physician.

general relaxation [L, *genus,* kind, *relaxare,* to ease], a slackening of strain or tension of the entire body, particularly of the muscles.

general symptom [L, *genus*; Gk, *symptoma,* that which happens], a symptom that affects the entire body rather than a specific organ or location.

generation /jen'ərā'shən/ [L, *generare,* to beget], **1.** the act or process of reproduction; procreation. **2.** a group of contemporary individuals that have descended through the same number of life cycles from a common ancestor. **3.** the period between the birth of one individual and the birth of its offspring.

generative /jen'ərā'tiv/ [L, *generare,* to beget], pertaining to activity that generates new physical or mental growth, such as creative problem solving.

generic /jəner'ik/ [L, *genus,* kind], **1.** pertaining to a genus. **2.** pertaining to a substance, product, or drug that is not protected by trademark. **3.** pertaining to the non-trademarked name assigned to the drugs by the U.S. Adopted Names Council.

generic equivalent, a drug product sold under its generic name whose active ingredients are identical in chemical composition to one or more others sold under trademark. Inactive ingredients may not be the same.

generic name, the official established nonproprietary name assigned to a drug. A drug is licensed under its generic name, and all manufacturers of the drug list it by its generic name.

generic nursing program, a program that prepares people with no professional nursing experience for entry into the field of nursing.

genesis /jen'əsis/ [Gk, origin], **1.** the origin, generation, or developmental evolution of anything. **2.** the act of producing or procreating.

gene splicing /jēn/, a process by which a segment of DNA is attached to or inserted into a strand of DNA from another source.

gene therapy, a procedure that involves injection of "healthy genes" into the bloodstream of a patient to cure or treat a hereditary disease or similar illness. Blood is withdrawn from the patient. The white cells are separated and cultured in a laboratory. Normal genes from a volunteer are inserted into modified viruses, which, in turn, transfer the normal gene into the chromosomes of the patient's white cells. The white cells containing the normal genes are finally injected into the patient's bloodstream.

genetic /jənet'ik/ [Gk, *genesis,* origin], **1.** pertaining to reproduction, birth, or origin. **2.** pertaining to genetics or heredity. **3.** pertaining to or produced by a gene; inherited.

genetic affinity, relationship by direct descent.

genetically significant dose (GSD) /jənet'iklē/, **1.** an arbitrary measure of the estimated annual gonadal radiation received by the population gene pool. In the United States, the estimated GSD is 20 mrad. The figure is not intended to suggest possible genetic effects of exposure to that level of radiation. **2.** an estimate of the genetic significance of gonad radiation doses, which takes into account the number of offspring expected for each individual on the basis of age and sex.

genetic association, a condition in which specific genotypes are associated with other factors, such as specific diseases.

genetic carrier, a person who carries an allele without exhibiting its effects. Such an allele is usually recessive, but it may also be dominant and latent, with symptoms that do not appear until adulthood.

genetic code, the information carried by DNA that determines the specific amino acids and their sequence in each protein synthesized by an organism. The code consists of the sequence of nucleotides in the DNA molecule of each chromosome in the nucleus of every cell. A change in the code may result in an incorrect sequence of the amino acids in the protein, causing a mutation.

genetic colonization, the process by which a parasite introduces into its host genetic information that induces the host to synthesize products solely for the use of the parasite.

genetic counseling[1], the process of determining the occurrence or risk of occurrence of a genetic disorder in a family and of providing information and advice about topics such as care of an affected child, prenatal diagnosis, termination of a pregnancy, sterilization, and artificial insemination.

genetic counseling[2], a nursing intervention from the Nursing Interventions Classification (NIC) defined as use of an interactive helping process focusing on assisting an individual, family, or group manifesting or at risk for developing or transmitting a birth defect or genetic condition to cope.

genetic counselor, a health professional academically and clinically prepared to communicate genetic, medical, and technical information about the occurrence, or risk of occurrence, of a genetic condition or birth defect.

genetic death, 1. the failure of an organism to survive as a result of its genetic makeup. **2.** the removal of an allele or genotype from the gene pool of a population or from a given familial descent because of the sterility, failure to reproduce, or death before sexual maturity of all individuals bearing that allele or genotype.

genetic drift, a gradual change in the allelic frequencies within a population as a result of chance. The smaller a population is, the greater is the tendency for variation within each generation so that eventually small, isolated, inbreeding groups become genetically quite different from their ancestors.

genetic engineering, the process of producing recombinant DNA for the purposes of altering and controlling the genotype and phenotype of organisms. Restriction enzymes are used to break a DNA molecule into fragments so that genes from another organism can be inserted into the DNA. Genetic engineering has been used to produce a variety of human proteins, including growth hormone, insulin, and interferon, in bacteria. At present, it represents a powerful tool for medical research but is possible only in microorganisms.

genetic equilibrium, the state within a population at which the frequency of alleles and genotypes does not change from generation to generation.

G

genetic homeostasis, the maintenance of genetic variability within a population through adaptation to varied or changing environments and conditions of life as a result of shifts or resistance to shifts in allelic frequencies.

genetic isolate, a group of individuals that are genetically separated by geographic, racial, social, cultural, or other barriers that prevent them from interbreeding with those outside the group.

geneticist /jənet′isist/, a scientist who specializes in the study or application of genetics.

genetic load, the average number of accumulated detrimental genes per individual within a population, including those caused by mutation and selection within a recent generation and those inherited from ancestors.

genetic map, the graphic representation of the linear arrangement of genes on a chromosome and the relative distances between them, in map units or morgans.

genetic marker, any specific gene that produces a readily recognizable genetic trait that can be used in family and population studies or in linkage analysis.

genetic polymorphism, the recurrence within a population of two or more discontinuous genetic variants of a specific trait in such proportions that they cannot be maintained simply by mutation. Examples include the sickle cell trait, the Rh factor, and the blood groups.

genetics /jənet′iks/, **1.** the science that studies the principles and mechanics of heredity, specifically the means by which traits are passed from parents to offspring and the causes of the similarities and differences between related organisms. **2.** the total genetic makeup of a particular individual, family, group, or condition.

genetic screening, the process of investigating a specific population of persons for the purpose of detecting the presence of disease, either incipient or overt.

gene transfer [Gk, *genein,* to produce; L, *transferre,* to bring across], a type of gene therapy in which a gene is transplanted from a donor organism into a recipient organism.

geniculate neuralgia /jənik′yəlāt/ [L, *geniculum,* little knee; Gk, *neuron,* nerve, *algos,* pain], a severe debilitating inflammatory condition of the geniculate ganglion of the facial nerve characterized by pain in the ear, loss of the sense of taste, facial paralysis, and a decrease in salivation and lacrimation. It sometimes follows herpes zoster infection.

genioglossus, one of the thick, fan-shaped extrinsic muscles that depress the central part of the tongue and protrude the anterior part of the tongue out of the oral fissure.

geniohyoideus /jē′nē·ōhī·oi′dē·əs/ [Gk, *genion,* chin, *hyoides,* Y-shaped], one of the four suprahyoid muscles that draw the hyoid bone and the tongue forward.

genitals /jen′itəlz/ [L, *genitalis*], the sex, or reproductive, organs visible on the outside of the body. In the female, they include the vulva, mons veneris, labia majora, labia minora, clitoris, and vaginal vestibule. The male genitals include the penis, scrotum, and testicles. —**genital,** *adj.*

genital stage /jen′itəl/ [L, *genitalis*; Fr, *stage,* trial period], in psychoanalysis, the final period in freudian psychosexual development, beginning with adolescence and continuing through the adult years when the genitals are the predominant source of pleasurable stimulation.

genital wart [L, *genitalis*; AS, *wearte*], a small soft, moist pink or red swelling of the genitals that becomes pedunculated and may be painless, caused by the human papillomavirus. The growth may be solitary, or a cauliflower-like group may be present in the same area of the genitalia. Atypical genital warts should be biopsied and examined as possible carcinomas because they are associated with cervical cancer.

genitourinary (GU) /jen′itōyŏŏr′iner′ē/ [L, *genitalis*; Gk, *ouron,* urine], referring to the genital and urinary systems of the body: the organ structures, functions, or both.

genitourinary fistula, an abnormal communication between organs of the urogenital system or between organs of the urogenital system and some other system.

genocide /jen′əsīd/, the systematic extermination of a national, ethnic, political, religious, or other population.

genogram /jē′nōgram/, a diagram that depicts family relationships over at least three generations.

genome /jē′nōm/ [Gk, *genein,* to produce], the complete set of genes in the chromosomes of each cell of a specific organism. —**genomic,** *adj.*

genome map, a graphic representation of the locations of genes in a genome.

genomic /jēnō′mik/, pertaining to the genome.

genomic imprinting, differential expression of a gene or genes as a function of whether they were inherited from the male or the female parent (e.g., a deletion on chromosome 15 that causes Prader-Willi syndrome if inherited from the father instead causes Angelman's syndrome if inherited from the mother).

genotoxic /jē′nōtok′sik/, capable of altering DNA, thereby causing cancer or mutation.

genotoxic carcinogens, cancer-causing agents that can alter DNA molecules.

genotype /jē′nōtīp′/ [Gk, *genos*, birth, *typos*, mark], **1.** the complete genetic constitution of an organism or group, as determined by the specific combination and location of the genes on the chromosomes. **2.** the alleles situated at one or more sites on homologous chromosomes. **3.** a group or class of organisms having the same genetic makeup; the type species of a genus. —**genotypic,** *adj.*

gentamicin sulfate /jen′təmī′sin/, an aminoglycoside antibiotic prescribed for the treatment of severe infections caused by organisms sensitive to gentamicin, especially gram-negative organisms.

gentian violet /jen′shən/, a topical antibacterial and antifungal agent used to treat superficial *Candida* infections of the skin and vagina. It is also effective against some superficial bacterial infections such as those caused by *Staphylococcus.*

gentiotannic acid /jen′shē-ōtan′ik/, a form of tannic acid once used as an astringent and in the treatment of burns but no longer recommended because of its hepatotoxicity.

Gentran 40, a trademark for a plasma volume extender (dextran 40).

Gentran 70, a trademark for a plasma volume extender (dextran 70).

genu /jē′nōō/ [L, knee], the knee or any angular structure resembling the flexed knee.

genupectoral position /jē′nōōpek′tərəl/ [L, *genu,* knee, *pectus,* breast, *positio*], knee-chest position. To assume the genupectoral position the person kneels so that the weight of the body is supported by the knees and chest, with the buttocks raised. The head is turned to one side and the arms are flexed so that the upper part of the body can be supported in part by the elbows.

genu recurvatum [L, *genu,* knee, *recurvare,* to bend back], a deformity in which the lower leg is hyperextended at the knee joint.

genus /jē′nəs/ *pl.* **genera** [L, kind], a subdivision of a family of organisms. A genus usually is composed of several closely related species. The genus *Homo* has only one species, *Homo sapiens* (humans).

genu valgum [L, *genu,* knee, *valgus,* bent inward], a deformity in which the legs are curved inward, so that the knees are close together and strike each other as the person walks, and the ankles are widely separated.

genu varum [L, knee, *varus,* bent outward], a deformity in which one or both legs are bent outward at the knee.

Geocillin, a trademark for an antibacterial (carbenicillin indanyl sodium).

geographic retinal atrophy, a pattern of well-demarcated epithelial atrophy of retinal pigment leading to vision loss, most often associated with age-related macular degeneration.

geographic tongue /jē′əgraf′ik/ [Gk, *ge,* earth, *graphein,* to record; AS, *tunge*], a common benign condition in which the dorsum of the tongue possesses multiple zones of erythema surrounded by slightly elevated yellow-white borders. The pattern of lesions can change in appearance every few days or weeks. Patients may experience no sensation, or tenderness with a burning sensation.

geometric unsharpness, image blur resulting from the finite size of the x-ray tube focal spot (as opposed to a point source).

geophagia, the practice of eating clay or dirt. A form of pica, the compulsion is thought by some to be associated with disorders of mineral balance.

geotrichosis /jē′ōtrikō′sis/ [Gk, *ge,* earth, *thrix,* hair, *osis,* condition], a condition associated with the fungus *Geotrichum candidum,* which can cause oral, bronchial, pharyngeal, and intestinal disorders. Geotrichosis most commonly occurs in immunosuppressed individuals with diabetes. Geotrichosis has been associated with allergic asthmatic reactions similar to allergic aspergillosis and a type of intestinal disorder characterized by abdominal pain, diarrhea, and rectal bleeding.

Gerbich blood group /gər′bich/, a blood group consisting of three high-prevalence erythrocytic antigens, Ge 2, Ge 3, and Ge 4, and five antigens of very low prevalence.

GERD, abbreviation for *gastroesophageal reflux disease.*

geriatric day care /jer′ē-at′rik/ [Gk, *geras,* old age; AS, *daeg*; L, *garrire,* chatter], an ambulatory health care facility for elderly people who require continual supervision or assistance. It usually offers a broad range of professional and community services to maximize functional independence of the patients.

Geriatric Depression Scale (GDS), a brief depression screening inventory composed of 30 items that require yes or no answers. A score of 11 or above indicates depressed individuals.

geriatric education for emergency medical services (GEMS), a continuing education program, developed by the American Geriatrics Society and the National Council of State Emergency Medical Services Training Coordinators, to train first responders, EMTs, paramedics, and other emergency care providers to deliver state-of-the-art prehospital care to older adults.

geriatrician /jer′ē-ətrish′ən/, a physician who has specialized postgraduate education and experience in the medical care of older persons.

geriatric nurse practitioner (GNP), a registered nurse with additional education obtained through a master's degree program in nursing that prepares the nurse to deliver primary health care to elderly adults.

geriatrics /jer'ē·at'riks/, the branch of medicine dealing with the physiologic characteristics of aging and the diagnosis and treatment of diseases affecting the aged.

germ /jurm/ [L, *germen*, sprout], **1.** *non-technical,* any microorganism, especially one that is pathogenic. **2.** a unit of living matter able to develop into a self-sufficient organism, such as a seed, spore, or egg. **3.** in embryology, the first stage in development, such as a spermatozoon or other germ cell.

German cockroach, *Blattella germanica,* a small light brown species found as a household pest in North America and Europe.

germanium (Ge) /jərmā'nē·əm/ [Germany], a metallic element with some nonmetallic semiconductor properties. Its atomic number is 32, and its atomic mass is 72.61.

germ cell, 1. a sexual reproductive cell in any stage of development, from the primordial embryonic form to the mature gamete. **2.** an ovum or a spermatozoon or any of their preceding forms. **3.** any cell undergoing gametogenesis.

germ-free animal, a laboratory animal raised under sterile conditions, free of exposure to microorganisms.

germicide /jur'misīd/ [L, *germen,* sprout, *caedere,* to kill], a drug that kills pathogenic microorganisms. —**germicidal,** *adj.*

germinal /jur'minəl/ [L, *germen,* sprout], pertaining to or characteristic of a germ cell or to the early stages of development.

germinal center [L, *germen,* sprout; Gk, *kentron,* center], an antigen-localizing follicle of lymphoid tissue, occupying the center of the lymphatic nodules of the spleen, tonsils, and lymph nodes. It reacts to antigens, enlarging and becoming filled with lymphoblasts and macrophages at the center of a ring of small lymphocytes.

germinal cords, the precursors to the embryonic ovary or testis, derived from the gonadal cords.

germinal epithelium, 1. the epithelial layer covering the genital ridge from which the gonads are derived in early embryonic development. **2.** the epithelial covering of the ovary, formerly thought to be the site of the formation of the oogonia.

germinal infection, an infection transmitted to a child by the ovum or sperm of a parent.

germinal stage, in embryology, the interval of time from fertilization to implantation during which the ovum undergoes cell division several times, travels to the uterus, and, in the form of a blastocyst, begins to implant itself in the endometrium.

germination /jur'minā'shən/ [L, *germen,* sprout], **1.** the initial growth and development of an organism from the time of fertilization to the formation of the embryo. **2.** the sprouting of a spore or the seed of a plant. —**germinate,** *v.*

germinoma /jur'minō'mə/, a neoplasm of the germinal tissue of the gonads, the mediastinum, or the pineal region. It is commonly associated with pituitary disorders.

germ layer, one of the three primordial cell layers formed during gastrulation in the early stages of embryonic development from which the entire range of body tissue is derived.

germ line, genetic material in a cell lineage that is passed down through the gametes before it is modified by somatic recombination or maturation.

germ plasm, 1. the part of a germ cell that contains the reproductive and hereditary material; the total of the DNA in a specific cell or organism. **2.** *nontechnical.* germ cells in any stage of development together with the tissues from which they originated.

germ theory [L, *germen,* sprout; Gk, *theoria,* speculation], the concept that all infectious and contagious diseases are caused by living microorganisms. The science of bacteriology developed after establishment of this theory.

geroderma /jer'ədur'mə/ [Gk, *geron,* old man, *derma,* skin], **1.** the atrophic skin of aging. **2.** skin that is thin and wrinkled as a result of a defective state of nutrition. **3.** any condition characterized by skin that is thin and wrinkled, resembling the skin of old age.

gerodontics /jer'ōdon'tiks/ [Gk, *geron,* old man, *odous,* tooth], the delivery of dental care to aging persons; the diagnosis, prevention, and treatment of dental problems peculiar to advanced age.

gerontic nursing, nursing care pertaining to an older person, a compromise between geriatric nursing (nursing care primarily for older persons who are ill) and gerontologic nursing (a more holistic view of the nursing care of older persons).

gerontogen /jeron'təjən/, an environmental agent that contributes to the aging process by accelerating the onset and/or rate of progression of aging.

Gerontological Society of America (GSA), an organization of scientific and academic professionals interested in studies of the nature of the aging process and the clinical manifestations of disease in the aging organism.

gerontologic rehabilitation nursing, a nursing specialty whose focus is helping elderly individuals affected by chronic illness or physical disability to adapt to their disabilities and to achieve their optimal level of physical, mental, and psychosocial well-being.

gerontology /jer′əntol′əjē/ [Gk, *geras,* old age, *logos,* science], the study of all aspects of the aging process, including the clinical, psychologic, economic, and sociologic issues encountered by older persons and their consequences for both the individual and society.

gerontotoxon, an abnormal white or gray opaque ring at the outer edge of the cornea. It results from deposits of cholesterol in the cornea or from degeneration of the cornea's supporting framework.

geropsychiatry /jer′ōsīkī′ətrē/ [Gk, *geras,* old age, *psyche,* mind], the study and treatment of psychiatric aspects of aging and mental disorders of elderly people or the functional/mental disorders of people in their 50s and 60s if they qualify.

Gerson diet, a detoxification diet, claimed to be useful in the treatment of cancer, allergies, and a wide variety of degenerative diseases, consisting of large quantities of organically grown fruits and vegetables, consumed mainly in the form of juice. The U.S. Food and Drug Administration has warned against this regimen.

Gerstmann's syndrome /gerst′mänz/ [Josef Gerstmann, Austrian neurologist, 1887–1969], a combination of finger agnosia, right-left disorientation, agraphia, acalculia, and often constructional apraxia. It is often associated with dominant parietal lobe lesions.

Gerstmann-Sträussler-Scheinker syndrome /gerst′män shtrois′ler shīn′ker/, a group of rare prion diseases, inherited as an autosomal-dominant trait but linked to different mutations of the prion protein gene. All forms of the syndrome have the common characteristics of cognitive and motor disturbances and the presence of numerous amyloid plaques in the brain.

Gesell Developmental Assessment [Arnold L. Gesell, American pediatrician and psychologist, 1880–1961], an evaluation program that provides information by direct observation on gross motor, fine motor, language, personal-social, and cognitive development.

Gestalt /gəshtält′/ *pl.* **Gestalts, Gestalten** [Ger, form], a single physical, psychologic, or symbolic configuration, pattern, or experience that consists of a number of elements and has an effect as a whole different from that of the sum of its parts.

Gestalt psychology, a school of psychology, originating in Germany, that maintains that a psychologic phenomenon is perceived as a total configuration or pattern, rising from the relationships among its constituent elements, rather than as discrete elements possessing attributes of their own, and that the pattern, or Gestalt, cannot be derived from the summation of its constituents. Thus learning is regarded as resulting from insight, defined as a process or reorganization, rather than from association or trial and error, and behavior is seen as an integrated response to a unitary situation rather than as a series of reflexes and sensations.

Gestalt therapy, a form of psychotherapy that stresses the unity of self-awareness, behavior, and experience.

gestate /jes′tāt/ [L, *gestare,* to bear], **1.** to carry a developing fetus in the womb. **2.** to grow and develop slowly toward maturity, such as a fetus in the womb.

gestation /jestā′shən/ [L, *gestare,* to bear], in a viviparous animal, the period from the fertilization of the ovum until birth. Gestation varies with the species.

gestational age /jestā′shənəl/ [L, *gestare* + *aetas,* time of life], the age of a fetus or a newborn, usually expressed in weeks dating from the first day of the mother's last menstrual period.

gestational assessment [L, *gestare,* to bear, *assidere,* to sit beside], calculation of the fetal age of the offspring, based on such factors as the menstrual history of the mother, the date when fetal heart sounds are first detected, and the evaluation of ultrasound data. The information is important in planning emergency care in the event of premature birth signs.

gestational diabetes mellitus (GDM), a disorder characterized by an impaired ability to metabolize carbohydrates, usually caused by a deficiency of insulin or insulin resistance, occurring in pregnancy. It disappears after delivery of the infant but, in a significant number of cases, returns years later as type 2 DM.

gestational hypertension, abnormally increased BP occurring in pregnancy, comprising the conditions preeclampsia and eclampsia.

gestational psychosis [L, *gestare,* to bear; Gk, *psyche,* mind, *osis,* condition], a psychotic episode that can be attributed to a pregnancy and resolves when pregnancy ends.

gestational sac, a pouch containing the fetus in extrauterine gestation.

gestation period [L, *gestare,* to bear; Gk, *peri,* near, *hodos,* way], the time span between conception and labor.

gestures in physical examination /jes'chərs/, physical appearance clues in diagnosis, such as a patient's pressing a clenched fist against the sternum as a "body language" message of the pain experienced during an MI.

Getman visuomotor theory [Gerald Getman], a concept that visual perception is based on developmental sequences of physiologic actions in children. The sequence of eight stages begins with innate response systems and advances to cognitive integration of perceptions, abstractions, and higher symbolic activity.

GFP, abbreviation for **green fluorescent protein.**

GFR, abbreviation for **glomerular filtration rate.**

GGT, abbreviation for **gamma-glutamyltransferase.**

GH, abbreviation for **growth hormone.**

Ghon focus, the primary parenchymal lesion of primary pulmonary TB in children.

Ghon's complex [Anton Ghon, Czechoslovakian pathologist, 1866–1936], a combination of pleural surface-healed granulomas, calcifications, or scars on the middle lobe of the lung together with hilar lymph node granulomas. The complex is evidence that a primary TB case has healed.

ghost cells [AS, *gast*; L, *cella,* storeroom], RBCs that have lost their hemoglobin so that only the plasma membranes are observed in microscopic examinations of urine samples.

GHRF, abbreviation for **growth hormone–releasing factor.**

GH-RH, abbreviation for **growth hormone–releasing hormone.**

GHRIH, abbreviation for *growth hormone release–inhibiting hormone.*

GI, abbreviation for **gastrointestinal.**

Gianotti-Crosti syndrome /jänot'ē kros'tē/ [Fernando Gianotti, Italian dermatologist, 1920–1984; Agostino Crosti, Italian dermatologist, 1896–1988], a generally benign and self-limited disease of young children that had previously been associated with hepatitis B virus now known to occur in other viral illnesses. It is characterized by the appearance of crops of usually nonpruritic, dusky or coppery red, flat-topped, firm papules forming a symmetric eruption on the face, buttocks, and limbs, including the palms and soles, and associated with malaise and low-grade fever.

giant axonal neuropathy, an autosomal-recessive neuropathy of childhood characterized by enlarged axons made up of masses of tightly woven neurofilaments.

giant cell /jī'ənt/ [L, *gigas,* huge, *cella,* storeroom], an abnormally large tissue cell that often contains more than one nucleus and may appear as a merger of several normal cells.

giant cell carcinoma, a malignant epithelial neoplasm characteristically containing many large anaplastic cells.

giant cell myeloma, a bone tumor of multinucleated giant cells that resembles osteoclasts scattered in a matrix of spindle cells. Myelomas of this kind may be benign or malignant.

giant chromosome, any of the excessively large chromosomes found in insects and certain other animals, including the lampbrush and polytene chromosomes.

giant condyloma, a destructive tumor resembling squamous cell carcinoma but actually a form of condyloma acuminatum, usually on the penis, but sometimes present elsewhere in the anogenital area in either men or women. It presents as a large verrucous to fungating, cauliflower-like mass that erodes the involved skin and progresses to penetrate and destroy deeper tissues.

giant follicular lymphoma, a nodular, well-differentiated lymphocytic malignant lymphoma in which nodules distort the normal structure of a lymph node.

giant hypertrophic gastritis, a rare disease characterized by large folds of nodular gastric rugae that may cover the wall of the stomach, causing anorexia, nausea, vomiting, and abdominal distress.

giant peristaltic contraction, a propulsive contraction of the bowel that normally occurs periodically in the distal small intestine and colon. The contractions are 1.5 to 2 times larger than normal in amplitude and 4 to 6 times longer in duration than usual.

Gianturco coil, a mechanism for occluding a patent ductus arteriosus.

Giardia /jē·är'dē·ə/ [Alfred Giard, French biologist, 1846–1908], a common genus of flagellate protozoans. Many species of *Giardia* normally inhabit the digestive tract and cause inflammation in association with other factors that produce rapid proliferation of the organism.

giardiasis /jē·ärdī'əsis/ [Alfred Giard; Gk, *osis,* condition], a diarrheal illness caused by infection with the protozoan *Giardia lamblia.* The source of infection is usually fecally contaminated water.

gibbus /gib'əs, jib'əs/ [L, hump], a hump, swelling, or enlargement on a body surface, usually confined to one side.

gibbus deformity, a form of structural kyphosis, usually secondary to TB infection of the thoracic vertebral body, in which the vertebral column becomes sharply angulated at the site of the lesion.

Gibson's murmur [George A. Gibson, Scottish physician, 1854–1913], a heart murmur that is heard continuously throughout the cardiac cycle in patients with patent ductus arteriosis. It waxes at the end of systole and wanes near the end of diastole and is often described as a "machinery-like" murmur.

Gibson walking splint, a kind of Thomas splint that enables a patient to be ambulatory.

Giemsa's stain /gē·em′səz/ [Gustav Giemsa, German chemist, 1867–1948; Fr, *teindre,* to dye], an azure dye used as a stain in the microscopic examination of the blood for certain protozoal parasites, viral inclusion bodies, and rickettsiae and, more routinely, in the preparation of a smear for a differential white cell count. It is modified and combined with Wright's stain to better detect organisms.

GIFT, abbreviation for **gamete intrafallopian transfer.**

gigantism /jigan′tizəm/ [L, *gigas,* giant], an abnormal condition characterized by excessive size and stature. It is caused most frequently by hypersecretion of growth hormone (GH) that occurs prior to the closure of the bone epiphyses; it occurs to a lesser degree in hypogonadism and in certain genetic disorders. Excessive linear growth often occurs in males with more than one Y chromosome, and it may also accompany Klinefelter's syndrome, Marfan's syndrome, and some cases of generalized lipodystrophy.

Gilbert's syndrome [Nicolas A. Gilbert, French physician, 1858–1927], a benign hereditary condition characterized by hyperbilirubinemia and jaundice.

Gilles de la Tourette's syndrome /zhēl də lä tŏŏrets′/ [George Gilles de la Tourette, French neurologist, 1857–1927], an abnormal condition characterized by facial grimaces, vocalizations, tics, and involuntary arm and shoulder movements. In adolescence the condition worsens. Coprolalia can develop. In adulthood the condition usually lessens and tends to wax and wane. Treatment with dopamine antagonists has been found to be very effective, demonstrating an organic cause for this syndrome.

Gillies' operation /gil′ēz/ [Harold D. Gillies, English surgeon, 1882–1960], a surgical procedure for reducing fractures of the zygoma and zygomatic arch by making an incision in the temporal hairline.

Gil-Vernet technique, a type of ureteroneocystostomy in which both ureters are excised from their normal attachments to the bladder and reattached medially near each other within the trigone.

ginger, a herb used for nausea, motion sickness, indigestion, and inflammation. Ginger does appear to be effective against motion sickness but does not help treat nausea from other causes. Its efficacy as an antiinflammatory drug has not been established. It is considered safe when consumed in food.

ginger paralysis /jin′jər/, a polyneuropathy that primarily affects motor nerves to the distal parts of the extremities. First observed in the 1930s during prohibition in the United States, it is caused by drinking an alcoholic extract of Jamaican ginger adulterated by a pesticide.

gingiva /jinjī′və/ *pl.* **gingivae** [L, gum], the gum tissues of the mouth, consisting of a mucous membrane with supporting fibrous tissue that overlies the crowns of unerupted teeth and encircles the necks of teeth that have erupted.—**gingival,** *adj.*

gingival /jin′jival/, pertaining to the gingivae.

gingival blanching [L, *gingiva;* Fr, *blanchir,* to whiten], the lightening of gum color, usually temporary, caused by stretching or pressure upon gum tissue and decreased blood supply.

gingival blood supply, the vascular supply to the gums. It rises from blood vessels that pass along the outer periosteum of bone and anastomose with vessels of the periodontal membrane as well as intraalveolar blood vessels.

gingival cavity, a tooth cavity that occurs in the third of the clinical crown nearest to the gum.

gingival color, the color of gum tissue. It is affected by the thickness and degree of keratinization of the epithelium, blood supply, pigmentation, medications, and periodontal, gingival, and systemic diseases.

gingival consistency, the combination of tactile and visual characteristics of healthy gum tissue. The tissue should be firm and resilient and should resemble smooth velvet or a finely or coarsely grained orange peel.

gingival corium, the most stable connective tissue of the gingiva, which lies between the periosteum and the lamina propria mucosae.

gingival crater, a depression in the gum tissue, especially in the area of the former apex of interdental papilla. It is commonly caused by necrotizing ulcerative gingivitis and food impaction against the tissue subjacent to the contact areas of adjacent teeth.

gingival crevice, a normal space located around a tooth between the wall of the unattached gum tissue and the enamel and/or cementum of the tooth.

gingival cyst, a developmental nonkeratinizing odontogenic cyst found in the oral soft tissue of adults.

gingival discoloration, a change in the normal color of the gum tissue, associated with inflammation, reduced blood supply, abnormal pigmentation, and other problems.

gingival disease, any disease of the gingivae, such as gingivitis. The American Academy of Periodontology classifies gingival disease as a major group of periodontal diseases and distinguishes two main subgroups: those gingival diseases induced by dental plaque and those attributed to other causes, which include viral infections, fungal infections, genetic predispositions, systemic conditions, allergic reactions, and traumatic lesions.

gingival festoon, the distinct rounding and enlargement of the margins of the gum tissue found in early gingival involvement.

gingival hormonal enlargement, swelling of the gums associated with poor oral hygiene and hormonal imbalance during pregnancy, puberty, or postmenopausal therapy.

gingival hyperplasia, an increase in the number of cells of the gum tissues, resulting in an overgrowth that may partially or totally cover the teeth; may be generalized or localized. Causes include hereditary and metabolic disorders, or drugs such as the anticonvulsants phenytoin and carbamazepine; cyclosporine, a potent immunosuppressant used for organ transplant recipients; calcium channel blockers, such as nifedipine and amlodipine, used for the treatment of hypertension; the antibiotic erythromycin; and oral contraceptives. While the cause is considered to be multifactorial, the presence of gingival inflammation due to poor oral hygiene can contribute to the development. The presence of malpositioned teeth or orthodontic bands can exaggerate the condition. Treatment includes surgical excision of the enlarged tissue, followed by meticulous oral hygiene. Compare **fibromatosis.**

gingival hypertrophy, an increase in the size of gum tissue encircling the teeth. It may be caused by gum inflammation and periodontal disease.

gingival line [L, *gingiva,* gum + *linea*], the scalloped line formed by the edge of the unattached gum tissue at the margin of the soft tissues beside the teeth.

gingival massage, the mechanical rubbing of the gum tissues for cleansing purposes, for improvement of tissue tone and blood circulation, and for keratinization of the surface epithelium.

gingival mat, the connective tissue of the gum, composed of coarse, broad collagen fibers that attach the gingivae to the teeth and hold the unattached gum close to the teeth.

gingival physiology, the function of the gum tissue as supportive and protective investments of the teeth and subjacent tissues.

gingival position, the level of the gum margin in relation to the teeth.

gingival shrinkage, the reduction in the mass and height of the gum tissue, especially as a result of the therapeutic elimination of subgingival deposits and curettage of the soft tissue wall of the gingival pocket.

gingival stippling, numerous small depressions in the surface of healthy gum tissue, producing an appearance that varies from that of smooth velvet to that of an orange peel.

gingivectomy /jin′jĭvek′təmē/ [L, *gingiva*; Gk, *ektomē*, excision], surgical removal of infected and diseased gum tissue, performed to arrest the progress of periodontal disease.

gingivitis /jin′jivī′tis/ [L, *gingiva*; Gk, *itis*, inflammation], inflammation of the gingiva, with symptoms that may include redness, swelling, and bleeding. Gingivitis is generally the result of poor oral hygiene and of the accumulation of bacterial plaque on the teeth, but it may be a sign of other conditions, such as DM, leukemia, hormonal changes, or vitamin deficiency. It is common in pregnancy, is usually painless, and may be acute or chronic. Research is finding associations between the occurrence of periodontal disease and heart disease, stroke, asthma, and low birth weight neonates.

gingivoplasty /jin′jivōplas′tē/ [L, *gingiva*; Gk, *plassein*, to shape], the surgical contouring of the gum tissues and interdental papillae to restore gingival tissue to more normal form and function.

gingivostomatitis /jin′jivōstō′mətī′tis/ [L, *gingiva*; Gk, *stoma*, mouth, *itis*, inflammation], multiple painful ulcers on the gums and mucous membranes of the mouth, the result of a herpesvirus infection.

ginkgo, a herbal product used for poor circulation, diabetes, vascular disease, cancer, inflammatory disorders, impotence, and degenerative nerve conditions. It is also used for age-related declines in cognition and memory. Ginkgo is generally considered to have some efficacy against dementia, sometimes estimated as being equivalent to a 6-month delay in disease progression.

ginseng, a herb used for physical and mental exhaustion, stress, viral infections, diabetes, sluggishness, fatigue, weak immunity, and convalescence. It may have some efficacy (e.g., better stress tolerance, reaction times, abstract thinking).

Giordano-Giovannetti diet /jôrdä′nō jō′vənet′ē/, a low-protein, low-fat, high-carbohydrate diet with controlled potassium and sodium intake, used in chronic renal insufficiency and liver failure. Protein is given only in the form of essential amino acids so that the body will use excess BUN to synthesize the nonessential amino acids for the production of tissue protein.

gipoma /gipō′mə/, a pancreatic tumor that causes changes in secretion of gastric inhibitory polypeptide.

girdle /gur′dəl/, any curved or circular structure, such as the hipline formed by the bones and related tissues of the pelvis.

girdle pad, a covering that fits over the iliac crests and sacrum to protect the hip area in contact sports.

GI tract, abbreviation for **gastrointestinal tract.**

Giuliani's sign [Emilio R. Giuliani, twentieth-century American cardiologist], a posterior chest thrill felt between the left scapula and spinal column in mitral insufficiency caused by anterior mitral leaf prolapse.

glabella /gləbəl′ə/ [L, glabrum, bald], a flat triangular area of bone between the two superciliary ridges of the forehead. It is sometimes used as a baseline for cephalometric measurements.

glabella tap, a tap on the glabella to test the glabella tap reflex. Normally the patient stops blinking after the second or third tap, but in Parkinson's disease and certain kinds of cerebral degeneration the blinking continues even after many taps.

glabrous skin /glā′brəs/ [L, glaber, smooth; AS, scinn], smooth, hairless skin.

glacial acetic acid /glā′shəl/, a clear, colorless liquid or crystalline substance (CH_3COOH) with a pungent odor. It is obtained by the destructive distillation of wood or from acetylene and water or by the oxidation of ethyl alcohol by aerobic bacteria, as in the production of vinegar. Glacial acetic acid is strongly corrosive and potentially flammable, having a low flash point.

gland [L, glans, acorn], any one of many organs in the body, comprising specialized cells that secrete or excrete materials not related to their ordinary metabolism. Some glands lubricate; others, such as the pituitary gland, produce hormones; hematopoietic glands, such as the spleen and certain lymph nodes, take part in the production of blood components.

glanders [OFr, glandres, neck gland swelling], an infection caused by the bacillus Burkholderia mallei, transmitted to humans from horses and other domestic animals. It is characterized by purulent inflammation of the mucous membranes and development of skin nodules that ulcerate.

glands of bile duct, tubuloacinar glands in the mucosa of the bile ducts and the neck of the gallbladder.

glandular epithelium [L, glandula, small gland; Gk, epi, above, thele, nipple], epithelium that contains glandular cells.

glandular hypospadias [L, glandula, small gland, hypo, under, spadōn, a rent], the most common type of hypospadias, in which the urethral orifice opens at the site of the frenum, which may be rudimentary or absent. The normal site of the urinary meatus is represented on the glans penis as a blind pit.

glandular tissue [L, glandula, small gland; OFr, tissu], a group of epithelial secreting cells composing a definitive glandular organ, such as the thyroid.

glans /glanz/ pl. **glandes** [L, acorn], **1.** a general term for a small rounded mass or a glandlike body. **2.** erectile tissue.

glans of clitoris [L, glans; Gk, kleitoris], the erectile tissue at the end of the clitoris. It comprises two corpora cavernosa enclosed in a dense, fibrous membrane and connected to the pubis and ischium.

glans penis, the conical tip of the penis that covers the end of the corpora cavernosa penis and the corpus spongiosum like a cap. The urethral orifice is normally located at the distal tip of the glans penis.

glare, a strong, dazzling light that may cause discomfort to the eye.

Glasgow Coma Scale, a quick, practical standardized system for assessing the degree of consciousness in the critically ill and for predicting the duration and ultimate outcome of coma, primarily in patients with head injuries. The system involves eye opening, verbal response, and motor response, all of which are evaluated independently according to a rank order that indicates the LOC and degree of dysfunction. A score of 15 indicates no impairment, 3 is compatible with brain death, and 7 is usually accepted as a state of coma.

Glasgow Outcome Scale, a functional assessment inventory based on five global categories: death, persistent vegetative state, severe disability, moderate disability, and good recovery. It measures outcome. It has been criticized as lacking sensitivity to functionally significant changes.

glass ionomer cement, a dental cement used for small restorations on the proximal surfaces of anterior teeth, for restoration of eroded areas at the gingival margin, as a base material under dental restorations, and as a luting agent for restorations and orthodontic bands.

glatiramer, an MS drug used to reduce the frequency of relapses in patients with relapsing-remitting MS.

glaucoma /glôkō′mə, glou-/ [Gk, cataract], an abnormal condition of elevated pressure within an eye that occurs when aqueous production exceeds aqueous outflow, resulting in damage to the optic nerve. Acute glaucoma occurs if the pupil in an eye with a narrow angle between the iris and cornea dilates markedly, causing obstruction of aqueous humor drainage from the anterior chamber. Primary open-angle glaucoma is much more common; it develops slowly and insidiously without a narrow angle. Peripheral visual field losses are most common, developing often without the patient's awareness until there is very serious disease. The obstruction is believed to occur within the trabecular meshworks.—**glaucomatous,** adj.

glaucomatocyclitic crisis /glôkom′-ətōsiklit′ik/, a recurrent rise in intraocular pressure in one eye, resembling acute angle-closure glaucoma, associated with minimal signs of uveitis.

glaucomatous halo /glôkom′ətəs/, **1.** an illusion of a circle of brightness surrounding a light, observed by patients with acute glaucoma, which is caused by edema of the corneal epithelium. **2.** a yellowish white ring surrounding the optic disc, a sign of atrophy of the choroid in glaucoma.

glaze /glāz/ [ME, glasen], **1.** to cover with a glossy, smooth surface or coating. **2.** a ceramic veneer added to a dental porcelain restoration after it has been fired, to give a completely nonporous, glossy, or semiglossy surface. **3.** the final firing (in air) of dental porcelain, when formation of a thin, vitreous, glossy surface takes place.

glenohumeral /glē′nōhyōō′mərəl/ [Gk, glene, joint socket; L, humerus, shoulder], pertaining to the glenoid cavity and the humerus at the shoulder joint.

glenohumeral joint, the shoulder joint, formed by the glenoid cavity of the scapula and the head of the humerus.

glenohumeral ligaments [Gk, glene, joint socket; humerus, shoulder], three thickened bands of connective tissue attached proximally to the anterior margin of the glenoid cavity and distally to the neck of the humerus.

glenoid cavity /glē′noid/ [Gk, glene, joint socket; eidos, form; L, cavum], a shallow socket with which the head of the humerus articulates below the acromium at the junction of the superior and axillary borders.

glenoid labrum, a fibrocartilaginous collar that deepens and expands the glenoid cavity.

glia cells /glī′ə, glē′ə/ [Gk, glia, glue; L, cella, storeroom], neural cells that have a connective-tissue-supporting function in the CNS.

gliadin /glī′ədin/ [Gk, glia, glue], a fraction of the gluten protein that is found in wheat and rye and to a lesser extent in barley and oats. Those with celiac disease are sensitive to this substance, and it is excluded from their diet.

gliadin and endomysial antibodies testing, a blood test to assist in the identification of celiac disease and to monitor disease status and dietary compliance.

glial cell line–derived neurotrophic factor (GDNF) /glī′əl/, a nerve growth drug that has been used in laboratory animals to reverse the progression of symptoms of Parkinson's disease and other brain diseases.

gliding [AS, glidan, to glide], **1.** one of the four basic movements allowed by the various joints of the skeleton. It is common to all movable joints and permits one surface to move smoothly over an adjacent surface, regardless of shape. **2.** a smooth, continuous movement.

gliding contusion, a brain injury caused by displacement of the gray matter of the cerebral cortex during angular acceleration of the head. Most of the damage occurs at the junction between the gray matter and the white matter. Such contusions are associated with diffuse axonal injuries and acute subdural hematomas.

gliding joint, a synovial joint in which articulation of contiguous bones allows only gliding movements, as in the wrist and the ankle.

gliding testis, an undescended testis that can reach the top of the scrotum but then glides back up.

gliding zone, an articular cartilage surface area immediately adjacent to a joint space.

glimepiride /glimep′irīd/, a sulfonylurea compound used as a hypoglycemic in treatment of type 2 DM.

glioblastoma multiforme /glī′ōblastō′mə mul′tifôr′mē/ [Gk, glia, glue, blastos, germ, oma, tumor; L, multus, many, forma, form], a malignant, invasive, rapidly growing pulpy or cystic tumor of the cerebrum or the spinal cord. The lesion spreads with pseudopod-like projections.

glioma /glī·ō′mə/ pl. **gliomas, gliomata** [Gk, glia + oma, tumor], any of the largest group of primary tumors of the brain, composed of malignant glial cells.

glioneuroma /glī′ōnōōrō′mə/ pl. **glioneuromas, glioneuromata** [Gk, glia + neuron, nerve, oma, tumor], a neoplasm composed of nerve cells and elements of their supporting connective tissue.

gliosarcoma /glī′ōsärkō′mə/ pl. **gliosarcomas, gliosarcomata** [Gk, glia + sarx, flesh, oma, tumor], a tumor composed of spindle-shaped cells in the delicate supporting connective tissue of nerve cells.

gliosis /glī·ō′sis/, a proliferation of astrocytes that may appear as a sign of healing after a CNS injury.

glipiZIDE /glip′izīd/, an oral antidiabetic drug prescribed as an adjunct to diet and exercise to lower blood glucose levels of patients with type 2 (non-insulin-dependent) DM.

Glisson's capsule /glis′ənz/ [Francis Glisson, English physician, 1597–1677; L, *capsula,* little box], the fibrous outer tissue sheath around lobules of the liver that carry branches of the hepatic artery, portal vein, and bile duct.

glitter cells [ME, *gliteren,* to shine], WBCs in which movement of granules is observed in their cytoplasm. They are seen in microscopic examination of urine samples in cases of pyelonephritis or disorders marked by low osmolality.

Gln, abbreviation for **glutamine.**

global aphasia /glō′bəl/ [L, *globus,* ball; Gk, *a + phasis,* without speech], a loss of ability to use or comprehend any form of written or spoken language. The condition involves both sensory and motor nerve tracts.

Global Assessment of Functioning (GAF) scale, a scale used to assess psychiatric status, measuring psychologic, social, and occupational functioning. It is widely used in studies of treatment effectiveness.

global price, in U.S. managed care, an all-inclusive price for services rendered. It may refer to comprehensive physician services alone or include both hospital and physician services, depending on the contractual agreement.

global warming, an ecologic model of world climate changes based on the **greenhouse effect,** exacerbated by burning of fossil fuels, massive deforestation, and conversion of cropland to industrial and other urban uses, all contributing to an increase in the earth's temperature.

globin /glō′bin/ [L, *globus,* ball], a group of four protein molecules that become bound by the iron in heme molecules to form hemoglobin or myoglobin.

globose nucleus, one of four deeply placed cerebellar nuclei located medially to the emboliform nucleus. It receives input from the intermediate zone of the cerebellar cortex, and its axons exit via the superior cerebellar peduncle.

globule /glob′yōōl/ [L, *globulus,* small ball], a small spheric mass.

globulin /glob′yōōlin/, one of a broad category of simple proteins classified by solubility, electrophoretic mobility, and molecular weight.

globulinuria /-ōōr′ē·ə/ [L, *globulus,* small ball; Gk, *ouron,* urine], the presence of globulin-class proteins in the urine.

globus hystericus /glō′bus/ [L, small ball; Gk, *hystera,* womb], a transitory sensation of a lump in the throat that cannot be swallowed or coughed up, often accompanying emotional conflict or acute anxiety.

globus pallidus /pal′idəs/ [L, small ball + pale], the smaller and more medial part of the lentiform nucleus of the brain, separated from the putamen by the lateral medullary lamina.

glomangioma /glōman′jē·ō′mə/ *pl.* **glomangiomas, glomangiomata** [L, *glomus,* ball of thread; Gk, *angeion,* vessel + *oma*] a benign tumor that develops as a cluster of blood cells in the skin.

glomerular disease, any of a group of diseases in which the glomerulus of the kidney is affected. Depending on the particular disease, there may be hyperplasia, atrophy, necrosis, scarring, or deposits in the glomeruli.

glomerular endothelium, another name for the entire visceral layer of the kidney.

glomerular filtration, the renal process whereby fluid in the blood is filtered across the capillaries of the glomerulus and into the urinary space of Bowman's capsule.

glomerular filtration rate (GFR) [L, *glomerulus,* small ball; Fr, *filtre*; L, *ratus*], a kidney function test in which results are determined from the amount of ultrafiltrate formed by plasma flowing through the glomeruli of the kidney. The amount may be calculated from inulin and creatinine clearance, serum creatinine, and BUN. The GFR can also be estimated from equations that include creatinine, age, gender, and ethnicity.

glomerular proteinuria, the most common kind of proteinuria, caused by glomerular disease and abnormal permeability of the glomerular capillaries to protein.

glomerulonephritis /glōmer′yōōlōnəfrī′tis/ [L, *glomerulus,* small ball; Gk, *nephros,* kidney + *itis*], an inflammation of the glomerulus of the kidney, characterized by proteinuria, hematuria, decreased urine production, and edema.

glomerulosclerosis /-sklərō′sis/ [L, *glomerulus,* small ball; Gk, *sklerosis,* a hardening, *osis,* condition], a severe kidney disease in which glomerular function of blood filtration is lost as fibrous scar tissue replaces the glomeruli. The disease commonly follows an infection or arteriosclerosis.

glomerulotubular balance, the balance between reabsorption of solutes in the proximal renal tubules and glomerular filtration, which must be as constant as possible. If the glomerular filtration rate rises or falls, the rate of tubular reabsorption must rise or fall proportionally. Balance is maintained by neural, hormonal, and other mechanisms.

glomerulus /glōmer′yŏŏləs/ pl. **glomeruli** [L, small ball], **1.** a tuft or cluster. **2.** a structure composed of blood vessels or nerve fibers, such as a renal glomerulus. —**glomerular,** adj.

glomus /glŏ′məs/ pl. **glomera** [L, ball of thread], a small group of arterioles connecting directly to veins and having a rich nerve supply.

glomus cell, 1. an epithelioid cell surrounding a coiled arteriovenous anastomosis of a glomus body. **2.** a modified smooth muscle cell.

glomus tumor, a frequently painful neoplasm involving the arteriovenous anastomoses of the skin.

glossectomy /glosek′təmē/ [Gk, glossa, tongue, ektomē, excision], the surgical removal of all or a part of the tongue.

glossitis /glosī′tis/ [Gk, glossa, tongue + itis], inflammation of the tongue. Acute glossitis, characterized by swelling, intense pain that may be referred to the ears, salivation, fever, and enlarged regional lymph nodes, may develop during an infectious disease or after a burn, bite, or other injury.

glossodynia /glos′ōdin′ē·ə/ [Gk, glossa + odyne, pain], pain in the tongue caused by acute or chronic inflammation, an abscess, an ulcer, or trauma.

glossoepiglottic /glos′ō·ep′iglot′ik/, pertaining to the epiglottis and the tongue.

glossolalia /glos′ōlā′lyə/ [Gk, glossa + lalein, to babble], speech in an unknown "language," as "speaking in tongues" during a state of religious ecstasy.

glossoncus /glosong′kəs/ [Gk, glossa + onkos, swelling], a local swelling or general enlargement of the tongue.

glossopathy /glosop′əthē/ [Gk, glossa + pathos, disease], a pathologic condition or disease of the tongue, such as acute inflammation caused by a burn, bite, injury, or infectious disease; enlargement resulting from congenital lymphangioma; or a disorder produced by mycotic infection, malignant lesion, or congenital anomaly.

glossopexy /glos′əpek′sē/ [Gk, glossa + pexis, fixation], an adhesion of the tongue to the lip.

glossopharyngeal /glos′ōfərin′jē·əl/ [Gk, glossa + pharynx, throat], pertaining to the tongue and pharynx.

glossopharyngeal breathing (GPB), a technique of forcing air into the lungs with the pharynx and tongue muscles. The technique can be taught to patients whose respiratory muscles are weak.

glossopharyngeal nerve, either of a pair of cranial nerves essential to the sense of taste, sensation in some viscera, and secretion from certain glands.

glossopharyngeal neuralgia, a disorder of unknown origin characterized by recurrent attacks of severe pain in the back of the pharynx, the tonsils, the base of the tongue, and the middle ear.

glossophytia /glos′əfit′ē·ə/ [Gk, glossa + phyton, plant], a condition of the tongue characterized by a blackish patch on the dorsum on which filiform papillae are greatly elongated and thickened like bristly hairs.

glossoplasty /glos′ōplas′tē/ [Gk, glossa + plassein, to mold], a surgical procedure or plastic surgery on the tongue performed to correct a congenital anomaly, repair an injury, or restore a measure of function after excision of a malignant lesion.

glossoptosis /glos′optō′sis/ [Gk, glossa + ptosis, falling], the retraction or downward displacement of the tongue.

glossopyrosis /glos′ōpīrō′sis/ [Gk, glossa + pyr, fire, osis, condition], a burning sensation in the tongue caused by chronic inflammation, exposure to extremely hot or spicy food, or psychogenic glossitis.

glossorrhaphy /glosôr′əfē/ [Gk, glossa + rhaphe, seam], the surgical suturing of a wound in the tongue.

glossotrichia /glos′ətrik′ē·ə/ [Gk, glossa + thrix, hair], a condition of the tongue characterized by a hairlike appearance of the papillae.

glossy skin [ONorse, glosa, smooth and shiny; AS, scinn], a shiny skin that is usually secondary to neuritis and may be associated with other integumentary disorders, including alopecia, skin fissuring, and ulceration. It usually begins as an erythematous area on an extremity.

glottal fry, the raspy or croaking quality of the voice in its lowest register. It results from loose closure of the glottis that allows air to bubble through.

glottal stop /glot′əl stop/, **1.** a speech sound made by closure of the glottis and then an explosive release. **2.** an abnormal sound substitution with a guttural quality.

glottis pl. **glottises, glottides** [Gk, opening to larynx], **1.** a slitlike opening between the true vocal cords. **2.** the phonation apparatus of the larynx, composed of the true vocal cords and the opening between them.—**glottal, glottic,** adj.

gloves, sterile or clean fitted coverings for the hands, usually with a separate sheath for each finger and thumb. Clean gloves are worn to protect health care personnel from urine, stool, blood, saliva, and drainage from wounds and lesions of patients and to protect patients from health care personnel who may have cuts. Sterile gloves are worn when there is contact with sterile instruments or a patient's sterile part.

glow curve, in thermoluminescence dosimetry, the graphic representation of the emitted light intensity that increases with the increasing phosphor temperature.

GLP-1, abbreviation for **glucagon-like peptide 1.**

Glu, abbreviation for **glutamic acid.**

glucagon /gloo′kəgon/ [Gk, *glykys,* sweet, *agaein,* to lead], a polypeptide hormone, produced by alpha cells in the islets of Langerhans, that stimulates the conversion of glycogen to glucose in the liver. Secretion of glucagon is stimulated by hypoglycemia and by growth hormone from the anterior pituitary.

glucagon-like peptide 1 (GLP-1), an appetite-suppressing substance found in the brain and intestine. In the brain, GLP-1 acts as a satiety signal. In the intestine, it slows emptying of the stomach and stimulates the release of insulin from the pancreas.

glucagonoma syndrome /gloo′kəgonō′mə/ [Gk, *glykys* + *agaein* + *oma,* tumor], a disease associated with a glucagon-secreting tumor of the islet cells of the pancreas. It is characterized by hyperglycemia, stomatitis, glossitis, anemia, weight loss, and a characteristic rash.

glucagon (recombinant), a form of recombinant DNA origin, having the same actions and uses as that of animal origin.

glucagon test, a blood test measuring the hormone glucason that is used to help diagnose glucagonoma, glucagon deficiency, DM, pancreatic insufficiency, renal failure, and other conditions.

glucocorticoid /gloo′kōkôr′təkoid/ [Gk, *glykys*; L, *cortex,* bark; Gk, *eidos,* form], an adrenocortical steroid hormone that increases gluconeogenesis, exerts an antiinflammatory effect, and influences many body functions. The three glucocorticoids are cortisol (hydrocortisone), corticosterone, and cortisone. Glucocorticoids promote the release of amino acids from muscle, mobilize fatty acids from fat stores, and increase the ability of skeletal muscles to maintain contractions and avoid fatigue.

glucogenesis, giving rise to or producing glucose.

Glucometer, a trademark for a battery-powered instrument used to calculate blood glucose from as little as one drop of blood.

gluconeogenesis /gloo′kōnē′ōjen′əsis/, the formation of glucose from glycerol and proteins rather than from carbohydrates.

Glucophage, a trademark for an oral antidiabetic agent (metformin hydrochloride).

glucosamine sulfate, the sulfate salt of glucosamine, prepared artificially as a nutritional supplement and as a popular remedy for osteoarthritis.

glucosan /gloo′kəsan/ [Gk, *glykys,* sweet], any of a large group of anhydrous polysaccharides that on hydrolysis yield a hexose, primarily anhydrides of glucose. The glucosans include cellulose, glycogen, starch, and the dextrins.

glucose /gloo′kōs/ [Gk, *glykys,* sweet], a simple sugar found in certain foods, especially fruits, and a major source of energy present in the blood and animal body fluids.

glucose electrode, a specialized electric terminal that contains incorporated enzyme for glucose determination.

glucose-galactose malabsorption, a disorder of transport clinically characterized by the neonatal onset of profuse, acidic, watery diarrhea leading to severe dehydration and death if untreated, resulting from a selective defect in the intestinal transport of glucose and galactose.

glucose intolerance, inability to properly metabolize glucose, a type of carbohydrate intolerance.

glucose-1-phosphate, an intermediate compound in carbohydrate metabolism.

glucose-6-phosphate, an intermediate compound in carbohydrate metabolism.

glucose-6-phosphate dehydrogenase (G6PD) deficiency, an inherited disorder characterized by red cells partially or completely deficient in G6PD, an enzyme critical in aerobic glycolysis. The disorder is associated with episodes of acute hemolysis under conditions of stress or in response to certain chemicals or drugs. The resulting anemia is a kind of non spherocytic hemolytic anemia. A sex-linked disorder, the defect is fully expressed in affected males despite a heterozygous pattern of inheritance.

glucose-6-phosphate dehydrogenase (G6PD) test, a blood test to diagnose G6PD deficiency in suspected individuals. Deficiency of this enzyme causes precipitation of hemoglobin and cellular membrane changes, possibly resulting in hemolysis of variable severity, a sex-linked trait carried on the X chromosome.

glucose tolerance test (GTT), a test of the body's ability to metabolize carbohydrates by administering a standard dose of glucose and measuring the blood and urine for glucose level at regular intervals thereafter. It is most often used to assist in the diagnosis of diabetes, hypoglycemia, or other disorders that affect carbohydrate metabolism.

glucosuria /gloo′kōsoor′ē·ə/ [Gk, *glykys* + *ouron,* urine], abnormal presence of glucose in the urine resulting from the ingestion of large amounts of carbohydrate or from a metabolic disease, such as DM. —**glucosuric,** *adj.*

glucosyl, **1.** pertaining to glucose. **2.** a glucose radical.

Glucotrol, a trademark for an oral antidiabetic drug (glipiZIDE).

glue sniffing [Gk, *gloios;* ME, *sniffen*], the practice of inhaling the vapors of toluene, a volatile organic compound used as a solvent in certain glues.

glutamate /glōō'təmāt/, a salt of glutamic acid. In addition to being one of the 20 major amino acids, it is a major excitatory amino acid of the CNS.

glutamic acid (Glu) /glōōtam'ik/ [L, *gluten,* glue, *amine,* ammonia, *acidus,* sour], a nonessential amino acid that occurs widely in a number of proteins. Preparations of glutamic acid are used as aids for digestion.

glutamic acid decarboxylase autoantibody, an antibody found in patients with insulin-dependent DM.

glutamic acidemia /glōōtam'ik as'idē'mē-ə/, an inherited disorder of amino acid metabolism that causes an excessive level of glutamic acid. The condition is characterized by mental and physical retardation, seizures, and fragile hair growth.

glutamic acid hydrochloride, a gastric acidifier prescribed for the treatment of hypoacidity.

glutamine (Gln) /glōō'təmēn/ [L, *gluten + amine,* ammonia], a nonessential amino acid found in the juices of many plants and in many proteins in the body. It functions as an amino donor for many reactions. It is also a nontoxic transport for ammonia.

glutaraldehyde /glōō'tāral'dəhīd/, a histologic fixative and sterilant for medical instruments.

glutargin /glōōtär'gin/, arginine glutamate.

glutaricaciduria /glōōtar'ikas'idyōō'rē-ə/, **1.** an autosomal-recessive disorder of amino acid metabolism characterized by accumulation and excretion of the dicarboxylic acid glutaric acid and occurring in two types. Type 1 is characterized by progressive dystonia and dyskinesia, hypoglycemia, mild ketosis and acidosis, opisthotonus, choreoathetosis, motor delay, mental retardation, hypotonia, and death within the first decade. Type II is caused by any of several related defects and is characterized by accumulation and excretion of various organic acids, hypoglycemia without ketosis, metabolic acidosis, and many phenotypic manifestations varying with the specific defect. A later age at onset is correlated with decreased severity, whereas neonatal onset may be

accompanied by congenital anomalies and is rapidly fatal. **2.** excretion of glutaric acid in the urine.

glutathione /glōō'təthī'ōn/ [L, *gluten;* Gk, *theione,* sulfur], a tripeptide of glutamic acid, cysteine, and glycine whose deficiency is commonly associated with hemolytic anemia. It functions by taking up and giving off hydrogen. It transports amino acids across cell membranes and conjugates to drugs enabling excretion.

gluteal /glōō'tē-əl/ [Gk, *gloutos,* buttocks], pertaining to the buttocks or to the muscles that form the buttocks.

gluteal fold, **1.** a fold of the buttock. **2.** the horizontal lower margin of the buttock at its junction with the thigh.

gluteal reflex, contraction of the gluteus muscles elicited by stroking the back.

gluteal region, the region overlying the gluteal muscles.

gluteal tuberosity, a ridge on the lateral posterior surface of the femur to which is attached the gluteus maximus.

gluten /glōō'tən/ [L, glue], the insoluble protein constituent of wheat and other grains.

gluteus /glōōtē'əs/, any of the three muscles that form the buttocks: the gluteus maximus, gluteus medius, and gluteus minimus. The gluteus maximus is a large muscle with an origin in the iliac, the sacrum, and the sacrotuberous ligament and an insertion in the gluteal tuberosity of the femur and the fascia lata. It acts to extend the thigh. The gluteus medius originates between the anterior and posterior gluteal lines of the ilium and inserts in the greater trochanter of the femur. It acts to abduct and rotate the thigh. The gluteus minimus originates between the inferior and anterior gluteal lines of the ilium and inserts in the greater trochanter of the femur. It acts to abduct the thigh.

Gly, abbreviation for **glycine.**

glyBURIDE /glī'bərīd/, an oral antidiabetic drug prescribed as an adjunct to diet and exercise to lower blood glucose levels of patients with type 2 (non–insulin-dependent) DM.

glycate, the product of a nonenzymatic reaction between a sugar and a free amino group of a protein.

glycemic index, a ranking of foods based on the response of postprandial blood glucose levels as compared with a reference food, usually either white bread or glucose.

glycerin /glis'ərin/ [Gk, *glykys,* sweet], a sweet, colorless oily fluid that is a pharmaceutic grade of glycerol. It is used as a moistening agent for chapped skin, as an ingredient of suppositories for constipation, and as a sweetening agent and vehicle for drug preparations.

glycerol (C₃H₈O₃) /glis′ərôl/ [Gk, *glykys,* sweet], an alcohol that is a component of fats.

glycerol kinase, an enzyme in the liver and kidneys that catalyzes the transfer of a phosphate group from adenosine triphosphate to form adenosine diphosphate and L-glycerol-3-phosphate.

glycine (Gly) /glī′sin/ [Gk, *glykys;* L, *amine,* ammonia], a nonessential amino acid occurring widely as a component of animal and plant proteins.

glycocholic acid /glīkōkol′ik/ [Gk, *glykys,* sweet; L, *acidus,* sour], a substance in bile, formed by glycine and cholic acid, that aids in digestion and absorption of fats.

glycogen /glī′kəjən/ [Gk, *glykys,* sweet, *genein,* to produce], a polysaccharide that is the major carbohydrate stored in animal cells. It is formed from repeating units of glucose and stored chiefly in the liver and, to a lesser extent, in muscle cells.

glycogenesis /glī′kōjen′əsis/, the synthesis of glycogen from glucose.

glycogenolysis /glī′kōjenol′isis/ [Gk, *glykys; genein + lysis,* loosening], the breakdown of glycogen to glucose.

glycogen storage disease [Gk, *glykys + genein;* L, *instaurare,* to renew, *dis,* opposite of; Fr, *aise,* ease], any of a group of inherited disorders of glycogen metabolism. An enzyme deficiency or defect in glycogen transport causes glycogen to accumulate in abnormally large amounts in various parts of the body.

glycogen storage disease, type Ib, a form of glycogen storage disease in which excessive amounts of glycogen are deposited in the liver and leukocytes. Some symptoms are similar to, but less severe than, those of glycogen storage disease, type Ia (von Gierke's disease). Additional symptoms include neutropenia and recurrent GI inflammatory disease.

glycolipid /glī′kōlip′id/ [Gk, *glykys,* sweet, *lipos,* fat], a compound that consists of a lipid and a carbohydrate, usually galactose, found primarily in the tissue of the nervous system.

glycolysis /glīkol′isis/ [Gk, *glykys + lysis,* loosening], a series of enzymatically catalyzed reactions by which glucose and other sugars are broken down to yield lactic acid (anaerobic glycolysis) or pyruvic acid (aerobic glycolysis). The breakdown releases energy in the form of adenosine triphosphate.

glycolytic myopathy, any metabolic myopathy resulting from a defect of glycolytic enzyme activity, marked by exercise intolerance and cramping, the accumulation of glycogen in muscle, and recurrent myoglobinuria.

glycometabolism /glī′kōmətab′əliz′əm/, the metabolism of sugar in the animal body.

glycopenia /-pē′nē-ə/, a deficiency of sugar in the blood or tissues.

glycopeptides /-pep′tīdz/, a class of peptides that contain sugars linked with amino acids, as in bacterial cell walls.

glycophorin /-fôr′in/, one of a group of proteins that project through the membrane of RBCs. The outside end of glycophorins carries antigen of the MNS blood group. The sialic acid component of glycophorins contributes to the negative charge of the outer erythrocyte plasma membrane.

glycoprotein /glī′kōprō′tēn/ [Gk, *glykys,* sweet, *proteios,* first rank], any of the large group of conjugated proteins in which the nonprotein substance is a carbohydrate. These include the mucins, the mucoids, and the chondroproteins.

glycoprotein IIb/IIIa, a transmembrane protein of platelets, an integrin that binds fibrinogen, von Willebrand factor, and other adhesive ligands and plays a role in platelet aggregation and thrombus formation.

glycopyrrolate /glī′kōpir′əlāt/, an anticholinergic prescribed as an adjunct to ulcer therapy and parenterally to reduce secretions before surgery.

glycoside /glī′kəsīd/ [Gk, *glykys,* sweet], any of several carbohydrates that yield a sugar and a nonsugar on hydrolysis. The plant *Digitalis purpurea* yields a glycoside used in the treatment of heart disease.

glycosphingolipids /glī′kōsfing′gōlip′ids/, compounds formed from carbohydrates and ceramide, a fatty substance, found in tissues of the CNS and also in erythrocytes.

glycosuria /glī′kōsŏŏr′ē-ə/ [Gk, *glykys + ouron,* urine], abnormal presence of a sugar, especially glucose, in the urine. It is a finding most routinely associated with DM.—**glycosuric,** *adj.*

glycosyl /glī′kōsil/, the radical formed from a saccharide, such as glucose, by removal of a specific hydroxyl group.

glycosylated hemoglobin (GHb/Hb A₁c) /glī′kō′silā′tid/, a hemoglobin A molecule with a glucose group on the N-terminal valine amino acid unit of the beta chain. The glycosylated hemoglobin concentration represents the average blood glucose level over the previous several weeks. The normal range is 1.8% to 4.0% for children; 2.2% to 4.8% for adults.

glycosylated hemoglobin (GHb, GHB) test, a blood test used to monitor diabetes treatment. It measures the amount of hemoglobin A₁c in the blood and provides an accurate long-term index of the patient's average blood glucose level.

glycosylation /glīkə′səlā′shən/, the formation of linkages with glycosyl groups, covalently attaching a carbohydrate to another molecule.

glycyrrhiza /glis′iri′zə/, licorice.

glycyrrhizic acid /glis′iriz′ik/, a sweet compound containing potassium and calcium salts derived from licorice root. It is used as an expectorant and as a flavoring for pharmaceutics.

gm, abbreviation for **gram.**

GM-2, a carbohydrate found in much larger quantities in cancer cells than in normal cells, used in some experimental cancer therapy. When it is mixed with bacille Calmette-Guérin and injected into melanoma patients, some patients make antibodies against the cancer cells.

GM-CSF, abbreviation for **granulocyte-macrophage colony–stimulating factor.**

GMENAC, abbreviation for **Graduate Medical Education National Advisory Committee.**

GMP, abbreviation for **guanosine monophosphate.**

GN, abbreviation for **graduate nurse.**

GNA, abbreviation for **Gay Nurses' Alliance.**

gnathic /nath′ik/ [L, *gnathos,* jaw], pertaining to the jaw or cheek.

gnathic index, the degree of prominence of the upper jaw, expressed as a percentage of the distance from basion to nasion.

gnathion /nā′thē·on/ [L, *gnathos,* jaw], the lowest point in the lower border of the mandible in the median plane. It is a common reference point in the diagnosis and orthodontic treatment of various kinds of malocclusion.

gnathodynamometer /nā′thōdī′nəmom′ətər/ [Gk, *gnathos* + *dynamis,* force, *metron,* measure], an instrument used for measuring the biting pressure of the jaws of an individual.

gnathodynia /nā′thōdin′ē·ə/ [Gk, *gnathos* + *odyne,* pain], pain in the jaw, such as that commonly associated with an impacted wisdom tooth.

gnathology /nāthol′əjē/ [Gk, *gnathos* + *logos,* science], a field of dental or medical study that deals with the entire chewing apparatus, including its anatomic, histologic, morphologic, physiologic, and pathologic characteristics.

gnathostatic cast /nā′thōstat′ik/ [Gk, *gnathos* + *statike,* weighing; ME, *casten*], a cast of the teeth trimmed so that its occlusal plane is in its normal oral attitude when the cast is set on a horizontal surface.

gnathostatics /nā′thōstat′iks/ [Gk, *gnathos* + *statike,* weighing], a technique of orthodontic diagnosis based on an analysis

of the relationships between the teeth and certain reference points on the skull.

Gnathostoma /nathos′tomə/ [Gk, *gnathos* + *stoma,* mouth], a genus of parasitic nematodes of the family Gnathostomatidae characterized by distinct jaws.

gnathostomiasis /nath′ōstōmī′əsis/ [Gk, *gnathos* + *stoma,* mouth, *osis,* condition], infection with the nematode *Gnathostoma spinigerum,* occurring when undercooked fish harboring the larvae is eaten. The larvae migrate, often in the subcutaneous tissue, causing a creeping eruption associated with intense eosinophilia. Occasionally they migrate to deeper tissues and cause abscesses or to the CNS, where they cause eosinophilic myeloencephalitis.

gnotobiotic /nō′tōbī·ot′ik/, pertaining to a germ-free animal or an animal or an environment in which all the microorganisms are known.

GNP, abbreviation for **geriatric nurse practitioner.**

GnRH, abbreviation for **gonadotropin-releasing hormone.**

goal /gōl/ [ME, *gol,* limit], the purpose toward which an endeavor is directed, such as the outcome of diagnostic, therapeutic, and educational management of a patient's health problem.

goal-oriented movements, voluntary movements that are organized around behavioral goals, environmental context, and task specificity, as distinguished from reflexive movements.

GOAT, abbreviation for **Galveston Orientation and Amnesia Test.**

goblet cell [ME, *gobelet,* small bowl], one of the many specialized epithelial cells that secrete mucus and form glands of the epithelium of the stomach, the intestine, and parts of the respiratory tract.

goiter /goi′ter/ [L, *guttur,* throat], an enlarged thyroid gland, usually evident as a pronounced swelling in the neck. The enlargement may be associated with hyperthyroidism, hypothyroidism, or normal levels of thyroid function.—**goitrous,** *adj.*

goitrogenic glycoside /goi′trəjen′ik/, a glycoside that may cause hyperthyroidism or a goiter.

gold (Au) [AS, *geolu,* yellow], a yellowish soft metallic element that occurs naturally as a free metal and as the telluride $AuAgTe_4$. Its atomic number is 79, and its atomic mass is 196.97. It is used as a dental restorative material.

gold-198, a radioactive gold antineoplastic prescribed for treatment of cancer of the prostate, cervix, and bladder and for reduction of fluid accumulation secondary to a cancer.

Goldblatt kidney, an abnormal kidney in which constriction of a renal artery leads to ischemia and release of renin, a pressor substance associated with hypertension.

gold compound, a drug containing gold salts, usually administered with other drugs in the treatment of rheumatoid arthritis. Gold is potentially toxic and is administered only under the supervision of a specialist in chrysotherapy.

Goldenhar's syndrome /gōl′dən·härz/ [Maurice Goldenhar, Swiss physician, 20th century], a congenital condition characterized by colobomas of the upper eyelid, dermoids on the eyeball, bilateral accessory auricular appendages anterior to the ears, and vertebral anomalies, frequently associated with characteristic facies, consisting of asymmetry of the skull, prominent frontal bossing, low hairline, mandibular hypoplasia, low-set ears, and sometimes smallness of the mouth on one side.

goldenseal, a perennial herb used for high BP, poor appetite, infections, menstrual problems, minor sciatic pain, and muscle spasms. It is also used as an eye wash and by some hoping to hide the presence of marijuana, cocaine, or other illicit drugs in the urine. Goldenseal is ineffective at masking illicit drugs in urine tests. There is insufficient reliable information to gauge its efficacy for other uses.

gold foil, pure gold that has been rolled and beaten into a very thin sheet, used for making foil pellets, which are a direct dental restorative material.

gold inlay, an intracoronal cast restoration of gold alloy that restores one or more tooth surfaces within the cusp prominences of a posterior tooth.

Goldman-Fox knife, a dental surgical instrument with a sharp cutting edge, designed for the incision and contouring of gingival tissue.

gold sodium thiomalate, an antirheumatic prescribed for the treatment of rheumatoid arthritis.

gold standard, 1. an accepted test that is assumed to be able to determine the true disease state of a patient, regardless of positive or negative test findings or sensitivities or specificities of other diagnostic tests used. **2.** an acknowledged measure of comparison of the superior effectiveness or value of a particular medication or other therapy as compared with that of other drugs or treatments.

golfer's elbow, an informal term for inflammation of the medial epicondyle of the humerus, associated with repeated use of the wrist flexors.

Golgi apparatus /gôl′jē/ [Camillo Golgi, Italian histologist and Nobel laureate, 1843–1926; L, *ad,* toward, *praeparare,* to prepare], one of many small membranous structures found in most cells, composed of various elements associated with the formation of carbohydrate side chains of glycoproteins, mucopolysaccharides, and other substances.

Golgi-Mazzoni corpuscles /gôl′jē matsō′nē/ [Camillo Golgi; Vittori Mazzoni, Italian physiologist, 1880–1940], a number of thin capsules enveloping terminal nerve fibrils in the subcutaneous tissue of the fingers.

Golgi's cells [Camillo Golgi; L, *cella,* storeroom], **1.** Golgi type I neurons, nerve cells having long axons that leave the local neurophil area of the parent cell body, traverse the white matter, and project to the rest of the nervous system. **2.** Golgi type II neurons, nerve cells with short trajectory axons, such as stellate cells of the cerebral and cerebellar cortex. They generally do not enter white matter but remain within the local neurophil in the cerebral and cerebellar cortices and the retina.

Golgi tendon organ [Camillo Golgi], a sensory nerve ending that is sensitive to both tension and excessive passive stretch of a skeletal muscle.

gomphosis /gomfō′sis/ *pl.* **gomphoses** [Gk, *gomphos,* bolt], an articulation by the insertion of a conical process into a socket, such as the insertion of a root of a tooth into an alveolus of the mandible or the maxilla. Gomphosis is not a connection between true bones but is considered a type of fibrous joint.

gonad /gō′nad/ [Gk, *gone,* seed], a gamete-producing gland such as an ovary or a testis.—**gonadal,** *adj.*

gonadal aplasia /gō′nədəl/, a congenital state in which there is defective development of the germinal tissues of the gonads.

gonadal cords, epithelial cells derived from the coelomic epithelium that penetrate the underlying mesenchyme, where they form cords.

gonadal dose, the amount of radiation received by the gonads as a result of a radiographic examination. It may vary from less than 1 mrad for a dental or chest radiograph to 225 mrad for a lumbar spine radiograph and 800 mrad for a fetus during pelvimetry.

gonadal dysgenesis, a general designation for a variety of conditions involving anomalies in the development of the gonads.

gonadal shield, a specially designed contact or shadow shield used to protect the gonadal area of a patient from the primary radiation beam during radiographic procedures. It is generally used for patients who are potentially reproductive.

gonadoblastoma /gō′nədōblastō′mə/ [Gk, *gone,* seed, *blastos,* germ, *oma,* tumor], a rare benign type of germ cell tumor, usually occurring in patients with gonadal dysgenesis, and often bilateral. It contains all gonadal elements and is frequently associated with an abnormal chromosomal karyotype. It may give rise to a dysgerminoma or other more malignant germ cell tumor.

gonadorelin acetate, the acetate ester of gonadorelin, having the same actions and uses as the hydrochloride salt. It is used in the treatment of delayed puberty, female infertility, and amenorrhea.

gonadotrophic /gō′nədōtrof′ik/, **1.** pertaining to genitalia. **2.** capable of influencing the gonads. **3.** relating to the state in which the gonads exert influence on the body.

gonadotropic /gō′nədōtrop′ik/, acting on or stimulating the gonads.

gonadotropin /gō′nədōtrop′in/ [Gk, *gone* + *trophe,* nourishment], a hormonal substance that stimulates the function of the testes and the ovaries. The gonadotropic follicle-stimulating hormone and luteinizing hormone are produced and secreted by the anterior pituitary gland. In early pregnancy, HCG is produced by the placenta and acts to sustain the function of the corpus luteum of the ovary, forestalling menstruation and thus maintaining pregnancy. Gonadotropins are prescribed to induce ovulation in infertility that is caused by inadequate stimulation of the ovary by endogenous gonadotropic hormones. Follicle-stimulating hormone and luteinizing hormone are also major gonadotropins in the testes, causing the Leydig cells to secrete testosterone and facilitating spermatogenesis.

gonadotropin-releasing hormone (GnRH) [Gk, *gone,* seed, *trope,* a turn; ME, *relesen;* Gk, *hormaein,* to set in motion], a decapeptide hypophysiotropic hormone secreted by the hypothalamus. It stimulates the release of luteinizing hormone and follicle-stimulating hormone by the anterior pituitary.

goniometer /gon′ē·om′ətər/, an instrument used to measure angles, particularly range-of-motion angles of a joint.

goniometry /gon′ē·om′ətrē/ [Gk, *gonia,* angle, *metron,* measure], a system for measuring angles during testing for various labyrinthine diseases that affect the sense of balance.—**goniometric,** *adj.*

gonion /gō′nē·on/ *pl.* **gonia** [Gk, *gōnia,* angle], an anthropometric landmark located at the most inferior, posterior, and lateral point on the external angle of the mandible, being the apex of the maximum curvature of the mandible, where the ascending ramus becomes the body of the mandible.

gonioscope /gō′nē·əskōp′/ [Gk, *gonia* + *skopein,* to look], a mirrored optic instrument used to examine the filtration angle of the anterior chamber of the eye. The mirrors permit visualization of the angle by means of a reflected image.

goniotomy /gōn′ē·ot′əmē/, an operation performed to remove any obstruction to the flow of aqueous humor in the front chamber of the eye. The procedure is commonly done in patients with congenital glaucoma.

gonococcal /gon′əkok′əl/ [Gk, *gone,* seed, *kokkos,* berry], pertaining to or resembling gonococcus.

gonococcal pyomyositis [Gk, *gone,* seed, *kokkos,* berry, *pyon,* pus, *mys,* muscle, *itis,* inflammation], an acute inflammatory condition of a muscle caused by infection with *Neisseria gonorrhoeae,* characterized by abscess formation and pain. It is an unusual form of gonorrhea and must be differentiated from sarcoma.

gonococcal salpingitis [Gk, *gone,* seed, *kokkos,* berry, *salpigx,* tube, *itis,* inflammation], an inflammation of the fallopian tubes caused by a gonococcal infection.

gonococcal urethritis [Gk, *gone,* seed, *kokkos,* berry, *ourethra,* urethra, *itis,* inflammation], inflammation of the urethra caused by an infection of *Neisseria gonorrhoeae.*

gonococcus /gon′əkok′əs/ *pl.* **gonococci** [Gk, *gone* + *kokkos,* berry], a gram-negative intracellular diplococcus of the species *Neisseria gonorrhoeae,* the cause of gonorrhea.

gonorrhea /gon′ərē′ə/ [Gk, *gone* + *rhoia,* flow], a common STD that most often affects the genitourinary tract and occasionally the pharynx or rectum. Infection results from contact with an infected person or with secretions containing the causative organism *Neisseria gonorrhoeae.* Urethritis; dysuria; purulent, greenish-yellow urethral or vaginal discharge; red or edematous urethral meatus; and itching, burning, or pain around the vaginal or urethral orifice are characteristic.—**gonorrheal, gonorrheic,** *adj.*

gonorrheal arthritis [Gk, *gone,* seed, *kokkos,* berry, *arthron,* joint, *itis,* inflammation], a blood-borne gonococcal infection of the joints. It may affect one or several joints, may occur as a chronic or acute form, and often leads to joint fusion. Infection may result in pus formation in an affected joint.

gonorrheal conjunctivitis, a severe, destructive form of purulent conjunctivitis caused by the gonococcus *Neisseria gonor-rhoeae.* Newborns receive routine prophy-laxis of a topical ophthalmic instillation of 1% solution of silver nitrate or an antibiotic ophthalmic ointment. The treatment has largely eradicated the infection in infants.

gonorrheal proctitis [Gk, *gone,* seed, *rhoia,* flow, *proktos,* anus, *itis,* inflam-mation], an inflammation of the rectum caused by an infection of gonorrhea.

Gonyaulax catenella /gon′ē·ô′laks/, a spe-cies of toxin-producing planktonic proto-zoa ingested by shellfish along the coasts of North America that causes shellfish poisoning.

Goodell's sign /gŏodelz′/ [William Goodell, American gynecologist, 1829–1894], softening of the uterine cervix, a probable sign of pregnancy.

good faith and fair dealing, 1. actions taken with the best interests of the patient in mind and without harmful intent. **2.** in employee relations, an implied covenant preventing an employer from terminating an employee solely to avoid paying the employee for services already performed.

Goodman's syndrome /good′mənz/ [Rich-ard M. Goodman, Israeli physician, 20th century], an autosomal-recessive form of acrocephalopolysyndactyly characterized also by congenital heart defects, sidewards deviation and abnormal flexion of digits, and ulnar deviation, but without unimpaired intelligence.

Goodpasture's syndrome /good′paschər/ [Ernest W. Goodpasture, American pathol-ogist, 1886–1960], a chronic relapsing pulmonary hemosiderosis, an autoimmune disease usually associated with glomeru-lonephritis and characterized by a cough with hemoptysis, dyspnea, anemia, and progressive renal failure.

Goodrich, Annie Warburton, an Ameri-can nursing educator who was instru-mental in advancing nursing from an apprenticeship to a profession. She was superintendent of nurses at several New York hospitals before going to Teachers College, Columbia University, in 1914. In 1923 she became dean of the newly formed School of Nursing at Yale University.

Good Samaritan legislation /səmar′itən/ [good Samaritan, from New Tes-tament parable; L, *lex,* law, *lator,* pro-poser], laws enacted in most states to protect physicians, dentists, nurses, and some other health professionals from lia-bility while rendering emergency medical or dental aid, unless there is proven willful wrong or gross negligence.

Gordon's elementary body [Mervyn H. Gordon, English physician, 1872–1953], a particle found in tissues

containing eosinophils, once thought to be the viral cause of Hodgkin's disease.

Gordon's reflex [Alfred Gordon, American neurologist, 1874–1953], **1.** an abnormal variation of Babinski's reflex, elicited by compressing the calf muscles, characterized by dorsiflexion of the great toe and fanning of the other toes. It is evidence of disease of the pyramidal tract. **2.** an abnormal reflex, elicited by compressing the forearm mus-cles, characterized by flexion of the fingers or of the thumb and index finger. It is seen in diseases of the pyramidal tract.

Gordon's syndrome /gôr′dənz/ [Richard D. Gordon, Australian physician, 20th cen-tury], a type of pseudohypoaldoteron-ism with hypertension and hyperkalemia but without salt wasting, thought to be caused by abnormally increased absorp-tion of chloride by the renal tubules.

Gorham's disease /gor′əmz/ [Lemuel Whittington Gorham, American physi-cian, 1885–1968], a gradual, but often complete, resorption of a bone or group of bones, which may be associated with multiple hemangiomas. It usually occurs in children or young adults.

Gosselin's fracture /gôslaNz′/ [Leon A. Gosselin, French surgeon, 1815–1847], a V-shaped break in the distal tibia, extend-ing to the ankle.

GOT, abbreviation for *glutamic-oxalo-acetic transaminase.*

gotu kola, a creeping herb taken sys-temically to treat venous insufficiency and for a variety of other reasons, including improving memory and intelligence. It is used topically to treat chronic wounds and psoriasis. It may be effective for its topical indications and for treating venous insuf-ficiency. There are insufficient reliable data for any of its other uses.

goundou /gōōn′dōō/ [West African], a condition characterized by bony exostoses of the nasal and maxillary bones, usually occurring as a late sequela of yaws in peo-ple in Africa and Latin America.

gout [L, *gutta,* drop], a disease associated with an inborn error of uric acid metabo-lism that increases production or interferes with excretion of uric acid. Excess uric acid is converted to sodium urate crystals that precipitate from the blood and become deposited in joints and other tissues. The great toe is a common site for the accumu-lation of urate crystals. The condition can cause exceedingly painful swelling of a joint, accompanied by chills and fever. The disorder is disabling and, if untreated, can progress to the development of destructive joint changes, such as tophi.

gouty /gou′tē/ [L, *gutta,* drop], pertain-ing to or resembling the condition of gout.

GP, abbreviation for **general practitioner.**

gp160, a glycoprotein found on the outer surface, or envelope, of the HIV. It is composed of gp120, which protrudes from the envelope, and gp41, which is embedded in the envelope.

GPB, abbreviation for **glossopharyngeal breathing.**

GPT, abbreviation for *glutamic-pyruvic transaminase.*

GPWW, abbreviation for **group practice without walls.**

gr, abbreviation for **grain.**

graafian follicle /grä´fē·ən, -grä´-/ [Reijnier de Graaf, Dutch physician, 1641–1673; L, *folliculus,* small bag], a mature ovarian vesicle, measuring about 10 to 12 mm in diameter, that ruptures during ovulation to release the ovum. Many primary ovarian follicles, each containing an immature ovum about 35 μm in diameter, are embedded near the surface of the ovary. Under the influence of the follicle-stimulating hormone, one ovarian follicle ripens into a graafian follicle during the proliferative phase of each menstrual cycle. The cavity of the follicle collapses when the ovum is released, and the remaining follicular cells greatly enlarge to become the corpus luteum.

gracile /gras´il/, long, slender, and graceful.

gracilis /gras´ilis/, the most superficial of the five medial femoral muscles. It functions to adduct the thigh and flex the leg and to assist in the medial rotation of the leg after it is flexed.

gradation of activity /gradā´shən/, therapeutic activities that are appropriately paced and modified to demand maximal capacities at any point in progression or regression of the patient's condition.

graded exercise test (GXT), a test given to a patient with cardiac disease during rehabilitation to assess prognosis and quantify maximal functional capacity.

gradient /grā´dē·ənt/ [L, *gradus,* step], **1.** the rate of increase or decrease of a measurable phenomenon, such as temperature or pressure. **2.** a visual representation of the rate of change of a measurable phenomenon; a curve.

gradient former, a device for the preparation of linear density gradient medium in a column for gradient electrophoresis.

gradient gel electrophoresis, gel electrophoresis performed in a concentration gradient gel with progressively decreasing pore size.

gradient magnetic field, a magnetic field that changes in strength in a given direction. Such fields are used in MRI to select a region for imaging and to encode the location of MRI signals received from the object being imaged.

gradient plate technique, a method for isolating antibiotic-resistant bacteria mutants by exposing an agar plate containing concentration gradient of antibiotic to an inoculation of bacteria to be tested.

graduated bath /graj͞oo·a´tid/ [L, *gradus,* step; AS, *baeth*], a bath in which the temperature of the water is slowly reduced.

graduated muscular contractions, controlled shortening of muscle units in properly timed and adequate response to a stimulus. The contractions may be induced by the CNS or by electric stimulation.

graduate medical education /graj͞oo·it/, formal medical education pursued after receipt of the doctor of medicine (M.D, D.O.) or other professional degree in the medical sciences.

Graduate Medical Education National Advisory Committee (GMENAC), a committee established by order of the Secretary of what is now the Department of Health and Human Services to study the personnel issues in medicine. The committee issued its final report in September 1980. Among its conclusions was that the supply of nurses in expanded roles, including nurse practitioners and nurse midwives, should be increased.

graduate nurse (GN) [L, *gradus,* step, *nutrix,* nurse], a nurse who is a graduate of an accredited school of nursing but not yet licensed.

Graduate Record Examination (GRE), an examination administered to graduates of institutions of higher learning. The scores are used as criteria for admission to master's and doctoral programs in many institutions and areas of specialization, including nursing.

GRAE, abbreviation for **generally recognized as effective.**

graft [Gk, *graphion,* stylus], a tissue or an organ taken from a site or a person and inserted into a new site or person, performed to repair a defect in structure. The graft may be temporary or permanent.

graft facilitation, a method for extending the survival of a graft by conditioning the recipient with an immunoglobulin-blocking factor, which suppresses graft rejection.

graft rejection, the immunologic destruction of transplanted organs or tissues. The rejection may be based on both cell-mediated and antibody-mediated immunity against cells of the graft by a histoincompatible recipient.

graft-versus-host disease (GVHD), a rejection response of certain grafts, especially of bone marrow. It is commonly associated with inadequate immunosuppressive therapy of the donor, which allows immunocompetent cells in the donated tissue to recognize the recipient's tissues as foreign and to attack them. Characteristic signs may include skin lesions with edema, erythema, ulceration, scaling, loss of hair, lesions of the joints and the heart, and hemolytic anemia.

Graham's law /grā'əmz/ [Thomas Graham, English chemist, 1805–1869], the law stating that the rate of diffusion of a gas through a liquid (or the alveolar-capillary membrane) is directly proportional to its solubility coefficient and inversely proportional to the square root of its density.

Graham Steell murmur [Graham Steell, British physician, 1851–1942], an early diastolic murmur heard in the second intercostal space to the left of the sternum. It is associated with pulmonary valve regurgitation in pulmonary hypertension.

grain (gr) [L, *granum*, seed], the smallest unit of mass in avoirdupois, troy, and apothecaries' weights, which is equal to 65 mg. The troy and apothecaries' ounces contain 480 grains; the avoirdupois ounce contains 437.5 grains.

gram (g, gm) [L, *gramma*, small weight], a unit of mass in the metric system equal to $^1/_{1000}$ kilogram, 15.432 grains, and 0.0353 ounce avoirdupois. 453.6 g = 1 lb. The preferred abbreviation is **g**.

gram-equivalent weight (gEq), an equivalent weight of a substance calculated as the gram mass that contains, replaces, or reacts (directly or indirectly) with the Avogadro number of hydrogen atoms.

gram-molecular mass, a mass in grams numerically equal to the molecular mass of a substance, or the sum of all the atomic masses in its molecular formula.

gram-negative [Hans C.J. Gram, Danish physician, 1853–1938; L, *negare*, to say no], having the pink color of the counterstain used in Gram's method of staining microorganisms. This property is a primary method of characterizing organisms in microbiology.

gram-positive [Hans C.J. Gram; L, *positivus*], retaining the violet color of the stain used in Gram's method of staining microorganisms. This property is a primary method of characterizing organisms in microbiology.

Gram's stain [Hans C.J. Gram], the method of staining microorganisms using a violet stain, followed by an iodine solution; decolorizing with an alcohol or acetone solution; and counterstaining with safranin. The retention of either the violet color of the stain or the pink color of the

counterstain serves as a primary means of identifying and classifying bacteria.

gram-variable, gram-positive bacteria that can become gram-negative after culturing.

grandiose /gran'dē-ōs'/ [L, *grandis*, great], **1.** pertaining to something or somebody imposing, impressive, magnificent; pompous and showy. **2.** pertaining to behavior or beliefs seen in a mania.

grand multipara /grand/ [L, *grandis*, great, *multus*, many, *parere*, to give birth], a woman who has carried six or more pregnancies to a viable stage.

grand rounds [L, *grandis* + *rotundus*, wheel], a formal conference in which an expert presents a lecture concerning a clinical issue intended to be educational for the listeners. In some settings, grand rounds may be formal teaching rounds conducted by an expert at the bedsides of selected patients.

granisetron /granis'etron/, an antiemetic used in conjunction with cancer chemotherapy or radiotherapy.

grant [ME, *granten*, to bestow a request], a monetary award given to an institution, a project, equipment, or an individual by a granting agency, the federal government, a foundation, a private business, or an institution to provide financial support for research, service, or training.

granular /gran'yələr/ [L, *granulum*, little grain], **1.** macroscopically resembling or feeling like sand. **2.** microscopically appearing to have a few or many particles within or on its surface, such as a stained granular leukocyte.—**granularity,** *n.*

granular cast [L, *granulum*, little grain; ONorse, *kasta*], a mass of pathologic debris composed of cells filled with protein and fatty granules.

granular degeneration, swelling of cells caused by accumulation of intracellular water in response to cell injury.

granular induration, fibrosis of an organ, characterized by the formation of localized granular areas, as seen in cirrhosis of the liver.

granulation tissue /gran'yəlā'shən/ [L, *granulum*, little grain], any soft pink fleshy projections that form during the healing process in a wound that does not heal by primary intention. The tissue consists of many capillaries surrounded by fibrous collagen.

granule /gran'yo̅o̅l/ [L, *granulum*, little grain], a particle, grain, or other small dry mass capable of free movement. Unlike powders, granules are usually free-flowing because of small surface forces involved.

granulitis /gran'yəlī'tis/ [L, *granulum*, little grain; Gk, *itis*, inflammation], acute miliary TB.

G

granulocyte /gran′yŏŏləsīt′/ [L, *granu-lum*; Gk, *kytos*, cell], a type of leuko-cyte characterized by the presence of cytoplasmic granules; includes basophils, eosinophils, neutrophils, and monocytes. —**granulocytic,** *adj.*

granulocyte colony–stimulating factor (G-CSF), a glycoprotein secreted by a variety of cells that stimulates the growth of hematopoietic stem cells and their dif-ferentiation into granulocytes. It is often used to treat patients who have become severely neutropenic as a result of chemo-therapy or irradiation.

granulocyte-macrophage colony–stimu-lating factor (GM-CSF), a glycoprotein secreted by macrophages that stimulates the growth of myeloid progenitor cells and their differentiation into granulocytes and macrophages.

granulocyte transfusion, the use of spe-cially prepared leukocytes for the treat-ment of severe granulocytopenia and for prophylaxis in the prevention of serious infection in patients with leukemia or those receiving cancer chemotherapy.

granulocytopenia /gran′yŏŏlōsī′tōpē′nē-ə/ [L, *granulum*; Gk, *kytos*, cell, *penia*, pov-erty], an abnormal decrease in the total number of granulocytes in the blood. —**granulocytopenic,** *adj.*

granulocytosis /gran′yŏŏlōsītō′sis/ [L, *granulum*; Gk, *kytos*, cell, *osis*, condi-tion], an abnormal increase in the total number of granulocytes in the blood.

granuloma /gran′yŏŏlō′mə/, *pl.* **granu-lomas, granulomata** [L, *granulum*; Gk, *oma*, tumor], a chronic inflammatory lesion characterized by an accumulation of macrophages; epithelioid macrophages, with or without lymphocytes; and giant cells into a single, discrete enlarged mass. Granulomas most often occur in the lungs. They may resolve spontaneously, remain static, become gangrenous, spread, or act as a focus of infection. Treatment depends on the cause and probable course of the particular granuloma.

granuloma annulare, a self-limited chronic skin disease of unknown cause that consists of reddish papules arranged in a ring. It most commonly occurs on the dis-tal portions of the extremities in children.

granuloma gluteale infantum, a skin condition of the neonate characterized by large elevated bluish or brownish-red nod-ules on the buttocks. It often occurs as a secondary reaction to the application of strong steroid salves over time.

granuloma inguinale, an STD char-acterized by ulcers of the skin and subcutaneous tissues of the groin and genitalia. It is caused by infection with

Calymmatobacterium granulomatis, a small gram-negative rod-shaped bacillus. Untreated, the lesions spread, deepen, multiply, and become secondarily infected. Streptomycin is usually effective in treating the infection.

granulomatosis /gran′yŏŏlōmətō′sis/ [L, *granulum*; Gk, *oma,* tumor, *osis,* condi-tion], a condition or disease character-ized by the development of granulomas.

granulomatous /gran′yəlom′ətəs/ [L, *granulum,* little grain], pertaining to or resembling granulomas.

granulomatous amebic encephalitis, chronic encephalitis, usually seen in debil-itated or immunocompromised patients, caused by infection with species of *Acan-thamoeba.* It is marked by the formation of granulomas. Headache, seizures, nausea, and vomiting frequently occur.

granulomatous gastritis, chronic gas-tritis with granulomas of the stomach mucosa.

granulomatous lipophagia [L, *granulum,* little grain; Gk, *lipos,* fat, *phagein,* to eat], a disease in which enlarged intesti-nal and mesenteric lymph spaces become filled with fats and fatty acids.

granulomatous prostatitis, prostatitis with granuloma formation, such as from infec-tion with *Mycobacterium tuberculosis,* parasites, or fungi.

granulopoiesis /gran′yŏŏlōpōr′ē′sis/, the production or formation of granulocytes.

granulopoietin /gran′yŏŏlō′pōr′ē′tin/, a glycoprotein secreted by monocytes that controls the production of granulocytes by bone marrow.

granulosa cell tumor /gran′yŏŏlō′sə/ [L, *granulum,* little grain], a fleshy ovar-ian tumor with yellow streaks that origi-nates in cells of the primordial membrana granulosa and may grow to a large size. Excessive production of estrogen may be associated with the tumor.

granulosa-lutein cells, lutein cells of the corpus luteum derived from granulosa cells.

granulosa-theca cell tumor, an ovarian tumor composed of granulosa (follicular) cells or theca cells or both. The tumor is associated with excessive production of estrogen and hyperplasia of the breast and endometrium.

granulosis /gran′yŏŏlō′sis/, any disorder characterized by an accumulation of gran-ules in an area of body tissue.

grapeseed, an herb used as a chronic disease preventative and as an antiinflammatory, as well as a source of essential fatty acids and antioxidant tocopherols. It is used orally for the prevention of atherosclerosis and can-cer and in folk medicine for the treatment of circulatory disorders. Grapeseed may improve venous tone; there are insufficient reliable data for any other indications.

graphanesthesia /graf′anəsthē′zhə/, inability to feel writing on the skin, usually caused by a CNS lesion.

graphesthesia /graf′esthē′zhə/, ability to feel writing on the skin.

graphing /graf′ing/, the organization of data consisting of two or more variables along horizontal and vertical axes of a graph to show relationships between specific quantities or other specific factors.

graphite /graf′īt/ [L, *graphites*, from Gk, *graphis* a writing instrument], a form of native mineralized carbon whose dust causes a form of pneumoconiosis.

graphite pneumoconiosis /noo′mōkō′nē·ō′sis/, silicosis resulting from inhalation of graphite dust.

GRAS, abbreviation for **generally recognized as safe.**

Grashey method, a positioning method for producing true anteroposterior (AP) x-ray images of the scapulohumeral joint. The patient faces the x-ray tube with the affected shoulder centered to the midline of the image receptor (IR). The affected elbow is flexed, and the forearm is placed across the patient's chest. The opposite shoulder is angled 45 degrees away from the IR, and the central ray is directed perpendicularly through the affected shoulder joint.

grasping forceps, any forceps for grasping tissue and exerting traction, having finger rings and a locking mechanism.

grasp reflex [ME, *graspen,* grab; L, *reflectere,* to bend back], a reflex induced by stroking the palm or sole with the result that the fingers or toes flex in a grasping motion. The reflex is a pathologic manifestation of diseases of the premotor cortex.

grass-line ligature [AS, *graes*; L, *linea,* thread, *ligare,* to bind], a fine cord made from the fibers of a grass-cloth plant, used in orthodontics for minor adjustments or movement of the teeth.

Graves' disease /grāvz/ [Robert J. Graves, Irish physician, 1796–1853], a multisystem autoimmune disorder characterized by pronounced hyperthyroidism, usually associated with an enlarged thyroid gland and exophthalmos (abnormal protrusion of the eyeball). Typical signs are nervousness, a fine tremor of the hands, weight loss, fatigue, breathlessness, palpitations, increased heat intolerance, increased metabolic rate, and GI motility. An enlarged thymus, generalized hyperplasia of the lymph nodes, blurred or double vision, localized myxedema, atrial arrhythmias, and osteoporosis may occur.

Graves' orbitopathy /grāvz/ [Robert J. Graves, Irish physician, 1796–1853; L, *orbita,* wheel track; Gk, *pathos,* disease], the dysthyroid orbitopathy seen in Graves' disease.

gravid /grav′id/ [L, *gravidus,* pregnant], pregnant; carrying fertilized eggs or a fetus. —**gravidity, gravidness,** *n.*

gravida /grav′idə/ [L, *gravidus,* pregnant], a woman who is pregnant.

gravida macromastia, overdevelopment of the breasts during pregnancy.

gravidum gingivitis /grav′idəm/ [L, *gravidus,* pregnant, *gingiva,* gums, *itis,* inflammation], a type of gum inflammation that is associated with plaque formation during pregnancy.

gravid uterus [L, *gravidus,* pregnant, *uterus,* womb], a pregnant uterus.

gravity /grav′itē/ [L, *gravis,* heavy], the universal effect of the attraction between any body of matter and any planetary body. The force of the attraction depends on the relative masses of the bodies and on the inverse of the square of the distance between them.

gravity-eliminated plane, a supported position or plane in which the effect of gravity is absorbed or neutralized. In evaluation of muscle strength, certain tests are conducted in the gravity-eliminated plane.

gravity goniometer, an instrument used for measuring joint angles, consisting of a device that rests on or is strapped to the part to be measured and a dial that rotates behind a weighted pointer that remains vertical by force of gravity.

gray (Gy), the SI unit of absorbed radiation dose. One gray equals the energy equivalent of 1 J/kg of matter; 1 Gy equals 100 rad.

gray column, any of the three longitudinally oriented thickenings in the spinal cord, composed of gray nervous tissue and containing the nerve cell bodies. They are commonly referred to as *horns* because in transverse sections of the spinal cord they have the appearance of horns.

gray matter, the gray nervous tissue found in the cortex of the cerebrum cerebellum and the core of the spinal cord. It is predominantly composed of neuron cell bodies and unmyelinated axons. Nuclei in the gray substance of the spinal cord function as centers for all spinal reflexes.

gray ramus communicans, the communicating branch of nerves that connects the sympathetic trunk or a ganglion to the anterior ramus and contains the postganglionic sympathetic fibers.

gray scale, the property in which intensity information in ultrasonography is recorded as changes in the brightness of the gray scale display.

gray scale display, in ultrasonography, a signal-processing method for selectively amplifying and displaying the level echoes from soft tissues at the expense of the larger echoes.

gray syndrome, a toxic condition in neonates, especially premature infants, caused by a reaction to chloramphenicol. The condition is named for the characteristic ashen-gray cyanosis, which is accompanied by abdominal distension, hypothermia, vomiting, respiratory distress, and vascular collapse.

GRE, abbreviation for **Graduate Record Examination.**

great auricular nerve [AS, large; L, *auricula,* little ear, *nervus,* nerve], one of a pair of cutaneous branches of the cervical plexus, arising from the second and third cranial nerves. It is distributed to the skin of the face and that of the mastoid process.

great cardiac vein, one of the five tributaries of the coronary sinus, beginning at the apex of the heart and ascending along the anterior interventricular sulcus to the base of the ventricles. The great cardiac vein drains the blood through its tributaries from the capillaries of the myocardium.

greater omentum [AS, *great,* large; L, *omentum,* entrails], a filmy, transparent double fold of the peritoneum, draping the transverse colon and coils of the small intestine. It is a readily movable structure that spreads easily into areas of trauma, often sealing hernias and walling off infections that would otherwise cause general peritonitis.

greater palatine artery, a branch of the maxillary artery that supplies anterior regions of the medial wall and adjacent floor of the nasal cavity.

greater petrosal nerve, a branch of the facial nerve that innervates all the salivary glands above the level of the oral fissure, as well as all mucus glands in the nose and the lacrimal gland in the orbit.

greater saphenous vein, one of a pair of the longest veins in the body, which contains 10 to 20 valves along its course through the leg and the thigh before ending in the femoral vein. It begins in the medial marginal vein of the dorsum of the foot.

greater sciatic foramen [AS, *great;* Gk, *ischiadikos,* hip joint; L,*foramen,* hole], a major route of communication between the pelvic cavity and the lower limb, formed by the greater sciatic notch in the pelvic bone, the sacrotuberous and sacrospinous ligaments, and the spine of the ischium.

greater sciatic notch [AS, *great,* large; Gk, *ischiadikos,* hip joint; OFr, *enochier,* notch], a notch on the posterior border of

the hip bone between the posterior inferior iliac spine and the spine of the ischium.

greater trochanter, a large projection of the femur, to which are attached various muscles, including the gluteus medius, gluteus maximus, and obturator internus.

great foramen, a passage in the occipital bone through which the spinal cord enters the spinal column.

great membrane, the external components of a membrane, such as the layer of carbohydrate molecules on the outer surface.

great vessel, one of the large arteries and veins entering and leaving the heart. They include the aorta, the pulmonary arteries and veins, and the superior and inferior vena cava.

Greenfield filter [L. Greenfield, twentieth-century American surgeon], a filter placed in the inferior vena cava under fluoroscopic guidance. It is used in patients who are particularly vulnerable to pulmonary embolism to prevent venous emboli from entering the pulmonary circulation.

Greenfield's disease [Joseph G. Greenfield, British pathologist, 1884–1958], a disorder of the white matter of the brain tissue, characterized by an accumulation of sphingolipid in both parenchymal and supportive tissues and a diffuse loss of myelination.

green fluorescent protein (GFP), a protein obtained from the jellyfish *Aequorea victoria* that emits a bright green fluorescence when illuminated. GFP is used to monitor gene expression, gene transfer across plasma membranes, and cell surface activity.

greenhouse effect, a theorized change in the earth's climate caused by accumulation of solar heat in the earth's surface and atmosphere. Human activity contributes increasing amounts of the so-called greenhouse gases, such as carbon dioxide, methane, and chlorofluorocarbon, to the atmosphere. Some of the particles and gases in the atmosphere also allow more sunlight to filter through to the earth's surface but reflect back much of the radiant infrared energy that otherwise would escape through the atmosphere back into space.

green soap [AS, *grene*; L, *sapo*], a soft soap made from vegetable oils with sodium or potassium hydroxide in concentrations adjusted to retain glycerol. The soap actually may be any color, depending on the oils added.

green soap tincture [AS, *grene*; L, *sapo,* soap, *tinctura,* dyeing], an alcoholic solution of green soap with lavender oil added.

greenstick fracture [AS, *grene* + *stician*], an incomplete fracture in which the bone is bent but broken only on the outer arc of the bend. Children, especially those with rickets, are particularly likely to have greenstick fractures.

green tea, a herb used to prevent cancer and heart disease, for hypercholesterolemia, and as an antidiarrheal. It is effective as an antidiarrheal, and there is some epidemiologic evidence of efficacy related to its other uses.

green tobacco sickness, a nicotine-induced illness of tobacco harvest workers, characterized by headache, dizziness, vomiting, and prostration.

grenz rays [Ger, *Grenze,* boundary; L, *radius,* ray], low-energy x-rays used for treatment of skin conditions.

Greulich-Pyle method /groi′lish pīl, grōō′lik/, a technique for evaluating the bone age of children by using a single frontal radiograph of the left hand and wrist.

Grey Turner's sign [George Grey Turner, English surgeon, 1877–1951], bruising of the skin of the loin in acute hemorrhagic pancreatitis.

grid [ME, *gredire,* grate], a device used during a radiographic examination to absorb radiation that is not heading along a straight line from the x-ray source to the film.

grid cutoff, an undesirable absorption of primary-beam x-rays by a grid, which prevents useful x-rays from reaching a radiographic film. It is an effect of improper grid positioning.

grid ratio, in radiology, the ratio of the height of the lead strips to the width of the interspacing of a grid.

grief [L, *gravis,* heavy], a nearly universal pattern of physical and emotional responses to bereavement, separation, or loss. The physical components are similar to those of fear, hunger, rage, and pain.

grief reaction, a complex of somatic and psychologic symptoms associated with extreme sorrow or loss, specifically the death of a loved one. Somatic symptoms include feelings of tightness in the throat and chest with choking and shortness of breath, abdominal distress, lack of muscular power, and extreme tiredness and lethargy. Psychologic reactions involve a generalized awareness of mental anguish and discomfort accompanied by feelings of guilt, anger, hostility, extreme restlessness, inability to concentrate, and lack of capacity to initiate and maintain organized patterns of activities.

grief resolution, a nursing outcome from the Nursing Outcomes Classification (NOC) defined as adjustment to actual or impending loss.

grief work facilitation, a nursing intervention from the Nursing Interventions Classification (NIC) defined as assistance with the resolution of a significant loss.

grief work facilitation: perinatal death, a nursing intervention from the Nursing Interventions Classification (NIC) defined as assistance with the resolution of a perinatal loss.

Grifulvin, a trademark for an antifungal (griseofulvin).

grinder's asthma /grīn′dərz/ [ME, *grinden,* to crush; Gk, panting], a condition characterized by asthmatic symptoms caused by inhalation of fine particles produced by industrial grinding processes.

grinding-in, a clinical corrective grinding of one or more natural or artificial teeth to improve centric and eccentric occlusions.

grip and pinch strength, the measurable ability to exert pressure with the hand, fingers, or both. It is measured by having a patient forcefully squeeze, grip, or pinch dynamometers; results are expressed in either pounds or kilograms of pressure.

gripes /grīps/ [AS, *gripan,* to grasp], severe and usually spasmodic pain in the abdominal region caused by an intestinal disorder.

Grisactin, a trademark for an antifungal (griseofulvin).

griseofulvin /gris′ē-ōful′vin/, an antifungal prescribed in the treatment of certain fungal infections of the skin, hair, and nails.

Griswald brace, an orthosis for the control of vertebral body compression fractures. It is designed with two anterior forces that are each equal to one-half the posterior force to extend the spine.

grocer's itch [AS, *gican,* itch], a dermatitis caused by contact with mites found in grain, cheese, or dried foods.

groin [ME, *grynde*], each of two areas where the abdomen joins the thighs; the inguinal area.

grommet /grom′et/, a tube inserted through the tympanic membrane for drainage of the middle ear.

Grönblad-Strandberg syndrome /grön′blad strand′bərg/ [Ester E. Grönblad, Swedish ophthalmologist, 1898–1942; James V. Strandberg, Swedish dermatologist, 1883–1942], an autosomal-recessive disorder of connective tissue characterized by premature aging and breakdown of the skin, gray or brown streaks on the retina, and hemorrhagic arterial degeneration, including retinal bleeding that causes vision loss. Angina pectoris and hypertension are common. Weak pulse, episodic cramplike pains in the calves, and fatigue with exertion may affect the extremities.

groove [AS, *grafan,* to dig], a shallow, linear depression in various structures throughout the body, as those that form channels for nerves along the bones, those in bones for the insertion of muscles, and those between certain areas of the brain.

G

grooved pegboard test, a method for evaluating psychomotor function by measuring how quickly a subject can insert pegs into gross holes.

Groshong catheter, a modification of the Hickman catheter with a valve that is closed when the catheter is not in use, used for long-term administration of substances such as antibiotics, total parenteral nutrition, or chemotherapeutic agents.

gross [OFr, *gros,* large], **1.** macroscopic, as in gross pathology; the study of tissue changes without magnification by a microscope. **2.** large or obese.

gross anatomy, the study of the organs or parts of the body large enough to be seen with the naked eye.

Grossman principle, in tomography, the principle that when the fulcrum or axis of rotation remains at a fixed point, the focal plane is changed by raising or lowering the table top through this point to the desired height.

gross motor skills [Fr, *gros,* big; L, *movere* Old Norse, *skilja,* to cut apart], the ability to use large muscle groups that coordinate body movements involved in activities such as walking, running, jumping, throwing, and maintaining balance.

gross sensory testing, an evaluation procedure that includes assessment of passive motion sense in the shoulder, elbow, wrist, and fingers and ability to localize touch stimuli to specific fingers.

gross visual skills, the general ability of a person to track a large, bright object side-to-side or up-to-down without jerkiness, nystagmus, or convergence and to discriminate among various basic shapes and colors.

ground [AS, *grund*], **1.** in electricity, a connection between the electric circuit and the ground, which becomes a part of the circuit. **2.** in psychology, the background of a visual field that can enhance or inhibit the ability of a patient to focus on an object.

grounding pad, an inactive electrode, part of a monopolar electrocautery, that is attached to the patient and returns the current distributed from the active electrode to the generator through an attached cable to complete the electrical circuit.

ground itch, pruritic papules, urticarial vesiculopustular lesions secondary to penetration of the skin by hookworm larvae.

ground state, 1. the lowest energy level of a physical system. **2.** the stable form of an atom or molecule.

group [Fr, *groupe,* cluster], in research, any set of items or people under study.

group dynamics [Fr, *groupe*; Gk, *dynamis,* force], the interactions and relationships

that take place among group members, as well as between the group and the rest of society. It includes interdependence of group members, collective problem solving and decision making, and group conformity.

grouper /grōōp′er/, any of various usually large marine fish of the genera *Epinephelus* and *Mycteroperca,* found in tropical waters. They are often eaten by humans but sometimes contain ciguatoxin and can cause ciguatera.

group function, in dentistry, the simultaneous contacting of opposing teeth in a segment or a unit, used to stabilize a full maxillary and mandibular denture.

group-model HMO, a health maintenance organization (HMO) in which a contract is established with multispecialty medical groups for medical services. The HMO is responsible for marketing and developing contracts with enrollees and hospitals. Care is provided at hospitals where the physicians have admitting privileges or at ancillary facilities with which the HMO subcontracts.

group practice, two or more physicians, advanced practice nurses, and/or physician's assistants who work together and share facilities. The physicians may practice different specialties. Physicians who are part of a group often are prohibited from becoming independent contractors and earning money by providing medical care outside the group.

group practice without walls (GPWW), a medical practice formed to share economic risk, expenses, and marketing efforts. Physicians retain separate offices and finances. Often a central site is established to house administrative services and some or all ancillary services.

group therapy, the application of psychotherapeutic techniques within a group of people (usually 10 or fewer) who experience similar difficulties. Generally a group leader directs the discussion of problems in an attempt to promote individual psychologic growth and favorable personality change. Group therapy has been found to be particularly effective in the treatment of various addictions.

growing fracture [AS, *growan*; L, *fractura,* to break], a fracture, usually linear, in which consecutive radiographic images show a gradual separation of the fracture edges over time. The separation is often caused by the pressure of soft tissues.

growing pains, 1. rheumatism-like pains that occur in the muscles and joints of children or adolescents as a result of fatigue, emotional problems, postural defects, and other causes that are not related to growth and that may be symptoms of various disorders. **2.** emotional and psychologic problems experienced during adolescence.

growth¹ [AS, *growan,* to grow], **1.** an increase in the size of an organism or any of its parts, as measured in increments of weight, volume, or linear dimensions, that occurs as a result of hyperplasia or hypertrophy. **2.** the normal progressive anatomic, physiologic development from infancy to adulthood that is the result of gradual and normal processes of accretion and assimilation. **3.** any abnormal localized increase of the size or number of cells, as in a tumor or neoplasm. **4.** a proliferation of cells, specifically a bacterial culture or mold.

growth², a nursing outcome from the Nursing Outcomes Classification (NOC) defined as normal increase in bone size and body weight during growth years.

growth charts, graphic displays of normal progressive changes in height, weight, and head circumference. They consider the range of growth as expressed in percentiles, or as standard deviation from the mean for average height, weight, and BMI for age.

growth curve, a graphic display of data showing proliferation of cell numbers in a culture as a function of time.

growth factor, any protein that stimulates the division and differentiation of specific types of cells.

growth factor receptor, a plasma membrane–spanning protein that binds with a specific growth factor on the external surface of a cell and transduces a signal that triggers cell division.

growth failure, a lack of normal physical and psychologic development that results from genetic, nutritional, pathologic, or psychosocial factors.

growth hormone (GH), a single-chain peptide secreted by the anterior pituitary gland in response to GH-releasing hormone. Its secretion is controlled in part by the hypothalamus. GH promotes protein synthesis in all cells, increases fat mobilization and use of fatty acids for energy, and decreases use of carbohydrates. Growth effects depend on the presence of thyroid hormone, insulin, and carbohydrate. Somatomedins, proteins produced chiefly in the liver, play a vital role in GH-induced skeletal growth.

growth hormone–releasing hormone (GH-RH), a neuropeptide released by the hypothalamus that travels to the anterior pituitary to stimulate growth hormone release.

growth hormone (GH) test, a blood test used to identify GH deficiency in adolescents who have short stature, delayed sexual maturity, or other growth deficiencies. It is also used to document the diagnosis of GH excess in gigantic or acromegalic patients and as a screening test for pituitary hypofunction.

growth phase, one of the stages in the growth of a neoplasm.

growth retardation, failure of an individual to develop at a normal rate of height and weight for his or her age.

Grünfelder's reflex /grYn′feldərz, grēn′-/, an involuntary dorsiflexion of the great toe with a fanlike spreading of the other toes, caused by continued pressure on the posterior lateral fontanel.

grunting [ME, *grunten*], abnormal, short, deep, hoarse sounds in exhalation that often accompany severe chest pain. The grunt occurs because the glottis briefly stops the flow of air, halting the movement of the lungs and their surrounding or supporting structures. Grunting is most often heard in a person who has pneumonia, pulmonary edema, or fractured or bruised ribs, or in newborns with atelectasis.

GSA, abbreviation for **Gerontological Society of America.**

GSD, abbreviation for **genetically significant dose.**

GSR, abbreviation for **galvanic skin response.**

gt, abbreviation for **gutta.**

GTP, abbreviation for **guanosinetriphosphate.**

GTPase, enzyme activity that catalyzes the hydrolysis of guanosine triphosphate to guanosine diphosphate and orthophosphate.

GTT, abbreviation for **glucose tolerance test.**

gtt, gtts, GTTS, abbreviation for **guttae.**

GU, abbreviation for **genitourinary.**

guaiac /gwī′ak/, a wood resin, formerly used as a reagent in laboratory tests for the presence of occult blood.

guaiac test, a test, using guaiac as a reagent, formerly performed on feces and urine for detecting occult blood in the intestinal and urinary tracts.

guaifenesin /gwī′əfen′əsin/, glyceryl guaiacolate, a white to slightly gray powder with a bitter taste and faint odor, widely used as an expectorant.

guanabenz acetate /gwan′abenz/, a centrally acting alpha₂-adrenergic agonist that decreases sympathetic nervous system tone. It is prescribed in the treatment of hypertension.

guanadrel /gwä′nädrel/, an adrenergic neuron blocking agent, used in the treatment of hypertension, used as the sulfate salt.

guanadrel sulfate /gwan′ədril/, an antihypertensive agent prescribed in the treatment of hypertension in patients who do not respond to first-line agents, usually in combination with a diuretic.

guanethidine sulfate /gwaneth′idēn/, a peripherally acting antiadrenergic antihypertensive prescribed in the treatment of moderate and severe hypertension.

guanine /gwan′ēn/, a purine base that is a component of DNA and RNA. In free or uncombined form, it occurs in trace amounts in most cells, usually as a product of the enzymatic hydrolysis of nucleic acids and nucleotides.

guanine deaminase, an enzyme that catalyzes the hydrolysis of guanine to xanthine and ammonia.

guanosine /gwan′ōsēn/, a nucleoside composed of guanine and a sugar, D-ribose. It is a major component of the nucleotides guanosine monophosphate and guanosine triphosphate and of RNA.

guanosine monophosphate (GMP), a nucleotide that plays an important role in various metabolic reactions and in the formation of RNA from DNA templates.

guanosine triphosphate (GTP), a high-energy nucleotide that functions in various metabolic reactions, such as the activation of fatty acids and the formation of peptide bonds in protein synthesis.

guaranine /gwərä′nin/, caffeine.

guardian ad litem /ad lī′təm/ [L, *ad litem,* to litigate], in law, a person who is appointed by a court to prosecute or defend a suit for an infant or an incapacitated person. A guardian ad litem is sometimes appointed when a person's life is in imminent danger and that person refuses treatment.

guardianship, a legal status that places the care and property of an individual in the hands of another person. Implementation of the law varies in different cases and jurisdictions.

Guarnieri's bodies /goō′ärnyer′ēz/ [Giuseppi Guarnieri, Italian physician, 1856–1918], acidophilic inclusion bodies that are formed in the cytoplasm of cells infected with cowpox or vaccinia virus.

Gubbay test of motor proficiency, a screening test for the identification of developmental dyspraxia.

gubernaculum, a fetal ligament that passes through the anterior abdominal wall and connects the inferior pole of each gonad with primordia of the scrotum in men and the labia majora in women.

Guedel's signs /goō′dəlz/ [Arthur E. Guedel, American anesthesiologist, 1883–1956], a system for describing the stages and planes of anesthesia based on physical signs observed in the patient. These stages are most applicable to inhalation anesthesia and are difficult to delineate when combination or modern anesthetics are given.

Guérin's fracture /gāraNz′/ [Alphonse F.M. Guérin, French surgeon, 1816–1895], a break in the maxilla.

guggul, a herb used for high low-density lipoprotein cholesterol, elevated triglycerides, and weight loss.

guided imagery[1] /gī′did/, a therapeutic technique in which the patient enters a relaxed state and focuses on an image related to the issue being confronted. The therapist uses the image as the basis of an interactive dialogue to help the person resolve the issue.

guided imagery[2], a nursing intervention from the Nursing Interventions Classification (NIC) defined as purposeful use of imagination to achieve particular state, outcome, or action or to direct attention away from undesirable sensations.

guide dog [ME, *guiden,* to guard; OE, *docga*], a dog trained to aid in the mobility of a blind or partially blind person. Guide dogs also may be trained to serve as "ears" for deaf persons.

guided reminiscence, in reminiscence therapy, the eliciting of recollections of past experiences by the use of open-ended questions.

guide plane [ME, *guiden,* to guard; L, *planum,* level ground], 1. a part of an orthodontic appliance that has an established inclined plane for changing the occlusal relation of the maxillary and mandibular teeth and for permitting their movement to normal positions. 2. a plane that is developed on the occlusal surfaces of occlusion rims for positioning the mandible in centric relation. 3. two or more parallel vertical surfaces of abutment teeth shaped to direct the path of placement and removal of a partial denture.

guide-shoe marks, a radiographic image artifact caused by pressure of the guide shoes, the curved metal lips that guide x-ray film in automatic developing systems.

guidewire /gīd′wī·ər/ [ME, *guiden,* to guard; AS, *wir*], a device used to position an IV catheter, endotracheal tube, central venous line, or gastric feeding tube or to localize a tumor during open breast biopsy.

guiding, in occupational therapy, a method in which therapists assist their patients in perceiving the environment by directing movement of their hands and bodies in functional activities.

Guillain-Barré syndrome /gēyan′bärā′/ [Georges Guillain, French neurologist, 1876–1951; Jean A. Barré, French neurologist, 1880–1967], an idiopathic, peripheral polyneuritis that occurs 1 to 3 weeks after a mild episode of fever associated with a viral infection or with immunization but that can also occur with no preceding illness. Symmetric pain and weakness affect the extremities, and paralysis may develop. The neuritis may spread to the trunk and face.

guilt [AS, *gylt,* delinquency], a feeling caused by tension between the ego and the superego when one falls below the standards set for oneself, or a remorseful awareness of having done something wrong.

guilt work facilitation, a nursing intervention from the Nursing Interventions Classification (NIC) defined as helping another to cope with painful feelings of actual or perceived responsibility.

guilty, in criminal law, a verdict by the court that to a moral certainty it is beyond reasonable doubt that the defendant committed the crime and is responsible for the offense as charged.

Gulf War syndrome, a group of medical and psychologic complaints, including fatigue, skin rash, memory loss, and headaches, experienced by men and women who served in the 1991 Persian Gulf War.

gum, a sticky excretion from certain plants.

gumboil [AS, *goma,* gum + *byl*], an abscess of the gingiva and periosteum resulting from injury, infection, or dental decay. The gum is characteristically red, swollen, and tender.

gumma /gum′ə/ *pl.* **gummas, gummata** [AS, *goma,* gum], **1.** a granuloma, characteristic of tertiary syphilis, varying from 1 mm to 1 cm in diameter. It is usually encapsulated and contains a central necrotic mass surrounded by inflammatory and fibrotic zones of tissue. **2.** a soft granulomatous lesion that sometimes accompanies TB.

Gunning's splint [Thomas B. Gunning, American dentist, 1813–1889; D, *splinte,* split], a splint used to support the maxilla and the mandible during jaw surgery.

gunshot fracture [ME, *gunne;* AS, *sceotan,* to shoot; L, *fractura,* break], a fracture caused by a bullet or similar missile.

gunshot wound (GSW), penetration of the body by a bullet, commonly marked by a small entrance wound and a larger exit wound. The wound is usually accompanied by damage to blood vessels, bones, and other tissues.

Gunson method, a method of radiographic examination of the pharynx and upper esophagus during swallowing.

Günther's disease /gun′thərz/ [Hans Günther, German physician, 1884–1956], a rare congenital disorder of porphyrin metabolism that is associated with sunlight-induced skin lesions.

gurgle [Fr, *gargouiller,* to gurgle], an abnormal coarse sound heard during auscultation, especially over large cavities or over a trachea nearly filled with secretions.

gurney /gur′nē/, a cot with wheeled legs, used in hospitals to transport patients.

gurry /gur′ē/, *informal.* the detritus incident to physical trauma or surgery, including body fluids, secretions, and tissue.

gustation /gustā′shən/ [L, *gustare,* to taste], the sense and act of tasting foods, beverages, or other substances.

gustatory /gus′tətôr′ē/ [L, *gustare,* to taste], pertaining to the act or sense of taste or the organs of taste.

gustatory hallucination [L, *gustare,* to taste, *alucinari,* wandering mind], a false taste sensation of either food or beverage on the mucous membrane lining the empty mouth.

gustatory papilla [L, *gustare,* to taste, *papilla,* nipple], any of the small tissue elevations in the mouth that contain sense organs of taste, such as the circumvallate papillae of the tongue.

gut [AS, *guttas*], **1.** intestine. **2.** *informal.* digestive tract. **3.** suture material manufactured from the intestines of sheep.

gut-associated lymphoid tissue, lymphoid tissue associated with the gut, including the tonsils, Peyer's patches, lamina propria of the GI tract, and appendix.

Guthrie's bacterial inhibition assay (GBIA) /guth′rēz/, a screening for phenylketonuria (PKU) used to detect the abnormal presence of phenylalanine metabolites in the blood.

Guthrie test /guth′rē/, a screening tool used with infants to determine the level of phenylalanine in the blood. Blood is placed on filter paper, which is then placed on agar plates with a strain of *Bacillus subtilis* that requires phenylalanine for growth. If there is excessive phenylalanine in the blood sample, a halo will form around the filter paper, and additional tests are required to determine the seriousness of the hyperphenylalaninemia.

gutta (gt) /gut′ə, gŏŏt′ä/ [L, drop], one drop, or about 1 minim, of a medication.

guttae (gtt, gtts, GTTS) [L, drops], the plural of **gutta,** more than one drop, as in **guttae pro auribus,** or eardrops, or **guttae ophthalmicae,** or eyedrops.

gutta-percha /gut′ə pur′chə/ [Malay, *getah-percha,* latex sap], the coagulated rubbery sap of various tropical trees, used for temporarily sealing the dressings of prepared tooth cavities.

gutta-percha point, a small cone of gutta-percha, which, along with endodontic sealer, may be used to fill a root canal or to determine the depth and topographic

G

characteristics of periodontal pockets and fistulas by means of radiography.

guttate psoriasis /gut´āt/ [L, *gutta,* drop; Gk, *itch*], an acute form of psoriasis that consists of teardrop-shaped red scaly papules and patches measuring 3 to 10 mm all over the body.

guttural /gut´ərəl/ [L, *guttur,* throat], pertaining to or belonging to the throat, including low-pitched, raspy voice quality.

Guyon tunnel [Felix J. Guyon, French surgeon, 1831–1920], a fibroosseous tunnel formed in part by the pisohamate ligament of the hand. It contains the ulnar artery and nerve and may be the site of a compression injury.

GVHD, abbreviation for **graft-versus-host disease.**

GVHR, abbreviation for *graft-versus-host reaction.*

Gy, abbreviation for the SI unit **gray.**

gymnema, a herb used to reduce high blood glucose levels. It may have some efficacy.

gyn, 1. *informal.* abbreviation for **gynecologist. 2.** abbreviation for **gynecology.**

gynandrous /gīnan´drəs, jī-/ [Gk, *gyne,* woman, *aner,* man], describing a man or a woman who has some of the physical characteristics usually attributed to the other sex.—**gynandry,** *n.*

gynecography /gī´nə-, jin´əkog´rəfē/, the radiographic examination of the female pelvic organs by means of intraperitoneal gas insufflation.

gynecoid obesity, obesity in which fat is localized in the lower half of the body, most frequently seen in women and having a better prognosis for morbidity and mortality than android obesity.

gynecoid pelvis /gī´nəkoid, jin´ək-/ [Gk, *gyne* + *eidos,* form; L, *pelvis,* basin], a type of pelvis characteristic of the normal female and associated with the smallest incidence of fetopelvic disproportion. The inlet is nearly round, the sacrum is parallel to the posterior aspect of the symphysis pubis, the sidewalls are straight, and the ischial spines are blunt and do not encroach on the space in the true pelvis.

gynecologic examination, pelvic examination.

gynecologic operative procedures [Gk, *gynaikos,* of a woman; L, *operari,* to work, *procedere,* to proceed], surgical intervention on the female reproductive system.

gynecologist /gī´nəkol´əjist, jī´-, jin´-/, a physician who specializes in the health care of women, including diseases of the reproductive organs and breasts.

gynecology (gyn) /gī´nəkol´əjē, jī´-, jin´-/ [Gk, *gyne* + *logos,* science], the study of diseases of the female reproductive organs, including the breasts. Unlike most specialties in medicine, gynecology encompasses surgical and nonsurgical expertise. It is frequently studied and practiced in conjunction with obstetrics.—**gynecologic, gynecological,** *adj.*

gynecomastia /gī´nəkōmas´tē-ə, jī´-, jin´-/ [Gk, *gyne* + *mastos,* breast], an abnormal enlargement of one or both breasts in males. The condition is usually temporary and benign. It may be caused by hormonal imbalance; a tumor of an adrenal gland, testis, or pituitary; use of medication that contains estrogens or steroidal compounds; or failure of the liver to inactivate circulating estrogen, as in alcoholic cirrhosis. Less commonly the gynecomastia may be caused by a hormone-secreting tumor of the breast, lung, or other organ.

Gyne-Lotrimin, a trademark for an antifungal (clotrimazole).

gynephobia /gī´nəfō´bē-ə, jī´-, jin´-/ [Gk, *gyne* + *phobos,* fear], an anxiety disorder characterized by a morbid fear of women or by a morbid aversion to the society of women.

gynogamone /gī´nōgam´ōn/ [Gk, *gyne* + *gamos,* marriage], a chemical secreted by female gametes that is believed to attract male gametes.

gypsum /jip´səm/, a mineral composed mainly of crushed calcium sulfate hemihydrate. It is the main ingredient in making plaster of paris surgical casts and impressions for dentures.

gyrase /jī´rās/, an enzyme that promotes the unwinding of the closed circular DNA helix of bacteria.

gyromagnetic ratio (γ), a value characteristic of any magnetic nucleus that determines the Larmor frequency, f_L, in a given magnetic field B ($f_L = \gamma_B$).

gyrus /jī´rəs/ /jī´rī/, *pl.* **gyri** [Gk, *gyro,* circle], one of the winding convolutions of the cerebral hemisphere of the brain. They are created by infolding of the cortex and are separated by the shallow grooves (sulci) or deeper grooves (fissures).

H

[H+], symbol for **hydrogen ion.**

h, **1.** abbreviation for **haustus. 2.** abbreviation for **hecto-. 3.** abbreviation for **height. 4.** abbreviation for *hora,* the Latin word for hour. **5.** abbreviation for *horizontal.* **6.** abbreviation for *hyperopia.* **7.** symbol for **Planck's constant.**

H, **1.** symbol for the element **hydrogen. 2.** abbreviation for **henry.**

¹**H,** symbol for **protium,** an isotope of hydrogen.

²**H,** symbol for **deuterium,** an isotope of hydrogen.

³**H,** symbol for **tritium,** an isotope of hydrogen.

H₀, symbol for **null hypothesis.**

HA, abbreviation for **hepatitis A.**

HA-1A, a genetically engineered antibody used in the treatment of gram-negative bacteremia and septic shock. The antibody binds to bacterial lipopolysaccharide.

HAAg, abbreviation for *hepatitis A antigen.*

HAART, abbreviation for **highly active antiretroviral therapy.**

Haas method, a technique for producing radiographic images of the interior of the skull. The patient rests the forehead and nose on the table so that the x-ray beam enters the skull near the base of the occipital bone and emerges on the frontal bone above the nasal bone.

habeas corpus /hā′bē·əs kôr′pəs/ [L, you have the body], a right retained by all psychiatric patients that provides for the release of individuals who claim they are being deprived of their liberty and detained illegally. A hearing for this determination takes place in a court of law, where the patient's sanity may be at issue.

habilitation /həbil′itā′shən/, the process of supplying a person with the means to develop maximum independence in ADL through training or treatment.

habit [L, *habitus,* condition], **1.** a customary or particular practice, manner, or mode of behavior. **2.** an involuntary pattern of behavior or thought. **3.** the habitual use of drugs or narcotics.

habitat /hab′itat/ [L, *habitare,* to dwell], a natural environment where an organism may live and grow normally.

habit spasm, an involuntary twitching or tic. It usually involves a small muscle group

of the face, neck, or shoulders and causes movements such as spasmodic blinking or rapid jerking of the head to the side.

habit tic [L, *habitus,* condition; Fr, *tic*], a brief recurrent movement of a muscle group, such as a blink, grimace, or sudden head turning, that is of psychogenic rather than organic origin.

habit training, the process of teaching a child how to adjust to the demands of the external world by forming certain habits, primarily those related to eating, sleeping, elimination, and dress.

habitual abortion /həbich′ōō·əl/ [L, *habituare,* to become used to], spontaneous termination of three successive pregnancies before the twentieth week of gestation.

habitual dislocation [L, *habitus,* condition + *dis* + *locare,* to place], a dislocation that recurs repeatedly after reduction.

habitual hyperthermia, a condition of unknown cause that occurs in young females, characterized by body temperatures of 99° F to 100.5° F regularly or intermittently for years, associated with fatigue, malaise, vague aches and pains, insomnia, bowel disturbances, and headaches.

habituation /həbich′ōō·ā′shən/ [L, *habituare,* to become used to], **1.** an acquired tolerance gained by repeated exposure to a particular stimulus. **2.** a decline and eventual elimination of a conditioned response by repetition of the conditioned stimulus. **3.** psychological and emotional dependence on a drug, tobacco, or alcohol that results from the repeated use of the substance but without the addictive, physiological need to increase dosage.

habitus /hab′itəs/, a person's appearance or physique, as an athletic habitus.

HACEK, acronym for *Haemophilus, Actinobacillus, Cardiobacterium, Eikenella,* and *Kingella,* microorganisms associated with infective endocarditis.

hacking cough [AS, *haeccan* + *cohettan*], a short, weak repeating cough, often caused by irritation of the larynx by a postnasal drip.

HAD, abbreviation for **HIV-associated dementia.**

Haemophilus /hēmof′iləs/ [Gk, *haima,* blood, *philein,* to love], a genus of gram-negative pathogenic bacteria, frequently found in the respiratory tract of humans and other animals.

Haemophilus influenzae, a small gram-negative nonmotile parasitic bacterium that occurs in two forms, encapsulated and nonencapsulated, and in six types, a, b, c, d, e, and f. *H. influenzae* is found in the throats of 30% of healthy, normal people. In children and in debilitated older people, severe destructive inflammation of the larynx, trachea, and bronchi may result from infection. Subacute bacterial endocarditis, purulent meningitis, and pneumonia also may be caused by it. Several *H. influenzae* B conjugate vaccines are available.

Haemophilus influenzae pneumonia, bacterial pneumonia caused by infection with *H. influenzae*, seen mainly in young children and debilitated or immunocompromised adults.

hafnium (Hf) /haf′nē-əm/ [Hafnia, Medieval Latin name of Copenhagen, Denmark], a hard, brittle silver-gray metallic element of the third transition series. Its atomic number is 72; its atomic mass is 178.49.

Hagedorn needle /hä′gedôrn/ [Werner Hagedorn, German physician, 1831–1894], a flat surgical needle with a cutting edge near its point and a very large eye at the other end.

Haglund's deformity [Sims E.P. Haglund, Swedish orthopedist, 1870–1937], a foot disorder characterized by an enlarged posterosuperior lateral aspect of the calcaneus, often associated with an inverted subtalar joint. It is a common cause of posterior Achilles bursitis.

Hainsworth, Margaret A., a nursing theorist who, with Mary Lermann Burke and Georgene Gaskill Eakes, developed the Theory of Chronic Sorrow to describe the ongoing feelings of loss that arise from illness, debilitation, or death.

hair [AS, *haer*], a filament of keratin consisting of a root and a shaft formed in a specialized follicle in the epidermis. Scalp hair grows at an average rate of 1 mm every 3 days, body and eyebrow hair at a much slower rate.

hair analysis [AS, *haer*; Gk, a loosening], chemical analysis of a hair sample to find possible evidence of exposure to a toxic substance. Molecules of lead compounds and other chemicals are absorbed and stored in hair shafts. Hair analysis is also used to determine possible causes of malnutrition. Samples for analysis are taken from areas close to the scalp to eliminate chances that toxic chemicals found in the hair may have been absorbed from air pollutants.

hair care, a nursing intervention from the Nursing Interventions Classification (NIC) defined as promotion of neat, clean, attractive hair.

hair cycle, the successive phases of the production and then loss of hair, consisting of anagen, catagen, and telogen.

hair follicle [AS, *haer*; L, *folliculus,* a small bag], a tube-like opening in the epidermis where the hair shaft develops and into which the sebaceous glands open.

hairline fracture [AS, *haer*; L, *linea* + *fractura*], a minor fracture that appears on x-ray film as a thin line between two segments of a bone. The segments remain in alignment, and the fracture may not extend completely through the bone. A fatigue hairline fracture may develop without apparent injury and in the absence of trauma.

hair transplantation, a form of dermatologic surgery and plastic surgery, performed to correct scalp hair deficiencies caused by hormonal changes, burns, or injuries. The procedure uses existing hair to fill in bald areas, either by grafting hair-bearing tissue over the bald area directly or by using micrografts of follicles to restore the hairline.

hairy-cell leukemia [AS, *haer*; L, *cella,* storeroom; Gk, *leukos,* white, *haima,* blood], an uncommon neoplasm of blood-forming tissues, characterized by pancytopenia, enlargement of the spleen, and many fine projections on the surface of reticulum cells in the blood and bone marrow. The disease usually appears in the fifth decade with an insidious onset and a variable course marked by anemia, thrombocytopenia, and spontaneous bruising.

hairy leukoplakia, a form of leukoplakia characterized by a white plaque that is markedly folded in appearance or smooth and is often visible on one or both lateral borders of the tongue. It is associated with severe immunodeficiency, occurs in HIV-infected patients, and is believed to result from the Epstein-Barr virus.

hairy nevus [AS, *haer*; L, *naevus,* birthmark], a mole, usually pigmented, that has hairs growing from it.

hairy tongue, a dark, pigmented overgrowth of the filiform papillae of the tongue that has a thickened, furry appearance. It is a benign and frequent side effect of use of some antibiotics.

halcinonide /həlsin′ənīd/, a topical glucocorticoid prescribed topically for the treatment of inflammation.

Halcion, a trademark for a hypnotic agent (triazolam).

Haldol, a trademark for a tranquilizer (haloperidol).

half-life (*t*-½) [AS, *haelf* + *lif*], **1.** the time required for a radioactive substance to lose 50% of its activity through decay. **2.** the amount of time required to reduce a drug level to half of its initial value. Usually the term refers to time necessary to reduce the plasma value to half of its initial value. After five half-lives, 97% of a single drug dose will be eliminated.

half-normal saline, a solution of 0.45% NaCl used for mucosal hydration. As the water in the solution evaporates, the saline concentration increases, achieving nearly normal saline concentration in the respiratory tract.

half-sibling, one of two or more children who have one parent in common (a half-brother or half-sister).

half-value layer (HVL), the amount of absorbing material required to attenuate a beam of radiation to half its original level.

halfway house, a specialized treatment facility, usually for psychiatric patients who no longer require complete hospitalization but who need some care and time to adjust to living independently. Halfway houses are also used for substance abuse recovery.

halisteresis /həlis′tərē′sis/ [Gk, *hals,* salt, *steresis,* absence of], a theoretic process of bone resorption in which bone salts are removed by humoral mechanisms and returned to body tissue fluids, leaving behind a decalcified bone matrix.

halitosis /hal′itō′sis/ [L, *halitus,* breath; Gk, *osis,* condition], offensive breath resulting from poor oral hygiene; dental or oral infections; ingestion of certain foods, such as garlic or alcohol, use of tobacco; or some systemic diseases.

Hallervorden-Spatz syndrome /hol′ərfôr′ dən shpots/ [Julius Hallervorden, German neurologist, 1882–1965; H. Spatz, German neurologist, 1888–1969], a progressive degenerative neurologic disease of children, with symptoms of parkinsonism. It is characterized by rigidity, athetosis, and dementia.

Hall, Lydia E. [1906–1969], a nursing theorist who presented her Care, Core, and Cure Model in "Nursing: What Is It?" in *The Canadian Nurse* (1964). Hall believed that nursing functions differently in three overlapping circles that constitute aspects of patients. She labeled the circles *the body* (the care), *the disease* (the cure), and *the person* (the core). Hall viewed nursing in relation to the core aspect as concerned with the therapeutic use of self in communicating with the patient.

hallucination /həloo′sinā′shən/ [L, *alucinari,* to wander in mind], a sensory perception that does not result from an external stimulus and that occurs in the waking state. It can occur in any of the senses and is classified accordingly as auditory, gustatory, olfactory, tactile, or visual.—**hallucinate,** /həloo′sənāt/ *v.*

hallucination management, a nursing intervention from the Nursing Interventions Classification (NIC) defined as promoting the safety, comfort, and reality orientation of a patient experiencing hallucinations.

hallucinatory neuralgia /həloo′sənətôr′ē/, a feeling of localized pain that persists after an episode of severe throbbing pain has subsided.

hallucinogen /həloo′sənəjen′, hal′əsin′əjən, hal′yəsin′əjən/ [L, *alucinari,* to wander in mind; Gk, *genein,* to produce], a substance that causes excitation of the CNS, characterized by hallucination, mood change, anxiety, sensory distortion, delusion, and depersonalization; increased pulse, temperature, and BP; and dilation of the pupils.

hallucinogenesis /-jen′əsis/ [L, *alucinari,* to wander in mind; Gk, *genein,* to produce], a cause or source of hallucinations.

hallucinosis /haloo′sinō′sis/ [L, *alucinari;* Gk, *osis,* condition], a pathologic mental state in which awareness consists primarily or exclusively of hallucinations.

hallux /hal′əks/ *pl.* **halluces** [L, *hallex,* large toe], the great toe.

hallux rigidus, a painful deformity of the great toe, limiting motion at the metatarsophalangeal joint.

hallux valgus, a deformity in which the great toe is angled away from the midline of the body toward the other toes. In some cases the great toe rides over or under the other toes.

hallux varus, a deformity in which the great toe is angled away from the other toes.

halobetasol /hal′oba′tāsol/, a very high potency synthetic corticosteroid used topically in the form of the propionate as an antiinflammatory and antipruritic agent.

halo effect, the beneficial effect of an interview or other encounter, as may occur in the course of a research project or a health care visit. It is the result of indefinable interpersonal factors present in the interaction.

halofantrine, an antimalarial.

Halog, a trademark for a topical glucocorticoid (halcinonide).

halogen /hal′ōjən/ [Gk, *hals,* salt, *genein,* to produce], any member of the group 17 (or group VIIA) in the periodic table: fluorine, chlorine, bromine, iodine, and astatine.

halogenated hydrocarbon /həloj′ənā′tid/ [Gk, *hals,* salt, *genein,* to produce, *hydor,* water; L, *carbo,* coal], a volatile liquid used as an inhalation anesthetic, administered in combination with oxygen and/or nitrous oxide. The only halogenated hydrocarbon used for anesthesia is halothane.

halogenoderma /hal′ōdur′mə/, skin changes caused by ingestion or injection of halogen, usually a bromide or an iodide.

halo nevus, a benign melanocyte that appears as a central brown mole surrounded by a circle of depigmented skin.

Over a period of months, the central nevus becomes flat and loses its pigment, leaving a round white macule. Eventually the halo repigments.

haloperidol /hal′ŏper′ədôl/, a butyrophenone antipsychotic. It is prescribed in the treatment of schizophrenia, in the control of tics and verbal utterance of Tourette's syndrome, in the treatment of severe behavioral problems in children and as a sleep aid.

halo sign [Gk, *halos*, circular floor; L, *signum*, mark], a halo effect produced in the radiograph of the fetal head between the subcutaneous fat and the cranium. It is said to be indicative of intrauterine death of the fetus.

Halotestin, a trademark for an androgen (fluoxymesterone).

halothane /hal′əthān/, an inhalation anesthetic prescribed for induction and maintenance of general anesthesia.

halothane-related hepatitis, an adverse reaction of some patients to inhalation of halothane, characterized by hepatitis and a severe fever that develops several days after exposure to the anesthetic.

halo vest [Gk, *halos*, circular floor; AS, *kasta*], an orthopedic device used to help immobilize the neck and head, providing traction to the cervical spine. It incorporates a vest, usually with shoulder straps, and metal bars within the cast that connect the vest to secure pins to a band around the skull. The halo is attached to the skull by pins or screws.

Halsted's forceps /hal′stedz/ [William S. Halsted, American surgeon, 1852–1922], 1. a small pointed hemostatic forceps. 2. a forceps with slender jaws for grasping arteries and other blood vessels.

Halsted's suture [William S. Halsted], the union of two adjoining skin surfaces by a suture placed through the subcuticular fascia.

HALT, abbreviation for **Hypertension and Lipid Trial.**

hamartoma, a new tissue growth resembling a tumor. It results from a defective overgrowth in tissue formation.

hamate bone /ham′āt/ [L, *hamatus*, hooked], a carpal bone that rests on the fourth and fifth metacarpal bones and projects a hooklike process, the hamulus, from its palmar surface.

hammer finger [AS, *hamer* + *finger*], a permanently flexed terminal phalanx caused by an injury to the extensor tendon.

hammer toe [AS, *hamer* + *ta*], a foot digit permanently flexed at the proximal phalangeal joint and hyperextended at the distal interphalangeal joint, producing a clawlike appearance. The anomaly may be present in more than one digit but is most common in the second toe.

Hampton's hump [Aubrey O. Hampton, American radiologist, 1900–1955], a soft tissue image in a radiograph of the lung that is a manifestation of a pulmonary infarction.

Ham's test, a rarely performed blood test used in the diagnosis of paroxysmal nocturnal hemoglobinuria.

hamstring muscle [AS, *hamm* + *streng*], any of the group of three muscles at the back of the thigh: medially the semimembranosus and the semitendinosus and laterally the biceps femoris.

hamstring reflex, a normal deep tendon reflex elicited by tapping one of the hamstring tendons behind the knee, causing contraction of the tendon and flexion of the knee.

hamstring tendon, one of the three tendons from the three hamstring muscles in the back of the thigh. The one lateral and the two medial hamstring tendons connect the hamstring muscles to the knee.

hamulus /ham′yo͞o·ləs/ *pl.* **hamuli** [L, little hook], 1. a general term denoting a hook-shaped process. 2. hook of the hamate.

hand [AS, *hand*], the part of the upper limb distal to the forearm. It is the most flexible part of the skeleton and has a total of 29 bones, 8 forming the carpus, 5 forming the metacarpus, 14 forming the phalangeal section, and 2 sesamoid bones.

handblock [AS, *hand*; Fr, *bloc*], a device made of a wood block several inches high with a firm handle that can assist a disabled patient in sitting push-ups, which can enhance transfers or mobility in bed.

hand condenser, in dentistry, an instrument for compacting amalgams or gold foil, using force applied by the operator, with or without supplementary force from a mallet wielded by an assistant.

handedness /han′didnes/ [AS, *hand* + *ness*, condition], a preference for use of either the left or right hand. The preference is related to cerebral dominance: left-handedness corresponds to dominance of the right side of the brain, and vice versa.

hand-foot-and-mouth disease, a viral infection usually caused by coxsackie A virus but also by enterovirus 71. It is characterized by the appearance of painful ulcers and vesicles on the mucous membranes of the mouth and on the hands and feet. The disease is very contagious and mainly affects children, including infants. It is spread with oral secretions or stool.

handicapped /han′dikapt/ [*hand in cap*, a seventeenth-century game with forfeits], referring to a person who has a congenital or acquired mental or physical defect that interferes with normal functioning of the body system or the ability to be self-sufficient in modern society.

handpiece /hand′pēs/, a handheld extraoral or intraoral device for holding rotary instruments in a dental engine or condensing points in mechanical condensing units. It can be driven by an arm, cable, belt, or tube to a power source, such as a motor; directly to a motor; or to an air-pressure driven motor.

hand scaling, the manual removal of plaque and calculus from the surface of a tooth by an instrument.

Hand's disease /handz/, a rare idiopathic condition in which lipids accumulate in the body and manifest as histiocytic granuloma in bone.

hanging drop preparation [ME, *hangen,* to hang; AS, *dropa,* to fall; L, *praeparer,* to make ready], a technique used for the examination and identification of certain microorganisms, such as spirochetes or trichomonads. A drop of a fluid specimen is placed on a glass coverslip, which is then inverted carefully and placed over the slide so that the drop is hanging from the slip into the concavity in the slide. The delicate structures and the method of movement characteristic of the species may then be viewed through the microscope.

hangman's fracture, a break in the posterior elements of the cervical vertebrae with dislocation of C2.

hangnail [AS, *angnaegl,* troublesome nail], a piece of partially disconnected epidermis of the cuticle or nail fold. Tearing the skin fragment causes a red, painful, easily infected sore.

hangover, a popular term for a group of symptoms, including nausea, thirst, fatigue, headache, and irritability, resulting from the heavy consumption of alcohol and certain drugs.

Hanhart's syndrome /hän′härts/ [Ernst Hanhart, Swiss physician, 1891–1973], any of several syndromes of variable inheritance, characterized chiefly by severe micrognathia, high nose root, small eyelid fissures, low-set ears, and variable absence of digits or limbs, usually below the elbow or knee.

Hanot's disease /hanōz′/ [Victor C. Hanot, French physician, 1844–1896], primary biliary cirrhosis.

Hansel stain, a stain used to detect eosinophils in urine or other body fluids, the eosinophils staining red against a background of blue.

Hansen's bacillus [Gerard H.A. Hansen, Norwegian physician, 1841–1912; L, *bacillum,* a small rod], the acid-fast *Mycobacterium leprae,* the cause of leprosy.

Hantaan virus, a virus of the genus *Hantavirus* that causes severe epidemic hemorrhagic fever in Asia.

Hantavirus, a genus of RNA viruses in the *Bunyaviridae* family, the cause of several different forms of hemorrhagic fever with renal syndrome. About half of all reported cases have been fatal. A *Hantavirus* infection begins with flulike symptoms and may be mistaken for other diseases. The disease can be spread by several common rodent species via rodent excreta.

hantavirus pulmonary syndrome, a sometimes fatal febrile illness caused by a virus of the genus *Hantavirus,* characterized by variable respiratory symptoms followed by acute respiratory distress, sometimes progressing to respiratory failure.

hapadnavirus /hapad′nəvī′rəs/, a family of viruses that can cause liver infections. One example is hepatitis B.

haploid /hap′loid/ [Gk, *haploos,* single, *eidos,* form], having only one complete set of nonhomologous chromosomes. —**haploidy,** *n.*

haploid nucleus [Gk, *haploos,* single, *eidos,* form; L, *nucleus,* nut], a nucleus possessing only half the normal somatic number of chromosomes. It may occur in a germ cell after meiosis and before fertilization.

Hapsburg jaw, a lower jaw that projects forward in advance of the upper jaw, resulting in a skeletal Class III malocclusion.

Hapsburg lip, an overdeveloped, thick lower lip, which often accompanies the Hapsburg jaw.

hapten /hap′tən/ [Gk, *haptein,* to grasp], a small molecule that acts as an antigen by combining with particular bonding sites on an antibody. By itself it cannot induce an immune response, but when bonded to a carrier protein it may cause an immune response.

haptics /hap′tiks/ [Gk, *haptein,* to grasp], the science concerned with studying the sense of touch.—**haptic,** *adj.*

haptoglobin /hap′tōglō′bin/ [Gk, *haptein,* to grasp; L, *globus,* ball], a plasma protein that irreversibly binds free hemoglobin and is removed by macrophages conserving iron. The quantity of haptoglobin is increased in certain chronic diseases and inflammatory disorders and is decreased or absent in hemolytic anemia.

haptoglobin test, a blood test primarily used to detect hemolysis. Abnormally low levels of haptoglobin may indicate hemolytic anemias whereas high levels are found in primary liver disease, many inflammatory diseases, acute MI, and some cancers.

harborage transmission /här′bərij/, a mode of infection transmission in which the organism does not undergo morphologic and physiologic changes in the vector.

hard chancre [AS, *heard;* Fr, *canker*], a syphilitic chancre or primary lesion that develops at the site of a syphilis infection. The lesion begins as a small red papule that gradually hardens and erodes into an extremely contagious, although painless

H

ulcer. A secretion exuded by the sore contains *Treponema pallidum*.

hard contact lens [AS, *heard*; L, *contingere*, to touch + *lentil*], a rigid gas-permeable contact lens that retains its form without support, in contrast with a soft contact lens.

hard data, information about a patient that is obtained by observation and measurement, including laboratory data, as opposed to information collected by interview of the patient or others.

hardening /här′dəning/ [AS, *heard*, hard], the procedure of rendering tissue firm, so that it may be more readily cut for purposes of microscopic examination.

hard fibroma, a neoplasm composed of fibrous tissue in which few cells are present.

hard metal disease, pneumoconiosis caused by inhalation of fine particles of cobalt, usually in conjunction with tungsten carbide. In early stages, reversible hyperplasia and metaplasia of the bronchial epithelium are seen. Later, subacute alveolitis and then chronic interstitial fibrosis develop.

hardness /härd′nəs/ [AS, *heard*, hard], the quality of firmness produced by cohesion of the particles composing a substance, as evidenced by its inflexibility or resistance to indentation, distortion, or scratching.

hardness of x-rays, the relative penetrating power of x-rays. In general, the hardness increases as the wavelength of the x-rays decreases.

hard palate [AS, *heard*, hard; L, *palatum*], the bony part of the roof of the mouth, continuous posteriorly with the soft palate and bounded anteriorly and laterally by the alveolar arches and the gums.

hard soap, a detergent soap made with olive oil and sodium hydroxide.

hard water [AS, *heard* + *waeter*], water that contains certain cations, particularly calcium and magnesium, that precipitate with soap solutions.

Hardy-Weinberg equilibrium principle /här′dē wīn′bərg/ [G.H. Hardy, English mathematician, 1877–1947; Wilhelm Weinberg, German physician, 1862–1937; L, *aequilibris,* equal weight, *principium,* a beginning], a principle stating that the frequency of alleles and genotypes remains relatively unchanged from generation to generation in a large, interbreeding population characterized by random mating, Mendelian inheritance, and the absence of migration, mutation, and selection.

harlequin color /här′lək(w)in/ [It, *arlecchino,* goblin; L, *color,* hue], a temporary flushing of the skin on one lower side of the body with pallor on the other side. Commonly seen in normal young infants, it disappears as the child matures.

harlequin fetus, an infant whose skin at birth is completely covered with thick, horny scales that resemble armor and are divided by deep red fissures. The condition is the most severe form of lamellar exfoliation of the newborn, and the infant is stillborn or dies within a few days of birth.

harlequin ichthyosis, the ichthyosis affecting a harlequin fetus.

Harrington rod /har′ingtən/ [Paul R. Harrington, American orthopedic surgeon, b. 1911], one of the rigid, contoured metal rods inserted surgically, along with metal hooks, in the posterior elements of the spine to provide distraction and compression in treatment of scoliosis and other deformities.

Harrison's groove [Edward Harrison, English physician, 1776–1838], a deformity of the thorax that develops as a result of the pull of the diaphragm on ribs weakened by rickets or some other calcium deficiency disorder.

Harris tube [Franklin Harris, American surgeon, b. 1895], a mercury-weighted single-lumen tube used for gastric and intestinal decompression; no longer in use because of the danger of mercury poisoning.

Hartmann's curet [Arthur Hartmann, German physician, 1849–1931], a curet used for the removal of adenoids.

Hartmann's pouch, a bulbous region of the neck of the gallbladder. When a gallstone lodges in this area, the gallbladder cannot empty normally and contractions of the gallbladder wall produce severe pain.

Hartnup's disease [Hartnup, family name of first patients diagnosed in England, 1956], a rare autosomal-recessive genetic metabolic disorder characterized by pellagra-like skin lesions, transient cerebellar ataxia, and hyperaminoaciduria. It is caused by defects in intestinal absorption and renal reabsorption of neutral amino acids.

Harvard pump, a trademark for a small pump that can be adjusted to deliver small amounts of medication in solution through an IV infusion set. It is commonly used to administer oxytocin in the induction or augmentation of labor.

Hashimoto's disease /hä′shimō′tōz/ [Hakaru Hashimoto, Japanese surgeon, 1881–1934], a progressive autoimmune thyroid disorder, characterized by the production of antibodies in response to thyroid antigens and the replacement of normal thyroid structures with lymphocytes and lymphoid germinal centers. The thyroid, typically enlarged, pale yellow, and lumpy on the surface, shows dense lymphocytic infiltration, and follicular hyperplasia. The goiter is usually asymptomatic, but occasionally patients have difficulty swallowing and a feeling of local pressure. The thymus is usually enlarged, and regional lymph nodes often show hyperplasia.

hashitoxicosis /hash′itok′siko′sis/, excessive functional activity of the thyroid gland in patients with Hashimoto's disease, in whom decreased thyroid function would ordinarily be expected.

hatchet /hach′ət/, a bibeveled or single beveled cutting dental hand instrument having its cutting edge in line with the axis of its blade. It is used for breaking down tooth structure undermined by caries, smoothing cavity walls, removing unsupported enamel, and sharpening line and point angles.

hatha yoga, the area of raja yoga best known in the West, based on physical purification and strengthening as a means of self-transformation. It encompasses a system of over 1000 asanas (postures), designed to promote mental and physical well-being and to allow the mind to focus and become free from distraction for long periods of meditation, along with pranayama (breath control).

haustrum /hôs′trəm/ pl. **haustra** [L, *haustor,* drawer], a general term denoting a recess or sacculation.

haustus (h) /hôs′təs/, a draught of medicine, a quantity ordered as a single dose.

HAV, abbreviation for *hepatitis A virus.*

Haverhill fever /hā′vəril/ [Haverhill, Massachusetts, disorder first diagnosed, 1925], a febrile disease, caused by infection with *Streptobacillus moniliformis,* usually transmitted by the bite of a rat but sometimes transmitted by secretion from the mouth or nose or urine of an infected rodent. Characteristically the wound from the bite heals, but within 10 days fever, chills, vomiting, headache, and muscle and joint pain develop, followed within 3 days by a rash.

haversian canal /havur′shən/ [Clopton Havers, English physician, 1650–1702], one of the many tiny longitudinal canals in bone tissue, averaging about 0.05 mm in diameter. Each contains blood vessels, connective tissue, nerve filaments, and occasionally lymphatic vessels.

haversian canaliculus /kan′əlik′yələs/ [Clopton Havers], any of the many tiny passages radiating from the lacunae of bone tissue to larger haversian canals.

haversian glands [Clopton Havers; L, *glans,* acorn], extrasynovial fat pads that may project into the joint space.

haversian lamella [Clopton Havers; L, *lamella,* a small plate], one of a series of lamellae (circular layers) arranged around the central haversian canal of an osteon, or cylindric unit of bone structure.

haversian system [Clopton Havers], a circular district of bone tissue, consisting of concentric rings of osteocytes and lamellae in the bone around a central blood vessel canal.

Hawley retainer /hô′lē/ [C.A. Hawley, American dentist, early 20th century], an orthodontic appliance consisting of a removable palatal wire and an acrylic biteplate resting against the palate, used to stabilize teeth after their movement or as a basis for tooth movement by providing anchorage for other attachments.

hawthorn, a herbal product used for poor circulation, chest pain, irregular heartbeat, high blood lipids, and high BP. Several studies have shown beneficial effects of hawthorn in heart failure; there are insufficient reliable data for its other uses.

Hawthorne effect /hô′thôrn/, a general unintentional but usually beneficial effect on a person, a group of people, or the function of the system being studied. It is the effect of an encounter, as with an investigator or health care provider, or of a change in a program or facility, as by painting of an office or change in the lighting system.

hayfever [AS,*heawan,*tohew;L,*febris,*fever], informal, an acute, seasonal, allergic rhinitis stimulated by tree, grass, or weed pollen.

Hayflick limits [Leonard Hayflick, American microbiologist, b. 1928; L, *limes,* border], the concept that the life span of living organisms is limited by the number of times that somatic cells will subdivide.

Hay-Wells syndrome /hā welz/ [R.J. Hay, British dermatologist, 20th century; Robert Stuart Wells, British dermatologist, 20th century], an autosomal-dominant syndrome of ectodermal dysplasia, cleft lip and palate, and ankyloblepharon. It is also characterized by hypodontia, palmar and plantar keratoderma, partial anhidrosis, sparse wiry hair, and sometimes otologic defects.

hazard /haz′ərd/ [Fr, *hasard,* chance], a condition or phenomenon that increases the probability of a loss. A hazard can increase the chances of a loss that may not necessarily result in an injury or illness. —**hazardous,** *adj.*

hazardous materials, substances or materials that have been determined by the government to pose an unreasonable risk to health, safety, or property when transported in commerce, such as toxins, marine pollutants, and substances at high temperatures.

Hb, abbreviation for **hemoglobin.**

HB, abbreviation for **hepatitis B.**

Hb A, abbreviation for **hemoglobin A.**

Hb A$_2$, abbreviation for **hemoglobin A$_2$.**

HBAg, abbreviation for *hepatitis B antigen.*

Hb C, abbreviation for **hemoglobin C.**

HBE, abbreviation for **His bundle electrogram.**

Hb F, abbreviation for **hemoglobin F.**

HBIG, abbreviation for **hepatitis B immune globulin.**

HBP, abbreviation for *high blood pressure*.

Hb S, abbreviation for **hemoglobin S.**

HBsAG, abbreviation for *hepatitis B surface antigen*.

Hb SC, abbreviation for **hemoglobin SC.**

HBV, abbreviation for *hepatitis B virus*.

HC, abbreviation for **hepatitis C.**

HCG, abbreviation for *human chorionic gonadotropin*.

H chain, heavy chain, any of the large polypeptide chains of five classes that, paired with the L or light chains, make up the antibody molecule of an immunoglobulin. Heavy chains bear the antigenic determinants that differentiate the classes of immunoglobulins.

HCl, 1. formula for **hydrochloric acid** or hydrogen chloride. 2. formula for *hydrogen chloride*.

HCP, abbreviation for *hereditary coproporphyria*.

HCV, abbreviation for *hepatitis C virus*.

HD, 1. abbreviation for **hepatitis D.** 2. abbreviation for **hemodialysis.**

HDCV, abbreviation for **human diploid cell rabies vaccine.**

H deflection, a deviation observed on the His bundle electrogram that represents activation of the bundle of His.

HDI, abbreviation for **high-definition imaging.**

HDL, abbreviation for **high-density lipoprotein.**

HDL-C, abbreviation for *high-density lipoprotein cholesterol*.

HDV, abbreviation for *hepatitis D virus*.

He, symbol for the element **helium.**

HE, abbreviation for **hepatitis E.**

head [AS, *heafod*], 1. the uppermost extremity, containing the brain, special sense organs, mouth, nose, ears, and related structures. Most of the tissues are enclosed within the skull, composed of 22 bones. 2. a rounded, usually proximal part of some long bones.

headache /hed′āk/ [AS, *heafod* + *acan*, to hurt], a pain in the head from any cause.

head and neck cancer, any malignant neoplasms of the upper aerodigestive tract, facial features, and structures in the neck, which appear as masses, ulcerations, or flat lesions that usually produce early symptoms.

head banging, a form of physical exertion observed during some temper tantrums. It usually occurs near the peak of excitement and may be associated with other physical or muscular movements.

head bobbing, a sign of respiratory distress in an infant. It occurs when the infant uses the scaleni and sternocleidomastoid muscles to assist ventilation.

head box, a clear plastic chamber that fits over a patient's head with an adjustable seal around the neck for mechanical ventilation. Humidified gas enters the chamber, and excess gas is released through an outlet valve. The device may help prevent the need for intubation.

head, eye, ear, nose, and throat (HEENT), a specialty in medicine concerned with the anatomic, physiologic, and pathologic characteristics of the head, eyes, ears, nose, and throat and with diagnosis and treatment of their disorders.

headgear /hed′gēr/, a harnesslike device fitting over the top of the head, back of the head, or both, serving as a source of resistance for extraoral anchorage for an orthodontic appliance.

head injury, any traumatic damage to the head resulting from blunt or penetrating trauma of the skull. Blood vessels, nerves, and meninges can be torn; bleeding, edema, and ischemia may result.

head of rib, the head of a rib that articulates with a vertebral body.

head process, a strand of cells that extends forward from the primitive node in the early stages of embryonic development in vertebrates. It is the precursor of the notochord.

heads-up tilt table test (HUTT), a method of evaluating children with neurocardiac syncope. After baseline signs are recorded with the patient in the supine position, the patient is tilted to an 80-degree angle for 30 minutes, or until neurocardiac syncope signs appear.

head-tilt, chin-lift airway technique, a method of providing maximum airway opening in an unconscious person. With the victim lying on his or her back, the rescuer pushes down on the victim's forehead with the palm of the hand, tilting the victim's head back. With the other hand, the rescuer lifts the victim's lower jaw near the chin. The technique opens the airway by moving the tongue away from the back of the throat and the epiglottis away from the opening of the trachea. This technique is not recommended if a cervical spine injury is suspected.

Heaftest/hēf′ [FrederickR.G.Heaf,English physician, 1894–1973], a tuberculin skin test that uses a multiple puncture technique.

healing [AS, *haelan*, to cure], the act or process in which the normal structural and functional characteristics of health are restored to diseased, dysfunctional, or damaged tissues, organs, or systems of the body.

healing by third intention, a method of closing a grossly contaminated wound in which wound is left open until contamination has been markedly reduced and inflammation has subsided and then is closed by first intention.

health [AS, *haelth*], a condition of physical, mental, and social well-being and the absence of disease or other abnormal condition. It is not a static condition. Constant change and adaptation to stress result in homeostasis.

health assessment, an evaluation of the health status of an individual by performing a physical examination after obtaining a health history. Various laboratory tests also may be ordered to confirm a clinical impression or to screen for dysfunction.

health behavior, an action taken by a person to maintain, attain, or regain good health and to prevent illness. Health behavior reflects a person's health beliefs. Some common health behaviors are exercising regularly, eating a balanced diet, and obtaining necessary inoculations.

health belief model, a conceptual framework that describes a person's health behavior as an expression of health beliefs. The model was designed to predict a person's health behavior, including the use of health services, and to justify intervention to alter maladaptive health behavior.

health beliefs, a nursing outcome from the Nursing Outcomes Classification (NOC) defined as personal convictions that influence health behaviors.

health beliefs: perceived ability to perform, a nursing outcome from the Nursing Outcomes Classification (NOC) defined as the personal conviction that one can carry out a given health behavior.

health beliefs: perceived control, a nursing outcome from the Nursing Outcomes Classification (NOC) defined as the personal conviction that one can influence a health outcome.

health beliefs: perceived resources, a nursing outcome from the Nursing Outcomes Classification (NOC) defined as the personal conviction that one has adequate means to carry out a health behavior.

health beliefs: perceived threat, a nursing outcome from the Nursing Outcomes Classification (NOC) defined as the personal conviction that a threatening health problem is serious and has potential negative consequences for lifestyle.

health care consumer, any actual or potential recipient of health care, such as a patient in a hospital, a client in a community mental health center, or a member of a prepaid health maintenance organization.

health care industry, the complex of preventive, remedial, and therapeutic services provided by hospitals and other institutions, nurses, doctors, dentists, medical administrators, government agencies, voluntary agencies, noninstitutional care facilities, pharmaceutic and medical equipment manufacturers, and health insurance companies.

health care information exchange, a nursing intervention from the Nursing Interventions Classification (NIC) defined as providing patient care information to other health professionals.

health care provider, any individual, institution, or agency that provides health services to health care consumers.

health care proxy [AS, *haelth*; ME, *caru,* sorrow; L, *procuratio,* a deputy], a person designated to make health care decisions for a patient who has become incapacitated.

health care system, the complete network of agencies, facilities, and all providers of health care in a specified geographic area. Nursing services are integral to all levels and patterns of care, and nurses form the largest number of providers in a health care system.

health certificate, a statement signed by a health care provider that attests to the state of health of a person.

health councils, in Canada, organizations that plan and allocate health care facilities to optimize limited funding resources.

health culture, a system that attempts to explain and treat sickness and to maintain health. Health cultures are a component of the larger culture or tradition of a people and may be a popular or folk system or a technical or scientific one.

health economics, a social system that studies the supply and demand of health care resources and the effect of health services on a population.

health education[1], educational programs directed to the general public that attempt to improve, maintain, and safeguard the health of the community.

health education[2], a nursing intervention from the Nursing Interventions Classification (NIC) defined as developing and providing instruction and learning experiences to facilitate voluntary adaptation of behavior conducive to health in individuals, families, groups, or communities.

health hazard [AS, *haelth*; OFr, *hasard*], a danger to health resulting from exposure to environmental pollutants, such as asbestos or ionizing radiation, or to a lifestyle choice, such as cigarette smoking or chemical abuse.

health history, in nursing and medicine, a collection of information obtained from the patient and from other sources concerning the patient's physical status as well as his or her psychologic, social, and sexual function. The history provides a data base on which a diagnosis, a plan for management of the diagnosis, treatment, care, and follow-up observation of the patient may be made.

health information administrator, a graduate of a baccalaureate degree program in health information management who contributes to the development or management of computer-based clinical and administrative record systems.

health information technician, a graduate of an associate degree program who performs tasks related to computer-based management of health care data.

Health Insurance Portability and Accountability Act (HIPAA), an act of Congress, passed in 1996, that affords certain protections to persons covered by health care plans, including continuity of coverage when changing jobs, standards for electronic health care transactions, and privacy safeguards for individually identifiable patient information.

health literacy enhancement, a nursing intervention from the Nursing Interventions Classification (NIC) defined as assisting individuals with limited ability to obtain, process, and understand information related to health and illness.

health maintenance, a systematic program or procedure planned to prevent illness, to maintain maximal function, and to promote health.

health maintenance organization (HMO), a type of group health care practice that provides basic and supplemental health maintenance and treatment services to voluntary enrollees, who prepay a fixed periodic fee that is set without regard to the amount or kind of services received. In addition to diagnostic and treatment services, including hospitalization and surgery, an HMO often offers supplemental services, such as dental, mental, and eye care, and prescription drugs.

health nurse, a community or visiting nurse assigned primarily to promote health maintenance and preventive health measures within the community.

health orientation, a nursing outcome from the Nursing Outcomes Classification (NOC) defined as personal commitment to health behaviors as lifestyle priorities.

health physicist, a health scientist who directs research, training, and management of programs in which patients and health professionals are exposed to potential hazards associated with the use of diagnostic and therapeutic equipment, such as radioactive materials.

health physics, the study of the effects of ionizing radiation on the body and the methods for protecting people from the undesirable effects of the radiation.

health policy, **1.** a statement of a decision regarding a goal in health care and a plan for achieving that goal. **2.** a field of study and practice in which the priorities and values underlying health resource allocation are determined.

health policy monitoring, a nursing intervention from the Nursing Interventions

Classification (NIC) defined as surveillance and influence of government and organization regulations, rules, and standards that affect nursing systems and practices to ensure quality care of patients.

health professional, any person who has completed a course of study in a field of health, such as a registered nurse, physical therapist, or physician. The person is usually licensed by a government agency or certified by a professional organization.

health promoting behavior, a nursing outcome from the Nursing Outcomes Classification (NOC) defined as personal actions to sustain or increase wellness.

health-related services, actions of a health facility other than providing medical care that may contribute directly or indirectly to the physical or mental health and well-being of patients, such as personal or social services.

health resources, all materials, personnel, facilities, funds, and anything else that can be used for providing health care and services.

Health Resources and Services Administration (HRSA), a U.S. federal agency with responsibility for improving health care access for people who are uninsured, isolated, or medically vulnerable. HRSA also oversees organ, tissue, and bone marrow donation. It supports programs that prepare against bioterrorism, compensates individuals harmed by vaccination, and maintains databases that protect against health care malpractice and health care waste, fraud, and abuse.

health risk, a disease precursor associated with a higher than average morbidity or mortality rate.

health risk appraisal, a process of gathering, analyzing, and comparing an individual's characteristics prognostic of health with those of a standard age group.

health screening[1], a program designed to evaluate the health status and potential of an individual. Health screening may include taking a personal and family health history and performing a physical examination, tests, laboratory tests, or radiologic examination and may be followed by counseling, education, referral, or further testing.

health screening[2], a nursing intervention from the Nursing Interventions Classification (NIC) defined as detecting health risks or problems by means of history, examination, and other procedures.

health seeking behavior, a nursing outcome from the Nursing Outcomes Classification (NOC) defined as personal actions to promote optimal wellness, recovery, and rehabilitation.

health service area, a geographic region designated under the U.S. National Health

Planning and Resources Development Act of 1974 for the effective planning and development of health services.

health supervision, health teaching, counseling, or monitoring of the status of a patient's health other than for physical care.

health system guidance, a nursing intervention from the Nursing Interventions Classification (NIC) defined as facilitating a patient's location and use of appropriate health services.

health systems agency (HSA), a body established under the terms of the U.S. National Health Planning and Resources Development Act of 1974. Health planning agencies are intended to provide networks of health planning and resource development services in each of several health service areas established by the Act.

health systems plan, a plan specifying long-range goals of a health services area. Health systems plans are prepared by health systems agencies.

health unit coordinator, a person who ensures the efficient operation of hospital and medical offices by performing administrative and clerical tasks.

healthy, a condition of physical, mental, and social well-being and of absence of disease or another abnormal condition.

Healthy People 2020, a government-sponsored statement of national health objectives in 28 focus areas designed to identify and reduce the most significant preventable health threats within the United States. The overall goals of the program are to increase the quality and length of life and to eliminate health disparities.

hearing [AS, *hieran*], the sense that enables sound to be perceived. It is a major function of the ear.

hearing aid, an electronic device that amplifies sound used by people with impaired hearing. The device consists of a microphone, a battery power supply, an amplifier, and a receiver. Newer, programmable hearing aids can be customized on the basis of the characteristics of an individual's hearing loss.

hearing compensation behavior, a nursing outcome from the Nursing Outcomes Classification (NOC) defined as actions to identify, monitor, and compensate for hearing loss.

hearing handicap, a measure of the impact of hearing loss on an individual's everyday experiences and the psychosocial impact of a hearing loss.

hearing impairment, loss of hearing that adversely affects an individual's ability to communicate.

hearing loss, an inability to perceive the normal range of sounds audible to an individual with normal hearing.

heart [AS, *heorte*], the muscular cone-shaped hollow organ, about the size of a clenched fist, that pumps blood throughout the body and beats normally about 70 times per minute by coordinated nerve impulses and muscular contractions. Enclosed in pericardium, it rests on the diaphragm between the lower borders of the lungs, occupying the middle of the mediastinum. It is covered ventrally by the sternum and the adjoining parts of the third to the sixth costal cartilages. The layers of the heart, starting from the outside, are the epicardium, the myocardium, and the endocardium. The chambers include two ventricles with thick muscular walls, making up the bulk of the organ, and two atria with thin muscular walls. A septum separates the ventricles and extends between the atria (interatrial septum), dividing the heart into the right and left sides.

heartbeat, a complete cycle of cardiac muscle contraction and relaxation.

heart block, an interference with the normal conduction of electrical impulses that control activity of the heart muscle. Heart block is usually specified by the location of the block and the type.

heartburn, a painful burning sensation in the esophagus just below the sternum. Heartburn is usually caused by the reflux of gastric contents into the esophagus but may result from gastric hyperacidity or peptic ulcer.

heart disease risk factor [AS, *heorte,* heart; L, *dis*; Fr, *aise,* ease, *risquer,* chance of injury; L, *facere,* to make], one of several hereditary, lifestyle, and environmental influences that increase one's chance of developing heart disease.

heart failure, a condition in which the heart cannot pump enough blood to meet the metabolic requirements of body tissues. Many of the symptoms associated with heart failure are caused by the dysfunction of organs other than the heart, especially the lungs, kidneys, and liver. Ventricular dysfunction is usually the basic disorder in CHF. It often triggers compensatory mechanisms that preserve cardiac output but produce symptoms and signs such as dyspnea, orthopnea, rales, and edema. Clinicians commonly divide associated heart failure into left-sided heart failure and right-sided heart failure.

heart-lung machine, an apparatus consisting of a pump and an oxygenator that takes over the functions of the heart and lungs, especially during open heart surgery. The blood is shunted from the venous system through an oxygenator and returned to the arterial circulation.

heart rate, the frequency with which the heartbeats, calculated by counting the number of QRS complexes or ventricular beats per minute.

H

heart scan, a radiographic scan of the heart, performed after the injection of a radioactive material into a vein. It is used for determining the size, shape, and location of the heart; for diagnosing pericarditis; and for viewing the chambers of the heart.

heart sound, a noise produced within the heart during the cardiac cycle that can be heard over the precordium. It may reveal abnormalities in cardiac structure or function. Cardiac auscultation is performed systematically from the apex to the base of the heart or from base to apex, using a stethoscope to listen, initially with the diaphragm and then with the bell of the instrument. Standard heart sounds include S_1, S_2, S_3, and S_4. Additional heart sounds include clicks, gallops, murmurs, rubs, and snaps.

heart surgery, any surgical procedure involving the heart, performed to correct acquired or congenital defects, replace diseased valves, open or bypass blocked vessels, or graft a prosthesis or a transplant. Two major types of heart surgery are closed and open. The closed technique is done through a small incision, without using the heart-lung machine. In the open technique the heart chambers are open and fully visible, and blood is detoured around the surgical field by the heart-lung machine.

heart transplantation [AS, *hoerte*; L, *transplantare*], the surgical removal of a donor heart and transfer of the organ to a recipient. The donor heart is usually obtained from an accident victim who was healthy before dying, and it is used to replace the severely diseased heart of another person. The heart is transplanted with anastomoses of the aorta, pulmonary artery, and pulmonary vein; venous return is provided by an anastomosis between the recipient's right atrium and that of the transplanted organ.

heart valve, one of the four structures within the heart that prevent backflow of blood by opening and closing with each heartbeat. The valves include two semilunar valves, the aortic and pulmonary; the mitral or bicuspid valve; and the tricuspid valve. The valves permit blood flow in only one direction.

heat/cold application, a nursing intervention from the Nursing Interventions Classification (NIC) defined as stimulation of the skin and underlying tissues with heat or cold for the purpose of decreasing pain, muscle spasms, or inflammation.

heat cramp [AS, *haetu* + *crammian*, to fill], any cramp or painful spasm of the voluntary muscles in the arm, leg, or abdomen caused by depletion in the body of both water and salt. It usually occurs after vigorous physical exertion in an extremely hot environment or under other conditions that cause profuse sweating and depletion of body fluids and electrolytes.

heated nebulization, a method of inhalation therapy that uses a heating device with a nebulizer that produces a spray with a higher water content than that of a cold atomizer. The mist may be administered through a mask or in a tent.

heat exhaustion, an abnormal condition characterized by weakness, vertigo, nausea, muscle cramps, and LOC, caused by depletion of body fluid and electrolytes that results from exposure to intense heat or inability to acclimatize to heat. Body temperature is near normal; BP may drop but usually returns to normal as the person is placed in a recumbent position. The skin is cool, damp, and pale.

heat exposure treatment, a nursing intervention from the Nursing Interventions Classification (NIC) defined as management of a patient overcome by heat due to excessive environmental heat exposure.

heat hyperpyrexia, a severe and sometimes fatal condition resulting from failure of the temperature-regulating capacity of the body, caused by prolonged exposure to sun or to high temperature. Reduction or cessation of sweating is sometimes an early symptom. Body temperature of 105° F (41° C) or higher, tachycardia, hot and dry skin, headache, altered mental status, and seizures may occur.

heat-labile [L, *labilis*, liable to slip], readily destroyed by heat.

heat-labile antibody, an immunoglobulin that loses its ability to interact with antigens when heated above 31° F (56° C).

heat rash, a finely papular or vesicular inflammation of the skin that results from prolonged exposure to heat and high humidity.

heat shock protein (HsP), an intracellular protein that increases in concentration during metabolic stress, such as exposure to heat.

heaves /hēvz/ [AS, *hebban,* to lift], **1.** a chronic pulmonary disease, similar to human pulmonary emphysema, characterized by wheezing, coughing, and dyspnea on exertion. **2.** *informal.* vomiting and retching.

heavy chain, a high-molecular-weight polypeptide that is part of an immunoglobulin molecule. Different types of heavy chains characterize the various categories of immunoglobulins, such as IgG and IgA.

heavy chain disease [AS, *heafig*; L, *catena,* chain, *dis,* opposite of; Fr, *aise,* ease], a plasma cell disorder characterized by a proliferation of immunoglobulin heavy chains. Effects tend to vary according to the predominant type of heavy chain. Alpha heavy chain disease mainly affects children living in the Middle East, causing diffuse abdominal lymphoma and malabsorption disorders. Most gamma heavy chain disease patients are elderly men who have symptoms resembling those of malignant lymphoma: enlarged liver and spleen, fever, anemia, and increased susceptibility to infections. Delta heavy chain disease is rare and marked by symptoms similar to those of multiple myeloma. Mu heavy chain disease presents symptoms of chronic lymphocytic leukemia, and treatment is symptomatic.

heavy function, increased functional activity of the teeth, which enhances occlusal force.

heavy metal, a metallic element with a specific gravity five or more times that of water. The heavy metals include antimony, arsenic, bismuth, cadmium, cerium, chromium, cobalt, copper, gallium, gold, iron, lead, manganese, mercury, nickel, platinum, silver, tellurium, thallium, tin, uranium, vanadium, and zinc. Small amounts of many of these elements are common and necessary in the diet. Large amounts of any of them may cause poisoning.

heavy metal nephropathy, the kidney damage resulting from any of various forms of heavy metal poisoning, usually in the form of tubulointerstitial nephritis.

heavy metal poisoning, poisoning caused by the ingestion, inhalation, or absorption of various toxic heavy metals.

heavy water, water in which the hydrogen component is deuterium. It has properties different from those of ordinary water. Because of its ability to absorb neutrons, heavy water is used as a moderator in nuclear reactions.

Heberden's node /hēˈbərdənz/ [William Heberden, English physician, 1710–1801; L, *nodus,* knot], an abnormal cartilaginous or bony enlargement of a distal interphalangeal joint of a finger, usually occurring in degenerative diseases of the joints.

hebetude /hebˈitōōdˈ/ [L, *hebeo,* to be blunt], a state of dullness or lethargy, characteristic of some forms of schizophrenia.

hectic fever, a fever that recurs each day, with profound sweating, chills, and facial flushing.

heedfulness of affected side, a nursing outcome from the Nursing Outcomes Classification (NOC) defined as personal actions to acknowledge, protect, and cognitively integrate affected body part(s) into self.

heel [AS, *hela*], the posterior part of the foot, formed by the largest tarsal bone, the calcaneus.

heel cup, a plastic device designed to help relieve pain of a heel spur or contusion by pushing the fat pad of the heel under the calcaneus to increase the cushioning effect.

heel effect, the x-ray intensity greater at the cathode end of the x-ray field and lower at the anode end because of absorption in the target material.

heel-knee test [AS, *hela* + *cneow,* knee; L, *testum,* crucible], a method of assessing coordination of movements of the extremities. In the test, the patient, lying supine, is asked to touch the knee of one leg with the heel of the other.

heel lift, a foot orthosis, usually made of sheets of cork, to correct a dysfunction that may result from anatomic limb length differences or decreased flexibility.

heel puncture [AS, *hela*; L, *punctura*], a method of obtaining a blood sample from a newborn or premature infant by a puncture in the lateral or medial areas of the plantar surface of the heel. Care must be exercised to prevent puncture of the posterior curvature of the heel and to make the puncture as shallow as feasible.

heel-shin test [AS, *hela* + *scinu,* shin; L, *testum,* crucible], a cerebellar test for assessing coordination of movements of the extremities. In the test, the patient, lying supine, is asked to pass the heel of one leg slowly down the shin of the other leg from the knee to the ankle.

HEENT, abbreviation for **head, eye, ear, nose, and throat.**

Hegar's dilators /hāˈgərz/ [Alfred Hegar, German gynecologist, 1830–1914], a series of bougies used to dilate the cervical canal and urethra.

Hegar's sign [Alfred Hegar; L, *signum,* sign], a softening of the isthmus of the uterine cervix that occurs early in gestation. It is a probable sign of pregnancy.

height (h, ht) /hīt/ [AS, *hiehtho*], the vertical measurement of a structure, organ, or other object from bottom to top, when it is placed or projected in an upright position.

height of contour, the greatest convexity of a tooth surface, viewed from a predetermined position.

Heimlich maneuver /hīmˈlik, -lish/ [H.J. Heimlich, American physician, b. 1920; Fr, *manjuvre,* work done by hand], an emergency procedure for dislodging a bolus of food or other obstruction from the trachea to prevent asphyxiation. The choking person is grasped from behind by the rescuer, whose fist, thumb side in, is placed just below the victim's xiphoid with the other hand placed firmly over the fist. The rescuer then pulls the fist firmly and abruptly upward into the epigastrium, forcing the obstruction up the trachea.

Heimlich sign [H.J. Heimlich; L, *signum*], a universal distress signal that a person is choking and unable to speak, made by grasping the throat with a thumb and index finger, thereby attracting the attention of others nearby.

Heimlich valve, a small, one-way valve used for chest drainage, emptying into a flexible collection device. It prevents return of gases or fluids into the pleural space. It can be used in many patients instead of a traditional water seal drainage system.

Heinz bodies /hīnts/ [Robert Heinz, German pathologist, 1865–1924], irregularly shaped bits of altered hemoglobin found in the RBCs of people who are hypersensitive to certain chemicals, such as aniline, phenylhydrazine, and primaquine.

Helen, Sister (Helen Bowden), a nurse who became the first director of the newly formed Bellevue Hospital Training School for Nurses in New York in 1873. Although she had not trained under Florence Nightingale, she set up the Bellevue school according to Nightingale's principles.

helical computed tomography, CT that combines continuous gantry rotation with continuous table movement to form a helical or spiral path of scan data. Because this method scans a volume of tissue rather than a series of individual slices of tissue, small lesions can be easily detected.

helical virus /hel'ikəl/, a virus in which the protein capsid appears in a coiled pattern.

Helicobacter /hel'ikōbak'tər/ [Gk, *helix* coil, *bakterion,* small staff], a genus of gram-negative, rod-shaped, microaerophilic bacteria of the family Spirillaceae, consisting of motile, spiral organisms with multiple sheathed flagella. The bacteria are found in the gastric mucosal layer; many people are infected without showing any symptoms.

Helicobacter pylori, a species of spiral or straight gram-negative bacteria with multiple sheathed flagella found in the gastric mucosa of humans and other animals and associated with gastric and peptic ulcers as well as gastric cancers.

Helicobacter pylori **antibodies test,** a test to detect the presence of *H. pylori.* The most accurate method of testing is microscopic examination of a gastric mucosal biopsy specimen. Other kinds of tests include breath test, rapid urease testing, and serologic testing.

Helicobacter pylori **gastritis,** gastritis caused by the presence of *H. pylori* in the stomach mucosa. *H. pylori* may be present for many years as chronic gastritis before finally causing an attack of acute gastritis.

helicopod gait /hel'ikōpod'/ [Gk, *helix,* coil, *pous,* foot], a manner of walking in which the feet trace half-circles. It is associated with some mental disorders.

helicotrema, a narrow slit at the apex of the cochlea where the two canals of the cochlear duct, the scala vestibuli and the scala tympani, communicate.

helium (He) /hē'lē-əm/ [Gk, *helios,* sun], a colorless, odorless gaseous element; the second lightest element. Its atomic number is 2, and its atomic mass is 4.00. Helium is one of the rare or inert gases and does not combine with other elements. The main physiologic and medical uses of helium are in respiratory therapy and testing and the prevention of nitrogen narcosis and decompression sickness in hyperbaric environments. Helium is also used in pulmonary function testing to calculate the diffusion and residual capacities of the lungs.

helium therapy, the use of helium-oxygen gas mixtures to treat patients with airway obstruction. Because of its low density, helium can negotiate an obstruction more easily than nitrogen can, so less driving pressure is required to move the gas mixture in and out of the lungs.

helix /hē'liks/ [Gk, coil], **1.** a coiled, spiral-like formation characteristic of many organic molecules such as DNA and certain proteins. **2.** the large outside rim of the auricle.

Hellerwork structural integration, a bodywork technique that consists of deep pressure on soft tissues to improve alignment, movement reeducation to avoid unnecessary stress on the body structure, and dialogue with a practitioner to enhance the individual's awareness of how attitude affects structure and movement pattern.

Hellin's law, a generalized formula for calculating the ratio of multiple births in any population, stating that if twin births occur at the rate of 1:N, then the rate of triplet births is approximately 1:N^2, the rate of quadruplet births is approximately 1:N^3, and so on. The value of N varies greatly but is generally close to 80.

HELLP syndrome /help/, abbreviation for a form of severe preeclampsia, a hypertensive complication of late pregnancy. The letters stand for *h*emolysis, *e*levated *l*iver function, and *l*ow *p*latelet level.

helmet cells, fragmented RBCs that have been "scooped out" so they resemble helmets. They are found in patients with micro angiopathic hemolytic anemia and thrombotic thrombocytopenic purpura. Helmet cells can also be seen in blood samples of people with prosthetic heart valves and in individuals with unstable hemoglobin conditions that produce Heinz bodies.

helminth /hel'minth/ [Gk, *helmins,* worm], a worm, especially one of the pathogenic parasites of the division Metazoa, including flukes, tapeworms, and roundworms.

helminthemesis /hel'minthem'əsis/ [Gk, *helmins,* worm, *emesis,* vomiting], the vomiting of intestinal worms.

helminthiasis /hel'minthī'əsis/ [Gk, *helmins,* worm, *osis,* condition], a parasitic infestation of the body by helminths that may be cutaneous, visceral, or intestinal. Ascariasis, bilharziasis, filariasis, hookworm, and trichinosis are common forms of the disease.

helminthic /helmin'thik/ [Gk, *helmins*, worm], pertaining to worms.

helminthology /hel'minthol'əjē/, a branch of medicine concerned with parasitic worms.

helper factor, a protein produced by helper T lymphocytes that stimulates proliferation of and antibody production by other lymphocytes.

helper T cell, a T lymphocyte that promotes the immune response of other lymphocytes to foreign antigens by releasing soluble proteins called helper factors. It is essential in determining B cell antibody class switching and maximizing bacteriocidal activity of phagocytes, as well as in growth and activation of cytotoxic T cells.

helper virus, a virus that allows the replication of a co-infecting defective virus by supplying or restoring viral gene activity or allowing the defective virus to form a protein coat. Hepatitis B acts as a helper virus to delta agent, a defective RNA virus.

helplessness /help'ləsnəs/, a feeling of loss of control or ability, usually after repeated failures, or of being immobilized or frozen by circumstances beyond one's control, with the result that one is unable to make autonomous choices.

Helsinki Accords /helsing'kē/, a declaration signed by the representatives of 35 member nations of the Conference on Security and Cooperation in Europe in Helsinki, Finland, on August 1, 1975. The Helsinki Accords grew from the precedent set by the judgments at the Nuremberg tribunals that crimes against humanity are offenses subject to criminal prosecution. The principle and the practice of informed consent in health care grew from this precedent.

Hemabate, a trademark for a prostaglandin abortifacient, also used to treat refractory postpartum bleeding (carboprost tromethamine).

hemacytometer /-he'məsītom'ətər/ [Gk, *haima*, blood, *kytos*, cell, *metron*, measure], a device for visually counting the number of cells in a known volume of blood or other fluid.

hemadsorption /hē'madsôrp'shən, hem'-/ [Gk, *haima*, blood; L, *ad*, to, *sorbere*, to swallow], the adherence of RBCs to other cells or surfaces; a process in which a substance or an agent, such as certain viruses and bacilli, adheres to the surface of an erythrocyte.

hemagglutination /hē'məglōō'tinā'shən, hem'-/ [Gk, *haima*; L, *agglutinare*, to glue], the agglutination of erythrocytes by an antigen-antibody reaction.

hemagglutination inhibition (HI), 1. the inhibition of virus-induced hemagglutination

as a procedure for identifying hemagglutinating viruses. 2. a method for measuring the concentration of soluble antigens in biologic specimens in which the specimen is incubated first with homologous antibodies and then with antigen-coated erythrocytes.

hemagglutinin [Gk, *haima*; L, *agglutinare*], a type of antibody that agglutinates RBCs. It is classified according to the source of cells agglutinated as autologous (from the same organism), homologous (from an organism of the same species), and xenogeneic (from an organism of a different species).

hemangiectasis, dilation of a blood vessel.

hemangioblast /hēman'jē-ōblast'/, an embryonic mesodermal cell that gives rise to vascular endothelium and blood-forming cells.

hemangioblastoma /hēman'jē-ōblastō'mə/ *pl.* **hemangioblastomas, hemangioblastomata** [Gk, *haima* + *angeion*, vessel, *blastos*, germ, *oma*, tumor], a brain tumor composed of a proliferation of capillaries and of disorganized clusters of capillary cells or angioblasts.

hemangioendothelioma /hēman'jē-ō-en'dō thē'lē-ō'mə/ *pl.* **hemangioendotheliomas, hemangioendotheliomata** [Gk, *haima* + *endon*, inside, *thele*, nipple, *oma*, tumor], 1. a tumor, consisting of endothelial cells, that grows around an artery or a vein. The benign form occurs in children and is usually cured by local excision. The tumor rarely becomes malignant. 2. malignant hemangioendothelioma.

hemangiofibroma /-fībrō'mə/ [Gk, *haima*, blood; L, *fibra*, fiber; Gk, *oma*, tumor], a tumor that has the characteristics of both a hemangioma and a fibroma.

hemangioma /hēman'jē-ō'mə/ *pl.* **hemangiomas, hemangiomata** [Gk, *haima* + *angeion*, small vessel + *oma*], a benign tumor consisting of a mass of blood vessels.

hemangioma-thrombocytopenia syndrome, a blood disorder usually occurring in the first few months of life in which severe thrombocytopenia and other evidence of intravascular coagulation are accompanied by rapidly expanding hemangiomas of the trunk, extremities, and abdominal viscera, sometimes associated with bleeding and anemia.

hemapoiesis /hem'əpō-ē'sis/ [Gk, *haima*, blood, *poiein*, to make], the formation of blood cells.

hemarthros /hem'är'thrəs/ [Gk, *haima*, blood, *arthron*, joint], the extravasation of blood into a joint.

hematemesis /hē'mətem'əsis, hem'-/ [Gk, *haima* + *emesis*, vomiting], vomiting of bright red blood, indicating rapid upper GI bleeding, commonly associated with esophageal varices or peptic ulcer.

H

hematinic /hem′ətin′ik/, a therapeutic agent that produces an increase in the number of erythrocytes and/or hemoglobin concentration in erythrocytes, such as iron or B complex vitamins.

hematinuria /hem′ətinŏŏr′e·ə/ [Gk, *haima*, blood, *ouron*, urine], a dark-colored urine resulting from the presence of hematin or hemoglobin.

hematocele /hem′ətōsēl′/, a cystlike accumulation of blood within the tunica vaginalis of the scrotum. It is usually caused by injury.

hematochezia /hem′ətōke′zhə/ [Gk, *haima* + *chezo*, feces], the passage of blood in the feces. The cause is usually bleeding in the colon or rectum, but it may result from the loss of blood higher in the digestive tract. Cancer, colitis, and ulcers are among causes of hematochezia.

hematocrit /hemat′ōkrit/ [Gk, *haima* + *krinein*, to separate], a measure of the packed cell volume of red cells, expressed as a percentage of the total blood volume. The normal range is between 43% and 49% in men and between 37% and 43% in women.

hematocyte /hem′ətōsīt/ [Gk, *haima*, blood, *kytos*, cell], a blood cell, particularly an RBC.

hematocytoblast /hem′ətōsī′təblast′/ [Gk, *haima*, blood, *kytos*, cell, *blastos*, germ], a large nucleated reticuloendothelial cell found in bone marrow. It is believed to be a common precursor of various blood elements.

hematogenesis /-jen′əsis/ [Gk, *haima*, blood, *genein*, to produce], the formation of blood cells or an increase in the production of blood elements.

hematogenous /hēmətoj′ənəs/ [Gk, *haima* + *genein*, to produce], originating or transported in the blood.

hematogenous pigment [Gk, *haima*, blood, *genein*, to produce; L, *pingere*, to paint], the red color of erythrocytes caused by the presence of hemoglobin.

hematogenous tuberculosis [Gk, *haima*, blood, *genein*, to produce; L, *tuberculum*, a small swelling; Gk, *osis*, condition], a form of TB that is blood borne.

hematoid /hem′ətoid/, bloodlike or resembling blood.

hematologic death syndrome /hem′ətō loj′ik/, a group of clinical signs and symptoms of radiation damage to the blood cells. The condition is characterized by nausea, vomiting, fever, diarrhea, infections, anemia, leukopenia, and hemorrhage. It can result from exposure to a dose of 200 to 1000 rad. The mean survival time for a person with hematologic death syndrome is estimated at between 10 and 60 days.

hematologic effect, the response of blood cells to radiation exposure. All types of blood cells are destroyed by radiation, and the degree of cell depletion increases with increasing dose.

hematologist /hē′mətol′əjist, hem′-/, a medical specialist in the field of blood and blood-forming tissues.

hematology /hē′mətol′əjē, hem′-/ [Gk, *haima* + *logos*, science], the scientific study of blood and blood-forming tissues. **—hematologic, hematological** *adj*.

hematoma /hē′mətō′mə, hem′-/ *pl*. **hematomas, hematomata** [Gk, *haima* + *oma*, tumor], a collection of extravasated blood trapped in the tissues of the skin or in an organ, resulting from trauma or incomplete hemostasis after surgery. The clot hardens, and the mass becomes palpable to the examiner and is often painful to the patient.

hematometra /hē′mətōme′trə/, an accumulation of fluid or menstrual blood in the uterine cavity.

hematometry /hem′ətom′ətrē/, an examination of a blood sample to determine the number, type, and properties of blood cells and platelets and the amount of hemoglobin.

hematomyelia /hē′mətōme′lē·ə/ [Gk, *haima* + *meylos*, marrow], the appearance of frank blood in the fluid of the spinal cord.

hematopathology /-pəthol′əjē/, the division of pathology that specializes in blood cell diseases and diseases of the blood forming organs.

hematoperitoneum /-per′itənē′əm/ [Gk, *haima*, blood, *peri*, near, *tenein*, to stretch], the effusion of blood into the peritoneal cavity.

hematophagous /hem′ətof′əgəs/, **1.** pertaining to the feeding on blood by insects or other parasites. **2.** the destruction of erythrocytes by phagocytes.

hematopoiesis /hē′mətōpō·ē′sis, hem′-/ [Gk, *haima* + *poiein*, to make], the normal formation and development of blood cells in the bone marrow. In severe anemia and other hematologic disorders, cells may be produced in organs outside the marrow (extramedullary hematopoiesis). **—hematopoietic,** *adj*.

hematopoietic, related to the formation of blood.

hematopoietic growth factor /-pō·et′ik/, one of a group of proteins, including erythropoietin, interleukins, and colony-stimulating factors, that promote the proliferation of blood cells.

hematopoietic malignancies, diseases such as leukemia that arise as a result of unregulated clonal proliferation of stem cells.

hematopoietic stem cell, an actively dividing cell that is capable of self-renewal and of differentiation into any blood cell lineage.

hematopoietic syndrome, a group of clinical features associated with effects of radiation on the blood and lymph tissues. It is characterized by nausea and vomiting, anorexia, lethargy, hemolysis and destruction of the bone marrow, and atrophy of the spleen and lymph nodes.

hematopoietic system [Gk, *haima,* blood, *poiein,* to make; L, *systema*], body organs and tissues involved in the formation and functioning of blood elements; includes the bone marrow and spleen.

hematospermia /-spur′mē·ə/, the presence of blood in the semen. Causes include vascular congestion, infection of the seminal vesicles, coitus interruptus, sexual abstinence, and frequent coitus. The condition is rarely serious.

hematoxylin-eosin /hē′mətok′silin/ [*Haematoxylon campechianum,* logwood; Gk, *eos,* dawn], a stain commonly used to treat tissue sections on microscope slides.

hematuria /hē′mətŏŏr′ē·ə, hem′-/ [Gk, *haima* + *ouron,* urine], abnormal presence of blood in the urine. It is symptomatic of many renal diseases and disorders of the genitourinary system.—**hematuric,** *adj.*

heme /hēm/ [Gk, *haima,* blood], the pigmented iron-containing nonprotein part of the hemoglobin molecule. Heme binds and carries oxygen in the RBCs, releasing it to tissues that give off excess amounts of CO_2.

heme iron, iron occurring in a heme complex, as in hemoglobin and myoglobin. Dietary sources of iron are meat, fish, and poultry.

hemeralopia /hem′ərəlō′pē·ə/ [Gk, *hemera,* day, *alaos,* blind, *ops,* eye], an abnormal visual condition in which bright light causes blurring of vision.—**hemeralopic,** *adj.*

hemiacephalus /hem′ē·āsef′ələs/ [Gk, *hemi,* half, *a,* without, *kephale,* head], a fetus in which the brain and most of the cranium are lacking.

hemiachromatosia /hem′ē·ak′rōmatō′zhə/, a state of being color-blind in only one half of the visual field.

hemialgia /hem′ē·al′jē·ə/, pain that affects one side of the body.

hemiamblyopia /hem′ē·am′blē·ō′pē·ə/ [Gk, *hemi,* half, *amblys,* dull, *ops,* eye], blindness in half of the normal visual field.

hemianalgesia /hem′ē·an′əljē′sē·ə/ [Gk, *hemi,* half, *a,* without, *algos,* pain], a loss of feeling or sensitivity to pain affecting half of the body or one side of the body.

hemianesthesia /hem′ē·an′esthē′zhə/ [Gk, *hemi* + *anaisthesia,* absence of feeling], a loss of feeling on one side of the body.

hemiarthroplasty /hem′ē·är′thrəplas′tē/, a surgical procedure for repair of an injured or diseased hip joint involving replacing the head of the femur with a prosthesis without reconstruction of the acetabulum.

hemiataxia /hem′ē·ətak′sē·ə/, a loss of muscle control affecting one side of the body, usually as a result of a stroke or cerebellar injury.

hemiazygous vein /hem′ē·əzī′gəs/ [Gk, *hemi* + *a,* without, *zygon,* yoke], one of the tributaries of the azygous vein of the thorax.

hemiblock, a failure to conduct a cardiac impulse down one division of the left bundle branch, such as an anterior superior or a posterior inferior hemiblock.

hemic /hem′ik, hē′mik/, pertaining to blood.

hemicellulose /hem′ēsel′yŏŏlōs/ [Gk, *hemi*; L, *cellula,* little cell], any of a group of polysaccharides that constitute the chief part of the skeletal substances of the cell walls of plants. They resemble cellulose but are soluble and more easily extracted and decomposed.

hemicephalia /-sefā′lyə/ [Gk, *hemi* + *kephale,* head], a congenital anomaly characterized by the absence of half of the cerebrum, caused by severe arrest of brain development in the fetus.

hemicephalus [Gk, *hemi,* half, *kephale,* head], a fetus with congenital absence of half of the cerebrum.

hemicolectomy /hem′ikōlek′təme/ [Gk, *hemi,* half, *kolon,* colon, *ektome,* excision], excision of approximately half of the colon.

hemicrania /-krā′nē·ə/ [Gk, *hemi* + *kranion,* skull], **1.** a headache, usually migraine, that affects only one side of the head. **2.** a congenital anomaly characterized by the absence of half of the skull in the fetus; incomplete anencephaly.

hemicraniectomy /-kran′ē·ek′təmē/ [Gk, *hemi,* half, *kranion,* skull, *ektomē,* excision], a surgical procedure in which part or all of one half of the skull is excised and reflected as a preliminary step to certain types of brain operations.

hemidiaphragm /-dī′əfram/, either the left or right functional half of the diaphragm. Although the diaphragm is a single anatomic unit, it is divided by the union of its central tendon and the pericardium into separate leaves. Each hemidiaphragm can function independently.

hemidystrophy /-dis′trəfē/, a condition in which the two sides of the body do not develop equally.

hemiectromelia /hem′ē·ek′trōmē′lyə/ [Gk, *hemi* + *ektosis,* miscarriage, *melos,* limb], a congenital anomaly characterized by the incomplete development of the limbs on one side of the body.—**hemiectromelus,** *n.*

hemiepilepsy /hem′ē·ep′əlepsē/, a form of epilepsy that affects only one side of the body.

hemigastrectomy /-gastrek'tɔmē/, surgical removal of one half of the body of the stomach.

hemigeusia, absence of the sense of taste on one side of the tongue.

hemiglossal /-glos'əl/, pertaining to one side of the tongue.

hemignathia /hem'ēnā'thē·ə/ [Gk, *hemi* + *gnathos,* jaw], **1.** a congenital anomaly characterized by incomplete development of the lower jaw on one side of the face. **2.** a condition of having only one jaw. —**hemignathus,** *n.*

hemihyperplasia /-hī'pərplā'zhə/ [Gk, *hemi* + *hyper,* excessive, *plassein,* to form], overdevelopment or excessive growth of half of a specific organ or part or all of the organs and parts on one side of the body.

hemihypertonia /-hī'pərtō'nē·ə/ [Gk, *hemi* + *hyper* + *tonikos,* stretching], exaggerated tension in the muscles on one side of the body, causing tonic contraction.

hemihypertrophy /-hīpur'trɔfē/ [Gk, *hemi* + *hyper* + *trophe,* nourishment], an unusual enlargement or overgrowth of half of the body or half of a body part.

hemihypoplasia /-hī'pōplā'zhə/ [Gk, *hemi* + *hypo,* under, *plassein,* to form], partial or incomplete development of half of a specific organ or part or all of the organs and parts on one side of the body.

hemilaminectomy /hem'ilam'inek'tɔmē/ [Gk, *hemi,* half; L, *lamina,* plate; Gk, *ektome,* excision], surgical removal of one side of the vertebral lamina.

hemilateral /-lat'ərəl/, pertaining to one side.

hemimelia /-mē'lyə/ [Gk, *hemi* + *melos*], a developmental anomaly characterized by the absence or gross shortening of the lower portion of one or more of the limbs.

hemiopia /hem'ē·ō'pē·ə/ [Gk, *hemi,* half, *ops,* eye], a condition involving only one eye or half the visual field.

hemipagus /hemip'əgəs/ [Gk, *hemi* + *pagos,* fixture], symmetric twins who are conjoined at the thorax.

hemiparesis /-pərē'sis/ [Gk, *hemi* + *paralyein,* to be palsied], muscular weakness of one half of the body.

hemiparesthesia /-per'esthē'zhə/ [Gk, *hemi,* half, *para,* beside, *aisthesis,* sensation], a numbness or other abnormal or impaired sensation that is experienced on only one side of the body.

hemiplegia/hem'iplē'jə/ [Gk,*hemi*+*plege,* stroke], paralysis of one side of the body. —**hemiplegic,** *adj.*

hemiplegic gait /-plē'jik/ [Gk, *hemi,* half, *plege,* stroke; ONorse, *gata,* a way], a manner of walking in which an affected limb moves in a semicircle with each step.

hemisection /-sek'shən/ [Gk, *hemi,* half; L, *sectare,* to cut], half of a body or other object divided along a longitudinal plane, producing two lateral halves.

hemisectomy /hem'ēsek'tāmē/, amputation of one root of a two-rooted mandibular tooth.

hemisomus /hem'isō'məs/ [Gk, *hemi* + *soma,* body], a fetus or individual in whom one side of the body is malformed, defective, or absent.

hemisphere /hem'isfir/ [Gk, *hemi* + *sphaira,* sphere], **1.** one half of a sphere or globe. **2.** the lateral half of the cerebrum or cerebellum. —**hemispheric,** *adj.*

hemispherectomy /hem''isfērek'tɔmē/, resection of one hemisphere of the brain, most often performed to treat intractable seizure disorders in children. Although this surgery results in some physical debilitation, it does not affect cognitive abilities.

hemiteras /hem'ēter'əs/ *pl.* **hemiterata** [Gk, *hemi* + *teras,* monster], any individual with a congenital malformation that is not so severe or disabling as to be classified as a teratic condition. —**hemiteratic,** *adj.*

hemithorax /-thôr'aks/, one side of the chest.

hemithyroidectomy /-thī'roidek'tɔmē/, surgical removal of one lobe of the thyroid gland.

hemivertebra /-vur'təbrə/, an abnormal condition characterized by the congenital failure of a vertebra to develop completely. It is possibly caused by the complete failure of the growth center of one vertebral body. Usually half of the vertebra involved is completely or partially developed, and the other half is absent. One or more vertebrae may be involved. The different conditions produce varying degrees of balanced or unbalanced scoliosis.

hemizona assay, an in vitro test of sperm function in which a human zona pellucida is divided in half and one half is incubated with sperm from a donor known to be normal and the other half with sperm from the patient being tested. The number of sperm bound to each half is calculated and that from the patient's sperm is divided by that from the donor's sperm. A figure of less than 0.60 indicates abnormal patient sperm.

hemizygote /-zī'gōt/ [Gk, *hemi* + *zygon,* yoke], an individual, organism, or cell that has only one allele for a specific characteristic. The trait specified by the allele is expressed regardless of whether the allele is dominant or recessive. —**hemizygosity,** *n.,* **hemizygous, hemizygous,** *adj.*

hemlock, the common name for *Conium maculatum,* a plant that is the source of a poisonous alkaloid, coniine. It is considered unsafe for any use, but an extract of the leaves and flowers of conium has been used as a respiratory sedative and its hydrochloride salts have been used as an antispasmodic.

Hemlock Society, a group that provides information about euthanasia and suicide for terminally ill patients.

hemobilinuria /hē′mōbil′inŏŏr′ē-ə/, the presence of the brown pigment urobilin in the blood and urine.

hemochromatosis /hē′mōkrō′mətō′sis, hem′-/ [Gk, *haima*, blood, *chroma*, color, *osis*, condition], an inherited disease of iron metabolism, characterized by excess iron deposits throughout the body.

hemoclip, a malleable metal clip used to ligate small blood vessels during surgery and to mark the location of body structures in radiographic procedures.

hemoconcentration /-kon′səntrā′shən/ [Gk, *haima*; L, *cum*, together with, *centrum*, center], an increase in the number of RBCs resulting from either a decrease in plasma volume or increased production of erythrocytes.

hemocyanin /hē′mōsī′ənin/, an oxygen-carrying protein molecule present in certain lower animals, particularly arthropods and mollusks. The molecule is similar to the hemoglobin molecule of human blood but uses copper atoms, rather than iron.

hemocytology /-sītol′əjē/ [Gk, *haima*, blood, *kytos*, cell, *logos*, science], the study of the components of blood.

hemodiafiltration /-dī′əfiltrā′shən/, a technique similar to hemofiltration, used to treat uremia by convective transport of the solute rather than diffusion.

hemodialysis /hē′mōdī′al′isis, hem′-/ [Gk, *haima* + *dia*, apart, *lysis*, loosening], a procedure in which impurities or wastes are removed from the blood, used in treating patients with renal failure and various toxic conditions. The patient's blood is shunted from the body through a machine for diffusion and ultrafiltration and then returned to the patient's circulation. Hemodialysis requires access to the patient's bloodstream, a mechanism for the transport of the blood to and from the dialyzer, and a dialyzer.

hemodialysis access, a nursing outcome from the Nursing Outcomes Classification (NOC) defined as functionality of a dialysis access site.

hemodialysis technician, a health professional who has received special training in the operation of hemodialysis equipment and treatment of patients with kidney failure.

hemodialysis therapy, a nursing intervention from the Nursing Interventions Classification (NIC) defined as management of extracorporeal passage of the patient's blood through a dialyzer.

hemodilution /-dilŏŏ′shən/ [Gk, *haima*, blood; L, *diluare*, to wash away], a condition in which the concentration of erythrocytes or other blood elements is lowered, usually resulting from an increase in plasma volume.

hemodynamic regulation, a nursing intervention from the Nursing Interventions Classification (NIC) defined as optimization of heart rate, preload, afterload, and contractility.

hemodynamics /-dīnam′iks/ [Gk, *haima* + *dynamis*, force], the study of the physical aspects of blood circulation, including cardiac function and peripheral vascular physiological characteristics.

Hemofil M, a trademark for human antihemophilic factor.

hemofiltration /-filtrā′shən/, a type of hemodialysis in which there is convective transport of the solute through ultrafiltration across the membrane.

hemofiltration therapy, a nursing intervention from the Nursing Interventions Classification (NIC) defined as the cleansing of an acutely ill patient's blood via a hemofilter controlled by the patient's hydrostatic pressure.

hemoglobin (Hb, Hgb) /hē′məglō′bən/ [Gk, *haima*; L, *globus*, ball], a complex protein-iron compound in the blood that carries oxygen to the cells from the lungs and carbon dioxide away from the cells to the lungs. Each erythrocyte contains 200 to 300 molecules of hemoglobin, each molecule of hemoglobin contains four groups of heme, and each group of heme can carry one molecule of oxygen. The normal concentrations of hemoglobin in the blood are 12 to 16 g/dL in women and 13.5 to 18 g/dL in men. In an atmosphere of high oxygen concentration, such as in the lungs, hemoglobin binds with oxygen to form oxyhemoglobin. In an atmosphere of low oxygen concentration, such as in the peripheral tissues of the body, oxygen is replaced by carbon dioxide to form carboxyhemoglobin. Hemoglobin releases the carboxyhemoglobin in the lungs for excretion and picks up more oxygen for transport to the cells.

hemoglobin A (Hb A), normal adult hemoglobin composed of alpha and beta globin chains.

hemoglobin A_2 (Hb A_2), a normal hemoglobin present in small amounts in adults, characterized by the substitution of delta chains for beta chains.

hemoglobin Bart's, an abnormal hemoglobin composed of four gamma chains having high oxygen affinity in homozygous alpha thalassemia.

hemoglobin C (Hb C), an abnormal type of hemoglobin characterized by the substitution of lysine for glutamic acid at position 6 of the beta chain of the hemoglobin molecule.

hemoglobin C disease, an inherited hemoglobinopathy caused by hemoglobin C.

hemoglobin E, a qualitative hemoglobinopathy in which lysine becomes substituted for glutamic acid at position 26 of the beta chain.

hemoglobin E disease [Gk, *haima,* blood; L, *globus,* ball; E; Gk, *dis,* not; Fr, *aise,* ease], a mild form of anemia caused by a genetic abnormality of the hemoglobin molecule.

hemoglobin electrophoresis, a test to identify various abnormal hemoglobins in the blood, including certain genetic disorders such as sickle cell anemia.

hemoglobinemia /hē′mōglō′binē′mē·ə, hem′-/, presence of free hemoglobin in the blood plasma.

hemoglobin F (Hb F), normal fetal hemoglobin. Hb F is replaced by hemoglobin A in the first weeks after birth. Hb F has an increased capacity to carry oxygen and is present in increased amounts in sickle cell disease, thalassemia, and hereditary persistence of hemoglobin F.

hemoglobin G, any of various abnormal hemoglobins with an amino acid substitution on the alpha chain. The most common one is hemoglobin G Philadelphia.

hemoglobin Gower, a normal hemoglobin present in early embryonic life and disappearing before birth. It occasionally consists entirely of epsilon chains, but the usual forms are hemoglobin Gower-1, consisting of two zeta and two epsilon chains, and hemoglobin Gower-2, consisting of two alpha and two epsilon chains.

hemoglobin H, hemoglobin composed of four beta chains, found in alpha-thalassemia. Infants may be born with a mixture of hemoglobin H and hemoglobin Bart's.

hemoglobin H disease, alpha-thalassemia in individuals heterozygous for hemoglobin H, characterized by chronic hemolytic anemia associated with splenomegaly. RBC hypochromia, anisocytosis, and poikilocytosis are accompanied by inclusion bodies detectable by supravital staining.

hemoglobin Kansas, an abnormal hemoglobin with threonine substituted for asparagine at position 102 of the beta chain, resulting in decreased oxygen affinity and cyanosis.

hemoglobin Köln, an unstable hemoglobin that has methionine substituted for valine at position 95 of the beta chain, usually resulting in hemolytic anemia with Heinz bodies in the erythrocytes.

hemoglobin M, hemoglobin in which the iron, normally in the bivalent ferrous state is oxidized the the trivalent ferric state, usually as a result of smoking or other inflammatory conditions, rarely an inherited hemoglobinopathy.

hemoglobin M disease [Gk, *haima,* blood; L, *globus,* ball; M; Gk, *dis,* not; Fr, *aise,* ease], a mild to moderate anemia in which a percentage of the hemoglobin contains iron in the Fe^{+++} state and is unable to combine with oxygen. The patient may experience cyanosis.

hemoglobinometer /-om′ətər/ [Gk, *haima,* blood; L, *globus,* ball; Gk, *metron,* measure], any of several types of instruments designed to measure the concentration of hemoglobin in a blood sample.

hemoglobinometry /hē′məglōbən′/, measurement of blood hemoglobin concentration, usually with a hemoglobinometer after the hemoglobin has been converted to cyanmethemoglobin or freed from red blood cells by sodium dodecyl sulfate.

hemoglobinopathy /hē′mōglō′binop′ə thē, hem′-/ [Gk, *haima;* L, *globus,* ball; Gk, *pathos,* disease], a group of inherited disorders characterized by structural variations of the hemoglobin molecule. An abnormality may occur in the heterozygous or the homozygous form.

hemoglobin Portland, a normal hemoglobin present in the fetus late in the first trimester of pregnancy, consisting of zeta and gamma chains. It disappears in utero.

hemoglobin S (Hb S), hemoglobinopathy characterized by the substitution of the amino acid valine for glutamic acid at position 6 in the beta chain of the hemoglobin molecule.

hemoglobin SC (Hb SC) disease, a genetic blood disorder in which two different abnormal alleles, one for hemoglobin S and one for hemoglobin C, are inherited. The disorder is characterized by a clinical course considerably less severe than that of sickle cell anemia despite the absence of normal hemoglobin.

hemoglobin SD disease, a genetically determined anemia in which the erythrocytes contain both hemoglobin S and hemoglobin D, with symptoms like those of mild sickle cell anemia.

hemoglobin Seattle, an abnormal hemoglobin in which glutamic acid replaces alanine at position 76 of the β chain, decreasing the hemoglobin molecule's affinity for oxygen.

hemoglobin (Hb, Hgb) test, a blood test that measures the total amount of hemoglobin in the peripheral blood, which reflects the number of RBCs in the blood. The test is normally performed as part of a CBC.

hemoglobinuria /-ōōr′ē-ə/ [Gk, *haima;* L, *globus,* ball; Gk, *ouron,* urine], abnormal presence in the urine of hemoglobin that is not attached to RBCs.—**hemoglobinuric,** *adj.*

hemogram /hē′məgram/ [Gk, *haima* + *gramma*, record], a written or graphic record of a differential blood count that emphasizes the size, shape, special characteristics, and numbers of the solid components of the blood.

hemolith /-lith/, a calculus in the wall of a blood vessel.

hemolysin /himol′əsin/ [Gk, *haima* + *lysis*, loosening], any one of the numerous substances that lyse or dissolve RBCs. Hemolysins are produced by bacterial strains and appear to aid the invasive power of bacteria.

hemolysis /himol′isis/ [Gk, *haima* + *lysis*, loosening], the breakdown of RBCs and the release of hemoglobin that occur normally at the end of the life span of a red cell. Hemolysis may occur in antigen-antibody reactions, metabolic abnormalities of the red cell that significantly shorten red cell life span, and mechanical trauma, such as cardiac prosthesis. Dilution of the blood by IV administration of excessive amounts of hypotonic solutions also results in hemolysis.—**hemolytic,** *adj.*

hemolytic anemia /-lit′ik/ [Gk, *haima* + *lysis* + *a*, without, *haima,* blood], a disorder characterized by acute or chronic premature destruction of red blood cells. Anemia may be partially compensated by bone marrow production.

hemolytic antibody, an antibody capable of causing membrane damage and lysis of red blood cells in the presence of complement.

hemolytic disease of the fetus and newborn, alloimmune hemolytic anemia caused by placental transfer.

hemolytic jaundice, a yellowish discoloration of the skin and conjunctiva caused by a breakdown of RBCs, which causes excessive amounts of bilirubin.

hemolytic uremic syndrome, a kidney disorder marked by renal failure, microangiopathic hemolytic anemia, and platelet deficiency. With conservative management, including dialysis, most infants and children recover. The prognosis in adults is uncertain.

hemoperfusion /-pərfyoo′zhən/, the perfusion of blood through a sorbent device, such as activated charcoal or resin beads, rather than through dialysis equipment. Hemoperfusion may be used in treating uremia, liver failure, and certain forms of drug toxicity.

hemopericardium /-per′ikär′dē-əm/ [Gk, *haima* + *peri,* near, *kardia,* heart], an accumulation of blood within the pericardial sac surrounding the heart.

hemoperitoneum /-per′itōnē′əm/ [Gk, *haima* + *peri,* around, *tenein,* to stretch], the presence of extravasated blood in the peritoneal cavity.

hemophil /hē′mōfil/ [Gk, *haima,* blood, *philein,* to love], **1.** bacteria of the genus *Haemophilus,* which thrive in culture media containing blood. **2.** an organism thriving on blood.

hemophilia /hē′mōfē′lyə, hem′-/ [Gk, *haima* + *philein,* to love], a group of hereditary bleeding disorders characterized by a deficiency of one of the factors necessary for coagulation of the blood. The primary presenting sign in hemophilia is excessive, poorly controlled bleeding. The clinical severity of the disorder varies with the extent of the deficiency.

hemophilia A, a hereditary blood disorder transmitted as an X-linked recessive trait and caused by a deficiency of coagulation factor VIII. Hemophilia A is considered the classic type of hemophilia.

hemophilia B, a hereditary blood disorder transmitted as an X-linked recessive trait and caused by a deficiency of factor IX. The condition is clinically similar to but less severe than hemophilia A.

hemophilia C, a hereditary blood disorder, transmitted as an X-linked recessive trait and caused by a deficiency of factor XI, the plasma thromboplastin antecedent. The condition is clinically similar to but may be less severe than hemophilia A.

hemopneumopericardium /hē′mōnoo̅′mōper′ikär′dē-əm/ [Gk, *haima,* blood, *pneuma,* air, *kardia,* heart], an accumulation of blood and air in the pericardium.

hemopneumothorax /hē′mōnoo̅′mōthôr′aks/ [Gk, *haima,* blood, *pneuma,* air, *thorax,* chest], an accumulation of blood and air in the pleural cavity.

hemoptysis /himop′tisis/ [Gk, *haima* + *ptyein,* to spit], coughing up of blood from the respiratory tract. Blood-streaked sputum often is present in minor URIs or bronchitis. More profuse bleeding may indicate *Aspergillus* infection, lung abscess, TB, or bronchogenic carcinoma.

hemorheology /-rē-ol′əjē/ [Gk, *haima,* blood, *rhoia,* flow, *logos,* science], the study of the effects of blood flow pressure on the cellular components of blood and on the walls of blood vessels.

hemorrhage /hem′ərij/ [Gk, *haima* + *rhegnynei,* to gush], a loss of a large amount of blood in a short period, either externally or internally. Hemorrhage may be arterial, venous, or capillary.—**hemorrhagic,** *adj.*

hemorrhage control, a nursing intervention from the Nursing Interventions Classification (NIC) defined as reduction or elimination of rapid and excessive blood loss.

hemorrhagic cholecystitis, cholecystitis with hemorrhage into the gallbladder. It is usually acalculous, but sometimes there are gallstones.

H

hemorrhagic cystitis, bladder inflammation with a large amount of blood in the urine secondary to chemotherapy, radiation, mechanical trauma, or passage of a kidney stone.

hemorrhagic diathesis /-raj'ik/, an inherited predisposition to any of a number of abnormalities characterized by excessive bleeding.

hemorrhagic disease of newborn, a bleeding disorder of neonates that is usually caused by a deficiency of vitamin K.

hemorrhagic fever, a group of viral infections characterized by fever, chills, headache, malaise, and respiratory or GI symptoms, followed by capillary hemorrhages and, in severe infection, by oliguria, kidney failure, hypotension, and possibly death.

hemorrhagic gastritis, a form of acute gastritis usually caused by a toxic agent such as alcohol, aspirin or other drugs, or bacterial toxins that irritate the lining of the stomach. Nausea, vomiting, and epigastric distress may persist after the irritant is removed.

hemorrhagic infarct [Gk, *haima,* blood, *rhegnynei,* to gush; L, *infarcire,* to stuff], an area of necrosis that has accumulated so much blood that it resembles a red, swollen bruise.

hemorrhagic jaundice [Gk, *haima,* blood, *rhegnynei,* to gush; Fr, *jaune,* yellow], a form of jaundice that occurs in Weil's syndrome or other forms of **leptospirosis** in which capillary injury and anemia are present.

hemorrhagic measles [Gk, *haima,* blood, *rhegnynei,* to gush; ME, *masalas*], a severe form of measles characterized by bleeding into the skin and mucous membranes.

hemorrhagic pericarditis [Gk, *haima,* blood, *rhegnynei,* to gush, *peri,* near, *kardia,* heart, *itis,* inflammation], inflammation of the pericardium accompanied by a bloody effusion. The condition is frequently caused by TB or a tumor.

hemorrhagic plague [Gk, *haima,* blood, *rhegnynei,* to gush; L, *plaga,* stroke], a severe form of bubonic plague in which bleeding occurs under the skin.

hemorrhagic pleurisy [Gk, *haima,* blood, *rhegnynei,* to gush + *pleuritis*], an inflammation of the pleura in which effusion of blood into the tissues occurs.

hemorrhagic purpura [Gk, *haima,* blood, *rhegnynei,* to gush; L, *purpura,* purple], bruises or purple skin discolorations of 1 cm diameter or greater associated with thrombocytopenia and prolonged bleeding time.

hemorrhagic shock, shock associated with the sudden and rapid loss of significant amounts of blood. Severe traumatic injuries often cause such blood losses. This results in inadequate perfusion to meet the metabolic demands of cellular function.

hemorrhagic urticaria [Gk, *haima,* blood, *rhegnynei,* to gush; L, *urtica,* nettle], a skin eruption characterized by bleeding in the wheals, usually as a complication of another disease such as nephritis. In some cases, the bleeding occurs first, and the wheals become superimposed.

hemorrhoid /hem'əroid/ [Gk, *haima* + *rhoia,* flow], a varicosity in the lower rectum or anus caused by congestion in the veins of the hemorrhoidal plexus.—**hemorrhoidal,** *adj.*

hemorrhoidal tag, an anal skin tag that was originally part of hemorrhoidal tissue.

hemorrhoidectomy /hem'əroidek'təmē/ [Gk, *haimorrhois,* a vein that discharges blood, *ektomē,* excision], the removal of dilated veins in the anal region to mitigate pain and bleeding. Most hemorrhoidectomies are outpatient procedures.

hemosalpinx /hē'mōsal'pinks/ [Gk, *haima,* blood, *salpinx,* tube], a collection of menstrual blood in a fallopian tube.

hemosiderin /hē'mōsid'ərin/ [Gk, *haima* + *sideros,* iron], an iron-rich pigment that is a product of red cell hemolysis. Iron is often stored in this form.

hemosiderosis /hē'mōsid'ərō'sis, hem'-/ [Gk, *haima* + *sideros,* iron, *osis,* condition], an increased deposition of iron in a variety of tissues, usually in the form of hemosiderin and usually without tissue damage.

hemostasis /himos'təsis, hē'məstā'sis/ [Gk, *haima* + *stasis,* halting], the process of maintaining the blood in a fluid state within the confines of the circulatory system.

hemostatic /-stat'ik/ [Gk, *haima* + *stasis,* halting], pertaining to a procedure, device, or substance that arrests the flow of blood.

hemotherapeutics /-ther'əpyōō'tiks/, a form of treatment that involves the use of fresh blood plasma or serum.

hemothorax /hē'mōthôr'aks, hem'-/ [Gk, *haima* + *thorax,* chest], an accumulation of blood and fluid in the pleural cavity, between the parietal and visceral pleura, usually the result of trauma. Hemothorax also may be caused by the rupture of small blood vessels in inflammation.

hemotroph /hē'mətrof/, the total nutritive substances supplied to the embryo from the maternal circulation after the development of the placenta.—**hemotrophic,** *adj.*

Henderson-Hasselbalch equation [Lawrence J. Henderson, American chemist, 1878–1942; Karl A. Hasselbalch, Danish biochemist, 1874–1962], the relationship among pH, the pK_a of a buffer system, and the ratio of the concentrations of the weak acid and its conjugate base.

Henderson, Virginia, a nursing theorist who introduced a holistic approach to the profession in 1966. The theory is based on the concepts that the body and mind are inseparable, no two individuals are alike, and the role of nursing is independent of the functions of the physician.

Henle's fissure /hen'lĕz/ [Friedrich Gustav Henle, German anatomist, 1809–1885], one of many patches of connective tissue between the muscle fibers of the heart.

Henoch-Schönlein purpura /hen'ŏkh shœn'līn/ [Eduard H. Henoch, German physician, 1820–1910; Johannes L. Schönlein, German physician, 1793–1864], a self-limited hypersensitivity vasculitis, chiefly of children, characterized by purpuric skin lesions that appear predominantly on the lower abdomen, buttocks, and legs and are usually associated with pain in the knees and ankles. Other joint involvement, GI bleeding, and hematuria are also common findings.

Henoch-Schönlein purpura nephritis, a type of glomerulonephritis sometimes seen with Henoch-Schönlein purpura. Clinical characteristics usually resemble those of IgA nephropathy, and a rapidly progressive form can lead to renal failure.

henry (H) [Joseph Henry, American physicist, 1797–1878], an International System unit of electrical inductance equal to 1 volt-second per ampere.

Henry's law [William Henry, English chemist, 1774–1836], in physics, a law stating that the solubility of a gas in a liquid is proportional to the pressure of the gas if the temperature is constant and the gas does not chemically react with the liquid.

Henschen method, a technique for positioning a patient's head in a true lateral position to produce a radiographic image of the mastoid and petrous portions of the head.

HEP, abbreviation for **hepatoerythropoietic porphyria.**

HEPA, abbreviation for *high-efficiency particulate air* filters.

hepadnavirus /hĕpad'năvi'rus/, any member of a family of DNA viruses that cause hepatitis B in humans and other animals.

heparin /hep'ərin/ [Gk, *hēpar,* liver], a naturally occurring mucopolysaccharide that acts in the body as an antithrombin factor to prevent intravascular clotting. In the form of sodium salt, heparin is used therapeutically as an anticoagulant.

heparin lock flush solution (USP) [Gk, *hēpar,* liver; OE, *loc;* ME, *fluschen;* L, *solutus,* dissolved], a sterile solution of heparin sodium, saline solution, and benzyl alcohol that is intended for use in maintaining patency in IV equipment. It is not used in anticoagulant therapy.

heparin rebound, the reactivation of heparin effect that occurs from 5 minutes to 5 hours after neutralization with protamine sulfate.

heparin sodium, an anticoagulant prescribed in the treatment and prophylaxis of a variety of thromboembolic disorders.

hepatectomy /hep'ətek'təmē/ [Gk, *hēpar,* liver, *ektomē,* excision], a surgical procedure performed to remove a portion of the liver.

hepatic /hepat'ik/ [Gk, *hēpar,* liver], pertaining to the liver.

hepatic acinus, a functional unit of the liver, smaller than a portal lobule; a diamond-shaped mass of liver parenchyma surrounding a portal tract.

hepatic adenoma, a rapidly growing tumor of the liver that may become very large and rupture, causing a lethal internal hemorrhage.

hepatic amebiasis, a disorder characterized by enlargement and tenderness of the liver that is often associated with amebic dysentery. The inflammation results from direct infection with ***Entamoeba histolytica,*** ingested in water or food contaminated with human feces.

hepatic amyloidosis, a type of primary amyloidosis in which amyloid fibrils invade the liver, causing hepatomegaly. The prognosis is grave, with many patients dying within a year.

hepatic bile, a "C" form of bile obtained from a duodenal drainage tube after the gallbladder has been emptied.

hepatic coma, a neuropsychiatric manifestation of extensive liver damage caused by chronic or acute liver disease. Either endogenous or exogenous waste toxic to the brain is not neutralized in the liver before being shunted back into the peripheral circulation of the blood, or substances required for cerebral function are not synthesized in the liver. The condition is characterized by variable consciousness, including lethargy, stupor, and coma; a tremor of the hands; personality change; memory loss; hyperreflexia; and hyperventilation. Respiratory alkalosis, mania, convulsions, and death may occur.

hepatic cord, a mass of cells arranged in irregular radiating columns and plates, spreading outward from the central vein of the hepatic lobule. Many such cords join to form the parenchyma of the liver lobule.

hepatic dyspepsia, a digestive difficulty caused by a liver disorder.

hepatic fistula, an abnormal passage from the liver to another organ or body structure.

hepatic insufficiency, a failure or partial failure of normal liver function.

hepatic ischemia, injury to liver cells resulting from a deficiency of blood or oxygen, caused by hypotension from decreased cardiac output, shock, or some other cause.

hepatic lobes [Gk, *hēpar,* liver, *lobos,* lobes], the large divisions of the liver: caudate, quadrate, left, and right.

hepatic node, a node in one of three groups of lymph glands associated with the abdominal and pelvic viscera supplied by branches of the celiac artery.

hepaticoduodenostomy /hepat'ikōdoō´ōdənos'təmē/, surgical establishment of a passageway between the hepatic duct and the duodenum.

hepaticoenterostomy /hepat'ikō·en'teros´təmē/, surgical establishment of a passageway between the hepatic duct and the intestine.

hepaticolithotomy /-lithot'əmē/, an incision made in the bile duct for the removal of gallstones.

hepaticolithotripsy /-lith'ətrip'sē/, a surgical procedure in which gallstones in the bile duct are crushed for removal.

hepatic portal vein, a large vein through which all venous blood from the GI system enters the inferior surface of the liver. The vein then ramifies like an artery to distribute blood to small endothelial-lined hepatic sinusoids, which form the vascular exchange network of the liver.

hepatic pulse, pulsation of the liver, such as may occur in tricuspid incompetence.

hepatic vein catheterization, the introduction of a long, fine catheter into a hepatic venule for the purpose of recording intrahepatic venous pressure.

hepatic veins [Gk, *hēpar,* liver; L, *vena*], the three main veins, the right, middle, and left, that drain the blood returned from the liver into the inferior vena cava.

hepatitis /hep'ətī´tis/ [Gk, *hēpar* + *itis,* inflammation], an inflammatory condition of the liver, characterized by jaundice, hepatomegaly, anorexia, abdominal and gastric discomfort, abnormal liver function, clay-colored stools, and tea-colored urine. The condition may be caused by bacterial or viral infection, parasitic infestation, alcohol, drugs, toxins, or transfusion of incompatible blood. The liver usually is able to regenerate its tissue, but severe hepatitis may lead to cirrhosis and chronic liver dysfunction.

hepatitis A (HA), a viral hepatitis caused by the hepatitis A virus, characterized by slow onset of signs and symptoms. The virus may be spread through fecally contaminated food or water. The infection is usually followed by complete recovery. A vaccine for immunization is available.

hepatitis A vaccine inactivated, an inactivated whole virus vaccine derived from an attenuated strain of hepatitis A virus grown in cell culture.

hepatitis B (HB), a viral hepatitis caused by HBV. The virus is transmitted by transfusion of contaminated blood or blood products, by sexual contact with an infected person, by the use of contaminated needles and instruments, or in utero. Severe infection may cause prolonged illness, destruction of liver cells, cirrhosis, increased risk of liver cancer, or death. A vaccine is available and recommended for infants, teenagers, and adults at risk for exposure.

hepatitis B immune globulin (HBIG), a passive immunizing agent prescribed for postexposure prophylaxis against infection by HBV.

hepatitis B vaccine, a vaccine prepared from the blood plasma of asymptomatic human carriers of hepatitis B virus. A series of three doses is recommended to achieve immunity. The vaccine is advised particularly for people who are likely to have contact with blood or fluids of affected people.

hepatitis B vaccine (recombinant), a genetically engineered vaccine produced in yeast cells by recombinant DNA technology.

hepatitis B vaccine inactivated, a preparation of formalin-treated hepatitis B surface antigen isolated from plasma of human carriers of hepatitis B. It has been superseded by the recombinant form of the vaccine in the United States.

hepatitis C (HC), a type of hepatitis transmitted most commonly by blood transfusion or percutaneous inoculation or, less commonly, by sexual intercourse. The disease progresses to chronic hepatitis in up to 80% of the patients acutely infected, culminating in cirrhosis.

hepatitis D (HD), a form of acute or chronic hepatitis, caused by the hepatitis delta virus, that occurs only in patients co-infected with hepatitis B. Hepatitis D virus relies on HBV replication and cannot replicate independently. The disease usually develops into a chronic state. It is transmitted sexually and through needle sharing.

hepatitis E (HE), a self-limited type of hepatitis acquired by ingestion of fecally contaminated water or food.

hepatitis F (HF), a hypothetical virus linked to hepatitis, possibly a mutation of HBV.

hepatitis G (HG), a form of hepatitis, caused by the hepatitis G virus, that is transmitted by infected blood or blood products. It can also be transmitted by sharing personal items contaminated with the virus, by vertical transmission (mother to newborn), and by various sexual activities. Infection is of widespread occurrence and causes generally asymptomatic to mild disease.

hepatitis virus studies, a series of tests used to detect antigens and antibodies to hepatitis B surface antigen, hepatitis B surface antibody, hepatitis B core antibody, hepatitis B e-antigen, hepatitis B e-antibody, and hepatitis C antibodies.

hepatization /hep′ətīzā′shən/ [Gk, *hepatizein,* like the liver], transformation of lung tissue into a solid mass resembling the liver, as in early pneumococcal pneumonia, in which consolidation and effusion of RBCs in the alveoli produce **red hepatization.** In later stages of pneumococcal pneumonia, when WBCs fill the alveoli, the consolidation becomes gray hepatization, or yellow hepatization, when infiltrated by fat deposits.

hepatoblastoma /hep′ətō′blastō′mə/, a cancer of the liver that tends to occur in children. Hepatoblastoma may be associated with precocious puberty.

hepatocarcinogen /-kärsin′əjən/, an agent that causes carcinoma of the liver.

hepatocele [Gk, *hēpar,* liver, *kele,* hernia], a hernia of a portion of the liver through the diaphragm or the abdominal wall.

hepatocellular jaundice /-sel′yələr/, jaundice resulting from disease or injury to liver cells.

hepatocholangitis /hep′ətōkō′lanjī′tis/, an inflammation of both the liver and the bile ducts.

hepatocyte /hep′ətōsīt/ [Gk, *hēpar* + *kytos,* cell], a parenchymal liver cell that performs all the functions ascribed to the liver.

hepatocyte growth factor (HGF), a potent mitogen and inducer of hepatocyte proliferation, produced in the liver by cells other than hepatic cells and in many other organs by cells of the mesenchyme. It is also multifunctional and regulates cell growth and motility.

hepatoduodenal ligament /hep′ətōdōō′ədē′nəl, -dōō·od′inəl/ [Gk, *hēpar* + L, *duodeni,* twelve fingers], the portion of the lesser omentum between the liver and the duodenum, containing the hepatic artery, the common bile duct, the portal vein, the lymphatics, and the hepatic plexus of nerves.

hepatoerythropoietic porphyria (HEP) /hep′ə·tō·ərith′rōpoi·et′ik/ [Gk, *hēpar,* liver; *erythros,* red; *poiein,* to make], a severe homozygous form of **porphyria cutanea tarda** (PCT) believed to result from an autosomal-dominant defect in the same enzyme activity as PCT. It is clinically identical to PCT, but onset is in early childhood, and activity of the affected enzyme in liver, erythrocytes, and fibroblasts is virtually absent.

hepatogastric ligament /hep′ətōgas′trik/ [Gk, *hēpar* + *gaster,* stomach], the portion of the lesser omentum between the liver and the stomach.

hepatogenous jaundice /hep′ətoj′ənəs/ [Gk, *hēpar,* liver, *genein,* to produce; Fr, *jaune,* yellow], a type of jaundice caused by a condition of the liver.

hepatogram /hep′ətōgram′/, **1.** a sphygmographic tracing of the liver pulse. **2.** a radiographic image of the liver.

hepatography /hep′ətog′rəfē/, **1.** the recording of the liver pulse. **2.** the radiographic or isotope scintigraphic visualization of the liver.

hepatojugular /hep′ətōjug′yŏōlər/ [Gk, *hēpar,* liver; L, *jugulum,* neck], pertaining to the liver and the jugular vein.

hepatojugular reflux [Gk, *hēpar;* L, *jugulum,* neck], an increase in jugular venous pressure when pressure is applied for 30 to 60 seconds over the abdomen, suggestive of right-sided heart failure.

hepatolenticular degeneration /həpat′-ōlentik′yŏōlər/ [Gk, *hēpar;* L, *lens,* lentil], an abnormal autosomal-recessive condition associated with defective copper metabolism in the body, characterized by decreased serum ceruloplasmin and copper levels and increased secretion of urinary copper. In individuals with this condition, tissue deposits of copper associated with hepatic cirrhosis, deep marginal pigmentation of the cornea, and extensive degeneration of the CNS, especially the basal ganglions, develop.

hepatolithiasis /-lithī′əsis/, the presence of stones in the liver.

hepatologist /hep′ətol′əjist/, a physician who specializes in diseases of the liver.

hepatology /hep′ətol′əjē/, the branch of medicine that is concerned primarily with diseases of the liver.

hepatoma /hep′ətō′mə/ *pl.* **hepatomas, hepatomata** [Gk, *hēpar* + *oma,* tumor], a primary malignant tumor of the liver characterized by hepatomegaly, pain, hypoglycemia, weight loss, anorexia, and ascites, as well as elevated serum alphafetoprotein levels, portal hypertension, and jaundice in the plasma.

hepatomegaly /hep′ətōmeg′əlē/ [Gk, *hēpar* + *megas,* large], abnormal enlargement of the liver that is usually a sign of disease. It may be caused by hepatitis or other infection; fatty infiltration, as in alcoholism; biliary obstruction; or malignancy.

hepatonecrosis /-nekrō′sis/, **1.** the death of liver cells. **2.** gangrene of the liver.

hepatopancreatic ampulla /-pan′krē·at′ik/ [Gk, *hēpar* + *pan,* all, *kreas,* flesh], the dilation formed by the junction of the pancreatic and bile ducts as they open into the lumen of the duodenum.

hepatopulmonary syndrome, arterial hypoxemia caused by pulmonary vasodilatation in conjunction with chronic liver

H

disease, usually occurring as a result of portal hypertension in cirrhosis.

hepatorenal /hep′ətōre′nəl/ [Gk, *hēpar,* liver; L, *ren,* kidney], pertaining to the liver and the kidneys.

hepatorenal syndrome, a type of kidney failure characterized by a gradual loss of function without signs of tissue damage. It is associated with hepatitis or cirrhosis of the liver.

hepatosplenomegaly /-splē′nōmeg′əlē/ [Gk, *hēpar,* liver + *splen* + *megas,* large], enlargement of the spleen and liver.

hepatotoxic /-tok′sik/, destructive to the liver.

hepatotoxicity /hep′ətōtoksis′itē/ [Gk, *hēpar* + *toxikon,* poison], the tendency of an agent, usually a drug or alcohol, to have a destructive effect on the liver.

hepatotropic /hep′ə-totrop′ik/, having a special affinity for or exerting a specific effect on the liver.

hepatotropic virus, a virus that primarily affects the liver, such as the hepatitis viruses.

Hepatovirus /hep′ə-tovi′rəs/, the hepatitis A viruses, a genus of picornaviruses.

hepatoxin /-tok′sin/, a poison that damages parenchymal cells of the liver.

heptachlor poisoning /hep′təklôr′/ [Gk, *hepar,* seven, *chloros,* green; L, *potio,* drink], a form of chlorinated organic insecticide poisoning.

heptavalent /hep′tivā′lənt/, pertaining to a chemical that has a valence of 7.

herb /(h)urb/ [L, *herba,* grass], **1.** any plant that is used for culinary or medicinal purposes. **2.** a leafy plant without a woody stem. **3.** a plant with aerial parts that do not persist from one year to the next.

herbalist /hur′bəlist/, **1.** a person who specializes in the study of herbs. **2.** a dealer in medicinal herbs.

herbal medicine, the use of medicinal products containing as active ingredients exclusively plant material and/or vegetable drug preparations used to treat various health conditions. Herbal medicine is a major form of treatment for more than 70% of the world's population.

herb bath [L, *herba,* grass; AS, *baeth*], a medicinal bath taken in water containing a decoction of aromatic herbs.

herbicide /er′-, her′bisīd/, an agent that is destructive to weeds or causes an alteration in their normal growth.

herbicide poisoning /her′bisīd/ [L, *herba,* grass, *caedere,* to kill], a poisoning caused by the ingestion, inhalation, or absorption of a substance intended for use as a weed killer or defoliant. Many of the commonly used agricultural herbicides can produce symptoms ranging from skin

irritation to hypotension, liver and kidney damage, and coma or convulsions.

herbivore /hərbivōr/ [L, *herba,* grass, *vorare,* to devour], an animal that subsists mostly or entirely on plants.—**herbivorous,** *adj.*

herb tea, a medicinal beverage prepared by the infusion of a water-soluble extract of leaves, roots, bark, or other parts of an herb. The vegetable matter is commonly macerated and steeped in boiling water, which is strained and served hot.

herd immunity [ME, *heord;* group; L, *immunis,* free from], the level of disease resistance of a community or population.

herd instinct [ME, *heord;* L, *instinctus,* impulse], the basic need of social animals, including humans, for the companionship of peers and a tendency to find compatibility with the behavioral standards of others in the group.

heritability /həred′itəbil′itē/ [L, *hereditas,* inheritance], the degree to which a specific trait is controlled by inheritance.

hereditary /həred′iter′ē/ [L, *hereditas,* inheritance], transmitted from parent to offspring; inborn; inherited.

hereditary angioedema, an inherited autosomal-dominant disorder characterized by the episodic appearance of nonpitting edema involving any part of the body.

hereditary ataxia, one of a group of inherited degenerative diseases of the spinal cord, cerebellum, and often other parts of the nervous system, characterized by tremor, spasm, muscle wasting, skeletal change, and sensory disturbances resulting in impaired motor activity.

hereditary hemochromatosis, an autosomal-recessive disorder of metabolism that involves the deposition of iron-containing pigments in the tissues. Iron accumulation is lifelong, with symptoms that include joint or abdominal pain, weakness, and fatigue appearing usually in the fifth or sixth decades of life.

hereditary hemorrhagic telangiectasia, a vascular anomaly, inherited as an autosomal-dominant trait, characterized by hemorrhagic telangiectasia of the skin and mucosa. Small red-to-violet lesions are found on the lips, oral and nasal mucosa, tongue, and tips of fingers and toes. The thin, dilated vessels may bleed spontaneously or as a result of only minor trauma, and this condition becomes progressively more severe. Bleeding from superficial lesions is often profuse and may result in severe anemia.

hereditary multiple exostoses, a rare familial dyschondroplastic disease in which bony protuberances form on the shafts of the long bones and eventually develop into caps of cartilage covering the ends of the bones. The affected joints lose their mobility, and the bones stop growing.

hereditary oral disease, any abnormal condition characterized by genetic defects of structures in or around the mouth, such as deformed dentition, ankyloglossia, hereditary gingival fibromatosis, or cleft palate.

hereditary renal adysplasia, an autosomal-dominant condition in which a kidney is severely dysplastic, nonfunctional, and often ectopic. If bilateral, as in the oligohydramnios sequence, the infant usually dies soon after birth.

heredity /hə·red′itē/ [L, *hereditas,* inheritance], **1.** the process by which particular traits or conditions are genetically transmitted from parents to offspring, causing resemblance of individuals related by descent. **2.** the total genetic constitution of an individual; the sum of the qualities inherited from ancestors and the potentialities of transmitting these qualities to offspring.

Hering-Breuer reflex /her′ing broi′ər/ [Heinrich E. Hering, German physiologist, 1866–1948; Joseph Breuer, Austrian physician, 1842–1925], a neural mechanism that terminates inspiration and initiates expiration.

Hermansky-Pudlak syndrome /hərmän′skē po͞od′läk/ [F. Hermansky, Czechoslovakian internist, 20th century; P. Pudlak, Czechoslovakian internist, 20th century], an autosomal-recessive form of oculocutaneous albinism with a hemorrhagic diathesis secondary to a platelet defect, and accumulation of a ceroid-like substance in the reticuloendothelial system, oral mucosa, and urine.

hermaphroditism /hərmaf′rədītiz′əm/ [Gk, *Hermaphroditos,* son of Hermes and Aphrodite], a rare condition resulting from a chromosomal abnormality in which both testicular and ovarian tissue exist in the same person.—**hermaphroditic,** *adj.*

hermetic /hərmet′ik/ [Gk, *Hermes*], from use in alchemy, pertaining to sealing a container to make it airtight.

hernia /hur′nē·ə/ [L, rupture], protrusion or projection of an organ through an abnormal opening in the muscle wall of the cavity that surrounds it.

hernial ring, a ring through which a hernia protrudes, such as a dilated internal inguinal ring.

hernial sac [L, *hernia,* rupture; Gk, *sakkos,* sack], a pouch of peritoneum into which organs or other tissues pass to form a hernia.

herniated /hur′nē·ā′tid/, pertaining to a tear or abnormal bulge of an organ or organ part through a retaining tissue.

herniated disk, a rupture of the fibrocartilage surrounding an intervertebral disk, releasing the nucleus pulposus that cushions the vertebrae above and below. The

resultant pressure on spinal nerve roots may cause considerable pain and damage the nerves, resulting in restriction of movement. The condition most frequently occurs in the lumbar region.

herniation /hur′nē·ā′shən/, a protrusion of a body organ or part of an organ through an abnormal opening in a membrane, muscle, or other tissue.

herniography /hur′nē·og′rəfē/, the radiographic examination of a hernia after it has been injected with a contrast medium.

herniorrhaphy /hur′nē·ôr′əfē/, the surgical repair of a hernia.

herniotomy /hur′nē·ot′əmē/ [L, *hernia;* Gk, *temnein,* to cut], a surgical procedure to reduce a hernia.

heroin /her′ō·in/ [Ger, *heroine,* originally trademark for diacetylmorphine], a morphine-like drug with no currently acceptable medical use in the United States. Heroin is included in Schedule I of the Controlled Substances Act of 1970. Like other opium alkaloids, it can produce analgesia, respiratory depression, GI spasm, and physical dependence. It produces its major effects on the CNS and bowel and alters the endocrine and autonomic nervous systems. Abstinence from heroin after relatively few exposures commonly produces acute withdrawal syndrome. Methadone is commonly used as a substitute drug in the treatment of heroin addiction.

herpangina /hur′panjī′nə/ [Gk, *herpein,* to creep; L, *angina,* quinsy], a viral infection, usually of young children, characterized by sore throat, headache, anorexia, and pain in the abdomen, neck, and extremities. Febrile convulsions and vomiting may occur in infants. Papules or vesicles may form in the pharynx and on the tongue, palate, or the tonsils. The cause is often infection by a strain of coxsackievirus.

herpes genitalis /hur′pēz jen′ital′is/ [Gk, *herpein,* to creep; L, *genitalis,* genitalia], a chronic infection caused by HSV2, usually transmitted by sexual contact. It causes painful vesicular eruptions on the skin and mucous membranes of the genitalia of males and females. When acquired during pregnancy, HSV2 may be transmitted through the placenta to the fetus and to the newborn by direct contact with infected tissue during birth. It can be a precursor of cervical cancer.

herpes gestationis [Gk, *herpein;* L, *gestare,* to bear], a generalized pruritic vesicular or bullous rash that appears in the second or third trimester of pregnancy and disappears several weeks after delivery. The lesions often recur with succeeding pregnancies and are associated with premature birth and increased fetal mortality rate.

H

herpes menstrualis [Gk, *herpein,* to creep; L, *menstruare*], a form of herpes simplex that tends to erupt during menstrual periods.

herpes simplex [Gk, *herpein*; L, *simplex,* uncomplicated], an infection caused by an HSV, which has an affinity for the skin and nervous system and usually produces small, transient, irritating, and sometimes painful fluid-filled blisters on the skin and mucous membranes. HSV1 (oral herpes, herpes labialis) infections tend to occur in the facial area, particularly around the mouth and nose; HSV2 (herpes genitalis) infections are usually limited to the genital region. The vesicles generally are associated with itching, pain, or similar discomfort.

herpes simplex encephalitis, a necrotizing inflammation of the brain that follows an infection with HSV. It is a common acute form of encephalitis and similar to other viral encephalitis infections. Repeated seizures occur early in the course, and there is severe hemorrhagic necrosis. The mortality rate varies, but even desperately ill patients may recover completely.

herpes simplex (HSV) test, a blood test or microscopic culture done to detect types 1 and 2 of the HSV. Culture is the more accurate of the two types of tests.

herpesvirus /hur'pēzvī'rəs/ [Gk, *herpein*; L, *virus,* poison], viruses from the family Herperviridae. At least seven species of herpesvirus are known to be infectious to humans: HSV 1 and 2, varicella zoster virus, Epstein-Barr virus, cytomegalovirus, human herpesvirus 6, and human herpesvirus 7.

herpesvirus simiae encephalomyelitis, an infection of the CNS by a B form of HSV that usually affects simians. Persons most likely to be infected by the monkey virus are veterinarians and animal laboratory workers.

herpes zoster /zos'tər/ [Gk, *herpein* + *zoster,* girdle], an acute infection caused by reactivation of the latent varicella zoster virus, which mainly affects adults. It is characterized by the development of painful vesicular skin eruptions that follow the underlying route of cranial or spinal nerves inflamed by the virus.

herpes zoster ophthalmicus, a form of herpes zoster causing pain and skin eruptions along the ophthalmic branch of the fifth cranial nerve. There also may be involvement of the third cranial nerve. The infection frequently leads to corneal ulceration or other ocular complications.

herpes zoster oticus, a herpes zoster infection of vestibulocochlear nerve ganglia and geniculate ganglion, causing severe pain in the external ear structures and pain or paralysis along the facial nerve. The disease also may cause hearing loss and vertigo.

herpetic encephalitis /hərpet'ik/ [Gk, *herpein,* to creep, *enkephalos,* brain, *itis,* inflammation], the most common form of acute encephalitis, caused by a herpesvirus and characterized by hemorrhagic necrosis of parts of the temporal and frontal lobes. Onset is over several days and involves fever, headache, seizures, stupor, and often coma, frequently with a fatal outcome.

herpetic neuralgia /hərpet'ik/ [Gk, *herpein,* to creep, *neuron,* nerve, *algos,* pain], a form of neuralgia with intractable pain that develops at the site of a previous eruption of herpes zoster.

herpetic sore throat, a herpes inflammation that develops in the region of the pharynx.

herpetic stomatitis [Gk, *herpein,* to creep, *stoma,* mouth, *itis,* inflammation], a form of inflammation of the mouth caused by a herpesvirus infection, also characterized by ulcers.

herpetic whitlow, cutaneous herpes simplex on the terminal segment of a finger, resulting in formation of deep coalescing vesicles with tissue destruction.

herpetiform /hərpet'ifôrm'/ [Gk, *herpein*; L, *forma,* form], having clusters of vesicles that resemble the skin lesions of some herpesvirus infections.

Herplex, a trademark for a topical antiviral (idoxuridine).

Hers' disease /herz, hurz/ [H.G. Hers, twentieth-century Belgian physiologist; L, *dis,* opposite of; Fr, *aise,* ease], an uncommon metabolic disorder of glycogen storage involving a deficiency of glycogen phosphorylase. It is characterized by hepatomegaly and an accumulation of abnormally large amounts of glycogen in the liver as a result of its inability to break down glycogen.

hertz (Hz) /hurts, herts/ [Heinrich R. Hertz, German physicist, 1857–1894], a unit of measurement of wave frequency equal to 1 cycle per second.

HERV, abbreviation for **human endogenous retroviruses.**

Herxheimer's reaction /herks'hī'mərz/ [Karl Herxheimer, German dermatologist, 1861–1944], an increase in symptoms after administration of a drug. The reaction was originally discovered in penicillin treatment of syphilis, but it has been found to occur with other diseases as well.

Herzog taping protocol, a procedure for immobilizing and balancing a foot with tape after a musculoskeletal injury.

Heschl's gyrus /hesh'əlz/ [Richard L. Heschl, Austrian pathologist, 1824–1881; Gk, *gyros,* turn], any of several small gyri that run transversely on the upper surface of the temporal operculum of the insula of the cortex.

hesperidin /hesper′idin/, a crystalline flavone glycoside present in most citrus fruits, especially in the spongy casing of oranges and lemons.

Hesselbach's hernia /hes′əlbaks, -bäkhs/ [Franz K. Hesselbach, German surgeon, 1759–1816], a protrusion of diverticula through the femoral sheath, usually associated with direct inguinal hernia.

hetastarch /het′əstärch/, a plasma volume expander prescribed to treat hypovolemia in shock and used in leukapheresis to help increase the yield of granulocytes.

heteroallele /het′ərō-əlēl′/ [Gk, *heteros*, different, *alleolon*, of one another], one of a pair of alleles at a specific locus on homologous chromosomes that differs from the other of the pair.—**heteroallelic**, *adj.*

heteroantibody /het′ərō-an′tibod′ē/, an antibody that recognizes an antigen from a species other than that of the antibody producer.

heteroantigen /he′tərō-an′təjən/, an antigen that originates in a different species and is foreign to the antibody producer.

heteroblastic /het′ərōblas′tik/ [Gk, *heteros* + *blastos*, germ], developing from different germ layers or kinds of tissue rather than from a single type.

heterocellular /-sel′yələr/, pertaining to a structure formed by more than one kind of cell.

heterocephalus /-sef′ələs/ [Gk, *heteros* + *kephale*, head], a malformed fetus that has two heads of unequal size.—**heterocephalic, heterocephalous**, *adj.*

heterochromatin /-krō′mətin/ [Gk, *heteros*, different, *chroma*, color], the part of a chromosome that is inactive in gene expression but may function in controlling metabolic activities, transcription, and cell division.—**heterochromatic**, *adj.*

heterochromatinization /-krō′mətīnəzā′shən/, the transformation of genetically active euchromatin into genetically inactive heterochromatin. It occurs during the inactivation of one of the X chromosomes in the mammalian female during the early stages of embryogenesis.

heterochromia iridis /het′ər-ōkrō′mē-ə ī′ridis/ [Gk, *heteros*, different, *chroma*, color, *iris*, rainbow], difference of color in the two irides or in different areas of the same iris.

heterochromosome /-krō′məsōm/, a sex chromosome.—**heterochromosomal**, *adj.*

heterocytotropic antibody /-sī′tətrop′ik/, an antibody of immunoglobulin class E that has a greater affinity for antigens when fixed to mast cells of a different species than that of the antibody producer.

heterodidymus /het′ərōdid′iməs/ [Gk, *heteros* + *didymos*, twin], a conjoined twin fetus in which the parasitic elements consist of a head, neck, and thorax attached to the thoracic wall of the autosite.

heteroduplex /-dōō′pleks/ [Gk, *heteros*; L, *duoplicare*, to double], a DNA molecule in which the two strands are derived from different individuals, with the result that some base pairs may not be complementary.

heteroduplex mapping, a method for determining the location of insertions, deletions, and other heterogeneities in the two strands of a DNA molecule.

heteroenzyme /het′ərō-en′zīm/, a functionally identical enzyme from a different species.

heteroeroticism /het′ərō-irot′isiz′əm/ [Gk, *heteros*, different, *eros*, love], sexual feeling or activity directed toward another individual.

heterofermentation /-fur′məntā′shun/, fermentation that produces major products that are different.

heterogametic /-gamet′ik/, pertaining to the sex that produces gametes of different kinds, in terms of their sex chromosomes. In human beings the male, who possesses X-bearing and Y-bearing sperm, is the heterogametic sex.

heterogeneic antigen, xenogeneic antigen.

heterogeneity /-jənē′itē/, **1.** a quality of being dissimilar in kind. **2.** a state of having different characteristics and qualities.

heterogeneous /het′əroj′ənəs/ [Gk, *heteros*, different, *genos*, kind], **1.** consisting of dissimilar elements or parts; unlike; incongruous. **2.** not having a uniform quality throughout.

heterogenesis /-jen′əsis/ [Gk, *heteros* + *genein*, to produce], reproduction that differs in successive generations, such as the alternation of sexual and asexual reproduction, so that offspring have characteristics different from those of the parents.

heterogenous /het′əroj′ənəs/ [Gk, *heteros* + *genos*, kind], **1.** having a nonuniform composition throughout. **2.** derived or developed from another source or from two different sources.

heterogenous vaccine [Gk, *heteros*, different, *genein*, to produce; L, *vaccinus*, cow], a vaccine made against the same species of pathogen from a source other than the patient's own tissues.

heteroimmunization /-im′yənīzā′shun/, immunization of an individual with antigens from a different species.

heteroinfection /-infek′shən/ [Gk, *heteros*, different; L, *inficere*, to stain], infection by a microorganism originating outside the body.

heterolactic acid fermentation /-lak′tik/, bacterial fermentation that produces a mixture of lactic acid and other products.

heterologous anaphylaxis /het′ərol′əgəs/ [Gk, *heteros,* differen, *logos,* relation, *ana,* again, *phylaxis,* protection], a form of passive anaphylaxis that results from the transfer of serum between two animals of different species.

heterologous tumor [Gk, *heteros* + *logos,* relation], a neoplasm consisting of tissue different from that of its site.

heterologous vaccine, a vaccine that confers protective immunity against a pathogen that shares cross-reacting antigens with the microorganisms in the vaccine.

heterometropia /-mətrō′pē·ə/ [Gk, *heteros,* different, *metron,* measure, *ops,* eye], a generally mild visual disorder in which one eye refracts differently from the other, causing slightly different images to be perceived by the right and left eyes.

heteronymous /het′əron′iməs/ [Gk, *heteros,* different, *onyma,* name], **1.** having different names; the opposite of synonymous. **2.** pertaining to an optic phenomenon in which two images are produced by one object. **3.** abnormal.

heterophil /het′ərofil′/ [Gk, *heteros* + *philein,* to love], having affinity for something unusual or abnormal, as an antibody that recognizes an antigen other than the one it is expected to challenge.

heterophil antibody test [Gk, *heteros* + *philein,* to love], a test for the presence of heterophil antibodies in the serum of patients suspected of having infectious mononucleosis, based on an agglutination reaction between heterophil antibodies in a person's serum and heterophil antigen.

heterophilic leukocyte /-fil′ik/ [Gk, *heteros,* different, *philein,* to love, *leukos,* white, *kytos,* cell], a neutrophil of certain animal species that takes an acid stain.

Heterophyes /het′erofi′ēz/, a genus of minute trematodes found in the middle third of the small intestine of humans and certain other mammals.

heteroplastic transplantation /-plas′tik/ [Gk, *heteros,* different, *plassein,* to mold; L, *transplantare*], the transfer of tissue from one animal to another of a different species.

heteroploid /het′ərəploid′/ [Gk, *heteros* + *ploos,* times, *eidos,* form], **1.** an individual, organism, strain, or cell that has a variation in the number of chromosomes characteristic of somatic cells of the species. **2.** pertaining to such an individual, organism, strain, or cell.—**heteroploidy,** *n.*

heteroploidy /het′ərəploi′dē/, the state or condition of having an abnormal number of chromosomes, either more or less than that characteristic of the somatic cell of the species.

heteropolymer /-pol′imir/ [Gk, *heteros* + *polys,* many, *meros,* part], a compound formed from subunits that are not all the

same, such as a protein composed of various amino acid subunits.

heterosexual /-sek′shəl/ [Gk, *heteros,* different; L, *sexus,* male or female], **1.** a person whose sexual desire or preference is for people of the opposite sex. **2.** pertaining to sexual desire or preference for people of the opposite sex.—**heterosexuality,** *n.*

heterosexual panic, an acute attack of anxiety that results in the frantic pursuit of heterosexual activity in response to unconscious or latent homosexual impulses.

heterosis /het′ərō′sis/ [Gk, *heteros* + *osis,* condition], the superiority of first-generation hybrid plants and animals with respect to one or more traits when compared with either of the parent strains or with corresponding inbred strains.

heterotaxy syndrome, a variable set of complex congenital anomalies of the GI and cardiovascular systems that results from heterotaxia of the abdominal and thoracic viscera.

heterotopic ossification /-top′ik/ [Gk, *heteros* + *topos,* place], a nonmalignant overgrowth of bone, frequently occurring after a fracture, that is sometimes confused with certain bone tumors when visualized on x-ray film.

heterotopic pain, pain that appears in the wrong part of the body, as pain originating in the gallbladder that may be felt in the right shoulder. The phenomenon seems to be caused by projection of sensory neurons from different parts of the body into the same regions of the CNS.

heterotopic pregnancy, a pregnancy that is both intrauterine and extrauterine.

heterotopic transplantation [Gk, *heteros,* different, *topos,* place; L, *transplantare*], the transfer of tissue from one part of a body of a donor to another area of the body of a recipient.

heterotransplant /-trans′plant/ [Gk, *heteros,* different; L, *transplantare*], the transfer of tissue from one animal to another of a different species.

heterotypic /het′ərōtip′ik/ [Gk, *heteros* + *typos,* pattern], pertaining to or characteristic of a type differing from the usual or the normal, specifically regarding the first meiotic division of germ cells in gametogenesis as distinguished from the second meiotic division or a mitotic division.

heterotypicchromosomes, anyunmatched pair of chromosomes, specifically the sex chromosomes.

heterotypic mitosis, the division of bivalent chromosomes, as occurs in the first meiotic division of germ cells in gametogenesis; a reduction division.

heterozygosis /het′ərōzīgō′sis/ [Gk, *heteros* + *zygotos,* yoked, joined], **1.** the formation of a zygote by the union of two gametes that have dissimilar pairs of alleles. **2.** the production of hybrids through crossbreeding.—**heterozygotic,** *adj.*

heterozygote /-zī′gōt/ [Gk, *heteros,* different, *zygotos,* yoked], an organism whose somatic cells have two different allelomorphic genes on the same locus of each pair of chromosomes. It can produce two different types of gametes.

heterozygote detection, the use of amniocentesis and other techniques to identify potential inherited X-linked recessive disorders.

heterozygous /het′ərəzī′gəs/ [Gk, *heteros* + *zygotos,* yoked], having two different alleles at corresponding loci on homologous chromosomes. An individual who is heterozygous for a trait has inherited an allele for that trait from one parent and an alternative allele from the other parent. An individual who is heterozygous for a genetic disease caused by a dominant allele manifests the disorder. A person who is heterozygous for a hereditary disorder produced by a recessive allele is asymptomatic or exhibits reduced symptoms of the disease. The offspring of a heterozygous carrier of a genetic disorder have a 50% chance of inheriting the allele associated with the disorder if the other parent does not carry the allele.

heuristic /hyŏŏris′tik/ [Gk, *heuriskein,* to discover], **1.** serving to stimulate interest for further investigation. **2.** pertaining to a teaching method in which the student is encouraged to learn through independent research and investigation.

HEV, abbreviation for *hepatitis E virus.*

hexachlorophene /hek′səklôr′əfēn/, a topical bacteriostatic cleansing agent used as an antiseptic scrub and as a disinfectant to clean inanimate objects of gram-positive bacteria. It is not effective against gram-negative bacteria.

hexadactyly /hek′sədak′təle/ [Gk, *hex,* six, *daktylos,* finger], the occurrence of six digits on the hand or foot.

Hexadrol, a trademark for a glucocorticoid (dexamethasone).

hexavalent /hek′sivā′lənt/, pertaining to a chemical with a valence of 6.

hexokinase /hek′səkī′nās/ [Gk, *hex,* six, *glykys,* sweet, *kinein,* to move, *ase,* enzyme], a transferase enzyme present in all tissue that catalyzes the transfer of a phosphate group from adenosine triphosphate to glucose 6-phosphate. It is also found in yeast.

hexosaminidase test, a blood test used to detect the presence of the enzyme hexosaminidase, which is present in Tay-Sachs disease and Sandhoff's disease, a variant of Tay-Sachs.

hexose /hek′sōs/ [Gk, *hex,* six, *glykys,* sweet], a monosaccharide that contains six carbon atoms in the molecule. Glucose, mannose, and fructose are the principal hexoses found in nature.

hexylcaine hydrochloride /hek′silkān/, a local anesthetic for use on intact mucous membranes of the respiratory, upper GI, and urinary tracts.

hexylresorcinol /hek′silrəsôr′sənol/, an antiseptic and anthelmintic.

Hf, symbol for the element **hafnium.**

HF, abbreviation for **hepatitis F.**

HFJV, abbreviation for **high-frequency jet ventilation.**

HFO, abbreviation for **high-frequency oscillation.**

HFV, abbreviation for **high-frequency ventilation.**

Hg, symbol for the element **mercury.**

HG, abbreviation for **hepatitis G.**

Hgb, abbreviation for **hemoglobin.**

HGE, abbreviation for *human granulocytic ehrlichiosis.*

HGF, 1. abbreviation for *human growth factor.* **2.** abbreviation for *hyperglycemic-glycogenolytic factor.*

HHCC, abbreviation for **Home Health Care Classification.**

HHCC system, a computerized classification system for home health care, assessing and classifying home health Medicare patients to predict their need for nursing and other home health care services and their outcomes of care.

HI, abbreviation for **hemagglutination inhibition.**

hiatal hernia, protrusion of a part of the stomach upward through the diaphragm. The major difficulty in symptomatic patients is gastroesophageal reflux.

hiatus /hī-ā′təs/ [L, *hiare,* to stand open], a usually normal opening in a membrane or other body structure.—**hiatal,** *adj.*

hiatus esophagus [L, *hiare,* to stand open; Gk, *oisophagos,* gullet], the opening in the diaphragm for the esophagus.

hibakusha /hē′bäkōō′shä/ [Japanese], people who were exposed to the atomic bomb explosions in Hiroshima and Nagasaki.

Hib disease, an infection caused by *Haemophilus influenzae* type B (Hib), which mainly affects children in the first 5 years of life. It is a leading cause of bacterial meningitis, as well as pneumonia, joint or bone infections, and throat inflammations. The infection can generally be prevented with a vaccine, given in infancy, usually at 2, 4, 6, and 12-18 months.

hibernation /hī′bərnā′shun/ [L, *hibernare,* to winter], a natural physiologic state or process wherein a generalized slowdown in metabolic and body functions produces a somnolescent condition and in which body temperature is maintained at a lower level than normal.

hibernoma /hī'bərnō'mə/ *pl.* **hibernomas, hibernomata** [L, *hibernus,* winter; Gk, *oma,* tumor], a benign tumor, usually on the hips or the back, composed of fat cells that are partly or entirely of fetal origin.

Hibiclens, a trademark for a topical antibiotic and cleanser for the skin and mucous membranes (chlorhexidine gluconate).

hiccup /hik'əp/, a characteristic sound that is produced by the involuntary contraction of the diaphragm, followed by rapid closure of the glottis. Hiccups have various causes, including indigestion, rapid eating, certain types of surgery, and epidemic encephalitis. They can also be caused by or associated with abdominal distension.

Hickman catheter /hik'mən/ [R.O. Hickman, American surgeon, 20th century], a type of central venous catheter used for the long term administration of substances via the venous system. It can be used for continuous or intermittent administration and may have either a single or a double lumen.

HICPAC, abbreviation for **Hospital Infection Control Practices Advisory Committee.**

hidradenitis suppurativa /hī'dradənī'tis sup'yŏŏrətē'və/ [Gk, *hydos,* water + *aden,* gland + *itis,* inflammation; L, *suppurare,* to form pus], a chronic suppurative and cicatricial disease of the apocrine gland–bearing areas caused by occlusion of the pores with secondary bacterial infection of apocrine sweat glands. It is characterized by the development of one or more tender red abscesses that enlarge and eventually break through the skin, yielding purulent and seropurulent drainage.

hidrosis /hidrō'sis, hī-/ [Gk, *hidros,* sweat], sweat production and secretion. —**hidrotic,** *adj.*

hieralgia /hī'əral'jə/ [Gk, *hieron,* sacrum, *algos,* pain], a painful sacrum.

high-altitude pulmonary edema [ME, *heigh,* high; L, *altitudo;* Gk, *oidema,* swelling], a form of pulmonary edema that occurs in people who move rapidly to higher altitudes. Fluid accumulates in the lungs as atmospheric pressure decreases.

high-calorie diet, a diet that provides 1000 or more calories a day beyond what is ordinarily recommended. It may be prescribed for nursing mothers, patients with severe weight loss caused by illness, or people with abnormally high metabolic rates or energy requirements.

high-copy number, a large number of repetitive copies of a gene, such as may be produced by cloning.

high-definition imaging (HDI), an ultrasound technique used in breast cancer diagnosis to determine without biopsy whether a lump is a solid tumor or a relatively harmless fluid-filled cyst.

high-density lipoprotein (HDL) [ME, *heigh,* high; L, *densus,* thick; Gk, *lipos,* fat, *proteios,* first rank], a plasma protein made mainly in the liver and containing about 50% lipoprotein (apoprotein) along with cholesterol, triglycerides, and phospholipid. It is involved in transporting cholesterol and other lipids to the liver to be disposed. Higher levels of high-density lipoprotein are associated with decreased cardiac risk profiles.

high-dose tolerance, the absence of an expected immunologic response after repeated injections of large amounts of an antigen.

high enema [ME, *heigh*; Gk, *einienai,* to send in], an enema that is inserted into the colon through a long catheter.

high-energy phosphate compound, a chemical compound containing an easily hydrolyzed phosphoric anhydride group. The hydrolysis of this group liberates considerable energy. Adenosine triphosphate is the most powerful and ubiquitous of the high-energy phosphate compounds found in the body.

highest intercostal vein [ME, *heigh*; L, *inter,* between, *costa,* rib, *vena,* vein], one of a pair of veins that drains the blood from the upper two or three intercostal spaces.

high-flow oxygen delivery system, a respiratory care apparatus that supplies inspired gases at a consistent preset oxygen concentration. It is generally not affected by changes in the ventilatory pattern.

high forceps, an obstetric procedure in which forceps are used to deliver a baby whose head is not engaged in the birth canal. It is no longer considered acceptable or meeting the standard of care.

high-Fowler's position [ME, *heigh,* high; George R. Fowler, American surgeon, 1848–1906], placement of the patient in a semisitting position by raising the head and trunk 90 degrees. The knees may or may not be flexed.

high-frequency hearing loss [ME, *heigh*; L, *frequens;* AS, *deaf*], a loss of ability to hear high-frequency sounds. It is most commonly associated with aging or noise exposure. Hearing loss may begin in early adulthood with a loss of hearing to frequencies in the range of 18 to 20 kHz.

high-frequency jet ventilation, a type of high-frequency ventilation characterized by delivery of gas through a small catheter in the endotracheal tube.

high-frequency oscillation, a type of high-frequency ventilation characterized by the use of active expiration.

high-frequency percussive ventilation, a type of high-frequency ventilation characterized by delivery of pressure-limited breaths in short bursts of gas from a venturi mask.

high-frequency positive pressure ventilation, a type of high-frequency ventilation characterized by low compressible volume circuit and tidal volume delivery of 3 to 4 mL per kg.

high-frequency ventilation (HFV), a technique for providing ventilatory support to patients at a rate of at least 60 breaths per minute with small tidal volumes. It may be used during intraoperative procedures such as laryngoscopy or bronchoscopy, as well as for ventilation in patients with a bronchopleural fistula or advanced respiratory distress syndrome or in respiratory distress of the neonate. Kinds of HFV include high-frequency jet ventilation (HFJV) and high-frequency oscillation (HFO). HFJV uses a high-pressure gas source that can produce short, rapid jets of gas through a small-bore cannula into the airway above the carina. HFO forces small impulses of gas into and out of the airway.

high-fructose corn syrup, a sweetener made by processing corn syrup to increase the level of fructose, usually to between 42% and 55% of the total sugar, with the balance being glucose. It is used extensively as a sweetener in processed foods and soft drinks, particularly soda and baked goods, but it is included also in many foods not normally thought of as sweet foods.

high labial arch, a labial arch wire adapted to lie gingival to the anterior tooth crowns with auxiliary springs that extend downward in contact with the teeth to be moved.

high-level wellness, a concept of optimal health that emphasizes the integration of body, mind, and environment to maximize the function of an individual.

high lithotomy, a suprapubic approach for surgical removal of urinary bladder stones that are not easily removed by ultrasonic crushing.

highly active antiretroviral therapy (HAART), the aggressive use of extremely potent antiretroviral agents in the treatment of HIV infection.

high-potassium diet, a diet that contains foods rich in potassium, including all leafy green vegetables, brussels sprouts, citrus fruits, bananas, dates, raisins, legumes, meats, and whole grains. It is indicated for any condition that causes loss of extracellular fluid and for patients who are receiving some diuretics, such as thiazide and furosemide, or corticosteroid therapy.

high-pressure liquid chromatography, a method of chromatography for separating and quantitating mixtures of substances in a solution.

high-protein diet, a diet that contains large amounts of protein, consisting largely of meats, fish, milk, legumes, and nuts. It may be indicated in protein depletion that results from any cause. It may be contraindicated in liver failure or when kidney function is so impaired that added protein could result in azotemia and acidosis.

high-residue diet /-rez′idyoo/ [ME, *heigh*; L, *residuum,* remaining; Gk, *diaita,* way of living], a diet that contains a greater than usual proportion of substances the digestive tract will not metabolize and absorb.

high-risk infant, any neonate, regardless of birth weight, size, or gestational age, who has a greater than average chance of morbidity or mortality, especially within the first 28 days of life. Risk factors include preconceptual, prenatal, natal, or postnatal conditions or circumstances that interfere with the normal birth process or impede adjustment to extrauterine growth and development.

high-risk pregnancy care, a nursing intervention from the Nursing Interventions Classification (NIC) defined as identification and management of a high-risk pregnancy to promote healthy outcomes for mother and baby.

high-speed handpiece, a handheld dental cutting instrument that rotates at up to 450,000 rpm.

high-vitamin diet, a dietary regimen that includes a variety of foods containing therapeutic amounts of all of the vitamins necessary for the metabolic processes of the body. It is often ordered in combination with other therapeutic diets that contain larger than usual amounts of protein or calories, especially when treating severe or chronic infection, malnutrition, or vitamin deficiency.

hilar /hī′lär/ [L, *hilum,* a trifle], pertaining to a hilum.

Hilgenreiner's line, a line connecting the superior aspect of the triradiate cartilages of the acetabula, used in radiographic assessment of the hip joint.

Hill-Burton Act, a 1946 amendment to the U.S. Public Health Service Act authorizing grants to states for surveying their hospital and public health center needs and for planning and constructing additional facilities.

Hill-Burton programs, a cluster of programs created by U.S. legislation included in the National Health Planning and Resources Development Act of 1974. The programs allow federal monetary assistance for modernization of health facilities, construction of outpatient health centers, construction of inpatient facilities in underserved areas, and conversion of existing health care facilities for the provision of new health services.

H

hilum /hī′ləm/ *pl.* **hila** [L, *hilum,* a trifle], a depression or recess at that part of an organ where vessels and nerves enter.

hilum of the lung, an area of the lung where the mediastinal pleura is continuous with the visceral pleura.

hindbrain /hīnd′brān/ [ME, *hind*; AS, *bragen*], the division in the brain of an embryo that eventually becomes the pons, the medulla oblongata, and the cerebellum.

hindgut /hīnd′gut/ [ME, *hind*; AS, *guttas*], the caudal part of the embryonic alimentary canal.

hinge axis, a line that passes through the left and right mandibular condyles and coincides with the center of rotation of the mandible. Determining the hinge axis is essential in constructing dental prostheses and in correcting occlusal interferences.

hinge axis-orbital plane, a reference plane for the diagnosis of various types of malocclusions and for the development of associated prostheses. It is usually determined by marking three points on a patient's skull. Two of the points, one on each side of the face, are located on the hinge axis. The third point is located on the face at the level of the orbital rim just beneath the eye.

hinged knee, an appliance designed to protect and support the knee during activity. It consists of an elastic sleeve with medial and lateral steel or aluminum bars hinged at the axis of the knee joint. The hinged bars are stabilized with leather or self-adhesive (Velcro) straps.

hinge joint [ME, *henge,* hinge, *jointe,* a connection], a synovial joint providing a connection in which articular surfaces are closely molded together in a manner that permits extensive motion in one plane.

HIPAA, abbreviation for **Health Insurance Portability and Accountability Act.**

hip-joint disease [AS, *hype*; L, *jungere,* to join; Gk, *dis,* not; Fr, *aise,* ease], any abnormal condition of the hip joint, such as **Legg-Calvé-Perthes disease** or congenital dislocation of the hip.

Hippel's disease [Eugen von Hippel, German ophthalmologist, 1867–1939], a familial disease, hereditary hemangioma confined mainly to the retina, first described by Hippel.

hippocampal /hip′ōkam′pəl/ [Gk, *hippokampos,* seahorse], pertaining to the hippocampus.

hippocampal commissure [Gk, *hippokampos,* seahorse; L, *commissura,* a joint], a thin triangular sheet of transverse fibers that connects the medial edges of the posterior pillars of the fornix in the brain.

hippocampal fissure, a fissure reaching from the posterior aspect of the corpus callosum to the tip of the temporal lobe.

hippocampal formation [Gk, *hippokampos,* seahorse; L, *formatio*], a part of the rhinencephalon, including the dentate gyrus, longitudinal striae, and hippocampus.

hippocampal gyrus [Gk, *hippokampos,* seahorse, *gyros,* turn], a convolution on the medial side of the temporal lobe of the cerebral cortex.

hippocampus /hip′ōkam′pəs/ *pl.* **hippocampi** [Gk, *hippokampos,* seahorse], a curved convoluted elevation of the floor of the inferior horn of the lateral ventricle of the brain.

Hippocrates /hipok′rətēz/, a Greek physician born about 460 BCE on the island of Cos, a center for the worship of Æsculapius. Called the "Father of Medicine," Hippocrates introduced a scientific approach to healing by seeking physical causes of disease rather than magic or mythic relationships used by members of the Æsculapian cults of the time.

hippocratic facies, a drawn, pinched, and pale appearance of the face, indicative of approaching death.

Hippocratic oath /hip′əkrat′ik/, an oath, attributed to Hippocrates, that serves as an ethical guide for the medical profession. It may be incorporated into the graduation ceremonies of medical colleges.

hippuric acid [Gk, *hippos,* horse, *ouron,* urine; L, *acidus,* sour], a detoxication product in the urine of some animals, used as a medication in the treatment of arthritic diseases.

hip replacement [AS, *hype*], substitution of an artificial ball and socket joint for the hip joint. Hip replacement is performed to relieve a chronically painful and stiff hip in advanced osteoarthritis, an improperly healed fracture, degenerative joint disease, or rheumatoid arthritis. During surgery the femoral head, neck, and part of the shaft are removed, and the contours of the socket are smoothed. A prosthesis of a durable, hard metal alloy or stainless steel is attached to the femur. A metal or a plastic acetabulum is implanted.

Hiprex, a trademark for a urinary antibacterial (methenamine hippurate).

Hirschberg's reflex /hursh′bərgz/, a diagnostic test for pyramidal tract disease. The test result is regarded as positive if inversion of the foot occurs when the sole is stroked at the base of the great toe.

Hirschfeld's method [Isador Hirschfeld, American dentist, 1881–1965], a toothbrushing technique in which the bristles are vigorously rotated in very small circles against the gingivae and the axial surfaces of the teeth at a slight incisal or occlusal angle.

Hirschsprung's disease /hirsh′sprŏōngz/ [Harald Hirschsprung, Danish physician, 1830–1916], the congenital absence of autonomic ganglia in the smooth muscle wall of the distal part of the colon, which causes poor or absent peristalsis in the involved segment of colon, accumulation of feces, and dilation of the bowel (megacolon). Symptoms include intermittent vomiting, diarrhea, and constipation. The abdomen may become distended to several times its normal size. The condition is usually diagnosed in infancy, but it may not be recognized until much later in childhood.

hirsutism /hur'sŌŌtiz'əm/ [L, *hirsutus,* hairy], excessive body hair in a masculine distribution pattern as a result of heredity, hormonal dysfunction, porphyria, or medication.—**hirsute,** *adj.,* **hirsuteness,** *n.*

hirsutoid papilloma of the penis /hur'sŌŌtoid/ [L, *hirsutus,* shaggy; Gk, *eidos,* form], a condition characterized by clusters of small white papules on the coronal edge of the glans penis.

His, abbreviation for **histidine.**

His bundle electrogram (HBE) [Wilhelm His, Jr., German physician, 1863–1934], a direct recording of the electrical activity in the atrioventricular bundle.

His-Purkinje system /his pərkin jē/ [Wilhelm His, Jr.; Johannes E. Purkinje, Czechoslovakian physiologist, 1787–1869], the conduction system in the heart from the atrioventricular bundle to the distal Purkinje fibers.

histaminase /histam'inās/, a soft tissue enzyme found in various body tissues. It catalyzes the decarboxylation of histamine and converts histamine into inactive imidazolacetic acid.

histamine /his'təmēn, -min/ [Gk, *histos,* tissue; L, *amine,* ammonia], a compound, found in all cells, that is produced by the breakdown of histidine. It is released in allergic inflammatory reactions.

histamine blocking agent, a substance that interferes with stimulation of cells by histamine, which is a substance produced by nearby cells to cause, among other things, inflammation and acid release in the stomach.

histamine headache, a headache associated with the release of histamine from the body tissues and marked by symptoms of dilated carotid arteries, fluid accumulation under the eyes, tearing or lacrimation, and rhinorrhea (runny nose). Symptoms include sudden sharp pain on one side of the head, involving the facial area from the neck to the temple.

histenzyme /histen'zīm/, a renal tissue enzyme that splits hippuric acid into glycine and benzoic acid.

histidine (His or H) /his'tidēn/ [Gk, *histos,* tissue], a basic amino acid found in many proteins and a precursor of histamine. It is an essential amino acid in infants.

histidinemia /his'tidinē'mē·ə/, an inherited metabolic disorder caused by an enzyme defect involving L-histidine ammonia lyase and affecting the amino acid histidine. The condition leads to retardation and nervous system disorders.

histioblast /his'tē-/, a tissue-forming cell.

histiocytic malignant lymphoma /his'tē-ō sit'ik/ [Gk, *histos* + *kytos,* cell], a lymphoid neoplasm containing undifferentiated primitive cells or differentiated reticulum cells.

histiocytosis X /his'tē-ōsītō'sis/, *obsolete,* a cluster of conditions encompassing benign eosinophilic granuloma and several malignant lymphomatous diseases.

histiotypic growth /his'tē-ōtip'ik/ [Gk, *histos* + *typos,* mark], the uncontrolled proliferation of cells, as occurs in tissue cultures, bacterial cultures, and molds.

histocompatibility /his'tōkəmpat'ibil'itē/ [Gk, *histos,* tissue; L, *compatibilis,* agreeing], a measure of the similarity of the antigens of a donor and a recipient of transplanted tissue.

histocompatibility antigen [Gk, *histos*; L, *compatibilis,* agreeable], one of a group of genetically determined antigens on the surface of many cells. They are the cause of most graft rejections that occur in organ transplantation.

histocompatibility complex, a group of genes whose products determine the compatibility of tissues or organs transplanted from one individual to another of the same species or from one species to another.

histocompatibility gene [Gk, *histos,* tissue; L, *compatibilis*; Gk, *genein,* to produce], a gene of the HLA complex that determines an antigen that governs histocompatibility of the donor and recipient of transplanted tissue.

histocompatibility locus, one of a set of positions on a chromosome occupied by a complex of genes that govern several tissue antigens.

histocyte /his'təsīt/ [Gk, *histion,* web, *kytos,* cell], a macrophage of connective tissue that plays a role in the body's immune system.

histogram /his'təgram'/ [Gk, *histos* + *gramma,* record], in research, a graph showing the values of one or more variables plotted against time or against frequency of occurrence.

histography /histog'rəfē/ [Gk, *histos* + *graphein,* to record], the process of describing or creating visualizations of tissues and cells.—**histographer,** *n.,* **histographic,** *adj.,* **histographically,** *adv.*

histoincompatible /his'tō·in'kəmpat'əbəl/, pertaining to host and donor tissues that have different genotypes and are therefore likely to induce an immune response, leading to rejection of a tissue graft or organ transplant.

histologic technician, an allied health professional who prepares tissue specimens of human and animal origin for a pathologist to examine for diagnostic, research, or teaching purposes.

histologist /histol′əjist/, a medical scientist who specializes in the study of the structure of organ tissues, including the composition of cells and their organization into various body tissues.

histology /histol′əjē/ [Gk, *histos* + *logos,* science], **1.** the science dealing with the microscopic identification of cells and tissue. **2.** the structure of organ tissues, including the composition of cells and their organization into various body tissues.—**histologic,** *adj.*

histolysis [Gk, *histos,* tissue, *lysis,* loosening], breakdown or dissolution of living organic tissue.—**histolytic,** *adj.*

histone /his′tōn/ [Gk, *histos,* tissue], any of a group of strongly basic, low–molecular weight proteins that are soluble in water and insoluble in dilute ammonia and combine with DNA to form nucleoproteins. They are found in the nucleus of eukaryotic cells, where they form a complex with DNA in the chromatin and function in regulating gene activity.

histopathology /his′tōpəthol′əjē/ [Gk, *histos,* tissue, *pathos,* disease, *logos,* science], the study of diseases involving the tissue cells.

histoplasma agglutinin /-plaz′mə/ [Gk, *histos* + *plasma,* a formation], a specific antibody that causes the clumping associated with fungal lung infections when it interacts with antigens.

Histoplasma capsulatum [Gk, *histos* + *plasma;* L, *capsula,* little box], a dimorphic fungal organism that is a single budding yeast at body temperature and a mold at room temperature. It is the causative organism in histoplasmosis.

histoplasmin test /-plaz′min/, a skin test for diagnosis of an infection caused by *Histoplasma capsulatum* fungus.

histoplasmosis /his′tōplazmō′sis/ [Gk, *histos* + *plasma* + *osis,* condition], an infection caused by inhalation of spores of the fungus *Histoplasma capsulatum.* Most cases are asymptomatic. Individuals who experience symptoms are usually either immunocompromised or have been exposed to a high inoculum. Primary histoplasmosis is characterized by fever, malaise, cough, and lymphadenopathy. Spontaneous recovery is usual; small calcifications remain in the lungs and affected lymph glands. Progressive histoplasmosis, the sometimes fatal disseminated form of the infection,

is characterized by ulcerating sores in the mouth and nose; enlargement of the spleen, liver, and lymph nodes; and severe and extensive infiltration of the lungs.

history /his′tərē/ [L, *historia,* inquiry], **1.** a record of past events. **2.** a systematic account of the medical, emotional, and psychosocial occurrences in a patient's life and of factors in the family, ancestors, and environment that may have a bearing on the patient's condition.

history of present illness, an account obtained during the interview with the patient of the onset, duration, and character of the present illness, as well as of any acts or factors that aggravate or ameliorate the symptoms.

histotechnologist, an allied health professional who prepares tissue specimens of human and animal origin for a pathologist to examine for diagnostic, research, or teaching purposes. Histotechnologists perform all functions of the histologic technician as well as identifying tissue structures, cell components, and their staining characteristics and relating them to physiologic functions; implementing and testing new techniques and procedures; making judgments concerning the results of quality control measures; instituting proper procedures to maintain accuracy; and sometimes supervising and teaching.

histotoxin /-tok′sin/ [Gk, *histos* + *toxikon,* poison], any substance that is poisonous to body tissues. Histotoxins are usually generated within the body rather than being introduced externally.

histrionic /his′trē·on′ik/ [L, *histrio,* actor], pertaining to exaggerated facial expressions, speech, or body movements, such as used on the stage.

histrionic paralysis [L, *histrio,* actor; Gk, *paralyein*], a condition in which paralysis of facial muscles results in dramatic, excitable behavior.

histrionic personality [L, *histrio,* actor, *persona,* role played], a personality characterized by behavioral patterns and attitudes that are overreactive, emotionally unstable, overly dramatic, and self-centered, exhibited as a means of attracting attention, either consciously or unconsciously.

histrionic personality disorder, a disorder characterized by dramatic, reactive, and intensely exaggerated behavior, which is typically self-centered. It results in severe disturbance in interpersonal relationships.

HIV, abbreviation for **human immunodeficiency virus.**

HIV-associated dementia (HAD), a usually rapidly progressive dementia that is the primary manifestation of encephalopathy caused by HIV type I infection. It is marked a variety of cognitive, motor, and behavioral abnormalities. Survival after the onset of dementia is usually three to six months but is occasionally longer.

HIV-associated fever of unknown origin, a fever of at least 38.3° C occurring on several occasions over a period of 4 weeks of outpatient care or 3 days of hospitalization in a patient with HIV infection, and for which a cause cannot be determined after 3 days of investigation, including 2 days of incubation of cultures.

HIV-associated nephropathy, renal pathology in patients infected with HIV, similar to focal glomerular sclerosis, with proteinuria, enlarged kidneys, and dilated tubules containing proteinaceous casts. It may progress to end-stage renal disease within weeks.

HIV-associated retinopathy, a usually asymptomatic microangiopathy affecting the retina, seen in HIV infection. It is manifested by transient cotton-wool exudate and occasionally hemorrhages, microaneurysms, and other lesions of the microvasculature.

Hivid, a trademark for an antiretroviral nucleoside analog (zalcitabine).

HIVNET, an international vaccine test network organized to conduct studies of prospective vaccines for HIV infection. It also supports behavioral and other studies of HIV infections.

HIV protease inhibitor /prō'tē·ās inhib'itor/ [*protein + -ase,* enzyme suffix; L, *inhibere,* to restrain], any of a group of antiretroviral drugs active against HIV that prevent protease-mediated cleavage of viral polyproteins, causing production of immature viral particles that are noninfective.

H$^+$,K$^+$-ATPase /ātēpē'ās/, a membrane-bound enzyme occurring on the secretory surfaces of parietal cells that uses the energy derived from the hydrolysis of adenosine triphosphate to drive the exchange of ions across the cell membrane, secreting acid into the gastric lumen. Protons and chloride ions are pumped against gradients across the apical membranes of activated parietal cells into the gastric lumen in exchange for potassium ions.

HLA, abbreviation for **human leukocyte antigen.**

HLA-A, abbreviation for *human leukocyte antigen A.*

HLA-B, abbreviation for *human leukocyte antigen B.*

HLA complex, antigens formed from genes on chromosome 6. HLA genes code for proteins that enable the immune system to differentiate tissues or proteins between "self" and "nonself." These loci are identified by numbers and letters, such as HLA-B27. Antigens are divided into three classes.

Class I antigens (HLA-A, -B, and -C) occur on the surface of all nucleated cells and platelets and are important in tissue transplantation. If donor and recipient human leucocyte antigen (HLA) antigens do not match, the nonself antigens are recognized and destroyed by killer T cells. Class II antigens occur only on immunocompetent cells and normally recognize foreign proteins. Class III antigens are nonhistocompatibility antigens, such as some complement components, that map in the HLA complex.

HLA-D, abbreviation for *human leukocyte antigen D.*

HLH, abbreviation for *human luteinizing hormone.*

HLHS, abbreviation for **hypoplastic left heart syndrome.**

HMD, abbreviation for *hyaline membrane disease.*

HME, abbreviation for *human monocytic erlichiosis.*

HMG-CoA reductase, a rate-controlling enzyme of cholesterol synthesis.

HMG-CoA reductase inhibitor, any of a a group of drugs that competitively inhibit the enzyme catalyzing the rate-limiting step in cholesterol biosynthesis and are used to lower plasma lipoprotein levels in the treatment of hyperlipoproteinemia.

HMO, abbreviation for **health maintenance organization.**

HMS Liquifilm, a trademark for an ophthalmic preparation containing a glucocorticoid (medrysone).

Ho, symbol for the element **holmium.**

H$_2$O, symbol for **water.**

hoarseness /hôrs'nəs/, an unnatural condition marked by a deep or rough, harsh, grating voice, indicating an inflammation of the throat and larynx.

Hodgkin's disease, Hodgkin's lymphoma /hoj'kinz/ [Thomas Hodgkin, English physician, 1798–1866], a malignant disorder characterized by painless, progressive enlargement of lymphoid tissue, usually first evident in cervical lymph nodes; splenomegaly; and the presence of Sternberg-Reed cells, large, atypical macrophages with multiple or hyperlobulated nuclei and prominent nucleoli. Symptoms include anorexia, weight loss, generalized pruritus, low-grade fever, night sweats, anemia, and leukocytosis.

Hodgson's disease /hoj'sənz/ [Joseph Hodgson, English physician, 1788–1869; Gk, *dis,* not; Fr, *aise,* ease], an aneurysmal dilation of the aorta.

Hoffmann's reflex [Johann Hoffmann, German neurologist, 1857–1919], an abnormal reflex elicited by sudden forceful flicking of the nail of the index, middle, or ring finger, which causes flexion of the thumb and of the middle and distal

phalanges of one of the other fingers. It is indicative of pyramidal tract disease above the level of the seventh or eighth cervical and first thoracic vertebrae.

holandric /holan′drik/ [Gk, *holos,* whole, *aner,* man], **1.** referring to genes located on the nonhomologous portion of the Y chromosome. **2.** pertaining to traits or conditions transmitted only through the paternal line.

holandric inheritance, the acquisition or expression of traits or conditions only through the paternal line, transmitted by genes located on the nonhomologous portion of the Y chromosome.

hold-relax, a technique of facilitating neuromuscular sensation and awareness, used in treating hypertonicity or motor dysfunction. It is often applied when there is muscle tightness on one side of a joint and when immobility is the result of pain.

holism /hō′lizəm/ [Gk, *holos,* whole], a philosophic concept in which an entity is seen as more than the sum of its parts.

holistic /hōlis′tik/ [Gk, *holos*], pertaining to the whole; considering all factors, as holistic medicine.

holistic counseling, an alternative form of psychotherapy that focuses on the whole person (mind, body, and spirit) and health.

holistic dentistry, dental practice that takes into account the effect of dental treatment and materials on the overall health of the individual.

holistic health /hōlis′tik/ [AS, *hal,* whole + *haelth*], a concept that concern for health requires a perspective of the individual as an integrated system rather than one or more separate parts.

holistic health care, a system of comprehensive or total patient care that considers the physical, emotional, social, economic, and spiritual needs of the person; his or her response to illness; and the effect of the illness on the ability to meet self-care needs.

Holliday-Segar formula, a method of estimating the daily caloric needs of the average hospital patient under conditions of bed rest, based on the body weight in kilograms of the patient.

hollow /hol′ō/ [OE, *holh*], a depressed area or concavity.

hollow cathode lamp [ME, *holwe;* Gk, *kata,* down, *hodos,* way + *lampas*], a lamp consisting of a metal cathode and an inert gas. When an electric current is passed through the cathode, electrons in the metal are excited so as to emit a line spectrum of specific wavelengths related to the metal of the cathode.

holmium (Ho) /hōl′mē·əm/ [L, *Holmia,* Stockholm, Sweden], a rare earth metallic element. Its atomic number is 67, and its atomic mass is 164.93.

holoacardius /hol′ō·ākär′dē·əs/ [Gk, *holos + kardia,* heart], a separate, grossly defective monozygotic twin fetus.

holoacardius acephalus, a grossly defective separate twin fetus that lacks a heart, a head, and most of the upper part of the body.

holoacardius acormus, a grossly defective, separate twin fetus in which the trunk is malformed and little more than the head is recognizable.

holoacardius amorphus, a malformed separate twin fetus in which there are no recognizable or formed parts.

holoarthritis /-ärthrī′tis/, a form of arthritis that involves all or most of the joints.

holoblastic /hol′əblas′tik/ [Gk, *holos + blastos,* germ], pertaining to an ovum that contains little or no yolk and undergoes total cleavage.

holocephalic /hō′lōsifal′ik/ [Gk, *holos + kephale,* head], pertaining to a malformed fetus in which several parts are deficient, although the head is complete.

holocrine /hol′əkrēn/ [Gk, *holos,* whole, *krienein,* to secrete], pertaining to the secretion of a gland or the gland itself as well as the accumulated gland secretions.

holocrine gland [Gk, *holos,* whole, *krienein,* to secrete], a gland whose discharge contains disintegrated or altered cells of the gland.

holoendemic /hol′ō·endem′ik/, pertaining to an intensely endemic disease area.

holoenzyme /hol′ō·en′zīm/ [Gk, *holos + en,* in, *zymos,* ferment], a complete enzyme-cofactor complex that gives rise to full catalytic activity.

holographic reconstruction /-graf′ik/, a method of producing three-dimensional images with diagnostic ultrasound equipment.

hologynic /hol′ōjin′ik/ [Gk, *holos + gyne,* female], **1.** referring to genes located on attached X chromosomes. **2.** pertaining to traits or conditions transmitted only through the maternal line.

hologynic inheritance, the acquisition or expression of traits or conditions only through the maternal line, transmitted by genes located on attached X chromosomes. The phenomenon is not known to occur in humans.

holoprosencephaly /hol′ōpros′ensef′əlē/ [Gk, *holos + pro,* before, *enkephalos,* brain], a congenital defect caused by the failure of the prosencephalon to divide into hemispheres during embryonic development. It is characterized by multiple midline facial defects, including cyclopia in severe cases.—**holoprosencephalic, holoprosencephalous,** *adj.*

Holter monitor [Norman J. Holter, American biophysicist, 1914–1983; L, *monere,* to remind], a trademark for a device for making prolonged ECG recordings (usually 24 hours) on a portable tape recorder while the patient conducts normal daily activities.

Holt-Oram syndrome /hōlt or'əm/ [Mary Clayton Holt, British cardiologist, 20th century; Samuel Oram, English cardiologist, 1913–1991], autosomal-dominant heart disease of varying severity, usually an atrial or ventricular septal defect, associated with skeletal malformation (hypoplastic thumb and short forearm).

Holtzman inkblot technique, a modification of the Rorschach test in which many more pictures of inkblots are used, the subject is permitted only one response to each design, and the scoring is predominantly objective rather than subjective.

Homans' sign [John Homans, American surgeon, 1877–1954; L, *signum*, mark], pain in the calf with dorsiflexion of the foot, indicating thrombophlebitis or thrombosis. It is not, however, a reliable indicator of either medical problem.

home assessment [AS, *ham*, village; L, *assidere*, to sit beside], an examination of the living area of a physically challenged person for the purposes of making recommendations about elimination of safety hazards and suggesting architectural or other modifications that would allow for independent functioning.

home care [AS, *ham*, village; L, *garrire*, to chatter], a health service provided in the patient's place of residence for the purpose of promoting, maintaining, or restoring health or minimizing the effects of illness and disability.

home health agency, an organization that provides health care in the home. Medicare certification for a home health agency in the United States requires provision of skilled nursing services and at least one additional therapeutic service.

Home Health Care Classification (HHCC), a system developed by Dr. Virginia Saba to assess and classify patients receiving home health care.

home health nurse, a registered nurse who visits patients in the home. The nurse works primarily in the area of secondary or tertiary care, providing hands-on care and educating the patient and family on care and prevention of future episodes.

homeless person, an individual who has no permanent home, haven, or domicile. Such individuals usually are indigent and depend on charity or public assistance for temporary lodging and medical care. An estimated 30% of homeless persons suffer from some type of mental disorder.

home maintenance assistance, a nursing intervention from the Nursing Interventions Classification (NIC) defined as helping the patient/family to maintain the home as a clean, safe, and pleasant place to live.

homeodynamics /hō′mē·ədīnam′iks/ [Gk, *homoios*, similar, *dynamis*, force], the constantly changing interrelatedness of body components while an overall equilibrium is maintained.

homeomorphous /-môr′fəs/, similar in appearance but different in composition.

Homeopathic Pharmacopoeia of the United States, one of the three official drug compendia specified in the Federal Food, Drug, and Cosmetic Act.

homeopathist /hō′mē·op′əthist/, a physician who practices homeopathy.

homeopathy /hō′mē·op′əthē/ [Gk, *homoios*, similar, *pathos*, disease], a system of therapeutics based on the theory that "like cures like." The theory was advanced in the late eighteenth century by Dr. Samuel Hahnemann, who believed that a large amount of a particular drug may cause symptoms of a disease whereas moderate dosage may reduce those symptoms; thus some disease symptoms could be treated by very small doses of medicine.—**homeopathic,** *adj.*

homeostasis /hō′mē·əstā′sis/ [Gk, *homoios* + *stasis*, standing still], a relative constancy in the internal environment of the body, naturally maintained by adaptive responses that promote healthy survival. Some of the key control mechanisms are the reticular formation in the brainstem and the endocrine glands.—**homeostatic,** *adj.*

homeotherapy /-ther′əpē/, the treatment or prevention of disease by homeopathic methods.

homeotic mutation /hō′mē·ot′ik/, a mutation that causes tissues to alter their normal differentiation pattern, producing integrated structures but in unusual locations.

homeotypic /hō′mē·ōtip′ik/ [Gk, *homoios* + *typos*, mark], pertaining to or characteristic of the regular or usual type, specifically regarding the second meiotic division of germ cells in gametogenesis as distinguished from the first meiotic division.

homeotypic mitosis, the separation of sister chromatids, as occurs in the second meiotic division of germ cells in gametogenesis.

Home's silver precipitation method, a technique for depositing silver in enamel and dentin by applying ammoniac silver nitrate solution and reducing with formalin or eugenol.

homicide /hom′isīd/ [L, *homo*, man, *caedere*, to kill], the death of one human being caused by another.

hominal physiology /hom′inəl/ [L, *hominis*, human; Gk, *physis*, nature, *logos*, science], the study of the specific physical and chemical processes involved in the normal functioning of humans; human physiology.

hominid /hom′inid/ [L, *homo*, man; Gk, *eidos*, form], pertaining to the primate family Hominidae, which includes humans.

homoblastic /hō″mōblas′tik/ [Gk, *homos* + *blastos*, germ], developing from the same germ layer or from a single type of tissue.

homocarnosine /hō″mōkär′nōsēn/, a dipeptide consisting of gamma-aminobutyric acid and histidine. In humans it is found in the brain but not in other tissues.

homochronous inheritance /hōmok′rōnəs/ [Gk, *homos* + *chronos*, time], the appearance of traits or conditions in offspring at the same age when they appeared in the parents.

homocysteine /-sis′tēn/, an amino acid containing sulfur and a homolog of cysteine, produced in the demethylation of methionine. It is also an intermediate product in the biosynthesis of cysteine from L-methionine via L-cystathionine in the breakdown of proteins. High levels of homocysteine are associated with an increased risk of collagen cardiovascular disorders.

homocysteine (HCY) test, a blood test used to detect levels of homocysteine, which, if elevated, may act as an independent risk factor for ischemic heart disease, cerebrovascular disease, peripheral arterial disease, and venous thrombosis.

homocystine /-sis′tin/, a disulfide analog of homocysteine produced by the oxidation of homocysteine.

homocystinemia /-sis′tinē″mē·ə/, an amino acid disorder that causes an excess of homocystine in the blood.

homocystinuria /hō″mōsis′tinoōr′ē·ə/ [Gk, *homos*; (cystine); Gk, *ouron*, urine], a rare biochemical abnormality characterized by the abnormal presence of homocystine, an amino acid, in the blood and urine, which is caused by any of several enzyme deficiencies in the metabolic pathway of methionine to cystine. Its clinical signs are similar to those of Marfan's syndrome.—**homocystinuric,** *adj.*

homogametic /hō″mōgamet′ik/ [Gk, *homos* + *gamete*, spouse], pertaining to the sex that produces gametes of only one kind, in terms of their sex chromosomes. In human beings, the female is the homogametic sex.

homogenate /hōmoj′ənit/, a tissue that is or has been made homogenous.

homogeneous /hō″mōjē′nē·əs/ [Gk, *homos* + *genos*, kind], **1.** consisting of similar elements or parts. **2.** having a uniform quality throughout.—**homogeneity,** *adj.*

homogenesis /hō″mōjē′nē·əs/ [Gk, *homos* + *genesis*, origin], reproduction by the same process in succeeding generations so that offspring are similar to the parents.

homogenized /hōmoj′ənīzd/ [Gk, *homos*, same, *genein,* to produce], the state of having undergone homogenization; having a uniform texture or consistency throughout.

homogenized milk [Gk, *homos* + *genos*, kind], milk that has been mechanically treated to reduce and emulsify the fat globules so that the cream cannot separate.

homogenous /hōmoj′ənəs/ [Gk, *homos* + *genos*, kind], having a likeness in form or structure as a result of a common ancestral origin.

homogentisic acid, a compound that is an intermediate product of the metabolism of tyrosine. It forms a melanin-like staining substance in the urine of people who have alkaptonuria.

homogeny /hōmoj′ənē/ [Gk, *homos* + *genos,* kind], a likeness in structure or form that results from a common ancestral origin.

homoiothermic /hom″ē·əthur′mik/ [Gk, *homos*, same, *therme*, heat], pertaining to the ability of warm-blooded animals to maintain a relatively stable internal temperature, regardless of the temperature of the environment. This ability is not fully developed in newborn humans.

homolateral /hō″mōlat′ərəl/, pertaining to the same side of the body.

homolateral limb synkinesis, a condition of hemiplegia in which there appears to be a mutual dependency between the affected upper and lower limbs. Efforts at flexion of an upper extremity cause flexion of the lower extremity.

homolog /hom′əlog/ [Gk, *homos*, same], **1.** any organ corresponding in function, origin, and structure to another organ, as the flippers of a seal that correspond to human hands. **2.** in chemistry, one of a series of compounds, each formed by an added common atom or atom combination.—**homologous,** *adj.*

homologous /hōmol′əgəs/ [Gk, *homos*, same, *logos*, relation], pertaining to corresponding attributes or similar in structure.

homologous anaphylaxis [Gk, *homos*, same, *logos*, relation, *ana*, back, *phylaxis*, protection], a form of passive anaphylaxis resulting from the transfer of serum between animals of the same species.

homologous chromosomes [Gk, *homos*, same, *chroma*, color, *soma*, body], any two chromosomes in a diploid somatic cell that are identical in size, shape, and gene loci. In humans there are 22 pairs of homologous chromosomes and 1 pair of sex chromosomes.

homologous graft [Gk, *homos*, same, *logos*, relation, *graphein*, stylus], a tissue removed from a donor for transplantation to a recipient of the same species.

homologous organs [Gk, *homos,* same, *logos,* relation,*organon,* instrument], body parts of different species (or sexes) that are structural equivalents, such as the arms of humans and the forelegs of dogs and cats.

homologous tumor, a neoplasm made up of cells resembling those of the tissue in which it is growing.

homonymous /hōmon′iməs/ [Gk, *homos,* same, *onyma,* name], having the same name or sound.

homonymous diplopia [Gk, *homos,* same, *onyma,* name, *diploos,* double, *opsis,* vision], a type of diplopia in which the image observed by the right eye is located to the right of the image observed by the left eye.

homonymous hemianopia [Gk, *homos* + *onyma,* name], blindness or defective vision in the right or left halves of the visual fields of both eyes.

homophobia /hō′mōfō′bē·ə/ [Gk, *homos,* same, *phobos,* fear], the fear of or prejudice against homosexuals.

homoplastic transplantation [Gk, *homos,* same, *plassein,* to mold; L, *transplantare,* to transplant], the homologous transplantation of tissue from one human to another or from one animal to another of the same species.

homoplasty /hō′məplas′tē/ [Gk, *homos* + *plassein,* to mold], having a likeness in form or structure acquired through similar environmental conditions or parallel evolution rather than resulting from common ancestral origin.—**homoplastic,** *adj.*

homopolymer /hō′mōpol′imir/ [Gk, *homos* + *poly,* many, *meros,* part], a compound formed from subunits that are the same, such as a carbohydrate composed of a series of glucose units.

homosalate /hō′mōsal′āt/, a sunscreen effective against ultraviolet B rays, applied topically to the skin.

Homo sapiens /hō′mō sā′pē·əns, sä′pē·ens/ [L, *homo,* human, *sapere,* to know or taste], the scientific name of the human species.

homosexual /-sek′shəl/ [Gk, *homos;* L, *sexus,* sex, gender], **1.** pertaining to or denoting the same sex. **2.** a person who is sexually attracted to members of the same sex.

homosexual panic, an acute attack of anxiety based on unconscious conflicts concerning gender identity and a fear of being homosexual.

homosexual sexual intercourse [Gk, *homos,* same; L, *sexus,* male or female, *intercursus,* interposition], sexual activity of members of the same sex ranging from feelings and fantasies to kissing and genital, oral, or anal contact.

homotopic pain /hō′mōtop′ik/, pain experienced at the point of injury.

homotype /hō′mōtīp/, any structure or body part, such as a hand or foot, that appears in reversed symmetry with a similar part.

homovanillic acid (HVA) /hō′mōvənil′ik/, an acid that is produced by the normal metabolism of dopamine and that may occur at an elevated level in urine in association with tumors of the adrenal gland.

homozygosis /hō′mōzīgō′sis/ [Gk, *homos* + *zygon,* yoke], **1.** the formation of a zygote by the union of two gametes that have one or more pairs of identical alleles. **2.** the production of purebred organisms or strains through inbreeding.

homozygote /hō′məzī′gōt/ [Gk, *homos,* same, *zygon,* yoke], an organism whose somatic cells have identical genes on the same locus on one of the chromosome pairs.

homozygous /hō′məzī′gəs/ [Gk, *homos* + *zygon,* yoke], having two identical alleles at corresponding loci on homologous chromosomes.

homunculus /hōmung′kyələs/, *pl.* **homunculi** [L, little man], **1.** a dwarf in whom all the body parts are proportionally developed and in which there is no deformity or abnormality. **2.** in early embryologic theories of development, primarily preformation, a minute and complete human being contained in each of the germ cells that after fertilization grows from the microscopic to normal size. **3.** a small anatomic model of the human form; a manikin. **4.** in psychiatry, a little man who possesses magical powers created by the imagination.

hook grasp, a type of prehension in which an object is grasped with the fingers alone.

hookworm [AS, *hok* + *wyrm*], *nontechnical.* a nematode of the genera *Ancylostoma, Necator,* and *Uncinaria.* Most hookworm infections in the western hemisphere are caused by the species *Necator americanus.*

hookworm disease [AS, *hok* + *wyrm*; Gk, *dis,* not; Fr, *aise,* ease], a roundworm infestation that may involve either of two important intestinal parasites of humans, *Ancylostoma duodenale* and *Necator americanus.* Both forms of the disease are characterized by abdominal pain and iron deficiency anemia. The worm enters the human body as a larva by penetrating the skin, traveling to the lungs via the circulatory system, and ascending the respiratory tract to the pharynx, where it is swallowed. In the intestinal tract, the hookworm attaches its mouth to the mucosa and subsists on the blood of the host.

hope, a nursing outcome from the Nursing Outcomes Classification (NOC) defined as optimism that is personally satisfying and life-supporting.

H

hope inspiration, a nursing intervention from the Nursing Interventions Classification (NIC) defined as enhancing the belief in one's capacity to initiate and sustain actions.

hops, a perennial herb used as a flavoring (e.g., beer), mild sedative, diuretic, and weak antibiotic. It is also used to improve appetite and to treat insomnia, hyperactivity, pain, fever, and jaundice. It may be effective against restlessness; there are insufficient reliable data on its efficacy for other indications.

hordeolum /hôrdēʹələm/ [L, *hordeum,* barley], a furuncle of the margin of the eyelid originating in the sebaceous gland of an eyelash.

horizon /hōrīʹzən/ [Gk, *horizein,* to encircle], a specific stage of human embryonic development determined by the appearance and ultimate formation of certain anatomic characteristics. The classification comprises 23 stages, each lasting 2 to 3 days, beginning with the fertilization of the ovum.

horizontal abdominal position /hôrizʹtəl/, prone position.

horizontal angulation [Gk, *horizein,* to encircle; L, *angularis,* angle], the angle within the occlusal plane, relative to a reference in the vertical or sagittal plane, at which the central x-ray beam is directed during radiography or dental imaging of oral structures.

horizontal fissure of the right lung, a cleft that marks the separation of the upper and middle lobes of the right lung.

horizontal plane [Gk, *horizein,* to encircle; L, *planum,* level ground], **1.** any plane of the erect body parallel to the horizon, dividing the body into upper and lower parts. **2.** a plane passing through a tooth at right angles to its long axis.

horizontal position, a position in which the patient lies on the back with the legs extended.

horizontal pursuit, a visual screening test in which the patient is asked to follow with both eyes a target moving in a horizontal plane while the examiner observes accuracy of alignment and supportive head movements.

horizontal resorption, a pattern of bone reduction in marginal periodontitis wherein the marginal crest of the alveolar bone between adjacent teeth remains level and the bases of the periodontal pockets are above the crest.

horizontal transmission, the spread of an infectious agent from one person or group to another, usually through contact with contaminated material.

horizontal vertigo, a giddiness or feeling of instability experienced while lying down, frequently caused by a labyrinthine disorder.

horizontal violence, violence directed toward one's peers.

hormic psychology /hôrʹmic/ [Gk, *hormaein,* to begin action], in psychology, the school that stresses the purposive, goal-oriented nature of human behavior.

hormonal /hôrʹmōnəl/ [Gk, *hormaein,* to set in motion], pertaining to or resembling hormones.

hormone /hôrʹmōn/ [Gk, *hormaein,* to set in motion], a complex chemical substance produced in one part or organ of the body that initiates or regulates the activity of an organ or a group of cells in another part. Hormones secreted by the endocrine glands are carried through the bloodstream to the target organ. Other hormones are released by organs for local effect, most commonly in the digestive tract.

hormone replacement therapy[1], the administration of sex hormones after menopause or hysterectomy or in amenorrhea. There are a number of indications, including the prevention of postmenopausal osteoporosis and coronary artery disease, and the induction of menses in amenorrhea.

hormone replacement therapy[2], a nursing intervention from the Nursing Interventions Classification (NIC) defined as facilitation of safe and effective use of hormone replacement therapy.

hormone-sensitive lipase, an enzyme that catalyzes the release of fatty acids from adipose tissues.

hormone therapy, the treatment of diseases with hormones obtained from endocrine glands or substances that simulate hormonal effects.

horn, a projection or protuberance on a body structure.

Horner's syndrome [Johann F. Horner, Swiss ophthalmologist, 1831–1886], a neurologic condition characterized by an ipsilateral miotic pupil, ptosis, and facial anhidrosis, which results from a lesion in the spinal cord, with damage to a cervical nerve or any ascending part of the sympathetic outflow to the face/head.

horny /hôrʹnē/, having the nature or appearance of a horn.

horse chestnut, a herbal product used for fever, fluid retention, frostbite, hemorrhoids, inflammation, lower extremity swelling, phlebitis, varicose veins, and wounds. Horse chestnut seeds may have efficacy in the treatment of varicose veins and other forms of venous insufficiency. There is insufficient reliable information regarding efficacy of the bark, flower, or leaf products for other indications.

horse serum [AS, *hors*; L, *serum,* whey], immune serum prepared from the blood of a horse that has developed immunity to toxins. Because many people are sensitive to horse serum, a skin test for sensitivity is recommended before passive immunization with horse antibodies.

horseshoe fistula /hôrs'shoo/ [AS, *hors* + *scoh,* shoe], an abnormal semicircular passage in the perianal area with both openings on the surface of the skin.

horseshoe kidney, a relatively common congenital anomaly characterized by an isthmus of parenchymal tissue connecting the two kidneys at the lower poles. The condition may cause obstruction of the ureters, hydronephrosis, and abdominal pain.

horsetail, a perennial herb that is likely unsafe and should not be used for any purpose. This herb is used as a diuretic, a genitourinary astringent, and an antihemorrhagic. It is also used for Bell's palsy and for healing broken bones. There are no studies confirming its efficacy.

hospice /hos'pis/ [L, *hospes,* host], a system of family-centered care designed to assist the terminally ill person to be comfortable and to maintain quality of life through the phases of dying.

hospital /hos'pitəl/ [L, *hospitium,* guesthouse], a health care facility that provides inpatient beds, continuous nursing services, and an organized medical staff.

hospital clinic, an ambulatory care site owned by a hospital where persons who do not require hospitalization receive medical care. It may be primary care or subspecialty care.

Hospital Infection Control Practices Advisory Committee (HICPAC), a committee established in 1991 by the U.S. government with members appointed by the Secretary of Health and Human Services. It provides advice and guidance related to isolation practices and serves as an advisory committee to the Centers for Disease Control and Prevention for updating guidelines and policy statements related to control of nosocomial infection.

hospitalism /hos'pitəliz'əm/, the physical or mental effects of hospitalization or institutionalization on patients, especially infants and children, in whom the condition is characterized by social regression, personality disorders, and stunted growth.

hospitalist /hos'pitəlist/, a physician specializing in hospital inpatient care.

host /hōst/ [L, *hospes*], **1.** an organism in which another, usually parasitic organism is nourished and harbored. A definitive host is one in which the adult parasite lives and reproduces. An intermediate host is one in which the parasite exists in its nonsexual, larval stage. A reservoir host is a primary animal host for organisms that are sometimes parasitic in humans and through

which humans may become infected. **2.** the recipient of a transplanted organ or tissue.

host defense mechanisms, a group of body protective systems, including physical barriers and the immune response, that normally guard against infection.

hostility /hostil'itē/ [L, *hostilis,* hostile], an emotional state characterized by enmity toward others and a desire to harm those at whom the antagonism is directed. The hostility may be expressed passively and actively.

host modulating therapy, efforts to control periodontal disease by directly targeting the host response.

hot bath [AS, *hat* + *baeth*], a bath in which the temperature of the water is gradually raised to about 106° F (41.11° C).

hot compress [AS, *hat*; L, *comprimere,* to press together], a heated pad of damp, thickly folded cloth applied to an area to reduce pain or inflammation.

hot flash, a transient sensation of warmth experienced by some women during or after menopause. Hot flashes result from autonomic vasomotor disturbances that accompany changes in the neurohormonal activity of the ovaries, hypothalamus, and pituitary.

hot line, a means of contacting a trained counselor or specific agency for help with a particular problem, such as a rape hot line or a battered child hot line. The person needing help calls a telephone number and speaks to a counselor, who remains anonymous and who offers emotional support, specific recommendations for action, and referral to other medical, social, or community services.

hot spot, 1. a site in a gene sequence at which mutations occur with an unusually high frequency. **2.** an area on a nuclear medicine image that represents an abnormally high absorption of radiation.

Hounsfield unit /hounz'fēld/ [Godfrey N. Hounsfield, 20th century English scientist], the numeric information contained in each pixel of a CT image. It is related to the composition and nature of the tissue imaged and is used to represent the density of tissue.

hourglass uterus [Gk, *hora*; AS, *glaes*], a uterus in which a segment of circular muscle fibers contracts during labor, causing constriction ring dystocia.

housekeeping department, a unit of a hospital staff responsible for cleaning the hospital premises and furnishings, including controlling pathogenic organisms.

housemaid's knee [AS, *hus* + *maeden* + *cneow,* knee], a chronic inflammation of the bursa in front of the kneecap, characterized by redness and swelling. It is caused by prolonged and repetitive pressure of the knee on a hard surface.

H

house organ, a publication designed for distribution to the employees or members of an institution or business.

house physician [AS, *hus*; Gk, *physikos*, natural], a physician on call and immediately available in a hospital or other health care facility.

house staff, the interns and residents who are employed at a hospital while receiving additional training after graduation from medical college.

house surgeon, a surgeon on call and immediately available on the premises of a hospital.

housewives' eczema [AS, *hus* + *wif*; Gk, *ekzein*, to boil over], an informal term for contact dermatitis of the hands caused and exacerbated by their frequent immersion in water and by the use of soaps and detergents.

Howell-Jolly bodies/hou'əljol'ē/ [William H. Howell, American physiologist, 1860–1945; Justin M.J. Jolly, French histologist, 1870–1953], deep purple spherical erythrocyte nucleic acid inclusions observed on microscopic examination of stained blood films. They are most commonly seen in people who have hemolytic or pernicious anemia, leukemia, thalassemia, or congenital absence of the spleen and in those who have had a splenectomy.

HPG, abbreviation for *human pituitary gonadotropin.*

HPL, abbreviation for **human placental lactogen.**

HPV, 1. abbreviation for **human papillomavirus. 2.** abbreviation for **human parvovirus.**

hr, abbreviation for *hour.*

H₁ receptor, a type of histamine receptor on vascular smooth muscle cells through which histamine mediates vasodilation.

H₂ receptor, a type of histamine receptor on various kinds of cells through which histamine mediates bronchial constriction in asthma and GI constriction in diarrhea.

H₁ receptor antagonist, any of a large number of agents that block the action of histamine by competitive binding to the H₁ receptor. Such agents also have sedative, anticholinergic, and antiemetic effects, and are used for the relief of allergic symptoms and as antiemetics, antivertigo agents, sedatives, and antidyskinetics in parkinsonism. This group is traditionally called the *antihistamines.*

H₂ receptor antagonist, an agent that blocks the action of histamine by competitive binding to the H₂ receptor. It is used to inhibit gastric secretion in the treatment of peptic ulcer.

HRF, 1. abbreviation for *histamine-releasing factor.* **2.** abbreviation for *homologous restriction factor.*

HRIG, abbreviation for *human rabies immune globulin* vaccine.

HRSA, abbreviation for **Health Resources and Services Administration.**

hs, h.s., abbreviation for the Latin *hora somni,* at bedtime.

HSA, abbreviation for **health systems agency.**

HsP, abbreviation for **heat shock protein.**

HSV, abbreviation for *herpes simplex virus.*

HSV1, abbreviation for *herpes simplex virus type 1.*

ht, abbreviation for **height.**

HTLV, abbreviation for *human T-cell lymphotropic virus.*

HTLV-I, abbreviation for **human T-cell lymphotropic virus type I.**

HTLV-II, abbreviation for **human T-cell lymphotropic virus type II.**

HTLV-III, abbreviation for *human T-cell lymphotropic virus type III.*

Hu antigen, a family of four RNA-binding proteins (HuD, HuC/ple21, Hel-N1, and Hel-N2) that are expressed in neurons and are believed to play an important role in the development and maintenance of the nervous system. They are also expressed in the cells of small cell lung carcinoma, sarcoma, and neuroblastoma, and antibodies to them are associated with neurologic paraneoplastic syndromes.

Hubbard tank [Carl P. Hubbard, American engineer, b. 1857; Port, *tanqu*], a water tank in which patients can perform underwater exercise. The patient's trunk and extremities are submerged on a stretcher.

huffing, forced expiration with an open glottis used to clear secretions from the airway when pain limits normal coughing.

HUGO /hyōō'gō/, an acronym for **Human Genome Organization.**

Huhner test /hōō'nər/ [Max Huhner, American urologist, 1873–1947], a test for male fertility in which a semen sample aspirated from the vagina within an hour after coitus is examined for spermatozoal activity.

human /hyōō'mən/ [L, *humanus*], a member of the genus *Homo* and particularly of the species *H. sapiens.*

human bite [L, *humanus*; AS, *bitan*], a wound caused by the piercing of skin by human teeth.

human chorionic somatomammotropin (HCS), a hormone produced by the syncytiotrophoblast during pregnancy. It regulates carbohydrate and protein metabolism of the mother to ensure delivery to the fetus of glucose for energy and protein for fetal growth.

human diploid cell rabies vaccine (HDCV), an inactivated rabies virus vaccine prepared from rabies virus grown in human diploid cell cultures. Active immunization with HDCV begins on the day of exposure, followed by four or five additional injections.

human ecology, the study of the interrelationships between people and their environments, as well as among individuals within an environment.

human endogenous retroviruses (HERV), retrovirus-like sequences found in the human genome, thought to constitute the remains of true retroviruses that were absorbed through evolution. At least one is thought to be linked to expression of tumor cells. They are also thought to be involved in autoimmune disorders.

Human Genome Organization (HUGO), an international group established in 1989 to coordinate activities concerned with the Human Genome Project, including the distribution of funding and dissemination of information.

human herpesvirus 6, a T-cell lymphotrophic virus belonging to the subfamily Betaherpesvirinae that has a high affinity for CD4 lymphocytes. It exists as two variants, A and B. Variant A is isolated mainly in immunocompromised individuals. Variant B causes roseola infantum.

human herpesvirus 7, a virus belonging to the subfamily Betaherpesvirinae, closely related to human herpesvirus 6, but not known to be associated with any disease.

human herpesvirus 8, a virus in the family Herpesviridae that has been implicated as the causative agent of Kaposi's sarcoma and primary effusion lymphoma.

human immunodeficiency virus (HIV) /im'yŏŏnō'difish'ənsē/ [L, *humanus* + *immunis,* free from, *de,* from, *facere,* to make, *virus,* poison], a retrovirus that causes AIDS. Retroviruses produce the enzyme reverse transcriptase, which allows the viral RNA genome to be transcribed into DNA inside the host cell. HIV is transmitted through contact with an infected individual's blood, semen, breast milk, cervical secretions, CSF, or synovial fluid. It infects CD4-positive helper T cells of the immune system and causes infection, with an incubation period that averages 10 years. With the immune system destroyed, AIDS develops as opportunistic infections.

human insulin, a biosynthetic product manufactured from *Escherichia coli* by recombinant DNA technology. It eliminates allergic reactions that occur with the use of animal insulins.

human investigations committee, a group established in a hospital, school, or university to review research proposals involving human subjects to protect the rights of the people to be studied and to ensure that ethical principles are appropriately followed.

humanism /hyŏŏ'məniz'əm/, a system of thought pertaining to the interests, needs, and welfare of human beings; the concept that human needs and values are of utmost importance.

humanistic existential therapy /hyŏŏ'mənis'tik/, a kind of psychotherapy that promotes self-awareness and personal growth by stressing current reality and by analyzing and altering specific patterns of response to help a person realize his or her potential.

humanistic nursing model, a conceptual framework in which the nurse-patient relationship is analyzed as a human-to-human event rather than a nurse-to-patient interaction.

humanistic psychology, a branch of psychology that emphasizes a person's struggle to develop and maintain an integrated, harmonious personality as the primary motivational force in human behavior.

human leukocyte antigen (HLA), any one of four significant histocompatibility antigens governed by genes of the HLA complex, specific loci on chromosome 6, designated HLA-A, HLA-B, HLA-C, and HLA-D. Each locus has several genetically determined alleles; each of these is associated with certain diseases or conditions. The HLA system is used to assess tissue compatibility.

human lymphocyte antigen B27 (HLA-B27) test, a blood test done as part of paternity investigations, to indicate tissue compatibility with tissue transplantation, and to assist in the diagnosis of Reiter's syndrome and other conditions.

human metapneumovirus, a species that causes respiratory infection in humans that is clinically similar to, but less severe than, that caused by respiratory syncytial virus.

human natural killer cell, a lymphocyte that is able to lyse tumor and virally infected cells as part of the body's natural defense against malignancy and invasion by pathogens.

human papillomavirus (HPV), a virus that is the cause of common warts of the hands and feet, as well as lesions of the mucous membranes of the oral, anal, and genital cavities. The virus can be transmitted through sexual contact, and specific types of the virus are a precursor to cancer of the cervix.

human papillomavirus (HPV) test, a fluid analysis of a cervical mucus specimen, performed to identify genital HPV in women who have abnormal Pap smears.

human parvovirus (HPV), a small single-stranded DNA virion that has been associated with several diseases, including

H

erythema infectiosum and aplastic crises of chronic hemolytic anemias.

human placental lactogen (HPL), a placental hormone that may be deficient in certain abnormalities of pregnancy.

human placental lactogen (HPL) test, a blood test to measure HPL, useful in monitoring placental function.

human rhinovirus 14, the common cold virus.

human T-cell lymphotropic virus type I (HTLV-I), a type C oncovirus, with an affinity for helper/inducer T lymphocytes, that causes chronic infection and is associated with adult T-cell leukemia and lymphoma and tropical spastic paraparesis.

human T-cell lymphotropic virus type II (HTLV-II), a type C oncovirus having extensive serologic cross-reactivity with HTLV-I, isolated from an atypical T-cell variant of hairy cell leukemia and also from patients with other hematologic disorders.

human T-cell lymphotrophic virus (HTLV) type I/II antibody test, a blood test to detect HTLV infection.

Humatin, a trademark for an amebicide (paromomycin sulfate).

Humatrope, a trademark for a brand of human synthetic growth hormone produced with recombinant DNA techniques. It is a polypeptide hormone with 191 amino acids in the same sequence as somatotropin.

humectant /hyōōmek′tənt/, a substance that promotes retention of moisture.

humeral stem, in arthroplasty of the shoulder or elbow, the part of the prosthesis that inserts into the end of the trimmed and prepared humerus.

humerus /hyōō′mərəs/ *pl.* **humeri** [L, shoulder], the bone of the upper arm, from the elbow to the shoulder joint where it articulates with the scapula. It comprises a body, a head, and a condyle. The nearly hemispheric head articulates with the glenoid cavity of the scapula and has a constriction called the surgical neck, frequently the seat of a fracture.—**humeral,** *adj.*

humidification /hyōōmid′ifikā′shən/ [L, *humidus,* moist, *facere,* to make], the process of increasing the relative humidity of the atmosphere around a patient through the use of aerosol generators or steam inhalers that exert an antitussive effect. Humidification acts by decreasing the viscosity of bronchial secretions.

humidifier /hyōōmid′ifī′ər/ [L, *humidus,* moist, *facere,* to make], a machine designed to adjust the amount of moisture in the atmosphere of a room or respiratory device.

humidifier lung, hypersensitivity pneumonitis caused by inhalation of air that has been passed through humidifiers, dehumidifiers, or air conditioners contaminated by any variety of fungi, amebas, or thermophilic bacteria.

humidity /hyōōmid′itē/ [L, *humidus,* moist], the level of moisture in the atmosphere, which varies with the temperature. The percentage is usually represented in terms of **relative humidity,** with 100% the point of air saturation, or the level at which the air can absorb no additional water.

humor[1] /hyōō′mər/ [L, *humidus,* moist], any body fluid or semifluid substance such as blood or lymph. The term is often used in reference to the aqueous humor or the vitreous humor of the eye.

humor[2], a nursing intervention from the Nursing Interventions Classification (NIC) defined as facilitating the patient to perceive, appreciate, and express what is funny, amusing, or ludicrous in order to establish relationships, relieve tension, release anger, facilitate learning, or cope with painful feelings.

humoral hypercalcemia of malignancy, hypercalcemia of malignancy caused by bone resorption mediated by circulating osteoclast-activating factors released from distant tumor cells.

humoral immunity /hyōō′mərəl/ [L, *humor,* liquid, *immunis,* freedom], a form of immunity mediated by circulating antibodies (IgA, IgB, and IgM), which coat the antigens and target them for destruction by polymorphonuclear neutrophils. Circulating antibodies are produced by plasma cells of the reticuloendothelial system. The interaction of antibody with antigen also activates the complement system.

humoral response, a hypersensitivity reaction mediated by B lymphocytes.

Humorsol, a trademark for an ophthalmic anticholinesterase agent (demecarium bromide).

Humulin, a trademark for a brand of human insulin of recombinant DNA origin.

hunger, a physical sensation usually associated with a craving or desire for food.

hunger contractions, strong contractions of the stomach usually associated with a desire for food.

hunger pain, epigastric cramps often associated with a desire for food.

hung-up reflex, a deep tendon reflex in which, after a stimulus is given and the reflex action takes place, the limb slowly returns to its neutral position.

Hunner's ulcer [Guy LeRoy Hunner, American surgeon, 1868–1957], a deep hemorrhagic lesion in the bladder associated with interstitial cystitis.

Hunter's syndrome [Charles Hunter, Canadian physician, 1873–1955; Gk, *syn,* together, *dromos,* course], a hereditary defect in mucopolysaccharide metabolism affecting only males, characterized by dwarfism, kyphosis, gargoylism, and mental retardation. It is transmitted as an X-linked recessive trait.

Huntington's disease [George S. Huntington, American physician, 1851–1916], a rare abnormal hereditary condition characterized by chronic progressive chorea and mental deterioration that results in dementia. An individual afflicted with the condition usually shows the first signs in the fourth decade of life and dies within 15 years.

Hurler's syndrome [Gertrude Hurler, German physician, 1889–1965], a type of mucopolysaccharidosis, transmitted as an autosomal-recessive trait, that produces severe mental retardation. Characteristic signs of the disease are enlargement of the liver and spleen, often with cardiovascular involvement. Facial characteristics include a low forehead and enlargement of the head, sometimes resulting from hydrocephalus. Corneal clouding is common, and the neck is short. Marked kyphosis is apparent at the dorsolumbar level, and the hands and the fingers are short and broad. Flexion contractures are common.

Hürthle cell adenoma /hirt′lə, hōōrth′lē/ [Karl W. Hürthle, German histologist, 1860–1945], a benign tumor of the thyroid gland composed of large cells with granular eosinophilic cytoplasm (Hürthle cells).

Hürthle cell carcinoma [Karl W. Hürthle], a malignant neoplasm of the thyroid gland composed of Hürthle cells. These tumors are encapsulated, resemble adenomas, and are locally invasive.

Hürthle cell tumor [Karl W. Hürthle], a neoplasm of the thyroid gland composed of large cells with granular eosinophilic cytoplasm (Hürthle cells) that may be benign (Hürthle cell adenoma) or malignant (Hürthle cell carcinoma).

Husted, Gladys L. and James H., nursing theorists who developed the Symphonological Bioethical Theory and the Symphonological Model for Ethical Decision Making. Symphonology is the system of ethics inherent in the mutual commitments and obligations agreed upon by the health care professional and the patient. Central to this implicit agreement are the needs of the patient. The model is designed to provide nurses and other health care professionals with theoretical guidelines for ethical delivery of care.

Hutch diverticulum, herniation of bladder mucosa through a weak point in the wall near the ureterovesical junction, often caused by chronically high intravesical pressure.

Hutchinson's freckle [Jonathan Hutchinson, English surgeon, 1828–1913], a tan patch on the skin that grows slowly and becomes mottled, dark, thick, and nodular. The lesion is usually seen on one side of the face of an elderly person.

Hutchinson's teeth [Jonathan Hutchinson], a characteristic of congenital syphilis in which the adult secondary central and lateral incisors are peg-shaped or screwdriver-shaped, widely spaced, and notched at the end, with a central crescent-shaped deformity.

Hutchinson's triad [Jonathan Hutchinson], the interstitial keratitis, notched teeth, and deafness characteristic of congenital syphilis.

Hutchison-type neuroblastoma [Robert G. Hutchison, English pediatrician, 1871–1960; Gk, *typos,* mark], a neuroblastoma that has metastasized to the cranium.

HUTT, abbreviation for **heads-up tilt table test.**

HVA, abbreviation for **homovanillic acid.**

HV interval /hī′tərvəl/, the conduction time of an impulse traveling through the His-Purkinje system. It is measured from the onset of the atrioventricular bundle potential to the onset of ventricular activation as recorded on an electrogram.

HVL, abbreviation for **half-value layer.**

hyaline /hī′əlin/ [Gk, *hyalos,* glass], pertaining to substances that are clear or glasslike.

hyaline bodies [Gk, *hyalos;* AS, *bodig*], **1.** the residue of colloidal degeneration found in some cells. **2.** globules of neurosecretory material found in the posterior lobe of the pituitary. **3.** deposits of homogenous eosinophilic material found in renal tubular epithelium and representing excess protein molecules that cannot be metabolized or transported.

hyaline cartilage [Gk, *hyalos,* glass; L, *cartilago*], a type connective tissue composed of specialized cells in a translucent, pearly blue matrix. Hyaline cartilage thinly covers the articulating ends of bones, connects the ribs to the sternum, and supports the nose, the trachea, and part of the larynx.

hyaline cast, a transparent cast composed of mucoprotein.

hyaline membrane [Gk, *hyalos,* glass; L, *membrana*], a fibrous covering of the alveolar membranes in infants, caused by a lack of pulmonary surfactant associated with prematurity and low-birth-weight delivery.

hyaline thrombus, a transparent mass of hemolyzed erythrocytes.

hyalinization /hī′əlin′izā′shən/ [Gk, *hyalos,* glass], the development of glassy homogenous material within a cell.

hyalinuria /-ŏŏr′ē-ə/ [Gk, *hyalos,* glass, *ouron,* urine], the presence of hyaline casts of protein in acidic urine, indicative of renal disease.

hyalohyphomycosis /hī'älōhī'fŏmīkō'sis/, a hyphomycosis caused by mycelial fungi with colorless walls, most of which are opportunistic.

hyaloid /hī'əloid/ [Gk, *hyalos,* glass, *eidos,* form], pertaining to or resembling hyaline.

hyaloid artery [Gk, *hyalos* + *eidos,* form], an embryonic blood vessel that branches to supply the vitreous body of the eye and develops part of the blood supply to the capsula vasculosa lentis. It disappears from the fetus in the ninth month of pregnancy.

hyaloid membrane [Gk, *hyalos,* glass; L, *membrana*], a surface layer of the vitreous body of the eye, at the interface between the primary and secondary vitreous and at the boundaries of the hyaloid canal.

hyaloplasm /hī'əlōplaz'əm/ [Gk, *hyalos* + *plasma,* formation], the portion of the cytoplasm that is clear and more fluid than the granular and reticular part.

hyaluronate /hī'əlŏŏrōnāt/, a salt, anion, or ester of hyaluronic acid.

hyaluronate sodium, the sodium salt of hyaluronic acid; a preparation obtained from chicken combs used as an analgesic in the treatment of osteoarthritis of the knee.

hyaluronate sodium derivative, a polymeric derivative of hyaluronate sodium, having the same actions and uses.

hyaluronic acid /hī'əlyŏŏron'ik/, a mucopolysaccharide formed by the polymerization of acetylglucosamine and glucuronic acid. Known as the cement substance of tissues, it forms a gel in intercellular spaces.

hyaluronidase /hī'əlyŏŏron'ədās/, an enzyme that hydrolyzes hyaluronic acid, a component of the extracellular matrix. It is prescribed to increase the absorption and dispersion of parenteral drugs that have extravasated (e.g., vesicant chemotherapeutics), for hypodermoclysis, and for improvement of resorption of radiopaque agents.

hybrid /hī'brid/ [L, *hybrida,* offspring], **1.** an offspring produced by mating organisms from different species, varieties, or genotypes. **2.** pertaining to such an offspring.

hybridization /hī'bridīzā'shən/, **1.** the process of producing hybrids by crossbreeding. **2.** the process of combining single-stranded nucleic acids from different sources to form stable, double-stranded molecules.

hybridoma /hī'bridō'mə/, a hybrid cell formed by the fusion of a myeloma cell and an antibody-producing cell. Hybridomas are used to produce monoclonal antibodies.

hybrid subtraction, a method for producing digitized radiographic images that requires at least four images. It uses both energy and temporal subtraction steps to mitigate patient motion artifacts.

Hycodan, a trademark for a fixed-combination antitussive/decongestant medication containing hydrocodone, chlorpheniramine, phenylephrine, caffeine, and acetaminophen.

Hycomine, a trademark for a fixed-combination drug containing an adrenergic (phenylpropanolamine hydrochloride) and an antitussive (hydrocodone bitartrate).

hydantoin /hīdan'tō·in/, any one of a group of anticonvulsant medications, chemically and pharmacologically similar to the barbiturates, that act to limit seizure activity and reduce the spreading of abnormal electrical excitation from the focus of the seizure.

hydatid /hī'dətid/ [Gk, *hydatis,* water drop], a cyst or cystlike structure that usually is filled with fluid, especially the cyst formed around the developing scolex of the dog tapeworm *Echinococcus granulosus.—***hydatic,** *adj.*

hydatid cyst, a cyst in the liver that contains larvae of the tapeworm *Echinococcus granulosus,* whose eggs are carried from the intestinal tract to the liver via the portal circulation. Patients are generally asymptomatic, except for hepatomegaly and a dull ache over the right upper quadrant of the abdomen.

hydatidiform /hī'dətid'ifôrm/ [Gk, *hydatis,* water drop; L, *forma*], having the appearance or form of a **hydatid.**

hydatid mole, an intrauterine neoplastic mass of grapelike enlarged chorionic villi. Characteristic signs are extreme nausea, uterine bleeding, anemia, hyperthyroidism, an unusually large uterus for the duration of pregnancy, absence of fetal heart sounds, edema, and high BP.

hydatidosis /hī'dətidō'sis/ [Gk, *hydatis* + *osis,* condition], infestation with the tapeworm *Echinococcus granulosus.*

Hydeltrasol, a trademark for a glucocorticoid (prednisoLONE sodium phosphate).

Hydeltra TBA, a trademark for a glucocorticoid (prednisoLONE tebutate).

Hydergine, a trademark for a fixed-combination drug containing various ergoloid mesylates.

hydradenitis /hī'dradənī'tis/ [Gk, *hydor,* water, *aden,* gland, *itis,* inflammation], an infection or inflammation of the sweat glands.

hydrALAZINE hydrochloride /hīdral'əzēn/, a vasodilator prescribed in the treatment of moderate to severe hypertension, primary pulmonary hypertension, and hypertension of preeclampsia, and during the treatment of CHF.

hydramnios /hīdram'nē·əs/ [Gk, *hydor* + *amnos,* lamb's caul], an abnormal condition of pregnancy characterized by an excess of amniotic fluid. It is associated with maternal disorders, including toxemia of pregnancy and DM, and some fetal disorders.

hydranencephaly /hīdran′ənsef′əlē/, a neurologic disorder in which the cerebral hemispheres are lacking, although the cerebellum, brainstem, and other CNS tissues may be intact. The newborn with hydranencephaly may have normal neurologic functions but does not develop.

hydrate /hī′drāt/ [Gk, hydor, water], 1. a combination of a substance with one or more water molecules. 2. a molecular association of a substance with water.

hydration[1] /hīdrā′shən/ [Gk, hydor, water], a chemical process in which water is added to a substance.

hydration[2], a nursing outcome from the Nursing Outcomes Classification (NOC) defined as adequate water in the intracellular and extracellular compartments of the body.

Hydrea, a trademark for an antineoplastic (hydroxyurea).

hydremic ascites /hīdrem′ik/ [Gk, hydor + haima, blood, askos, bag], an abnormal accumulation of fluid within the peritoneal cavity accompanied by hemodilution, as in protein calorie malnutrition.

hydroa /hīdrō′ə/ [Gk, hydor + oon, egg], an unusual vesicular and bullous skin condition of childhood that recurs each summer after exposure to sunlight, sometimes accompanied by itching, lichenification, and scars.

hydroalcoholic /hī′drō-al′kähol′ik/, pertaining to or containing both water and alcohol.

hydrobilirubin /hī′drōbil′iroo′bin/ [Gk, hydor, water; L, bilis, bile, ruber, red], a reddish-brown bile pigment produced by the reduction of bilirubin.

hydrocarbon /-kär′bən/ [Gk, hydor; L, carbo, charcoal], any of a large group of organic compounds whose molecules are composed of hydrogen and carbon, many of which are derived from petroleum.

hydrocele /hī′drōsēl′/ [Gk, hydor + kele, hernia], an accumulation of fluid in any saclike cavity or duct, specifically in the tunica vaginalis testis or along the spermatic cord. The condition is caused by inflammation of the epididymis or testis or by lymphatic or venous obstruction in the cord. Congenital hydrocele is caused by failure of the canal between the peritoneal cavity and the scrotum to close completely during prenatal development.

hydrocephalic cry /-səfal′ik/, an involuntary loud nighttime cry of a child who has acquired hydrocephalus.

hydrocephalocele, a hernia consisting of a watery sac of brain tissue protruding through a fissure into the skull.

hydrocephalus /-sef′ələs/ [Gk, hydor + kephale, head], a pathologic condition characterized by an abnormal accumulation of CSF, usually under increased pressure, within the cranial vault and subsequent dilation of the ventricles. Interference with the normal flow of CSF may result from increased secretion of the fluid, obstruction within the ventricular system (noncommunicating or intraventricular hydrocephalus), or defective resorption from the cerebral subarachnoid space (communicating or extraventricular hydrocephalus), caused by developmental anomalies, infection, trauma, or brain tumors.—**hydrocephalic** /-səfal′ik/ adj., n.

hydrochloric acid (HCl) /-klôr′ik/ [Gk, hydor + chloros, green], an aqueous solution of hydrogen chloride or hydrogen ions and chloride ions. Hydrochloric acid is secreted in the stomach and is a major component of gastric juice.

hydrochlorothiazide /-klôr′ōthī′əzīd/, a thiazide diuretic prescribed in the treatment of mild to moderate hypertension and edema caused by CHF or protein loss by the kidney (nephritic syndrome).

hydrocholeretics /-kō′ləret′iks/ [Gk, hydor + chloe, bile, eresis, removal], drugs that stimulate the production of bile with a low specific gravity or with a minimal proportion of solid constituents.

Hydrocil Instant, a trademark for a laxative (psyllium hydrophilic mucilloid).

hydrocodone bitartrate /-kō′dōn/, an opioid antitussive and analgesic prescribed in the treatment of cough and moderate to severe pain.

hydrocolloid, a gelatinous colloid in which water is the dispersion material. It is used in dentistry as an impression material.

hydrocortisone /-kôr′tisōn/, a topical corticosteroid prescribed for the treatment of skin inflammation.

hydrocortisone enema, an aqueous solution of hydrocortisone administered rectally as an antiinflammatory in treatment of ulcerative colitis.

hydrocortisone probutate, an ester of hydrocortisone used topically for the relief of inflammation and pruritus in corticosteroid-responsive dermatoses.

Hydrocortone, a trademark for a glucocorticoid (hydrocortisone acetate).

HydroDiuril, a trademark for a diuretic (hydrochlorothiazide).

hydroflumethiazide /-floo′methī′əzīd/, a diuretic. It is prescribed in the treatment of mild to moderate hypertension and edema due to CHF or protein loss in the urine (nephrotic syndrome).

hydrofluoric acid /hī′drōflŏŏr′ik/, a term applied to aqueous solutions of hydrogen fluoride, an organic acid used in dilute

hydrogel, a gel in which water is the dispersion medium.

hydrogen (H) /hī′drəjən/ [Gk, *hydor* + *genein,* to produce], a gaseous monovalent element. Its atomic number is 1, and its atomic mass is 1.008. It is the simplest and the lightest of the elements and is a colorless, odorless, highly flammable diatomic gas. Hydrogen is a component of numerous compounds, many of them produced by the body. As a component of water, hydrogen is crucial in the metabolic interaction of acids, bases, and salts within the body and in the fluid balance necessary for the body to survive.

hydrogenase /hī′drōjənās′/ [Gk, *hydor,* water, *genein,* to produce, *ase,* suffix indicating an enzyme], an enzyme that catalyzes reduction of molecules by combining them with two atoms of hydrogen.

hydrogen bonding, the attractive force of compounds in which a hydrogen atom covalently linked to an electronegative element such as oxygen, nitrogen, or fluorine has a large degree of positive character relative to the electronegative atom, thereby causing the compound to possess a large dipole and to associate strongly with other like molecules.

hydrogen cyanide (HCN), an extremely poisonous colorless, toxic, volatile liquid or gas with the aroma of bitter almonds. It occurs naturally in almonds and in the stone pits of peaches, plums, and other fruits. Inhalation of the gas can cause death within a minute.

hydrogen donor, a compound that gives up hydrogen (usually H^+, a proton) to another compound.

hydrogen ion [H⁺], a positively charged hydrogen atom or proton.

hydrogen ion [H⁺] concentration of blood, a measure of blood pH and its effect on the ability of the hemoglobin molecule to hold oxygen.

hydrogen peroxide, a disinfectant and sterilizing agent without antiseptic properties because it is rapidly inactivated by enzymes in the skin. However, the frothing that occurs is beneficial because it loosens debris in wounds.

hydrogen sulfide poisoning, poisoning by excessive exposure to hydrogen sulfide gas, seen primarily in those who work with petroleum or petrochemicals. It is characterized by metabolic acidosis and anoxia. Severe cases may result in coma with death from respiratory paralysis.

hydrokinetics /-kinet′iks/ [Gk, *hydor,* water, *kinesis,* motion], the study of movement of fluids.

hydrolase /hī′drōlās/, an enzyme that cleaves ester bonds by the addition of water.

hydrolysis /hīdrol′isis/ [Gk, *hydor* + *lysis,* loosening], the chemical alteration or decomposition of a compound with water.

hydrolytic /-lit′ik/ [Gk, *hydor,* water, *lysis,* loosening], pertaining to or having the ability to produce hydrolysis.

hydrolyze /hī′drōlīz/ [Gk, *hydor,* water, *lysis,* loosening], 1. to cause or bring about hydrolysis. 2. to cause a substance to split into component parts by the addition of water.

hydrometer /hīdrom′ətər/ [Gk, *hydor* + *metron,* measure], a device that determines the specific gravity or density of a liquid by a comparison of its weight with that of an equal volume of water. A calibrated hollow glass device is placed in the liquid being examined, and the depth to which the device settles in the liquid is noted.

hydromorphone hydrochloride /-môr′fōn/, an opioid analgesic used to treat moderate to severe pain.

hydromyelia /hī′drōmī·ē′lē·ə/ [Gk, *hydor,* water; *myelos,* marrow], a pathologic condition characterized by dilation of the central canal of the spinal cord with increased fluid accumulation.

hydronephrosis /hī′drōnefrō′sis/ [Gk, *hydor* + *nephros,* kidney, *osis,* condition], distension of the pelvis and calyces of the kidney by urine that cannot flow past an obstruction in a ureter. Ureteral obstruction may be caused by a tumor, a calculus lodged in the ureter, inflammation of the prostate gland, or edema caused by a UTI. Symptoms include pain in the flank and, in some cases, hematuria, pyuria, and hyperpyrexia.—**hydronephrotic,** *adj.*

hydropenia /-pē′nē·ə/, 1. the process of removing water from a living thing. 2. the condition resulting from lack of water in the body tissues.

hydropericarditis, inflammation of the pericardium accompanied by excessive accumulation of serous fluid.

hydroperitoneum /-per′itənē′əm/, an accumulation of fluid in the peritoneum.

hydrophilic /-fil′ik/ [Gk, *hydor* + *philein,* to love], pertaining to the property of attracting or associating preferentially with water molecules, possessed by polar radicals or ions.

hydrophobia /-fō′bē·ə/ [Gk, *hydor* + *phobos,* fear], 1. one of the later symptoms of rabies infection. 2. a morbid, extreme fear of water.

hydrophobiaphobia, a morbid fear of hydrophobia, with symptoms that may simulate those of rabies.

hydrophobic [Gk, *hydor* + *phobos,* fear], pertaining to the property of repelling or preferentially excluding water molecules, a quality possessed by nonpolar radicals or molecules that are more soluble in organic solvents than in water.

hydrophone /hī′drəfōn/, a small-diameter probe with a piezoelectric element, usually about 0.5 mm in diameter, at one end. When placed in an ultrasound beam, the hydrophone produces an electric signal.

hydrophthalmos, a type of glaucoma characterized by enlargement and distension of the fibrous coats of the eyeball.

hydropic /hīdrop′ik/ [Gk, *hydrops*], **1.** pertaining to the condition of dropsy. **2.** containing an excess of water or watery fluid.

Hydropres, a trademark for a fixed-combination drug containing a diuretic (hydrochlorothiazide) and an antihypertensive (reserpine).

hydrops /hī′drops/ [Gk, dropsy], an abnormal accumulation of clear watery or serous fluid in a body tissue or cavity.

hydrops fetalis, massive edema in the fetus or newborn, usually in association with severe erythroblastosis fetalis. Severe anemia and effusions of the pericardial, pleural, and peritoneal spaces also occur.

hydrops gravidarum [Gk, *hydor,* water; L, *gravidus,* pregnant], edema caused by pregnancy.

hydroquinone /hī′drōkwin′ōn/, a dermatologic bleaching agent prescribed to reduce pigmentation of the skin in certain conditions in which an excess of melanin causes hyperpigmentation.

hydrosalpinx /hī′drōsal′pingks/ [Gk, *hydor* + *salpinx,* tube], an abnormal condition of the fallopian tube in which it is cystically enlarged and filled with clear fluid. It is the result of an infection that has previously occluded the tube at both ends.

hydrosis [Gk, *hydor,* water, *osis,* condition], pertaining to the production of sweat.

Hydro-Sphere Nebulizer, a trademark for a type of nebulizer in which a source gas enters a hollow sphere coated with a film of water. The gas exits through slits at the top of the sphere as an aerosol jet, carrying particles of fluid from the sphere's surface.

hydrostatic /-stat′ik/ [Gk, *hydor,* water, *statos,* standing], pertaining to fluids at rest or in equilibrium and the pressure they exert.

hydrostatic dosimetry, the weighing of a person under water to determine the ratio of lean tissue to body fat.

hydrostatic pressure, the pressure exerted by a liquid.

hydrostatics, the study of pressures in liquids at rest or in equilibrium.

hydrotherapy /-ther′əpē/ [Gk, *hydor* + *therapeia,* treatment], the use of water in

the treatment of various disorders. Hydrotherapy may include continuous tub baths, wet sheet packs, or shower sprays.

hydrothorax /-thôr′aks/ [Gk, *hydor* + *thorax,* chest], a noninflammatory accumulation of serous fluid in one or both pleural cavities.

hydrotropism /-trō′pizəm/ [Gk, *hydor* + *trope,* turning], the tendency of a cell or organism to turn or move in a certain direction under the influence of a water stimulus.

hydrous /hī′drəs/ [Gk, *hydor,* water], pertaining to a substance or object that contains water or is moist.

hydroxide (OH⁻) /hīdrok′sīd/, an ion.

hydroxyamphetamine hydrobromide /hī drok′sē-əmfet′əmēn/, an adrenergic agonist prescribed for short-term dilation of the pupil for ophthalmoscopy and as a diagnostic aid in Horner's syndrome.

hydroxyandrosterone /hīdrok′sē-andros′ tərōn/ [Gk *hydor* + *andros,* male, *stereos,* solid], a sex hormone secreted by the testes and adrenal glands.

hydroxyapatite /hīdrok′sē-ap′ətīt/, an inorganic compound composed of calcium, phosphate, and hydroxide, found in the bones and teeth in a crystallized lattice-like form that gives these structures rigidity.

hydroxychloroquine sulfate /-klôr′əkwīn/, a drug initially developed to treat malaria that also has efficacy against autoimmune diseases. It is prescribed in the treatment of malaria and the suppression of acute paroxysmal attacks of the disease; in the treatment of extraintestinal, usually hepatic, amebiasis; and in conjunction with salicylate to reduce symptoms of lupus erythematosus and rheumatoid arthritis.

17-hydroxycorticosteroid /-kôr′tikos′təroid/, any steroid hydroxylated at carbon-17 secreted by adrenal glands and occasionally measured in the urine in a test for determining adrenal function and diagnosing hypoadrenalism or hyperadrenalism.

17-hydroxycorticosteroids test (17-OCHS), an obsolete 24-hour urine test formerly used to detect abnormal levels of 17-OCHS. Elevated levels are seen in hyperfunction of the adrenal gland (Cushing's syndrome), while low levels are seen in hypofunction (Addison's disease).

11-hydroxyetiocholanolone /hīdrok′sē-ē′ tē-ōkolan′əlōn/, a sex hormone secreted by the testes and adrenal glands.

5-hydroxyindoleacetic acid (5-HIAA) /hī drok′sē-in′dōlē-əset′ik/, an acid produced by serotonin metabolism, measured in the blood and urine to aid in the diagnosis of certain kinds of tumors. It commonly rises above normal levels in whole blood in association with asthma, diarrhea, rapid heartbeat, and other symptoms and is elevated in the urine of patients with carcinoid syndrome.

5-hydroxyindoleacetic acid test, a 24-hour urine test used to detect and follow the clinical course of patients with carcinoid tumors, which may grow in the appendix, intestine, lung, or any tissue derived from the neuroectoderm.

hydroxyl (OH) /hīdrok′sil/, a monovalent radical consisting of an oxygen and a hydrogen atom.

hydroxyproline /-prō′lēn/, an amino acid whose level in the urine is elevated in diseases of the bone and certain genetic disorders such as Marfan's syndrome.

hydroxypropyl cellulose /hīdrok′sēprō′il sel′u-lōs/, a water-soluble derivative of cellulose, used as a pharmaceutic aid and also applied topically to the conjunctiva to protect and lubricate the cornea in the treatment of dry eye.

hydroxyurea /hīdrok′siyŏŏrē′ə/, an antineoplastic prescribed in the treatment of a variety of neoplasms and other conditions involving the blood, and by itself or as a radiosensitizer for the treatment of other cancers, including those involving the brain, head and neck, lungs, kidneys, ovaries, and prostate.

hydrOXYzine hydrochloride /hīdrok′səzēn/, an antihistamine prescribed for the relief of anxiety, nervous tension, hyperkinesis, itching, and motion sickness.

hygiene /hī′jēn/ [Gk, *Hygieia*, the goddess of health], **1.** the principles and science of the preservation of health and prevention of disease. **2.** sanitation.

hygienist /hī′jənist, hījē′nist/ [Gk, *Hygieia*], one who practices the principles and laws of **hygiene.**

hygroma /hīgrō′mə/ pl. **hygromes, hygromata** [Gk, *hygros*, moist; *oma*, tumor], a sac, cyst, or bursa distended with a fluid.

hygrometer /hīgrom′ətər/ [Gk, *hygros*, moist, *metron*, measure], an instrument that directly measures relative humidity of the atmosphere or the proportion of water in a specific gas or gas mixture, without extracting the moisture.

hygroscopic humidifier /-skop′ik/, a humidifying device attached to the tubing circuit of a mechanical ventilator or anesthesia gas machine to maintain a constant rate of humidity in the trachea.

Hygroton, a trademark for a diuretic (chlorthalidone).

Hylorel, a trademark for an antihypertensive (guanadrel sulfate).

hymen /hī′mən/ [Gk, membrane], a fold of mucous membrane, skin, and fibrous tissue that covers the introitus of the vagina.

hymenal /hī′mənəl/ [Gk, *hymen*, membrane], pertaining to the hymen.

hymenal tag, normal redundant hymenal tissue protruding from the floor of the vagina during the first weeks after birth.

hymenectomy /hī′mənek′təmē/ [Gk, *hymen*, membrane, *ektomē*, excision], the surgical excision of a membrane, particularly the hymen.

hymenolepiasis, heavy infestation by *Hymenolepis nana,* a rat tapeworm that may cause abdominal pain, bloody stools, and disorders of the nervous system, especially in children. Contaminated food spreads the disease.

Hymenolepis /hī′mənol′əpis/ [Gk, *hymen*, membrane, *lepis*, rind], a genus of tapeworms of the family Hymenolepididae, which parasitize birds and mammals, including humans.

hymenotomy /hī′mənot′əmē/ [Gk, *hymen* + *temnein*, to cut], the surgical incision of the hymen.

hyoepiglottic ligament, a ligament that extends from the midline of the epiglottis anterosuperiorly to the body of the hyoid bone.

hyoglossal /hī′ōglos′əl/ [Gk, *hyoeides,* upsilon, U-shaped *glossa,* tongue], pertaining to the tongue and the horseshoe-shaped hyoid bone at the base of the tongue immediately above the thyroid cartilage.

hyoglossal membrane, a widening of the lingual septum connecting the root of the tongue to the hyoid bone.

hyoglossus /-glos′əs/ [Gk, *hyoeides* + *glossa,* tongue], a depressor muscle of the tongue that arises from the hyoid bone.

hyoid arch [Gk, *hyoeides;* L, *arcus,* bow], the second pharyngeal or branchial arch. It is present in typical form in the embryo, but the skeletal elements develop into the stapes and styloid process of the temporal bone of the adult.

hyoid bone /hī′oid/ [Gk, *hyoeides,* upsilon, U-shaped; AS, *ban,* bone], a single U-shaped bone suspended from the styloid processes of the temporal bones. The body of the hyoid is square and flat. Its ventral surface is convex and angled cranially. Two greater wings of the bone attach to the lateral thyroid ligaments, and the body of the bone attaches to various muscles, such as the hypoglossus and the sternohyoideus.

hyoscyamine /hī′əsī′əmēn/, an anticholinergic/antispasmodic prescribed in the treatment of hypermotility of the GI and lower urinary tracts and used preoperatively to reduce secretions and block vagal inhibitory effects on the heart.

hypalgesia /hī′paljē′zē·ə/ [Gk, *hypo,* below, *algesis,* pain], the perception of a painful stimulus to a degree that varies significantly from a normal perception of the same stimulus.

hypaxial muscles, muscles of the limbs and trunk.

Hyperab, a trademark for a passive immunizing agent (rabies immune globulin).

hyperacidity /hī′pərəsid′itē/ [Gk, *hyper,* excess; L, *acidus,* sour], an excessive amount of acidity, as in the stomach.

hyperactivity /-aktiv′itē/ [Gk, *hyper*; L, *activus,* active], any abnormally increased motor activity or function involving either the entire organism or a particular organ, as the heart or thyroid.

hyperactivity level, a nursing outcome from the Nursing Outcomes Classification (NOC) defined as the severity of patterns of inattention or impulsivity in a child from 1 year through 17 years of age.

hyperacuity /-akyo͞o′itē/ [Gk, *hyper* + *akouein,* to hear], excessive sensitivity to sounds.

hyperadenosis /-ad′ənō′sis/ [Gk, *hyper* + *aden,* gland, *osis,* condition], a condition characterized by enlarged glands.

hyperalbuminemia /-albyo͞o′minē′mē·ə/, an excessive amount of albumin in the blood.

hyperalgia /-al′jə/, extreme sensitivity to pain.

hyperalimentation /-al′iməntā′shən/ [Gk, *hyper*; L, *alimentum,* nourishment], overfeeding or the ingestion or administration of an amount of nutrients that exceeds the demands of the appetite.

hyperalkalinity /-al′kəlin′itē/, a condition of excessive alkalinity.

hyperammonemia /hī′pəram′ōnē′mē·ə/ [Gk, *hyper* + (ammonia) + *haima,* blood], abnormally high levels of ammonia in the blood. Untreated, the condition leads to hepatic encephalopathy characterized by asterixis, vomiting, lethargy, coma, and death.

hyperammonuria /hī′peram′ōnu′re·ə/, increased excretion of ammonia in the urine, as with hyperammonemia.

hyperbaric chamber /-ber′ik/ [Gk, *hyper,* excess, *baros,* weight, *kamara,* arched roof], an airtight chamber containing an oxygen atmosphere under high pressure. A patient may be placed in the chamber for the treatment of certain infections, tumors, and cardiovascular diseases in which atmospheric oxygen pressures up to three times normal may have therapeutic value.

hyperbaric oxygen, oxygen under greater than atmospheric pressure.

hyperbaric oxygenation [Gk, *hyper* + *baros,* weight, *oxys,* sharp, *genein,* to produce], the administration of oxygen at greater than normal atmospheric pressure. The technique is used to overcome the natural limit of oxygen solubility in blood. Hyperbaric oxygenation has been used to treat carbon monoxide poisoning,

air embolism, smoke inhalation, acute cyanide poisoning, decompression sickness, clostridial myonecrosis, and certain cases of blood loss or anemia in which increased oxygen transport may compensate in part for hemoglobin deficiency.

hyperbaric solution [Gk, *hyper,* excess, *baros,* weight], a type of spinal anesthetic that has a specific gravity greater than that of CSF so it will settle into the lowest parts of the spinal canal.

hyperbarism /-ber′izəm/, any disorder resulting from exposure to increased ambient pressure, usually caused by sudden exposure to or a significant increase in pressure.

hyperbetalipoproteinemia /hī′pərbā′təlip′ōprō′tēnē′mē·ə/ [Gk, *hyper* + *beta,* second letter of Greek alphabet, *lipos,* fat, *proteios,* first rank, *haima,* blood], type II hyperlipoproteinemia, a genetic disorder of lipid metabolism in which there are abnormally high levels of serum cholesterol and the appearance of xanthomas on the tendons of the heels, knees, and fingers.

hyperbilirubinemia /hī′pərbil′iro͞o′binē′mē·ə/ [Gk, *hyper*; L, *bilis,* bile, *ruber,* red; Gk, *haima,* blood], greater than normal amounts of the bile pigment bilirubin in the blood, often characterized by jaundice, anorexia, and malaise. Hyperbilirubinemia is most often associated with liver disease or biliary obstruction, but it also occurs when there is excessive destruction of RBCs.

hyperbilirubinemia of the newborn, an excess of bilirubin in the blood of the neonate. It is usually caused by a deficiency of an enzyme that results from physiologic immaturity, or by increased hemolysis, especially that produced by blood group incompatibility, which, in severe cases, can lead to kernicterus.

hypercalcemia /hī′pərkalsē′mē·ə/ [Gk, *hyper*; L, *calx,* lime; Gk, *haima,* blood], greater than normal amounts of calcium in the blood, most often resulting from excessive bone resorption and release of calcium, as occurs in hyperparathyroidism, metastatic tumors of bone, Paget's disease, and osteoporosis. Clinically, patients with hypercalcemia experience confusion, anorexia, abdominal pain, muscle pain, and weakness.—**hypercalcemic,** *adj.*

hypercalcemia of malignancy, abnormal elevation of serum calcium associated with malignant tumors, resulting from osteolysis caused by bone metastases or by the action of circulating osteoclast-activating factors released from distant tumor cells.

hypercalcemic nephropathy /-kalsē′mik/ [Gk, *hyper*; L, *calx,* lime Gk, *haima,* blood, *nephros,* kidney, *pathos,* disease], a progressive disorder of kidney function caused by an excessive level of calcium in the blood. The calcium causes cumulative functional and histologic abnormalities that lead to a decreased glomerular filtration rate and kidney failure.

hypercalciuria /hī′pərkal′sēyŏŏr′ē-ə/ [Gk, *hyper;* L, *calx,* lime; Gk, *ouron,* urine], the presence of abnormally great amounts of calcium in the urine, resulting from conditions such as sarcoid, hyperparathyroidism, or certain types of arthritis that are characterized by augmented bone resorption. Concentrated amounts of calcium in the urinary tract may form kidney stones.—**hypercalciuric,** *adj.*

hypercapnia /hī′pərkap′nē-ə/ [Gk, *hyper* + *kapnos,* vapor], greater than normal amounts of carbon dioxide in the blood.

hypercapnic acidosis /-kap′nik/ [Gk, *hyper* + *kapnos,* vapor; L, *acidus,* sour, *osis,* condition], an excessive acidity in body fluids caused by an increase in carbon dioxide tension in the blood. The condition may be secondary to pulmonary insufficiency. As carbon dioxide accumulates in the blood, its acidity increases.

hypercarotenemia /hī′pər′kar′ətinē′mē-ə/ an excessive amount of carotene in the blood usually associated with a yellow discoloration of the skin.

hyperchloremia /-klôrē′mē-ə/ [Gk, *hyper* + *chloros,* green, *haima,* blood], an excessive level of chloride in the blood that results in acidosis.

hyperchlorhydria /-klôrhid′rē-ə/ [Gk, *hyper* + *chloros* + *hydor,* water], the excessive secretion of hydrochloric acid by cells lining the stomach.

hypercholesterolemia /-kōles′tərōlē′mē-ə/ [Gk, *hyper* + *chole,* bile, *stereos,* solid, *haima,* blood], a condition in which greater than normal amounts of cholesterol are present in the blood. High levels of cholesterol and other lipids may lead to the development of atherosclerosis.

hyperchromia /-krō′mē-ə/ [Gk, *hyper* + *chroma,* color], an increase of hemoglobin in the erythrocytes.

hyperchylomicronemia /-kī′lōmī′krōnē′mē-ə/ [Gk, *hyper* + *chylos,* juice, *mikros,* small, *haima,* blood], type I hyperlipoproteinemia, a rare congenital deficiency of an enzyme essential to fat metabolism. Fat accumulates in the blood as chylomicrons. The condition affects children and young adults, in whom xanthomas in the skin, hepatomegaly, and abdominal pain develop. Pancreatitis is the most significant complication.

hypercoagulability /-kō-ag′yələbil′itē/ [Gk, *hyper;* L, *coagulare,* to curdle, *habilis,* able], a tendency of the blood to coagulate more rapidly than normal.

hyperdipsia, intense thirst of relatively brief duration.

hyperdynamic circulation, abnormally increased circulatory volume with low vascular resistance and often tachycardia.

hyperdynamic syndrome /-dīnam′ik/ [Gk, *hyper* + *dynamis,* force], a cluster of symptoms that signals the onset of septic shock, often including a shaking chill, rapid rise in temperature, flushing of the skin, galloping pulse, and alternating rise and fall of the BP.

hyperemesis /hī′perem′əsis/ [Gk, *hyper,* excess; *emesis,* vomit], excessive vomiting.

hyperemesis gravidarum /hī′pərem′isis/ [Gk, *hyper* + *emesis,* vomiting; L, *gravida,* pregnant], an abnormal condition of pregnancy characterized by protracted vomiting, weight loss, and fluid and electrolyte imbalance. If the condition is severe and intractable, brain damage, liver and kidney failure, and death may result.

hyperemesis lactentium, a condition of excessive vomiting by infants.

hyperemia /hī′pərē′mē-ə/ [Gk, *hyper* + *haima,* blood], an excess of blood in part of the body, caused by increased blood flow, as in the inflammatory response, local relaxation of arterioles, or obstruction of the outflow of blood from an area. Skin overlying a hyperemic area usually becomes reddened and warm.—**hyperemic,** *adj.*

hyperesthesia /-esthē′zhə/, an extreme sensitivity of one of the body's sense organs, such as pain or touch receptors in the skin.

hyperextension /-exten′shən/ [Gk, *hyper;* L, *extendere,* to stretch out], movement at a joint to a position beyond the joint's normal maximum extension.

hyperextension bed, a bed used in pediatric orthopedics to maintain any correction achieved by suspension of a body part and to increase the ROM of the hips after an operative muscle release procedure.

hyperflexia /-flek′shə/ [Gk, *hyper;* L, *flectere,* to bend], the forcible overflexion or bending of a limb.

hyperfunction /-fungk′shən/ [Gk, *hyper;* L,*functio,* performance], increased function of any organ or system.

hypergenesis /-jen′əsis/ [Gk, *hyper* + *genesis,* origin], excessive growth or overdevelopment. The condition may involve the entire body, as in gigantism, or any part, or it may result in the formation of extra parts, such as additional fingers or toes.—**hypergenetic,** *adj.*

hypergenetic teratism /-jənet′ik/ [Gk, *hyper* + *genesis* + *teras,* monster], a congenital anomaly in which there is excessive growth of a part, an organ, or the entire body, as in gigantism.

hypergenitalism /-jen′itəliz′əm/, the presence of abnormally large external genitalia. The condition is usually associated with precocious puberty.

hyperglobulinemia /-glob′yəlinē′mē-ə/ [Gk, *hyper*; L, *globulus,* small globe, *haima,* blood], an excess of globulin in the plasma.

hyperglycemia /hī′pərglīsē′mē-ə/ [Gk, *hyper* + *glykys,* sweet, *haima,* blood], a greater than normal amount of glucose in the blood. Most frequently associated with DM, the condition may occur in newborns, after the administration of glucocorticoid hormones, and with an excess infusion of IV solutions containing glucose.

hyperglycemia management, a nursing intervention from the Nursing Interventions Classification (NIC) defined as preventing and treating above-normal blood glucose levels.

hyperglycemic-hyperosmolar nonketotic syndrome /-glīsē′mik/ [Gk, *hyper* + *glykys* + *hyper* + *osmos,* impulse; L, *non,* not (ketone); Gk, deep sleep], a diabetic syndrome caused by hyperosmolarity of extracellular fluid and resulting in severe osmotic diuresis causing dehydration.

hyperglyceridemia /-glī′səridē′mē-ə/ [Gk, *hyper* + *glykys* + *haima,* blood], an excess of glycerides, particularly triglycerides, in the blood.

hyperglycinemia, an increased concentration of glycine in the blood.

hyperglycogenolysis /-glī′kōjənol′isis/, excessive breaking down of glycogen to glucose in animal tissue.

hyperglycosuria /-glī′kōsŏŏr′ē-ə/, an excess of sugar in the urine.

hypergonadism /-gō′nədiz′əm/ [Gk, *hyper* + *gone,* seed], excessive secretion of hormones from the ovaries or testes.

hyperhidrosis /hī′pərhidrō′sis, -hidrō′sis/ [Gk, *hyper* + *hidros,* perspiration], excessive perspiration often caused by heat, hyperthyroidism, strong emotion, menopause, or infection.

hyperimmune /-imyŏŏn′/ [Gk, *hyper*; L, *immunis,* freedom], having a greater-than-normal immunity because of an unusual abundance of antibodies.

hyperimmune globulin, any of various immune globulin preparations especially high in antibodies against certain specific diseases.

hyperimmune plasma, plasma containing high levels of antibodies.

hyperimmunoglobulinemia D, an abnormal elevation of IgD in the serum.

hyperimmunoglobulinemia D syndrome (HIDS), a periodic fever inherited as an autosomal-recessive trait, caused by mutations in the gene for mevalonate kinase and having onset usually before 1 year of age. It is characterized by attacks of high fever preceded by chills, occurring at intervals of approximately 4 to 8 weeks and lasting 4 to 6 days, often accompanied by headache, arthritis and arthralgia, erythematous lesions, and hepatosplenomegaly. Serum IgD levels are continuously high.

hyperinsulinism /-in′səliniz′əm/ [Gk, *hyper*; L, *insula,* island], an excessive amount of insulin in the body. It may be caused by administration of an insulin dose greater than required or the presence of an insulin-secreting tumor in the islets of Langerhans or insulin reference. If there is hypoglycemia, symptoms include hunger, shakiness, and diaphoresis.

hyperirritability /-irit′əbil′itē/ [Gk, *hyper*; L, *irritare,* to tease], excessive excitability or sensitivity; exaggerated response to a stimulus.

hyperkalemia /hī′pərkəlē′mē-ə/ [Gk, *hyper*; L, *kalium,* potassium; Gk, *haima,* blood], greater than normal amounts of potassium in the blood. This condition is seen frequently in acute renal failure, massive trauma, major burns, and Addison's disease. Early signs are nausea, diarrhea, and muscle weakness.

hyperkeratinization /-ker′ətinīzā′shən/ [Gk, *hyper,* excessive, *keras,* horn], an abnormal horny thickening of the epithelium of the palms and soles.

hyperkeratosis /-ker′ətō′sis/ [Gk, *hyper* + *keras,* horn, *osis,* condition], overgrowth of the cornified epithelial layer of the skin.

hyperketonemia /-kē′tōnē′mē-ə/, an abnormally high level of ketone bodies in the blood.

hyperketonuria /-kē′tōnŏŏr′ē-ə/, an abnormally high level of ketone bodies in the urine.

hyperlactation /-laktā′shən/, a condition in which lactation continues beyond the usual period of breastfeeding.

hyperlipemia /-lipē′mē-ə/, cloudy or opaque plasma caused by fat particles called chylomicrons seen subsequent to a fat-laden meal caused by a lipoprotein lipase deficiency or a defect in the conversion of low-density lipoprotein to high-density lipoprotein.

hyperlipidemia /-lip′idē′mē-ə/ [Gk, *hyper* + *lipos,* fat, *haima,* blood], an excess of lipids, including glycolipids, lipoproteins, and phospholipids, in the plasma.

hyperlipidemia type I, a condition of elevated blood lipid levels, characterized by an increase in both cholesterol and triglycerides and caused by the presence of chylomicrons. It is inherited as an autosomal-recessive trait and has a low risk of atherosclerosis. It results in recurrent bouts of acute pancreatitis.

hyperlipidemia type IV, a relatively common form of hyperlipoproteinemia characterized by a slight elevation in cholesterol levels, a moderate elevation of triglyceride levels, and an elevation of the normal triglyceride carrier protein (very low-density lipoprotein) level. It is associated with an increased risk for coronary atherosclerosis.

hyperlipidemia type V, a condition of elevated blood lipid levels, characterized by slightly increased cholesterol level, greatly increased triglyceride level, elevation of the triglyceride carrier protein (very low-density lipoprotein) level, and above normal levels of chylomicrons. It is a genetically heterogenous disorder that apparently does not increase the risk of atherosclerosis.

hyperlipoproteinemia /hī′pərlip′ōprō′tēnē′mē·ə/ [Gk, *hyper* + *lipos,* fat, *proteios,* first rank, *haima,* blood], any of a large group of inherited and acquired disorders of lipoprotein metabolism characterized by greater than normal amounts of certain protein-bound lipids and other fatty substances in the blood and usually low levels of high-density lipoprotein cholesterol.

hypermagnesemia /hī′pərmag′nisē′mē·ə/ [Gk *hyper* + *magnesia,* magnesium, *haima,* blood], a greater than normal amount of magnesium in the plasma, found in people with kidney failure and in those who use large doses of drugs containing magnesium such as antacids. Toxic levels of magnesium cause cardiac arrhythmias and depression of deep tendon reflexes and respiration.

hypermature cataract /-məchŏŏr′/ [Gk, *hyper*; L, *maturare,* to make ripe; Gk, *katarrhaktes,* portcullis], an opaque lens that has lost water and has become soft and reduced in size.

hypermetabolic state /-met′əbol′ik/, an abnormally increased rate of metabolism, as in a high fever or hyperthyroidism.

hypermetabolism /-mətab′əliz′əm/, increased metabolism, usually accompanied by excessive body heat.

hypermetaplasia /-met′əplā′zhə/, an abnormal increase in the rate of transformation of one kind of tissue into another, as in the development of tumors.

hypermetria /hī′pərmē′trē·ə/ [Gk, *hyper* + *metron,* measure], an abnormal form of dysmetria characterized by a dysfunction of the power to control the range of muscular action and causing movements that overreach the intended goal of the affected individual.

hypermnesia /hī′pərmnē′zhə/, an extraordinarily good state of memory.

hypermobility /-mōbil′itē/ [Gk, *hyper*; L, *mobilis,* movable], an abnormally wide range of movement of the joints.

hypermorph /hī′pərmôrf′/ [Gk, *hyper* + *morphe,* form], **1.** a person whose arms and legs are disproportionately long in relation to the trunk and whose sitting height is disproportionately short compared with the standing height. **2.** a mutant allele that has an increased effect on the expression of a trait.

hypermotility /-motil′itē/, an excessive movement of the involuntary muscles, particularly in the GI tract.

hypernasality /hī′pərnāzal′itē/ [Gk, *hyper,* excess; L, *nasus,* nose], excessively nasal speech resonance, which may result in unintelligible speech. The cause is velopharyngeal dysfunction with emission of too much air through the nose.

hypernatremia /hī′pərnatrē′mē·ə/ [Gk, *hyper*; L, *natrium,* sodium], a greater than normal concentration of sodium in the blood, caused by excessive loss of water and electrolytes that results from polyuria, diarrhea, excessive sweating, inadequate water intake, or a large intake of salt. People with hypernatremia may become mentally confused, have seizures, and lapse into coma.

hyperopia (h) /-ō′pē·ə/ [Gk, *hyper* + *ops,* eye], farsightedness, or an inability of the eye to focus on nearby objects. It results from an error of refraction in which rays of light entering the eye are brought into focus behind the retina.

hyperorchidism /-ôr′kidiz′əm/ [Gk, *hyper,* excessive, *orchis,* testis], excessive endocrine activity of the testes.

hyperornithinemia /-ôr′nithinē′mē·ə/, a metabolic disorder involving the amino acid ornithine, which tends to accumulate in the tissues, causing seizures and retardation.

hyperosmia /-oz′mē·ə/, an abnormally increased sensitivity to odors.

hyperosmolarity /-oz′məler′itē/ [Gk, *hyper* + *osmos,* impulse], a state or condition of abnormally increased osmolarity.—**hyperosmolar,** *adj.*

hyperosmotic /-osmot′ik/, pertaining to a solution that has a higher solute concentration than another solution.

hyperostosis frontalis interna, thickening of the inner table of the frontal bone, which may be associated with hirsutism and obesity.

hyperoxaluria /-ok′səlŏŏr′ē·ə/, an excessive level of oxalic acid or oxalates, primarily calcium oxalate, in the urine. An excess of oxalates may lead to the formation of renal calculi and renal failure.

hyperoxemia /-okse̅′me̅·ə/ [Gk, *hyper,* excess, *oxys,* sharp, *haima,* blood], increased oxygen content of the blood.

hyperoxia /-ok′se̅·ə/, abnormally high oxygen tension in the blood.

hyperoxygenation /-ok′sijənā′shən/ [Gk, *hyper* + *oxys,* sharp, *genein,* to produce], the use of high concentrations of inspired oxygen before and after endotracheal aspiration.

hyperparathyroidism /-per′əthī′roidiz′əm/ [Gk, *hyper* + *para,* beside, *thyreos,* shield, *eidos,* form], an abnormal endocrine condition characterized by hyperactivity of any of the four parathyroid glands with excessive secretion of parathyroid hormone, which causes increased resorption of calcium from the skeletal system and increased absorption of calcium by the kidneys and GI system. The condition may be primary, originating in one or more of the parathyroid glands and usually caused by an adenoma, or secondary, resulting from an abnormal hypocalcemia-producing condition in another part of the body, which causes a compensatory hyperactivity of the parathyroid glands.

hyperperistalsis /-per′istal′sis/ [Gk, *hyper,* excess, *peristellein,* to clasp], a state of excessive motility of the waves of alternate contractions and relaxations that propel contents forward through the digestive tract.

hyperphenylalaninemia /hī′pərfen′ilal′əni ne̅′me̅·ə/ [Gk, *hyper* + (phenylalanine) + *haima,* blood], an abnormally high concentration of phenylalanine in the blood. This symptom may be the result of one of several defects in the metabolic process of breaking down phenylalanine.

hyperphoria /hī′pərfôr′e̅·ə/ [Gk, *hyper* + *pherein,* to bear], the tendency of an eye to deviate upward.

hyperphosphoremia /-fos′fəre̅′me̅·ə/, an abnormally high level of phosphorus compounds in the blood.

hyperpigmentation /-pig′məntā′shən/ [Gk, *hyper*; L, *pigmentum,* paint], darkening of the skin. Causes include heredity, drugs, exposure to the sun, trauma, and adrenal insufficiency.

hyperpituitarism /-pityo̅o̅′itəriz′əm/ [Gk, *hyper,* excess; L, *pituita,* phlegm], overactivity of the anterior lobe of the pituitary gland, resulting in increased secretion of its hormones.

hyperplasia /hī′pərplā′zhə/ [Gk, *hyper* + *plassein,* to mold], an increase in the number of cells of a body part that results from an increased rate of cellular division.

hyperplastic gingivitis [Gk, *hyper,* excess, *plassein,* to mold; L, *gingiva,* gum; Gk, *itis,* inflammation], inflammation and enlargement of the gums caused by an increase in the number of cells, usually because of bacterial plaque accumulation.

hyperploid /hī′pərploid/ [Gk, *hyper* + *eidos,* form], **1.** an individual, organism, strain, or cell that has one or more chromosomes in excess of the haploid number or of an exact multiple of the haploid number characteristic of the species. **2.** pertaining to such an individual, organism, strain, or cell.—**hyperploidy,** *adj.*

hyperploidy /hī′pərploi′de̅/, any increase in chromosome number that involves individual chromosomes rather than entire sets, resulting in more than the normal haploid number characteristic of the species, as in Down syndrome.

hyperpnea /hī′pərpne̅′ə/ [Gk, *hyper* + *pnoe,* blowing], an exaggerated deep, rapid, or labored respiration. It occurs normally with exercise and abnormally with aspirin overdose, pain, fever, hysteria, or any condition in which the supply of oxygen is inadequate.—**hyperpneic, hyperpnoic,** *adj.*

hyperpolarized helium /-pō′lərīzd/, a gas used in MRI studies of respiratory disorders to produce images of the air spaces in the lungs.

hyperprolactinemia /-prōlak′tine̅′me̅·ə/ [Gk, *hyper*; L, *pro,* before, *lac,* milk; Gk, *haima,* blood], an excessive amount of prolactin in the blood, usually caused by a pituitary adenoma but sometimes caused by endocrine side effects related to certain antipsychotic medications. In women it is usually associated with galactorrhea and secondary amenorrhea; in men it may be a factor in gynecomastia, decreased libido, and impotence.

hyperprolinemia /hī′pərprō′line̅′me̅·ə/, an autosomal-recessive aminoacidopathy characterized by an excess of proline in the body fluids and occurring as two types. Type 1 is associated with renal disease and type 2 with mental retardation and convulsions.

hyperproteinemia /-prō′te̅ne̅′me̅·ə/ [Gk, *hyper,* excessive, *proteios,* first rank, *haima,* blood], an abnormally high concentration of protein in the blood.

hyperpyrexia /hī′pərpīrek′se̅·ə/ [Gk, *hyper* + *pyressein,* to be feverish], an extremely elevated temperature that sometimes occurs in acute infectious diseases, especially in young children. Malignant hyperpyrexia, characterized by a rapid rise in temperature, tachycardia, tachypnea, sweating, rigidity, and blotchy cyanosis, occasionally occurs in patients undergoing general anesthesia.—**hyperpyretic,** *adj.*

hyperreactivity /-re̅′aktiv′ite̅/ [Gk, *hyper*; L, *re,* again, *activus,* active], an abnormal condition in which responses to stimuli are exaggerated.

hyperreflection /-riflek'shən/, a compulsion to devote excessive attention to oneself.

hyperreflexia /-riflek'sē·ə/ [Gk, *hyper*; L, *reflectere*, to bend back], increased reflex reactions.

hypersensibility /-sen'səbil'itē/, excessive ability to perceive or feel, as excessive sensibility to pain.

hypersensitivity /-sen'sətiv'itē/ [Gk, *hyper*; L, *sentire*, to feel], an abnormal condition characterized by an exaggerated response of the immune system to an antigen.—**hypersensitive,** *adj.*

hypersensitivity pneumonitis, an inflammatory form of interstitial pneumonia that results from an immunologic reaction in a hypersensitive person. The reaction may be provoked by a variety of inhaled organic dusts, often those containing fungal spores. A wide variety of symptoms may occur, including asthma, fever, chills, malaise, and muscle aches, which usually develop 4 to 6 hours after exposure.

hypersensitivity reaction, an inappropriate and excessive response of the immune system to an allergen. Hypersensitivity reactions are classified into four types according to the components of the immune system involved in their mediation. A type I or immediate hypersensitivity reaction occurs rapidly, within several minutes, on reexposure to an antigen, and is the result of interaction of IgE and the antigen; anaphylaxis is a particularly severe type I hypersensitivity reaction. A type II or cytotoxic hypersensitivity reaction is one of tissue or cell damage resulting from antibody-antigen interactions on cell surfaces. A type III or immune complex–mediated hypersensitivity reaction is a local or general inflammatory response caused by formation of circulating antigen-antibody complexes and their disposition in tissues. A type IV hypersensitivity reaction is one initiated by antigen-specific T lymphocytes; this type takes 1 or more days to develop and the hypersensitivity can be transferred by lymphocytes but not by serum.

hypersensitization /-sen'sitīzā'shən/ [Gk, *hyper*, excess; L, *sentire*, to feel], a state of increased reactivity or sensitivity to a stimulus.

hypersomnia /hī'pərsom'nē·ə/ [Gk, *hyper*; L, *somnus,* sleep], **1.** sleep of excessive depth or abnormal duration, usually caused by psychologic rather than physical factors and characterized by a state of confusion on awakening. **2.** extreme drowsiness, often associated with lethargy.

3. a condition characterized by periods of deep, long sleep.

hypersplenism /hī'pərsplē'nizəm/ [Gk, *hyper* + *splen,* spleen], a syndrome consisting of splenomegaly and a deficiency of one or more types of blood cells. Causes may include portal hypertension, the lymphomas, the hemolytic anemias, malaria, TB, and various connective tissue and inflammatory diseases. Patients complain of abdominal pain of the left upper and middle quadrant and often experience a sensation of fullness after small meals secondary to an enlarged spleen pressing against the stomach.

Hyperstat, a trademark for an emergency vasodilator (diazoxide).

hypersthenic /hī'pərsthen'ik/, **1.** pertaining to a condition of excessive strength or tonicity of the body or a body part. **2.** pertaining to a body type characterized by massive proportions.

hypersystole /-sis'təlē/, abnormal force or duration of ventricular contraction.

hypertaurodontism /hī'pərtô'rōdon'tizəm/ [Gk, *hyper,* excess; L, *taurus,* bull; Gk, *odous,* tooth], taurodontism in which the tooth roots do not branch.

hypertelorism /hī'pərtel'əriz'əm/ [Gk, *hyper* + *tele,* far, *horizo,* separate], a developmental defect characterized by an abnormally wide space between two organs or parts.

hypertension /-ten'shən/ [Gk, *hyper*; L, *tendere,* to stretch], a common disorder that is a known cardiovascular disease risk factor, characterized by elevated BP over the normal values of 120/80 mm Hg in an adult over 18 years of age. This elevation in BP can be divided into three classes of hypertension. Prehypertension describes BP measurements of greater than 120 mm Hg systolic or 80 mm Hg diastolic and less than 130 mm Hg systolic or 90 mm Hg diastolic. Stage 1 hypertension is defined by a BP of over 130 mm Hg systolic or 90 mm Hg diastolic but less than 160 mm Hg systolic or 100 mm Hg diastolic. Stage 2 hypertension is defined by a BP greater than 160 mm Hg systolic or 100 mm Hg diastolic. Essential hypertension, the most common kind, has no single identifiable cause, but risk for the disorder is increased by obesity, a high serum sodium level, hypercholesterolemia, and a family history of high BP. Known causes of secondary hypertension include sleep apnea, chronic kidney disease, primary aldosteronism, renovascular disease, chronic steroid therapy, Cushing's syndrome, pheochromocytoma, coarctation of the aorta, and thyroid or parathyroid disease. The incidence of hypertension is higher in men than in women and is twice as great in African-Americans as in Caucasians. People with mild or moderate hypertension may be asymptomatic or may experience suboccipital headaches, especially on rising; tinnitus; lightheadedness; ready fatigability; and palpitations. With sustained hypertension, arterial walls become thickened, inelastic, and resistant to blood flow, and the left ventricle becomes distended and hypertrophied as a result of its efforts to maintain normal circulation against the increased resistance. Inadequate blood supply to the coronary arteries may cause angina or MI. Left ventricular hypertrophy may lead to CHF. Malignant hypertension, characterized by a diastolic pressure higher than 120 mm Hg, severe headaches, blurred vision, and confusion, may result in fatal uremia, MI, CHF, or a CVA.

Hypertension and Lipid Trial (HALT), a study to assess the efficacy and safety of alpha-adrenergic blockers in patients with hypertension.

hypertensive /-ten′siv/ [Gk, *hyper,* excessive; L, *tendere,* to stretch], pertaining to high BP, its cause, or its effects.

hypertensive arteriosclerosis, a form of arteriosclerosis complicated by a buildup of the muscular and elastic tissues of the arterial walls caused by hypertension.

hypertensive crisis [Gk, *hyper;* L, *tendere,* to stretch; Gk, *krisis,* turning point], a sudden, severe increase in BP to a level exceeding 200/120 mm Hg.

hypertensive encephalopathy [Gk, *hyper;* L, *tendere,* to stretch; Gk, *enkephalos,* brain, *pathos,* disease], a set of symptoms, including headache, lethargy, vision changes, convulsions, and coma, secondary to end organ damage from critically elevated systolic or diastolic BP.

hypertensive retinopathy [Gk, *hyper;* L, *tendere,* to stretch, *rete* + *net,* web; Gk, *pathos,* disease], a condition in which retinal changes occur in association with arterial hypertension. The changes may include blood vessel alterations, hemorrhages, exudates, and retinal edema.

hyperthermia /hī′pərthur′mē-ə/ [Gk, *hyper* + *therme,* heat], **1.** a much higher than normal body temperature induced therapeutically or iatrogenically. **2.** *nontechnical.* malignant hyperthermia. **3.** the use of various heating methods, such as electromagnetic therapy, to produce temperature elevations of a few degrees in cells and tissues. It is believed to lead to an antitumor effect.

hyperthyroidism /-thī′roidiz′əm/ [Gk, *hyper* + *thyreos,* shield, *eidos,* form], a condition characterized by hyperactivity of the thyroid gland. The gland is usually enlarged, secreting greater than normal amounts of thyroid hormones, and the metabolic processes of the body are accelerated. Nervousness, exophthalmos, tremor, constant hunger, weight loss, fatigue, heat intolerance, palpitations, and diarrhea may develop.

hypertonia /-tō′nē-ə/, **1.** abnormally increased muscle tone or strength. The condition is sometimes associated with genetic disorders and may be expressed in arm or leg deformities. **2.** a condition of excessive pressure, such as the intraocular pressure of glaucoma.

hypertonic /hī′pərton′ik/ [Gk, *hyper* + *tonos,* stretching], **1.** pertaining to a solution that causes cells to shrink. **2.** a solution that increases the degree of osmotic pressure on a semipermeable membrane.

hypertonic bladder [Gk, *hyper,* excess, *tonos,* tone; AS, *blaedre*], a condition of excessive tension in the detrusor muscle of the bladder, usually caused by an irritant such as a calculus or occurring after surgery.

hypertonic contracture, prolonged muscle contraction that results from continuous nerve stimulation in spastic paralysis.

hypertonicity /-tənis′itē/ [Gk, *hyper,* excess, *tonos,* tone], **1.** excessive tone, tension, or activity. **2.** in ophthalmology, increased intraocular pressure. **3.** excessive tension of the arteries or muscles. **4.** increase in osmotic pressure.

hypertonic saline, a saline solution that contains 1% to 23.4% sodium chloride (compared with normal saline solution at 0.9%).

hypertonus /-tō′nəs/, an excessive level of skeletal muscle tension or activity.

hypertrophic /-trof′ik/ [Gk, *hyper,* excess, *trophe,* nourishment], pertaining to an increase in size, structure, or function.

hypertrophic cardiomyopathy, an abnormal condition characterized by gross hypertrophy of the interventricular septum and left ventricular free wall of the heart. Ventricular hypertrophy results in impaired diastolic filling and reduced cardiac output. Signs and symptoms, such as fatigue and syncope, are often associated with exercise when the demand for increased cardiac output cannot be met.

hypertrophic catarrh [Gk, *hyper* + *trophe,* nourishment, *kata,* down, *rhoia,* flow], a chronic condition characterized by inflammation and discharge from a mucous membrane, accompanied by the thickening of the mucosal and submucosal tissue.

hypertrophic cirrhosis, a stage of cirrhosis characterized by an overgrowth of liver tissue.

hypertrophic gastritis, a premalignant condition characterized by inflammation of the gastric mucosa associated with gastric albumin wasting. Symptoms include epigastric pain, nausea, vomiting, weight loss, and abdominal distension. It is differentiated from other forms of gastritis by the presence of prominent rugae (folds), enlarged glands, excess mucus production, and nodules on the wall of the stomach. This condition often accompanies peptic ulcer, Zollinger-Ellison syndrome, or gastric hypersecretion.

hypertrophic gingivitis [Gk, *hyper,* excess, *trophe,* nourishment], inflammation and enlargement of the gums resulting from an increase in the size of cells, usually because of an underlying systemic disorder.

hypertrophic scarring, excessive overgrowth of dense collagen tissue at the site of a healed skin defect.

hypertrophic subaortic stenosis, a form of hypertrophic cardiomyopathy, in which the left ventricle is hypertrophied (commonly with disproportionate involvement of the interventricular septum) and the cavity is small. It is marked by obstruction to left ventricular outflow.

hypertrophy /hīpur'trəfē/ [Gk, *hyper* + *trophe,* nourishment], an increase in the size of an organ caused by an increase in the size of the cells rather than the number of cells.—**hypertrophic,** *adj.*

hypertrophy of heart [Gk, *hyper,* excess, *trophe,* nourishment; AS, *heorte*], an increase in the size of the heart resulting from enlargement of the heart muscle, but without an increase in the capacity of the heart chambers.

hyperuricosuria /hī'per'urikō'shurē-ə/, an excess of uric acid or urates in the urine.

hypervalinemia /hī'pərval'inē'mē-ə/, **1.** an autosomal-recessive aminoacidopathy, probably caused by a defect in an enzyme necessary for valine catabolism, characterized by elevated levels of valine in the plasma and urine and by failure to thrive. **2.** elevated levels of valine in the plasma. Hypervalinemia is often associated with maple sugar urine disease.

hyperventilation /-ven'tilā'shən/ [Gk, *hyper*; L, *ventilare,* to fan], a pulmonary ventilation rate greater than that metabolically necessary for gas exchange, resulting from an increased respiration rate, an increased tidal volume, or both. Hyperventilation causes an excessive intake of oxygen and elimination of carbon dioxide and may cause hyperoxygenation. Hypocapnia and respiratory alkalosis then occur, leading to dizziness, faintness, numbness of the fingers and toes, possibly syncope, and psychomotor impairment.

hyperventilation tetany, a nervous disorder characterized by muscle twitches, cramps, or spasms caused by abnormally low blood levels of CO_2 from forced overbreathing.

hyperviscosity /-viskos'itē/ [Gk, *hyper,* excess; L, *viscosus,* sticky], extreme viscosity or thickness of fluid.

hyperviscosity syndrome, several syndromes associated with increased thickness and slowed flow rate of blood. One type, which results from serum hyperviscosity, is caused by increased proteins and is characterized by neurologic and ocular disorders. Another type is polycythemia, causing organ congestion, reduced capillary perfusion, and increased cardiac effort. A third group includes conditions in which the deformability of erythrocytes is impaired, such as sickle cell anemia.

hypervitaminosis /-vī'təminō'sis/, an abnormal condition resulting from excessive intake of toxic amounts of one or more vitamins, especially over a long period.

hypervolemia /-vōlē'mē-ə/ [Gk, *hyper*; L, *volumen,* paper roll; Gk, *haima,* blood], an increase in the amount of intravascular fluid, particularly in the volume of circulating blood or its components.

hypervolemia management, a nursing intervention from the Nursing Interventions Classification (NIC) defined as reduction in extracellular and/or intracellular fluid volume and prevention of complications in a patient who is fluid-overloaded.

hypesthesia /hī'pisthē'zhə/ [Gk, *hypo,* under, *aisthesis,* feeling], a decrease in sensation in response to stimulation of the sensory nerves or body organs or areas they innervate.—**hypesthetic,** *adj.*

hypha /hī'fə/ *pl.* **hyphae** [Gk, *hyphe,* web], a threadlike structure in the mycelium in a fungus.

hyphema /hīfē'mə/ [Gk, *hypo,* under, *haima,* blood], a hemorrhage into the anterior chamber of the eye, usually caused by a blunt trauma. Glaucoma may result from recurrent bleeding.

hyphomycosis /hi'fomiko'sis/, any infection caused by an imperfect fungus of the form-class Hyphomycetes. The group has been divided into hyalohyphomycosis and phaeohyphomycosis on the basis of the color of the mycelium and wall of the fungus. It is a disease of horses and mules, rarely of humans.

hypnagogic hallucination /hip'nəgoj'ik/ [Gk, *hypnos,* sleep, *agogos,* leading], a vivid image that occurs while falling asleep.

hypnagogue /hip'nəgog/ [Gk, *hypnos* + *agogos,* leading], an agent or substance that tends to induce sleep or the feeling of dreamy sleepiness, as occurs before falling asleep. —**hypnagogic,** *adj.*

hypnoanalysis /hip'nə·anal'isis/ [Gk, *hypnos* + *analyein,* to loosen], the use of hypnosis as an adjunct to other techniques in psychoanalysis.

hypnogenic zone /hip'nəjen'ik/, a specific area on the body that, when stimulated with pressure, can cause a person to enter a hypnotic state.

hypnopomic hallucination, an image perceived while awakening from sleep.

hypnosis[1] /hipnō'sis/ [Gk, *hypnos,* sleep], a passive, trancelike state that resembles normal sleep during which perception and memory are altered, resulting in increased responsiveness to suggestion. The condition is usually induced by the monotonous repetition of words and gestures while the subject is completely relaxed.

hypnosis[2], a nursing intervention from the Nursing Interventions Classification (NIC) defined as assisting a patient to achieve a state of attentive, focused concentration with suspension of some peripheral awareness to create changes in sensation, thoughts, or behavior.

hypnotherapy /hip'nəther'əpē/ [Gk, *hypnos* + *therapeia,* treatment], the induction of a specific altered state (trance) for memory retrieval, relaxation, or suggestion. Hypnotherapy is often used to alter habits (e.g., smoking, obesity), treat biologic mechanisms such as hypertension or cardiac arrhythmias, deal with the symptoms of a disease, alter an individual's reaction to disease, and affect an illness and its course through the body.

hypnotic /hipnot'ik/ [Gk, *hypnos,* sleep], a class of drugs often used as sedatives.

hypnotic sleep /hipnot'ik/ [Gk, *hypnos,* sleep; ME, *slep*], sleep induced by hypnosis through the administration of hypnotic medicines.

hypnotic suggestion [Gk, *hypnos,* sleep; L, *suggerere,* to suggest], a suggestion implanted in the mind of a person under hypnosis.

hypnotic trance, an artificially induced sleeplike state, as in hypnosis.

hypnotism /hip'nətiz'əm/ [Gk, *hypnos,* sleep], the study or practice of inducing hypnosis.

hypnotist /hip'nətist/, one who practices hypnotism.

hypnotize /hip'nətīz/, **1.** to put into a state of hypnosis. **2.** to fascinate, entrance, or control through personal charm.

hypoacidity /hī'pō·əsid'itē/, a deficiency of acid.

hypoactivity /-aktiv'itē/ [Gk, *hypo,* under; L, *activus,* active], any abnormally diminished activity of the body or its organs, such as decreased cardiac output, thyroid secretion, or peristalsis.

hypoacusis /-əkoō'sis/ [Gk, *hypo,* under, *akouein,* to hear], a reduced sensitivity to sounds.

hypoalbuminemia /-alboō'minē'mē·ə/, a condition of abnormally low levels of albumin in the blood.

hypoalimentation /-al'imentā'shən/ [Gk, *hypo*; L, *alimentum,* nourishment], a condition of insufficient or inadequate nourishment.

hypoallergenic /-al'ərjen'ik/ [Gk, *hypo,* under, *allos,* other, *ergein,* to work], having a lowered potential for producing an allergic reaction.

hypobarism /-ber'izəm/, air pressure that is significantly less than the sea level normal of 760 mm Hg.

hypobetalipoproteinemia /hī'pōbā'təlip'ōprō'tēnē'mē·ə/ [Gk, *hypo* + *beta,* second letter of Greek alphabet, *lipos,* fat, *proteios,* first rank, *haima,* blood], an inherited disorder in which there are less than normal amounts of beta-lipoprotein in the serum.

hypoblast /hī'pōblast/ [Gk, *blastos,* germ], the lower layer of the bilaminar embryonic disk in a human embryo, present during the second week. It gives rise to the endoderm.

hypocalcemia /hī'pōkalsē'mē·ə/ [Gk, *hypo*; L, *calx,* lime; Gk, *haima,* blood], a deficiency of calcium in the serum that may be caused by hypoparathyroidism, vitamin D deficiency, kidney failure, acute pancreatitis, or inadequate amounts of plasma magnesium and protein. Mild hypocalcemia is asymptomatic. Severe hypocalcemia is characterized by cardiac arrhythmias and tetany with hyperparesthesia of the hands, feet, lips, and tongue.— **hypocalcemic,** *adj.*

hypocalcemic tetany /-kalsē'mik/ [Gk, *hypo,* under; L, *calx,* calcium, *haima,* blood, *tetanos,* convulsive tension], a disease caused by an abnormally low level of calcium in the blood. It is characterized by hyperexcitability of the neuromuscular system and results in carpopedal spasms. A common cause is a deficiency of parathyroid hormone secretion.

hypocalciuria /-kal'siuðōr'ē·ə/ [Gk, *hypo,* under; L, *calx,* lime; Gk, *ouron,* urine], a diminished level of calcium in the urine.

hypocapnia /-kap'nē·ə/, an abnormally low arterial carbon dioxide level.

hypochloremia /-klôrē'mē·ə/ [Gk, *hypo* + *chloros,* green, *haima,* blood], a decrease in the chloride level in the blood serum. The condition may result from prolonged gastric suctioning.

hypochloremic alkalosis /-klôr·ē′mik/, a metabolic disorder resulting from an increase in blood bicarbonate level secondary to loss of chloride from the body.

hypochlorhydria /-klôrhid′rē·ə/ [Gk, *hypo* + *chloros*, green, *hydor*, water], a deficiency of hydrochloric acid in gastric secretions.

hypochlorite poisoning /-klôr′īt/, toxic effects of ingestion of or skin contact with household or commercial bleaches or similar chlorinated products. Symptoms include pain and inflammation of the mouth and digestive tract, vomiting, and breathing difficulty. Skin contact may produce blisters.

hypochlorous acid /-klôr′əs/ [Gk, *hypo* + *chloros*, green; L, *acidus*, sour], a compound, HOC1, that is stable only in the form of a dilute aqueous solution formed by dissolving chlorine gas in water to yield a greenish-yellow solution. It is used as a bleaching agent and disinfectant.

hypocholesteremia /-kəles′tərē′mē·ə/, an abnormally low level of cholesterol in the blood.

hypochondriac /-kon′drē·ak/ [Gk, *hypo*, under, *chondros*, cartilage], **1.** pertaining to the regions of the upper abdomen beneath the lower ribs and lateral to the epigastric region. **2.** a person who is so preoccupied with matters of ill health that the state of mind itself becomes a disability.—**hypochondriacal** /-kəndrī′əkəl/, *adj.*

hypochondriac region [Gk, *hypo* + *chondros*, cartilage; L, *regio*, direction], the part of the abdomen in the upper zone on both sides of the epigastric region and beneath the cartilages of the lower ribs.

hypochondriasis /hī′pōkəndrī′əsis/ [Gk, *hypo* + *chondros*, cartilage, *osis*, condition], a chronic abnormal concern about the health of the body. It is characterized by extreme anxiety, depression, and an unrealistic interpretation of real or imagined physical symptoms as indications of a serious illness or disease despite rational medical evidence that no disorder is present.

hypochondroplasia /-kon′drōplā′zhə/, an inherited form of dwarfism that resembles a mild form of achondroplasia.

hypochromic /hī′pōkrō′mik/ [Gk, *hypo* + *chroma*, color], pale staining red blood cells with broadened central zone of pallor most often associated with hypochromic, microcytic anemia, thalassemia, and anemia of chronic inflammation.

hypochromic anemia, a decrease in hemoglobin characterized by hypochromic, microcytic red blood cells such as iron deficiency anemia, thalassemia and anemia of chronic inflammation.

hypocitraturia /hī′pōsitratu′re·ə/, excretion of urine containing an abnormally

small amount of citrate, an important cause of the formation of oxalate urinary calculi.

hypocycloidal motion /-sī′kloidəl/, a complex circular movement of the x-ray tube and film during the acquisition of CT images. It is used to blur structures outside the focal plane and eliminate ghost images.

hypocythemia, deficiency in the number of RBCs.

hypodermic /-durmik/ [Gk, *hypo* + *derma*, skin], pertaining to the area below the skin.

hypodermic implantation [Gk, *hypo*, under, *derma*, skin; L, *implantare*, to set into], the introduction of a solid medicine under the skin, usually on the chest or abdominal wall, to ensure local action or slow absorption.

hypodermic needle, a short, thin hollow needle that attaches to a syringe for injecting a drug or medication under the skin or into vessels and for withdrawing a fluid for examination.

hypodermic syringe [Gk, *hypo*, under, *derma*, skin, *syrigx*, tube], an instrument designed to direct fluid under the skin through a fine hollow needle.

hypodermic tablet, a compressed or molded dosage form of a medication that can be dissolved for IV administration.

hypodermoclysis /hī′pōdərmok′lisis/ [Gk, *hypo* + *derma*, skin, *klysis*, flushing out], the injection of an isotonic or hypotonic solution into subcutaneous tissue to supply a continuous and large amount of fluid, electrolytes, and nutrients. The procedure is used to replace the loss or inadequate intake of water and salt during illness or surgery or after shock or hemorrhage. It is performed only when a patient is unable to take fluids intravenously, orally, or rectally.

hypodipsia /-dip′sē·ə/, a condition in which homeostasis is threatened by an abnormally low fluid intake. It is often related to dysfunction of the thirst osmoreceptor in the anterior hypothalamus.

hypofibrinogenemia /-fī′brinōjənē′mē·ə/ [Gk, *hypo*; L, *fibra*, fiber; Gk, *genein*, to produce, *haima*, blood], plasma fibrinogen deficiency. It may be inherited or acquired, as in disseminated intravascular coagulation or liver disease.

hypofunction /-fungk′shən/ [Gk, *hypo*, under; L, *functio*, performance], a diminished or inadequate level of activity of an organ system or its parts.

hypogammaglobulinemia /-gam′əglōb′byəli nē′mē·ə/ [Gk, *hypo* + *gamma*, third letter in Greek alphabet; L, *globus*, small sphere; Gk, *haima*, blood], lower than normal concentration of plasma gamma globulin, usually the result of increased protein catabolism or loss of protein via the urine. It is associated with a decreased resistance to infection.

hypogastric /-gas′trik/ [Gk, *hypo,* under, *gaster,* stomach], pertaining to the hypogastrium.

hypogastric pain, pain in the lower abdomen.

hypogastric plexus, a complex of nerve fibers in the pelvic area near the termination of the aorta and the beginning of the common iliac artery.

hypogenitalism /-jen′itəliz′əm/ [Gk, *hypo;* L, *genitalis,* fruitful], a condition of retarded sexual development caused by a defect in male or female hormonal production in the testis or ovary.

hypogeusia /-goō′zē-ə/, reduced taste.

hypoglossal /-glos′əl/ [Gk, *hypo,* under, *glossa,* tongue], pertaining to nerves or other structures under the tongue.

hypoglossal nerve [Gk, *hypo* + *glossa,* tongue], either of a pair of cranial nerves essential for swallowing and for moving the tongue.

hypoglossus /-glos′əs/, **1.** a muscle that retracts and pulls down the side of the tongue. **2.** the hypoglossal nerve.

hypoglycemia /hī′pōglīsē′mē-ə/ [Gk, *hypo* + *glykys,* sweet, *haima,* blood], a low level of glucose in the blood. It may be caused by administration of too much insulin, excessive secretion of insulin by the islet cells of the pancreas, or dietary deficiency. The condition may cause weakness, headache, hunger, visual disturbances, ataxia, anxiety, personality changes, and, if untreated, delirium, coma, and death.

hypoglycemia management, a nursing intervention from the Nursing Interventions Classification (NIC) defined as preventing and treating low blood glucose levels.

hypoglycemic /-glīsē′mik/ [Gk, *hypo,* under, *glykys,* sweet, *haima,* blood], pertaining to or resembling a state of low blood glucose level.

hypoglycemic agent, any of various synthetic drugs that lower the blood glucose level and are used to treat type 2 DM. They may stimulate synthesis of insulin by pancreatic beta cells, inhibit glucose production, facilitate transport of glucose to muscle cells, and sometimes increase the number of receptor sites where insulin can be bound and can initiate the process of breaking down glucose. Patients should be advised that these drugs are not a cure for diabetes but only a means of controlling it.

hypoglycemic coma [Gk, *hypo,* under, *glykys,* sweet, *koma,* deep sleep], LOC that results from abnormally low blood glucose levels.

hypoglycogenolysis /-glī′kōjənol′isis/, a metabolic disorder in which deficient or defective splitting of glycogen molecules results in decreased formation of glucose.

hypogonadism /-gō′nədiz′əm/, a deficiency in the secretory activity of the ovary or testis. The condition may be primary or caused by a gonadal dysfunction involving the Leydig's cells in the male, or it may occur secondary to a hypothalamus or pituitary disorder.

hypoinsulinism /-in′səliniz′əm/ [Gk, *hypo,* under; L, *insula,* island (of Langerhans)], a deficiency of insulin secretion by cells of the pancreas, with associated signs and symptoms of diabetes.

hypokalemia /hī′pōkəlē′mē-ə/ [Gk, *hypo;* L, *kalium,* potassium; Gk, *haima,* blood], a condition in which an inadequate amount of potassium, the major intracellular cation, is found in the circulating bloodstream. Hypokalemia is characterized by abnormal ECG findings, weakness, confusion, mental depression, and flaccid paralysis. The cause may be starvation, treatment of diabetic acidosis, adrenal tumor, or diuretic therapy. —**hypokalemic,** *adj.*

hypokalemic alkalosis /-kalē′mik/, a pathologic condition resulting from the accumulation of base or the loss of acid from the body, associated with a low level of serum potassium.

hypokalemic nephropathy, nephropathy with hypokalemia, interstitial nephritis, swelling and vacuolization of proximal renal tubules, and progressive renal failure, resulting from long-term conditions such as oncotic overloading of the kidney filtration mechanisms by sugars.

hypokalemic periodic paralysis [Gk, *hypo,* under; L, *kalium,* potassium; Gk, *peri,* near, *hodos,* way, *paralyein,* to be palsied], a state of recurring attacks of muscular weakness associated with low blood levels of potassium.

hypokinetic /-kinet′ik/ [Gk, *hypo,* under, *kinesis,* movement], pertaining to diminished power of movement or motor function, which may or may not be accompanied by a mild form of paralysis.

hypolipoproteinemia /hī′pōlip′ōprō′tēnē′mē-ə/ [Gk, *hypo* + *lipos,* fat, *proteios,* first rank, *haima,* blood], a group of defects of lipoprotein metabolism that cause varying complexes of signs. Primary, or hereditary, hypolipoproteinemia factors include abnormal transport of triglycerides in the blood, low levels of high-density lipoproteins, and abnormal fat deposits in the body, especially in the kidneys and the liver. The condition also may be secondary to anemia, malabsorption syndromes, or malnutrition.

hypomagnesemia /hī′pōmag′nisē′mē·ə/, an abnormally low concentration of magnesium in the blood plasma, which causes nausea, vomiting, muscle weakness, tremors, tetany, and lethargy. Tachycardia and arrhythmia may also occur. Mild hypomagnesemia is usually the result of inadequate absorption of magnesium in the kidney or intestine. A more severe form is associated with malabsorption syndrome, protein malnutrition, and parathyroid disease.

hypomania /-mā′nē·ə/ [Gk, *hypo* + *mania,* madness], a mild degree of mania characterized by optimism; excitability; energetic, productive behavior; marked hyperactivity and talkativeness; heightened sexual interest; quick anger and irritability; and a decreased need for sleep.—**hypomaniac,** *n.,* **hypomanic,** *adj.*

hypometria /hī′pōmē′trē·ə/ [Gk, *hypo* + *metron,* measure], an abnormal form of dysmetria, characterized by a dysfunction of the power to control the range of muscular action, resulting in movements that fall short of the intended goals of the affected individual.

hypomobility /-mōbil′itē/, a decrease in the normal movement of a joint or body part, as may result from an articular surface dysfunction or from disease or injury that affects a bone, muscle, or joint.

hypomorph /hī′pōmôrf/ [Gk, *hypo* + *morphe,* form], **1.** a person whose arms and legs are disproportionately short in relation to the trunk and whose sitting height is disproportionately tall compared with the standing height. **2.** a mutant allele that has a reduced effect on the expression of a trait but does not cause abnormal development.

hypomotility /-mōtil′itē/ [Gk, *hypo,* under; L, *motare,* to move frequently], a state of diminished motility or loss of power to move about.

hyponasality /hī′pōnazal′itē/ [Gk, *hypo,* under; L, *nasus,* nose], a speech characteristic caused by insufficient resonance of air in the nasal cavity, so that speakers sound as if they have a cold.

hyponatremia /hī′pōnatrē′mē·ə/ [Gk, *hypo*; L, *natrium,* sodium; Gk, *haima,* blood], a lower-than-normal concentration of sodium in the blood, caused by inadequate excretion of water or by excessive water in the circulating bloodstream. In a severe case the person may experience water intoxication, with confusion and lethargy, leading to muscle excitability, convulsions, and coma.

hypoosmolality [Gk, *hypo* + *osmos,* impulse], a state or condition of abnormally reduced osmolality.

hypoosmotic /hī′pō·ozmot′ik/, pertaining to a solution that has a lower solute concentration than another solution.

hypoosmotic swelling, swelling of sperm in a hypoosmotic solution.

hypoparathyroidism /-per′əthī′roidiz′əm/ [Gk, *hypo* + *para,* beside, *thyreos,* shield, *eidos,* form], a condition of insufficient secretion of the parathyroid glands. It can be caused by primary parathyroid dysfunction or by elevated serum calcium level.

hypoperistalsis /-per′istal′sis/ [Gk, *hypo,* under, *peristellein,* to clasp], a state of abnormally slow motility of waves of alternate contraction and relaxation that impel contents forward through the digestive tract.

hypopharyngeal /-fərin′jē·əl/ [Gk, *hypo* + *pharynx,* throat], **1.** pertaining to the hypopharynx. **2.** situated below the pharynx.

hypopharynx /-fer′ingks/, the inferior portion of the pharynx, between the epiglottis and the larynx. It corresponds to the height of the epiglottis and is a critical dividing point in separating solids and fluids from air entering the region.

hypophonia /-fō′nē·ə/ [Gk, *hypo,* under, *phone,* voice], a weak or whispered voice.

hypophoria /-fôr′ē·ə/, a type of strabismus in which the patient may not show signs of ocular muscle imbalance until the affected eye is covered, resulting in a downward deviation.

hypophosphatasia /hī′pōfos′fətā′zhə/ [Gk, *hypo* + *phosphoros,* lightbearing], congenital absence of alkaline phosphatase, an enzyme essential to the calcification of bone tissue. Complications include vomiting, growth retardation, and often death in infancy. Children who survive have numerous skeletal abnormalities and suffer from dwarfism.

hypophosphatemic rickets /hī′pōfos′fatē′mik/, a rare familial disorder characterized by impaired resorption of phosphate in the kidneys and poor absorption of calcium in the small intestine, which result in osteomalacia, retarded growth, skeletal deformities, and pain.

hypophyseal /-fizē′əl, -fiz′ē·əl/ [Gk, *hypo,* under, *phyein,* to grow], pertaining to the hypophysis.

hypophyseal hormones, pituitary hormones that are associated with body growth and exercise effects, such as luteinizing hormone, growth hormone, and antidiuretic hormone.

hypophyseal portal system, a set of vessels (arteries and capillaries) that carry blood and regulatory hormones from the hypothalamus to the adenohypophysis, where the target cells of the releasing hormones are located.

hypophysectomy /hīpof′əsek′təmē/ [Gk, *hypo* + *phyein*, to grow, *ektomē*, excision], surgical removal of the pituitary gland. It may be performed to slow the growth and spread of endocrine-dependent malignant tumors or to excise a pituitary tumor. The gland is removed only if other treatment, such as x-ray therapy, radioactive implants, or cryosurgery, fails to destroy all pituitary tissue.—**hypophysectomize,** *v.*

hypophyseoprivic /-fiz′ē-ōpriv′ik/ [L, *privus,* deprived], pertaining to a deficiency of hormone secretions by the hypophysis. The condition may be caused by functional inactivity or surgical removal of the gland.

hypophysial fossa, the deep central area of the sella turcica that contains the pituitary gland.

hypophysis /hīpof′isis/ [Gk, *hypo,* under, *phyein,* to grow], the pituitary body (gland). The anterior lobe is sometimes identified as the adenohypophysis and the posterior lobe as the neurohypophysis.

hypopigmentation /-pig′məntā′shən/ [Gk, *hypo*; L, *pigmentum,* paint], unusual lack of skin color, but not complete lack of pigment as seen in albinism.

hypopituitarism /-pityo͞o′iteriz′əm/ [Gk, *hypo*; L, *pituita,* phlegm], an abnormal condition caused by diminished activity of the pituitary gland resulting in decreased secretion of its hormones. The manifestations depend on the hormone(s) and target tissues involved.

hypoplasia /hī′pōplā′zhə/ [Gk, *hypo* + *plassein,* to mold], underdevelopment of an organ or a tissue, usually resulting from the presence of a smaller-than-normal number of cells.—**hypoplastic,** *adj.*

hypoplastic anemia /-plas′tik/, anemias characterized by inadequately functioning bone marrow.

hypoplastic left heart syndrome (HLHS), any of a group of congenital anomalies consisting of hypoplasia or atresia of the left ventricle and of the aortic or mitral valve or both and hypoplasia of the ascending aorta. It is characterized by respiratory distress and extreme cyanosis, with cardiac failure and death in early infancy.

hypoploid /hī′pəploid/ [Gk, *hypo* + *eidos,* form], **1.** an individual, organism, strain, or cell that has fewer than the haploid number or than an exact multiple of the haploid number of chromosomes characteristic of the species. **2.** pertaining to such an individual, organism, strain, or cell. —**hypoploidy,** *n.*

hypoploidy /hī′pōploi′dē/, any decrease in chromosome number that involves individual chromosomes rather than entire sets, so that fewer than the normal haploid

number of chromosomes characteristic of the species are present, as in Turner's syndrome.

hypopnea /hīpop′nē·ə, hī′pōnē′ə/ [Gk, *hypo* + *pnoe,* breath], abnormally shallow and slow respiration. In well-conditioned athletes it may be appropriate. Otherwise it is characteristic of damage to the brainstem.

hypopotassemia /-pot′əsē′mē·ə/ [Gk, *hypo*; D, *potasch,* potash; Gk, *haima,* blood], a deficiency of potassium in the blood.

hypoproliferative anemias /-prolif′ərətiv′/, a group of anemias caused by inadequate production of erythrocytes. The condition is associated with protein deficiencies, renal disease, and myxedema.

hypoproteinemia /hī′pōprō′tēnē′mē·ə/ [Gk, *hypo* + *proteios,* first rank, *haima,* blood], abnormally decreased plasma protein, accompanied by edema, nausea, vomiting, diarrhea, and abdominal pain. It may be caused by renal failure and burns.

hypoprothrombinemia /hī′pōprōthrom′bi nē′mē·ə/ [Gk, *hypo*; L, *pro,* before; Gk, *thrombos,* lump, *haima,* blood], abnormally reduced plasma prothrombin, characterized by bleeding, poor clot formation, prolonged prothrombin and partial thromboplastin times. Usually caused by inadequate synthesis of prothrombin in the liver or vitamin K deficiency or most often by anticoagulant therapy.

hypopyon /hīpō′pē·on/ [Gk, *hypo* + *pyon,* pus], the presence of leukocytes and an accumulation of pus in the anterior chamber of an eye, which appears as a whitish or gray fluid between the cornea and the iris. It may occur as a complication of a penetrating wound to the eye, conjunctivitis, herpetic keratitis, or corneal ulcer.

hyporeflexia /-riflek′sē·ə/ [Gk, *hypo*; L, *reflectere,* to bend back], decreased reflex reactions.

hyposalivation /-sal′ivā′shən/ [Gk, *hypo*; L, *saliva,* spittle], a decreased flow of saliva associated with dehydration, radiation therapy of the salivary gland regions, anxiety, menopause, the use of drugs such as atropine and antihistamines, vitamin deficiency, inflammation or infection of the salivary glands, or various syndromes.

hyposensitization, a form of immunotherapy that can either reduce or eliminate hypersensitivity.

hypospadias /hī′pōspā′dē·əs/ [Gk, *hypo,* under, *spadōn,* a rent], a developmental anomaly in the male in which the urethra opens on the underside of the penis or on the perineum.

hypospermatogenesis /hī′pōspər′matojen′ə sis/, abnormally decreased production of spermatozoa.

H

hypostatic /-stat′ik/ [Gk, *hypo* + *stasis,* standing still], pertaining to an accumulation of deposits of substances or congestion in a body area that results from a lack of activity.

hypostatic lung collapse [Gk, *hypo,* under, *stasis,* standing still; AS, *lungen;* L, *collabi,* to fall together], a disorder in which fluids or suspended solids pool or settle in a part of the lung, resulting in congestion.

hypostatic pneumonia, a type of pneumonia in which fluids tend to settle in one area of the lungs, increasing the susceptibility to infection.

hyposthenic /hī′pōsthen′ik/, **1.** pertaining to a lack of strength or muscle tone. **2.** a body type characterized by a slender build.

hypotelorism /hī′pōtel′əriz′əm/ [Gk, *hypo* + *tele,* far, *horizo,* separate], a developmental defect characterized by an abnormally decreased distance between two organs or parts.

hypotension /-ten′shən/ [Gk, *hypo;* L, *tendere,* to stretch], an abnormal condition in which the BP is not adequate for normal perfusion and oxygenation of the tissues. An expanded intravascular space, hypovolemia, or diminished cardiac output may be the cause.

hypotensive /-ten′siv/ [Gk, *hypo,* under; L, *tendere,* to stretch], pertaining to abnormally low BP.

hypothalamic amenorrhea /-thalam′ik/ [Gk, *hypo* + *thalamos,* chamber], cessation of menses caused by disorders that inhibit the hypothalamus from initiating the cycle of neurohormonal interactions of the brain, pituitary, and ovary necessary for ovulation and subsequent menstruation.

hypothalamic hormones, a group of hormones secreted by the hypothalamus, including vasopressin, oxytocin, and releasing and inhibitory hormones that act on the anterior pituitary.

hypothalamic obesity [Gk, *hypo,* under, *thalamos,* chamber; L, *obesitas,* fatness], obesity caused by damage or a functional disturbance involving the hypothalamus.

hypothalamic-pituitary-adrenal axis, the combined system of neuroendocrine units that in a negative feedback network regulates the adrenal gland's hormonal activities.

hypothalamus /hī′pōthal′əməs/ [Gk, *hypo* + *thalamos,* chamber], a part of the diencephalon of the brain, forming the floor and part of the lateral wall of the third ventricle. It activates, controls, and integrates the peripheral autonomic nervous system, endocrine processes, and many somatic functions, such as body temperature, sleep, and appetite.—**hypothalamic,** *adj.*

hypothenar eminence /hīpoth′ənär, hī′pōthē′när/ [Gk, *hypo* + *thenar,* palm], a fleshy pad on the ulnar side of the palm of the hand.

hypothermal /-thur′məl/ [Gk, *hypo,* under, *therme,* heat], **1.** pertaining to a condition in which the body temperature is significantly below normal as a result of external exposure to cold or has been reduced markedly for surgical or therapeutic purposes. **2.** pertaining to temperatures that are tepid to slightly warm.

hypothermia /hī′pōthur′mē·ə/ [Gk, *hypo* + *therme,* heat], **1.** an abnormal and dangerous condition in which the temperature of the body is below 95° F (35° C), usually caused by prolonged exposure to cold and/or damp conditions. Respiration is shallow and slow, and the heart rate is faint and slow. The person may appear to be dead. **2.** the deliberate and controlled reduction of body temperature with cooling mattresses or ice as preparation for some surgical procedures.

hypothermia blanket, a covering or pad used to lower the body temperature to decrease metabolism and oxygen consumption during a surgical procedure.

hypothermia induction, a nursing intervention from the Nursing Interventions Classification (NIC) defined as attaining and maintaining core body temperature below 35° C and monitoring for side effects and/or prevention of complications.

hypothermia therapy, the reduction of a patient's body temperature to counteract high prolonged fever caused by an infectious or neurologic disease or, less frequently, as an adjunct to anesthesia in heart or brain surgery.

hypothermia treatment, a nursing intervention from the Nursing Interventions Classification (NIC) defined as rewarming and surveillance of a patient whose core body temperature is below 35° C.

hypothesis /hīpoth′isis/ [Gk, groundwork], in research, a statement derived from a theory that predicts the relationship among variables representing concepts, constructs, or events.

hypothyroid /-thī′roid/ [Gk, *hypo,* under, *thyreos,* shield, *eidos,* form], pertaining to or resembling thyroid deficiency.

hypothyroidism /-thī′roidiz′əm/ [Gk, *hypo* + *thyreos,* shield, *eidos,* form], a condition characterized by decreased activity of the thyroid gland. It may be caused by surgical removal of all or part of the gland, overdosage with antithyroid medication, decreased effect of thyroid-releasing hormone secreted by the hypothalamus, decreased secretion of TSH by the pituitary gland, atrophy of the thyroid gland itself, or peripheral resistance to thyroid hormone. Manifestations include weight gain; cold, pale, dry, rough hands and feet; reduced attention span with memory impairment, slowed speech, and loss of initiative; swelling in the extremities and around the eyes, eyelids, and face; menstrual irregularities; muscle aches and weakness; joint aches and stiffness; clumsiness; hyperstiff reflexes; decreased pulse; decreased BP; agitation; depression; and paranoia.

hypotonia /-tŏ′nē·ə/ [Gk, *hypo,* under, *tonos,* stretching], a condition of diminished tone or tension that may involve any body structure.

hypotonic /hī′pŏtŏn′ik/ [Gk, *hypo,* under, *tonos,* stretching], **1.** pertaining to a lower or lessened tone or tension in any body structure, as in paralysis. **2.** a solution having a lower concentration of solute than another solution, hence exerting less osmotic pressure than that solution. **3.** pertaining to a solution that causes cells to swell.

hypotonic saline [Gk, *hypo,* under, *tonos,* tone; L, *sal,* salt], a saline solution that is less than isotonic in strength.

hypoventilation /-ven′tilā′shən/ [Gk, *hypo;* L, *ventilare,* to fan], an abnormal condition of the respiratory system that occurs when the volume of air that enters the alveoli and takes part in gas exchange is not adequate for the body's metabolic needs. It is characterized by cyanosis, polycythemia, increased $PaCO_2$, and generalized decreased respiratory function. The results of hypoventilation are hypoxia, hypercapnia, pulmonary hypertension with cor pulmonale, and respiratory acidosis.

hypovolemia /-vōlē′mē·ə/ [Gk, *hypo;* L, *volumen,* whirl; Gk, *haima,* blood], an abnormally low circulating blood volume.—**hypovolemic,** *adj.*

hypovolemia management, a nursing intervention from the Nursing Interventions Classification (NIC) defined as expansion of intravascular fluid volume in a patient who is volume-depleted.

hypovolemic shock /-vōlēmik/, a state of physical collapse and prostration caused by massive blood loss, about one fifth or more of total blood volume. The common signs include low BP, thready pulse, clammy skin, tachycardia, rapid breathing, and reduced urinary output. The associated blood losses may stem from GI bleeding, internal or external hemorrhage, or excessive reduction of intravascular plasma volume and body fluids. Disorders that may cause hypovolemic shock are dehydration from excessive perspiration, severe diarrhea, protracted vomiting, intestinal obstruction, peritonitis, acute pancreatitis, and severe burns, which deplete body fluids.

hypoxemia /hī′poksē′mē·ə/ [Gk, *hypo + oxys,* sharp, *genein,* to produce, *haima,* blood], an abnormal deficiency in the concentration of oxygen in arterial blood. Symptoms of acute hypoxemia are cyanosis, restlessness, stupor, coma, Cheyne-Stokes respiration, apnea, increased BP, tachycardia, and an initial increase in cardiac output that later falls, producing hypotension and ventricular fibrillation or asystole. Chronic hypoxemia stimulates RBC production by the bone marrow, leading to secondary polycythemia.

hypoxia /hīpok′sē·ə/ [Gk, *hypo + oxys,* sharp, *genein,* to produce], inadequate oxygen tension at the cellular level, characterized by tachycardia, hypertension, peripheral vasoconstriction, dizziness, and mental confusion. The tissues most sensitive to hypoxia are the brain, heart, pulmonary vessels, and liver.

hypoxic drive /-hīpok′sik/, stimulation of respiration by low PaO_2, mediated through the carotid and aortic bodies.

hypsibrachycephaly /hips′ibrakisef′əlē/ [Gk, *hypsi,* high, *brachys,* short, *kephale,* head], the condition of having a skull that is high with a broad forehead.—**hypsibrachycephalic,** *adj., n.*

hysterectomy /his′tərek′təmē/ [Gk, *hystera,* womb, *ektomē,* excision], surgical removal of the uterus, performed to remove fibroid tumors of the uterus or to treat chronic PID, severe recurrent endometrial hyperplasia, uterine hemorrhage, and precancerous and cancerous conditions of the uterus. Types of hysterectomy include total hysterectomy, in which the uterus and cervix are removed, and radical hysterectomy, in which ovaries, oviducts, lymph nodes, and lymph channels are removed with the uterus and cervix.—**hysterectomize,** *v.*

hysteresis /his′tərē′sis/ [Gk, *hysterein,* to be late], **1.** a lagging or retardation of one of two associated phenomena or a failure to act in unison. **2.** the influence of the previous condition or treatment of the body on its subsequent response to a given force.

hysteria /histir′ē·ə/ [Gk, *hystera,* womb], a general state of tension or excitement in a person or a group, characterized by unmanageable fear and temporary loss of control over the emotions.

hysteric /hister′ik/ [Gk, *hystera,* womb], pertaining to or resembling hysteria.

hysteric amaurosis [Gk, *hystera + amauroein,* to darken], monocular or, more rarely, binocular blindness that follows an emotional shock. It may last for hours, days, or months.

hysteric ataxia [Gk, *hystera,* womb, *ataxia,* without order], a loss of control over voluntary movements in walking or standing although the involved muscles function normally when the person is lying or sitting.

hysteric chorea [Gk, *hystera,* womb, *choreia,* dance], a condition in which an individual has choreiform movements, although the actions are psychogenic rather than the result of true chorea.

hysteric convulsion, a violent involuntary contraction and relaxation of the skeletal muscles marked by spasmodic muscular contractions with no organic cause.

hysteric dyspepsia, difficulty in digestion caused by emotional disturbances.

hysteric lethargy [Gk, *hystera* + *lethargia,* drowsiness], a sleep induced by hypnosis.

hysteric paralysis [Gk, *hystera,* womb, *paralyein,* to be palsied], a loss of movement or muscular weakness that is psychogenic rather than the result of an identifiable organic defect.

hysteric syncope, a temporary LOC or a fainting spell caused by emotional agitation.

hysteric tremor [Gk, *hystera,* womb; L, *tremere,* to tremble], **1.** a fine, rhythmic shaking in one extremity or of a generalized nature that may be an expression of fear, anxiety, or hysteria. **2.** a coarse irregular shaking that increases with voluntary movements. **3.** a shaking that is transient and caused by exposure to drugs or toxic substances rather than an organic disorder.

hysteric vertigo, a giddiness or loss of stability, often with a sensation of rotation, with no organic cause.

hysterogram /his′tərōgram′/ [Gk, *hystera* + *gramma,* record], a radiographic image of a uterus made after the injection of a contrast medium into the uterine cavity.

hysterography /his′tərog′rəfē/ [Gk, *hystera,* womb, *graphein,* to record], the use of x-ray film and other instruments to make a medical assessment of the condition of the uterus.

hysterolaparotomy /his′tərōlap′ərot′əmē/ [Gk, *hystera* + *lapara,* loin, *temnein,* to cut], abdominal hysterectomy or hysterotomy.

hystero-oophorectomy /-ō′əfərek′təmē/ [Gk, *hystera,* womb, *oophoron,* ovary, *ektomē,* excision], the surgical removal of the uterus and both ovaries.

hysterosalpingogram /his′tərō′salping′gō gram′/ [Gk, *hystera* + *salpinx,* tube, *gramma,* record], an x-ray film of the uterus and the fallopian tubes using gas or a radiopaque substance introduced through the cervix to allow visualization of the cavity of the uterus and the passageway of the tubes.

hysterosalpingography /his′tərōsal′ping· gog′rəfē/, a method of producing radiographic images of the uterus and fallopian tubes as part of the diagnosis of abnormalities in the reproductive tract of a nonpregnant woman.

hysterosalpingo-oophorectomy /-salping′ gō-ō′əfərek′təmē/ [Gk, *hystera* + *salpinx,* tube, *oophoron,* ovary, *ektomē,* excision], surgical removal of one or both ovaries and oviducts along with the uterus, performed commonly to treat malignant neoplastic disease of the reproductive tract and chronic endometriosis. To prevent the severe symptoms of sudden menopause in premenopausal women, a portion of one ovary is left, unless a malignancy is present.

hysteroscope /his′tərōskōp′/ [Gk, *hystera,* womb, *skopein,* to look to view], an endoscope used in direct visual examination of the canal of the uterine cervix and the cavity of the uterus.

hysteroscopy /his′təros′kepē/ [Gk, *hystera* + *skopein,* to look], direct visual inspection of the cervical canal and uterine cavity through a hysteroscope. Hysteroscopy is performed to examine the endometrium, to secure a specimen for biopsy, to remove an IUD, or to excise cervical polyps. —**hysteroscope,** *n.,* **hysteroscopic,** *adj.*

hysterotome /his′tərotōm′/ [Gk, *hystera,* womb, *temnein,* to cut], a surgical knife used for certain procedures involving the uterus.

hysterotomy /his′tərot′əmē/ [Gk, *hystera* + *temnein,* to cut], surgical incision of the uterus, performed as a method of abortion in a pregnancy beyond the first trimester of gestation in which a saline injection abortion was incomplete or in which a tubal sterilization is to be done with the abortion.

hysterovaginoenterocele /-vaj′inō-en′tər ōsēl′/ [Gk, *hystera,* womb; L, *vagina,* sheath; Gk, *enteron,* bowel, *kele,* hernia], a hernia involving the uterus, vagina, and intestines.

Hytone, a trademark for a glucocorticoid (hydrocortisone).

Hz, abbreviation for **hertz.**

HZV, abbreviation for **herpes zoster virus.**

I, 1. symbol for *inspired gas.* 2. symbol for the element **iodine.**

131I, symbol for *radioactive iodine, isotopic (atomic) mass 131.*

132I, symbol for *radioactive iodine, isotopic (atomic) mass 132.*

IABC, abbreviation for **intraaortic balloon counterpulsation.**

IABP, abbreviation for **intraaortic balloon pump.**

IADL, abbreviation for **instrumental activities of daily living.**

IADR, abbreviation for **International Association for Dental Research.**

IAH, abbreviation for **idiopathic diffuse alveolar hemorrhage.**

I & O, abbreviation for *intake and output.*

iatrogenic /ī′atrōjen′ik, yat-/ [Gk, *iatros,* physician, *genein,* to produce], caused by treatment or diagnostic procedures. —**iatrogenesis, iatrogeny,** *n.*

iatrogenic diabetes mellitus, a form of diabetes that develops as an adverse effect of treatment for a different medical problem.

iatrogenic pneumothorax, a condition in which air or gas is present in the pleural cavity as a result of mechanical ventilation, tracheostomy tube placement, or other therapeutic intervention.

iatrology, the science of medicine.

iatropic /ī′atrop′ik/ [Gk, *iatros,* physician, *trepein,* to turn], describing a need to see a physician.

iatropic stimulus, the symptoms that induce a patient to seek professional health care.

I band [ME, *band,* flat strip], an isotropic band within a striated muscle fiber that appears dark in polarized light but light when stained.

ibandronate, a bone-resorption inhibitor and electrolyte modifier used to prevent and treat osteoporosis.

IBC, abbreviation for **iron-binding capacity.**

IBD, abbreviation for *inflammatory bowel disease.*

ibritumomab tiuxetan, an immunoconjugate of ibritumomab and the linker-chelator tiuxetan. It is used as part of a regimen for non-Hodgkin's lymphoma in conjunction with the monoclonal antibody rituximab and the radiopharmaceuticals indium-111 and yttrium-90.

IBS, abbreviation for **irritable bowel syndrome.**

ibuprofen /ī′byōō′prōfin/, a COX-1 OTC nonsteroidal antiinflammatory agent used for the treatment of fever, headaches, and pain from rheumatoid arthritis and osteoarthritis, muscle aches, and menstrual cramps.

ibutilide /ību′tilīd/, a cardiac depressant used in treatment of atrial arrhythmias, administered by IV infusion as the fumarate salt.

ibutilide fumarate, a drug used to treat heart arrhythmias. It is prescribed in an effort to convert atrial fibrillation and atrial flutter of recent onset to normal sinus rhythm.

IC, 1. abbreviation for **inspiratory capacity.** 2. abbreviation for **interstitial cystitis.**

ICA, abbreviation for **islet cell antibody.**

ICD, abbreviation for **implantable cardioverter-defibrillator.**

ICD, abbreviation for *International Classification of Diseases.*

ice burn, partial-thickness thermal necrosis of the skin caused by prolonged therapy entailing applications of ice.

Iceland disease /īs′land/, a group of symptoms associated with effects of a viral infection of the nervous system, including muscular pain and weakness, depression, and sensory changes.

Iceland moss, *Cetraria islandica,* a lichen native to Iceland.

I-cell disease, a form of lysosomal disease characterized by progressive mental deterioration, heart disease, and respiratory failure in the first 10 years of life. A number of lysosomal enzymes are lacking and fibroblasts display numerous coarse inclusions.

ice pack [ME, *is + pakke*], a container of crushed ice placed on the body to reduce tissue temperature, relieve pain, soothe inflamed tissue, or control bleeding.

ICF, 1. abbreviation for **intermediate care facility.** 2. abbreviation for **intracellular fluid.**

ICF/MR, abbreviation for *intermediate care facility for the mentally retarded.*

ICH, abbreviation for **intracerebral hemorrhage.**

ichor /ī′kôr/, a thin, watery fluid discharged from a sore.

ichthyoid /ik′thē·oid/ [Gk, *ichthys,* fish, *eidos,* form], pertaining to objects or structures that are fish-shaped or fishlike.

ichthyosis /ik′thē·ō′sis/ [Gk, *ichthys,* fish, *osis,* condition], any of several inherited dermatologic conditions in which the skin is dry and hyperkeratotic, resembling fish scales. It usually appears at or shortly after birth and may be part of one of several rare syndromes.—**ichthyotic,** *adj.*

ichthyosis hystrix [Gk, *ichthys,* fish, *osis,* condition, *hystrix,* porcupine], a localized form of epidermolytic hyperkeratosis having the appearance of linear epidermal nevi.

ichthyosis vulgaris [Gk, *ichthys* + *osis,* L *vulgaris,* common], a hereditary skin disorder characterized by large, dry dark scales that cover the face, neck, scalp, ears, back, and extensor surfaces but not the flexor surfaces of the body.

ICN, abbreviation for **International Council of Nurses.**

icon /ī′kon/, an image on the screen of a computer terminal representing a specific command or point for data entry.

ICP, abbreviation for **intracranial pressure.**

ICSH, abbreviation for *interstitial cell–stimulating hormone.*

ICSI, abbreviation for *intracytoplasmic sperm injection.*

ictal /ik′təl/ [Gk, *ikteros,* jaundice], pertaining to a sudden acute onset, as convulsions of an epileptic seizure.

icteric /ikter′ik/ [Gk, *ikteros,* jaundice], pertaining to or resembling jaundice.

icterogenic /ik′tərōjen′ik/, causing jaundice.

icterus gravis neonatorum /ik′tərəs/ [Gk, *ikteros,* jaundice; L, *gravis,* weight, *neonatus,* newborn], a hemolytic jaundice of the newborn caused by incompatibility between the mother's serum and the infant's red corpuscles.

icterus neonatorum, a jaundiced condition in a newborn.

ictus /ik′təs/ *pl.* **ictuses, ictus** [L, stroke], **1.** a seizure. **2.** a cerebrovascular accident.—**ictal, ictic,** *adj.*

ICU, abbreviation for **intensive care unit.**

id [L, it], **1.** in freudian psychoanalysis, the part of the psyche functioning in the unconscious that is the source of instinctive energy, impulses, and drives. **2.** the true unconscious.

ID, abbreviation for **infectious disease.**

idarubicin, an antibiotic and antineoplastic used in combination with other antineoplastics for acute myelocytic leukemia in adults.

IDDM, abbreviation for *insulin-dependent diabetes mellitus.*

idea [Gk, form], any thought, concept, intention, or impression that exists in the mind as a result of awareness, understanding, or other mental activity.

ideal body weight (IBW), the weight statistically determined on actuarial tables to be associated with the lowest mortality for an average individual, adjusting for some combination of height, age, frame size, and gender.

ideal gas law /īdē′əl/ [Gk, *idea,* form, *chaos,* gas; AS, *lagu,* law], the rule that $PV = nRT$, with the product of pressure (P) and volume (V) equal to the product of the number of moles of gas (n), absolute temperature (T), and a gas constant (R).

idealized image /īdē′əlīzd/, a concept of a person characterized by a sense of perfection and admiration. It results in unrealistically high and unattainable goals.

idea of influence, an idea held less firmly than a delusion, often seen in paranoid disorders, that external forces or persons are controlling one's thoughts, actions, and feelings.

idea of persecution, an idea held less firmly than a delusion, often seen in paranoid disorders, that one is being threatened, discriminated against, or mistreated by other persons or external forces.

idea of reference, a delusion that the statements, events, or actions of others, usually interpreted as deprecatory, refer to oneself. It is often seen in paranoid disorders.

ideational apraxia /ī′dē·ā′shənəl/ [Gk, *idea,* form, *a* + *prassein,* not to do], a condition in which the conceptual process is lost, often because of a lesion in the submarginal gyrus of the parietal lobe. The individual is unable to formulate a plan of movement and does not know the proper use of an object because of a lack of perception of its purpose.

identification /īden′tifikā′shən/ [L, *idem,* the same, *facere,* to make], an unconscious defense mechanism by which a person patterns his or her personality on that of another person, assuming the person's qualities, characteristics, and actions. The process is a normal function of personality development and learning.

identity[1] /īden′titē/, a component of self-concept characterized by one's persisting consciousness of being oneself, separate and distinct from others. Identity diffusion, or identity confusion, is a lack of clarity and consistency in one's perception of the self, which produces a high degree of anxiety.

identity[2], a nursing outcome from the Nursing Outcomes Classification (NOC) defined as: distinguishes between self and nonself and characterizes one's essence.

identity crisis [L, *idem,* the same; Gk, *krisis,* turning point], a period of confusion concerning an individual's sense of self and role in society, which occurs most frequently in the transition from one stage of life to the next. It is often expressed by isolation, negativism, extremism, and rebelliousness.

identity disorder of childhood, a mental disturbance of childhood in which the person is abnormally uncertain and concerned about long-term goals such as career choice or sexual preference.

ideology /ī′de·ol′əjē/ [Gk, *idea*], a scheme of ideas or systematic organization of ideas associated with doctrine and philosophy.

ideomotor apraxia /īdē′əmō′tor/ [Gk, *idea*; L, *motare,* to move about; Gk, *a + prassein,* not to do], the inability to translate an idea into motion, resulting from some interference with the transmission of the appropriate impulses from the brain to the motor centers. There is no loss of the ability to perform an action automatically, such as tying the shoelaces, but the action cannot be performed on request.

ideophobia /-fō′bē·ə/ [Gk, *idea + phobos,* fear], an anxiety disorder characterized by the irrational fear or distrust of ideas or reason.

idiogram /id′ē·əgram′/, a diagram or graphic representation of a karyotype, showing the number, relative sizes, and morphologic characteristics of the chromosomes of a species, individual, or cell.

idiojunctional rhythm /-jungk′shənəl/ [Gk, *idios,* own; L, *jungere,* to join; Gk, *rhythmos*], a heart rhythm emanating from the junction of the atrioventricular (AV) node and the AV bundle but without retrograde conduction to the atria.

idiopathic (diffuse) alveolar hemorrhage (IAH), bleeding into the alveoli of the lungs caused by any of a number of disorders.

idiopathic disease, a disease that develops without an apparent or known cause, although it may have a recognizable pattern of signs and symptoms and may be curable.

idiopathic edema, edema of unknown cause, usually affecting women, occurring intermittently over a period of years, and usually worse during the premenstrual phase. It is associated with increased aldosterone secretion.

idiopathic gangrene [Gk, *idios,* own, *pathos,* disease + *gaggraina*], a gangrenous condition of unknown cause.

idiopathic guttate hypomelanosis /hī′pō mel′ənō′sis/, one or many drop-shaped hypopigmented macules of unknown origin.

idiopathic hemosiderosis, the accumulation of iron-containing deposits in cells of the lungs as a result of bleeding in the lungs.

idiopathic hypercalciuria, elevated urine calcium of unknown cause, often with formation of renal calculi.

idiopathic hypoventilation, a disorder of unknown cause associated with deficient ventilation of the alveoli of the lungs.

idiopathic midline destructive disease (IMDD), a disorder of unknown cause characterized by ulceration and necrosis of the midline facial tissues and obstruction of the upper airways.

idiopathic necrotizing crescentic glomerulonephritis, an autoimmune disorder that causes intracapsular hemorrhage and cellular crescent formation in the renal glomerulus.

idiopathic nephrotic syndrome [Gk, *idios,* own, *pathos,* disease, *nephros,* kidney], a kidney disease of unknown origin characterized by hematuria, albuminuria, edema, and hypertension resulting from damaged glomerular capillaries.

idiopathic neuralgia [Gk, *idios,* own, *pathos,* disease, *neuron,* nerve, *algos,* pain], a form of neuralgia that occurs without any identifiable structural nerve lesion.

idiopathic pericarditis [Gk, *idios,* own, *pathos,* disease, *peri,* near, *kardia,* heart, *itis,* inflammation], inflammation of the pericardium of unknown cause.

idiopathic postpartum renal failure, kidney failure that begins 1 day to several weeks after delivery that follows an uneventful gestation. Symptoms include oliguria or anuria, which progresses to azotemia, with complications of hemolytic anemia or coagulopathy.

idiopathic pulmonary fibrosis [Gk, *idios,* own, *pathos,* disease; L, *pulmoneus,* of the lungs, *fibra,* fiber], a disorder of unknown cause characterized by fibrosis of the lungs. It may follow an earlier inflammation or disease, such as TB or pneumoconiosis.

idiopathic pulmonary hemorrhage, bleeding in the lungs without a known cause. It may be a cause of secondary spontaneous pneumothorax.

idiopathic reactive hypoglycemia, a condition of diminished blood glucose level that occurs after the ingestion of carbohydrates and has no known cause. It is controversial as to whether this is a real disease.

idiopathic scoliosis, an abnormal condition characterized by a lateral curvature of the spine. The main factors in diagnosing idiopathic scoliosis are the degree, balance, and rotational component of the curvature. The rotational component may contribute to rib cage deformities and impingement on the pulmonary and cardiac systems. The signs commonly associated with scoliosis include unlevel shoulders, a prominent scapula, a prominent breast, a prominent flank area, an unlevel or prominent hip, poor posture, and an obvious curvature.

I

Neurologic deficits are commonly associated with severe curvature and vary according to the extent to which the curvature has impinged on the spinal cord.

idiopathic steatorrhea [Gk, *idios*, own, *pathos*, disease, *stear*, fat, *rhoia*, flow], excess fat in the stools, particularly as in celiac disease in adults.

idiopathic tetanus [Gk, *idios*, own, *pathos*, disease, *tetanos*, convulsive tension], **1.** a tetanus infection of unknown cause. **2.** a tetanus infection occurring without a wound.

idiopathic ventricular tachycardia, an accelerated heart rhythm (greater than 100 beats/min) that originates in a focus within a ventricle but is of unknown cause.

idiopathy /id′ē·op′əthē/, any primary disease that arises without an apparent cause. —**idiopathic,** *adj.*

idiosyncrasy /-sin′krəsē/ [Gk, *idios* + *synkrasis*, mixing together], **1.** a physical or behavioral characteristic or manner that is unique to an individual or a group. **2.** an individual's unique hypersensitivity to a particular drug, food, or other substance. —**idiosyncratic,** *adj.*

idiosyncratic drug effect [Gk, *idios*, own, *sygkrasis*, mixing together; Fr, *drogue*], an uncommon response to a drug because of a genetic predisposition.

idiotope /id′ē·ətōp′/, an antigenic determinant on a variable region of an immunoglobulin molecule.

idiotrophic /-trof′ik/, describing an organism capable of choosing its own food.

idiot savant /idē·ō′ savänt′/, an individual with mental retardation who is nonetheless capable of performing certain unusual mental feats, primarily those involving music, puzzle solving, or manipulation of numbers.

idiotype /id′ē·ətīp′/ [Gk, *idios* + *typos*, mark], the portion of an immunoglobulin molecule that confers the molecule's unique character, most often including its antigen-binding site.

idioventricular /-ventrik′yələr/ [Gk, *idios*; L, *ventriculus*, little belly], originating in a ventricle.

idioventricular rhythm [Gk, *idios*, own; L, *ventriculus*, little belly; Gk, *rhythmos*], an independent cardiac rhythm caused by a repeated discharge of impulses at a rate of less than 100 beats/min from a focus within a ventricle.

IDL, abbreviation for **intermediate-density lipoprotein.**

IDM, abbreviation for *infant of a diabetic mother.*

idoxuridine /ī′doksyŏŏr′ədēn/, an ophthalmic antiviral prescribed for the treatment of herpes simplex keratitis.

id reaction, the autosensitization resulting from any inflammatory condition that causes pruritus and vesicular lesions. These secondary lesions are caused by circulating antigens and are usually distant from the primary infection.

IDSA, abbreviation for *Infectious Disease Society of America.*

idursulfase, a rarely used enzyme replacement used to treat mucopolysaccharidosis II.

I:E ratio, the ratio of the duration of inspiration to the duration of expiration. A range of 1:1.5 to 1:2 for an adult is considered acceptable for mechanical ventilation.

ifosfamide, an antineoplastic alkylating agent used to treat testicular cancer, soft tissue sarcoma, Ewing's sarcoma, non-Hodgkin's lymphoma, lung sarcoma, and pancreatic sarcoma.

Ig, abbreviation for **immunoglobulin.**

IgA, abbreviation for **immunoglobulins A, D, E, G,** and **M.**

IgA deficiency, a selective lack of IgA, a major antibody in the saliva and in the mucous membranes of the intestines and the bronchi. It protects against bacterial and viral infections. IgA deficiency is inherited and is associated with autoimmune abnormalities. It is common in patients with rheumatoid arthritis and in those with SLE. Common symptoms are respiratory allergies associated with chronic sinopulmonary infection, GI diseases, autoimmune diseases, and malignant tumors.

IgD, abbreviation for **immunoglobulin D.**

IgE, abbreviation for **immunoglobulin E.**

IGF, abbreviation for **insulin-like growth factor.**

IgG, abbreviation for **immunoglobulin G.**

IgM, abbreviation for **immunoglobulin M.**

ignipeditis /ig′nēpedī′tis/ [L, *ignis*, fire, *pes*, foot], a burning pain in the soles of the feet caused by peripheral neuritis.

IGT, abbreviation for **impaired glucose tolerance.**

I.H., abbreviation for **infectious hepatitis.**

IL-1, abbreviation for **interleukin-1.**

IL-2, abbreviation for **interleukin-2.**

IL-3, abbreviation for **interleukin-3.**

IL-4, abbreviation for **interleukin-4.**

IL-5, abbreviation for **interleukin-5.**

IL-6, abbreviation for **interleukin-6.**

IL-7, abbreviation for **interleukin-7.**

IL-8, abbreviation for **interleukin-8.**

IL-9, abbreviation for **interleukin-9.**

IL-10, abbreviation for **interleukin-10.**

IL-11, abbreviation for **interleukin-11.**

IL-12, abbreviation for **interleukin-12.**

IL-13, abbreviation for **interleukin-13.**

IL-14, abbreviation for **interleukin-14.**

IL-15, abbreviation for **interleukin-15.**

ILD, abbreviation for **interstitial lung disease.**

Ile, abbreviation for **isoleucine.**

ileal atresia, atresia of the ileum, the most common type of intestinal atresia.

ileal bypass /ilʹē·əl/ [L, *ileum,* intestine; AS, *bi,* near; Fr, *passer*], a surgical procedure for treating obesity by anastomosing the upper portion of the small intestine to a more distal segment of the small intestine, thereby bypassing much of the length of the ileum that normally absorbs nutrients.

ileal conduit [Fr, *conduire,* to guide], a method of urinary diversion using intestinal tissue. The ureters are implanted in a section of dissected ileum. This section is sutured closed on one end. The other end is drawn through the abdominal wall (right lower quadrant) to create a stoma. The patient wears a pouch to collect the urine.

ileal intussusception, intussusception involving two segments of the ileum.

ileal neobladder, a neobladder made from a section of ileum.

ileectomy /ilʹē·ekʹtəmē/, surgical removal of the ileum.

ileitis /ilʹē·īʹtis/ [L, *ileum,* intestine; Gk, *itis*], inflammation of the ileum.

ileoanal /ilʹē·ō·āʹnal/, pertaining to or connecting the ileum and the anus.

ileoanal anastomosis /ilʹē·ō·āʹnal/, a surgical procedure in which the colon and rectum are removed but the anus and anal sphincter are left intact. An anastomosis is formed between the lower end of the small intestine and the anus.

ileoanal reservoir, a pouch for the collection of feces, created surgically in a two-stage operation. The first stage involves removal of the rectal mucosa, an abdominal colectomy, and construction of a fecal reservoir from loops of ileum. A temporary ileostomy is created at this time to allow the ileoanal reservoir to heal. Several months later the ileostomy is closed so that discharge of feces through the anus is possible.

ileocecal /ilʹē·ōsēʹkəl/ [L, *ileum,* intestine, *caecus,* blind], pertaining to both the ileum and the cecum and the region where they are joined.

ileocecal fold, two flaps surrounding the opening of the ileum into the large intestine where the cecum and ascending colon join together. The flaps project into the lumen of the large intestine and come together at their end, forming ridges. Musculature from the ileum continues into each flap, forming a sphincter. Possible functions of the ileocecal fold include preventing reflux from the cecum to the ileum and regulating the passage of contents from the ileum to the cecum.

ileocecal intussusception, intussusception at the ileocecal junction, with the cecum being drawn back into the ileum.

ileocecal lip of ileal orifice, the inferior of the two lips forming the ileal orifice.

ileocecal orifice, ostium ileale.

ileocecal valve [L, *ileum,* intestine, *caecus,* blind, *valvarum,* folding door], the sphincter muscle between the ileum of the small intestine and the cecum of the large intestine. It consists of two flaps that project into the lumen of the large intestine, immediately above the vermiform appendix, preventing food from reentering the small intestine.

ileocecocystoplasty /ilʹē·ōseʹkosisʹtəplasʹtē/, augmentation cystoplasty using an isolated segment of the ileum and cecum for the graft.

ileocolic intussusception, intussusception at the ileocecal junction, with the distal ileum being drawn forward into the colon.

ileocolic lip of ileal orifice, the superior of the two lips forming the ileal orifice.

ileocolic node /ilʹē·ōkolʹik/ [L, *ileum;* Gk, *kolon,* colon; L, *nodus,* knot], a node in one of three groups of superior mesenteric lymph glands, forming a chain of approximately 15 nodes around the ileocolic (mesenteric) artery.

ileocolitis /-kōlīʹtis/, an inflammation of the ileum and colon.

ileocystoplasty /-sisʹtəplasʹtē/ [L, *ileum;* Gk, *kystis,* bag, *plassein,* to mold], a surgical procedure in which the bladder is reconstructed by using a segment of the ileum for the bladder wall.

ileocystostomy /-sistosʹtəmē/ [L, *ileum;* intestine; Gk, *kystis,* bag, *stoma,* mouth], a surgical procedure to form a passage to direct urine through the abdominal wall by using a segment of small intestine as a tube from the bladder.

ileorectal /-rekʹtəl/, pertaining to the ileum and rectum.

ileosigmoid knotting, a severe type of volvulus consisting of twisting together of the ileum and the sigmoid colon.

ileosigmoidostomy /-sigʹmoidosʹtəmē/, surgical formation of a passageway between the ileum and the sigmoid colon.

ileostomate /ilʹē·osʹtəmāt/, a person who has undergone an ileostomy.

ileostomy /ilʹē·osʹtəmē/ [L, *ileum;* Gk, *stoma,* mouth, *temnein,* to cut], surgical formation of an opening of the ileum onto the surface of the abdomen, through which fecal matter is emptied. The operation is performed in advanced or recurrent ulcerative colitis, Crohn's disease, or cancer of the large bowel.

ileum /ilʹē·əm/ *pl.* **ilea** [L, intestine], the lower-third distal portion of the small intestine, extending from the jejunum to the cecum. It ends in the right iliac fossa, opening into the medial side of the large intestine. —**ileac, ileal,** *adj.*

ileus /il′ē·əs/ [L; Gk, *eilein*, to pack close together], an obstruction of the intestines, such as an adynamic ileus caused by immobility of the bowel or a mechanical ileus in which the intestine is blocked by mechanical means.

iliac circumflex node /il′ē·ak/ [L, *ilium,* flank, *circum,* around, *flectere,* to bend, *nodus,* knot], a node in one of the seven clusters of parietal lymph nodes of the abdomen. This node is one of a group found along the course of the deep iliac circumflex vessels.

iliac crest [L, *ilia,* intestines; ME, *creste*], the upper elevated margins of the ilium.

iliac fascia, the portion of the endoabdominal fascia that is attached with the iliacus to the crest of the ilium and passes under the inguinal ligament into the thigh.

iliac horns, accessory bony spurs on the posterior of the ilium, one of the symptoms of nail-patella syndrome.

iliac part of iliopsoas fascia, the part of the fascia that invests the iliac muscle.

iliac tuberosity, a rough elevation of the posterior iliac crest to which the posterior sacroiliac ligaments are attached. It is also a point of origin of the erector spinae and multifidus muscles.

iliacus /il′ē·əkəs/ [L, *ilium,* flank], a flat triangular muscle that covers the inner curved surface of the iliac fossa. It acts to flex and laterally rotate the thigh.

iliocostalis, the most laterally placed column of erector spinae muscles, including the iliocostalis lumborum, iliocostalis thoracis, and iliocostalis cervicis.

iliofemoral /il′ē·ōfem′ərəl/, pertaining to the ilium and femur.

iliofemoral ligament [L, *ilium* + *femur,* thigh + *ligamentum*], a triangular band of connective tissue attached by its apex to the anterior inferior spine of the ilium and acetabular margin and by its base to the intertrochanteric line of the femur.

iliofemoral thrombosis, an abnormal vascular condition in which a clot develops in the iliofemoral circulation.

iliohypogastric nerve, a nerve with branches that innervate the posterolateral gluteal skin and the skin in the pubic region, as well as the abdominal musculature.

ilioinguinal /il′ē·ō·ing′gwinəl/ [L, *ilium* + *inguen,* groin], pertaining to the hip and inguinal regions.

ilioinguinal nerve, a nerve that provides cutaneous innervation to the upper medial thigh, the root of the penis and the anterior

surface of the scrotum in men, or the mons pubis and labia majora in women. Through its course, it also supplies branches to the abdominal musculature.

iliolumbar artery, a branch of the posterior trunk of the internal iliac artery that supplies muscle and bone.

iliolumbar ligament /-lum′bər/ [L, *ilium* + *lumbus,* loin, *ligare,* to bind], one of a pair of ligaments forming part of the connection between the vertebral column and the pelvis. Each iliolumbar ligament attaches to a transverse process of the fifth lumbar vertebra and laterally to the ilium and inferiorly passes to the base of the sacrum.

iliopectineal line /-pek′tənəl/ [L, *ilium* + *pectus,* breast + *linea*], a bony ridge on the inner surface of the ilium and pubic bones that divides the true and false pelves.

iliopsoas /il′ē·ōsō′əs/ [L, *ilium*; Gk, *psoa,* loin muscle], one of the pair of muscle complexes that flex the thigh and the lumbar vertebral column.

iliopsoas abscess [L, *ilium*], a collection of pus in the iliopsoas muscle, possibly tuberculous in origin, that spreads from the thoracic or lumbar spine to the upper leg muscles. It is usually caused by staphylococcus infection.

iliopubic eminence, a diffuse enlargement just anterior to the acetabulum, marking the junction of the ilium with the superior ramus of the pubis.

iliorenal bypass, a technique of renal revascularization involving insertion of a saphenous vein graft between an iliac artery and a renal artery to serve as a passage around an occluded segment of renal artery.

iliotibial tract /-tib′ē·əl/ [L, *ilium,* flank, *tibia,* shinbone], a band of connective tissue that extends from the iliac crest to the knee and links the gluteus maximus to the tibia.

ilium /il′ē·əm/ *pl.* **ilia** [L, flank], the uppermost of the three bones that make up the innominate bone. The ilium forms the superior part of the acetabulum and provides attachment for several muscles, including the obturator internus, the gluteals, the iliacus, and the sartorius. —**iliac,** *adj.*

illegal abortion, an abortion performed contrary to the laws regulating abortion. Illegal abortions are often associated with life-threatening complications.

illegitimate /il′ejit′imit/ [L, *in,* not, *lex,* law], **1.** not authorized by law. **2.** abnormal.

illicit /ilis′it/ [L, *in,* not, *lex,* law], pertaining to an act that is unlawful or otherwise not permitted.

illiterate /ilit′ərit/, unable to read and write.

illness [ME, unhealthy condition], an abnormal process in which aspects of the social, physical, emotional, or intellectual condition and function of a person are diminished or impaired, compared with that person's previous condition.

illness behavior, the manner in which individuals monitor the structure and functions of their own bodies, interpret symptoms, take remedial action, and make use of health care facilities.

illness experience, the process of being ill. A commonly used model is Suchman's stages of illness, comprising five stages: stage I, experiencing a symptom; stage II, assuming a sick role; stage III, making contact for health care; stage IV, being dependent (a patient); and stage V, recovering or being rehabilitated.

illness prevention, 1. a system of health education programs and activities directed to protecting patients from real or potential health threats, minimizing risk factors, and promoting healthy behavior. **2.** actions taken by individuals to prevent illness in themselves and/or their families.

illumination /iloo'minā'shən/ [L, *illuminare,* to make light], the lighting up of a part of the body or of an object under a microscope for the purpose of examination.—**illuminate,** *v.*

illusion /iloo'zhən/ [L, *illudere,* to mock], a false interpretation of an external sensory stimulus, usually visual or auditory, such as a mirage in the desert or voices on the wind.

Ilosone, a trademark for an antibacterial (erythromycin estolate).

IM, abbreviation for **intramuscular.**

image /im'ij/ [L, *imago,* likeness], **1.** a representation or visual reproduction of the likeness of someone or something, such as a painting, photograph, or sculpture. **2.** an optic representation of an object, such as that produced by refraction or reflection. **3.** a person or thing that closely resembles another; semblance. **4.** a mental picture, representation, idea, or concept of an objective reality. **5.** in psychology, a mental representation of something previously perceived and subsequently modified by other experiences.

image acquisition time, the time required to acquire the data used in producing an MRI. It does not include the time involved in constructing the image from the data.

image compression, reduction of the space required to store or time required to transfer a digital image.

image detector, any recording medium used in radiology, such as film or a cathode ray tube.

image foreshortening, a type of shape distortion in which a radiographic image appears shorter and wider than the actual structure it represents. It results from misalignment of the x-ray tube relative to the patient, of the patient relative to the film, or of the tube relative to the film.

image format, the manner in which a digital image is stored, such as on a computer disk, magnetic tape, or film.

image intensifier, an electronic device used to produce a fluoroscopic image with a low-radiation exposure. A beam of x-rays passing through the patient is converted into a pattern of electrons in a vacuum tube. The electrons are accelerated and concentrated onto a small fluorescent screen, where they present a bright image, which is generally displayed on a video monitor.

image matrix, an arrangement of columns or rows of cells, or pixels, forming a digital image.

image receptor (IR), a device that changes the x-ray beam into a visible image. An image receptor may be a radiographic film and cassette, a phosphorescent screen, or a special detector placed in a table or upright bucky diaphragm.

imagery /im'ijrē/ [L, *imago*], in psychiatry, the formation of mental concepts, figures, ideas; any product of the imagination.

imagination /imaj'inā'shən/ [L, *imaginare,* to picture to oneself], **1.** the ability to form, or the act or process of forming, mental images or conscious concepts of things that are not immediately available to the senses. **2.** in psychology, the ability to reproduce images or ideas stored in the memory by the stimulation or suggestion of associated ideas or to regroup former ideas and concepts to form new images and ideas.

imaging /im'ijing/ [L, *imago*], the formation of a mental picture or representation of someone or something using the imagination.

imago /imā'gō/ [L, likeness], in analytic psychology, an unconscious, usually idealized mental image of a significant individual, such as one's mother, in a person's early formative years.

imatinib /imā'tinib'/, an inhibitor acting specifically on an abnormal enzyme form that is created by the Philadelphia chromosome abnormality and present in chronic myeloid leukemia.

imbalance /imbal'əns/ [L, *im,* not, *bilanx,* having two scales], **1.** lack of balance between opposing muscle groups. **2.** an abnormal balance of fluid and electrolytes in the body tissues. **3.** the unequal distribution of subjects in a population group. **4.** a lack of balance in a person with mental abilities that are remarkable in one area but deficient in others, as an idiot savant.

imbricate /im'brikāt/ [L, *imbrex,* roofing tile], to build a surface with overlapping layers of material. Surgeons may imbricate with layers of tissue when closing a

wound or other opening in a body part.—
imbrication, n.

IMDD, abbreviation for **idiopathic midline destructive disease.**

Imferon, a trademark for an injectable
hematinic (iron dextran).

imiglucerase, an analog of a human
enzyme produced by recombinant DNA
technology. It is prescribed as enzyme
replacement therapy for patients with type
I Gaucher disease.

iminoglycinuria /im′inōglī′sinŏŏr′ē·ə/, a
benign familial condition characterized by
the abnormal urinary excretion of the imino
acids glycine, proline, and hydroxyproline.

imipenem-cilastatin sodium /im′ipē′nəm
sil′əstat′in/, a broad-spectrum parenteral
antibiotic prescribed for the treatment of
infections caused by susceptible organisms in the lower respiratory or urinary
tracts, skin, abdomen, reproductive organs,
bones, or joints. It is also used in the treatment of endocarditis and septicemia.

imipramine hydrochloride /imip′rəmēn/,
a tricyclic antidepressant prescribed in the
treatment of mental depression.

imiquimod /im′ikwim′od/, a biologic
response modifier used topically in the
treatment of venereal warts of the external
genitalia and perianal region.

immature baby /iməchŏŏr′/ [L, *im,* not,
maturus, ripe], a term sometimes applied
to an infant who weighs less than 1134 g
(2.5 lb) and who is significantly underdeveloped at birth.

immature cataract [L, *im + maturus,* ripe;
Gk, *katarrhaktes*], a cataract at an early
stage of development when the lens, partially opaque, absorbs fluid and increases
by swelling. Only part of the lens is opaque.

immature erythrocyte [L, *im + maturus,*
ripe; Gk, *erythros,* red, *kytos,* cell], A
nucleated precursor red blood cell in the
erythrocyte series: pronormoblast, basophilic normoblast, polychromatophilic
normoblast, or orthochromic normoblast.
The orthochromic normoblast appears on
peripheral blood films of newborns, in
uncompensated hemolytic anemia, and in
hematologic neoplasms.

immediate auscultation /imē′dē·it/ [L,
im + medius, middle, *auscultare,* to lis-
ten], a method of examining a patient by
placing an ear or stethoscope on the skin
directly over the body part being studied.

immediate automatism, a state in which
a person acts spontaneously and automatically and later has no recollection of the
behavior.

immediate denture [L, *im + medius + dens,*
tooth], a removable artificial denture
that is placed in the mouth immediately
after the surgical removal of all remaining

teeth at the same appointment as the tooth
extractions to maintain normal appearance,
act as a compression and protective dressing, and allow the ability to chew food.

immediate hypersensitivity, an allergic
reaction that occurs within minutes after
exposure to an allergen and is mediated by
antibodies.

**immediate postoperative fit (IPOF) pros-
thesis,** a temporary or preparatory prosthesis, such as a pylon.

immediate posttraumatic automatism, a
posttraumatic state in which a person acts
spontaneously and automatically and later
has no recollection of the behavior.

immersion /imur′zhən/ [L, *im + mergere,*
to dip], the placing of a body or an object
into water or other liquid so that it is completely covered by the liquid.—**immerse,** v.

immersion foot, an abnormal condition
of the feet characterized by damage to the
muscles, nerves, skin, and blood vessels,
caused by prolonged exposure to dampness
or by prolonged immersion in cold water.

Immerslund-Gräsbeck   syndrome, a
familial form of megaloblastic anemia and
cobalamin deficiency. It is characterized by
selective intestinal malabsorption of vitamin B_{11}, uninfluenced by intrinsic factor.

immiscible /imis′əbəl/ [L, *im + miscere,*
to mix], not capable of being mixed,
such as oil and water.

immobility consequences: physiological, a
nursing outcome from the Nursing Outcomes
Classification (NOC) defined as the extent of
compromise in physiological functioning
due to impaired physical mobility.

**immobility consequences: psychocogni-
tive,** a nursing outcome from the Nursing
Outcomes Classification (NOC) defined as
the severity of compromise in psychocog-
nitive functioning due to impaired physical
mobility.

immobilization /imō′bəlīzā′shən/, **1.** fixation of a body part so that it cannot move
during surgery or after setting of a fracture.
2. prolonged inactivity of an individual,
as with bed rest or neurologic injury such
as coma, paraplyia, or quadraplyia.—
immobile, *adj.*

immobilization test, a procedure for
identifying antibodies to motile microorganisms by measuring the ability of the
antibodies to restrict the motility of the
microorganisms.

immotile cilia syndrome /imō′til/ [L, *im
+ motilis,* movable, *cilia,* eyelashes; Gk,
syn, together, *dromos,* course], a condition in which cilia, the hairlike processes
of epithelial cells, fail to function normally. As a result, the patient has difficulty
in filtering dust and other airborne debris
from the respiratory system.

immune /imyo͞on′/ [L, *immunis,* free from], having resistance to infection by a certain pathogen.

immune cytolysis, cell destruction mediated by a specific antibody, which activates the compliment system, resulting in rupture of the cell membrane.

immune deviation, modification of an immune response to an antigen caused by a previous exposure to the same antigen.

immune elimination, 1. a method for determining antibody response by measuring the rate of removal of labeled antigens from the circulation. **2.** an accelerated removal of antigens as a result of their binding to antibodies.

immune exclusion, the prevention of an antigen from entering the body by a specific immune response.

immune gamma globulin, passive immunizing agent obtained from pooled human plasma. It is prescribed for immediate short-lived protection against measles, poliomyelitis, chickenpox, serum hepatitis after transfusion, hepatitis A, and other disease-causing organisms to which the person has been recently exposed or may be exposed and as replacement therapy for patients with agammaglobulinemia or hypogammaglobulinemia.

immune hemolysis, the destruction of RBCs caused by the formation of specific antigen-antibody complexes in the presence of complement.

immune human globulin, a sterile solution of globulins derived from adult human blood that is used as a passive immunizing agent.

immune hypersensitivity response, a nursing outcome from the Nursing Outcomes Classification (NOC) defined as the severity of inappropriate immune responses.

immune neutropenia, neutrophil destruction caused by antibodies specific for neutrophil antigenic determinants, as often occurs in autoimmune diseases.

immune protein [L, *immunis,* free from; Gk, *proteios,* first rank], a protein, such as an antibody or antitoxin, that contributes to the immunity of a host.

immune recognition, the activation of a T or B cell by an antigen.

immune response, a defense function of the body that protects the body against invading pathogens, foreign tissues, and malignancies. It consists of the humoral response and the cell-mediated immune response.

immune status, a nursing outcome from the Nursing Outcomes Classification (NOC) defined as natural and acquired appropriately targeted resistance to internal and external antigens.

immune system, a system of tissues, organs, and cells that protects the body against pathogenic organisms and other foreign bodies. The principal components of the immune system include the bone marrow, the thymus, and the lymphoid tissues. The system also uses peripheral organs, such as the lymph nodes, the spleen, and the lymphatic vessels.

immune thrombocytopenic purpura /-sī′təpē′nik/ [Gk, *thrombos* + *kytos,* cell, *penia,* poverty; L, *purpura,* purple], mucocutaneous bleeding of thrombocytopenia, caused by a platelet membrane-specific autoantibody that shortens the platelet lifespan. It is diagnosed by exclusion of drug effects, inflammatory disorder, thrombotic thrombocytopenic purpura, DIC, or hematologic disorder. It affects middle-aged adults and is more prevalent in women than in men. Acute immune thrombocytopenic purpura is a side effect of viral infection in children 2 to 6 years of age, and although the thrombocytopenia is profound, the disorder resolves spontaneously within a few weeks. Also known as **autoimmune thrombocytopenic purpura,** once called *idiopathic thrombocytopenic purpura.*

immunity /imyo͞o′nitē/ [L, *immunis,* free from], **1.** in civil law, exemption from a duty or an obligation generally required by law, as an exemption from taxation or from penalty for wrongdoing or protection against liability. **2.** the quality of being insusceptible to or unaffected by a particular disease or condition.—**immune,** *adj.*

immunization /im′yənīzā′shən/ [L, *immunis,* free], **1.** a process that increases an organism's reaction to an antigen, thereby improving the organism's ability to resist or overcome infection. **2.** a technique used to induce an immune response to a specific disease in humans by exposing the individual to an antigen in order to raise antibodies to that antigen.

immunization behavior, a nursing outcome from the Nursing Outcomes Classification (NOC) defined as personal actions to obtain immunization to prevent a communicable disease.

immunization/vaccination management, a nursing intervention from the Nursing Interventions Classification (NIC) defined as monitoring immunization status, facilitating access to immunizations, and providing immunizations to prevent communicable disease.

immunoablative /im′mu-no·ab′lätiv/, immunosuppressant with removal and destruction of a cell population, such as in the ablative step preceding bone marrow transplantation.

immunoabsorbent /im′yənō′absôr′bənt/, a gel or other inert substance used to absorb antibodies from a solution or to purify them.

immunoabsorption /im'yənō·absôrp'shən/, **1.** removal of a specific group of antibodies by antigens. **2.** removal of antigen by interaction with specific antibodies.

immunoadsorbent /im'yənō·adsôr'bənt/, an insoluble preparation of antigens or antibodies used to bind homologous antibodies or antigens and remove them from a mixture of substances.

immunoassay /im'yənō·as'ā/ [L, *immunis*; Fr, *essayer*, to try], a commonly employed assay in which a solid-phase target antigen is designed to bind with an antibody in vitro to reveal its presence. When a conjugated antihuman immunoglobulin is added, it binds the antibody of interest. The conjugate, usually an enzyme, then reacts with its substrate to generate color or fluorescence that is proportional to antibody concentrations. See also **enzyme-linked immunosorbent assay** (ELISA), **radioimmunoassay, sandwich technique.**

immunoaugmentative therapy, an alternative cancer treatment that proposes that cancer cells can be arrested by the use of four different blood proteins. This approach is also proposed to restore the immune system and can be used as an adjunctive therapy.

immunobead /im'yənōbēd'/, a tiny, inert plastic sphere coated with antigens or antibody, used for immunoassays, such as the isolation of B cells from T cells.

immunobead assay, an assay for any of various types of antibodies or antigens, using immunobeads coated with a corresponding antigen or antibody that aggregates or agglutinates in the presence of the one in question.

immunoblastic lymphoma /-blas'tik/, a proliferation of immunoblasts involving the lymph nodes.

immunoblotting /-blot'ing/, a method for identifying antigens. The antigens are allowed to adhere to cellulose sheets and are identified by staining with labeled antibodies. The method is also used to detect monoclonal proteins.

immunochemistry, the study of the chemical properties of antigens and antibodies, complement, and T-cell receptors.

immunochemotherapy /-kem'ōther'əpē/, a combination of biotherapy and chemotherapy.

immunocompetence /-kom'pətəns/, the ability of an immune system to mobilize and deploy its antibodies and other responses to stimulation by an antigen. —**immunocompetent,** *adj.*

immunocomplex, a multimolecular complex formed when an antibody binds to a specific antigen. The complex is capable of activating complement and is a factor in diseases such as arthritis, vasculitis, serum sickness, and glomerulonephritis.

immunocomplex assay, a laboratory assessment of the amounts of components in multimolecular antigen-antibody complexes. The assay is used in various diagnostic tests for collagen-vascular disorders, glomerulonephritis, vasculitis, hepatitis, and neoplastic diseases.

immunocomplex hypersensitivity [L, *immunis,* free from, *complexus,* embrace; Gk, *hyper,* excess; L, *sentire,* to feel], a complement-dependent, immediate-acting, humoral hypersensitivity to certain soluble antigens. It occurs when antibodies (IgG or IgM) bind to circulating antigens, forming immune complexes, which are deposited in tissues and induce tissue injury or dysfunctional responses.

immunocomplex-mediated hypersensitivity reaction, type III hypersensitivity reaction.

immunocompromised /-kom'prəmīzd'/ [L, *immunis,* free from, *compromittere,* to promise mutually], pertaining to an immune response that has been weakened by a disease or an immunosuppressive agent.

immunocompromised host, an individual whose immune response is weakened as a result of an immunodeficiency disorder or exposure to immunosuppressive drugs or irradiation.

immunodeficiency disease /-difish'ənsē/, any of a group of diseases caused by a defect in the immune system and generally characterized by susceptibility to infections and chronic diseases. Such diseases are sometimes classified as B-cell (antibody) deficiencies, T-cell (cellular) deficiencies, combined T- and B-cell deficiencies, defects of cell movement, and defects of microbicidal activity.

immunodeficient /-difish'ənt/ [L, *immunis* + *de,* from, *facere,* to make], pertaining to an abnormal condition of the immune system in which cellular or humoral immunity is inadequate and resistance to infection is decreased.

immunodiagnostic /-dī'əgnos'tik/ [L, *immunis;* Gk, *dia,* through, *gnosis,* knowledge], pertaining to or characterizing a diagnosis based on an antigen-antibody reaction.

immunodiffusion /-difyōō'zhən/ [L, *immunis* + *diffundere,* to spread], a technique for the identification and quantification of any of the immunoglobulins. It is based on the presence of a visible precipitate that results from an antigen-antibody combination under certain circumstances. Gel diffusion is a technique that involves evaluation of the precipitin reaction in a clear gel. Electroimmunodiffusion is a gel diffusion to which an electric field is applied, accelerating the reaction. Double gel diffusion is a technique that permits identification of antibodies in mixed specimens.

immunoelectroadsorption /im'yənō'ilek'trō·adsôrp'shən/, an antibody assay technique in which antigens are adsorbed onto a metal-coated glass slide with an electric current. Serum containing antibodies is then applied to the slide.

immunoelectron microscopy /im'yənō'ilek'tron/, electron microscopy of specimens labeled with antibodies that have been conjugated with gold. The gold makes the antibody labels electron-dense.

immunoelectrophoresis /-ilek'trōfôrē'sis/ [L, *immunis*; Gk, *elektron*, amber, *pherein*, to bear], a technique that combines electrophoresis and immunodiffusion to separate and allow identification of complex proteins. The proteins in the test serum are spread out in agar and separated by electrophoresis. Wells or troughs are then cut into the agar, and parts of antibody are placed in the troughs and allowed to diffuse toward the separated proteins. A visible precipitin will form in a series of arcs in the agar when an antigen-antibody reaction occurs. —**immunoelectrophoretic,** *adj.*

immunoenhancement /im'yənō'enhans'mənt/, the augmentation of immune responsiveness by immunization or other means.

immunoferritin /-fer'itin/, an antibody labeled with ferritin used to identify specific antigens in electron microscopy.

immunoferritin technique, a method of labeling antibody molecules with ferritin, an electron-dense material. The ferritin renders the sites of antibody attachment visible in electron microscopy.

immunofixation /-fiksā'shən/, a process by which antigens in a protein mixture are separated on an electrophoretic gel and identified by the application of labeled antibodies.

immunofixation electrophoresis, a blood or urine test used to detect monoclonal gammopathies.

immunofluorescence /-floores'əns/ [L, *immunis* + *fluere*, to flow], a technique used for the rapid identification of an antigen by exposing it to known antibodies tagged with the fluorescent dye fluorescein and observing the characteristic antigen-antibody reaction of precipitation. —**immunofluorescent,** *adj.*

immunogen /imyoo'nəjən/ [L, *immunis*; Gk, *genein*, to produce], any agent or substance capable of provoking an immune response or producing immunity. —**immunogenic,** *adj.*

immunogenetics /-jənet'iks/, a branch of medicine concerned with the role of genetics in tissue transplantation and immunologic response.

immunoglobulin (Ig) /-glob'yəlin/ [L, *immunis* + *globus*, small sphere], any of five structurally distinct classes of proteins that function as antibodies in the serum and external secretions of the body. In response to specific antigens, immunoglobulins are formed in the bone marrow, spleen, and all lymphoid tissues except the thymus.

immunoglobulin A (IgA), one of the most prevalent of the five classes of antibodies produced by the body. It is found in all secretions of the body and is the major antibody in the tears, saliva, mucous membranes lining the intestines, and bronchi. IgA combines with a protein in the mucosa and defends body surfaces by seeking out foreign microorganisms and triggering an antigen-antibody reaction.

immunoglobulin D (IgD), one of the five classes of antibodies produced by the body. It is found in small amounts in serum tissue. Although its precise function is not known, IgD increases in quantity during allergic reactions to milk, insulin, penicillin, and various toxins.

immunoglobulin E (IgE), one of the five classes of antibodies produced by the body. It is concentrated in the lungs, skin, and mucous membranes. It provides the primary defense against environmental antigens and is believed to be responsive to immunoglobulin A. IgE reacts with certain antigens to trigger the release of chemical mediators that cause anaphylactic hypersensitivity reactions characterized by wheal and flare.

immunoglobulin electrophoresis, a blood test done to detect and identify the various immunoglobulins. Serum immunoelectrophoresis is used to detect and monitor the course of diseases.

immunoglobulin G (IgG), one of the five classes of antibodies produced by the body. It is synthesized in response to invasions by bacteria, fungi, and viruses. IgG crosses the placenta and protects the fetus against red cell antigens and white cell antigens.

immunoglobulin M (IgM), one of the five classes of antibodies produced by the body and the largest in molecular structure. It is found in circulating fluids and is the first immunoglobulin produced when the body is challenged by antigens. IgM triggers the increased production of immunoglobulin G and the complement fixation required for effective immune response. It is the dominant antibody in ABO blood group incompatibilities.

immunohematology /-hem'ətol'əjē/ [L, *immunis;* Gk, *haima,* blood, *logos,* science], the study of antigen-antibody reactions and their effects on blood.

immunoincompetence /im'yənō'inkom'pə təns/, the inability to develop an immune reaction.

immunologically competent cell, a cell of the lymphoid series that can react with antigen to produce antibody or to become active in cell-mediated immunity or delayed hypersensitivity reactions.

immunologic barrier /-loj'ik/, an apparent protection against an immune response afforded by certain areas of the body as demonstrated by the prolonged survival of foreign grafts in those areas.

immunologic disease [L, *immunis,* free from; Gk, *logos,* science; L, *dis;* Fr, *aise,* ease], any condition caused by an abnormal immune system.

immunologic granuloma, a small, organized, compact collection of mononuclear phagocytes that develops within 2 or 3 weeks after the introduction of a foreign material, provoking an inflammatory response.

immunologic infertility, any of several types of female factor infertility believed to be caused by presence of antibodies that interfere with functioning of the sperm.

immunologic model of aging, an idea that a decline in the function of T cells and B cells causes normal cells to be unrecognized as such, thereby triggering immune reactions against an individual's own tissues.

immunologic pregnancy test, a method of detecting pregnancy through an increase in the concentration of HCG in the plasma or urine.

immunologic surveillance [L, *immunis,* free from; Gk, *logos,* science; Fr, *surveiller,* to watch over], the constant monitoring by the immune system of microorganisms, foreign tissue, and diseases caused by altered cells, especially cancer cells.

immunologic test [L, *immunis + testum,* crucible], a test based on the principles of antigen-antibody reactions.

immunologist /im'yənol'əjist/, a specialist in immunology.

immunology /im'yənol'əjē/ [L, *immunis;* Gk, *logos,* science], the study of the reaction of tissues of the immune system of the body to antigenic stimulation.

immunomodulator /-mod'yəlā'tər/ [L, *immunis + modulus,* little measure], a substance that alters the immune response by augmenting or reducing the ability of the immune system to produce antibodies or sensitized cells that recognize and react with the antigen that initiated their production. Immunomodulators include corticosteroids, cytotoxic agents, thymosin, and immunoglobulins.—**immunomodulation,** *n.*

immunopathology /-pəthol'əjē/, **1.** the study of disease processes that have an immunologic cause. **2.** injury induced by antibodies or other products of an immune response.

immunophenotypic analysis /-fē'nōtip'ik/, a method for dividing lymphomas and leukemias into clonal subgroups on the basis of differences in cell surfaces and cytoplasmic antigens.

immunopotency /-pō'tənsē/ [L, *immunis + potentia,* power], the ability of an antigen to elicit an immune response.

immunoprecipitation /-prisip'itā'shən/, a procedure used to isolate target molecules with which antibodies react.

immunoproliferative disorder, a condition characterized by the continuous proliferation of a subset of immune cells, such as lymphocytes or plasma cells, that is associated with autoimmune and immunoglobulin disorders.

immunoproliferative small intestine disease (IPSID), a disorder characterized by a small, diffuse lesion composed of cells that have features of plasma cells, histiocytes, and atypical lymphocytes. The disease mainly affects the duodenum and proximal jejunum. Patients experience diarrhea, weight loss, abdominal pain, and clubbing of the fingers and toes.

immunoprophylaxis /-prō'filak'sis/, the introduction of active immunization through vaccines or passive immunization through antisera.

immunoradiometricassay/-rā'dē-ōmet'rik/, a method for measuring certain plasma proteins by using radiolabeled antibodies.

immunoreactant, a substance that participates in an immune response; an antigen or antibody.—**immunoreactive,** *adj.*

immunoregulation /-reg'yəlā'shən/, control of the immune response, as by manipulation of pathways involving suppressor and contrasuppressor T cells.

immunoregulatory hormones /-reg'yə lətôr'ē/, chemical substances secreted by endocrine glands and lymphocytes that influence activities of the immune system.

immunosecretory disorders, a group of disorders characterized by monoclonal proliferation of immunoglobulin-producing cells that resemble lymphocytes or plasma cells. The group includes primary amyloidosis, cryoglobulinemia, heavy chain disease, benign monoclonal gammopathy, multiple myeloma, and plasma cell dyscrasias.

immunoselection /-silek'shən/ [L, *immunis + seligere,* to select], the survival of certain cells as a result of their lack of surface antigens that would otherwise make them vulnerable to attack and destruction by antibodies.

immunosorbent /-sôr′bənt/, a substance containing attached antigens used to remove homologous antibodies from a solution.

immunostimulant /-stim′yələnt/, an agent that induces an immune response at the site of injection, a response that sometimes can be beneficial in the treatment of cancer and other diseases.

immunosuppression /-səpresh′ən/ [L, *immunis* + *supprimere*, to press down], **1.** the administration of agents that significantly interfere with the ability of the immune system to respond to antigenic stimulation by inhibiting cellular and humoral immunity. Immunosuppression may be deliberate, such as in preparation for bone marrow or other transplantation to prevent rejection by the host of the donor tissue, or incidental, such as often results from chemotherapy for the treatment of cancer. **2.** an abnormal condition of the immune system characterized by markedly inhibited ability to respond to antigenic stimuli.—**immunosuppressed,** *adj.*

immunosuppressive /-səpres′iv/, **1.** pertaining to a substance or procedure that lessens or prevents an immune response. **2.** an immunosuppressive agent.

immunotherapy /-ther′əpē/ [L, *immunis*; Gk, *therapeia*, treatment], the application of immunologic knowledge and techniques to prevent and treat disease. Examples are the administration of increasing doses of allergens in the treatment of allergies, the use of immunostimulants and immunosuppressants, the transfer of immunocompetent cells and tissues from one person to another, and the use of interferon for its antiviral and antitumor properties. —**immunotherapeutic,** *adj.*

immunotoxin (IT) /-tok′sin/, a toxin that is attached to a monoclonal antibody and used to destroy a specific type of target cell.

Imodium, a trademark for an antidiarrheal (loperamide hydrochloride).

Imovax, a trademark for a rabies virus vaccine (rabies human diploid cell vaccine).

impacted /impak′tid/ [L, *impingere,* to drive against], tightly or firmly wedged in a limited amount of space.—**impact,** *v.*, **impaction,** *n.*

impacted cerumen, accumulated cerumen forming a solid mass that adheres to the wall of the external auditory canal.

impacted fracture, a bone break in which the adjacent fragmented ends of the fractured bone are wedged together.

impacted tooth, a tooth so positioned against another tooth, bone, or soft tissue that its complete and normal eruption is impossible or unlikely.

impaction /impak′shən/ [L, impactio, a pressing together], **1.** an obstacle or malposition that prevents a tooth from erupting. **2.** the presence of a large or hard fecal mass in the rectum or colon.

impaired glucose tolerance (IGT) /imperd′/ [L, *impejorare,* to make worse; Gk, *glykys,* sweet; L, *tolerare,* to endure], a condition in which fasting plasma glucose levels are higher than normal but lower than those diagnostic of DM.

impairment [L, *impejorare,* to make worse], any disorder in structure or function resulting from anatomic, physiologic, or psychologic abnormalities that interfere with normal activities.

impedance /impē′dəns/ [L, *impedire,* to entangle], a form of electric resistance observed in an alternating current that is analogous to the classic electric resistance that occurs in a direct current circuit.

impedance plethysmography, a technique for detecting blood vessel occlusion that determines volumetric changes in the limb by measuring changes in its girth as indicated by changes in the electric impedance of mercury-containing polymeric silicone (Silastic) tubes in a pressure cuff. The technique does not accurately indicate the presence or absence of partially obstructing thrombi in major vessels.

imperative conception /imper′ətiv/ [L, *imperare,* to command], a thought or impression that appears spontaneously in the mind and cannot be eliminated, such as an obsession.

imperforate /impur′fərit/ [L, *im,* not, *perforare,* to pierce], lacking a normal opening in a body organ or passageway.

imperforate anus, any of several congenital developmental malformations of the anorectal portion of the GI tract. The most common form is anal agenesis, in which the rectal pouch ends blindly above the surface of the perineum. An anal fistula is present in 80% to 90% of cases. Other forms include anal stenosis, in which the anal aperture is small, and anal membrane atresia, in which the anal membrane covers the aperture, creating an obstruction.

imperforate hymen [L, *im* + *perforare,* to pierce; Gk, *hymen,* membrane], a hymen that completely encloses the external orifice of the vagina.

impermeable /impur′mē·əbəl/ [L, *im,* not, *permeare,* to pass through], of a tissue, membrane, or film, preventing the passage of a substance through it.

impetigo /im′pətī′gō/ [L, *impetus,* attack], a streptococcal, staphylococcal, or combined infection of the skin beginning as focal erythema and progressing to pruritic vesicles, erosions, and honey-colored crusts. Lesions usually form on the face and spread locally. The disorder is highly contagious through contact with the discharge from the lesions.— **impetiginous** /im'petij'inəs/, *adj*.

impetigo contagiosa [L, *impetus*, attack; *contingere*, to touch], an acute contagious superficial infection of the skin. It is characterized by vesicles that rupture, leaving a purulent exudate that dries into golden crusts.

impetigo herpetiformis [L, *impetus*, attack; Gk, *herpein*, to creep; L, *forma*], a rare skin disorder that mainly affects pregnant women, beginning as an eruption in the genitofemoral area and spreading to other areas. The eruptions are usually irregular or circular groups of pustules that tend to coalesce.

impingement injection test /impinj'mənt/, an appraisal of shoulder injury in which the injection of 10 mL of lidocaine into the subacromial space reduces the painful arc of abduction by more than 50%.

impingement sign, a painful arc produced by forceful abduction of the internally rotated arm against the acromion in evaluation of a shoulder injury.

impingement syndrome, a progressive condition of shoulder pain and dysfunction, usually caused by repetitive placement of the arm in overhead positions. The disorder is a common sports injury.

implant /im'plant, implant'/ [L, *implantare*, to set into], **1.** in radiotherapy, an encapsulated radioactive substance embedded in tissue for therapy. **2.** in surgery, material inserted or grafted into an organ or structure of the body. The implant may be of tissue, such as in a blood vessel graft, or of an artificial substance, such as in a hip prosthesis, a cardiac pacemaker, or a container of radioactive material.

implantable cardioverter-defibrillator (ICD), a surgically implanted electric device that automatically terminates lethal ventricular arrhythmias by delivering low-energy shocks to the heart, restoring proper rhythm when the heart begins beating rapidly or erratically.

implantation, in embryology, the process involving the attachment, penetration, and embedding of the blastocyst in the lining of the uterine wall during the early stages of prenatal development.

implantation dermoid cyst, a tumor derived from embryonal tissues, caused by an injury that forces part of the ectoderm into the body.

implantation endometriosis [L, *implantare*, to set into; Gk, *endon*, within, *metra*, womb, *osis*, condition], ectopic endometrial tissue prevalent throughout the peritoneal cavity.

implant denture, complete or partial denture that includes a subperiosteally or intraperiosteally implanted framework in contact with alveolar bone. The denture attaches to one or more posts that project from the framework through the connective tissues and mucous membranes.

implanted infusion port, a self-sealing silicone septum encased in a metal or plastic case with an attached silicone catheter that is threaded intravenously. It is implanted subcutaneously and used for long-term venous access for infusion of medications, parenteral nutrition, or IV solutions.

implanted suture [L, *implantare*, to set into + *sutura*], a suture formed by inserting pins on opposite sides of a wound and drawing the edges of the wound together by winding thread tightly around the pins.

implant restoration, 1. a single- or multiple-tooth implant crown or bridge that replaces a missing tooth or teeth. **2.** use of an elastomeric material to physically record a prepared tooth impression.

implementation /im'pləməntā'shən/ [L, *implere*, to fill], a deliberate action performed to achieve a goal, such as carrying out a plan in caring for a patient. It is the fourth step, or phase, of the nursing process.

implementation mechanism, the means by which innovations are transferred from the planners to the units of service.

implementing /im'pləmen'ting/ [L, *implere*, to fill], in five-step nursing process, a category of nursing behavior in which the actions necessary for accomplishing the health care plan are initiated and completed. Implementing includes performing or assisting in the performance of the patient's ADL, if necessary; counseling and teaching the patient or the patient's family; giving care to achieve patient comfort and therapeutic goals and to optimize the patient's achievement of health goals; supervising and evaluating the work of staff members; and recording and exchanging information relevant to the patient's continued health care.

implied consent /implīd'/ [L, *implicare*, to involve, *consentire*, to feel], the granting of permission for health care without a formal agreement between the patient and health care provider. An example is an appointment made with a physician by a patient with a physical complaint; it is implied that by making the appointment the patient gives consent to the physician to make a diagnosis and offer treatment.

implosion /implō'zhən/ [L, *im* + *plaudere*, to strike], **1.** a bursting inward. **2.** a psychiatric treatment for people disabled by phobias and anxiety in which the person is desensitized to anxiety-producing stimuli by repeated intense exposure in imagination or reality, until the stimuli are no longer stressful.—**implode,** v.

impotence /im′pətəns/ [L, *im,* not, *potentia,* power], **1.** weakness. **2.** inability of the adult male to achieve penile erection or, less commonly, to ejaculate after achieving an erection. Functional impotence has a psychologic basis. Organic impotence includes vasculogenic, neurogenic, endocrinic, and anatomic factors. Anatomic impotence results from physically defective genitalia. Atonic impotence involves disturbed neuromuscular function.—**impotent,** adj.

impregnate /impreg′nāt/ [L, *impregnare,* to make pregnant], **1.** to inseminate and make pregnant; to fertilize. **2.** to saturate or mix with another substance.—**impregnable,** adj., **impregnation,** n.

impression /impresh′ən/ [L, *imprimere,* to press into], **1.** in dentistry and prosthetic medicine, a mold of a part of the mouth or other part of the body from which a replacement or prosthesis may be formed. **2.** in the medical record, the examiner's diagnosis or assessment of a problem, disease, or condition. **3.** a strong sensation or effect on the mind, intellect, or feelings. **4.** a slight indentation or depression, as one produced in the surface of one organ by pressure exerted by another.

impression material [L, *imprimere,* to press into, *materia,* stuff], any substance used for making impressions of teeth and oral structures to produce dental restorations.

imprinted gene, a gene whose expression has been affected by genomic imprinting so that only a single allele functions, the other being turned off by epigenetic mechanisms during embryonic development.

imprinting [Fr, *empreindre,* to impress], in ethology, a special type of learning that occurs at critical points during the early stages of development in animals. It involves behavioral patterning and social attachment, is characterized by rapid acquisition and irreversibility, and is usually species-specific.

imprisonment /impriz′ənment/ [Fr, *emprisonner,* to confine], in law, the act of confining, detaining, or arresting a person or in any way restraining personal liberty and preventing free exercise of movement.

impulse /im′puls/ [L, *impellere,* to drive], **1.** in psychology, a sudden irresistible, often irrational inclination, urge, desire, or action resulting from a particular feeling or mental state. **2.** in physiology, the electrochemical process involved in neural transmission.—**impulsive,** adj.

impulse-conducting system [L, *impellere,* to drive, *conducere,* to conduct; Gk, *systema*], the Purkinje fibers within the heart muscle that conduct impulses controlling the contractions of the atria and ventricles.

impulse control disorder, a behavior in which the individual fails to resist performing a potentially harmful act.

impulse control training, a nursing intervention from the Nursing Interventions Classification (NIC) defined as assisting the patient to mediate impulsive behavior through application of problem-solving strategies to social and interpersonal situations.

impulse self-control, a nursing outcome from the Nursing Outcomes Classification (NOC) defined as the self-restraint of compulsive or impulsive behaviors.

impulsion /impul′shən/ [L, *impellere,* to drive], an urge to act without consideration of consequences.

Imuran, a trademark for an immunosuppressive (azathioprine).

IMV, abbreviation for **intermittent mandatory ventilation.**

In, symbol for the element **indium.**

inactivated measles virus vaccine /inak′tivā′tid/ [L, *in,* not + *activus;* OE, *masala,* blister; L, *virus,* poison, *vaccinus,* of a cow], a measles vaccine virus that has been treated so that it is no longer capable of replication. It is an alternative to live attenuated measles vaccine, which may be contraindicated for some individuals.

inactive colon /inak′tiv/ [L, *in,* not, *activus,* active; Gk, *kolon,* colon], hypotonicity of the bowel that results in decreased contractions and propulsive movements and a delay in the normal 12-hour transit time of luminal contents from the cecum to the anus. Colonic inactivity may be caused by acquired or congenital megacolon, anticholinergic drugs, depression, faulty habits of elimination, inadequate fluid intake, lack of exercise, a low-residue or starvation diet, neuroendocrine response to surgical stress, prolonged bed rest, or a neurologic disease such as diabetic visceral neuropathy, MS, parkinsonism, and spinal cord lesions. Normal motility of the colon is frequently compromised by the continued use of laxatives.

inactive electrode, in electrocautery, the electrode through which current distributed through the active electrode is returned to the generator.

inadequate personality /inad′əkwit/ [L, *in,* not, *adaequare,* to equal, *personalis,* of a person], a personality characterized by a lack of physical stamina, emotional immaturity, social instability, poor judgment, reduced motivation, ineptness—especially in interpersonal relationships—and an inability to adapt or react effectively to new or stressful situations.

inamrinone lactate /am′rinōn/, an IV cardiac inotropic drug prescribed in the short-term management of CHF in patients who do not respond to therapy with digitalis, diuretics, and vasodilators.

inanimate /inan′imit/ [L, *in,* not, *animus,* life spirit], not alive; lacking signs of life.

inanition /in′ənish′ən/ [L, *inanis,* empty], **1.** an exhausted condition resulting from lack of food and water or a defect in assimilation; starvation. **2.** a state of lethargy characterized by a loss of vitality or vigor in all aspects of social, moral, and intellectual life.

inborn /in′bôrn/ [L, *in,* within; AS, *beran,* to bear], innate; acquired or occurring during intrauterine life, with reference to both normally inherited traits and developmental or genetically transmitted anomalies.

inborn error of metabolism, one of many rare abnormal metabolic conditions caused by an inherited defect of a single enzyme or other protein. Although people with such diseases are defective in only one protein, they generally display a large number of physical signs that are characteristic of the genetic trait and are related to excesses or deficiencies of the substrate on which the enzyme acts.

inborn lysosomal disease, one of many inherited disorders of metabolism involving degradative enzymes normally located in lysosomes. The condition leads to storage of abnormal amounts of lysosomal agents.

inbreeding /in′brēding/ [L, *in,* within; AS, *bredan,* to reproduce], the production of offspring by the mating of closely related organisms, the most extreme form being self-fertilization, which occurs in certain plants and animals. Inbreeding increases the chance that recessive alleles for both desirable and undesirable traits will become homozygous and be expressed phenotypically.

incandescent [L, *incandescere,* to begin to glow], hot to the point of glowing or emitting intense light rays, as an incandescent light bulb.

incapacitating agents, drugs that interfere with the inability to think clearly or cause unconsciousness or some other altered state of consciousness.

incarcerate /inkar′sərāt/ [L, *in,* within, *carcerare,* to imprison], to trap, imprison, or confine, such as a loop of intestine in an inguinal hernia.

incarcerated hernia [L, *in + carcerare,* to imprison, *hernia,* rupture], a loop of bowel with ends occluded so that solids cannot pass. The herniated bowel will not return to its normal position without manipulation or surgery.

incentive spirometry /insen′tiv/, a method of encouraging voluntary deep breathing by providing visual feedback about inspiratory volume. Incentive spirometry reduces the risk of atelectasis and pulmonary consolidation.

inception /insep′shən/ [L, *incipere,* to begin], the origin or beginning of anything.

incest /in′sest/ [L, *incestum,* defiled], sexual intercourse between persons too closely related to marry legally. —**incestuous,** *adj.*

incidence /in′sidəns/ [L, *incidere,* to happen], **1.** the number of times an event occurs. **2.** in epidemiology, the number of new cases in a particular period.

incidence rate, the rate of new cases of a disease in a specified population over a defined period.

incidental additives /in′siden′təl/ [L, *incidere,* to happen, *additio,* something added], material added to food by the use of pesticides, herbicides, or chemicals used in food processing.

incident report, a document, usually confidential, describing any accident or deviation from policies or orders involving a patient, employee, visitor, or student on the premises of a health care facility.

incident reporting, a nursing intervention from the Nursing Interventions Classification (NIC) defined as written and verbal reporting of any event in the process of patient care that is inconsistent with desired patient outcomes or routine operations of the health care facility.

incineration /insin′ərā′shən/ [L, *incinerare,* to burn to ashes], the removal or reduction of waste materials by burning.

incipient /insip′ē-ənt/ [L, *incipire,* to commence], coming into existence; at an initial stage; beginning to appear; such as a symptom or disease.

incipient dental caries, the earliest detectable signs of tooth decay. At this stage, the lesion has not penetrated the dentin.

incisal /insī′zəl/ [L, *incidere,* to cut into], **1.** cutting. **2.** pertaining to the cutting edge of an anterior tooth.

incisal angle /insī′səl/ [L, *incidere,* to cut into, *angulus,* corner], the angle between the hinge axis-orbital plane and the discluding surface of the maxillary incisors.

incisal guide pin, a metal rod, attached to the upper member of a dental articulator, that touches the incisal guide table to maintain the established vertical separation of the upper and lower members of the articulator.

incision /insizh′ən/ [L, *incidere,* to cut into], a cut produced surgically by a sharp instrument that creates an opening into an organ or space in the body.

incisional hernia /inish′ənəl/ [L, *incidere,* to cut into, *hernia,* rupture], a herniation through a surgical scar.

incision site care, a nursing intervention from the Nursing Interventions Classification (NIC) defined as cleansing, monitoring, and promotion of healing in a wound that is closed with sutures, clips, or staples.

incisor /insī′zər/, one of the four front teeth in each dental arch. The crown of each incisor is chisel shaped and has a sharp cutting edge. Its labial surface is convex, smooth, and highly polished; its lingual surface is concave and, in many individuals, is marked by an inverted V-shaped basal ridge near the gingiva of the maxillary arch. The neck of an incisor is constricted, and the root is single, long, and conic. The upper incisors are larger and stronger than the lower.

incisura /in′sisyoo̅′rə/ [L, *incidere,* to cut into], a notch or incision on an organ or body part.

inclusion /inkloo̅′zhən/ [L, *in,* within, *claudere,* to shut], **1.** the act of enclosing or the condition of being enclosed. **2.** a structure within another, such as an inclusion in the cytoplasm of the cells.

inclusion bodies, normal or abnormal objects of various shapes and sizes observed in the nucleus or cytoplasm of blood cells or other tissue cells.

inclusion body myositis, a progressive inflammatory myopathy primarily involving muscles of the pelvic region and legs, usually seen in older people. The muscles are infiltrated by mononuclear inflammatory cells, sarcoplasmic vacuoles, masses of filaments and filamentous microtubules, and sometimes eosinophilic bodies.

inclusion conjunctivitis, an acute purulent conjunctival infection caused by *Chlamydia* organisms. It occurs in two forms: the infection in infants is characterized by bilateral chemosis, redness, and purulent discharge. The adult variety is unilateral, less severe, and less purulent and is associated with preauricular lymphadenopathy.

inclusion dermoid cyst, a tumor derived from embryonal tissues, caused by the inclusion of foreign tissue when a developmental cleft closes.

inclusiveness principle /inkloo̅′sivnəs/ [L, *in,* within, *claudere,* to shut, *principium,* a beginning], a rule that response to various objects in the environment is proportional to the amount of stimulus provided by each object.

inclusive rate /inkloo̅′siv/, a method of calculating inpatient hospital charges in which a fixed amount covers all services, regardless of number or intensity.

incoercible /in′kō·ur′sibəl/, pertaining to something that cannot be restrained or willfully terminated, as a siege of hiccups.

incoercible vomiting, vomiting that is intractable or uncontrollable.

incoherent /in′kōhir′ənt/ [L, *in,* not, *cohaere,* to hold together], **1.** disordered; without logical connection; disjointed; lacking orderly continuity or relevance. **2.** unable to express one's thoughts or ideas in an orderly, intelligible manner, usually as a result of emotional stress.

incompatibility /in′kəmpat′ibil′itē/ [L, *in,* not, *compatibilis,* agreeing], transfusion of a mismatched red blood cell unit, for instance, giving blood group A donor cells to a blood group O recipient, resulting in a transfusion reaction.

incompatible /in′kəmpat′əbəl/ [L, *in,* not, *compatibilis,* agreeing], unable to coexist. A tissue transplantation may be rejected because recipient and donor antibody factors are incompatible.

incompetence /inkom′pətəns/ [L, *in,* not, *competentia,* capable], **1.** lack of ability to function. **2.** in law, inability to function at a safe level or to provide care that is consistent with standards of practice. —**incompetent,** *adj.*

incompetency /inkomp′ətənsē/, legal status of a person declared in a court hearing to be unable to provide for his or her own needs and protection.

incompetent cervix [L, *in,* not, *competentia,* capable, *cervix,* neck], in obstetrics, a condition characterized by painless dilation of the cervical os of the uterus before term without labor or contractions of the uterus. Miscarriage or premature delivery may result.

incomplete abortion /in′kəmplēt′/ [L, *in,* not, *complere,* to fill, *ab,* away from, *oriri,* to be born], termination of pregnancy in which the products of conception are not entirely expelled or removed. It often causes hemorrhage that may require surgical evacuation by curettage, oxytocics, and blood replacement.

incomplete dislocation [L, *in* + *complere,* to fill + *dis* + *locare,* to place], a partial abnormal separation of the articular surfaces of a joint.

incomplete fracture, a bone break in which the crack in the osseous tissue does not completely traverse the width of the affected bone but may angle off in one or more directions.

incomplete hemianopia, loss of only a part of the half of the visual field.

incomplete hernia [L, *in* + *complere,* to fill up, *hernia,* rupture], a hernia that has not yet protruded through a weak spot or opening.

incomplete protein, a food that is inadequate in one or more of the nine amino acids essential for normal growth and maintenance of tissue when used as the sole source of protein and adequate energy is available.

incongruent communication /inkong′groo̅·ənt/, a communication pattern in which the sender gives conflicting messages on verbal and nonverbal levels and the listener does not know which message to accept.

inconspicuous penis, a categorical term denoting a penis that appears to be abnormally small, although the shaft can be abnormal or normal in size.

incontinence /inkon'tinəns/ [L, *incontinentia,* inability to retain], the inability to control urination or defecation.—**incontinent,** *adj.*

incontinentia pigmenti /inkon'tinen'shə pigmen'tī/, a male-lethal X-linked dominant syndrome with onset at birth or shortly thereafter, characterized by the presence of brown or slate-brown bands, whorls, swirls, or splatter-like hyperpigmented cutaneous lesions, preceded by vesiculobullous and verrucous inflammatory changes, often associated with developmental anomalies involving other structures.

incontinentia pigmenti achromians, a congenital neurocutaneous syndrome, not present at birth but appearing in early life, characterized by the presence of peculiar whorled, linear, and splatter-like patterns of hypopigmentation, and often associated with other abnormalities, including hair loss and ocular, musculoskeletal, and mental disturbances. It is unrelated to incontinentia pigmenti.

Increlex, a trademark for mecasermin.

increment /ing'krəmənt/ [L, *incresere,* to grow], **1.** an increase or gain. **2.** the act of growing or increasing. **3.** the amount of an increase or gain in intrauterine pressure as uterine contractions begin in labor. —**incremental,** *adj.*

incremental line /ing'krəmen'təl/, **1.** one of a series of lines showing successive layers deposited in a tissue. **2.** a very fine line of cementum that follows the contours of a tooth.

incremental lines of Ebner [Victor von Ebner, Austrian histologist, 1842–1925], delicate lines seen on ground sections of a tooth, demarcating increments of dentin.

incrustation, hardened exudate, scale, or scab.

incubation period /in'kyəbā'shən/ [L, *incubare,* to lie on; Gk, *peri,* around, *hodos,* way], **1.** the time between exposure to a pathogenic organism and the onset of symptoms of a disease. **2.** the time required to induce the development of an embryo in an egg or to induce the development and replication of tissue cells or microorganisms being grown in culture media or other special laboratory environment. **3.** the time allowed for a chemical reaction or process to proceed.

incubator /in'kyəbā'tər/, an apparatus used to provide a controlled environment, especially temperature.

incudectomy /in'kyōōdek'təmē/ [L, *incus,* anvil; Gk, *ektomē,* excision], surgical removal of the incus, performed to treat conductive hearing loss that results from necrosis of the tip of the incus. The defective incus is excised and replaced with a bone chip graft so that sound vibrations are again transmitted.

incurable /inkyōō'rəbəl/, not responding to medical or surgical treatment.

incus /ing'kəs/ *pl.* **incudes** [L, anvil], one of the three ossicles in the middle ear, resembling an anvil. It transmits sound vibrations from the malleus to the stapes.

IND, abbreviation for **investigational new drug.**

indanedione derivative /indane'dē·ōn/, one of a small group of oral anticoagulants designed for long-term therapeutic use in patients who cannot tolerate other oral anticoagulants.

indemnify /indem'nifī/, to protect against loss or injury by compensating for the loss or injury.

indentation /in'dəntā'shən/ [L, *in,* within, *dens,* tooth], a notch, pit, or depression in the surface of an object, such as toothmarks on the tongue or skin.—**indent,** *v.*

independence /in'dəpen'dəns/ [L, *in,* not, *de,* from, *pendere,* to hang], **1.** the state or quality of being independent; autonomy; freedom from the influence, guidance, or control of a person or a group. **2.** a lack of requirement or reliance on another for physical existence or emotional needs. —**independent,** *adj.*

independent living center, rehabilitation facility in which disabled persons can receive special education and training in the performance of all or most ADL with a particular handicap.

independent practice, in nursing, the practice of certain aspects of professional nursing that are encompassed by applicable licensure and law and require no supervision or direction from others. Nurses in independent practice may have an office in which they see patients and charge fees for service. In all nursing settings, state practice acts define certain aspects of nursing practice that are independent and may define those that must be done only under supervision or direction of another individual, usually a physician.

Independent Practice Association (IPA), a U.S. type of physician alliance in which the physicians own the practice, as opposed to physicians employed by an entity such as a health maintenance organization.

independent variable, in research, a variable that is manipulated by the researcher and evaluated by its measurable effect on the dependent variable or variables.

Inderal, a trademark for a nonselective beta-adrenergic blocking agent (propranolol).

indeterminate cleavage /in'ditur'minit/ [L, *in,* not, *determinare,* to fix limits; AS, *cleofan,* to split], mitotic division of the fertilized ovum into blastomeres that have similar developmental potential and, if isolated, can give rise to a complete individual embryo.

index /in'deks/ *pl.* **indexes, indices** [L, that which points out], **1.** the second digit of the hand, the finger adjacent to the thumb. **2.** a unit-less quantity, usually a ratio of two measurable quantities having the same dimensions, or such a ratio multiplied by 100. **3.** a core or mold used in dentistry to record or maintain the relative position of a tooth or teeth to one another and/or to a cast, to ensure reproduction in the dental prosthesis of their original position. **4.** a directory, in particular an alphabetized list of terms, each term accompanied by page numbers or other notations telling where it appears in a given work or set of works.

index astigmatism [L, *indicare,* to make known + *a* + *stigma,* point], an astigmatism caused by unequal refractive indices in different parts of the lens.

index case [L, *indicare,* to make known], in epidemiology, the first case of a disease, as contrasted with subsequent cases.

Index Medicus, an index published monthly by the National Library of Medicine, which lists articles from the medical, nursing, and allied health literature from throughout the world by subject and by author.

index myopia, a kind of nearsightedness caused by a variation in the index of refraction of the eye media.

India ink test, a test used to detect *Cryptococcus* in wet preparations of patient specimens. The capsule of the yeast resists colorization by the India ink, resulting in clear organisms against dark background.

Indiana pouch, a type of continent urinary diversion in which part of the ileum and cecum is modified to form a pouch with modification of the ileocecal orifice to maintain continence.

Indian Health Service, a bureau of the Department of Health and Human Services for providing public health and medical services to Native Americans and Alaska natives in the United States. In Canada, the services are provided by the Ministry of Indian Affairs.

indican /in'dikən/ [Gk, *indikon,* indigo], a substance (potassium indoxyl sulfate) produced in the intestine by the decomposition of tryptophan, absorbed by the intestinal wall, and excreted in the urine. Its level may be elevated in the urine of patients on high-protein diets or those suffering from GI disease.

indication /in'dikā'shən/ [L, *indicare,* to make known], a reason to prescribe a medication or perform a treatment. A bacterial infection may be an indication for the prescription of a specific antibiotic; appendicitis is an indication for appendectomy. **—indicate,** *v.*

indicator /in'dikā'tər/, a tape, paper, tablet, or other substance that is used to test for a specific reaction because it changes in a predictable visible way.

indicator-dilution method, a method for measuring blood volume. A known amount of a substance that dissolves freely in blood but does not leave the capillaries is injected intravenously. After a few minutes a sample of blood is withdrawn, and the volume of blood in the body is calculated from the concentration of the substance in the sample, sample's volume, and the hematocrit.

indifference-to-pain syndrome /indif'ərəns/, a congenital lack of pain sensitivity caused by defective development of sensory nerve endings in the skin.

indigence /in'dijəns/ [L, *indigere,* to need], a condition of having insufficient income to pay for adequate medical care without depriving oneself or one's dependents of food, clothing, shelter, or other living essentials.

indigenous /indij'ənəs/ [L, *indigena,* a native], native to or occurring naturally in a specified area or environment, as certain species of bacteria in the human digestive tract.

indigestible /in'dijes'təbəl/ [L, *in,* not, *digerere,* to separate], pertaining to a food substance that cannot be broken down within the digestive tract and converted into an absorbable nutrient.

indinavir, an antiretroviral protease inhibitor prescribed in the treatment of HIV infection.

indirect anaphylaxis [L, *in,* not, *directus,* straight; Gk, *ana,* again, *phylaxis,* protection], an exaggerated reaction of hypersensitivity to one of a person's own antigens that occurs because the antigen has been altered in some way.

indirect calorimetry, the measurement of the amount of heat generated in an oxidation reaction by determining the intake or consumption of oxygen or by measuring the amount of carbon dioxide or nitrogen released and translating these quantities into a heat equivalent.

indirect Coombs' test, a blood test used during blood compatibility crossmatching to detect the presence of circulating antibodies against RBCs. The major purpose of this test is to determine whether the patient has serum antibodies (besides the major ABO/Rh system) to RBCs that he or she is about to receive by blood transfusion.

indirect laryngoscopy [L, *in,* not, *directus,* straight; Gk, *larynx* + *skopein,* to view], a method of examining the larynx with a mirror.

indirect nursing care functions, liaison nurse activities used to solve problems with a consultee who is responsible and accountable for implementing and evaluating any recommended changes.

indirect ophthalmoscope, an ophthalmoscope with a biconvex lens that produces a reversed direct stereoscopic image.

indirect provider reimbursement, a method of payment to an agency for health services delivered by providers, such as nurses.

indirect restorative method, a technique for fabricating a restoration on a cast of the original tooth, such as the indirect construction of an inlay. After a die is made from an impression of the prepared tooth, a wax pattern is formed and the inlay is cast. The cast inlay is then fitted and finished on the die and then cemented into the tooth.

indirect retainer, that part of a removable partial denture that resists movement of a free-end denture base away from its tissue support by means of lever action on the opposite side of the fulcrum line.

indirect vision [L, *in* + *directus,* straight, *visio,* seeing], a visual sensation caused by stimulation of the extramacular part of the retina.

indium (In) [L, *indicum,* indigo], a silvery metallic element with some nonmetallic chemical properties. Its atomic number is 49, and its atomic mass is 114.82. It is used in electronic semiconductors.

indium 111 in ibritumomab tiuxetan, a chelate of indium 111 and the immunoconjugate ibritumomab tiuxetan, used in the treatment of non-Hodgkin's lymphoma.

individual immunity /in′divij′oo·əl/ [L, *individuus,* indivisible, *immunis,* free from], a form of natural immunity not shared by most other members of the race and species. It probably occurs as the result of an infection that was not recognized when it occurred.

individual-model HMO, a health maintenance organization (HMO) in which individual physicians contract directly and independently with the HMO.

individual psychology, a modified system of psychoanalysis, developed by Alfred Adler, that views maladaptive behavior and personality disorders as resulting from

a conflict between the desire to dominate and feelings of inferiority.

Indocin, a trademark for a nonsteroidal antiinflammatory agent (indomethacin).

indocyanine green /in′dōsī′ənēn/, a dye occurring as an olive-brown, dark green, dark blue, or black powder, used intravenously as a diagnostic aid in the determination of blood volume, cardiac output, and hepatic function.

indocyanine green clearance, the hepatic clearance of indocyanine green, calculated in liver function tests.

indole /in′dōl/, a volatile chemical produced during serotonin metabolism. It is partly responsible for the odor of the feces.

indoleacetic acid /in′dōləsē′tik, -əset′ik/, a major terminal metabolite of tryptophan that is present in very small amounts in normal urine and excreted in elevated quantities by patients with carcinoid tumors.

indolent /in′dələnt/ [L, *in* + *dolere,* to suffer pain], **1.** pertaining to an organic disorder that is accompanied by little or no pain. **2.** slow to heal or grow, e.g., wounds that heal very slowly.

indomethacin /in′dōmeth′əsin/, a nonsteroidal antiinflammatory agent prescribed in the treatment of arthritis, gout attacks, and certain other inflammatory conditions.

induce /ind(y)oos′/ [L, *inducere,* to lead in], to cause or stimulate the start of an activity, as an enzyme induces a metabolic activity.—**inducer, induction,** *n.*

induced abortion, an intentional termination of pregnancy before the fetus has developed enough to live if born. The type of procedure depends on stage of pregnancy and may be either medical or surgical in nature.

induced fever, a deliberate elevation of body temperature by application of heat or by inoculation with a fever-producing organism to kill heat-sensitive pathogens.

induced lethargy, a trancelike state produced during hypnosis.

induced mutation [L, *inducere,* to lead in, *mutare,* to change], a mutation that is produced by treatment with a physical or chemical agent that affects the DNA molecules of a living organism.

induced phagocytosis [L, *inducere,* to lead in; Gk, *phagein,* to eat, *kytos,* cell], the ingestion of microorganisms and other foreign particles by cells of the reticuloendothelial system because of a stimulus from the microorganisms or particles.

induced psychotic disorder, a severe mental disturbance in which there is a withdrawal from reality, resulting from exposure to a toxic agent such as a drug or hallucinogen.

induced trance, a somnambulistic state resulting from hypnotism.

induced vomiting [L, *inducere,* to lead in; *vomere,* to vomit], vomiting produced by administration of ipecac syrup, soapy water, or handwashing liquid detergent or by insertion of a finger or blunt instrument into the throat. Vomiting may be medically indicated in cases of ingestion of noncaustic poisons but may also be self-induced by patients afflicted with bulimia.

inducer /indo͞oʹsər/, a substance, usually a substrate of a specific enzyme, that combines with and inactivates the repressor produced by a regulator gene in bacteria.

induction /indukʹshən/ [L, *inducere,* to lead in], the process of stimulating and determining morphogenetic differentiation in a developing embryo through the action of chemical substances transmitted from one embryonic part to another.

induction chemotherapy, chemotherapy as the initial treatment for cancer, especially as part of combined modality therapy.

induction of anesthesia, 1. the administration of a drug or combination of drugs at the beginning of an anesthetic that results in a state of general anesthesia. 2. the process of causing general anesthesia by the administration of pharmaceutics.

induction of labor, an obstetric procedure in which labor is initiated artificially by means of amniotomy or administration of oxytocics.

induction phase, the period during which a normal cell becomes transformed into a cancerous cell.

induction therapy, the first therapeutic measure used to treat a disease, especially when combined modality therapy is planned.

inductive approach /indukʹtiv/, the analysis of data and examination of practice problems within their own context rather than from a predetermined theoretic basis.

inductor /indukʹtər/ [L, *inducere,* to lead in], in embryology, a tissue or cell that emits a chemical substance that stimulates some morphogenetic effect in the developing embryo.

induration /inʹdyərāʹshən/ [L, *indurare,* to make hard], hardening of a tissue, particularly the skin, caused by edema, inflammation, or infiltration by a neoplasm.—**indurated,** *adj.*

indurative myocarditis /inʹdyərāʹtiv/ [L, *indurare,* to make hard; Gk, *mys,* muscle, *kardia,* heart, *itis,* inflammation], inflammation of the myocardium that leads to a hardening of the muscles of the heart walls.

industrial health [L, *industria,* diligence; ME, *helthe*], the health concerns associated with the workplace, such as exposure to asbestos, mining and milling dusts, and metal and acid vapors; lighting; and ergonomic factors.

industrial psychology [L, *industria,* diligence], the application of psychologic principles and techniques to the problems of business and industry, including the selection of personnel, the motivation of workers, and the development of training programs.

indwelling catheter /inʹdwelling/ [L, *in,* within; AS, *dwellan,* to remain], any catheter designed to be left in place for a prolonged period.

inebriant /inēʹbrē-ənt/ [L, *inebriare,* to make drunk], a substance that induces inebriation or intoxication, as does ethanol.

inebriate /inēʹbrē-āt/, to make intoxicated.

inert /inurtʹ/ [L, *iners,* idle], 1. not moving or acting, such as inert matter. 2. of a chemical substance, not taking part in a chemical reaction. 3. of a medical ingredient, not active pharmacologically; serving only as a bulking, binding, or sweetening agent or other excipient in a medication.

inert gas, neutral monotomic elements with completely filled outer electron shells. These elements are all gaseous and extremely nonreactive. The inert gases are argon, helium, and neon.

inertia /inurʹshə/ [L, idleness], 1. the tendency of a body at rest to remain at rest unless acted on by an outside force, and the tendency of a body in motion to remain at motion in the direction in which it is moving unless acted on by an outside force. 2. an abnormal condition characterized by a general inactivity or sluggishness, such as colonic inertia or uterine inertia.

inertial impaction /inurʹshəl/, the deposition of large aerosol particles on the walls of an airway conduit. The impaction tends to occur where the airway direction changes.

inevitable abortion /inevʹitəbəl/ [L, *inevitabilis,* unavoidable], a condition of pregnancy in which spontaneous termination is imminent and cannot be prevented. It is characterized by bleeding, uterine cramping, dilation of the cervix, and presentation of the conceptus in the cervical os.

in extremis, in the extremity, or at the point of death.

infant /inʹfənt/ [L, *infans,* unable to speak], 1. a child who is in the earliest stage of extrauterine life, a time extending from the first month after birth to approximately 12 months of age, when the baby is able to assume an erect posture. 2. in law, a person not of full legal age; a minor. 3. pertaining to infancy; in an early stage of development.—**infantile,** *adj.*

infant botulism, an intoxication by neurotoxins produced by *Clostridium botulinum* that occurs in children less than 6 months of age. The condition is character-ized by severe hypotonicity of all muscles, constipation, lethargy, and feeding dif-ficulties, and it may lead to respiratory insufficiency. The botulism neurotoxin is usually found in the GI tract rather than in the blood, indicating that it is probably produced in the gut rather than ingested.

infant care, a nursing intervention from the Nursing Interventions Classification (NIC) defined as provision of developmen-tally appropriate family-centered care to the child under 1 year of age.

infant death, the death of a live-born infant between the ages of 1 month and 1 year of age.

infant feeder, a device for nourishing small or weak babies who cannot suck hard enough to get milk from the breast or a bottle. The feeder resembles a bulb syringe with a long soft nipple on the end.

infanticide /infan′tisīd/ [L, *infans,* unable to speak, *caedere,* to kill], **1.** the killing of an infant or young child. **2.** one who takes the life of an infant or young child. —**infanticidal,** *adj.*

infantile /in′fəntīl/ [L, *infans,* unable to speak], **1.** of, relating to, or characteris-tic of infants or infancy. **2.** lacking matu-rity, sophistication, or reasonableness. **3.** affected with infantilism. **4.** being in a very early stage of development.

infantile amnesia, in psychology, the inability to remember events from early childhood.

infantile arteritis, a disorder in infants and young children characterized by inflammation of many arteries in which atherosclerotic lesions are rarely present.

infantile autism, a pervasive develop-mental disorder characterized by abnormal emotional, social, and linguistic develop-ment in a child. Symptoms include abnor-mal ways of relating to people, objects, and situations. It may result from organic brain dysfunction, in which case it occurs before 3 years of age.

infantile cerebral ataxic paralysis [L, *infans,* unable to speak, *cerebrum,* the brain; Gk, *ataxia,* without order, *paraly-ein,* to be palsied], a form of congenital diplegia, characterized by cerebral malde-velopment, ataxia, spasticity of the legs, and possibly mental deficiency.

infantile cirrhosis, a progressive fibrous liver disorder caused by protein malnutrition.

infantile colic [L, *infans,* unable to speak; Gk, *kolikos,* pain in the colon], a descrip-tive term for a suggested intestinal cause of discomfort in a newborn; specific causes and mechanisms have not been defined. The typical infantile colic patient eats and

gains weight but may also appear exces-sively hungry. Aerophagia caused by cry-ing may lead to flatulence and abdominal distension.

infantile cortical hyperostosis, a famil-ial disorder characterized in an infant by subperiosteal bone formation over many bones, causing swellings and tenderness in the affected areas. The child also tends to be feverish and irritable. The mandible is most commonly involved. It disappears during childhood.

infantile dwarf, a person whose men-tal and physical development is greatly retarded as a result of various causes, such as genetic or developmental defects.

infantile encephalitis [L, *infans,* unable to speak; Gk, *enkephalos,* brain, *itis,* inflam-mation], any of a group of brain inflam-mation conditions affecting infants. The cause may be a direct viral infection or a secondary encephalitis that is a complica-tion of measles, chickenpox, rubella, or other diseases.

infantile hemiplegia, paralysis of one side of the body that may occur at birth as a result of a cerebral hemorrhage, in utero as a result of lack of oxygen, or during a febrile illness in infancy.

infantile hydrocele [L, *infans;* Gk, *hydor,* water, *kele,* hernia], an accumulation of fluid in the tunica vaginalis. It may be pres-ent at birth or acquired.

infantile myofibromatosis, a condition present at birth or occurring soon after, characterized by solitary or multiple, firm, rubbery, spherical or ovoid nodules in the skin and subcutaneous tissue. The nodules are composed of myofibroblasts and may undergo ulceration and calcification. In about half of patients, skeletal fibromas also occur. Visceral involvement may occur and is highly lethal.

infantile neuroaxonal dystrophy, pro-gressive hereditary degenerative encephalopathy transmitted as an autoso-mal-recessive trait, beginning in infancy with muscular hypotonia and arrest of development in late infancy, followed by dementia, blindness, spasticity, and ataxia. Pathologically it is characterized by wide-spread focal swellings and degeneration of the axons with scattered globular bodies in the brain.

infantile scurvy, a nutritional disease caused by an inadequate dietary supply of vitamin C, which may occur because cow's milk unfortified with vitamin C is the prin-cipal food in an infant's diet.

infantile spasms, a syndrome of severe myoclonus appearing in the first 18 months of life and associated with general cere-bral deterioration. It is marked by severe flexion spasms of the head, neck, and trunk and extension of the arms and legs.

infantile spinal paralysis [L, *infans,* unable to speak + *spina;* Gk, *paralyein,* to be palsied], acute anterior poliomyelitis, a viral infection characterized by nonspecific illnesses, aseptic meningitis, and flaccid weakness of muscle groups.

infantile uterus, a uterus that has failed to attain adult characteristics.

infantilism /infan′tiliz′əm/ [L, *infans,* unable to speak], 1. a condition in which various anatomic, physiologic, and psychologic characteristics of childhood persist in the adult. It is characterized by mental retardation, underdeveloped sexual organs, and usually small stature. 2. a condition, usually of psychologic rather than organic origin, characterized by speech and voice patterns in an older child or adult that are typical of very young children.

infant mortality, the statistical rate of infant death during the first year after live birth, expressed as the number of such deaths per 1000 live births in a specific geographic area or institution in a given period.

infant of chemically dependent mother, a newborn who shows withdrawal symptoms, usually within the first 24 hours of life, most commonly caused by maternal antepartum dependence on heroin, methadone, diazepam, phenobarbital, or alcohol. Characteristic symptoms include tremors, irritability, hyperactive reflexes, increased muscle tone, twitching, increased mucus production, nasal congestion, respiratory distress, excessive sweating, elevated temperature, vomiting, diarrhea, and dehydration.

infarct /infärkt′/ [L, *infarcire,* to stuff], a localized area of necrosis in a tissue resulting from anoxia. It is caused by an interruption in the blood supply to the area or, less frequently, by circulatory stasis produced by the occlusion of a vein that ordinarily carries blood away from the area. Some infarcts are pale and white because of the lack of circulation. Others may resemble a red, swollen bruise because of hemorrhage and an accumulation of blood in the area.

infarct extension, an MI that has spread beyond the original area, usually as a result of the death of cells in the ischemic margin of the infarct zone.

infarction /infärk′shən/ [L, *infarcire,* to stuff], the development and formation of an infarct.

infect [L, *inficere,* to stain], to transmit a pathogen that may induce development of an infectious disease in another person.

infected abortion, a spontaneous or induced termination of an immature pregnancy in which the products of conception

have become infected, causing fever and requiring antibiotic therapy and evacuation of the uterus.

infected hydronephrosis, a dilation of the renal pelvis and calyces that has become complicated by bacterial infection.

infection /infek′shən/ [L, *inficere,* to stain], 1. the invasion of the body by pathogenic microorganisms that reproduce and multiply, causing disease by local cellular injury, secretion of a toxin, or antigen-antibody reaction in the host. 2. a disease caused by the invasion of the body by pathogenic microorganisms. —**infectious,** *adj.*

infection control[1], programs of disease surveillance, generally within health care facilities, designed to investigate, prevent, and control the spread of infections and their causative microorganisms. Infection control can include the policies and procedures of a hospital or other health facility to minimize the risk of spreading of nosocomial or community-acquired infections to patients or members of the staff.

infection control[2], a nursing intervention from the Nursing Interventions Classification (NIC) defined as minimizing the acquisition and transmission of infectious agents.

infection control committee, a group of hospital health professionals composed of infection control personnel, with medical, nursing, administrative, and occasionally dietary and housekeeping department representatives, who plan and supervise infection control activities.

infection control: intraoperative, a nursing intervention from the Nursing Interventions Classification (NIC) defined as preventing nosocomial infection in the operating room.

infection control nurse, a registered nurse who is assigned responsibility for surveillance and infection prevention, education, and control activities.

infection protection, a nursing intervention from the Nursing Interventions Classification (NIC) defined as prevention and early detection of infection in a patient at risk.

infection severity, a nursing outcome from the Nursing Outcomes Classification (NOC) defined as the severity of infection and associated symptoms.

infection severity: newborn, a nursing outcome from the Nursing Outcomes Classification (NOC) defined as the severity of infection and associated symptoms during the first 28 days of life.

infectious /infek′chəs/, 1. capable of causing an infection. 2. caused by an infection.

infectious arthritis [L, *inficere*, to stain; Gk, *arthron*, joint, *itis*, inflammation], arthritis caused by bacteria, rickettsiae, mycoplasmas, viruses, fungi, or parasites.

infectious bulbar paralysis [L, *inficere*, to stain, *bulbus*, swollen root; Gk, *paralyein*, to be palsied], a herpesvirus disease of animals that may cause a mild pruritus when transmitted to humans.

infectious disease (ID) [L, *inficere*, to stain + *dis;* Fr, *aise*, ease], any clinically evident communicable disease, or one that can be transmitted from one human being to another or from animal to human by direct or indirect contact.

infectious endocarditis, endocarditis caused by infection with microorganisms, especially bacteria and fungi.

infectious gastritis, any type of inflammation of the gastric mucosa, usually chronic, caused by a bacterial infection in the stomach, the most common type being *Helicobacter pylori* gastritis. Many cases are asymptomatic, but symptoms can include dyspepsia and GI bleeding. In immunocompromised patients, gastritis may occur as a complication of TB, syphilis, or other conditions.

infectious granuloma [L, *inficere*, to stain, *granulum*, little grain; Gk, *oma*, tumor], a lumpy lesion of granuloma tissue that may develop in diseases such as TB, syphilis, and actinomycosis.

infectious isolation [L, *inficere*, to stain; It, *isolare*, to detach], a practice of confining a patient with a particularly virulent disease to an isolated room or other area to reduce the risk of contact and spread of the disease among hospital personnel.

infectious mononucleosis [L, *inficere*, to stain; Gk, *monos*, single; L, *nucleus*, nut; Gk, *osis*, condition], an acute herpesvirus infection caused by the Epstein-Barr virus. The hallmark signs are profound fatigue, a fever that peaks in the late afternoon at 101° F to 105° F (38.3° C to 40.6° C), severely painful and exudative pharyngitis, and symmetric lymphadenopathy. Splenomegaly is usually present in the second or third week. Mild hepatomegaly may also be present.

infectious myringitis, an inflammatory contagious condition of the eardrum caused by viral or bacterial infection. It is characterized by the development of painful vesicles on the eardrum, very often linked to otitis media.

infectious nucleic acid, DNA or, more commonly, viral RNA that is able to infect the nucleic acid of a cell and to induce the host to produce viruses.

infective tubulointerstitial nephritis [L, *inficere*, to stain, *tubulus*, tubule, *interstitium,* space between], an acute inflammation of the kidneys caused by an infection by *Escherichia coli* or another pyogenic pathogen. The condition is characterized by chills, fever, nausea and vomiting, flank pain, dysuria, proteinuria, and hematuria. The kidney may become enlarged, and parts of the renal cortex may be destroyed.

infectivity /infektiv′itē/ [L, *inficere*, to stain], the ability of a pathogen to spread rapidly from one host to another.

inferior /infir′ē·ər/ [L, *inferus,* lower], **1.** situated below a given point of reference, as the feet are inferior to the legs. **2.** of poorer quality or value.

inferior alveolar artery, an artery that descends with the inferior alveolar nerve from the first or mandibular part of the maxillary artery to the mandibular foramen.

inferior aperture of minor pelvis, an irregular aperture bounded by the coccyx, the sacrotuberous ligaments, part of the ischium, the sides of the pubic arch, and the pubic symphysis.

inferior aperture of thorax, an irregular opening bounded by the twelfth thoracic vertebra, the eleventh and twelfth ribs, and the edge of the costal cartilages as they meet the sternum.

inferior carotid triangle [L, *inferior,* lower; Gk, *karos,* heavy sleep; L, *triangulus,* three-cornered], a triangular area bounded by the midline of the neck, the superior belly of the omohyoid muscle above, and the sternocleidomastoid muscle behind.

inferior cervical ganglion, a ganglion at the lower end of the cervical part of the sympathetic trunk that combines with the first thoracic ganglion to form the stellate ganglion.

inferior conjunctival fornix, the space in the fold of conjunctiva created by the reflection of the conjunctiva covering the eyeball and the lining of the lower eyelid.

inferior gastric node, a node in one of two groups of gastric lymph glands, lying between the two layers of the lesser omentum along the pyloric half of the greater curvature of the stomach.

inferior gluteal artery, a large terminal trunk of the internal iliac artery that contributes to the blood supply of the gluteal region and anastomoses with a network of vessels around the hip joint.

inferior gluteal nerve, a nerve that supplies the gluteus maximus.

inferiority complex /infir′ē·ôr′itē/, **1.** a personal feeling or sense of being inadequate. It is largely unconscious and influences attitudes and behaviors. **2.** in psychoanalysis, a complex characterized by striving for unrealistic goals motivated by an unresolved Oedipus complex. **3.** *informal.* a feeling of being inferior.

inferior kidney, inferior segment of kidney; the renal segment located most inferiorly.

inferior mesenteric artery, a visceral branch of the abdominal aorta, supplying the left half of the transverse colon, all of the descending and iliac colons, and most of the rectum.

inferior mesenteric node, a node in one of the three groups of visceral lymph glands serving the viscera of the abdomen and the pelvis. The inferior mesenteric nodes drain the descending colon, the iliac and sigmoid parts of the colon, and the upper part of the rectum. Their efferent vessels pass to the preaortic nodes.

inferior mesenteric vein, the vein in the lower body that returns the blood from the rectum, the sigmoid and descending colons, and part of the transverse colon.

inferior olivary nucleus [L, *inferior,* lower, *oliva,* olive, *nucleus,* nut kernel], a small purse-shaped collection of nerve cells lying posterolateral to the pyramid, just below the level of the pons. It is a source of cerebellar climbing fibers.

inferior orbital fissure, a groove in the inferolateral wall of the orbit that contains the infraorbital and zygomatic nerves and the infraorbital vessels.

inferior phrenic artery, a small visceral branch of the abdominal aorta that arises from the aorta itself, the renal artery, or the celiac artery. It supplies the diaphragm.

inferior rectal plexus, the subcutaneous portion of the rectal venous plexus, below the pectinate line.

inferior right lateral flexure of rectum, the fourth bend of the rectum, where it deviates laterally to the right.

inferior sagittal sinus, one of the six venous channels of the posterior dura mater, draining blood from the brain into the internal jugular vein.

inferior subscapular nerve /sub skap′yo͞olər/, one of three small nerves that arise from the posterior cord of the brachial plexus. It supplies part of the subscapularis.

inferior thyroid vein, one of the few veins that arise in the venous plexus on the thyroid gland and form a plexus ventral to the trachea, under the sternothyroideus muscle.

inferior ulnar collateral artery, one of a pair of branches of the deep brachial arteries, carrying blood to the muscles of the forearm.

inferior vena cava, the large vein that returns deoxygenated blood to the heart from parts of the body below the diaphragm. The vessel receives blood from the two common iliacs, the lumbar veins, and the testicular veins.

inferior vesical artery, an artery in men that supplies branches to the bladder, ureter, seminal vesicle, and prostate.

inferolateral /in′fərōlat′ərəl/ [L, *inferus,* lower, *latus,* side], pertaining to a location situated below and to the side.

inferomedial /in′fərōmē′dē·əl/ [L, *inferus,* lower, *medius,* middle], pertaining to a location situated below and toward the center.

infertile /infur′təl/ [L, *in,* not, *fertilis,* fruitful], denoting the inability to produce offspring.

infertility /in′furtil′itē/, the condition of being unable to produce offspring. This condition may be present in one or both sex partners and may be temporary and reversible. The cause may be physical, or it may result from psychologic or emotional problems. The condition is classified as primary, in which pregnancy has never occurred, and secondary, when there have been one or more pregnancies.

infest /infest′/, to attack, invade, and subsist on the skin or in the internal organs of a host.

infestation /in′festā′shən/ [L, *infestare,* to attack], the presence of animal parasites in the environment, on the skin, or in the hair of a host.

infiltrate /infil′trāt/, **1.** to penetrate the interstices of a tissue or substance. **2.** the material or solution so deposited.

infiltration /in′filträs′hən/ [L, *in,* within, *filtare,* to strain through], the process whereby a fluid passes into the tissues, such as when a local anesthetic is administered or an IV infusion infiltrates.

infiltrative disorder /infil′trətiv/, a condition caused by the diffusion or accumulation in cells or tissues of substances not normally found in those cells or tissues.

infirmary /infur′mərē/ [L, *infirmus,* weak], a place that provides care for sick or infirm persons.

inflammation [L, *inflammare,* to set afire], the protective or destructive response of body tissues to irritation or injury. Inflammation may be acute or chronic. Its cardinal signs are redness (rubor), heat (calor), swelling (tumor), and pain (dolor), often accompanied by loss of function.

inflammatory autobullectomy, spontaneous regression of a bulla caused by inflammation in patients with bullous emphysema.

inflammatory cell, a neutrophil, macrophage, monocyte, eosinophil, or basophil that participates in the inflammatory response to a foreign substance.

inflammatory dysmenorrhea [L, *inflammare;* Gk, *dys* + *men,* month, *rhein,* to flow], menstrual pain that accompanies pelvic infection, fibroids, or endometritis.

inflammatory fracture [L, *inflammare,* to set afire, *fractura,* break], a break in bone tissue weakened by inflammation.

inflammatory response, a tissue reaction to injury or an antigen that may include pain, swelling, itching, redness, heat, and loss of function.

inflammatory scoliosis [L, *inflammare;* Gk, *skoliosis,* curvature], a form of scoliosis caused by muscle spasms associated with acute inflammation.

inflatable splint /inflā′təbəl/ [L, *in,* within, *flare,* to blow; ME, *splente*], a tubular device that is placed around a patient's extremity and inflated with air to maintain rigidity.

inflection, the act of bending inward or the state of being bent inward.

infliximab, a monoclonal antibody used to treat moderate to severe fistulizing Crohn's disease.

influenza /in′floo·en′zə/ [It, influence], a highly contagious infection of the respiratory tract caused by orthomyxovirus and transmitted by airborne droplet infection. Symptoms include sore throat, cough, fever, muscular pains, and weakness. The incubation period is brief (from 1 to 3 days), and the onset is usually sudden, with chills, fever, respiratory symptoms, headache, myalgia, and extreme fatigue.

influenza A virus, influenza B virus, influenza C virus, species in the genera *Influenzavirus A, Influenzavirus B,* and *Influenzavirus C.*

influenza-like illness, nonspecific respiratory illness whose symptoms resemble those of influenza but which are usually caused not by influenza virus infection but by other viruses or by bacteria.

Influenzavirus /in′floo·en′zävi′rus/, former genus name for the viruses that cause influenza, now found to be two different genera, which are named *Influenzavirus A* and *Influenzavirus B.*

Influenzavirus A, a genus of viruses of the family Orthomyxoviridae, containing the agent of influenza A.

Influenzavirus B, a genus of viruses of the family Orthomyxoviridae, containing the agent of influenza B.

Influenzavirus C, a genus of viruses of the family Orthomyxoviridae, containing the agent of influenza C.

influenza-virus vaccine, an active immunizing agent prescribed for immunization against influenza.

informal admission, a type of admission to a psychiatric hospital in which there is no formal or written application and the patient is free to leave at any time.

information processing, a nursing outcome from the Nursing Outcomes Classification (NOC) defined as the ability to acquire, organize, and use information.

informed consent [L, *informare,* to give form, *consentire,* to sense], permission obtained from a patient to perform a specific test or procedure. Informed consent is required before most invasive procedures are performed and before a patient is admitted to a research study.

infraclavicular fossa /in′frəkləvik′yələr/, a small pocket or indentation just below the clavicle on both sides of the body.

infraclusion /in′frəkloo′zhən/ [L, *infra,* below, *occludere,* to close up], malocclusion in which a tooth has failed to erupt fully and reach the line of occlusion and is out of contact with the opposing tooth.

infraction fracture /infrak′shən/ [L, *infractio,* a breaking, *fractura,* break], a neoplastic fracture characterized by a small radiolucent line in radiographs and most commonly associated with a disorder of metabolism.

infradentale /in′frədentā′lē/, a bone measurement landmark, being the highest anterior point on the gingiva between the mandibular central incisors.

infradian rhythm /in′frā′dē·ən/ [L, *infra,* below, *dies,* day; Gk, *rhythmos*], a biorhythm that has a period shorter than 24 hours.

infraglenoid tubercle, a large triangular roughening inferior to the glenoid cavity in the scapula that is the site of attachment for the long head of the triceps brachii muscle.

infrahyoid /in′frəhī′oid/, pertaining to the area below the hyoid bone, particularly the group of muscles attached to it.

inframammary fold (IMF), the angle of deflection where the breast tissue meets the chest wall below the breast.

inframammary region, the part of the pectoral region inferior to the breast, bordered inferiorly by the hypochondriac region of the abdomen.

inframaxillary, 1. pertaining to the mandible, or lower jaw. 2. lying below the maxilla, or upper jaw.

infranodal block /in′frənō′dəl/ [L, *infra,* below, *nodus,* knot; Fr, *bloc*], a type of atrioventricular (AV) block caused by an abnormality below the AV node, either in the bundle of His or in both bundle branches. The condition is often the result of arteriosclerosis, degenerative diseases, a defect in the conduction system, or a tumor. Symptoms include frequent episodes of fainting and a pulse rate of 20 to 40 beats/min.

infranodal disease, a cardiac disorder involving the electrical conduction system of the heart below the atrioventricular node.

infraorbital /in'frə·ôr'bitəl/ [L, *infra,* below, *orbita,* wheeltrack], pertaining to the area beneath the floor of the bony cavity in which the eyeball is located.

infraorbital foramen [L, *infra,* below, *orbita,* wheeltrack, *foramen,* hole], an opening on the anterior aspect of the maxilla. Through it pass the inferior orbital nerves and blood vessels.

infrapatellar fat pad /in'frəpətel'ər/, an area of palpable soft tissue in front of the joint space on either side of the patellar tendon.

infrared radiation /in'frəred'/ [L, *infra;* AS, *read,* red; L, *radiare,* to emit rays], electromagnetic radiation with wavelengths between about 700 nm and 1 mm, or longer than those of visible light but shorter than those of microwaves and radio waves. Infrared radiation that strikes the body surface is perceived as heat.

infrared therapy, treatment by exposure to various wavelengths of infrared radiation. Infrared treatment is performed to relieve pain and to stimulate circulation of blood.

infrared thermography, measurement of temperature through the detection of infrared radiation emitted by heated tissue.

infrasonics /in'frəson'iks/, sound frequencies that are below the range of human hearing.

infraspinous fossa, a large triangular region of the posterior scapula below the spine.

infraspinous muscle /in'frəspīnās/ [L, *infra,* below *spina,* spine], the muscle arising from the infraspinous fossa and inserting in the greater tubercle of the humerus. It functions to rotate the humerus laterally.

infraversion /in'frəver'zhən/ [L, *infra,* below, *vertere,* to turn], **1.** the downward deviation of one eye. **2.** conjugate downward rotation of both eyes.

infundibular stalk /in'fundib'yələr/ [L, *infundibulum,* funnel; ME, *stalke*], an elongated funnel-shaped structure that connects the hypothalamus with the pituitary gland.

infundibulopelvic ligament, the suspensory ligament of the ovary.

infundibulum /in'fundib'yələm/ *pl.* **infundibula** [L, funnel], a funnel-shaped structure or passage, such as the cavity formed by the fimbriae tubae at the distal end of the fallopian tubes.

infundibulum of gallbladder, the tapering part of the gallbladder, ending at the neck.

infusate /infyoo'sāt/, a parenteral fluid slowly introduced into a patient over a specific period.

infusate contamination, the introduction of pathogens into a sterile container, the contents of which are to be infused through a sterile setup with tubing into a patient's intravascular system during surgery or other procedures.

infused oil, a mixture comprised of an herb's volatile oils and another oil.

infusion /infyoo'zhən/ [L, *in,* within, *fundere,* to pour], **1.** the introduction of a substance, such as a fluid, electrolyte, nutrient, or drug, directly into a vein or interstitially by means of gravity flow. **2.** the substance introduced into the body by infusion. **3.** the steeping of a substance, such as an herb, to extract its medicinal properties. **4.** a liquid preparation made by pouring water over plant parts (such as dried or fresh leaves, flowers, and fruits) and allowing the mixture to steep. —**infuse,** *v.*

infusion pump, an apparatus designed to deliver measured amounts of a drug or IV solution through IV injection over time. Some kinds of infusion pumps can be implanted surgically.

ingestion /injes'chən/ [L, *in,* within, *gerere,* to carry], the oral taking of substances into the body. The term is generally applied to both nutrients and medications.

ingrown hair [L, *in,* within; AS, *growen,* to grow + *haer*], a hair that fails to follow the normal follicle channel to the surface, with the free end becoming embedded in the skin. The hair then acts like a foreign body, and inflammation and suppuration follow.

ingrown toenail, a toenail whose distal lateral margin grows or is pressed into the skin of the toe, causing an inflammatory reaction.

inguinal /ing'gwinəl/ [L, *inguen,* groin], pertaining to the groin.

inguinal canal, the tubular passage through the lower muscular layers of the abdominal wall that contains the spermatic cord in the male and the round ligament in the female. It is a common site for hernias.

inguinal falx, the inferior terminal portion of the common aponeurosis of the internal abdominal oblique and the transverse abdominis. It is inserted into the crest of the pubis, just below the superficial inguinal ring, and strengthens that part of the anterior abdominal wall.

inguinal hernia, a hernia in which a loop of intestine enters the inguinal canal. In a male it sometimes fills the entire scrotal sac.

inguinal ligament, a band of fibrous tissue that spans the gap between the anterior superior iliac spine and the pubic tubercle.

I

inguinal node, any of the approximately 18 nodes in the group of lymph glands in the upper femoral triangle of the thigh.

inguinal part of ductus deferens, a middle part of the ductus deferens, located within the inguinal canal.

inguinal region, the part of the abdomen surrounding the inguinal canal, in the lower zone on both sides of the pubic region.

inguinal ring, either of the two apertures of the inguinal canal, the internal end opening into the abdominal wall and the external end opening into the aponeurosis of the obliquus externus abdominis above the pubis.

inguinal ring, external, superficial inguinal ring.

inguinal ring, internal, deep inguinal ring.

inguinal triangle, a triangular area in the lower abdominal wall bounded laterally by the inferior epigastric artery, medially by the rectus abdominis muscle, and inferiorly by the inguinal ligament.

inguinocrural hernia /ing'gwinōkrōō'rəl/ [L, *inguen,* groin, *crus,* thigh, *hernia,* rupture], an inguinal hernia that has turned from the inguinal canal laterally over the groin.

INH, abbreviation for *isonicotinic acid hydrazide.*

inhalant /inhā'lənt/, a substance introduced into the body by inhalation. It may be a medication, such as an aerosol, administered in respiratory therapy or a volatile chemical that is abused, such as toluene, used in glue sniffing.

inhalation administration of medication /in'hələ'shən/ [L, *in,* within, *halare,* to breathe], the administration of a drug by inspiration of the vapor released from a fragile ampule packed in a fine mesh that is crushed for immediate administration. The medication is absorbed into the circulation through the mucous membrane of the nasal passages.

inhalational challenge test, a type of challenge test done to determine reactivity to drugs or causative allergens in allergic asthma, in which a dilute concentrate of the suspected substance is inhaled and the patient is assessed for bronchial reactivity.

inhalation anesthesia, anesthesia achieved by the inhalation of an anesthetic gas or a vapor. Among the principal inhalation anesthetics are nitrous oxide, desflurane, sevoflurane, and isoflurane.

inhalation injury, damage to the pulmonary parenchyma caused by inhalation of substances such as very hot air, toxic gas, asbestos, and chemical products of plastic manufacture.

inhalation therapy, a treatment in which a substance is introduced into the respiratory tract with inspired air. Oxygen, water, and various drugs may be administered by techniques of inhalation therapy.

inhalation toxicity, a severe neuromuscular disorder with symptoms like those of Parkinson's disease, caused by prolonged inhalation of manganese dust.

inhale /inhāl'/ [L, *in,* within, *halare,* to breathe], to breathe in or to draw in with the breath.

inhaler [L, *in* + *halare,* to breathe], a device for administering medications to be inhaled, such as vapors, fine powders, or volatile substances. An inhaler also may be designed to administer anesthetic gases.

inherent /inhir'ənt/ [L, *inhaerere,* to cling to], inborn, innate; natural to an environment.

inherent rate, the frequency of impulse formation attributed to a given pacemaker location within the heart.

inheritance /inher'itəns/ [L, *in,* within, *hereditare,* to inherit], **1.** the acquisition or expression of traits or conditions by transmission of genetic material from parents to offspring. **2.** the sum of the genetic qualities or traits transmitted from parents to offspring; the total genetic makeup of a fertilized ovum.—**inherited,** *adj.,* **inherit,** *v.*

inherited disorder /inher'itid/, any disease or condition that is genetically determined and involves either a single gene mutation, multifactorial inheritance, or a chromosomal aberration.

inherited trait [L, *in,* within, *hereditare,* to inherit; Fr, *trait,* a draft], a distinguishing quality or characteristic that is transmitted genetically from one generation to the next.

inhibin /inhib'in/, a gonadal hormone that inhibits activity of the follicle-stimulating hormone secreted by the anterior pituitary gland.

inhibiting gene /inhib'iting/ [L, *inhibere,* to restrain; Gk, *genein,* to produce], a gene that prevents the expression of another gene.

inhibition /in'hibish'ən/ [L, *inhibere,* to restrain], **1.** in psychology, the unconscious restraint of a behavioral process, usually resulting from the social or cultural forces of the environment; the condition inducing such restraint. **2.** in psychoanalysis, the process in which the superego prevents the conscious expression of an unconscious instinctual drive, thought, or urge. **3.** in physiology, the restraint, checking, or arrest of the action of an organ or cell or the reduction of a physiologic activity by antagonistic stimulation. **4.** in chemistry, the stopping or slowing of the rate of a chemical reaction.

inhibition assay, an immunoassay in which an excess of antigens prevents or inhibits the completion of either the initial or the indicator phase of the reaction.

inhibition of reflexes [L, *inhibere,* to restrain, *reflectere,* to bend back], **1.** the prevention of a reflex action, requiring a series of biochemical mechanisms to restrict the flow of excitatory impulses at presynaptic and postsynaptic points in the system. **2.** a negative reflex effect that may become established during differential conditioning. The negative conditioned reflex represents an inhibition of a conditioned reflex.

inhibitor /inhib′itər/, a drug or other agent that prevents or restricts a certain action.

inhibitor of apoptosis protein (IAP), any of a class of proteins that play a regulatory role in apoptosis in many species by inhibiting caspase activity, which in turn blocks apoptosis.

inhibitory /inhib′itôr′ē/ [L, *inhibere,* to restrain], tending to stop or slow a process, such as a neuron that suppresses the intensity of a nerve impulse.

inhibitory enzyme [L, *inhibere,* to restrain; Gk, *en,* within, *zyme,* ferment], an enzyme that blocks rather than catalyzes a chemical reaction.

initial contact stance stage /inish′əl/ [L, *initium,* beginning, *contigere,* to touch], one of the five stages in the stance phase of walking or gait, specifically associated with the moment when the foot touches the ground or floor and the leg prepares to accept the weight of the body.

initiation codon /inish′ē·ā′shən kō′don/ [L, *initium,* beginning, *caudex,* book], the triplet of nucleotides, usually adenine-uracil-guanine or, in some cases, guanine-uracil-guanine, that in eukaryotes and archea code for methionine, and in bacteria code for formylmethionine, the first amino acids in all protein sequences.

initiator /inish′ē·ā′tər/, a cocarcinogenic factor that causes a usually irreversible genetic mutation in a normal cell and primes it for uncontrolled growth. Examples are radiation, aflatoxins, urethane, and nitrosamines.

injectable contraceptive /injek′təbəl/, medroxyprogesterone acetate, a progestin used as a contraceptive, administered intramuscularly at a dose sufficient to prevent ovulation. The muscle into which the hormone is injected serves as a depot from which the hormone is slowly released, so that injections need to be given only every 3 months. This is a very convenient and highly effective method of contraception.

injectable silicone [L, *in* + *jacere,* to throw, *silex,* silicon], polymeric organic compounds of silicone that are used in plastic surgery. The silicones are injected beneath the skin for cosmetic benefits.

injection /injek′shən/ [L, *in,* within, *jacere,* to throw], **1.** the act of forcing a liquid into the body by means of a needle and syringe. **2.** the substance injected. **3.** redness and swelling observed in the physical examination of a part of the body, caused by dilation of the blood vessels secondary to an inflammatory or infectious process.—**inject,** *v.*

injection cap, a rubber diaphragm under a plastic cap. It permits needle insertion into a catheter or vial.

injunction /injungk′shən/ [L, *injungere,* to enjoin], a court order that prevents a party from performing a specified act.

injury severity score (ISS), an evaluation system developed to predict the outcomes of traumas, including mortality and length of hospital stay.

inlay /in′lā/ [L, *in,* within; AS, *lecan,* lay], **1.** material, such as bone or skin, inserted into a tissue defect. **2.** in dentistry, a restoration made outside of a tooth to correspond with the form of a prepared cavity and then cemented into the tooth.

inlay splint [L, *in,* within; AS, *lecan,* lay], a casting for fixing or supporting one or more approximating teeth. It is composed of either a single casting or two or more inlays soldered together.

inlet [L, *in,* within; ME, *leten*], a passage leading into a cavity, such as the pelvic inlet that marks the brim of the pelvic cavity.

in loco parentis /in lō′kō pəren′tis/ [L, in the parents' place], the assumption by a person or institution of the parental obligations of caring for a child without adoption.

innate /in′āt, ināt′/ [L, *innatus,* inborn], **1.** existing in a person from birth; inborn; hereditary; congenital. **2.** a natural and essential characteristic of something or someone; inherent. **3.** originating in or produced by the intellect or the mind.

inner cell mass [AS, *innera,* within; L, *cella,* storeroom, *massa,* lump], a cluster of cells localized around the animal pole of the blastocyst of placental mammals from which the embryo develops.

inner ear, the complex inner structure of the ear, containing receptors for hearing and balance. The maculae and crystae cells help maintain equilibrium; the organ of Corti cells translate sound vibrations into impulses for the sense of hearing. The auditory receptor cells are innervated by the cochlear nerve.

inner layer of glomerular capsule, the visceral layer of glomerular capsule.

innervate /in'ərvāt/ [L, *in* + *nervus*], to supply a body part or organ with nerves or nervous stimuli.

innervation /in'ərvā'shən/ [L, *in,* within, *nervus,* nerve], the distribution or supply of nerve fibers or nerve impulses to a body part.—**innervate,** *v.*

inner zone of renal medulla, the part of the renal medulla farthest in from the cortex, containing the innermost part of the loop of Henle and of the medullary collecting tubule.

innocent /in'əsənt/ [L, *innocens,* harmless], benign, innocuous, or functional; not malignant, such as an innocent heart murmur.

innocuous /inok'yoo̅·əs/ [L, *innocuus,* harmless], pertaining to use of a substance or procedure that causes no ill effects.

innominate /inom'ināt/ [L, *innominatum,* nameless], without a name or unnamed. The term is traditionally applied to certain anatomic structures, often identified by their descriptive name, such as the hip bone.

innominate artery, one of the three arteries branching from the arch of the aorta.

innominate bone, the hip bone. It consists of the ilium, ischium, and pubis and unites with the sacrum and coccyx to form the pelvis.

innominate substance, a region of the forebrain that lies ventral to the anterior half of the lentiform nucleus. It contains the basal forebrain, which receives afferent input from the reticular formation, hypothalamus, and limbic cortex.

innominate vein, a large vein on either side of the neck that is formed by the union of the internal jugular and subclavian veins. The two veins drain blood from the head, neck, and upper extremities and unite to form the superior vena cava.

Inocor, a trademark for a cardiac inotropic drug (inamrinone lactate).

inoculation /inok'yəlāshən/ [L, *inoculare,* to graft], (medical term) the introduction of a substance (inoculum) into the body to produce or to increase immunity to the disease or condition associated with the substance.

inoculum /inok'yoo̅ləm/ *pl.* **inocula** [L, *inoculare,* to graft], a substance introduced into the body to cause or to increase immunity to a specific disease or condition. It may be a toxin; a live, attenuated, or killed virus or bacterium; or an immune serum.

inoperable /inop'ərəbəl/ [L, *in* + *operari,* to work], pertaining to a medical condition that would not benefit from surgical intervention or for which the risk outweighs the benefits.

inorganic /in'ôrgan'ik/ [L, *in,* not; Gk, *organikos,* natural], in chemistry, pertaining to a chemical compound that is not primarily based on or derived from hydrocarbons.

inorganic acid, a compound containing no carbon that is composed of hydrogen and one or more electronegative elements, such as chlorine.

inorganic chemistry, the study of the properties and reactions of all chemical elements and compounds other than hydrocarbons or their derivatives.

inorganic dust, dry, finely powdered particles of an inorganic substance, especially dust, which, when inhaled, can cause abnormal conditions of the lungs.

inorganic phosphorus, phosphorus that may be measured in the blood as phosphate ions.

inoscopy, the diagnosis of disease by artificial digestion and examination of the fibers or fibrinous matter of the sputum, blood, effusions, etc.

inosine /in'əsēn, -sīn/, a nucleoside derived from animal tissue, especially intestines. It has been used in the treatment of cardiac disorders and is now under investigation in studies of cancer and virus chemotherapy.

inosiplex /inō'sipleks/, a form of inosine that acts as a stimulator of the immune system. It is currently under investigation for use in cancer therapy, in the treatment of herpesvirus and rhinovirus infections, and in immune restoration in pre-AIDS patients.

inositol /inō'sətōl, inos'-/, an isomer of glucose that occurs widely in plant and animal cells. Although inositol has no current therapeutic use, it is an essential cell constituent.

inotropic /in'ōtrop'ik/ [Gk, *inos,* fiber, *trope,* turning], pertaining to the force or energy of muscular contractions, particularly those of the heart.

inotropic agent, a substance that influences the force of muscular contractions; an agent that increases the force of muscular contractions of the heart.

inpatient /in'pāshənt/ [L, *in,* within, *patior,* to suffer], **1.** a patient who has been admitted to a hospital or other health care facility for at least an overnight stay. **2.** pertaining to the treatment or care of such a patient or to a health care facility to which a patient may be admitted for 24-hour care.

inpatient care unit, a unit of a hospital organized for medical and continuous nursing services for a group of inpatients who are usually grouped according to diagnosis or other common characteristics, such as maternity or surgical patients.

inquest /in′kwest/ [L, *in,* within, *quaerere,* to seek], a legal inquiry or examination.

INR, abbreviation for *International Normalized Ratio.*

insane /insān′/ [L, *in,* not, *sanus,* sound], a legal term describing unsound, diseased, or deranged mental functioning, particularly as it pertains to a person who is unable to provide adequate self-care if there is a need to protect the patient and the public from each other. In the United States, the precise definition of this legal term varies from state to state.

insanity /insan′itē/ [L, *in,* not, *sanus,* sound], *informal.* a term used more in legal and social than in medical terminology. It refers to those mental illnesses that are of such a serious or debilitating nature as to interfere with one's capability of functioning within the legal limits of society and performing the normal ADL.

insatiable /insā′shē-əbəl/ [L, *insatiatus,* not satisfied], pertaining to an appetite for food or other needs that cannot be satisfied.

insect bite [L, *in,* within, *secare,* to cut], the bite of any parasitic or venomous arthropod such as a louse, flea, mite, tick, or arachnid. Many arthropods inject venom that produces poisoning or severe local reaction, saliva that may contain viruses, or substances that produce mild irritation.

insecticide /insek′tisīd/, a chemical agent that kills insects.

insemination /insem′inā′shən/, the injection of semen into the vagina. It may involve an artificial process unrelated to sexual intercourse.

insenescence /in′sines′əns/ [L, *insenescere,* to begin to grow old], 1. the process of aging. 2. the state of being chronologically old but retaining the vitality of a young person.

insensible /insen′sibəl/ [L, *in + sentire,* to feel], 1. pertaining to a person who is unconscious for any reason. 2. pertaining to a person who is apathetic or deprived of normal sense perceptions.

insensible perspiration [L, *in,* not, *sentire,* to feel, *per,* through, *spirare,* to breathe], the loss of body fluid by evaporation, such as normally occurs during respiration.

insensible water loss, the amount of fluid lost on a daily basis from the lungs, skin, respiratory tract, and water excreted in the feces. The exact amount cannot be measured, but it is estimated to be between 40 and 600 mL in an adult under normal circumstances.

insertion /insur′shən/ [L, *inserere,* to introduce], in anatomy, the place of attachment, such as that of a muscle to the bone it moves.

insertion site, the point in a vein where a needle or catheter is inserted.

inservice education [L, *in,* within, *servus,* a slave, *educare,* to rear], a program of instruction or training that is provided by an agency or institution for its employees.

insheathed /inshēthd′/ [L, *in,* within; AS, *scaeth,* sheath], enclosed within a sheath.

insidious /insid′ē-əs/ [L, *insidiosus,* cunning], describing a development that is gradual, subtle, or imperceptible.

insight /in′sīt/ [L, *in,* within; AS, *gesihth,* sight], 1. the capacity of comprehending the true nature of a situation or of penetrating an underlying truth. 2. an instance of penetrating or comprehending an underlying truth, primarily through intuitive understanding. 3. in psychology, a type of self-understanding encompassing both intellectual and emotional awareness of the unconscious nature, origin, and mechanisms of one's attitudes, feelings, and behavior.

insipid /insip′id/ [L, *in + sapidus,* savory], dull, tasteless, or lifeless.

in situ /in sī′tōō, sit′ōō/ [L, *in,* within, *situs,* position], 1. in the natural or usual place. 2. describing a cancer that has not metastasized or invaded neighboring tissues.

insoluble /insol′yəbəl/ [L, *in,* not, *solubilis,* soluble], unable to be dissolved, usually in a specific solvent, such as a substance that is insoluble in water.

insoluble fiber, fiber that is not soluble in water, composed mainly of lignin, cellulose, and hemicelluloses and primarily found in the bran layers of cereal grains. Its actions include increasing fecal bulk and decreasing free radicals in the GI tract.

insomnia /insom′nē-ə/ [L, *in,* not, *somnus,* sleep], chronic inability to sleep or to remain asleep throughout the night; wakefulness; sleeplessness.

insomniac /insom′nē-ak/, 1. a person with insomnia. 2. pertaining to, causing, or associated with insomnia. 3. characteristic of or occurring during a period of sleeplessness.

inspiration /in′spirā′shən/ [L, *inspirare,* to breathe in], the act of drawing air into the lungs. The major muscle of inspiration is the diaphragm, the contraction of which creates a reduced pressure in the chest, causing the lungs to expand and air to flow inward.—**inspiratory,** *adj.*

inspiratory capacity (IC), the maximum volume of gas that can be inhaled from the end of a resting exhalation.

inspiratory dyspnea [L, *inspirare,* to breathe in; Gk, *dys,* without, *pnoia,* breath], a form of breathing difficulty caused by an obstruction in the larynx, trachea, or bronchi. The patient attempts to compensate for this deficiency with prolonged, deep inspirations.

inspiratory gas flow rate, the amount of gas delivered per minute to a patient's lungs by mechanical ventilation.

inspiratory hold, either of two kinds of modification in an inhalation produced by intermittent positive-pressure breathing: (1) a pressure hold, in which a preset pressure is reached and held for a designated period, or (2) a volume hold, in which a predetermined volume is delivered and then held for a designated period.

inspiratory muscle fatigue, weakness or exhaustion of the muscles that produce inspiration, resulting in a condition of threatened acute respiratory failure.

inspiratory reserve volume (IRV), the maximum volume of gas that can be inhaled beyond a normal resting inspiration.

inspiratory resistance muscle training, exercises that require inhalation against some type of resisting force, such as abdominal breathing practice with the Pflex or threshold inspiratory muscle trainer.

inspiratory waveform, one of several flow patterns during inspiration associated with mechanical ventilation. one of several flow patterns during inspiration associated with mechanical ventilation. These patterns include a square wave, in which the inspiratory flow rises rapidly to a preset level and stays at that level until expiration begins; a sinusoidal wave, in which the flow gradually increases and decreases throughout inspiration; and a descending ramp wave, in which the flow increases very rapidly and then decreases gradually until the end of inspiration. The last pattern is most similar to normal breathing.

inspirometer /in′spirom′ətər/ [L, *inspirare,* to breathe in; Gk, *metron,* measure], an apparatus used to measure the volume, force, and frequency of a patient's inspirations.

inspissate /inspis′āt/ [L, *inspissare,* to thicken], of a fluid, to thicken or harden through the absorption or evaporation of liquid, such as milk in an inspissated milk duct.—**inspissation,** *n.*

instillation /in′stilā′shən/ [L, *instillare,* to drip], **1.** a procedure in which a fluid is slowly introduced into a cavity or passage of the body and allowed to remain for a specific length of time before being drained or withdrawn. **2.** a solution so introduced.—**instill,** *v.*

instinct /in′stingkt/ [L, *instinctus,* impulse], an inborn psychologic need, such as life instincts of hunger, thirst, and

sex, as well as the destructive and aggressive death instincts.

institutionalism syndrome /in′stityōō′shə nəliz′əm/, a condition characterized by apathy, withdrawal, submissiveness, and lack of initiative. The person may resist leaving a hospital, even when the surroundings are barely adequate, because it is familiar and predictable.

institutionalize /in′stityōō′shənəlīz′/ [L, *instituere,* to put in place], to place a person in an institution for psychologic or physical treatment or for the protection of the person or society.—**institutionalization,** *n.,* **institutionalized,** *adj.*

institutional licensure /in′stityōō′shənəl/ [L, *instituere,* to put in place, *licere,* to be permitted], a procedure in which individual licensure for almost all health professions would be abandoned and the responsibility for assessing professional competence would fall to the health care facility where the health professional is used.

institutional review board (IRB), an organizational committee that reviews and approves biomedical research that uses humans as subjects.

instructive series, a test consisting of a series of x-ray films performed on the abdomen of patients with suspected bowel obstruction, paralytic ileus, perforated viscus, abdominal abscess, kidney stones, appendicitis, or foreign body ingestion.

instrument /in′strəmənt/ [L, *instrumentum,* tool], a surgical tool or device designed to perform a specific function, such as cutting, dissecting, grasping, holding, retracting, or suturing.

instrumental activities of daily living (IADL) /in′strəmen′təl/, the activities often performed by a person who is living independently in a community setting during the course of a normal day, such as managing money, shopping, telephone use, travel in community, housekeeping, preparing meals, and taking medications correctly.

instrumental labor [L, *instrumentum,* tool, *labor,* work], child delivery in which the use of instruments, such as forceps or perforators, is required.

instrumentation /in′strəməntā′shən/, the use of instruments for treatment and diagnosis.

insufficiency /in′səfish′ənsē/ [L, *in,* not, *sufficere,* to be adequate], inability to perform a necessary function adequately.

insufficient sleep syndrome /in′səfish′ənt/, a neurologic disorder in which individuals persistently fail to obtain enough sleep to support normal wakefulness.

insufflate /in′səflāt, insuf′lāt/ [L, *insufflare,* to blow into], to blow a gas or powder into a tube, cavity, or organ to allow visual examination, to remove an obstruction, or to apply medication. —**insufflation,** *n.*

insufflator /in'səflā'tər/ [L, *insufflare,* to blow into], an apparatus used to blow air or gas into a body cavity.

insulation /in'səlā'shən/, a nonconducting substance that offers a barrier to the passage of heat or electricity.

insulin /in'səlin/ [L, *insula,* island], **1.** a naturally occurring polypeptide hormone secreted by the beta cells of the islets of Langerhans in the pancreas in response to increased levels of glucose in the blood as well as to the parasympathetic nervous system and other stimuli. The hormone acts to regulate the metabolism of glucose and the processes necessary for the intermediary metabolism of fats, carbohydrates, and proteins. Insulin lowers the blood glucose level and promotes transport of glucose into the muscle cells and other tissues. Inadequate secretion of insulin causes elevated blood glucose and triglyceride levels, and ketonemia, as well as the characteristic signs of DM. **2.** a pharmacologic preparation of the hormone administered in treating DM. The various preparations of insulin available for prescription vary in onset, intensity, and duration of action. They are termed quick-acting, intermediate-acting, and long-acting. Most replacement insulin is given by subcutaneous injection in individualized dosage schedules and insulin pumps, but insulin also can be replaced intravenously.

insulin allergy, a hypersensitivity reaction to insulin, usually a reaction to its protein components. More purified insulins have now been developed that are less likely to cause an allergic reaction and other complications.

insulin antibody test, a blood test used to detect the presence of insulin antibodies, which develop in nearly all patients treated with exogenous insulin. These antibodies may reduce the amount of insulin available for glucose metabolism and may contribute to insulin resistance.

insulinase, an enzyme that inactivates insulin.

insulin aspart, a rapid-acting analog of human insulin created by recombinant DNA technology, in which an aspartate residue has been substituted for the usual proline at position 28 on the insulin B chain. It is administered subcutaneously for the treatment of DM.

insulin assay, a blood test used to diagnose insulinoma and to evaluate patients with fasting hypoglycemia. It is often

combined with a fasting plasma glucose test to increase its accuracy.

insulinemia /in'səlinēmē·ə/ [L, *insula,* island; Gk, *haima,* blood], an abnormally high level of insulin in the blood.

insulin glargine, an analog of human insulin produced by recombinant DNA technology, differing from human insulin in that the asparagine at position A21 is replaced by glycine and two arginines are added to the C-terminus of the B-chain. It is administered subcutaneously for once-daily insulin replacement therapy.

insulin human zinc suspension, an intermediate-acting insulin consisting of a sterile suspension of insulin human in buffered water with the addition of a suitable zinc salt such that the solid phase of the suspension contains a 7:3 ratio of crystalline to amorphous insulin.

insulin hypoglycemic test, a postoperative procedure for determining the completeness of vagotomy for peptic ulcer disease. Insulin is administered to cause hypoglycemia. If vagotomy is complete, the acid output from the stomach should be less than before surgery.

insulin injection sites, body tissue areas that allow optimal use of subcutaneous injections of insulin. Repeated use of the same injection site can lead to localized tissue damage, resulting in malabsorption of insulin. These problems are minimized by systematic rotation of injection sites within the selected anatomic area.

insulin kinase, an enzyme, assumed to be present in the liver, that activates insulin.

insulin-like growth factor (IGF), hormones that stimulate protein synthesis and sulfation. IGF I and II play a role in uterine and placental growth and early fetal growth during pregnancy.

insulin lipodystrophy [L, *insula,* island; Gk, *lipos,* fat; *dys,* bad, *trophe,* nourishment], the loss of local fat deposits in patients with diabetes, as a complication of repeated insulin injections into the same subcutaneous tissue.

insulin lispro, a pancreatic hormone used to treat ketoacidosis types I and II and types 1 and 2 DM.

insulinogenic /in'səlin'ōjen'ik/ [L, *insula;* Gk, *genein,* to produce], promoting the production and release of insulin by the islets of Langerhans in the pancreas.

insulinoma /in'səlinō'mə/ *pl.* **insulinomas, insulinomata** [L, *insula;* Gk, *oma,* tumor], a tumor, usually benign, of the insulin-secreting cells of the islets of Langerhans. A majority are benign. Surgical resection of the tumor may be possible, thus limiting the development of hypoglycemia.

insulin pump [L, *insula,* island; ME, *pumpe*], a portable, battery-powered instrument that delivers a measured amount of insulin through the abdominal wall. It can be programmed to deliver varied doses of insulin according to the body's needs at the time.

insulin reaction, the adverse effects caused by excessive levels of circulating insulin causing hypoglycemia.

insulin rebound, extreme fluctuations in blood glucose levels as a result of overreaction of the body's homeostatic feedback mechanisms for control of glucose metabolism. When exogenous insulin is given, the hypoglycemia triggers an outpouring of glucagon and epinephrine, both of which raise the blood glucose concentration markedly, so that, although the patient may actually have periods of hypoglycemia, urine and blood glucose tests will show hyperglycemia.

insulin resistance, a cause of type 2 DM characterized by a need for an increased amount of insulin per day to control hyperglycemia and ketosis. The cause is associated with decreased or ineffective glucose transporter proteins with insulin-sensitive cells or insulin binding by high levels of antibody.

insulin shock, a condition of severe hypoglycemia caused by an overdose of insulin, decreased intake of food, or excessive exercise. It is characterized by sweating, trembling, chilliness, nervousness, irritability, hunger, hallucination, numbness, and pallor. Uncorrected, it progresses to convulsions, coma, and death.

insulin tolerance test, a test of the body's ability to use insulin, in which insulin is given and blood glucose is measured at regular intervals.

insulintropin /in'səlintrop'in/ [L, *insula,* island], a naturally occurring hormone produced in the intestines when food is ingested. It causes the release of insulin from the pancreas, which in turn regulates blood glucose levels.

insulitis /in'səli'tis/, a lymphocytic infiltration of the pancreatic beta cells in the islets of Langerhans. The condition is associated with the development of type 1 DM.

insurance authorization, a nursing intervention from the Nursing Interventions Classification (NIC) defined as assisting the patient and provider to secure payment for health services or equipment from a third party.

intake [L, *in,* within; AS, *tacan,* to take], **1.** the process in which a person is admitted to a clinic or hospital or is signed in for an office visit. The reason for the visit and various identifying data about the patient are noted. **2.** in nursing, the amount of food or fluid ingested in a given period, measured and noted in milliliters or grams per 8-, 12-, or 24-hour period.

Intal, a trademark for an antiasthmatic mast cell inhibitor agent (cromolyn sodium).

integral dose /in'təgrəl/ [L, *integrare,* to make whole; Gk, *dosis,* giving], the total amount of energy absorbed by a patient or object during exposure to radiation.

Integrated Group Without Walls /in'təgrā'tid/, a network of physicians who have merged legally but continue to practice individually.

Integrated Health Care Delivery System, a managed care system in the United States that includes a hospital organization that provides acute patient care, a multispecialty medical care delivery system, the capability of contracting for any other needed services, and a payer.

Integrated Multispecialty Group, a managed care system similar to a single-specialty medical group, except that various specialties and usually primary care are also provided.

integrated system, **1.** in managed care, a legal partnership between groups of physicians and hospitals that contract and share risk while working together. **2.** a group of interconnected units that form a functioning computer system.

integrating dose meter /in'təgrā'ting/, a device that measures the total amount of radiation administered to a patient during a radiotherapy exposure. It is usually placed on the patient's skin and may terminate the exposure when the desired amount is reached.

integration /in'təgrā'shən/ [L, *integrare,* to make whole], **1.** the act or process of unifying or bringing together. **2.** in psychology, the organization of all elements of the personality into a coordinated functional whole that is in harmony with the environment.—**integrate,** *v.*

integration of self, one of the components of high-level wellness. It is a prerequisite for the achievement of maturity and is characterized by the integration of mind, body, and spirit into one harmoniously functioning unit.

integrin /integ'rin/, **1.** a protein that links the outside of a cell with its interior. **2.** a heterodimeric molecule involved in cell-substrate and cell-cell adhesion.

integument /integ'yŏŏmənt/ [L, *integumentum,* a covering], a covering or skin.—**integumentary,** *adj.*

integumentary system /integ'yəmen'tərē/, the skin and its appendages, hair, nails, and sweat and sebaceous glands.

integumentary system assessment, an evaluation of the general condition of a patient's integument and of factors or abnormalities that may contribute to the presence of a dermatologic disorder.

intellect /in'təlekt/ [L, *intellectus*, perception], **1.** the power and ability of the mind for knowing and understanding, as contrasted with feeling or with willing. **2.** a person possessing a great capacity for thought and knowledge.—**intellectual,** *adj., n.*

intellectualization /in'təlek'choo-əlizā'shən/ [L, *intellectus;* Gk, *izein,* to cause], **1.** in psychiatry, a defense mechanism in which reasoning is used as a means of blocking a confrontation with an unconscious conflict and the emotional stress associated with it. **2.** the overuse of abstract thinking or generalizations to control or minimize painful feelings.

intelligence /intel'ijəns/ [L, *intelligentia,* perception], **1.** the potential ability to acquire, retain, and apply experience, understanding, knowledge, reasoning, and judgment in coping with new experiences and solving problems. **2.** the manifestation of such ability.—**intelligent,** *adj.*

intelligence quotient (IQ), a numeric expression of a person's intellectual level as measured against the statistical average of his or her age group. On several of the traditional scales, it is determined by dividing the mental age, derived through psychologic testing, by the chronologic age and multiplying the result by 100. Average IQ is considered to be 100.

intelligence test, any of a variety of standardized tests designed to determine the mental age of an individual by measuring the relative capacity to absorb information and to solve problems.

intemperance /intem'pərəns/ [L, *in,* not, *temperare,* to moderate], excessive indulgence in eating, drinking, or other life-style functions.

intensifying screen /inten'sifi'ing/ [L, *intensus,* tighten, *facere,* to make; ME, *screne*], a device consisting of fluorescent material, which is placed in contact with the film in a radiographic cassette. Radiation interacts with the fluorescent phosphor, releasing light photons. These photons expose the film with greater efficiency than would the radiation alone. Thus, patient exposure to radiation can be reduced.

intensity-modulated radiation therapy (IMRT), a specialized method of delivering radiation so that the beam enters the body from many different angles to get to the tumor with pinpoint accuracy while sparing much of the surrounding healthy tissue.

intensive care /inten'siv/ [L, *intensus,* tighten, *garrire,* to chatter], constant complex health care as provided in various acute life-threatening conditions such as multiple trauma, severe burns, or MI or after certain kinds of surgery.

intensive care unit (ICU), a hospital unit in which patients requiring close monitoring and intensive care are kept. An ICU contains highly technical and sophisticated monitoring devices and equipment and is staffed by personnel to deliver critical care.

intention /inten'shən/ [L, *intendere,* to aim], a kind of healing process. Healing by primary intention is the initial union of the edges of a wound, progressing to complete healing without granulation. Healing by secondary intention is wound closure in which the edges are separated, granulation tissue develops to fill the gap, and epithelium grows in over the granulations, producing a scar. Healing by tertiary intention is wound closure in which granulation tissue fills the gap between the edges of the wound, with epithelium growing over the granulation at a slower rate and producing a larger scar than results from healing from second intention. Suppuration is also usually found.

intentional additives, substances that are deliberately added in the manufacture of food or pharmaceutic products to improve or maintain flavor, color, texture, or consistency or to enhance or conserve nutritional value.

intention tremor, fine, rhythmic purposeless movements that tend to increase during voluntary movements.

interactional model /-ak'shənəl/ [L, *inter,* between, *agere,* to do], a therapy model that views the family as a communication system comprising interlocking subsystems of family members. Family dysfunction occurs when the rules governing family interaction become vague and ambiguous. The therapeutic goal is to help the family clarify the rules governing their relationships.

interactionist theory /-ak'shənist/, an aging theory that views age-related changes as resulting from the interactions among the individual characteristics of the person, the circumstances in society, and the history of social interaction patterns of the person.

interaction processes, a component of the theory of effective practice. The processes consist of a series of interactions between a nurse and a patient. The series occurs in a sequence of actions and reactions until the patient and the nurse both understand what is wanted and the desired behavior or act is achieved.

interactive guided imagery, the focusing of a patient's attention on a target visual stimulus to produce a specific physiologic change that can promote healing.

I

interalveolar /-alvē′ələr/ [L, *inter,* between, *alveolus,* little hollow], pertaining to the area between alveoli.

interalveolar septum, 1. the tissue between adjacent pulmonary alveoli, consisting of a dense capillary network covered on both sides by thin alveolar epithelial cells. **2.** a bony partition between adjacent tooth sockets.

interarticular /-ärtik′yələr/ [L, *inter,* between, *articulus,* joint], pertaining to the areas between two joints or between facing surfaces of a joint.

interarticular fibrocartilage [L, *inter* + *articulus,* joint], one of four kinds of fibrocartilage, consisting of flattened fibrocartilaginous plates between the articular cartilage of the most active joints, such as the sternoclavicular, wrist, and knee joints. The fibrocartilaginous plates absorb shocks and increase mobility.

interarytenoid fold, a fold of mucosa forming the base of the rima glottidis at the bottom of the interarytenoid notch.

interatrial /in′tərā′trē-əl/ [L, *inter,* between, *atrium,* hall], situated between the atria of the heart.

intercalary /intur′kəler′ē, in′tərkal′ərē/ [L, *intercalare,* to insert], occurring between two others, such as the absence of the middle part of a bone with the proximal and distal parts present.

intercalate /intur′kəlāt/ [L, *intercalare*], to insert between adjacent surfaces or structures.—**intercalation,** *n.*

intercalated disks /intur′kəlātəd/, dense bands running between myocardial cells both transversely and longitudinally, forming a stepped configuration. They contain intercellular junctions that link adjacent cells both electrically and mechanically.

intercapillary /in′tərkap′ilarē/ [L, *inter,* between, *capillaris,* hairlike], among or between capillaries.

intercapillary glomerulosclerosis /-kap′iler′ē/ [L, *inter* + *capillaris,* hairlike, *glomerulus,* small ball; Gk, *sklerosis,* a hardening], an abnormal condition characterized by degeneration of the renal glomeruli. It is associated with diabetes and often produces albuminuria, nephrotic edema, hypertension, and renal insufficiency.

intercavernous sinuses /-kav′ərnəs/ [L, *inter,* between, *caverna,* cavity, *sinus,* curve], the cavities through which the cavernous sinuses of the dura mater communicate.

intercellular /-sel′yələr/ [L, *inter* + *cella,* storeroom], pertaining to the area between or among cells.

intercellular bridge, a structure that connects adjacent cells, occurring primarily in the epithelium and other stratified

squamous epithelia. It consists of slender strands of cytoplasm that project from the surfaces of adjacent cells and merge at the desmosome.

interceptive orthodontics /in′tərsep′tiv/, that phase of orthodontics concerned with elimination of a condition that might lead to the development of malocclusion.

intercerebral /-ser′əbrəl/ [L, *inter,* between, *cerebrum,* brain], pertaining to the area between the left and right cerebral hemispheres.

interchondral articulation, the articulation of the cartilage of adjacent ribs, mainly between the costal cartilages of ribs VII to X but sometimes involving the costal cartilages of ribs V and VI. Interchondral joints provide indirect anchorage to the sternum and contribute to the formation of a smooth inferior costal margin. They are usually synovial, and the thin fibrous capsules are reinforced by interchondral ligaments.

interclavicular /-kləvik′yələr/ [L, *inter,* between, *clavicula,* little key], pertaining to the area between the clavicles.

interconceptional gynecologic care /-kənsep′shənəl/ [L, *inter* + *concipere,* to take in], health care of a woman during her reproductive years, between pregnancies, and 6 weeks after delivery.

intercondylar fracture /-kon′dilər/ [L, *inter;* Gk, *kondylos,* knuckle], a longitudinal fracture of the humerus between its two condyles.

intercostal /-kos′təl/ [L, *inter* + *costa,* rib], pertaining to the space between two ribs.

intercostal bulging, the visible expansion of the soft tissues between the ribs that occurs when increased expiratory effort is needed to exhale, as in asthma, CF, or obstruction of an airway by a foreign body.

intercostal muscles, the muscles between adjacent ribs. They are designated as external and internal and function as secondary ventilatory muscles.

intercostal neuralgia, pain in the intercostal spaces of the chest wall, involving intercostal nerves.

intercostal node, a node in one of three groups of thoracic parietal lymph nodes situated near the dorsal parts of the intercostal spaces. The nodes are associated with lymphatic vessels that drain the posterolateral area of the chest.

intercostal space [L, *inter,* between, *costa,* rib + *spatium*], the region between the ribs.

intercostobrachial nerve, a branch of the second intercostal nerve that contributes to cutaneous innervation of the medial surface of the upper arm.

intercristal /-kris′təl/ [L, *inter + crista,* ridge], pertaining to the space between two crests.

intercurrent disease /-kur′ənt/ [L, *inter-currere,* to run between], a disease that develops in and may alter the course of another disease.

interdental canal /-den′təl/ [L, *inter + dens,* tooth], a channel in the alveolar process of the mandible, between the roots of the medial and lateral incisors, for the passage of anastomosing blood vessels between the sublingual and inferior dental arteries.

interdental gingiva, the supporting gingival tissues, containing prominent horizontal collagen fibers, that normally fill the space between two approximating teeth.

interdental groove, a linear vertical depression on the surface of the interdental papillae, which functions as a channel for the egress of food from the interproximal areas.

interdental spillway, a channel formed by the interproximal contours of adjoining teeth and their investing tissues.

interdigestive migrating motor complex /-dijes′tiv/, a pattern of small bowel cyclic motor activity that follows completion of food digestion and absorption.

interdigestive period, a period of relative inactivity in the alimentary tract between two periods of digestive activity.

interest tests, psychologic tests designed to clarify an individual's vocational potential or to compare an individual's performance with the average scores of a specific population.

interfemoral /in′tərfem′ərəl/ [L, *inter,* between, *femur,* thigh], between the thighs.

interference /-fir′əns/ [L, *inter + ferire,* to strike], the effect of a component on the accuracy of measurement of the desired analyte.

interferent /-fir′ənt/ [L, *inter + ferire,* to strike], any chemical or physical phenomenon that can interfere with or disrupt a reaction or process.

interferential current therapy /-fərən′shəl/, a form of electric stimulation therapy using two or three distinctly different currents that are passed through a tissue from surface electrodes. Portions of each current are canceled by the other, resulting in the application of a different net current to the target tissue.

interferon /-fir′on/ [L, *inter + ferire,* to strike], a natural glycoprotein formed by cells exposed to a virus or another foreign particle of nucleic acid. It induces the production of translation inhibitory protein (TIP) in noninfected cells. TIP blocks translation of viral RNA, thus giving other cells protection against both the original and other viruses. Interferon is species specific.

interferon alfa-2a, a synthetic form of interferon-α that acts as a biologic response modifier, used as an antineoplastic in the treatment of hairy cell leukemia and AIDS-related Kaposi's sarcoma.

interferon alfa-2a, recombinant, a parenteral antineoplastic drug administered in the treatment of AIDS-related Kaposi's sarcoma, hairy cell and chronic myelogenous leukemia, and chronic hepatitis C. It also has a variety of unlabeled or investigational uses.

interferon alfa-2b, a synthetic form of interferon-α that acts as a biologic response modifier, used in the treatment of venereal warts, hepatitis B, and chronic hepatitis C and as an antineoplastic in the treatment of hairy cell leukemia, malignant melanoma, non-Hodgkin's lymphomas, multiple myeloma, mycosis fungoides, and AIDS-related Kaposi's sarcoma.

interferon alfa-2b, recombinant, a parenteral antineoplastic drug with indications, contraindications, and adverse effects similar to those of interferon alpha-2a, recombinant.

interferon alfacon-1, a recombinant type I interferon used to treat chronic hepatitis C infections. It is being used investigationally to treat hairy cell leukemia in combination with granulocyte colony–stimulating factor.

interferon alfa-n1 lymphoblastoid, a recombinant type 1 interferon used to treat chronic hepatitis C infections.

interferon alfa-n3, a highly purified mixture of natural human interferon proteins that acts as a biologic response modifier, used in the treatment of venereal warts.

interferon-alpha, the major interferon produced by virus-induced leukocyte cultures. It is used in the experimental treatment of hairy cell leukemia and other selected neoplasias.

interferon-beta, the major interferon produced by double-stranded RNA-induced fibroblast cultures. The major producer cells are fibroblasts, epithelial cells, and macrophages, and its major activity is antiviral.

interferon beta-1a, an antiviral and immune system regulator prescribed in the treatment of relapsing forms of MS.

interferon beta-1b, a synthetic modified form of interferon-beta used as a biologic response modifier in the treatment of relapsing forms of MS.

interferon beta-2, a cytokine derived from T cells that stimulate B cells to proliferate in vitro but, unlike B cell differentiation factors, does not stimulate antibody secretion.

interferon gamma, a small, species-specific glycoprotein produced by mitogen-stimulated T cells. It possesses antiviral activity and plays a central role in the immunoregulatory processes.

interferon gamma-1b, a synthetic form of interferon-beta that acts as a biologic response modifier and antineoplastic. It is used to reduce the frequency and severity of serious infections associated with chronic granulomatous disease.

interferon nomenclature, a system recommended by the International Interferon Nomenclature Committee for identifying interferon compounds. For a specific interferon, the name consists of "interferon" followed by a Greek letter (spelled out), a dash, an arabic number, and a lowercase letter.

interim rate /in′tərim/ [L, meanwhile + *ratum,* calculate], a method of third-party payment for costs of hospital services in which an amount is paid periodically pending an accounting of actual costs at the end of a designated period.

interior /intir′ē·ər/ [L, inner], **1.** situated inside; inward. **2.** an inner part or cavity.

interiorization /intir′ē·ərīzā′shən/ [L, *interior,* inner; Gk, *izein,* to cause], the merging of reflex and cognitive processes as a response to the environment.

interior mesenteric artery [L, inner; Gk, *mesos,* middle, *enteron,* intestine, *arteria,* airpipe], a visceral branch of the abdominal aorta, supplying the left half of the transverse colon, all of the descending and iliac colons, and most of the rectum.

interkinesis /in′tərkinē′sis, -kīnē′sis/ [L, *inter;* Gk, *kinein,* to move], the interval between the first and second nuclear divisions in meiosis.

interlace mode /-lās′/, a process whereby a conventional video camera tube produces 2 fields of 262.5 lines each in 17 ms to form a 525-line video frame in 33 ms. Each field represents repeated adjacent active traces and horizontal retraces of the electron beam across a video screen.

interleukin /-loo′kin/, one of a large group of proteins produced mainly by T cells and in some cases by mononuclear phagocytes or other cells. Interleukins participate in communication among leukocytes and are important in the inflammatory response. Most interleukins direct other cells to divide and differentiate.

interleukin-1 (IL-1), a protein with numerous immune system functions, including activation of resting T cells, endothelial cells, and macrophage; mediation of inflammation, and stimulation of the synthesis of lymphokines, collagen, and collagenases. IL-1 can also induce fever, sleep, adrenocorticotropic hormone release, and nonspecific resistance to infection.

interleukin-2 (IL-2), a protein with various immunologic functions, including the ability to initiate proliferation of activated T cells. IL-2 is used in the laboratory to grow T-cell clones with specific helper, cytotoxic, and suppressor functions.

interleukin-3 (IL-3), an immune-response protein that supports the growth of pluripotent bone marrow stem cells and is a growth factor for mast cells.

interleukin-4 (IL-4), an immune-response protein that is a growth factor for activated B cells, resting T cells, and mast cells.

interleukin-5 (IL-5), a cytokine produced by helper T cells. It stimulates B cells and eosinophils and facilitates the differentiation of B cells that secrete IgA.

interleukin-6 (IL-6), a cytokine derived from fibroblasts, macrophages, and tumor cells. It is an antiviral protein that is also used in the treatment of some types of cancer.

interleukin-7 (IL-7), a cytokine produced by bone marrow stromal cells that causes lymphoid stem cells to differentiate into progenitor B and T cells and stimulates the killing of foreign cells by T cells and monocytes.

interleukin-8 (IL-8), a cytokine produced by various cell types involved in inflammation that attracts and activates neutrophils.

interleukin-9 (IL-9), a glycoprotein that helps induce the growth of some helper T-cell clones but not of cytotoxic T-cell clones.

interleukin-10 (IL-10), a protein expressed by CD4 and CD8 T cells, monocytes, macrophages, and activated B cells. It inhibits cytokine synthesis and suppresses the functions of macrophages and natural killer T cells.

interleukin-11 (IL-11), a cytokine produced by bone marrow stromal cells. It induces IL-6–dependent murine plasmacytoma cells to proliferate and plays an important role in early platelet hematopoiesis.

interleukin-12 (IL-12), a protein produced by activated T cells that stimulates cell-mediated killing by natural killer cells and lymphocytes. It promotes the maturation of cytotoxic T cells.

interleukin-13 (IL-13), a protein produced by activated T cells that inhibits inflammatory cytokine production by peripheral blood monocytes. It suppresses cell-mediated immune responses and promotes B-cell differentiation.

interleukin-14 (IL-14), a protein produced by follicular dendritic cells, germinal T cells, and some malignant B cells. It enhances the proliferation of B cells and induces memory B-cell production and maintenance.

interleukin-15 (IL-15), a growth factor that enhances peripheral blood T-cell production.

interlobular duct /-lob'yələr/ [L, *inter + lobulus,* small lobe], any duct connecting or draining the lobules of a gland.

interlobular ductules, interlobular bile ducts: small channels between the hepatic lobules, draining into the biliary ductules.

interlobular pleurisy, encysted pleurisy between the lobes of the lung.

interlocked twins [L, *inter*; AS, *loc,* a fastening], monozygotic twins so positioned in the uterus that the neck of one becomes entwined with that of the other during presentation, making vaginal delivery impossible.

intermaxillary segment, median palatine process.

intermediary /-mē'dē·er'ē/ [L, *inter + mediare,* to divide], a private insurance company or public or private agency selected by health care providers to pay claims under the Medicare program.

intermediary metabolism [L, *inter,* between, *mediary,* to divide; Gk, *metabole,* change], the metabolic processes involved in the synthesis of cellular components between digestion of food and excretion of waste products.

intermediate-acting insulin [L, *inter + mediare,* to divide, *activus,* active], a preparation of synthetic human or pork insulin to which zinc has been added under specific chemical conditions that has an intermediate range of action.

intermediate care /-mē'dē·it/, **1.** a level of medical care for certain chronically ill or disabled individuals in which room and board are provided but skilled nursing care is not. **2.** a unit for patients who do not require intensive care but who are not yet ready to be kept in a regular medical-surgical unit.

intermediate care facility (ICF), a health facility that provides medically related services to persons with a variety of physical or emotional conditions requiring institutional facilities but without the degree of care provided by a hospital or skilled nursing facility.

intermediate care unit, a transitional unit for patients from critical care units that provides close monitoring and provision of noncritical care before discharge.

intermediate cuneiform bone, the smallest of the three cuneiform bones of the foot, located between the medial and lateral cuneiform bones.

intermediate-density lipoprotein (IDL), a lipid-protein complex with a density between those of very low-density lipoprotein and low-density lipoprotein. The product has a relatively short half-life and is normally in the blood in very low concentrations.

intermediate host, any animal in which the larval or intermediate stage of a parasite develops but does not sexually reproduce. Humans are intermediate hosts for malaria parasites.

intermediate left lateral flexure of rectum, the third bend of the rectum, where it deviates laterally to the left.

intermediate mass, the connecting mass of nervous tissue between two lobes of the diencephalon.

intermediate nerve, the smaller root of the facial nerve, lying between the main root and the vestibulocochlear nerve. It consists of parasympathetic and sensory fibers, and its branches supply the lacrimal, nasal, palatine, submandibular, and sublingual glands, as well as the anterior two thirds of the tongue.

intermenstrual /-men'strōō·əl/ [L, *inter + menstruum,* menstrual fluid], pertaining to the time between menstrual periods.

intermenstrual fever, the normal slight elevation of temperature that marks ovulation, usually occurring about 14 days before the onset of menses.

intermittent /-mit'ənt/ [L, *inter + mittere,* to send], occurring at intervals; alternating between periods of activity and inactivity, such as rheumatoid arthritis, which is marked by periods of signs and symptoms followed by periods of remission.

intermittent assisted ventilation (IAV), a system of respiratory therapy in which assisted ventilation is combined with spontaneous breathing.

intermittent compression, external compression used to control and reduce accumulation of lymph in body tissues. Devices to provide intermittent compression in an on-off timing sequence include inflated pressure sleeves and linear compression pumps. Intermittent compression is also used to decrease acute bleeding.

intermittent explosive disorder, a mental disturbance beginning in childhood and characterized by discrete episodes of violence and aggressive behavior or destruction of property in otherwise normal individuals.

intermittent fever, a fever that recurs in cycles of paroxysms and remissions, such as in malaria.

intermittent hydrosalpinx [L, *inter,* between, *mittere,* to send; Gk, *hydor,* water, *salpinx,* tube], a fluid accumulation in a fallopian tube. The fluid is released periodically through the uterine cavity.

intermittent incontinence [L, *inter,* between, *mittere,* to send, *incontinentia,* inability to retain], urinary incontinence that occurs only when there is pressure on the bladder or exertion of muscular effort.

intermittent mandatory ventilation (IMV), a mode of mechanical ventilation in which the patient is allowed to breathe independently except during certain prescribed intervals, when a ventilator delivers a breath either under positive pressure or in a measured volume.

intermittent positive-pressure breathing (IPPB), a form of assisted or controlled respiration produced by a ventilatory apparatus in which compressed gas is delivered under positive pressure into a person's airways until a preset pressure is reached. Passive exhalation is allowed through a valve, and the cycle begins again as the flow of gas is triggered by inhalation. The specific pressure and volume and the use of nebulizing or other attachments are ordered individually.

intermittent pulse [L, *inter,* between, *mittere,* to send, *pulsare,* to beat], a pulse in which an occasional beat is absent. It tends to occur with second-degree heart block or extrasystole.

intermittent torticollis [L, *inter,* between, *mittere,* to send, *tortus,* twisted, *collum,* neck], intermittent, powerful spasms of the neck muscles, usually the sternocleidomastoid muscle, drawing the head to one side.

intermittent tremor [L, *inter,* between, *mittere,* to send, *tremere,* to tremble], a rhythmic involuntary shaking that occurs intermittently.

intern /in′turn/ [L, *internus,* inward], **1.** a physician in the first postgraduate year, learning medical practice under supervision before beginning a residency program. **2.** any immediate postgraduate trainee in a clinical program. **3.** to work as an intern.

internal /intur′nəl/ [L, *internus,* inward], within or inside. **—internally,** *adv.*

internal abdominal oblique muscle, one of a pair of anterolateral muscles of the abdomen. It functions to compress the abdominal contents and assists in micturition, defecation, emesis, parturition, and forced expiration. Both sides acting together serve to flex the vertebral column. One side acting alone bends the vertebral column laterally and rotates it.

internal acoustic meatus, an opening in the petrous portion of the temporal bone through which the facial, intermediate, and vestibulocochlear nerves and the labyrinthine artery pass.

internal aperture of tympanic canaliculus, the upper opening of the tympanic channel in the temporal bone, leading to the tympanum.

internal bleeding [L, *internus,* inward; AS, *blod*], any hemorrhage from an internal organ or tissue, such as intraperitoneal bleeding into the peritoneal cavity or intestinal bleeding into the bowel.

internal carotid artery, each of two arteries starting at the bifurcation of the common carotid arteries, opposite the cranial border of the thyroid cartilage, through which blood circulates to many structures and organs in the head.

internal carotid plexus, a network of nerves on the internal carotid artery, formed by the internal carotid nerve. The internal carotid plexus supplies sympathetic fibers to the branches of the internal carotid artery, the tympanic plexus, the nerves of the cavernous sinus, and the cranial parasympathetic ganglia through which the fibers pass.

internal cervical os, an internal opening of the uterus that corresponds to the slight constriction or isthmus of that organ about midway in its length. The internal cervical os separates the body of the uterus from the cervix.

internal fertilization, the union of gametes within the body of the female after insemination.

internal fistula, an abnormal passage between two internal organs or structures.

internal fixation, any method of holding together the fragments of a fractured bone without the use of appliances external to the skin. After open reduction of the fracture, smooth or threaded pins, Kirschner wires, screws, plates attached by screws, or medullary nails may be inserted through an appropriate incision to stablize the fragments.

internal hemorrhage, bleeding into a serous cavity, a hollow viscus, or tissues.

internal hemorrhoid, a fold of mucous membrane at the anorectal junction, caused by edema or dilation of the interior rectal vein.

internal hernia, a protrusion of an intraperitoneal viscus into a recess or compartment within the peritoneal cavity.

internal iliac artery, a division of the common iliac artery, supplying the walls of the pelvis, the pelvic viscera, the genital organs, and part of the medial thigh.

internal iliac node, a node in one of seven groups of parietal lymph nodes serving the abdomen and the pelvis. Their afferent vessels drain lymph from the pelvic viscera, the buttocks, and the dorsal portions of the thighs. Their efferent vessels end in the common iliac nodes.

internal iliac vein, one of the pair of veins in the lower body that join the external iliac vein to form the two common iliac veins.

internal injury [L, *internus*, inward + *injuria*], any hurt, wound, or damage to the viscera.

internalization /intur′nəlīzā′shən/ [L, *internus;* Gk, *izein,* to cause], the process of adopting within the self, either unconsciously or consciously through learning and socialization, the attitudes, beliefs, values, and standards of another person or more generally of the society or group to which one belongs.

internal jugular catheter, a central venous catheter inserted through the internal jugular vein.

internal jugular vein, one of a pair of veins in the neck. Each vein collects blood from one side of the brain, the face, and the neck, and both unite with the subclavian vein to form the brachiocephalic vein.

internal mammary artery bypass, a surgical procedure to correct a coronary artery obstruction. The internal mammary artery in situ and still attached to the subclavian artery is anastomosed to the coronary artery beyond the obstruction.

internal medicine, the branch of medicine concerned with the study of the physiologic and pathologic characteristics of the internal organs and with the medical diagnosis and treatment of disorders of these organs.

internal os, the internal opening of the cervical canal.

internal pterygoid muscle, one of the four muscles of mastication. It acts to close the jaws.

internal pudendal artery, a branch of the anterior trunk of the internal iliac artery in the pelvis with branches that supply the rectum and perineum and the erectile tissues of the penis and clitoris.

internal rotation, 1. the turning of a limb about its axis of rotation toward the midline of the body. 2. medial rotation.

internal secretion [L, *internus,* inward, *secernere,* to separate], a type of secretion in which substances pass directly from a gland into the bloodstream.

internal sphincter muscle of urethra, a circular layer of smooth muscle fibers that surrounds the internal urethral orifice in males and acts to close the it. No such structure exists in females.

internal standard, an element or compound added in a known amount to yield a signal against which an instrument or an analyte to be measured can be calibrated.

internal strangulation [L, *internus,* inward, *strangulare,* to choke], a state of extreme constriction of an organ, such as a loop of intestine trapped in an opening, resulting in an interruption in the blood supply and ischemia.

internal thoracic artery, one of a pair of arteries that arise from the first portions of the subclavian arteries and descend to the margin of the sternum. The artery supplies the pectoral muscles, the breasts, the pericardium, and the abdominal muscles.

internal thoracic vein, one of a pair of veins that accompanies the internal thoracic artery, receiving tributaries that correspond to those of the artery.

International Association for Dental Research (IADR), an international organization concerned with research in dentistry and the exchange of information regarding such research.

International Classification of Diseases (ICD), an official list of categories of diseases, physical and mental, issued by the World Health Organization. It is used primarily for statistic purposes in the classification of morbidity and mortality data.

International Commission on Radiation Protection (ICRP), a nongovernmental organization founded in England in 1928 to provide general guidance on the safe use of radiation sources, including appropriate protective measures and codes of practice for medical radiology. The ICRP was reorganized in 1950 to include effects of nuclear energy.

International Council of Nurses (ICN), the oldest international health organization. It is a federation of nurses' associations from 112 countries and was one of the first health organizations to develop strict policies of nondiscrimination on the basis of nationality, race, creed, color, politics, sex, or social status. The objectives of the ICN include promotion of national associations of nurses, improvement of standards of nursing and competence of nurses, improvement of the status of nurses within their countries, and provision of an authoritative international voice for nurses.

International Normalized Ratio (INR), a comparative rating of a patient's prothrombin time (PT) ratio, used as a standard for monitoring the effects of warfarin. The INR indicates what the patient's PT ratio would have been if measured by using the primary World Health Organization International Reference reagent.

International Red Cross Society, an international philanthropic organization based in Geneva, Switzerland, concerned primarily with the humane treatment and welfare of the victims of war and calamity and with the neutrality of hospitals and medical personnel in times of war.

International Sign Language, a sign language composed of a blending of vocabulary signs from numerous different countries, sometimes used at international meetings and events of deaf persons.

International Society of Surgery (ISS), an international professional organization of surgeons.

International System of Units (SI), an internationally accepted scientific system of expressing length, mass, and time in base units (IU) of meters, kilograms, and seconds, replacing the old centimeter-gram-second system. The SI system includes as standard measurements the ampere, kelvin scale, candela, and mole.

International Union Against Cancer (UICC) [Fr, *Union Internationale Contre le Cancer*], an international, nongovernmental organization founded in 1933 addressing all aspects of cancer control.

International Unit (IU, I.U.), a unit of measure in the International System of Units.

interneuron /-nŏŏr′on/, a nerve cell whose axon and dendrite lie entirely within the CNS and whose function is to relay impulses within the CNS.

internist /intur′nist, in′turnist/ [L, *internus*, inward], a physician who specializes in internal medicine.

internship /in′turnship′/, a period of apprenticeship for a medical school graduate who serves in a hospital for a specified period before beginning a professional practice. Some hospitals offer internships for new graduates in nursing or for senior nursing students.

internuncial neuron /-nun′sē·əl/ [L, *inter* + *nuntius*, messenger], a connecting neuron in a neural pathway, usually serving as a link between two other neurons.

interocclusal record /-əklōō′səl/, an imprint of the positional relation of opposing teeth or jaws to each other, made on the surfaces of occlusal rims or teeth with a material such as plaster of paris, wax, zinc oxide-eugenol paste, or acrylic resin.

interoceptive /in′tərōsep′tiv/ [L, *internus*, inward, *capere*, to take], pertaining to stimuli originating from within the body that are related to the functioning of the internal organs or the receptors they activate.

interoceptor /-sep′tər/ [L, *internus* + *capere*, to take], any sensory nerve ending located in cells in the viscera that responds to stimuli originating from within the body in relation to the function of the internal organs, such as digestion, excretion, and BP.

interosseous /-os′ē·əs/ [L, *inter,* between, *os,* bone], pertaining to an area between bones or a structure, such as a ligament, connecting two bones.

interparoxysmal /-per′əksis′məl/ [L, *inter,* between, *paroxysmos,* irritation], pertaining to something that happens between paroxysms.

interperiosteal fracture /in′tərper′ē·os′tē·əl/ [L, *inter;* Gk, *peri,* around, *osteon,* bone], an incomplete fracture in which the periosteum is not disrupted.

interpersonal /-pur′sənəl/ [L, *inter,* between + *personalis*], pertaining to the interactions of individuals.

interpersonal psychiatry [L, *inter* + *persona,* mask], a theory of psychiatry introduced by Harry Stack Sullivan (1892–1949) that stresses the nature and quality of relationships with significant others as the most critical factor in personality development.

interpersonal therapy, a kind of psychotherapy that views faulty communications, interactions, and interrelationships as basic factors in maladaptive behavior.

interphase /in′tərfās′/ [L, *inter;* Gk, *phasis,* phase], the stage in the cell cycle during which the cell is not dividing, the chromosomes are not individually distinguishable, and such biochemical and physiologic activities as DNA synthesis occur.

interpleural space /-plŏŏr′əl/ [L, *inter,* between; Gk, *pleura,* rib; L, *spatium*], the potential space of the mediastinum between the two pleural linings, which contains serous fluid.

interpolated premature ventricular contraction /intur′pəlā′tid/ [L, *interpolare,* to refurbish], a ventricular extrasystole that occurs between two consecutive sinus-conducted beats. It is not followed by a compensatory pause.

interpolation /intur′pəlā′shən/, **1.** the transfer of tissues, as in plastic surgery or transplantation. **2.** in statistics, the introduction of an estimated intermediate value of a variable between known values.

interpubic disk /-pyŏŏ′bik/ [L, *inter* + *os pubis,* pubic bone; Gk, *diskos,* flat plate], the fibrocartilaginous plate connecting the opposed surfaces of the bodies of the pubic bones.

interpulse interval /-puls´/, the time elapsed between successive nerve impulses; the reciprocal of impulse frequency.

interradicular space /-radik´yəlor/ [L, *inter* + *radix*, root + *spatium*], the area between the roots of a multirooted tooth, normally occupied by a bony septum and the periodontal membrane.

interrogatories /in´tərog´ətôr´ēz/ [L, *inter* + *rogare*, to ask], in law, a series of written questions submitted to a witness or other person having information of interest to the court. The answers are transcribed and are sworn to under oath. Interrogatories are used during the pretrial period as a means of discovery.

interrupted suture /in´tərup´tid/ [L, *interrumpere*, to sever + *sutura*], a single suture tied separately, as distinguished from a continuous suture.

intersection syndrome, a condition of pain, crepitus, and a squeaky sensation in the dorsal radial forearm. It occurs most commonly among weight lifters and rowers.

intersex /in´tərseks´/ [L, *inter* + *sexus*, sex, gender], any individual who has anatomic characteristics of both sexes or whose external genitalia are ambiguous or inappropriate for either the normal male or female.

intersexuality /-sek´shōō·al´itē/ [L, *inter* + *sexus*, male or female], the condition in which an individual has both male and female anatomic characteristics to varying degrees or in which the appearance of the external genitalia is ambiguous or differs from that characteristic of the gonadal or genetic sex.—**intersexual,** *adj.*

intersphincteric groove, an indistinct groove in the anal canal, forming the lower border of the pecten analis, marking the change between the subcutaneous part of the external anal sphincter and the border of the internal anal sphincter.

interspinales, the true segmental muscles of the back.

interspinal ligament /-spī´nəl/ [L, *inter* + *spina*, spine, *ligare*, to bind], one of many thin, narrow membranous ligaments that connect adjoining spinous processes of the vertebrae and extend from the root of each process to the apex.

interspinous /-spī´nəs/ [L, *inter* + *spina*, spine], pertaining to the space between any spinous processes.

interstitial /in´tərstish´əl/ [L, *inter* + *sistere*, to stand], pertaining to the space between cells, as interstitial fluid, or between organs.

interstitial cell–stimulating hormone (ICSH), a hormone secreted by the anterior pituitary gland that stimulates the production of testosterone by the Leydig cells of the testis.

interstitial cystitis (IC), an inflammation of the bladder, believed to be associated with an autoimmune or allergic response. The bladder wall becomes inflamed, ulcerated, and scarred, causing frequent painful urination. Hematuria often occurs.

interstitial emphysema, a form of emphysema in which air or gas escapes into the interstitial tissues of the lung after a penetrating injury or a rupture in an alveolar wall. Because the alveoli must be decompressed, there is danger that the pleura will be torn, causing a pneumothorax.

interstitial fibroid [L, *interstitium,* space between, *fibra,* fiber; Gk, *eidos,* form], a fibrous tumor that develops in the muscular wall of the uterus and tends to grow inward.

interstitial fluid, an extracellular fluid that fills the spaces between most of the cells of the body and provides a substantial portion of the liquid environment of the body. Formed by filtration through the blood capillaries, it is drained away as lymph.

interstitial growth, an increase in size by hyperplasia or hypertrophy within the interior of a part or structure that is already formed.

interstitial implantation, in embryology, the complete embedding of the blastocyst within the endometrium of the uterine wall.

interstitial inflammation [L, *interstitium,* space between, *inflammare,* to set afire], an inflammation in an area of connective tissues.

interstitial keratitis, an uncommon inflammation within the layers of the cornea. The first symptom is a diffuse haziness. Blood vessels may grow into the area and cause permanent opacities. The causes are syphilis, TB, leprosy, and vascular hypersensitivity.

interstitial lung disease (ILD), a respiratory disorder characterized by a dry, unproductive cough and dyspnea on exertion. The patient may have swallowing disorders or joint and muscle pain and a history of industrial exposure to inorganic dusts such as asbestos or silica. X-ray films usually show fibrotic infiltrates in the lung tissue, usually in the lower lobes, often resulting from an immune reaction to an inhaled substance. However, ILD may result from viral, bacterial, or other infections; uremic pneumonitis; cancer; a congenital or inherited disorder; or circulatory impairment.

interstitial mastitis [L, *interstitium,* space between; Gk, *mastos,* breast], an inflammation of the connective tissue between ducts of the breast.

interstitial nephritis, inflammation of the interstitial tissue of the kidney, including the tubules. Acute interstitial nephritis is an immunologic adverse reaction to certain drugs, often sulfonamide or methicillin. Acute renal failure, fever, rash, and proteinuria are characteristic of this condition. Chronic interstitial nephritis is a syndrome of interstitial inflammation and structural changes, sometimes associated with such conditions as ureteral obstruction, pyelonephritis, exposure of the kidney to a toxin, rejection of a transplant, and certain systemic diseases. Gradually renal failure, nausea, vomiting, weight loss, fatigue, and anemia develop.

interstitial pneumonia, a condition of diffuse, chronic inflammation of the lungs beyond the terminal bronchioles, characterized by fibrosis and collagen formation in the alveolar walls and by the presence of large mononuclear cells in the alveolar spaces. The symptoms are progressive dyspnea, clubbing of the fingers, cyanosis, and fever. X-ray films of the lungs show patchy shadows and mottling, as in bronchopneumonia. Later stages of the disease reveal bronchiectasis, dilation of the bronchi, and shrinkage of the lungs.

interstitial therapy, radiotherapy in which needles or wires that contain radioactive material are implanted directly into tumor areas.

interstitial tissue [L, *interstitium,* space between; OFr, *tissu*], the connective and supporting tissue within and surrounding major functional elements of an organ.

interstitial tubal pregnancy, a kind of tubal pregnancy in which implantation occurs in the proximal interstitial portion of one of the fallopian tubes.

interstitium /-stish′ē-əm/, the space between cells in a tissue.

intertransverse ligament /-transvurz′/ [L, *inter* + *transversus,* cross-direction], one of many fibrous bands connecting the transverse processes of vertebrae.

intertrigo /in′tərtrī′gō/ [L, *inter* + *terere,* to scour], an erythematous irritation of opposing skin surfaces caused by friction, moisture, warmth, or sweat retention. Common sites are the axillae, the folds beneath large or pendulous breasts, and the inner aspects of the thighs.—**intertriginous,** *adj.*

intertrochanteric crest /in′tərtrō′kanter′ik/ [L, *inter* + *trochanter,* runner, *crista,* ridge], one of a pair of ridges along the thigh bones, curving obliquely from the greater to the lesser trochanter.

intertrochanteric fracture, a crack in the proximal femur between the greater and the lesser trochanters.

intertrochanteric line, a line that runs across the anterior surface of the thigh bone from the greater to the lesser trochanter, winding around the medial surface and ending in the linea aspera. The proximal half of the intertrochanteric line is the attachment for the iliofemoral ligament; the distal half holds the vastus medialis muscle.

intertuberous diameter /-tōō′bərəs/ [L, *inter* + *tuber,* swelling; Gk, *dia,* across, *metron,* measure], the distance between the ischial tuberosities, a factor used in determining the dimensions, including the narrowest diameter, of the pelvic outlet.

interureteral /in′terure′teral/, situated between the ureters.

interval /in′tərval/ [L, *intervallum,* space between], a space between things or events, or a break or interruption in an otherwise continuous flow.

interval health history [L, *intervallum,* space between], a kind of health history that notes the general condition of a client during the period between visits and is not limited to facts relevant to a particular condition. The interval health history provides an ongoing account of a person's health, serving to bring the data base up to date.

intervention /in′tərven′shən/ [L, *inter* + *venire,* to come], any act performed to prevent harming of a patient or to improve the mental, emotional, or physical function of a patient. A physiologic process may be monitored or enhanced, or a pathologic process may be arrested or controlled. Independent intervention is any health care activity pertaining to aspects of professional practice that are encompassed by licensure and law and require no supervision or direction from others. Interdependent intervention refers to any health care activity carried out by one health care professional in collaboration with another.

interventional cardiology, the subspecialty of cardiology that uses intravascular catheter-based techniques with fluoroscopy to treat coronary artery, valvular, and congenital cardiac disease.

interventricular /-ventrik′yələr/ [L, *inter,* between, *ventriculus,* little belly], pertaining to the location between the ventricles, as the septum of the heart.

interventricular septum [L, *inter,* between, *ventriculus,* little belly, *saeptum,* fence], the wall between the ventricles of the heart.

intervertebral /in′tərvur′təbrəl/ [L, *inter* + *vertebra,* back joint], pertaining to the space between any two vertebrae, such as the fibrocartilaginous disks.

intervertebral disk, one of the fibrous, broad, and flattened disks found between adjacent spinal vertebrae, except the axis and the atlas. The disks vary in size, shape, thickness, and number, depending on the location in the back and on the particular vertebrae they separate.

intervertebral foramen, any of the passages between adjacent vertebrae through which the spinal nerves and vessels pass.

intervertebral ganglion [L, *inter,* between, *vertebra,* back joint; Gk, *ganglion,* knot], the ganglionic enlargement of a spinal nerve root between adjacent vertebrae.

interview /in′tərvyo͞o/, a verbal interaction with a patient initiated for a specific purpose and focused on a specific content area. A problem-seeking interview is an inquiry that focuses on gathering data to identify problems the patient needs to resolve. A problem-solving interview focuses on problems that have been identified by the patient or health care professional.

intervillous space /in′tərvil′əs/ [L, *inter* + *villus,* hair + *spatium*], one of many spaces between the chorionic villi of the endometrium of the gravid uterus, beneath the placenta. The intervillous spaces act as small reservoirs for oxygenated maternal blood.

intestinal, pertaining to the intestines.

intestinal absorption [L, *intestinum,* intestine, *absorbare,* to swallow], the passage of the products of digestion from the lumen of the small intestine into the blood and lymphatic vessels in the wall of the gut. The surface area of the intestine is greatly increased by the presence of finger-like projections, called villi, each of which contains capillaries and a lymphatic vessel, or lacteal.

intestinal angina, chronic vascular insufficiency of the mesentery caused by atherosclerosis and resulting ischemia of the smooth muscle of the small bowel.

intestinal apoplexy, the sudden occlusion of one of the three principal arteries to the intestine by an embolism or a thrombus. This condition leads rapidly to necrosis of intestinal tissue and is often fatal.

intestinal atresia [L, *intestinum;* Gk, *a* + *tresis,* boring], a pathologic obstruction of the continuous lumen of the intestinal tract caused by a defect of development in utero.

intestinal bypass [L, *intestinum;* AS, *bi;* Fr, *passer;* Gk, *cheirourgos*], a surgical procedure to shorten the digestive tract, usually by anastomosing the jejunum to the ilium. It is performed so that less intestinal surface will be available to absorb nutrients from the digested food passing through or to bypass a blocked or diseased portion of the intestine.

intestinal colic [L, *intestinum;* Gk, *kolikos,* colonic pain], spasmodic pain in intestinal disorders.

intestinal dyspepsia, an abnormal condition characterized by impaired digestion associated with a disorder that originates in the intestines.

intestinal fistula, an abnormal passage from the intestine to other internal organs or to an external abdominal opening or stoma, usually created surgically for the exit of feces after removal of a malignant or severely ulcerated segment of the bowel.

intestinal flora [L, *intestinum* + *flos,* flower], the natural bacterial content of the inside of the digestive tract.

intestinal flu, a viral gastroenteritis, usually caused by infection by an enterovirus. It is characterized by abdominal cramps, diarrhea, nausea, and vomiting.

intestinal fluke [L, *intestinum;* AS, *floc*], any internal parasite of the genera *Fasciolopsis, Heterophyes,* and *Metagonimus* in North America and of other genera in Asia and in tropical countries. They enter the body through the mouth as encysted larvae in aquatic vegetation or freshwater fish. Symptoms of intestinal fluke infestation usually include abdominal pain and obstruction and diarrhea.

intestinal gas [L, *intestinum*], gas in the digestive tract arising from three sources— swallowed air, gas produced by digestive processes, and blood gases diffused into the intestinal lumen. Gases produced in the intestine and diffused from blood are mainly hydrogen, most of which is a bacterial fermentation product of ingested carbohydrates, carbon dioxide, and methane.

intestinal juices, the secretions of glands lining the intestine.

intestinal obstruction, any obstruction that results in failure of the contents of the intestine to progress through the lumen of the bowel. The most common cause is a mechanical blockage resulting from adhesions, impacted feces, tumor of the bowel, hernia, intussusception, volvulus, or the strictures of inflammatory bowel disease. Obstruction of the small bowel may cause severe pain, vomiting of fecal matter, dehydration, and eventually a drop in BP. Obstruction of the colon causes less severe pain, marked abdominal distension, and constipation.

intestinal perforation [L, *intestinum* + *perforare,* to pierce], the escape of digestive tract contents into the peritoneal cavity as the result of trauma or a disease condition such as a ruptured appendix or perforated

I

ulcer. The condition inevitably leads to peritonitis.

intestinal pseudoobstruction [L, *intestinum,* intestine; Gk, *pseudes,* false; L, *obstruere,* to build against], a condition characterized by constipation, colicky pain, and vomiting, but without evidence of organic obstruction apparent at laparotomy.

intestinal strangulation, the arrest of blood flow to the bowel, causing edema, cyanosis, and gangrene of the affected loop of bowel. This condition is usually caused by a hernia, intussusception, or volvulus. Early signs of intestinal strangulation resemble those of intestinal obstruction.

intestinal tonsil, one of a group of lymphatic nodules forming a single layer in the mucous membrane of the ileum opposite the mesenteric attachment.

intestinal tract [L, *intestinum + tractus*], the segments of the small and large intestines between the pyloric valve and the rectum.

intestinal tube [L, *intestinum + tubus*], a tube into the intestines, inserted for therapeutic measures.

intestine /intes′tin/ [L, *intestinum*], the part of the alimentary canal extending from the pyloric opening of the stomach to the anus. It includes the small and large intestines. —**intestinal,** *adj.*

intima /in′timə/ *pl.* **intimae** [L, *intimus,* innermost], the innermost layer of a structure, such as the lining membrane of an artery, vein, lymphatic vessel, or organ. —**intimal,** *adj.*

intimal fibroplasia, a type of fibromuscular dysplasia that affects mainly children and young adult men, characterized by short localized areas of smooth stenosis of the tunica intima, either symmetric or asymmetric.

intimal sclerosis [L, *intimus,* innermost; Gk, *sklerosis,* hardening], a hardening of the innermost layer of a blood vessel wall.

intolerance /intol′ərəns/ [L, *in,* not, *tolerare,* to bear], a condition characterized by inability to absorb or metabolize a nutrient or medication. Exposure to the substance may cause an adverse reaction, as in lactose intolerance.

intoxicant /intok′sikənt/ [L, *in;* Gk, *toxikon,* poison], any agent that can cause intoxication or poisoning.

intoxication /intok′sikā′shən/ [L, *in,* within; Gk, *toxikon,* poison], **1.** the state of being poisoned by a drug or other toxic substance. **2.** the state of being inebriated as a result of an excessive consumption of alcohol. **3.** a state of mental or emotional hyperexcitability, usually euphoric.

intraabdominal infection /in′trə·abdom′inəl/, a disease caused by organisms,

usually bacterial or fungal, situated within the cavity of the abdomen.

intraabdominal pressure [L, *intra,* within, *abdomen,* belly], the degree of pressure within the abdominal cavity.

intraaortic balloon pump (IABP) /in′trə·ā·ôr′tik/ [L, *intra;* Gk, *aeirein,* to rise], a counterpulsation device that provides temporary cardiac assist in the management of refractory left ventricular failure that may follow MI or occur in preinfarction angina. The balloon is attached to a catheter inserted into the aorta and is automatically inflated during diastole and deflated during systole.

intraarterial /in′trə·ärtir′ē·əl/, pertaining to a structure or action inside an artery.

intraarticular /in′trə·ärtik′yələr/ [L, *intra + articulus,* joint], within a joint.

intraarticular fracture, a fracture involving the articular surfaces of a joint.

intraarticular injection, the injection of a medication into a joint space, usually to reduce inflammation, such as in bursitis or fibromyositis.

intraarticular ligament, a ligament that forms part of the joints between 16 of the 24 ribs, dividing the joints into two cavities, each containing a synovial membrane. Each intraarticular ligament consists of a short, flattened band of fibers inside the joint, attached by one extremity to the rib and by the other to the intervertebral disk.

intraatrial /in′trə·ā′trē·əl/ [L, *intra + atrium,* hall], pertaining to the space or substance within an atrium of the heart.

intraatrial block, delayed or abnormal conduction of the cardiac impulse within the atria. It is identified on an ECG by a prolonged and often a notched P wave.

intracanalicular fibroma /-kan′əlik′yələr/ [L, *intra + canaliculus,* small channel], a tumor containing glandular epithelium and fibrous tissue, occurring in the breast.

intracanalicular papilloma /-kənik′yələr/, a benign warty growth in certain glands, especially the breast.

intracapsular fracture /-kap′syələr/ [L, *intra + capsula,* little box], a fracture within the capsule of a joint.

intracardiac /-kar′dē·ak/ [L, *intra,* within; Gk, *kardia,* heart], pertaining to the interior of the heart chambers.

intracardiac electrogram, a record of changes in the electric potentials of specific cardiac loci as measured by electrodes placed within the heart via cardiac catheters. It is used for loci that cannot be assessed by body surface electrodes.

intracardiac lead /lēd/ [L, *intra;* Gk, *kardia,* heart; AS, *laedan,* lead], **1.** an ECG conductor in which the exploring electrode is placed within one of the cardiac chambers, usually by means of cardiac catheterization. **2.** *informal.* a tracing produced by such a lead on an ECG.

intracatheter /-kath′ətər/ [L, *intra;* Gk, *katheter,* something lowered], a thin, flexible plastic catheter introduced through a stainless steel needle and threaded into a blood vessel to infuse blood, fluid, or medication.

intracavernosal injection, introduction of a hypodermic needle into the corpus cavernosum of the penis in order to administer a medication. It is used for treatment of erectile dysfunction.

intracavitary /in′trəkav′itər′ē/ [L, *intra* + *cavum,* cave], pertaining to the space within a body cavity.

intracavitary therapy, a kind of radiotherapy in which one or more radioactive sources are placed, usually with the help of an applicator or holding device, within a body cavity to irradiate the walls of the cavity or adjacent tissues.

intracellular /-sel′yələr/ [L, *intra,* within, *cella,* storeroom], **1.** pertaining to the interior of a cell. **2.** within a cell.

intracellular fluid (ICF) [L, *intra* + *cella,* storeroom, *fluere,* to flow], a fluid within cell membranes throughout most of the body, containing dissolved solutes that are essential to electrolyte balance and to healthy metabolism.

intracerebral /-ser′əbrəl/ [L, *intra* + *cerebrum,* brain], pertaining to the area or substance within the cerebrum.

intracerebral hematoma, a localized collection of extravasated blood within the cerebrum, associated with a cerebral laceration resulting from a contusion.

intracerebral hemorrhage (ICH), a type of hemorrhagic stroke in which bleeding directly into the brain occurs. It is most often caused by hypertension and is associated with increased ICP. ICH usually occurs in the basal ganglia, thalamus, pons, and cerebral and cerebellar white matter.

intracistronic /in′trəsistron′ik/ [L, *intra* + *cis,* this side, *trans,* across], within a cistron.

intracoronal retainer /-kôr′ənəl/ [L, *intra* + *corona,* crown], **1.** a cast restoration, such as an inlay, that lies largely within the contour of the tooth crown. **2.** a direct retainer used in the construction of removable partial dentures. It consists of a female portion within the coronal segment of the crown of an abutment and a male portion attached to the denture proper.

intracostal /-kos′təl/, pertaining to the inner surface of a rib.

intracranial /-krā′nē·əl/ [L, *intra,* within; Gk, *kranion,* skull], pertaining to the area within the cranium (the bony skull).

intracranial aneurysm, localized dilation of any of the cerebral arteries. Characteristics of the condition include sudden severe headache, stiff neck, photophobia, nausea, vomiting, and sometimes LOC. Rupture of an intracranial aneurysm produces a mortality rate approaching 50%, and survivors face a high risk of recurrence.

intracranial hemorrhage [L, *intra,* within; Gk, *kranion,* skull, *haima,* blood], a hemorrhage within the cranium.

intracranial pressure (ICP), pressure that occurs within the cranium.

intracranial pressure (ICP) monitoring, a nursing intervention from the Nursing Interventions Classification (NIC) defined as measurement and interpretation of patient data to regulate intracranial pressure.

intractable /intrak′təbəl/ [L, *intractabilis,* hard to manage], having no relief, such as a symptom or a disease that is not relieved by the therapeutic measures used.

intractable pain [L, *intractabilis,* hard to manage, *poena,* penalty], pain that is not relieved by ordinary medical, surgical, and nursing measures. The pain is often chronic and persistent and can be psychogenic in nature.

intracutaneous /-kyo͞otā′nē·əs/ [L, *intra* + *cutis,* skin], within the skin.

intracystic papilloma /-sis′tik/ [L, *intra;* Gk, *kystis,* bag], a benign epithelial tumor formed within a cystic adenoma.

intracytoplasmic sperm injection (ICSI), a micromanipulation technique used in male factor infertility in which a single spermatocyte is inserted into an oocyte by micropuncture.

intradermal /-dur′məl/ [L, *intra,* within; Gk, *derma,* skin], in the skin.

intradermal injection, the introduction of a hypodermic needle into the dermis for the purpose of instilling a substance, such as a serum or vaccine.

intradermal test [L, *intra;* Gk, *derma,* skin], a procedure used to identify suspected allergens by subcutaneously injecting the patient with small amounts of extracts of the suspected allergens. The injections are made at spaced intervals. The patient is concurrently injected with the diluent alone as a control procedure. The test result is positive if within 15 to 30 minutes the injection of extract produces a wheal surrounded by erythema and the control injection produces no symptoms. The intradermal test is started with highly diluted solutions; if the initial test result is negative, the procedure is repeated with stronger solutions.

intradialytic hypotension, hypotension sometimes seen as a complication of hemodialysis.

intradiscal electrothermal therapy, a minimally invasive procedure for the treatment of discogenic low back pain.

intraductal /-duk′təl/, within a duct.

intraductal carcinoma [L, *intra* + *ductus,* duct], a neoplasm that occurs most often in the breast but can occur elsewhere, as in the salivary glands.

intraductal papilloma, a small benign epithelial tumor in a milk duct of the breast, occasionally marked by bleeding from the nipple.

intradural lipoma [L, *intra* + *dura,* hard], a fatty tumor in or beneath the dura mater of the spine or sacrum that tends to infiltrate the dorsal column and roots of spinal nerves, causing pain and dysfunction.

intraepidermal carcinoma /in′trə·ep′idu r′məl/ [L, *intra;* Gk, *epi,* above, *derma,* skin], a neoplasm of squamous epidermal cells that does not proliferate into the basal area and often occurs in many sites simultaneously.

intraepidermal vesicle, a fluid-filled blister-like cavity within the epidermis, usually less than 1 cm in diameter.

intrafollicular insemination (IFI), method of assisted reproductive technology in which semen is injected into a follicle.

intrafusal muscle fiber /-fyo͞o′zəl/, the striated muscle fiber within a muscle spindle.

intrahepatic cholestasis, a result of some condition inside the liver, such as an infection, sepsis, cirrhosis, an abscess, a tumor, or a complication from medication.

intrahepatic cholestasis of pregnancy, a type of intrahepatic cholestasis sometimes seen during the third trimester of pregnancy, characterized by severe itching, hepatomegaly, and sometimes jaundice. It clears up after delivery.

intraluminal /-lo͞o′minəl/, **1.** within the lumen of any tubular structure or organ. **2.** between or among tubes.

intraluminal coronary artery stent, a device permanently inserted into a coronary artery to maintain patency of the lumen of the vessel.

intramammary abscess /-mam′ərē/, a collection of pus within a mammary gland.

intramural /-myo͞o′rəl/ [L, *intra,* within, *murus,* wall], pertaining to events or structures within the walls of an organ, body part, or cavity.

intramural part of male urethra, the short, most proximal part of the urethra, running almost vertically down from the bladder to where it enters the prostate.

intramural part of ureter, the short distal portion of the ureter after it bends to run obliquely through the wall of the bladder.

intramuscular (IM) /-mus′kyələr/ [L, *intra,* within, *musculus,* muscle], pertaining to the interior of muscle tissue.

intramuscular injection [L, *intra* + *musculus*], the introduction of a hypodermic needle into a muscle to administer a medication.

intraocular /-ok′yələr/ [L, *intra* + *oculus,* eye], pertaining to structures or substances within the eyeball.

intraocular lens (IOL), a plastic artificial lens inserted into the capsule of the lens after cataract removal.

intraocular pressure, the internal pressure of the eye, regulated by resistance to the flow of aqueous humor through the fine sieve of the trabecular meshwork.

intraoperative /-op′ərətiv′/ [L, *intra* + *operari,* to work], pertaining to the period during a surgical procedure.

intraoperative hyperthermia [L, *intra* + *operari,* to work], hyperthermia delivered as a therapeutic measure to internal sites that have been exposed by a surgical procedure.

intraoperative radiotherapy (IORT), the use of a single high dose of radiation at the time of surgery as adjuvant therapy in tumor resection.

intraoperative ultrasound, a diagnostic technique that uses a portable ultrasound device to scan the spinal cord during spinal surgery. Intraoperative ultrasound can distinguish between syrinxes, or fluid-filled cysts, and neoplastic growths in nervous system tissue.

intraoral orthodontic appliance /in′trə·ôr′əl/ [L, *intra* + *oralis,* mouth], a device placed inside the mouth to correct or alleviate malocclusion.

intraosseous /in′trə·os′ē·əs/ [L, *intra,* within, *os,* bone], pertaining to the interior of bone.

intraosseous infusion, the injection of blood, medications, or fluids into bone marrow rather than into a vein. The technique may be performed in emergency treatment of a child when IV infusion is not feasible.

intraparietal sulcus /-perī′ətəl/ [L, *intra* + *paries,* wall, *sulcus,* groove], an irregular groove on the convex surface of the parietal lobe that marks the division of the inferior and superior parietal lobules of the cerebrum.

intrapartal care¹ /-pär′təl/ [L, *intra* + *partus,* birth], care of a pregnant woman from the onset of labor to the completion of the fourth stage of labor with the expulsion of the placenta.

intrapartal care², a nursing intervention from the Nursing Interventions Classification (NIC) defined as monitoring and management of stages one and two of the birth process.

intrapartal care: high-risk delivery, a nursing intervention from the Nursing Interventions Classification (NIC) defined as assisting vaginal birth of multiple or malpositioned fetuses.

intrapartal period, the period spanning labor and birth.

intrapartum /-pär′təm/, pertaining to the period of labor and birth.

intrapartum hemorrhage, copious bleeding, usually caused by abruptio placentae or placenta previa during labor.

intraperiosteal fracture /in′trəper′ē·os′tē·əl/ [L, *intra;* Gk, *peri,* around, *osteon,* bone], a fracture that does not rupture the periosteum.

intraperitoneal insemination (IPI), method of assisted reproductive technology in which semen is injected into the peritoneal cavity.

intrapleural space /-plŏŏr′əl/ [L, *intra,* within; Gk, *pleura,* rib; L, *spatium*], the cavity of the pleura.

intrapsychic conflict /-sī′kik/ [L, *intra;* Gk, *psyche,* mind], an emotional clash of opposing impulses within oneself.

intrapulmonary /-pul′məner′ē/ [L, *intra,* within, *pulma,* lung], pertaining to the interior of the lungs.

intrapulmonary shunt [L, *intra* + *pulmoneus,* relating to the lung], in respiratory therapy, a condition in which a region of the lungs is perfused with little or no ventilation. It is indicated by a low ratio of QS/QT, in which QS represents the difference between end capillary oxygen content and mixed venous oxygen content and QT represents cardiac output. The condition may occur in atelectasis, pneumonia, pulmonary edema, and adult respiratory distress syndrome.

intrarenal azotemia, an elevated blood urea concentration caused by a reduced glomerular filtration rate resulting in acute or chronic diseases of the renal parenchyma.

intrarenal hemodynamics /-rē′nəl/ [L, *intra* + *ren,* kidney], the pattern of blood flow or distribution in the various parts of the kidney. Normally the renal cortex and outer medulla receive the major part of renal blood flow.

intraspinal hypodermic /-spī′nəl/ [L, *intra,* within, *spina,* spine, *hypo,* under, *derma,* skin], pertaining to the injection of a substance into the spinal canal.

intrathecal /in′trəthē′kəl/ [L, *intra* + *theca,* sheath], pertaining to a structure, process, or substance within a sheath, such as within the spinal canal.

intrathecal injection, the introduction of a hypodermic needle into the subarachnoid space for the purpose of instilling a material for diffusion throughout the spinal fluid.

intrathoracic goiter /-thôras′ik/ [L, *intra;* Gk, *thorax,* chest; L, *guttur,* throat], an enlargement of the thyroid gland that protrudes into the thoracic cavity.

intrathoracic kidney, an ectopic kidney that partially or completely protrudes above the diaphragm into the posterior mediastinum.

intratubal insemination (ITI), method of ART in which washed semen is injected into the fallopian tube.

intrauterine /in′trəyŏŏ′tərin/ [L, *intra,* within, *uterus,* womb], pertaining to the inside of the uterus.

intrauterine device (IUD) [L, *intra* + *uterus,* womb; Fr, *devise*], a contraceptive device consisting of a bent strip of radiopaque plastic with a fine monofilament tail. The addition of copper wire and/or bands increases the effectiveness. Progesterone-filled IUDs are also available. The mechanism of action is not known. Insertion into the cervix is performed during or just after menstruation when the cervix is slightly open and menstruation assures that a pregnancy does not exist.

intrauterine fracture, a fracture that occurs during fetal life.

intrauterine growth curve, a line on a standardized graph representing the mean weight for gestational age through pregnancy to term.

intrauterine growth retardation, an abnormal process in which the development and maturation of the fetus are impeded or delayed more than two deviations below the mean for gestational age, sex, and ethnicity.

intrauterine insemination (IUI), artificial insemination in which specially washed sperm is injected through the cervix directly into the uterus.

intrauterine transfusion, direct transfer of Rh-negative blood cells into a fetus in utero in cases of isoimmunization.

intravascular /-vas′kyələr/ [L, *intra* + *vasculum,* little vessel], pertaining to the inside of a blood vessel.

intravascular coagulation test, a test for detecting coagulation of blood within the blood vessels.

intravascular fluid, a term sometimes used to refer to that part of the extracellular fluid that is within the blood vessels, i.e., the plasma.

intravenous (IV) /-vē′nəs/ [L, *intra* + *vena,* vein], pertaining to the inside of a vein, as of a thrombus or an injection, infusion, or catheter.

intravenous bolus, a relatively large dose of medication administered into a vein in a short period, usually within 1 to 30 minutes. The IV bolus is commonly used when rapid administration of a medication is needed, when drugs that cannot be diluted, and when the therapeutic purpose is to achieve a peak drug level in the bloodstream of the patient.

intravenous catheter [L, *intra,* within, *vena,* vein; Gk, *katheter,* a thing inserted], a catheter that is inserted into a vein for supplying medications or nutrients directly into the bloodstream or for diagnostic purposes such as studying BP.

intravenous cholangiography (IVC), in diagnostic radiology, a procedure for outlining the major bile ducts. A radiopaque contrast material is injected intravenously, and serial radiographic films are taken.

intravenous controller, any of several devices that automatically deliver IV fluid at selectable flow rates. The controller is commonly equipped with a rate selector, drop sensor, and alarm. When the infusion does not flow at the prescribed rate, the drop alarm emits a visual and an audible signal.

intravenous digital subtraction angiography (IV-DSA), a procedure for the radiographic visualization of arteries after injection of a radiopaque contrast medium into a vein.

intravenous fat emulsion, a preparation of 10% fat administered into a vein to help maintain the weight of an adult patient or the weight and growth of a younger patient. Such fat emulsions are prepared from refined soybean oil and egg-yolk phospholipids and may contain such major fatty acids as linoleic, oleic, palmitic, and linolenic acids. IV fat emulsions are often administered when hyperalimentation is not sufficient to maintain adequate treatment of a patient or when the patient needs calories but cannot tolerate the high percentage of dextrose contained in hyperalimentation solutions.

intravenous feeding, the administration of nutrients through a vein or veins.

intravenous infusion, 1. a solution administered into a vein through an infusion set that includes a plastic or glass vacuum bottle or bag containing the solution and tubing connecting the bottle to a catheter or a needle in the patient's vein. **2.** the process of administering a solution intravenously.

intravenous infusion filter, any of the numerous devices used to help ensure the purity of an IV solution. IV filters strain the solution to remove such contaminants as dissolved impurities (detergents, proteins, and polysaccharides), extraneous salts, microorganisms, particles, precipitates, and undissolved drug powders.

intravenous infusion technique, the calculations for determining the delivery rate of IV fluid for the individual patient and the necessary spiking of the container and priming of the tubing before venipuncture and fluid administration.

intravenous injection, a hypodermic injection into a vein for the purpose of instilling a single dose of medication, injecting a contrast medium, or beginning an IV infusion of blood, medication, or a fluid solution, such as saline or dextrose in water.

intravenous (IV) insertion, a nursing intervention from the Nursing Interventions Classification (NIC) defined as insertion of a needle into a peripheral vein for the purpose of administering fluids, blood, or medications.

intravenous (IV) therapy, 1. the administration of fluids into a vein through a needle or small-caliber catheter. Ongoing assessment and attention to patient comfort are important. **2.** a nursing intervention from the Nursing Interventions Classification (NIC) defined as administration and monitoring of intravenous fluids and medications.

intravenously, through a vein.

intravenous medication [L, *intra,* within, *vena,* vein, *medicare,* medicine], a pharmaceutic delivered directly into the bloodstream via a vein.

intravenous peristaltic pump, any one of several devices for administering IV fluids by exerting pressure on the IV tubing rather than on the fluid itself. Most peristaltic pumps operate with normal IV tubing and deliver fluid at a selectable cubic centimeter per hour rate. An alarm sounds when the infusion does not flow at the prescribed rate.

intravenous piston pump, any of several devices that accurately control the infusion of IV fluids by piston action. Most IV piston pumps can be operated by battery, as well as by electric current, and require special tubing. Some models are portable. IV piston pumps are commonly equipped with controls that allow selectable flow rates and indicators that display flow rates, dose limits, and cumulative fluid volumes. Such pumps commonly monitor the patient's skin for infiltration by IV fluid and are equipped with infiltration and flow alarms. The IV piston pump monitors the actual volume of IV fluid administered instead of counting drops of fluid.

intravenous pump, a pump designed to regulate the rate of flow of a fluid administered through an IV catheter.

intravenous pyelography (IVP), a radiographic technique for examining the structure and function of the urinary system. A contrast medium is injected intravenously, and serial x-ray films are taken as the medium is cleared from the blood by the kidneys. The renal calyces, renal pelvis, ureters, and urinary bladder are all visible on the radiographs.

intravenous syringe pump, any one of several devices that automatically compress a syringe plunger at a controlled rate. Such devices are used with disposable syringes that can deliver blood, medications, or nutrients by IV, arterial, or subcutaneous routes. IV syringe pumps can deliver small volumes of fluid at rates as low as 0.01 mL/hour. They are often used in the treatment of infants and are especially useful in the care of ambulatory patients.

intravenous team, a group of registered nurses and licensed practical nurses with special training who administer IV therapy.

intravenous (IV) therapy, the administration of fluids or drugs, or both, into the general circulation through a venipuncture.

intraventricular /-ventrik'yələr/ [L, *intra* + *ventriculus,* little belly], pertaining to the space within a ventricle or to the conduction system within the walls of a ventricle.

intraventricular block, altered conduction of the cardiac impulse within the ventricles. The block can occur as a right bundle branch block, left bundle branch block, hemiblock, left anterior or posterior fascicular block, or bifascicular block. Intraventricular blocks are identified on an ECG when the QRS duration is greater than normal.

intraventricular conduction defect, a delay in conduction of a ventricular impulse within the ventricles that does not correspond to either a right bundle branch block or a left bundle branch block.

intraventricular pressure [L, *intra,* within, *ventriculus,* little belly], the pressure of the blood within the ventricles of the heart. It varies with the phase of the cardiac cycle.

intraventricular sulcus, one of the two sulci (anterior and posterior) that separate the two ventricles of the heart. The anterior intraventricular sulcus contains the anterior interventricular artery and the great cardiac vein. The posterior interventricular sulcus contains the posterior interventricular artery and the middle cardiac vein.

intravesical pressure, the pressure exerted on the contents of the urinary bladder, being the sum of the intraabdominal pressure from outside the bladder and the detrusor pressure exerted by the bladder wall musculature itself.

intravesical ureterocele, a ureterocele located entirely inside the bladder. It may be either orthotopic or ectopic.

intrinsic /intrin'sik/ [L, *intrinsecus,* inside], **1.** denoting a natural or inherent part or quality. **2.** originating from or situated within an organ or tissue.

intrinsic asthma, a nonseasonal, nonallergic form of asthma, which usually first occurs later in life than allergic asthma and tends to be chronic and persistent rather than episodic. Precipitating factors include inhalation of irritating pollutants. Intrinsic asthma may also be triggered by exposure to cold, damp weather; sudden inhalation of cold, dry air; physical exercise; violent coughing or laughing; respiratory infections, such as the common cold; or psychologic factors, such as anxiety.

intrinsic factor, a substance secreted by the gastric mucosa that is essential for the intestinal absorption of cyanocobalamin. A deficiency of intrinsic factor causes pernicious anemia.

intrinsic minus hand deformity, an abnormality that results from interruption of the ulnar and median nerves at the wrist. It causes metacarpophalangeal joint hyperextension and interphalangeal joint flexion.

intrinsic muscles, muscles that are entirely within the body part or segment moved by them, as the tongue muscles.

intrinsic muscles of the tongue, the superior longitudinal, inferior longitudinal, transverse, and vertical muscles, which alter the shape of the tongue by lengthening and shortening it, curling and uncurling its apex and edges, and flattening and rounding its surface.

intrinsic pathway of coagulation, an in vitro sequence of reactions leading to fibrin formation, beginning with the contact activation of factor XII, followed by the sequential activation of factors XI, IX, and VIII, and resulting in the activation of factor X, which in activated form initiates the common pathway of coagulation.

intrinsic PEEP, intrinsic positive endexpiratory pressure.

intrinsic positive end-expiratory pressure (intrinsic PEEP), elevated positive endexpiratory pressure and dynamic pulmonary hyperinflation caused by insufficient expiratory time or a limitation on expiratory flow. It cannot be routinely measured by a ventilator's pressure monitoring system but only by an expiratory hold maneuver done by the clinician. Its presence increases the work required to trigger the ventilator, causes errors in the calculation of pulmonary compliance, may cause hemodynamic compromise, and complicates interpretation of hemodynamic measurements.

introitus /intrō'itəs/ [L, *intro,* inside, *ire,* to go], an entrance or orifice in a cavity

introjection /-jek'shən/ [L, *intro* + *jacere*, to throw], an ego defense mechanism whereby an individual unconsciously incorporates into his own ego structure the qualities of another person.

intromission /-mish'ən/, the insertion of one object into another, such as the introduction of the penis into the vagina.

intron /in'tron/ [L, *intra*, within, *regin*, region], a sequence of nucleotides in eukaryotic DNA that does not code for amino acids and interrupts the coding sequence of a gene.

Intron A, a trademark for a parenteral antineoplastic (interferon alfa-2b, recombinant).

Intropin, a trademark for an adrenergic (DOPamine hydrochloride).

introspection /-spek'shən/ [L, *introspicere,* to look into], **1.** the act of examining one's own thoughts and emotions. **2.** a tendency to look inward and view the inner self.—**introspective,** *adj.*

introsusception /-susep'shən/ [L, *intro,* inside, *suscipere,* to receive], the telescoping or invagination of one segment of the digestive tract into another segment, usually a lower segment. The process can cause obstruction and strangulation of the bowel.

introversion /-vur'zhən/ [L, *intro* + *vertere,* to turn], **1.** the tendency to direct one's interests, thoughts, and energies inward or toward things concerned with the self. **2.** the state of being totally or primarily concerned with one's own intrapsychic experience.

introvert /in'trəvurt/ [L, *intro* + *vertere,* to turn], **1.** a person whose interests are directed inward and who is shy, withdrawn, emotionally reserved, and self-absorbed. **2.** to turn inward or to direct one's interests and thoughts toward oneself.

introverted personality /-vur'tid/ [L, *intro,* inside, *vertere,* to turn + *personalis*], a personality that is preoccupied with inner thoughts and fantasies rather than with the outer world of people and things.

intrusion /in·trōō'zhən/ [L, *intrudere,* to push or force in], an orthodontic technique of depressing a tooth back into the occlusal plane or attempting to prevent its eruption or elongation during correction of an excessive overbite.

intubate /in'tyōōbāt/ [L, *in,* within, *tubus,* tube], to catheterize or insert a tube into an organ or body part.

intubation [L, *in,* within, *tubus,* tube, *atio,* process], passage of a tube into a body aperture, specifically the insertion of a breathing tube through the mouth or nose into the trachea to ensure a patent airway for the delivery of anesthetic gases and oxygen or both. Blind intubation is the insertion of a breathing tube without the use of a laryngoscope.

intussusception /in'təsəsep'shən/ [L, *intus,* within, *suscipere,* to receive], prolapse of one segment of bowel into the lumen of another segment. This kind of intestinal obstruction may involve segments of the small intestine, the colon, or the terminal ileum and cecum. Intussusception occurs most often in infants and small children and is characterized by abdominal pain, vomiting, and presence of bloody mucus in the stool.

intussusceptum, the portion of the intestine that has been invaginated within another part in intussusception.

inulin /in'yōōlin/, a fructose-based starch derived from rhizomes of plants from the *Compositae* family. It is used as a diagnostic aid in tests of kidney function, specifically glomerular filtration. It is not metabolized or absorbed by the body. It is freely filtered by the glomeruli of the kidney but is neither secreted nor reabsorbed by the tubules, making its clearance equivalent to the glomerular filteration rate.

inulin clearance, a test of the rate of filtration of a starch, inulin, in the glomerulus of the kidney. Inulin is given by mouth, and the glomerular filtration rate can be estimated from the amount of inulin that appears in the urine.

inunction /inungk'shən/ [L, *in,* within, *ungere,* to smear], **1.** the rubbing of a drug mixed with an oil or fatty substance into the skin, with absorption of the active ingredient. **2.** any compound so applied.

in utero /inyōō'tərō/, inside the uterus.

invagination /invaj'ənā'shən/ [L, *in,* within, *vagina,* sheath], **1.** a condition in which one part of a structure telescopes into another, as the intestine during peristalsis. If the invagination is extensive or involves a tumor or polyp, it may cause an intestinal obstruction. **2.** surgery for repair of a hernia by replacement of the contents of the hernial sac in the abdominal cavity. —**invaginate,** *v.*

invariable behavior /inver'ē·əbəl/ [L, *in,* not, *variare,* to vary], behavior that results from physiologic response to a stimulus and is not modified by individual experience, such as a reflex.

invasion /invā'zhən/ [L, *in,* within, *vadere,* to go], the process by which malignant cells move through the basement membrane and gain access to blood vessels and lymphatic channels.

invasion of privacy, in law, the violation of another person's right to be left alone and free of unwarranted publicity and intrusion.

invasive /invā′siv/ [L, *in,* within, *vadere,* to go], characterized by a tendency to spread, infiltrate, and intrude.

invasive carcinoma, a malignant neoplasm composed of epithelial cells that infiltrate and destroy surrounding tissues and may metastasize.

invasive hemodynamic monitoring, a nursing intervention from the Nursing Interventions Classification (NIC) defined as measurement and interpretation of invasive hemodynamic parameters to determine cardiovascular function and regulate therapy as appropriate.

invasive procedure [L, *in* + *vadere,* to go, *procedere,* to proceed], a diagnostic or therapeutic technique that requires entry of a body cavity or interruption of normal body functions. Examples are the Pap test and colonoscopy.

invasive thermometry, measurement of tissue temperature using probes placed directly into the tissue.

Invega, a trademark for **paliperidone.**

inverse anaphylaxis /invurs′, in′vurs/, an exaggerated reaction of hypersensitivity induced by an antibody rather than by an antigen.

inverse I:E ratio, an inspiratory/expiratory ratio in mechanical ventilation in which the duration of inspiration is prolonged relative to that of expiration. This condition is sometimes instituted to improve oxygenation.

inverse square law, a law stating that the amount of radiation reaching a surface is inversely proportional to the square of the distance between the source and the surface.

Inversine, a trademark for a ganglionic blocking agent (mecamylamine hydrochloride).

inversion /invur′zhən/ [L, *invertere,* to turn over], **1.** an abnormal condition in which an organ is turned inside out, such as a uterine inversion. **2.** a chromosomal defect in which a segment of a chromosome breaks off and then reattaches to the chromosome in the reverse orientation, causing the genes carried on that part of the chromosome to be in an abnormal position and sequence.

inversion recovery (IR), a magnetic resonance pulse sequence designed to emphasize T_1 differences.

inversion traction, a positional form of traction for the prevention and treatment of back disorders. Special equipment is used to lengthen the spinal column while the patient is in an inverted position.

invert /in′vurt/ [L, *invertere,* to turn over], to turn something upside down or inside out.

invertebrate /invur′təbrit/, an animal that lacks a vertebral column.

invert sugar [L, *invertere,* to turn over; Gk, *sakcharon*], a mixture of equal amounts of dextrose and fructose, obtained by hydrolyzing sucrose. It is used in solution as a parenteral nutrient.

investigational device exemption (IDE) /inves′tigā′shənəl/ [L, *investigare,* to search for], an agreement through which the federal government permits the testing of new medical devices.

investigational new drug (IND), a drug not yet approved for marketing by the U.S. Food and Drug Administration and available only for use in experiments to determine its safety and effectiveness.

investing fascia, a layer of fascia that closely invests a muscle or ligament.

Invirase, a trademark for an antiretroviral protease inhibitor (saquinavir).

invisible differentiation /inviz′ibəl/ [L, *in,* not, *visibilis,* visible, *differentia,* difference], in embryology, a fixed determination for specialization and diversification that exists in embryonic cells but is not yet visibly apparent.

in vitro /in vē′trō/ [L, *in,* within, *vitreus,* glassware], occurring in a laboratory apparatus.

in vitro fertilization (IVF), a method of fertilizing human ova outside the body by collecting the mature ova and placing them in a dish with a sample of spermatozoa. After an incubation period of 48 to 72 hours, the fertilized ova are injected into the uterus through the cervix.

in vitro susceptibility testing, a laboratory trial of the sensitivity of microorganisms, particularly fungi, to potential therapeutic chemicals.

in vivo /in vē′vō/ [L, *in,* within, *vivo,* alive], occurring in an organism.

in vivo fertilization, a method of fertilization of an ovum within a fallopian tube of a fertile female donor for transplantation into an infertile recipient.

in vivo tracer study, a diagnostic procedure in which a series of images of an administered radioactive tracer demonstrates normal or abnormal structures or processes as the tracer passes through a patient's body.

involucrum /in′vəloo′krəm/ *pl.* **involucra** [L, *involvere,* to wrap up], a sheath or coating, such as that encasing a sequestrum of necrotic bone.

involuntary /invol′ənter′ē/ [L, *in,* not, *voluntas,* will], occurring without conscious control or direction.

involuntary patient, a person admitted to a psychiatric facility against his or her will.

involution /in′vəloo′shən/ [L, *involvere,* to wrap up], **1.** a normal process of turning or rolling inward characterized by a decrease in the size of an organ caused by a decrease in the size of its cells, such as postpartum involution of the uterus. **2.** in embryology, a developmental process in which a group of cells grows over the rim at the border of the organ or part and, rolling inward, rejoins the organ or part to form a tube, such as in the heart or bladder.

inward aggression /in'wərd/ [AS, *inweard*], destructive behavior that is directed against oneself.

iodide /ī'ədīd/ [Gk, *ioeides*, violet], an anion of iodine. Sodium and potassium iodide are the salts most commonly used in medicine.

iodinated serum albumin /ī'ədinā'tid/, a sterile, buffered, isotonic solution containing radioiodinated normal human serum used in diagnostic tests of blood volume and cardiac output. It is adjusted to provide not more than 1 mCi of radioactivity per milliliter.

iodine (I) /ī'ədīn/ [Gk, *ioeides*, violet], a nonmetallic element of the halogen group. Its atomic number is 53; its atomic mass is 126.90. Iodine is an essential micronutrient or trace element. Almost 80% of the iodine present in the body is in the thyroid gland, mostly in the form of thyroglobulin. Iodine deficiency can result in goiter or cretinism. Iodine is found in seafood, iodized salt, and some dairy products. It is used as a contrast agent for blood vessels in CT scans. Radioisotopes of iodine are used in radioisotope scanning procedures and in palliative treatment of cancer of the thyroid.

iodine poisoning [Gk, *ioeides*, violet; L, *potio*, drink], toxic effects of ingesting iodine. Symptoms include burning pain in the mouth and esophagus, abdominal pain, vomiting, diarrhea, delirium, shock, nephritis, laryngeal edema, and circulatory collapse.

iodism /ī'ədiz'əm/ [Gk, *ioeides* + *ismos*, process], a condition produced by excessive amounts of iodine in the body. It is characterized by increased lacrimation and salivation, rhinitis, weakness, and skin eruption.

iodize /ī'ədīz/ [Gk, *ioeides* + *izein*, to cause], to treat or impregnate with iodine or an iodide.

iodized oil, an iodine addition product of vegetable oil. It is used as a radiopaque contrast medium in various diagnostic procedures.

iodized salt [Gk, *ioeides*, violet; AS, *sealt*], table salt to which potassium or sodium iodide has been added to protect against goiter, particularly in regions where soil and drinking water have low iodine content.

iododerma /ī·ō'dōdur'mə/ [Gk, *ioeides* + *derma*, skin], a skin rash caused by a hypersensitivity to ingested iodides. The lesions may be acneiform, bullous, or fungating.

iodophor /ī·ōdəfôr/ [Gk, *ioeides* + *phoros*, bearer], an antiseptic or disinfectant that combines iodine with another agent, such as a detergent.

iodopsin /ī'ōdop'sin/ [Gk, *ioeides* + *optikos*, vision], a photosensitive chemical in the cones of the retina that reacts in association with other chemicals and plays a part in color vision. Iodopsin is more stable when exposed to bright light than rhodopsin, which is found in the rods of the retina.

iodoquinol /ī'ōdō'kwinol/, an amebicide prescribed in the treatment of intestinal amebiasis. It is also used as a preventative in high-risk people.

iodotherapy /ī·ō'dōther'əpē/, a treatment that uses iodine or an iodide.

ion /ī'ən, ī'on/ [Gk, *ienai*, to go], an atom or group of atoms that has acquired an electrical charge through the gain or loss of an electron or electrons.

ion exchange chromatography, the process of separating and analyzing different substances according to their affinities for chemically stable but very reactive synthetic exchangers, which are composed largely of polystyrene and cellulose. Ion exchange chromatography is often used to separate components of nucleic acids and proteins elaborated by various structures throughout the body.

ionic bonding /ī·on'ik/ [Gk, *ienai*; ME, *band*, to bind], an electrostatic force between ions. Ionic compounds do not form true molecules; in aqueous solution they separate into their hydrated constituent ions.

ionic dissociation, a phenomenon whereby ions in ionic compounds in an aqueous solution are freed from their mutual attractions and distribute themselves uniformly throughout the solvent.

ionic strength, the sum of the concentrations of all ions in a solution multiplied by the square of their charge.

ionization /ī'ənīzā'shən/ [Gk, *ienai* + *izein*, to cause], the process in which a neutral atom or molecule gains or loses electrons and thus acquires a negative or positive electrical charge.

ionization chamber, a small cavity filled with air that collects the ionic charge liberated during irradiation.

ionization constant (K), after establishment of ionic equilibrium, the product of the molar concentration of the ions divided by the molar concentration of the nonionized molecules.

ionize /ī′ənīz/ [Gk, *ienai* + *izein,* to cause], to separate or change into ions.

ionized calcium, the ionized, unbound, noncomplexed fraction of serum calcium that is biologically active.

ionizing energy /ī′ənī′zing/, the average energy lost by ionizing radiation in producing an ion pair in a gas.

ionizing radiation, high-energy electromagnetic waves (such as x-rays and gamma rays) and particles (such as alpha and beta particles, neutrons, protons, and heavy nuclei) that cause substances in their paths to dissociate into ions. Ionizing radiation directly affects living organisms by killing cells or retarding their development and by producing gene mutations and chromosome breaks.

ionizing radiation injury [Gk, *ion,* going; L, *radiare,* to shine + *injuria*], damage or ill effects suffered by exposure to ionizing radiation, including cellular harm resulting from radiation for diagnostic or therapeutic application. The risk of cell death or injury from radiation depends on the type of tissue cells, the stage of cell division at the time of exposure, the intensity and time span of exposure, and the type of radiation administered.

ion-selective electrode, a potentiometric electrode that develops a potential in the presence of one ion (or class of ions) but not in the presence of a similar concentration of other ions.

iontophoresis /ī·on′tōfōrē′sis/ [Gk, *ion,* going, *pherein,* to carry], the introduction of ions of soluble salts into the tissues by direct current.

iontophoretic pilocarpine test [Gk, *ienai* + *pherein,* to carry], a sweat test used in the diagnosis of CF. Pilocarpine iontophoresis is used to stimulate production of sweat, which is absorbed from the forearm in a previously weighed gauze pad. The sweat sample is then analyzed for concentrations of sodium and chloride electrolytes.

ion transfer, a method of transporting chemicals across a membrane by using an electric current as a driving force.

iopromide /ī′opro′mīd/, a nonionic, low-osmolality radiopaque medium used for cardiovascular imaging, excretory urology, and contrast enhancement in CT.

iota /ī·ō′tə/, I, ι, the ninth letter of the Greek alphabet. Iota is also used to refer to something tiny, such as one iota.

ioversol /ī′over′sol/, a nonionic contrast medium used in angiography and urography and for contrast enhancement in CT.

Iowa trumpet /ī′owə/, a trademark for a kind of needle guide used in performing a pudendal block. It consists of a long, thin cylinder through which a needle may be passed. A ring is attached to the proximal end of the guide, allowing the operator to hold it securely.

ioxilan /iok′slan/, a low-viscosity, low-osmolality, nonionic contrast agent used in arteriography, excretory urography, and CT.

IPA, abbreviation for **independent practice association.**

IPAA, abbreviation for *International Psychoanalytical Association.*

IPA-Model HMO, a health maintenance organization (HMO) that contracts with an independent practice association (IPA) for physician services. The IPA processes and adjudicates claims. The HMO provides enrollees and hospital contracts.

IPA paradigm shift, an independent practice association that takes on the role of the health maintenance organization and contracts with its participating providers but is neither a payer nor a provider.

ipecac /ip′əkak/, an emetic prescribed to cause emesis in certain types of recent poisonings and drug overdoses.

IPOF, abbreviation for **immediate postoperative fit prosthesis.**

ipomea /ipəmē′ə/, a resin prepared from the dried root of *Ipomoea orizabensis,* formerly used as a cathartic.

IPPB, abbreviation for **intermittent positive-pressure breathing.**

IPPB unit, a pressure-cycled ventilator providing a flow of air into the lungs at a predetermined pressure, used to prevent postoperative atelectasis, to promote full expansion of the lungs, to improve oxygenation, and to administer nebulized medications into the respiratory passages.

IPPV, abbreviation for *intermittent positive-pressure ventilation.*

Iprivask, a trademark for desirudin.

IPSID, abbreviation for **immunoproliferative small intestine disease.**

ipsilateral [L, *ipse,* same, *latus,* side], affecting the same side of the body.

IPSP, abbreviation for *inhibitory postsynaptic potential.*

IPV, abbreviation for *poliovirus vaccine inactivated.*

IQ, abbreviation for **intelligence quotient.**

Ir, symbol for the element **iridium.**

IR, 1. abbreviation for **image receptor. 2.** abbreviation for *intervential radiology.*

IRB, abbreviation for **institutional review board.**

irbesartan, an antihypertensive used to treat hypertension, either alone or in combination with other drugs. It is also used investigationally to treat heart failure and hypertension in patients with diabetic nephropathy caused by type 2 DM.

Iressa, a trademark for **gefitinib.**

Ir g, abbreviation for *immune response function gene*.

iridectomy /ĭ'rĭdek'təmē/ [Gk, *iris,* rainbow, *ektomē,* excision], surgical removal of part of the iris of the eye. It is performed most often to restore drainage of the aqueous humor in glaucoma or to remove a foreign body or a malignant tumor.

iridemia /ĭ'rĭdē'mē.ə/, hemorrhage from the iris.

iridescence /ir'ides'əns/ [L, *iridescere,* to shine like a rainbow], the property of light interference or ability to break up light waves into colors of the spectrum.

iridium (Ir) /irĭd'ē-əm/ [Gk, *iris,* rainbow], a silvery-bluish metallic element. Its atomic number is 77; its atomic mass is 192.22.

iridology /ĭ'ridol'əjē/ [Gk, *iris,* rainbow, *logos,* science], the science that specializes in relations between disease and the shape, color, and other individual characteristics of the iris. There is considerable controversy over its validity.

iridopathy /ĭ'ridop'əthē/, any disease of the iris.

iridoplegia /ĭ'ridōplē'jə/ [Gk, *iris,* rainbow, *plege,* stroke], a condition of paralysis of the sphincter muscle of the iris or the dilator muscle or both.

iridotomy /ĭ'ridot'əmē/ [Gk, *iris* + *temnein,* to cut], a surgical incision into the iris of the eye. It is performed to relieve occlusion of the pupil, to enlarge the pupil in cataract extraction, or to treat postoperative glaucoma.

irinotecan, an antineoplastic hormone used to treat metastatic carcinoma of the colon or rectum.

iris /ī'ris/ [Gk, rainbow], an annular colored membrane shaped like a disc, suspended in aqueous humor between the cornea and the crystalline lens of the eye and enclosing a circular pupil. Smooth muscle fibers of the iris contract and relax to allow more or less light to enter the eye through the pupil. The periphery of the iris is continuous with the ciliary body and is connected to the cornea by the pectinate ligament.—**iridic,** *adj.*

iritis /ĭrī'tis/ [Gk, *iris* + *itis*], an inflammatory condition of the iris of the eye characterized by pain, lacrimation, photophobia, and, if severe, diminished visual acuity. On ophthalmic examination the eye looks cloudy, the iris bulges, and the pupil is contracted.

iron (Fe) /ī'ərn/ [AS, *iren*], a common metallic element essential for the synthesis of hemoglobin. Its atomic number is 26; its atomic mass (weight) is 55.85. Iron salts and complexes are used to treat iron-deficiency anemias.

iron-binding capacity (IBC), the extent to which transferrin in the serum of a given patient can bind serum iron.

iron deficiency anemia, a microcytic hypochromic anemia caused by inadequate supplies of iron needed to synthesize hemoglobin. Symptoms are pallor, fatigue, anorexia, malaise, and weakness. Laboratory diagnosis includes hemoglobin, hematocrit, transferrin saturation, ferritin, and serum iron concentration.

iron dextran, an injectable hematinic prescribed in the treatment of iron deficiency anemia that is not responsive to oral iron therapy.

iron level and total iron-binding capacity test, a blood test used to diagnose iron deficiency anemia and hemochromatosis (iron overload or poisoning), among other conditions.

iron metabolism, a series of processes involved in the entry of iron into the body and its absorption, transport, storage, use in the formation of hemoglobin and other iron compounds, and eventual excretion. Iron normally enters through the intestinal mucosa and is oxidized from ferrous to ferric iron in the process. The rate at which iron enters is modulated by this absorption mechanism. When iron stores are high, iron no longer passes through but is trapped by the mucosal cells of the intestine to be eliminated. Once in the blood, iron cycles between the plasma and the reticuloendothelial or erythropoietic system. For hemoglobin synthesis, plasma iron is delivered to the normoblast, where it remains up to 4 months, functioning in the hemoglobin molecules of a mature red cell. Senescent red cells then deteriorate. The iron is released from the hemoglobin by the reticuloendothelial system to reenter the transport pool for recycling.

iron overload, an excess of iron in the body.

iron poisoning [AS, *iren;* L, *potio,* drink], toxic effects of ingesting iron salts, particularly ferrous sulfate and ferrous chloride. Ferrous sulfate tablets, sometimes mistaken for candy, can cause vomiting, collapse, and liver necrosis. Ferrous chloride, a corrosive substance, causes vomiting, diarrhea, and hemorrhage when taken internally. Iron encephalopathy has resulted from excessive use of iron preparations.

iron-polysaccharide, polysaccharide-iron complex.

iron-rich food, any food item containing a relatively large amount of iron. One of the best sources of dietary iron is liver. Oysters, clams, heart, kidney, lean meat, seafood, and iron-fortified foods are other good sources. Leafy green vegetables, whole grains, and legumes are among the best plant sources.

iron salt poisoning, poisoning caused by overdose of ferric or ferrous salt, characterized by vomiting, bloody diarrhea, cyanosis, and gastric and intestinal pain.

iron-storage disease, an abnormal accumulation of iron in the parenchyma of many organs, as in hemosiderosis.

iron sucrose, a complex of ferric hydroxide, $Fe(OH)_3$, in sucrose, used intravenously to treat iron deficiency anemia in hemodialysis patients receiving supplemental erythropoietin therapy.

iron transport, the process whereby iron is carried from the intestinal mucosa to sites of use and storage. Iron binds with transferrin and shuttles to storage and utilization sites.

irradiation /irā'dē·ā'shən/ [L, *irradiare,* to beam upon], exposure to any form of radiant energy, such as heat, light, or x-rays. Radioactive sources of radiant energy, such as x-rays or isotopes of iodine or cobalt, are used diagnostically to examine internal body structures. The same or similar sources of radioactivity in larger amounts are used to destroy microorganisms or tissue cells that have become cancerous. Infrared or ultraviolet light may be used to produce heat in body tissues for pain relief or to treat acne, psoriasis, or other skin ailments. Ultraviolet light is also used to identify certain bacteria and toxic molds.—**irradiate,** *v.*

irrational /irash'ənəl/ [L, *irrationalis,* contrary to reason], pertaining to events, conditions, or behavior that may be considered unreasonable.

irreducible /ir'əd(y)ōō'sibəl/ [L, *in,* not, *reducere,* to bring back], unable to be returned to the normal position or condition, as an irreducible hernia.

irregular pulse /ireg'yələr/ [L, *in,* not, *regula,* rule, *pulsare,* to beat], a variation in the force or rhythm of impulses in an artery, caused by cardiac arrhythmia.

irreversible /ir'əvur'sibəl/ [L, *irrevertere,* to not turn back], pertaining to a situation or condition that cannot be reversed.

irreversible shock, a condition in which shock does not respond to available forms of treatment and in which recovery is impossible as a result of massive cellular damage.

irrigate /ir'igāt/ [L, *irrigare,* to supply water], to flush with a fluid, usually with a slow, steady pressure on a syringe plunger. It may be done to cleanse a wound or to clear tubing.

irrigation /ir'igā'shən/, the process of washing out a body cavity or wounded area with a stream of water or other fluid. It is also used to cleanse a tube or drain inserted into the body such as an indwelling catheter.—**irrigate,** *v.*

irrigator /ir'igā'tər/, an apparatus with a flexible tube for flushing or washing out a body cavity.

irritability /ir'itəbil'itē/ [L, *irritare,* to tease], a condition of abnormal excitability or sensitivity.

irritable bowel syndrome (IBS) [L, *irritare,* to tease; OFr, *boel;* Gk, *syn,* together, *dromos,* course], abnormally increased motility of the small and large intestines, of unknown origins. Most of those affected are young adults, who complain of diarrhea and, occasionally, pain in the lower abdomen. The pain is usually relieved by passing flatus or stool. In diagnosing irritable bowel syndrome, other more serious conditions, such as dysentery, lactose intolerance, and the inflammatory bowel diseases, must be ruled out.

irritant /ir'itənt/ [L, *irritare,* to tease], an agent that produces inflammation or irritation.

irritant poison [L, *irritare,* to tease, *potio,* drink], any of a large number of toxic substances in the environment that can cause pain in the digestive tract, diarrhea, vomiting, abdominal cramps, and urinary tract disorders. Some irritant chemicals are industrial gases, which may leak into the atmosphere.

irritation fibroma /ir'itā'shən/, a localized, peripheral, tumorlike enlargement of connective tissue caused by prolonged irritation. It commonly develops on the gums or the buccal mucosa.

IRV, abbreviation for **inspiratory reserve volume.**

Irving technique, a method of tubal ligation in which the uterine tubes are ligated and severed and the proximal ends are sewn into the myometrium.

Isaacs' syndrome /ī'zəks/ [H. Isaacs, neurologist, 20th century], progressive muscle stiffness and spasms, with continuous muscle fiber activity similar to that seen with neuromyotonia.

ischemia /iske'mē·ə/ [Gk, *ischein,* to hold back, *haima,* blood], a decreased supply of oxygenated blood to a body part. The condition is often marked by pain and organ dysfunction, as in ischemic heart disease.—**ischemic,** *adj.*

ischemic heart disease /iske'mik/, a pathologic condition caused by lack of oxygen in cells of the myocardium.

ischemic lumbago, a pain in the lower back and buttocks caused by vascular insufficiency, as in occlusion of the abdominal aorta.

ischemic pain, unpleasant, often excruciating pain associated with decreased blood flow caused by mechanical obstruction, constricting orthopedic casts, or insufficient blood flow that results from injury or surgical trauma. Ischemic pain caused by occlusive arterial disease is often severe and may not be relieved, even with narcotics. The ischemic pain of partial arterial occlusion is not as severe as the abrupt, excruciating pain associated with complete occlusion, such as by an embolus or thrombus.

ischemic paralysis, loss of motor control in a body area caused by an interruption in the blood supply to the area's muscles or nerves.

ischemic penumbra, an area of moderately ischemic brain tissue surrounding an area of more severe ischemia. Theoretically, blood flow to this area may be enhanced to prevent the spread of a cerebral infarction.

ischemic pericarditis [Gk, *ischein,* to hold back, *haima,* blood, *peri,* near, *kardia,* heart, *itis,* inflammation], inflammation of the pericardium caused by interruption of its blood supply during MI.

ischemic stroke, a cerebrovascular disorder caused by deprivation of blood flow to an area of the brain, generally as a result of thrombosis, embolism, or reduced BP.

ischial spines /is′kē-əl/ [Gk, *ischion,* hip joint; L, *spina,* thorn], two relatively sharp posterior bony projections into the pelvic outlet from the ischial bones that form the lower border of the pelvis.

ischial tuberosity [Gk, *ischion,* hip joint; L, *tuber,* swelling], a rounded protuberance of the lower part of the ischium. It forms a bony area on which the human body rests when in a sitting position.

ischioanal fossae, gutters in the anal triangle, one on each side of the anal aperture, formed by the levator ani muscles and adjacent pelvic walls as the two structures diverge inferiorly.

ischiocavernosus, one of two muscles that cover the crura of the penis and clitoris and force blood from the crura into the body of the erect penis and clitoris.

ischiococcygeal muscle, a muscle originating in the ischial spine and innervated by the third and fourth sacral nerves.

ischiofemoral ligament, a ligament that reinforces the posterior aspect of the fibrous membrane that encloses the hip. It is attached medially to the ischium, just posteroinferior to the acetabulum, and laterally to the ischial tuberosity deep to the iliofemoral ligament. It helps to stabilize the hip joint and reduce the amount of muscle energy required to maintain a standing position.

ischium /is′kē-əm/ *pl.* **ischia** [L; Gk, *ischion,* hip joint], one of the three parts of the hip bone, which joins the ilium and the pubis

to form the acetabulum. The ischium comprises the dorsal part of the hip bone and is divided into the body of the ischium, which forms the posteroinferior two fifths of the acetabulum, and the ramus, which joins the inferior ramus of the pubis.

ISCLT, abbreviation for *International Society of Clinical Laboratory Technologists.*

Isentress, a trademark for raltegravir.

ISG, abbreviation for **immune serum globulin.**

ISH, abbreviation for **isolated systolic hypertension.**

Ishihara chart, the pseudoisochromatic chart used in the Ishihara test.

Ishihara color test /ish′ēhä′rə/ [Shinobu Ishihara, Japanese ophthalmologist, 1879–1963], a test of color vision that uses a series of plates on which are printed pseudoisochromatic round dots in a variety of colors and patterns. People with normal color vision are able to discern specific numbers or patterns on the plates; the inability to pick out a given number or shape is symptomatic of a specific deficiency in color perception.

Ishihara test /ish′ē-hä rə/, a test for color vision made by the use of a series of pseudoisochromatic plates or charts.

ISID, abbreviation for *International Society of Infectious Diseases.*

ISIS, abbreviation for *International Study of Infarct Survival.*

island /ī′lənd/ [OE, *īegland,* island], a cluster of cells or an isolated piece of tissue.

islets of Langerhans /lang′gərhanz/ [L, *insula,* island; Paul Langerhans, German pathologist, 1847–1888], clusters of cells within the pancreas that produce insulin, glucagon, and pancreatic polypeptide. They form the endocrine part of the gland, and their hormonal secretions released into the bloodstream are balanced, important regulators of carbohydrate metabolism.

islet /ī′lət/ [MFr, *islette,* little island], a cluster of cells or an isolated piece of tissue.

islet cell antibody (ICA) /ī′lit/ [MFr, *islette,* little island], an immunoglobulin that reacts with cytoplasmic components of all of the cells in the pancreatic islets. These antibodies occur in about 60% to 70% of newly diagnosed patients with insulin-dependent DM, providing strong evidence for an autoimmune origin and pathogenesis of the disease.

islet cell tumor, any tumor of the islands of Langerhans.

isoagglutination /ī′sō-əglo͞o′tinā′shən/ [Gk, *isos,* equal; L, *agglutinate,* to glue], the clumping of erythrocytes by agglutinins from the blood of another individual of the same species.

isoagglutinin /ī'sō-əglŏŏ'tinin/ [Gk, *isos,* equal; L, *agglutinate,* to glue], an antibody that causes agglutination of erythrocytes in other members of the same species that carry an antigen on their erythrocytes.

isoantibody /ī'sō-an'tibod'ē/ [Gk, *isos* + *anti,* against; AS, *boding,* body], an antibody to isoantigens found in other members of the same species.

isoantigen /ī'sō-an'tijən/ [Gk, *isos* + *anti,* against; AS, *boding,* body; Gk, *genein,* to produce], a substance present in some members of a species that stimulates production of antibodies in other members of the species.

isobar /ī'səbär/ [Gk, *isos* + *barrios,* weight], **1.** a line connecting points of equal pressure on a graph. **2.** in nuclear medicine, one of a group of nuclides having the same total number of neutrons and protons in the nucleus but so proportioned that their atomic numbers have different values.

isobaric /-bär'ik/ [Gk, *isos,* equal, *barrios,* weight], **1.** pertaining to two substances or solutions of the same specific gravity. **2.** pertaining to two isotopes that have the same mass number but different atomic numbers. **3.** having the same barometric pressure.

isobutyl alcohol ($C_4H_{10}O$) /ī'sobyŏŏ'til/ [Gk, *isos* + *butyrin,* butter, *hyl,* matter; AR, *alcohol,* essence], a clear colorless liquid that is miscible with ethyl alcohol or ether.

isocapnic /-kap'nik/, pertaining to a level of carbon dioxide in the tissues that remains steady despite changing levels of ventilation.

isocarboxazid /-kärbok'səzid/, a monoamine oxidase inhibitor prescribed in the treatment of mental depression.

isochromosome /-krō'məsōm/, a chromosome whose arms are of equal length.

isocrotic, describing the separation of a mixture by chromatography using a single solvent or solvent mixture.

isodiametric, measuring the same in all diameters.

isodose chart /ī'sədōs/ [Gk, *isos* + *dosis,* giving, *charta,* paper], a graphic representation of the distribution of radiation in a medium in which lines are drawn through points receiving equal doses.

isodynamic law /ī'sōdīnam'ik/, the rule that for energy purposes different foods may replace one another in accordance with their caloric values, as determined when burned in a calorimeter.

isoeffect lines /ī'sō-ifekt'/, lines on a graph representing doses of radiation that have tumoricidal effects in normal tissues.

isoelectric /ī'sō·ilek'trik/ [Gk, *isos* + *electron,* amber], pertaining to the electric baseline of an ECG.

isoelectric focusing, the ordering and concentration of substances according to their isoelectric points.

isoelectric period, a period in physiologic activity, such as nerve conduction or muscle contraction, when there is no variation in electric potential.

isoelectric point, the pH at which a molecule containing two or more ionizable groups is electrically neutral. The average number of positive charges equals the average number of negative charges.

isoenzyme /ī'sō·en'zīm/ [Gk, *isos* + *en,* in, *syme,* ferment], a chemically distinct form of an enzyme. The various forms are distinguishable in analysis of blood samples, which aids in the diagnosis of disease.

isoetharine mesylate /ī'sō·eth'ərēn/, a beta-adrenergic bronchodilator prescribed in the treatment of bronchial asthma, bronchitis, and emphysema.

isoexposure line /ī'sō·ikspō'zhər/, an imaginary line representing positions of equal exposure to radiation around a fluoroscopic instrument.

isoflows /ī'sōflōz/, a measure of early small airway dysfunction in a patient made by comparing forced expiratory flow rates of air and of helium at fixed points in time.

isogamete /ī'sōgam'ēt/ [Gk, *isos* + *gamete,* wife], a reproductive cell of the same size and structure, as the one with which it unites.—**isogametic,** *adj.*

isogamy /īsog'əmē/ [Gk, *isos* + *gamos,* marriage], sexual reproduction in which there is fusion of gametes of the same size and structure, such as in certain algae, fungi, and protists.—**isogamous,** *adj.*

isogenesis /-jen'əsis/ [Gk, *isos* + *genein,* to produce], development from a common origin and according to similar processes.—**isogenetic, isogenic,** *adj.*

isograft /ī'səgraft'/ [Gk, *isos* + *graphion,* stylus], surgical transplantation of histocompatible tissue between genetically identical individuals, such as identical twins.

isohydric shift [Gk, *isos* + *hydor,* water; AS, *sciftan,* to divide], the series of reactions in RBCs in which CO_2 is taken up and oxygen is released without the production of excess hydrogen ions.

isoimmunization /ī'sō·im'yənīzā'shən/, the development of antibodies against antigens from the same species, such as anti-Rh antibodies in an Rh-negative person.

isokinetic /-kinet'ik/, pertaining to a concentric or eccentric contraction that occurs at a set speed against a force of maximal resistance produced at all points in the ROM.

isokinetic exercise [Gk, *isos,* equal, *kinesis,* motion; L, *exercere,* to keep at work], a form of exercise in which maximum force is exerted by a muscle at each point throughout the active ROM as the muscle contracts. The effort of the patient to resist the movement is measured.

isolate /ī′səlāt/ [It, *isolare,* to detach], **1.** to separate a pure chemical substance from a mixture. **2.** to derive from any source a pure culture of a microorganism. **3.** to prevent an individual from having contact with the rest of a population.

isolated systolic hypertension (ISH), a type of hypertension in which only the systolic BP is elevated. The condition, which usually affects the elderly, increases the risk of stroke or heart attack.

isolation /-lā′shən/ [L, *insula,* island], the separation of a seriously ill patient from others to prevent the spread of an infection or to protect the patient from irritating environmental factors.

isolation incubator, an incubator bed regularly maintained for premature or other infants who require isolation.

isolation precautions, special precautionary measures, practices, and procedures used in the care of patients with contagious or communicable diseases. The Centers for Disease Control and Prevention provides explicit and comprehensive guidelines for control of the spread of infectious disease in the care of hospitalized patients, with the type of disease dictating the kind of precautions necessary.

isolation ward [It, *isolare,* to detach; ME, *warden*], a room or section of a hospital in which certain categories of patients, particularly those infected with acute contagious diseases, can be treated with a minimum of contact with the rest of the patients and hospital personnel.

Isolette, a trademark for a self-contained incubator unit that provides a controlled heat, humidity, and oxygen microenvironment for the isolation and care of premature and low–birth weight neonates.

isoleucine (Ile) /ī′sōloo̅′sēn/ [Gk, *isos* + *leukos,* white], an amino acid that occurs in most dietary proteins and is essential for proper growth in infants and for nitrogen balance in adults.

isologous graft /īsol′əgəs/ [Gk, *isos,* equal, *logos,* relation, *graphion,* stylus], a tissue transplant between two individuals who are genetically identical, as identical twins.

isomeric /-mer′ik/ [Gk, *isos,* equal, *meros,* part], pertaining to a chemical phenomenon in which two compounds of the same chemical formula may differ in chemical and physical properties. The difference is the result of the arrangement of atoms in the respective molecules, either the connections between the atoms or their arrangements in three-dimensional space.

isomers /ī′səmərz/, compounds that have the same formula but different structures, resulting in different properties.

isometheptene hydrochloride /-məthep′tēn mu′kāt/, an antispasmodic and vasoconstrictor drug that is a component in some fixed-combination drugs used to treat migraines.

isometheptene mucate /ī′somothep′tēn mu′kāt/, a vasoconstrictor that acts on dilated carotid and cerebral vessels, used in combination with dichloralphenazone and acetaminophen in treatment of migraine and tension headache.

isometric /ī′səmet′rik/ [Gk, *isos* + *metron,* measure], maintaining the same length or dimension.

isometric contraction [Gk, *isos,* equal, *metron,* measure; L, *contractio,* a drawing together], muscular contraction not accompanied by movement of the joint. Resistance applied to the contraction increases muscle tension without producing movement of the joint.

isometric exercise, a form of active exercise in which muscle tension is increased while pressure is applied against stable resistance.

isometric growth, an increase in size of different organs or parts of an organism at the same rate.

isoniazid /ī′sonī′əzid/, a tuberculostatic antibacterial prescribed for prophylaxis to those who have been exposed to TB and used in combination with other agents in the treatment of TB caused by mycobacteria sensitive to the drug.

isophane insulin suspension /ī′səfān/ [Gk, *isos* + *phanein,* to show; L, *insula,* island, *suspendere,* to hang up], a modified form of protamine zinc insulin suspension. It is an intermediate-acting insulin that is a stable, commonly prescribed preparation.

isopropyl alcohol (C_3H_8O) /ī′sōprō′pil/, a clear, colorless bitter aromatic liquid that is miscible with water, ether, chloroform, and ethyl alcohol. A solution of approximately 70% isopropyl alcohol in water is used as a rubbing compound.

isoproterenol hydrochloride /ī′sōprəter′ənol/, a beta-adrenergic stimulant used as a bronchodilator and as a cardiac stimulant.

Isoptin, a trademark for a calcium channel blocker or calcium ion antagonist (verapamil).

Isopto Atropine, a trademark for an anticholinergic (atropine sulfate).

Isopto Carbachol, a trademark for a cholinergic (carbachol).

Isopto Carpine, a trademark for a cholinergic (pilocarpine hydrochloride).

Isopto Cetamide, a trademark for an antibacterial (sulfacetamide sodium).

Isopto Homatropine, a trademark for an anticholinergic (homatropine hydrobromide).

Isopto Hyoscine, a trademark for an anticholinergic (scopolamine hydrobromide).

Isordil, a trademark for an antianginal agent (isosorbide dinitrate).

isosmotic /ī′sozmot′ik/, pertaining to a solution that has the same solute concentration (osmolality) as another solution.

isosorbide dinitrate /-sôr′bīd/, an antianginal agent prescribed as a coronary vasodilator in the treatment of angina pectoris and CHF and esophageal spasm caused by GI reflux.

isosorbide mononitrate, an active metabolite of isosorbide dinitrate, having the same actions and uses.

Isospora /īsos′pərə/ [Gk, *isos,* equal, *sporos,* seed], a genus of coccidian protozoa found in birds, amphibians, reptiles, and mammals, including humans, that infects the epithelial cells of the small intestine. It is the least common cause of coccidiosis.

isosporiasis /īsos′pərī′əsis/, infection with *Isospora.*

isotachophoresis /-tak′ōfôrē′sis/ [Gk, *isos* + *tachos,* speed, *pherein,* to bear], the ordering and concentration of substances of intermediate effective mobilities between an ion of high effective mobility and one of much lower effective mobility, followed by their migration at a uniform speed.

isothermal /-thur′məl/ [Gk, *isos,* equal, *therme,* heat], having the same temperature.

isotones /ī′sətōnz′/, atoms that have the same number of neutrons but different numbers of protons.

isotonic /ī′səton′ik/ [Gk, *isos* + *tonikos,* stretching], pertaining to a solution that causes no change in cell volume.

isotonic exercise, a form of active exercise in which muscles contract and cause movement. There is no significant change in resistance throughout the movement, so the force of contraction remains constant. Such exercise greatly enhances joint mobility and helps improve muscle strength and tone.

isotonicity law /ī′sətonis′itē/, a law that describes a state of equal osmotic pressure in extracellular body fluids that results from equal concentrations of electrolytes and other solute particles in the fluid.

isotope /ī′sətōp/ [Gk, *isos* + *topos,* place], one of two or more forms of an atom having the same number of protons in the atomic nucleus but different numbers of neutrons and thus a different atomic mass. Many isotopes are used in diagnostic and therapeutic procedures.

isotopic tracer /ī′sətop′ik/ [Gk, *isos* + *topos,* place; Fr, *tracer,* to track], an isotope or mixture of isotopes of an element incorporated into a sample to permit observation of the course of the element through a chemical, physical, or biologic process. The observations may be made by measuring the radioactivity or the abundance of the isotope.

isotretinoin /-tratin′ō·in/, an antiacne agent. Subject to significant restrictions, it is prescribed for the treatment of severe cystic acne.

isotype /ī′sətīp/, an antigenic determinant that occurs in all members of a subclass of an immunoglobulin class. An antigenic determinant that is isotypic in one subclass may appear as an allotypic marker in another class.

isovaleric acid /-vəler′ik/ [Gk, *isos;* L, *valeriana,* herb, *acidus,* sour], a fatty acid with a pungent taste and disagreeable odor that is found in valerian and other plant products, as well as in cheese. It also occurs as a metabolite of the amino acid leucine and is found in the sweat of feet and in the urine of patients with smallpox, hepatitis, and typhus. Isovaleric acidemia occurs in patients who have abnormally high levels of isovaleric acid in the blood and urine as a result of an inherited deficiency of the enzyme isovaleryl coenzyme A dehydrogenase.

isovolume pressure-flow curve /-vol′yəm/, a curve on a graph describing the relationship of driving pressure to the resulting volumetric flow rate in the airways at any given lung inflation.

isovolumic contraction /-vəloo′mik/ [Gk, *isos;* L, *volumen,* paper roll, *contractio,* drawing together], the early phase of systole, in which the myocardial muscle fibers have begun to shorten but have not developed enough pressure in the ventricles to overcome the aortic and pulmonary end-diastolic pressures and open the aortic and pulmonary valves.

isoxsuprine hydrochloride /īsok′səprēn/, a peripheral vasodilator prescribed for the symptomatic relief of cerebrovascular insufficiency and improvement of circulation in arteriosclerosis, Raynaud's disease, and Buerger's disease.

isradipine /israd′ipēn/, a calcium channel blocking agent used alone or with a thiazide diuretic for the treatment of hypertension.

ISS, 1. abbreviation for **International Society of Surgery. 2.** abbreviation for **injury severity score.**

isthmus /is′məs/ *pl.* **isthmuses, isthmi** [Gk, *isthmos,* a narrow connection, passage, or constriction], a constriction between two larger parts of an organ or anatomic structure, such as the isthmus of the thyroid.

isthmus of gastric gland, the part of a gastric gland immediately adjacent to the opening into the gastric pit.

isthmus of thyroid [Gk, *isthmos* + *thyreos* + *eidos*, form], a part of the thyroid gland, anterior to the trachea, which joins the two lateral lobes of the gland.

Isuprel, a trademark for a beta-adrenergic stimulant (isoproterenol).

IT, abbreviation for **immunotoxin.**

itch [AS, *giccan*], **1.** to feel a sensation, usually on the skin, that makes one want to scratch. **2.** a tingling, annoying sensation on an area of the skin that makes one want to scratch it. **3.** the pruritic condition of the skin caused by infestation with the parasitic mite *Sarcoptes scabiei.* —**itchy,** *adj.*

itch mite [AS, *giccan* + *mite*], a tiny arachnid with piercing and sucking mouthparts. At least three genera of itch mites are recognized: *Chorioptes, Notoedres,* and *Sarcoptes.*

ITP, abbreviation for **immune thrombocytopenic purpura.**

IU, I.U., abbreviation for **International Unit.**

IUD, abbreviation for **intrauterine device.**

IUPC, abbreviation for *intrauterine pressure catheter.*

IV, **1.** abbreviation for **intravenous** or **intravenously.** **2.** *informal.* equipment consisting of a bottle or bag of fluid, infusion set with tubing, and IV catheter, used in IV therapy. **3.** IV administration of fluids or medication by injection into a vein.

IVAC pump, a trademark for a portable IV pump that electronically regulates and monitors the flow of IV fluid. It is usually attached to the IV stand.

IVC, abbreviation for **intravenous cholangiography.**

Ivemark's syndrome /ē′vəmärks,ĭ′v′märks/, a congenital defect in which organs on the left side of the body are a mirror image of their counterparts on the right side.

IVF, abbreviation for **in vitro fertilization.**

IVP, abbreviation for **intravenous pyelography.**

IVT, abbreviation for *intravenous transfusion.*

IV-type traction frame, a metal structure for holding traction equipment. It consists of two metal uprights, one at each end of the bed, which support an overhead metal bar.

Ivy method [Robert H. Ivy, American surgeon, 1881–1947], a test of bleeding time in which a BP cuff on the upper arm is inflated to 40 mm of mercury and a small wound is made with a scalpel and a template on the volar surface of the arm. Normal adult Ivy bleeding time is 1 to 9 minutes.

ixabepilone, a miscellaneous antineoplastic used to treat breast cancer.

Ixempra, a trademark for ixabepilone.

Ixodes /iksō′dēz/ [Gk, sticky], a genus of parasitic hard-shelled ticks associated with the transmission of a variety of infections, such as Rocky Mountain spotted fever, Lyme disease, ehrlichiosis, and babesiosis.

ixodiasis /ik′sōdī′əsis/, **1.** skin lesions created by the bites of ixodid ticks. **2.** any tick-transmitted disease.

ixodid /iksod′id, iksō′did/, pertaining to hard ticks of the family Ixodidae.

Iyengar yoga, a style of yoga that emphasizes correct body alignment in the asanas (postures) and holding the asanas for extended periods of time.

J, abbreviation for **joule.**

Jaccoud's dissociated fever /zhäko͞oz'/ [Sigismond Jaccoud, French physician, 1830–1913], a form of febrile meningitic fever accompanied by a paradoxic slow pulse rate.

jacket [Fr, *jaquette*], a supportive or confining therapeutic casing or garment for the torso. It is also used to prevent edema in the extremities.

jacket restraint, an orthopedic device used to help immobilize the trunk of a patient in traction and to discourage the patient from sitting up in bed. The jacket restraint is attached to both sides of the bedspring frame by means of buckled webbing straps that are sewn into the side seams of the restraint.

jackknife position /jak'nīf/, an anatomic position in which the patient is placed on the stomach with the hips flexed and the knees bent at a 90-degree angle and the arms outstretched in front of the patient. Examination and instrumentation of the rectum are facilitated by this position.

jackscrew /jak'skro͞o/, a threaded device used in orthodontic appliances for the separation or approximation of teeth or jaw segments.

Jackson crib, a removable orthodontic appliance retained in position by crib-shaped wires.

jacksonian epilepsy /jakso͞o'nē·ən/, epilepsy characterized by focal motor seizures with unilateral clonic movements that start in one group of muscles and spread systematically to adjacent groups, reflecting the march of the epileptic activity through the motor cortex. The seizures are due to a discharging focus in the contralateral motor cortex.

jacksonian seizure, a series of focal seizures with unilateral clonic movements that start in one group of muscles and spread systematically to adjacent groups, reflecting the march of the epileptic activity through the motor cortex.

Jackson's sign [John H. Jackson, English neurologist, 1835–1911], in hemiparesis, an observation that during quiet respiration the movement of the paralyzed side of the chest may be greater than that of the opposite side.

Jackson tracheostomy tube, a trademark for a silver tracheostomy tube with a rubber cuff built onto the tube. The design is intended to prevent accidental migration of the cuff off the end of the tube, causing interference with airflow to the patient.

jackstone calculus, a urinary calculus with six spikes like those of the toy in the game of jacks.

Jacquemier's sign /zhäkmē·āz'/ [Jean M. Jacquemier, French obstetrician, 1806–1879], a deepening of the color of the vaginal mucosa just below the urethral orifice. It may sometimes be noted after the fourth week of pregnancy.

jactitation /jak'titā'shən/ [L, *jactare*, show off, display], twitchings or spasms of muscles or muscle groups, as observed in the restless body movements of a patient with a severe fever.

JADA, abbreviation for *Journal of the American Dental Association.*

JAMA /jä'mä, jam'ə, jā'ā'em'ā'/, abbreviation for *Journal of the American Medical Association.*

jamais vu /zhämävY', -vē', -vo͞o'/ [Fr, never seen], the sensation of being a stranger when with a person one knows or when in a familiar place. The phenomenon occurs occasionally in healthy people but more frequently in those who have temporal lobe epilepsy.

Janeway lesion /jān'wä/ [Edward G. Janeway, American physician, 1841–1911; L, *laedere,* to injure], a small erythematous or hemorrhagic macule on the palms or soles. It is diagnostic of subacute bacterial endocarditis.

janiceps /jan'əseps/ [L, *Janus,* two-faced Roman god, *caput,* head], a conjoined twin fetus in which the heads are fused, with the faces looking in opposite directions.

Jansky-Bielschowsky disease /yahn'skē byelschov'skē/, the late infantile form of neuronal ceroid lipofuscinosis, occurring between 2 and 4 years of age and characterized by abnormal accumulation of lipofuscin. It begins as myoclonic seizures and progresses to neurologic and retinal degeneration and death, usually by the age of 8 to 12 years.

Januvia, a trademark for sitagliptin.

721

Japanese encephalitis (JE), a severe epidemic infection of brain tissue seen in East and Southeast Asia and the South Pacific. It is characterized by shaking chills, paralysis, and weight loss. Symptoms include headache, fever, neck stiffness, tremors, seizures, spastic paralysis, and coma. Mortality rate ranges widely. Various neurologic and psychiatric sequelae are common.

Japanese spotted fever, an acute infection occurring in Japan caused by *Rickettsia japonica,* and transmitted by Ixodidae. It is characterized by fever and headache and the appearance of an eschar and rash.

JAPHA /jaf′ə, jä′ə′pē″ach′ä′/, abbreviation for *Journal of the American Public Health Association.*

jar, 1. *v.* to shake or jolt. 2. *n.* a cylindrical container.

Jarcho-Levin syndrome /jär′kō lev′in/ [Saul Wallenstein Jarcho, American physician, 1906–2000; Paul M. Levin, American physician, 20th century], an autosomal-recessive disorder consisting of multiple vertebral defects, short thorax, rib abnormalities, camptodactyly, syndactyly, and, occasionally, urogenital abnormalities. Death from respiratory insufficiency usually occurs in infancy.

jargon (jar.) /jär′gən/ [Fr, *jargonner,* to speak indistinctly], 1. incoherent speech or gibberish. 2. a terminology used by scientists, artists, or others of a professional subculture that is not understood by the general population. 3. a state in child language acquisition characterized by strings of babbled sounds paired with gestures.

jargon aphasia [Fr, *jargonner*; Gk, *a + phasis,* speech], a form of speech in which several words are combined in a single word but in a jumbled manner with incorrect accents or words mixed with neologisms. Although outwardly incomprehensible, the speech may be meaningful when analyzed by a psychotherapist.

Jarisch-Herxheimer reaction /jä′rish herks′hīmər/ [Adolph Jarisch, Austrian dermatologist, 1850–1902; Karl Herxheimer, German dermatologist, 1861–1944], a transient, short-term immunologic reaction commonly seen after antibiotic treatment of early and later stages of syphilis and less often in other diseases, such as borreliosis, brucellosis, typhoid fever, and trichinosis. Manifestations include fever, chills, headache, myalgias, and exacerbation of cutaneous lesions.

Jarotzky's treatment /jərot′skēz/ [Alexander Jarotzky, Russian physician, b. 1866], therapy of gastric ulcer consisting of a bland diet of egg whites, fresh butter, bread, milk, and noodles.

Jarvik-7 [Robert K. Jarvik, American cardiologist, b. 1946], an artificial heart designed by R.K. Jarvik for use in humans. The Jarvik-7 was an early model that depended on air pressure to drive the ventricles.

jaundice /jôn′dis, jän′dis/ [Fr, *jaune,* yellow], a yellow discoloration of the skin, mucous membranes, and sclerae of the eyes, caused by greater than normal amounts of bilirubin in the blood. Persons with jaundice may experience nausea, vomiting, and abdominal pain and may pass dark urine and clay-colored stools. Jaundice is a symptom of many disorders, including liver diseases, biliary obstruction, and the hemolytic anemias. Physiologic jaundice commonly develops in newborns and disappears after a few days. —**jaundiced,** *adj.*

jaw [AS, *ceowan,* to chew], a common term used to describe the maxillae and the mandible and the soft tissue that covers these structures, which contain the teeth and form the framework for the mouth.

jaw jerk, an abnormal reflex elicited by tapping the chin with a rubber hammer while the mouth is half open and the jaw muscles are relaxed. A quick snapping shut of the jaw implies damage to the area of cerebral cortex governing motor activity of the fifth cranial nerve.

jaw relation, any relation of the mandible to the maxilla.

jaw-winking, an involuntary facial movement phenomenon in which the eyelid droops, usually on one side of the face, when the jaw is closed but rises when the jaw is opened or when the jaw is moved from side to side.

J chain, a polypeptide chain that holds IgAdimers and IgM pentamers together.

J/deg, abbreviation for *joules per degree.*

JE, abbreviation for **Japanese encephalitis.**

Jefferson fracture, a fracture characterized by bursting of the ring of the first cervical vertebra.

jejunal atresia, atresia of the jejunum, a type of intestinal atresia.

jejunal feeding tube, a hollow tube inserted into the jejunum through the abdominal wall for administration of liquefied foods to patients who have a high risk of aspiration.

jejunectomy /jij′ōōnek′təmē/, the surgical removal of all or part of the jejunum.

jejunocolostomy /jijōō′nōkəlos′təmē/, the surgical creation of an anastomosis between the jejunum and colon.

jejunogastric intussusception, the prolapse of an anastomosed jejunum into the stomach; a complication sometimes seen after gastrojejunostomy.

jejunostomy /jij͞o͞onos′təmē/, a surgical procedure to create an artificial opening to the jejunum through the abdominal wall. It may be a permanent or a temporary opening.

jejunotomy /jij͞o͞onot′əmē/, a surgical incision in the jejunum.

jejunum /jij͞o͞o′nəm/ pl. **jejuna** [L, jejunus, empty], the intermediate or middle of the three parts of the small intestine, connecting proximally with the duodenum and distally with the ileum.—**jejunal,** adj.

jelly, a semisolid nonliquid colloidal solution.

jellyfish sting [L, gelare, to congeal; AS, fisc + stingan], a wound caused by skin contact with a jellyfish, a sea animal with a bell-shaped gelatinous body and numerous suspended long tentacles containing stinging structures. In most cases, a tender, red welt develops on the affected skin. In some cases, depending on the sensitivity of the person and the species of jellyfish, severe localized pain and nausea, weakness, excessive lacrimation, nasal discharge, muscle spasm, perspiration, difficulty in swallowing, and dyspnea may occur.

Jendrassik's maneuver /yendrä′shiks/ [Ernst Jendrassik, Hungarian physician, 1858–1921; Fr, manoeuvre, action], in neurology, a diagnostic maneuver in which the patient hooks the flexed fingers of the two hands together and forcibly tries to pull them apart, used to overcome the voluntary suppression of reflexes. While this tension is being exerted, the lower extremity reflexes are tested.

jerk, **1.** a sudden abrupt motion such as a thrust, yank, push, or pull. **2.** a quick muscular contraction induced when a tendon over a bone is tapped.

jerk nystagmus, a slow drift of the eyes in one direction, followed by a rapid recovery movement in the other direction.

jerks, a form of choromania, or morbid desire to make rhythmic movements, sometimes associated with emotional fervor.

jet humidifier, a humidifier that increases the surface area for exposure of water to gas by breaking the water into small aerosol droplets. Gas issuing from the unit has a maximum amount of water vapor and a minimum of liquid water particles.

jet lag [L, jacere, to throw; Scand, lagga, to fall behind], a condition of desynchrony with disruption of the normal circadian rhythm, caused by rapid travel across several time zones. It is characterized by fatigue, insomnia, and disturbances in body function.

jet nebulizer [L, nebula, mist], a humidifier that uses Bernoulli's principle to convert a pool of liquid into a fine mist of aerosol particles.

Jeune's syndrome /zhœnz, zh͞o͞onz/ [Mathis Jeune, French pediatrician, b. 1910], a form of lethal short-limbed dwarfism characterized by constriction of the upper thorax and occasionally by polydactylism. It is inherited as an autosomal-recessive trait.

jeweler's forceps, a thumb forceps with very fine, pointed tips, used for microvascular and ophthalmic procedures.

jimson weed /jim′sən/, a common name for Datura stramonium, a poisonous plant with large, trumpet-shaped flowers. Its chief components are the anticholinergics hyosciamine and scopolamine.

jitters, **1.** irregularities in ultrasound echo locations caused by mechanical or electronic disturbances. **2.** a very uneasy, nervous feeling.

J/kg, abbreviation for joules per kilogram.

Jobst garment, a trademark for a type of pressure wrap applied to control hypertrophic scar formation or lymphedema.

JOD, abbreviation for juvenile-onset diabetes.

Jod-Basedow phenomenon /jod′ bä′zədō′/ [Ger, Jod, iodine; Karl A. von Basedow, German physician, 1799–1854], thyrotoxicosis that may occur when dietary iodine is given to a patient with endemic goiter in an area of environmental iodine deficiency. The phenomenon may also occur when large doses of iodine are given to patients with nontoxic multinodular goiter in areas with sufficient environmental iodine.

Joffroy's reflex /zhôfrô·äz′, jof′roiz/ [Alexis Joffroy, French physician, 1844–1908], a reflex contraction of the gluteus muscles produced when firm pressure is applied to the buttocks of patients with spastic paralysis of the lower limbs.

Joffroy's sign [Alexis Joffroy], **1.** an upward direction of a patient's gaze, caused by the absence of facial muscle contraction in ophthalmic goiter. **2.** an inability to perform simple mathematic exercises such as addition or multiplication, caused by an organic brain disease.

jogger's heel [ME, joggen, to shake; AS, hela, heel], a painful condition characterized by bruising, bursitis, fasciitis, or calcaneal spurs that results from repetitive and forceful striking of the heel on the ground. It is common among joggers and distance runners.

Johnson, Dorothy E. [American nurse, 1919–1999], a nursing theorist who developed a behavioral systems model presented in Conceptual Models for Nursing Practice (Riehl and Roy, eds., 1973). The patient is a behavioral system with seven interrelated subsystems. Each subsystem has structural and functional requirements. Johnson considered that problems in nursing are caused by disturbances in the structure or functions of the subsystems or the system.

Johnson's method, a technique for filling root canals, in which gutta-percha cones are dissolved in a chloroform-rosin solution in the root canal to form a plastic mass. The plastic material is forced toward the apex of the root canal, and more is added until the canal is sealed.

joint [L, *jungere,* to join], any one of the articulations between bones. Each is classified according to structure and movability as fibrous, cartilaginous, or synovial. Fibrous joints are immovable, cartilaginous joints are slightly movable, and synovial joints are freely movable.

joint and several liability, in law, a condition in which several persons share the liability for a plaintiff's injury and may be found liable individually or as a group.

joint appointment, 1. a faculty appointment to two institutions within a university or system, as to the schools of nursing and medicine of the same university. **2.** in academic nursing, the appointment of a member of the faculty of a university to a clinical service of an associated service institution.

joint capsule [L, *jungere,* to join, *capsula,* little box], a fibrous saclike structure of connective tissue that envelops the end of bones in a diarthrodial joint and contains synovial fluid.

joint chondroma, a cartilaginous mass that develops in the synovial membrane of a joint.

joint conference committee, a hospital organization composed of the governing board, administration, and medical staff representatives whose purpose is to facilitate communication between the groups.

joint instability, an abnormal increase in joint mobility.

joint mouse, a small movable stone formed in or near a joint, usually a knee.

joint movement, a nursing outcome from the Nursing Outcomes Classification (NOC) defined as active range of motion of all joints with self-initiated movement.

joint movement: ankle, a nursing outcome from the Nursing Outcomes Classification (NOC) defined as active range of motion of the ankle with self-initiated movement.

joint movement: elbow, a nursing outcome from the Nursing Outcomes Classification (NOC) defined as active range of motion of the elbow with self-initiated movement.

joint movement: fingers, a nursing outcome from the Nursing Outcomes Classification (NOC) defined as active range of motion of the fingers with self-initiated movement.

joint movement: hip, a nursing outcome from the Nursing Outcomes Classification (NOC) defined as active range of motion of the hip with self-initiated movement.

joint movement: knee, a nursing outcome from the Nursing Outcomes Classification (NOC) defined as active range of motion of the knee with self-initiated movement.

joint movement: neck, a nursing outcome from the Nursing Outcomes Classification (NOC) defined as active range of motion of the neck with self-initiated movement.

joint movement: passive, a nursing outcome from the Nursing Outcomes Classification (NOC) defined as joint movement with assistance.

joint movement: shoulder, a nursing outcome from the Nursing Outcomes Classification (NOC) defined as active range of motion of the shoulder with self-initiated movement.

joint movement: spine, a nursing outcome from the Nursing Outcomes Classification (NOC) defined as active range of motion of the spine with self-initiated movement.

joint movement: wrist, a nursing outcome from the Nursing Outcomes Classification (NOC) defined as active range of motion of the wrist with self-initiated movement.

joint planning, the development by two or more health care providers of a strategic plan to serve the health care needs of an area while sharing clinical or administrative services or data but not assets.

joint practice, 1. the practice of one or more physicians, nurses, and other health professionals, usually private, who work as a team, sharing responsibility for a group of patients. **2.** in inpatient nursing, the practice of making joint decisions about patient care by committees of the physicians and nurses working on a division.

joint protection, the use of orthotics with therapeutic exercise to prevent damage or deformity of a joint during rehabilitation to restore power and ROM.

Jones criteria /jōnz/, a standardized set of guidelines for the diagnosis of rheumatic fever, as recommended by the American Heart Association.

Joubert's syndrome /zhoo·bärz'/ [Marie Joubert, Canadian neurologist, 20th century], an autosomal-recessive syndrome consisting of partial or complete agenesis of the cerebellar vermis, with hypotonia, episodic hyperpnea, mental retardation, and abnormal eye movements. Most patients die in infancy.

joule (J) /jool/ [James P. Joule, English physicist, 1818–1889], a unit of energy or work in the meter-kilogram-second system and the SI system. It is equivalent to 10^7 ergs or 1 watt second and 100 rad.

journaling, a nursing intervention from the Nursing Interventions Classification (NIC) defined as promotion of writing as a means to provide opportunities to reflect upon and analyze past events, experiences, thoughts, and feelings.

J-pouch, a fecal reservoir formed surgically by folding over the lower end of the ileum in an ileoanal anastomosis.

JRA, abbreviation for **juvenile rheumatoid arthritis.**

Judd method, a technique for positioning a patient for radiographic examination of the atlas and odontoid process.

judgment /juj′mənt/ [L, *judicare*, to judge], **1.** in law, the final decision of the court regarding the case before it. **2.** the reason given by the court for its decision; an opinion. **3.** an award, penalty, or other sentence of law given by the court. **4.** the ability to recognize the relationships of ideas and to form correct conclusions from those data as well as from those acquired from experience.

judgment call *slang.* a decision based on experience, especially a judgment that resolves a serious problem in which the data are inconclusive or equivocal.

jugal /jōō′gəl/ [L, *jugum*, yoke], pertaining to structures attached or yoked, as the zygomatic bone or malar bone.

jugular /jug′yələr/ [L, *jugulum*, neck], **1.** pertaining to or involving the throat. **2.** *informal.* the jugular vein.

jugular foramen [L, *jugulum*, neck, *foramen*, hole], one of a pair of openings between the lateral part of the occipital bone and the petrous part of the temporal bones in the skull. The foramen contains the inferior petrosal sinus; the transverse sinus; some meningeal branches of the occipital and ascending pharyngeal arteries; and the glossopharyngeal, vagus, and accessory nerves.

jugular fossa, a deep depression adjacent to the interior surface of the petrosa of the temporal bone of the skull.

jugular notch of the sternum, the large notch in the manubrium of the sternum.

jugular process, a portion of the occipital bone that projects laterally from the squamous part to the temporal bone. On its anterior border, a deep notch forms the posterior and medial boundary of the jugular foramen.

jugular pulse, a pulsation in the jugular vein caused by conditions that inhibit diastolic filling of the right side of the heart.

jugular trunk, one of the two lymphatic vessels, right and left, that drain the head and neck.

jugular tubercle, a large rounded mound of the occipital bone medial to the jugular foramen.

jugular venous pressure (JVP), BP in the jugular vein, which reflects the volume and pressure of venous blood. An elevated JVP is typically a sign of CHF.

jugum /jōō′gəm/ [L, yoke], a ridge or furrow joining two points.

juice /jōōs/ [L, *jus*, broth], any fluid secreted by the tissues of animals or plants. In humans, it usually refers to the secretions of the digestive glands.

juice therapy, the use of concentrated nutritional elixirs of fruit extracts and vegetables for nutritional maintenance, illness prevention, detoxification, and adjunctive treatment of allergies, digestive disorders, rheumatoid arthritis, skin diseases, and other conditions such as hypotension and hypertension, bronchitis, obesity, and insomnia.

jumentous /jōōmen′təs/ [L, *jumentum*, beast of burden], having a strong animal odor, especially that of a horse. The term is used to describe the odor of urine associated with certain disease conditions.

jumping disease, any of several culture-specific disorders characterized by exaggerated responses to small stimuli, muscle tics including jumping, automatic obedience even to dangerous suggestions, and sometimes coprolalia or echolalia. It is unclear whether the responses are neurogenic or psychogenic in origin. An example is Gilles de la Tourette's syndrome.

jumping Frenchmen of Maine syndrome, a form of jumping disease observed in a group of lumbermen of French-Canadian descent working in a remote area of Maine. Affected individuals had exaggerated startle responses, automatic obedience, and often echolalia. It is believed to have represented a form of operant conditioning rather than a true disease.

junction /jungk′shən/ [L, *jungere*, to join], an interface or meeting place for tissues or structures.

junctional bigeminy /jungk′shənəl/ [L, *jungere*, to join, *bis*, twice, *geminus*, twin], cardiac arrhythmia in which each sinus beat is followed by a junctional beat after a constant delay.

junctional epithelium [L, *jungere*, to join; Gk, *epi* + *thele*, nipple], an area of epithelial soft tissue surrounding the abutment post of a tooth.

junctional extrasystole [L, *jungere*, to join, *extra*, beyond; Gk, *systole*, contraction], a premature heartbeat that usually arises from the junction of the atrioventricular (AV) node and the AV bundle, the primary junctional pacing site, but may also arise from within the AV bundle.

junctional parenchymal defect, on ultrasound of the kidney, an echogenic mass sometimes seen in the parenchyma, resembling a cortical scar but indicating only a benign collection of fat at the junction where two of the fetal lobes of the kidney fuse.

junctional rhythm, a cardiac rhythm usually originating at the junction of the atrioventricular (AV) node and the AV bundle. It may be a normal escape rhythm (rate between 40 and 60 beats/min) or an active focus (rate 60 beats/min or greater).

junctional tachycardia, a junctional rhythm with a rate greater than 100 beats/min. The mechanism may be enhanced normal automaticity, abnormal automaticity, or triggered activity caused by digitalis toxicity.

junction lines, vertical lines that appear in the mediastinum on a posterior-anterior projection radiographic image of the chest.

junction nevus [L, *jungere*, to join, *naevus*, birthmark], a hairless flat or slightly raised brown skin blemish arising from pigment cells at the epidermal-dermal junction. Malignant change may be signaled by increase in size, hardness or darkening, bleeding, or appearance of satellite discoloration around the nevus.

juncture, a joint or union of two parts.

juniper tar /jōō′nipər/ [L, *juniperus*; AS, *teoru*], a dark, oily liquid obtained by the destructive distillation of the wood of *Juniperus oxycedrus* trees, used as an antiseptic stimulant in ointments for skin disorders.

jurisprudence /jōō′risprōō′dəns/ [L, *jus*, law, *prudentia*, knowledge], the science and philosophy of law.

justice [L, *justus*, sufficient], **1.** a principle of fair and equal treatment for all, with due reward and honor. **2.** in research, equitable distribution of benefits and burdens of research. **3.** the treatment of people in a nonprejudicial manner.

juvenile /jōō′vənəl, -vənīl′ [L, *juvenus*, youthful], **1.** a young person; youth; child; youngster. **2.** pertaining to, characteristic of, or suitable for a young person; youthful. **3.** physiologically underdeveloped or immature. **4.** denoting psychologic or intellectual immaturity; childish.

juvenile alveolar rhabdomyosarcoma, a rapidly growing tumor of striated muscle occurring in children and adolescents, chiefly in the extremities. The prognosis is grave.

juvenile delinquency, persistent antisocial, illegal, or criminal behavior by children or adolescents to the degree that it cannot be controlled or corrected by the parents. It endangers others in the community, and it becomes the concern of a law enforcement agency.

juvenile delinquent, a person who performs illegal acts and who has not reached an age at which treatment as an adult can be accorded under the laws of the community having jurisdiction.

juvenile glaucoma [L, *juvenus*, young; Gk, *glaukos*, bluish-gray], increased intraocular tension in a young adult caused by developing structural defects that restrict the outflow of fluid.

juvenile laryngeal respiratory papillomatosis, multiple squamous cell tumors that develop in the larynx, usually in young children. The growths are transmitted by a papilloma virus and may be acquired from the mother.

juvenile myoclonic syndrome, a condition in which myoclonic seizures begin to appear around the time of puberty. The myoclonic jerks are often associated with sleep deprivation and photosensitivity.

juvenile periodontitis, an abnormal, extremely invasive condition characterized by severe localized pocketing and bone loss in the dental alveoli of children and adolescents, generally associated with poor oral hygiene and inadequate nutrition.

juvenile rheumatoid arthritis (JRA), a form of rheumatoid arthritis, usually affecting the larger joints of children younger than 16 years of age and often accompanied by systemic manifestations. As bone growth in children is dependent on the epiphyseal plates of the distal epiphyses, skeletal development may be impaired if these structures are damaged.

juvenile spinal muscular atrophy, a disorder beginning in childhood in which progressive degeneration of anterior horn and medullary nerve cells leads to skeletal muscle wasting. The condition usually begins in the legs and pelvis.

juvenile xanthogranuloma, a skin disorder characterized by groups of yellow, red, or brown papules or nodules on the extensor surfaces of the arms and legs, and in some cases on the eyeball, meninges, and testes. The lesions typically appear in infancy or early childhood and usually disappear in a few years.

juxtaarticular /juk′stə·ärtik′yələr/ [L, *juxta*, near, *articulus*, joint], pertaining to a location near a joint.

juxtacrine /juks′təkrin/, describing a hormonal relationship in which the secretory cell is adjacent to an effector cell.

juxtaglomerular /-glōmer′ələr/ [L, *juxta*, near, *glomerulus*, small ball], pertaining to an area near or adjacent to the afferent and efferent arterioles of the kidney glomerulus.

juxtaglomerular apparatus, a collection of cells located beside each renal glomerulus. It is involved in the secretion of renin and erythropoietin in response to BP changes and is important in autoregulation of certain kidney functions.

juxtaglomerular cells [L, *juxta,* near, *glomerulus,* small ball, *cella,* storeroom], smooth myoepithelioid cells lining the glomerular end of the afferent arterioles in the kidney that are in opposition to the macula densa region of the early distal tubule. These cells synthesize and store renin and release it in response to decreased renal perfusion pressure, increased sympathetic nerve stimulation of the kidneys, or decreased sodium concentration in fluid in the distal tubule.

juxtamedullary /-med′əler′ē/, near the border of a medulla.

juxtamedullary cortex, the part of the renal cortex nearest to the medulla.

juxtamedullary glomerulus, a renal glomerulus located particularly close to the corticomedullary border.

juxtamedullary nephron, one whose proximal convoluted tubule is close to the corticomedullary border and whose loop of Henle extends deep into the renal medulla.

juxtaposition /-pəzish′ən/, the placement of objects side by side or end to end.

JVP, abbreviation for **jugular venous pressure.**

k, abbreviation for *kilo,* 1000, or 10^3.

K, 1. symbol for **ionization constant. 2.** symbol for **Kelvin scale. 3.** symbol for the element **potassium** (kalium). **4.** abbreviation for **kilobyte. 5.** symbol in electronics for 1024 (2^{10}). **6.** abbreviation for **katal.**

K_m, symbol for *Michaelis-Menten constant.*

kA, abbreviation for *kiloampere.*

kainate /kī′nāt/, a non-NMDA (*N*-methyl-D-aspartate) receptor agonist. The natural mineral is used as a fertilizer.

kala-azar /kä′lə äzär′/ [Hindi, *kala,* black; Assamese, *azar,* fever], a chronic and potentially fatal disease caused by the protozoan *Leishmania donovani,* transmitted to humans, particularly to children, by the bite of the sand fly. Signs and symptoms include anemia, hepatomegaly, splenomegaly, irregular fever, suppression of bone marrow, and emaciation. Patients are also susceptible to secondary bacterial infections.

kalemia /kəlē′mē·ə/, the presence of potassium in the blood.

kalium (K) /kā′lē·əm/ [Ar, *quali,* potash], potassium.

kaliuresis /kal′iyŏŏrē′sis/, the excretion of potassium in the urine.

kallak /kal′ak/, a pustular skin disease observed among Eskimos.

kallikrein-kinin system /kalik′rē·in-/, a proposed hormonal system that functions within the kidney, with the enzyme kallikrein in the renal cortex mediating production of bradykinin, which acts as a vasodilator peptide.

Kallmann's syndrome[1] [Franz J. Kallmann, American psychiatrist, 1897–1965], a condition characterized by the absence of the sense of smell. It is caused by agenesis of the olfactory bulbs and secondary hypogonadism related to a decrease of luteinizing hormone–releasing hormone.

Kallmann's syndrome[2] /kahl′mahns/, a type of hypogonadotropic hypogonadism caused by failure of fetal gonadotropin-releasing hormone neurons to migrate to the thalamus, usually associated with anosmia or hyposmia.

kanamycin /kan′əmī′sin/, an antibacterial substance derived from *Streptomyces kanamyceticus.*

kanamycin sulfate, an aminoglycoside antibiotic prescribed in the treatment of certain severe infections (especially those caused by gram-negative aerobes) and as second line therapy for TB.

kangaroo care, a nursing intervention from the Nursing Interventions Classification (NIC) defined as promoting closeness between parent and physiologically stable preterm infant by preparing the parent and providing the environment for skin-to-skin contact.

Kanner's syndrome [Leo Kanner, Austrian-born American child psychiatrist, 1894–1981], a form of infantile psychosis with an onset in the first 30 months of life. It is characterized by infantile autism.

Kantian theory, the ethical theory of the 18th-century German philosopher Immanuel Kant. It focuses on the rightness or wrongness of actions in and of themselves, rather than on the consequences of those actions.

Kantrex, a trademark for an antibacterial (**kanamycin sulfate**).

Kaochlor, a trademark for an electrolyte replacement solution (potassium chloride).

kaolin /kā′əlin/ [Chin, *kao-ling,* high ridge], an adsorbent used internally to treat diarrhea, often in combination with pectin. Kaolin in an ointment base is also used topically as an absorbent and a protective emollient.

kaolinosis /kā′əlinō′sis/, a form of pneumoconiosis acquired by inhaling clay dust (kaolin).

Kaon Cl, a trademark for an electrolyte replacement solution (potassium chloride).

Kaopectate, a trademark for an antidiarrheal fixed-combination drug containing an adsorbent (kaolin) and an emollient (pectin).

Kaposi's disease /kap′əsēz/ [Moritz K. Kaposi, Austrian dermatologist, 1837–1902; L, *dis;* Fr, *aise,* ease], a rare inherited skin disorder that begins in childhood and involves mainly exposed skin areas. Exposure to sunlight results in erythema and vesiculation, followed by increased pigmentation and telangiectasia, skin ulcers, warts, and malignant epitheliomas.

Kaposi's sarcoma (KS, ks) [Moritz K. Kaposi], a malignant, multifocal neoplasm of reticuloendothelial cells that begins as soft brownish or purple papules on the feet or hard palate and slowly spreads in the skin, metastasizing to the lymph nodes and viscera. It occurs most often in men and is associated with diabetes, malignant lymphoma, AIDS, or other disorders.

kappa /kap′ə/, K, κ, the tenth letter of the Greek alphabet, used to denote (in chemistry) the tenth carbon atom in a chain, one of two light chains in an immunoglobulin molecule, a type of killer particle present in certain strains of *Paramecium,* and a visual axis angle.

kappa chain, a type of light polypeptide chain of immunoglobulin molecules.

kappa light chain, one of two kinds of smaller peptide chains present in an immunoglobulin molecule.

karaya powder /kär′äyä/ [Hindi, *karayal,* resin; L, *pulvis,* dust], a dried form of *Sterculia urens* or other species of *Sterculia,* used as a bulk cathartic. Methylcellulose has largely replaced this drug in modern use. Externally it is used as a drying agent for stage I and stage II pressure ulcers.

Kardex, a trademark for a card-filing system that allows quick reference to the particular needs of each patient for certain aspects of nursing care.

Kartagener's syndrome /kärtag′ənərz/, an inherited disorder characterized by bronchiectasis, chronic paranasal sinusitis, and transposed viscera, usually dextrocardia.

karyocyte /ker′ē·əsīt′/ [Gk, *karyon,* nut, *kytos,* cell], a normoblast, or developing RBC, with a nucleus condensed into a homogenous staining body. It is normally found in the red bone marrow.

karyogamy /ker′ē·og′əmē/ [Gk, *karyon,* nut, *gamos,* marriage], the fusion of cell nuclei, as in conjugation and zygosis. —**karyogamic,** *adj.*

karyogenesis /ker′ē·ōjen′əsis/ [Gk, *karyon* + *genein,* to produce], the formation and development of the nucleus of a cell. —**karyogenetic,** *adj.*

karyokinesis /ker′ē·ōkine′sis, -kīne′sis/ [Gk, *karyon* + *kinesis,* motion], the division of the nucleus and equal distribution of nuclear material during mitosis and meiosis.—**karyokinetic,** *adj.*

karyoklasis /ker′ē·ok′ləsis/ [Gk, *karyon* + *klasis,* breaking], **1.** the disintegration of a cell nucleus or nuclear membrane. **2.** the interruption of mitosis.—**karyoclastic, karyoklastic,** *adj.*

karyology /ker′ē·ol′əjē/ [Gk, *karyon* + *logos,* science], the branch of cytology that concentrates on the study of the cell nucleus, especially the structure and function of the chromosomes.—**karyologic,** *adj.,* **karyologist,** *n.*

karyolymph /ker′ē·əlimf′/ [Gk, *karyon* + *lympha,* water], the clear, usually nonstaining, fluid substance of a cell nucleus. It consists primarily of proteinaceous, colloidal material in which the nucleolus, chromatin, linin, and various submicroscopic particles are dispersed.—**karyolymphatic,** *adj.*

karyolysis /ker′ē·ol′isis/ [Gk, *karyon* + *lysis,* loosening], the dissolution of a cell nucleus. It occurs normally, both as a form of necrobiosis and during the generation of new cells through mitosis and meiosis.

karyolytic /ker′ē·əlit′ik/, **1.** pertaining to karyolysis. **2.** something that causes the destruction of a cell nucleus.

karyomegaly /ker′ē·ōmeg′əlē/ [Gk, *karyon,* nut, *megas,* large], an increase in the nuclear size of tissue cells.

karyomere /ker′ē·əmir′/ [Gk, *karyon* + *meros,* part], **1.** a saclike structure containing an unequal portion of the nuclear material after atypical mitosis. **2.** a segment of a chromosome.

karyometry /ker′ē·om′ətrē/, the measurement of the nucleus of a cell.—**karyometric,** *adj.*

karyomit /ker′ē·əmit′/ [Gk, *karyon* + *mitos,* thread], **1.** a single chromatin fibril of the network within the nucleus of a cell. **2.** a chromosome.

karyomitome /ker′ē·om′itōm/ [Gk, *karyon* + *mitos,* thread], the fibrillar chromatin network within the nucleus of a cell.

karyomorphism /-môr′fizəm/ [Gk, *karyon* + *morphe,* form], the shape or form of a cell nucleus, especially that of a leukocyte.—**karyomorphic,** *adj.*

karyon /ker′ē·on/ [Gk, nut], the nucleus of a cell.—**karyontic,** *adj.*

karyophage /ker′ē·ōfāj′/ [Gk, *karyon* + *phagein,* to eat], an intracellular protozoan parasite that destroys the nucleus of the cell it infects.—**karyophagic, karyophagous,** *adj.*

karyopyknosis /-piknō′sis/ [Gk, *karyon* + *pyknos,* thick], the state of a cell in which the nucleus has shrunk and the chromatin has condensed into solid masses.—**karyopyknotic,** *adj.*

karyorrhexis /-rek′sis/ [Gk, *karyon* + *rhexis,* rupture], the disintegration of the nucleus in a cell.—**karyorrhectic,** *adj.*

karyosome /ker′ē·əsōm′/ [Gk, *karyon* + *soma,* body], a dense, irregular mass of chromatin filaments in a cell nucleus.

karyospheric /-sfer′ik/ [Gk, *karyon* + *sphaira,* ball], **1.** a spheric nucleus. **2.** pertaining to such a nucleus.

karyostasis /ker′ē·os′təsis/ [Gk, *karyon* + *stasis,* standing], the resting stage of the nucleus between cell division.—**karyostatic,** *adj.*

karyotype /ker′ē·ətīp′/ [Gk, *karyon* + *typos,* mark], **1.** the number, form, size, and arrangement within the nucleus of the somatic chromosomes of an individual or species, as determined by a

K

microphotograph taken during metaphase of mitosis. **2.** a diagrammatic representation of the chromosome complement of an individual or species, in which the chromosomes are arranged in pairs in descending order of size and according to the position of the centromere.—**karyotypic,** *adj.*

Kasabach method /kas′əbak/, in radiology, a technique for positioning a patient for radiographic examination of the odontoid process.

Kashin-Bek disease [Nikolai I. Kashin, Russian orthopedist, 1825–1872; E.V. Bek; L, *dis*; Fr, *aise,* ease], a form of osteoarthrosis afflicting mainly children living in China, Korea, and eastern Siberia. It is believed to be caused by eating foods made with wheat contaminated by a fungus, *Fusarium sporotrichiella.*

kat, abbreviation for **katal.**

katadidymus /kat′ədid′əməs/ [Gk, *kata,* down, *didymos,* twin], conjoined twins united in the lower part of the body and separated at the top.

katal (K, kat) /kat′al/ [Gk, *kata,* down], an enzyme unit in moles per second defined by the SI system: 1 K= 1 mol/s = 6.6×10^9 U.

Katz index /kats/, a tool for assessing a patient's ability to perform ADL.

kava, herb that is useful for nervous anxiety, restlessness, sleep disturbances, and stress, although there are safety concerns following several reports of hepatotoxicity and liver failure occurring with relatively normal doses used for a short term.

Kay Ciel, a trademark for an electrolyte replacement solution (potassium chloride).

Kayser-Fleischer ring /kī′zər flī′shər/ [Bernhard Kayser, German ophthalmologist, 1869–1954; Bruno Fleischer, German ophthalmologist, 1874–1904], a gray-green to red-gold pigmented ring at the outer margin of the cornea, pathognomonic of hepatolenticular degeneration.

Kazanjian's operation /kasan′jē-ənz/ [Varaztad J. Kazanjian, Armenian-born maxillofacial surgeon in U.S., 1879–1974], a surgical procedure for extending the vestibular sulcus to improve the prosthetic foundation of toothless dental ridges.

kb, 1. abbreviation for **kilobase.**
2. abbreviation for **kilobyte.**

kbp, abbreviation for **kilobase pair.**

kbs, abbreviation for *kilobits per second.*

kcal, abbreviation for **kilocalorie.**

kCi, abbreviation for *kiloCurie.*

KCl, symbol for **potassium chloride.**

KE, abbreviation for **kinetic energy.**

Kearns-Sayre syndrome /kernz sār/ [Thomas P. Kearns, American ophthalmologist, b. 1922; George P. Sayre, American pathologist, b. 1911], progressive ophthalmoplegia, pigmentary degeneration of

the retina, myopathy, ataxia, and cardiac conduction defect, with onset before the age of 20 years. Almost all patients have large mitochondrial DNA deletions, and ragged red fibers are seen on muscle biopsy.

K-edge, a discontinuity in the absorption coefficient at an energy level corresponding to the binding energy of K-shell electrons.

keel, in prosthetics, a device in a stored-energy foot prosthesis, that bends the foot upward when weight is applied to the toe.

kefir /kef′ər/ [Russ, fermented milk], a slightly effervescent, acidulous beverage prepared from the milk of cows, sheep, or goats through fermentation by kefir grains, which contain yeasts and lactobacilli. It is an important source of the bacteria necessary in the GI tract to synthesize vitamin K.

Keflex, a trademark for an antibacterial (cephalexin).

Kefzol, a trademark for an antibacterial (cefazolin sodium).

Keith-Wagener-Barker classification system [Norman M. Keith, Canadian physician, b. 1885; Henry P. Wagener, American physician, b. 1890; N.W. Barker, 20th century American physician], a method of classifying the degree of hypertension in a patient on the basis of retinal changes. The stages are group 1, identified by constriction of the retinal arterioles; group 2, constriction and sclerosis of the retinal arterioles; group 3, characterized by hemorrhages and exudates in addition to group 2 conditions; and group 4, papilledema of the retinal arterioles.

Kellgren's syndrome /kel′grinz/ [Henry Kellgren, Swedish physician, 1827–1916], a form of osteoarthritis affecting the proximal and distal interphalangeal joints, the first metatarsophalangeal and carpometacarpal joints, the knees, and the spine. The absence of rheumatoid factor and rheumatoid nodules and the lack of systemic involvement differentiate this syndrome from rheumatoid arthritis.

Kelly clamp [Howard A. Kelly, American gynecologist, 1858–1943; AS, *clam,* to fasten], a curved hemostat without teeth, used primarily for grasping vascular tissue in gynecologic procedures.

Kelly plication, an operation for correction of stress incontinence in women. The connective tissue between the vagina and the urethra and the floor of the bladder are sutured to form a wide shelf of firm tissue supporting the urethra and bladder.

Kelly's pad, a horseshoe-shaped inflatable rubber drainage pad used in a bed or on the operating table.

keloid /kē′loid/ [Gk, *kelis,* spot, *eidos,* form], an overgrowth of collagenous scar tissue at the site of a skin injury, particularly a wound or a surgical incision.

The new tissue is elevated, rounded, and firm.—**cheloidal, keloidal,** *adj.*

keloid acne [Gk, *kelis,* spot, *eidos,* form, *akme,* point], pyoderma in and around the pilosebaceous structures, resulting in keloid scarring.

keloidosis /kē′loidō′sis/ [Gk, *kelis* + *eidos,* form, *osis,* condition], habitual or multiple formation of keloids.

keloid scar [Gk, *kelis,* spot, *eidos,* form, *eschara,* scab], an overgrowth of tissue in a scar at the site of skin injury, particularly a wound or a surgical incision. The amount of tissue growth is in excess of that necessary to repair the wound and is partially caused by an accumulation of collagen at the site.

kelp [ME, *culp*], **1.** any of the brown seaweed species of *Laminaria* found on the Atlantic coast of Europe. **2.** the ashes of *Laminaria* seaweed burned in a process of extracting iodine and potassium salts.

Kelvin scale (K) [Lord Kelvin (William Thomson), British physicist, 1824–1907], an absolute temperature scale calculated in Celsius units from the point at which molecular activity apparently ceases, −273.151° C. To convert Celsius degrees to Kelvin, add 273.15.

Kemadrin, a trademark for an antiparkinsonian skeletal muscle relaxant (procyclidine hydrochloride).

Kenalog, a trademark for a glucocorticoid (triamcinolone acetonide).

Kennedy classification [Edward Kennedy, American dentist, b. 1883], a method of classifying partial edentulous conditions and partial dentures, based on the position of the spaces once occupied by the missing teeth in relation to the remaining teeth. It is useful in the construction of and planning for removable partial dentures.

Kent bundle [Albert F.S. Kent, English physiologist, 1863–1958; AS, *byndel,* to bind], an accessory pathway between an atrium and a ventricle outside of the conduction system. This congenital anomaly causes Wolff-Parkinson-White syndrome.

kerasin /ker′əsin/ [L, *cera,* wax], a cerebroside, found in brain tissue, that consists of a fatty acid, galactose, and sphingosine.

keratectomy /ker′ətek′təmē/ [Gk, *keras,* horn, *ektomē,* excision], surgical removal of a part of the cornea, performed to excise a small, superficial lesion that does not warrant a corneal graft.

keratic /kərat′ik/ [Gk, *keras,* horn; L, *icus,* like], **1.** pertaining to keratin. **2.** pertaining to the cornea.

keratic precipitate, a group of inflammatory cells deposited on the endothelial surface of the cornea after trauma or inflammation, sometimes obscuring vision.

keratin /ker′ətin/ [Gk, *keras,* horn], a fibrous sulfur-containing protein that is the primary component of the epidermis, hair, nails, enamel of the teeth, and horny tissue of animals. The protein, insoluble in most solvents, including gastric juice, is often used as a coating for pills that must pass through the stomach unchanged to be dissolved in the intestines.

keratin cyst, an epithelial cyst containing keratin.

keratinization /-īzā′shən/ [Gk, *keras* + *izein,* to cause], a process by which epithelial cells lose their moisture and are replaced by horny tissue.

keratinize /ker′ətinīz/, to make or become horny tissue.

keratinocyte /kerat′inōsīt′/ [Gk, *keras* + *kytos,* cell], an epidermal cell that synthesizes keratin and other proteins and sterols. These cells constitute 95% of the epidermis, being formed from undifferentiated, or basal, cells at the dermal-epidermal junction.

keratinophilic /kerat′inōfil′ik/, describing a type of fungi that uses keratin as a substrate.

keratitis /ker′ətī′tis/, any inflammation of the cornea.—**keratic,** *adj.*

keratoacanthoma /ker′ətō·ak′anthō′mə/ *pl.* **keratoacanthomas, keratoacanthomata** [Gk, *keras* + *akantha,* thorn, *oma,* tumor], a benign, rapidly growing, flesh-colored papule or nodule of the skin with a central plug of keratin. The lesion is most common on the face and the back of the hands and arms. Biopsy is often necessary to differentiate it from a squamous carcinoma.

keratocele /ker′ətōsēl′/, a hernia of Descemet's membrane through an ulcer in the outer layers of the cornea.

keratoconjunctivitis /ker′ətōkənjungk′tiv ī′tis/ [Gk, *keras;* L, *conjunctivus,* connecting, Gk, *itis,* inflammation], inflammation; of the cornea and the conjunctiva.

keratoconjunctivitis sicca, dryness of the cornea caused by a deficiency of tear secretion in which the corneal surface appears dull and rough and the eye feels gritty and irritated. The condition may be associated with erythema multiforme, Sjögren's syndrome, trachoma, and vitamin A deficiency.

keratoconus /ker′ətōkō′nəs/ [Gk, *keras* + *konos,* cone], a noninflammatory protrusion of the central or paracentral region of the cornea. It may result in marked astigmatism.

keratocyst /ker′ətōsist′/, a thin-walled, tooth-forming cyst lined by keratinizing epithelium.

keratoderma /ker′ətōdur′mə/ [Gk, *keras,* horn, *derma,* skin], **1.** a horny skin or covering. **2.** hypertrophy of the horny layer of the skin.

K

keratoderma blennorrhagica /-dʉrmə/, the development of hyperkeratotic skin lesions of the palms, soles, and nails. The condition tends to occur in some patients with Reiter's syndrome.

keratodermatitis /-dʉr´mətī´tis/, an inflammation and proliferation of the cells of the horny layer of the skin.

keratoectasia /ker´ətō·ektā´zhə/, a forward bulging or protrusion of the cornea.

keratoepithelioplasty /-ep´ithē´lē·əplas´tē/, a surgical procedure for the repair of corneal epithelial defects. The defective cornea is removed and replaced with small pieces of donor cornea, which proliferate and replace the original tissue.

keratogenesis /-jen´əsis/, the formation of horny tissue caused by the growth of keratin-producing cells.

keratogenic /-jen´ik/, pertaining to an agent that induces a growth of horny tissue.

keratogenous /ker´ətoj´ənəs/, pertaining to development of the horny layer of the skin or the growth of cells that produce keratin.

keratoglobus /-glō´bəs/, a congenital anomaly characterized by distension of the eyeball or the anterior segment of the eye.

keratohyalin /-hī´əlin/ [Gk, *keras* + *hyalos*, glass], a substance in the granules found in keratinocytes of the epidermis.

keratoid /ker´ətoid/ [Gk, *keras*, horn, *eidos*, form], resembling horny or corneal tissue.

keratoiritis /ker´ətōīrī´tis/, an inflammation of the cornea in association with iritis.

keratolysis /ker´ətol´ə·sis/ [Gk, *keras* + *lysis*, loosening], the loosening and shedding of the outer layer of the skin, which may occur normally by exfoliation or as a congenital condition in which the skin is shed at periodic intervals.—**keratolytic,** *adj.*

keratoma /ker´ətō´mə/, a hard, thick, epidermal growth caused by hypertrophy of the horny layer of the skin.

keratomalacia /-məlā´shə/ [Gk, *keras* + *malakia*, softness], a condition characterized by xerosis and ulceration of the cornea, resulting from severe vitamin A deficiency. Early symptoms include night blindness; photophobia; swelling and redness of the eyelids; and drying, roughness, pain, and wrinkling of the conjunctiva. In advanced deficiency, Bitot's spots appear; the cornea becomes dull, lusterless, and hazy, and without adequate therapy it eventually softens and perforates, resulting in blindness.

keratomycosis /-mīkō´sis/, a fungal disease of the cornea.

keratopathy /ker´ətop´əthē/ [Gk, *keras* + *pathos*, disease], any noninflammatory disease of the cornea.

keratophakia /-fā´kē·ə/, the surgical implantation of donor cornea to the anterior cornea to modify a refractive error.

keratorhexis /ker´ətorek´sis/, rupture of the cornea.

keratosis /ker´ətō´sis/ [Gk, *keras* + *osis*, condition], any skin lesion in which there is overgrowth and thickening of the cornified epithelium.—**keratotic,** *adj.*

keratosis follicularis, a group of several skin disorders characterized by keratotic papules that coalesce to form brown or black, crusted, wartlike patches. These vegetations may spread widely, ulcerate, and become covered with a purulent exudate.

kerion /kir´ē·on/ [Gk, honeycomb], an inflamed, boggy granuloma or secondary infected lesion that develops as an immune reaction to a superficial fungus infection, generally in association with *Tinea capitis* of the scalp.

Kerley lines /kur´lē/ [Peter J. Kerley, English radiologist, 1900–1979], lines resembling interstitial infiltrate that appear on chest x-ray images and are associated with certain disease conditions, such as CHF and pleural lymphatic engorgement.

KERMA, 1. abbreviation for *kinetic energy released in material,* a quantity that describes the transfer of energy from a photon to a medium as the ratio of energy transferred per unit mass at each point of interaction. 2. acronym for *kinetic energy released in matter,* a unit of quantity referring to the kinetic energy transferred from photons to charged particles, such as electrons in Compton interactions, per unit mass. The SI unit for the KERMA is the gray, and the special unit is the rad.

kernicterus /kərnik´tərəs/ [Ger, *kern,* kernel; Gk, *ikteros,* jaundice], an abnormal toxic accumulation of bilirubin in CNS tissues caused by hyperbilirubinemia.

Kernig's sign /ker´niks/ [Vladimir M. Kernig, Russian physician, 1840–1917], a diagnostic sign for meningitis marked by a loss of the ability of a supine patient to completely straighten the leg when it is fully flexed at the knee and hip.

kerosene poisoning /ker´əsēn/ [Gk, *keros,* wax; L, *potio,* drink], a toxic condition caused by the ingestion of kerosene or the inhalation of its fumes. Symptoms after ingestion include drowsiness, fever, a rapid heartbeat, tremors, and severe pneumonitis if the fluid is aspirated. Vomiting is not induced.

Ketalar, a trademark for a general anesthetic (ketamine hydrochloride).

ketamine hydrochloride /kē´təmēn/, a nonbarbiturate general anesthetic induction agent administered parenterally to achieve dissociative anesthesia. It is a potent somatic analgesic and is particularly useful for brief, minor surgical procedures.

Ketek, a trademark for telithromycin.

ketoacidosis /kē′tōas′idō′sis/ [Gk, *keton,* form of acetone; L, *acidus,* sour; Gk, *osis,* condition], acidosis accompanied by an accumulation of ketones in the body, resulting from extensive breakdown of fats because of faulty carbohydrate metabolism. It occurs primarily as a complication of DM and is characterized by a fruity odor of acetone on the breath, mental confusion, dyspnea, nausea, vomiting, dehydration, weight loss, and, if untreated, coma.—**ketoacidotic,** *adj.*

ketoaciduria /-as′idō̄r′ē-ə/ [Gk, *keton;* L, *acidus,* sour; Gk, *ouron,* urine], presence in the urine of excessive amounts of ketone bodies, occurring as a result of uncontrolled DM, starvation, or any other metabolic condition in which fats are rapidly catabolized.—**ketoaciduric,** *adj.*

17-ketoandrosterone /-andros′tərōn/, a metabolite of a sex hormone secreted by the testes and adrenal glands that may be measured in the urine to assess hormonal and adrenal functions.

ketoconazole /-kō′nəzōl/, an antifungal agent prescribed for the treatment of candidiasis, coccidioidomycosis, histoplasmosis, and other fungal diseases.

17-ketoetiocholanolone /kē′tō-ē′tē-ōkəlan′əlōn/, a metabolite of a sex hormone secreted by the testes and adrenal glands that may be measured in the urine to assess hormonal and adrenal functions.

ketogenesis /-jen′əsis/ [Fr, *keton;* Gk, *genein,* to produce], the formation or production of ketone bodies.

ketogenic amino acid /-jen′ik/, an amino acid whose carbon skeleton serves as a precursor for ketone bodies.

ketogenic diet, a diet high in fats (often as medium chain triglycerides) and proteins and low in carbohydrates, often indicated in the treatment of epilepsy.

ketone /kē′tōn/ [Fr, *acetone*], an organic chemical compound characterized by having in its structure a carbonyl, or keto, group, $=CO$, attached to two alkyl groups. It is produced by oxidation of secondary alcohols.

ketone alcohol [Gk, *keton;* Ar, *alkohl,* essence], an alcohol containing the ketone group.

ketone bodies, two products of lipid pyruvate metabolism, beta-hydroxybutyric acid and aminoacetic acid, from which acetone may arise spontaneously. Ketone bodies are produced from acetyl-CoA in the liver and are oxidized by the muscles.

ketone group, the chemical carbonyl group of a ketone (i.e., with two alkyl groups attached to it).

ketonemia /kē′tōnē′mē-ə/, the presence of ketones, mainly acetone, in the blood. It is characterized by the fruity breath odor of ketoacidosis.

ketoprofen /-prō′fən/, an NSAID with analgesic and antipyretic actions. It is prescribed for the treatment of rheumatoid arthritis and osteoarthritis and other conditions causing mild to moderate pain.

ketose /kē′tōs/ [Gk, *keton + glykys,* sweet], the chemical form of a monosaccharide in which the carbonyl group is a ketone.

ketosis /kitō′sis/ [Gk, *keton + glykys,* sweet; *osis,* condition], the abnormal accumulation of ketones in the body as a result of excessive breakdown of fats caused by a deficiency or inadequate use of carbohydrates. Fatty acids are metabolized instead, and the end products, ketones, begin to accumulate. This condition is seen in starvation, occasionally in pregnancy if the intake of protein and carbohydrates is inadequate, and most frequently in DM. It is characterized by ketonuria, loss of potassium in the urine, and a fruity odor of acetone on the breath. —**ketotic,** *adj.*

17-ketosteroid /kē′tōstir′oid, kētō′stəroid/, any of the adrenal cortical hormones, or ketosteroids, that has a ketone group attached to its seventeenth carbon atom. These hormones are commonly measured in the blood and urine to aid the diagnoses of Addison's disease; Cushing's syndrome, stress, and endocrine problems associated with precocious puberty, feminization in men, and excessive hair growth.

17-ketosteroids (17-KS) test, a 24-hour urine test that is useful in diagnosing adrenocortical dysfunction. It is used to detect levels of 17-KS, which are metabolites of the testosterone and nontestosterone androgenic sex hormones secreted from the adrenal cortex and the testes.

ketotic /kētot′ik/ [Fr, *acetone*], **1.** pertaining to the presence of ketone in the body. **2.** denoting the presence of a carbonyl group in a chemical compound.

ketotifen /ke′toti′fen/, a noncompetitive H_1-receptor antagonist and mast cell stabilizer used as the fumarate salt, administered orally in the chronic treatment of children with mild atopic asthma and topically to the conjunctiva as an antipruritic in the treatment of allergic conjunctivitis.

keV, abbreviation for *kiloelectron volts,* an energy unit equivalent to 1000 electron volts.

key points of control, areas of the body, the shoulder and pelvic girdles, that can be handled by a therapist in a specific manner to change an abnormal pattern, to reduce spasticity throughout the body, and to guide the patient's active movements.

key ridge, the lowest point of the zygomaticomaxillary ridge.

kG, abbreviation for **kilogauss.**

kg cal, abbreviation for **kilogram calorie.**

K

khat, herbal product used for obesity and gastric ulcers, and as a stimulant to offset depression and fatigue. Its efficacy for these indications is unproven due to insufficient reliable data. Khat causes a psychologically addicting euphoria and cannot be legally imported into the U.S.

kHz, abbreviation for **kilohertz.**

kidney [ME, *kidnere*], one of a pair of bean-shaped, purplish brown urinary organs in the dorsal part of the abdomen; one is located on each side of the vertebral column between the twelfth thoracic and third lumbar vertebrae. In most individuals the right kidney is slightly lower than the left. Each kidney is about 11 cm long, 6 cm wide, and 2.5 cm thick. The kidneys filter the blood and eliminate wastes in the urine through a complex filtration network and resorption system comprising more than 2 million nephrons. The nephrons are composed of glomeruli and renal tubules that filter blood under high pressure, removing urea, salts, and other soluble wastes from blood plasma and returning the purified filtrate to the blood. More than 1183 L of blood pass through the kidneys every day. The kidneys remove water as urine and return water that has been filtered to the blood plasma, thus helping to maintain the water balance of the body.

kidney cancer, a malignant neoplasm of the renal parenchyma or renal pelvis. Factors associated with an increased incidence of disease are exposure to aromatic hydrocarbons or tobacco smoke. The characteristic symptoms include hematuria, flank pain, fever, and a palpable mass.

kidney disease, any one of a large group of conditions, including infectious, inflammatory, obstructive, vascular, and neoplastic disorders of the kidney. Characteristics of kidney disease are hematuria, persistent proteinuria, pyuria, edema, dysuria, and pain in the flank. Specific symptoms vary with the type of disorder. Among the special diagnostic tests for kidney disorders are excretory urography, IV pyelography, tests of the glomerular filtration rate, biopsy, and ultrasound examination.

kidney function, a nursing outcome from the Nursing Outcomes Classification (NOC) defined as filtration of blood and elimination of metabolic waste products through the formation of urine.

Kielland's rotation /kē′lands/ [Christian Kielland, Norwegian obstetrician, 1871–1941], an obstetric procedure in which Kielland's forceps are used in turning the head of the fetus from an occiput posterior or occiput transverse position to an occiput anterior position.

Kiesselbach's plexus /kē′səlbäkhs′, -bäks′/ [Wilhelm Kiesselbach, German laryngologist, 1839–1902], a convergence of small fragile arteries and veins located superficially on the anterosuperior part of the nasal septum.

Kikuchi's lymphadenitis /kēkōō′chēz/ [M. Kikuchi, Japanese pathologist, 20th century], a benign, self-limited syndrome of lymphadenopathy, usually in the neck. Characteristics include patchy necrotizing lesions of the paracortex and proliferation of distinctive histiocytes, plasmacytoid monocytes, and lymphoblasts surrounded by karyorrhectic debris. Some consider it a self-limited form of SLE.

killed vaccine [ME, *killen;* L, *vaccinus,* of a cow], a vaccine prepared from dead microorganisms, generally used to provide immunization from organisms that are too virulent to be used in the living attenuated state. The immune system reacts to the presence of the pathogen in the same manner, whether the organism is alive or dead. However, immunity produced by a live, attenuated vaccine is usually more effective.

killer T cells, antigen-stimulated T lymphocytes or cytotoxic T cells that attack foreign antigens directly and destroy cells that bear those antigens.

killer yeast, a strain of yeast cells that contains a toxic protein that destroys other yeast strains.

kilobase (kb), a length of nucleic acid equal to 1000 bases or nucleotides.

kilobase pair (kbp), a length of DNA or double-stranded RNA equal to 1000 base pairs.

kilocalorie (kcal) /-kəl′ərē/ [Gk, *chilioi,* thousand; L, *calor,* heat], a unit of heat equal to 1000 small calories or 4186 joules.

kilogram (kg) /-gram/ [Gk, *chilioi,* thousand; Fr, *gramme*], a unit for the measurement of mass in the metric system. One kilogram is equal to 1000 grams or to 2.2046 pounds avoirdupois.

kilohertz (kHz) /-hurts/ [Gk, *chilioi,* thousand; *hertz,* Heinrich R. Hertz, German physicist, 1857–1894], unit of frequency equal to 1000 (10^3) hertz.

kiloliter (kL) /-lē′tər/ [Gk, *chilioi,* thousand; Fr, *litre*], unit of volume equivalent to 1057 quarts, 1000 liters, or 1 cubic meter (1 m^3).

kilometer (km) /-mē′tər/ [Gk, *chilioi,* thousand, *metron*], measure equivalent to 1000 meters (about 0.62 mile).

kilovolt (kV) /-volt/ [Gk, *chilioi,* thousand; volt, Count Alessandro Volta, Italian scientist, 1745–1827], measure of electric potential, 1000 volts.

kilovolt peak (kVp), a measure of the maximum electrical potential in kilovolts across an x-ray tube.

kinanesthesia /kin′anesthē′zhə/, **1.** an inability to perceive the movement or position of one's body parts. The condition is observed as a sign of ataxia. **2.** loss of movement sense.

kinase /kī′nās/ [Gk, *kinesis*, motion; *ase*, enzyme], **1.** an enzyme that catalyzes the transfer of a phosphate group or another high-energy molecular group to an acceptor molecule. **2.** an enzyme that activates a preenzyme (zymogen).

kind firmness, in psychology, a direct, clear, and confident approach to a patient in which rules and regulations are calmly cited in response to infractions and requests.

kindred /kin′drid/, a group of genetically related individuals.

kinematic face-bow /kin′əmat′ik/, an adjustable caliper-like device used for precisely locating the axis of rotation of a mandible through the sagittal plane.

kinematics /kin′əmat′iks, kī-′/ [Gk, *kinema*, motion], the description, measurement, and recording of body motion without regard to the forces acting to produce the motion. The most common types of motions studied in kinematics are flexion, extension, adduction, abduction, internal rotation, and external rotation. Kinematics is especially important in orthopedics, rehabilitation medicine, and physical therapy.

kineplasty, amputation in which the stump is formed in such a way that the muscles are able to produce motion in a prosthesis.

kinesia /kīnē′zhə/ [Gk, *kinein*, to move], a condition caused by erratic or rhythmic motions in any combination of directions, such as in a boat or a car. Severe cases are characterized by nausea, vomiting, vertigo, and headache; mild cases by headache and general discomfort.

kinesic behavior /kīnē′sik/, nonverbal cues of communication that help to achieve and maintain bonds of attachments between people.

kinesics /kīnē′siks/ [Gk, *kinesis*, motion], the study of body position, posture, movement, and facial expression in relation to communication.

kinesiologic electromyography /kinē′sē-əloj′ik/, the study of muscle activity involved in body movements.

kinesiology /-ol′əjē/ [Gk, *kinesis* + *logos*, science], the scientific study of muscular activity and the anatomy, physiology, and mechanics of the movement of body parts.

kinesiotherapist, a health care professional who, under the direction of a physician, treats the effects of disease, injury, and congenital disorders through the use of rehabilitative exercise and education alone.

kinesiotherapy, a specialized area of medicine in which exercise and movement are used as the primary form of rehabilitation. It is typically used in the treatment of amputees.

kinesis /kīnē′sis, kinē′sis/, physical movement or force, particularly when induced by a stimulus.

kinesthesia /kin′esthē′zhə/ [Gk, *kinesis*, motion, *aisthesis*, feeling], the perception of one's own body parts, weight, and movement.

kinesthetic memory /kin′esthet′ik/, the recollection of movement, weight, resistance, and position of the body or parts of the body.

kinesthetic sense [Gk, *kinesis*, motion; L, *sentire*, to feel], an ability to be aware of muscular movement and position. By providing information through receptors about muscles, tendons, joints, and other body parts, the kinesthetic sense helps control and coordinate activities such as walking and talking.

kinetic analysis /kinet′ik/, analysis in which the change of the monitored parameter with time is related to concentration, such as change of absorbance per minute, to determine the rate of a reaction.

kinetic energy (KE) [Gk, *kinesis*, motion + *energeia*], the energy possessed by an object by virtue of its motion. It is expressed by the formula $KE = (\frac{1}{2})mv^2$, where m represents the mass of the object and v is its velocity.

kinetic hallucination [Gk, *kinesis*, motion; L, *allucinari*, wandering mind], a false perception of body movement.

kinetic proofreading, 1. a molecular activity in which an enzyme distinguishes correct substrates. **2.** a mechanism that permits a ribosome to make correct codon-anticodon interactions.

kinetic reflex [Gk, *kinesis*, motion; L, *reflectere*, to bend back], a postural response resulting from stimulation of the vestibular apparatus.

kinetics /kinet′iks/ [Gk, *kinesis*; L, *icus*, like], the study of the forces that produce, arrest, or modify the motions of the body. Newton's first and third laws of motion are especially applicable to kinetics. Newton's first law states that bodies at rest stay at rest and bodies in motion keep moving unless they are acted on by an unbalancing force. Newton's third law states that every action force has a reaction force that is equal in magnitude but opposite in direction. These two laws apply to the forces produced by muscles that act on joints. The reaction forces of the muscles contribute to equilibrium and the motion of the body.

kinetoplasm /kīnet′ōplaz′əm/, the most highly contractile part of a cell.

kinetotherapeutic bath /kinet′ōthur′əpyoo′tik/ [Gk, *kinesis* + *therapeutike*, medical practice; AS, *baeth*], a bath in which underwater exercises are performed to strengthen weak or partially paralyzed muscles.

K

King-Devick test /kingdev'ik/, a tool for evaluation of saccade, consisting of a series of charts of numbers. The charts become progressively more difficult to read in a flowing manner because of increasing space between the numbers.

King, Imogene [1923–2007], a nursing theorist who introduced her theory of goal attainment in her book, *Toward a Theory for Nursing* (1971). King defines nursing as a process of human interactions between nurse and patients who communicate to set goals and then agree to meet the goals. She suggests that the patient's and the nurse's perceptions, judgments, and actions lead to reaction, interaction, and transaction, which she calls the process of nursing.

kin group, family members who are related genetically or by marriage.

kinin /kī'nin/, any of a group of polypeptides with varying physiologic activity, such as contraction of visceral smooth muscle, vascular permeability, and vasodilation.

kinky hair disease [Du, *kink,* short twist; AS, *haer;* L, *dis;* Fr, *aise,* ease], an inherited condition characterized by short, sparse, poorly pigmented hair with shafts that are twisted and broken. Other mental and physical disorders are usually associated with the disease.

Kinsbourne's syndrome /kinz'born/, a neurologic disorder of unknown cause with onset between ages 1 and 3 years, characterized by myoclonus of trunk and limbs and by nonrhythmic horizontal and vertical oscillations of the eyes, with ataxia of gait and intention tremor.

kinship model family group, a family unit comprising the biologic parents and their offspring. It is like a nuclear family but more closely tied to an extended family.

Kinyoun stain, a modification of the Ziehl-Neelsen acid-fast stain where organisms are stained cold by using carbolfuchsin. It is often used for detection of mycobacteria, *Nocardia,* and oocysts of some parasites.

Kirkland knife [Olin Kirkland, American periodontist, 1876–1969; AS, *cnif*], a surgical knife with a heart-shaped blade that is sharp on all edges. It is used for a primary gingivectomy incision.

Kirklin staging system, a system for determining the prognosis of colon cancer on the basis of the extent to which the tumor has penetrated the bowel area.

Kirlian photography, a photographic technique in which a high-voltage current passed over a subject in contact with photographic film or paper produces an image surrounded by a luminous radiation, or aura.

Kirschner's wire /kursh'nərz/ [Martin Kirschner, German surgeon, 1879–1942; AS, *wir*], a threaded or smooth metallic wire available in three diameters and 22.86 cm long. The wire is used in internal fixation of fractures or for skeletal traction.

Kite method, a technique for positioning a patient for radiographic examination of congenital clubfoot.

kiting /kī'ting/, *informal.* the improper and illegal practice of altering a drug prescription to indicate that more of a drug was prescribed than was actually ordered by the physician.

KJ, abbreviation for *knee jerk.*

kL, abbreviation for *kiloliter.*

Klebsiella /kleb'zē·el'ə/ [Theodore A.E. Klebs, German bacteriologist, 1834–1913], a genus of diplococcal bacteria that appear as small, plump rods with rounded ends. Several respiratory diseases, including bronchitis, sinusitis, and some forms of pneumonia, are caused by infection by species of *Klebsiella.*

Klebsiella pneumoniae [Theodore A.E. Klebs; Gk, *pneumon,* lung], a species of gram-negative, nonmotile bacteria found in soil, water, cereal grains, and the intestinal tract of humans and other animals. It is associated with several pathologic conditions, including pneumonia. It is commonly implicated in nosocomial UTIs, especially in immunocompromised patients.

Klebs-Löeffler bacillus /klebz' lef'lər/ [Theodore A.E. Klebs; Friederich A J. Löeffler, German bacteriologist, 1852–1915; L, *bacillum,* small rod], the gram-positive asporogenic bacteria *Corynebacterium diphtheriae* that has three cultural types according to severity of the cases.

Kleine-Levin syndrome /klīn' lev'in/ [Willi Kleine, 20th century German psychiatrist; Max Levin, Russian-born American neurologist, b. 1901], a disorder of unknown cause often associated with psychotic conditions that is characterized by episodic sleep, abnormal hunger, and hyperactivity.

kleptolagnia /klep'tōlag'nē·ə/ [Gk, *kleptein,* to steal, *lagneia,* lust], sexual excitement or gratification produced by stealing.

kleptomania /-mā'nē·ə/ [Gk, *kleptein,* to steal, *mania,* madness], an anxiety disorder characterized by an abnormal, uncontrollable, and recurrent urge to steal. The objects are taken not for their monetary value, immediate need, or utility but because of a symbolic meaning usually associated with some unconscious emotional conflict; they are usually given away, returned surreptitiously, or kept and hidden. —**kleptomaniac,** *n.*

Klinefelter's syndrome /klīn'feltərz/ [Harry F. Klinefelter, American physician, 1912–1990], a condition of gonadal defects appearing in males after puberty, with an extra X chromosome in at least one cell line. Characteristics are small firm testes, long legs, gynecomastia, poor social adaptation, subnormal intelligence, chronic pulmonary disease, and varicose veins. The severity of the abnormalities increases with greater numbers of X chromosomes.

Klippel-Feil syndrome /klipel' fel, klip'əl fīl/ [Maurice Klippel, French neurologist, 1858–1942; Andre Feil, French neurologist, b. 1884], a condition of short neck and limited neck movements because of congenital fusion of the cervical vertebrae or reduction in the number of cervical vertebrae.

Klippel-Trénaunay syndrome /klipel' trānönā'/ [Maurice Klippel, French neurologist, 1858–1942; Paul Trénaunay, French physician, 20th century], a rare condition usually affecting one extremity, characterized by hypertrophy of the bone and related soft tissues, large cutaneous hemangiomas, persistent nevus flammeus, and skin varices.

Kloehn headgear, an extraoral orthodontic appliance consisting of a cervical strap and a long outer bow, used to retract maxillary teeth or to reinforce tooth anchorage during retraction.

Klonopin, a trademark for an anticonvulsant (clonazepam).

Klor, a trademark for an electrolyte replacement solution (potassium chloride).

Klorvess, a trademark for an electrolyte replacement solution (potassium chloride).

Klumpke's palsy /kloomp'kēz/ [Augusta Dejerine-Klumpke, French neurologist, 1859–1927], atrophic paralysis of the forearm and hand. It is present at birth and involves the seventh and eighth cervical nerves and the first thoracic nerve. The condition may be accompanied by Horner's syndrome, ptosis, and miosis because of involvement of sympathetic nerves.

K-Lyte/Cl, a trademark for an electrolyte replacement solution (potassium chloride).

km, abbreviation for **kilometer.**

kneading /nē'ding/ [AS, *cnedan*], a grasping, rolling, and pressing movement, as is used in massaging the muscles.

knee /nē/ [AS, *cneow*], a joint complex that connects the thigh with the lower leg. It consists of three condyloid joints, 12 ligaments, 13 bursae, and the patella.

knee-ankle interaction, one of the five major kinetic determinants of gait, which helps to minimize the displacement of the body's center of gravity during the walking cycle. The knee and the foot work simultaneously to lower the body's center of gravity. When the heel of the foot is in contact with the ground, the foot is dorsiflexed, and the knee is fully extended so that the associated limb is at its maximum length with the center of gravity at its lower point. Plantar flexion of the foot with the initiation of knee flexion maintains the center of gravity in its forward progression at about the same level, also helping to minimize the vertical displacement of the center of gravity.

knee-elbow position [AS, *cneow* + *elboga*], a position in which a patient being examined rests on the knees and elbows with the head supported on the hands.

knee-hip flexion, one of the five major kinetic determinants of gait, which allows the passage of body weight over the supporting extremity during the walking cycle. Knee-hip flexion occurs during the stance and swing phases of the cycle. The knee first locks into extension as the heel of the weight-bearing limb strikes the ground and is unlocked by final flexion and initiation of the swing phase in the walking cycle. Hip flexion is synchronized with these movements, which help minimize the vertical displacement of the body's center of gravity in the act of walking.

knee joint, the complex, hinged joint at the knee, regarded as three articulations in one, comprising condyloid joints connecting the femur and the tibia and a partly arthrodial joint connecting the patella and the femur. The knee joint and its ligaments permit flexion, extension, and, in certain positions, medial and lateral rotation.

knee replacement, the surgical insertion of a hinged prosthesis performed to relieve pain and restore motion to a knee severely affected by osteoarthritis, rheumatoid arthritis, or trauma. The diseased surfaces are removed, and tricompartmental implants are inserted to replace the opposing femorotibial joint and the patellofemoral joint.

knee sling, a leg support in sling form used under the knee for Russell's traction.

knife needle /nīf/ [AS, *cnif* + *neal*], a slender surgical knife with a needle point, used in the discission of a cataract and other ophthalmic procedures such as goniotomy and goniopuncture.

knockout mouse, a mouse that has had a specific gene artificially deleted from its genome.

Knoop hardness test /noop/ [Frederick Knoop, 20th century American metallurgist], a method of assessing surface hardness by measuring resistance to the penetration of an indenting tool made of diamond. The test is commonly used for testing the hardness of teeth.

knot /not/ [AS, *cnotta*], in surgery, the interlacing of the ends of a ligature or suture so that they remain in place without slipping or becoming detached. The ends of the suture are passed twice around each other before being pulled taut to form a simple surgeon's knot.

K

knowledge: arthritis management, a nursing outcome from the Nursing Outcomes Classification (NOC) defined as the extent of understanding conveyed about arthritis, its treatment, and the prevention of complications.

knowledge: asthma management, a nursing outcome from the Nursing Outcomes Classification (NOC) defined as the extent of understanding conveyed about asthma, its treatment, and the prevention of complications.

knowledge: body mechanics, a nursing outcome from the Nursing Outcomes Classification (NOC) defined as the extent of understanding conveyed about proper body alignment, balance, and coordinated movement.

knowledge: breastfeeding, a nursing outcome from the Nursing Outcomes Classification (NOC) defined as the extent of understanding conveyed about lactation and nourishment of an infant through breastfeeding.

knowledge: cancer management, a nursing outcome from the Nursing Outcomes Classification (NOC) defined as the extent of understanding conveyed about the cause, type, progress, symptoms, and treatment of cancer.

knowledge: cancer threat reduction, a nursing outcome from the Nursing Outcomes Classification (NOC) defined as the extent of understanding conveyed about causes, prevention, and early detection of cancer.

knowledge: cardiac disease management, a nursing outcome from the Nursing Outcomes Classification (NOC) defined as the extent of understanding conveyed about heart disease, its treatment, and the prevention of complications.

knowledge: child physical safety, a nursing outcome from the Nursing Outcomes Classification (NOC) defined as the extent of understanding conveyed about safely caring for a child from 1 year through 17 years of age.

knowledge: conception prevention, a nursing outcome from the Nursing Outcomes Classification (NOC) defined as the extent of understanding conveyed about prevention of unintended pregnancy.

knowledge: congestive heart failure management, a nursing outcome from the Nursing Outcomes Classification (NOC) defined as the extent of understanding conveyed about heart failure, its treatment, and the prevention of exacerbations.

knowledge: depression management, a nursing outcome from the Nursing Outcomes Classification (NOC) defined as the extent of understanding conveyed about depression and interrelationships among causes, effects, and treatments.

knowledge: diabetes management, a nursing outcome from the Nursing Outcomes Classification (NOC) defined as the extent of understanding conveyed about diabetes mellitus, its treatment, and the prevention of complications.

knowledge: diet, a nursing outcome from the Nursing Outcomes Classification (NOC) defined as the extent of understanding conveyed about recommended diet.

knowledge: disease process, a nursing outcome from the Nursing Outcomes Classification (NOC) defined as the extent of understanding conveyed about a specific disease process and prevention of complications.

knowledge: energy conservation, a nursing outcome from the Nursing Outcomes Classification (NOC) defined as the extent of understanding conveyed about energy conservation techniques.

knowledge: fall prevention, a nursing outcome from the Nursing Outcomes Classification (NOC) defined as the extent of understanding conveyed about prevention of falls.

knowledge: fertility promotion, a nursing outcome from the Nursing Outcomes Classification (NOC) defined as the extent of understanding conveyed about fertility testing and the conditions that affect conception.

knowledge: health behavior, a nursing outcome from the Nursing Outcomes Classification (NOC) defined as the extent of understanding conveyed about the promotion and protection of health.

knowledge: health promotion, a nursing outcome from the Nursing Outcomes Classification (NOC) defined as the extent of understanding conveyed about information needed to obtain and maintain optimal health.

knowledge: health resources, a nursing outcome from the Nursing Outcomes Classification (NOC) defined as the extent of understanding conveyed about relevant health care resources.

knowledge: hypertension management, a nursing outcome from the Nursing Outcomes Classification (NOC) defined as the extent of understanding conveyed about high blood pressure, its treatment, and the prevention of complications.

knowledge: illness care, a nursing outcome from the Nursing Outcomes Classification (NOC) defined as the extent of understanding conveyed about illness-related information needed to achieve and maintain optimal health.

knowledge: infant care, a nursing outcome from the Nursing Outcomes Classification (NOC) defined as the extent of understanding conveyed about caring for a baby from birth to first birthday.

knowledge: infection management, a nursing outcome from the Nursing Outcomes Classification (NOC) defined as the extent of understanding conveyed about infection, its treatment, and the prevention of complications.

knowledge: labor & delivery, a nursing outcome from the Nursing Outcomes Classification (NOC) defined as the extent of understanding conveyed about labor and vaginal delivery.

knowledge: medication, a nursing outcome from the Nursing Outcomes Classification (NOC) defined as the extent of understanding conveyed about the safe use of medication.

knowledge: multiple sclerosis management, a nursing outcome from the Nursing Outcomes Classification (NOC) defined as the extent of understanding conveyed about multiple sclerosis, its treatment, and the prevention of relapses or exacerbations.

knowledge: ostomy care, a nursing outcome from the Nursing Outcomes Classification (NOC) defined as the extent of understanding conveyed about maintenance of an ostomy for elimination.

knowledge: pain management, a nursing outcome from the Nursing Outcomes Classification (NOC) defined as the extent of understanding conveyed about causes, symptoms, and treatment of pain.

knowledge: parenting, a nursing outcome from the Nursing Outcomes Classification (NOC) defined as the extent of understanding conveyed about the provision of a nurturing and constructive environment for a child from 1 year through 17 years of age.

knowledge: personal safety, a nursing outcome from the Nursing Outcomes Classification (NOC) defined as the extent of understanding conveyed about the prevention of unintentional injuries.

knowledge: postpartum maternal health, a nursing outcome from the Nursing Outcomes Classification (NOC) defined as the extent of understanding conveyed about maternal health in the period following the birth of an infant.

knowledge: preconception maternal health, a nursing outcome from the Nursing Outcomes Classification (NOC) defined as the extent of understanding conveyed about maternal health prior to conception to ensure a healthy pregnancy.

knowledge: pregnancy, a nursing outcome from the Nursing Outcomes Classification (NOC) defined as the extent of understanding conveyed about promotion of a healthy pregnancy and prevention of complications.

knowledge: pregnancy & postpartum sexual functioning, a nursing outcome from the Nursing Outcomes Classification (NOC) defined as the extent of understanding conveyed about sexual function during pregnancy and postpartum.

knowledge: prescribed activity, a nursing outcome from the Nursing Outcomes Classification (NOC) defined as the extent of understanding conveyed about prescribed activity and exercise.

knowledge: preterm infant care, a nursing outcome from the Nursing Outcomes Classification (NOC) defined as the extent of understanding conveyed about the care of a premature infant born 24 to 37 weeks (term) gestation.

knowledge: sexual functioning, a nursing outcome from the Nursing Outcomes Classification (NOC) defined as the extent of understanding conveyed about sexual development and responsible sexual practices.

knowledge: substance use control, a nursing outcome from the Nursing Outcomes Classification (NOC) defined as the extent of understanding conveyed about controlling the use of addictive drugs, toxic chemicals, tobacco, or alcohol.

knowledge: treatment procedure, a nursing outcome from the Nursing Outcomes Classification (NOC) defined as the extent of understanding conveyed about a procedure required as part of a treatment regimen.

knowledge: treatment regimen, a nursing outcome from the Nursing Outcomes Classification (NOC) defined as the extent of understanding conveyed about a specific treatment regimen.

knowledge: weight management, a nursing outcome from the Nursing Outcomes Classification (NOC) defined as the extent of understanding conveyed about the promotion and maintenance of optimal body weight and fat percentage congruent with height, frame, gender, and age.

knuckle /nuk'əl/, the dorsal aspect of any interphalangeal joint, but especially of the metacarpophalangeal joints of the flexed fingers. By extension the term is sometimes applied to any anatomic structure of similar appearance, such as an extruded loop of intestine in a hernia.

Kocher's forceps /kō'kərz/ [Emil T. Kocher, Swiss surgeon, 1841–1917], a kind of surgical forceps that has notched jaws, interlocking teeth, and thick curved or straight powerful handles.

Koch's bacillus /kōks/ [Robert Koch, German bacteriologist, 1843–1910; L, *bacillum,* small rod], the *Mycobacterium tuberculosis* microorganism.

Koch's phenomenon [Robert Koch; Gk, *phainomenon,* anything seen], a tuberculin reaction that occurs when a culture of tubercle bacilli is injected into the skin of subjects already infected with the disease.

Koch's postulates [Robert Koch; L, *postulare,* to demand], the prerequisites for experimentally establishing that a specific microorganism causes a particular disease. The following conditions must be met: (1) the microorganism must be observed in all cases of the disease; (2) the microorganism must be isolated and grown in pure culture; (3) microorganisms from the pure culture, when inoculated into a susceptible animal, must reproduce the disease; and (4) the microorganism must be observed in and recovered from the experimentally diseased animal.

Koebner phenomenon /kōb′nər/ [Heinrich Koebner, Polish dermatologist, 1838–1904; Gk, *phainomenon,* something observed], the development of isomorphic lesions at the site of an injury, occurring in psoriasis, lichen nitidus, lichen planus, and verruca plana.

KOH, chemical formula for **potassium hydroxide.**

koilonychia /koi′lōnik′ē·ə/ [Gk, *koilos,* hollow, *onyx,* nail], a condition in which nails are thin and concave from side to side.

Kolcaba, Katharine, a nursing theorist who developed the Theory of Comfort to help nurses design interventions to increase the physical, psychospiritual, environmental, and social comfort of the patient.

Konakion, a trademark for a vitamin K formulation (phytonadione).

Kopan's needle /kō′pənz/, a long biopsy needle used to locate the position of a breast tumor on x-ray film.

Koplik's spots /kop′liks/ [Henry Koplik, American pediatrician, 1858–1927], small red spots with bluish-white centers on the lingual and buccal mucosa, characteristic of measles. The rash of measles usually erupts a day or two after the appearance of Koplik's spots.

Korányi's sign /kôr′ənyēz/ [Friedrich von Korányi, Hungarian physician, 1828–1913; L, *signum*], a paravertebral area of dullness found posteriorly on the side opposite a pleural effusion.

Korean hand acupuncture, a system of acupuncture in which the hand is considered to be a representation of the entire body, and stimulation of specific points on the hand is used to obtain effects in distant areas of the body.

Korotkoff sounds /kôrot′kôf/ [Nicolai Korotkoff, Russian physician, 1874–1920], sounds heard during the taking of a BP reading with a sphygmomanometer and stethoscope. As air is released from the cuff, pressure on the artery is reduced, and the blood is heard pulsing through the vessel.

Korsakoff's psychosis /kôr′səkôfs/ [Sergei S. Korsakoff, Russian psychiatrist, 1854–1900], a form of amnesia often seen in chronic alcoholics that is characterized by a loss of short-term memory and an inability to learn new skills.

kosher [Heb, *kasher,* fit or proper], pertaining to the preparation and serving of foods according to Jewish dietary laws (e.g., keeping dairy and meat separate in cooking and ingesting). Kosher foods include common fruits, vegetables, and cereals, as well as tea and coffee. Foods that are not kosher include pork, birds of prey, and seafood that lacks fins and scales.

Kostmann's syndrome /kost′mahnz/, infantile genetic agranulocytosis.

Kr, symbol for the element **krypton.**

K-ras gene, a type of oncogene.

Kraske position /kras′kə/ [Paul Kraske, Swiss surgeon, 1851–1930], an anatomic position in which the patient is prone, with hips flexed and elevated, head and feet down. The position is used for renal surgery.

kraurosis /krôrō′sis/ [Gk, *krauros,* dry, *osis,* condition], a thickening and shriveling of the mucous membranes, particularly the female genitalia.

kraurosis vulvae, a skin disease of aged women characterized by dryness, itching, and atrophy of the external genitalia.

Krause's corpuscles [Wilhelm J.F. Krause, German anatomist, 1833–1910; L, *corpusculum,* little body], any of a number of sensory end organs in the conjunctiva of the eye; mucous membranes of the lips and tongue; epineurium of nerve trunks, the penis, and the clitoris; and synovial membranes of certain joints. Krause's corpuscles are tiny cylindric oval bodies. They contain a soft, semifluid core in which the axon terminates either in a bulbous extremity or in a coiled mass.

Krukenberg's tumor /krōō′kənbərgz/ [Friedrich E. Krukenberg, German pathologist, 1871–1946], a neoplasm of the ovary that is a metastasis of a GI malignancy, usually stomach cancer.

krypton (Kr) /krip′ton/, a generally inert rare gaseous element present in air. Its atomic number is 36, and its atomic mass is 83.80.

KS, ks, abbreviation for **Kaposi's sarcoma.**

KUB, abbreviation for *kidney, ureter, and bladder;* a term used in a radiographic examination to determine the location, size, shape, and malformation of the kidneys, ureters, and bladder.

Kuchendorf method /kōō′kəndôrf/, in radiology, a technique for positioning a patient for radiographic examination of the patella. The patella is placed against the image receptor and is moved laterally to reduce superimposition.

kudzu, a herb used to reduce alcohol cravings and to treat alcohol hangovers and menopausal symptoms. Its efficacy is unproven.

Kufs' disease /koofs/ [H. Kufs, German psychiatrist, 1871–1955], an adult form of hereditary cerebral sphingolipidosis (amaurotic familial idiocy), characterized by cerebromacular degeneration, hypertonicity, and progressive spastic paralysis.

Kümmell's disease /kim'əlz/ [Hermann Kümmell, German surgeon, 1852–1937; L, *dis;* Fr, *aise,* ease], a set of symptoms that develop after a compression fracture of the vertebrae with spinal injury. They include spinal pain, intercostal neuralgia, kyphosis, and weakness in the legs.

kundalini yoga, a style of yoga whose purpose is controlled release of latent kundalini energy.

kunecatechins, a topical keratolytic used to treat external genital and perianal warts.

Küntscher nail /kʌoon'chər, kin'chər/ [Gerhard Küntscher, German surgeon, 1902–1972; AS, *naegel*], a stainless steel nail used in orthopedic surgery for the fixation of fractures of the long bones, especially the femur.

Kupffer cells /koop'fərz/ [Karl W. von Kupffer, German anatomist, 1829–1902], specialized cells of the reticuloendothelial system lining the sinusoids of the liver. Kupffer cells filter bacteria and other small foreign proteins out of the blood.

kurtosis /kerto'sis/, the degree of peakedness or flatness of a probability distribution, relative to the normal distribution with the same variance.

kuru /koo'roo/ [New Guinea, trembling with fear], a slow, progressive, fatal infection of the CNS that was endemic to natives of the New Guinea highlands. Disease was transmitted by ritual cannibalism of brain tissue during funeral rites. No new cases have been recorded since cessation of the cannibalism. This disease is a model for prion diseases such as BSE and variant CJD.

Kussmaul breathing /koos'moul/ [Adolf Kussmaul, German physician, 1822–1902; AS, *braeth*], abnormally deep, very rapid sighing respirations characteristic of diabetic ketoacidosis.

Kussmaul's coma [Adolf Kussmaul; Gk, *koma,* deep sleep], a diabetic coma characterized by acidosis and deep breathing or extreme hyperpnea.

Kussmaul's sign [Adolf Kussmaul; L, *signum,* mark], **1.** a paradoxic rise in venous pressure with distension of the jugular veins during inspiration, as seen

in constrictive pericarditis or mediastinal tumor. **2.** conditions of convulsions and coma associated with a GI disorder caused by absorption of a toxic substance.

kV, abbreviation for **kilovolt.**

Kveim reaction [Morten A. Kveim, Norwegian physician, 1892–1966; L, *re,* again, *agere,* to act], a reaction, used in a diagnostic test for sarcoidosis, to an intradermal injection of antigen derived from a lymph node known to be sarcoid.

kVp, abbreviation for **kilovolt peak.**

kVp test cassette, in radiology, a light-proof box containing a copper filter, a series of stepwedges, and an optical attenuator, used to test the accuracy of kVp settings for peak electrical potential across an x-ray tube.

kwashiorkor /kwä'shē·ôr'kôr/ [Afr], a malnutrition disease, primarily of children, caused by severe protein deficiency that usually occurs when the child is weaned from the breast. Symptoms are retarded growth, changes in skin and hair pigmentation, diarrhea, loss of appetite, nervous irritability, lethargy, edema, anemia, fatty degeneration of the liver, necrosis, dermatoses, and fibrosis, often accompanied by infection and multivitamin deficiencies.

Kwell, a trademark for a pediculicide and scabicide (gamma benzene hexachloride).

Kyasanur Forest disease, a flavovirus infection transmitted by the bite of a tick that is harbored by shrews and other forest animals in western tropical India. Characteristics of the infection include fever, headache, muscle ache, cough, abdominal and eye pain, and photophobia.

kymography /kēmog'rəfē/ [Gk, *kyma,* wave, *graphein,* to record], a technique for graphically recording motions of body organs, such as the heart and the blood vessels.

kyphos /kī'fəs/ [Gk, *kyphos,* hunchbacked], the exaggeration or angulation from the normal position of the thoracic vertebral column that is associated with kyphosis.

kyphoscoliosis /kī'fōskō'lē·ō'sis/ [Gk, *kyphos,* hunchbacked, *skolios,* curved, *osis,* condition], an abnormal condition characterized by an anteroposterior and a lateral curvature of the spine.—**kyphoscoliotic,** *adj.*

kyphosis /kīfō'sis/ [Gk, *kyphos,* hunchbacked], an abnormal condition of the vertebral column, characterized by increased convexity in the curvature of the thoracic spine as viewed from the side. It may be caused by rickets or TB of the spine.—**kyphotic,** *adj.*

K

L, 1. symbol for *kinetic potential*. 2. abbreviation for **Lactobacillus**. 3. abbreviation for **lambert**. 4. abbreviation for *Latin*. 5. abbreviation for **liter**. 6. abbreviation for **lung**.

L&A, abbreviation for reaction of the pupil to *light and accommodation*.

La, symbol for the element **lanthanum**.

LA, abbreviation for **left atrium**.

lab, abbreviation for **laboratory**.

label [ME, band], 1. a substance with a special affinity for an organ, tissue, cell, or microorganism in which it may become deposited and fixed. 2. an atom or molecule attached to either a ligand or binding protein and capable of generating a signal for monitoring in the binding reaction. 3. to deposit and fix a substance, tissue, cell, or microorganism. 4. to attach a radioisotope to a compound for the purpose of tracing it during a physiologic action in the body.

labeled compound, a chemical substance in which part of the molecules are labeled with a radionuclide or isotope so that observations of the radioactivity or isotopic composition make it possible to follow the compound or its fragments through physical, chemical, or biologic processes.

labeling, 1. the providing of information on a drug, food, device, or cosmetic to the purchaser or user. Regulations for labeling are provided by the Food and Drug Administration. The label must contain directions for use, unless such directions are exempted by regulation, as well as warnings or contraindications. 2. the assignment of a word or term to a form of behavior. 3. the act of classifying a patient according to a diagnostic category. Labeling can be misleading because not all patients conform to defined characteristics of standard diagnostic categories.

la belle indifference /lä bel indifäräNs'/ [Fr, nice indifference], an air of unconcern displayed by some patients toward their physical symptoms. It is believed the physical symptoms may relieve anxiety and result in secondary gains in the form of sympathy and attention given by others.

labetalol hydrochloride /ləbet'əlol/, an antihypertensive drug with beta and alpha blocking properties, prescribed for the treatment of moderate to severe hypertension.

labia /lā'bē·ə/ *sing*. **labium** [L, lip], 1. the lips. 2. the fleshy liplike edges of an organ or tissue. 3. the folds of skin at the opening of the vagina.—**labial,** *adj*.

labial arch wire, an arch wire of high tensile strength whose arms come through the embrasure between the canine and lateral incisors in the maxillary arch, and between the canines and first premolar in the mandibular arch. It is used primarily for moving teeth in the lingual direction and for retruding the anterior teeth and closing spaces.

labial bar /lā'bē·əl/, a bar that is installed labially or buccally to the dental arch and connects bilateral parts of a mandibular removable partial denture.

labial flange, the part of a denture that occupies the outer vestibule of the mouth.

labial glands [L, *labium,* lip, *glans,* acorn], small mucous or serous glands embedded in the lips.

labial notch, a depression in the border of a denture that accommodates the labial frenum.

labial vestibule, that portion of the vestibule of the mouth that lies between the lips and the teeth and gingivae or residual alveolar ridges.

labia majora, *sing*. **labium majus** /mā'jəs/, two long lips of skin, one on each side of the vaginal orifice, outside the labia minora. They extend from the anterior labial commissure to the posterior labial commissure and form the lateral boundaries of the pudendal cleft.

labia minora /minôr'ə/, *sing*. **labium minus** /mē'nəs/, two thin folds of skin between the labia majora, extending from the clitoris backward on both sides of the vaginal orifice, ending between it and the labia majora.

labile /lā'bil/ [L, *labilis,* slipping], 1. unstable; characterized by a tendency to change or be altered or modified. 2. in psychiatry, characterized by rapidly shifting or changing emotions, as in bipolar disorder and certain types of schizophrenia; emotionally unstable.—**lability,** *n*.

labiodental /lā'bē·ōden'təl/ [L, *labium,* lip, *dens,* tooth], 1. pertaining to the labial, or lip-facing, surfaces of the 12 anterior teeth. 2. pertaining to the sounds of speech that require a special coordination of teeth and lips.

labiolingual fixed orthodontic appliance /lā′bē·ōling′-gwəl/ [L, *labium,* lip, *lingua,* tongue], an appliance for correcting or improving malocclusion that is anchored to the maxillary and mandibular first permanent molars. The appliance has labial arches that fit into horizontal buccal tubes attached to anchor bands and lingual arches that are fastened to the lingual side of the anchor bands.

labioversion /lā′bē·ōver′zhən/ [L, *labium,* lip, *vertere,* to turn], displacement of a tooth labially from the line of occlusion.

labor [L, work], the time and the processes that occur during parturition from the beginning of cervical dilation to the delivery of the placenta.

laboratory (lab) /lab′ərətôr′e/ [L, *laborare,* to labor], **1.** a facility, room, building, or part of a building in which scientific research, experimentation, testing, or other investigative activities are carried out. **2.** pertaining to a laboratory.

laboratory data interpretation, a nursing intervention from the Nursing Interventions Classification (NIC) defined as critical analysis of patient laboratory data in order to assist with clinical decision making.

laboratory diagnosis, a diagnosis arrived at after study of secretions, excretions, or tissue through chemical, microscopic, or bacteriologic means or by biopsy.

laboratory error, any error made by the personnel in a clinical laboratory in performing a test, interpreting data, or reporting or recording the results. The general procedure is to repeat the test when an abnormal result is found.

laboratory medicine, the branch of medicine in which specimens of tissue, fluid, or other body substance are examined outside of the person, usually in the laboratory. Some fields of laboratory medicine are chemistry, cytology, hematology, histology, and pathology.

Laboratory Response Network (LRN), a network of federal, state, and local laboratories, established in 1999 by the Centers for Disease Control and Prevention, whose purpose is to provide the laboratory infrastructure and capacity to respond to biologic and chemical terrorism and other public health emergencies.

laboratory test, a procedure, usually conducted in a laboratory, that is intended to detect, identify, or quantify one or more significant substances, evaluate organ functions, or establish the nature of a condition or disease.

labor coach, a person who assists a woman in labor and delivery by closely attending to her emotional needs and encouraging her to use properly the breathing patterns, concentration techniques, body positions, and massage techniques that were taught in a program of psychophysical preparation for childbirth. The task of a labor coach is to decrease or eliminate the use of analgesia or anesthesia.

labored breathing, abnormal respiration characterized by evidence of increased effort, including the use of accessory muscles of respiration in the chest wall, stridor, grunting, or nasal flaring.

labor induction, a nursing intervention from the Nursing Interventions Classification (NIC) defined as initiation or augmentation of labor by mechanical or pharmacological methods.

labor pains [L, *labor,* work, *poena,* penalty], pain associated with contraction of the uterus in labor.

labor suppression, a nursing intervention from the Nursing Interventions Classification (NIC) defined as controlling uterine contractions prior to 37 weeks of gestation to prevent preterm birth.

labyrinthectomy /lab′ərinthek′təmē/, the surgical excision of the aural labyrinth.

labyrinthine /lab′ərin′thin/ [Gk, *labyrinthos,* maze], pertaining to or resembling a labyrinth or maze, such as the structure of the inner ear.

labyrinthine righting, one of the five basic neuromuscular reactions involved in a change of body positions. The change stimulates cells in the semicircular canals of the inner ear, causing neck muscles to respond by automatically adjusting the head to the new position.

labyrinthitis /lab′ərinthī′tis/ [Gk, *labyrinthos,* maze, *itis*], inflammation or dysfunction of the labyrinthine canals of the inner ear, resulting in vertigo.

laceration /las′ərā′shən/ [L, *lacerare,* to tear], **1.** the act of tearing or slashing. **2.** a torn, jagged wound.—**lacerate,** *v.,* **lacerated,** *adj.*

laceration of cervix [L, *lacerare,* to tear, *cervix,* neck], a wound or irregular tear of the cervix uteri during childbirth.

laceration of the perineum [L, *lacerare,* to tear; Gk, *perineos*], a wound or irregular tear of the perineal tissues during childbirth.

lacertus /ləser′təs/ [L, lizard, because of a fancied resemblance], a general term for certain fibrous attachments of muscles.

lacrimal /lak′riməl/ [L, *lacrima,* tear], pertaining to tears.

lacrimal apparatus, a network of structures of the eye that secrete tears and drain them from the surface of the eyeball. These parts include the lacrimal glands, lacrimal ducts, lacrimal canals, lacrimal sacs, and nasolacrimal ducts.

lacrimal artery, an artery arising from the ophthalmic artery on the lateral side of the optic nerve that supplies the lacrimal gland, muscles, the anterior ciliary branch to the eyeball, and the lateral sides of the eyelid.

lacrimal bone, one of the smallest and most fragile bones of the face, located at the anterior part of the medial wall of the orbit. It unites with the maxilla to form the groove for the lacrimal sac.

lacrimal caruncle, the small, reddish, fleshy protuberance that fills the triangular space between the medial margins of the upper and lower eyelids.

lacrimal duct, one of a pair of channels through which tears pass from the lacrimal lake to the lacrimal sac of each eye.

lacrimal fold [L, *lacrima,* tear; AS，*fealdan*], a valvelike fold of mucous membrane at the lower part of the nasolacrimal duct.

lacrimal gland, one of a pair of glands situated superiorly and laterally to the eye bulb in the lacrimal fossa of the frontal bone. The watery secretion from the gland consists of the tears, slightly alkaline and saline, that moisten the conjunctiva.

lacrimal groove, a groove formed by the lacrimal bone and the frontal process of the maxilla that contains the lacrimal sac.

lacrimal lake, an accumulation of fluid secreted by the lacrimal gland. It is drained by the lacrimal canaliculi.

lacrimal papilla, the small conic elevation on the medial margin of each eyelid, supporting an apex pierced by the punctum lacrimale through which tears emerge to moisten the conjunctiva.

lacrimal punctum, an opening through which fluid enters each lacrimal canaliculum.

lacrimal reflex [L, *lacrima,* tear, *reflectere,* to bend back], a release of tears in response to stimulation or irritation of the cornea or conjunctiva.

lacrimal sac, the upper end of each of the two nasolacrimal ducts. Each sac is lodged in a deep groove formed by the lacrimal bone and the frontal process of the maxilla. The lacrimal sacs fill with tears secreted by the lacrimal glands and conveyed through the lacrimal ducts.

lacrimation /lak′rimā′shən/, **1.** the normal continuous secretion of tears by the lacrimal glands. **2.** an excessive amount of tear production, as in crying or weeping.

lacrimator /lak′rimā′tər/, an agent that stimulates the secretion of tears.

lacrimotomy /lak′rimot′əmē/, a surgical incision in the lacrimal gland.

La Crosse encephalitis, encephalitis caused by the La Crosse virus, transmitted by *Aedes triseriatus,* seen primarily in children, chiefly in the Midwestern United States.

lactalbumin /lak′talbyoo͞o′min/ [L, *lac,* milk, *albus,* white], a simple, highly nutritious protein found in milk.

lactam /lak′təm/, a cyclic amide created by the elimination of a molecule of water from aminocarboxylic acid.

lactase /lak′tās/ [L, *lac*; Fr, *diastase,* enzyme], an enzyme that catalyzes the hydrolysis of lactose to glucose and galactose.

lactase deficiency, an inherited abnormality in which the amount of the digestive enzyme lactase is inadequate for the normal digestion of milk products, resulting in lactose intolerance (except for the bacterial breakdown of lactose in the large intestine).

lactate /lak′tāt/, an anion of lactic acid.

lactate dehydrogenase (LDH), an enzyme that is found in the cytoplasm of almost all body tissues, where its main function is to catalyze the oxidation of L-lactate to pyruvate. It is assayed as a measure of anaerobic carbohydrate metabolism and as one of several serum indicators of MI and muscular dystrophies.

lactate dehydrogenase (LDH) test, a blood test used to detect levels of lactate dehydrogenase, which is widely distributed throughout the body. Disease or injury to body tissues such as the heart, liver, RBCs, kidneys, skeletal muscles, brain, and lungs will result in higher-than-normal blood levels.

lactation /laktā′shən/ [L, *lac,* milk, *atio,* process], the process of synthesis and secretion of milk from the breasts in the nourishment of an infant or child.

lactation consultant, a health care professional, often with advanced certification, who provides education and management related to breastfeeding.

lactation counseling, a nursing intervention from the Nursing Interventions Classification (NIC) defined as use of an interactive helping process to assist in maintenance of successful breastfeeding.

lactation suppression, a nursing intervention from the Nursing Interventions Classification (NIC) defined as facilitating the cessation of milk production and minimizing breast engorgement after giving birth.

lacteal /lak′tē·əl/, referring to the tiny vessels in the villi of the wall of the small intestine through which chylomicrons are absorbed and released into the lymphatic system.

lacteal fistula, an abnormal passage opening into a lacteal duct.

lacteal vessel, one of the many central intestinal capillaries in the villi of the small intestine. They open into the lymphatic vessels in the submucosa. The capillary passes chyle to the lymph circulation via the thoracic duct to the blood vascular system.

lactic /lak′tik/ [L, *lac* + *icus,* like], referring to milk and milk products.

lactic acid, a three-carbon organic acid produced by anaerobic respiration. L-Lactic acid in muscle and blood is a product of glucose and glycogen metabolism; D-lactic acid is produced by the fermentation of dextrose by a species of micrococcus; a mixture of both D- and L-isomers is found in the stomach, in sour milk, and in certain foods prepared by bacterial fermentation such as sauerkraut.

lactic acid fermentation, 1. the anaerobic production of lactic acid from glucose. **2.** the souring of milk.

lactic acidosis, a disorder characterized by an accumulation of lactic acid in the blood, resulting in a lowered pH in muscle and serum.

lactic acid test, a blood test that measures lactate levels, which are a fairly sensitive and reliable indicator of tissue hypoxia.

lactiferous /laktif′ərəs/ [L, *lac* + *ferre,* to carry], pertaining to a structure that produces or conveys milk, such as the tubules of the breasts.

lactiferous duct, one of many channels that carry milk from the lobes of each breast to the nipple.

lactiferous glands [L, *lac,* milk, *ferre,* to carry, *glans,* acorn], glands that secrete or convey milk.

Lactinex, a trademark for a GI, fixed-combination drug containing *Lactobacillus acidophilus* and *Lactobacillus bulgaricus,* used to reestablish normal GI flora after antibiotic therapy.

lactitol /lak′t-tol/, a disaccharide analogue of lactulose, used as a sweetener. It is also a laxative and is used to treat constipation.

Lactobacillus **(L)** /lak′tōbəsil′əs/ [L, *lac* + *bacillum,* small rod], any one of a group of nonpathogenic gram-positive rod-shaped bacteria that produce lactic acid from carbohydrates.

Lactobacillus acidophilus [L, *lac,* milk, *bacillum,* small rod, *acidus,* sour; Gk, *philein,* to love], a bacterium present in the intestinal tract and vagina, as well as in milk and dairy products. The strain is used to manufacture a fermented milk product. Generally considered to be beneficial because it produces vitamin K, lactase, and other antimicrobial substances when ingested.

Lactobacillus bulgaricus, a genus of bacteria used in the production of yogurt.

lactoferrin /lak′tō·fer′in/, an iron-binding protein present in neutrophil granules.

lactoferrin assay, a test of a fecal sample to detect inflammatory WBCs in the intestinal tract. It is used to help diagnose bacterial enteritis, acute Crohn's disease, and acute ulcerative colitis.

lactogen /lak′təjən/ [L, *lac*; Gk, *genein,* to produce], a drug or other substance that enhances the production and secretion of milk.—**lactogenic,** *adj.*

lacto-ovo-vegetarian /lak′tō ōv′ō vej′ əter′ē·ən/, a person whose diet consists primarily of foods of vegetable origin but also includes some animal products such as eggs *(ovo),* milk, and cheese *(lacto)* but no meat, fish, or poultry.

lactoperoxidase /-pərok′sidās/, an enzyme found in milk and saliva. It is believed to inhibit a number of microorganisms, functioning in a nonspecific immunity role.

lactose /lak′tos/ [L, *lac*; Gk, *glykys,* sweet], a disaccharide found in the milk of all mammals. On hydrolysis, lactose yields the monosaccharides glucose and galactose.

lactose intolerance, a sensitivity disorder resulting in the inability to digest lactose from milk products because of an inadequate production of or defect in the enzyme lactase. Symptoms of the disorder are bloating, flatus, nausea, diarrhea, and abdominal cramps.

lactose tolerance test, a blood test performed to detect lactose intolerance.

lactosuria /lak′təsŏŏr′ē·ə/ [L, *lac*; Gk, *glykys,* sweet, *ouron,* urine], the presence of lactose in the urine, a condition that may occur in late pregnancy or during lactation.

lactotherapy /-ther′əpē/ [L, *lac,* milk; Gk, *therapeia,* treatment], any treatment that depends on a diet consisting exclusively or almost exclusively of milk.

lactotoxin /-tok′sin/, any toxic base occurring in milk as a result of decomposition of its proteins.

lactotroph /lak′totrōf′/, a type of acidophil in the adenohypophysis that secretes prolactin.

lactovegetarian /-vej′əter′ē·ən/, one whose diet consists of milk and milk products *(lacto)* in addition to foods of vegetable origin but does not include eggs, meat, fish, or poultry.

lactulose /lak′tyəlōs/, a nonabsorbable synthetic disaccharide, 4-0-beta-D-galactopyranosyl-D-fructose, $C_{12}H_{22}O_{11}$. It is hydrolyzed in the colon by bacteria primarily to lactic acid. It is used as a cathartic in chronic constipation and in the treatment of hepatic coma.

lacuna /ləkyōō′nə/ *pl.* **lacunae** [L, pit], **1.** a hollow within a structure, especially a bony tissue, in which lie osteoblasts. **2.** a gap, as in the field of vision.

lacunar /lakyōō′nər/ [L, *lacuna,* pit], pertaining to or characterized by the presence of pits, depressions, hollows, or spaces.

lacunar ligament, a crescent-shaped extension of fibers at the medial end of the inguinal ligament that passes backward to attach to the pecten pubis on the superior ramus of the pubic bone.

lacunar state, a pseudobulbar disorder characterized by the appearance of small, smooth-walled cavities in the brain tissue. The condition usually follows a series of small strokes.

lacus lacrimalis /lā′kəs lak′rimā′ləs/ [L, *lacus,* lake, *lacrimalis,* tears], a triangular space separating the medial ends of the upper and the lower eyelids at the inner canthus where the tears collect.

LAD, 1. abbreviation for *left anterior descending.* **2.** abbreviation for **leukocyte adhesion deficiency.**

Ladd's bands, a series of peritoneal folds in patients in whom the cecum ends up in the midabdomen. These folds extend to the right undersurface of the liver and compress the duodenum.

LADME /lad′mē/, an abbreviation for the time course of drug distribution, representing the terms *liberation, absorption, distribution, metabolism,* and *elimination.*

Laënnec's catarrh /lā′əneks′/ [René T.H. Laënnec, French physician, 1781–1826; Gk, *kata,* down, *rhoia,* flow], a form of bronchial asthma characterized by the expectoration of small, viscous, beadlike bodies of sputum. These bodies, called Laënnec's pearls, are formed in the bronchioles.

Laënnec's cirrhosis [René T.H. Laënnec; Gk, *kirrhos,* yellow-orange, *osis,* condition], a fibrotic form of cirrhosis precipitated by alcohol abuse.

Laetrile /lā′ətril/, a substance composed primarily of amygdalin, a cyanogenic glycoside derived from apricot pits. Laetrile has been offered as a cancer medication despite clinical studies by the National Cancer Institute that failed to show benefits from its use. It is not approved by the Food and Drug Administration (FDA).

laf, abbreviation for **laminar air flow.**

lag, the afterglow of an image on a screen or television camera, caused by phosphorescence.

lag of accommodation, the dioptric value in which the accommodative stimulus exceeds the accommodative response.

lagophthalmos /lag′əfthal′məs/ [Gk, *lagos,* hare, *ophthalmos,* eye], an abnormal condition in which an eye may not be fully closed because of a neurologic, muscular, or mechanical disorder.

lag phase [Dan, *lakke,* go slowly; Gk, *phasis,* appearance], a time span during which bacteria injected into a fresh medium have not begun to multiply, although they may enlarge.

laity /lā′itē/ [Gk, *laikos,* of the people], a nonprofessional segment of the population,

as viewed from the perspective of a member of a particular profession. A clergyman may regard a physician as a member of the laity and vice versa.

LAK, abbreviation for *lymphokine-activated killer.*

laked blood /lākt/ [Fr, *laque,* a deep red color], blood that is clear, red, and homogeneous because of hemolysis of the RBCs, as may occur in poisoning and severe extensive burns.

La Leche League International /lälech′ā/ [Sp, *la leche,* the milk], an organization that promotes breastfeeding and provides education about it.

lallation /lalā′shən/ [L, *lallare,* to babble], **1.** babbling, repetitive, unintelligible utterances, such as the babbling of an infant and the mumbled speech of schizophrenics, alcoholics, and the severely mentally retarded. **2.** a speech disorder characterized by a defective pronunciation of words containing the sound /l/ or by the use of the sound /l/ in place of the sound /r/.

lalophobia /lal′ōfō′bē-ə/ [Gk, *lalia,* speech, *phobos,* fear], a morbid dread of talking caused by fear and anxiety that one will stammer or stutter.

lamarckism /ləmärk′izəm/ [Jean B.P. de Lamarck, French naturalist, 1744–1829; Gk, *ismos,* practice], a theory postulating that organic evolution results from structural changes in plants and animals caused by adaptation to environmental conditions and that these acquired characteristics are transmitted to offspring.—**lamarckian,** *adj., n.*

Lamaze method /ləmäz′/ [Fernand Lamaze, French obstetrician, 1890–1957], a method of psychophysical preparation for childbirth developed in the 1950s. It requires classes, practice at home, and coaching during labor and delivery. The classes, given during pregnancy, teach the physiology of pregnancy and childbirth, exercises to develop strength in the abdominal muscles and control of isolated muscles of the vagina and perineum, and techniques of breathing and relaxation to promote control and relaxation during labor.

lambda /lam′də/, **1.** Λ, λ, the eleventh letter of the Greek alphabet. **2.** a posterior fontanel of the skull marking the point where the sagittal and lambdoidal sutures meet.

lambda chain, a type of light polypeptide chain found in immunoglobulin molecules.

lambda light chain, one of two kinds of smaller polypeptide chains present in an immunoglobulin molecule.

lambda wave, a low-voltage occipital wave recorded by electroencephalography during visual activity.

lambdoid /lam′doid/, having the shape of the Greek letter lambda.

lambdoidal suture /lamdoi'dəl/, the interdigitating connection between the occipital bone and the parietal bones of the skull.

lambert (L) /lom'bert, lam'bərt/ [J.H. Lambert, German physicist, 1728–1777], a unit of luminance or brightness of a perfectly diffusing surface, whether emitting or reflecting, equal to a total luminous flux of one lumen per square centimeter.

lamella /ləmel'ə/ pl. **lamellae** [L, small plate], **1.** a thin leaf or plate, as of bone. **2.** a medicated disk of glycerin and an alkaloid, for insertion under the eyelid, where it dissolves and is absorbed for local application.

lamellar /ləmel'ər/ [L, lamella, small plate], pertaining to or characterized by lamella.

lamellar exfoliation [L, lamella + ex, without, folium, leaf], a congenital skin disorder transmitted as an autosomal-recessive trait in which a parchmentlike scaly membrane that covers the infant peels off within 24 hours of birth. Complete healing or a progressively less severe process of reforming and shedding of the scales then occurs.

lameness /lām'nəs/ [ME, lama, to break], a condition of diminished function, particularly because of a foot or leg injury. The term may also be applied to a stiff or painful back that makes walking difficult.

Lamictal, a trademark for an anticonvulsant drug (lamotrigine).

lamina /lam'inə/ pl. **laminae** [L, thin plate], any thin, flat layer of membrane or other bulkier tissue. It may be structureless or part of a structure, as the laminae of the vertebral arch.

lamina densa, a layer of epithelial basal lamina that appears dark in electron micrographs.

lamina dura, 1. a sheet of compact alveolar bone that lies adjacent to the periodontal membrane, the lining of the tooth socket. **2.** a radiographic term used to identify the radiopaque lining of an alveolus.

lamina lucida, an electron-dense layer of the basal lamina lying between the lamina densa and the adjoining cell layer divided in the pulmonary alveolus and renal glomerulus into the internal and external laminae rarae.

lamin antibody /lam'in/, a type of immunoglobulin found in the serum of some patients with autoimmune diseases, including SLE.

lamina propria, a layer of connective tissue that lies just under the epithelium of a mucous membrane.

laminar air flow (laf) /lam'iner/ [L, lamina, plate; Gk, aer; AS, flowan], a system of circulating filtered air in parallel-flowing planes in hospitals or other health care facilities. The system reduces the risk of airborne contamination and exposure to chemical pollutants in surgical theaters, food preparation areas, hospital pharmacies, and laboratories.

lamina rara, in the renal glomerulus and pulmonary alveolus, one of the layers of lamina lucida surrounding the lamina densa. The lamina rara externa is on the epithelial side and the lamina rara interna is on the endothelial side.

Laminaria /lam'iner'ē·ə/ [L, lamina, plate], a type of seaweed that swells on absorption of water.

laminaria tent, a cone of dried seaweed that swells as it absorbs water and therefore is used to dilate the cervix nontraumatically in preparation for induced abortion or induced labor.

laminated thrombus /lam'inā'tid/, a blood clot composed of blood platelets, fibrin, clotting factors, and cellular elements arranged in layers, apparently formed at different times.

laminectomy /lam'inek'təmē/ [L, lamina; Gk, ektomē, excision], surgical removal of the bony arches of one or more vertebrae. It is performed to treat compression fractures, dislocations, herniated nucleus pulposus, and cord tumors and to stimulate the spinal cord. Spinal fusion with cages, rods, screws, and/or bone graft is used to stabilize the spine if several laminae are removed.—**laminectomize,** v.

laminin /lam'inin/, any of several large glycoproteins consisting of three polypeptide subunits and found in basement membranes. It is involved in neurite regeneration.

laminotomy /-ot'əmē/, the surgical division of the lamina of a vertebral arch.

lamivudine (3TC) /lämiv'udēn/, a nucleoside analog that inhibits reverse transcriptase and is used as an antiviral agent in treatment of hepatitis B infection and, in combination with zidovudine, in treatment of HIV infection and AIDS.

lamotrigine /lämo'trijēn/, an anticonvulsant drug prescribed as adjunct therapy in the treatment of partial seizures in epilepsy patients over the age of 16 and as an adjunct therapy in children less than 16 years of age with generalized seizures associated with Lennox-Gastaut syndrome. It is not approved for use in children less than 2 years of age.

lampbrush chromosome [Gk, lampas, torch; AS, bryst, bristle], an excessively large type of chromosome found in the oocytes of many animals. It has long,

L

threadlike, projecting loops, giving it a hairy, brushlike appearance.

lance [L, *lancea,* spear], to incise a furuncle or an abscess to release accumulated pus.

Lancefield's classification [Rebecca C. Lancefield, American bacteriologist, 1895–1981], a serologic classification of streptococci based on their antigenic characteristics.

lancet /lan′sit/ [L, *lancea,* lance], a short pointed blade used to obtain a drop of blood for a capillary sample.

lancinating /lan′sinā′ting/ [L, *lancea,* lance], sharply cutting or tearing, such as lancinating pain.

Landau-Kleffner syndrome /län′dou klef′nər/ [William M. Landau, American neurologist, 20th century; F.R. Kleffner, American neurologist, 20th century], an epileptic syndrome of childhood characterized by partial or generalized seizures, psychomotor abnormalities, and language regression that can progress to mutism. The EEG from bilateral temporal regions is abnormal.

Landau reflex /län′dou/, a normal response of infants when held in a horizontal prone position to maintain a convex arc with the head raised and the legs slightly flexed.

landmark /land′mark/ [AS *land* + *meark,* mark], a readily recognizable anatomic structure used as a point of reference in establishing the location of another structure or in determining certain measurements.

landmark position [AS, *land* + *meark,* mark; L, *positio*], the correct placement of the hands on the chest in CPR.

Langer-Giedion syndrome /lang′ər zhēdē·ôN′/ [Leonard O. Langer, Jr., American physician, b. 1928; A. Giedion, Swiss physician, 1888–1968], an inherited disorder characterized by mental retardation, microcephaly, multiple exostosis, characteristic facies with bulbous nose, sparse hair, cone shaped epiphyses, loose redundant skin, joint laxity, and other anomalies.

Langerhans' cells /lung′ərhuns, lang′ərhans/ [Paul Langerhans, German pathologist, 1847–1888], a stellate dendritic cell found mostly in the stratum spinosum of the epidermis. It is believed to have an immune function.

Langer's muscle /läng′ərz/ [Carl Ritter von Edenberg von Langer, Austrian anatomist, 1819–1887], muscular fibers from the insertion of the pectoralis major muscle over the bicipital groove to the insertion of the latissimus dorsi.

language /lang′gwij/ [L, *lingua,* tongue], a defined set of characters that, when used alone or in combinations, form a meaningful set of words and symbols that are used for communication.

language delay, the failure of language to develop at the expected age.

language disorder, a partial or complete disruption in the ability to understand and produce the conventional symbols or words that comprise one's native language.

lanolin /lan′əlin/ [L, *lana,* wool, *oleum,* oil], a fatlike substance from the wool of sheep. It contains about 25% water as a water-in-oil emulsion and is used as an ointment base and an emollient for the skin.

Lanoxin, a trademark for a cardiac glycoside (digoxin).

lanreotide, an antigrowth hormone used to treat acromegaly in patients having an inadequate response to other treatments.

lansoprazole, an antiulcer agent and proton pump inhibitor used to treat gastroesophageal reflux disease (GERD), severe erosive esophagitis, poorly responsive systemic GERD, and pathologic hypersecretory conditions (Zollinger-Ellison syndrome, systemic mastocytosis, multiple endocrine adenomas). It is also a potentially effective treatment for duodenal and gastric ulcers and for maintenance of healed duodenal ulcers.

lanthanum (La)[1] /lan′thənəm/ [Gk, *lanthanein,* to escape notice], a rare earth metallic element. Its atomic number is 57; its atomic mass is 138.91.

lanthanum[2], a phosphate binder used to treat end-stage renal disease.

lanuginous /lənoo̅′jinəs/ [L,*lanugo,*down], pertaining to lanugo.

lanugo /lanyoo̅′go/ [L, down], **1.** the soft, downy hair covering a normal fetus beginning in the fifth month of gestation and almost entirely shed by the ninth month. **2.** the fine, soft hair covering all parts of the body except palms, soles, and areas where other types of hair are normally found.

lanulous /lan′yoo̅ləs/ [L, *lana,* wool, *osus,* filled with], downy or covered with short, fine wooly hair, such as the skin of a fetus.

lap, abbreviation for **laparotomy.**

LAP, 1. abbreviation for *left atrial pressure.* **2.** abbreviation for **leukocyte alkaline phosphatase. 3.** abbreviation for **leucine aminopeptidase test.**

laparectomy /lap′ərek′təmē/, the surgical excision of tissue from the abdomen wall, usually performed to correct muscle laxity.

laparoenterostomy /lap′ərō·en′təros′təmē/ [Gk, *lapara,* loin, *enteron,* bowel, *stoma,* mouth], the surgical installation of a tube through an external opening in the abdomen to drain the bowel. A similar procedure may be used to supply nutrients to a patient with an upper digestive tract obstruction.

laparoenterotomy /lap′ərō·en′tərot′əmē/ [Gk, *lapara*, loin, *enteron*, bowel, *temnein*, to cut], a surgical incision in the intestine through the abdominal wall.

laparohysterectomy/-his′tərek′təmē/ [Gk, *lapara*, loin, *hystera*, womb, *ektomē*, excision], a hysterectomy performed by making an excision through the abdominal wall.

laparohystero-oophorectomy /-his′tərō-/, the surgical removal of the uterus and ovaries through a small incision in the abdominal wall.

laparohysterosalpingo-oophorectomy/-his′tərō′salping′gō-/, the surgical removal of the uterus, ovaries, and fallopian tubes through a small incision in the abdominal wall.

laparomyitis /-mī·ī′tis/, an inflammation of the abdominal or lumbar muscles.

laparosalpingo-oophorectomy /-salping′gō-/, the surgical removal of the ovaries and fallopian tubes through a small incision in the abdominal wall.

laparoscope /lap′ərəskōp′/ [Gk, *lapara*, loin, *skopein*, to look], a type of endoscope consisting of an illuminated tube with an optical system. It is inserted through the abdominal wall for examining the peritoneal cavity.—**laparoscopic,** *adj.,* **laparoscopy,** *n.*

laparoscopic-assisted vaginal hysteroscopy /-skop′ik/, a procedure for viewing the inner surface of the uterus with a specially designed endoscope inserted through the cervix.

laparoscopic biopsy, biopsy of the abdominal organs performed with instruments introduced through a laparoscope for the removal of tissue.

laparoscopic gastric banding (LGB), gastric banding performed through a laparoscope.

laparoscopic nephrectomy, a minimally invasive type of nephrectomy performed with laparoscopic techniques.

laparoscopic sterilization [Gk, *lapara,* loin, *skopein,* to view; L, *sterilis,* barren], the process of rendering a woman incapable of reproduction by inserting a specialized endoscope through a small incision in the abdominal wall through which clips are affixed to occlude the fallopian tubes or electrocoagulation and severance are performed.

laparoscopy /lap′əros′kəpē/, a technique to examine the abdominal cavity with a laparoscope through one or more small incisions in the abdominal wall, usually at the umbilicus.

laparotomy (lap) /lap′ərot′əmē/ [Gk, *lapara + temnein,* to cut], any surgical incision into the abdominal wall, usually performed under general or regional anesthesia, often on an exploratory basis. —**laparotomize,** *v.*

lapatinib, a miscellaneous antineoplastic used to treat advanced breast cancer in patients with tumors that overexpress HER2 protein and who have received previous chemotherapy.

lapboard [ME, *lappa + bord,* plank], a flat board placed over the lap to serve as a temporary desk or table.

lapis /lap′is/ [L, stone], any substance that does not easily volatilize, as lapis dentalis, or tooth tartar.

Laplace's law /läpläs′/ [Pierre S. de Laplace, French physicist, 1749–1827], a principle of physics that the tension on the wall of a sphere is the product of the pressure times the radius of the chamber and the tension is inversely related to the thickness of the wall.

laporotomy sponge, a radiopaque pad used as an absorbent and as a covering for the viscera.

large for gestational age (LGA) infant, an infant whose fetal growth was accelerated and whose size and weight at birth fall above the 90th percentile of appropriate for gestational age infants, whether delivered prematurely, at term, or later than term. Factors other than genetic influences that cause accelerated intrauterine growth include maternal DM and Beckwith's syndrome. A major problem is that preterm LGA infants, because of their size, are not recognized as high-risk neonates with immature organ system development.

large intestine [L, *largus,* abundant, *intestinum*], the part of the digestive tract comprising the cecum; appendix; ascending, transverse, descending, and sigmoid colons; and rectum.

lariat structure /ler′ē·ət/, a ring of intron segments that has been spliced out of a messenger RNA molecule by enzymes. Some introns form a long tail attached to the ring, giving the structure the appearance of a microscopic cowboy lariat.

Larmor frequency [Joseph Larmor, Irish physicist, 1857–1942], the frequency of the precession of a charged particle when its motion comes under the influence of an applied magnetic field and a central force.

Larodopa, a trademark for an antiparkinsonian agent (levodopa).

Laron dwarfism /läröN′/ [Zvi Laron, Israeli endocrinologist, b. 1927], an autosomal-recessive syndrome of skeletal growth retardation resulting from impaired ability to synthesize insulin-like growth factor I, usually because of growth hormone receptor defects.

laronidase, a rarely used miscellaneous drug used to treat mucopolysaccharidosis I.

L

Larsen's syndrome /lär'sənz/ [Loren Joseph Larsen, American orthopedic surgeon (1914–2001)], a rare genetic disorder characterized by cleft palate, flattened facies, multiple congenital dislocations, and foot deformities.

larva /lär'və/ *pl.* **larvae** [L, specter], the early immature form of an animal, which undergoes metamorphosis to an adult form. It is one of the growth stages for some insects; the state between the egg and the pupolarval stage is the feeding stage in the growth process. —**larval**, *adj.*

laryngeal artery, either of the two arteries, superior and inferior, that are responsible for the major blood supply to the larynx.

laryngeal cancer [Gk, *larynx*; L, *cancer, crab*], a malignant neoplastic disease characterized by a tumor arising from the epithelium of the structures of the larynx. Chronic alcoholism and heavy use of tobacco increase the risk of developing the cancer. Persistent hoarseness is usually the first sign. Advanced lesions may cause a sore throat, dyspnea, dysphagia, and cervical adenopathy.

laryngeal catheterization, the insertion of a catheter into the larynx for the purpose of removing secretions or introducing gases.

laryngeal inlet, the opening connecting the larynx and pharynx.

laryngeal mask airway, a device for maintaining a patent airway without tracheal intubation, consisting of a tube connected to an oval inflatable cuff that seals the larynx.

laryngeal polyp [Gk, *larynx* + *poly,* many, *pous,* foot], a polyp on the vocal cords that causes hoarseness, resulting from vocal abuse or smoking.

laryngeal prominence, the bulge at the front of the neck produced by the thyroid cartilage of the larynx.

laryngeal reflex [Gk, *larynx*; L, *reflectere,* to bend back], a cough reflex caused by irritation of the fauces and larynx.

laryngeal vertigo [Gk, *larynx*; L, *vertere,* to turn], a short episode of dizziness or unconsciousness after a paroxysmal attack of coughing or laryngeal spasm.

laryngeal web, a common congenital malformation of the larynx that may be thin and translucent or thicker and more fibrotic. It is spread between the vocal folds near the anterior commissure. It may cause hoarseness, aphonia, and other symptoms.

laryngectomy /ler'injek'təmē/ [Gk, *larynx* + *ektomē,* excision], surgical removal of the larynx performed to treat cancer of the larynx. In a partial laryngectomy only the vocal cords are removed. If the malignancy is extensive, the entire larynx is removed, along with the hyoid, epiglottis, false cords, true cords, cricoid cartilage,

and two or three rings of the trachea. The trachea is sutured to the skin of the neck, and the patient breathes through his or her neck. Speech loss is permanent after total laryngectomy.—**laryngectomize,** *v.*

laryngismus stridulus, a sudden laryngeal spasm with cyanosis and inhalation accompanied by a crowing sound, usually seen in children at night.

laryngitis /ler'injī'tis/ [Gk, *larynx* + *itis*], inflammation of the mucous membrane lining the larynx, accompanied by edema of the vocal cords with hoarseness or loss of voice, occurring as an acute disorder caused by a cold, by irritating fumes, by sudden temperature changes or as a chronic condition resulting from excessive use of the voice, heavy smoking, or exposure to irritating fumes.

laryngocele /ləring'gōsēl'/, an abnormal air-containing cavity connected to the laryngeal ventricle. It is caused by a protrusion of the mucous membrane of the ventricle and may displace and enlarge the false vocal cord, resulting in hoarseness and airway obstruction. Because a laryngocele is also a potential reservoir of infection, it is usually excised.

laryngologist /ler'ing·gol'əjist/, a physician who specializes in the diagnosis and treatment of disorders of the larynx.

laryngology /ler'ing·gol'əjē/ [Gk, *larynx* + *logos,* science], the branch of medicine that specializes in the causes and treatments of disorders of the larynx.

laryngopharyngeal reflux, a complication of gastroesophageal reflux caused by reflux from the esophagus into the pharynx, characterized by a variety of intermittent chronic symptoms, including hoarseness, cough, throat clearing, and dysphagia.

laryngopharyngitis /ləring'gōfer'injī'tis/ [Gk, *larynx* + *pharynx,* throat + *itis*], inflammation of the larynx and pharynx.

laryngopharyngography /lering'gōfer'ing·gog'rəfē/ [Gk, *larynx* + *pharynx* + *graphein,* to record], the radiographic examination of the larynx and pharynx.

laryngopharynx /lering'gōfer'ingks/ [Gk, *larynx* + *pharynx,* throat], one of the three regions of the throat, extending from the hyoid bone to the esophagus.—**laryngopharyngeal,** *adj.*

laryngoplastic phonosurgery, phonosurgery that restructures the cartilaginous framework of the larynx.

laryngoscope /ləring'gəskōp/, an endoscope for examining the larynx.

laryngoscopy /ler'ing·gos'kəpē/ [Gk, *larynx* + *skopein,* to view], the use of a laryngoscope to view the larynx.—**laryngoscopic,** *adj.*

laryngospasm /ləring′gōspaz′əm/ [Gk, *larynx* + *spasmos*, spasm], a spasmodic closure of the larynx.

laryngotomy /ler′ing·got′əmē/ [Gk, *larynx* + *temnein*, to cut], a surgical incision into the larynx through the cricovocal membrane. It is usually an emergency procedure that is performed when a standard tracheotomy cannot be done.

laryngotracheal tube, the embryonic endodermal tube that is split off from the primordium of the oropharynx and esophagus when the tracheoesophageal septum divides the cranial part of the foregut. It constitutes the primordium of the larynx, trachea, bronchi, and lungs.

laryngotracheitis /-trā′kē·ī′tis/, an inflammation of the larynx and trachea.

laryngotracheobronchitis (LTB) /lering′gō trā′kē·ō′brong- kī′tis/ [Gk, *larynx*; L, *trachea*; Gk, *bronchos*, windpipe, *itis*], an inflammation of the major respiratory passages, usually causing hoarseness, nonproductive cough, dyspnea, and, in severe cases, significant airway obstruction.

laryngotracheoesophageal cleft, a cleft between the larynx and the upper trachea resulting from incomplete separation of these structures during embryonic development, with respiratory manifestations including respiratory distress with feeding, flaccid aryepiglottic folds, chronic cough, and increased oral secretions. It is frequently associated with other congenital anomalies of the respiratory system or GI tract. Complications include failure to thrive and recurrent aspiration pneumonia.

laryngotracheotomy /-trā′kē·ot′əmē/, a surgical incision into the larynx and trachea.

larynx /ler′ingks/ [Gk], the organ of voice that is part of the upper air passage connecting the pharynx with the trachea. The larynx forms the caudal portion of the anterior wall of the pharynx and is lined with mucous membrane that is continuous with that of the pharynx and the trachea. It is composed of three single cartilages and three paired cartilages, all connected by ligaments and moved by various muscles. —**laryngeal,** *adj.*

LAS, abbreviation for **lymphadenopathy syndrome.**

laser /lā′zər/, abbreviation for *light amplification by stimulated emission of radiation,* a source of intense monochromatic radiation of the visible, ultraviolet, or infrared portions of the spectrum. Lasers are used in surgery to divide or cause adhesions or to destroy or fix tissue in place.

laser angioplasty, the opening of an occluded artery with laser energy delivered to the site through a fiberoptic probe.

laser bronchoscopy, bronchoscopy performed with the aid of a laser beam directed through fiberoptic equipment, used in the diagnosis and treatment of bronchial disorders, tracheobronchial tumors, and subglottic stenosis.

laser iridotomy, a procedure for the treatment of closed-angle glaucoma in which the patient has intermittent periods of increased intraocular pressure. The angle-closure mechanism is controlled by creating an opening in the iris. Specific techniques vary with the type of laser used.

laser pain management, the use of lasers to relieve pain. This treatment has been applied effectively to specific acupuncture points where there is no anatomic dysfunction at the base of the pain.

laser precautions, a nursing intervention from the Nursing Interventions Classification (NIC) defined as limiting the risk of laser-related injury to the patient.

laser prostatectomy, removal of the prostate after it has been exposed to a laser either by direct contact with vaporization or by an indirect system that causes coagulation necrosis.

laser trabeculoplasty, an application of argon or selective laser energy to the trabecular meshwork to increase aqueous outflow in the treatment of glaucoma. The procedure may be recommended when intraocular pressure increases despite administration of topical agents. The eye is anesthetized with a topical anesthetic. The trabecular network is viewed through an antireflective-coated four-mirror gonioprism. A power setting and exposure time are selected to blanch the anterior trabecular meshwork with laser energy without causing bubble formation. A potential complication is a temporary increase in intraocular pressure, which is treated with drugs. The effects of laser trabeculoplasty are not always long lasting.

LASIK /lā′sik/, acronym for *laser-assisted in situ keratomileusis,* a retractive surgery on the cornea in which the excimer laser and microkeratome are combined for correction of distance vision. The microkeratome is used to shave a thin slice and create a hinged flap in the cornea, the flap is reflected back, the exposed cornea is reshaped by the laser, and the flap is replaced, without sutures, to heal back into position.

Lasix, a trademark for a diuretic agent (furosemide).

Lassa fever /lä′sə/ [Lassa, Nigeria; L, *febris,* fever], a highly contagious disease of West Africa caused by an arenavirus. It is characterized by fever, pharyngitis, dysphagia, and ecchymoses. Pleural effusion, edema and renal involvement, mental disorientation, confusion, and death from cardiac failure often ensue. Stringent precautions are taken against the spread of infection.

last sacraments [ME, *laste*; L, *sacramentum*, solemn oath], a religious ceremony performed by a member of the clergy on behalf of a person about to die.

latanoprost /la·tan′ō·prost′/, an agent applied topically to the conjunctiva for treatment of open-angle glaucoma and ocular hypertension.

latchkey children, minors who are often at home alone because their parents are at work.

latency period /lā′tənse/ [L, *latere,* to be concealed; Gk, *peri* + *hodos,* way], **1.** the period between contact with a pathogen and development of symptoms. **2.** the time between stimulus and response.

latency stage [L, *latere,* to be concealed; Fr, *estage,* stage], in psychoanalysis, a period in psychosexual development occurring between early childhood and puberty when sexual motivation and expression are repressed or transferred, through sublimation, to the feelings and behavioral patterns expected as typical of the age.

latent /lā′tənt/ [L, *latere,* to be concealed], dormant; existing as a potential. For example, TB may be latent for extended periods of time and become active under certain conditions.

latent allergy, allergy that does not have overt symptoms but may be detected by tests.

latent energy [L, *latere,* to be concealed; Gk, *energeia*], the energy contained in an object as a result of its position in space, its internal structure, and stresses imposed on it.

latent heat [L, *latere,* to be concealed; AS, *haetu*], the heat absorbed by a substance when it changes from a solid to a liquid or from a liquid to a gas without an accompanying rise in temperature.

latent image, an invisible image produced in a film emulsion by x-rays or visible light that can be converted into a visible image by development.

latent learning [L, *latere,* to be concealed; ME, *lernen*], learning acquired unintentionally. It may remain in the subconscious, or be latent, until a need for the knowledge arises.

latent malaria [L, *latere,* to be concealed; It, *mal* + *aria,* bad air], a continuing infection without clinical symptoms, resulting from a balance established between the parasite and the body's immune system.

latent period, the interval between the time of exposure to an injurious dose of radiation and the response.

latent phase, the early stage of labor that is characterized by irregular, infrequent, and mild contractions and little or no dilation of the cervix or descent of the fetus.

latent syphilis [L, *latere,* to be concealed; Gk, *syn,* together, *philein,* to love], a stage of syphilis infection in which no clinical symptoms appear, although serologic tests indicate the presence of the syphilis spirochete. Latent syphilis occurs in two phases following secondary syphilis. The early phase occurs within 1 year of infection, and the late phase occurs after 1 year of infection. Late latent syphilis is noninfectious.

latent tetany [L, *latere,* to be concealed; Gk, *tetanos,* convulsive tension], a form of tetany that is elicited only by mechanical or electric stimuli.

late-phase hypersensitivity reaction, an inflammatory response in immunoglobulin E allergic diseases. It begins 2 to 4 hours after exposure to an antigen, peaks at 6 to 12 hours, and disappears after 24 hours.

lateral /lat′ərəl/ [L, *latus,* side], **1.** pertaining to the side. **2.** away from the midsagittal plane. **3.** farther from the midsagittal plane. **4.** to the right or left of the midsagittal plane. **5.** pertaining to a speech sound produced by passing air along one or both sides of the tongue, such as /l/.

lateral antebrachial cutaneous nerve, a continuation of the musculocutaneous nerve that innervates the skin over the radial side of the forearm and sometimes an area of skin of the back of the hand; its modality is sensory.

lateral aortic node, a lumbar lymph node in any of three clusters of nodes serving the pelvis and abdomen.

lateral aperture of the fourth ventricle, an opening between the end of each lateral recess of the fourth ventricle and the subarachnoid space.

lateral atlantoaxial joint, either of a pair of joints, one on each side of the body, formed by the inferior articular surface of the atlas and the superior surface of the axis.

lateral cerebral sulcus, a deep cleft marking the division of the temporal from the frontal and parietal lobes of the brain.

lateral condensation method, a technique for filling root canals, in which a preselected master gutta-percha cone is sealed into the apex of the root and other auxiliary gutta-percha cones are forced laterally and compacted with a spreader hand instrument until the canal is filled.

lateral corticospinal tract, a group of nerve fibers in the lateral funiculus of the spinal cord, originating in the cerebral cortex, that control voluntary movement of the body.

lateral cuneiform bone, one of the three cuneiform bones of the foot. It is located in the center of the front row of tarsal bones.

lateral decentering, in radiology, an error in positioning of the tube head or a focused grid, resulting in partial grid cutoff over the entire film.

lateral flexures of rectum, the three lateral bends in the rectum.

lateral geniculate body, one of two elevations of the lateral posterior thalamus receiving visual impulses from the retina via the optic nerves and tracts and relaying the impulses to the calcarine (visual) cortex.

lateral horn, a small hornlike projection of gray matter into the white matter of the spinal cord, located between the anterior and posterior horns or columns.

lateral humeral epicondylitis, inflammation of the tissue at the lower end of the humerus at the elbow joint, caused by the repetitive flexing of the wrist against resistance. It may result from athletic activity or manual manipulation of tools or other equipment.

lateral incisal guide angle, the inclination of the incisal guide of a dental articulator in the frontal plane.

lateralis, lateral, a term denoting a structure situated farther from the median plane of the body or the midline of an organ.

lateralization /lat′ərəl′īzā′shən/, the tendency for certain processes to be more highly developed on one side of the brain than the other, such as development of spatial and musical thoughts in the right hemisphere and verbal and logical processes in the left hemisphere in most persons.

lateral ligament of the ankle, one of the three ligaments on the lateral side of the ankle: the anterior talofibular ligament, the posterior talofibular ligament, and the calcaneofibular ligament.

lateral lobes of thyroid gland [L, *latus,* side; Gk, *lobos* + *thyreos,* shield; L, *glans,* acorn], the left and right lobes of a thyroid gland, situated in front of the neck. The two conical lobes lying on either side of and attached to the larynx are connected by a narrow isthmus.

lateral nystagmus [L, *latus,* side; Gk, *nystagmos,* nodding], an involuntary jerky movement in which the eyes move from side to side.

lateral pectoral nerve, one of a pair of branches from the brachial plexus that, with the medial pectoral nerve, supplies the pectoral muscles.

lateral pectoral region, the most lateral part of the pectoral region, bounded laterally by the axillary region.

lateral pelvic displacement, one of the five major kinetic determinants of gait. It helps to synchronize the rhythmic movements of walking and is produced by the horizontal shift of the pelvis or relative hip abduction.

lateral pinch, a grasp in which the thumb is opposed to the middle phalanx of the index finger.

lateral pivot shift test, a test of the integrity of the anterior cruciate ligament. The patient lies prone with the hip flexed and the knee extended; the examiner gradually flexes the knee while pushing the outside of the knee medially and internally rotating the tibia.

lateral plantar nerve, one of the two terminal branches of the tibial nerve that innervates all but three intrinsic muscles in the sole of the foot and a strip of skin on the lateral side of the anterior two thirds of the sole and the adjacent plantar surfaces of the fifth toe and lateral half of the fourth.

lateral projection, a radiographic representation of the body produced by an x-ray beam that travels from the left to the right side of the body, or vice versa.

lateral pubovesical ligament, the lateral branch of the pubovesical ligament in the female, extending from the bladder neck to the tendinous arch of the pelvic fascia.

lateral recumbent position, the posture assumed by the patient lying on the left side with the right thigh and knee drawn up.

lateral region, the part of the abdomen in the middle zone on both sides of the umbilical region.

lateral resolution, the resolution of objects in a plane perpendicular to the axis of an ultrasound beam. It is a measure of the ability of the system to detect closely separated objects such as adjacent blood vessels.

lateral rocking, a sideways rocking of the body used to move the body forward or backward when normal muscle action is not possible. The technique is used by some handicapped patients to move the body to or from the edge of a chair or to a different sitting position on a bed.

lateral rotation, a turning away from the midline of the body.

lateral sacral artery, one of two arteries that originate from the posterior division of the internal iliac artery and give rise to branches that pass into the anterior sacral foramina to supply related bone and soft tissues, structures in the vertebral canal, and skin and muscle posterior to the sacrum.

lateral sinus [L, *latus,* side, *sinus,* hollow], one of the transverse bilateral sinuses of the dura mater that lie along the attached margin of the tentorium cerebelli. They receive the superior sagittal and straight sinuses and drain into the internal jugular veins.

lateral spinal curvature [L, *latus,* side, *spina,* backbone, *curvatura,* bend], a bending or abnormal curve of the vertebral column to the right or left side.

lateral sural cutaneous nerve, a branch of the common fibular nerve that innervates skin over the upper lateral leg.

lateral umbilical fold, a fold in the peritoneum produced by a slight protrusion of the inferior epigastric artery and the interfoveolar ligament.

lateral ventricle [L, *latus,* side, *ventriculus,* little belly], a cavity in each cerebral hemisphere that communicates with the third ventricle through the interventricular foramen.

late rickets [Gk, *rhachis,* backbone], a form of rickets in which bone changes because of a kidney defect that results in a vitamin D or calcium deficiency. The disorder tends to affect older children.

lateroconal fascia, the lateral part of the renal fascia where its anterior and posterior parts join. This extends on either side posteriorly to the ascending and descending colon and is continuous with the parietal peritoneum.

lateroduction /lat′ərōduk′shən/, **1.** muscular action in movement to one side or the other. **2.** a turning away from the midline.

laterognathism /lat′ərōnath′izəm/, an asymmetric mandible resulting from irregular growth and development, fractures, tumors, or soft tissue atrophy or hypertrophy.

laterotorsion /-tôr′shən/, **1.** displacement of the uterus to one side. **2.** a twisting of the uterus to one side.

lateroversion /-vur′zhən/, the act of turning over or being deflected from one side to the other.

latex /lā′teks/ [L, liquid], an emulsion or fluidlike sap produced in special cells or vessels of certain plants. Latex contains resins, proteins, and other substances and is a source of rubber.

latex allergy, anaphylactic hypersensitivity to soluble proteins in latex, seen most often in patients sensitized by repeated exposure to latex.

latex fixation test [L, *latex,* fluid, *figere,* to fasten], a serologic test used in the diagnosis of rheumatoid arthritis in which antigen-coated latex particles agglutinate with rheumatoid factors in a slide specimen of serum or synovial fluid.

latex precautions, a nursing intervention from the Nursing Interventions Classification (NIC) defined as reducing the risk of a systemic reaction to latex.

Lathrop, Rose Hawthorne, (1851–1926), an American nurse who was a daughter of Nathaniel Hawthorne. She established a home in New York for patients with incurable cancer, mostly those who were poor and not accepted in hospitals because of the nature of their disease. Later she became a member of the Third Order of St. Dominic and founded the order of sisters called Servants of Relief for Incurable Cancer. The order founded hospitals wherever there was sufficient need and offered quality care to their patients.

Latin American medical practices, an ethnomedical system representing many healing practices throughout Latin America. The etiology of illness is framed in terms of imbalance, which can be between hot and cold in the body, between parts of the body, between patients and the social environment, or between patients and the spiritual realm. This system has been used to treat susto (fear), believed to cause the soul to become dislodged from the body, resulting in illness; empacho, a GI disorder believed to be caused by blockage in the stomach or intestine; and mal de ojo (evil eye), characterized by fever, irritability, headache, and weeping, generally affecting children.

latissimus dorsi /latis′iməs dôr′sī/ [L, widest + *dorsum,* the back], one of a pair of large triangular muscles on the thoracic and lumbar areas of the back. The latissimus dorsi extends, adducts, and rotates the arm medially; draws the shoulder back and down; and, with the pectoralis major, draws the body up when climbing.

latitude [L, *latitudio,* breadth], the ability of an x-ray imaging system to produce acceptable images over a range of exposures. If a system has wide latitude, it is possible to image parts of the body that vary in thickness or density with only one exposure.

LATS, abbreviation for **long-acting thyroid stimulator.**

LATS-P, abbreviation for **long-acting thyroid stimulator protector.**

lattice formation [OFr, *lattis,* geometric design], a three-dimensional cross-linked structure formed by the reaction of polyvalent antigens with antibodies.

latus /lā′təs/ [L], broad, wide.

laudanum /lôd′ənəm/ [Gk, *landanon,* gum resin], a tincture of opium made from a solution of macerated raw opium and 50% alcohol.

Lauenstein method, a technique for positioning a patient for radiographic examination of the hip joint. The knee of the affected leg is flexed, and the thigh is drawn up to nearly a right angle.

laughing gas /laf′ing/, *informal.* nitrous oxide, a side effect of which is laughter or giggling when administered in low doses.

Launois' syndrome /lonwah′/, pituitary gigantism.

Laurence-Moon-Bardet-Biedl syndrome /lôr′əns mōōn′ bärdā′ bē′dəl/ [John Z. Laurence, English ophthalmologist, 1829–1870; Robert C. Moon, American ophthalmologist, 1844–1933; Georges Bardet, French physician, b. 1885; Artur Biedl, Czechoslovakian physician, 1869–1933], a hereditary condition characterized by obesity, hypogenitalism, mental deficiency, polydactylism, and retinitis pigmentosa.

Laurence-Moon syndrome /lô'rəns mōōn/ [John Zachariah Laurence, British ophthalmologist, 1830–1874; Robert C. Moon, American ophthalmologist, 1844–1914], an autosomal-recessive disorder characterized by mental retardation, pigmentary retinopathy, hypogonadism, and spastic paraplegia.

laureth-9 /law'reth/, a compound used as a spermicide, surfactant, and sclerosing agent.

lavage /ləväzh'/ [Fr, washing], **1.** the process of washing out an organ, usually the bladder, bowel, paranasal sinuses, or stomach, for therapeutic purposes. **2.** to perform a lavage.

law [AS, *lagu*], **1.** in a field of study, a rule, standard, or principle that states a fact or a relationship between factors, such as Dalton's law regarding partial pressures of gas. **2.** a rule, principle, or regulation established and promulgated by a government to protect or restrict the people affected; the field of study concerned with such laws; the collected body of the laws of a people, derived from custom and from legislation.

Law method, in radiology, any of several techniques for positioning a patient for radiographic examination of the facial bones, mastoid process, and relationship of the teeth to the maxillary sinuses.

law of definite composition, in chemistry, a law stating that a given compound is always made of the same elements present in the same proportion.

law of dominance, formerly considered as a separate principle of Mendel's laws of inheritance, but in modern genetics it is incorporated as part of the first mendelian law, the law of segregation.

law of initial value, the physiologic and psychologic principle that states that, with a given intensity of stimulation, the degree of change produced tends to be greater when the initial value of that variable is low. The higher the initial level of functioning, the smaller is the change that can be produced.

law of universal gravitation, in physics, the law stating that the force with which bodies are attracted to each other is directly proportional to the masses of the objects and inversely proportional to the square of the distance by which they are separated.

lawrencium (Lr) /lôren'sē-əm/ [Ernest O. Lawrence, American physicist, 1901–1958], a synthetic transuranic metallic element. Its atomic number is 103; its atomic mass is 257.

laws of cure, in homeopathy, the four general directions in which cure of a disease moves: from above downward, from inside outward, from more vital to less vital organs, and in reverse order of symptom appearance.

lax, 1. abbreviation for **laxative. 2.** a condition of relaxation or looseness.

laxative (lax) /lak'sətiv/ [L, *laxare*, to loosen], **1.** pertaining to a substance that causes evacuation of the bowel by a mild action. **2.** a laxative agent that promotes bowel evacuation by increasing the bulk of the feces, softening the stool, or lubricating the intestinal wall.

laxative regimen, a diet that ensures an adequate intake of high-fiber bulk foods, including fruits and vegetables, to avoid chronic constipation. The regimen is supplemented with fluids and physical exercise.

lay referral system, an illness referral system through which a person passes from the first recognition of an abnormality to an announcement to the family, to members of the community, to traditional or culturally recognized healers, and then to the regular medical system that includes nurses and physicians. Depending on the culture and the medical care available, some steps may be omitted.

lazy leukocyte syndrome, an immunodeficiency disease of children characterized by recurrent stomatitis, gingivitis, otitis media, and low-grade fever with severe neutropenia.

lb [L, *libra*], abbreviation for **pound.**

lb ap, abbreviation for *apothecary pound,* equal to 5760 grains or 374.4 g as opposed to the English pound with 7000 grains or 455 g.

lb avdp, abbreviation for *avoirdupois pound.*

LBBB, abbreviation for **left bundle branch block.**

lbd, abbreviation for *lower back disorder.*

lbf, abbreviation for *pound-force.*

lbf/ft², abbreviation for *pound-force per square foot.*

lbf/in², abbreviation for *pound-force per square inch.*

lbm, abbreviation for **lean body mass.**

lbp, 1. abbreviation for **low back pain. 2.** abbreviation for *low blood pressure.*

LBW, abbreviation for *low birth weight.*

LCAT, abbreviation for *lecithin-cholesterol acetyltransferase.*

LCBF, abbreviation for **local cerebral blood flow.**

LCD, abbreviation for **liquid crystal display,** a video display device that is more compact than and uses less electrical power than the conventional cathode ray tube (CRT). An LCD is composed of electrically sensitive liquid crystals laminated between layers of plastic. Application of small electrical currents alters the orientation of the crystals, producing the image.

L chain, abbreviation for *light chain.*

LCMRG, abbreviation for **local cerebral metabolic rate of glucose** utilization.

LD, abbreviation for **lethal dose.**

LD$_{50}$, symbol for *median lethal dose.*

LDH, abbreviation for **lactate dehydrogenase.**

LDL, abbreviation for **low-density lipoprotein.**

LE, abbreviation for *lupus erythematosus.*

leaching /lē'ching/, removal of the soluble contents of a substance by running water or another liquid through it, leaving the insoluble part behind.

lead /lēd/ [AS, *laedan,* to lead], an electric connection attached to the body to record electric activity, especially of the heart or brain.

lead (Pb) /led/ [ME, *leed*], a common soft blue-gray metallic element. Its atomic number is 82, and its atomic mass is 207.19. In its metallic form, lead is used as a protective shielding against x-rays. Lead is poisonous, a characteristic that has led to a reduction in the use of lead compounds as pigments for paints and inks.

lead apron /led/ [AS, *led*; Fr, *napperon*], a protective shield of lead and rubber that may be worn by a patient, radiologic technologist or radiologist, or both during exposure to x-rays or other diagnostic radiation. It is intended to guard against excessive exposure of the reproductive and other vital body organs to ionizing radiation.

lead-containing eyeglasses /led/, glasses that provide radiation shielding for the eyes of radiographic personnel. They are particularly useful during fluoroscopic procedures or angiographic examinations.

lead encephalopathy /led/ [AS, *led*; Gk, *enkephalos,* brain, *pathos,* disease], a condition of brain structure and function as a result of lead poisoning, including exposure to tetraethyl lead. Children are commonly afflicted after eating chips of lead-based paints. The untreated disorder is characterized by delirium, convulsions, mania, cortical blindness, and coma.

lead equivalent /led/, the thickness of lead required to achieve the same shielding effect against radiation, under specified conditions, as that provided by a given material.

leadership [AS, *leadan,* to lead, *scieppan,* to shape], the ability to influence others in the attainment of goals.

lead nephropathy, kidney damage that accompanies lead poisoning. Lead deposits appear in the epithelium of the proximal tubules and as nuclear inclusions in cells. In time this leads to tubulointerstitial nephritis with chronic renal failure and other symptoms.

lead pipe fracture /led/, a linear fracture that is produced on the side of a bone opposite from the side of impact with a hard object. The point of impact is marked by a compression of bony tissue.

lead-pipe rigidity /led/, a state of stiffness and inflexibility that remains uniform throughout the range of passive movement. It is associated with diseases of the basal ganglia.

lead poisoning /led/, a toxic condition caused by the ingestion or inhalation of lead or lead compounds. Many children have developed the condition as a result of eating flaked lead paint. Poisoning also occurs from the ingestion of water from lead pipes and lead salts in certain foods and wines, the use of pewter or earthenware glazed with a lead glaze, and the use of leaded gasoline. Inhalation of lead fumes is common in industry. Toxicity leads to three major clinical syndromes: cerebral (hyperactivity, behavior problems, learning problems, neurologic disability, and/or mental retardation); neuromuscular (peripheral neuritis, paresthesias, and poor coordination); and alimentary (anorexia, abdominal cramping, weight loss, intestinal spasm, and rigidity of abdominal wall). Lead exposure in pregnant women can retard fetal development.

lead shielding /led/, the use of aprons and other devices containing lead as protective measures against radiation. A layer of lead 1 mm thick can attenuate 99% of x-rays of 50 kVp and 94% of x-rays of 100 kVp.

leakage /le'kaj/, the escape of something through a break in a barrier or wall.

leakage radiation /lē'kij/ [ONorse, *leka,* to drip; L, *radiare,* to emit rays], radiation, exclusive of the primary beam, that is emitted through the housing of equipment used in radiation therapy and radiography.

leak point pressure, the pressure at which leakage occurs through the urethra as the bladder fills, used as a measure of strength of the urethral sphincters.

lean body mass (lbm) [ME, *lenen,* slender; AS, *bodig*; ME, *massa,* lump], the combination of cell solids, extracellular and intracellular water, and mineral mass of the body.

learned helplessness /lurnd/, a behavioral state and personality trait of a person who believes that he or she is ineffectual, his or her responses are futile, and control over reinforcers in the environment has been lost. It may be seen in depression.

learning [AS, *leornian,* to learn], **1.** the act or process of acquiring knowledge or some skill by means of study, practice, or experience. **2.** knowledge, wisdom, or a skill acquired through systematic study or instruction. **3.** in psychology, the modification of behavior through practice, experience, or training.

learning curve, a graphic presentation of the effects of a specified method of teaching or training on the ability of a subject to learn, as shown by improved performance in a particular task.

learning disability, an abnormal condition often affecting children of normal or above-average intelligence, characterized by difficulty in learning such fundamental procedures as reading, writing, and numeric calculation.

learning-disabled adult, an adult with a nonspecific difficulty in the learning process, commonly resulting from developmental lag rather than brain damage or demonstrable illness.

learning environment, the sum of the internal and external circumstances and influences surrounding and affecting a person's learning.

learning facilitation, a nursing intervention from the Nursing Interventions Classification (NIC) defined as promoting the ability to process and comprehend information.

learning readiness enhancement, a nursing intervention from the Nursing Interventions Classification (NIC) defined as improving the ability and willingness to receive information.

learning theory [AS, *leornian,* to learn; Gk, *theoria,* speculation], a group of concepts and principles that attempts to explain the learning process. One concept, Guthrie's contiguous conditioning premise, postulates that each response becomes permanently linked with stimuli present at the time so that contiguity rather than reinforcement is a part of the learning process.

Leber's congenital amaurosis /lāʹbərz/ [Theodor von Leber, German ophthalmologist, 1840–1917; L, *congenitus,* born with; Gk, *amauroein,* to darken], a rare kind of blindness or severely impaired vision caused by a defect transmitted as an autosomal-recessive trait and occurring at birth or shortly thereafter. The eyes appear normal externally, but pupillary constriction to light is sluggish or absent, and electroretinographic responses are decreased or absent. Pendular nystagmus, photophobia, cataract, and keratoconus may be present; the ophthalmic disorder may be associated with mental retardation and epilepsy.

Leber's plexus /lāʹbərz/ [Theodor Leber], a venous plexus in the ciliary region connected with the canal of Schlemm.

Leboyer method of delivery /ləboiyāʹ/ [Frederick LeBoyer, French obstetrician, b. 1918], a psychophysical approach to delivery with the goal of minimizing the trauma of birth by gently and pleasantly introducing the newborn to life outside the womb. It has four aspects: a gentle controlled delivery in a quiet dimly lit room, avoidance of pulling on the head, avoidance of overstimulation of the infant's sensorium, and encouragement of maternal-infant bonding.

LE cell, a neutrophil that has phagocytosed the nucleus of another leukocyte that has already been altered by interacting with the LE factor in the bloodstream.

lecithin /lesʹithin/ [Gk, *lekithos,* yolk], phosphatidylcholine, a phospholipid common in plants and animals. It is an essential component of all cell membranes and for fat metabolism and is used in the processing of foods, pharmaceutical products, cosmetics, and inks.

lecithin-cholesterol acetyltransferase (LCAT) deficiency, an autosomal-recessive disorder characterized by an accumulation of unesterified cholesterol in the tissues, corneal opacity, hemolytic anemia, proteinuria, renal insufficiency, and premature atherosclerosis. It is caused by a deficiency of LCAT activity.

lecithin/sphingomyelin ratio (L/S ratio), the ratio of two components of amniotic fluid, used for predicting fetal lung maturity. The normal ratio in amniotic fluid is 2:1 or greater when fetal lungs are mature.

lecithoblast /lesʹithəblast′/, an embryonic cell, the primitive entoderm of a two-layered blastodisc.

lecithoprotein /lesʹithəprōʹtēn/, a compound formed by lecithin and a protein.

lectin /lekʹtin/, a protein in seeds and other parts of certain plants that binds with glycoproteins and glycolipids on the surface of animal cells, causing agglutination.

Ledercillin VK, a trademark for a bacterial antibiotic (penicillin V potassium).

leech therapy, a nursing intervention from the Nursing Interventions Classification (NIC) defined as application of medicinal leeches to help drain replanted or transplanted tissue engorged with venous blood.

Leeuwenhoekia australiensis [Anton van Leeuwenhoek, Dutch microscopist, 1632–1723; Australia], a mite indigenous to New South Wales that burrows into the skin, producing severe irritation.

leeway space, the amount by which the space occupied by the deciduous canine and first and second deciduous molars exceeds that occupied by the canine and premolar teeth of the secondary dentition.

Lee-White method [Roger I. Lee, American physician, b. 1881; Paul D. White, American physician, 1886–1973; Gk, *meta,* beyond, *hodos,* way], a method of determining the length of time required for a clot to form in a test tube of venous blood.

L

leflunomide, a pyrimidine synthesis inhibitor with antiinflammatory effects used to treat rheumatoid arthritis.

left atrioventricular orifice, the opening between the left atrium and ventricle of the heart.

left atrium (LA), the uppermost chamber on the left side of the heart. It receives blood from the pulmonary veins.

left brachiocephalic vein [ME, *left,* weak; Gk, *brachys,* short, *kephale,* head], a vessel that starts in the root of the neck at the junction of the internal jugular and the subclavian veins on the left side and runs obliquely across the thorax to join the right brachiocephalic vein and form the superior vena cava.

left bundle branch block (LBBB), the failure of the cardiac impulse to propagate down the left bundle branch from the bundle of His, resulting in early activation of the right side of the septum and the right ventricular myocardium.

left common carotid artery, the longer of the two common carotid arteries, arising from the aortic arch and having cervical and thoracic parts.

left coronary artery, one of a pair of branches from the ascending aorta, arising in the left posterior aortic sinus, dividing into the left interventricular artery and the circumflex branch, and supplying both ventricles and the left atrium.

left-handedness /left han′didnes/, a natural tendency by some persons to favor the use of the left hand in performing certain tasks.

left-heart failure, an abnormal cardiac condition characterized by the impairment of the left side of the heart and elevated pressure and congestion in the pulmonary veins and capillaries. Left-heart failure may be related to right-heart failure, because both sides of the heart are part of a circuit and the impairment of one side will eventually affect the other. It is most commonly caused by coronary artery disease, hypertension, or aortic stenosis.

left hepatic duct, the duct that drains the bile from the left lobe of the liver into the common bile duct.

left lateral recumbent position [ME, *left*; L, *latus,* side, *recumbere,* to lie down + *positio*], a position in which the patient lies on the left side with the upper knee and thigh drawn upward.

left pulmonary artery, the shorter and smaller of two arteries conveying venous blood from the heart to the lungs, rising from the pulmonary trunk, and connecting to the left lung.

left subclavian artery, an artery, divided into three parts, that arises from the aortic arch to supply the vertebral column, spinal cord, ear, and brain.

left-to-right shunt, 1. a diversion of blood from the left side of the heart to the right, such as a septal defect. 2. a diversion of blood from the systemic to the pulmonary circulation, such as from a patent ductus arteriosus.

left ventricle (LV), the thick-walled chamber of the heart that pumps blood through the aorta and the systemic arteries, the capillaries, and back through the veins to the right atrium. It has walls about three times thicker than those of the right ventricle and contains a mitral valve with two flaps that controls the flow of blood from the left atrium.

left ventricular assist device (LVAD), a mechanical pump that temporarily and artificially aids the natural pumping action of the left ventricle.

left ventricular failure, heart failure in which the left ventricle fails to contract forcefully enough to maintain a normal cardiac output and peripheral perfusion. Pulmonary congestion and edema develop from back pressure of accumulated blood in the left ventricle. Signs include breathlessness, crackles, dyspnea, orthopnea, pallor, sweating, and peripheral vasoconstriction. The heart is usually enlarged.

left ventricular veins, rarely occurring smallest cardiac veins emptying into the left ventricle of the heart.

leg /leg/ [ONor, *leggr*], 1. that section of the lower limb between the knee and ankle. 2. in common usage, the entire lower limb.

legacy /leg′əsē/ [L, *legatum,* bequest], something that is handed down from the past or intended to be bestowed on future generations.

legal [L, *lex,* law], actions or conditions that are permitted or authorized by law.

legal blindness [L, *lex,* law; ME, *blend,* sightless], a state of visual acuity in which no better than 20/200 is measured in the better eye with corrective lenses or a visual field of not more than 20 degrees is obtained.

leg cylinder cast [ONor, *leggr*; Gk, *kylindros*; ONorse, *kasta*], an orthopedic device of plaster of paris or fiberglass used to immobilize the leg in treating fractures from the ankle to the middle femur. It is used especially for repairing knee fractures and dislocations, for treating soft tissue trauma around the knee, for maintaining postoperative positioning and immobilization of the knee, and for correcting or maintaining correction of knee deformities. The cast extends from the upper thigh to the ankle. The foot is not encased.

legionellosis /lē′jənelō′sis/, infection with a species of *Legionella,* which may cause any of several illnesses, including **Legionnaires' disease.**

Legionnaires' disease /lē'jənerz'/ [American Legion], an acute bacterial pneumonia caused by infection with *Legionella pneumophila*. It is characterized by an influenza-like illness followed within a week by high fever, chills, muscle aches, and headache. The symptoms may progress to dry cough, pleurisy, and sometimes diarrhea. Contaminated air-conditioning cooling towers and warm, stagnant water supplies, including water vaporizers, water sonicators, whirlpool spas, and showers, may be sources of organisms. Person-to-person contagion has not occurred. Risk of infection is increased by the presence of other conditions, such as cardiopulmonary diseases.

Legionnaires' disease antibody test, a blood test to diagnose Legionnaires' disease.

Leigh disease /lē/ [Archibald Denis Leigh, British neuropathologist, 1915–1998], an encephalopathy causing neuropathologic damage like that of the Wernicke-Korsakoff syndrome. It occurs in two forms: the infantile form is characterized by degeneration of gray matter with necrosis and capillary proliferation in the brainstem; hypotonia, seizures, and dementia; anorexia and vomiting; slow or arrested development; and ocular and respiratory disorders. Death usually occurs before age 3. The adult form usually first manifests as bilateral optic atrophy with central scotoma and color blindness; then there is a quiescent period of up to 30 years before late symptoms appear, such as ataxia, spastic paresis, clonic jerks, grand mal seizures, psychic lability, and mild dementia.

Leiner's disease /lī'nərz/ [Karl Leiner, Austrian pediatrician, 1871–1930], an infant condition of generalized dermatitis, with scaling and erythema, as well as seborrheic dermatitis of the scalp, generalized lymphadenopathy, and diarrhea.

Leininger, Madeleine, a nursing theorist who is credited with the foundation of transcultural nursing and the resultant nursing research, education, and practice in this subfield of nursing. The most complete account of transcultural care theory is found in her book *Care: The Essence of Nursing and Health* (1984). A basic tenet of Leininger's theory is that human beings are inseparable from their cultural background and social structure.

leiomyofibroma /lī'ōmī'ōfī'brō'mə/ *pl.* **leiomyofibromas, leiomyofibromata** [Gk, *leios,* smooth, *mys,* muscle; L, *fibra,* fiber; Gk, *oma,* tumor], a tumor consisting of smooth muscle cells and fibrous connective tissue, commonly occurring in the uterus in middle-aged women.

leiomyoma /lī'ōmī·ō'mə/, *pl.* **leiomyomas, leiomyomata** a benign smooth-muscle tumor occurring most commonly in the uterus, stomach, esophagus, or small intestine.

leiomyoma cutis, a neoplasm of the smooth muscles of the skin. The lesion is characterized by many small, tender, red nodules.

leiomyoma uteri, a benign neoplasm of the smooth muscle of the uterus. The tumor is characteristically firm, well-circumscribed, round, and gray-white.

leiomyosarcoma /-särkō'mə/ [Gk, *leios,* smooth, *mys,* muscle, *sarx,* flesh, *oma,* tumor], a sarcoma that contains large spindle cells of unstriated muscle.

Leishman-Donovan body /lēsh'mən don'əvən/ [William B. Leishman, English pathologist, 1865–1926; Charles Donovan, Irish physician, 1863–1951], the resting stage of an intracellular nonflagellated protozoan parasite *(Leishmania donovani)* that causes kala-azar.

Leishmania /lēshmā'nē·ə/ [William B. Leishman], a genus of protozoan parasites. These organisms are transmitted to humans by any of several species of sand flies.

leishmaniasis /lēsh'mənī'əsis/ [William B. Leishman], infection with any species of protozoan of the genus *Leishmania*. The diseases caused by these organisms may be cutaneous, mucocutaneous, or visceral. A typical infection may begin with a cutaneous sore and progress to ulceration of the mouth, palate, and nose. Some cases are accompanied by a febrile illness. There are three major types of leishmaniasis: **American leishmaniasis,** the form found in Central America and South America, **kala-azar,** and **cutaneous.—leishmanial,** *adj.*

leisure participation, a nursing outcome from the Nursing Outcomes Classification (NOC) defined as the use of relaxing, interesting, and enjoyable activities to promote well-being.

lemniscal system /lemnis'kəl/ [Gk, *lemniskos,* fillet, *systema*], a part of the somatosensory network of large-diameter myelinated A fibers. It includes the dorsal columns and the neospinothalamic tract extending from the spinal cord to the thalamus and cortex.

lemniscus /lemnis'kəs/ [Gk, *lemniskos,* fillet], a band or tract of CNS fibers, particularly the ascending axons of secondary sensory neurons leading to the thalamus.

lemon balm, a perennial herb used for abdominal gas and cramping, and for cold sores. There is evidence of efficacy.

lenalidomide, an antianemic, biologic response modifier hormone used to treat transfusion-dependent anemia due to low or intermediate-1-risk myelodysplastic syndrome and to treat multiple myeloma in combination with dexamethasone.

Lenègre's disease /lenågråz/ [Jean Lenègre, 20th century French cardiologist, 1904–1972], sclerodegeneration of the conduction system of the heart that eventually results in complete heart block.

length of stay (LOS), the period of time a patient remains in a hospital or other health care facility as an inpatient.

Lennox-Gastaut syndrome /len'oks gåstō'/ [William G. Lennox, American neurologist, 1884–1960; Henri Gastaut, French biologist, 1915–1995], a condition in which a variety of generalized seizures, such as tonic, atonic, absence, tonic-clonic, akinetic, and myoclonic, begin to appear in the first 5 years of life. Seizures are often intractable and may require multiple antiepileptic medications. Mental retardation is often present.

lens [L, lentil], **1.** a curved transparent piece of plastic or glass that is shaped, molded, or ground to refract light in a specific way, as in eyeglasses, microscopes, or cameras. **2.** *informal.* the crystalline lens of the eye.—**lenticular,** *adj.*

lens capsule, the clear thin elastic capsule that surrounds the lens of the eye.

lens implant, an artificial lens that is usually implanted at the time of cataract extraction but may also be used for patients with extreme myopia, diplopia, ocular albinism, and certain other abnormalities.

Lente Insulin, a trademark for an intermediate-acting insulin.

lenticonus /len'tikō'nəs/, an abnormal spheric or conic protrusion on the lens of the eye. It is a congenital defect found in Alport's syndrome.

lenticular nucleus /lentik'yələr/ [L, *lens*, lentil, *nucleus*, nut], biconvex basal ganglia of the cerebrum, composed of lateral putamen and medial globus pallidus tissue as part of the corpus striatum.

lentiform /len'tifôrm/ [L, *lens* + *forma*], pertaining to or resembling a lentil shape, such as the lens of the eye.

lentigo /lentī'gō/ *pl.* **lentigines** [L, freckle], a tan or brown macule on the skin brought on by sun exposure, usually in a middle-aged or older person. It is benign, and no treatment is necessary, although, in some cases it may mimic melanoma and should be biopsied.

lentigo maligna melanoma, a neoplasm developing from Hutchinson's freckle on the face or other exposed surfaces of the skin in elderly patients. It is asymptomatic, flat, and tan or brown, with irregular darker spots and frequent hypopigmentation. It is one of the major clinical types of melanoma.

lentivirus /len'tivī'rəs/, any member of a genus of retroviruses that have long incubation periods and cause chronic, progressive, usually fatal diseases in humans and other animals.

LEOPARD syndrome, a hereditary syndrome transmitted as an autosomal-dominant trait, consisting of multiple lentigines, asymptomatic cardiac defects, and typical coarse facies. It may also be associated with pulmonary stenosis, sensorineural hearing loss, skeletal changes, ocular hypertelorism, and abnormalities of the genitalia.

Leopold's maneuver [Christian G. Leopold, German physician, 1846–1911], a series of four steps used in palpating the abdomen of a pregnant woman to determine position and presentation of the fetus.

lepirudin, a direct thrombin inhibitor used to treat heparin-induced thrombocytopenia and other thromboembolic conditions.

leprechaunism /lep'rəkän'izəm/, a rare lethal familial condition marked by slow physical and mental development, the elfin facies suggested by the name (wide-set eyes, low-set ears, and hirsutism), and severe endocrine disorders, such as enlargement of the clitoris and breasts in females and of the phallus in males.

lepromin test /leprō'min/, a skin sensitivity test used to distinguish between the lepromatous and tuberculoid forms of leprosy. The test consists of an intradermal injection of lepromin, which is prepared from heat-sterilized *Mycobacterium leprae.*

leprosarium /lep'rōser'ē·əm/ [Gk, *lepra*, leprosy], a hospital for persons who have leprosy.

leprosy /lep'rəsē/ [Gk, *lepra*], a chronic communicable disease caused by *Mycobacterium leprae* that may take either of two forms, depending on the degree of immunity of the host. Tuberculoid leprosy, seen in those with high resistance, presents as thickening of cutaneous nerves and anesthetic, saucer-shaped skin lesions. Lepromatous leprosy, seen in those with little resistance, involves many body systems, with widespread plaques and nodules in the skin, iritis, keratitis, destruction of nasal cartilage and bone, testicular atrophy, peripheral edema, and involvement of the reticuloendothelial system. Blindness may result.—**lepromatous, leprotic, leprous,** *adj.*

leptin /lep'tin/ [Gk, thin], a peptide secreted by adipose tissue. Leptin inhibits neuropeptide Y and is thought to be an appetite suppressant.

leptocytosis /lep'tōsītō'sis/ [Gk, *leptos,* thin, *kytos,* cell, *osis,* condition], a hematologic disorder in which target cells are present in the blood. Thalassemia, some forms of liver disease, and hemoglobin C disease are associated with leptocytosis.

leptomeninges /lep'tōminin'jēz/ [Gk, *leptos* + *meninx*, membrane], the arachnoid membrane and the pia mater, two of the three layers covering the brain and spinal cord.

leptomeningitis /-men'inji'tis/, an inflammation of the arachnoid and pia mater layers of the meninges.

leptonema /lep'tənē'mə/ [Gk, *leptos* + *nema*, thread], the threadlike chromosome formation in the leptotene stage in the first meiotic prophase of gametogenesis, before the beginning of synapsis.

Leptospira /-spī'rə/ [Gk, *leptos* + *speira*, coil], a genus of the family Leptospiraceae, order Spirochaetales; tightly coiled microorganisms having spirals with hooked ends. The spirochete thrives in the urine of infected animals, especially rodents; is pathogenic to humans and other mammals; and may cause hepatitis, jaundice, skin hemorrhages, fever, renal failure, mental status changes, and muscular illness.

Leptospira **agglutinin,** an agglutinin found in the blood of patients with leptospirosis.

leptospirosis /lep'tōspīrō'sis/ [Gk, *leptos* + *speira* + *osis,* condition], an acute infectious disease caused by several serotypes of the spirochete *Leptospira interrogans*. Clinical symptoms may include hepatitis, jaundice, hemorrhage into the skin, fever, chills, renal failure, meningitis with mental status changes, and muscular pain.

leptotene /lep'tətēn/ [Gk, *leptos* + *tainia,* ribbon], the initial stage in the first meiotic prophase in gametogenesis, in which the chromosomes condense and become visible as single, thin filaments.

leptotrichosis /lep'totriko'sis/, infection with a species of *Leptotrichia.*

leptotrichosis conjunctivae, name given to Parinaud's oculoglandular syndrome when caused by infection with *Leptotrichia.*

Leriche's syndrome /lərēshs'/ [René Leriche, French surgeon, 1879–1955], a vascular disorder marked by gradual occlusion of the terminal aorta, bilateral iliac arteries, or both; intermittent claudication in the buttocks, thighs, or calves; absence of pulsation in femoral arteries; pallor and coldness of the legs; gangrene of the toes; and, in men, impotence.

lesbian /lez'bē·ən/ [Gk, island of Lesbos, home of Sappho], **1.** a female homosexual. **2.** pertaining to the sexual preference or desire of one woman for another. **—lesbianism,** *n.*

Lesch-Nyhan syndrome /lesh' nī'han/ [Michael Lesch, American pediatrician, b. 1939; William L. Nyhan, Jr., American pediatrician, b. 1926], a hereditary disorder of purine metabolism, characterized by mental retardation, self-mutilation of the fingers and lips by biting, impaired renal function, and abnormal physical development.

Leser-Trélat sign /lā'zər trälä'/ [Edmund Leser, German surgeon, 1828–1916; Ulysse Trélat, French surgeon, 1828–1890], a condition of malignant cells present in the skin. It is characterized by the sudden onset of multiple seborrheic keratoses, with pruritus or enlargement of preexisting keratosis in older adults. It is associated with adenocarcinoma of the stomach, breast cancer, and lung cancer.

lesion /lē'zhen/ [L, *laesus,* an injury], **1.** a wound, injury, or pathologic change in body tissue. **2.** any visible, local abnormality of the tissues of the skin, such as a wound, sore, rash, or boil. A lesion may be described as benign, cancerous, gross, occult, or primary.

lesser occipital nerve [AS, *losian,* to lose; L, *occiput,* back of the head, *nervus,* nerve], one of a pair of cutaneous branches of the cervical plexus, arising from the second cervical nerve and ascending along the side of the head behind the ear to supply the skin. It communicates with the posterior auricular branch of the facial nerve.

lesser omentum [AS, *losian,* to lose; L, *omentum,* entrails], a membranous extension of the peritoneum from the peritoneal layers covering the ventral and the dorsal surfaces of the stomach and the first part of the duodenum.

lesser petrosal nerve, a small nerve originating in the tympanic plexus that carries preganglionic parasympathetic fibers to the otic ganglion.

lesser sciatic foramen, an opening positioned below the attachment of the pelvic floor formed by the lesser sciatic notch of the pelvic bone, the ischial spine, the sacrospinous ligament, and the sacrotuberous ligament. It acts as a route of communication between the perineum and the gluteal region.

lesser sciatic notch [AS, *losian,* to lose; Gk, *ischiadikos,* hip joint; OFr, *enochier*], a notch on the posterior border of the ischium of the hip bone. It is smooth, is coated with cartilage, and has several ridges corresponding to subdivisions of the obturator internus tendon.

lesser trochanter, one of a pair of conic projections on the shaft of the femur, just below the neck. It is the site of insertion of the psoas major muscle.

LET, abbreviation for **linear energy transfer.**

L

Letairis, a trademark for ambrisentan.

let-down, a sensation in the breasts of lactating women that often occurs as the milk flows into the ducts. It may occur when the infant begins to suck or when the mother hears the baby cry or even thinks of nursing the child.

lethal /lē'thəl/, deadly, capable of causing death.

lethal allele, an allele that produces a phenotypic effect that causes the death of the organism at any stage of life. The allele may be dominant, incompletely dominant, or recessive.

lethal dose (LD), the amount of toxin that produces death in all members of a species population within a specified period of time.

lethal equivalent [L, *letum,* death, *aequus,* equal, *valere,* to be strong], a recessive allele carried in the heterozygous state that would be lethal in the homozygous state, or any combination of alleles, each with slightly deleterious effects, that are equivalent to such an allele.

lethality /lēthal'itē/, the probability that a person threatening suicide will succeed, based on the method described, the specificity of the plan, and the availability of the means.

lethargy /leth'ərjē/ [Gk, *lethargos,* forgetful], the state or quality of dullness, prolonged sleepiness, sluggishness, or serious drowsiness.—**lethargic,** *adj.*

letrozole, an antineoplastic nonsteroidal aromatase inhibitor used to treat metastatic breast cancer in postmenopausal women.

Letterer-Siwe syndrome /let'ərər zē'və/ [Erich Letterer, German pathologist, 1895–1982; Sture A. Siwe, Swedish physician, 1897–1966], any of a group of acquired malignant neoplastic diseases of unknown origin, characterized by histiocytic elements. The syndrome, fatal when untreated, occurs in infancy. Anemia, hemorrhage, splenomegaly, lymphadenopathy, and localized tumefactions over bones are usually present.

Leu, abbreviation for **leucine.**

leucine (Leu) /lōō'sēn/ [Gk, *leukos,* white], a white crystalline essential amino acid required for optimal growth in infants and nitrogen equilibrium in adults. It cannot be synthesized by the body and is obtained by the hydrolysis of food protein during digestion.

leucine aminopeptidase (LAP) test, a blood or 24-hour urine test that detects levels of LAP, used primarily in diagnosing liver, pancreas, and small intestine disorders and in the differential diagnosis of increased levels of alkaline phosphatase.

leucinosis /lōō'sinō'sis/ [Gk, *leukos* + *osis,* condition], a condition in which the pathways for the degradation of leucine are blocked and large amounts of the amino acid accumulate in body tissue, producing leucine in the urine.

leucovorin calcium /lōō'kəvôr'in/, a reduced form of folic acid that can be used immediately for nucleic acid synthesis. It is prescribed in the treatment of an overdose of a folic acid antagonist and certain cases of megaloblastic anemia. It is also used for leucovorin "rescue" after high-dose methotrexate therapy in osteosarcoma to diminish the toxicity of the methotrexate.

leukapheresis /lōō'kəfərē'sis/ [Gk, *leukos* + *aphairesis,* removal], a donation process by which blood is withdrawn from a vein, white blood cells are selectively removed, and the remaining blood is reinfused into the donor. It is a treatment or supportive care measure in patients with leukocytopenia.

leukemia /lōōkē'mē·ə/ [Gk, *leukos* + *haima,* blood], A group of malignant neoplasms of hematopoietic tissues characterized by diffuse replacement of bone marrow or lymph nodes with proliferative white blood cell precursors. Peripheral blood WBC counts become elevated, and immature or variant forms appear in the peripheral blood. Leukemia may be chronic or acute, lymphoid, myeloid, or erythroid. In some chronic leukemias, when untreated, the WBC count becomes grossly elevated and the blood may appear whitish, giving leukemia its name.—**leukemic,** *adj.*

leukemia cutis, a condition of the skin in which yellow-brown, red, or purple nodular lesions form localized or general diffuse infiltrations.

leukemia inhibitory factor (LIF), a cytokine named for its ability to suppress the spontaneous proliferation of lymphoid stem cells.

leukemic hiatus, a condition observed in acute myelogenous leukemia in which there are numerous myeloblasts and a number of mature neutrophils in the peripheral blood, with few or no intermediate forms.

leukemoid /lōōkē'moid/, resembling leukemia.

leukemoid reaction [Gk, *leukos* + *eidos,* form; L, *re,* again, *agere,* to act], a clinical syndrome resembling leukemia in which the WBC is elevated in response to an allergy, inflammatory disease, infection, poison, hemorrhage, burn, or severe physical stress.

Leukeran, a trademark for an antineoplastic (chlorambucil).

leukoagglutinin /lōō'kō·aglōō'tinin/, an antibody that causes WBCs to adhere to one another.

leukoagglutinin test, a blood test to determine whether WBC incompatibility is the source of transfusion reaction in patients who have undergone complete compatibility testing.

leukoblast /loo'kəblast/ [Gk, *leukos,* white, *blastos,* germ], an immature leukocyte.

leukocyte /loo'kəsīt/ [Gk, *leukos* + *kytos,* cell], a blood cell that participates in immunity and inflammation. Five categories of leukocytes are classified by nuclear appearance and the presence or absence of granules in the cytoplasm. Lymphocytes have no granules or a few scattered azurophilic granules. The granulocytes are monocytes, neutrophils, basophils, and eosinophils.—**leukocytic,** *adj.*

leukocyte adhesion deficiency (LAD), an autosomal inherited disorder caused by a defective integrin molecule (CD18) that is important for cellular adhesion. This defect causes neutrophils to be immotile and unable to phagocytose. Patients with LAD have recurring bacterial infections and impaired wound healing, which may lead to necrosis and gangrene.

leukocyte alkaline phosphatase (LAP), an enzyme present in lymphocytes that is elevated in various diseases such as cirrhosis and polycythemia and in certain infections. It may be measured in the blood to detect these disorders and to differentiate chronic myelogenous (myelocytic) leukemia from leukemoid reactions.

leukocyte emigration, the passage (diapedesis) of leukocytes through the endothelial gap junctions of blood vessels in inflammation.

leukocytic, pertaining to white blood cells. See **leukocyte.**

leukocytoclastic vasculitis /loo'kəsī'təklas'-tik/, an allergic inflammation of blood vessels, characterized by deposits of fragmented cells, nuclear dust, necrotic debris, and fibrin staining in the vessels.

leukocytogenesis /-jen'əsis/, the origin and development of leukocytes.

leukocytosis /loo'kōsītō'sis/ [Gk, *leukos* + *kytos,* cell, *osis,* condition], an abnormally elevated total peripheral white blood cell count, often associated with bacterial infection. Extreme elevations may be associated with leukemia.

leukocyturia /loo'kəsītoor'ē-ə/, the presence of WBCs in the urine.

leukoderma /loo'kōdur'mə/ [Gk, *leukos* + *derma,* skin], localized loss of skin pigment.

leukodystrophy /-dis'trəfē/ [Gk, *leukos,* white, *dys* + *trophe,* nourishment], a disease of the white matter of the brain, characterized by demyelination.

leukoencephalopathy /loo'kō-ən·sef'əlop'-əthē/ [Gk, *leukos,* white, *enkephalos,* brain, *pathos,* disease], any of a group of diseases affecting the white matter of the brain, especially of the cerebral hemispheres, and occurring as a rule in infants and children.

leukoerythroblastic /loo'kō-erith'rōblas'tik/ [Gk, *leukos* + *erythros,* red, *blastos,* germ, *a* + *haima,* not blood], the presence of immature red blood cells and granulocytes in the peripheral blood and bone marrow, often associated with primary myelofibrosis and other myeloproliferative neoplasms.

leukonychia /loo'kōnik'ē-ə/ [Gk, *leukos* + *onyx,* nail], a benign condition in which white patches appear under the nails. Trauma, infection, and many disorders can cause white spots or streaks on nails.

leukopenia /loo'kōpē'nē-ə/ [Gk, *leukos* + *penes,* poor], an abnormal decrease in the total peripheral blood white cell count, often associated with chemotherapy or radiation. Leukopenia may result from an idiosyncratic drug reaction and may be seen in acute myeloblastic leukemia. —**leukopenic,** *adj.*

leukophoresis /loo'kōfərē'sis/ [Gk, *leukos* + *phoresis,* being transmitted], a laboratory procedure in which blood is drawn and WBCs are separated from the blood and the RBCs are returned to the patient.

leukoplakia /loo'kōplā'kē-ə/ [Gk, *leukos* + *plakos,* plate], a precancerous, slowly developing change in a mucous membrane characterized by thickened, white, firmly attached patches that are slightly raised and sharply circumscribed.

leukoplakic vulvitis /-plā'kik/ [Gk, *leukos,* white, *plakos,* plate, *vulva* + *itis,* inflammation], a condition in which the skin of the vulva becomes thick and white, develops bleeding fissures, and later becomes atrophic. The condition may progress to cancer.

leukopoiesis /loo'kōpō-ē'sis/ [Gk, *leukos* + *poiein,* to make], Production of white blood cells. Monocytes, neutrophils, basophils, and eosinophils are produced from bone marrow myeloblasts. Lymphocytes develop from lymphoblastic precursors in peripheral lymphoid tissue. –**leukopoietic,** *adj.*

leukorrhea /loo'kōrē'ə/ [Gk, *leukos* + *rhoia,* flow], a white discharge from the vagina. Normally, vaginal discharge occurs in regular variations of amount and consistency during the course of the menstrual cycle. A greater than usual amount is normal in pregnancy, and a decrease is to be expected after delivery, during lactation, and after menopause.

leukostasis, increased blood viscosity and tendency to clotting, seen in leukemia that is accompanied by hyperleukocytosis.

leukotoxin /lōō'kətok'sin/ [Gk, *leukos* + *toxikon*, poison], a substance that can inactivate or destroy leukocytes.—**leukotoxic,** *adj.*

leukotrienes /lōō'kətrī'ēnz/, a class of biologically active compounds that occur naturally in leukocytes and produce allergic and inflammatory reactions similar to those of histamine. They are thought to play a role in the development of allergic and autoallergic diseases such as asthma, rheumatoid arthritis, inflammatory bowel disease, and psoriasis.

leukovirus /lōō'kəvī'rus/ [Gk, *leukos,* white; L, *virus,* poison], a former genus composed of RNA tumor viruses now included in the family Retroviridae.

leuprolide acetate /lōō'prōlīd/, an analog of gonadotropin-releasing hormone. It is an agonist administered at levels that desensitize the pituitary gland from responding to it or to endogenous gonadotropin-releasing hormone, thereby preventing pituitary stimulation of sex hormone production by the ovaries or testes. It is used for the palliative treatment of advanced prostatic cancer, in the management of endometriosis, and for the treatment of children with central precocious puberty.

levalbuterol, an adrenergic beta-2-agonist used in the treatment and prevention of bronchospasm (reversible obstructive airway disease).

levamisole, an immunomodulator used as an adjuvant treatment in combination with fluorouracil after surgical resection in patients with Dukes' stage C colon cancer.

levator /livā'tər/ *pl.* **levatores** [L, *levare,* to lift up], **1.** a muscle that raises a structure of the body, as the levator ani raises parts of the pelvic diaphragm. **2.** a surgical instrument used to lift depressed bony fragments in fractures of the skull and other bones.

levator anguli oris, a deeply placed oral muscle arising from the maxilla that elevates the corner of the mouth and may help deepen the furrow between the nose and the corner of the mouth during sadness.

levator ani, one of a pair of muscles of the pelvic diaphragm that stretches across the bottom of the pelvic cavity like a hammock, supporting the pelvic organs. It functions to support and slightly raise the pelvic floor. The pubococcygeus draws the anus toward the pubis and constricts it.

levatores costarum, muscles of the thoracic wall that together with muscles between the vertebrae and ribs posteriorly alter the position of the ribs and sternum and so change thoracic volume during breathing.

levator labii superioris, an oral muscle arising from the maxilla just superior to the infraorbital foramen that deepens the furrow between the nose and the corner of the mouth during sadness.

levator labii superioris alaeque nasi, an oral muscle medial to the levator labii superioris that arises from the maxilla next to the nose and inserts into both the alar cartilage of the nose and the skin of the upper lip. It may assist in flaring the nares.

levator palpebrae superioris, one of the three muscles of the eyelid, also considered an extrinsic muscle of the eye. It is innervated by the oculomotor nerve. It elevates the upper eyelid and is the antagonist of the orbicularis oculi.

levator scapulae, a muscle of the dorsal and lateral aspects of the neck. It acts to raise the scapula and pull it toward the midline.

levator veli palatini, one of the muscles originating from the base of the skull that elevate the palate above neutral position and close the pharyngeal isthmus between the nasopharynx and oropharynx.

LeVeen shunt [Harry H. LeVeen, American surgeon, 1914–1997], a tube that is surgically implanted to connect the peritoneal cavity and the superior vena cava to drain accumulated fluid from the peritoneal cavity. It is used in cirrhosis of the liver, right-sided heart failure, or abdominal cancer.

level of activities [OFr, *livel*; L, *activus*], pertaining to the hierarchy of nervous system activity that determines the level responsible for certain functions while also being controlled by a higher level, as in the sequence of events in a reflex action.

level of consciousness (LOC) [OFr, *livel*; L, *conscire,* to be aware of], a degree of cognitive function involving arousal mechanisms of the reticular formation of the brain. The usual standard levels include coma, in which the patient does not appear to be aware of the environment; stupor, in which the patient is vaguely aware of the environment; drowsiness, in which the patient responds to stimuli but may be slow to react; and alert wakefulness.

level of inquiry [OFr, *livel*: L, *inquirere,* to ask about], in nursing research, one of the levels in a rank-ordered system of classification and organization of the questions to be answered in a research study.

levels of care, a classification of health care service levels by the kind of care given, the number of people served, and the people providing the care.

lever /lĕ'vər, lev'ər/ [L, *levare,* to lift up], any one of the numerous bones and associated joints of the body that act as a simple machine so that force applied to one end of the bone tends to rotate the bone in the direction opposite from that of the applied force.

levetiracetam, an anticonvulsant used to treat partial onset seizures.

Levine, Myra Estrin [1920–1996], a nursing theorist who developed a framework for nursing practice with the formulation of Four Conservation Principles: energy, structural integrity, personal integrity, and social integrity. The first edition of her book discussing the conservation principles, *Introduction to Clinical Nursing,* was published in 1969. Levine's model stresses nursing interventions and interactions based on the scientific background of these principles.

Levin tube /lev'in/ [Abraham L. Levin, American physician, 1880–1940], a plastic catheter introduced through the nose and used in gastric intubation for gastric decompression or gavage feeding.

levitation /lev'itā'shən/ [L, *levitas,* lightness, *atus,* process], in psychiatry, a hallucinatory sensation of floating or rising in the air.—**levitate,** *v.*

Levitra, a trademark for vardenafil.

levobetaxolol /le'vobatak'sälol/, a cardioselective beta-adrenergic blocking agent used in the form of hydrochloride salt, administered topically to the conjunctiva in treatment of glaucoma and ocular hypertension.

levobunolol /le'vobu'nolol/, a beta-adrenergic blocking agent used in the treatment of glaucoma and ocular hypertension, applied topically to the conjunctiva as the hydrochloride salt.

levobupivacaine, a local anesthetic used for local and regional anesthesia, for pain management, and for continuous epidural analgesia.

levocabastine /le'vokab'ästēn/, an antihistamine applied topically to the conjunctiva as the hydrochloride salt to treat seasonal allergic conjunctivitis.

levocardia /-kär'dē-ə/, a congenital anomaly in which the viscera are transposed to the opposite side of the body, except for the heart, which is in its normal position.

levocarnitine /-kär'nitēn/, an oral drug prescribed for treatment of primary systemic carnitine deficiency.

levocetirizine, a low-sedating antihistamine used to treat perennial or seasonal rhinitis, allergy symptoms, and chronic idiopathic urticaria.

levodopa /lĕ'vōdō'pə/, an antiparkinsonian agent prescribed in the treatment of Parkinson's disease, juvenile forms of Huntington's disease when rigidity is the main feature, and chronic manganese poisoning.

Levo-Dromoran, a trademark for an opioid analgesic (levorphanol tartrate).

levofloxacin, an antiinfective used to treat acute sinusitis, acute chronic bronchitis, community-acquired pneumonia, uncomplicated skin infections, complicated UTIs, and acute pyelonephritis caused by *Streptococcus pneumoniae, Haemophilus influenzae, H. parainfluenzae,* and *Moraxella catarrhalis.*

levomethadyl /le'vometh'ädil/, an opioid analgesic used as an adjunct in the treatment of opioid addiction.

Levophed Bitartrate, a trademark for an adrenergic (norepinephrine bitartrate).

levorphanol tartrate /lĕ'vôrfă'nol/, an opioid analgesic prescribed for the treatment of pain and preoperative analgesia.

levothyroxine sodium /-thī'roksēn/, a thyroid hormone prescribed in the treatment of hypothyroidism.

levotorsion /lev'itôr'shən/, the rotation to the left of the upper pole of the cornea of one or both eyes.

Lev's disease [Maurice Lev, American pathologist, 1908–1994], fibrosis or calcification of the conduction system of the heart that results in varying degrees of heart block in patients with normal myocardium and coronary arteries.

Lewis blood group system, a blood-group system based on antigens present in soluble forms in blood and secretions. The antigens are adsorbed from the plasma onto the red cell membrane. The expressed Lewis phenotype is based on whether the patient is a secretor or nonsecretor of the Lewis gene product.

lewisite /lōō'isīt/ [Winford L. Lewis, American chemist, 1878–1943], 2-chlorovinyl arsine, a poisonous blister gas used in World War I, that causes irritation of the lungs, dyspnea, damage to the tissues of the respiratory tract, tears, and pain.

Lewy bodies /lā'wē, lōō'ē/ [Frederick H. Lewy, German neurologist, 1885–1950], concentric spheres found inside vacuoles in midbrain and brainstem neurons in patients with idiopathic parkinsonism, Alzheimer's disease, and other neurodegenerative conditions.

Lexiva, a trademark for fosamprenavir.

lexor retinaculum of the hand, the thick fibrous band of antebrachial fascia that wraps the carpal canal surrounding the tendons of flexor muscles of the forearm at the distal ends of the radius and the ulna.

Leyden-Möbius muscular dystrophy /lī'dənmœ'bē-əs, mē'bē-əs/, a form of

L

limb-girdle muscular dystrophy that begins in the pelvic girdle.

Leydig cells /lī′dig/ [Franz von Leydig, German anatomist, 1821–1908], **1.** cells of the interstitial tissue of the testes that secrete testosterone. **2.** mucous cells that do not pour their secretions out over the surface of the epithelium.

Leydig cell tumor, a generally benign neoplasm of interstitial cells of a testis that may cause gynecomastia in adults and precocious sexual development if the lesion occurs before puberty.

LF, abbreviation for *low frequency.*

LFA, abbreviation for *left frontoanterior fetal position.*

LFP, abbreviation for *left frontoposterior fetal position.*

LFT, abbreviation for **liver function test.**

LGA, abbreviation for **large for gestational age.**

LGL, abbreviation for *Lown-Ganong-Levine.*

LGV, abbreviation for **lymphogranuloma venereum.**

LH, abbreviation for **luteinizing hormone.**

Lhermitte's sign /ler′mits/ [Jacques J. Lhermitte, French neurologist, 1877–1959], sudden, transient, electric-like shocks spreading down the body when the head is flexed forward, occurring chiefly in MS but also in compression disorders of the cervical spinal cord.

LH-RH, abbreviation for **luteinizing hormone–releasing hormone.**

Li, symbol for the element **lithium.**

liability /lī′əbil′itē/ [L, *ligare,* to bind], **1.** something one is obligated to do or an obligation required to be fulfilled by law, usually financial in nature. **2.** the amount of money required to fulfill a financial obligation.

liaison nursing /lē-ā′zən/, an arrangement with clinical specialists in psychiatric nursing whereby nurses and health professionals in other disciplines obtain consultation services in medical-surgical, parent-child, and geriatric settings.

libel /lī′bal/ [L, *libellus,* little book], a false accusation written, printed, or typewritten or presented in a picture or a sign that is made with malicious intent to defame the reputation of a person who is living or the memory of a person who is dead, resulting in public embarrassment, contempt, ridicule, or hatred.

liberation /lib′ərā′shən/ [L, *liber,* free], the process of drug release from the dosage form.

libido /libē′dō, librī′dō/, **1.** the psychic energy or instinctual drive associated with sexual desire, pleasure, or creativity. **2.** in

psychoanalysis, the instinctual drives of the id. **3.** lustful desire or striving. —**libidinal, libidinous,** *adj.* —**libidinize,** *v.*

Libman-Sacks endocarditis /lib′mən saks′/ [Emanuel Libman, American physician, 1872–1946; Benjamin Sacks, American physician, 1896–1939], the most common manifestation of lupus erythematosus, characterized by warty lesions that develop near the heart valves but rarely affect valvular action.

Librax, a trademark for a GI, fixed-combination drug containing an anticholinergic (clidinium bromide) and a sedative (chlordiazepoxide hydrochloride).

Libritabs, a trademark for an antianxiety agent (chlordiazepoxide hydrochloride).

Librium, a trademark for an antianxiety agent (chlordiazepoxide hydrochloride).

lice [AS, *lus*], any of the small wingless insect order of Phthiraptera. Lice are ectoparasites of birds and mammals and may spend their entire life cycle on a single host, attaching eggs to the hair shafts or feathers. They transfer to humans by direct contact. Three forms that infect humans are the head louse, *Pediculus humanus capitis;* the body louse, *Pediculus humanus corporis;* and the crab louse, *Phthirus pubis.*

license, an agency- or government-granted permission issued to a health care professional to engage in a given occupation on finding that the applicant has attained the degree of competency and met the educational requirements necessary to ensure that the public health, safety, and welfare are reasonably well-protected.

licensed counselor, a mental health provider who has fulfilled certain standards of education and supervised practice and who has passed the National Counselor Examination of the National Board for Certified Counselors.

licensed marriage and family therapist (LMFT), a person who has earned a master's or PhD in marriage and family therapy from an accredited graduate program and has completed at least 1000 hours of supervised clinical practice and scored successfully on the National Certification Examination.

licensed practical nurse (LPN) /lī′sənst/ [L, *licere,* to be allowed; Gk, *praktikos,* fit for action; L, *nutrix,* nurse], *U.S.* a person educated in basic nursing techniques and direct patient care whose qualifications and education have been examined by a state board of nursing and who has legal authorization to practice. The course of education usually lasts 1 year. Once licensed, a licensed practical nurse practices under the supervision of a registered nurse.

licensed psychologist, a person who has earned a PhD in psychology from an accredited graduate school, has completed 2 to 3 years of postgraduate training with special emphasis on the diagnosis and treatment of psychologic disorders, and is licensed in the state in which he or she practices.

licensure /lī′sənshŏŏr/ [L, *licere,* to be allowed], the granting of permission by a competent authority (usually a government agency) to an organization or individual to engage in a practice or activity that would otherwise be illegal.

lichen amyloidosis /lī′kən/, a common form of amyloidosis characterized by symmetric distribution over the skin of translucent yellowish-brown dome-shaped pruritic papules.

lichen aureus, a rare type of chronic pigmented purpura in which the patient has a single red or rust-colored lesion on the lower limb, usually over a perforating vein.

lichenification /līken′ifikā′shən/ [Gk, *leichen,* lichen, *facere,* to make], thickening and hardening of the skin, often resulting from the irritation caused by repeated scratching of a pruritic lesion. **—lichenified,** *adj.*

lichen nitidus [Gk, *leichen*; L, *nitidus,* bright], a rare skin disorder characterized by numerous flat, glistening, pale, discrete papules measuring 2 to 3 mm in diameter.

lichenoid eczema /lī′kənoid/, a chronic inflammatory cutaneous condition characterized by skin thickening and accentuated skin lesions.

lichen planus, a nonmalignant, chronic, pruritic skin disease of unknown cause that is characterized by small flat purplish polygonal papules or plaques with fine gray lines on the surface.

lichen sclerosis et atrophicus, a chronic skin disease characterized by white flat papules and black hard follicular plugs. In advanced cases the papules tend to coalesce into large white patches of thin pruritic skin. Lesions often occur on the torso and in the anogenital regions.

lichen simplex chronicus, a form of dermatitis characterized by a patch of pruritic confluent papules. Factors, such as scratching, contribute to its chronicity.

licorice, an herb that grows in shrub form in many subtropical areas, used for allergies, arthritis, asthma, constipation, esophagitis, gastritis, hepatitis, inflammatory conditions, peptic ulcers, poor adrenal function, and poor appetite. Its efficacy for these indications is not proven, but its active ingredients (glycyrrhizin and glycyrrhetinic acid) alter prostaglandin synthesis, are agonists at mineralocorticoid receptors, and prolong the half-life of cortisol.

Lidex, a trademark for a glucocorticoid (fluocinonide).

lidocaine hydrochloride /lī′dəkān/, a local anesthetic agent prescribed for topical administration or local injection into skin or mucous membranes. It is used parenterally as an antiarrhythmic agent.

lie [AS, *licgan,* position], the relationship between the long axis of the fetus and the long axis of the mother. In a longitudinal lie, the fetus is lying lengthwise, or vertically, in the uterus, whereas in a transverse lie, the fetus is lying crosswise, or horizontally.

Lieberkühn's glands /lē′bərkēnz/ [Johann N. Lieberkühn, German anatomist, 1711–1756; L, *glans,* acorn], tubular glands between the bases of the villi of the small intestine and on the surface of the epithelium of the large intestine. They secrete a watery fluid.

lie detector [AS, *leogan,* untruth; L, *detegere,* to uncover], an electronic device or instrument used to detect lying or anxiety in regard to specific questions.

lienal vein /lī′ənəl, lē-ē′nəl/ [L, *lien,* spleen, *vena*], a large vein of the lower body that unites with the superior mesenteric vein to form the portal vein. It returns blood from the spleen.

lienography /lē′ənog′rəfē/, the radiographic examination of the spleen after it has been injected with a contrast medium.

LIF, abbreviation for **leukemia inhibitory factor.**

LiF, symbol for **lithium fluoride.**

life [AS, *lif*], the energy that enables organisms to grow, reproduce, absorb and use nutrients, evolve, and in some organisms, achieve mobility, express consciousness, and demonstrate a voluntary use of the senses.

life costs [AS, *lif*: L, *constare,* constant], the mortality, morbidity, and suffering associated with a given disease or medical procedure.

life cycle, 1. the interval of time from conception to natural death. **2.** the series of stages from any stage of one generation to the same stage of the next generation.

life expectancy, the probable number of years a person will live after a given age, as determined by mortality in a specific geographic area. It may be individually qualified by the person's condition or race, sex, age, or other demographic factors.

life extension [AS, *lif,* life; L, *extenere,* to stretch out], the process of extending the life span of an individual or population by intervention that promotes better use of preventive medicine and use of established diagnostic and therapeutic facilities.

life island, a plastic bubble enclosing a bed, used to provide a germ-free environment for patients with a specific kind of immune deficit.

life review, 1. in psychiatry, a progressive return to consciousness of past experiences. 2. reminiscences that occur in old age as a consequence of the realization of the inevitability of death.

lifesaving measure, any medical intervention that is implemented when a patient's life is threatened.

life science, the study of the laws and properties of living matter.

life space, a term introduced by American psychologist Kurt Lewin to describe simultaneous influences that may affect individual behavior. The totality of the influences make up the life space.

life span, the length of life of an individual or the average length of life in a population or species.

lifestyle-induced health problems, diseases with natural histories that include conscious exposure to certain health-compromising or risk factors.

life support [AS, *lif,* life; L, *supportare,* to bring up to], the use of any therapeutic technique, device, or technology to maintain physical life functions.

lifetime reserve [AS, *lif* + *tid,* time; L, *re, again, servare,* to keep], a lifetime total of days of inpatient hospitalization benefits that may be drawn on by a patient who has exhausted the maximum benefits allowed under Medicare for a single spell of illness.

Li-Fraumeni cancer syndrome /lē′ frômen′ē/ [Frederick P. Li; Joseph F. Fraumeni, Jr.; 20th century American epidemiologists], a type of familial breast carcinoma affecting young women and associated with soft-tissue sarcomas and other cancers in close relatives.

lift assessment [AS, *lyft,* loft; L, *assidere,* to sit beside], the selection of the most appropriate lift method to use when moving a patient, as from the bed to a chair.

ligament /lig′əmənt/ [L, *ligare,* to bind], 1. one of many predominantly white, shiny, flexible bands of fibrous tissue binding joints together and connecting the articular bones and cartilages to facilitate movement. 2. a layer of serous membrane with little or no tensile strength, extending from one visceral organ to another, such as the ligaments of the peritoneum. —**ligamentous,** *adj.*

ligamental tear /lig′əmen′təl/ [L, *ligare,* to bind; AS, *teran,* to destroy], a complete or partial rupture of a ligament caused by an injury to a joint, as by a sudden twisting motion or a forceful blow. Ligamental tears may occur at any joint but are most common in the knees.

ligament of the head of the femur, a flat band of delicate connective tissue that attaches at one end to the fovea on the head of the femur and at the other end to the acetabular fossa, transverse acetabular ligament, and margins of the acetabular notch. It carries a small branch of the obturator artery, which contributes to the blood supply of the head of the femur.

ligament of the neck of the rib, one of five ligaments of each costotransverse joint, consisting of short, strong fibers passing from the neck of the rib to the transverse process of the adjacent vertebra.

ligament of the tubercle of the rib, one of the five ligaments of each costotransverse joint, comprising a short thick fasciculus passing obliquely from the transverse process of a vertebra to the tubercle of the associated rib.

ligand /lig′ənd, lī′gənd/ [L, *ligare,* to bind], 1. a molecule, ion, or group bound to the central metal atom of a chemical compound, such as the oxygen molecule in oxyhemoglobin, which is bound to the central iron atom. 2. an organic molecule attached to a specific site on a cell surface or to a tracer element. The binding is reversible in a competitive binding assay. It may be the analyte or a cross-reactant.

ligase chain reaction, a type of DNA amplification that uses DNA ligase to link chains and amplify the template containing the sequence in question.

ligases /lī′gāsəz/ [L, *ligare;* Fr, *diastase,* enzyme], a group of enzymes that catalyze the formation of a bond between substrate molecules coupled with the breakdown of a pyrophosphate bond in adenosine triphosphate or a similar donor molecule.

ligation /līgā′shən/ [L, *ligare,* to bind], the procedure of tying off a blood vessel or duct with a suture or wire ligature. It may be performed to stop or prevent bleeding during surgery, to stop spontaneous or traumatic hemorrhage, to prevent passage of material through a duct as in tubal ligation, or to treat varicosities. —**ligate,** *v.*

ligation clip, a small V-shaped clip made from stainless steel, platinum, titanium, or an absorbable material, used to ligate bleeding vessels.

ligature /lig′əchər/ [L, *ligare,* to bind], 1. a suture. 2. a wire, as used in orthodontia.

ligature needle, a long, thin curved needle used for passing a suture underneath an artery for ligation of the vessel.

ligature wire [L, *ligare,* to bind; AS, *wir*], a soft, thin wire used in dental procedures, particularly to connect brackets or attachments on orthodontic appliances.

light [AS, *leoht*], **1.** electromagnetic radiation of the wavelength and frequency that stimulate visual receptor cells in the retina to produce nerve impulses that are perceived as vision. **2.** electromagnetic radiation with wavelengths shorter than ultraviolet light and longer than infrared light, the range of visible light generally in the range of 400 to 800 nm.

light-adapted eye [AS, *leoht*; L, *adaptatio*; AS, *eage*], an eye that has been exposed to bright light long enough for chemical and physiologic changes to take place, such as bleaching of the rhodopsin or visual purple. The loss of cone sensitivity to light may require increased light intensity to obtain the same degree of visual acuity.

light bath, the exposure of the patient's uncovered skin to the sun or to actinic light rays from an artificial source for therapeutic purposes.

light chain deficiency, an immunodeficiency disease, such as megaloblastic anemia, that is associated with an alteration in the kappa or lambda light chains of immunoglobulins.

light chain disease, a type of multiple myeloma in which plasma cell tumors produce only monoclonal light chain proteins. Persons with light chain disease may develop lytic bone lesions, hypercalcemia, impaired kidney function, and amyloidosis.

light chain (L, chain), immunoglobulin subunit of about 22,000 daltons molecular weight.

lightening /lī'təning/ [AS, *leoht*, light], a subjective sensation reported by many women late in pregnancy as the fetus settles lower in the true pelvis, leaving more space in the upper abdomen.

light film fault [AS, *leoht*, light, *filmen*, membrane; L, *fallere*, to deceive], a defect in a radiograph photograph that appears as a barely distinct and inadequate image.

light headedness, a condition of feeling giddy, faint, delirious, or slightly dizzy.

light microscope [AS, *leoht*; Gk, *mikros*, small, *skopein*, to view], a microscope that uses visible light to view objects too small for the naked eye to see.

light reflex, the mechanism by which the pupil of the eye constricts in response to direct or consensual stimulation with light.

light scatter, light dispersion in any direction by suspended particles in a solution. The degree of scattering depends on the size and shape of the particles.

light therapy [AS, *leoht*; Gk, *therapeia*, treatment], the use of natural light or light of specified wavelengths to treat disease. The eye is generally the initial entry point for the light because of its direct connection to the brain. Light therapy has been used primarily for ADD, cataracts, conjunctivitis, headaches, head trauma, hyperactivity, lazy eye, macular degeneration, migraine, night blindness, poor eyesight, stroke, and vision disorders. It has also been effective in treating eczema, fever, psoriasis, addictions, allergies, anxiety, autism, bronchitis, childbirth, glaucoma, insomnia, muscle spasm, PMS, stress, and strep throat. Light therapy complements many other treatments for these and other conditions.

light-touch palpation [AS, *leoht*; Fr, *toucher*; L, *palpare*, to touch gently], a method of examination in which the abdomen is gently depressed 1 to 2 cm to determine the size and position of abdominal organs.

ligneous /lig'nē-əs/ [L, *ligum*, wood], woody or resembling wood in texture or other characteristics.

lignin /lig'nin/ [L, *lignum*, wood], an insoluble polysaccharide that with cellulose and hemicellulose forms the chief part of the skeletal substances of the cell walls of plants. It provides bulk in the diet necessary for proper GI functioning.

limb /lim/ [AS, *lim*], **1.** an appendage or extremity of the body, such as an arm or leg. **2.** a branch of an internal organ, such as a loop of a nephron.

limb-girdle muscular dystrophy [AS, *lim*, limb, *gyrdel*], a form of muscular dystrophy transmitted as an autosomal-recessive trait. The characteristic weakness and degeneration of the muscles begins in the shoulder girdle or the pelvic girdle. The condition is progressive, regardless of the area in which it is first manifest.

limbic /lim'bik/ [L, *limbus*, edge], pertaining to something that is marginal or at a junction between structures.

limbic lobe [L, *limbus*, edge; Gk, *lobos*, lobe], the marginal section of the cerebral hemispheres on the medial aspects. It forms a ring of neural tissue around the hypothalamus and some nuclei.

limbic system [L, *limbus*, edge], a group of structures within the rhinencephalon of the brain that are associated with various emotions and feelings such as anger, fear, sexual arousal, pleasure, and sadness. The structures of the limbic system include the cingulate gyrus, the isthmus, the hippocampal gyrus, the uncus, and the amygdala. The function of the system is incompletely understood.

limb lead /lēd/ [AS, *lim*, limb, *laeden*, lead], an ECG electrode that is attached to an arm or a leg.

L

Limbrel, a trademark for flavocoxid.

limbus /lim′bəs/, an edge or border, such as the corneal limbus at the edge of the cornea bordering the sclera.

lime [AS, *lim*], **1.** any of several oxides and hydroxides of calcium. **2.** a citrus fruit yielding a juice with a high ascorbic acid content. Lime juice was one of the first effective agents to be used in the treatment of scurvy.

limitation of motion /lim′itā′shən/ [L, *limes*, limit], the restriction of or reduction to a normal ROM of a body part, caused by disease or injury.

limited fluctuation method of dosing [L, *limes*, limit, *fluctuare*, to wave], a method of drug administration in which the dose is not allowed to rise or fall beyond specified maximum and minimum limits.

limiting charge, the maximum amount that can be charged in the United States for the services of a physician who does not accept the restrictions on fees established by Medicare laws.

limiting resolution, in CT, the spatial frequency at a modulation transfer function equal to 0.1. The absolute object size that can be resolved by a scanner is equal to the reciprocal of the spatial frequency.

limit of stability, the greatest distance in any direction a person can lean away from a midline vertical position without falling, stepping, or reaching for support.

limit setting, a nursing intervention from the Nursing Interventions Classification (NIC) defined as establishing the parameters of desirable and acceptable patient behavior.

limp [ME, not firm], an abnormal pattern of ambulation in which the two phases of gait are markedly asymmetric.

LINAC, abbreviation for **linear accelerator.**

Lincocin, a trademark for an antibacterial agent (lincomycin hydrochloride).

lincomycin hydrochloride /lin′kəmī′sin/, a macrolide antibiotic prescribed in the treatment of certain infections caused by susceptible bacteria, especially streptococci and staphylococci.

lindane /lin′dān/, a gamma-benzene hexachloride prescribed in the treatment of pediculosis and scabies.

Lindbergh pump [Charles A. Lindbergh, American technician, 1902–1974; ME, *pumpe*], a pump used to preserve an organ of the body by perfusing its tissues with oxygen and other essential nutrients, usually during the transport of an organ from a donor to a recipient.

line [L, *linea*], **1.** a connection between two points. **2.** a stripe, streak, or narrow ridge, often imaginary, that serves to connect reference points or to separate various parts of the body, as the hairline or nipple line. **3.** a black absorption line in a continuous spectrum passing through a medium. **4.** an accretion line in the enamel of a tooth marking successive layers of calcification. **5.** a catheter or wire that may be inserted in a vein, as an IV line. **6.** the base line of an ECG when neither positive nor negative potentials are recorded. **7.** line of sight.

linea /lin′ē·ə/ [L, line], a line defining anatomic features.

linea alba [L, *linea*, line, *albus*, white], the white part of the anterior abdominal aponeurosis in the middle line of the abdomen, made of connective tissue representing the fusion of three aponeuroses into a single tendinous band extending from the xiphoid process to the symphysis pubis. It contains the umbilicus.

linea arcuata, the curved tendinous band in the sheath of the rectus abdominis below the umbilicus. It inserts into the linea alba.

linea aspera, the posterior crest of the femur that extends proximally into three ridges to which are attached various muscles, including the gluteus maximus, pectineus, and iliacus.

lineae albicantes, lines, white to pink or gray, that occur on the abdomen, buttocks, breasts, and thighs and are caused by the stretching of the skin and weakening or rupturing of the underlying elastic tissue.

linea nigra /lin′ē·ə nīgrə/, a dark line appearing longitudinally on the abdomen of a pregnant woman during the latter 24 weeks of term. It usually extends from the symphysis pubis midline to the umbilicus.

linear /lin′ē·ər/ [L, *linea*, line], pertaining to a line or lines, particularly straight lines.

linear accelerator (LINAC) [L, *linea*, line, *accelerare*, to quicken], an apparatus for accelerating charged subatomic particles used in radiotherapy, physics research, and the production of radionuclides.

linear array, a contiguous sequence of identical discrete detectors, either gas-filled ionization chambers or solid-state semiconductors, used with a fan beam x-ray generator. The detectors read off once for each x-ray pulse. The resulting electronic signal is digitized and stored in a computer memory.

linear energy transfer (LET), the rate at which energy is transferred from ionizing radiation to soft tissue. It is expressed in terms of kiloelectron volts per micrometer (keV/μm) of track length in soft tissue.

linear flow velocity, the velocity of a particle carried in a moving stream, usually measured in centimeters per second.

linear fracture, a fracture that extends parallel to the long axis of a bone but does not displace the bone tissue.

linear IgA bullous disease, a condition characterized by linear deposits of immunoglobulin A binding to the area of the lamina lucida. Tense bullae are frequent, and the vesicles are likely to occur on the face, thighs, feet, and flexures.

linearity /lin′ē·er′itē/, the principle that the density of a radiographic exposure is determined by the product of the current and the exposure time.

linear morphea, linear scleroderma.

linear regression, a statistical procedure in which a straight line is established through a data set that best represents a relationship between two subsets or two methods.

linear scan, an ultrasound scan in which the transducer moves at a constant speed along a straight line at right angles to the ultrasound beam.

linear staining, the use of fluorescein-labeled goat or rabbit antiimmunoglobulins to produce smooth-staining patterns for study by immunofluorescence microscopy.

linear tomography, tomography that produces a blurring pattern consisting of indistinguishable linear streaks or blurs over the focal-plane image. The pattern is caused by elongation of structures outside the focal plane.

linea semilunaris, the slightly curved line on the ventral abdominal wall, approximately parallel to the median line and lying about halfway between the median line and the side of the body. It marks the lateral border of the rectus abdominis and is visible as a shallow groove when that muscle is tensed.

linea terminalis, a hypothetical line dividing the upper, or false, pelvis from the lower, or true, pelvis.

line compensator, a device that monitors electric power for medical devices such as x-ray equipment and adjusts for voltage fluctuations.

line density, in ultrasonography, the number of scan lines used to generate an image.

line focus principle, the principle that states that viewing a sloped surface at an angle reduces its apparent size. In an x-ray tube, the angling of the anode results in the effective focal spot being smaller than the actual focal spot.

line of demarcation [L, linea + de + marcare, to mark], a line that indicates a change in the condition of tissues, such as the boundary between gangrenous and healthy tissues.

line of gravity, an imaginary line that extends from the center of gravity to the base of support.

line pair (lp), a factor that determines the spatial frequency of CT and radiographic images. It consists of two parallel lines or bars separated by a space. As the number of line pairs per centimeter increases, the fidelity of the image decreases.

line spread function (LSF), a graph obtained from the image of a narrow line, which quantifies the amount of blur produced by an imaging system.

Lineweaver-Burk transformation /lī′n-wēvər burk′/ [Hans Lineweaver, American chemist, 1907–2009; Dean Burk, American scientist, 1904–1988; L, transformare, to change shape], a method of converting experimental data from studies of enzyme activity so that they can be displayed on a linear plot.

linezolid /līnez′olid/, a synthetic antibacterial of the oxazolidinone class, effective against gram-positive organisms and used for the treatment of community-acquired and nosocomial pneumonia, skin and soft tissue infections, and bacteremia.

lingual /ling′gwəl/ [L, lingua, tongue], pertaining to or resembling the tongue.

lingual artery [L, lingua, tongue], one of a pair of arteries that arises from the external carotid arteries and supplies the tongue and surrounding muscles.

lingual bar, a bar that is installed on the tongue side of the dental arch and connects bilateral parts of a mandibular removable partial denture.

lingual crib, an orthodontic appliance consisting of a wire frame suspended behind the maxillary incisors, used to obstruct undesirable thumb and tongue habits that can produce malocclusions, especially in children.

lingual flange, the part of a mandibular denture that occupies the space adjacent to the residual ridge and next to the tongue.

lingual gingiva [L, lingua, tongue, gingiva, gum], the gum tissue covering the teeth on the surfaces facing the tongue.

lingual goiter, a tumor at the back of the tongue formed by an enlargement of the primordial thyrolingual duct.

lingualis leukoplakia [L, lingua, tongue; Gk, leukos, white, plax, plate], a chronic inflammatory lesion characterized by smooth thick white patches on the surface of the tongue, generally attributed to excessive use of alcohol and tobacco. The lesions may be a precursor of epithelioma.

lingual nerve, a major branch of the mandibular nerve that carries general sensation from the oral part of the tongue, the mucosa on the floor of the oral cavity, and gingiva associated with the lower teeth. It also carries parasympathetic and taste fibers from the oral part of the tongue that are part of the facial nerve.

lingual pain, a pain in the tongue, which may be caused by biting the tongue, heavy metal poisoning, Vincent's stomatitis, or infiltration of the lingual muscles by a neoplasm.

lingual rest, a metallic extension attached to the tongue side of an anterior tooth to provide support or indirect retention for a removable partial denture.

lingual thyroid, residual thyroid tissue at the base of the tongue that failed to descend into the neck during embryologic development.

lingual tonsil, a mass of lymphoid follicles near the root of the tongue.

lingula /ling′gyələ/ [L, small tongue], any anatomic structure that resembles a tongue.

lingula of the lung [L, *lingula,* small tongue; AS, *lungen*], a tonguelike projection from the costal surface of the upper lobe of the left lung.

lingulectomy /ling′gyəlek′təmē/, a surgical excision of the lingula of the left lung.

linguoocclusion /ling′gwōklō′zhən/ [L, *lingua,* tongue, *occludere,* to close up], malocclusion in which the tooth is lingual to the line of the normal dental arch.

linguoversion /ling′gwōver′zhən/ [L, *lingua,* tongue, *vertere,* to turn], displacement of a tooth lingually from the line of occlusion.

liniment /lin′imənt/ [L, *linere,* to smear], a preparation, usually containing an alcoholic, oily, or soapy vehicle, that is rubbed on the skin as a counterirritant.

linin /li′nin/ [Gk, *linon,* flax], the faintly staining threads seen in the nuclei of cells, with granules of chromatin attached to the threads.

linitis /lini′tis/ [Gk, *linon,* flax, *itis,* inflammation], inflammation of cellular tissue of the stomach, seen frequently in adenocarcinoma of the stomach.

linitis plastica, a diffuse fibrosis and thickening of the wall of the stomach, resulting in a rigid, inelastic organ. Causes of this condition include infiltrating undifferentiated carcinoma, syphilis, and Crohn's disease involving the stomach.

linkage /ling′kij/ [Gk, *linke,* connection], **1.** in genetics, the location of two or more genes on the same chromosome so that they do not segregate independently during meiosis but tend to be transmitted together as a unit. The closer the loci of the genes, the more likely they are to be inherited as a group and associated with a specific trait. **2.** in psychology, the association between a stimulus and the response it elicits. **3.** in chemistry, the bond between two atoms or radicals in a chemical compound or the lines used to designate valency connections between the atoms in structural formulas.

linkage disequilibrium, a nonrandom association of two genes on the same chromosome.

linkage group, a group of genes that tend to be inherited as a unit because they are located on the same chromosome. Without crossing over, all of the genes on a given chromosome constitute a linkage group, and the number of linkage groups in an organism is equal to the number of autosomes in a haploid cell.

linked genes [ME, *linke;* Gk, *genein,* to produce], genes that are located so close together on the same chromosome that they tend to be transmitted as a linkage group.

linker [ME, *linke,* connection], a small segment of synthetic DNA used to join DNA fragments in cloning.

linoleic acid /lin′əlē′ik/ [Gk, *linon,* flax, *oleum,* oil], a colorless to straw-colored essential fatty acid with two unsaturated bonds, occurring in many vegetable oils such as corn, soy, and safflower oils.

linolenic acid /lin′ōlen′ik/ [Gk, *linon,* flax, *oleum,* oil], an unsaturated essential fatty acid occurring in triglycerides of canola, soy, linseed, and other vegetable oils.

Lioresal, a trademark for an antispastic agent (baclofen).

liothyronine sodium /lī′ōthī′rənēn/, a synthetic thyroid hormone prescribed in the treatment of primary hypothyroidism, myxedema, simple goiter, cretinism, and secondary hypothyroidism.

liotrix /lī′ətriks/, a uniform mixture of the thyroid hormones T_3 and T_4 prescribed in the treatment of hypothyroid conditions.

lip [AS, *lippa*], **1.** either the upper or lower fleshy structure surrounding the opening of the oral cavity. **2.** any rimlike structure bordering a cavity or groove.

LIP, abbreviation for **lymphocytic interstitial pneumonia.**

lipase /lī′pās, lip′ās/ [Gk, *lipos,* fat; Fr, *diastase,* enzyme], any of several enzymes produced by the organs of the digestive system that catalyze the breakdown of lipids through the hydrolysis of the linkages between fatty acids and glycerol in triglycerides and phospholipids.

lipase test, a blood test whose results are used most often to diagnose acute pancreatitis but also are useful in helping to diagnose renal failure, intestinal infarction or obstruction, and several other conditions.

lipectomy /lipek′təmē/ [Gk, *lipos* + *ektomē,* excision], an excision of subcutaneous fat, as from the abdominal wall.

lipedema /lip′ədē′mə/, a condition in which fat deposits accumulate in the lower extremities from the hips to the ankles, accompanied by symptoms of tenderness in the affected areas.

lipemia /lipē′mē-ə/ [Gk, *lipos* + *haima,* blood], chylomicrons in plasma causing the plasma to appear cloudy. It occurs following a heavy or fatty meal or may indicate a metabolic lipid disorder.

lipid /lip'id, lī'pid/ [Gk, *lipos,* fat, *eidos,* form], any of a structurally diverse group of organic compounds that are insoluble in water but soluble in alcohol, chloroform, ether, and other solvents. Some lipids are stored in the body and serve as an energy reserve but are elevated in various diseases such as atherosclerosis.

lipidosis /lip'idō'sis/ [Gk, *lipos + osis,* condition], a general term that includes several rare familial disorders of fat metabolism. The chief characteristic of these disorders is the accumulation of abnormal levels of certain lipids in the body.

lipid pneumonia, an inflammation of the spongy tissue of the lung caused by inhalation of oil droplets into the alveoli.

lipiduria /lip'idōōr'ē·ə/, the presence of lipids (fatty bodies) in the urine.

lipoatrophic diabetes /lip'ō·atrof'ik/, an inherited disease characterized by a total loss of subcutaneous body fat, insulin-resistant DM, acanthosis nigricans, hypermetabolism, hepatomegaly, and hypertrophied musculature. It is associated with a disorder of the hypothalamus that results in excessive blood levels of growth hormone and adrenocorticotropic-releasing hormone.

lipoatrophy /lip'ō·at'rəfē/, a breakdown of subcutaneous fat at the site of an insulin injection. It usually occurs after several injections at the same site.

lipochrome /lip'əkrōm/ [Gk, *lipos + chroma,* color], any of the naturally occurring pigments that contain a lipid and give a yellow color to fats, such as carotene.

lipodystrophia progressiva /-distrō'fē·ə/ [Gk, *lipos + dys,* bad, *trophe,* nourishment; L, *progredior,* to go forth], an abnormal accumulation of fat around the buttocks and thighs and a progressive, symmetric disappearance of subcutaneous fat from areas above the pelvis and on the face.

lipodystrophy /lip'ōdis'trəfē/ [Gk, *lipos + dys,* bad, *trophe,* nourishment], any abnormality in the metabolism or deposition of fats.

lip of hip fracture, a break in the posterior lip of the acetabulum, often associated with displacement of the hip.

lipofuscin /lip'əfus'in/, a class of fatty pigments consisting mostly of oxidized fats that are found in abundance in the cells of adults.

lipogenesis /-jen'əsis/ [Gk, *lipos,* fat, *genein,* to produce], the production and accumulation of fat.

lipogranuloma /lip'ōgran'yōōlō'mə/ pl. **lipogranulomas, lipogranulomata** [Gk,

lipos; L, *granulum,* little grain; Gk, *oma,* tumor], a nodule of necrotic, fatty tissue associated with granulomatous inflammation or a foreign-body reaction around a deposit of injected material containing an oily substance.

lipohypertrophy /lip'ōhīpur'trəfē/, a buildup of subcutaneous fat tissue at a site where insulin has been injected continuously.

lipoic acid /lipō'ik/, a bacterial growth factor found in liver and yeast.

lipoid /lip'oid/, resembling a lipid.

lipolysis /lipol'isis/, the breakdown or destruction of fats.

lipolytic /-lit'ik/, pertaining to the chemical breakdown of fat.

lipolytic digestion, a phase of food digestion in which fat molecules are split into glycerol and fatty acids.

lipoma /lipō'mə/ pl. **lipomas, lipomata** [Gk, *lipos + oma,* tumor], a benign tumor consisting of mature fat cells. —**lipomatous,** *adj.*

lipoma annulare colli, a diffuse, symmetric accumulation of fat around the neck, not a true lipoma.

lipoma arborescens, a fatty tumor of a joint, characterized by a treelike distribution of fat cells.

lipoma capsulare, a benign neoplasm characterized by the abnormal presence of fat cells in the capsule of an organ.

lipoma fibrosum, a fatty tumor containing masses of fibrous tissue.

lipomatosis /lip'ōmətō'sis/ [Gk, *lipos + oma,* tumor, *osis,* condition], a disorder characterized by abnormal tumorlike accumulations of fat in body tissues.

lipomatosis dolorosa, a disorder characterized by the abnormal accumulation of painful or tender fat deposits.

lipomatosis gigantea, a condition characterized by massive deposits of fat.

lipomatous /lipō'mətəs/ [Gk, *lipos,* fat, *oma,* tumor], pertaining to or resembling a benign tumor made up of mature fat cells.

lipomatous myxoma, a tumor containing fatty tissue that arises in connective tissue.

lipomatous nephritis, a rare condition in which the renal nephrons are replaced by fatty tissue. Kidney failure may result.

lipometabolism /-metab'əliz'əm/ [Gk, *lipos,* fat, *metabole,* change], the chemical processes involved in building up or breaking down fat molecules.

lipomyoma /-mī·ō'mə/ [Gk, *lipos,* fat; *mys,* muscle, *oma,* tumor], a tumor that combines characteristics of a lipoma and myoma.

lipomyxoma /lip'ōmiksō'mə/ pl. **lipomyxomas, lipomyxomata** [Gk, *lipos + myxa,* mucus, *oma,* tumor], a myxoma that contains fat cells.

L

lipophilia /-fĭl′yə/   [Gk, *lipos*, fat, *philein*, to love], a tendency to attract or absorb fat.

lipoprotein /lip′ōprō′tēn/   [Gk, *lipos* + *proteios*, first rank], a conjugated protein in which lipids form an integral part of the molecule. They are synthesized primarily in the liver; contain varying amounts of triglycerides, cholesterol, phospholipids, fat-soluble vitamins, and protein; and are classified according to their composition and density.

lipoprotein electrophoresis,   a blood test performed on patients with rare lipid profiles to predict coronary arteriosclerotic heart disease.

lipoprotein lipase (LPL),   an enzyme that plays a key role in breaking down triglycerides present in chylomicrons and very low–density lipoprotein particles, releasing their fatty acids for entry into tissue cells.

lipoproteins test (HDL, LDL, and VLDL),   a blood test, performed as part of a lipid profile, to identify persons who are at risk for developing heart disease and to monitor therapy if abnormalities are found.

liposarcoma /lip′ōsärkō′mə/ *pl.* **liposarcomas, liposarcomata** [Gk, *lipos* + *sarx,* flesh, *oma,* tumor], a malignant growth of primitive fat cells that occurs in the deep soft tissue of the extremities and retroperitoneum.

liposoluble /-sol′yəbəl/   [Gk, *lipos,* fat; L, *solubilis*], soluble in fats.

liposomal cytarabine,   a suspension of cytarabine molecules encapsulated in liposomes. It is a sustained-release preparation that is injected intrathecally in the treatment of meningitis associated with lymphoma.

liposomal daunorubicin,   an aqueous solution of the citrate salt of daunorubicin encapsulated within specifically constructed liposomes. It is used in the treatment of advanced Kaposi's sarcoma associated with AIDS.

liposomal doxorubicin,   doxorubicin hydrochloride encapsulated within liposomes, used in the treatment of Kaposi's sarcoma associated with AIDS.

liposome /lip′əsōm/   [Gk, *lipos,* fat, *soma,* body], a small, spheric particle consisting of a bilayer of phospholipid molecules surrounding an aqueous solution.

liposuction /-suk′shən/,   plastic surgery that removes adipose tissue with a suction pump device. It is used primarily to remove or reduce localized areas of fat around the abdomen, breasts, legs, face, and upper arms where the skin is contractile enough to redrape in a normal manner.

Liquaemin Sodium,   a trademark for an anticoagulant (heparin sodium).

liquefaction /lik′wəfak′shən/   [L, *liquere,* to flow, *facere,* to make], the process in which a solid or a gas is made liquid.

liquefactive degeneration /lik′wəfak′tiv/,   dissolution of tissues, resulting from hydrolytic enzymes released by leukocytes and tissue cells. It occurs in the skin of patients with lichen planus and lupus erythematosus.

liquid /lik′wid/   [L, *liquere,* to flow], a state of matter, intermediate between solid and gas, in which the molecules move freely among themselves and the substance flows freely with little application of force. Liquids have a fixed volume, but assume the shape of the vessel in which they are contained.

liquid crystal display (LCD),   a thin membrane containing liquid crystals, used for displays in computers and monitoring equipment.

liquid diet,   a diet consisting of foods that can be served in liquid or strained form but that may include custard, ice cream, pudding, tapioca, and soft-cooked eggs. It is prescribed in acute infections, in acute inflammatory conditions of the GI tract, and for patients unable to consume other soft or semifluid foods, usually after surgery.

liquid glucose,   a thick, syrupy odorless and colorless or yellowish liquid obtained by the incomplete hydrolysis of starch, primarily consisting of dextrose with dextrins, maltose, and water.

liquid scintillation counter,   a device for measuring radioactivity, usually beta particles, emitted from a sample dispersed in a liquid scintillation cocktail.

liquor /lik′ər/,   **1.** any fluid or liquid such as liquor amnii, the amniotic fluid. **2.** an alcoholic beverage.

lisdexamfetamine,   a CNS stimulant used to treat ADD with hyperactivity.

Lisfranc's fracture /lisfrangks′/   [Jacques Lisfranc, French surgeon, 1790–1847], a fracture dislocation of the foot in which one or all of the proximal metatarsals are displaced.

Lister, Joseph [Scottish surgeon, 1827–1912], the surgeon who introduced the use of antiseptic surgery in London hospitals in 1867. Lister operations were performed under a spray of diluted carbolic acid, instruments were dipped in carbolic acid, and wounds were dressed with gauze similarly treated.

lisp,   the mispronunciation of one or more of the sibilant consonant sounds, usually /s/ and /z/.

Listeria monocytogenes /lister′ē·ə mon′ōsī toj′inēz/ [Joseph Lister; Gk, *mono,* single, *kytos,* cell, *genein,* to produce], a common species of gram-positive, motile bacillus that causes listeriosis and a noninvasive food-borne diarrheal disease.

listeriosis /listir´ē·ō´sis/ [Joseph Lister; Gk, *osis*, condition], an infectious disease caused by a genus of gram-positive motile bacteria that are nonsporulating. It is transmitted by direct contact between infected animals and humans, through ingesting contaminated meat and dairy products, by inhalation of dust, or by contact with mud, sewage, or soil contaminated with the organism. The disorder is characterized in mild cases by fever, myalgia, nausea, and diarrhea and in severe cases by circulatory collapse, shock, endocarditis, hepatosplenomegaly, and a dark red rash over the trunk and legs. Fever, bacteremia, malaise, and lethargy are commonly seen. The signs of infection and the severity of the disease vary according to the site of infection and the age and condition of the person. Pregnant women characteristically experience a mild brief episode of illness, but fetal infection acquired through the placental circulation in utero is usually fatal.

Liston's forceps [Robert Liston, Scottish surgeon, 1794–1847], a kind of bone-cutting forceps.

liter (L) /lē´tər/ [Fr], a derived unit of volume equivalent to 1.057 quarts and defined as the volume occupied by a mass of 1 kg of water at standard temperature and pressure.

Lithane, a trademark for an antimanic drug (lithium carbonate).

lithiasis /lithī´əsis/ [Gk, *lithos*, stone, *osis*, condition], the formation of calculi in the hollow organs or ducts of the body. Lithiasis occurs most commonly in the gallbladder, kidney, and lower urinary tract. It may be asymptomatic, but more often the condition is extremely painful.

lithium (Li) /lith´ē·əm/ [Gk, *lithos*, stone], a silver-white alkali metal occurring in various compounds such as petalite and spodumene. Its atomic number is 3; its atomic mass is 6.94. Lithium is the lightest known metal and one of the most reactive elements. Its salts are used in the treatment of manias, but the mechanisms by which these compounds help to stabilize psychologic moods are not understood.

lithium carbonate, an antimanic agent prescribed in the treatment of manic episodes of manic-depressive disorder.

lithium fluoride (LiF), a compound commonly used for thermoluminescent dosimetry.

Lithobid, a trademark for an antimanic drug (lithium carbonate).

lithogenesis /lith´əjen´əsis/ [Gk, *lithos*, stone, *genein*, to produce], the origin of the formation of a calculus.

lithopedion /lith´əpē´dē·ən/ [Gk, *lithos* + *paidion*, child], a fetus that has died during an ectopic pregnancy and has become calcified or ossified.

Lithostat /lith´ostat/, a trademark for a preparation of a urease inhibitor used in treatment of kidney stones and UTIs (acetohydroxamic acid).

Lithotabs, a trademark for an antimanic drug (lithium carbonate).

lithotomy /lithot´əmē/ [Gk, *lithos* + *temnein*, to cut], **1.** the surgical excision of a calculus, especially one from the urinary tract. **2.** a position in OR in which the patient is supine with legs raised and abducted to expose the perineal region. The legs are placed in stirrups to maintain the position.

lithotomy forceps, a forceps for the extraction of a calculus, usually from the urinary tract.

lithotomy position, the position assumed by the patient lying supine with the hips and knees flexed and the thighs abducted and rotated externally.

lithotripsy /lith´ətrip´sē/ [Gk, *lithos*, stone, *tribein*, to wear away], a procedure for eliminating a calculus in the renal pelvis, ureter, bladder, or gallbladder. It may be crushed surgically or by using a noninvasive method such as a pulsed dye laser. The fragments may then be expelled or washed out.

lithotrite /lith´ətrīt/ [Gk, *lithos*; L, *terere*, to rub], an instrument for crushing a stone in the urinary bladder. —**lithotrity,** *n.*

litigant /lit´əgənt/ [L, *litigare*, to go to law], in law, a party to a lawsuit.

litigate /lit´əgāt/, in law, to carry on a suit or to contest.

litigious paranoia [L, *litigare*, to go to law; Gk, *paranous*, madness], a form of paranoia in which the person seeks legal proof or justification for systematized delusions.

litmus paper /lit´məs/ [ONorse, *litmosi*, coloring herb; L, *papyrus*, paper], absorbent paper coated with litmus, a blue dye, that is used to determine pH. Acid substances or solutions turn blue litmus to red. Alkaline substances or solutions do not cause a color change in blue litmus.

litter [Fr, *lit*, bed], a stretcher.

live attenuated measles virus vaccine /əten´yoo̅·ā´tid/, a vaccine prepared from live strains of measles virus that have been cultured under conditions that cause them to lose their virulence without losing their ability to induce immunity. The vaccine is not recommended for pregnant women or others who may have certain medical conditions that tend to diminish immunity.

live attenuated vaccine, a vaccine prepared from live microorganisms or functional viruses whose disease-producing ability has been weakened but whose immunogenic properties have not.

live birth [AS, *libben,* to be alive; ONorse, *byrth*], the birth of a newborn, irrespective of the duration of gestation, that exhibits any sign of life, such as respiration, heartbeat, umbilical pulsation, or movement of voluntary muscles.

livedo /livē′dō/ [L, *liveo,* bluish spot], a blue or reddish mottling of the skin that worsens in cold weather and is probably caused by arteriolar spasm.

livedo reticularis, a disorder accentuated by exposure to cold and presenting with a characteristic reddish-blue mottling with a typical "fishnet" appearance. The condition involves the entire leg and, less often, the arms.

live measles and mumps virus vaccine, a vaccine prepared from live strains of measles and mumps viruses. The vaccine is commonly combined with live rubella viruses such as measles, mumps, and rubella vaccine and administered to normal infants at the age of 15 months.

live oral poliovirus vaccine, a vaccine prepared from three strains (trivalent) of live polioviruses. Primary immunization with the vaccine usually begins at the age of 2 months.

liver [AS, *lifer*], the largest gland of the body and one of its most complex organs. It is located in the upper cranial, right part of the abdominal cavity. It has a soft solid consistency, is shaped like an irregular hemisphere, and is dark reddish-brown. The liver is divided into four lobes, contains as many as 100,000 lobules, and is served by two distinct blood supplies. The hepatic artery conveys oxygenated blood to the liver, and the hepatic portal vein conveys nutrient-filled blood from the stomach and the intestines. More than 500 functions of the liver have been identified. Some of the major functions are the production of bile by hepatic cells; the secretion of glucose, proteins, vitamins, fats, and most of the other compounds used by the body; the processing of hemoglobin for vital use of its iron content; and the conversion of poisonous ammonia to urea. The hepatic cells also detoxify numerous ingested substances, such as alcohol, nicotine, and other poisons, as well as various toxic substances produced by the intestine.

liver abscess [L, *abscedere,* to go away; AS, *lifer*], an abscess in the liver cells, usually caused by an amebic infection, bacterial infection, or trauma. It is characterized by sweats and chills, pain, nausea, and vomiting.

liver biopsy, a diagnostic procedure in which a special needle is introduced into the liver under local anesthesia to obtain a specimen for pathologic examination.

liver cancer, a malignant neoplastic disease of the liver. Primary tumors are associated with cirrhosis of the liver in 70% of the cases. Other risk factors include hemochromatosis, hepatitis, schistosomiasis, exposure to vinyl chloride or arsenic, and possibly nutritional deficiencies. Alcoholism may be a predisposing factor, but nonalcoholic cirrhosis is a greater risk than alcoholic cirrhosis. Aflatoxins in moldy grain and peanuts appear to be linked to high rates of hepatocellular carcinoma. Characteristics of liver cancer are abdominal bloating, anorexia, weakness, dull upper abdominal pain, ascites, mild jaundice, and a tender enlarged liver; in some cases tumor nodules are palpable on the liver surface.

liver disease, any one of a group of disorders of the liver. Characteristics of liver disease are jaundice, anorexia, hepatomegaly, ascites, and impaired consciousness.

liver failure [AS, *lifer*; L, *fallere,* to deceive], a condition in which the liver fails to fulfill its function or is unable to meet the demands made on it. Anorexia, fatigue, and weakness are common symptoms of liver cell failure, whereas jaundice indicates a biliary obstruction, and fever may accompany viral or alcoholic liver diseases.

liver fluke [AS, *lifer* + *floc*], a parasitic trematode belonging to the class Trematoda with six genera that may infest the liver. The most important species affecting humans in industrialized countries is *Clonorchis sinensis,* which is usually acquired by eating freshwater fish containing the encysted larvae. Infestations are most likely to result from ingestion of raw, dried, salted, or pickled freshwater fish and can be prevented by thorough cooking of such fish.

liver function test (LFT), one of several tests used to evaluate various functions of the liver, including metabolism, storage, filtration, and excretion. Kinds of liver function tests include alanine aminotransferase test, alkaline phosphatase test, prothrombin time, and serum bilirubin.

liver scan, a noninvasive technique of visualizing the size, shape, and consistency of the liver and for assessing the liver's functional status. It involves IV injection of a radioactively labeled compound that is readily taken up and trapped in the Kupffer cells of the liver. Liver scans are useful for diagnosing three-dimensional lesions such as abscesses and tumors, for performing biopsies, and for evaluating hepatomegaly, jaundice, and ascites.

liver segments, the eight regions of the liver based on blood supply and biliary drainage.

liver spot *nontechnical.* a variably pigmented lentigo occurring on the exposed skin of older Causasians.

liver transplantation, a treatment for end-stage hepatic dysfunction in which a donor liver is matched to the blood group to the recipient. The transplanted organ may be introduced as an auxiliary liver or as a total replacement. The procedure requires five anastomoses and many units of blood. Because of a shortage of child-size livers, pediatric transplants often are performed with a segment of an adult liver. Common postoperative complications include acute graft rejection, infection, hepatic complications (bile leakage, abscess formation, hepatic thrombosis), acute renal failure, giant emphysematous blebs, and fungal infections.

livid /liv'id/ [L, *lividus,* bluish], pertaining to an injury that is congested and has a bluish discoloration.

lividity /livid'itē/ [L, *lividus,* bluish], a tissue condition of being red or blue because of venous congestion, as in a contusion.

living related donor, an organ donor who is a close blood relative of the recipient.

living unrelated donor, one who is not a close blood relative of the recipient.

living will [AS, *libben* + *willa,* wish], **1.** an advance declaration by a patient that, if determined to be hopelessly and terminally ill, the person does not want to be connected to life support equipment. **2.** a written agreement between a patient and physician to withhold heroic measures if the patient's condition is found to be irreversible.

livor mortis /lī'vər/, a purple discoloration of the skin in some dependent body areas following death as a result of blood cell destruction.

lizard /liz'ərd/ [L, *lacerta*], a scaly-skinned reptile with a long body and tail and two pairs of legs. The large Gila monster and the beaded lizard are the only North American lizards known to be venomous. The symptoms of their bites are similar to those of the bites from poisonous snakes.

LLD, abbreviation for **lower level discriminator.**

LLE, abbreviation for *left lower extremity.*

LLQ, abbreviation for *left lower quadrant* of the abdomen.

LMA, abbreviation for *left mentoanterior fetal position.*

L.M.D., abbreviation for *licensed medical doctor.*

LMFT, abbreviation for **licensed marriage and family therapist.**

LMP, 1. abbreviation for *last menstrual period.* **2.** abbreviation for *left mentoposterior fetal position.*

LMT, abbreviation for *left mentotransverse fetal position.*

LMWH, abbreviation for **low-molecular-weight heparin.**

Loa /lo'ə/, a genus of nematodes of the superfamily Filarioidea. *L. loa* is a threadlike species 2.5 to 5 cm long found in West Africa. It inhabits the subcutaneous connective tissue of the human body and is seen especially as an eye worm about the orbit and under the conjunctiva. It causes itching and occasionally edematous swellings (Calabar swellings).

LOA, abbreviation for *left occipitoanterior fetal position.*

load, a departure from normal body values for parameters such as water content, salt concentration, and heat. A positive load indicates a higher-than-normal value, whereas a negative load indicates a below-normal value.

loading, 1. the administration of a substance in sufficient quantity to test a patient's ability to metabolize or absorb it. **2.** the exertion of force on a muscle or ligament to increase its strength.

loading response stance stage [AS, *lad, support;* L, *responsum,* reply], one of the five stages of the stance phase of walking or gait, specifically associated with the moment when the leg reacts to and accepts the weight of the body.

loads [AS, *lad,* support], *slang.* a fixed combination of a sedative hypnotic (glutethimide) and a major opioid analgesic (codeine), which is taken orally by drug abusers for a euphoric effect reported to be similar to that produced by heroin but longer lasting.

Loa loa /lō'ä lō'ä/, a parasitic worm of western and central Africa that causes loiasis.

lobar bronchus /lō'bär/ [Gk, *lobos,* lobe, *bronchos,* windpipe], a bronchus extending from a primary bronchus to a segmental bronchus into one of the lobes of the right or left lung.

lobar buds, secondary bronchial buds.

lobar nephronia, acute pyelonephritis.

lobar pneumonia, a severe infection of one or more of the five major lobes of the lungs that, if untreated, eventually results in consolidation of lung tissue. The disease is characterized by fever, chills, cough, rusty sputum, rapid shallow breathing, cyanosis, nausea, vomiting, and pleurisy. *Streptococcus pneumoniae* is the usual cause. Complications include lung abscess, atelectasis, empyema, pericarditis, and pleural effusion.

lobate /lō′bāt/, organized in lobes or rounded divisions.

lobe /lōb/ [Gk, *lobos*], **1.** a roundish projection of any structure. **2.** a part of any organ, demarcated by sulci, fissures, or connective tissue, as the lobes of the brain, liver, and lungs.—**lobar, lobular,** *adj.*

lobectomy /lōbek′təmē/ [Gk, *lobos* + *ektomē*, excision], the surgical excision of one or more lobes of a lung. It is performed to remove a malignant tumor or large benign tumor and to treat uncontrolled bronchiectasis, trauma with hemorrhage, congenital anomalies, or intractable TB.—**lobectomize,** *v.*

lobe of ear [Gk, *lobos*, lobe; AS, *eare*], the lower part of the auricle that contains no cartilage.

lobotomy /lōbot′əmē/ [Gk, *lobos* + *temnein,* to cut], a neurosurgical procedure (craniotomy) in which the nerve fibers in the bundle of white matter in the frontal lobe of the brain are severed to interrupt the transmission of various affective responses. Severe intractable depression and pain are among the indications for the operation. It is seldom performed because it has many unpredictable and undesirable effects, including personality change, aggression, socially unacceptable behavior, incontinence, apathy, and lack of consideration for others.

lobular carcinoma /lob′yələr/ [Gk, *lobos* + *karkinos,* crab, *oma,* tumor], a neoplasm that often forms a diffuse mass and accounts for a small percentage of breast tumors.

lobule /lob′yo͞ol/, a small lobe, such as the soft lower pendulous part of the external ear.—**lobular,** *adj.*

LOC, 1. abbreviation for **level of consciousness. 2.** abbreviation for *loss of consciousness.*

local [L, *locus,* place], **1.** pertaining to a small circumscribed area of the body. **2.** pertaining to a treatment or drug applied locally. **3.** *informal.* a local anesthetic.

local adaptation syndrome (LAS), the localized response of a tissue, organ, or system that occurs as a reaction to stress.

local anaphylaxis [L, *locus,* place; Gk, *ana* + *phylaxis*], a hypersensitivity reaction in which injections of an antigen result in localized swellings and necrosis of the skin and subcutaneous tissues.

local anesthesia, the infiltration of a local anesthetic medication to induce the absence of sensation into a small area of the body. The anesthetic may be applied topically to the surface of the skin or membrane or injected subcutaneously or intradermally. Advantages include low cost, ease of administration, low toxicity, and rapid recovery.

local anesthetic, a medication used to prevent the transmission of impulses through nerves to eliminate sensation in a defined area of the body. It can also prevent motor and atonomic function in this area. The effect is transient (time limited). Drugs available for local anesthesia are classified as members of the ester or the amide family.

local cerebral blood flow (LCBF), in PET, a parametric image of blood flow through the brain expressed as milliliters per minute per 100 g of brain tissue.

local cerebral metabolic rate of glucose utilization (LCMRG), in PET, a parametric image of brain activity expressed as milligrams of glucose used per minute per 100 g of brain tissue.

local control, the arrest of cancer growth at the site of origin.

local hypothermia, the heating of a local area of tissue to therapeutic temperatures.

local immunity, a state of protection against disease in a particular organ, tissue, or anatomic site mediated by localized antibodies or lymphoid cells.

local infection [L, *locus,* place, *inficere,* to stain], an infection involving bacteria that invade the body at a specific point and remain there, multiplying, until eliminated.

localization /lō′kəlīzā′shən/ [L, *locus,* place], **1.** the designation of a particular site for a lesion or organ function. **2.** the determination of the site of a biologic function. **3.** the assignment of a position to an object detected by radiography.—**localize,** *v.*

localization film [L, *locus,* place; Gk, *izein,* to cause; AS, *filmen,* membrane], a radiographic film taken to confirm a treatment effect or to view the position of an intracavitary or interstitial implant, especially for the purpose of computing the radiation dose delivered.

localizer image, an image used to localize a specific body part in CT.

local lesion [L, *locus,* place, *laesio,* hurting], **1.** a lesion anywhere on the body that does not spread. **2.** a lesion of the CNS characterized by distinctive local symptoms.

local osteolytic hypercalcemia (LOH), a syndrome of malignancy-associated hypercalcemia resulting from the action of locally acting osteolytic factors released in conjunction with tumor deposits adjacent to bone.

local paralysis, a loss of motor control that is confined to a single muscle, muscle group, or part of the body.

local reaction [L, *locus,* place, *re + agere,* to act], a reaction to treatment that occurs at the site at which it was administered.

locant /lō′kənt/, a number or letter code that locates the position of an atom, radical, or compound in the structure of a more complex molecule.

location [L, *locus,* place, *atus,* process], a specific place in the memory of a computer where a unit of information is stored.

lochia /lō′kē-ə/ [Gk, *lochos,* childbirth], the discharge that flows from the vagina after childbirth. During the first 2 to 4 days after delivery, the lochia is red or brownish red (lochia rubra) and is made up of blood, endometrial decidua, fetal lanugo, vernix, and sometimes meconium, and it has a fleshy odor. About the third day the amount of blood diminishes. The placental site exudes serous material, erythrocytes, lymph, cervical mucus, and microorganisms from the superficial layer called lochia serosa. During the next 10 to 14 days, bacteria appear in large numbers along with mucinous decidual material and epithelial cells, causing the lochia to appear whitish yellow (lochia alba). This may continue for 3 to 6 weeks into the postpartum period.—**lochial,** *adj.*

locked-in syndrome [ME, *loc*; Gk, *syn,* together, *dromos,* course], a paralytic condition, caused by bilateral destruction of the medulla oblongata or pons, in which a person may be conscious and alert but unable to communicate except by eye movements or blinking (e.g., pseudocoma). The condition renders the individual unable to speak or move any of the limbs.

locked knee [AS, *loc + cneow*], a condition in which the knee is fixed in either a flexed or an extended position, often caused by longitudinal splitting of the medial meniscus.

locking point [AS, *loc,* lock; L, *punctum,* puncture], a point on the body at which light pressure can be applied to help a weak or debilitated patient maintain a desired posture or position. A basic locking point is the body's center of gravity, at the level of the second sacral vertebra, where mild pressure can assist a patient in standing or walking erect.

locomotion [L, *locus,* place, *motio,* movement], movement or the ability to move from one place or position to another.

locomotor [L, *locus + motio*], pertaining to locomotion.

loculate /lok′yŏŏlāt/ [L, *loculus,* little place], divided into small spaces or cavities.

loculation /lok′yəla′shən/, the presence of numerous small spaces or cavities.

loculus /lok′yŏŏləs/ [L, little place], a small chamber, pocket, or cavity, such as the interior of a polyp.

locum tenens /lō′kəm ten′ənz/ [L, *locus,* place, *tenere,* to hold], a physician who is contacted to work on a temporary basis to fill in for a vacancy, vacation, or extended leave.

locus *pl.* **loci** /lō′sī, lō′kē/ [L, place], a specific place or position, such as the locus of a particular gene on a chromosome.

locus ceruleus [L, *locus,* place, *caeruleus,* sky-blue], a deeply pigmented group of several thousand neurons in the floor of the fourth ventricle. It is part of a major norepinephrine pathway of the CNS.

locus of control [L, *locus,* place; Fr, *controle*], a center of perceived responsibility for one's behavior. Individuals with an internal locus of control believe that they can control events related to their life, whereas those with an external locus of control tend to believe that real power resides in forces outside themselves and determines their life.

locus of infection, a site in the body where an infection originates.

lodoxamide /lō·dok′sämīd/, a mast cell stabilizer that inhibits immediate hypersensitivity, applied topically to the eye for treatment of allergen-induced conjunctivitis, keratitis, and keratoconjunctivitis.

Loestrin, a trademark for an oral contraceptive containing an estrogen (ethinyl estradiol) and a progestin (norethindrone acetate).

Löffler's syndrome /lef′lərz/ [Wilhelm Löffler, Swiss physician, 1887–1972], a benign, idiopathic disorder marked by episodes of pulmonary eosinophilia, transient opacities in the lungs, anorexia, breathlessness, fever, and weight loss. Recovery is spontaneous and prompt.

logotherapy /log′ōther′əpē/ [Gk, *logos,* word, *therapeia,* treatment], a treatment modality based on the application of humanistic and existential psychology to assist a patient in finding meaning and purpose in life and unique life experiences.

log roll [ME, *logge*; L, *roto,* turn around], a maneuver used to turn a reclining patient from one side to the other or completely over without flexing the spinal column. The arms of the patient are folded across the chest and the legs extended. A draw sheet under the patient is manipulated by attending health care team members or nursing personnel to facilitate the procedure.

LOH, abbreviation for **local osteolytic hypercalcemia.**

loiasis /lō·ī′əsis/, a form of filariasis caused by the worm *Loa loa*. The worms may migrate in subcutaneous tissue, producing localized inflammation known as Calabar swellings. The disease is acquired through the bite of an infected African deer fly.

loin [ME, *loyn,* flank], a part of the body on each side of the spinal column between the false ribs and the hip bones.

loin pain–hematuria syndrome, a syndrome of intense loin pain, either unilateral or bilateral, lasting from a few days to weeks, followed by hematuria, usually seen in young women. The cause is unknown, but some cases have been linked to treatment with estrogen compounds.

lomefloxacin /lo'mĕflok'säsin/, a broad-spectrum antibiotic effective against a wide range of aerobic gram-negative and gram-positive organisms.

lomefloxacin hydrochloride, the hydrochloride salt of lomefloxacin, administered orally in the treatment of bronchitis and the treatment and prevention of UTIs.

Lomotil, a trademark for an antidiarrheal fixed-combination drug containing an antiperistaltic (diphenoxylate hydrochloride) and an anticholinergic (atropine sulfate).

lomustine /lōmus'tēn/, an antineoplastic alkylating agent prescribed in the treatment of a variety of malignant neoplastic diseases, including brain tumors and Hodgkin's disease.

Lonalac, a trademark for a low-sodium nutritional supplement.

loneliness severity, a nursing outcome from the Nursing Outcomes Classification (NOC) defined as the severity of emotional, social, or existential isolation response.

long-acting drug [AS, *lang;* L, *agere,* to do; Fr, *drogue,* drug], a pharmacologic agent with a prolonged effect because of a formulation resulting in the slow release of the active principle or the continued absorption of small amounts of the dosage of the drug over an extended period.

long-acting insulin, a preparation of insulin modified by an interaction with zinc under specific chemical conditions and supplied as a suspension with a prolonged action. An injection of the preparation takes effect within 8 hours, reaches a peak of action in 16 to 24 hours, and has a duration of action of more than 36 hours.

long-acting thyroid stimulator (LATS), an immunoglobulin, probably an autoantibody, that exerts a prolonged stimulatory effect on the thyroid gland, causing rapid growth of the gland and excess activity of thyroid function, resulting in hyperthyroidism.

long-acting thyroid stimulator protector (LATS-P), an antibody that inhibits the neutralization of long-acting thyroid stimulator and is found in the serum of persons with Graves' disease.

long-arm cast [AS, *lang + earm,* arm; ONorse, *kasta*], an orthopedic cast applied to immobilize the arm from the hand to the upper arm.

long below-knee (BK) amputation, transtibial amputation in which the division is in the distal third of the tibia.

long bone, any of the bones that contribute to the height or length of an extremity, particularly the bones of the legs and arms.

longevity /lonjev'itē/ [L, *longus,* long, *aevum,* age], the number of years an average person of a particular age is expected to continue living. It is determined by statistical tables based on mortality rates of various population groups.

longissimus /lonjis'iməs/ [L, longest, very long], a general term denoting a long structure, as a muscle.

longitudinal /lon'jətoo'dənəl/ [L, *longitudo,* length], **1.** pertaining to a measurement in the direction of the long axis of an object, body, or organ, such as the longitudinal arch of the foot. **2.** pertaining to a scientific study that is conducted over a long period of time.

longitudinal diffusion, the diffusion of solute molecules in the direction of flow of the mobile phase.

longitudinal dissociation, the insulation of parallel pathways of cardiac impulses from each other, usually in the atrioventricular junction.

longitudinal fissure [L, *longitudo,* length, *fissura,* cleft], the largest and deepest groove between the medial surfaces of the cerebral hemispheres.

longitudinal presentation [L, *longitudo,* length, *praesentare,* to show], the normal presentation of a fetus, with the long axis of the infant body parallel to that of the mother.

longitudinal sound waves, pressure waves formed by the oscillation of particles or molecules parallel to the axis of wave propagation. The compression and expansion of such waves at high frequencies is the principle on which ultrasonography is based.

long-leg cast, an orthopedic cast applied to immobilize the leg from the toes to the upper thigh.

long-leg cast with walker, an orthopedic cast applied to immobilize the leg from the toes to the upper thigh in treating certain leg fractures. This type of cast is the same as the long-leg cast but incorporates a rubber walker, enabling the patient to walk while the leg is encased in the cast and when weight-bearing ambulation is allowed.

long QT syndrome, an inherited cardiac disorder characterized by prolongation of the QT interval. The disorder is associated with ventricular tachycardia, cardiac arrhythmias, syncope, and sudden death.

long-scale contrast, a high-kilovolt radiographic image containing a wide range and great number of shades of gray with little difference in the adjacent tones.

long-term care (LTC), the provision of medical, social, and personal care services on a recurring or continuing basis to persons with chronic physical or mental disorders.

long terminal repeats, identical nucleotide sequences occurring at each end of a proviral genome or a transposon and believed to be essential for integration of the molecule into host DNA.

long-term memory, the ability to recall sensations, events, ideas, and other information for long periods of time without apparent effort.

long thoracic nerve, one of a pair of supraclavicular branches from the roots of the brachial plexus.

long thoracic nerve injury, damage to the nerve (C5-7) that innervates the serratus muscle, which anchors the apex of the scapula to the posterior of the rib cage. Symptoms include an abnormally prominent scapula and difficulty in flexing the outstretched arm above the shoulder level, protracting the shoulder, or performing scapula abduction and adduction.

long tract signs, neurologic signs such as clonus, muscle spasticity, or bladder involvement that usually indicate a lesion in the middle or upper parts of the spinal cord or in the brain.

longus capitis, a muscle that flexes the head.

longus colli, a muscle that flexes the neck anteriorly and laterally, with slight rotation to the opposite side.

Loniten, a trademark for an antihypertensive (minoxidil).

loop [ME, *loupe*], **1.** a fine wire which, when energized with electricity, becomes a curved surgical instrument. It is used in loop excision procedures. **2.** curve or bend in a tube or tube-like structure.

loop colostomy [ME, *loupe*; Gk, *kolon*, colon, *stoma*, mouth], a type of temporary colostomy performed as part of the surgical treatment for repair of some colon diseases. The procedure involves bringing an intact segment of colon proximal to the repair through an abdominal incision and suturing it onto the abdomen.

loop excision, the surgical removal of dysplastic tissue cells with a small wire loop. The technique is used to remove intraepithelial neoplasms from the uterine cervix.

loop of Henle /hen'lē/ [ME, *loupe;* Friedrich Gustave Henle, German anatomist, 1809–1885], the U-shaped part of a renal tubule, consisting of a thin descending limb and a thick ascending limb.

loose anagen hair syndrome, a syndrome of unknown cause, usually seen in children, in which scalp hair can be plucked easily and painlessly during the anagen part of the hair cycle, resulting from defective anchorage of the hair shaft to the follicle. There is also slowing of hair growth.

loose body, a fragment of solid tissue in a body cavity or joint.

loose fibrous tissue [ME, *lous,* not fastened], a constrictive, pliable fibrous connective tissue consisting of interwoven elastic and collagenous fibers, interspersed with fluid-filled areolae.

looseness of association (LOA) [ME, *lous,* not fastened], in psychiatry, a disturbance of thinking in which the association of ideas and thought patterns becomes so vague, fragmented, diffuse, and unfocused as to lack any logical sequences or relationship to any preceding concepts or themes.

loose-pack joint position, a point in the ROM of a joint at which articulating surfaces are the least congruent and the supporting structures are the most lax.

Looser's zones /lō′zərz/ [Emil Looser, Swiss physician, 1877–1936], transverse translucent bands, sometimes symmetric, seen radiographically in the cortex of bones affected with osteomalacia or certain other deficiency diseases.

Lo/Ovral, a trademark for an oral contraceptive containing an estrogen (ethinyl estradiol) and a progestin (norgestrel).

LOP, abbreviation for *left occipitoposterior fetal position.*

loperamide hydrochloride /lōper′əmīd/, an antiperistaltic agent prescribed in the treatment of diarrhea.

Lopid, a trademark for a lipid-regulating agent (gemfibrozil).

lopinavir /lopin′ävir/, an HIV protease inhibitor, an antiviral agent used in combination with ritonavir in the treatment of HIV infection.

Lopressor, a trademark for a beta-adrenergic receptor blocking agent used in the treatment of hypertension (metoprolol tartrate).

Loprox, a trademark for an antifungal (ciclopirox olamine).

loratadine /lärat′ädēn/, a nonsedating antihistamine (H_1 receptor antagonist) used for treatment of allergic rhinitis and chronic idiopathic urticaria and as a treatment adjunct in asthma.

L

lorazepam /lôrā′zəpam/, a benzodiazepine tranquilizer prescribed in the treatment of anxiety, nervous tension, and insomnia and given intravenously to abort status epilepticus and for preanesthesia.

lordoscoliosis /lôr′dōskō′lē·ō′sis/ [Gk, *lordos*, bent, *skoliosis*, curvature], a combination of lordosis and scoliosis.

lordosis /lôrdō′sis/ [Gk, *lordos*, bent forward, *osis*, condition], an abnormal anterior concavity of the lumbar part of the back.

lordotic pelvis /lôrdot′ik/ [Gk, *lordos*, bent forward; L, *pelvis*, basin], a deformed pelvis that bends forward in the lumbar region and is associated with lordosis.

LOS, abbreviation for **length of stay.**

losartan, an antihypertensive agent used to treat hypertension, either alone or in combination with other drugs.

loss of consortium [ME, *lossen*, to lose; L, *consortionis*, companionship], in law, a claim for damages sought in recompense for the loss of conjugal relations, including society, affection, and assistance, and impairment or loss of sexual relations.

LOT, abbreviation for *left occipitotransverse fetal position.*

loteprednol /lo′tĕpred′nol/, a corticosteroid applied topically to the conjunctiva in the treatment of seasonal allergic conjunctivitis, postoperative inflammation, and ocular inflammatory disorders.

lotion [L, *lotio*, a washing], a liquid preparation applied externally to protect the skin or to treat a dermatologic disorder.

Lotrimin, a trademark for an antifungal (clotrimazole).

loupe /lo͞op/ [Fr, magnifying glass], a magnifying lens mounted in a frame worn on the head, as used to examine the eyes.

louse bite, a minute puncture wound produced by a louse that may transmit typhus, trench fever, and relapsing fever. Secondary infection may result from scratching the affected area.

low back pain (lbp) [ME, *low*; AS, *baec*; L, *poena*, penalty], local or referred pain at the base of the spine caused by a sprain, a strain, osteoarthritis, ankylosing spondylitis, a neoplasm, or a herniated intervertebral disk. Low back pain is a common complaint and is often associated with poor posture, obesity, sagging abdominal muscles, sitting for prolonged periods of time, or improper body mechanics.

low-birth weight (LBW) infant, a newborn whose weight at birth is less than 2500 g, regardless of gestational age.

low-calcium diet, a diet that restricts the use of calcium and eliminates most of the dairy foods, all breads made with milk or dry skimmed milk, and deep-green leafy vegetables. It is prescribed for patients with absorptive hypercalciuria.

low-caloric diet, a diet that is prescribed to limit calorie intake, usually to cause a reduction in body weight. Such diets may be designated as a very low–calorie diet, 1000-calorie diet, or other specific numbers of calories.

low cervical cesarean section, a surgical procedure to deliver a baby through a transverse incision in the thin supracervical part of the lower uterine segment, behind the bladder and the bladder flap. This incision bleeds less during surgery and heals with a stronger scar than the higher vertical scar of the classic cesarean section.

low-cholesterol diet, a diet that restricts foods containing animal fats and saturated fatty acids, egg yolk, cream, butter, milk, muscle and organ meats, and shellfish. It is indicated for persons with high serum cholesterol levels, cardiovascular disorders, obesity, hyperlipidemia, hypercholesterolemia, or hyperlipoproteinemia.

low-density lipoprotein (LDL), a plasma protein provided from very low–density lipoprotein (VLDL) or by the liver, containing relatively more cholesterol and triglycerides than protein. It is derived in part, if not completely, from the intravascular breakdown of the VLDLs and delivers lipids and cholesterol to the body tissues.

low-density lipoprotein (LDL) receptor disorder, an inherited autosomal-dominant trait characterized by an abnormality in clearance of LDL, caused by a defect in LDL receptor activity.

low-dose tolerance, a temporary and incomplete immunosuppression induced by the administration of subimmunogenic doses of soluble antigen. The tolerance is achieved in the neonatal period, when lymphoid cells have not matured enough to activate a response.

lower esophageal sphincter, the terminal few centimeters of the esophagus, near the esophagogastric junction, which normally remain constricted except during swallowing and prevent reflux of gastric contents into the esophagus.

lower extremity monitoring, a nursing intervention from the Nursing Interventions Classification (NIC) defined as the collection, analysis, and use of patient data to categorize risk and prevent injury to the lower extremities.

lower extremity suspension [ME, *low*; L, *extremitas* + *suspendere*, to hang], an orthopedic procedure used in the treatment of bone fractures and the correction of orthopedic abnormalities of the lower limbs. Traction equipment, including metal frames, ropes, and pulleys, is applied to relieve the weight of the involved lower limb rather than to exert traction pull.

lower level discriminator (LLD), an electronic device used in nuclear medicine to discriminate against all radionuclide pulses whose heights are below a given level.

lower motor neuron dysarthria, a disorder of articulation caused by weakness or paralysis of the articulatory muscles and marked by a rasping, monotonous voice and, in advanced forms, shriveling and flaccidity of the tongue and laxness and tremulousness of the lips, seen in advanced cases of lesions of motor nuclei of the lower pons or medulla oblongata.

lower motor neuron paralysis, paralysis resulting from an injury or lesion that damages the cell bodies or axons, or both, of the lower motor neurons, which are located in the anterior horn cells of the spinal cord and the spinal and peripheral nerves. In partial transection of the spinal cord, function is altered in varying degrees, depending on the areas innervated by the nerves involved.

lower pole ureter, the ureter draining the lower pole of a duplex kidney.

lower respiratory tract, one of the two divisions of the respiratory system. The lower respiratory tract includes the left and right bronchi and the alveoli where the exchange of oxygen and carbon dioxide occurs during the respiratory cycle. The bronchi divide into smaller bronchioles in the lungs, the bronchioles into alveolar ducts, the ducts into alveolar sacs, and the sacs into alveoli.

Lowe's syndrome [Charles U. Lowe, American pediatrician, 1921–2012], a sex-linked condition in males characterized by progressive mental deterioration, renal tubular dysfunction, and cortical cataracts with or without glaucoma.

low-fat diet [ME, *low;* AS, *faett;* Gk, *diaita,* life-style], a diet containing limited amounts of fat and consisting chiefly of easily digestible foods of high carbohydrate content. It includes all vegetables, lean meats, fish, fowl, pasta, cereals, and whole wheat or enriched bread. Experts recommend that no more than 30% of one's daily calories should come from fatty foods and that no more than 10% should come from saturated fats.

low-fat milk, milk containing 1% to 2% fat, making it an intermediate in fat content between whole and skimmed milk.

low-flow oxygen delivery system, respiratory care equipment that allows the patient to inhale some ambient air along with the delivered oxygen. As the patient's ventilatory pattern changes, different amounts of air are mixed with the constant flow of oxygen, thus causing the inspired oxygen concentration to vary.

low forceps [ME, *low*; L, *forceps,* pair of tongs], an obstetric operation in which forceps are used to deliver a baby whose head is on the pelvic floor. It is commonly required for the delivery of mothers whose expulsive powers have been weakened by analgesia, anesthesia, or fatigue.

low-grade fever, an oral temperature that is above 98.6° F (37° C) but lower than 100.4° F (38° C) for 24 hours.

low-grade infection [ME, *lah*; L, *gradus,* degree, *inficere,* to stain], a subacute or chronic infection with mild fever and no pus production.

low-molecular-weight heparin (LMWH), a class of drugs used to prevent potentially fatal blood clots in patients undergoing surgery or patients at risk for blood clots. LMWH has an advantage over regular heparin in that predictable plasma levels are achieved, obviating the need for regular monitoring of prothrombin time and partial thromboplastin time.

Lown-Ganong-Levine (LGL) syndrome /loun gənong′ lavēn′/ [Bernard Lown, American physician, b. 1921; William F. Ganong, American physiologist, 1924–2007; S.A. Levine, American physician, 1891–1966], a disorder of the atrioventricular (AV) conduction system marked by ventricular preexcitation. Part or all of the AV nodal connection is bypassed by an abnormal connection between the atria and the bundle of His.

low-power field, the low magnification field of vision under a light microscope.

low-protein diet [ME, *lah*, low; Gk, *proteios,* first rank, *diaita,* way of living], a diet proportionally low in protein, usually designed for persons who must restrict protein intake because of a metabolic abnormality associated with kidney failure or a liver disease.

low-purine diet, a diet used as adjunct therapy for gout patients who suffer from a painful accumulation of salts of uric acid in the joints. Purine-rich foods are primary sources of uric acid. They include meat, poultry, fish, and particularly organ meats such as liver, kidney, and sweetbreads.

low-residue diet, a diet that will leave a minimal residue in the lower intestinal tract after digestion and absorption. It consists of tender meats, poultry, fish, eggs, white bread, pasta, simple desserts, clear soups, tea, and coffee. The diet is prescribed in cases of diverticulitis, GI irritability or inflammation, and before and after GI surgery. Because it is lacking in

L

calcium, iron, and vitamins, it should be used only for a limited time or with nutrient supplementation.

low-saturated-fat diet, a diet that limits sources of saturated fats from animal meats, egg yolks, butter, and full-fat dairy foods. Two plant sources of saturated fat, coconut oil and palm oil, must also be limited.

low-sodium diet, a diet that restricts the use of sodium chloride plus other compounds containing sodium, such as baking powder or soda, monosodium glutamate, sodium citrate, sodium propionate, and sodium sulfate. It is indicated in hypertension, edematous states (especially when associated with cardiovascular disease), renal or liver disease, and therapy with corticosteroids. The degree of sodium restriction depends on the severity of the condition.

low-vision therapist, a doctor of optometry or ophthalmology who diagnoses and treats ocular and vision problems that cannot be corrected fully by pharmacologic means or surgery, conventional eye glasses, or contact lenses.

loxapine /lok′səpēn/, an antipsychotic agent prescribed in the treatment of schizophrenia.

Loxitane, a trademark for an antipsychotic (loxapine succinate).

Loxosceles /loksos′ēlēz/, a genus of six-eyed spiders, some of which have poisonous bites.

lp, abbreviation for **line pair.**

LP, abbreviation for **lumbar puncture.**

LPL, abbreviation for **lipoprotein lipase.**

Lpm, abbreviation for *liters per minute.*

LPN, abbreviation for **licensed practical nurse.**

LPS Act, a California law named for sponsors of the legislation (*L*anterman, *P*etris, and *S*hort) that provides for the protection and treatment of persons judged to be "gravely disabled" and thus unable to provide food, clothing, or shelter for themselves. The legislation was designed to safeguard the constitutional rights of persons threatened with involuntary commitment on the basis of a psychiatric diagnosis. Some other states have similar laws.

Lr, symbol for the element **lawrencium.**

LRN, abbreviation for **Laboratory Response Network.**

LSD, abbreviation for *lysergic acid diethylamide.*

LSF, abbreviation for **line spread function.**

L-shaped kidney, a fused kidney in which one renal mass is vertical and the other is inferior to it in a transverse position. This can be either a variety of horseshoe kidney or a type of crossed renal ectopia.

L-spine, abbreviation for **lumbar spine.**

L/S ratio, the lecithin/sphingomyelin ratio, used in a test for fetal lung maturity.

LTB, abbreviation for **laryngotracheobronchitis.**

LTC, abbreviation for **long-term care.**

LTH, abbreviation for *luteotropic hormone.*

L-Trp, abbreviation for *L-tryptophan.*

Lu, symbol for the element **lutetium.**

lubb /lub/, a syllable used to represent the first heart sound in auscultation, which is longer and lower pitched than the second heart sound.

lubb-dupp, an imitation of the two basic sounds heard in the cardiac cycle. Lubb represents the first sound (S_1) and is made by the closure of the mitral and tricuspid valves. It is lower in pitch and lasts slightly longer than the second sound, dupp (S_2), which is made by the closure of the aortic valve.

lubiprostone, a miscellaneous GI agent used to treat chronic idiopathic constipation.

lubricant /loo′brikənt/ [L, *lubricans,* making slippery], a fluid, ointment, or other agent capable of diminishing friction and making a surface slippery.

lubricating enema /loo′brəkā′ting/ [L, *lubricans,* making slippery; Gk, *enienai,* to send in], an enema used to lubricate the anal canal after surgery for hemorrhoids or to prevent fecal impaction. The enema solution may be made with warm olive or mineral oil.

Lucentis, a trademark for **ranibizumab.**

lucid /loo′sid/ [L, *lucidus,* clear], clear, rational, and able to be understood.

lucid interval, a period of relative mental clarity between periods of irrationality, especially in organic mental disorders such as delirium and dementia.

lucidity /loosid′itē/ [L, *lucidus,* clear], pertaining to clarity of mind, perception, or intelligibility.

lucid lethargy, a mental state characterized by a loss of will; an inability to act, even though the person is conscious and intellectual function is normal.

lucifugal /loosif′yəgəl/, repelled by bright light.

Lucio's leprosy phenomenon [R. Lucio, Mexican physician, 1819–1866], an acute form of diffuse lepromatous infection of the skin, characterized by intensely red, tender plaques, particularly on the legs.

lucipetal /loosip′ətəl/, attracted to bright light.

Ludiomil, a trademark for an antidepressant (maprotiline hydrochloride).

Ludwig's angina /lood′vigz/ [Wilhelm F. von Ludwig, German surgeon, 1790–1865;

L, *angina,* quinsy], a severe, potentially life-threatening form of cellulitis in the region of the submandibular gland. Inflammatory edema may distort the floor of the mouth and make swallowing difficult.

LUE, abbreviation for *left upper extremity.*

Luer-Lok connection, a connection between extracorporeal equipment for peritoneal dialysis and the intraabdominal catheter, using two rigid tubes that screw together.

Luer-Lok syringe /lōō′ərlōk′/, a glass or plastic syringe for injection having a simple screw lock mechanism that securely holds the needle in place.

Lufyllin, a trademark for a respiratory smooth muscle relaxant (dyphylline).

Lugol's solution [Jean G.A. Lugol, French physician, 1786–1851; L, *solutus,* unbound], an aqueous solution of iodine (5%) and potassium iodide (10%) that paradoxically suppresses the thyroid function, used in preparation for thyroidectomy and during treatment of thyrotoxic crisis.

Lukes-Collins classification [L.J. Lukes; R.D. Collins, 20th century American pathologists], a system of identifying non-Hodgkin's lymphomas according to B cell, T cell, true, and unclassifiable types. B-cell types include lymphocytic, plasmacytic, follicular cell lymphomas, and B-cell–derived immunoblastic lymphoma. T-cell types include T-cell–derived immunoblastic lymphoma and convoluted cell lymphoma. True types are of histiocytic origin.

lukewarm bath [ME, *luke*; AS, *wearm, baeth*], a bath in which the temperature of the water is between 90° F and 96° F.

LUL, abbreviation for *left upper lobe* of lung.

lumbago /lumbā′gō/ [L, *lumbus,* loin], pain in the lumbar region caused by a muscle strain, rheumatoid arthritis, osteoarthritis, or a herniated intervertebral disk. Ischemic lumbago, characterized by pain in the lower back and buttocks, is caused by vascular insufficiency, as in terminal aortic occlusion.

lumbar /lum′bər, lum′bär/ [L, *lumbus,* loin], pertaining to the part of the body between the thorax and the pelvis.

lumbar lordosis, the dorsally concave curvature of the lumbar spinal column when seen from the side.

lumbar nerves, the five pairs of spinal nerves rising in the lumbar region of the vertebral column. They become increasingly large the more caudal their origin and pass laterally and downward under the cover of the psoas major or between its fasciculi and form part of the lumbar plexus.

lumbar node, a node in one of the seven groups of parietal lymph nodes serving the abdomen and the pelvis.

lumbar plexus, a network of nerves formed by the ventral anterior primary divisions of the first three and the greater part of the fourth lumbar nerves. It is located on the inside of the posterior abdominal wall, either dorsal to the psoas major or among its fibers and ventral to the transverse processes of the lumbar vertebrae.

lumbar puncture (LP), a diagnostic or therapeutic procedure in which a hollow needle and stylet are introduced into the subarachnoid space of the lumbar part of the spinal canal to obtain CSF. Strict aseptic technique is used. Diagnostic indications include measuring of CSF pressure; obtaining CSF for laboratory analysis; and injecting oxygen or a radiopaque substance for radiographic visualization of the spinal canal and meninges and brain. Therapeutic indications for lumbar puncture include removing blood or pus from the subarachnoid space, injecting sera or drugs, withdrawing CSF to reduce ICP, introducing a local anesthetic to induce spinal anesthesia, and placing a small amount of the patient's blood in the subarachnoid space to form a clot to patch a hole in the dura to prevent leak of CSF into the epidural space.

lumbar radiculopathy, compression and irritation of nerve roots in the lumbar region, with resultant pain in the lower back and lower limbs.

lumbar rib, a rudimentary rib that articulates with the transverse process of the first lumbar vertebra.

lumbar spine (L-spine), that portion of the spine comprising the lumbar vertebrae.

lumbar subarachnoid peritoneostomy, a surgical procedure to drain CSF in hydrocephalus, usually in the newborn. It may be used when a temporary shunt is needed. A lumbar laminectomy is performed, and then a polyethylene tube is passed from the subarachnoid space around the flank and into the peritoneum.

lumbar subarachnoid ureterostomy, a surgical procedure to drain CSF through the ureter to the bladder in hydrocephalus, usually in the newborn. A lumbar laminectomy and a left nephrectomy are performed, after which a polyethylene tube is passed from the lumbar subarachnoid space through the paraspinal muscles and into the free ureter.

lumbar veins, four pairs of veins that collect blood by dorsal tributaries from the loins and abdominal tributaries from the walls of the abdomen.

lumbar vertebra, one of the five largest segments of the movable part of the vertebral column, distinguished by the absence of a foramen in the transverse process and by vertebral bodies without facets between the sacrum and thoracic vertebrae. The body of each lumbar vertebra is flattened or slightly concave superiorly and inferiorly and is deeply constricted ventrally at the sides.

lumbocostal /lum′bŏkos′tǎl/, pertaining to the lumbar region and ribs.

lumbodorsal fascia, the extensive subdivision of the vertebral fascia that sheaths the sacrospinalis muscle. It spreads caudally to become the glistening white lumbar aponeurosis and the origin of the latissimus dorsi. Medially it attaches to the sacrum, laterally to the ribs and the intercostal fascia, and cranially to the nuchal ligament.

lumbosacral /lum′bŏsā′krǎl/ [L, *lumbus,* loin, *sacrum,* sacred], pertaining to the lumbar vertebrae and the sacrum.

lumbosacral plexus [L, *lumbus,* loin, *sacrum,* sacred, *plexus,* braided], the combination of all the ventral anterior primary divisions of the lumbar, sacral, and coccygeal nerves. The lumbar and sacral plexuses supply the lower limb. The sacral nerves also supply the perineum through the pudendal plexus and the coccygeal area through the coccygeal plexus.

lumbrical plus deformity /lum′brikǎl/, a complication of rheumatoid arthritis in which the lumbricals (muscles in the hands and feet) become contracted. A main effect of the dysfunction is metacarpophalangeal joint flexion and interphalangeal joint extension.

lumen /lōō′mǎn/ *pl.* **lumina, lumens** [L, light], **1.** a tubular space or the channel within any organ or structure of the body. **2.** a unit of luminous flux that equals the flux emitted in a unit solid angle by a point source of one candle intensity.—**lumenal, luminal,** *adj.*

luminance, the brightness of a light-emitting source.

luminescence /lōō′mines′ǎns/ [L, *lumen,* light, *escens,* beginning], **1.** the emission of light by a material after excitation by some stimulus. **2.** the emission of light by intensifying-screen phosphors after x-ray interaction.

luminiferous /lōō′minif′ǎrǎs/ [L, *lumen,* light, *ferre,* to bear], pertaining to a medium that will transmit light.

luminophore /lōō′min′ǎfôr/, **1.** an organic compound or chemical grouping that emits light. **2.** a substance that emits light when illuminated.

lumpectomy /lumpek′tǎmē/ [ME, *lump,* mass; Gk, *ektomē,* excision], surgical excision of a tumor without removing large amounts of surrounding tissue.

lumpy jaw [ME, *lump,* mass, *ceowan,* to chew], *nontechnical.* actinomycosis of cows.

lunar, crescent-shaped.

lunar month /lōō′nǎr/ [L, *luna,* moon; AS, *monath,* month], a period of 4 weeks or 28 days, approximately the time required for the moon to revolve about the earth.

lunate bone /lōō′nāt/ [L, *luna,* moon; AS, *ban*], the carpal bone in the center of the proximal row of carpal bones between the scaphoid and triangular bones.

Lunesta, a trademark for *eszopiclone.*

lung (L) [AS, *lungen*], one of a pair of light, spongy organs in the thorax, constituting the main component of the respiratory system. The two highly elastic lungs are the main mechanisms in the body for inhaling (inspiring) air from which oxygen is extracted for the arterial blood system and for exhaling carbon dioxide dispersed from the venous system. The right lung is divided into three lobes; the left lung, two lobes. Each lung is composed of an external serous coat, which comprises the thin, visceral pleura; a subserous layer of areolar tissue that contains many elastic fibers and invests the entire surface of the organ; and the parenchyma, which is composed of secondary lobules divided into primary lobules, each of which consists of blood vessels, lymphatics, nerves, and an alveolar duct connecting with air spaces.

lung abscess [AS, *lungen*; L, *abscedere,* to go away], a complication of an inflammation and infection of the lung, often caused by aspiration of infected material from the mouth. On a chest x-ray, it is characterized by a cavity containing an air-fluid line.

lung biopsy, a test to obtain a specimen of pulmonary tissue for histologic examination to diagnose pulmonary parenchymal disease.

lung cancer, a pulmonary malignancy attributable in the majority of cases to cigarette smoking. Other predisposing factors are exposure to acronitrile, arsenic, asbestos, beryllium, chloromethyl ether, chromium, coal products, ionizing radiation, iron oxide, mustard gas, nickel, petroleum, uranium, and vinyl chloride. Lung cancer develops most often in scarred or chronically diseased lungs. It is usually far advanced when detected, because metastases may precede detection of the primary lesion in the lung. Symptoms of lung cancer include persistent cough, hoarseness, dyspnea, purulent or blood-streaked sputum, chest pain, and repeated attacks of bronchitis or pneumonia.

lung capacity, a lung volume that is the sum of two or more of the four primary, nonoverlapping lung volumes. Lung capacities are functional residual capacity, inspiratory capacity, total lung capacity, and vital capacity.

lung compliance, a measure of the ease of expansion of the lungs and thorax, determined by pulmonary volume and elasticity. A high degree of compliance indicates a loss of elastic recoil of the lungs, as in old age or emphysema. Decreased compliance means that a greater change in pressure is needed for a given change in volume, as in atelectasis, edema, fibrosis, pneumonia, or absence of surfactant. Dyspnea on exertion is the main symptom of diminished lung compliance.

lung fluke [AS, *lungen,* lung + *floc*], a parasitic flatworm of the genus and species *Paragonimus westermani.* It may enter the body as encysted larvae in crabs and crayfish. Symptoms of infestation include peribronchiolar distress and hemoptysis.

lung scan, a radiographic examination of a lung and its function.

lung surfactant, a detergent-like agent that reduces the surface tension of the liquid film covering the inner lining of the pulmonary alveoli.

lung transplantation, the transfer of an entire pulmonary organ system to a new site. The procedure may be performed as a combined cardiopulmonary transplantation.

lunula /lōōn′yələ/ *pl.* **lunulae** [L, *luna,* moon], a semilunar structure, such as the crescent-shaped pale area at the base of a fingernail or toenail.

lupoid, resembling systemic lupus erythematosus.

lupoid hepatitis, an autoimmune form of hepatitis with the histologic appearance of chronic active hepatitis. Many patients show lupoid cells in the blood without SLE.

Lupron, a trademark for a parenteral antineoplastic drug (leuprolide acetate).

lupus anticoagulant, an antibody specific for phospholipoproteins or phospholipid components of coagulation factors found in patients with SLE. It causes an increase in partial thromboplastin time and is associated with arterial and venous thrombosis, fetal loss, and thrombocytopenia.

lupus band test, a direct immunofluorescent method of visualizing a band of immunoglobulins and complement at the dermal-epidermal junction of involved skin in patients with SLE.

lupus pernio, a cutaneous form of sarcoidosis, characterized by smooth, shiny plaques on the face, fingers, and toes, clinically resembling frostbite.

lupus vulgaris, a rare cutaneous form of TB in which areas of the skin become ulcerated and heal slowly, leaving deeply scarred tissue. The disease is not related to SLE.

LUQ, abbreviation for *left upper quadrant* of the abdomen.

Luride, a trademark for a chemical prophylactic that reduces dental caries (sodium fluoride).

lusus naturae /lōō′səs/ [L, *lusus,* sport, *natura,* nature], a congenital anomaly; teratism.

lute /lōōt/ [L, *lutum,* mud], **1.** a substance such as cement, wax, or clay that coats a surface or joint area to make a tight seal. **2.** to coat or seal with such a substance.

luteal /lōō′tē·əl/, pertaining to the corpus luteum or its functions or effects.

luteal hormone [L, *luteus,* yellow; Gk, *hormaein,* to set in motion], a hormone produced by the **corpus luteum.**

luteal phase, the third phase of the human menstrual cycle, when the ovarian follicle ruptures and transforms into the corpus luteum.

luteal phase deficiency, female infertility or early miscarriage caused by inadequate secretion of progesterone during the luteal phase of the menstrual cycle or poor endometrial lining response to progesterone levels. It is associated with an abnormality in pituitary gland function.

lutein /lōō′tē·in/ [L, *luteus,* yellow], a yellow-red crystalline carotenoid pigment found in plants with carotenes and chlorophylls.

luteinization /lōō′tē·in′izā′shən/ [L,*luteus,* yellow], the formation of the corpus luteum from an ovarian follicle that had recently discharged an ovum. The process involves the hypertrophy of the follicular lutein cells and the development of blood vessels and connective tissue at the site.

luteinizing hormone (LH) /lōō′tē·inī′zing/ [L,*luteus,* yellow; Gk, *izein,* to cause, *hormein,* to begin activity], a glycoprotein hormone produced by the anterior pituitary gland. It stimulates the secretion of sex hormones by the ovary and the testes and is involved in the maturation of spermatozoa and ova. In males, it induces the secretion of testosterone by the interstitial cells of the testes. In females, LH, working together with follicle-stimulating hormone, stimulates the growing follicle in the ovary to secrete estrogen.

luteinizing hormone (LH) and follicle-stimulating hormone (FSH) assay, a blood test used in the evaluation of infertility. An LH assay is an easy way to determine if ovulation has occurred. The LH assay and FSH test also are used to

L

determine whether a gonadal insufficiency is primary (a problem with the ovary or testicle) or secondary (caused by pituitary insufficiency resulting in reduced levels of FSH and LH).

luteinizing hormone–releasing hormone (LH-RH), a neurohormone of the hypothalamus that stimulates and regulates the pituitary gland's release of the luteinizing hormone.

luteinizing hormone surge, a sharp increase in serum levels of luteinizing hormone seen around the middle of the menstrual cycle about 1 to 2 days before ovulation.

luteoma /lōō'tē-ō'mə/ *pl,* **luteomas, luteomata** [L, *luteus;* Gk, *oma,* tumor], **1.** a granulosa or theca cell tumor whose cells resemble those of the corpus luteum. **2.** a unilateral or bilateral nodular hyperplasia of ovarian lutein cells, occasionally developing during the last trimester of pregnancy.

lutetium (Lu) /lōōtē'shē-əm/ [L, *Lutetia,* Paris], a rare earth metallic element. Its atomic number is 71, and its atomic mass is 174.97.

Luvox, a trademark for an antidepressant drug (fluvoxamine maleate).

lux (lx), a unit of illumination equivalent to one lumen per square meter of surface when measured at right angles to the direction of the light.

luxated joint /luk'sātid/, a dislocated joint in which there is no contact between articular surfaces.

luxation /luksā'shən/ [L, *luxare,* to dislocate], dislocation.

LV, abbreviation for **left ventricle.**

LVAD, abbreviation for **left ventricular assist device.**

LVN, abbreviation for *licensed vocational nurse.*

LWD, abbreviation for *living with disease.*

lx, abbreviation for **lux.**

lyases /lē'āsez/ [Gk, *lyein,* to loosen; Fr, *disastase,* enzyme], a group of enzymes that reversibly split carbon bonds with carbon, nitrogen, or oxygen without hydrolysis or oxygen reduction reactions.

lycopene /lī'kəpēn/ [Gk, *lykopersikon,* tomato], a red crystalline unsaturated hydrocarbon that is the carotenoid pigment in tomatoes and various berries and fruits. It is considered the primary substance from which all natural carotenoid pigments are derived.

lycopenemia /lī'kōpēnē'mē-ə/, a condition characterized by a high concentration of the carotenoid pigment lycopene in the blood, the result of ingesting large amounts of tomato products and other lycopene-rich fruits. Lycopenemia patients may develop a yellowish skin color.

lye poisoning /lī/ [AS, *leah,* lye; L, *potio,* drink], toxic effects of ingesting caustic soda or sodium hydroxide (NaOH), a powerful alkali. If the chemical has a pH above 11.5, the chemical burn damage to the mouth and throat is usually irreversible. An alkali burn can be more serious than an acid burn because an acid is usually neutralized by the tissues it contacts.

lying-in [AS, *licgan,* lying; L, *in*], **1.** designating the time before, during, and after childbirth. **2.** designating a hospital that provides care for women in childbirth and the puerperium. **3.** the condition of being in confinement, or childbed.

Lyme disease /līm/ [Lyme, Connecticut, where originally described], an infection caused by the spirochete, *Borrelia burgdorferi,* transmitted by the bite of infected *Ixodes* ticks. The disease first manifests itself as a red skin macule or papule at the bite site with accompanying flulike symptoms, such as headache, fever, chills, muscle aches, and fatigue. In about 50% of cases, other lesions develop soon after onset. Lymphadenopathy, neck pains, and hepatosplenomegaly are also often present in early disease. After weeks or months, neurologic abnormalities such as meningitis, meningoencephalitis, neuritis, and radiculopathies appear in about 15% of all cases. Myocardial abnormalities such as atrioventricular block, myopericarditis, and cardiomegaly occur in 8% of cases. Joint inflammation, pain, and arthritis develop in 50% of cases as long as 2 years after transmission.

Lyme disease test, a Western blot–specific blood test to isolate the spirochete *Borrelia burgdorferi,* which causes Lyme disease.

Lyme disease vaccine (recombinant OspA), a preparation of outer surface protein A, a cell surface lipoprotein of *Borrelia burgdorferi,* produced by recombinant technology.

lymph /limf/ [L, *lympha,* water], a thin watery fluid originating in organs and tissues of the body that circulates through the lymphatic vessels and is filtered by the lymph nodes. Lymph enters the bloodstream at the junction of the internal jugular and subclavian veins. Lymph contains chyle, erythrocytes, and leukocytes, most of which are lymphocytes.

lymphadenectomy, surgical removal of a lymph node or nodes.

lymphadenitis /limfad'inī'tis, lim'fəd-/ [L, *lympha;* Gk, *aden,* gland, *itis,* inflammation], an inflammatory condition of the lymph nodes, usually the result of systemic neoplastic disease, bacterial infection, or other inflammatory condition. The nodes may be enlarged, hard, smooth or irregular, and red and may feel hot.

lymphadenopathy /limfad′inop′əthē/, any disorder characterized by a localized or generalized enlargement of the lymph nodes or lymph vessels.

lymphadenopathy syndrome (LAS), a persistent, generalized swelling of the lymph nodes. It is often a part of the AIDS-wasting syndrome.

lymphangiectasia /limfan′jē·ektā′zhə/ [L, *lympha*; Gk, *angeion,* vessel, *ektasis,* stretching], dilation of the smaller lymphatic vessels, usually resulting from obstruction in the larger vessels.

lymphangiogram /limfan′jē·əgram′/ [L, *lympha,* water; Gk, *angeion,* vessel, *gramma,* record], a radiographic visualization of a part of the lymphatic system.

lymphangiography, an x-ray done with contrast dye that is especially useful in patients suspected of having lymphoma, metastatic tumor, or Hodgkin's disease. It is also used to demonstrate the extent and level of lymphatic metastasis, to stage lymphoma patients, to evaluate the results of chemotherapy or radiation therapy, and to evaluate patients with chronic leg swelling.

lymphangioma /limfan′jē·ō′mə/ *pl.* **lymphangiomas, lymphangiomata** [L, *lympha*; Gk, *angeion,* vessel, *oma,* tumor], a benign yellowish-tan tumor on the skin, composed of a mass of dilated lymph vessels.

lymphangioma cavernosum, a tumor formed by dilated lymphatic vessels and filled with lymph mixed with coagulated blood.

lymphangioma circumscriptum, a benign skin lesion that develops from superficial hypertrophic lymph vessels.

lymphangioma simplex, a growth formed by moderately dilated lymph vessels in a circumscribed area on the skin.

lymphangiosarcoma /limfan′jē·ō′särkō′mə/ [L, *lympha,* water; Gk, *angeion,* vessel, *sarx,* flesh, *oma,* tumor], a tumor arising from the lymphatic vessels.

lymphangioscintigraphy (LAS) /limfan′ jē·ō ·sintig′rəfē/, scintigraphic evaluation of primary and secondary lymphedema by means of radioactive tracers.

lymphangitis /lim′fanjī′tis/ [L, *lympha*; Gk, *angeion,* vessel + *itis*], an inflammation of one or more lymphatic vessels, usually resulting from an acute streptococcal infection of one of the extremities. It is characterized by fine red streaks extending from the infected area to the axilla or groin and by fever, chills, headache, and

myalgia. The infection may spread to the bloodstream.

lymphatic /limfat′ik/ [L, *lympha* + *icus,* form], **1.** pertaining to the lymphatic system of the body, consisting of a vast network of tubes transporting lymph. **2.** pertaining to any of the vessels associated with the lymphatic network.

lymphatic capillary plexus, one of the numerous networks of lymphatic capillaries that collect lymph from the intercellular fluid and constitute the beginning of the lymphatic system. The lymphatic vessels arise from the capillary plexuses, which vary in size and number in different regions and organs of the body.

lymphatic follicles of rectum, concentrations of lymphoid tissue in the tunica mucosa of the rectum.

lymphatic follicles of stomach, small lymphocytic aggregates in the interstitial tissue of the lamina propria of the stomach, especially in the pyloric region.

lymphatic organ [L, *lympha,* water; Gk, *organon,* instrument], any body structure composed of lymphatic tissue, such as the thymus, spleen, tonsils, and lymph nodes.

lymphatic system, a vast, complex network of capillaries, thin vessels, valves, ducts, nodes, and organs that helps protect and maintain the internal fluid environment of the entire body by producing, filtering, and conveying lymph and producing various blood cells. The lymphatic network also transports fats, proteins, and other substances to the blood system and restores 60% of the fluid that filters out of the blood capillaries into interstitial spaces during normal metabolism. Small semilunar valves throughout the lymphatic network help to control the flow of lymph and, at the junction with the venous system, prevent venous blood from flowing into the lymphatic vessels. The lymph collected throughout the body drains into the blood through two ducts situated in the neck. Various body dynamics such as respiratory pressure changes, muscular contractions, and movements of organs surrounding lymphatic vessels combine to pump the lymph through the lymphatic system. The system also includes specialized lymphatic organs such as the tonsils, the thymus, and the spleen.

lymphatic vasculitis, a condition of blood vessel necrosis in which the vessels acquire fibrinoid deposits and are infiltrated by lymphocytes.

lymphatic vessels [L, *lympha,* water, *vascellum,* little vase], fine, thin-walled, transparent valved channels distributed through most tissues. They are often distinguished by their beaded appearance,

L

which is caused by an irregular lumen. The collecting branches form two systems, one generally running with the superficial veins and the other below the deep fascia and including the intestinal lacteals. They drain through a thoracic duct and a right lymphatic duct into the venous system near the base of the neck.

lymphedema /lim'fĭdē'mə/ [L, *lympha*; Gk, *oidema*, swelling], a primary or secondary condition characterized by the accumulation of lymph in soft tissue and the resultant swelling caused by inflammation, obstruction, or removal of lymph channels. Congenital lymphedema (Milroy's disease) is a hereditary disorder characterized by chronic lymphatic obstruction. Lymphedema praecox occurs in adolescence, chiefly in females, and causes puffiness and swelling of the lower limbs, apparently because of hyperplastic development of lymph vessels. Secondary lymphedema may follow surgical removal of lymph channels in mastectomy, obstruction of lymph drainage caused by malignant tumors, or the infestation of lymph vessels with adult filarial parasites.—**lymphedematose, lymphedematous,** *adj.*

lymph node [L, *lympha* + *nodus*, knot], one of the many small oval structures that filter the lymph and fight infection and in which lymphocytes, monocytes, and plasma cells are formed. The lymph nodes are of different sizes, some as small as pinheads, others as large as lima beans. Each node is enclosed in a capsule; is composed of a lighter-colored cortical part and a darker medullary part; and consists of closely packed lymphocytes, reticular connective tissue laced by trabeculae, and three kinds of sinuses: subcapsular, cortical, and medullary. Lymph flows into the node through afferent lymphatic vessels. Most lymph nodes are clustered in areas such as the mouth, the neck, the lower arm, the axilla, and the groin.

lymph nodule [L, *lympha*, water, *nodulus*, small knot], any of the small densely packed spheric nodes or aggregations of lymph cells embedded in the reticular meshwork of the lymphatic system, mainly in the tonsils, spleen, and thymus.

lymphoblast /lim'fəblast/, a large, immature cell that develops into a lymphocyte after an antigenic or mitogenic challenge.—**lymphoblastic,** *adj.*

lymphocele /lim'fəsēl/, a tumor that contains lymph from injured lymph vessels.

Lymphocryptovirus /lim'fokrip'tovī'rus/, a genus of herpesviruses that includes the Epstein-Barr virus and species affecting nonhuman primates.

lymphocyte /lim'fəsīt/ [L, *lympha*; Gk, *kytos,* cell], a family of mononuclear, nonphagocytic white blood cells that circulate in blood, lymph, and peripheral lymphatic tissues. Lymphocytes are categorized as B and T lymphocytes and natural killer cells and are responsible for humoral and cellular immunity and tumor surveillance.

lymphocyte activation, the stimulation of lymphocytes by antigens or mitogens, rendering them metabolically active and causing them to differentiate into effector cells.

lymphocyte immune globulin, an immunosuppressant used to prevent rejection of organ transplants and to treat aplastic anemia.

lymphocyte immunophenotyping, a blood test used to detect the progressive depletion of CD4 T lymphocytes, which is associated with an increased likelihood of clinical complications from AIDS. Test results can also indicate if an AIDS patient is at risk for developing opportunistic infections.

lymphocyte transformation, **1.** the morphologic changes accompanying lymphocyte activation, in which small, resting lymphocytes are transformed into lymphoblasts. **2.** an in vitro immunity test process in which a patient's lymphocytes are placed in a culture with an antigen. The rate of transformation, in terms of proliferation and enlargement of T memory cells, is measured by the uptake of radioactive thymidine by the lymphocytes, indicating protein synthesis.

lymphocytic choriomeningitis /lim'fəsit'ik/ [L, *lympha*; Gk, *kytos,* cell, *chorion,* skin, *meninx,* membrane, *itis,* inflammation], an arenavirus infection of the meninges and the CSF. It is caused by the lymphocytic choriomeningitis virus and characterized by fever, headache, and stiff neck often complicated by aseptic meningitis.

lymphocytic gastritis, chronic gastritis with large numbers of T lymphocytes in the epithelium of the stomach. It may be associated with celiac disease or *Helicobacter pylori* infection.

lymphocytic hypophysitis, the massive infiltration of the pituitary gland by lymphocytes and plasma cells, with destruction of the normal parenchyma.

lymphocytic interstitial pneumonia (LIP), a diffuse respiratory disorder characterized by fibrosis and accumulation of lymphocytes in the lungs. It is commonly associated with lymphoma.

lymphocytopenia /lim'fōsī'təpē'nē-ə/ [L, *lympha*; Gk, *kytos,* cell, *penes,* poor], a decreased number of lymphocytes in the peripheral circulation, associated with immunodeficiency, neoplasm, or chemotherapy.

lymphocytosis /lim′fōsītō′sis/, a proliferation of lymphocytes, as occurs in certain chronic diseases and during convalescence from acute infections.

lymphocytotoxic antibody /lim′fōsītətok′sik/, an antibody that induces the cell-killing activity of killer lymphocytes on combining with a certain antigen.

lymphocytotrophic /-trof′ik/, having an affinity for lymphocytes.

lymphoepithelioma /lim′fō·ep′ithē′lē·ō′mə/ [L, *lympha;* Gk, *epi,* above, *thele,* nipple, *oma,* tumor], a poorly differentiated neoplasm developing from the epithelium overlying lymphoid tissue in the nasopharynx.

lymphogenesis /-jen′əsis/, the formation of lymph.

lymphogranulomatosis /-gran′yəlō′mətō′sis/ [L, *lympha,* water, *granulum,* small grain; Gk, *oma,* tumor, *osis,* condition], an infectious granuloma of the lymphatic system. The term is used to identify several inflammatory, granulomatous, or sarcomatous disorders, such as Hodgkin's disease, sarcoidosis, and lymphadenoma venereum.

lymphogranuloma venereum (LGV) /-gran′yəlō′mə/ [L, *lympha* + *granulum,* small grain; Gk, *oma,* tumor; L, *Venus,* goddess of love], an STD caused by a strain of the bacterium *Chlamydia trachomatis* that primarily infects the lymphatics. It is characterized by ulcerative genital lesions, marked swelling of the lymph nodes in the groin, headache, fever, and malaise. Ulcerations of the rectal wall occur less commonly.

lymphoid /lim′foid/ [L, *lympha,* water; Gk, *eidos,* form], pertaining to lymph or lymphatics.

lymphoid aplasia, failure of development of lymphoid tissue, as in severe combined immunodeficiency.

lymphoid interstitial pneumonia (LIP), a form of pneumonia that involves the lower lobes with extensive alveolar infiltration by mature lymphocytes, plasma cells, and histiocytes. It is associated with HIV infection, especially in children; dysproteinemia; and Sjögren's syndrome. This is an AIDS-defining illness in children.

lymphoid system, the lymphoid tissue of the body considered collectively. It can be divided into primary (or central) lymphoid tissues—the thymus and bone marrow, where lymphocytes differentiate from stem cells—and secondary (or peripheral) tissues—the lymph nodes, spleen, and gut-associated lymphoid tissue (tonsils, Peyer's patches)—where lymphocytes take part in immune responses.

lymphoid tissue [L, *lympha,* water; Gk, *eidos,* form; OFr, *tissu*], tissue that consists of lymphocytes on a framework of reticular cells and fibers, as the tonsils and adenoids.

lymphokine /lim′fōkīn/ [L, *lympha;* Gk, *kinesis,* motion], one of the chemical factors produced and released by T lymphocytes that attract macrophages to the site of infection or inflammation and prepare them for attack.

lymphokine-activated killer (LAK) cells, nonspecific cytotoxic cells that are generated in the presence of interleukin-2 and the absence of antigen. They are distinct from human natural killer cells, peripheral T lymphocytes, or memory cytotoxic thymus-derived lymphocytes. LAK cell infusions have been used investigationally for the treatment of cancer.

lympholysis /limfol′əsis/ [L, *lympha;* Gk, *lysein,* to loosen], cellular destruction of lymphocytes, especially of certain ones in the process of an immune response. **—lympholytic,** *adj.*

lymphoma /limfō′mə/ *pl.* **lymphomas, lymphomata** [L, *lympha;* Gk, *oma,* tumor], a type of neoplasm of lymphoid tissue that originates in the reticuloendothelial and lymphatic systems. It is usually malignant but in rare cases may be benign. It usually responds to treatment. Two main kinds of lymphomas are Hodgkin disease and non-Hodgkin lymphoma (NHL). The various lymphomas differ in degree of cellular differentiation and content, but the manifestations are similar in all types. Characteristically the appearance of a painless enlarged lymph node or nodes is followed by weakness, fever, weight loss, and anemia. With widespread involvement of lymphoid tissue, the spleen and liver usually enlarge; and GI disturbances, malabsorption, and bone lesions frequently develop.**—lymphomatoid,** *adj.*

lymphoma staging, a system for classifying lymphomas according to the extent of the disease for the purpose of treatment and prognosis. Stage I is characterized by the involvement of a single lymph node region or one extralymphatic organ or site. Stage II is characterized by the involvement of two or more lymph node regions on the same side of the diaphragm or a localized involvement of an extralymphatic organ or site plus one or more regions on the same side of the diaphragm. In stage III, lymph nodes on both sides of the diaphragm are affected, and there may be involvement of the spleen or localized involvement of an extralymphatic organ or site. Stage IV is typified by diffuse or disseminated involvement of one or more extralymphatic organs or sites with or without associated lymph node involvement.

lymphomatoid granulomatosis /limfō'mətoid/, a condition of unknown cause in which lymphocytes and plasma cells infiltrate the blood vessels, producing an angiocentric lesion. It most often affects the lungs, causing chest pains, cough, and shortness of breath.

lymphopoiesis /-pō·ē'sis/ [L, *lympha,* water; Gk, *poien,* to make], formation and production of lymphocytes, primarily in peripheral lymphoid tissue.—**lymphopoietic** /-pō·et'ik/, *adj.*

lymphoproliferative /-prōlif'ərətiv'/ [L, *lympha,* water, *prolles,* offspring, *ferre,* to bear], pertaining to the proliferation of lymphoid tissue.

lymphoproliferative syndrome induced, a group of malignant neoplasms associated with infections by human T cell leukemia-lymphoma virus. The neoplasms arise from the clonal proliferation of lymphoid cells. The most common lymphoid leukemias include lymphoblastic leukemia, which can be rapidly fatal if untreated.

lymphoreticular malignancy /-retik'yələr/, a disease of the lymphoreticular system commonly associated with cell-mediated immune deficiencies in which patients have a scarcity of normal WBCs.

lymphoreticular system, the tissues of the lymphoid and reticuloendothelial systems considered together as one system.

lymphoreticulosis /-retik'yəlō'sis/ [L, *lympha + reticulum,* little net; Gk, *osis,* condition], subacute granulomatous inflammation of lymphoid tissue with proliferation of macrophages. The disorder is characterized by the formation of an ulcerated papule at the site of the scratch, fever, and tender lymphadenopathy, sometimes progressing to suppuration.

lymphorrhagia, an escape of lymph from a damaged vessel.

lymphorrhoid /limfôr'oid/, a dilated lymph vessel.

lymphosarcoma cell leukemia /-särkō'mə/ [L, *lympha;* Gk, *sarx,* flesh, *oma,* tumor], a malignancy of blood-forming tissues characterized by many lymphosarcoma cells in the peripheral circulation that tend to infiltrate surrounding tissues.

lymphoscintigraphy /-sintig'rəfē/, a diagnostic technique using scintillation scanning of technetium-99m antimony trisulfide colloid in a noninvasive test for primary and secondary lymphedema. The radiopharmaceutical is injected subcutaneously in the interdigital space of the hands and feet.

lymphotrophy /limfot'rəfē/, the nourishment of cells by lymph, particularly in areas lacking adequate blood vessels.

lymph sinuses [L, *lympha,* water, *sinus,* hollow], continuous small endothelial-lined spaces just below the capsule of the lymph node. The sinuses slow the flow of lymph through the nodes.

Lyon hypothesis /lī'ən/ [Mary L. Lyon, English geneticist, b. 1925], a hypothesis stating that only one of the two X chromosomes in a female is functional, the other having become inactive early in development.

lyonization /lī'ənīzā'shən/ [Mary L. Lyon; Gk, *izein,* to cause], the process of random inactivation of one of the X chromosomes in the cells of females to compensate for the presence of the double X gene dose.

Lyon's ring [Mary L. Lyon], a type of congenital uropathy in females in which submeatal or distal urethral stenosis causes enuresis, dysuria, and recurring infections.

lyophilic /lī'ōfil'ik/ [Gk, *lyein,* to dissolve, *philein,* to love], pertaining to substances having an affinity for stability, in solution. Lyophilic substances are used to stabilize colloids.

lyophilize, to freeze-dry a substance under vacuum conditions.

Lyrica, a trademark for pregabalin.

Lys, abbreviation for **lysine.**

lysate /lī'sāt/, a product of dissolution of matter by lysis, as in the destruction of proteins by hydrolysis.

lysemia /līsē'mē·ə/, the disintegration of RBCs, accompanied by the release of hemoglobin in the plasma.

lysergide /līsur'jīd/, a psychotomimetic, semisynthetic derivative of ergot that acts at multiple sites in the CNS from the cortex to the spinal cord. In susceptible individuals, as little as 20 to 25 mg of the potent drug may cause pupillary dilation, increased BP, hyperreflexia, tremor, muscle weakness, piloerection, and increased body temperature. Larger doses also produce dizziness, drowsiness, paresthesia, euphoria or dysphoria, and synesthesias. Colors may be heard, sounds visualized, and time is felt to pass slowly. Psychologic dependence may develop, and use of lysergide is associated with significant hazards such as panic, serious depression, paranoid behavior, and prolonged psychotic episodes.

Lysholm method, any of several techniques for positioning a patient for radiographic examination of the cranial base, the mastoid and petrous regions of the temporal bone, the optic foramen, and the orbital fissure.

lysin /lī'sin/, a specific complement-fixing antibody that initiates the lysis of cells.

lysine (Lys) /lī′sēn, lī′sin/, an essential amino acid needed for proper growth in infants and for maintenance of nitrogen balance in adults.

lysine intolerance, a congenital disorder resulting in the inability to hydrolyze lysine because of an enzyme deficiency or defect. It is characterized by weakness, vomiting, and coma.

lysinemia /lī′sinē′mē·ə/, a condition caused by an inborn error of metabolism and resulting in the inability to hydrolyze lysine because of an enzyme defect or deficiency. It is characterized by muscle weakness and mental retardation.

lysine monohydrochloride, a salt of the amino acid lysine, used as a dietary supplement to increase the use of vegetable proteins such as those of corn, rice, and wheat.

lysinogen /līsin′əjən/, an antigen that stimulates the production of a specific lysin.

lysinurea /lī′sinŏŏr′ē·ə/, the presence of lysine in the urine.

lysinuria /li′snu′re·ä/, an aminoaciduria consisting of excessive lysine in the urine, such as in hyperlysinemia.

lysis /lī′sis/ [Gk, lysein, to loosen], **1.** destruction or dissolution of a cell or molecule through the action of a specific agent. Cell lysis is frequently caused by a lysin.—**lytic,** adj. **2.** gradual diminution in the symptoms of a disease. **3.** surgery performed to free adhesions of tissues. —**lyse,** v.

Lysodren, a trademark for an antineoplastic (mitotane).

lysogenesis /lī′səjen′əsis/ [Gk, lysein, loosening, genein, to produce], the formation of lysins.

lysokinase /lī′sōkī′nās/, an enzyme that serves as an activating agent for the production of plasmin.

lysosome /lī′səsōm/ [Gk, lysein + soma, body], a cytoplasmic, membrane-bound particle that contains hydrolytic enzymes that function in intracellular digestive processes. If the hydrolytic enzymes are released into the cytoplasm, they cause self-digestion of the cell so that lysosomes may play an important role in certain self-destructive diseases characterized by the wasting of tissue, such as muscular dystrophy.

lysotype /lī′sətīp/, a bacterial species type determined by its reaction to certain phages.

lysozyme /lī′səzīm/ [Gk, lysein + en, within, zyme, ferment], an enzyme with antiseptic actions that destroys some foreign organisms. It is found in granulocytic and monocytic blood cells and is normally present in saliva, sweat, breast milk, and tears.

lytes /līts/, an informal abbreviation of electrolytes, especially the levels of potassium, sodium, phosphorus, magnesium, and calcium in the blood, as determined by laboratory testing.

L

M

m, 1. abbreviation for **meter.** 2. abbreviation for **milli-.** 3. symbol for **muscle.** 4. abbreviation for **minim.**

M, 1. abbreviation for **mega.** 2. abbreviation for **molar.** 3. abbreviation for *distant metastasis* in the tumor, node, metastasis (TNM) system for staging malignant neoplastic disease.

M$_r$, symbol for *relative molecular mass.*

mA, abbreviation for **milliampere.**

MA, abbreviation for **mental age.**

M.A., abbreviation for *Master of Arts* degree.

MAA, abbreviation for **methacrylic acid.**

Maass, Clara [1876–1901], an American nurse who volunteered for military service at the outbreak of the Spanish-American War. She worked at army camps where soldiers were dying of yellow fever and then volunteered to go to Havana to participate in experiments to determine the cause of that disease. She was bitten by a mosquito and died 10 days later of yellow fever. She was one of the first nurses to be inducted into the Hall of Fame of the American Nurses Association.

MAB, abbreviation for **monoclonal antibodies.**

mabp, abbreviation for *mean arterial blood pressure.*

MAC, 1. abbreviation for **membrane attack complex.** 2. abbreviation for **microcystic adnexal carcinoma.** 3. abbreviation for **midupper arm circumference.** 4. abbreviation for **minimum alveolar concentration.** 5. abbreviation for *Mycobacterium avium* complex.

MAC awake, end-tidal concentration of an anesthetic agent at which 50% of patients appropriately respond to verbal commands (such as "open your eyes"). It applies only to inhalation agents and is affected by adjunctive needs, age, hypothermia, and sedatives.

mace /mās/, the oil-containing, red, fibrous wrapping of the nutmeg kernel. Dried and ground, it is used as an aromatic spice and flavoring. Historical medicinal uses include the treatment of gastrointestinal disorders and as an analgesic.

Mace, a trademark for a chemical causing tearing and eye pain. The name is an abbreviation formed by letters in

methylchloroform-2-chloro*ace*tophenone, which is dispersed from a pressurized container to immobilize an attacker.

macerate /mas′ərāt/ [L, *macerare,* to soften], to soften something solid by soaking.

maceration /-ā′shən/, the softening and breaking down of skin resulting from prolonged exposure to moisture.

Machado-Joseph disease /mächä′dō jō′səf/ [Machado and Joseph, afflicted families], a progressive degenerative disease of the CNS occurring in families of Portuguese-Azorean descent, inherited as an autosomal-dominant trait. There are four major types: *Type I,* with pyramidal and extrapyramidal deficits; *Type II,* with cerebellar, pyramidal, and extrapyramidal deficits; *Type III,* with cerebellar deficits and distal sensorimotor neuropathy; and *Type IV,* with parkinsonism and distal sensory neuropathy.

machismo /mächis′mō/, in psychology, a concept of the male that includes both desirable traits of courage and fearlessness and the dysfunctional behaviors of heavy drinking, seduction of women, and abusive spouse behavior.

Macleod, John J., co-winner, with Sir Frederick G. Banting, of the 1923 Nobel prize for medicine and physiology, for their discovery of insulin.

macrencephaly /mak′rənsef′əlē/ [Gk, *makros,* large, *enkephalos,* brain], a congenital anomaly characterized by abnormal largeness of the brain.—**macrencephalic,** *adj.*

macroadenoma /mak′rō.ad′ənō′mə/, a glandular tumor more than 10 mm in diameter.

macroamylase /-am′ilās/, a form of serum amylase in which the enzyme is bound to a globulin. Because the resulting complex is too large for renal clearance, plasma amylase levels are increased.

macroamylasemia /mak′rō.am′ilāsē′mē.ə/, the presence of macroamylase in the blood.

macrobiosis /-bī′ō′sis/ [Gk, *makros,* long, *bios,* life], a long life.

macrobiotic diet /-bī.ot′ik/, a restrictive dietary regimen consisting of grains and unprocessed foods.

macroblepharia /mak′rōblifer′ē.ə/ [Gk, *makros* + *blepharon,* eyelid], the condition of having abnormally large eyelids.

macrocephaly /mak′rōsef′əlē/ [Gk, *makros* + *kephale*, head], a congenital anomaly characterized by abnormal largeness of the head and brain in relation to the rest of the body, resulting in some degree of mental and growth retardation.—**macrocephalic, macrocephalous,** *adj.*, **macrocephalus,** *n.*

macrocyte /mak′rəsīt/ [Gk, *makros* + *kytos*, cell], an erythrocyte that exceeds 9 μm in diameter on a peripheral blood film, associated with an MCV greater than 100 fL. Macrocytes are seen in liver disease, alcoholism, megaloblastic anemia with folate or cobalamin deficiency, and in myelodysplastic syndromes.

macrocytic /mak′rōsit′ik/ [Gk, *makros* + *kytos*; L, *icus,* form], of a cell, larger than normal, such as the erythrocytes in macrocytic anemia.

macrocytic anemia, anemia characterized by impaired erythropoiesis and macrocytes on a peripheral blood film. Macrocytic anemia is seen in liver disease, alcoholism, megaloblastic anemia with folate or cobalamin deficiency, and in myelodysplastic syndromes.

macrocytosis /mak′rōsītō′sis/ [Gk, *makros* + *kytos* + *osis,* condition], an abnormal proliferation of macrocytes in the peripheral blood film.

Macrodantin, a trademark for a urinary antibacterial (nitrofurantoin).

Macrodex, a trademark for a plasma expander (dextran).

macrodrip /mak′rōdrip/ [Gk, *makros*; AS, *drypan,* to fall in drops], in IV therapy, an apparatus that is used to deliver measured amounts of IV solutions at specific flow rates based on the size of drops of the solution. The size of the drops is controlled by the fixed diameter of a plastic delivery tube.

macroelement, a chemical element required in relatively large quantities for the normal physiologic processes of the body. Macroelements include carbon, hydrogen, oxygen, nitrogen, potassium, sodium, calcium, chloride, magnesium, phosphorus, and sulfur.

macrogamete /-gam′ēt/ [Gk, *makros* + *gamete,* spouse], a large nonmotile female gamete of certain thallophytes and sporozoa, specifically the malarial parasite *Plasmodium.*

macrogametocyte /-gamē′təsīt/ [Gk, *makros* + *gamete* + *kytos,* cell], an enlarged merozoite that undergoes meiosis to form the mature female gamete during the sexual phase of the life cycle of certain thallophytes and sporozoa, specifically the malarial parasite *Plasmodium.*

macrogenitosomia /mak′rōjen′itōsō′mē·ə/ [Gk, *makros*; L, *genitalis,* genitalia; Gk, *soma,* body], a congenital condition in which the genitalia are abnormal because of an excess of androgen during fetal development. It is characterized in boys by enlarged external genitalia and in girls by pseudohermaphroditism.

macroglobulin /-glob′yəlin/, a globular serum protein with a molecular mass above 400 kilodaltons such as the proteinase inhibitor alpha$_2$-macroglobulin.

macroglobulinemia /mak′rōglob′yōōlinē′mē·ə/ [Gk, *makros*; L, *globulus,* small ball; Gk, *haima,* blood], plasma presence of a high-molecular-weight globulin such as alpha$_2$-macroglobulin or an immunoglobulin of the IgM isotype. Macroglobulins raise plasma viscosity and are associated with monoclonal gammopathies of undetermined significance.

macroglossia /mak′rōglos′ē·ə/ [Gk, *makros* + *glossa,* tongue], an excessively large tongue. It is seen in certain syndromes of congenital defects, including Down syndrome.

macrognathia /mak′rōnā′thē·ə/ [Gk, *makros* + *gnathos,* jaw], an abnormally large growth of the jaw.—**macrognathic,** *adj.*

macromolecule /-mol′əkyōōl/ [Gk, *makros*; L, *moles,* mass], a molecule of colloidal size, such as a protein, nucleic acid, or polysaccharide.—**macromolecular,** *adj.*

macronodular adrenal disease /-nod′yələr/, a form of Cushing's syndrome characterized by massively enlarged adrenal glands.

macronucleus /-nōō′klē·əs/ [Gk, *makros*; L, *nucleus,* nut], **1.** a large nucleus that occupies a relatively large portion of the cell. **2.** in protozoa, the larger of two nuclei in each cell, governing cell metabolism and growth.

macronutrient /-nōō′triənt/ [Gk, *makros*; L, *nutriens,* food that nourishes], nutrient required in the greatest amounts: carbohydrate, protein, fat or lipid, and water.

macroovalocyte /mak′rō·o′vəlosīt/, an enlarged, oval erythrocyte seen in megaloblastic anemia.

macropenis, abnormal largeness of the penis.

macrophage /mak′rəfāj/ [Gk, *makros* + *phagein,* to eat], a granular mononuclear phagocyte that circulates as a monocyte in the blood and resides in all tissues.

macrophage activating factor (MAF) [Gk, *makros,* large, *phagein,* to eat; L, *activus,* active, *facere,* to make], a lymphokine released from a sensitized leukocyte that induces changes in the appearance and function of macrophages and makes them active against certain antigens.

macrophage colony–stimulating factor (M-CSF), a glycoprotein growth factor

M

that induces committed bone marrow stem cells to differentiate and mature into mono-nuclear phagocytes.

macrophage migration inhibiting factor [Gk, *makros*, large, *phagein*, to eat; L, *migrare*, to wander, *inhibere*, to restrain, *facere*, to make], a lymphokine produced by leukocytes that immobilizes macrophages after contact with an antigen.

macroprolactinoma /-prōlak'tino'mə/, a prolactin secreting pituitary tumor more than 10 mm in diameter that causes serum prolactin levels higher than 500 ng/mL. Bromocriptine is used with some success to shrink tumor size before surgery. Frequent monitoring of endocrine status is indicated for the remainder of the patient's life after therapy.

macropsia /makrop'sē-ə/ [Gk, *makros*, large, *opsis*, vision], hallucination in which objects seem larger than they actually are. It may be related to seizure activity, a retinal abnormality, or migraine.

macroreentry circuit /mak'rōrē-en'trē/ [Gk, *makros*; L, *re*, again; Fr, *entree*, entry], a relatively large pathway for the reactivation of myocardial tissue by the same impulse. An example is a reentry circuit that uses one bundle branch for antegrade conduction and another for retrograde conduction to produce the highly malignant bundle branch reentry ventricular tachycardia.

macroscopic /-skop'ik/ [Gk, *makros*, large, *skopein*, to view], large enough to be examined with the naked eye.

macroshock, shock from an electric current of 1 milliampere (mA) or greater. Currents of 1 to 15 mA produce a tingling sensation and some muscle contraction, those of 15 to 100 mA can cause a painful shock, those of 100 to 200 mA can cause cardiac fibrillation or respiratory arrest, and those above 200 mA may produce rapid burning and destruction of tissue.

macrosis /makrō'sis/ [Gk, *makros*, large, *osis*, condition], an increase in the size or volume of an object.

macrotear /-ter/, significant damage to soft tissues caused by acute trauma.

macula /mak'yələ/ *pl.* **maculae** [L, spot], a small pigmented area or a spot that appears separate or different in color from the surrounding tissue.

macula albida [L, *macula*, spot, *albidare*, to make white], small white areas in the serous membranes of the pericardium or in the peritoneum or pleura.

macula atrophica, a condition of cutaneous atrophy characterized by the appearance of small glistening white spots on the skin.

macula densa [L, *macula*, spot, *densus*, thick], a thickening in the wall of a distal tubule of the kidney nephron at a point where it is in contact with the afferent glomerulus and in direct opposition to the juxtaglomerular cells. It may be part of a negative feedback system for sodium.

macula folliculi, a spot on the wall of an ovary where a mature follicle will rupture to release an ovum.

macula lutea, an oval yellow spot at the optical "center" of the retina 2 mm from the optic nerve. It contains a pit, no blood vessels, and the fovea centralis, which contains only retinal cones. Central high-acuity vision occurs when an image is focused directly on the fovea centralis of the macula lutea.

macular degeneration (MD) /mak'yələr/ [L, *macula*, spot, *degenerare*, to deviate], a progressive deterioration of the maculae of the retina. The condition may occur as a primary disorder or may be an effect of several diseases, such as retinitis pigmentosa.

macular dystrophy, any of a variety of eye disorders that damage the central part of the retina. Several of the disorders are related to gene mutations that affect older adults.

macular rash [L, *macula*, spot; OFr, *rasche*], a skin eruption in which the lesions are flat and less than 1 cm in diameter.

macula solaris [L, *macula*, spot, *solaris*, sun], a freckle.

macule /mak'yōōl/ [L, *macula*, spot], **1.** a small flat blemish or discoloration that is level with the skin surface. **2.** a gray scar on the cornea that is visible without magnification.—**macular,** *adj.*

maculopapular rash /mak'yəlōpap'yə lər/ [L, *macula*, spot, *papula*, pimple; OFr, *rasche*], a skin eruption characterized by distinctive macules and papules.

maculopathy /mak'yəlop'əthē/ [L, *macula*, spot; Gk, *pathos*, disease], a form of macular degeneration primarily involving the macula lutea.

MAD, abbreviation for **multiple autoimmune disorder.**

Madigan prostatectomy, a type of perineal prostatectomy.

Madura foot /maj'ŏŏr'e/ [Madura, India; AS, *fot*, foot], a progressive destructive tropical fungal infection of the foot.

maedi/visna virus, a lentivirus that is the causal agent of a type of pneumonia in sheep.

MAF, abbreviation for **macrophage activating factor.**

mafenide acetate /maf'ənīd/, a topical antibiotic prescribed in the treatment of second- and third-degree burns to prevent infection by susceptible microorganisms such as *Pseudomonas aeruginosa*.

Maffucci's syndrome, a congenital disorder characterized by the proliferation of cartilage at the ends of long bones and by benign, blood-filled tumors of the skin or viscera.

magaldrate /mag'əldrāte/, an antacid containing a combination of magnesium and aluminum compounds, prescribed in the treatment of hypersensitivity and stomach upset associated with heartburn, sour stomach, or acid indigestion.

magical thinking /maj'ikəl/, in psychology, a belief that merely thinking about an event in the external world can cause it to occur. It is regarded as a form of regression to an early phase of development.

magic-bullet approach [Gk, *magikos*, sorcerer; Fr, *boulette*, small ball; L, *ad*, toward, *prope*, near], **1.** a therapeutic or diagnostic method that makes use of a specific relationship between a drug and a disease or organ. **2.** in clinical medicine, the administration of a specific drug to cure or ameliorate a given disease or condition. **3.** in traditional diagnostic radiology, the administration of a specific dye to facilitate the radiographic visualization of a given organ. **4.** in nuclear medicine, the administration of a specific radionuclide tagged to an appropriate carrier to provide a scintillation camera image of a given organ or structure.

Magill forceps, angled forceps used to guide a tracheal tube into the larynx or a nasogastric tube into the esophagus under direct vision. It is also used to place pharyngeal packs and remove foreign bodies.

magnesemia /mag'nəsē'mē·ə/, the presence of magnesium in the blood.

magnesium (Mg) /magnē'sē·əm, magnē'zhəm/ [Gr, *magnesia*; L, lodestone], a silver-white mineral element. Its atomic number is 12, and its atomic mass is 24.32. Magnesium is the second most abundant cation of the intracellular fluids in the body. It is essential for many enzyme activities and the interaction of intracellular particles and binding of macromolecules to subcellular organelles. It also is important to neurochemical transmissions and muscular excitability.

magnesium alginate, the magnesium salt of alginic acid, administered orally as a component of an antacid used in the treatment of gastroesophageal reflux disease.

magnesium chloride, an electrolyte replenisher and a pharmaceutical necessity for hemodialysis and peritoneal dialysis fluids.

magnesium gluconate, the gluconate salt of magnesium, administered orally in the prevention of hypomagnesemia.

magnesium lactate, the lactate salt of magnesium, administered orally in the prevention of hypomagnesemia.

magnesium salicylate, the magnesium salt of salicylic acid, used as an analgesic, antipyretic, antiinflammatory, and antirheumatic.

magnesium silicate, $MgSiO_3$, a silicate salt of magnesium. The most common hydrated forms found in nature are asbestos and talc.

magnesium sulfate, a salt of magnesium prescribed parenterally to prevent seizures, especially in preeclampsia and acute nephritis in children, and orally to treat constipation and heartburn and to correct magnesium deficiency.

magnesium test, a blood test used to measure levels of magnesium, an electrolyte that is critical in nearly all metabolic processes.

magnetic field /magnet'ik/ [Gk, *magnesia*, lodestone; AS, *feld*], the region around any magnet in which its effects can be detected.

magnetic field therapy, the placement of magnets directly on the skin, stimulating living cells and increasing blood flow by ionic currents created from polarities on the magnets. Trigger points for magnets are acupuncture points where the action of the magnets serves to activate the tendinomuscular system to readily and widely transmit electrical stimuli. Common physiologic responses include vasodilation, analgesia, antiinflammatory action, spasmolytic activity, accelerated healing, and antiedema activity.

magnetic flux (N), a quantitative measure of a magnetic field.

magnetic lines of force [Gk, *magnesia*, lodestone; L, *linea*, line, *fortis*, strong], theoretic lines of magnetism that surround a magnet or fill a magnetic field. The presence of the magnetic force along the imaginary lines can be demonstrated by inserting a sensitive material such as iron filings into the lines of magnetic effect.

magnetic moment [Gk, *magnesia*, lodestone, *momentum*, movement], a measure of the net magnetic field produced by an elementary particle or an atomic nucleus spinning about its own axis. Such fields are the basis for MRI.

magnetic permeability, the ratio of the magnetism induced in a body to the strength of the magnetic field of induction.

magnetic resonance (MR), a phenomenon in which the atomic nuclei of certain materials placed in a strong, static magnetic field absorb radio waves supplied by a transmitter at particular frequencies. The energy of the radio waves promotes the nuclei from a low-energy state, in which the nuclear spin is aligned parallel to the magnetic field, to

M

a higher-energy state, in which the nuclear spin has a component transverse or opposed to the field. These nuclei occasionally revert to the lower-energy state by emitting photons at characteristic (resonance) frequencies, providing information about the local magnetic field at the nuclei.

magnetic resonance angiography, the use of special MR imaging pulses to visualize the vascular system and identify regions of nonflowing blood.

magnetic resonance imaging (MRI) [Gk, *magnesia,* lodestone; L, *resonare,* to sound again, *imago,* image], medical imaging based on the resonance of atomic nuclei in a strong magnetic field. MRI is the method of choice for a growing number of disease processes. Among its advantages are its superior soft-tissue contrast resolution, ability to image in multiple planes, and lack of ionizing radiation hazards. MRI is regarded as superior to CT for most CNS abnormalities, particularly those of the posterior fossa, brainstem, and spinal cord. It has also become an important tool in musculoskeletal and pelvic imaging.

magnetic resonance urography, imaging of the urinary tract using MRI, such as to detect obstructions and dilations during pregnancy when other methods are ineffective or undesirable.

magnetic susceptibility, a measure of the ability of a substance to become magnetized.

magnetization /mag'nətīzā'shən/ [Gk, *magnesia,* lodestone *izein,* to cause], the magnetic polarization of a material produced by a magnetic field (magnetic moment per unit volume).

magnetron /mag'nətron/ [Gk, *magnesia,* lodestone, *trum,* device], a source of microwave energy used in medical linear accelerators to accelerate electrons to the therapeutic energies.

magnification /mag'nifikā'shən/, in psychology, cognitive distortion in which the effects of one's behavior are magnified.

magnification factor, the size of a radiographic, photographic, or microscopic image divided by the object size. In radiography, it is equal to the source-to-image receptor distance divided by the source-to-object distance.

MAHA, abbreviation for **microangiopathic hemolytic anemia.**

Mahaim fiber [I. Mahaim, twentieth-century French physician, 1897–1965], one of the conductive tracts in cardiac tissue running between the atrioventricular (AV) node or the AV bundle and the muscle of the ventricular septum. The fibers conduct early excitation impulses.

Mahoney, Mary Eliza, the first African-American nurse. Mahoney did private nursing in the Boston area and was active in furthering intergroup relationships and improving the role of the African-American nurse in the community. A medal in her name, established after her death, was first presented in 1936. It is given to an African-American nurse in recognition of outstanding contribution to the nursing profession.

mainstreaming /mān'strēming/ [OE, *maegan,* strength; ME, *strem*], **1.** the system of educating children with disabilities in regular classrooms, with special assistance as needed. **2.** the return of persons recovering from mental illness to the community.

maintenance dose /mān'tənəns/ [Fr, *maintenir,* to uphold; Gk, *dosis,* giving], the amount of drug required to keep a desired mean steady-state concentration in the tissues.

Mainz pouch, any of several continent urinary diversion surgeries using a section of the rectum and sigmoid colon to create a pouch for maintenance of continence.

maitake, an herbal product derived from a mushroom that is native to Japan, used as an immunostimulant and as a treatment for diabetes, hypertension, high cholesterol, and obesity. It is probably safe, but there is no reliable information related to efficacy.

Majocchi's granuloma /mäjok'ēz/ [Domenico Majocchi, Italian dermatologist, 1849–1929; L, *granulum,* small grain; Gk, *oma,* tumor], a rare type of tinea corporis that involves the follicle and affects the lower legs. It is caused by the fungus *Trichophyton,* which infects the hairs of the affected site and raises spongy granulomas.

major connector, a metal plate or bar used for joining the two halves of a removable partial denture.

major depressive disorder, a major disorder of mood characterized by a persistent dysphoria, anxiety, irritability, fear, brooding, appetite and sleep disturbances, weight loss, psychomotor agitation or retardation, decreased energy, feelings of worthlessness or guilt, difficulty in concentrating or thinking, possible delusions and hallucinations, and thoughts of death or suicide.

Major Diagnostic Category, a group of similar diagnosis-related groups, such as all those affecting a given organ system of the body.

major duodenal papilla, the common entrance in the duodenum for the bile and pancreatic ducts.

major histocompatibility antigen, one of a group of proteins encoded by genes of the major histocompatibility complex on chromosome 6.

major medical insurance, insurance coverage designed to offset the costs of prolonged or catastrophic illness and injury.

major surgery, a surgical procedure that is extensive, involving removal of organs, and/or life-threatening.

making weight, in sports medicine, the practice of rapid weight loss based on the belief that training at a heavier body weight, then dropping weight shortly before competition, gives an athlete an advantage.

mal /mal, mäl/ [L, *malus*, bad], an illness or disease, such as grand mal.

malabsorption /mal′əbsôrp′shən/ [L, *malus* + *absorbere*, to swallow], impaired absorption of nutrients from the GI tract. It occurs in celiac disease, sprue, dysentery, diarrhea, inflammatory bowel disease, and other disorders.

malabsorption syndrome, a complex of symptoms resulting from disorders in the intestinal absorption of nutrients, characterized by anorexia, weight loss, abdominal bloating, muscle cramps, bone pain, and steatorrhea. Anemia, weakness, and fatigue occur because iron, folic acid, and vitamin B_{12} are not absorbed in sufficient amounts.

malacia /məlā′shə/ [Gk, *malakia*, softness], **1.** a morbid softening or sponginess in any part or any tissue of the body. **2.** a craving for spicy foods such as mustard, hot peppers, or pickles.—**malacic,** *adj.*

maladaptation /mal′adəptā′shən/ [L, *malus* + *adaptatio*], faulty intrapersonal adjustment to stress or change.—**maladaptive,** *adj.*

maladjusted /mal′adjus′tid/ [L, *malus,* bad, *adjuxtare*, to bring together], appearing unable to maintain effective relationships needed to fit into the environment and showing irritability, depression, and other psychogenic conditions.

malady /mal′ədē/ [ME, *maladie,* sick], a disease or illness.

malaise /məlāz′/ [Fr, discomfort], a vague uneasy feeling of body weakness, distress, or discomfort, often marking the onset of and persisting throughout a disease.

malalignment /mal′əlīn′mənt/ [L, *malus* + *ad,* to, *linea,* line], a failure of parts of the body to align normally, such as the teeth in the dental arch.

malar /mā′lər/ [L, *mala,* cheek], pertaining to the cheek or the cheekbone.

malaria /məler′ē-ə/ [It, *mal,* bad, *aria,* air], a severe infectious illness caused by one or more of at least four species of the protozoan genus *Plasmodium.* The disease is transmitted by a bite from an infected *Anopheles* mosquito, by blood transfusion from an infected patient, or by the use of a contaminated or an infected hypodermic needle. Malaria is characterized by chills and fever, anemia, an enlarged spleen, myalgia, arthralgia, weakness, and vomiting. Splenomegaly, anemia, thrombocytopenia, hypoglycemia, pulmonary or renal dysfunction, and neurosis may also occur. —**malarial,** *adj.*

malarial parasite /məler′ē-əl/ [It, *mal aria,* bad air; Gk, *parasitos,* guest], one of four known species of *Plasmodium* that may be injected into the human bloodstream by an anopheline mosquito to begin the cycle of malarial disease.

Malarone /mal′ä-rōn /, a trademark for a combination preparation of proguanil and atovaquone, an antimalarial agent.

Malassezia /mal′əsē′zē-ə/ [Louis C. Malassez, French physiologist, 1842–1910], a genus of fungi. *Malassezia furfur* causes tinea versicolor. *M. ovalis* is a nonpathogenic organism found in sebaceous areas.

malathion poisoning /malā′thē-on, məl′əthī′on/, a toxic condition caused by the ingestion or absorption through the skin of malathion, an organophosphorus insecticide. Symptoms include vomiting, nausea, salivation, tearing, abdominal cramps, headache, dizziness, weakness, confusion, convulsions, and respiratory difficulties.

mal de Meleda /mal də mel′ədä/ [Fr, *meleda,* sickness], a chronic, autosomal-recessive form of keratoderma of the palms and soles of the feet, in which the hyperkeratosis spreads to involve the dorsal aspects of the hands and feet and other areas of the body, with erythematous, scaling, malodorous cutaneous lesions that may cause deep fissuring.

male [L, *mas*], **1.** pertaining to the sex that produces sperm cells and fertilizes the female egg to beget offspring; masculine. **2.** a male person.

male catheterization, the passage of a catheter through the male urethra for the purpose of draining the urinary bladder. The male patient is placed in a supine position with the legs extended. The catheter is inserted 17.5 to 22.5 cm or until urine flows. Sterile technique is important throughout the procedure to prevent the introduction of infectious organisms into the bladder.

male factor infertility, infertility of a couple caused by a problem in the male's reproductive system, such as anejaculation, aspermatogenesis, or azoospermia.

male menopause [L, *mas,* male, *men,* month; Gk, *pauein,* to cease], a late middle-age

M

psychogenic condition affecting some men, who experience anxiety over diminished potency, increased fatigue, thinning and graying hair, and other signs of aging.

male pattern alopecia [L, *mas,* male; ME, *patron;* Gk, *alopex,* fox mange], a common form of baldness in males, beginning at the frontal scalp and spreading gradually until only a fringe remains around the back of the head. Individual differences are determined by heredity, androgenic stimulation, and aging.

male reproductive system assessment, an evaluation of the condition of the patient's genitalia, reproductive history, and past and present genitourinary infections and disorders.

male sexual dysfunction, impaired or inadequate ability of a man to carry on his sex life to his own satisfaction. Symptoms include difficulties in starting and maintaining an erection, premature ejaculation, inability to ejaculate, and loss of desire.

male sterility [L, *mas* + *sterilis,* barren], the inability of a man to produce sperm. Causes may include environmental factors, such as exposure to heat or radiation, or physiologic factors, such as undescended testes, varicocele, prolonged fever, endocrine disorders, cancer chemotherapy, vasectomy, and abuse of alcohol or marijuana.

male urethra, a canal extending from the neck of the bladder to the urinary meatus, measuring about 20 cm in length, and presenting a double curve when the penis is flaccid.

malfeasance /malfē′zəns/ [Fr, *malfaire,* to do evil], performance of an unlawful, wrongful act.

malformation /mal′fôrmā′shən/ [L, *malus,* bad, *forma,* shape], an anomalous structure in the body.

malfunction /mal′fungk′shən/ [L, *malus,* bad, *functio,* performance], **1.** the inability to function normally. **2.** not to function normally.

Malgaigne's fracture of pelvis /malgā′nyəz/ [Joseph F. Malgaigne, French surgeon, 1806–1865], breaks in multiple pelvic bones with associated upper displacement of the hemipelvis.

malicious prosecution /məlish′əs/ [L, *malitia,* wickedness, *prosequi,* to pursue], in law, a suit begun in malice and pursued without sufficient cause.

malign /məlīn/ [ME, *malignen,* deceptive], to show ill will or maliciousness; to act viciously; to harm.

malignant /məlig′nənt/ [L, *malignus,* bad disposition], **1.** tending to become worse and to cause death. **2.** describing a cancer, anaplastic, invasive, and metastatic. —**malignancy,** *n.*

malignant astrocytoma, a high-grade astrocytoma, such as glioblastoma multiforme.

malignant atrophic papulosis, a form of cutaneous lymphocytic vasculitis. The skin disease shows erythematous papules with characteristic porcelain-white centers and elevated borders. The early signs are followed by perforated intestinal ulcers, leading to peritonitis; occluded arterioles; and progressive neurologic disability.

malignant dysentery [L, *malignus,* bad disposition; Gk, *dys,* bad, *enteron,* bowel], a potentially fatal form of dysentery in which symptoms are severe.

malignant granuloma [L, *malignus,* bad disposition, *granulum,* little grain, *oma,* tumor], a malignant lymphoma, such as Hodgkin's disease, or a lymphosarcoma.

malignant hypertension, the most lethal form of hypertension. It is a fulminating condition characterized by severely elevated BP that commonly damages the intima of small vessels, the brain, the retina, the heart, and the kidneys. Many patients with this condition exhibit signs of hypokalemia and alkalosis and have aldosterone secretion rates even higher than those associated with primary aldosteronism.

malignant hyperthermia (MH), a rare genetic hypermetabolic condition characterized by severe hyperthermia and rigidity of the skeletal muscles, occurring in affected people exposed to inhalation anesthetics and succinylcholine, a nondepolarizing muscle relaxant.

malignant hyperthermia precautions, a nursing intervention from the Nursing Interventions Classification (NIC) defined as prevention or reduction of hypermetabolic response to pharmacological agents used during surgery.

malignant mesenchymoma, a sarcoma that contains mesenchymal elements.

malignant neoplasm, a tumor that tends to grow, invade, and metastasize. The tumor usually has an irregular shape and is composed of poorly differentiated cells.

malignant transformation, the changes that a normal cell undergoes as it becomes a cancerous cell.

malignant tumor, a neoplasm that characteristically invades surrounding tissue, metastasizes to distant sites, and contains anaplastic cells.

malingering /məling′gəring/ [Fr, *malingre,* puny, weak], a willful and deliberate feigning of the symptoms of a disease or injury to gain some consciously desired end.—**malinger,** *v.,* —**malingerer,** *n.*

malleable /mal′ē·əbəl/ [L, *malleare,* to beat], able to be pressed, hammered, or otherwise forced into a shape without breaking.

malleolar fold, one of two folds, the anterior and posterior, on the surface of the tympanic membrane.

malleolus /məlē′ələs/ pl. **malleoli** [L, little hammer], a rounded bony process, such as the protuberance on each side of the ankle.

mallet deformity [ME, maillet, maul], a loss of the ability to extend the distal joint of a finger or toe. It may be caused by severe damage such as rupture of the terminal tendon.

mallet fracture, a fracture in which the dorsal base of a distal phalanx of the hand or foot is torn away. The fracture disrupts the associated extensor apparatus and causes dropped flexion of the distal segment.

malleus /mal′ē-əs/ pl. **mallei** [L, hammer], one of the three ossicles in the middle ear, resembling a hammer, with a head, neck, and three processes. It is connected to the tympanic membrane and transmits sound vibrations to the incus.

Mallory body /mal′ərē/ [Frank B. Mallory, American pathologist, 1862–1941; AS, bodig, body], an eosinophilic cytoplasmic inclusion, alcoholic hyalin, found in the liver cells. It is typically, but not always, associated with acute alcoholic liver injury.

Mallory-Weiss syndrome [G. Kenneth Mallory, American pathologist, b. 1926; Soma Weiss, American physician, 1899–1942], a condition characterized by massive bleeding after a tear in the mucous membrane at the junction of the esophagus and the stomach. The laceration is usually caused by protracted vomiting, most commonly in alcoholics or in people whose pylorus is obstructed.

malnutrition /mal′nōōtrish′ən/ [L, malus, bad, nutrire, to nourish], any disorder of nutrition. It may result from an unbalanced, insufficient, or excessive diet or from impaired absorption, assimilation, or use of foods.

malocclusion /mal′əklōō′zhən/ [L, malus + occludere, to shut up], abnormal contact between the teeth of the upper jaw and those of the lower jaw.

malonic acid (CH₂(COOH)₂) /məlō′nik/, a white crystalline, highly toxic substance used as an intermediate compound in the production of barbiturates.

malpighian body /malpig′ē-ən/ [Marcello Malpighi, Italian physician, 1628–1694; AS, bodig, body], **1.** the renal corpuscle, which includes a glomerulus with Bowman's capsule. **2.** lymphoid tissue surrounding the arteries of the spleen.

malpighian corpuscle [Marcello Malpighi; L, corpusculum, little body], one of a number of small, round, deep-red bodies in the cortex of the kidney, each communicating with a renal tubule. The corpuscles are part of a filtering system through which nonprotein components of blood plasma enter the tubules for urinary excretion.

malposition /mal′pəzish′ən/, a wrong or faulty placement of a body part, such as in an untreated fracture.

malpractice /malprak′tis/ [L, malus; Gk, praktikos, practical], in law, professional negligence that is the proximate cause of injury or harm to a patient, resulting from a lack of professional knowledge, experience, or skill that can reasonably be expected in others in the profession in similar circumstances or from a failure to exercise reasonable care or judgment in the application of professional knowledge, experience, or skill.

malpresentation /malpres′əntā′shən/ [L, malus, bad, praesentare, to show], an abnormal position of the fetus in the birth canal.

malrotated kidney, a kidney that failed to rotate properly during its ascent from the pelvis in prenatal development, usually with the hilum facing anteriorly instead of anteromedially.

malrotation /mal′rōtā′shən/, **1.** any abnormal rotation of an organ or body part, such as the vertebral column or a tooth. **2.** a failure of the intestinal tract or other viscera to undergo normal rotation during embryonic development.

malt /môlt/ [AS, mealt], a preparation obtained from germinated grain, such as barley, that contains partially degraded starch and protein with nutritive and digestive properties.

maltitol /mawl′titol/, a hydrogenated, partially hydrolyzed starch used as a sweetener.

malt soup extract, an extract of malt from barley grains, containing also a small amount of polymeric carbohydrates, proteins, electrolytes, and vitamins, administered orally as a bulk-forming laxative.

malunion /malyōō′nyən/ [L, malus + unus, one], an imperfect union of previously fragmented bone or other tissue. Causes of bone malunion include osteomyelitis and improper immobilization of a fracture.

mamillary body /mam′iler′ē/ [L, mamilla, nipple; AS, bodig, body], either of the two small round masses of gray matter in the hypothalamus located close to one another in the interpeduncular space. They may be involved with olfactory reflexes.

mammary /mam′ərē/ [L, mamma, breast], pertaining to the breast.

mammary glands [L, mamma, breast, glans, acorn], lactiferous glands within the breasts. Glandular tissue forms a radius

M

of lobes containing alveoli, each lobe having a system of ducts for the passage of milk from the alveoli to the nipple.

mammary region, the part of the pectoral region surrounding the mammary gland.

mammogram /mam′əgram/ [L, *mamma*; Gk, *gramma*, record], an x-ray film of the soft tissues of the breast.

mammography /mamog′rəfē/, the radiographic examination of the soft tissues of the breast. It is used to identify various benign and malignant neoplastic processes and may show conclusively that a lesion is malignant.

Mammography Quality Standards Act (MQSA), an act passed into law in the United States in 1992, which requires all mammography facilities to be accredited.

mammoplasty /mam′əplas′tē/ [L, *mamma*; Gk, *plassein*, to mold], plastic reshaping of the breasts, performed to reduce or lift large or sagging breasts, to enlarge small breasts, or to reconstruct a breast after removal of a tumor.

mammothermography /mam′ōthərmog′rəfē/ [L, *mamma*; Gk, *therme*, heat, *graphein*, to record], a diagnostic procedure in which the breast is examined for abnormal growths by means of a heart-sensitive probe that detects regional differences in blood flow.

managed care, a health care system in which there is administrative control over primary health care services in a medical group practice. The intention is to eliminate redundant facilities and services and to reduce costs. Health education and preventive medicine are emphasized. Patients may pay a flat fee for basic family care but may be charged additional fees for secondary care services.

managed care organization (MCO), an organization that combines the functions of health insurance, delivery of care, and administration.

management service organization (MSO), an entity that under contract provides services such as a facility, equipment, staffing, contract negotiation, administration, and marketing. Services may be provided to solo practitioners or groups.

Mandelamine, a trademark for an antibacterial (methenamine mandelate).

mandible /man′dibəl/ [L, *mandere*, to chew], a large U-shaped bone constituting the lower jaw. It contains the lower teeth and consists of a horizontal part, a body, and two perpendicular rami that join the body at almost right angles.—**mandibular,** *adj.*

mandibular arch /mandib′yələr/ [L, *mandere*, to chew, *arcus*, bow], the first visceral arch from which the lower jawbone develops.

mandibular block, regional anesthesia of the lower jaw produced by injection of a local analgesic near the third division of the trigeminal nerve.

mandibular canal [L, *mandere*, to chew, *canalis*, channel], a passage or channel that extends from the mandibular foramen on the medial surface of the ramus of the mandible to the mental foramen. It holds mandibular blood vessels and a part of the mandibular branch of the trigeminal nerve.

mandibular foramen, the opening on the medial surface of the ramus for the transmission of the inferior alveolar nerve and vessels.

mandibular fossa [L, *mandere*, to chew, *fossa*, ditch], a prominent depression in the inferior surface of the squamous part of the temporal bone at the base of the zygomatic process, in which the condyle of the mandible rests.

mandibular nerve, the largest of the three branches of the trigeminal nerve. Its branches innervate the ear, the cheek, the skin and mucous membrane of the lower lip, the skin of the chin, the teeth and related gingivae, the tongue, and the muscles of the cheek and jaw.

mandibular notch, a depression in the inferior border of the mandible, anterior to the attachments of the masseter muscle, where the external facial muscles cross the inferior border of the mandible.

mandibular process [L, *mandere*, to chew + *processus*], **1.** the upper alveolar part of the mandible. **2.** the projection of the upper posterior part of the ramus of the mandible bearing the condyle.

mandibular ramus [L, *mandere*, to chew, *ramus*, branch], a broad quadrilateral part of the mandible projecting upward from the posterior end of the body behind the lower teeth. It has two surfaces, four borders, and two processes.

mandibular sling, the connection between the mandible and the maxilla, formed by the masseter and the pterygoideus at the angle of the mandible.

mandibular spine, a protuberance on the mandibular ramus to which the sphenomandibular ligament is attached.

mandibular symphysis, a small vertical ridge that marks the fusion of the left and right parts of the mandible.

mandibulofacial dysostosis /mandib′yəlo fā′shəl/ [L, *mandere* + *facies*, face; Gk, *dys*, bad, *osteon*, bone], an abnormal hereditary condition characterized by an antimongoloid slant of the palpebral fissures, coloboma of the lower lid, micrognathia and hypoplasia of the zygomatic arches, and microtia.

Mandol, a trademark for a cephalosporin antibiotic (cefamandole nafate).

mandrel /man′drəl/ [Fr, *mandrin*, boring tool], the shaft of an object, such as a dental polishing disk, cutting device, or sharpening stone, which is inserted into a handpiece or lathe and supports the object while it rotates.

maneuver /mənōō′vər/ [Fr, *manœvre*, action], **1.** an adroit or skillful manipulation or procedure. **2.** in obstetrics, a manipulation of the fetus, performed to aid in delivery.

mangafodipir /mang′gäfo′dīpir/, a contrast-enhancing agent used to improve the images obtained in MRI of hepatic lesions.

manganese (Mn) /mang′gənēs/ [L, *manganesium*, associated with magnesium], a common metallic element found in trace amounts in tissues of the body, where it aids in the functions of various enzymes. Its atomic number is 25, and its atomic mass is 54.938.

manganese nodule, a small node produced by microbial reduction of manganese oxides.

mange /mānj/, a cutaneous disease of domestic and wild animals caused by skin-burrowing mites.

mania /mā′nē·ə/ [Gk, madness], a mood characterized by an unstable expansive emotional state; extreme excitement; excessive elation; hyperactivity; agitation; overtalkativeness; flight of ideas; increased psychomotor activity, fleeting attention; and sometimes violent, destructive, and self-destructive behavior, delusions, or hallucinations.

manifest image, the change on an x-ray film that becomes visible when the latent image undergoes appropriate chemical processing.

manipulation /mənip′yəlā′shən/ [L, *manipulare*, to work with the hands], the skillful use of the hands in therapeutic or diagnostic procedures, such as palpation, reduction of a dislocation, turning a fetus, or various treatments in physical therapy and osteopathy.

mannitol /man′itol/, a poorly metabolized sugar used as an osmotic diuretic and in kidney function tests. It is prescribed to promote diuresis, to decrease intraocular and ICP, to promote the excretion of poisons and other toxic wastes, and to evaluate renal function.

mannose /man′ōs/, a monosaccharide sugar of the aldose group, found as part of many glycolipids and glycoproteins.

mannosidosis /man′ōsidō′sis/, a lysosomal storage disease caused by an enzymatic defect in the metabolism of mannose-containing glycoproteins, resulting in accumulation of oligosaccharides. Characteristics include coarse facies, upper respiratory congestion and infections, profound mental retardation, hepatosplenomegaly, cataracts, radiographic signs of skeletal abnormalities, and gibbus deformity.

manometer /mənom′ətər/ [Gk, *manos*, thin, *metron*, measure], a device for measuring the pressure of a fluid, consisting of a tube marked with a scale and containing a relatively incompressible fluid such as mercury. The level of the fluid in the tube varies with the pressure of the fluid being measured.

manometry /mənom′ətrē/ [Gk, *manos*, thin, *metron*, measure], **1.** the science of pressure movements of liquids or gases. **2.** a technique for measuring changes in the pressure of a gas or liquid that result from a biologic or chemical action.

Mansonella /man′sənel′ə/, a genus of nematodes of the superfamily Filarioidea. *M. ozzardi* and *M. perstans* are two species that parasitize humans and cause mild symptoms.

Mansonella ozzardi /man′sənel′ə/, a relatively benign parasitic nematode that infects humans. The larvae live in the bloodstream, and adult worms are found in the visceral mesenteries.

mansonellosis /man′sənelō′sis/, a rare tropical infectious disease caused by nematodes of the genus *Mansonella*. It can cause skin rashes, muscle and joint pains, neurologic disorders, and skin lumps.

mantle cell lymphoma /man′təl/, a rare form of non-Hodgkin's lymphoma having a usually diffuse pattern. It mainly affects people over 50 years of age and runs an indolent course, although it may metastasize to the spleen or liver.

Mantoux test /mantōō′/ [Charles Mantoux, French physician, 1877–1947], a tuberculin skin test that consists of intradermal injection of a purified protein derivative of the tubercle bacillus. A hardened, raised red area of 8 to 10 mm, appearing 24 to 72 hours after injection, is a positive reaction. This method is the most reliable means of testing tuberculin sensitivity.

manual lymph drainage, the application of light rhythmic strokes, similar to those used in effleurage, to the skin and superficial fascia in the direction of the heart to increase the drainage of lymph from the involved structures.

manual rotation /man′yōō·əl/ [L, *manualis*, hand, *rotare*, to turn], an obstetric maneuver in which a baby's head is turned by hand from a transverse to an anteroposterior position in the birth canal to facilitate delivery.

manubriosternal articulation /mənōō′brē·ōstur′nəl/ [L, *manubrium*, handle; Gk, *sternum*, chest; L, *articularis*, joints], the

M

fibrocartilaginous connection between the manubrium and the body of the sternum.

manubrium /mənōō'brē·əm/ [L, handle], the most anterior of the three bones of the sternum, presenting a broad quadrangular shape that narrows caudally at its articulation with the superior end of the body of the sternum.—**manubrial,** *adj.*

manudynamometer /man'ōōdī'nəmom'ətər/ [L, *manus,* hand; Gk, *dynamis,* force, *metron,* measure], a device for measuring the force or extent of thrust.

many-tailed bandage [AS, *manig,* many, *taegel,* tail; Fr, *bande,* strip], **1.** a broad, evenly shaped bandage with both ends split into strips of equal size and number. As the bandage is placed on the abdomen, chest, or limb, the ends may be overlapped and secured. **2.** an irregularly shaped bandage with torn or cut ends that are secured together.

MAO, abbreviation for **monoamine oxidase.**

MAO inhibitor, abbreviation for **monoamine oxidase inhibitor,** also abbreviated **MAOI.**

Maolate, a trademark for a skeletal muscle relaxant (chlorphenesin carbamate).

MAP, 1. abbreviation for *medical aid post.* **2.** abbreviation for **mean arterial pressure.**

maple bark disease [AS, *mapul;* ONorse, *bark;* L, *dis,* opposite of; Fr, *aise,* ease], a hypersensitivity pneumonitis caused by exposure to the mold *Cryptostroma corticale,* found in the bark of maple trees. In the susceptible person the condition may be acute, accompanied by fever, cough, dyspnea, and vomiting, or chronic, characterized by fatigue, weight loss, dyspnea on exertion, and a productive cough.

maple syrup urine disease [AS, *mapul;* Ar, *sharab;* Gk, *ouron,* urine], an inherited metabolic disorder in which an enzyme necessary for the breakdown of the amino acids valine, leucine, and isoleucine is lacking. The disease is usually diagnosed in infancy. It is recognized by the characteristic maple syrup odor of the urine and by hyperreflexia.

mapping [L, *mappa,* napkin], the process of locating the relative position of genes on a chromosome through the analysis of genetic recombination.

maprotiline hydrochloride /maprō'tilēn/, a tetracyclic antidepressant similar to the tricyclics.

map unit [L, *mappa,* napkin, *unus,* one], an arbitrary unit of measure used to express the distance between genes on a chromosome. It is calculated from the percentage of recombinations that occur between specific genes so that 1% of crossing over represents one unit on a genetic map.

marasmic kwashiorkor /məraz'mik/ [Gk, *marasmos,* a wasting; Afr], a malnutrition disease, primarily of children, resulting from the deficiency of both calories and protein. The condition is characterized by severe tissue wasting, dehydration, loss of subcutaneous fat, lethargy, and growth retardation.

marasmoid /məraz'moid/, resembling marasmus.

marasmus /məraz'məs/ [Gk, *marasmos,* a wasting], a condition of extreme malnutrition and emaciation, occurring chiefly in young children. It is characterized by progressive wasting of subcutaneous tissue and muscle. Marasmus results from a lack of adequate calories and proteins and is seen in children with failure to thrive and in individuals in a state of starvation. Less commonly it results from an inability to assimilate or use protein because of a defect in metabolism.

marathon encounter group /mer'əthon/ [Marathon, Greece; L, *in,* in, *contra,* against; Fr, *groupe*], an intensive group experience that accelerates self-awareness and promotes personal growth and behavioral change through the continuous interaction of group members for a period ranging from 16 to more than 40 hours.

maraviroc, an antiretroviral used to treat CCR5-tropic HIV in combination with other antiretroviral agents.

Marax, a trademark for a fixed-combination respiratory drug containing a smooth muscle relaxant (theophylline), an adrenergic (epHEDrine sulfate), and an antihistamine (hydrOXYzine hydrochloride).

Marburg virus disease /mär'bərg/, a severe febrile viral disease characterized by rash, hepatitis, pancreatitis, and severe GI hemorrhages. The disease is caused by the Marburg virus, a member of the Filoviridae family.

Marcaine Hydrochloride, a trademark for a local anesthetic (bupivacaine hydrochloride).

march /märch/, the progression of electrical activity through the motor cortex.

march foot [Fr, *marcher,* to walk; AS, *fot*], an abnormal condition of the foot caused by excessive use, such as in a long march. The forefoot is swollen and painful, and one or more of the metatarsal bones may be broken.

march hemoglobinuria, a rare abnormal condition, characterized by the presence of hemoglobin in the urine, that occurs after strenuous physical exertion or prolonged exercise such as marching or distance running.

Marchiafava-Micheli disease /mär'kyəfä'və mikä'lē/ [Ettore Marchiafava, Italian physician, 1847–1935; F. Micheli, Italian physician, 1872–1929], a rare disorder of unknown origin characterized by episodic hemoglobinuria, which occurs usually, but not always, at night.

Marchi's globule /mär'kēz/ [Vittoria Marchi, Italian physician, 1851-1908], fragments and particles of broken-up myelin that stain by Marchi's method, seen in degeneration of the spinal cord.

Marchi's method, a laboratory staining procedure for demonstrating degenerated nerve fibers.

Marcus Gunn pupil sign [Robert Marcus Gunn, English ophthalmologist, 1850–1909], paradoxic dilation of the pupils in an ophthalmologic examination in response to afferent visual stimuli.

Marezine, a trademark for an antiemetic (cyclizine hydrochloride).

Marfan's syndrome /märfäNz'/ [Bernard-Jean A. Marfan, French pediatrician, 1858–1942], a hereditary condition that affects the musculoskeletal system and is often associated with abnormalities of the cardiovascular system and of the eyes. Its major musculoskeletal effects include muscular underdevelopment, ligamentous laxity, joint hypermobility, and bone elongation. The extremities of individuals with Marfan's syndrome are very long and spider-like, with greatly extended hands, feet, and fingers. Most adult patients are over 6 feet (1.8 meters) tall and have asymmetric skulls. Pathologic alterations of the cardiovascular system appear to produce fragmentation of the elastic fibers in the media of the aorta, which may lead to aneurysm. Ocular changes include a variety of disorders, including dislocation of the lens. No specific treatment is available, and symptomatic management of the associated problems is the usual alternative.

marginal gingiva /mär'jənəl/ [L, *margo,* margin, *gingiva,* gum], the uppermost part of the free gingiva. It overlaps the neck and base of the crown of the tooth.

marginal gyrus [L, *margo,* margin; Gk, *gyros,* turn], the superior frontal convolution on the surface of the cerebral hemispheres.

marginal peptic ulcer [L, *margo,* margin; Gk, *peptein,* to digest; L, *ulcus,* ulcer], an ulcer that develops postoperatively at the surgical anastomosis of the stomach and jejunum.

marginal placenta previa, placenta previa in which the placenta is implanted in the lower uterine segment, with its margin touching or spreading to some degree over the internal os of the uterine cervix. During labor, as the cervix dilates, bleeding may occur from the separation of the edge of the placenta from the uterus beneath it.

marginal ridge, an elevation of enamel that forms the proximal boundary of the occlusal surface of a tooth.

marginal sinus [L, *margo* + *sinus,* hollow], a sinus that may encircle the placenta.

marginal sinus rupture, a detachment of the placenta from the implantation site. It may be complete, partial, or marginal in abruptio placentae.

margin of safety, an index of a drug's effectiveness and safety. It is calculated as the amount of drug that is lethal to 1% of animals (LD_1) divided by the amount of drug that causes a beneficial effect in 99% of the animals (ED_{99}).

Marie's hypertrophy [Pierre Marie, French neurologist, 1853–1940; Gk, *hyper,* excess, *trophe,* nourishment], chronic enlargement of the joints caused by periostitis.

Marin Amat's syndrome [Manuel Marin Amat, Spanish ophthalmologist, b. 1879], an involuntary facial movement in which the eyes close when the mouth opens or when the jaws move in mastication. The phenomenon results from a facial nerve paralysis.

Marinesco-Sjögren syndrome /märēnes' kōshur'gren/ [Georges Marinesco, Romanian neurologist, 1863–1938; Karl Gustav Torsten Sjögren, Swedish physician, b. 1896], a hereditary syndrome transmitted as an autosomal-recessive trait, consisting of cerebellar ataxia, mental and somatic growth retardation, congenital cataracts, inability to chew, thin brittle fingernails, and sparse, incompletely keratinized hair.

Marinol, a trademark for an oral antiemetic (dronabinol).

marital rape [L, *rapere,* to seize], forcible sexual intercourse with a spouse.

marital therapy, a type of family therapy aimed at understanding and treating one or both members of a couple in the context of a distressed relationship, but not necessarily addressing the discordant relationship itself.

mark [AS, *mearc*], any nevus or birthmark.

markers [AS, *mearc*], body language movements that serve as indicators and punctuation marks in interpersonal communication.

Maroteaux-Lamy syndrome /märōtō' lämē'/ [Pierre Maroteaux, French physician, b. 1926; Maurice Emile Joseph Lamy, French physician, 1895–1975], a mucopolysaccharidosis characterized biochemically by the predominance of the

M

mucopolysaccharide dermatan sulfate in the urine and the presence of coarse granules in the leukocytes and clinically by Hurler-like signs with normal intelligence.

Marplan, a trademark for an antidepressant (isocarboxazid).

marriage therapy, a subset of marital therapy that focuses specifically on enhancing and preserving the bond of marriage between two people.

Marseilles fever /märsälz', märsä'/ [Marseille, France; L, *febris,* fever], a disease caused by *Rickettsia conorii* transmitted by the brown dog tick *(Rhipicephalus sanguineus).* Characteristic symptoms are chills, fever, an ulcer covered with a black crust at the site of the tick bite, and a rash appearing on the second to fourth day.

Marshall-Marchetti-Krantz procedure, a surgical procedure performed to correct stress incontinence. The vesicourethropexy involves a retropubic incision and suturing of the urethra, vesicle neck, and bladder to the posterior surface of the pubic bone.

marsupialize /märsōō'pē·əlīz/ [L, *marsupium,* pouch; Gk, *izein,* to cause], to form a pouch surgically to treat a cyst when simple removal would not be effective, such as in a pancreatic or a pilonidal cyst. The cyst sac is opened and emptied. Its edges are sutured to adjacent tissues, and a drain is left in place.

Martinsen, Kari, a nursing theorist who proposed a philosophy of caring in reaction to social and health care inequalities and what she considered nursing's uncritical adoption of science as the basis for nursing. It involves a collectivist vision of humanity in which the individual is dependent upon the community and creation, or nature, and caring rather than control should be the guiding philosophy. As it relates to nursing, caring is simultaneously relational, practical, and moral.

MAS, abbreviation for **mobile arm support.**

mAs, abbreviation for **milliampere-second.**

masculine /mas'kyəlin/ [L, *masculinus,* male], having the characteristics of a male.

masculinization /mas'kyəlin′īzä'shən/ [L, *masculinus*; Gk, *izein,* to cause], the normal development or induction of male sex characteristics.—**masculinize,** *v.*

MASER /mā'sər/, abbreviation for *microwave amplification by stimulated emission of radiation.*

MASH /mash/, abbreviation for *mobile army surgical hospital.*

mask [Fr, *masque*], **1.** to obscure, as in symptomatic treatment that may conceal the development of a disease. **2.** to cover, as does a skin-toned cosmetic that may hide a pigmented nevus. **3.** a cover worn over the nose and mouth to prevent inhalation of toxic or irritating materials, to control delivery of oxygen or anesthetic gas, or (by medical personnel) to shield a patient during aseptic procedures from pathogenic organisms normally exhaled from the respiratory tract.

masked residue, the amino acid part of a peptide that is not accessible for activity after a condensation reaction.

mask image, a radiographic image made either before or immediately after contrast material has been injected but before it reaches the anatomic site being examined. The image thus produced is stored in a computer and then subtracted electronically from a series of additional images. The technique enhances the image of the tissues being studied.

masking, **1.** the covering or concealing of a disorder by a second condition. An example is a person's beginning a weight-loss diet while an undiagnosed wasting disease such as cancer has developed. The loss of body weight is attributed to the diet. **2.** the unconscious display of a personality trait that conceals a behavioral aberration.

masking agent, a cosmetic preparation for covering nevi, surgical scars, and other blemishes.

masklike facies [Fr, *masque*; L, *facies,* face], an immobile expressionless face with staring eyes and slightly open mouth. It is sometimes associated with parkinsonism or psychiatric conditions.

Maslow's hierarchy of needs /mas'lōz/ [Abraham H. Maslow, American psychiatrist, 1908–1970; Gk, *hierarches,* position of authority; AS, *nied,* obligation], in psychology, a hierarchic categorization of the basic needs of humans. The most basic needs on the scale are the physiologic or biologic needs, such as the need for air, food, or water. Of second priority are the safety needs. The subsequent order of needs in the hierarchic progression are the need to belong, to love, and to be loved; the need for self-esteem; and ultimately the need for self-actualization.

masochism /mas'ōkiz'əm/ [Leopold von Sacher-Masoch, Austrian author, 1836–1895], pleasure or gratification derived from receiving physical, mental, or emotional abuse.—**masochistic,** *adj.*

masochist /mas'ōkist/ [Leopold von Sacher-Masoch], a person who derives pleasure or gratification from masochistic acts or abuse.

mass (*m*) [L, *massa*], **1.** the physical property of matter that gives it weight and inertia. **2.** in pharmacology, a mixture from which pills are formed. **3.** an aggregate of cells clumped together, such as a tumor.

mass action law, **1.** the mathematic description of reversible reactions that attain equilibrium, generally regarded as applicable to competitive assay. **2.** the rate of a chemical reaction that is proportional to the active masses of the resulting substances.

massage¹ /məsäzh, məsäj′/ [Fr, *masser,* to stroke], the manipulation of the soft tissue of the body through stroking, rubbing, kneading, or tapping, to increase circulation, to improve muscle tone, and to relax the patient. The most common sites for massage are the back, knees, elbows, and heels.

massage², a nursing intervention from the Nursing Interventions Classification (NIC) defined as stimulation of the skin and underlying tissues with varying degrees of hand pressure to decrease pain, produce relaxation, and/or improve circulation.

massage therapist, a person who performs massages to relieve pain and enhance healing.

massage therapy, the manipulation of the soft tissues of the body for the purpose of normalizing them, thereby enhancing health and healing. Massage therapy includes a number of methods, such as acupressure, classical Western massage, and shiatsu.

masseter /masē′tər/ [Gk, one who chews], the thick rectangular muscle in the cheek that functions to close the jaw. It is one of the four muscles of mastication.

masseteric nerve, a branch of the anterior trunk of the mandibular nerve that supplies the masseter muscle.

mass fragment [L, *massa,* lump, *frangere,* to shatter], in mass spectrometry, a degraded part of a molecule containing one or more charges.

mass hysteria [ME, *maiour,* great; Gk, *hystera,* womb], an episode of psychogenic illness affecting a large group of individuals at the same time. An example is the witchcraft trials of the 17th century.

massive lung collapse, a condition in which an entire lung or one of its lobes becomes airless, frequently as a result of an obstruction in a bronchus.

massive transfusion syndrome [L, *multus,* many, *plica,* fold, *transfundere,* to pour through; Gk, *syn,* together, *dromos,* course], a hemorrhagic reaction to massive transfusions of platelet-poor stored blood. For an adult, transfusion of 10 units of blood in a 24-hour period is a massive transfusion. Platelet concentrates and/or fresh frozen plasma may be given to correct the deficiency.

mass number (A), the sum of the number of protons and neutrons in the nucleus of an atom or isotope.

mass reflex, an abnormal condition, seen in patients with transection of the spinal cord, characterized by a widespread nerve discharge. Stimulation below the level of the lesion results in flexor muscle spasms, incontinence of urine and feces, priapism, hypertension, and profuse sweating. A mass reflex may be triggered by scratching or other painful stimulus to the skin, overdistension of the bladder or intestines, cold weather, prolonged sitting, or emotional stress.

mass spectrometer, an analytic instrument for identifying a substance by sorting a stream of charged particles (ions) according to their mass.

mass spectrometry, in chemistry, a technique for the analysis of a substance in which the molecule is subjected to bombardment by high-energy electrons or atoms to cause ionization and fragmentation to give a series of ions in the gas phase that constitutes the fragmentation pattern observed by using a mass spectrometer.

mass spectrum, a characteristic pattern obtained from a mass spectrometer.

mass transfer, the movement of mass from one phase to another.

mass transfer-area coefficient (MTAC), the permeability of a dialysis membrane multiplied by the available area of the membrane, calculated as the clearance rate by diffusion when there is no ultrafiltration and when there is not yet any solute in the dialysate.

MAST, abbreviation for **military antishock trousers.**

mastalgia /mastal′jə/ [Gk, *mastos,* breast, *algos,* pain], pain in the breast caused by congestion or "caking" during lactation, an infection, or fibrocystic disease, especially during or before menstruation, or by advanced cancer. —**mastalgic,** *adj.*

mast cell [Ger, *Mast,* fattening; L, *cella,* storeroom], a constituent of connective tissue containing large basophilic granules that contain heparin, serotonin, bradykinin, and histamine.

mast cell leukemia, a malignant neoplasm of leukocytes characterized by connective tissue mast cells in circulating blood.

mast cell tumor [Ger, *Mast,* fattening; L, *cella,* storeroom + *tumor*], a connective tissue tumor composed of mast cells.

mastectomy /mastek′təmē/ [Gk, *mastos,* breast, *ektomē,* excision], the surgical removal of one or both breasts, most commonly performed to remove a malignant tumor. In a simple mastectomy the breast

M

is removed without lymph node dissection. In a radical mastectomy some of the muscles of the chest are removed with the breast, together with lymph nodes in the axilla. In a modified radical mastectomy the involved breast and all axillary contents (axillary, pectoral, and superior apical nodes) are removed, but the pectoral muscles are preserved.

master problem list, a list of a patient's problems that serves as an index to his or her record. Each problem, the date when it was first noted, the treatment, and the desired outcome are added to the list as each becomes known.

master's degree program in nursing, a postgraduate program in a school of nursing in a university setting that grants the degree Master of Science in Nursing to successful candidates. Nurses with this degree function in leadership roles in clinical nursing, as consultants in various settings, in faculty positions in schools of nursing, and as nurse practitioners in various specialties.

mastery /mas'tərē/ [L, *magister,* chief], command or control of a situation.

mastication /mas'tikā'shən/ [L, *masticare,* to chew], chewing, tearing, or grinding food with the teeth while it becomes mixed with saliva.

masticatory movement /mas'tikətôr'ē/, motion of the lower jaw in chewing.

masticatory system [L, *masticare,* to chew; Gk, *systema*], the combination of structures involved in chewing, including the jaws, teeth and supporting structures, mandibular and maxillary musculature, TMJs, tongue, lips, cheeks, oral mucosa, blood supply, and cranial nerves.

mastigophora, protozoa having flagella.

mastigophoran /mas'tigof'ärahn/, any member of the subphylum Mastigophora.

mastitis /mastī'tis/ [Gk, *mastos,* breast, *itis,* inflammation], an inflammatory condition of the breast, usually caused by streptococcal or staphylococcal infection. Acute mastitis, most common in the first 2 months of lactation, is characterized by pain, swelling, redness, axillary lymphadenopathy, fever, and malaise. Chronic tuberculous mastitis is rare; when it occurs, it represents extension of TB from the lungs and ribs beneath the breast.

mastocarcinoma /mas'təkär'sinō'mə/, carcinoma of the mammary gland.

mastocytoma /mas'təsītō'mə/, a tumor that contains mast cells.

mastocytosis /mas'təsītō'sis/ [Ger, *Mast,* fattening; Gk, *kytos,* cell, *osis,* condition], local or systemic overproduction of mast cells, which in rare instances may infiltrate liver, spleen, bones, the GI system, and skin.

mastoid /mas'toid/ [Gk, *mastos,* breast, *eidos,* form], **1.** pertaining to the mastoid process of the temporal bone. **2.** breast-shaped.

mastoid antrum, a cavity continuous with mastoid cells. It is separated from the middle cranial fossa above by the tegmen tympani.

mastoid cells [Gk, *mastos,* breast, *eidos,* form; L, *cella,* storeroom], air cells in the mastoid process of the temporal bone.

mastoidectomy /mas'toidek'təmē/ [Gk, *mastos + eidos,* form, *ektomē,* excision], surgical excision of a part of the mastoid part of the temporal bone, frequently performed to treat cholesteatoma. It may also be performed to treat chronic suppurative otitis media or mastoiditis when systemic antibiotics are ineffective. In a simple mastoidectomy diseased mastoid bone is removed while the ossicles, eardrum, and canal wall are left intact, and the eardrum is incised to drain the middle ear. In a radical procedure the eardrum and most middle ear structures are removed. The stapes is left intact so that a hearing aid may be used. The opening to the eustachian tube is plugged. In a modified radical procedure the eardrum and some of the ossicles are saved, and the patient has more hearing than after a radical mastoidectomy.

mastoid fontanel, a posterolateral fontanel that is usually not palpable.

mastoiditis /mas'toidī'tis/ [Gk, *mastos + eidos,* form, *itis,* inflammation], an infection of one of the mastoid bones, usually an extension of a middle ear infection. It is characterized by earache, fever, headache, and malaise. Residual hearing loss may follow the infection.

mastoid process, the irregular conic projection of the caudal, posterior part of the temporal bone, serving as the attachment for various muscles, including the sternocleidomastoideus, splenius capitis, and longissimus capitis.

mastopathy /mastop'əthē/, any disease of the breast.

mastopexy, a reconstructive procedure in cosmetic surgery to lift the breasts.

masturbation /mas'tərbā'shən/ [L, *masturbari,* to masturbate], sexual activity in which the penis or clitoris is stimulated, usually to orgasm, by means other than coitus.—**masturbate,** *v.,* **masturbatic, masturbatory,** *adj.*

mat, 1. abbreviation for **maternity. 2.** abbreviation for **maturity. 3.** abbreviation for **maternal.**

matching layer, a layer of material placed in front of an ultrasound transducer to improve the efficiency of energy transfer into and out of a patient.

materia /mətir′ē·ə/, matter or material.

materia alba /mətir′ē·ə al′bə/ [L, white matter], a whitish or cream-colored cheesy mass deposited around the necks of the teeth, composed of food debris, mucin, and dead epithelial cells.

material fact /mətir′ē·əl/ [L, *materia*, matter + *factum*], **1.** in law, a fact that establishes or refutes an element essential to the complaint, charge, or defense. **2.** a fact that would be important to a reasonable person in deciding whether to engage in a transaction or not.

materia medica (mat. med.), 1. the study of the origins, preparation, uses, and effects of drugs and other substances used in medicine. **2.** a substance or a drug used in medical treatment.

matern., 1. abbreviation for **maternal. 2.** abbreviation for **maternity.**

maternal (mat, matern.) /mətur′nəl/ [L, *maternus,* motherhood], **1.** inherited, derived, or received from a mother. **2.** motherly in behavior. **3.** related through the mother's side of the family, such as a maternal grandfather.

maternal and child health (MCH) services, various facilities and programs organized for the purpose of providing medical and social services for mothers and children. Medical services include prenatal and postnatal services, family planning care, and pediatric care in infancy.

maternal antibody, an antibody transmitted from mother to fetus via the placenta. Such antibodies can provide immunity for the fetus and the newborn for up to 6 months after birth. They may also cause hemolytic anemia in newborns in cases of Rh or ABO blood group incompatibility between mother and child.

maternal death, the death of a woman during the childbearing cycle.

maternal deprivation syndrome [L, *maternus,* motherhood, *deprivare,* to deprive; Gk, *syn,* together, *dromos,* course], a condition characterized by developmental retardation that occurs as a result of physical or emotional deprivation. It is seen primarily in infants. Typical symptoms include lack of physical growth, with weight below the third percentile for age and size; malnutrition; pronounced withdrawal; silence; apathy; irritability; and a characteristic posture and body language, featuring unnatural stiffness and rigidity with a slow response reaction to others. Causes of the syndrome are usually multiple and complex, involving such factors as parental indifference; emotional instability or insecurity of the mother; lack of or delayed development of the mother-child attachment process; unrealistic expectations or disappointment

concerning the sex, appearance, or adaptability of the child; or unfavorable socioeconomic conditions within the family.

maternal immunity, protection against disease acquired by a fetus through the passage of maternal antibodies via the placenta.

maternal-infant bonding, the complex process of attachment of a mother to her newborn. In the first minutes and hours after birth, a sensitive period occurs during which the baby and the mother become intimately involved with each other through behaviors and stimuli that are complementary and that provoke further interactions. The mother touches the baby and holds it en face to achieve eye-to-eye contact. The infant looks back eye to eye. The mother and the baby move in turn to the voice and sounds of the other, a process known as entrainment. Physically the mother provides her body heat for the baby's warmth and comfort. Thus the extended contact in the newborn period satisfies physical and emotional needs of the mother and baby.

maternal inheritance, the transmission of traits or conditions controlled by cytoplasmic factors within the ovum that are not self-replicating and are determined by genes within the nucleus.

maternal microchimerism, persistence of cells derived from the mother in her offspring.

maternal mortality, 1. the death of a woman as a result of childbearing. **2.** the number of maternal deaths per 100,000 live births.

maternal placenta [L, *maternus,* motherhood, *placenta,* flat cake], the part of the placenta that develops from the decidua basalis of the uterus and is usually shed along with the fetal elements.

maternal screen testing, a blood or urine screen for birth defects and genetic disorders, administered in early pregnancy. It is most important for women over 35 years of age and those who have previously delivered children with birth defects.

maternal serum alpha-fetoprotein (MSAFP) test, a test of a pregnant woman's blood designed to indicate an increased risk for fetal open neural tube defects, such as spina bifida. It may also indicate an increased risk for Down syndrome.

maternal status: antepartum, a nursing outcome from the Nursing Outcomes Classification (NOC) defined as the extent to which maternal well-being is within normal limits from conception to the onset of labor.

maternal status: intrapartum, a nursing outcome from the Nursing Outcomes

M

Classification (NOC) defined as the extent to which maternal well-being is within normal limits from onset of labor to delivery.

maternal status: postpartum, a nursing outcome from the Nursing Outcomes Classification (NOC) defined as the extent to which maternal well-being is within normal limits from delivery of placenta to completion of involution.

maternity cycle [L, *maternus,* motherhood; Gk, *kyklos,* circle], the antepartal, intrapartal, and postpartal periods of pregnancy and the puerperium, from conception to 6 weeks after birth.

maternity (mat, matern.) /mətur′nitē/ [L, *maternus,* motherhood], motherhood; the character and quality of a mother.

maternity nursing, nursing care provided to women and their families during pregnancy and parturition and through the first days of the puerperium.

mat gold [Fr, *mat,* dull; AS, *geolu,* yellow], a noncohesive form of pure gold.

mating /mā′ting/ [D, *mate,* companion], the pairing of individuals of the opposite sex, primarily for purposes of reproduction.

mat. med., abbreviation for **materia medica.**

matrifocal family /mat′rifō′kəl/ [L, *mater,* mother, *focus,* hearth, *familia,* household], a family unit composed of a mother and her children. Biologic fathers may have a temporary place in the family during the first years of the children's lives, but they maintain a more permanent position in their own original families.

matrix /mā′triks, mat′riks/ [L, womb], **1.** an intercellular substance. **2.** a basic substance from which a specific organ or kind of tissue develops. **3.** a form used in shaping a tooth surface in dental procedures. **4.** in analytic chemistry, material of no interest in an analysis that may have an effect on the analysis. **5.** a rectangular arrangement of elements into rows and columns, often used to display a digital image.

matrix band, a cylindrical copper or stainless steel band or short tube that is seated over a tooth. The band may be filled with impression compound, which flows into a prepared cavity in order to obtain an impression, or it may be used to aid in the placement and contouring of restorative materials.

matrix metalloproteinase, any of a group of endopeptidases that hydrolyze proteins of the extracellular matrix.

matrix retainer, a mechanical device used to secure the ends of a matrix band around a tooth.

matroclinous inheritance /mātrō′klinəs/ [L, *mater,* mother; Gk, *klinein,* to incline], a form of heredity in which the traits of the offspring have been transmitted from the mother.

matter [L, *materia*], **1.** anything that has mass and occupies space. **2.** any substance not otherwise identified as to its constituents, such as gray matter, pus, or serum exuding from a wound.

Mattis Dementia Rating Scale (DRS), a widely used tool for evaluation of cognitive function dementia in adults over the age of 55 years who have brain dysfunction. It measures overall cognitive functioning on five subscales and can be used at lower ability levels than can be tested by most other methods.

Matulane, a trademark for an antineoplastic (procarbazine hydrochloride).

maturation /mach′ərā′shən/ [L, *maturare,* to ripen], **1.** the process or condition of attaining complete development. In humans, it is the unfolding of full physical, emotional, and intellectual capacities that enable a person to function at a higher level of competency and adaptability within the environment. **2.** the final stages in the meiotic formation of germ cells in which the number of chromosomes in each cell is reduced to the haploid number characteristic of the species. **3.** suppuration.—**maturate,** *v.*

maturational crisis /mach′ərā′shənəl/, a transitional or developmental period within a person's life, such as puberty, when psychologic equilibrium is upset.

mature /məchoor′/ [L, *maturus,* ripe], **1.** to become fully developed; to ripen. **2.** fully developed or ripened.

maturity (mat) /məchoo′ritē/ [L, *maturus,* ripe], **1.** a state of complete growth or development, usually designated as the period of life between adolescence and old age. **2.** the stage at which an organism is capable of reproduction.

max, 1. abbreviation for *maxima.* **2.** abbreviation for *maximum.*

maxilla /maksil′ə/ *pl.* **maxillae** [L, *mala,* jaw], one of a pair of large bones (often referred to as one bone) that form the upper jaw and teeth, consisting of a pyramidal body and four processes: the zygomatic, frontal, alveolar, and palatine.

maxillary /mak′səler′ē/ [L, *maxilla,* upper jaw], pertaining to the upper jawbone.

maxillary arch [L, *maxilla,* upper jaw, *arcus,* bow], the curved bony ridge of the upper jawbone, in the shape of a horseshoe, including the dentition and supporting structures.

maxillary artery [L, *maxilla,* upper jaw; Gk, *arteria,* airpipe], either of two larger terminal branches of the external carotid arteries that rise from the neck of the mandible near the parotid gland and divide into six branches, supplying the deep structures of the face.

maxillary nerve, the second division of the trigeminal nerve, a purely sensory nerve that branches into a zygomaticotemporal branch, a zygomaticofacial branch, and the large infraorbital nerve, which in turn has multiple branches that supply the face.

maxillary process [L, *maxilla,* upper jaw + *processus*], **1.** the alveolar process of the upper jaw that contains the tooth sockets. **2.** the frontal process that extends upward to articulate with the frontal and nasal bones. **3.** the palatine process that helps form the hard palate. **4.** the zygomatic process, or anterior surface, that articulates with the zygomatic bone.

maxillary sinus, one of a pair of large air cells forming a pyramidal cavity in the body of the maxilla.

maxillary tuberosity, a rounded eminence on the posterior surface of the body of the maxilla, behind the root of the third molar.

maxillary vein, one of a pair of deep veins of the face, accompanying the maxillary artery. Each maxillary vein is a tributary of the internal and external jugular veins.

maxillodental /mak′silōden′təl/, pertaining to or affecting the upper jaw and teeth.

maxillofacial /mak′silōfā′shəl/ [L, *maxilla,* upper jaw, *facies,* face], pertaining to the maxilla and face.

maxillofacial prosthesis [L, *maxilla,* upper jaw, *facies,* face], a prosthetic replacement for part, or all, of the upper jaw, nose, or cheek. It is applied when surgical repair alone is inadequate.

maxillofacial syndrome, a congenital defect of fetal ossification characterized by anteroposterior shortening of the maxilla and various other anomalies, including mandibular prognathism, slanting of the eyes, and malformation of the auricles.

maxillofacial trauma, injury to the jaw and face. Fractures requiring reconstructive surgery tend to occur most frequently in motor vehicle collisions and short falls.

maxillolacrimal suture /-lak′riməl/, a line of union between the anterior border of the lacrimal bone and the frontal process of the maxilla.

maxillomandibular /maksil′ōmandib′yo͞olər/, pertaining to the upper and lower jaws.

maxillomandibular fixation [L, *maxilla,* upper jaw, *mandere,* to chew, *figere,* to fasten], stabilization of fractures of the face or jaw by temporarily connecting the maxilla and mandible by wires, elastic bands, or metal splints.

maxillotomy /mak′silot′əmē/ [L, *maxilla,* upper jaw; Gk, *tomē,* a cutting], surgical sectioning of the maxilla that allows movement of all or a part of the maxilla into the desired position.

maximal acid output (MAO), on the pentagastrin test, the output of gastric acid for 1 hour after administration of pentagastrin, expressed as mmol/hr.

maximal diastolic membrane potential, the most-negative transmembrane potential achieved by a cardiac cell during repolarization.

maximal expiratory flow rate (MEFR), the rate of the most rapid flow of gas from the lungs during a forced expiration after a full inspiration.

maximal expiratory pressure (MEP), the greatest pressure of expired air achieved by a person after a full inspiration.

maximal midexpiratory flow rate (MMFR), the rate of the most rapid flow of gas during the middle half (in terms of volume) of a forced expiration after a full inspiration. It is measured in pulmonary function tests to detect and evaluate COPDs.

maximal treadmill test (MTT), an exercise stress test in which subjects increase their heart rate during exercise to 80% to 90% of the maximal rate, which is estimated from each subject's age and sex. Newer methods of stress testing produce the same physiologic effect of exercise on the heart by using drugs such as dipyridamole rather than exercise to "stress" the heart.

maximum breathing capacity (MBC) /mak′səməm/ [L, *maximus,* greatest; AS, *braeth*; L, *capacitas*], the maximum volume of gas that a person can inhale and exhale per minute by breathing as quickly and deeply as possible.

maximum inspiratory pressure (MIP) /mak′səməm/ [L, *maximus,* greatest, *inspirare,* to breathe in, *premere,* to press], the maximum pressure within the alveoli of the lungs that occurs during a full inspiration.

maximum intensity projection (MIP), a three-dimensional image processing method used in CT and magnetic resonance.

maximum oxygen uptake, the greatest volume of oxygen per minute that can be absorbed from the lungs by the blood.

maximum permissible dose (MPD, M.P.D.), the largest amount of ionizing radiation a person may receive according to radiation protection guidelines for persons working with radioactive materials or x-rays. It is 5 rem per year or a lifetime accumulation of 1 rem times the age of the person.

maximum voluntary isometric contraction (MVIC), the peak force produced

M

by a muscle as it contracts while pulling against an immovable object.

maximum voluntary ventilation (MVV), the maximum volume of gas that a person can inhale and exhale by voluntary effort per minute by breathing as quickly and deeply as possible. It is measured in pulmonary function tests.

maxofacial surgery, posttrauma and/or reconstructive and plastic surgery to the jaws and midface region.

Mayer's reflex /mā′orz/ [Karl Mayer, Austrian neurologist, 1862–1932], a normal reflex elicited by grasping the ring finger and flexing it at the metacarpophalangeal joint of a person whose hand is relaxed with thumb abducted. The normal responses are adduction and apposition of the thumb.

May-Hegglin anomaly, a rare autosomal-dominant inherited blood cell disorder characterized by thrombocytopenia and granulocytes with blue-colored RNA containing cytopathic inclusions, similar to Döhle's bodies.

mazindol /mā′zindōl/, an anorexiant prescribed over a short-term period to decrease appetite in the treatment of exogenous obesity.

mb, abbreviation for *millibar*.

M.B., abbreviation for *Bachelor of Medicine*.

mbar, abbreviation for *millibar*.

MBC, abbreviation for **maximum breathing capacity.**

MBD, M.B.D., abbreviation for *minimal brain dysfunction*.

mbp, abbreviation for *mean blood pressure*.

mbt, abbreviation for *mean body temperature*.

mc, abbreviation for *millicycle*.

mC, abbreviation for **millicoulomb.**

Mc, abbreviation for *megacycle*.

MC, 1. abbreviation for *medical certificate*. 2. abbreviation for *Medical Corps*.

MCAD, abbreviation for *medium-chain acyl-CoA dehydrogenase*, an enzyme involved in degradation of medium–chain length fatty acids. Deficiency of the enzyme is characterized by recurring episodes of hypoglycemia, vomiting, and lethargy, with urinary excretion of medium-chain dicarboxylic acids, minimal ketogenesis, and low plasma and tissue levels of carnitine.

McArdle's disease /məkär′dəlz/ [Brian McArdle, English neurologist, b. 1911], an inherited glycolic storage disease marked by an absence of myophosphorylase B and abnormally large amounts of glycogen in skeletal muscle. It is milder than other glycogen storage diseases, characterized by muscle fatigability and stiffness after exercise.

MCAT, abbreviation for **Medical College Aptitude Test.**

McBurney's incision /makbur′nēz/ [Charles McBurney, American surgeon, 1845–1913], a surgical wound that begins 2 to 5 cm above the anterior superior iliac spine and runs parallel to the external oblique muscle of the abdomen. This incision is used for an appendectomy.

McBurney's point [Charles McBurney; L, *pungere,* to puncture], a site of extreme sensitivity in acute appendicitis, situated in the normal area of the appendix midway between the umbilicus and the anterior iliac crest in the right lower quadrant of the abdomen.

McBurney's sign [Charles McBurney], a reaction of the patient indicating severe pain and extreme tenderness when McBurney's point is palpated. Such a reaction indicates appendicitis.

McCall's festoon /məkôlz′/, in dentistry, a ring-shaped enlargement of the gingival margin on the vestibular surface (buccal or labial) of canines and premolars. It may be associated with occlusal trauma.

MCFA, abbreviation for **medium-chain fatty acid.**

mcg, abbreviation for **microgram.**

MCH, 1. abbreviation for *maternal and child health services*. 2. abbreviation for **mean corpuscular hemoglobin.**

M.Ch., abbreviation for *Master of Surgery*.

MCHC, abbreviation for **mean corpuscular hemoglobin concentration.**

mCi, abbreviation for **millicurie.**

mCi-hr, abbreviation for *millicurie hour*.

McManus, R. Louise, a nurse who established the first national testing service for the nursing profession.

McMurray's sign /makmur′ēz/ [Thomas P. McMurray, English surgeon, 1887–1949], an audible click heard when rotating the tibia on the femur, indicating injury to meniscal structures.

MCO, abbreviation for **managed care organization.**

M component, an abnormal immunoglobulin that appears in large numbers in patients with macroglobulinemia, heavy chain disease, and multiple myeloma.

MCP, abbreviation for **metacarpophalangeal.**

M-CSF, abbreviation for **macrophage colony–stimulating factor.**

MCTD, abbreviation for **mixed connective tissue disease.**

MCV, abbreviation for **mean corpuscular volume.**

Md, symbol for the element **mendelevium.**

MD, 1. abbreviation for **muscular dystrophy.** 2. abbreviation for **macular degeneration.**

M.D., abbreviation for *Doctor of Medicine*.

MDA, 1. abbreviation for *Muscular Dystrophy Association*. 2. abbreviation for *methylenedioxyamphetamine*.

MDEC tube, a multipurpose diagnostic and enteroclysis triple-lumen intestinal tube used in the management of small bowel disorders.

MDI, abbreviation for **metered dose inhaler.**

MDMA, abbreviation for *3,4-methylene-dioxymethamphetamine*.

MDR, abbreviation for **minimum daily requirement.**

M.D.V., abbreviation for *Doctor of Veterinary Medicine*.

Me, abbreviation for **methyl.**

MEA, abbreviation for **multiple endocrine adenomatosis.**

Meals on Wheels, a program designed to deliver hot meals to elderly, physically disabled, or other people who lack the resources to provide nutritionally adequate meals for themselves on a daily basis.

mean [ME, *mene,* in the middle], occupying a position midway between two extremes of a set of values or data. The arithmetic mean is a value that is derived by dividing the total of a set of values by the number of items in the set. The geometric mean is a value between the first and last of a set of values organized in a geometric progression.

mean arterial pressure (MAP), the arithmetic mean of the BP in the arterial part of the circulation. It is calculated by adding the systolic pressure reading to two times the diastolic reading and dividing the sum by 3.

mean cell hemoglobin concentration (MCHC), the average percentage of hemoglobin per red blood cell computed as the ratio of the hemoglobin to the hematocrit. The MCHC adult reference interval is 32% to 36% in adults.

mean cell hemoglobin (MCH), an estimate of the mass of hemoglobin in an average erythrocyte, computed as the ratio of the hemoglobin concentration and the red blood cell count. The MCH reference interval is 28 to 32 picograms.

mean cell volume (MCV), average volume of each red cell, computed as the ratio of hematocrit to the red blood cells count. The MCV reference interval is 80 to 100 fL.

mean marrow dose (MMD), the estimated average annual somatic radiation received by each person in the United States. The figure is 77 mrad and represents a weighted average for people exposed to radiation and those not exposed during the period. It is expressed in terms of bone marrow because irradiation of that tissue is assumed to be a cause of leukemia.

mean platelet volume (MPV) test, a blood test that measures the volume of a large number of platelets as determined by an automated analyzer. The MPV is very useful in the differential diagnosis of thrombocytopenic disorders.

measles /mē′zəlz/ [ME, *meseles,* skin spots], an acute, highly contagious viral disease involving the respiratory tract and characterized by a spreading maculopapular cutaneous rash. It occurs primarily in young children who have not been immunized and in teenagers or young adults who are inadequately immunized. Measles is transmitted by direct contact with droplets spread from the nose, throat, and mouth of infected people, usually in the prodromal stage of the disease. An incubation period of 7 to 14 days is followed by the prodromal stage, characterized by fever, malaise, coryza, cough, conjunctivitis, photophobia, anorexia, and the pathognomonic Koplik's spots, which appear 1 to 2 days before onset of the rash.

measles and rubella virus vaccine live, an active immunizing agent prescribed for immunization against measles and rubella.

measles, mumps, and rubella virus vaccine live (MMR), an active immunizing agent prescribed for simultaneous immunization against measles, mumps, and rubella.

measles virus, a paramyxovirus that is the cause of measles.

measurement /mezh′ərment/ [L, *mensura*], the determination, expressed numerically, of the extent or quantity of a substance, energy, or time.

measure of central tendency, in descriptive statistics, an indication of the middle point of distribution for a particular group. Measures include the mean average score, the median, and the mode.

measure of variability, in descriptive statistics, a mathematic determination of how much the performance of the group as a whole deviates from the mean or median. The most frequently used measure of variability is the standard deviation.

meatal stenosis, stenosis of the urinary meatus, seen most often in boys or men as a complication of circumcision and meatitis.

meatorrhaphy /mē′ətôr′əfē/ [L, *meatus,* channel; Gk, *rhaphe,* suture], the suturing of the cut end of the urethra to the glans penis after surgery to enlarge the urethral meatus.

meatoscopy /mē′ətos′kəpē/ [L, *meatus;* Gk, *skopein,* to look], the visual

M

examination of any meatus, especially the urethra, usually performed with the aid of a speculum or endoscope.

meatus /mē·ā′təs/ *pl.* **meatuses** [L, channel], an opening or tunnel through any part of the body.

Mebaral, a trademark for a sedative used as an anticonvulsant (mephobarbital).

mebendazole /məben′dəzōl/, an anthelmintic prescribed in treatment of pinworm, whipworm, roundworm, and hookworm infestations.

MEC, abbreviation for *minimum effective concentration,* or the minimum inhibitory concentration that allows a drug to be active. The drug is effective at any level above this threshold value.

mecamylamine hydrochloride /mek′əmil′əmēn/, a ganglionic blocking agent prescribed in the management of severe essential hypertension and uncomplicated malignant hypertension.

mecasermin, a biologic response modifier and insulin-like growth factor used to treat growth failure in children with severe primary insulin-like growth factor–1 deficiency or with growth hormone (GH) gene deletion who have developed neutralizing antibodies to GH.

mechanical advantage [Gk, *mechane,* machine; L, *abante,* superior position], the ratio of the output force developed by a muscle to the input force applied to the body structure that the muscle moves.

mechanical condenser, a device that delivers automatically controlled impacts for condensing restorative material in the filling of tooth cavities.

mechanical dead airspace [Gk, *mechane*; AS, *dead*; Gk, *aer*; L, *spatium*], the volume of air that fills the breathing circuits of a mechanical ventilator. The mechanical dead space may be increased if necessary to control hypocapnia and respiratory alkalosis.

mechanical heart-lung, a device connected to the circulatory system to maintain oxygenated blood flow during surgery that requires interruption of normal heart-lung functions.

mechanical restraint [Gk, *mechane*; L, *restringere,* to confine], a device made of fabric that hinders a patient's movement, such as a safety vest, hand straps, mittens, or a stretcher equipped with belts.

mechanical ventilation management: invasive, a nursing intervention from the Nursing Interventions Classification (NIC) defined as assisting the patient receiving artificial breathing support through a device inserted into the trachea.

mechanical ventilation management: non-invasive, a nursing intervention

from the Nursing Interventions Classification (NIC) defined as assisting a patient receiving artificial breathing support that does not necessitate a device inserted into the trachea.

mechanical ventilation response: adult, a nursing outcome from the Nursing Outcomes Classification (NOC) defined as the alveolar exchange and tissue perfusion are effectively supported by mechanical ventilation.

mechanical ventilation weaning response: adult, a nursing outcome from the Nursing Outcomes Classification (NOC) defined as the respiratory and psychologic adjustment to progressive removal of mechanical ventilation.

mechanical ventilatory weaning, a nursing intervention from the Nursing Interventions Classification (NIC) defined as assisting the patient to breathe without the aid of a mechanical ventilator.

mechanism /mek′əniz′əm/, 1. an instrument or process by which something is done, results, or comes into being. 2. a machine or machinelike system. 3. a stimulus-response system. 4. a habit or drive.

mechanism of injury, the circumstance in which an injury occurs, for example, sudden deceleration, wounding by a projectile, or crushing by a heavy object.

mechanoreceptor /mek′ənō′risep′tər/ [Gk, *mechane,* machine; L, *recipere,* to receive], any sensory nerve ending that responds to mechanical stimuli, such as touch, pressure, sound, and muscular contractions.

mechlorethamine hydrochloride /mek′lōreth′əmēn/, an antineoplastic alkylating agent prescribed in the treatment of a variety of neoplasms, especially lymphomas, and of malignant effusions.

Meckel's cartilage /mek′elz/ [Johann Friedrich Meckel, German anatomist, 1781–1833], a cartilaginous bar in the embryo. From it or its sheath, the sphenomandibular ligament, the malleus, and the incus develop.

Meckel's diverticulum [Johann F. Meckel, German anatomist, 1781–1833], an anomalous sac protruding from the wall of the ileum. It is congenital, resulting from the incomplete closure of the yolk stalk. The diverticulum is usually asymptomatic, but the condition is suggested by signs of appendicitis in infancy; by sudden and painless bleeding in the sac, usually in childhood; or by symptoms of intestinal obstruction.

Meckel's diverticulum nuclear scan, a nuclear scan to detect Meckel's diverticulum.

meclizine hydrochloride /mek′lizēn/, an antihistamine prescribed in the prevention and treatment of motion sickness.

meclofenamate sodium /mek'lōfen'əmāt/, a nonsteroidal antiinflammatory agent prescribed in the treatment of rheumatoid arthritis, osteoarthritis dysmenorrhea, and other mild to moderate pain.

Meclomen, a trademark for an antiinflammatory agent (meclofenamate sodium).

meconium /mikō'nē-əm/ [Gk, mekon, poppy], a material that collects in the intestines of a fetus and forms the first stools of a newborn. It is thick and sticky, usually greenish to black, and composed of secretions of the intestinal glands, some amniotic fluid, and intrauterine debris, such as bile pigments, fatty acids, epithelial cells, mucus, lanugo, and blood. The presence of meconium in the amniotic fluid during labor may indicate fetal distress and may lead to a lack of oxygen and developmental delays.

meconium aspiration, the inhalation of meconium by a fetus or newborn. It can block the air passages and cause failure of the lungs to expand or other pulmonary dysfunction, such as pneumonia or emphysema.

meconium ileus, obstruction of the small intestine in the newborn caused by impaction of thick, dry, tenacious meconium, usually at or near the ileocecal valve. Symptoms include abdominal distension, vomiting, failure to pass meconium within the first 24 to 48 hours after birth, and rapid dehydration with associated electrolyte imbalance.

meconium periorchitis, a rare condition seen in infant boys after meconium peritonitis has healed, characterized by a hydrocele of meconium in the scrotum that gradually hardens and often resolves spontaneously in time.

meconium peritonitis, peritonitis resulting from perforation of the bowel into the peritoneal cavity in utero or shortly after birth. This causes escape of the meconium into the peritoneal cavity.

meconium plug syndrome, obstruction of the large intestine in the newborn caused by thick, rubbery meconium that may fill the entire colon and part of the terminal ileum. Symptoms include failure to pass meconium within the first 24 to 48 hours after birth, abdominal distension, and vomiting if complete intestinal blockage occurs.

med, 1. abbreviation for medical. **2.** abbreviation for **medicine. 3.** abbreviation for minimum effective dose. **4.** abbreviation for **median.**

MED, 1. abbreviation for minimum effective dose. **2.** abbreviation for **minimal erythema dose.**

medcard /med'kärd/, in nursing, a small card listing the name, dose, and schedule of administration of each patient's medications, used in dispensing drugs to each patient.

medevac, abbreviation for medical evacuation.

MEDEX /med'eks/, **1.** an educational program accredited by the American Medical Association for training military personnel with medical experience to become physician's assistants. **2.** a physician's assistant who has gained medical experience during a military service and further training in a physician's assistant program.

medial /mē'dē-əl/ [L, medius, middle], **1.** pertaining to, situated in, or oriented toward the midline of the body. **2.** pertaining to the tunica media, the middle layer of a blood vessel wall.

medial antebrachial cutaneous nerve, a nerve of the arm that arises from the medial cord of the brachial plexus, medial to the axillary artery. Its branches innervate the skin from the biceps to the wrist.

medial brachial cutaneous nerve, a nerve of the arm arising from the medial cord of the brachial plexus and distributed to the medial side of the arm. It supplies the skin of the arm as far as the olecranon.

medial calcaneal nerve, a nerve that innervates skin on the medial surface and sole of the heel.

medial circumflex femoral artery, an artery that passes medially around the shaft of the femur and near the margin of the adductor brevis, giving off a small branch, which enters the hip joint through the acetabular notch and anastomoses with the acetabular branch of the obturator artery, then divides into two major branches deep to the quadratus femoris muscle. One of these branches ascends to the trochanteric fossa and connects with branches of the gluteal and lateral circumflex femoral arteries. The other branch passes laterally to participate with other arteries to form an anastomotic network of vessels around the hip.

medial cuneiform bone, the largest of three cuneiform bones of the foot, situated on the medial side of the tarsus, between the scaphoid bone and the first metatarsal. It serves as the attachment for various ligaments, the tendons of the tibialis anterior, and the peroneus longus.

medial fibroplasia, the most common type of fibromuscular dysplasia, seen mainly in adult women, characterized on an angiogram by areas of the artery wall having protruding aneurysms alternating with stenosis and thinning.

medial geniculate body, one of a pair of areas on the posterior dorsal thalamus that relay auditory impulses from the lateral lemniscus to the auditory cortex.

M

medialis /mē'dē·ā'lis/ [L, *medius*, middle], pertaining to the middle or to the median plane.

medial labial frenulum, a fold of mucosa on the inner surface of both lips that connects the lip to the adjacent gum.

medial malleolus, the rounded process of the tibia forming the internal surface of the ankle joint.

medial palpebral arteries, small branches of the ophthalmic artery that supply the medial area of the upper and lower eyelids.

medial pectoral nerve, a branch of the brachial plexus that, with the lateral pectoral nerve, supplies the pectoral muscles.

medial plantar nerve, the major sensory nerve in the sole of the foot.

medial posterior intertransverse muscles of neck, small muscles passing between the posterior tubercles of adjacent cervical vertebrae, close to the vertebral body. They act to bend the vertebral column laterally.

medial puboprostatic ligament, a thickening of the superior fascia of the pelvic diaphragm in the male that extends laterally from the prostate to the tendinous arch of the pelvic fascia and continues forward and medially from the tendinous arch to the pubis.

medial pubovesical ligament, the medial branch of the pubovesical ligament in the female, a forward continuation of the tendinous arch of the pelvic fascia to the pubis.

medial rotation, a turning toward the midline of the body.

medial umbilical ligament, a remnant of the embryologic urachus that continues from the apex of the bladder superiorly up the anterior abdominal wall to the umbilicus.

median (med) /mē'dē·ən/ [L, *medius*, middle], in statistics, the number representing the middle value of the scores in a sample. In an odd number of scores arrayed in ascending order, it is the middle score. In an even number of scores so arrayed, it is the average of the two central scores.

median antebrachial vein /an'tēbrā'kē·əl/, a superficial vein of the upper limb that drains the venous plexus on the palmar surface of the hand.

median aperture of fourth ventricle, an opening between the roof of the fourth ventricle and the subarachnoid space.

median arcuate ligament, a tendinous arch that connects the crura of the diaphragm.

median atlantoaxial joint, one of three points of articulation of the atlas and the axis. It allows rotation of the axis and the skull, the extent of rotation limited by the alar ligaments.

median basilic vein, one of the superficial veins of the upper limb, often formed as one of two branches from the median cubital vein. It is commonly used for venipuncture, phlebotomy, or IV infusion.

median cephalic vein, a vein sometimes present as the lateral branch, ending in the cephalic vein, of a bifurcation of the median antebrachial vein.

median effective dose (ED$_{50}$), the dose of a drug that may be expected to cause a specific intensity of effect in half of the patients to whom it is given.

median jaw relation, any jaw relation that exists when the mandible is in the median sagittal plane.

median lethal dose (MLD, LD$_{50}$), the amount of a substance or of radiation sufficient to kill one half of a population of organisms within a specified period.

median nerve, one of the terminal branches of the brachial plexus that extends along the radial parts of the forearm and the hand and supply various muscles and the skin of these parts.

median palatine suture, the line of junction between the horizontal parts of the palatine bones that extends from both sides of the skull to form the posterior part of the hard palate.

median plane, a vertical plane that divides the body into right and left halves and passes approximately through the sagittal suture of the skull.

median rhomboid glossitis, a red, depressed, diamond-shaped area on the dorsum of the tongue, frequently irritated by alcohol, hot drinks, or spicy foods.

median sternotomy, a chest surgery technique in which an incision is made from the suprasternal notch to below the xiphoid process. The sternum is then opened with a saw and a sternal retractor is inserted. The procedure is used in coronary artery bypass and valve replacement operations.

median toxic dose (TD$_{50}$), the dosage that may be expected to cause a toxic effect in half of the patients to whom it is given.

mediastinal /mē'dē·əstī'nəl/ [L, *mediastinus*, midway], pertaining to a median septum or space between two parts of the body.

mediastinal cyst, a congenital cyst arising in the mediastinum.

mediastinitis, an inflammation of the mediastinum.

mediastinoscopy /mē'dē·as'tinos'kəpē/ [L, *mediastinus*, midway; Gk, *skopein*, to view], an examination of the mediastinum through an incision in the suprasternum, by using an endoscope with light and lenses.

mediastinum /mē′dē·əstī′nəm/ *pl.* **mediastina** [L, *mediastinus,* midway], a part of the thoracic cavity in the middle of the thorax, between the pleural sacs containing the two lungs. It extends from the sternum to the vertebral column and contains all the thoracic viscera except the lungs. It is enclosed in a thick extension of the thoracic subserous fascia.—**mediastinal,** *adj.*

mediate /mē′dē·āt/ [L, *medio,* in the middle], **1.** to cause a change, as in stimulation by a hormone. **2.** to settle a dispute, as in collective bargaining. **3.** situated between two places, things, parts, or terms. **4.** in psychology, an event that follows one process or event and precedes another. —**mediating,** *adj.,* **mediator,** *n.*

mediated transport, the movement of a solute across a membrane with the assistance of a transport agent, such as a protein, that is specific for certain solutes.

medic, abbreviation for **paramedic.**

Medicaid /med′ikād/, a U.S. federally funded state-operated program of medical assistance to people with low incomes, authorized by Title XIX of the Social Security Act. Under broad federal guidelines, the individual states determine benefits, eligibility, rates of payment, and methods of administration.

Medicaid mill, *informal.* a health program or facility that solely or primarily serves people eligible for Medicaid. Such facilities are found mainly in depressed areas where few other health services are available.

medical assistant [L, *medicare,* to heal, *assistere,* to stand by], a person who, under the direction of a physician, performs various routine administrative and nontechnical clinical tasks in a hospital, clinic, or similar facility.

medical care, the provision by a physician of services related to the maintenance of health, prevention of illness, and treatment of illness or injury.

medical care plan [L, *medicare,* to heal; OE, *caru,* sorrow, *planus,* floor], a long-range program of professional medical guidance designed to meet specific health objectives.

medical center, **1.** a health care facility. **2.** a hospital, especially one staffed and equipped to care for many patients and for a large number of kinds of diseases and dysfunctions, using sophisticated technology.

Medical College Admission Test (MCAT), an examination taken by persons applying to medical school. The score attained is an important criterion for acceptance.

medical consultation, a procedure whereby, on request by one physician, another physician reviews a patient's medical history, examines the patient, and makes recommendations as to care and treatment. The medical consultant often is a specialist with expertise in a particular field of medicine.

medical corpsman /kôr′man/ [L, *medicare,* to heal, *corpus,* body], a member of a military medical unit.

medical decision level, the concentration of analyte or body fluid sample being analyzed, at which some medical action is indicated for proper patient care.

medical diagnosis [L, *medicare;* Gk, *dia,* through, *gnosis,* knowledge], the determination of the cause of a patient's illness or suffering by the combined use of physical examination, patient interview, laboratory tests, review of the patient's medical records, knowledge of the cause of observed signs and symptoms, and differential elimination of similar possible causes.

medical diathermy [L, *medicare;* Gk, *dia,* through, *therme,* heat], the application of high-frequency electrical currents to generate therapeutic heat in diseased tissues.

medical directive, a general term for documents that provide direction on the type of care a person desires.

medical director, a physician who is usually employed by a hospital to serve in a medical and administrative capacity as head of the organized medical staff.

medical emergency kit, a package of drugs and devices that may be used to deal with life-threatening medical situations. The kit may include positive pressure ventilation equipment, an oxygen tank, cardiac and other medications, airway management supplies, dressings, IV fluids, suction, and splints.

medical engineering, a field of study of biomedical engineering and technologic concepts applied to develop equipment and instruments required in health care delivery.

Medic Alert, a nonprofit U.S. organization that maintains a huge database of information about individuals who are taking one or more medications for a chronic disorder. The database also includes emergency telephone numbers for physicians treating the patients and provides bracelets or pendants to alert paramedics, interns, or other emergency medical personnel of the medical condition and prescription drugs taken by the patient, who may be unconscious or confused after an accident or episode of illness.

medical ethics [L, *medicare;* Gk, *ethikos*], the moral conduct and principles that govern members of the medical profession.

medical futility, 1. a judgment that further medical treatment of a patient would have no useful result. 2. a medical treatment whose success is possible although reasoning and experience suggest that it is highly improbable.

medical illustrator, an artist who creates visual material designed to record and communicate medical, biologic, and related knowledge. A medical illustrator requires a strong foundation in biology, anatomy, physiology, pathology, general medicine, and the visual arts.

medical indigency /in'dijen'sē/, the lack of financial reserves adequate to pay for medical care, especially that of a person or family able to manage other basic living expenses.

medical jurisprudence [L, *medicare* + *jus,* law, *prudentia,* knowledge], the interaction of medicine with civil and criminal law.

medical laboratory technician (MLT), a person who, under the supervision of a medical technologist or physician, performs microscopic and bacteriologic tests of human blood, tissue, and fluids for diagnostic and research purposes.

medical model, the traditional approach to the diagnosis and treatment of illness as practiced by physicians in the Western world. The medical model is focused on the physical and biologic aspects of specific diseases and conditions.

medical nutrition therapy, the assessment of the nutrition status of a patient followed by nutrition therapy ranging from diet modification to administration of enteral or parenteral nutrition.

medical outcomes study, an evaluation of comparable medical care approaches and their relative prognoses.

medical pathology [L, *medicare*; Gk, *pathos,* disease, *logos,* science], the study of diseases not readily treated by surgical procedures.

medical record [L, *medicare*; ME, *recorden,* to report], that part of a client's health record that is made by physicians and is a written or transcribed history of various illnesses or injuries requiring medical care; inoculations; allergies; treatments; prognosis; and frequently health information about parents, siblings, occupation, and military service. The record may be reviewed by a physician in diagnosing the condition.

medical record administrator, a person who oversees maintenance of records of patients' medical histories, diagnoses, treatment, and outcome for a condition that meets medical, administrative, legal, ethical, regulatory, and institutional requirements.

medical record technician, a health professional responsible for maintaining components of health information systems consistent with the medical, administrative, ethical, legal, accreditation, and regulatory requirements of the health care delivery system.

medical secretary, a person who prepares and maintains medical records and performs related secretarial duties.

medical snatch bag *informal.* a light, compact, waterproof, and shockproof container of emergency medical equipment for advanced prehospital care. It should provide all that is required to relieve an obstructed airway, provide artificial ventilation, arrest hemorrhage from a peripheral site, and establish an IV access for infusion.

medical staff, physicians and dentists who are approved and given privileges to provide health care to patients in a hospital or other health care facility.

medical staff, courtesy, physicians and dentists who meet certain qualifications of the medical staff of a hospital but who admit patients only occasionally or act as consultants. They are ineligible to participate in medical staff activities.

medical staff, honorary, physicians and dentists, usually retired, who are recognized by the hospital medical staff for their noteworthy contributions but who may not admit patients to the hospital or participate in medical staff activities.

medical-surgical nursing, the nursing care of adult patients whose conditions or disorders are treated medically, pharmacologically, or surgically.

medical transcriptionist, a health professional who prepares a written record of patient data dictated by a physician. A certified medical transcriptionist is one who has met the qualifying standards of the American Association of Medical Transcription.

medical waste, any discarded biologic product such as blood or tissue removed from ORs, morgues, laboratories, or other medical facilities. The term may also be applied to bedding, bandages, syringes, and similar materials that have been used in treating patients and to animal carcasses or body parts used in research.

Medical Women's International Association (M.W.I.A.), an international professional organization of women physicians.

medicamentosus /med'ikəmen'tōsəs/ [L, *medicamentum,* drug], pertaining to a drug, particularly to an adverse reaction attributed to a medication.

Medicare /med'iker/, 1. a federally funded national health insurance program in the United States for people over 65 years of age or who meet other criteria. Part A provides basic protection against costs of medical, surgical, and psychiatric hospital care. Part B is a voluntary medical insurance program financed in part from federal funds and in part from premiums contributed by enrollees. Medicare was authorized by Title XVIII of the Social Security Act of 1965. **2.** in Canada, the name of the national health insurance program.

medicate /med′ikāt/ [L, *medicare,* to heal], to treat an illness by administering drugs.

medicated bougie /med′ikātid/ [L, *medicare,* to heal; Fr, candle], a bougie containing a medicated agent.

medicated enema, a medication administered via an enema. It is usually used preoperatively with patients scheduled for bowel surgery or may be used to treat infections locally.

medicated tub bath, a therapeutic bath in which medication is dispersed in water, usually in the treatment of dermatologic disorders.

medication /med′ikā′shən/ [L, *medicare,* to heal], **1.** a drug or other substance that is used as a medicine. **2.** the administration of a medicine.

medication administration, a nursing intervention from the Nursing Interventions Classification (NIC) defined as preparing, giving, and evaluating the effectiveness of prescription and nonprescription drugs.

medication administration: ear, a nursing intervention from the Nursing Interventions Classification (NIC) defined as preparing and instilling otic medications.

medication administration: enteral, a nursing intervention from the Nursing Interventions Classification (NIC) defined as delivering medications through a tube inserted into the gastrointestinal system.

medication administration: eye, a nursing intervention from the Nursing Interventions Classification (NIC) defined as preparing and instilling ophthalmic medications.

medication administration: inhalation, a nursing intervention from the Nursing Interventions Classification (NIC) defined as preparing and administering inhaled medications.

medication administration: interpleural, a nursing intervention from the Nursing Interventions Classification (NIC) defined as administration of medication through an interpleural catheter for reduction of pain.

medication administration: intradermal, a nursing intervention from the Nursing Interventions Classification (NIC) defined as preparing and giving medications via the intradermal route.

medication administration: intramuscular (IM), a nursing intervention from the Nursing Interventions Classification (NIC) defined as preparing and giving medications via the intramuscular route.

medication administration: intraosseous, a nursing intervention from the Nursing Interventions Classification (NIC) defined as insertion of a needle through the bone cortex into the medullary cavity for the purpose of short-term, emergency administration of fluid, blood, or medication.

medication administration: intraspinal, a nursing intervention from the Nursing Interventions Classification (NIC) defined as the administration and monitoring of medication via an established epidural or intrathecal route.

medication administration: intravenous (IV), a nursing intervention from the Nursing Interventions Classification (NIC) defined as preparing and giving medications via the intravenous route.

medication administration: nasal, a nursing intervention from the Nursing Interventions Classification (NIC) defined as preparing and giving medications via nasal passages.

medication administration: oral, a nursing intervention from the Nursing Interventions Classification (NIC) defined as preparing and giving medications by mouth.

medication administration: rectal, a nursing intervention from the Nursing Interventions Classification (NIC) defined as preparing and inserting rectal suppositories.

medication administration: skin, a nursing intervention from the Nursing Interventions Classification (NIC) defined as preparing and applying medications to the skin.

medication administration: subcutaneous, a nursing intervention from the Nursing Interventions Classification (NIC) defined as preparing and giving medications via the subcutaneous route.

medication administration: vaginal, a nursing intervention from the Nursing Interventions Classification (NIC) defined as preparing and inserting vaginal medications.

medication administration: ventricular reservoir, a nursing intervention from the Nursing Interventions Classification (NIC) defined as administration and monitoring of medication through an indwelling catheter into the lateral ventricle of the brain.

M

medication error, any incorrect or wrongful administration of a medication, such as a mistake in dosage or route of administration, failure to prescribe or administer the correct drug or formulation for a particular disease or condition, use of outdated drugs, failure to observe the correct time for administration of the drug, or lack of awareness of adverse effects of certain drug combinations.

medication management, a nursing intervention from the Nursing Interventions Classification (NIC) defined as facilitation of safe and effective use of prescription and over-the-counter drugs.

medication order, a written order by a physician, dentist, nurse practitioner, or other designated health professional for a medication to be dispensed by a pharmacy for administration to a patient.

medication prescribing, a nursing intervention from the Nursing Interventions Classification (NIC) defined as prescribing medication for a health problem.

medication reconciliation, a nursing intervention from the Nursing Interventions Classification (NIC) defined as comparison of the patient's home medications with the admission, transfer, and/or discharge orders to ensure accuracy and patient safety.

medication response, a nursing outcome from the Nursing Outcomes Classification (NOC) defined as therapeutic and adverse effects of prescribed medication.

medicinal treatment, therapy of disorders based chiefly on the use of appropriate pharmacologic agents.

medicine (med) [L, *medicina,* art of healing], **1.** a drug or a remedy for illness. **2.** the art and science of the diagnosis, treatment, and prevention of disease and the maintenance of good health. **3.** the art or technique of treating disease without surgery. Two major divisions of medicine are academic medicine and clinical medicine.—**medical,** *adj.*

medicolegal /med′ĭkōlē′gəl/ [L, *medicina,* art of healing, *lex,* law], pertaining to both medicine and law. Medicolegal considerations, decisions, definitions, and policies provide the framework for informed consent, professional liability, and many other aspects of current practice in the health care field.

Medigap /med′igap/, a health insurance policy sold by a private insurance company to fill gaps in coverage of a person's original Medicare plan.

Medihaler-Epi, a trademark for an adrenergic (epINEPHrine bitartrate).

mediocarpal /mē′dē·ōkär′pəl/ [L, *medius,* middle; Gk, *karpos,* wrist], between the two rows of bones of the carpus.

mediolateral /mē′dē·ōlat′ərəl/ [L. *medius,* middle, *latus,* side], pertaining to the middle and to one side.

meditation /med′itā′shən/ [L, *meditari,* to consider], a state of consciousness in which the individual eliminates environmental stimuli from awareness so that the mind has a single focus, producing a state of relaxation and relief from stress.

meditation facilitation, a nursing intervention from the Nursing Interventions Classification (NIC) defined as facilitating a person to alter his/her level of awareness by focusing specifically on an image or thought.

meditation therapy, a method of achieving relaxation and consciousness expansion by focusing on a mantra or a key word, sound, or image while eliminating outside stimuli from one's awareness.

medium /mē′dē·əm/ *pl.* **media** [L, *medius,* middle], a substance through which something moves or through which it acts. For example, a culture medium is a substance that provides a nutritional environment for the growth of microorganisms or cells. A dispersion medium is the substance in which a colloid is dispersed. A refractory medium is the transparent tissues and fluid of the eye that refract light.

medium-chain fatty acid (MCFA), a fatty acid having a chain length roughly 8 to 12 carbons long. It is absorbed directly into the portal blood, bypassing the lymphatic system.

medium-chain triglyceride (MCT), a glycerine ester combined with medium-chain triglycerides distinguished from other triglycerides by having 8 to 10 carbon atoms. Once hydrolyzed, these fatty acids can be absorbed directly into the portal system.

medius /mē′dē·əs/ [L], in the middle; a term used in reference to a structure lying between two other structures that are anterior and posterior, superior and inferior, or internal and external in position.

MEDLARS /med′lärs/, abbreviation for *Medical Literature Analysis and Retrieval System,* a computerized literature retrieval service of the National Library of Medicine in Bethesda, Maryland.

MEDLINE /med′līn/, a U.S. National Library of Medicine computer database that contains over 19 million references to life sciences journal articles. It is the primary component of PubMed®. The NLM Medical Subject Headings (MeSH®) are used for indexing.

MedRC, abbreviation for *medical reserve corps.*

Medrol, a trademark for a glucocorticoid (methylPREDNISolone disodium phosphate).

Medrol Acetate, a trademark for a glucocorticoid (methylPREDNISolone acetate).

medroxyPROGESTERone acetate /medrok′sēprōjes′tərōn/, a progestin prescribed in endometrial and renal carcinomas and in the treatment of menstrual disorders caused by hormone imbalance. It is given as a depot injection for contraception (Depo-Provera).

medrysone /med′risōn/, a glucocorticoid that decreases the infiltration of leukocytes at the site of inflammation.

Med.Sc.D., abbreviation for *Doctor of Medical Science.*

Med Tech, abbreviation for *medical technician.*

medulla /mədul′ə/ *pl.* **medullas, medullae** [L, marrow], the most internal part of a structure or organ, such as the renal medulla.

medulla oblongata, a bulbous continuation of the spinal cord just above the foramen magnum and separated from the pons by a horizontal groove. It is one of three parts of the brainstem and contains the cardiac, vasomotor, and respiratory centers of the brain.

medulla of the kidney [L, *medulla,* marrow; ME, *kidenei*], a part of the parenchyma of the kidney, beneath the cortex, including the renal pyramids and columns. An inner layer contains the papillae, and the outer part contains the thick ascending limbs of the loop of Henle.

medullary /med′əlerē, mədul′erē, med′yəler′ē/ [L, *medulla,* marrow], **1.** pertaining to the medulla of the brain. **2.** pertaining to the bone marrow. **3.** pertaining to the spinal cord.

medullary carcinoma, a soft malignant neoplasm of the epithelium containing little or no fibrous tissue.

medullary cystic disease, a chronic familial disease of the kidney, characterized by the slow onset of uremia. The disease appears in young children or adolescents who pass large volumes of dilute urine with greater than normal amounts of sodium.

medullary sponge kidney, a congenital defect of the kidney, leading to cystic dilation of the collecting tubules. People with this defect often develop a kidney stone or an infection of the kidney caused by urinary stasis.

medullated /med′yəlā′tid/ [L, *medulla,* marrow], enclosed by a marrow-like substance, such as the myelin sheath of a nerve fiber.

medulloblastoma /mədul′ōblastō′mə/ [L, *medulla*; Gk, *blastos,* germ, *oma,* tumor],

a poorly differentiated malignant neoplasm composed of tightly packed cells of spongioblastic and neuroblastic lineage. The tumor usually arises in the cerebellum, is extremely radiosensitive, and grows rapidly.

mefenamic acid /mef′ənam′ik/, a nonsteroidal antiinflammatory agent and analgesic prescribed in the treatment of mild to moderate pain including dysmenorrhea.

mefloquine /mef′ləkēn/, an antimalarial for the prophylaxis and treatment of malaria caused by chloroquine-resistant strains of *Plasmodium falciparum,* or *P. vivax.*

Mefoxin, a trademark for a cephalosporin antibiotic (cefoxitin sodium).

MEFR, abbreviation for **maximal expiratory flow rate.**

Megace, a trademark for an antineoplastic progestational agent (megestrol acetate).

megacolon /meg′əkōlən/ [Gk, *megas* + *kolon,* colon], abnormal massive dilation of the colon that may be congenital, toxic, or acquired. Congenital megacolon (Hirschsprung's disease) is caused by the absence of autonomic ganglia in the smooth muscle wall of the colon. Toxic megacolon is a grave complication of ulcerative colitis and may cause perforation of the colon, septicemia, and death. Acquired megacolon is the result of a chronic refusal to defecate, which usually occurs in children who are psychotic or mentally retarded. The colon becomes dilated by an accumulation of impacted feces.

megacystis, an abnormally enlarged urinary bladder.

megadose /meg′ədōs/, a dose that greatly exceeds the amount usually prescribed or recommended.

megadyne /meg′ədīn/, a unit of force equal to one million dynes.

megaesophagus /meg′ə·isof′əgəs/ [Gk, *megas* + *oisophagos,* gullet], abnormal dilation of the lower segments of the esophagus caused by distension resulting from the failure of the cardiac sphincter to relax and allow the passage of food into the stomach.

megahertz (MHz) /meg′əhurts/ [Gk, *megas,* large, *hertz,* a number of cycles per second], a unit of frequency equal to a million cycles per second.

megakaryocyte /meg′əker′ē·əsīt′/ [Gk, *megas,* large, *karyon,* nut, *kytos,* cell], bone marrow cell measuring 35 to 160 um in diameter and having a multilobed nucleus. Megakaryocytes are platelet precursors.—**megakaryocytic,** *adj.*

megakaryocytic leukemia /meg′əker′ē·ō sit′ik/ [Gk, *megas* + *karyon,* nut, *kytos,* cell], a rare malignancy of blood-forming tissue in which megakaryocytes proliferate in the bone marrow and circulate in the blood in large numbers.

M

megalencephaly /meg′əlensef′əlē/ [Gk, *megas* + *enkephalos*, brain], a condition characterized by pathologic parenchymal overgrowth of the brain. In some cases, generalized cerebral hyperplasia is associated with mental retardation or a brain disorder, such as epilepsy.—**megalencephalic, megalencephalous,** *adj.*

megaloblast /meg′əlōblast′/ [Gk, *megas* + *blastos*, germ], abnormally large nucleated immature erythrocyte that develops in the bone marrow in megaloblastic anemias associated with deficiency of vitamin B_{12}, or folic acid.—**megaloblastic,** *adj.*

megaloblastic anemia /-blas′tik/, a hematologic disorder characterized by the production of macrocytes in folate and vitamin B_{12} deficiency.

megalocornea, an inherited disorder in which the corneal diameter is enlarged.

megalocystis /meg′əlōsis′tis/ [Gk, *megas* + *kystis*, bag], an abnormal condition primarily affecting girls, characterized by an enlarged and thin-walled bladder.

megalocyte /meg′əlōsīt/, an extremely large erythrocyte.

megalocytic interstitial nephritis, an early stage of malacoplakia of the urinary tract in which there are no Michaelis-Gutmann bodies.

megalomania /meg′əlōmā′nē·ə/ [Gk, *megas* + *mania*, madness], an abnormal mental state characterized by delusions of grandeur in which one believes oneself to be a person of great importance, power, fame, or wealth.

megaloureter /meg′əlōyōŏrē′tər/ [Gk, *megas* + *oureter*, ureter], an abnormal condition characterized by marked dilation of one or both ureters, resulting from dysfunctional peristaltic action of the smooth muscle in the ureters.

megaureter, congenital dilatation of the ureter.

megaureter-megacystis syndrome, chronic ureteral dilation associated with hypotonia and dilation of the bladder and gaping of the ureteral orifices, permitting vesicoureteral reflex of urine and resulting in chronic pyelonephritis.

megavitamin therapy /-vī′təmin/, a type of treatment that involves the administration of large doses of certain vitamins and minerals.

megestrol acetate /məjes′trōl/, an antineoplastic progestational agent prescribed to treat endometrial cancer and more commonly to palliate advanced endometrial and breast cancer. It is also used to stimulate appetite and to promote weight gain in cachexia patients.

meibomian gland /mēbō′mē·ən/ [Heinrich Meibom, German physician, 1638–1700], one of several sebaceous glands that secrete sebum from their ducts on the posterior margin of each eyelid. The glands are embedded in the tarsal plate of each eyelid.

Meige's disease /mezh′əz/ [Henri Meige, French physician, 1866–1940], dystonia of facial and oromandibular muscles with blepharospasm, grimacing mouth movements, and protrusion of the tongue, usually occurring in older women.

Meigs' syndrome /megz/ [Joe V. Meigs, American gynecologist, 1892–1963], ascites and hydrothorax associated with a fibroma of the ovaries or other pelvic tumor.

meiocyte /mī′əsīt/ [Gk, *meiosis,* becoming smaller, *kytos,* cell], any cell undergoing meiosis.

meiogenic /mī′əjen′ik/ [Gk, *meiosis* + *genein,* to produce], producing or causing meiosis.

meiosis /mī·ō′sis/ [Gk, becoming smaller], the division of a sex cell as it matures into two and then four haploid cells. The nucleus of each receives one half of the number of chromosomes present in the somatic cells of the species.—**meiotic** /mī·ot′ik/, *adj.*

Meissner's corpuscle /mīs′nərz/ [Georg Meissner, German anatomist, 1829–1905; L, *corpusculum,* little body], any one of a number of small, special pressure-sensitive sensory end organs with a connective tissue capsule and tiny stacked plates in the dermis of the hand and foot, the front of the forearm, the skin of the lips, the mucous membrane of the tongue, the palpebral conjunctiva, and the skin of the mammary papilla.

Meissner's plexus [Georg Meissner; L, *plaited*], small aggregations of ganglion cells located in the submucosa of the intestine.

melancholia /mel′angkō′lē·ə/ [Gk, *melas,* black, *chole,* bile], a severe form of depression.

melaniferous /mel′ənif′ərəs/ [Gk, *melas,* black; L, *ferre,* to bear], pertaining to a black pigment.

melanin /mel′ənin/ [Gk, *melas,* black], a black or dark brown pigment that occurs naturally in the hair, skin, and iris and choroid of the eye.

melanin test, a test for detecting melanin in the urine of patients with malignant melanomas.

melanism /mel′əniz′əm/ [Gk, *melas,* black], an abnormal deposit of dark brown to black melanin pigment in the skin, hair, and other tissues.

melanoameloblastoma /mel′ənō·am′əlōblastō′mə/, a benign neoplasm appearing as a blue-black lesion on the anterior maxilla of infants. The growth is of neuroectodermal origin and consists of small round undifferentiated tumor cells and larger melanin-producing cells.

melanoblast /mel'ənōblast'/ [Gk, *melas,* black, *blastos,* germ], an epithelial tissue cell containing black granules. It develops into a melanocyte.

melanoblastoma /mel'ənō·blastō'mə/, a tumor of poorly differentiated melanin-producing cells.

melanocarcinoma /-kär'sinō'mə/, a malignant melanoma.

melanocyte /mel'ənōsīt', mələn'ōsīt/ [Gk, *melas* + *kytos,* cell], a body cell capable of producing melanin. Melanocytes are distributed throughout the basal cell layer of the epidermis and form melanin pigment from tyrosine, an amino acid.

melanocyte-stimulating hormone (MSH), a polypeptide hormone, secreted by the pars intermedia of the pituitary gland, that controls the intensity of pigmentation in pigmented cells. It is synthesized on the same large precursor polypeptide as adrenocorticotropic hormone and the enkephalins.

melanocytic nevus /-sit'ik/, a congenital pigmented lesion of the skin caused by a disorder involving melanocytes.

melanoderma /mel'ənōdur'mə/ [Gk, *melas* + *derma,* skin], any abnormal darkening of the skin caused by increased deposits of melanin or the salts of iron or silver.

melanoma /mel'ənō'mə/ *pl.,* **melanomas, melanomata** [Gk, *melas* + *oma,* tumor], any of a group of malignant neoplasms that originate in the skin and that are composed of melanocytes. A melanocytic nevus may be acquired or congenital. The congenital melanocytic nevus is regarded as more likely to develop into a malignant melanoma, primarily because of its larger size. Smaller melanomas tend to develop from a pigmented nevus over several months or years. They may be sporadic and occur most commonly in fair-skinned people having light-colored eyes. A previous sunburn increases a person's risk. Any black or brown spot having an irregular border; pigment appearing to radiate beyond that border; a red, black, and blue coloration observable on close examination; or a nodular surface is suggestive of melanoma and is usually excised for biopsy. Melanomas may metastasize and are among the most malignant of all skin cancers. Prognosis depends on the kind of melanoma; its size, depth of invasion, and location; and the age and condition of the patient.

melanomatosis /-mətō'sis/, **1.** a condition characterized by many widespread melanoma lesions. **2.** the development of melanomas throughout the body.

melanosis coli /mel'ənō'sis/, an abnormal condition in which the mucous membrane of the colon is pigmented with melanin.

melanosome /mel'ənōsōm'/, one of the oval pigment granules within melanocytes that synthesize melanin.

melanotic carcinoma /mel'ənot'ik/, a malignant pigmented skin cancer.

melanuria /mel'ənōōr'ē·ə/, urine that has a dark color caused by the presence of melanin or other pigments.

melasma gravidarum /məlaz'mə/ [Gk, *melas,* black; L, *gravida,* pregnant], a dark pigment or discoloration that may appear on the skin of pregnant women.

MELAS syndrome, abbreviation for *mitochondrial encephalopathy, lactic acidosis,* and *stroke-like episodes,* constituting a familial syndrome of maternal (mitochondrial) inheritance.

melatonin, a dietary supplement, also known as N-acetyl-5-methoxytryptamine. It is used for jet lag and insomnia, for cancer protection, and as an oral contraceptive. Melatonin is effective for treating jet lag and has shown benefit when used in combination therapy for various cancers. It is not very effective for insomnia. There are insufficient data related to its efficacy for other uses.

melena /məlē'nə, mol'ənə/ [Gk, *melas,* black], abnormal black tarry stool that has a distinctive odor and contains digested blood. It usually results from bleeding in the upper GI tract and is often a sign of peptic ulcer or small bowel disease.

melena neonatorum [Gk, *melas,* black, *neos,* new; L, *natus,* born], the passage of dark tarry stools by a newborn. The cause is usually the alteration of blood pigment associated with hemorrhage.

melioidosis /mel'ē·oidō'sis/ [Gk, *melis,* distemper, *eidos,* form, *osis,* condition], an infection caused by the gram-negative bacillus *Burkholderia pseudomallei.* Acute melioidosis is fulminant and usually characterized by pneumonia, empyema, lung abscess, septicemia, and liver or spleen involvement. Chronic melioidosis is associated with osteomyelitis, multiple abscesses of the internal organs, and development of fistulas from the abscesses.

Melkersson-Rosenthal syndrome /mel'kərson rō'zentäl/ [Ernst Gustaf Melkersson, Swedish physician, 1898–1932; Curt Rosenthal, German psychiatrist, 20th century], an autosomal-dominant condition characterized chiefly by chronic noninflammatory facial swelling, localized particularly to the lips, with recurrent facial palsy and sometimes fissured tongue.

M

Associated ophthalmic symptoms may include lagophthalmos, blepharochalasis, swollen eyelids, burning sensation of the eyes, corneal opacities, retrobulbar neuritis, and exophthalmos.

Mellaril, a trademark for an antipsychotic agent (thioridazine).

melon-seed body /mel′ən/, a small, fibrous, loose body in a joint or tendon sheath.

meloxicam /melok′sikam/, an NSAID used in the treatment of osteoarthritis.

melphalan /mel′fələn/, an antineoplastic alkylating agent prescribed in the treatment of malignant neoplastic diseases, including palliative treatment of multiple myeloma and nonresectable ovarian carcinoma.

melting, 1. the liquefaction effect of heat. **2.** the thermal denaturation of double-stranded DNA into two component strands. **3.** conversion of the solid to the liquid phase.

melting point (mp) [AS, *meltan*; L, *punctus,* pricked], a characteristic temperature at which the solid and liquid forms of a substance are in equilibrium. The mp of ice is 32° F, or 0° C, at one atmosphere pressure.

memantine, an anti-Alzheimer agent used to treat minor to severe dementia in Alzheimer's disease.

membrana tectoria /membrā′nə/ [L, *membrana,* thin skin, *tectorium,* a covering], **1.** the broad, strong ligament covering the dens and helping to connect the axis to the occipital bone of the skull. **2.** a spiral membrane projecting from the vestibular lip of the cochlea over the organ of Corti.

membrane /mem′brān/ [L, *membrana,* thin skin], a thin layer of tissue composed of epithelial cells and connective tissue that covers a surface, lines a cavity, or divides a space in the body.

membrane attack complex (MAC), a cluster of complement components that creates a pore in the plasma membrane of a cell, leading to the lysis of a cell.

membrane conductance, the degree of permeability of a cellular membrane to certain ions; the reciprocal of the membrane resistance.

membrane diffusion coefficient, a factor that relates the quantitative characteristics of alveolar-capillary membranes to total pulmonary diffusing capacity.

membrane potential [L, *membrana + potentia*], the difference in electric polarization or charge between two sides of a membrane or cell wall.

membrane responsiveness, the relationship between the membrane potential and the maximal rate of rise of the action potential.

membranoproliferative glomerulonephritis (MPGN) /mem′brənō′prōlif′ərətiv′/, a chronic form of glomerulonephritis, characterized by mesangial cell proliferation, irregular thickening of glomerular capillary walls, thickening of the mesangial matrix, and low serum levels of complement.

membranous /mem′brənəs/ [L, *membrana*], resembling or consisting of a membrane.

membranous dysmenorrhea [L, *membrana*; Gk, *dys,* bad, *men,* month, *rhein,* to flow], a form of spasmodic pain associated with menstruation, in which a cast of the uterine cavity is passed.

membranous labyrinth [L, *membrana + labyrinthos,* a maze], a network of three fluid-filled membranous semicircular ducts suspended within the bony semicircular canals of the inner ear, associated with the sense of balance.

membranous pharyngitis [L, *membrana*; Gk, *pharynx,* throat], a diphtheric inflammation of the pharynx with the formation of a false membrane in the throat.

memory¹ /mem′ərē/ [L, *memoria*], **1.** the mental faculty or power that enables one to retain and to recall, through unconscious associative processes, previously experienced sensations, impressions, ideas, concepts, and all information that has been consciously learned. **2.** the reservoir of all past experiences and knowledge that may be recollected or recalled at will. **3.** the recollection of a past event, idea, sensation, or previously learned knowledge.

memory², a nursing outcome from the Nursing Outcomes Classification (NOC) defined as the ability to cognitively retrieve and report previously stored information.

memory cells, T and B lymphocytes that mediate immunologic memory. They are believed to retain information that permits a subsequent antigenic challenge to be followed by a more rapid efficient immunologic reaction than that seen with the first exposure.

memory image, a sensation, impression, or sense perception as it is recalled in the memory.

memory training, a nursing intervention from the Nursing Interventions Classification (NIC) defined as facilitation of memory.

mem retinoscopy, a type of dynamic retinoscopy in which the fixation target is a series of letters on the retinoscope or a card with letters at a normal reading distance.

MEN, abbreviation for **multiple endocrine neoplasia.**

menadione /men′ədi·ōn/, vitamin K₃. A synthetic fat-soluble provitamin that can be chemically converted in the body to active vitamin K. It is used as a source of vitamin K in the treatment of hypoprothrombinemia associated with vitamin K deficiency.

menarche /menär′kē/ [Gk, *men,* month, *archaios,* from the beginning], the first menstruation and the commencement of cyclic menstrual function.

menarcheal age /menär′kē·əl/ [Gk, *men,* month, *archaios,* beginning; L, *aetas,* age], the age at which menstruation begins. The normal range is from 9 to 17 years of age.

mendelevium (Md) /men′dəlē″vē·əm/ [Dimitrii Ivanovich Mendeleev, Russian chemist, 1834–1907], a synthetic element in the actinide group. Its atomic number is 101. The atomic mass of its most stable isotope is 256.

mendelism /men′dəliz′əm/ [Gregor J. Mendel, Austrian geneticist, 1822–1884], the concept of inheritance derived from the application of Mendel's laws.—**mendelian,** *adj.*

Mendel's laws [Gregor J. Mendel], the basic principles of inheritance based on breeding experiments on garden peas by the 19th-century Austrian monk Gregor Mendel. These principles are usually stated as the law of segregation and the law of independent assortment. According to the law of segregation, each trait of a species is represented in the somatic cells by a pair of units, now known as genes, which are segregated during meiosis so that each gamete receives only one gene for each trait. According to the law of independent assortment, the members of a gene pair on different chromosomes segregate independently from other pairs during meiosis so that the gametes show all possible combinations of genes.

Mendelson's syndrome [Curtis L. Mendelson, American obstetrician, b. 1913], a respiratory condition caused by the aspiration of acidic gastric contents into the lungs. It is marked by bronchoconstriction and destruction of the tracheal mucosa, progressing to a syndrome resembling acute respiratory distress syndrome.

Mendel's reflex /men′dəlz/ [Kurt Mendel, German neurologist, 1874–1946], percussion of the top of the foot normally causing dorsal flexion of the second to fifth toes but in certain organic nervous conditions causing plantar flexion of the toes.

Ménière's disease /mānē·erz′/ [Prosper Ménière, French physician, 1799–1862], a chronic disease of the inner ear characterized by recurrent episodes of vertigo; progressive sensorineural hearing loss, which may be bilateral; and tinnitus.

meningeal artery, one of the arteries that supply the dura mater. All are small except the middle meningeal artery, which supplies the greatest part of the dura.

meninges /minin′jēz/ *sing.* **meninx** [Gk, *meninx,* membrane], the three membranes enclosing the brain and the spinal cord, comprising the dura mater, the pia mater, and the arachnoid membrane. —**meningeal,** *adj.*

meningioma /minin′jē·ō′mə/ *pl.* **meningiomas, meningiomata** [Gk, *meninx,* membrane, *oma,* tumor], a mesenchymal fibroblastic tumor of the membranes enveloping the brain and spinal cord. The tumors may be nodular, plaquelike, or diffuse lesions that invade the skull, causing bone erosion and compression of brain tissue.

meningism /minin′jizəm/ [Gk, *meninx* + *ismos,* process], an abnormal condition characterized by irritation of the brain and spinal cord and by symptoms that mimic those of meningitis, but with no actual inflammation of the meninges.

meningismus /men′injis′məs/ [Gk, *meninx,* membrane], a condition in which the patient shows signs of meningitis but examination reveals no pathologic changes in the meninges. The condition is associated with cases of pneumonia in small children.

meningitis /minin′jī″tis/ *pl.* **meningitides** [Gk, *meninx* + *itis,* inflammation], any infection or inflammation of the membranes covering the brain and spinal cord. It is usually purulent and involves the fluid in the subarachnoid space. The most common causes in adults are bacterial infection with *Streptococcus pneumoniae, Neisseria meningitidis,* or *Haemophilus influenzae.* The onset is usually sudden and characterized by severe headache, stiffness of the neck, irritability, malaise, and restlessness. Nausea, vomiting, delirium, and complete disorientation may develop quickly. Temperature, pulse rate, and respirations are increased. Residual damage may include deafness, blindness, paralysis, and mental retardation. Hydrocephalus may also may develop.

meningocele /mining′gōsēl′/ [Gk, *meninx* + *kele,* hernia], a saclike protrusion of either the cerebral or spinal meninges through a congenital defect in the skull or the vertebral column. It forms a hernial cyst that is filled with CSF but does not contain neural tissue. The anomaly is designated a cranial meningocele or spinal meningocele, depending on the site of the defect.

meningococcal meningitis /mining′gōkok·əl/, bacterial meningitis caused by infection with *Neisseria meningitidis,* an acute infectious disease with seropurulent meningeal

M

inflammation. It usually appears in epidemics, and symptoms are those of acute cerebral and spinal meningitis, usually with an eruption of cutaneous erythematous, herpetic, or hemorrhagic spots.

meningococcal polysaccharide vaccine /-kok′əl/, one of four active immunizing agents against group A, group C, group Y, or group W-135 meningococcal organisms. It is prescribed for immunization against meningococcal meningitis, with the serogroup matched according to the local outbreak.

meningococcemia /mining′gōkoksē′mē·ə/ [Gk, *meninx* + *kokkos*, berry, *haima*, blood], a disease caused by *Neisseria meningitidis* in the bloodstream, subsequently causing vasculitis. Onset is sudden, with chills, pain in the muscles and joints, headache, petechiae, sore throat, and severe prostration. Tachycardia is present, respirations and pulse rate are increased, and fever is intermittent.

meningococcus /mining′gōkok′əs/ *pl.* **meningococci** /-kok′sī/ [Gk, *meninx* + *kokkos*, berry], a bacterium of the genus *Neisseria meningitidis*, a nonmotile gram-negative diplococcus, frequently found in the nasopharynx of asymptomatic carriers, that may cause septicemia or epidemic cerebrospinal meningitis.—**meningococcal,** *adj.*

meningoencephalitis /-ensef′əlī′tis/ [Gk, *meninx,* membrane, *enkephalos,* brain, *itis,* inflammation], an inflammation of both the brain and the meninges, usually caused by a bacterial infection.

meningoencephalocele /mining′gō·ensef′əlōsēl′/ [Gk, *meninx* + *enkephalos,* brain, *kele,* hernia], a saclike cyst containing brain tissue, CSF, and meninges that protrudes through a congenital defect in the skull.

meningoencephalomyelitis /mining′gō·ensef′əlōmī′əlī′tis/, a combined inflammation of the brain, spinal cord, and meninges.

meningoencephalopathy /mining′gō·ensef′əlop′əthē/, a noninflammatory disease of the brain and its membranes.

meningomyelitis /-mī′əlī′tis/ [Gk,*meninx,* membrane, *myelos,* marrow, *itis,* inflammation], an inflammation of the spinal cord and its surrounding membranes.

meningovascular neurosyphilis /-vas′kyələr/ [Gk, *meninx,* membrane; L, *vasculum,* little vessel; Gk, *neuron,* nerve, *syn,* together, *philein,* to love], a neurosyphilis inflammation of the supporting and nutrient tissues of the CNS.

meniscectomy /men′isek′təmē/ [Gk, *meniskos,* crescent, *ektomē,* excision], surgical excision of one of the crescent-shaped cartilages of the knee joint. It is performed when

a torn cartilage results in chronic pain and in instability or locking of the joint.

meniscus /minis′kəs/ *pl.* **menisci** [Gk, *meniskos,* crescent], **1.** the interface between a liquid and air. **2.** a lens with both convex and concave aspects. **3.** a curved, fibrous cartilage in the knees and other joints.

Menkes' kinky hair syndrome /men′kēz/ [John H. Menkes, American neurologist, b. 1928; D, *kinke,* tight twist; AS, *haer*], a familial disorder affecting the normal absorption of copper from the intestine, characterized by the growth of sparse, kinky hair. Infants with the syndrome suffer cerebral degeneration, retarded growth, and early death.

menometrorrhagia /men′ōmet′rōrā′jē·ə/ [L, *men,* month; Gk, *metra,* womb, *rhegnyai,* to burst forth], excessive menstrual and uterine bleeding other than that caused by menstruation. It is a combination of metrorrhagia and menorrhagia and may be a sign of a urogenital malignancy.

menopause /men′əpôz′/ [L, *men,* month; Gk, *pausis,* to cease], strictly, the cessation of menses, but commonly referring to the period of the female climacteric. Menses stop naturally with the decline of cyclic hormonal production and function usually between 45 and 55 years of age but may stop earlier in life as a result of illness, surgery, or for unknown reasons. As the production of ovarian estrogen and pituitary gonadotropins decreases, ovulation and menstruation become less frequent and eventually stop. Fluctuations in the circulating levels of these hormones occur as the levels decline. Hot flashes are a common symptom of menopause.

menorrhagia /men′ərā′jē·ə/ [L, *men;* Gk, *rhegnyai,* to burst forth,], abnormally heavy or long menstrual periods. Menorrhagia occurs occasionally during the reproductive years of most women's lives. If the condition becomes chronic, anemia from recurrent excessive blood loss may result.—**menorrhagic,** *adj.*

menorrhea /men′ôrē′ə/ [L, *men;* Gk, *rhoia,* flow], the normal discharge of blood and tissue from the uterus.

menostasis /minos′təsis/ [L, *men;* Gk, *stasis,* stand still], an abnormal condition in which the products of menstruation cannot escape the uterus or vagina because of stenosis, an occlusion of the cervix or the introitus of the vagina.—**menostatic,** *adj.*

menotropins /men′ōtrop′inz/ [L, *men;* Gk, *trepein,* to turn], a preparation of gonadotropic hormones from the urine of postmenopausal women. It is prescribed with chorionic gonadotropin to induce ovulation, development of multiple ovarian follicles for in vitro fertilization and to stimulate spermatogenesis in males.

menoxenia /men'okse'ne-ə/ [L, *men*; Gk, *xenos*, strange], any abnormality relating to menstruation.

menses /men'sēz/ [L, *men,* month], the normal flow of blood and decidua that occurs during menstruation. The first day of the flow of the menses is the first day of the menstrual cycle.

menstrual age [L, *menstrualis,* monthly, *aetas,* lifetime], the age of an embryo or fetus as calculated from the first day of the last menstrual period.

menstrual colic [L, *menstrualis,* monthly; Gk, *kolikos,* colon pain], a form of dysmenorrhea characterized by abdominal pain during or immediately before menstruation.

menstrual cramps, low abdominal pain that may range from a colicky feeling to a constant dull ache. The pain may radiate to the lower back and legs. Menstrual cramps are often associated with the beginning of menses.

menstrual cycle, the recurring cycle of change in the endometrium during which the decidual layer of the endometrium is shed, then regrows, proliferates, is maintained for several days, and sheds again at menstruation. The average length of the cycle, from the first day of bleeding of one cycle to the first of another, is 28 days. The duration and character vary greatly among women.

menstrual phase, the fourth phase of the human menstrual cycle, following the luteal phase and occurring only if fertilization has not taken place. The corpus luteum regresses and is shed through menstruation, and growth begins for the ovarian follicle, leading to the follicular phase of the next menstrual cycle.

menstrual sponge, a small sponge to which a loop of string may be attached. It is inserted into the vagina to absorb the menstrual flow. Once removed, it may be washed, squeezed dry, and reused as necessary throughout menstruation. Menstrual sponges are not commonly used.

menstruation /men'strōō·ā'shən/ [L, *menstruare,* to menstruate], the periodic discharge through the vagina of a bloody secretion containing tissue debris from the shedding of the endometrium from the nonpregnant uterus. The average duration of menstruation is 4 to 5 days, and it recurs at approximately 28-day intervals throughout the reproductive life of nonpregnant women.—**menstruate,** *v.*

mental¹ /men'təl/ [L, *mens,* mind], **1.** of, relating to, or characteristic of the mind or psyche. **2.** existing in the mind; performed or accomplished by the mind.

3. of, relating to, or characterized by a disorder of the mind. **4.** slang term used to describe clients believed to have a mental health disorder.

mental² [L, *mentum,* chin], pertaining to the chin.

mental age (MA), the age level at which one functions intellectually, as determined by standardized psychologic and intelligence tests and expressed as the age at which that level is average.

mental disorder, any disturbance of emotional equilibrium, as manifested in maladaptive behavior and impaired functioning, caused by genetic, physical, chemical, biologic, psychologic, or social and cultural factors.

mental foramen [L, *mentum,* chin], an opening on the lateral part of the body of the mandible, inferior to the second premolar, through which the mental nerve and blood vessels pass.

mental handicap, any mental defect or characteristic resulting from a congenital abnormality, traumatic injury, or disease that impairs normal intellectual functioning and prevents a person from participating normally in activities appropriate for a particular age group.

mental health (MH), a relative state of mind in which a person is able to cope with and adjust to the recurrent stresses of everyday living in an acceptable way.

Mental Health Association, a voluntary nonprofessional agency dedicated to the improvement of mental health facilities and services in community clinics and hospitals, the recruitment and training of volunteers, and the promotion of mental health legislation.

mental health consultation, any interaction between two or more health care professionals related to a specific issue of mental health.

mental health service, any one of a group of government, professional, or lay organizations operating at a community, state, national, or international level to aid in the prevention and treatment of mental disorders.

mental hygiene, the study of the development of healthy mental and emotional habits, attitudes, and behavior and the prevention of mental illness.

mental image, any concept or sensation produced in the mind through memory or imagination.

mentalis, a muscle that arises from the mandible just inferior to the incisor teeth and helps position the lip during pouting or drinking from a cup. It raises and protrudes the lower lip as it wrinkles the skin on the chin.

M

mentality /mental'itē/ [L, *mens*, mind], **1.** the functional power and capacity of the mind. **2.** intellectual character.

mental protuberance, a midline swelling on the base of the mandible on its anterior surface where the two sides of the mandible come together.

mental retardation, a disorder characterized by subaverage general intellectual function with deficits or impairments in the ability to learn and to adapt socially. The cause may be genetic, biologic, psychosocial, or traumatic.

mental ridge [L, *mentum,* chin; AS, *hyrcg*], a dense elevation that extends from the symphysis menti (the center front of the mandible) to the premolar area on the anterolateral aspect of the body of the mandible.

mental status, the degree of competence shown by a person in intellectual, emotional, psychologic, and personality functioning as measured by psychologic testing with reference to a statistical norm.

mental status examination, a diagnostic procedure for determining the mental status of a person. The trained interviewer poses certain questions in a carefully standardized manner and evaluates the verbal responses and behavioral reactions.

mental tubercle [L, *mentum,* chin], one of a bilateral pair of prominences on the lower border of the body of the mandible.

mentation /mentā'shən/ [L, *mens*, mind, *atus,* process], any mental activity, including conscious and unconscious processes.

menthol /men'thol/ [L, *menta*, mint], a topical antipruritic with a cooling effect that relieves itching. It is an ingredient in many topical creams and ointments.

mentholated camphor /men'thəlā'tid/, a mixture of equal parts of camphor and menthol, used as a local counterirritant.

menton /men'ton/ [L, *mentum,* chin], the most inferior point on the chin in the lateral view of a cephalogram. It is a cephalometric landmark used in orthodontic treatment.

mentor /men'tər/ [Gk, *Mentor,* mythic educator], **1.** a more experienced, trusted adviser or counselor who offers helpful guidance to less experienced colleagues. **2.** a person who enters into a relationship with a new nurse to provide him or her with a source of support and information as he or she learns new roles.

mentum /men'təm/ [L, chin], **1.** the chin, especially of the fetus. **2.** a fetal reference point in designating the position of the fetus with respect to the maternal pelvis.

MEP, 1. abbreviation for **maximal expiratory pressure. 2.** abbreviation for *mean effective pressure.*

mepenzolate bromide /mepen'zəlāt/, an anticholinergic/antispasmodic agent prescribed as an adjunct in treating peptic ulcer and preoperatively to reduce respiratory secretions.

Mepergan, a trademark for a fixed-combination CNS drug containing an opioid analgesic (meperidine hydrochloride) and an antihistamine (promethazine hydrochloride).

meperidine hydrochloride /meper'idēn/, an opioid analgesic used to treat moderate to severe pain and to relieve pain and anxiety before or after surgery.

mephobarbital /mef'ōbär'bitol/, an anticonvulsant and sedative prescribed in the treatment of anxiety, nervous tension, insomnia, and epilepsy.

Mephyton, a trademark for a vitamin K product (phytonadione).

meprobamate /miprō'bəmāt/, an antianxiety agent prescribed in the treatment of anxiety and tension.

mEq, abbreviation for **milliequivalent.**

mEq/L, abbreviation for **milliequivalent per liter.**

meradimate /merad'imāt/, an absorber of ultraviolet A radiation, used topically as a sunscreen.

meralgia /miral'jə/ [Gk, *meros,* thigh, *algos,* pain], the presence of pain in the thigh.

meralgia paresthetica /per'esthet'ikə/, a condition characterized by pain, paresthesia, and numbness on the lateral surface of the thigh in the region supplied by the lateral femoral cutaneous nerve. The cause of the condition is ischemia of the nerve caused by its entrapped position in the inguinal ligament.

mercaptopurine /mərkap'təpyōō'rēn/, an antineoplastic and immunosuppressive; a purine antimetabolite. It is prescribed in the treatment of malignant neoplastic diseases, especially as maintenance therapy for acute lymphocytic leukemia.

Mercer, Ramona T., a nursing theorist who developed the Maternal Role Attainment model presented in her book *First-Time Motherhood: Experiences from Teens to Forties* (1986). Maternal role attainment is an interactional and developmental process. It occurs over a period during which the mother becomes attached to her infant, acquires competence in the care-giving tasks, and expresses pleasure and gratification in her role. The focus of Mercer's work went beyond the concept of the "traditional" mother to encompass a variety of mothering roles.

mercurial /mərkyōōr'ē·əl/, **1.** pertaining to mercury, particularly a medicine containing the element mercury. **2.** pertaining to an adverse effect associated with the administration of a mercurial medication, such as a mercurial tremor caused by mercury poisoning.

mercurial diuretic, any one of several diuretic agents that contain mercury in an organic chemical form. The principal use for the drugs is in treating edema of cardiac origin, ascites associated with cirrhosis, or oliguria in the nephrotic stage of glomerulonephritis. Immediate fatal reactions have occurred, usually as a result of ventricular failure after intravascular injection and transient high concentration of mercury in the blood. Because of the toxicity of these drugs, current practice usually recommends their replacement with more convenient and less toxic diuretics.

mercury (Hg) /mur′kyərē/ [L, *Mercurius,* mythic messenger of the gods], a metallic element. Its atomic number is 80; its atomic mass is 200.59. It is the only common metal that is liquid at room temperature. Mercury is produced commercially and is used in dental amalgams, thermometers, barometers, and other measuring instruments. It forms many poisonous compounds.

mercury bichloride, an extremely poisonous compound formerly used in treatment of syphilis but now used only as a disinfectant.

mercury dilators, an esophageal dilator system consisting of a series of mercury-filled tubes of graded diameter for dilating the cardioesophageal sphincter.

mercury nephropathy, acute tubular necrosis caused by mercury poisoning after ingestion of inorganic mercury salts.

mercury poisoning, a toxic condition caused by the ingestion or inhalation of mercury or a mercury compound. The chronic form, resulting from inhalation of the vapors or dust of mercurial compounds or from repeated ingestion of very small amounts, is characterized by irritability, excessive saliva, loosened teeth, gum disorders, slurred speech, tremors, and staggering. Symptoms of acute mercury poisoning include a metallic taste in the mouth, thirst, nausea, vomiting, severe abdominal pain, bloody diarrhea, and renal failure that may result in death.

mercury thermometer [L, *Mercurius,* mythic messenger of the gods; Gk, *thermē,* heat, *metron,* measure], a thermometer in which the expandable indicator is mercury.

Merkel cell carcinoma /mer′kəl, mur′kəl/ [Friedrich S. Merkel, German anatomist and physiologist, 1845–1919], a rapidly growing malignant skin tumor that tends to occur on sun-exposed surfaces of older Caucasian individuals.

meroanencephaly /mer′ō·an′ənsef′əlē/ [Gk, *meros,* part; *a, enkephalos,* not brain], congenital absence of part of the brain, usually the forebrain and midbrain.

meroblastic /mer′əblas′tik/ [Gk, *meros* + *blastos,* germ], pertaining to or characterizing an ovum that contains a large amount of yolk and in which cleavage is restricted to the yolk-free part of the cytoplasm.

merocrine gland /mer′əkrin/ [Gk, *meros,* part, *krinein,* to separate; L, *secernere,* to separate], a gland in which the secreting cell remains intact while producing and releasing the secretory product.

meromelia /mer′əmē′lyə/ [Gk, *meros* + *melos,* limb], **1.** an abnormality of development in which the upper part of the arm or leg is missing so that hands or feet are attached to the body like stumps, generally resulting from the use of thalidomide during pregnancy. **2.** a general designation for the congenital absence of any part of a limb. It is used in reference to such conditions as adactyly, hemimelia, or phocomelia.

meropenem /mer′əpen′əm/ [Gk, *meros* + *zoon,* animal], a miscellaneous antiinfective used to treat serious infections caused by *Streptococcus pneumoniae,* group A beta-hemolytic streptococci, enterococcus, *Klebsiella, Proteus, Escherichia coli, Pseudomonas aeruginosa, Bacteroides fragilis,* and *B. thetaiotaomicron.* It is also used to treat appendicitis and peritonitis caused by the *viridans* group of streptococci, as well as bacterial meningitis.

merozoite /mer′əzō′īt/ [Gk, *meros* + *zoon,* animal], an organism produced from segmentation of a schizont during the asexual reproductive phase of the life cycle of a sporozoon, specifically the malarial parasite *Plasmodium.*

merozygote /mer′əzī′gōt/, an incomplete zygote that contains only part of the genetic material of one of the parents. It occurs during conjugation in bacteria.

MERRF syndrome, abbreviation for *myoclonus with epilepsy and with ragged red fibers,* a familial syndrome of maternal (mitochondrial) inheritance.

Merrifield's knife, a surgical knife with a long, narrow, triangular blade set into a shank, used for gingivectomy incisions.

Meruvax II, a trademark for an active immunizing agent (live rubella virus vaccine).

mesalamine, an active metabolite of sulfasalazine, used in the prophylaxis and treatment of inflammatory bowel disease and ulcerative proctitis.

mesangial /mesan′jē·əl/, pertaining to the mesangium.

mesangium /mesan′jē·əm/, a cellular network in the renal glomerulus that helps support the capillary loops.

M

mescaline /mes′kəlēn, -lin/ [Mex, *mezcal*], a psychoactive agent with effects similar to LSD. Closely related chemically to epinephrine, mescaline causes heart palpitations, diaphoresis, pupillary dilation, and anxiety. It is a Schedule I substance.

mescalism /mes′kəliz′əm/ [Mex, *mezcal*], a type of chemical dependence on the effects of mescal, an intoxicant spirit obtained from a species of cactus (agave).

mesencephalon /mes′ensef′əlon/ [Gk, *mesos,* middle, *enkephalos,* brain], one of the three parts of the brainstem, lying just below the cerebrum and just above the pons. It consists primarily of white substance with some gray substance around the cerebral aqueduct.—**mesencephalic** /mes′ensifal′ik/, *adj.*

mesenchymal chondrosarcoma /meseng′kəməl/ [Gk, *mesos,* middle, *enchyma,* infusion, *chondros,* cartilage, *sarx,* flesh, *oma,* tumor], a rare malignant, highly vascular tumor of soft tissue that develops in many sites.

mesenchyme /mes′engkīm/ [Gk, *mesos + enchyma,* infusion], a diffuse network of tissue derived from the embryonic mesoderm. It consists of stellate cells embedded in gelatinous ground substance with reticular fibers.—**mesenchymal,** *adj.*

mesenchymoma /mes′engkimō′mə/ [Gk, *mesos + enchyma,* infusion, *oma,* tumor], a mixed mesenchymal neoplasm composed of two or more cellular elements that are not usually associated and fibrous tissue.

mesenteric /mes′enter′ik/ [Gk, *mesos,* middle, *enteron,* intestine], pertaining to the mesentery, the double layer of peritoneum suspending the intestine from the posterior abdominal wall.

mesenteric angina, severe pain and discomfort after a heavy meal resulting from diminished blood supply and concomitant lack of oxygen caused by the narrowing of the celiac and mesenteric artery openings.

mesenteric axis, a line passing transversely between a portion of the GI tract and its adjacent mesentery.

mesenteric ischemia, ischemia in an area of the intestine supplied by a mesenteric artery. It may be either occlusive or nonocclusive and may progress to a mesenteric infarction.

mesenteric node [Gk, *mesos + enteron,* intestine; L, *nodus,* knot], a node in one of three groups of superior mesenteric lymph glands serving parts of the intestine.

mesenteric panniculitis, inflammation with variable fibrosis of mesenteric fat, usually of the small intestine, causing a solid mass that may displace or obstruct the intestine.

mesenteroaxial volvulus, the less common of the two types of gastric volvulus,

in which the stomach twists transversely around its mesenteric axis. This type is more common in children.

mesentery proper /mez′ənter′ē/ [Gk, *mesos + enteron,* intestine; L, *propius,* more suitable], a broad fan-shaped fold of peritoneum suspending the jejunum and the ileum from the dorsal wall of the abdomen. The root of the mesentery proper is connected to certain structures ventral to the vertebral column. The intestinal border of the mesentery proper separates to enclose the intestine. The cranial part of the mesentery suspends the small intestine and various nerves and arteries.

MeSH /mesh/, an abbreviation derived from *Medical Subject Headings,* the list of medical terms used by the U.S. National Library of Medicine (NLM) for its computerized system of storage and retrieval of published medical reports.

mesh graft, a partial- or split-thickness skin graft that has had multiple slits cut into it. The slits allow the graft to be stretched to several times its original size for coverage of a larger area on the recipient.

MeSH terms, subject headings.

mesiobuccoocclusal /mē′zē-ōbuk′ō-ōkloo′zəl/ [Gk, *mesos,* middle; L, *bucca,* cheek, *occludere,* to close up], pertaining to the angle formed by the mesial, buccal, and occlusal surfaces of a tooth.

mesiocclusion /mē′zē-okloo′zhən/ [Gk, *mesos;* L, *occludere,* to close up], an occlusal relationship in which the lower teeth are positioned mesially to the upper teeth.

mesiodens /mē′zē-ədenz/ [Gk, *mesos;* L, *dens,* tooth], a supernumerary erupted or unerupted tooth that develops between two maxillary central incisors.

mesiolinguoocclusal, pertaining to the angle formed by the mesial, lingual, and occlusal surfaces of a tooth.

mesioversion /mē′zē-ōvur′zhən/ [Gk, *mesos;* L, *vertere,* to turn], **1.** a condition in which one or more teeth are closer than normal to the midline. **2.** a condition in which the maxilla or mandible is positioned more anteriorly than normal.

mesmerism /mez′məriz′əm/ [Franz A. Mesmer, Austrian physician, 1734–1815], a practice of hypnotism introduced by Mesmer, who believed human health was affected by "celestial magnetic forces." Mesmer was regarded as a fraud by the medical profession, but his work led to serious studies of the health effects of the power of suggestion.

mesoblastic nephroma, a renal tumor similar to Wilms' tumor but appearing earlier in infancy and with more infiltration of surrounding tissue.

mesocolic node /mes′ōkol′ik/ [Gk, *mesos* + *kolon*, colon; L, *nodus*, knot], a node in one of three groups of superior mesenteric lymph glands, proliferating between the layers of the transverse mesocolon, close to the transverse colon.

mesocolopexy /mes′ōkō′ləpek′sē/ [Gk, *mesos* + *kolon*, colon, *pexis*, fixation], suspension or fixation of the mesocolon.

mesoderm /mes′ōdurm/ [Gk, *mesos* + *derma*, skin], in embryology, the middle of the three cell layers of the developing embryo. It lies between the ectoderm and the endoderm. Bone, connective tissue, muscle, blood, vascular and lymphatic tissue, and the pleurae of the pericardium and peritoneum are all derived from the mesoderm.

mesoduodenum /-dŏŏ′ədē′nəm/ [Gk, *mesos*, middle; L, *duodeni*, 12 fingers long], a fold of tissue that joins the duodenum to the wall of the abdomen of the fetus. The membrane sometimes persists in later life as the duodenal mesentery.

mesoepididymis /mez′ō·ep′idid′imis/ [Gk, *mesos*, middle, *epi*, above, *didymos*, pair], a fold of tunica vaginalis that sometimes connects the epididymis with the testicle.

mesogastric /-gas′trik/ [Gk, *mesos*, middle, *gaster*, belly], pertaining to the mesogastrium, a mesentery of the embryonic stomach.

mesogluteus /mez′ōglŏŏ′tē·əs/ [Gk, *mesos*, middle, *gloutos*, buttocks], the middle gluteal muscle, which abducts and rotates the thigh medially.

mesojejunum /mez′ōjəjŏŏ′nəm/ [Gk, *mesos*, middle; L, *jejunus*, empty], the mesentery of the jejunum.

mesomere /mez′əmir/ [Gk, *mesos*, middle, *meros*, part], a row of bastomere between the macromere and micromere of the embryo. It develops into the renal tubules.

mesomerism /mesom′erizəm/, the existence of organic chemical structures that cannot be accurately represented by a single structural formula, the actual formula lying intermediate between several possible representations that differ only in the position of electrons.

mesomorph /mes′əmôrf′/ [Gk, *mesos* + *morphe*, form], a person whose physique is characterized by a predominance of muscle, bone, and connective tissue, structures that develop from the mesodermal layer of the embryo.

mesonephric duct /-nef′rik/ [Gk, *mesos* + *nephros*, kidney; L, *ducere*, to lead], in embryology, a duct that in the male gives rise to the ducts of the reproductive system

(ductus epididymidis, ductus deferens, seminal vesicle, ejaculatory duct). In the female it persists vestigially as Gartner's duct.

mesonephric tubule, any of the embryonic renal tubules composing the mesonephros. They function as excretory structures during the early embryonic development of humans and other mammals but are later incorporated into the reproductive system. In males the tubules give rise to the efferent and aberrant ductules of the testes, the appendix epididymis, and the paradidymis; in females to the epoöphoron, paroöphoron, and vesicular appendices.

mesonephros /-nef′rəs/ *pl.* **mesonephra, mesonephroi** [Gk, *mesos* + *nephros*, kidney], the second type of excretory organ to develop in the vertebrate embryo. It consists of a series of twisting tubules that arise from the nephrogenic cord caudal to the pronephros and that at one end form the glomerulus and at the other connect with the excretory mesonephric duct.—**mesonephric, mesonephroid,** *adj.*

mesoridazine /mez′ərid′əzēn/, a phenothiazine antipsychotic prescribed in the treatment of schizophrenia.

mesosalpinx /mes′ōsal′pingks/ [Gk, *mesos* + *salpinx*, tube], the superior, free border of the broad ligament in which the uterine tubes lie.

mesotaurodontism /mez′ōtô′rōdon′ tizəm/ [Gk, *mesos*, middle; L, *taurus*, bull; Gk, *odous*, tooth], taurodontism in which the tooth roots branch only in the middle.

mesothelial /mez′ōthē′lē·əl/, pertaining to the mesothelium cell layer.

mesothelioma /mes′ōthē′lē·ō′mə/ *pl.* **mesotheliomas, mesotheliomata** [Gk, *mesos* + *epi*, above, *thele*, nipple, *oma*, tumor], a rare malignant tumor of the mesothelium of the pleura or peritoneum, associated with exposure to asbestos.

mesothelium /mes′ōthē′lē·əm/ [Gk, *mesos* + *epi*, above, *thele*, nipple], a layer of cells that line the body cavities of the embryo and continue as a layer of squamous epithelial cells covering the serous membranes of the adult.

messenger RNA (mRNA) /mes′ənjər/ [ME, *messangere*, message bearer; *RNA*, ribonucleic acid], in molecular genetics, an RNA fraction that carries information from DNA to the protein-synthesizing ribosomes of cells. mRNA contains codons that are eventually encoded into amino acids via the translation process.

Mestinon, a trademark for a neuromuscular blocking agent (pyridostigmine bromide).

mestranol /mes′trənōl/, an estrogen prescribed in fixed-combination drugs with a progestin as an oral contraceptive.

M

Met, abbreviation for the amino acid **methionine.**

MET, abbreviation for **metabolic equivalent of task.**

meta-analysis, a systematic method of evaluating statistical data based on results of several independent studies of the same problem.

metabiosis /met′əbī-ō′sis/, **1.** a condition in which the growth and metabolism of one organism alters the environment to allow the growth of another organism. **2.** the parasitic dependence of the existence of one organism on that of another.

metabolic /met′əbol′ik/ [Gk, *metabole,* change], pertaining to **metabolism.**

metabolic acidosis, acidosis (blood pH below 7.4) in which excess acid is added to the body fluids or bicarbonate is lost from them. In starvation and in uncontrolled DM, glucose is not present or is not available for oxidation for cellular nutrition. This glucose lack causes breakdown of fats for energy, resulting in acidic ketone bodies. The body uses plasma bicarbonate to neutralize these acids. Metabolic acidosis also occurs when oxidation takes place without adequate oxygen, as in heart failure or shock. Severe diarrhea, renal failure, ingestion of toxic substances (e.g., antifreeze and large doses of aspirin) and lactic acidosis also may result in metabolic acidosis. Hyperkalemia may accompany the condition.

metabolic alkalosis, an abnormal condition characterized by the significant loss of acid in the body or by increased levels of base bicarbonate. Loss of acid may be caused by excessive vomiting, insufficient replacement of electrolytes, hyperadrenocorticism, or Cushing's disease. Increased levels of base bicarbonate may have various causes, such as the ingestion of excessive amounts of bicarbonate of soda or other antacids during the treatment of peptic ulcers, or the administration of excessive volumes of IV fluids containing high concentrations of bicarbonate. Signs and symptoms of metabolic alkalosis may include apnea, headache, lethargy, muscle cramps, hyperactive reflexes, tetany, shallow and slow respirations, irritability, nausea, vomiting, and atrial tachycardia.

metabolic balance [Gk, *metabole,* change; L, *bilanx,* having two scale trays], an equilibrium between the intake of nutrients and their eventual loss through absorption or excretion. In a positive balance the intake of a nutrient exceeds its loss; in a negative balance a nutrient is used or excreted faster than it is consumed in the diet.

metabolic body size, an estimate of the active tissue mass of a person, calculated by the body weight in kilograms to the 0.75 power.

metabolic cirrhosis, cirrhosis of the liver associated with a metabolic disorder such as Wilson's disease.

metabolic component, the bicarbonate component of plasma.

metabolic disorder, any pathophysiologic dysfunction that results in a loss of metabolic control of homeostasis in the body.

metabolic equivalent of task (MET), a unit of measurement of heat production by the body. One MET is equal to 50 kcal per hour per square meter of body surface of a resting individual.

metabolic failure, the severe and usually rapid failure of mental and physical functions, resulting in death.

metabolic myopathy, myopathy as a result of disordered metabolism, usually caused by genetic defects or hormonal dysfunction.

metabolic pathway, a series of consecutive biochemical reactions or steps through which digested food is transformed into basic nutrients such as amino acids, free fatty acids, and simple carbohydrates.

metabolic rate, the amount of energy liberated or expended in a given unit of time. Energy is stored in the body in energy-rich phosphate compounds (adenosine triphosphate, adenosine monophosphate, and adenosine diphosphate) and in proteins, fats, and complex carbohydrates.

metabolic syndrome, a combination including at least three of the following: abdominal obesity, hypertriglyceridemia, low level of high-density lipoproteins, hypertension, and high fasting plasma glucose level. It is associated with an increased risk for development of DM and cardiovascular disease.

metabolic tolerance, the ability of the body to limit a drug's effects by increasing the rate at which it is broken down or eliminated.

metabolic waste products [Gk, *metabole,* change; L, *vastare,* to destroy, *producere,* to produce], the products of metabolic activity after oxygen and nutrients have been supplied to a cell. These mainly include water and carbon dioxide, along with sodium chloride and soluble nitrogenous salts, which are excreted in urine, feces, and exhaled air.

metabolism /mətab′əliz′əm/ [Gk, *metabole,* change, *ismos,* process], the aggregate of all chemical processes that take place in living organisms, resulting in growth, generation of energy, elimination of wastes, and other body functions as they relate to the distribution of nutrients in the blood after digestion. Metabolism takes place in two steps: anabolism, the constructive phase, in which smaller molecules (such as amino acids) are converted to larger molecules (such as proteins), and catabolism, the destructive phase, in which larger molecules (such as glycogen) are converted to smaller molecules (such as glucose). The metabolic rate is customarily expressed (in calories) as the heat liberated in the course of metabolism.

metabolite /mitab′əlīt/ [Gk, *metabole,* change], a substance produced by metabolic action or necessary for a metabolic process. An essential metabolite is one required for a vital metabolic process.

metabolize /mətab′əlīz/ [Gk, *metabole,* change], to undergo metabolism, the breaking down of carbohydrates, proteins, and fats into smaller units; reorganizing those units as tissue building blocks or as energy sources; and eliminating waste products of the processes.

metacarpal phalanx /-kär′pəl/ [Gk, *meta + karpos,* wrist, *phalanx,* line of soldiers], the hands and fingers, particularly phalanges that articulate with carpal bones.

metacarpophalangeal (MCP) /-kar′pōfəlan′jē·əl/ [Gk, *meta,* beyond, *karpos,* wrist, *phalanx,* line of soldiers], pertaining to the metacarpal bones of the hand and the phalanges of fingers, as in metacarpophalangeal joints.

metacarpophalangeal (MCP) joint dislocation [Gk, *meta + karpos + phalanx*; L, *jungere,* to join, *dis + locare,* to place], the dislocation of a finger at the junction with the metacarpal bone, usually with damage to tendons and other structures.

metacarpus /-met′əkär′pəs/ [Gk, *meta,* beyond, *karpos,* wrist], the middle part of the hand, consisting of five slender bones, metacarpals I through V, numbered from the thumb side. Each metacarpal consists of a body and two extremities. —**metacarpal,** *adj., n.*

metacentric /met′əsen′trik/ [Gk, *meta + kentron,* center], pertaining to a chromosome in which the centromere is located near the center so that the arms of the chromosome are of approximately equal length.

metachromasia /-krōmā′zhē·ə/ [Gk, *meta,* beyond, *chroma,* color], a tissue staining phenomenon in which cells being examined acquire a color other than that of the dye used. Cartilage cells, for example, may appear red after being stained with a blue dye. The cause is an interaction between the dye molecules and the acidic radicals of the tissue cells.

metachromatic lipids /-krōmat′ik/ [Gk, *meta,* beyond, *chroma,* color, *lipos,* fat], lipid molecules that accumulate in the CNS, peripheral nerves, and internal organs of infants who inherit a lipidosis disorder.

metachromatic stain [Gk, *meta + chroma,* color; OFr, *desteindre,* to dye], a basic dye, such as toluidine, that can stain substances a different color than that of the stain.

metacommunication /-kəmyōō′nikā′shən/ [Gk, *meta*; L, *communicare,* to inform], stimulus surrounding verbal communication that indicates how verbal information should be interpreted. It may support or contradict verbal communication.

metagenesis /met′əjen′əsis/ [Gk, *meta + genein,* to produce], the regular alternation of sexual with asexual methods of reproduction within the same species. —**metagenetic, metagenic,** *adj.*

metal [Gk, *metallon,* a mine], any element that conducts heat and electricity, is malleable and ductile, and forms positively charged ions (cations).

metal fume fever, an occupational disorder caused by the inhalation of fumes of metallic oxides and characterized by symptoms similar to those of influenza.

metallesthesia /met′əlesthē′zhə/ [Gk, *metallon,* a mine, *aisthesia,* perception], an ability to identify a metal through the sense of touch.

metalloid /met′əloid/, **1.** any element with both metallic and nonmetallic properties, such as silicon, boron, or arsenic. **2.** resembling a metal.

metalloprotein /mətal′ōprō′tēn/, a protein that contains one or more metal atoms.

metallurgy /met′əlur′jē/ [Gk, *metallon,* a mine, *ergein,* to work], the theoretic and applied sciences of the nature and uses of metals.

metals, agents that consist of metallic poisons, such as arsenic, mercury, and thallium. Exposure to metallic poisons can be by inhalation or ingestion. Heavy metals can affect many systems, and large doses or prolonged exposure can lead to death.

metamorphopsia /met′əmôrfop′sē·ə/ [Gk, *meta + morphe,* form, *opsis,* sight], a defect in vision in which objects are seen as distorted in shape, which results from disease of the retina or imperfection of the media.

metamorphosis /met′əmôr′fəsis/ [Gk, *meta + morphe,* form], a change in shape or structure, especially a change from one stage of development to another, such as the transition from the larval to the adult stage.

metamyelocyte /met′əmī′əlōsīt/ [Gk, *meta + myelos,* marrow, *kytos,* cell], a stage in the development of the granulocyte

M

series of leukocytes, between the myelocyte stage and the neutrophilic band.

metanephric blastema, a mass of intermediate mesodermal cells around the distal end of the ureteric bud that gives rise to nephrons in the permanent kidney.

metanephrine /met'ənef'rin/, one of the two principal urinary metabolites of epinephrine and norepinephrine in the urine, the other being vanillylmandelic acid.

metanephrogenic /met'ənef'rəjen'ik/ [Gk, *meta* + *nephros,* kidney, *genein,* to produce], capable of forming the metanephros, or fetal kidney.

metanephros /-nef'rəs/ *pl.* **metanephra, metanephroi** [Gk, *meta* + *nephros,* kidney], the third, and permanent, excretory organ to develop in the vertebrate embryo. It consists of a complex structure of secretory and collecting tubules that develop into the kidney.

metaphase /met'əfāz/ [Gk, *meta* + *phasis,* appearance], the second of the four stages of nuclear division in mitosis and in each of the two divisions of meiosis, during which the chromosomes become arranged in the equatorial plane of the spindle to form the equatorial plate, with the centromeres attached to the spindle fibers in preparation for separation.

metaphyseal dysostosis /mətaf'ize'əl disostō'sis, met'əfiz'ē·əl disostō'sis/ [Gk, *meta* + *phyein,* to grow, *dys,* bad, *osteon,* bone], a condition characterized by abnormal mineralization of the metaphyseal area of the bones, resulting in dwarfism. Metaphyseal dysostosis is classified as the Gansen, Schmidt, or Spahar-Hartmann type or as cartilage-hair hypoplasia. The Gansen type is characterized by metaphyseal alterations similar to those of achondroplasia but not involving the skull or the epiphyses of the long bones. The Schmidt type is characterized by developmental changes from the weight-bearing age to approximately 5 years of age. The Spahar-Hartmann type is characterized by skeletal changes and severe bowleg. Cartilage-hair hypoplasia is characterized by severe dwarfism and hair that is sparse, short, and brittle. Mental retardation is not usually associated with metaphyseal dysostosis.

metaphyseal dysplasia, a condition characterized by disordered modeling of the long bones, in which the metaphyseal circumference is enlarged and the medullary area is reduced. Metaphyseal dysplasia most often affects the distal femur or the proximal tibia.

metaphysis /mətaf'əsis/ [Gk, *meta* + *phyein,* to grow], a region of a growing long bone in which diaphysis and epiphysis converge.—**metaphyseal,** *adj.*

metaplasia /met'əplā'zhə/, the reversible conversion of normal tissue cells into another, less differentiated cell type in response to chronic stress or injury.

metaproterenol sulfate /met'əprōter'i nōl/, a beta₂-receptor agonist bronchodilator prescribed in the treatment of bronchial asthma and COPD when a delayed onset but prolonged effect is desired.

metaraminol bitartrate /met'äram'inol/, an adrenergic vasopressor prescribed in the treatment of hypotension and shock.

metarubricyte /-rōō'brisīt/ [Gk, *meta*; L, *ruber,* red; Gk, *kytos,* cell], a red blood cell precursor, the last nucleated stage of red blood cell production.

metastable state, a transient energy state of an atom with a half-life longer than 10^{-12} seconds (e.g., Technetium-99m).

metastasis /mətas'təsis/ *pl.* **metastases** [Gk, *meta* + *stasis,* standing], **1.** an active process by which tumor cells move from the primary location of a cancer by severing connections from the original cell group and establishing remote colonies. Because malignant tumors have no enclosing capsule, cells may escape, become emboli, and be transported by the lymphatic circulation or the bloodstream to implant in lymph nodes and other organs far from the primary tumor. **2.** a tumor that develops away from the site of origin. —**metastasize (metas)** /mətas'təsīz/, *v.* **metastatic,** *adj.*

metastatic abscess /-stat'ik/ [Gk, *meta,* beyond, *stasis,* standing; L, *abscedere,* to go away], any secondary abscess that develops at a point distant from an original infection, resulting from transportation of infectious particles to other locations via the bloodstream.

metastatic calcification [Gk, *meta* + *stasis,* standing; L, *calx,* lime, *facere,* to make], the pathologic process whereby calcium salts accumulate in previously healthy tissues, caused by excessive levels of blood calcium.

metastatic endometriosis [Gk, *meta,* beyond, *stasis,* standing, *endon,* within, *metra,* womb, *osis,* condition], extraperitoneal lesions that resemble metastases from a carcinoma.

metastatic survey [Gk, *meta,* beyond, *stasis,* standing; OFr, *surveoir,* to examine], a method of monitoring the spread of a cancer by taking a series of periodic x-ray films.

metatarsal /met'ətär'səl/ [Gk, *meta* + *tarsos,* flat surface], **1.** pertaining to the metatarsus of the foot. **2.** any one of the five bones making up the metatarsus.

metatarsalgia /met'ətärsal'jə/ [Gk, *meta* + *tarsos* + *algos,* pain], a painful condition around the metatarsal bones caused by an abnormality of the foot or by recalcification of degenerated heads of metatarsal bones.

metatarsal phalanx /-tär′səl/ [Gk, *meta* + *tarsos,* flat surface, *phalanx,* line of soldiers], the bones of the foot and toes.

metatarsal stress fracture, a break or rupture of a metatarsal bone caused by prolonged running or walking. The condition is often difficult to diagnose with x-ray films.

metatarsus /-tär′səs/ [Gk, *meta* + *tarsos,* flat surface], a part of the foot, consisting of five bones numbered I to V from the medial side. Each bone has a long, slender body; a wedge-shaped proximal end; a convex distal end; and flattened, grooved sides for the attachment of ligaments. —**metatarsal,** *adj.*

metatarsus valgus, a congenital deformity of the foot in which the forepart rotates outward away from the midline of the body and the heel remains straight.

metatarsus varus, a congenital deformity of the foot in which the forepart rotates inward toward the midline of the body and the heel remains straight.

metathalamus /met′əthal′əməs/ [Gk, *meta* + *thalamos,* chamber], one of five parts of the diencephalon. The medial geniculate body acts as a relay station for nerve impulses between the inferior brachium and the auditory cortex. The lateral geniculate body is a superficial oval bulge at the posterior end of the thalamus, which accommodates the terminal ends of the fibers of the optic tract. Relay cells project to the visual cortex. —**metathalamic,** *adj.*

metaxalone /metak′səlōn/, a skeletal muscle relaxant prescribed as an adjunct in the treatment of acute skeletal muscle spasm.

metazoa /-zō′ə/ [Gk, *meta* + *zoon,* animal], a classification that includes animals that have tissues and organs. All animals except sponges are metazoa.

Metchnikoff's theory /mech′nikofs/ [Elie Metchnikoff, Russian-French biologist, 1845–1916; Gk, *theoria,* speculation], the theory that living cells ingest microorganisms. The theory proved correct, as seen in the process of phagocytosis and the ingestion of injurious microbes by leukocytes.

meteorism [Gk, *meteorizein,* to hold up], accumulation of gas in the abdomen or the intestine, usually with distension.

meteorotropism /mē′tē-ərətrō′pizəm/ [Gk, *meteoros,* high in the air, *trope,* turning], a reaction to meteorologic influences shown by various biologic occurrences, such as sudden death, attacks of arthritis, and angina. —**meteorotropic,** *adj.*

meter (m) /mē′tər/ [Gk, *metron,* measure], a metric unit of length equal to 39.37 inches.

metered dose inhaler (MDI) /mē′tərd/, a device designed to deliver a measured dose of an inhaled drug. It usually consists of a canister of aerosol spray, mist, or fine powder that releases a specific dose each time it is pushed against a dispensing valve. It is intended to reduce the risk of overmedication by the patient.

metformin /metfor′min/, a hypoglycemic agent that potentiates the action of insulin, used in the treatment of type 2 DM.

methacholine /meth′äko′lēn/, a cholinergic agonist, having a longer duration of action than acetylcholine and predominantly muscarinic effects. It has vasodilator and cardiac vagomimetic effects but has largely been replaced by other drugs. It is also used in bronchial challenge tests.

methacholine challenge /meth′əko′lēn/, a method of measuring airway activity by an inhalation challenge test. The patient inhales a saline aerosol as a control, followed by increasing concentrations of methacholine chloride, a cholinergic drug. The test is used to confirm the diagnosis of asthma when symptoms are not present. This is a potentially dangerous test and should be performed only by qualified personnel, with resuscitation equipment readily available.

methacrylic acid (MAA) /meth′əkril′ik/, an organic acid obtained from Roman chamomile oil. The methyl ester of methacrylic acid is used in medical and dental products. A copolymer is used in tablet coatings.

methadone hydrochloride, an opioid analgesic used for anesthesia or as a substitute for heroin, permitting withdrawal without development of acute abstinence syndrome. Methadone does not produce marked euphoria, sedation, or narcosis.

methamphetamine hydrochloride /meth′amfet′əmēn/, a CNS stimulant that is prescribed in the treatment of attention deficit/ hyperactivity disorder, and short-term for the reduction of the appetite in exogenous obesity. An unlabeled use is for the treatment of narcolepsy.

methandriol /methan′drē-ol/, an anabolic hormone used as adjunctive therapy in senile and postmenopausal osteoporosis.

methane (CH₄) /meth′ān/, a simple hydrocarbon in the form of colorless gas, produced by the anaerobic decomposition of organic matter.

methanol (CH3OH) /meth′ənol/, a clear, colorless, toxic liquid distillate of wood miscible with water, other alcohols, and ether. It is widely used as a solvent and in the production of formaldehyde.

M

methanol poisoning, a toxic effect of ingestion, inhalation, or absorption through the skin of methanol (methyl alcohol, wood alcohol) that may impair the CNS; cause severe acidosis, blindness, and shock; and result in death.

methazolamide /meth′əzō′ləmīd/, a carbonic anhydrase inhibitor prescribed in the treatment of glaucoma.

methemoglobin /met′hēməglō′bin, met·he′ məglō′bin/, a form of hemoglobin in which the iron component has been oxidized from the ferrous to the ferric state. Methemoglobin cannot carry oxygen.

methemoglobinemia /-ē′mē·ə/, the presence of methemoglobin in the blood.

methemoglobin test, a blood test to detect methemoglobinemia.

methemoglobinuria /-ōōr′ē·ə/ [Gk, *meta,* beyond, *haima,* blood; L, *globus,* ball; Gk, *ouron,* urine], the presence of methemoglobin in the urine.

methenamine hippurate and mandelete /methē′nəmēn/, a urinary antibacterial prescribed in the treatment of UTIs.

methenamine silver stain, a specialized stain consisting of methenamine and silver nitrate used in histologic examinations for the detection of fungi. This stain is the best for detecting fungi in specimens but is very time-consuming and mainly used in histology labs.

Methergine, a trademark for an oxytocic (methylergonovine maleate).

methimazole /məthim′əzōl/, an orally administered antithyroid drug prescribed in the treatment of hyperthyroidism.

methionine (Met) /methī′ənēn/, an essential amino acid needed for proper growth in infants and for maintenance of nitrogen balance in adults. It is a source for methyl groups and sulfur in the body.

methocarbamol /meth′əkär′bəmol/, a skeletal muscle relaxant prescribed in the relief of skeletal muscle spasm.

method /meth′əd/ [Gk, *meta,* beyond, *hodos,* way], a technique or procedure for producing a desired effect, such as a surgical procedure, a laboratory test, or a diagnostic technique.

methodology /meth′ədol′əjē/ [Gk, *meta + hodos + logos,* science], **1.** a system of principles or methods of procedure in any discipline such as education, research, diagnosis, or treatment. **2.** the section of a research proposal in which the methods to be used are described.—**methodologic,** *adj.*

methohexital sodium /meth′ōhek′sitōl/, an IV barbiturate of short duration used for the induction of anesthesia in short surgical procedures like cardioversion or electroconvulsive therapy.

methotrexate /meth′ōtrek′sāt/, an antineoplastic antimetabolite. It is prescribed in the treatment of a variety of malignant neoplastic diseases of the blood and organs and in the treatment of psoriasis, and it is widely used as an immunosuppressive agent for the treatment of autoimmune diseases such as rheumatoid arthritis.

methoxsalen /methok′sələn/, a pigmentation agent used topically for unresponsive psoriasis and enhancement of pigmentation or for repigmentation in vitiligo and administered orally prior to longwave ultraviolet irradiation of severe recalcitrant psoriasis.

methscopolamine bromide /meth′skōpō′ ləmēn/, an anticholinergic/antispasmodic prescribed in the treatment of hypermotility of the GI tract and as an adjunct in treatment of peptic ulcer.

methsuximide /methsuk′simīd/, an anticonvulsant prescribed in the treatment of refractory absence seizures.

methyclothiazide /məthī′klōthī′əzīd, meth′ əklōthī′əzīd/, a diuretic prescribed in the treatment of mild to moderate hypertension and edema.

methyl (Me) /meth′il/, the chemical radical CH_3.

methylate /meth′ilāt/ [Gk, *methy,* wine, *hyle,* matter], **1.** an organic compound in which the hydrogen atom of methanol is replaced by a metal. **2.** to add a methyl group, CH_3, to a chemical compound.

methylation /-lā′shən/ [Gk, *methy,* wine, *hyle,* matter], **1.** the introduction of a methyl group, CH_3, to a chemical compound. **2.** the addition of methyl alcohol and naphtha to ethanol to produce denatured alcohol.

methyl blue, a blue dye of the triarylmethane class, $C_{37}H_{27}N_3O_9S_3Na_2$; used, alone or in combination with water blue as a biologic stain.

methyldopa /-dō′pə/, an alpha$_2$ receptor agonist that acts in the CNS to decrease sympathetic nervous system outflow. It is prescribed for the reduction of hypertension in moderate to severe cases.

methylene blue /meth′ələn/, a bluish-green crystalline substance used as a histologic stain and as a laboratory indicator. It is also used in the treatment of cyanide poisoning and methemoglobinemia.

methylergonovine maleate /-ərgon′əvēn/, a synthetic ergot alkaloid prescribed as an oxytocic to prevent or to treat postpartum uterine atony, hemorrhage, or subinvolution.

3-methylfentanyl, a potent heroin substitute and so-called designer drug.

methylmalonicacidemia /meth′əlməlon′ik as′idē′mē·ə/, **1.** an autosomal-recessive aminoacidopathy characterized by an excess of the carboxylic acid methylmalonic acid in the blood and urine, with metabolic ketoacidosis, hyperammonemia, and excess glycine in the blood and urine, presenting in infancy as failure to thrive, persistent vomiting and dehydration, respiratory distress, and hypotonia. **2.** an excess of methylmalonic acid in the blood.

methylphenidate hydrochloride /-fen′idāt/, a CNS stimulant prescribed in the treatment of attention deficit/hyperactivity disorder in children and, more recently, adults and for narcolepsy in adults.

methylPREDNISolone /-prednis′əlōn/, a glucocorticoid prescribed as an antiinflammatory drug and as an immunosuppressant to treat autoimmune disease, cancer, and other disease involving cells of the immune system. It is also administered to suppress graft-versus-host disease following bone marrow transplantation.

methylTESTOSTERone /meth′iltəstos′tə rōn/, an androgen prescribed in the treatment of testosterone deficiency and in palliation of female breast cancer.

methysergide maleate /meth′isur′jīd/, a vasoconstrictor prescribed for relief of migraine headache.

Meticorten, a trademark for a glucocorticoid (predniSONE).

metipranolol /met′ipran′älol/, a beta-adrenergic blocking agent, applied topically to the conjunctiva in the treatment of glaucoma and ocular hypertension.

metoclopramide hydrochloride /met′ əklō′prəmīd/, a GI motility agent prescribed to stimulate motility of and increase the tone of gastric contractions of the upper GI tract and to prevent emesis.

metolazone /mətō′lazōn/, a diuretic prescribed for the treatment of edema and mild to moderate high BP.

"me-too" drug *informal.* a drug product that is similar, identical, or closely related to a drug for which a manufacturer has obtained a new drug application. The drug is placed on the market by a company or companies other than the holder of the application. Clinical trials required of the original manufacturer are not required of the new supplier, but information regarding the manufacture, bioavailability, and labeling of the product is required to complete the abbreviated procedure for approval by the U.S. Food and Drug Administration.

metopic /mətō′pik/, pertaining to the forehead.

metoprolol tartrate /metop′rəlol/, an antiadrenergic; a beta₁-receptor antagonist. It is prescribed in the treatment of hypertension and angina pectoris and to prevent MI and atrial flutter or fibrillation. It also has proven benefits for patients with CHF when used in combination with other

drugs. Unlabeled uses include migraine prophylaxis and treatment of essential tremor and ventricular arrhythmias.

metralgia /mətral′jə/ [Gk, *metra,* womb, *algos,* pain], tenderness or pain in the uterus.

metric /met′rik/, pertaining to a system of measurement that uses the meter as a basis.

metric equivalent [Gk, *metron,* measure; L, *aequus,* equal, *valare,* to be strong], any value in metric units of measurement that equals the same value in English units, for example, 2.54 cm equals 1 inch, and 1 L equals 1.0567 quarts.

metric system, a decimal system of measurement based on the meter (39.37 inches) as the unit of length, on the gram (15.432 grains) as the unit of weight or mass, and, as a derived unit, on the liter (0.908 U.S. dry quart or 1.0567 U.S. liquid quart) as the unit of volume.

metritis /mətrī′tis/ [Gk, *metra,* womb, *itis,* inflammation], inflammation of the walls of the uterus.

metrocarcinoma /met′rōkär′sinō′mə/ [Gk, *metra,* womb, *karkinos,* crab, *oma,* tumor], a cancer of the uterus.

metromalacia, abnormal softening of the uterus.

metronidazole /met′rənī′dəzōl/, an antimicrobial with activity against anaerobic bacteria and protozoa. It is prescribed in the treatment of a variety of infections, including amebiasis, trichomoniasis, anaerobic infections, antibiotic-induced infections, pseudomembranous colitis, and bacterial vaginosis.

metronoscope /mətron′əskōp/, **1.** a device that exposes a small amount of reading matter to the eyes for brief preset periods. It is used in testing and in aiding individuals to increase reading speed. **2.** an apparatus that exercises the eyes rhythmically to improve binocular coordination.

metroplasty /mē′trəplas′tē/ [Gk, *metra,* womb], reconstructive surgery on the uterus.

metrorrhagia /met′rōrä′jē·ə/ [Gk, *metra,* womb, *rhegnynai,* to burst forth], uterine bleeding other than that caused by menstruation. It may be caused by uterine lesions and may be a sign of a urogenital malignancy.

metyrapone /metir′əpōn/, a diagnostic test drug used to test hypothalamic and pituitary function.

metyrosine /mətir′əsēn/, an inhibitor of tyrosine hydroxylase, the rate-limiting enzyme for catecholamine synthesis. It is prescribed in the treatment of pheochromocytoma before surgery and may be used for long-term therapy if surgery is contraindicated.

M

mev, MeV, abbreviation for *million electron volts,* the equivalent of 3.82×10^{-14} small calories, or 1.6×10^{-6} ergs.

mevalonate kinase /məval'ənāt/, an enzyme in the liver and in yeast. It catalyzes the transfer of a phosphate group from adenosine triphosphate to produce adenosine diphosphate and 5-phosphomevalonate.

Mexican typhus [Gk, *typhos,* fever], a form of epidemic typhus carried by lice in Mexico.

mexiletine hydrochloride /mek'silē'tin/, an oral antiarrhythmic drug prescribed for the treatment of symptomatic ventricular arrhythmias and suppression of premature ventricular contractions.

Mexitil, a trademark for an oral antiarrhythmic drug (mexiletine hydrochloride).

Meyenburg complexes, groups of hamartomas in the bile ducts.

Meyer, Adolf /mi'er/ [1866–1950], Swiss-born psychiatrist in the United States who directed the development of the Henry Phipps Psychiatric Clinic at Johns Hopkins University. His major contributions include propounding the theory of psychobiology, standardizing case histories, and reforming mental health institutions.

Meynet's node /mānāz'/, any of the numerous nodules that may develop within the capsules surrounding joints and in tendons affected by rheumatic diseases, especially in children.

Mezlin, a trademark for a semisynthetic penicillin antibiotic (mezlocillin sodium).

mezlocillin sodium /mezlos'ilin/, a semisynthetic penicillin antibiotic prescribed for the treatment of lower respiratory tract, intraabdominal, urinary tract, gynecologic, and skin infections and bacterial septicemia caused by susceptible strains of multiple microorganisms.

mF, abbreviation for *millifarad.*

MFCC, abbreviation for *Marriage, Family, and Child Counselor.*

MFD, abbreviation for *minimum fatal dose.*

mg, abbreviation for **milligram.**

Mg, 1. symbol for the element **magnesium.** 2. abbreviation for *megagram.*

MH, 1. abbreviation for **malignant hyperthermia.** 2. abbreviation for **mental health.**

MHC, abbreviation for *major histocompatibility complex.*

MHD, abbreviation for **minimum hemolytic dose.**

MHz, abbreviation for **megahertz.**

MI, abbreviation for **myocardial infarction.**

miasma /mī-az'mə/ [Gk, *miainein,* defilement], an unwholesome, polluted atmosphere or environment, such as a marsh or swamp containing rotting organic matter.

MIC, abbreviation for **minimal inhibitory concentration.**

mica /mī'kə/, an aluminum silicate mineral that occurs in thin laminated scales.

micafungin, a systemic antifungal used in the treatment of esophageal candidiasis and susceptible candida species *(Candida albicans, C. glabrata, C. krusei, C. parapsilosis,* and *C. tropicalis)* and in prophylaxis of candida infections in patients undergoing hepatopoietic stem cell transplantation.

micatosis /mī'kətō'sis/, a form of pneumoconiosis caused by inhalation of mica particles.

micellar chromatography /mīsel'ər/, a method of monitoring minute quantities of drugs in whole body fluids by using micellar or colloidal compounds to keep proteins in solution. The technique eliminates the need to remove proteins that usually interfere with chromatographic analysis of blood serum, urine, or saliva.

Michaelis-Menten kinetics [Leonor Michaelis, American biochemist, 1875–1949; Maud L. Menten, Canadian physician in U.S. practice, 1879–1960], a method of transforming drug plasma levels into a linear relationship by using the parameters of drug concentration and a constant, K_m, which is a measure of enzyme-substrate affinity. This is necessary when drug elimination mechanisms are saturable rather than proceeding by first-order kinetics.

miconazole nitrate /mīkon'əzōl/, an antifungal used topically to treat certain fungal infections of the skin and vagina.

mircencephalon /mī'krənsef'əlon/, an abnormally small brain.—**mircencephalic,** *adj., n.*

microabrasion /mi'kro·ābra'zhun/, removal of minute amounts of dental enamel by using an abrasive compound in order to correct enamel defects or remove caries.

microabscess /mī'krō·ab'ses/ [Gk, *mikros,* small; L, *abscedere,* to go away], a very small abscess.

microadenoma /mī'krō·ad'ənō'mə/, a pituitary adenoma less than 10 mm in diameter.

microaerophile /mī'krō·er'ōfil/ [Gk, *mikros,* small; *aer,* air, *philein,* to love], a microorganism that requires free oxygen for growth but at a lower concentration than that contained in the atmosphere. —**microaerophilic,** *adj.*

microaerotonometer /mī'krō·er'ətonom'ətər/ [Gk, *mikros + aer,* air, *tonos,* tension, *metron,* measure], instrument for measuring the volume of gases in blood or other fluids.

microaggregate recipient set /mi'krō·ag'rəgāt/ [Gk, *mikros;* L, *ad,* to, *gregare,* to collect, *recipere,* to receive; AS, *settan*], a device composed of plastic components for the IV delivery of large volumes of stored whole blood or of packed blood cells.

microalbumin test, a urine test to detect a greater than normal albumin concentration in the blood, an early indication of renal disease.

microalbuminuria /mī′krō·al′boomĭnoor′ē·ə/, the urinary excretion of small amounts of albumin, below the detection level of routine dipstick analysis. The condition is an early indicator of altered glomerular permeability in diabetes.

microampere /mī′krō·am′pir/, one millionth of an ampere.

microanalysis /mī′krō·anal′isis/, **1.** analysis of minute quantities of material. **2.** identification of substances by examination under a microscope.

microaneurysm /mi′krō·an′yəriz′əm/ [Gk, *mikros* + *aneurysma,* a widening], a microscopic aneurysm characteristic of thrombotic purpura.

microangiopathic hemolytic anemia (MAHA) /mī′krō·anjē·əpath′ik/, a condition in which narrowing or obstruction of small blood vessels results in distortion and fragmentation of erythrocytes, hemolysis, and anemia.

microangiopathy /mī′krō·an′jē·op′əthē/ [Gk, *mikros* + *angeion,* vessel, *pathos,* disease], a disease of the small blood vessels. Examples are diabetic microangiopathy, in which the basement membrane of capillaries thickens, and thrombotic microangiopathy, in which thrombi form in the arterioles and capillaries.

microbe /mī′krōb/, a microorganism. —**microbial,** *adj.*

microbial ecology /mīkrō′bē·əl/, the branch of biology that deals with the interaction of microorganisms with their environment.

microbial pesticides, pathogenic microorganisms that are toxic to a particular bacterium, insect, or other pest.

microbicide /mīkrō′bisīd/ [Gk, *mikros,* small, *bios,* life; L, *cadere,* to kill], any drug, chemical, or other agent that can kill microorganisms.

microbiological assay /-bī·əloj′ik/, **1.** the use of microorganisms for measuring the activity of organic compounds. **2.** the calculation of the purity of nutritional factors such as vitamins by measuring the growth of certain bacteria.

microbiology /mī′krōbī·ol′əjē/ [Gk, *mikros* + *bios,* life, *logos,* science], the branch of biology that is concerned with the study of microorganisms, including bacteria, archaea, viruses, algae, protozoa, and fungi, and their effect on humans.—**microbiologic, microbiological,** *adj.*

microbiology technologist, a medical technologist who specializes in the identification of bacteria and other microorganisms found in patient tissues and other specimens.

microblast /mī′krōblast′/ [Gk, *mikros,* small, *blastos,* germ], a very small immature RBC.

microbody /mī′krōbod′ē/, any of the round membrane-bound granular cytoplasmic particles containing enzymes and other substances, originating in the endoplasmic reticulum of vertebrate liver and kidney cells and other cells, and in protozoa, yeast, and many cell types of higher plants.

microbrachia /mī′krōbrā′kē·ə/ [Gk, *mikros* + *brachion,* arm], a developmental defect characterized by abnormal smallness of the arms.—**microbrachius,** *n.*

microcarrier /-ker′ē·ər/, microscopic bead or sphere that increases the surface area in a tissue culture for the attachment and yield of anchorage-dependent cells.

microcephaly /mī′krōsef′əlē/ [Gk, *mikros* + *kephale,* head], a congenital anomaly characterized by abnormal smallness of the head in relation to the rest of the body and by underdevelopment of the brain, resulting in some degree of mental retardation. The head is more than two standard deviations below the average circumference size for age, sex, race, and period of gestation. The facial features are generally normal. —**microcephalic, microcephalous,** *adj.,* **microcephalic, microcephalus,** *n.*

microcheiria /mī′krōkī′rē·ə/ [Gk, *mikros* + *cheir,* hand], a developmental defect characterized by abnormal smallness of the hands. The condition is usually associated with other congenital malformations or with bone and muscle disorders.

microcide /mī′krəsīd/, an antimicrobial flavoprotein enzyme. It has antibacterial activity only in the presence of glucose and oxygen as it reduces the oxygen to hydrogen peroxide.

microcirculation /-sur′kyələ′shən/, the flow of blood throughout the system of smaller vessels of the body, particularly the capillaries.

microcurie (μCi) /mī′krōkyoor′ē/ [Gk, *mikros* + *curie,* Marie Curie], a unit of radioactivity equal to one millionth of a curie, or 3.70×10^4 disintegrations per second.

microcystic adnexal carcinoma (MAC), a form of adnexal tumor that often appears on the face as a yellow, indurated plaque with ill-defined margins.

microcyte /mī′krəsīt/ [Gk, *mikros* + *kytos,* cell], an abnormally small erythrocyte

M

with a mean cell volume of less than 80 fL, often occurring in iron deficiency anemia and thalassemia.

microcythosis [Gk, *mikros,* small, *kytos,* cell], an excessive number of microcytes in the blood.

microcytic /mī′krōsit′ik/ [Gk, *mikros* + *kytos,* cell], (of a cell) pertaining to a smaller-than-normal cell.

microcytic anemia, a hematologic disorder characterized by abnormally small erythrocytes, usually associated with iron deficiency anemia, thalassemia, or anemia of chronic inflammation.

microcytosis /mī′krōsītō′sis/ [Gk, *mikros* + *kytos* + *osis,* condition], a hematologic condition characterized by erythrocytes that are smaller than normal. Microcytosis is found in iron deficiency anemia, thalassemia, and anemia of chronic inflammation.—**microcytic,** *adj.*

microdactyly /mī′krōdak′təlē/ [Gk, *mikros* + *dactylos,* finger], a developmental defect characterized by abnormal smallness of the fingers and toes. The condition is usually associated with bone and muscle disorders.

microdermabrasion, a cosmetic procedure in which all or part of the stratum corneum is removed by light abrasion, used to improve the appearance of sun-damaged skin, treat hyperpigmentation, and reduce or remove scars.

microdrepanocytic /mī′krōdrep′ənosit′ik/ [Gk, *mikros* + *drepane,* sickle, *kytos,* cell], pertaining to a blood disorder marked by the presence of both microcytes and drepanocytes, such as occurs in sickle cell thalassemia.

microdrip /mī′krōdrip′/, in IV therapy, an apparatus for delivering relatively small measured amounts of IV solutions at specific flow rates over time. The size of the drops is controlled by the fixed diameter of the plastic delivery tube.

microelectrode /mī′krō-ilek′trōd/, an electrode with a very small tip for use in brain studies. The device can be inserted without membrane damage into nervous tissue to record the bioelectrical activity of a simple neuron.

microencapsulation /mī′krō-enkap′syəlā′shən/ [Gk, *mikros* + *en,* in; L, *capsula,* little box], a laboratory technique used in the bioassay of hormones in which certain antibodies are encapsulated with a perforated membrane. The antibodies cannot escape through the tiny perforations, but hormones that bind with the antibodies may enter the structure to bind with them.

microencephaly /mī′krō-ensef′əlē/ [Gk, *mikros,* small, *egkephalos,* brain], the condition of being born with an abnormally small brain.

microequivalent /mī′krō-ikwiv′ələnt/, one millionth of an equivalent, the amount of a substance that corresponds to its equivalent mass in micrograms.

microfarad (μF) /mī′krōfer′əd/ [Gk, *mikros farad,* Michael Faraday], a unit of capacitance that equals one millionth of a farad.

microfiche /mī′krōfēsh′/ [Gk, *mikros;* Fr, *fiche,* peg], a sheet of microfilm that contains several separate photographic reproductions. The sheet is a convenient size for filing and enables large amounts of data to be stored in a relatively small space.

microfilament /-fil′əmənt/, any of the finest of the fibrous cellular filaments, such as the tonofibrils, found in the cytoplasm of most cells, that function primarily as a supportive system.

microfilaria /mī′krōfiler′ē-ə/ *pl.* **microfilariae** [Gk, *mikros;* L, *filum,* thread], the prelarval form of any filarial worm.

microfilm /mī′krəfilm/, a strip of 16 mm or 35 mm film that contains photographic reproductions of pages of books, documents, or other library or medical records in greatly reduced size. The film is viewed through a machine that enlarges the photographic images to normal reading size.

microgamete /-gam′ēt/, the small motile male gamete of certain thallophytes and sporozoa, specifically the malarial parasite *Plasmodium.* It corresponds to the sperm of the higher animals.

microgametocyte /-gamē′təsīt/ [Gk, *mikros* + *gamete,* spouse, *kytos,* cell], an enlarged merozoite that undergoes meiosis to form the mature male gamete during the sexual phase of the life cycle of certain thallophytes and sporozoa.

microgenitalia /-jen′itā′lē-ə/, a condition characterized by abnormally small external genitalia.

microglia /mīkrog′lē-ə/ [Gk, *mikros* + *glia,* glue], small migratory interstitial cells that form part of the CNS. They serve as phagocytes that collect waste products of the nerve tissue of the body.

microglossia /mī′krōglos′ē-ə/ [Gk, *mikros,* small, *glōssa,* tongue], undersized tongue.

micrognathia /mī′krōnā′thē-ə/ [Gk, *mikros* + *gnathos,* jaw], underdevelopment of the jaw, especially the mandible.—**micrognathic,** *adj.*

microgram (μg, mcg) /mī′krəgram/, a unit of measurement of mass equal to one millionth (10^{-6}) of a gram.

microgyria /mī′krōjī′rē-ə/ [Gk, *mikros* + *gyros,* turn], a developmental defect of the brain in which the convolutions are abnormally small, resulting in structural malformation of the cortex. The condition is usually associated with mental retardation and physical defects.

microgyrus /mī′krōjī′rəs/ pl. **microgyri**, an underdeveloped, malformed convolution of the brain.

microhematocrit, a hematocrit determination performed using less than a milliliter of whole blood in a capillary tube spun by a high-speed centrifuge.

microhm /mī′krōm/ [Gk, mikros; ohm, George Ohm], a unit of electric resistance equal to one millionth of an ohm.

microinjection /mī′krō·injek′shən/, the injection of tiny amounts of a substance into a cell by using micromanipulation instruments.

microinjector /mī′krō·injek′tər/, an instrument that delivers tiny amounts of a substance into a cell.

microinvasive carcinoma /mī′krō·invā′siv/ [Gk, mikros; L, in, within, vadere, to go], a squamous epithelial neoplasm that has penetrated the basement membrane, the first stage in invasive cancer.

microkeratome /mī′krō·kər′ə·tōm/ [Gk, mikros + keratome], an instrument for removing a thin slice, or creating a thin hinged flap, on the surface of the cornea.

microleakage /mī′krō·lē′kij/ [Gk, mikros; ONorse leka, to drip], leakage of minute amounts of fluids, debris, and microorganisms through the microscopic space between a dental restoration or its cement and the adjacent surface of the cavity preparation; it may progress through the dentin into the pulp.

microlevel interventions /-lev′əl/, health-generating changes performed at the individual level, such as in conditioning or stimulus control therapies.

microliter (μL) /mī′krəlē′tər/, a unit of liquid volume equal to one millionth of a liter, or 1 mm³.

microlith /mī′krəlith/ [Gk, mikros + lithos, stone], a small rounded mass of mineral matter or calcified stone.

micromanipulation /-mənip′yəlā′shən/, surgical displacement or dissection of very small tissues by using either miniature instruments or mechanical devices that translate large motions into smaller movements.

micromanipulator /-mənip′yəlā′tər/, a guidance accessory to a microscope that performs displacement or dissection of very small tissues.

micromelic dwarf /-mē′lik/ [Gk, mikros + melos, limb], a dwarf whose limbs are abnormally short.

micrometer (μm) /mīkrom′ətər/, **1.** an instrument used for measuring small angles or distances on objects being observed through a microscope or telescope. **2.** a

unit of measurement that equals one thousandth (10^{-3}) of a millimeter.

micromyeloblastic leukemia /mī′krōmī′əlōblas′tik/ [Gk, mikros + myelos, marrow, blastos, germ], a malignant neoplasm of blood-forming tissues, characterized by the proliferation of small myeloblasts distinguishable from lymphocytes only by special staining techniques and microscopic examination.

micron (μ, mu) /mī′kron/ [Gk, mikros, small], in physical chemistry, a colloidal particle with a diameter between 0.2 and 10 μg.

Micronase, a trademark for an oral antidiabetic drug (glyburide).

microneurography /-nyŏŏrog′rəfē/, the recording of impulse conduction in individual nerve fibers by means of a microelectrode. The technique is used in studies of the relationship between body mass and the sympathetic nervous system.

micronodular /-nod′yələr/, characterized by the presence of very small nodules.

micronodular adrenal disease, a rare form of Cushing's syndrome caused by multiple bilateral small, pigmented autonomous adrenocorticotropic hormone–independent cortisol-secreting adenomas.

Micronor, a trademark for an oral contraceptive containing a progestin (norethindrone).

micronucleus /-nōō′klē·əs/, **1.** a small nucleus. **2.** the smaller of two nuclei in some protozoa. It functions in sexual reproduction.

micronutrient /-nōō′trē·ənt/, any dietary element essential only in minute amounts for the normal physiologic processes of the body.

microorganism /-ôr′gəniz′əm/ [Gk, mikros + organon, instrument], any tiny, usually microscopic entity capable of carrying on living processes. It may be pathogenic.

microphage /mī′krəfāj/ [Gk, mikros + phagein, to eat], a neutrophil capable of ingesting small things such as bacteria. —**microphagic,** adj.

microphallus /-fal′əs/ [Gk, mikros + phallos, penis], an abnormally small penis.

microphthalmos /mī′krəfthal′məs/ [Gk, mikros + ophthalmos, eye], a developmental anomaly characterized by abnormal smallness of one or both eyes. When the condition occurs in the absence of other ocular defects, it is called pure microphthalmos or nanophthalmos. —**microphthalmic,** adj.

micropodia /-pō′dē·ə/ [Gk, mikros + pous, foot], a developmental anomaly characterized by abnormal smallness of the feet. The condition is often associated with

M

other congenital malformations or with bone and skeletal disorders.

microprolactinoma /-prōlak'tinō'mə/, a prolactin-secreting pituitary tumor less than 10 mm in diameter.

microprosopus /mī'krōprō'səpəs, -prəsō' pəs/ [Gk, *mikros* + *prosopon,* face], a fetus having an abnormally small or underdeveloped face.

micropsia /mīkrop'sē·ə/ [Gk, *mikros* + *opsis,* sight], a condition of vision in which a person perceives objects as smaller than they really are.—**microptic,** *adj.*

micropuncture /mī'krōpunk'cher/, **1.** the creation of minute openings by piercing. **2.** in renal physiology, the process by which nephron segments are pierced.

microreentry /-rē·en'trē/ [Gk, *mikros*; L, *re,* again; Fr, *entree,* entry], the reactivation of myocardial tissue by an impulse transmitted along a very small circuit within the conductive tissue of the heart.

microscope /mī'krəskōp'/ [Gk, *mikros,* small, *skopein,* to view], an instrument with lenses for viewing very small objects.

microscopic /mī'krəskop'ik/ [Gk, *mikros* + *skopein,* to look], **1.** pertaining to a microscope. **2.** very small; visible only when magnified and illuminated by a microscope.

microscopic anatomy, the study of the microscopic structure of the tissues and cells.

microscopy /mīkros'kəpē/ [Gk, *mikros* + *skopein,* to look], a technique for observing minute materials using a microscope.

microshock /mī'krəshok/, **1.** shock from an electric current of less than 1 milliampere. It may not be felt. **2.** the passage of current directly into the cardiac tissue.

microsomal enzymes /-sō'məl/, a group of enzymes associated with a certain particulate fraction of liver homogenate that plays a role in the metabolism of many drugs.

microsome /mī'krəsōm/, a fragment of endoplasmic reticulum associated with ribosomes, found in cells that have been homogenized and ultracentrifuged.

microsomia /-sō'mē·ə/ [Gk, *mikros* + *soma,* body], the condition of having an abnormally small and underdeveloped yet otherwise perfectly formed body with normal proportionate relationships of the various parts.

microsphere /mī'krəsfir'/, **1.** a centrosome. **2.** a microscopic globule of radiolabeled material.

microspherocytosis /-sfir'əsītō'sis/, anemia characterized by the presence of microcytes and spherocytes in a peripheral blood film. Spherocytes are red blood cells that are spherical in suspension that lack a central zone of pallor, and whose diameter is reduced on a peripheral blood film.

Microsporida /mī'krōspor'idə/ [Gk, *mikros* + *sporos,* seed], an order of parasitic protozoa found in invertebrates, especially arthropods, in lower vertebrates, and, rarely, in higher vertebrates.

microsporidiosis /mī'krō·spōrid'ē·ō'sis/, infection with protozoa of the order Microsporida, usually seen in immunocompromised patients, usually characterized by diarrhea and wasting.

Microsporum /-spôr'əm/ [Gk, *mikros* + *sporos,* seed], a genus of dermatophytes of the family Moniliaceae. One species is *M. audouinii,* which causes epidemic tinea capitis in children.

microstomia /-stō'mē·ə/ [Gk, *mikros,* small, *stoma,* mouth], the condition of having an abnormally small mouth.

microsurgery /-sur'jərē/ [Gk, *mikros,* small, *cheirourgos,* surgery], surgery that involves dissection and manipulation of minute tissue structures under a microscope.

microsurgical epididymal sperm aspiration (MESA), retrieval of sperm from the epididymis by using microsurgical techniques, done in men with obstructive azoospermia.

microtear /mī'krəter'/, minor damage to soft tissue.

microthermy /-thur'mē/ [Gk, *mikros* + *therme,* heat], the use of heat generated by radio wave conversion in physical therapy.

microthrombus /mī'krōthrom'bəs/ *pl.* **microthrombi** [Gk, *mikros,* small, *thrombos,* lump], a small thrombus located in a capillary or other small blood vessel.

microtia /mīkrō'shī·ə/, underdevelopment or complete absence of the auricle of the ear, with a blind or absent external canal.

microtome /mī'krətōm/ [Gk, *mikros* + *temnein,* to cut], a device that cuts specimens of tissue prepared in paraffin blocks into extremely thin slices for microscopic study.

microtrauma /-trô'mə/, a very slight injury or lesion.

microtuboplasty, the surgical repair of an occluded fallopian tube, performed with micro instruments and a microscope.

microtubule, a hollow cylindric structure that occurs widely within plant and animal cells. Microtubules increase in number during cell division.

microtubule organizing center (MTOC), region of eukaryotic cells such as a centrosome or basal body from which microtubules grow.

microvascular /-vas'kyələr/, pertaining to the portion of the circulatory system that is composed of the capillary network.

microvilli /-vil´ī/ [Gk, *mikros,* small; L, *villus,* shaggy hair], tiny hairlike folds in the plasma membrane that extend from the surface of many absorptive or secretory cells.

microwave [Gk, *mikros;* AS, *wafian,* wave], electromagnetic radiation with a wavelength of 1 mm to 30 cm.

microwave interstitial system /mī´krəwāv/, a microwave-generated hyperthermia system that creates a heat field in certain accessible tumors no more than 2 inches beneath the skin. The treatment can be monitored on a video terminal that shows location of the tumor and heat applicators.

microwave thermography, measurement of temperature through the detection of microwave radiation emitted from heated tissue.

Micruroides /mi´krooroi´dēz/, a genus of venomous coral snakes found in Mexico and the southwestern United States.

Micrurus /mikroo´rus/, a genus of venomous coral snakes, including a species found in the southeastern United States and south into Central America.

micturition reflex /mik´chərish´ən/ [L, *micturire,* to urinate, *reflectere,* to bend back], a normal reaction to a rise in pressure within the bladder, resulting in contraction of the bladder wall and relaxation of the urethral sphincter, allowing urination. Voluntary inhibition normally prevents incontinence; urination follows withdrawal of the inhibition.

micturition syncope [L, *micturire,* to urinate; Gk, *syn,* together, *koptein,* to cut], a temporary LOC that tends to affect some adult males after arising from a reclining posture to urinate in an upright posture. The effect is caused by a brief interruption of blood flow to the brain.

MICU, abbreviation for *medical intensive care unit.*

MID, abbreviation for **minimal infecting dose.**

Midamor, a trademark for a diuretic (amiloride hydrochloride).

midarm muscle circumference, a calculation made by subtracting the triceps skin fold from the midupper arm circumference measurement.

midaxillary line /midak´siler´ē/, an imaginary vertical line that passes midway between the anterior and posterior axillary folds.

midazolam hydrochloride /midaz´əlam/, a short-acting benzodiazepine CNS depressant; a benzodiazepine anxiolytic. It is prescribed for preoperative sedation and impairment of memory of preoperative events, and for conscious sedation before short diagnostic endoscopic or dental procedures.

midbody, 1. the middle of the body, or the midregion of the trunk. 2. a mass of granules that appears in the middle of the spindle during mitotic anaphase.

midclavicular line /mid´kləvik´yŏŏlər/ [AS, *midd;* L, *clavicula,* little key, *linea,* line], in anatomy, an imaginary line that extends downward over the trunk from the midpoint of the clavicle, dividing each side of the anterior chest into two parts.

middle adult [AS, *middel;* L, *adultus,* grown up], an individual in the transitional age span between young adult and elderly, approximately 45 to 65 years of age.

middle cardiac vein, one of the five tributaries of the coronary sinus that drain blood from the capillary bed of the myocardium. It receives tributaries from both ventricles, and ends in the right extremity of the coronary sinus.

middle cerebral artery, the largest of the cerebral arteries and the vessel most commonly affected by CVA.

middle cervical ganglion, a ganglion at the level of the sixth cervical vertebra. Branches from this ganglion pass to spinal nerves C7 to T1, the vertebral artery, and the heart as the middle cardiac nerve.

middle ear, the tympanic cavity with the auditory ossicles contained in an irregular space in the temporal bone. It is separated from the external ear by the tympanic membrane and from the inner ear by the oval window. The auditory (eustachian) tube carries air from the posterior nasopharynx into the middle ear.

middle lobe syndrome, localized atelectasis of the middle lobe of the right lung, characterized by chronic infection, cough, dyspnea, wheezing, and obstructive pneumonitis. Asymptomatic obstruction of the bronchus may occur. The condition arises when the cuff of lymphatic glands that surrounds the middle lobe bronchus becomes enlarged as a result of nonspecific or tuberculous inflammation during childhood.

middle mediastinum, the widest part of the mediastinum, containing the heart, ascending aorta, lower half of the superior vena cava, pulmonary trunk, and phrenic nerves.

middle molecule, any molecule with an atomic mass between 350 and 2000 daltons. These molecules accumulate in the body fluids of patients with uremia.

middle-old, persons from 75 to 84 years of age.

middle sacral artery, a small visceral branch of the abdominal aorta, descending to the fourth and fifth lumbar vertebrae, the sacrum, and the coccyx.

middle suprarenal artery, one of a pair of small visceral branches of the

M

abdominal aorta, arising opposite the superior mesenteric artery and supplying the suprarenal gland.

middle temporal artery, one of the branches of the superficial temporal artery on each side of the head.

middle temporal gyrus [AS, *middel*; L, *tempus*, time; Gk, *gyros*, turn], the middle of three gyri of the temporal area of the surface of the brain. It runs horizontally between the inferior and superior temporal sulci of the temporal lobe.

middle umbilical fold, the fold of peritoneum over the urachal remnant within the abdomen.

midface /mid'fās/, the middle of the face, including the nose, nasion, and glabella.

mid forceps [AS, *midd*; L, *forceps,* pair of tongs], an obstetric operation in which forceps are applied to the baby's head when it has reached the midplane of the mother's pelvis. In some cases such as severe fetal distress, mid forceps may be the most rapid and safest means of delivery.

midgut [AS, *midd* + *guttas*], the central portion of the embryonic alimentary canal, between the foregut and the hindgut. It is connected to the yolk sac during early prenatal development and eventually gives rise to some of the small intestine and part of the large intestine.

midgut loop, a U-shaped loop of intestine that temporarily forms during the period of rapid elongation and rotation of the midgut in embryonic development. It projects into the proximal part of the umbilical cord, to which it is attached via the yolk stalk; with further development, it retracts into the abdomen, rotating further.

midgut volvulus, volvulus neonatorum involving the entire part of the intestines derived from the midgut.

midlife transition, a period between early adulthood and middle adulthood that occurs between 40 and 45 years of age.

midline /mid'līn/ [AS, *midd*; L, *linea,* line], an imaginary line that divides the body into right and left halves.

midoccipital /mid'oksip'itəl/, pertaining to the center of the occiput.

midodrine, a vasopressor used to treat orthostatic hypotension.

midparental height /-pəren'təl/, the average height of both parents at 25 to 45 years of age.

midposition /mid'pəzish'ən/, the end-expiratory or end-tidal level or position of the lung-chest system under any given condition. It determines the functional residual capacity.

Midrin, a trademark for a fixed-combination CNS drug containing an adrenergic (isometheptene mucate), a hypnotic

(dichloralphenazone), and an analgesic (acetaminophen), used in the treatment of tension and vascular headaches.

midstance /mid'stanz/ [AS, *midd*; L, *stare,* to stand], one of the five stages in the stance phase of walking, or gait, directly associated with the period of single-leg support of body weight or the period during which the body advances over the stationary foot.

midsternum /midstur'nəm/ [AS, *midd*; Gk, *sternon,* chest], the body of the sternum.

midstream catch urine specimen [AS, *midd* + *stream*; L, *captere,* to capture], a urine specimen collected during the middle of a flow of urine, after the urinary opening has been carefully cleaned.

midupper arm circumference (MAC), a measurement of the circumference of the arm at a midpoint between the tip of the acromial process of the scapula and the olecranon process of the ulna.

midwife [AS, *midd* + *wif*], **1.** in traditional use, a (female) person who assists women in childbirth. **2.** according to the International Confederation of Midwives, World Health Organization, and Federation of International Gynecologists and Obstetricians, "a person who, having been regularly admitted to a midwifery educational program fully recognized in the country in which it is located, has successfully completed the prescribed course of studies in midwifery and has acquired the requisite qualifications to be registered and/or legally licensed to practice midwifery." **3.** a nurse midwife or Certified Nurse Midwife.

midwifery /mid'wif(ə)rē/ [AS, *midd* + *wif*], the employment of a person who is qualified by special training and experience to assist a woman in childbirth.

MIF, abbreviation for *macrophage inhibition factor.*

mifepristone /mif'əpris'tōn/, an antiprogestin used with misoprostol or other prostaglandins that induces abortion if taken within the first 7 weeks of pregnancy.

MIF test, abbreviation for *migration inhibitory factor test.*

miglitol, an oral hypoglycemic used to treat type 2 DM.

miglustat, a rarely used miscellaneous agent used to treat adults with mild to moderate type 1 Gaucher disease.

migraine /mī'grān/ [Gk, *hemi,* half, *kranion,* skull], a recurring headache characterized by unilateral onset, severe throbbing pain, photophobia, phonophobia, and autonomic disturbances during the acute phase, which may last for hours or days. The disorder occurs more frequently in women than in men, and a predisposition to migraine may be inherited. The exact mechanism responsible for the disorder is not known, but the head pain may be related to dilation of extracranial blood vessels, which may be the result of chemical changes that cause spasms of intracranial vessels. Allergic reactions, excess carbohydrates, iodine-rich foods, alcohol, bright lights, or loud noises may trigger attacks, which often occur during a period of relaxation after physical or psychic stress.

migrainous cranial neuralgia /mī'grānəs, mīgrā'nəs/ [Gk, *hemi,* half, *kranion,* skull; L, *osus,* having], a variant of migraine most common in middle-aged men, characterized by closely spaced episodes of excruciating throbbing unilateral headaches often accompanied by dilation of temporal blood vessels, flushing, sweating, lacrimation, rhinorrhea, ptosis, and facial edema. Repeated episodes usually occur in clusters within a few days or weeks and may be followed by a relatively long remission period.

migrating phlebitis /mī'grāting/ [L, *migrare,* to wander; Gk, *phleps,* vein, *itis,* inflammation], a form of phlebitis characterized by inflammation in one part of a vein and, after remission, in another part of the vein.

migration /mīgrā'shən/ [L, *migrare,* to wander], the passage of the ovum from the ovary into a fallopian tube and then into the uterus.

migratory polyarthritis /mī'grətôr'ē/, arthritis that progressively affects a number of joints and finally settles in one or more. It occurs in persons with gonorrhea and develops a few days to a few weeks after the onset of gonorrheal urethritis. Large joints are most affected.

migratory thrombophlebitis, an abnormal condition in which multiple thromboses appear in both superficial and deep veins. It may be associated with malignancy, especially carcinoma of the pancreas, often preceding other evidence of cancer by several months.

Mikulicz's syndrome /mik'yōolich'ēz/ [Johann von Mikulicz-Radecki, Polish surgeon, 1850–1905], an abnormal bilateral enlargement of the salivary and lacrimal glands found in a variety of diseases, including leukemia, TB, and sarcoidosis.

mild [AS, *milde,* soft], gentle, subtle, or of low intensity such as a mild infection.

mildew /mil'dyōo/, a visible growth of any of numerous species of saprophytic fungi.

milia neonatorum [L, *milium,* millet; Gk, *neo,* new; L, *natus,* born], a nonpathologic dermatologic condition characterized by minute epidermal cysts consisting of keratinous debris that occur on the face and occasionally on the trunk of the newborn.

miliaria /mil'ē·er'ē·ə/ [L, *milium,* millet], minute vesicles and papules, often with surrounding erythema, caused by occlusion of sweat ducts during times of exposure to heat and high humidity.

miliaria profunda, the deepest type of miliaria, with occlusion of the ducts at the dermoepidermal junction. It occurs following severe, recurrent miliaria rubra and is seen primarily in hot, humid climates. Because large numbers of sweat glands are inactivated, it can lead to heat intolerance or heat stress, as in tropical anhidrotic asthenia.

miliary /mil'ē·er'ē/ [L, *milium,* millet], describing a condition marked by the appearance of very small lesions the size of millet seeds.

miliary carcinosis, a condition characterized by numerous cancerous nodules resembling miliary tubercles.

miliary fever [L, *milium,* millet, *febris*], an inflammatory skin eruption caused by sweat retention.

miliary tuberculosis, extensive dissemination by the bloodstream of tubercle bacilli. In children it is associated with high fever, night sweats, and often meningitis, pleural effusions, or peritonitis. A similar illness may occur in adults but with a less abrupt onset and occasionally with weeks or months of nonspecific symptoms such as weight loss, weakness, and low-grade fever. Multiple small opacities resembling millet seeds may be evident on chest x-ray films.

milieu /milyœ', milyōō'/ *pl.* **milieus, milieux** [Fr, middle], the environment, surroundings, or setting.

milieu extérieur /ekstærē·œr'/, the external or physical surroundings of an organism, including the social environment, especially the home, school, and recreational facilities, which play a dominant role in personality development.

milieu intérieur /äNterē·œr'/, the basic concept in physiology that multicellular organisms exist in an aqueous internal environment composed of the blood, lymph, and interstitial fluid that bathes all cells and provides a medium for the elementary exchange of nutrients and waste material. All fundamental processes necessary for the maintenance and life of the tissue elements depend on the stability and balance of this environment.

milieu therapy[1], a type of psychotherapy model in which the total environment is used in treating mental and behavioral disorders. It is primarily conducted in

M

a hospital or other institutional setting, where the entire facility acts as a therapeutic community. The emphasis is on providing pleasant physical surroundings, structured activities, and a stable social environment where behavior modification and personal growth are promoted through patient-group interaction; staff support and understanding; and a total, humanistic approach.

milieu therapy², a nursing intervention from the Nursing Interventions Classification (NIC) defined as use of people, resources, and events in the patient's immediate environment to promote optimal psychosocial functioning.

military antishock trousers (MAST) [L, *ante,* opposed; Fr, *choc;* Gael, *triubhas,* trews], a garment designed to produce pressure on the lower part of the body, thereby preventing the pooling of blood in the legs and abdomen. The trousers are used to combat shock and stabilize fractures, promote hemostasis, increase peripheral vascular resistance, and permit autotransfusion of small amounts of blood. They also are used in emergencies in the treatment of hemorrhagic shock.

military attitude, in obstetrics, a fetal position in which the fetal head is not flexed and the cervical spine is in extension.

milium /mil′ē-əm/ *pl.* **milia** [L, millet], a minute white cyst of the epidermis caused by obstruction of hair follicles and eccrine sweat glands. One variety is seen in newborns and disappears within a few weeks. Another type is found primarily on the faces of middle-aged women.

milk [AS, *meoluc*], a liquid secreted by the mammary glands or udders of mammalian animals that suckle their young. Milk is a basic food containing carbohydrate (in the form of lactose); protein (mainly casein, with small amounts of lactalbumin and lactoglobulin); suspended fat; the minerals calcium and phosphorus; and the vitamins A, riboflavin, niacin, thiamine, and, when the milk is fortified, vitamin D.

milk-alkali syndrome, a condition of alkalosis caused by the excessive ingestion of milk, antacid medications containing calcium, or other sources of absorbable alkaline substances. The condition results in hypercalcemia, hypocalciuria, and calcium deposits in the kidneys and other tissues. The patient may experience symptoms of nausea, headache, weakness, and kidney damage.

milk ejection reflex, a normal reflex in a lactating woman elicited by tactile stimulation of the nipple, resulting in release of milk from the glands of the breast.

milker's nodule, a smooth brownish-red papilloma of the fingers or palm that

begins as a macule and progresses through a vesicular stage to become a nodule. The disease is acquired from pustular lesions on the udder of a cow infected with poxvirus.

milk fever *nontechnical.* postpartum fever that begins with the onset of lactation. Continued high readings above 100.4° F may indicate infection.

milk globule, a spheric droplet of fat in milk that tends to separate out as cream.

milking, a procedure used to express the contents of a duct or tube to test for tenderness or to obtain a specimen for study. The examiner compresses the structure with a finger and moves the finger firmly along the duct or tube to its opening.

Milkman's syndrome [Louis A. Milkman, American radiologist, 1895–1951], a form of osteomalacia characterized by the appearance on x-ray film of multiple bilateral, symmetric stripes in hypocalcified long bones and in the pelvis and scapula. The stripes indicate pseudofractures.

milk of magnesia, a laxative and antacid containing magnesium hydroxide used to relieve constipation and less commonly, acid indigestion.

milk thistle, a herb used to protect against alcoholic cirrhosis and hepatitis and as an antiinflammatory. Standardized extracts have shown some efficacy for cirrhosis in clinical trials.

Miller-Abbott tube [Thomas G. Miller, American physician, 1886–1981; William O. Abbott, American physician, 1902–1943], a long, small-caliber double-lumen catheter once widely used in intestinal intubation for decompression. One lumen ends in a perforated metal tip, and the other in a collapsible balloon. These tubes are radiopaque and can therefore be seen on a radiogram.

Miller's syndrome /mil′ər/ [Marvin Miller, American pediatrician, 20th century], a syndrome of extensive facial and limb defects, characterized by malar hypoplasia, downslanting palpebral fissures, micrognathia, cleft lip and palate, cup-shaped ears, lower lid ectropion, postaxial limb deficiencies, and syndactyly.

milliampere (mA) /mil′ēam′pir/ [L, *mille,* thousand; Andre Ampere], a unit of electric current that is one thousandth of an ampere.

milliampere-second (mAs), a measure of electric charge obtained by multiplying the electric current in milliamperes by the time in seconds.

millicoulomb (mC) /-kyōō′lōm/ [L, *mille,* thousand; Charles A. de Coulomb], a unit of electric charge that is one thousandth of a coulomb.

millicurie (mCi) /-kŏŏr′ē/ [L, *mille,* thousand; Marie Curie], a unit of radioactivity equal to one thousandth of a curie, or 3.70 × 10[7] disintegrations per second.

milliequivalent (mEq) /-ikwiv'ələnt/ [L, *mille* + *aequus*, equal, *valere*, to be strong], **1.** the number of grams of solute dissolved in 1 mL of a normal (1 N) solution. **2.** one thousandth of a gram equivalent.

milliequivalent per liter (mEq/L), one thousandth of 1 equivalent of a specific substance dissolved in 1 L of solution or plasma.

milligram (mg) /-gram/ [L, *mille*; Fr, *gramme*, small weight], a metric unit of mass equal to one thousandth (10^{-3}) of a gram.

milliliter (mL) /-lē'tər/ [L, *mille*; Fr, *litre*, a measure], a metric unit of volume that is one thousandth (10^{-3}) of a liter, or 1 cm³.

millimeter (mm) /-mē'tər/, a metric unit of length equal to one thousandth (10^{-3}) of a meter.

millimole (mmol, mM) /-mōl/ [L, *mille* + *moles*, mass], a unit of metric measurement that is equal to one thousandth (10^{-3}) of a mole.

Millin operation, a formerly common method of radical retropubic prostatectomy.

milliosmol /mil'ē·oz'mōl/, one thousandth of an osmole. —**milliosmolar,** *adj.*

millipede /mil'ipēd'/ [L, *mille* + *pes*, foot], a many-legged wormlike arthropod. Certain species squirt irritating fluids that may cause dermatitis.

millirad (mrad) /-rad/, a unit of absorbed dose of ionizing radiation equal to one thousandth of a rad.

millirem (mrem), a unit of ionizing radiation dose equal to one thousandth of a rem.

milliroentgen (mr, mR) /mil'irent'gən, -jən/ [L, *mille*, thousand; Wilhelm K. Roentgen], a unit of radiation equal to one thousandth of a roentgen.

millisecond (msec) /-sek'ənd/ [L, *mille,* thousand; ME, *seconde,* small part], one thousandth of a second.

millivolt (mV, mv) /-vōlt/ [L, *mille,* thousand; Alessandro Volta], a unit of electromotive force equal to one thousandth of a volt.

Milroy's disease /mil'roiz/ [William Forsyth Milroy, American physician, 1855–1942], congenital hereditary lymphedema of the legs caused by chronic lymphatic obstruction, sometimes involving additional areas, including the arms, trunk, and face.

Miltown, a trademark for a sedative (meprobamate).

Milwaukee brace /milwô'kē/ [Milwaukee, Wisconsin; OFr, *bracier,* to embrace], an orthotic device that helps immobilize the torso and neck of a patient in the treatment or correction of scoliosis, lordosis, or kyphosis. It is usually constructed of strong but light metal and fiberglass bars lined with rubber to protect against abrasion. The bars hold the trunk and neck erect while controlling cervical flexion and hip movements.

mimicry /mim'ikrē/ [Gk, *mimetikos,* imitation], **1.** the effort of one species or organism to resemble another to obtain an offensive or defensive advantage. **2.** an autonomic nervous system phenomenon in which facial expressions may be the unwilled and largely unconscious expression of feelings and ideas.

mimic spasm /mim'ik/ [Gk, *mimetikos,* imitative, *spasmos,* spasm], involuntary stereotyped movements of a small group of muscles such as of the face. The spasm is usually psychogenic and may be aggravated by stress or anxiety but is generally controllable.

min, 1. abbreviation for **minim. 2.** abbreviation for *minute.*

Minamata disease /min'əmä'tə/, a severe degenerative neurologic disorder caused by the ingestion of seed grain heated with alkyl compounds of mercury or seafood taken from waters polluted with industrial wastes contaminated with soluble mercuric salts.

mind [AS, *gemynd*], **1.** the part of the brain that is the seat of mental activity and that enables one to know, reason, understand, remember, think, feel, react to, and adapt to external and internal stimuli. **2.** the totality of all conscious and unconscious processes of the individual that influence and direct mental and physical behavior. **3.** the faculty of the intellect or understanding, in contrast to emotion and will.

mind-body medicine, a holistic approach to medicine that takes into account the effect of the mind on physical processes, including the effects of psychosocial stressors and conditioning, particularly as they affect the immune system. Many of the therapeutic techniques used have as their purpose increasing the body's natural resistance to disease by managing the stressors.

mindfulness meditation, a technique of meditation in which distracting thoughts and feelings are not ignored but are rather acknowledged and observed nonjudgmentally as they arise to create a detachment from them and gain insight and awareness.

mineral /min'ərəl/ [L, *minera,* mine], **1.** an inorganic substance occurring naturally in the earth's crust, having a characteristic chemical composition and (usually) crystalline structure. **2.** in nutrition, a compound containing a metal,

M

nonmetal, radical, or phosphate that is needed for proper body function and maintenance of health. The needed substance is usually ingested as a part of such a compound, such as table salt (sodium chloride), instead of as a free element.

mineralization /-īzā'shən/ [L, *minera*; Gk, *izein*, to cause], the addition of any mineral to the body.

mineralocorticoid /min'əral'ōkôr'tikoid/ [L, *minera* + *cortex*, bark; Gk, *eidos*, form], a hormone, secreted by the adrenal cortex, that maintains normal blood volume, promotes sodium and water retention, and increases urinary excretion of potassium and hydrogen ions. Trauma and stress increase mineralocorticoid secretion.

mineral oil, a laxative, stool softener, emollient, and pharmaceutical aid used as a solvent. It is prescribed to prevent constipation, to treat mild constipation, to prepare the bowel for surgery or examination, and to act as a solvent for various preparations.

miner's elbow [L, *minera*; AS, *elboga*], an inflammation of the olecranon bursa, caused by resting the weight of the body on the elbow, as in some coal mining activities. The condition is sometimes seen in schoolchildren who lean on their elbows.

Minerva cast /minur'və/ [L, *Minerva*, Roman goddess of wisdom; ONorse, *kasta*], an orthopedic cast applied to the trunk and head, with spaces cut out for the face and ears. It is used to immobilize the head and part of the trunk in the treatment of torticollis, cervical and thoracic injuries, and cervical spinal infections.

minim (m, min) /min'im/ [L, *minimus*, smallest], a measurement of volume in the apothecaries' system, originally one drop (of water). It is now standardized to 0.06 mL; 60 minims equals 1 fluid dram.

minimal bactericidal concentration, the lowest concentration of drug that results in a 99.9% reduction in the initial bacterial density.

minimal care unit /min'iməl/ [L, *minimus*, smallest], a unit for the treatment of inpatients who are ambulatory and able to meet many of their own daily living needs but require minimal nursing care.

minimal change disease, a kidney disorder characterized by subtle changes in renal function, including albuminuria and presence of lipid droplets in the proximal tubules. It mainly affects small children but also occurs in adults with idiopathic nephrotic syndrome. It may or may not progress to glomerulonephritis.

minimal infecting dose (MID), the smallest amount of infective material that usually produces infection.

minimal inhibitory concentration (MIC), the lowest concentration of an antibiotic medication in the blood that is effective against a bacterial infection.

minimally invasive surgery, surgery done with only a small incision or no incision at all, such as through a cannula with a laparoscope or endoscope.

minimal occlusive volume (MOV), the volume to which an endotracheal or tracheostomy tube cuff must be inflated to obliterate an air leak during the inspiratory phase of ventilation.

Mini-Mental State Examination (MMSE), a brief psychologic test designed to differentiate among dementia, psychosis, and affective disorders.

minimization /min'imīzā'shən/ [L, *minimum*, smallest; Gk, *izein*, to cause], in psychology, cognitive distortion in which the effects of one's behavior are underestimated.

minimum alveolar concentration (MAC) /min'iməm/, the smallest concentration of a gas that is measured in the alveoli of the lungs.

minimum daily requirement (MDR) [L, *minimum*; OE, *daeglie*; L, *requirere*, to seek], the daily human requirement of nutrients for health and for prevention of a deficiency disease. The figures, established by the U.S. Food and Drug Administration, are generally extrapolated from experimental animal studies and include an added margin for safety.

minimum dose [L, *minimum*, smallest; Gk, *dosis*, giving], the smallest amount of a drug or other substance needed to produce a desired or specified effect.

minimum hemagglutinating dose, the smallest amount of hemagglutinating agent that causes a complete hemagglutinating reaction in a standard volume of RBCs.

minimum hemolytic dose (MHD), the smallest amount of a reagent that produces complete lysis of a specified amount of RBCs.

minimum lethal dose (MLD) [L, *minimum*, smallest; *lethum*, death; Gk, *dosis*, giving], the smallest dose of a drug, relative to body weight, that will kill an experimental animal. The MLD may vary with the species of animal tested.

Minipress, a trademark for an antihypertensive (prazosin hydrochloride), an alpha₁ receptor blocking agent.

miniprotein /min'iprō'tēn/, a protein that has been reduced to half its natural size without loss of its ability to function.

Minnesota Multiphasic Personality Inventory (MMPI), a commonly used psychologic test used clinically for evaluating personality and detecting various disorders.

Minocin, a trademark for an antibacterial (minocycline hydrochloride).

minocycline hydrochloride /min′əsī′klēn/, a tetracycline antibiotic prescribed for infections caused by gram-positive and gram-negative bacteria, rickettsiae, anthrax, and other microorganisms.

minor /mī′nər/ [L, smaller], in law, a person not of legal age; a person beneath the age of majority.

minor arterial circle of iris, the small artery encircling the outer circumference of the iris.

minor connector, a device that links the major connector or base of a removable partial denture to other denture units such as rests and direct and indirect retainers.

minor duodenal papilla, the entrance into the duodenum for the accessory pancreatic duct and the junction of the foregut and midgut. It is just below the major duodenal papilla.

minor hysteria [Gk, *hystera,* womb], a mild disorder that may be expressed in emotional outbursts, repressed anxieties, or conversion of unconscious conflicts into physical symptoms.

minor surgery, surgical procedure for minor problems or injuries that are not considered life-threatening or hazardous.

minoxidil /mīnok′sidil/, a vasodilator prescribed in the treatment of severe refractory hypertension and as a topical solution for the treatment of androgenic alopecia in both males and females.

mint, a herb used as a flavoring and medicinally for GI disorders. Peppermint oil may exert beneficial effects in irritable bowel syndrome.

Mintezol, a trademark for an anthelmintic (thiabendazole).

minute ventilation /min′it/ [L, *minus,* very small], the total lung ventilation per minute, the product of tidal volume and respiration rate. It is measured by expired gas collection for a period of 1 to 3 minutes.

miosis /mī·ō′sis/ [Gk, *meiosis,* becoming less], **1.** contraction of the sphincter muscle of the iris, causing the pupil to become smaller. **2.** an abnormal condition characterized by excessive constriction of the sphincter muscle of the iris, resulting in pinpoint pupils.

miotic /mē·ot′ik/, **1.** pertaining to miosis. **2.** causing constriction of the pupil of the eye. **3.** any substance or pharmaceutical that causes constriction of the pupil of the eye. Such agents are used in the treatment of glaucoma.

MIP, **1.** abbreviation for **maximum inspiratory pressure. 2.** abbreviation for **maximum intensity projection.**

miracidium /mir′əsid′ē·əm/ *pl.* **miracidia** [Gk, *meirakidion,* youthfulness], the ciliated larva of a parasitic trematode that hatches from an egg and can survive only by penetrating and further developing within a host snail.

mirage /miräzh′/ [L, *mirari,* to look at], an optical illusion caused by the refraction of light through air layers of different temperatures, such as the illusionary sheets of water that appear to shimmer over stretches of hot sand and pavement.

MIRL, abbreviation for *membrane inhibitor of reactive lysis.*

mirror image /mir′ər/ [L, *mirare,* to look at + *imago*], **1.** an image formed by a reflection in a plane mirror. **2.** a kind of reversed asymmetry of characteristics often found in sets of monozygotic twins. **3.** chemical molecules with the same composition but with asymmetric arrangement of the atoms.

mirror speech [L, *mirari,* to look at; AS, *spaec,* speech], an abnormal manner of speaking characterized by the reversal of the order of syllables in a word.

mirtazapine, an antidepressant prescribed to treat depression, dysthymic disorder, and bipolar disorder with either depression or agitation.

miscible /mis′ibəl/ [L, *miscere,* to mix], able to be mixed or blended with another substance.

misdemeanor /mis′dəmē′nər/ [AS, *missan,* to miss; ME, *demenen,* conduct], in criminal law, an offense that is considered less serious than a felony and carries a lesser penalty, usually a fine or imprisonment for less than 1 year.

misfeasance /misfē′zəns/ [AS, *missan,* to miss; L, *facere,* to make], an improper performance of a lawful act, especially in a way that may cause damage or injury.

Mishel, Merle H., a nursing theorist who developed the Uncertainty in Illness Theory, which asserts that uncertainty is initially a neutral cognitive state representing the inability of the patient with chronic or life-threatening conditions to interpret the outcome of events related to the illness and that nursing interventions must help patients adapt and cope productively with this uncertainty, integrating it into their lives and improving quality of life.

misogamy /misog′əmē/ [Gk, *misein,* to hate, *gamos,* marriage], an aversion to marriage.—**misogamic,** **misogamous,** *adj.,* **misogamist,** *n.*

misogyny /misoj′inē/ [Gk, *misein,* to hate, *gyne,* women], an aversion to women. —**misogynist,** *n.,* **misogynistic,** *adj.*

M

misopedia /mis′ōpē′dē-ə/ [Gk, *misein* + *pais,* children], an aversion to children. —**misopedic,** *adj.,* **misopedist,** *n.*

missed abortion [OE, *missan,* to be lacking; L, *ab,* away from, *oriri,* to be born], a condition in which a dead immature embryo or fetus is not expelled from the uterus for 2 months or more. The uterus diminishes in size, and symptoms of pregnancy abate; maternal infection and blood clotting disorders may follow.

missed period [OE, *missan,* to be lacking; Gk, *peri* + *hodos,* way], an unexplained interruption in the menstrual cycle.

missile fracture [L, *mittere,* to throw], a penetration fracture caused by a projectile, such as a bullet or a piece of shrapnel.

mistura /mistyōō′trə/ [L, mixture], any of a number of mixtures of drugs, usually containing suspensions of insoluble substances intended for internal use.

mite /mīt/ [AS], a minute arachnid with a flat, almost transparent body and four pairs of legs. Many species of these relatives of ticks and spiders are parasitic, including the chigger and *Sarcoptes scabiei,* which cause localized pruritus and inflammation.

Mithracin, a trademark for an antineoplastic (plicamycin).

mitleiden /mit′līdən/ [Ger, *mit,* with, *leiden,* to suffer], psychosomatic symptoms sometimes experienced by expectant fathers.

mitochondrion /mī′tōkon′drē-on/ *pl.* **mitochondria** [Gk, *mitos,* thread, *chondros,* cartilage], a rodlike, threadlike, or granular organelle that functions in aerobic respiration and occurs in varying numbers in all eukaryotic cells except mature erythrocytes. Mitochondria provide the principal source of cellular energy through oxidative phosphorylation and adenosine triphosphate synthesis. They also contain the enzymes involved with electron transport and the citric acid and fatty acid cycles.—**mitochondrial,** *adj.*

mitogen /mī′təjən, mit′-/ [Gk, *mitos* + *genein,* to produce], an agent that triggers mitosis.—**mitogenic,** *adj.*

mitogenesia /mī′tōjənē′zhə/ [Gk, *mitos* + *genein,* to produce], production resulting from mitosis.

mitogenesis /mī′tōjen′əsis/, the induction of mitosis in a cell.—**mitogenetic,** *adj.*

mitogenetic radiation /-jənet′ik/, the force or specific energy that is supposedly given off by cells undergoing division.

mitogenic factor /-jen′ik/, a lymphokine that is released from activated T lymphocytes and that stimulates the production of normal unsensitized lymphocytes.

mitome /mī′tōm/, the reticular network sometimes observed within the cytoplasm and nucleoplasm of fixed cells.

mitomycin /mī′təmī′sin/, an antineoplastic antibiotic prescribed in the treatment of malignant neoplastic diseases, including disseminated adenocarcinoma of the stomach and pancreas, bladder cancer, and colon cancer.

mitosis /mītō′sis, mit-/ [Gk, *mitos,* thread], a type of cell division that occurs in somatic cells and results in the formation of two genetically identical daughter cells containing the diploid number of chromosomes characteristic of the species. Mitosis is the process by which the body produces new cells for both growth and repair of injured tissue.—**mitotic,** *adj.*

mitotane /mī′tətān/, an antineoplastic that destroys normal and neoplastic adrenal cortical cells. It is prescribed in the treatment of carcinoma of the adrenal cortex and has an unlabeled use for treating Cushing's syndrome.

mitotic figure [Gk, *mitos;* L, *figura,* form], any chromosome or chromosome aggregation during any of the stages of mitosis.

mitotic index, the number of cells per unit (usually 1000 cells) undergoing mitosis during a given time. The ratio is used primarily as an estimation of the rate of tissue growth.

mitoxantrone, a synthetic antineoplastic antibiotic. It is prescribed in combination with other approved drugs in the initial treatment of acute nonlymphocytic leukemia in adults, and has activity against other leukemias, lymphoma, and breast cancer.

mitral /mī′trəl/ [L, *mitra,* turban], **1.** pertaining to the mitral valve of the heart. **2.** shaped like a miter.

mitral atresia, a congenital absence of the mitral valve associated with transposition of the great vessels or hypoplastic left heart syndrome.

mitral commissurotomy [L, *mitra,* turban, *commissura,* joining together; Gk, *temnein,* to cut], a closed-heart surgical procedure in which the mitral valve is divided at the junction of its cusps for the treatment of mitral valve stenosis.

mitral gradient, the difference in pressure in the left atrium and left ventricle during diastole.

mitral murmur [L, *mitra,* turban, *murmur,* humming], a heart murmur caused by a defective mitral valve.

mitral regurgitation, a backflow of blood from the left ventricle into the left atrium in systole across a diseased mitral valve. The condition may result from congenital valve abnormalities, rheumatic fever, mitral valve prolapse, endocardial fibroelastosis, myocarditis, myocardiopathy, or dilation of the left ventricle as a result of severe anemia. Symptoms include dyspnea, fatigue, intolerance of exercise, systolic murmur, and heart palpitations. CHF may ultimately occur.

mitral valve, a bicuspid valve situated between the left atrium and the left ventricle; the only valve with two, rather than three, cusps. The mitral valve allows blood to flow from the left atrium into the left ventricle but prevents blood from flowing back into the atrium. Ventricular contraction in systole forces the blood against the valve, closing the two cusps and ensuring the flow of blood from the ventricle into the aorta.

mitral valve prolapse (MVP) syndrome, protrusion of one or both cusps of the mitral valve back into the left atrium during ventricular systole.

mitral valve stenosis, an obstructive lesion in the mitral valve caused by adhesions on the leaflets of the valve, usually the result of recurrent episodes of rheumatic endocarditis or age-related calcification of the valve leaflets. Hypertrophy of the left atrium develops and may be followed by right-sided heart failure and pulmonary edema.

mittelschmerz /mit′əlshmerts/ [Ger, *mitte,* middle, *Schmerz,* pain], abdominal pain in the region of an ovary during ovulation, which usually occurs midway through the menstrual cycle. Present in many women, mittelschmerz is useful for identifying ovulation, thus pinpointing the fertile period of the cycle.

Mittendorf's dot, an eye anomaly characterized by the presence of a small, dense, floating opacity behind the posterior lens capsule. It is a remnant of the hyaloid artery that was present in the eye during embryonic development. The object usually does not affect vision.

mivacurium, a nondepolarizing neuromuscular blocker used to facilitate endotracheal intubation and skeletal muscle relaxation during mechanical ventilation, surgery, or general anesthesia.

mixed anxiety-depressive disorder, a mental disorder characterized by symptoms of depression and of anxiety, but not meeting the full criteria for either a depressive disorder or an anxiety disorder.

mixed cell malignant lymphoma [L, *miscere,* to mix], a lymphoid neoplasm containing lymphocytes and histiocytes (macrophages).

mixed cell sarcoma, a tumor consisting of two or more cellular elements, excluding fibrous tissue.

mixed connective tissue disease (MCTD), a systemic disease characterized by the combined symptoms of various collagen diseases such as synovitis, polymyositis, scleroderma, and SLE.

mixed culture [L, *miscere,* to mix, *colere,* to cultivate], a laboratory culture that contains two or more different strains of organisms.

mixed dentition, dentition containing both deciduous and secondary teeth. It usually occurs between 6 and 13 years of age.

mixed dust pneumoconiosis, pneumoconiosis that is caused by more than one type of dust.

mixed glioma, a tumor, composed of glial cells, that contains more than one kind of cell, the most common being nonneural cells of ectodermal origin.

mixed hearing loss, hearing loss that is both conductive and sensorineural in nature.

mixed infection, an infection by several microorganisms, as in some abscesses, pneumonia, and infections of wounds. Numerous combinations of bacteria, viruses, and fungi may be involved.

mixed leukemia, a malignancy of blood-forming tissues characterized by the proliferation of more than one predominant cell line.

mixed lymphocyte culture (MLC) reaction, an assay of the function of T cells. It is used primarily for histocompatibility testing before grafting.

mixed neoplasm [L, *miscere,* to mix; Gk, *neos,* new, *plasma,* something formed], a tumor or growth involving two germinal layers of tissue.

mixed nerve [L, *miscere,* to mix + *nervus*], a nerve that contains both sensory and motor fibers.

mixed receptive-expressive language disorder, a communication disorder involving both the expression and the comprehension of language, either spoken or signed. Patients have difficulties with language production and also have trouble understanding words, sentences, or specific types of words.

mixed sleep apnea, a condition marked by signs and symptoms of both central sleep apnea and obstructive sleep apnea.

mixed triglyceride breath test, a breath test for pancreatic function, in which a mixture of synthetic triglycerides labeled with carbon-13 is administered to the fasting patient and levels of labeled carbon dioxide in the breath are subsequently measured at regular time intervals. Excessively low carbon dioxide indicates inadequate pancreatic lipase in the intestine.

mixed tumor, a growth composed of more than one kind of neoplastic tissue.

M

mixed vaccine, an immunizing preparation that protects against more than one kind of pathogen, such as the diphtheria, tetanus, and pertussis vaccine.

mixed venous blood, blood that is composed of the venous blood from the heart and all systemic tissues in proportion to their venous returns. In the absence of abnormalities, mixed venous blood is present in the main pulmonary artery.

mixture /miks'chər/ [L, *miscere*, to mix], **1.** a substance composed of ingredients that are not chemically combined and do not necessarily occur in a fixed proportion. **2.** in pharmacology, a liquid containing one or more medications in suspension. The proportions of the ingredients are specific to each mixture.

mL, abbreviation for **milliliter.**

MLC, abbreviation for *mixed lymphocyte culture.*

MLD, abbreviation for **minimum lethal dose.**

MLT, abbreviation for **medical laboratory technician.**

MLVA, abbreviation for **multiple-locus variable number of tandem repeat analysis.**

mm, abbreviation for **millimeter.**

mM, abbreviation for **millimolar.**

mm³, abbreviation for **cubic millimeter.**

MMFR, abbreviation for **maximal mid-expiratory flow rate.**

MMIH syndrome, abbreviation for *megacystis-microcolon-intestinal hypoperistalsis syndrome.*

M-mode, motion modulation in diagnostic ultrasonography. It is a variation of B-mode ultrasound used in ECHO.

mmol, abbreviation for **millimole.**

MMPI, abbreviation for **Minnesota Multiphasic Personality Inventory.**

MMR, abbreviation for **measles, mumps, and rubella virus vaccine live.**

MMWR, abbreviation for *Morbidity and Mortality Weekly Report.*

Mn, symbol for the element **manganese.**

mnemonics [Gk, *mnemonikos*], a system of memory training that links a new concept or image with one already established in the memory, such as associating the numbers of a combination lock with a birthday or telephone number.

MNL, abbreviation for **mononuclear leukocyte.**

Mo, symbol for the element **molybdenum.**

Moban, a trademark for an antipsychotic agent (molindone hydrochloride).

mobile arm support (MAS) /mō'bəl, mōbēl'/, a forearm support device that enables people with upper extremity disabilities to fulfill some ADL, by helping to move the hand into position for self-feeding. It may also be used as a training device and may be mounted on a wheelchair.

mobile unit, an easily transportable radiography unit designed for use outside a radiology department.

mobility¹ /mōbil'itē/ [L, *mobilis*, movable], the velocity a particle or ion attains for a given applied voltage; a relative measure of how quickly an ion may move in an electric field.

mobility², a nursing outcome from the Nursing Outcomes Classification (NOC) defined as the ability to move purposefully in one's own environment independently with or without an assistive device.

Mobitz I heart block /mō'bits/ [Woldemar Mobitz, German physician, 1889–1951; AS, *hoerte*, heart; Fr, *bloc*, block], second-degree or partial atrioventricular (AV) block in which the P-R interval increases progressively until the propagation of an atrial impulse to the ventricles does not occur. Mobitz I heart block is caused by abnormal conduction of the cardiac impulse in the AV node and may be precipitated by increased vagal tone, AV nodal ischemia, or digitalis therapy.

Mobitz II heart block, second-degree or partial atrioventricular block, characterized by the sudden nonconduction of an atrial impulse and a periodic dropped beat without prior or subsequent lengthening of the P-R interval. This kind of block usually results from bilateral impaired conduction in the bundle branches. It may be caused by anterior MI, myocarditis, drug toxicity, electrolyte disturbances, rheumatoid nodules, and various degenerative diseases.

Möbius' syndrome /mē'bē·əs/ [Paul J. Möbius, German neurologist, 1853–1902], a rare developmental disorder characterized by congenital bilateral facial palsy usually associated with oculomotor or other neurologic dysfunctions, speech disorders, and various anomalies of the extremities.

moccasin /mok'äsin/, any of several species of snakes of the genus *Agkistrodon*.

Moctanin, a trademark for a gallstone-dissolving agent (monooctanoin).

modafinil, a cerebral stimulant used to treat narcolepsy.

modality /mōdal'itē/, **1.** the method of application of a therapeutic agent or regimen. **2.** a sensory entity, such as the sense of vision or taste.

mode /mōd/ [L, *modus*, measure], a value or term in a set of data that occurs more frequently than other values or terms.

model /mod'əl/ [L, *modulus*, small measure], in nursing research, a symbolic representation of the interrelations exhibited by a phenomenon within a system or a process. The model is presented as a conceptual framework or a theory that explains a phenomenon and allows predictions to be made about a patient or a process.

Model HMO Act, a comprehensive health maintenance organization (HMO) statute adopted by several states. It requires that enrollees be entitled to receive copies of individual and group contracts and documented evidence of coverage describing the essential services and features of the HMO. It also requires filing of a premium rate schedule or method used to determine rates and establishment of a grievance procedure to resolve enrollee complaints.

modeling /mod'əling/, a technique used in behavior therapy in which a person learns a desired response by observing and imitating the behavior.

Modeling and Role Modeling, a theory developed by the nursing theorists Helen C. Erickson, Evelyn M. Tomlin, and Mary Ann P. Swain. Their book, *Modeling and Role Modeling: A Theory and Paradigm for Nursing,* was published in 1983. The term *modeling* refers to the development of an understanding of the client's world. Role modeling is the nursing intervention, or nurturance, that requires unconditional acceptance. Role modeling provides a framework for understanding the way clients structure their world. Erickson, Tomlin, and Swain view nursing as a self-care model based on the client's perception of the world and adaptations to stressors.

moderator band /mod'ərā'tər/ [L, *moderari,* to restrain; AS, *bindan,* to bind], a thick bundle of muscle in the central part of the right ventricle of the heart.

modesty, propriety of dress, speech, and conduct in relations between patients and health care personnel, including draping and covering of the patient to the greatest extent possible, depending on the type of care or examination.

Modicon, a trademark for an oral contraceptive containing an estrogen (ethinyl estradiol) and a progestin (norethindrone).

modification /mod'ifikā'shən/, **1.** a process whereby a substance is changed from one form to another. **2.** a change in an organism that is acquired or learned but does not involve inheritance.

modified barium swallow, radiologic examination performed while the person swallows barium-coated substances, done to assess quality of the swallowing mechanisms of the mouth, pharynx, and esophagus.

modified jaw thrust /mod'ifīd/, an upper airway control maneuver to maintain an open airway of an unconscious person in cases of potential spinal injury. In such persons, in-line stabilization of the head and neck can be obtained primarily by forward jaw thrust with minimum head extension.

modified milk [L, *modus,* measure, *facere,* to make], cow's milk in which the protein content has been reduced and the fat content increased to correspond to the composition of breast milk.

modified plantigrade position, a position used in physical therapy to prepare the patient for independent standing and walking. The person stands with feet flat on the ground and the upper limbs leaning on a table or similar structure to support a large part of the weight.

modified radical mastectomy, a surgical procedure in which a breast is completely removed with the underlying pectoralis minor and some of the adjacent lymph nodes. The pectoralis major is not excised.

modifying gene /mod'ifī'ing/ [L, *modus,* measure; Gk, *genein,* to produce], a gene that alters or influences the expression function of another gene, including the suppression or reduction of the usual function of the modified gene.

modiolus, a central column of bone around which the cochlea twists.

modulation /mod'yəlā'shən/, an alteration in the magnitude or any variation in the duration of an electrical current. Modulation, which affects physiologic responses to various waveforms, may be continuous, interrupted, pulsed, or surging.

modulation transfer function (MTF) [L, *modulus,* small measure, *transferre,* to carry, *functio,* performance], a quantitative measure of the ability of an imaging system to reproduce patterns that vary in spatial frequency.

modulator /mod'ula'tər/, a specific inductor or agent that brings out characteristics peculiar to a definite region.

MODY, abbreviation for *maturity-onset diabetes of youth.*

Moeller's glossitis /mel'ərz/ [Julius O.L. Moeller, German surgeon, 1819–1887], a form of chronic glossitis, characterized by burning or pain in the tongue and increased sensitivity to hot or spicy foods.

moexipril, an angiotensin-converting enzyme inhibitor prescribed in the treatment of high BP alone or in combination with diuretics and in the treatment of left ventricular dysfunction after MI.

mohel /mō'əl, môhāl'/, in Judaism, ordained to circumcise.

Mohr's syndrome /mor/ [Otto Lous Mohr, Norwegian geneticist, 1886–1967], an autosomal-recessive disorder characterized

M

by brachydactyly, clinodactyly, polydactyly, syndactyly, and bilateral polysyndactyly of the big toe; by cranial, facial, lingual, palatal, and mandibular anomalies; and by episodic neuromuscular disturbances.

moiety /moi′itē/ [L, *medietas,* middle], a part of a molecule that exhibits a particular set of chemical and pharmacologic characteristics.

moist crackle [OFr, *moiste,* fresh; ME, *krakelen*], an adventitious breathing sound heard on auscultation when air bubbles through fluid or secretions in the bronchi or trachea.

moist heat [OFr, *moiste;* AS, *haetu*], the use of hot water, towels soaked in hot water, aquathermia pads, hot water bottles, or hot water vapors to reduce inflammation and pain, stimulate circulation, and/or relieve symptoms as directed by a physician. Hot towels should be wrung out to remove surplus moisture and should not be too hot to be held in the hands of the person applying moist heat.

moist rale, one heard over fluid in the bronchial tubes.

molality /mōlal′itē/ [L, *moles,* mass], the number of moles of solute per kilogram of water or other solvent. It refers to the solution concentration.

molar (*M*) /mō′lər/ [L, *moles,* mass], **1.** any of the 12 teeth, 6 in each dental arch, located posterior to the premolars. **2.** (M) pertaining to the concentration of a solution, expressed as the number of moles of solute per liter of solution.

molarity /mōler′itē/ [L, *moles,* mass], the number of moles of solute per liter of solution. It refers to the concentration of the solution.

molar pregnancy, pregnancy in which a hydatid mole develops from the trophoblastic tissue of the early embryonic stage of development. The signs of pregnancy are all exaggerated: the uterus grows more rapidly than is normal, morning sickness is often severe and constant, BP is likely to be elevated, and blood levels of chorionic gonadotropins are extremely high. The uterus must be evacuated because the mole may develop into choriocarcinoma.

molar solution, a solution that contains 1 mole of solute per liter of solution.

mold, **1.** a hollow form for casting or shaping an object, as a prosthesis. **2.** fungi that grows on moist organic matter, breaking it down.

molding /mōl′ding/ [ME, *moulde,* shaping], the natural process by which a baby's head is shaped during labor as it is squeezed into and through the birth passage by the forces of labor. Most of the changes caused by molding resolve

themselves during the first few days of life.

mole[1] [L, mass], *informal.* **1.** a pigmented nevus. **2.** in obstetrics, a hydatid mole.

mole[2] [L, *molecula,* small mass], the standard unit used to measure the amount of a substance. A mole of a substance is the amount containing the same number of elementary particles as there are atoms in 12 g of carbon 12, typically 6.02×10^{23} particles.

molecular biology /məlek′yələr/ [L, *molecula,* small mass; Gk, *bios,* life, *logos,* science], the branch of biology that deals with the physical and chemical interactions of molecules involved in life functions.

molecular genetics [L, *molecula,* small mass; Gk, *genesis,* origin], the branch of genetics that focuses on the chemical structure and the functions, replication, and mutations of the molecules involved in the transmission of genetic information, namely DNA and RNA.

molecular hybridization, in molecular biology, formation of a partially or wholly complementary nucleic acid duplex by association of single strands, usually between DNA and RNA strands or previously unassociated DNA strands, but also between RNA strands, used to detect and isolate specific sequences, measure homology, or define other characteristics of one or both strands.

molecular mass, the mass of a molecule of a substance as compared with the mass of an atom of carbon-12. It is equal to the sum of the masses of its constituent atoms and is measured in daltons.

molecular mimicry, an antigenic similarity between unrelated macromolecules, believed to play a role in the pathogenesis of rheumatic fever and other diseases.

molecular pathology [L, *molecula,* small mass; Gk, *pathos,* disease, *logos,* science], the branch of the science of disease that is concerned with the health effects of specific molecules.

molecular sieve, **1.** a crystalline chemical separation device with molecular size pores that adsorbs small but not large molecules. **2.** a cross-linked polymer that forms a porous sieve used as a supporting medium for chromatographic separation of mixtures of solutes.

molecular stutter, a gene defect in which the three-nucleotide code for an amino acid is repeated, missing, or jumbled, causing the gene either to fail to make a specific protein or to make a protein that does not function properly. In Huntington's disease, for example, the code for glutamine may be repeated 40 or 50 times in a row in the defective gene. The longer the string of repeats, the earlier the symptoms develop.

molecular taxonomy, the classification of organisms on the basis of the distribution and composition of chemical substances in them.

molecule /mol′əkyool/ [L, *molecula,* small mass], the smallest unit that exhibits the properties of an element or compound. A molecule is composed of two or more atoms that are covalently bonded.

mole percent, a percentage calculation expressed in terms of moles of a substance in a mixture or solution rather than in terms of molecular mass.

mole volume, the volume occupied by one mole of a substance, which may be a solid, liquid, or gas. It is numerically equal to the molecular mass divided by the density.

molindone hydrochloride /mol′indōn/, an antipsychotic agent prescribed in the treatment of schizophrenia.

molluscum contagiosum /məlus′kəm/ [L, *molluscus,* soft], a disease of the skin and mucous membranes caused by a poxvirus, characterized by scattered flesh-toned or white papules. Palms of the hands and soles of the feet are not affected.

Moloney test [Paul J. Moloney, Canadian physician, 1870–1939], a skin test for sensitivity to diphtheria toxoid.

mol wt, abbreviation for **molecular weight.**

molybdenum (Mo) /məlib′dənəm/ [Gk, *molybdos,* lead], a grayish metallic element. Its atomic number is 42; its atomic mass is 95.94. Molybdenum is poisonous if ingested in large quantities. It is used as an additive in certain steels.

molybdenum-99, the radionuclide that is the parent of technetium-99 and as such is present as a generator in most nuclear medicine departments.

monad /mon′ad, mō′nəd/, **1.** a unicellular, free-living organism. **2.** a monovalent element or radical. **3.** a haploid set of chromosomes in a spermatid or ootid.

monarthritis /mon′ärthrī′tis/ [Gk, *monos,* single, *arthron,* joint, *itis,* inflammation], arthritis affecting only one joint.

monarticular /mon′ärtik′yələr/ [Gk, *monos,* single; L, *articulus,* joint], pertaining to only one joint.

monascus, a natural product derived from red yeast grown on rice, used to help maintain acceptable cholesterol levels.

monaural /monôr′əl/ [Gk, *monos,* single; L, *auris,* ear], pertaining to one ear.

Mönckeberg's arteriosclerosis /meng′kəbərgz/ [Johann G. Mönckeberg, German pathologist, 1877–1925], a form of arteriosclerosis in which extensive calcium deposits are found in the tunica media of the artery with little obstruction of the lumen.

Mongolian spot /mong·gō′lē·ən/ [*Mongol,* Asian ethnic group; ME, *spotte,* stain], a benign bluish-black macule, between 2 and 8 cm, occurring over the sacrum and on the buttocks of some newborns. It usually disappears during early childhood.

monilethrix /mōnil′əthriks/ [L, *monile,* necklace; Gk, *thrix,* hair], an autosomal-dominant condition in which the hairs exhibit multiple constrictions, with a beading effect, and are brittle, rarely reaching an inch in length before breaking.

moniliform /mōnil′ifôrm/, resembling a string of beads.

Monistat, a trademark for an antifungal (miconazole nitrate).

monitor /mon′ətər/ [L, *monere,* to warn], **1.** to observe and evaluate a function of the body closely and constantly. **2.** a mechanical device that provides a visual or audible signal or a graphic record of a particular function, such as a cardiac monitor.

monitrice /mon′itris/ [Fr, female instructor], a labor coach, usually a registered nurse, who provides emotional support and leads the mother through labor and delivery.

monkeypox, an epidemic human disease caused by exposure to a monkeypox virus, with symptoms resembling those of smallpox. The virus is related antigenically to smallpox and vaccinia organisms.

mono, abbreviation for **mononucleosis.**

monoamine /mon′ō·am′in/, an amine containing one amine group.

monoamine oxidase (MAO), an enzyme that catalyzes the oxidation of amines.

monoamine oxidase inhibitor (MAOI, MAO inhibitor), any of a chemically heterogeneous group of drugs used primarily in the treatment of depression. These drugs also exert an antianxiety effect, especially anxiety associated with phobia. MAO inhibitors are also sometimes used in the treatment of migraine headache and hypertension. The effects of the drugs vary greatly from patient to patient, and their specific actions leading to clinical benefits are poorly understood.

monobasic acid /mon′ōbā′sik/, an acid with only one replaceable hydrogen atom such as hydrochloric acid.

monobasic potassium phosphate, the monopotassium salt, KH_2PO_4, used as a buffering agent in pharmaceutical preparations and, alone or in combination with other phosphate compounds, as an electrolyte replenisher and urinary acidifier and for prevention of kidney stones.

M

monobasic sodium phosphate, a mono-sodium salt of phosphoric acid, used in buffer solutions. Used alone or in combination with other phosphate compounds, it is given intravenously as an electrolyte replenisher, orally or rectally as a laxative, and orally as a urinary acidifier and for prevention of kidney stones.

monobenzone /-ben'zōn/, a depigmenting agent prescribed in final depigmentation in extensive vitiligo.

monoblast /mon'əblast/ [Gk, *monos,* single, *blastos,* germ], earliest identifiable immature monocyte. Increased production of monoblasts in the marrow and the presence of these forms in the peripheral circulation occur in acute monoblastic leukemias and tuberculosis.—**monoblastic,** *adj.*

monoblastic leukemia /-blas'tik/, a malignancy of blood-forming organs, characterized by the proliferation of monoblasts and monocytes.

monocarboxylic acid /mon'ōkär'boksil'ik/, a carboxylic acid with a single carboxyl group.

monochromatic /-krōmat'ik/, **1.** pertaining to a single color or a single wavelength of light. **2.** describing a person who is totally color blind. **3.** pertaining to a substance that has only one color or stains with only one color.

monochromaticity /-krō'mətis'itē/, the specificity of light in a single defined wavelength. If the specificity is in the visible light spectrum, it is only one color.

Monocid, a trademark for a cephalosporin-type antibiotic (cefonicid sodium).

monoclonal /mon'əklō'nəl/ [Gk, *monos* + *klon,* twig], pertaining to or designating a group of identical cells or organisms derived from a single cell or organism.

monoclonal antibody (MAB) [Gk, *monos,* single, *klon,* twig + *anti;* AS, *bodig,* body], an antibody produced in a laboratory from a single clone of B lymphocytes. All MABs produced from the same clone are identical and have the same antigenic specificity.

monocrotic pulse /-krot'ik/ [Gk, *monos,* single, *krotein,* to strike; L, *pulsare,* to beat], a pulse characterized by a single wave.

monocular diplopia /monok'yələr/ [Gk, *monos,* single; L, *oculus,* eye; Gk, *diploos,* double, *opsis,* vision], a condition in which a double image is perceived with one eye. The cause is a disorder in the refracting medium of the eye, such as a cataract, or partial dislocation of the lens. In rare cases, more than two images may be seen with one eye.

monocular strabismus [Gk, *monos,* single; L, *oculus,* eye; Gk, *strabismos*], strabismus that is confined to one particular eye.

monocular vision [Gk, *monos,* single; L, *oculus,* eye, *visio,* seeing], a condition of seeing with or using only one eye at a time.

monocutaneous candidiasis, a cellular immunodeficiency disorder associated with fungal *(Candida)* infections of the skin, mucous membranes, nails, and hair.

monocyte /mon'əsīt/ [Gk, *monos* + *kytos,* cell], a granular peripheral blood mononuclear leukocyte, 13 to 25 μm in diameter with a lobulated nucleus, containing chromatin material with a lacy pattern and abundant gray-blue cytoplasm filled with fine, bluish granules.—**monocytic,** *adj.*

monocytic leukemia /mon'əsit'ik/, a malignancy of blood-forming tissues in which the predominant cells are monocytes. The disease has an erratic course characterized by malaise, fatigue, fever, anorexia, weight loss, splenomegaly, bleeding gums, dermal petechiae, anemia, and lack of responsiveness to therapy. There are two forms: Schilling's leukemia, in which most of the cells are monocytes that probably arise from the reticuloendothelial system, and the more common Naegeli's leukemia, in which a large number of the cells resemble myeloblasts.

monocytopenia /-sī'təpē'nē-ə/, an abnormally low number of monocytes in the peripheral blood.

monocytosis /mon'ōsītō'sis/, an increased proportion of monocytes in the circulation.

monodactylism /-dak'tiliz'əm/ [Gk, *monos,* single, *daktylos,* finger or toe], a congenital defect in which the person is born with only one finger on the hand or one toe on the foot.

monofactorial inheritance /-faktôr'ē-əl/ [Gk, *monos;* L, *factare,* to make], the acquisition or expression of a trait or condition that depends on the transmission of a single specific gene.

monogamy /mənog'əmē/, **1.** the practice of being married to no more than one person at a time. **2.** in biology, the habit of pairing with only one mate.

monohybrid /-hī'brid/ [Gk, *monos;* L, *hybrida,* mixed offspring], pertaining to or describing an individual, organism, or strain that is heterozygous for only one specific trait or for the single trait or gene locus under consideration.

monohybrid cross, the mating of two individuals, organisms, or strains that have different alleles for only one specific trait or in which only one particular characteristic or gene locus is being followed.

monohydric alcohol /-hī'drik/, an alcohol containing one hydroxyl group.

monoiodotyrosine /mon′ō-ī·ō′dōtī′rəsin/, an iodinated amino acid involved in the synthesis of thyroxine and triiodothyronine.

monokaryotic /-ker′ē·ot′ik/, having a single nucleus.

monolayer /-lā′ər/, a sheet of cells one cell thick such as may be formed on the surface of a culture vessel.

monomer /mon′əmər/ [Gk, *monos* + *meros*, part], a molecule that repeats itself to form a polymer, such as a molecule of fibrin monomer that polymerizes to form fibrin in the blood-clotting process. **—monomeric,** *adj.*

monomolecular elimination reaction (E1) /-məlek′yələr/, a first-order chemical kinetic reaction in which only one molecule is involved in the slow step reaction.

monomphalus /mənom′fələs/ [Gk, *monos* + *omphalos*, navel], conjoined twins that are united at the umbilicus.

mononeuropathy /-nŏŏrop′əthē/ [Gk, *monos* + *neuron*, nerve, *pathos*, disease], any disease or disorder that affects a single nerve trunk. Some common causes of disorders involving single nerve trunks are electric shock, radiation, and fractured bones that may compress or lacerate nerve fibers. Casts and tourniquets that are too tight may also damage a nerve by compression or by ischemia.

mononeuropathy multiplex, a peripheral nerve disorder characterized by numbness, pain, and weakness in several areas of the body. The symptoms may develop suddenly in the region supplied by one peripheral nerve and days later in the region of another nerve.

mononuclear /-nyŏŏ′klē·ər/ [Gk, *monos,* single; L, *nucleus,* nut kernel], pertaining to one nucleus, such as a monocyte.

mononuclear leukocyte, a WBC, including lymphocytes and monocytes, with a single nucleus.

mononucleosis (mono) /mon′ōnŏŏ′klē·ō′sis/ [Gk, *monos,* single; L, *nucleus,* nut kernel; Gk, *osis,* condition], an abnormal increase in the number of mononuclear leukocytes in the blood.

mononucleosis spot test, a rapid slide blood test performed to aid in the diagnosis of infectious mononucleosis, a disease caused by the Epstein-Barr virus (EBV). Abnormal findings may indicate chronic EBV infection, chronic fatigue syndrome, some forms of chronic hepatitis, and Burkitt's lymphoma.

monooctanoin /mon′ō·ok′tənō′in/, a gallstone-dissolving agent used to dissolve cholesterol gallstones.

monoovular twins, identical twins.

monophagia /-fā′jə/, the practice of eating only one kind of food.

monophasic /-fā′sik/, having one phase, part, aspect, or stage.

monopodial symmelia, a congenital anomaly characterized by the fusion of the lower extremities and the presence of one foot.

monopolar electrocautery, an electrocautery in which current is applied through a handheld active electrode and travels back to the generator through an inactive electrode attached to the patient (the grounding pad), so that the patient is part of the electrical circuit.

Monopril, a trademark for an angiotensin-converting enzyme inhibitor (fosinopril).

monopus /mon′əpəs/ [Gk, *monos* + *pous,* foot], a fetus or individual with the congenital absence of a foot or leg.

monorchid /monôr′kid/, a male who has monorchism.

monorchism /mon′ôrkiz′əm/ [Gk, *monos* + *orchis,* testicle, *ismos,* state], a condition in which only one testicle has descended into the scrotum.—**monorchidic,** *adj.*

monosaccharide /-sak′ərīd/ [Gk, *monos* + *sakcharon,* sugar], a simple carbohydrate consisting of a single basic sugar unit with the general formula $Cn(H_2O)n$, with n ranging from 3 to 8.

monosodium glutamate (MSG) /-sō′dē·əm/, a food flavor enhancer derived from naturally occurring salt of glutamic acid and a cause of Chinese restaurant syndrome. It is also used in the treatment of encephalopathies associated with liver disorders.

monosodium urate monohydrate, the monosodium salt of uric acid, deposited as needle-shaped crystals in the joints and other sites in gout.

monosome /mon′əsōm/ [Gk, *monos* + *soma,* body], **1.** an unpaired X or Y chromosome. **2.** the single, unpaired chromosome in monosomy.

monosomy /mon′əsō′mē/ [Gk, *monos* + *soma,* body], a chromosomal aberration characterized by the absence of one chromosome from the normal diploid complement.—**monosomic,** *adj.*

monospecific /-spəsif′ik/ [Gk, *monos;* L, *species,* form, *facere,* to make], pertaining to an antibody that binds to only one type of antigen.

monosymptomatic demyelinating disease, acute occurrence of any one of a number of symptoms that suggest a diagnosis of MS. Persons who have such an attack may or may not develop MS.

monosynaptic reflex /-sinap′tik/ [Gk, *monos,* single, *synaptein,* to join; L, *reflectere,* to bend back], a reflex requiring only one afferent and one efferent neuron.

M

monotherapy /mon'ŏther'əpē/ [Gk, *monos*, single, *therapeia*, treatment], treatment of a condition by means of a single drug.

monotropy /mənot'rəpē/ [Gk, *monos* + *trepein*, to turn], a phenomenon in which a mother appears to be able to bond with only one infant at a time. When one twin is taken home from the hospital earlier than the other, the mother often reports that she does not feel that the baby discharged later is hers.—**monotropic,** *adj.*

monovalent /-vā'lənt/, **1.** describing an atom or radical having the valence or combining power of one hydrogen atom. **2.** describing a serum antibody capable of combining with only one antigen or complement.

monovulatory /mənŏ'vyələtôr'ē/ [Gk, *monos*; L, *ovulum*, small egg, *orius*, characterized by], routinely releasing one ovum during each ovarian cycle.

monozygotic (MZ) /-zīgŏ'tik/ [Gk, *monos* + *zygon*, yoke], pertaining to or developed from a single fertilized ovum, or zygote, such as occurs in identical twins. —**monozygosity,** *n.,* **monozygous,** *adj.*

monozygotic twins, two offspring born of the same pregnancy and developed from a single fertilized ovum that splits into equal halves during an early cleavage phase in embryonic development, giving rise to separate fetuses. Such twins are always of the same sex, have the same genetic constitution, possess identical blood groups, and closely resemble each other in physical, psychologic, and mental characteristics.

Monro-Kellie doctrine /mənrō' kel'ē/ [Alexander Monro, Scottish anatomist and surgeon, 1733–1817; George Kellie, Scottish anatomist, late 18th century], the doctrine that the CNS and its accompanying fluids are enclosed in a rigid container whose total volume tends to remain constant. An increase in volume of one component, (e.g., brain, blood, or CSF) will elevate pressure and decrease the volume of one of the other elements.

mons /mons/ [L, mountain], a mound or slight elevation.

Monsel's solution /monselz'/, a reddish-brown aqueous solution of basic ferric sulfate, prepared from ferrous sulfate and nitric acid and used as an astringent and hemostatic.

Monson curve [George S. Monson, American dentist, 1869–1933; L, *curvus,* a bend], the curve of occlusion in which each tooth cusp and incisal edge lie on the surface of a sphere 8 inches (20 cm) in diameter, with its center in the region of the glabella.

mons veneris /ven'əris/ [L, *mons,* mountain; *venus,* love], a pad of fatty tissue and thick skin that overlies the symphysis pubis in the woman.

Monteggia's fracture /montej'əz/ [Giovanni B. Monteggia, Italian physician, 1762–1815], a break in the ulna, associated with radial dislocation or rupture of the annular ligament and resulting in the angulation or overriding of ulnar fragments.

montelukast, a leukotriene receptor used to treat chronic asthma.

Montenegro test /mon'tənā'grō/, a test used in the diagnosis of cutaneous leishmaniasis, in which killed *Leishmania* antigens are injected intradermally. A positive reaction is indicated by the appearance of a palpable nodule in 48 to 72 hours.

Montercaux fracture /monterkō'/, a break in the neck of the fibula associated with the dislocation of the ankle mortise joint.

Montgomery strap /montgom'ərē/, a band of adhesive tape featuring a lace-up design, used to secure dressings that must be changed frequently.

mood, a prolonged subjective emotional state that influences one's whole personality and perception of the world. Examples are sadness, elation, and anger.

mood-congruent psychotic features /-kon'grōō'ənt/ [AS, *mod,* mind; L, *congruere,* to come together], the characteristics of a psychosis in which the content of hallucinations or delusions is consistent with an elevated, expansive mood or with a depression.

mood disorder [AS, *mod,* mind; L, *dis* + *ordo,* rank], a variety of conditions characterized by a disturbance in mood as the main feature, which may be a sign of a major depressive disorder or dysthymic reaction or be symptomatic of a bipolar disorder. Other mood disorders may be caused by a general medical condition.

mood equilibrium, a nursing outcome from the Nursing Outcomes Classification (NOC) defined as appropriate adjustment of prevailing emotional tone in response to circumstances.

mood management, a nursing intervention from the Nursing Interventions Classification (NIC) defined as providing for safety, stabilization, recovery, and maintenance of a patient who is experiencing dysfunctionally depressed or elevated mood.

mood swing, an oscillation between periods of feelings of well-being and depression. Occasional "blue" periods are not regarded as abnormal.

moon face [AS, *mona,* moon; L, *facies,* face], a condition characterized by a rounded, puffy face. It occurs in people treated with large doses of corticosteroids.

The features return to normal when the medication is stopped.

Moore, Ruth Ella /mor/ [1903–1994], the first African-American woman to earn a PhD in bacteriology. Her areas of research were blood groups and the family Enterobacteriaceae.

Moore's fracture [Edward M. Moore, American surgeon, 1814–1902], a break in the distal radius with associated dislocation of the ulnar head, which causes the styloid process to be secured under the annular ligaments of the wrist.

Moore, Shirley M., a nursing theorist who, with Cornelia M. Ruland, developed the Peaceful End of Life Theory, which asserts that nurses are integral to the creation of peaceful end-of-life care, which includes freedom from suffering, emotional support, closeness to and participation by significant others, and treatment with empathy and respect.

MOPP /mop/, abbreviation for a combination drug regimen used in the treatment of cancer, containing three antineoplastics, *M*ustargen (mechlorethamine hydrochloride), *O*ncovin (vinCRIStine sulfate), Matulane (*p*rocarbazine hydrochloride), and *p*redniSONE (a glucocorticoid). MOPP is prescribed in the treatment of Hodgkin's disease.

Moraxella, a genus of the Neisseriaceae family of gram-negative nonmotile cocci. They are found as pathogens and parasites on the mucous membranes of warm-blooded animals.

Moraxella catarrhalis, a species of aerobic nonmotile bacteria found in both the normal and the diseased nasopharynx. It is a cause of otitis media and respiratory diseases.

Moraxella lacunata, a species of nonmotile cocci that causes corneal infections and subacute conjunctivitis or angular conjunctivitis in humans.

morbid [L, *morbidus,* diseased], **1.** pertaining to a pathologic or diseased condition, either physical or mental. **2.** preoccupied with unwholesome ideas.

morbidity /môrbid'itē/ [L, *morbidus,* diseased], **1.** an illness or an abnormal condition or quality. **2.** in statistics, the rate at which an illness or abnormality occurs, calculated by dividing the number of people who are affected within a group by the entire number of people in that group. **3.** the rate at which an illness occurs in a particular area or population.

Morbidity and Mortality Weekly Report (MMWR), a weekly epidemiologic report on the incidence of communicable diseases and deaths in 120 urban areas of the United States. It is published by the Centers for Disease Control and Prevention in Atlanta, Georgia.

morbidity rate [L, *morbidus,* diseased, *ratum,* calculation], the number of cases of a particular disease occurring in a single year per a specified population unit, as *x* cases per 1000. It also may be calculated on the basis of age groups, sex, occupation, or other population unit.

morbidity statistics [L, *morbidus,* diseased, *status,* condition], a branch of statistics that is concerned with the disease rate of a population or geographic region.

morbid obesity [L, *morbidus,* diseased, *obesitas,* fatness], an excess of body fat, or weight of 100 pounds over IBW that increases the risk of developing cardiac and endocrine disturbances, as well as some kinds of cancer.

morbilliform /môrbil'ifôrm/ [L, *morbilli,* little disease, *forma,* form], describing a skin condition that resembles the erythematous maculopapular rash of measles.

mordant /môr'dənt/, a substance capable of deepening the reaction of a biologic specimen to a stain. The chief mordants are alum, aniline, oil, and phenol.

Morgagni's globule /môrgan'yēz/ [Giovanni B. Morgagni, Italian anatomist, 1682–1771], a minute opaque sphere that may form from fluid coagulation between the eye lens and its capsule, especially in cataract.

Morgagni's tubercle [Giovanni B. Morgagni], one of several small soft nodules on the surface of each of the areolas in women. The tubercles are produced by large sebaceous glands just below the surface of the areolae.

morgan /môr'gən/ [Thomas H. Morgan, American biologist, 1866–1945], a unit of measure used in mapping the relative distances between genes on a chromosome. The measurement uses the total crossover value as the basic unit so that 1 morgan equals 100% crossing over or 1 centimorgan equals 1% recombination.

Morganella morganii, urease-producing bacteria found in UTIs and enteric bacteriosis.

morgue /môrg/ [Fr, mortuary], a unit of a hospital with facilities for the storage and autopsy of the dead.

moribund /môr'ibund/ [L, *moribundus,* dying], near death or in the act of dying.

moricizine /mori'sizēn/, a phenothiazine derivative. The hydrochloride salt is used in treatment of ventricular arrhythmias.

morinda, an evergreen shrub used for headache; arthritis; and digestive, heart, and liver conditions. There are no reliable data regarding efficacy.

Morita therapy /môrē'tä/ [Shomei Morita, twentieth-century Japanese

M

physician], an alternative therapy that has as its focus the symptoms of the patient. Its goal is character building, which enables the patient to live responsibly and constructively, even if the symptoms persist.

morning-after pill [AS, *morgen* + *aefter* + *pilian,* to peel], *informal.* initially referred to a large dose of an estrogen given orally, over a short period, to a woman within 24 to 72 hours after sexual intercourse to prevent conception. Mifepristone is an alternative and effective method of preventing pregnancy with fewer side effects.

morning dip, a significant decline in maximal expiratory flow rate observed in some asthmatic patients during the early morning.

morning ptosis, a temporary paralysis of the upper eyelid on awakening from sleep.

morning stiffness [OE, *morgen* + *stif*], a period of muscular stiffness after awakening in the morning, a common complaint of patients with arthritis or similar musculoskeletal disorders.

Moro reflex /môr'ō/ [Ernst Moro, German pediatrician, 1874–1951], a normal mass reflex in a young infant (up to 3 to 4 months of age) elicited by a sudden loud noise, such as by striking the table next to the child, or raising the head slightly and allowing it to drop. A normal response consists of flexion of the legs, an embracing posture of the arms, and usually a brief cry.

morphea /môr'fē·ə/ [Gk, *morphe,* form], a skin disease consisting of patches of yellowish or ivory-colored hard, dry, smooth skin.

morphine /môr'fēn/ [Gk, *Morpheus,* god of sleep], a white crystalline alkaloid derived from the opium poppy, *Papaver somniferum.* Morphine acts on the CNS to produce both depression and euphoric stimulation. Its principal therapeutic value is for the relief of moderate to severe pain. Morphine rarely provides total relief of pain, but in most cases it reduces the level of suffering. Patients with severe pain may become drowsy and relaxed but seldom achieve the sensation of euphoria. Repeated use of morphine leads to tolerance, necessitating increased dosage levels to get the same degree of pain relief.

morphine poisoning, adverse effect of injection or ingestion of opioids, marked by symptoms of pinpoint pupils, drowsiness, and shallow respiration.

morphine sulfate, an opioid analgesic prescribed to relieve moderate to severe pain, including that from MI and dyspnea caused by the left heart failure, and as a preanesthetic.

morphine tartrate, a white crystalline powder used in injections of morphine. It is more soluble in water than morphine itself and is used in various parenteral preparations.

morphinism /môr'finiz'əm/, a pathologic state caused by morphine addiction.

morphogen /môr'fəjen/, **1.** a soluble substance that controls the embryonic differentiation of a cell or tissue. **2.** a substance secreted by one group of cells that causes a specific change in the growth and differentiation of a different group.

morphogenesis /môr'fəjen'əsis/ [Gk, *morphe* + *genein,* to produce], the development and differentiation of the structures and form of an organism, specifically the changes that occur in the cells and tissue during embryonic development.

morphogenetic /-jənet'ik/, in embryology, pertaining to a substance or hormone that acts as an evocator in differentiation.

morphology /môrfol'əjē/ [Gk, *morphe* + *logos,* science], the study of the physical shape and size of a specimen, plant, or animal.—**morphologic** /môr'fəloj'ik/, *adj.*

morphometry /môrfom'ətrē/, the measurement of the structures and parts of organisms.

Morquio's disease /môrkē'ōz/ [Luis Morquio, Uruguayan physician, 1867–1935], a familial form of mucopolysaccharidosis that results in abnormal musculoskeletal development in childhood. Dwarfism, hunchback, enlarged sternum, and knock-knees may occur.

mortal [L, *mortalis,* perishable], **1.** subject to death. **2.** causing death.

mortality [L, *mortalis,* perishable], **1.** the condition of being subject to death. **2.** the death rate, which reflects the number of deaths per unit of population in any specific region, age group, disease, or other classification, usually expressed as deaths per 1000, 10,000, or 100,000.

mortar /môr'tər/ [L, *mortarium*], a cup-shaped vessel in which materials are ground or crushed by a pestle in the preparation of drugs.

mortinatality /môr'tinātal'itē/ [L, *mors,* death, *natus,* birth], the stillbirth rate. It is calculated by multiplying the number of stillbirths by 1000 and dividing by the total number of births per year.

mortise joint /môr'tis/ [ME, *mortays,* fixed in; L, *jungere,* to join], the articulatio talocruralis joint of the ankle.

Morton's disease [Thomas G. Morton, American surgeon, 1835–1903; L, *dis*; Fr, *aise,* ease], a form of foot neuralgia caused by a falling metatarsal arch, which puts pressure on the digital branches of the lateral plantar nerve.

Morton's plantar neuralgia [Thomas G. Morton; L, *planta,* foot sole; Gk, *neuron,* nerve, *algos,* pain], a severe throbbing pain that affects the anastomotic nerve branch between the medial and lateral plantar nerves.

Morton's syndrome [Dudley J. Morton, American orthopedist, 1884-1960; Gk, *syn,* together, *dromos,* course], a congenital foreshortening of the first metatarsal segment, causing pain and deformity of the front part of the foot.

mortuary /môr′chəwer′ē/ [L, *mortuarium,* tomb], a building where the bodies of deceased persons are held for identification, postmortem examination, and preparation for burial or cremation.

morula /môr′ələ/ *pl.* **morulas, morulae** [L, *morulus,* blackberry], a solid, spheric mass of cells resulting from the cleavage of the fertilized ovum in the early stages of embryonic development.—**morular,** *adj.*

Morvan's disease, a form of syringomyelia with tissue changes in the extremities, such as a paresthesia of the forearms and hands and progressive painless ulceration of the fingertips.

mosaic /mōzā′ik/ [L, *Musa,* goddess of the arts], **1.** an individual or organism that developed from a single zygote but that has two or more kinds of genetically different cell populations. Mosaicism may result from a mutation, crossing over, or, more commonly in humans, nondisjunction of chromosomes during early embryogenesis, which causes a variation in the number of chromosomes in the cells. The type of chromosomal aberration and the fraction of cells that are affected depend on the cleavage stage at which the causative event occurred. The degree of clinical involvement depends on the type of tissue containing the abnormality and may vary from near normal to full manifestation of a syndrome. **2.** a fertilized ovum that undergoes determinate cleavage.—**mosaicism,** *n.*

mosaic bone, bone tissue appearing to be made up of many tiny pieces cemented together, as seen on microscopic examination of an x-ray film of the affected bone. It is characteristic of Paget's disease.

mosaic development, a kind of embryonic development occurring in the blastocyst. The fertilized ovum undergoes determinate cleavage, developing according to a precise, unalterable plan in which each blastomere has a characteristic position and limited developmental potency and is a precursor of a specific part of the embryo.

mosaicism /mōzā′isiz′əm/ [L, *Musa,* goddess of the arts], in genetics, a condition in which an individual or an organism that

develops from a single zygote has two or more cell populations that differ in genetic constitution.

mosaic wart, a group of contiguous plantar warts.

mosquito bite /məskē′tō/ [L, *musca,* a fly; AS, *bitan,* to bite], a bite of a blood-sucking arthropod of the subfamily Culicidae that may result in a systemic allergic reaction in a hypersensitive person, an infection, or, most often, a pruritic wheal.

mosquito forceps, a small hemostatic forceps.

Mössbauer spectrometer /mes′bou·ər, mœs′bou·ər/ [Rudolf L. Mössbauer, German physicist, b. 1929], an instrument that can detect small changes between an atomic nucleus and its environment, such as caused by alterations in temperature, pressure, or chemical state.

most probable number, a statistical value representing the viable bacterial population in a sample through the use of dilution and multiple tube inoculations.

mother fixation [AS, *modor,* mother; L, *figere,* to fasten], an arrest in psychosexual development characterized by an abnormally persistent, close, and often paralyzing emotional attachment to one's mother.

motilin /mōtil′in/, a peptide hormone secreted by enterochromaffin cells of the intestinal tract. It stimulates GI motility and pepsin secretion.

motility /mō′tilitē/ [L, *motare,* to move often], spontaneous but unconscious or involuntary movement.—**motile,** *adj.*

motivation[1] /mō′tivā′shən/ [L, *movere,* to move], conscious or unconscious needs, interests, rewards, or other incentives that arouse, channel, or maintain a particular behavior.

motivation[2], a nursing outcome from the Nursing Outcomes Classification (NOC) defined as the inner urge that moves or prompts an individual to positive action(s).

motivational conflict /mō′tivā′shənəl/ [L, *movere,* to move, *alis,* relating to, *confluere,* to come together], a conflict resulting from the arousal of two or more motives that direct behavior toward incompatible goals.

motoneuron /mō′tōnŏŏr′on/ [L, *movere,* to move; Gk, *neuron,* nerve], a motor neuron. Its function is to produce muscle contractions.

motor [L, *movere,* to move], **1.** pertaining to motion, the body apparatus involved in movement, or the brain functions that direct purposeful activities. **2.** pertaining to a muscle, nerve, or brain center that produces or subserves motion.

M

motor aphasia, the inability to say remembered words, caused by a cerebral lesion in the inferior frontal gyrus of the left hemisphere. The condition most commonly is the result of a stroke.

motor apraxia, the inability to carry out planned movements or to handle small objects, although cognizant of the proper use of the object. The condition results from a lesion in the premotor frontal cortex on the opposite side of the affected limb.

motor area, a portion of the cerebral cortex that includes the precentral gyrus and the posterior part of the frontal gyri and that causes the contraction of the voluntary muscles on stimulation with electrodes. Normal voluntary activity requires associations between the motor area and other parts of the cortex; removal of the motor area from one cerebral hemisphere causes paralysis of voluntary muscles, especially of the opposite side of the body.

motor ataxia, an inability to perform coordinated movements.

motor control, the systematic transmission of nerve impulses from the motor cortex to motor units, resulting in coordinated contractions of muscles.

motor coordination, the harmonious functioning of body parts that involve movement, including gross motor movement, fine motor movement, and motor planning.

motor depressant [L, *movere,* to move, *deprimere,* to press down], a drug or agent that reduces the normal functioning level of motor neurons, mainly in voluntary muscles.

motor endplate, a large special synaptic contact between motor axons and each skeletal muscle fiber. Each muscle fiber forms one end plate.

motor fiber, one of the fibers (axons) in the cranial and spinal nerves that transmit impulses to and cause contraction of muscle fibers.

motor hallucination [L, *movere,* to move, *alucinari,* wandering mind], the subjective experience of movement when there is no movement.

motor image, a visual concept of one's bodily movements, real or imagined.

motor learning, the process of improving motor skills through practice, with long-lasting changes in the capability for responding. The cerebellum and basal nuclei play a major role in such coordination.

motor nerve, an efferent nerve that conveys impulses to motor end plates or another terminal and is mainly responsible for stimulating muscles and glands.

motor neuron, one of various efferent nerve cells that transmit nerve impulses from the brain or from the spinal cord to muscular or glandular tissue.

motor neuron disease [L, *movere,* to move, *neuron,* nerve + *dis;* Fr, *aise,* ease], any disease of a motor neuron, with degeneration of anterior horn cells, motor cranial nerve nuclei, and pyramidal tracts.

motor neuron paralysis, an injury to the spinal cord that causes damage to the motor neurons and results in various degrees of functional impairment depending on the site of the lesion.

motor nucleus [L, *movere,* to move, *nucleus,* nut kernel], the nucleus of a motor nerve or a collection of motor neurons.

motor pathway [L, *movere,* to move; AS, *paeth*], the route of motor nerve impulses, from the central neuron to a muscle or gland.

motor planning, the ability to plan and execute skilled nonhabitual tasks.

motor point, 1. a point at which a motor nerve enters a muscle. **2.** any point on the skin over a muscle at which electric stimulation (via electrode) causes contraction of the muscle.

motor protein, protein that moves along a surface, propelled by the energy of adenosine triphosphate hydrolysis.

motor root [L, *movere,* to move; AS, *rot*], the proximal end of a motor nerve at its attachment to the spinal cord.

motor seizure, abnormal electrical activity that arises initially in a localized motor area of the cerebral cortex. The manifestations depend on the site of the abnormal electrical activity, such as tonic contractures of the thumb caused by excessive discharges in the motor area of the cortex controlling the first digit or chewing movements resulting from discharges in the lower part of the motor strip controlling mastication.

motor sense, the feeling or perception enabling a person to accomplish a purposeful movement, presumably achieved by evoking a sensory engram or memory of the pattern for that specific movement.

motor speech areas [L, *movere,* to move; AS, *spaec;* L, *area,* vacant place], the regions of the cerebral hemispheres that are associated with motor control of speech.

motor tract [L, *movere,* to move + *tractus*], an efferent nerve pathway that conveys impulses controlling movement.

motor unit, a functional structure consisting of a motor neuron and the muscle fibers it innervates.

motor unit recruitment, the bringing into activity of additional motor neurons, which causes additional muscle fibers to contract. As more units are recruited and as the frequency of discharge increases, muscle tension increases.

mottle [ME, *motley,* mixed colors], an effect observed in radiographic imaging when the dose of radiation used is reduced to a level where individual quantum effects can be seen.

mounting /mount′ing/, the preparation of specimens and slides for study.

mourning /môr′ning/ [AS, *murnan,* to mourn], a response to the loss of a loved person or object. It is through mourning that grief is resolved.

mouse-tooth forceps, a kind of dressing forceps that has one or more fine sharp points on the tip of each blade. The tips turn in, and the delicate teeth interlock.

mouth [AS, *muth*], **1.** the nearly oval oral cavity at the superior, anterior end of the digestive tube, bounded anteriorly by the lips and containing the tongue and the teeth. It consists of the vestibule and the oral cavity proper. The vestibule, situated in front of the teeth, is bounded externally by the lips and the cheeks, internally by the gums and the teeth. The vestibule receives the secretion from the parotid salivary glands. The oral cavity proper is bounded by the alveolar arches and the teeth, communicates with the pharynx, and is roofed by the hard and the soft palates. The tongue forms the greater part of the floor of the cavity. **2.** an orifice.

mouth breathing, breathing through the mouth instead of the nose, usually because of some obstruction of the nasal passages.

mouth guard, a soft plastic intraoral appliance that covers the palate and all the occlusal surfaces of the teeth. It is worn in contact sports to limit damage to tissues of the mouth, lips, and other oral surfaces.

mouth rinse /mouth′rins/, a solution for cleaning or treating the oral mucosa and controlling dental caries. A typical therapeutic mouth rinse may contain sodium fluoride, glycerine, alcohol, detergents, and other ingredients.

mouthstick /mouth′stik/, a device that is gripped with the teeth and can be used to type, push buttons, turn pages, operate power wheelchairs, or modify environmental control units and other equipment using head movements. It is commonly used by individuals who have a high-level (C4 and up) tetraplegia.

mouth-to-mouth resuscitation, a procedure in artificial resuscitation, performed most often with cardiac massage. The victim's nose is sealed by pinching the nostrils closed, the head is extended, and air is breathed by the rescuer through the mouth into the lungs.

mouth-to-nose resuscitation, a procedure in artificial resuscitation in which the mouth of the victim is covered and held closed and air is breathed through the victim's nose.

mouthwash /mouth′wôsh/, a medicated liquid used for cleaning the oral cavity and treating mucous membranes of the mouth. Many OTC mouthwashes contain alcohol, which may contribute to surface softening and increased wear of dental resins and composite materials.

MOV, abbreviation for **minimal occlusive volume.**

movement decomposition [L, *movere,* to move, *de,* away, *componere,* to assemble], a distortion in voluntary movement in which motion occurs in a distinct sequence of isolated steps rather than in a normal smooth, flowing pattern.

movement disorder, any of numerous neurologic disorders characterized by disturbances of muscular movement, distinguished as either hyperkinetic (conditions such as chorea, dystonia, hemiballismus, myoclonus, stereotypy, tic, and tremor) or hypokinetic (conditions such as akinetic mutism, psychomotor retardation, and the stiff-man syndrome).

movement therapy, a movement-based therapeutic technique that aids in release of expressions or feelings and aids in promoting feeling and awareness.

moving grid, an x-ray grid that is continuously moved or oscillated throughout the exposure of a radiographic film.

moxibustion /mok′səbus′chən/ [Jpn, *moe kusa,* burning herb; L, *comburere,* to burn up], a method of producing analgesia or altering the function of a body system by igniting moxa, wormwood, or another combustible, slow-burning substance and holding it as near the point on the skin as possible without causing pain or burning. It is also sometimes used with acupuncture.

moxifloxacin, an antiinfective used to treat acute bacterial sinusitis caused by *Streptococcus pneumoniae, Haemophilus influenzae,* and *Moraxella catarrhalis;* acute bacterial exacerbation of chronic bronchitis from *S. pneumoniae, H. influenzae, H. parainfluenzae, Klebsiella pneumoniae, Staphylococcus aureus,* and *M. catarrhalis;* and community-acquired pneumonia from *S. pneumoniae, H. influenzae, Mycoplasma pneumoniae, Chlamydia pneumoniae,* and *M. catarrhalis.*

moxifloxacin hydrochloride, the hydrochloride salt of moxifloxacin used in the treatment of bacterial exacerbation of chronic bronchitis, acute sinusitis, community-acquired pneumonia, and skin and

M

skin structure infections caused by susceptible organisms.

moyamoya disease /moi′əmoi′ə/, a cerebrovascular disorder in which the main cerebral arteries at the base of the brain are replaced by a fine network of vessels. It is caused by progressive stenosis of the large-caliber vessels and development of a collateral network. It is characterized by convulsions, hemiplegia, mental retardation, and subarachnoid hemorrhage. Patients who survive into adulthood are susceptible to massive intracerebral hemorrhage caused by rupture of the fragile network of new vessels. Few patients live beyond 30 years of age.

6-MP, abbreviation for *6-mercaptopurine.*

MPD, M.P.D., abbreviation for **maximum permissible dose.**

MPGN, abbreviation for **membranoproliferative glomerulonephritis.**

M.P.H., abbreviation for *Master of Public Health.*

MPL + PRED, an anticancer drug combination of melphalan and predniSONE.

MPO, abbreviation for **myeloperoxidase.**

MPR, abbreviation for **multiplanar reformatting.**

MPS, abbreviation for **mucopolysaccharidosis.**

MPS I, abbreviation for *mucopolysaccharidosis I.*

MPS II, abbreviation for *mucopolysaccharidosis II.*

MPS IV, abbreviation for *mucopolysaccharidosis IV.*

MQF, abbreviation for *mobile quarantine facility.*

MQSA, abbreviation for **Mammography Quality Standards Act.**

mr, mR, abbreviation for **milliroentgen.**

mrad, abbreviation for **millirad.**

mrem, abbreviation for **millirem.**

MRI, abbreviation for **magnetic resonance imaging.**

mRNA, abbreviation for **messenger RNA.**

MRSA, abbreviation for *methicillin-resistant* Staphylococcus aureus.

MS, abbreviation for **multiple sclerosis.**

M.S., 1. abbreviation for *Master of Science.* 2. abbreviation for *Master of Surgery.*

MSAFP, abbreviation for *maternal serum alpha-fetoprotein.*

msec, abbreviation for **millisecond.**

MSG, abbreviation for **monosodium glutamate.**

MSH, abbreviation for **melanocyte-stimulating hormone.**

MSLT, abbreviation for **multiple sleep latency test.**

MS/MS, abbreviation for **tandem mass spectrometry.**

MSN, abbreviation for *Master of Science in Nursing.*

MSO, abbreviation for **management service organization.**

M.T., abbreviation for *medical technologist.*

MTOC, abbreviation for **microtubule organizing center.**

MTT, abbreviation for **maximal treadmill test.**

MTX + MP + CTX, an anticancer drug combination of methotrexate, mercaptopurine, and cyclophosphamide.

mu /myo͞o, mo͞o/, 1. μ, M, the twelfth letter of the Greek alphabet. 2. μ, symbol for **micron.**

Mucha-Habermann disease /mo͞o′kä hä′bermän/ [Viktor Mucha, Austrian dermatologist, 1877–1919; Rudolf Habermann, German dermatologist, 1884–1941], an acute or subacute, sometimes relapsing, widespread macular, papular, or vesicular eruption that tends to crusting, necrosis, and hemorrhage, which heals and leaves pigmented depressed scars, followed by the development of a new crop of lesions.

Much's granules /mo͞oks, mo͞okhs/ [Hans C. Much, German physician, 1880–1932], granules and rods, found in TB sputum, that stain with Gram's stain but not by the usual methods for acid-fast bacilli.

mucilage /m(y)o͞o′səlij/, 1. a sticky mixture of carbohydrates produced by plant cell activity. 2. a thick aqueous solution of a gum used for suspending insoluble substances and for increasing viscosity.

mucin /myo͞o′sin/ [L, *mucus,* slime], a mucopolysaccharide, the chief ingredient in mucus. Mucin is present in most glands that secrete mucus and is the lubricant protecting body surfaces from friction or erosion.

mucinoid /myo͞o′sinoid/ [L, *mucus;* Gk, *eidos,* form], resembling mucin.

mucinous carcinoma /myo͞o′sinəs/, an epithelial neoplasm characterized by a sticky gelatinous consistency caused by copious mucin secretion.

mucocele /myo͞o′kōsēl/ [L, *mucus,* slime; Gk, *koilia,* cavity], dilation of a cavity with accumulated mucus secretion.

mucocutaneous /myo͞o′kōkyo͞otā′nē·əs/ [L, *mucus + cutis,* skin, *osus,* having], pertaining to the mucous membrane and the skin.

mucocutaneous lymph node syndrome (MLNS), an acute febrile illness, primarily of young children, characterized by inflamed mucous membranes of the mouth; "strawberry tongue"; cervical lymphadenopathy; polymorphous rash on the trunk; and edema, erythema, and desquamation of the skin on the extremities. Other commonly associated findings include arthralgia, diarrhea, otitis, pneumonia, photophobia, meningitis, and ECG changes.

mucoepidermoid carcinoma /myo͞o′kō·ep′idur′moid/ [L, *mucus*; Gk, *epi*, above, *derma*, skin, *eidos*, form], a malignant neoplasm of glandular tissues, especially the ducts of the salivary glands. The tumor contains mucinous and epidermoid squamous cells.

mucogingival junction /myo͞o′kōjinjī′vəl/ [L, *mucus* + *gingiva*, gum, *jungere*, to join], the scalloped linear area of the gums that separates the gingiva from the alveolar mucosa.

mucoid /myo͞o′koid/ [L, *mucus*; Gk, *eidos*, form], **1.** resembling mucus. **2.** pertaining to a group of glycoproteins, including colloid and ovomucoid, similar to the mucins, primarily differing in solubility.

mucoid cyst [L, *mucus*; Gk, *eidos*, form, *kytis*, bag], a cyst formed by an overgrowth of a mucous gland or by the spread of mucus into the interstitial tissues.

mucolipidosis /myo͞o′kōlip′idō′sis/, any of a group of metabolic disorders characterized by an accumulation of mucopolysaccharides and lipids in the tissues, but without an excess of mucopolysaccharides in the urine.

mucolipidosis IV, an autosomal-recessive disorder characterized by psychomotor retardation and severe visual impairment, initially manifest in infancy or childhood as corneal clouding. Sialic acid–containing gangliosides are accumulated as a result of deficient ganglioside sialidase activity. However, the deficiency is not believed to be the primary defect.

mucolytic /myo͞o′kəlit′ik/ [L, *mucus*; Gk, *lysis*, loosening], **1.** exerting a destructive effect on mucus. **2.** any agent that dissolves or destroys mucus.

mucomembranous /myo͞o′kəmem′brə nəs/ [L, *mucus* + *membrana*, thin skin, *osus*, having], pertaining to a mucous membrane, such as that of the small intestine or the bladder.

Mucomyst, a trademark for a mucolytic (acetylcysteine), also the antidote for acute acetaminophen poisoning.

mucopolysaccharidase /myo͞o′kōpol′esak′əridās′/, an enzyme that breaks down molecules of polysaccharides.

mucopolysaccharide /myo͞o′kōpol′esak′ərīd/ [L, *mucus*; Gk, *polys*, many, *sakcharon*, sugar], a polysaccharide containing hexosamine and sometimes occurring with protein, such as mucins.

mucopolysaccharidosis (MPS) /myo͞o′kōpol′esak·ar′idō′sis/ *pl.* **mucopolysaccharidoses** [L, *mucus*; Gk, *polys*, many, *sakcharon*, sugar, *osis*, condition], one of a group of genetic disorders characterized by greater than normal accumulations of mucopolysaccharides in the tissues, with other symptoms specific to each type. The disorders are numbered MPS I through MPS VII. All types are characterized by pronounced skeletal deformity (especially of the face), mental and physical retardation, and decreased life expectancy.

mucoprotein /myo͞o′kōprō′tēn, -tē·in/ [L, *mucus*; Gk, *proteios*, first rank], a compound, present in all connective and supporting tissue, that contains polysaccharides combined with protein. It is relatively resistant to denaturation.

mucopurulent /myo͞o′kōpyo͝or′yələnt/ [L, *mucus* + *purulentus*, pus], characteristic of a combination of mucus and pus.

Mucorales, an order of perfect fungi of the class Zygomycetes, made up of bread molds and related fungi. Genera *Absidia*, *Mucor*, and *Rhizopus* can cause opportunistic mucormycosis in humans.

mucosal immune system /myo͞okō′səl/, the lymphoid tissues of the mucosal surfaces lining the GI, respiratory, and urogenital tracts.

mucosal neuroma syndrome /mo͞oko′säl no͝oro′mä/, multiple endocrine neoplasia, type III.

mucosal prolapse, prolapse of the mucosa in part of the GI tract. In the colon it sometimes occurs with congenital megacolon.

mucositis /myo͞o′kōsī′tis/, any inflammation of a mucous membrane, such as the lining of the mouth and throat.

mucous membrane /myo͞o′kəs/ [L, *mucus* + *membrana*, thin skin], any one of four major kinds of thin sheets of tissue that cover or line various parts of the body. Mucous membrane lines cavities or canals of the body that open to the outside, such as the linings of the mouth, the digestive tube, the respiratory passages, and the genitourinary tract. It consists of a surface layer of epithelial tissue covering a deeper layer of connective tissue and protects the underlying structure, secretes mucus, and absorbs water, salts, and other solutes.

mucous plug, in obstetrics, a collection of thick mucus in the uterine cervix that is often expelled at the onset of dilation of the cervix, just before labor begins or in its early hours.

mucus /myo͞o′kəs/ [L, *slime*], the viscous, slippery secretions of mucous membranes and glands, containing mucin, WBCs, water, inorganic salts, and

M

exfoliated cells.—**mucoid,** *adj.,* **mucous** /myŏŏ′kəs/, *adj.*

mucus extravasation phenomenon, extravasation of mucus from a damaged minor salivary gland excretory duct into the surrounding connective tissue, followed by an inflammatory reaction. It is visible as a small nodule or vesicle on the oral mucosa.

mucus retention cyst, a mucus-containing epithelium-lined cavity caused by blockage of a salivary gland duct with mucus, visible as a small nodule on the oral mucosa.

mucus trap suction apparatus, a catheter containing a trap to prevent mucus being aspirated from the trachea of a newborn from entering the mouth of the person operating the device. Mucus traps are also found in adult respiratory equipment.

mud bath, the application of warm mud to the body for therapeutic purposes.

mud fever, a type of leptospirosis occurring in the summer and autumn in Germany and Russia, caused by *Leptospira interrogans.* It is transmitted to humans by the field mouse *Microtus arvalis* and affects mainly workers in swamps or flooded fields.

μF, abbreviation for **microfarad.**

MUGA, abbreviation for *multigated acquisition* scan.

μg, abbreviation for **microgram.**

mulberry molar, a malformed first molar characterized by dwarfing of the cusps and hypertrophy of the enamel surrounding the cusp with agglomeration of masses of globules, giving it the appearance of a mulberry.

mulibrey nanism /mul′ibrī/, a rare genetic disorder, transmitted as an autosomal-recessive trait, characterized by dwarfism, constrictive pericarditis, muscular hypotonia, anomalies of the skull and face, and characteristic yellow dots in the ocular fundus. The name of the condition is an abbreviation composed of the first two letters of the anatomic sites of the principal defects: *mu*scle, *li*ver, *br*ain, and *ey*es.

müllerian duct /miler′ē-ən, mYl-/ [Johannes P. Müller, German physiologist, 1801–1858], one of a pair of embryonic ducts that become the fallopian tubes, uterus, and vagina in females and that atrophy in males.

Müller's law /mil′ərz, mYl-/ [Johannes P. Müller], the principle that each type of sensory nerve cell normally responds to only one specific stimulus and gives rise to one sensation. A cell may be excited artificially by other forms of stimuli, but the sensation evoked will be the same.

Müller's maneuver [Johannes P. Müller], an inspiratory effort against a closed airway or glottis. The effort decreases intrapulmonary and intrathoracic pressures and expands pulmonary gas.

multibacillary /mul′tĭbas′ĭlare/, having numerous bacilli.

multicellular /-sel′yələr/, **1.** consisting of more than one cell. **2.** containing many cavities.

multicomponent virus /-kəmpō′nənt/, a virus that occurs in two or more different particles. Each particle contains only one part of the viral genome.

multidisciplinary care conference, a nursing intervention from the Nursing Interventions Classification (NIC) defined as planning and evaluating patient care with health professionals from other disciplines.

multidisciplinary health care team /-dis′ipliner′ē/, a group of health care workers who are members of different disciplines, each providing specific services to the patient.

multidrug resistance, 1. the resistance of tumor cells to more than one chemotherapeutic agent. **2.** the resistance of bacteria, especially *Mycobacterium tuberculosis,* against more than two of the antibiotics that were once effective.

multidrug-resistant organisms, antimicrobial resistance, such as in methicillin-resistant *Staphylococcus aureus* and vancomycin-resistant enterococcus.

multifactorial /-faktôr′ē-əl/ [L, *multus,* many, *facere,* to make], pertaining to or characteristic of any condition or disease resulting from the interaction of many factors, specifically the interaction of several genes, usually polygenes, with or without the involvement of environmental factors.

multifactorial inheritance, the tendency to develop a physical appearance, disease, or condition that is a condition of many genetic and environmental factors, such as stature and BP.

multifidus, a group of transversospinales muscles that span the length of the vertebral column. They are best developed in the lumbar region.

multifocal /-fō′kəl/ [L, *multus* + *focus,* hearth], characterized by more than two ectopic foci that pace the heart. The foci may be atrial or ventricular.

multifocal atrial tachycardia, an atrial rhythm with a rate exceeding 100 beats/min caused by multifocal atrial activity and characterized by at least three different shapes of P′ waves on the ECG. It is often associated with chronic obstructive lung disease.

multifocal motor neuropathy, an acquired, autoimmune neuropathy characterized by progressive, asymmetric muscle weakness, affecting especially the arms, with little or no sensory deficit.

multiform /mul′tifôrm/ [L, *multus,* many + *forma*], an organ, tissue, or other object that may appear in more than one shape.

multigenerational model /-jen′ərā′shənəl/, a model of family therapy that focuses on reciprocal role relationships over a period and thus takes a longitudinal approach. The family is viewed as an emotional system in which patterns of interacting and coping can be passed down from one generation to the next and can cause stress to the family members onto whom they are projected.

multigenerational transmission process, the repetition of relationship patterns, including divorce, suicide, and alcoholism, associated with emotional dysfunction that can be traced through several generations of the same family.

multigravida /mul′tigrav′idə/ [L, *multus* + *gravidus,* pregnancy], a woman who has been pregnant more than once.

multihospital system /-hos′pitəl/, a group of two or more hospitals owned, sponsored, or managed by a central organization.

multiinfarct dementia /-infärkt′/ [L, *multus* + *infarcire,* to stuff, *de,* away, *mens,* mind], a form of organic brain disease characterized by the rapid deterioration of intellectual functioning, caused by vascular disease. Symptoms include emotional lability; disturbances in memory, abstract thinking, judgment, and impulse control; and focal neurologic impairment, such as gait abnormalities, pseudobulbar palsy, and paresthesia.

multilocular cyst /-lok′yələr/ [L, *multus* + *loculus,* little place; Gk, *kystis,* bag], **1.** a cyst containing several loculi or spaces. **2.** a hydatid cyst with many small irregular cavities that may contain scoleces but generally little fluid.

multilocular cyst of kidney, a thick-walled cyst in the kidney, found in clusters and usually unilaterally. In children it contains blastema and may develop into a Wilms' tumor. A variety in adults has more fibrous tissue than the juvenile variety.

multipara /multip′ərə/ *pl.* **multiparae** [L *multus* + *parere,* to bear], a woman who has delivered more than one viable infant.

multiparity /-per′itē/ [L, *multus,* many, *parere,* to give birth], the status of a mother of more than one child.

multiparous /multip′ərous/ [L, *multus,* many, *parere,* to give birth], having given birth to more than one child.

multipenniform /-pen′ifôrm/ [L, *multus* + *penna,* feather + *forma*], of a body structure, having a shape resembling a pattern of many feathers.

multiphase generator /-fāz′/, a generator of x-rays that operates on more than single-phase power. It usually has three phases, which greatly increases the rate at which it produces x-rays.

multiphasic screening /-fā′sik/ [L, *multus* + *phasis,* appearance; ME, *scren*], a technique of screening populations for diseases that combines a battery of screening tests. The technique serves to identify any of several diseases being screened for in a population.

multiplanar reformatting (MPR), a technique used in two-dimensional tomographic imaging (CT and MRI) to generate sagittal, coronal, and oblique views from axial sections.

multiple autoimmune disorder (MAD) /mul′tipəl/, a condition in which a patient exhibits symptoms of at least two of a group of diseases including Addison's disease, autoimmune thyroid disease, mucocutaneous candidiasis, hypoparathyroiditis, and insulin-dependent diabetes.

multiple carboxylase deficiency, an autosomal-recessive inherited amino-acidopathy caused by deficiency of either of two enzymes necessary for activity of several biotin-containing carboxylases. It is characterized by metabolic ketoacidosis, excretion of organic acids in the urine, hyperammonemia, and variable manifestation of breathing difficulties, hypotonia, seizures, ataxia, alopecia, skin rash, and developmental delay. The neonatal form may progress rapidly to coma; the juvenile form is characterized additionally by sensorineural deafness and optic atrophy.

multiple endocrine adenomatosis (MEA), a condition characterized by functioning tumors in more than one endocrine gland. The disorder is commonly associated with Zollinger-Ellison's syndrome and may involve the pituitary, pancreas, and parathyroid glands. It is also seen in multiple endocrine neoplasia type I.

multiple endocrine neoplasia (MEN), a hereditary hormonal disorder that occurs in an autosomal-dominant pattern. The endocrine neoplasms may be expressed as hyperplasia, adenoma, or carcinoma and may develop synchronously or metachronously.

multiple endocrine neoplasia, type I, a type of multiple endocrine neoplasia that includes tumors of the pituitary, parathyroid glands, and pancreatic islet cells, often with peptic ulcers and sometimes the Zollinger-Ellison syndrome.

multiple endocrine neoplasia, type II, a type of multiple endocrine neoplasia characterized by medullary carcinoma of the thyroid, pheochromocytoma, and hyperplasia of the parathyroid glands.

multiple family therapy [L, *multus* + *plica,* fold], psychotherapy in which several

M

families meet weekly to confront and deal with problems or issues that they have in common.

multiple fission, cell division in which the nucleus first divides into several equal parts and then the cytoplasm divides into as many cells as there are nuclei. It is a common form of asexual reproduction in certain acellular organisms.

multiple fracture, 1. a fracture break that extends several fracture lines in one bone. 2. the fracture of several bones at one time or from the same injury.

multiple lipomatosis, a rare inherited disorder characterized by discrete localized subcutaneous deposits of fat in the tissues of the body.

multiple-locus variable number of tandem repeat analysis (MLVA), a laboratory tool designed to recognize tandem repeats and other qualities in the genome of an individual to provide a high resolution DNA fingerprint for the purpose of identification.

multiple mononeuropathy, an abnormal condition characterized by dysfunction of several individual nerve trunks. It may be caused by various diseases, such as DM and some inflammatory immunologic disorders.

multiple mucosal neuroma syndrome, a condition in which multiple submucosal neuromas or neurofibromas of the lips, tongue, and eyelids. The disease affects young persons and may be associated with tumors of the thyroid or adrenal medulla or with subcutaneous neurofibromatosis.

multiple myeloma, a malignant neoplasm of the bone marrow.

multiple peripheral neuritis, acute or subacute disseminated inflammation or degeneration of symmetrically distributed peripheral nerves, characterized initially by numbness, tingling in the extremities, hot and cold sensations, and slight fever, progressing to pain, weakness, diminished reflexes, and in some cases, flaccid paralysis. The disorder may be caused by toxic substances.

multiple pregnancy, a pregnancy in which there is more than one fetus in the uterus at the same time.

multiple pterygium syndrome, an autosomal-recessive syndrome characterized by pterygia of the neck, axillae, and popliteal, antecubital, and intercrural areas, accompanied by hypertelorism, cleft palate, micrognathia, ptosis of eyelids, and short stature. Skeletal abnormalities include camptodactyly, syndactyly, clubfoot, and flatfoot in which the bottom of the foot resembles a rocker, as well as vertebral fusion and rib anomalies. Cryptorchidism is present in males, and labia majora are absent in females.

multiple sclerosis (MS) [L, *multus* + *plica,* fold; Gk, *sklerosis,* hardening], a progressive disease characterized by disseminated demyelination of nerve fibers of the brain and spinal cord. It begins slowly, usually in young adulthood, and continues throughout life with periods of exacerbation and remission. The first signs are often paresthesias, or abnormal sensations in the extremities or on one side of the face. Other early signs are muscle weakness, vertigo, and visual disturbances, such as nystagmus, diplopia (double vision), and partial blindness. Later in the course of the disease there may be extreme emotional lability, ataxia, abnormal reflexes, and difficulty in urinating.

multiple sclerosis self-management, a nursing outcome from the Nursing Outcomes Classification (NOC) defined as personal actions to manage multiple sclerosis and prevent disease progression.

multiple sleep latency test (MSLT), a test of the propensity to fall asleep, often used to diagnose narcolepsy. The subject is given five 20-minute nap opportunities at 2-hour intervals, usually after an overnight polysomnogram.

multiple sulfatase deficiency, an autosomal-recessive lysosomal storage disease in which a deficiency of at least nine lysosomal and microsomal sulfatases leads to accumulation of sulfate-containing glycolipids, mucopolysaccharides, and steroids. Neurologic deterioration is rapid.

multipolar mitosis /-pō'lər/ [L, *multus* + *polus,* pole], cell division in which the spindle has three or more poles and results in the formation of a corresponding number of daughter cells.

multiskilled worker, a health team member with at least the education of a nurse assistant who has been trained to perform selected nursing skills and selected skills from the allied health professions under the supervision of a registered nurse. Duties may include, but are not limited to, bedmaking, bathing, assisting with elimination needs, performing phlebotomy, and recording ECGs.

multisource drug /mul'tisôrs/ [L, *multus;* OFr, *sourse,* origin], a pharmaceutical that can be purchased under any of several trademarks from different manufacturers or distributors.

multispecific /-spes'ifik/, pertaining to an antibody that binds to more than one type of antigen.

multisynaptic /-sinap'tik/ [L, *multus;* Gk, *synaptein,* to join], pertaining to a nervous process or system of nerve cells requiring a series of synapses.

multivalent /mul'tiva̅'lənt/ [L, *multus* + *valere*, to be strong], in immunology, able to act against more than one strain of organism.

multivalent vaccine [L, *multus*, many, *valere*, value, *vaccinus*, cow], a vaccine prepared from several antigenic types within a species.

μm, abbreviation for **micrometer.**

mummification /mum'ifika̅'shən/ [Per, *mum*, wax; L, *facere*, to make], a dried-up state, such as occurs in dry gangrene or a dead fetus in utero.

mummified fetus /mum'ifi̅d/, a fetus that has died in utero and has shriveled and dried.

mumps [D, *mompen*, to sulk], an acute viral disease, characterized by a swelling of the parotid glands, caused by a paramyxovirus. It is most likely to affect children between 5 and 15 years of age, but it may occur at any age. In adulthood the infection may be severe. The mumps paramyxovirus is present in the saliva of the affected individual and is transmitted in droplets or by direct contact.

mumps orchitis, an inflammatory disorder of the testis characterized by swelling with fever, malaise, and acute parotitis. It usually occurs in postpubertal men with a recent history of mumps and may result in testicular atrophy.

Mumpsvax, a trademark for an active immunizing agent (live mumps virus vaccine).

mumps virus, a paramyxovirus that causes mumps and sometimes tenderness and swelling of the testes, pancreas, ovaries, or other organs.

mumps virus vaccine live, an active immunizing agent that can be prescribed for immunization against mumps. MMR (mumps/measles/rubella) is generally the preferred vaccine for children and adults.

Münchausen's syndrome /mun'chousənz/ [Baron von Münchausen, German adventurer and confabulator, 1720–1797], an unusual condition characterized by habitual pleas for treatment and hospitalization for a symptomatic but imaginary acute illness. The affected person may logically and convincingly present the symptoms and history of a real disease.

Münchausen's syndrome by proxy [Baron von Münchausen], a variation of Münchausen's syndrome in which the parent persistently fabricates or induces illness in a child with the intent of keeping in contact with hospitals and physicians. The child may endure dozens of surgeries and hospitalizations for illness induced by the parent.

mural /myoo'rəl/ [L, *murus*, wall], **1.** pertaining to something that is found on or against the wall of a cavity. **2.** a painting on a wall.

mural thrombus [L, *murus*, wall], a thrombus that originates in the wall of a cavity, particularly on a diseased patch of endocardium.

muriatic acid /moo're̅·at'ik/ [L, *muria*, brine, *acidus*, sour], hydrochloric acid.

murine typhus /myoo're̅n/ [L, *mus*, mouse; Gk, *typhos*, stupor], an acute arbovirus infection caused by *Rickettsia typhi* and transmitted by the bite of an infected flea. The disease is similar to epidemic typhus but less severe. It is characterized by headache, chills, fever, myalgia, and rash.

murmur /mur'mər/ [L, a humming], a gentle blowing, fluttering, or humming sound, such as a heart murmur.

muromonab-CD3 /myoo'rəmon'ab/, a parenteral immunosuppressant drug, a monoclonal antibody that interferes with the function of the T-cell antigen recognition receptors. It is used in the control of acute renal transplant rejection and to control liver or pancreas rejection or graft-versus-host disease when conventional methods are unsuccessful.

Murphy's sign, a test for gallbladder disease in which the patient is asked to inhale while the examiner's fingers are hooked under the liver border at the bottom of the rib cage. The inspiration causes the gallbladder to descend onto the fingers, producing pain if the gallbladder is inflamed.

muscarine /mus'kəre̅n/ [L, *musca*, fly], a choline-related alkaloid present in the poisonous mushroom *Amanita muscaria*. It is similar pharmacologically to acetylcholine, although it is not used in therapeutics.

muscarinic /mus'kərin'ik/ [L, *musca*, fly], **1.** stimulating the postganglionic parasympathetic receptor. **2.** pertaining to the poisonous activity of muscarine.

muscle (m) /mus'əl/ [L, *musculus*], a kind of tissue composed of fibers or cells that is able to contract, causing movement of body parts and organs. Muscle fibers are richly vascular, excitable, conductive, and elastic. There are two basic kinds — striated muscle and smooth muscle. The myocardium is sometimes classified as a third (cardiac) kind of muscle, but it is basically a striated muscle.

muscle albumin, albumin present in muscle.

muscle biopsy [L, *musculus*; Gk, *bios*, life, *opsis*, view], an examination of surgically removed muscle tissue for diagnosis.

muscle bridge, a band of myocardial tissue over one or more of the large epicardial

M

coronary vessels. It may cause constriction of the artery during systole.

muscle cell, any contractile cell peculiar to muscle. Smooth muscle cells are elongated spindle-shaped cells containing a single nucleus and longitudinally arranged myofibrils.

muscle cramp, a sudden intermittent pain in almost any part of the body. It may involve involuntary contractions of variable duration and be accompanied by spasms. Cramps may develop in striated muscle as a result of exertion, high temperature, and excessive loss of sodium, potassium, and magnesium through perspiration. Cramps can also be associated with arthritic conditions and exposure to cold.

muscle excitability /eksī'təbil'itē/, the ability of a muscle fiber to respond rapidly to a stimulating agent.

muscle fiber, any of the cells of skeletal or cardiac muscle tissue.

muscle guarding, a protective response in muscle that results from pain or fear of movement.

muscle receptor, a sensory organ that responds to muscle stretch or tension, including muscle spindles and tendon organs.

muscle reeducation, the use of physical therapeutic exercises to restore muscle tone and strength after an injury or disease.

muscle relaxant, an agent that reduces the contractility of muscle fibers. Curare derivatives and succinylcholine compete with acetylcholine and block neural transmission at the myoneural junction. These drugs are used during anesthesia, in the management of patients undergoing mechanical ventilation, and in shock therapy, to reduce muscle contractions in pharmacologically or electrically induced seizures.

muscle-setting exercise, a method of maintaining muscle strength and tone by alternately contracting and relaxing a skeletal muscle or group of skeletal muscles without moving the associated body part.

muscles of mastication, a group of muscles—the masseter, pterygoideus lateralis, pterygoideus medialis, and temporalis—responsible for movement of the jaws during the process of chewing.

muscles of ventilation [L, *musculus* + *respirare,* to breathe], muscles that provide inspiration, partly by increasing the volume of the chest cavity so that air is drawn into the lungs, including the diaphragm and external intercostal muscles. They are aided during forced breathing by the scalenus muscles, levatores costarum, sternocleidomastoid, pectoralis major, platysma myoides, and serratus

superior posterior. Muscles of forced expiration include the external and internal oblique, rectus abdominis, and transverse abdominis.

muscle spindle [L, *musculus*; AS, *spinel*], a specialized proprioceptive sensory organ composed of a bundle of fine striated intrafusal muscle fibers innervated by gamma nerve fibers. Their nuclei are gathered together near the center of each fiber to form a nuclear sac, which is surrounded in turn by sensory, annulospiral nerve endings, all enclosed in a fibrous sheath.

muscle testing, a method of evaluating the contractile unit, including the muscle, tendons, and associated tissues, of a moving part of the body by neurologic or resistance testing. The tests may include shortened, middle, and lengthened range-of-motion ability; isokinetic measurement of muscle strength, power, and endurance; and functional tests, such as jogging or specific agility drills, as well as radiography, arthroscopy, electromyography, and other medical tests.

muscular /mus'kyələr/ [L, *musculus*], **1.** pertaining to a muscle. **2.** characteristic of well-developed musculature.

muscular atrophy, a condition of motor unit dysfunction, usually the result of a loss of efferent innervation.

muscular branch of the deep brachial artery, one of several similar branches of the deep brachial artery, supplying certain arm muscles such as the coracobrachialis, biceps brachii, and brachialis.

muscular dystrophy (MD) [L, *musculus*; Gk, *dys,* bad, *trophe,* nourishment], a group of genetically transmitted diseases characterized by progressive atrophy of symmetric groups of skeletal muscles without evidence of involvement or degeneration of neural tissue. In all forms of muscular dystrophy an insidious loss of strength with increasing disability and deformity occurs, although each type differs in the groups of muscles affected, the age at onset, the rate of progression, and the mode of genetic inheritance.

muscular fatigue, a condition in which a muscle loses its ability to contract as a result of overactivity. It is usually a period after stimulation during which the muscle is unresponsive to a second stimulus.

muscular incompetence [L, *musculus* + *incompetens*], a failure of a cardiac valve to close properly because of a dysfunction of the papillary muscles of the heart.

muscular sarcoidosis, the formation of epithelioid tubercles in the skeletal muscles, characterized by interstitial inflammation, fibrosis, atrophy, and damage to the muscle fibers as the tubercles form within and replace normal muscle cells.

muscular system, all of the muscles of the body, including the smooth, cardiac, and striated muscles, considered as an interrelated structural group.

muscular tone [L, *musculus*; Gk, *tonos,* stretching], a normal degree of tension in muscles at rest.

muscular tremor [L, *musculus* + *tremor,* shaking], minute regular involuntary contraction of individual muscle fasciculi. If the tremors are mild and occasional, the cause may be physiologic. Profuse, persistent, or recurrent widespread muscular twitching often indicates a motor neuron disorder.

musculature /mus′kyəlā′chər/, the arrangement and condition of the muscles.

musculocutaneous nerve /mus′kyəlōkyo͞otā′nē·əs/ [L, *musculus* + *cutis,* skin, *osus,* having], one of the terminal branches of the brachial plexus. It is formed on each side by division of the lateral cord of the plexus into two branches. Various branches and filaments supply different structures, such as the biceps, the brachialis, the humerus, and the skin of the forearm.

musculophrenic artery, a terminal branch of the internal thoracic artery whose branches supply the superior part of the anterolateral abdominal wall.

musculoskeletal /mus′kyo͝olōskel′ətəl/ [L, *musculus*; Gk, *skeletos,* dried up], pertaining to the muscles and skeleton.

musculoskeletal system, all of the muscles, bones, joints, and related structures, such as the tendons and connective tissue, that function in the movement of body parts and organs.

musculoskeletal system assessment, an evaluation of the condition and functioning of the patient's muscles, joints, and bones and of factors that may contribute to abnormalities in these body structures.

musculus trigoni vesicae urinariae superficialis, the superficial layer of the trigonal muscles, continuous proximally with the muscles of the ureteral wall.

musculus uvulae, a muscle that elevates and retracts the uvula, thickening the central part of the soft palate and helping the levator veli palatini muscles close the pharyngeal isthmus between the nasopharynx and oropharynx.

mush bite, a procedure for making simultaneous tooth impressions used in the construction of study models or full or partial dentures. The patient draws his or her upper and lower jaws together into a block of softened wax, thus indicating the spatial relationship between the maxilla and mandible.

mushroom [ME, *mucheron*], the fruiting body of the fungus of the class Basidomycetes, especially edible members of the order Agaricales, commonly known as field mushrooms or meadow mushrooms. Mushrooms contain some protein and minerals, but they are composed largely of water.

mushroom poisoning, a toxic condition caused by the ingestion of certain mushrooms, particularly species of the genus *Amanita*. Muscarine in *A. muscaria* produces intoxication in a few minutes to 2 hours. Symptoms include lacrimation, salivation, sweating, vomiting, labored breathing, abdominal cramps, diarrhea, and in severe cases convulsions, coma, and circulatory failure. More deadly but slower-acting phalloidin in *A. phalloides* and *A. verna* causes similar symptoms, as well as liver damage, renal failure, and death.

mushroom worker's lung, a type of farmer's lung seen in those working on mushroom farms, caused by inhalation of mold spores from mushroom beds.

music therapist, a health professional trained to use music within a therapeutic relationship to address a client's needs, such as facilitating movement and physical rehabilitation, motivating the client to cope with treatment, providing emotional support, and providing an outlet for expressing feelings.

music therapy[1] [Gk, *mousike,* music, *therapeia,* treatment], a form of adjunctive psychotherapy in which music is used as a means of recreation and communication, especially with autistic children, and as a means to elevate the mood of depressed and psychotic patients.

music therapy[2], a nursing intervention from the Nursing Interventions Classification (NIC) defined as using music to help achieve a specific change in behavior, feeling, or physiology.

Musset's sign /mo͝osāz′/ [Alfred de Musset, French poet, 1810–1857], a rhythmic movement of the head and neck synchronous with each ventricular systole.

mustard gas /mus′tərd/, a poisonous gas used in chemical warfare during World War I. It causes corrosive destruction of the skin and mucous membranes, often resulting in permanent respiratory damage and death.

mustard plaster [L, *mustum*; Gk, *emplastron*], a counterirritant made from dried mustard, flour and a small amount of water and spread onto a fabric base that is placed on the skin. It must be used with care because it can cause burns.

Mustargen, a trademark for an antineoplastic (mechlorethamine hydrochloride).

mutacism /myōō'təsiz'əm/, mimmation, or the incorrect use of the /m/ sound.

mutagen /myōō'təjən/ [L, *mutare*, to change, *genein*, to produce], any chemical or physical environmental agent that induces a genetic mutation or increases the mutation rate.—**mutagenic**, *adj.*, **mutagenicity**, *n.*

mutagenesis /myōō'təjen'əsis/, the induction or occurrence of a genetic mutation.

Mutamycin, a trademark for an antineoplastic (mitomycin).

mutant /myōō'tənt/ [L, *mutare*, to change], **1.** any individual or organism with genetic material that has undergone mutation. **2.** relating to or produced by mutation.

mutant gene, any gene that has undergone a change, such as the loss, gain, or exchange of genetic material, that affects the normal transmission and expression of a trait.

mutase /myōō'tās/, any enzyme that catalyzes the shifting of a chemical group or radical from one position to another within the same molecule or occasionally from one molecule to another.

mutation /myōōtā'shən/ [L, *mutare*, to change], an unusual change in a gene occurring spontaneously or by induction. The change affects the original expression of the gene. If a mutation occurs in the genome of a gamete, the mutation may be transmitted to later generations.—**mutate**, *v.*, **mutational**, *adj.*

mutein /myōō'tē·in, m(y)ōō'tēn/, a protein molecule that results from a mutation.

mutism /myōō'tizəm/ [L, *mutus*, mute], the inability to speak because of a physical defect or emotional problem.

muton /myōō'ton/, the smallest DNA segment whose alteration can result in a mutation.

mutual goal setting, a nursing intervention from the Nursing Interventions Classification (NIC) defined as collaborating with the patient to identify and prioritize care goals, then developing a plan for achieving those goals.

mutually exclusive categories /myōō'chōō·əlē/, categories on a research instrument that are sufficiently precise to allow each subject, factor, or variable to be classified uniquely, such as male/female.

mutual support group, a type of group in which members organize to solve their own problems. It is led by the group members themselves who share a common goal and use their own strengths to gain control over their lives.

MV, **1.** abbreviation for *megavolt*. **2.** abbreviation for *minute volume*.

mv, mV, abbreviation for **millivolt**.

MVIC, abbreviation for **maximum voluntary isometric contraction**.

mVO₂, symbol for *myocardial oxygen consumption*.

MVP, abbreviation for *mitral valve prolapse*.

MVV, abbreviation for **maximum voluntary ventilation**.

M.W.I.A., abbreviation for **Medical Women's International Association**.

MX gene, a human gene that helps the body resist viral infections. When exposed to interferon, the MX gene inhibits the production of viral protein and nucleic acid necessary for the proliferation of new viral particles.

myalgia /mī·al'jə/ [Gk, *mys*, muscle, *algos*, pain], diffuse muscle pain, usually accompanied by malaise.

myalgic asthenia /mī·al'jik/ [Gk, *mys* + *algos*, pain, *a* + *sthenos*, without strength], a condition characterized by a general feeling of fatigue and muscular pain, often resulting from or associated with psychologic stress.

Myambutol, a trademark for an antitubercular (ethambutol hydrochloride).

myasthenia /mī'əsthē'nē·ə/ [Gk, *mys* + *sthenos*, without strength], a condition characterized by an abnormal weakness of a muscle or a group of muscles that may be the result of a systemic myoneural disturbance, such as in myasthenia laryngitis, which involves the vocal cord tensor muscles.—**myasthenic**, *adj.*

myasthenia gravis, an abnormal condition characterized by chronic fatigability and muscle weakness, especially in the face and throat, caused by the inability of receptors at the myoneural junction to depolarize because of a deficiency of acetylcholine.

myasthenia gravis crisis, an acute exacerbation of the muscular weakness characterizing the disease, triggered by illness, infection, surgery, emotional stress, or an overdose or insufficiency of anticholinesterase medication.

myasthenic crisis /mī'asthen'ik/, an acute episode of muscular weakness.

Mycamine, a trademark for micafungin.

mycelium /mīsē'lē·əm/ *pl.* **mycelia** [Gk, *mykes*, fungus, *helos*, nail], a mass of interwoven, branched, threadlike filaments that makes up most fungi.

mycetoma /mī'sətō'mə/ [Gk, *mykes* + *oma*, tumor], a severe fungal infection involving skin, subcutaneous tissue, fascia, and bone.

Mycitracin, a trademark for a fixed-combination topical drug containing antibacterials (polymyxin B sulfate, bacitracin, and neomycin sulfate).

mycobacteria /mī′kōbaktir′ē-ə/ [Gk, *mykes* + *bakterion*, small rod], acid-fast microorganisms belonging to the genus *Mycobacterium.*—**mycobacterial,** *adj.*

mycobacteriosis /mī′kōbak′tire-ō′sis/ [Gk, *mykes* + *bakterion* + *osis,* condition], a TB-like disease caused by mycobacteria other than *Mycobacterium tuberculosis.*

Mycobacterium /mī′kōbaktir′ē-əm/ [Gk, *mykes* + *bakterion,* small rod], a genus of rod-shaped acid-fast bacteria having two significant pathogenic species: *Mycobacterium leprae* and *M. tuberculosis. M. avium* complex or *M. avium-intracellulare* disseminated infection may occur in AIDS.

Mycobacterium avium **complex (MAC) disease,** systemic disease caused by infection with organisms of the *Mycobacterium avium-intracellulare* complex in patients with HIV infection. Manifestations include bacteremia, fever, chills, fatigue, night sweats, weight loss, abdominal pain, anemia, and elevated alkaline phosphatase.

Mycobacterium avium-intracellulare, a complex of slow-growing organisms that cause TB in birds and swine and are associated with human pulmonary disease, lymphadenitis in children, and serious systemic disease in immunocompromised patients.

Mycobacterium bovis, a species of bacteria that causes TB in cattle and other animals and is transmitted to humans by the ingestion of raw milk contaminated by the microorganism.

Mycobacterium kansasii, a species of slow-growing photochromogenic bacteria that causes TB-like pulmonary infection in humans. It affects the joints, gonads, spinal fluid, lymph nodes, and viscera. The incidence of this infection has increased with the advent of AIDS.

Mycobacterium leprae, a species of bacteria that causes leprosy.

Mycobacterium marinum, a species of bacteria that causes a form of TB in cold-blooded animals, including saltwater fish. The bacterium is also found in swimming pools and aquariums and is associated with skin lesions in humans.

Mycolog, a trademark for a topical fixed-combination drug containing a glucocorticoid (triamcinolone acetonide).

mycology /mīkol′əjē/ [Gk, *mykes* + *logos,* science], the study of fungi and fungoid diseases.—**mycologic,** *adj.,* **mycologist,** *n.*

mycophenolate mofetil, an immunosuppressant prescribed to prevent rejection of organ transplants and for prophylaxis of organ rejection in allogenic cardiac transplants.

mycophenolic acid /mī′kōfino′lik/, a bacteriostatic and fungistatic crystalline immunosuppressant obtained from *Penicillium brevicompactum* and related species.

Mycoplasma /mī′kōplaz′mə/ [Gk, *mykes* + *plassein,* to mold], a genus of ultramicroscopic organisms lacking rigid cell walls and considered to be the smallest free-living organisms. Some are saprophytes, some are parasites, and many are pathogens.

mycoplasma pneumonia, a contagious disease of children and young adults caused by *Mycoplasma pneumoniae.* It is characterized by symptoms of URI, dry cough, and fever.

mycosis /mīkō′sis/ [Gk, *mykes* + *osis,* condition], any disease caused by a fungus.—**mycotic,** *adj.*

mycosis fungoides /fung·goi′dēz/, a rare chronic lymphomatous skin malignancy resembling eczema or a cutaneous tumor that is followed by microabscesses in the epidermis and lesions simulating those of Hodgkin's disease in lymph nodes and viscera.

Mycostatin, a trademark for an antifungal (nystatin).

mycotic /mīkot′ik/ [Gk, *mykes,* fungus], pertaining to a disease caused by a fungus.

mycotic aneurysm, a localized dilation in the wall of a blood vessel caused by the growth of a fungus. It usually occurs as a complication of bacterial endocarditis.

mycotic endocarditis /mīkot′ik en′do·kär·dī′tis/ [Gk, *mykes,* fungus, *endon,* within, *kardia,* heart, *-itis,* inflammatory disease suffix], infectious endocarditis caused by a fungal infection, most commonly *Candida albicans* and species of *Aspergillus* and *Histoplasma.* Symptoms are usually subacute.

mycotic granuloma of the larynx, a chronic throat condition characterized by white patches on an otherwise bright red mucous membrane. In the southwestern United States, it is associated with histoplasmosis of the larynx. It may also be caused by candidiasis as a complication of chemotherapy or an altered immune state.

mycotoxicosis /mī′kōtok′sikō′sis/ [Gk, *mykes* + *toxikon,* poison, *osis,* condition], a systemic poisoning caused by toxins produced by fungal organisms.

mycotoxin /mī′kōtok′sins/, a poison produced by fungi that are harmful to other organisms.

mydriasis /midrī′əsis/ [Gk, *mydros,* hot mass], **1.** dilation of the pupil of the eye caused by contraction of the dilator muscle of the iris, a muscular sheath that radiates

M

outward like the spokes of a wheel from the center of the iris around the pupil. **2.** an abnormal condition characterized by contraction of the dilator muscle, resulting in widely dilated pupils.—**mydriatic** /mid′rē·at′ik/, *adj.*

mydriatic and cycloplegic agent /mid′rē·at′ik/ [Gk, *mydros* + *kyklos*, circle, *plege*, stroke], any one of several ophthalmic pharmaceutical preparations that dilate the pupil and paralyze the ocular muscles of accommodation. These drugs are used in diagnostic and refractive examination of the eye, before and after various procedures in eye surgery, in some tests for glaucoma, and in the treatment of anterior uveitis and certain kinds of glaucoma.

myectomy, excision of part of a muscle.

myectomy/myotomy, a surgical method of treating total or near-total intestinal aganglionosis. It combines circular excision of seromuscular tissue from a short segment of bowel and a longitudinal myotomy with creation of a stoma, resulting in a short length of functional intestine that will support increasing amounts of enteral nutrition.

myelacephalus /mī′əlāsef′ələs/ [Gk, *myelos*, marrow, *a* + *kephale*, without head], a fetus, usually a separate monozygotic twin, whose form and parts are barely recognizable; a slightly differentiated amorphous mass.—**myelacephalous,** *adj.*

myelatelia /mī′əlatē′lē·ə/ [Gk, *myelos* + *atelia*, unfinished], any developmental defect involving the spinal cord.

myelauxe /mī′əlôk′sē/ [Gk, *myelos* + *auxe*, increasing], a developmental anomaly characterized by hypertrophy of the spinal cord.

myelencephalon /mī′əlensef′əlon/, the lower part of the embryonic hindbrain, from which the medulla oblongata develops.

myelin /mī′əlin/ [Gk, *myelos*, marrow], a lipoproteinaceous substance constituting the sheaths of various nerve fibers throughout the body and enveloping the axis of myelinated nerves. It is largely composed of phospholipids and protein, which gives the fibers a white, creamy color.—**myelinic,** *adj.*

myelinated /mī′əlinā′tid/, of a nerve, having a myelin sheath.

myelination /mī′əlinā′shən/ [Gk, *myelos*; L, *atio*, process], the process of furnishing or taking on myelin.

myelin globule, a fatlike droplet found in some sputum.

myelinic neuroma, a neuroma neoplasm composed of myelinated nerve fibers.

myelinization /mī′əlinīzā′shən/ [Gk, *myelos* + *izein*, to cause], development of the myelin sheath around a nerve fiber.

myelinolysis /mī′əlinol′isis/ [Gk, *myelos* + *lysein*, to loosen], a pathologic process that dissolves the myelin sheaths around certain nerve fibers, such as those of the pons in alcoholic and undernourished people who are afflicted with central pontine myelinolysis.

myelin sheath, a segmented fatty lamination composed of myelin that wraps the axons of many nerves in the body. Various diseases such as MS can destroy myelin wrappings.

myelitis /mī′əlī′tis/, an abnormal condition characterized by inflammation of the spinal cord with associated motor or sensory dysfunction.—**myelitic,** *adj.*

myeloablation /mī′əlō·ablā′shən/ [Gk, *myelos*, marrow; L, *ab*, *latus* carried away], severe myelosuppression.

myeloblast /mī′əloblast′/ [Gk, *myelos* + *blastos*, germ], earliest precursors of the granulocytic leukocytes. The cytoplasm appears light blue, scanty, and nongranular when seen in a stained blood smear through a microscope.—**myeloblastic,** *adj.*

myeloblastic leukemia /-blas′tik/, a malignant neoplasm of blood-forming tissues, characterized by many myeloblasts in the circulating blood and tissues.

myeloblastomatosis /mī′əloblas′tōmətō′sis/ [Gk, *myelos* + *blastos* + *oma*, tumor, *osis*, condition], abnormal localized clusters of myeloblasts in the peripheral circulation.

myeloblastosis /mī′əloblastō′sis/ [Gk, *myelos* + *blastos* + *osis*, condition], an excess of myeloblasts in the blood.

myeloclast /mī′əloclast′/ [Gk, *myelos* + *klastos*, broken], a cell that breaks down the myelin sheaths of nerves.

myelocyst /mī′əlōsist′/ [Gk, *myelos* + *kystis*, cyst], any benign cyst formed from the rudimentary medullary canals that give rise to the vertebral canal during embryonic development.

myelocyte /mī′əlōsīt′/ [Gk, *myelos* + *kytos*, cell], the third of the maturation stages of the granulocytic leukocytes normally found in the bone marrow. Granules are visible in the cytoplasm. The nuclear material of the myelocyte is denser than that of the myeloblast. Myelocytes appear on peripheral blood films in chronic myelogenous leukemia or in severe infection.—**myelocytic,** *adj.*

myelocythemia /mī′əlōsīthē′mē·ə/ [Gk, *myelos* + *kytos* + *haima*, blood], an excessive presence of myelocytes in the circulating blood, such as in myelocytic leukemia.

myelocytoma /mī′əlō′sītō′mə/ [Gk, *myelos + kytos,* cell, *oma,* tumor], a localized cluster of myelocytes in the peripheral vasculature that may occur in myelocytic leukemia.

myelodiastasis /mī′əlōdī·as′təsis/ [Gk, *myelos + diastasis,* separation], disintegration and necrosis of the spinal cord.

myelodysplasia /mī′əlōdisplā′zhə/ [Gk, *myelos + dys,* bad, *plassis,* formation], **1.** a general designation for the defective development of any part of the spinal cord. The term is used primarily to describe abnormalities without gross superficial defects. **2.** dysplasia of the myelocytes and other elements in bone marrow.

myelofibrosis /mī′əlōfībrō′sis/, the replacement of bone marrow with fibrous tissue. The condition may be associated with anemia, thrombocytopenia, myeloid metaplasia, new bone formation, polycythemia vera, and other abnormalities.

myelogenesis /-jen′əsis/ [Gk, *myelos + genein,* to produce], **1.** the formation and differentiation of the nervous system, in particular of the brain and spinal cord, during prenatal development. **2.** the development of the myelin sheath around the nerve fiber.

myelogenous /mī′əloj′ənəs/, pertaining to the cells produced in bone marrow or to the tissue from which such cells originate.

myelogeny /mī′əloj′ənē/ [Gk, *myelos + genein,* to produce], the formation and differentiation of the myelin sheaths of nerve fibers during the prenatal and postnatal development of the CNS.

myelogram /mī′əlōgram′/, **1.** an x-ray film taken after the injection of a radiopaque medium into the subarachnoid space to demonstrate any distortions of the spinal cord, spinal nerve roots, and subarachnoid space. **2.** a graphic representation of a count of the different kinds of cells in a stained preparation of bone marrow.

myelography /mī′əlog′rəfē/ [Gk, *myelos + graphein,* to record], a radiographic process by which the spinal cord and the spinal subarachnoid space are viewed and photographed after the introduction of a contrast medium.—**myelographic,** *adj.*

myeloid /mī′əloid/ [Gk, *myelos + eidos,* form], **1.** pertaining to the bone marrow. **2.** pertaining to the spinal cord. **3.** pertaining to myelocytic forms that do not necessarily originate in the bone marrow.

myeloid metaplasia, a disorder in which bone marrow tissue develops in abnormal sites. Characteristics of the condition are anemia, splenomegaly, immature blood cells in the circulation, and hematopoiesis in the liver and spleen.

myeloidosis /mī′əloidō′sis/ [Gk, *myelos + eidos,* form, *osis,* condition], an abnormal condition characterized by general hyperplasia of the myeloid tissue.

myeloma /mī′əlō′mə/ [Gk, *myelos + oma,* tumor], an osteolytic neoplasm consisting of a profusion of cells typical of the bone marrow that may develop in many sites and cause extensive destruction of the bone. Intense pain and spontaneous fractures are common.

myeloma cast, a urinary cast containing Bence Jones protein and desquamated cells of the tubular epithelium, seen with multiple myeloma in the condition known as myeloma kidney.

myeloma kidney disease, a kidney disorder often characterized by irreversible renal failure.

myelomalacia /mī′əlōmələ′shə/ [Gk, *myelos + malakia,* softening], an abnormal softening of the spinal cord, caused primarily by inadequate blood supply.

myelomeningocele /mī′əlō′məning′gōsēl/ [Gk, *myelos + menix,* membrane, *kele,* hernia], a developmental defect of the CNS in which a hernial sac containing a portion of the spinal cord, its meninges, and CSF protrudes through a congenital cleft in the vertebral column. The condition is caused primarily by failure of the neural tube to close during embryonic development, although in some instances it may result from the reopening of the tube as a result of an abnormal increase in CSF pressure.

myelomere /mī′əlōmir′/ [Gk, *myelos + meros,* part], any of the embryonic segments of the brain or spinal cord during prenatal development.

myelopathy /mī′əlop′əthē/, **1.** any disease of the spinal cord. **2.** any disease of the myelopoietic tissues.

myeloperoxidase (MPO) /mī′əlōpərok′si dās/, a peroxidase enzyme occurring in phagocytic cells that can oxidize halide ions, producing a bactericidal effect.

myelopoiesis /mī′əlō′pō·ē′sis/ [Gk, *myelos + poiein,* to form], the formation and development of bone marrow or the cells that originate from it.—**myelopoietic** /-pō·et′ik/, *adj.*

myeloproliferative neoplasms /mī′əlōprōlif′ərətiv′/, a family of chronic malignant bone marrow and blood diseases caused by mutations that generate clones of myelocytic or erythrocytic precursors and platelet precursors.

myeloradiculodysplasia /mī′əlō′rədik′yə lō′dis′plā′zhə/ [Gk, *myelos;* L, *radiculus,* small root; Gk, *dys,* bad, *plassein,* to form], any developmental abnormality of the spinal cord and spinal nerve roots.

myeloschisis /mī′əlos′kəsis/ [Gk, *myelos* + *schisis*, cleft], a developmental defect characterized by a cleft spinal cord that results from the failure of the neural plate to fuse and form a complete neural tube.

myenteric plexus /mī′enter′ik/ [Gk, *mys*, muscle, *enteron*, bowel; L, *plexus*, plaited], a group of autonomic nerve fibers and ganglion cells in the muscular coat of the intestine.

myesthesia /mī′esthē′zhə/, perception of any sensation in a muscle, such as touch, direction, proprioception, contraction, relaxation, or extension.

myiasis /mī′yəsis/ [Gk, *myia*, fly, *osis*, condition], infection or infestation of the body by the larvae of flies, usually through a wound or an ulcer, but rarely through intact skin.

Myleran, a trademark for an antineoplastic (busulfan).

Mylicon, a trademark for an antiflatulent (simethicone).

mylohyoideus /mī′lōhī·oi′dē·əs/ [Gk, *myle*, mill, *hyoeides*, upsilon, U-shaped], one of a pair of flat triangular muscles that form the floor of the cavity of the mouth. It acts to raise the hyoid bone and the tongue.

myocardial infarction (MI) /mī′ōkär′dē·əl/ [Gk, *mys*, muscle, *kardia*, heart; L, *infarcire*, to stuff], necrosis of a portion of cardiac muscle caused by an obstruction in a coronary artery resulting from atherosclerosis, a thrombus, or a spasm. The onset is characterized by a crushing, viselike chest pain that may radiate to the left arm, neck, jaw, or epigastrium and sometimes stimulates the sensation of acute indigestion or a gallbladder attack. The patient usually becomes ashen, clammy, short of breath, nauseated, faint, and anxious and often feels that death is imminent. Typical signs are tachycardia, a barely palpable pulse, low BP, mildly elevated temperature, cardiac arrhythmia, and elevation of the ST segment and Q wave on the ECG.

myocardial insufficiency, inadequate functioning of the heart muscle.

myocardial ischemia, a condition of insufficient blood flow to the heart muscle via the coronary arteries, often resulting in chest pain (angina pectoris).

myocardial perfusion, the flow of blood to the heart muscle.

myocardiograph /mī′ōkär′dē·əgraf′/, a tracing device for recording the activity of heart muscle.

myocarditis /mī′ōkärdī′tis/ [Gk, *mys* + *kardia* + *itis*, inflammation], inflammation of the myocardium. It may be caused by viral, bacterial, or fungal infection; serum sickness; rheumatic fever; or a chemical agent; or it may be a complication of a collagen disease. Myocarditis most frequently occurs in an acute viral form and is self-limited, but it may lead to acute heart failure.

myocardium /mī′ōkär′dē·əm/ [Gk, *mys*, muscle, *kardia*, heart], a thick contractile middle layer of uniquely constructed and arranged muscle cells that forms the bulk of the heart wall. The myocardium contains a minimum of other tissue, except blood vessels, and is covered interiorly by the endocardium. The contractile tissue of the myocardium is composed of fibers with the characteristic cross-striations of muscular tissue. The fibers are about one third as large in diameter as those of skeletal muscle and contain more sarcoplasm. They branch frequently and are interconnected to form a network that is continuous, except where the bundles and the laminae are attached at their origins and insertions into the fibrous trigone of the heart. Most of the myocardial fibers function to contract the heart. —**myocardial,** *adj.*

myoclonic seizure, a seizure characterized by a brief episode of myoclonus (brief lightning-like jerks), with immediate recovery and often without LOC.

myoclonus /mī′ōklō′nəs/ [Gk, *mys*, muscle, *klonos*, contraction], a spasm of a muscle or a group of muscles. —**myoclonic,** *adj.*

myocutaneous flap /mī′ōkyōō·tā′nē·əs/ [Gk, *mys*, muscle; L, *cutis*, skin], a compound flap of skin and muscle with adequate vascularity to permit sufficient tissue to be transferred to the recipient site.

myocyte /mī′əsīt/, a muscle cell.

myodiastasis /mī′ōdī·as′təsis/ [Gk, *mys* + *diastasis*, separation], an abnormal condition in which there is separation of muscle bundles.

myoedema /mī′ō·idē′mə/ *pl.* **myoedemas, myoedemata,** muscle edema.

myoelectric, pertaining to the electric property of muscle.

myofascial /mī·ōfa′shē·əl/, pertaining to a muscle and its sheath of connective tissue, or fascia.

myofascial pain, jaw muscle distress associated with chewing or exercise of the masticatory muscles.

myofascial release, a set of massage techniques used to relieve muscle pain resulting from abnormally tight fascia.

myofibril /-fī′bril/ [Gk, *mys*; L, *fibrilla*, small fiber], a slender striated strand within skeletal and cardiac muscle fibers and composed of bundles of myofilaments.

myofilament /mī′ōfil′ə·mənt/ [Gk, *mys*, L, *filare*, to spin], any of the numerous ultramicroscopic threadlike structures occurring in bundles in the myofibrils of striated muscle fibers. The thick filaments of myosin and the thin filaments of actin are together responsible for the contractile properties of muscle.

myogelosis /mī′ōjəlō′sis/ [Gk, *mys*; L, *gelare,* to freeze; Gk, *osis*], a condition in which there are hardened areas or nodules within muscles, especially the gluteal muscles.

myogenic /mī′ōjen′ik/ [Gk, *mys* + *genesis,* origin], generated by muscles. The term usually refers to rhythmic activity in cardiac and smooth muscles, which do not require neural input to initiate and maintain contractions.

myoglobin /mī′ōglō′bin/ [Gk, *mys*; L, *globus,* ball], a ferrous globin complex in muscle consisting of one heme molecule containing one iron molecule attached to a single globin chain. Myoglobin is responsible for the red color of muscle and for its ability to store oxygen.

myoglobin test, a blood test that detects levels of myoglobin, an oxygen-binding protein found in cardiac and skeletal muscle. Measurement of myoglobin is an index of damage to the myocardium in MI or reinfarction, and also an indicator of disease or trauma of the skeletal muscle.

myoglobinuria /-glō′binōōr′ē·ə/ [Gk, *mys*; L, *globus*; Gk, *ouron,* urine], the presence of myoglobin in the urine. The condition usually occurs after massive muscle injury, physical trauma, or electric injury.

myoglobinuric renal failure /-glō′bi nōōr′ik/, a kidney disease in which large amounts of filtered myoglobin coalesce in the tubules, obstructing nephronal flow and producing epithelial cell injury.

myoma /mī·ō′mə/ *pl.* **myomas, myomata** [Gk, *mys* + *oma,* tumor], a common benign fibroid tumor of the uterine muscle. Menorrhagia, backache, constipation, dysmenorrhea, dyspareunia, and other symptoms develop in proportion to the size, location, and rate of growth of the tumor.

myomectomy /mī′ōmek′təmē/, the surgical removal of muscle tissue.

myometritis /mī′ōmətrī′tis/, an inflammation or infection of the myometrium of the uterus.

myometrium /mī′ōmē′trē·əm/ *pl.* **myometria** [Gk, *mys* + *metra,* womb], the muscular layer of the wall of the uterus.

myonecrosis /mī′ōnekrō′sis/ [Gk, *mys* + *necrosis,* death], the death of muscle fibers. Progressive or clostridial myonecrosis is caused by the anaerobic bacteria of the genus *Clostridium.* Seen in deep wound infections, progressive

myonecrosis is accompanied by pain, tenderness, a brown serous exudate, and a rapid accumulation of gas within the muscle tissue.

myoneural /mī′ōnōōr′əl/ [Gk, *mys* + *neuron,* nerve], pertaining to a muscle fiber and the synapse of the motor neuron, especially a nerve ending in a muscle.

myopathy /mī·op′əthē/ [Gk, *mys* + *pathos,* disease], an abnormal condition of skeletal muscle characterized by muscle weakness, wasting, and histologic changes within muscle tissue, as seen in any of the muscular dystrophies. A myopathy is distinct from a muscle disorder caused by nerve dysfunction. —**myopathic,** *adj.*

myope /mī′ōp/, an individual who is nearsighted or afflicted with myopia.

myopia /mī·ō′pē·ə/ [Gk, *myops,* nearsighted], a condition of nearsightedness caused by the elongation of the eyeball or by an error in refraction so that parallel rays are focused in front of the retina. —**myopic,** *adj.*

myorrhaphy /mī·ôr′əfē/ [Gk, *mys* + *rhaphe,* suture], suturing of a wound in a muscle.

myorrhexis /mī′ərek′sis/ [Gk, *mys* + *rhexis,* rupture], the tearing of any muscle.—**myorrhectic,** *adj.*

myosarcoma /mī′ōsärkō′mə/ [Gk, *mys* + *sarx,* flesh, *oma,* tumor], a malignant tumor of muscular tissue.

myosin /mī′əsin/ [Gk, *mys* + *in,* within], a protein that makes up close to one half of the total protein in muscle tissue. The interaction between myosin and actin is essential for muscle contraction.

myositis /mī′əsī′tis/, inflammation of muscle tissue, usually of voluntary muscle. Causes of myositis include infection, trauma, and infestation by parasites.

myositis fibrosa, an uncommon inflammation of the muscles, characterized by abnormal formation of connective tissue.

myositis ossificans /əsif′əkanz/, a rare inherited disease in which muscle tissue is replaced by bone.

myositis ossificans progressiva, a progressive disease, beginning in early life, in which the muscles are gradually converted into bony tissue.

myositis purulenta, any bacterial infection of muscle tissue. This condition may result in the formation of an abscess or multiple abscesses.

myositis trichinosa /trik′ənō′sə/, inflammation of the muscles resulting from infection by the parasite *Trichinella spiralis.*

myostasis /mī′ōstā′sis/ [Gk, *mys* + *stasis,* standing], a condition of muscle weakness

M

in which the resting length of the muscle is shorter than normal, which reduces the maximal tension the muscle can develop when it contracts.—**myostatic,** *adj.*

myostroma /mī′əstrō′mə/ [Gk, *mys* + *stroma,* covering], the framework of muscle tissue.

myotenotomy /-tenot′əmē/ [Gk, *mys* + *tenon,* tendon, *temnein,* to cut], surgical division of the whole or part of a muscle by cutting through its main tendon.

myotherapy /-ther′əpē/, a technique of corrective muscle exercises involving pressure on fingers and joints to relieve pain or spasms.

myotome /mī′ətōm/ [Gk, *mys* + *temnein,* to cut], **1.** the muscle plate of an embryonic somite that develops into a voluntary muscle. **2.** a group of muscles innervated by a single spinal segment. **3.** an instrument for cutting or dissecting a muscle.

myotomic muscle /-tom′ik/, any of the numerous muscles of the trunk of the body, derived from the myotomes and divided into the deep muscles of the back and the thoracoabdominal muscles.

myotomy /mī·ot′əmē/ [Gk, *mys* + *temnein,* to cut], the dissection or cutting of a muscle, performed to gain access to underlying tissues or to relieve constriction in a sphincter such as in severe esophagitis or pyloric stenosis.

Myotonachol, a trademark for a cholinergic (bethanechol chloride).

myotonia /mī′ətō′nē·ə/ [Gk, *mys* + *tonos,* tone], any condition in which a muscle or a group of muscles does not readily relax after contracting.—**myotonic,** *adj.*

myotonia congenita /konjen′itə/, a rare mild and nonprogressive form of myotonic myopathy evident early in life. The only effects of the disorder are hypertrophy and stiffness of the muscles.

myotonic muscular dystrophy /-ton′ik/, a severe form of muscular dystrophy marked by ptosis, facial weakness, and dysarthria. Weakness of the hands and feet precedes that in the shoulders and hips.

myotonic myopathy, any of a group of disorders characterized by increased skeletal muscle tone and decreased relaxation of muscle after contraction.

myotube /mī′otōōb/, a developing muscle cell or fiber with a centrally located nucleus.

myringectomy /mir′injek′təmē/ [L, *myringa,* eardrum; Gk, *ektomē,* excision], excision of the tympanic membrane.

myringitis /mir′injī′tis/ [L, *myringa;* Gk, *itis*], inflammation or infection of the tympanic membrane.

myringomycosis /miring′gōmīkō′sis/ [L, *myringa;* Gk, *mykes,* fungus, *osis,* condition], a fungal infection of the tympanic membrane.

myringoplasty /miring′gōplas′tē/ [L, *myringa;* Gk, *plassein,* to mold], surgical repair of perforations of the eardrum with a tissue graft, performed to correct hearing loss. The openings in the eardrum are enlarged, and the grafting material is sutured over them.

myringotomy /mir′ing·got′əmē/ [L, *myringa;* Gk, *temnein,* to cut], surgical incision of the eardrum, performed to relieve pressure and release pus or fluid from the middle ear.

Mysoline, a trademark for an anticonvulsant (primidone).

mysophobia /mē′sə-/ [Gk, *mysos,* anything disgusting, *phobos,* fear], an anxiety disorder characterized by an overreaction to the slightest uncleanliness or an irrational fear of dirt, contamination, or defilement. —**misophobic, mysophobic,** *adj.*

myxedema /mik′sədē′mə/ [Gk, *myxa,* mucus, *oidema,* swelling], the most severe form of hypothyroidism. It is characterized by swelling of the hands, face, feet, and periorbital tissues and may lead to coma and death.

myxofibroma /mik′sōfibrō′mə/ [Gk, *myxa;* L, *fibra,* fiber; Gk, *oma,* tumor], a fibrous tumor that contains myxomatous tissue.

myxoma /miksō′mə/ [Gk, *myxa* + *oma,* tumor], a neoplasm of the connective tissue, characteristically composed of stellate cells in a loose mucoid matrix crossed by delicate reticulum fibers. These tumors may grow to enormous size and may occur under the skin but are also found in bones, the genitourinary tract, and the retroperitoneal area.—**myxomatous,** *adj.*

myxopoiesis /mik′sōpō·ē′sis/ [Gk, *myxa* + *poiein,* to make], the production of mucus.

myxosarcoma /mik′sōsärkō′mə/ [Gk, *myxa* + *sarx,* flesh, *oma,* tumor], a sarcoma that contains some myxomatous tissue.

myxovirus /mik′sōvī′rəs/ [Gk, *myxa;* L, *virus,* poison], any of a group of medium-size RNA viruses that are further divided into orthomyxoviruses and paramyxoviruses. The viruses that cause influenza, mumps, and parainfluenza are myxoviruses.

MZ, abbreviation for **monozygotic.**

N, 1. symbol for the element **nitrogen.** 2. abbreviation for **normal.** 3. abbreviation for *node* in the TNM system for staging malignant neoplastic disease. 4. symbol for **magnetic flux.** 5. abbreviation for the amino acid **asparagine.**

N/1, symbol for **normal solution.**

n, 2n, 3n, 4n, symbols for the haploid, diploid, triploid, and tetraploid number of chromosomes in a cell, organism, strain, or individual.

N_A, symbol for **Avogadro's number.**

nA, abbreviation for *nanoampere,* one billionth of an ampere.

Na, chemical symbol for the element **sodium.**

nabilone, an antiemetic used to prevent nausea and vomiting associated with cancer chemotherapy in those who have not responded to other treatment.

nabothian cyst /nabōʹthē·ən/ [Martin Naboth, German physician, 1675–1721; Gk, *kystis,* bag], a cyst formed in a nabothian gland of the uterine cervix. The cyst, which is pearly white and firm, seldom results in adverse or pathologic effects.

nabothian gland /nabōʹthē·ən/ [Martin Naboth; L, *glans,* acorn], one of many small, mucus-secreting glands of the uterine cervix.

NAD, abbreviation for *no appreciable disease.*

NADH, abbreviation for *nicotine adenine dinucleotide, reduced.*

nadir /nāʹdər/, the lowest point, such as the blood count after it has been depressed by chemotherapy.

nadolol /nadʹolol/, a beta-adrenergic blocking agent prescribed for long-term management of angina pectoris, for hypertension, and for migraine prophylaxis.

NADPH, abbreviation for *nicotine adenine disphosphonucleotide, reduced.*

NADPH oxidase defect, a disorder in patients with chronic granulomatosis disease. It is caused by an abnormality in the enzyme (nicotinamide adenine dinucleotide phosphate oxidase) that catalyzes the conversion of oxygen to superoxide anions and hydrogen peroxide in phagocytes. Phagocytes with the abnormal enzyme are unable to destroy invading microorganisms.

Naegleria /nāglērʹē·ə/ [F.P.O. Nägler, Austrian bacteriologist, 20th century], a genus of free-living protozoa found in freshwater, soil, and sewage. Certain species, especially *N. fowleri,* are capable of facultative parasitism, and some strains are highly pathogenic and may cause a highly fatal primary amebic meningoencephalitis.

naegleriasis /nāʹglərīʹəsis/, infection with *Naegleria.*

nafcillin sodium /nafsilʹin/, an antibiotic prescribed in the treatment of infections caused by penicillinase-producing staphylococci.

Naffziger sign /nafʹzigər/ [Howard C. Naffziger, American surgeon, 1884–1961], a diagnostic sign for sciatica or a herniated intervertebral disk. Nerve root irritation is produced by the examiner through external jugular venous compression.

Naffziger's syndrome [Howard C. Naffziger], a condition of cervical vertebral muscle spasms secondary to intervertebral disk disease, cervical rib disease, or other disorders. The spasms compress the major nerve plexus of the arm, causing the patient to experience pain in the neck, shoulder, arm, and hand.

Naffziger's test /nafʹzigərz/, (for nerve root compression) manual compression of the jugular veins bilaterally. An increase or aggravation of pain or sensory disturbance over the distribution of the involved nerve root confirms the presence of an extruded intervertebral disk or other mass.

Nägele's rule /nāʹgələz/ [Franz K. Nägele, German obstetrician, 1778–1851; L, *regula,* model], a method for calculating the estimated date of delivery based on a mean length of gestation. Three months are subtracted from the first day of the last normal menstrual period, and 1 year plus 7 days are added to that date.

Nager's acrofacial dysostosis /nāʹgərz/ [Felix R. Nager, Swiss physician, 1877–1959; Gk, *akron,* extremity; L, *facies,* face; Gk, *dys,* bad, *osteon,* bone, *osis,* condition], an abnormal congenital condition characterized by limb deformities such as radioulnar synostosis, hypoplasia, and the absence of the radius or of the thumbs.

Naglazyme, a trademark for galsulfase.

Nahrungs-Einheit-Milch (nem) /nä'rŏŏngz ĭn'hītmilsh, milkh/ [Ger, *Nahrung,* food, *Einheit,* unit, *Milch,* milk], a nutritional unit in Pirquet's system of feeding that is equivalent to 1 g of breast milk.

nail [AS, *naegel*], **1.** a flattened elastic structure with a horny texture at the end of a finger or a toe. Each nail is composed of a root, body, and free edge at the distal extremity. The root fastens the nail to the finger or the toe by fitting into a groove in the skin and is closely molded to the surface of the dermis. The nail matrix beneath the body and the root projects longitudinal vascular ridges. The matrix firmly attaches the body of the nail to the underlying connective tissue. The whitish lunula near the root contains irregularly arranged papillae that are less firmly attached to the connective tissue than the rest of the matrix. The cuticle is attached to the surface of the nail just ahead of the root. **2.** any of various metallic nails used in orthopedics to fasten together bones or pieces of bone.

nailbed [AS, *naegle,* nail, *bedd,* bed], the dermis beneath the nail. It appears through the clear nail as a series of longitudinal ridges.

nail biting, the habit of excessive biting and chewing one's fingernails and periungual skin, sometimes leading to cutaneous injury. The condition is commonly associated with body manipulations of anxious children. It is also considered a form of motor discharge of inner tension.

nail care, a nursing intervention from the Nursing Interventions Classification (NIC) defined as promotion of clean, neat, attractive nails and prevention of skin lesions related to improper care of nails.

nail fold, a fold of skin supporting a nail at its base.

nail groove [AS, *naegle;* D, *groeve,* groove], a shallow depression between the nailbed and the nail wall.

nail-patella syndrome, a hereditary syndrome consisting of dystrophy of the nails, absence or hypoplasia of the patella, hypoplasia of the lateral side of the elbow joint, and bilateral iliac horns.

nail plate, the rigid outer part of a nail. It extends about 8 mm under the nail fold and arises from the nailbed.

nail plate avulsion, a partial or complete removal of the nail plate without disruption of the underlying matrix cells.

nalbuphine, a synthetic opioid agonist and antagonist used to treat moderate to severe pain.

Nalebuff arthrodesis, surgical fixation of the wrist accomplished with the use of a Steinmann pin.

Nalfon, a trademark for an antiinflammatory agent (fenoprofen calcium).

nalidixic acid /nal'idik'sik/, an antibacterial prescribed in the treatment of certain UTIs.

nalmefene /nal'mefēn'/, an opioid antagonist, used as the hydrochloride salt in the treatment of opioid overdose and postoperative opioid depression.

naloxone hydrochloride /nal'əksŏn/, an opioid antagonist prescribed for reversal of respiratory depression and other opioid effects in patients receiving opioid analgesics and in patients who have abused heroin, morphine, or other synthetic opioids.

naltrexone hydrochloride /naltrek'sŏn/, an oral opioid antagonist prescribed to block the effects of opioid analgesics, including heroin, morphine, and methadone, in patients recovering from addiction and to treat ethanol dependence.

Namaqualand hip dysplasia, an autosomal-dominant genetic defect found in children of African heritage. It is characterized by a growth failure in the femoral epiphysis, resulting in pain and early degenerative arthritis of the hip.

Namenda, a trademark for memantine.

NAMI, abbreviation for **National Alliance for the Mentally Ill.**

NANB, abbreviation for *non-A, non-B hepatitis.*

NANDA, abbreviation for **North American Nursing Diagnosis Association,** a professional organization of registered nurses created in 1982. The purpose of the organization is "to develop, refine, and promote a taxonomy of nursing diagnostic terminology of general use to the professional." This organization is now called **NANDA International** with an abbreviation of **NANDA-I.** This organization no longer uses North American Nursing Diagnosis as its full name.

nandrolone /nan'drəlŏn/, an anabolic steroid prescribed to treat metastatic breast cancer in females and to increase hemoglobin and red cell mass in the management of the anemia of renal insufficiency.

nanism /nā'nizəm, nan'-/ [Gk, *nanos,* dwarf], an abnormal smallness or underdevelopment of the body; dwarfism.

nanocephaly /nā'nōsef'əlē, nan'-/ [Gk, *nanos + kephale,* head], a developmental defect characterized by abnormal smallness of the head.—**nanocephalous,** *adj.,* **nanocephalus,** *n.*

nanocormia /nā'nōkôr'mē-ə/ [Gk, *nanos + kormos,* trunk], abnormal disproportionate smallness of the trunk of the body in comparison with the head and limbs. —**nanocormus,** *n.*

nanocurie (nCi) /nan'əkyŏŏr'ē/ [Gk, *nanos,* dwarf; Marie and Pierre Curie], a unit of radiation equal to one billionth of a curie.

nanogram (ng) /nan'əgram/ [Gk, *nanos*; Fr, *gramme*, small weight], one billionth (10^{-9}) of a gram.

nanomelia /nä'nōmē'lyə, nan'-/ [Gk, *nanos* + *melos*, limb], a developmental defect characterized by abnormally small limbs in comparison with the size of the head and trunk.—**nanomelous,** *adj.,* **nanomelus,** *n.*

nanometer (nm) /nan'əmē'tər/ [Gk, *nanos* + *metron*, measure], a unit of length equal to one billionth of a meter.

nanophthalmos /nä'nofthal'məs, nan'-/ [Gk, *nanos* + *ophthalmos*, eye], the condition in which one or both eyes are abnormally small, although other ocular defects are not present.

nanosecond (ns) /nan'əsek'ənd/ [Gk, *nanos*, dwarf; L, *secundus*, second], one billionth (10^{-9}) of a second.

nanosomus /nä'nōsō'məs/ [Gk, *nanos* + *soma*, body], a person of very short stature; a dwarf.

nanotechnology /-teknol'əjē/, technology at the level of atoms, molecules, and molecular fragments, including manipulating them and creating new structures.

nanukayami /nä'nōōkäyä'mē/ [Jpn], an acute, infectious disease caused by one of the serotypes of the spirochete *Leptospira*.

nanus /nä'nəs/, a pygmy.—**nanoid** /nä' noid/, *adj.*

napalm /nä'päm/, abbreviation for *napthenate palmitate*, a form of jellied gasoline used in warfare.

napalm burn [AS, *baernan*, burn], a thermal burn caused by contact with flaming **napalm.**

nape [ME], the back of the neck.

naphazoline hydrochloride /nəfaz'əlēn/, an adrenergic vasoconstrictor prescribed in the treatment of nasal congestion and as an ophthalmic vasoconstrictor to decrease redness and itching.

naphthalene poisoning /naf'thələn/ [Gk, *naptha*, flammable liquid; L, *potio*, drink], a toxic condition caused by the ingestion of naphthalene or paradichlorobenzene that may cause increased heart rate, nausea, vomiting, headache, abdominal pain, spasm, and convulsions. Naphthalene and paradichlorobenzene are common ingredients in mothballs, moth crystals, and toilet bowl deodorizers. Paradichlorobenzene is also used as an insecticide in agriculture.

napkin ring tumor [ME, *nappekin*, tablecloth, *hring*, band; L, *tumor*, swelling], a tumor that encircles a tubular structure of the body, usually impairing its function and constricting its lumen to some degree.

NAP-NAP, abbreviation for **National Association of Pediatric Nurse Associates/Practitioners.**

NAPNES, abbreviation for **National Association for Practical Nurse Education and Services.**

napping [ME, *nappen*, to doze], periods of sleep, usually during the day, which may last from 15 to 60 minutes without attaining the level of deep sleep.

Naprosyn, a trademark for a nonsteroidal antiinflammatory, antipyretic, and analgesic agent (naproxen).

naproxen /naprok'sən/, a nonsteroidal antiinflammatory agent prescribed for the relief of fever, migraine headache, inflammatory symptoms of rheumatoid arthritis and osteoarthritis, and mild to moderate pain and for treatment of primary dysmenorrhea, ankylosing spondylitis, tendinitis, bursitis, and acute gout.

NAPT, abbreviation for *National Association of Physical Therapists*.

Naqua, a trademark for a diuretic and antihypertensive agent (trichlormethiazide).

naratriptan, a migraine agent used in the acute treatment of migraine with or without aura.

narc, abbreviation for **narcotic.**

Narcan, a trademark for an opioid antagonist (naloxone hydrochloride).

narcissism /när'sisiz'əm/ [Gk, *Narcissus*, mythic youth in love with himself], **1.** an abnormal interest in oneself, especially in one's own body and sexual characteristics; self-love. **2.** in psychoanalysis, sexual self-interest that is a normal characteristic of the phallic stage of psychosexual development, occurring as the infantile ego acquires a libido. Narcissism in the adult is abnormal.

narcissistic personality, a disposition characterized by behavior and attitudes that indicate an abnormal love of the self.

narcissistic personality disorder /när'sisis'tik/, a psychiatric diagnosis characterized by an exaggerated sense of self-importance and uniqueness, an abnormal need for attention and admiration, preoccupation with grandiose fantasies concerning the self, and disturbances in interpersonal relationships, usually involving the exploitation of others and a lack of empathy.

narcoanalysis /när'kōənal'isis/, an interview conducted while the patient is deeply sedated with medication so that inhibitions are reduced and responses will be more truthful.

narcohypnosis /-hipnō'sis/ [Gk, *narke*, stupor, *hypnos*, sleep], hypnosis induced with the aid of a narcotic drug such as sodium amobarbital or sodium pentothal.

narcolepsy /när'kəlep'sē/ [Gk, *narke*, stupor, *lambanein*, to seize], a syndrome characterized by sudden sleep attacks, cataplexy, sleep paralysis, and visual or auditory hallucinations at the onset of sleep. Persons with narcolepsy experience an uncontrollable desire to sleep, sometimes many times in one day. Episodes may last from a few minutes to several hours. Momentary loss of muscle tone occurs during waking hours (cataplexy) or while the person is asleep.

narcoleptic /närˈkəlepˈtik/, **1.** pertaining to a condition or substance that causes an uncontrollable desire for sleep. **2.** a narcoleptic drug. **3.** a person suffering from narcolepsy.

Narcon, abbreviation for *Narcotics Anonymous.*

narcosis /närkōˈsis/ [Gk, *narkosis,* numbness], a state of insensibility or stupor caused by opioid drugs.

narcotic (narc) /narkotˈik/ [Gk,*narkotikos,* benumbing], **1.** pertaining to a substance that produces insensibility or stupor. **2.** a narcotic drug. Narcotic analgesics, derived from opium or produced synthetically, alter perception of pain; induce euphoria, mood changes, mental clouding, and deep sleep; depress respiration and the cough reflex; constrict the pupils; and cause smooth muscle spasm, decreased peristalsis, emesis, and nausea. Repeated use of narcotics may result in physical and psychologic dependence.

narcotic addict, a person who is psychologically and physically dependent on narcotic drugs, a condition in which the drug may be present in the body in amounts great enough to be toxic or sufficient to alter behavior.

narcotic poisoning [Gk, *narkotikos,* be numbing; L, *potio,* drink], the toxic effects of a narcotic drug that depresses the brain centers, causing unconsciousness or coma. Narcotic drugs are generally derived from opium, but other drugs, including alcohol, can produce similar effects.

narcotize /närˈkətiz/, to subject to the influence of narcotics.

Nardil, a trademark for an antidepressant (phenelzine sulfate).

nares /nerˈēz/, *sing.* **naris,** the pairs of anterior and posterior openings to the nasal cavity that allow the passage of air to the pharynx and ultimately the lungs during respiration.

nas, abbreviation for **nasal.**

nasal (nas) /näˈzəl/ [L, *nasus,* nose], **1.** pertaining to the nose and the nasal cavity. **2.** a speech sound produced by having air flow through the nose, such as /n/, /ng/, or /m/.—**nasally,** *adv.*

nasal airway, a flexible, curved piece of rubber or plastic, with one wide, trumpetlike end and one narrow end that can be inserted through the nose into the pharynx.

nasal balloon tamponade, a procedure for the control of posterior epistaxis in which a nasal balloon is inserted into the nasal cavity and filled with saline solution. Alternatively, a Foley catheter can be placed through the nostril and used in the same manner.

nasal cannula, a device for delivering oxygen by way of two small tubes that are inserted into the nares.

nasal cartilage [L, *nasus,* nose + *cartilago*], a flat plate of cartilage in the lower anterior part of the nasal septum.

nasal cavity, one of a pair of cavities that open on the face through the pear-shaped anterior nares and communicate posteriorly with the pharynx.

nasal decongestant, a drug that provides temporary relief of nasal symptoms in acute and chronic rhinitis and sinusitis. Most are OTC products. Prolonged use or dosage greater than recommended on the package may cause rebound vasodilation and severe congestion (rhinitis medicamentosa).

nasal drip, a method of slowly infusing liquid into a dehydrated infant by means of a catheter inserted through the nose down the esophagus.

nasal fin, a thickened platelike ectodermal structure between the lateral and medial nasal prominences that thins to form the oronasal membrane.

nasal fossa, one of the pair of approximately equal chambers of the nasal cavity that are separated by the nasal septum and open externally through the nares and internally into the nasopharynx through the internal nares. Each fossa is divided into an olfactory region, consisting of the superior nasal concha and part of the septum, and a respiratory region, constituting the rest of the chamber.

nasal fracture reduction, repair of the paired nasal bones or cartilage. Reduction can be closed or open. Closed reduction is usually performed by digital and instrumental manipulation with the patient under topical and local anesthesia. When the fracture is severe, open reduction under general anesthesia with interosseous wire fixation of bone fragments may be necessary.

nasal glioma, a neoplasm characterized by the ectopic growth of neural tissue in the nasal cavity.

nasal instillation of medication, the instillation of a medicated solution into the nostrils by an atomized spray from a squeeze bottle or a nasal inhaler. The patient holds one nostril closed while spraying the medication into the opposite nostril. Nasal spray is administered to the patient in a sitting position.

nasalis /nāzal′is/ [L, *nasus*, nose], one of the three muscles of the nose, divided into a transverse part and an alar part. The transverse part serves to depress the cartilaginous part of the nose and to draw the alar toward the nostril. The alar part serves to dilate the nostril.

nasal obstruction [L, *nasus*, nose + *obstruere*], a narrowing of the nasal cavity, thereby reducing the breathing capacity, caused by an irregular or deviated septum, nasal polyps, foreign bodies, or enlarged turbinates. Sinusitis is a common complication.

nasal placode, an oval area of thickened ectoderm on either ventrolateral surface of the head of the early embryo, constituting the first indication of the olfactory organ.

nasal polyp, a rounded, elongated piece of pulpy, dependent mucosa that projects into the nasal cavity.

nasal septum, the partition dividing the nostrils. It is composed of bone and cartilage covered by mucous membrane.

nasal sinus, any one of the numerous cavities in various bones of the skull, lined with ciliated mucous membrane continuous with that of the nasal cavity. The nasal sinuses are divided into frontal sinuses, ethmoidal air cells, sphenoidal sinuses, and maxillary sinus.

Nasarel, a trademark for an intranasal steroid antiinflammatory agent (flunisolide).

nascent /nas′ənt, nā′sənt/ [L, *nasci*, to be born], **1.** just born; beginning to exist; incipient. **2.** in chemistry, pertaining to any substance liberated during a chemical reaction, which, because of its uncombined state, is more reactive.

nascent oxygen, oxygen that has just been liberated from a chemical compound.

nasion /nā′zē·on/ [L, *nasus*, nose], **1.** the anthropometric reference point at the front of the skull where the midsagittal plane intersects a horizontal line tangential to the highest points in the superior palpebral sulci. **2.** the depression at the root of the nose that indicates the junction of the intranasal and the frontonasal sutures.

nasociliary nerve, usually the first branch of the ophthalmic nerve. It branches into the communicating branch with the ciliary ganglion; the long ciliary nerves, which are sensory to the eyeball but may also contain sympathetic fibers for pupillary dilation; the posterior ethmoidal nerve, which supplies the posterior ethmoidal air cells and the sphenoid sinus; the infratrochlear nerve, which distributes to the medial part of the upper and lower eyelids, the lacrimal sac, and the skin of the upper half of the nose; and the anterior ethmoidal nerve,

which supplies the anterior cranial fossa, nasal cavity, and skin of the lower half of the nose.

nasogastric /nā′zōgas′trik/ [L, *nasus*, nose; Gk, *gaster*, stomach], pertaining to the nose and stomach.

nasogastric back wall echo, in ultrasonography, an echo from the posterior surface of the nasal cavity.

nasogastric intubation, the placement of a nasogastric tube through the nose into the stomach to relieve gastric distension by removing gas, gastric secretions, or food; to instill medication, food, or fluids; or to obtain a specimen for laboratory analysis.

nasogastric suction, the removal by suction of solids, fluids, or gases from the GI tract through a tube inserted into the stomach or intestines via the nasal cavity.

nasogastric tube (NG tube), any tube passed into the stomach through the nose.

nasojejunal tube /nā′zōjijōō′nəl/, a mercury-weighted tube inserted through the nose to allow natural peristaltic movement from the pylorus into the jejunum.

nasolabial /nā′zōlā′bē·əl/ [L, *nasus*, nose, *labium*, lip], pertaining to the nose and lip.

nasolabial reflex [L, *nasus*, nose, *labium*, lip], a sudden backward movement of the head, arching of the back, and extension and stretching of the limbs that occur in infants in response to a light touch to the tip of the nose with an upward sweeping motion.

nasolacrimal /nā′zōlak′riməl/ [L, *nasus* + *lacrima*, tear], pertaining to the nasal cavity and associated lacrimal ducts.

nasolacrimal duct, a channel that carries tears from the lacrimal sac to the nasal cavity.

nasolacrimal groove [L, *nasus*, nose, *lacrima*, tear; D, *groeve*, a shallow depression], a groove on the nasal surface of the upper jaw.

nasomandibular fixation /nā′zōmandib′yōōlər/ [L, *nasus* + *mandere*, to chew, *figere*, to fasten], a type of maxillomandibular fixation to stabilize fractures of the jaw by using maxillomandibular splints connected to a wire through a hole drilled in the anterior nasal spine of the maxillary bone.

nasomental reflex /-men′təl/ [L, *nasus*, nose, *mentum*, chin, *reflectere*, to bend back], a reflex elicited by tapping the side of the nose, thereby causing contraction of the mentalis muscle with elevation of the lower lip and wrinkling of the skin of the chin.

nasopalatine nerve, the largest of the nasal nerves, which passes across the roof

N

nasopharyngeal /nā´zōferin´jē-əl/, pertaining to the cavity of the nose and the nasal parts of the pharynx.

nasopharyngeal angiofibroma [L, *nasus;* Gk, *pharynx,* throat], a benign tumor of the nasopharynx consisting of fibrous connective tissue with many vascular spaces. Typical signs are nasal and eustachian tube obstruction, adenoidal speech, and dysphagia.

nasopharyngeal cancer, a malignant neoplastic disease of the nasopharynx. Depending on the site of a nasopharyngeal tumor, there may be nasal obstruction, otitis media, hearing loss, sensory or motor nerve damage, bony destruction of the skull, or deep cervical lymphadenopathy. Squamous cell and undifferentiated carcinomas are the most common lesions.

nasopharyngography /-fer´ingog´rəfē/ [L, *nasus;* Gk, *pharynx,* throat, *graphein,* to record], radiographic imaging and examination of the nasopharynx.

nasopharyngoscopy /nā´zōfer´ing·gos´kəpē/ [L, *nasus;* Gk, *pharynx,* throat, *skopein,* to look], a technique in physical examination in which the nose and throat are visually examined by using a laryngoscope, a fiberoptic device, a flashlight, and a dilator for the nares.—**nasopharyngoscopic,** *adj.*

nasopharynx /nā´zōfer´ingks/ [L, *nasus;* Gk, *pharynx,* throat], the uppermost of the three regions of the throat (pharynx), situated behind the nasal cavity and extending from the posterior nares to the level above the soft palate. On the posterior wall of the nasopharynx, opposite the posterior nares, are the pharyngeal tonsils. —**nasopharyngeal,** *adj.*

nasotracheal tube /-trā´kē-əl/ [L, *nasus;* Gk, *tracheia,* rough artery; L, *tubus*], a catheter inserted through the nasal cavity into the trachea. It is commonly attached to a mechanical ventilator or a resuscitator bag to administer oxygen.

Nasu-Hakola disease, a rare autosomal-recessive syndrome of bone cysts with presenile dementia.

natal /nā´təl/, **1.** [L, *natus*] pertaining to birth. **2.** pertaining to the nates, or buttocks.

natalizumab, an MS agent and monoclonal antibody used to treat ambulatory patients with relapsing-remitting MS who have not responded to other treatments. An unlabeled use is for the treatment of Crohn's disease.

natamycin /nat´ämi´sin/, a polyene antibiotic used in topical treatment of fungal keratitis, blepharitis, and conjunctivitis.

nateglinide /näteg´linīd/, an antidiabetic agent that lowers blood glucose concentrations by stimulating the release of insulin from pancreatic islet beta cells. It is administered orally in the treatment of type 2 DM, either alone or in combination with metformin.

nates /nā´tēz/ *sing.* **natis** [L, buttocks], the fleshy hillocks at the lower posterior part of the torso comprising fat and the gluteal muscles.

National Alliance for the Mentally Ill (NAMI), a national organization for family members of patients with mental illness.

National Association for Practical Nurse Education and Services (NAPNES), an organization concerned with the education of practical nurses and with the services provided by licensed practical nurses in the United States.

National Association of Pediatric Nurse Associates/Practitioners (NAP-NAP), an organization of nurses who are prepared by education or experience to give primary care to pediatric patients in the United States. NAP-NAP works in conjunction with the American Academy of Pediatrics.

National Board of Surgical Technology & Surgical Assisting (NBSTSA), an organization established in 1974 that administers the national certification examinations for surgical technologists and surgical assistants, and designates the CST® and CFA® credentials to candidates who successfully pass the exam.

National Cancer Institute (NCI), an institute of the National Institutes of Health that leads a national effort to reduce the burden of cancer morbidity and mortality by stimulating and supporting scientific discoveries through basic and clinical biomedical research and training. It conducts and supports programs to understand the causes of cancer; prevent, detect, diagnose, treat, and control cancer; and disseminate information to the practitioner, patient, and public in general.

National Center for Chronic Disease Prevention and Health Promotion (NCCD-PHP), an organizational component of the Centers for Disease Control and Prevention, charged with preventing premature death and disability from chronic diseases and promoting healthy personal behaviors.

National Center for Environmental Health (NCEH), an organizational component of the Centers for Disease

Control and Prevention, charged with providing national leadership in prevention and control of disease and death resulting from the interaction between people and their environment.

National Center for Health Statistics (NCHS), an organizational component of the Centers for Disease Control and Prevention, charged with providing statistical information that will guide actions and policies to improve the health of the American people.

National Center for HIV, STD, and TB Prevention (NCHSTP), an organizational component of the Centers for Disease Control and Prevention, charged with providing national leadership in preventing and controlling HIV infection, STDs, and TB.

National Center for Infectious Diseases (NCID), an organizational component of the Centers for Disease Control and Prevention, charged with preventing illness, disability, and death caused by infectious diseases in the United States and around the world.

National Center for Injury Prevention and Control (NCIPC), an organizational component of the Centers for Disease Control and Prevention, charged with preventing death and disability from nonoccupational injuries, including those that are unintentional and those that result from violence.

National Center for Research Resources (NCRR), an institute of the National Institutes of Health that advances biomedical research and improves human health through research projects and shared resources that create, develop, and provide a comprehensive range of human, animal, technologic, and other resources.

National Center on Birth Defects and Developmental Disabilities (NCBDDD), an organizational component of the Centers for Disease Control and Prevention, charged with providing national leadership for preventing birth defects and developmental disabilities and for improving the health and wellness of people with disabilities.

National Center on Minority Health and Health Disparities (NCMHD), an institute of the National Institutes of Health whose mission is to reduce and ultimately eliminate health disparities between racial and ethnic minorities (and other groups, such as the urban and rural poor) and society as a whole. It does this by conducting and supporting basic, clinical, and behavioral research and offering emerging programs, training, and information dissemination in this area.

National Certification Board for Therapeutic Massage and Bodywork, an agency that offers certification to therapeutic massage and bodywork practitioners who meet eligibility criteria, pass a certification exam, uphold a national code of ethics and standard of practice, and demonstrate continued education in their field.

National Committee for Quality Assurance (NCQA), a U.S. independent nonprofit accrediting body for managed health care organizations. Its focus is on improving quality of care in the managed care industry by assessing compliance of health plans to NCQA-developed standards for quality improvement, utilization management, credentialing processes, member rights and responsibilities, preventive services, and record management.

National Council Licensure Examination (NCLEX), a comprehensive integrated examination, developed and administered by the National Council of State Boards of Nursing, designed to test basic competency for nursing practice. The exam is administered by the individual boards of nursing that are members of the National Council of State Boards of Nursing and can be offered to candidates for licensure as registered nurses or as practical/vocational nurses.

National Council of State Boards of Nursing, an organization through which boards of nursing from all 50 states, the District of Columbia, Guam, American Samoa, The Commonwealth of the Northern Mariana Islands, Puerto Rico, and the Virgin Islands act and counsel together on matters of common interest and concern related to the safe and effective practice of nursing in the interest of public health, safety, and welfare, including the development of nurse licensure examinations.

National Eye Institute (NEI), one of several institutes of the National Institutes of Health. NEI was established in 1968 to support research in the normal functioning of the human eye and visual system, the pathology of visual disorders, and the rehabilitation of the visually handicapped.

National Formulary (NF, N.F.), a publication containing the official standards for the preparation of various pharmaceuticals not listed in the *United States Pharmacopeia.* It is revised every 5 years.

national health insurance, a health insurance program in many countries other than the United States that is financed by taxes and administered by the government to provide comprehensive health care that is accessible to all citizens of that nation.

National Health Planning and Resources Development Act of 1974, U.S. congressional legislation (PL 93-641) that established a nationwide network of health systems agencies. The act provides for the coordination and direction of national health policy through state and regional regulatory agencies.

National Health Service Corps (NHSC), a program of the U.S. Public Health Service (USPHS) in which health care personnel are placed in areas that are underserved. The Corps was established by the Emergency Health Personnel Act of 1970. Nurses, physicians, and dentists serve in rural and urban areas, usually as employees of local health care agencies.

National Heart, Lung, and Blood Institute (NHLBI), an institute of the National Institutes of Health whose mission is to provide leadership for a national program in diseases of the heart, blood vessels, lungs, and blood, as well as blood resources and sleep disorders. It also has administrative responsibility for the NIH Women's Health Initiative.

National Human Genome Research Institute (NHGRI), an institute of the National Institutes of Health (NIH) that supports the NIH component of the human genome project.

National Immunization Program (NIP), an organizational component of the Centers for Disease Control and Prevention, charged with preventing disease, disability, and death from vaccine-preventable diseases in children and adults.

National Institute for Occupational Safety and Health (NIOSH), an organizational component of the Centers for Disease Control and Prevention, charged with ensuring safety and health for all people in the workplace through research and prevention.

National Institute of Allergy and Infectious Diseases (NIAID), an institute of the National Institutes of Health whose mission is to understand, treat, and ultimately prevent infectious, immunologic, and allergic disorders affecting human beings.

National Institute of Arthritis and Musculoskeletal and Skin Diseases (NIAMS), an institute of the National Institutes of Health that supports research into the causes, treatment, and prevention of arthritis, musculoskeletal diseases, and skin diseases.

National Institute of Biomedical Imaging and Bioengineering (NIBIB), an institute of the National Institutes of Health whose mission is to improve health by promoting fundamental discoveries, design and development, translation, and assessment of technological capabilities in biomedical imaging and bioengineering.

National Institute of Child Health and Human Development (NICHHD), a branch of the National Institutes of Health that is concerned with all aspects of the growth, development, and health of the children of the United States. It conducts research on fertility, pregnancy, growth, development, and medical rehabilitation, striving to ensure that every child is born healthy and wanted and grows up free from disease and disability.

National Institute of Dental and Craniofacial Research (NIDCR), an institute of the National Institutes of Health that provides leadership for a national research program designed to understand, treat, and ultimately prevent infectious and inherited craniofacial, oral, and dental diseases and disorders.

National Institute of Diabetes and Digestive and Kidney Diseases (NIDDK), an institute of the National Institutes of Health that conducts and supports basic and applied research and provides leadership for a national program in diabetes, endocrinology, and metabolic diseases; digestive diseases and nutrition; and kidney, urologic, and hematologic diseases.

National Institute of Environmental Health Sciences (NIEHS), an institute of the National Institutes of Health whose mission is to reduce the burden of human illness and dysfunction from environmental causes by defining how environmental exposures, genetic susceptibility, and age interact to affect the individual's health.

National Institute of General Medical Sciences (NIGMS), an institute of the National Institutes of Health whose mission is to support biomedical research that is not targeted at specific diseases, resulting in increased understanding of life and laying the foundation for advances in disease diagnosis, treatment, and prevention.

National Institute of Mental Health (NIMH), an institute of the National Institutes of Health whose mission is to provide national leadership in the understanding, treatment, and prevention of mental illnesses through basic research on the brain and behavior, and through clinical, epidemiologic, and services research.

National Institute of Neurological Disorders and Stroke, an institute of the National Institutes of Health whose mission is to reduce the burden of neurologic diseases by supporting and conducting research (both basic and clinical) on the normal and diseased nervous system, fostering the training of investigators in the neurosciences, and seeking better understanding, diagnosis, treatment, and prevention of neurologic disorders.

National Institute of Nursing Research (NINR), an institute of the National Institutes of Health that supports clinical and basic research to establish a scientific basis for the care of individuals across the life span in a variety of ways.

National Institute of Standards and Technology (NIST), a federal agency in the Department of Commerce that sets accurate measurement standards for commerce, industry, and science in the United States. The NIST compares and coordinates its standards with those of other countries.

National Institute on Aging (NIA), an institute of the National Institutes of Health that leads a national program of research on the biomedical, social, and behavioral aspects of the aging process; the prevention of age-related diseases and disabilities; and the promotion of a better quality of life for older Americans.

National Institute on Alcohol Abuse and Alcoholism, an institute of the National Institutes of Health that conducts research focused on improving the treatment and prevention of alcoholism and alcohol-related problems.

National Institute on Deafness and Other Communication Disorders, an institute of the National Institutes of Health that conducts and supports biomedical research and research training on normal mechanisms, diseases, and disorders of hearing, balance, smell, taste, voice, speech, and language.

National Institute on Drug Abuse (NIDA), an institute of the National Institutes of Health that seeks to bring the power of science to bear on drug abuse and addiction through support and conduct of research across a broad range of disciplines, with rapid and effective dissemination of results of the research.

National Institutes of Health (NIH), an agency of the U.S. Department of Health and Human Services made up of several institutions and constituent divisions, including the Bureau of Health Manpower Education, the National Library of Medicine, the National Cancer Institute, and several research institutes and divisions. NIH is divided into two parts: one part is responsible for funding of biomedical research outside of NIH, and the other conducts research.

National League for Nursing (NLN), an organization concerned with the improvement of nursing education and nursing service and the provision of health care in the United States. Among its many activities are preadmission and achievement tests for nursing students and compilation of statistical data on nursing personnel and trends in health care delivery.

National League for Nursing Accrediting Commission (NLNAC), a corporation established in 2001 that is a wholly-owned subsidiary of the National League for Nursing and is responsible for accreditation of nursing education schools and programs in the United States.

National Library of Medicine (NLM), a library and information resource center that is part of the National Institutes of Health. It collects, organizes, and makes available biomedical science information to investigators, educators, and practitioners and carries out programs designed to strengthen medical library services in the United States. It offers a free search engine, PubMed, and its electronic databases include MEDLINE and MEDLINEplus.

National Male Nurses Association (NMNA), an organization that promotes the interests and practice of male nurses in the United States.

National Marrow Donor Program (NMDP), a coordinating center for bone marrow transplants, providing links with national and international registries of prospective volunteer donors of human leukocyte antigen–compatible bone marrow tissue.

National Organization of Victim Assistance, a private nonprofit organization in the United States of victims and witness assistance practitioners, criminal justice professionals, researchers, former victims, and others committed to the recognition of victims' rights and services.

National Society of Critical Care Nurses of Canada (NSCCN), an organization of Canadian critical care nurses, established originally in 1975 as the Toronto Chapter of the American Association of Critical-Care Nurses. The group became an independent Canadian organization in 1983.

National Student Nurses Association (NSNA), an organization of students in the field of nursing in the United States. Among its purposes are the improvement of nursing education to improve health care, aid in the development of the nursing student, and encourage optimal achievement in the professional role of the nurse and the health care of people.

Native American medicine, therapies used by many Native American Indian tribes that include their own healing herbs and ceremonies using components with a spiritual emphasis. An individual's connection to Nature and Mother Earth and communion with the spirit world is either in or out of harmony. The unique energies of the eight directions of the medicine wheel, as well as the sky, sun, moon, and earth, all play an integral part in Native American cosmology. Symptoms of illness are seen as connected with the spirit, and energy is then used as a catalyst to help patients come back into harmony.

natremia /nātrē′mē·ə/ [L, *natrium,* sodium; Gk, *haima,* blood], the presence of sodium in the blood.

natriuresis /nā′trēyo͞orē′sis/ [L, *natrium,* sodium; Gk, *ouresis,* urination], the excretion of greater-than-normal amounts of sodium in the urine. The condition may result from the administration of natriuretic diuretic drugs or from various metabolic or endocrine disorders.

natriuretic /nā′trēyo͞oret′ik/, **1.** pertaining to the process of natriuresis. **2.** a substance that inhibits the resorption of sodium ions from the glomerular filtrate in the kidneys, thus allowing more sodium to be excreted with the urine.

natriuretic peptides test, a blood test to predict CHF, MI, systemic hypertension, cor pulmonale, or heart transplant rejection.

natural antibody /nach′(ə)rəl/ [L, *natura,* nature; Gk, *anti;* AS, *bodig,* body], an antibody that is present in serum in the absence of an apparent specific antigen contact.

natural childbirth [L, *natura,* nature; AS, *cild,* child; ME, *bwith,* birth], labor and parturition accomplished by a mother with little or no medical intervention. Prerequisites include normal gestation, an adequate birth canal, strong maternal motivation, physical and emotional preparation, and constant and intensive support of the mother during labor and birth.

natural dentition, the entire array of natural teeth in the dental arches at any given time, consisting of deciduous or secondary dentitions or a mixture of the two.

natural family planning method, any of several methods of conception control that do not rely on a medication or a physical device for effectiveness in avoiding pregnancy. Some of the methods are also used to pinpoint the time of ovulation to increase the chance of fertilization when artificial insemination or extraction of an oocyte for in vitro fertilization is to be performed.

natural foods, foods that have been grown, processed, packaged, and stored without the use of chemical additives.

natural immunity, a usually inherent, nonspecific form of immunity to a specific disease.

naturalistic illness /nach′ərəlis′tik/, an illness thought to be caused by impersonal factors such as a disturbance in the Asian yin and yang equilibrium.

natural killer cell [L, *natura;* ME, *kullen,* to kill, *cella,* storeroom], a lymphocyte that lacks B or T cell markers. It is the effector cell of antibody-dependent cell-mediated cytotoxicity; it recognizes antibodies on target cells and lyses those cells through a cell-cell interaction that does not require complement.

natural law, a doctrine that holds there is a natural moral order or law inherent in the structure of the universe.

natural network, in psychiatric nursing, a patient's natural contacts in the community, including church and social groups, friends, family, and occupation that support the person's function outside the institutional environment.

natural pacemaker, any cardiac pacing site in the heart tissues, as opposed to an artificial pacemaker.

natural radiation, radioactivity that emanates from the soil, groundwater, or cosmic sources. Cosmic radiation includes actinic radiation from the sun and neutrinos from beyond the solar system.

natural selection, the natural evolutionary processes by which the organisms that are best adapted to an environment tend to survive and propagate whereas those that are unfit are less likely to do so.

Naturetin, a trademark for a diuretic (bendroflumethiazide).

nature versus nurture /nur′chər/, a name given to a long-standing controversy as to the relative influences of genetics versus the environment in the development of personality. Nature is represented by instincts and genetic factors, and nurture is represented by social influences.

naturopath /nach′ərōpath′/, a person who practices naturopathy.

naturopathic medicine, a philosophy of medicine that presumes that there is an inherent healing power in nature and in every human being. This major health system includes practices that emphasize diet, nutrition, homeopathy, and various mind-body therapies. Emphasis is placed on self-healing and treatment through changes in lifestyle and the use of prevention techniques that promote health. Naturopathic doctors are licensed in about one quarter of all states in the United States.

naturopathy /nach′ərop′əthē/ [L, *natura;* Gk, *pathos,* disease], a system of therapeutics based on natural foods, light, warmth, massage, fresh air, regular exercise, and the avoidance of medications. Advocates believe that illness can be healed by the natural processes of the body.

Nauheim bath /nou′hīm/ [Nauheim, Germany; AS, *baeth*, bath], a bath taken in water through which carbon dioxide is bubbled, followed by systematic exercises, used in the treatment of cardiac conditions.

nausea /nô′zē·ə, nô′zhə/ [Gk, *nausia*, seasickness], a sensation accompanying the urge but not always leading to vomiting. Common causes are seasickness and other motion sicknesses, early pregnancy, intense pain, emotional stress, gallbladder disease, food poisoning, CNS tumors, and various enteroviruses.—**nauseate**, *v.*, **nauseous**, *adj.*

nausea and vomiting of pregnancy, a common condition of early pregnancy, characterized by recurrent or persistent nausea, often in the morning, that may result in vomiting, weight loss, anorexia, general weakness, and malaise. The causes of the condition are poorly understood. It usually does not begin before the sixth week after the last menstrual period and ends by the twelfth to the fourteenth week of pregnancy.

nausea management, a nursing intervention from the Nursing Interventions Classification (NIC) defined as prevention and alleviation of nausea.

nausea & vomiting control, a nursing outcome from the Nursing Outcomes Classification (NOC) defined as personal actions to control nausea, retching, and vomiting symptoms.

nausea & vomiting: disruptive effects, a nursing outcome from the Nursing Outcomes Classification (NOC) defined as the severity of observed or reported disruptive effects of nausea, retching, and vomiting on daily functioning.

nausea & vomiting severity, a nursing outcome from the Nursing Outcomes Classification (NOC) defined as the severity of nausea, retching, and vomiting symptoms.

nauseous /nô′shəs, nô′zē·əs/ [Gk, *nausia*, seasickness], pertaining to feelings of nausea or reaction to things that may stimulate nausea.

Navane, a trademark for an antipsychotic agent (thiothixene).

Navelbine, a trademark for a chemotherapeutic mitotic inhibitor (vinorelbine).

navicular /navik′yələr/, boat-shaped; sunken.

navicular pads, tarsal supports for flat feet. They are inserted directly under the arch of the foot.

Nb, symbol for the element **niobium.**

n.b., abbreviation for the Latin *nota bene,* "note well."

NBCOT, abbreviation for *National Board for Certification in Occupational Therapy.*

NBNA, abbreviation for *National Black Nurses Association.*

NBRC, abbreviation for *National Board for Respiratory Care.*

NBSTSA, abbreviation for **National Board of Surgical Technology & Surgical Assisting.**

NCBDDD, abbreviation for **National Center on Birth Defects and Developmental Disabilities.**

NCCAM, abbreviation for *National Center for Complementary and Alternative Medicine,* part of the National Institutes of Health.

NCCDPHP, abbreviation for **National Center for Chronic Disease Prevention and Health Promotion.**

NCDRH, abbreviation for **National Center for Devices and Radiological Health.**

NCEH, abbreviation for **National Center for Environmental Health.**

NCHS, abbreviation for **National Center for Health Statistics.**

NCHSTP, abbreviation for **National Center for HIV, STD, and TB Prevention.**

NCI, abbreviation for the **National Cancer Institute.**

nCi, abbreviation for **nanocurie.**

NCID, abbreviation for **National Center for Infectious Diseases.**

NCIPC, abbreviation for **National Center for Injury Prevention and Control.**

NCLEX CAT, abbreviation for *National Council Licensure Examination through computerized adaptive testing.*

NCLEX-PN, abbreviation for *National Council Licensure Examination for Practical Nurses.*

NCLEX-RN, abbreviation for *National Council Licensure Examination for Registered Nurses.*

NCMHD, abbreviation for **National Center on Minority Health and Health Disparities.**

NCQA, abbreviation for **National Committee for Quality Assurance.**

NCRR, abbreviation for **National Center for Research Resources.**

Nd, symbol for the element **neodymium.**

N.D., abbreviation for *Doctor of Naturopathy.*

NDA, abbreviation for *National Dental Association.*

NDHA, abbreviation for *National Dental Hygienists' Association.*

Ne, symbol for the element **neon.**

NE, abbreviation for **niacin equivalent.**

Neal-Robertson litter, a modified spine board for transporting trauma patients with spinal injuries.

near-death experience [ME, *nere* + *deth;* L, *experientia,* trial], the subjective observations of people who have been either close to clinical death or have

N

recovered after having been declared dead. Many claim to have witnessed similar episodes of passing through a tunnel toward a bright light and encountering people who had preceded them in death.

near drowning [ME, *nere*, almost, *drounen*, to drown], a pathologic state in which the victim has survived exposure to circumstances that usually cause drowning. CPR is performed immediately if the patient is without pulse and/or respiration. Hospitalization is always indicated.

nearest neighbor analysis, a biochemical method used to estimate the frequency with which specific pairs of bases are located next to one another.

nebivolol, an antihypertensive.

nebula /neb'yələ/ *pl.* **nebulae** [L, cloud], **1.** a slight corneal opacity or scar that seldom obstructs vision and that can be seen only by oblique illumination. **2.** a murkiness in the urine. **3.** an oily concoction that is applied with an atomizer. **4.** mass of interstellate dusts.

nebulization /neb'yəlīzā'shən/ [L, *nebula*, cloud; Gk, *izein*, to cause], a method of administering a drug by spraying it into the respiratory passages of the patient.

nebulize /neb'yəlīz/, to vaporize or disperse a liquid in a fine spray.

nebulizer /neb'yəlī'zər/, a device for producing a fine spray.

NEC, abbreviation for **necrotizing enterocolitis.**

Necator americanus /nekā'tər/ [L, *necare*, to kill], a species of nematode that is an intestinal parasite and causes hookworm disease.

necatoriasis /nek'ətərī'əsis/ [L, *necare*, to kill; Gk, *osis*, condition], hookworm disease, specifically that caused by *Necator americanus*, the most common North American hookworm. The larvae live in the soil; they reach the human digestive tract through contaminated food and water or through the skin of the feet and legs, attach to mucosa in the small bowel, and suck blood from the human host. Most infections are asymptomatic. Symptoms, if present, include diarrhea, nausea, abdominal pain, and hypochrome microcyte iron deficiency anemia in the more severe cases.

necessity /nĕses'te/, something necessary or indispensable.

neck [AS, *hnecca*], a constricted section, such as the part of the body that connects the head with the trunk. Other such constrictions are the neck of the humerus and the neck of the uterus.

neck dissection, surgical removal of the cervical lymph nodes, performed to prevent the spread of malignant tumors of the head and neck.

neck of femur [AS, *hnecca;* L, *femur*, thigh], the part of the long bone of the thigh between the head and the greater and lesser trochanters.

neck of gastric gland, a constricted area of a gastric gland just interior to the isthmus.

neck righting reflex, 1. an involuntary response in newborns in which turning the head to one side while the infant is supine causes rotation of the shoulders and trunk in the same direction. The reflex enables the child to roll over from the supine to the prone position. **2.** any tonic reflex associated with the neck that maintains body orientation in relation to the head.

neck ring, a metal ring at the neck of a cervicothoracolumbosacral orthosis. It opens posteriorly for ease in putting on or removing the orthosis and is an attachment for a throat mold and occiput pads.

neck shaft angle, an angle created by the intersection of a line through the femoral shaft and a line through the femoral head and neck.

necrobiosis /nek'rōbī·ō'sis/, **1.** the death of a small area of cells in a large area of living tissue. **2.** the normal death of tissue cells as a result of changes associated with development, aging, atrophy, or degeneration.—**necrobiotic,** *adj.*

necrobiosis lipoidica /lipoi'dikə/ [Gk, *nekros,* dead, *bios,* life, *lipos,* fat, *eidos,* form], a skin disease characterized by thin, shiny, yellow-to-red plaques on the shins or forearms. Telangiectases, crusting, and ulceration of these plaques may occur. Necrobiosis lipoidica is usually associated with DM.

necrobiotic granulomas, granulomas that share some of the characteristics of both immunologic and nonimmunologic collections of mononuclear phagocytes. Relatively acellular areas of the skin become necrobiotic, and the collagen assumes a homogenous, amorphous appearance.

necrogenic /nek'rōjen'ik/ [Gk, *nekros,* dead, *genein,* to produce], **1.** capable of causing death, as of cells or tissue. **2.** originating or caused by infected dead matter.

necrology (necrol) /nekrol'əjē/ [Gk, *nekros,* dead, *logos,* science], the study of the causes of death, including the compilation and interpretation of mortality statistics.

necrolysis /nekrol'isis/ [Gk, *nekros* + *lysis,* loosening], disintegration or exfoliation of dead tissue.—**necrolytic,** *adj.*

necrophilia /nek'rōfil'yə/ [Gk, *nekros* + *philein,* to love], **1.** a morbid liking for being with dead bodies. **2.** a morbid desire to have sexual contact with a dead body, usually of men to perform a sexual act with a dead woman.—**necrophile, necrophiliac,** *n.*

necrophobia [Gk, *nekros,* dead, *phobos,* fear], a morbid fear of death and dead bodies.

necrosis /nekrō′sis/ [Gk, *nekros* + *osis,* condition], localized tissue death that occurs in groups of cells in response to disease or injury. In coagulation necrosis, blood clots block the flow of blood, causing tissue ischemia distal to the clot. In gangrenous necrosis, ischemia combined with bacterial action causes putrefaction to set in.

necrotaxis /nek′rōtak′sis/, the attraction of leukocytes to dead or dying cells.

necrotic /nekrot′ik/, pertaining to the death of tissue in response to disease or injury.

necrotic arachnidism, tissue destruction caused by spider venom.

necrotizing /nek′rōtī′zing/ [Gk, *nekros,* death], causing the death of tissues or organisms.

necrotizing enteritis [Gk, *nekros* + *izein,* to cause, *enteron,* intestine + *itis*], acute inflammation of the small and large intestine by the bacterium *Clostridium perfringens,* characterized by severe abdominal pain, bloody diarrhea, and vomiting.

necrotizing enterocolitis (NEC), an acute inflammatory bowel disorder that occurs primarily in preterm or low-birth-weight neonates. It is characterized by ischemic necrosis of the GI mucosa that may lead to perforation and peritonitis. The cause of the disorder is unknown, although it appears to be a defect in host defenses with infection resulting from normal GI flora rather than from invading organisms.

necrotizing ulcerative gingivitis (NUG), an inflammatory destructive disease of the gingivae that has a sudden onset with periods of remission and exacerbation. It is marked by ulcers of the gingival papillae that become covered by sloughed necrotic tissue and circumscribed by linear erythema. Foul-smelling breath, increased salivation, bone destruction, lymphadenopathy, and spontaneous gingival hemorrhage are additional features. It may extend to other parts of the oral mucosa, with lesions involving the palate or pharynx.

necrotizing ulcerative periodontitis (NUP), an inflammatory destructive disease of the gingiva that progresses to destruction of the periodontium.

necrotizing vasculitis, an inflammatory condition of blood vessels, characterized by necrosis, fibrosis, and proliferation of the inner layer of the vascular wall. Some cases result in occlusion and infarction. Necrotizing vasculitis may occur in rheumatoid arthritis and is common in SLE, periarteritis nodosa, and progressive systemic sclerosis.

nedocromil /ned′okro′mil/, an NSAID administered by inhalation in the treatment of bronchial asthma.

nedocromil sodium, the sodium salt of nedocromil, administered topically to the conjunctiva in the treatment of allergic conjunctivitis.

needle bath [AS, *naedl,* needle], a shower in which fine jets of water are sprayed over the body.

needle biopsy, the removal of a segment of living tissue for microscopic examination by inserting a hollow needle through the skin or the external surface of an organ or tumor and rotating it within the underlying cellular layers.

needle filter, a device, usually made of plastic, used for filtering medications that are drawn into a syringe before administration.

needle holder, a surgical forceps used to hold and pass a suturing needle through tissue.

needlestick injuries, accidental skin punctures resulting from contact with hypodermic syringe needles, IV cannula stylets, needles used to "piggyback" IV infusions, and needles used for drawing blood or administering parenteral injections. The contact may occur accidentally during efforts to inject a patient or as a result of carelessly touching discarded medical waste. Such injuries can be dangerous, particularly if the needle has been used in treatment of a patient with a severe blood-borne infection.

NEEP, abbreviation for **negative end-expiratory pressure.**

Neer and Horowitz classification system, a method of classifying proximal humeral fractures in children on the basis of the degree of separation of the epiphysis from the shaft.

Neer classification system, a method of classifying femoral supracondylar and intercondylar fractures. The system ranges from *type I* for minimal displacement to *type III* for conjoined supracondylar and shaft fractures. The Neer system is also applied to humeral head and neck fractures.

nefazodone hydrochloride /nefa′zodōn/, an antidepressant drug prescribed in the treatment of mental depression in adults.

negative (neg) /neg′ətiv/ [L, *negare,* to deny], **1.** of a laboratory test, indicating that a substance or a reaction is not present. **2.** of a sign, indicating on physical examination that a finding is not present, often meaning that there is no pathologic change. **3.** of a substance, tending to carry or carrying a negative chemical charge.

negative anxiety, in psychology, an emotional and psychologic condition in which anxiety prevents a person's normal functioning and interrupts the person's ability to perform the usual ADL.

negative balance, a state in which the amount of water or an electrolyte excreted from the body is greater than that ingested.

negative catalysis, a decrease in the rate of any chemical reaction caused by a substance that is not consumed and not affected by the reaction.

negative electrode [L, *negare,* to deny; Gk, *elektron,* amber, *hodos,* way], a cathode, or the negative pole of an electric current or of a battery or dry cell.

negative end-expiratory pressure (NEEP), the application of subatmospheric pressure to a patient's airway on exhalation during mechanical ventilation. The technique counterbalances the increase in mean intrathoracic pressure caused by intermittent positive-pressure breathing and is intended to reduce intrathoracic pressure for venous return to the right atrium.

negative feedback, 1. in physiology, a decrease in function in response to a stimulus. For example, the secretion of follicle-stimulating hormone decreases as the amount of circulating estrogen increases. **2.** *informal.* a critical, derogatory, or otherwise negative response from one person to what another person has communicated.

negative identity, the assumption of a persona that is at odds with the accepted values and expectations of society.

negative pathognomonic symptom /pəthog'nəmon'ik/ [L, *negare,* to deny; Gk, *pathos,* disease, *gnomen,* index, *symptoma,* that which happens], any symptom that is not usually found in a specific condition and that, if present, would not be compatible with the diagnosis.

negative pi meson pion, a form of electromagnetic radiation emitted from a proton linear accelerator.

negative pi meson radiotherapy, a form of radiotherapy using a beam of subatomic particles known as negative pi mesons, or pions, emitted by a proton linear accelerator. When the particles are beamed at a tumor, they cause the atomic nuclei of malignant cells to explode and scatter intensely radioactive subatomic particles through the tumor.

negative pressure, a pressure less than ambient atmospheric pressure, as in a vacuum, at an altitude above sea level, or in a hypobaric chamber.

negative pressure isolation rooms, isolation rooms used for patients with an airborne transmitted disease. Airflow goes from the corridor into the patient's room. As the room air is exhausted, it is vented to the outside.

negative reinforcement, a form of behavior modification in which the removal of something after an operant (behavior) decreases the probability of the operant's recurrence.

negative reinforcer, in psychology, a stimulus that, when presented immediately after occurrence of a particular behavior, decreases the rate of occurrence of the behavior.

negative relationship, in research, an inverse relationship between two variables. As one variable increases, the other decreases.

negative sequence, the sequence of bases on the strand of a double-stranded nucleic acid that is complementary to the positive-sense strand. In DNA it is the template strand on which the mRNA is synthesized.

negative staining, a technique in which an electron-dense substance is mixed with a specimen, resulting in an electron microscopic image in which the specimen appears translucent against an opaque or dark background.

negative symptom, diminishing or absence of a characteristic of normal health as an indication of disease, such as the flat affect or mutism sometimes seen in schizophrenia.

negativism /neg'ətiviz'əm/ [L, *negare,* to deny], a behavioral attitude characterized by opposition, resistance, or the refusal to cooperate with even the most reasonable request, and the tendency to act in a contrary manner.

negatron /neg'ətron/, an electron or beta particle with a single negative charge.

NegGram, a trademark for an antibacterial (nalidixic acid).

neglect /nəglekt'/, a condition that occurs when a parent or guardian fails to provide minimal physical and emotional care for a child or other dependent person.

neglect cessation, a nursing outcome from the Nursing Outcomes Classification (NOC) defined as evidence that the victim is no longer receiving substandard care.

neglect recovery, a nursing outcome from the Nursing Outcomes Classification (NOC) defined as the extent of physical, emotional, and spiritual healing following the cessation of substandard care.

negligence /neg′lijens/ [L, *negligentia*, carelessness], in law, the commission of an act that a prudent person would not have done or the omission of a duty that a prudent person would have fulfilled, resulting in injury or harm to another person.

negligence per se, in law, a finding of negligence rendered in judgment of a professional action or inaction in violation of a statute or so at odds with common sense that beyond any doubt no prudent person would have been guilty of it.

Negri bodies /nā′grē/ [Adelchi Negri, Italian physician, 1876–1912; AS, *bodig*], intracytoplasmic inclusion bodies found in the brain and CNS cells of rabies victims.

NEI, abbreviation for **National Eye Institute.**

Neisseria /nīser′ē-ə/ [Albert L.S. Neisser, Polish dermatologist, 1855–1916], a genus of aerobic to facultatively anaerobic bacteria of the family Neisseriaceae. The gram-negative cocci, which appear in pairs with adjacent sides flattened, are among the normal flora of the genitourinary and upper respiratory tracts. Pathogenic species include gonococcus and meningococcus forms.

Neisseriaceae /nī′serē-ā′si-ē/ [Albert L.S. Neisser], a family of four genera of gram-negative aerobic cocci and rod-shaped bacteria occurring singly or in pairs, chains, or clusters. The genera are *Actinobacter, Kingella, Moraxella,* and *Neisseria.*

Neisseria gonorrhoeae [Albert L.S. Neisser; Gk, *gone,* seed, *rhoia,* flow], a gram-negative, nonmotile diplococcal bacterium usually seen microscopically as flattened pairs within the cytoplasm of neutrophils. It is the causative organism of gonorrhea.

Neisseria sicca [Albert L.S. Neisser], a species of dry or slimy white-to-yellow bacteria normally found in the human nasopharynx and in saliva and sputum.

NEJM, abbreviation for *New England Journal of Medicine.*

nelarabine, an antineoplastic used to treat T-cell lymphoblastic leukemia, and T-cell lymphoblastic lymphoma after relapse or treatment failure with at least two chemotherapeutic agents.

Nélaton's dislocation /nālätôNz′/ [Auguste Nélaton, French surgeon, 1807–1873], a dislocation of the ankle in which the distal ends of the tibia and fibula are separated and the talus is forced upward between the tibia and fibula.

nelfinavir, an antiviral used alone or in combination with other drugs to treat HIV.

Nelson's syndrome [Donald H. Nelson, American physician, b. 1925], a pituitary adenoma that may follow bilateral adrenalectomy for Cushing's syndrome. It is characterized by a marked increase in the secretion of adrenocorticotropic hormone and melanocyte-stimulating hormone by the pituitary gland and visual problems because of optic chiasm compression.

nemaline myopathy /nem′əlēn/ [Gk, *nēma,* thread], a nonprogressive myopathy of uncertain inheritance, characterized histologically by abnormal threadlike structures in muscle cells and clinically by hypotonia with diffuse weakness of the limbs and trunk, usually beginning in infancy.

nematocides /nəmat′əsīdz/ [Gk, *nema,* thread, *eidos,* form; L, *caedere,* to kill], chemical pesticides that are used to kill nematode worms.

nematocyst /nem′ətōsist′/ [Gk, *nema,* thread, *eidos,* form, *kystis,* bag], a capsule containing a barbed, thread-like process found in certain cells on the external surface of cnidarians, such as the Portuguese man-of-war and jellyfish. The nematocysts of some cnidarians can penetrate the skin and inject a poison, causing painful and potentially fatal injury.

nematode /nem′ətōd/ [Gk, *nema + eidos,* form], a multicellular, parasitic animal of the phylum Nematoda. All roundworms belong to the phylum.

nematodiasis /nem′ətōdī′əsis/ [Gk, *nema,* thread, *eidos,* form, *osis,* condition], an infestation of nematode worms.

Nembutal, a trademark for a barbiturate (pentobarbital).

neoadjuvant therapy /nē′ō-ad′jəvənt/, a preliminary cancer treatment, such as chemotherapy or radiation, that usually precedes another phase of treatment.

neoantigen /-an′tijən/ [Gk, *neos,* new, *anti,* against, *genein,* to produce], a new specific antigen that develops in a tumor cell.

neobehaviorism /-bihā′vē-əriz′əm/ [Gk, *neos;* ME, *behaven,* behavior], a school of psychology based on the general principles of behaviorism but broader and more flexible in concept. It stresses experimental research and laboratory analyses in the study of overt behavior and in various subjective phenomena that cannot be directly observed and measured, such as love and personality.

neobehaviorist /-ist/, a disciple of the school of neobehaviorism.

neobladder /nē′oblad′er/, a continent urinary reservoir made from a detubularized segment of bowel or stomach, with implantation of ureters and urethra. It is used to replace the bladder after cystectomy.

neoblastic /-blas′tik/ [Gk, *neos + blastos,* germ], pertaining to a new tissue or development within a new tissue.

N

neocerebellum /-ser′əbel′əm/, those parts of the cerebellum that receive input via the corticopontocerebellar pathway.

neocortex /-kôr′teks/ [Gk, *neos*, new; L, *cortex*, bark], the most recently evolved part of the brain. In humans the neocortex includes all of the cerebral cortex except for the hippocampal and piriform areas.

NeoDecadron, a trademark for a topical fixed-combination drug containing a glucocorticoid (dexamethasone phosphate) and an antibacterial (neomycin sulfate).

neodymium (Nd), a rare earth metal element with the atomic number of 60.

neoglottis /-glot′is/, a vibrating structure that replaces the glottis in alaryngeal speech, such as after a laryngectomy.

neologism /nē·ol′əjiz′əm/ [Gk, *neos* + *logos*, word], **1.** a word or term newly coined or used with a new meaning. **2.** in psychiatry, a word coined by a psychotic or delirious patient that is meaningful only to the patient.

neomycin sulfate /ne′ōmī′sin/, an aminoglycoside antibiotic prescribed orally to treat infections of the intestine, to prepare the GI tract for surgery. It is prescribed topically to treat skin infections.

neon (Ne) /nē′on/ [Gk, *neos*, new], a colorless odorless gaseous element and one of the inert gases. Its atomic number is 10; its atomic mass is 20.18. Neon has no compounds and occurs in the atmosphere in the ratio of about 18 parts per million.

neonatal /-nā′təl/ [Gk, *neos*; L, *natus*, born], the period of time covering the first 28 days after birth.

neonatal abstinence syndrome, a behavioral pattern of irritability, tremulousness, and inconsolability exhibited in newborns exposed to heroin and methadone. Following treatment during the neonatal period, the abnormal signs usually resolve.

Neonatal Behavioral Assessment Scale (NBAS), a scale for evaluating the neurologic condition and behavior of a newborn by assessing his or her alertness, motor maturity, irritability, consolability, and interaction with people. It consists of a series of 27 reaction tests, including response to inanimate objects, pinprick, light, and sound.

neonatal breathing, respiration in newborns. It begins when pulmonary fluid in the lungs is expelled by compression of the thorax during delivery and resorbed from the alveoli into the bloodstream and lymphatics. As air enters the lungs, the chest and lungs recoil to a resting position, but forceful inspirations are necessary to keep the lungs inflated. The control of rhythm breathing is not fully developed at birth.

neonatal death, the death of a live-born infant during the first 28 days after birth. Early neonatal death is usually considered to be one that occurs during the first 7 days.

neonatal developmental profile, an evaluation of the developmental status of a newborn based on a gestational age inventory, a neurologic examination, and a Neonatal Behavioral Assessment score.

neonatal hepatitis, hepatitis of unknown cause with onset in the first few weeks of life. It is characterized by the transformation of hepatocytes into polynuclear giant cells and by conjugated hyperbilirubinemia with jaundice. Most patients recover completely; some develop chronic disease or fatal cirrhosis.

neonatal intensive care unit (NICU), a hospital unit containing a variety of sophisticated mechanic devices and special equipment for the management and care of premature and seriously ill newborns.

neonatal mortality, the statistical rate of death during the first 28 days after live birth, expressed as the number of such deaths per 1000 live births in a specific geographic area or institution in a given time.

neonatal period, the interval from birth to 28 days of age. It represents the time of the greatest risk to the infant.

neonatal pustular melanosis, a transient skin condition of the neonate characterized by vesicles present at birth that become pustular. The lesions contain neutrophils rather than eosinophils.

neonatal thermoregulation, the regulation of the body temperature of a newborn, which may be affected by evaporation, conduction, radiation, and convection.

neonatal unit, a unit of a hospital that provides care and treatment of newborns through the age of 28 days, and longer if necessary.

neonatal vital signs monitor, equipment in a specialized NICU that measures mean BP and mean heart rate from a plastic BP cuff, with values digitally displayed on a monitor.

neonatal volvulus, volvulus in the newborn, usually cecal volvulus or midgut volvulus.

neonatology /nē′ōnātol′əjē/ [Gk, *neos*; L, *natus*, born; Gk, *logos*, science], the branch of medicine that concentrates on the care of the neonate and specializes in the diagnosis and treatment of the disorders of the newborn.—**neonatologic,** *adj.,* **neonatologist,** *n.*

neonatorum encephalitis /-nātôr′əm/ [Gk, *neos*, new; L, *natus*, born; Gk, *enkephalos*, brain, *itis*, inflammation], a brain inflammation that develops in the first 4 weeks of life.

neoplasia /nē″ōplā′zhə/ [Gk, *neos* + *plassein*, to mold], the new and abnormal development of cells that may be benign or malignant. —**neoplastic** /-plas′tik/, *adj.*

neoplasm /nē′ōplaz′əm/ [Gk, *neos* + *plasma*, formation], any abnormal growth of new tissue, benign or malignant. —**neoplastic**, *adj.*

neoplastic fracture, a fracture resulting from a weakness in bone tissue caused by a benign or malignant tumor.

neoplastic pericarditis [Gk, *neos,* new, *plasma,* formation, *peri,* around, *kardia,* heart, *itis,* inflammation], inflammation of the pericardium, usually secondary to a malignant tumor within the area.

neoplastic transformation, conversion of a tissue with a normal growth pattern into a malignant tumor.

neoplasty /nē″ōplas′tē/ [Gk, *neos,* new, *plassein,* to mold], a plastic surgery procedure to restore a part or add a new part.

Neosporin, a trademark for a topical, fixed-combination drug containing antibacterials (polymyxin B sulfate, neomycin sulfate, and bacitracin zinc).

neostigmine bromide /nē′ōstig′mēn/, a reversible acetylcholinesterase inhibitor prescribed in situations in which it is desirable to potentiate the effects of neuronally released acetylcholine, such as the treatment of myasthenia gravis and postoperative urinary retention, and to reverse the effects of nondepolarizing neuromuscular blockers.

neostriatum /-strī″ā′təm/, the most recently evolved part of the corpus striatum, consisting of the caudate nucleus and putamen. The neostriatum receives input from the entire cerebral cortex and other brain areas and provides output to the basal nuclei.

Neo-Synephrine, a trademark for a vasoconstrictor (phenylephrine hydrochloride).

neoteny /nē·ot′ənē/ [Gk, *neos,* new, *teinein,* to stretch], the attainment of sexual maturity during the larval stage of development, such as in certain amphibians.

nephelometer /nef′əlom′ətər/ [Gk, *nephele,* cloud, *metron,* measure], a photometric apparatus used to determine the concentration of solids suspended in a liquid or a gas, such as the number of bacteria in a specimen.

nephelometry /nef′əlom′ətrē/, a technique for detecting proteins in body fluids based on the tendency of proteins to scatter light in identifiable ways. —**nephelometric, nephelometrical,** *adj.*

nephrectomy /-ek′təmē/ [Gk, *nephros,* kidney, *ektomē,* excision], the surgical removal of a kidney, performed to remove a tumor or otherwise diseased kidney. In the patient with renal failure, the kidney may

be the cause of extreme hypertension, and therefore one or both kidneys are removed.

nephritic /nəfrit′ik/ [Gk, *nephros,* kidney, *itis,* inflammation], pertaining to an inflammation of the kidney.

nephritic factor, a protein found in the serum of patients with membranoproliferative glomerulonephritis. It activates alternative complement pathways.

nephritic gingivitis [Gk, *nephros* + *itis,* inflammation, *gingiva,* gum; Gk, *itis,* inflammation], inflammation of the mouth and gingiva associated with kidney failure, accompanied by pain, the odor of ammonia, and increased salivation.

nephritic syndrome, a group of signs and symptoms of a urinary tract disorder, including hematuria, hypertension, and renal failure.

nephritis /nəfrī′tis/ [Gk, *nephros* + *itis,* inflammation], any one of a large group of diseases of the kidney characterized by inflammation and abnormal function.

nephroangiosclerosis /nef′rō·an′jē·ō′skle rō′sis/ [Gk, *nephros* + *angeion,* vessel, *skleros,* hard, *osis,* condition], necrosis of the renal arterioles associated with hypertension. This condition is present in a small number of hypertensive individuals between 30 and 50 years of age. Early signs are headaches, blurring of vision, and a diastolic BP greater than 120 mm Hg. Examination of the retina reveals hemorrhages, vascular exudates, and papilledema. The heart is usually enlarged, especially the left ventricle. Proteins and RBCs are found in the urine. Heart and kidney failure may occur if the disease remains untreated.

nephrocalcinosis /nef′rōkal′sinō′sis/ [Gk, *nephros;* L, *calx,* lime; Gk, *osis,* condition], an abnormal condition of the kidneys in which deposits of calcium form in the parenchyma at the site of previous inflammation or degenerative change.

nephrocystitis /-sistī′tis/, an inflammation involving both the kidney and the urinary bladder.

nephrocystosis /-sistō′sis/, the formation of cysts in the kidney.

nephrogenic /nef′rōjen′ik/ [Gk, *nephros* + *genein,* to produce], **1.** generating kidney tissue. **2.** originating in the kidney.

nephrogenic ascites, the abnormal presence of fluid in the peritoneal cavity of patients undergoing hemodialysis for renal failure. The cause of this type of ascites is unknown.

nephrogenic cord, either of the paired longitudinal ridges of tissue that lie along the dorsal surface of the coelom in the early developing vertebrate embryo. It gives rise to the structures making up the embryonic urogenital system.

N

nephrogenic diabetes insipidus, an abnormal condition in which the kidneys do not concentrate the urine, resulting in polyuria, polydipsia, and very dilute urine. The secretion of antidiuretic hormone (ADH) by the pituitary is normal, and all kidney function is normal, except the lack of response to ADH.

nephrogenic rests, remnants of renal blastema tissue found in or around the kidney, sometimes precursors of Wilms' tumor.

nephrogenous /nəfroj′ənəs/, pertaining to the formation and development of the kidneys.

nephrogram /nef′rōgram/, a radiograph of the kidney.

nephrography /nəfrog′rəfē/, the radiographic examination of the kidney.

nephrohypertrophy /-hīpur′trəfē/ [Gk, *nephros,* kidney, *hyper,* excessive, *trophe,* nourishment], enlargement of the kidney.

nephrolith, a calculus formed in a kidney. —**nephrolithic,** *adj.*

nephrolithiasis /nef′rōlithī′əsis/, a disorder characterized by the presence of calculi in the kidney.

nephrolithotomy /-lithot′əmē/, the surgical removal of renal calculi.

nephrology /nəfrol′əjē/ [Gk, *nephros + logos,* science], the study of the anatomy, physiology, and pathology of the kidney. —**nephrologic,** *adj.*

nephrolytic /-lit′ik/ [Gk, *nephros + lysis,* loosening], pertaining to the destruction of a kidney.

nephron /nef′ron/ [Gk, *nephros,* kidney], a structural and functional unit of the kidney, resembling a microscopic funnel with a long stem and two convoluted tubular sections. Each kidney contains about 1.25 million nephrons. All nephrons have a renal corpuscle and renal tubules. Juxtamedullary nephrons also have loops of Henle. Each renal corpuscle consists of a glomerulus of renal capillaries enclosed within Bowman's capsule. Urine is formed in the renal corpuscles and renal tubules by filtration, reabsorption, and secretion.

nephronia /nəfrō′nē·ə/, an inflammation of intrarenal connective tissue that occurs in a small percentage of patients with UTIs.

nephroparalysis /-pəral′isis/ [Gk, *nephros,* kidney, *paralyein,* to be palsied], a paralysis of the kidney resulting in a cessation of its functions.

nephropathic cystinosis, one of the types of cystinosis that involves kidney damage and ophthalmic symptoms.

nephropathy /nefrop′əthē/ [Gk, *nephros + pathos,* disease], any disorder of the kidney, including inflammatory, degenerative, and sclerotic conditions.

nephropexy /nef′rəpek′sē/ [Gk, *nephros + pexis,* fixation], a surgical operation to fixate a floating or ptotic kidney.

nephroptosis /nef′räptō′sis/ [Gk, *nephros + ptosis,* falling], a downward displacement or dropping of a kidney.

nephrorrhaphy /nəfrôr′əfē/ [Gk, *nephros + rhaphe,* suture], an operation that sutures a floating kidney in place.

nephroscope /nef′rəskōp/ [Gk, *nephros + skopein,* to look], a fiberoptic instrument used specifically for visualization of the kidney and the disintegration and removal of renal calculi.

nephrostoma /-stō′mə/ *pl.* **nephrostomas, nephrostomata** [Gk, *nephros + stoma,* mouth], the funnel-shaped ciliated opening of the excretory tubules into the coelom of the early developing vertebrate embryo.—**nephrostomic,** *adj.*

nephrostomy /nəfros′təmē/, a surgical procedure in which a flank incision is made so that a catheter can be inserted into the kidney pelvis to drain the kidney, often done to relieve obstruction.

nephrostomy catheter, a catheter used with percutaneous nephrostomy, as for drainage.

nephrotic syndrome /nəfrot′ik/ [Gk, *nephros;* L, *icus,* like], an abnormal condition of the kidney characterized by marked proteinuria, hypoalbuminemia, and edema. It occurs in glomerular disease and thrombosis of a renal vein and as a complication of many systemic diseases, DM, amyloidosis, SLE, and multiple myeloma. The presenting symptoms include anorexia, weakness, proteinuria, hypoalbuminuria, and edema. —**nephrotic,** *adj.*

nephrotome /nef′rətom/ [Gk, *nephros + tome,* section], a zone of segmented mesodermal tissue in the developing vertebrate embryo. It is the primordial tissue for the urogenital system and gives rise to the nephrogenic cord.

nephrotomography /-təmog′rəfē/ [Gk, *nephros + tome,* section, *graphein,* to record], sectional radiographic examination of the kidneys.

nephrotomy /nəfrot′əmē/ [Gk, *nephros + temnein,* to cut], a surgical procedure in which an incision is made in the kidney.

nephrotoxicity, the quality of being destructive to kidney cells.—**nephrotoxic,** *adj.*

nephrotoxin /-tok′sin/, a toxin with specific destructive properties for the kidneys.

nephroureterolithiasis /nef′rōyōōrē′tərō′ lithī′əsis/, the presence of calculi in the kidneys and ureters.

Neptazane, a trademark for a carbonic anhydrase inhibitor (methazolamide).

neptunium (Np) /nept(y)o͞o′nē-əm/ [planet Neptune], a transuranic, metallic element. Its atomic number is 93; its atomic mass is 237.

Neri's sign /nā′rēz/ [Vincenzo Neri, Italian neurologist, 20th century], a sign of organic hemiplegia, consisting of the spontaneous bending of the knee of the affected side as the leg is passively lifted, the patient being in the dorsal position. With the patient standing, forward bending of the trunk will cause flexion of the knee on the affected side in lumbosacral and iliosacral lesions.

Nernst equation [Hermann W. Nernst, German physicist, 1864–1941; L, *aequare,* to make equal], an expression of the relationship between the electric potential across a membrane and the ratio between the concentrations of a given species of permeant ion on either side of the membrane.

nerve /nurv/ [L, *nervus*], one or more bundles of impulse-carrying fibers, myelinated or unmyelinated or both, that connect the brain and the spinal cord with other parts of the body. Nerves transmit afferent impulses from receptor organs toward the brain, spinal cord, and efferent impulses peripherally to the effector organs. Each nerve consists of an epineurium enclosing fasciculi of nerve fibers; each fasciculus is surrounded by its own sheath of connective tissue, or epineurium.

nerve accommodation, the ability of nerve tissue to adjust to a constant source and intensity of stimulation so that some change in either intensity or duration of the stimulus is necessary to elicit a response beyond the initial reaction.

nerve agents, chemicals that interfere with the proper functioning of the nervous system. They are highly potent, and very small amounts can have serious effects. Exposure is by inhalation or by skin or eye contact. Nerve agents can also be mixed with water and can be used to poison water supplies.

nerve cable graft, a multistrand free nerve graft, taken from elsewhere in the body, to bridge a large gap in one of the main nerves in the forearm.

nerve compression, an abnormal condition and type of mononeuropathy, characterized by nerve damage and muscle weakness, atrophy, or paresthesias over time. Any nerve that passes over a rigid prominence is vulnerable, and the degree of damage depends on the magnitude and duration of the compressive force.

nerve conduction test, an electrodiagnostic test of the integrity of the peripheral nerves. It involves placing an electrical stimulator over a nerve and measuring the time required for an impulse to travel over a measured segment of the nerve. The test is used in the diagnosis of nerve entrapment syndrome radiculopathies and polyneuropathies.

nerve endings, the fine branchlike terminations of peripheral neurons. Sensory endings are effectively dendrites lying far from the neuronal cell body, and motor nerve endings are the effectors of axons.

nerve entrapment, an abnormal condition and type of mononeuropathy, characterized by nerve damage and muscle weakness or atrophy. The peripheral nerve trunks are especially vulnerable to entrapment in which repeated compression results in significant impairment. Nerves that pass over rigid prominences or through narrow bony and fascial canals are particularly prone to entrapment. The common signs of this disorder are pain and muscular weakness.

nerve excitability [L, *nervus,* nerve, *excitare,* to rouse], the readiness of a nerve cell to respond to a stimulus.

nerve fiber, a slender process, the axon of a neuron. Each fiber is classified as myelinated or unmyelinated. Myelinated fibers are further designated as A or B fibers; C fibers are unmyelinated. The A fibers are somatic. B fibers are more finely myelinated than A fibers. They are both afferent and efferent and are mainly associated with visceral innervation. The unmyelinated C fibers are efferent postganglionic autonomic fibers and afferent fibers that conduct impulses of prolonged, burning pain sensation from the viscera and periphery.

nerve graft, the transplantation of all or part of a nerve. The procedure may be performed in cases in which the gap in a severed nerve is too large to be repaired by suture alone. The graft provides a pathway that encourages the regrowth of severed axons from the central stump of the damaged nerve. Donor material may consist of heterografts, homografts, or autografts.

nerve growth factor (NGF), a protein whose hormone-like action affects differentiation, growth, and maintenance of neurons.

nerve plexus [L, *nervus,* nerve, *plexus,* plaited], an interwoven network of nerves, such as the lumbar plexus.

nerve root, the part of a nerve adjacent to the center to which it is connected.

nerve root impingement, the abnormal protrusion of body tissue into the space occupied by a spinal nerve root. Causes may include disk herniation, tissue prolapse, and inflammation.

nerve sheath [L, *nervus,* nerve; AS, *scaeth*], any of several types of coatings or coverings for nerve fibers and nerve tracts.

N

Kinds of nerve sheaths include endoneurial, medullary, myelin, neurilemma, and notochordal.

nervimotor /ner'vi·mō'tər/ [L, *nervus*, nerve, *motare*, to move], pertaining to a motor nerve.

nervous emesis [L, *nervus*; Gk, *emesis*, vomiting], vomiting that is functional and psychogenic. The condition is most common among young women and is regarded as a psychologic representation of a desire to reject something.

nervous prostration [L, *nervus* + *prosternere*, to throw down], a condition of irritable weakness and depression, which may be psychogenic or the result of a severe prolonged illness or exhausting experience.

nervous system [L, *nervus*, nerve; Gk, *system*], the extensive, intricate network of structures that activates, coordinates, and controls all the functions of the body. It is divided into the CNS, composed of the brain and spinal cord, and the peripheral nervous system, which includes the cranial nerves and the spinal nerves. These morphologic subdivisions combine and communicate to innervate the somatic and visceral parts of the body with the afferent and efferent nerve fibers.

nervous tachypnea [L, *nervus*; Gk, *tachys*, rapid, *pnoia*, breath], a neurotic symptom characterized by quick, shallow breathing.

Nesacaine, a trademark for a long-acting local anesthetic (chloroprocaine).

nesiritide, a vasodilator used to treat acutely decompensated CHF.

nested nails, a pair of nails placed side by side in the medullary canal of long bones during orthopedic surgery.

nested variable, a variable located entirely within another variable, such as the rate of a given disease in one specific city.

net charge, the arithmetic sum of positive and negative charges.

net protein utilization (NPU), a measure of protein quality based on the percentage of ingested nitrogen that is retained by the body. Because NPU does not take into account differences in the digestibility of proteins, it gives a poorly digested but good-quality protein a false low value.

net radiation, the arithmetic difference between solar radiation received and outgoing terrestrial radiation.

nettle, a perennial herb used as a diuretic and as a treatment for hay fever. It shows some evidence of efficacy for these indications.

nettle rash [AS, *netele*, nettle; Fr, *rasche*, scurf], a fine, urticarial eruption resulting from skin contact with stinging nettle,

a common weed with leaves containing histamine. It is characterized by stinging and itching that lasts from a few minutes to several hours.

Network Design Group, a Medicare-specific oversight group that maintains a log of enrollee complaints related to service and quality of care issues reported to the Centers for Medicare and Medicaid Services. It participates in investigation of complaints.

networking, 1. the process of developing and using an interaction format with professional colleagues and agencies. 2. in psychiatric nursing, the process of developing a set of agencies and professional personnel who are able to create a system of communication and support for psychiatric patients, usually those recently discharged from inpatient psychiatric facilities. 3. a network of supportive contacts or services, such as the Women's Health Network.

network-model HMO, a managed care system analogous to the group-model health maintenance organization (HMO), but with services provided at multiple sites by multiple groups so that a wider geographic area is served.

net wt, abbreviation for *net weight*.

Neufeld nail /nyōō'fəld/ [Alonzo J. Neufeld, American surgeon, b. 1906], an orthopedic nail with a V-shaped tip and shank used for fixating an intertrochanteric fracture. The nail is driven into the neck of the femur until it reaches a round metal plate screwed onto the side of the femur.

Neufeld roller traction, a traction device for a fractured femur, consisting of a cast for the calf and thigh hinged at the knee. The cast is suspended by a line that passes from the anterior midthigh, around a pulley, to a spring attached to the anterior midleg.

Neuman, Betty, a nursing theorist who developed the Neuman Systems Model, first published in 1972. In this model, the client is presented as a whole person, an open system in constant change and in reciprocal interaction with the environment.

neural /nŏōr'əl/ [Gk, *neuron*, nerve], pertaining to nerve cells and their processes.

neural cell-adhesion molecule, an immunoglobulin that functions as a molecular recognition molecule.

neural crest, the ectodermally derived cells along the outer surface of each side of the neural tube in the early stages of embryonic development. The cells migrate laterally throughout the embryo and give rise to spinal, cranial, enteric, and sympathetic ganglia; pigment cells; Schwann cells; and the adrenal medulla.

neural ectoderm, the part of the embryonic ectoderm that develops into the neural tube.

neural fold, either of the paired longitudinal elevations resulting from the invagination of the neural plate in the early developing embryo. The folds unite to enclose the neural groove and form the neural tube.

neuralgia /nŏŏral'jə/   [Gk, *neuron* + *algos,* pain], an abnormal condition characterized by severe stabbing pain, caused by a variety of disorders affecting the nervous system.—**neuralgic,** *adj.*

neuralgic amyotrophy /nŏŏral'jik ā'mīot'rəfē/, a brachial plexus disorder characterized by sudden pain and muscle weakness in the upper limbs and sometimes by muscular wasting or atrophy. The cause is unknown.

neural groove, the longitudinal depression that occurs between the neural folds during the invagination of the neural plate to form the neural tube in the early stages of embryonic development.

neural plate, a thick layer of ectodermal tissue that lies along the central longitudinal axis of the early developing embryo and gives rise to the neural tube and subsequently to the brain, spinal cord, and other tissues of the CNS.

neural tube, the longitudinal tube, lying along the central axis of the early developing embryo, that gives rise to the brain, spinal cord, and other neural tissue of the CNS.

neural tube defect (NTD), any of a group of congenital malformations involving defects in the skull and spinal column that are caused primarily by the failure of the neural tube to close during embryonic development. The defect may occur at any point along the neural axis or extends the entire length of the spinal column. The amount of deformity and disability depends on the degree of neural involvement, the most severe defect being complete cranioschisis, or the total absence of the skull and defective brain development. Other cerebral dysplasias resulting from the failure of the cranial end of the neural tube to fuse are meningoencephalocele and cranial meningocele. Most neural tube malformations are caused by incomplete fusion of one or more laminae of the vertebral column, with varying degrees of tissue protrusion and neural involvement. Adequate folate levels during the first month after conception are important in preventing neural tube defects.

neural tube formation, the various processes and stages involved in the embryonic development of the neural tube.

neuraminic acid /nŏŏr'əmin'ik/, a nine-carbon amino acid formed from mannosamine and pyruvate.

neuraminidase /nŏŏr'əmē'nədās/, an enzyme that catalyzes the cleavage of *N*-acetyl neuraminic acid from mucopolysaccharides. A hereditary deficiency of the enzyme causes sialidosis and is associated with galactosialidosis, which is characterized by mental retardation and skeletal changes.

neuraminidase spikes, projections from surfaces of influenza viruses containing neuraminidase that are involved in the release of viruses from infected cells.

neurapraxia /nŏŏr'əprak'sē·ə/, the interruption of nerve conduction without loss of continuity of the axon.

neurasthenia /nŏŏr'əsthē'nē·ə/   [Gk, *neuron* + *a* + *sthenos,* without strength], **1.** an abnormal condition that often follows depression, characterized by nervous exhaustion and a vague functional fatigue. **2.** in psychiatry, a stage in the recovery from a schizophrenic experience during which the patient is listless and apparently unable to cope with routine activities and relationships.—**neurasthenic,** *adj.*

neurectomy /nŏŏrek'təmē/   [Gk, *neuron,* nerve, *ektomē,* excision], the surgical excision of a nerve segment.

neurenteric canal /nŏŏr'ənter'ik/   [Gk, *neuron* + *enteron,* intestine; L, *canalis,* channel], a tubular passage between the posterior part of the neural tube and the archenteron in the early embryonic development of lower animals.

neurilemma /nŏŏr'əlem'ə/   [Gk, *neuron* + *lemma,* sheath], a layer of cells composed of one or more Schwann cells that forms the segmented myelin sheaths of peripheral nerve fibers. It is necessary for regeneration of peripheral nerves when they have been severed.—**neurilemmal, neurilemmatic, neurilemmatous,** *adj.*

neurinoma /nŏŏr'inō'mə/   *pl.* **neurinomas, neurinomata** [Gk, *neuron* + *oma,* tumor], a tumor of the nerve sheath. It is usually benign but may undergo malignant change.

neuritic plaque /nŏŏrit'ik/, an extracellular deposit consisting of beta-amyloid protein mixed with branches of dying nerve cells in the brain of a patient with Alzheimer's disease.

neuritis /nŏŏrī'tis/   *pl.* **neuritides** [Gk, *neuron* + *itis,* inflammation], an abnormal condition characterized by inflammation of a nerve. Some of the signs of this condition are neuralgia, hypesthesia, anesthesia,

N

paralysis, muscular atrophy, and defective reflexes.

neuroacanthocytosis /nŏŏr′ō·əkan′thōsītō′sis/ [Gk, *neuron,* nerve, *akantha,* thorn, *kytos,* cell, *osis,* condition], an autosomal-recessive syndrome characterized by tics, chorea, and personality changes, with acanthocytes in the blood.

neuroanatomy /nŏŏr′ō·ənat′əmē/, the branch of biology that is concerned with the structure of the nervous system.

neuroarthropathy /-ärthrop′əthē/ [Gk, *neuron + arthron,* joint, *pathos,* disease], a condition in which a disease of a joint is secondary to a disease of the nervous system.

neurobiology /-bī′ol′əjē/, a branch of biology that is concerned with the anatomy and physiology of the nervous system.

neuroblast /nŏŏr′əblast/ [Gk, *neuron + blastos,* germ], any embryonic cell that develops into a functional neuron; an immature nerve cell. —**neuroblastic,** *adj.*

neuroblastoma /nŏŏr′ōblastō′mə/ *pl.* **neuroblastomas, neuroblastomata** [Gk, *neuron + blastos,* germ, *oma,* tumor], a highly malignant tumor composed of primitive ectodermal cells derived from the neural plate during embryonic life. The tumor may originate in any part of the sympathetic nervous system but is most common in the adrenal medulla. Neuroblastomas metastasize early and widely to lymph nodes, liver, lungs, and bone. Symptoms may include an abdominal mass, respiratory distress, and anemia. Hormonally active adrenal lesions may cause irritability, flushing, sweating, hypertension, and tachycardia.

neurobrucellosis /-brōō′səlō′sis/, a serious complication of a brucellosis infection that affects the nervous system and may cause meningitis, stroke, cranial nerve lesions, or mycotic aneurysms.

neurocardiogenic syncope, a particularly serious type of vasovagal attack, the cause of which is unknown.

neurocentral /-sen′trəl/ [Gk, *neuron + kentron,* center], pertaining to the centrum and the developing vertebrae in the early stages of embryology.

neurocentrum /-sen′trəm/ [Gk, *neuron;* L, *centrum,* center], the embryonic mesodermal tissue that subsequently gives rise to the vertebrae.

neuro check [Gk, *neuron;* ME, *chek,* stop], *nontechnical.* a brief neurologic assessment ordered by the physician to be performed every 4 hours on patients who may have evolving disease, such as stroke. The LOC is evaluated as alert and oriented, lethargic, stuporous, or comatose. The movements of the extremities are determined to be voluntary or involuntary. The pupils of the eyes are observed for equality of dilation, reactivity to light, and ability to accommodate.

neurochemistry /-kem′istrē/, a branch of neurology that is concerned with the biochemistry of the nervous system.

neurocirculatory asthenia /-sur′kyələtôr′ē/ [Gk, *neuron;* L, *circulare,* to go around; Gk, *a + sthenos,* without strength], a psychosomatic disorder characterized by nervous and circulatory irregularities, including dyspnea, palpitation, giddiness, vertigo, tremor, precordial pain, and increased susceptibility to fatigue.

neurocoele /nॅŏor′əsēl/ [Gk, *neuron + koilos,* hollow], a system of cavities in the CNS of humans and other vertebrate animals. It consists of the ventricles of the brain and the central canal of the spinal cord.

neurocytolysin /-sītol′isin/, a toxic substance in snake venom that destroys nerve cell membranes.

neurocytolysis /-sītol′isis/, the destruction of nerve cells.

neurocytoma /nŏŏr′ōsītō′mə/ [Gk, *neuron + kytos,* cell, *oma,* tumor], a tumor composed of undifferentiated nerve cells that are usually ganglionic.

neurodermatitis /-dur′məti′tis/ [Gk, *neuron + derma,* skin, *itis,* inflammation], a nonspecific, pruritic skin disorder seen in anxious, nervous individuals. Excoriations and lichenification occur on easily accessible, exposed areas of the body such as the forearms and forehead.

neurodevelopmental adaptation /-dəvel′əpmen′təl/, a type of therapy that emphasizes the inhibition/integration of primitive postural patterns and promotes the development of normal postural reactions and achievement of normal tone. The therapy is used in the treatment of children with CP.

neuroectoderm /nŏŏr′ō·ek′tədurm/ [Gk, *neuron + ektos,* outside, *derma,* skin], the part of the embryonic ectoderm that gives rise to the central and peripheral nervous systems, including some glial cells. —**neuroectodermal,** *adj.*

neuroelectric therapy, the use of a low-amperage electric current to stimulate nerve endings. The action may stimulate endogenous neurotransmitters, such as endorphins that produce symptomatic relief. A kind of neuroelectric therapy is transcutaneous electric nerve stimulation.

neuroendocrine /nॅŏor′ō·en′dəkrin/ [Gk, *neuron,* nerve, *endon,* within, *krinein,* to secrete], pertaining to or resembling the effects produced by endocrine glands strongly linked with the nervous system.

neuroendoscope /nŏŏr′o·en′doskōp′/, an endoscope for examining and performing various interventions in the CNS.

neuroendoscopy, the use of a neuroendoscope with the aid of a neuronavigation system to examine the CNS and perform minimally invasive neurosurgical procedures.

neuroepithelioma /nŏŏr′ō·ep′ithē′lē·ō′mə/ [Gk, *neuron* + *epi,* upon, *thele,* nipple, *oma,* tumor], an uncommon neoplasm of neuroepithelium in a sensory nerve.

neurofibril /-fī′bril/, a threadlike structure found in the cytoplasm of a neuron.

neurofibrillary tangles /-fī′briler′ē/, an intracellular clump of neurofibrils made of insoluble protein in the brain of a patient with Alzheimer's disease.

neurofibroma /nŏŏr′ōfībrō′mə/ *pl.* **neurofibromas, neurofibromata** [Gk, *neuron;* L, *fibra,* fiber; Gk, *oma,* tumor], a fibrous tumor of nerve tissue resulting from the abnormal proliferation of Schwann cells. Multiple growths in the peripheral nervous system are often associated with abnormalities in other tissues.

neurofibromatosis /nŏŏr′ōfī′brōmətō′sis/ [Gk, *neuron;* L, *fibra,* fiber; Gk, *oma,* tumor, *osis,* condition], a congenital condition transmitted as an autosomal-dominant trait, characterized by numerous neurofibromas of the nerves and skin, café-au-lait spots on the skin, and developmental anomalies of the muscles, bones, and viscera.

neurofilament /nŏŏr′ōfil′əment/ [Gk, *neuron,* nerve; L, *filare,* to spin], a cytoplasmic filament approximately 10 nm in diameter occurring in the neurons. It has a cytoskeletal function and may be involved in the intracellular transport of metabolites.

neurogen /nŏŏr′əjən/ [Gk, *neuron* + *genein,* to produce], a substance within the early developing embryo that stimulates the primary organizer to initiate the formation of the neural plate, which gives rise to the primary axis of the body.

neurogenesis /-jen′əsis/ [Gk, *neuron* + *genesis,* origin], the formation of the tissue of the nervous system.—**neurogenetic,** *adj.*

neurogenic /-jen′ik/ [Gk, *neuron* + *genesis,* origin], **1.** pertaining to the formation of nervous tissue. **2.** pertaining to the stimulation of nervous energy. **3.** originating in the nervous system.

neurogenic arthropathy, an abnormal condition associated with neural damage, characterized by the gradual and usually painless degeneration of a joint.

neurogenic bladder, dysfunction of the urinary bladder caused by a lesion of the nervous system.

neurogenic claudication, claudication accompanied by pain and paresthesias in the back, buttocks, and lower limbs that is relieved by stooping, caused by mechanical disturbances resulting from posture or by ischemia of the cauda equina.

neurogenic fracture, a fracture associated with the destruction of the nerve supply to a specific bone.

neurogenic hoarseness, a sign of unilateral vocal cord paralysis. It is asymptomatic, but there may be excessive air escape during speech as a result of incomplete closure of the glottis. Extra effort is required to generate enough air flow to make speech sounds. Untreated, there is a danger of aspiration pneumonia.

neurogenic impotence, penile erectile dysfunction caused by neurologic disorders. The disorders may involve the parasympathetic sacral spinal cord or the peripheral efferent autonomic fibers to the penis.

neurogenic shock, a form of shock that results from peripheral vascular dilation.

neuroglia /nŏŏrog′lē·ə/ [Gk, *neuron* + *glia,* glue], the supporting or nonneuronal tissue cells of the central and peripheral nervous system. They perform the less specialized functions of the nerve network. —**neuroglial,** *adj.*

neurography /nŏŏrog′rəfē/, **1.** the study of the action potentials of the nerves. **2.** a technique for visualization of peripheral nerve activity by graphic representation of data obtained by media contrast radiographics or by electric recording.

neurohormone /nŏŏr′əhôr′mōn/, a hormone produced in neurosecretory cells such as those of the hypothalamus and released into the bloodstream, the CSF, or intercellular spaces of the nervous system. The product may or may not be a true systemic hormone such as epinephrine. When the hormone is not a true hormone, it may be a cell product that induces the release of a tropic hormone, which in turn stimulates an endocrine gland to release a systemic hormone.

neurohypophyseal hormone /-hī′pōfiz′ē·əl/ [Gk, *neuron* + *hypo,* under, *phyein,* to grow], a hormone secreted by the posterior pituitary gland.

neurohypophysis /-hīpof′isis/ [Gk, *neuron* + *hypo,* under, *phyein,* to grow], the posterior lobe of the pituitary gland that is the release point of antidiuretic hormone and oxytocin. Nervous stimulation from the hypothalamus controls the release of the substances into the blood.

neuroimmunology /nŏŏr′ō·im′yōōnol′əjē/ [Gk, *neuron;* L, *immunis,* freedom; Gk, *logos,* science], the study of relationships between the immune and nervous systems, such as autoimmune activity in neurologic diseases.

neurol, abbreviation for **neurology.**

neurolepsis /-lep′sis/ [Gk, *neuron* + *lepsis,* seizure], an altered state of consciousness, as induced by a neuroleptic agent, characterized by quiescence, reduced motor activity, decreased anxiety, and indifference to the surroundings. Sleep may occur, but usually the person can be aroused and can respond to commands.

neurolepsy /nŏŏr′əlep′sē/, a mental state characterized by the blocking of autonomic reflexes, as in hypnosis or antipsychotic drug–induced disorders.

neuroleptanalgesia /-lept′anəljē′zē·ə/ [Gk, *neuron* + *lepsis,* seizure, *a* + *algos,* without pain], a form of analgesia achieved by the concurrent administration of a neuroleptic such as droperidol and an analgesic such as fentanyl. Anxiety, motor activity, and sensitivity to painful stimuli are reduced; the person is quiet and indifferent to surroundings and is able to respond to commands.

neuroleptanesthesia /-lept′anəsthē′zhə/ [Gk, *neuron* + *lepsis,* seizure, *anaisthesia,* lack of feeling], a form of anesthesia achieved by the administration of a neuroleptic agent, a narcotic analgesic, and nitrous oxide with oxygen. Induction of anesthesia is slow, but consciousness returns quickly after the inhalation of nitrous oxide is stopped.

neuroleptic /-lep′tik/ [Gk, *neuron* + *lepsis,* seizure], pertaining to neurolepsis.

neuroleptic anesthesia [Gk, *neuron,* nerve, *lepsis,* seizure, *anaisthesia,* lack of feeling], a form of anesthesia induced by an injection of a butyrophenone derivative with a narcotic analgesic.

neuroleptic drug, a substance that produces a sedating or tranquilizing effect.

neuroleptic malignant syndrome [Gk, *neuron,* nerve, *lepsis,* seizure; L, *malignus,* bad disposition; Gk, *syn,* together, *dromos,* course], a condition characterized by hypertonicity, pallor, dyskinesia, fever, incontinence, unstable BP, and pulmonary congestion. It is caused by the administration of neuroleptic drugs at normal or high doses. Reaction to these drugs is idiosyncratic.

neurolinguistic programming, a complementary therapeutic strategy based on the premise that thought is a representation of sensory experience and that behavior can be modified to achieve a desired result by changing the patient's thought patterns and mental strategies to give the patient more choices in problem solving. It is used for behavior modification and the management of psychosomatic disorders and stress.

neurolinguistics /nŏŏr′oling·gwis′tiks/ [Gk, *neuron;* L, *lingua,* tongue], the study of language acquisition, processing, and production at the neurologic level.

neurological status, a nursing outcome from the Nursing Outcomes Classification (NOC) defined as the ability of the peripheral and central nervous system to receive, process, and respond to internal and external stimuli.

neurological status: autonomic, a nursing outcome from the Nursing Outcomes Classification (NOC) defined as the ability of the autonomic nervous system to coordinate visceral and homeostatic function.

neurological status: central motor control, a nursing outcome from the Nursing Outcomes Classification (NOC) defined as the ability of the central nervous system to coordinate skeletal muscle activity for body movement.

neurological status: consciousness, a nursing outcome from the Nursing Outcomes Classification (NOC) defined as arousal, orientation, and attention to the environment.

neurological status: cranial sensory/ motor function, a nursing outcome from the Nursing Outcomes Classification (NOC) defined as the ability of the cranial nerves to convey sensory and motor impulses.

neurological status: peripheral, a nursing outcome from the Nursing Outcomes Classification (NOC) defined as the ability of the peripheral nervous system to transmit impulses to and from the CNS.

neurological status: spinal sensory/motor function, a nursing outcome from the Nursing Outcomes Classification (NOC) defined as the ability of the spinal nerves to convey sensory and motor impulses.

neurologic assessment /-loj′ik/ [Gk, *neuron* + *logos,* science; L, *icus,* like, *adsidere,* to approximate], an evaluation of the patient's neurologic status and symptoms. If alert and oriented, the patient is asked about instances of weakness, numbness, headaches, pain, tremors, nervousness, irritability, or drowsiness. Information is elicited regarding loss of memory, periods of confusion, hallucinations, and episodes of LOC. The patient's general appearance, facial expression, attention span, responses to verbal and painful stimuli, emotional status, coordination, balance, cognition, and ability to follow commands are noted. Assessment of cranial nerves and deep tendon reflexes is included. If the patient is disoriented, stuporous, or comatose, demonstrated signs of these states are recorded. Diagnostic aids that may be required for a complete evaluation include a lumbar puncture, CBC, myelogram, MRI, echoencephalogram, brain scan, CT, and determinations of glucose, fluid, and electrolyte levels.

neurologic examination, a systematic examination of the nervous system, including an assessment of mental status, of the function of each of the cranial nerves, of sensory and neuromuscular function, of the reflexes, and of proprioception and other cerebellar functions.

neurologic monitoring, a nursing intervention from the Nursing Interventions Classification (NIC) defined as collection and analysis of patient data to prevent or minimize neurologic complications.

neurology (neurol) /nŏŏrol′əjē/ [Gk, *neuron* + *logos,* science], the field of medicine that deals with the nervous system and its disorders.—**neurologic, neurological,** *adj.* **neurologist,** *n.*

neuroma /nŏŏrō′mə/ *pl.* **neuromas, neuromata** [Gk, *neuron* + *oma,* tumor], a benign neoplasm composed chiefly of neurons and nerve fibers, usually arising from a nerve tissue. Pain radiating from the lesion to the periphery of the affected nerve is usually intermittent but may become continuous and severe.

neuroma cutis, a neoplasm in the skin that contains nerve tissue and may be extremely sensitive to painful stimuli.

neuromatosis /nŏŏr′ōmətō′sis/ [Gk, *neuron* + *oma,* tumor, *osis,* condition], a neoplastic disease characterized by numerous neuromas.

neuromechanism /-mek′əniz′əm/, a neurologic system whose components work together to produce a CNS function.

neuromodulator, a substance that alters nerve impulse transmission.

neuromotor /nŏŏr′ōmō′tər/ [Gk, *neuron,* nerve; L, *mover,* to move], pertaining to both the nerves and muscles or to nerve impulses transmitted to muscles.

neuromuscular /nŏŏr′ōmus′kyŏŏlər/ [Gk, *neuron;* L, *musculus,* muscle], pertaining to the nerves and muscles.

neuromuscular blockade, the inhibition of a muscular contraction activated by the nervous system, possibly resulting in muscle weakness or paralysis.

neuromuscular blocking agent, a chemical substance that interferes locally with the transmission or reception of impulses from motor nerves to skeletal muscles. Nondepolarizing agents competitively block the transmitter action of acetylcholine at the motor end plate. Depolarizing blocking agents also compete with acetylcholine for cholinergic receptors of the motor end plate, but work by first activating the receptor and then blocking its ability to be reset for subsequent stimulation. Neuromuscular blocking agents are used

to induce muscle relaxation in anesthesia, endotracheal intubation, and electroshock therapy and as adjuncts in the treatment of tetanus, encephalitis, and poliomyelitis.

neuromuscular electric stimulator (NMES), a device for improving or modulating muscular activation. The NMES generates electric pulses that produce controlled muscle contractions similar to those that occur physiologically. Unless nerve degeneration has occurred, muscles that are weak or paralyzed because of CNS involvement should contract when NMES is applied. The procedure may be tested first on an uninvolved muscle on the same or another extremity to establish a normal response.

neuromuscular junction, the area of contact between the ends of a large myelinated nerve fiber and a fiber of skeletal muscle.

neuromuscular spindle, any one of a number of small bundles of delicate muscular fibers enclosed by a capsule, in which sensory nerve fibers terminate. The nerve fibers end as naked axons encircling the intrafusal fibers with flattened expansions or ovoid disks.

neuromyal transmission /-mī′əl/ [Gk, *neuron* + *mys,* muscle; L, *transmittere,* to transmit], the passage of excitation from a motor neuron to a muscle fiber at the neuromuscular junction.

neuromyelitis /nŏŏr′ōmī′əlī′tis/ [Gk, *neuron* + *myelos,* marrow, *itis,* inflammation], an abnormal condition characterized by inflammation of the spinal cord and peripheral nerves.

neuron /nŏŏr′on/ [Gk, nerve], the basic nerve cell of the nervous system, containing a nucleus within a cell body and extending one or more processes. Neurons can be classified according to the direction in which they conduct impulses or according to the number of processes they extend. Sensory neurons transmit nerve impulses toward the spinal cord and the brain. Motor neurons transmit nerve impulses from the brain and the spinal cord to the muscles and the glandular tissue. Multipolar neurons, bipolar neurons, and unipolar neurons are classified according to the number of processes they extend to the different kinds of neurons. As the generators and carriers of nerve impulses, neurons function according to electrochemical processes involving positively charged sodium and potassium ions and the changing electrical potential of the extracellular and the intracellular fluid of the neuron.—**neuronal,** *adj.*

neuronal antibody, an antibody found in the CSF of many SLE patients with neuropsychiatric manifestations and in some SLE patients without such manifestations.

neuronal sprouting, the growth of axons or dendrites from a damaged neuron or from an intact neuron that projects to an area denervated by damage to other neurons.

neuronitis /nŏŏr′ənī′tis/ [Gk, *neuron* + *itis,* inflammation], inflammation of a nerve or a nerve cell, especially the cells and the roots of the spinal nerves.

neuroparalysis /-pərəl′isis/, loss of muscle power as a result of a disorder involving the part of the nervous system affecting the muscle.

neuropathic joint disease /-path′ik/ [Gk, *neuron* + *pathos,* disease], a chronic progressive degenerative disease of one or more joints, characterized by swelling, joint instability, hemorrhage, heat, and atrophic and hypertrophic changes in the bone. The disease is the result of an underlying neurologic disorder, such as tabes dorsalis from syphilis, diabetic neuropathy, leprosy, or congenital absence or depression of pain sensation.

neuropathic pain, pain that results from direct stimulation of the myelin or nervous tissue of the peripheral or central nervous system (except for sensitized C fibers), generally felt as burning or tingling and often occurring in an area of sensory loss. It is seen commonly in patients with uncontrolled diabetes.

neuropathic pain syndrome, a condition of autonomic hyperactivity that results in sharp, stinging, or stabbing pain. The disorder is usually noninflammatory but may result in the destruction of peripheral nerve tissue. It may also be accompanied by changes in skin color, temperature, and edema.

neuropathy /nŏŏrop′əthē/ [Gk, *neuron* + *pathos,* disease], inflammation or degeneration of the peripheral nerves.—**neuropathic,** *adj.*

neuropeptide /nŏŏr′ōpep′tīd/, any of several types of molecules found in brain tissue, composed of short chains of amino acids including endorphins, enkephalins, vasopressin, and others. They are often localized in axon terminals at synapses and are classified as putative neurotransmitters, although some are also hormones.

neuropeptide Y (NPY), a natural substance that acts on the brain to stimulate eating. Laboratory animals injected with NPY greatly overeat. Substances that block the NPY receptor reduce the appetite. Leptin, a hormone that stimulates weight loss, reduces the output of NPY from the hypothalamus, a major production center.

neurophysin /-fiz′in/, one of a group of proteins released from the posterior pituitary gland at the same time as the hormone vasopressin or oxytocin. It is cleared from a larger protein of which vasopressin or oxytocin is a part.

neuroplasticity /-plastis′itē/, the capacity of the nervous system for adaptation or regeneration after trauma.

neuroplasty /nŏŏr′əplas′tē/ [Gk, *neuron, nerve, plassein,* to mold], plastic surgery to repair a nerve.

neuroplegia /nŏŏr′ōplē′jē·ə/ [Gk, *neuron* + *plege,* stroke], nerve paralysis caused by disease, injury, or the effect of neuroleptic drugs.

neuropore /nŏŏr′ōpôr/ [Gk, *neuron* + *poros,* pore], the opening at each end of the neural tube during early embryonic development, leading from the central canal of the neural tube to the exterior.

neuropraxia /-prak′sē·ə/ [Gk, *neuron, nerve, prassein,* to do], a condition in which a nerve remains in place after a severe injury, although it no longer transmits impulses.

neuroprotection /nŏŏr′ōprōtek′shən/, protection against neurotoxicity.

neuroprotective /nŏŏr′opro-tek′tiv/, guarding or protecting against neurotoxicity.

neuropsychiatrist /-sīkī′ətrist/, a physician who deals with the relationship between neurologic processes and psychiatric disorders.

neuropsychiatry /-sīkī′ətrē/, a branch of medicine that deals with problems of psychiatry as it relates to the neurophysiology of brain functions.

neuroradiography /-rā′dē·og′rəfē/, the radiographic examination of the tissues of the nervous system.

neuroradiology /-rā′dē·ol′əjē/, the branch of radiology concerned with diagnosing diseases of the nervous system.

neurorrhaphy /nŏŏrôr′əfē/ [Gk, *neuron, nerve, rhaphe,* suture], a surgical procedure to suture a severed nerve.

neurosarcoidosis /-sär′koidō′sis/, a granulomatous disease that may involve any part of the nervous system but most commonly affects the cranial and spinal nerves. Cranial nerve involvement may result in facial paralysis, whereas spinal nerve involvement may manifest as mononeuritis multiplex. If the CNS is affected, the vasculature of the brain may be damaged, resulting in stroke.

neurosarcoma /-särkō′mə/ [Gk, *neuron* + *sarx,* flesh, *oma,* tumor], a malignant neoplasm composed of nerve, connective, and vascular tissues.

neuroscience /nŏŏr′ōsī′əns/ [Gk, *neuron,* nerve; L, *scientia*], the study of neurology and related subjects, including neuroanatomy, neurophysiology, neuropharmacology, and neurosurgery.

neurosis /nŏŏrō'sis/ *pl.* **neuroses,** former name for a category of mental disorders in which the symptoms are distressing to the person, reality testing is intact, behavior does not violate gross social norms, and there is no apparent organic cause.

neuroskeleton /-skel'ətən/ [Gk, *neuron,* nerve, *skeletos,* dried up], the parts of the skeleton that surround or otherwise protect the nervous system, particularly the skull and vertebrae.

neurosome /nŏŏr'ōsōm/ [Gk, *neuron,* nerve, *soma,* body], **1.** the body of a neuron. **2.** any of the minute particles found in the protoplasm of a neuron.

neurosurgery /-sur'jərē/ [Gk, *neuron* + *cheirourgia,* surgery], any surgery involving the brain, spinal cord, or peripheral nerves. Brain surgery is performed to treat a wound, vascular disorders, or epilepsy; remove a tumor or foreign body; relieve pressure in intracranial hemorrhage or hydrocephaly; excise an abscess; treat parkinsonism; or relieve pain. Kinds of spinal surgery include fusion and laminectomy. Surgery on the peripheral nerves is performed to remove a tumor, relieve pain, or reconnect a severed nerve.

neurosyphilis /-sif'ilis/ [Gk, *neuron* + *sys,* hog, *philein,* to love], infection of the CNS by *Treponema pallidum,* the causative agent of syphilis, which may invade the meninges and cerebrovascular system. **—neurosyphilitic,** *adj.*

neurotendinous /-ten'dinəs/ [Gk, *neuron,* nerve; L, *tendo,* tendon], pertaining to both nerves and tendons.

neurotendinous spindle [Gk, *neuron;* L, *tendo,* tendon; AS, *spinel,* spindle], a capsule containing enlarged tendon fibers, found chiefly near the junctions of tendons and muscles.

neurotensin /-ten'sin/, a peptide neurotransmitter found in various parts of the brain. It is involved in vasodilation, hypotension, and pain perception.

neurotensinoma /-ten'sinō'mə/, a neuroendocrine tumor of the GI tract. Its major secreted product is neurotensin. The tumor originates in nonbeta islet cells, but unlike other neuroendocrine tumors, it has no distinguishing clinical features.

neurotic /n(y)ŏŏrot'ik/ [Gk, *neuron* + *osis,* condition; L, *icus,* like], **1.** pertaining to neurosis. **2.** pertaining to the nerves. **3.** one who is afflicted with a neurosis. **4.** *informal.* an emotionally unstable person.

neurotic personality [Gk, *neuron,* nerve, *osis,* condition; L, *personalis,* of a person], a disposition characterized by traits

and tendencies that increase the likelihood of a specific neurotic behavior. For example, the orderly, cautious, meticulous person may be prone to development of an obsessive-compulsive disorder.

neurotmesis /nŏŏr'ōtmē'sis/ [Gk, *neuron* + *tmesis,* cutting apart], a peripheral nerve injury in which the nerve is completely disrupted by laceration or traction.

neurologic /nŏŏr'ōtōloj'ik/, pertaining to the study of the elements of the ear as they relate to the brain and nervous system.

neurotology /nŏŏr'ōtol'əjē/, a branch of otology concerned with those parts of the nervous system related to the ear, especially the inner ear and associated brainstem structures.

neurotomy /nŏŏrot'əmē/, the surgical severing of a nerve or nerves.

neurotoxic /nŏŏr'ōtok'sik/, having a poisonous effect on nerves and nerve cells, such as when ingested lead degenerates peripheral nerves.

neurotoxicity /-toksis'itē/ [Gk, *neuron,* nerve, *toxikon,* poison], the ability of a drug or other agent to destroy or damage nervous tissue.

neurotoxin /nŏŏr'ōtok'sin/ [Gk, *neuron* + *toxikon,* poison], a toxin that acts directly on the tissues of the CNS, traveling along the axis cylinders of the motor nerves to the brain. The toxin may be secreted in the venom of certain snakes, or it may be present on the spines of a shell or in the flesh of fish or shellfish; it may be produced by certain bacteria or by the cellular disintegration of certain bacteria.

neurotransmitter /-transmit'ər/ [Gk, *neuron;* L, *transmittere,* to transmit], a chemical that modifies or results in the transmission of nerve impulses between synapses. Neurotransmitters are released from synaptic knobs into synaptic clefts and bridge the gap between presynaptic and postsynaptic neurons. When a nerve impulse reaches a synaptic knob, thousands of neurotransmitter molecules squirt into the synaptic cleft and bind to specific receptors. This flow allows an associated diffusion of potassium and sodium ions that causes an action potential.

neurotripsy /-trip'sē/, the surgical crushing of a nerve.

neurotrophic /-trof'ik/, pertaining to the nourishment of nerve cells.

neurotropic viruses /-trop'ik/ [Gk, *neuron,* nerve, *tropein,* to turn, *virus,* poison], viruses with an unexplained attraction to nerve tissue. The predilection also applies to certain toxic chemicals.

neurotropism /nŏŏrot'rəpiz'əm/ [Gk, *neuron,* nerve, *trepein,* to turn], **1.** the tendency for certain microorganisms, poisons, and nutrients to be attracted to nervous tissue. **2.** the tendency of basic dyes to be attracted to nervous tissue.

Neurpro, a trademark for rotigotine.

neurula /nŏŏr′ələ/ *pl.* **neurulas, neurulae** [Gk, *neuron,* nerve], an early embryo during the period of neurulation when the nervous system tissue begins to differentiate. The embryo at this level of growth represents a third stage in embryonic development. In humans the neurula stage occurs from about 19 to 26 days after fertilization.

neurulation /-ā′shən/ [Gk, *neuron;* L, *atus,* process], the development of the neural plate and the processes involved with its subsequent closure to form the neural tube during the early stages of embryonic development.

neutral /n(y)ŏŏ′trəl/ [L, *neutralis,* neuter], the state exactly between two opposing values, qualities, or properties. For example, in electricity a neutral state is one in which there is neither a positive nor a negative charge. In chemistry a neutral state is one in which a substance is neither acid nor alkaline.

neutralization /-īzā′shən/ [L, *neutralis;* Gk, *izein,* to cause], the interaction between an acid and a base that produces a solution that is neither acidic nor basic. The usual products of neutralization are a salt and water.—**neutralize,** *v.*

neutral rotation, the position of a limb that is turned neither toward nor away from the body's midline. When a person is supine and the leg is neutrally rotated, the toes should point straight up.

neutral thermal environment, an environment created by any method or apparatus to maintain the normal body temperature to minimize oxygen consumption and caloric expenditure, such as in an incubator for a premature infant.

neutron /n(y)ŏŏ′tron/ [L, *neuter,* neither; Gk, *elektron,* amber], in physics, an elementary particle that is a constituent of the nuclei of all elements except the isotopic form of hydrogen ^{1}H. It has no electric charge and has approximately the same mass as a proton.

neutron activation analysis, the analysis of elements in a specimen performed by exposing it to neutron irradiation. The irradiation converts many elements in the specimen to radioactive forms that can be identified by their emissions of radiation. The method has limited application to human and animal studies.

neutropenia /nŏŏ′trōpē′nē·ə/ [L, *neuter,* neither; Gk, *penia,* poverty], an abnormal decrease in the number of neutrophils in the blood. The decrease may be relative or absolute. Neutropenia is associated with acute leukemia, infection, rheumatoid arthritis, vitamin B_{12} deficiency, and chronic splenomegaly.

neutropenic fever of unknown origin, a fever of at least 38.3° C occurring on several occasions in a patient whose neutrophil level is lower than 500/mm^3 or is expected to fall below that level within 1 or 2 days, the cause of which cannot be determined after 3 days of investigation, including 2 days of incubation of cultures.

neutrophil /nŏŏ′trəfil/ [L, *neuter;* Gk, *philein,* to love], a polymorphonuclear, granular leukocyte that stains easily with neutral dyes. Neutrophils are the circulating WBCs essential for phagocytosis and proteolysis by which bacteria, cellular debris, and solid particles are removed and destroyed. A neutrophil count less than or equal to 500 uL may be life-threatening.

neutrophilia /-fil′yə/, an elevated number of neutrophils in the blood, a common cause of leukocytosis.

Neviaser procedure, the surgical transfer of a coracoacromial ligament to the clavicle for the repair of an acromioclavicular separation.

nevirapine, an antiretroviral nonnucleoside reverse transcriptase inhibitor prescribed in combination for the treatment of HIV infection.

nevoid basal cell carcinoma syndrome /nē′void/, an inherited form of premalignant skin lesion. It is an autosomal-dominant trait, but the cause is unknown. It is associated with other abnormalities of the skin or bone, the nervous system, the eyes, and the reproductive system. It affects persons under the age of 20 years and is accompanied by palmar pits, mandibular cysts, bifid ribs, and other birth defects.

nevoid neuroma [L, *naevus,* birthmark; Gk, *eidos,* form], a tumor of nerve tissue that contains numerous small blood vessels.

nevus /nē′vəs/ [L, *naevus,* birthmark], a pigmented skin blemish that is usually benign but may become cancerous.

nevus flammeus /flam′ē·əs/, a flat capillary hemangioma that is present at birth and that varies from pale red to deep reddish purple. It most commonly occurs on the occiput and rarely causes any problems. The depth of the color depends on whether the superficial, middle, or deep dermal vessels are involved.

nevus sebaceus of Jadassohn, a congenital skin neoplasm with several cutaneous tissue elements. The most common location is the scalp, face, or neck. It may appear as a yellow or tan waxy patch of alopecia at birth. During puberty the lesion becomes raised, thick, and verrucous.

Untreated, the lesion may remain benign or become a malignant growth in later life.

New Ballard Score, a system of newborn assessment of gestational maturation. It provides a valid estimation of postnatal maturation for preterm infants with gestational ages greater than 20 weeks.

newborn [AS, *niwe*, new, *boren*, to bear], a human infant from the time of birth through the 28th day of life. At birth, the gestational age and birth weight are assessed and the newborn classified accordingly, for example, large for gestational age, preterm (premature), or low birth weight.

newborn adaptation, a nursing outcome from the Nursing Outcomes Classification (NOC) defined as the adaptative response to the extrauterine environment by a physiologically mature newborn during the first 28 days.

newborn care, a nursing intervention from the Nursing Interventions Classification (NIC) defined as management of neonate during the transition to extrauterine life and subsequent period of stabilization.

newborn intrapartal care, care of the newborn in the delivery area during the time after birth before the mother and infant are transferred to the postpartum unit.

newborn monitoring, a nursing intervention from the Nursing Interventions Classification (NIC) defined as measurement and interpretation of physiologic status of the neonate the first 24 hours after delivery.

new drug, a drug for which the U.S. Food and Drug Administration requires premarketing approval.

New England Journal of Medicine (NEJM), a weekly professional medical journal that publishes findings of medical research and articles about controversial political and ethical issues in the practice of medicine.

new growth, a neoplasm or tumor.

Newman, Margaret A. [b. 1933], a nursing theorist who defined three approaches to the discovery of nursing theory: "borrowing" theories from related disciplines, analyzing nursing practice situations in search of conceptual relationships, and creating new conceptual systems from which theories can be derived.

newton /n(y)ōōʹtən/ [Isaac Newton, English scientist, 1642–1727], a unit of force in the SI system that imparts an acceleration to 1 kilogram of mass of 1 meter per second per second.

new tuberculin [ME, *newe;* L, *tuber,* swelling], an extract of the tubercle bacillus from which all soluble material has been removed and glycerin added.

Nexavar, a trademark for sorafenib.

nexus /nekʹsəs/ *pl.* **nexus** [L, bond], a bond, especially one between members of a series or group.

Nezelof's syndrome /nezʹəlofs/ [Christian Nezelof, French physician, b. 1922], an abnormal condition characterized by absent T-cell function, deficient B-cell function, fairly normal immunoglobulin levels, and little or no specific antibody production. The cause is unknown. Patients with Nezelof's syndrome have progressively severe, recurrent, and eventually fatal infections.

nF, abbreviation for *nanofarad.*

NF1, a gene associated with neurofibromatosis. The gene is normally part of a family that helps regulate the timing of cell divisions. It may become defective, leading to neurofibromatosis expression, when an itinerant sequence of a DNA molecule becomes wedged in the NF1 gene.

NF, N.F., abbreviation for *National Formulary.*

ng, abbreviation for *nanogram.*

NGF, abbreviation for **nerve growth factor.**

NG tube, abbreviation for **nasogastric tube.**

NGU, abbreviation for **nongonococcal urethritis.**

NHGRI, abbreviation for **National Human Genome Research Institute.**

NHSC, abbreviation for **National Health Service Corps.**

Ni, symbol for the element **nickel.**

NIA, abbreviation for **National Institute on Aging.**

niacin /nīʹəsin/, a white, crystalline water-soluble vitamin of the B complex, usually occurring in various plant and animal tissues as nicotinamide. It functions as a coenzyme necessary for the breakdown and use of all major nutrients and is essential for a healthy skin, normal functioning of the GI tract, maintenance of the nervous system, and synthesis of the sex hormones. It may be used therapeutically to help reduce high blood cholesterol levels.

niacinamide /nīʹəsinʹəmīd/, a B complex vitamin. It is closely related to niacin but has no vasodilating action.

niacin equivalent (NE), units used to express niacin content of food. It represents preformed niacin plus tryptophan equivalents (60 mg tryptophan = 1 mg niacin).

NIAMS, abbreviation for **National Institute of Arthritis and Musculoskeletal and Skin Diseases.**

NIB, abbreviation for *National Institute for the Blind.*

NIBIB, abbreviation for **National Institute of Biomedical Imaging and Bioengineering.**

N

NIC, abbreviation for **Nursing Interventions Classification.**

niCARdipine /nĭkär′dĭpĭn/, a calcium channel blocker. It causes vasodilation and is prescribed as an antihypertensive and antianginal agent.

niche /nĭch/ [Fr, recess], a defect in an otherwise even surface, especially a depression or recess in the wall of an organ as seen on a radiograph or by the unaided eye.

NICHHD, abbreviation for **National Institute of Child Health and Human Development.**

Nicholas procedure, a surgical method for repairing severe injuries to the ligaments of the knee. It involves five procedures: medial meniscectomy, medial collateral ligament repair, vastus medialis advancement, semitendinosus advancement, and pes anserinus transfer.

nick [ME, *nyke*, notch], a split in a single strand of DNA that can be made with the enzyme deoxyribonuclease or with ethidium bromide.

nickel (Ni) [Ger, *Kupfernickel,* copper demon], a silver-white metallic element. Its atomic number is 28, and its atomic mass is 58.71. Many people are allergic to nickel. Nickel carbonyl, an extremely toxic volatile liquid, may produce serious lung damage if inhaled. Nickel is now a suspected carcinogen.

nickel dermatitis, an allergic contact dermatitis caused by the metal nickel. Exposure comes usually from jewelry, wristwatches, metal clasps, and coins. Sweating increases the degree of rash.

nick translation, a method of labeling DNA in the laboratory by using the enzyme DNA polymerase.

Nicobid, a trademark for two coenzymes, a water-soluble vitamin (B_3) (niacin and niacinamide).

Nicola procedure, the surgical transfer of the long head of the biceps tendon through the humeral head for chronic anterior shoulder dislocation.

Nicorette, a trademark for a nicotine resin complex (nicotine polacrilex).

nicotine /nik′ətēn/ [Jean Nicot de Villemain, French ambassador to Portugal, 1530–1600], a colorless, rapidly acting toxic substance in tobacco that is one of the major contributors to the ill effects of smoking. It is used as an insecticide in agriculture and as a parasiticide in veterinary medicine. Ingestion of large amounts causes salivation, nausea, vomiting, diarrhea, headache, vertigo, slowing of the heartbeat, and, in acute cases, paralysis of respiratory muscles.

nicotine nasal spray, a product approved by the U.S. Food and Drug Administration for aiding tobacco smoking cessation in adults. One dose of the nasal spray administers 1 mg of nicotine directly into the nasal membranes. Because of the risk of becoming dependent on the nasal spray, it is recommended that patients not use it for more than 6 months.

nicotine poisoning, poisoning from intake of nicotine. Nicotine poisoning is characterized by stimulation of the central and autonomic nervous systems, followed by depression of these systems. In fatal cases, death occurs from respiratory failure.

nicotine polacrilex /pōlak′rĭleks/, a chewing gum (nicotine resin complex) source of nicotine as an adjunct for smoking cessation. It may be prescribed as an aid for patients who are trying to quit cigarette smoking.

nicotine replacement therapy, the use of chewing gum, lozenges, and skin patches as a substitute for tobacco smoke sources to satisfy nicotine cravings.

nicotine withdrawal syndrome, physiologic and psychologic effects of tobacco dependence that make it difficult for addicted smokers to cease use of nicotine. Withdrawal symptoms may be diminished by substituting nicotine chewing gum and transdermal nicotine skin patches for cigarettes.

NICU, abbreviation for **neonatal intensive care unit.**

NID, abbreviation for *National Institute for the Deaf.*

NIDA, abbreviation for *National Institute on Drug Abuse.*

nidation /nīdā′shən/ [L, *nidus,* nest], the process by which an embryo burrows into the endometrium of the uterus.

NIDCD, abbreviation for **National Institute on Deafness and Other Communication Disorders.**

NIDCR, abbreviation for *National Institute of Dental and Craniofacial Research.*

NIDDM, abbreviation for **non–insulin-dependent diabetes mellitus.**

nidus /nī′dəs/ [L, nest], a point or origin, focus, or nucleus of a disease process.

Niebauer prosthesis /nē′bou·ər/, a Silastic prosthesis for interphalangeal and thumb joint replacement.

Niemann-Pick disease /nē′mon pik/ [Albert Niemann, German pediatrician, 1880–1921; Ludwig Pick, German pediatrician, 1868–1935], an inherited disorder of lipid metabolism in which there are accumulations of sphingomyelin in the bone marrow, spleen, and lymph nodes. The disease begins in infancy or childhood and is characterized by enlargement of liver and spleen, anemia, lymphadenopathy, and progressive mental and physical deterioration.

NIFEdipine /nifed'ipēn/, a calcium channel blocker prescribed for the treatment of vasospastic and effort-associated angina, pulmonary hypertension, and hypertension (sustained-release form only).

Nightingale, Florence, considered the founder of modern nursing. After limited formal training in nursing in Germany and Paris, she became superintendent in 1853 of a small hospital in London. Her outstanding success in reorganizing the hospital led the British government to request that she head a mission to the Crimea, where Britain was fighting a war with Russia. After her return to England in 1856, she wrote *Notes on Hospitals* and *Notes on Nursing* and founded a training school for nurses at St. Thomas' Hospital. The graduates became matrons of the most important hospitals in Great Britain, thus raising the standards of nursing across the nation and eventually around the world. Although she was, by then, bedridden much of the time, she carried on her work on the sanitary reform of India, conducted a study of midwifery, helped establish visiting nurse services, and worked for the reform of the poor laws in which she proposed separate institutions for the sick, the insane, the incurable, and children. One of Florence Nightingale's outstanding contributions was significantly decreasing the infection-related death rate through cleanliness.

Nightingale pledge, a statement of principles for the nursing profession, formulated by a committee in 1893. It is as follows: "I solemnly pledge myself before God and in the presence of this assembly: To pass my life in purity and to practice my profession faithfully. I will abstain from whatever is deleterious and mischievous, and will not take or knowingly administer any harmful drug. I will do all in my power to elevate the standard of my profession, and will hold in confidence all personal matters committed to my keeping and all family affairs coming to my knowledge in the practice of my profession. With loyalty will I endeavor to aid the physician in his work, and devote myself to the welfare of those committed to my care."

Nightingale ward, a hospital ward designed by Florence Nightingale that limited the number of beds to permit the circulation of air and to enhance general cleanliness and the comfort of patients. Three sides of the ward were windowed to admit light and fresh air. Although multiple-bed wards are now obsolete in hospital design, the concerns and benefits that impelled Miss Nightingale to create them remain central to hospital planning.

nightingalism /nī'ting·gā'lizəm/, an ideology emphasizing self-sacrifice on the part of a nurse whose primary concern is the welfare of the patient, with minimum personal attention to the needs of the nurse.

nightmare /nīt'mer/ [AS, *niht,* night, *mara,* incubus], a dream occurring during rapid eye movement sleep that arouses feelings of intense inescapable fear, terror, distress, or extreme anxiety and that usually awakens the sleeper.

night splint, any splint or similar device applied to the affected extremity. It is used only at night.

nightstick fracture, an undisplaced fracture of the ulnar shaft caused by a direct blow.

night sweat [AS, *niht* + *swaetan*], sweating that occurs with a nocturnal fever, as in a wasting disease like pulmonary TB.

night terrors [AS, *niht;* L, *terrour*], a form of dissociated sleep, usually in children, in which there may be repeated episodes of abrupt awakening from sleep with signs of panic and anxiety. The subject may have only fragmentary dream images of a threatening nature.

night vision [AS, *niht,* L, *visio,* seeing], a capacity to see dimly lit objects. It stems from a chemophysical phenomenon associated with the retinal rods. The rods contain the highly light-sensitive chemical rhodopsin, or visual purple, which is essential for the conduction of optic impulses in subdued light. Night vision is sharpest at the periphery of the retina because of the concentration of rods.

nightwalking [AS, *niht;* ME, *walken*], a disorder occurring during nonrapid eye movement sleep in which the subject usually sits up in bed briefly, then gets up and walks around, opening doors, eating, and so on, and eventually returns to bed. The person has no memory of the event the next day.

NIGMS, abbreviation for **National Institute of General Medical Sciences.**

NIH, abbreviation for **National Institutes of Health.**

nihilistic delusion /nī'hilis'tik/ [L, *nihil,* nothing, *icus,* form of, *deludere,* to deceive], a persistent denial of the existence of particular things or of everything, including oneself, as seen in various forms of schizophrenia.

Nikolsky's sign /nikol'skēz/ [Petr V. Nikolsky, Russian dermatologist, 1858–1940], easy separation of the stratum corneum layer of the epidermis from the basal cell layer by rubbing apparently normal skin areas, found in pemphigus and a few other bullous diseases.

nilotinib, a miscellaneous antineoplastic used to treat chronic- and accelerated-phase

Philadelphia chromosome–positive chronic myelogenous leukemia that is resistant to or intolerant of imatinib.

Nilstat, a trademark for an antifungal (nystatin).

nilutamide, an antineoplastic hormone used to treat stage D2 metastatic prostatic carcinoma in combination with surgical castration.

NIMH, abbreviation for **National Institute of Mental Health.**

nimodipine /nĭmōd′əpēn/, a calcium channel blocking agent used as a vasodilator in the treatment of neurologic deficits associated with subarachnoid hemorrhage from a ruptured intracranial aneurysm.

NINR, abbreviation for **National Institute of Nursing Research.**

niobium (Nb) /nī-ō′bē·əm/ [Gk, *Niobe*, mythic daughter of Tantalus and Amphion], a silver-gray metallic element. Its atomic number is 41, and its atomic mass is 92.906.

NIOSH, abbreviation for **National Institute for Occupational Safety and Health.**

NIP, abbreviation for **National Immunization Program.**

nipple [ME, *neb,* beak], a small cylindric, pigmented structure that projects just below the center of each breast. The tip of the nipple has about 20 tiny openings to the lactiferous ducts. The skin of the nipple is surrounded by the lighter pigmented skin of the areola. In pregnancy the skin of the nipple darkens but loses some of its pigmentation when lactation is completed.

nipple cancer, an inflammatory malignant neoplasm of the nipple and areola that is usually associated with carcinoma in deeper breast structures. It represents only a small percentage of breast cancers.

nipple discharge, spontaneous exudation of material from the nipple. It may be normal, such as colostrum in pregnancy, or it may be a sign of endocrinologic, neoplastic, or infectious disease.

nipple shield, a device to protect the nipples of a lactating woman. The shield is usually made of soft latex, is 4 or 5 cm wide, and has a tab on one side with which the mother may hold it. The baby nurses from an opening at the center of the shield. It is most often used to allow sore or cracked nipples to heal while maintaining lactation.

Nipride, a trademark for a direct-acting vasodilator used for controlled lowering of BP (sodium nitroprusside).

Nirschl procedure /nur′shəl/, a surgical procedure for treating chronic inflammation of the elbow. It involves excision of a segment from the hypercapsular tendon of the extensor carpi radialis brevis and

removal of the head of the anterolateral condyle.

nirvanic state /nirvä′nik, nirvan′ik/, in Buddhist meditation, a state in which mental processes cease, often leading to a radical alteration of the personality.

NIS, abbreviation for *Nursing Information System.*

nisoldipine, a calcium channel blocker that causes vasodilation and is prescribed, either alone of in combinations, for the management of hypertension.

Nissl body /nis′əl/ [Franz Nissl, German neurologist, 1860–1919], any one of the large granular structures in the cytoplasm of nerve cells that stains with basic dyes and contains ribonucleoprotein.

NIST, abbreviation for **National Institute of Standards and Technology.**

NIST standard, a radioactive source standardized or certified or both by the National Institute of Standards and Technology.

nit, the egg of a parasitic insect, particularly a louse.

nitazoxanide, an antiprotozoal agent used to treat diarrhea caused by *Cryptosporidium parvum* or *Giardia lamblia.*

nitisinone, an orphan drug used to treat hereditary tyrosinemia type 1.

nitr, 1. abbreviation for **nitrocellulose. 2.** abbreviation for **nitroglycerin.**

nitrate /nī′trāt/ [Gk, *nitron,* soda], **1.** the ion NO_3^-. **2.** a salt of nitric acid.

nitric acid (HNO$_3$) /nī′trik/ [Gk, *nitron*, soda; L, *acidus*, sour], a colorless, highly corrosive liquid that may give off suffocating brown fumes of nitrogen dioxide on exposure to air. Traces of nitric acid may be found in rainwater during a thunderstorm. Commercially prepared nitric acid is a powerful oxidizing agent with many industrial uses and is occasionally used as a cauterizing agent for the removal of warts. Organic nitrates or polyol esters of nitric acid such as nitroglycerin and amyl nitrite are effective vasodilators often used in relieving angina.

nitric oxide (NO)[1], a colorless gas and stable free radical commonly found in tissues of humans and other mammals. It participates in many biologic functions, such as neurotransmission, vasodilation, cytotoxicity of macrophages, lipid-lowering therapy, inhibition of platelet aggregation, smooth muscle action, and penile erection. It may improve oxygenation in patients with high-altitude pulmonary edema. NO deprivation may lead to high BP and the formation of atherosclerotic plaque. On contact with air, NO is quickly converted to the very poisonous nitrogen dioxide (NO_2).

nitric oxide (NO)[2], a respiratory inhalant used in combination with other agents and ventilatory support in the treatment of full-term and near-term (>34 weeks) neonates with hypoxic respiratory failure associated with pulmonary hypertension.

nitrite /nī'trīt/ [Gk, *nitron,* soda], an ester or salt of nitrous acid used as a vasodilator and antispasmodic. Among the most widely used nitrites in medicine are amyl, ethyl, potassium, and sodium nitrite.

nitritoid reaction /nī'tritoid/, a group of adverse effects, including hypotension, flushing, light-headedness, and fainting, produced by administration of arsenicals or gold. The reaction is similar to that caused by administration of nitrites.

nitrobenzene poisoning /nī'trōben'zēn/, a toxic condition caused by the absorption into the body of nitrobenzene, a pale yellow, oily liquid used in the manufacture of aniline, shoe dyes, soap, perfume, and artificial flavors. Nitrobenzene, especially its vapors, is extremely toxic. Symptoms of acute poisoning include headache, drowsiness, nausea, ataxia, cyanosis, and, in extreme cases, respiratory failure. Chronic exposure to nitrobenzene may cause headache, fatigue, loss of appetite, and anemia.

Nitro-Bid, a trademark for a coronary vasodilator (nitroglycerin).

nitrocellulose (nitr) /-sel'yəlōs/, a mixture of nitrate esters of cellulose made by treating cotton with nitric and sulfuric acids. Solutions in a mixture of ether and alcohol are used as "plastic skin" under the name of collodion.

nitrofuran /-fyoo'ran/, one of a group of synthetic antimicrobials used to treat infections caused by protozoa or by certain gram-positive or gram-negative bacteria. Two agents commonly prescribed are furazolidone, used to treat bacterial and protozoal diarrhea and enteritis, and nitrofurantoin, used to treat UTIs caused by *Escherichia coli* and other enteric pathogens of the urinary tract.

nitrofurantoin /nī'trōfyŏŏran'tō·in, -fyoo'rəntō'in/, a urinary antibacterial prescribed in the treatment of UTIs caused by some gram-negative bacteria and a few gram-positive bacteria. Some of the more common causes of UTIs are resistant to it.

nitrofurazone /-fyoo'rəzōn/, a topical antibacterial prescribed in the prophylaxis and treatment of infections in second- and third-degree burns and of the skin and mucous membranes.

nitrogen (N) /nī'trəjən/ [Gk, *nitron,* soda, *genein,* to produce], a gaseous nonmetallic element. Its atomic number is 7; its atomic mass is 14.008. It exists as a diatomic molecule, N_2. Nitrogen constitutes approximately 78% of the atmosphere and is a component of all proteins and a major component of most organic substances in living cells. Nitrogen is essential to the synthesis of necessary proteins, particularly nitrogen-containing compounds or amino acids derived directly or indirectly from plant food.

nitrogen balance, the relationship between the amount of nitrogen taken into the body, usually as food, and that excreted from the body in urine and feces. Most of the body's nitrogen is incorporated into protein. Positive nitrogen balance, which occurs when the intake of nitrogen is greater than its excretion, implies tissue formation and growth. Negative nitrogen balance, which occurs when more nitrogen is excreted than is taken in, indicates wasting or destruction of tissue.

nitrogen cycle [Gk, *nitron,* soda, *genein,* to produce, *kyklos,* circle], the circulation of nitrogen through natural processes in either of two ways: from the soil to organisms that excrete nitrogen products back into the soil or by bacterial fixation of atmospheric nitrogen through other organisms that decay and release the element back into the atmosphere.

nitrogen dioxide (NO_2), a brownish irritating gas that can be released from silage and the reaction of nitric acid with metals. It may produce symptoms of pulmonary damage in workers who perform ensilage tasks. Some studies indicate that measurable changes in pulmonary function occur when healthy individuals are exposed to NO_2 concentrations of two to three parts per million.

nitrogen fixation, the process by which free nitrogen in the atmosphere is converted by biologic or chemical means to ammonia and to other forms usable by plants and animals. Biologic nitrogen fixation is the more important process and is accomplished by microorganisms in the soil.

nitrogen narcosis, a condition of depressed CNS functions as a result of high partial pressure of nitrogen.

nitrogen washout curve, a curve obtained by plotting the concentration of nitrogen in expired alveolar gas during oxygen breathing as a function of time. As a person inhales pure oxygen after breathing ambient air, the nitrogen concentration in exhaled air decreases. In healthy subjects, the concentration is less than 2% after 4 minutes.

nitroglycerin (nitr) /-glis'ərin/, a potent smooth muscle relaxant and vasodilator used in transdermal patches and in a paste as well as in oral and sublingual tablets. It is prescribed for the prevention or relief of

N

angina pectoris. There are recommended limits to the amount of nitroglycerin use before calling for emergency assistance (no more than 3 sublingual tablets at 5-minute intervals). The drug should not be used continuously because tolerance develops within 24 to 48 hours. Nitroglycerin is also used to treat pulmonary hypertension, to help treat CHF following acute MI, and to treat hypertensive emergencies during cardiovascular surgery.

nitroglycerin tablets, tablets of glyceryl trinitrate, a volatile ester prepared by the action of nitric and sulfuric acids on glycerol. A tablet placed under the tongue provides prompt relief of chest pain from angina, and sustained release forms are available for preventing angina.

nitromersol /-mur′sol/, an organic mercurial antiseptic that is not a highly effective germicide, sometimes used for the disinfecting of surgical instruments and as an antiseptic on the skin and mucous membranes.

nitrosamines /nīt′rəsam′ēnz/, potentially carcinogenic compounds produced by reactions of nitrites with amines or amides normally present in the body. Nitrites are produced by bacteria in saliva and in the intestine from nitrates normally present in vegetables and in nitrate-treated fish, poultry, and meats.

nitrosourea /nītrō′sōyŏŏrē′ə/, one of a group of alkylating drugs used as antineoplastic drugs in the chemotherapy of brain tumors, multiple myeloma, Hodgkin's disease, adenocarcinomas, hepatomas, chronic leukemias, lymphomas, myelomas, and cancers of the breast and ovaries. They have been less successful in therapy for cancers of the lungs, head, neck, and GI tract.

Nitrospan, a trademark for a coronary vasodilator (nitroglycerin).

Nitrostat, a trademark for a coronary vasodilator (nitroglycerin).

nitrous acid (HNO₂), a weak acid and clinical laboratory reagent formed by the action of strong acids on inorganic nitrites. An aqueous solution of nitrous acid gradually decomposes into nitric oxide and nitric acid.

nitrous oxide (N₂O, NOx) /nī′trəs/, a colorless, odorless, sweet-tasting, weak anesthetic gas used in dentistry, surgery, and childbirth. It must be delivered with oxygen to prevent anoxia. Nitrous oxide alone does not provide enough anesthesia for surgery, for which it is supplemented with other anesthetic agents.

Nix, a trademark for a topical pediculicide (permethrin).

Nizoral, a trademark for an antifungal agent (ketoconazole).

NLM, abbreviation for **National Library of Medicine.**

NLN, abbreviation for **National League for Nursing.**

NLNAC, abbreviation for **National League for Nursing Accrediting Commission.**

nm, abbreviation for **nanometer.**

N-m, abbreviation for *newton meter.*

N/m², abbreviation for *newton per square meter.*

NMDP, abbreviation for **National Marrow Donor Program.**

NMDS, abbreviation for **nursing minimum data set.**

NMES, 1. abbreviation for **neuromuscular electric stimulator.** 2. abbreviation for *neuromuscular electrical stimulation.*

NMNA, abbreviation for **National Male Nurses Association.**

NMR, abbreviation for *nuclear magnetic resonance.*

NNRTIs, abbreviation for **nonnucleoside reverse transcriptase inhibitors.**

No, symbol for the element **nobelium.**

NO, abbreviation for **nitric oxide.**

N₂O, symbol for **nitrous oxide.**

Noack's syndrome /no′äks/ [Margot Noack, German physician, b. 1909], an autosomal-dominant type of acrocephalopolysyndactyly.

nobelium (No) /nōbel′ē·əm/ [Alfred Nobel Institute, Stockholm, Sweden], a synthetic, transuranic metallic element. Its atomic number is 102, and the atomic mass of its most stable isotope is 259.

NOC, abbreviation for **Nursing Outcomes Classification.**

Nocardia /nōkär′dē·ə/ [Edmund I.E. Nocard, French veterinarian, 1850–1903], a genus of weakly gram-positive aerobic bacteria, some species of which are pathogenic, such as *Nocardia asteroides.*

nocardiosis /nōkär′dē·ō′sis/ [Edmund I.E. Nocard; Gk, *osis,* condition], infection with *Nocardia* species, most often *N. asteroides.* It can cause pneumonia, often with cavitation, and chronic abscesses in the brain and subcutaneous tissues, and it can cause cutaneous disease through wounds contaminated with soil. The organism enters via the respiratory tract and spreads by the bloodstream, especially in immunocompromised persons.

nocebo /nōsē′bō/, an adverse, nonspecific side effect occurring in conjunction with a medication but not directly resulting from the pharmacologic action of the medication.

nociceptive /nō′səsep′tiv/ [L, *nocere,* to injure, *capere,* to receive], pertaining to a neural receptor for painful stimuli.

nociceptive reflex [L, *nocere,* to injure, *capere,* to receive, *reflectere,* to bend back], a reflex caused by a painful stimulus.

nociceptive stimulus [L, *nocere,* to injure, *capere,* to receive, *stimulus,* goad], a painful, sometimes detrimental or injurious, stimulus.

nociceptor /nō′sĕsep′tər/, a somatic and visceral free nerve ending of thinly myelinated and unmyelinated fibers. It usually reacts to tissue injury but also may be excited by endogenous chemical substances.

no code [AS, *na,* not; L, *caudex,* book], a note written in the patient record and signed by a qualified, usually senior or attending physician instructing the staff of the institution not to attempt to resuscitate a particular patient in the event of cardiac or respiratory failure. This instruction is usually given only when a patient is so gravely ill that death is imminent and inevitable.

noct., abbreviation for the Latin word *nocte,* meaning "at night."

nocturia /noktŏŏr′ē·ə/ [L, *nocturnus,* by night; Gk, *ouron,* urine], excessive urination at night. It may be a symptom of renal or prostatic disease or bladder outlet obstruction. The condition may also occur in people who drink excessive amounts of fluids, particularly alcohol or coffee, before bedtime or in older patients who have excess body fluids that are mobilized by lying down.

nocturnal /noktur′nəl/ [L, *nocturnus,* by night], **1.** pertaining to or occurring during the night. **2.** describing an individual or animal that is active at night and sleeps during the day.

nocturnal emission, involuntary emission of semen during sleep, usually in association with an erotic dream.

nocturnal enuresis [L, *nocturnus,* by night; Gk, *enourein*], involuntary urination while asleep at night.

nocturnal myoclonus, a sleep disorder that usually affects older adults and is marked by thrashing or kicking movements. The condition may be exacerbated by the use of tricyclic depressants used to induce sleep.

nocturnal penile tumescence (NPT) [L, *nocturnus,* by night, *penile,* pertaining to the penis, *tumescere,* to begin to swell], a normal condition of penile erection that occurs during sleep throughout most of the lifetime of a male. The occurrence of NPT is important in the diagnosis of impotence, because it indicates that impotence may be psychogenic.

nodal /nō′dəl/ [L, *nodus,* knot], pertaining to a node.

nodal event /nō′dəl/, an occurrence that may cause anxiety, such as birth, death, divorce, marriage, or a child leaving home.

node /nōd/ [L, *nodus,* knot], **1.** a small rounded mass. **2.** a lymph node.

nodular /nod′yələr/ [L, *nodus,* knot], of a structure or mass, small, firm, and knotty.

nodular circumscribed lipomatosis, a condition in which circumscribed, encapsulated lipomas are distributed around the neck symmetrically, randomly, or like a collar. The adipose deposits may be painful and tender.

nodular cutaneous angiitis, inflammation of small arteries accompanied by skin lesions.

nodular fasciitis, an inflammation of the fascia that causes the formation of nodules.

nodular goiter [L, *nodus,* knot; Gk, *guttur,* throat], an enlarged goiter that contains nodules.

nodular hyperplasia of the liver, the presence of a regenerative nodule or nodules in the liver.

nodular melanoma, a melanoma that is uniformly pigmented, usually bluish-black and nodular and sometimes surrounded by an irregular halo of pale, unpigmented skin. The lesion is always raised and may be dome-shaped or polypoid.

nodule /nod′yōōl/ [L, *nodulus,* small knot], **1.** a small node. **2.** a small node-like structure.

noise-induced hearing loss, a gradual loss of hearing caused by exposure to loud noise over an extended period of time. The hearing loss is sensorineural in nature and greatest in the higher frequencies. Although an early hearing loss may be temporary, it becomes permanent with increased exposure to noise.

noise pollution, an unwanted noise level in the environment, causing discomfort and possibly threatening health.

nok, abbreviation for *next of kin.*

Nolvadex, a trademark for an antiestrogen (tamoxifen).

noma /nō′mə/ [Gk, *nome,* distribution], an acute, necrotizing ulcerative process involving mucous membranes of the mouth or genitalia, most commonly seen in severely malnourished, debilitated persons. There are rapid spreading and painless destruction of bone and soft tissue accompanied by a putrid odor caused by oral anaerobic bacteria, especially *Fusobacterium nucleatum.*

nomenclature /nō′mənklā′chər, nōmen′-/ [L, *nomen,* name, *clamare,* to call], a consistent, systematic method of naming used in a scientific discipline to denote classifications and to avoid ambiguities in names, such as binomial nomenclature in biology and chemical nomenclature in chemistry.

Nomina Anatomica, the book of official international nomenclature for anatomy as designated by the International Congress of Anatomists.

nominal aphasia /nom′inəl/ [L, *nomen;* Gk, *a + phasis,* without speech], a type of language disorder in which the person uses incorrect names in identifying objects. Minor episodes may result from anxiety, fatigue, or senility. Severe cases can indicate a focal lesion on the left side of the brain.

nomogram /nom′əgram, nō′mə-/ [Gk, *nomos,* law, *gramma,* a record], **1.** a graphic representation, by any of various systems, of a numeric relationship. **2.** a graph on which several variables are plotted so that the value of a dependent variable can be read on the appropriate line when the values of the other variables are given.

nonabsorbable surgical sutures /nonəbsôr′bəbəl/ [L, *non,* not + *absorbere;* Gk, *cheirourgos,* surgeon; L, *sutura*], sutures of silk, nylon, steel, or other materials that resist absorption. They are used mainly in deep tissues, where it is important for them to remain in place.

nonadaptive immunity /-adap′tiv/, an immune response that persists after repeated exposure to the same antigen.

nonadherent cell /-ədhir′ənt/, a cell such as a lymphocyte that will not adhere to a smooth surface of laboratory equipment.

nonadherent dressing [L, *non + adhesio,* sticking to; OFr, *dresser,* to arrange], a dressing designed specifically not to stick to the dried secretions of a wound.

nonadhesive skin traction /-ədhē′siv/ [L, *non,* not, *adhesio,* sticking to], a type of skin traction in which the therapeutic pull of traction weights is applied over the body structure involved with foam-backed traction straps that do not stick to the skin. Nonadhesive skin traction straps may be easily removed to facilitate skin care and are usually used when continuous traction is not required. The straps decrease the patient's vulnerability to skin breakdown by spreading the traction pull over a wide area of skin surface.

nonbacterial prostatitis, prostatitis with pain and increased numbers of inflammatory cells but without history of UTI.

nonbacterial thrombotic endocarditis /-baktir′ē·əl/ [L, *non;* Gk, *bakterion,* small rod], one of the three main types of endocarditis, characterized by various kinds of lesions affecting the heart valves, most often on the left side of the heart. The disease may be the first step in the development of bacterial endocarditis, and the lesions may cause peripheral arterial embolisms, resulting in death.

noncellulose polysaccharides /-sel′yəlōs/, food substances such as hemicellulose, pectins, gums, mucilages, and algal products that absorb water and swell to a larger bulk. They slow emptying of food from the stomach, bind bile acids, provide fermentation material for the colon, and prevent spastic colon pressure.

noncompetitive inhibition /-kəmpet′itiv/, in pharmacology, a form of inhibition in which a substance (drug) occupies a receptor and cannot be displaced from the receptor by increasing the number of other molecules through the principle of mass action. The drug is irreversibly bound to the receptor.

non compos mentis /non kom′pos men′tis/ [L, not of sound mind], a legal term applied to a person declared to be mentally incompetent.

nondepolarizing blocking agent, a compound that causes paralysis of skeletal muscle by blocking neural transmission at the myoneural junction. It acts by competitive binding to the cholinergic receptors of the motor end plate without depolarizing the postsynaptic membrane.

nondirective therapy /-direk′tiv/ [L, *non + digere,* to direct], a psychotherapeutic approach in which the psychotherapist refrains from giving advice or interpretation as the client is helped to identify conflicts and to clarify and understand feelings and values.

nondisjunction /-disjungk′chən/ [L, *non + disjungere,* to disjoint], failure of homologous pairs of chromosomes to separate during the first meiotic division or of the two chromatids of a chromosome to split during anaphase of mitosis or the second meiotic division. The result is an abnormal number of chromosomes in the daughter cells.

nonessential amino acid /-esen′shəl/, any amino acids that are not essential to the diet because the body can synthesize their molecules from other amino acids.

nonfeasance /nonfē′zəns/ [L, *non + facere,* to do], a failure to perform a task, duty, or undertaking that one has agreed to perform or that one had a legal duty to perform.

nongonococcal urethritis (NGU) /-gon′əkok′əl/ [L, *non;* Gk, *gone,* seed, *kokkos,* berry], an infectious condition of the urethra in males that is characterized by mild dysuria and a small to moderate amount of penile discharge. The discharge may be white or clear, thin or mucoid, or, less often, purulent. The infection is often caused by the obligate intracellular parasite *Chlamydia trachomatis.* Women exposed to the exudate during coitus may develop a hypertrophic erosion of the cervix and purulent cervical mucus.

nonheme iron /non′hēm/, one of two forms of dietary iron. It is less efficiently absorbed than heme iron. All plant food sources and 60% of animal food sources contain nonheme iron.

nonhemolytic jaundice /-hē'məlit'ik/ [L, *non;* Gk, *haima,* blood, *lysein,* to loosen; Fr, *jaune,* yellow], a form of jaundice that is caused by a liver disease rather than the destruction of RBCs.

Non-Hodgkin's lymphoma (NHL) /-hoj'kənz/, Solid tumors of peripheral lymphoid tissue classified by histologic features and lymphocyte morphology. Distinguished from Hodgkin lymphoma, a proliferation of Reed-Sternberg cells with accumulation of reactive peripheral blood cells. Non-Hodgkin lymphoma prevalence peaks at 50 years of age and may be mild or aggressively malignant, depending upon cell category.

nonigravida /nō'nigrav'idə/ [L, *nonus,* nine, *gravidus,* pregnancy], indicating a woman pregnant for the ninth time.

noni juice, the juice of *Morinda citrifolia.*

noninfective valvular mass /-infek'tiv/, a growth or swelling on one of the heart valves associated with autoimmune diseases or with cardiac or extracardiac malignancies. Such masses are frequently asymptomatic and are discovered only at autopsy.

noninflammatory diarrhea /-inflam'ətôr'ē/, a profuse watery diarrhea without fever or vomiting that begins 6 to 24 hours after ingesting food contaminated by bacterial toxins produced by either *Clostridium perfringens* or *Bacillus cereus.* The food poisoning usually involves raw meat or other proteinaceous foods exposed to warm temperatures for several hours.

noninvasive /-invā'siv/ [L, *non* + *in,* into, *vadere,* to go], pertaining to a diagnostic or therapeutic technique that does not require the skin to be broken or a cavity or organ of the body to be entered.

noninvasive ventilation, mechanical ventilation that does not use an artificial airway, such as positive pressure ventilation with a nasal or face mask.

nonionic /-ī-on'ik/, pertaining to compounds without a net negative or positive charge.

nonionizing radiation /-ī'ənīz'ing/ [L, *non;* Gk, *ion,* going, *izein,* to cause], radiation for which the mechanism of action in tissue does not directly ionize atomic or molecular systems through a single interaction.

nonipara /nōnip'ərə/ [L, *nonus,* nine, *parere,* to bear], a woman who has given birth to nine offspring.

nonketotic hyperglycinemia /nonkētot'ik/, a usually fatal autosomal-recessive aminoacidopathy with accumulation of glycine in body fluids, particularly the blood,

urine, and CSF. It has neonatal onset and is characterized by lethargy, metabolic acidosis with ketosis, absence of cerebral development, seizures, myoclonic jerks, and frequently coma and respiratory failure.

nonmyelinated nerve fiber /-mī'əlinā'tid/ [L, *non;* Gk, *myelos,* marrow; L, *nervus,* nerve, *fibra,* fiber], a nerve fiber that lacks the fatty myelin insulating sheath. Such fibers form the gray matter of the nervous system, as distinguished from the white matter of myelinated fibers.

nonnucleoside reverse transcriptase inhibitors (NNRTIs), a class of antiretroviral drugs that inhibit HIV replication by blocking the reverse transcriptase enzyme essential for viral replication.

nonnutritive sucking, a nursing intervention from the Nursing Interventions Classification (NIC) defined as provision of sucking opportunities for the infant.

nonnutritive sweetener /-noo'tritiv/, a chemical additive such as saccharin, acesulfame, or sucralose that gives a sweet taste to foods without significant calories. The sugar substitute is either not metabolized or so intensely sweet that the calorie count is negligible.

nonossifying fibroma /-os'ifī'ing/, sharply circumscribed, eccentrically located lesion in the metaphyses of long bones in children. Microscopic examination reveals whorl patterns of spindle cells, fibrous tissue, numerous xanthoma cells, and occasional giant cells.

nonosteogenic fibroma /non'ostē-əjen'ik/, a common bone lesion characterized by degeneration and proliferation of the medullary and cortical tissue near the ends of the diaphyses of the large long bones of the lower extremities.

nonpalpable testis /-pal'pəbəl/, a testis that cannot be felt and may be intraabdominal or absent.

nonparametric test of significance /-per'əmet'rik/ [L, *non;* Gk, *para,* beside, *metron,* measure], in statistics, one of several tests that use a qualitative approach to analyze rank order data and incidence data that cannot be assumed to have a normal distribution. Kinds of nonparametric tests of significance include chi-square and Spearman's rho.

nonparous /-per'əs/ [L, *non* + *parere,* to bear], indicating a woman who has never given birth to a child.

nonpenetrating wound /-pen'ətrā'ting/ [L, *non,* not, *penetrare,* to penetrate; AS, *wund*], a wound that does not break the surface of the skin.

nonpermissive host /-pərmis'iv/, an animal or cell that resists the replication of an infectious agent.

N

nonpolar /-pō′lər/ [L, *non* + *polus,* pole], pertaining to molecules that have low polarity and have a hydrophobic affinity, tending to exclude or avoid water.

nonpolar solvent /-pō′lər/, a liquid solvent without significant partial charges on any atoms, as in the hydrocarbons, or where the polar bonds are arranged in such a way that the effects of their partial charges cancel out, as in carbon tetrachloride.

nonproductive cough /-prəduk′tiv/ [L, *non* + *producere,* to produce], a sudden, noisy expulsion of air from the lungs that may be caused by irritation or inflammation and does not remove sputum from the respiratory tract. Intratracheal suctioning may be necessary when secretions cause severe respiratory difficulty and coughing is unproductive.

nonproprietary name /-prəprī′ətər′ē/ [L, *non* + *proprietas,* owner, *nomen,* name], the chemical or generic name of a drug or device, as distinguished from a brand name or trademark.

nonprotein nitrogen (NPN) /-prō′tēn/ [L, *non;* Gk, *proteios,* first rank, *nitron,* soda, *genein,* to produce], the nitrogen in the blood that is not a constituent of protein, such as the nitrogen associated with urea, uric acid, creatine, and polypeptides.

nonrebreather /non′rēbrēth′ər/, a breathing system having one-way valves so that exhaled carbon dioxide is expelled from the system and not inhaled again.

nonresponse bias, in epidemiology, errors that may develop when a part of those selected and identified as study subjects cannot or will not participate in the study. The bias may occur when the group of nonrespondents differs systematically from respondents with respect to exposure or disease status. To minimize this bias, a high participation rate is necessary, or a survey is made of nonresponders to determine whether or how they might differ with regard to the risk of disease or exposure.

nonreversible inhibitor /-rivur′səbəl/ [L, *non* + *revertere,* to turn back, *inhibere,* to restrain], an effector substance that binds permanently to an active site of an enzyme, inhibiting the normal catalytic activity of the enzyme.

nonsecretor /-səkrē′tər/ [L, *non* + *secernere,* to separate], a person who does not secrete ABO blood group substances in mucous secretions of the saliva or gastric juice. The condition is genetically determined.

nonseg., abbreviation for *nonsegmented.*

nonseminomatous testicular tumors /-sem′inom′ətəs/, any of a variety of histologic types of testicular carcinoma, including embryonal cell carcinoma, teratocarcinoma, and tumors with mixed elements.

nonsense mutation, a mutation in which one of the three terminator codons in the mRNA used to signal the end of a polypeptide appears in the middle of a genetic message and causes premature termination of transcription and release of incomplete, generally nonfunctional polypeptides from the ribosome.

nonshivering thermogenesis /-shiv′əring/, a natural method by which newborns can produce body heat by increasing their metabolic rate.

non–small cell carcinoma, a general term comprising all lung carcinomas except small cell carcinoma, including adenocarcinoma of the lung, large cell carcinoma, and squamous cell carcinoma.

non–small cell carcinoma of lung, a major category of histologic types of lung carcinomas, including adenocarcinoma of the lung, large-cell carcinoma, and squamous cell carcinoma.

nonspecific binding (NSB) /-spəsif′ik/, in ligand binding assay, the part of a tracer used in a competitive-binding assay that is found in the bound fraction, independent of the binding reaction.

nonspecific immunosuppression, a therapy, including the use of immunosuppressive drugs and high doses of radiation, that blunts or abolishes the response of the immune system to all antigens.

nonspecific urethritis (NSU) [L, *non,* not, *species,* form], inflammation of the urethra of unknown origin. Onset of symptoms is often related to sexual intercourse. The condition is noted by urethral discharge in men and by reddening of the urethral mucosa in women.

nonspecific vaginitis [L, *non,* not, *species,* form, *facere,* to make, *vagina,* sheath; Gk, *itis,* inflammation], a term formerly used for any vaginal inflammation for which no specific pathogen could be identified.

nonspecular reflection, diffuse ultrasound reflections (scatter) at rough surfaces or irregular boundaries.

nonsteroidal antiinflammatory drug (NSAID) /-stir′oidəl/, any of a group of drugs having antipyretic, analgesic, and antiinflammatory effects. They counteract or reduce inflammation by inhibiting COX, the enzyme responsible for prostaglandin synthesis. NSAIDs may be indicated in the treatment of mild to moderate pain, rheumatoid arthritis, osteoarthritis, ankylosing spondylosis, gouty arthritis, fever, nonrheumatic inflammation, and dysmenorrhea.

nonstress test (NST) /non'stres/,   an evaluation of the fetal heart rate response to natural contractile activity or to an increase in fetal activity.

nonsuppurative osteomyelitis /-sup'yər ā'tiv/,   TB of the bone.

nonthrombocytopenic purpura /-throm' bōsī'təpē'nik/,   a disorder characterized by purplish or reddish skin areas. The condition does not involve a decrease in the number of platelets.

nontoxic /-tok'sik/,   not poisonous.

nontreponemal antigen test,   any of various tests detecting serum antibodies to reagin (cardiolipin and lecithin) derived from host tissue in the diagnosis of the *Treponema pallidum* infection of syphilis.

nontropical sprue /-trop'ikəl/   [L, *non,* not; Gk, *tropikos,* of the solstice; D, *sprouw*],   a malabsorption syndrome resulting from an inborn inability to digest foods that contain gluten.

nonulcerative blepharitis /-ul'sərativ'/ [L, *non + ilcus,* ulcer; Gk, *blepharon,* eyelid, *itis,* inflammation],   a form of blepharitis characterized by greasy scales on the margins of the eyelids around the lashes and hyperemia and thickening of the skin. Nonulcerative blepharitis is often associated with seborrheic dermatitis.

nonunion /-yōō'nyən/,   pertaining to a fractured bone that fails to heal properly.

nonvascularized graft,   a graft in which the blood supply to the grafted tissue is not maintained.

nonverbal communication /-vur'bəl/,   the transmission of a message without the use of words. It may involve any or all of the five senses.

nonviable /-vī'əbəl/   [L, *non + vita,* life],   unable to exist independently after birth.

nonvital pulp [L, *non,* not, *vita,* life, *pulpa,* flesh],   dead dental pulp caused by a disease or trauma that interferes with the blood supply.

Noonan's syndrome,   the phenotype of Turner's syndrome (webbed neck, ptosis, hypogonadism, congenital heart disease, and short stature) without gonadal dysgenesis.

nootropic /nō-ətrop'ik/,   a chemical designed to increase brain metabolism.

Norcuron,   a trademark for an IV neuromuscular blocking drug (vecuronium bromide).

norepinephrine (NE) /nôr'epinef'rin/,   an adrenergic hormone (catecholamine) that acts to increase BP by vasoconstriction but does not affect cardiac output. It is synthesized by the adrenal medulla, the peripheral sympathetic nerves, and the CNS. It is available as a drug, levarterenol, which is used to maintain the BP in acute hypotension secondary to trauma, heart disease, or vascular collapse.

norepinephrine bitartrate,   a commercial preparation of an endogenous agonist of alpha-1, alpha-2, and beta-1 adrenergics. It is prescribed in the treatment of shock that persists after hypovolemia has been corrected.

no response (NR),   the condition for which the maximum decrease in treated tumor volume is less than 50%.

norethindrone /nôreth'indrōn/,   a progestin prescribed in the treatment of abnormal uterine bleeding and endometriosis and used alone or as a component in oral contraceptive medications.

norethindrone acetate and ethinyl estradiol,   a combination oral contraceptive containing a progestin (norethindrone) and an estrogen (ethinyl estradiol). It is prescribed for contraception, the treatment of acne and moderate to severe vasomotor symptoms in menopause, and the prevention of osteoporosis in postmenopausal women at high risk. Unlabeled uses include hypermenorrhea, endometriosis, and female hypogonadism.

Norflex,   a trademark for a skeletal muscle relaxant with anticholinergic properties (orphenadrine citrate).

norfloxacin /nôrflok'səsin/,   an oral antibacterial drug prescribed for the treatment of bacterial UTIs, sexually transmitted gonorrhea, and proctitis.

Norgesic Forte,   a trademark for a fixed-combination drug containing a muscle relaxant with anticholinergic activity (orphenadrine citrate), aspirin, and caffeine, used for the relief of mild to moderate pain of acute musculoskeletal disorders.

norgestimate /nôrjes'təmāt/,   a synthetic progestational agent used in combination with an estrogen component as an oral contraceptive.

norgestrel /nôrjes'trəl/,   a progestin prescribed alone or in combination with estrogen as a contraceptive.

Norinyl,   a trademark for several formulations of oral contraceptives containing a progestin (norethindrone) and an estrogen (mestranol or ethinyl estradiol).

norm [L, *norma,* rule],   **1.** a measure of a phenomenon generally accepted as the ideal standard performance against which other measures of the phenomenon may be measured. **2.** abbreviation for **normal.**

norma basalis /nôr'mə basā'lis/   [L, rule; Gk, *basis,* foundation],   the inferior surface of the base of the skull with the mandible removed, formed by the palatine bones, the vomer, the pterygoid processes, and parts of the sphenoid and temporal bones.

normal (N, norm) /nôr'məl/ [L, *norma, rule*], **1.** describing a standard, average, or typical example of a set of objects or values. **2.** describing a chemical solution in which 1 L contains 1 g of a substance or the equivalent in replaceable hydrogen ions. **3.** describing people in a nondiseased population. **4.** a gaussian distribution.

normal dental function, the correct and healthy action of opposing teeth during chewing.

normal distribution, in statistics, a theoretic distribution frequency of variable data usually represented graphically by a bell-shaped curve that reaches a peak about the mean.

normal human serum albumin, an isotonic preparation of pooled human serum albumin for treating hypoproteinemia, hypovolemia, and threatened or existing shock.

normalization promotion, a nursing intervention from the Nursing Interventions Classification (NIC) defined as assisting parents and other family members of children with chronic illnesses or disabilities in providing normal life experiences for their children and families.

normal last shoes, orthopedic shoes for infants and children constructed with a normal sole.

normal phase, a chromatographic mode in which the mobile phase is less polar than the stationary phase.

normal pressure hydrocephalus [L, *norma,* rule, *premere,* to press; Gk, *hydor,* water, *kephale,* head], a condition in which there is dilation of the ventricles without an increase in ICP. Classic symptoms are gait disturbance, memory/cognitive problems, and urinary incontinence.

normal saline, physiologic or normal saline solution.

normal saline solution [L, *norma,* rule + *sal* + *solutus,* dissolved], a 0.9% w/v (grams of solute per mL of solution) sterile solution of sodium chloride in water that is isotonic with blood and injectable intravenously.

normal sinus rhythm (NSR) [L, *norma,* rule, *sinus,* hollow; Gk, *rhythmos*], the normal heartbeat initiated by the pacemaker in the sinus node, with a heart rate of 60 to 100 beats/min.

normal solution (N/I, N) [L, *norma,* rule, *solutus,* dissolved], a solution that contains the gram-equivalent weight of a reagent per liter.

normal strain, a quantity described by the quotient of the change of length of a line and its original length.

normal stress, in physics, a quantity described by the quotient of distributed force and area when the force is perpendicular to the area.

normal temperature [L, *norma,* rule + *temperatura*], for a normal person at rest, an oral temperature of 98.6° F or 37° C. Actual "normal" temperatures may range a fraction of a degree or increments of a whole degree higher or lower because of effects of sleep, exercise, eating, sleeping, metabolism, and the ambient temperature. Rectal temperature also averages a fraction of a degree higher than oral temperatures, and axillary readings are usually lower than oral temperatures.

normoblast /nôr'məblast/ [L, *norma;* Gk, *blastos,* germ], a nucleated precursor cell in the bone marrow of the adult circulating erythrocyte. After the extrusion of the nucleus of the normoblast, the young erythrocyte becomes known as a reticulocyte and enters the circulating blood. **—normoblastic,** *adj.*

normochromic /nôr'məkrō'mik/ [L, *norma;* Gk, *chroma,* color], pertaining to a blood cell having normal color caused by the presence of an adequate amount of hemoglobin.

normocyte /nôr'məsīt/ [L, *norma;* Gk, *kytos,* cell], an ordinary, normal adult RBC of average size having a diameter of 7 μm.**—normocytic,** *adj.*

Normodyne, a trademark for an antihypertensive drug (labetalol hydrochloride).

normoglycemic /-glīsē'mik/, pertaining to a normal blood glucose level.

normotensive /-ten'siv/, pertaining to the condition of having normal BP. Normal BP is typically 120/80 but may be lower in younger individuals or athletes.**—normotension,** *n.*

normoventilation /-ven'tilā'shən/, the alveolar ventilation rate that produces an alveolar carbon dioxide pressure of about 40 mm Hg at any metabolic rate.

normoxia /nôrmok'sē-ə/, an ambient oxygen pressure of about 150 (plus or minus 10) torr, or the partial pressure of oxygen in atmospheric air at sea level.

Noroxin, a trademark for an oral antibacterial drug (norfloxacin).

Norpace, a trademark for an antidysrhythmic cardiac depressant (disopyramide phosphate).

Norpramin, a trademark for an antidepressant (desipramine hydrochloride).

Nor-QD, a trademark for an oral contraceptive containing a progestin (norethindrone) but no estrogen.

North American blastomycosis, an infection caused by inhaling the fungus

Blastomyces dermatitidis. It may resemble bacterial pneumonia. Painless, well-demarcated, verrucous or ulcerated lesions occur on the face and hands. The disease may progress to involve bones and the brain; many viscera are infected in fatal cases.

North American coral snake antivenin, antivenin to *Micrurus fulvius.*

North Asian tick-borne rickettsiosis, an infection, acquired in the Eastern Hemisphere, caused by *Rickettsia sibirica,* transmitted by ticks. It resembles Rocky Mountain spotted fever. Usual findings include a generalized maculopapular rash involving palms and soles, fever, and lymph node enlargement.

Northern blot test, an electrophoretic test for identifying the presence or absence of particular mRNA molecules and nucleic acid hybridization.

Norton risk scale /nor′tən/, a tool for estimating a patient's risk for developing pressure ulcers.

nortriptyline hydrochloride /nôrtrip′tilēn/, a tricyclic antidepressant prescribed in the treatment of mental depression. Unlabeled uses include chronic pain, anxiety, enuresis, and attention deficit/hyperactivity disorder.

Norvir, a trademark for a protease inhibitor (ritonavir).

Norwalk agent [Norwalk, Ohio, site where first identified], a virus that produces gastroenteritis symptoms. The infection is transmitted from one person to another and is involved in 40% of the nonbacterial diarrhea cases in children and adults.

Norwegian scabies [Norway; L, *scabere,* to scratch], a severe infestation of human skin by an itch mite, *Sarcoptes scabiei.* The condition is associated with intense itching, crusting and scaling of the skin, and insect egg burrows that appear as discolored lines in the affected skin areas.

nose [AS, *nosu*], the structure that protrudes from the anterior part of the face and serves as a passageway for air to and from the lungs. The nose filters the air, warming, moistening, and chemically examining it for impurities that might irritate the mucous lining of the respiratory tract. The nose also contains receptor cells for smell, and it aids the faculty of speech. The external part, which protrudes from the face, is considerably smaller than the internal part, which lies over the roof of the mouth. The hollow interior part is separated into a right and left cavity by a septum. Each cavity is divided into the superior, middle, and inferior meatuses

by the projection of nasal conchae. The external part of the nose is perforated by two nostrils (anterior nares), and the internal part by two posterior nares.

nosebleed [AS, *nosu;* ME, *blod,* blood], abnormal hemorrhage from the nose.

nose drops, a medicated solution to be dropped into the nose.

NOSIE, abbreviation for **nurses' observation scale for inpatient evaluation.**

nosocomial /nos′əkō′mē·əl/ [Gk, *nosokomeian,* hospital], **1.** pertaining to a hospital. **2.** pertaining to a secondary disorder associated with hospitalization but unrelated to the primary condition of the patient.

nosocomial fever of unknown origin, a fever of at least 38.3° C occurring on several occasions in a hospitalized patient in whom neither fever nor infection was present on admission, and for which a cause cannot be determined after 3 days of investigation, including 2 days of incubation of cultures.

nosocomial infection, an infection acquired at least 72 hours after hospitalization, often caused by *Candida albicans, Escherichia coli,* hepatitis viruses, herpes zoster virus, *Pseudomonas,* or *Staphylococcus.*

nosology /nōsol′əjē/ [Gk, *nosos,* disease, *logos,* science], the science of classifying diseases.

notch [Fr, *noche*], an indentation or depression in a bone or other organ, such as the cardiac notch.

nothing by mouth (NPO) [L, *nil per os,* nothing by mouth], a patient care instruction advising that the patient is prohibited from ingesting food, beverage, or medicine. It is usually posted above the bed of a patient who is about to undergo surgery or special diagnostic procedures requiring that the digestive tract be empty or who is unable to tolerate food and fluids by mouth.

no-threshold curve, a linear dose-response curve that assumes that there is no detectable threshold below which there is no harm. As applied in nuclear medicine, there is no identifiable concentration of radiation below which no response curve occurs.

notifiable [L, *nota,* mark, *facere,* to make], pertaining to certain conditions, diseases, and events that must, by law, be reported to a governmental agency, such as birth, death, smallpox, certain other communicable diseases, and certain violations of public health regulations.

notifiable diseases, diseases that are classified as reportable by each state

N

and territorial health department, which also prescribes the manner and time of reporting.

notochord /nō'tōkôrd/ [Gk, *noton,* back, *chorde,* cord], an elongated strip of mesodermal tissue that originates from the primitive node and extends along the dorsal surface of the developing embryo beneath the neural tube. In humans and other higher vertebrates, the structure is replaced by vertebræ, although a remnant of it remains as part of the nucleus pulposus of the intervertebral disks. —**notochordal,** *adj.*

notochordal canal /no'tōkôr'dəl/ [Gk, *noton* + *chorde,* cord; L, *canalis,* channel], a tubular passage that extends from the primitive pit into the head process during the early stages of embryonic development in mammals.

notogenesis /nō'tōjen'əsis/ [Gk, *noton* + *genein,* to produce], the formation of the notochord.—**notogenetic,** *adj.*

notomelus /nətom'ələs/ [Gk, *noton* + *melos,* limb], a congenital malformation in which one or more accessory limbs are attached to the back.

Nott retinoscopy, a type of dynamic retinoscopy in which the fixation target is 40 cm from the eye. The test is first done with the object farther away than the target distance and then continued while the target is moved toward the patient until neutrality is observed.

nourish /nur'ish/ [L, *nutrire,* to suckle], to furnish or supply the essential foods or nutrients for maintaining life.

nourishment /nur'ishmənt/, **1.** the act or process of nourishing or being nourished. **2.** any substance that nourishes and supports the life and growth of living organisms.

Novahistine, a trademark for a fixed-combination drug containing an antihistamine (chlorpheniramine maleate) and an adrenergic decongestant (pseudoepHEDrine).

Novantrone, a trademark for a synthetic antineoplastic anthracenedione (mitoxantrone).

Novocain, a trademark for a local anesthetic (procaine hydrochloride).

NOx, abbreviation for a mixture of oxides of nitrogen, including nitric oxide, nitrogen dioxide, and nitrous oxide.

Noxafil, a trademark for posaconazole.

noxious /nok'shəs/ [L, *noxius,* harm], harmful, injurious, or detrimental to health.

Noyes test /noiz/, an orthopedic knee test performed with the knee extended and the thigh relaxed. The knee is partially dislocated anterolaterally. As the knee is gradually flexed, the dislocation is reduced at about 30 degrees of flexion.

Np, symbol for the element **neptunium.**

NP, abbreviation for **nurse practitioner.**

NPH Iletin, a trademark for an insulin suspension (isophane).

NPH Insulin, a trademark for an insulin suspension (isophane).

NPN, abbreviation for **nonprotein nitrogen.**

NPO, abbreviation for **nothing by mouth.**

n-**propyl alcohol (C₃H₇OH)** /en'prō'pil/, a clear, colorless liquid used as a solvent for resins.

NPT, abbreviation for **nocturnal penile tumescence.**

NPU, abbreviation for **net protein utilization.**

NPY, abbreviation for **neuropeptide Y.**

NR, 1. abbreviation for **no response. 2.** abbreviation for *nodal rhythm.*

NREM, abbreviation for *nonrapid eye movement.*

NRTI, abbreviation for **nucleoside reverse transcriptase inhibitor.**

NSAIA, abbreviation for *nonsteroidal antiinflammatory analgesic.*

NSAID, abbreviation for **nonsteroidal antiinflammatory drug.**

NSB, abbreviation for **nonspecific binding.**

NSCCN, abbreviation for **National Society of Critical Care Nurses of Canada.**

n-s/m², abbreviation for *newton second per square meter.*

NSNA, abbreviation for **National Student Nurses Association.**

NSR, abbreviation for **normal sinus rhythm.**

NSU, abbreviation for **nonspecific urethritis.**

N-telopeptide test (NTx), a urine test that detects levels of N-telopeptide, a biochemical marker of bone metabolism and the most sensitive and specific indicator of bone resorption. It is used primarily to monitor the effect of antiresorptive therapy in women with osteoporosis.

NTP, ntp, abbreviation for *normal temperature and pressure.*

nu /n(y)ōō/, N, ν, the thirteenth letter of the Greek alphabet.

Nubain, a trademark for a synthetic opioid analgesic (nalbuphine hydrochloride), used as an adjunct to anesthesia.

nuc, abbreviation for *nuclear.*

nucha /nōō'kə/ *pl.* **nuchae** [Fr, *nuque,* nape], the nape, or back of the neck. —**nuchal,** *adj.*

nuchal cord /nōō'kəl/ [Fr, *nuque,* nape; Gk, *chorde*], an abnormal but common condition in which the umbilical cord is wrapped around the neck of the fetus in utero or of the baby as it is being born. It is usually possible to slip the loop or loops of cord gently over the child's head.

nuchal ligament, the fibrous membrane that reaches from the external occipital protuberance and median nuchal line to the spinous process of the seventh vertebra.

nuchal line, one of the curved lines that extend laterally from the external occipital protuberance, a midline projection visible on the occipital bone.

nuchal rigidity, a resistance to flexion of the neck, a condition seen in patients with meningitis.

nuchocephalic reflex /noo̅ˈkəsefalˈik/, a test for diffuse cerebral dysfunction, such as in senility. When the shoulders are turned to the left or the right, the head fails to turn in the same direction within a half-second.

nuclear envelope, a double membrane that surrounds the nucleus of a eukaryotic cell.

nuclear family /n(y)oo̅ˈkle̅-ər/ [L, *nucleus,* nut kernel, *familia,* household], a family unit consisting of the biologic parents and their offspring.

nuclear isomer, one of two or more nuclides with the same number of neutrons and protons in the nucleus (the same atomic number, or Z, and the same atomic mass, or A) but existing in different energy states.

nuclear medicine, a medical discipline that uses radiation emitted by radioactive isotopes in the diagnosis and treatment of disease. Forms of radiation important in nuclear medicine include alpha and beta particles, gamma rays, and x-rays. Radioactive elements used in nuclear medicine, called radionuclides or radiopharmaceuticals, are produced artificially. Radiopharmaceuticals are used as tracers for assessing the structure, function, secretion, excretion, and volume of a particular organ or tissue. They are also used to analyze biologic specimens and to treat specific diseases such as thyroid cancer. An important component of nuclear medicine is imaging, which involves administering radiopharmaceuticals to a patient orally, intravenously, or by inhalation to localize a specific organ or system and its structure and function.

nuclear medicine technologist, an allied health professional who uses radioactive and stable nuclides to make diagnostic evaluations of the anatomic or physiologic conditions of the body and who provides therapy with unsealed radioactive sources.

nuclear physics, the study of atomic nuclei and their reactions.

nuclear problem, in psychology, an underlying reason for an individual's reaction to a precipitating event.

nuclear radiology, the branch of radiology that uses radioactive materials in the diagnosis and treatment of health disorders.

nuclear scanning, a diagnostic technique that uses an injected, ingested, or inhaled radioactive material and a scanning device to determine the size, shape, location, and function of various body parts.

nuclear spin, an intrinsic form of angular momentum possessed by atomic nuclei containing an odd number of nucleons (protons or neutrons).

nuclear transplantation, the transfer of the nucleus of one cell into the cytoplasm of another.

nucleic acid /noo̅kle̅ˈik/ [L, *nucleus* + *acidus,* sour], a high-molecular-weight polymeric compound composed of nucleotides, each consisting of a purine or pyrimidine base, a ribose or deoxyribose sugar, and a phosphate group. Nucleic acids are involved in the determination and transmission of genetic characteristics.

nucleic acid amplification, amplification of a specific nucleic acid sequence, such as to test for the presence of a given virus or bacteria in a sample.

nucleic acid amplification technique, any of various in vitro methods by which a DNA or RNA sequence is amplified, making it more readily detectable for various procedures or tests. The original, and still most commonly used, is the polymerase chain reaction.

nucleic acid test, any of various tests that use molecular biology techniques to detect and identify microorganisms, including viruses, on the basis of their nucleic acids. It includes culture confirmation tests, which identify organisms grown in culture, and direct tests, which can identify the organisms directly in a specimen.

nucleocapsid /noo̅kle̅-ōkapˈsid/ [L, *nucleus; capsa,* box], a viral enclosure consisting of a capsid or protein coat and a nucleic acid that it surrounds. Some viruses consist solely of bare nucleocapsids; others have more complex enclosures.

nucleochylema /noo̅kle̅-ōkīle̅ˈmə/ [L, *nucleus;* Gk, *chylos,* juice, *haima,* blood], the ground substance of the nucleus, as distinguished from that of the cytoplasm.

nucleocytoplasmic /noo̅kle̅-ōsiˈtōplasˈmik/ [L, *nucleus;* Gk, *kytos,* cell, *plasma,* something formed], of or relating to the nucleus and cytoplasm of a cell.

N

nucleocytoplasmic ratio, the ratio of the volume of a nucleus of a cell to the volume of the cytoplasm. The proportion is usually constant for a specific cell type, and an increase is indicative of malignant neoplasms.

nucleohistone /nōō′klē·ōhis′tōn/ [L, *nucleus;* Gk, *histos,* tissue], a complex consisting of DNA and a histone protein that is the basic constituent of the chromatin in a cell nucleus.

nucleolar organizer /nōōklē′ələr/ [L, *nucleolus,* little nut kernel; Gk, *organon,* instrument, *izein,* to cause], a part of the nucleus of the cell, thought to consist of heterochromatin, that is responsible for the formation of the nucleolus.

nucleolus /nōōklē′ələs/ pl. **nucleoli** [L, little nut kernel], any one of the small, dense structures composed largely of RNA that are situated within the cytoplasm of cells. Nucleoli are essential in the formation of ribosomes that synthesize cell proteins.

nucleon /n(y)ōō′klē·on/, a collective term applied to protons and neutrons within the nucleus.

nucleophilic /-fil′ik/, pertaining to some molecules, particularly nucleic acids and proteins, having electrons that can be shared and thus form bonds with alkylating agents.

nucleoplasm /nōō′klē·əplaz′əm/ [L,*nucleus;* Gk, *plasma,* something formed], the protoplasm of the nucleus as contrasted with that of the cell. —**nucleoplasmic,** *adj.*

nucleoplasmin, an acidic protein found in the nucleus that binds to histone and participates in nucleosome assembly.

nucleoprotein /-prō′tēn/ [L, *nucleus;* Gk, *proteios,* first rank], a molecule in which protein is combined with nucleic acid in a cell nucleus.

nucleoside /nōō′klē·əsīd′/, a component of a nucleotide that consists of a nitrogenous base linked to a pentose sugar.

nucleoside analog, a structural analog of a nucleoside, a category that includes both purine analogs and pyrimidine analogs.

nucleoside monophosphate kinase, a liver enzyme that catalyzes the reversible transfer of a phosphate group from adenosine triphosphate, producing adenosine diphosphate and a nucleoside diphosphate.

nucleoside reverse transcriptase inhibitors (NRTIs), a class of antiretroviral drugs that mimic one or more of the components of DNA or RNA and interrupt the viral replication process. The drugs (nucleoside analogs) work by being incorporated into the DNA made by the viral reverse transcriptase enzyme that is essential for viral replication. Examples of nucleoside analogs include zidovudine and didanosine.

nucleosome /nōō′klē·əsōm′/ [L, *nucleus;* Gk, *soma,* body], any one of the repeating DNA-histone complexes that appear as beadlike structures at distinct intervals along a chromosome.

5′-nucleotidase /nōō′klē·ot′idās/, an enzyme, elevated in some liver disorders and cancer of the pancreas. It is widely distributed throughout the body but is found in high concentrations in the liver and pancreas.

5′-nucleotidase test, an infrequently performed blood test used to help diagnose liver disease, particularly cholestasis. It is used to confirm liver disease when alkaline phosphatase test results are uncertain.

nucleotide /nōō′klē·ətīd′/, a compound consisting of one or more phosphate groups, a pentose sugar, and a nitrogenous base. Chains of nucleotides form DNA and RNA; free nucleotides, such as adenosine triphosphate and guanosine triphosphate, are important energy carriers in all cells.

nucleus /n(y)ōō′klē·əs/ pl. **nuclei** [L, nut kernel], 1. the central controlling body within a living cell, usually a spheric unit enclosed in a membrane and containing genetic codes for maintaining life systems of the organism and for issuing commands for growth and reproduction. 2. a group of nerve cells of the CNS having a common function, such as supporting the sense of hearing or smell. 3. the center of an atom about which electrons rotate. 4. the central element in an organic chemical compound or class of compounds.—**nuclear,** *adj.*

nuclide /nōō′klīd/ [L, *nucleus,* nut kernel], a species of atom characterized by the constitution of its nucleus, in particular by the number of protons and neutrons.

nudge control, a mechanical device on a prosthesis that can be pressed by the chin to lock or unlock one or more joints of the prosthesis.

NUG, abbreviation for **necrotizing ulcerative gingivitis.**

Nuhn's gland /noonz/ [Anton Nuhn, German anatomist, 1814–1889], a gland on the inferior surface and near the apex and midline of the tongue.

nuke, a slang term for **nucleoside analog.**

null cell [L, *nullus,* not one, *cella,* storeroom], a lymphocyte that develops in the bone marrow and lacks the characteristic surface markers of the B and T cells (surface immunoglobulin or the pan-T antigen).

null hypothesis (H₀), in research, a hypothesis that predicts that an observed difference is due to chance alone and not a systematic cause.

nulligravida /nul'igrav'ədə/, a woman who has never been pregnant.

nullipara /nulip'ərə/ *pl.* **nulliparae** [L, *nullus,* not one, *parere,* to bear], a woman who has not given birth to a viable infant. The designation "para 0" indicates nulliparity.

nulliparity /nul'iper'itē/ [L, *nullus,* none, *parere,* to bear], the status of a woman who has never borne a child.

nulliparous /nulip'ərəs/ [L, *nullus,* none, *parere,* to bear], never having given birth.

num, abbreviation for *number, numeral.*

numbness /num'nəs/ [ME, *nomen,* loss of feeling], a partial or total lack of sensation in a body part, resulting from any factor that interrupts the transmission of impulses from the sensory nerve fibers.

numeric pain scale /n(y)o͞omer'ik/, a pain assessment system in which patients are asked to rate their pain on a scale from 1 to 10, with 10 representing the worst pain they have experienced or could imagine.

numeric taxonomy, a system of classifying organisms on the basis of the overall similarities of the measurable phenotypic characters they share. The system is used to classify strains of bacteria, as well as to separate closely related species of plants and animals.

nummular dermatitis /num'yələr/ [L, *nummuli,* petty cash; Gk, *derma,* skin, *itis,* inflammation], a skin disease characterized by coin-shaped, vesicular, or scaling eczema-like lesions, commonly on the forearms and front of the calves.

Numorphan, a trademark for an opioid analgesic (oxymorphone hydrochloride).

Nupercainal, a trademark for a local anesthetic (dibucaine hydrochloride).

Nuremberg tribunal [Nuremberg, Germany; L, *tribunus,* platform for administration of justice], an international tribunal planned and implemented by the United Nations War Crimes Commission to detect, apprehend, try, and punish people accused of war crimes. In preparation for the prosecution of World War II criminals, a set of principles to govern the participation of human beings in medical research, known as the Nuremberg code, was devised. The principle and practice of informed consent was reinforced by the precedent set in the trials in which Nazi physicians were declared guilty of crimes against humanity in performing experiments on human beings who were not volunteers and did not consent.

nurse [L, *nutrix*], **1.** a person educated and licensed in the practice of nursing; one who is concerned with "the diagnosis and treatment of human responses to actual or potential health problems" (American Nurses Association). The practice of the nurse includes data collection, diagnosis, planning, treatment, and evaluation within the framework of the nurse's singular concern with the patient's response to the problem, rather than to the problem itself. The concerns of the nurse are thus broader and less discrete and circumscribed than the traditional concerns of medicine. The nurse may be a generalist or a specialist and, as a professional, is ethically and legally accountable for the nursing activities performed and for the actions of others to whom the nurse has delegated responsibility. **2.** to provide nursing care.

nurse anesthetist, a registered nurse qualified by advanced study in an accredited program in the specialty of nurse anesthesia to manage patient care during the administration of anesthesia in selected surgical situations.

nurse cell, a cell that transfers nutrients to an oocyte via a cytoplasmic bridge.

nurse-client interaction, any process in which a nurse and a client exchange or share information, verbally or nonverbally. It is fundamental to communication and is an essential component of the nursing assessment.

nurse-client relationship, a therapeutic relationship between a nurse and a client built on a series of interactions and developing over time. It is time-limited and goal-oriented and has three phases. During the first phase, the phase of establishment, the nurse establishes the structure, purpose, timing, and context of the relationship and expresses an interest in discussing this initial structure with the client. During the middle, developmental phase of the relationship, the nurse and the client get to know each other better and test the structure of the relationship to be able to trust one another. The last phase, termination, ideally occurs when the goals of the relationship have been accomplished, when both the client and the nurse feel a sense of resolution and satisfaction.

nurse clinician, a nurse who is prepared to identify and diagnose problems of clients by using increased knowledge and skills gained through advanced study in a specific area of nursing practice.

nurse coordinator, a registered nurse who coordinates and manages the activities of nursing personnel engaged in specific nursing services, such as obstetrics or surgery, for one or more patient care units.

Nurse Corps, the branch within each of the armed services comprising the nurses within that service, such as the Army

N

Nurse Corps. In each of the armed services, the members of the Nurse Corps have the rank, title, responsibilities, and status of commissioned officer.

nurse educator, a registered nurse whose primary area of interest, competence, and professional practice is the education of nurses at university level.

nurse midwife, a registered nurse qualified by advanced education and clinical experience in obstetric and neonatal care and certified by the American College of Nurse Midwives. The nurse midwife manages the perinatal care of women having a normal pregnancy, labor, and childbirth.

nurse practice act, a statute enacted by the legislature of each of the states or by the appropriate officers of the districts or possessions. The act delineates the legal scope of the practice of nursing within the geographic boundaries of the jurisdiction. The purpose of the act is to protect the public.

nurse practitioner (NP), a registered nurse who has advanced education in nursing (a master's of science in nursing) and clinical experience in a specialized area of nursing practice. NPs collaborate with other health care providers to deliver primary care to patients with common acute or stable chronic medical conditions in ambulatory care settings. Some NPs also function in a specialty, tertiary, or long-term care setting. NPs may offer a variety of services, such as complete physical examinations, health assessments, and patient education. In many states, NPs may obtain prescriptive authority. Some insurance organizations recognize NPs as primary health care providers and allow direct reimbursement for their services.

nursery diarrhea /nur'sərē/ [L, *nutrix*, nurse; Gk, *dia*, through, *rhein*, to flow], diarrhea of the newborn. In nurseries, outbreaks of diarrhea caused by *Escherichia coli, Salmonella,* echoviruses, or adenoviruses are potentially life-threatening to the infant. The most serious aspect of the disease is fluid loss, leading to dehydration and electrolyte imbalance.

nurse's aide, a person who is employed to carry out basic nonspecialized tasks in the care of patients, such as bathing and feeding, making beds, and transporting patients, under the supervision and direction of a registered nurse.

nurses' observation scale for inpatient evaluation (NOSIE), a systematic, objective behavioral rating scale that is applied by nurses to patient behavior.

nurses' registry, an employment agency that provides nurses to work in temporary positions at facilities.

nurses' station, an area in a clinic, unit, or ward in a health care facility that serves as the administrative center for nursing care for a particular group of patients. It is usually centrally located and may be staffed by a unit secretary or clerk who assists with paperwork, telephone, and other communication. Before going on duty, nurses usually meet there to receive daily assignments, review the patients' charts, and update the files.

nursing, 1. the practice in which a nurse assists "the individual, sick or well, in the performance of those activities contributing to health or its recovery (or to a peaceful death) that he would perform unaided if he had the necessary strength, will or knowledge. And to do this in such a way as to help him gain independence as rapidly as possible" (Virginia Henderson). **2.** "the diagnosis and treatment of human responses to actual or potential health problems" (American Nurses Association). There are four principal characteristics that further define nursing care: the phenomena that concern nurses; the use of theories to observe the need for nursing intervention and to plan nursing action; the nursing action taken; and an evaluation of the effects of the actions relative to the phenomena. This definition of nursing provides a framework for the nursing process, including data collection, diagnosis, planning, treatment, and evaluation. A nursing diagnosis is derived from the data collected concerning the health status of the client. A plan for nursing care incorporates goals derived from the nursing diagnosis and the priorities and approaches to achieve the goals as indicated by the nursing diagnosis. Nursing actions, which are selected and performed with the client's participation, provide for promotion, maintenance, or restoration of the client's health and serve to maximize the client's health care abilities. The progress or lack of progress toward the goal is mutually determined by the client and the nurse, resulting in reassessment, reordering of priorities, establishment of new goals, and revision of the plan for nursing care. **3.** the professional practice of a nurse. **4.** the process of acting as a nurse, of providing care that encourages and promotes the health of the person or persons being served.

nursing assessment, an identification by a nurse of the needs, preferences, and abilities of a patient. Assessment includes an interview with observation of a patient by the nurse and considers the symptoms and signs of the condition, the patient's verbal and nonverbal communication, the patient's medical and social history, and any other information available. Among the physical aspects assessed are vital signs, skin color and condition, motor and sensory nerve function, nutrition, rest, sleep, activity, elimination, and consciousness. Assessment is extremely important because it provides the scientific basis for a complete nursing care plan.

nursing assistant, a person trained in basic nursing techniques and direct patient care who practices under the supervision of a registered nurse.

nursing audit, a review of the patient record designed to identify, examine, or verify the performance of certain specified aspects of nursing care using established criteria. A concurrent nursing audit is performed during ongoing nursing care. A retrospective nursing audit is performed after discharge from the care facility, using the patient's record. Often a nursing audit and a medical audit are performed collaboratively, resulting in a joint audit.

nursing care plan, a plan based on a nursing assessment and a nursing diagnosis carried out by a nurse. It has four essential components: identification of the nursing care problems or nursing diagnoses and statement of the nursing approach to solve those problems; statement of the expected benefit to the patient; statement of the specific actions by the nurse that reflect the nursing approach and achieve the goals specified; and evaluation of the patient's response to nursing care and readjustment of that care as required. A written nursing care plan should be a part of every patient's chart.

nursing diagnosis, a statement of a health problem or of a potential problem in the client's health status that a nurse is licensed and competent to treat. Four steps are required in the formulation of a nursing diagnosis. A database is established by collecting information from all available sources, including interviews with the client and the client's family, a review of any existing records of the client's health, observation of the client's response to any alterations in health status, a physical assessment, and a conference or consultation with others concerned in the client's care. The database is continually updated. The second step includes analysis of the client's responses to the problems, healthy or unhealthy, and classification of those responses as psychologic, physiologic, spiritual, or sociologic. The third step is the organization of the data so that a tentative diagnostic statement can be made that summarizes the pattern of problems discovered. The last step is confirmation of the sufficiency and accuracy of the

database by evaluation of the appropriateness of the diagnosis to nursing intervention and by the assurance that, given the same information, most other qualified practitioners would arrive at the same nursing diagnosis. In use, each diagnostic category has three parts: the term that concisely describes the problem, the probable cause of the problem, and the defining characteristics of the problem.

nursing differential, an allowance added to payments to hospitals for services rendered to Medicaid patients in recognition of the cost of providing nursing services to such patients that is greater than the cost to the general patient population.

nursing director, a nurse whose function is the administrative and clinical leadership of the nursing service of a division of a health care facility, such as a nursing director of maternal and infant care nurses.

nursing ethics [L, *nutrix,* nurse; Gk, *ethikos,* character], the values or moral principles governing relationships between the nurse and patient, the patient's family, other members of the health professions, and the general public.

nursing goal, a general goal of nursing involving activities that are desirable but difficult to measure, such as self-care, good nutrition, and relaxation.

nursing health history, data collected about a patient's level of wellness, changes in life patterns, sociocultural role, and mental and emotional reactions to illness.

nursing intervention, any act by a nurse that implements the nursing care plan or any specific objective of that plan such as turning a comatose patient to avoid the development of decubitus ulcers or teaching insulin injection technique to a patient with diabetes before discharge from the hospital. The patient may require intervention in the form of support, limitation, medication, or treatment for the current condition or to prevent the development of further stress.

nursing intervention model, in nursing research, a conceptual framework used to determine appropriate nursing interventions. The model is a holistic representation of the patient and the health care system. The goal is to learn what nursing interventions would be most effective for the particular problem within the particular health care system.

Nursing Interventions Classification (NIC), a comprehensive, standardized system to classify treatments performed by nurses. It is a clinical tool developed by a research team at the University of Iowa that describes and defines the knowledge base for nursing curricula and practice. There are at present 542 nursing

N

interventions that describe the treatments nurses perform. Each intervention has been labeled, defined, and given a list of appropriate activities. The full range of activities that nurses perform on behalf of patients are included, both independent and collaborative interventions, and both direct and indirect care. A taxonomy is provided to help the nurse find what is most relevant to her or his practice area. NIC interventions have been linked to NANDA diagnoses. It is considered part of the clinical decision making of the nurse to decide and document the nursing diagnoses, desired outcomes, interventions used, and outcomes achieved. The NIC system provides a standardized language to document interventions.

nursing licensure compact, an agreement between two or more states or other jurisdictions that the licensing of a type of nursing or a nursing specialty in one place will be valid in the other.

nursing minimum data set (NMDS), a minimum set of items of information with uniform definitions and categories concerning the specific dimension of nursing, which meets the information needs of multiple data users in the health care system. It is the first attempt to standardize the collection of essential nursing data.

nursing objective, a specific aim planned by a nurse to decrease a person's stress, to improve the ability to adapt, or both. A nursing objective may be physical, emotional, social, or cultural and may involve the person's family, friends, and other patients. It is the purpose of any specific nursing order or nursing intervention.

nursing observation, an objective evaluation made by a nurse of the various aspects of a client's condition. It includes the person's general appearance, emotional affect, nutritional status, habits, and preferences, as well as body temperature, skin condition, and any abnormal processes, including those of which the client complains.

nursing orders, specific instructions for implementing the nursing care plan, including the patient's preferences, timing of activities, details of health education necessary for the particular patient, role of the family, and plans for care after discharge. Nursing orders must be signed by the professional nurse who writes them.

Nursing Outcomes Classification (NOC), a comprehensive, standardized system to classify outcomes of nursing interventions. It is a clinical tool developed by a research team at the University of Iowa that describes and defines the knowledge base for nursing curricula and practice. At present, NOC includes 330 nursing outcomes for use for individual patients or individual family caregivers in the home.

nursing process, the process that serves as an organizational framework for the practice of nursing. It encompasses all of the steps taken by the nurse in caring for a patient: assessment, nursing diagnosis, planning, implementation, and evaluation. The rationale for each step is founded in nursing theory.

nursing process model, a conceptual framework in which the nurse-patient relationship is the basis of the nursing process. The nursing process is represented as dynamic and interpersonal, the nurse and the patient being affected by each other's behavior and by the environment around them. Each successful two-way communication is termed a "transaction" and can be analyzed to discover the factors that promote transactions.

nursing research, a detailed systematic study of a problem in the field of nursing. Nursing research is practice- or discipline-oriented and is essential for the continued development of the scientific base of professional nursing practice.

Nursing Research, a bimonthly refereed journal containing papers and other materials concerning nursing research. The goal of the journal is to stimulate research in nursing and disseminate research findings.

nursing rounds, chart rounds, walking rounds, teaching rounds, or grand rounds that are held specifically for nurses and that focus on nursing care.

nursing specialty, a nurse's selected professional field of practice, such as surgical, pediatric, obstetric, or psychiatric nursing.

nursing theorist, a person who develops integrated concepts or frameworks of nursing roles, functions, objectives, and activities and their relationships to clients and the roles of other health professionals.

nursing theory, an organized framework of concepts and purposes designed to guide the practice of nursing.

nursology /nursol′əjē/ [L, *nutrix,* nurse; Gk, *logos,* science], a conceptual framework for the study and practice of nursing. Nursology is intended to provide a model for nursing methods and research. The nurse and the patient have the opportunity to grow, and the science of nursing may emerge from the "angular" investigations and syntheses.

NursoyTM, a trademark for a hypoallergenic nutritional supplement for infants.

nurture /nur′chər/, to feed, rear, foster, or care for, such as in the nourishment, care, and training of growing children.

nutation /nōōtā'shən/ [L, *nutare,* to nod], the act of nodding, especially involuntary nodding as occurs in some neurologic disorders.

nutcracker phenomenon, compression of the left renal vein between the aorta and the superior mesenteric artery, causing hypertension in the kidney with flank pain and sometimes fever and gross hematuria.

nutmeg poisoning, a toxic effect of ingesting the dried kernels of the seeds of nutmeg (*Myristica fragrans*) or its volatile oils. The oils contain terpenes and myristicin, which have stimulant and carminative effects. A dose of one to three kernels may produce convulsions for up to 60 hours.

nutraceuticals /nōō'trāsōō'tikalz/, **1.** functional foods. **2.** foods thought to have a beneficial effect on human health.

Nutramigen, a trademark for a milk-substitute formula that is prepared from a soy isolate base and is lactose-free. It is prescribed for infants with galactosemia and as a protein supplement for people with lactose intolerance.

nutrient /nōō'trē-ənt/ [L, *nutriens,* food that nourishes], a chemical substance that provides nourishment and affects the nutritive and metabolic processes of the body.

nutrient artery of the humerus, one of a pair of branches of the deep brachial arteries, arising near the middle of the arm and entering the nutrient canal of the humerus.

nutrient density, the relative ratio obtained by dividing a food's contribution to the needs for a nutrient by its contribution to calorie needs.

nutrient enema [L, *nutriens;* Gk, *enienai,* injection], the introduction of saline or glucose into the body via the rectum.

nutrient supplements, vitamins and other nutrients that may not be necessary for healthy adults with an adequate intake of proper nutrients but that may be needed under certain circumstances for elderly adults or persons in a debilitated or undernourished state.

nutriment /nōō'trimənt/ [L, *nutriens,* food that nourishes], any substance that nourishes and aids the growth and development of the body.

nutrition /n(y)ōōtrish'ən/ [L, *nutriens*], **1.** nourishment. **2.** the sum of the processes involved in the taking in of nutrients and their assimilation and use for proper body functioning and maintenance of health. **3.** the study of food and drink as related to the growth and maintenance of living organisms.

nutritional /n(y)ōōtrish'ənəl/ [L, *nutrire,* to nourish], pertaining to the quality of food or eating behavior that provides nourishment through assimilation of food to tissues.

nutritional anemia [L, *nutrire,* to nourish; Gk, *a + haima,* without blood], a disorder characterized by the inadequate production of hemoglobin or erythrocytes caused by a nutritional deficiency of iron, folic acid, or vitamin B_{12} or other nutritional disorders.

nutritional care, the substances, procedures, and setting involved in ensuring the proper intake and assimilation of nutriments, especially for the hospitalized patient.

nutritional counseling, a nursing intervention from the Nursing Interventions Classification (NIC) defined as use of an interactive helping process focusing on the need for diet modification.

nutritional monitoring, a nursing intervention from the Nursing Interventions Classification (NIC) defined as collection and analysis of patient data to prevent or minimize malnourishment.

nutritional science, a body of science that relates to the processes involved in nutrition.

nutritional status, a nursing outcome from the Nursing Outcomes Classification (NOC) defined as the extent to which nutrients are available to meet metabolic needs.

nutritional status: biochemical measures, a nursing outcome from the Nursing Outcomes Classification (NOC) defined as body fluid components and chemical indices of nutritional status.

nutritional status: energy, a nursing outcome from the Nursing Outcomes Classification (NOC) defined as the extent to which nutrients and oxygen provide cellular energy.

nutritional status: food and fluid intake, a nursing outcome from the Nursing Outcomes Classification (NOC) defined as the amount of food and fluid taken into the body over a 24-hour period.

nutritional status: nutrient intake, a nursing outcome from the Nursing Outcomes Classification (NOC) defined as nutrient intake to meet metabolic needs.

nutrition base, a person's normal nutritional requirements before modification to accommodate a specific condition.

nutritionist /n(y)ōōtrish'ənist/ [L, *nutrire,* to nourish], a professional who has completed academic degrees of BS, MS, EdD, or PhD in foods and nutrition.

nutrition management, a nursing intervention from the Nursing Interventions Classification (NIC) defined as assisting with or providing a balanced dietary intake of foods and fluids.

nutrition therapy, a nursing intervention from the Nursing Interventions

N

Classification (NIC) defined as administration of food and fluids to support metabolic processes of a patient who is malnourished or at high risk for becoming malnourished.

Nutting, Mary Adelaide, a Canadian-born American nursing educator and reformer. As head of Johns Hopkins School of Nursing in Baltimore beginning in 1894, she improved course content and teaching facilities, instituted a 6-month preparatory course, reduced the 12-hour day to 8 hours, and abolished the monthly payment system to students. At Teachers College, Columbia University, she created and developed the Department of Nursing and Health and became the first professor of nursing in the world. With Lavinia Dock, she wrote *History of Nursing* (published 1907–1912), a classic in nursing literature.

Nuvigil, a trademark for armodafinil.

nux vomica /nuks′ vom′ikə/ [L, *nux*, nut, *vomere*, to vomit], the dried ripe seeds of a small Asian tree, *Strychnos nux vomica,* a source of the alkaloids strychnine and brucine. The seeds are powdered, and the strychnine content is reduced to a little more than 1% by the addition of lactose for use as a bitter tonic and nerve stimulant. It is unsafe at this concentration. Homeopathic remedies of nux vomica are much more diluted and are considered safe.

nV, abbreviation for **nanovolt.**

nvm, abbreviation for *nonvolatile matter.*

NVMA, abbreviation for *National Veterinary Medical Association.*

nyctalopia /nik′təlō′pē·ə/ [Gk, *nyx*, night, *alaos*, obscure, *ops*, eye], poor vision at night or in dim light resulting from decreased synthesis of rhodopsin, vitamin A deficiency, retinal degeneration, or a congenital defect.—**nyctalopic,** *adj.*

nyctophobia /nik′tō-/ [Gk, *nyx* + *phobos,* fear], an anxiety reaction characterized by an obsessive, irrational fear of darkness.

nymphomania /nim′fəmā′nē·ə/ [Gk, *nymphe,* maiden, *mania,* madness], a psychosexual disorder of women characterized by an insatiable desire for sexual satisfaction, often resulting from an unconscious conflict concerning personal adequacy.

nymphomaniac /-mā′nē·ak/, **1.** a person with or displaying characteristics of an individual possessing an insatiable desire for sexual satisfaction. **2.** pertaining to or exhibiting nymphomania.—**nymphomaniacal** /nim′fəmənī′əkəl/, *adj.*

nystagmus /nīstag′məs/ [Gk, *nystagmos,* nodding], involuntary, rhythmic movements of the eyes. The oscillations may be horizontal, vertical, rotary, or mixed. Jerking nystagmus, characterized by faster movements in one direction than in the opposite direction, is more common than pendular nystagmus, in which the oscillations are approximately equal in rate in both directions. Labyrinthine vestibular nystagmus, most frequently rotary, is usually accompanied by vertigo and nausea. Vertical nystagmus is considered pathognomonic of disease of the tegmentum of the brainstem; nystagmus occurring only in the abducting eye is said to be a sign of MS. Seesaw nystagmus, in which one eye moves up and the other down, may be observed in bilateral hemianopia.—**nystagmic,** *adj.*

nystatin /nis′tətin/, an antifungal antibiotic prescribed in oral, topical, and vaginal formulations for the treatment of fungal infections of the GI tract, skin, and vagina.

O, symbol for the element **oxygen.**

Ω, symbol for *ohm.*

O₂, symbol for *oxygen molecule.*

OASDHI, abbreviation for **Old Age, Survivors, Disability and Health Insurance Program.**

oat cell carcinoma [AS, *ate,* oat; L, *cella,* storeroom; Gk, *karkinos,* crab, *oma,* tumor], a malignant, usually bronchogenic epithelial neoplasm consisting of small, tightly packed round, oval, or spindle-shaped epithelial cells that stain darkly and contain neurosecretory granules and little or no cytoplasm. Tumors produced by these cells do not form bulky masses but usually spread along submucosal lymphatics. Many malignant tumors of the lung are of this type.

oatmeal bath, a colloid treatment for pruritus and other skin disorders. The procedure may consist of covering the patient with a layer of muslin containing oatmeal and pouring warm water over the fabric. The bath has a soothing effect. In a variation of the therapy, starch is substituted for oatmeal.

OAWO, abbreviation for **opening abductory wedge osteotomy.**

ob., abreviation for the Latin word *obit,* "died."

OB *informal.* **1.** abbreviation for **obstetrician. 2.** abbreviation for **obstetrics.**

obduction /əbduk′shən/ [L, *obductio,* a covering], a forensic medical autopsy.

Ober and Barr procedure, a surgical method for treating weak biceps muscles by transfer of the brachioradialis muscle.

Ober procedure, a surgical method for treating paralytic clubfoot by transfer of the posterior tibial tendon to the third cuneiform or metatarsal.

Obersteiner-Redlich zone /ō′bərshtī′nər räd′lish, ō′bərstē′nər red′lik/ [H. Obersteiner, Austrian neurologist, 1847–1942; Emil Redlich, Austrian neurologist, 1866–1930], a thin line of demarcation between fibers of the peripheral nervous system and the spinal cord or brainstem. It is produced by a basal lamina separating the Schwann cells and collagen of the peripheral nervous system from the neuroglia of the CNS.

Ober test [Frank R. Ober, American surgeon, 1861–1925], an examination for tightness in the tensor fasciae latae, a muscle that flexes and rotates the thigh.

The patient lies on one side with the lower hip and knee flexed on the table and the upper hip extended while the knee is flexed. Inability to place the upper knee on the table indicates tightness in the muscle.

obese /ōbēs′/ [L, *obesus,* swollen], pertaining to a corpulent or excessively heavy individual. A body mass index of greater than or equal to 30.0 indicates obesity. Because the "average" human body is approximately 25% fat, the proportion may be doubled for a medically defined obese person.

obesity /ōbē′sitē/ [L, *obesitas,* fatness], an abnormal increase in the proportion of fat cells, mainly in the viscera and subcutaneous tissues of the body. Obesity may be exogenous or endogenous. Hyperplastic obesity is caused by an increase in the number of fat cells in the increased adipose tissue mass. Hypertrophic obesity results from an increase in the size of the fat cells in the increased adipose tissue mass. The manifestation of obesity is excess body weight for height.

obex /ō′beks/, a small triangular membrane formed at the caudal angle of the rhomboid fossa or fourth ventricle.

obfuscation /ob′fəskā′shən/ [L, *obfuscare,* to darken], the act of making something confused, clouded, or obscure.

OBG, abbreviation for *obstetrics and gynecology.*

OB-Gyn *informal.* abbreviation for *obstetrics and gynecology.*

object /ob′jəkt/, in psychology, something through which an instinct can achieve its goal; in psychoanalytic terms, a person other than self.

object blindness, an inability to recognize objects or analyze spatial relationships. The condition is associated with lesions of the right cerebral hemisphere in right-handed patients.

object constancy, the ability to perceive an object as unchanging even under different conditions of observation.

objective /əbjek′tiv/ [L, *objectare,* to set against], **1.** a goal. **2.** pertaining to a phenomenon or clinical finding that is observed; not subjective.

objective data collection, the process in which data relating to the client's problem are obtained through direct physical examination, including observation, palpation, percussion, and auscultation, and by laboratory analyses and radiologic and other studies.

objective lens, a lens that accepts light from the output phosphor of a radiographic image-intensifier tube and converts the light into a parallel beam for recording an image on film.

objective sign [L, *objectum,* something cast before; *signum,* sign], a clinical observation that can be seen, heard, measured, or otherwise recorded by an examining physician, nurse, or other health care provider.

objective symptom [L, *objectum,* something cast before; Gk, *symptoma,* that which happens], a symptom accompanied by signs that tend to confirm the patient's physical complaint and enable the examining physician, nurse, or other health care provider to deduce the cause.

objective tinnitus, a noise produced in the ear that can be heard by another person, particularly someone using a stethoscope.

object permanence, a capacity to perceive that something exists even when it is not seen.

object relations, emotional bond between one person and another, as contrasted with interest in and love for the self.

obligate /ob′ligit, -gāt/ [L, *obligare,* to bind], characterized by the ability to survive only in a particular set of environmental conditions.

obligate aerobe, an organism that cannot grow in the absence of oxygen.

obligate anaerobe, an organism that cannot grow in the presence of oxygen, such as *Clostridium tetani, C. botulinum,* and *C. perfringens.*

obligatory water loss /əblig′ətôr′ē/, the volume of water required for daily urinary excretion of metabolic waste products. This amount of water loss is necessary to maintain normal health.

oblique /əblēk′/ [L, *obliquus,* slanted], a slanting direction or any variation from the perpendicular or the horizontal.

oblique bandage, a circular bandage applied spirally in slanting turns, usually to a limb.

oblique fiber, any of the collagenous filaments that are bundled together, extending from the alveolus to the cementum of the tooth in an apical direction on lateral view.

oblique fissure of the lung, 1. the groove marking the division of the lower and middle lobes in the right lung. 2. the groove marking the division of the upper and the lower lobes in the left lung.

oblique fracture, a slanted fracture of the shaft along the bone's long axis.

oblique popliteal ligament, an extension of the tendon of semimembranosus that reinforces the fibrous membrane of the knee joint posteromedially.

oblique presentation [L, *obliquus,* slanted, *praesentare,* to show], a presentation in which the long axis of the fetus is oblique to the long axis of the mother.

obliquity of pelvis /əblik′witē/ [L, *obliquus,* aslant], an abnormal tilt of the pelvis with respect to the spinal column.

obliteration /əblit′ərā′shən/ [L, *obliterare,* to efface], the removal or loss of function of a body part by surgery, disease, or degeneration.

obliterative phlebitis /əblit′ərətiv′/ [L, *obliterare,* to efface; Gk, *phleps,* vein, *itis,* inflammation], a form of phlebitis in which the inflammation results in permanent closure of the vessel.

OBS, abbreviation for *organic brain syndrome.*

observation [L, *observare,* to watch], 1. the act of watching carefully and attentively. 2. a report of what is seen or noticed, such as a nursing observation.

observation hip, a condition in which a patient experiences a limp, pain in the hip, and limited hip motion. Causes include toxic synovitis, infection, and avascular necrosis.

obsession [L, *obsidere,* to haunt], a persistent and recurrent thought or idea with which the mind is continually and involuntarily preoccupied and that cannot be expunged by logic or reasoning.

obsessive-compulsive/əbses′iv/ [L,*obsidere,* to haunt, *compellere,* to impel], 1. characterized by or relating to the tendency to perform repetitive acts or rituals or think repetitive thoughts, usually as a means of releasing tension or relieving anxiety. 2. describing a person who has an obsessive-compulsive disorder.

obsessive-compulsive disorder (OCD), an anxiety disorder characterized by recurrent and persistent thoughts, ideas, and feelings or repetitive acts sufficiently severe to cause marked distress, consume considerable time, or significantly interfere with the patient's occupational, social, or interpersonal functioning.

obsolescence /ob′səles′əns/ [L, *obsolescere,* to decay], 1. to fall into disuse because of age or loss of function. 2. a state of being useless.

obstetric anesthesia [L, *obstetrix,* midwife; Gk, *anaisthesia,* lack of feeling], any of various procedures used to provide anesthesia for childbirth. It includes local anesthesia for episiotomy or episiotomy repair; regional anesthesia for labor or delivery, such as by paracervical block or pudendal block; or, for a wider block, epidural, spinal, caudal, or saddle block. Anesthesia for cesarean section may be achieved with an epidural or spinal block or by general anesthesia.

obstetric forceps, forceps used to assist delivery of the fetal head. They vary in weight, length, shape, and mechanism of action, but all consist of a pair of instruments comprising a handle, a shank, and a blade. The several styles of forceps are designed to assist in various clinical situations. The station of the fetus in the pelvis, the position of the head in relation to the pelvis, the size of the fetus, and the preference of the operator all affect the choice of forceps.

obstetrician (OB) /ob′stətrish′ən/, a physician who specializes in the branch of medicine concerned with pregnancy and childbirth.

obstetrics (OB) /əbstet′riks/ [L, *obstetrix*, midwife], the branch of medicine concerned with pregnancy and childbirth, including the study of the physiologic and pathologic function of the female reproductive tract and the care of the mother and fetus throughout pregnancy, childbirth, and the immediate postpartum period. —**obstetric,** *adj.*

obstipation /ob′stipā′shən/ [L, *obstipare*, to press], **1.** a condition of extreme and persistent constipation caused by obstruction in the intestinal system. **2.** a process of blocking.—**obstipant,** *n.,* **obstipate,** *v.*

obstruction /əbstruk′shən/ [L, *obstruere*, to build against], **1.** something that blocks or clogs. **2.** the act of blocking or preventing passage. **3.** the condition of being obstructed or clogged.—**obstruct,** *v.,* **obstructive,** *adj.*

obstruction series, a test consisting of a series of x-ray films performed on the abdomen of patients with suspected bowel obstruction, paralytic ileus, perforated viscus, abdominal abscess, kidney stones, appendicitis, or foreign body ingestion.

obstructive airway disease /əbstruk′tiv/, any respiratory disease characterized by air trapping caused by either decreased airway diameter or increased airway secretions, or both. It includes chronic bronchitis and emphysema.

obstructive anuria [L, *obstruere*, to build against; Gk, *a + ouron*, without urine], an almost complete absence of urination caused by blockage of the urinary tract.

obstructive biliary cirrhosis [L, *obstruere*, to build against, *bilis*, bile; Gk, *kirrhos*, yellow-orange, *osis*, condition], a form of secondary cirrhosis in which a stricture develops in the bile ducts. The condition may develop after cholecystectomy, gallstones, or a tumor.

obstructive constipation [L, *obstruere*, to build against, *constipare*, to crowd together], a condition in which feces are retained in the intestine because of a blockage in the lumen.

obstructive hydroureter, megaureter in the segment proximal to an obstruction, such as that caused by aperistalsis that interferes with passage of urine.

obstructive nephropathy, nephropathy caused by obstruction of the urinary tract (usually the ureter), with hydronephrosis, slowing of the glomerular filtration rate, and tubular abnormalities.

obstructive sleep apnea, a form of sleep apnea involving a physical obstruction in the upper airways. The condition tends to affect mainly obese people, particularly those with secondary pulmonary insufficiency or a constitutional defect, but a nonobese person with a congenital abnormality of the upper airways may also be affected. The condition is usually marked by recurrent sleep interruptions, snoring, choking and gasping spells on awakening, and drowsiness caused by loss of normal sleep. Uncorrected, the disorder often leads to central sleep apnea, pulmonary failure, and cardiac abnormalities.

obstructive uropathy, any pathologic condition that blocks the flow of urine. The condition may lead to impairment of kidney function and an increased risk of urinary infection.

obtund /obtund′/ [L, *obtundere*, to blunt], **1.** to deaden pain. **2.** to render insensitive to unpleasant or painful stimuli by reducing the LOC, such as by anesthesia or a strong opioid analgesic. —**obtundation, obtundity,** *n.,* **obtunded, obtundent,** *adj.*

obtundation /ob′tundā′shən/ [L, *obtundere,* to blunt, *atus,* process], a greatly reduced LOC. The patient is not yet comatose but is close, arousing only with very strong stimulus.

obturation /ob′t(y)ərā′ahən/ [L, *obturare,* to stop up], an obstruction of an opening, such as an intestinal blockage.

obturator /ob′tərā′tər, ob′tyərā′tər/ [L, *obturare,* to close], **1.** a device used to block a passage or a canal or to fill in a space such as a prosthesis implanted to bridge the gap in the roof of the mouth in a cleft palate. **2.** *nontechnical.* an obturator muscle or membrane. **3.** a device that is placed into a large-bore cannula during insertion to prevent potential blockage by residual tissues.

obturator artery, an artery that supplies the adductor region of the thigh.

obturator canal, a passageway between the pelvic cavity and the adductor region of the thigh formed in the superior aspect of the obturator foramen between bone, a connective tissue membrane, and muscles that fill the foramen. The upper margin of the canal is marked by the obturator groove.

O

obturator externus, the flat, triangular muscle covering the outer surface of the anterior wall of the pelvis. It functions to rotate the thigh laterally.

obturator foramen, a large opening on each side of the lower part of the hip bone, formed posteriorly by the ischium, superiorly by the ilium, and anteriorly by the pubis.

obturator internus, a muscle that covers a large area of the inferior aspect of the lesser pelvis, where it surrounds the obturator foramen. It functions to rotate the thigh laterally and to extend and abduct the thigh when it is flexed.

obturator membrane, a tough fibrous membrane that covers the obturator foramen of each side of the pelvis.

obturator muscles [L, *obturare,* to close + *musculus*], a pair of thigh muscles, the external and internal obturators. The external obturator flexes and rotates the thigh laterally, and the internal obturator abducts and rotates the thigh laterally.

obturator nerve, a branch of the lumbar plexus that supplies the adductor region of the thigh.

obturator sign [L, *obturare,* to close, *signus,* sign], a sign of appendicitis or other peritoneal inflammation. The internal rotation of the right leg with the leg flexed to 90 degrees at the hip and knee and a resultant tightening of the internal obturator muscle may cause abdominal discomfort indicative of, for example, appendicitis.

obv, abbreviation for **obverse.**

OC, abbreviation for **oral contraceptive.**

OCA, abbreviation for **oculocutaneous albinism.**

occ, abbreviation for **occipital.**

occipital (occ) /oksip'itəl/, **1.** pertaining to the back of the head. **2.** situated near the occipital bone, such as the occipital lobe of the brain.

occipital anchorage, an orthodontic anchorage in which the resistance is borne by the top and back of the head and the force transmitted to the teeth by means of the headgear and heavy elastics connected with attachment on the teeth.

occipital artery, one of a pair of tortuous branches from the external carotid arteries that divides into six branches and supplies parts of the head and scalp.

occipital bone, the cuplike bone at the back of the skull, marked by a large opening, the foramen magnum, that communicates with the vertebral canal. The occipital bone articulates with the two parietal bones, the two temporal bones, the sphenoid, and the atlas.

occipital condyles, paired structures on each anterolateral border of the foramen magnum that articulate with the atlas.

occipital condyle syndrome, a condition characterized by a stiff neck and severe localized occipital pain that intensifies with neck flexion. It is associated with unilateral involvement of the twelfth nerve, dysarthria, and dysphagia.

occipitalization /oksip'italī′zā′shən/, a process of bony ankylosis of the atlas with the occipital bone.

occipital lobe, one of the five lobes of each cerebral hemisphere, occupying a relatively small pyramidal part of the occipital pole. The occipital lobe lies beneath the occipital bone and presents medial, lateral, and inferior surfaces.

occipital sinus, the smallest of the cranial sinuses and one of six posterior superior venous channels associated with the dura mater.

occipitobregmatic /oksip'itōbregmat′ik/ [L, *occiput,* back of the head; Gk, *bregma,* front of the head], pertaining to the occiput and the bregma.

occipitofrontal /oksip'itōfrun′təl/ [L, *occiput* + *frons,* forehead], pertaining to the occiput and the frontal bone of the skull.

occipitofrontalis /oksip'itōfrəntal′is/, one of a pair of thin, broad muscles covering the top of the skull, consisting of an occipital belly and a frontal belly connected by an extensive aponeurosis. It is the muscle that draws the scalp and raises the eyebrows.

occipitomastoid suture, the articulation across the lower part of the calvaria between the temporal bone and the occipital bone.

occiput /ok'sipət/ *pl.* **occipita** /oksip'itə/, **occiputs** the back part of the head.

occluded /əkl⎯oo̅′did/ [L, *occludere,* to close up], closed, plugged, or obstructed.

occlusal /əkl⎯oo̅′səl/ [L, *occludere,* to close up], pertaining to a closure, such as the contact between the teeth of the upper and lower jaws.

occlusal adjustment, the intentional mechanical grinding of the biting surfaces of teeth to improve the contact of or relationship between opposing tooth surfaces, their supporting structures, the muscles of mastication, and the TMJs.

occlusal contouring, the modification by grinding of occlusal tooth irregularities such as uneven marginal ridges and extruded or malpositioned teeth.

occlusal form, the shape of the occluding surfaces of a tooth, a row of teeth, or any dentition.

occlusal harmony, a combination of healthy and nondisruptive occlusal relationships between the teeth and their supporting structures, the associated neuromuscular mechanisms, and the TMJs.

occlusal plane [L, *occludere*, to close up, *planum*, level ground], a plane passing through the occlusal or biting surfaces of the teeth. It represents the mean of the curvature of the occlusal surface.

occlusal radiograph, an intraoral radiograph or dental image made with the film or image receptor placed on the occlusal surfaces of one of the arches. It shows the relationship of teeth to underlying structures in the alveolar process, such as cysts and abscesses.

occlusal recontouring, the reshaping of an occlusal surface of a natural or artificial tooth.

occlusal relationship, the relationship of the mandibular teeth to the maxillary teeth when they are in a defined contact position.

occlusal rest, an indent created on the top surface of a posterior tooth to support a removable partial denture.

occlusal rest angle, the angle formed by an occlusal rest with its upright minor connector of a removable partial denture framework.

occlusal spillway, a natural groove that crosses a cusp ridge or a marginal ridge of a tooth.

occlusal surface [L, *occludere*, to close up, *superficies*, surface], the surfaces of a tooth in one arch that makes contact or near contact with the corresponding surface of a tooth.

occlusal trauma, injury to a tooth and surrounding structures caused by malocclusive stresses, including trauma, TMJ dysfunction, and bruxism.

occlusion /əklōō′zhən/ [L, *occludere*, to close up], **1.** in anatomy, a blockage in a canal, vessel, or passage of the body; the state of being closed. **2.** in dentistry, any contact between the incising or masticating surfaces of the maxillary and mandibular teeth.—**occlude,** v., **occlusive,** adj.

occlusion rim, an artificial dental structure with occluding surfaces attached to temporary or permanent denture bases, used for recording the relation of the maxilla to the mandible and for positioning the teeth.

occlusive /əklōō′siv/, pertaining to something that effects an occlusion or closure.

occlusive dressing, a dressing that prevents air from reaching a wound or lesion and that retains moisture, heat, body fluids, and medication. It may consist of a sheet of thin plastic affixed with transparent tape.

occlusive mesenteric infarction, mesenteric infarction caused by occlusion of one of the mesenteric arteries, such as by a thrombus or by mechanical compression.

occlusive mesenteric ischemia, mesenteric ischemia caused by occlusion of one of the mesenteric arteries, such as by a thrombus or mechanical compression.

occult /əkult′/ [L, *occultare*, to hide], hidden or difficult to observe directly.

occult blood, blood that is not obvious on examination and is from a nonspecific source, with obscure signs and symptoms. It may be detected by means of a chemical test or by microscopic or spectroscopic examination.

occult blood test [L, *occultare*, to hide; AS, *blod*; L, *testum*, crucible], a test for the presence of microscopic amounts of blood in the feces secondary to bleeding in the digestive tract. Benign and malignant GI tumors, ulcers, inflammatory bowel disease, arteriovenous malformations, diverticulosis, and hematobilia can cause the appearance of occult blood in the stool, as can swallowed blood from oral or nasal pharyngeal bleeding.

occult carcinoma, a small carcinoma that does not cause overt symptoms. The carcinoma may remain localized, be discovered only incidentally at autopsy after death resulting from another cause, or metastasize and be discovered as a result of metastatic disease.

occult ectopic ACTH syndrome, a medical condition that mimics the clinical and biochemical picture of Cushing's disease. The cause is usually a tumor that secretes adrenocorticotropic hormone in the lungs, thymus, pancreas, adrenal medulla, or thyroid gland.

occult fracture, a fracture that cannot be detected by radiographic standard examination until several weeks after injury. The break is most likely to occur in the ribs, tibia, metatarsals, hip, or navicular.

occupancy /ok′yəpənsē′/ [L, *occupare*, to take possession of], the ratio of average daily hospital census to the total number of beds maintained during the reporting period.

occupancy factor (T), the level of human occupancy of an area adjacent to a source of radiation. It is used to determine the amount of shielding required in the walls. T is rated as full, for an office or laboratory next to an x-ray facility; partial, for corridors and restrooms; or occasional, for stairways, elevators, closets, and outside areas.

occupational accident /ok′yəpā′shənəl/ [L, *occupare*, to take possession of, *accidere*, to happen], an injury to an employee that occurs in the workplace. Occupational accidents account for over 95% of occupational disabilities.

occupational asthma, an abnormal condition of the respiratory system resulting from exposure in the workplace to allergenic or other irritating substances.

occupational deafness, a loss of hearing resulting from noise levels in the workplace.

occupational dermatoses, skin disorders associated with exposure to toxic chemicals

O

or other agents in the workplace. An estimated 80% of cases of contact dermatitis are the result of exposure to chemical irritants.

occupational disability, a condition in which a worker is unable to perform the functions required to complete a job satisfactorily because of an occupational disease or an occupational accident.

occupational disease, a disease that results from a particular type of employment, usually from the effects of long-term exposure to specific substances or continuous or repetitive physical acts.

occupational health, the ability of a worker to function at an optimum level of well-being at a worksite as reflected in terms of productivity, work attendance, disability compensation claims, and employment longevity.

occupational history, a part of the health history in which questions are asked about the person's occupation, source of income, effects of the work on the worker's health or the worker's health on the job, the duration of the job, and to what degree the occupation satisfies the person.

occupational lung disease, any of a group of abnormal conditions of the lungs caused by the inhalation of dusts, fumes, gases, or vapors in an environment where a person works.

occupational medicine, a field of preventive medicine concerned with the medical problems and practices relating to occupations and especially to the health of workers in various industries.

occupational performance tasks, activities that can be used to measure the potential ability or actual proficiency in the handling of certain objects and use of skills related to a given occupation.

occupational socialization, the adaptation of an individual to a given set of job-related behaviors, particularly the expected behavior that accompanies a specific job.

occupational stress, a disorder associated with a job or work.

occupational therapist (OT), an allied health professional who is nationally certified to practice occupational therapy. The OT uses purposeful activity and interventions to maximize the independence and health of any client who is limited by physical injury or illness, cognitive impairment, psychosocial dysfunction, mental illness, or a developmental or learning disability. Services include the assessment, treatment, and education of the client or family; interventions directed toward developing daily living skills, work readiness, or work performance; and facilitation of the development of sensory-motor, perceptual, or neuromuscular functioning or ROM.

occupational therapy (OT), a health rehabilitation profession designed to help people of all ages with physical, developmental, social, or emotional deficits regain and build skills that are important for functional independence, health, and well-being.

occupational therapy aide, a person who, under the supervision of an occupational therapist (OT) or OT assistant, performs clerical and other treatment-related tasks necessary for the implementation of occupational therapy programs.

occurrence policy /əkur'əns/ [L, *occurere,* to run, *politica,* pertaining to the state], a professional liability insurance policy that covers the holder during the period an alleged act of malpractice occurred. Occurrence policies are said to have a "long tail," because the statute of limitations on malpractice allegations is unlimited.

OCD, abbreviation for **obsessive-compulsive disorder.**

ochre mutation, a genetic alteration that causes the synthesis of polypeptide chain to terminate prematurely because the triplet of nucleotides that normally codes for the next amino acid in chain becomes uracil-adenine-guanine, the sequence that signals the end of the chain. It is one of three possible nonsense mutations.

ochronosis /ō'krənō'sis/ [Gk, *ochros,* yellow, *osis*], an inherited error of protein metabolism characterized by an accumulation of homogentisic acid, resulting in degenerative arthritis and brown-black pigment deposited in connective tissue and cartilage.

OCN, abbreviation for *Oncology Certified Nurse.*

OCT, abbreviation for **oxytocin challenge test.**

octacosanol, a dietary supplement used for herpes, inflammation of the skin, amyotrophic lateral sclerosis (ALS), and physical endurance. It is probably not effective for ALS, and there are insufficient reliable data for other indications.

octan /ok'tan/, occurring at 7-day intervals, or every 8th day.

octanoic acid breath test, a breath test for gastric emptying. The patient is administered a test meal containing octanoic acid labeled with carbon-13, and the breath is assessed at intervals for levels of labeled carbon dioxide. Excessive carbon dioxide is seen when gastric emptying is inadequate.

octigravida /ok'tigrav'ədə/ [L, *octo,* eight, *gravidus,* pregnancy], a woman who is pregnant for the eighth time.

octinoxate /oktin'ok-sāt/, an absorber of ultraviolet B radiation, used topically as a sunscreen.

octisalate /ok′tīsal′āt/, a substituted salicylate that absorbs ultraviolet light in the UVB range, used as a sunscreen.

octocrylene /ok′to-kril′ēn/, a sunscreen that absorbs ultraviolet rays in the UVB range.

octopus /ok′təpəs/, any of numerous carnivorous marine mollusks having eight tentacles.

octreotide, an antidiarrheal and hormone. The two brand names of this drug are used for different purposes. Sandostatin is used to treat acromegaly, carcinoid tumors, and vasoactive intestinal peptide tumors (VIPomas). Sandostatin LAR Depot is used for long-term maintenance of acromegaly, carcinoid tumors, and VIPomas.

octreotide scan, a nuclear scan performed to detect neuroendocrine tumors, both primary and metastatic.

ocul., abbreviation for the Latin word *oculis,* "pertaining to the eyes."

ocular /ok′yələr/ [L, *oculus,* eye], **1.** pertaining to the eye. **2.** an eyepiece of an optic instrument.

ocular dysmetria, a visual disorder in which the eyes are unable to fix the gaze on an object or follow a moving object with accuracy. It is a sign of cerebellar disease.

ocular herpes [L, *oculus,* eye; Gk, *herpein,* to creep], a herpesvirus infection of the eye.

ocular hypertelorism, a developmental defect involving the frontal region of the cranium, characterized by an abnormally widened bridge of the nose and increased distance between the eyes.

ocular hypertension, a condition of intraocular pressure that is higher than normal but that has not resulted in a constricted visual field or increased cupping of the optic nerve head.

ocular hypotelorism, a developmental defect involving the frontal region of the cranium, characterized by an abnormal narrowing of the bridge of the nose and decreased distance between the eyes, with resulting convergent strabismus.

ocular melanoma, malignant melanoma arising from the structures of the eye, usually the choroid, ciliary body, or iris, and occurring most often in the fourth and fifth decades of life; the most common site of metastasis is the liver, and such metastasis is followed rapidly by death.

ocular myopathy, slowly progressive weakness of ocular muscles, characterized by decreased mobility of the eye and drooping of the upper lid. The disorder may be unilateral or bilateral and may be caused by damage to the oculomotor nerve, an intracranial tumor, or a neuromuscular disease.

ocular refraction [L, *oculus,* eye, *refringere,* to break apart], an examination of vision to determine the need for corrective lenses.

oculocephalic reflex /ok′yəlō′səfal′ik/ [L, *oculus*; Gk, *kephale,* head; L, *reflectere,* to bend backward], a test of the integrity of brainstem function. When the patient's head is quickly moved to one side and then to the other, the eyes will normally lag behind the head movement and then slowly assume the midline position. Failure of the eyes to either lag properly or revert back to the midline indicates a lesion on the ipsilateral side at the brainstem level.

oculocerebral-hypopigmentation syndrome /ok′yələ-sərē′brəl/ [L, *oculus,* eye, *cerebrum,* brain], an autosomalrecessive syndrome marked by cutaneous hypopigmentation, microphthalmos, small opaque corneas, gingival hypertrophy, and cerebral defect manifested by spasticity, mental and physical retardation, and athetoid movements.

oculocutaneous albinism (OCA) /ok′yo͞olōkyo͞otā′-nē·əs/, a human albinism occurring in 10 types, all distinguished in their incidence and genetic, biochemical, and clinical characteristics but having in common varying degrees of decreased melanotic pigment of the skin, hair, and eyes; hypoplastic foveas; photophobia; nystagmus; and decreased visual acuity.

oculoglandular syndrome /ok′yəlōglan′dyələr/ [L, *oculus,* eye], a unilateral granulomatous form of conjunctivitis. It is associated with a visibly enlarged and tender ipsilateral lymph node and a history of cat-scratch disease.

oculogyric crisis /ok′yəlōjī′rik/ [L, *oculus* + *gyrare,* to turn around], a paroxysm in which the eyes are held in a fixed position, usually up and sideways, for minutes or several hours, often occurring in postencephalitic patients with signs of parkinsonism. Oculogyric crises may be precipitated by emotional stress and neuroleptic overdose, and patients with the disorder frequently show psychiatric symptoms.

oculomotor /-mō′tər/ [L, *oculus,* eye, *motor,* mover], pertaining to movements of the eyeballs.

oculomotor nerve [L, *oculus* + *motor,* mover], one of a pair of cranial nerves essential for eye movements, supplying certain extrinsic and intrinsic eye muscles.

oculomotor nucleus [L, *oculus,* eye, *motor,* mover, *nucleus,* nut kernel], a nucleus of a third cranial nerve arising in the midbrain.

Ocusert Pilo, a trademark for an acetylcholinesterase inhibitor used to treat glaucoma (pilocarpine).

OD, 1. abbreviation for *oculus dexter,* a Latin phrase meaning "right eye."

2. abbreviation for *Doctor of Optometry.*

3. abbreviation for **overdose.**

odaxetic /ō′dakset′ik/ [Gk, *odaxein,* a biting pain], causing a tactile sensation of itching or biting.

OD'd /ōdēd′/, *slang.* overdosed, usually referring to a person who has suffered adverse effects from an excessively large dose of a drug of abuse.

Oddi's sphincter [Ruggero Oddi, Italian surgeon, 1864–1913; Gk, *sphigein,* to bind], a band of circular muscle fibers around the lower part of the common bile duct and pancreatic duct, near the common duct junction with the duodenum.

odontectomy /ō′dontek′tōmē/ [Gk, *odous,* tooth, *ektomē,* cut out], the extraction of a tooth by removal of the bone from around the roots before force is applied.

odontiasis /ō′dontī′əsis/, the process of teething.

odontitis /ō′dontī′tis/ [Gk, *odous + itis,* inflammation], abnormal enlargement of a tooth pulp, usually resulting from inflammation of the odontoblasts (cells responsible for dentin formation) rather than of the mature, or erupted, tooth. It may be caused by infection, tumor, or trauma.

odontoblast /ōdon′təblast′/ [Gk, *odous,* tooth, *blastos,* germ], one of the connective tissue cells in the periphery of the dental pulp that develops into the primary and secondary dentin of a tooth.

odontodysplasia /-displā′zhə/ [Gk, *odous + dys,* bad, *plasis,* forming], an abnormality in the development of the teeth, characterized by deficient formation of enamel and dentin.

odontogenesis /-jen′əsis/ [Gk, *odous,* tooth, *genein,* to produce], the origin and formation of developing teeth.

odontogenic /ōdon′tōjen′ik/ [Gk, *odous + genein,* to produce], **1.** pertaining to the generation of teeth. **2.** developing in tissues that produce teeth.

odontogenic cyst, 1. a cyst derived from epithelium, usually containing fluid or semisolid material, that develops along lines of embryonic fusion or during various stages of tooth formation and development and is nearly always enclosed within bone. **2.** any of a variety of lesions of mouth tissues, including the relatively common dentigerous cyst, which is associated with the crown of an unerupted third molar or maxillary cuspid.

odontogenic fibroma, a benign neoplasm of the jaw derived from the embryonic part of the tooth germ, dental follicle, or dental papilla or from the periodontal membrane.

odontogenic fibrosarcoma, a malignant neoplasm of the jaw that develops in a mesenchymal component of a tooth or tooth germ.

odontogenic keratocyst, a distinctive developmental odontogenic cyst which arises from the dental lamina, containing clear fluid and a cheesy material resembling keratin debris. This usually asymptomatic lesion can occur at any age and is found upon radiographic or dental imaging. Large lesions may present with pain, swelling, or drainage.

odontogenic myxoma, a rare tumor of the jaw that may develop from the mesenchyme of the tooth germ.

odontoid process [Gk, *odous + eidos,* form; L, *processus*], the toothlike projection that rises perpendicularly from the upper surface of the body of the second cervical vertebra (axis) and that serves as a pivot point for the rotation of the atlas (first cervical vertebra), enabling the head to turn.

odontology /ō′dontol′əjē/ [Gk, *odous + logos,* science], the scientific study of the anatomy and physiology of the teeth and of the surrounding structures of the oral cavity.

odontoma /ō′dontō′mə/ [Gk, *odous + oma,* tumor], a benign tumor consisting of cementum, dentin, enamel, and pulp tissue that may be arranged in the form of teeth.

odor /ō′dər/ [L, a smell], a scent or smell. The sense of smell is activated when airborne molecules stimulate receptors of the first cranial nerve.

odoriferous /ō′dərif′ərəs/ [L, *odor,* smell, *ferre,* to bear], pertaining to something that produces a smell, particularly one that is strong or offensive.

odorous /ō′dərəs/ [L, *odor,* smell], pertaining to something that has an odor, smell, or fragrance.

ODTS, abbreviation for **organic dust toxic syndrome.**

odynacusis [Gk, *odyne,* pain, *akouein,* to hear], a painful sensitivity to noise.

odynophagia /od′inōfā′jə/ [Gk, *odyne,* pain, *phagein,* to swallow], a severe sensation of burning squeezing pain while swallowing caused by irritation of the mucosa or a muscular disorder of the esophagus.

Oedipus complex /ed′ipəs, ē′dəpəs/ [Gk, *Oedipus,* mythic king who slew his father and married his mother], **1.** in psychoanalysis, a child's desire for a sexual relationship with the parent of the opposite sex, usually with strong negative feelings for the parent of the same sex. **2.** a son's desire for a sexual relationship with his mother.

OEM, abbreviation for *optical electron microscope.*

OER, abbreviation for **oxygen enhancement ratio.**

o/f, symbol for *oxidation/fermentation.*

off-center grid, in radiology, a focused grid that is perpendicular to the central-axis x-ray beam but is shifted laterally, resulting in a cutoff across the entire grid.

off-cycle time, in managed care, a time during which open enrollment in a health plan is usually not permitted.

off-focus radiation, in radiology, x-rays produced by stray electrons that interact at positions on the anode at points other than the focal spot.

Office of the Inspector General (OIG) of the United States, an agency within the U.S. Department of Health and Human Services that enforces Medicare regulations and investigates and prosecutes charges of Medicare fraud and abuse.

off-level grid, in radiology, a grid that is not perpendicular to the central-axis x-ray beam. The cause is often a malpositioned x-ray tube rather than an improperly positioned grid.

ofloxacin /oflak'səsin/, a fluoroquinolone antibiotic used to treat lower respiratory tract infections, genitourinary infections, skin and skin structure infections, and conjunctivitis.

Ogden classification system, a system for categorizing 17 different kinds of epiphyseal fractures.

Ogden plate, a long metal plate used for fixing long bone fractures. It is designed to accommodate preexisting intramedullary devices, such as rods or the stem of a prosthesis, and has slots that can accept encircling bands.

Ogen, a trademark for an estrogen (estropipate).

Ogsten line, a line drawn through the knee from the adduction tubercle to the intercondylar notch, used as a guide for transection of the condyle in the surgical repair of knock-knee.

OH, symbol for **hydroxyl.**

o.h., abbreviation for the Latin term *omni hora,* "hourly."

OHD, abbreviation for *organic heart disease.*

OHF, abbreviation for **Omsk hemorrhagic fever.**

ohm (Ω) [Georg S. Ohm, German physicist, 1787–1854], a unit of measurement of electric resistance. One ohm is the resistance of a conductor in which an electric potential of 1 volt produces a current of 1 ampere.

Ohm's law [Georg S. Ohm], the principle that the strength or intensity of an unvarying electric current is directly proportional to the electromotive force and inversely proportional to the resistance of the circuit.

OIG, abbreviation for **Office of the Inspector General of the United States.**

oil [L, *oleum*], any of a large number of greasy liquid substances not miscible in water.

oil-in-water emulsion, an emulsion in which oil is the dispersed liquid and an aqueous solution is the continuous phase.

Water can be used to dilute such an emulsion or to remove it.

oil retention enema, an enema containing about 200 to 250 mL of an oil-based solution given to soften a fecal mass.

ointment [L, *unguentum,* a salve], a semisolid, externally applied preparation, usually containing a drug. Various ointments are used as local analgesic, anesthetic, antibiotic, astringent, depigmenting, irritant, and keratolytic agents.

ointment base, a vehicle for the medicinal substances carried in an ointment.

olanzapine, an antipsychotic and neuroleptic used to treat psychotic disorders.

Old Age, Survivors, Disability and Health Insurance Program (OASDHI), a benefit program, administered by the U.S. Social Security Administration, that provides cash benefits to workers who are retired or disabled, their dependents, and survivors, commonly referred to as Social Security. The program also provides health insurance benefits for people over 65 and disabled people under 65, commonly referred to as Medicare.

old dislocation, a dislocation in which inflammatory changes have occurred.

Older Americans Act Amendment of 1987, U.S. federal legislation authorizing support of Title III nutrition services for state and county programs on aging. The services include both congregate and home-delivered meals, with related nutrition education.

Older Americans Resources and Services Scale, a scale of instrumental ADLs, consisting of eight questions designed to assess the person's degree of involvement with family and society.

old-old, persons 85 years of age and older.

old tuberculin [ME, *ald*, L, *tubercle*], the original formula for an extract of the tubercle bacillus used in the treatment of TB by Koch.

oleandrism /ō'lē·an'drizəm/, a toxic effect of ingesting or inhaling the cardiac glycoside contained in the roots, bark, flowers, and seeds of oleander *(Nerium oleander),* an evergreen ornamental shrub. Symptoms range from nausea and vomiting to bradycardia and cardiac arrest.

olecranon /olek'rənon/ [Gk, *olekranon,* tip of the elbow], a proximal projection of the ulna that forms the tip of the elbow and fits into the olecranon fossa of the humerus when the forearm is extended at the proximal extremity of the ulna.

olecranon bursa, the bursa of the elbow.

olecranon fossa, the depression in the posterior surface of the humerus that receives the olecranon of the ulna when the forearm is extended.

O

olefin /ō'ləfin/ [L, *oleum*, oil, *facere*, to make], any of a group of unsaturated aliphatic hydrocarbons containing one or more double bonds in the carbon chain.

oleic acid /ōlē'ik/ [L, *oleum*, oil, *acidus*, sour], a colorless, monounsaturated fatty acid occurring in almost all natural fats.

oleoresin /ō'lē-ōrez'in/ [L, *oleum*, oil + *resin*], 1. any natural combination of a resin and a volatile oil such as exudes from pines and other plants. 2. a compound prepared by exhausting a drug by percolation with a volatile solvent, such as acetone, alcohol, or ether, and evaporating the solvent.

oleovitamin /ō'lē-ōvī'təmin/, a preparation of fish-liver oil or edible vegetable oil that contains one or more of the fat-soluble vitamins or their derivatives.

oleovitamin A, an oily preparation, usually fish-liver oil or fish-liver oil diluted with an edible vegetable oil, containing the natural or synthetic form of vitamin A.

Olestra, a trade name for a synthetic fat substitute derived from sucrose and eight acids of vegetable oils. Olestra adds no calories or fats to the food into which it is incorporated. Because the molecules of Olestra are larger and more tightly packed than those of ordinary fats, they cannot be broken down by digestive enzymes and cannot enter the bloodstream. Adverse effects reported include cramping and loose stools in some people and inhibition of absorption of some vitamins.

olfaction /olfak'shən/ [L, *olfacere*, to smell], 1. the act of smelling. 2. the sense of smell.—**olfactory,** *adj.*

olfactory bulb [L, *olfactus,* sense of smell, *bulbus,* swollen root], the area of the forebrain where the olfactory nerves terminate and the olfactory tracts arise.

olfactory center [L, *olfactus,* sense of smell; Gk, *kentron*], the part of the brain responsible for the subjective appreciation of odors, a complex group of neurons located near the junction of the temporal and parietal lobes.

olfactory cortex [L, *olfactus,* sense of smell, *cortex,* bark], the part of the cerebral cortex, including the pyriform lobe and the hippocampus formation, that is concerned with the sense of smell.

olfactory foramen, one of several openings in the cribriform plate of the ethmoid bone.

olfactory hallucination [L, *olfactus,* sense of smell, *alucinari,* to wander mentally], a condition in which an individual has false perceptions of odors, which are usually repugnant or offensive. The hallucinations are sometimes associated with guilt feelings.

olfactory lobe [L, *olfactus,* sense of smell; Gk, *lobos,* lobe], a structure involved in the sense of smell in lower animals. Vestiges of the tissue are found in the cerebral hemispheres of humans.

olfactory nerve, one of a pair of nerves associated with the sense of smell. The area in which the olfactory nerves arise is situated in the most superior part of the mucous membrane that covers the superior nasal concha. The olfactory sensory endings are modified epithelial cells, and the least specialized of the special senses. The olfactory nerves connect with the olfactory bulb and the olfactory tract, which are components of the part of the brain associated with the sense of smell.

olfactory organ [L, *olfactus,* sense of smell], the apparatus in the mucous membrane of the nose responsible for the sense of smell. It includes the sensory nerve endings and the olfactory bulb of the brain.

olfactory receptors [L, *olfactus,* sense of smell, *recipere,* to receive], bipolar nerve cells located in the nasal epithelium. Axons of the cells become receptors of the olfactory nerve.

oligemia /ol'ijē'mē-ə/ [Gk, *oligos,* little, *haima,* blood], a condition of hypovolemia or reduced circulating intravascular volume.

oligoclonal banding /ol'igōklō'nəl/, a process by which CSF IgG is distributed, after electrophoresis, in discrete bands. Approximately 90% of MS patients show oligoclonal banding.

oligodactyly /ol'igōdak'tilē/ [Gk, *oligos* + *dactylos,* finger], a congenital anomaly characterized by the absence of one or more of the fingers or toes.—**oligodactylic,** *adj.*

oligodendrocyte /ol'igōden'drəsīt/ [Gk, *oligos* + *dendron,* tree, *kytos,* cell], a type of neuroglial cell with dendritic projections that coil around axons of neural cells.

oligodendroglia /ol'igōdendrog'lē-ə/, one of three types of glial cells that, with the nerve cells, compose the CNS and are characterized by sheetlike processes that wrap around individual axons to form a myelin sheath of nerve fibers.

oligodendroglioma /ol'igōden'drōglī-ō'mə/ *pl.* **oligodendrogliomas, oligodendrogliomata** [Gk, *oligos* + *dendron,* tree, *glia,* glue, *oma,* tumor], an uncommon brain tumor composed of nonneural ectodermal cells that form part of the supporting connective tissue around nerve cells.

oligodontia /ol'igōdon'shə/ [Gk, *oligos* + *odous,* tooth], a genetically determined dental defect characterized by the development of fewer than the normal number of teeth.

oligogenic /ol'igōjen'ik/ [Gk, *oligos* + *genein,* to produce], pertaining to hereditary characteristics produced by one or only a few genes.

oligohydramnios /-hidram'nē·əs/ [Gk, *oligos* + *hydor*, water, *amnion*, fetal membrane], an abnormally small amount or absence of amniotic fluid.

oligomeganephronia /ol'igōmeg'ənefrō'nē·ə/ [Gk, *oligos* + *megas*, large, *nephros*, kidney], a type of congenital renal hypoplasia associated with chronic renal failure in children. The condition is characterized by a decreased number of functioning nephrons and hypertrophy of other renal elements without the presence of aberrant tissue.—**oligomeganephronic**, *adj.*

oligomenorrhea /-men'ōrē'ə/ [Gk, *oligos*; L, *men*, month; Gk, *rhoia*, flow], abnormally light or a reduction in menstruation. —**oligomenorrheic**, *adj.*

oligonucleotide /-nōō'klē·ətīd'/, a compound formed by linking a small number of nucleotides.

oligopeptide /-pep'tīd/, a peptide composed of fewer than 20 amino acids.

oligosaccharide /-sak'ərīd/, a compound formed by a small number of monosaccharide units.

oligospermia /ol'igōspur'mē·ə/ [Gk, *oligos* + *sperma*, seed], an insufficient number of spermatozoa in the semen.

oligotroph /ol'igətrof'/, an organism that can survive in a nutrient-poor environment.

oliguria /ol'igyōōr'ē·ə/ [Gk, *oligos* + *ouron*, urine], a diminished capacity to form and pass urine, such that the end products of metabolism cannot be excreted efficiently. It is usually caused by imbalances in body fluids and electrolytes, renal lesions, or urinary tract obstruction.—**oliguric**, *adj.*

olisthy /ōlis'thē/ [Gk, *olisthanein*, to slip], the slippage of a bone from its normal anatomic site, as in a slipped disk. —**olisthetic**, *adj.*

olivary body /ol'iver'ē/ [L, *oliva*; AS, *bodig*], an olivary nucleus on the medulla oblongata, part of an aggregate of small, densely packed nerve cells.

olivopontocerebellar /ol'ivōpon'tōser'ibel'ər/ [L, *oliva*, olive, *pons*, bridge, *cerebellum*, small brain], pertaining to the olivae, the middle peduncles, and the cerebellum.

olivopontocerebellar atrophy (OPCA), a group of hereditary ataxias characterized by mixed clinical features of pure cerebellar ataxia, dementia, Parkinson-like symptoms, spasticity, choreoathetosis, retinal degeneration, myelopathy, and peripheral neuropathy.

Ollier's dyschondroplasia /ol'ē·āz'/ [Louis X.E.L. Ollier, French surgeon, 1830–1900; Gk, *dys*, bad, *chondros*, cartilage, *plasis*, formation], a rare disorder of bone development in which the epiphyseal tissue responsible for growth spreads through the bones, causing abnormal irregular growth and deformity.

olmesartan medoxomil, an antihypertensive agent.

olopatadine /o'lopat'ahdēn/, a histamine H₁ receptor antagonist used as the hydrochloride salt in the topical treatment of allergic conjunctivitis.

o.m., abbreviation for the Latin term *omni mane,* "every morning."

Omaha System, a method of community health nursing practice, documentation, and data management based on a nursing process model. It incorporates three standardized schemes: the problem classification scheme, the intervention scheme, and the problem rating scale for outcomes.

omalgia /ōmal'jə/ [Gk, *omos,* shoulder, *algos,* pain], pain in the shoulder.

omalizumab, a monoclonal antibody used to treat moderate to severe persistent asthma.

omarthritis /ō'märthrī'tis/, inflammation of the shoulder joint.

ombudsman /om'bədzmən/ [ONorse, *umbothsmathr,* commission man], a person who investigates and mediates patients' problems and complaints in relation to a hospital's services.

omega /ōmĕ'gə, ōmā'gə, om'əgə/, Ω, ω, the 24th letter of the Greek alphabet.

omega-3 fatty acid, a fatty acid with a double bond located at the third carbon atom away from the omega (methyl) end of the molecule. Major sources are coldwater fish and vegetable oils. Omega-3 fatty acids appear to have protective functions in preventing the formation of blood clots and reducing the risk of coronary heart disease.

omega-6 fatty acid, an unsaturated fatty acid in which the double bond closest to the omega (methyl) end of the molecule occurs at the sixth carbon from that end. Major sources are vegetable and seed oils.

omega-9 fatty acid, a polyunsaturated fatty acid found in animal and vegetable fats.

omega-oxidation, a metabolic pathway of fatty acid oxidation involving the carbon atom farthest removed from the original carboxyl group.

omental appendix, a peritoneal accumulation of fat associated with the colon.

omental bursa, a cavity in the peritoneum behind the stomach, the lesser omentum, and the lower border of the liver and in front of the pancreas and duodenum.

omental foramen, a restricted opening connecting the two sacs of the peritoneum.

omentectomy /ō'mentek'təmē/, the surgical excision of a portion of the omentum or the complete omentum.

omentum /ōmen'təm/ *pl.* **omenta, omentums** [L, membrane of the bowels], an extension of the peritoneum that enfolds one or more organs adjacent to the stomach.—**omental,** *adj.*

omicron /ōm'ikron/, O, o, the 15th letter of the Greek alphabet.

omission /ōmish'ən/ [L, *omittere,* to neglect], in law, intentional or unintentional neglect to fulfill a duty required by law.

Ommaya reservoir, a device placed under the scalp and used to deliver anticancer drugs to the CSF.

omnifocal lens /om'nēfō'kəl/ [L, *omnis,* all, *focus,* hearth + *lentil*], an eyeglass lens designed for both near and far vision with the reading part in a variable curve.

Omnipen, a trademark for an antibacterial (ampicillin).

omnipotence /omnip'ətəns/, in psychology, an infantile perception that the outside world is part of the organism and within it, which leads to a primitive feeling of all-powerfulness.

omnivorous /omniv'ərəs/ [L, *omnis,* all, *vorare,* to devour], eating both plants and animals.

omn. noct., abbreviation for the Latin term *omni nocte,* "every night."

omn. quad. hor., abbreviation for the Latin term *omni quadrante hora,* "every quarter of an hour."

omohyoid, a muscle that depresses and fixes the hyoid bone.

omophagia /om'ōfā'jē·ə/ [Gk, *ōmos,* raw, *phagein,* to eat], the eating of raw foods, particularly raw meat or fish.

omphalic /omfal'ik/ [Gk, *omphalos,* navel], pertaining to the umbilicus.

omphalitis /om'fəlī'tis/, an inflammation of the umbilical stump marked by redness, swelling, and purulent exudate in severe cases. This condition is rare in developed countries.

omphalocele /om'fəlōsēl'/ [Gk, *omphalos* + *kele,* hernia], congenital herniation of intraabdominal viscera through a defect in the abdominal wall around the umbilicus.

omphalogenesis /-jen'əsis/ [Gk, *omphalos* + *genesis,* origin], the formation of the umbilicus or yolk sac during embryonic development.—**omphalogenetic,** *adj.*

omphalomesenteric fistula, an abnormal passageway between the umbilicus and the terminal ileum, formed by persistence of the intraembryonic part of the yolk stalk.

omphalosite /om'falōsīt'/ [Gk, *omphalos* + *sitos,* food], the underdeveloped parasitic member of unequal conjoined twins united by the vessels of the umbilical cord.

OMS, abbreviation for *Organisation Mondiale de la Santé.*

Omsk hemorrhagic fever (OHF) /ômsk/, an acute infection seen in regions of the former U.S.S.R., caused by a flavivirus transmitted by the bite of an infected tick or by handling infected muskrats. It is characterized by fever, headache, epistaxis, GI and uterine bleeding, and other hemorrhagic manifestations.

o.n., abbreviation for the Latin term *omni nocte,* "every night."

onanism /ō'nəniz'əm/, coitus interruptus; withdrawal of the penis just before ejaculation during sexual intercourse.

Oncaspar, a trademark for an oncolytic agent (pegaspargase).

Onchocerca /ong'kōsər'kə/ [Gk, *onkos,* tumor, *kerkos,* tail], a genus of nematode parasites of the superfamily Filarioidea that infect humans and ruminants. The adults live and breed in subcutaneous fibroid nodules. The young (the microfilariae) are carried by the lymph and are found chiefly in the skin, subcutaneous connective tissues, and eyes. It is the cause of human onchocerciasis and is transmitted by the bites of buffalo gnats.

onchocerciasis /ong'kōsərkī'əsis, sī'əsis/ [Gk, *onkos,* swelling, *kerkos,* tail, *osis,* condition], a form of filariasis common in Central and South America and Africa, characterized by subcutaneous nodules, pruritic rash, and eye lesions.

oncofetal protein /-fē'təl/ [Gk, *onkos;* L, *fetus,* pregnant; Gk, *proteios,* first rank], a protein normally produced by fetal tissue and also by cancerous tissues in adult life.

oncogene /ong'kōjēn/ [Gk, *onkos* + *genein,* to produce], a potentially cancer-inducing gene. Under normal conditions such genes play a role in the growth and proliferation of cells, but, when altered in some way by a cancer-causing agent such as radiation, a carcinogenic chemical, or an oncogenic virus, they may cause the cell to be transformed to a malignant state.

oncogenesis /ong'kōjen'əsis/ [Gk, *onkos* + *genesis,* origin], the process initiating and promoting the development of a neoplasm through the action of biologic, chemical, or physical agents.

oncogenic /ong'kōjen'ik/ [Gk, *onkos,* swelling, *genein,* to produce], pertaining to the origin and development of tumors or cancer.

oncogenic viruses, an epidemiologic class of viruses that are acquired by close contact or injection and cause usually persistent infection. They may induce cell transformation and malignancy.

oncogenous osteomalacia /ongkoj'ənəs/, a bone disorder caused by mesenchymal tumors. Patients may have normal-to-low serum calcium levels, a low serum phosphorus level, and an elevated serum alkaline phosphatase level.

oncologic emergencies /ong'kōloj'ik/, cancer-related disorders that require emergency medical or surgical care. An example is superior vena cava syndrome.

oncologist /ongkol'əjist/, a physician who specializes in the study and treatment of neoplastic diseases, particularly cancer.

oncology /ongkol'əjē/ [Gk, *onkos,* swelling, *logos,* science], **1.** the branch of medicine concerned with the study of malignancy. **2.** the study of cancerous growths.

Oncology Nursing Society (ONS), an organization of nurses interested or specializing in cancer patient nursing.

oncolysis /ongkol'isis/, **1.** the destruction or disposal of neoplastic cells. **2.** the reduction of a swelling or mass.

oncolytic /ong'kōlit'ik/, pertaining to the destruction of tumor cells.

oncoscint scan, a nuclear scan used to detect recurrent metastatic colorectal or ovarian cancer.

oncotic /ongkot'ik/ [Gk, *onkos,* a swelling], pertaining to or resulting from the presence of a swelling.

oncotic pressure [Gk, *onkos,* a swelling; L, *premere,* to press], the osmotic pressure of a colloid in solution, such as when there is a higher concentration of protein in the plasma on one side of a cell membrane than in the neighboring interstitial fluid.

oncotic pressure gradient, the difference between the osmotic pressure of blood and that of tissue fluid or lymph. It is an important force in maintaining fluid balance between the vascular space and the interstitium.

Oncovin, a trademark for an antineoplastic (vinCRIStine sulfate).

Oncovirinae /ong'kōvir'inē/, a subfamily of RNA viruses, including types A, B, C, and D genera of oncoviruses. They are classified on the basis of morphology and type of host.

oncovirus /ong'kōvī'rəs/ [Gk, *onkos;* L, *virus,* poison], a member of a family of viruses associated with leukemia and sarcoma in animals and, possibly, in humans.

Ondine's curse /ondēnz'/ [L, *Undine,* mythic water nymph; ME, *curs,* invocation], apnea caused by loss of automatic control of respiration. The term refers to a syndrome in patients with a defect in central chemoreceptor responsiveness to carbon dioxide. The patient is able to breathe voluntarily but has hypercapnia and hypoxemia.

one-and-a-half spica cast, an orthopedic cast that covers the trunk cranially to the nipple line, one leg caudally as far as the toes, and the other leg caudally as far as the knee. For stability, a diagonal crossbar connects the parts of the cast encasing the legs.

one gene/one enzyme hypothesis, a general rule, proposed in 1941 by G. Beadle and E. Tatum, that each gene in a chromosome controls the synthesis of one enzyme. A modification of this idea, the one gene/one polypeptide hypothesis, accommodates the fact that all gene products are polypeptides but not all polypeptides are enzymes. A further modification, the one cistron/one polypeptide concept, accommodates alternate splicing and alternative promoter sequences.

one gene/one polypeptide, a principle that each gene in a chromosome determines a particular polypeptide. An exception allows many genes to specify only functional RNA.

one-to-one care, a method of organizing nursing services in an inpatient care unit by which one registered nurse assumes responsibility for all nursing care provided one patient for the duration of one shift.

one-to-one relationship, a mutually defined, collaborative goal-directed client-therapist relationship for the purpose of psychotherapy.

one-way speaking valve, a valve, placed on the end of a tracheostomy tube, that opens during inhalation and closes during exhalation, so that the exhaled air is directed through the vocal cords and out the mouth and nose, allowing a person who has had a tracheostomy to speak.

onlay [AS, *ana,* up, *licagan,* to lie], **1.** a cast type of metal restoration retained by friction and mechanical forces in a prepared tooth, used for restoring one or more of the tooth's cusps and adjoining occlusal surfaces. **2.** an occlusal rest part of a removable partial denture, extended to cover the entire occlusal surface of a tooth.

onlay graft, a bone graft in which the transplanted tissue is laid directly onto the surface of the recipient bone.

online, access to information directly connected with and accessible to a computer.

on/off phenomenon, a periodic loss of the efficacy of levodopa in the treatment of Parkinson's disease, without obvious relationship to the timing of levodopa administration.

ONS, abbreviation for **Oncology Nursing Society.**

onset of action, the time required after administration of a drug for a response to be observed.

ontogenetic /on'tōjənet'ik/, **1.** of, relating to, or acquired during ontogeny. **2.** describing an association based on visible morphologic characteristics and not necessarily indicative of a natural evolutionary relationship.

ontogeny /ontoj'ənē/ [Gk, *ontos,* being, *genein,* to produce], the development of one organism from a single-celled ovum to the time of birth, including all phases of differentiation and growth.

onychia /ōnĭk′ē·ə/ [Gk, *onyx,* nail], inflammation of the nailbed.

onychodystrophy [Gk, *onyx,* nail, *dys,* bad, *trophe,* nourishment], a condition of malformed or discolored fingernails or toenails.

onychogryphosis /on′ikōgrifō′sis/ [Gk, *onyx* + *gryphein,* to curve, *osis,* condition], thickened, curved, clawlike overgrowth of fingernails or toenails.

onycholysis /on′ikol′isis/ [Gk, *onyx* + *lysein,* to loosen], separation of a nail from its bed, beginning at the free margin, associated with psoriasis, dermatitis of the hand, fungal infection, *Pseudomonas* infection, and many other conditions.

onychomycosis /on′ikō′mīkō′sis/ [Gk, *onyx* + *mykes,* fungus, *osis,* condition], any fungal infection of the nails.

onychosis [Gk, *onyx,* nail, *osis,* condition], a condition of atrophy or dystrophy of the nails, usually caused by a dermatosis such as a fungal infection.

onychotillomania /on′ikōtil′əmā′nē·ə/ [Gk, *onyx,* nail, *tillein,* to pluck, *mania,* madness], a nervous habit of picking at the nails to the point of tissue damage (i.e., bleeding).

onychotomy /on′ikot′əmē/, a surgical incision into a nailbed.

oob, abbreviation for *out of bed.*

oobe, abbreviation for **out-of-body experience.**

ooblast /ō′əblast/ [Gk, *oon,* egg, *blastos,* germ], a female germ cell from which a mature ovum is developed.

oocyesis /ō′əsī·ē′sis/ [Gk, *oon* + *kyesis,* pregnancy], an ectopic ovarian pregnancy.

oocyst /ō′əsist/ [Gk, *oon* + *kystis,* bag], a stage in the development of sporozoa consisting of a zygote enclosed by cyst wall.

oocyte /ō′əsīt/ [Gk, *oon* + *kytos,* cell], a primordial or incompletely developed ovum.

oocyte donation, a method of assisted reproductive technology in which an oocyte from a fertile woman is aspirated for incubation in the uterus of a woman who has female factor infertility, such as after oophorectomy or premature menopause.

oocytin /ō′əsī′tin/, the substance in a spermatozoon that stimulates the formation of the fertilization membrane after penetration of an ovum.

oogamy /ō·og′əmē/ [Gk, *oon* + *gamos,* marriage], **1.** sexual reproduction by the fertilization of a large nonmotile female gamete by a smaller, actively motile male gamete, such as occurs in certain algae and the malarial parasite *Plasmodium.* **2.** heterogamy.—**oogamous,** *adj.*

oogenesis /ō′əjen′əsis/ [Gk, *oon* + *genesis,* origin], the formation of the female gametes, or ova.—**oogenetic,** *adj.*

oogonium /ō′əgō′nē·əm/ *pl.* **oogonia** [Gk, *oon* + *gonos,* offspring], the precursor cell from which an oocyte develops in the fetus during intrauterine life.

ookinesis /ō′əkinē′sis/ [Gk, *oon* + *kinesis,* movement], the chromsomal movement occurring in the nucleus of the egg cell during maturation and fertilization. —**ookinetic,** *adj.*

ookinete /ō′əkinēt′/ [Gk, *oon* + *kinein,* to move], the motile elongated zygote that is formed by the fertilization of the macrogamete during the sexual reproductive phase of the life cycle of a sporozoan, specifically the malarial parasite *Plasmodium.*

oophoralgia /ō′əfôral′jə/ [Gk, *oophoron,* ovary, *algos,* pain], a pain in an ovary.

oophorectomy /ō′əfôrek′təmē/ [Gk, *oophoron,* ovary, *ektomē,* excision], the surgical removal of one or both ovaries. It is performed to remove a cyst or tumor, excise an abscess, treat endometriosis, or in breast cancer to remove the source of estrogen, which stimulates some types of cancer. In premenopausal women, one ovary or a part of one ovary may be left intact unless a malignancy is present. The operation routinely accompanies a hysterectomy in menopausal or postmenopausal women.

oophoritis /ō′əferī′tis/, an inflammatory condition of one or both ovaries, usually occurring with salpingitis or another infection.

oophorosalpingectomy /ō′əfôr′əsal′pinjek′təmē/ [Gk, *oophoron* + *salpinx,* tube, *ektomē,* excision], the surgical removal of one or both ovaries and the corresponding fallopian tubes, performed to remove a cyst or tumor, excise an abscess, or treat endometriosis.

oophorosalpingitis /ō′əfôr′əsal′pinjī′tis/ [Gk, *oophoron,* ovary, *salpinx,* tube, *itis,* inflammation], an inflammation involving both the ovary and the fallopian tube.

ooplasm /ō′əplaz′əm/ [Gk, *oon* + *plasma,* something formed], the cytoplasm of the egg, or ovum, including the yolk in lower animals.

oosperm /ō′əspurm/ [Gk, *oon* + *sperma,* seed], a fertilized ovum; the cell resulting from the union of the pronuclei of the spermatozoon and the ovum after fertilization; a zygote.

ootid /ō′ətid/ [Gk, *ootidion,* small egg], the nearly mature ovum after penetration by the spermatozoon and completion of the second meiotic division but before the fusion of the pronuclei to form the zygote.

OP, **1.** abbreviation for *operative procedure.* **2.** abbreviation for **outpatient.**

opacity /ōpas′itē/ [L, *opacitus*, shadiness], pertaining to an opaque quality of a substance or object, such as cataract opacity.

opalescent /ō′pəl·es′ənt/, showing a milky iridescence, like an opal.

opal mutation, a genetic alteration that causes the synthesis of a polypeptide chain to terminate prematurely because of the triplet of nucleotides that normally codes for the next amino acid in the chain becomes uracil-adenine-guanine, the sequence that signals the end of the chain. It is one of the three possible nonsense mutations.

opaque /ōpāk′/ [L, *opacus*, obscure], **1.** pertaining to a substance or surface that neither transmits nor allows the passage of light. **2.** neither transparent nor translucent.

OPD, abbreviation for *Outpatient Department.*

open amputation [AS, *offan*, open; L, *amputare*, to cut away], a kind of amputation in which a straight, guillotine cut is made without skin flaps. Open amputation is performed if an infection is probable, developing, or recurrent.

open bite, an abnormal dental condition in which the anterior teeth in the maxilla do not occlude those in the mandible in any mandibular position.

open-cavity tympanomastoidectomy, tympanomastoidectomy with removal of the posterior wall of the ear canal, such as radical mastoidectomy and modified radical mastoidectomy.

open-chain exercise, exercise in which the distal aspect of the extremity is free in space and not in contact with the ground.

open charting, a system of medical record keeping in which the patient has access to his or her chart.

open circuit, an electric circuit in which current flow ceases.

open-circuit breathing system, a breathing apparatus used in cardiopulmonary therapy in which rebreathing does not occur. Gas is inspired through a breathing branch or limb that is connected to a gas source or open to the ambient atmosphere. Expired gas flows through a directional valve into a collecting reservoir or into the ambient atmosphere.

open dislocation, a joint displacement accompanied by a break in the skin.

open-drop anesthesia, the oldest and simplest anesthetic technique. It is no longer used in the United States. A volatile liquid anesthetic agent such as ether is dripped, one drop at a time, onto a porous cloth or mask held over the patient's face. It is difficult to control the anesthetic depth and pollution of the OR.

open-enrollment period, a time during which individuals can enroll in a health care plan.

open fracture grading system, a system for dividing open fractures into five categories, ranging from a clean wound that communicates to the fracture site and measures less than 1 cm to a fracture requiring repair of arteries.

open heart surgery, any heart surgery in which the chest is opened, including minimally invasive surgery.

opening abductory wedge osteotomy (OAWO), a procedure for treating a bunion deformity, in which a bone graft is used to open the wedge cut into the bone and bring the first metatarsal closer to the second.

opening of ileocecal valve, the slitlike or oval orifice in the ileocecal valve, seen in the cadaver. It has two flaps or lips, one above and one below, that form the valve and project at thickened folds into the lumen of the large intestine. In the living individual this structure is the ostium ileale.

opening pressure, the amount of pressure measured in a manometer after insertion of a spinal needle into the subarachnoid space.

opening wedge osteotomy, a procedure for treating bunion deformity in which a proximal cut is made in the metatarsal to reduce the deformity. It is performed with or without tendon transfers.

open magnetic resonance imaging (open MRI), a procedure that allows visualization of soft-tissue structures of the body. Because the patient is not enclosed within the magnetic resonance unit, claustrophobic reactions do not occur with open MRI, but the scan does take substantially longer to complete.

open medical staff, in managed care, the opening of hospital medical staff membership to all physicians in the community who meet membership and clinical privilege requirements.

open MRI, abbreviation for **open magnetic resonance imaging.**

open operation, a surgical procedure that provides a full view of the structures or organs involved through membranous or cutaneous incisions.

open-panel HMO, a health maintenance organization (HMO) in which physicians treat both HMO and private patients.

open PHO, a physician-hospital organization in which all physicians on the hospital medical staff can participate.

open pneumothorax [AS, *open*; Gk, *pneuma*, air, *thorax*, chest], the presence of air or gas in the chest as a result of an open wound in the chest wall.

open reduction [AS, *open*; L, *reducere*, to lead back], a surgical procedure for reducing a fracture or dislocation by exposing the skeletal parts involved.

open system, a system that interacts with its environment.

open-wedge osteotomy, a straight cut made across a bone, leaving a wedge-shaped gap in the bone.

open wound [AS, *open* + *wund*], a wound that disrupts the integrity of the skin.

operable /op′ərəbəl/ [L, *operare,* to work], amenable to surgical intervention.

operant /op′ərənt/ [L, *operare,* to work], any act or response occurring without an identifiable stimulus.

operant conditioning, a form of learning used in behavior therapy in which the person undergoing therapy is rewarded for the correct response and punished for the incorrect response.

operant level, the frequency or form of a performance under baseline conditions before any systematic conditioning procedures are introduced.

operating field, an isolated area in which surgery is performed.

operating microscope /op′ərā′ting/ [L, *operare*; Gk, *mikros,* small, *skopein,* to look], a binocular microscope used in delicate surgery, especially surgery of the eye or ear. The standing type of operating microscope has a motorized zoom system operated by a foot pedal that quickly changes the magnification. The operating microscope that attaches to a surgeon's head has interchangeable lenses for different magnifications.

operating room (OR, O.R.), **1.** a room in a health care facility in which surgical procedures requiring anesthesia are performed. **2.** *informal.* a suite of rooms or an area in a health care facility in which patients are prepared for and undergo surgery.

operating telescope, a magnifying lens that gives low magnification and a wide field of vision.

operation /op′ərā′shən/, any surgical procedure.

operationalization of behavior /op′ərā′sh ənəlīzā′shən/, in psychology, the stating of a patient's complaints or problems in specific, observable behavioral terms.

operative cholangiography /op′ərətiv′/ [L, *operare*; Gk, *chole,* bile, *angeion,* vessel, *graphein,* to record], a procedure for radiographically outlining the major bile ducts during surgery by injecting radiopaque contrast medium directly into the ducts.

operative dentistry, the phase of dentistry concerned with restoration of parts of the teeth that are defective through disease, trauma, or abnormal development to a state of normal function, health, and esthetics, including preventive, diagnostic, biologic, mechanical, and therapeutic techniques, as well as material and instrument science and application.

operator gene /op′ərā′tər/ [L, *operare*; Gk, *genein,* to produce], a section of bacterial DNA that regulates the transcription of structural genes in an operon by interacting with a repressor protein.

operatory /op′ərətor′ē/ [L, *operare,* to work], the dental surgical working area of a dental office, in which treatment is provided to patients.

operculum /ōpur′kyŏŏləm/ *pl.* **opercula, operculums** [L, lid], a lid or covering such as the mucus plug that blocks the cervix of the gravid uterus.—**opercular,** *adj.*

operon /op′əron/ [L, *operare,* to work], a section of bacterial DNA consisting of an operator gene and one or more structural genes with related functions. Transcription of the structural genes is controlled by the operator gene in conjunction with a regulator gene.

ophth, abbreviation for **ophthalmology.**

ophthalmia /ofthal′mē·ə/ [Gk, *ophthalmos,* eye], severe inflammation of the conjunctiva or the deeper parts of the eye.

ophthalmia neonatorum /nē′ōnətôr′əm/, a purulent conjunctivitis and keratitis of the newborn resulting from exposure of the eyes to chemical, chlamydial, bacterial, or viral agents. Chemical conjunctivitis usually occurs as a result of the instillation of silver nitrate in the eyes of a newborn to prevent a gonococcal infection.

ophthalmic /ofthal′mik/ [Gk, *ophthalmos,* eye], pertaining to the eye.

ophthalmic administration of medication, the administration of a drug by instillation of a cream, an ointment, or a liquid drop preparation in the conjunctival sac.

ophthalmic dispensing optician, an allied health professional who adapts and fits corrective eyewear, including eyeglasses and contact lenses, as prescribed by an ophthalmologist or optometrist.

ophthalmic laboratory technician, a person who, working from a prescription written by an ophthalmologist or optometrist, cuts, grinds, edges, and finishes lenses and fabricates eyewear.

ophthalmic medical technician, an allied health professional who assists ophthalmologists by collecting data and administering treatment ordered by the ophthalmologist. These specialists are qualified to take medical histories; administer diagnostic tests; make anatomic and functional ocular measurements; test ocular functions, including visual acuity, visual fields, and sensorimotor functions; administer topical ophthalmic medications; and instruct the patient in home care and the use of contact lenses. Ophthalmic medical technologists perform all duties performed by technicians but are expected to do so at a higher level of expertise.

ophthalmic nerve [Gk, *ophthalmos*, eye; L, *nervus*, nerve], the first division of the trigeminal nerve (CN V), supplying sensory innervation to the forehead, scalp, lacrimal gland, eye, and side of the nose.

ophthalmic solution, a specially prepared sterile preparation free of foreign particles for instillation of a medication into the eye.

ophthalmic vein, one of two venous channels in the orbit, the superior ophthalmic vein and the inferior ophthalmic vein, that communicate with the cavernous sinus. This communication can be a route by which infections spread from outside to inside the cranial cavity.

ophthalmitis /of'thalmī'tis/ [Gk, *ophthalmos*, eye, *itis*, inflammation], an inflammation of the eye.

ophthalmodynamometer /-din'əmom'ətər/ [Gk, *ophthalmos*, eye, *dynamis*, force, *metron*, measure], an instrument for measuring pressure on the sclera while the fundus is studied with an ophthalmoscope. It may be used to measure BPs in the ophthalmic artery.

ophthalmodynia /-din'ē·ə/ [Gk, *ophthalmos*, eye, *odyne*, pain], a pain in the eye.

ophthalmologist /of'thalmol'əjist/, a physician who specializes in ophthalmology.

ophthalmology (ophth) /of'thalmol'əjē/ [Gk, *ophthalmos* + *logos*, science], the branch of medicine concerned with the study of the physiology, anatomy, and pathology of the eye and the diagnosis and treatment of disorders of the eye. —**ophthalmologic, ophthalmological,** *adj.*

ophthalmopathy /of'thalmop'ə·thē/ [Gk, *ophthalmos*, eye, *pathos*, disease], any disease of the eye.

ophthalmoplasty /ofthal'mōplas'tē/ [Gk, *ophthalmos*, eye, *plassein*, to mold], plastic surgery of the eye or the area around the eye.

ophthalmoplegia /ofthal'məplē'jē·ə/ [Gk, *ophthalmos* + *plege*, stroke], an abnormal condition characterized by paralysis of the motor nerves of the eye. Bilateral ophthalmoplegia of rapid onset is associated with acute myasthenia gravis, acute thiamin deficiency, botulism, and acute inflammatory cranial polyneuropathy.

ophthalmoscope /ofthal'məskōp/ [Gk, *ophthalmos* + *skopein*, to look], a device for examining the interior of the eye. It includes a light, a mirror with a single aperture through which the examiner views, and a dial holding several lenses of varying strengths.

ophthalmoscopy /of'thalmos'kəpē/, the technique of using an ophthalmoscope to examine the eye.

ophthalmospasm /ofthal'mōspaz'əm/ [Gk, *ophthalmos*, eye + *spasmos*], a sudden involuntary contraction of the eyeball.

opiate /ō'pē·it/ [Gk, *opion*, poppy juice], **1.** a drug that contains opium, derivatives of opium, or any of several semisynthetic or synthetic drugs with opium-like activity. **2.** *informal.* any soporific or opioid drug. **3.** pertaining to a substance that causes sleep or relief of pain. Morphine and related opiates may produce unwanted side effects such as respiratory depression, nausea, vomiting, dizziness, and constipation.

opiate poisoning [Gk, *opion*, poppy juice; L, *potio*, drink], toxic effects of a potent opioid, including depression of the brain centers, causing unconsciousness and a failure to breathe. Acute intoxication is characterized by euphoria, flushing, itching, and constriction of pupils, followed by reduced rate of respiration, hypotension, lowered body temperature, and abnormally slow heartbeat.

opiate receptor [Gk, *opion*, poppy juice; L, *recipere*, to receive], transmembrane proteins that bind to endogenous opioid neuropeptides and exogenous morphine and similar natural or synthetic compounds. The receptors are found in high concentrations in the dorsal horn of the spinal cord and in the brain regions involved with pain modulation or pain transmission (e.g., periaqueductal gray matter). Endogenous agonists at these receptors include endorphins, enkephalins, and dynorphins.

opinion /əpin'yən/ [L, *opinari*, to suppose], **1.** in law, a statement by the court, usually in writing, of the reasoning behind its decision or judgment in a particular case. **2.** a statement prepared for a client by an attorney that represents the attorney's understanding of the law as it pertains to a legal question posed by the client.

opioid /ō'pē·oid/ [Gk, *opion*, poppy juice, *eidos*, form], strictly speaking, pertaining to natural and synthetic chemicals that have opium-like effects similar to morphine though they are not derived from opium. Examples include endorphins or enkephalins produced by body tissues or synthetic methadone. Morphine and related drugs are often included in this category because the term narcotic has lost its original meaning.

opioid antagonist, a drug used primarily in the treatment of opioid-induced mureceptor–mediated respiratory depression. The opioid antagonist naloxone is administered parenterally, whereas naltrexone is administered orally.

opioid receptor, any of a number of types of receptors for opiates and opioids; at least seven different types are postulated at different locations in the body, grouped into three major classes (δ, κ, and μ) according

O

to the specific substances they bind to and to the specific physiologic effect or effects that binding causes or inhibits.

opisthion /ō·pis'thē·on/ [Gk, *opisthion*, rear, posterior], a landmark located at the midpoint of the posterior border of the foramen magnum.

opisthorchiasis /ō'pisthôrkī'əsis/ [Gk, *opisthen*, behind, *orchis*, testicle, *osis*, condition], infection with one of the species of *Opisthorchis* liver flukes.

opisthotonos /ō'pisthot'ənəs/ [Gk, *opisthios*, posterior, *tonos*, straining], a prolonged severe spasm of the muscles causing the back to arch acutely, the head to bend back on the neck, the heels to bend back on the legs, and the arms and hands to flex rigidly at the joints. It is related to meningitis.

opium /ō'pē·əm/ [Gk, *opion*, poppy juice], a milky exudate from the unripe capsules of *Papaver somniferum* and *Papaver album* yielding 9.5% or more of anhydrous morphine. It is an opioid analgesic, a hypnotic, and an astringent.

opium alkaloid, one of several alkaloids isolated from the milky exudate of the unripe seed pods of *Papaver somniferum*. Two of the alkaloids, codeine and morphine, are used clinically for the relief of pain, but their use entails the risk of physical or psychologic dependence. Morphine is the standard against which the analgesic effect of newer drugs for relief of pain is measured. The opium alkaloids and their semisynthetic derivatives, including heroin, act on the CNS, producing analgesia, change in mood, drowsiness, and mental slowness. In usual doses the analgesic effects are achieved without LOC.

opium tincture, an analgesic and antidiarrheal prescribed in the treatment of intestinal hyperactivity, cramping, and diarrhea.

Oppenheim reflex /op'ənhīm/ [Herman Oppenheim, German neurologist, 1858–1919], a variation of Babinski's reflex, elicited by firmly stroking downward on the anterior and medial surfaces of the tibia, characterized by extension of the great toe and fanning of other toes. It is a sign of pyramidal tract disease.

opponens digiti minimi, a muscle that originates from the hook of the hamate and from the adjacent flexor retinaculum and inserts into the medial margin and palmar surface of the fifth metacarpal, rotating it toward the palm.

opponens pollicis, the largest of the three thenar muscles. It rotates and flexes the first metacarpal on the trapezium, so bringing the pad of the thumb into a position facing the pads of the fingers.

opportunistic infection [L, *opportunus*, convenient, *icus*, form], **1.** an infection caused by normally nonpathogenic organisms in a host whose resistance has been decreased by disorders such as DM, HIV infection, or cancer; a surgical procedure such as a CSF shunt or a cardiac or urinary tract catheterization; or immunosuppressive drugs. Long-term use of antibiotics or other drugs may also affect the immune system. **2.** an unusual infection with a common pathogen such as cellulitis, meningitis, or otitis media.

opportunistic pathogen, an organism that exists harmlessly as part of the normal human body environment and does not become a health threat until the body's immune system fails.

opposition [L, *opponere*, to oppose], the relation between the thumb and the other digits of the hand for the purpose of grasping objects between the thumb and fingers.

oprelvekin /ō·prel've·kin/, recombinant interleukin-11, used as a stimulator of hematopoiesis to prevent thrombocytopenia after myelosuppressive chemotherapy.

opscan, abbreviation for *optical scanning*.

opsin, a protein that combines with retinal to form visual pigments (rhodopsin and iodopsin) in the photoreceptor cells of the retina.

opsonin /op'sənin/ [Gk, *opsonein*, to supply food], an antibody or complement split product that, on attaching to foreign material, microorganisms, or other antigens, enhances phagocytosis of that substance by leukocytes and other macrophages.—**opsonize,** *v.*

opsonization /op'sənizā'shən/ [Gk, *opsonein* + *izein*, to cause], the action of opsonin.

optic [Gk, *optikos*, sight], pertaining to the eyes or to sight.

optic activity /op'tik/, the rotation of the plane of polarized light clockwise or counterclockwise. Substances that rotate the plane of polarized light to the right are dextrorotatory; those that rotate the plane to the left are levorotatory.

optical biopsy, any technique that uses the interaction of light and tissue to provide information about the tissue.

optically stimulated luminescence dosimeter (OSL dosimeter), a personal radiation monitoring device similar to the thermoluminescence dosimeter but using aluminum oxide to absorb the energy of x-rays and a laser rather than heat to release the stored energy and measure the dose of ionizing radiation received.

optic atrophy, wasting of the optic disc resulting from degeneration of fibers of the optic nerve and optic tract. Optic atrophy may be caused by a congenital defect, inflammation, occlusion of the central retinal artery or internal carotid artery, alcohol, arsenic, lead, tobacco, or other toxic substances. Degeneration of the disc may accompany arteriosclerosis, diabetes, glaucoma, hydrocephalus, pernicious anemia, and various neurologic disorders.

optic brightener, a compound that absorbs ultraviolet light and emits visible light.

optic chiasm [Gk, *optikos,* sight, *chiasma,* crossed lines], a point near the thalamus and hypothalamus where parts of each optic nerve cross over.

optic coupling, the attachment of the crystal window of a scintillator to the window of a photomultiplier tube. It maximizes the transmission of light from the scintillator to the interior of the photomultiplier tube.

optic cup, a two-layered embryonic cavity that develops in early pregnancy. The cells of the optic cup differentiate to form the retina that first develops its layers of rods and cones in the central part of the cup. The outer layer of the cup persists as the pigmented layer of the retina; the inner layer develops the nervous elements and the supporting fibers of the retina.

optic density, a number describing the blackening of an x-ray film in any specified location. In general, the optic density is the logarithm of the ratio of incident light intensity to the intensity of light transmitted through that area and is measured with a densitometer.

optic disc, the small blind spot on the surface of the retina, located about 3 mm to the nasal side of the macula. It is the point where the fibers of the retina leave the eye and become part of the optic nerve. It is the only part of the retina that is insensitive to light.

optic foramen [Gk, *optikos,* sight; L, *foramen,* hole], an aperture in the root of the lesser wing of the sphenoid bone transmitting the optic nerve.

optic glioma, a slow-growing tumor on the optic nerve or in the chiasm, composed of glial cells. Symptoms may include loss of vision, secondary strabismus, exophthalmos, and ocular paralysis.

optician /optish′ən/ [Gk, *optikos,* sight], a person who grinds and fits eyeglasses and contact lenses by prescription.

optic illusion [Gk, *optikos,* sight; L, *illudere,* to mock], a false visual image derived from a misinterpretation of sensory stimuli caused by physical or psychologic factors or both.

optic nerve, one of a pair of nerves that transmit visual impulses. It consists mainly of coarse myelinated fibers that arise in the retinal ganglionic layer, traverse the thalamus, and connect with the visual cortex. The visual cortex functions in the perception of light, shade, and objects. The optic nerve fibers correspond to a tract of fibers within the brain.

optic neuritis [Gk, *optikos,* sight, *neuron,* nerve, *itis,* inflammation], inflammation, degeneration, or demyelinization of an optic nerve caused by a wide variety of diseases. Loss of vision is the cardinal symptom.

optic neuropathy [Gk, *optikos,* sight, *neuron,* nerve, *pathos,* disease], a disease, generally noninflammatory, of the eye, characterized by dysfunction or destruction of the optic nerve tissues. Causes include an interruption in the blood supply, compression by a tumor or aneurysm, a nutritional deficiency, and toxic effects of a chemical. The disorder, which can lead to blindness, usually affects only one eye.

optic radiation [Gk, *optikos,* sight; L, *radiare,* to shine], a system of fibers from the lateral geniculate body of the thalamus that pass through the sublenticular part of the internal capsule to the striate area.

optic righting, one of the five basic neuromuscular reactions that enable a person to change body positions. It involves a reflex that automatically orients the head to a new optical or visual fixation point, depending on the body position change.

optic righting reflex [Gk, *optikos,* sight; AS, *riht;* L, *reflectere,* to bend back], a reflex that restores normal posture and head position with the help of visual clues.

optics /op′tiks/ [Gk, *optikos,* sight], **1.** in physics, a field of study that deals with the electromagnetic radiation of wavelengths shorter than radio waves but longer than x-rays. **2.** in physiology, a field of study that deals with vision and the process by which the functions of the eye and the brain are integrated in the perception of shapes, patterns, movements, spatial relationships, and color.

optic stalk, one of a pair of slender embryonic structures that become the optic nerve.

optic system assessment, an evaluation of the patient's eyes, vision, and current and past disorders or injuries that may be responsible for abnormalities in the individual's optic system.

optic thermometer, a temperature-measuring device in which the properties of transmission and reflection of visible light are temperature-dependent, the detection of which can be related to tissue temperature.

optic tract [Gk, *optikos,* sight; L, *tractus*], a flat band of nerve fibers running backward and laterally around each cerebral peduncle from the optic chiasma to the lateral geniculate body.

optic vesicle, an early embryonic outgrowth from the ventrolateral wall of the forebrain. Its cells develop into the retina and optic nerve of the eye.

Optimine, a trademark for an antihistamine (azatadine maleate).

optional water loss /op'shənəl/, a volume of average daily water loss, in addition to obligatory water loss, depending on physical activities, climate, and other factors.

optokinetic /op'tōkinet'ik/ [Gk, *optikos,* sight, *kinesis,* motion], pertaining to movement of the eyeballs in response to the movement of objects across the visual field, such as in optokinetic nystagmus.

optometric vision therapy, a treatment plan prescribed to correct or improve specific dysfunctions of the vision system. It includes, but is not limited to, the treatment of strabismus, other dysfunctions of binocularity, amblyopia, accommodation, ocular motor function, and visual-motor and visual-perceptual abilities.

optometric vision therapy technician (OVTT), an allied health professional, supervised by an optometrist, who participates in evaluating clients and in planning and implementing optometric vision therapy programs.

optometrist /optom'ətrist/ [Gk, *optikos,* sight, *metron,* measure], a person who practices optometry.

optometry /optom'ətrē/ [Gk, *optikos,* sight, *metron,* measure], the practice of primary eye care, including testing the eyes for visual acuity, prescribing corrective spectacles or contact lenses and topical medications, and managing binocular vision disorders.

OPV, abbreviation for **oral poliovirus vaccine.**

OR, O.R., abbreviation for **operating room.**

ora /ôr'ə/ *pl.* **orae** [L], an edge or margin.

oral /ôr'əl/ [L, *oralis,* the mouth], pertaining to the mouth.

oral administration of medication, the administration of a tablet, a capsule, an elixir, or a solution or other liquid form of medication by mouth.

oral airway, a curved tubular device of rubber, plastic, or metal placed in the oropharynx during general anesthesia and other situations in which the LOC is impaired. Its purpose is to maintain free passage of air and keep the tongue from obstructing the trachea.

oral and maxillofacial surgery [L, *oralis,* mouth; Gk, *cheirourgos,* surgeon], one of the nine recognized dental specialties. Oral and maxillofacial surgery is the specialty of dentistry which includes the diagnosis, surgical and adjunctive treatment of diseases, injuries, and defects involving both the functional and esthetic aspects

of the hard and soft tissues of the oral and maxillofacial region.

oral cancer, a malignant neoplasm on the lip or in the mouth that occurs at an average age of 60 with a frequency eight times higher in men than in women. Predisposing factors are alcoholism; heavy use of tobacco; poor oral hygiene; ill-fitting dentures; syphilis; Plummer-Vinson syndrome; betel nut chewing; and, in lip cancer, pipe smoking and overexposure to sun and wind. Premalignant leukoplakia or erythroplasia or a painless nonhealing ulcer may be the first sign of oral cancer; localized pain usually occurs later, but lymph nodes may be involved early in the course. Almost all oral tumors are epidermoid carcinomas.

oral cavity [L, *oralis,* pertaining to mouth, *cavum,* cavity], the space within the mouth, containing the tongue and teeth.

oral character, in psychoanalysis, a kind of personality that exhibits patterns of behavior originating in the oral and first phase of infancy. This personality is characterized by optimism, self-confidence, and carefree generosity reflecting the pleasurable aspects of the stage; or pessimism, futility, anxiety, and sadism as manifestations of frustrations or conflicts occurring during the period.

oral contraceptive (OC), oral hormone medication for contraception. The two major sex hormones in females are estrogens and progestins. When synthetic forms of these hormones are taken, they inhibit the production of gonadotropin-releasing hormone by the hypothalamus. The pituitary therefore does not secrete gonadotropins to stimulate follicular maturation and ovulation. Progestin-only oral contraceptives generally do not block ovulation. Instead they cause the cervical mucus to remain thick, which prevents the entry of sperm into the uterus and fallopian tubes. The pregnancy rate when oral contraceptives are used correctly is less than 0.2% a year.

oral decongestant, a drug such as pseudoephedrine prescribed for the relief of nasal congestion. Oral decongestants do not appear to cause nasal swelling after long periods of use. They are commonly combined with antihistamines for the treatment of allergic rhinitis.

oral dosage, the administration of a medicine by mouth.

oral eroticism, in psychoanalysis, a libidinal fixation or regression to the oral stage of psychosexual development.

oral examination [L, *oralis,* mouth, *examinatio,* weighing], a clinical, visual, and tactile inspection and investigation of the hard and soft structures of the oral cavity for purposes of assessment, diagnosis, planning, treatment, and evaluation.

oral-facial-digital (OFD) syndrome, type I, an X-linked dominant disorder lethal in males characterized by camptodactyly, polydactyly, and syndactyly; cranial, facial, lingual, and dental anomalies; and mental retardation, familial trembling, alopecia, and seborrhea of the face and milia.

oral-facial-digital (OFD) syndrome, type III, an autosomal-recessive disorder characterized by postaxial hexadactyly of the hands and feet; ocular, lingual, and dental anomalies; and profound mental retardation.

oral health maintenance, a nursing intervention from the Nursing Interventions Classification (NIC) defined as maintenance and promotion of oral hygiene and dental health for the patient at risk for developing oral or dental lesions.

oral health promotion, a nursing intervention from the Nursing Interventions Classification (NIC) defined as promotion of oral hygiene and dental care for a patient with normal oral and dental health.

oral health restoration, a nursing intervention from the Nursing Interventions Classification (NIC) defined as promotion of healing for a patient who has an oral mucosa or dental lesion.

oral hygiene[1], the condition or practice of maintaining the tissues and structures of the mouth. Oral hygiene includes brushing the tongue and teeth to remove food particles and residue, bacteria, and plaque; massaging the gums with a toothbrush, dental floss, or water irrigator to stimulate circulation and remove foreign matter; and cleansing dentures and ensuring their proper fit to prevent irritation.

oral hygiene[2], a nursing outcome from the Nursing Outcomes Classification (NOC) defined as the condition of the mouth, teeth, gums, and tongue.

oral hypoglycemic agent, an oral antidiabetic agent commonly used in the treatment of type 2 DM. Oral hypoglycemic agents are not prescribed as a substitute for diet and exercise but rather as adjunctive therapy.

oral mucosa, the mucous membrane of the cavity of the mouth, including the gums.

oral pathology, the branch of pathology that deals with the structural and functional changes in cells, tissues, and organs of the oral cavity that cause or are caused by disease.

oral poliovirus vaccine (OPV), an attenuated preparation of live poliovirus that confers immunity to poliomyelitis. Replaced by inactivated poliovirus vaccine, OPV supplies in the United States will be limited once existing supplies are depleted. It was routinely prescribed for immunization against poliomyelitis, but its use is now limited to treatment in areas with outbreaks of paralytic polio.

oral prophylaxis [L, *oralis,* mouth; Gk, *prophylax,* advance guard], the science and practice of preventing the onset of diseases of the teeth and adjoining mouth tissues. It involves removing bacterial plaque, food debris, stains, and calculus from the crowns and roots with hand scaling or ultrasonic scaling instruments and hand or electric polishers.

oral rehydration solutions (ORS) [L, *oralis,* mouth, *re + hydor,* water, *solutus,* dissolved], solutions of electrolytes and glucose used in oral rehydration therapy. The recommended electrolytes include NaCl, KCl, and trisodium citrate.

oral rehydration therapy (ORT), the adjustment of water, glucose, and electrolyte balance in a dehydrated patient by giving fluids with measured amounts of essential ingredients by mouth.

oral sadism, in psychoanalysis, a sadistic form of oral eroticism manifested by such behavior as biting, chewing, and other aggressive impulses associated with eating habits.

oral stage, in psychoanalysis, according to Freud, the initial stage of psychosexual development occurring in the first 12 to 18 months of life, when the feeding experience and other oral activities are the predominant source of pleasurable stimulation.

oral temperature [L, *oralis,* mouth, *temperatura*], the body temperature as recorded by a clinical thermometer placed in the mouth. It is normally around 98.6° F (37° C), but it may vary within a fraction of a degree, depending on the individual and such factors as time of day, sleep, and exercise and whether measured before or after a meal.

oral tolerance therapy, a treatment in which a patient ingests a foreign protein in an attempt to develop tolerance to that protein when it is encountered as an antigen. In addition to inhibiting allergic reactions, the therapy may suppress immune responses in general.

Orap, a trademark for an oral neuroleptic drug (pimozide).

ora serrata retinae, the irregular, serrated demarcation between the retina and the ciliary body. It is the most anterior peripheral part of the retina.

orb /ôrb/ [L, *orbis,* circle], describing something spheric or globelike.

orbicular /ôrbik′yələr/ [L, *orbiculus,* little circle], pertaining to something round.

orbicular bone [L, *orbiculus,* little circle; AS, *ban*], a knob on the end of the long process of the incus that articulates with the stapes.

O

orbicularis ciliaris /ôrbik'yŏōlär'is/ [L, *orbiculus,* little circle; *cilium,* eyelash], one of the two zones of the ciliary body of the eye, extending from the ora serrata of the retina to the ciliary processes at the margin of the iris.

orbicularis oculi, the muscular body of the eyelid, encircling the eye and comprising the palpebral, orbital, and lacrimal muscles. The palpebral muscle functions to close the eyelid gently; the orbital muscle functions to close it more energetically, such as in winking.

orbicularis oris, the muscle surrounding the mouth. It consists partly of fibers derived from other facial muscles such as the buccinator that are inserted into the lips and partly of fibers proper to the lips. It serves to close and purse the lips.

orbicularis pupillary reflex, a normal phenomenon elicited by forceful closure of the eyelids or attempting to close them while they are held apart, resulting first in constriction and then dilation of the pupil.

orbit /ôr'bit/ [L, *orbita,* wheel track], one of a pair of bony, conical cavities in the skull that accommodate the eyeballs and associated structures, such as the eye muscles, nerves, and blood vessels. **—orbital,** *adj.*

orbital aperture /ôr'bitəl/, an opening in the cranium to the orbit of the eye.

orbitale /ôrbitā'lē/ [L, *orbitalis,* pertaining to the orbit], an anthropometric landmark, the lowest point on the inferior margin of the orbit.

orbital fat, a semifluid adipose cushion that lines the bony orbit supporting the eye. Selective loss of fatty tissue caused by hormonal imbalances may produce "bulging" of the eye. Traumatic loss of the fat causes a sunken appearance of the eye.

orbital fissure [L, *orbita,* wheel track, *fissura,* cleft], the space between the floor and lateral wall of the orbit, serving as a conduit for nerves and blood vessels.

orbital myositis, an inflammation of the external ocular muscles. The process, which is generally autoimmune, may be associated with pain, forward displacement of the eyeball, and paralysis of the ocular muscles.

orbital pseudotumor, a specific inflammatory reaction of the orbital tissues of the eye, characterized by exophthalmos and edematous congestion of the eyelids.

orbitography /ôr'bitog'rəfē/, the radiographic examination of the bony cavity containing the eye.

orbitomeatal line /ôr'bitŏ'mē-ā'təl/ [L, *orbita,* wheel track, *meatus,* passage], a positioning line used in radiography of the skull that passes through the outer canthus of the eye and the center of the external auditory meatus.

orbitopathy /ôrbitop'əthē/ [L, *orbita,* wheel track; Gk, *pathos,* disease], disease affecting the orbit and its contents.

Orbivirus /ôr'bivī'rəs/ [L, *orbis,* ring], a genus of the Reoviridae family of viruses that contains double-stranded RNA. Insects are hosts for orbiviruses. Orbiviruses are primarily animal pathogens; only 7 out of 100 of these are linked to clinical human disease.

orchidectomy /ôr'kidek'təmē/ [Gk, *orchis,* testis, *ektomē,* excision], surgical removal of one or both testes. It may be indicated for serious disease or injury to the testis or to control cancer of the prostate by removing a source of androgenic hormones.

orchiopexy /ôr'kē-ōpek'sē/ [Gk, *orchis* + *pexis,* fixation], an operation to mobilize an undescended testis, bring it into the scrotum, and attach it so that it will not retract.

orchioplasty /ôr'kē-ōplas'tē/ [Gk, *orchis,* testis, *plassein,* to mold], a surgical procedure involving a testis.

orchitis /ôrkī'tis/ [Gk, *orchis* + *itis,* inflammation], inflammation of one or both of the testes, characterized by swelling and pain. The condition is often caused by mumps, syphilis, or TB.**—orchitic,** *adj.*

ordered pairs [L, *ordo,* series, *par,* equal], pertaining to graph coordinates in which the first number of the pair represents a distance along the x (horizontal) axis and the second number is plotted along the y (vertical) axis.

orderly /ôr'dərlē/, **1.** an attendant who assists in the care of hospital patients. **2.** in order; with regular arrangements, method, or system.**—orderliness,** *adj.*

order of procedure, the sequence in which the required steps are taken to complete an operation, such as preparation of the patient and preparation of the cavity and restoration of a tooth.

order transcription, a nursing intervention from the Nursing Interventions Classification (NIC) defined as transferring information from order sheets to the nursing patient care planning and documentation system.

Orem, Dorothea E. [1914-2007], author of the Self-Care Nursing Model, a nursing theory introduced in 1959. The Orem theory describes the role of the nurse in helping a person experiencing inabilities in self-care. The goal of the Orem system is to meet the patient's self-care demands until the family and/or patient is capable of providing care. The process is divided into three categories: universal, which consists of self-care to meet physiological and psychosocial needs; developmental, the self-care required when one goes through developmental stages; and health deviation, the self-care required when one has a deviation from a healthy status.

Orencia, a trademark for abatacept.

Oretic, a trademark for a diuretic (hydrochlorothiazide).

orexigenic /ŏrek′sijen′ik/ [Gk, *orexis*, longing, *genein*, to produce], a substance that increases or stimulates the appetite.

oreximania /ŏrek′simā′nē-ə/ [Gk, *orexis* + *mania*, madness], a condition characterized by a greatly increased appetite and excessive eating resulting from an unrealistic or exaggerated fear of becoming thin.

orexis/ŏrek′sis/ [Gk,longing], **1.** desire, appetite. **2.** the aspect of the mind involving feeling and striving as contrasted with the intellectual aspect.

orf [AS], a contagious viral skin disease acquired from infected sheep and goats, characterized by painless vesicles that may progress to red, weeping nodules and finally to crusting and healing.

Orfadin, a trademark for nitisinone.

organ [Gk, *organon,* instrument], a structural part of a system of the body that is composed of tissues and cells that enable it to perform a particular function, such as the liver or spleen.

organ albumin, albumin characteristic of a particular organ.

organelle /ôrgənel′/ [Gk, *organon,* instrument], **1.** any one of various specialized macromolecular structures bound within most cells, such as the mitochondria. **2.** any one of the tiny structures of protozoa associated with locomotion, metabolism, and other processes.

organic /ôrgan′ik/ [Gk, *organikos*], **1.** any chemical compound containing carbon other than simple metal carbonate, hydrogen carbonate, or cyanides. **2.** pertaining to an organ.

organic chemistry, the branch of chemistry concerned with the composition, properties, and reactions of chemical compounds containing carbon, specifically, the study of the hydrocarbons and their derivatives.

organic disease [Gk, *organikos*; L, *dis*; Fr, *aise,* ease], any disease associated with detectable or observable changes in one or more body organs.

organic dust, dried particles of plants, animals, fungi, or bacteria that are fine enough to be wind-borne.

organic dust toxic syndrome (ODTS), any nonallergic, noninfectious respiratory illness caused by inhalation of organic dust, as from moldy silage, hay, or other agricultural products. Symptoms include shaking chills or sweats, cough or shortness of breath, headache, anorexia, and myalgia.

organic evolution, the theory that all existing forms of animal and plant life have descended with modification from previous simpler forms or from a single cell; the origin and perpetuation of species.

organic foods, foods that have been produced and processed without the use of commercial chemicals such as fertilizers or pesticides or synthetic substances that enhance color or flavor.

organic headache, a headache caused by any of a wide variety of intracranial disorders, including sinus or ear infections, brain tumors, and subdural hematomas.

organic mental disorder (OMD), any of a *DSM-IV* class of psychiatric disorders characterized by progressive deterioration of the mental processes and caused by permanent brain damage or temporary brain dysfunction.

organic mental syndrome, former term for a constellation of psychologic or behavioral signs and symptoms associated with brain dysfunction of unknown or unspecified cause and grouped according to symptoms. Designating certain conditions as having an organic basis, possibly implying that others do not, is currently discouraged.

organic mood syndrome, a term used in a former system of classification, denoting an organic mental syndrome characterized by the presence of manic or depressive mood disturbance caused by a specific organic factor and not associated with delirium. Such disorders are now mainly classified as *substance-induced mood disorders* and *mood disorders due to a general medical condition.*

organic murmur, an abnormal cardiac sound caused by congenital or acquired heart disease.

organic personality syndrome, a term used in a former system of classification, denoting an organic mental syndrome characterized by a marked change in behavior or personality, caused by a specific organic factor and not associated with delirium or dementia. The most common causes are space-occupying lesions of the brain, head trauma, and cerebrovascular disease.

organic psychosis [Gk, *organikos* + *psyche*, mind, *osis*, condition], a condition characterized by a loss of contact with reality caused by an alteration in brain tissue function.

organic solvents, chemicals, such as benzene, that damage tissues by dissolving fats and oils. Exposure is mainly by inhalation but may also occur by ingestion or by skin or eye contact.

organic vertigo [Gk, *organikos*; L, *vertigo,* dizziness], vertigo that is associated with a CNS disorder such as cerebellar lesions or tabes dorsalis.

O

organification /ôrgan'ifikā'shən/, a process in the thyroid gland whereby iodide is oxidized and incorporated into tyrosyl residues (tyrosine) of thyroglobulin. Organification is catalyzed by the enzyme thyroid peroxidase.

organism /ôr'gəniz'əm/ [Gk, *organon,* instrument], an entity capable of carrying on life functions.

organization center /ôr'gənīzā'shən/ [Gk, *organon + izein,* to cause], a focal point within the developing embryo from which the organism grows and differentiates.

organizer /ôr'gənī'zər/ [Gk, *organon + izein,* to cause], in embryology, any part of the embryo that induces morphologic differentiation in some other part.

organoaxial volvulus, the more common of the two types of gastric volvulus, in which the stomach twists around its longitudinal axis.

organocarbamate insecticide poisoning /ôr'gənō-kär'bəmāt/, an adverse reaction to pesticides derived from esters of carbonic acid. Some of those insecticides are formulated in methyl alcohol, acquiring its added toxicity. The effects are similar to those of organophosphate insecticides, but the toxicity is less, and the duration of effects is shorter. The organocarbamate insecticides rarely produce overt CNS effects.

organochlorine insecticide poisoning /-klôr'ēn/, an adverse reaction to DDT-like pesticides such as chlordane and methoxychlor. Symptoms include CNS system disorders, convulsions, increased myocardial irritability, and depressed respiration.

organ of Corti [Gk, *organon;* Alfonso Corti, Italian anatomist, 1822–1888], the true organ of hearing, a spiral structure within the cochlea containing hair cells that are stimulated by sound vibrations. The hair cells convert the vibrations into nerve impulses that are transmitted by the cochlear part of the vestibulocochlear nerve to the brain.

organogenesis /-jen'əsis/ [Gk, *organon + genesis,* origin], in embryology, the formation and differentiation of organs and organ systems during embryonic development.—**organogenetic,** *adj.*

organoid /ôr'gənoid/ [Gk, *organon + eidos,* form], 1. resembling an organ. 2. any structure that resembles an organ in appearance or function, specifically an abnormal tumor mass.

organoid neoplasm, a growth that resembles a body organ.

organomegaly /-meg'əlē/ [Gk, *organon,* instrument, *megas,* large], abnormal enlargement of an organ, particularly an organ of the abdominal cavity.

organophosphate, any of a class of anticholinesterase chemicals used in certain pesticides and war gases. They act by causing irreversible inhibition of cholinesterase.

organophosphate insecticide poisoning /-fos'fāt/, an adverse reaction to organophosphate pesticides such as malathion, chlorothion, and nerve gas agents. Symptoms include nausea, vomiting, abdominal cramping, headache, blurred vision, and excessive salivation.

organophosphorus /ôr'ganō-fäs'fārus/, a compound containing phosphorus bound to an organic molecule. Some are used as insecticides and others are nerve gases; they are highly toxic acetylcholinesterase inhibitors.

organophosphorus compound poisoning, poisoning, often fatal, by excessive exposure to an organophosphorus compound. There are usually neurologic symptoms, such as axonopathy and paralysis.

organotherapy /-ther'əpē/ [Gk, *organon + therapeia,* treatment], the treatment of disease by administering animal endocrine glands or their extracts. Whole glands are no longer implanted, but substances derived from animal organs are widely used.—**organotherapeutic,** *adj.*

organotypic growth /ôr'gənōtip'ik/ [Gk, *organon + typos,* mark], the controlled reproduction of cells, such as that which occurs in the normal growth of tissues and organs.

organ procurement, a nursing intervention from the Nursing Interventions Classification (NIC) defined as guiding families through the donation process to ensure timely retrieval of vital organs and tissue for transplant.

organ specificity, a term describing a substance or activity that is identified with a specific organ, commonly applied to enzymes that function in particular organ systems.

orgasm /ôr'gasəm/ [Gk, *orgein,* to be lustful], the sexual climax, a series of strong involuntary contractions of the muscles of the genitalia, accompanied in males by ejaculation of semen, experienced as exceedingly pleasurable, set off by sexual excitation of critical intensity.—**orgasmic,** *adj.*

orgasmic maturity /ôrgas'mik/, the physiological maturity of the reproductive system that enables the individual to complete the adult sexual response cycle.

orgasmic platform [Gk, *orgein;* Fr, *plateforme,* a flat form], congestion of the lower vagina during sexual intercourse.

orient /ôr'ē-ənt/ [L, *oriens,* rising sun], 1. to make someone aware of new surroundings, including people and their roles; the layout of a facility; and its routines, rules, and services. 2. to help a person become aware of a situation or simply of reality, such as when a patient recovers from anesthesia.—**orientation**, *n.*, **oriented**, *adj.*

Oriental medical practices, a term referring to ancient forms of medicine that focus on prevention and secondarily treat disease with an emphasis on maintaining balance through the body by stimulating a constant, smooth-flowing Qi energy. Herbs, acupuncture, massage, diet, and exercise are also used.

orientation /ôr′ē-əntā′shən/ [L, *oriens* + *itio*, process], **1.** the direction of a fragment of nucleic acid inserted into a vector. The orientation of the fragment may be the same as that of the genetic map of the vector (the n orientation) or opposite (the u orientation). **2.** the awareness of one's physical environment with regard to time, place, and the identity of other people; the ability to adapt to such an existing or new environment.

orientation and mobility specialist, a human services professional who specializes in helping the visually impaired and legally blind to acclimate to their physical environments.

Orientia tsutsugamushi /ôr′e·enshe′ə tsōōtsōōgəmōō′she/ [L, *oriens*, east; Jpn, *tsutsuga*, illness, *mushi*, tick], a species of organisms, formerly known as *Rickettsia tsutsugamushi*, that causes scrub typhus.

orifice /ôr′ifis/ [L, *orificium*, opening], the entrance or outlet of any body cavity.—**orificial**, *adj.*

ori gene /ôr′ē/, in molecular genetics, the site or region in which DNA replication starts.

origin /ôr′ijin/ [L, *origo*, source], the more fixed or most proximal attachment of two points of a muscle.

Orimune, a trademark for an active immunizing agent (live oral poliovirus vaccine).

Orinase, a trademark for an oral sulfonylurea antidiabetic (TOLBUTamide).

Orlando (Pelletier), Ida Jean, (1926–2007), a nursing theorist who first described her nursing process theory in *The Dynamic Nurse-Patient Relationship* (1972). Her theory stresses the reciprocal relationship between the nurse and patient and the use of the nursing process to meet the patient's need and thus alleviate distress. Three elements—patient behavior, nurse reaction, and nursing actions—comprise a nursing situation. Her contribution as a theorist has advanced nursing from personal and automatic responses to disciplined and professional practice responses.

orlistat, a lipase inhibitor used to manage obesity.

Ornish diet, a vegetarian diet containing 10% of calories from fat, 20% from protein, and 70% from carbohydrates, used in combination with stress reduction techniques and moderate exercise for the prevention and treatment of cardiovascular disease.

ornithine /ôr′nithēn/, an amino acid, not a constituent of proteins, that is produced as an important intermediate substance in the urea cycle.

ornithine carbamoyltransferase, an enzyme in the blood that increases in patients with liver and other diseases.

ornithine carbamoyltransferase (OCT) deficiency, an X-linked aminoacidopathy involving the biosynthesis of urea. Characteristic signs include hyperammonemia, neurologic abnormalities, and orotic aciduria.

Ornithodoros /ôr′ōfer′ings/ [Gk, *ornis*, bird, *doros*, leather bag], a genus of ticks, some species of which are vectors for the spirochetes of relapsing fevers.

orofacial /ôr′ōfā′shəl/ [L, *os, oris,* mouth, *facies,* face], pertaining to the mouth and face.

oropharyngeal dysphagia /ôr′ōfərin′jē·əl/, difficulty in either the oral or pharyngeal phases of swallowing, such as in chewing, initiating the swallow, or propelling the bolus through the pharynx to the esophagus. It is caused by multiple neurologic, structural, or other medical conditions.

oropharynx /ôr′ōfer′ingks/ [L, *oris,* mouth; Gk, *pharynx,* throat], one of the three anatomic divisions of the pharynx that lies posterior to the mouth and is continuous above with the nasopharynx and below with the laryngopharynx. It extends behind the mouth from the soft palate above to the level of the hyoid bone below and contains the palatine and lingual tonsils.—**oropharyngeal**, *adj.*

orotic acid /ôrot′ik/, a pyrimidine synthesized in the cell from carboxyl phosphate and aspartic acid via condensation, dehydration, and oxidation.

orotic aciduria, a rare autosomal-recessive inherited disorder of pyrimidine metabolism. It includes signs and symptoms of macrocytic hypochromic anemia with megaloblastic changes in bone marrow, leukopenia, retarded growth, and urinary excretion of large amounts of orotic acid.

orphan disease /ôr′fən/, any rare health disorder for which no treatment has been developed.

orphan drug /ôr′fən/ [Gk, *orphanos,* without parents; ME, *drogge*], a term that generally refers to drugs needed to treat rare diseases but can encompass any pharmaceutic product available to physicians and patients in countries other than the United States that has not been "adopted" by a domestic pharmaceutic manufacturer

O

or distributor. The U.S. Orphan Drug Act of 1983 offers federal financial incentives to commercial and nonprofit organizations to develop and market drugs previously unavailable in the United States for rare diseases affecting less than 200,000 people.

orphan virus [Gk, *orphanos*, without parents; L, *virus*, poison], a virus that has been isolated and identified, although it has not been associated with any particular disease.

orphenadrine citrate /ôrfen′ədrēn/, a skeletal muscle relaxant with anticholinergic and antihistaminic activity. It is prescribed in the treatment of severe muscle strain.

ORS, abbreviation for **oral rehydration solutions.**

ORT, abbreviation for **oral rehydration therapy.**

ortho, abbreviation for *orthopedic.*

orthochromatic /or′thōkrōmat′ik/, denoting a photographic emulsion sensitive to all colors except red.

orthoclase ceramic feldspar /ôr′thəkläs/ [Gk, *orthos,* straight, *klassis,* breaking, *keramikos,* pottery], a plentiful clay in the solid crust of the earth, used to fill space and give body to fused dental porcelain.

Orthoclone OKT3, a trademark for an immunosuppressant drug (muromonab-Cd3).

orthodontic appliance /-don′tik/ [Gk, *orthos + odous,* tooth], any device used to modify tooth position.

orthodontic band, a thin metal ring, usually made of stainless steel, that is fitted over a tooth and bonded or cemented to it, for securing orthodontic attachments to the tooth.

orthodontics and dentofacial orthopedics /ôr′thədon′tiks/ [Gk, *orthos + odous,* tooth], the specialty of dentistry concerned with the diagnosis and treatment of malocclusion and irregularities of the teeth.

orthodontist /-don′tist/, a dentist who is concerned with the diagnosis, prevention, and correction of malocclusion of the teeth.

orthodromic conduction /ôr′thədrom′ik/ [Gk, *orthos + dromos,* course; L, *conducere,* to connect], the conduction of a neural impulse in the normal direction, from a synaptic junction or a receptor forward along an axon to its termination with depolarization.

orthogenesis /ôr′thəjen′əsis/ [Gk, *orthos + genesis,* origin], the theory that evolution is controlled by intrinsic factors within the organism and progresses according to a predetermined course rather than in several directions as a result of natural selection and other environmental factors.—**orthogenetic,** *adj.*

orthogenic /-jen′ik/ [Gk, *orthos + genein,* to produce], **1.** pertaining to orthogenesis; orthogenetic. **2.** pertaining to the treatment and rehabilitation of children who are mentally or emotionally disturbed.

orthogenic evolution, change within an animal or plant induced solely by an intrinsic factor, independent of any environmental elements.

orthognathic surgery, reconstruction of the mandible, the maxilla, or both, performed to repair acquired or congenital facial defects like cleft palate.

Orthohepadnavirus /or′thohepad′nahvi′rus/, a genus of hepadnaviruses that includes HBV.

orthokinetic cuff /-kinet′ik/ [Gk, *orthos,* straight, *kinesis,* movement; ME, *cuffe*], an elastic covering for a muscle that provides tactile stimulation sufficient to induce contraction and that restricts contraction of an opposing muscle.

orthokinetics /-kinet′iks/ [Gk, *orthos,* straight, *kinesis,* movement], **1.** a therapy for hypertrophic osteoarthritis in which an effort is made to change muscular action from one group to another to protect a joint. **2.** a therapy for spasticity that uses an orthotic device to enable contraction of one muscle while inhibiting its antagonist. **3.** the movement of microscopic particles in the same direction during sedimentation as a result of the effect of gravity on brownian motion.

orthologous genes /ôrthol′əgəs/, genes in different species that are similar in their nucleotide sequences, suggesting that they originated from a common ancestral gene.

orthomolecular medicine, a system for the prevention and treatment of disease based on the theory that each person's biochemical environment is genetically determined and specific to the individual. Therapy is provided by supplementation with substances naturally present in the body, such as vitamins, minerals, trace elements, and amino acids, in amounts that are optimized for each individual to correct nutritional deficiencies and the resulting biochemical abnormalities.

orthomyxovirus /ôr′thəmik′sōvī′rəs/ [Gk, *orthos + mykes,* fungus; L, *virus,* poison], a member of a family of viruses that includes several organisms responsible for human influenza infection.

Ortho-Novum, a trademark for oral contraceptives containing an estrogen (ethinyl estradiol or mestranol) and a progestin (norethindrone).

orthopantogram /ôr′thəpan′təgram/ [Gk, *orthos + pan,* all, *gramma,* record], a radiograph that is taken extraorally and shows a panoramic view of the entire dentition, alveolar bone, and other adjacent structures on a single film.

orthopedic nurse /-pē′dik/ [Gk, *orthos + pais,* child], a nurse whose primary area of interest, competence, and professional practice is the branch of nursing concerned with the prevention and correction of disorders of the locomotor system, including the skeleton, muscles, joints, and related tissues.

orthopedic oxford, a hard leather shoe with a leather or rubber sole, sometimes with a steel shank between the floor of the shoe and the sole, and with firmly constructed sides that support the foot in an upright position. The shoe is constructed so that assistive devices can be added.

orthopedics /-pē′diks/ [Gk, *orthos,* straight, *pais,* child], a branch of health care that is concerned with the prevention and correction of disorders of the musculoskeletal system of the body.

orthopedic surgery [Gk, *orthos,* straight, *pais,* child, *cheirourgia,* surgery], the branch of medicine that is concerned with the treatment of the musculoskeletal system, mainly by manipulative and operative methods.

orthopedic traction, a procedure in which a patient is maintained in a device attached by ropes and pulleys to weights that pull on an extremity or body part while countertraction is maintained. Traction is applied most often to reduce and immobilize fractures, but it also is used to overcome muscle spasm, stretch adhesions, correct certain deformities, and help release arthritic contractures.

orthopedist /-pē′dist/, a physician who specializes in orthopedics.

orthopnea /ôrthop′nē-ə/ [Gk, *orthos* + *pnoia,* breath], an abnormal condition in which a person must sit or stand to breathe deeply or comfortably. It occurs in many disorders of the cardiac and respiratory systems.—**orthopneic** /ôr′thopnē′ik/, *adj.*

orthopneic position [Gk, *orthos,* straight, *pnoia,* breath; L, *positio*], a body position that enables a patient to breathe comfortably. Usually it is one in which the patient is sitting up and bent forward with the arms supported on a table or chair arms.

orthopoxvirus /ôr′thopoksvī′rəs/, any member of a genus of poxviruses, including the viruses that cause human smallpox and vaccinia.

orthopsychiatry /-sīkī′ətrē/ [Gk, *orthos* + *psyche,* mind, *iatreia,* treatment], the branch of psychiatry that specializes in correcting incipient and borderline mental and behavioral disorders, especially in children, and in developing preventive techniques to promote mental health and emotional growth and development.

orthoptic /ôrthop′tik/ [Gk, *orthos* + *ops,* eye], **1.** pertaining to normal binocular vision. **2.** pertaining to a procedure or

technique for correcting the visual axes of eyes improperly coordinated for binocular vision.

orthoptic examination, an ophthalmoscopic examination of the binocular function of the eyes. A stereoscopic instrument presents a slightly different picture to each eye. The examiner notes the degree to which the pictures are combined by the normal process of fusion. If the person has diplopia, separate pictures are seen. If the person has suppression amblyopia, only one picture is seen.

orthoptic training [Gk, *orthos,* straight, *ops,* eye; ME, *trainen*], a type of therapy for correction of squint or other ocular muscle disorders by the use of eye exercises.

orthoptist /ôrthop′tist/ [Gk, *orthos* + *ops,* eye], a person qualified by postsecondary training and successful completion of an examination by the American Orthoptist Council who, under the supervision of an ophthalmologist, tests eye muscles and teaches exercise programs designed to correct eye coordination defects.

orthoroentgenography /ôr′thōrent′gənog′rəfē/, a radiographic method for measuring disparity of limb length. Three separate radiographs are made of the hip, knee, and ankle (for the leg) or the shoulder, elbow, and wrist (for the arm) to produce an image of the whole limb.

orthoscopy /ôrthos′kəpē/ [Gk, *orthos,* straight, *skopein,* to view], the use of an orthoscope for examining the fundus of the eye.

orthosis /ôrthō′sis/ [Gk, *orthos,* straight], a force system designed to control, correct, or compensate for a bone deformity, deforming forces, or forces absent from the body. Orthosis often involves the use of special braces.—**orthotic** /ôrthot′ik/, *adj., n.*

orthostasis /-stā′sis/, maintenance of an upright standing posture. In some medical tests a patient may need to maintain orthostasis for a long period to stimulate a rise in aldosterone concentration.

orthostatic /-stat′ik/ [Gk, *orthos* + *statikos,* standing], pertaining to an erect or standing position.

orthostatic hypotension, abnormally low BP that occurs when an individual suddenly assumes the standing posture. It can produce dizziness and fainting.

orthostatic intolerance, an abnormal response to standing upright that results from decreased BP and inadequate blood flow to the brain, characterized by a variety of symptoms including lightheadedness, palpitations, tremulousness, visual disturbances, and syncope. The cause is unknown but may be related to

O

abnormalities in the autonomic regulation of cardiovascular function.

orthostatic proteinuria, presence of protein in the urine, especially in teenagers who have been standing for a long period. It disappears when they recline and is of no pathologic significance.

orthotics /ôrthot′iks/ [Gk, *orthos,* straight], the design and use of external appliances to support a paralyzed muscle, promote a specific motion, or correct a musculoskeletal deformity.

orthotist /ôr′thətist/ [Gk, *orthos,* straight], a person who designs, fabricates, and fits braces or other orthopedic appliances prescribed by physicians. A certified orthotist is one who passed the examination of the American Orthotist and Prosthetic Association.

orthotonos /ôrthot′ənəs/ [Gk, *orthos* + *tonos,* tension], a straight, rigid posture of the body caused by a tetanic spasm, resulting from strychnine poisoning or tetanus infection. The neck and all other parts of the body are in a position of extension but not as severely as in opisthotonos.

orthotopic liver transplantation [Gk, *ortho,* straight, *topos,* place], a graft of liver tissue occurring at its natural place or on the proper part of the body.

orthotopic neobladder, a urinary reservoir fashioned from a bowel segment that is in the normal anatomic position of the bladder, with discharge of urine through the urethra.

orthotopic ureterocele, a ureterocele occurring in a ureter in the proper position in the trigone of the bladder. It may be small and asymptomatic or large and extending deeply into the bladder.

orthovoltage /-vōl′tij/ [Gk, *orthos,* straight; Count Alessandro Volta], the energy range of 100 to 350 kiloelectron volts supplied by some x-ray generators used for radiation therapy. Such generators have been replaced in many health facilities by equipment that operates in the megaelectron volt range.

Ortolani's sign /ôr′təlä′nē/ [Marius Ortolani, twentieth-century Italian surgeon], a click heard in a test for a congenital dislocated hip. It is noted in infancy when the hip slips into or out of the socket.

Ortolani's test [Marius Ortolani; L, *testum,* crucible], a procedure used to evaluate the stability of the hip joints in newborns and infants. The baby is placed on his back, and the hips and knees are flexed at right angles and abducted until the lateral aspects of the knees are touching the table. Internal and external rotation are attempted, and symmetry of mobility is evaluated. A click or a popping sensation (Ortolani's sign) may be felt if the joint is unstable.

Orudis, a trademark for a nonsteroidal antiinflammatory agent (ketoprofen).

Os, symbol for the element **osmium.**

OS, abbreviation for *oculus sinister,* a Latin phrase meaning "left eye."

Osborne and Cotterill procedure, the surgical correction of a chronic dislocated elbow by means of capsular reefing, the folding in or overlapping of soft tissue followed by surgical suture to make the joint tighter.

Osborn wave, an abnormal, upward deflection in the ECG occurring at the junction of the QRS complex and the S-T segment. It is often found in ECGs of patients with moderate hypothermia and becomes more pronounced as body temperature declines.

osc, 1. abbreviation for **oscillator. 2.** abbreviation for **oscilloscope.**

oscheitis /os′kē·ī′tis/, an inflammation of the scrotum.

oscillation (HFO) /os′ilā′shən/ [L, *oscillare,* to swing], **1.** a back and forth motion. **2.** vibration or the effects of a mechanical or electric vibrator.

oscillator (osc) /os′ilā′tər/ [L, *oscillare,* to swing], an electric or other device that produces oscillations, vibrations, or fluctuations, such as an alternating electric current generator.

oscillopsia /os′silop′sē·ə/, abnormal jerky eye movements associated with MS. They create a subjective sensation that the environment is oscillating.

oscilloscope (osc) /osil′əskōp/ [L, *oscillare,* to swing; Gk, *skopein,* to look], an instrument that displays a visual representation of electrical variations on the fluorescent screen of a cathode ray tube. The graphic representation is produced by a beam of electrons on the screen. The beam is focused or directed by a magnetic field that is influenced in turn by a source such as an amplified current produced by heart contractions. As used in cardiology, the oscilloscope can function as a continuous ECG.

oseltamivir, an antiviral used to treat type A influenza.

Osgood osteotomy /oz′good/, a surgical procedure for correcting the malrotation of a femur.

Osgood-Schlatter disease /-shlat′ər/ [Robert B. Osgood, American surgeon, 1873–1956; Carl Schlatter, Swiss surgeon, 1864–1934], inflammation or partial separation of the tibial tubercle caused by chronic irritation, usually as a result of overuse of the quadriceps muscle. The condition is seen primarily in muscular, athletic adolescent boys and is characterized by swelling and tenderness over the tibial tubercle that increase with exercise or any activity that extends the leg.

OSHA /ō′shä/, abbreviation for *Occupational Safety and Health Administration,* the federal agency that regulates worker safety.

OSL dosimeter, abbreviation for **optically stimulated luminescence (dosimeter).**

Osler's nodes /ōs′lərz/ [William Osler, American-British physician, 1849–1919], tender, reddish or purplish subcutaneous nodules of the soft tissue on the ends of fingers or toes, seen in subacute bacterial endocarditis and usually lasting only 1 or 2 days. The nodes represent bacterial embolisms from the infected heart valve.

osm, 1. abbreviation for **osmosis. 2.** abbreviation for *osmotic.*

osmethesia /os′məthē″zhə/ [Gk, *osme,* odor, *aisthesis,* feeling], the ability to perceive and distinguish odors; the sense of smell.

osmium (Os) /oz′mē·əm/ [Gk, *osme,* odor], a hard, grayish, pungent-smelling metallic element. Its atomic number is 76; its atomic mass is 190.2. Used to produce alloys of extreme hardness, it is highly toxic, and is slowly converted to the highly volatile, pungent-smelling, extremely toxic osmium tetroxide (OsO_4) in air.

osmoceptors /oz′mōsep′tərz/ [Gk, *osme;* L, *recipere,* to receive], receptors in the anterior hypothalamus that respond to osmotic pressure, thereby regulating thirst and production of the antidiuretic hormone.

osmolal gap /ozmōl′əl/, a difference between the observed and calculated osmolalities in serum analysis. The calculated osmolar values include sodium concentration multiplied by 2, plus glucose and BUN.

osmolality /oz′mōlal′itē/, the osmotic pressure of a solution expressed in osmols or milliosmols per kilogram of water.

osmolal solution, the solute concentration expressed in the number of osmoles per kilogram of solvent.

osmolar /osmō′lər/, pertaining to the osmotic characteristics of a solution of one or more molecular substances, ionic substances, or both, expressed in osmoles or milliosmoles.

osmolarity /oz′mōler′itē/, the osmotic pressure of a solution expressed in osmoles or milliosmoles per liter of the solution.

osmolar solution, the solute concentration expressed in the number of osmoles per liter of solution.

osmole /os′mōl/ [Gk, *osmos,* impulse, *osis,* condition + mole (molecule)], the quantity of a substance in solution in the form of molecules, ions, or both (usually expressed in grams) that has the same osmotic pressure as one mole of an ideal nonelectrolyte.—**osmolal,** *adj.*

osmology /ozmol′əjē/ [Gk, *osme,* odor, *ōsmos,* impulse, *logos,* science], **1.** the science of the sense of smell and the production and composition of odors. **2.** the branch of science that is concerned with osmosis.

osmometer /ozmom′ə·tər/ [Gk, *ōsmos,* impulse, *metron,* measure], **1.** a device for measuring the acuity of the sense of smell. **2.** a device for measuring osmotic pressure either directly or indirectly. It was formerly used to assess the extent of dehydration or blood loss.

osmometry /ozmom′ətrē/ [Gk, *ōsmos,* impulse, *metron,* measure], the field of study that deals with the phenomenon of osmosis and the measurement of osmotic forces.—**osmometric,** *adj.*

Osmone-Clarke procedure, a surgical method for correcting splayfoot. It involves soft tissue release of the medial and lateral foot with peroneus brevis tendon transfer.

osmoreceptor /-risep′tər/ [Gk, *ōsmos,* impulse; L, *recipere,* to receive], **1.** a neuron in the hypothalamus that is sensitive to the relative fluid/solute concentration in the blood plasma and that regulates the secretion of antidiuretic hormone. **2.** a receptor of smell stimuli.

osmoreceptor cell, a cell that recognizes changes in extracellular fluid osmolality.

osmoregulation /-reg′yəlā′shən/ [Gk, *ōsmos,* impulse; L, *regula,* rule], the act of influencing or controlling the speed and extent of osmosis.

osmosis (osm) /ozmō′sis, os-/ [Gk, *ōsmos,* impulse, *osis,* condition], the movement of a pure solvent, such as water, through a differentially permeable membrane from a solution that has a lower solute concentration to one that has a higher solute concentration. Movement across the membrane continues until the concentrations of the solutions equalize.—**osmotic (osm)** /ozmot′ik/, *adj.*

osmotic diarrhea, a form of diarrhea associated with water retention in the bowel resulting from an accumulation of nonabsorbable water-soluble substances. An excessive intake of hexitols, sorbitol, and mannitol (used as sugar substitutes in candies, chewing gum, and dietetic foods) can result in slow absorption and rapid small intestine motility, leading to osmotic diarrhea. It may also occur in infants if they intake an undiluted concentrated form of formula.

osmotic diuresis, diuresis resulting from the presence of certain nonabsorbable substances in tubules of the kidney, such as mannitol, urea, or glucose.

osmotic fragility, a sensitivity to changes in osmotic pressure characteristic of RBCs. Exposed to a hypotonic

O

concentration of sodium in solution, red cells take in increasing quantities of water, swell until the capacity of the cell membrane is exceeded, and burst. Exposed to a hypertonic concentration of sodium in a solution, red cells give up intracellular fluid, shrink, and break up.

osmotic pressure, 1. the pressure exerted on a differentially permeable membrane separating a solution from a solvent, the membrane being impermeable to the solutes in the solution and permeable only to the solvent. 2. the pressure exerted on a differentially permeable membrane by a solution containing one or more solutes that cannot penetrate the membrane, which is permeable only by the solvent surrounding it.

osmotic transfection, a method of inserting foreign DNA molecules into cells by putting cells into a dilute solution that causes them to rupture. The cell membranes quickly repair themselves. During the rupture period the alien DNA is added to the fluid and absorbed into the cell nuclei.

osphresis /osfrē'sis/ [Gk, smell], olfaction; the sense of smell.

osseointegrated implant /os'ē·ō·in'tegrā təd/ [Gk, osteon, bone; L, integrare, to make whole], an endosteal implant containing pores into which osteoblasts and supporting connective tissue can migrate.

osseous /os'ē·əs/ [L, os, bone], bony; consisting of or resembling bone.

osseous labyrinth [L, os, bone; Gk, labyrinthos, maze], the bony part of the internal ear, which transmits sound vibrations from the middle ear to the eighth cranial nerve. It is composed of three cavities: the vestibule, the semicircular canals, and the cochlea, All three cavities contain perilymph, in which a membranous labyrinth is suspended.

ossicle /os'ikəl/ [L, ossiculum, little bone], a small bone such as the malleus, the incus, or the stapes, all of which are ossicles of the middle ear.—**ossicular,** adj.

ossiferous /osif'ərəs/ [L, os, bone, ferre, to bear], pertaining to the formation of bone or bone tissue.

ossification /os'ifikā'shən/ [L, os + facere, to make], the development of bone. Intramembranous ossification is that preceded by membrane, such as in the process initially forming the roof and sides of the skull. Intracartilaginous endochondral ossification is that preceded by rods of cartilage, such as that forming the bones of the limbs.

ossify /os'ifī/ [L, os + facere, to make], to develop into bone.

ossifying fibroma /os'ifī'ing/ [L, os + facere, to make], a slow-growing, benign neoplasm, occurring most often in the

jaws, especially the mandible. The tumor is composed of bone that develops within fibrous connective tissue.

ostealgia /os'tē·al'jə/ [Gk, osteon, bone, algos, pain], any pain that is associated with an abnormal condition within a bone, such as osteomyelitis.—**ostealgic,** adj.

osteitis /os'tē·ī'tis/ [Gk, osteon + itis, inflammation], an inflammation of bone caused by infection, degeneration, or trauma. Symptoms include swelling, tenderness, dull aching pain, and redness in the skin over the affected bone.

osteitis fibrosa cystica, an inflammatory degenerative condition in which normal bone is replaced by cysts and fibrous tissue. It is usually associated with hyperparathyroidism.

ostemia /ostē'mē·ə/, an abnormal congestion of blood in a bone.

ostempyesis /os'təmpī·ē'sis/, an accumulation of pus within a bone.

osteo /os'tē·ō/, 1. abbreviation for **osteopath.** 2. abbreviation for **osteopathy.** 3. pertaining to bone osteology.

osteoanagenesis /os'tē·ō·an'əjen'əsis/ [Gk, osteon + ana, again, genesis, origin], the regeneration or formation of bone tissue.

osteoaneurysm /-an'yəriz'əm/, a dilation of the wall of a blood vessel within a bone.

osteoarthritis /os'tē·ō'ärthrī'tis/ [Gk, osteon + arthron, joint, itis, inflammation], a form of arthritis in which one or many joints undergo degenerative changes, including subchondral bony sclerosis, loss of articular cartilage, and proliferation of bone spurs (osteophytes) and cartilage in the joint.

osteoarthropathy /-ärthrop'əthē/ [Gk, osteon + arthron, joint, pathos, disease], any disorder affecting bones and joints.

osteoarthrosis /-arthrō'sis/, a condition of chronic arthritis, usually mechanical, without inflammation.

osteoarticular /-artik'yələr/, pertaining to or affecting bones and joints.

osteoarticular brucellosis, a form of brucellosis that affects mainly the weight-bearing joints.

osteoarticular graft, a transplant of bone that contains a joint surface.

osteoblast /os'tē·ō·blast'/ [Gk, osteon + blastos, germ], a bone-forming cell that is derived from the embryonic mesenchyme and, during the early development of the skeleton, differentiates from a fibroblast to function in the formation of bone tissue.—**osteoblastic,** adj.

osteoblastoma /-blastō'mə/ pl. **osteoblastomas, osteoblastomata,** small, benign, fairly vascular tumor of poorly formed bone and fibrous tissue, occurring most frequently in the vertebrae, femur, tibia, or bones of the upper extremities in children and young adults. The tumor may cause pain, erosion, and resorption of native bone.

osteocachexia /-kəkek′sē·ə/, a chronic disease that causes bone wasting, usually caused by malnutrition.

osteocalcin /-kal′sin/, a protein found in the extracellular matrix of bone and dentin. It is involved in regulating mineralization in the bones and teeth.

osteocarcinoma /-kär′sinō′mə/ [Gk, *osteon,* bone, *karkinos,* crab, *oma,* tumor], cancer of the bone.

osteochondral graft /-kon′drəl/, a transplant containing both bone and cartilage.

osteochondritis /-kəndrī′tis/ [Gk, *osteon,* bone, *chondros,* cartilage, *itis,* inflammation], a disease of the epiphyses, or bone-forming centers of the skeleton, that begins with necrosis and tissue fragmentation and is followed by repair and regeneration.

osteochondritis dissecans [Gk, *osteon,* bone, *chondros,* cartilage; L, *dissecare,* to cut apart], a joint disorder in which a piece of cartilage and neighboring bone tissue become detached from an articular surface.

osteochondrofibroma /-kon′drōfībrō′mə/, a tumor containing tissues of osteoma, chondroma, and fibroma.

osteochondroma /os′tē·ōkondrō′mə/ [Gk, *osteon* + *chondros,* cartilage, *oma,* tumor], a benign tumor composed of bone and cartilage. The onset is usually in childhood. It affects more males than females.

osteochondromatosis /-kon′drōmətō′sis/, the transformation of synovial villi into bone and cartilage masses, causing loose bodies in the joints. It usually develops in joints affected by injury or degenerative disease.

osteochondropathy /-kəndrop′əthē/, a condition affecting both bone and cartilage and characterized by abnormal enchondral ossification.

osteochondrosarcoma /-kon′drōsärkō′mə/ [Gk, *osteon,* bone, *chondros,* cartilage, *karkinos,* crab, *oma,* tumor], a cancer of the bone and cartilage.

osteochondrosis /-kondrō′sis/ [Gk, *osteon* + *chondros,* cartilage, *osis,* condition], a disease affecting the ossification centers of bone in children. It is initially characterized by degeneration and necrosis, followed by regeneration and recalcification.

osteochondrosis dissecans /dis′əkanz/, the formation of a separate center of bone and cartilage on an epiphyseal surface. The stray fragment may remain in place, be absorbed, or break off and become a loose body.

osteoclasia /-klā′zhə/ [Gk, *osteon* + *klasis,* breaking], **1.** the destruction and absorption of bony tissue by osteoclasts, such as during growth or the healing of fractures.

2. the degeneration of bone through disease.

osteoclasis /os′tē·ōk′ləsis/, the intentional surgical fracture of a bone to correct a deformity.

osteoclast /os′tē·əklast′/ [Gk, *osteon* + *klasis,* breaking], **1.** a large type of multinucleated bone cell with a large amount of acidophilic cytoplasm that functions to absorb and remove osseous tissue. During bone healing of fractures, or during certain disease processes, osteoclasts excavate passages through the surrounding tissue by enzymatic action. **2.** a surgical instrument used in the fracturing or refracturing of bones for therapeutic purposes such as correction of a deformity.

osteoclast activating factor, a lymphokine that promotes the resorption of bone.

osteoclastic /-klas′tik/, **1.** pertaining to osteoclasts. **2.** destructive to bone.

osteoclastoma /os′tē·ōklastō′mə/ *pl.* **osteoclastomas, osteoclastomata** [Gk, *osteon* + *klasis,* breaking, *oma,* tumor], a giant cell tumor of the bone that occurs most frequently at the end of a long bone and appears as a mass surrounded by a thin shell of new periosteal bone. The lesion may be malignant and may cause local pain, loss of function, weakness, and pathologic fracture.

osteocope /os′tē·əkōp/, a painful, syphilitic bone disease.

osteocystoma /-sistō′mə/, a cystic tumor in a bone.

osteocyte /os′tē·əsīt/ [Gk, *osteon* + *kytos,* cell], a bone cell; a mature osteoblast that has become embedded in the bone matrix. It occupies a small cavity and sends out protoplasmic projections that anastomose with those of other osteocytes to form a system of minute canals within the bone matrix.—**osteocytic,** *adj.*

osteodensitometer /-den′sitom′ətər/ [Gk, *osteon,* bone; L, *densus,* thick; Gk, *metron,* measure], an apparatus for measuring the density of bone tissue.

osteodentin /-den′tin/, dentin that resembles bone. It is found chiefly in the teeth of fish and certain other animals but also occurs occasionally in humans when odontoblasts are entrapped by rapidly developing secondary dentin.

osteodermia /-dur′mēə/, a condition in which skeletal changes occur in the skin, such as a bony tumor of the skin.

osteodiastasis /-dī·as′təsis/, an abnormal separation of bones.

osteodynia /-din′ē·ə/, bone pain.

osteodystrophy /-dis′trəfē/ [Gk, *osteon* + *dys,* bad, *trophe,* nourishment], any generalized defect in bone development, usually associated with disturbances in

O

calcium and phosphorus metabolism and renal insufficiency, such as in renal osteodystrophy.

osteoenchondroma /os'tē·ō·en'kəndrō'mə/, a benign bone and cartilage tumor within a bone.

osteofibrochondrosarcoma /-fī'brōkon'drō särkō'mə/, a malignant tumor containing bone, cartilage, and fibrous tissues.

osteofibroma /-fī'brō'mə/ [Gk, *osteon*, bone; L, *fibra*, fiber; Gk, *oma*, tumor], a tumor composed of both bony and fibrous tissues.

osteogenesis /-jen'əsis/ [Gk, *osteon* + *genesis*, origin], the origin and development of bone tissue. —**osteogenetic, osteogenic, osteogenous**, *adj*.

osteogenesis imperfecta, a genetic disorder involving defective development of the connective tissue. It is characterized by abnormally brittle and fragile bones that are easily fractured by the slightest trauma.

osteogenic, composed of or originating from any tissue involved in the development, growth, or repair of bone.

osteohalisteresis /-hal'istərē'sis/, a condition of soft bones caused by a loss or deficiency of mineral elements.

osteoid /os'tē·oid/ [Gk, *osteon* + *eidos*, form], pertaining to or resembling bone.

osteolipochondroma /-lip'ōkəndrō'mə/, a cartilage tumor with bone and fat elements.

osteolipoma /-lipō'mə/, a fatty tumor containing bone elements.

osteology /os'tē·ol'əjē/ [Gk, *osteon*, bone, *logos*, science], the branch of medicine concerned with the development and diseases of bone tissue.

osteolysis /os'tē·ol'isis/ [Gk, *osteon* + *lysis*, loosening], the degeneration and dissolution of bone caused by disease, infection, or ischemia. The condition commonly affects the terminal bones of the hands and feet and is seen in disorders involving blood vessels, such as Raynaud's disease. —**osteolytic**, *adj*.

osteolytic hypercalcemia /-lit'ik/, a malignancy associated with excess calcium in the blood. It may be caused by either widespread skeletal metastases or extensive bone marrow involvement by a primary hematologic tumor.

osteoma /os'tē·ō'mə/ *pl.* **osteomas, osteomata**, a tumor of bone tissue.

osteomalacia /-mələ'shə/ [Gk, *osteon* + *malakia*, softening], an abnormal condition of lamellar bone, characterized by a loss of calcification of the matrix and resulting in softening of the bone. It is accompanied by weakness, fracture, pain, anorexia, and weight loss. The condition is the result of an inadequate amount of phosphorus and calcium available in the blood for mineralization of the bones.

osteomesopyknosis /-mez'ōpikno'sis/, a genetic disorder characterized by osteosclerosis of the axial spine, pelvis, and proximal areas of long bones.

osteomyelitis /-mī'əli'tis/ [Gk, *osteon* + *myelos*, marrow, *itis*, inflammation], local or generalized infection of bone and bone marrow, usually caused by bacteria introduced by trauma or surgery, by direct extension from a nearby infection, or via the bloodstream. Staphylococci are the most common causative agents. —**osteomyelitic**, *adj*.

osteomyelodysplasia /os'tē·ōmī'əlō'displā' zhə/ [Gk, *osteon*, bone, *myelos*, marrow, *dys* + *plasis*, forming], a loss of bone tissue through absorption of minerals, usually associated with leukopenia and sometimes with fever. It may result from an excess of parathyroid hormone.

osteon /os'tē·on/ [Gk, bone], the basic central structural unit of compact bone, consisting of the haversian canal and its concentric rings of 4 to 20 lamellae.

osteonal bone /os'tē·ō'nəl/, bone tissue composed of tiny chalky tubes with an arteriole running down the middle and circular laminations of bone concentric with an artery. It is seen in mature adults.

osteonecrosis /os'tē·ō'nəkrō'sis/ [Gk, *osteon* + *nekros*, dead, *osis*, condition], the destruction and death of bone tissue, such as from ischemia, infection, malignant neoplastic disease, or trauma. —**osteonecrotic**, *adj*.

osteoonychodysplasia /os'tē·ō·on'i·kō·dis· plā'zhə/ [Gk, *osteon*, bone, *onyx*, nail, *dys*, bad, *plassein*, to form], abnormal development of nails and bones.

osteopath (osteo) /os'tē·ōpath'/, a physician who specializes in osteopathy.

osteopathology /-pathol'əjē/ [Gk, *osteon*, bone, *pathos*, disease, *logos*, science], the study of bone diseases.

osteopathy (osteo) /os'tē·op'əthē/ [Gk, *osteon* + *pathos*, disease], a therapeutic approach to the practice of medicine that uses all the usual forms of medical diagnosis and therapy, including drugs, surgery, and radiation, but that places greater emphasis on the influence of the relationship between the organs and the musculoskeletal system than traditional medicine does. Osteopathic physicians recognize and correct structural problems using manipulation. —**osteopathic**, *adj*.

osteopenia /-pē'nē·ə/ [Gk, *osteon* + *penes*, poverty], a condition of subnormally mineralized bone, usually the result of a rate of bone lysis that exceeds the rate of bone matrix synthesis.

osteoperiosteal graft /-per'ē·os'tē·əl/, a bone graft that includes the periosteal membrane covering the bone.

osteopetrosis /os′tē·ōpētrō′sis/ [Gk, *osteon* + *petra*, stone, *osis*, condition], an inherited disorder characterized by a generalized increase in bone density, probably caused by faulty bone resorption resulting from a deficiency of osteoclasts. In its most severe form, the bone marrow cavity is obliterated, causing severe anemia, marked deformities of the skull, and compression of the cranial nerves, which may result in deafness and blindness and lead to an early death. A milder, benign form is characterized by short stature, fragile bones that fracture easily, and a tendency to develop osteomyelitis.—**osteopetrotic,** *adj.*

osteophlebitis /-fləbī′tis/, an inflammation of the veins that are a part of the vascular system of bones.

osteophyte /os′tē·əfīt/, a bony outgrowth, usually found around a joint. It is commonly seen in degenerative joint disease.

osteoplastica /-plas′tikə/, a form of bone inflammation associated with cystic fibrosis.

osteoplasty /o′stē·əplas′tē/ [Gk, *osteon,* bone, *plassein,* to mold], plastic surgery performed on bone tissue.

osteopoikilosis /os′tē·ōpoi′kilō′sis/ [Gk, *osteon* + *poikilos,* mottled, *osis,* condition], an inherited condition of the bones characterized by multiple areas of dense calcification throughout the osseous tissue. It is a benign condition, usually without symptoms, and of unknown cause. —**osteopoikilotic,** *adj.*

osteoporosis /os′tē·ōpərō′sis/ [Gk, *osteon* + *poros,* passage, *osis,* condition], a disorder characterized by abnormal loss of bone density and deterioration of bone tissue, with an increased fracture risk. It occurs most frequently in postmenopausal women, sedentary or immobilized individuals, and patients on long-term steroid therapy.—**osteoporotic,** *adj.*

osteoporosis of disuse [Gk, *osteon,* bone, *poros,* passage, *osis,* condition; L, *dis,* not; ME, *usen,* to act], a decrease in bone mass that occurs in sedentary people or patients confined to bed for a long period.

osteosarcoma /os′tē·ō′särkō′mə/ [Gk, *osteon* + *sarx,* flesh + *oma*], a malignant tumor of the bone, composed of anaplastic cells derived from mesenchyme.

osteosclerosis /os′tē·ōsklerō′sis/ [Gk, *osteon* + *skleros,* hard, *osis,* condition], an abnormal increase in the density of bone tissue. The condition occurs in a variety of disease states and is commonly associated with ischemia, chronic infection, and tumor formation. It also may be caused by faulty bone resorption as a result of some abnormality involving osteoclasts.—**osteosclerotic,** *adj.*

osteosuture /-sŌŌ′chər/, the surgical repair of a fractured bone by wiring or suturing the fragments together.

osteosynovitis /-sin′ōvī′tis/ [Gk, *osteon,* bone, *syn,* together; L, *ovum,* egg; Gk, *itis,* inflammation], an inflammation of the synovial membrane of a joint and the surrounding bone tissue.

osteosynthesis /-sin′thəsis/, the surgical fixation of a bone using any internal mechanical means. It is usually performed in the treatment of fractures.

osteotabes /-tā′bēz/, a condition usually affecting infants in which bone marrow cells are destroyed and the marrow disappears.

osteotelangiectasia /-telan′jē·əktā′zhə/, a sarcoma of the bone characterized by dilated capillaries.

osteothrombophlebitis /-throm′bōfləbī′tis/, a progressive inflammation of small venules and intact bone often accompanied by clot formation.

osteothrombosis /-thrəmbō′sis/, a blockage of blood vessels in bone tissue.

osteotome /os′tē·ətōm/ [Gk, *osteon* + *temnein,* to cut], a surgical instrument for cutting through bone.

osteotomy /os′tē·ot′əmē/ [Gk, *osteon* + *temnein,* to cut], the sawing or cutting of a bone. Kinds of osteotomy include block osteotomy, in which a section of bone is excised; cuneiform osteotomy to remove a bone wedge; and displacement osteotomy, in which a bone is redesigned surgically to alter the alignment or weight-bearing stress areas.

osteotripsy /-trip′sē/, any percutaneous reduction of a bony prominence or callus.

ostomate /os′təmāt/ [L, *ostium,* mouth], a person who has undergone an ostomy.

ostomy /os′təmē/ [L, *ostium,* mouth], informal. a surgical procedure in which an incision or stoma is surgically created in the wall of the abdomen to allow the passage of urine from the bladder or of intestinal contents from the bowel. An ostomy procedure may be performed to correct an anatomic defect, relieve an obstruction, or permit treatment of a severe infection or injury of the urinary or intestinal tract. Each procedure is named for the anatomic location of the ostomy, such as a colostomy, ureterostomy, cecostomy, or cystostomy.

ostomy care[1], the management and support of a patient with a surgical opening created in the bladder, ileum, or colon for the temporary or permanent passage of urine or feces, necessitated by carcinoma, intestinal obstruction, trauma, or severe ulceration distal to the site of the incision. In most cases the opening is covered with a temporary disposable bag in the OR.

ostomy care[2], a nursing intervention from the Nursing Interventions Classification (NIC) defined as maintenance of elimination through a stoma and care of surrounding tissue.

ostomy irrigation, a procedure for cleansing of, stimulating of, and regulating evacuation of an artificially created orifice. Fluids used in irrigation include tap water and saline or medicated solutions. Loop and double-barrel colostomies require a sequential irrigation of the proximal loop, distal loop, and rectum to prevent the accumulation of discharge.

ostomy self-care, a nursing outcome from the Nursing Outcomes Classification (NOC) defined as the personal actions to maintain an ostomy for elimination.

os trigonum /os trĭgŏ′nəm/, a small foot bone just posterior to the talus.

OT, 1. abbreviation for **occupational therapist. 2.** abbreviation for **occupational therapy.**

otalgia /ōtal′jə/, a pain in the ear.

OTC, abbreviation for **over the counter.**

Othello syndrome /ōthel′ō/ [Othello, jealous Shakespearean character], a psychopathologic condition characterized by suspicion of a spouse's infidelity and morbid jealousy. This condition may be accompanied by rage and violence and is frequently associated with paranoia.

otic /ō′tik, ot′ik/ [Gk, *ous*, ear], pertaining to the ear.

otics /ō′tiks, ot′iks/, a group of drugs used locally to treat inflammation of the external ear canal or to remove excess cerumen.

otic vertigo, a sensation of rotation motion caused by an inner ear disease. Its subcategories are Ménière's disease, inner ear dysfunction, fistula or other pressure sensitivity, unilateral paresis, and benign paroxysmal positional vertigo.

otitic /ōtit′ik/ [Gk, *ous*, ear], pertaining to otitis.

otitis /ōtī′tis/ [Gk, *ous* + *itis,* inflammation], inflammation or infection of the ear.

otitis externa, inflammation or infection of the external canal or the auricle of the external ear. Major causes are allergy, bacteria, fungi, viruses, and trauma. Allergy to nickel or chromium in earrings and to chemicals in hair sprays, cosmetics, hearing aids, and medications, particularly sulfonamides and neomycin, is common. *Staphylococcus aureus, Pseudomonas aeruginosa,* and *Streptococcus pyogenes* are common bacterial causes. Herpes simplex and herpes zoster viruses are frequently implicated.

otitis mastoidea [Gk, *ous,* ear, *itis,* inflammation, *mastos,* breast, *eidos,* form], an inflammation of the middle ear associated with a mastoid infection.

otitis media, inflammation or infection of the middle ear. Acute otitis media is most often caused by *Haemophilus influenzae, Moraxella catarrhalis,* or *Streptococcus pneumoniae.* Chronic otitis media is usually caused by gram-negative bacteria such as *Proteus, Klebsiella,* and *Pseudomonas.* Allergy, *Mycoplasma* infections, and several viruses also may be causative factors. Organisms gain entry to the middle ear through the eustachian tube. Obstruction of the eustachian tube and accumulation of exudate may increase pressure within the middle ear, forcing infection into the mastoid bone or rupturing the tympanic membrane. Symptoms of acute otitis media include a sense of fullness in the ear, diminished hearing, pain, and fever. Usually only one ear is affected.

otitis sclerotica [Gk, *ous,* ear, *itis,* inflammation, *sclerosis,* hardening], a sclerosing type of inflammation of the middle ear.

otoacoustic emissions, echoes emitted by the outer hair cells of the inner ear. These echoes are used to evaluate the integrity of the inner ear and to screen hearing in newborns.

otocephalus /ō′tōsef′ələs/, a fetus with otocephaly.

otocephaly /ō′tōsef′əlē/ [Gk, *ous* + *kephale,* head], a congenital malformation characterized by the absence of the lower jaw, defective formation of the mouth, and union or close approximation of the ears on the front of the neck.—**otocephalic, otocephalous,** *adj.*

otocranial debris, otoliths that have been dislodged by trauma and may move about in the semicircular canals when the head changes position.

otolaryngologist /-ler′ing·gol′əjist/ [Gk, *ous* + *larynx* + *logos,* science], a physician who specializes in the diagnosis and treatment of diseases and injuries of the ears, nose, and throat.

otolaryngology /-ler′ing·gol′əjē/ [Gk, *ous* + *larynx* + *logos,* science], a branch of medicine dealing with the diagnosis and treatment of diseases and disorders of the ears, nose, throat, and adjacent structures of the head and neck.

otolith /ō′təlith/ [Gk, *ous,* ear, *lithos,* stone], **1.** a calculus in the middle ear. **2.** any of the crystals of calcium carbonate attached to the hair cells of the inner ear as gravity orientation receptors.

otolith righting reflex [Gk, *ous* + *lithos,* stone], an involuntary response in newborns in which tilting of the body when the infant is in an erect position causes the head to return to the upright position.

otologist /ōtol′əjist/, a physician trained in the diagnosis and treatment of diseases and other disorders of the ear.

otology /ōtol′əjē/ [Gk, *ous* + *logos*, science], the study of the ear, including the diagnosis and treatment of its diseases and disorders.

otomycosis /ō′tōmīkō′sis/, a lesion of the external ear caused by a fungus infection.

otoplasty /ō′təplas′tē/ [Gk, *ous* + *plassein*, to mold], a common procedure in reconstructive plastic surgery in which, for cosmetic reasons, some of the cartilage in the ears is removed to bring the auricle and pinna closer to the head.

otopyosis /ō′təpi·ō′sis/, a pus-producing inflammation of the ear, occurring either in the tympanic cavity or the external auditory meatus.

otorrhea /ō′tərē′ə/ [Gk, *ous* + *rhoia*, flow], any discharge from the external ear. Otorrhea may be serous, sanguinous, or purulent or contain CSF.—**otorrheal, otorrheic, otorrhetic,** *adj.*

otosclerosis /ō′tōsklərō′sis/ [Gk, *ous* + *skleros*, hard, *osis*, condition], a hereditary condition of unknown cause in which irregular ossification occurs in the ossicles of the middle ear, especially of the stapes, causing hearing loss.

otoscope /ō′təskōp′/ [Gk, *ous* + *skopein*, to look], an instrument used to examine the external ear, the eardrum, and, through the eardrum, the ossicles of the middle ear. It consists of a light, a magnifying lens, a speculum, and sometimes a device for insufflation.

otoscopy /ōtos′kəpē/ [Gk, *ous,* ear, *skopein,* to view], an inspection of the tympanic membrane and other parts of the outer ear with an otoscope.

ototoxic hearing loss, hearing loss caused by ingestion of toxic substances.

ototoxicity /ō′tōtok′sisitē/ [Gk, *ous* + *toxikon,* poison], the harmful effects of certain substances on the eighth cranial nerve or the organs of hearing and balance. Common ototoxic drugs include the aminoglycoside antibiotics, aspirin, furosemide, and quinine.—**ototoxic,** *adj.*

OTR, abbreviation for *occupational therapist, registered.*

Otrivin, a trademark for a nasal adrenergic vasoconstrictor (xylometazoline hydrochloride).

Otto pelvis /ot′ō/ [Adolph W. Otto, German surgeon, 1786–1845], a type of hip dislocation that involves a gradual central displacement of the femur. The cause is unknown.

O.U., abbreviation for *oculus uterque,* a Latin phrase meaning "each eye."

oubain /wäbā′in/, a crystalline glycoside derived from the seeds of *Strophanthus gratus* and the wood of *Acocanthera oubaio.* It blocks Na$^+$,K$^+$-ATPase similarly to strophanthin-K and the digitalis glycosides, and is often used in pharmacologic studies because of its greater solubility in water. It is used as an arrow poison in Africa.

Ouchterlony double diffusion [Orjan T.G. Ouchterlony, Swedish bacteriologist, b. 1914], a form of gel diffusion technique in which antigen and antibody in separate cells are allowed to diffuse toward each other.

ounce (oz) /ouns/ [L, *uncia,* one twelfth], a unit of mass equal to $^1/_{16}$ of a pound avoirdupois or 28.349 grams.

outbreak /out′brāk/, in epidemiology, the occurrence of infection with a particular disease in a small, localized group, such as the population of a village. The term is sometimes used more broadly to refer to an epidemic or a pandemic.

outbreeding [AS, *ut,* out, *bredan,* to breed], the production of offspring by the mating of unrelated individuals, which can lead to superior hybrid traits or strains.

outcome [AS, *ut* + *couman,* to come], the condition of a patient at the end of therapy or a disease process, including the degree of wellness and the need for continuing care, medication, support, counseling, or education.

outcome criteria, standards that focus on observable or measurable results of nursing and other health service activities.

outcome data, information collected to evaluate the capacity of a client to function at a level described in the outcome statement of a nursing care plan or in standards for patient care.

outcome measure, a measure of the quality of medical care, the standard against which the end result of the intervention is assessed.

outer zone of renal medulla, the part of the renal medulla nearest to the cortex. It contains part of the distal straight tubule and the medullary collecting tubule.

outlet [AS, *ut* + *laetan,* to permit], an opening through which something can exit, such as the pelvic outlet.

outlet contracture, an abnormally small pelvic outlet. It may be anteroposterior or transverse and is of significance in childbirth because it may impede or prevent passage of a baby through the birth canal.

outlier, 1. in managed care, a case in which costs exceed the allowable amount for the specific diagnosis or treatment. The outlier amount is typically specified in advance in the contract between the provider and payer. **2.** in research, an observation that differs from all others, suggesting that a gross error has occurred in sampling, measurement, or analysis.

outline form [AS, *ut* + *lin,* thread], the shape of the cavosurface of a prepared tooth cavity before the tooth surface or surfaces are restored.

out-of-body experience (oobe), a sensation that the mind has separated temporarily from the body. The feeling tends to occur when the patient is asleep, in a trance, or unconscious as during surgery. The person visualizes his or her body as an impersonal observer might. In some cases the person visualizes objects or persons who are beyond the range of normal senses. Occasionally a patient near death learns after awakening that he or she has been declared clinically dead during the moments of the experience.

out of phase, pertaining to a series of events or actions that are not synchronous with a previously established periodic process or phenomenon. An oscillation or periodic process that runs in an opposite direction or pattern is sometimes described as 180 degrees out of phase.

out-of-plan services, services given to a patient by a provider outside the managed care system. The patient may be responsible for a larger co-payment than if the services were received within the plan.

outpatient (OP) [AS, *ut*; L, *patientia,* endurance], **1.** a patient, not hospitalized, who is being treated in an office, clinic, or other ambulatory care facility. **2.** pertaining to a health care facility for patients who are not hospitalized or to the treatment or care of such a patient.

output [AS, *ut + putian,* to put], **1.** the total of any and all measurable liquids lost from the body, including urine, vomitus, and diarrhea; drainage from wounds and fistulas; and those removed by suction equipment. The output is recorded as a means of monitoring a patient's fluid and electrolyte balance. **2.** the end product of a system.

output amplifier, an apparatus used to increase the amplitude of the voltage output of a generator and control it at a specific level.

outreach program, a system of delivery of services to geropsychiatric clients, particularly mentally ill older adults in rural environments. Outreach programs can diagnose and treat homebound clients with physical limitations or major psychiatric illnesses who are socially isolated.

ova and parasites test /ōˈvä/, a microscopic examination of feces for detecting parasites, such as amebas or worms and their ova, which are indicators of parasitic disorders.

oval foramen, **1.** an opening in the septum between the right and the left atria in the fetal heart. This opening provides a bypass for blood that would otherwise flow to the fetal lungs. **2.** an oval foramen

situated laterally to the foramen rotundum of the sphenoid bone.

ovalocytes /ōˈvələsīts′/ [L, *ovalis,* egg-shaped; Gk, *kytos,* cell], elliptical or oval-shaped red blood cells with pale centers occasionally found in patients with hereditary elliptocytosis.

oval window /ōˈvəl/ [L, *ovum;* ME, *windoge*], an aperture in the wall of the middle ear, leading to the inner ear. The footplate of the stapes vibrates in the oval window, transmitting sound waves to the cochlea.

ovarian /ōverˈē-ən/ [L, *ovum,* egg], pertaining to the ovary.

ovarian artery, a slender branch of the abdominal aorta, arising caudal to the renal arteries, and supplying an ovary.

ovarian carcinoma, a malignant neoplasm of the ovaries rarely detected in the early stage and usually far advanced when diagnosed. It occurs frequently in the fifth decade of life. Risk factors of the disease are infertility, nulliparity or low parity, delayed childbearing, repeated spontaneous abortion, endometriosis, group A blood type, previous history of breast or colorectal cancer, and exposure to chemical carcinogens such as asbestos and talc. Characteristic of the disease as it advances are abdominal swelling and discomfort, abnormal vaginal bleeding, weight loss, dysuria or abnormal frequency of urination, constipation, and a palpable ovarian mass, especially in postmenopausal women. In many cases the cancer spreads over the surface of the peritoneum, and, early in the course of the lesion, tumor cells invade the lymphatic vessels under the diaphragm and the paraaortic nodes. Approximately half of the tumors diagnosed are unresectable.

ovarian cyst, a globular sac filled with fluid or semisolid material that develops in or on the ovary. It may be transient and physiologic or pathologic.

ovarian fimbria, the longest of the processes that make up the uterine fimbria tube, extending along the free border of the mesosalpinx. It is fused to the ovary, so that the ostium of the tube relates to the ovary.

ovarian follicle [L, *ovum + folliculus,* small bag], a cavity or recess in an ovary containing a liquor that divides the follicular cells into layers and surrounds an ovum.

ovarian hyperstimulation, ovarian enlargement with exudation of fluid and protein.

ovarian pregnancy, a rare type of ec-top-ic pregnancy in which the conceptus is implanted within the ovary.

ovarian reserve, the number and quality of oocytes in the ovaries of a woman of childbearing age.

ovarian varicocele, a varicose swelling of the veins of the uterine broad ligament.

ovarian vein, one of a pair of veins that emerge from convoluted plexuses in the broad ligament near the ovaries and the uterine tubes. The veins from each plexus ascend and unite to form single veins. The right ovarian vein opens into the inferior vena cava, and the left ovarian vein into the renal vein.

ovariocele /ōver'ē·əsēl/, a hernia of an ovary or protrusion of an ovary through the vaginal wall.

ovariocentesis /ōver'ē·ōsentē'sis/, surgical puncture of an ovary and drainage of an ovarian cyst.

ovariohysterectomy /-his'tərek'təmē/, the surgical removal of the uterus and ovaries.

ovary /ō'vərē/ [L, *ovum,* egg], one of the paired female gonads found on each side of the lower abdomen, beside the uterus in a fold of the broad ligament. At ovulation, an egg is expelled from a follicle on the surface of the ovary under the stimulation of the gonadotrophic hormones follicle-stimulating hormone (FSH) and luteinizing hormone (LH). The remainder of the follicle (corpus luteum) secretes the hormones estrogen and progesterone, which regulate the menstrual cycle by a negative-feedback system in which an increase in estrogen decreases the secretion of FSH by the pituitary gland and an increase in progesterone decreases the secretion of LH. Each ovary is normally firm and smooth and resembles an almond in size and shape.

Ovcon, a trademark for an oral contraceptive containing an estrogen (ethinyl estradiol) and a progestin (norethindrone acetate).

overactive bladder, a condition characterized by a nearly constant urge to urinate.

overbite /ō'vərbīt/ [AS, *ofer,* over, *bitan,* to bite], increased vertical overlapping of the lower teeth by the upper teeth, usually measured perpendicular to the occlusal plane.

overclosure /-klō'zhər/ [AS, *ofer;* L, *claudere,* to close], an abnormal condition in which the mandible rises beyond the point of normal occlusal contact, caused by drifting of teeth, loss of occlusal vertical dimension, change in tooth shapes through grinding, or loss of teeth.

overcompensation /-kom'pənsā'shən/ [AS, *ofer;* L, *compensare,* to weigh together], an exaggerated attempt to overcome a real or imagined physical or psychologic deficit. The attempt may be conscious or unconscious.

overdenture /-den'chər/ [AS, *ofer;* L, *dens,* tooth], a complete or partial removable denture supported by retained roots or teeth to provide improved support, stability, and tactile and proprioceptive sensation and to reduce bone resorption.

overdose (OD) /-dōs/, an excessive use of a drug, resulting in adverse reactions ranging from mania or hysteria to coma or death.

overdrive suppression /-drīv/ [AS, *ofer + drifan,* to drive], the inhibitory effect of a faster cardiac pacemaker on a slower one.

overeruption /-irup'shən/, the projection of a tooth beyond the normal occlusal plane.

overflow /-flō/ [AS, *ofer + flowan*], the flooding or excessive discharge of a fluid, such as urine, saliva, or bile.

overflow incontinence [AS, *ofer + flowan;* L, *incontinentia,* inability to retain], an overflow of urine from a distended paralyzed bladder.

overgrafting /-graf'ting/, placing an additional transplant over a previously healed tissue graft. It is sometimes performed to strengthen a split-thickness graft or to replace epithelium that may have been lost.

overgrowth [AS, *ofer;* ME, *growen*], an excessive growth, usually applied to organ or tissue development.

overhang /-hang/ [AS, *ofer + hangian,* to hang], an excess of dental filling material that projects beyond the margin of a tooth cavity preparation.

overhydration /-hīdrā'shən/, an excess of water in the body.

overinclusiveness /-inklōō'sivnəs/ [AS, *ofer;* L, *includere,* to include], a type of association disorder observed in some schizophrenia patients. The individual is unable to think in a precise manner because of an inability to keep irrelevant elements outside perceptual boundaries.

overjet /-jet/ [AS, *ofer;* Fr, *jeter,* to throw], increased projection of the upper teeth in front of the lower teeth, usually measured parallel to the occlusal plane.

overlap /-lap'/, to extend over and cover part of an existing surface or structure.

overlay /ō'vərlā/, to add to an existing condition or structure; to lay on top of something.

overlearning /-lur'ning/, the practice of an ability that continues beyond the point where performance meets a specified standard.

overload /-lōd/, **1.** a burden greater than the capacity of the system designed to move or process it. **2.** in physiology, any factor or influence that stresses the body beyond its natural limits and may impair its health.

overnutrition /-nōōtrish'ən/, a condition of excess nutrient and energy intake over time. Overnutrition may be regarded as a form of malnutrition when it leads to morbid obesity.

overoxygenation /-ok'sijənā'shən/ [AS, *ofer*; Gk, *oxys*, sharp, *genein*, to produce; L, *atio*, process], an abnormal condition in which the oxygen concentration in the blood and other tissues of the body is greater than normal. The condition is characterized by a fall in BP, decreased vital capacity, fatigue, errors in judgment, paresthesia of the hands and feet, anorexia, nausea, vomiting, and hyperemia.

overresponse /-rispons'/, an abnormally strong reaction to a stimulus.

overriding /-rī'ding/ [AS, *ofer* + *ridan*], **1.** the slipping of either part of a fractured bone past the other. **2.** extending beyond the usual position.

overripe cataract /-rīp/ [AS, *ofer*; OE, *reap*], a cataract in which a completely opaque lens solidifies and shrinks.

oversensing /-sen'sing/, the sensation of stimuli, such as magnetism or static electricity, that are not normally detected by the sense organs.

overshoot /ō'vərshoot/, **1.** to go beyond or exceed a target or goal. **2.** an upper part of a structure that extends beyond the lower part.

over the counter (OTC), of a drug, available to the consumer without a prescription.

overtone, **1.** any tone produced by voice or a musical instrument that is of a higher frequency than the lowest or fundamental tone of a sound. **2.** a harmonic.

overweight /-wāt/ [AS, *ofer* + *gewiht*, weight], **1.** more than normal in body weight after adjustment for height, body build, and age, or 10% to 20% above the person's "desirable" body weight. **2.** a body mass index between 25.0 and 29.9.

overwintering /-win'təring/, persistence of seasonal infectious agents beyond their normal period of activity, particularly warm weather pathogen vectors that remain operative into the winter months.

ovicidal /ō'visī'dəl/, causing destruction of an ovum.

ovicide /ō'visīd/, an agent that destroys ova.

oviferous /ōvif'ərəs/ [L, *ovum*, egg, *ferre*, to bear], bearing or capable of producing ova (egg cells).

oviparous /ōvip'ərəs/ [L, *ovum* + *parere*, to bring forth], giving birth to young by laying eggs.

oviposition /ō'vipəsish'ən/ [L, *ovum* + *ponere*, to place], the act of laying or depositing eggs by a female oviparous animal.

ovipositor /ō'vipos'itər/ [L, *ovum* + *ponere*, to place], a specialized organ, found primarily in insects, for depositing eggs on plants or in the soil. It may be modified into a stinger, as in worker bees and wasps.

ovocenter /ō'vəsen'tər/ [L, *ovum* + *centrum*, center], the centrosome of a fertilized ovum.

ovoflavin /ō'vəflā'vin/ [L, *ovum* + *flavus*, yellow], a riboflavin derived from the yolk of eggs.

ovoglobulin /ō'vəglob'yōōlin/ [L, *ovum* + *globulus*, small sphere], a globulin protein derived from the whites of eggs.

ovoid /ō'void/, egg-shaped, oval.

ovoid arch [L, *ovum*; Gk, *eidos*, form; L, *arcus*, bow], a dental arch that curves smoothly from the molars on one side to those on the opposite side to form half an oval.

ovomucin /ō'vəmyōō'sin/ [L, *ovum* + *mucus*, slime], a glycoprotein derived from the whites of eggs.

ovomucoid /ō'vəmyōō'koid/ [L, *ovum* + *mucus*, slime; Gk, *eidos*, form], pertaining to a glycoprotein, similar to mucin, derived from the whites of eggs.

ovotestis /ō'vətes'tis/ [L, *ovum* + *testis*, testicle], a gonad that contains both ovarian and testicular tissue; a hermaphroditic gonad.—**ovotesticular**, *adj.*

ovoviviparous /ō'vəvivip'ərəs/ [L, *ovum* + *vivus*, living, *parere*, to bring forth], bearing young in eggs that are hatched within the body, as in some reptiles and fishes.

Ovral, a trademark for an oral contraceptive containing a progestin (norgestrel) and an estrogen (ethinyl estradiol).

Ovrette, a trademark for an oral contraceptive containing a progestin (norgestrel).

OVTT, abbreviation for **optometric vision therapy technician**.

ovulation /ov'yəlā'shən/ [L, *ovum* + *atio*, process], expulsion of an ovum from the ovary on spontaneous rupture of a mature follicle as a result of cyclic ovarian and pituitary endocrine function. It usually occurs on or about the eleventh to the fourteenth day before the next menstrual period and may cause brief, sharp lower abdominal pain on the side of the ovulating ovary.—**ovulate** /ov'yə'lāt/, *v.*

ovulation method of family planning, a natural method of family planning that uses observation of changes in the character and quantity of cervical mucus to determine the time of ovulation during the menstrual cycle. Because pregnancy occurs with fertilization of an ovum extruded from the ovary at ovulation, the method is used to increase or decrease the woman's chance of becoming pregnant by causing or avoiding insemination by spontaneous or artificial means during the fertile period associated with ovulation. The cyclic changes in gonadotropic hormones, especially estrogen, cause changes in the quantity and character of cervical mucus. Daily close monitoring of the mucus is necessary even after several cycles because the length of the "safe" and "unsafe" periods and the time of ovulation vary from cycle to cycle, as they do from woman to woman.

ovulatory /ov′yələtôr′ē/ [L, *ovum*], pertaining to ovulation.

ovulatory phase, the second phase of the human menstrual cycle, during which the luteinizing hormone surges, the follicle-stimulating hormone surges, and ovulation occurs.

ovulocyclic /ov′yəlōsī′klik/, pertaining to recurrent events associated with the ovulatory cycle.

ovulocyclic porphyria, episodes of acute abnormalities of porphyrin metabolism that tend to recur in the premenstrual period.

ovum /ō′vəm/ *pl.* **ova** [L, egg], **1.** an egg. **2.** the secondary oocyte (female germ cell) extruded from the ovary at ovulation.

owl-eye cell, an enlarged cell infected by cytomegalovirus and containing large inclusion bodies, found mainly in the renal epithelium.

Owren's disease [Paul A. Owren, Norwegian hematologist, 1905–1990], a rare congenital bleeding disorder caused by a deficiency of coagulation factor V.

oxacillin sodium /ok′səsil′in/, a penicillinase-resistant penicillin antibiotic prescribed in the treatment of severe bacterial infections caused by penicillinase-producing staphylococci.

oxalate ($C_2O_4^{2-}$) /ok′səlāt/, an anion of oxalic acid.

oxalated blood /ok′səlā′tid/, blood to which a soluble ester of oxalic acid has been added to prevent coagulation.

oxalemia /ok′səlē′mē·ə/, elevated levels of oxalates in the blood.

oxalic acid ($H_2C_2O_4$) /oksal′ik/, a member of a family of dibasic acids found in many common plants, such as buckwheat, wood sorrel, and rhubarb. It is an important reagent and is used in bleaching and drying. Poisonous if ingested, oxalic acid is used in veterinary medicine as a hemostatic. In dietary intake of foods containing oxalic acid, the substance binds with calcium and is sometimes found in renal calculi and the urine of patients with hyperoxaluria.

oxaliplatin, an antineoplastic agent used to treat metastatic carcinoma of the colon or rectum in combination with 5-FU/leucovorin.

oxalosis /ok′səlō′sis/, a condition in which calcium oxalate crystals accumulate in the kidneys, heart, and other organs and urinary excretion of oxalate increases. Oxalosis-inducing agents include oxalic

acid, methoxyflurane, ethylene glycol, and ascorbic acid.

oxaluric acid /ok′səlŏŏr′ik/, a compound derived from uric acid or from parabanic acid, which occurs in normal urine.

oxandrolone /oksan′drəlōn/, an androgen prescribed in the treatment of bone pain accompanying osteoporosis and for the stimulation of weight gain after extensive surgery or trauma or when a pathophysiologic reason exists for failure to maintain normal weight.

oxaprozin /ok′säpro′zin/, an NSAID used in treatment of arthritis.

oxazepam /oksā′zəpam/, a benzodiazepine tranquilizer prescribed to relieve anxiety and nervous tension and manage ethanol withdrawal. It has unlabeled use for treatment of simple partial seizures.

oxazolidinone /ok′səzō·lid′inōn/, any of a class of synthetic antibacterial agents effective against gram-positive organisms.

oxcarbazepine /oks′kär-baz′e-pēn/, an anticonvulsant used in the treatment of partial seizures.

oxiconazole /ok′si-kon′äzōl/, a topical antifungal agent used as the nitrate salt in the treatment of athlete's foot and ringworm.

oxidant /ok′sidənt/ [Gk, *oxys*, sharp], an oxidizing agent.

oxidase /ok′sidās/ [Gk, *oxys*, sharp], an enzyme that induces biologic oxidation by activating the oxygen in molecules containing the element, such as hydrogen peroxide.

oxidation /ok′sidā′shən/ [Gk, *oxys*, sharp, *genein*, to produce; L, *atio*, process], **1.** any process in which the oxygen content in a compound or the number of bonds to oxygen (or other electronegative element, such as a halogen) in a compound is increased. **2.** any reaction in which the positive valence of a compound or a radical is increased because of a loss of electrons. **3.** any process in which the hydrogen content in a compound or the number of bonds to hydrogen (or other element of low electronegativity, such as a metal) is decreased.—**oxidative,** *n.,* **oxidize,** *v.*

oxidation-reduction reaction, a chemical change in which electrons are removed (oxidation) from an atom, ion, or molecule, accompanied by a simultaneous transfer of electrons (reduction) to another. The reaction may also involve the transfer of electronegative atoms (e.g., oxygen) or atoms of low electronegativity (e.g., hydrogen or metal) from one molecule to another.

oxidative phosphorylation /ok′sidā′tiv/, an ATP-generating process in which oxygen serves as the final electron acceptor. The process occurs in mitochondria and is the major source of adenosine triphosphate generation in aerobic organisms.

oxidative stress, 1. any of various pathologic changes seen in living organisms in response to excessive levels of cytotoxic oxidants and free radicals in the environment. **2.** use of antioxidant intake in the diet to provide both preventive and therapeutic advantage and reduce the damaging effects of free radicals on cellular constituents.

oxidative water [Gk, *oxys,* sharp, *genein,* to produce; L, *ativus,* related to], water produced by the oxidation of molecules of food substances, such as the conversion of glucose to water and carbon dioxide.

oxide /ok'sīd/, **1.** a compound of oxygen and another element or radical. **2.** a dianion of oxygen, O^{2-}.

oxidize /ok'sidīz/ [Gk, *oxys,* sharp, *genein,* to produce, *izein,* to cause], of an element or compound, to combine or cause to combine with oxygen, to remove hydrogen, or to increase the valence of an element through the loss of electrons. —**oxidation,** *n.,* **oxidizing,** *adj.*

oxidizing agent, a compound that readily gives up oxygen or accepts hydrogen or electrons from another compound.

oxidoreductase /ok'sidō'riduk'tās/, an enzyme that catalyzes a reaction in which one substance is oxidized while another is reduced. An example is alcohol dehydrogenase.

oximeter /oksim'ətər/, a device used to measure oxyhemoglobin in arterial blood.

oximetry, a photodiagnostic method of monitoring arterial blood oxygen saturation (SaO_2). Oximetry is commonly used to titrate levels of oxygen on hospitalized patients. It is used for monitoring the patient's oxygenation status during the perioperative period or any other time of heavy sedation, during mechanical ventilation, and in many clinical situations such as pulmonary rehabilitation programs and stress testing.

oxprenolol /oks-pren'älol/, a nonselective beta-adrenergic blocking agent used in the treatment of hypertension, hypertrophic cardiomyopathy, cardiac arrhythmias, and MI.

Oxsoralen, a trademark for a pigmentation agent (methoxsalen).

oxtriphylline /oks'trəfil'ēn/, a bronchodilator prescribed in the treatment of bronchial asthma, bronchitis, and emphysema.

oxyacoia, an abnormal hearing acuity. Increased sensitivity to sound is sometimes associated with paralysis of the stapedius muscle.

oxybutynin chloride /ok'sibōō'tinin/, an anticholinergic prescribed in the treatment of neurogenic bladder.

oxycalorimeter /ok'sēkal'ôrim'ətər/, an apparatus that measures the heat of combustion of organic materials in terms of oxygen consumed. Each liter of oxygen is roughly equivalent to 5 kilocalories,

oxycellulose /ok'sēsel'yəlōs/, **1.** cellulose that has been oxidized so that all or most of the glucose residues have been converted to glucuronic acid residues for use as an absorbent in chromatography. **2.** cellulose that has been partially oxidized for use as a local hemostatic.

oxycephaly /ok'sisef'əlē/ [Gk, *oxys* + *kephale,* head], a congenital malformation of the skull in which premature closure of the coronal and sagittal sutures results in accelerated upward growth of the head, giving it a long, narrow appearance with the top pointed or conic.—**oxycephalous,** *adj.,* **oxycephalus,** *n.*

oxycodone hydrochloride /ok'sikōdōn/, an opioid analgesic used to treat moderate to severe pain, often in combination with nonopioid analgesics.

oxygen (O) /ok'səjən/ [Gk, *oxys,* sharp, *genein,* to produce], a tasteless, odorless, colorless gas essential for human respiration. Its atomic number is 8, and its atomic mass is 15.9994. Oxygen makes up approximately 20% of the atmosphere. In anesthesia, oxygen functions as a carrier gas for the delivery of anesthetic agents to tissues. In respiratory therapy, oxygen is administered to increase the amount circulating in the blood. Overdose of oxygen can cause irreversible toxicity in people with pulmonary abnormalities, especially when complicated by chronic carbon dioxide retention.

oxygenation /ok'səjənā'shən/, the process of combining or treating with oxygen. —**oxygenate,** *v.*

oxygen capacity of blood, the maximum amount of oxygen that can combine chemically with a given amount of hemoglobin in blood. It does not include oxygen dissolved in plasma.

oxygen concentration in blood, the concentration of oxygen in a blood sample, including both oxygen combined with hemoglobin and oxygen dissolved in the plasma.

oxygen consumption, the amount of oxygen used by the body per minute. For normal aerobic metabolism, it is about 250 mL/min.

oxygen cost of breathing, the rate at which the respiratory muscles consume oxygen as they ventilate the lungs.

oxygen debt, the quantity of oxygen that the lungs take up during recovery from exercise or apnea that is in excess of the quantity needed for resting metabolism before the exercise or apnea.

oxygen delivery system, a device that delivers oxygen through the upper airways to the lungs at concentrations above that of ambient air. There are two general types: high flow and low flow.

oxygen dissociation curve, graphic expression of the affinity of hemoglobin for oxygen as a function of the partial pressure of oxygen. Dissociation is influenced by pH, temperature, and carbon dioxide pressure. Formerly called *oxyhemoglobin dissociation curve.*

oxygen enhancement ratio (OER), a measure of tumor sensitivity to the presence or absence of oxygen, expressed as the ratio of radiation dose required to produce a given effect with no oxygen present to the dose required to produce the same effect in 1 atmosphere of air.

oxygen hood, a device placed over the head of a patient to deliver high concentrations of oxygen.

oxygen mask, a device used to administer oxygen, shaped to fit snugly over the mouth and nose and secured in place with a strap or held with the hand. The mask has inspiratory and expiratory valves allowing oxygen to be inhaled or pumped into the respiratory tract and carbon dioxide to be exhaled into the environment.

oxygen P50, the oxygen pressure necessary for 50% saturation of hemoglobin at body temperature and at pH 7.4 or for 40 mm Hg of carbon dioxide pressure. The P50 is used as a measure of hemoglobin affinity for oxygen.

oxygen radicals [Gk, *oxys,* sharp; L, *radix,* root], a substituent group of chemical elements rich in oxygen but incapable of prolonged existence in a free state. Oxygen radicals are used in some types of therapy.

oxygen saturation, 1. the fraction of the hemoglobin molecules in a blood sample that are saturated with oxygen at a given partial pressure of oxygen. 2. percentage of hemoglobin-bound oxygen compared to total capacity of the hemoglobin.

oxygen store, the total quantity of oxygen stored in various body compartments, including the lungs, arterial and venous blood, and tissues. In a 70-kg human, blood contains about 800 mL of oxygen as oxyhemoglobin, muscles contain about 150 mL as oxymyoglobin, alveolar gas contains a few hundred milliliters, and about 50 mL is dissolved in the tissues.

oxygen tension, the partial pressure of oxygen molecules dissolved in a liquid, such as blood plasma.

oxygen tent [Gk, *oxys,* sharp; ME, *tente*], a canopy that encloses the head and neck of a patient and provides humidified oxygen.

oxygen therapy[1], any procedure in which oxygen is administered to a patient to relieve hypoxia. The method selected depends on the condition of the patient and the cause of hypoxia.

oxygen therapy[2], a nursing intervention from the Nursing Interventions Classification (NIC) defined as administration of oxygen and monitoring of its effectiveness.

oxygen tolerance, an increased capacity to withstand the toxic effects of abnormally high oxygen tension as a result of any adaptive change occurring within an organism.

oxygen toxicity, a condition of oxygen overdosage that can result in pathologic tissue changes, such as retinopathy of prematurity or bronchopulmonary dysplasia. It can also decrease the hypoxic drive to breathe.

oxygen transport, the process by which oxygen is absorbed by red blood cell hemoglobin in the lungs and carried to the peripheral tissues. Hemoglobin combines with oxygen when present at a high concentration, such as in the lungs, and releases oxygen when the concentration is low, such as in the peripheral tissues.

oxyhemoglobin /ok'sēhē'məglō'bin, -hem'-/ [Gk, *oxys* + *genein,* to produce, *haima,* blood; L, *globus,* ball], the product of combining hemoglobin with oxygen. The loosely bound complex dissociates easily when the concentration of oxygen is low.

oxymesterone /ok'sēmes'tərōn/, an androgen and anabolic steroid involved in tissue building.

oxymetazoline hydrochloride /ok'sēmətaz'əlēn/, an adrenergic vasoconstrictor prescribed topically in the treatment of nasal congestion and for the relief of eye redness caused by minor eye irritation.

oxymetholone /ok'sēmeth'əlōn/, an anabolic steroid prescribed in the treatment of anemias caused by antineoplastic drugs.

oxymorphone hydrochloride /ok'sēmôr'fōn/, an opioid analgesic prescribed for relief of moderate to severe pain, as a preoperative medication, and to support anesthesia.

oxyntic cell, a hydrochloric acid–producing cell of the stomach.

oxyopia /ok'sē·ō'pē·ə/ [Gk, *oxys* + *opsis* vision], unusual acuteness of vision. A person with normal (20/20) vision when standing 20 feet from the standard Snellen eye chart can read the seventh line of letters, each of which is an eighth of an inch high. An individual with oxyopia can read smaller letters at that distance.

oxyphil cell /ok'səfil/, a cell of the parathyroid glands that takes up acidic stains and has a dark nucleus and fine, granular cytoplasm. Such cells occur singly or in small groups and increase in number with age.

oxytalan /ok′sētal′ən, oksit′ələn/, a type of connective tissue fiber particular to the periodontal membrane.

oxytetracycline /ok′sētet′rəsī′klēn/, a tetracycline antibiotic prescribed in the treatment of bacterial and rickettsial infections.

oxytetracycline calcium, a tetracycline antibiotic.

oxytocia /ok′sētō′shə/, rapid childbirth.

oxytocic /ok′sitō′sik/ [Gk, oxys + tokos, birth], **1.** pertaining to a substance that is similar to the hormone oxytocin. **2.** any one of numerous drugs that stimulate the smooth muscle of the uterus to contract. These drugs are used to induce or augment labor at term, control postpartum hemorrhage, correct postpartum uterine atony, produce uterine contractions after cesarean section or other uterine surgery, and induce therapeutic abortion.

oxytocin¹ /ok′sitō′sin/, an oxytocic prescribed to stimulate contractions in inducing or augmenting labor and to contract the uterus to control postpartum bleeding.

oxytocin², a polypeptide secreted by magnocellular neurons in the hypothalamus and stored as a posterior pituitary hormone along with vasopressin. It promotes uterine contractions and milk ejection and contributes to the second stage of labor.

oxytocin challenge test, a stress test for the assessment of intrauterine function of the fetus and the placenta. It is performed to evaluate the ability of the fetus to tolerate continuation of pregnancy or the anticipated stress of labor and delivery. A dilute IV infusion of oxytocin is begun, regulated by an infusion pump. The uterine activity is monitored with a tocodynamometer, and the fetal heart rate is monitored with an ultrasonic sensor as the uterus is stimulated to contract by the oxytocin. The fetal heart rate is observed for variability and for the timing of any marked variation from the normal in relation to uterine contractions. Decelerations of the fetal heart rate in certain repeating patterns may indicate fetal distress.

oxyuricide /ok′sē-ōō′risīd/, an agent that destroys pinworms.

oz, abbreviation for **ounce.**

oz ap [L, uncia], abbreviation for apothecary ounce, a unit of weight equal to 31.1035 grams.

ozena /ōzē′nə/ [Gk, ozein, to have an odor], a condition of the nose characterized by atrophy of the nasal conchae and mucous membranes. Symptoms include crusting of nasal secretions, discharge, and, especially, a very offensive odor. Ozena may follow chronic inflammation of the nasal mucosa.

ozone (O₃) [Gk, ozein, to have an odor], an allotropic form of oxygen consisting of molecules containing three oxygen atoms. Ozone is formed when oxygen is present in an electric discharge, as might occur in a lightning storm. Ozone is used as a bleaching, cleaning, and oxidizing agent and has a faint, chlorine-like odor.

ozone hole, a seasonal depletion of the steady-state ozone concentration in the stratosphere, particularly over Antarctica.

ozone shield, the layer of ozone that hangs in the atmosphere from 20 to 40 miles above the surface of the earth and protects the earth from excessive ultraviolet radiation.

ozone sickness, an abnormal condition caused by the inhalation of ozone that may seep into jet aircraft at altitudes over 40,000 feet. It is characterized by headaches, chest pains, itchy eyes, and sleepiness. It is more prevalent early in the year and occurs more often over the Pacific Ocean.

oz t [L, uncia], abbreviation for troy ounce, a unit of weight equal to 31.103 grams.

P, 1. abbreviation for *power*. **2.** abbreviation for **pressure**.

P, 1. symbol for the element **phosphorus**. **2.** symbol for *after*, or *post*. **3.** in genetics, symbol for *first parental generation*. **4.** symbol for *first pulmonic sound*.

p, symbol for *gas partial pressure*.

p-, symbol for **para-**.

p17, symbol for a protein that lines the interior of the HIV envelope.

P1E1, P2E1, P3E1, P4E1, P6E1, trademarks for fixed-combination ophthalmic drugs containing a cholinergic (pilocarpine hydrochloride) and an adrenergic (epinephrine bitartrate). The numbers indicate the percentage of each ingredient in the solution; for example, P2E1 contains 2% pilocarpine hydrochloride and 1% epinephrine bitartrate.

P₂, symbol for *second pulmonic sound*.

p24, symbol for a protein that surrounds the RNA and reverse transcriptase of the HIV.

P₅₀, the partial pressure of oxygen at which hemoglobin is half-saturated with bound oxygen.

P & A, 1. abbreviation for *percussion and auscultation*. **2.** abbreviation for *posterior and anterior*.

pA, abbreviation for *picoampere*.

Pa, 1. symbol for *pascal*. **2.** symbol for the element **protactinium**.

PA, 1. abbreviation for **physician assistant**. **2.** abbreviation for **pulmonary artery**.

P-A,p-a, abbreviation for **posteroanterior**.

PABA, abbreviation for **paraaminobenzoic acid**, a topical sunscreen.

pabulin /pab′yəlin/ [L, *pabulum*, food], products of fat and protein digestion found in the blood after a meal.

pabulum /pab′yələm/ [L, food], any substance that is food or nutrient.

PAC, abbreviation for **premature atrial complex**.

pacchionian foramen /pak′ē·ō′nē·ən/ [Antonio Pacchioni, Italian anatomist, 1665–1720], a thick opening in the center of the diaphragm of sella through which the infundibulum passes.

PACE /pās/, abbreviation for **Program of All-Inclusive Care of the Elderly.**

PACE II, an interdisciplinary assessment and planning system that focuses on evaluation of the physical health of nursing home residents. It includes checklists of defined (diagnosed) conditions, abnormal laboratory or other findings, risk factors, and other impairments and disabilities.

pacemaker [L, *passus,* step; AS, *macian,* to make], **1.** the sinoatrial node composed of specialized nervous tissue located at the junction of the superior vena cava and the right atrium. It initiates the contractions of the atria, which transmit the impulse on to the atrioventricular (AV) node, thereby initiating the contraction of the ventricles. An ectopic or idioventricular pacemaker, originating in the atria, AV node, or ventricle, may cause contractions in cases of abnormal heart functioning. **2.** an electric apparatus used in most cases to increase the heart rate in severe bradycardia by electrically stimulating the heart muscle. A pacemaker may be permanent or temporary, emit the stimulus at a constant and fixed rate, or fire only on demand.

pacemaker management: permanent, a nursing intervention from the Nursing Interventions Classification (NIC) defined as care of the patient receiving permanent support of cardiac pumping through the insertion and use of a pacemaker.

pacemaker management: temporary, a nursing intervention from the Nursing Interventions Classification (NIC) defined as temporary support of cardiac pumping through the insertion and use of temporary pacemakers.

pachyblepharon /-blef′əron/ [Gk, *pachy,* thick], a thickening of the tarsal border of the eyelid.

pachycheilia /-kī′lē·ə/, an abnormal thickening or swelling of the lips.

pachycholia /-kō′lē·ə/, a thickening of the bile.

pachychromatic /-krōmat′ik/, characterized by coarse chromatin filaments.

pachychymia /-kī′mē·ə/, thickness of the partially digested food moving from the stomach into the duodenum.

pachydactyly /pak′ēdak′tilē/ [Gk, *pachy* + *daktylos,* finger], an abnormal thickening of the fingers or toes.—**pachydactylic, pachydactylous,** *adj.*

971

pachyderma /-dur′mə/, an overgrowth or thickening of the skin and subcutaneous tissues.

pachyderma alba /-dur′mə/ [Gk, *pachy* + *derma*, skin; L, *albus*, white], an abnormal state in which the buccal mucosa has an appearance suggestive of whitened elephant hide.

pachyderma laryngis, an overgrowth of epithelium in the posterior glottis, sometimes affecting the vocal cords.

pachyderma vesicae, a potentially malignant condition of white plaques in the mucous membrane at the base of the bladder.

pachydermoperiostosis /-dur′moper′e·os to′sis/, a syndrome characterized by a thickening and folding of the facial skin, clubbing of the fingers, and new bone formation over the ends of the long bones.

pachyglossia /-glos′e·ə/, an abnormal thickening of the tongue.

pachygnathy /-gnoth′e/, an abnormal thickening of the jaw.—**pachygnathous,** *adj.*

pachygyria /-ji′re·ə/, a broadening and flattening of the gyri of the brain.

pachyleptomeningitis /-lep′təmin′inji′ tis/, an inflammation of all the membranes of the brain and spinal cord.

pachylosis /-lo′sis/, a condition of rough, dry, and thickened skin.

pachymenia /-me′ne·ə/, an abnormal thickness of the skin or other membranes. —**pachymenic,** *adj.*

pachymeningitis /-min′inji′tis/, an inflammation of the dura mater.

pachymeningopathy /-mining′gopath′e/, an abnormality, other than inflammation, involving the dura mater.

pachymeninx /-me′ninks/ *pl.* **pachymeninges** [Gk, *pachys,* thick, *meninx,* membrane]. See **dura mater.**

pachymeter /pakim′ətər/ [Gk, *pachy* + *metron,* measure], an instrument used to measure thickness, especially of a thin structure, such as a membrane or a tissue.

pachynema /pak′ine′mə/ [Gk, *pachy* + *nema,* thread], the postsynaptic tetradic chromosome formation that occurs in the pachytene stage of the first meiotic prophase of gametogenesis.

pachynsis /pakin′sis/, any thickening of tissues having a pathologic cause.

pachyonychia /pak′e·onik′e·ə/, an abnormal thickness of the fingernails or toenails.

pachyonychia congenita [Gk, *pachy* + *onyx,* nail; L, *congenitus,* born with], a congenital deformity characterized by abnormal thickening and raising of the nails on the fingers and toes and hyperkeratosis of the palms of the hands and soles of the feet.

pachyotia /pak′e·o′shə/, an abnormal thickness of the auricle of the ears.

pachypelviperitonitis /-pel′veper′itəni′tis/, pelvic peritonitis associated with a thickening of the tissues.

pachyperitonitis /-per′itəni′tis/, an inflammation and abnormal thickening of the tissues of the peritoneum.

pachypleuritis /-plŏori′tis/, an inflammation and thickening of the pleural membranes.

pachysalpingoovaritis /-salping′go·o′veri′ tis/, an inflammation and thickening of the tissues of the ovaries and fallopian tubes.

pachysomia /-so′me·ə/ [Gk, *pachys,* thick, *soma,* body], an abnormal thickening of the soft tissues of the body.

pachytene /pak′iten/ [Gk, *pachy* + *tainia,* ribbon], the third stage in the first meiotic prophase of gametogenesis, in which the paired homologous chromosomes form tetrads. The bivalent pairs become short and thick and intertwine so that four chromatids are visible.

pachyvaginalitis /-vaj′inəli′tis/, an inflammation and thickening of the membrane covering the testis and epididymis.

pachyvaginitis /-vaj′ini′tis/, chronic inflammation and thickening of the walls of the vagina.

pacifier /pas′ifi′ər/ [L, *pacificare,* to bring peace], **1.** an agent that soothes or comforts. **2.** a nipple-shaped object used by infants and children for sucking.

pacing [L, *passus,* step], setting of the heart's rhythm by the sinus node, by another site in the heart, or by an artificial electric stimulator.

pacing wire [L, *passus,* step; AS, *wir*], the electrical connection between a pulse generator and a pacing electrode in a cardiac pacemaker.

Pacini's corpuscles /päse′nēz/ [Filippo Pacini, Italian anatomist, 1812–1883; L, *corpusculum,* little body], special sensory end organs resembling tiny white bulbs. Each is attached to the end of a single nerve fiber in the subcutaneous, submucous, and subserous connective tissue of many parts of the body, especially the palm of the hand, sole of the foot, genital organs, joints, and pancreas. They are pressure-sensitive and vibration-sensitive, contain numerous concentric layers around a central core, and in cross section resemble an onion.

pacinitis /pas′ini′tis/, an inflammation of Pacini's corpuscles.

pack [ME, *pakke,* bundle], **1.** a treatment in which the entire body or a part of it is wrapped in wet or dry towels or in ice for various therapeutic purposes, as with cold packs for reducing high temperatures and swellings. **2.** a tampon. **3.** the act of applying a dressing or dental cement to a surgical wound. **4.** a surgical dressing to cover a wound or to fill the cavity left from extraction of a tooth, especially a wisdom tooth.

package insert (P.I.), a leaflet that, by order of the U.S. Food and Drug Administration (FDA), must be placed inside the package of every prescription drug. The leaflet must include the trademark for the drug, its generic name, and its mechanism of action; state its indications, contraindications, warnings, precautions, adverse effects, and dosage forms; and include instructions for the recommended dose, time, and route of administration.

packed cells [ME, *pakke,* bundle; L, *cella,* storeroom], a preparation of blood cells separated from liquid plasma, often administered in severe anemia to restore adequate levels of hemoglobin and RBCs without overloading the vascular system with excess fluids.

packed cell volume (PCV) [ME, *pakke*; L, *cella,* storeroom, *volumen,* paper roll], percentage of packed red blood cells in a centrifuged column of whole blood.

packer, an instrument for tamponing or introducing a pack of gauze into a wound.

packing [ME, *pakke*], **1.** material used to fill a wound or cavity. **2.** the act of inserting material into a wound or cavity, especially a wound with tunneling.

paclitaxel, an anticancer drug derived from the bark of the rare, slow-growing Pacific yew tree. It is used in the treatment of ovarian cancer.

PaCO₂, abbreviation for **partial pressure of carbon dioxide in arterial blood.**

PACS, acronym for *picture archiving and communications system,* a network of computers used by radiology departments that replaces film with digital images. It provides archives for storage of multimodality images, integrates images with patient database information, facilitates laser printing of images, and displays both images and patient information at work stations throughout the network.

pad [D, *paden,* cushion], **1.** a mass of soft material used to cushion shock, prevent wear, or absorb moisture, such as the abdominal pads used to absorb discharges from abdominal wounds. **2.** in anatomy, a mass of fat that cushions various structures, such as the infrapatellar pad lying below the patella.

PAD, 1. abbreviation for **peripheral arterial disease. 2.** abbreviation for **pulsatile assist device.**

p. ae [L, *partes* + *aequales*], symbol for *equal parts.*

pagetoid /paj′ətoid/, resembling Paget's disease.

Paget's disease /paj′əts/ [James Paget, English surgeon, 1814–1899], a common nonmetabolic disease of bone of unknown cause, usually affecting middle-aged and elderly people and characterized by excessive bone destruction and unorganized bone repair.

Pagliaro combined modality treatment, the use of chemotherapy in combination with surgery or irradiation or both in the treatment of cancer.

pagophagia /pā′gōfā′jē·ə/ [Gk, *pagos,* frost, *phagein,* to eat], an abnormal condition characterized by a craving to eat enormous quantities of ice. It is associated with a lack of the nutrient iron.—**pagophagic, pagophagous,** *adj.*

PAHA, abbreviation for **paraaminohippuric acid.**

PAHA sodium clearance test, a procedure formerly used for detecting kidney damage or certain muscle diseases that determined the rate at which the kidneys removed the sodium salt of para-aminohippuric acid from the blood and urine.

PAHO, abbreviation for *Pan American Health Organization.*

PAI, abbreviation for *plasminogen activator inhibitor.*

PAI-1, abbreviation for **plasminogen activator inhibitor 1.**

pain [L, *poena,* punishment], an unpleasant sensation caused by noxious stimulation of the sensory nerve endings. It is a subjective feeling and an individual response to the cause. Pain is a cardinal symptom of inflammation and is valuable in the diagnosis of many disorders and conditions. It may be mild or severe, chronic, acute, lancinating, burning, dull or sharp, precisely or poorly localized, or referred.

pain: adverse psychological response, a nursing outcome from the Nursing Outcomes Classification (NOC) defined as the severity of observed or reported adverse cognitive and emotional responses to physical pain.

pain and suffering, in law, an element in a claim for damages that allows recovery for the mental and physical pain, suffering, distress, and trauma that an individual has endured as a result of injury.

pain assessment, an evaluation of the reported pain and the factors that alleviate or exacerbate it, as well as the response to treatment of pain. The patient is asked to describe the cause of the pain, if known; its intensity, location, and duration; the events preceding it; the pattern usually followed for handling pain; previous treatments and effectiveness; allergies; and ways in which the pain has affected the ADL. Intensity of pain is often assessed using pain scales (numeric or face scales). Key aspects in evaluating pain intensity are the size of the area, the tenderness within the pain area, and the effects of movement and pressure on the pain.

pain control, a nursing outcome from the Nursing Outcomes Classification (NOC) defined as personal actions to control pain.

pain: disruptive effects, a nursing outcome from the Nursing Outcomes Classification (NOC) defined as the severity of observed or reported disruptive effects of chronic pain on daily functioning.

pain intervention, the attempt to relieve pain by various measures. Effective pain intervention depends on proper evaluation of the type of pain the patient is experiencing, the physical and psychologic origins of the pain, and the behavioral patterns commonly associated with different kinds of pain. The most common method of pain intervention is the administration of narcotics, such as morphine, but many authorities believe that the exclusive use of pain-killing drugs without consideration and implementation of psychologic aids is too narrow an approach. Acute pain, occurring in the first 24 to 48 hours after surgery, is often difficult to relieve, and narcotics seldom alleviate it completely. Mild pain may best be relieved by comfort measures and the distraction afforded by television, visitors, reading, and other passive activities. Moderate pain may best be relieved by a combination of comfort measures and drugs. Cognitive dissonance, often used to ameliorate moderate pain, encourages the patient to reflect on pleasant experiences and describe them to health care personnel. Intervention to relieve severe pain often includes the administration of narcotics, purposeful interaction between the patient and attending hospital personnel, reduction of environmental stimuli, increased comfort measures, and "waking imagined analgesia," in which the patient is encouraged to concentrate on and become distracted by former pleasant experiences.

pain level, a nursing outcome from the Nursing Outcomes Classification (NOC) defined as the severity of observed or reported pain.

pain management, a nursing intervention from the Nursing Interventions Classification (NIC) defined as alleviation of pain or a reduction in pain to a level of comfort that is acceptable to the patient.

pain mechanism, the network that communicates unpleasant sensations and the perceptions of noxious stimuli throughout the body in association with physical disease and trauma involving tissue damage.

The gate control theory of pain is an attempt to explain the role of the nervous system in the pain response. It states that pain signals that reach the nervous system excite a group of small neurons that form a "pain pool." When the total activity of these neurons reaches a minimum level, a theoretic gate opens up and allows the pain signals to proceed to higher brain centers. The areas in which the gates operate are considered to be in the spinal cord dorsal horn and the brainstem. The pattern theory holds that the intensity of a stimulus evokes a specific pattern, which is interpreted by the brain as pain. This perception is the result of the intensity and frequency of stimulation of a nonspecific end organ. Some authorities believe that bradykinin and histamine, two chemical substances produced by the body, cause pain. It is known that after histamine and some other naturally occurring chemical substances are released in the body, pain sensations travel along fast-conducting and slow-conducting nerve fibers. These pain-transmitting neuropathways communicate the pain sensation to the dorsal root ganglia of the spinal cord and synapse with certain neurons in the posterior horns of the gray matter. The pain sensation is then transmitted to the reticular formation and the thalamus by neurons that form the anterolateral spinothalamic tract. It is then conveyed to various areas of the brain, such as the cortex and the hypothalamus, by synapses at the thalamus. The immediate reaction to pain is transmitted over the reflex arc by sensory fibers in the dorsal horn of the spinal cord and by synapsing motor neurons in the anterior horn. This anatomic pattern of sensory and motor neurons allows the individual to move quickly at the touch of some harmful stimulus such as extreme heat or cold.

pain receptor, any one of the many free nerve endings throughout the body that warn of potentially harmful changes in the environment, such as excessive pressure or temperature. The free nerve endings constituting most of the pain receptors are located chiefly in the epidermis and in the epithelial covering of certain mucous membranes. They also appear in the stratified squamous epithelium of the cornea, in the root sheaths and in the papillae of the hairs, and around the bodies of sudoriferous glands. The terminal ends of pain receptors consist of unmyelinated nerve fibers that often anastomose into small knobs between the epithelial cells. Any kind of stimulus, if it is intense enough, can stimulate the pain receptors in the skin and the mucosa, but only radical changes in pressure and certain chemicals can stimulate the pain receptors in the viscera.

paint [Fr, *peindre*], **1.** to apply a medicated solution to the skin, usually over a wide area. **2.** a medicated solution that is applied in this way.

pain threshold, the point at which a stimulus, usually one associated with pressure or temperature, activates pain receptors and produces a sensation of pain. Individuals with low pain thresholds experience pain much sooner and faster than those with higher thresholds.

pair, 1. two corresponding items similar in form and function. **2.** one object composed of two joined interdependent parts.

PAL, abbreviation for *posterior axillary line.*

palatable /pal′ətəbəl/ [L, *palatum*, palate], pleasant to the taste.

palatal /pal′ətəl/ [L, *palatum*, palate], **1.** pertaining to the palate or palate bone. **2.** pertaining to the lingual surface of a maxillary tooth.

palatal shelf, lateral palatine process.

palate /pal′it/ [L, *palatum*], the bony muscular partition between the oral and nasal cavities that forms the roof of the mouth. It is divided into the hard palate and the soft palate.—**palatal, palatine** /pal′ətīn/, *adj.*

palatine aponeurosis, the major structural element of the soft palate to which other muscles of the palate attach. It is attached anteriorly to the margin of the hard palate, but it is unattached posteriorly, where it ends in a free margin.

palatine arch [L, *palatum + arcus*, bow], the vault-shaped muscular structure forming the soft palate between the mouth and the nasopharynx. An opening in the arch connects the mouth with the oropharynx; the uvula is suspended from the middle of the posterior border of the arch.

palatine bone, one of a pair of bones of the skull, forming the posterior part of the hard palate, part of the nasal cavity, and the floor of the orbit of the eye.

palatine foramina, the openings in the palatine canal. The greater palatine foramina transmit the greater palatine nerve and vessels to the hard palate. The lesser palatine foramina distribute the lesser palatine nerve and vessels to the soft palate.

palatine raphe, a medial longitudinal ridge of the mucosa of the hard palate that ends anteriorly in a small oval elevation, the incisive papilla.

palatine ridge, any one of the four to six transverse ridges on the anterior surface of the hard palate.

palatine rugae, the numerous transverse folds of the mucosa of the hard palate.

palatine suture, any one of a number of thin wavy lines marking the joining of

the palatine processes that form the hard palate.

palatine tonsil, one of a pair of almond-shaped masses of lymphoid tissue between the palatoglossal and the palatopharyngeal arches on each side of the fauces. They are covered with mucous membrane and contain numerous lymph follicles and various crypts.

palatine torus, a bony ridge along the hard palate at the line of fusion of the left and right jawbone segments.

palatine uvula, an elongated process that hangs from the middle of the back edge of the soft palate.

palatitis, an inflammation of the hard palate.

palatoglossal /pal′ətoglos′əl/ [L, *palatum*, palate; Gk, *glossa*, tongue], pertaining to both the palate and the tongue.

palatoglossus /-glos′əs/, the muscle that underlies the glossopalatine arch. The palatoglossus muscles depress the palate, move the arches toward the midline like curtains, and elevate the back of the tongue. These actions help close the fauces.

palatognathous /pal′ətog′nəthəs/, pertaining to a cleft palate.

palatograph /pal′ətōgraf′/, a device that records the movement of the palate while the person is speaking.

palatomaxillary /-mak′siler′ē/ [L, *palatum + maxilla*, jaw], pertaining to the palate and the maxilla.

palatonasal /-nā′zəl/ [L, *palatum + nasus*, nose], pertaining to the palate and the nose.

palatopharyngeal /-ferin′jē-əl/, pertaining to the palate and pharynx.

palatopharyngeus /-ferin′jē-əs/, a muscle with an origin at the back of the soft palate and an insertion on the posterior border of the thyroid cartilage and the wall of the pharynx. It acts to raise the pharynx.

palatopharyngoplasty /-fering′gōplas′tē/, the surgical excision of palatal and oropharyngeal tissues. The procedure may be performed to treat cases of snoring or sleep apnea thought to be caused by obstructions in the nose or pharynx.

palatopharyngorrhaphy, surgical repair of defects in the uvula, soft palate, and pharynx.

palatoplasty /pal′ətōplas′tē/, plastic surgery of the palate.

palatoplegia /-plē′jē-ə/, paralysis of the soft palate.

palatorrhaphy /pal′ətôr′əfē/, the surgical repair of a cleft palate.

palatosalpingeus /-salpin′jē-əs/, the tensor muscle of the soft palate. It arises from the scaphoid fossa of the sphenoid bone.

palatoschisis /pal′ətos′kisis/, a cleft palate.

P

pale infarct [L, *pallidus,* pallid, *infarcire,* to stuff], a wedge of dead tissue that is white because of an absence of blood.

paleocerebellum /pal′ē·ōser′əbel′əm/, the phylogenetically oldest part of the cerebellum, including the vermis, which connects the cerebellar hemispheres, and the flocculus, or lobule on the posterior lobe.

paleocortex /-kôr′teks/, the phylogenetically oldest part of the cerebral cortex, particularly the olfactory bulb.

paleogenetic /-jənet′ik/ [Gk, *palaios,* long ago, *genesis,* origin], **1.** a trait or structure of an organism or species that originated in a previous generation. **2.** relating to the development of such a trait or structure.

paleokinetic /-kinet′ik/, pertaining to primitive reflexes and other automatic muscular movements.

paleopathology /-pathol′əjē/, the science of disease in ancient eras based on the condition of remains of mummies, skeletons, and other archaeologic findings.

palikinesia /pal′ikīnē′zhə/, a condition in which involuntary movements are constantly repeated.

palilalia /pal′ilā′lyə/ [Gk, *palin,* again, *lalein,* to babble], an abnormal condition characterized by the increasingly rapid repetition of the same word or phrase, usually at the end of a sentence.

palindrome /pal′indrōm′/ [Gk, *palin* + *dromos,* course], a segment of DNA in which identical or almost identical sequences of bases run in opposite directions of the complementary strands.

palindromia /pal′indrō′mē·ə/, the recurrence of a disease.

palingenesis /pal′injen′əsis/ [Gk, *palin* + *genesis,* origin], **1.** the regeneration of a lost part. **2.** the hereditary transmission of ancestral structural characteristics.—**palingenetic, palingenic,** *adj.*

paliperidone, an antipsychotic used to treat schizophrenia.

palivizumab, a monoclonal antibody used to prevent serious lower respiratory tract disease caused by respiratory syncytial virus in pediatric patients.

palladium (Pd) /pəlā′dē·əm/ [Gk, *Pallas Athena,* mythic goddess and protector of Troy], a hard silvery metallic element. Its atomic number is 46, and its atomic mass is 106.42. Highly resistant to tarnish and corrosion, palladium is used in high-grade surgical instruments and in dental inlays, bridgework, and orthodontic appliances.

pallanesthesia /pal′anesthē′zhə/, a condition characterized by an inability to sense vibrations.

pallesthesia /pal′esthē′zhə/ [Gk, *pallein,* to quiver], hypersensitivity to vibration,

particularly that caused by a tuning fork placed on a bony prominence.

palliate /pal′ē·āt/ [L, *palliare,* to cloak], to soothe or relieve.—**palliation,** *n.,* **palliative,** *adj.*

palliative treatment /pal′ē·ətiv′/ [L, *palliare,* to cloak, *tractare,* to handle], therapy designed to relieve or reduce intensity of uncomfortable symptoms but not to produce a cure. Some kinds of palliative treatment are the use of narcotics to relieve pain in a patient with advanced cancer, the creation of a colostomy to bypass an inoperable obstructing lesion of the bowel, and the debridement of necrotic tissue in a patient with metastatic malignancy.

pallid /pal′id/ [L, *pallidus,* pale], lacking color.

pallidectomy /pal′idek′təmē/ [L, *pallidus,* pale; Gk, *exome,* cutting out], the destruction of all or part of the globus pallidus by chemicals or freezing in the treatment of Parkinson's disease.

pallidotomy /pal′idot′əmē/, the surgical production of lesions in the globus pallidus for the treatment of extrapyramidal disorders.

pallor /pal′ər/ [L, *paleness*], an unnatural paleness or absence of color in the skin.

palm /päm/ [L, *palma*], the flexor anterior surface of the hand, beyond the wrist to the base of the fingers, exclusive of the thumb and finger.—**palmar,** *adj.*

palm and sole system of identification, a method of identifying individuals by the patterns of ridges in the skin of the palms of the hands and soles of the feet.

palmar /pal′mər/ [L, *palma*], pertaining to the palm.

palmar aponeurosis [L, *palma;* Gk, *apo,* from, *neuron,* nerve], a sheet of fascia under the skin of the palm and surrounding the muscles.

palmar crease, a normal groove across the palm of the hand.

palmar erythema, an inflammatory redness of the palms of the hands.

palmar grasp reflex [L, *palma,* palm; ONorse, *grapa,* grab], a flexion of the fingers caused by stimulation of the palm of the hand. The reflex is present at birth and usually disappears by 6 months of age.

palmar interossei, the four unipennate muscles originating from the metacarpals of the digits with which each is associated. They adduct the thumb and the index, ring, and little fingers at the metacarpophalangeal joints.

palmaris longus /pəlmer′is/, a long, slender, superficial fusiform muscle of the forearm, lying on the medial side of the flexor carpi radialis that functions to flex the hand.

palmar metacarpal artery, any one of several arteries arising from the deep palmar arch that supply the fingers.

palmar pinch, a thumbless grasp in which the tips of the other fingers are pressed against the palm of the hand.

palmar reflex, a reflex that curls the fingers when the palm of the hand is tickled.

palmature /pal′məchər/ [L, *palma*], an abnormal condition in which the fingers are webbed.

Palmer notation, a system for designating teeth in which the mouth is divided into quadrants and the teeth in each quadrant are numbered from 1 to 8, starting with the central incisor and ending with the third molar. The system is no longer in general use.

palmitic acid $(CH_3(CH_2)_{14}COOH)$ /palmit′ik/ [L, *palma*], a saturated fatty acid that commonly occurs in animal and vegetable fats and oils. It is a carboxylic acid used in the production of soaps and candles.

palmitin /pal′mitin/, a triglyceride consisting of palmitic acid present in palm oil and other vegetable and animal fats.

palmomental reflex /pal′məmen′təl/ [L, *palma* + *mentum*, chin, *reflectere*, to bend back], an abnormal neurologic sign, elicited by scratching the palm of the hand at the base of the thumb, characterized by contraction of the muscles of the chin and corner of the mouth on the same side of the body as the stimulus.

palmoplantar erythrodysesthesia, hand-foot syndrome.

palmoscopy /palmos′kəpē/, detection of the pulse or heartbeat.

palonosetron, an antiemetic agent used to prevent nausea and vomiting associated with cancer chemotherapy.

palpable /pal′pəbəl/ [L, *palpare*, to touch gently], perceivable by touch.

palpation /palpā′shən/ [L, *palpare*, to touch gently], a technique used in physical examination in which the examiner feels the texture, size, consistency, and location of certain body parts with the hands.—**palpate,** *v.*

palpatory percussion /pal′pətôr′ē/ [L, *palpare*, to touch gently, *percutere*, to strike hard], a technique in physical examination in which the vibrations produced by percussion are evaluated by using light pressure of the flat of the examiner's hand.

palpebral fissure /pal′pəbrəl/ [L, *palpebra*, eyelid, *fissura*, cleft], the opening between the margins of the upper and lower eyelids.

palpebra superior /pal′pəbrə/ *pl.* **palpebrae superiores,** the upper eyelid, larger and more movable than the lower eyelid and furnished with an elevator muscle.

palpebrate /pal′pəbrāt/, **1.** to wink or blink. **2.** having eyelids.

palpitate /pal′pitāt/ [L, *palpitare*, to flutter], to pulsate rapidly, as in the unusually fast beating of the heart under various conditions of stress and in certain heart problems.

palpitation /pal′pitā′shən/ [L, *palpitare*, to flutter], a pounding or racing of the heart. It is associated with normal emotional responses and with heart disorders. —**palpitate,** *v.*

PALS, abbreviation for **pediatric advanced life support.**

palsy /pôl′zē/ [Gk, *para*, beyond, *lysis*, loosening], an abnormal condition characterized by paralysis.

Paltauf's nanism /päl′toufs/ [Arnold Paltauf, Czechoslovakian physician, 1860–1893; Gk, *nanos*, dwarf], dwarfism associated with excessive production or growth of lymphoid tissue.

Pamelor /päm′e-lôr/, a trademark for a tricyclic antidepressant preparation of (nortriptyline hydrochloride).

pamidronate disodium, the disodium salt of pamidronate, used in the treatment of malignancy-associated hypercalcemia, osteitis deformans, and osteolytic bone metastases associated with breast cancer and myeloma.

Pamine, a trademark for an anticholinergic (methscopolamine bromide).

p-aminohippurate /ə-mē′nō-hip′yə-rāt/, a salt, conjugate base, or ester of *p*-aminohippuric acid. The sodium salt is used to measure effective renal plasma flow and to determine the functional capacity of the tubular excretory mechanism.

pampiniform /pampin′ifôrm/ [L, *pampinus*, vine tendril, *plexus*, plaited], having the shape of a tendril.

pampiniform plexus [L, *pampinus*, vine tendril, *plexus*, plaited], a network of veins in the spermatic cord that drains the testes into the testicular vein in the lower abdomen.

panacea /pan′əsē′ə/ [Gk, *pan*, all, *akeia*, remedy], **1.** a universal remedy. **2.** an ancient name for a herb or liquid potion with healing properties. **3.** a remedy for all disease; a cure-all.

panacinar emphysema /pan′əsin′ər/ [Gk, *pan*, all; L, *acinus*, grape], one of the principal types of emphysema, characterized by relatively uniform enlargement of air spaces throughout the terminal bronchioles and alveoli.

Panafil, a trademark for a fixed-combination topical drug containing an enzyme (papain).

panagglutinable /pan′əgloo′tinəbəl/, pertaining to RBCs that are agglutinable by the sera of all blood groups of the same species.

P

panagglutinin /pan'əgloo'tinin/, an antibody that causes clumping (agglutination) of RBCs of all blood groups of a species.

pananencephaly /panan'ensef'əlē/, pain that affects all parts of the body.

panangiitis /panan'jē·ī'tis/, an inflammation that affects all layers of a blood vessel.

panarteritis /-är'tərī'tis/ [Gk, *pan*, all, *arteria*, artery, *itis*, inflammation], an inflammation that involves all the tissue layers of an artery.

panarthritis /-ärthrī'tis/ [Gk, *pan* + *arthron*, joint], an abnormal condition characterized by the inflammation of many joints in the body.—**panarthritic**, *adj.*

panatrophy /panat'rəfē/, **1.** a general atrophy of all parts of a body or structure. **2.** a rare disorder associated with atrophy of cutaneous and subcutaneous tissue. It is characterized by prominence of underlying body structures as all levels of skin and subcutaneous tissue are reduced in thickness.

panbronchiolitis /panbrong'kē·əlī'tis/, chronic inflammation and obstruction of the bronchioles caused by the accumulation of foam cells. It usually leads to bronchiectasis.

pancake kidney /pan'kāk/ [ME, *panne*, pan, *kaka*, cake + *kidnere*], a congenital anomaly in which the left and right kidneys are fused into a single mass in the pelvis. The fused kidney has two collecting systems and two ureters and frequently becomes obstructed because of its abnormal position.

pancarditis /-kärdī'tis/ [Gk, *pan* + *kardia*, heart, *itis*, inflammation], an abnormal condition characterized by inflammation of the entire heart, including the endocardium, myocardium, and pericardium.

Pancoast's syndrome /pan'cōsts/ [Henry K. Pancoast, American radiologist, 1875–1939], **1.** a combination of signs associated with a tumor in the apex of the lung. The signs include neuritic pain in the arm, atrophy of the muscles of the arm and the hand, and Horner's syndrome. **2.** an abnormal condition caused by osteolysis in the posterior part of one or more ribs, sometimes involving associated vertebrae.

pancolectomy /-kōlek'təmē/ [Gk, *pan* + *kolon*, colon, *ektomē*, excision], the excision of the entire colon, necessitating an ileostomy.

pancreas /pan'krē·əs/ [Gk, *pan*, all, *kreas*, flesh], an elongated grayish pink lobulated gland that stretches transversely across the posterior abdominal wall in the epigastric and hypochondriac regions of the body and secretes various substances, such as digestive enzymes, insulin, and glucagon. A compound, mixed gland composed of exocrine and endocrine tissue, it contains a main duct that runs the length of the organ, draining

smaller ducts and emptying into the duodenum at the major duodenal papilla.

pancreas scan, a radiographic scan of the pancreas after the IV injection of a radiopaque contrast medium, used for detecting various abnormalities, such as tumors, cysts, and infections.

pancreatalgia /pan'krē·ətal'jə/, pain in or near the pancreas.

pancreatectomy /pan'krē·ətek'təmē/ [Gk, *pan* + *kreas* + *ektomē*, excision], the surgical removal of all or part of the pancreas, performed to excise a cyst or tumor, treat pancreatitis, or repair trauma. If the entire pancreas is removed, a brittle type of diabetes develops, requiring precise management of both diet and insulin dosage.

pancreatemphraxis /pan'krē·at'emfrak'sis/, hypertrophy or congestion of the pancreas caused by an obstruction in the pancreatic duct.

pancreatic abscess, an infection characterized by a collection of pus in or around the pancreas.

pancreatic autodigestion, premature breakdown of pancreatic zymogens into digestive enzymes that digest pancreatic tissue, causing acute pancreatitis.

pancreatic buds, two outgrowths, one dorsal and one ventral, from the endodermal lining of the caudal part of the embryonic foregut that fuse and develop into the pancreas.

pancreatic cancer [Gk, *pan* + *kreas*; L, *cancer*, crab], a malignant neoplastic disease of the pancreas, characterized by anorexia, flatulence, weakness, dramatic weight loss, epigastric or back pain, jaundice, pruritus, a palpable abdominal mass, recent onset of diabetes, and clay-colored stools if the pancreatic and biliary ducts are obstructed. About 90% of pancreatic tumors are adenocarcinomas; two thirds are in the head of the pancreas. Cancer of the pancreas has a poor prognosis.

pancreatic collum, neck of pancreas; a constricted portion marking the junction of the head and body of the pancreas.

pancreatic diabetes [Gk, *pan*, all, *kreas*, flesh, *diabainein*, to pass through], DM caused by a deficiency of insulin production by the islet cells of the pancreas.

pancreatic diverticulum, one of a pair of membranous pouches arising from the embryonic duodenum. These two diverticula later form the pancreas and its ducts.

pancreatic dornase, an enzyme from beef pancreas that has been used as a mucolytic for URIs and CF.

pancreatic duct, the primary secretory channel of the pancreas.

pancreatic enzyme, any one of the enzymes secreted by the pancreas in the process of digestion. The most important are trypsin, chymotrypsin, steapsin, and amylopsin.

pancreatic enzyme digestion, the action of pancreatic enzymes in the process of breaking down food into its constituents.

pancreatic enzyme therapy, replacement therapy for conditions of pancreatic insufficiency with malabsorption, such as CF.

pancreatic hormone, any one of several chemical compounds secreted by the pancreas, associated with the regulation of cellular metabolism. Major hormones secreted by the pancreas are insulin, glucagon, somatostatin, and pancreatic polypeptide.

pancreatic insufficiency, a condition characterized by inadequate production and secretion of pancreatic hormones or enzymes. It usually occurs secondary to a disease process destructive to pancreatic tissue. Nutritional malabsorption, anorexia, poorly localized upper abdominal or epigastric pain, malaise, and severe weight loss often occur. Alcohol-induced pancreatitis is the most common form of the condition.

pancreatic juice, the fluid secretion of the pancreas, produced by the stimulation of food in the duodenum. It contains water, protein, inorganic salts, and enzymes. The juice is essential in breaking down proteins into their amino acid components, reducing dietary fats to glycerol and fatty acids, and converting starch to simple sugars.

pancreaticoduodenal /pan′krē·at′ikōdoo′ədē′nəl/, pertaining to the pancreas and duodenum.

pancreaticoduodenectomy /pan′krē·ətō doo′ədanek′təmē/ [Gk, *pan + kreas*; L, *duodeni,* twelve fingers; Gk, *ektomē,* excision], a surgical procedure in which the head of the pancreas, the entire duodenum, a portion of the jejunum, the distal third of the stomach, and the lower half of the common bile duct are excised, usually to relieve obstruction caused by tumors, often malignant. Continuity is reestablished between the biliary, pancreatic, and GI systems.

pancreaticolienal node /pan′krē·at′ikōli′ē′nəl/ [Gk, *pan + kreas*; L, *lien,* spleen, *nodus,* knot], a node in one of three groups of lymph glands associated with branches of the abdominal and pelvic viscera that are supplied by branches of the celiac artery.

pancreatic rest, ectopic pancreatic tissue, usually in the stomach or small intestine, forming a polyplike lesion.

pancreatin /pan′krē·ətin′, -krē·ā′tin/, a concentrate of pancreatic enzymes from swine or beef cattle prescribed as an aid to digestion to replace endogenous pancreatic enzymes in CF and after pancreatectomy.

pancreatitis /pan′krē·ətī′tis/ [Gk, *pan + kreas + itis,* inflammation], an inflammatory condition of the pancreas that may be acute or chronic. Acute pancreatitis is generally the result of damage to the biliary tract, as by alcohol, trauma, infectious disease, or certain drugs. It is characterized by severe abdominal pain (generally epigastric or upper left) radiating to the back, fever, anorexia, nausea, and vomiting. There may be jaundice if the common bile duct is obstructed. The causes of chronic pancreatitis are similar to those of the acute form. When the cause is alcohol abuse, there may be calcification and scarring of the smaller pancreatic ducts. Abdominal pain, nausea, and vomiting occur, as well as steatorrhea and creatorrhea, caused by the diminished output of pancreatic enzymes. Pancreatic insulin production may be diminished, and DM develops in some patients.

pancreatoduodenostomy /-doo′ədanos′ təmē/, a surgical procedure to establish a fistula or duct from the pancreas into the duodenum.

pancreatogastrostomy /-gastros′təmē/, the surgical establishment of a fistula or duct from the pancreas to the stomach.

pancreatogenic /-jen′ik/, originating in the pancreas.

pancreatography /pan′krē·ətog′rəfē/ [Gk, *pan + kreas + graphein,* to record], visualization of the pancreas or its ducts by radiography after injection of a contrast medium into the ducts at surgery or via an endoscope, or by ultrasonography, CT, or radionuclide imaging.

pancreatojejunostomy /-jij′oonos′təmē/, the surgical establishment of a fistula or duct from the pancreas to the jejunum.

pancreatolith /pan′krē·at′əlith/, a stone or calculus in the pancreas.

pancreatolithiasis /pan′kre·ətolithī′əsis/, the presence of calculi in the pancreas or pancreatic duct.

pancreatolithotomy /-lithot′əmē/, the surgical removal of pancreatic calculi.

pancreatolysis /pan′krē·ətol′isis/, destruction of the pancreas by pancreatic enzymes.

pancreatomegaly /-meg′əlē/, an abnormal enlargement of the pancreas.

pancreatopathy /pan′krē·ətop′əthē/, any disease of the pancreas.

pancreatotomy /pan′krē·ətot′əmē/, a surgical incision in the pancreas.

pancreatropic /pan′krē·ətrop′ik/, exerting an influence on the pancreas.

pancreolauryl test, for pancreatic function, the oral administration of fluorescein dilaurate and the monitoring of its cleavage to yield lauric acid as a measure of pancreatic esterase activity.

P

pancuronium bromide /pan′kyərō′nē-əm/, a skeletal muscle relaxant; a nondepolarizing neuromuscular blocker. It is prescribed as an adjunct to anesthesia and mechanical ventilation.

pancytopenia /pan′sītəpē′nē-ə/ [Gk, *pan* + *kytos*, cell, *penia*, poverty], simultaneous reduction in red blood cell, white blood cell, and platelet counts.—**pancytopenic,** *adj.*

p and a, abbreviation for *percussion and auscultation,* as noted in the patient's chart after physical examination of the chest.

pandemia /-dē′mē-ə/ [Gk, *pan,* all, *demos,* people], a disease epidemic that affects all or most of a population group.

pandemic /-dē′mik/ [Gk, *pan* + *demos,* people], of a disease, occurring throughout the population of a country, a people, or the world.

pandiastolic /-dī′əstol′ik/ [Gk, *pan* + *dia,* through, *stellein,* to set], pertaining to the complete diastole.

panencephalitis /pan′ənsef′əlī′tis/ [Gk, *pan* + *enkephale,* brain, *itis,* inflammation], inflammation of the entire brain characterized by an insidious onset, a progressive course with deterioration of motor and mental functions, and evidence of a viral cause.

panendoscope /-en′dəskōp′/ [Gk, *pan* + *endon,* within, *skopein,* to look], a cystoscope that allows a wide view of the interior of the bladder and urethra with a special lens system.

panesthesia /-esthē′zhə/ [Gk, *pan* + *aisthesis,* feeling], the total of all sensations experienced by an individual at one time.

pang, a sudden severe but temporary pain.

pangenesis /-jen′əsis/ [Gk, *pan* + *genesis,* origin], an idea that each cell and particle of a parent reproduces itself in progeny.

panhidrosis, perspiration over the entire body.

panhypopituitarism /panhī′pōpitoo′itəriz′əm/ [Gk, *pan* + *hypo,* under, *pituita,* phlegm], generalized insufficiency of pituitary hormones, resulting from damage to or deficiency of the gland.

panhysterectomy /pan′histərek′təmē/ [Gk, *pan* + *hystera,* uterus, *ektomē,* excision], complete surgical removal of the uterus and cervix.

panic /pan′ik/, an intense, sudden, and overwhelming fear or feeling of anxiety that produces terror and immediate physiologic changes that result in paralyzed immobility or senseless, hysteric behavior.

panic attack [Gk, *panikos,* of the god Pan; Fr, *attaquer*], an episode of acute anxiety that occurs unpredictably, with feelings of intense apprehension or terror accompanied by dyspnea, dizziness, sweating, trembling, and chest pain or palpitations.

The attack may last several minutes and may occur again in certain situations.

panitumumab, a miscellaneous antineoplastic used to treat metastatic colon cancer expressing epidermal growth factor receptor.

panivorous /paniv′ərəs/ [L, *panis,* bread, *vorare,* to devour], pertaining to the practice of subsisting exclusively on bread. —**panivore,** *n.*

panmyelosis /panmī′əlō′sis/, a pathologic condition characterized by a proliferation of bone marrow cells of all types.

Panner's disease, a rare form of osteochondrosis in which abnormal bony growth occurs in the capitulum of the humerus.

panniculitis /pənik′yəlī′tis/ [L, *panniculus,* piece of cloth; Gk, *itis,* inflammation], a chronic inflammation of subcutaneous fat in which the skin becomes hardened, particularly over the abdomen and thorax. Small subcutaneous masses of hard tissue are found in the affected areas.

panniculus /pənik′yələs/ *pl.* **panniculi** [L, small garment], a membranous layer; the many sheets of fascia covering various structures in the body.

pannus /pan′əs/ [L, cloth], an abnormal condition of the cornea, which has become vascularized and infiltrated with granular tissue just beneath the surface. Pannus may develop in the inflammatory stage of trachoma or after a detached retina, glaucoma, iridocyclitis, or other degenerative eye disorder.

panography /pənog′rəfē/, a method of tomography that visualizes curved surfaces of the body at any depth. In dentistry it is accomplished by simultaneous radiography or dental imaging of the maxillary and mandibular dental arches and associated structures along two axes of rotation. A panoramic image is recorded on an intensifying screen that rotates with the radiation source around the patient's head. The image is converted to digital form to be viewed on a computer screen.

panophthalmitis /pan′ofthalmī′tis/ [Gk, *pan* + *ophthalmos,* eye, *itis,* inflammation], an inflammation of the entire eye, usually caused by virulent pyogenic organisms, such as strains of meningococci, pneumococci, streptococci, anthrax bacilli, and clostridia. Initial symptoms are pain, fever, headache, drowsiness, edema, and swelling. As the infection progresses, the iris appears muddy and gray, the aqueous humor becomes turbid, and precipitates form on the posterior surface of the cornea.

panoptic /panop′tik/ [Gk, *pan,* all, *opsis,* vision], pertaining to the enhanced visual effect produced by stains applied to microscopic specimens.

panoramic radiograph /pan'ôram'ik/ [Gk, *pan* + *horama,* view; L, *radiare,* to emit rays; Gk, *graphein,* to record], an x-ray image of a curved body surface, such as the upper and lower jaws, on a single film.

panotitis /pan'ōtī'tis/, a general inflammation of the ear, including the middle ear.

PanOxyl, a trademark for a keratolytic (benzoyl peroxide).

panphobia /-fō'bē·ə/ [Gk, *pan* + *phobos,* fear], an anxiety disorder characterized by an irrational fear of everything.—**panophobic,** *adj.*

panplegia /panplē'jē·ə/, paralysis of all four extremities.

pansclerosis /pan'sklərō'sis/, a general hardening of a tissue or body part.

pansystolic /-sistol'ik/, pertaining to the entire systole.

pantanencephaly /pantan'ensef'əlē/, a congenital absence of all or nearly all brain tissue.

panthenol /pan'thənôl/, **1.** an alcohol converted in the body to pantothenic acid. **2.** a viscous liquid derived from pantothenic acid.

panting [Fr, *panteler,* to gasp], a ventilatory pattern characterized by rapid, shallow breathing. Panting usually moves gas back and forth in the anatomic dead space at a high flow rate, which evaporates water and removes heat but produces little or no alveolar ventilation and does not cause hypocapnia.

pantograph /pan'təgraf/, **1.** a jointed device for copying a plane figure to any desired scale. **2.** a device that incorporates a pair of face-bows fixed to the jaws, used for inscribing centrically related points and arcs leading to the points on segments relatable to the three craniofacial planes.

pantomograph /pantom'əgraf/. See **panoramic radiograph.**

pantomography /-mog'rəfē/ [Gk, *pan* + *graphein,* to record], panoramic radiography or dental imaging for obtaining simultaneous radiographs or images of the maxillary and mandibular dental arches and related structures.

pantoprazole /pantō'prə-zōl/, a gasric acid pump inhibitor used to treat erosive esophagitis associated with gastroesophageal reflux disease and hypersecretion associated with Zollinger-Ellison syndrome or other neoplastic conditions.

pantoscopic /pan'təskop'ik/, pertaining to bifocal eyeglasses designed for both reading and distance viewing. The bottom half is for close vision, and the top half is for far vision.

pantothenic acid /pan'təthen'ik/, a member of the vitamin B complex. It is widely distributed in plant and animal tissues and may be an important element in human nutrition.

pantropic virus, a virus that affects or has an affinity for many different kinds of tissue or organs.

PaO₂, symbol for **partial pressure of oxygen in arterial blood.**

PAO₂, symbol for *partial pressure of alveolar oxygen.*

pap, 1. any soft, soggy food. **2.** porridge or gruel.

papain /pəpā'ēn/, an enzyme from the fruit of *Carica papaya,* the tropical melon tree. It has been prescribed for enzymatic debridement of wounds and promotion of healing.

Papanicolaou (Pap) test /pap'ənik'əlou/ [George N. Papanicolaou, Greek physician in U.S. practice, 1883–1962], a simple smear method of examining stained exfoliative cells. It is used most commonly to detect cancers of the cervix, but it may be used for tissue specimens from any organ. A smear is usually obtained during a routine pelvic examination annually beginning at 18 years of age. The technique permits early diagnosis of cancer and has contributed to a lower death rate from cervical cancer.

papaverine hydrochloride /pəpav'ərēn/, a vasodilator prescribed in the treatment of cardiovascular or visceral spasms.

papaya /pəpī'ə/, the fruit of the tropical *Carica papaya* (pawpaw) tree and the source of the proteolytic enzyme papain used in blood group serologic evaluation. Papain is also used to prevent adhesions.

paper, a material produced in sheets, usually from wood pulp or other cellulose products. It can be adapted for many purposes, such as litmus paper for testing acidity, filter paper, and articulating carbon paper used to record points of contact between teeth of the upper and lower jaws.

paper chromatography [Gk, *papyros,* papyrus], the separation of a mixture into its components by filtering it through a strip of special paper.

paper point, in root canal therapy, a cone of variable width and taper, usually made of paper or a paper product, used to dry or maintain a liquid disinfectant in the canal.

paper radioimmunosorbent test (PRIST), a technique for determining total IgE levels in patients with type I hypersensitivity reactions.

papilla /pəpil'ə/ *pl.* **papillae** [L, nipple], **1.** a small nipple-shaped projection, such as the conoid papillae of the tongue and the papillae of the dermis, that extend from collagen fibers, the capillary blood vessels, and sometimes the nerves of the dermis. **2.** the optic papilla, a round white disc in the fundus oculi, which corresponds to the entrance of the optic nerve.

P

papillary /pap'əle'rē/ [L, *papilla*, nipple], pertaining to a papilla.

papillary adenocarcinoma, a malignant neoplasm characterized by small papillae of vascular connective tissue covered by neoplastic epithelium that projects into follicles, glands, or cysts. The tumor is most common in the ovaries and thyroid gland.

papillary adenocystoma lymphomatosum, an unusual tumor, consisting of epithelial and lymphoid tissues, that develops in the area of the parotid and submaxillary glands.

papillary adenoma, a benign epithelial tumor in which the membrane lining the glandular tissue forms papillary processes that project into the alveoli or grow out of a cavity's surface.

papillary carcinoma, a malignant neoplasm characterized by finger-like projections.

papillary duct, any one of the thousands of straight collecting renal tubules that descend through the medulla of the kidney and join with others to form the common ducts opening into the renal papillae.

papillary muscle, any one of the rounded or conical muscular projections attached to the chordae tendineae in the ventricles of the heart. The papillary muscles vary in number. The two main muscles are the anterior papillary muscle and the posterior papillary muscle. The papillary muscles are associated with the atrioventricular valves that they help open and close.

papillate /pap'ilit/, marked by papillae or nipple-like prominences.

papilledema /pap'iləde̅'mə/ pl. **papilledemas, papilledemata** [L, *papilla*; Gk, *oidema*, swelling], swelling of the optic disc, visible on ophthalmoscopic examination of the fundus of the eye, caused by increase in ICP. The meningeal sheaths that surround the optic nerves from the optic disc are continuous with the meninges of the brain; therefore, increased ICP is transmitted forward from the brain to the optic disc in the eye to cause swelling.

papilliform /pəpil'ifôrm/, shaped like a nipple.

papillitis /pap'ili'tis/ [L, *papilla*; Gk, *itis*, inflammation], **1.** inflammation of a papilla, such as the lacrimal papilla. **2.** inflammation of the optic disc.

papilloadenocystoma /pap'ilō'ad'əno̅'sistō'mə/, a benign epithelial tumor in which the lining develops in numerous small folds.

papillocarcinoma [L, *papilla*, nipple; Gk, *oma*, tumor, *karkinos*, crab, *oma*, tumor], a malignant tumor in which there are papillary outgrowths.

papilloma /pap'ilō'mə/ [L, *papilla*; Gk, *oma*, tumor], a benign epithelial neoplasm characterized by a branching or lobular tumor.

papillomatosis /pap'ilōmətō'sis/ [L, *papilla*; Gk, *oma*, tumor, *osis*, condition], an abnormal condition characterized by widespread development of nipple-like growths.

papillomavirus /pap'ilō'məvī'rəs/ [L, *papilla*; Gk, *oma*, tumor; L, *virus*, poison], the virus that causes warts in humans.

Papillon-Lefèvre syndrome /pä'pēyôN' ləfev'rə/ [M.M. Papillon, French dermatologist, 20th century; Paul Lefèvre, French dermatologist, 20th century], an autosomal-recessive disorder occurring between the first and fifth years of life, characterized by palmoplantar keratoderma resembling psoriasis, which may also involve the elbows, knees, tibias, external malleoli, and other areas; ectopic calcifications of the skull; and periodontitis and premature shedding of both the deciduous and secondary teeth.

papilloretinitis /pap'ilōret'ini'tis/ [L, *papilla* + *rete*, net; Gk, *itis*, inflammation], an inflammatory occlusion of a retinal vein.

papillotomy /pap'ilot'əmē/, a surgical incision in the papilla of the duodenum.

papovavirus /pap'əvavī'rəs/ [(abbreviation) *pa*pilloma/*po*lyoma *va*cuolating *virus*], one of a group of small DNA viruses, some of which may be potentially cancer-producing. The human wart is caused by a kind of papovavirus, but it very rarely undergoes malignant transformation.

Pappenheimer bodies [A.M. Pappenheimer, U.S. pathologist, 1878–1955], red blood cell inclusions composed of ferric iron.

pappus /pap'əs/ [Gk, *pappos*, down], the first growth of beard, characterized by downy hairs.

papula /pap'yələ/ [L, *papula*, pimple], a small superficial elevation of the skin.

papular scaling disease [L, *papula*, pimple; AS, *scealu*], any of a group of skin disorders characterized by discrete raised, dry, scaling lesions.

papular urticaria [L, *papula*, pimple, *urtica*, nettle], a persistent cutaneous eruption representing a hypersensitivity reaction to insect bites, seen primarily in atopic children, and characterized by crops of small urticarial papules and wheals and transitional forms of these lesions, which may become secondarily infected or lichenified as a result of rubbing and scratching.

papulation /pap'yəlā'shən/ [L, *papula*, pimple, *atus*, process], the development of papules.

papule /pap'yo͞ol/ [L, *papula*, pimple], a small, solid, raised skin lesion less than 1 cm in diameter, such as that found in lichen planus and nonpustular acne. —**papular**, *adj.*

papuloerythematous /pap'yəlō·er'ithem'ə təs/, pertaining to an eruption of papules on an erythematous surface.

papulopustular /pap'yəlōpus'tyələr/, pertaining to a skin eruption of both pustules and papules.

papulosis /pap'yəlō'sis/, a widespread occurrence of papules over the body.

papulosquamous /pap'yəlōskwā'məs/ [L, *papula,* pimple, *squama,* scale], pertaining to a skin eruption that is both papular and scaly.

papulovesicular /pap'yəlō·vesik'yələr/, pertaining to a skin rash characterized by both papules and vesicles.

papyraceous /pap'irā'shəs/ [Gk, *papyros,* paper], having a paper-like quality.

Paquelin's cautery /pak'əlinz/ [Claude A. Paquelin, French physician, 1836–1905; Gk, *kauterion,* branding iron], a cauterizing device consisting of a platinum loop through which a heated hydrocarbon is passed.

Paquin technique, a type of ureteroneocystostomy in which the ureter is excised from its attachment to the bladder and reattached in a more posteromedial position.

par, a pair, specifically a pair of cranial nerves, such as the par nonum, or ninth pair.

PAR, abbreviation for **pulmonary arteriolar resistance.**

para /par'ə/ [L, *parere,* to bear], a woman who has produced an infant regardless of whether the child was alive or stillborn. The term is used with numerals to indicate the number of pregnancies carried to more than 20 weeks' gestation, such as para 2, indicating two pregnancies.

paraactinomycosis /per'ə·ak'tinō'mīkō'sis/, a chronic pulmonary infection similar to actinomycosis. The infection is caused by bacteria of the genus *Nocardia.*

paraaminobenzoic acid ($H_2NC_6H_4COOH$) **(PABA)** /per'ə·amē'nōbenzō'ik/, a substance often associated with the vitamin B complex, found in cereals, eggs, milk, and meat and present in detectable amounts in blood, urine, spinal fluid, and sweat. It is widely used as a sunscreen that forms a partial chemical conjugation with constituents of the horny layer and that resists removal by water and sweat. PABA is a sulfonamide antagonist and may be an effective agent for the treatment of scleroderma, dermatomyositis, and pemphigus.

paraaminohippuric acid (PAHA, PHA) /per'ə·amē'nōhipōōr'ik/, the *p*-aminobenzamide derivative of glycerin. Its sodium salt is used for measuring effective renal plasma flow and determining kidney function.

paraaminosalicylic acid (PAS, PASA) /per'ə·amē'nōsal'isil'ik/, a bacteriostatic agent prescribed for the treatment of pulmonary and extrapulmonary TB. It has unlabeled indications for Crohn's disease.

paraballism /per'əbôl'izəm/ [Gk, *ballismos,* jumping about], involuntary jerking movements of the legs.

parabiosis /-bī·ō'sis/, the fusion of two eggs or embryos, resulting in conjoined twins.

parabolic /-bol'ik/, in ultrasonics, pertaining to flow conditions in blood vessels. Under parabolic flow, blood cells in the middle of the vessels move the fastest, with a gradual decrease in flow velocity for points farther away from the center.

paracanthoma /-kənthō'mə/, a tumor that develops from the abnormal overgrowth of the prickle cell layer of the skin.

paracellular transport, transport of molecules around cells and through tight junctions in an epithelial cell layer.

paracelsian method /-sel'sē·ən/ [Philippus Aureolus Paracelsus, Swiss alchemist and physician, 1493–1541], the use of chemical agents such as sulfur, iron, lead, and arsenic in the treatment of disease.

paracenesthesia /-sen'esthē'zhə/, any abnormality in the general sense of well-being.

paracentesis /per'əsentē'sis/ [Gk, *para* + *kentesis,* puncturing], a procedure in which fluid is withdrawn from a body cavity. An incision is made in the skin, and a hollow trocar, cannula, or catheter is passed through the incision into the cavity to allow outflow of fluid into a collecting device. Paracentesis is most commonly performed to remove excessive accumulations of ascitic fluid from the abdomen.

paracentesis thoracis [Gk, *para* + *kentesis,* puncturing, *thorax,* chest], the aspiration of fluid or air or both through a needle inserted into the pleural cavity.

paracentral /-sen'trəl/ [Gk, *para* + *kentron*], close to a center or a central part.

paracervical /-sur'vikəl/ [Gk, *para*; L, *cervix,* neck], pertaining to the area adjacent to the cervix.

paracervical block, a form of regional anesthesia in which a local anesthetic is injected into each side of the uterine cervix to block nerves innervating the uterine cervix. Paracervical block is not the anesthesia of choice for labor and delivery, given the high incidence of fetal bradycardia and its efficacy in only the first stage of labor, but it is an option during abortion and other gynecologic procedures.

paracervix /-sur'viks/, the connective tissue of the pelvic floor, extending from the uterine cervix.

P

paracholera /-kol′ərə/, an infectious disease with symptoms similar to those of cholera but not caused by the true infectious agent, *Vibrio cholerae.*

parachute reflex /per′əsho͞ot/, a variation of the Moro reflex whereby an infant is tested for motor nerve development by suspending him or her in the prone position and then dropping him or her a short distance onto a soft surface. If the motor nerve development is normal, the infant at 4 to 6 months will extend the arms, hands, and fingers on both sides of the body in a protective movement.

paracme /perak′mē/, **1.** the phase of a fever or disease marked by a subsidence of symptoms. **2.** the point of involution, beyond the prime of life.

paracoccidioidomycosis /per′əkoksid′ē·oi′dōmīkō′sis/ [Gk, *para* + *kokkos,* berry, *eidos,* form, *mykes,* fungus, *osis,* condition], a chronic, occasionally fatal fungal infection caused by *Paracoccidioides brasiliensis.* It is characterized by ulcers of the oral cavity, larynx, and nose. Other effects include large, draining lymph nodes; cough; dyspnea; weight loss; and skin, genital, and intestinal lesions.

paracolic gutters, depressions formed between the lateral margins of the ascending and descending colon and the posterolateral abdominal wall through which material can pass from one region of the peritoneal cavity to another.

paracolitis /-kōlī′tis/, an inflammation of the outer, peritoneal coat of the colon.

paracolpium /-kol′pē·əm/, the connective and other tissues around the vagina.

paracortex /-kôr′teks/, the thymus-dependent area of a lymph node between the subscapular cortex and the medullary cord.

paracrine /per′əkrēn/, an endocrine function in which effects of a hormone are localized to adjacent or nearby cells.

paracusis /per′əko͞o′sis/, a disorder involving the sense of hearing, including distortions of pitch.

paracystitis /-sistī′tis/, an inflammation of the connective tissues around the urinary bladder.

paradenitis /-dēnī′tis/, an inflammation of tissues around a gland.

paradidymal /-did′iməl/ [Gk, *para,* beside, *didymos,* twin], **1.** pertaining to the paradidymis. **2.** beside the testis.

paradidymis /per′ədid′imis/ *pl.* **paradidymides** [Gk, *para* + *epi,* above, *didymos,* twin], a rudimentary structure in the male, situated on the spermatic cord of the epididymis, that consists of vestigial remains of the caudal part of the embryonic mesonephric tubules. A similar vestigial structure, the paroophoron, is found in the female.

paradigm /per′ədīm, -dim/, a pattern that may serve as a model or example.

paradipsia /-dip′sē·ə/, an abnormal desire for fluids unrelated to body needs.

paradoxic /-dok′sik/ [Gk, *paradoxos,* strange], pertaining to a person, situation, statement, or act that may appear to have inconsistent or contradictory qualities or that may be true but appears to be absurd or unbelievable.

paradoxic aciduria, a metabolic alkalosis condition that may involve an exchange of sodium and hydrogen ions for potassium. It may occur with prolonged nasogastric suctioning or repeated vomiting.

paradoxic breathing [Gk, *paradoxos;* AS, *braeth*], a condition in which a part of the lung deflates during inspiration and inflates during expiration. The condition usually is associated with a chest trauma, such as an open chest wound or rib cage damage.

paradoxic bronchospasm, a constriction of the airways after treatment with a sympathomimetic bronchodilator.

paradoxic intention, a logotherapeutic technique that encourages a patient to do what he or she fears and if possible to exaggerate it to the point of humor. The technique is used in the treatment of phobias.

paradoxic pupillary reflex, the response of a pupil to light that is the reverse of a normal reflex, as when the pupil contracts in a darkened room. It can be a sign of severe congenital visual deficit.

paradoxic thrombosis syndrome, a condition of arterial and venous clots that may develop after a period of heparin therapy. It is thought to be caused by the production of antiplatelet antibodies that induce clotting.

paraffin /per′əfin/ [L, *parum,* little, *affinis,* related], any of a group of hydrocarbons or hydrocarbon mixtures of the paraffin series as indicated by the formula, $C_nH_{(2n+2)}$. Examples are methane gas, kerosene, and paraffin wax.

paraffin bath [L, *parum,* little, *affinis,* related], the application of heat to a specific area of the body through the use of paraffin. The part is quickly immersed in heated liquid wax and then withdrawn so that the wax solidifies to form an insulating layer. The procedure is repeated until the layer is 5 to 10 mm thick, and then the entire area is wrapped in an insulating material, such as a loose-fitting plastic bag or paper towels. The technique is used primarily for patients with arthritis and rheumatism or any joint condition.

paraffin method, in surgical pathology, a method used in preparing a selected part of tissue for pathologic examination. The tissue is fixed, dehydrated, and infiltrated by and embedded in paraffin, forming a block that is cut with a microtome into slices 8 μm thick. This method, which is more commonly used than the frozen section method, is slower and therefore not used during surgery.

paraffinoma /per′əfinŏ′mə/, a tumor caused by the prosthetic or therapeutic injection of paraffin beneath the skin.

paraffin section [L, *parum,* little, *affinis,* related + *sectio*], a histologic section cut from tissue that has been embedded in paraffin wax.

Paraflex, a trademark for a skeletal muscle relaxant (chlorzoxazone).

parafollicular C cell /-folik′yəlar/, a calcitonin-secreting cell located between follicles.

Parafon Forte, a trademark for a skeletal muscle relaxant used for the relief of painful musculoskeletal conditions (chlorzoxazone).

paraganglioma /-gang′glē·ō′mə/, a tumor derived from the chromoreceptor tissue of a paraganglion.

paraganglion /-gang′glē·on/ *pl.* **paraganglia** [Gk, *para* + *ganglion,* knot], any one of the small groups of chromaffin cells associated with the ganglia of the sympathetic nerve trunk and situated outside the adrenal medulla, most often near the sympathetic ganglia along the aorta and its branches. The paraganglia secrete the hormones epinephrine and norepinephrine.

parageusia /-jōō′sē·ə/, a disorder involving the sense of taste.

paragonimiasis /per′əgon′imī′əsis/ [Gk, *para* + *gonimos,* generative, *iasis,* condition], chronic infection by the lung fluke *Paragonimus westermani.* It is characterized by hemoptysis, bronchitis, and occasionally abdominal masses; pain and diarrhea; ocular pathologic conditions; cerebral involvement with paralysis; or seizures. The disease is acquired by ingesting cysts in infected freshwater crabs or crayfish, the intermediate hosts.

parahippocampal gyrus, a convolution on the inferior surface of each cerebral hemisphere, lying between the hippocampal and collateral sulci.

parahormone /-hôr′mōn/, a substance produced through normal metabolism that may exert an influence on a remote organ even though it is not a true hormone.

parahypnosis /-hipnō′sis/ [Gk, *para* + *hypnos,* sleep], a form of disordered sleep that is observed in hypnosis and narcosis.

parainfectious /par′ə-in-fek′shəs/, pertaining to manifestations of infectious disease that are caused by the immune response to the infectious agent.

parainfluenza virus /per′ə·in′flōō′en′zə/ [Gk, *para*; It, *influenza,* influence], a myxovirus with four serotypes, causing respiratory infections in infants and young children and, less commonly, in adults. Type 1 and type 2 parainfluenza viruses may cause laryngotracheobronchitis or croup; type 3 is a cause of croup, tracheobronchitis, bronchiolitis, and bronchopneumonia in children; and types 1, 3, and 4 are associated with pharyngitis and the common cold.

parakeratosis /-ker′ətō′sis/, an abnormal formation of horn cells of the epidermis caused by the persistence of nuclei, incomplete formation of keratin, and moistness and swelling of the horn cells. It is observed as scaling in many conditions such as psoriasis.

parakinesia /-kinē′zhə/ [Gk, *para* + *kinesis,* movement], an abnormality of movement resulting from a nerve disorder in a muscle, such as an irregularity of one of the ocular muscles.

paraldehyde /peral′dəhīd/, a clear, colorless, strong-smelling liquid obtained by the polymerization of acetaldehyde with a small amount of sulfuric acid. It is used as a solvent and may be administered orally, intravenously, intramuscularly, or rectally to induce hypnotic states or sedation.

paralinguistic cues, nonverbal elements, such as intonation, body posture, gestures, and facial expression, that modify the meaning of verbal communication.

parallax /per′əlaks/ [Gk, *parallelos,* side-by-side], the apparent displacement of an object at different distances from the eyes when viewed by both eyes together. It is the basis of stereoscopic vision and depth perception.

parallel grid /per′əlel/ [Gk, *parallelos,* side-by-side; ME, *gredire*], in radiography, an x-ray grid that has lead strips oriented parallel to each other.

parallelogram condenser /per′əlel′əgram/ [Gk, *parallelos* + *gramma,* record; L, *condensare,* to make thick], an instrument with an end shaped like a rectangle or parallelogram, used for compacting amalgams in filling teeth.

parallel play [Gk, *parallelos*; AS, *plegan,* to play], a form of play among a group of children, primarily toddlers, in which each engages in an independent activity that is similar to but not influenced by or shared with the others.

parallel talk, a form of speech used during children's play therapy in which the clinician verbalizes activities of the child without requiring answers to questions. The clinician repeats utterances of the child correctly and may parallel the child's actions.

parallergic /per'alur'jik/, having a nonspecific sensitivity to allergens as a result of a prior sensitization with a specific allergen.

Paralympics /per'əlim'piks/ [*paraplegic + Olympics*], an international competitive wheelchair sports event, usually held in association with the official quadrennial Olympic Games.

paralysis /pəral'isis/ *pl.* **paralyses** [Gk, *paralyein*, to be palsied], the loss of muscle function, loss of sensation, or both. It may be caused by a variety of problems such as trauma, disease, and poisoning. Paralyses may be classified according to the cause, muscle tone, distribution, or body part affected.—**paralytic,** *adj.*

paralytic ileus [Gk, *paralyein*, to be paralyzed, *eilein*, to twist], a decrease in or absence of intestinal peristalsis. It may occur after abdominal surgery or peritoneal injury or be associated with severe pyelonephritis; ureteral stone; fractured ribs; MI; extensive intestinal ulceration; heavy metal poisoning, porphyria; retroperitoneal hematomas, especially those associated with fractured vertebrae; or any severe metabolic disease. The most common overall cause of intestinal obstruction, paralytic ileus is mediated by a hormonal component of the sympathoadrenal system.

paralytic incontinence [Gk, *paralyein*, to be palsied; L, *incontinentia*, inability to retain], urinary or fecal incontinence resulting from loss of or impaired motor nerve control of the sphincter muscles.

paralytic mydriasis [Gk, *paralyein*, to be palsied, *mydriasis*, pupil enlargement], an area of depressed vision that is on the periphery of the field.

paralytic poliomyelitis [Gk, *paralyein*, to be palsied, *polios*, gray, *myelos*, marrow, *itis*, inflammation], a flaccid paralysis of the limbs resulting from damaged lower motor neurons. Progressive bulbar paralysis with respiratory and vasomotor failure may result when the brainstem nuclei are involved.

paralytic stroke [Gk, *paralyein*, to be palsied; AS, *strac*], a sudden attack of paralysis caused by disease or injury to the brain or spinal cord.

paralyze /per'əlīz/ [Gk, *paralyein*, to be palsied], **1.** to produce or enter into a state of paralysis. **2.** to cause loss of muscle power.

paramagnetic /pār'amagnet'ik/, being attracted by a magnet and assuming a position parallel to that of a magnetic force, but not becoming permanently magnetized.

paramagnetic substance, a substance with positive magnetic susceptibility resulting from the presence of unpaired atomic electrons (e.g., gadolinium chelates). These substances enhance magnetic relaxation and are often used as contrast agents in MRI.

paramedic (medic) /-med'ik/ [Gk, *para*; L, *medicina*, art of healing], a person who acts as an assistant to a physician or in place of a physician until the physician is available.—**paramedical,** *adj.*

paramedical personnel, health care workers other than physicians, dentists, podiatrists, and nurses who have special training in the performance of supportive health care tasks.

paramesonephric duct /per'əmēz'ōnef' rik/ [Gk, *para + mesos*, middle, *nephros*, kidney], one of a pair of embryonic ducts that develops into the uterus and the uterine tubes.

parameter /pəram'ətər/ [Gk, *para + metron*, measure], **1.** a value or constant used to describe or measure a set of data representing a physiologic function or system, as in the use of acid-base relationships of the blood as parameters for evaluating the function of a patient's respiratory system. **2.** a statistical value of a population group. **3.** *informal.* limit or boundary.

parametric imaging /-met'rik/ [Gk, *para + metron*, measure; L, *imago*, image], **1.** a diagnostic procedure in which an image of an administered radioactive tracer is derived mathematically such as by dividing one image by another. **2.** in PET, a procedure in which a physiologic parameter such as blood flow is mapped according to anatomic position.

parametric statistics, statistics that assume that a population has a symmetric, such as a gaussian or normal, distribution.

parametritis /per'əmetri'tis/ [Gk, *para + metra*, womb, *itis*, inflammation], an inflammatory condition of the tissue of the structures around the uterus.

parametrium /per'əmē'trē-əm/ *pl.* **parametria** [Gk, *para + metra*, womb], the lateral extension of the uterine subserous connective tissue into the broad ligament.

paramnesia /per'amnē'zhə/ [Gk, *para + amnesia*, forgetfulness], **1.** a perversion of memory in which one believes that one remembers events and circumstances that never actually occurred. **2.** a condition in which words are remembered and used without comprehension of their meaning.

paramyloidosis /peram'iloidō'sis/, **1.** an accumulation of amyloid-like protein in the tissues. **2.** any of several hereditary forms of amyloidosis characterized by sensory changes and muscle atrophy caused by amyloid deposits in somatic and visceral nerves.

paramyxovirus /-mik'sōvī'rəs/ [Gk, *para + myxa*, mucus; L, *virus*, poison], a member of a family of viruses that includes the organisms that cause parainfluenza, mumps, and some respiratory infections.

paranasal /-nā'zəl/ [Gk, *para*; L, *nasus*, nose], pertaining to an area near or alongside the nose.

paranasal sinus, any one of the air cavities in various bones around the nose, such as the frontal sinus in the frontal bone lying deep to the medial part of the superciliary ridge and the maxillary sinus within the maxilla between the orbit, the nasal cavity, and the upper teeth.

paraneoplastic cerebellar degeneration, the most common paraneoplastic syndrome affecting the brain, occurring most commonly with ovarian and breast carcinoma and Hodgkin's disease, characterized pathologically by severe loss of Purkinje's cells and clinically by insidious and progressive truncal and appendicular ataxia, dysarthria, nystagmus, and occasionally dementia.

paraneoplastic syndromes /-nē'ōplas'tik/ [Gk, *para* + *neos*, new, *plassein*, to mold, *syn*, together, *dromos*, course], the indirect effects of a tumor that occur distant to the tumor or metastatic site. They may result from the production of active proteins, polypeptides, or inactive hormones by the tumor.

paranesthesia /peran'esthē'zhə/, anesthesia affecting the lower half of the body.

paranoia /par'ənoi'ə/ [Gk, *para* + *nous*, mind], in psychiatry, a condition characterized by an elaborate, overly suspicious system of thinking. It often includes delusions of persecution and grandeur usually centered on one major theme, such as a financial matter, a job situation, an unfaithful spouse, or another problem, such as being followed or monitored by the CIA, FBI, or outer space aliens.

paranoid /per'ənoid/ [Gk, *para* + *nous*, mind, *eidos*, form], **1.** pertaining to or resembling paranoia. **2.** a person afflicted with a paranoid disorder. **3.** *informal.* a person, or pertaining to a person, who is overly suspicious or exhibits persecutory trends or attitudes.

paranoid disorder, a mental disorder characterized by an impaired sense of reality and persistent delusions.

paranoid ideation, an exaggerated, sometimes grandiose, belief or suspicion, usually not of a delusional nature, that one is being harassed, persecuted, or treated unfairly.

paranoid personality, a personality characterized by paranoia.

paranoid personality disorder, a psychiatric disorder characterized by extreme suspiciousness and distrust of others to the degree that one blames them for one's mistakes and failures and goes to abnormal lengths to validate prejudices, attitudes, or biases.

paranoid reaction, a psychopathologic condition that may be associated with delirium or dementia and characterized by the gradual formation of delusions, usually of a persecutory nature and often accompanied by related hallucinations. Other manifestations of senile degeneration, such as memory loss and confusion, may not accompany the reaction.

paranoid schizophrenia, a form of schizophrenia characterized by persistent preoccupation with illogical, absurd, and changeable delusions, usually of a persecutory, grandiose, or jealous nature, accompanied by related hallucinations. The symptoms include extreme anxiety, exaggerated suspiciousness, aggressiveness, anger, argumentativeness, and hostility, which may lead to violence.

paranoid state, a transitory abnormal mental condition characterized by illogical thought processes and generalized suspicion and distrust, with a tendency toward persecutory ideas or delusions.

paranormal /-nôr'məl/ [Gk, *para*; L, *normalis*, rule], pertaining to phenomena that cannot be explained by normal scientific investigation.

paraoperative, pertaining to the accessories essential to operative surgery, such as sterilization and the care of instruments and gloves.

paraparesis /-pərē'sis/ [Gk, *para* + *paresis*, paralysis], a partial paralysis, usually affecting only the lower extremities.

parapedesis /-pedē'sis/, any secretion or excretion through an abnormal passageway.

paraperitoneal /-per'itənē'əl/, near or beside the peritoneum.

paraperitoneal nephrectomy [Gk, *para* + *peri* + *tenein*, to stretch, *nephros*, kidney, *ektome*, excision], the surgical removal of the kidney through an extraperitoneal incision.

parapertussis /per'əpərtus'is/ [Gk, *para*; L, *per*, very, *tussis*, cough], an acute bacterial respiratory infection caused by *Bordetella parapertussis*, having symptoms closely resembling those of pertussis. It is usually milder than pertussis, although it can be fatal. It is possible to be infected with both *B. parapertussis* and *B. pertussis* at the same time.

parapharyngeal abscess /per'əfərin'jē-əl/ [Gk, *para* + *pharynx*, throat; L, *abscedere*, to go away], a suppurative infection of tissues adjacent to the pharynx, usually a complication of acute pharyngitis or tonsillitis. Infection may spread to the jugular vein, where it may cause thrombophlebitis and septic emboli.

paraphasia /-fā'zhə/ [Gk, *para* + *phrasein*, to utter], **1.** a condition in which a

P

person hears and comprehends words but is unable to speak correctly. Incoherent words are substituted for intended words. **2.** speech that is incoherent, unintelligible, and apparently incomprehensible but may be meaningful when carefully interpreted by a psychotherapist.

paraphia /pəˈrāˈfēˈə/ [Gk, *para,* apart from or against, *haphē,* touch], a disorder of the sense of touch.

paraphilia /perˈəfilˈyə/ [Gk, *para* + *philein,* to love], sexual perversion or deviation; a condition in which the sexual instinct is expressed in ways that are socially prohibited or unacceptable or are biologically undesirable, such as sexual relations with a nonconsenting partner.—**paraphiliac,** *adj., n.*

paraphimosis /perˈəfīmōˈsis/ [Gk, *para* + *phimoein,* to muzzle], a condition characterized by an inability to replace the foreskin in its normal position after it has been retracted behind the glans penis. Caused by a narrow or inflamed foreskin, the condition may lead to gangrene.

paraphrenia /-frēˈnēˈə/, a psychiatric condition that is primary to an affective illness or organic mental disorder. Gross disturbances of affect, volition, and function, which are characteristic of schizophrenia, are not prominent, but paranoid delusions and hallucinations are always present.

paraplasm /perˈəplazˈəm/ [Gk, *para* + *plassein,* to mold], any abnormal growth or malformation.—**paraplasmic,** *adj.*

paraplastic /-plasˈtik/ [Gk, *para* + *plassein,* to mold], **1.** misshapen or malformed. **2.** showing abnormal formative power; of the nature of a paraplasm.

paraplegia /perˈəplēˈjēˈə/ [Gk, *para* + *plege,* stroke], paralysis characterized by motor or sensory loss in the lower limbs and trunk. The signs and symptoms of paraplegia may develop immediately from trauma and include the loss of sensation, motion, and reflexes below the level of the lesion. Depending on the level of the lesion and whether damage to the spinal cord is complete or incomplete, the patient may lose bladder and bowel control, and sexual dysfunctions may develop. Paraplegia less commonly results from nontraumatic lesions such as scoliosis, spina bifida, or neoplasms.—**paraplegic,** *adj., n.*

paraplegic /-plēˈjik/ [Gk, *para* + *plege,* stroke], pertaining to a person affected by paraplegia or a condition resembling paraplegia.

parapneumonic empyema, thoracic empyema occurring as a complication of pneumonia.

parapraxia /-prakˈsēˈə/ [Gk, *para* + *praxis,* doing], **1.** the abnormal performance of purposive actions, such as performance of one movement occurring in place of another intended movement. **2.** forgetfulness with a tendency to misplace things.

paraproctitis /-proktīˈtis/, an inflammation affecting the tissues around the rectum and anus.

paraprostatitis /-prosˈtətīˈtis/, an inflammation of the tissues around the prostate gland.

paraprotein /-prōˈtēn/, any of the incomplete monoclonal immunoglobulins that occur in plasma cell disorders.

parapsoriasis /perˈəsərīˈəsis/ [Gk, *para* + *psorian,* to itch], a group of chronic skin diseases resembling psoriasis, characterized by maculopapular, erythematous scaly eruptions without systemic symptoms.

parapsychology /-sīkolˈəjē/ [Gk, *para* + *psyche,* mind, *logos,* science], a branch of psychology concerned with the study of alleged psychic phenomena such as clairvoyance, extrasensory perception, and telepathy.

paraquat poisoning /perˈəkwot/ [Gk, *para*; L, *quaterni,* four each, *potio,* drink], a toxic condition caused by the ingestion of paraquat dichloride, a highly poisonous pesticide. Characteristically, progressive pulmonary fibrosis and damage to the esophagus, kidneys, and liver develop several days after ingestion. After fibrosis begins, death is inevitable, usually within 3 weeks.

pararectal fossa, either of two cavities formed by folds of the peritoneum, one on either side of the rectum, varying in size according to distension of the rectum. In males this is continuous with the rectovesical pouch, and in females it is continuous with the rectouterine pouch.

parareflexia /-rəflexˈsēˈə/, any abnormal condition of the reflexes.

pararenal fat, a layer of fat that accumulates posteriorly and posterolaterally to each kidney.

parasacral /-sāˈkrəl/ [Gk, *para* + *sacrum*], pertaining to the area around the sacrum.

parasalpingitis /-salˈpinjīˈtis/, an inflammation of the tissues around the fallopian tubes.

parasite /perˈəsīt/ [Gk, *parasitos,* guest], an organism living in or on and obtaining nourishment from another organism. A facultative parasite may live on a host but is capable of living independently. An obligate parasite is one that depends entirely on its host for survival.
—**parasitic,** *adj.*

parasitemia /perˈəsītēˈmēˈə/ [Gk, *parasitos* + *haima,* blood], the presence of parasites in the blood.

parasitic fetus /-sitˈik/ [Gk, *parasitos*; L, *icus,* like, *fetus,* pregnant], the smaller, usually malformed member of conjoined, unequal, or asymmetric twins that is attached to and dependent on the more normal fetus for growth and development.

parasitic fibroma, a pedunculated uterine fibroid deriving part of its blood supply from the omentum.

parasitic glossitis, a mycosis of the tongue, characterized by a black or brown furry patch on the posterior dorsal surface. The patch is composed of hypertrophied filiform papillae that measure about 1 cm in length and are easily broken. This condition may occur as the result of poor oral hygiene, the use of broad-spectrum antibiotics, or radiation treatment of the neck and head. The condition produces no discomfort.

parasitic hemoptysis [Gk, *parasitos*, guest, *haima*, blood, *ptyein*, to spit], the spitting of bright red blood caused by a parasitic infection. The condition usually involves the lung fluke *(Paragonimus)* or tapeworms *(Echinococcus)*.

parasitism /per'əsitiz'əm/ [Gk, *parasitos*, guest], the relationship between two different organism types whereby one organism (the parasite) receives benefits from the other organism (the host) by inducing damage to it.

parasympathetic /-sim'pəthet'ik/ [Gk, *para + sympathein*, to feel with], pertaining to the craniosacral division of the autonomic nervous system, consisting of the oculomotor, facial, glossopharyngeal, vagus, and pelvic nerves. The actions of the parasympathetic division are mediated by the release of acetylcholine and primarily involve the protection, conservation, and restoration of body resources. Reactions to parasympathetic stimulation are highly localized and tend to counteract the adrenergic effects of sympathetic nerves. Parasympathetic fibers slow the heart; stimulate peristalsis; promote the secretion of lacrimal, salivary, and digestive glands; induce bile and insulin release; dilate peripheral and visceral blood vessels; constrict the pupils, esophagus, and bronchioles; and relax sphincters during micturition and defecation. Postganglionic parasympathetic fibers extend to the uterus, vagina, oviducts, and ovaries in females and to the prostate, seminal vesicles, and external genitalia in males, innervating blood vessels of pelvic organs in both sexes; stimulation of these nerves causes vasodilation in the clitoris and labia minora and erection of the penis.

parasympathetic ganglion [Gk, *para + sympathein*, to feel with, *ganglion*, knot], a cluster of nerve cell bodies of the parasympathetic division of the autonomic nervous system. The nerves are functionally antagonistic to those of the sympathetic division.

parasympathomimetic /per'əsim'pəthō'mimet'ik/ [Gk, *para + sympathein*, to feel with, *mimesis*, imitation], **1.** pertaining to a substance producing effects similar to those caused by stimulation of a parasympathetic nerve. **2.** an agent whose effects mimic those resulting from stimulation of parasympathetic nerves, especially those produced by acetylcholine.

parasynovitis /-sinəvī'tis/, an inflammation of the tissues around a joint.

parasystole [Gk, *para + systole*, contraction], an independent ectopic rhythm whose pacemaker cannot be discharged by impulses of the dominant (usually the sinus) rhythm because an area of depressed conduction surrounds the parasystolic focus. In the classic parasystole, the interectopic intervals are exact multiples of a common denominator reflecting the protected status of the parasystolic focus; however, the ectopic focus is usually influenced by the phasic events around its protection zone (modulated parasystole). Thus the sinus rhythm may modulate the parasystolic rhythm so that criteria for absolute, undisturbed regularity are not fulfilled. Fusion beats are common because of the simultaneous discharge of the ventricles by both the sinus and the parasystolic impulses.

parataxic distortion /per'ətak'sik/ [Gk, *para + taxis*, arrangement], **1.** a defense mechanism in which current interpersonal relationships are perceived and judged according to a mode of reference established by an earlier experience. **2.** Harry S. Sullivan's term for inaccuracies in judgment and perception.

parataxic mode, a term introduced by H.S. Sullivan to identify a childhood perception of the physical and social environment as being illogical, disjointed, and inconsistent. The parataxic mode may persist into adulthood in some individuals.

parathion poisoning /per'əthī'on/ [Gk, *para + thio*, phosphate, *on*; L, *potio*, drink], a toxic condition caused by the ingestion, inhalation, or absorption through the skin of the highly toxic organophosphorus insecticide parathion. Symptoms include nausea, vomiting, abdominal cramps, confusion, headache, lack of muscular control, convulsions, and dyspnea.

parathyroidectomy /-thī'roidek'təmē/ [Gk, *para + thyreos*, shield, *eidos*, form, *ektomē*, excision], the surgical removal of the parathyroid gland.

parathyroid gland /-thī'roid/ [Gk, *para + thyreos*, shield, *eidos*, form; L, *glans*, acorn], any one of several small structures, usually four, attached to the dorsal surfaces of the lateral lobes of the thyroid gland. The parathyroid glands secrete parathyroid hormone, which helps maintain the blood calcium concentration and ensures normal neuromuscular irritability, blood clotting, and cell membrane permeability.

parathyroid hormone (PTH), a hormone secreted by the parathyroid glands that acts to maintain a constant concentration of calcium in the extracellular fluid. The hormone regulates absorption of calcium from the GI tract; mobilization of calcium from the bones; deposition of calcium in the bones; and excretion of calcium in the breast milk, feces, sweat, and urine.

parathyroid hormone (PTH) test, a blood test that is useful in establishing a diagnosis of hyperparathyroidism and distinguishing nonparathyroid from parathyroid causes of hypercalcemia.

parathyroid scan, a nuclear scan used to determine the number of parathyroid glands involved in hyperparathyroidism. Enlargement of all four glands indicates parathyroid hyperplasia. Enlargement of only one indicates adenoma or cancer.

parathyroid tetany [Gk, *para + thyreos,* shield, *tetanos,* convulsive tension], a form of tetany (hypocalcemia) that is caused by a deficiency of parathyroid secretion.

parathyrotropic /-thī′rōtrop′ik/, stimulating the growth or rate of activity of the parathyroid glands.

paratrichosis /-trikō′sis/, an abnormality in the distribution, growth, and quantity of scalp hair.

paratriptic /-trip′tik/, pertaining to an agent that causes chafing.

paratrooper fracture /-trōō′pər/ [Fr, *parasol + troupe,* company; L, *fractura,* break], a break in the distal tibia and its malleolus, commonly occurring when an individual jumps from an elevated platform and lands feet first on the ground, subjecting the ankles to extreme force.

paratyphlitis /-tiflī′tis/ [Gk, *para + typhlos* blind, *itis,* inflammation], an inflammation of the tissues around the cecum and vermiform appendix.

paratyphoid fever /-tī′foid/ [Gk, *para + typhos,* stupor, *eidos,* form; L, *febris,* fever], a bacterial infection, caused by any *Salmonella* species other than *S. typhi,* characterized by symptoms resembling typhoid fever, although somewhat milder.

paraurethral duct /per′əyōōrē′thrəl/ [Gk, *para + ourethra,* urethra; L, *ducere,* to lead], one of a pair of ducts that drain the bulbourethral glands into the vestibule of the vagina.

paravaccinia virus /-vaksin′ē-ə/, a member of a subgroup of pox viruses that can infect humans through direct contact with

infected livestock. It is related to the smallpox virus and is the cause of pseudocowpox, which produces milker's nodules.

paravaginitis /-vaj′inī′tis/, an inflammation of the tissues around the vagina.

paravertebral /-vur′təbrəl/ [Gk, *para;* L, *vertebra,* joint], pertaining to the area alongside the spinal column or near a vertebra.

paravertebral block [Gk, *para;* L, *vertebra;* OFr, *bloc*], **1.** the blocking of transmission of somatic impulses by the spinal nerves by injection of a local analgesic solution near the point of their emergence. **2.** the blocking of the paravertebral sympathetic chain of nerves anterolateral to the vertebral bodies.

paravertebral sympathetic trunk, the trunk formed by ascending and descending postganglionic fibers, together with all the ganglia, that extends the entire length of the vertebral column on each side and enables the visceral motor fibers of the sympathetic part of the autonomic division of the peripheral nervous system to be distributed to peripheral regions innervated by all spinal nerves.

paravesical fossa, the fossa formed by the peritoneum on each side of the urinary bladder, into which the obturator canal opens. In females it is the lateral part of the vesicouterine pouch.

paravesical spaces, a pair of subdivisions of the extraperitoneal space found lateral to the prevesical space.

paraxial /perak′sē-əl/, pertaining to an organ or other structure located near the axis of the body.

parchment skin /pärch′mənt/ [Fr, *parchemin;* AS, *scinn*], thin, wrinkled, or stretched skin that is exceptionally fragile.

paregoric /per′əgôr′ik/, a camphorated tincture of opium prescribed in the treatment of diarrhea and as an analgesic.

parencephalitis /per′ensef′əlī′tis/, an inflammation of the cerebellum.

parencephalocele /per′ensef′əlōsēl′/, a protrusion of the cerebellum through a hole in the cranium.

parenchyma /pəreng′kimə/ [Gk, *para + enchyma,* infusion], the functional tissue or cells of an organ or gland, as distinguished from supporting or connective tissue.

parenchymal cell /pəreng′kiməl/, any cell that is a functional element of an organ, such as a hepatocyte.

parenchyma of prostate, glandular substance consisting of small compound tubulosaccular or tubuloalveolar glands that makes up the bulk of the prostate. It is surrounded by muscular substance and permeated by muscular strands.

parenchymatous /per'əngkim'ətəs/ [Gk, *para + enchyma,* infusion], pertaining to or resembling the functional tissues of an organ or gland.

parenchymatous neuritis [Gk, *para + enchyma,* infusion; L, *osus,* like], any inflammation affecting the substance, axons, or myelin of the nerve.

parenchymatous salpingitis, an inflammation and thickening of the fallopian tubes.

parent [L, *parens*], a mother or father; one who bears offspring.—**parental,** *adj.*

parental generation (P₁) /pəren'təl/, the initial cross between two varieties in a genetic sequence; the parents of any individual belonging to a first generation.

parental grief, the behavioral reactions that characterize the grieving process and result in the resolution of grief at the loss of a child from expected or unexpected death. The immediate reactions are shock and disbelief, followed by acute grief and, in the case of sudden, unexpected death, extreme feelings of guilt and remorse.

parent education, thoughtful conveyance of information enabling the parent to provide high-quality childrearing.

parent education: adolescent, a nursing intervention from the Nursing Interventions Classification (NIC) defined as assisting parents to understand and help their adolescent children.

parent education: child-rearing family, a nursing intervention from the Nursing Interventions Classification (NIC) defined as assisting parents to understand and promote the physical, psychological, and social growth and development of their toddler, preschooler, or school-age child or children.

parent education: infant, a nursing intervention from the Nursing Interventions Classification (NIC) defined as instruction on nurturing and physical care needed during the first year of life.

parent ego state, in transactional analysis, an ego state that incorporates the feelings and behavior learned from parents or other authority figures; a part of the self that offers advice like that of one's own parents, containing messages that emphasize what one "ought to" or "should not" do.

parenteral /pəren'tərəl/ [Gk, *para + enteron,* bowel], pertaining to treatment other than through the digestive system.—**parenterally,** *adv.*

parenteral absorption, the taking up of substances within the body by structures other than the digestive tract.

parenteral dosage, pertaining to a medication administered by a route that bypasses the GI tract, such as a drug given by injection.

parenteral nutrition, the administration of nutrients by a route other than the alimentary canal, such as subcutaneously, intravenously, intramuscularly, or intradermally. The parenteral fluids usually consist of physiologic saline solution with glucose, amino acids, electrolytes, vitamins, and medications. They may not be nutritionally complete but maintain fluid and electrolyte balance during the immediate postoperative period and in other conditions, such as shock, coma, malnutrition, and chronic renal and hepatic failures.

parent figure [L, *parens + figura,* form], **1.** a parent or a substitute parent or guardian who cares for a child, providing the physical, social, and emotional requirements necessary for normal growth and development. **2.** a person who symbolically represents an ideal parent, having those attributes that one conceptualizes as necessary for forming the perfect parent-child relationship.

parent image, a conscious and unconscious concept that a child forms concerning the roles and characteristics of the personality of the mother and father.

parent-infant attachment, a nursing outcome from the Nursing Outcomes Classification (NOC) defined as parent and infant behaviors that demonstrate an enduring affectionate bond.

parenting: adolescent physical safety, a nursing outcome from the Nursing Outcomes Classification (NOC) defined as parental actions to prevent physical injury in an adolescent from 12 years through 17 years of age.

parenting: early/middle childhood physical safety, a nursing outcome from the Nursing Outcomes Classification (NOC) defined as parental actions to avoid physical injury of a child from 3 years through 11 years of age.

parenting: infant/toddler physical safety, a nursing outcome from the Nursing Outcomes Classification (NOC) defined as parental actions to avoid physical injury of a child from birth through 2 years of age.

parenting performance, a nursing outcome from the Nursing Outcomes Classification (NOC) defined as parental actions to provide a child with a nurturing and constructive physical, emotional, and social environment.

parenting promotion, a nursing intervention from the Nursing Interventions Classification (NIC) defined as providing parenting information, support, and coordination of comprehensive services to high-risk families.

parenting: psychosocial safety, a nursing outcome from the Nursing Outcomes

Classification (NOC) defined as parental actions to protect a child from social contacts that might cause harm or injury.

Parents Anonymous, a self-help group for parents who have abused their children or who feel that they are prone to maltreat them. The organization offers support and guidance, provides a forum for discussing mutual problems, and furnishes distressed parents with a positive mechanism for coping with anger by talking to another member rather than by releasing their emotions on the child.

Parents Without Partners, a self-help group for single parents, including those who are separated, divorced, or widowed.

paresis /pərē′sis, per′isis/ [Gk, *paralyein*, to be palsied], **1.** motor weakness or partial paralysis related in some cases to local neuritis. **2.** a late manifestation of neurosyphilis, characterized by generalized paralysis, tremulous incoordination, transient seizures, Argyll Robertson pupils, and progressive dementia caused by degeneration of cortical neurons. —**paretic,** *adj.*

paresthesia /per′esthē′zhə/ [Gk, *para* + *erethizein,* to excite], any subjective sensation, experienced as numbness, tingling, or a "pins and needles" feeling. Paresthesias often fluctuate according to such influences as posture, activity, rest, edema, congestion, or underlying disease.

paretic /peret′ik/ [Gk, *paresis,* paralysis], pertaining to or resembling partial paralysis.

paricalcitol, a vitamin D analog used to treat hypoparathyroidism.

paries /per′i·ēz/ *pl.* **parietes,** the wall of a hollow organ or cavity in the body.

parietal /pərī′ətəl/ [L, *paries,* wall], **1.** pertaining to the outer wall of a cavity or organ. **2.** pertaining to the parietal bone of the skull or the parietal lobe of the cerebrum.

parietal abdominal fascia, the fascia lining the wall of the abdominal cavity.

parietal bone, one of a pair of bones forming the sides of the cranium. Each parietal bone has two surfaces, four borders, and four angles and articulates with five bones: the opposite parietal, occipital, frontal, temporal, and sphenoid.

parietal cells [L, *paries,* wall, *cella,* storeroom], the cells on the periphery of the gastric glands of the stomach. They are located on the basement membrane beneath the chief cells and secrete hydrochloric acid.

parietal layer of glomerular capsule, the layer of the glomerular capsule opposite the visceral layer, with the urinary space in between. It is composed of simple squamous epithelium.

parietal lobe, a part of each cerebral hemisphere that occupies the parts of the lateral and medial surfaces that are covered by the parietal bone. On the lateral surface of the hemisphere, the parietal lobe is separated from the frontal lobe by the central sulcus and from the temporal lobe by an imaginary line that extends from the posterior ramus of the lateral sulcus toward the occipital pole. It is concerned with language mechanisms and general sensory functions.

parietal lymph node, any one of the small oval glands that filter the lymph coursing through the lymphatic vessels in the walls of the thorax or through the lymphatic vessels associated with the larger blood vessels of the abdomen and the pelvis.

parietal pain, a sharp sensation of distress in the parietal pleura, aggravated by respiration and thoracic movements and caused by pneumonia, empyema, pneumothorax, asbestosis, TB, neoplasm, or the accumulation of fluid resulting from heart, liver, or kidney disease. Pain arising from the parietal pleura lining the chest wall is perceived over the involved area, but that arising from the central part of the diaphragm is referred to the posterior shoulder area; pain from the costal parts of the diaphragm is referred to the adjacent thoracic wall.

parietal pelvic fascia, the layer of fascia surrounding the abdominal cavity, composed of transversalis fascia, the fascia covering muscle associated with the upper regions of the pelvic bones, and similar fascia covering the muscles of the pelvic cavity.

parietal pericardium [L, *paries,* wall; Gk, *peri* + *kardia,* heart], an outer layer of the serous pericardium that is not in direct contact with the heart muscle.

parietal peritoneum, the portion of the largest serous membrane in the body that lines the abdominal wall.

parietal pleura, the outer layer of the pleura, lining the walls of the thoracic cavity.

parietomastoid suture, the suture at which the mastoid part of the temporal bone articulates superiorly with the parietal bone.

parietooccipital /pərī′ətō·oksip′itəl/ [L, *paries* + *occiput,* back of the head], pertaining to the parietal and occipital bones or cerebral lobes.

parietooccipital sulcus, a groove on each cerebral hemisphere marking the division of the parietal and occipital lobes of the cerebrum.

parietotemporal /-tem′pərəl/ [L, *paries,* wall, *tempus,* temple], pertaining to the temporal and parietal bones of the cranium.

parietovisceral /-vis′ərəl/, pertaining to the abdominal wall and abdominal organs.

Parinaud's oculoglandular syndrome /per′ənōz/ [Henri Parinaud, French ophthalmologist, 1844–1905], a term often used to refer to conjunctivitis that is usually unilateral, follicular, and followed by enlargement of the preauricular lymph nodes and tenderness. The syndrome is caused by a wide range of tularemia, cat-scratch fever, and lymphogranuloma venereum.

pari passu /per′ē pas′ōō/ [L, *par,* equal, *passus,* step], at the same time or in equal proportions.

parity /per′itē/ [L, *parere,* to give birth], **1.** in obstetrics, the classification of a woman by the number of live-born children and stillbirths she has delivered at more than 20 weeks of gestation. Commonly parity is noted with the total number of pregnancies and represented by the letter *P* or the word *para.* **2.** in epidemiology, the classification of a woman by the number of live-born children she has delivered.

parkinsonian, pertaining to to or resembling Parkinson's disease.

parkinsonian facies [James Parkinson, English physician, 1755–1824; L, *facies,* face], a masklike and immobile facial expression, usually occurring with Parkinson's disease. Infrequent blinking also occurs.

parkinsonian tremor [James Parkinson; L, *tremor,* shaking], a mild resting tremor with slow, regular oscillations of three to six per second, exacerbated by fatigue, cold, or emotion. The tremors usually, but not always, cease during voluntary movement of the affected part and during sleep.

parkinsonism /pär′kənsəniz′əm/ [James Parkinson], a neurologic disorder characterized by tremor, muscle rigidity, hypokinesia, a slow shuffling gait, and difficulty in chewing, swallowing, and speaking, caused by various lesions in the extrapyramidal motor system. Signs and symptoms of parkinsonism resemble those of idiopathic Parkinson's disease and may develop during or after acute encephalitis and in syphilis, malaria, poliomyelitis, and carbon monoxide poisoning.

Parkinson's disease [James Parkinson], a slowly progressive degenerative neurologic disorder characterized by resting tremor, pill rolling of the fingers, a masklike facies, shuffling gait, forward flexion of the trunk, loss of postural reflexes, and muscle rigidity and weakness. It is usually an idiopathic disease of people over 60 years of age. Typical pathologic changes are destruction of neurons in basal ganglia, loss of pigmented cells in the substantia nigra, and depletion of dopamine in the caudate nucleus, putamen, and pallidum, structures in the neostriatum that normally contain high levels of the neurotransmitter dopamine. Signs and symptoms of Parkinson's disease, which include resting tremor, bradykinesias, drooling, increased appetite, intolerance to heat, oily skin, emotional instability, and defective judgment, are increased by fatigue, excitement, and frustration.

Parkinson's mask [James Parkinson; Fr, *masque*], an expressionless face with eyebrows raised and smoothing but immobility of the facial muscles.

Parlodel, a trademark for a dopamine receptor agonist (bromocriptine).

Parnate, a trademark for an antidepressant (tranylcypromine sulfate).

parole /pərōl′/, in psychiatry, a system of supervision of a patient who has been physically released from a hospital setting but is still listed as an inpatient and may be returned to the hospital without further court action.

paromomycin sulfate /per′əmōmī′sin/, an oral antiamebic aminoglycoside antibiotic prescribed in the treatment of intestinal amebiasis, tapeworms, and *Cryptosporidium.* It is used preoperatively to suppress intestinal flora.

paromphalocele /perom′fəlōsēl′/, a hernia or tumor near the umbilicus.

paronychia /per′onik′ē·ə/ [Gk, *para* + *onyx,* nail], an infection of the fold of skin at the margin of a nail.

paroophoritis /per′ō·of′ərī′tis/ [Gk, *para* + *oon,* egg, *pherein,* to bear, *itis,* inflammation], **1.** inflammation of the paroophoron. **2.** inflammation of the tissues surrounding the ovary.

paroophoron /per′ō·of′əron/ [Gk, *para* + *oon,* egg, *pherein,* to bear], a small vestigial remnant of the mesonephros, consisting of a few rudimentary tubules lying in the broad ligament between the epoophoron and the uterus. A similar vestigial structure, the aberrant ductule, is found in the male.

parosmia /pəroz′mē·ə/ [Gk, *para* + *osme,* smell], any dysfunction or perversion concerning the sense of smell.

parosteitis /per′ostē·ī′tis/, an inflammation of the tissues adjacent to or associated with a bone.

parosteosis /per′ostē·ō′sis/, the development of bone in an abnormal location, such as in the area of the periosteum or in the skin.

parotid /pərot′id/ [Gk, *para* + *ous,* ear], near the ear.

parotid abscess, a collection of pus in a parotid salivary gland.

parotid duct [Gk, *para* + *ous,* ear; L, *ducere,* to lead], a tubular canal, about

P

7 cm long, that extends from the anterior part of the parotid gland near the ear to the mouth.

parotidectomy /pərot′idek′təmē/ [Gk, *para + ous + ektomē*, excision], the surgical removal of the parotid gland.

parotid gland [Gk, *para + ous*, ear; L, *glans*, acorn], one of the largest pairs of salivary glands that lie at the side of the face just below and in front of the external ear. The main part of the gland is superficial, somewhat flattened, and quadrilateral. It is enclosed in a capsule continuous with the deep cervical fascia.

parotitis /per′ətī′tis/ [Gk, *para + ous*, ear, *itis*, inflammation], inflammation or infection of one or both parotid salivary glands.

parous /per′əs/, having borne one or more viable offspring.

parovarian /per′ōver′ē·ən/ [Gk, *para*; L, *ovum*, egg], pertaining to residual tissues in the area near the fallopian tubes and the ovary.

paroxetine, a selective serotonin reuptake inhibitor prescribed in the treatment of mental depression, obsessive-compulsive disorder, panic disorders, and anxiety disorders, including social anxiety and general anxiety. Unlabeled uses include treatment of impulse control disorders, PMS, and vasomotor symptoms of menopause.

paroxysm /per′əksiz′əm/ [Gk, *paroxynein*, to stimulate], **1.** a marked, usually episodic increase in symptoms. **2.** a convulsion, fit, seizure, or spasm.—**paroxysmal**, *adj.*

paroxysmal AV nodal reentry tachycardia [Gk, *paroxysmos*, irritation; L, *nodus*, knot; Gk, *tachys*, fast, *kardia*, heart], a type of paroxysmal supraventricular tachycardia usually initiated by a premature atrial complex and sustained by an atrioventricular nodal reentry mechanism. A vagal maneuver is usually successful in restoring sinus rhythm.

paroxysmal cold hemoglobinuria (PCH), a rare autoimmune hemolytic anemia disorder marked by hemolysis minutes or hours after exposure to cold.

paroxysmal cough [Gk, *paroxysmos*, irritation; AS, *cohhetan*, cough], a severe attack of coughing, as may accompany whooping cough, bronchiectasis, or a lung injury.

paroxysmal hemoglobinuria, the sudden passage of hemoglobin in urine, occurring after local or general exposure to low temperatures, as in paroxysmal cold hemoglobinuria.

paroxysmal nocturnal dyspnea (PND), a disorder characterized by sudden attacks of respiratory distress that awaken the person, usually after several hours of sleep in a reclining position. This occurs because of increased fluid central circulation with reclining position. It is most commonly caused by pulmonary edema resulting from CHF. The attacks are often accompanied by coughing, a feeling of suffocation, cold sweat, and tachycardia with a gallop rhythm.

paroxysmal nocturnal hemoglobinuria (PNH), an acquired hemolytic anemia caused by a clonal stem cell mutation that results in an absence of glycosylphosphatidylinositol-anchored proteins, including decay-accelerating factor (DAF) and CD55. Red cells lacking DAF and CD55 have an increased susceptibility to complement activation and lysis, resulting in intravascular hemolysis and hemoglobinuria, especially during sleep.

paroxysmal supraventricular tachycardia, an ectopic heart rhythm with a rate of 170 to 250 beats/min. It begins abruptly with a premature atrial or ventricular beat and is supported by an atrioventricular (AV) nodal reentry mechanism or by an AV reentry mechanism involving an accessory pathway.

paroxysmal ventricular tachycardia [Gk, *paroxysmos*, irritation; L, *ventriculus*, little belly; Gk, *tachys + kardia*], a rapid heartbeat of sudden onset and termination caused by a quick succession of discharges from an ectopic site in a ventricle.

pars /pärs/ *pl.* **partis** [L, part], a part, such as the pars abdominalis esophagi.

Parse, Rosemarie Rizzo, a nursing theorist who, in her *Man-Living-Health: A Theory of Nursing* (1981), synthesized Martha E. Rogers' principles and concepts (Science of Unitary Human Beings) and the work of existential phenomenologists. Parse's view of nursing is based on humanism as opposed to positivism. Her theory addresses the unity of humans' lived experience, the lived experience of health. Humans choose from options and bear responsibility for choices. Parse proposes that nursing is a human science and rejects the traditional view of nursing as an emerging natural science.

pars flaccida, the thin and slack part of the tympanic membrane superior to the anterior and posterior malleolar folds.

pars interarticularis, a region of the vertebra between the superior and inferior facet joints that is susceptible to trauma.

pars planitis /pärz plänī′tis/, **1.** a granulomatous uveitis of the ciliary disk (pars plana of the ciliary body). **2.** intermediate uveitis.

pars tensa, the thick and taut part of the tympanic membrane.

part [L, *pars*], a part of a larger area, such as the condylar part of the occipital bone.

part. aeq., abbreviation for the Latin phrase *partes aequales,* meaning "in equal parts."

parthenogenesis /pär′thənōjen′əsis/ [Gk, *parthenos,* virgin, *genesis,* origin], a type of nonsexual reproduction in which an organism develops from an unfertilized ovum, as in many simpler animals. The development of the unfertilized ovum may be artificially induced through mechanical or chemical stimulation.—**parthenogenetic, parthenogenic,** *adj.*

partial anodontia, partial absence of the teeth. It is a relatively common congenital condition characterized by absence of one or more teeth because of absence of their anlage, which is seldom associated with other anomalies.

partial cleavage /pär′shəl/, mitotic division of only part of a fertilized ovum, usually the activated cytoplasmic part surrounding the nucleus.

partial crown, a restoration that replaces some but not all surfaces of a tooth.

partial denture [L, *pars,* part, *dens,* tooth], a dental prosthesis, either fixed or removable, used to replace one or more missing teeth.

partial dislocation [L, *pars* + *dis* + *locare,* to place], the partial, abnormal separation of the articular surfaces of a joint.

partial hospitalization program, an organizational entity that provides therapeutic services to patients who use only day or night hospital services or adult day health services rather than regular inpatient hospitalization services.

partial liquid ventilation, ventilatory support in which the lungs are filled to the level of the functional residual capacity with a liquid perfluorocarbon. Mechanical ventilation is then superimposed, and oxygen and carbon dioxide are transferred through the liquid.

partially acid-fast /pär′shəlē/, capable of retaining the stain carbolfuchsin during mild acid decolorization. This ability is found in bacteria of the genus *Nocardia,* because of the presence of unusual long-chain fatty acids in their cell walls.

partially edentulous arch, a dental arch in which one or more but not all natural teeth are missing.

partial placenta previa, placenta previa in which the placenta is implanted in the lower uterine segment and partially covers the internal os of the uterine cervix. As the cervix dilates in labor, the part of the placenta that lies over the cervix is separated, causing bleeding from the villous spaces of the uterine wall. Depending on the degree of separation, the bleeding may be scant or severe, resulting in hemorrhage that is life-threatening to the mother and the baby.

partial pressure, the pressure exerted by any one gas in a mixture of gases or in a liquid, with the pressure directly related to the concentration of that gas to the total pressure of the mixture. The concentration of oxygen in the atmosphere represents approximately 21% of the total atmospheric pressure, calculated at 760 mm Hg under standard conditions. Therefore the partial pressure of atmospheric oxygen is about 160 mm Hg (760×0.21).

partial pressure of carbon dioxide in arterial blood (PaCO$_2$), the part of total blood gas pressure exerted by carbon dioxide. It decreases during heavy exercise, during rapid breathing, or in association with uncontrolled diabetes. It increases with chest injuries or respiratory disorders.

partial pressure of oxygen in arterial blood (PaO$_2$), the part of total blood gas pressure exerted by oxygen gas. It is lower than normal in patients with asthma, obstructive lung disease, or certain blood diseases and in healthy individuals during vigorous exercise.

partial response, the condition in which the maximum decrease in treated tumor volume is at least 50% but less than 100%.

partial shadowing, in ultrasonics, a manifestation of decreased echo signal amplitudes returning from regions lying beyond an object in which the attenuation is higher than the average attenuation in adjacent overlying regions.

partial thromboplastin time (PTT), a test for detecting coagulation defects of the intrinsic system by adding activated partial thromboplastin to a sample of test plasma and to a control sample of normal plasma. The time required for the formation of a clot in test plasma is compared with that in the normal plasma. A delayed clotting time suggests an abnormality in one or more factors of the intrinsic system. PTT is one of the basic tests used to measure specific factor activity and to detect hemophilias. It can be used to monitor liver function and the activity of the anticoagulant heparin.

partial volume artifact, an artifact caused by a mixture of tissues with different attenuation coefficients within any given voxel.

partial zona dissection (PZD), an older micromanipulation technique used in male factor infertility. A cut is made into the zona pellucida and spermatozoa are inserted.

participant, a subject in a research project.

participation in health care decisions, a nursing outcome from the Nursing Outcomes Classification (NOC) defined as personal involvement in selecting and

P

evaluating health care options to achieve a desired outcome.

particle /pär'tikəl/ [L, *particula,* small part], **1.** any fundamental unit of matter. **2.** a minute fragment or speck.

particulate /pärtik'yəlit/, pertaining to a minute discrete particle or fragment of a substance or material.

parts per million (PPM, ppm), the ratio of the amount of one substance to the amount of another, expressed as a unit of solute dissolved in 1 million units of solution. It may be further expressed in terms of mass-to-mass, volume-to-volume, or another relationship of units of measure.

parturient /pärt(y)ōō'rē·ənt/ [L, *parturire,* to desire to bring forth], pertaining to the act of childbirth.

parturition /pär't(y)ōōrish'ən/ [L, *parturire,* to desire to bring forth], the process of giving birth.

part. vic, abbreviation for the Latin term *partes vicibus,* meaning "divided doses."

paruresis, the inhibition of urination as a result of psychologic or other reasons.

paruria /pərōōr'ē·ə/, any defect of the urination process.

parvovirus B19 /pär'vōvī'rəs/, a small single-stranded DNA virus of the Parvoviridae family that infects humans, causing erythema infectiosum, aplastic crisis in hemolytic anemia, and other disorders.

parvovirus B19 antibody test, a blood test used to detect the presence of antibodies to the B19 parvovirus, a known human pathogen.

parvule /pär'vyōōl/, a very small pill.

PAS, PASA, abbreviation for **paraaminosalicylic acid.**

PASCAL /poskul', paskal'/ [Blaise Pascal, French scientist, 1623–1662], a higher-level computer compiler language, used to teach programming.

Pascal's principle /poskuls', paskals'/ [Blaise Pascal], in physics, a law stating that a confined liquid transmits pressure applied to it from an external source equally in all directions. Pascal's principle provides the basis for all hydraulic devices.

PASG, abbreviation for *pneumatic antishock garment.*

passage /pas'ij/, **1.** an opening, channel, route, or gap. **2.** the movement of something from one place to another, as in evacuation of the bowels.

pass facilitation, a nursing intervention from the Nursing Interventions Classification (NIC) defined as arranging a leave for a patient from a health care facility.

passiflora /pas'iflôr'ə/, the passion flower, *Passiflora incarnata,* a climbing herb. It has flowers and fruiting tops that are the source of medications used as antispasmodics and sedatives and for the treatment of burns, dysmenorrhea, hemorrhoids, and insomnia.

passion flower, a herbal product derived from a perennial climbing vine. It is used orally for the treatment of insomnia and restlessness and GI disturbances associated with nervousness. It is used topically for the treatment of hemorrhoids, burns, and inflammation. Other traditional uses include treatment of menopause, pain, palpitations, arrhythmias, and hypertension. It may be effective in relieving nervousness; there are insufficient reliable data regarding its effectiveness for other indications.

passive [L *passivus*], pertaining to behavior that subordinates the individual's own interests to the demands of others.

passive-aggressive personality [L, *passivus* + *aggressus,* combative, *persona,* character], a personality characterized by a chronically negativistic disposition with passive resistance and aggression with forceful actions or attitudes expressed in an indirect, nonviolent manner such as pouting, obstructionism, procrastination, inefficiency, stubbornness, and forgetfulness.

passive-aggressive personality disorder, a *DSM-IV* psychiatric disorder characterized by the indirect expression of resistance to occupational or social demands. It results in persistent pervasive ineffectiveness, lack of self-confidence, poor interpersonal relationships, and pessimism that can lead in severe cases to major depression, alcoholism, or drug dependence.

passive carrier [L, *passivus;* OFr, *carier*], **1.** a healthy person whose body carries the causal organisms of an infectious disease although the person has not contracted the disease and remains symptomless. **2.** a person who carries a gene associated with a hereditary trait although the trait is not expressed in the person.

passive clot, a clot that forms in an aneurysm when circulation is interrupted.

passive congestion [L, *passivus* + *congerere,* to heap together], an excessive amount of blood accumulation in an organ as a result of increased venous pressure.

passive-dependent personality [L, *passivus;* Fr, *dependre,* to depend; L, *persona,* character], a personality characterized by helplessness, indecisiveness, and a tendency to cling to and seek support from others.

passive euthanasia, the ending of life by the deliberate withholding of drugs or other life-sustaining treatment.

passive exercise, repetitive movement of a part of the body as a result of an externally applied force or of a voluntary effort to move another part of the body. Passive exercise can be used to prevent contractures and maintain joint mobility but does not promote muscle maintenance.

passive expiration [L, *passivus* + *expirare*, to breathe out], normal exhalation that occurs without direct muscular effort, as during normal tidal breathing. Air is expelled from the lungs as a result of the recoil effect of elastic tissues in the chest, lungs, and diaphragm.

passive immunity, a form of acquired immunity resulting from antibodies that are transmitted naturally through the placenta to a fetus, through the colostrum to an infant, or artificially by injection of antiserum for treatment or prophylaxis. Passive immunity is not permanent.

passive incontinence [L, *passivus* + *incontinentia*], urine overflow that may occur when the bladder is paralyzed and greatly distended.

passive lingual arch, an orthodontic appliance that may help maintain tooth space and dental arch length when bilateral primary molars are prematurely lost.

passive lung collapse [L, *passivus*; AS, *lungen*; L, *collabi*], a condition of dyspnea, cough, and hemoptysis with pigmented cells, caused by an obstructed blood flow from the lungs to the heart.

passive motion [L, *passivus*; *motio*], involuntary motion caused by an external force rather than by voluntary muscular effort.

passive movement, the moving of parts of the body by an outside force without voluntary action or resistance by the individual.

passive play, play in which a person does not participate actively. For younger children such activity may include watching and listening to others, observing other children or animals, listening to stories, or looking at pictures. Older children are passively entertained by games and toys that require concentration and intellectual skill.

passive range of motion (PROM), the moving of a joint through its range of motion without exertion by the subject, usually done by an examiner who moves the person's body part manually.

passive recoil, the return of elastic tissue to its normal length and position when applied tension on the tissue is released.

passive sensitization [L, *passivus* + *sentire*, to feel], a temporary form of sensitization induced by injecting serum from a sensitized individual.

passive smoking, the inhalation by nonsmokers of the smoke from other people's cigarettes, pipes, or cigars. The amount of such smoke is enough to aggravate respiratory illnesses and contribute to serious diseases.

passive stretching, stretching that involves only noncontractile elements such as ligaments. Examples are manipulation of a muscle, such as during therapeutic massage or during isometric exercises.

passive symptom [L, *passivus*; Gk, *symptoma*, that which happens], a symptom that attracts little or no attention.

passive transfer, the conferring of immunity to a nonimmune host by injection of antibody or lymphocytes from an immune or sensitized donor.

passive transport, the movement of small molecules across the membrane of a cell by diffusion. Passive transport is essential to various processes of metabolism, such as the intake of digestive products by the cells lining the intestines.

passivity /pəsiv′itē/ [L, *passivus*], a maladaptive mental state of submission, dependence, or inactivity.

Passy-Muir valve, a one-way speaking valve for use with tracheostomy tubes. Its normal position at rest is closed, so that it is open only during inhalation and closes during exhalation, allowing air to pass through the vocal folds for phonation.

paste /pāst/, a topical semisolid formulation containing a pharmacologically active ingredient in a fatty base, a viscous or mucilaginous base, or a mixture of starch and petrolatum.

Pasteur effect /pastŏŏr′, pästœr′/ [Louis Pasteur, French chemist, 1822–1895], the inhibiting effect of oxygen on carbohydrate fermentation by living cells.

Pasteurella /pas′tərel′ə/ [Louis Pasteur], a genus of gram-negative bacilli or coccobacilli, including species pathogenic to humans and domestic animals.

pasteurellosis /pas′tərelō′sis/ [Louis Pasteur], a local wound infection, caused by the gram-negative bacillus *Pasteurella multicida*, which may be acquired through the bite or scratch of an infected animal, usually a cat.

pasteurization /pas′tərīzā′shən/ [Louis Pasteur; Gk, *izein*, to cause], the process of applying heat, usually to milk or cheese, for a specified period for the purpose of killing or retarding the development of pathogenic bacteria.—**pasteurize,** *v.*

pasteurized milk /pas′tərīzd/ [Louis Pasteur; Gk, *izein*, to cause; AS, *moluc*, milk], milk that has been treated by heat to destroy pathogenic bacteria. By law, pasteurization requires a temperature of 145° to 150° F for not less than 30 minutes, followed by a temperature of 161° F for 15 seconds, followed by immediate cooling.

P

Pasteur, Louis [French chemist, 1822–1895], promoter of the germ theory of infection and developer of the pasteurization process to kill pathogenic organisms in milk. Pasteur also developed several vaccines and pioneered the development of stereochemistry by separating mirror image isomers.

Pasteur treatment [Louis Pasteur], a method of preventing rabies by daily injections of attenuated cultures of rabies virus cultured in the CNS tissues of rabbits. The treatment, developed by Pasteur, is no longer used.

past health [ME, *passen,* to pass; AS, *hoelth,* sound body], in a health history, an overall summary of the person's general health to date, including past injuries, allergies, surgical procedures, immunizations, hospitalizations, and obstetric and psychiatric history.

Pastia's lines /pas′te·əz/ [Chessec Pastia, twentieth century Romanian physician], lines of hyperpigmentation seen in the body folds in scarlet fever.

pastille /pastēl′, pas′til/, **1.** a gelatin-based sweetened and molded medication impregnated with a therapeutic substance intended to be sucked. **2.** a chemically treated paper disk that undergoes color changes when exposed to radiation. **3.** a small mass containing aromatic substances and benzoic acid that is burned for fumigation.

pastoral counseling department /pas′tərəl/ [L, *pastor,* shepherd], the hospital chaplaincy service.

past pointing [OFr, *passer;* L, *punctus,* pricked], the inability to place a finger on another part of the body accurately, indicating a lack of coordination in voluntary movements.

patch [ME, *pacche*], a small spot of surface tissue that differs from the surrounding area in color or texture or both and is not elevated above it.

patch test, a skin test for identifying allergens, especially those causing contact dermatitis. The suspected substance (food, pollen, animal fur) is applied to an adhesive patch that is placed on the patient's skin. Another patch, with nothing on it, serves as a control. After a certain period (usually 24 to 48 hours) both patches are removed. If the skin under the suspect patch is red and swollen and the skin under the control area is not, the test result is said to be positive, and the person is probably allergic to that substance.

patella /pətel′ə/ [L, small dish], a flat, large, sesamoid bone at the front of the knee joint, having a pointed apex that attaches to the patellar ligament.

patellar /pətel′ər/ [L, *patella,* small dish], pertaining to the patella.

patellar-bearing supracondylar/suprapatellar (PTBSC/SP) socket, a type of patellar-tendon below-the-knee bearing prosthesis with a socket that extends in front, medially, and laterally to accommodate both the patella and the femoral condyles. The higher socket increases knee stability, and a suspension strap is not required.

patellar bursa [L, *patella,* small dish; Gk, *byrsa,* wineskin], any of the fluid-filled connective tissue sacs around the knee cap.

patellar ligament [L, *patella* + *ligare,* to bind], the central part of the common tendon of the quadriceps femoris. The ligament is a strong, flat ligamentous band attached proximally to the apex and the adjoining margins of the patella and distally to the tuberosity of the tibia.

patellar reflex, a deep tendon reflex, elicited by a sharp tap on the tendon just distal to the patella, normally characterized by contraction of the quadriceps muscle and extension of the leg at the knee.

patellar tendon–bearing (PTB) prosthesis, an ankle-foot orthosis that provides prolonged stretch to the posterior leg musculature and may create extension force at the knee joint.

patellar tendon–bearing supracondylar (PTB/SC) socket, a lower-leg prosthesis with supracondylar and suprapatellar suspension.

patellectomy /pat′əlek′təmē/ [L, *patella,* small dish; Gk, *ektomē,* excision], the surgical removal of the patella.

patency /pā′tənsē/ [L, *patens,* open], a state of being open or exposed.

patent /pā′tənt/ [L, *patens,* open], open and unblocked, such as a patent airway or a patent anus.

patent ductus arteriosus (PDA), an abnormal opening between the pulmonary artery and the aorta caused by failure of the fetal ductus arteriosus to close after birth. It is seen primarily in premature infants. The defect allows blood from the aorta to flow into the pulmonary artery and to recirculate through the lungs, where it is reoxygenated and returned to the left atrium and left ventricle, placing an increased workload on the left side of the heart and causing increased pulmonary vascular congestion and resistance. Clinical manifestations include cardiomegaly, especially of the left atrium and left ventricle; dilated ascending aorta; bounding pulses resulting from increased systolic pressure; tachycardia; and a typical machinery-like murmur that is heard during all of systole and most of diastole.

patent medicine [L, *patens,* open + *medicina*], a drug available to the general public without a prescription. The ingredients and contraindications are usually listed on the label or wrapper.

patent urachus, a congenital anomaly in which the urachus remains patent from the bladder to the umbilicus, with a channel that may be small or large and leakage of urine at the umbilicus.

paternal /pətur'nəl/ [L, *pater,* father], pertaining to fatherhood, characteristic of a father, or related through a father.

paternity test /pətur'nitē/ [L, *pater + testum,* crucible], a test based on genetic blood groups and used mainly to exclude or confirm the possibility that a particular man could be the father of a specific child.

Paterson-Parker dosage system [James R.K. Paterson, English radiologist; H.M. Parker, twentieth-century American-English physicist], a radiotherapy system that uses sources of specific relative loadings arranged according to defined rules, which lead to a homogenous dose in the implanted region.

path [AS, *paeth*], a route or course along which something moves, such as a circuit of the nervous system that is followed by sensory or motor nerve impulses.

path., 1. abbreviation for **pathologic. 2.** abbreviation for **pathology.**

pathetic /pəthet'ik/, pertaining to something that engenders emotions of sympathy, pity, and sadness.

pathfinder, a thin, flexible cylindric instrument containing a series of filiform guides, used to locate strictures.

pathogen /path'əjən/ [Gk, *pathos,* disease, *genein,* to produce], any microorganism capable of producing disease.—**pathogenic,** *adj.*

pathogenesis /-jen'əsis/ [Gk, *pathos + genesis,* origin], the source or cause of an illness or abnormal condition.

pathogenic /-jen'ik/ [Gk, *pathos,* disease, *genein,* to produce], capable of causing or producing a disease.

pathogenicity /-jənis'itē/, the ability of a pathogenic agent to produce a disease.

pathogenic occlusion, an abnormal closure of the teeth, capable of producing pathologic changes in the teeth, supporting tissues, and related structures.

pathognomonic /pathog'nəmon'ik/ [Gk, *pathos + gnomon,* index], of a sign or symptom, specific to a disease or condition, such as Koplik's spots on the buccal and lingual mucosa, which are indicative of measles.

pathologic (path.) /-loj'ik/ [Gk, *pathos + logos,* science], pertaining to a condition that is caused by or involves a disease process.

pathologic amenorrhea [Gk, *pathos,* disease, *logos,* science, *a + men,* month, *rhoia,* to flow], a stoppage or absence of menstrual discharge from the uterus as a reult of a disease.

pathologic anatomy, in applied anatomy, the study of the structure and morphologic characteristics of the tissues and cells of the body as related to disease.

pathologic diagnosis, a diagnosis arrived at by an examination of the substance and function of the tissues of the body, especially of the abnormal developmental changes in the tissues by histologic techniques of tissue examination.

pathologic histology [Gk, *pathos,* disease, *logos,* science, *histos,* tissue, *logos,* science], the study of the effects of disease on the structure, composition, and function of tissues.

pathologic microorganisms [Gk, *pathos,* disease, *logos,* science, *mikros,* small, *organon,* instrument, *ismos,* condition], any microscopic life form, from a virus to a nematode, that has the potential to cause disease.

pathologic mitosis, any cell division that is atypical, asymmetric, or multipolar and results in an unequal number of chromosomes in the nuclei of the daughter cells. It is indicative of malignancy.

pathologic myopia, a type of severe, progressive nearsightedness characterized by changes in the fundus of the eye, posterior staphyloma, and deficient corrected acuity.

pathologic physiology, 1. the study of the physical and chemical processes involved in the functioning of diseased tissues. **2.** the study of the modification of the normal functioning processes of an organism caused by disease.

pathologic reflex [Gk, *pathos,* disease, *logos,* science; L, *reflectere,* to bend back], any abnormal reflex that is caused by a lesion in or an organic disease of the nervous system.

pathologic retraction ring, a ridge that may form around the uterus at the junction of the upper and lower uterine segments during the prolonged second stage of an obstructed labor. The ring, which may be seen and felt abdominally, is a warning of impending uterine rupture.

pathologic sleep [Gk, *pathos,* disease, *logos,* science; AS, *slaep*], excessive sleep associated with a neurologic disorder such as encephalitis lethargica, or sleeping sickness.

pathologic triad, the combination of three respiratory disease conditions: bronchospasm, retained secretions, and mucosal edema.

pathologist /pəthol'əjist/, a physician specializing in the study of disease. A pathologist usually specializes in autopsy or in clinical or surgical pathology.

P

pathologists' assistant, an allied health professional who, under the direct supervision of a licensed pathologist, participates in autopsies and in the examination, dissection, and processing of tissue specimens.

pathology (path.) /pəthol'əjē/ [Gk, *pathos,* disease, *logos,* science], the study of the characteristics, causes, and effects of disease, as observed in the structure and function of the body. Cellular pathology is the study of cellular changes in disease. **Clinical pathology** is the study of disease by the use of laboratory tests and methods. —**pathologic,** *adj.*

pathophysiology /-fiz'ē·ol'əjē/ [Gk, *pathos,* disease, *physis,* nature, *logos,* science], the study of the biologic and physical manifestations of disease as they correlate with the underlying abnormalities and physiologic disturbances. —**pathophysiologic,** *adj.*

pathosis, a disease condition.

pathway [AS, *paeth* + *weg*], **1.** a network of neurons that provides a transmission route for nerve impulses from any part of the body to the spinal cord and the cerebral cortex or from the CNS to the muscles and organs. **2.** a chain of chemical reactions that produces various compounds in critical sequence, such as the Embden-Meyerhof pathway.

patient (pt.) /pā'shənt/ [L, *pati,* to suffer], **1.** a recipient of a health care service. **2.** a health care recipient who is ill or hospitalized. **3.** a client in a health care service.

patient assignment, a specialty capitation method in which patients choose a provider in each specialty represented. Capitation payments are then distributed accordingly to the providers selected.

patient care committee, a hospital staff organization, composed of medical, nursing, and other health professionals, with responsibility for monitoring all patient care practices to ensure that predetermined standards are met.

patient care technician, a health technician working under the supervision of a registered nurse, physician, or other health professional to provide basic patient care. Duties may include taking vital signs, obtaining blood and urine samples, performing basic diagnostic tests, and assisting the physician as needed.

patient compensation fund, a fund usually established by state law, commonly financed by a surcharge on malpractice premiums, and used to pay malpractice claims.

patient contracting, a nursing intervention from the Nursing Interventions Classification (NIC) defined as negotiating an agreement with a patient that reinforces a specific behavior change.

patient-controlled analgesia (PCA), a drug-delivery system that dispenses a preset intravascular dose of a narcotic analgesic when the patient pushes a switch on an electric cord. The device consists of a computerized pump with a chamber containing the drug. A lockout interval automatically inactivates the system if a patient tries to increase the amount of narcotic within a preset period.

patient-controlled analgesia (PCA) assistance, a nursing intervention from the Nursing Interventions Classification (NIC) defined as facilitating patient control of analgesic administration and regulation.

patient day (P.D.), a unit in a system of accounting used by health care facilities and health care planners. Each day represents a unit of time during which the services of the institution or facility are used by a patient; thus 50 patients in a hospital for 1 day would represent 50 patient days.

patient dumping, the premature discharge of Medicare or indigent patients from hospitals for economic reasons. A 1986 U.S. federal rule requires hospitals to advise Medicare patients on admission for treatment of their right to challenge what they consider to be premature discharge after treatment.

patient interview, a systematic interview of a patient, the purpose of which is to obtain information that can be used to develop an individualized plan for care.

patient mix, 1. the distribution of demographic variables in a patient population, often represented by the percentage of a given race, age, sex, or ethnic derivation. **2.** the distribution of indications for admission in a patient population, such as surgical, maternity, or trauma.

patient plan of care, a document developed after the patient assessment that identifies the nursing diagnoses to be addressed in the hospital or clinic. The plan of care includes the objectives, nursing interventions, and time frame for accomplishment and evaluation.

patient record, a collection of documents that provides an account of each episode in which a patient visited or sought treatment and received care or a referral for care from a health care facility. The record is confidential and is usually held by the facility, and the information in it is released only to the patient or with the patient's written permission.

patient representative services, hospital services provided by designated staff members relating to the investigation and mediation of patients' complaints and the promotion and protection of patients' rights.

patient rights protection, a nursing intervention from the Nursing Interventions Classification (NIC) defined as protection of health care rights of a patient, especially a minor, incapacitated, or incompetent patient unable to make decisions.

Patient's Bill of Rights, a list of the patient's rights promulgated by the American Hospital Association. It offers some guidance and protection to patients by stating the responsibilities that a hospital and its staff have toward them and their families during hospitalization, but it is not a legally binding document.

Patient Self-Determination Act, an act mandating that individuals enrolled in health care facilities are informed in writing on admission of their rights to formulate advance directives and to consent to or refuse treatment.

Patient Zero, an individual identified by the Centers for Disease Control and Prevention (CDC) as the person who introduced HIV in the United States. According to CDC records, Patient Zero, an airline steward, infected nearly 50 other persons before he died of AIDS in 1984.

Patrick test, a test for pain or dysfunction in the hip and sacroiliac joints in which overpressure is applied at the knee during flexion, abduction, and external rotation of the hip. While applying pressure on the knee, the examiner also applies counterpressure at the opposite anterior superior iliac spine.

patrilineal /pat′rilin′ē·əl/ [L, *pater,* father, *linea,* line], pertaining to a line of descent through the male members of the family.

patten /pat′ən/, a metal support worn on a shoe to prevent weight-bearing on the opposite leg.

patterning /pat′ərning/ [ME, *patron*], the method of treatment or act of establishing a system or pattern of stimuli that will evoke a new set of responses. The process is commonly used to retrain people who have suffered a brain injury that disrupts normal sensory-motor activities.

patulous /pat′yələs/ [L, *patulus,* open], pertaining to something that is open or spread apart.

paucibacillary /paw′səbas′əlärē/, containing just a few bacilli.

pau d'arco, a herbal product harvested from an evergreen flowering tree native to Florida, the West Indies, Mexico, and Central/South America. This herb is used for cancer, inflammation, and infection. This herb is possibly unsafe when used orally in typical dosages, and there is insufficient data regarding its efficacy for any indications.

Paul-Bunnell test [John R. Paul, American physician, 1893–1971; Walls W. Bunnell,

American physician, 1902–1966], an old term for a blood test for heterophil antibodies, used for confirming a diagnosis of infectious mononucleosis.

pauresis /pôrē′sis/, the inhibition of urination for psychologic or other reasons.

Pautrier microabscess /pôtrēyā′/ [Lucien M.A. Pautrier, French dermatologist, 1876–1959; Gk, *mikros,* small; L, *abscedere,* to go away], an accumulation of intensely staining mononuclear cells in the epidermis, characterizing malignant lymphoma of the skin, especially mycosis fungoides.

Pauwels' fracture /pou′əlz/ [Friedrich Pauwels, twentieth-century German surgeon; L, *fractura,* break], a break in the proximal femoral neck with varying degrees of angulation.

Pavabid, a trademark for a smooth muscle relaxant (papaverine hydrochloride).

Pavlik harness, a device used to correct hip dislocations in infants with developmental dysplasia of the hip, consisting of a set of straps that hold the hips in flexion and abduction.

Pavlov, Ivan Petrovich /pav′lôv, pä′vlôf/, (1849–1936), a Russian physiologist who discovered a pattern of conditioned stimulus-reflex learning, the manner in which the physiologic mechanism of digestion is controlled by the nervous system, and a theory of the causes and treatment of human neuroses.

pavor /pā′vôr/ [L, quaking], a reaction to a frightening stimulus, characterized by excessive terror.

pavor diurnus /dī·ur′nəs/, a sleep disorder occurring in children during daytime sleep in which they cry out in alarm and awaken in fear and panic.

pavor nocturnus /noktur′nəs/, a sleep disorder occurring in children during nighttime sleep in which they cry out in alarm and awaken in fear and panic.

Pavulon, a trademark for a neuromuscular blocking agent (pancuronium bromide).

PAWP, abbreviation for *pulmonary artery wedge pressure.*

Paxil, a trademark for a selective serotonin reuptake inhibitor (paroxetine).

Payr's clamp /pī′ərz/ [Erwin Payr, German surgeon, 1871–1946; AS, *clam,* fastener], a heavy clamp used in GI surgery.

Pb, symbol for the element **lead.**

PBL, abbreviation for *peripheral blood lymphocytes.*

PC, 1. abbreviation for *professional corporation.* 2. abbreviation for the Latin *post cibum,* "after meals."

p.c., abbreviation for the Latin *post cibum,* "after meals."

PCB, abbreviation for **polychlorinated biphenyl.**

pcc, abbreviation for *precipitated calcium carbonate.*

PCC, abbreviation for **prothrombin complex concentrate.**

PCCM, abbreviation for **primary care case management.**

PCH, abbreviation for **paroxysmal cold hemoglobinuria.**

PCI, abbreviation for **percutaneous coronary intervention.**

PCIS, abbreviation for *Patient Care Information System,* an online computer system that contains full medical care data on all the residents or the patients in a facility.

PCLN, abbreviation for **psychiatric consultation liaison nurse.**

PCOS, abbreviation for **polycystic ovary syndrome.**

P.C.P., abbreviation for **primary care physician,** used by house staff or others to distinguish a patient's primary physician from university faculty, attending specialist physicians, or house staff.

PCP, 1. abbreviation for **phencyclidine hydrochloride. 2.** abbreviation for **Pneumocystis pneumonia. 3.** abbreviation for **primary care physician.**

PCR, 1. abbreviation for **polymerase chain reaction. 2.** abbreviation for **protein catabolic rate.**

PCT, abbreviation for **porphyria cutanea tarda.**

PCWP, abbreviation for *pulmonary capillary wedge pressure.*

PD, abbreviation for **peritoneal dialysis.**

Pd, symbol for the element **palladium.**

p.d., abbreviation for the Latin *per diem,* "by the day."

P.D., PD, 1. abbreviation for **patient day. 2.** abbreviation for *Doctor of Pharmacy.* **3.** abbreviation for *prism diopter.* **4.** abbreviation for *pupil diameter.* **5.** abbreviation for *pupillary distance.* **6.** abbreviation for **pulse duration.**

PDA, 1. abbreviation for **patent ductus arteriosus. 2.** abbreviation for *personal digital assistant.*

PDL, abbreviation for **periodontal ligament.**

PDR, abbreviation for **Physicians' Desk Reference.**

PE, abbreviation for **pulmonary embolism.**

PEA, abbreviation for **pulseless electrical activity.**

peak [ME, *pec*], the amount of medication in the blood that represents the highest level during a drug administration cycle.

peak acid output (PAO), on the pentagastrin test, after administration of pentagastrin, the sum of the two highest 15-minute outputs of gastric acid multiplied by 2, expressed in mmol/hr.

peak and trough specimens, serum samples collected to determine the level of an antibiotic or other pharmaceutical agent in the blood. Peak specimens, which represent the highest level, are generally collected ½ hour after the dose is given intravenously or 1 hour after it is given intramuscularly. Trough specimens, representing the lowest level, are generally collected approximately half an hour before the next dose.

peak compressional pressure, in ultrasonics, the temporal maximum positive-pressure in a medium during the passage of a pulsed sound wave. It is expressed in pascals or megapascals.

peak concentration, the maximum amount of a substance or force, such as the highest concentration of a drug measured after it is administered.

peak expiratory flow, the greatest rate of airflow that can be achieved during forced expiration beginning with the lungs fully inflated.

peak flow meter, an instrument for measuring the flow of air in the early part of forced expiration.

peak height velocity, a point in pubescence in which the tempo of growth is the greatest.

peak level, the highest concentration, usually in the blood, that a substance reaches during the period under consideration, such as the highest blood glucose level attained during a glucose tolerance test.

peak method of dosing, the administration of a drug dosage so that a specified maximum level is reached to produce a desired effect, such as lowering the BP.

peak mucus sign, a lubricative, cloudy-to-clear white cervical mucus that occurs during periods of high estrogen levels, particularly at the time of ovulation.

peak refractional pressure, in ultrasonics, the temporal maximum negative pressure in a medium occurring during the passage of a pulsed ultrasound wave. It is expressed in pascals or megapascals.

Pean clamp, a curved or straight hemostatic clamp with serrations along the entire length of the jaw.

pear-shaped bladder, a urinary bladder with widening of the inferior section, seen in conditions including pelvic lipomatosis, perivesical hematoma or urinoma, and lymphoma or lymphocyst.

Pearson's product movement correlation [Karl Pearson, English mathematician, 1857–1936], in statistics, a statistical test of the relationship between two variables measured in interval or ratio scales. Correlations computed fall between +1.00 and −1.00.

peau d'orange /pō dôräNzh′/ [Fr, skin of orange], a dimpling of the skin that gives it the appearance of the skin of an orange. It is common in advanced breast cancer.

pecten /pek′tən/, **1.** a ridge extending laterally from the pubic tubercle, to which the pectineal part of the inguinal ligament is attached. **2.** a vascular pleated membrane that extends from the optic disc to the vitreous humor in some animals.

pectenitis /pek′tənī′tis/, an inflammation of the anal canal, causing interference with the anal sphincter muscle.

pectin /pek′tin/ [Gk, *pektos,* congealed], a gelatinous carbohydrate substance found in fruits and succulent vegetables and used as the setting agent for jams and jellies and as an emulsifier and stabilizer in many foods. It also adds to the diet bulk necessary for proper GI functioning.

pectinate muscles, the ridges that cover the walls of the atrium proper and the right auricle.

pectineal ligament, the fibers that extend from the lacunar ligament along the pectineal line of the pelvic brim.

pectineal line, a ridge on the superior ramus of the pubic bone.

pectineus /pektin′ē·əs/ [L, *pecten,* comb], the most anterior of the five medial femoral muscles. It functions to flex and adduct the thigh and to rotate it medially.

pectoral /pek′tərəl/ [L, *pectus,* breast], pertaining to the thorax or chest.

pectoralgia /pek′tôral′jə/, a pain in the thorax.

pectoralis major /pek′tərä′lis, pek′tərəlis′/ [L, *pectus,* breast], a large muscle of the upper chest wall that acts on the joint of the shoulder. It serves to flex, adduct, and medially rotate the arm in the shoulder joint.

pectoralis minor, a thin triangular muscle of the upper chest wall beneath the pectoralis major. It functions to rotate the scapula, to draw it down and forward, and to raise the third, fourth, and fifth ribs in forced inspiration.

pectoriloquy /pek′təril′əkwē/, a phenomenon in which voice sounds, including whispers, are transmitted clearly through the pulmonary structures and are clearly audible through a stethoscope. It is often a sign of lung consolidation.

pedagogy /ped′əgōj′ē/ [Gk, *pais,* child, *agogos,* leader], the art and science of teaching children, based on a belief that the purpose of education is the transmittal of knowledge.

pedal /ped′əl/ [L, *pes,* foot], pertaining to the foot.

Pediaflor, a trademark for a dental preparation (sodium fluoride) used in prophylaxis against dental caries in children.

Pedialyte, a trademark for a balanced solution containing various electrolytes.

pediatric advanced life support (PALS), a system of critical care procedures and facilities, such as the intensive care nursery for the basic and advanced treatment of seriously ill or injured infants and children. It includes the neonatal resuscitation program as recommended by the American Academy of Pediatrics and the American Heart Association.

pediatric anesthesia [Gk, *pais,* child, *iatreia,* treatment], a subspecialty of anesthesiology dealing with the anesthesia of neonates, infants, and children up to 12 years of age.

pediatric dentistry, the branch of dentistry devoted to the diagnosis and treatment of dental problems affecting children.

pediatric dosage, the determination of the correct amount, frequency, and total number of doses of a medication to be administered to a child or infant. Various formulas have been devised to calculate pediatric dosage from a standard adult dose, although the most reliable method is to use the proportional amount of body surface area to body weight, based on one of the formulas.

pediatric hospitalization, the confinement of a child or infant in a hospital for diagnostic testing or therapeutic treatment.

pediatrician /pē′dē·ətrish′ən/ [Gk, *pais,* child, *iatreia,* treatment], a physician who specializes in the development and care of infants and children and in the treatment of their diseases.

pediatric nurse practitioner (PNP), a nurse practitioner who, by advanced study and clinical practice, such as in a master's degree program or certificate program in pediatric nursing, has gained advanced knowledge in the nursing care of infants and children.

pediatric nursing, the branch of nursing concerned with the care of infants and children.

pediatric nutrition, the maintenance of a proper, well-balanced diet, consisting of the essential nutrients and the adequate caloric intake necessary to promote growth and sustain the physiologic requirements at the various stages of a child's development. Nutritional needs vary considerably with age, level of activity, and environmental conditions, and they are directly related to the rate of growth.

pediatrics /pē′dē·at′triks/, a branch of medicine concerned with the development and care of infants and children. Its specialties are the particular diseases of children and their treatment and prevention. —**pediatric,** *adj.*

pediatric surgery, the special preparation and care of the child undergoing surgical procedures for injuries, deformities, or disease.

P

pedicle [L, *pediculus,* little foot], a narrow stalk, stem, or tube of tissue attached to a tumor, skin flap, bone, or organ.

pedicle clamp /ped′ikəl/ [L, *pediculus,* little foot; ME, *clam,* fastener], a locking surgical forceps used for compressing blood vessels or pedicles of tumors during surgery.

pedicle flap operation, a surgical procedure for grafting gingival tissue from a donor site to the site of an isolated defect, usually a tooth surface denuded of attached gingiva.

pedicle of vertebral arch, one of the paired parts of the vertebral arch that connect a lamina to the vertebral body.

pediculicide /pədik′yŏŏlisīd′/ [L, *pediculus,* little foot, *caedere,* to kill], any of a group of drugs that kill lice.

pediculosis /pədik′yŏŏlō′sis/ [L, *pediculus + osis,* condition], an infestation with blood-sucking lice. Pediculosis capitis is infestation of the scalp with lice. Pediculosis corporis is infestation of the skin of the body with lice. Pediculosis palpebrarum is infestation of the eyelids and eyelashes with lice. Pthirus pubis (formerly called pediculosis pubis) is infestation of the pubic hair region with lice. An OTC treatment is available with pyrethrin- or permethrin-containing topical agents.

pediculous /pədik′yələs/ [L, *pediculus*], infested with sucking lice.

Pediculus humanus capitis, a species of head louse.

Pediculus humanus corporis, a species of body lice.

pedicure /ped′ikyŏŏr/, care of the feet, especially trimming of the toenails.

pedigree /ped′əgrē/ [Fr, *pied de grue,* crane's foot pattern], **1.** line of descent; lineage; ancestry. **2.** a chart that shows the genetic makeup of a person's ancestors, used in the mendelian analysis of an inherited characteristic or disease in a particular family.

pedogenesis /pē′dōjen′əsis/ [Gk, *pais,* child, *genesis,* origin], the production of offspring by young or larval forms of animals, often by parthenogenesis, as in certain amphibians.—**pedogenetic,** *adj.*

pedophilia /ped′əfil′ē-ə/ [Gk, *pais,* child, *philein,* to love], **1.** an abnormal interest in children. **2.** in psychiatry, a psychosexual disorder in which the fantasy or act of engaging in sexual activity with prepubertal children is the preferred or exclusive means of achieving sexual excitement and gratification.—**pedophilic,** *adj.*

peduncle /pədung′kəl/ [L, *pes,* foot], a stemlike connecting part, such as the pineal peduncle or a peduncle graft.—**peduncular, pedunculate,** *adj.*

pedunculated /pədung′kyəlā′tid/ [L, *pes,* foot], pertaining to a structure with a stalk or peduncle.

pedunculotomy /pədung′kyəlot′əmē/, a surgical incision in a cerebral peduncle.

pedunculus /pədung′kyələs/ [L, *pes,* foot], a stalk, stem, or stalklike anatomic structure.

peeling, the loss of all or part of the epidermis, as may occur after a sunburn or exposure to a chemical.

PEEP, abbreviation for **positive end-expiratory pressure.**

peeping testis, an undescended testis in the peritoneal cavity that moves slightly across the internal inguinal ring.

peer [L, *par,* equal], a person deemed an equal for the purpose at hand. A peer is usually a companion or associate of roughly the same age or level of mental endowment.

peer review[1], an appraisal by professional co-workers of equal status of the way an individual nurse or other health professional conducts practice, education, or research. The appraisal uses accepted standards as measures against which performance is weighed.

peer review[2], a nursing intervention from the Nursing Interventions Classification (NIC) defined as systematic evaluation of a peer's performance compared with professional standards of practice.

Peganone, a trademark for an anticonvulsant (ethotoin).

pegaptanib, a miscellaneous ophthalmic agent that binds to vascular endothelial growth factor, thereby inhibiting angiogenesis. It is used in the treatment of neovascular age-related macular degeneration. It may be used alone or with photodynamic therapy.

pegaspargase, a modified version of the enzyme L-asparaginase used in cancer chemotherapy. It is prescribed in the treatment of acute lymphoblastic leukemia, during a blast crisis of chronic lymphocytic leukemia and during salvage therapy in non-Hodgkin's lymphoma. It may also be effective in those who are hypersensitive to other forms of the enzyme.

pegfilgrastim /peg-filgras′tim/, a long-acting colony-stimulating factor produced by recombinant technology and used as an adjunct in patients with bone marrow suppression caused by antineoplastic therapy.

peginterferon alfa-2a, a covalent conjugate of recombinant interferon alfa-2a and polyethylene glycol, used in the treatment of chronic infection by hepatitis C virus.

peginterferon alfa-2b, a covalent conjugate of recombinant interferon alfa-2b and polyethylene glycol, used in the treatment of chronic infection by hepatitis C virus.

pegvisomant, a rarely used miscellaneous agent used to treat acromegaly in those patients who have an inadequate response to other treatment.

PEL, abbreviation for **permissible exposure limit.**

Pel-Ebstein fever /pel eb'stēn/ [Pieter K. Pel, Dutch physician, 1852–1919; Wilhelm Ebstein, German physician, 1836–1912], a fever recurring in cycles of several days or weeks, characteristic of Hodgkin's disease or other malignant lymphomas.

Pelger-Huët anomaly /pel'gər hyŌŌ'ət/ [Karel Pelger, Dutch physician, 1885–1931; G.J. Huët, Dutch physician, 1879–1970; Gk, *anomalia,* irregular], an inherited disorder characterized by granulocytes with unusually coarse nuclear material and dumbbell-shaped or peanut-shaped nuclei.

pelidnoma /pel'idnō'mə/, a circumscribed elevated dark patch on the skin.

peliosis hepatitis /pel'ē·ō'sis/, the presence of blood-filled cavities in the liver. The cavities may become lined by endothelium and may be found in patients who are infected with HIV or who use oral contraceptives or anabolic steroids.

Pelizaeus-Merzbacher disease /pā'lētsä′ŌŌs merts′bä·kər/ [Friedrich Pelizaeus, German physician, 1850–1917; Ludwig Merzbacher, German physician, 1875–1942], an X-linked leukoencephalopathy, occurring in early life and running a slowly progressive course into adolescence or adulthood. It is marked by nystagmus, ataxia, tremor, choreoathetoid movements, parkinsonian facies, dysarthria, and mental deterioration. Pathologically, there is diffuse demyelination in the white substance of the brain, which may involve the brainstem, cerebellum, and spinal cord.

pellagra /pəlā′grə, pəlag′rə/ [It, *pelle,* skin, *agra,* rough], a disease resulting from a deficiency of niacin or tryptophan or a metabolic defect that interferes with the conversion of the precursor tryptophan to niacin. It is characterized by scaly dermatitis, especially of the skin exposed to the sun; glossitis; inflammation of the mucous membranes; diarrhea; and mental disturbances, including depression, confusion, disorientation, hallucination, and delirium.—**pellagrous,** *adj.*

pellagra sine pellagra /sī′nē, sē′nə/, a form of pellagra in which the characteristic dermatitis is not present.

Pellegrini's disease /pel′əgrē′nēz/ [Augusto Pellegrini, Italian surgeon, 1877–1958], ossification of the upper part of the medial collateral ligament, sometimes accompanied by bony growth at the internal condyle of the femur. The condition usually follows a leg injury.

pellet /pel'it/, a pilule or very small pill.

pellicle /pel′ikəl/, **1.** a thin film or skin. **2.** a scum or crust on a solution.

pelotherapy /pē′lōther′əpē/, the treatment of certain conditions with baths or packs of mud, peat, or earth on part or all of the body surface.

pelvic abscess [L, *pelvis,* basin, *abscedere,* to go away], a pus-producing lesion in the pelvic peritoneum, usually originating in the rectouterine pouch.

pelvic axis, an imaginary curved line that passes through the centers of the various anteroposterior diameters of the pelvis.

pelvic bones [L, *pelvis,* basin; AS, *ban*], a combination of the ilium, ischium, and pubis.

pelvic brim, the curved top of the bones of the hip extending from the anterosuperior iliac crest in front on one side around and past the sacrum to the crest on the other side. Below the brim is the pelvis.

pelvic cellulitis, bacterial infection of the parametrium, occurring after childbirth or spontaneous therapeutic abortion. It represents an extension of infection via the blood vessels and lymphatics from a primary wound infection in the external genitalia, perineum, vagina, cervix, or uterus. It is characterized by fever, uterine subinvolution, chills and sweats, abdominal pain that spreads laterally, and, if untreated, the formation of a large abscess and signs of peritonitis.

pelvic classification, 1. a process in which the anatomic and spatial relationships of the bones of the pelvis are evaluated, usually to assess the adequacy of the pelvic structures for vaginal delivery. **2.** one of the types in a classification system of the pelvis.

pelvic congestion syndrome, an abnormal gynecologic condition characterized by chronic low back pain, dysuria, dysmenorrhea, vague lower abdominal pain, vaginal discharge, and dyspareunia.

pelvic diameter [L, *pelvis,* basin; Gk, *diametros,* measuring across], **1.** at the rim of the pelvis, a line from the lumbosacral angle to the symphysis pubis. **2.** at the pelvic outlet, a line from the tip of the coccyx to the lower border of the symphysis pubis.

pelvic diaphragm, the inferior aspect of the body wall, stretched like a hammock across the pelvic cavity and comprising the levator ani and the coccygeus muscles. It holds the abdominal contents, supports the pelvic viscera, and is pierced by the anal canal, the urethra, and the vagina.

pelvic examination, a diagnostic procedure in which the external and internal genitalia are physically examined by

P

inspection, palpation, percussion, and auscultation. It should be performed regularly throughout a woman's life.

pelvic exenteration /eksen'tərā'shən/, the surgical removal of all reproductive organs and their lymph nodes and en bloc removal of the rectum, distal sigmoid colon, urinary bladder, distal ureters, internal iliac vessels, entire pelvic floor, with accompanying pelvic peritoneum, levator muscles, and perineum. Pelvic exenteration is the preferred treatment for recurrent or persistent carcinoma of the cervix after radiation therapy.

pelvic floor, the soft tissues enclosing the pelvic outlet.

pelvic floor electrical stimulation (PFES), functional electrical stimulation of the muscles of the pelvic floor, delivered through a vaginal or rectal probe, used in the treatment of stress incontinence.

pelvic girdle [L, *pelvis,* basin; AS, *gyrdel*], a bony ring formed by the hip bones, the sacrum, and the coccyx.

pelvic hematoma, an accumulation of blood in the soft tissues of the pelvis, as may occur during childbirth.

pelvic inflammatory disease (PID), any inflammatory condition of the female pelvic organs, especially one caused by bacterial infection. Characteristics of the condition include fever; foul-smelling vaginal discharge; pain in the lower abdomen; abnormal uterine bleeding; pain with coitus; and tenderness or pain in the uterus, affected ovary, or fallopian tube on bimanual pelvic examination. If an abscess has already developed, a soft, tender fluid-filled mass may be palpated. Severe PID is usually very painful; the woman may be prostrate and require narcotic analgesia. Recurrent or severe PID often results in scarring of the fallopian tubes, obstruction, and infertility.

pelvic inlet, in obstetrics, the inlet to the true pelvis, bounded by the sacral promontory, the horizontal rami of the pubic bones, and the top of the symphysis pubis. Because the infant must pass through the inlet to enter the true pelvis and be born vaginally, the anteroposterior, transverse, and oblique dimensions of the inlet are important measurements to be made in assessing the pelvis in pregnancy.

pelvic lipomatosis, deposition of fat around the pelvic cavity. As it progresses, the fat may compress the pelvic organs, causing urinary tract, kidney, or other symptoms.

pelvic minilaparotomy /min'ēlap'ərot' əmē/, a surgical operation in which the lower abdomen is entered through a small suprapubic incision. It is performed most often for tubal sterilization but also for diagnosis and treatment of ectopic pregnancy, ovarian cyst, endometriosis, and

infertility. It may be performed as a faster and less expensive alternative to laparoscopy, often on an outpatient basis.

pelvic muscle exercise, a nursing intervention from the Nursing Interventions Classification (NIC) defined as strengthening and training the levator ani and urogenital muscles through voluntary, repetitive contraction to decrease stress, urge, or mixed types of urinary incontinence.

pelvic outlet, the space surrounded by the bones of the lower part of the true pelvis. In women the shape and size of the pelvis vary and are of importance in childbirth.

pelvic pain, pain in the pelvis, as occurs in appendicitis, oophoritis, and endometritis.

pelvic part of ductus deferens, the distal part of the ductus deferens, where it is within the pelvic cavity and terminates at the ampulla ductus deferentis.

pelvic pole, the end of the axis at which the breech of the fetus is located.

pelvic presentation [L, *pelvis,* basin, *praesentare,* to show], a breech presentation.

pelvic rotation, one of the five major kinematic determinants of gait, involving the alternate rotation of the pelvis to the right and left of the body's central axis. Pelvic rotation occurs during the stance phase of gait and involves a medial to lateral circular motion. During normal locomotion or walking, considered a progressive sinusoidal movement, pelvic rotation serves to minimize the vertical displacement of the body's center of gravity.

pelvic rotunda [L, *pelvis,* basin, *rotundus,* wheel], a part of the ear appearing as a funnel-shaped depression of the tympanum above the fenestra cochlea.

pelvic tilt, one of the five major kinematic determinants of gait that lowers the pelvis on the side of the swinging lower limb during the walking cycle. Through the action of the hip joint, the pelvis tilts laterally downward, adducting the lower limb in the stance phase of gait and abducting the opposite extremity in the swing phase of gait. The knee joint of the nonweightbearing limb flexes during its swing phase to allow the pelvic tilt. Pelvic tilt helps minimize the vertical displacement of the body's center of gravity, thus conserving energy during walking.

pelvic ultrasonography, an ultrasound examination of a woman performed to identify paracervical, endometrial, or ovarian pathology or the risk of fetal abnormalities.

pelvifemoral /pel'vēfem'ərəl/ [L, *pelvis,* basin, *femur,* thigh], pertaining to the structures of the hip joint, especially the muscles and the area around the bony pelvis and the head of the femur that make up the pelvic girdle.

pelvimeter /pelvim′ətər/ [L, *pelvis,* basin; Gk, *metron,* measure], a device for measuring the diameter and capacity of the pelvis.

pelvimetry /pelvim′ətrē/, the act or process of determining the dimensions of the bony birth canal.

pelvis /pel′vis/ *pl.* **pelves** [L, basin], the lower part of the trunk of the body, composed of four bones, the two innominate bones laterally and ventrally and the sacrum and coccyx posteriorly. It is divided into the greater or false pelvis and the lesser or true pelvis by an oblique plane passing through the sacrum and the pubic symphysis. The greater pelvis is the expanded part of the cavity situated cranially and ventrally to the pelvic brim. The lesser pelvis is situated distally to the pelvic brim, and its bony walls are more complete than those of the greater pelvis. The inlet and outlet of the pelvis have three important diameters: anteroposterior, oblique, and transverse. The pelvis of a woman is usually less massive but wider and more circular than that of a man.—**pelvic,** *adj.*

pelvisacral /pel′visā′krəl/, pertaining to the pelvis and sacrum.

pelvospondylitis ossificans /pel′vōspon′di lī′tis/, inflammation of the pelvic part of the spine with deposits of bony material between the sacral vertebrae.

PEM, abbreviation for **protein-energy malnutrition.**

pemetrexed, an antineoplastic-antimetabolite used in combination with cisplatin in the treatment of malignant pleural mesothelioma and as a single agent in the treatment of non–small cell lung cancer.

pemirolast /pĕ-mir′o-last/, a mast cell stabilizer that inhibits type I hypersensitivity reactions, administered topically to the conjunctiva to prevent pruritus associated with allergic conjunctivitis.

pemphigoid /pem′figoid/ [Gk, *pemphix,* bubble, *eidos,* form], a bullous disease resembling pemphigus, distinguished by thicker walled bullae arising from erythematous macules or urticarial bases. It may rarely be associated with an internal malignancy.

pemphigus /pem′figəs, pemfī′gəs/ [Gk, *pemphix,* bubble], an uncommon, severe disease of the skin and mucous membranes, characterized by thin-walled bullae arising from apparently normal skin or mucous membrane. The bullae rupture readily, leaving raw patches. The person loses weight, becomes weak, and is subject to major infections.

pemphigus vulgaris [Gk, *pemphix,* bubble; L, *vulgus,* common], a chronic progressive autoimmune disease that is often fatal, characterized by the formation of bullae on otherwise normal oral mucosal membrane.

penbutolol /pen-bu′tah-lol/, a beta-adrenergic blocking agent with intrinsic sympathomimetic activity, used as an antihypertensive in the form of the sulfate salt.

penciclovir /pen-si′klo-vir/, a compound that inhibits viral DNA synthesis in herpesviruses 1 and 2, used in the treatment of recurrent herpes labialis.

Pender, Nola J. [b. 1941], a nursing theorist who first presented her Health Promotion Model for nursing in her book *Health Promotion in Nursing Practice* (1982). She developed the idea that promoting optimal health supersedes preventing disease. Pender's theory identifies cognitive-perceptual factors in the individual, such as importance of health, perceived benefits of health-promoting behaviors, and perceived barriers to health-promoting behaviors. A major assumption in Pender's theory is that health, as a positive high-level state, is assumed to be a goal toward which an individual strives.

pendular nystagmus [L, *pendulus,* hanging down; Gk, *nystagmos,* nodding], an undulating involuntary movement of the eyeball.

pendulous /pen′dələs/, hanging loose or lacking proper support.

pendulous abdomen [L, *pendulus,* hanging down + *abdomen*], an abnormal condition in which the anterior abdominal wall becomes relaxed and allows the abdomen to hang down over the pubic region.

penetrance /pen′ətrəns/ [L, *penetrare,* to penetrate], the regularity with which an allele is expressed in a person who carries it. If an allele always produces its effect on the phenotype, it is fully penetrant.—**penetrant,** *adj.*

penetrate /pen′ətrāt/ [L, *penetrare*], **1.** to enter or pierce a barrier. **2.** pertaining to the degree to which x-rays pass through matter.

penetrating wound /pen′ətrā′ting/ [L, *penetrare*; AS, *wund*], a wound that breaks the skin and enters into a body area, organ, or cavity.

penetration /pen′ətrā′shən/, **1.** a piercing or entering. **2.** intellectual discernment. **3.** a stage in establishment of a viral infection in which the viral genetic material enters the host cell through fusion, phagocytosis, or injection.

penicillamine /pen′isil′əmēn/, a chelating agent prescribed for the treatment of Wilson's disease and cystinuria. It can be prescribed to bind with and remove heavy metals from the blood when there is poisoning resulting from metals such as copper, lead, mercury, arsenic, and gold. It is also prescribed as a palliative in the treatment of systemic sclerosis and rheumatoid arthritis when other medications have failed.

penicillic acid /pen′isil′ik/, an antibiotic compound isolated from various species of the fungus *Penicillium*.

penicillin /pen′isil′in/ [L, *penicillus*, paintbrush], any one of a group of antibiotics derived from cultures of species of the fungus *Penicillium* or produced semisynthetically. Various penicillins administered orally or parenterally for the treatment of bacterial infections exert their antimicrobial action by inhibiting the biosynthesis of cell wall mucopeptides during active multiplication of the organisms. The penicillins include penicillin G (benzylpenicillin), penicillin V (phenethicillin), cloxacillin, dicloxacillin, methicillin, nafcillin, oxacillin, ampicillin, amoxicillin carbenicillin, piperacillin, and ticarcillin.

penicillinase /pen′əsil′ənās/, an enzyme elaborated by certain bacteria, including many strains of staphylococci, that inactivates penicillin and thereby promotes resistance to the antibiotic. A purified preparation of penicillinase is used in the treatment of adverse reactions to penicillin.

penicillinase-producing *Neisseria gonorrhoeae* (PPNG), strains of *Neisseria gonorrhoeae* that are resistant to the effects of penicillin through the production of penicillinase.

penicillinase-producing staphylococci, strains of staphylococcal organisms that elaborate the penicillin-inactivating enzyme penicillinase and thereby resist the bactericidal action of the antibiotic.

penicillin G benzathine, a long-acting depot form of penicillin used primarily for the treatment of syphilitic infection outside the CNS. It is given by deep IM injection to achieve steady concentrations in the plasma and to slow systemic absorption from the repository in the muscle over a period of 12 hours to several days. It may be administered as prophylaxis against susceptible strains of bacteria, primarily gram-positive bacteria.

penicillin G potassium, a narrow-spectrum antibacterial for parenteral use. It is prescribed in the treatment of many gram-positive bacterial infections (generally excluding *Staphylococcus*), some gram-negative infections (e.g., *Neisseria*), syphilis, and some anaerobes.

penicillin V, a narrow spectrum bacterial antibiotic for oral administration prescribed for prophylaxis against rheumatic fever and in the treatment of ear, nose, throat, skin, and UTIs caused by susceptible bacterial strains (primarily gram-positive bacteria).

penicilliosis /pen′isil′ē·ō′sis/ [L, *penicillus*, paintbrush; Gk, *osis*, condition], pulmonary infection caused by fungi of the genus *Penicillium*.

Penicillium /pen′isil′ē·əm/ [L, *penicillus*, paintbrush], a genus of imperfect fungi, some species of which have been tentatively linked to disease in humans, most notably in immunocompromised patients. Penicillin G is obtained from *Penicillium chrysogenum* and *P. notatum*.

penile /pē′nīl/ [L, penis], pertaining to the penis.

penile cancer /pē′nīl/ [L, *penis*, penis, *cancer*, crab], a rare malignancy of the penis generally occurring in uncircumcised men and associated with genital herpesvirus infection and poor hygiene. It is often mistaken for a venereal wart. Leukoplakia or the flat-topped papules of balanitis xerotica obliterans may be premalignant lesions, and the velvety red painful papules of Queyrat's erythroplasia are penile squamous cell carcinoma in situ. Cancer of the penis usually presents as a local mass or a bleeding ulcer and metastasizes early in its course.

penile curvature, abnormal curving of the penis to one side when erect.

penile prosthesis [L, *penis*; Gk, *prosthesis*, addition], a device that can be surgically implanted in the penis to treat erectile dysfunction.

penis /pē′nis/ [L, male sex organ], the external reproductive organ of a man, homologous with the clitoris of a woman. It is attached with ligaments to the front and sides of the pubic arch and is composed of three cylindric masses of cavernous tissue covered with skin. The corpora cavernosa penis surrounds a median mass called the corpus spongiosum penis, which contains the greater part of the urethra.

penis envy, literally, female envy of the male penis, but generally a female wish for male attributes, position, and advantages. It is believed by some psychologists to be a significant factor in female personality development.

penniform /pen′ifôrm/ [L, *penna*, feather, *forma*, form], pertaining to the shape of a feather, especially the patterns of muscular fasciculi that correlate with the ROM and the power of muscles.

penoscrotal fusion, a developmental anomaly in which the penis is fused to the scrotum.

penoscrotal transposition, a developmental anomaly in which the two halves of the scrotum are found lateral to the shaft of the penis or sometimes higher, often accompanied by hypospadias.

Penrose drain [Charles B. Penrose, American surgeon, 1862–1925; AS, *draehen*, teardrop], a thin rubber tube used as a surgical drain device.

pentachlorophenol poisoning /pen′təklôr′ō fē′nol/, a toxic effect of skin absorption of sodium pentachlorophenate, an antimildew agent sometimes used in laundering. The condition has affected newborns with occasionally fatal symptoms of fever and profuse sweating, caused by skin contact with pentachlorophenate residue on diapers and nursery linens.

pentad /pen′tad/, **1.** a pentavalent chemical element. **2.** a relationship among five things.

pentadactyl /pen′tədak′til/ [Gk, *pente,* five, *daktylos,* fingers or toes], having five fingers per hand and five toes per foot.

pentagastrin test, for gastric function, a test comparing basal acid output with a peak acid output. After the patient fasts overnight, a basal acid output and its pH are obtained for secretion of stomach acid. Then pentagastrin is administered into the stomach through a nasogastric tube and maximal acid output and peak acid output values are obtained.

pentalogy of Cantrell /pental′əjē kantrel′/ [Gk, *pente,* five, *logos,* word; James R. Cantrell, American physician, 20th century], a cleft in the inferior part of the sternum associated with midline abdominal defects such as omphalocele and defective pericardium and diaphragm with communication between the pericardial and peritoneal cavities and with cardiac anomalies such as ventricular septal defect or, less often, atrial septal defect, tetralogy of Fallot, or left ventricular diverticulum.

Pentam 300, a trademark for an antiprotozoal agent (pentamidine isethionate).

pentamidine isethionate, a parenteral antiprotozoal drug prescribed in the treatment and prevention of pneumonia caused by *Pneumocystis jirovecii,* particularly in patients who have human immunodeficiency syndrome. It can also be used to treat trypanosomiasis and visceral leishmaniasis.

Pentatrichomonas hominis /pen′tətrik′ə mō′nəs/, a species of parasitic protozoan flagellate, formerly part of the genus *Trichomonas,* that lives symbiotically in the colon of humans.

pentavalent /pəntav′ələnt/ [Gk, *pente,* five; L, *valere,* to have worth], **1.** a chemical radical or element that has a valency of 5. **2.** pertaining to a body formed by the association of five chromosomes held together by chiasmata at the first division of meiosis.

pentazocine hydrochloride /pentā′zəsēn/, an agonist/antagonist opioid analgesic that stimulates kappa opioid receptors and blocks the mu opioid receptors. It is prescribed for the relief of moderate to severe pain.

pentobarbital /pen′təbär′bitol/, a sedative and hypnotic prescribed as a preoperative sedative, to induce coma during treatment of increased ICP, and to abort status epilepticus unresponsive to other medications.

pentosan /pen′to-san′/, a carbohydrate derivative used as an antiinflammatory, in the form of pentosan polysulfate sodium, in the treatment of interstitial cystitis.

pentosan polysulfate sodium, a polysulfated derivative of a xylose-containing, glucuronate-substituted pentosan, having fibrinolytic and anticoagulant actions. It is used as an antiinflammatory in the treatment of interstitial cystitis.

pentose /pen′tōs/ [Gk, *pente,* five; L, *osus,* having], a monosaccharide made of carbohydrate molecules, each containing five carbon atoms. It is produced by the body and is elevated after the ingestion of certain fruits, such as plums and cherries, and in certain rare diseases.

Pentothal Sodium, a trademark for a barbiturate drug (thiopental sodium).

pentoxifylline /pentok′sēfil′ēn/, a drug that lowers blood viscosity by making RBCs even more flexible. It is prescribed for the treatment of intermittent claudication associated with chronic occlusive arterial limb disease, but should not be used as a replacement for other types of medications used for peripheral vascular disease because its efficacy is marginal. There are several unlabled uses for the drug where decreased blood viscosity could be advantageous, including cerebrovascular disease and diabetic neuropathy.

Pen-Vee K, a trademark for an antibiotic (penicillin V potassium).

Pepcid, a trademark for an H_2 receptor antagonist used as antiulcer medication (famotidine).

Peplau, Hildegard E. [1909–1999], a pioneer in nursing theory development and a proponent in the 1950s of the concept that nursing is an interpersonal process. In a 1952 work, Peplau wrote that the nurse-patient relationship occurs in phases during which the nurse functions as a resource person, a counselor, and a surrogate. The four phases of the process are orientation, identification, exploitation, and resolution. The nurse assists in orientation when a patient with a need seeks help. Identification assures the patient that the nurse can understand his or her situation. Exploitation begins when the patient uses the services available. Resolution is marked as old needs are met and newer ones emerge.

peplos /pep′los/, a lipoprotein coat that may surround a virion.

peppermint, the dried leaves and flowering tops of the herb *Mentha piperita.* A source of a volatile oil, it is used as a carminative and antiemetic.

P

peppermint oil, a volatile oil from fresh aboveground parts of the flowering plant of peppermint *(Mentha piperita),* used as a flavoring agent for drugs and as a gastric stimulant and carminative.

pepper spray, an aerosolized form of oleoresins from capsicum, highly irritant to the skin and mucous membranes. It is used similarly to tear gas.

Pepper's syndrome [William Pepper, American physician, 1874–1947], a neuroblastoma of the adrenal glands that usually metastasizes to the liver.

pep pills *slang.* amphetamines, diet pills, or any other stimulant.

pepsin /pep'sin/ [Gk, *pepsis,* digestion], an enzyme secreted in the stomach that catalyzes the hydrolysis of protein. Preparations of pepsin obtained from pork and beef stomachs are sometimes used as digestive aids.

pepsinogen /pəpsin'əjən/ [Gk, *pepsis* + *genein,* to produce], a zymogenic substance secreted by pyloric and gastric chief cells. It is converted to the enzyme pepsin in an acidic environment, as in the presence of hydrochloric acid produced in the stomach.

pepsinuria /pep'sinŏŏr'ē-ə/ [Gk, *pepsis,* digestion, *ouron,* urine], the presence of pepsin in urine.

peptic /pep'tik/ [Gk, *peptein,* to digest], pertaining to digestion or to the enzymes and secretions essential to digestion.

peptic ulcer, a sharply circumscribed loss of the mucous membrane of the stomach, duodenum, or any other part of the GI system exposed to gastric juices containing acid and pepsin. Acute ulcers are almost always multiple and superficial and may be totally asymptomatic. Chronic ulcers are deep, single, persistent, and symptomatic. Characteristically ulcers cause a gnawing pain in the epigastrium that does not radiate to the back, is not aggravated by a change in position, and has a temporal pattern that mimics the diurnal rhythm of gastric acidity.

peptidase /pep'tidās/ [Gk, *peptein,* to digest, *ase,* enzyme suffix], a protein-splitting enzyme that breaks peptides into amino acids. It occurs naturally in plants, yeasts, certain microorganisms, and digestive juices.

peptide /pep'tīd/ [Gk, *peptein,* to digest], a molecular chain compound composed of two or more amino acids joined by peptide bonds.

peptidergic /pep'tidur'jik/, using small peptides as neurotransmitters.

peptogenic /pep'təjen'ik/, pertaining to an agent that produces peptones or pepsin.

peptone /pep'tōn/, a derived protein, which may be produced by hydrolysis of a native protein with an acid or enzyme.

Peptostreptococcus /pep'təstrep'təkok'əs/, a genus of gram-positive anaerobic chemoorganotrophic bacteria that occur in pairs or chains. The potentially pathogenic organisms are found in normal and pathologic female genital tracts and in the intestinal and respiratory tracts of normal humans. They have been associated with a variety of disorders ranging from appendicitis to putrefactive wounds.

Peptostreptococcus anaerobius, a potentially pathogenic species of anaerobic bacterium found throughout the body, including the mouth, the intestinal and respiratory tracts, and body cavities, particularly the vagina.

peracephalus /pur'əsef'ələs/ *pl.* **peracephali** [L, *per,* completely; Gk, *a* + *kephale,* not head], a fetus or individual with a malformed head.

peracetic acid /per'ah-se'tik/, peroxyacetic acid, CH_3COOOH, a strong oxidizing agent sometimes used for sterilization.

per an., abbreviation for the Latin phrase *per annum,* "yearly."

perceived severity /pərsēvd'/ [L, *percipere,* to perceive, *severus,* serious], in health belief model, a person's perception of the seriousness of the consequences of contracting a disease.

perceived susceptibility, in health belief model, a person's perception of the likelihood of contracting a disease.

percentage depth dose /pərsen'tij/ [L, *per,* completely, *centum,* hundred; ME, *dep,* deep; L, *dosis,* something given], the amount of therapeutic radiation delivered at a specified dose, expressed as a percentage of the skin dose.

percentile, the 100th part of a statistical distribution. A percentile rank of 80 indicates that 20% of the total number of cases scored above and 80% scored below in whatever characteristics were being studied.

percent solution, a relationship of a quantity of solute to the quantity of solution, multiplied by 100, expressed in terms of mass of solute per mass of solution. An example of a 5% by mass solution is 5 g of glucose dissolved in 95 g of water, forming 100 g of solution.

percent systole [L, *per* + *centum;* Gk, *systole,* contraction], the fraction of the duration of each heartbeat that is devoted to the contraction of the ventricles.

percept /pur'sept/ [L, *percipere,* to perceive], the mental impression of an object that is gained through the use of the senses.

perception /pərsep'shən/ [L, *percipere,* to perceive], **1.** the conscious recognition and interpretation of sensory stimuli that serve as a basis for understanding, learning, and knowing or for motivating a particular action or reaction. **2.** the result or product of the act of perceiving.—**perceptive, perceptual,** *adj.*

perceptivity /pur′səptiv′ītē/, the ability to receive sense impressions.

perceptual constancy /pərsep′cho͞o·əl/ [L, *percipere,* to perceive, *cum,* together with, *stare,* to stand], in Gestalt psychology, the phenomenon in which an object is seen in the same way under varying circumstances.

perceptual defect, any of a broad group of disorders or dysfunctions of the CNS that interfere with the conscious mental recognition of sensory stimuli. Such conditions are caused by lesions at specific sites in the cerebral cortex that may result from any illness or trauma affecting the brain at any age or stage of development.

perceptual deprivation, the absence of or decrease in meaningful groupings of stimuli, which may result from a constant background noise or constant inadequate illumination.

perceptual monotony, a mental state characterized by a lack of variety in the normal pattern of everyday stimuli.

Percodan, a trademark for a fixed-combination medication containing aspirin and an opioid analgesic (oxycodone) used to treat moderate to severe pain.

Percogesic, a trademark for a fixed-combination drug containing an antihistamine (phenyltoloxamine citrate) and an analgesic (acetaminophen) used to treat mild to moderate pain.

percolation /pur′kəlā′shən/ [L, *percolare,* to strain], **1.** the act of filtering any liquid through a porous medium. **2.** in pharmacology, the removal of the soluble parts of a crude drug by passing a liquid solvent through it.

per con., abbreviation for the Latin phrase *per contra,* "the other side."

per contiguum, spreading from one body structure to a contiguous area.

per continuum, describing the spread of an inflammation or other disease process from one body part to another through continuous tissue.

percuss /pərkus′/ [L, *percutere,* to strike hard], to perform percussion by striking, for example, the thoracic or abdominal wall, thereby producing sound vibrations that aid in diagnosis.

percussion /pərkush′ən/ [L, *percutere,* to strike hard], a technique in physical examination of tapping the body with the fingertips or fist to evaluate the size, borders, and consistency of some of the internal organs and to discover the presence and evaluate the amount of fluid in a body

cavity. Immediate or direct percussion is percussion performed by striking the fingers directly on the body surface. Indirect, mediate, or finger percussion involves striking a finger of one hand on a finger of the other hand as it is placed over the organ.—**percuss,** *v.,* **percussible,** *adj.*

percussor /pərkus′ər/ [L, a striker], a small hammer-like diagnostic tool having a rubber head that is used to tap the body lightly in percussion.

percutaneous /pur′kyo͞otā′nē·əs/ [L, *per + cutis,* skin], performed through the skin, such as a biopsy; aspiration of fluid from a space below the skin using a needle, catheter, and syringe; or instillation of a fluid in a cavity or space by similar means.

percutaneous absorption, the process of absorption through the skin from topical application.

percutaneous catheter, a catheter inserted through the skin rather than through an orifice, such as a central venous catheter or one used for hemodialysis or peritoneal dialysis.

percutaneous catheter placement, a technique in which an intracatheter is introduced through the skin into an artery and placed at a site or structure to be studied by selective angiography and other diagnostic procedures.

percutaneous coronary intervention (PCI), the management of coronary artery occlusion by any of various catheter-based techniques, such as percutaneous transluminal coronary angioplasty, atherectomy, angioplasty using the excimer laser, and implantation of coronary stents and related devices.

percutaneous endoscopic gastrostomy (PEG), the creation of a new opening in the stomach for enteral tube feedings. It can also be used for gastric decompression. PEG is accomplished by puncturing the abdominal wall after the stomach has been distended. A tube is then inserted through the abdominal wall into the stomach under endoscopic guidance.

percutaneous epididymal sperm aspiration, retrieval of sperm from the epididymis by using fine-needle aspiration, done in men with obstructive azoospermia.

percutaneous nephrolithotomy, a uroradiologic procedure performed to extract stones from within the kidney or proximal ureter by percutaneous surgery after the stones have been visualized radiologically.

percutaneous nephroscope, a thin fiberoptic probe that can be inserted into the kidney through an incision in the skin. Light transmitted along the fibers allows visualization of the inside of the kidney. The device is equipped with a tool that can be used to grasp and remove small kidney stones.

P

percutaneous transhepatic biliary drainage, drainage of the biliary tree by the introduction of a catheter through the liver and into the biliary tree under radiologic guidance.

percutaneous transhepatic cholangiography (PTC), the radiographic examination of the structure of the bile ducts. A contrast medium is injected through a needle passed directly into a hepatic duct.

percutaneous transluminal angioplasty (PTA), a procedure for dilating blood vessels in the treatment of peripheral artery disease. Under fluoroscopic guidance a balloon-tipped catheter is inserted into a stenotic artery and the balloon is inflated. The inflated balloon may dilate the artery by stretching its elastic fibers or by flattening accumulation of plaque.

percutaneous transluminal coronary angioplasty (PTCA), a technique in the treatment of atherosclerotic coronary heart disease and angina pectoris in which some plaques in the arteries of the heart are flattened against the arterial walls, resulting in improved circulation. The procedure involves threading a catheter through the vessel to the atherosclerotic plaque, inflating and deflating a small balloon at the tip of the catheter several times, and then removing the catheter. The procedure is performed under radiographic or ultrasonic visualization.

percutaneous transluminal renal angioplasty (PTRA), percutaneous transluminal angioplasty to enlarge the lumen of a sclerotic renal artery, preserve renal function, and treat renovascular hypertension.

per diem rate /pər dē′əm, dī′əm/ [L, *per diem,* daily, *ratus,* reckoned], an established rate of payment for hospital services.

per discharge payment, a payment method in which costs of resources used for the entire hospital stay are the responsibility of the hospital. The hospital is then compensated according to a contractually determined amount per discharge.

perencephaly /per′ensef′əlē/, a condition characterized by one or more cerebral cysts.

Perez reflex /pərez′, per′ez/ [Bernard Perez, French physician, 1836–1903; L, *reflectere,* to bend back], the normal response of an infant to cry, flex the limbs, and elevate the head and pelvis when supported in a prone position with a finger pressed along the spine from the sacrum to the neck.

perfectionism /pərfek′shəniz′əm/ [L, *perficere,* to complete], a subjective state in which a person pursues an extremely high standard of performance and in many cases demands the same standards of others. Failure to attain the goals may lead to feelings of defeat and other adverse psychologic consequences.

perflation /pərflā′shən/, a method of opening a passage or cavity entrance with air pressure.

perfluorocarbon /pərflŏŏr′ōkär′bən/, any of a group of chemicals with limited capacity for transporting oxygen through the circulatory system. They can be used for certain blood substitute purposes, regardless of the blood type of the patient. They are stable at room temperatures, have a pH of 7.4, and are free of infectious pathogens.

perforans /pur′fôrənz/ [L, *perforare,* to pierce], penetrating. The term applies mainly to nerves, muscles, or other anatomic features that penetrate other structures or nerves of the musculocutaneous tissues.

perforate [L, *perforare,* to pierce], **1.** /pur′fôrāt/ to pierce, punch, puncture, or otherwise make a hole. **2.** /pur′fôrit/ riddled with small holes. **3.** /pur′fôrit/ (of the anus) having a normal opening; not imperforate.—**perforation,** *n.*

perforating arteries, three arteries that branch from the deep artery of the thigh as it descends anterior to the adductor brevis muscle. All three penetrate through the adductor magnus near its attachment to the linea aspera to enter and supply the posterior compartment of thigh. The ascending and descending branches of the vessels interconnect to form a longitudinal channel that participates in forming an anastomotic network of vessels around the hip and inferiorly anastomoses with branches of the popliteal artery behind the knee.

perforating capsular plexus, a vascular plexus around the renal capsule, supplied by the perforating radiate, inferior suprarenal, renal, and testicular or ovarian arteries.

perforating cutaneous nerve, a nerve that originates in the sacral plexus and penetrates directly through the sacrotuberous ligament to course to the skin over the inferior aspect of the buttocks.

perforating fracture, an open fracture caused by a projectile, making a small surface wound.

perforating radiate arteries, small arteries that are continuations of the cortical radiate arteries and perforate the renal capsule.

perforating ulcer /pur′fôrā′ting/ [L, *perforare,* to pierce + *ilcus*], **1.** an ulcer that penetrates the thickness of a wall or membrane, such as a peptic ulcer of the digestive tract. **2.** a deep, painless ulcer, often on the sole of the foot, of a person whose skin is insensitive because of a disease such as diabetes.

perforation /pur′fôrā′shən/ [L, *perforare,* to pierce], a hole or opening made through the entire thickness of a membrane or other tissue or material.

perforation of stomach or intestines, a condition in which disease or injury has resulted in a leakage of digestive tract contents into the peritoneal cavity. A common cause is a ruptured appendix or perforating peptic ulcer. Immediate surgical intervention is needed to prevent peritonitis.

perforation of the uterus, a puncture of the uterus, as may be caused by a curet or by an intrauterine contraceptive device.

perfusion /pərfyōō′zhən/ [L, *perfundere,* to pour over], **1.** the passage of a fluid through a specific organ or an area of the body. **2.** a therapeutic measure whereby a drug intended for an isolated part of the body is introduced via the bloodstream.

perfusionist /pərfyōō′zhənist/ [L, *perfundere,* to pour over], an allied health professional who assists in performing procedures that involve extracorporeal circulation, such as during open-heart surgery or hypothermia.

perfusion lung scan, a radiographic examination of the lungs and their function, performed after an IV injection of a radioactive material. It is performed to detect areas of lung perfusion as an aid in the diagnosis of pulmonary embolism.

perfusion rate, the rate of blood flow through the capillaries per unit mass of tissue, expressed in milliliters per minute per 100 g.

perfusion technologist, a person who, under the supervision of a physician, operates a heart-lung machine used for cardiopulmonary bypass during surgery.

per gene, a gene that is associated with circadian rhythms of some animal species. Mutations of the per gene result in alterations of their biorhythms. A similar DNA sequence occurs in the human genome, but its effect on human circadian rhythms is unknown.

pergolide /per′golīd/, a long-acting ergot derivative with dopaminergic properties used in the treatment of parkinsonism.

Pergonal, a trademark for human menopausal gonadotropin used to treat anovulation and infertility.

periacinous /pere′as′inus/, near or around a small saclike dilation, particularly in the lung or a gland.

Periactin, a trademark for an antihistamine and antipruritic used to treat rash and other symptoms of allergies (cyproheptadine hydrochloride).

periadenitis /per′e-ad′ənī′tis/, an inflammation of tissues around a gland.

perianal /per′i-a′nəl/ [Gk, *peri,* around; L, *anus*], pertaining to the area around the anus.

perianal abscess [Gk, *peri,* around; L, *anus* + *abscedere,* to go away], a focal purulent subcutaneous infection in the region of the anus.

periaortic /per′i-a-ôr′tik/ [Gk, *peri,* around, *aerein,* to raise], pertaining to the area around the aorta.

periaortitis /per′i-a′ôrtī′tis/, an inflammation of the adventitia or surrounding tissues of the aorta.

periapical /per′i-ap′ikəl/ [Gk, *peri*; L, *apex,* top], pertaining to the tissues surrounding the apex of a tooth root, including the periodontal membrane and the alveolar bone.

periapical abscess, an infection around the root of a tooth, usually a result of spreading of dental caries leading to pulpal necrosis. The abscess may perforate into the oral cavity or maxillary sinus; extend into nearby bone, causing osteomyelitis; or more often, spread to soft tissues, causing cellulitis and a swollen face.

periapical fibroma, a mass of benign connective tissue that may form at the apex of a tooth with normal pulp.

periapical infection, infection surrounding the root of a tooth, often accompanied by toothache.

periapical radiograph, a dental x-ray film or dental imaging used to detect changes in the bone surrounding the roots of the teeth.

periappendicitis decidualis /per′i-apen′di sī′tis/, an inflammation of the vermiform appendix with the presence of decidual cells in the peritoneum of the appendix. It occurs in cases of right tubal pregnancy with adhesions between the appendix and the fallopian tubes.

periappendicular /per′i-ap′ndik′yələr/ [Gk, *peri,* around; L, *appendere,* to hang upon], pertaining to the area around the appendix.

periarterial /per′i-artir′e-əl/ [Gk, *peri,* around, *arteria,* airpipe], pertaining to the area around an artery.

periarteritis /per′i-är′tərī′tis/ [Gk, *peri* + *arteria,* airpipe, *itis,* inflammation], inflammation of the outer coat of one or more arteries and the tissue surrounding them.

periarteritis nodosa, a progressive polymorphic disease of the connective tissue that is characterized by numerous large and palpable nodules or clusters of visible nodules along segments of middle-sized arteries, particularly near points of bifurcation. The disease causes occlusion of vessels, resulting in regional ischemia, hemorrhage, necrosis, and pain. Early signs of the disease include tachycardia, fever, weight loss, and pain in the viscera.

periarthritis /per′i-ärthrī′tis/, inflammation of tissues around a joint.

periarticular /per′i-ärtik′yələr/ [Gk, *peri,* around; L, *articulus,* joint], pertaining to the area around a joint.

P

peribronchial /-brong'kē·əl/, surrounding a bronchus.

peribronchiolar /-brong'kē·ō'lər/ [Gk, *peri*, around; L, *bronchiolus*], pertaining to the area around the bronchioles.

pericalyceal /per'ikal'isē'əl/, near or around a renal calyx.

pericardiac /-kär'dē·ak/ [Gk, *peri*, around, *kardia*, heart], **1.** pertaining to the pericardium. **2.** pertaining to the area around the heart.

pericardial adhesion /-kär'dē·əl/ [Gk, *peri*, around, *kardia*, heart; L, *adhesio*, sticking to], an attachment of the pericardium to the heart muscle, sometimes restricting the muscle's action. The condition may be general or localized and may involve adhesion between the two layers of pericardium (internal adhesive pericarditis) or between one layer and surrounding tissues (external adhesive pericarditis).

pericardial artery [Gk, *peri* + *kardia*, heart, *arteria*, airpipe], one of several small vessels branching from the thoracic aorta, supplying the dorsal surface of the pericardium.

pericardial effusion [Gk, *peri*, around, *kardia*, heart; L, *effundere*, to pour out], the escape of blood or other fluid into the pericardium.

pericardial friction rub [Gk, *peri*, around, *kardia*, heart; L, *fricare*, to rub; ME, *rubben*], the rubbing together of inflamed membranes of the pericardium, as may occur in pericarditis or after MI. It produces a sound audible on auscultation.

pericardiectomy /per'i·kär'dē·ek'tə·mē/ [Gk, *peri*, around, *kardia*, heart, *ektomē*, excision], excision of the pericardium.

pericardiocentesis /per'ikär'dē·ō'sintē'sis/ [Gk, *peri* + *kardia*, heart, *kentesis*, pricking], a procedure for drawing fluid in the pericardial space between the serous membranes by surgical puncture and aspiration of the pericardial sac.

pericardioperitoneal canals, a pair of passages in the embryo, connecting the primordial pericardial and peritoneal cavities.

pericardiotomy /-kär'di·ot'əmē/, a surgical incision in the pericardium.

pericarditis /per'ikärdī'tis/ [Gk, *peri* + *kardia*, heart, *itis*, inflammation], inflammation of the pericardium associated with trauma, malignant neoplastic disease, infection, uremia, MI, collagen disease, or unknown causes. The first stage is characterized by fever, substernal chest pain that radiates to the shoulder or neck, dyspnea, a dry, nonproductive cough, a rapid and forcible pulse, a pericardial friction rub, and a muffled heartbeat over the apex. The patient becomes increasingly anxious, tired, and orthopneic. If treatment is not effective, the condition may progress to the extremely grave second stage, in which a serofibrinous effusion develops within the pericardium, restricting cardiac activity. If the effusion is purulent (caused by bacterial infection) a high fever, sweat, chills, and prostration also occur. The heart sounds become muffled, weak, and distant on auscultation, and a bulge is visible on the chest over the precordial area.

pericardium /per'ikär'dē·əm/ *pl.* **pericardia** [Gk, *peri* + *kardia*, heart], a fibroserous sac that surrounds the heart and the roots of the great vessels. It consists of the serous pericardium and the fibrous pericardium. The serous pericardium consists of the parietal layer, which lines the inside of the fibrous pericardium, and the visceral layer, which adheres to the surface of the heart. Between the two layers is the pericardial space containing a few drops of pericardial fluid, which lubricates opposing surfaces of the space and allows the heart to move easily during contraction. The fibrous pericardium, which constitutes the outermost sac and is composed of tough, white fibrous tissue lined by the parietal layer of the serous pericardium, fits loosely around the heart and attaches to large blood vessels emerging from the top of the heart but not to the heart itself. It is relatively inelastic and protects the heart and the serous membranes.—**pericardial,** *adj.*

pericholangitis /per'əkō'lanjī'tis/ [Gk, *peri* + *chole*, bile, *angeion*, vessel, *itis*, inflammation], an inflammatory condition of the tissues surrounding the bile ducts in the liver. Pericholangitis is a complication of ulcerative colitis and portal hypertension.

perichondrial bone /-kon'drē·əl/ [Gk, *peri*, around, *chondros*, cartilage; AS, *ban*], bone that forms in the perichondrium of the cartilaginous template.

perichondrium /-kon'drē·əm/, a fibrous, irregular connective tissue sheath and membrane surrounding both hyaline and elastic cartilages.

perichrome /per'ikrōm/, a nerve cell in which the stainable chromophil substance is scattered throughout the cytoplasm.

pericolic abscess, an abscess just outside the colon as a result of perforation complicating diverticulitis.

pericolitis /-kōlī'tis/, an inflammation of the connective tissue around the colon.

pericoronitis /-kôr'ənī'tis/, inflammation of the gum tissue around the crown of a tooth, usually associated with the eruption of a third molar.

pericranium /-krā'nē·əm/, the connective tissue membrane that surrounds the skull.

pericystium /-sis'tē·əm/, the tissues around a gallbladder or urinary bladder.

periderm /per'idurm/, the outermost layer of flattened epidermis on an embryo or fetus during the first 6 months of gestation.

perididymitis /-did'imī'tis/, an inflammation of the tunica vaginalis testis.

periencephalitis /per'i·ensef'əlī'tis/, an inflammation of the membranes and surface of the brain, including the cortex.

perifocal /-fō'kəl/, pertaining to tissues situated around a focus of infection.

perifollicular /-folik'yələr/ [Gk, peri, around; L, folliculus, small bag], pertaining to the area around a follicle.

perifolliculitis /-folik'yəlī'tis/ [Gk, peri; L, folliculus, small bag; Gk, itis, inflammation], inflammation of the tissue surrounding a hair follicle.

periglottic /-glot'ik/, around the tongue, particularly the base of the tongue.

periglottis /-glot'is/, the mucous membrane of the tongue.

perihepatitis /per'ihep'ətī'tis/, inflammation of the peritoneal capsule of the liver and other nearby tissues.

periimplantoclasia /per'i·implan'tōklā'zhə/, a pathologic tissue reaction surrounding implanted foreign material, characterized by local inflammation.

perikaryon /per'iker'ē·on/ [Gk, peri + karyon, nut], the cytoplasm of a cell body exclusive of the nucleus and any processes, specifically the cell body of a neuron.—**perikaryontic,** adj.

perilymph /per'ilimf/ [Gk, peri; L, lympha, water], the clear fluid separating the osseous labyrinth from the membranous labyrinth in the internal ear.

perimenopause /-men'əpôs/, a span of 4 to 6 years preceding menopause when menstrual cycles and blood flow may be irregular. As estrogen levels decline, osteoporosis begins to develop and women are at increased risk for cardiovascular disease.

perimeter /pərim'ətər/ [Gk, peri, around; metron, measure], **1.** the circumference, outer edge, or periphery of an object. **2.** an instrument for measuring visual fields. **3.** an instrument for measuring the circumference of teeth.

perimetrium /per'imē'trē·əm/ [Gk, peri + metra, womb], the serous membrane enveloping the uterus.

perimetry /pərim'ətrē/, the determination and mapping of the limits of the visual field.

perimolysis /-mol'isis/, decalcification of the teeth caused by exposure to gastric acid in patients with chronic vomiting, as may occur in anorexia or bulimia.

perinatal /per'inā'təl/ [Gk, peri; L, natus, birth], pertaining to the time and process of giving birth or being born.

perinatal AIDS, AIDS acquired by infants and children from their mothers during pregnancy, during delivery, or from ingesting infected breast milk.

perinatal death, 1. the death of a fetus weighing 500 g or more at 22 or more weeks of gestation. **2.** the death of an infant between birth and the end of the neonatal period.

perinatal mortality, the statistical rate of fetal and infant death, including stillbirth, from 28 weeks of gestation to the end of the neonatal period of 4 weeks after birth. Perinatal mortality is usually expressed as the number of deaths in a given period per 1000 live births in a specific geographic area or program.

perinatal period, an interval extending approximately from the 28th week of gestation to the 28th day after birth.

perinatal physiology, the physiology of the process of giving birth or being born.

perinatologist /-nātol'əjəst/, a physician who specializes in the diagnosis and treatment of disorders of pregnancy, childbirth, and the puerperium in the mother and child.

perinatology /-nātol'əgē/ [Gk, peri; L, natus, birth; Gk, logos, science], a branch of medicine concerned with the study of the anatomic and physiologic characteristics of mothers and their unborn and newborns, with the diagnosis and treatment of disorders occurring in them during pregnancy, childbirth, and the puerperium.—**perinatologic,** adj.

perindopril, an antihypertensive.

perineal artery, an artery that originates near the anterior end of the pudendal canal and gives off a transverse perineal branch and a posterior scrotal or labial artery to surrounding skin and tissue.

perineal body [Gk, perineos, perineum; AS, bodig], a mass of tissue composed of muscle and fascia between the vagina and rectum in females and between the scrotum and rectum in males.

perineal care[1] [Gk, perineos, perineum], a cleansing procedure prescribed for cleansing the perineum after various obstetric and gynecologic procedures.

perineal care[2], a nursing intervention from the Nursing Interventions Classification (NIC) defined as maintenance of perineal skin integrity and relief of perineal discomfort.

perineal membrane, a thick triangular fascial sheet that fills the space between the arms of the pubic arch and has a free posterior border.

perineal pad [Gk, perineos, perineum], a cushion of soft material used to cover the perineum to absorb the menstrual flow or to protect a wound or incision.

P

perineal raphe, a ridge along the median line of the perineum that runs forward from the anus. In the male, it is continuous with the raphe of the scrotum and the raphe of the penis.

perineocele /per′inē′əsēl/, a hernia in the perineal area, around the rectum.

perineorrhaphy /per′inē·ôr′əfē/ [Gk, *perineos* + *rhaphe,* suture], a surgical procedure in which an incision, tear, or defect in the perineum is repaired by suturing.

perineostomy /per′inē·os′təmē/, the surgical creation of an opening between the urethra and the skin of the perineal region.

perineotomy /per′inē·ot′əmē/ [Gk, *perineos* + *temnein,* to cut], a surgical incision into the perineum.

perinephric abscess /-nef′rik/ [Gk, *peri,* around, *nephros,* kidney; L, *abscedere,* to go away], an abscess that develops in the fatty tissue around a kidney. It is usually secondary to an abscess originating earlier in the cortex of the organ.

perinephrium /-nef′rē·əm/, the connective tissue around the kidneys.

perineum /per′inē′əm/ [Gk, *perineos*], the part of the body situated dorsal to the pubic arch and the arcuate ligaments, ventral to the tip of the coccyx, and lateral to the inferior rami of the pubis and the ischium and the sacrotuberous ligaments. The perineum supports and surrounds the distal parts of the urogenital and GI tracts of the body.—**perineal,** *adj.*

perinocele, a hernia in the perineum.

perinodal fiber /-nō′dəl/ [Gk, *peri;* L, *nodus,* knot], any of the atrial fibers surrounding the atrioventricular or sinus node.

period /pir′ē·od/, **1.** an interval of time. **2.** one of the stages of a disease. **3.** in physics, the duration of a single cycle of a periodic wave or event.

periodic /pir′ē·od′ik/ [Gk, *peri* + *hodos,* way], of an event or phenomenon, recurring at regular or irregular intervals. —**periodicity,** *n.*

periodic apnea of the newborn, a normal condition in the full-term newborn, characterized by an irregular pattern of rapid breathing followed by a brief period of apnea, usually associated with rapid eye movement sleep.

periodic deep inspiration, an occasional deep breath that may be 1.5 times the normal tidal volume. The process helps prevent atelectasis.

periodic fever [Gk, *peri,* around, *hodos,* way; L, *febris*], a hereditary illness with intermittent episodes of fever accompanied by abdominal or pleuritic pain. Onset occurs between 10 and 20 years of age. Some cases are complicated by symptoms of arthritis, splenomegaly, and renal amyloidosis that may progress to a fatal kidney disorder.

periodic hyperinflation, a normal phenomenon of unconscious sighing or deep breathing. It tends to occur most frequently during periods of physical inactivity.

periodicity /pir′ē·ədis′itē/ [Gk, *periodikos,* periodical], events or episodes that tend to repeat at predictable intervals. For example, filarial worms may appear in cutaneous blood vessels at night but not in daylight hours, and malaria may cause paroxysms at 24-, 48-, or 72-hour intervals, depending on the species of pathogen.

periodic table, a systematic arrangement of the chemical elements. An earlier version was devised in 1869 by Dmitri Ivanovich Mendeleev (Russian chemist, 1834–1907). By arranging the elements in order of their atomic weights, he was able to show relationships, such as valency, that occurred at regular intervals and was able to predict the properties of elements still undiscovered in the 19th century.

periodontal /per′ē·ōdon′təl/ [Gk, *peri* + *odous,* tooth], pertaining to the supporting structures of a tooth, including the cementum, alveolar bone, and gingiva.

periodontal abscess [Gk, *peri,* around, *odous,* tooth; L, *abscedere,* to go away], an infection in the area around a tooth. It is usually classified according to its location in the periodontal tissues, such as lateral, lateral alveolar, parietal, or peridental.

periodontal cyst, a fluid-filled, epithelium-lined sac at the apex of a tooth that has an infected pulp or, less often, is lateral to a tooth root.

periodontal disease, a pathologic condition of the tissues that support a tooth or teeth, such as an inflammation of the periodontal membrane or periodontal ligament.

periodontal index, a measure of an individual's periodontal condition. It is determined by adding scores based on the condition of the gingiva and dividing the sum by the number of teeth present. Individuals with clinically normal gingiva have an index of 0 to 0.2. The index reaches a maximum of 8.0 in persons with severe terminal destructive periodontitis.

periodontal ligament (PDL), the fibrous tissue that surrounds a tooth and attaches the tooth to the alveolus. It is composed of many bundles of collagenous tissue arranged in groups, between which lies loose connective tissue interwoven with blood vessels, lymphatic vessels, and nerves.

periodontal pocket [Gk, *peri,* around, *odous,* tooth; Fr, *pochette*], a pathologic increase in the depth of the gingival crevice or sulcus surrounding a tooth at the gingival margin.

periodontal probe [Gk, *peri,* around, *odous,* tooth; L, *probare,* to test], **1.** a slender, tapered, flat, or cylindric instrument with indentations spaced in millimeters, designed for introduction into the gingival sulcus for the purpose of measuring its depth. **2.** a slender, tapered instrument with or without millimeter indentations for measuring furcations of the roots of premolars and molars.

periodontics /-don´tiks/ [Gk, *peri,* around, *odous,* tooth], the branch of dentistry concerned with the diagnosis, treatment, and prevention of diseases of the periodontium.

periodontist /-don´tist/, a dentist who specializes in treating the supporting structures of the teeth.

periodontitis /per´ē-ō´dontī´tis/, inflammation of the periodontium caused by a complex reaction initiated when subgingival plaque bacteria are in close contact with the epithelium of the gingival sulcus.

periodontium /per´ē-ōdon´shē·əm/ *pl.* **periodontia** [Gk, *peri,* around; *odous,* tooth], the tissues that invest or help invest and support the teeth, including the periodontal ligament, gingivae, cementum, and alveolar and supporting bone.

periodontoclasia [Gk, *peri* + *odous,* tooth, *klasis,* breaking], the loosening of secondary teeth caused by breakdown and absorption of the supporting bone.

periodontosis /-dontō´sis/ [Gk, *peri* + *odous,* tooth, *osis,* condition], a rare disease that affects young people, especially women, and is characterized by idiopathic destruction of the periodontium without inflammation.

perioperative /per´i·op´ərativ/ [Gk, *peri,* around; L, *operari,* to work], pertaining to the time before, during, and after surgery.

perioperative nursing [Gk, *peri;* L, *operari,* to work, *nutrix,* nurse], nursing care provided to surgery patients before and during the procedure and in the recovery room.

perioperative nursing data set, a nursing language specialized for vocabulary that addresses the perioperative patient experience from preadmission until discharge.

periorbita /per´i·ôr´bitə/ [Gk, *peri;* L, *orbita,* wheeltrack], the periosteum of the orbit of the eye. It is continuous with the dura mater and the sheath of the optic nerve.

periorbital /per´i·ôr´bitəl/, pertaining to the area surrounding the socket of the eye.

periosteal /per´i·os´tē·əl/ [Gk, *peri,* around, *osteon,* bone], pertaining to the periosteum, the membrane covering the bone.

periosteal layer, the outer layer of the dura mater; the periosteum of the cranial cavity. It is firmly attached to the skull and

is continuous with the periosteum on the outer surface of the skull at the foramen magnum and other intracranial foramina.

periosteum /per´i·os´tē·əm/ [Gk, *peri* + *osteon,* bone], a thick fibrous vascular membrane covering the bones, except at their extremities. It consists of an outer layer of collagenous tissue containing a few fat cells and an inner layer of fine elastic fibers. Periosteum is permeated with the nerves and blood vessels that innervate and nourish underlying bone.

periostitis /per´i·ostī´tis/ [Gk, *peri* + *osteon,* bone, *itis,* inflammation], inflammation of the periosteum. The condition is caused by chronic or acute infection or trauma and is characterized by tenderness and swelling of the affected bone, pain, fever, and chills.

peripatetic /-patet´ik/ [Gk, *peripatein,* to walk about], pertaining to an ambulatory typhoid patient.

peripelvic extravasation, extravasation of urine into the area around the renal pelvis.

peripheral /pərif´ərəl/ [Gk, *periphereia,* circumference], pertaining to the outside, surface, or surrounding area of an organ, other structure, or field of vision.

peripheral acrocyanosis of the newborn, a normal transient condition of the newborn, characterized by pale cyanotic discoloration of the hands and feet, especially the fingers and toes.

peripheral angiography [Gk, *peri,* around, *phereia,* boundary, *angeion,* vessel, *graphein,* to record], the study of the peripheral blood vessels by radiography after radiopaque dye is injected into the circulation.

peripheral arterial disease (PAD), a systemic form of atherosclerosis producing symptoms in the cardiac, cerebral, and renal vascular systems. Blood flow is restricted by an intraarterial accumulation of soft deposits of lipids and fibrin that harden over time, particularly at bends or bifurcations of the arterial walls. Patients generally are not aware of the changes until the diameter of the arterial lumen has been reduced by half. Early symptoms include intermittent claudication and ischemic rest pain.

peripheral arteriovenography, the radiographic examination of the blood vessels in the peripheral parts of the body, such as the arms and legs, after the injection of a contrast medium into these vessels.

peripheral blood stem cells, stem cells that circulate in the peripheral blood rather than the bone marrow. Their numbers can be artificially increased by exposure to hematopoietic growth factors so that they can be harvested for peripheral blood stem cell transplantation.

P

peripheral giant cell granuloma, a relatively common oral tumor-like growth consisting of multinucleated giant cells which resemble osteoclasts or believed to be formations of mononuclear phagocytes. The lesion can be sessile or pedunculated, can develop at any age, and is caused by local irritation or trauma.

peripheral lesion [Gk, *perphereia*; L, *laesio,* hurting], an injury to any tissues distal to the main organ systems. It is usually traumatic and interrupts the flow of impulses between the site of the lesion and the nerve root or plexus.

peripherally inserted central catheter (PICC), a long catheter introduced through a vein in the arm, and then through the subclavian vein into the superior vena cava or right atrium to administer parenteral fluids or medications or to measure central venous pressure.

peripherally inserted central (PIC) catheter care, a nursing intervention from the Nursing Interventions Classification (NIC) defined as insertion and maintenance of a peripherally inserted central catheter either midline or centrally located.

peripheral motor neuron [Gk, *periphereia*; L, *motor,* mover; Gk, *neuron,* nerve], an effector neuron located outside the CNS, usually in a ganglion of a sympathetic or parasympathetic nervous system.

peripheral nervous system, the motor and sensory nerves and ganglia outside the brain and spinal cord. The system consists of 12 pairs of cranial nerves, 31 pairs of spinal nerves, and their various branches in body organs. Sensory, or afferent, peripheral nerves transmitting information to the CNS and motor, or efferent, peripheral nerves carrying impulses from the brain usually travel together but separate at the cord level into a posterior sensory root and an anterior motor root. Fibers innervating the body wall are designated somatic; those supplying internal organs are termed visceral. The autonomic system includes the peripheral nerves involved in regulating cardiovascular, respiratory, endocrine, and other automatic body functions. Nerves in the sympathetic or thoracolumbar division of the autonomic system secrete norepinephrine and cause peripheral vasoconstriction, cardiac acceleration, coronary artery dilation, bronchodilation, and inhibition of peristalsis. Parasympathetic nerves, which constitute the craniosacral division of the autonomic system, secrete acetylcholine; cause peripheral vasodilation, cardiac inhibition, and bronchoconstriction; and stimulate peristalsis.

peripheral neuropathy, any functional or organic disorder of the peripheral nervous system.

peripheral odontogenic fibroma, a fibrous connective tissue tumor associated with the gingival margin and believed to originate from the periodontium. It is a localized form of fibromatosis and commonly contains areas of calcification.

peripheral ossifying fibroma, a relatively common gingival growth of mesenchymal cells from the periosteum or the periodontal ligament.

peripheral pulse [Gk, *periphereia*; L, *pulsare,* to beat], the series of waves of arterial pressure caused by left ventricular systoles as measured in the limbs.

peripheral scotoma [Gk, *periphereia* + *skotos,* darkness, *oma,* tumor], a lost area of the visual field that is located peripherally and does not involve the central 30 degrees of vision.

peripheral sensation management, a nursing intervention from the Nursing Interventions Classification (NIC) defined as prevention or minimization of injury or discomfort in the patient with altered sensation.

peripheral vascular disease (PVD), any abnormal condition that affects the blood vessels and lymphatic vessels, except those that supply the heart. Different kinds and degrees of PVD are characterized by a variety of signs and symptoms, such as numbness, pain, pallor, elevated BP, and impaired arterial pulsations. PVD in association with bacterial endocarditis may involve emboli in terminal arterioles and produce gangrenous infarctions of distal parts of the body, such as the tip of the nose, the pinna of the ear, the fingers, and the toes. Large emboli may occlude peripheral vessels and cause atherosclerotic occlusive disease.

peripheral vascular resistance, a resistance to the flow of blood determined by the tone of the vascular musculature and the diameter of the blood vessels.

peripheral vision, a capacity to see objects in the outer aspects of the field of view caused by reflected light waves that fall on areas of the retina distant from the macula.

peripheral zone, a large area of the prostate, just beneath the capsule, covering the posterior and lateral aspects and composed mainly of acinar glandular tissue. Its ducts drain into the prostatic urethra along most of its length.

periphery /pərif′ərē/ [Gk, *peri,* around, *phereia,* boundary], **1.** parts or areas near or outside a perimeter or boundary. **2.** the outer body parts, such as the skin or limbs.

perirectal /-rek′təl/ [Gk, *peri,* around; L, *rectus,* straight], pertaining to the area around the rectum.

perirenal fat, an accumulation of extraperitoneal fat that completely surrounds the kidney.

perirenal hematoma, a hematoma resulting from a perirenal hemorrhage.

perirenal hemorrhage, hemorrhage from the kidney into the perirenal space, such as from trauma, vasculitis, aneurysm, tumor, renal infarct, or cyst.

perirenal space, the part of the retroperitoneal space that is within the renal fascia and contains the kidney, perirenal fat, adrenal gland, and proximal ureter.

perisinusitis /-sī′nəsī′tis/ [Gk, *peri,* around; L, *sinus,* hollow], an inflammation of the structures around a sinus.

peristalsis /-stal′sis, -stôl′sis/ [Gk, *peri + stalsis,* contraction], the coordinated, rhythmic serial contraction of smooth muscle that forces food through the digestive tract, bile through the bile duct, and urine through the ureters.

peristaltic /-stal′tik, -stôl′tik/ [Gk, *peri + stalsis,* contraction], pertaining to peristalsis.

peristaltic rush, a powerful wave of contractile activity that travels long distances down the small intestine, caused by intense irritation or unusual distension.

peristomal /per′istō′məl/, pertaining to the area of skin surrounding a stoma in the abdominal wall.

peritoneal abscess [Gk, *peri + teinein;* L, *abscedere,* to go away], an abscess in the peritoneal cavity, the result of peritonitis and usually complicated by adhesions.

peritoneal cavity [Gk, *peri + teinein,* to stretch], the potential space between the parietal and visceral layers of the peritoneum, which are normally in contact.

peritoneal dialysis (PD), a dialysis procedure performed to correct an imbalance of fluid or of electrolytes in the blood or to remove toxins, drugs, or other wastes normally excreted by the kidney. The peritoneum is used as a diffusible membrane.

peritoneal dialysis solution, a solution of electrolytes and other substances that is introduced into the peritoneum to remove toxic substances from the body in some patients with renal failure.

peritoneal dialysis therapy, a nursing intervention from the Nursing Interventions Classification (NIC) defined as administration and monitoring of dialysis solution into and out of the peritoneal cavity.

peritoneal endometriosis [Gk, *peri + teinein,* to stretch, *endon,* within, *metra,* womb], ectopic endometrial tissue found in the pelvic cavity.

peritoneal equilibration test, the calculation of the ratio of plasma to dialysis solution concentrations of solutes, such as creatinine and glucose, after a certain specific dwell time.

peritoneal fluid, a naturally produced fluid in the abdominal cavity that lubricates surfaces, thereby preventing friction between the peritoneal membrane and internal organs.

peritoneoscopy /-tō′nē·os′kəpē/ [Gk, *peri + teinein + skopein,* to view], the use of an endoscope to inspect the peritoneum through a stab incision in the abdominal wall.

peritoneum /per′itənē′əm/ [Gk, *peri + teinein,* to stretch], an extensive serous membrane that lines the entire abdominal wall of the body and is reflected over the contained viscera. It is divided into the parietal peritoneum and the visceral peritoneum. In men, the peritoneum is a closed membranous sac. In women, it is perforated by the free ends of the uterine tubes. The free surface of the peritoneum is smooth mesothelium, lubricated by serous fluid that permits the viscera to glide easily against the abdominal wall and against one another. The mesentery of the peritoneum fans out from the main membrane to suspend the small intestine. Other parts of the peritoneum are the transverse mesocolon, the greater omentum, and the lesser omentum.—**peritoneal,** *adj.*

peritonitis /per′itənī′tis/ [Gk, *peri + teinein,* to stretch, *itis,* inflammation], an inflammation of the peritoneum produced by bacteria or irritating substances introduced into the abdominal cavity by a penetrating wound or perforation of an organ in the GI tract or the reproductive tract. Peritonitis is caused most commonly by rupture of the appendix but also occurs after perforations of intestinal diverticula, peptic ulcers, gangrenous gallbladders, gangrenous obstructions of the small bowel, or incarcerated hernias, as well as ruptures of the spleen, liver, ovarian cyst, or fallopian tube, especially in ectopic pregnancy. Characteristic signs and symptoms include abdominal distension, rigidity and pain, rebound tenderness, decreased or absent bowel sounds, nausea, vomiting, and tachycardia. The patient has chills and fever; breathes rapidly and shallowly; is anxious, dehydrated, and unable to defecate; and may vomit fecal material.

peritonitis meconium [Gk, *peri + teinein, itis,* inflammation, *mekon,* poppy], a condition of peritonitis in a newborn resulting from rupture of the digestive tract. The inflammation is caused by leakage of meconium into the peritoneal cavity.

peritonsillar /-ton′silər/ [Gk, *peri;* L, *tonsilla*], pertaining to the area around a tonsil.

peritonsillar abscess [Gk, *peri;* L, *tonsilla,* tonsil, *abscedere,* to go away], an infection

P

of tissue between the tonsil and pharynx, usually after acute follicular tonsillitis. The symptoms include dysphagia, pain radiating to the ear, and fever. Redness and swelling of the tonsil and adjacent soft palate are present.

peritubular capillary, any of the capillaries around the proximal and distal convoluted tubules of the kidney.

periumbilical /per'i·umbil'ikəl/ [Gk, *peri,* around, *umbilicus,* navel], pertaining to the area around the umbilicus.

periungual /per'i·ung'gwəl/ [Gk, *peri;* L, *unguis,* nail], pertaining to the area around the fingernails or the toenails.

periurethral zone, a narrow area of the prostate consisting of the short ducts adjacent to the prostatic urethra.

periurethritis /per'-u'rĕ-thri'tis/, inflammation of the tissue around the urethra; spongiositis.

perivascular goiter /per'ivas'kyōōlər/ [Gk, *peri;* L, *vasculum,* little vessel, *guttur,* throat], an enlargement of the thyroid gland surrounding a large blood vessel.

perivascular spaces [Gk, *peri,* around; L, *vasculum,* little vessel, *spatium,* space], spaces that surround blood vessels as they enter the brain. They communicate with the subarachnoid space.

perivertebral /-vur'təbrəl/ [Gk, *peri,* around, *vertebra,* joint], pertaining to the area around a vertebra.

perivesical spaces, subdivisions of the extraperitoneal space found anterior to the urinary bladder.

perivitelline /-vitel'ēn/ [Gk, *peri;* L, *vitellus,* yolk], surrounding the vitellus or yolk mass.

perivitelline space, the space between a mammalian ovum and the zona pellucida, into which the polar bodies are released at the time of maturation.

Perkin's line, a line through the anterior inferior iliac spine, perpendicular to Hilgenreiner's line, used in radiographic assessment of the hip joint.

perle /purl, perl/ [Fr, pearl], a soft gelatin capsule filled with liquid medicine.

perlèche, single or multiple fissures and cracks at the corner of the mouth on one side or both sides, which in advanced stages may spread to the lips and cheeks. Causes include primary or superimposed infection with microorganisms, such as *Candida albicans,* staphylococci, or streptococci; poor hygiene; drooling of saliva; overclosure of the jaws in patients without teeth or with ill-fitting dentures; and riboflavin deficiency.

perlingual /pərling'gwəl/ [L, *per* + *lingua,* tongue], pertaining to the administration of drugs through the tongue, which absorbs substances through its surface.

permanent pacemaker [L, *permanere,* to remain, *passus,* step; ME, *maken*], any electric pacemaker implanted inside a patient's body for permanent use.

permeability /pur'mē·əbil'itē/ [L, *permeare,* to pass through], the degree to which one substance allows another substance to pass through it.—**permeable,** *adj.*

per member per month (PMPM), usual unit of measure for capitation payments that payers provide to providers, both hospitals and physicians. These payments also include ancillary service use.

permethrin /pərmeth'rin/, a topical pediculicide and scabicide used for the treatment of head lice and their nits, for the treatment of scabies, and as prophylaxis when there are epidemics of lice.

permissible dose /pərmis'ibəl/ [L, *permittere,* to permit, *dosis,* something given], the maximum amount of radiation that may be expected to produce no significantly harmful results if given to an individual in a specified period.

permissible exposure limit (PEL), an occupational health standard instituted to safeguard workers against exposure to toxic material in the workplace. PELs are the result of the 1970 U.S. Occupational Safety and Health Act, which established the Occupational Safety and Health Administration (OSHA), the policing and enforcing arm of the act, and the National Institute for Occupational Safety and Health (NIOSH), which represents the research arm. OSHA publishes PELs and short-term exposure limits based on recommendations of NIOSH.

permissive hypercapnia, ventilation that allows $PaCO_2$ to rise slowly over time as the pH becomes normalized. The goal is to reduce tidal volume and rate while preventing volutrauma.

Permitil, a trademark for a tranquilizer (fluphenazine hydrochloride).

pernicious /pərnish'əs/ [L, *perniciosus,* destructive], potentially injurious, destructive, or fatal unless treated.

pernicious anemia [L, *perniciosus,* destructive; Gk, *a* + *haima,* not blood], a progressive megaloblastic macrocytic anemia that results from a lack of intrinsic factor essential for the absorption of cyanocobalamin (vitamin B_{12}). The maturation of RBCs in bone marrow becomes disordered, the posterior and lateral columns of the spinal cord deteriorate, the WBC count is reduced, and the polymorphonuclear leukocytes become multilobed. Extreme weakness, numbness and tingling in the extremities, fever, pallor, anorexia, and loss of weight may occur.

pernicious vomiting [L, *perniciosus,* destructive, *vomere,* to vomit], a severe life-threatening episode of vomiting that may occur during pregnancy.

perobrachius /pē′rōbrā′kē·əs/ [Gk, *peros,* damaged, *brachion,* arm], a fetus or individual with malformed arms.

perochirus /pē′rōkī′rəs/ [Gk, *peros* + *cheir,* hand], a fetus or individual with malformed hands.

perodactylus /pē′rōdak′tiləs/, a fetus or an individual with a deformity of the fingers or the toes, especially the absence of one or more digits.

perodactyly /pē′rōdak′tilē/ [Gk, *peros* + *daktylos,* finger], a congenital anomaly characterized by a deformity of the digits, primarily the complete or partial absence of one or more of the fingers or toes.

peromelia /pē′rōmē′lyə/ [Gk, *peros* + *melos,* limb], a congenital anomaly characterized by the malformation of one or more of the limbs. —**peromelus,** *n.*

peroneal /per′ənē′əl/ [Gk, *perone,* brooch], pertaining to the outer part of the leg, over the fibula and the peroneal nerve.

peroneal muscular atrophy, symmetric weakening or atrophy of the foot and ankle muscles and hammer toes. Affected individuals usually have high plantar arches and an awkward gait, caused by weak ankle muscles.

peroneus brevis /per′ənē′əs/ [Gk, *perone;* L, *brevis,* short], the smaller of the two lateral muscles of the leg, lying under the peroneus longus. It pronates and plantar flexes the foot.

peroneus longus, the more superficial of the two lateral muscles of the leg. The muscle pronates and plantar flexes the foot.

peronia /pərō′nē·ə/ [Gk, *peros,* damaged], a congenital malformation or developmental anomaly.

peropus /pərō′pəs/ [Gk, *peros* + *pous,* foot], a fetus or individual with malformed feet, often in association with some defect of the legs.

per os /pər os′/ [L], by mouth.

perosomus /pē′rōsō′məs/ [Gk, *peros* + *soma,* body], a fetus or individual whose body, especially the trunk, is severely malformed.

perosplanchnia /pē′rōsplangk′nē·ə/ [Gk, *peros* + *splanchnon,* viscera], a congenital anomaly characterized by the malformation of the viscera.

peroxisome /pərok′sisōm/, any of the microbodies present in vertebrate animal cells, especially liver and kidney cells, which are rich in the enzymes peroxidase, catalase, ᴅ-amino acid oxidase, and, to a lesser extent, urate oxidase. Their functions are not fully understood, but they participate in metabolic oxidations involving hydrogen peroxide, purine

metabolism, cellular lipid metabolism, and gluconeogenesis.

perphenazine /pərfen′əzēn/, a phenothiazine derivative used as an antipsychotic and antiemetic/antivertigo agent. It is prescribed in the treatment of schizophrenia and in the control of severe nausea and vomiting in adults. Unlabeled uses include treatment of ethanol withdrawal, Huntington's chorea, Tourette's syndrome, spasmodic torticollis, and dementia in the elderly.

per primam intentionem [L], by primary (first) intention.

per pro., abbreviation for the Latin term *per procurationem,* "on behalf of."

per rectum [L], by rectum.

PERRLA /pur′lə/, abbreviation for *pupils equal, round, react to light, accommodation.* While performing an assessment of the eyes, one evaluates the size and shape of the pupils, their reaction to light, and their ability to accommodate.

Persantine, a trademark for an inhibitor of platelet aggregation (dipyridamole).

per se [L], by itself, or of itself.

per secundum intentionem [L], by second intention.

perseveration /pur′səvərā′shən/ [L, *persevero,* to persist], the involuntary and pathologic persistence of the same verbal response or motor activity, regardless of the stimulus or its duration. It is caused by a neurologic deficit.

Persian Gulf syndrome, a diffuse collection of symptoms reported by many veterans of the 1991 Persian Gulf war. Symptoms vary widely, but include fatigue, joint pain, headache, and sleep disturbances. Musculoskeletal and connective tissue diseases are also common. The specific cause is unknown, but explanations include exposure to chemicals from burning oil wells, insecticides, and poisons linked to inoculations against biologic warfare or to chemical weapons used by the Iraqi army.

persistent cloaca /pərsis′tənt/ [L, *persistere,* to persist, *cloaca,* sewer], a congenital anomaly in which the intestinal, urinary, and reproductive ducts open into a common cavity, a result of the failure of the urorectal septum to form during prenatal development.

persistent vegetative state, a state of wakefulness accompanied by an apparent complete lack of cognitive function, experienced by some patients in an irreversible coma. Vegetative functions and brainstem reflexes are intact, but the cortex is permanently damaged.

persona /pərsō′nə/ *pl.* **personae** [L, mask], in analytic psychology, the personality façade or role that a person assumes

P

and presents to the outer world to satisfy the demands of the environment or society or to express some intrapsychic conflict.

personal and social history /pur′sənəl/, in a health history, an account of the personal and social details of a person's life that serves to identify the person. Place of birth, religion, race, marital status, number of children, military status, occupational history, and place of residence are the usual components of this part of the history.

personal autonomy, a nursing outcome from the Nursing Outcomes Classification (NOC) defined as the personal actions of a competent individual to exercise governance in life decisions.

personal care services, the services performed by health care workers to assist patients in meeting the requirements of daily living.

personal health status, a nursing outcome from the Nursing Outcomes Classification (NOC) defined as the overall physical, psychological, social, and spiritual functioning of an adult 18 years or older.

personality /pur′sənal′itē/ [L, *personalis,* role], **1.** the composite of the behavioral traits and attitudinal characteristics by which one is recognized as an individual. **2.** the behavior pattern each person develops, both consciously and unconsciously, as a means of adapting to a particular environment and its cultural, ethnic, national, and provincial standards.

personality disorder, a *DSM-IV* psychiatry disorder characterized by disruption in relatedness. It is manifested in any of a large group of mental disorders characterized by rigid, inflexible, and maladaptive behavior patterns and traits that impair a person's ability to function in society by severely limiting adaptive potential.

personality test, any of a variety of standardized tests used in the evaluation or assessment of various facets of personality structure, emotional status, and behavioral traits.

personal orientation, 1. a continually evolving process in which a person determines and evaluates the relationships that appear to exist between him or her and other people. **2.** the assessment of those relationships derived by a person.

personal protective equipment (PPE), a part of standard precautions for all health care workers to prevent skin and mucous membrane exposure when in contact with blood and body fluid of any patient. Personal equipment includes protective laboratory clothing, disposable gloves, eye protection, and face masks.

personal resiliency, a nursing outcome from the Nursing Outcomes Classification (NOC) defined as the positive adaptation

and function of an individual following significant adversity or crisis.

personal safety behavior, a nursing outcome from the Nursing Outcomes Classification (NOC) defined as personal actions that prevent physical injury to self.

personal space, the area surrounding an individual that is perceived as private by the individual, who may regard a movement into the space by another person as intrusive. Personal space boundaries vary somewhat in different cultures, but in general they are regarded as a distance of about 1 meter (3 feet) around the individual.

personal unconscious, in analytic psychology, the thoughts, ideas, emotions, and other mental phenomena acquired and repressed during one's lifetime.

personal well-being, a nursing outcome from the Nursing Outcomes Classification (NOC) defined as the extent of positive perception of one's health status.

personal zone, an individual protective zone in which the boundaries may contract or expand according to contextual characteristics, usually between 18 inches and 4 feet.

person year, a statistical measure representing one person at risk of development of a disease during a period of 1 year.

perspiration /pur′spirā′shən/ [L, *per* + *spirare,* to breathe], **1.** the act or process of perspiring; the excretion of fluid by the sweat glands through pores in the skin. **2.** the fluid excreted by the sweat glands. It consists of water containing sodium chloride, phosphate, urea, ammonia, and other waste products. Perspiration serves as a mechanism for excretion and for regulation of body temperature.

per tertiam intentionem [L], by tertiary (third) intention.

Perthes disease, osteochondrosis of the head of the femur in children, characterized initially by epiphyseal necrosis or degeneration, followed by regeneration or recalcification.

Pertofrane, a trademark for an antidepressant (desipramine hydrochloride).

perturbation /pur′tərbā′shən/ [L, *per* + *turbare,* to disturb], a cause or a condition of disturbance, disorder, or confusion.

pertussis /pərtus′is/ [L, *per* + *tussis,* cough], an acute, highly contagious respiratory disease characterized by paroxysmal coughing that ends in a loud whooping inspiration. It occurs primarily in infants and in children less than 4 years of age who have not been immunized. The causative organism, *Bordetella pertussis,* is a small, nonmotile gram-negative coccobacillus. Transmission occurs directly by contact or by inhalation of infectious particles, usually spread by coughing and sneezing, and indirectly by contact with freshly contaminated articles.

pertussis immune globulin, a passive immunizing agent against whooping cough prescribed for immediate but short-lived immunization against whooping cough.

pertussis vaccine, an active immunizing agent prescribed for immunization against pertussis when the administration of diphtheria, pertussis, and tetanus vaccine is contraindicated.

per vaginam [L], via the vagina.

perversion /pərvur′shən/ [L, *pervertere,* to turn about], **1.** any deviation from what is considered normal or natural. **2.** the act of causing a change from what is normal or natural. **3.** *informal.* in psychiatry, any of a number of sexual practices that deviate from what is considered normal adult behavior.

pervert /pur′vərt/ [L, *pervertere*], **1.** *informal.* a person whose sexual pleasure is derived from stimuli almost universally regarded as unnatural, such as a fetishist or sadomasochist. **2.** one whose sexual behavior deviates from a social or statistical norm but is not necessarily pathologic.

pes /pēz, pās/ *pl.* **pedes** [L, foot], the foot or a footlike structure.

pes equinus [L, *pes,* foot, *equinus,* pertaining to a horse], a deformity of the foot in which the toes are extremely flexed, walking is done on the dorsal surface of the toes, and the heel does not touch the ground.

pessary /pes′ərē/ [Gk, *pessos,* oval stone], a device inserted in the vagina to treat uterine prolapse, uterine retroversion, or cervical incompetence. It is used in the treatment of women whose advanced age or poor general condition precludes surgical repair. Pessaries are also used in younger women in evaluating symptomatic uterine retroversion and in managing cervical incompetence in pregnancy. A pessary must be removed, usually daily, for cleaning.

pessary management, a nursing intervention from the Nursing Interventions Classification (NIC) defined as placement and monitoring of a vaginal device for treating stress urinary incontinence, uterine retroversion, genital prolapse, or incompetent cervix.

pessimism /pes′imiz′əm/ [L, *pessimus,* worst], the inclination to anticipate the worst possible results from any action or situation or to emphasize unfavorable conditions, even when progress or gain might reasonably be expected.—**pessimist,** *n.*

pesticide poisoning /pes′tisīd/ [L, *pestis,* plague, *caedere,* to kill, *potio,* drink], a toxic condition caused by the ingestion

or inhalation of a substance used for the eradication of pests.

pestilence /pes′tiləns/ [L, *pestilentia,* infectious disease], any epidemic of a virulent infectious or contagious disease.

pes valgus [L, *pes,* foot, *valgus,* bent outward], deviation of the foot outward at the talocalcanean joint.

PET /pet/, abbreviation for **positron emission tomography.**

petaling /pet′əling/, a process of smoothing the raw or ragged edges of a plaster cast to prevent skin irritation.

petechiae /pētē′kē·ē/ *sing.* **petechia** [It, *petecchie,* flea bites], tiny purple or red spots appearing on the skin as a result of tiny hemorrhages within the dermal or submucosal layers.—**petechial,** *adj.*

petechial fever /pitē′kē·əl/ [It, *petecchie;* L, *febris,* fever], any febrile illness accompanied by small petechiae on the skin, such as seen with meningococcemia or in the late stage of typhoid fever.

petechial hemorrhage [It, *petecchie;* Gk, *haima,* blood, *rhegnynei,* to gush], a small discrete hemorrhage under the skin.

petit pas gait /pet′ē pä, ptē pä′/, a manner of walking with short, mincing steps and shuffling with loss of associated movements. It is seen in cases of parkinsonism as well as in diffuse cerebral disease resulting from multiple small infarcts.

Petren's gait /pet′rənz/, a hesitant form of walking in which a patient takes a few steps, halts, and then takes a few more steps. In some cases the patient must be encouraged to begin the next brief walking period.

Petri dish /pē′trē, pä′trē/ [Julius R. Petri, German bacteriologist, 1852–1921], a shallow circular glass dish used to hold solid culture media.

petrification /pet′rifikā′shən/, the process of becoming calcified or stonelike.

pétrissage /pā′trisäzh′/ [Fr, *petrir,* to knead], a technique in massage in which the skin is gently lifted and squeezed. Pétrissage promotes circulation and relaxes muscles.

petrolatum /pet′rəlā′təm/ [L, *petra,* rock, *oleum,* oil], a purified mixture of semisolid hydrocarbons obtained from petroleum and commonly used as an ointment base or skin emollient.

petrolatum gauze, absorbent gauze permeated with white petrolatum.

petroleum distillate poisoning /pətrō′lē·əm/, a toxic condition caused by the ingestion or inhalation of a petroleum distillate, such as fuel oil, lubricating oil, glue used in making model airplanes or the like, and various solvents. Nausea, vomiting, chest pain, dizziness, and severe depression of the CNS characterize the condition.

P

Severe or fatal pneumonitis may occur if the substance is aspirated. Therefore induced emesis is contraindicated.

petroleum jelly, a nonliquid colloidal solution or gel of soft paraffin. It is used as a topical soothing medication for burns and abrasions.

petrosal sinuses, channels, superior and inferior, that drain the cavernous sinuses into the transverse sinuses. The superior petrosal sinuses receive cerebral and cerebellar veins whereas the inferior petrosal sinuses receive cerebellar veins and veins from the internal ear and brainstem. Basilar sinuses connect the inferior petrosal sinuses to each other and to the vertebral plexus of veins.

petrosphenoidal fissure /pet'rōsfēnoi'dəl/ [L, petra, rock; Gk, sphen, wedge, eidos, form], a fissure on the floor of the cranial fossa between the posterior edge of the great wing of the sphenoid bone and the petrous part of the temporal bone.

petrous /pet'rəs/ [L, petra, rock], resembling a rock or stone.

PET scan, positron emission tomography, or the image obtained from it.

Peutz-Jeghers syndrome /poits jeg'ərz/ [J.L.A. Peutz, Dutch physician, 1886–1957; Harold J. Jeghers, American physician, b. 1904], an inherited disorder transmitted as an autosomal-dominant trait, characterized by multiple intestinal polyps and abnormal mucocutaneous pigmentation, usually over the lips and buccal mucosa.

Peyer's patches, one of a group of solitary nodules or groups of lymph nodes forming a single layer in the mucous membrane of the ileum opposite the mesenteric attachment. In most individuals, they appear in the distal ileum, but they also appear in the jejunum of a few individuals.

peyote /pā·ō'tē/ [Aztec, peyotl], a cactus from which a hallucinogenic drug, mescaline, is derived.

Peyronie's disease /pārōnēz'/ [François de la Peyronie, French physician, 1678–1747], a disease of unknown cause resulting in fibrous induration of the corpora cavernosa of the penis. The chief symptom of Peyronie's disease is painful erection.

Pezzer's catheter /pezäz/ [Oscar M. de Pezzer, French surgeon, 1853–1917], a self-retaining catheter with a bulbous tip.

pF, abbreviation for picofarad.

Pfizerpen-AS, a trademark for an antibacterial in Canada (penicillin G procaine).

PFT, abbreviation for **pulmonary function test.**

PG, abbreviation for **prostaglandin.**

PGI₂, abbreviation for **prostacyclin.**

PGY, abbreviation for postgraduate year, describing medical school graduates during their postgraduate training as interns

(PGY-1, first year), residents (PGY-2, -3, -4), or fellows (PGY-4, -5).

pH, abbreviation for potential hydrogen, a scale representing the relative acidity (or alkalinity) of a solution, in which a value of 7.0 is neutral, below 7.0 is acid, and above 7.0 is alkaline. The numeric pH value indicates the relative concentration of hydrogen ions in the solution compared with that of a standard (1 molar) solution.

Ph, symbol or abbreviation for **phenyl, C_6H_5.**

Ph¹, symbol for **Philadelphia chromosome.**

PHA, 1. abbreviation for **paraaminohippuric acid.** 2. abbreviation for **phytohemagglutinin.**

phacolytic glaucoma, an abnormal condition characterized by an acute autoimmune reaction of the eye. It is caused by hypersensitivity of the eye to the protein of the crystalline lens and commonly follows trauma to the crystalline lens or cataract surgery. Associated symptoms include swelling and inflammation of the eye, severe pain, and blurred vision. The substance of the lens is invaded by polymorphonuclear cells and mononuclear phagocytes.

phacomalacia /fak'ōmələ'shə/ [Gk, phalos, lens, malkia, softness], an abnormal condition of the eye in which the lens becomes soft as a result of the presence of a soft cataract.

phaeohyphomycosis /fē'ōhī'fōmīkō'sis/, an opportunistic fungal infection, other than mycetoma and chromoblastomycosis, caused by the dematiaceous, or darkly pigmented, molds.

phage typing /fāj/ [Gk, phagein, to eat, typos, mark], the identification of bacteria by testing their vulnerability to bacterial viruses.

phagocyte /fag'əsīt/ [Gk, phagein + kytos, cell], a cell that is able to surround, engulf, and digest microorganisms and cellular debris. **Fixed noncirculating phagocytes** include the fixed macrophages. **Free circulating phagocytes** include the polymorphonuclear neutrophils. —**phagocytic,** adj.

phagocytic /-sit'ik/ [Gk, phagein, to eat, kytos, cell], pertaining to phagocytes or phagocytosis.

phagocytosis /fag'əsītō'sis/ [Gk, phagein + kytos + osis, condition], the process by which certain cells engulf and destroy microorganisms and cellular debris. The process includes five steps: (1) invagination, (2) engulfment, (3) internalization and formation of the phagocyte vacuole, (4) fusing of lysosomes to digest the phagocytosed material, and (5) release of digested microbial products. —**phagocytize,** v.

phagolysosome, a cytoplasmic body formed by the fusion of a phagosome, or ingested particle, with a lysosome containing hydrolytic enzymes. The enzymes digest most of the material within the phagosome.

phagosome /fag′əsōm/, a membrane-bound cytoplasmic vesicle within the phagocyte that engulfs it. The vesicle contains phagocytized materials and may fuse with a lysosome, forming a phagolysosome.

phakomatosis /fak′ōmətō′sis/ *pl.* **phakomatoses** [Gk, *phako*, lens, *oma*, tumor, *osis*, condition], in ophthalmology, any of several hereditary syndromes characterized by benign tumor-like nodules of the eye, skin, and brain. The four disorders designated phakomatoses are neurofibromatosis, tuberous sclerosis, encephalotrigeminal angiomatosis, and cerebroretinal angiomatosis.

phal, 1. abbreviation for **phalanges. 2.** abbreviation for **phalanx.**

phalangeal /fəlan′jē·al/ [Gk, *phalanx*, line of soldiers], pertaining to a phalanx.

phalanx (phal) /fā′langks/ *pl.* **phalanges** /phal/ [Gk, line of soldiers], any of the 14 tapering bones composing the fingers of each hand and the toes of each foot. They are arranged in three rows at the distal end of the metacarpus and the metatarsus. The fingers each have three phalanges; the thumb has two. Toes 2 through 5 each have three phalanges; the great toe has two.

phallic /fal′ik/ [Gk, *phallos*, penis], pertaining to the penis or penis-shaped.

phallic stage [Gk, *phallos*, penis; L, *stare*, to stand], in psychoanalysis, the period in psychosexual development occurring between 3 and 6 years of age when emerging awareness and self-manipulation of the genitals are the predominant source of pleasurable experience.

phallic symbol [Gk, *phallos*, penis, *symbolon*, sign], in psychoanalysis, any object that may be thought to resemble a penis.

phalloidine /faloi′din/, a poison present in the mushroom *Amanita phalloides*. Ingestion of phalloidine results in bloody diarrhea, vomiting, severe abdominal pain, kidney failure, and liver damage.

phalloplasty /fal′ōplas′tē/, a surgical procedure to lengthen, thicken, reconstruct, or otherwise reshape the penis. It may be performed to correct congenital defects, such as epispadias.

phantasm /fan′taz′əm/ [Gk, *phantasma*, vision], an illusory image, such as an optical illusion of something that does not exist.

phantom /fan′təm/ [Gk, *phantasma*, vision], a mass of material similar to human tissue used to investigate the interaction of radiation beams with human beings. Phantom materials can range from water to complex chemical mixtures that faithfully mimic the human body as it would interact with radiation.

phantom image, an image that appears in a CT scan but is not actually in the focal plane. It is created by the incomplete blurring or fusion of the blurred margins of some structures characteristic of the type of tomographic motion used.

phantom limb syndrome, a phenomenon common after amputation of a limb in which sensation or discomfort is experienced in the missing limb.

phantom tumor, a swelling resembling a tumor, usually caused by muscle contraction or gaseous distension of the intestines.

phantom vision, a sense perception occurring in the form of a visual illusion or hallucination. It is usually regarded as a pseudohallucination in that the person sensing the perception is aware that the phenomenon is illusory.

phar, 1. abbreviation for **pharmacy. 2.** abbreviation for **pharmacology. 3.** abbreviation for **pharmaceutical.**

Phar.B., abbreviation for *Bachelor of Pharmacy.*

Phar.D., abbreviation for *Doctor of Pharmacy.*

pharmaceutical (phar) /fär′məsoo̅′tik/ [Gk, *pharmakeuein*, to give drugs], **1.** pertaining to pharmacy or drugs. **2.** a drug.

pharmaceutical chemistry (Pharm Chem), the science dealing with the composition and preparation of chemical compounds used in medical diagnoses and therapies.

pharmaceutical necessity, a substance having slight or no value therapeutically but used in the preparation of various pharmaceuticals, including preservatives; solvents; ointment bases; and flavoring, coloring, diluting, emulsifying, and suspending agents.

pharmacist /fär′məsist/ [Gk, *pharmakon*, drug], a person who formulates, dispenses, and provides clinical information on drugs or medications to health professionals and patients.

pharmacodynamics /-dīnam′iks/ [Gk, *pharmakon*, drug, *dynamis*, power], the study of how a drug acts on a living organism, including the pharmacologic response observed relative to the concentration of the drug at an active site in the organism.

pharmacogenetics /-jənet′iks/ [Gk, *pharmakon*, drug, *genesis*, origin], the study of the effect of the genetic factors belonging to a group or an individual on the response of the group or the individual to certain drugs.

P

pharmacognosy, the study of chemicals taken from natural sources to be used as drugs or in the preparation of drugs.

pharmacokinetics /fär′məkōkinet′iks/ [Gk, *pharmakon* + *kinesis*, motion], the study of the action of drugs within the body, including the mechanisms of drug absorption, distribution, metabolism, and excretion; onset of action; duration of effect; biotransformation; and effects and routes of excretion of the metabolites of the drug.

pharmacologic agent /-loj′ik/, any oral, parenteral, or topical substance used to alleviate symptoms and treat or control a disease process or aid recovery from an injury.

pharmacologic vagotomy, the use of medications to curtail functions of the vagus nerve.

pharmacologist /fär′məkol′əjist/, a specialist in the preparation, properties, uses, and actions of drugs.

pharmacology (phar) /-kol′əjē/ [Gk, *pharmakon* + *logos*, science], the study of the preparation, properties, uses, and actions of drugs.

pharmacopoeia /fär′məkəpē′ə/ [Gk, *pharmakon* + *poiein*, to make], **1.** a compendium containing descriptions, recipes, strengths, standards of purity, and dosage forms for selected drugs. **2.** the available stock of drugs in a pharmacy. **3.** the total of all authorized drugs available within the jurisdiction of a given geographic or political area.

pharmacotherapy /-ther′əpē/ [Gk, *pharmakon,* drug + *therapeia*], the use of drugs to treat diseases.

pharmacy (phar) /fär′məsē/ [Gk, *pharmakon*], **1.** the study of preparing and dispensing drugs. **2.** a place for preparing and dispensing drugs.

pharmacy technician, a person who prepares and dispenses prescriptions under the supervision of a pharmacist.

Pharm Chem, abbreviation for **pharmaceutical chemistry.**

pharyngeal /ferin′jē·əl/ [Gk, *pharynx,* throat], pertaining to the pharynx.

pharyngeal aponeurosis [Gk, *pharynx,* throat, *apo,* from, *neuron,* sinew], a sheet of connective tissue immediately beneath the mucosa of the pharynx.

pharyngeal bursa, a blind sac at the base of the pharyngeal tonsil.

pharyngeal membrane, a thin fold of ectoderm and endoderm that separates the pharyngeal pouches from the branchial clefts in a developing embryo.

pharyngeal nerve, a nerve that supplies the mucosa and glands of the nasopharynx.

pharyngeal suction catheter, a device that allows direct visualization of a pharyngeal suctioning procedure.

pharyngitis /fer′injī′tis/ [Gk, *pharynx* + *itis,* inflammation], inflammation or infection of the pharynx, usually causing symptoms of a sore throat. Some causes of pharyngitis are diphtheria, HSV, infectious mononucleosis, and streptococcal infection.

pharyngobasilar fascia, a thick layer of fascia that lines the inner surface of the pharyngeal wall and, with the buccopharyngeal fascia, reinforces the pharyngeal wall where muscle is deficient, particularly above the level of the superior constrictor where the pharyngeal wall is formed almost entirely of fascia.

pharyngoconjunctival fever /fəring′gōkon′jungktī′vəl/ [Gk, *pharnyx;* L, *conjunctivus,* connecting, *febris,* fever], an adenovirus infection characterized by fever, sore throat, and conjunctivitis. Contaminated water in lakes and swimming pools is a common source of infection.

pharyngoesophageal constriction, the narrowing where the pharynx ends and the cervical esophagus begins, the site of the pharyngoesophageal sphincter.

pharyngoplasty /fəring′gōplas′tē/ [Gk, *pharynx,* throat, *plassein,* to mold], surgical repair of the pharynx.

pharyngoscope /fəring′gəskōp/ [Gk, *pharynx* + *skopein,* to view], an endoscopic device for examining the lining of the pharynx.

pharyngoscopy /fer′ing·gos′kəpē/ [Gk, *pharynx,* throat, *skopein,* to view], the examination of the throat with a pharyngoscope.

pharyngotonsillitis /-ton′silī′tis/ [Gk, *pharynx;* L, *tonsilla;* Gk, *itis,* inflammation], an inflammation involving the pharynx and the tonsils.

pharynx /fer′inks/ *pl.* **pharynxes, pharynges** [Gk], the throat, a tubular structure that extends from the base of the skull to the esophagus and is situated immediately in front of the cervical vertebrae. The pharynx serves as a passageway for the respiratory and digestive tracts and changes shape to allow the formation of various vowel sounds. The pharynx is composed of muscle, is lined with mucous membrane, and is divided into the nasopharynx, the oropharynx, and the laryngopharynx. It contains the openings of the right and left auditory tubes, the openings of the two posterior nares, the fauces, the opening into the larynx, and the opening into the esophagus. It also contains the pharyngeal tonsils, the palatine tonsils, and the lingual tonsils.

phase /fāz/ [Gk, *phasis,* appearance], in a periodic function, such as rotational or sinusoidal motion, the position relative to a particular part of the cycle.

phase 0, in cardiology, the upstroke of the action potential.

phase 1, in cardiology, the initial rapid repolarization phase of the action potential, seen in ventricular and His-Purkinje action potentials.

phase 2, in cardiology, the plateau of the action potential, occurring during repolarization.

phase 3, in cardiology, the terminal rapid repolarization phase of the action potential.

phase 4, in cardiology, the period of electrical diastole. A graph of phase 4 shows a gradual upward slope in a pacemaker cell, whereas phase 4 in a nonpacemaker cell is flat.

phase-contrast microscopy, a type of light microscopy in which a special condenser and objective with a phase-shifting ring are used to visualize small differences in refractive index as differences in intensity or contrast. It is useful in viewing unstained specimens that appear transparent.

phased array /fāzd/, an array transducer assembly that has very thin rectangular elements arranged side by side. It relies on electronic beam steering to sweep sound beams over a sector-shaped scanned region. Beam steering is done using electronic time delays in the transmitting and receiving circuits.

phase microscope, a microscope with a special condenser and objective containing a phase-shifting ring that allows the viewer to see small differences in refraction indexes as differences in image intensity or contrast.

phase of maximum slope, the time of rapid cervical dilation and rapid fetal descent in the active phase of labor.

phase one study, a clinical trial to assess the risk that may arise from administering a new treatment modality. A phase two study evaluates the clinical effectiveness of the new modality, and a phase three study compares its effectiveness with that of the best existing treatment.

phasic /fā'zik/ [Gk, *phasis*], **1.** pertaining to a process proceeding in stages or phases. **2.** pertaining to a type of afferent or sensory nerve receptor of the proprioceptive system that responds to rate versus length changes in a muscle spindle.

Ph.D., abbreviation for *Doctor of Philosophy.*

Phe, abbreviation for the amino acid **phenylalanine.**

phenacetin /fənas'itin/, an analgesic no longer marketed because of its carcinogenic properties.

Phenaphen with Codeine, a trademark for an analgesic-antipyretic (acetaminophen and codeine).

phenazopyridine hydrochloride /fen'əzōpī'ridēn/, a urinary tract analgesic prescribed to reduce the pain of cystitis or other UTIs or to relieve the pain following clinical procedures of the urinary tract.

phencyclidine hydrochloride (PCP) /fensī'klidēn/, a piperidine derivative administered parenterally to achieve neuroleptic anesthesia. Because of its marked hallucinogenic properties, it is not used therapeutically in the United States.

phendimetrazine tartrate /fen'dīmet'rəsēn/, a sympathomimetic amine used as an anorectic agent. It is prescribed to reduce appetite during the first few weeks of dieting during treatment of exogenous obesity. Its beneficial effects slowly disappear over 3 to 12 weeks.

phenelzine sulfate /fē'nəlzēn/, a monoamine oxidase inhibitor prescribed in the treatment of depression, especially atypical endogenous depression and depression associated with adverse life events.

Phenergan, a trademark for a phenothiazine derivative (promethazine).

phenobarbital /fē'nəbär'bital/, a barbiturate anticonvulsant and sedative-hypnotic prescribed in the treatment of seizure disorders and as a long-acting sedative.

phenobarbital-phenytoin serum levels /-fen'itō'in/, the concentration of phenobarbital and phenytoin in the serum, monitored to maintain concentrations sufficient to control seizures but not high enough to cause toxic reactions.

phenocopy /fē'nōkop'ē/ [Gk, *phainein,* to appear; L, *copia,* plenty], a phenotypic trait or condition that is induced by environmental factors but closely resembles a phenotype usually produced by a specific genotype. The trait is neither inherited nor transmitted to offspring. Because phenocopies may present problems in genetic screening and genetic counseling, all exogenous factors must be ruled out before any congenital trait or defect is labeled hereditary.

phenol /fē'nol/ [Gk, *phainein,* to appear; L, *oleum,* oil], any of a large number and variety of chemical products closely related in structure to the alcohols and containing a hydroxyl group attached to a benzene ring.

phenol block, neurolytic alcohol or block using hydroxybenzene (phenol), intended to anesthetize a particular nerve permanently. The technique is sometimes used to control spasticity in specific muscle groups or to block transmission of nerve impulses in chronic pain conditions such as cancers.

phenol camphor, an oily mixture of camphor and phenol, used as an antiseptic and toothache remedy.

phenol coefficient, a measure of the disinfectant activity of a given chemical in relation to carbolic acid.

phenolphthalein /fē′nolthal′ē·in, -thā′lēn/,
1. a cathartic and pH indicator with a
range of 8.5 (colorless) to 9.0 (red). 2. an
indicator of hydrogen ion in urine and gastric juice.

phenol poisoning, corrosive poisoning
caused by the ingestion of compounds
containing phenol, such as carbolic acid,
creosote, cresol, guaiacol, and naph-
thol. Characteristic signs are burns of the
mucous membranes; weakness; pallor;
pulmonary edema; seizures; and respiratory, circulatory, cardiac, and renal failure.

phenolsulfonphthalein /fē′nəlsul′fonfthal′ē
·in/, a bright red water-soluble triphenyl-
methane dye used as an indicator at pH 7.7.

phenomenon /finom′ənən/ *pl.* **phenomena**
[Gk, *phainomenon,* something seen], a
sign that is often associated with a specific
illness or condition and is therefore diagnostically important.

phenothiazine /fē′nōthī′əzēn/, a yellow to
green crystalline compound that is a source
of dyes and is used in veterinary medicine to
treat infestations of threadworms and roundworms. It is too toxic for human use, but
derivatives of phenothiazine are used in antipsychotic and antihistamine medications.

phenothiazine derivatives, any of a
group of drugs that have a three-ring structure in which two benzene rings are linked
by a nitrogen and a sulfur. They represent
the largest and oldest group of antipsychotic compounds in clinical medicine.
This group of drugs largely revolution-
ized the practice of psychiatric medicine,
a process that is now continuing with the
introduction of the newer atypical antipsychotics such as risperidone and olanzapine.
Unlike the barbiturates, which act exclusively on the CNS, the phenothiazines
exert significant influence on many organ
systems of the body at once.

phenotype /fē′nətīp/ [Gk, *phainein,* to
appear, *typos,* mark], 1. the complete
observable characteristics of an organism or group, including anatomic, physiologic, biochemical, and behavioral traits,
as determined by the interaction of genetic
makeup and environmental factors. 2. a
group of organisms that resemble each
other in appearance.—**phenotypic,** *adj.*

phenoxybenzamine hydrochloride /fē
nok′sēben′zəmēn/, an irreversible (noncompetitive) alpha₁-adrenergic receptor
blocker producing long-lasting blockade.
It is prescribed in the control of pheochromocytoma and other instances of hypertensive crisis. If tachycardia is excessive,
concomitant administration of propranolol
may be necessary.

phentermine hydrochloride /fen′tərmēn/,
a sympathomimetic amine used as an

anorectic agent. It is prescribed as a short-
term adjunct to decrease appetite during
treatment of obesity with a regimen of
caloric reduction, exercise, and behavioral
modification.

phentolamine /fentol′əmēn/, an alpha₁-
adrenergic receptor blocker prescribed
in the control of symptoms of pheochromocytoma before and during surgery and
for dermal necrosis and sloughing after
extravasation of parenteral drugs with
alpha-adrenergic effects (e.g., norepinephrine, epinephrine, dopamine).

phenyl (Ph) /fē′nil, fen′il/, a monovalent
organic radical, C_6H_5, derived from benzene.

phenylacetic acid /fen′iləsē′tik/, a catabo-
lite of phenylalanine, excessively formed
and excreted, sometimes conjugated with
glutamine, in phenylketonuria.

phenylalanine (Phe) /fen′ilal′ənēn/, an
essential amino acid necessary for the
normal growth and development of infants
and children and for normal protein metabolism throughout life. It is abundant in
milk, eggs, and other common foods.

phenylalaninemia /fen′ilal′əninē′mē·ə/,
the presence of phenylalanine in the blood.

phenylephrine hydrochloride /-ef′rēn/,
an alpha-adrenergic agonist prescribed for
maintenance of BP and used locally as a
nasal or ophthalmic vasoconstrictor.

phenylethyl alcohol ($C_6H_5CH_2CH_2OH$)
/-eth′il/, a colorless fragrant liquid with a
burning taste, used as a bacteriostatic agent
and preservative in medicinal solutions.

phenylketonuria (PKU) /fen′əlkē′tŏn
yŏŏr′ē·ə, fē′nəl-/, abnormal presence of
phenylketone and other metabolites of
phenylalanine in the urine, characteristic
of an inborn metabolic disorder caused by
the absence or a deficiency of phenylalanine hydroxylase, the enzyme responsible
for the conversion of the amino acid phenylalanine into tyrosine. Accumulation
of phenylalanine is toxic to brain tissue.
Untreated individuals have very fair hair,
eczema, a mousy odor of the urine and
skin, and progressive mental retardation.
—**phenylketonuric,** *adj.*

phenylketonuria (PKU) test, a blood or
urine test performed to determine the presence of PKU in infants.

phenylpyruvic acid /fen′ilpīrōō′vik/, a
product of the metabolism of phenylalanine. The presence of phenylpyruvic acid in
the urine is indicative of phenylketonuria.

phenyl salicylate, the salicylic ester of
phenol.

phenyltoloxamine citrate /fen′iltəlok′sə
mēn/, an antihistamine usually used in a
fixed-combination drug with an analgesic.

phenytoin /fen′ətŏ′in/, a drug that alters
cells' membrane conductances of Na^+ and

Ca^{2+}, ions whose conductances are important during the function of excitable nerve, heart, and muscle tissues. It is prescribed as an anticonvulsant for the treatment and prevention of tonic-clonic seizures, complex partial seizures, and seizures resulting from head trauma or surgery. It has as an unlabeled use as antiarrhythmic agent, particularly in digitalis-induced ventricular arrhythmias.

pheochromocytoma /fē'ōkrō'mōsītō'mə/ *pl.* **pheochromocytomas,** **pheochromocytomata** [Gk, *phaios,* dark, *chroma,* color, *kytos,* cell, *oma,* tumor], a vascular tumor of chromaffin tissue of the adrenal medulla or sympathetic paraganglia, characterized by hypersecretion of epinephrine and norepinephrine, causing persistent or intermittent hypertension. Typical signs include headache, flushing, palpitation, sweating, nervousness, hyperglycemia, nausea, vomiting, and syncope. Weight loss, myocarditis, cardiac arrhythmia, and heart failure may occur.

pheochromocytoma suppression and provocative testing, a blood test to diagnose pheochromocytoma, consisting of either the administration of glucagon to provoke a rise in catecholamine levels or the administration of clonadine to suppress catecholamine levels.

pheromone /fer'əmōn/ [Gk, *pherein,* to carry, *hormaein,* to stimulate], a substance secreted by an organism that elicits a particular response from another individual of the same species, usually of the opposite sex.

phi /fī/, Φ, φ, the twenty-first letter of the Greek alphabet.

Phialophora /fī'älof'ərə/, a genus of imperfect fungi. *P. verrucosi* is a cause of chromoblastomycosis and *P. jeanselmei* is a cause of maduromycosis.

Philadelphia chromosome (Ph¹) [Philadelphia, Pennsylvania], a translocation of the long arm of chromosome 22, often seen in the abnormal myeloblasts, erythroblasts, and megakaryoblasts of patients who have chronic myelocytic leukemia.

philtrum /fil'trəm/, the vertical groove in the center of the upper lip.

phimosis /fīmō'sis/ [Gk, muzzle], tightness of the prepuce of the penis that prevents the retraction of the foreskin over the glans. The condition is usually congenital but may be the result of infection.

phimosis vaginalis /vaj'inā'lis/, congenital narrowness or closure of the vaginal opening.

pHisoHex, a trademark for a detergent containing a topical antibiotic (hexachlorophene).

phlebectomy /fləbek'təmē/ [Gk, *phleps,* vein, *ektomē,* excision], the surgical removal of a vein or part of a vein.

phlebogram /fleb'əgram/ [Gk, *phleps,* vein, *gramma,* record], **1.** a radiograph obtained by phlebography. **2.** a graphic representation of the venous pulse obtained by phlebography.

phlebograph /fleb'əgraf/, a device for producing a graphic record of the venous pulse.

phlebography /fləbog'rəfē/ [Gk, *phleps* + *graphein,* to record], **1.** the radiographic examination of veins injected with a radiopaque contrast medium. **2.** the graphic recording of the venous pulse.

phlebography of the lower extremities, an x-ray study with contrast dye designed to identify and locate thrombi within the venous system of the lower extremities.

phlebostasis /fləbäs'tə-səs/, an abnormally slow flow of blood in the veins, which are usually distended.

phlebostatic axis /-stat'ik/ [Gk, *phleps* + *stasis,* standing still], the approximate location of the right atrium, found at the intersection of the midaxillary and a line drawn from the fourth intercostal space at the right side of the sternum.

phlebothrombosis /fleb'ōthrombō'sis/ [Gk, *phleps* + *thrombos,* lump, *osis,* condition], an abnormal condition in which a clot forms within a vein. It is usually caused by hemostasis, hypercoagulability, or occlusion. In contrast to that in thrombophlebitis, the wall of the vein is not inflamed.

phlebotomist /fləbot'əmist/ [Gk, *phleps,* vein + *ektomē*], a person with special training in the practice of drawing blood.

phlebotomize /fləbot'əmīz/ [Gk, *phleps,* vein, *ektomē,* excision], to open a vein to remove blood.

phlebotomus fever /fləbot'əməs/ [Gk, *phleps* + *tomos,* cutting; L, *febris,* fever], an acute mild infection caused by one of five distinct arboviruses transmitted to humans by the bite of an infected sandfly, characterized by rapidly developing fever, headache, eye pain, conjunctivitis, myalgia, and occasionally a macular or urticarial rash.

phlebotomy /fləbot'əmē/ [Gk, *phleps* + *temnein,* to cut], the incision of a vein for the letting of blood, as in collecting blood from a donor. Phlebotomy is the chief treatment for polycythemia vera and may be performed every 2 to 3 months or more frequently if required. The procedure is sometimes used to decrease the amount of circulating blood and pulmonary engorgement in acute pulmonary edema.

phlebotomy: arterial blood sample, a nursing intervention from the Nursing Interventions Classification (NIC) defined as obtaining a blood sample from

P

an uncannulated artery to assess oxygen and carbon dioxide levels and acid-base balance.

phlebotomy: blood unit acquisition, a nursing intervention from the Nursing Interventions Classification (NIC) defined as procuring blood and blood products from donors.

phlebotomy: cannulated vessel, a nursing intervention from the Nursing Interventions Classification (NIC) defined as aspirating a blood sample through an indwelling vascular catheter for laboratory tests.

phlebotomy: venous blood sample, a nursing intervention from the Nursing Interventions Classification (NIC) defined as removal of a sample of venous blood from an uncannulated vein.

phlegm /flem/ [Gk, *phlegma,* mucus, sluggishness], thick mucus secreted by the tissues lining the airways of the lungs.

phlegmasia alba dolens [Gk, *phlegmone,* inflammation; L, *albus,* white, *dolens,* painful], thrombophlebitis of the femoral vein, resulting in pain and edema of the leg. It may occur after childbirth or a severe febrile illness.

phlegmatic /flegmat′ik/ [Gk, *phlegma,* mucus, sluggishness], pertaining to a person who may be dull or apathetic, or calm and composed to an extent that excitation is difficult.

phlegmon /fleg′mon/ [Gk, *phlegmone,* inflammation], an inflammation of connective tissue.

phlegmonous gastritis /fleg′mənəs/ [Gk, *phlegmone* + *osis,* condition], a rare but severe form of gastritis involving the connective tissue layer of the stomach wall. It occurs as a complication of systemic infection, peptic ulcer, cancer, surgery, or other severe stress and represents an acute abdominal emergency.

phlyctenular keratoconjunctivitis /flik ten′yələr/ [Gk, *phlyktaina,* blister], an inflammatory condition of the cornea, characterized by tiny ulcerating nodules. It is seen most often in children as a response to allergens found in *Mycobacterium tuberculosis,* gonococci, *Candida albicans,* or various parasites.

PHO, abbreviation for **physician-hospital organization.**

phobia /fō′bē-ə/ [Gk, *phobos,* fear], an obsessive, irrational, and intense fear of a specific object, such as an animal or dirt; of an activity, such as meeting strangers or leaving the familiar setting of the home; or of a physical situation, such as heights and open or closed spaces. Typical manifestations of phobia include faintness, fatigue, palpitations, perspiration, nausea, tremor, and panic.—**phobic,** *adj.*

phobiac /fō′bē-ak/, a person who exhibits or is afflicted with a phobia.

phobic desensitization [Gk, *phobos,* fear; L, *de* + *sentire,* to feel], a method of resolving an ego dystonic or uncomfortable behavior pattern by gradual reentry into the emotionally upsetting life situation in stages, first in fantasy and then in real life.

phobic state, a condition characterized by extreme anxiety resulting from the excessive, irrational fear of a particular object, situation, or activity.

phocomelia /fō′kəmē′lyə/ [Gk, *phoke,* seal, *melos,* limb], a developmental anomaly characterized by absence of the upper part of one or more of the limbs so that the feet or hands or both are attached to the trunk of the body by short, irregularly shaped stumps, resembling the fins of a seal.—**phocomelic,** *adj.*

phocomelic dwarf /fō′kəmē′lik/, a dwarf in whom the long bones of any or all of the extremities are abnormally short.

phocomelus /fōkom′ələs/, an individual who has phocomelia.

phonation /fōnā′shən/ [Gk, *phone,* sound; L, *atio,* process], the production of voice through the vibration of the vocal folds of the larynx coupled with airflow directed upward from the lungs.

phonetics /fōnet′iks/ [Gk, *phone,* voice], **1.** the science of speech sounds used in language. **2.** a written code used by speech-language pathologists and linguists to represent speech sounds.

phonic, pertaining to voice, sounds, or speech.

phonocardiogram /fō′nōkär′dē-əgram′/, a graphic recording obtained from a phonocardiograph.

phonocardiograph /-kär′dē-əgraf′/ [Gk, *phone,* sound, *kardia,* heart, *graphein,* to record], an electroacoustic device that produces graphic heart sound recordings using a system of microphones and associated recording equipment. Phonocardiographs are used in the diagnosis and monitoring of heart disorders.—**phonocardiographic,** *adj.*

phonocardiography /-kär′dē-og′rəfē/ [Gk, *phone* + *kardia* + *graphein,* to record], the recording of heart sounds and murmurs by a phonocardiograph.

phonologic disorder /fōnəloj′ik/, a communication disorder of unknown cause, characterized by failure to use age- and dialect-appropriate sounds in speaking, with errors in the selection, production, or articulation of sounds. The most common errors are omissions, substitutions, and distortions of speech sounds.

phonology /fōnol′əjē/, the study of speech sounds, particularly the principles governing the way speech sounds are used in a given language.

phonophoresis /fō′nōfərē′sis/, a therapeutic technique in which ultrasound waves are used to force topical medicines, such as hydrocortisone, aspirin, and lidocaine, into subcutaneous tissues. Because of the risk that the patient may be hypersensitive to the medication, the technique is used with caution.

phonoreceptor /-risep′tər/ [Gk, *phone,* sound; L, *recipere,* to receive], a device for receiving sound impulses.

phoropter /for-op′ter/, an instrument for evaluation of vision, with lenses placed on dials in a unit that is positioned in front of the patient.

phosphatase /fos′fətāz/, an enzyme that acts as a catalyst in chemical reactions involving phosphorus. It is essential in the calcification of bone.

phosphate (PO_4^{3-}) /fos′fāt/, **1.** an anion of phosphoric acid. **2.** a salt of phosphoric acid. Phosphates are extremely important in living cells, particularly in the storage and use of energy and the transmission of genetic information.

phosphate binder, a substance that binds phosphate in the blood, removing it from circulation. It is used in treatment of hyperphosphatemia, in patients with end-stage renal disease or hypoparathyroidism.

phosphate-bond energy, the Gibbs energy for hydrolysis of a phosphate compound; a measure of relative phosphorylation power.

phosphatemia /fos′fətē′mē·ə/ [Gk, *phosphoros,* bringer of light, *haima,* blood], a condition of excessive levels of phosphates in the blood.

phosphate (PO_4) test, a blood test used to detect hyperphosphatemia and hypophosphatemia. Abnormal phosphate levels are associated with many conditions.

phosphatide /fos′fətīd/, phosphatidic acid or any of its esters. Phosphatidic acid (diacylglycerol phosphate) consists of glycerol esterified to phosphoric acid and to two fatty acids. Phosphatides are major components of cell membranes.

phosphaturia /fos′fətōōr′ē·ə/ [Gk, *phosphoros,* bringer of light, *ouron,* urine], an excessive level of phosphates in the urine.

phosphoglycerate kinase /fos′fōglis′ərāt/, an enzyme that catalyzes the reversible transfer of a phosphate group from adenosine triphosphate to D-3-phosphoglycerate, forming D-1,3-biphosphoglycerate. The reaction is one of the steps in gluconeogenesis.

Phospholine Iodide, a trademark for a cholinergic (echothiophate iodide).

phospholipase /fos′fōli′pās/, any of a group of enzymes that catalyze the hydrolysis of phospholipids. Various phospholipases digest cell membranes, aid in the synthesis of prostaglandins, and help produce arachidonic acid, one of the essential fatty acids.

phospholipid /fos′folip′id/ [Gk, *phos,* light, *pherein,* to bear, *lipos,* fat], a phosphorus-containing lipid. Two kinds of phospholipids are phosphatides and sphingomyelins.

phospholipid transfer protein (PLTP), an ubiquitous protein having multiple functions in lipoprotein metabolism. In plasma, it plays an important role in high-density lipoprotein (HDL) metabolism by mediating the transfer of phospholipids from triglyceride-rich lipoproteins to HDL and the transfer of phospholipids between HDL molecules.

phosphomevalonate kinase /fos′fōməval′ə nāt/, an enzyme that catalyzes the transfer of a phosphate group from adenosine triphosphate to produce adenosine diphosphate and 5-pyrophosphomevalonate.

phosphorescence /fos′fōres′əns/ [Gk, *phos,* light, *pherein,* to bear], **1.** a glow of yellow phosphorus caused by slow oxidation. **2.** the emission of visible light without accompanying heat as observed in phosphorus that has been exposed to radiation, which continues beyond a few nanoseconds after radiation has ceased.

phosphoric acid (H_3PO_4) /fosfôr′ik/, a clear, colorless, odorless liquid that is irritating to the skin and eyes and moderately toxic if ingested. It is used in the production of fertilizers, soaps, detergents, animal feeds, and certain drugs.

phosphorus (P) /fos′fərəs/ [Gk, *phos,* light, *pherein,* to bear], a nonmetallic chemical element occurring extensively in nature as a component of phosphate rock. Its atomic number is 15, and its atomic mass is 30.975. Phosphorus is essential for the metabolism of protein, calcium, and glucose. The body uses phosphorus in its combined forms, which are obtained from such nutritional sources as milk, cheese, meat, egg yolk, whole grains, legumes, and nuts. A nutritional deficiency of phosphorus can cause weight loss, anemia, and abnormal growth.

phosphorus poisoning, a toxic condition caused by the ingestion of white or yellow phosphorus, sometimes found in rat poisons, certain fertilizers, and fireworks. Intoxication is characterized initially by nausea, throat and stomach pain, vomiting, diarrhea, and an odor of garlic on the breath. After a few days of apparent recovery, nausea, vomiting, and diarrhea recur with renal and hepatic dysfunction.

phosphorylase /fosfôr′ilās/ [Gk, *phosphoros,* bringer of light; *ase,* enzyme suffix], any of a group of physiologically

P

important enzymes that catalyze reactions between phosphates and glycogen or other starch components, yielding glucose 1-phosphate.

phosphorylation /fosfôr′ilā′shən/, the process of attaching a phosphate group to a protein, sugar, or other compound.

phot /fot/ [Gk, *phos*, light], the centimeter-gram-second unit of illumination, being one lumen per square centimeter.

photic /fō′tik/ [Gk, *phos*, light], pertaining to light.

photic epilepsy [Gk, *phos*, light, *epilepsia*, seizure], a condition in which epileptic attacks may be triggered by flickering light.

photoablation /fō′tō·a-blā′shun/, volatilization of tissue by ultraviolet rays emitted by a laser.

photoaging /fō′tō·āj′ing/, premature aging of the skin caused by long-term exposure to sunlight or other ultraviolet radiation.

photoallergic /-əlur′gik/ [Gk, *phos*, light, *allos*, other, *ergein*, to work], exhibiting a delayed hypersensitivity reaction after exposure to light.

photoallergic contact dermatitis, a papulovesicular, eczematous, or exudative skin reaction that occurs 24 to 48 hours after exposure to light in a previously sensitized person. The sensitizing substance concentrates in the skin and requires chemical alteration by light to become an active antigen.

photoallergy /-al′ərjē/ [Gk, *phos*, light, *allos*, other, *ergein*, to work], a sensitivity to light that causes allergic reactions.

photobiology /-bī·ol′əjē/, the study of the effects of light on organisms.

photochemistry /fō′tōkem′istrē/ [Gk, *phos*, light, *chemeia*, alchemy], the branch of chemistry that deals with the chemical properties or effects of light rays or other radiation.

photochemotherapy /-kē′mōther′əpē/ [Gk, *phos* + *chemeia*, alchemy, *therapeia*, treatment], a kind of chemotherapy in which the effect of the administered drug is enhanced by exposing the patient to light.

photochromogen /-krō′məjen/, **1.** a pigment that develops as a result of exposure to light. **2.** a type of mycobacterium that is nonpigmented in the dark but produces a yellow pigment on constant exposure to light.

photodisintegration /-disin′təgrā′shən/, the emission of a nuclear fragment caused by the interaction of a high-energy x-ray with an atomic nucleus.

photoelectron /-ilek′tron/ [Gk, *phos*, light, *elektron*, amber], any electron that is discharged when light strikes a metal surface.

photokinetic /-kinet′ik/ [Gk, *phos*, light, *kinesis*, movement], pertaining to any movement that is stimulated by light rays.

photometer /fotom′ətər/ [Gk, *phos* + *metron*, measure], an instrument that measures light intensity.

photomultiplier /-mul′tiplī′ər/ [Gk, *phos*, light; L, *multiplex*, many folds], a device used in many radiation detection applications that converts low levels of light into electrical pulses.

photon /fō′ton/ [Gk, *phos*, light], the smallest quantity of electromagnetic energy. It has no mass and no charge but travels at the speed of light. Photons may occur in the form of x-rays, gamma rays, or quanta of light.

photophobia /-fō′bē·ə/ [Gk, *phos* + *phobos*, fear], **1.** abnormal sensitivity to light, especially by the eyes. The condition is prevalent in albinism and various diseases of the conjunctiva and cornea and may be a symptom of such disorders as measles, psittacosis, encephalitis, Rocky Mountain spotted fever, and Reiter's syndrome. **2.** in psychiatry, a morbid fear of light with an irrational need to avoid bright places.—**photophobic,** *adj.*

photopic vision /fōtop′ik/, daylight vision, which depends primarily on the function of the retinal cone cells.

photoprotective /-prətek′tiv/, protective against the potential adverse effects of ultraviolet light.

photoreaction /-rē·ak′shən/ [Gk, *phos*; L, *re*, again, *agere*, to act], any chemical reaction that is stimulated by the influence of light.

photoreceptor /-risep′tər/ [Gk, *phos*, light; L, *recipere*, to receive], a nerve cell that is receptive to light stimuli.

photoreceptor layer [L, *columna*, column; AS, *lecgan*], the layer of rods and cones in the retina.

photorefractive /fo′to-re-frak′tiv/, pertaining to the refraction of light.

photorefractive keratectomy (PRK) /-refrak′tiv/, a surgical procedure in which an excimer laser is used to reshape the human cornea to improve the refractive properties of the eye and reduce or eliminate the need for eyeglasses. Rather than cutting, the laser shaves off preprogrammed outer layers of corneal tissue.

photoscan /fō′toskan/, a radiograph that shows the distribution of a radiopharmaceutical in the body.

photosensitive /-sen′sitiv/ [Gk, *phos*; L, *sentire*, to feel], pertaining to increased reactivity of the skin to sunlight caused by a disorder, such as albinism or porphyria, or, more frequently, by the use of certain drugs. Relatively brief exposure to sunlight or to an ultraviolet lamp may cause edema, papules, urticaria, or acute burns in susceptible individuals.

photosensitivity /-sen'sitiv'itē/, **1.** sensitivity of a cell to light. **2.** any abnormal response to exposure to light, specifically, a skin reaction requiring the presence of a sensitizing agent and exposure to sunlight or its equivalent.

photosensitization /-sen'sitĭzā'shən/ [Gk, *phos,* light; L, *sentire,* to feel], the process of rendering an organism sensitive to the effects of light.—**photosensitizer,** *n.*

photostimulable phosphor, a material used to capture radiographic images in computed radiography systems.

photosynthesis /fōtōsin'thəsis/ [Gk, *phos* + *synthesis,* putting together], a process by which plants, algae, and some bacteria containing chlorophyll synthesize organic compounds, chiefly carbohydrates, from atmospheric carbon dioxide and water, using light for energy and liberating oxygen in the process.—**photosynthetic,** *adj.*

phototherapy /-ther'əpē/ [Gk, *phos* + *therapeia* treatment], the treatment of disorders by the use of light, especially ultraviolet light. Ultraviolet light may be used in the therapy of acne, pressure ulcers and other indolent ulcers, psoriasis, and hyperbilirubinemia.—**phototherapeutic,** *adj.*

phototherapy in the newborn, a treatment for hyperbilirubinemia and jaundice in the newborn that involves the exposure of an infant's bare skin to intense fluorescent light. The blue range of light accelerates the excretion of bilirubin in the skin, decomposing it by photooxidation.

phototherapy: mood/sleep regulation, a nursing intervention from the Nursing Interventions Classification (NIC) defined as the administration of doses of bright light in order to elevate mood and/or normalize the body's internal clock.

phototherapy: neonate, a nursing intervention from the Nursing Interventions Classification (NIC) defined as use of light therapy to reduce bilirubin levels in newborn infants.

phototoxic /-tok'sik/ [Gk, *phos* + *toxikon,* poison], characterized by a rapidly developing nonimmunologic reaction of the skin when it is exposed to a photosensitizing substance and light.

phototoxic contact dermatitis, a rapidly appearing, sunburn-like response of areas of skin that have been exposed to the sun after contact with a photosensitizing substance. Hyperpigmentation may follow the acute reaction.

phren /fren/ [Gk, mind], **1.** the diaphragm. **2.** the mind.

phrenetic /frənet'ik/ [Gk, *phren*], frenzied, delirious, maniacal.

phrenic /fren'ik/ [Gk, *phren,* mind], **1.** pertaining to the diaphragm. **2.** pertaining to the mind.

phrenic nerve, one of a pair of branches of the cervical plexus, arising from the first four cervical nerves and passing to the diaphragm. It contains about half as many sensory as motor fibers and is generally known as the motor nerve to the diaphragm, although the lower thoracic nerves also help innervate the diaphragm.

phrenicoceliac part of suspensory muscle of duodenum, a band of skeletal muscle that passes from the right crus of the diaphragm to join the celiacoduodenal part (pars coeliacoduodenalis) and attach to the celiac trunk.

phrenology [Gk, *phren,* mind], the study of the conformation of the skull based on the assumption that mental faculties are localized in particular sites on the surface of the brain. According to phrenologists, intelligence or other faculties of a person may be mirrored through elevations in the skull overlying the particular area of the brain.

PHSP, abbreviation for **physician health service plan.**

Phthirus /thī'rəs/ [Gk, *phtheir,* louse], a genus of blood-sucking lice that includes the species *P.* the crab louse.

phthisis /tis'is, thī'sis/ [Gk, *phthisis,* wasting away], any wasting disease involving all or part of the body, such as pulmonary TB.

phycologist /fēkol'əjist/, a person who specializes in the study of algae.

phycology /fēkol'əjē/ [Gk, *phykos,* seaweed, *logos,* science], the branch of science concerned with algae.

phycomycosis /fī'kōmīkō'sis/ [Gk, *phykos* + *mykes,* fungus, *osis,* condition], a fungal infection caused by a species of the order Phycomycetes. These organisms are common in the soil and are not usually pathogenic.

phylactic /filak'tik/ [Gk, *phylax,* guard], **1.** serving to protect. **2.** something that produces phylaxis.

phylogenetic /fī'lōgənet'ik/ [Gk, *phylon,* tribe, *genesis,* origin], **1.** relating to or acquired during phylogeny. **2.** based on a natural evolutionary relationship, such as a system of classification.

phylogeny /filoj'ənē/ [Gk, *phylon* + *genesis*], the development of the structure of a particular race or species as it evolved from earlier forms of life.

phylum /fī'ləm/ [Gk, *phylon,* tribe], a major subdivision of a kingdom of organisms, representing one or more classes.

Physalia /fisā'lēə/, a genus of marine invertebrates of the phylum Cnidaria.

physiatrist /fiz'ē·at'rist/, a physician specializing in physical medicine and rehabilitation who has been certified by the American Board of Physical Medicine and

P

Rehabilitation after completing residency and other requirements.

physiatry /fizī′ətrē/, the branch of medicine that deals with the prevention, diagnosis, and treatment of disease or injury and the rehabilitation from resultant impairments and disabilities by using physical agents such as light, heat, cold, water, electricity, therapeutic exercise, mechanical apparatus, and sometimes pharmaceutical agents.

physical abuse /fiz′ikəl/ [Gk, *physikos*, natural; L, *abuti*, to abuse], one or more episodes of aggressive behavior, usually resulting in physical injury with possible damage to internal organs, sense organs, the CNS, or the musculoskeletal system of another person.

physical aging, a nursing outcome from the Nursing Outcomes Classification (NOC) defined as normal physical changes that occur with the aging process.

physical allergy, a hypersensitive reaction to physical factors such as cold, heat, light, or trauma. Common characteristics include pruritus, urticaria, and angioedema. Usually specific antibodies are found in people having physical allergies.

physical assessment, the part of the health assessment representing a synthesis of the information obtained in a physical examination. It involves the detailed examination of the body from head to toe using the techniques of observation/inspection, palpation, percussion, and auscultation.

physical chemistry, the natural science dealing with the relationship between chemical and physical properties of matter.

physical dependence, substance dependence in which there is evidence of tolerance, withdrawal, or both.

physical diagnosis, the diagnostic process accomplished by the study of the physical manifestations of health, disease, and illness revealed in the physical examination, as guided by the patient's complete history and supported by various laboratory tests.

physical examination, an investigation of the body to determine its state of health, using any or all of the techniques of inspection, palpation, percussion, auscultation, and smell. The physical examination, history, and initial laboratory tests constitute the data base on which a diagnosis is made and on which a plan of treatment is developed.

physical fitness[1], the ability to carry out daily tasks with alertness and vigor, without undue fatigue, and with enough energy reserve to meet emergencies or to enjoy leisure time pursuits.

physical fitness[2], a nursing outcome from the Nursing Outcomes Classification (NOC) defined as the ability to perform physical activities with vigor.

physical injury severity, a nursing outcome from the Nursing Outcomes Classification (NOC) defined as severity of injuries from accidents and trauma.

physical maturation: female, a nursing outcome from the Nursing Outcomes Classification (NOC) defined as normal physical changes in the female that occur with the transition from childhood to adulthood.

physical maturation: male, a nursing outcome from the Nursing Outcomes Classification (NOC) defined as normal physical changes in the male that occur with the transition from childhood to adulthood.

physical restraint, a nursing intervention from the Nursing Interventions Classification (NIC) defined as application, monitoring, and removal of mechanical restraining devices or manual restraints used to limit physical mobility of a patient.

physical science, the study of the properties and behavior of nonliving matter.

physical sign [Gk, *physikos,* natural; L, *signum*], an objective indicator found during physical diagnosis or detected by inspection, palpation, percussion, or auscultation.

physical therapist (PT), a person who is licensed in the examination, evaluation, and treatment of physical impairments through the use of special exercise, application of heat or cold, and other physical modalities. The goal is to assist persons who are physically challenged to maximize independence and improve mobility, self-care, and other functional skills necessary for daily living.

physical therapy (PT), the treatment of disorders with physical agents and methods, such as massage, manipulation, therapeutic exercises, cold, heat (including paraffin, shortwave and microwave diathermy and ultrasonic heat), hydrotherapy, electrical stimulation, and light to assist in habilitating or rehabilitating patients and in restoring function after an illness or injury.

physical therapy assistant (PTA), a person who, under the supervision of a physical therapist, assists in carrying out patient treatment programs, providing treatment that improves mobility, relieves pain, and prevents or lessens physical disabilities of patients.

physician /fizish′ən/ [Gk, *physikos,* natural], a health professional who has earned a degree of Doctor of Medicine (M.D.) or Doctor of Osteopathy (D.O.) after completing an approved course of study at an approved medical school. Satisfactory completion of National Board Examinations, usually given during both the second and the final years of medical school and after graduation, is also required. An M.D. or D.O. usually enters a hospital internship or residency program for at least 2 years of postgraduate training before beginning practice or further training in a specialty. To practice medicine, an M.D. or D.O. is required to obtain a license from the state in which professional services will be performed.

physician assistant (PA), a person academically and clinically prepared to practice medicine under the supervision of a licensed doctor of medicine or osteopathy. Within the physician-PA relationship, PAs exercise autonomy in medical decisions and provide a wide range of diagnostic and therapeutic services.

physician extender, a health care provider who is not a physician but who performs medical activities typically performed by a physician. It is most commonly a nurse practitioner or physician assistant.

physician health service plan (PHSP), in the United States, a general term relating to an arrangement for provision of professional (physician) services only.

physician-hospital organization (PHO), in the United States, a management service organization in which the partners are physicians and hospitals. The PHO organization contracts for physician and hospital services.

Physician's Desk Reference (PDR), a compendium compiled annually, containing information supplied by their manufacturers about drugs, primarily prescription drugs and products used in diagnostic procedures in the United States.

physician support, a nursing intervention from the Nursing Interventions Classification (NIC) defined as collaborating with physicians to provide quality patient care.

physicist /fis′isist/, a scientist who specializes in physics.

physics /fiz′iks/ [Gk, *physikos,* natural], the study of matter and energy, particularly as related to motion and force.

physiognomy /fiz′ē·og′nəmē/ [Gk, *physis,* nature, *gnosis,* knowledge], a method of judging the personality and other characteristics of a client by studying the face and general carriage of the body.

physiologic age [Gk, *physis,* nature, *logos,* science; L, *aetas,* age], the age of the body as determined by its stage of development in terms of functional norms for various systems.

physiological /fiz′ē·əloj′ik/ [Gk, *physis,* nature, *logos,* science], pertaining to physiology, particularly normal functions as opposed to the pathological.

physiologic albuminuria [Gk, *physis,* nature, *logos,* science; L, *albus,* white; Gk, *ouron,* urine], the presence of albumin in the urine in the absence of any disease.

physiologic amenorrhea [Gk, *physis,* nature, *logos,* science, *a + men,* month, *rhoia,* to flow], an absence of menstruation having a nonpathologic cause, such as pregnancy, lactation, menopause, or a prepubertal state of maturity.

physiologic antidote [Gk, *physis + logos + anti,* against, *dotos,* that which is given], a drug that has the opposite effect on the body from that caused by a poisonous or toxic substance.

physiologic contracture [Gk, *physis + logos,* science; L, *contractio,* drawing together], a temporary condition in which muscles may contract and shorten for a considerable period. Drugs, temperature extremes, and local accumulation of lactic acid are possible causes.

physiologic flexion, an excessive amount of flexor tone that is normally present at birth because of the existing level of CNS maturation and fetal positioning in the uterus.

physiologic hypertrophy, a temporary increase in the size of an organ or part caused by normal physiologic functions, such as occurs in the walls of the uterus and in the breasts during pregnancy.

physiologic incompatibility, a condition in which substances, such as drugs, may have mutually antagonistic effects on the body.

physiologic jaundice [Gk, *physis,* nature, *logos,* science; Fr, *jaune,* yellow], a simple jaundice of newborns that involves the breaking down of the excessive number of RBCs that may be present at birth.

physiologic motivation, a body need, such as for food or water, that initiates behavior directed toward satisfying the particular need.

physiologic occlusion, 1. a closure of the teeth that complements and enhances the functions of the masticatory system. 2. a closure of the teeth that produces no pathologic effects on the stomatognathic system, normally dissipating the stresses placed on the teeth and creating a balance between the stresses and the adaptive capacity of the supporting tissues. 3. an acceptable occlusion in a healthy gnathic system.

physiologic psychology, the study of the interrelationship of physiologic and psychologic processes, especially the effects of a change from normal to abnormal.

physiologic retraction ring, a ridge around the inside of the uterus that forms during the second stage of normal labor at the junction of the thinned lower uterine segment and thickened upper segment. It forms as a result of progressive lengthening of the muscle fibers of the lower segment and concomitant shortening of the muscle fibers of the upper segment.

P

physiologic salt solution, a normal saline solution, usually consisting of a sterile 0.9% w/v solution of sodium chloride in distilled water. It is isotonic with normal body fluids.

physiologic tetanus, a state of sustained muscular contraction without periods of relaxation caused by repetitive stimulation of the motor nerve trunk at frequencies so high that individual muscle twitches are fused and cannot be distinguished from one another.

physiologic tremor [Gk, *physis* + *logos;* L, *tremor,* shaking], any shaking or trembling caused by physiologic factors, such as fatigue, fear, or cold.

physiologist /fiz′ē·ol′ə·jist/ [Gk, *physis,* nature, *logos,* science], a person who specializes in the science of living organisms.

physiology /fiz′ē·ol′əjē/ [Gk, *physis* + *logos,* science], **1.** the study of the processes and function of the human body. **2.** the study of the physical and chemical processes involved in the functioning of organisms and their parts.

physiopathologic /fiz′ē·ə·path′əloj′ik/ [Gk, *physis,* nature, *pathos,* disease, *logos,* science], pertaining to the physiologic approach to disease.

physique /fizēk′/, the body structure and development of a person.

physostigmine salicylate, an acetylcholinesterase inhibitor prescribed as a miotic agent for the treatment of glaucoma and administered systemically for treating the toxic effects of excessive cholinergic receptors blockade (e.g., due to atropine poisoning).

phytanic acid storage disease /fītan′ik/, a rare genetic disorder of lipid metabolism in which phytanic acid accumulates in the plasma and tissues. The condition is characterized by ataxia, peripheral neuropathy, retinitis pigmentosa, and abnormalities of the bone and skin.

phytochemical, the active chemical components present in a plant that account for its medicinal properties.

phytogenesis /fī′tōjen′əsis/ [Gk, *phyton,* plant, *genein,* to produce], the origin and evolution of algae and plants.

phytogenous /fītoj′ənəs/ [Gk, *phyton,* plant, *genein,* to produce], **1.** produced by or originating in algae or plants. **2.** pertaining to phytogenesis.

phytohemagglutinin (PHA) /fī′tōhem′ə gloo′tinin/ [Gk, *phyton,* plant, *haima,* blood; L, *agglutinare,* to glue], a hemagglutinin that is derived from a plant, specifically the lectin obtained from the red kidney bean.

phytohemagglutinin test, a test to identify genetic carriers of CF, performed by exposing WBCs to phytohemagglutinin.

A normal reaction involves a noticeable increase in cell protein.

phytonadione, an agent used to promote the production of prothrombin to treat hypoprothrombinemia.

pi /pī/, **1.** Π, π, the sixteenth letter of the Greek alphabet. **2.** in mathematics, the ratio of a circle's circumference to its diameter.

P.I., **1.** in patient records, abbreviation for *present illness.* **2.** abbreviation for *International Pharmacopeia.* **3.** in research, abbreviation for *principal investigator.* **4.** in pharmacology, abbreviation for *package insert.*

pia, abbreviation for **pia mater.**

pia-arachnoid /pī′ə·arak′noid/ [L, *pia,* tender; Gk, *arachne,* spider, *eidos,* form], pertaining to both the pia mater and arachnoid layers of the meninges covering the brain and spinal cord.

piagetian /pī′äzhe′ən/, pertaining to the theories and viewpoints of Piaget.

Piaget, Jean /zhän pē·äzhā′/ [1896–1980], a Swiss psychologist and genetic epistemologist who established the Genevan school of developmental psychology. From his original training in zoology and his early work in testing schoolchildren in the laboratory, Piaget developed a premise that human intelligence is an extension of biologic adaptation. He assumed that human intelligence evolves in a series of stages that are related to age. At each successive stage, intellectual adaptation is more general and shows a higher level of logical organization.

pia mater (pia) /pē′ə mā′tər, pī′ə/ [L, *pia,* tender, *mater,* mother], the innermost of the three meninges covering the brain and the spinal cord. It is closely applied to both structures and carries a rich supply of blood vessels, which nourish the nervous tissue.

pica /pī′kə/ [L, magpie], a craving to eat nonfood substances, such as dirt, clay, chalk, glue, ice, starch, or hair. The appetite disorder may occur with some nutritional deficiency states (particularly iron deficiency), with pregnancy, and in some forms of mental illness.

Pick's disease[1] [Arnold Pick, Czech neurologist, 1851–1924], a form of dementia that may occur in middle age. This disorder mainly affects the frontal and temporal lobes of the brain and characteristically produces slow disintegration of intellect, personality, and emotions and degeneration of cognitive abilities.

Pick's disease[2] [Friedel Pick, Czech physician, 1867–1926], constrictive inflammation of the mediastinum and pericardium, leading to chronic venous congestion and cirrhosis.

pickwickian syndrome /pikwik′ē·ən/ [*The Pickwick Papers* by Charles

Dickens], an abnormal condition characterized by obesity, decreased pulmonary function, somnolence, and polycythemia.

picogram (pg) /pī'kəgram/, a unit of measure equal to one trillionth of a gram, or 10^{-12} gram.

picornavirus /pīkôr'nəvī'rəs/ [It, *pico,* small; *RNA,* ribonucleic acid; L, *virus,* poison], a member of a group of small RNA viruses that are ether-resistant. The two main genera are *Enterovirus* and *Rhinovirus.* These viruses cause poliomyelitis, herpangina, aseptic meningitis, encephalomyocarditis, and foot-and-mouth disease.

picosecond (ps), a unit of measure equal to one trillionth of a second (10^{-12} sec).

picrotoxin /pik'rōtok'sin/ [Gk, *pikros,* bitter; *toxikon,* poison], a CNS stimulant obtained from the seeds of *Anamirta cocculus,* formerly used as an antidote for acute barbiturate poisoning.

PID, abbreviation for **pelvic inflammatory disease.**

PIE, abbreviation for **pulmonary infiltrate with eosinophilia.**

piebald /pī'bôld/ [L, *pica,* magpie; ME, *balled,* smooth], **1.** having patches of white hair or skin caused by an absence of melanocytes in those nonpigmented areas. It is a hereditary condition. **2.** having two colors: black and white or brown and white; mottled.—**piebaldism,** *n.*

Piedmont fracture /pēd'mənt/, an oblique break in the distal radius, with fragments of bone pulled into the ulna.

piedra /pē·ā'drə/, fungal disease of the hair shaft characterized by the presence of small black or white nodules. Black piedra is caused by *Piedria bortae.* White piedra is caused by *Trichosporon beigelii.*

Pierre Robin's syndrome /pyer rob'inz, pyer rōbans'/ [Pierre Robin, French histologist, 1867–1950], a complex of congenital anomalies, including a small mandible, cleft lip, cleft palate, other craniofacial abnormalities, and defects of the eyes and ears, including glaucoma. Intelligence is usually normal.

piezochemistry /pī·ē'zō·kem'istrē/ [Gk, *piezein,* to press, *chemeia* alchemy], a branch of chemistry concerned with reactions that occur under pressure.

piezoelectric activity, the changing of electric surface charges of a structure that force the structure to change shape.

piezoelectric effect /pī'ē·zō·ilek'trik/ [Gk, *piezein,* to press, *elektron* amber; L, *effectus*], **1.** the generation of a voltage across a solid when a mechanical stress is applied. **2.** the dimensional change resulting from the application of a voltage. **3.** in ultrasound, the conversion of one form of energy into another, such as the conversion

of electrical energy into mechanical energy.

pigeon breast /pij'ən/ [L, *pipio,* young bird; AS, *broest,* breast], a congenital structural defect characterized by a prominent anterior projection of the xiphoid and the lower part of the sternum and by a lengthening of the costal cartilages. It may cause cardiorespiratory complications but rarely warrants surgical correction.—**pigeon-breasted,** *adj.*

pigeon breeder's lung, a respiratory disorder caused by acquired hypersensitivity to antigens in bird droppings. It is characterized by chills, fever, and difficult breathing.

piggyback port [AS, *piken,* pick; ME, *pakke,* pack; L, *portus,* haven], a special coupling in the primary IV tubing that allows a supplementary, or piggyback, solution to run into the IV system.

pigment /pig'mənt/ [L, *pigmentum,* paint], **1.** any organic coloring material produced in the body, such as melanin. **2.** any colored, paintlike medicinal preparation applied to the skin surface.—**pigmentary, pigmented,** *adj., pigmentation, n.*

pigmentary retinopathy /pig'məntər ē/, a disorder of the retina characterized by deposits of pigment and increasing loss of vision.

pigmented villonodular synovitis /pig'mən tid/, a disease of the joints characterized by finger-like proliferative growths of synovial tissue, with hemosiderin deposition within the synovial tissue.

pigment layers, the parts of the eye comprising the pigmented strata of the ciliary body, iris, and retina.

pigtail stent, a ureteral stent with a curl near the end like that of a pig's tail to maintain it in place.

pil, abbreviation for the Latin words *pilula,* "pill," and *pilulae,* "pills."

pilar cyst /pī'lər/ [L, *pilus,* hair; Gk, *kystis,* bag], an epidermoid cyst of the scalp. The cyst originates from the middle part of the epithelium of a hair follicle.

Pilates method, a gentle but focused exercise-based system that tones, stretches, and strengthens the body in a non-impact, balanced system of body-mind exercise and mobilizes the body to move with maximum efficiency and minimum effort. This method can achieve an improvement of body alignment and breathing, increased body awareness, and efficient and graceful movement.

pili annulati [L, *pilus,* hair, *annulus,* ring], a condition in which the individual hairs appear to be marked by alternating bands of white as a result of some barrier in the hair that prevents passage of light and causes the rays to be reflected back, giving the appearance of white bands.

piliform /pī'lifôrm/ [L, *pilus,* hair], having the appearance of hair.

pi lines /pī/, radiograph artifacts that result from dirt or chemical stains on a processing roller.

pillion fracture /pil'yən/ [Gael, *pillean,* couch; L, *fractura,* break], a T-shaped break in the distal femur with displacement of the condyles posterior to the femoral shaft, caused by a severe blow to the knee.

pilocarpine and epinephrine /pī'lōkär'pēn/, a fixed-combination drug used in the treatment of glaucoma, containing a cholinergic (pilocarpine hydrochloride) and an adrenergic (epinephrine bitartrate) vasoconstrictor.

pilocarpine and physostigmine, a fixed-combination drug used in the treatment of glaucoma, containing a cholinergic (pilocarpine hydrochloride) and a short-acting cholinesterase inhibitor (physostigmine salicylate). Both ingredients reduce intraocular pressure.

pilocarpine hydrochloride, a cholinergic derived from the leaves of the jaborandi tree and other species of *Pilocarpus.* It is used mainly in a topical ophthalmic preparation as a miotic to contract the pupil in cases of glaucoma. Pilocarpine is administered orally to increase saliva production in patients with xerostomia.

pilomotor reflex /pī'lōmō'tər/ [L, *pilus,* hair, *motor,* mover, *reflectere,* to bend back], erection of the hairs of the skin caused by contraction of small involuntary arrector muscles (arrectores pilorum) in response to a chilly environment, emotional stimulus, or skin irritation.

pilonidal /pī'lənī'dəl/ [L, *pilus,* hair, *nidus,* nest], a growth of hair in a cyst or other internal structure.

pilonidal cyst [L, *pilus + nidus,* nest], a cyst that often develops in the sacral region of the skin. Pilonidal cysts may sometimes be recognized at birth by a depression, sometimes by a hairy dimple in the midline of the back in the sacrococcygeal area.

pilonidal cystectomy, a procedure performed to remove an abscessed pilonidal cyst with sinus tracts.

pilonidal fistula, an abnormal channel containing a tuft of hair, situated most frequently over or close to the tip of the coccyx but also occurring in other regions of the body.

pilonidal sinus [L, *pilus + nidus + sinus,* curve], a cavity or sinus containing hair, in a dermoid cyst or the deepest layers of the skin. In most instances the hair originates in another area and becomes lodged in the sinus.

pilosebaceous /pī'lōsibā'shəs/ [L, *pilus + sebum,* fat], pertaining to a hair follicle and its oil gland.

pilus /pē'ləs/ *pl.* **pili** [L, hair], **1.** a hair or hairlike structure. **2.** in microbiology, a fine filamentous appendage found on certain bacteria and similar to flagellum, except that it is shorter, straighter, and found in greater quantities in the organism.

Pima, a trademark for an expectorant (potassium iodide).

pimozide /pim'əzīd/, an antipsychotic agent from the diphenylbutylpiperidine class. It is prescribed for the suppression of motor and phonic tics associated with Gilles de la Tourette's syndrome.

pimple [ME, *pinple*], a small papule, pustule, or furuncle.

pin [AS, *pinn*], **1.** in orthopedics, to secure and immobilize fragments of bone with a nail. **2.** in dentistry, a small metal rod or peg, used as a support in rebuilding a tooth.

pinch, a compression or squeezing of the end of the thumb in opposition to the end of one or more of the fingers.

pinch graft [Fr, *pince*; Gk, *graphion,* stylus], a small, circular, deep graft of skin only a few millimeters in diameter. It is cut so that the center is of whole skin but the edges consist of only epidermis.

pinch meter, a type of dynamometer that measures the strength of a finger pinch.

pincushion distortion, 1. inward bowing of gridded straight lines in an image as a result of lens distortion. **2.** the image of a square object thus resembling a pincushion or pillow. **3.** a distortion of a fluoroscopic image associated with the use of image intensifier tubes.

pindolol /pin'dəlol/, a beta-adrenergic blocker with intrinsic sympathomimetic activity. It is prescribed in the treatment of hypertension, alone or concomitantly with a diuretic.

pineal /pin'ē-əl/ [L, *pineus,* pine cone], **1.** pertaining to the pineal body. **2.** resembling a pine cone.

pineal body [L, *pineus,* pine cone; AS, *bodig,* body], a cone-shaped structure in the brain, situated between the superior colliculi, the pulvinar, and the splenium of the corpus callosum. Its precise function has not been established.

pinealectomy /pin'ē-əlek'təme/ [L, *pineus*; Gk, *ektomē,* excision], the surgical removal of the pineal body.

pineal hyperplasia syndrome, an abnormal condition caused by overgrowth of the pineal gland. It is characterized by severe insulin resistance, dry skin, thick nails, hirsutism, early dentition, and sexual precocity.

pinealoma /pin′ē·əlō′mə/ *pl.* **pinealomas, pinealomata** [L, *pineas*; Gk, *oma*, tumor], a rare neoplasm of the pineal body in the brain, characterized by hydrocephalus, pupillary changes, gait disturbances, headache, nausea, and vomiting.

pineal peduncle [L, *pineus*, pine cone, *peduncle*, small foot], the stalk of the pineal body.

pineal tumor, a neoplasm of the pineal body.

pine tar [L, *pinus*, pine; AS, *teoru*, tar], a topical antieczematic and a rubefacient. It is a common ingredient in creams, soaps, and lotions used in the treatment of chronic skin conditions, such as eczema or psoriasis.

pinguecula /ping·gwe′kyŌŌ·lə/ *pl.* **pingueculae** [L, somewhat fatty], a yellowish spot of proliferation on the bulbar conjunctiva near the junction of the sclera and cornea, usually on the nasal side, likely related to ultraviolet light exposure and chronic environmental irritation. It is seen in elderly people.

pinhole pupil [ME, *pyn* + *hol*; L, *pupilla*, little girl], a very small pupil, which may be a congenital condition, an effect of the use of miotics, or the result of an inflamed iris.

pinhole retention [ME, *pyn* + *hol*; L, *retinere*, to hold], retention developed by drilling one or more holes, 2 to 3 mm in depth, in suitable areas of a cavity preparation to supplement resistance and retention form.

pinhole test, 1. a test performed on a person who has diminished visual acuity to distinguish a refractive error from organic disease. Several pinholes, 0.5 to 2 mm in diameter, are punched in a card. The patient selects one and looks through it with one eye at a time, without wearing corrective lenses. If visual acuity is improved, the defect is refractive; if not, it is organic. The pinhole effect results from blocking peripheral light waves, which are most distorted by refractive error. **2.** a test to determine the size of the focal spot of an x-ray tube. **3.** a test to trace the path of x-ray movement.

Pin-Indexed Safety System (PISS), 1. a subsection of the American Standard Safety System that applies only to valve outlets of small cylinders and employs a yoke and pin connection. **2.** a system for identifying connectors for certain small cylinders of medical gases that have flush valve outlets rather than threaded outlets.

pinocyte /pī′nəsīt′/ [Gk, *pinein*, to drink, *kytos*, cell], a cell that can absorb liquids by pinocytosis.—**pinocytic,** *adj.*

pinocytosis /pī′nōsītō′sis/ [Gk, *pinein* + *kytos* + *osis*, condition], the process

by which extracellular fluid is taken into a cell. The plasma membrane develops a saccular indentation filled with extracellular fluid and then pinches off the indentation, forming a vesicle or vacuole of fluid within the cell.

pinprick test, a test of a person's ability to detect a cutaneous pain sensation and to differentiate such sensations from pressure stimuli. The test is performed with a pin or needle gently applied to a skin area where it cannot be observed by the subject. The application of the pin is alternated with the pressing of a dull object against the skin.

pinta /pēn′tə/ [Sp, spot], an infection of the skin caused by *Treponema carateum*. The bacterium gains entry into the body through a break in the skin. The primary lesion is a slowly enlarging papule with regional lymph node enlargement, followed in 1 to 12 months by a generalized red to slate-blue macular rash.

pin track infection [ME, *pyn* + *trak,* trace; L, *inficere,* to taint], an abnormal condition associated with skeletal traction or external fixation devices and characterized by infection of superficial, deeper, or soft tissues or by osteomyelitis. These infections may develop at skeletal traction pin sites.

PIO₂, symbol for *partial pressure of inspired oxygen.*

pioglitazone, an oral antidiabetic drug prescribed to treat stable type 2 DM.

pion /pī′on/ [Gk, *pi,* 16th letter of Greek alphabet, *meson,* nuclear particle], any of a family of subatomic particles that can be created in nuclear reactions. Pions are unstable but can exist long enough to be formed into beams and used in certain types of medical therapy, such as the treatment of brain tumors.

pipecuronium /pip′ĕ-ku-ro′ne-um/, a nondepolarizing neuromuscular blocking agent used as an adjunct to anesthesia, inducing skeletal muscle relaxation and facilitating management of patients on mechanical ventilation.

pipestem ureter, stenosis and calcification of a ureter, seen as a complication of renal TB that has spread into the ureter.

pipette /pīpet′, pipet′/ [Fr, little pipe], **1.** a calibrated transparent open-ended tube of glass or plastic used for measuring or transferring small quantities of a liquid or gas. **2.** use of a pipette to dispense liquid.

Pipracil, a trademark for an antibiotic (piperacillin sodium).

piriform /pir′ifôrm/ [L, *pirum,* pear + *forma*], pear-shaped.

piriform aperture [L, *pirum,* pear, *forma,* form, *apertura,* opening], the

P

piriformis /pir′ifôr′mis/ [L, *pirum* + *forma*], a flat pyramidal muscle lying almost parallel with the posterior margin of the gluteus medius. It functions to rotate the thigh laterally and to abduct and help extend it.

Pirogoff's amputation [Nikolai I. Pirogoff, Russian surgeon, 1810–1881], an ankle joint amputation in which the posterior process of the calcaneum is retained at the skin flap and opposed to the cut end of the tibia.

Pirquet's test /pirkäz′/ [Clemens P. von Pirquet, Austrian physician, 1874–1929], a tuberculin skin test that consists of scratching the tuberculin material onto the skin.

pisiform /pī′sifôrm, pē′-/ [L, *pisum*, pea + *forma*], pea-shaped.

pisiform bone [L, *pisa*, pea, *forma*, form; AS, *ban*, bone], a small pea-shaped spheroidal carpal bone in the proximal row of carpal bones.

Piskacek's sign /pis′kəcheks/ [Ludwig Piskacek, Austrian obstetrician, 1854–1933], asymmetric enlargement of the body of the pregnant uterus as a result of its enlargement in the cornual region, usually over the site of implantation.

pisohamate ligament, the ligament that connects the pisiform bone to the hamate. It is an extension of the flexor carpi ulnaris.

pisometacarpal ligament, the ligament that connects the pisiform bone to the fifth metacarpal.

PISS, abbreviation for **Pin-Index Safety System.**

pistol-shot sound, a sharp slapping sound heard by auscultation over the femoral pulse of a patient with aortic incompetence. It is caused by a large-volume pulse with a sharp rise in pressure.

pit and fissure cavity [AS, *pytt*; L, *fissura*, cleft, *cavum*, cavity], a cavity or area of decay that starts in a tiny groove or fault in tooth enamel, usually on an occlusal surface of a molar or premolar.

pitch [ME, *picchen*], **1.** the highness or lowness of a tone or sound depending on the rate of vibration of the sound source. **2.** in helical CT, the ratio of table advancement per 360-degree rotation of the x-ray tube to the detector collimator.

pithing /pith′ing/ [AS, *pitha*], the destruction of the CNS of an experimental animal in preparation for physiologic research. It is usually done by inserting a blunt probe through a foramen.

Pitocin, a trademark for an oxytocic (oxytocin).

Pitressin, a trademark for an antidiuretic hormone (vasopressin).

pitting [AS, *pytt*], **1.** small, punctate indentations in fingernails or toenails, often a result of psoriasis. **2.** an indentation that remains for a short time after pressing edematous skin with a finger. **3.** small depressed scars in the skin or other organ of the body. **4.** the removal by the spleen of material from within erythrocytes without damage to the cells.

pitting edema [AS, *pytt*; Gk, *oidema*, swelling], an edema characterized by a condition in which a finger pressed into the skin over an accumulation of fluid will result in a temporary depression in the skin. Normal skin and subcutaneous tissues quickly rebound when the pressure is released.

pituicyte /pit(y)ōō′isīt/ [L, *pituita*, phlegm; Gk, *kytos*, cell], a primary cell of the posterior lobe of the pituitary gland.

pituitarism /pit(y)ōō′itəriz′əm/ [L, *pituita*, phlegm], any condition caused by a defect or failure of the pituitary gland.

pituitary /pit(y)ōō′iter′ē/, pertaining to the pituitary gland.

pituitary dwarf [L, *pituita*, phlegm; AS, *dweorge*], a dwarf whose retarded development is caused by a deficiency of growth hormone resulting from hypofunction of the anterior lobe of the pituitary. The body is properly proportioned, with no facial or skeletal deformities, and mental and sexual development is normal.

pituitary eunuchism, a form of failure of sexual development and impotence resulting from disease or dysfunction of the pituitary gland.

pituitary gland [L, *pituita*, phlegm], an endocrine gland suspended beneath the brain in the pituitary fossa of the sphenoid bone, supplying numerous hormones that govern many vital processes. The anterior lobe of the gland is composed of polygonal cells related to the production of seven hormones: growth hormone, prolactin, TSH, follicle-stimulating hormone, luteinizing hormone, adrenocorticotropic hormone, and melanocyte-stimulating hormone. The posterior lobe is morphologically an extension of the hypothalamus and the source of antidiuretic hormone and oxytocin.

pituitary myxedema [L, *pituita*; Gk, *myxa*, mucus, *oidema*, swelling], a type of hypothyroid condition secondary to an anterior pituitary disease.

pituitary nanism, a type of dwarfism associated with hypophyseal infantilism.

pituitary snuff lung, a type of hypersensitivity pneumonitis that sometimes occurs among users of pituitary snuff. Symptoms of the acute form of the disease include chills, cough, fever, dyspnea, anorexia, nausea, and vomiting. The chronic form of the disease is characterized by fatigue, chronic cough, weight loss, and dyspnea on exercise.

pituitary stalk, a structure that connects the pituitary gland with the hypothalamus.

pit viper [AS, *pytt*; L, *vipera,* snake], any one of a family of venomous snakes found in the Western Hemisphere and Asia, characterized by a heat-sensitive pit between the eye and nostril on each side of the head and hollow perforated fangs that are usually folded back in the roof of the mouth. With the exception of coral snakes, all indigenous poisonous snakes in the United States are pit vipers.

pityriasis /pitərī′əsis/ [Gk, *pityron,* bran], any of a number of skin diseases that have in common lesions that resemble dandruff-like scales without obvious signs of inflammation.

pityriasis alba [Gk, *pityron,* bran; L, *albus,* white], a common idiopathic dermatosis characterized by round or oval finely scaling patches of hypopigmentation, usually on the cheeks. The lesions are sharply demarcated and occasionally pruritic and are found primarily in children and adolescents. The condition may recur, but spontaneous clearing is the usual prognosis.

pityriasis lichenoides, a rare, self-limited skin disease with discolored papular lesions, encompassing a spectrum from pityriasis lichenoides et varioliformis acuta to pityriasis lichenoides chronica.

pityriasis rosea, a self-limited skin disease in which a slightly scaling pink macular rash spreads over the trunk and other unexposed areas of the body. A characteristic feature is the herald patch, a larger, more scaly lesion that precedes the diffuse rash by several days. Mild itching is the only symptom. The disease lasts 4 to 8 weeks and rarely recurs.

pityriasis rubra pilaris [Gk, *pityron,* bran; L, *ruber,* red, *pilus,* hair], a chronic inflammatory cutaneous disease characterized by tiny acuminate, reddish brown follicular papules topped by central horny plugs in which are embedded hairs; disseminated yellowish pink scaling patches; and often solid confluent hyperkeratosis of the palms and soles with a tendency to fissuring.

pivot joint /piv′ət/ [Fr, hinge; L, *jungere,* to join], a synovial joint in which movement is limited to rotation. The joint is formed by a pivot-like process that may turn within a ring composed partly of bone and partly of ligament.

pivot transfer, the movement of a person from one site to another, such as from a bed to a wheelchair, when there is a loss of control of one side of the body or when one side of the body is immobile. The person is helped to a position on the strong side of the body with both feet on the floor, heels behind the knees, and knees lower than the hips. The person stands with the weight on the strong leg, pivots on it, and carefully lowers the body into the wheelchair.

PJC, abbreviation for *premature junctional complex.*

PK, abbreviation for **psychokinesis.**

pK$_a$, the negative logarithm of the ionization constant of an acid, a measure of the strength of an acid. The lower the pK$_a$, the stronger the acid.

PKA, abbreviation for **protein kinase.**

PKD, abbreviation for **polycystic kidney disease.**

PK test, abbreviation for **Prausnitz-Küstner test.**

PKU, abbreviation for **phenylketonuria.**

placebo /pləsē′bō/ [L, shall please], an inactive substance, such as saline solution, distilled water, or sugar, or a less than effective dose of a harmless substance, such as a water-soluble vitamin, prescribed as if it were an effective dose of a needed medication. Placebos are used in experimental drug studies to compare the effects of the inactive substance with those of the experimental drug. They are also prescribed for patients who cannot be given the medication they request or who, in the judgment of the health care provider, do not need that medication.

placebo effect, a physical or emotional change occurring after a substance is taken or administered that is not the result of any special property of the substance. The change may reflect the expectations of the patient.

placement /plās′mənt/ [Fr, *placer,* to place], the positioning of a dental prosthesis, such as a removable denture in its planned site on the dental arch.

placement path, the direction of insertion and removal of a removable partial denture on its supporting oral structures.

placenta /pləsen′tə/ [L, flat cake], a highly vascular fetal organ that exchanges with the maternal circulation, mainly by diffusion of oxygen, carbon dioxide, and other substances. It begins to form on approximately the eighth day of gestation when the blastocyst touches the wall of the uterus and adheres to it. At term the normal placenta is one-seventh to one-fifth of the weight of the infant. The maternal surface is lobulated and has a dark red rough, liver-like appearance. The fetal surface is smooth and shiny, covered with the fetal membranes, and marked by the large white blood vessels beneath the membranes that fan out from the centrally inserted umbilical cord. The time between the infant's birth and the expulsion of the placenta is the third and last stage of labor.

P

placenta accreta, a placenta that invades the uterine muscle, making separation from the muscle difficult.

placental /pləsen'təl/ [L, *placenta,* flat cake], pertaining to the placenta.

placental bruit [L, *placenta,* flat cake; Fr, *bruit,* noise], a humming noise caused by fetal circulation, heard in the pregnant uterus. It is synchronized with the mother's pulse.

placental dystocia, a prolonged or otherwise difficult delivery of the placenta.

placental hormone, one of the hormones produced by the placenta, which include human placental lactogen, chorionic gonadotropin, estrogen, progesterone, and a thyrotropin-like hormone.

placental infarct, a localized ischemic hard area on the fetal or maternal side of the placenta.

placental insufficiency, an abnormal condition of pregnancy, manifested clinically by a retarded rate of fetal and uterine growth. Some of the abnormalities that can result in placental insufficiency are abnormal implantation of the placenta, multiple pregnancy, abnormal attachments of the umbilical cord or anomalies of the cord itself, and abnormalities of the placental membranes.

placental membrane, a layer of tissue in the placenta between the fetal and maternal blood systems. The membrane regulates the diffusion of materials between the two systems.

placental scan, a scan of the uterus of a pregnant woman, performed after an IV injection of a contrast medium, used for locating the fetus and placenta and for detecting intrauterine bleeding.

placental stage of labor, the third stage of labor, when the placenta and membranes are expelled from the uterus after the birth of the child.

placental thrombosis [L, *placenta,* flat cake; Gk, *thrombos,* lump, *osis,* condition], intravascular coagulation that occurs in the placenta and veins of the uterus.

placental transmission [L, *placenta,* flat cake; L, *transmittere,* to transmit], the transference of a drug or other substance across the placenta.

placenta praevia /prē'vē·ə/, a condition of pregnancy in which the placenta is implanted abnormally in the uterus so that it impinges on or covers the internal os of the uterine cervix. It is the most common cause of painless bleeding in the third trimester of pregnancy. Even slight dilation of the internal os can cause enough local separation of an abnormally implanted placenta to result in bleeding. If severe hemorrhage occurs, immediate cesarean section is usually required to stop the bleeding and to save the mother's life; it is performed regardless of the stage of fetal maturity.

placenta praevia partialis, a placenta that partially obstructs the internal cervical os.

placenta souffle [L, *placenta,* flat cake; Fr, *souffle,* puff], a soft blowing or humming sound produced by fetal circulation at the placenta.

placenta succenturiate, an accessory placenta.

plafon fracture, a fracture that involves the buttress part of the malleolus of a bone.

plagiocephaly /plā'jē-ōsef'əlē/ [Gk, *plagios,* askew, *kephale,* head], a congenital malformation of the skull in which premature or irregular closure of the coronal or lambdoidal sutures results in asymmetric growth of the head, giving it a twisted, lopsided appearance.—**plagiocephalic, plagiocephalous,** *adj.*

plague /plāg/ [L, *plaga,* blow], an infectious disease transmitted by the bite of a flea from a rodent infected with the bacillus *Yersinia pestis.* Plague is primarily an infectious disease of rats. The rat fleas feed on humans only when their preferred rodent hosts, usually rats, have been killed by the plague in a rat epizootic. Therefore epidemics occur after rat epizootics.

plague vaccine, an active immunizing agent prepared with killed plague bacilli. It is prescribed for immunization against plague after probable exposure or as protection for travelers in endemic areas, such as Southeast Asia.

plaintiff /plān'tif/ [ME, *plaintif,* one who complains], in law, a person who files a lawsuit initiating a legal action.

planar view, a two-dimensional view of a process or function.

planar xanthoma /plā'nər/ [L, *planum,* level; Gk, *xanthos,* yellow, *oma,* tumor], a yellow or orange flat macule or slightly raised papule containing foam cells and occurring in clusters in localized areas, such as the eyelids. These lesions may be widely distributed over the body.

Planck's constant (h) /plangks/ [Max Planck, German physicist, 1858–1947], a fundamental physical constant that relates the energy of radiation to its frequency. It is expressed as 6.63×10^{-27} erg-seconds or 6.63×10^{-34} joule-seconds.

plane [L, *planum,* level], **1.** a flat surface determined by three points in space. **2.** an extension of a longitudinal section through an axis, such as the coronal, horizontal, transverse, frontal, and sagittal planes, used to identify the position of various parts of the body in the study of anatomy. **3.** the act of paring or rubbing away. **4.** a superficial incision in the wall of a cavity or between tissue layers, especially in plastic surgery.—**planar,** *adj.*

planigraphic principle /plan'igraf'ik/, a rule of tomography in which the fulcrum or axis of rotation is raised or lowered to alter the level of the focal plane, but the tabletop height remains constant.

plankton /plangk'tən/ [Gk, *planktos*, wandering], nearly microscopic floating or weakly swimming organisms (both photosynthetic and nonphotosynthetic) found in lakes and oceans that provide the initial level in the food chain for aquatic animals.

planned change, an alteration of the status quo by means of a carefully formulated program that follows four steps: unfreezing the present level, establishing a change relationship, moving to a new level, and freezing at the new level.

planned parenthood, a philosophic framework central to the development of contraceptive methods, contraceptive counseling, and family planning programs and clinics. Advocates hold that it is the right of each woman to decide when to conceive and bear children and that contraceptive and gynecologic care and information should be available to her to help her become or prevent becoming pregnant.

planning [L, *planum*], in five-step nursing process, a category of nursing behavior in which a strategy is designed to achieve the goals of care for an individual patient, as established in assessing and analyzing. Planning includes developing and modifying a care plan for the patient, cooperating with other personnel, and recording relevant information.

planoconcave lens, a lens with one plane and one concave side.

planoconvex lens, a lens with one plane and one convex side.

plant /plant/, any multicellular eukaryotic organism that performs photosynthesis to obtain its nutrition. Plants comprise one of the five kingdoms in the most widely used classification of living organisms.

plantago seed /plantä'gō/, a bulk-forming laxative derived from *Plantago psyllium* seeds, prescribed in the treatment of constipation and nonspecific diarrhea.

plantar /plan'tər/ [L, *planta*, sole], pertaining to the sole of the foot.

plantar aponeurosis, the tough fascia surrounding the muscles of the soles of the feet.

plantar arch [L, *planta*, sole, *arcus*, bow], the hollow on the sole of the foot.

plantar calcaneocuboid joint, a synovial joint between the facet on the anterior surface of the calcaneus and the corresponding facet on the posterior surface of the cuboid that allow sliding and rotating movements involved with inversion and eversion of the foot. It also contributes to pronation and supination of the forefoot on the hindfoot.

plantar calcaneonavicular ligament, a broad, thick ligament of the foot that spans the space between the sustentaculum tali and the navicular bones, supports the head of the talus, and resists depression of the medial arch of the foot.

plantar flexion [L, *planta*, sole, *flectere*, to bend], a toe-down motion of the foot at the ankle. It is measured in degrees from the 0-degree position of the foot at rest on the ground with the body in a standing position.

plantar grasp reflex, a reflex characterized by the flexion of the toes when the sole of the foot is stroked gently. It is present in babies at birth but should disappear after 6 weeks.

plantaris / planter'is, plantä'ris/ [L, *planta*], one of three superficial muscles at the back of the leg, between the soleus and the gastrocnemius. It plantarflexes the foot and the leg.

plantar neuroma, a tumor or growth of nerve cells and nerve fibers on the sole of the foot.

plantar reflex, the normal response, elicited by firmly stroking the outer surface of the sole from heel to toes, characterized by flexion of the toes.

plantar wart, a painful verrucous lesion on the sole of the foot, primarily at points of pressure, such as over the metatarsal heads and the heel. Caused by the common wart virus, it appears as a soft central core and is surrounded by a firm hyperkeratotic ring resembling a callus.

plantigrade /plan'tigräd/ [L, *planta*, sole, *gradi*, to walk], **1.** pertaining to or characterizing the human gait; walking on the sole of the foot with the heel touching the ground. **2.** a position in which an individual is standing flexed at the hips and bearing some weight through the upper extremities.

plant toxin [ME, *plante*; Gk, *toxikon*, poison], any poisonous substance derived from a plant, such as ricin, which is produced by castor-oil seeds.

plaque /plak/ [Fr, plate], **1.** a flat, often raised patch on the skin or any other organ of the body. **2.** a patch of atherosclerosis. **3.** a usually thin film on the teeth. It is made up of mucin and colloidal material found in saliva and often secondarily invaded by bacteria.

Plaquenil Sulfate, a trademark for an antimalarial, antiarthritic, and lupus erythematosus suppressant agent (hydroxychloroquine sulfate).

plasma /plaz'mə/ [Gk, something formed], the watery straw-colored fluid part of the

P

lymph and the blood in which the leukocytes, erythrocytes, and platelets are suspended. Plasma is made up of water, electrolytes, proteins, glucose, fats, bilirubin, and gases and is essential for carrying the cellular elements of the blood through the circulation, transporting nutrients, maintaining the acid-base balance of the body, and transporting wastes from the tissues.

plasma cell, a lymphoid or lymphocyte-like cell found in the bone marrow, connective tissue, and sometimes the blood. Plasma cells are involved in the immunologic mechanism.

plasma cell leukemia, an unusual neoplasm of blood-forming tissues in which the predominant cells are plasmacytes. The disease may develop with multiple myeloma or arise independently.

plasma cell tumor, a plasma cell dyscrasia.

plasmacytoma /plaz′məsītō′mə/ *pl.* **plasmacytomas, plasmacytomata,** a focal neoplasm containing plasma cells that may develop in the bone marrow, as in multiple myeloma, or outside the bone marrow, as in tumors of the viscera and the mucosa of the nasal, oral, and pharyngeal areas.

plasma exchange [Gk, *plassein,* to mold; L, *ex* + *cambire,* to change; Gk, *therapeia,* treatment], a method of treating certain diseases by removing a part of the patient's plasma and replacing it with albumin, plasma, or other fluids.

plasma expander, a substance, usually a high-molecular-weight dextran, that is administered intravenously to increase the oncotic pressure of a patient.

plasma membrane, the outer covering of a cell, often having projecting microvilli and containing the cellular cytoplasm. The plasma membrane is so thin and delicate that it is barely visible with a light microscope. The membrane controls the exchange of materials between the cell and its environment by various processes, such as osmosis, phagocytosis, pinocytosis, and secretion.

plasmapheresis /plaz′məfərē′sis/, the removal of plasma from previously withdrawn blood by centrifugation, reconstitution of the cellular elements in an isotonic solution, and reinfusion of this solution into the donor or another client who needs RBCs rather than whole blood.

plasma protein, any of the proteins, including albumin, fibrinogen, prothrombin, and the gamma globulins. These substances help maintain water balance that affects osmotic pressure, increase blood viscosity, and help maintain blood pressure.

plasma refilling rate, in hemodialysis, the rate at which plasma that has been

withdrawn and dialyzed flows back into the patient's circulatory system.

plasma renin activity, the action of the enzyme renin (produced by the kidney), measured in plasma to aid in the diagnosis of adrenal disease associated with hypertension.

plasma renin assay (PRA), a blood test that measures the rate of generation of angiotensin. The most commonly used renin assay, it is a screening procedure for detecting essential, renal, or renovascular hypertension, and it is also performed to diagnose and separate primary from secondary hyperaldosteronism.

plasma volume, the total volume of plasma in the body, elevated in diseases of the liver and spleen and in vitamin C deficiency and lowered in Addison's disease, dehydration, and shock.

plasma volume extender [Gk, *plassein;* L, *volumen,* paper roll, *extendere,* to stretch], an IV solution of dextran, proteins, or other substances used to treat shock caused by blood volume loss.

plasmid /plaz′mid/ [Gk, *plasma,* something formed], in a bacterium, a small, circular molecule of DNA that is separate from the bacterial chromosome. Plasmids often carry genes that affect the ability of bacteria to respond to environmental challenges. Plasmids may be passed from one bacterium to another and are replicated in later generations of any bacterium carrying them. Molecular geneticists often use plasmids to insert specific genes into the chromosomes of bacteria and other organisms.

plasminogen activator, the enzyme that converts plasminogen to plasmin.

plasminogen activator inhibitor 1 (PAI-1) test, a blood test to determine the level of PAI-1. Increased levels are indicative of acute coronary syndrome, coronary artery disease, restenosis after coronary angioplasty, infection, inflammation, trauma, type 1 diabetes, insulin resistance syndrome, or pregnancy. Decreased levels are indicative of bleeding disorders.

plasminogen test, a blood test used to diagnose suspected plasminogen deficiency in patients who present with multiple thromboembolic episodes. Abnormal levels of plasminogen are also characteristic of disseminated intravascular coagulation, primary fibrinolysis, cirrhosis and other severe liver diseases, pregnancy, eclampsia, and some inflammatory conditions.

Plasmodium /plazmō′dē-əm/ *pl.* **plasmodia** [Gk, *plasma* + *eidos,* form], a genus of protozoa, several species of which cause malaria, transmitted to humans by the bite of an infected *Anopheles* mosquito.

plasmosome /plaz′məsōm/ [Gk, *plasma* + *soma,* body], the true nucleolus of a cell as distinguished from the karyosomes in the nucleus.

plaster [Gk, *emplastron*], **1.** any composition of a liquid and a powder that hardens when it dries, used in shaping a cast to support a fractured bone as it heals. **2.** a home remedy consisting of a semisolid mixture applied to a part of the body as a counterirritant or for other therapeutic reasons, such as a mustard plaster.

plaster cast [Gk, *emplastron,* plaster; ONorse, *kasta*], a traditional cast used to encase and immobilize a part of the body, made from a gauze roll impregnated with plaster of paris. The gauze is dipped in warm water and wrapped around the body part.

plaster of paris [Gk, *emplastron,* plaster; Paris, France], a white powder, calcium sulfate hemihydrate, which is mixed with water to make a paste that can be molded to encase a body part.

plastic /plas′tik/ [Gk, *plastikos*], **1.** tending to build up tissues or to restore a lost part. **2.** conformable; capable of being molded. **3.** a high-molecular-weight polymeric material, usually organic, capable of being molded, extruded, drawn, or otherwise shaped and then hardened into a form. **4.** material that can be molded.

plasticity /plastis′itē/ [Gk, *plassein,* to mold], the quality of being plastic or formative.

plastic surgery [Gk, *plassein,* to mold, *cheirourgia,* surgery], surgery to heal, reconstruct, restore function, and correct disfigurement or scarring resulting from trauma or acquired or congenital lesions or defects.

plate [Fr, *plat,* flat dish], **1.** a flat structure or layer, such as a thin layer of bone or the frontal plate between the sides of the ethmoid cartilage and the sphenoid bone in the fetus. **2.** a single partitioning unit of a chromatographic system.

platelet aggregation, platelet cohesion, mediated by glycoprotein membrane receptors and fibrinogen, part of a sequential mechanism leading to the initiation and formation of a thrombus or hemostatic plug.

platelet aggregation test, a blood test that can detect diseases that affect either platelet number or function, thereby prolonging bleeding time. This test can provide information about prolonged platelet aggregation times, connective tissue disorders, such as lupus erythematosus, recent cardiopulmonary or dialysis bypass, various myeloproliferative diseases, primary protein disease, von Willebrand's disease, uremia, and congenital disorders such as Wiskott-Aldrich syndrome, Bernard-Soulier syndrome, and glycogen storage disorders.

platelet antibody detection test, a blood test used to detect immune-mediated destruction of platelets. Such destruction can cause paroxysmal hemoglobinuria as well as immunologic thrombocytopenia.

platelet count, a blood test that is performed on all patients who develop petechiae, spontaneous bleeding, or increasingly heavy menses. It is also used to monitor the course of the disease or therapy for thrombocytopenia or bone marrow failure.

plateletpheresis /plat′litfer′əsis/ [Fr, *platelet*; Gk, *aphairesis,* to carry away], collection of platelets from a donor using the apheresis technique.

platelets /plat′lits/ [Fr, small plate], the smallest cells in the blood. They are formed in the red bone marrow, and some are stored in the spleen. Platelets are disk-shaped, contain no hemoglobin, and are essential for the coagulation of blood and in maintenance of hemostasis.

platinized gold foil /plat′inīzd/ [Sp, *plata,* silver; AS, *geolu,* gold; L, *folium,* leaf], a thin sheet of platinum sandwiched between two sheets of gold, used for making parts of dental restorations requiring greater hardness than that obtained with other materials, such as copper amalgam.

Platinol, a trademark for an antineoplastic (cisplatin).

platinum (Pt) /plat′ənəm/ [Sp, *plata,* silver], a silver-white soft metallic element. Its atomic number is 78; its atomic mass is 195.09. Platinum is used in dentistry and is a good catalyst for a variety of chemical reactions.

platinum foil, a very thin sheet of pure platinum that has a high fusing point, making it an ideal matrix in various soldering procedures for fabricating orthodontic appliances and dentures.

Platyhelminthes /plat′ihelmin′thēz/ [Gk, *platys,* broad, *helmins,* worm], a phylum of flatworms that includes parasitic tapeworms (class Cestoda) and flukes (classes Monogenea and Trematoda), as well as mostly free-living species, such as planarians (class Turbellaria).

platypelloid pelvis /plat′əpel′oid/ [Gk, *platys,* broad, *pella,* bowl, *eidos,* form; L, *pelvis,* basin], a rare type of pelvis in which the inlet is round like the gynecoid type in the anterior section, but the posterior section is foreshortened by its flat and heavy border. The sacrum is hollow and inclines posteriorly, and the sidewalls are convergent. In the midplane the transverse diameter is much wider than the narrowed anteroposterior diameter. Vaginal delivery is not usually possible in the 3% of women who have platypelloid pelves.

P

platysma /plətiz'mə/ [Gk, *platys*, broad], one of a pair of platelike, wide muscles at the side of the neck. The platysma serves to draw down the lower lip and the corner of the mouth.

play [AS, *plegan*, sport], any spontaneous or organized activity that provides enjoyment, entertainment, amusement, or diversion. It is essential in childhood for the development of a normal personality and as a means for physical, intellectual, and social development. Play provides an outlet for releasing tension and stress, as well as a means for testing and experimenting with new or fearful roles or situations.

play participation, a nursing outcome from the Nursing Outcomes Classification (NOC) defined as the use of activities by a child from 1 year through 11 years of age to promote enjoyment, entertainment, and development.

play therapy, a form of psychotherapy in which a child plays in a protected and structured environment with games and toys provided by a therapist, who observes the behavior, affect, and conversation of the child to gain insight into thoughts, feelings, and fantasies.

pleasure principle /plezh'ər/ [Fr, *plaisir*, pleasure; L, *principium*], in psychoanalysis, the need for immediate gratification of instinctual drives.

pledget /plej'ət/, a small flat compress made of cotton gauze, or a tuft of cotton wool, lint, or a similar synthetic material, used to wipe the skin, absorb drainage, or clean a small surface.

Plegine, a trademark for an anorexiant (phendimetrazine tartrate).

pleiotropic gene /plī'ətrop'ik/, a gene that produces many effects in the phenotype.

pleiotropy /plī·ot'rəpē/ [Gk, *pleion*, more, *trepein*, to turn], the production by a single gene of a complex of unrelated phenotypic effects. The effects may be a manifestation of a particular disorder, such as the cluster of symptoms in Marfan's syndrome, aortic aneurysm, dislocation of the optic lens, skeletal deformities, and arachnodactyly, any or all of which may be present.—**pleiotropic,** *adj.*

Plenaxis, a trademark for abarelix.

pleocytosis /plē'ōsītō'sis/, presence of a greater than normal number of cells in the CSF.

plerocercoid /plir'ōsur'koid/, the second larval stage of the cestode *Diphyllobothrium latum*. It develops in the second intermediate host, a freshwater fish, and is infective to humans if ingested.

plethora /pleth'ərə/ [Gk, *plethore*, fullness], a term applied to the beefy red coloration of a newborn. The "boiled lobster" hue of the infant's skin is caused by an unusually high proportion of erythrocytes per volume of blood.—**plethoric,** *adj.*

plethysmogram /pləthiz'məgram/ [Gk, *plethynein*, to increase, *gramma*, to record], a tracing produced by a plethysmograph.

plethysmograph /pləthiz'məgraf/, an instrument for measuring and recording changes in the size and volume of extremities and organs by measuring changes in their blood volume.—**plethysmographic,** *adj.*

plethysmography /pleth'izmog'rəfē/ [Gk, *plethynein*, to increase, *graphein*, to record], the measurement of changes in the volume of organs or other body parts, particularly those changes resulting from blood flow.

pleura /plŏŏr'ə/ *pl.* **pleurae** [Gk, rib], a delicate serous membrane enclosing the lung, composed of a single layer of flattened mesothelial cells resting on a delicate membrane of connective tissue. The pleura divides into the visceral pleura, which covers the lung, dipping into the fissures between the lobes, and the parietal pleura, which lines the chest wall, covers the diaphragm, and reflects over the structures in the mediastinum.—**pleural,** *adj.*

pleural biopsy, the removal of pleural tissue for histologic examination after exudative fluid indicative of infection, neoplasm, or TB is obtained by thoracentesis or when a pleural-based tumor, reaction, or thickening is indicated by a chest x-ray.

pleural cavity [Gk, *pleura*, rib; L, *cavum*, cavity], the space within the thorax that contains the lungs.

pleural effusion, an abnormal accumulation of fluid in the intrapleural spaces of the lungs. It is characterized by chest pain, dyspnea, adventitious lung sounds, and nonproductive cough.

pleural space, the potential space between the visceral and parietal layers of the pleurae. The space contains a small amount of fluid that acts as a lubricant, allowing the pleurae to slide smoothly over each other as the lungs expand and contract with respiration.

pleurisy /plŏŏr'əsē/ [Gk, *pleura* + *itis*, inflammation], inflammation of the parietal pleura of the lungs. It is characterized by dyspnea and stabbing pain, leading to restriction of ordinary breathing with spasm of the chest on the affected side. A pleural friction rub may be heard on auscultation. Common causes include bronchial carcinoma, lung or chest wall abscess, pneumonia, pulmonary infarction, and TB. The condition may result in permanent adhesions between the pleura and adjacent surfaces.—**pleuritic,** *adj.*

pleurisy with effusion [Gk, *pleura* + *itis,* inflammation; L, *effundere,* to pour out], pleurisy in which there is an accumulation of fluid in the intrapleural space.

pleurodynia /plŏŏr′ōdin′ē·ə/ [Gk, *pleura* + *odyne,* pain], acute inflammation of the intercostal muscles and the muscular attachment of the diaphragm to the chest wall. It is characterized by sudden, severe pain and tenderness, fever, headache, and anorexia. These symptoms are aggravated by movement and breathing.

pleuropericardial folds, a pair of small ridges that originate along the lateral body walls in the fifth week of embryonic development and project into the cranial ends of the pericardioperitoneal canals to divide the pleural cavities from the pericardial cavity. They later develop into the pleuropericardial membranes.

pleuropericardial rub /-per′ikär′dē·əl/ [Gk, *pleura* + *peri,* around, *kardia,* heart; ME, *rubben,* to scrape], an abnormal coarse, grating sound heard on auscultation of the lungs during late inspiration and early expiration. It occurs when the visceral and parietal pleural surfaces rub against each other. A pleuropericardial rub indicates primary inflammatory, neoplastic, or traumatic pleural disease, or inflammation secondary to infection or neoplasm.

pleuroperitoneal hiatus, a posterolateral opening in the fetal diaphragm. Its failure to close leaves a congenital posterolateral defect that may become a site for a congenital diaphragmatic hernia.

pleuropneumonia /plŏŏr′ōnŏŏmō′nē·ə/ [Gk, *pleura* + *pneumon,* lung], **1.** a combination of pleurisy and pneumonia. **2.** an infection of cattle resulting in inflammation of both the pleura and lungs, caused by microorganisms of the *Mycoplasma* group.

pleuropneumonia-like organism (PPLO), a group of filterable organisms of the genus *Mycoplasma* similar to *M. mycoides,* the cause of pleuropneumonia in cattle.

pleurothotonos /plŏŏr′əthot′ənəs/ [Gk, *pleurothen,* side of the body, *tonos,* tension], an involuntary severe prolonged contraction of the muscles of one side of the body, resulting in an acute arch to that side. It is usually associated with tetanus infection or strychnine poisoning.—**pleurothotonic,** *adj.*

plexiform neuroma /plek′sifôrm/ [L, *plexus,* braided, *forma,* form; Gk, *neuron,* nerve, *oma,* tumor], a neoplasm composed of twisted bundles of nerves.

pleximeter /pleksim′ətər/ [Gk, *plessein,* to strike, *metron,* measure], a mediating device, such as a percussor or finger, used to receive light taps in percussion.

plexus /plek′səs/ *pl.* **plexuses** [L, braided], a network of intersecting nerves and blood vessels or of lymphatic vessels.

plica /plī′kə/ *pl.* **plicae** [L, plicare, to fold], a fold of tissue within the body, such as the plicae transversales of the rectum.—**plical,** *adj.*

plicamycin /plī′kəmī′sin/, an antineoplastic agent prescribed primarily in the treatment of malignant tumors of the testis. It is also prescribed in the treatment of hypercalcemia and hypercalciuria associated with cancer.

plication /plīkā′shən/, any operation that involves folding, shortening, or decreasing the size of a muscle or hollow organ by taking in tucks.

plication of stomach [L, *plicare,* to fold; Gk, *stomakhos,* gullet], a surgical treatment for obesity in which tucks are created in the wall of the stomach.

pliers /plī′ərz/, small tong-jawed pincers for bending metals or holding small objects. Various forms are often used in dentistry.

Plimmer's bodies [Henry G. Plimmer, English biologist, 1857–1918], small round encapsulated bodies found in cancers and once thought to be the causative parasites.

ploidy /ploi′dē/ [Gk, *eidos,* form], the status of a cell nucleus in regard to the number of complete chromosome sets it contains.

plug [D, *plugge,* stopper], a mass of tissue cells, mucus, or other matter that blocks a normal opening or passage of the body, such as a cervical plug.

plugger, an instrument for condensing or consolidating a filling material, such as a dental amalgam into a tooth restoration.

plumbism /plum′izəm/ [L, *plumbum,* lead], a chronic form of lead poisoning caused by absorption of lead or lead salts.

Plummer's disease [Henry S. Plummer, American physician, 1874–1937], goiter characterized by a hyperfunctioning nodule or adenoma and thyrotoxicosis.

Plummer-Vinson syndrome /plum′ər vin′sən/ [Henry S. Plummer; Porter P. Vinson, American physician; 1890–1959], a rare disorder associated with severe and chronic iron deficiency anemia, characterized by glossitis, koilonychia, and dysphagia caused by esophageal webs at the level of the cricoid cartilage.

pluripara /plŏŏrip′ərə/ [L, *plus,* more, *parere,* to bear], a woman who has borne three or more children.

plutonium (Pu) /plŏŏtō′nē·əm/ [planet *Pluto*], a synthetic transuranic metallic element. Its atomic number is 94, and the atomic mass of its longest-lived isotope is

P

242. A highly toxic, heavy metal, plutonium is used in nuclear power plants, and was used in the assembly of early nuclear weapons.

plyometrics, bounding or high-velocity exercise that entails eccentric and rapid concentric contractions, such as jumping or weighted ball throwing and catching.

pm, abbreviation for *picometer.*

Pm, symbol for the element **promethium.**

P.M.D., abbreviation for *private medical doctor.*

PMDD, abbreviation for **premenstrual dysphoric disorder.**

pmh, abbreviation for *past medical history.*

PMI, abbreviation for **point of maximum impulse.**

PMN, abbreviation for **polymorphonuclear.**

PMS, pms, abbreviation for **premenstrual syndrome.**

PMT, abbreviation for *premenstrual tension.*

PND, 1. abbreviation for **paroxysmal nocturnal dyspnea. 2.** abbreviation for **postnasal drip.**

pneopneic reflex /nē′ōnē′ik/ [Gk, *pnoe,* breath; L, *reflectere,* to bend back], a change in the normal breathing rhythm when an irritating gas is introduced into the lungs.

pneumatic /noomat′ik/ [Gk, *pneuma,* air], pertaining to air or gas.

pneumatic condenser [Gk, *pneuma,* air; L, *condensare,* to thicken], a pneumatic device that delivers compacting blows of variable force to restorative material used in filling tooth cavities.

pneumatic heart driver, a mechanical device that regulates compressed air delivery to an artificial heart, controlling heart rate, percent systole, and delay in systole.

pneumatic lithotripsy, lithotripsy in which a rigid probe is inserted through the ureter and pneumatic pressure is applied directly to the calculus.

pneumatic retinopexy, a treatment for retinal detachment involving injection of gas into the posterior vitreous cavity in such a way that the gas bubble presses against the area of torn retina, forcing it back into place.

pneumatic tourniquet precautions, a nursing intervention from the Nursing Interventions Classification (NIC) defined as applying a pneumatic tourniquet while minimizing the potential for patient injury from use of the device.

pneumatocele /noomat′əsēl/, **1.** a thin-walled cavity in the lung parenchyma caused by partial airway obstruction. **2.** a hernial protrusion of lung tissue. **3.** a

tumor or sac containing gas, especially of the scrotum.

pneumatogram /noomat′əgram/ [Gk, *pneuma,* air, *gramma,* to record], a tracing made by a pneumograph of chest movements during breathing.

pneumobelt /noo′mōbelt/, a corset with an inflatable bladder that fits over the abdominal area. The bladder is connected by a hose to a ventilator that delivers positive pressure at an adjustable rate and pressure. It is used to assist in the respiratory rehabilitation of patients with high cervical injuries.

pneumocentesis /-sentē′sis/ [Gk, *pneumon,* lung, *kentesis,* pricking], a procedure in which a lung is punctured to drain fluid contents.

pneumocephalus /noo′mō·sef′ə·ləs/ [Gr, *pneuma,* air, *kephalē,* head], the presence of air in the intracranial cavity.

pneumococcal /noo′mōkok′əl/ [Gk, *pneumon,* lung, *kokkos,* berry], pertaining to bacteria of the genus *Pneumococcus.*

pneumococcal heptavalent conjugate vaccine, a preparation of capsular polysaccharides from the seven serotypes of *Streptococcus pneumoniae* most commonly isolated from children 6 years of age or younger, coupled to a nontoxic variant of diphtheria toxin, used as an active immunizing agent for infants and children at risk for pneumococcal disease.

pneumococcal meningitis [Gk, *pneumon,* lung, *kokkos,* berry, *meninx,* membrane, *itis,* inflammation], meningitis caused by pneumococcal infection.

pneumococcal nephritis, nephritis or glomerulonephritis from infection with *Streptococcus pneumoniae,* usually as a complication of pneumonia or empyema.

pneumococcal pneumonitis, inflammation of the lungs caused by an infection of pneumococcal bacteria.

pneumococcal vaccine, an active immunizing agent containing antigens of the 23 types of *Pneumococcus* associated with more than 98% of the cases of pneumococcal pneumonia in the U.S. and Europe. It is prescribed for persons over 2 years of age who are at high risk of development of severe pneumococcal pneumonia, all adults over 65 years of age, and immunocompromised adults.

pneumococcal vaccine polyvalent, a preparation of purified capsular polysaccharides from the 23 serotypes of *Streptococcus pneumoniae* causing the majority of pneumococcal disease, used as an active immunizing agent in persons more than 2 years of age.

pneumococcus /noo′mōkok′əs/ *pl.* **pneumococci** [Gk, *pneumon* + *kokkos,* berry], a gram-positive diplococcal bacterium of the species *Streptococcus pneumoniae,* the most common cause of bacterial pneumonia.

pneumoconiosis /nōō′mōkō′ne·ō′sis/ [Gk, *pneumon* + *konis,* dust, *osis,* condition], any disease of the lung caused by chronic inhalation of dust, usually mineral dust of occupational or environmental origin.

pneumoconstriction /nōō′mōkənstrik′shən/, an area of collapsed lung tissue that results from mechanical stimulation of an exposed part of the lung. It is produced by local reflex muscular closure of alveolar ducts and alveoli.

Pneumocystis jirovecii /nōō′mōsis′tis/, a microorganism that causes pneumocystosis, a type of interstitial cell pneumonitis.

Pneumocystis pneumonia (PCP) [Gk, *pneuma,* air, *kystis,* bag, *pneumon,* lung], a type of interstitial plasma cell pneumonia in which the alveoli become honeycombed with an acidophilic material. The patient may or may not be febrile but usually is weak, dyspneic, and cyanotic.

pneumocystosis /nōō′mōsistō′sis/ [Gk, *pneuma,* air, *kystis,* bag, *osis,* condition], infection with the fungus *Pneumocystis jirovecii,* usually seen in patients with HIV infection; premature, malnourished infants; or debilitated or immunosuppressed people, particularly those with hematologic malignancies. It is characterized by fever, cough, tachypnea, and frequently cyanosis.

pneumoencephalography /nōō′mō·ensef′əlog′rəfē/ [Gk, *pneuma,* air, *enkephalos,* brain, *graphein,* to record], a procedure for the radiographic visualization of the ventricular space, basal cisterns, and subarachnoid space overlying the cerebral hemispheres of the brain. Air, helium, or oxygen is injected into the lumbar subarachnoid space after the intermittent removal of the CSF by lumbar puncture. —**pneumoencephalographic,** *adj.*

pneumograph /nōō′məgraf/, a device that records breathing movements by means of an inflated coil around the chest. It mainly measures the ventilatory cycle rather than the amplitude of breathing movements.

pneumohemothorax /-hem′ōthôr′aks/ [Gk, *pneuma,* air, *haima,* blood, *thorax,* chest], an accumulation of air and blood in the pleural cavity.

pneumolysin /nōōmol′isin/, virulence factor produced by *Streptococcus pneumoniae* associated with cytolysis.

pneumomediastinum /nōō′mōmē′dē·əst ī′nəm/ [Gk, *pneuma,* air, *mediastinus,* midway], the presence of air or gas in the mediastinal tissues. In infants it may lead to pneumothorax or pneumopericardium,

especially in those with respiratory distress syndrome or aspiration pneumonitis. In older children the condition may result from bronchitis, acute asthma, pertussis, CF, or bronchial rupture from cough or trauma.

pneumonectomy /nōō′mənek′təmē/ [Gk, *pneumon,* lung, *ektomē,* excision], the surgical removal of all or part of a lung.

pneumonia /nōōmō′ne·ə/ [Gk, *pneumon,* lung], an acute inflammation of the lungs, often caused by inhaled pneumococci of the species *Streptococcus pneumoniae.* The alveoli and bronchioles of the lungs become plugged with a fibrous exudate. Pneumonia may be caused by other bacteria, as well as by viruses, rickettsiae, and fungi.

pneumonic plague /nōōmon′ik/ [Gk, *pneumon,* lung; L, *plaga,* stroke], a highly virulent and rapidly fatal form of plague characterized by bronchopneumonia. There are two forms: primary pneumonic plague, which results from involvement of the lungs in the course of bubonic plague, and secondary pneumonic plague, which results from the inhalation of infected particles of sputum from a person having pneumonic plague.

pneumonitis /nōō′mənī′tis/ *pl.* **pneumonitides** [Gk, *pneumon* + *itis*], inflammation of the lung. Pneumonitis may be caused by a virus or may be a hypersensitivity reaction to chemicals or organic dusts, such as bacteria, bird droppings, or molds. It is usually an interstitial, granulomatous, fibrosing inflammation of the lung, especially of the bronchioles and alveoli. Dry cough is a common symptom.

pneumonopathy /nōō′mənop′əthē/, any disease or disorder involving the lungs.

pneumonopleuritis /-plŏōrī′tis/, a combined disorder of pneumonia and pleurisy.

pneumonotherapy /-ther′əpē/, the treatment of lung disease.

pneumopericardium /-per′ikär′dē·əm/, the presence of air or gas in the pericardial sac.

pneumoperitoneum /nōō′mōper′itənē′əm, -per′itənē′əm/ [Gk, *pneuma,* air, *peri,* around, *teinein,* to stretch], the presence of air or gas within the peritoneal cavity of the abdomen. It may be spontaneous, such as from rupture of a hollow, gas-containing organ, or induced for diagnostic or therapeutic purposes.

pneumoperitonitis /nōō′mōper′itənī′tis/, an acute inflammation of the peritoneal cavity accompanied by the presence of air or gas.

pneumotachometer /-takom′ətər/, a device that measures the flow of respiratory gases in liters per minute.

P

pneumothorax /nōo̅′mōthôr′aks/ [Gk, *pneuma*, air, *thorax*, chest], the presence of air or gas in the pleural space, causing a lung to collapse. Pneumothorax may be the result of an open chest wound that permits the entrance of air, the rupture of an emphysematous vesicle on the surface of the lung, or a severe bout of coughing. It may also occur spontaneously without apparent cause. The onset is accompanied by a sudden sharp chest pain, followed by difficult, rapid breathing; decreased breath sounds and cessation of normal chest movements on the affected side; tachycardia; a weak pulse; hypotension; diaphoresis; an elevated temperature; pallor; dizziness; and anxiety.

PNF, abbreviation for **proprioceptive neuromuscular facilitation.**

PNH, abbreviation for **paroxysmal nocturnal hemoglobinuria.**

PNP, abbreviation for **pediatric nurse practitioner.**

Po, symbol for the element **polonium.**

p.o., PO, abbreviation for the Latin phrase *per os,* "by mouth"; a route for administration of medications.

PO₂, symbol for *partial pressure of oxygen.*

pocket /pok′ət/, a saclike space.

pockmark [AS, *pocc* + *meark*], a pitted scar on the skin, usually the result of acne or a smallpox or chickenpox pustule at the site.

podalic /pōdal′ik/ [Gk, *pous,* foot], pertaining to the feet.

podalic version, the shifting of the position of a fetus to position the feet at the outlet during labor.

podiatrist /pədī′ətrist/, a health professional who diagnoses and treats disorders of the feet.

podiatry /pədī′ətrē/ [Gk, *pous* + *iatros,* healer], the diagnosis and treatment of diseases and other disorders of the feet.

podofilox /pädəfil′loks/, a corrosive preparation of podophyllotoxin that inhibits cell mitosis and is used for topical treatment of venereal warts.

podophyllotoxin /pä′dəfil′ətok′sin/ [Gk, *pous* + *phyllon,* leaf, *toxikon,* poison], any one of a group of substances derived from the roots of *Podophyllum peltatum,* a common plant species known as mayapple or American mandrake. Podophyllin, a resinous preparation of podophyllotoxin, is prescribed in the topical treatment of condyloma acuminatum and other types of warts. Several podophyllotoxin derivatives have been used as purgatives.

POEMS syndrome, a multisystem syndrome combining *p*olyneuropathy *o*rganomegaly, *e*ndocrinopathy, *m*onoclonal gammopathy component, and *s*kin changes. It may be linked to a dysproteinemia such as the presence of unusual monoclonal proteins and light chains.

poetry therapy, a form of bibliotherapy in which a selected poem is used to evoke feelings and responses for discussion in a therapeutic setting.

pogonion /pōgō′nē·on/ [Gk, diminutive of *pōgōn,* beard], the most anterior point in the contour of the chin in the sagittal plane.

poikilocytosis /poi′kilō′sītō′sis/ [Gk, *poikilos,* variation, *kytos,* cell, *osis,* condition], an abnormal degree of variation in the shape of the erythrocytes in the blood.

poikiloderma atrophicans vasculare /-dur′mə/ [Gk, *poikilos,* variation, *derma,* skin, *a* + *trophe,* not nourishment; L, *vasculum,* little vessel], an abnormal skin condition characterized by hyperpigmentation or hypopigmentation, telangiectasia, and atrophy of the epidermis.

poikiloderma of Civatte, a common benign progressive dermatitis characterized by erythematous patches on the face and neck that become dry and scaly. As the condition progresses, pigment is deposited around the hair follicles, extending down the lateral aspects of the neck.

point [L, *punctus,* pricked], a small spot or designated area.

point behavior [L, *punctus,* pricked; AS, *bihabban,* to behave], the orientation of body parts in a certain direction within a quantum of space.

point forceps, a dental instrument used to hold filling cones during their placement in root canal filling.

point lesion, a disruption of single chemical bonds caused by effects of ionizing radiation on a macromolecule.

point mutation [L, *punctus,* pricked, *mutare,* to change], a mutation in which only a single nucleotide of DNA is changed.

point of maximum impulse (PMI), the place where the apical pulse is palpated as strongest, often in the fifth intercostal space of the thorax, just medial to the left midclavicular line.

point-of-service plan, in the United States, a plan in which the member may seek care outside the network or directly from preferred providers with initial evaluation by a primary care provider but must pay a deductible and/or copayment.

point system, in the United States, a specialty capitation method in which points are assigned for each patient seen in specific diagnostic or service categories. Periodically points are totaled, and income distributed proportionately.

poise /poiz/ [Jean L.M. Poiseuille, French physiologist, 1799–1869], a unit of liquid or gas (fluid) viscosity expressed in terms of grams per centimeter per second ($g \times cm^{-1} \times sec^{-1}$). The centipoise, or $^1/_{100}$ of a poise, is more commonly used.

poison /poi'zən/ [L, *potio,* drink], any substance that impairs health or destroys life when ingested, inhaled, or absorbed by the body in relatively small amounts. Clinically all poisons are divided into those that respond to specific treatments or antidotes and those for which there is no specific treatment.—**poisonous,** *adj.*

poison center, a telephone service for toxicology experts providing emergency treatment advice for all kinds of poisonings, 24 hours a day. Poison control centers also provide poison prevention information to the community and education about recognition and treatment of poison exposures for health care providers. There are more than 500 poison control centers in the United States; 65 of them are officially certified and are members of the American Association of Poison Control Centers.

poisoning, 1. the act of administering a toxic substance. **2.** the condition or physical state produced by the ingestion of, injection of, inhalation of, or exposure to a poisonous substance. Identification of the poison ingredients and presentation of a container label are critical to expeditious diagnosis and treatment.

poisoning treatment, the symptomatic and supportive care given a patient who has been exposed to or who has ingested a toxic drug, commercial chemical, or other dangerous substance. In the case of oral poisoning, a primary effort should be directed toward recovery of the toxic substance before it can be absorbed into the body tissues. If vomiting does not occur spontaneously, it should be induced after first identifying the poison, if possible, and calling a poison control center. If the poison is a petroleum distillate, such as kerosene, or a caustic or corrosive substance, vomiting should not be induced. In certain cases an antidote may be administered to render the poison inert or to prevent its absorption, as by giving a mild solution of vinegar or citrus juice to neutralize an alkali.

poison ivy, any of several species of climbing vine of the genus *Rhus,* characterized by shiny three-pointed leaves. It is common in North America and causes severe allergic contact dermatitis in many people. Localized vesicular eruption with itching and burning results.

poison ivy dermatitis [L, *potio,* drink; ME, *ivi;* Gk, *derma,* skin, *itis,* inflammation], an allergic contact dermatitis caused by exposure to a nonvolatile oil,

toxicodendrol, present in the leaves and other plant parts of poison ivy.

poison oak, any of several species of shrub of the genus *Rhus,* common in North America. Skin contact results in allergic dermatitis in many people.

poison sumac /soo͞o'mak/, a shrub of the genus *Rhus,* common in North America. Skin contact results in allergic dermatitis in many people.

Poland's syndrome /pō'ləndz/ [Alfred Poland, British physician, 1820–1872], unilateral absence of the sternocostal head of the pectoralis major muscle and ipsilateral syndactyly.

polar [L, *polus,* pole], pertaining to molecules that have atoms bearing substantial partial electric charges that are not distributed symmetrically. These molecules are hydrophilic, and tend to attract or aggregate with water. Polar substances tend to dissolve in polar solvents.

Polaramine, a trademark for an antihistaminic (dexchlorpheniramine maleate).

polar body, one of the small cells produced during the two meiotic divisions in the maturation of a female gamete, or ovum. Polar bodies are nonfunctional and incapable of being fertilized.

polarity /pōler'itē/ [L, *polus*], **1.** the existence or manifestation of opposing qualities, tendencies, or emotions, such as pleasure and pain, love and hate, and masculinity and femininity. The concept is central to various psychotherapeutic approaches. **2.** in physics, the distinction between a negative and a positive electric charge.

polarity therapy, a bodywork technique that combines tissue manipulation with theories of vital energy derived from ayurveda and acupuncture. It is believed that energy blockages within the body result in imbalances, which in turn manifest as pain. Manipulation, using light touch and medium and deep pressure, is used to release these energy blockages and restore balance.

polarization /pō'lərizā'shən/ [L, *polus;* Gk, *izein,* to cause], the concentration, within a population or group, of members' interests, beliefs, and allegiances around two conflicting positions.

polarization microscope [L, *polus,* pole; Gk, *mikros,* small, *skopein,* to view], a microscope that uses polarized light for special diagnostic purposes, such as examining crystals of chemicals found in patients with gout and related disorders.

polarized light /po'lərīzd/ [L, *polus;* AS, *leoht*], light that is propagated in such a way that the radiation waves occur in only one direction in the vibration plane and not at random.

P

polarographic oxygen analyzer /pō′lərō graf′ik/, an electrochemical device used to analyze the proportion of oxygen molecules in respiratory care systems. The oxygen is measured in terms of an electron current produced after it acquires electrons from a negative electrode in a hydroxide bath.

pole [L, *polus*], **1.** in biology, an end of an imaginary axis drawn through the symmetrically arranged parts of a cell, organ, ovum, or nucleus. **2.** one of a pair of opposite forces or attractants, as in magnetism or electricity. **3.** in anatomy, the point on a nerve cell at which a dendrite originates. —**polar,** *adj.*

poles of kidney, either end of an axis through the length of a kidney. They are designated as the upper pole of the kidney (extremitas superior renis) and the inferior pole of the kidney (extremitas inferior renis).

***pol* gene,** a segment of a retrovirus, such as HIV, that encodes its reverse transcriptase enzyme.

policy /pol′isē/ [Gk, *politeia,* the state], a principle or guideline that governs an activity and that employees or members of an institution or organization are expected to follow.

polioencephalitis /pō′lē·ō′ensef′əlī′tis/ [Gk, *polios,* gray, *enkephalos,* brain, *itis*], an inflammation of the gray matter of the brain caused by infection of the brain by a poliovirus.

polioencephalomeningomyelitis /pō′lē· ō′ensef′əlō′məning′gōmī′əlī′tis/ [Gk, *polios,* gray, *enkephalos,* brain, *meninx,* membrane, *myelos,* marrow, *itis,* inflammation], an inflammation caused by a poliovirus that involves the gray matter of the brain and spinal cord and also the meninges.

polioencephalomyelitis /pō′lē·ō′ensef′əlo mī′əlī′tis/ [Gk, *polios* + *enkephalos* + *myelos,* marrow, *itis*], inflammation of the gray matter of the brain and the spinal cord, caused by infection by a poliovirus.

polioencephalopathy /pō′lē·ō′ensef′əlop′ə thē/ [Gk, *polios,* gray, *enkephalos,* brain, *pathos,* disease], a pathologic condition caused by a poliovirus affecting the gray matter of the brain.

poliomyelitis /pō′lē·ōmī′əlī′tis/ [Gk, *polios* + *myelos,* marrow, *itis,* inflammation], an infectious disease caused by one of the three polioviruses. It is transmitted from person to person through fecal contamination or oropharyngeal secretions. Asymptomatic, mild, and paralytic forms of the disease occur. Asymptomatic infection has no clinical features, but it confers immunity. Abortive poliomyelitis lasts only a few hours and is characterized by minor illness with fever, malaise, headache, nausea, vomiting, and slight abdominal discomfort. Nonparalytic poliomyelitis is longer lasting and is marked by meningeal irritation with pain and stiffness in the back and by all the signs of abortive poliomyelitis. Paralytic poliomyelitis begins as abortive poliomyelitis. The symptoms abate, and for several days the person seems well. Malaise, headache, and fever recur; pain, weakness, and paralysis develop. The peak of paralysis is reached within the first week. In spinal poliomyelitis, viral replication occurs in the anterior horn cells of the spine, causing inflammation, swelling, and, if severe, destruction of the neurons. The large proximal muscles of the limbs are most often affected. Bulbar poliomyelitis results from viral multiplication in the brainstem. Bulbar and spinal poliomyelitis often occur together.

poliosis /pō′lē·ō′sis/ [Gk, *polios* + *osis,* condition], depigmentation of the hair on the scalp, eyebrows, eyelashes, mustache, beard, or body. The condition may be inherited and generalized or acquired and localized in patches.

poliovirus /-vī′rəs/ [Gk, *polios*; L, *virus,* poison], a member of the family Picornaviridae and the causative organism of poliomyelitis. This very small RNA virus has three serologically distinct types. Infection or immunization with one type does not protect against the others.

poliovirus vaccine, a vaccine prepared from poliovirus to confer immunity to it. The inactivated poliovirus vaccine (IPV) is a suspension of three strains of polioviruses that have been inactivated in formalin so that normal activity of the organisms has been destroyed. IPV is given subcutaneously at 2 months, 4 months, between 6 and 18 months, and between 4 and 6 years, and is the form of vaccination recommended in the United States. A trivalent live oral form of vaccine, TOPV, is no longer used in the United States because of rare vaccine-associated paralysis after administration. TOPV is nevertheless the treatment of choice in areas of the world where polio is still endemic.

polishing [L, *polire,* to make smooth], **1.** creation of a smooth and glossy finish on a surface, as of a tooth, dental restoration, or denture. **2.** a tendency of patients with right temporal lobe lesions to deny dysphoric affect and minimize socially disapproved behavior while exaggerating other qualities.

Politano-Leadbetter technique, a type of ureteroneocystostomy in which the ureter is excised from its attachment to the bladder and reattached in a more medial and superior position.

political nursing /pəlit′ikəl/ [Gk, *politia,* the state, *nutrix,* nurse], the use of knowledge about power processes and strategies to influence the nature and direction of health care and professional nursing.

pollenogenic, pertaining to a plant that produces pollen or something that is produced by pollen.

pollex /pol′eks/ *pl.* **pollices** [L], **1.** the thumb. **2.** the big toe.

pollutant /pəloō′tənt/ [L, *polluere,* to befoul], an unwanted substance that occurs in the environment, usually with health-threatening effects. Pollutants may exist in the atmosphere as gases or fine particles that may be irritating to the lungs, eyes, and skin; in drinking water as dissolved or suspended substances; and in foods or beverages as carcinogens or mutagens.

polonium (Po) /pəlō′nē·əm/ [Polonia, Poland], a radioactive element that is one of the disintegration products of uranium. Its atomic number is 84, and its atomic mass is approximately 210.

polus /pō′ləs/ *pl.* **poli** [L, pole], either of the opposite ends of any axis; the official anatomic designation for the extremity of an organ.—**polar,** *adj.*

polyacrylamide /-akril′əmīd/, a polymer of acrylamide and usually some cross-linking derivative.

polyamine /pol′ē·am′ēn/, any compound that contains two or more amine groups, such as spermidine, spermine, and putrescine that are normally found in human tissue. Many polyamines function as essential growth factors in microorganisms such as in DNA synthesis and gene expression.

polyanionic /pol′ē·an′ī·on′ik/ [Gk, *polys,* many, *ana,* not, *jenai,* to go], pertaining to multiple negative electric charges.

polyarteritis /pol′ē·är′tərī′tis/ [Gk, *polys* + *arteria,* airpipe, *itis,* inflammation], an abnormal inflammatory condition of several arteries.

polyarteritis nodosa, a severe and poorly understood collagen vascular disease in which widespread inflammation and necrosis of small and medium-sized arteries and ischemia of the tissues they serve occur. Any organ or organ system may be affected. The disease is characterized by fever, abdominal pain, weight loss, neuropathy, and, if the kidneys are affected, hypertension, edema, and uremia. Mortality rate is high, especially if there is kidney involvement.

polyarthralgia /pol′ē·ärthral′jə/ [Gk, *polys* + *arthron,* joint, *algos,* pain], pain in several joints simultaneously.

polyarthritis /-ärthrī′tis/, an inflammation that involves more than one joint.

polyarticular /-ärtik′yələr/ [Gk, *polys,* many, *articulus,* joint], pertaining to many joints.

polycarboxylate cement /pol′ēkärbok′silāt/, a dental cement used as a luting agent for cementing restorations and as a cavity lining.

polychlorinated biphenyls (PCBs) /-klôr′i nā′tid/, a group of more than 30 isomeric compounds used in plastics, insulation, and flame retardants and varying in physical form from oily liquids to crystals and resins. All are potentially toxic and carcinogenic.

polychondritis /pol′ēkon·drī′tis/ [Gk, *polys,* many, *chondros,* cartilage, *itis,* inflammation], inflammation involving many cartilages of the body.

polychromatic /-krōmatik/ [Gk, *polys* + *chroma,* color], a light of many colors or wavelengths. The term is usually applied to white light, although it may also refer to a defined part of the spectrum.

polychromatophil /pol′ēkrōmat′əfil/, any cell or structure that may be stained by several different dyes.

polychromatophilia /pol′ēkrō′matəfil′yə/ [Gk, *polys* + *chroma* + *philein,* to love], an elevated reticulocyte count on a peripheral blood film stained with new methylene blue dye or an increase in the number of polychromatophilic red blood cells on a Wright-stained blood film.

Polycillin, a trademark for an antibacterial **(ampicillin).**

polyclonal /pol′ēklō′nəl/ [Gk, *polys* + *klon,* cutting], pertaining to or designating a group of cells or organisms derived from several cells.

Polycose, a trademark for an easily digestible and rapidly absorbed nutritional supplement for oral and tube feeding containing glucose polymers. It is not formulated for use as the sole source of nutrition.

polycystic /-sis′tik/ [Gk, *polys* + *kystis,* bag], characterized by the presence of many cysts.

polycystic kidney disease (PKD), an abnormal condition in which the kidneys are enlarged and contain many cysts. There are two unrelated hereditary diseases in which there is massive enlargement of the kidney with cyst formation. *Autosomal dominant polycystic kidney disease* (ADPKD), formerly called adult polycystic kidney disease, is the most common type of cystic disease of the kidneys. It is usually manifested during the third decade of life. Renal failure may appear by the fifth decade, with terminal failure occurring in the next 10 years, although in some cases it never appears. Although there is rarely any liver dysfunction accompanying

P

this disorder, cyst formation in the liver does occur. *Autosomal recessive polycystic kidney disease* (ARPKD), formerly called childhood polycystic kidney disease, is diagnosed at birth or in the first 10 years of life and is much less common than the autosomal dominant form. Both the kidney and the liver are involved, causing renal failure and liver failure with portal hypertension Characteristic symptoms early in the process include pain, hematuria, urinary tract infection, kidney stones, and obstructive uropathy with anuria.

polycystic liver, congenital cystic disease of the liver.

polycystic ovary syndrome (PCOS), an endocrine disturbance characterized by anovulation, amenorrhea, hirsutism, and infertility. It is caused by increased levels of testosterone, estrogen, and luteinizing hormone (LH) and decreased secretion of follicle-stimulating hormone (FSH). The depressed but continuous production of FSH associated with this disorder causes continuous partial development of ovarian follicles. Numerous follicular cysts may develop. The increased level of estrogen associated with this abnormality raises the risk of cancers of the breast and endometrium.

polycythemia /polˈē·sīˈthēˈmē·ə/ [Gk, *polys* + *kytos*, cell, *haima*, blood], an increase in the number of erythrocytes in the blood that may be primary or secondary to pulmonary disease, heart disease, or prolonged exposure to high altitudes.

polycythemia rubra vera (PV) [Gk, *polys,* many, *kytos,* cell, *haima,* blood; L, *ruber,* red, *verus,* true], a condition of unknown cause characterized by a marked increase in the RBC count, packed cell volume, cellular hemoglobin, leukocytes, platelets, and total blood volume. The skin and mucous membranes acquire a maroon or plum color, and hepatomegaly, splenomegaly, hypertension, and neurologic symptoms develop. The condition is associated with an F chromosome defect.

polydactyly /-dakˈtilē/ [Gk, *polys* + *daktylos,* finger], a congenital anomaly characterized by the presence of more than the normal number of fingers or toes.

polydipsia /polˈēˈdipˈsēˈə/ [Gk, *polys* + *dipsa,* thirst], **1.** excessive thirst. It is characteristic of several different conditions, including DM, diabetes insipidus, and nephrogenic diabetes insipidus. Polyuria resulting from other forms of renal dysfunction also leads to polydipsia. The condition also may be psychogenic in origin. **2.** *informal.* alcoholism.

polyelectrolyte /polˈē·ilekˈtrəlīt/ [Gk, *polys* + *elektron,* amber, *lytos,* soluble], a

substance with many charged or potentially charged groups.

polyene, a chemical compound with a carbon chain of four or more atoms and several conjugated double bonds.

polyesthesia /polˈē·esthēˈzhə/ [Gk, *polys* + *aisthesis,* feeling], a sensory disorder involving the sense of touch in which a stimulus to one area of the skin is also felt at nonstimulated sites.

polyestradiol phosphate /-esˈtrədīˈôl/, an antineoplastic estrogen compound. It is not available in the United States, but is prescribed elsewhere as palliative therapy for advanced inoperable prostate cancer.

polyethylene /polˈē·ethˈilēn/, a strong but flexible synthetic resin produced by the polymerization of ethylene. Polyethylene materials have been used in surgery.

polyethylene glycol, a polymer of ethylene oxide and water, available in liquid form or as waxy solids used in various pharmaceutical preparations as a water-soluble ointment base. Polyethylene glycol is also used as a laxative.

polygene /polˈējēnˈ/ [Gk, *polys* + *genein,* to produce], any of a group of nonallelic genes that individually exert a small effect but interact in a cumulative manner to produce a particular characteristic, usually of a quantitative nature such as size, weight, skin pigmentation, or degree of intelligence.—**polygenic,** *adj.*

polyglandular autoimmune syndromes, a group of disorders manifested by subnormal functioning of more than one endocrine gland. Type I is characterized by the appearance of mucocutaneous candidiasis, often occurring in childhood, and is associated with hypoparathyroidism and adrenal insufficiency. It occurs in siblings, without involvement of other generations in the family. Type II involves primary adrenal insufficiency and primary thyroid failure occurring in the same patient for unclear reasons. Many of these patients have an autoimmune disorder and form antibodies against cellular fractions of many endocrine glands.

polyglandular deficiency syndrome, primary failure of any combination of endocrine glands, including the adrenals, thyroid, gonads, parathyroids, and endocrine pancreas. It is often accompanied by autoimmune abnormalities that affect systems other than the endocrine system.

polyglucosan /-glooˈkəsan/ [Gk, *polys* + *glykys,* sweet], a large molecule consisting of many anhydrous polysaccharides.

polygraph /polˈē·grafˈ/ [Gk, *polys* + *graphein,* to write], an apparatus for simultaneously recording several mechanical or electrical impulses, such as blood pressure, pulse and respiration, and variations in electrical resistance of the skin; popularly known as **lie detector.**

polyhedral, having many sides or surfaces.

polyhybrid /-hī′brid/ [Gk, *polys;* L, *hybrida,* offspring of mixed parents], pertaining to or describing an individual, organism, or strain that is heterozygous for more than three specific traits or gene pairs or that is the offspring of parents differing in more than three specific gene pairs.

polyhybrid cross, the mating of two polyhybrid individuals, organisms, or strains.

polyleptic /pol′elep′tik/ [Gk, *polys + lambanein,* to seize], describing any disease or condition marked by numerous remissions and exacerbations.

polymenorrhea, an abnormally frequent recurrence of the menstrual cycle.

polymerase /pəlim′ərās/, any enzyme that catalyzes polymerization, especially of nucleotides to polynucleotides.

polymerase chain reaction (PCR), a rapid technique for in vitro amplification of specific DNA or RNA sequences, allowing small quantities of short sequences to be analyzed without cloning. The process can be used to make prenatal diagnoses of genetic diseases and to identify an individual by analysis of a single tissue cell.

polymerization /pəlim′əriza′shən/, the act or process of forming a compound (polymer), usually of high molecular weight, by the combination of simpler molecules (monomers).

polymerize /pol′əmərīz′/ [Gk, *polys,* many, *meros,* parts], to convert two or more molecules into a polymer.

polymethacrylate cement, a cement used in surgery and dentistry, consisting of an acrylic resin formed by the polymerization of methyl methacrylate monomers.

polymicrobial /-mīkrō′bē·əl/ [Gk, *polys,* many, *mikros,* small, *bios,* life], pertaining to a number of species of microbes.

polymicrobic infection /-mīkrō′bik/ [Gk, *polys,* many, *mikros,* small, *bios,* life; L, *inficere,* to stain], an infection involving more than one species of pathogen.

polymorphic /-môr′fik/ [Gk, *polys,* many, *morphe,* form], pertaining to the ability to assume two or more distinct forms, such as the existence of two or more forms of chromosomes or hemoglobins in a population.

polymorphism /pol′ēmôr′fizəm/ [Gk, *polys + morphe,* form], **1.** the state or quality of existing or occurring in several different forms. **2.** the state or quality of appearing in different forms at different stages of development.—**polymorphic,** *adj.*

polymorphocytic leukemia /pol′ēmôr′fəs it′ik/ [Gk, *polys + morphe + kytos,* cell, *leukos,* white, *haima,* blood], a neoplasm of blood-forming tissues in which mature segmented granulocytes are predominant.

polymorphonuclear /pol′ēmôr′fōnŏŏ′klē·ər/ [Gk, *polys + morphe;* L, *nucleus,* nut kernel], having a nucleus with a number of segments connected by fine threads of nuclear membrane.

polymorphonuclear neutrophil, a neutrophil with a segmented nucleus.

polymorphous /pol′ēmôr′fəs/ [Gk, *polys + morphe,* form], occurring in many varying forms, possibly changing in structure or appearance at different stages.

polymorphous light eruption, a common recurrent superficial vascular reaction to sunlight or ultraviolet light in susceptible individuals. Within 1 to 4 days after exposure to the light, small erythematous papules and vesicles appear on otherwise normal skin, and then disappear within 2 weeks.

polymyalgia rheumatica /-mī·al′jə/ [Gk, *polys + mys,* muscle, *algos,* pain, *rheuma,* flux], a chronic, episodic, inflammatory disease of the large arteries that usually develops in people over 60 years of age. The disease primarily affects the arteries in muscles. It is characterized by pain and stiffness of the back, shoulder, or neck that is usually more severe on rising in the morning. There may also be a cranial headache, which affects the temporal and occipital arteries, causing a severe throbbing headache. Serious complications of polymyalgia rheumatica include arterial insufficiency, coronary occlusion, stroke, and blindness. Patients with the disease usually have a high ESR.

polymyositis /pol′ēmī′ōsī′tis/ [Gk, *polys + mys,* muscle, *itis,* inflammation], inflammation of many muscles, usually accompanied by deformity, edema, insomnia, pain, sweating, and tension. Some forms of polymyositis are associated with malignancy.

polymyxin B sulfate, an antibiotic prescribed for ocular infections.

polyneuralgia /-nŏŏral′jə/ [Gk, *polys,* many, *neuron,* nerve, *algos,* pain], a type of neuralgia that affects several nerves at the same time.

polyneuritis /-nŏŏrī′tis/ [Gk, *polys,* many, *neuron,* nerve, *itis,* inflammation], an inflammation involving many nerves.

polyneuropathy /-nŏŏrop′əthē/ [Gk, *polys,* many, *neuron,* nerve, *pathos,* disease], a condition in which many peripheral nerves are afflicted with a disorder.

polynuclear, having many nuclei.

polyopia /pol′ē·ō′pē·ə/ [Gk, *polys + ops,* eye], a defect of sight in which one

P

object is perceived as many images; multiple vision. The condition can occur in one or both eyes.

polyp /pol'ip/ [Gk, *polys* + *pous,* foot], a small tumorlike growth that projects from a mucous membrane surface.

polypapilloma /-pap'ilo'mə/ [Gk, *polys,* many; L, *papilla,* nipple; Gk, *oma*], multiple papillomas, or stalked tumors.

polypeptide /pol'ē'pep'tīd/, a long chain of amino acids joined by peptide bonds. Polypeptides may be formed by partial hydrolysis of proteins or synthesized from free amino acids. Very long polypeptides are usually called proteins.

polyphagia /pol'ēfā'jē-ə/ [Gk, *polys* + *phagein,* to eat], excessive, uncontrolled eating.

polypharmacy /-fär'məsē/, the use of a number of different drugs, possibly prescribed by different doctors and filled in different pharmacies by a patient who may have one or several health problems.

polyploid /pol'əploid/ [Gk, *polys* + *plous,* times], **1.** an individual, organism, strain, or cell that has more than twice the haploid number of chromosomes characteristic of the species. The multiple of the haploid number is denoted by the appropriate prefix, as in triploid, tetraploid, pentaploid, hexaploid, heptaploid, octaploid, and so on. **2.** pertaining to such an individual, organism, strain, or cell.

polyploidy /pol'iploi'dē/, the state or condition of having more than two complete sets of chromosomes.

polypoid [Gk, *polys,* many, *pous,* foot, *eidos,* form], like a polyp or tumor on a stalk.

polyposis /-pōsis/ [Gk, *polys* + *pous,* foot, *osis,* condition], an abnormal condition characterized by the presence of numerous polyps on a part.

polyposis coli [Gk, *polys,* many, *pous,* foot, *osis,* condition, *kolikos* colon], a condition of multiple polyps in the large intestine.

polyradiculitis /pol'ērədik'yōōli'tis/ [Gk, *polys;* L, *radicula,* rootlet; Gk, *itis*], inflammation of many nerve roots, such as found in Guillain-Barré syndrome.

polysaccharide /-sak'ərīd/ [Gk, *polys* + *sakcharon,* sugar], a carbohydrate polymer that is formed from three or more molecules of simple carbohydrates. Examples of polysaccharides are dextrin and insulin.

polysaccharide-iron complex, ferric iron complexed to a low-molecular-weight polysaccharide prepared by extensive hydrolysis of starch, used as an oral hematinic.

polysome /pol'isōm/ [Gk, *polys* + *soma,* body], a group of ribosomes joined by a molecule of messenger RNA containing a portion of the genetic code that is to

be translated. Polysomes are found in the cytoplasm during protein synthesis.

polysomnographic technologist, a person who monitors sleep studies and records the relevant physiological variables.

polysomnography /pol'ē·som·nog'rə·fē/ [Gk, *polys,* many; L, *somnus,* sleep; Gk, *graphein,* to write or record], the polygraphic recording during sleep of multiple physiological variables, both directly and indirectly related to the state and stages of sleep, to assess possible biological causes of sleep disorders.

polysomy /pol'isō'mē/, the presence of more than two copies of a chromosome in an otherwise diploid somatic cell as the result of chromosomal nondisjunction during meiosis.

Polysporin, a trademark for an ophthalmic and topical fixed-combination antibiotic ointment containing two antibacterials (**polymyxin B sulfate** and **bacitracin**).

polysulfide polymer /pol'ēsul'fīd/, an elastomeric synthetic rubber used in dentistry as an impression material for fixed partial prosthodontic structures, inlays for single quadrants, and dental impressions.

polysynaptic /-sinap'tik/ [Gk, *polys,* many, *synaptein,* to join], pertaining to nerve cells that end in synapses.

polysyndactyly /-sindak'tilē/ [Gk, *polys,* many, *syn,* together, *daktylos,* finger or toe], multiple webbing or fusion between fingers or toes.

polytene chromosome /pol'itēn/ [Gk, *polys* + *tainia,* band], an excessively large type of chromosome consisting of a large number of copies of the chromosome bundled side by side. Polytene chromosomes are produced by repeated rounds of DNA synthesis without mitosis and are found primarily in the salivary glands of certain insects.

polythiazide /-thī'az'īd/, a thiazide diuretic prescribed as adjunctive therapy in the treatment of hypertension and edema.

polyunsaturated /-unsach'ərā'tid/ [Gk, *polys,* many; AS, *un,* not; L, *saturare,* to fill], pertaining to a chemical compound containing more than one double or triple bond that can be opened to accept more atoms into the molecule, thereby making the compound saturated.

polyuria /pol'ēyōōr'ē-ə/ [Gk, *polys* + *ouron,* urine], the excretion of an abnormally large quantity of urine. Some causes of polyuria are diabetes insipidus, DM, use of diuretics, excessive fluid intake, and hypercalcemia.

polyvalent, denoting the capacity of an element to combine with two or more atoms.

polyvalent vaccine /-vā'lənt/ [Gk, *polys,* many; L, *valere,* worth, *vaccinus,* of a cow], a vaccine prepared from several different antigens of a species.

Poly-Vi-Flor, a trademark for an oral fixed-combination pediatric drug containing several vitamins and sodium fluoride.

polyvinyl chloride (PVC) /-vī'nil/, a tasteless, odorless, clear hard resin with many industrial uses. Workers in its manufacture are at risk primarily because of the toxicity of its parent compound, vinyl chloride. It releases hydrochloric acid when burned. Excessive inhalation of its dust can cause pneumoconiosis.

polyvinylidene fluoride (PVF₂) /-vīnil'idēn/, a commonly used piezoelectric material in a hydrophone. It is also used in imaging transducers.

Pomeroy technique, a method of tubal ligation in which a loop of fallopian tube is picked up and ligated at its base with an absorbable suture, about 5 cm from the uterine cornua, and the tied loop is then resected.

POMP /pomp/, an abbreviation for a combination drug regimen used in the treatment of cancer, containing three antineoplastics, *P*urinethol (mercaptopurine), *O*ncovin (vincristine sulfate), and *m*ethotrexate, and *p*rediSONE (a glucocorticoid).

Pompe's disease [J.C. Pompe, twentieth-century Dutch physician; L, *dis,* opposite of; Fr, *aise,* ease], a rare genetic disorder that is a form of muscle glycogen storage disease, characterized by generalized accumulation of glycogen resulting from a deficiency of acid maltase (alpha-1,4-glucosidase). It is usually fatal in infants, causing cardiac or respiratory failure. Children with Pompe's disease appear mentally retarded and hypotonic, seldom living beyond 20 years of age. In adults, muscle weakness is progressive, but the disease is not fatal.

POMR, abbreviation for **problem-oriented medical record.**

pons /ponz/ *pl.* **pontes** [L, bridge], **1.** a prominence on the ventral surface of the brainstem, between the medulla oblongata and the cerebral peduncles of the midbrain. The pons consists of white matter and a few nuclei and is divided into a ventral part and a dorsal part. The ventral part consists of transverse fibers separated by longitudinal bundles and small nuclei. The dorsal part comprises the tegmentum, which is a continuation of the reticular formation of the medulla containing the nuclei of several cranial nerves. **2.** any slip of tissue connecting two parts of a structure or an organ of the body.

Ponstel, a trademark for an antiinflammatory and analgesic (mefenamic acid).

pontic /pon'tik/ [L, *pons,* bridge], the suspended member of a removable partial denture or fixed bridge, such as an artificial tooth, usually occupying the space previously occupied by the natural tooth crown.

pontine micturition center, a center in the pons that contributes to control of the bladder and inhibition of tension of the urethral sphincters.

pontine nucleus [L, *pons,* bridge, *nucleus,* nut kernel], nerve cells in the basilar part of the pons where impulses are relayed between the cerebrum and cerebellum.

Pontocaine, a trademark for a local anesthetic (tetracaine hydrochloride).

PONV, abbreviation for **postoperative nausea and vomiting.**

pooled plasma [AS, *pol;* Gk, *plasma,* something formed], plasma pooled from many donors and used to prepare plasma protein derivatives. Source plasma is plasma collected specifically for the manufacture of derivatives; recovered plasma is plasma separated from whole blood donations.

poorly differentiated lymphocytic malignant lymphoma, a lymphoid neoplasm containing cells resembling lymphoblasts that have a fine nuclear structure and one or more nucleoli.

popliteal /poplit'ē-əl, pop'litē'əl/ [L, *poples,* ham of the knee], pertaining to the area behind the knee.

popliteal artery [L, *poples,* ham of the knee; Gk, *arteria,* airpipe], a continuation of the femoral artery, extending from the opening in the abductor magnus, passing through the popliteal fossa at the knee, dividing into 10 branches, and supplying various muscles of the thigh, leg, and foot.

popliteal fossa, the hollow at the posterior part of the knee.

popliteal node, a node in one of the groups of lymph glands in the leg. Approximately seven small popliteal nodes are embedded in the fat of the popliteal fossa at the back of the knee.

popliteal pterygium syndrome, 1. a congenital syndrome consisting chiefly of popliteal webs, cleft palate, lower lip pits, and dysplasia of the toenails. **2.** popliteal webbing associated with cleft lip and palate, fistula of the lower lip, syndactyly, nail dysplasia, and clubfoot.

popliteal pulse, the pulsation of the popliteal artery, best palpated with the patient lying prone with the knee flexed.

population /pop'yəlā'shən/ [L, *populus,* the people], **1.** an interbreeding group of individuals characterized by genetic continuity through several generations. **2.** a group of individuals collectively occupying a particular geographic locale. **3.** any

P

group that is distinguished by a particular trait or situation. **4.** any group from which samples may be measured for some variable characteristic for statistical purposes.

population at risk, a group of people who share a characteristic that causes each member to be susceptible to a particular event, such as nonimmunized children who are exposed to poliovirus.

population genetics, a branch of genetics that applies mendelian inheritance to groups and studies the frequency of alleles and genotypes in breeding populations.

poractant alfa, a lung surfactant extract used in the treatment (rescue) of respiratory distress syndrome in premature infants.

porcelain /por'sə·lən/, a white, translucent, dense ceramic material produced by fusing under high temperature a mixture of feldspar, kaolin, quartz, whiting, and other substances.

porcine /pôr'sīn/ [L, *porcinus*, pig-like], obtained from or related to hogs, such as porcine insulin.

porcine graft [L, *porcinus*, pig-like; Gk, *graphion*, plant stylus], a temporary biologic heterograft made from the skin of a pig.

porfimer, a miscellaneous antineoplastic used to treat completely obstructing esophageal cancer and endobronchial non–small cell lung cancer.

poriomania /pôr′ē·ōmā′nē·ə/, a tendency to leave home impulsively or to be a vagabond.

porion /por′ē·on/ [Gk. *poros*, passage], the most lateral point on the roof of the bony external acoustic meatus, vertically over the middle of the meatus.

pork tapeworm infection [L, *porcus*, pig, hog (male); AS, *taeppe*, tape, *wyrm*, worm; L, *inficere*, to stain], an infection of the intestine or other tissues caused by adult and larval forms of the tapeworm *Taenia solium*. The pork tapeworm is unique in that it can use humans as both intermediate hosts for larvae and definitive hosts for the adult worm. Humans are usually infected with the adult worm after eating contaminated undercooked pork.

porosis /pərō′sis/ [Gk, *poros*, passage], a condition of thinning bone tissue, particularly its supporting connective tissue, as in osteoporosis.

porous /pôr′əs/ [Gk, *poros*, passage], pertaining to something with pores or openings.

porphobilinogen /pôr′fōbilin′əjən/, a chromogen substance that is an intermediate in the biosynthesis of heme and porphyrins. It appears in the urine of people with porphyria.

porphyria /pôrfir′ē·ə/ [Gk, *porphyros*, purple], a group of inherited disorders in which there is abnormally increased production of substances called porphyrins. Two major classifications of porphyria are erythropoietic porphyria, characterized by the production of large quantities of porphyrins in the blood-forming tissue of the bone marrow, and hepatic porphyria, in which large amounts of porphyrins are produced in the liver. Clinical signs common to both classifications of porphyria are photosensitivity, abdominal pain, and neuropathy.

porphyria cutanea tarda (PCT), the most common form of porphyria, characterized by cutaneous photosensitivity that causes scarring bullae, hyperpigmentation, facial hypertrichosis, and sometimes sclerodermatous thickenings and alopecia; it is frequently associated with alcohol abuse, liver disease, or hepatic siderosis. Urinary levels of uroporphyrin and coproporphyrin are increased, and activity of a specific enzyme involved in heme biosynthesis is decreased.

porphyrin /pôr′fərin/ [Gk, *porphyros*, purple], any iron- or magnesium-free pyrrole derivative occurring in many plant and animal tissues.

porphyrinogen /pôr′f-rin′ō-jen/, the reduced form of a porphyrin. The porphyrinogens are the functional intermediates in the biosynthesis of heme and, if oxidized to their corresponding porphyrins, such as occurs in porphyrias, are irreversibly removed from the biosynthetic pathway and accumulate in tissue.

porphyrins and porphobilinogens test, a quantitative analysis of urinary porphyrins and porphobilinogens to screen for porphyria.

portacaval shunt /pôr′təkă′vəl/ [L, *porta*, gateway, *cavus*, cavity; ME, *shunten*], a shunt created surgically to increase blood flow from the portal circulation by carrying it into the vena cava.

Portagen, a trademark for a nutritional supplement containing protein, carbohydrate, and fat.

portal /pôr′təl/ [L, *porta*, gateway], an entrance.

portal circulation [L, *porta*, gateway, *circulare*, to go around], the pathway of blood flow from the GI tract and spleen to the liver via the portal vein and its tributaries.

portal fissure [L, *porta* + *fissura*, cleft], a fissure on the visceral surface of the liver along which the portal vein, the hepatic artery, and the hepatic ducts pass.

portal hypertension, an increased venous pressure in the portal circulation caused by compression or occlusion in the portal or hepatic vascular system. It results in splen-o-megaly, large collateral veins, ascites, and, in severe cases, systemic hypertension and esophageal varices.

portal of entry, the route by which an infectious agent enters the body, such as through nonintact skin.

portal system, arrangement of blood vessels in which blood exiting one tissue is immediately carried to a second tissue before being returned to the heart and lungs for oxygenation and redistribution.

portal vein, a vein from the small intestine that ramifies in the liver and ends in capillary-like sinusoids that convey the blood to the inferior vena cava through the hepatic veins. The right branch of the portal vein enters the right lobe of the liver, and the left branch enters the left lobe.

Porter-Silber reaction [Curt C. Porter, American biochemist, b. 1914; Robert H. Silber, American biochemist, b. 1915], a reaction, visible as a change in color to yellow, that indicates the amount of adrenal steroids (the 17-hydroxycorticosteroids) excreted per day in the urine. The test is used to evaluate adrenocortical function but is now largely supplanted by immunoassay techniques.

portoenterostomy /pôr′tō·en′təros′təmē/ [L, *porta*; Gk, *enteron*, bowel, *stoma*, mouth, *temnein*, to cut], construction of a bile drainage system with an intestinal conduit to correct biliary atresia. There are several procedural approaches, such as anastomosis of the jejunum by a Roux-en-Y loop to the portal fissure region to establish bile flow from the bile ducts to the intestine. The procedure is indicated in patients younger than 3 months of age.

Portuguese man-of-war /por′chəgēs/, any member of the genus *Physalia,* in the phylum Cnidaria. All species have a large purple air sac that allows them to float on the surface of the water, and from which many long tentacles of stinging polyps hang. The tentacles are equipped with nematocysts that are able to penetrate the skin of humans, causing intense pain. Paralysis can result from numerous stings.

posaconazole, a systemic antifungal used for prevention of aspergillus, *Candida* infection, and oropharyngeal candidiasis in the immunocompromised.

position /pəzish′ən/ [L, *positio*], **1.** any one of many postures of the body, such as the anatomic position. **2.** in obstetrics, the relationship of an arbitrarily chosen fetal reference point, such as the occiput, on the presenting part of the fetus to its location in the maternal pelvis.

positional behavior /pəzish′ənəl/, the orientation of the body regions to claim a quantum of space. Positional behavior involves four body regions: head and neck, upper torso, pelvis and thighs, and lower legs and feet.

positional vertigo, a severe but brief episode of vertigo associated with a change of body position.

positioner /pəzish′ənər/, a resilient rubbery and plastic removable appliance fitted over the occlusal surfaces of the teeth to obtain limited tooth movement and stabilization, usually at the end of orthodontic treatment.

positioning, a nursing intervention from the Nursing Interventions Classification (NIC) defined as deliberative placement of the patient or a body part to promote physiological and/or psychological well-being.

positioning: intraoperative, a nursing intervention from the Nursing Interventions Classification (NIC) defined as moving the patient or body part to promote surgical exposure while reducing the risk of discomfort and complications.

positioning: neurologic, a nursing intervention from the Nursing Interventions Classification (NIC) defined as achievement of optimal, appropriate body alignment for the patient experiencing or at risk for spinal cord injury or vertebral irritability.

positioning: wheelchair, a nursing intervention from the Nursing Interventions Classification (NIC) defined as placement of a patient in a properly selected wheelchair to enhance comfort, promote skin integrity, and foster independence.

position sense, a variety of muscular senses by which the position or attitude of the body or its parts is perceived.

positive /poz′itiv/ [L, *positivus*], **1.** of a laboratory test result, indicating that a substance or a reaction is present. **2.** of a sign, indicating on physical examination that a finding is present, often meaning that there is pathologic change. **3.** of a substance, tending to carry or carrying a positive chemical charge.

positive balance, a state in which the amount of water or an electrolyte excreted from the body is less than that ingested.

positive end-expiratory pressure (PEEP), positive airway pressure applied at the end of the exhalation phase during mechanical ventilation. Each successive breath begins from a new baseline. Air is delivered in cycles of constant pressure through the respiratory cycle. PEEP is used for the relief of respiratory distress secondary to prematurity, pancreatitis, shock, pulmonary edema, trauma, surgery, or other conditions in which spontaneous respiratory efforts are inadequate and arterial levels of oxygen are deficient.

positive feedback, 1. in physiology, an increase in function in response to a stimulus. For example, micturition increases after the flow of urine has started. **2.** *informal.* an encouraging, favorable, or otherwise positive response from one person to what another person has communicated.

positive identification, the unconscious modeling of one's personality on that of another who is admired and esteemed.

positive pressure, 1. a greater-than-ambient atmospheric pressure. **2.** any technique in which compressed gas or air is delivered to the airways at greater-than-ambient pressure.

positive pressure ventilation (PPV), any of numerous types of mechanical ventilation in which gas is delivered into the airways and lungs under positive pressure, producing positive airway pressure during inspiration. it may be done via either an endotracheal tube or a nasal mask.

positive relationship, in research, a direct relationship between two variables in which as one increases, the other can be expected to increase.

positive sequence, the sequence of the bases on the strand of a double-stranded nucleic acid that encodes the product. In DNA it is the strand that encodes the RNA, having thus the same base sequence except changing T for U in the RNA.

positive signs of pregnancy, three unmistakable signs of pregnancy: fetal heart tones, heard on auscultation; fetal skeleton, seen on x-ray film or ultrasonogram; and fetal parts, felt on palpation.

positive symptom, a symptom of the acute phase of schizophrenia.

positron /pos′itron/, a positively charged particle emitted from neutron-deficient radioactive nuclei; the antiparticle of an electron.

positron emission tomography (PET) [L, *positivus*; Gk, *elektron,* amber; L, *emittere,* to send out; Gk, *tome,* section, *graphein,* to record], a computerized radiographic technique that uses radioactive substances to examine the metabolic activity of various body structures. The patient either inhales or is injected with a metabolically important substance such as glucose, carrying a radioactive element that emits positively charged particles, or positrons. When the positrons combine with electrons normally found in the cells of the body, gamma rays are emitted. The PET device detects the gamma rays and constructs color-coded images that indicate the intensity of metabolic activity throughout the organ involved.

postanesthesia care, a nursing intervention from the Nursing Interventions Classification (NIC) defined as monitoring and management of the patient who has recently undergone general or regional anesthesia.

postanesthesia care unit (PACU), an area adjoining the OR to which surgical patients are taken for nursing assessment and care while recovering from anesthesia. Vital signs, adequacy of ventilation, LOC, surgical site, and levels of pain are carefully monitored as the patient recovers consciousness.

postaxial /pōst·ak′sē·əl/ [L, *post,* after Gk, *axon,* axis], posterior to an axis. In anatomic usage, this refers to the medial (ulnar) aspect of the upper limb and the lateral (fibular) aspect of the lower limb.

postcaval shunt /-kā′vəl/ [L, *post,* after + *vena cava*; ME, *shunten*], any of several surgical anastomoses of the portal and systemic circulations to relieve symptoms of portal hypertension.

postcentral gyrus /-sen′trəl/ [L, *post,* after; Gk, *kentron,* center, *gyros,* turn], a convolution of the brain immediately posterior to the central sulcus of the cerebrum.

postcoital /-kō′itəl/ [L, *post,* after, *coire,* to come together], after sexual intercourse.

postcoital contraceptive, one that blocks or terminates pregnancy after sexual intercourse.

postcoital test, for infertility, examination of secretions aspirated from the vaginal fornix and endocervical canal after coitus to determine the number and condition of spermatozoa present and the extent to which they have penetrated the cervical mucus.

postcommissurotomy syndrome /-kəmis′yərot′əmē/ [L, *post,* after, *commissura,* a union; Gk, *temnein,* to cut], a condition of unknown cause occurring within the first few weeks after cardiac valvular surgery, characterized by intermittent episodes of pain and fever, which may last weeks or months and then resolve spontaneously.

postconcussion syndrome /-kənkush′ən/ [L, *post* + *concussio,* shake violently], a condition that follows head trauma, characterized by dizziness, poor concentration, headache, hypersensitivity, and anxiety.

postdate pregnancy /-dāt′/ [L, *post,* after + *data* + *praegnans,* bearing child], a pregnancy that lasts more than 42 weeks.

postdural puncture headache (PDPH), headache following procedures involving puncture of the dura mater, such as lumbar puncture and spinal anesthesia. It is thought to be caused by leakage of CSF at the puncture site, with settling of the brain and stretching of the intracranial nerves.

posterior /postir′ē·ər/ [L, behind], **1.** in the back part of a structure, such as the dorsal surface of the human body. **2.** the back part of something. **3.** toward the back.

posterior Achilles bursitis, a painful heel condition caused by inflammation of the bursa between the Achilles tendon and the calcaneus. It is commonly associated with Haglund's deformity.

posterior antebrachial cutaneous nerve, a nerve that branches off from the radial nerve, innervates the skin of the dorsal aspect of the forearm, and has a general sensory modality.

posterior atlantoaxial ligament, one of five ligaments connecting the atlas to the axis.

posterior atlantooccipital membrane, one of a pair of thin, broad fibrous sheets that form part of the atlantooccipital joint between the atlas and the occipital bone.

posterior auricular artery, one of a pair of small branches from the external carotid arteries, dividing into auricular and occipital branches and supplying parts of the ear, scalp, and other structures in the head.

posterior circumflex humeral artery, an artery that originates from the third part of the axillary artery and supplies related muscles and the glenohumeral joint in the posterior scapular region.

posterior costotransverse ligament, one of the five ligaments of each costotransverse joint, comprising a fibrous band passing from the neck of each rib to the base of the vertebra above.

posterior drawer sign, an orthopedic test used to determine laxity of the posterior cruciate ligament of the knee. The patient is positioned with hips at 45 degrees and knees flexed at 90 degrees while the examiner stabilizes the foot and pushes the tibia backward. Also, with both the hips and knees flexed at 90 degrees, the examiner holds the heels together and observes the knees to compare the relative posterior sag of the tibia.

posterior ethmoidal artery, an artery that supplies the ethmoidal air cells and the nasal cavity.

posterior ethmoidal nerve, a nerve that supplies the posterior ethmoidal air cells and the sphenoid sinus.

posterior fontanel, a small triangular area between the occipital and parietal bones at the junction of the sagittal and lambdoidal sutures.

posterior fossa, a depression on the posterior surface of the humerus, above the trochlea, that lodges the olecranon of the ulna when the elbow is extended.

posterior horn [L, behind + *cornu,* horn], the horn-shaped projection of gray matter in the posterior region of the spinal cord.

posterior kidney, the posterior segment of the kidney; the renal segment located most posteriorly.

posterior liver, a term used to refer to the posterior region that is not part of either the left part or the right part of the liver but is coextensive with the caudate lobe.

posterior longitudinal ligament, a thick strong ligament attached to the dorsal surfaces of the vertebral bodies, extending from the occipital bone to the coccyx.

posterior median fissure, a narrow groove in the closed part of the medulla oblongata.

posterior mediastinal node, a node in one of three groups of thoracic visceral nodes, connected to the part of the lymphatic system that serves the esophagus, pericardium, diaphragm, and convex surface of the liver.

posterior mediastinum, the irregularly shaped lower part of the mediastinum, parallel with the vertebral column. It contains the bifurcation of the trachea, two primary bronchi, the esophagus, the thoracic duct, many large lymph nodes, and various vessels.

posterior nares, a pair of posterior internal openings in the nasal cavity connecting it with the nasopharynx and allowing the inhalation and exhalation of air.

posterior neuropore, the embryonic opening at the inferior end of the neural tube from neural canal to exterior.

posterior palatal seal area, the area of soft tissues along the junction of the hard and soft palates on which displacement, within the physiologic tolerance of the tissues, can be applied by a denture to aid its retention.

posterior parietal artery, an artery that originates at the terminal part of middle cerebral artery and serves the posterior parietal lobe of the brain.

posterior ramus, a branch of each spinal nerve. Collectively, the posterior rami innervate the back.

posterior rhizotomy [L, behind; Gk, *rhiza,* root, *temnein,* to cut], a surgical procedure for cutting the posterior, or sensory, nerve root for the relief of intractable pain or to relieve spasms from neurologic causes.

posterior sagittal anorectoplasty, plastic surgery to create a functional anus and rectum in children with imperforate anus or other anorectal malformations.

posterior spinal arteries, one of two arteries that originate in the cranial cavity, usually arising directly from a terminal branch of each vertebral artery, and descend along the spinal cord, each as two branches that bracket the posterolateral sulcus and the connection of posterior roots with the spinal cord.

P

posterior subcapsular cataract [L, *capsula;* Gk, *katarrhaktes,* waterfall], a visual opacity caused by a thickening of the epithelial cells lining the capsule. The condition is frequently the result of the aging process or a disease that involves surrounding eye tissues.

posterior temporal artery, the posterior temporal branch of middle cerebral artery, originating in the middle cerebral artery and supplying the cortex of the posterior temporal lobe.

posterior tibial artery, one of the divisions of the popliteal artery, supplying various muscles of the lower leg, foot, and toes.

posterior tibialis pulse, the pulse of the posterior tibialis artery palpated on the medial aspect of the ankle, just posterior to the prominence of the malleolus.

posterior tooth, any of the maxillary and mandibular premolars and molars of the deciduous or secondary dentition, or of prostheses.

posterior uveitis, uveitis involving the posterior segment of the eye.

posterior vein of left ventricle, one of the five tributaries of the coronary sinus that drain blood from the capillary bed of the myocardium.

posteroanterior (P-A, p-a) /pos'tərō·antir'ē·ər/ [L, *posterus,* coming after, *anterior,* before], the direction from back to front.

posteroexternal /pos'tərō·ekster'nəl/ [L, *posterus,* coming after, *externus,* outward], situated on the outer side of a posterior aspect.

posteroinferior /-infir'ē·ər/ [L, *posterus,* coming after, *inferior,* lower], pertaining to a position that is both lower and behind.

posterolateral /-lat'ərəl/ [L, *posterus,* coming after, *latus,* side], pertaining to a position behind and to the side.

posterolateral sulcus, a shallow depression on each side of the posterior surface of the spinal cord that marks where the posterior rootlets of the spinal nerve enter the cord.

posterolateral thoracotomy, a chest surgery technique in which an incision is made in the submammary fold, below the tip of the scapula, and continued posteriorly upward. It requires division of the trapezius, rhomboideus, latissimus dorsi, and serratus anterior muscles.

posteromedial /pos'tərōmē'dē·əl/ [L, *posterus,* coming after, *medius,* middle], situated toward the middle of the posterior surface.

posteromedial central arteries of posterior communicating artery, branches of the posterior communicating artery that supply the medial surface of the thalamus and the walls of the third ventricle.

posteroparietal /pos'tərōpərī'ətəl/ [L, *posterus,* coming after, *paries,* wall], situated at the posterior part of the parietal bone.

posterosuperior /pos'tərōsōōpēr'ē·ər/ [L, *posterus,* coming after, *superior,* higher], situated posteriorly and superiorly.

postganglionic /-gang'glē·on'ik/ [L,*post,* after; Gk, *ganglion,* knot], distal to a ganglion.

postganglionic fiber, the axon of a nerve cell whose cell body is situated in a ganglion.

postganglionic neuron [L, *post,* after; Gk, *ganglion,* knot, *neuron,* nerve], a neuron that is distal to or beyond a ganglion.

posthepatic jaundice /pōst'hepat'ik/ [L, *post,* after; Gk, *hepar,* liver; Fr, *jaune,* yellow], jaundice caused by obstruction of the bile ducts.

posthumous /pos'chəməs/ [L, *post,* after, *humare,* to bury], after a person's death.

posthypnotic suggestion /-hipnot'ik/ [L, *post,* after; Gk, *hypnos,* sleep; L, *suggerere,* to suggest], an action suggested to a hypnotized subject during a trance that the subject carries out on awakening from the trance. The action is in response to a cue, and the subject usually does not know why he or she is performing it.

postictal /pōst'iktəl/ [L, *post;* Gk, *ikteros,* jaundice], **1.** after a seizure. **2.** confused. **—postictus,** *n.*

postinfectious /-infek'shəs/ [L, *post* + *inficere,* to stain], after an infection.

postinfectious glomerulonephritis, the acute form of glomerulonephritis, which may follow 1 to 6 weeks after a streptococcal infection, most often in childhood. Characteristics of the disease are hematuria, oliguria, edema, and proteinuria, especially in the form of granular casts.

postinfectious psychosis [L, *post,* after, *inficere,* to stain; Gk, *psyche,* mind, *osis,* condition], psychotic behavior that follows a severe infection, such as pneumonia, scarlet fever, malaria, uremia, or typhoid fever.

postlumbar puncture headache /-lum'bar/ [L, *post,* after, *lumbus,* loin + *punctura;* AS, *heafod* + *acan*], a headache that occurs within a few hours of a lumbar puncture and usually lasts 1 or 2 days to several weeks. It may be accompanied by nausea and vomiting and improves when the patient lies down.

postmastectomy exercises /-məstek'təmē/ [L, *post;* Gk, *mastos,* breast, *ektomē,* excision], exercises essential to the prevention of shortening of the muscles, prevention of contracture of the joints, and improvement in lymph and blood circulation after mastectomy. Brushing the teeth and hair is encouraged as effective exercise. Other exercises are usually taught, including four specific exercises: climbing the wall, arm swinging, rope pulling, and elbow spreading.

postmature infant, an infant born after the end of the 42nd week (288 days) of gestation, bearing the physical signs of placental insufficiency. Characteristically the baby has dry, peeling skin; long fingernails and toenails; and folds of skin on the thighs and sometimes on the arms and buttocks. Hypoglycemia and hypokalemia are common. Postmature infants often look as if they have lost weight in utero.

postmaturity /-məcho͞oʹritē/ [L, *post* + *maturare,* to become ripe], **1.** overdevelopment or maturity. **2.** beyond the normal date for maturity, as in a postmature infant.

postmenopausal /-menʹəpôʹsəl/ [L, *post* + *men,* month; Gk, *pauein,* to cease], pertaining to the period of life after the menopause.

postmenopausal hemorrhage, bleeding from the uterus after menopause.

postmenopausal vaginitis [L, *post,* after, *men,* month; Gk, *pauein,* to cease; L, *vagina,* sheath; Gk, *itis,* inflammation], an inflammation caused by degenerative changes in the vaginal mucosa after menopause.

postmortem /môrʹtəm/ [L, *post* + *mors,* death], after death.

postmortem care, a nursing intervention from the Nursing Interventions Classification (NIC) defined as providing physical care of the body of an expired patient and support for the family viewing the body.

postmortem cesarean section [L, *post,* after, *mors,* death, *secare,* to cut, *sectio*], delivery of a fetus by incision into the uterus after death of a woman.

postmortem examination [L, *post,* after, *mors,* death + *examinatio*], an examination of a body after death by a person trained in pathology.

postmortem graft [L, *post,* after, *mors,* death; Gk, *graphion,* stylus], the transplanting of a cornea, artery, or other body part from a dead person to repair a defect in a living body.

postmortem lividity, the black and blue discoloration of the skin of a cadaver, resulting from an accumulation of deoxygenated blood in subcutaneous vessels.

postmyocardial infarction syndrome /-mīʹəkärʹdē·əl/ [L, *post;* Gk, *mys,* muscle, *kardia,* heart; L, *infarcire,* to stuff], a condition that may occur days or weeks after an acute MI. It is characterized by chest pain, fever, pericarditis with a friction rub, pleurisy, pleural effusion, joint pain, and elevated WBC count and sedimentation rate. It tends to recur and often provokes severe anxiety, depression, and fear that another heart attack is occurring.

postnasal /-nāʹzəl/ [L, *post,* after, *nasus,* nose], pertaining to the region posterior to the nasal cavity.

postnasal drip (PND) [L, *post* + *nasus,* nose; AS, *dryppan*], a drop-by-drop discharge of nasal mucus into the posterior pharynx caused by rhinitis, chronic sinusitis, or hypersecretion by the nasopharyngeal mucosa. It is often accompanied by a feeling of obstruction, an unpleasant taste, and fetid breath.

postnecrotic cirrhosis /-nekrotʹik/ [L, *post;* Gk, *nekros,* dead; *kirrhos,* yellowish, *osis,* condition], a nodular form of cirrhosis that may follow hepatitis or other inflammation of the liver.

postoperative (post-op) /-opʹərətiv/ [L, *post* + *operari,* to work], pertaining to the period of time after surgery. It begins with the patient's emergence from anesthesia and continues through the time required for the acute effects of the anesthetic and surgical procedures to abate.

postoperative atelectasis, a form of atelectasis in which collapse of lung tissue is caused by the depressant effects of anesthetic drugs or the inability to breathe deeply or cough effectively because of pain. Deep breathing and coughing are encouraged at frequent postoperative intervals to prevent this condition.

postoperative bed, a surface prepared for a patient who is weak or unconscious, as when recovering from anesthesia. The bed is in the flat position. The bottom sheet may be covered with a cotton bath blanket that is tucked tightly beneath the mattress. The top linen is fan-folded to the far side of the bed and not tucked in. The bed is made in this way to simplify transferring a patient from a stretcher into the bed.

postoperative care, the management of a patient after surgery. The postanesthesia care nurse performs the immediate postoperative procedures, and the clinical unit nurse provides ongoing care, emotional support, and instructions for the patient and family.

post operative cholangiography, in diagnostic radiology, a procedure for outlining the major bile ducts. A radiopaque contrast material is injected into the common bile duct via a T-tube inserted during surgery. It is usually performed after a cholecystectomy to discover any residual calculi.

postoperative ileus [L, *post* + *operari,* to work; Gk, *eilein,* to twist], an absence of normal intestinal function caused by a loss of peristaltic muscular action of the intestine after surgery.

postoperative nausea and vomiting (PONV), nausea and vomiting occurring after a surgical procedure.

postoperative paresthesia, prolonged paresthesia after surgery with a local anesthetic, usually around the mouth, resulting from injury of the mental nerve or mandibular nerve.

postparalytic /-per´əlit´ik/ [L, *post*; Gk, *paralyein,* to be palsied], pertaining to the period after paralysis.

postpartal care¹ /-pär´təl/ [L, *post + partus,* birth], care of the mother and her newborn during the first few days of the puerperium.

postpartal care², a nursing intervention from the Nursing Interventions Classification (NIC) defined as monitoring and management of the patient who has recently given birth.

postpartum /pōstpär´təm/, after childbirth.

postpartum blues [L, *post,* after, *partus,* birth; ME, *bleu*], an emotional effect of childbirth experienced by mothers, consisting mainly of transient feelings of sadness for a period of about 72 hours. If the symptom persists for a longer period, the diagnosis of depression may apply. The condition may require psychotherapy, use of antidepressant medications, or both.

postpartum depression [L, *post + partus + deprimere,* to press down], an abnormal psychiatric condition that occurs after childbirth, typically from 3 days to 6 weeks after birth. It is characterized by symptoms that range from mild "postpartum blues" to an intense suicidal depressive psychosis.

postpartum hemorrhage [L, *post,* after, *partus,* birth; Gk, *haima,* blood, *rhegnynai,* to burst forth], excessive bleeding (a loss of more than 500 mL of blood) after childbirth.

postpartum iliofemoral thrombophlebitis [L, *post,* after, *parturs,* birth, *ilia,* flank, *femur,* thigh; Gk, *thrombos,* lump, *phleps,* vein, *itis,* inflammation], thrombophlebitis involving the iliofemoral artery after childbirth.

postpartum maternal health behavior, a nursing outcome from the Nursing Outcomes Classification (NOC) defined as personal actions to promote health of a mother in the period following birth of an infant.

postpartum pituitary necrosis [L, *post + partus + pituita,* phlegm; Gk, *nekros,* dead, *osis,* condition], an infarct of the pituitary resulting from hypovolemia and shock in the immediate postpartum period. The condition causes a state of hypopituitarism. Lactation may not develop, pubic and axillary hair may be lost, and symptoms of hypoglycemia and amenorrhea are experienced.

postpartum psychosis [L, *post,* after, *partus,* birth; Gk, *psyche,* mind], an episode of psychosis, which may be depressive, after childbirth. Because the condition usually develops in the month after childbirth, endocrinologic factors are believed to be a cause.

postperfusion syndrome /-pərfyōō´zhən/ [L, *post + perfundere,* to pour over], a cytomegalovirus (CMV) infection occurring between 2 and 4 weeks after the transfusion of fresh blood containing CMV. It is characterized by prolonged fever, hepatitis, rash, atypical lymphocytosis, and occasionally jaundice.

postpericardiotomy syndrome /pōst´peri kär´dē-ot´əmē/ [L, *post*; Gk, *peri,* around, *kardia,* heart, *temnein,* to cut], a condition that sometimes occurs days or weeks after pericardiotomy, characterized by symptoms of pericarditis, often without any fever. It appears to be an autoimmune response to damaged cells of the myocardium and pericardium.

postpill amenorrhea /-pill´/ [L, *post + pilla,* ball; Gk, *a,* not, *men,* month, *rhoia,* flow], failure of normal menstrual cycles to resume within 3 months after discontinuation of oral contraception.

postpoliomyelitis muscular atrophy (PPMA) /-pō´lē-ōmī´əlī´tis/ [L, *post,* after; Gk, *polios,* gray, *myelos,* marrow, *itis,* inflammation; L, *musculus*; Gk, *a,* not, *trophe,* nourishment], a recurrence of muscular weakness and other neuromuscular symptoms in people who recovered from acute paralytic polio many years earlier. The condition may or may not affect the same muscles that were damaged in the earlier polio attack.

postpolycythemic myeloid metaplasia /-pol´isīthē´mik/ [L, *post*; Gk, *polys,* many, *kytos,* cell, *haima,* blood, *myelos,* marrow, *eidos,* form, *meta,* with, *plassein,* to mold], a late development in polycythemia vera, characterized by anemia caused by sclerosis of the bone marrow. The production of RBCs occurs only in the liver and spleen.

postprandial, after a meal.

postprandial glucose test, a blood test in which a meal acts as a glucose challenge to the body's metabolism. It is an easily performed screening test for DM.

postprandial pain [L, *post,* after, *prandium,* meal, *poena,* penalty], pain that occurs after a meal.

post procedure recovery, a nursing outcome from the Nursing Outcomes Classification (NOC) defined as the extent to which an individual returns to baseline function after a procedure(s) requiring anesthesia or sedation.

postprocessing /-pros´əsing/, in ultrasonics, manipulation and conditioning of signals and image data after they emerge from the scan converter and before they are displayed. Postprocessing is used to change the assignment of image brightness versus echo signal amplitude in memory.

postpubertal panhypopituitarism /-pyoo′bərtəl/ [L, *post* + *pubertas,* maturation; Gk, *pan,* all, *hypo,* below, *pituita,* phlegm], insufficiency of pituitary hormones, caused by pituitary necrosis resulting from a blood clot in the artery supplying the gland or trauma to the gland. The disorder is characterized initially by weakness, lethargy, loss of libido, intolerance to cold, and, in females, by failure to lactate and amenorrhea. It leads eventually to loss of axillary and pubic hair, bradycardia, hypotension, premature wrinkling of the skin, and atrophy of the thyroid and adrenal glands.

postpuberty /-pyoo′bərtē/ [L, *post* + *pubertas,* maturation], a period of approximately 1 to 2 years after puberty during which skeletal growth slows and the physiologic functions of the reproductive years are established.—**postpuberal, postpubertal, postpubescent,** *adj.*

postrenal anuria /-rē′nəl/ [L, *post* + *renes,* kidney; Gk, *a* + *ouron,* not urine], cessation of urine production caused by obstruction of the ureters or urethra.

poststeroid lobular panniculitis [L, *panniculus,* piece of cloth], subcutaneous nodules that may develop in a layer of fatty connective tissue in children 1 to 13 days after discontinuation of steroid therapy. The condition resolves spontaneously or without readministration of the medication.

poststeroid panniculitis /pos′təroid pənik′yəli′tis/ [L, *panniculus,* piece of cloth], subcutaneous nodules that may develop in children after withdrawal of corticosteroid treatment for rheumatic fever or nephrotic syndrome. The condition resolves spontaneously or with readministration of the medication.

postsynaptic /-sinap′tik/ [L, *post;* Gk, *synaptein,* to join], **1.** situated after a synapse. **2.** occurring after a synapse has been crossed.

posttransfusion syndrome /-transfyoo′zhən/ [L, *post,* after, *transfundere,* to pour through; Gk, *syn,* together, *dromos,* course], a complex of adverse reactions that may accompany or follow IV administration of blood or blood components. Reactions may include hemolytic effects, headache and back pain, allergies to an unknown component in donor blood, circulatory overloading, effects of cold blood that chill the patient's cardiovascular system, and effects of microaggregates in stored blood.

posttransplant diabetes, glucose intolerance or overt hypoglycemia that first appears after an organ transplant. Some cases are steroid diabetes caused by use of steroid immunosuppressive agents.

posttraumatic /-trômat′ik/ [L, *post,* after, Gk, *trauma,* wounded], pertaining to any emotional, mental, or physiological consequences after a major illness or injury.

posttraumatic amnesia [L, *post;* Gk, *trauma,* wound], a period of amnesia between a brain injury resulting in memory loss and the point at which the functions concerned with memory are restored.

posttraumatic osteoporosis [L, *post,* after; Gk, *trauma,* wound, *osteon,* bone, *poros,* passage, *osis,* condition], a loss of bone density that develops after an injury or other severe health episode.

posttraumatic stress disorder (PTSD), a *DSM-IV* psychiatric disorder characterized by an acute emotional response to a traumatic event or situation involving severe environmental stress, such as a natural disaster or military combat.

postulate /pos′chəlāt/ [L, *postulare,* to demand], a hypothesis that is offered as true without proof or as a basis for argument or debate.

postural background movements /pos′chərəl/ [L, *ponere,* to place], the spontaneous body adjustments, requiring vestibular and proprioceptive integration, that maintain the center of gravity, keep the head and body in alignment, and stabilize body parts.

postural drainage, the use of positioning to drain secretions from specific segments of the bronchi and the lungs into the trachea. Coughing usually expels secretions from the trachea. Pillows and raised sections of the hospital bed are used to support or elevate parts of the body. The procedure is begun with the patient level, and the head is gradually lowered to a full Trendelenburg's position. Inhalation through the nose and exhalation through the mouth are encouraged. Simultaneously the nurse or other health care provider may use cupping and vibration over the affected area of the lungs to dislodge and mobilize secretions. The person is then helped to a position conducive to coughing and is asked to breathe deeply at least three times and to cough at least twice.

postural reflex [L, *ponere,* to place, *reflectere,* to turn back], any of several reflexes associated with maintaining normal body posture.

posture /pos′chər/ [L, *ponere,* to place], the position of the body with respect to the surrounding space. A posture is determined and maintained by coordination of the various muscles that move the limbs, by proprioception, and by the sense of balance.

postvaccinal encephalitis /-vak'sinəl/ [L, *post,* after, *vaccinus,* of a cow; Gk, *enkephalos,* brain, *itis,* inflammation], acute encephalitis after vaccination, especially with smallpox vaccine or the Semple rabies vaccine.

postvaccinal encephalomyelitis [L, *post,* after, *vaccinus,* of a cow; Gk, *enkephalos,* brain, *myelos,* marrow, *itis,* inflammation], acute encephalomyelitis after vaccination.

postviral fatigue syndrome /-vīrəl/ [L, *post,* after, *virus,* poison, *fatigare,* to tire; Gk, *syn,* together, *dromos,* course], a condition after a viral infection of chronic muscle fatigue unrelieved by rest. Other symptoms may include visual and hearing difficulties, low-grade fever, stiff neck, urinary frequency, and insomnia.

potable water /pō'təbəl/ [L, *potare,* to drink], water that can be consumed without concern for adverse health effects. It does not have to taste good.

potassemia /pŏt'əsē'mēə/ [D, *potasschen,* potash; Gk, *haima,* blood], an excess of potassium in the blood.

potassium (K) /pətas'ē·əm/ [D, *potasschen,* potash], an alkali metal element. Its atomic number is 19, and its atomic mass is 39.10. Potassium in the body constitutes the predominant intracellular cation, helping to regulate neuromuscular excitability and muscle contraction. Sources of potassium in the diet are whole grains, meat, legumes, fruit, and vegetables.

potassium and sodium phosphate, any of various preparations containing both sodium and potassium phosphate in some combination of the monobasic and dibasic salts of each. It is used as electrolyte replenishers, urinary acidifier, and antiurolithic.

potassium channel blocking agent, any of a class of antiarrhythmic agents that inhibit the movement of potassium ions through potassium channels, thus prolonging repolarization of the cell membrane.

potassium chloride (KCl), a white crystalline salt used as a substitute for table salt in the diet of people with cardiovascular disorders, in administration of the potassium ion, and as a constituent of Ringer's solution. It is prescribed in the treatment of hypokalemia resulting from a variety of causes and of digitalis intoxication.

potassium hydroxide (KOH), a white, soluble, highly caustic compound. Occasionally used in solution as an escharotic for bites of rabid animals, KOH has many laboratory uses as an alkalinizing agent, including the preparation of clinical specimens for examination for fungi under the microscope.

potassium iodide, an expectorant prescribed in the treatment of chronic bronchitis, bronchiectasis, asthma, and other pulmonary disease with excess mucus formation and of various thyroid disorders.

potassium phosphates, a combination of monobasic and dibasic potassium phosphates used as an electrolyte replenisher.

potassium pump, a mechanism that involves energy-dependent pumping of potassium or the active transport of the potassium ion (K^+) across a biologic membrane using the energy of K^+-activated adenosine triphosphatase.

potency /pō'tənsē/ [L, *potentia,* power], **1.** in embryology, the range of developmental possibilities of which an embryonic cell or part is capable, regardless of whether the stimulus for growth or differentiation is natural, artificial, or experimental. **2.** a measure of the strength of the active chemical components contained in a herb or herbal preparation.

potent /pō'tənt/ [L, *potentia,* power], powerful or strong.

potential /pəten'shəl/ [L, *potentia*], an expression of the energy involved in transferring a unit of electrical charge. The gradient or slope of a potential causes the charge to move.

potential abnormality of glucose tolerance, a classification that includes people who have never had abnormal glucose tolerance but who have an increased risk of diabetes or impaired glucose tolerance. Factors associated with an increased risk of type 1 DM include having circulating islet cell antibodies, being a monozygotic twin or sibling of a type 1 diabetes patient, and being the offspring of a type 1 diabetes patient. Factors associated with an increased risk of type 2 DM include being a first-degree relative of a type 2 diabetes patient (particularly in a family in which there are several generations with type 2 diabetes), giving birth to a neonate weighing more than 9 pounds (4.086 kilograms), being a member of a racial or ethnic group with a high prevalence of diabetes, such as some Native American groups, and being an obese adult.

potential difference, the difference in electric potential between two points.

potential energy [L, *potentia,* power; Gk, *energeia*], the energy contained in a body as a result of its position in space, internal structure, and stresses imposed on it.

potential life, a criterion used by the U.S. Centers for Disease Control and Prevention to gauge premature death rates. Among younger individuals, it is based on an assumption that the person would have lived to 65 years of age if life had not been interrupted by a particular disease or injury. For older people the system is based on years of potential life lost before 85 years of age.

potential trauma, a change in tissue that may occur because of existing malocclusion or dental disharmony.

potentiate /pōten′shē·āt/, to increase the strength or degree of activity of something.

potentiation /pōten′shē·ā′shən/ [L, *potentia*], a synergistic action in which the effect of two drugs given simultaneously is greater than the sum of the effects of each drug given separately.

potentiometer /pōten′shē·om′ətər/ [L, *potentia;* Gk, *metron,* measure], a voltage-measuring device.

Potter-Bucky grid [Hollis E. Potter; Gustav Bucky; twentieth-century American radiologists; ME, *gredire,* grate], an x-ray grid that oscillates during the exposure of a radiographic film, blurring the grid lines.

Pott's fracture [Percival Pott, English physician, 1713–1788], a break in the fibula near the ankle, often accompanied by a break in the malleolus of the tibia or a rupture of the internal lateral ligament.

potty chair [AS, *pott;* ME, *chaire*], a small chair that has an open seat over a removable pot, used for the toilet training of young children.

pouch [OFr, *pouche*], any small saclike appendage or pocket such as Rathke's pouch in the embryonic roof cavity.

poultice /pōl′tis/ [L, *puls,* porridge], a soft moist pulp spread between layers of gauze or cloth and applied hot to a surface to provide heat or to counter irritation.

pound (lb) [L, *pondus,* weight], a unit of measure equal to 16 ounces, avoirdupois; 0.45359 kg; 7000 grains.

P. ovale, abbreviation for *Plasmodium ovale.*

poverty /pov′ərtē/ [L, *paupertas*], **1.** a lack of material wealth needed to maintain existence. **2.** a loss of emotional capacity to feel love or sympathy.

povidone /pō′vidōn/, a polymerized form of vinylpyrrolidone, a white hygroscopic powder readily soluble in water, used as a dispersing and suspending agent in drugs. It also has been used as a blood volume extender and, in a complex with iodine, as a topical antiseptic.

povidone-iodine /pō′vidōn ī′ədīn/, an antiseptic microbicide prescribed as a topical microbicide for disinfection of wounds, as a preoperative surgical scrub, for vaginal infections, and for antiseptic treatment of burns. A drop is also often placed into the eyes of neonates to prevent ophthalmia neonatorum.

Powassan virus infection [Powassan, Ontario], an uncommon form of encephalitis caused by a tickborne arbovirus found in eastern Canada and the northern United States.

powder, the dried product of an extraction process in which a substance is first mixed with a solvent such as alcohol or water. Then the solvent is removed completely.

power centric, the position of the mandible during a forceful bite.

power mode, a method of color flow processing and display in which the Doppler signal amplitude or the signal intensity, averaged over a small interval, is displayed rather than the average Doppler frequency. Velocity and flow direction are not displayed, and artifacts do not affect the image.

power of attorney [Fr, *pouvoir;* OFr, *atorne,* legal agent], a document authorizing one person to take legal actions on behalf of another, to act as an agent for the grantor.

power stroke, a working stroke with a dental scaling instrument, used for splitting or dislodging calculus from the surface of a tooth or tooth root.

pox [ME, *pokkes,* pustules], **1.** any of several vesicular or pustular exanthematous diseases terminating in scars. **2.** the pitlike scars of smallpox or chickenpox. **3.** *archaic.* syphilis.

poxvirus /poksvī′rəs/ [ME, *pokkes;* L, *virus,* poison], a member of a family of viruses that includes the organisms that cause molluscum contagiosum, smallpox, and vaccinia.

PP, abbreviation for (Latin) *punctum proximum,* "near the point of accommodation."

PPD, abbreviation for **purified protein derivative.**

PPE, abbreviation for **personal protective equipment.**

PPLO, abbreviation for **pleuropneumonia-like organism.**

PPM, ppm, abbreviation for **parts per million.**

PPMA, abbreviation for **postpoliomyelitis muscular atrophy.**

PPNG, abbreviation for **penicillinase-producing** *Neisseria gonorrhoeae.*

PPO, abbreviation for **preferred provider organization.**

PPS, abbreviation for **prospective payment system.**

PPV, abbreviation for **positive pressure ventilation.**

Pr, symbol for the element **praseodymium.**

PR, abbreviation for **prosthion.**

practice guideline, a detailed description of a process of patient care management that will facilitate improvement or maintenance of health status or slow the decline in health status in certain chronic

P

clinical conditions. The purpose of a practice guideline is to assist health care providers to identify preferred treatment by providing linkages among diagnoses, treatments, and outcomes and by describing alternatives available for each patient.

practice models /prak'tis/ [Gk, *praktikos,* practical], the patterns by which health care services are made available to people in different settings.

practice setting, the context or environment within which nursing care is given.

practice theory, in nursing research, a theory that describes, explains, and prescribes nursing practice in general. It serves as the basis for specific items in the curriculum of nursing education and for the development of theories in the administration of nursing and nursing education.

practicing /prak'tising/, the second subphase of the separation-individuation phase in Mahler's system of preoedipal development, when the child is able to move away from the mother and return to her for emotional nurturing.

practicing medicine without a license, in law, practicing activities defined under state law in the medical practice act without physician supervision, direction, or control.

practitioner /praktish'ənər/ [Gk, *praktikos*], a person qualified to practice in a special professional field, such as a nurse practitioner.

Prader-Willi syndrome /prä'dər wil'ē/ [A. Prader; H. Willi; twentieth-century Swiss physicians; Gk, *syn,* together, *dromos,* course], a congenital metabolic condition characterized by hypotonia, hyperphagia, marked obesity, hypogonadism, and mental retardation.

praecox [L, premature], pertaining to something that occurred at an earlier stage of life or development.

praevia /prē'vē·ə/ [L], having occurred at an earlier time or in front of a place.

pragmatic /pragmat'ik/, pertaining to a belief that ideas are valuable only in terms of their consequences.

pragmatism /prag'mətiz'əm/ [Gk, *pragma,* deed], a philosophy concerned with actual practice and practical results as opposed to theory and speculation.

pralidoxime chloride /pral'ədok'sēm/, a cholinesterase reactivator prescribed as an antidote for organophosphate poisoning and drug overdosage in the treatment of myasthenia gravis.

pramipexole, an agent used to treat parkinsonism.

pramlintide, an antidiabetic that modulates and slows stomach emptying, prevents postprandial rise in plasma glucagon,

decreases appetite, and leads to decreased caloric intake and weight loss. It is used as an adjunct to insulin therapy to treat uncontrolled type 1 or type 2 diabetes.

Pramosone, a trademark for a fixed-combination topical drug containing a glucocorticoid (hydrocortisone acetate) and a topical anesthetic (pramoxine hydrochloride) used to treat perianal pain and swelling.

pramoxine hydrochloride /prəmok'sēn/, a local anesthetic for the relief of pain and itching associated with dermatoses, anogenital pruritus, hemorrhoids, anal fissure, and minor burns.

prandial /pran'dē·əl/ [L, *prandium,* meal], pertaining to a meal.—**prandiality,** *n.*

praseodymium (Pr) /prā'sē·ōdim'ē·əm/ [Gk, *prasaios,* light-green, *didymos,* twin], a rare earth metallic element. Its atomic number is 59; its atomic mass is 140.91.

Prausnitz-Küstner test (PK test) /prous'nits kist'nər/ [Otto C. Prausnitz, German hygienist, 1876–1963; Heinz Küstner, German gynecologist, 1897–1963], a skin test formerly used to measure the presence of IgE. It is no longer used because of the high risk of transfer of hepatitis or blood-borne diseases such as AIDS.

pravastatin /prav'əstat'in/, an antihyperlipidemic agent that acts by inhibiting cholesterol synthesis, used as the sodium salt in the treatment of hypercholesterolemia and other forms of dyslipidemia and to lower the risks associated with atherosclerosis and coronary heart disease.

praxis [Gk, action], **1.** a concept that deals with actions and overt behavior or the performance of an action to the exclusion of metaphysical thought. **2.** the ability to plan and then execute movement.

prazepam /praz'əpam/, a benzodiazepine derivative used to treat anxiety. It is not available in the United States, but it is prescribed elsewhere for the treatment of anxiety disorders or the short-term relief of symptoms of anxiety, and has several unlabeled uses, including alcohol and opiate withdrawal, spasticity, and partial seizures.

prazosin hydrochloride /prä'zəsin/, an antihypertensive, peripherally acting, alpha$_1$-adrenergic blocker prescribed to treat hypertension and to decrease afterload in congestive heart disease. Unlabeled uses include treatment of benign prostatic hyperplasia and Raynaud's phenomenon.

PRE, abbreviation for **progressive resistance exercise.**

preadmission certification /prē'ədmish'ən/, a system whereby physicians are required to obtain advance approval for nonemergency admission of Medicare, Medicaid, and managed care patients to hospitals, as well as most third-party payers. The system is intended to determine whether the patient can be treated as an outpatient or in another, less expensive manner than hospitalization. Emergency admissions require post hoc approval.

preagonal ascites /prē·ag′ənəl/ [L, *prae,* before; Gk, *agon,* struggle, *askos,* bag], a rapid accumulation of fluid within the peritoneal cavity, representing the transudation of serum from the circulatory system.

prealbumin test (PAB, TBPA), a blood, 24-hour urine, or CSF analysis. It is useful as a marker of nutritional status and is a sensitive indicator of protein synthesis and catabolism.

preanal /prē·ā′nəl/, located anterior to the anus.

preaortic node /prē′ā·ôr′tik/ [L, *prae;* Gk, *aerein,* to raise; L, *nodus,* knot], a node in one of the three sets of lumbar lymph nodes that serve various abdominal viscera supplied by the celiac, superior mesenteric, and inferior mesenteric arteries. The preaortic nodes lie ventral to the aorta and are divided into the celiac nodes, superior mesenteric nodes, and inferior mesenteric nodes. Most of the efferent vessels from the preaortic nodes unite to form the lymphatic intestinal trunk that enters the cisterna chyli.

preauricular /prē′ôrik′yələr/, located anterior to the auricle of the ear.

precancerous /-kan′sərəs/ [L, *prae* + *cancer,* crab], pertaining to a stage of abnormal tissue growth that is likely to develop into a malignant tumor.

precautionary labels /prikô′shənər′ē/, information and identification that must be applied to the containers of all hazardous chemicals, including flammables, combustibles, corrosives, carcinogens, and potential carcinogens.

prececocolic fascia, an extension sometimes found in the parietal abdominal fascia, crossing anterior to the cecum adjacent to the ascending colon.

precedent /pres′ədənt/ [L, *praecedere,* to go before], a previously adjudged decision that serves as an authority in a similar case.

precentral gyrus /-sen′trəl/ [L, *prae;* Gk, *kentron,* center, *gyros,* turn], a convolution of the cerebral hemisphere immediately anterior to the central sulcus of the cerebrum in each hemisphere. It is the location of the motor strip that controls voluntary movements of the contralateral side of the body.

preceptor: employee, a nursing intervention from the Nursing Interventions Classification (NIC) defined as assisting and supporting a new or transferred employee through a planned orientation to a specific clinical area.

preceptorship /-sep′tərship′/ [L, *prae* + *capere,* to take up], **1.** the position of teacher or instructor. **2.** a defined period of time in which two people (a nurse with a student nurse or an experienced nurse with a new graduate) work together so that the less experienced person can learn and apply knowledge and skills in the practice setting with the help of the more experienced person.

preceptor: student, a nursing intervention from the Nursing Interventions Classification (NIC) defined as assisting and supporting learning experiences for a student.

precertification, authorization for a specific medical procedure before it is done or for admission to an institution for care. It is required for payment by most U.S. managed care organizations.

precession /-sesh′ən/ [L, *praecedere,* to go before], a comparatively slow gyration of the axis of a spinning body, such that the axis traces out a cone, caused by the application of a torque.

precipitant /-sip′ətənt/ [L, *praecipitare,* to cast down], a substance that causes another substance to settle, separate, or deposit from a solution, such as a reagent that causes certain metals to precipitate.

precipitate /prəsip′itāt, -tit/ [L, *praecipitare,* to cast down], **1.** to cause a substance to separate or to settle out of solution. **2.** a substance that has separated from or settled out of a solution. **3.** occurring hastily or unexpectedly.

precipitate delivery /-sip′itit/, childbirth that occurs with such speed or in such a situation that the usual preparations cannot be made.

precipitating factor /-sip′itā′ting/, an element that causes or contributes to the occurrence of a disorder.

precipitation /-sip′itā′shən/ [L, *praecipitare,* to cast down], a process whereby solid particles are made to settle out of a solution so that they can be separated from other dissolved substances.

precipitin /prəsip′itin/ [L, *praecipitare;* Gk, *anti,* against; AS, *bodig,* body; Gk, *genein,* to produce], an antibody that causes formation of an insoluble complex when combined with a specific soluble antigen.

precision attachment /prisizh′ən/ [L, *praecidere,* to cut short], a device using a close fitting male and female portion to adjoin fixed or removable partial dentures to the crown of an abutment tooth or a restoration.

precision rest /prisish′ən/ [L, *praecidere,* to cut short; AS, *rest*], a rigid denture support consisting of two tightly fitting parts, the insert of which rests firmly against the gingival part of the device.

P

preclinical /-klin'ikəl/ [L, *prae*; Gk, *kline*, bed], a stage in a disease when a specific diagnosis cannot be made because adequate signs and symptoms have not yet developed.

precocious /-kō'shəs/ [L, *praecoquere*, to mature early], pertaining to the early, often premature, development of physical or mental qualities.

precocious dentition, an abnormal acceleration of the eruption of the deciduous or secondary teeth, usually associated with an endocrine imbalance.

precocious puberty [L, *praecoquere*, to mature early + *pubertas*], abnormally early development of sexual maturity. It is usually marked by early breast development and ovulation in girls before 8 years of age and the production of mature sperm in boys before 10 years of age.

precognition /-kognish'ən/, the alleged intuitive foreknowledge of events.

preconception counseling, a nursing intervention from the Nursing Interventions Classification (NIC) defined as screening and providing information and support to individuals of childbearing age before pregnancy to promote health and reduce risks.

preconscious /-kon'shəs/ [L, *prae*, before, *conscire*, to be aware], **1.** before the development of self-consciousness and self-awareness. **2.** in psychiatry, the mental function in which thoughts, ideas, emotions, or memories not in immediate awareness can be brought into the consciousness without encountering any intrapsychic resistance or repression. **3.** the mental phenomena capable of being recalled, although not present in the conscious mind.

precordial movement, any motion of the anterior wall of the thorax localized in the area over the heart. Variations of precordial movements include apical impulse, left ventricular thrust, and right ventricular thrust.

precordial pain [L, *prae*, before, *cor*, heart; *poena*, penalty], pain in the chest wall over the heart.

precordium /-kôr'dē·əm/ [L, *prae*, before, *cor*, heart], the part of the front of the chest wall that overlies the heart and the epigastrium. —**precordial,** *adj.*

Precose, a trademark for an antidiabetic agent (acarbose).

precursor /-kur'sər/ [L, *prae* + *currere*, to run], **1.** something preceding, or coming before, another. **2.** a prognostic characteristic or feature of a patient's health data, such as a radiographic or laboratory finding, that is associated with a higher or lower risk of death than the average.

precursor therapy, a type of treatment involving the use of nutrients that may influence neurologic clinical conditions. An example is the use of choline, a B complex vitamin precursor of acetylcholine, in the treatment of tardive dyskinesia.

predeciduous dentition /-disid'yoo̅·əs/ [L, *prae* + *decidere*, to fall off], the epithelial structures in the mouth of the infant before the eruption of the primary teeth.

prediastole /-dī·as'təlē/ [L, *prae*, before; Gk, *dia* + *stellein*, to set], the part of the cardiac cycle between late systole and the early diastole.

prediastolic murmur /-dī·əstol'ik/ [L, *prae*; Gk, *dia* + *stellein*, to set; L, *murmur*, humming], a murmur heard during cardiac systole.

predictive hypothesis /-dik'tiv/ [L, *prae* + *dicere*, to say; Gk, foundation], in research, a hypothesis that predicts the nature of a relationship among the variables to be studied.

predictive validity, validity of a test or a measurement tool that is established by demonstrating the ability of a test or measure to predict the results of an analysis of the same data made with another test instrument or measurement tool.

predisposing cause /-dispō'sing/ [L, *prae* + *disponere*, to arrange + *causa*], any condition that enhances the specific cause of a disease, such as susceptibility caused by hereditary or lifestyle factors.

predisposing factor [L, *prae* + *disponere*, to dispose], any conditioning factor that influences both the type and the amount of resources that the individual can elicit to cope with stress. It may be biologic, psychologic, genetic, or sociocultural.

predisposition /-dis'pəzish'ən/ [L, *prae* + *disponere*, to dispose], a state of being particularly susceptible.

prednicarbate /pred'n-kär'bāt/, a synthetic corticosteroid used topically for the relief of inflammation and pruritus in certain dermatoses.

prednisoLONE /prednis'əlōn/, a glucocorticoid prescribed as treatment for inflammation of the skin, conjunctiva, and cornea and for immunosuppression.

predniSONE /pred'nisōn/, a glucocorticoid prescribed in the treatment of severe inflammation and for immunosuppression.

predonated autologous blood, blood donated before surgery or another invasive procedure for use in a possible autotransfusion.

preeclampsia /prē'iklamp'sē·ə/ [L, *prae*; Gk, *ek*, out, *lampein*, to flash], an abnormal condition of pregnancy characterized by the onset of acute hypertension after the 24th week of gestation. The classic triad of preeclampsia is hypertension, proteinuria, and edema. Preeclampsia is classified as mild or severe. It commonly causes abnormal metabolic function, including negative nitrogen balance, increased CNS irritability, hyperactive reflexes, compromised renal function, hemoconcentration, and alterations of fluid and electrolyte balance. Complications include premature separation of the placenta, hypofibrinogenemia, hemolysis, cerebral hemorrhage, ophthalmologic damage, pulmonary edema, hepatocellular changes, fetal malnutrition, and lowered birth weight. The most serious complication is eclampsia, which can result in maternal and fetal death.

preexcitation /prē'eksitā'shən/ [L, *prae* + *excitare*, to arouse], activation of part of the ventricular myocardium earlier than would be expected if the activating impulses traveled only down the normal routes and had experienced a normal delay within the atrioventricular (AV) node. Preexcitation may be a result of either Wolff-Parkinson-White syndrome or Lown-Ganong-Levine syndrome. The degree of preexcitation is determined by the speed at which the impulse traverses the atrial tissue and the accessory pathway or the AV node.

preexisting condition /prē'iksis'ting/ [L, *prae* + *existere*, to have reality + *conditio*], any injury, disease, or disability that may have occurred at some time in the past and may predispose an individual to limited health in the future.

preferential anosmia /pref'əren'shəl/ [L, *praeferens*, being preferred; Gk, *a* + *osme*, not smell], the inability to smell certain odors. The condition is often caused by psychologic factors concerning either a particular smell or the situation in which the smell occurs.

preferred provider organization (PPO) /prēfurd'/ [L, *praeferre*, to put before], an organization of physicians, hospitals, and pharmacists whose members discount their health care services to subscriber patients.

preformation /-fôrmā'shən/ [L, *prae* + *formatio*, formation], an early theory in embryology in which the organism is contained in minute and complete form within the germ cell and after fertilization grows from microscopic to normal size.

preformed water /-fôrmd'/ [L, *prae* + *forma*, form; AS, *waeter*], the water that is contained in foods.

prefrontal lobotomy /-frôn'təl/ [L, *prae* + *frons*, forehead; Gk, *lobos*, lobe, *temnein*, to cut], a surgical procedure in which connecting fibers between the prefrontal lobes of the brain and the thalamus are severed. It formerly was an accepted procedure for treating schizophrenic patients with uncontrollable, destructive behavior.

preg, abbreviation for **pregnancy.**

pregabalin, an anticonvulsant used to treat neuropathic pain associated with diabetic peripheral neuropathy, partial-onset seizures, and postherpetic neuralgia.

preganglionic neuron /-gang'glē·on'·ik/ [L, *prae*; Gk, *gagglion*, knot, *neurom*, nerve], a neuron whose axon terminates in contact with another nerve cell located in a peripheral ganglion.

Pregestimil, a trademark for a hypoallergenic nutritional supplement for infants.

pregnancy (preg) /preg'nənsē/ [L, *praegnans*, pregnant], the gestational process, comprising the growth and development within a woman of a new individual from conception through the embryonic and fetal periods to birth. Pregnancy lasts approximately 266 days (38 weeks) from the day of fertilization, but it is clinically considered to last 280 days from the first day of the last menstrual period.

pregnancy gingivitis, an enlargement or hyperplasia of the gingivae caused by hormonal imbalance during pregnancy.

pregnancy rate, in statistics, the ratio of pregnancies per 100 woman-years, calculated as the product of the number of pregnancies in the women observed multiplied by 12 (months), divided by the product of the number of women observed multiplied by the number of months observed.

pregnancy termination care, a nursing intervention from the Nursing Interventions Classification (NIC) defined as management of the physical and psychological needs of the woman undergoing a spontaneous or elective abortion.

pregnanediol /pregnān'dē·ol/, a crystalline, biologically inactive compound in the urine of women during pregnancy or during the secretory phase of the menstrual cycle. A dihydroxy derivative of the saturated steroid pregnane, pregnanediol is the end product of metabolism of progesterone in the urine.

pregnanediol test, an infrequently used 24-hour urine test that evaluates progesterone production by the ovaries and placenta. It is useful in documenting whether ovulation has occurred, and if so, when.

pregnant /preg'nənt/ [L, *praegnans*], gravid, with child.

prehensile /prēhen'sil/ [L, *prehendre*, to seize], able to grasp.

prehension /-hen'shən/, the use of the hands and fingers to grasp, pick up objects, or pinch.

prehospital care, any initial medical care given an ill or injured patient by a paramedic or other person before the patient reaches the hospital ED.

P

preimplantation genetic diagnosis (PGD), in assisted reproductive technology, the determination of chromosomal abnormalities in the embryo before it is transferred to the uterus.

preinfarction angina /prē'infärc'shən/ [L, *prae + infarcire,* to stuff, *angina,* quinsy], angina pectoris before MI.

prekallikrein /prekal'ikre'in/, a plasma protein that is the proenzyme of plasma kallikrein. It is cleaved to its active enzyme form by activated coagulation factor XII.

preload /prē'lōd/ [L, *prae;* AS, *lad*], the stretch of ventricular muscle fibers at end diastole. It is reflected by the ventricular pressure and volume at that part of the cardiac cycle.

preload filling pressure, the load on the ventricular muscle fibers at the end of diastole or just before contraction. The preload on the heart is estimated by the left ventricular filling pressure.

premalignant fibroepithelioma /prēmalig'nənt/ [L, *prae + malignus,* bad disposition, *fibra,* fiber; Gk, *epi,* above, *thele,* nipple, *oma,* tumor], an elevated white-flesh-colored sessile neoplasm formed of interlacing ribbons of epithelial cells on a hyperplastic mesodermal stroma. The tumor occurs most often on the lower trunk of older people.

Premarin, a trademark for conjugated estrogens.

Premarin with Methyltestosterone, a trademark for a fixed-combination hormonal drug containing Premarin and an androgen (methyltestosterone).

premarket approval (PMA) /-mar'kit/, permission given by the federal government to equipment manufacturers to sell their devices to the medical profession.

premature /-məchoor'/ [L, *praematurus,* too soon], **1.** not fully developed or mature. **2.** occurring before the appropriate or usual time. —**prematurity,** *n.*

premature alopecia [L, *praematurus,* too soon; Gk, *alopex,* fox mange], acquired baldness in a person who is not old.

premature atrial complex (PAC), an atrial depolarization that occurs earlier than expected. It is indicated electrocardiographically by an early P' wave followed by a normal QRS complex. PACs may be the result of atrial enlargement or ischemia or may be caused by stress, caffeine, or nicotine.

premature beat [L, *praematurus,* too soon; AS, *beatan*], an ECG deflection or complex that occurs earlier than expected in the ongoing rhythm pattern.

premature complex, any ECG deflection representing either the ventricles or atria that occurs early with respect to the dominant rhythm.

premature ejaculation, uncontrollable, untimely ejaculation of semen during sexual intercourse, often caused by anxiety.

premature infant, any neonate, regardless of birth weight, born before 37 weeks of gestation. Predisposing factors associated with prematurity include multiple pregnancy, toxemia, chronic disease, acute infection, sensitization to blood incompatibility, any severe trauma that may interfere with normal fetal development, substance abuse, and teenage pregnancy.

premature rupture of membranes, the spontaneous rupture of the amniotic sac before the onset of labor.

premature systole [L, *praematurus;* Gk, *systole,* contraction], a ventricular contraction that occurs too early as a result of a discharge of an ectopic focus in the atria, atrioventricular junction, or ventricle.

premature ventricular complex (PVC), a ventricular depolarization that occurs earlier than expected. It appears on the ECG as an early, wide QRS complex without a preceding related P wave. PVCs may be idiopathic or caused by stress, electrolyte imbalance, ischemia, hypoxemia, hypercapnia, ventricular enlargement, or a toxic reaction to drugs. Frequent PVCs may be a precursor of ventricular tachycardia or fibrillation.

prematurity /-məchoor'ritē/ [L, *praematurus,* too soon], pertaining to an event that occurs before the usual or expected time, such as a premature birth.

premed /-med'/, abbreviation for *premedical student.*

premedication /-med'ikā'shən/ [L, *prae + medicare,* to heal], **1.** any sedative, tranquilizer, hypnotic, or anticholinergic medication administered before anesthesia to relieve anxiety and decrease pain. **2.** the administration of such medications. —**premedicate,** *v.*

premenarchal /-mənär'kəl/ [L, *prae,* before, Gk, *men,* month; Gk, *archaios,* from the beginning], before the start of the first menstrual period.

premenopausal /-men'əpô'səl/ [L, *prae + Gk, men,* month; Gk, *pauein,* to cease], before the start of menopause.

premenstrual /-men'stroo'əl/ [L, *prae,* before, *menstrualis,* monthly], before the start of menstruation each month.

premenstrual dysphoric disorder (PMDD), a mental health condition in women that begins 1 or 2 weeks before menstrual flow. Symptoms include depression, tension, mood swings, irritability, decreased interest, difficulty in concentrating, fatigue, changes in appetite or sleep, physical symptoms, and a sense of being overwhelmed.

premenstrual syndrome (PMS, pms) [L, *prae* + *menstrualis,* monthly, *tendere,* to stretch], a syndrome of nervous tension, irritability, weight gain, edema, headache, mastalgia, dysphoria, sleep changes, and lack of coordination occurring during the last few days of the menstrual cycle before the onset of menstruation.

premenstrual syndrome (PMS) management, a nursing intervention from the Nursing Interventions Classification (NIC) defined as the alleviation/attenuation of physical and/or behavioral symptoms occurring during the luteal phase of the menstrual cycle.

premise /prem'is/ [L, *prae* + *mittere,* to send], a proposition that is presented as the basis of an argument and usually established beforehand.

premolar /prēmō'lər/ [L, *prae* + *mola,* mill], one of eight teeth, four in each dental arch, located lateral and posterior to the canine teeth and in front of the molars. They are smaller and shorter than the canine teeth. The upper premolars are larger than the lower premolars.

premonition /-mənish'ən/, a sense of an impending event without prior knowledge of it.

premonitory /-mon'iter'ē/ [L, *prae* + *monere,* to warn], an early symptom or sign of a disease. The term is commonly used to describe minor symptoms that precede a major health problem.

premorbid personality /-môr'bid/, a personality characterized by early signs or symptoms of a mental disorder. The specific defects may indicate whether the condition will progress to schizophrenia, a bipolar disorder, or another type of condition.

prenatal /-nā'təl/ [L, *prae* + *natus,* birth], occurring or existing before birth, referring to both the care of the woman during pregnancy and the growth and development of the fetus.

prenatal care, a nursing intervention from the Nursing Interventions Classification (NIC) defined as monitoring and management of patient during pregnancy to prevent complications of pregnancy and promote a healthy outcome for both mother and infant.

prenatal development, the entire process of growth, maturation, differentiation, and development that occurs between conception and birth. On approximately the 14th day before the next expected menstrual period, ovulation usually occurs. If the egg is fertilized, it immediately begins the course to fetal maturity and birth. During the first 14 days the fertilized ovum undergoes cell division several times, becoming a morula and then a blastocyst that is able to implant in the uterine wall. From the beginning of the third to the end of the seventh week of embryonic development, implantation deepens and completes. From the 8th to the 10th week the fetus continues to grow and development is rapid. By the 12th week the facial features are formed and the eyelids are present but not yet closed because they have not divided into upper and lower eyelids. The palate is fusing, a neck connects the large head and the body, and tooth buds and nailbeds have begun to form. Identification of the external genitalia is possible for the first time. From the 13th to the 16th week the arms, legs, and trunk grow rapidly, and the fetus is active. Scalp hair develops. The skeleton of the fetus is calcified and may be seen on a x-ray film. A sonogram sometimes detects respiratory movements. Between the 17th and the 20th weeks of pregnancy the mother usually first feels the baby move. At 28 weeks subcutaneous fat begins to develop, fingernails and toenails are present, the eyelids are separate, the eyes may open, scalp hair is well developed, and in males the testes are at the internal inguinal ring or below. In a modern NICU most of the babies born at 28 weeks survive. At 40 weeks the average fetus weighs 7¼ pounds and is between 19 and 22 inches long.

prenatal diagnosis, any of various diagnostic techniques to determine whether a developing fetus in the uterus is affected with a genetic disorder or other abnormality. Such procedures as radiographic examination and ultrasound scanning can be used to follow fetal growth and detect structural abnormalities; amniocentesis enables fetal cells to be obtained from the amniotic fluid for culture and biochemical assay for detection of metabolic disorders and chromosomal analysis; fetoscopy enables fetal blood to be withdrawn from a blood vessel of the placenta and examined for disorders such as thalassemia, sickle cell anemia, and Duchenne's muscular dystrophy.

prenatal health behavior, a nursing outcome from the Nursing Outcomes Classification (NOC) defined as personal actions to promote a healthy pregnancy and a healthy newborn.

prenatal surgery, any surgical procedure that is performed on a fetus. The technique has been used to correct hydrocephalus, urinary tract obstructions, and many other conditions.

preoccupation /prē·ok'yəpā'shən/, a state of being self-absorbed or engrossed in one's own thoughts to a degree that hinders effective contact with or relationship to external reality.

P

pre-op /prē·op′/, abbreviation for **preoperative.**

preoperational thought phase /prē·op′ə rā′shənəl/ [L, *prae* + *operari,* to work; AS, *thot;* Gk, *phainein,* to show], a piagetian phase of child development, during the period of 2 to 7 years of age, when the child focuses on the use of language as a tool to meet his or her needs.

preoperative (pre-op) /prē·op′ərətiv′/ [L, *prae* + *operari,* to work], pertaining to the period before a surgical procedure. Commonly the preoperative period begins with the first preparation of the patient for surgery and ends with the induction of anesthesia in the operating suite.

preoperative care, the preparation and management of a patient before surgery. The patient's NPO status, nutritional and hygienic state, medical and surgical history, allergies, current medication, physical handicaps, signs of infection, and elimination habits are recorded. The patient's understanding of the operative, preoperative, and postoperative procedures; the patient's ability to verbalize anxieties; and the family's knowledge of the planned surgery are ascertained and education provided. The accuracy of the patient's signed informed consent is verified, requests in the physician's preoperative orders are fulfilled, and the patient's identification bands and blood type are checked. Vital signs are recorded, and any abnormalities of the ECG, chest radiographic study, or laboratory tests are reported to the surgeon and anesthesiologist. If needed, the number of matched blood units required to be held for a possible blood transfusion is determined. When ordered, an enema is given, a bowel preparation is completed, a nasogastric tube or indwelling catheter is inserted, and parenteral fluids are administered. If preoperative sedation is administered, the side rails of the bed are raised. Before transfer to the OR with the completed chart, the patient voids, and any dentures, contact lenses, jewelry, and valuables are removed for safekeeping.

preoperative coordination, a nursing intervention from the Nursing Interventions Classification (NIC) defined as facilitating preadmission diagnostic testing and preparation of the surgical patient.

prep, 1. abbreviation for *prepare.* **2.** abbreviation for *preparation,* particularly when referring to preparation for surgery.

preparatory prosthesis /prep′ərətôr′ē/, a temporary artificial limb that is fitted to the stump soon after amputation. It permits ambulation and biomechanical adaptation during the first several weeks after surgery.

preparatory sensory information, a nursing intervention from the Nursing

Interventions Classification (NIC) defined as describing in concrete and objective terms the typical sensory experiences and events associated with an upcoming stressful health care procedure/treatment.

preparedness /preper′ednes/, the state of being ready beforehand for a given event.

prepared tooth cavity /priperd′/ [L, *praeparare,* to make ready, *cavum,* cavity], a tooth cavity that has been carved with a compressed-air handpiece and other hand instruments to receive and retain a restoration.

prepartum /-pär′təm/, before childbirth.

prepatellar /-pətel′ər/ [L, *prae,* before, *patella,* small dish], pertaining to the area in front of the patella.

prepatellar bursa [L, *prae* + *patella,* small dish; Gk, *byrsa,* wineskin], a bursa between the tendon of the quadriceps muscle group and the lower part of the femur continuous with the cavity of the knee joint.

prepatellar bursitis [L, *prae,* before + *patella:* Gk, *byrsa,* wineskin, *itis,* inflammation], an inflammation of the bursa in front of the patella and beneath the skin over the site.

prepayment /-pā′mənt/ [L, *prae* + *pacere,* to pacify], the payment in advance for health care services by subscribers to a third-party insurance program.

preperitoneal hernia, an interstitial hernia located between the parietal peritoneum and the transversalis fascia.

preprandial /-pran′dē·əl/ [L, *prae* + *prandium,* meal], before a meal.

preprocedure readiness, a nursing outcome from the Nursing Outcomes Classification (NOC) defined as the readiness of a patient to safely undergo a procedure requiring anesthesia or sedation.

preprocessing /prēpros′əsing/, in ultrasonics, conditioning and manipulation of echo signals before their storage in the scan memory.

prepubertal panhypopituitarism /-pyo͞o′bərtəl/ [L, *prae* + *pubertas,* maturity; Gk, *pan,* all, *hypo,* under, *pituita,* phlegm], insufficiency of pituitary hormones, caused by damage to the gland usually associated with a suprasellar cyst or craniopharyngioma, occurring in childhood. The disorder is characterized by dwarfism with normal body proportions; subnormal sexual development; impaired thyroid and adrenal function; and yellow, wrinkled skin. Diabetes insipidus is frequently present, and there may be bitemporal hemianopia or complete blindness, but the patient's mentality is usually normal. Radiographic pictures show delayed fusion of the epiphyses and suprasellar calcification, and the sella turcica is often destroyed.

prepuberty /-pyo͞o′bərtē/ [L, *prae + pubertas,* maturity], the period immediately before puberty, lasting approximately 2 years. It is characterized by preliminary physical changes, such as accelerated growth and appearance of secondary sex characteristics that lead to sexual maturity. —**prepuberal, prepubertal,** *adj.*

prepubescence /prē′pyo͞obes′əns/, the state of being prepubertal.—**prepubescent,** *adj.*

prepuce /prē′pyo͞os/ [L, *praeputium,* foreskin], a fold of skin that forms a retractable cover, such as the foreskin of the penis or the fold around the clitoris.—**prepucial, preputial,** *adj.*

prerenal /-rē′nəl/ [L, *prae,* before, *ren,* kidney], **1.** pertaining to the area in front of the kidney. **2.** pertaining to events occurring before reaching the kidney.

prerenal anuria [L, *prae + renes,* kidneys; Gk, *a + ouron,* not urine], cessation of urine production that results when the BP in the kidney is too low to maintain glomerular filtration pressure.

prerenal uremia [L, *prae,* before, *ren,* kidney; Gk, *ouron,* urine, *haima,* blood], a condition of kidney failure in which the primary cause may be outside the kidney, as in CHF or some severe cases of alkalosis.

presacral fascia, a layer of parietal pelvic fascia between the sacrum and the rectum in which the superior and inferior hypogastric plexuses are embedded.

presacral space, a subdivision of the extraperitoneal space found between the urinary bladder and the sacrum.

presbycardia /prez′bekär′dē-ə/ [Gk, *presbys,* old man, *kardia,* heart], an abnormal cardiac condition that especially affects elderly individuals and may be associated with heart failure in the presence of other complications such as heart disease, fever, anemia, mild hyperthyroidism, and excess fluid administration. Presbycardia may be associated with decreased myocardial elasticity and with mild fibrotic changes of the heart valves, but the basis for these changes and the associated pigmentation of the heart is not known.

presbycusis /-ko͞o′sis/ [Gk, *presbys + akousis,* hearing], hearing loss associated with aging.

presbyopia /prez′bē-ō′pē-ə/ [Gk, *presbys + ops,* eye], a refractive condition in which the accommodative ability of the eye cannot meet the accommodative demand for near work. It results from a loss of elasticity of the lens of the eye. The condition commonly develops with advancing age.—**presbyopic,** *adj.*

presbyopic /prez′bē-op′ik/ [Gk, *presbys,* old man, *ops,* eye], pertaining to

a decrease in accommodation of the lens as one grows older and resulting in a shift toward hyperopia or farsightedness.

preschizophrenic state /prē′skit′səfren′ik, prē′-/ [L, *prae;* Gk, *schizein,* to split, *phren,* mind], a period before psychosis is evident when the patient deviates from normal behavior but does not demonstrate psychotic symptoms of delusions, hallucinations, or stupor.

prescreen /-skrēn/ [L, *prae;* ME, *screen*], **1.** to evaluate a person or a group of people to identify those who are at greater risk of development of a specific condition in order to select those who are in particular need of special diagnostic procedures or health care. **2.** *informal.* a rapid, superficial examination of a person who does not appear to be acutely ill. It may include taking a medical history.

prescribe /priskrīb′/ [L, *prae + scribere,* to write], **1.** to write an order for a drug, treatment, or procedure. **2.** to recommend or encourage a course of action.

prescription /priskrip′shən/, an order for medication, therapy, or therapeutic device given by a properly authorized person, which ultimately goes to a person properly authorized to dispense or perform the order. A prescription is usually in written form; can be emailed from a secure encrypted computer system, written, phoned, or faxed; and includes the patient's name and address, the date, the Rx symbol (superscription), the medication prescribed (inscription), directions to the pharmacist or other dispenser (subscription), the acceptability of dispensing generic, directions to the patient that must appear on the label, prescriber's signature, and in some instances, an identifying number.

prescription drug [L, *prae + scribere;* Fr, *drogue*], a drug that can be dispensed to the public only with an order given by a properly authorized person. The designation of a medication as a prescription drug is made by the U.S. Food and Drug Administration.

prescriptive intervention mode /priskrip′tiv/ [L, *praescriptus,* prescribed, *intervenire,* to come between, *modus,* measure], a therapeutic situation in which the health professional tells the patient explicitly how to solve a problem so that less collaboration between the consultant and patient is needed.

prescriptive theory, a theory that comprises a description of a specific activity, a statement of the goal of the activity, and an analysis of the elements of the activity, which together constitute a prescription for reaching the goal.

P

presence¹ /prez'əns/, a mode of being available in a situation with the wholeness of one's individual being; a gift of self that can be given freely, invoked, or evoked.

presence², a nursing intervention from the Nursing Interventions Classification (NIC) defined as being with another, both physically and psychologically, during times of need.

presenile /-sē'nīl/ [L, *prae*, before, *senex*, aged], pertaining to a condition in which a person manifests signs of aging in early or middle life.

presenile dementia, dementia occurring in younger persons, usually in persons age 65 or younger. Because most cases are the result of Alzheimer's disease, the term is sometimes used to denote the early-onset form of dementia of the Alzheimer type; it has also been used more generally to denote Alzheimer's disease.

present health [L, *praesentare*, to show; AS, *haelth*], in a health history, a succinct chronologic account of any recent changes in the health of the patient and of the circumstances or symptoms that prompted the person to seek health care.

presenting part /prəsen'ting/ [L, *praesentare* + *pars*, part], the part of the fetus that lies closest to the internal os of the cervix.

preservative /prisur'vətiv/ [L, *praeservare*, to keep], a chemical or other agent that reduces the rate of decomposition of a substance.

presomite embryo /prēsō'mīt/ [L, *prae*; Gk, *soma*, body, *en*, in, *bryein*, to grow], an embryo in any stage of development before the appearance of the first pair of somites (segments), which in humans usually occurs around 19 to 21 days after fertilization of the ovum.

pressor /pres'ər/ [L, *premere*, to press], describing a substance that tends to cause a rise in BP.

pressure acupuncture, a system of acupuncture involving the application of pressure, such as by the tip of a finger, to certain specified points of the body.

pressure area, an oral area that is subject to excessive displacement of soft tissue by a prosthesis.

pressure control ventilation, positive-pressure ventilation in which breaths are augmented by air at a rate and fixed amount of pressure, with tidal volume not being fixed. It is used particularly for patients with acute respiratory distress syndrome.

pressure cycling, the delivery of gas under positive pressure during inspiration until an adjustable, preselected pressure has been reached.

pressure diuresis, increased urinary excretion of water when there is an increase of arterial pressure, a compensatory mechanism to maintain BP within the normal range.

pressure dressing, a bandage or cloth material firmly applied to exert pressure to stop bleeding, prevent edema, and provide support for varicose veins. It also is commonly used in the treatment of burns and after skin grafting.

pressure edema, 1. edema of the lower extremities caused by pressure of a pregnant uterus against the large veins of the area. 2. edema of the fetal scalp after cephalic presentation.

pressure management, a nursing intervention from the Nursing Interventions Classification (NIC) defined as minimizing pressure to body parts.

pressure natriuresis, increased urinary excretion of sodium along with water when there is an increase of arterial pressure, a compensatory mechanism to maintain BP within the normal range.

pressure (P) /presh'ər/ [L, *premere*, to press], a force, or stress, applied to a surface by a fluid or an object, usually measured in units of mass per unit of area, such as pounds per square inch. Other units include mm Hg, bar, and atm.

pressure point, 1. a point over an artery where the pulse may be felt. Pressure on the point may be helpful in stopping the flow of blood from a wound distal to it. 2. a site that is extremely sensitive to pressure, such as the phrenic pressure point along the phrenic nerve between the sternocleidomastoid and the scalenus anticus on the right side.

pressure-sensitive adhesive (PSA), a drug-delivery device that uses polymers that are permanently tacky at room temperature and adhere to the skin when slight pressure is applied.

pressure support ventilation (PSV), the augmentation of spontaneous breathing effort with a specific amount of positive airway pressure. The patient initiates the inspiratory flow and sets his or her own respiration rate and tidal volume.

pressure transducer, an electronic device that converts pressure (such as BP) into electrical signals that can be recorded graphically and monitored.

pressure trigger, a trigger for initiating assisted ventilation, consisting of a mechanism for measuring pressure and starting assisted ventilation when pressure reaches a given level.

pressure ulcer, an inflammation, sore, or ulcer in the skin over a bony prominence, most frequently the sacrum, elbows, heels, outer ankles, inner knees, hips, shoulder blades, and occipital bone. It results from ischemic hypoxia of the tissues caused by prolonged pressure on them. Pressure ulcers are most often seen in aged, debilitated, immobilized, or cachectic patients. Prevention of pressure ulcers is a cardinal aspect of nursing care.

pressure ulcer care¹, the management and prevention of pressure ulcers. Prevention of pressure ulcers begins with an understanding of proper body positioning, the importance of turning and repositioning, and the need for suitable support surfaces for sleeping and for sitting. Bedfast patients should be repositioned at least every two hours, and chairfast patients should be repositioned every 15 minutes. Bed linen should be kept dry and wrinkle-free. To avoid shear, a sheet or mechanical lift is used to move a patient. Skin should be inspected at least once daily for redness or discoloration, and each time the patient is repositioned the bony areas should be inspected. A prophylactic measure is daily skin care, in which all areas are washed, rinsed, and dried thoroughly, and lotion is gently applied to bony prominences. Topical wound management involves debridement, wound cleansing, the application of dressings, and possibly adjunct therapy (electric stimulation, hyperbaric oxygen, ultrasound). Clinical Practice Guidelines for Treatment of Pressure Ulcers may be obtained from the U.S. Department of Health and Human Services, Agency for Health Care Policy and Research (AHCPR). Normal saline is recommended for cleaning most pressure ulcers. The pressure ulcer wound bed should be moist. Devices such as heat lamps and hair dryers should not be used.

pressure ulcer care², a nursing intervention from the Nursing Interventions Classification (NIC) defined as facilitation of healing in pressure ulcers.

pressure ulcer prevention, a nursing intervention from the Nursing Interventions Classification (NIC) defined as the prevention of pressure ulcers for an individual at high risk for developing them.

pressure ventilator, a mechanical ventilator in which gas delivery is limited by a predetermined pressure.

presternal region, the region of the thorax overlying the sternum, bounded laterally by the pectoral regions.

presumptive signs /prēsump′tiv/ [L, *praesumere,* to take beforehand; *signum,* mark], manifestations that indicate a pregnancy, although they are not necessarily positive. Presumptive signs may include cessation of menses and morning sickness.

preswing stance stage /prē′swing/ [L, *prae;* AS, *swingan,* to fling; L, *stare,* to stand; OFr, *estage,* stage], one of the five

stages in the stance phase of walking or gait, a brief transitional period of double-limb support during which one leg is rapidly relieved of body-bearing weight and prepared for the swing forward.

presymptomatic disease /-simp′tomat′ik/ [L, *prae;* Gk, *symptoma,* a happening], an early stage of disease when physiologic changes have begun but no signs or symptoms are observed.

presynaptic /-sinap′tik/ [L, *prae;* Gk, *synaptein,* to join], **1.** situated near or before a synapse. **2.** before a synapse is crossed.

presystole /-sis′təlē/ [L, *prae,* before; Gk, *systole,* contraction], the interval in the cardiac cycle immediately before systole. **—presystolic,** *adj.*

presystolic murmur (psm) [L, *prae,* before; Gk, *systole,* contraction; L, *murmur,* humming], a heart murmur heard immediately before systole in cases of mitral valve stenosis.

preterm /prēturm′/ [L, *prae,* before; Gk, *terma,* limit], **1.** events before a specific date. **2.** pertaining to a shorter-than-normal period of gestation.

preterm birth, any birth that occurs before the thirty-seventh week of gestation.

preterm contractions, irregular tightening of the pregnant uterus that begins in the first trimester and increases in frequency, duration, and intensity as pregnancy progresses. Contractility of uterine muscle increases in pregnancy. Near term, strong preterm contractions are often difficult to distinguish from the contractions of true labor.

preterm infant organization, a nursing outcome from the Nursing Outcomes Classification (NOC) defined as extrauterine integration of physiological and behavioral function by the infant born at 24 to 37 (term) weeks of gestation.

preterm labor, labor that occurs earlier in pregnancy than normal, either before the fetus has reached a weight of 2000 to 2500 g or before the 37th or 38th week of gestation. No single measure of fetal weight or gestational age is used universally to designate preterm birth; local or institutional policy dictates which of several standards is applied. Incidence is higher for African-American women, for women who have not had adequate prenatal care or have an abnormal obstetric history, and for women who smoke or whose diet is deficient in protein or calories. Predisposing conditions include maternal infection, low weight gain, uterine bleeding, multiple gestation, polyhydramnios, uterine abnormalities, incompetent cervix, premature rupture of membranes, and intrauterine fetal growth retardation. If preterm labor itself constitutes a threat to the fetus, the outcome of pregnancy may be improved if labor can be inhibited.

pretibial /prĕtib´ē·əl/ [L, *prae* + *tibia,* shinbone], pertaining to the area of the leg in front of the tibia.

pretibial fever, an acute infection caused by *Leptospira autumnalis.* It is characterized by headache, chills, fever, enlarged spleen, myalgia, low WBC count, and rash on the anterior surface of the legs.

prevalence /prev´ələns/ [L, *praevalentia,* a powerful force], in epidemiology, the number of all new and old cases of a disease or occurrences of an event during a particular period. —**prevalent,** *adj.*

prevention /-ven´shən/ [L, *praevenire,* to anticipate], in nursing care, any action directed to preventing illness and promoting health to eliminate the need for secondary or tertiary health care.

preventive /-ven´tiv/ [L, *praevenire,* to anticipate], pertaining to hindering the occurrence of an illness or decreasing the incidence of a disease.

preventive care, a pattern of nursing and medical care that focuses on disease prevention and health maintenance. It includes early diagnosis of disease, discovery, and identification of people at risk for development of specific problems, counseling, and other necessary intervention to avert a health problem.

preventive dentistry [L, *praevenire,* to anticipate, *dens,* tooth], the science of the care required to prevent disease of the teeth and supporting structures.

preventive medicine [L, *praevenire,* to anticipate + *medicina*], the branch of medicine that is concerned with the prevention of disease and methods for increasing the power of the patient and community to resist disease and prolong life.

preventive nursing [L, *praevenire,* to anticipate, *nutrix,* nurse], the branch of nursing concerned with general health promotion, teaching of early recognition and treatment of disease, encouragement of lifestyle modification, and prevention of further deterioration of the disabled.

preventive psychiatry, the use of theoretic knowledge and skills to plan and implement programs designed to achieve primary, secondary, and tertiary prevention of the onset of psychiatric disorders.

preventive treatment, a procedure, measure, substance, or program designed to prevent a disease from occurring or a mild disorder from becoming more severe. Various diseases are prevented by immunizations with vaccines, antiseptic measures, the avoidance of smoking, regular exercise, prudent diet, adequate rest, correction of congenital anomalies, and screening programs for the detection of preclinical signs of disorders.

prevertebral ganglia, collections of postgangionic sympathetic neuronal cell bodies in recognizable aggregations along the abdominal prevertebral plexus. They play a critical role in the innervations of the abdominal viscera.

previllous embryo /prēvil´əs/ [L, *prae* + *villus,* hairy; Gk, *en,* in, *bryein,* to grow], an embryo of a placental mammal at any stage before the development of the chorionic villi, which in humans occurs between the first and second months after fertilization.

previous abnormality of glucose tolerance /prē´vē·əs/, an obsolete classification that includes people who previously had DM or impaired glucose tolerance but whose fasting and postprandial plasma glucose levels have returned to normal.

prevocational evaluation /-vōkā´shənəl/, an evaluation of the abilities and limitations of a patient undergoing rehabilitation for a disabling disorder. The goal is to find eventual employment in a sheltered workshop or in the general community.

prevocational training, a rehabilitation program designed to prepare a patient for the performance of useful paid work in a sheltered setting or community. It may involve training in basic work skills and counseling as required for a typical employment setting.

Prezista, a trademark for darunavir.

PRF, abbreviation for **pulse repetition frequency.**

priapism /prī´əpiz´əm/ [Gk, *priapos,* phallus], an abnormal condition of prolonged or constant penile erection, often painful and seldom associated with sexual arousal. It may result from localized infection, a lesion in the penis or the CNS, or the use of certain drugs. It sometimes occurs in men who have acute leukemia or sickle cell anemia.

priapitis /prī´əpī´tis/, inflammation of the penis.

prilocaine hydrochloride /pril´ōkān/, a local anesthetic agent of the amide family, used for nerve block, epidural, and regional anesthesia. It is not used for spinal or topical anesthesia.

prima facie rights /prī´mə fā´shē·ə/, rights on the surface, or face, that may be overridden by stronger conflicting rights or by other values.

primal scream therapy /prī´məl/, a non-mainstream form of psychotherapy developed by Arthur Janov that focuses on repressed pain of infancy or childhood. The goal of the therapy is to enable the patient to surrender his or her anxiety defenses and "become real."

primaquine phosphate /prī'məkwin/, an antimalarial drug that is prescribed in the treatment of malaria and prevention of relapse during recovery from the disease. It eradicates the tissue schizonts of *Plasmodium vivax* and *P. ovale* infections.

primary /prī'marē/ [L, *primus,* first], **1.** first in order of time, place, development, or importance. **2.** not derived from any other source or cause; specifically, the original condition or set of symptoms in disease processes, such as a primary infection or a primary tumor. **3.** in chemistry, referring to the first and simplest compound in a related series, formed by the substitution of one of two or more atoms or of a group in a molecule.

primary abscess [L, *primus* + *abscedere,* to go away], an abscess that develops at the original point of infection by a pus-producing microorganism.

primary amebic meningoencephalitis, a rare and often fatal acute, febrile, purulent meningoencephalitis caused by usually free-living soil and water amebas of the genera *Naegleria* and *Acanthamoeba.* Infection caused by *Naegleria* is generally seen in young persons who swim or bathe in contaminated freshwater, the pathogens gaining access to the CNS by penetrating the nasal mucosa and cribriform plate and then following the olfactory bulbs and nerves to the brain and meninges. *Acanthamoeba* infections are more often seen in older or immunocompromised persons and are sometimes associated with spontaneous recovery.

primary amputation, amputation performed after severe trauma, after the patient has recovered from shock, and before infection occurs.

primary apnea, a self-limited condition characterized by an absence of respiration. It may follow a blow to the head and is common immediately after birth in the newborn who breathes spontaneously when the carbon dioxide level in the circulation reaches a certain value.

primary atelectasis, failure of the lungs to expand fully at birth, most commonly seen in premature infants or those narcotized by maternal anesthesia. The infant is usually cared for in an incubator, in which the temperature and humidity may be closely monitored.

primary biliary cirrhosis, a chronic inflammatory condition of the liver characterized by generalized pruritus; enlargement and hardening of the liver; weight loss; and diarrhea with pale, bulky stools. Petechiae, epistaxis, or hemorrhage resulting from hypoprothrombinemia may also be evident. Jaundice, dark urine, pale stools, and cutaneous xanthosis may occur in the later stages of this disease.

primary bronchial buds, two outgrowths from the respiratory diverticulum, which ultimately become the right and left primary bronchi and also give rise to the secondary bronchial buds.

primary bronchus, one of the two main air passages that branch from the trachea and convey air to the lungs as part of the respiratory system. The right primary bronchus enters the right lung nearly opposite the fifth thoracic vertebra. The left primary bronchus divides into bronchi for the superior and anterior lobes of the lung.

primary carcinoma, a neoplasm at the site of origin.

primary care, the first contact in a given episode of illness that leads to a decision regarding a course of action to resolve the health problem.

primary care case management (PCCM), in the United States, a situation in which primary care receives concurrent utilization management review, and discharge planning is used to minimize resource consumption while maintaining quality of care.

primary care physician (PCP, P.C.P.) [L, *primus;* ME, *caru,* sorrow; Gk, *physikos,* natural], a physician who usually is the first health professional to examine a patient and who recommends secondary care physicians, medical or surgical specialists with expertise in the patient's specific health problem, if further treatment is needed.

primary cell, an irreversible (nonrechargeable) electromotive force cell.

primary cell culture, a cell line derived directly from the parent tissue. Cells in primary culture have the same karyotype and chromosome number as those in the original tissue.

primary colors, a small number of fundamental colors. In visual science these are red, green, and blue, the colors specifically picked up by the retinal cones. In painting and printing, the primary colors are red, blue, and yellow.

primary curvature of vertebral column, a dorsally convex part of the spinal (vertebral) column.

primary cutaneous melanoma, a malignant neoplasm on the skin at the site of origin.

primary dental caries, dental caries developing in a tooth that was previously unaffected.

primary dentition, the set of 20 teeth that appears normally during infancy, consisting of four incisors, two canines, and four molars in each jaw. The primary teeth are usually shed between the ages of 6 and 13

P

years, although the timing varies greatly from person to person.

primary dermatitis [L, *primus;* Gk, *derma,* skin, *itis,* inflammation], skin eruption caused by a substance that can produce cell damage on initial contact, as opposed to that which develops as a sensitivity reaction to an allergen.

primary effusion lymphoma, a B-cell lymphoma associated with human herpesvirus 8 infection, characterized by the occurrence of lymphomatous effusions in body cavities without the presence of a solid tumor.

primary endometriosis [L, *primus;* Gk, *endon,* within, *metra,* womb, *osis,* condition], an ingrowth of the muscle walls of the uterus by the mucous membrane lining of the organ.

primary fissure, a fissure that marks the division of the anterior and posterior lobes of the cerebellum.

primary gain, a benefit, primarily relief from emotional conflict and freedom from anxiety, attained through the use of a defense mechanism or other psychologic process.

primary gangrene [L, *primus;* Gk, *gangraina*], a form of gangrene that occurs without preceding inflammation.

primary health care, a basic level of health care that includes programs directed at the promotion of health, early diagnosis of disease or disability, and prevention of disease. Primary health care is provided in an ambulatory facility to limited numbers of people, often those living in a particular geographic area. It includes continuing health care, as provided by a family nurse practitioner.

primary hemorrhage [L, *primus;* Gk, *haima,* blood, *rhegnynei,* to burst forth], a hemorrhage immediately after an injury.

primary iritis [L, *primus;* Gk, *iris,* rainbow, *itis,* inflammation], an inflammation of the iris that results from a source within the body, such as a systemic disease.

primary lateral sclerosis, a slowly progressing degenerative brain disease characterized by weakness, spasticity, hyperreflexia, and a positive Babinski sign. It involves neurons of the motor cortex but not the brainstem or spinal cord neurons.

primary lesion [L, *primus* + *laesio,* hurting], a sore or wound that develops at the point of inoculation of the disease, usually applied to a syphilis chancre.

primary nurse, a nurse who is responsible for the planning, implementation, and evaluation of the nursing care of one or more clients 24 hours a day for the duration of the hospital stay.

primary nursing, a system for the distribution of nursing care in which care of one patient is managed for the entire 24-hour day by one nurse who directs and coordinates nurses and other personnel; schedules all tests, procedures, and daily activities for that patient; and cares for that patient personally when on duty. In acute care the primary care nurse may be responsible for only one patient; in intermediate care the primary care nurse may be responsible for three or more patients.

primary oocyte, an oocyte that has begun but not completed the first maturation division. It is derived from an oogonium by differentiation near the time of birth.

primary organizer, the part of the dorsal lip of the blastopore that is self-differentiating and induces the formation of the neural plate that gives rise to the main axis of the embryo.

primary palate, a shelf formed from the medial nasal process of an embryo that separates the primitive nasal cavity from the oral cavity.

primary physician, 1. the physician who usually takes care of a patient. **2.** the physician who first sees a patient for the care of a given health problem. **3.** a family practice physician or general practitioner.

primary prevention, a program of activities directed at improving general well-being while also involving specific protection for selected diseases, such as immunization against measles.

primary processes, in psychoanalytic theory, unconscious processes, originating in the id, that obey laws different from those of the ego. These processes occur in the least disguised form in infancy and in the dreams of the adult.

primary progressive aphasia, a speech disorder seen with certain degenerative brain diseases, consisting of deterioration of speech and language ability over a period of years without significant loss of memory or of ability to understand language.

primary relationships, relationships with intimates, close friends, and family.

primary sclerosing cholangitis, a progressive chronic fibrosing inflammation of the bile ducts of unknown cause, occurring most commonly in young men and frequently in association with chronic ulcerative colitis.

primary sensation, a feeling or impression resulting directly from a particular stimulus.

primary sequestrum, a piece of dead bone that completely separates from sound bone during the process of necrosis.

primary sex character, an inherited trait directly concerned with the reproductive function of the primary sex organs of the individual.

primary shock, a state of physical collapse comparable to fainting. It is usually mild, self-limited, and of short duration.

primary sterility [L, *primus + sterilis,* barren], the inability to produce offspring caused by a functional failure of the ovaries or testes.

primary triad, in A.T. Beck's theory of depression, the three major cognitive patterns that force the individual to view self, environment, and future in a negative manner.

primary tuberculosis, the childhood form of TB, most commonly occurring in the lungs, the posterior pharynx, or, rarely, the skin. Infants lack resistance to the disease and are readily infected and especially vulnerable to rapid and extensive spread of infection through the body. In childhood the disease is usually brief and benign, characterized by regional lymphadenopathy, calcification of the tubercles, and residual immunity.

primate /prī′māt, prī′mit/ [L, *primus,* first], a member of the order of mammals that includes lemurs, monkeys, apes, and humans. Most primates have large brains, stereoscopic vision, and hands and feet developed for grasping.

Primaxin, a trademark for a broad-spectrum parenteral antibiotic (imipenem-cilastatin sodium).

prime mover /prīm/ [L, *primus + movere,* to move], a muscle that acts directly to produce a desired movement amid other muscles acting simultaneously to produce the same movement indirectly. Most movements of the body require the combined action of numerous muscles.

primer /prī′mər/, **1.** a short piece of DNA or RNA complementary to a given DNA sequence that acts as a point at which replication can proceed, as in a polymerase chain reaction. **2.** a molecule, such as a small polymer, that induces the synthesis of a larger molecule.

primidone /prī′mədōn/, an anticonvulsant prescribed in the treatment of seizure disorders. It has an unlabeled use for treating familial (essential) tremor.

primigravida /prim′igrav′idə/ [L, *primus + gravidus,* pregnancy], a woman pregnant for the first time.—**primigravid,** *adj.*

primipara /primip′ərə/ *pl.* **primiparae** [L, *primus + parere,* to bear], a woman who has given birth to one viable infant, indicated by the notation *para 1* on the patient's chart.

primiparity /prim′iper′itē/ [L, *primus + parere,* to bear], the condition of having borne one child.

primiparous /primip′ərəs/ [L, *primus + parere,* to bear], pertaining to a woman who has borne one child.

primitive /prim′itiv/ [L, *primivus*], **1.** undeveloped; undifferentiated; rudimentary; showing little or no evolution. **2.** embryonic; formed early in the course of development; existing in an early or simple form.

primitive groove, a furrow in the posterior region of the embryonic (primordial) disk. It indicates the cephalocaudal axis that results from the active involution of cells forming the primitive streak.

primitive heart tube, the primordium of the heart, formed by fusion of the two lateral endocardial tubes.

primitive node, a knoblike accumulation of cells at the cephalic end of the primitive streak in the early stages of embryonic development in humans and higher animals.

primitive pit, a minute indentation at the anterior end of the primitive groove in the early developing embryo. It probably functions as an opening into the notochordal canal in humans and higher animals and into the neurenteric canal in lower animals.

primitive reflex, any reflex normal in an infant or fetus. Its presence in an adult usually indicates serious neurologic disease.

primitive ridge, a ridge that bounds the primitive groove in the early stages of embryonic development.

primitive streak, a dense area on the central posterior region of the embryonic disk. It is formed by the morphogenetic movement of a rapidly proliferating mass of cells that spreads between the ectoderm and endoderm, giving rise to the mesoderm layer.

primordial /prīmôr′dē·əl/ [L, *primordium,* origin], **1.** characteristic of the most undeveloped or earliest state, specifically those cells or tissues that are formed in the early stages of embryonic development. **2.** first or original; primitive.

primordial cyst, one of three kinds of follicular cysts, consisting of an epithelium-lined sac that contains fluid and appears radiographically as a light area in the affected jaw. It develops from a dental enamel organ before the formation of hard tissue.

primordial dwarf, a person of extremely short stature who is otherwise perfectly formed, with the usual proportions of body parts and normal mental and sexual development.

primordial germ cell, any of the large spheric diploid cells that are formed in the early stages of embryonic development and are precursors of the oogonia and spermatogonia.

primordial image, in analytic psychology, the archetype or original parent, representing the source of all life.

primordial oocyte, an oocyte very early in its development.

primordium /prīmôr′dē-əm/*pl.* **primordia** [L, origin], the first recognizable stage in the embryonic development and differentiation of a particular organ, tissue, or structure.

principal /prin′sipəl/ [L, *principalis,* first in rank], first in authority or importance.

Principen, a trademark for an antibacterial (ampicillin).

principle /prin′sipəl/ [L, *principium,* foundation], **1.** a general truth or established rule of action. **2.** a prime source or element from which anything proceeds. **3.** a law on which others are founded or from which others are derived.

principle of infinitesimal dose, one of the fundamental principles of homeopathy, stating that the more a remedy is diluted (even to the point that none of the medicinal substance is likely to be present), the more powerful and longer-lasting will be its effect.

principles of instrumentation, six rules for the use of mirrors and other hand-driven and motor-driven devices in dentistry and dental hygiene: (1) grasp, (2) fulcrum, (3) insertion, (4) adaptation and angulation, (5) activation (lateral pressure and working stroke), and (6) rest.

Prinivil, a trademark for an angiotensin-converting enzyme inhibitor used for hypertension (lisinopril).

P-R interval, the interval from the beginning of the P wave to the beginning of the QRS complex on an ECG. It represents the atrioventricular conduction time, which normally is between 0.12 and 0.20 second.

Prinzmetal's angina [Myron Prinzmetal, American cardiologist, 1908–1994], chest pain caused by reversible, severe coronary artery spasm. It is associated with ST segment elevation that reverts to normal within minutes. The S-T segment elevation indicates total occlusion of the epicardial coronary artery.

prion /prī′on/, one of several kinds of proteinaceous particles believed to be responsible for transmissible neurodegenerative diseases, including scrapie in sheep and kuru and Creutzfeldt-Jakob disease in humans. Because prions lack detectable nucleic acid, they are not inactivated by the usual procedures for destroying viruses. They also do not trigger an immune response.

prion disease, any of a group of fatal degenerative diseases of the nervous system caused by abnormalities in the metabolism of prion protein. These diseases are unique in that they may be transmitted genetically as an autosomal-dominant trait or by infection with abnormal forms of the protein (prions). Infectious forms of the disease result from ingestion of infected tissue or the introduction of infected tissue into the body.

priority /prī·ôr′itē/ [L, *prius,* previously], actions established in order of importance or urgency to the welfare or purposes of the organization, patient, or other person at a given time.

Priscoline, a trademark for a peripheral vasodilator (tolazoline hydrochloride).

prism /priz′əm/ [Gk, *prisma,* that which is seen through], **1.** a solid of glass, plastic, or a similar substance with a triangular or polygonal cross section, which splits up a ray of light into its constituent colors and turns or deflects light rays toward its base. Prisms are used to correct deviations of the eyes, because they alter the apparent situation of objects. **2.** enamel prism, or calcified rods, surrounded by organic prism cuticle joined together to form tooth enamel. **3.** an adverse prism or verger prism used to test and train ocular muscles.

prismatic colors /prizmat′ik/, the seven rainbow hues (red, orange, yellow, green, blue, indigo, and violet) produced from white light when it is reduced to its component wavelengths by the dispersion effect of a prism.

privacy /prī′vəsē/, a culturally specific concept defining the degree of one's personal responsibility to others in regulating behavior that is regarded as intrusive. Some privacy-regulating mechanisms are physical barriers (closed doors or drawn curtains, such as around a hospital bed) and interpersonal types (lowered voices or cessation of smoking).

private duty nurse /prī′vit/, a nurse who may work in an institution, caring for a patient on a fee-for-service basis. The private duty nurse is not a member of the institution staff. Private duty care also occurs in the home.

private practice, the work of a professional health care provider who is independent of economic or policy control by professional peers, except for licensing and other legal restrictions.

privileged communication /priv′ilijd/, a legal term used in court-related proceedings concerning the right to reveal information that belongs to the person who spoke. It may prevent the listener from disclosing the information without the permission of the speaker. Privileged communication may exist between a patient and a health professional only if the law specifically establishes it.

privileges /priv′ilij′əs/ [L, *privilegium,* private law], authority granted to a physician or dentist by a hospital governing board to provide patient care in the hospital. Clinical privileges are limited to the individual's professional license, experience, and competence. Emergency privileges may be granted by a hospital governing board or chief executive officer in an emergency and without regard to the physician's or dentist's regular service assignment or status. Temporary privileges may be granted a physician or dentist to provide health care to patients for a limited period or to a specific patient.

Privine, a trademark for an alpha-1 adrenergic agonist (naphazoline hydrochloride).

PRK, abbreviation for **photorefractive keratectomy.**

PRL, abbreviation for **prolactin.**

prn, p.r.n., in prescriptions, abbreviation for *pro re nata,* a Latin phrase meaning "as needed." The administration times are determined by the patient's needs.

Pro, abbreviation for **proline.**

probability /prob′əbil′itē/ [L, *probabilitas*], **1.** a measure of the likelihood that something will occur. **2.** a mathematic ratio of the number of times something will occur to the total number of possible occurrences.

probable signs /prob′əbəl/ [L, *probabalis,* credible, *signum,* mark], clinical signs that there is a definite likelihood of pregnancy. Examples are enlargement of the abdomen, Goodell's sign, Hegar's sign, Braxton Hicks' sign, and positive hormonal test results.

Pro-Banthine, a trademark for an anticholinergic (propantheline bromide).

probe, **1.** any device used to explore an opening such as a sinus or wound. Common types of probes include a probe with a blunt leading end, a drum probe with a sounding device for the detection of metallic foreign particles, and an eyed probe with a small opening at one end for introducing a guiding thread along a fistula. **2.** any device or agent, such as a radioactively tagged isotope or a molecular DNA fragment probe, inserted into a medium to obtain information about a structure or substance. **3.** a Doppler probe used to detect blood flow in a vessel. **4.** the act of exploring or investigating an action or unfamiliar matter.

probenecid /prōben′əsid/, a uricosuric and adjunct to antibiotics prescribed in the treatment of gout and as an adjunct to prolong the activity of penicillin or cephalosporins in some infections, such as gonorrhea.

problem /prob′ləm/ [Gk, *proballein,* to throw forward], any health care condition that requires diagnostic, therapeutic, or educational action. It also refers, in nursing, to any unmet or partially met basic human need.

problem-oriented medical record (POMR), a method of recording data about the health status of a patient in a problem-solving system. The POMR preserves the data in an easily accessible way that encourages ongoing assessment and revision of the health care plan by all members of the health care team. A database is collected before beginning the process of identifying the patient's problems. The database consists of all available information. The physical examination or health assessment makes up the second major part of the database. The next section of the POMR is the master problem list. The formulation of the problems on the list is similar to the assessment phase of the nursing process. Each problem as identified represents a conclusion or a decision resulting from examination, investigation, and analysis of the database. The third major section of the POMR is the initial plan, in which each separate problem is named and described, usually on the progress note in a subjective, objective, assessment, and plan (SOAP) format. A discharge summary is formulated and written, relating the overall assessment of progress during treatment and the plans for follow-up or referral. The summary allows a review of all the problems initially identified and encourages continuity of care for the patient.

problem-solving approach to patient-centered care, in nursing, a conceptual framework that incorporates the overt physical needs of a patient with covert psychologic, emotional, and social needs. It provides a model for caring for the whole person as an individual, not as an example of a disease or medical diagnosis. Nursing is defined within this model as a problem-solving process. The patient is viewed as a person who is in an impaired state, less than usually able to perform self-care activities.

procainamide hydrochloride /prōkān′əmīd/, an antiarrhythmic agent prescribed in the treatment of a variety of cardiac arrhythmias, including premature ventricular contractions, ventricular tachycardia, and atrial fibrillation.

procaine hydrochloride /prō′kān/, a local anesthetic of the ester family administered for local anesthesia by infiltration and injection and for caudal, epidural, and other regional anesthetic procedures. It is not used for topical anesthesia.

procarbazine hydrochloride /prōkär′bəzēn/, an antineoplastic prescribed in the treatment of a variety of neoplasms, including Hodgkin's disease, lymphomas, brain tumors, and lung cancer.

Procardia, a trademark for a calcium channel blocker (nifedipine).

Procaryotae /prōker′ē·ō′tē/, in bacteriology, a kingdom of bacteria, viruses, and blue-green algae that includes all microorganisms in which the nucleoplasm has no basic protein and is not surrounded by a nuclear membrane. The kingdom has two divisions: cyanobacteria, which includes the blue-green bacteria, and bacteria.

procedure /prəsē′jər/ [L, *procedere,* to proceed], the sequence of steps to be followed in establishing some course of action.

procercoid /prōsur′koid/, the first stage in the life cycle of certain tapeworms that develop from the coracidium stage of *Diphyllobothrium latum.*

procerus /prəsir′əs/ [L, stretched], one of three muscles of the nose. The procerus functions to draw down the eyebrows and wrinkle the nose.

process /pros′əs/ [L, *processus*], **1.** a series of related events that follow in sequence from a particular state or condition to a conclusion or resolution. **2.** a natural growth that projects from a bone or other part. **3.** to put through a particular series of interdependent steps, as in preparing a chemical compound.

process criteria, standards identified by the American Nurses Association that focus on nursing activities.

process recording, in nursing education, a system used for teaching nursing students to understand and analyze verbal and nonverbal interaction. The conversation between nurse and patient is written on special forms or in a special format and then studied by the nursing instructor to discover and to help the student nurse identify patterns of difficulty in communicating with the patient.

processus vaginalis peritonei /prəses′əs/ [L, *processus,* process, *vagina,* sheath; Gk, *peri,* around, *teinein,* to stretch], a diverticulum of the peritoneal membrane that during embryonic development extends through the inguinal canal. In males it descends into the scrotum to form the processus vaginalis testis; in females it is usually completely obliterated.

prochlorperazine /-klôrper′əzēn/, a phenothiazine antipsychotic and antiemetic.

procidentia /-siden′shə/ [L, *procidere,* to fall forward], the prolapse of an organ. The term is usually applied to a prolapsed uterus.

procoagulant /-kō·ag′yələnt/, an inactive coagulation protein that becomes activated

during the coagulation process to form a serine protease or cofactor and produce a fibrin clot. Prothrombin is an example.

procreation /-krē·ā′shən/ [L, *procreare,* to create], the entire reproductive process of producing offspring.—**procreate,** *v.*

proctalgia /proktal′jə/ [Gk, *proktos,* anus, *algos,* pain], a neurologic pain in the anus or lower rectum.

proctalgia fugax [Gk, *proktos* + *algos,* pain; L, *fugax,* fleeting], periodic pain in the anus, possibly muscular in origin, that follows a pattern and is sometimes relieved by food and drink.

proctitis /proktī′tis/ [Gk, *proktos,* anus, *itis*], inflammation of the rectum and anus caused by infection, trauma, drugs, allergy, or radiation injury. Acute or chronic, it is accompanied by rectal discomfort and the repeated urge to pass feces and inability to do so. Pus, blood, or mucus may be present in the stools, and tenesmus may occur.

proctocolectomy /prok′tōkəlek′təmē/, a surgical procedure in which the anus, rectum, and colon are removed. An ileostomy is created for the removal of digestive tract wastes. The procedure treats severe, intractable ulcerative colitis or Crohn's disease.

Proctocort, a trademark for an anorectal preparation containing a glucocorticoid (hydrocortisone).

proctodeum /proktō′dē·əm/ *pl.* **proctodea** [Gk, *proktos* + *hodiaos,* a route], a depression of the ectoderm, behind the urorectal septum of the developing embryo, that forms the anus and anal canal when the cloacal membrane ruptures.—**proctodaeal, proctodeal,** *adj.*

proctodynia /-din′ē·ə/ [Gk, *proktos* + *odyne,* pain], pain in or around the anus.

proctologist /proktol′əjist/, a physician who specializes in proctology.

proctology /proktol′əjē/ [Gk, *proktos* + *logos,* science], the branch of medicine concerned with treating disorders of the colon, rectum, and anus.

proctoplasty /prok′təplas′tē/ [Gk, *proktos,* anus, *plassein,* to mold], a plastic surgery procedure performed on the anus and rectum.

proctoscope /prok′təskōp′/ [Gk, *proktos* + *skopein,* to look], an instrument used to examine the rectum and the distal part of the colon. It consists of a light mounted on a tube or speculum.

proctoscopy /proktos′kəpē/, the examination of the rectum with an endoscope inserted through the anus.

proctosigmoidoscopy /prok′tōsig′moidos′kəpē/ [Gk, *proktos* + *sigmoid* + *skopein,* to view], the use of a sigmoidoscope to examine the rectum and pelvic colon.

procumbency /prōkum'bensē/ [L, *procumbere*, to lean forward], excessive inclination of the incisor teeth toward the lips.

procyclidine hydrochloride /prōsī'klədēn/, an anticholinergic prescribed in the treatment of parkinsonism and drug-induced extrapyramidal dysfunction. It also controls sialorrhea resulting from neuroleptic medication.

prodromal /-drō'məl/ [Gk, *pro,* before, *dromos,* course], pertaining to early symptoms that may mark the onset of a disease.

prodromal labor [Gk, *prodromos,* running before; L, *labor,* work], the early period in parturition before uterine contractions become forceful and frequent enough to result in progressive dilation of the uterine cervix.

prodromal.

prodromal myopia, an optical condition in which the ability to do close work without eyeglasses returns but usually as a symptom of developing cataracts.

prodromal phase, a clear deterioration in function before the active phase of a mental disturbance. It is not caused by a disorder in mood or a psychoactive substance. It includes some residual phase symptoms.

prodromal rash, a rash that precedes a potentially more serious skin eruption caused by an infectious disease.

prodromal symptom [Gk, *pro* + *dromos,* course, *symptoma,* that which happens], a symptom that may be the first indication of the onset of a disease.

prodrome /prō'drōm/ [Gk, *prodromos,* running before], **1.** an early sign of a developing condition or disease. **2.** the earliest phase of a developing condition or disease.—**prodromal,** *adj.*

prodrug /prō'drug/, an inactive or partially active drug that is metabolically changed in the body to an active drug.

product evaluation, a nursing intervention from the Nursing Interventions Classification (NIC) defined as determining the effectiveness of new products or equipment.

product evaluation committee /prod'əkt/, a hospital committee composed of medical, nursing, purchasing, and administrative staff members whose purpose is to evaluate health care–related products and advise on their procurement.

productive cough /prəduk'tiv/ [L, *producere;* AS, *cohhetan,* to cough], a sudden, noisy expulsion of air from the lungs that effectively removes sputum from the respiratory tract and helps clear the airways, permitting air to reach the alveoli. Deep breathing, with contraction of the diaphragm and intercostal muscles and forceful exhalation, promotes productive coughing in patients with respiratory infections.

Profenal, a trademark for an oral nonsteroidal antiinflammatory analgesic (suprofen).

professional corporation (PC) /prəfesh'ənəl/ [L, *professio,* profession], a corporation formed according to the law of a particular state for the purpose of delivering a professional service.

professional liability, the legal obligation of health care professionals, or their insurers, to compensate patients for injury or suffering caused by acts of omission or commission by the professionals. Professional liability is a better characterization of the responsibility of all professionals to their patients than is the concept of malpractice, but the idea of professional liability is central to malpractice.

professional network, in psychiatric nursing, the network of professional resources available to support the psychiatric outpatient in the community. The network may include a therapist, hospital day treatment program, social work agency, and other agencies.

professional organization, an organization whose members share a professional status, created to deal with issues of concern to the professional group or groups involved.

Professional Standards Review Organization (PSRO), an organization formed under the U.S. Social Security Act Amendments of 1972 to review the services provided under Medicare, Medicaid, and Maternal Child Health programs. Review is conducted by physicians to ascertain the need for the program and to ensure that it is carried out in accord with certain criteria, norms, and standards, and in institutional situations, in a proper setting.

profile /prō'fīl/ [L, *profilare,* to outline], a short sketch, diagram, or summary relating to a person or thing.

profunda /prōfun'də/ [L, *profundus,* deep], pertaining to structures, mainly blood vessels, that are deeply embedded in tissues.

profuse sweat /prəfyōōs'/ [L, *profundere,* to pour out; AS, *swaetan*], excessive perspiration.

progenitive /-jen'itiv/ [Gk, *pro,* before, *genein,* to produce], capable of producing offspring; reproductive.

progenitor /-jen'itor/ [Gk, *pro* + *genein*], **1.** a parent or ancestor. **2.** someone or something that begets or creates.

progeny /proj'ənē/ [L, *progenies*], **1.** offspring; an individual or organism resulting from a particular mating. **2.** the descendants of a known or common ancestor.

progeria /prōjir'ē-ə/ [Gk, *pro* + *geras,* old age], an abnormal congenital condition characterized by premature aging, appearance in childhood of gray hair and

P

wrinkled skin, small stature, absence of pubic and facial hair, and posture and habitus of an aged person. Death usually occurs before 20 years of age.

progestagen-only contraceptive, an oral contraceptive consisting only of a small dose of a progestational agent to be taken every day.

progestational /prō′jestā′shənəl/ [Gk, *pro;* L, *gestare,* to bear], pertaining to a drug with effects similar to those of progesterone, the hormone produced by the corpus luteum and adrenal cortex during the luteal phase of the menstrual cycle that prepares the uterus for reception of the fertilized ovum.

progestational agent [L, *pro + gestare,* to bear, *agere,* to do], any chemical having the same action as progesterone produced by the corpus luteum and the placenta.

progesterone /prəjes′tərōn/, a natural progestational hormone used to prevent endometrial hyperplasia in nonhysterectomized, postmenopausal women who are receiving conjugated estrogen tablets; to treat dysfunctional uterine bleeding caused by hormonal imbalances; as a contraceptive in IUDs; and in intravaginal gel for women using assisted reproductive technology.

progesterone assay, a blood test that is useful in documenting whether ovulation has occurred, and if so, when. Repeated assays may also be used to monitor the status of the placenta in high-risk pregnancy and progesterone supplementation in patients with an inadequate luteal phase.

progesterone receptor assay, a tumor-specimen analysis used primarily to determine the prognosis and treatment of breast cancer.

progestin /-jes′tin/, 1. progesterone. 2. any of a group of hormones, natural or synthetic, secreted by the corpus luteum, placenta, or adrenal cortex that have a progesterone-like effect on the uterine endometrial lining to prepare it for implantation of the blastocyst.

progestogen /-jes′təjən/, any natural or synthetic progestational hormone.

proglottid /prōglot′id/ [Gk, *pro + glossa,* tongue], a sexual segment of an adult tapeworm, containing both male and female reproductive organs.

prognathism /prog′nəthiz′əm/ [Gk, *pro + gnathos,* jaw], an abnormal facial configuration in which one or both jaws project forward.—**prognathic,** *adj.*

prognosis /prognō′sis/ [Gk, *pro + gnosis,* knowledge], a prediction of the probable outcome of a disease based on the condition of the person and the usual course of the disease as observed in similar situations.

prognostic /prognos′tik/ [Gk, *pro + gnosis,* knowledge], pertaining to signs and symptoms that may indicate the outcome of an illness or injury.

prognosticate /prognos′tikāt/ [Gk, *pro,* before, *gnosis,* knowledge], to forecast or predict from facts, present indications, or signs, such as the course a disease may take and the final outcome.

prognostic indicators, factors, such as staging, tumor type, and laboratory studies, that may indicate treatment effectiveness and outcomes.

Prograf, a trademark for an immunosuppressive drug (tacrolimus).

program development, a nursing intervention from the Nursing Interventions Classification (NIC) defined as planning, implementing, and evaluating a coordinated set of activities designed to enhance wellness or to prevent, reduce, or eliminate one or more health problems for a group or community.

programmable pacemaker /-gram′əbəl/ [Gk, *pro + graphein,* to record; L, *passus,* step; ME, *maken*], an electronic pacemaker with multiple settings that can be changed after implantation.

programmed aging theory, 1. a theory of aging that states that life expectancy is predetermined and timed for individual species, with cells programmed to divide a certain number of times. Functional changes in the cells cause aging of the cells and thus the organism. 2. any of various theories of aging based on timed functional changes.

programmed pacing, control of the heart rate by a programmable pacemaker.

Program of All-inclusive Care of the Elderly (PACE) /pās/, a U.S. federally supported program of comprehensive care with a primary objective of keeping clients in the community as long as medically, socially, and financially possible. It is a team approach in which professionals assess client needs, develop a care plan, integrate primary care and other services, and arrange for implementation of services. PACE is sponsored by one or more facilities and community groups and receives funds from Medicare, Medicaid, and private donations.

progravid /-grav′id/ [L, *pro + gravid,* pregnant], before pregnancy.

progression /-gresh′ən/, a carcinogenic process whereby cells genetically altered by initiators undergo a second (nongenetic) cell expansion that allows uncontrollable growth.

progressive /-gres′iv/ [L, *progredi,* to advance], describing the course of a disease or condition in which the characteristic signs and symptoms become more prominent and severe, such as progressive muscular atrophy.

progressive assistive exercise, an exercise designed to improve the strength of a muscle group progressively by gradually decreasing assistance required of a therapist for an active motion, thereby increasing the patient's active effort.

progressive bulbar paralysis [L, *progredi,* to advance, *bulbus,* swollen root; Gk, *paralyein,* to be palsied], a motor neuron disease characterized by weakness of the laryngeal, pharyngeal, tongue, and facial muscles. The patient experiences progressive dysarthria and dysphagia.

progressive familial intrahepatic cholestasis, an autosomal-recessive type of intrahepatic cholestasis of hepatocellular origin. Affected children often develop cirrhosis by age 10 and die during adolescence.

progressive muscle relaxation, a nursing intervention from the Nursing Interventions Classification (NIC) defined as facilitating the tensing and releasing of successive muscle groups while attending to the resulting differences in sensation.

progressive myopia [L, *progredi;* Gk, *myops,* nearsighted], a condition in which myopia increases, continuing into adulthood.

progressive ophthalmoplegia [L, *progredi*], a form of ocular muscle paralysis that usually begins with ptosis and gradually involves all of the extraocular muscles.

progressive patient care, a system of care in which patients are placed in units on the basis of their needs for care as determined by the degree of illness rather than in units based on a medical specialty.

progressive relaxation, a technique for combating tension and anxiety by systematically tensing and relaxing muscle groups.

progressive resistance exercise (PRE), a method of increasing the strength of a weak or injured muscle by gradually increasing the resistance against which the muscle works, such as by using graduated weights.

progressive scan mode, a method of cathode ray tube scanning in which all lines are scanned successively.

progressive supranuclear palsy [L, *supra,* above, *nucleus,* nut kernel; Gk, *paralyein*], a rare progressive neurologic disorder of unknown cause occurring in middle age, more often in men. It is characterized by paralysis of eye muscles, ataxia, neck and trunk rigidity, pseudobulbar palsy, and parkinsonian facies. Dementia and inappropriate emotional responses also are common.

progress notes [L, *progredi* + *nota,* mark], in the patient record, notes made by a nurse, physician, social worker, physical therapist, and other health care professionals that describe the patient's condition and the treatment given or planned. Progress notes may follow the problem-oriented medical record format. The physician's progress notes usually focus on the medical or therapeutic aspects of the patient's condition and care. The nurse's progress notes usually focus on the objectives stated in the nursing care plan.

proguanil /prōgwahn′il/, an antimalarial agent. Its use in the United States is limited because of the development of drug-resistant malarial parasites.

proinsulin /prō·in′s(y)əlin/ [L, *pro* + *insula,* island], a single-chain peptide molecule that is a precursor of insulin.

projectile vomiting /-jek′til/, expulsive vomiting that is extremely forceful, and the vomitus is expelled some distance.

projection /-jek′shən/ [L, *projectio,* thrown forward], **1.** a protuberance; anything that thrusts or juts outward. **2.** the act of perceiving an idea or thought as an objective reality. **3.** in psychology, an unconscious defense mechanism by which an individual attributes his or her own unacceptable traits, ideas, or impulses to another.

projection reconstruction imaging, the techniques used in MRI to obtain a cross-sectional image of an object. Such an image is computer-reconstructed from a series of magnetic resonance profiles recorded all around an object by rotating the gradient field superimposed on the static magnetic field.

projective test /-jek′tiv/ [L, *projectio,* thrown forward], a kind of diagnostic, psychologic, or personality test that uses unstructured or ambiguous stimuli such as inkblots, a series of pictures, abstract patterns, or incomplete sentences to elicit responses that reflect a projection of various aspects of the individual's personality.

prokaryocyte /prōker′ē·əsīt/ [Gk, *protos,* first, *karyon,* nut, *kytos,* cell], a cell without a true nucleus and with nuclear material scattered throughout the cytoplasm. Prokaryocytic organisms include bacteria, viruses, mycoplasmas, actinomycetes, and blue-green algae.

prokaryon /prōker′ē·on/ [Gk, *protos* + *karyon,* nut], a region within a bacterial cell that contains most of the bacterial DNA. It is not separated from the rest of the cell by a membrane.

prokaryosis /-ker′ē·ō′sis/ [Gk, *protos* + *karyon* + *osis,* condition], the condition of having a prokaryon.

P

prokaryote /prōkăr′ē-ōt/ [Gk, *protos* + *karyon*], a unicellular organism that does not contain a true nucleus surrounded by a double membrane; a bacterium. Division usually occurs through simple fission. —**prokaryotic,** *adj.*

prokaryotic cell, one without a true nucleus.

prokinetic /prō′kinet′ik/, stimulating movement or motion, such as a drug that promotes GI motility.

prolactin (PRL) /prōlak′tin/ [Gk, *pro,* before, *lac,* milk], a hormone produced and secreted into the bloodstream by the anterior pituitary gland. It stimulates the development and growth of the mammary glands after the glands have been prepared by estrogen, progesterone, thyroxine, insulin, growth hormone, glucocorticoids, and human placental lactogen. After parturition, prolactin, together with glucocorticoids, is essential for the initiation and maintenance of milk production.

prolactin levels test, a blood test that is helpful for monitoring the disease activity of pituitary adenomas.

prolapse /prō′laps, prōlaps′/ [L, *prolapsus,* falling], the dropping, falling, sinking, or sliding of an organ from its normal position or location in the body.

prolapsed cord /prōlapst′/, an umbilical cord that protrudes beside or ahead of the presenting part of the fetus.

prolapsed hemorrhoid [L, *prolapsus,* falling; Gk, *haimorrhois,* a vein that loses blood], an internal hemorrhoid that protrudes through the anal orifice.

prolapsed ureterocele, an intravesical ureterocele that extends beyond the bladder neck down into the urethra, usually seen in females.

prolapse of anus [L, *prolapsus,* falling + *anus*], the protrusion of the mucous membrane of the anus through the external sphincter.

prolapse of rectum [L, *prolapsus,* falling, *rectus,* straight], a protrusion of the mucous membrane of the lower part of the rectum through the anal orifice.

prolapse of uterus [L, *prolapsus,* falling, *uterus,* womb], the descent of the uterine cervix into the vagina, partly into the vagina, or outside the vagina.

Prolastin, a trademark for alpha₁-antitrypsin (alpha₁-proteinase inhibitor, human).

proliferation /-lif′ərā′shən/ [L, *proles,* offspring, *ferre,* to bear], the reproduction or multiplication of similar forms. The term is usually applied to increases of cells or cysts.— **proliferate,** *v.,* **proliferative, prolific,** *adj.*

proliferation inhibiting factor, a lymphokine that restricts cell division in tissue cultures.

proliferative glomerulonephritis, any of various types of glomerulonephritis accompanied by proliferation of endothelial or mesangial cells in the glomeruli, including acute, diffuse, membranoproliferative, mesangial proliferative, and rapidly progressive glomerulonephritis.

proliferative phase /-lif′ərativ/, the phase of the menstrual cycle after menstruation. Under the influence of follicle-stimulating hormone from the pituitary, the ovary produces increasing amounts of estrogen, causing the lining of the uterus to become dense and richly vascular.

prolific /-lif′ik/ [L, *proles,* offspring, *ferre,* to bear], highly productive.

proline (Pro) /prō′lēn/, a nonessential amino acid found in many proteins of the body, particularly collagen.

prolonged gestation /-longd′/ [L, *prolongare,* to lengthen, *gestare,* to bear], a pregnancy that lasts longer than the usual period of 41 weeks.

prolonged release [Gk, *pro,* before, *longus,* long], a term applied to a drug that is designed to deliver a dose of a medication over an extended period. The most common device for this purpose is a soft, soluble capsule containing minute pellets of the drug for release at different rates in the GI tract, depending on the thickness and nature of the oil, fat, wax, or resin coating on the pellets.

Proloprim, a trademark for an antibacterial (trimethoprim).

PROM, abbreviation for **passive range of motion.**

promastigote /prōmas′tigōt/, the flagellate stage of a trypanosome. It is found in the insect intermediate host or in culture.

promethazine hydrochloride /-meth′əzēn/, a phenothiazine antiemetic, antihistamine, and sedative prescribed in the treatment of motion sickness, nausea, rhinitis, itching, and skin rash and as an adjunct to anesthesia and pain control.

promethium (Pm) /-mē′thē-əm/ [L, *Prometheus,* mythic character who gave fire to humans], a radioactive rare earth metallic element. Its atomic number is 61; its atomic mass is 145.

prominence /prom′inəns/ [L, *prominentia,* sticking out], any protuberance or projection of a structural feature.

promontory of the sacrum /prom′əntôr′ē/ [L, *promontorium,* headland], the superior projecting part of the sacrum at its junction with the L5 vertebra.

promoter /-mō′tər/ [L, *promovere,* to move forward], **1.** a DNA sequence that initiates transcription of the genetic code. **2.** a cocarcinogen that encourages cells altered by initiators to reproduce more rapidly than normal, increasing the probability of malignant transformation.

prompted voiding, a nursing intervention from the Nursing Interventions Classification (NIC) defined as promotion of urinary continence through the use of timed verbal toileting reminders and positive social feedback for successful toileting.

prompt insulin zinc suspension [L, *promptus,* ready], a fast-acting noncrystalline semilente insulin prescribed in the treatment of DM when a prompt, intense, and short-acting response is desired.

promyelocyte /prōmī′shən/, precursor in the bone marrow myelocytic series that is intermediate in development between a myeloblast and a myelocyte. The cytoplasm contains prominent primary granules. Appears in peripheral blood in acute promyelocytic leukemia.

pronation /prōnā′shən/ [L, *pronare,* to bend forward], **1.** assumption of a prone position, one in which the ventral surface of the body faces downward. **2.** of the arm, the rotation of the forearm so that the palm of the hand faces downward or backward. **3.** of the foot, the lowering of the medial edge of the foot by turning it outward and through abduction in the tarsal and metatarsal joints.—**pronate,** *v.*

pronator quadratus /prōnā′tər/, a muscle of the forearm. It functions to pronate the forearm and hand.

pronator reflex [L, *pronare* + *reflectere,* to bend back], a reflex elicited by holding the patient's hand vertically and tapping the distal end of the radius or ulna, resulting in pronation of the forearm.

pronator syndrome [L, *pronare,* to bend forward; Gk, *syn,* together, *dromos,* course], the compression of the median nerve in the forearm between the two heads of the pronator teres muscle.

pronator teres /ter′əs/, a superficial muscle of the forearm. It functions to pronate the hand.

prone /prōn/ [L, *pronare,* to bend forward], **1.** having a tendency or inclination. **2.** of the body, being in horizontal position when lying face downward.

proneness profile /prōn′nəs/ [L, *pronare,* to bend forward, *profilare,* to outline], a screening process that evaluates the probability of developmental problems in the early years of a child's life. Several of the variables in the proneness profile that appear to be significant in selecting the infants who are at risk are the perinatal health status of the mother and infant, especially complications of pregnancy, delivery, the neonatal period, and the puerperium; characteristics of the mother, especially her temperament, educational

level, perception of the life situation, and perception of the infant; characteristics of the infant, including alertness, activity pattern, and responsiveness; and behaviors of the infant and caregiver as they interact.

prone-on-elbows, a body position in which the person rests the upper part of the body on the elbows while lying face down. The position is used as an initial rehabilitation exercise in training a person with a cerebellar dysfunction to achieve various goals.

pronephric duct /-nef′rik/ [Gk, *pro,* before, *nephros,* kidney; L, *ducere,* to lead], one of the paired ducts that connects the tubules of each of the pronephros with the cloaca in the early developing vertebrate embryo.

pronephric tubule, any of the segmentally arranged excretory units of the pronephros in the early developing vertebrate embryo.

pronephros /-nef′rəs/ *pl.* **pronephroi** [Gk, *pro* + *nephros,* kidney], the earliest and simplest kind of excretory organ in the developing vertebrate embryo. In humans and other mammals the structure is nonfunctional.—**pronephric,** *adj.*

prone posture [L, *pronare,* to bend forward, *ponere,* to place], a posture assumed by lying flat with the face forward in response to certain disorders of the spine or viscera.

pronucleus /-nōō′klē·əs/ *pl.* **pronuclei** [Gk, *pro;* L, *nucleus,* nut kernel], the nucleus of an ovum or a spermatozoon after fertilization but before fusion of the chromosomes to form the nucleus of the zygote.

propagation /prop′əgā′shən/ [L, *propagare,* to generate], the process of increasing or causing to increase.

propantheline bromide /-pan′thəlēn/, an anticholinergic/antispasmodic prescribed as an adjunct in peptic ulcer therapy, irritable bowel syndrome, and pancreatitis and for spasm of the ureters or urinary bladder.

proparacaine hydrochloride /prōper′əkān/, a rapid-acting topical anesthetic of the amide family used for tonometry, gonioscopy, removal of foreign objects from the eye, and other minor ophthalmologic procedures and preoperatively for major eye surgery.

prophase /prō′fāz/ [Gk, *pro* + *phasis,* appearance], the first of four stages of nuclear division in mitosis and in each of the two divisions of meiosis.

prophylactic /prō′filak′tik/ [Gk, *prophylax,* advance guard], **1.** preventing the spread of disease. **2.** an agent that prevents the spread of disease. **3.** a popular name for condom.—**prophylactically,** *adv.*

prophylactic odontomy, the surgical removal of harmful pits and fissures in the

P

posterior primary and secondary molars to prevent the formation of caries in those areas.

prophylaxis /prō′filak′sis/ [Gk, *prophylax,* advance guard], prevention of or protection against disease, often involving the use of a biologic, chemical, or mechanical agent to destroy or prevent the entry of infectious organisms.

Propionibacterium /prō′pē·on′ēbaktir′ē·əm/ [Gk, *pro* + *pion,* fat, *bakterion,* small rod], a genus of nonmotile anaerobic gram-positive bacteria found on the skin of humans, in the intestinal tract of humans and animals, and in dairy products. *Propionibacterium acnes* is common in acne pustules.

propionic acid /prō′pē·on′ik/, an aliphatic carboxylic acid, methylacetic acid, a chemical component of sweat. It can be formed by fermentation of sugars by several species of bacteria.

propionicacidemia /prō′pē·on′ikas′idē′mē·ə/ [Gk, *pro* + *pion,* fat; L, *acidus,* sour; Gk, *haima,* blood], a rare inherited metabolic defect caused by the failure of the body to metabolize the amino acids threonine, isoleucine, and methionine, characterized by lethargy and mental and physical retardation. Acidosis results from the accumulation of propionic acid in the body.—**propionicacidemic,** *adj.*

propionic fermentation [Gk, *pro* + *pion;* L, *fermentare,* to cause to ferment], the production of propionic acid by the action of certain bacteria on sugars or lactic acid.

Proplex T, a trademark for human clotting factor IX.

propofol /prō′pə-fol/, a short-acting sedative and hypnotic used as a general anesthetic and adjunct to anesthesia.

proportional /prəpôr′shənəl/, pertaining to the relationship between two quantities when a fractional variation of one is always accompanied by the same fractional change in the other.

proportional gas detector, a device for measuring alpha and beta forms of radioactivity.

proportional mortality [L, *pro* + *portio,* part, *mortalis,* subject to death], a statistical method of relating the number of deaths from a particular condition to all deaths within the same population group for the same period.

proposition /prop′əzish′ən/ [L, *proponere,* to place forward], 1. a statement of a truth to be demonstrated or an operation to be performed. 2. to bring forward or offer for consideration, acceptance, or adoption.

propositus /prōpoz′itəs/ [L, *proponere,* to place forward], a person from whom a genealogic lineage is traced, as is done

to discover the pattern of inheritance of a familial disease or a physical trait.

propoxyphene hydrochloride, an analgesic prescribed for the relief of mild to moderate pain.

propranolol hydrochloride /-pran′əlol/, a nonselective beta-adrenergic receptor blocking agent prescribed in the treatment of hypertension angina pectoris, catecholamine-induced cardiac arrhythmias, pheochromocytoma, essential tremor, and migraine headache and for various unlabeled uses such as treatment of anxiety and aggressive behavior.

proprietary /-prī′əter′ē/ [L, *proprietas,* property], 1. pertaining to an institution or other organization that is operated for profit. 2. pertaining to a product, such as a drug or device, that is made for profit.

proprietary hospital, a hospital operated as a profit-making organization.

proprietary medicine, any pharmaceutical preparation or medicinal substance that is protected from commercial competition because its ingredients or method of manufacture is kept secret or protected by trademark or copyright.

proprioception /prō′prē·əsep′shən/ [L, *proprius,* one's own, *capere,* to take], sensation pertaining to stimuli originating from within the body related to spatial position and muscular activity or to the sensory receptors that they activate.

proprioceptive /prō′prē·əsep′tiv/ [L, *proprius,* one's own, *capere,* to take], pertaining to the sensations of body movements and awareness of posture, enabling the body to orient itself in space without visual clues.

proprioceptive impulse, a nerve impulse that originates with a sensory ending in muscle, joint, or tendon. Such impulses provide information to the CNS about the relative position of body parts.

proprioceptive neuromuscular facilitation (PNF), an activity, such as a therapeutic technique, that helps initiate a proprioceptive response in a patient.

proprioceptive reflex [L, *proprius* + *capere,* to take, *reflectere,* to bend back], any reflex initiated by stimulation of proprioceptors, such as the increase in respiratory rate and volume induced by impulses arising from muscles and joints during exercise.

proprioceptive sensation [L, *proprius* + *capere* + *sentire,* to feel], the feeling of body movement and position, including motion of the arms and legs, resulting from stimuli received by special sense organs in the muscles, tendons, joints, and inner ear.

proprioceptor /prō′prē·əsep′tər/ [L, *proprius* + *capere*], any sensory nerve ending, such as those located in muscles, tendons, joints, and the vestibular apparatus, that responds to stimuli originating from within the body related to movement and spatial position.

proptosis /proptō'sis/ [L, *pro* + *ptosis,* falling], a bulging, protrusion, or forward displacement of a body organ or area.

propulsion /prə-pŭl'shən/ [L, *propellere,* to drive forward], **1.** the process of pushing forward. **2.** the tendency of some patients, particularly those afflicted with nervous disorders, to push or fall forward while walking as their center of gravity is displaced.

propylene glycol (CH₃CHOHCH₂OH) /prop'ilĕn/, a colorless viscous liquid used as a solvent in the preparation of certain medications. It also inhibits the growth of fungi and microorganisms and is used commercially as an antifreeze.

propylthiouracil /prō'pilthī'əyŏŏr'əsil/, an inhibitor of thyroid hormone biosynthesis prescribed in treatment of hyperthyroidism and thyrotoxic crisis and in preparation for thyroidectomy.

prorenin /prōren'in/, the inactive precursor of renin, stored in the juxtaglomerular cells of the kidney and activated by cleavage to renin.

proscribe /prōskrīb'/, to forbid.—**proscriptive,** *adj.*

prosector /-sek'tər/ [L, *prosecare,* to cut off], a person who, under the supervision of a pathologist, performs gross dissections and prepares autopsy specimens for pathologic examination.

prosencephalon /pros'ensef'əlon/ [Gk, *pro* + *enkephalon,* brain], the anterior primitive cerebral vesicle which further divides into diencephalon and telencephalon.—**prosencephalic,** *adj.*

Pro Sobee, a trademark for a commercial milk-substitute formula that is prepared from a soy isolate base and is lactose-free. It is prescribed for infants with galactosemia and people with lactose intolerance. It is supplemented with other nutrients, is fortified with vitamins and minerals, and is available in both powder and liquid forms.

prosopopilary virilism /pros'əpōpī'lərē/, a heavy growth of facial hair.

prosopospasm /pros'əpōspaz'əm/ [Gk, *prosopon,* face + *spasmos*], a spasm of the facial muscles, such as may occur in tetanus.

prosoposternodidymus /pros'əpōstur'nə did'əməs/ [Gk, *prosopon,* face, *sternon,* chest, *didymos,* twin], a fetus consisting of conjoined twins united laterally from the head through the sternum.

prosopothoracopagus /pros'əpōthôr'əkop'ə gəs/ [Gk, *prosopon* + *thorax,* chest, *pagos,* fixed], conjoined symmetric twins who are united laterally in the frontal plane from the thorax through most of the head region.

prospective medicine /-spek'tiv/ [L, *proscipere,* to look forward, *medicina,* art of healing], the early identification of pathologic or potentially pathologic processes and the prescription of intervention to stop them.

prospective payment system (PPS), a payment mechanism for reimbursing hospitals for inpatient health care services in which a predetermined rate is set for treatment of specific illnesses. The system was originally developed by the U.S. federal government for use in treatment of Medicare recipients.

prospective reimbursement, a method of payment to an agency for health care services to be delivered that is based on predictions of what the agency's costs will be for the coming year.

prospective study, an analytic study designed to determine the relationship between a condition and a characteristic shared by some members of a group. The population selected is healthy at the beginning of the study. Some of the members of the group share a particular characteristic, such as cigarette smoking. The researcher follows the population group over a period of time, noting the rate at which a condition, such as lung cancer, occurs in the smokers and in the nonsmokers. Prospective studies produce a direct measure of risk called the *relative risk.*

prostacyclin (PGI₂) /pros'təsī'klin/, a prostaglandin. It inhibits the vasoconstrictor effect of angiotensin and stimulates renin release and has been used to treat pulmonary hypertension.

prostaglandin (PG) /pros'təglan'din/ [Gk, *prostates,* standing before; L, *glans,* acorn], one of several potent unsaturated fatty acids that act in exceedingly low concentrations on local target organs. Prostaglandins are produced in small amounts and have a large array of significant effects. Some of the pharmacologic uses of the prostaglandins are termination of pregnancy and treatment of asthma and gastric hyperacidity.

prostaglandin endoperoxide synthase /pros'tə-glan'din en'doperok'sīd sin'thāas/, an enzyme of the oxidoreductase class that has both COX and peroxidase activities, which together catalyze part of the synthesis of prostaglandins and thromboxanes from arachidonic acid.

prostaglandin inhibitor, an agent that prevents the production of prostaglandins. An example is an NSAID.

prostanoic acid /pros'tənō'ik/, a 20-carbon aliphatic carboxylic acid that is the basic framework for prostaglandin molecules, which differ according to the location of hydroxyl and keto substitutions at various positions along the molecule.

P

prostate /pros'tāt/ [Gk, *prostates*, standing before], a gland in men that surrounds the neck of the bladder and the proximal part of the urethra and produces a fluid that becomes part of semen. A firm structure normally about the size of a chestnut, the prostate is located in the pelvic cavity, below the inferior part of the symphysis pubis and ventral to the rectum, through which it can be felt, especially when it is enlarged. A depression on its cranial border accommodates the entry of the two ejaculatory ducts from the seminal vesicles. The prostate is composed of glandular and muscular tissue and contracts during ejaculation of seminal fluid. —**prostatic,** *adj.*

prostate cancer, the most common invasive cancer among American males, rarely occurring before the age of 39 and most often affecting men between the ages of 60 and 79. Ninety-five percent are adenocarcinomas; the remaining types are transitional cell carcinoma, squamous cell carcinoma, sarcoma, and ductal carcinoma. The cause is unknown, but it is believed to be hormone-related.

prostatectomy /pros'tətek'təmē/ [Gk, *prostates + ektomē,* excision], surgical removal of a part of the prostate gland, such as that performed for benign prostatic hypertrophy, or the total excision of the gland, as performed for malignancy.

prostate-specific antigen (PSA), a protein produced by the prostate that may be present at elevated levels in patients with cancer or other disease of the prostate.

prostate-specific antigen (PSA) test, a blood test used to detect prostatic cancer and to monitor the patient's response to therapy. The PSA velocity monitors the change in PSA with time, and the percent-free PSA is assessed as an independent predictor of prostate cancer risk.

prostatic calculus [Gk, *prostates,* standing before; L, *calculus,* pebble], a solid calcification formed in the prostate. Typically small and multiple, prostatic calculi are often the product of chronic prostatitis and are usually composed of calcium carbonate and/or calcium phosphate. They are not clinically significant.

prostatic catheter, a catheter used in male urinary bladder catheterization to pass an enlarged prostate gland obstructing the urethra.

prostatic ductule /duk'tyŌŌl/ [Gk, *prostates;* L, *ductulus,* little duct], any of 12 to 20 tiny excretory tubes that convey the alkaline secretion of the prostate and open into the floor of the prostatic part of the urethra.

prostatic fascia, a condensation of fascia around the anterior and lateral region of the prostate that contains and surrounds the prostatic plexus of veins.

prostatic fluid, the secretion of the prostate gland, which contributes to formation of the semen.

prostatic syncope [Gk, *prostates,* standing before, *syn,* together, *koptein,* to cut], a temporary LOC caused by restricted cerebral blood flow that may occur during a digital rectal examination of the prostate.

prostatic urethral polyps, presence of numerous polyps in the prostatic urethra, sometimes causing obstruction, seen in male children as a developmental anomaly and in older males in some inflammatory reactions.

prostatic utricle, the part of the urethra in men that forms a cul-de-sac about 6 mm long behind the middle lobe of the prostate. It is homologous with the uterus in women.

prostatism /pros'tətiz'əm/ [Gk, *prostates,* standing before], an abnormal condition of the prostate, particularly an enlargement of the gland resulting in obstructed urinary flow.

prostatitis /pros'tətī'tis/ [Gk, *prostates + itis,* inflammation], an inflammation of the prostate gland, usually the result of infection. The patient complains of burning, urinary frequency, and urgency.

prostatomegaly /pros'tətōmeg'əlē/ [Gk, *prostates + megas,* large], hypertrophy of the prostate.

prosthesis /prosthē'sis/ *pl.* **prostheses** [Gk, addition], **1.** an artificial replacement for a missing body part, such as an artificial limb or total joint replacement. **2.** a device designed and applied to improve function, such as a hearing aid.

prosthesis care, a nursing intervention from the Nursing Interventions Classification (NIC) defined as care of a removable appliance worn by a patient and the prevention of complications associated with its use.

prosthetic heart valve /prosthet'ik/ [Gk, *prosthesis,* addition; AS, *hoerte;* L, *valva,* door, leaf], an artificial heart valve.

prosthetics /prosthet'iks/ [Gk, *prosthesis,* addition], the design, construction, and attachment of artificial limbs or other systems to assume the function of missing body parts.

prosthetist /pros'thətist/, a person who fabricates and fits artificial limbs and similar devices prescribed by a physician.

prosthion (PR) /pros'thē·on/ [Gk, *prosthios,* foremost], the point of the maxillary alveolar process that projects most anteriorly in the midline of the maxilla, used for measuring upper facial height and determining the gnathic index.

prosthodontics /pros'thədon'tiks/ [Gk, *prosthesis + odous,* tooth], a branch of dentistry devoted to the construction of artificial appliances that replace missing teeth or restore parts of the face.

Prostigmin, a trademark for a cholinergic (neostigmine bromide).

Prostin VR Pediatric, a trademark for a proprietary form of prostaglandin (alprostadil).

prostration /prostrā′shən/ [L, *prosternere,* to throw down], **1.** a condition of extreme exhaustion and inability to exert oneself further, as in heat prostration or nervous prostration. **2.** lying face down in front of something or someone to show reverence.—**prostrate,** *adj.*

protactinium (Pa) /-taktin′ē·əm/ [Gk, *protos,* first, *aktis,* ray], a radioactive element. Its atomic number is 91, and its atomic mass is 231.04. Its decay products are actinium and an alpha particle.

protamine sulfate /prō′təmēn/, a heparin antagonist derived from fish sperm. It is prescribed to diminish or reverse the anticoagulant effect of heparin, particularly in cases of heparin overdosage.

protamine zinc insulin (PZI) suspension, a long-acting insulin that is absorbed slowly at a steady rate and is used to maintain baseline levels of insulin. Combination therapy with regular insulin may be necessary for adequate control.

protanopia /-tənō′pē·ə/, a form of color blindness in which the person is unable to distinguish shades of red.

protaxic mode of experience /-tak′sik/, in psychology, a type of primitive experience characterized by sensations, feelings, and fragmented images of short duration that are not logically connected.

protease /prō′tē·ās/, an enzyme that is a catalyst in the breakdown of peptide bonds that join the amino acids in a protein.

protease inhibitor, a substance that blocks activity of endopeptidase (protease), such as in a virus.

protectin /protek′tin/, a membrane-bound protein, CD59, that protects normal bystander cells from lysis after complement activation in nearby bacteria or immune complexes.

protective /-tek′tiv/ [L, *protegere,* to cover], guarding another person from danger or injury and providing a safe environment.

protective isolation [L, *protegere,* to cover in front; It, *isolare,* detached], **1.** the practice of confining a patient with a virulent infectious disease in a separate area so that contact with other people can be minimized. **2.** the practice of placing a highly susceptible person, such as an immunodeficient patient, in a separate area where the risk of contact with pathogenic microorganisms can be controlled.

protein /prō′tē·in, prō′tēn/ [Gk, *proteios,* first rank], any of a large group of naturally occurring complex organic nitrogenous compounds. Each is composed of large combinations of amino acids (usually 50 or more) containing the elements carbon, hydrogen, nitrogen, oxygen, and occasionally sulfur, phosphorus, iron, iodine, or other essential constituents of living cells. Protein is the major source of building material for muscles, blood, skin, hair, nails, and the internal organs. It is necessary for the formation of many hormones, enzymes, and antibodies, and may act as a source of energy. Rich dietary sources are meat, poultry, fish, eggs, milk, and cheese. Nuts and legumes, including navy beans, chick-peas, soybeans, and split peas, are also good sources but are incomplete proteins because they do not contain all the essential amino acids in adequate amounts. Protein deficiency causes abnormal growth and tissue development in children, leading to kwashiorkor, whereas in adults it results in lack of vigor and stamina, weakness, mental depression, poor resistance to infection, impaired healing of wounds, and slow recovery from disease. Excessive intake of protein may in some conditions result in fluid imbalance.

proteinase /prō′tē·inās/ [Gk, *proteios,* first rank, *ase,* enzyme suffix], a proteolytic enzyme that splits protein molecules at central linkages.

protein catabolic rate (PCR), a calculation derived by multiplying 6.25 times the amount of nitrogen in grams excreted in the urine over a given time period, which represents the amount of protein catabolized by the body in excess of protein synthesis. In a healthy steady state of nitrogen balance, it approximates the amount of protein in the diet.

protein C–protein S test, a blood test performed to determine the activity of proteins C and S. Deficient activity of one or both of these proteins is associated with liver disease, severe malnutrition, hypercoagulability, autoimmune diseases, and intervascular thrombosis.

protein/creatinine ratio, the ratio of protein to creatinine in the urine, calculated as a measure of proteinuria.

proteinemia /prō′tē·inē′mē·ə/ [Gk, *proteios,* first rank, *haima,* blood], an excessive level of protein in the blood.

protein-energy malnutrition (PEM), a wasting condition resulting from a diet inadequate in either protein or energy (calories) or both. These inadequacies are major problems for children in developing countries.

protein hydrolysate injection, a fluid and nutrient replenisher prescribed to correct a negative nitrogen balance and to

P

provide parenteral nutrition in other clinical situations.

protein kinase (PKA), a protein that catalyzes the transfer of a phosphate group from adenosine triphosphate to produce a phosphoprotein.

protein metabolism, the processes whereby protein foods are used by the body to make tissue proteins, together with the processes of breakdown of tissue proteins in the production of energy. Food proteins are first broken down into amino acids, then absorbed into the bloodstream, and finally used in body cells to form new proteins.

protein sensitization [Gk, *proteios,* first rank; L, *sentire,* to feel], a reaction that follows parenteral introduction of a foreign protein into the body. Symptoms of varying severity, including serum sickness, occur when the same foreign protein is reintroduced into the body at a later date.

protein truncation test, a method for detection of one or more translation termination mutations in a gene that cause a truncated, usually inactive, protein to be synthesized. The appropriate genomic DNA or mRNA is isolated, amplified by polymerase chain reaction, and used as a template for in vitro transcription and translation.

proteinuria /prō'tēnyŏŏr'ē·ə/ [Gk, *proteios* + *ouron,* urine], the presence in the urine of abnormally large quantities of protein, usually albumin. Persistent proteinuria is usually a sign of renal disease or renal complications of another disease.

proteolipid /prō'tē·ōlip'id/ [Gk, *proteios* + *lipos,* fat], a type of lipoprotein in which lipid material forms more than half of the molecule. It is insoluble in water and occurs primarily in the brain.

proteolysis /prō'tē·ol'isis/ [Gk, *proteios* + *lysis,* loosening], a process in which water added to the peptide bonds of proteins breaks down the protein molecule into simpler substances. Numerous enzymes may catalyze this process.

Proteus /prō'tē·əs/ [Gk, *Proteus,* mythic god who changed shapes], a genus of motile, gram-negative bacilli often associated with nosocomial infections, normally found in feces, water, and soil. *Proteus* may cause UTIs, pyelonephritis, wound infections, diarrhea, bacteremia, and endotoxic shock.

Proteus mirabilis, a species of anaerobic, motile, rod-shaped bacteria found in putrid meat, abscesses, and fecal material. It is a leading cause of UTIs.

Proteus morganii, a species of bacteria associated with infectious diarrhea in infants.

Proteus syndrome /prō'tē·us/, a rare congenital disorder with highly variable manifestations, including partial gigantism of the hands and feet with hypertrophy of the palms and soles, nevi, hemihypertrophy, subcutaneous tumors, macrocephaly and other skull abnormalities, and abdominal or pelvic lipomatosis.

Proteus vulgaris, a species of bacteria that is a frequent cause of UTIs. The bacteria are found in feces, water, and soil.

prothrombin, /prō-'thräm-bən/ a plasma protein that is converted to the active form, factor IIa, or thrombin, when cleaved by factor Xa bound to factor Va. Thrombin then cleaves fibrinogen to fibrin, which forms the fibrin clot.

prothrombinemia /-ē'mē·ə/ [L, *pro,* before; Gk, *thrombos,* lump, *haima,* blood], the presence of prothrombin in the blood.

prothrombin time (PT), a one-stage test for detecting certain plasma coagulation defects caused by a deficiency of factors V, VII, or X. Thromboplastin and calcium are added to a sample of the patient's plasma and simultaneously to a sample from a normal control. The amount of time required for clot formation in both samples is observed.

protist, a member of the kingdom Protista, which includes eukaryotic, mostly unicellular organisms with animal-like (protozoa), plantlike (algae), or funguslike (slime molds) modes of nutrition.

protium (^{1}H) /prō'tēəm/, ordinary, or light, hydrogen, as opposed to **deuterium** (^{2}H) or **tritium** (^{3}H).

protocol /prō'təkôl/ [Gk, *protos,* first, *kolla,* glued page], a written plan specifying the procedures to be followed in giving a particular examination, conducting research, or providing care for a particular condition.

proton /prō'ton/ [Gk, *protos,* first], a positively charged particle that is a fundamental component of the nucleus of all atoms. The number of protons in the nucleus of an atom equals the atomic number of the element.

proton density, a measure of proton concentration, or the number of atomic nuclei per given volume. It is one of the major determinants of magnetic resonance signal strength in hydrogen imaging.

proton pump inhibitor, an agent that inhibits gastric acid secretion by blocking the action of hydrogen and potassium ions and adenosine triphosphatase at the secretory surface of gastric parietal cells.

Protopam Chloride, a trademark for a cholinesterase reactivator (pralidoxime chloride).

protopathic sensibility /prō'təpath'ik/, pertaining to the somatic sensations of fast localized pain; slow, poorly localized pain; and temperature.

protoplasmic /-plaz'mik/ [Gk, *protos,* first, *plasma,* something formed], pertaining to or composed of protoplasm, the substance of which animal and vegetable cells are formed.

protoplast /prō′təplast/ [Gk, *protos* + *plassein,* to mold], **1.** in biology, the protoplasm of a cell without its containing membrane. **2.** a first entity or an original. —**protoplastic,** *adj.*

protoporphyria /prō′tōpôrfir′ē·ə/ [Gk, *protos* + *porphyros,* purple, *haima,* blood], increased levels of protoporphyrin in the blood and feces.

protoporphyrin /prō′tōpôr′firin/ [Gk, *protos* + *porphyros*], a kind of porphyrin that combines with iron and protein to form various important organic molecules, including catalase, hemoglobin, and myoglobin.

prototaxic mode /prō′tətak′sik/ [Gk, *protos* + *taxis,* arrangement, *modus,* measure], a stage in infancy, according to H.S. Sullivan's theory, characterized by a lack of differentiation between the self and the environment.

prototype /prō′tətīp/ [Gk, *protos,* first, *typos,* mark], the primary or original form of an object or organism.

protozoal infection /-zō′əl/, any disease caused by single-celled organisms of the subkingdom Protozoa.

protozoon /prō′təzō′ən/ pl. **protozoa** [Gk, *protos* + *zoon,* animal], a unicellular protist that ingests food. Protozoa include free-living forms, such as amebas and paramecia, as well as parasites. Approximately 30 protozoa are pathogenic to humans, including *Plasmodium,* which causes malaria, and *Trypanosoma,* which causes sleeping sickness.—**protozoal, protozoan,** *adj.*

protracted dose /prōtrak′tid/ [L, *pro,* before, *trahere,* to draw, *dosis,* something given], a low amount of therapeutic radiation delivered continuously over a relatively long period.

protriptyline hydrochloride /-trip′tilēn/, a tricyclic antidepressant prescribed in the treatment of endogenous depression marked by withdrawal and anergy.

Protropin, a trademark for a synthetic human growth hormone (somatrem).

protrusion /-trōō′zhən/ [L, *protrudere,* to push forward], a state or condition of being forward or projecting.

protrusive incisal guide angle /-trōō′siv/, the inclination of the incisal guide of a dental articulator in the sagittal plane.

protuberance /-t(y)ōō′bərəns/ [L, *pro* + *tuberare,* to swell], an anatomic landmark that appears as a blunt projection, eminence, or swelling such as the chin, buttock, or bulge of the frontal bone above the eyebrow.

proud flesh [AS, *prud* + *flaesc*], excessive granulation tissue.

Proventil, a trademark for a bronchodilator (albuterol).

Provera, a trademark for a progestin (medroxyPROGESTERone acetate).

provider, a hospital, clinic, health care professional, or group of health care professionals who provide a service to patients.

Provincial/Territorial Nurses Association (PTNA), an association of Canadian nurses organized at the provincial or territorial level. The Canadian Nurses' Association is a federation of the 11 PTNAs.

provirus /-vī′rəs/, a stage of viral replication in which the viral genetic information has been integrated into the genome of the host cell.

provitamin /prōvī′təmin/, a precursor to a vitamin; a substance found in certain foods that in the body may be converted into a vitamin.

provocative diagnosis /-vok′ətiv/ [L, *provocare,* to call forth; Gk, *dia,* through, *gnosis,* knowledge], a diagnosis in which the identity and cause of an illness are discovered by inducing an episode of the condition.

prox, abbreviation for **proximal.**

proxemics /proksē′miks/ [L, *proximus,* nearest], the study of spatial distances between people and their effect on interpersonal behavior, especially in relation to population density, placement of people within an area, territoriality, personal space, and the opportunity for privacy.

proximal (prox) /prok′siməl/ [L, *proximus*], nearer to a point of reference or attachment, usually the trunk of the body, than other parts of the body.

proximal cavity, a cavity that occurs on the mesial or distal surface of a tooth.

proximal contact [L, *proximus,* nearest, *contingere,* to touch], contact between the distal surface of one tooth and the mesial surface of an adjacent tooth.

proximal contour, the shape or form of the mesial or the distal surface of a tooth.

proximal dental caries, decay that may occur in the mesial or distal surface of a tooth.

proximal part of prostatic urethra, the first portion of the prostatic urethra, up to and including the seminal colliculus.

proximal radioulnar articulation, the pivot joint between the circumference of the head of the radius and the ring formed by the radial notch of the ulna and the annular ligament. The joint allows the rotary movements of the head of the radius in pronation and supination.

proximal renal tubular acidosis (RTA), an abnormal condition characterized by excessive acid accumulation and bicarbonate excretion. It is caused by the defective resorption of bicarbonate in the proximal tubules of the kidney and the resulting flow of excessive bicarbonate into the distal tubules, which normally secrete hydrogen ions. This disruption impedes the formation of titratable acids and ammonium for excretion and ultimately leads to metabolic acidosis.

proximate /prok'simit/ [L, *proximus,* nearest], the nearest to a point of origin or attachment.

proximate cause [L, *proximus,* nearest], a legal concept of cause-and-effect relationships in determining, for example, whether an injury would have resulted from a particular cause.

proximity principle /proksim'itē/ [L, *proximus + principium,* origin], a rule that when two or more objects are close to each other, they may be seen as a perceptual unit.

Prozac, a trademark for an oral antidepressant (fluoxetine hydrochloride).

PrP, abbreviation for *prion protein,* a virus-like infectious agent associated with Creutzfeldt-Jakob disease.

prune-belly syndrome, a syndrome in which the lower part of the rectus abdominis muscle and the lower and medial parts of the oblique muscles are absent, the bladder and ureters are usually greatly dilated, the kidneys are small and dysplastic with hydronephrosis, and the testes are undescended. The abdomen is protruding and thin-walled, with wrinkled skin.

prurigo /prŏŏrī'gō/ [L, an itch], any of a group of chronic inflammatory conditions of the skin characterized by severe itching and multiple dome-shaped small papules capped by tiny vesicles. As a result of repeated scratching, crusting and lichenification may occur. Some causes of prurigo are allergies, drugs, endocrine abnormalities, malignancies, and parasites. A mild form of the disease is called prurigo mitis; a more severe form, prurigo agria or prurigo ferox.—**pruriginous,** *adj.*

pruritic urticarial papules and plaques of pregnancy (PUPPP) /prŏŏrit'ik/, small, semisolid, intensely itching blisters that may appear on the abdomen of a pregnant woman and spread peripherally. They begin in the third trimester and resolve spontaneously after delivery.

pruritus /prŏŏrī'təs/ [L, *prurire,* to itch], the symptom of itching, an uncomfortable sensation leading to the urge to scratch. Scratching may result in secondary infection. Some causes of pruritus are allergy, infection, jaundice, chronic renal disease, lymphoma, and skin irritation. —**pruritic,** *adj.*

pruritus ani, a common chronic condition of itching of the skin around the anus. Some causes are candidal infection, contact dermatitis, external hemorrhoids, pinworms, psoriasis, and psychogenic illness.

pruritus management, a nursing intervention from the Nursing Interventions Classification (NIC) defined as preventing and treating itching.

pruritus vulvae, itching of the external genitalia of a female. The condition may become chronic and result in lichenification, atrophy, and occasionally malignancy. Some causes of pruritus vulvae are contact dermatitis, lichen sclerosus et atrophicus, psychogenic pruritus, trichomoniasis, and vaginal candidiasis.

Prussian blue /prush'ən/ [Prussia, Germany; ME, *blew*], a chemical stain used on microscopic preparations. It demonstrates the presence of copper by developing a bright blue color.

ps, abbreviation for **picosecond.**

PSA, 1. abbreviation for **pressure-sensitive adhesive.** 2. abbreviation for **prostate-specific antigen.**

P sac, abbreviation for *pericardial cavity.*

psammoma /samō'mə/ *pl.* **psammomas, psammomata** [Gk, *psammos,* sand, *oma,* tumor], a neoplasm containing small calcified granules (psammoma bodies) that occurs in the meninges, choroid plexus, pineal body, and ovaries.

psammoma body, a round layered mass of calcareous material occurring in benign and malignant epithelial and connective tissue neoplasms and in some chronically inflamed tissue.

pseudarthritis /soo'därthrī'tis/ [Gk, *pseudes,* false, *arthron,* joint, *itis,* inflammation], musculoskeletal pain that does not involve the joints.

pseudesthesia /soo'desthē'zhə/ [Gk, *pseudes,* false, *aisthesis,* feeling], a sensation experienced without an external stimulus or a sensation that does not correspond to the causative stimulus, such as phantom limb pain occurring after an amputation.

pseudoacanthosis nigricans /-ak'ənthō'sis/, a condition of pigmented velvety thickening of the flexural skin, often with skin tags. It occurs most commonly in obese persons with dark complexions or in persons with endocrine disorders and is secondary to maceration of the skin from sweating.

pseudoagraphia /soo'dō·ə·graf'ē·ə/ [Gk, *pseudes,* false; *a + graphein,* not to write], a type of dysgraphia in which the patient can copy writing but cannot write to express ideas.

pseudoainhum /soo'dō·īn'yoom/, ringlike constrictions around the digits, limbs, or trunk occurring both congenitally and in association with a wide variety of disorders. The most severe cases of congenital pseudoainhum result in autoamputation in utero.

pseudoallele /-əlēl'/ [Gk, *pseudes* + *allelon*, of one another], one of two or more closely linked genes on a chromosome that appear to function as a single allelic pair but occupy distinct, nearly corresponding loci on homologous chromosomes.—**pseudoallelic,** *adj.,* **pseudoallelism,** *n.*

pseudoaneurysm /-an'yəriz'əm/, **1.** a dilation of an artery caused by damage to one or more layers of the artery as a result of arterial trauma or rupture of a true aneurysm. **2.** a tortuosity of a blood vessel or cavity resulting from a herniated infarction.

pseudoankylosis /-ang'kilō'sis/ [Gk, *pseudes,* false, *ankylosis,* joint stiffness], fixation of a joint caused by inflexibility of body structures outside the joint.

pseudoanodontia /-an'ōdon'shə/, an absence of teeth caused by failure of the teeth to erupt.

pseudoanorexia /-an'ərek'sē·ə/ [Gk, *pseudes* + *a* + *orexis,* without appetite], a condition in which an individual eats secretly while claiming a lack of appetite and inability to eat.

pseudoataxia /-ətak'sē·ə/ [Gk, *pseudes,* false, *ataxia,* without order], a loss of control over voluntary movements that does not involve an organic lesion.

pseudobulbar paralysis /-bul'bər/ [Gk, *pseudes,* false; L, *bulbus,* swollen root; Gk, *paralyein,* to be palsied], a condition resembling progressive bulbar paralysis, with dysarthria and dysphagia, but in which weakness of the bulbar muscles is of the upper motor neuron type. It may result from multiple bilateral infarcts of the cerebral cortex.

pseudocephalocele /-sef'ələlōsēl'/, a noncongenital cerebral hernia resulting from a skull injury or disease.

pseudochancre /-shang'kər/, an indurated genital sore resembling or simulating a chancre.

pseudochondroplasia /-əkon'drōplā'zhə/, a hereditary condition resembling achondroplasia but developing after birth.

pseudochylous ascites /-kī'los/ [Gk, *pseudes* + *chylos,* juice, *askos,* bag], the abnormal accumulation in the peritoneal cavity of a milky fluid that resembles chyle. It is indicative of an abdominal tumor or infection.

pseudoclaudication/-klō'dikā'shən/, painful cramps that are not caused by peripheral artery disease but rather by spinal, neurologic, or orthopedic disorders, such as spinal stenosis, diabetic neuropathy, or arthritis.

pseudocyesis /-sī·ē'sis/ [Gk, *pseudes* + *kyesis,* pregnancy], a condition in which a woman believes that she is pregnant when she is not. The condition may be psychogenic in origin or caused by a tumor or endocrine dysfunction.

pseudocyst /sōō'dəsist/ [Gk, *pseudes* + *kystis,* bag], a space or cavity containing gas or liquid but without a lining membrane. Pseudocysts commonly occur after pancreatitis when digestive juices break through the normal ducts of the pancreas and collect in spaces lined by fibroblasts and surfaces of adjacent organs.

pseudodementia /-dimen'shə/, a syndrome that mimics dementia. It needs to be differentiated from depression.

pseudoephedrine hydrochloride /-ef'əd rēn/, an adrenergic agonist that acts as a vasoconstrictor and decongestant. It is prescribed for the relief of nasal congestion.

pseudoepitheliomatous keratotic and micaceous balanitis, a rare, white, plaquelike, hyperkeratotic lesion of the glans penis that may be premalignant and progress to a verrucous type of carcinoma.

pseudofracture /-frak'chər/ [Gk, *pseudes,* false; L, *fractura*], radiological evidence of a thickened periosteum and new bone formation over what looks like an incomplete fracture.

pseudogene /sōō'dōjēn'/ [Gk, *pseudes* + *genein,* to produce], a DNA sequence that resembles a gene and may be derived from one but lacks a genetic function.

pseudoglandular period, the period or phase of prenatal lung development lasting from about the 6th to the 16th week. Repeated branching of bronchi and bronchioles takes place to form primordial conductive airways, and the lungs resemble exocrine glands. Fetuses delivered during this phase are not viable because the lungs are not yet capable of respiration.

pseudo-Graefe's sign, slow descent of the upper lid on looking down, and quick ascent on looking up. It is seen in conditions other than Graves' disease.

pseudogynecomastia /-gī'nəcōmas'tē·ə/, enlarged breasts in a male caused by fat accumulation.

pseudohermaphrodite /-hərmaf'redīt/ [Gk, *pseudes,* false, *Hermaphroditos,* son of Hermes and Aphrodite], a person who has either male or female gonads but external genitalia of the opposite sex, or both.

pseudohermaphroditism /-hərmaf'rəditi z'əm/ [Gk, *pseudes* + *Hermaphroditos,* son of Hermes and Aphrodite], a condition in which a person exhibits the somatic characteristics of both sexes though possessing the physical characteristics of either males (testes) or females (ovaries).

pseudo-Hurler polydystrophy, a disorder similar to but milder than I-cell disease

P

(mucolipidosis II) and thought to result from the same enzyme deficiency but to a lesser extent.

pseudohyperkalemia /-hī′pərkəlē′mē·ə/, a laboratory artifact indicating an elevated blood potassium level caused by potassium released in vitro from cells in the blood sample.

pseudohyperparathyroidism /-hī′pərper′ə thī′roidiz′əm/, signs of hypercalcemia in a cancer patent in the absence of primary hyperparathyroidism or skeletal metastases.

pseudohypertension /-hī′pərten′shən/, a BP reading that erroneously appears elevated as a result of arterial compliance.

pseudohypertrophy /-hīpur′trəfē/, abnormal enlargement of an organ or body structure caused by an overgrowth of fatty and fibrous tissues.

pseudohypoaldosteronism /-hī′pōaldos′ tərōn′izəm/, **1.** a hereditary disorder of infancy characterized by severe salt and water depletion and other signs of aldosterone deficiency, even though normal or elevated amounts of aldosterone are secreted. Causes include aldosterone receptor defects and renal dysfunction. **2.** the endocrine abnormality associated with sodium-losing nephropathy, usually resulting from chronic pyelonephritis, seen primarily in adults.

pseudohyponatremia /-hī′pōnātrē′mē·ə/, a decreased sodium concentration that does not correspond to a true hypotonic disorder. It may result instead from volume displacement by massive hyperlipidemia or hyperproteinemia.

pseudohypoparathyroidism /-hī′pōper′ə thī′roidiz′əm/, a condition of end-organ resistance characterized by hypocalcemia, growth failure, and skeletal abnormalities such as short fingers.

pseudoileus /sōō′dō·il′ē·əs/, **1.** a condition resembling an intestinal obstruction caused by paralysis of a part of the bowel wall. **2.** an adynamic bowel obstruction.

pseudoisochromatic /sōō′dō·ī′sōkrōmat′ik/, pertaining to visual test materials in which dots that differ in color appear to be a similar color to a person with color blindness.

pseudojaundice /-jôn′dis/ [Gk, *pseudes;* Fr, *jaune,* yellow], a yellow discoloration of the skin that is not caused by hyperbilirubinemia. The excessive ingestion of carotene results in a form of pseudojaundice.

pseudolymphoma /-limfō′mə/, a benign disorder of lymphoid cells or histiocytes that produces clinical features of a malignant lymphoma.

pseudolysogeny /-līsoj′ənē/, a condition in which a bacteriophage is carried in a culture of a bacterial strain by infecting susceptible variants of the strain.

pseudomamma /-mam′ə/, a glandular structure resembling a nipple or mammary gland, sometimes found in a dermoid ovarian cyst.

pseudomania /-mā′nē·ə/, **1.** a condition in which a person claims to have committed crimes of which he or she is really innocent. **2.** a deliberately pretended condition of mental illness.

pseudomegacolon /-meg′əkō′lon/, a dilation of the colon in an adult patient.

pseudomembrane /-mem′brān/ [Gk, *pseudes,* false; L, *membrana*], a membrane consisting of coagulated fibrin, bacteria, and leukocytes that forms in the throats of diphtheria patients.

pseudomembranous /-mem′brənəs/, describing a false membrane, as occurs in diphtheria.

pseudomembranous colitis /-mem′brənəs/ [Gk, *pseudes;* L, *membrana,* thin skin], a diarrheal disease frequently found in hospitalized patients who have received antibiotics that caused overgrowth of the anaerobic spore-forming toxin *Clostridium difficile.* Patients have profuse watery diarrhea, fever, and cramping and are found to have exudates of the colon on endoscopy.

pseudomembranous stomatitis, a severe inflammation of the mouth that produces a membrane-like exudate. The inflammation may be caused by various bacteria or by chemical irritants. It may produce dysphagia, pain, fever, and swelling of the lymph glands.

pseudomenstruation /-men′strōō·ā′shən/, bleeding from the uterus that resembles menstruation but is not associated with the usual changes in endometrial tissues.

pseudomnesia /sōō′dōmnē′zhə/, a memory aberration in which a patient claims to remember events that actually have not taken place.

pseudomonad /sōō′dōmō′nad, sōōdom′ə nad/, a bacterium of the genus *Pseudomonas.*

Pseudomonas /sōōdom′ənas/ [Gk, *pseudes* + *monas,* unit], a genus of gram-negative bacteria that includes several free-living species in soil and water and some opportunistic pathogens. Pseudomonads are notable for their fluorescent pigments and their resistance to disinfectants and antibiotics.

Pseudomonas aeruginosa [Gk, *pseudes,* false, *monas,* unity], a species of gram-negative nonspore-forming motile bacteria that may cause various human diseases ranging from purulent meningitis to nosocomial infected wounds.

pseudomutuality /-mōō′tyōō·al′itē/ [Gk, *pseudes;* L, *mutuus,* reciprocal], in psychotherapy, an atmosphere maintained by family members in which surface harmony and a high degree of agreement with one another hide deep and destructive intrapsychic and interpersonal conflicts.

pseudomyopia /-mī·ō′pē·ə/, overaccommodation during distance viewing that results in distance blur.

pseudomyxoma /-miksō′mə/, a mucus-rich tumor.

pseudomyxoma peritonei, the presence in the peritoneal cavity of mucoid matter from a ruptured ovarian cyst or a ruptured mucocele of the appendix.

pseudopapilledema /-pap′ilēdē′mə/, a congenitally swollen optic disc that resembles papilledema but with no retinal hemorrhages or exudates or any systemic signs of increased intraocular pressure.

pseudoparalysis /-pərəl′isis/, a condition in which a person appears to be unable to move the arms or legs but has no "true" paralysis. In infants the condition may be caused by pain in joints resulting from a disease such as rickets or scurvy.

pseudoparaplegia /-per′əplē′jə/, a form of psychogenic paralysis.

pseudoparesis /-pərē′sis/, a form of psychogenic paralysis.

pseudopelade /-pelād′, -pē′lād/, a scarring type of alopecia, preceded by folliculitis, in which one or more areas of baldness may appear and spread to become joined, forming an area of smooth finger-like projections that are slightly depressed in the skin.

pseudopericarditis /-per′ikärdī′tis/, an auscultation sound resembling a friction rub when the diaphragm of a stethoscope is over the apex beat. It is actually caused by the movement of tissue in the intercostal space.

pseudophakia /-fā′kē·ə/, artificial lens implantation after cataract surgery.

pseudophakodonesis /-fā′kōdōnē′sis/, excessive movement by an intraocular lens implant.

Pseudophyllidea /-filid′ē·ə/, an order of tapeworms with an aquatic life cycle. The scolex usually has two opposing sucking organs.

pseudopod /sōō′dəpod/ [Gk, *pseudes,* false, *pous,* foot], a temporary cytoplasmic process of an ameba that can be extended to propel the organism or to engulf food.

pseudopolyp /-pol′ip/, a projecting mass of granulation tissue that may develop in ulcerative colitis and become covered by regenerating epithelium.

pseudoprognathism /-prog′nəthiz′əm/, a condition in which the mandible is forced forward from its normal position by an occlusal disorder.

pseudopseudohypoparathyroidism /sōō′dōsōō′dōhī′pōpar′əthī′roidizəm/, an incomplete form of pseudohypoparathyroidism characterized by the same

constitutional features but by normal levels of calcium and phosphorus in the serum.

pseudopsychosis /-sīkō′sis/, a condition such as malingering that may resemble a true mental and behavioral disorder.

pseudopterygium /sōō′dopterij′ē·əm/, a fold of conjunctiva that has become attached to the cornea after an injury or disease.

pseudoptosis /sōō′doptō′sis/, an abnormally small palpebral fissure.

pseudopuberty /-p(y)ōō′bərtē/, the appearance of somatic and functional changes in an individual before the chronologic age of puberty.

pseudoretinitis pigmentosa /-ret′ini′tis/, a pigmentary mottling of the retina that may follow an eye injury.

pseudosarcoma /-särkō′mə/, a spindle cell epithelioma on skin that has been exposed to irradiation.

pseudostrabismus /-strəbiz′məs/, an appearance of strabismus caused by an epicanthal fold of skin, which narrows the visible width of the sclera medial to the iris.

pseudostratified /-stra′tifīd/ [Gk, *pseudes,* false, *stratum,* cover], pertaining to a type of layered epithelium in which the nuclei of adjacent cells are at different levels.

pseudotabes /-tā′bēz/, any neuropathy with symptoms like those of tabes dorsalis.

pseudotruncus arteriosus /-trung′kəs/, a condition in which blood is carried to the pulmonary arteries by collateral vessels.

pseudotubercle /-t(y)ōō′bərkəl/, a nodule that resembles a TB granule but is caused by a microorganism other than *Mycobacterium tuberculosis.*

pseudotuberculosis /-t(y)ōōbur′kyəlō′sis/, a pulmonary condition with symptoms resembling those of TB but not caused by *Mycobacterium tuberculosis.*

pseudotumor /-t(y)ōō′mər/ [Gk, *pseudes;* L, *tumor,* swelling], a false tumor.

pseudotumor cerebri, a condition characterized by increased ICP, headache, blurring of the optic disc margins, vomiting, and papilledema without neurologic signs, except palsy of the sixth cranial nerve.

pseudovitamin /-vī′təmin/, a substance that has a chemical structure similar to that of a vitamin but lacks the physiologic effects.

psi /sī/, Ψ, ψ, the twenty-third letter of the Greek alphabet.

p.s.i., abbreviation for *pounds per square inch.*

psia, abbreviation for *pounds per square inch, absolute.*

psig, abbreviation for *pounds per square inch, gauge.*

psilocin /sī′ləsin/, one of several indole-derived psychomimetic drugs. It is related chemically to psilocybin.

P

psilocybin /sī′lōsī′bin, -sib′in/, a psychedelic drug and an active ingredient of various Mexican hallucinogenic mushrooms of the genus *Psilocybe mexicana*. It can produce altered states of mood and consciousness and has no acceptable medical use in the United States. Psilocybin is controlled under Schedule I of the Controlled Substances Act of 1970, which bans the prescription of psilocybin.

psittacosis /sit′əkō′sis/ [Gk, *psittakos*, parrot], an infectious illness caused by the bacterium *Chlamydia psittaci*, characterized by respiratory pneumonia–like symptoms and transmitted to humans inhaling dried secretions from infected birds, especially pet birds and poultry. The clinical manifestations of the disease are extremely variable and resemble those of a great number of infectious diseases, but fever, cough, anorexia, and severe headache are almost always present.

psm, abbreviation for **presystolic murmur.**

psoas major /sō′əs/ [Gk, *psoa*, loin], a long muscle that acts to flex and rotate the thigh and to flex and laterally bend the spine.

psoas minor, a long, slender muscle of the pelvis, ventral to the psoas major, that functions to flex the spine.

psoas part of iliopsoas fascia, the part of the fascia that invests the psoas major muscle.

psomophagia /sō′mōfā′jē·ə/, the swallowing of food that has not been chewed properly.

psoralen-type photosensitizer /sôr′ələn/, any one chemical compound that contains photosensitizing psoralen and that reacts on exposure to ultraviolet light to increase the melanin in the skin. Some psoralen-type photosensitizers produced as pharmaceuticals are methoxsalen and trioxsalen; both are used to enhance skin pigmentation or tanning in the treatment of skin diseases such as psoriasis and vitiligo.

psorelcosis /sôr′əlkō′sis/, an ulceration of the skin caused by scabies.

psorenteritis /sôr′enterī′tis/, an inflammation of the intestines.

psoriasis /sərī′əsis/ [Gk, itch], a chronic skin disorder characterized by circumscribed red patches covered by thick, dry silvery adherent scales.—**psoriatic** /sôr′ē·at′ik/, *adj.*

psoriasis universalis [Gk, *psoriasis,* itch; L, *universus,* on the whole], a severe attack of psoriasis in which most or all of the skin is involved.

psoriatic arthritis /sôr′ē·at′ik/, a form of arthritis associated with psoriatic lesions of the skin and nails, particularly at the distal interphalangeal joints of the fingers and toes.

PSRO, abbreviation for **Professional Standards Review Organization.**

PSS, abbreviation for *progressive systemic sclerosis.*

PSSO, 1. abbreviation for *peer specialist second opinion.* 2. abbreviation for *physician support services organization.*

PSV, abbreviation for **pressure support ventilation.**

PSW, abbreviation for **psychiatric social worker.**

psych, abbreviation for **psychology.**

psychataxia /sī′kətak′sē·ə/, a condition of mental confusion and inability to concentrate or fix attention.

psyche /sī′kē/ [Gk, mind], 1. the aspect of one's mental faculty that encompasses the conscious and unconscious processes. 2. the vital mental or spiritual entity of the individual as opposed to the body or soma. 3. in psychoanalysis, the total components of the id, ego, and superego, including all conscious and unconscious aspects.

psychedelic /sī′kədel′ik/ [coined in 1956 by Humphry Osmond from Gk, *psyche + deloun,* to reveal], 1. describing a mental state characterized by altered sensory perception and hallucination, accompanied by euphoria or fear, usually caused by the deliberate ingestion of drugs or other substances known to produce this effect. 2. describing any drug or substance that causes this state, such as mescaline or psilocybin.

psychiatric consultation liaison nurse (PCLN), an advanced practice nurse with a master's degree in psychiatric nursing. The practice focuses on emotional, spiritual, developmental, cognitive, and behavioral responses of patients with actual or potential physical dysfunction.

psychiatric emergency service [Gk, *psyche + iatreia,* treatment], a hospital service that provides immediate initial evaluation and treatment to mentally ill patients on a 24-hour-a-day basis.

psychiatric foster care, a service for discharged psychiatric patients who receive observation and care in an approved foster home.

psychiatric home care, a service whereby a discharged psychiatric patient is provided observation and care in his or her place of residence. Many state laws require that the client be homebound.

psychiatric hospital, a health care facility providing inpatient and outpatient therapeutic services to clients with behavioral or emotional illnesses.

psychiatric inpatient unit, a hospital ward or similar area used for the treatment of inpatients who require psychiatric care.

psychiatric nurse practitioner, a nurse practitioner who, by advanced study and clinical practice, such as in a master's program in psychiatric nursing, has gained expert knowledge in the care and prevention of mental disorders.

psychiatric nursing, the branch of nursing concerned with the prevention, care, and cure of mental disorders and their sequelae. Psychiatric nurses work in many settings; their responsibilities vary with the setting and with the level of expertise, experience, and training of the individual nurse.

psychiatric social worker (PSW), a social worker who specializes in or works exclusively with the mentally ill.

psychiatrist /sīkī′ətrist/ [Gk, *psyche, mind, iatreia,* treatment], a physician with additional medical training and experience in the diagnosis, prevention, and treatment of mental disorders.

psychiatry /sīkī′ətrē/ [Gk, *psyche* + *iatreia,* treatment], the branch of medical science that deals with the causes, treatment, and prevention of mental, emotional, and behavioral disorders.—**psychiatric,** *adj.*

psychic /sī′kik/ [Gk, *psyche,* mind], a practitioner of the systematic study of parapsychology, a category of alleged psychologic phenomena that cannot be explained by scientific thinking.

psychic blindness [Gk, *psyche,* mind; AS, *blind*], a somatoform disorder that is manifested by the total or partial loss of vision in eyes that are organically normal. Despite the symptoms claimed, the patient usually reacts to light and avoids objects that might cause injury.

psychic energy, mental energy such as thinking, perceiving, and remembering.

psychic impotence [Gk, *psyche,* mind; L, *in* + *potentia,* power], a functional disorder of the male who is unable to perform sexual intercourse despite normal genitalia and sexual desire. The term generally applies to an inability to achieve and maintain an erection, but the disorder may be manifested in other forms such as premature ejaculation or the need for certain conditions.

psychic infection [Gk, *psyche;* L, *inficere,* to stain], the spread of psychic effects or influences on others on a small scale, as in folie à deux, or on a large scale, as in the spread of hysteria or panic in a crowd.

psychic pain [Gk, *psyche,* mind; L, *poena,* penalty], a functional pain that, in the absence of any organic cause, is usually associated with feelings of acute anxiety. In some cases, the person may experience hallucinations or obsessions.

psychic suicide, the termination of one's own life without the use of physical means or agents, such as by an older person who becomes sufficiently depressed to lose "the will to live."

psychic trauma, an emotional shock or injury or a distressful situation that produces a lasting impression, especially on the subconscious mind. Some causes of psychic trauma may include abuse or neglect in childhood, rape, and loss of a loved one.

psychoacoustics /sī′kō·əkōōs′tiks/, the branch of science concerned with the physical features of sound as it relates to the psychological and physiological aspects of the sense of hearing in the unimpaired ear.

psychoactive /sī′kō·ak′tiv/ [Gk, *psyche,* mind; L, *activus*], pertaining to a drug or other agent that affects such normal mental functioning as mood, behavior, or thinking processes, such as stimulants, sedatives, or hallucinogens.

psychoanalysis /sī′kō·ənal′isis/ [Gk, *psyche* + *analyein,* to separate parts], a branch of psychiatry founded by Sigmund Freud, devoted to the study of the psychology of human development and behavior. From its systematized method for investigating the processes of the mind evolved a system of psychotherapy based on the concepts of a dynamic unconscious. By using such techniques as free association, dream interpretation, and analysis of defense mechanisms, emotions and behavior are traced to the influence of repressed instinctual drives in the unconscious.

psychoanalyst /sī′kō·an′əlist/, a psychotherapist, usually a psychiatrist, who has had special training in psychoanalysis and who applies the techniques of psychoanalytic theory.

psychoanalytic /sī′kō·an′əlit′ik/, 1. pertaining to psychoanalysis. 2. using the techniques or principles of psychoanalysis.

psychobiology /-bī′ol′əjē/ [Gk, *psyche* + *bios,* life, *logos,* science], 1. the study of biochemical foundations of thought, mood, emotion, affect, and behavior. 2. personality development and functioning in terms of the interaction of the body and the mind. 3. a school of psychiatric thought that stresses total life experience, including biologic, emotional, and sociocultural factors, in assessing the psychologic makeup or mental status of an individual.—**psychobiologic,** *adj.*

psychodiagnosis /-dī′agnō′sis/ [Gk, *psyche,* mind + *dia* + *gnosis,* knowledge], the study of a personality through observations of behavior and mannerisms, combined with various tests.

psychodrama /-dram′ə/, a form of group psychotherapy, originated by J.L. Moreno, in which people act out their emotional problems through improvisational dramatizations.

psychodynamics /-dīnam′iks/ [Gk, *psyche* + *dynamis,* power], the study of the forces that motivate behavior.

P

psychoendocrinology /sī′kō·en′dōkrin ol′əjē/, the study of the relationship between endocrinology and psychology.

psychoesthesia, a sensation of cold perceived although the body is warm.

psychogalvanic /-galvan′ik/, pertaining to the effects of psychologic influences on the electrical properties of skin.

psychogender /-jen′dər/, the psychologic sex as expressed in gender attitudes of a person as distinguished from biologic or somatic sex.

psychogenesis /sī′kōjen′əsis/ [Gk, *psyche* + *genesis,* origin], **1.** the development of the mind or of a mental function or process. **2.** the development or production of a physical symptom or disease having a mental or psychic origin rather than an organic cause. **3.** the development of emotional states, either normal or abnormal, from the interaction of conscious and unconscious psychologic forces.

psychogenic /sī′kōjen′ik/ [Gk, *psyche* + *genein,* to produce], **1.** originating within the mind. **2.** referring to any physical symptom, disease process, or emotional state that is of psychologic rather than physical origin.

psychogenic pain [Gk, *psyche,* mind; L, *poena,* penalty], a functional pain that does not have any known organic cause.

psychogenic pain disorder, a *DSM-IV* psychiatric disorder characterized by persistent pain for which there is no apparent organic cause. The condition is often accompanied by other sensory or motor dysfunction, such as paresthesia or muscle spasm.

psychogenic vomiting, vomiting that is stimulated by anxiety and emotional distress.

psychogeusic /-jōō′sik/, pertaining to the psychologic influences in taste.

psychograph /si′kōgraf/, **1.** a chart for recording graphically the personality traits of an individual. **2.** a written description of the mental functioning of an individual.

psychokinesia /sī′kōkinē′zhə, -kīnē′zhə/ [Gk, *psyche* + *kinesis,* motion], impulsive behavior resulting from deficient or defective inhibitions without benefit of processing between the stimulus and the response.

psychokinesis (PK) /sī′kōkinē′sis, -kīnē′sis/ [Gk, *psyche* + *kinesis,* motion], the alleged direct influence of the mind or will on matter to produce motion in objects without the intervention of the physical senses or a physical force.

psychokinetics /sī′kōkinet′iks, -kīnet′iks/, the study of psychokinesis.

psycholinguistics /-ling·gwis′tiks/, the study of language as a form of behavior, including language development, speech, and personality.

psychological miscarriage, an absence or deficiency of a mother's love for her infant or absence of mother-child bonding.

psychological test [Gk, *psyche* + *logos,* science; L, *testum,* crucible], any of a group of standardized tests designed to measure or ascertain such characteristics of an individual as intellectual capacity, motivation, perception, role behavior, values, level of anxiety or depression, coping mechanisms, and general personality integration.

psychologist /sīkol′əjist/, a person who specializes in the study of the structure and function of the brain and related mental processes of animals and humans. A clinical psychologist is one who is qualified by graduate study in psychology and training in clinical psychology and who provides testing and counseling services to patients with mental and emotional disorders.

psychology (psych) /sīkol′əjē/ [Gk, *psyche* + *logos,* science], **1.** the study of behavior and of the functions and processes of the mind, especially as related to the social and physical environment. **2.** a profession that involves the practical applications of knowledge, skills, and techniques in the understanding of, prevention of, or solution to individual or social problems, especially in regard to the interaction between the individual and the physical and social environment. **3.** the mental, motivational, and behavioral characteristics and attitudes of an individual or group of individuals. —**psychologic,** *adj.,* **psychologically,** *adv.*

psychometrician /sī′kōmətrish′ən/ [Gk, *psyche,* mind, *metron,* measure], a specialist who performs quantitative estimation or measurement of personality and intelligence.

psychometrics /sī′kōmet′riks/ [Gk, *psyche* + *metron,* measure], the development, administration, or interpretation of psychologic and intelligence tests.

psychomotor /-mō′tər/ [Gk, *psyche;* L, *motare,* to move about], pertaining to or causing voluntary movements usually associated with neural activity.

psychomotor and physical development of infants, a branch of pediatric psychiatry that is concerned with the development of skills requiring coordination of sensory processes and motor activities, including infant reflexes, developmental timetables, and emotional and behavioral disorders.

psychomotor development, the progressive attainment by the child of skills that involve both mental and muscular activity, such as the ability of the infant to turn over, sit, or crawl at will and of the toddler to walk, talk, control bladder and bowel functions, and begin solving cognitive problems.

psychomotor domain, the area of observable performance of skills that require some degree of neuromuscular coordination.

psychomotor energy, a nursing outcome from the Nursing Outcomes Classification (NOC) defined as the personal drive and energy to maintain activities of daily living, nutrition, and personal safety.

psychomotor learning, the acquisition of ability to perform motor skills.

psychomotor retardation, a generalized slowing of motor activity related to a state of severe depression or dementia.

psychomotor seizure, a temporary impairment of consciousness, characterized by psychic symptoms, loss of judgment, automatic behavior, and abnormal acts. It is often associated with temporal lobe disease. No apparent convulsions occur, but there may be LOC or amnesia for the episode. During the seizure the individual may appear drowsy, intoxicated, or violent and may commit asocial acts or crimes, but normal activities, such as driving a car, typing, or eating, may continue at an automatic level.

psychoneuroimmunology /-nōōr′ō·imyōō nol′əjē/, a discipline that studies the relationships between psychologic states and the immune response.

psychooncology /sī′kō·ongkol′əjē/, the psychologic effects of cancer, particularly the psychosocial needs of the patient and the patient's family.

psychopath /sī′kōpath/ [Gk, *psyche* + *pathos,* disease], a person who has an antisocial personality disorder.—**psychopathic** /sī′kōpath′ik/, adj.

psychopathia sexualis /sī′kōpā′thē·ə sek′shōō·al′is/ [Gk, *psyche* + *pathos,* disease; L, *sexus,* male or female], a mental disease characterized by sexual perversion.

psychopathologist /-pəthol′əjist/, one who specializes in the study and treatment of mental disorders.

psychopathology /-pəthol′əjē/, **1.** the study of the causes, processes, and manifestations of mental disorders. **2.** the behavioral manifestation of any mental disorder.

psychopathy /sīkōp′əthē/, any disease of the mind, congenital or acquired, not necessarily associated with subnormal intelligence.

psychopharmaceutical /-fär′məsōō′tikəl/, a drug used in the treatment of mental health disorders.

psychopharmacology /-fär′məkol′əjē/ [Gk, *psyche* + *pharmakon,* drug, *logos,* science], **1.** the scientific study of the effects of drugs on behavior and normal and abnormal mental functions. **2.** the use of these drugs in the treatment of mental illness.

psychophysical /-fiz′ikəl/, pertaining to the psychosocial and physical aspects of a client's health and illness.

psychophysical preparation for childbirth, a program that prepares women for giving birth by teaching them the physiologic characteristics of the process, exercises to improve muscle tone and physical stamina, and various techniques of breathing and relaxation to promote control and comfort during labor and delivery.

psychophysics /-fiz′iks/ [Gk, *psyche* + *physikos,* natural], the branch of psychology concerned with the relationships between physical stimuli and sensory responses.

psychophysiologic /-fiz′ē·əloj′ik/ [Gk, *psyche* + *physikos,* natural], pertaining to physical symptoms, usually under the control of the autonomic nervous system, with emotional origins and involving a single organ system; psychosomatic.

psychophysiologic disorder, any of a large group of mental disorders that are characterized by the dysfunction of an organ or organ system controlled by the autonomic nervous system and that may be caused or aggravated by emotional factors.

psychophysiology /-fiz′ē·ol′əjē/, **1.** the study of physiology as it relates to various aspects of psychologic or behavioral function. **2.** the study of mental activity by physical examination and observation.

psychoprophylactic preparation for childbirth /-prō′filak′tik/, a system of prenatal education for giving birth using the Lamaze method of natural childbirth.

psychoprophylaxis /-prō′filak′sis/, a type of psychotherapy that is directed to prevention of emotional disorders.

psychorelaxation /-re′laksā′shən/, the systematic desensitization to stress and anxiety by the practice of general body relaxation.

psychosensory /-sen′sərē/, pertaining to the perception and interpretation of sensory stimuli.

psychosexual /-sek′shōō·əl/ [Gk, *psyche;* L, *sexus,* male or female], pertaining to the psychologic and emotional aspects of sex.—**psychosexuality,** *n.*

psychosexual development, in psychoanalysis, the emergence of the personality through a series of stages from infancy to adulthood. Each stage is relatively fixed in time and characterized by a dominant mode of achieving libidinal pleasure through the interaction of the person's biologic drives and the environmental restraints.

psychosexual disorder, any condition characterized by abnormal sexual attitudes, desires, or activities resulting from psychologic rather than organic causes.

P

psychosis /sīkō′sis/ *pl.* psychoses [Gk, *psyche* + *osis,* condition], any major mental disorder of organic or emotional origin characterized by a gross impairment in reality testing; the individual incorrectly evaluates the accuracy of his or her perceptions and thoughts and makes incorrect references about external reality, even in the face of contrary evidence. It is often characterized by regressive behavior, inappropriate mood and affect, and diminished impulse control.

psychosocial /-sō′shəl/ [Gk, *psyche*; L, *socialis,* partners], pertaining to a combination of psychologic and social factors.

psychosocial adjustment: life change, a nursing outcome from the Nursing Outcomes Classification (NOC) defined as the adaptive psychosocial response of an individual to a significant life change.

psychosocial assessment, an evaluation of a person's mental health, social status, and functional capacity within the community.

psychosocial development, in child development, a description devised by Erik Erikson of the normal serial development of trust, autonomy, initiative, industry, identity, intimacy, generativity, and ego integrity. The development begins in infancy and progresses as the infantile ego interacts with the environment. For the child to reach a new stage successfully, the tasks of the preceding one should be fully mastered.

psychosomatic /sī′kōsəmat′ik/ [Gk, *psychosome* + *soma,* body], **1.** pertaining to psychosomatic medicine. **2.** relating to, characterized by, or resulting from the interaction of the mind or psyche and the body. **3.** relating to the expression of an emotional conflict through physical symptoms.

psychosomatic approach, the interdisciplinary or holistic study of physical and mental disease from a biologic, psychosocial, and sociocultural point of view.

psychosomatic medicine, the branch of medicine concerned with the interrelationships between mental and emotional reactions and somatic processes, in particular the manner in which intrapsychic conflicts influence physical symptoms.

psychosomatic pain [Gk, *psyche,* mind, *soma,* body; L, *poena,* penalty], pain that is caused in part by psychologic factors.

psychosomatogenic /-sōmat′əjen′ik/, pertaining to factors that cause or lead to the development of psychophysiologic coping measures as learned responses to stressors.

psychostimulant /-stim′yələnt/, an agent that increases psychomotor activity in most patients. It improves concentration and impulse control in attention deficit hyperactivity disorder.

psychosurgery /-sur′jərē/ [Gk, *psyche* + *cheirourgia*], surgical interruption of certain nerve pathways in the brain, performed to treat selected cases of chronic unremitting anxiety, agitation, or obsessional neuroses. Psychosurgery is performed when the condition is severe and when alternative treatments, such as psychotherapy, drugs, and electroshock, have proved ineffective.

psychosynthesis /-sin′thəsis/, a form of psychotherapy that focuses on three levels of the unconscious—lower, middle, and higher unconscious, or superconscious. The goal of the treatment is the re-creation or integration of the personality.

psychotherapeutic drugs /-ther′əp(y)ōō′tik/ [Gk, *psyche,* mind, *therapeutike,* medical practice; Fr, *drogue*], drugs that are prescribed for their effects in relieving symptoms of anxiety, depression, or other mental disorders.

psychotherapeutics /-tiks/ [Gk, *psyche* + *therapeia,* treatment], the treatment of personality disorders by means of psychotherapy.

psychotherapist /-ther′əpist/, one who practices psychotherapy, including psychiatrists, licensed psychologists, psychiatric nurses, psychiatric social workers, and individuals trained in counseling.

psychotherapy /-ther′əpē/ [Gk, *psyche* + *therapeia,* treatment], any of a large number of related methods of treating mental and emotional disorders by psychologic techniques rather than by physical means.

psychotic /sīkot′ik/ [Gk, *psyche* + *osis,* condition], **1.** pertaining to psychosis. **2.** a person exhibiting the characteristics of a psychosis. **3.** not in contact with reality.

psychotic insight, a stage in the development of a psychosis that follows an initial experience of confusion, bizarreness, and apprehension, characterized by an insight that enables the patient to interpret the external world in terms of a delusional system of thinking. The factors that had previously been confusing become a part of the systematized pattern of the delusion, which, although irrational to an observer, is perceived by the patient as the attainment of exceptionally lucid thinking.

psychotogenic /sīkot′əjen′ik/, pertaining to an agent that is capable of inducing symptoms of psychosis.

psychotomimetic /sīkot′ōmimet′ik/, a drug or other substance whose effects mimic the symptoms of psychosis, such as hallucinations.

psychotropic /-trop′ik/ [Gk, *psyche* + *trepein,* to turn], exerting an effect on the mind or modifying mental activity, as in psychotropic medications.

psychotropic drugs, drugs that affect the psychic functions, behavior, or experience of a person using them.

psychroesthesia /sī′krō·esthē′zhə/, **1.** a chill. **2.** a sensation of cold although the body is warm.

psychrometer /sīkrom′ətər/, an instrument for calculating the degree of humidity in the atmosphere by comparing the temperatures of two thermometers, one with a wet bulb, one dry. The difference in temperature between the two thermometers indicates the relative humidity.

psychrometry /sīkrom′ətrē/, the calculation of relative humidity and water vapor pressure from psychrometer data and barometric pressure.

psychrophore /sī′krəfôr/, a double-lumen catheter through which cold water is circulated.

psyllium husk, the cleaned, dried seed coat from the seeds of *Plantago* species, used as a bulk-forming laxative.

Pt, symbol for the element **platinum.**

PT, 1. abbreviation for **physical therapist. 2.** abbreviation for **physical therapy. 3.** abbreviation for **prothrombin time.**

pt., 1. abbreviation for *pint.* **2.** abbreviation for **patient.**

PTA, 1. abbreviation for **percutaneous transluminal angioplasty. 2.** abbreviation for **plasma thromboplastin antecedent. 3.** abbreviation for **physical therapy assistant.**

PTB, abbreviation for **patellar-tendon–bearing prosthesis.**

PTB/SC, abbreviation for **patellar tendon–bearing supracondylar socket.**

PTCA, abbreviation for **percutaneous transluminal coronary angioplasty.**

pterion /tir′ē·on/, a point near the sphenoid fontanel of the skull, at the junction of the greater wing of the sphenoid, squamous, temporal, frontal, and parietal bones. It also intersects the course of the anterior division of the middle meningeal artery.

pterygium /tərij′ē·əm/ [Gk, *pterygion,* wing], a thick triangular patch of pale hypertrophied tissue that extends medially from the nasal border of the cornea to the inner canthus of the eye.

pterygoid /ter′igoid/ [Gk, *pteryx,* wing, *eidos,* form], pertaining to a winglike structure.

pterygoid fossa, a depression that separates the medial and lateral plates of each pterygoid process.

pterygoid hamulus, a hooklike projection at the inferior end of each medial plate of the pterygoid process.

pterygoid plexus, one of a pair of extensive networks of veins between the temporalis and the pterygoideus lateralis muscles,

extending between surrounding structures in the infratemporal fossa. It communicates with the facial vein through the deep facial and angular veins.

pterygoid process [Gk, *pteryx,* wing, *eidos,* form; L, *processus*], any one of the paired processes of the sphenoid bone.

pterygomandibular /ter′igōmandib′yələr/ [Gk, *pteryx,* wing, *eidos,* form; L, *mandere,* to chew], pertaining to the pterygoid process and the mandible.

pterygomandibular raphe, a tendinous band between the pterygoid hamulus superiorly and the mandible inferiorly. It is the point of attachment for the buccinators and superior pharyngeal constrictor muscles.

pterygomaxillary /-mak′siler′ē/ [Gk, *pteryx,* wing, *eidos,* form; L, *maxilla,* jaw], pertaining to the sphenoid bone and the maxilla.

pterygomaxillary notch, a fissure at the junction of the maxilla and the pterygoid process of the sphenoid bone.

pterygopalatine fossa, a space shaped like a teardrop between the bones on the lateral side of the skull immediately posterior to the maxilla. It is a major site of distribution for the maxillary nerve and for the terminal part of the maxillary artery.

PTH, abbreviation for **parathyroid hormone.**

PTNA, abbreviation for **Provincial/ Territorial Nurses Association.**

ptomaine /tō′mān/ [Gk, *ptoma,* corpse], an imprecise term introduced in the 19th century to identify a group of nitrogenous substances found in putrefied proteins. Because injection of the substances produced toxic reactions, the ptomaines were once regarded as poisonous. Later studies showed that the same substances were produced by the normal digestion of proteins in the human intestine without toxic effects.

ptomainemia /tō′mānē′mē·ə/, a condition caused by the presence of a ptomaine, a potentially toxic amine, in the blood.

ptosis /tō′sis/ [Gk, *falling*], an abnormal condition of one or both upper eyelids in which the eyelid droops because of a congenital or acquired weakness of the levator muscle or paralysis of the third cranial nerve.

ptotic kidney /tot′ik/, a kidney that is abnormally situated in the pelvis, usually over the sacral promontory behind the peritoneum.

PTSD, abbreviation for **posttraumatic stress disorder.**

PTT, abbreviation for **partial thromboplastin time.**

ptyalin /tī′əlin/ [Gk, *ptyalon,* spittle], a starch-digesting enzyme present in saliva. It hydrolyzes starch and glycogen.

ptyalism /tī′əliz′əm/ [Gk, *ptyalon,* spittle], excessive salivation, such as sometimes occurs in the early months of pregnancy. It is also a clinical sign of mercury poisoning.

ptyocrinous /tī·ok′rinəs/, pertaining to the secretion of the contents of a unicellular gland in the form of extruded granules.

Pu, symbol for the element **plutonium.**

pubarche /pyo͞obär′kē, pyo͞o′bärkē/ [L, *puber,* ripe, *arch,* beginning], onset of puberty. It is marked by the beginning of the development of secondary sexual characteristics.

pubertal /p(y)o͞o′bərtəl/ [L, *pubertas,* age of maturity], pertaining to puberty.

puberty /p(y)o͞o′bərtē/ [L, *pubertas,* age of maturity], the period of life at which the ability to reproduce begins. It is a stage of development when genitalia reach maturity and secondary sex characteristics appear. The onset normally occurs in females between 9 and 13 years of age with the development of breasts and menarche. In males, puberty usually occurs between 12 and 14 years of age and is characterized by the ejaculation of sperm.

puberulic acid /pyo͞o͞ober′yo͞olik/, an antibiotic isolated from the mold *Penicillium puberulum* that prevents the replication of gram-positive bacteria.

pubescent /p(y)o͞obes′ənt/ [L, *pubescere,* to reach puberty], pertaining to the beginning of puberty.

pubescent uterus [L, *pubescere,* to reach puberty, *uterus,* womb], a uterus in which the cervix and body remain of equal length, the premenstruation state, in adult life.

pubic /p(y)o͞o′bik/ [L, *pubis*], pertaining to or involving the region of the pubic symphysis.

pubic hair /p(y)o͞o′bik/ [L, *pubis*; AS, *haer*], hair of the pubic region.

pubic ligament, either of the two ligaments, superior and inferior, associated with the pubic symphysis.

pubic region [L, *pubes,* signs of maturity, *regio,* territory], the most inferior part of the abdomen in the lower zone between the right and left inguinal regions and below the umbilical region.

pubic symphysis, the slightly movable interpubic joint of the pelvis, consisting of two pubic bones separated by a disk of fibrocartilage and connected by two ligaments.

pubiotomy /p(y)o͞o′bi·ot′əmē/, the separation of the pubic bone, performed to increase the capacity of the pelvis to permit passage of a fetus.

pubis /pyo͞o′bis/ *pl.* **pubes** [L, *pubis*], one of a pair of pubic bones that, with the ischium and the ilium, form the hip bone.

The pubis forms one fifth of the acetabulum and is divisible into the body, the superior ramus, and the inferior ramus.

public health [L, *publicus,* of the people; AS, *haelth*], a field of medicine that deals with the physical and mental health of the community, particularly in such areas as water supply, waste disposal, air pollution, and food safety.

public health nursing, a field of nursing that is concerned with the health needs of the community as a whole. Public health nurses may work with families in the home, in schools, at the workplace, in government agencies, and at major health facilities.

public sector, in health care, typically, government at the federal, state, provincial, and local levels; may refer to other community organizations and lobbying groups.

publish or perish [L, *publicare,* to make public, *perire,* to come to naught], *informal.* a practice followed in many academic institutions in which a contract for employment is renewed only if a candidate has demonstrated scholarship by having work published in a book or in a reputable refereed professional or scientific journal. This work is required in addition to whatever obligations for teaching or professional practice are entailed in the position.

pubocapsular /p(y)o͞o′bōkap′sələr/, pertaining to the pubis and articular capsule of the hip joint.

pubocervical ligament, a condensation of fascia that extends from the cervix to the anterior pelvic wall. It is thought to help stabilize the uterus in the pelvic cavity.

pubococcygeal /pyo͞o′bōkoksij′ē·əl/ [L, *pubis*; Gk, *kokkyx,* cuckoo's beak], pertaining to the pubis and the coccyx.

pubococcygeus exercises /pyo͞o′bōkoksij′ē ·əs/ [L, *pubis*; Gk, *kokkyx,* cuckoo's beak; L, *exercere,* to make strong], a regimen of isometric exercises in which a woman executes a series of voluntary contractions of the muscles of her pelvic diaphragm and perineum in an effort to increase the contractility of her vaginal introitus or to improve retention of urine. The exercise involves the familiar muscular squeezing action that is required to stop the urinary stream while voiding; that action is performed in an intensive, repetitive, and systematic way throughout each day.

pubofemoral ligament, a triangular ligament anteroinferior to the hip joint. Its base is attached medially to the iliopubic eminence, adjacent bone, and obturator membrane.

puboprostatic /p(y)o͞o′bōprostat′ik/, relating to the pubis and prostate gland.

pubovaginal sling, a support constructed of rectoabdominal fascia or synthetic mesh used to stabilize the bladder in treatment of stress incontinence.

pudendal /p(y)ōōden′dəl/, pertaining to or supplying the pudendum.

pudendal block /p(y)ōōden′dəl/ [L, *pudendus,* shameful; Fr, *bloc,* lump], a form of regional anesthetic block administered to provide anesthesia of the perineum, which is particularly useful during the expulsive second stage of labor. Pudendal block anesthetizes the perineum, vulva, clitoris, labia majora, and perirectal area without affecting the muscular contractions of the uterus.

pudendal nerve, one of the branches of the pudendal plexus that supplies the external genital structures and the pelvic region.

pudendal plexus, a network of motor and sensory nerves formed by the anterior branches of the second, the third, and all of the fourth sacral nerves. It is often considered part of the sacral plexus. The pudendal plexus lies in the posterior hollow of the pelvis.

pudendum /p(y)ōōden′dəm/ *pl.* **pudenda** [L, *pudendus,* shameful], the external genitalia, especially of women. In a woman, it comprises the mons veneris, the labia majora, the labia minora, the vestibule of the vagina, and the vestibular glands. In a man, it comprises the penis, scrotum, and testes.—**pudendal,** *adj.*

puericulture /py‿oo′ərikul′chər/ [L, *pueri,* children, *colere,* to cultivate], the rearing and training of children.—**puericulturist,** *n.*

puerile /pyōō′əril, -īl/ [L, *puerilis,* childish], pertaining to children or childhood; juvenile.—**puerility,** *n.*

puerilism /pyōō′əriliz′əm/ [L, *puerilis,* childish], childishness, particularly when manifested in an older adult.

puerpera /pyōō·er′pərə/ [L, *puerpus,* childbirth], a woman who has just given birth.

puerperal /pyōō·er′pərəl/ [L, *puerpus,* childbirth], **1.** pertaining to the period immediately after childbirth. **2.** pertaining to a woman (a puerpera) who has just given birth to an infant.

puerperal eclampsia [L, *puerpus,* childbirth; Gk, *ek,* out, *lampein,* to flash], a condition of coma and convulsive seizures occurring after childbirth. It is associated with hypertension, edema, and proteinuria.

puerperal fever, a syndrome associated with systemic bacterial infection and septicemia that occurs after childbirth, usually as a result of unsterile obstetric technique. It is characterized by endometritis, fever, tachycardia, uterine tenderness, and foul lochia. If it is untreated, prostration, renal failure, bacteremic shock, and death may

occur. The causative organism is most often one of the hemolytic streptococci.

puerperal mania, a rare acute mood disorder that sometimes occurs in women after childbirth, characterized by a severe manic reaction.

puerperal mastitis [L, *puerpus,* childbirth; Gk, *mastos,* breast, *itis,* inflammation], a form of acute mastitis in a nursing mother.

puerperal phlebitis [L, *puerpus,* childbirth; Gk, *phleps,* vein, *itis,* inflammation], an inflammation that begins in a uterine vein after childbirth and spreads to other veins, particularly the iliac and femoral veins.

puerperal sepsis, an infection acquired during the puerperium.

puerperium /pyōō′ərpir′ē·əm/ [L, *puerperus*], the time after childbirth, lasting approximately 6 weeks, during which the anatomic and physiologic changes brought about by pregnancy resolve and a woman adjusts to the new or expanded responsibilities of motherhood.

PUFA, abbreviation for *polyunsaturated fatty acid.*

puff [ME *puf*], a short, soft, blowing sound heard on auscultation.

puffer fish /puf′er fish/, any of several species of marine fish of genera *Fugu, Sphaeroides, Tetraodon,* and others, which when disturbed can inflate themselves to a spherical shape. Their flesh contains tetrodotoxin and can cause fatal tetrodotoxism.

Pulex /pyōō′leks/ [L, flea], a genus of fleas, some species of which transmit arthropod-borne infections, such as plague and epidemic typhus.

pulmoaortic /pōol′mō·ā·ôr′tik/, pertaining to the lungs and aorta.

pulmonary /pōol′məner′ē/ [L, *pulmo,* lungs], pertaining to the lungs or the respiratory system.

pulmonary alveolar proteinosis [L, *pulmoneus,* lungs, *alveolus,* little hollow; Gk, *proteios,* first rank, *osis,* condition], a condition in which the air sacs of the lungs become filled with protein and lipids, progressing to respiratory failure.

pulmonary angiography [L, *pulmoneus,* lungs; Gk, *angeion,* vessel, *graphein,* to record], the radiographic examination of the blood vessels of the lungs after the injection of radiopaque contrast medium into the pulmonary circulation. It is used to detect pulmonary emboli.

pulmonary arteriolar resistance (PAR), pressure loss per unit of blood flow from the pulmonary artery to a pulmonary vein.

pulmonary artery (PA) [L, *pulmoneus,* lungs; Gk, *arteria,* airpipe], one of two arteries, the left one supplying the left lung and the right one supplying the right lung.

P

pulmonary artery catheter [L, *pulmoneus,* lungs; Gk, *arteria + katheter,* a thing lowered], any of various cardiac catheters for measuring pulmonary arterial pressures, introduced into the venous system through a large vein and guided by blood flow into the superior vena cava, the right atrium and ventricle, and the pulmonary artery.

pulmonary atresia [L, *pulmoneus,* lungs; Gk, *a + tresis,* without perforation], a congenital heart defect of the right ventricular outflow tract. One form consists of an intact ventricular septum with an interatrial communication and a persistent patent ductus arteriosus. A more extreme form is the four-defect tetralogy of Fallot.

pulmonary atrium, any of the spaces at the end of an alveolar duct into which alveoli open.

pulmonary candidiasis [L, *pulmones,* lungs; L, *candidus,* white; Gk, *iasis,* disease suffix], a type of fungal pneumonia caused by infection with *Candida* species, seen especially in immunocompromised patients or those with malignancies.

pulmonary circulation [L, *pulmoneus,* lungs + *circulare*], the blood flow through the network of vessels between the heart and the lungs for the oxygenation of blood and removal of carbon dioxide.

pulmonary congestion [L, *pulmoneus,* lungs, *congerere,* to heap together], an excessive accumulation of fluid in the lungs, usually associated with either an inflammation or CHF.

pulmonary disease, any abnormal condition of the respiratory system, characterized by cough, chest pain, dyspnea, hemoptysis, sputum production, stridor, or adventitious sounds. Obstructive respiratory disease is the result of a reduction of airway size that impedes air flow and is characterized by reduced expiratory flow rates and increased total lung capacity. Restrictive respiratory disease is caused by conditions that limit lung expansion, such as fibrothorax, obesity, a neuromuscular disorder, kyphosis, scoliosis, spondylitis, or surgical removal of lung tissue. Characteristics of restrictive respiratory disease are decreased forced expired vital capacity and total lung capacity, with increased work of breathing and inefficient exchange of gases. Acute restrictive conditions are the most common pulmonary cause of acute respiratory failure.

pulmonary dysmaturity syndrome, a respiratory disorder of premature infants in which the lungs contain focal emphysematous blebs and thickened alveolar walls. The infants commonly die of hypoxia.

pulmonary edema, the accumulation of extravascular fluid in lung tissues and alveoli, caused most commonly by CHF.

Serous fluid is pushed through the pulmonary capillaries into alveoli and quickly enters bronchioles and bronchi. Signs and symptoms of pulmonary edema include tachypnea; labored, shallow respirations; restlessness; apprehensiveness; air hunger; cyanosis; and blood-tinged or frothy, pink sputum. The peripheral and neck veins are usually engorged, BP and heart rate are increased, and the pulse may be full and pounding or weak and thready. There may be edema of the extremities, adventitious breath sounds in the lungs, respiratory acidosis, and profuse diaphoresis.

pulmonary embolism (PE), the blockage of a pulmonary artery by fat, air, tumor tissue, or a thrombus that usually arises from a peripheral vein (most frequently one of the deep veins of the legs). It is characterized by dyspnea, anxiety, sudden chest pain, shock, and cyanosis. Analysis of blood gases reveals arterial hypoxia and hypocapnia.

pulmonary emphysema, a chronic obstructive disease of the lungs, marked by an overdistension of the alveoli and destruction of the supporting alveolar structure.

pulmonary function laboratory, an area of a hospital or other health facility used for examination and evaluation of patients' respiratory function.

pulmonary function test (PFT), a procedure for determining the capacity of the lungs to exchange oxygen and carbon dioxide efficiently. There are two general kinds of respiratory function tests. One measures ventilation, or the ability of the bellows action of the chest and lungs to move gas in and out of alveoli. The other kind measures the diffusion of gas across the alveolar capillary membrane and the perfusion of the lungs by blood. Basic ventilation studies are performed with a spirometer and recording device as the patient breathes through a mouthpiece and connecting tube; a nose clip prevents nasal breathing. Bronchospirometric measurements of the ventilation and oxygen consumption of each lung separately are performed using a specially constructed double-lumen catheter with two balloons; one balloon is inflated to seal off the contralateral lung when the other lung is tested. Arterial blood gas studies, including determinations of the acidity, partial pressure of carbon dioxide and of oxygen, and oxyhemoglobin saturation, provide information on the diffusion of gas across the alveolar capillary membrane and the adequacy of oxygenation of tissues.

pulmonary groove, a depression on each side of the vertebral bodies that accommodates the posterior part of the lung.

pulmonary hypertension, a condition of abnormally high BP within the pulmonary circulation.

pulmonary infarction (PI) [L, *pulmoneus,* lungs, *infarcire,* to stuff], necrosis in a part of a lung caused by an obstruction in a branch of a pulmonary artery.

pulmonary infiltrate with eosinophilia (PIE), a hypersensitivity reaction characterized by infiltration of alveoli with eosinophils and large mononuclear cells, edema, and inflammation of the lungs. The simplest form of the condition, in which patchy, migratory infiltrates cause minimal symptoms, is a self-limited reaction elicited by helminthic infections and by certain drugs. A more prolonged illness, characterized by fever, night sweats, cough, dyspnea, weight loss, and more severe tissue reaction, occurs in certain drug allergies and in bacterial, fungal, and parasitic infections.

pulmonary insufficiency [L, *pulmoneus,* lungs, *in + sufficere,* to suffice], a failure of the pulmonary valve to close properly.

pulmonary ligament, a thin, bladelike fold of pleura extending from the hilum to the mediastinum that may stabilize the position of the inferior lobe of the lung and may also accommodate the down-and-up translocation of structures in the root during breathing.

pulmonary opening, opening of pulmonary trunk, pulmonary orifice.

pulmonary orifice, orifice of pulmonary trunk, the opening between the pulmonary trunk and the right ventricle of the heart.

pulmonary oxygen toxicity [L, *pulmoneus,* lungs; Gk, *toxikon,* poison], a form of oxygen poisoning caused by breathing air having an oxygen concentration of 50% or higher for 12 to 24 hours. Pathophysiologic effects include pulmonary capillary endothelial damage and alveolar epithelial cell destruction. Clinical manifestations include cough, substernal pain, nausea, vomiting, and atelectasis.

pulmonary pleura, the part of the pleural membrane that covers the lungs, as distinguished from the parietal layer of pleura that lines the inner aspect of the thoracic cavity.

pulmonary renal syndrome, antiglioblastoma multiforme nephritis.

pulmonary stenosis, an abnormal cardiac condition generally characterized by concentric hypertrophy of the right ventricle with relatively little increase in diastolic volume. When the ventricular septum is intact, this condition may be caused by valvular stenosis, infundibular stenosis, or both; it produces a pressure difference during systole between the right ventricular cavity and the pulmonary artery.

pulmonary sulcus tumor, a destructive invasive neoplasm that develops at the apex of the lung and infiltrates the ribs, vertebrae, and brachial plexus.

pulmonary trunk, the short, wide vessel that conveys venous blood from the right ventricle of the heart to the lungs.

pulmonary tuberculosis, infection of the lungs by *Mycobacterium tuberculosis.* The first infection is usually quiescent, but it may develop later into tuberculous pneumonia and other conditions.

pulmonary valve, a cardiac structure composed of three semilunar cusps that close during each heartbeat to prevent blood from flowing back into the right ventricle from the pulmonary trunk. The cusps are separated by sinuses that resemble tiny buckets when they are closed and filled with blood. When the sinuses collapse from the ejection of ventricular blood, they open the valve and allow deoxygenated blood to flow through the pulmonary artery and on to the lungs.

pulmonary vascular resistance (PVR), the resistance in the pulmonary vascular bed against which the right ventricle must eject blood.

pulmonary vein, one of two pairs of large vessels that return oxygenated blood from each lung to the left atrium of the heart.

pulmonary wedge pressure (PWP), the pressure produced by an inflated latex balloon against the inner wall of a pulmonary artery. A pulmonary artery catheter (PA catheter) or similar balloon-tipped catheter is inserted through a subclavian, jugular, or femoral vein to the vena cava and on through the right atrium and ventricle to the pulmonary artery. The balloon is inflated briefly, during which time it measures left ventricular diastolic pressure.

pulmonary Wegener's granulomatosis, a rare fatal disease of young or middle-aged men, characterized by granulomatous lesions of the respiratory tract, focal necrotizing arteritis, and finally widespread inflammation of body organs.

pulmonologist /pŏŏl'mənol'əjist/ [L, *pulmo,* lung], an individual skilled in pulmonology.

pulmonology /pŏŏl'mōnol'əjē/ [L, *pulmo,* lung], the science concerned with the anatomy, physiology, and pathology of the lungs.

pulp [L, *pulpa,* flesh], any soft, coherent, solid, spongy tissue, such as that contained within the spleen, the pulp chamber of the tooth, or the distal subcutaneous pads of the fingers and the toes.—**pulpy,** *adj.*

pulp abscess [L, *pulpa,* flesh, *abscedere,* to go away], an abscess that develops in the pulp cavity of a tooth.

P

pulpaceous /pulpāʹshəs/, pertaining to a substance that is pulpy or macerated.

pulpal /pulʹpəl/, pertaining to pulp.

pulp canal, the space occupied by the nerves, blood vessels, and lymphatic vessels in the radicular part of the tooth.

pulp cavity, the space in a tooth bounded by the dentin and containing the dental pulp. It is divided into the pulp chamber and the pulp canal.

pulpectomy /pulpekʹtəmē/ [L, *pulpa*, flesh; Gk, *ektomē*, excision], the surgical removal of all or part of the pulp of a tooth.

pulpifaction /pulʹpifak′shən/, the act of reducing something to a pulp.

pulpitis /pulpīʹtis/, infection or inflammation of the dental pulp.

pulpless tooth /pulpʹləs/, a tooth in which the dental pulp is necrotic or has been removed.

pulpotomy /pulpotʹəmē/, root canal therapy consisting of partial excision of the dental pulp.

pulpy nucleus, the central part of each intervertebral disk, consisting of a pulpy elastic substance that loses some of its resiliency with age.

pulsate /pulʹsāt/ [L, *pulsare*, to beat], to throb or vibrate rhythmically, as the heart does during its contraction-relaxation cycle.

pulsatile /pulʹsətil/ [L, *pulsare,* to beat], pertaining to an activity characterized by a rhythmic pulsation.

pulsatile assist device (PAD), a flexible, valveless balloon conduit contained within a rigid, plastic cylinder that is inserted into the arterial circulation to provide pulsatile perfusion during a cardiopulmonary bypass.

pulsatility index /pulʹsətilʹitē/, a measure of the variability of blood velocity in a vessel, equal to the difference between the peak systolic and minimum diastolic velocities, divided by the mean velocity during the cardiac cycle.

pulsating exophthalmos /pulʹsāting/ [L, *pulsare,* to beat; Gk, *ex* + *ophthalmos,* eye], an eye disorder characterized by a bulging, pulsating eyeball, caused by an arteriovenous aneurysm involving the internal carotid artery and the cavernous sinus of the orbit.

pulsation /pəl·sāʹshən/ [L, *pulsatio*], a throb or rhythmic beat, as of the heart.

pulse [L, *pulsare,* to beat], **1.** a rhythmic beating or vibrating movement. **2.** a brief electromagnetic wave. **3.** the regular, recurrent expansion and contraction of an artery produced by waves of pressure caused by the ejection of blood from the left ventricle of the heart as it contracts. The pulse is easily detected on superficial arteries, such as the radial and carotid arteries, and corresponds to each beat of the heart.

pulsed Doppler, a type of Doppler device involving the transmission of a short-duration burst of sound into the region to be examined.

pulse deficit, a condition in which a peripheral pulse rate is less than the ventricular contraction rate as auscultated at the apex of the heart or seen on the ECG, indicating a lack of peripheral perfusion.

pulsed laser, a laser that emits short bursts of energy at fixed intervals rather than a continuous stream of energy.

pulse duration (P.D., PD), in ultrasonics, a measure of the time a transducer oscillates for each pulse. The shorter the pulse duration, the better the axial resolution.

pulse-echo response profile, a graph of the amplitude of an ultrasound echo from a small reflector versus the distance from the reflector beam axis. The reflector is scanned perpendicular to the axis of the ultrasound transducer beam.

pulse-echo ultrasound, a diagnostic technique in which short-duration ultrasound pulses are transmitted into the region to be studied, and echo signals resulting from scattering and reflection are detected and displayed. The depth of a reflective structure is inferred from the delay between pulse transmission and echo reception.

pulse generator, the power source for a cardiac pacemaker system, usually fueled by lithium, supplying impulses to the implanted electrodes, either at a fixed rate or in some programmed pattern.

pulse height analyzer, a device that accepts or rejects electronic pulses according to their amplitude or energy.

pulseless electrical activity (PEA), continued electrical rhythmicity of the heart in the absence of effective mechanical function. It may be caused by the uncoupling of ventricular muscle contraction from electrical activity or may be a result of cardiac damage with respiratory failure and cessation of cardiac venous return.

pulse MR, a magnetic resonance (MR) technique that uses radiofrequency pulses and Fourier transformation of the MR signal. Pulse MR has largely replaced older, continuous-wave techniques.

pulse oximeter, a device that measures the amount of saturated hemoglobin in the tissue capillaries to determine respiratory function. The cliplike device may be used on either the earlobe or the fingertip.

pulse point, one of the sites on the surface of the body where arterial pulsations can be easily palpated. The most commonly used pulse point is over the radial artery at the wrist. Other pulse points include the temporal artery in front of the ear, the common carotid artery at the lower level of the thyroid cartilage, the facial artery at the lower margin of the jaw, and the femoral, popliteal, posterior tibialis, and dorsalis pedis pulse points.

pulse pressure, the difference between the systolic and diastolic BPs, normally 30 to 50 mm Hg.

pulser /pul′sər/, a component of an ultrasound instrument that provides signals for exciting the piezoelectric transducer in order to transmit an ultrasound beam.

pulse rate [L, *pulsare* + *reri*, to calculate], the number of pulse beats per minute, normally the same as the heart rate.

pulse repetition frequency (PRF), in ultrasonics, the number of acoustic pulses transmitted per second.

pulse sequence, the sequence of radiofrequency pulses and magnetic gradients used to generate an MRI.

PULSES profile, an assessment tool that measures six functions and factors to evaluate the degree of independence possessed by a disabled individual. The score is used in the assessment of progress made in rehabilitation as well as to help identify the severity of disability. The six are: *P*hysical condition (i.e., general health), *U*pper limb function, *L*ower limb function, *S*ensory function, *E*xcretory function, and *S*upport (e.g., social, psychologic, financial support).

pulse wave [L, *pulsare*, to beat; AS, *wafian*], a transient increase in BP that spreads like a wave through the arterial system. It begins with the ejection of blood by the ventricles during systole.

pulsus alternans /pul′səs ôl′tərnanz/ [L, *pulsare* + *alternare*, to alternate], a pulse characterized by a regular alternation of weak and strong beats without changes in the pulse rate.

pulsus paradoxus, an abnormally large decrease in systolic BP and pulse wave amplitude during inspiration.

pulsus parvus et tardus [L, *pulsus,* beat, *parvus,* small, *tardus,* slow], a small pulse with low pressure that rises and falls gradually. The condition occurs in aortic stenosis.

pulsus tardus [L, *pulsus,* beat, *tardus,* slow], a pulse with a gradual rise and fall in amplitude.

pultaceous, pertaining to a substance that is pulpy or macerated.

pulverize /pul′vərīz/ [L, *pulvis,* dust], to reduce to a fine powder.

pulverulent /pulver′ələnt/, having the form of a fine powder.

pulvule /pul′vyŏŏl/ [L, *pulvis,* dust], a proprietary type of capsule containing a dose of a drug in powder form.

pumice /pum′is/ [L, *pumex*], a very finely divided volcanic rock, used in powdered or solid form for smoothing or polishing surfaces.

pump [ME, *pumpe*], **1.** an apparatus used to move fluids or gases by suction or by positive pressure, such as an infusion pump or stomach pump. **2.** a physiologic mechanism by which a substance is moved, usually by active transport across a cell membrane, such as a sodium-potassium pump. **3.** to move a liquid or gas by suction or positive pressure.

pump oxygenator [ME, *pumpe*; Gk, *oxys,* sharp, *genein,* to produce], a device that pumps oxygenated blood through the body during cardiopulmonary surgery.

punch biopsy [L, *pungere,* to prick; Gk, *bios,* life, *opsis,* view], the removal of living tissue for microscopic examination, usually bone marrow aspirates from the sternum, by means of a punch.

punchdrunk syndrome, a condition resulting from repeated cerebral concussions, characterized by an abnormal gait, slow movement, tremor, and slurred or halting speech.

punch forceps, a surgical instrument used to cut out a disk of dense or resistant tissue, such as bone and cartilage. The ends of the blades of the punch forceps are perforated to grip the involved tissue.

punctate /pungk′tāt/ [L, *punctum,* point], marked with elevated or colored dots or punctures.

punctiform /pungk′tifôrm/, of very small size, as is a bacterial colony in a solid medium.

punctum /pungk′təm/, a physiologic area or point.

punctum caecum, blind spot.

punctum lacrimale /lak′rimā′lē/ *pl.* **puncta lacrimalia** [L, *punctum,* prick, *lacrima,* tear], a minute circular aperture in the medial opening into the nasolacrimal sac. The puncta drains the tears that travel from the lacrimal glands through the lacrimal ducts to the conjunctiva.

puncture /pungk′chər/ [L, *punctura*], **1.** to prick or pierce a surface, as with a needle or knife. **2.** a wound or opening made by piercing.

puncture of the antrum [L, *punctura*; Gk, *antron,* cave], a cavity or hollow, as is made in piercing the wall of the maxillary sinus to drain pus.

puncture wound [L, *punctura*; AS, *wund*], a traumatic injury caused by skin penetration by an object, such as a knife, nail, or slender fragment of metal, wood, glass, or other material.

Punnett square [Reginald C. Punnett, English geneticist, 1875–1967; OFr, *esquarre*],

P

a matrix that shows all of the possible combinations of male and female gametes when one or more pairs of independent alleles are crossed.

P.U.O., abbreviation for *pyrexia of unknown origin*.

pupa /pyōō'pə/ [L, doll], a stage between the larval and adult stages in the life cycle of many insects, including flies, butterflies, and beetles.

pupil /pyōō'pəl/ [L, *pupa*, doll], a circular opening in the iris of the eye, located slightly to the nasal side of the center of the iris. The pupil lies posterior to the cornea and the anterior chamber of the eye and is anterior to the lens. Its diameter changes with contraction and relaxation of the muscular fibers of the iris as the eye responds to changes in light, emotional states, and autonomic stimulation. —**pupillary,** *adj.*

pupillary /pyōō'piler'ē/ [L, *pupilla*], pertaining to the pupil.

pupillary ruff, a brown wrinkled rim on the edge of the pupil, derived from posterior pigment epithelium of the iris.

pupillometry /pyōō'pilom'ətrē/, the measurement of the pupil.

pupillomotor /pyōō'pilōmō'tər/, pertaining to the autonomic nerve fibers of the smooth muscles of the iris.

PUPP /pup/, abbreviation for **pruritic urticarial papules and plaques of pregnancy.**

PUPs, abbreviation for *previously untreated patients,* usually infants participating in clinical trials.

pure /pyōōr/, **1.** free of contamination by extraneous matter. **2.** a state in which a substance contains nothing other than itself.

purgative /pur'gətiv/ [L, *purgare,* to purge], a strong medication usually administered by mouth to promote evacuation of the bowel or to produce several bowel movements.

purge /purj/ [L, *purgare*], **1.** to evacuate the bowels, as with a cathartic. **2.** a cathartic. **3.** to make free of an unwanted substance.—**purgative,** *n., adj.*

purified cotton, cotton freed from impurities, bleached, and sterilized. It is used as a surgical dressing.

purified protein derivative (PPD) /pyōō'rifīd/, a dried form of tuberculin used in testing for past or present infection with tubercle bacilli. This product is usually introduced into the skin during such tests and may produce a tuberculin reaction (wheal) within 48 to 72 hours.

purine /pyōō'rēn/ [L, *purus,* pure, *urina,* urine], any one of a large group of nitrogenous compounds. Purines are produced as end products in the digestion of certain proteins in the diet, but some are synthesized in the body. Purines are also present in many medications and other substances, including caffeine, theophylline, and various diuretics, muscle relaxants, and myocardial stimulants.

purine base [L, *purus,* pure], any of the purine derivatives found in animal waste products or in nucleic acids. They include hypoxanthine, xanthine, and uric acid (waste products), and adenine and guanine (nucleic acids).

purine-free diet, a diet that excludes foods that are rich sources of purines. Foods high in purines include organ meats, such as liver, kidney, and sweetbreads, as well as red meats, poultry, and fish.

purine-low diet, a diet that excludes some foods rich in purines, particularly anchovies, meat extracts, sardines, and organ meats.

Purinethol, a trademark for an antineoplastic (mercaptopurine).

Purkinje's cells /pərkin'jēz, pur'kinjēz, -jāz/ [Johannes E. Purkinje, Czech physiologist, 1787–1869], large neurons with dendrites that extend to the molecular lay and provide the only output from the cerebellar cortex after the cortex processes sensory and motor impulses from the rest of the nervous system.

Purkinje's fiber [Johannes E. Purkinje], one of the myocardial fibers that are the termination of the bundle branches. The fibers comprise part of the conduction system of the heart.

Purkinje's network [Johannes E. Purkinje], a complex fibrous network of large muscle cells that spread through the right and the left ventricles of the heart and carry the impulses that contract those chambers almost simultaneously.

purposeful activity /pur'pəsfōol/, activity that depends on consciously planned and directed involvement of the person.

purpura /pur'pyərə/ [L, purple], any of several bleeding disorders characterized by hemorrhage into the tissues, particularly beneath the skin or mucous membranes, producing ecchymoses or petechiae. —**purpuric,** *adj.*

purpura rheumatica [L, *purpura,* purple; Gk, *rheum,* flow], a distinctive clinical sign associated with hemorrhages of the skin and other tissues. The lesions are red or purple and do not blanch on pressure. Purpura is related to either a disorder of the blood or an abnormality affecting the blood vessels.

purpura senilis /senē'lis/ [L, *purpura,* purple, *senilis,* aged], a skin condition affecting older people and characterized by fragile blood vessel walls that rupture on minimal trauma.

pursed-lip breathing /purst-/, respiration characterized by deep inspirations followed by prolonged expirations through pursed lips. It is done to increase expiratory airway pressure, improve oxygenation of the blood, and help prevent early airway closure.

purse-string suture [L, *sutura*], a continuous suture placed in a circle about a round wound. The opening is closed by tightly drawing the ends of the suture together.

purulence /pyŏŏr'(y)ələns/ [L, *purulentus,* pus formation], the condition of producing or discharging pus.

purulent /pyŏŏr'(y)ələnt/ [L, containing pus], producing or containing pus.

purulent conjunctivitis [L, *purulentus,* pus formation, *conjunctivus,* connecting; Gk, *itis,* inflammation], an inflammation of the conjunctiva caused by suppurative microorganisms, including species of streptococci, gonococci, and pneumococci.

purulent diarrhea [L, *purulentus,* pus formation; Gk, *dia* + *rhein,* to flow], diarrhea in which stools contain pus, a sign of a purulent GI tract infection.

purulent inflammation [L, *purulentus,* pus formation, *inflammare,* to set afire], an inflammation that is accompanied by the formation of pus.

purulent iritis [L, *purulentus,* pus formation; Gk, *iris,* rainbow, *itis,* inflammation], an inflammation of the iris accompanied by the formation of pus.

purulent keratitis [L, *purulentus,* pus formation; Gk, *keras,* horn, *itis,* inflammation], a severe form of keratitis leading to disintegration of the cornea if untreated. The condition commonly begins with a bacterial infection of the lacrimal sac, occurs frequently in elderly patients who have poor nutrition, and spreads into a pus-producing ulcer.

purulent pancreatitis [L, *purulentus,* pus formation; Gk, *pan,* all, *kreas,* flesh, *itis,* inflammation], inflammation of the pancreas accompanied by pus formation.

purulent rhinitis [L, *purulentus,* pus formation; Gk, *rhis,* nose, *itis,* inflammation], an infection of the nasal mucosa that is accompanied by pus formation. The condition is often secondary to a systemic infection, such as measles.

purulent synovitis [L, *purulentus,* pus formation; Gk, *syn,* together; L, *ovum,* egg], an inflammation of the synovial membrane of a joint with pus formation in the cavity.

pus [L, corrupt matter], a creamy, viscous fluid exudate that is the result of fluid remains of necrosis of tissues. It is usually pale yellow to yellow green, sometimes whitish, and sometimes bloody. Its main constituent is an abundance of polymorphonuclear leukocytes. Bacterial infection is its most common cause.

pus cell, a necrotic polymorphonuclear leukocyte, a major component of pus.

pus in urine [L,*pus*; Gk, *ouron,* urine], the presence of pus in a urine sample, indicating a UTI anywhere from the kidneys to the urethra.

pustular psoriasis [L, *pustula,* blister; Gk, *psoriasis,* itch], a severe form of psoriasis consisting of bright red patches and sterile pustules all over the body. Crops of lesions lasting 4 to 7 days occur every few days in cycles over weeks or months. Fever, leukocytosis, and hypoalbuminemia are associated.

pustule /pus'chŏŏl/ [L, *pustula*], a small circumscribed elevation of the skin containing fluid that is usually purulent. —**pustular,** *adj.*

putamen /pyŏŏtā'mən/ [L, *putamen,* husk], a part of the lentiform nucleus that is lateral to the globus pallidus. It is associated with the corpus striatum and receives connections from the suppressor centers of the cortex.

putrefaction /pyŏŏ'trəfak'shən/ [L, *puter,* rotten, *facere,* to make], the decay of enzymes, especially proteins, that produces foul-smelling compounds such as ammonia, hydrogen sulfide, and mercaptans.

putrefactive /-fak'tiv/ [L, *puter,* rotten, *facere,* to make], causing, promoting, or relating to putrefaction.

putrefy /pyŏŏ'trəfī/ [L, *puter,* rotten, *facere,* to make], to decay, with the production of foul-smelling substances, especially putrescine and mercaptans associated with the decomposition of animal tissues and proteins.

putrescine /pyŏŏ'tresēn/, a foul-smelling toxic ptomaine produced by the decomposition of the amino acid ornithine during the decay of animal tissues, bacillus cultures, and fecal bacteria.

putrid /pyŏŏ'trid/ [L, *putridus,* rotten], decomposed.

putromaine /pyŏŏtrŏ'mān/, any toxin produced by the decay of food within a living body.

PUVA, an abbreviation for a psoriatic photochemotherapy treatment consisting of a medication called *p*soralen plus *u*ltraviolet light of *A* (long) wavelength.

P value, in research, the statistical probability of the occurrence of a given finding by chance alone in comparison with the known distribution of possible findings, considering the kinds of data, the technique of analysis, and the number of observations.

PVC, 1. abbreviation for **polyvinyl chloride.** 2. abbreviation for **premature ventricular complex.**

PVP-I, abbreviation for **povidone-iodine.**

PVR, abbreviation for **pulmonary vascular resistance.**

pW, abbreviation for *picowatt.*

PWA, abbreviation for *person with AIDS.*

P wave, the component of the cardiac cycle shown on an ECG as an inverted U-shaped curve that follows the T wave and precedes the QRS complex. It represents atrial depolarization.

P′ wave (P prime wave), a P wave that is generated from a site other than the sinus node; an ectopic P wave.

PWP, abbreviation for **pulmonary wedge pressure.**

pyelitis /pī′əlī′tis/, an inflammation of the renal pelvis, often accompanied by symptoms such as pain and tenderness in the loins, irritability of the bladder, bloody or purulent urine, and a peculiar pain on flexion of the thigh.

pyelogram /pī′əlōgram′/ [Gk, *pyelos,* pelvis, *gramma,* record], a radiographic picture of the kidneys and ureters taken after the IV or intraureteral injection of a radiopaque contrast medium. It shows the size and location of the kidneys, the outline of the ureters and bladder, the filling of the renal pelves, the patency of the urinary tract, and any cysts or tumors within the kidneys.

pyelointerstitial backflow, backflow of fluid from the renal pelvis into interstitial tissue under certain conditions of back pressure.

pyelolithotomy /pī′əlō′lithot′əmē/, a surgical procedure in which renal calculi are removed from the pelvis of the ureter.

pyelonephritis /pī′əlōnəfrī′tis/ [Gk, *pyelos* + *nephros,* kidney, *itis,* inflammation], a diffuse pyogenic infection of the pelvis and parenchyma of the kidney. Acute pyelonephritis is usually the result of an infection that ascends from the lower urinary tract to the kidney. The onset of acute pyelonephritis is rapid and characterized by fever, chills, pain in the flank, nausea, and urinary frequency. Chronic pyelonephritis develops slowly after bacterial infection of the kidney.

pyelonephritis of pregnancy, a renal infection during pregnancy characterized by dilatation of the renal pelvis and the ureters. Some degree of ureteric obstruction may be caused by the gravid uterus.

pyeloplasty /pī′əlōplas′tē/, the surgical reconstruction of the kidney pelvis.

pyelorostomy, the surgical establishment of a fistula from the abdominal surface to the stomach at a point near the pylorus.

pyelosinus backflow, backflow of fluid from the renal pelvis into the renal sinus under certain conditions of back pressure.

pyelovenous backflow, backflow of fluid from the renal pelvis into the venous system under certain conditions of back pressure.

pyemesis /pī·em′əsis/, the action of vomiting purulent material.

pyemic embolism /pī-ē′mik/ [Gk, *pyon,* pus, *haima,* blood, *embolos,* plug], an infective embolus producing an abscess.

pygeum, an herbal product used for benign prostate hypertrophy for which there is some evidence of efficacy, and as an antiinflammatory medication, for which there are insufficient reliable data regarding efficacy.

pygmalianism /pigmā′lē·əniz′əm/ [Gk, *Pygmalion,* mythic sculptor who fell in love with his statue], a psychosexual abnormality in which the individual directs erotic fantasies to an object that he or she has created.

pygmy /pig′mē/ [L, *pygmaeus,* dwarf], an extremely small person whose body parts are proportioned accordingly.

pygoamorphus /pī′gō·əmôr′fəs/ [Gk, *pyge,* buttocks, *a* + *morphe,* not form], asymmetric, conjoined twins in which the parasitic member is represented by an undifferentiated amorphous mass attached to the autosite in the sacral region.

pygodidymus /pī′gōdid′əməs/ [Gk, *pyge,* buttocks, *didymos,* twin], 1. a malformed fetus that has a double pelvis and hips. 2. conjoined twins who are fused in the cephalothoracic region but separated at the pelvis.

pygomelus /pīgom′ələs/ [Gk, *pyge* + *melos,* limb], a malformed fetus that has an extra limb or limbs attached to the buttock.

pygopagus /pīgop′əgəs/ [Gk, *pyge* + *pegos,* fixed], conjoined twins consisting of two fully formed or nearly formed fetuses united in the sacral region so that they are positioned back to back.

pyknic /pik′nik/ [Gk, *pyknos,* thick], describing a body structure characterized by short, round limbs; a full face with a broad head and thick shoulders; a short neck; stockiness; and a tendency to obesity.

pyknodysostosis /pik′nōdis′ostō′sis/ [Gk, *pyknos,* thick, *dys,* bad, *osteon,* bone, *osis,* condition], an autosomal-recessive symptom complex consisting of dwarfism, osteopetrosis, partial agenesis of terminal digits of hands and feet, cranial anomalies, frontal and occipital bossing, and hypoplasia of the angle of the mandible.

pyknosis /piknō′sis/, the condensation of nuclear material into a solid, darkly staining mass in a dying cell thickness, especially shrinking of cells through degeneration.

pyla /pī′lə/, the opening between the third ventricle and the cerebral aqueduct.

pylethrombophlebitis /pī′ləthrom′bōfləbī′tis/, inflammation of the portal vein with formation of a thrombus.

pylon /pī′lon/ [Gk, gate], an artificial lower limb, often a narrow vertical support consisting of a socket with wooden side supports and a rubber-clad peg end. It may be used as a temporary prosthesis.

pyloric /pīlôr′ik/ [Gk, pyle, gate, ouros, guard], pertaining to the pylorus, the opening between the stomach and duodenum.

pyloric antrum, that part of the stomach between the pyloric canal and the body of the stomach.

pyloric canal, the narrow, constricted region of the pyloric part of the stomach.

pyloric constriction, the constriction at the distal end of the pylorus, overlying the pyloric orifice, marking the junction of the stomach and duodenum.

pyloric obstruction and dilation /pīlôr′ik/ [Gk, pyle, gate and ouros guard; L, obstruere, to build against, dilatare, to widen], a reaction of the stomach to pyloric obstruction, which increases the resistance to the expulsion of partly digested food from the stomach. As a result, the stomach may become hypertrophied, then dilated. Excessive consumption of food and beverages contributes to the condition.

pyloric orifice [Gk, pyle, gate, ouros, guard; L, orificium, opening], the opening of or passage between the stomach into the duodenum, lying to the right of the midline at the level of the upper border of the first lumbar vertebra.

pyloric sphincter, a sphincter at the opening from the stomach into the duodenum. It is usually closed, opening only for a moment when a peristaltic wave passes over it.

pyloric stenosis, a narrowing of the pyloric sphincter at the outlet of the stomach, causing an obstruction that blocks the flow of food into the small intestine.

pyloroduodenitis /pīlôr′ōdoo′ədəni′tis/, an inflammation of the pylorus and the duodenum.

pyloromyotomy /pīlôr′ōmī·ot′əmē/ [Gk, pyle + ouros + mys, muscle, temnein, to cut], the incision of the longitudinal and circular muscle of the pylorus, which leaves the mucosa intact but separates the incised muscle fibers. It is the treatment of choice for hypertrophic pyloric stenosis.

pyloroplasty /pīlôr′əplas′tē/ [Gk, pyle + ouros + plassein, to mold], a surgical procedure performed to relieve the pyloric stenosis by widening the pyloric outlet.

pylorospasm /pīlôr′əspaz′əm/ [Gk, pyle + ouros + spasmos], a spasm of the pyloric sphincter of the stomach, as occurs in pyloric stenosis.

pylorostomy /pī′lôros′təmē/, the surgical establishment of a fistula from the abdominal surface to the stomach at a point near the pylorus.

pylorotomy /pī′lôrot′əmē/ [Gk, pyle, gate, ouros, guard, temnein, to cut], a surgical incision of the pylorus, usually performed to remove an obstruction.

pylorus /pīlôr′əs/ pl. **pylori, pyloruses** [Gk, pyle, gate, ouros, guard], a narrow, nearly tubular part of the stomach that angles to the right from the body of the stomach toward the duodenum. —**pyloric,** adj.

pyocele, an accumulation of pus in the scrotum.

pyocolpos, an accumulation of pus in the vagina.

pyocyanic /pī′ōsī·an′ik/, pertaining to pus that is blue or to an organism that produces blue pus, such as Pseudomonas pyocyanea.

pyocyanin /pī′ōsī′ənin/, a blue or blue-green pigment that may be extracted from Pseudomonas aeruginosa with chloroform.

pyocyst /pī′əsist/ [Gk, pyon, pus, kytos, cell], a pus-filled cyst.

pyocystitis /-sistī′tis/, an inflammation involving a pus-filled cyst within the urinary bladder.

pyoderma /pī′ōdur′mə/ [Gk, pyon, pus, derma, skin], any purulent skin disease, such as impetigo.

pyoderma gangrenosum, a rapidly evolving, idiopathic, chronic debilitating skin disease that usually accompanies a systemic disease, especially chronic ulcerative colitis, and is characterized by irregular, boggy, blue-red ulcers with undermined borders surrounding purulent necrotic bases.

pyogenic /pī′əjen′ik/ [Gk, pyon + genein, to produce], pus-producing.

pyogenic exotoxin, extracellular toxin secreted by Streptococcus pyogenes that may be associated with fever and the development of renal failure, respiratory distress, and necrosis.

pyogenic granuloma, a small nonmalignant mass of excessive granulation tissue, usually found at the site of an injury. Most often a dull red, it contains numerous capillaries, bleeds readily, and is very tender. It may be attached by a narrow stalk.

pyogenic infection [Gk, pyon, pus, genein, to produce; L, inficere, to stain], any infection that results in pus production.

pyogenic microorganisms [Gk, *pyon,* pus, *genein,* to produce, *mikros,* small, *organon,* instrument], microorganisms that produce pus. They include species of bacilli, clostridia, gonococci, meningococci, pseudomonads, staphylococci, and streptococci.

pyohemothorax /-hem'ōthôr'aks/ [Gk, *pyon,* pus, *haima,* blood, *thorax,* chest], an accumulation of pus and blood in the pleural cavity.

pyonephrolithiasis /-nef'rōlithī'əsis/, an accumulation of pus and calculi in the kidney.

pyophylactic /-filak'tik/ [Gk, *pyon,* pus, *phylax,* protector], providing protection against purulent infections, such as administering an antibiotic before the onset of an infection.

pyophysometra /-fī'sōmē'trə/, an accumulation of pus and gas in the uterus.

pyopneumopericardium /pī'ōnōo͞o'mōper'ikär'dē·əm/, the presence of pus and air or gas in the pericardial sac.

pyopneumoperitonitis /pī'ōnōo͞o'mōper'itənī'tis/, inflammation of the peritoneal cavity caused by an accumulation of air and pus in the cavity.

pyopyelectasis /-pī'əlek'təsis/, a dilation of the renal pelvis of the kidney resulting from an accumulation of pus.

pyorrhea /pī'ərē'ə/ [Gk, *pyon* + *rhoia,* flow], **1.** a discharge of pus. **2.** a purulent inflammation of the tissues surrounding the teeth.—**pyorrheal,** *adj.*

pyosalpinx /pī'ōsal'pingks/ [Gk, *pyon* + *salpinx,* tube], an accumulation of pus in a fallopian tube.

pyospermia, a complication of chronic prostatitis marked by pus in the seminal fluid.

pyostatic /-stat'ik/, arresting the formation of pus.

pyostomatitis /-stō'mətī'tis/, an inflammation of the mouth.

pyothorax /-thôr'aks/, **1.** a collection of pus in the pleural cavity. **2.** purulent pleurisy.

pyoureter /pī'ōyoͦo͞or'ətər, -yoͦo͞orē'tər/, the presence of pus in the ureter.

pyoverdin /-vur'din/, a yellow pigment produced by some strains of *Pseudomonas aeruginosa.*

pyramid /pir'əmid/ [Gk, *pyramis*], a mass of tissue rising to an apex, such as the pyramids of the cerebellum and kidneys.

pyramidal /piram'idəl/ [Gk, *pyramis*], pertaining to the shape of a pyramid.

pyramidal cell [Gk, *pyramis*; L, *cella,* storeroom], a neuron with a pyramid-shaped cell body in the gray matter of the cerebral cortex.

pyramidalis /piram'idā'lis/, one of a pair of anterolateral muscles of the abdomen,

contained in the lower end of the sheath of the rectus abdominis. It functions to tense the linea alba.

pyramidal nucleus [Gk, *pyramis*; L, *nucleus,* nut kernel], a band of gray matter lying between the olivary nucleus and the midline that projects fibers contralaterally to the vermis part of the cerebellum.

pyramidal tract, a pathway composed of groups of nerve fibers in the white matter of the spinal cord through which motor impulses are conducted to the anterior horn cells from the opposite side of the brain. These descending fibers regulate the voluntary and reflex activity of the muscles through the anterior horn cells.

pyramidotomy /piram'idot'əmē/, the surgical severance of pyramidal tracts in the treatment of disorders associated with involuntary muscle contractions.

pyrantel pamoate /pīran'təl/, an anthelmintic prescribed in the treatment of infestation by roundworms or pinworms.

pyrazinamide /pī'rəzin'əmīd/, an antimycobacterial prescribed in combination chemotherapy in the treatment of TB of hospitalized patients who fail to respond to other medications.

pyrenemia /pī'rənē'mē·ə/, a condition in which nucleated erythrocytes are present in the blood.

pyrethrin and piperonyl butoxide /pī'rəthrin, piper'ənil/, a fixed-combination scabicide and pediculicide prescribed in the treatment of infestations of head, body, and pubic lice.

pyretic /pīre'tik/ [Gk, *pyretos,* fever], pertaining to or characterized by fever.

pyretogenic /pī'rətojen'ik/ [Gk, *pyretos,* fever, *genein,* to produce], inducing, causing, or resulting from a fever.

Pyridium, a trademark for a urinary tract analgesic (phenazopyridine hydrochloride).

pyridostigmine bromide /pir'idōstig'mēn/, an acetylcholinesterase inhibitor that prolongs the effects of neuronally released acetylcholine. It is prescribed in the treatment of myasthenia gravis and is used as an antagonist to nondepolarizing muscle relaxants, such as curare.

pyridoxal phosphate /pir'ədok'səl/, an enzyme that acts with pyridoxamine phosphate and transaminase to catalyze the reversible transfer of an amino group from an alpha-amino acid to an alpha-keto acid, especially alpha-ketoglutaric acid. Such processes are essential to metabolism.

pyridoxamine phosphate /pir'ədok'səmēn/, an enzyme that participates with pyridoxal phosphate and transaminase in the reversible transfer of an amino group from an alpha-amino acid to an alpha-keto acid.

pyridoxine /pir′ədok′sēn/, a water-soluble white crystalline vitamin that is part of the B complex. It is derived from pyridine and converted in the body to pyridoxal and pyridoxamine for synthesis. It functions as a coenzyme essential for the synthesis and breakdown of amino acids, the conversion of tryptophan to niacin, the breakdown of glycogen to glucose 1-phosphate, the production of antibodies, the formation of heme in hemoglobin, the formation of hormones important in brain function, the proper absorption of vitamin B_{12}, the production of hydrochloric acid and magnesium, and the maintenance of the balance of sodium and potassium, which regulates body fluids and the functioning of the nervous and musculoskeletal systems.

pyrimethamine /pir′imeth′əmēn/, an antimalarial prescribed in the treatment of malaria and toxoplasmosis.

pyrimidine /pərim′ədēn/, an organic compound of heterocyclic nitrogen found in nucleic acids and in many drugs, including the antiviral drugs acyclovir, ribavirin, and trifluridine.

pyrogen /pī′rəjən/ [Gk, *pyr,* fire, *genein,* to produce], any substance or matter that tends to cause a rise in body temperature, such as some bacterial toxins.—**pyrogenic,** *adj.*

pyroglobulin /pī′rōglob′yəlin/, an immunoglobulin that precipitates irreversibly when heated. Pyroglobulins are often present in the blood of patients with diseases such as multiple myeloma.

pyroglutamic acid /pi′roglootam′ik/, an uncommon amino acid derivative.

pyrolagnia /pī′rōlag′nē·ə/ [Gk, *pyr* + *lagneia,* lust], sexual stimulation or gratification from watching or setting fires.

pyrolysis /pīrol′isis/, the decomposition of a chemical compound by the application of heat.

pyromania /pī′rōmā′nē·ə/ [Gk, *pyr* + *mania,* madness], an impulse-control disorder characterized by an uncontrollable urge to set fires.

pyromaniac /pī′rōmā′nē·ak/, **1.** a person having or displaying characteristics of pyromania. **2.** pertaining to or exhibiting pyromania.

pyropoikilocytosis /pī′rōpoi′kilō′sītō′sis/, a recessive inherited disorder characterized by severe hemolysis, irregular shapes of RBCs, and sensitivity of blood cells to fragmentation in vitro after minor temperature variations.

pyrotherapy /pī′rōther′əpē/, a method of treatment in which the temperature of a patient is raised to a fever level.

pyrrole (C_4H_4NH) /pirōl′, pir′ōl/ [Gk, *pyrrhos,* red], a five-membered heterocyclic aromatic substance occurring naturally in many compounds in the body.

pyruvate carboxylase /pī′rōōvāt kär bok′səlās/, an enzyme that catalyzes the irreversible carboxylation of pyruvate, a reaction necessary for gluconeogenesis from lactate or amino acids forming pyruvate and also providing four-carbon compounds for the citric acid cycle.

pyruvate dehydrogenase complex /pī′rōōvāt dēhī′drōjənās/, a multienzyme complex, consisting of at least three distinct enzymes, which catalyzes the formation of acetyl coenzyme A from pyruvate and coenzyme A.

pyruvate kinase /pī′rəvāt/, an enzyme essential for anaerobic glycolysis in RBCs. It catalyzes the transfer of a phosphate group from adenosine triphosphate to produce adenosine diphosphate.

pyruvate kinase deficiency, a congenital hemolytic anemia transmitted as an autosomal-recessive trait. The homozygous condition is characterized by severe chronic hemolysis. The heterozygous form is usually asymptomatic and of no clinical significance, although mild to severe anemia may occur.

pyruvic acid /pīrōō′vik/, a compound formed as an end product of glycolysis, the anaerobic stage of glucose metabolism.

pyuria /pīyŏōr′ē·ə/, the presence of an excessive number of WBCs in the urine, typically more than four leukocytes per high-power field count. It is generally a sign of an infection in the urinary tract but can reflect inflammation from chemical or radiation causes. Bacterial pyuria usually is caused by infection of the bladder and urethra.

PZI, abbreviation for **protamine zinc insulin.**

P

Q

Q, 1. symbol for *blood volume*. 2. symbol for *quantity*. 3. symbol for **coulomb**.

Q̇, symbol for *rate of blood flow*.

q2h, in prescriptions, abbreviation for *quaque secunda hora,* a Latin phrase meaning "every 2 hours."

q3h, in prescriptions, abbreviation for *quaque tertia hora,* a Latin phrase meaning "every 3 hours."

q4h, in prescriptions, abbreviation for *quaque quarta hora,* a Latin phrase meaning "every 4 hours."

q6h, in prescriptions, abbreviation for *quaque sex hora,* a Latin phrase meaning "every 6 hours."

q8h, in prescriptions, abbreviation for *quaque octa hora,* a Latin phrase meaning "every 8 hours."

Q angle, the angle of incidence of the quadriceps muscle relative to the patella. The Q angle determines the tracking of the patella through the trochlea of the femur. As the angle increases, the chance of patellar compression problems increases.

QCT, abbreviation for **quantitative computed tomography.**

q.d., 1. in prescriptions, abbreviation for *quaque die* /dēˈā/, a Latin phrase meaning "every day." 2. abbreviation for *quartile deviation.*

qdrnt, abbreviation for **quadrant.**

Q fever [L, *febris*], an acute febrile illness, usually respiratory, caused by the rickettsia *Coxiella burnetii (Rickettsia burnetii).* The disease is spread through contact with infected domestic animals, by inhaling the rickettsiae from their hides, drinking their contaminated milk, or being bitten by a tick harboring the organism. Onset is abrupt, and high fever may persist for 3 weeks or more. Treatment with tetracycline is usually effective in 36 to 48 hours. Because Q fever is transmitted by inhalation of rickettsiae it is considered a bioterrorism agent and is classified as a category B agent by the CDC.

q.h., in prescriptions, abbreviation for *quaque hora,* a Latin phrase meaning "every hour."

Qi, in traditional Chinese medicine, the vital energy of the human body.

qid, q.i.d, in prescriptions, abbreviation for *quater in die* /dēˈā/, a Latin phrase meaning "four times a day."

Qi Gong, a form of Chinese exercise stimulation therapy that proposes to improve health by redirecting mental focus, breathing, coordination, and relaxation. The goal is to rebalance the body's own healing capacities by activating proposed electric or energetic currents that flow along meridians located throughout the body.

q.l., abbreviation for the Latin phrase *quantum libet,* "as much as one pleases."

qli, abbreviation for *quality of life index.*

Q-R interval, the period from the start of the QRS complex to the peak of the R wave on an ECG.

QRS complex, a series of waveforms on an ECG that represents both normal and abnormal depolarization of ventricular muscle cells. It is composed of Q, R, and S waves: a Q wave is the negative deflection before the first R wave, an R wave is any positive deflection, and an S wave is the negative deflection after an R wave. If there is no R wave, the totally negative complex is designated QS.

QRST complex [L, *complexus*], a series of waveforms on an ECG, consisting of the QRS complex, the S-T segment and the T wave. It represents depolarization and repolarization of the ventricular muscle cells.

q.s., in prescriptions, abbreviation for *quantum sufficit,* a Latin phrase meaning "quantity required."

Q-switched laser, a laser containing a switching device that causes the laser to produce very high intensity impulses of very short duration.

Q-switching, a laser technique used in glaucoma surgery to achieve high-peak power in nanosecond pulses of energy.

qt, abbreviation for **quart.**

Q-T interval, the period from the beginning of the QRS complex to the end of the T wave on an ECG. It reflects the refractory period of the heart. A long Q-T interval is associated with the life-threatening ventricular tachycardia known as torsades de pointes.

Quaalude, a trademark for a sedative-hypnotic (methaqualone). It is no longer distributed in the United States.

quad, 1. abbreviation for *quadriceps.* 2. abbreviation for *quadrilateral.* 3. abbreviation for **quadrant.** 4. abbreviation for **quadriplegia.**

quad cane, a cane adapted for increased stability by providing a four-legged rectangular base of support.

quad coughing /kwod/, a form of assisted coughing for patients with CNS disorders who are unable to generate sufficient force to clear respiratory secretions. After a maximal inspiration, the patient coughs while an assistant exerts gentle upward and inward pressure with both hands on the abdomen. The increased intraabdominal pressure produces a more forceful cough.

quadrangular bandage /kwodrang′gələr/, a towel or other large rectangular sheet of cloth folded over for use as a wrapping for a wound of the abdomen, chest, or head.

quadrant (qdrnt, quad) /kwod′rənt/ [L, *quadrans,* a fourth part], **1.** one quarter of a circle. **2.** one quarter of an anatomic area formed by the division of the area by imaginary vertical and horizontal lines bisecting each other.

quadrantanopsia /kwodran′tənop′sē-ə/, a loss of vision in a quarter section of the visual field of one or both eyes. The cause may vary with the quadrant affected.

quadrantectomy /kwod′rantek′təmē/, a partial mastectomy in which a tumor and at least a 1-inch margin of surrounding tissue along with the pectoralis muscle fascia are excised in one quadrant of a breast.

quadrant streak, a technique for microbial inoculation in which a single colony is isolated on a culture plate divided into four sections.

quadriceps femoris /kwod′riseps/ [L,*quattuor,* four, *caput,* head, *femur,* thigh], the large extensor muscle of the anterior thigh, composed of the rectus femoris, the vastus lateralis, the vastus medialis, and the vastus intermedius. It functions to extend the leg.

quadrigeminal /kwod′rijem′inəl/ [L,*quadrigeminum,* fourfold], **1.** in four parts. **2.** a fourfold increase in size or frequency. **3.** having four symmetric parts.

quadrigeminal pulse, a pulse in which a pause occurs after every fourth beat.

quadrilateral socket /kwod′rilat′ərəl/, a four-sided prosthetic socket design for people with above-the-knee amputations. The posterior brim is designed to fit directly beneath the ischial tuberosity so that the person literally sits on it.

Quadrinal, a trademark for a respiratory, fixed-combination drug containing a smooth muscle relaxant (theophylline calcium salicylate), an adrenergic (epHEDrine hydrochloride), an expectorant (potassium iodide), and a sedative-hypnotic (phenobarbital).

quadriplegia (quad) /kwod′rəplē′jē-ə/ [L, *quattuor,* four; Gk,*plege,* stroke], paralysis of the arms, legs, and trunk of the body below the level of an associated injury to the spinal cord. This disorder is usually caused by spinal cord injury, especially in the area of the fifth to the seventh vertebrae. Automobile accidents and sporting mishaps are common causes. This condition affects about 150,000 Americans, the majority of whom are men between 20 and 40 years of age. Signs and symptoms commonly include flaccidity of the arms and the legs and the loss of power and sensation below the level of the injury. Cardiovascular complications also may develop from any injury that damages the spinal cord above the fifth cervical vertebra because of an associated block of the sympathetic nervous system. A major cause of death from such injury is respiratory failure. Other symptoms may include low body temperature, bradycardia, impaired peristalsis, and autonomic dysreflexia. Diagnosis is based on a complete physical and neurologic examination with radiographic pictures of the head, chest, and abdomen to rule out underlying injuries. Spinal x-ray examinations and CT scores and MRI are usually done to evaluate the extent of the injury.

quadrivalent /kwod′rivā′lənt/, a chemical element or radical with a valence of four.

quadruped /kwod′rŏŏped′/ [L, *quattuor,* four, *pes,* foot], **1.** any four-footed animal. **2.** a human whose body weight is supported by both arms as well as both legs.

quadruplet /kwod′rŏŏplit, kwodrŏŏ′plit/ [L, *quadruplex,* fourfold], any one of four offspring born of the same gestation period during a single pregnancy.

quadrupole mass filter, a four-pole magnet system used to separate charged mass fragments in a mass spectrometer.

qual anal, abbreviation for **qualitative analysis.**

quale /kwā′lē/ *pl.* **qualia** [L, *qualis,* what kind], **1.** the quality of a particular thing. **2.** a quality considered as an independent entity. **3.** in psychology, a feeling, sensation, or other conscious process that has its unique particular quality, regardless of its external meaning or frame of reference.

qualified /kwol′ifīd/ [L, *qualis,*], pertaining to a health professional or health facility that is formally recognized by an appropriate agency or organization as meeting certain standards of performance related to the professional competence of an individual or the eligibility of an institution to participate in an approved health care program.

qualitative /kwol′itā′tiv/ [L, *qualis*], pertaining to the quality, value, or nature of something.

Q

qualitative analysis (qual anal) [L, *qualis,* what kind; Gk, *analysis,* a loosening], **1.** in chemistry, the study of a sample of material to determine what chemical substances are present. **2.** in research, the analysis and interpretation of data that cannot be analyzed by statistical methods.

qualitative test, a test that determines the presence or absence of a substance.

quality /kwol'itē/ [L, *qualis*], **1.** a descriptive specification of the penetrating nature of an x-ray beam. It is influenced by kilovoltage and filtration: a higher kilovoltage produces more penetration; filtration removes selected wavelengths and "hardens" the beam. **2.** in phonetics, refers to the nature of phonation produced by the vocal folds. Disorders of voice quality include hoarseness, harshness, breathiness, and glottal fry.

quality assessment measures, formal systematic organizational evaluation of overall patterns or programs of care, including clinical, consumer, and systems evaluation.

quality control, a method of repeated assay of known standard materials and monitoring reaction parameters to ensure precision and accuracy.

quality factor, a term that expresses the biologic damage that radiation can produce. Doses of different types of radiation can be set equal to one another if the actual absorbed dose is multiplied by the quality factor. The product is called the dose equivalent, measured in sieverts or rem.

quality management, **1.** in health care, any evaluation of services provided and the results achieved as compared with accepted standards. In one form of quality assurance, various attributes of health care such as cost, place, accessibility, treatment, and benefits are scored in a two-part process. **2.** a system of review of selected hospital medical/nursing records by medical/nursing staff members, performed for the purposes of evaluating the quality and effectiveness of medical/nursing care in relation to accepted standards.

quality monitoring, a nursing intervention from the Nursing Interventions Classification (NIC) defined as systematic collection and analysis of an organization's quality indicators for the purpose of improving patient care.

quality of life[1] [L, *qualis,* what kind; AS, *lif*], a measure of the optimum energy or force that endows a person with the power to cope successfully with the full range of challenges encountered in the real world. The term applies to all individuals, regardless of illness or handicap, on the job, at home, or in leisure activities.

quality of life[2], a nursing outcome from the Nursing Outcomes Classification (NOC) defined as the extent of positive perception of current life circumstances.

quantitative /kwon'titā'tiv/ [L, *quantus,* how much], capable of being measured.

quantitative analysis [L, *quantum,* how much; Gk, *analysis,* a loosening], **1.** in chemistry, the determination of the amounts of constituents in a sample of material. Kinds of quantitative analysis include gravimetric analysis, volumetric analysis, and spectrophotometric analysis. **2.** in research, the use of statistical methods to analyze data.

quantitative computed tomography (QCT), a type of computed tomography that calculates and displays bone density in three dimensions. QCT is used mainly for lumbar spine studies but can also be applied in hip and peripheral bone mineral evaluations.

quantitative test [L, *quantum,* how much, *testum,* crucible], a test that determines the amount of a substance per unit volume or unit weight.

quantitative ultrasound, an ultrasound technique for assessing bone mineral density. Its main advantage is the complete absence of radiation; a disadvantage is the confounding influence of soft tissue.

quantum theory /kwon'təm/ [L, *quantum,* how much; Gk, *theoria,* speculation], in physics, the theory dealing with the interaction of matter and electromagnetic radiation, particularly at the atomic and subatomic levels, according to which radiation consists of small units of energy called quanta.

quarantine /kwor'əntēn/ [It, *quarantina,* forty], **1.** isolation of people with communicable disease or those exposed to communicable disease during the contagious period in an attempt to prevent spread of the illness. **2.** the practice of detaining travelers or vessels coming from places of epidemic disease, originally for 40 days, for the purpose of inspection or disinfection.

quart (qt) /kwôrt/ [L, *quartus,* fourth], a unit of volume fluid measure equivalent to ¼ gallon, 2 pints, 32 ounces, or 946.24 milliliters. The British Imperial quart is equal to 40 ounces, or 1.136 L, and the American quart for dry measure is 1.101 L.

quartan /kwôr'tən/ [L, *quartanus,* relating to the fourth], recurring on the fourth day, or at about 72-hour intervals.

quartan malaria, a form of malaria, caused by the protozoan *Plasmodium malariae,* characterized by febrile paroxysms that occur every 72 hours.

quartile /kwôr'təl, kwôr'tīl/ [L, *quartus,* fourth], one-fourth of the distribution of scores. The first quartile would be the lowest 25% of scores, the second quartile would represent the 26% to 50% range of scores, and so on.

quartz crystal therapy, an alternative therapy that involves placement of a four- or six-sided quartz crystal over a chakra, or major energy station, of the body such as the brow, throat, heart, stomach, abdomen, base of the spine, or near the skull to act as a destressor and to support the immune system.

quasispecies /quah′ze-spe′sēz/, a swarm of virus with similar genetic structure sharing a host with other quasispecies of different genetic makeup. Usually all quasispecies in one host are descended from a single ancestor strain.

quaternary /kwot′əner″ē, kwətur′nərē/ [L, *quattuor,* four], 1. pertaining to a chemical compound in which four atoms or groups of elements are bonded to one atom, such as a quaternary ammonium compound in which four organic radicals are substituted for the four hydrogen molecules on an ammonium ion. 2. fourth-level structure in proteins as in the structure of hemoglobin made up of two alpha-globulins and two beta-globulins.

quaternary ammonium derivative, a substance whose chemical structure has four carbon groups attached to a positively charged nitrogen atom. When the quaternary ammonium ion has more than about 16 carbon atoms, it is usually a strong emulsifying agent, highly water soluble but relatively insoluble in lipids.

quazepam /kwah′zē-pam/, a benzodiazepine used as a sedative and hypnotic in the treatment of insomnia.

Queckenstedt's test /kwek′ənstets/ [Hans H.G. Queckenstedt, German physician, 1876–1918], a test for an obstruction in the spinal canal in which the jugular veins on each side of the neck are compressed alternately. Normally occlusion of the veins of the neck causes an immediate rise in spinal fluid pressure; if the vertebral canal is blocked, no rise occurs.

Queensland tick typhus, an infection caused by *Rickettsia australis,* occurring in Australia, transmitted by ticks, and resembling mild Rocky Mountain spotted fever. Treatment includes the administration of chloramphenicol or tetracycline. Prevention depends on avoiding tick bites and on the prompt removal of attached ticks.

Quelidrine, a trademark for a fixed-combination respiratory drug containing adrenergics (phenylephrine hydrochloride and epHEDrine hydrochloride), an antihistaminic (chlorpheniramine maleate), an antitussive (dextromethorphan hydrobromide), and an expectorant (ammonium chloride).

quellung reaction /kwel′ung/ [Ger, *Quellung,* swelling; L, *re,* again, *agere,* to act], the swelling of the capsule of a bacterium, seen in the laboratory when the organism is exposed to specific antisera. This phenomenon is used to identify the genera, species, or subspecies of the bacteria causing a disease.

quenching /kwen′ching/, 1. a process of removing or reducing an energy source such as heat or light. 2. stopping or diminishing a chemical or enzymatic reaction. 3. decreasing counting efficiency in beta liquid scintillation caused by interfering materials. 4. preventing emission of light from fluorescent compounds.

Quengel cast /kwen′gəl/, a two-section orthopedic cast for immobilizing the lower extremity from the foot or ankle to below the knee and the upper thigh to just above the knee. The two parts of the cast are connected by hinges at knee level, medially and laterally. The Quengle cast is used for the gradual correction of knee contractures.

quercetin /kwur′sitin/, a yellow, crystalline, flavonoid pigment found in oak bark, the juice of lemons, asparagus, and other plants. It is used to reduce abnormal capillary fragility.

querulous paranoia /kwer′(y)ələs/ [L, *queri,* to complain; Gk, *para,* beside, *nous,* mind], a form of paranoia characterized by extreme discontent and habitual complaining, usually about imagined slights by others.

Quervain's disease /kervănz′, kerveNz′/ [Fritz de Quervain, Swiss surgeon, 1868–1940; L, *dis;* Fr, *aise,* ease], chronic tenosynovitis of the abductor pollicis longus and extensor pollicis brevis muscles of the thumb.

Questran, a trademark for an ion exchange resin used to lower blood cholesterol levels (cholestyramine resin).

quetiapine, an antipsychotic/neuroleptic prescribed in the treatment of psychotic disorders.

Quibron, a trademark for a fixed-combination respiratory drug containing a smooth muscle relaxant (theophylline) and an expectorant (guaifenesin).

quick connect [ME, *quic,* living; L, *connectere,* to bind], a plastic or similar connecting device that is attached to or implanted in a patient who will be joined to an electromechanical or other apparatus.

quickening /kwik′(ə)ning/ [ME, *quic,* living], the first feeling by a pregnant woman of movement of her baby in utero, usually occurring between 16 and 20 weeks of gestation.

quick pulse, a pulse that strikes the finger smartly and leaves it quickly.

quiescent /kwī·es′ənt/, **1.** inactive, quiet, or at rest. **2.** latent. **3.** dormant.

quiet alert /kwī′ət/, a period when a neonate is calm and attentive, with eyes open, ready to become acquainted with an adult person. Newborns spend about 10% of their time in this state.

Quigley traction /kwig′lē/, a type of traction for lateral malleolar and trimalleolar fractures in which a stockinette is placed around the leg and ankle and attached to an overhead frame, thus suspending the leg by the ankle.

Quinaglute, a trademark for a cardiac antiarrhythmic (quinidine gluconate).

Quincke's disease /kwing′kēz/ [Heinrich I. Quincke, German physician, 1842–1922; L, dis; Fr, aise, ease], angioedema, a potentially fatal chronic condition of subcutaneous edema, abdominal pain, urticaria, and laryngeal edema.

Quincke's pulse [Heinrich I. Quincke], an abnormal alternate blanching and reddening of the skin or nails that may be observed in several ways, such as by pressing the front edge of the fingernail and watching the blood in the nailbed recede and return. This pulsation is characteristic of aortic insufficiency and other abnormal conditions but may also occur in otherwise normal individuals.

Quinidex, a trademark for a cardiac antiarrhythmic (quinidine sulfate).

quinidine /kwin′əden, -din/, an antiarrhythmic agent administered as a bisulfate, gluconate, polygalacturonate, or sulfate salts. It is prescribed in the treatment of atrial flutter, atrial fibrillation, premature ventricular contractions, and tachycardias.

quinine /kwī′nīn/ [Sp, quina, bark], a white, bitter, crystalline alkaloid made from cinchona bark. It was formerly used in antimalarial medications and replaced when chloroquine became available. It is once again being used to treat some cases of chloroquine-resistant malaria.

quinoline /kwin′o-lēn/, an amine or alkaloid derivable from quinine, coal tar, and various other sources, which has antiseptic, antipyretic, and antimalarial properties.

quinolone /kwin′əlōn/, any of a class of antibiotics that act by interrupting the replication of DNA molecules in bacteria. An example is ciprofloxacin.

quintan /kwin′tən/ [L, quintanus, relating to the fifth], recurring on the fifth day, or at about 96-hour intervals.

quintessence /kwintes′əns/ [L, quinta + essentia, the fifth essence], **1.** a highly concentrated extract of any substance. **2.** a tincture or extract containing the most essential components of plant materials.

quintuplet /kwin′tŏŏplit, kwintŏŏ′plit/ [L, quintuplex, fivefold], any one of five offspring born of the same gestation period during a single pregnancy.

quinupristin /kwinu′pris-tin/, a semisynthetic antibacterial effective against a variety of gram-positive organisms. It is used in conjunction with dalfopristin in the treatment of serious bacteremia caused by vancomycin-resistant *Enterococcus faecium* and complicated skin and skin structure infections caused by *Streptococcus pyogenes* or methicillin-sensitive *Staphylococcus aureus*.

quotidian /kwōtid′ē-ən/ [L, quotidianus, daily], occurring every day; for example, a malarial fever with daily attacks.

quotient /kwō′shənt/, the number obtained by dividing one number by another.

quot. op. sit, abbreviation for the Latin phrase *quoties opus sit,* "as often as necessary."

q.v., 1. abbreviation for the Latin phrase *quantum vis,* "as much as you please." **2.** abbreviation for the Latin phrase *quod vide,* "which see."

Q wave, the first negative component of the QRS complex on an ECG. Lengthening of the wave indicates MI.

r, 1. abbreviation for *right*. 2. symbol for *resistance ohm*.

R, 1. abbreviation for **resolution.** 2. abbreviation for **respiratory exchange ratio.** 3. abbreviation for **roentgen.** 4. symbol for *gas constant*. 5. abbreviation for **respiration.** 6. abbreviation for the amino acid **arginine.**

R$_f$, 1. symbol for a ratio used in paper and thin-layer chromatography, representing the distance from the origin to the center of the separated zone divided by the distance from the origin to the solvent front. 2. abbreviation for **radiofrequency.**

R$_i$, symbol for *inhibitory receptor* molecule.

R$_s$, symbol for *stimulatory receptor* molecule.

R$_x$, symbol for the Latin *recipe*, "take."

Ra, symbol for the element **radium.**

RA, 1. abbreviation for *rheumatoid arthritis*. 2. abbreviation for *right atrium*.

rabeprazole, a proton pump inhibitor prescribed to treat gastroesophageal reflux disease (GERD), severe erosive esophagitis, poorly responsive systemic GERD, pathologic hypersecretory conditions such as Zollinger-Ellison syndrome, systemic mastocytosis, multiple endocrine adenomas, and active duodenal ulcers.

rabid /rab'id/ [L, *rabidus*, raving], 1. pertaining to or suffering from rabies. 2. displaying signs of madness, agitation, delirium, hallucinations, and bizarre behavior.

rabies /rā'bēz/ [L, *rabere*, to rave], an acute, usually fatal viral disease of the CNS of mammals. It is transmitted from animals to people through infected saliva. The reservoir of the virus is chiefly wild animals, including skunks, bats, foxes, and raccoons, and unvaccinated dogs and cats. After introduction into the human body, often by a bite of an infected animal, the virus travels along nerve pathways to the brain and later to other organs. An incubation period ranges from 10 days to 1 year and is followed by a prodromal period characterized by fever, malaise, headache, paresthesia, and myalgia. After several days, severe encephalitis, delirium, agonizingly painful muscular spasms, seizures, paralysis, coma, and death ensue. Few nonfatal cases have been documented in humans; survival in those cases has been the result of intensive supportive nursing and medical care.—**rabid** /rab'id/, *adj*.

rabies immune globulin (RIG), a solution of antirabies immune globulin. It is used in conjunction with human diploid cell culture rabies vaccine for possible protection against rabies in persons suspected of exposure to rabies.

rabies-neutralizing antibody test, a blood test performed on those who work with animals and have received the human diploid cell rabies vaccine and on those who may have been exposed to the rabies virus.

rabies vaccine, a sterile suspension of killed rabies virus prepared from duck embryo. It is prescribed for immunization and postexposure prophylaxis against rabies.

rabies virus group [L, *rabere*, to rave, *virus*, poison; It, *gruppo*, knot], the genus of viruses that includes the organism that causes rabies in humans, the *lyssa* virus.

raccoon eyes, ecchymotic areas surrounding both eyes, suggestive of a basilar skull fracture or childhood neuroblastoma.

race [It, *razza*], 1. a vague unscientific term for a group of genetically related people who share certain physical characteristics. 2. a distinct ethnic group characterized by traits that are transmitted through their offspring.

racemic /rāsē'mik/ [L, *racemus*, bunch of grapes], pertaining to a compound made up of equal amounts of dextrorotatory and levorotatory isomers, rendering it optically inactive under polarized light.

racemose /ras'əmōs'/ [L, *racemus*], like a bunch of grapes. The term is used in describing a structure in which many branches terminate in nodular cystlike forms such as pulmonary alveoli.

racemose aneurysm, a pronounced dilation of lengthened and tortuous blood vessels, which may form a tumor.

rachial /rā'kē·əl/ [Gk, *rhachis*, backbone], pertaining to the spinal column.

rachialgia /rā'kē·al'jə/ [Gk, *rhachis*, backbone, *algos*, pain], pain in the vertebral column.

rachiopagus /rā'kē·op'əgəs/ [Gk, *rhachis*, backbone, *pagos*, fixed], conjoined symmetric twins united back to back along the spinal column.

R

rachiresistance /rā'kēresis'təns/ [Gk, *rhachis*, backbone], a failure to respond adequately to spinal anesthesia.

rachischisis /rəkis'kəsis/ [Gk, *rhachis* + *schizein*, to split], a congenital fissure of one or more vertebrae.

rachitic, 1. pertaining to rickets. 2. resembling or suggesting the condition of one afflicted with rickets.

rachitic dwarf, a person whose retarded growth is caused by rickets.

rachitis /rəkī'tis/ [Gk, *rhachis* + *itis*, inflammation], 1. rickets. 2. an inflammatory disease of the vertebral column.

rachitis fetalis annularis, congenital enlargement of the epiphyses of the long bones.

rachitis fetalis micromelia, congenital shortening of the long bones.

racial immunity /rā'shəl/ [It, *razza*; L, *immunis*, free], a form of natural immunity shared by most of the members of a genetically related population.

rad /rad/, abbreviation for **radiation absorbed dose.**

radappertization /rad'apur'tizā'shən/, the irradiation of food for the destruction of *Clostridium botulinum.*

radarkymography /rā'därkīmog'rəfē/ [radar + Gk, *kyma*, wave, *graphein*, to record], a technique for showing the size and outline of the heart, using a radar tracking device and a fluoroscopic screen to display images produced by electric impulses passed over the chest surface.

Radford nomogram [Edward P. Radford, Jr., American physiologist, b. 1922], a mathematic chart device used in respiratory therapy to estimate combined tidal volumes and rates for mechanical ventilation. It is based on the three parameters of body weight, sex, and respiratory rate.

radial /rā'dē-əl/ [L, *radius*, ray], pertaining to the radius.

radial artery [L, *radius*, ray], an artery in the forearm, starting at the bifurcation of the brachial artery and passing in 12 branches to the forearm, wrist, and hand.

radial keratotomy (RK), a surgical procedure in which a series of tiny shallow incisions is made in the cornea to flatten it, thereby reducing refractive error. It usually corrects mild-to-moderate myopia.

radial nerve, the largest branch of the brachial plexus, arising on each side as a continuation of the posterior cord. It supplies the skin of the arm and forearm and their extensor muscles.

radial nerve palsy, a type of mononeuropathy characterized by radial nerve damage with symptoms of forearm muscle weakness and sensory loss. It may be caused by excessive compression of the radial nerve against a hard surface in individuals insensitized by the intake of alcohol or sedatives. It may also be caused by the repeated compression of the nerve by various weights. Time and the withdrawal of causative compression usually ensure full recovery.

radial notch of ulna, the narrow lateral depression in the coronoid process of the ulna that receives the head of the radius.

radial paralysis [L, *radius*; Gk, *paralyein*], paralysis of muscles supplied by the radial nerve, mainly the wrist and finger extensors.

radial pulse, the pulse of the radial artery palpated at the wrist over the radius. The radial pulse is the one most often taken, because of the ease with which it is palpated.

radial recurrent artery, a branch of the radial artery arising just distal to the elbow, ascending between the branches of the radial nerve, and supplying several muscles of the arm and the elbow.

radial reflex, a normal reflex elicited by tapping over the distal radius, with the response being flexion of the forearm.

radial symmetry, a form of symmetry in which body parts are arranged around a central axis, as found in animals such as jellyfish and sea urchins.

radial tuberosity, a large blunt projection on the medial surface of the radius for the attachment of the biceps brachii tendon.

radiant /rā'dē-ənt/ [L, *radiare*, to emit rays], pertaining to any object that emits rays or is the center of rays that spread outward.

radiant energy [L, *radiare*, to emit rays; Gk, *energeia*], energy emitted as electromagnetic radiation such as radio waves, infrared radiation, visible light, ultraviolet light, x-rays, and gamma rays.

radiant heat, a form of infrared energy that is emitted in electromagnetic waves from a central source. It proceeds outward in wavelengths greater than those of visible light. Objects absorbing the energy experience a rise in temperature.

radiate /rā'dē-āt/ [L, *radiare*, to emit rays], to diverge or spread from a common point or center.

radiate crown, 1. a network of fibers that weaves through the internal capsule of the cerebral cortex and intermingles with the fibers of the corpus callosum. 2. an aggregate of cells that surrounds the zona pellucida of the ovum.

radiate ligament, a ligament that connects the head of a rib with a vertebra and an associated intervertebral disk.

radiation /rā'dē·ā'shən/ [L, *radiatio*],
1. the emission of energy, rays, or waves.
2. the use of a radioactive substance in the
diagnosis or treatment of disease.

radiation absorbed dose (rad), the standard unit of absorbed dose of ionizing radiation. One rad is equal to 0.01 J/kg of matter.

radiation burn, a burn resulting from
exposure to radiant energy in the form of
sunlight, x-rays, or nuclear emissions or
explosion. Ionizing radiation can produce
tissue damage directly by striking a vital
molecule such as DNA.

radiation caries, tooth decay triggered by
exposure of the head to ionizing radiation. It
especially affects the cementoenamel junction and the coronal root area. Radiation
makes the teeth more susceptible to caries by
decreasing salivation, reducing the vitality of
dental tissues, and altering oral bacteria.

radiation cataract [L, *radiare,* to emit rays;
Gk, *katarrhaktes,* portcullis], a cataract
that is caused by excessive exposure of
the eye to x-rays or other types of radiation that cause a change in the protein molecules of the lens.

radiation cystitis, inflammatory changes
in the urinary bladder caused by ionizing
radiation.

radiation dermatitis [L, *radiare,* to emit
rays; Gk, *derma,* skin, *itis,* inflamma-
tion], an acute or chronic inflammation
of the skin caused by exposure to ionizing
radiation, as in cancer radiation therapy.
Symptoms, which may not appear until
3 weeks after exposure, include redness,
blistering, and sloughing of the skin. In
severe cases the condition can progress to
scarring, fibrosis, and atrophy.

radiation detector, a device for detecting
the presence and sometimes the amount of
radiation.

**Radiation Effects Research Foundation
(RERF),** an organization that studies the
long-term effects of the atomic bombings
of Hiroshima and Nagasaki during World
War II on survivors.

radiation exposure, a measure of the ionization produced in air by x-rays or gamma
rays. It is the sum of the electric charges on
all ions of one sign that are produced when
all electrons liberated by the radiation in
a volume of air are completely stopped,
divided by the mass of air in that volume.
The unit of exposure is the roentgen. Acute
radiation exposure is exposure of short
duration to intense ionizing radiation, usually occurring as the result of an accidental
spill of radioactive material.

**radiation exposure, emergency proce-
dures,** first-aid treatment of a person
who has received external body radiation
through exposure to radioactive material or

internal radiation contamination by inhaling
or ingesting radioactive material. External
radiation exposure is treated initially by
cleansing and surgical isolation to protect
others. One who has inhaled or ingested
radioactive material should be given emergency treatment similar to a person who has
been exposed to chemical poisons. Body
wastes should be collected and checked
for radiation levels. If the victim has also
suffered a wound, care must be taken to
avoid cross-contamination of exposed surfaces. In general, except for taking special
precautions to control the spread of radiation effects, the patient should be given any
lifesaving emergency treatment needed, and
personnel handling the patient should wear
surgical gowns, caps, and gloves.

radiation force, a small steady force that
is produced when a sound beam strikes a
reflecting or absorbing surface. It is proportional to the acoustic power.

radiation hygiene, the art and science
of protecting human beings from injury
by radiation. It reduces clinical exposure
from external radiation through protective
barriers of radiation-absorbing material,
ensures safe distances between people and
radiation sources, reduces radiation exposure times, or uses combinations of all
these measures.

radiation leakage, radiation going out
through the x-ray tube housing in all directions other than that of the useful beam.

radiation nephritis, kidney damage
caused by ionizing radiation. Symptoms
include glomerular and tubular damage,
hypertension, and proteinuria, sometimes
leading to renal failure.

radiation oncologist, a physician with
special training in the use of ionizing radiation in the treatment of cancers.

radiation oncology, the study of the treatment of cancer using ionizing radiation.

radiation protection, the use of devices,
equipment, distance, and barriers to reduce
the risk of exposure to ionizing radiation
in a health care facility, research center,
or industrial site where radiation-emitting
devices are operated.

radiation risk, a hazard to health resulting from exposure to natural and synthetic
radioactive materials. Radiation sources
include cosmic rays, radon, radium, and
other radionuclides in the soil; nuclear
reactors, accelerators, and weapons; uranium mining and milling; and diagnostic
and therapeutic x-ray devices.

radiation safety committee, an organization responsible for monitoring and
maintaining a safe radiation environment
in institutions where radiation is produced
and/or used.

R

radiation sensitivity, a measure of the response of tissue to ionizing radiation.

radiation sickness, an abnormal condition resulting from exposure to ionizing radiation. Moderate exposure may cause headache, nausea, vomiting, anorexia, and diarrhea; long-term exposure may result in sterility, fetal damage in pregnant women, leukemia or other forms of cancer, alopecia, and cataracts.

radiation symbol, a universal symbol consisting of three red wedges arranged at positions 120 degrees apart around a central red circle on a yellow background. The symbol identifies sources or containers of radioactive materials and areas of potential radiation exposure.

radiation therapist, an allied health professional who administers radiation therapy services to patients and observes patients during treatment. Duties may include tumor localization, dosimetry, patient follow-up, patient education, and record keeping.

radiation therapy management, a nursing intervention from the Nursing Interventions Classification (NIC) defined as assisting the patient to understand and minimize the side effects of radiation treatments.

radiation toxicity, the degree of virulence of a given exposure or dose of ionizing radiation.

radical /rad′ikəl/ [L, *radix*, root], **1.** an atom or group of atoms that contains an unpaired electron. A radical does not exist freely in nature except for O_2, NO, and NO_2. **2.** pertaining to drastic therapy such as the surgical removal of an organ, limb, or other part of the body.

radical dissection, the surgical removal of tissue in an extensive area surrounding the operative site. Most often it is performed to identify and excise all tissue that may possibly be malignant to decrease the chance of recurrence and often includes adjacent lymph nodes.

radical mastectomy, surgical removal of an entire breast; pectoral muscles; axillary lymph nodes; and all fat, fascia, and adjacent tissues. It is one surgical treatment for breast cancer.

radical neck dissection, dissection and removal of all lymph nodes and removable tissues under the skin of the neck, performed to prevent the spread of malignant tumors of the head and neck that have a reasonable chance of being controlled.

radical nephrectomy, the surgical removal of a kidney, usually performed in the treatment of cancer of the kidney.

radical retropubic prostatectomy, radical prostatectomy through the retropubic space via a suprapubic incision.

radical surgery [L, *radix*, root; Gk, *cheirourgia*, surgery], surgery that is usually extensive and complex and intended to correct a severe health threat such as a rapidly growing cancer.

radical therapy, **1.** a treatment intended to cure, not palliate. **2.** a definitive extreme treatment; not conservative, such as radical mastectomy rather than simple or partial mastectomy.

radicidation /rā′disidā′shən/, the irradiation of food to inactivate nonsporing pathogens of *Salmonella* and other microorganisms.

radicular /rədik′yələr/ [L, *radix*, root], pertaining to a root such as a spinal nerve root or radical.

radicular artery, arteries arising from the segmental spinal arteries at every vertebral level. They supply the anterior and posterior roots of the spine.

radicular cyst [L, *radix*, root; Gk, *kystis*. bag], a cyst with a wall of fibrous connective tissue and a lining of stratified squamous epithelium that is attached to the root apex of a tooth with dead pulp or a defective root canal filling.

radicular retainer, a type of retainer, such as a dowel crown, that lies within the body of a tooth, usually in the root.

radicular retention, resistance to displacement of a dental prosthesis developed by placing a metal projection into the root canal of a pulpless tooth.

radiculitis /rədik′yəlī′tis/ [L, *radix*, root; Gk, *itis*, inflammation], an inflammation involving a spinal nerve root, resulting in pain and hyperesthesia.

radiculopathy /rədik′yəlop′əthē/ [L, *radix*, root; Gk, *pathos*, disease], a disease involving a spinal nerve root.

radioactive /rā′dē-ōak′tiv/ [L, *radius*, ray, *activus*, active], giving off radiation as the result of the disintegration of atomic nuclei.

radioactive contamination, the undesirable addition of radioactive material to the body or part of the environment such as clothing or equipment. Contamination of the body by beta radiation may occur through the ingestion, inhalation, or absorption of a beta emitter. Instruments, drapes, surgical gloves, and clothing that come in contact with serous fluids, blood, and urine of patients containing beta or gamma radiation emitters may be contaminated.

radioactive contrast medium, a solution or colloid containing radioactive material used for visualizing soft tissue structures.

radioactive decay, the disintegration of the nucleus of an unstable nuclide by the spontaneous emission of charged particles, photons, or both.

radioactive element, an element subject to spontaneous degeneration of its nucleus accompanied by the emission of alpha particles, beta particles, or gamma rays. All elements with atomic numbers greater than 83 are radioactive.

radioactive implant, a small container holding a radioactive isotope that is embedded in tissues for purposes of interstitial radiotherapy.

radioactive iodine (RAI), a radioactive isotope of iodine used in diagnostic radiology and radiotherapy, especially in the treatment of some thyroid conditions. A common form is ^{131}I.

radioactive iodine excretion, the elimination by the body of radioactive iodine (RAI) administered in a test of thyroid function and in the treatment of hyperthyroidism. Most RAI is excreted in urine, but small amounts may be found in sputum, perspiration, feces, and vomitus.

radioactive iodine excretion test, a method of evaluating thyroid function that entails measuring the amount of radioactive iodine (RAI) in urine after the patient is given an oral tracer dose of RAI in the form of the isotope ^{131}I. After administration of the tracer, a scintillation detector is placed over the patient's neck at 2, 6, and 24 hours to measure the amount of RAI accumulated by the thyroid; the amount excreted is assayed in urine collected for 24 hours after the oral dose.

radioactive iodine uptake (RAIU), the absorption and incorporation by the thyroid of radioactive iodine (RAI), administered orally as a tracer dose in a test of thyroid function and as larger doses for the treatment of hyperthyroidism.

radioactive tracer, a molecule containing a radioactive atom, which can be followed through a physiologic system with radiation detectors.

radioactivity /-activ′ĭtē/, the emission of alpha or beta particles or gamma radiation as a consequence of nuclear disintegration.

radioallergosorbent test (RAST) /rā′dē·ō′ alur′gōsôr′bənt/ [L, *radius*; Gk, *allos,* other, *ergein,* to work; L, *absorbere,* to swallow], a test in which a technique of radioimmunoassay is used to identify and quantify IgE in serum that has been mixed with any of 45 known allergens. If an atopic allergy to a substance exists, an antigen-antibody reaction occurs with characteristic conjugation and clumping.

radiobiology /-bī·ol′əjē/ [L, *radius*; Gk, *bios,* life, *logos,* science], the branch of the natural sciences dealing with the effects of radiation on biologic systems. —**radiobiologic,** *adj.*

radiocarcinogenesis /-kär′sinəjen′əsis/, the production of cancer by exposure to ionizing radiation.

radiocarpal articulation /-kär′pəl/ [L, *radius*; Gk, *karpos,* wrist], the condyloid joint at the wrist that connects the radius and distal surface of an articular disk with the scaphoid, lunate, and triangular bones. The joint involves four ligaments and allows all movements but rotation.

radiochemistry /-kem′istrē/ [L, *radius*; Gk, *chemiea,* alchemy], the branch of chemistry that deals with the properties and behavior of radioactive materials and the use of radionuclides in the study of chemical and biologic problems.

radiocolloids /rā′dē·ōkol′oidz/, radioisotopes in pure form in solution, which tend to act more like colloids than solutes.

radiocurable /-kyōō′rəbəl/, pertaining to the susceptibility of tumor cells to destruction by ionizing radiation.

radiofrequency (rf) /-frē′kwənsē/ [L, *radius* + *frequens*], the part of the electromagnetic spectrum with frequencies lower than about 10^{10} Hz, used to produce magnetic resonance images.

radiofrequency ablation, unmodulated, high-frequency, alternating current flow that is applied to heart tissue to raise its temperature and injure cells for the purpose of destroying ectopic foci and accessory pathways. Radiofrequency ablation of accessory pathways is a cure for the arrhythmias associated with Wolff-Parkinson-White syndrome and is successfully used in atrial flutter and idiopathic ventricular tachycardia. It has replaced surgical ablation.

radiofrequency pulse, a short burst of electromagnetic radiation in the radiofrequency range, used in combination with magnetic gradients to generate a magnetic resonance image.

radiofrequency (rf) signal, 1. an electric signal whose frequency is in the rf range. 2. a signal within an ultrasound instrument between the transducer terminals and components where rectification and filtering occur.

radiofrequency therapy, the use of radiofrequency ablation for therapeutic purposes, such as the treatment of pain syndromes and arrhythmias.

radiograph /rā′dē·əgraf′/, an x-ray image.

radiographer /rā′dē·og′rəfər/, an allied health professional who performs diagnostic examinations on patients using a variety of modalities, including radiography, computed tomography, magnetic resonance imaging, mammography, and cardiovascular interventional technology. In addition to the technical duties of evaluating radiographs,

R

evaluating equipment performance, and managing a quality assurance program, radiographers also play significant roles in patient assessment and education.

radiographic grid /-graf'ik/, a device consisting of parallel strips of radiopaque materials alternating with strips of radiolucent materials. It is used to reduce the amount of scatter radiation reaching an x-ray film.

radiographic magnification, a procedure used to improve visualization of fine blood vessels and small bony structures during x-ray imaging. Magnification is achieved by increasing the distance of the object from the radiographic image receptor or by decreasing the distance of the x-ray source from the image receptor.

radiographic position, the specific position of the body or a body part in relation to the image receptor during x-ray imaging.

radiographic projection, the path taken by an x-ray beam as it passes through the body.

radiographic view, the body image as seen by the image receptor of a radiographic imaging system. It is the opposite of the radiographic projection.

radiography /rā'dē-og'rəfē/ [L, *radius*; Gk, *graphein*, to record], the production of shadow images on photographic emulsion through the action of ionizing radiation.—**radiographic,** *adj.*

radiohumeral /rā'dē-ōhyōō'mərəl/ [L, *radius* + *humerus*, shoulder], pertaining to the radius and humerus.

radioimmunoassay (RIA) /rā'dē-ō-im'yənō-as'ā/ [L, *radius* + *immunis*, free; Fr, *essayer*, to try], a technique in radiology used to determine the concentration of an antigen, antibody, or other protein in the serum.

radioimmunofluorescence assay (RIFA) /rā'dē-ō-im'yənō-flŏōres'əns/, a test for the presence of antibodies sometimes used to confirm the results of ELISA or other methods.

radioimmunosorbent test (RIST) /rā'dē-ō-im'yənōsôr'bənt/ [L, *radius* + *immunis* + *absorbere*, to swallow], a test that uses serum IgE to detect allergies to various substances such as certain cosmetics, animal fur, dust, and grasses.

radioimmunotherapy /ra'dē-ō im-mu'nother'ah-pe/, use of radionuclides to deliver monoclonal antibodies to targeted cancer cells.

radioiodine /rā'dē-ō-ī'ədīn/, a radioactive isotope of iodine used in nuclear medicine and radiotherapy. A common form of radioiodine is ^{131}I.

radioiodine uptake, uptake of radioiodine from the blood by the thyroid gland.

radioiodine uptake test, one of the most common thyroid function tests. A known quantity of radioiodine is administered, and 6 and 24 hours later the percentage that has been absorbed by the thyroid gland is calculated. An increased uptake indicates hyperthyroidism and a decreased uptake indicates hypothyroidism.

radioisotope /rā'dē-ō-ī'sətōp/ [L, *radius*; Gk, *isos*, equal, *topos*, place], a radioactive form of an element, which may be used for therapeutic and diagnostic purposes.

radioisotope scan, a two-dimensional representation of the gamma rays emitted by a radioisotope, showing its concentration in a body site such as the thyroid gland, brain, or kidney.

Radiological Society of North America (RSNA), a professional organization of radiologists. The group originated the certification of operators of x-ray equipment in 1920 but is no longer involved in such certification.

radiologic anatomy /-loj'ik/ [L, *radius*; Gk, *logos*, science], in applied anatomy, the study of the structure and morphology of the tissues and organs of the body based on their x-ray visualization.

radiologic technologist, a person who, under the supervision of a physician radiologist, operates radiologic equipment and assists radiologists and other health professionals and whose competence has been tested and approved by the American Registry of Radiologic Technologists.

radiologic units, units used to measure radiation, including roentgens, rads, rems, and curies.

radiologist /rā'dē-ol'əjist/, a physician who specializes in radiology. A certified radiologist is one whose competence has been tested and approved by the American Board of Radiology.

radiology /-ol'əjē/ [L, *radius* + *logos*, science], the branch of medicine concerned with radioactive substances and with the diagnosis and treatment of disease by visualizing any of the various sources of radiant energy. Three subbranches of radiology are diagnostic radiology, imaging using external sources of radiation; nuclear medicine, imaging radioactive materials that are placed into body organs; and therapeutic radiology, the treatment of cancer using radiation.—**radiologic,** *adj.*

radiolucency /-lōō'sənsē/ [L, *radiare* + *lucere*, to shine], the ability of materials of relatively low atomic number to allow most x-rays to pass through them, producing dark images on x-ray film.

radiolucent /-lōō'sənt/ [L, *radiare,* to emit rays, *lucere,* to shine], pertaining to materials that allow x-rays to penetrate with a minimum of absorption.

radionecrosis /-nəkrō′sis/, tissue death caused by radiation.

radionuclide /-nōō′klīd/ [L, *radiare* + *nucleus*, nut kernel], an isotope that undergoes radioactive decay.

radionuclide angiocardiography, the radiographic examination of cardiac blood vessels after an IV injection of a radiopharmaceutical.

radionuclide imaging, the noninvasive examination of various parts of the body, especially the heart, using a radiopharmaceutical such as thallium-201 and a detection device such as a gamma camera, rectilinear scanner, or positron camera.

radiopacity /-pas′itē/ [L, *radiare,* to emit rays, *opacus,* obscure], the ability to stop or reduce the passage of x-rays.

radiopaque /-pāk′/ [L, *radiare* + *opacus,* obscure], not permitting the passage of x-rays or other radiant energy.

radiopaque contrast medium, a substance that stops the passage of x-rays and is used to outline the interior of hollow organs such as heart chambers, blood vessels, respiratory passages, and the biliary tract in x-ray or fluoroscopic pictures.

radiopathology /-pəthol′əjē/, a branch of medicine involving both pathology and radiology and concerned with the effects of ionizing radiation on body tissues.

radiopharmaceutical /-fär′məsōō′tikəl/ [L, *radiare;* Gk, *pharmakeuein,* to give a drug], a drug that contains radioactive atoms. Kinds of radiopharmaceuticals are **diagnostic radiopharmaceutical, research radiopharmaceutical,** and **therapeutic radiopharmaceutical.**

radiopharmacist /-fär′məsist/, a person responsible for formulating and dispensing prescribed radioactive tracers and for the clinical aspects of radiopharmacy. Radiopharmacists are required to receive training in radioactive tracer techniques, in the safe handling of radioactive materials, in the preparation and quality control of drugs for administration to humans, and in the basic principles of nuclear medicine.

radiopharmacy /-fär′məsē/ [L, *radiare;* Gk, *pharmakeuein,* to give a drug], a facility for the preparation and dispensing of radioactive drugs and for the storage of radioactive materials, inventory records, and prescriptions of radioactive substances. The radiopharmacy is usually the correlation point for radioactive wastes, the unit responsible for waste disposal or storage, and a center for clinical investigations using radioactive tracers.

radioprotectant /rā′dē·opro-tek′tant/, **1.** providing protection against the toxic effects of ionizing radiation. **2.** radioprotector.

radioprotective drugs /-prətek′tiv/ [L, *radiare,* to emit rays, *protegere,* to cover; Fr, drogue], pharmaceuticals that protect the body against ionizing radiation. An example is Lugol's solution, an aqueous solution of iodine used to supply iodine internally, thereby blocking the uptake of radioactive iodine.

radioprotector /rā′dē·ōprōtek′ter/, an agent that provides protection against the toxic effects of ionizing radiation.

radioresistance /-risis′təns/ [L, *radiare* + *resistare,* to withstand], the ability of cells, tissues, organs, organisms, chemical compounds, or any other substances to remain unchanged by radiation.

radioresistant /-risis′tənt/, unchanged by or protected against damage by radioactive emissions such as x-rays, alpha particles, or gamma rays.

radioresponsive /-rispon′siv/, responding to radiation, whether harmful or beneficial.

radiosensitive /-sen′sitiv/ [L, *radiare* + *sentire,* to feel], capable of being changed by or reacting to radioactive emissions such as x-rays, alpha particles, or gamma rays.

radiosensitivity /-sen′sitiv′itē/, the relative susceptibility of cells, tissues, organs, organisms, or any other substances to the effects of radiation. Cells of self-renewing tissues, such as those in the crypts of the intestine, are the most radiosensitive. Least radiosensitive are cells that have lost the ability to divide, such as neurons.

radiosensitizers /-sen′siti′zərs/ [L, *radiare* + *sentire;* Gk, *izein,* to cause], drugs that enhance the killing effect of radiation on cells.

radiotherapist /-ther′əpist/, a health professional who specializes in the use of radiation, including the application of radiopharmaceuticals, in the treatment of disease.

radiotherapy /-ther′əpē/ [L, *radiare,* to emit rays; Gk, *therapeia,* treatment], the treatment of neoplastic disease by using x-rays or gamma rays to deter the proliferation of malignant cells by decreasing the rate of mitosis or impairing DNA synthesis.

radioulnar articulation /-ul′nər/ [L, *radius,* ray, *ulna,* elbow, arm], the articulation of the radius and ulna, consisting of a proximal articulation, a distal articulation, and three sets of ligaments.

radium (Ra) /rā′dē·əm/ [L, *radius,* ray], a radioactive metallic element of the alkaline earth group. Its atomic number is 88. Four radium isotopes occur naturally and have different atomic masses: 223, 224, 226, and 228.

R

radium-226, a radioactive isotope used for most of the 20th century to fill the needles and tubes required for brachytherapy. It is now being replaced by cesium-137 and cobalt-60, which have similar energy characteristics but are not subject to hazardous leakage as radium sources sometimes are.

radium insertion, the introduction of metallic radium (Ra) into a body cavity, such as the uterus or cervix, to treat cancer.

radium therapy [L, *radius,* ray; Gk, *therapeia,* treatment], the use of radium and its radioactive emissions to treat disease.

radius /rā′dē·əs/ *pl.* **radii** [L, ray], one of the outer, shorter bones of the forearm lying parallel to the ulna and partially revolving around it. Its proximal end is small and forms a part of the elbow joint. The distal end is large and forms a part of the wrist joint.

radon (Rn) /rā′don/ [L, *radiare,* to emit rays], a radioactive, chemically inert, gaseous element. Its atomic number is 86; its atomic mass is 222. A decay product of radium, radon is used in radiation cancer therapy.

radon-222, a radioactive decay product of radium-226 that has been used to fill permanent implants in tumors. It is being replaced by the more manageable radionuclide iodine-125.

radon daughters, ions that are decay products of radon. They are regarded as a potential health hazard by the U.S. Environmental Protection Agency because they tend to adhere to surfaces, such as the alveoli of the lungs, where they can cause ionizing radiation damage.

radon seed, a small, sealed tube of glass or gold containing radon and visible radiographically, for insertion into body tissues in the treatment of malignancies.

ragweed /rag′wēd/ [ME, *ragge,* rag; AS, *weod,* herb, grass, weed], any of various species of plants of the genus *Ambrosia* whose pollen can cause hay fever.

RAI, abbreviation for **radioactive iodine.**

RAIU, abbreviation for **radioactive iodine uptake.**

RA latex test, abbreviation for *rheumatoid arthritis latex test.*

rale, a common abnormal respiratory sound heard on auscultation of the chest during inspiration, characterized by discontinuous bubbling noises. Although the term rale is commonly used, the American Thoracic Society now prefers **crackle,** as this term is more descriptive of the actual sound heard.

raloxifene, a selective estrogen receptor modulator (SERM) prescribed to prevent osteoporosis in postmenopausal women.

raltegravir, an antiretroviral. It is used to treat HIV in combination with other retrovirals.

ramelteon, a sedative-hypnotic with antianxiety properties. It is used to treat insomnia.

ramification /ram′ifikā′shən/ [L, *ramus,* branch, *facere,* to make], a branching, distribution.

rampant dental caries, dental caries that involve several teeth, appear suddenly, and often progress rapidly.

Ramsay Hunt syndrome [James Ramsay Hunt, American neurologist, 1872–1937], a neurologic condition resulting from invasion of the seventh nerve ganglia and the geniculate ganglion by varicella zoster virus, characterized by severe ear pain, facial nerve paralysis, vertigo, hearing loss, and often mild generalized encephalitis. Treatment usually includes the prescription of corticosteroid drugs.

ramus /rā′məs/ *pl.* **rami** [L, branch], a small branchlike structure extending from a larger one or dividing into two or more parts such as a branch of a nerve or artery or one of the rami of the blood vessel or nerve.—**ramification,** *n.,* **ramify,** *v.*

ramus of mandible, a quadrilateral process projecting upward from the posterior part of either side of the mandible.

Ranchos Los Amigos Scale, a scale of cognitive functioning, developed as a behavioral rating scale to aid in assessment and treatment of head-injured persons. Eight levels of cognitive functioning are identified, from I (no response) to VIII (purposeful and appropriate behavioral response).

rancidity /ransid′itē/, the unpleasant taste and smell of fatty foods that have undergone decomposition, liberating butyric acid and other volatile lipids.

random controlled trial [ME, *randoun,* run violently; Fr, *contrôle,* check, *trier,* to grind], a study plan for a proposed new treatment in which subjects are assigned on a random basis to participate either in an experimental group receiving the new treatment or in a control group that does not.

randomization [ME, *randoun,* run violently], the process of assigning subjects or objects to a control or experimental group on a random basis.

random mating [ME, *randoun,* run violently + *gemate*], a pairing of subjects when each individual has an equal chance of mating with those of other genetic backgrounds.

random sampling [ME, *randoun,* run violently; L, *exemplum*], a method of sampling for a study in which each individual has the same chance of being selected and the choice of a particular individual does not affect the chances of the others.

random selection, a method of choosing subjects for a research study in which all members of a particular group have an equal chance of being selected.

random voided specimen, a voided urine specimen obtained at any point of a 24-hour period.

Ranexa, a trademark for ranolazine.

range /rānj/ [OFr, *ranger,* to arrange in a row], the interval between the lowest and highest values in a series of data.

range abnormalities, uncertainties in the actual range from which Doppler signals or echo signals originate. In pulsed Doppler instruments a high pulse repetition frequency can result in range ambiguities.

range equation, a relationship between the distance to a reflector and the time it takes for a pulse of ultrasound to propagate to the reflector and return to the transducer.

range of accommodation [OFr, *ranger;* L, *accommodatio*], the distance between the farthest point at which an object can be seen clearly with accommodation fully relaxed and the nearest distance at which an object can be observed with full accommodation, measured in meters or centimeters.

range of motion (ROM) [OFr, *ranger;* L, *motio*], the extent of movement of a joint, measured in degrees of a circle.

range-of-motion exercise [OFr, *ranger,* to arrange in a row; L, *motio,* movement], any body action involving the muscles, joints, and natural movements such as abduction, adduction, extension, flexion, pronation, supination, and rotation. Such exercises are usually applied actively or passively in the prevention and treatment of orthopedic deformities, in the assessment of injuries and deformities, and in athletic conditioning.

ranibizumab, an ophthalmic drug that binds to the receptor binding site of active forms of vascular endothelial growth factor A. This drug is used in the treatment of neovascular macular degeneration.

ranitidine /ranit′idēn/, a histamine H_2 receptor antagonist. It is prescribed in the treatment of gastroesophageal reflux disease and gastric hypersecretory conditions.

Rankine scale [William J.M. Rankine, Scottish physicist, 1820–1870], an absolute temperature scale calculated in degrees Fahrenheit. Absolute zero on the Rankine scale is −460° F, equivalent to −273° C.

rank sum test, a nonparametric statistic test for ordinal data, testing the null hypothesis that two samples are drawn from the same population against the alternative hypothesis that the two samples are drawn from two populations having probability distributions of the same shape but different locations.

ranolazine, an antianginal. It is used in combination with other antianginals (such as amlodipine, beta blockers, or nitrates) to treat chronic stable angina pectoris in those who have not responded to other treatment options.

ranula /ran′yŏŏlə/ *pl.* **ranulae** [L, *rana,* frog], a large mucocele in the floor of the mouth, usually caused by obstruction of the ducts of the sublingual salivary glands and less commonly caused by obstruction of the ducts of the submandibular salivary glands.

Ranvier's nodes /ränvē·āz′, räN-/ [Louis A. Ranvier, French pathologist, 1835–1922], constrictions in the medullary substance of a nerve fiber at more or less regular intervals.

rape [L, *rapere,* to seize], a sexual assault, homosexual or heterosexual, the legal definitions for which vary from state to state. Rape is a crime of violence or one committed under the threat of violence, and its victims are treated for medical and psychologic trauma.

rape counseling, counseling by a trained person provided to a victim of rape. Rape counseling ideally begins at the time the crime is first reported, as in an ED. Initially the counselor offers sensitive support for the victim by accepting the victim in a nonprejudicial, noncritical way. Counseling personnel may provide supportive services and advocacy and liaison between the victim and medical, legal, and law enforcement authorities. This involves staying with the victim during medical examination, during police or district attorney's questioning, and throughout the criminal justice process.

rape-trauma treatment, a nursing intervention from the Nursing Interventions Classification (NIC) defined as the provision of emotional and physical support immediately following a reported rape.

raphe /rā′fē/ [Gk, *rhaphe,* seam], a crease, ridge, or seam of the halves of various symmetric parts, such as the abdominal raphe of the linea alba or the raphe penis, which appears as a narrow dark streak on the inferior surface of the penis.

raphe nuclei, a subgroup of the reticular nuclei of the brainstem, found in narrow longitudinal sheets along the raphe of the medulla oblongata, pons, and mesencephalon. They include many neurons that synthesize serotonin. Their ascending fibers project to parts of the limbic system, and their descending fibers project to other brainstem nuclei, the medulla oblongata, and the pons.

raphe of tongue [Gk, *rhaphe,* seam; AS, *tunge*], a fibrous wall that forms a line of union between the right and left sides of the tongue.

R

rapid grower /rap′id/, a saprophytic mycobacterium in group IV of the Runyon classification system that grows within 3 to 5 days.

rapid plasma reagin test (RPR test), an agglutination examination used in screening for syphilis. The test detects two groups of antibodies. The first is a nontreponemal antibody (reagin) directed against a lipoidal agent resulting from the *Treponema pallidum* infection. The second is an antibody directed against the *T. pallidum* organism itself.

rapid pulse [L, *rapidus*, rush, *pulsare*, to beat], a pulse faster than normal.

rapport /rapôr′/ [Fr, agreement], a sense of mutuality and understanding; harmony, accord, confidence, and respect underlying a relationship between two persons, which is an essential bond between a therapist and patient.

rapprochement /räprôshmäN′/ [Fr, *rapprocher*, to bring together], in psychology, the third subphase of the separation-individuation phase of Mahler's system of preoedipal development. This stage is characterized by a rediscovery of and reestablishment with the mother or a significant nurturer.

Raptiva, a trademark for efalizumab.

raptus /rap′təs/ [L, *rapere*, to seize], **1.** a state of intense emotional or mental excitement, often characterized by uncontrollable activity or behavior resulting from an irresistible impulse; ecstasy; rapture. **2.** any sudden or violent seizure or attack.

rare-earth element [L, *rarus*, thin; AS, *earthe*; L, *elementum*], a metallic element having an atomic number between 57 and 71 inclusively.

rare-earth screen, an x-ray-intensifying screen made of rare-earth elements such as yttrium and gadolinium. Such screens enable lower radiation doses to be used while producing acceptable film densities.

rarefaction /rer′əfak′shən/, reductions of density of a medium at a location in the medium accompanying the cyclic pressure reductions during the passage of a sound wave.

RAS, abbreviation for **reticular activating system.**

rasagiline, an antiparkinson agent used alone or with levodopa to treat idiopathic Parkinson's disease.

rasburicase, an antineoplastic, antimetabolite used to reduce uric acid levels in children with leukemia and lymphoma and in chemotherapy patients with solid tumor malignancies.

rash [OFr, *rasche*, scurf], a skin eruption. Kinds of rashes are **butterfly rash, diaper rash, drug rash,** and **heat rash.**

Rashkind procedure /rash′kind/ [William J. Rashkind, American physician, b. 1922; L, *procedere*, to go forth], the enlargement of an opening in the cardiac septum between the right and left atria. It is performed to relieve CHF in newborns with certain congenital heart defects by improving the oxygenation of the blood.

Rasmussen's aneurysm /rahs′moosənz/ [Fritz Waldemar Rasmussen, Danish physician, 1834–1877], dilation of a pulmonary artery in a tuberculous cavity. Rupture causes hemorrhage and hemoptysis.

raspberry leaves, a herbal product harvested from the raspberry plant, found worldwide. This herb is used to facilitate childbirth, as a uterine tonic, and as a treatment for dysmenorrhea, fever, and vomiting, but there are insufficient reliable data regarding effectiveness.

raspberry tongue /raz′berē/, a dark red tongue with a smooth surface and prominent papillae, seen after shedding of the white coating characteristic of the early stage of scarlet fever.

RAST, abbreviation for **radioallergosorbent test.**

rat-bite fever [AS, *raet* + *bitan*, to bite], either of two distinct infections transmitted to humans commonly by the bite of a rat or mouse, but also via contact with excretions of the mouth, nose, or urine of an infected animal. It is characterized by fever, headache, malaise, nausea, vomiting, and rash. In the United States the disease is more commonly caused by *Streptobacillus moniliformis*. Its unique features are a rash on palms and soles, painful joints, prompt healing of the wound, and a duration of 2 weeks. If left untreated, severe complications may occur, such as infection of the heart valves. Penicillin administered intramuscularly is effective in treating either form of the disease.

rate [L, *ratus*, reckoned], a numeric ratio, often used in the compilation of data concerning the prevalence and incidence of events, in which the number of actual occurrences appears as the numerator and the number of possible occurrences appears as the denominator. Standard rates are stated in conventional units of population such as neonatal mortality per 1000 or maternal mortality per 100,000.

rate-pressure product, the heart rate multiplied by the systolic BP. It is a clinical indicator of myocardial oxygen demand.

rate-responsive pacer, an electronic pacemaker whose rate can be adjusted as required to meet physiologic demands.

Rathke's pouch /rät′kēz/ [Martin H. Rathke, German anatomist, 1793–1860; OFr, *pouche*], a depression that forms in the roof of the mouth of an embryo, anterior to the buccopharyngeal membrane, around the fourth week of gestation. The walls of the diverticulum develop into the anterior lobe of the pituitary gland.

rating of perceived exertion (RPE), a scale for quantifying perceived exertion, with 6 being extremely light exertion and 20 being extremely hard. The American College of Sports Medicine (ACSM) has recalibrated the scale from 1 to 10. The ACSM has also established minimal guidelines pertaining to the frequency, intensity, and duration of exercise needed to produce a training effect.

ratio /rā′shō/ [L, a reckoning], the relationship of one quantity to one or more other quantities expressed as a proportion of one to the others and written either as a fraction $^8/_3$ or linearly (8:3).

rational /rash′ənəl/ [L, *rationalis,* reasonable], **1.** pertaining to a measure, method, or procedure based on reason. **2.** pertaining to a therapeutic method based on an understanding of the cause and mechanisms of a specific disease and the potential effects of the drugs or procedures used in treating the disorder. **3.** sane; capable of normal reasoning or behavior.

rationale /rash′ənal′/ [L, *rationalis,* reasonable], a system of reasoning or a statement of the reasons used in explaining data or phenomena.

rational emotive therapy (RET), a form of cognitive therapy, originated by Albert Ellis, that emphasizes a reorganization and challenge of one's cognitive and emotional functions, a redefinition of one's problems, and a change in one's attitudes to develop more effective and suitable patterns of behavior.

rationalization /rash′ənəlīzā′shən/, the most commonly used defense mechanism in which an individual justifies ideas, actions, or feelings with seemingly acceptable reasons or explanations. It is often used to preserve self-respect, reduce guilt feelings, or obtain social approval or acceptance.

ratio solution, the relationship of a solute to a solution expressed as a proportion, such as 1:1000, or parts per thousand.

rattle [ME, *ratelen*], an abnormal sound heard by auscultation of the lungs in some forms of pulmonary disease. It consists of a coarse vibration, more intense than a crackle, very much like a rhonchus, caused by the movement of moisture and the separation of the walls of small air passages during respiration.

rattlesnake [ME, *ratelen*; AS, *snacan,* to creep], a poisonous pit viper with a series of loosely connected, horny segments at the end of the tail that make a noise like a rattle when shaken. They have a hematoxin in their venom, and they are responsible for most of the poisonous snake bites in the United States. Immediate treatment includes keeping the victim quiet and immobilizing the bite area at the level of the heart. Antivenin is available.

rauwolfia alkaloid [Leonhard Rauwolf, sixteenth century German botanist], any one of more than 20 alkaloids derived from the root of a climbing shrub, *Rauwolfia serpentina,* indigenous to India and the surrounding area. Formerly used as an antipsychotic agent, it is today confined to the treatment of hypertension and tranquilizing alkaloid drugs such as reserpine.

rauwolfia serpentina, the dried root from *Rauwolfia serpentina.* It is prescribed in the treatment of mild hypertension and agitation due to psychosis.

Rauzide, a trademark for a cardiovascular, fixed-combination drug containing a diuretic (bendroflumethiazide) and an antihypertensive (rauwolfia serpentina).

raw data, the information obtained by radio reception of a magnetic resonance signal as stored by a computer. Specific computer manipulation of the data is required to construct an image.

ray [L, *radius*], a beam of radiation, such as heat or light, moving away from a source.

rayl /rāl/ [John W.S. Rayleigh, English physicist, 1842–1919], the unit for characteristic acoustic impedance. Its fundamental units are $kg/m^2/s$.

Rayleigh scatterer /rā′lē/ [John W. S. Rayleigh, English physicist, 1842–1919], reflecting objects whose dimensions are much smaller than the ultrasonic wavelength. The scattered intensity from a volume of Rayleigh scatterers increases rapidly with increasing frequency, being related to frequency raised to the fourth power.

Ray, Marilyn Anne, a nursing theorist who introduced the Theory of Bureaucratic Caring, which emphasizes the interconnectedness of nursing care and health care organizations. The theory emphasizes the holistic nature of an organization rather than simple cause-effect relationships of individual actions. Spiritual-ethical caring by nurses, the ultimate goal of which is the promotion of well-being through caring, has a positive effect on health care organizations and can become an economic resource.

Raynaud's phenomenon /rānōz′/ [Maurice Raynaud, French physician, 1834–1881], intermittent attacks of ischemia of the extremities of the body, especially the fingers, toes, ears, and nose, caused by exposure to cold or by emotional stimuli. The attacks are characterized by severe blanching of the extremities, followed by

R

cyanosis, then redness; they are usually accompanied by numbness, tingling, burning, and often pain. Normal color and sensation are restored by heat. The condition is called Raynaud's disease when there is a history of symptoms for at least 2 years with no progression of symptoms and no evidence of an underlying cause.

Rb, symbol for the element **rubidium.**

RBBB, abbreviation for **right bundle branch block.**

RBC, abbreviation for *red blood cell.*

RBE, abbreviation for **relative biologic effectiveness.**

RBRVS, abbreviation for **resource-based relative value scale.**

RCEEM, abbreviation for **Recognized Continuing Education Evaluation Mechanism.**

R.C.P., abbreviation for **Royal College of Physicians.**

RCPSC, abbreviation for **Royal College of Physicians and Surgeons of Canada.**

R.C.S., abbreviation for **Royal College of Surgeons.**

RD, abbreviation for **registered dietitian.**

RDAs, abbreviation for **recommended dietary allowances.**

RDH, abbreviation for *Registered Dental Hygienist.*

rdi, abbreviation for *recommended daily intake.*

RDS, abbreviation for **respiratory distress syndrome of the newborn.**

Re, symbol for the element **rhenium.**

reabsorption /rē′əbsôrp′shən/, the process of something being absorbed again, such as the removal of calcium from the bone back into the blood.

reacher /rē′chər/, an assistive device with a pincer-type claw and an extended handle that can be used by persons with upper extremity disabilities or those who lose the ability to bend and stoop to reach and grasp objects overhead or on the floor.

Reach to Recovery [AS, *reacan,* to reach; ME, *recoveren,* to get back], a national volunteer organization that offers counseling and support to women with breast cancer and their families. Many of the members have had mastectomies themselves.

reaction /rē·ak′shən/ [L, *re,* again, *agere,* to act], a response to a substance, treatment, or other stimulus such as an antigen-antibody reaction, an allergic reaction, or an adverse pharmacologic reaction. —**react,** *v.,* **reactive,** *adj.*

reaction formation, an unconscious defense mechanism in which a person expresses toward another person or situation feelings, attitudes, or behaviors that are the opposite of what would normally be expected.

reaction time [L, *re,* again, *agere,* to act; AS, *tima*], the interval between the application of a stimulus and the beginning of a response.

reactivate /rē·ak′tivāt/ [L, *re + activus*], to make active again, as in adding fresh serum to restore the potency of an original supply of the serum.

reactivation /rē·ak′tivā′shən/, the restoration of impaired biologic activity caused by chemical reaction, thermal application, genetic recombination, or helper elements.

reactivation tuberculosis, a form of secondary TB that recurs as a result of the activation of a dormant endogenous infection. Causes of the reactivation may include loss of immunity, hormonal changes, or poor nutrition.

reactive airways disease, any of several conditions characterized by wheezing and allergic reactions, the most common being asthma, bronchiolitis, and chronic obstructive lung disease.

reactive arthritis /rē·ak′tiv/ [L, *re + activus,* active], arthritis after an infection such as urethritis caused by *Chlamydia trachomatis* or enteritis caused by *Campylobacter, Salmonella, Shigella,* or *Yersinia.*

reactive decision /rē·ak′tiv/ [L, *re + activus*], in psychology, a decision made by an individual in response to the influence or goals of others.

reactive depression, an obsolete term for an emotional condition characterized by an acute feeling of despondency, sadness, and depressive dysphoria caused by some identifiable external situation or environmental stress. It is generally relieved when the circumstance is altered or the conflict understood and resolved.

reactive gastritis, gastric inflammation caused by presence of a harmful substance, such as an NSAID, bile refluxing from the duodenum, or a toxic chemical (chemical gastritis). It may be either acute or chronic.

reactive hypoglycemia, low levels of glucose in the circulating blood (45 to 50 mg/dL) in an arterialized specimen after ingestion of carbohydrates in patients who have had stomach surgery, causing food to travel quickly into the intestine.

reactive inflammation [L, *re + activus + inflammare,* to set afire], an inflammation that develops as a reaction to an antigen.

reactive psychosis, in psychiatry, a psychotic episode that results from a specific set of external circumstances.

reactive schizophrenia, a form of schizophrenia caused by environmental factors rather than organic changes in the brain. Disease onset is usually rapid; symptoms are of brief duration, and the affected individual appears well immediately before and after the schizophrenic episode.

reactor /rē·ak′tər/, **1.** in psychology, a family therapist who lets a family in therapy take the lead and then follows in that direction. **2.** in radiology, a cubicle in which radioisotopes are artificially produced.

reading [AS, *raedan*], the linear process in which the genetic information contained in a nucleotide sequence is decoded, as in the translation of the messenger RNA into a sequence of amino acids in a polypeptide.

reading disorder, a language disorder in which one's reading ability is significantly below intellectual capacity. Tests show that the problem does not involve mental retardation, chronologic age, or inadequate schooling but is marked by faulty oral reading, slow reading, and reduced comprehension.

Read method [Grantley Dick-Read, English obstetrician, 1890–1959], a method of psychophysical preparation for childbirth. It was the first "natural childbirth" program, a term coined by Dr. Read in the 1930s. Basically Read held that childbirth is a normal, physiologic procedure and that the pain of labor and delivery is of psychologic origin—the fear-tension-pain syndrome. He countered women's fears with education about the physiologic process, encouraged a positive welcoming attitude, corrected false information, and led tours of the hospital. To decrease tension he developed a series of breathing exercises for use during the various stages of labor. To foster relaxation and optimal physical function in labor and recovery after delivery, he incorporated a series of physical exercises to be performed regularly in classes and in practice at home during pregnancy.

readthrough [AS, *raedan* + *thurh*, through], transcription beyond the normal termination sequence in a DNA template, caused by the occasional failure of RNA polymerase to respond to the end-point signal.

reagent /rē·ā′jənt/ [L, *re*, again, *agere*, to act], a chemical substance known to react in a specific way. A reagent is used to detect or synthesize another substance in a chemical reaction.

reagent strip, a strip of paper impregnated with a reagent to a given substance, used in testing for that substance in a body fluid or other secretion.

reagin /rē′ăjin/ [L, *re* + *agere*], an antibody associated with human atopy such as asthma and hay fever. It attaches to mast cells and basophils and sensitizes the skin and other tissues. **2.** a nonspecific, nontreponemal antibody-like substance found in the serum of individuals with syphilis.—**reaginic,** *adj.*

reaginic antibody /rē′əgin′ik/, an IgE antibody that is more numerous in hypersensitive individuals.

reagin-mediated disorder, a hypersensitivity reaction, such as hay fever or an allergic response to an insect sting, produced by reaginic (IgE) antibodies and causing degranulation and the release of histamine, bradykinin, serotonin, and other vasoactive amines. An initial sensitizing dose of the antigen induces the formation of specific IgE antibodies, and their attachment to mast cells and basophils results in hypersensitivity to a subsequent challenging dose of the antigen. Reactions range from a simple wheal and flare on the skin to life-threatening anaphylactic shock, depending on the size and route of entrance of the sensitizing dose and the challenging dose, the number and distribution of IgE antibodies, the responsiveness of the host, the timing of exposure to the allergen, and the tissues in which the antigen-antibody reaction occurs.

REAL classification, a classification of lymphomas using histologic criteria division based on B cell, neoplasm, T or NK neoplasms, and Hodgkin's disease.

reality /rē·al′itē/ [L, *res*, factual], the culturally constructed world of perception, meaning, and behavior that members of a culture regard as true.

reality orientation¹, a formal activity that uses specific approaches to assist confused or disoriented persons toward an awareness of reality, or the "here and now" as by emphasizing, for example, the time, day, month, year, situation, and weather.

reality orientation², a nursing intervention from the Nursing Interventions Classification (NIC) defined as promotion of patient's awareness of personal identity, time, and environment.

reality principle, an awareness of the demands of the environment and the need for an adjustment of behavior to meet those demands, expressed primarily by the renunciation of immediate gratification of instinctual pleasures to obtain long-term and future goals.

reality testing, an ego function that enables one to differentiate between external reality and any inner imaginative world and to behave in a manner that exhibits an awareness of accepted norms and customs. Impairment of reality testing is indicative of a disturbance in ego functioning that may lead to psychosis.

reality therapy, a form of psychotherapy developed by William Glassner. The aims are to help define and assess basic values within the framework of a current situation and to evaluate the person's present behavior and future plans in relation to those values.

R

real time [L, *res*, factual; AS, *tid*, tide], an application of computerized equipment that allows data to be processed with relation to ongoing external events, so that the operators can make immediate diagnostic or other decisions based on the current data output. Ultrasound scanning uses real-time control systems.

real-time scanning, the imaging of an entire object, or a cross-sectional slice of the object, at a single moment. To produce such an image, the data must be recorded quickly over a very short time rather than by accumulation over a longer period.

reamer [AS, *ryman*, to make room], **1.** a tool with a straight or spiral cutting edge, used in a rotating motion to enlarge a hole or clear an opening. **2.** in dentistry, an instrument with a tapered and loosely spiraled metal shaft, used for enlarging, shaping, and cleaning root canals.

reapproximate /rē′əprok′simāt/ [L, *re*, again, *approximare*, to come near], to rejoin tissues separated by surgery or trauma so that their anatomic relationship is restored.—**reapproximation,** *n.*

reasonable accommodation /rē′zənəbəl/, an interpretation of the U.S. Americans With Disabilities Act regarding responsibility of an employer to provide an adequate work environment for a disabled but otherwise competent employee. The rule may apply in making facilities accessible, restructuring jobs, reassigning disabled employees to vacant positions, modifying work schedules, acquiring or modifying equipment, and adjusting training materials and examinations. The employer may not be required to provide reasonable accommodation if it can be shown to impose an "undue hardship" on the business operation.

reasonable care [L, *rationalis*], the degree of skill and knowledge used by a competent health practitioner in treating and caring for the sick and injured.

reasonable charge, 1. in Medicare, the lowest customary charge by a physician for a service. **2.** the prevailing charge by a group of physicians in the area for a particular service.

reasonable cost, the amount a medical insurer will reimburse for a particular health service based on the cost to the provider for delivering that service.

reasonable person, in law, a hypothetic person who possesses the qualities that are used as an objective standard on which to judge a defendant's action in a negligence suit.

reasonably prudent person doctrine /rē′zənəblē′/, a concept that a person of ordinary sense will use ordinary care and skill in meeting the health care needs of a patient.

reattachment /rē′ətach′mənt/ [L, *re*, again; OFr, *attachier*], **1.** the rejoining of accidentally severed body parts. **2.** the rejoining of periodontal membrane fibers to the cementum of a tooth and the alveolar bone to restore a loosened tooth.

rebase /rēbās′/ [L, *re*, again, *basis*, base], a process of refitting a denture by replacing or adding to its base material without changing the occlusal relationships of the teeth.

rebirthing /rēbur′thing/, a form of psychotherapy developed by Leonard Orr that focuses on the breath and breathing apparatus. The goal of treatment is to overcome the trauma of the birth-damaged breathing apparatus so the person is able to use the breath as a supportive and creative part of life.

rebound /rē′bound/ [Fr, *rebondir*, to bounce], **1.** recovery from illness. **2.** a sudden contraction of muscle after a period of relaxation, often seen in conditions in which inhibitory reflexes are lost.

rebound congestion, swelling and congestion of the nasal mucosa that follows the vasodilator effects of decongestant medications.

rebound phenomenon [OFr, *rebondir*; Gk, *phainomenon*, anything seen], a renewal of reflex activity after the stimulus that triggered the original action has been removed. It may be indicative of a lesion of the cerebellum.

rebound tenderness, a sign of inflammation of the peritoneum in which pain is elicited by the sudden release of the fingertips pressing on the abdomen.

rebreather, 1. a breathing apparatus that allows the breathing of a combination of supplied oxygen and exhaled or room air. **2.** a reservoir mask that allows room air to flow in through ports so that it is mixed with supplied oxygen.

rebreathing /rēbrē′thing/ [L, *re*; AS, *braeth,* breath], breathing in a closed system. Exhaled gas mixes with the gas in the system, and some of this mixture is then reinhaled. Rebreathing may result in progressively decreasing concentrations of oxygen and progressively increasing concentrations of carbon dioxide in the blood.

rebreathing bag, in anesthesia, a flexible bag attached to a mask. It may function as a reservoir for anesthetic gases during surgery or for oxygen during resuscitation.

recalcification /rēkal′sifikā′shən/ [L, *re* + *calx,* lime, *facere,* to make], the restoration of lost calcium salts in the body needed for normal neuromuscular excitability, excitation-coupling contraction in cardiac and smooth muscle stimulus-secretion coupling, maintenance of tight junctions between cells, blood clotting, and compressional strength of bone.

recannulate /rēkan'yəlāt/ [L, *re* + *cannula*, small reed], to make a new opening through an organ or tissue, such as opening a passage through an occluded blood vessel.

recapitulation concept /rē'kəpit'yələ' shən/ [L, *re* + *capitulum*, small head], the notion, formulated by German naturalist Ernst Heinrich Haeckel (1834–1919), that an organism during the course of embryonic development passes through stages that resemble the structural form of species from which it evolved. It is summarized by the statement "ontogeny recapitulates phylogeny." The concept is now regarded as an oversimplification.

receiver /risē'vər/ [L, *recipere*, to receive], **1.** in communication theory, the person or persons to whom a message is sent. **2.** the part of a hearing aid that converts electric signals to acoustic signals.

receiver operating characteristic (ROC) curve, a curve that plots the true-positive fraction versus false-positive fraction. One use is to evaluate imaging performance.

receiving sensitivity pattern /risē'ving/, the spatial response of an ultrasound transducer as an echo detector. For a single-element transducer it is essentially the same as the transmitted beam. For transducer arrays it can be quite different from the transmitted beam.

receptive aphasia /risep'tiv/, a form of sensory aphasia marked by impaired comprehension of language.

receptor /risep'tər/ [L, *recipere*, to receive], **1.** a chemical structure, usually of protein or carbohydrate, on the surface of a cell that combines with an antigen to produce a discrete immunologic component. **2.** a sensory nerve ending that responds to various kinds of stimulation. **3.** a specific cellular protein that must first bind a hormone before cellular response can be elicited.

receptor site [L, *recipere*, to receive + *situs*], a location on a cell surface where certain molecules such as enzymes, neurotransmitters, or viruses attach to interact with cellular components.

receptor theory of drug action, the concept that certain drugs produce their effects by acting specifically at a receptor site on a cell or within the cell or its membrane.

recess /rē'ses, rises'/ [L, *recedere*, to retreat], a small hollow cavity, such as the epitympanic recess in the middle ear or the retrocecal recess extending as a small pocket behind the cecum.

recessive /rises'iv/ [L, *recedere*], pertaining to or describing a gene, the effect of which is masked or hidden if there is a dominant gene at the same locus.

recessive allele, the member of a pair of alleles that lacks the ability to express itself in the presence of a dominant allele at the same locus. It is expressed only in the homozygous state.

recessive trait, an inherited characteristic that is determined by a recessive allele.

recidivism (recid) /risid'iviz'əm/ [L, *recidivus*, falling back], a tendency by an ill person to relapse or return to a hospital.

recipient /risip'ē-ənt/ [L, *recipere*, to receive], a person who receives a blood transfusion, tissue graft, or organ.

reciprocal beat /risip'rəkəl/, an atrial or ventricular complex on an ECG resulting from return of an impulse to its chamber of origin.

reciprocal change, a change detected electrocardiographically in a wall of the heart opposite the site of an MI. In acute inferior wall infarction, reciprocal changes are considered a sign of more extensive myocardial damage.

reciprocal force, a force applied by an orthodontic anchorage in which the resistance of one or more teeth and their adnexa is used to move one or more opposing teeth and their adnexa.

reciprocal inhibition, the theory in behavior therapy that, if an anxiety-producing stimulus occurs simultaneously with a response that diminishes anxiety, the stimulus may cause less anxiety.

reciprocal roentgens, the reciprocal of the number of roentgens needed to produce a density of 1 on x-ray film. It is used to define the speed of the film.

reciprocal translocation, the mutual exchange of genetic material between two nonhomologous chromosomes.

reciprocation /risip'roka'shən/, the means by which one part of a removable partial denture framework is made to counter the effect created by another part of the framework.

reciprocity /res'ipros'itē/ [Fr, *réciprocité*], a mutual agreement to exchange privileges, dependence, or relationships. An example is an agreement between two governing bodies to accept the medical credentials of nurses or physicians licensed in either community.

Recklinghausen's canal /rek'linghou'sənz/ [Friedrich D. von Recklinghausen, German pathologist, 1833–1910], the small lymph space in the connective tissues of the body.

Recklinghausen's tumor [Friedrich D. von Recklinghausen], a benign tumor, derived from smooth muscle containing connective tissue and epithelial elements, that occurs in the wall of the oviduct or posterior uterine wall.

reclining /riklī'ning/, leaning backward. **—recline,** *v.*

R

recognition site /rek'əgnish'ən/, a location on a nucleic acid or protein to which a specific ligand binds.

Recognized Continuing Education Evaluation Mechanism (RCEEM), a control process for checking that educational activities meet certain standards and establishing programs for evaluating educational opportunities and activities.

recombinant /rēkom'binənt/ [L, re, again, combinare, to combine], **1.** a molecule, a cell, or an organism that results from the recombination of genes, regardless of whether naturally or artificially induced. **2.** pertaining to such a molecule, a cell, or an organism.

recombinant DNA, a DNA molecule in which rearrangement of the genes has been experimentally induced. Enzymes are used to break isolated DNA molecules into fragments that are then rearranged in the desired sequence. DNA sequences from another organism of the same or a different species may also be introduced into the molecule, which is then replicated, resulting in both genotypic and phenotypic alterations in the organism that carries the recombinant DNA.

recombinant factor VIII concentrate, a concentrate of factor VIII prepared by recombinant DNA technology used to treat bleeding in hemophilia A patients (factor VIII deficiency).

recombinant Lyme test, a method of identifying infection by Borrelia burgdorferi, the bacterium that causes Lyme disease. A protein (P-39) specific to the bacterium, produced through recombinant DNA techniques and cloning in other bacteria, is the key component in the test. It causes a strong reaction in blood cells from persons with a B. burgdorferi infection.

recombinant vaccine, a suspension of attenuated viruses or killed microorganisms developed through recombinant DNA techniques.

recombination /rē'kombinā'shən/ [L, re + combinare], **1.** the formation of new arrangements of genes within the chromosomes as a result of independent assortment of unlinked genes, crossing over of linked genes, or intracistronic crossing over of nucleotides. **2.** the coupling of oppositely charged ions liberated by ionizing radiation. Ionic recombination lowers the total number of charges collected by a dosimeter, thus causing the radiation dose to be underestimated.

Recombivax HB, a trademark for a hepatitis B vaccine (recombinant).

recommended dietary allowances (RDAs) /rek'əmen'did/ [L, re + commendere, to commend], levels of daily intake of essential nutrients judged by the Food and Nutrition Board of the National Research Council to be adequate to meet the known nutrient needs of practically all healthy people.

recon /rē'kon/ [L, re + combinare; Gk, ion, going], the smallest genetic unit that is capable of recombination, thought to be a triplet of nucleotides.

reconstitution /rē'konstit(y)ōō'shən/ [L, re + constituere, to establish], the continuous repair of tissue damage.

reconstruction time /rē'kənstruk'shən/, the period between the end of a CT scan and the appearance of an image.

reconstructive mammaplasty, breast reconstruction after mastectomy.

record /rek'ərd/, a written form of communication that permanently documents information relevant to the care of a patient.

recorded detail /rikôr'did/, the sharpness of structural lines as recorded on a radiograph.

Recovery, Inc. /rikuv'əry/, a self-help group that provides support for persons with mental illness.

recovery room, an area adjoining the operating room to which surgical patients are taken while recovering from anesthesia, before being returned to their rooms.

recreational drug, any substance with pharmacologic effects that is taken voluntarily for personal pleasure or satisfaction rather than for medicinal purposes. The term is generally applied to alcohol, barbiturates, amphetamines, THC, PCP, cocaine, and heroin; however, it also includes caffeine in coffee and cola beverages.

recreational therapist, a person who uses recreational activities to reduce the effects of disability or illness so that patients can function more effectively in their families and communities.

recreational therapy /rē'krē·ā'shonəl/ [L, recreare, to renew], a form of adjunctive treatment in which games or other group activities are used as a means of modifying maladaptive behavior, awakening social interests, or improving the ability to interact and function in socially acceptable ways.

recreation therapy, a nursing intervention from the Nursing Interventions Classification (NIC) defined as purposeful use of recreation to promote relaxation and enhancement of social skills.

recrudescence /rē'krōōdes'əns/ [L, re + crudescere, to become hard], a return of symptoms of a disease during a period of recovery.

recrudescent /-ənt/ [L, re + crudescere, to become hard], the return of disease symptoms after a period of remission.

recrudescent hepatitis, a form of acute viral hepatitis marked by a relapse during the period of recovery.

recruitment /rikroōt′mənt/, **1.** the perception of a rapid growth of loudness, commonly seen in sensorineural hearing losses that are cochlear in nature. The impaired ear cannot hear faint sounds but hears intense sounds as loudly as a normal ear. **2.** in muscle contractions, the ability to recruit additional motor units into action as the need to overcome resistance increases.

rectal abscess /rek′təl/ [L, *rectus*, straight, *abscedere*, to go away], an abscess in the perianal area.

rectal alimentation [L, *rectus,* straight, *alimentum,* nourishment], the delivery of nourishment in concentrated form by injection or instillation through the rectum.

rectal anesthesia [L, *rectus*, straight], general anesthesia achieved by the insertion, injection, or infusion of an anesthetic agent into the rectum. This procedure is sometimes used in children and other patients who may be uncooperative or unable to tolerate medications. Absorption is unpredictable.

rectal instillation of medication, the instillation of a medicated suppository, cream, or gel into the rectum. Some conditions treated by this method are constipation, pruritus ani, and hemorrhoids. Occasionally a drug may be given in a medicated enema.

rectal prolapse management, a nursing intervention from the Nursing Interventions Classification (NIC) defined as prevention and/or manual reduction of rectal prolapse.

rectal reflex, the normal response (defecation) to the presence of an accumulation of feces in the rectum.

rectal speculum, a speculum that enlarges the diameter of the rectum for an examination.

rectal stenosis, stenosis or stricture of the rectum.

rectal temperature [L, *rectus,* straight + *temperatura*], body temperature as measured by a clinical thermometer placed in the rectum. Rectal temperatures average 0.5° to 0.75° F (0.3° to 0.4° C) higher than oral temperatures.

rectal thermometer [L, *rectus*; Gk, *thermē,* heat, *metron,* measure], a clinical thermometer suitable for measuring body temperature in the rectum.

rectal ultrasound of the prostate, an ultrasound used to diagnose cancer and to help stage rectal cancers.

rectification /rek′tifikā′shən/, **1.** the conversion of alternating current into pulsating direct current. **2.** a step in echo signal processing in a pulse-echo ultrasound instrument in which radiofrequency signals, which oscillate both above and below zero volts, are converted.

rectifier /rek′tifī′ər/, an electric device that converts alternating current into pulsating direct current.

rectilinear scanner /rek′tilin′ē·ər/, a device that generates an image of an anatomic structure by detecting radioactivity within the structure.

rectocele /rek′təsēl′/ [L, *rectus*; Gk, *koilos,* hollow], a protrusion of the rectum and posterior wall of the vagina into the vagina caused by weakening of the muscles of the vagina and pelvic floor by childbearing, old age, or surgery. It may reflect a congenital weakness in the wall. If severe, it may result in dyspareunia and difficulty in evacuating the bowel.

rectosacral fascia, the fusion of the inferior part of the presacral fascia with the visceral fascia on the posterior aspect of the rectum.

rectosigmoid /rek′tōsig′moid/ [L, *rectus*; Gk, *sigma,* the letter S, *eidos,* form], pertaining to the part of the large intestine that includes the lower part of the sigmoid and the upper part of the rectum.

rectosigmoidoscopy /-sig′moidəs′kəpē/ [L, *rectus*, straight; Gk, *sigma,* the letter S, *eidos,* form, *skopein,* to view], the examination of the rectum and pelvic colon with a sigmoidoscope.

rectosigmoid sphincter, circular muscle fibers in the wall of the large intestine at the junction of the sigmoid colon and rectum.

rectovaginal fistula /-vaj′ənəl/ [L, *rectus*, straight, *vagina,* sheath, *fistula,* pipe], an abnormal passage or opening between the rectum and the vagina.

rectovaginal ligament, one of the four main uterine support ligaments. It helps hold the uterus in position by maintaining traction on the cervix.

rectovaginal septum, a band of loose connective tissue between the vagina and the ampulla of the rectum.

rectovesical /-ves′ikəl/ [L, *rectus*, straight, *vesica,* bladder], pertaining to the rectum and bladder.

rectovesical septum, a partition that separates the posterior surface of the vagina from the rectum.

rectum /rek′təm/ *pl.* **rectums, recta** [L, *rectus*], the lower part of the large intestine, about 12 cm long, continuous with the descending sigmoid colon, proximal to the anal canal. It follows the sacrococcygeal curve and ends in the anal canal. —**rectal,** *adj.*

rectus abdominis /rek′təs/, one of a pair of anterolateral muscles of the abdomen, extending the whole length of the ventral aspect of the abdomen. It functions to flex the vertebral column, tense the anterior

R

abdominal wall, and assist in compressing the abdominal contents.

rectus femoris, a fusiform muscle of the anterior thigh, one of the four parts of the quadriceps femoris. With the quadriceps group, it functions to extend the lower leg.

rectus muscle [L, straight, *musculus*], a muscle of the body that has a relatively straight form.

recumbent /rikum′bənt/ [L, *recumbere,* to lie down], lying down or leaning backward.—**recumbency,** *n.*

recuperate /rikoo̅′pərāt/ [L, *recupare,* to regain], to recover one's health and strength.

recuperation /rikoo̅′pərā′shən/ [L, *recupare,* to regain], the process of recovering health and strength.

recurrence /rikur′əns/ [L, *recurrere,* to run back], the reappearance of a sign or symptom of a disease after a period of remission.

recurrence risk, the chance that a disease found in one member of a proband will appear in other members of the same pedigree.

recurrent /rikur′ənt/ [L, *recurrere,* to run back], a disease sign or symptom that returns periodically.

recurrent bandage [L, *recurrere,* to run back], a strip of cloth that is wrapped several times around itself, usually applied to the head or amputated limb.

recurrent caries, an acidic destruction of dental tissues which have previously experienced such destruction and have already received dental restoration.

recurrent respiratory papillomatosis, the recurrent growth of benign squamous cell papillomas in the larynx and trachea, caused by the human papillomavirus, and leading to severe narrowing of the airway that may require frequent treatments. Onset is in childhood or early adulthood.

recurvatum /rē′kərvā′təm/ [L, *recurvare,* to bend back], backward thrust, or bending, for example, of the knee caused by weakness of the quadriceps or a joint disorder.

red blood cell cast, a urine sediment cast that contains red blood cells, signifying bleeding in the kidney, seen in glomerulonephritis.

red blood cell (RBC) count [AS, *read* + *blod*; L, *cella,* storeroom; Fr, *conter,* to count], a count of the erythrocytes in a specimen of whole blood, commonly made with an electronic counting device. The normal concentrations of red blood cells in the whole blood of males are 4.6 to 6.2 million/mm^3; in females the concentrations are 4.2 to 5.4 million/mm^3.

red blood cell indices, a series of mathematical parameters that characterize the red cell population in terms of volume, hemoglobin mass, and hemoglobin concentration. Derived mathematically from the red cell count, hemoglobin, and hematocrit values, the indices are useful in making differential diagnoses of several kinds of anemia.

red blood cell (RBC) survival study, a nuclear scan that is often performed on patients with hemolytic anemia. The test is carried out in two parts. The first determines the half-life of the RBC within the circulation, and the second images the spleen, liver, and pericardium.

Red Book of the American Academy of Pediatrics, a book published by the American Academy of Pediatrics, Inc., that serves as the standard reference source of immunization procedures for children and adolescents.

red cell indexes, a series of relationships that characterize the red cell population in terms of size, hemoglobin content, and hemoglobin concentration. Derived mathematically from the red cell count and hemoglobin and hematocrit values, the indexes are useful in making differential diagnoses of several kinds of anemia.

red clover, a preparation of the flower heads of *Trifolium pratense,* used internally for coughs and respiratory symptoms and externally for chronic skin conditions, such as psoriasis and eczema; it is also used in traditional Chinese medicine.

red-green blindness, red-green color blindness, popular names for any imperfect perception of red and green tints, including all of the most common types of color vision deficiency.

redia /rē′dē-ə/, an elongated second or third larval stage of a trematode that develops in a sporocyst and matures into numerous cercariae.

red infarct [AS, *read;* L, *infarcire,* to stuff], a pathologic change that occurs in brain tissue that has been rendered ischemic by lack of blood. With restricted blood flow, diapedesis of RBCs occurs into the parenchyma of the brain without actually producing a well-formed hematoma but only infiltration of erythrocytes.

red marrow [AS, *read* + *mearh,* marrow], the red vascular substance consisting of connective tissue and blood vessels containing primitive blood cells, macrophages, megakaryocytes, and fat cells. It is found in the cavities of many bones, including flat and short bones, bodies of the vertebrae, sternum, ribs, and articulating ends of long bones. Red marrow manufactures and releases leukocytes, erythrocytes, and thrombocytes into the bloodstream.

red neck syndrome, an allergic reaction to a rapid infusion of the antimicrobial agent vancomycin. It is characterized by flushing, pruritus, and erythema of the head and upper body resulting from histamine release.

redon /rē'don/, the smallest unit of DNA capable of recombination. It may be as small as one base pair.

redox, an abbreviation for *reduction-oxidation* (reaction).

reduce /rid(y)oōs'/ [L, *reducere,* to lead back], **1.** in surgery, to restore a part to its original position after displacement, as in the reduction of a fractured bone by bringing ends or fragments back into alignment. **2.** to decrease the amount, size, extent, or number of something, as of body weight.

reducible hernia /rid(y)oō'səbəl/ [L, *reducere,* to lead back, *hernia,* rupture], a hernia in which the protruding tissues can be manipulated into a normal position.

reducing agent /rid(y)oō'sing/ [L, *reducere,* to lead back, *agere,* to do], a substance that donates electrons to another substance in a chemical reaction.

reduction /riduk'shən/ [L, *reducere*], **1.** the addition of hydrogen to a substance. **2.** the removal of oxygen from a substance. **3.** the decrease in the valence of the electronegative part of a compound. **4.** the addition of one or more electrons to a molecule or atom of a substance. **5.** the correction of a fracture, hernia, or luxation. **6.** the reduction of data, as in converting interval data to an ordinal or nominal scale of measurement.

reductionism/riduk'shəniz'əm/, an approach that tries to explain a form of behavior or an event in terms of a specific category of phenomena, such as biologic, psychologic, or cultural, negating the possibility of an interrelation of causal phenomena.

reduction ureteroplasty, surgical tapering or plication of the ureter for treatment of megaureter.

Reed, Pamela G., a nursing theorist who developed the Self-Transcendence Theory. Self-transcendence is the expansion of a person's concept of self through introspection, interaction with other people and the surrounding environment, integration of the past and future, and spirituality. It is based on the belief that, to maintain a sense of well-being, older adults must continue their cognitive development during the process of aging.

Reed-Sternberg cell [Dorothy M. Reed, American pathologist, 1874–1964; Karl Sternberg, Austrian pathologist, 1872–1935], one of a number of large, abnormal, multinucleated reticuloendothelial cells in the lymphatic system found in Hodgkin's disease. The number and proportion of Reed-Sternberg cells identified are the basis for the histopathologic classification of Hodgkin's disease.

reentry /rē·en'trē/ [L, *re,* again; Fr, *entrée*], in cardiology, the reactivation of myocardial tissue for the second or subsequent time by the same impulse. Reentry is one of the most common arrhythmogenic mechanisms.

refeeding /rēfēd'ing/, restoration of normal nutrition after a period of fasting or starvation.

refeeding syndrome, moderate to severe electrolyte and fluid shifts occurring during a period of refeeding. Hypophosphatemia is common, and heart failure sometimes occurs.

refereed journal /ref'ərēd'/ [L, *referre,* to bring back, *diurnalis,* daily record], a professional or literary journal in which articles or papers are selected for publication by a panel of referees who are experts in the field.

reference electrode /ref'ərəns/ [L, *referre,* to bring back; Gk, *elektron,* amber, *hodos,* way], an electrode that has an established potential and is used as a reference against which other potentials may be measured.

reference group, a group with which a person identifies or wishes to belong.

reference interval, distribution of test results that are normal for a selected population of healthy persons. Reference intervals are interpreted according to age, sex, and race. Also called *reference range, normal range.*

referential index deletion /ref'ərən'shəl/, a neurolinguistic programming term that pertains to the omission of the specific person being discussed.

referral[1] /rifur'əl/ [L,*referre,*to bring back], a process whereby a patient or the patient's family is introduced to additional health resources in the community, as in helping a patient find an appropriate community health nurse after discharge from a hospital.

referral[2], a nursing intervention from the Nursing Interventions Classification (NIC) defined as arrangement for services by another care provider or agency.

referred pain /rifurd'/ [L, *referre* + *poena,* punishment], pain felt at a site different from that of an injured or diseased organ or body part. Angina, the pain of coronary artery insufficiency, may be felt in the left shoulder, arm, or jaw.

referred sensation, a feeling or impression that occurs at a site other than where the stimulus is initiated.

refined birth rate /rifīnd/ [L, *re* + *finire,* to finish], the ratio of total births to the total female population, considered during a period of 1 year.

refl, abbreviation for *reflexive.*

R

reflecting /riflek'ting/, a communication technique in which the listener picks up the feeling or tone of the patient's message and repeats it back to the patient. It encourages the patient to continue with clarifying comments and is a means of assisting patients to better understand their own thoughts and feelings.

reflection /riflek'shən/ [L, *reflectere*, to bend back], **1.** a form of reentry in myocardial tissue in which, after encountering delay in one fiber, an impulse enters a parallel fiber and returns retrogradely to its source. **2.** the return or reentry of ultrasound waves where there is a discontinuity in the characteristic acoustic impedance along the propagation path.

reflective layer /riflek'tiv/, a thin layer of magnesium oxide or titanium oxide between the phosphor and the base of an intensifying screen used in radiography. Its function is to intercept and redirect isotropically emitted light from the phosphor to the x-ray film.

reflex /rē'fleks/ [L, *reflectere*, to bend back], **1.** a backward or return flow of energy or of an image, as a reflection. **2.** a reflected action, particularly an involuntary action or movement.

reflex action, the involuntary functioning or movement of any organ or body part in response to a particular stimulus.

reflex apnea, involuntary cessation of respiration caused by irritating, noxious vapors or gases.

reflex arc [L, *reflectere*, to bend back, *arcus*, bow], a simple neurologic unit of a sensory neuron that carries a stimulus impulse to the spinal cord, where it connects with a motor neuron that carries the reflex impulse back to an appropriate muscle or gland.

reflex center [L, *reflectere*, to bend back; Gk, *kentron*], any part of the nervous system in which reception of afferent impulses results in a discharge of efferent impulses leading to some change in a muscle or gland.

reflex dyspepsia, an abnormal condition characterized by impaired digestion associated with the disease of an organ not directly involved with digestion.

reflex emesis [L, *reflectere*, to bend back; Gk, *emesis*, vomiting], vomiting or gagging that is induced by touching the mucous membrane of the throat or as a result of other noxious stimuli.

reflex hammer [L, *reflectere*, to bend back; AS, *hamer*], a percussion mallet with a rubber head used to tap tendons, nerves, or muscles to elicit reflex reactions.

reflex incontinence, the urinary incontinence that accompanies detrusor hyperreflexia.

reflex inhibiting pattern (RIP), a conscious set of neuromuscular actions directed toward inhibition of a natural reflex. Examples include actions taken to suppress a sneeze and the learned inhibitions of toilet training.

reflexology /rē'fleksol'əjē/, a bodywork technique that uses reflex points on the hands and feet. Pressure is applied at points that correspond to various body parts with the intention of eliminating blockages thought to produce pain or disease.

reflex seizure, an epileptic seizure in response to a sensory stimulus, which may be tactile, visual, auditory, or musical.

reflex sympathetic dystrophy (RSD), a diffuse, persistent pain involving central reorganization of sensory processing. It is characterized by vasomotor disorders, limited joint mobility, and trophic changes. The condition usually follows an injury to an afferent pathway and affects an extremity.

reflex tachycardia [L, *reflectere*, to bend back; Gk, *tachys*, fast, *kardia*, heart], a rapid heart sinus rhythm caused by a variety of autonomic nervous system effects such as BP changes, fever, or emotional stress.

reflex vasodilation [L, *reflectere*, to bend back, *vas*, vessel, *dilatare*, to spread out], any blood vessel dilation that results from stimulation of vasodilator nerves or inhibition of vasoconstrictors of the sympathetic nervous system, including epinephrine-type drugs.

reflux /rē'fluks/ [L, *refluere*, to flow back], an abnormal backward or return flow of a fluid.

reflux esophagitis, esophageal irritation and inflammation that result from reflux of the stomach contents into the esophagus.

reflux laryngitis, a burning sensation in the hypopharynx and larynx caused by nocturnal gastric reflux. It occurs most commonly in older patients who sleep in the recumbent position.

refraction /rifrak'shən/ [L, *refringere*, to break apart], **1.** the change of direction of energy as it passes from one medium to another of different density. **2.** an examination to determine and correct refractive errors of the eye. **3.** in ultrasonography, the phenomenon of bending wave fronts as the acoustic energy propagates from the medium of one acoustic velocity to a second medium of differing acoustic velocity. **4.** pertaining to the recovery period after an action potential either in muscular or nervous tissue.—**refractive,** *adj.*

refraction of eye [L, *refringere*, to break apart; AS, *eage*], the deflection of light from a straight path through the eye by various ocular tissues, including the cornea, lens, aqueous humor, and vitreous body.

refractive error /rifrak′tiv/, a defect in the ability of the lens of the eye to focus an image accurately, as occurs in nearsightedness and farsightedness.

refractive index, a numeric expression of the refractive power of a medium, as compared with that of air, which has a refractive index value of 1. The refractive index is related to the number, charge, and mass of vibrating particles in the material through which light is passing.

refractive keratotomy (RK), a surgical procedure in which a varying number of radial or perpendicular incisions are made to flatten the cornea, resulting in the elimination or reduction of myopia or astigmatism. This type of refractive surgery has been largely replaced by newer methods.

refractometer /rē′fraktom′ətər/ [L, *refringere,* to break apart; Gk, *metron,* measure], an instrument for measuring the refractive index of a substance and used primarily for measuring the refractivity of solutions.

refractoriness /rifrak′tôrines′/, the property of excitable tissue that determines how closely together two action potentials can occur.

refractory /rifrak′tərē/ [L, *refringere*], **1.** pertaining to a disorder that is resistant to treatment. **2.** property of conductive tissue to return to original related state in preparation for a second stimulus.

refractory period, the time from phase 0 to the end of phase 3 of the action potential, divided into effective and relative. In pacing terminology, the period during which a pulse generator is unresponsive to an input signal of specified amplitude.

reframing /rēfrā′ming/, changing the conceptual and/or emotional viewpoint in relation to which a situation is experienced and placing it in a different frame that fits the "facts" of a concrete situation equally well, thereby changing its entire meaning.

Refsum's syndrome /ref′s‿oomz/ [Sigvald Refsum, Norwegian physician, 1907 –1991], a rare hereditary disorder of lipid metabolism in which phytanic acid cannot be broken down. It is characterized by ataxia, abnormalities of the bones and skin, peripheral neuropathy, cardiomyopathy, deafness, and retinitis pigmentosa. Foods containing phytanic acid must be avoided to prevent progressive deterioration.

refusal of treatment, the right of a patient to refuse treatment after the physician has informed the patient of the diagnosis, prognosis, available alternative interventions, risks and benefits of those options, and risk and probable outcome of no intervention.

regeneration /rijen′ərā′shən/, the process of repair, reproduction, or replacement of lost or injured cells, tissues, or organs.

regimen /rej′imən/ [L, guidance], a strictly regulated therapeutic program such as a diet or exercise schedule.

regional /rē′jənəl/ [L, *regio,* territory], pertaining to a geographic area such as a regional medical facility or to a part of the body such as regional anesthesia.

regional anatomy, the study of the structural relationships among the organs and the parts of the body.

regional anesthesia, anesthesia provided by injecting a local anesthetic to block a group of sensory nerve fibers. The tissues are anesthetized layer by layer, as the surgeon approaches the deeper structures of the body. Regional anesthesia has largely replaced local anesthesia for major procedures.

regional control, the control of cancer in sites that represent the first stages of spread from the local origin.

regional hyperthermia, the elevation of temperature over an extended volume of tissue.

regionalization /rē′jənalīzā′shən/, in health care planning, the organization of a system for the delivery of health care within a region to avoid costly duplication of services and to ensure availability of essential services.

regional medical program (RMP), a program of community health planning that includes all the medical resources available in a region that may be mobilized to meet a specific medical objective. The RMP was authorized by the Health, Disease, Cancer and Stroke Amendments passed by the U.S. Congress in 1965.

region of interest (ROI), an area on a digital image that circumscribes a desired anatomic location. Image processing systems permit drawing of ROIs on images.

region of recombination, the first stage of amplitude of an electric signal in a gas-filled radiation detector, when the voltage is very low. No electrons are attracted to the central electrode, and ion pairs produced in the chamber will recombine.

regiospecific, a chemical reaction favoring a single positional or structural isomer.

register /rej′istər/ [L, *regerere,* to bring back], in CT, a device in the central processing unit that stores information for future use.

registered dietitian (RD) /rej′istərd/, a professional trained in foods and the management of diets (dietetics) who is credentialed by the Commission on Dietetic Registration of the American Dietetic Association. Credentialing is based on completion of a BS or MS degree, an

R

approved dietetic internship, and passing a registration examination.

registered nurse (RN), 1. In the United States, a nurse who has completed a course of study at a state-approved school of nursing and passed the National Council Licensure Examination (NCLEX-RN). A registered nurse may use the initials RN after the signature. RNs are licensed to practice by individual states. 2. In Canada, *Canada.* a nurse who has completed a course of study at an approved school of nursing and who has taken and passed an examination administered by the Canadian Nurses Association Testing Service, called the Comprehensive Examination for Nurse Registration Licensure.

registered record administrator (RRA), a medical record administrator who has successfully completed the credentialing examination conducted by the American Medical Record Association.

registered respiratory therapist (RRT), an allied health professional who has successfully completed the registry examination of the National Board for Respiratory Care and who specializes in scientific knowledge and theory of clinical problems of respiratory care. Usually a 2- or 4-year college affiliation leading to an associate or bachelor's degree is required.

registered technologist (RT), a medical professional who is certified by the American Registry of Radiologic Technologists or equivalent certifying agency in one or more of the following disciplines: radiography, nuclear medicine, radiation therapy, mammography, CT, MRI, cardiovascular interventional technology, or quality management.

registrar /rej'isträr/, an administrative officer whose responsibility is to maintain the records of an institution.

registration /rej'istrā'shən/ [L, *registratio*], 1. a learning or memory recording made in the CNS of an impression resulting from a stimulus. 2. the recording of vital personal information such as health data. 3. the recording of professional qualification information relevant to government licensing regulations.

registry /rej'istrē/ [L, *regerere*, to bring back], 1. an office or agency in which lists of nurses and records pertaining to nurses seeking employment are maintained. 2. in epidemiology, a listing service for incidence data pertaining to the occurrence of specific diseases or disorders, such as a tumor registry.

Regitine, a trademark for an alpha-adrenergic blocking agent (phentolamine hydrochloride).

regression /rigresh'ən/ [L, *regredi*, to go back], 1. a retreat or backward movement

in conditions, signs, or symptoms. 2. a return to an earlier, more primitive form of behavior. 3. a tendency in physical development to become more typical of the population than of the parents.—**regress,** *v.*

Regroton, a trademark for a fixed-combination cardiovascular drug containing a diuretic (chlorthalidone) and an antihypertensive (reserpine).

regular diet /reg'yələr/ [L, *regula*, rule], a full, well-balanced diet containing all of the essential nutrients needed for optimal growth, tissue repair, and normal functioning of the organs.

regular insulin, a fast-acting insulin prescribed in the treatment of DM when the desired action is relatively prompt, intense, and short-acting. It can be mixed with long-acting forms of insulin.

regulative development /reg'yələtiv/ [L, *regula*, rule], a type of embryonic development in which the fertilized ovum undergoes indeterminate cleavage, producing blastomeres that have similar developmental potencies and are each capable of giving rise to a single embryo. Determination of the particular organs and parts of the embryo occurs during later stages of development and is influenced by inductors and intercellular interaction.

regulator /reg'yələtər/, in genetics, the part of a DNA molecule undergoing replication that controls the replication and coordinates with cell division.

regulator gene /reg'yələtər/, a gene that regulates or suppresses the activity of one or more structural genes.

regulatory HIV gene, one of a set of genes in the genome of HIV that influence the expression of other HIV genes. One regulatory gene *(tat)* stimulates expression, a second *(nef)* may inhibit expression, and a third *(rev)* provides feedback to the others.

regulatory sequence /reg'yələtôr'ē/ [L, *regula* + *sequi*, to follow], a series of DNA nucleotides that regulates the expression of a gene.

regurgitant murmur /rigur'jitənt/ [L, *re* + *gurgitare*, to flow back, *murmur*, humming], a heart murmur caused by the backflow of blood through the partly closed cusps of a defective valve.

regurgitation /rēgur'jitā'shən/ [L, *re*, again, *gurgitare*, to flow back], 1. the backward flow from the normal direction, as the return of swallowed food into the mouth. 2. the backward flow of blood through a defective heart valve, named for the affected valve, as in **aortic regurgitation.**

regurgitation jaundice [L, *re* + *gurgitare*, to flow back; Fr, *jaune*, yellow], jaundice caused by bile pigment entering the blood and lymphatic systems as a result of biliary obstruction.

rehabilitation (rehab) /rē´habil´itā´shən/ [L, *re* + *habitalas*, aptitude], the restoration of an individual or a part to normal or near normal function after a disabling disease, injury, addiction, or incarceration. —**rehabilitate**, *v.*

rehabilitation center, a facility providing therapy and training for rehabilitation. The center may offer occupational therapy, physical therapy, vocational training, and special training such as speech therapy.

rehabilitation counselor, a human services professional who assists persons with disabilities to become or remain productive and self-sufficient. The counselor may help clients deal with personal, environmental, and societal problems; arrange for medical and psychologic services; and arrange vocational assessment, training, and job placement.

rehabilitation teacher, a human services professional who teaches the blind and visually impaired independent living skills, as well as communication skills using Braille and assistive technology.

Rehfuss stomach tube /rā´fəs/ [Martin E. Rehfuss, American physician, 1887–1964], a specially designed gastric tube with a graduated syringe, used for withdrawing specimens of the contents of the stomach for study after a test meal.

rehydration /rē´hīdrā´shən/ [L, *re*; Gk, *hydor*, water], restoration of normal water balance in a patient by giving fluids orally or intravenously.

Reid's base line [Robert W. Reid, Scottish anatomist, 1851–1939], the base line of the skull, a hypothetic line extending from the inferior orbital ridge to the center of the aperture of the external auditory meatus.

Reifenstein's syndrome /rī´fənstīnz/ [Edward C. Reifenstein, Jr., American physician, 1908–1975], male hypogonadism of unknown origin, marked by azoospermia, undescended testes, gynecomastia, testosterone deficiency, and elevated gonadotropin titers.

reiki /rā´kē/, an Eastern healing tradition whose purpose is to rebalance the complex energy systems that compose the body when they have become out of balance. The reiki practitioner is trained to channel energy from the universal energy source, which flows through his or her hands to the body of the receiver. The result is the rebalancing of mind and body, the strengthening of body and spirit, the opening of energy blockages, the creation of a sense of well-being, and the healing of illnesses.

reiki therapy /rā´kē/, a complementary therapy in which a trained practitioner places his or her hands on or above a specific body area and transfers what is called "universal life energy" to the patient. That energy, it is claimed, provides strength, harmony, and balance necessary to treat health disturbances. The therapy, derived from an ancient Buddhist practice, involves a total of 15 hand positions covering all the body systems.

reimbursement /rē´imburs´mənt/ [L, *re* + *im*, in; Fr, *bourse*, purse], a method of payment, usually by a third-party payer, for medical treatment or hospital costs.

reimplantation /rē´im·plan·tā´shən/, the planting back of tissue or a structure, such as a tooth, in the site from which it was previously lost or removed.

reinfection /rē´infek´shən/, a second infection by the same microorganism, either after recovery or during the original infection.

reinforcement /rē´infôrs´mənt/ [L, *re*; Fr, *enforcir*, to strengthen], in psychology, a process in which a response is strengthened by the fear of punishment or the anticipation of reward.

reinforcement-extinction, a process of socialization in which one learns to engage in certain behaviors (reinforcement) or to avoid certain behaviors (extinction). The anticipated result is that the reinforced behaviors become habitual and those that undergo extinction disappear.

reinforcer /rē´infôr´sər/, in psychology, a consequence that increases the probability that an operant will recur.

Reiter's syndrome /rī´tərz/ [Hans Reiter, German physician, 1881–1969], an arthritic disorder predominantly of adult males, resulting from infection with *Shigella flexneri, Salmonessa, Yersinia,* enterocolitis, or *Chlamydia.* It most often affects the ankles, feet, and sacroiliac joints and is usually associated with conjunctivitis and urethritis. The onset may be marked by unexplained diarrhea and low-grade fever, followed in 2 to 4 weeks by conjunctivitis. Superficial ulcers may form lesions on the palms and the soles. Arthritis usually persists after the conjunctivitis and urethritis subside, but it may become episodic. Treatment includes a short course of tetracycline to treat the infection and phenylbutazone to relieve pain and inflammation in the joint.

reject analysis /rē´jekt/, the study of rejected radiographs to determine the cause for their being discarded.

rejection /rijek´shən/ [L, *re* + *jacere*, to throw], **1.** an immunologic attack against organisms or substances that the immune system recognizes as foreign, including grafts and transplants. **2.** the act of excluding or denying affection to another person.

rejunctive /rijungk′tiv/, in contextual psychotherapy, pertaining to a relationship that is characterized by moves toward trustworthy relatedness.

rejuvenation /rējōō′vənā′shən/ [L, *re* + *juvenis*, youth], the restoration of youthful health and vitality.

relapse /rilaps′/ [L, *relabi*, to slide back], **1.** to exhibit again the symptoms of a disease from which a patient appears to have recovered. **2.** the recurrence of a disease after apparent recovery.

relapsing [L, *relabi*, to slide back], pertaining to the return of disease after a period of apparent recovery.

relapsing fever, any one of several acute infectious diseases, marked by recurrent febrile episodes, caused by various strains of the spirochete *Borrelia*. The disease is transmitted by both lice and ticks and is often seen during wars and famines. The first episode usually starts with a sudden high fever (104° to 105° F, or 40° to 40.56° C), accompanied by chills, headache, neuromuscular pains, and nausea. A rash may appear over the trunk and extremities, and jaundice is common during the later stages. Each attack lasts 2 or 3 days and culminates in a crisis of high fever, profuse sweating, and a rise in heart and respiratory rate. This is followed by an abrupt drop in temperature and a return to normal BP. People typically relapse after 7 to 10 days of normal temperature but eventually recover completely. In louseborne disease there is usually only a single relapse; in tickborne disease several successively milder relapses may occur.

relapsing polychondritis, a rare disease of unknown cause resulting in inflammation and destruction of cartilage with replacement by fibrous tissue. Autoimmunity may be involved in this condition. Most commonly the ears and noses of middle-aged people are affected with episodes of tender swelling, often accompanied by fever, arthralgias, and episcleritis. Corticosteroids suppress the activity of the disease.

relation searching /rilā′shən/ [L, *relatio*], in nursing research, a study design used to discover and describe relationships between and among variables.

relationship therapy /rilā′shənship/ [L, *relatio*; AS, *scieppan*, to shape], a therapy that is based on a totality of client-therapist relationship and encourages the growth of self in the client.

relative biologic effectiveness (RBE) /rel′ətiv/ [L, *relatio*], a measure of the cell-killing ability of a particular radiation compared with that of 250 keV x-rays. The ratio of the number of cells killed with the test radiation over the number killed with the 250 keV radiation is the RBE.

relative centrifugal force (RCF), a method of comparing the force generated by various centrifuges based on the speeds of rotation and distances from the center of rotation.

relative growth, the comparison of the various increases in size of similar organisms, tissues, or structures at different time intervals.

relative humidity (r/h), the amount of moisture in the air compared with the maximum the air could contain at the same temperature.

relative risk, the ratio of the chance of a disease developing among members of a population exposed to a factor compared to a similar population not exposed to the factor.

relative sterility [L, *relatio* + *sterilis*, barren], a condition of infertility in which one or more factors tend to reduce the chances of becoming pregnant.

relative value unit (RVU), a comparable service measure used by hospitals to permit comparison of the amounts of resources required to perform various services within a single department or between departments.

relax /rilaks′/ [L, *relaxare*, to ease], to reduce tension or anxiety.

relaxant /rilak′sənt/ [L, *relaxare*, to ease], a drug or other agent that tends to reduce tension, as a muscle relaxant or bowel relaxant.

relaxation /rē′laksā′shən/ [L, *relaxare*, to ease], **1.** a reducing of tension, as when a muscle relaxes between contractions. **2.** in MRI, the return of excited nuclei to their normal unexcited state by the release of energy.

relaxation oven, a part of the xerographic plate conditioner system used to eliminate ghost images in mammograms. The plate is heated in the oven so that any residual electrostatic charge on the surface will be removed.

relaxation response, a protective mechanism against stress that brings about decreased heart rate, lower metabolism, and decreased respiratory rate. It is the physiologic opposite of the "fight or flight," or stress, response.

relaxation therapy¹, treatment in which patients are taught to perform breathing and relaxation exercises and to concentrate on a pleasant situation. Some patients learn through relaxation therapy to relax taut muscles at will, to abort migraine attacks, or to reduce their BP.

relaxation therapy², a nursing intervention from the Nursing Interventions Classification (NIC) defined as use of techniques to encourage and elicit relaxation for the purpose of decreasing undesirable signs and symptoms such as pain, muscle tension, or anxiety.

relaxation time, in MRI, the characteristic time it takes for a sample of atoms, whose nuclei have first been aligned along a static magnetic field and then excited to a higher-energy state by a radiofrequency (rf) signal to return to a lower-energy equilibrium state.

relaxin /rilak'sin/, a hormone obtained from the corpora lutea of swine and used to relax the pelvic ligaments and dilate the cervix during labor. The medication has also been used to treat dysmenorrhea.

release therapy /rilēs'/ [ME, *relesen*, to release], a type of pediatric psychotherapy used to treat children with stress and anxiety related to a specific recent event.

releasing hormone (RH), one of several peptides produced by the hypothalamus and secreted directly into the anterior pituitary gland via a connecting vein. Each of the releasing hormones stimulates the pituitary to secrete a specific tropic hormone. Thus corticotropic-releasing hormone stimulates the pituitary to secrete adrenocorticotropic hormone, whereas growth hormone–releasing hormone stimulates the secretion of growth hormone.

releasing stimulus, in psychology, an action or behavior by one individual that serves as a cue to trigger a response in others. An example is yawning by one person, which results in yawning by others in the group.

reliability /rilī'əbil'itē/ [L, *religare*, to fasten behind], in research, the extent to which a test measurement or device produces the same results with different investigators, observers, or administration of the test over time.

relief area [L, *relevare*, to lighten], the part of the tissue surface under a prosthesis on which pressure is reduced or eliminated.

relieve /rē·lēv'/ [L, *relevare*, to lighten], to mitigate or remove pain or distress.

relieving factor /rilē'ving/, an agent that alleviates a symptom.

religiosity /rilij'ē·os'itē/ [L, *religiosus*], a psychiatric symptom characterized by the demonstration of excessive or affected piety.

religious addiction prevention, a nursing intervention from the Nursing Interventions Classification (NIC) defined as prevention of a self-imposed controlling religious lifestyle.

religious ritual enhancement, a nursing intervention from the Nursing Interventions Classification (NIC) defined as facilitating participation in religious practices.

reline /rēlīn'/ [L, *re + linea*], the resurfacing of the tissue side of a denture with new base material.

relocation stress reduction, a nursing intervention from the Nursing Interventions Classification (NIC) defined as assisting the individual to prepare for and cope with movement from one environment to another.

rem /rem, är'ē'em'/, abbreviation for *roentgen equivalent man,* a dose of ionizing radiation that produces in humans the same effect as one roentgen of x-radiation or gamma radiation.

REM /rem, är'ē·em'/, abbreviation for **rapid eye movement.**

remasking /rēmas'king/, in digital fluoroscopy, the production of one or more additional mask images if the first is inadequate because of patient motion, noise, or other factors.

remedial /rimē'dē·əl/ [L, *remediare*, to cure], designed to improve or cure.

remifentanil, an opiate agonist analgesic used in combination with other drugs in general anesthesia and as a primary anesthetic in general surgery.

reminiscence /rem'inis'əns/ [L, *reminisci*, to remember], the recollection of past personal experiences and significant events.

reminiscence therapy[1], a psychotherapeutic technique in which self-esteem and personal satisfaction are restored, particularly in older persons, by encouraging patients to review past experiences of a pleasant nature. It is used in Alzheimer's disease when initially long-term memory stores are more intact than short-term and in other forms of dementia.

reminiscence therapy[2], a nursing intervention from the Nursing Interventions Classification (NIC) defined as using the recall of past events, feelings, and thoughts to facilitate pleasure, quality of life, or adaptation to present circumstances.

remission /rimish'ən/ [L, *remittere*, to abate], the partial or complete disappearance of the clinical and subjective characteristics of a chronic or malignant disease. Remission may be spontaneous or the result of therapy.

remittent fever /rimit'ənt/ [L, *remittere + febris*, fever], diurnal variations of an elevated temperature with exacerbations and remissions but never a return to normal.

remnant radiation /rem'nənt/ [L, *remanere*, to remain], the radiation that passes through an object and can produce an image on an x-ray film.

remodeling /rēmod'əling/ [L, *re + modus*, to copy again], the process of changing a body part or area, as in reconstructive surgery.

remote afterloading /rimōt'/ [L, *removere*, to remove], a radiotherapy technique in which an applicator, such as an acrylic mold of an area to be irradiated, is placed in or on the patient and then loaded from a safe source with a high-activity radioisotope. Remote afterloading is used

R

in the treatment of head, neck, vaginal, and cervical tumors.

remotivation /rē'mōtivā'shən/ [L, *re* + *motus*, movement], the use of special techniques that stimulate patients to become motivated to learn and interact.

remotivation group, a treatment group that is organized with the purpose of stimulating the interest, awareness, and communication of withdrawn and institutionalized mental patients.

removable lingual arch /rimoo'vəbəl/ [L, *removere*, to remove], an orthodontic arch wire designed to fit the lingual surface of the teeth and aid their orthodontic movement.

removable orthodontic appliance, a device placed inside the mouth to correct or alleviate malocclusion and designed to be removed or replaced by the patient.

removable partial denture, a partial denture made so that it can readily be removed from the mouth.

removable rigid dressing, a dressing similar to a cast used to encase the stump of an amputated limb. It is usually applied to permit the fitting of a temporary prosthesis so that ambulation can begin soon after surgery.

renal /rē'nəl/ [L, *ren*, kidney], pertaining to the kidney.

renal acidosis [L, *ren*, kidney, *acidus*, sour; Gk, *osis*, condition], an excessive increase in the H+ ions in body fluids because of impaired kidney function. The acidosis can result from excessive loss of bicarbonate or from the inability to excrete phosphoric and sulfuric acid.

renal aminoaciduria, aminoaciduria caused by defective transport mechanisms for amino acids in the renal tubules.

renal anemia, anemia occurring as a complication of chronic kidney disease, mainly caused by deficiency of erythropoietin in the blood.

renal angiography, a radiographic examination of the renal artery and associated blood vessels after the injection of a contrast medium.

renal anuria, cessation of urine production caused by intrinsic renal disease.

renal artery, one of a pair of large, visceral branches of the abdominal aorta. The renal arteries supply the kidneys, suprarenal glands, and the ureters.

renal biopsy, the removal of kidney tissue for microscopic examination. It is conducted to establish the diagnosis of a renal disorder and to aid in determining the stage of the disease, the appropriate therapy, and the prognosis. An open biopsy involves an incision, permits better visualization of the kidney, and carries a lower risk of hemorrhage. A closed or percutaneous biopsy performed by aspirating a specimen of tissue with a needle requires a shorter period of recovery and is less likely to cause infection.

renal calculus, a concretion occurring in the kidney.

renal calyx, the first unit in the system of ducts in the kidney carrying urine from the renal pyramid of the medulla to the renal pelvis for excretion through the ureters. There are two divisions: the minor renal calyx, with several others, drains into a larger major renal calyx, which in turn joins other major calyces to form the renal pelvis.

renal capsule, [L, *ren*, kidney, *capsula*, little box], the investing tissue around the kidney, divided into the fibrous renal capsule and the adipose renal capsule.

renal cast, a cast formed from gelled protein precipitated in the renal tubules and molded to the tubular lumen. Pieces of these casts break off and are washed out with the urine. In renal disease, casts may be seen containing RBCs or WBCs.

renal cell carcinoma, a malignant neoplasm of the kidney.

renal colic, sharp, severe pain in the lower back over the kidney, radiating forward into the groin. Renal colic usually accompanies forcible dilation of a ureter, followed by spasm as a stone is lodged or passed through it.

renal cortex, the highly vascularized granular outer layer of the kidney, containing approximately 1.25 million glomeruli and convoluted tubules that filter body wastes from the blood, reclaim useful materials, and dispose of the remainder as urine.

renal cortical necrosis, necrosis of the renal cortex caused by ischemia, often following acute tubular necrosis. It is usually seen as a complication of an obstetric condition such as abruptio placentae, septic abortion, preeclampsia, retained fetus, or amniotic fluid embolism.

renal dialysis [L, *ren*, kidney; Gk, *dia* + *lysis*, loosening], a process of diffusing blood across a semipermeable membrane to remove substances that a normal kidney would eliminate, including poisons, drugs, urea, uric acid, and creatinine. Renal dialysis may restore electrolytes and acid-base imbalances.

renal diet, a diet prescribed in chronic renal failure and designed to control intake of protein, potassium, sodium, phosphorus, and fluids, depending on individual conditions. Carbohydrates and fats are the principal sources of energy. Protein is limited; the amount is determined by the patient's condition and is usually supplied from milk, eggs, and meat.

renal dwarf, a dwarf in whom retardation of growth is caused by renal failure.

renal failure, inability of the kidneys to excrete wastes, concentrate urine, and conserve electrolytes. The condition may be acute or chronic. Acute renal failure is characterized by oliguria and by the rapid accumulation of nitrogenous wastes in the blood (azotemia). It results from hemorrhage, trauma, burn, toxic injury to the kidney, acute pyelonephritis or glomerulonephritis, or lower urinary tract obstruction. Chronic renal failure may result from many other diseases. The early signs include sluggishness, fatigue, and mental dullness. Later, anuria, convulsions, GI bleeding, malnutrition, and various neuropathies may occur. The skin may turn yellow-brown. CHF and hypertension are frequent complications, the results of hypervolemia.

renal failure index (RFI), an assessment of acute renal failure that compares the sodium clearance with the creatinine clearance. A value below 1.0 indicates renal failure because of prerenal azotemia, and a value above 2.0 suggests that it is caused by acute tubular necrosis.

renal fascia, a membranous condensation of extraperitoneal fascia that encloses the perirenal fat surrounding the kidney.

renal glycosuria [L, *ren,* kidney; Gk, *glykys,* sweet, *ouron,* urine], a familial condition characterized by lowered renal threshold to sugar. Blood glucose levels may be normal, although sugar is excreted in the urine.

renal hematuria [L, *ren,* kidney; Gk, *haima,* blood, *ouron,* urine], presence of blood in the urine because of a kidney disorder.

renal hypercalciuria, hypercalciuria caused by primary renal wasting of calcium, which stimulates production of parathyroid hormone to increase calcium resorption in the intestine. This type is not linked to formation of renal calculi.

renal hypertension, hypertension resulting from aortic or renal artery atherosclerosis or from kidney disease, including chronic glomerulonephritis, chronic pyelonephritis, renal carcinoma, and renal calculi. Untreated renal hypertension is likely to result in kidney damage and cardiovascular disease.

renal insufficiency [L, *ren,* kidney; *in + sufficere,* to suffice], partial kidney function failure characterized by less than normal urine excretion.

renal nanism, dwarfism associated with infantile renal osteodystrophy.

renal osteodystrophy, a condition resulting from chronic renal failure and characterized by uneven bone growth and demineralization.

renal parenchyma, the functional tissue of the kidney, consisting of the nephrons.

renal pelvis [L, *ren + pelvis,* basin], a funnel-shaped dilation that drains urine from the kidney into the ureter.

renal plasma flow (RPF), the amount of plasma that perfuses the kidneys per unit time. Approximately 90% of the total constitutes the *effective renal plasma flow;* the portion that perfuses functional renal tissue, such as the glomeruli.

renal pseudotumor, any mass in the kidney that is normal tissue but mimics something abnormal, such as in Bertin's column hypertrophy or a dromedary hump.

renal pyramid [L, *ren,* kidney; Gk, *pyramis*], any one of several conical masses of tissue that form the kidney medulla. The pyramids consist of the loops of Henle and the collecting tubules of the nephrons.

renal replacement lipomatosis, asymmetric fatty change in the kidney where renal parenchyma has become replaced by fatty tissue, such as with an infection or presence of a calculus. Symptoms include decreased renal function with inflammation, pain, pyuria, and sometimes pyelonephritis.

renal revascularization, surgical correction of occlusion of a renal artery.

renal rickets, a condition characterized by rachitic changes in the skeleton and caused by chronic nephritis.

renal scan, a radiographic scan of the kidneys performed after the IV injection of a radioactive substance. It is used to assess renal perfusion and function, particularly in renal failure and renovascular hypertension and after kidney transplantation.

renal sclerosis [L, *ren,* kidney; Gk, *skerosis,* hardening], arteriosclerosis or fibrosis of the arterioles of the kidney.

renal sinus cyst, a cyst in a renal sinus, usually derived from aberrant lymphatic vessels, occurring either alone or in groups. They may be asymptomatic or may expand to cause pelvic compression and local deformity with pain, hematuria, infection, and pyuria.

renal sinus lipomatosis, increased fat in the renal sinuses. A symmetric, usually asymptomatic, increase is seen in obesity, steroid therapy, and the atrophy that accompanies the aging process. An asymmetric increase known as *renal replacement lipomatosis,* which can have severe symptoms, occurs when infection destroys part of the renal parenchyma.

renal transplantation [L, *ren,* kidney *+ transplantare*], the surgical transfer of a complete kidney from a donor to a recipient.

renal tuberculosis, disease of the kidney caused by *Mycobacterium tuberculosis,* usually from bacillemia in cases

R

of pulmonary tuberculosis. Pathologic changes include granulomatous inflammation and caseous necrosis of kidney tissue.

renal tubular acidosis (RTA), an abnormal condition associated with persistent dehydration, metabolic acidosis, hypokalemia, hyperchloremia, and nephrocalcinosis. It is caused by the kidney's inability to conserve bicarbonate and to adequately acidify the urine. Common signs and symptoms of RTA, especially in children, include anorexia, vomiting, constipation, retarded growth, excessive urination, nephrocalcinosis, and rickets. RTA can also cause UTIs and pyelonephritis.

renal tubule [L, *ren*, kidney, *tubulus*, small tube], the part of the kidney's nephron that leads from the glomerulus to the collecting tubules. It consists of a looping segment and two convoluted sections. These canals resorb selected materials back into the blood and secrete, collect, and conduct urine.

renal vein renin assay, a blood test used to diagnose renovascular hypertension. It is very helpful in determining whether a stenosis seen on a renal angiogram is significantly contributing to hypertension.

Renese, a trademark for a thiazide diuretic (polythiazide).

renin /rē′nin/ [L, *ren*, kidney], a renal proteolytic enzyme, produced by and stored in the juxtaglomerular apparatus that surrounds each arteriole as it enters a glomerulus. The enzyme affects the BP by catalyzing the change of angiotensinogen to angiotensin I, which is then converted to angiotensin II, a strong pressor.

renin-angiotensin system, the regulation of sodium balance, fluid volume, and BP. In response to reduced perfusion, renin is secreted, which hydrolyzes a plasma globulin to release angiotensin I, which is rapidly hydrolyzed to angiotensin II, a powerful vasoconstrictor; angiotension II also stimulates aldosterone secretion, which causes sodium retention, an increase in BP, and restoration of renal perfusion, which shuts off the signal for renin release (negative feedback).

rennin /ren′in/ [ME, *rennen*, to run], a milk-curdling enzyme that occurs in the gastric juices of infants and is also contained in the rennet produced in the stomach of calves and other ruminants. It is an endopeptidase that converts casein to paracasein and was formerly used extensively as a curdling agent by the cheese industry.

renogram /rē′nəgram/, a radiographic image resulting from a renal scan.

renoprotective /re′no-pro-tek′tiv/, protecting the kidney against harmful effects, such as of a drug or other chemical.

Renshaw cells /ren′shô/ [B. Renshaw, American neurologist, b. 1911; L, *cella*, storeroom], small cells that reduce motor neuron discharge through a feedback circuit involving axon collaterals that excite interneurons. The system prevents rapid repeated firing of motor neurons.

ReoPro, a trademark for a preparation of an antithrombotic agent (abciximab).

reovirus /rē′ōvī′rəs/ [*respiratory enteric orphan*; L, *virus*], any one of three ubiquitous, double-stranded RNA viruses found in the respiratory and alimentary tracts in healthy and sick people. Reoviruses have been implicated in some cases of upper respiratory tract disease and infantile gastroenteritis.

repaglinide, an antidiabetic prescribed to treat stable type 2 DM.

repeat /rĕ-pēt′/, something done or occurring more than once, particularly over and over.

repercussion /rē′pərkush′ən/ [L, *repercussio*, rebounding], **1.** in obstetrics, ballottement. **2.** being driven back by a powerful resistance. **3.** the reduction of a swelling or tumor.

reperfusion /rē′pərfyōō′zhən/, the opening of blocked arteries to reestablish blood flow, either through thrombolytic therapy or percutaneous transluminal angioplasty.

repetition compulsion /rep′ətish′ən/ [L, *repetere*, to repeat], an unconscious need to revert to and repeat earlier situations, behavior patterns, and acts to experience previously felt emotions or relationships.

repetition time (TR), in magnetic resonance pulse sequences, the time interval before the basic pulse sequence is repeated.

repetitive stress injury /ripet′ətiv/, tissue damage associated with tasks that require repeated movements of the hands, legs, or trunk, such as meat cutting, computer keyboarding, or playing musical instruments. Effects include chronic nerve and joint pain, spine damage, and carpal tunnel syndrome. Among recommended preventive measures are frequent rest breaks and ergonomic improvements for the workplace.

replacement /riplās′mənt/ [Fr, *replacer*, to put in place again], the substitution of a missing part or substance with a similar structure or substance, such as the replacement of an amputated limb with a prosthesis or the replacement of lost blood with donor blood.

replacement therapy, 1. the use of a medicinal product to replace a natural hormone or enzyme that the body is no longer able to produce in sufficient amounts. **2.** a psychotherapeutic technique of replacing abnormal behavior with healthy, constructive activities.

replication /rep′likā′shən/ [L, *replicare,* to fold back], **1.** a process of duplicating, reproducing, or copying; literally, a folding back of a part to form a duplicate. **2.** in research, the exact repetition of an experiment performed to confirm the initial findings. **3.** in genetics, the duplication of the polynucleotide strands of DNA or the synthesis of DNA.—**replicate,** *v.*

replicator /rep′likā′tər/ [L, *replicare*], a segment of DNA that initiates and controls the replication of the molecule.

replicon /rep′lákon/ [L, *replicare*], a segment of DNA that is undergoing replication.

repolarization /rēpō′lərīzā′shən/ [L, *re* + *polus,* pole; Gk, *izein,* to cause], the process by which the membrane potential of a neuron or muscle cell is restored to the cell's resting potential. In a cardiac muscle cell, the repolarization process begins after phase 0 of the action potential and is completed by the end of phase 3. It encompasses the effective and relative refractory periods and correlates with the Q-T interval on the ECG.

report /ripôrt′/ [L, *re* + *portare,* to carry], in nursing, the transfer of information from the nurses on one shift to the nurses on the following shift or before the transfer of a patient from one unit to another. Report is given systematically at the time of change of shift.

reportable diseases /ripôr′təbəl/, diseases that must be reported by the health care provider to public health authorities, given their contagious nature. They include but are not limited to malaria, poliomyelitis, typhus, yellow fever, cholera, bubonic plague, STDs, and AIDS.

repositioning /rē′pəzish′əning/ [L, *reponere,* to put back], the restoration of an organ or body part to its natural position, as reposing an inverted uterus or changing the position of the jaws.

representative group /rep′rəsen′tətiv/, a group of individuals whose members represent all the various sectors of a community.

repression /ripresh′ən/ [L, *reprimere,* to press back], **1.** the act of restraining, inhibiting, or suppressing. **2.** in psychoanalysis, an unconscious defense mechanism whereby unacceptable thoughts, feelings, ideas, impulses, or memories, especially those concerning some traumatic past event, are pushed from the consciousness because of their painful guilt association or disagreeable content and are submerged in the unconscious, where they remain dormant but operant.—**repress,** *v.,* **repressive,** *adj.*

repressive-inspirational approach /ripres′iv/, a psychotherapeutic approach used in some groups to discourage the breaking down of defense mechanisms. Members are encouraged to focus on positive feelings and group strengths.

repressor /ripres′ər/ [L, *reprimere,* to press back], a protein produced by a regulator gene in a bacterial genome. It binds to a sequence of nucleotides in an operator gene, blocking the transcription of one or more structural genes.

reproduction /rē′prəduk′shən/ [L, *re* + *producere,* to produce], **1.** the sum of the cellular and genetic phenomena by which organisms produce offspring similar to themselves so that the species is perpetuated. **2.** the creation of a similar structure, situation, or phenomenon; duplication; replication. **3.** the recalling of a former idea or impression or of something previously learned.

reproductive /rē′prəduk′tiv/ [L, *re* + *producere,* to produce], pertaining to the process of reproduction.

reproductive endocrinology, the study of the maternal female hormone system, including the activities of the hypothalamus, pituitary, and ovaries from puberty through menopause.

reproductive system, the male and female gonads, associated ducts and glands, and external genitalia that function in the procreation of offspring. In women, these include the ovaries, fallopian tubes, uterus, vagina, clitoris, and vulva. In men, they include the testes, epididymis, vas deferens, seminal vesicles, ejaculatory duct, prostate, and penis.

reproductive technology management, a nursing intervention from the Nursing Interventions Classification (NIC) defined as assisting a patient through the steps of complex infertility treatment.

repulsion /ripul′shən/ [L, *repellere,* to drive away], **1.** the act of repelling, disjoining. **2.** a force that separates two bodies or things. **3.** in genetics, the situation in linked inheritance in which the alleles of two or more mutant genes are located on homologous chromosomes so that each chromosome of the pair carries one or more mutant and wild-type genes, which are located close enough to be inherited together.

request for proposal (RFP) /rikwest′/ [L, *requaerere,* to require, *propronere,* to propound], a solicitation by a funding agency for proposals to accomplish a particular goal. The RFP lists the requirements a project must meet to receive funding.

required arch length /rikwī′ərd/ [L, *requaerere,* to require], the sum of the mesiodistal widths of all the natural teeth in a dental arch. It represents the minimum arch length that can accommodate all of the teeth in the arch.

RES, abbreviation for **reticuloendothelial system.**

R

Rescriptor, a trademark for an antiretroviral nonnucleoside reverse transcriptase inhibitor (delaviridine).

Rescue Remedy, a trademark for a Bach remedy composed of the essences of five flowers (cherry plum, clematis, impatiens, rock rose, and star of Bethlehem) used for the acute treatment of stress.

research /risurch′, rē′surch/ [Fr, *rechercher,* to investigate], the diligent inquiry or examination of data, reports, and observations in a search for facts or principles.

research data collection, a nursing intervention from the Nursing Interventions Classification (NIC) defined as collecting research data.

research instrument, a testing device for measuring a given phenomenon, such as a paper and pencil test, a questionnaire, an interview, research tool, or a set of guidelines for observation.

research measurement, an evaluation of the quantity or incidence of a given variable as obtained by using a research instrument.

research radiopharmaceutical, a drug that is labeled with a small quantity of a radioactive tracer to allow its biodistribution to be studied; it may later be used in a nonradioactive form.

resection /risek′shən/, the cutting out of a significant part of an organ or structure. Resection of an organ may be partial or complete.

reserpine /res′ərpēn/, a depleter of biogenic amines (e.g., norepinephrine, dopamine) from nerve terminals. It is prescribed in the treatment of mild to moderate high BP and has unlabeled uses for tardive dyskinesia and certain neuropsychiatric disorders.

reserve /rizurv′/ [L, *reservare,* to save], a potential capacity to maintain vital body functions in homeostasis by adjusting to increased need, such as cardiac reserve, pulmonary reserve, and alkali reserve.

reserve capacity [L, *reservare,* to save; Gk, *aer*], the volume of air that can be exhaled with maximum effort after completion of a normal expiration.

reservoir /rez′ərvwär/ [Fr, réservoir], a chamber or receptacle for holding or storing a fluid.

reservoir bag, a component of an anesthesia machine in which gas accumulates, forming a reserve supply of gas for use during manual control of ventilation. It serves as a visible monitor of respiratory rate and depth.

reservoir host, a nonhuman host that serves as a means of sustaining an infectious organism as a potential source of human infection. Wild monkeys are reservoir hosts for the yellow fever virus.

reservoir of infection, a continuous source of infectious disease. People, animals, and plants may be reservoirs of infection.

resident /rez′idənt/ [L, *residere,* to remain], **1.** a physician in one of the postgraduate years of clinical training after the first, or internship, year. The length of residency varies according to the specialty. **2.** a person who receives inpatient care in a long-term care facility.

resident bacteria, bacteria living in a specific area of the body.

residential care facility /rez′iden′shəl/, a facility that provides custodial care to persons who, because of physical, mental, or emotional disorders, are not able to live independently.

residual /rizij′ oo·əl/ [L, *residuum,* remainder], **1.** pertaining to the part of something that remains after an activity that removes the bulk of the substance. **2.** in psychology, an aftereffect of an experience that influences latent behavior.

residual cyst, an odontogenic cyst that remains in the jaw after the removal of a tooth or by incomplete removal of all cystic material from the cystic area.

residual dental caries, any decayed material remaining in a prepared tooth cavity.

residual function [L, *residuum,* remainder, *functio,* performance], the remaining ability to function after a serious illness or injury.

residual limb, the portion of a limb remaining after an amputation.

residual ridge, the part of the alveolar ridge that remains after the alveolar process has disappeared after extraction of the teeth.

residual schizophrenia [L, *residuum*], a form of schizophrenia in which the essential features of delusions, hallucinations, incoherence, or gross disorganization are much less prominent.

residual urine, urine that remains in the bladder after urination.

residual volume (RV) /rez′id(y) oo/ [L, *residuum,* remainder, *volumen,* papyrus roll], the amount of air remaining in the lungs at the end of a maximum expiration.

residue-free diet /rez′id(y) oo/ [L, *residuum,* remainder; AS, *freo*; Gk, *diaita,* way of life], a diet free of nondigestible cellulose or fiber, such as found in semisolid bland food.

resilience /rizil′yəns/ [L, *resilere,* to spring back], **1.** a concept that proposes a recurrent human need to weather periods of stress and change successfully throughout life. The ability to weather each period of disruption and reintegration leaves the person better able to deal with the next change. **2.** the ability of a body to return to its original form after being stretched or compressed.

resiliency promotion, a nursing intervention from the Nursing Interventions Classification (NIC) defined as assisting individuals, families, and communities in development, use, and strengthening of protective factors to be used in coping with environmental and societal stressors.

resin /rez′in/ [L, *resina*], **1.** a mixture of carboxylic acids, essential oils, and terpenes (hydrocarbons of the formula $C_{10}H_{16}$), occurring as exudations on various trees and shrubs or produced synthetically. Most are soft and sticky but harden after exposure to cold. **2.** any of a variety of solid or semisolid amorphous substances that are insoluble in organic solvents but not in water. Orally administered bile acid–binding resins such as cholestyramine and colestipol interrupt the normal enterohepatic circulation of bile acids and increase their excretion in the stool.

res ipsa loquitur /räs′ ip′sə lok′witŏor/ [L, the thing speaks for itself], a legal concept that is important in many malpractice suits, describing a situation in which an injury occurred when the defendant was solely and exclusively in control and in which the injury would not have occurred had due care been exercised.

resistance /rizis′təns/ [L, *resistere,* to withstand], **1.** an opposition to a force, such as the resistance offered by the constriction of peripheral vessels to the blood flow in the circulatory system. **2.** the frictional force that opposes the flow of an electric charge, as measured in ohms. **3.** in respiratory therapy, the process or power of acting against a force placed on it, pertaining to thoracic resistance, tissue resistance, and airway resistance.

resistance form, the shape given to a prepared tooth cavity to impart strength and durability to the masticatory dislodging forces of a dental restoration and remaining tooth structure.

resistance-inducing factor (RIF), an agent that interferes with multiplication of a virus or other pathogen.

resistance to flow, the pressure differential required to produce a given rate of flow of a gas or liquid through a vessel.

resistance training, any method or form of strength training used to resist, overcome, or bear force.

resistance vessels, the blood vessels, including small arteries, arterioles, and metarterioles that form the major part of the total peripheral resistance to blood flow.

resistant /rizis′tənt/, pertaining to the ability of a microorganism to remain unaffected by an antimicrobial agent.

resistive magnet /resis′tiv/, a simple electromagnet in which electricity passing through coils of wire produces a magnetic field.

resocialization /rēsō′shəlīzā′shən/ [L, re + socialis, partners; Gk, izein, to cause], the reintegration of a client into family and community life after critical or long-term hospitalization.

resolution (R) [L, re + solvere, to solve], **1.** the state of having made a firm determination or decision on a course of action. **2.** the ability of an imaging process to distinguish adjacent structures in an object. It is an important measure of image quality. **3.** the ability of a chromatographic system to separate two adjacent peaks.

resolving power /rizol′ving/, **1.** the ability to separate closely migrating substances, as in electrophoresis. **2.** the ability to distinguish closely positioned objects as distinct entities.

resolving time, the minimum time between radiation-induced ionizations that can be detected by a Geiger-Müller-type scintillation device.

resonance [L, *vocalis* + *resonare,* to sound again], **1.** an echo or other sound produced by percussion of an organ or cavity of the body during a physical examination. **2.** the process of energy absorption by an object that is tuned to absorb energy of a specific frequency only. Other frequencies do not affect the object. **3.** modification of the laryngeal tone as it passes through the pharynx and oral cavity to produce an increase in the intensity and quality of the sound.—**resonant,** *adj.*

resonance frequency, **1.** in an ultrasound transducer, the frequency for which the response of a transducer to an ultrasound beam is a maximum. **2.** the frequency at which the transducer most efficiently converts electric signals to mechanical vibrations. **3.** in magnetic resonance, the frequency at which a nucleus absorbs radio energy when placed in a magnetic field.

resonant /rez′ənənt/ [L, *resonare,* to sound again], pertaining to a sound that vibrates on percussion or is amplified by sympathetic vibrations in another medium.

resonating /rez′ōnā′ting/ [L, *resonare,* to sound again], pertaining to vibrations or pulsations that are synchronous with a source of sound waves or electromagnetic oscillations.

resorb /risôrb′/ [L, *resorbere,* to swallow again], to absorb again.

resorbent /risôr′bənt/ [L, *resorbere*], a material or agent that is used to absorb blood or other substances.

resorcinated camphor /rizôr′sinā′tid/, a mixture of camphor and resorcinol, used for the treatment of pediculosis and itching.

R

resorcinol /rizôr′sinol/, an antiseptic substance used as a keratolytic agent in the dermatoses.

resorption /risôrp′shən/ [L, *resorbere,* to swallow again], **1.** the loss of substance or bone by physiologic or pathologic means. **2.** the cementoclastic and dentinoclastic action that may occur on a tooth root.

resource-based relative value scale (RBRVS), a system for a Medicare fee schedule designed to address the promise of compensation to a physician for the time involved in giving physical and mental status examinations and obtaining patient history from family members.

Respbid, a trademark for a smooth muscle relaxant (theophylline).

Res. Phys., abbreviation for *resident physician.*

respiration (R) /res′pirā′shən/ [L, *respirare,* to breathe], **1.** the molecular exchange of oxygen and carbon dioxide within the body's tissues. **2.** the process of moving air into and out of the lungs. The rate varies with the age and condition of the person.—**respiratory,** *adj.*

respiration of infants [L, *respirare,* to breathe, *infans,* unable to speak], a rate of breathing that averages 40 to 50 breaths per minute at birth and declines to 15 to 20 breaths per minute at puberty.

respiration rate [L, *respirare,* to breathe, *ratum,* rate], the rate of breathing. It is typically from 40 to 50 breaths per minute for newborns, 20 to 25 breaths per minute for older children, and 12 to 20 breaths per minute for teenagers and adults. The rate may be more rapid in fever, acute pulmonary infection, diffuse pulmonary fibrosis, gas gangrene, left ventricular failure, thyrotoxicosis, and states of tension. Slower breathing rates may result from head injury, coma, or narcotic overdose.

respirator /res′pirā′tər/ [L, *respirare*], an apparatus used to modify air for inspiration or to improve pulmonary ventilation. The term is commonly used to mean a ventilator.

respiratory, pertaining to respiration.

respiratory acidosis, an abnormal condition characterized by a low plasma pH resulting from reduced alveolar ventilation. Respiratory acidosis can result from disorders such as airway obstruction, medullary trauma, neuromuscular disease, chest injury, pneumonia, pulmonary edema, emphysema, and cardiopulmonary arrest. It may also be caused by the suppression of respiratory reflexes with narcotics, sedatives, hypnotics, or anesthetics. Some common signs and symptoms of respiratory acidosis are headache, dyspnea, fine tremors, tachycardia, hypertension, and vasodilation. Treatment seeks to remove or inhibit the underlying causes of associated hypoventilation. Any airway obstructions are immediately removed. Mechanical ventilation and oxygen therapy may be used, and IV bronchodilators and sodium bicarbonate may be administered. Ineffective treatment of acute respiratory acidosis can lead to coma and death.

respiratory alkalosis, an abnormal condition characterized by a high plasma pH resulting from increased alveolar ventilation. The hyperventilation may be caused by pulmonary problems such as acute asthma, pulmonary vascular disease, and pneumonia, or by nonpulmonary problems such as aspirin toxicity, anxiety, fever, metabolic acidosis, inflammation of the CNS, gram-negative septicemia, and hepatic failure. Deep and rapid breathing at rates as high as 40 breaths per minute is a major sign of respiratory alkalosis. Other symptoms are light-headedness, dizziness, peripheral paresthesia, tingling of the hands and feet, muscle weakness, tetany, and cardiac arrhythmia.

respiratory arrest, the cessation of breathing.

respiratory assessment, an evaluation of the condition and function of a person's respiratory system. Background information pertinent to the evaluation includes allergies, recent exposure to infection, immunizations, exposure to environmental irritants, previous respiratory disorders and operations, preexisting chronic conditions, medication currently taken, the person's smoking habits, and the family history. The person is asked if he or she coughs, wheezes, is short of breath, tires easily, or experiences chest or abdominal pain, chills, fever, excessive sweating, dizziness, or swelling of feet and hands. Signs of confusion; anxiety; restlessness; flaring nostrils; cyanotic lips, gums, ear lobes, or nails; clubbing of extremities; fever; anorexia; and a tendency to sit upright are noted if present. The person's breathing is closely observed for evidence of slow, rapid, irregular, shallow, or Cheyne-Stokes respiration; hyperventilation; and a long expiratory phase or periods of apnea, as well as for retractions in the suprasternal, supraclavicular, substernal, or intercostal areas during breathing. The presence of tachycardia, bradycardia, or sinus arrhythmia or evidence of CHF such as crackles, rhonchi, edema, hepatosplenomegaly, abdominal distension, or pain is recorded. The thorax is examined for scoliosis, kyphosis, funnel or barrel chest, or unequal shoulder height and is palpated for indications of thoracic expansion, tracheal deviation, crepitations, or fremitus. Percussion is performed to evaluate resonance, hyperresonance, tympany, and dull or flat sounds. Crackles, rhonchi, wheezing, friction rubs, the transmission of spoken words through the chest wall, and decreased or absent breath sounds are detected by auscultation. Valuable diagnostic aids include a chest x-ray examination; CBC; ECG; pulmonary function tests, and bronchoscopy; determination of blood gases and electrolytes; studies of sputum, throat, or nasopharyngeal cultures; and gastric washings, lung scans, and biopsies.

respiratory burn, tissue damage to the respiratory system resulting from the inhalation of a hot gas or burning particles, as may occur in a fire or explosion.

respiratory care practitioner, a health professional with special training and experience in the treatment and rehabilitation of patients with respiratory disorders. The respiratory care practitioner typically does not diagnose but must be competent with patient assessment in a variety of clinical settings.

respiratory center, a group of nerve cells in the pons and medulla of the brain that controls the rhythm of breathing in response to changes in levels of oxygen, carbon dioxide, and hydrogen ions in the blood and CSF. Such changes activate central and peripheral chemoreceptors, which send impulses to the respiratory center, triggering an increase or a decrease in the breathing rate.

respiratory component (αPCO_2), the acid component of an acid-base control system that is modified by the respiratory status.

respiratory depressant [L, *respirare,* to breathe, *depremere,* to press down], a drug or other agent that diminishes normal breathing functions. Most respiratory depressants, such as alcohol and opiates, act by depressing the CNS.

respiratory depression [L, *respirare,* to breathe, *depremere,* to press down], respiration that has a rate below 12 breaths per minute or that fails to provide full ventilation and perfusion of the lungs.

respiratory distress syndrome of the newborn (RDS), an acute lung disease of the newborn, occurring most often in premature infants, characterized by airless alveoli, inelastic lungs, a respiration rate greater than 60 breaths per minute, nasal flaring, intercostal and subcostal retractions, grunting on expiration, and peripheral edema. It is caused by a deficiency of pulmonary surfactant, resulting in overdistended alveoli and at times hyaline membrane formation, alveolar hemorrhage, severe right-to-left shunting of blood, increased pulmonary resistance, decreased cardiac output, and severe hypoxemia. Signs and symptoms usually appear within 6 hours of birth. Possible complications include intraventricular hemorrhage, tension pneumothorax, retinopathy of prematurity, bronchopulmonary dysplasia, apnea, patent ductus arteriosus, CHF, neurologic sequelae, necrotizing enterocolitis, pneumonia, sepsis, and/or death.

respiratory diverticulum, a pouchlike evagination from the foregut that gives rise to the trachea, bronchi, and the branches that form the tracheobronchial tree.

respiratory exchange ratio (R), the ratio of the amount of carbon dioxide produced to the amount of oxygen consumed or taken up.

respiratory failure, the inability of the cardiovascular and pulmonary systems to maintain an adequate exchange of oxygen and carbon dioxide in the lungs. Respiratory failure may be caused by a failure in oxygenation or in ventilation. Oxygenation failure is characterized by refractory hypoxemia and occurs in diseases that affect the alveoli or interstitial tissues of the lungs. Ventilatory failure, characterized by increased arterial tension of carbon dioxide, occurs in acute conditions in which retained pulmonary secretions cause increased airway resistance and decreased lung compliance. Respiratory failure in preexisting chronic lung diseases may be precipitated by added stress, as with cardiac failure, surgery, anesthesia, or upper respiratory tract infections. Treatment of respiratory failure includes clearing the airways by suction, bronchodilators, or tracheostomy or endotracheal tube with ventilator support; antibiotics for infections that are usually present; anticoagulants for pulmonary thromboemboli; and electrolyte replacement in fluid imbalance. Oxygen may be administered in some cases; in others it may further decrease the respiratory reflex by removing the stimulus of a decreased level of oxygen.

respiratory insufficiency, a failure of the respiratory system to maintain adequate ventilation and perfusion of the lungs.

respiratory monitoring, a nursing intervention from the Nursing Interventions Classification (NIC) defined as collection and analysis of patient data to ensure airway patency and adequate gas exchange.

respiratory muscles, the muscles that produce volume changes of the thorax during breathing. The inspiratory muscles include the hemidiaphragms, external intercostals, scaleni, sternomastoids, trapezius, pectoralis major, pectoralis minor, subclavius, latissimus dorsi, serratus anterior, and muscles that extend the back. The expiratory muscles are the internal intercostals, the abdominals, and the muscles that flex the back.

respiratory quotient (RQ), the ratio of the volume of carbon dioxide produced to the volume of oxygen consumed per unit of time by the body under steady-state conditions.

respiratory rhythm, a regular, oscillating cycle of inspiration and expiration, controlled by neuronal impulses transmitted between the respiratory centers in the brain and the muscles of inspiration in the chest and diaphragm.

respiratory standstill, the cessation of respiratory movements.

respiratory status, a nursing outcome from the Nursing Outcomes Classification (NOC) defined as movement of air in and out of the lungs and exchange of carbon dioxide and oxygen at the alveolar level.

respiratory status: airway patency, a nursing outcome from the Nursing Outcomes Classification (NOC) defined as open, clear tracheobronchial passages for air exchange.

respiratory status: gas exchange, a nursing outcome from the Nursing Outcomes Classification (NOC) defined as alveolar exchange of carbon dioxide and oxygen to maintain arterial blood gas concentrations.

respiratory status: ventilation, a nursing outcome from the Nursing Outcomes Classification (NOC) defined as movement of air in and out of the lungs.

respiratory syncytial virus (RSV, RS virus), a member of a subgroup of myxoviruses that in tissue culture cause formation of giant cells or syncytia. It is a common cause of epidemics of acute bronchiolitis, bronchopneumonia, and the common cold in young children and sporadic acute bronchitis and mild upper respiratory tract infections in adults. Symptoms of infection with this virus include fever, cough, and severe malaise. Treatment includes rest, high humidity, and adequate fluid intake, and, in severe cases, oxygen and ribavirin aerosol.

respiratory syncytial virus immune globulin (RSV-IGIV), an immune serum used in children less than 2 years of age with bronchopulmonary dysplasia or in those born prematurely to prevent serious lower respiratory tract infection caused by respiratory syncytial virus.

respiratory syncytial virus immune globulin intravenous, a preparation of IgG from pooled adult human plasma selected for high titers of antibodies against respiratory syncytial virus. It is used for passive immunization of infants and children less than 24 months of age.

respiratory therapist, a graduate of a program approved by the Commission on Accreditation of Allied Health Education Programs designed to qualify the person for the registry examination of the National Board for Respiratory Care.

respiratory therapy (RT), 1. any treatment that maintains or improves the ventilatory function of the respiratory tract. 2. *informal.* the department in a health care facility that provides respiratory therapy for the patients of the facility.

respiratory therapy technician, a graduate of a program approved by the Commission on Accreditation of Allied Health Education Programs, designed to qualify the person for the technician certification examination of the National Board for Respiratory Care. The program requires a special curriculum of basic sciences with supervised clinical experience.

respiratory therapy technician, certified (CRTT), an allied health professional who administers general respiratory care. Duties can include collection and review of clinical data; examination of the patient by inspection, palpation, percussion, and auscultation; and assembling and maintaining equipment used in respiratory care.

respiratory tract, the complex of organs and structures that performs the pulmonary ventilation of the body and the exchange of oxygen and carbon dioxide between ambient air and blood circulating through the lungs. It also warms the air passing into the body and assists in the speech function by providing air for the larynx and the vocal cords.

respiratory tract infection, any infectious disease of the upper or lower respiratory tract. URIs include the common cold, laryngitis, pharyngitis, rhinitis, sinusitis, and tonsillitis. Lower respiratory tract infections include bronchitis, bronchiolitis, pneumonia, and tracheitis.

respiratory zone, the air sacs where gas exchange actually occurs in the lungs, usually below the seventeenth division of bronchi.

respirometer /res′pirom′ətər/ [L, *respirare*, to breathe; Gk, *metron*, measure], an instrument used to analyze the quality of a patient's respirations.

respite care[1] /res′pit/ [L, *respicere*, to look back], 1. short-term health services to the dependent older adult, either at home or in an institutional setting. 2. the provision of temporary care for a patient who requires specialized or intensive care or supervision that is normally provided by his or her family at home, providing the family with relief from demands of the patient's care.

respite care[2], a nursing intervention from the Nursing Interventions Classification (NIC) defined as provision of short-term care to provide relief for family caregiver.

respite time /res′pit/, relief time from responsibilities for the care of a patient, an individual, or a family member.

respondeat superior /respon′dē·at/ [L, let the master answer], the concept that an employer may be held liable for torts committed by employees acting within the scope of their employment.

responder /rispon′dər/ [L, *respondere,* to promise in return], a person whose tumor shrinks in volume by at least 50% as a result of chemotherapy, radiation, or other treatment.

response /rispons′/ [L, *responsum,* reply], **1.** a reaction of an organism to a stimulus. **2.** in psychology, a category of negative punishment in which the reinforcer is lost or withdrawn after an operant.

response time, the period between the application of a stimulus and the response of a cell or cells.

rest¹ [AS, *restan,* to rest], an extension from a prosthesis that provides vertical support for a dental restoration.

rest², a nursing outcome from the Nursing Outcomes Classification (NOC) defined as quantity and pattern of diminished activity for mental and physical rejuvenation.

rest area, a prepared surface on a tooth or fixed restoration into which an arm or a removable partial denture fits.

resting cell, a cell that is not undergoing division.

resting membrane potential, the transmembrane voltage that exists when a neuron or muscle cell is not producing an action potential.

resting potential [AS, *rest;* L, *potentia,* power], the electric potential across a nerve cell membrane before it is stimulated to release the charge. The resting potential for a neuron is between 50 and 100 mV, with the excess of negatively charged ions inside the cell membrane.

resting tremor, an involuntary tremor occurring when the person is at rest; It is one of the signs of Parkinson's disease.

restitution /res′tit(y)oo͞o′shən/, the spontaneous turning of the fetal head to the right or left after it has extended through the vulva.

rest jaw relation, the postural relation of the mandible to the maxilla when the patient is resting comfortably in the upright position.

rest joint position, the position of a joint where the joint surfaces are relatively incongruent and the support structures are relatively lax. The position is used extensively in passive mobilization procedures.

restless legs syndrome [AS, *restlaes;* ONorse, *leggr*], a benign condition of unknown origin characterized by an irritating sensation of uneasiness, tiredness, and itching deep within the muscles of the leg, especially the lower part of the limb, accompanied by twitching and sometimes pain. The only relief is walking or moving the legs.

restoration /res′tôrā′shən/ [L, *restaurare,* to restore], any tooth filling, inlay, crown, partial or complete denture, or prosthesis that restores or replaces missing tooth structure, entire teeth, or oral tissues.

restoration contour, the profile of the surfaces of teeth that have been restored.

restoration of cusps, a reduction and inclusion of tooth cusps within a tooth cavity preparation and their restoration to functional occlusion with an artificial dental material.

restorative /ristôr′ətiv/ [L, *restaurare*], pertaining to the power or ability to restore or renew a person to a normal state of health or consciousness.

Restoril, a trademark for a hypnotic agent (temazepam).

restraint /ristrānt′/ [L, *restringere,* to confine], any one of numerous mechanical devices or chemical agents used to hinder or restrict a patient's movement. Examples of mechanical restraints are specially designed slings, jackets, or diapers.

restraint in bed [L, *restringere,* to confine; AS, *bedd*], the confinement of a person to bed rest by the use of mechanical, physical, or chemical means, if needed.

restraint of trade, an illegal act that interferes with free competition in a commercial or business transaction so as to restrict the production of a product or the provision of a service, affect the cost of a product or a service, or control the market in any way to the detriment of the consumers or purchasers of the service or product.

restriction endonuclease /ristrik′shən en′dōnoo͞o′klē·ās/ [L, *restringere*; Gk, *endon,* within; L, *nucleus,* nut kernel; Fr, *diastase,* enzyme], an enzyme that cleaves DNA at a specific site. Each of the many endonucleases isolated from various bacteria acts at a different site.

restriction fragment, a fragment of DNA produced by cleavage by a specific endonuclease.

restriction fragment length polymorphism (RFLP), a difference in the DNA sequences of homologous chromosomes as revealed by different lengths of the restriction fragments produced by enzymatic digestion of a selected region of chromosomes. RFLPs are believed to be inherited according to mendelian laws and have been used to locate the genes associated with several inherited disorders, including Huntington's disease.

restrictive cardiomyopathy, a form of heart disease characterized by diastolic noncompliance or poor compliance of the ventricles, as in constrictive pericarditis.

restrictive disease, a respiratory disorder characterized by restriction of expansion of the lungs or chest wall, resulting in diminished lung volumes and capacities.

resuscitation[1] /risus′itā′shən/ [L, *resuscitare,* to revive], the process of sustaining the vital functions of a person in respiratory or cardiac failure while reviving him or her, using techniques of artificial respiration and cardiac massage, correcting acid-base imbalance, and treating the cause of failure.—**resuscitate,** *v.*

resuscitation[2], a nursing intervention from the Nursing Interventions Classification (NIC) defined as administering emergency measures to sustain life.

resuscitation: fetus, a nursing intervention from the Nursing Interventions Classification (NIC) defined as administering emergency measures to improve placental perfusion or correct fetal acid-base status.

resuscitation: neonate, a nursing intervention from the Nursing Interventions Classification (NIC) defined as administering emergency measures to support newborn adaptation to extrauterine life.

resuscitator /risus′itā′tər/, an apparatus for pumping air into the lungs. It consists of a mask snugly applied over the mouth and nose, a reservoir for air, and a manually or electrically powered pump.

RET, abbreviation for **rational emotive therapy.**

retail dentistry /rē′tāl/ [ME, *retailen,* to divide into pieces], the practice of fee-for-service dentistry in an exclusively retail environment, such as a shopping center or a department store, with the specific intention of attracting the customers of that retail environment and by using the marketing techniques of the retailers involved.

retained placenta /ritānd′/ [L, *retinere,* to hold, *placenta,* flat cake], the failure of the placenta to be delivered during an appropriate period, usually 30 minutes, following birth of the infant.

retainer [L, *retinere,* to hold], **1.** the part of a dental prosthesis that connects an abutment tooth with the suspended part of a bridge. It may be an inlay, a partial crown, or a complete crown. **2.** an appliance for maintaining teeth and jaw positions gained by orthodontic procedures. **3.** the part of a fixed prosthesis that attaches a pontic to the abutment teeth. **4.** any clasp, attachment, or device for fixing or stabilizing a dental prosthesis.

retake /rē′tāk/, the repeat of a radiograph because of inadequate technical quality, patient motion, mispositioning of the body part, or equipment malfunction.

retardation /rē′tärdā′shən/ [L, *retardare,* to check], the slowing down of any mental or physical activity or failure of intellectual abilities to develop normally, as in mental retardation. Psychomotor retardation may occur in depression, and a conditioned response to an unconditioned stimulus may be retarded in appearance.

retarded /ritär′did/ [L, *retardare,* to check], of physical, intellectual, social, or emotional development, abnormally slow.—**retard** /ritärd′/, *v.*

retarded dentition, an abnormal delay in the eruption of the deciduous or secondary teeth resulting from malnutrition, malposition of the teeth, a hereditary factor, or a metabolic imbalance such as hypothyroidism.

retarded depression, the depressive phase of bipolar disorder.

retarded ejaculation, the inability of a male to ejaculate after having achieved an erection. This often accompanies the aging process.

retch [AS, *hraecan,* to spit], a strong, wrenching attempt to vomit that does not bring up anything.

rete /rē′tē/ [L, net], a network, especially of arteries or veins.—**retial** /rē′tē·əl/, *adj.*

retention /riten′shən/, **1.** a resistance to movement or displacement. **2.** the ability of the digestive system to hold food and fluid. **3.** the inability to urinate or defecate. **4.** the ability of the mind to remember information acquired from reading, observation, or other processes. **5.** the inherent property of a dental restoration to maintain its position without displacement under axial stress. **6.** a characteristic of proper tooth cavity preparation in which provision is made for preventing vertical displacement of the cavity filling. **7.** a period of treatment during which an individual wears an appliance to maintain teeth in positions to which they have been moved by orthodontic procedures.—**retain,** *v.*

retention cyst [L, *retinere,* to hold; Gk, *kystis,* bag], a cyst caused by blockage of the excretory duct of a gland so that glandular secretions are retained.

retention enema [L, *retinere,* to hold; Gk, *enienai,* to send in], a medicinal or nutrient enema specially formulated so that it will remain in the bowel without stimulating the nerve endings that would ordinarily result in evacuation.

retention form, the provision made in a prepared tooth cavity to hold in place a restoration and to prevent its displacement.

retention groove, a depression formed by the opposing vertical constrictions in a prepared tooth cavity, which improves the holding ability of a restoration.

retention of urine, an abnormal, involuntary accumulation of urine in the bladder as a result of a loss of muscle tone in the bladder, neurologic dysfunction or damage to the bladder, obstruction of the urethra, or administration of a narcotic analgesic.

retention pin, a small metal pin that extends from a metal casting into the dentin of a tooth to improve the holding ability of a tooth restoration.

retention procedure, a method established by state laws or mental health codes for committing a person to a psychiatric institution. Most states recognize four types of retention: emergency, informal, involuntary, and voluntary admission.

retention time (t$_a$), 1. in chromatography, the amount of time elapsed from the injection of a sample into the chromatographic system to the recording of the peak (band) maximum of the component in the chromatogram. 2. the length of time a compound is retained on a chromatography column.

retention with overflow [L, *retinere*, to hold; AS, *ofer* + *flowan*], a complication of bladder outlet obstruction in which the bladder is full but is not emptied completely. Urine dribbles out with a sense of urgency, or uncontrollable intermittent leakage occurs.

reteplase /ret′əplās/, a recombinant form of tissue plasminogen activator. It is used as a thrombolytic agent in treatment of MI.

reticular /ritik′yələr/ [L, *reticulum*, little net], of a tissue or surface, having a netlike pattern or structure.

reticular activating system (RAS), a functional system in the brain essential for wakefulness, attention, concentration, and introspection. A network of nerve fibers in the thalamus, hypothalamus, brainstem, and cerebral cortex contributes to the system.

reticular formation, a small, thick cluster of neurons nestled within the brainstem, including the medulla that controls the LOC and other vital functions of the body. The reticular formation constantly monitors the state of the body through connections with the sensory and motor tracts.

reticular membrane, a netlike membrane over the organ of Corti; the free ends of the outer acoustic hair cells pass through its apertures.

reticular nuclei, nuclei found in the reticular formation of the brainstem, primarily in longitudinal columns in three groups: the median column reticular nuclei, the medial column reticular nuclei, and the lateral column reticular nuclei. The term also encompasses several other nuclei that are not in any of the three columns, such as the reticular nucleus of the thalamus.

reticulation film fault /ritik′yəlā′shən/ [L, *reticulum* + *atio,* process], a defect in a radiograph or photograph that appears as a network of corrugations. It is usually caused during film development by an excessive temperature difference between any two of the three darkroom solutions.

reticulin /ritik′yəlin/ [L, *reticulum*], an albuminoid substance found in the connective fibers of reticular tissue.

reticulocyte /ritik′yələsīt′/ [L, *reticulum*; + Gk, *kytos*, cell], an immature erythrocyte characterized by a meshlike pattern of nucleic acids when stained using new methylene blue dye.

reticulocyte count, a count of the number of reticulocytes in a whole blood specimen, used in determining bone marrow activity. The reticulocyte count is lowered in hemolytic diseases and chronic infection; it is elevated after hemorrhage or during recovery from anemia.

reticulocytopenia /ritik′yəlōsī′təpē′nē·ə/ [L, *reticulum*; Gk, *kytos*, cell, *penia,* poverty], a decrease below the reference interval lower limit of 0.5% in the number of reticulocytes in a blood sample.

reticulocytosis /-sītō′sis/, an increase over the reference interval upper limit of 2.0% in the number of reticulocytes in the circulating blood that may represent a normal increase in activity of the bone marrow in response to blood loss.

reticuloendothelial cells /ritik′yəlō·en·dōthē′lē·əl/ [L, *reticulum*; Gk, *endon*, within, *thele,* nipple], albuminoid or scleroprotein cells lining vascular and lymph vessels and capable of phagocytosing bacteria, viruses, and colloidal particles or of forming immune bodies against foreign particles.

reticuloendothelial system (RES), a functional rather than anatomic system of the body involved primarily in defense against infection and in disposal of the products of the breakdown of cells. It is made up of macrophages; the Kupffer cells of the liver; and the reticulum cells of the lungs, bone marrow, spleen, and lymph nodes.

reticuloendothelioma /-thē′lē·ō′mə/, a tumor consisting of cells of the reticuloendothelial system.

reticuloendotheliosis /ritik′yəlō·en·dōthē′lē·ō′sis/, an abnormal condition characterized by increased growth and proliferation of the cells of the reticuloendothelial system.

reticulogranular /-gran′yələr/ [L, *reticulum* + *granulum,* little grain], pertaining to a cloudy appearance of the lungs on a chest radiograph of a patient with respiratory distress syndrome.

retina /ret′inə/ [L, *rete*, net], a 10-layered, delicate nervous tissue membrane of the eye, continuous with the optic nerve, that receives images of external objects and transmits visual impulses through the optic nerve to the brain. It consists of the outer pigmented layer and the nine-layered retina proper. These

R

nine layers, starting with the most internal, are the internal limiting membrane, the stratum opticum, the ganglion cell layer, the inner plexiform layer, the inner nuclear layer, the outer plexiform layer, the outer nuclear layer, the external limiting membrane, and the layer of rods and cones. The outer surface of the retina is in contact with the choroid; the inner surface with the vitreous body.

Retin-A, a trademark for an antiacne medication (tretinoin).

retinaculum /ret'inak'yələm/, pl. **retinacula** [L, halter], **1.** a structure that retains an organ or tissue. **2.** an instrument for retracting tissues during surgery.

retinal /ret'inəl, ret'inal'/ [L, rete], **1.** an aldehyde precursor of vitamin A produced by the enzymatic dehydration of retinol. **2.** pertaining to the retina.

retinal detachment, a separation of the retina from the retinal pigment epithelium in the back of the eye. It usually results from a hole or tear in the retina that allows the vitreous humor to leak between the choroid and the retina. In most cases, retinal detachment develops slowly. The first symptom is often the sudden appearance of a large number of floating spots loosely suspended in front of the affected eye. The person may not seek help because the number of spots tends to decrease during the days and weeks after the detachment. The person may also notice a curious sensation of flashing lights as the eye is moved. Because the retina does not contain sensory nerves that relay sensations of pain, the condition is painless. If the process of detachment is not halted, total blindness of the eye ultimately results. Surgery is usually required to repair the hole and prevent leakage of vitreous humor that separates the retina from its source of nourishment, the choroid.

retinal fissure, a ventral groove formed by invagination of the optic cup and its stalk by vascular mesenchyme from which the hyaloid vessels develop.

retinene /ret'inin/ [L, rete], either of the two carotenoid pigments found in the rods of the retina that are precursors of vitamin A and are activated by light.

retinitis /ret'ini'tis/ [L, rete, net; Gk, itis, inflammation], an inflammation of the retina.

retinitis pigmentosa [L, rete, net; Gk, itis, inflammation; L, pigmentum, paint], a group of diseases, often hereditary, characterized by bilateral primary degeneration of the retina, beginning in childhood and progressing to blindness by middle age. Clinical signs include night blindness, reduced visual fields, depigmentation of the retinal pigment epithelium, and macular degeneration.

retinoblastoma /ret'inōblastō'mə/ pl. **retinoblastomas, retinoblastomata** [L, rete; Gk, blastos, germ, oma, tumor], a congenital hereditary neoplasm developing from retinal germ cells. Characteristic signs are diminished vision, strabismus, retinal detachment, and an abnormal pupillary reflex. The rapidly growing tumor may invade the brain and metastasize to distant sites. Treatment includes removal of the eye and as much of the optic nerve as possible, followed by radiation and chemotherapy.

retinochoroiditis /-kôr'oidī'tis/ [L, rete, net; Gk, chorion, skin, itis, inflammation], an inflammation of the retina and choroid coat of the eye.

retinodialysis /ret'inō'dī·al'isis/ [L, rete; Gk, dia, through, lysis, loosening], a separation or tear in the retina in its anterior part, in the area of the ora serrata, just behind the ciliary body.

retinoid /ret'inoid/ [L, rete, net; Gk, eidos, form], **1.** resembling the retina. **2.** pertaining to any of a group of compounds whose molecules contain 20 carbon atoms structurally related to retinal, retinol, and other substances, some of which exhibit vitamin A activity. **3.** resinlike or having a resemblance to resin.

retinol /ret'inol/ [L, rete], one form of vitamin A. It is found in the retinas of mammals.

retinol equivalent (RE), a unit used for quantifying the vitamin A value of sources of vitamin A, both including preformed retinoids in animal foods and precursor carotenoids in plant foods. RE is defined as 3.3 International Units of vitamin A.

retinopathy /ret'inop'əthē/ [L, rete; Gk, pathos, disease], a group of noninflammatory eye disorders. Major contributing conditions include diabetes, hypertension, and atherosclerotic vascular disease.

retinopexy /ret'inopek'se/, restoring of the retina to its proper anatomic location.

retinoschisis /ret'inos'kisis/ [L, rete, net, schisis, cleavage], splitting of the retina: in the juvenile form the splitting occurs in the nerve fiber layer (stratum opticum), and in the adult form in the outer plexiform layer. The disorder is usually more benign and slowly progressive than retinal detachment.

retinoscope /ret'inəskōp'/ [L, rete, net, Gk, skopein, to view], an instrument used in retinoscopy to determine errors of refraction.

retinoscopy /ret'inos'kəpē/ [L, rete, net; Gk, skopein, to view], a procedure for examining the eyes for possible errors of refraction. The examiner shines a light into the eye through the pupillary opening and notes the movements of reflex from the fundus, which will vary with the type of refractive error.

retirement center /ritī′ərmənt/ [Fr, *retirer,* to withdraw; Gk, *kentron,* center], a facility or organized program to provide social services and activities for senior citizens who generally do not require ongoing health care.

retract /ritrakt′/ [L, *retractare,* to draw back], to shrink, make shorter, or pull back.

retracted nipple [L, *retractare,* to draw back; ME, *neb*], a nipple drawn inward, resulting from cancer or adhesions below the skin surface or a natural condition present at birth.

retractile mesenteritis /rē′trak′til/ [L, *retractare,* to draw back; Gk, *mesos,* middle; *enteron,* intestine; *itis,* inflammation], inflammation of the mesentery producing thickening, sclerosis, and retraction and occasionally resulting in distortion of intestinal loops.

retraction /ritrak′shən/ [L, *retractare,* to draw back], **1.** the displacement of tissues to expose a part or structure of the body. **2.** a distal movement of the teeth. **3.** a distal or retrusive position of the teeth, dental arch, or jaw.

retraction of the chest, the visible sinking in of the soft tissues of the chest between and around the firmer tissue of the cartilaginous and bony ribs, as occurs with increased inspiratory effort or obstruction at some level of the respiratory tract.

retractor /ritrak′tər/ [L, *retractare*], an instrument for holding back the edges of tissues and organs to maintain exposure of the underlying anatomic parts, particularly during surgery.

retroanterograde amnesia /ret′rō·anter′ō grād/ [L, *retro,* backward, *antero,* foremost; *gradus,* step; Gk, *amnesia,* forgetfulness], a memory disorder in which current events may be assigned to the past and past events may be regarded as current.

retroaortic node /ret′rō·ā·ôr′tik/ [L, *retro,* backward; Gk, *aerein,* to raise], a node in one of three sets of lumbar lymph nodes that serve various structures in the abdomen and pelvis.

retroauricular /ret′rō·ôrik′yələr/ [L, *retro,* backward, *auricula,* little ear], pertaining to a location behind the ear.

retrobulbar /-bul′bər/ [L, *retro,* backward, *bulbus,* swollen root], **1.** pertaining to the area behind the pons (posterior to the medulla oblongata). **2.** pertaining to the area behind the eyeball.

retrobulbar block, a block performed by injection of a local anesthetic into the retrobulbar space to anesthetize and immobilize the eye.

retrobulbar neuritis [L, *retro,* backward, *bulbus,* swollen root; Gk, *neuron + itis,* inflammation], a form of neuritis that involves the optic nerve or the optic disc.

retrobulbar pupillary reflex, an abnormal response of a pupil to light. After initial constriction of the pupil, dilation occurs as the stimulus continues. It is a sign of retrobulbar neuritis.

retrocalcaneal space, the space between the posterior calcaneus and the calcaneal tendon, occupied by the calcaneal bursa.

retrocecal /-sē′kəl/ [L, *retro,* backward, *caecus,* blind], pertaining to the region behind the cecum.

retroclusion /ret′rōkloo′zhən/, a method of controlling hemorrhage from an artery by compressing it between tissues on either side. A needle is inserted through the tissues above the bleeding vessel, then turned around and down so that it also passes through the tissues beneath the artery.

retrofilling /ret′rōfil′ing/, a method of root canal therapy in which the canal is filled from the apex, which has been surgically exposed.

retroflexion /-flek′shən/ [L, *retro + flectere,* to bend], an abnormal position of an organ in which the organ is tilted back acutely and folded over on itself.

retroflexion of the uterus, a condition in which the body of the uterus is bent backward at an angle with the cervix, whose position usually remains unchanged.

retrognathia /ret′rōnā′thē·ə/ [L, *retro,* backward; Gk, *gnathos,* jaw], a condition in which either or both jaws recede with respect to the frontal plane of the forehead.

retrognathism /ret′rōnā′thizəm/ [L, *retro*; Gk, *gnathos,* jaw], a facial abnormality in which a jaw, usually the mandible, or both jaws are posterior to their normal facial positions.

retrograde /ret′rəgrād/ [L, *retro + gradus,* step], **1.** moving backward; moving in the opposite direction to that which is considered normal. **2.** degenerating; reverting to an earlier state or worse condition. **3.** catabolic.

retrograde amnesia, the loss of memory for events occurring before a particular time in a person's life, usually before the event that precipitated the amnesia.

retrograde cystoscopy, a technique for radiographically examining the bladder in which a catheter is inserted through the urethra into the bladder. A radiopaque medium is introduced, filling the bladder, and the contour of the bladder is observed, using serial x-ray films or fluoroscopy.

retrograde ejaculation [L, *retro,* backward, *gradus,* step, *ejaculari,* to throw out], an ejaculation of semen in a reverse direction into the urinary bladder. It may result from surgery or medication.

retrograde filling, a restoration placed in the apical part of a tooth root to seal the apex of a previously treated root canal.

R

retrograde flow [L, *retro,* backward; AS, *flowan*], the flow of fluid in a direction other than normal, as in regurgitation.

retrograde infection, an infection that spreads along a tubule or duct against the flow of secretions or excretions, as in the urinary and lymphatic systems.

retrograde menstruation, a backflow of menstrual discharge through the uterine cavity and fallopian tubes into the peritoneal cavity.

retrograde pyelography, a radiologic technique for examining the structures of the collecting system of the kidneys that is especially useful in locating a urinary tract obstruction. A radiopaque contrast medium is injected through a urinary catheter into the ureters and the calyces of the pelves of the kidneys.

retrograde urethrography, radiographic examination of the urethra after suspicion of obstruction of its external orifice and injection of contrast material that travels in a retrograde direction toward the bladder. It is used for evaluation of strictures, diverticula, and trauma.

retrograde Wenckebach /veng′kəbäk, -bäk/ [Karel F. Wenckebach, Dutch-Austrian physician, 1864–1940], a delay in the conduction of impulses from the ventricles or atrioventricular junction to the atria. The delay increases progressively until an impulse fails to reach the atria.

retrogression /-gresh′ən/ [L, *retro* + *gradi,* to step], a return to a less complex state, condition, or behavioral adaptation; degeneration; deterioration.

retroinguinal space, the subdivision of the extraperitoneal space bounded by the peritoneum above and the fascia transversalis below.

retrolental fibroplasia /-len′təl/ [L, *retro* + *lentil,* lens, *fibra,* fiber; Gk, *plassein,* to mold], **1.** a formation of fibrous tissue behind the lens of the eye, resulting in blindness. **2.** a severe form of retinopathy in premature infants associated with complete retinal detachment. It can be prevented by timely administration of retinal laser therapy.

retromammary space, a layer of loose connective tissue separating the breast from the deep fascia, providing some degree of movement over underlying surfaces.

retromolar pad /-mō′lər/ [L, *retro* + *mola,* mill; D, *paden,* cushion], a mass of soft tissue, usually pear-shaped, that marks the distal termination of the mandibular residual ridge.

retromylohyoid space /ret′rōmī′lōhī′oid/ [L, *retro*; Gk, *myle,* mill, *hyoeides,* U-shaped; L, *spatium*], the part of the alveolingual sulcus that is distal to the distal end of the mylohyoid ridge.

retroperitoneal /-per′itənē′əl/ [L, *retro*; Gk, *peri,* around, *teinein,* to stretch], pertaining to organs closely attached to the posterior abdominal wall and partly covered by peritoneum, rather than suspended by that membrane.

retroperitoneal abscess, a collection of pus between the peritoneum and the posterior abdominal wall.

retroperitoneal fibrosis, a chronic inflammatory process, usually of unknown cause, in which fibrous tissue surrounds the large blood vessels in the lower lumbar area. It frequently causes constriction of the midportion of the ureters, which may lead to hydronephrosis and azotemia. Symptoms include low-back and abdominal pain, weakness, weight loss, fever, and, with urinary tract involvement, frequency of urination, hematuria, polyuria, or anuria.

retroperitoneal hematoma, hematoma resulting from a retroperitoneal hemorrhage.

retroperitoneal hemorrhage, hemorrhage from the kidney into the retroperitoneal space, such as from trauma, vasculitis, an aneurysm, a tumor, a renal infarct, or a cyst.

retroperitoneal lymph node dissection, surgical removal of lymph nodes bilaterally behind the peritoneum, and the lymph channels and fat around both renal pedicles, the vena cava, and the aorta, including the bifurcation of the aorta. The dissection is usually performed in an attempt to eliminate sites of lymphoma or metastases from malignancies originating in pelvic organs or genitalia.

retroperitoneum /-per′itənē′əm/ [L, *retro,* backward; Gk, *peri* + *teinein,* to stretch], the space behind the peritoneum.

retropharyngeal abscess /-fərin′jē·əl/ [L, *retro*; Gk, *pharynx,* throat], a collection of pus in the tissues behind the pharynx accompanied by difficulty in swallowing, fever, and pain. Occasionally the airway becomes obstructed. Treatment includes appropriate parenteral antibiotics and surgical drainage. Tracheostomy may be necessary.

retroplacental /-pləsen′təl/, behind the placenta.

retrospective chart audit /-spek′tiv/ [L, *retro* + *spicere,* to look], a format for an audit developed by the Joint Commission on Accreditation of Healthcare Organizations. The audit involves several steps that outline a procedure for evaluating the effectiveness of the care given at a particular institution and for correcting any deficiencies found by reviewing the patient's records after discharge and comparing the data with standards held to be adequate by the Commission.

retrospective study, a study in which a search is made for a relationship between one (usually current) phenomenon or condition and another that occurred in the past.

retrosternal /-stur'nəl/ [L, *retro*, backward; Gk, *sternon*, chest], behind the sternum.

retrouterine /re'trōyoo'tərin/, behind the uterus.

retroversion /-vur'zhən/ [L, *retro* + *vertere*, to turn], **1.** a common condition in which an organ is tipped backward, usually without flexion or other distortion. Uterine retroversion is measured as first-, second-, or third-degree, depending on the angle of tilt with respect to the vagina. **2.** an abnormal condition in which the teeth or other maxillary and mandibular structures are posterior to their normal positions.—**retrovert,** *v.*

Retrovir, a trademark for an antiretroviral drug (zidovudine).

retrovirus /-vī'rəs/ [L, *retro* + *virus*], any of a family of RNA viruses containing an enzyme, reverse transcriptase in the virion. The genetic information of the virus is stored in a molecule of single-stranded RNA. After entering the target cell, the virus uses reverse transcriptase to direct the cell to make viral DNA. Retroviruses are enveloped and assemble their capsids in the cytoplasm of the host cell. Retroviruses are used in laboratory research to import foreign DNA into a cell. They are transmitted by sexual contact with an infected person, through exposure to infected blood or blood products, and perinatally from an infected mother to the child. HIV, which causes AIDS, is a retrovirus.

Rett's syndrome /ret/ [Andreas Rett, Austrian physician, 1924–1997], a pervasive developmental disorder affecting the gray matter of the brain, occurring exclusively in females and present from birth. It is progressive and is characterized by autistic behavior, ataxia, dementia, seizures, and loss of purposeful use of the hands, with cerebral atrophy, mild hyperammonemia, and decreased levels of biogenic amines.

reuptake /re·up'tāk/, reabsorption of a previously secreted substance.

revaccination /rēvak'sinā'shən/, an immunization that is repeated although the original was successful.

revascularization /rēvas'kyələr'izā'shən/ [L, *re* + *vasculum*, small vessel; Gk, *izein*, to cause], the restoration by surgical means of blood flow to an organ or a tissue, as in bypass surgery.

reverberation /rivur'bərā'shən/, **1.** the phenomenon of multiple reflections within a closed system. **2.** an artifact in ultrasound caused by multiple echoes from parallel tissue interfaces.

Reverdin's needle /reverdaNz'/ [Jaques L. Reverdin, Swiss surgeon, 1842–1929], a

surgical needle with an eye that can be opened and closed with a slide.

reversal film /rivur'səl/, in radiology, a reverse-tone duplicate of an x-ray image, showing black changed to white and white to black. It is produced by exposing single-emulsion subtraction film through a standard x-ray film.

reverse Barton's fracture /rivurs'/ [L, *revertere*, to turn back; John R. Barton, American surgeon, 1794–1871], a break in the volar articular surface of the radius with associated displacement of the carpal bones and radius.

reverse curve, a convex curve of dental occlusion, as viewed in the frontal plane.

reversed bandage /rivurst'/, a roller bandage that is reversed on itself with a half twist so that it lies smoothly, conforming to the contour of the extremity.

reversed phase, a chromatographic mode in which the mobile phase is more polar than the stationary phase.

reverse isolation, isolation procedures designed to protect a patient from infectious organisms that might be carried by the staff, other patients, or visitors or on droplets in the air or on equipment or materials. Handwashing, gowning, gloving, sterilization, or disinfection of materials brought into the area and other details of housekeeping vary with the reason for the isolation and the usual practices of the hospital.

reverse peristalsis, peristalsis that propels the contents in a direction opposite to the normal outward direction.

reverse transcriptase (RT) /revers' transkrip'tās/, an enzyme of RNA viruses that catalyzes the transcription of RNA to DNA, which is then incorporated into the genome of the host cell. This is the reverse of the usual mechanism for replication of genetic information; in the presence of this enzyme, it is the RNA that serves as the template for DNA copies. It is one mechanism by which reproduction of cancer cells is facilitated.

reverse transcriptase inhibitor, a compound that inhibits the enzyme used by retroviruses to synthesize complementary DNA from viral RNA inside host cells.

reverse Trendelenburg [Friedrich Trendelenburg, German surgeon, 1844–1924.], a position in which the lower extremities are lower than the body and head, which are elevated on an inclined plane.

reversible /rivur'sibəl/, able to return to its original state or condition, as in a chemical reaction.

reversible brain syndrome, any of a group of acute brain disorders characterized by a disruption of cognition, as in delirium. The symptoms widely vary. The disorder is related to a variety of biologic stressors. Recovery is likely.

reversible obstructive airway disease, a condition characterized by bronchospasm reversible by intervention, as in asthma.

reversible vascular hyperplasia, a variation of Kaposi's sarcoma in which HIV may induce cells to produce a chemical growth factor. The growth factor, in turn, makes lymphatic endothelial cells proliferate. The process may cascade as each new Kaposi's sarcoma cell produces more growth factor.

reversion /rivur′zhən/, **1.** the appearance in offspring of traits expressed in previous, but not recent, generations. **2.** a return to an original phenotype by mutation or reinstatement of the original genotype.

review of systems (ROS) /rivyo͞o′/ [Fr, *revoir,* to see again], in a health history, a system-by-system review of the body functions. The ROS is begun during the initial interview with the patient and completed during the physical examination, as physical findings prompt further questions.

Revised Trauma Score, a system of combining cardiopulmonary assessment with the Glasgow Coma Score in estimating the degree of injury and the prognosis in a trauma patient. The cardiopulmonary factors included are respiratory rate and systolic BP.

Revlimid, a trademark for lenalidomide.

Reyataz, a trademark for atazanavir.

Reye's syndrome /rāz′/ [Ralph D.K. Reye, Australian pathologist, 1912–1978], a combination of acute encephalopathy and fatty infiltration of the internal organs that may follow acute viral infections. This syndrome has been associated with influenza B, chickenpox (varicella), the enteroviruses, and the Epstein-Barr virus. It usually affects people under 18 years of age, characteristically causing an exanthematous rash, vomiting, and confusion about 1 week after the onset of a viral illness. In the late stage there may be extreme disorientation followed by coma, seizures, and respiratory arrest. Mortality varies between 20% and 80%, depending on the severity of symptoms. The cause of Reye's syndrome is unknown; however, there appears to be an association with the administration of aspirin. Therefore aspirin is given to infants and children only if prescribed by a physician, and should not be given in cases of chickenpox or suspected influenza.

rf, 1. abbreviation for **radiofrequency. 2.** abbreviation for **rheumatic fever.**

Rf, 1. symbol for the element **rutherfordium. 2.** in chromatography, abbreviation for *retardation factor* or *ratio to (solvent) front.*

RF, abbreviation for **rheumatic fever.**

R factor, an episome in bacteria that is responsible for drug resistance and is transmissible to progeny and to other bacterial cells by conjugation. The part of the episome involved in replication and transmission is called resistance transfer factor.

RFP, abbreviation for **request for proposal.**

RGP, abbreviation for **rigid gas permeable contact lens.**

Rh, 1. abbreviation for *rhesus.* **2.** symbol for the chemical element **rhodium.**

r/h, 1. abbreviation for **relative humidity. 2.** abbreviation for *roentgens per hour.*

rhabdomyoblast /rab′dōmī′əblast/ [Gk, *rhabdos,* rod, *mys,* muscle, *blastos,* germ], large round spindle-shaped cells with cross striations, found in some rhabdomyosarcomas.

rhabdomyolysis /rab′dōmī·ol′isis/, a paroxysmal, potentially fatal syndrome caused by the breakdown of skeletal muscle fibers, characterized by the presence of myoglobin in the urine. It may result from untreated compartment syndrome. It is also associated with acute renal failure.

rhabdomyoma /rab′dōmī·ō′mə/ *pl.* **rhabdomyomas, rhabdomyomata** [Gk, *rhabdos,* rod, *mys,* muscle, *oma*], a tumor of striated muscle that may occur in the uterus, vagina, pharynx, tongue, or heart.

rhabdomyosarcoma /rab′dōmī′ōsärkō′mə/ *pl.* **rhabdomyosarcomas, rhabdomyosarcomata** [Gk, *rhabdos* + *mys,* muscle, *sarx,* flesh, *oma*], a highly malignant tumor derived from primitive striated muscle cells that occurs most frequently in the head and neck and is also found in the genitourinary tract, extremities, body wall, and retroperitoneum. In some cases the onset is associated with trauma. The initial symptoms depend on the site of tumor development and indicate local tissue or organ destruction such as dysphagia, vaginal bleeding, hematuria, or obstructed flow of urine. Surgical excision is rarely possible because the tumor is poorly encapsulated and tends to spread. Amputation of an affected limb or extremity may be curative. Radiotherapy and chemotherapy may greatly increase the length of survival.

rhabdosphincter /rab′dōsfingk′tər/, a sphincter composed of striated muscle fibers.

rhabdovirus /rab′dōvī′rəs/ [Gk, *rhabdos;* L, *virus,* poison], a member of a family of viruses that includes the organism causing rabies.

rhagades /rag′ədēz/ [Gk, chinks], cracks or fissures in skin that has lost its elasticity, especially common around the mouth.

Rh antiserum [Rh, rhesus; Gk, *anti,* against; L, *serum,* whey], a serum that contains Rh antibodies.

rhd, 1. abbreviation for *radioactive health data.* **2.** abbreviation for **rheumatic heart disease.**

rhe /rē/, **1.** an absolute unit of fluidity in the centimeter-gram-second system. **2.** the reciprocal of the unit of viscosity expressed as ¹/poise or ¹/centipoise.

rhegmatogenous /regˈmɝtojˈɝnəs/ [Gk, *rhegma,* breakage, *gen,* producing], arising from a tear or rupture in an organ.

rhegmatogenous retinal detachment, a separation of the retina associated with a hole, break, or tear in the sensory layer of the retina. The detachment occurs secondary to the passage of vitreous fluid through the break.

rhenium (Re) /rēˈnē·əm/ [L, *Rhenus,* Rhine], a hard, brittle metallic element. Its atomic number is 75, and its atomic mass is 186.21. Rhenium has a high melting point and is used in x-ray tube anodes and in thermometers for measuring high temperatures.

rheobase /rēˈəbās/, the least amount of electricity that will produce a stimulated response.

rheoencephalogram /rēˈō·ensefˈəlōgramˈ/, a graphic representation of the changes in electric conductivity of the head caused by blood flowing through vessels in the head.

rheogram /rēˈəgram/, a plot of shear stress versus the shear flow of a fluid.

rheology /rē·olˈəjē/, the study of the flow and deformation of matter.

Rheomacrodex, a trademark for a plasma expander (dextran 40).

rheometry /rē·omˈətrē/ [Gk, *rheos,* current, *metron,* measure], a technique for measuring the velocity of blood flow.

rheostat /rēˈəstat/ [Gk, *rheos,* current, *statikos,* causing to stand], a variable-resistance electrical device that can be adjusted to control the strength of a current.

rheostosis /rēˈostōˈsis/, a condition of bone overgrowth marked by streaks in the bones.

rhestocythemia /resˈtōsīthēˈmē·ə/, the presence of damaged RBCs in the peripheral circulation.

rheum /rōōm/ [Gk, *rheuma,* flow], a watery or mucous discharge from the skin or mucous membranes.

rheumatic, pertaining to rheumatism.

rheumatic aortitis, an inflammatory condition of the aorta, occurring in rheumatic fever. It is characterized by disseminated focal lesions that may progressively form patches of fibrosis.

rheumatic arteritis, a complication of rheumatic fever characterized by generalized inflammation of arteries and arterioles. Fibrin mixed with cellular debris may invade, thicken, and stiffen vessel walls and the affected vessels may be surrounded by hemorrhage and exudate.

rheumatic carditis [Gk, *rheuma,* flux, *kardia,* heart, *itis,* inflammation], pericarditis, myocarditis, and endocarditis that may be associated with acute rheumatic fever.

rheumatic endocarditis [Gk, *rheuma,* flux, *endon,* within, *kardia,* heart, *itis,* inflammation], inflammation of the endocardium in association with acute rheumatic fever.

rheumatic fever (rf), systemic inflammatory disease that may develop as a delayed reaction to an inadequately treated infection of the upper respiratory tract by group A beta-hemolytic streptococci. The disease usually occurs in young school-age children and may affect the brain, heart, joints, skin, or subcutaneous tissues. The onset is usually sudden, often occurring 1 to 5 symptom-free weeks after recovery from a sore throat or scarlet fever. Early symptoms generally include fever, joint pain, nosebleeds, abdominal pain, and vomiting. The major manifestations of this disease include migratory polyarthritis affecting numerous joints and carditis, which causes palpitations, chest pain, and in severe cases symptoms of cardiac failure. Affected individuals may also develop leukocytosis, moderate anemia, and proteinuria. Recurrences of rheumatic fever are common. Except for carditis, all the manifestations of the disease usually subside without any permanent effects. Management includes bed rest and severe restriction of normal activity. Penicillin is often administered, even if throat cultures are negative, and steroids or salicylates may be used, depending on the severity of any associated carditis and arthritis.

rheumatic heart disease (rhd), damage to heart muscle and heart valves caused by episodes of rheumatic fever. When a susceptible person acquires a group A beta-hemolytic streptococcal infection, an autoimmune reaction may occur in heart tissue, resulting in permanent deformities of heart valves or chordae tendineae. Involvement of the heart may be evident during acute rheumatic fever, or it may be discovered long after the acute disease has subsided.

rheumatic nodules [Gk, *rheuma,* flux; L, *nodulus,* small knot], aggregations of fibroblasts and lymphoid cells that may accumulate in soft tissues and over bony prominences of patients afflicted with rheumatoid arthritis and rheumatic disorders.

rheumatic scoliosis [Gk, *rheuma,* flux, *skoliosis,* curvature], a form of scoliosis associated with muscle spasms and acute inflammation.

rheumatid /rōōˈmətid/ [Gk, *rheuma,* flux], a skin eruption that sometimes occurs with rheumatic disorders.

rheumatism /rōōˈmətizˈəm/ [Gk, *rheuma,* flux], *nontechnical.* **1.** any of a large number of inflammatory conditions of the bursae, joints, ligaments, or muscles

R

characterized by pain, limitation of movement, and structural degeneration of one or more parts of the musculoskeletal system. **2.** the syndrome of pain, limitation of movement, and structural degeneration of elements in the musculoskeletal system, as may occur in gout, rheumatoid arthritis, SLE, ankylosing spondylitis, and many other diseases.—**rheumatic, rheumatoid,** *adj.*

rheumatoid arteritis /rōō'matoid/ [Gk, *rheuma,* flux, *arteria,* airpipe, *itis,* inflammation], inflammation of the arterial walls associated with a rheumatic disorder.

rheumatoid arthritis (RA) [Gk, *rheuma,* flux, *eidos,* form, *arthron,* joint, *itis,* inflammation], a chronic, inflammatory, destructive, and sometimes deforming collagen disease that has an autoimmune component, usually first appearing in patients, most often women, are between 36 and 50 years of age. It is characterized by symmetric inflammation of synovial membranes and increased synovial exudate, leading to thickening of the membranes and swelling of the joints. The course of the disease is variable but is most frequently marked by alternating periods of remission and exacerbation. Clinical data, mainly from radiographic studies and physical examination, classify the progress of the disease into four stages. Stage I, representing early effects, is based on x-ray films showing the onset of bone changes. Stage II, moderate rheumatoid arthritis, is assigned to cases in which there is evidence of some muscle atrophy and loss of mobility, in addition to x-ray findings. Stage III, severe rheumatoid arthritis, is marked by joint deformity, extensive muscle atrophy, soft tissue lesions, and definite bone and cartilage destruction. Stage IV includes all the stage III clinical signs plus fibrous or bony ankylosis. Rheumatoid arthritis may also be classified on the basis of functional capacity: class I, no loss of function; class II, minor impairment of functional capacity with some pain and immobility; class III, capacity limited to a few tasks; and class IV, confinement to bed or a wheelchair. The diagnostic criteria listed by the American Rheumatism Association include morning stiffness, joint pain or tenderness, swelling of at least two joints, subcutaneous nodules (called arthritic nodules and usually found at pressure points such as the elbows), structural changes in joints seen on x-ray film, a positive rheumatoid factor agglutination test, decreased precipitation of mucin from synovial fluid, and characteristic histologic changes on pathologic examination of the fluid, both blood serum and synovial fluid. Higher titers of rheumatoid factor are correlated with more severe forms of the disease. Rheumatoid arthritis is not always progressive, deforming, or debilitating; most patients may continue in their jobs.

rheumatoid coronary arteritis, an abnormal condition characterized by a thickening of the tunica intima of the coronary arteries, which may produce coronary insufficiency. Rheumatoid coronary arteritis is a collagen disease that causes inflammation and fibrinoid degeneration of connective tissue. It is commonly treated with glucocorticoids.

rheumatoid factor (RF), antiglobulin antibodies often found in the serum of patients with a clinical diagnosis of rheumatoid arthritis. They may also be found in such widely divergent diseases as TB, parasitic infections, leukemia, and connective tissue disorders.

rheumatoid factor (RF) test, a blood test whose results are positive in approximately 80% of patients with rheumatoid arthritis. RF is not a useful disease marker because its presence does not disappear in patients who are experiencing a remission from the disease symptoms.

rheumatologist /rōō'matol'ə'jist/, a specialist in the treatment of disorders of the connective tissue.

rheumatology /-ol'əjē/ [Gk, *rheuma,* flux, *logos,* science], the study of disorders characterized by inflammation, degeneration, or metabolic derangement of connective tissue and related structures of the body.

Rh factor, refers to the D antigen, found on the erythrocytes of 85% of the Caucasian population and varying frequencies in other populations. Rh-positive or Rh-negative refers to the presence or absence of the D antigen, but many other antigens are also part of this system, most notably C, c, E, and e. D is the most immunogenic antigen outside the ABO system; therefore D-negative recipients should receive only D-negative donor blood to avoid exposure and immunization to D. D-negative mothers who carry D-positive infants should receive Rh immune globulin to prevent immunization during pregnancy and delivery.

Rh genes [Rh, rhesus; Gk, *genein,* to produce], Rh antigens on the red cell membrane produced by allelic genes at two closely linked loci on chromosome 1, RhD and RhCE.

rhinalgia /rīnal'jə/, pain involving the nose.

Rh incompatibility, The agglutination (clumping together) of red blood cells as a result of mixing different antigens (agglutinogens) present on the surface of the cells. This agglutination is an immune reaction and depends on the formation of antibodies against the specific agglutinogen

(Rh factor) present on the red blood cells and in blood from a transfusion or fetal tissues. The immune reaction does not occur immediately, but depends on the gradual formation of antibodies.

rhinedema /rī′nedē′mə/, a fluid accumulation in the mucous membrane of the nose.

rhinencephalon /rī′nensef′əlon/ pl. **rhinencephala** [Gk, rhis, nose, encephalon, brain], a part of each cerebral hemisphere that contains the limbic system, which is associated with the emotions. —**rhinencephalic**, adj.

rhinenchysis /rī′nenkī′sis, rīnen′kisis/, douching of the nasal cavity.

rhinitis /rīnī′tis/ [Gk, rhis + itis, inflammation], inflammation of the mucous membranes of the nose, usually accompanied by swelling of the mucosa and a nasal discharge. It may be complicated by sinusitis.

Rhinocort, a trademark for a nasal corticosteroid (budesonide).

rhinoentomophthoromycosis /ri′no-en′to-mof′tho-ro-mi-ko′sis/, the usual form of an infection by Conidiobolus coronatus, marked by development of large polyps in the subcutaneous tissues of the nose and paranasal sinuses. Orbital involvement with unilateral blindness may follow.

rhinolaryngitis /-ler′injī′tis/ [Gk, rhis, nose, larynx, throat, itis, inflammation], an inflammation of the mucous membranes of the nose and throat.

rhinolith /rī′nəlith/, a concretion in the nasal cavity.

rhinolithiasis /rī′nəlithī′əsis/, the formation of concretions in the nasal cavity.

rhinologist /rīnol′əjist/, a physician who specializes in the diagnosis and treatment of disorders of the nose.

rhinology /rīnol′əjē/, a branch of medicine specializing in the diagnosis and treatment of disorders involving the nose.

rhinomanometer /rī′nōmanom′ətər/, a device for measuring the air pressure in the nose. It is used in the diagnosis of nasal obstruction.

rhinomycosis /rī′nōmīkō′sis/, a fungal infection of the mucous membrane of the nose.

rhinopathy /rīnop′əthē/ [Gk, rhis + pathos, disease], any disease or malformation of the nose.

rhinophycomycosis /rī′nōfī′kōmīkō′sis/, an infection of the nasal and paranasal sinuses caused by the phycomycete Entomophthora coronata. The infection often spreads to surrounding tissues, including the eye and brain.

rhinophyma /rī′nōfī′mə/ [Gk, rhis+phyma, tumor], a form of rosacea in which there is sebaceous hyperplasia, redness, prominent vascularity, swelling, and distortion of the skin of the nose. Treatment includes dermabrasion, electrosurgery, plastic surgery, and laser resurfacing.

rhinoplasty /rī′nəplas′tē/ [Gk, rhis + plassein, to mold], a procedure in plastic surgery in which the structure of the nose is changed or shaped. Bone or cartilage may be removed, tissue grafted from another part of the body, or synthetic material implanted. The procedure is most frequently performed for cosmetic reasons.

rhinorrhagia /rī′nôrā′jə/ [Gk, rhis, nose, rhegnynein, to gush forth], a profuse nosebleed.

rhinorrhea /rī′nôrē′ə/ [Gk, rhis + rhoia, flow], 1. the free discharge of a thin watery nasal fluid. 2. the flow of CSF from the nose after an injury to the head.

rhinosalpingitis /rī′nōsal′pinjī′tis/, an inflammation of the mucous membranes of the nose and eustachian tube.

rhinoscleroma /rī′nosklirō′mə/, a chronic inflammation in the nose, spreading to the larynx and pharynx. The cause is an infection of Klebsiella rhinoscleromatis.

rhinoscope /rī′nəskōp/, an instrument for examining the nasal passages through the anterior nares or through the nasopharynx.

rhinoscopy /rīnos′kəpē/ [Gk, rhis + skopein, to look], an examination of the nasal passages to inspect the mucosa and detect inflammation, deformities, or asymmetry, as in deviation of the septum. The nasal passages may be examined anteriorly by introducing a speculum into the anterior nares or posteriorly by introducing a rhinoscope through the nasopharynx. —**rhinoscopic**, adj.

rhinosporidiosis /rī′nōsporid′ē-ō′sis/ [Gk, rhis + sporo, seed, osis, condition], an infection caused by the fungus Rhinosporidium seeberi. It is characterized by fleshy red polyps on the mucous membranes of the nose, conjunctiva, nasopharynx, and soft palate. The disease may be acquired by swimming or bathing in infected water. The most effective treatment is electrocautery.

rhinostenosis /rī′nōstənō′sis/, an abnormal narrowing of a nasal passage.

rhinotomy /rīnot′əmē/ [Gk, rhis + temnein, to cut], a surgical procedure in which an incision is made along one side of the nose, performed to drain accumulated pus from an abscess or a sinus infection.

rhinovirus /rī′nōvī′rəs/ [Gk, rhis; L, virus, poison], any of about 100 serologically distinct, small RNA viruses that cause about 40% of acute respiratory illnesses. Infection is characterized by dry scratchy throat, nasal congestion, malaise, and headache. Fever is minimal. Nasal discharge lasts 2 or 3 days.

rhizoid /rī′zoid/, resembling a root or serving to anchor.

R

rhizome, an underground plant stem, growing more or less horizontally, that usually has roots on its underside and bears buds.

rhizomelia /rī'zōme'lyə/ [Gk, *rhizo,* root, *melos,* limb], **1.** a disorder of the hips and shoulders. **2.** an anomaly in the length of the arms and legs of an individual.

rhizomelic /rī'zəmel'ik/ [Gk, *rhizo,* root, *melos,* limb], pertaining to the hips and shoulder.

rhizomeningomyelitis /rī'zōmining'gōmī'-əlī'tis/, an inflammation of the nerve roots, meninges, and spinal cord.

Rhizopus /rī'zōpəs/, a genus of fungi that includes some species identified as a cause of zygomycosis in humans.

rhizotomy /rīzot'əmē/, the surgical resection of the dorsal root of a spinal nerve, performed to relieve pain and sometimes to decrease spasms.

rho /rō/, P, ρ, the seventeenth letter of the Greek alphabet.

Rhodesian trypanosomiasis /rōde'zhən/, an acute form of African trypanosomiasis, caused by the parasite *Trypanosoma brucei rhodesiense.* The disease may progress rapidly, causing encephalitis, coma, and death in only a few weeks.

Rh₀(D) immunoglobulin, a passive immunizing agent. It is prescribed to prevent Rh sensitization after abortion, miscarriage, ectopic pregnancy, or normal birth to an Rh-negative mother of an Rh-positive infant or fetus.

rhodium (Rh) /rō'dē·əm/ [Gk, *rhodon,* rose], a grayish-white metallic element. Its atomic number is 45; its atomic mass is 102.91.

rhodopsin /rōdop'sin/ [Gk, *rhodon,* rose, *opsis,* vision], the purple pigmented compound in the rods of the retina, formed by a protein, opsin, and a derivative of vitamin A, retinal. Rhodopsin gives the outer segments of the rods a purple color and adapts the eye to low-density light. The compound breaks down when struck by light, and this chemical change triggers the conduction of nerve impulses.

Rhodotorula /rō'dətôr'yələ/, a genus of yeasts, including species such as *R. rubra* that have been identified as causes of endocarditis and septicemia, particularly in immunocompromised patients.

rhoencephalography, a technique for monitoring blood flow in the brain by recording pulsatile changes in the electric impedance of the brain.

RhoGAM, a trademark for an immune globulin (Rh₀ [D] immune globulin).

rhombencephalon /rom'bensef'əlon/ [Gk, *rhombos,* parallelogram, *enkephalos,* brain], the most caudal of the three primary vesicles of the embryonic brain.

rhomboid /rom'boid/ [Gk, *rhombos,* rhombus, *eidos,* form], resembling the shape of an oblique equilateral parallelogram, as a rhomboid muscle.

rhomboidal sinus /rom'boidəl/, an opening in the central canal of the lumbar spinal cord.

rhomboideus major /romboi'dē·əs/ [Gk, *rhombos,* rhombus, *eidos,* form], a muscle of the upper back below and parallel to the rhomboideus minor. With the rhomboideus minor, it functions to draw the scapula toward the vertebral column while supporting it and drawing it slightly upward.

rhomboideus minor, a muscle of the upper back, above and parallel to the rhomboideus major. With the rhomboideus major, it acts to draw the scapula toward the vertebral column while supporting the scapula and drawing it slightly upward.

rhombomere /rom'bəmir/, any of the nine segments of the embryonic neural tube.

rhonchus /rong'kəs/ *pl.* **rhonchi** [Gk, *rhonchos,* snore], an abnormal sound heard on auscultation of an airway obstructed by thick secretions, muscular spasm, neoplasm, or external pressure. The continuous rumbling sound is more pronounced during expiration and characteristically clears on coughing.

rhotacism /rō'təsizm/, a speech disorder consisting of imperfect pronunciation of the /r/ sound.

r-HuEPO, abbreviation for *recombinant human erythropoietin.*

rhus /rus/, any member of the genus *Rhus.*

Rhus, a genus of vines and shrubs of the family Anacardiaceae, many of which are poisonous. The most important toxic species are *R. radicans* L. (poison ivy), *R. diversiloba* L. (western poison oak), *R. quercifolia* (eastern poison oak), and *R. vernix* L. (poison sumac).

rhus dermatitis /rōōs/ [Gk, *rhous,* sumac], a form of contact dermatitis caused by exposure to an allergenic oil, toxicodendrol, present in any part of a plant of the genus *Rhus* such as poison ivy or poison sumac. Contact can result in severe itching, rashes, and blistering. Even the smoke of burning rhus plants may be toxic.

rhythm /rith'əm/ [Gk, *rhythmos*], the relationship of one impulse to neighboring impulses as measured in time, movement, or regularity of action.

rhythm method, old popular name for natural family planning.

rhytid /ri'tid/ *pl.* **rhytides,** skin wrinkle.

rhytidoplasty /ritid'ōplas'tē/ [Gk, *rhytis,* wrinkle, *plassein,* to mold], a procedure in reconstructive plastic surgery in which the skin of the face is tightened, wrinkles are removed, and the skin is made to appear firm and smooth.

rhytidosis /rit′idō′sis/ [Gk, *rhytis,* wrinkle, *osis,* condition], a wrinkling, especially of the cornea.

RIA, abbreviation for **radioimmunoassay.**

rib [AS, roof], one of the 12 pairs of arches of bone forming a large part of the thoracic skeleton. The first seven ribs on each side are called true ribs because they articulate directly with the sternum and vertebrae. The remaining five ribs are called false ribs. The first three attach ventrally to ribs above; the last two are free at their ventral extremities and are called floating ribs.

ribavirin /rī′bəvir′in/, an aerosol antiviral drug prescribed for the treatment of respiratory syncytial virus infections for the lower respiratory tract in infants and small children.

rib fracture, a break in a bone of the thoracic skeleton. It may be caused by a blow or crushing injury, by violent coughing or sneezing, or occur as the result of a pathologic fracture secondary to metastatic disease. The ribs most commonly broken are the fourth to eighth. If the bone is splintered or the fracture is displaced, sharp fragments may pierce the lung, causing hemothorax or pneumothorax. The patient with a fractured rib suffers pain, especially on inspiration, and usually breathes rapidly and shallowly. The site of the break is generally very tender to the touch, and the crackling of bone fragments rubbing together may be heard on auscultation. Breath sounds may be absent, decreased, or accompanied by rales and rhonchi. The patient is observed for signs of hemoptysis, hemothorax, flail chest, atelectasis, pneumothorax, and pneumonia.

riboflavin /rī′bōflā′vin/ [*ribose*; L, *flavus,* yellow], a yellow crystalline water-soluble pigment, one of the heat-stable components of the B vitamin complex. It combines with specific flavoproteins and functions as a coenzyme in the oxidative processes of carbohydrates, fats, and proteins. Small amounts of riboflavin are found in the liver and kidneys, but it is not stored to any great degree in the body and must be supplied regularly in the diet. Deficiency of riboflavin is rare.

ribonuclear protein (RNP) /rī′bōnoo̅′klē-ər/ [*ribose*; L, *nucleus,* nut kernel; Gk, *proteios,* first rank], a conjugated protein consisting of a protein molecule and a nucleic acid.

ribonuclease (RNase) /-noo̅′klē-ās/, a class of endonucleases that hydrolyze RNA.

ribonucleic acid (RNA) /rī′bōnoo̅klē′ik/ [*ribose*; L, *nucleus,* nut kernel, *acidus,* sour], a nucleic acid, found in both the nucleus and cytoplasm of cells, that plays several roles in the translation of the genetic code and the assembly of proteins.

ribonucleoside /rī′bōnoo̅′klē-əsīd′/, a nucleoside in which the sugar component is ribose. The ribonucleosides of RNA are adenosine, cytidine, guanosine, and uridine.

ribonucleotide /-noo̅′klē-ətīd′/, a class of nucleotides in which the pentose is D-ribose.

ribose /rī′bōs/, a 5-carbon sugar that occurs as a component of RNA.

ribosomal RNA (rRNA) /rī′bōsō′məl/, the RNA of ribosomes and polyribosomes.

ribosome /rī′bəsōm/ [*ribose*; Gk, *soma,* body], an organelle composed of RNA and protein that functions in the synthesis of protein. Ribosomes interact with messenger RNA and transfer RNA to link amino acid into a polypeptide chain in a sequence determined by the sequence of nucleotides in the messenger RNA.

ribosome-inactivating protein (RIP), one of a variety of enzymes that cleave the N-glycosidic bond of adenine in a specific ribosomal RNA sequence. Type 1 RIPs are single-chain proteins. Some type 2 RIPs, such as ricin, possess a galactose-specific lectin domain that binds to cell surfaces, making them potent toxins.

ribosuria /rī′bəsoor′ē-ə/, the presence of ribose in the urine, usually a sign of muscular dystrophy.

rib shaking, a procedure in physiotherapy in which constant, downward pressure is applied with an intermittent shaking motion of the hands on the rib cage over the area being drained. It is done with the flat part of the palm of the hand over the lung segment being drained.

rib vibration, a procedure in physiotherapy similar to rib shaking but done with a downward vibrating pressure with the flat part of the palm during exhalations.

RICE, abbreviation for *rest, ice, compression, elevation,* referring to the treatment for sprains and strains.

rice diet [Gk, *oryza,* rice, *diaita,* way of living], a diet consisting only of rice, fruit, fruit juices, and sugar, supplemented with vitamins and iron. Salt is forbidden. It is prescribed for the treatment of hypertension, chronic renal disease, and obesity.

Richards, Linda, a nurse considered to be the first American-trained nurse, a graduate of the first class of the New England Hospital for Women and Children. She is credited with being the first to keep written records on patients, a practice she started when she worked as night superintendent at Bellevue Hospital in New York under Sister Helen.

Richter's hernia /rik′tərz, rish′tərs/ [August G. Richter, German surgeon,

R

1742–1812], a small nonpalpable visceral protrusion involving only a part of the intestinal wall.

ricin /rī′sin/, a poison made from waste produced in processing castor beans. It can take the form of a powder, mist, or pellet, or can be dissolved in water or weak acid and can be used as a poison by ingestion, inhalation, or injection. As little as 500 micrograms can be fatal. There is no antidote. Treatment consists of minimizing exposure and supportive care.

rickets /rik′əts/ [Gk, *rachis*, backbone, *itis*, inflammation], a condition caused by the deficiency of vitamin D, seen primarily in infancy and childhood and characterized by abnormal bone formation. Symptoms include soft pliable bones causing such deformities as bowlegs and knock-knees, nodular enlargements on the ends and sides of the bones, muscle pain, enlarged skull, chest deformities, spinal curvature, enlargement of the liver and spleen, profuse sweating, and general tenderness of the body when touched. Prophylaxis and treatment include a diet rich in calcium, phosphorus, and vitamin D and adequate exposure to sunlight.—**rachitic,** *adj.*

Rickettsia /riket′sē-ə/ *pl.* **rickettsiae** [Howard T. Ricketts, American pathologist, 1871–1910], a genus of microorganisms that combine aspects of both bacteria and viruses. They can be observed with a light microscope, divide by fission, and may be controlled with antibiotics. They also exist as viruslike intracellular parasites, living in the intestinal tracts of insects such as lice. Rickettsial diseases have been responsible for many of history's worst epidemics. The various species are distinguished on the basis of similarities in the diseases they cause. Rickettsial diseases are uncommon in parts of the world where insect and rodent populations are well controlled.—**rickettsial,** *adj.*

rickettsial disease [Howard T. Ricketts; L, *dis*; Fr, *aise,* ease], an infection caused by a species of *Rickettsia*. Examples include Rocky Mountain spotted fever and typhus.

rickettsialpox /riket′sē-əlpoks′/ [Howard T. Ricketts; ME, *pokkes,* pustules], a mild, acute infectious disease caused by *Rickettsia akari* and transmitted from mice to humans by mites *(Allodermanyssus sanguineus)*. It is characterized by an asymptomatic crusted primary lesion, chills, fever, headache, malaise, myalgia, and a rash resembling chickenpox. Chloramphenicol or tetracycline hastens recovery.

rickettsiosis /riket′sē-ō′sis/ *pl.* **rickettsioses** [Howard T. Ricketts; Gk, *osis,* condition], any of a group of infectious diseases caused by microorganisms of the genus *Rickettsia*.

Ridaura, a trademark for an oral disease-modifying antirheumatoid drug (auranofin).

rider's bone [AS, *ridan,* to ride, *ban,* bone], a bony deposit that sometimes develops in horseback riders on the inner side of the lower end of the tendon of the adductor muscle of the thigh.

rider's sprain [OFr, *espreindre,* to force out], a sprain of the adductor muscles of the thigh resulting from horseback riding.

ridge /rij/ [AS, *hyrcg*], a projection or projecting structure, such as the gastrocnemial ridge or crest on the posterior surface of the femur, giving attachment to the gastrocnemius muscle.

ridge extension, an intraoral surgical operation for deepening the labial, buccal, or lingual sulci.

ridge lap, the part of an artificial tooth that is adjacent to or approximates the residual ridge. Proper ridge lap can give the appearance of a natural tooth.

Rieder's cell leukemia /rē′dərz/ [Hermann Rieder, German pathologist, 1858–1932], a malignant neoplasm of blood-forming tissues characterized by the presence in blood of large numbers of atypical myeloblasts with immature cytoplasm and relatively mature lobulated, indented nuclei.

Riehl-Sisca, Joan, a nursing theorist who presented her symbolic interactionism theory in Riehl and Sister Callista Roy's book, *Conceptual Models for Nursing* (1980). The Riehl Interaction Model uses the nursing process in implementing nursing care. In symbolic interactionism theory, people interpret each other's actions based on the meaning attached to the action before reacting. It is a process of interpretation between the stimulus and response. Riehl's emphasis is on the assessment and interpretation of the patient's actions by the nurse, who then makes predictions about the patient's behavior.

RIF, abbreviation for **resistance-inducing factor.**

rifabutin /rif′ah-bu′tin/, an antibacterial used for the prevention of disseminated *Mycobacterium avium* complex disease in patients with advanced HIV infection.

Rifadin, a trademark for an antibacterial (rifampin).

rifampin /rif′əmpin/, an antibacterial. It is prescribed in combination for the treatment of TB, staphylococcal infections, and *Legionella* pneumonia, and in meningococcal meningitis and *Haemophilus influenzae* prophylaxis.

rifamycin /rif′ah-mi′sin/, any of a family of antibiotics biosynthesized by a strain of *Streptomyces mediterranei,* effective against a broad spectrum of bacteria. They are used for the initial treatment and retreatment of pulmonary TB and for prevention of meningococcal infections in close contacts of patients with *Neisseria meningitidis* infections.

rifapentine, an antitubercular prescribed to treat pulmonary tuberculosis. It must be used in combination with at least one other antitubercular.

rifaximin, a miscellaneous antiinfective used to treat traveler's diarrhea caused by *Escherichia coli* in adults and children older than 12 years of age.

Rift Valley fever, a bunyavirus infection of Egypt and east Africa spread by mosquitoes or by handling infected sheep, buffalo, goats, camels, and cattle. It is characterized by abrupt fever, chills, headache, and generalized aching, followed by epigastric pain, anorexia, loss of taste, and photophobia. The disease is of short duration, and recovery is usually complete. There is no specific treatment. A killed virus vaccine that provides protection for 2 years is available for those at risk.

RIG, abbreviation for **rabies immune globulin.**

Riga-Fede disease /rē′gä fā′dā/ [Antonio Riga, Italian physician, 1832–1919; Francesco Fede, Italian pediatrician, 1832–1913], an ulceration of the lingual frenum in some infants, caused by abrasion of the frenum by natal or neonatal teeth.

right atrial catheter, an indwelling IV catheter inserted centrally or peripherally and threaded into the superior vena cava and right atrium.

right atrioventricular orifice, the opening between the right atrium and ventricle of the heart.

right brachiocephalic vein [AS, *riht*; Gk, *brachion,* arm, *kephale,* head], a vessel, about 2.5 cm long, that starts in the root of the neck at the junction of the internal jugular and subclavian veins on the right side and descends vertically from behind the sternal end of the clavicle to join the left brachiocephalic vein and form the superior vena cava.

right bundle branch block (RBBB), impaired transmission or absence of transmission of electric impulses from the atrioventricular (AV) bundle of His to the right ventricle. RBBB is often associated with right ventricular hypertrophy, especially in athletes and individuals under 40 years of age. In older individuals, RBBB is commonly caused by coronary artery disease.

right common carotid artery, the shorter of the two common carotid arteries, arising from the brachiocephalic trunk, passing obliquely from the level of the sternoclavicular articulation to the upper border of the thyroid cartilage and dividing into the right internal and external carotids.

right coronary artery, one of a pair of branches of the ascending aorta, arising in the right posterior aortic sinus, passing along the right side of the coronary sulcus, dividing into the right interventricular artery and a large marginal branch. It supplies both ventricles, the right atrium, and the sinoatrial node.

right-handedness, a natural tendency to favor the use of the right hand.

right-hand rule, a principle of physics in which the direction of current flow in a wire is related to the position of the imaginary lines of force of the magnetic field about the wire.

right-heart failure, an abnormal cardiac condition characterized by the impairment of the right side of the heart and congestion and elevated pressure in the systemic veins and capillaries. The most common cause of right-heart failure is left-heart failure. Right ventricular infarction, pulmonic stenosis, and pulmonary hypertension can also result in right-heart failure.

right hepatic duct, the duct that drains bile from the right lobe of the liver into the common bile duct.

righting reflex [AS, *riht*; L, *reflectere,* to bend back], any one of the neuromuscular responses to restore the body to its normal upright position when it has been displaced. The righting reflexes involve complicated mechanisms and processes associated with the structures of the internal ear. The fibers of the vestibular branch of the eight cranial nerve transmit impulses to the brain, producing a sense of position. Also activating righting reflexes are proprioceptors in muscles and tendons and visual nerve impulses.

right lymphatic duct, a vessel that conveys lymph from the right upper quadrant of the body into the bloodstream in the neck at the junction of the right internal jugular and right subclavian veins.

right part of liver, the part that receives blood from the right branches of the hepatic portal vein and hepatic artery proper and whose bile flows out through the right hepatic duct.

right pulmonary artery, the longer and slightly larger of the two arteries conveying venous blood from the heart to the lungs. It arises from the pulmonary trunk, bends to the right behind the aorta, and divides into two branches at the root of the right lung.

right subclavian artery, a large artery that arises from the brachiocephalic artery. It has several important branches: the axillary, vertebral thoracic, and internal thoracic arteries and the cervical and costocervical trunks, which perfuse the right side of the upper body.

right-to-know laws, laws that require employers to inform workers regarding health effects of materials they must handle,

R

including toxic chemicals and radioactive substances. Under the authority of the U.S. Occupational Safety and Health Act of 1970, the National Institute for Occupational Safety and Health periodically revises recommendations or limits of exposure to potentially hazardous substances in the workplace. It also recommends appropriate preventive measures designed to reduce or eliminate adverse health effects of these hazards and publishes its recommendations in a variety of public documents.

right-to-left shunt [ME, *shunten*], a shunt in which unoxygenated venous blood bypasses the lungs and directly enters the arterial system, as in the tetralogy of Fallot and other conditions.

right umbilical vein, the right of the two veins in the umbilical cord that carry blood from the placenta to the sinus venosus of the heart in the early embryo. It degenerates during the seventh week.

right ventricle, the relatively thin-walled chamber of the heart that pumps blood received from the right atrium into the pulmonary arteries to the lungs for oxygenation. The right ventricle is shorter and rounder than the long conical left ventricle.

rigid gas-permeable (RGP) contact lens, a contact lens made of rigid plastic that transmits oxygen to the cornea, which increases the comfort of the lens. RGP lenses hold their shape better and offer clearer vision than soft lenses, are more durable, and are less prone to harbor bacteria and protein deposits. However, they cause discomfort on initial wearing and require a short adaptation period.

rigidity /rijid′itē/ [L, *rigere,* to be stiff], a condition of hardness, stiffness, or inflexibility.—**rigid,** *adj.*

rigidus /rij′idəs/ [L, stiff], a deformity characterized by limited motion, especially dorsiflexion of the great toe.

rigor /rig′ər/ [L, stiffness], **1.** a rigid condition of the body tissues, as in rigor mortis. **2.** a violent attack of shivering that may be associated with chills and fever.

rigor mortis /môr′tis/, the rigid stiffening of skeletal and cardiac muscle shortly after death.

riluzole, a glutamate antagonist used to treat amyotrophic lateral sclerosis.

rim [OE, *rima,* edge], an outer edge, which may be curved or circular, as on an occluding surface built on a temporary or permanent denture base.

rima /rī′mə/, a cleft or fissure.

Rimactane, a trademark for an antibacterial (rifampin).

rimantadine /ri-man′tah-dēn/, an antiviral agent used in prophylaxis and treatment of influenza A.

rimexolone /rimek′sah-lōn/, a corticosteroid used in topical treatment of inflammation after eye surgery and of uveitis affecting the anterior structures of the eye.

rimose /rī′mōs/, having many clefts or fissures.

Rimso-50, a trademark for a urinary tract antiinflammatory agent (dimethyl sulfoxide).

rimula /rim′yələ/ [L, small cleft], a very small fissure in the brain or spinal cord.

ring [AS, *hring*], **1.** a circular band surrounding a central opening. **2.** a closed chainlike linkage of atoms.

ring centriole, a common misnomer for the anulus of the spermatozoon, which is not actually a centriole.

ring chromosome [AS, *hring*], a circular chromosome formed by the fusion of the two ends. It is the primary type of chromosome found in bacteria.

ring-down artifact, in sonography, an echo pattern caused by reverberation in a bubble or other soft tissue entity.

ring-down time, in ultrasonics, the time required for vibration of the transducer element at its resonance frequency to decrease to a negligible level following excitation.

ringed sideroblast /sid′əroblast′/ [Gk, *sideros,* iron, *blastos,* germ], an iron-rich nucleated red blood cell precursor in the bone marrow characterized by a perinuclear ring of siderotic granules.

Ringer's lactate solution, a fluid and electrolyte replenisher prescribed for correction of extracellular volume and electrolyte depletion.

ring removal from swollen finger, a technique for taking off a tightly fitting ring. It consists of slipping the end of a string under the ring while moving the ring toward the hand. The rest of the string is then wound around the swollen part of the finger a number of times, after which the string is unwound from the hand side, gradually easing the ring toward the finger tip.

Rinne tuning fork test /rin′ə/ [Heinrich A. Rinne, German otologist, 1819–1868], a method of distinguishing conductive from sensorineural hearing loss. The base of a vibrating tuning fork is placed against the patient's mastoid bone. The ear not being tested is masked. When the patient no longer hears the sound, the time it was heard is noted, and the fork is positioned about ½ inch from the ipsilateral external auditory meatus. The time sound is heard is again noted. Air-conducted sound should be heard twice as long as bone-conducted sound after bone conduction stops. In sensorineural loss the sound is heard relatively longer by air conduction; in conductive hearing loss the sound is heard longer by bone conduction.

Riopan, a trademark for a fixed combination medication containing an antacid (magaldrate) and an antiflatulent (simethicone).

riot control agents, chemical agents normally used for crowd control. They are used as liquids or aerosols and exposure is by inhalation or by contact with the eyes or skin. They incapacitate by irritating the skin and mucous membranes and causing respiratory distress. High doses can cause blindness and death. Treatment is by removal of clothing and removing the agent from the skin and eyes.

RIP, 1. abbreviation for **reflex inhibiting pattern.** 2. abbreviation for **ribosome-inactivating protein.**

ripe cataract [OE, *ripan*; Gk, *katarrhaktes*, portcullis], a mature cataract that produces swelling and opacity of the entire lens.

risedronate, a bone-resorption inhibitor prescribed to treat Paget's disease.

risk-benefit analysis, the consideration as to whether a medical or surgical procedure, particularly a radical approach, is worth the risk to the patient as compared to possible benefits if the procedure is successful.

risk control, a nursing outcome from the Nursing Outcomes Classification (NOC) defined as personal actions to prevent, eliminate, or reduce modifiable health threats.

risk control: alcohol use, a nursing outcome from the Nursing Outcomes Classification (NOC) defined as personal actions to prevent, eliminate, or reduce alcohol use that poses a threat to health.

risk control: cancer, a nursing outcome from the Nursing Outcomes Classification (NOC) defined as personal actions to detect or reduce the threat of cancer.

risk control: cardiovascular health, a nursing outcome from the Nursing Outcomes Classification (NOC) defined as personal actions to eliminate or reduce threats to cardiovascular health.

risk control: drug use, a nursing outcome from the Nursing Outcomes Classification (NOC) defined as personal actions to prevent, eliminate, or reduce drug use that poses a threat to health.

risk control: hearing impairment, a nursing outcome from the Nursing Outcomes Classification (NOC) defined as personal actions to prevent, eliminate, or reduce threats to hearing function.

risk control: hyperthermia, a nursing outcome from the Nursing Outcomes Classification (NOC) defined as personal actions to prevent, detect, or reduce the threat of high body temperature.

risk control: hypothermia, a nursing outcome from the Nursing Outcomes Classification (NOC) defined as personal actions to prevent, detect, or reduce the threat of low body temperature.

risk control: infectious process, a nursing outcome from the Nursing Outcomes Classification (NOC) defined as personal actions to prevent, eliminate, or reduce the threat of infection.

risk control: sexually transmitted diseases (STDs), a nursing outcome from the Nursing Outcomes Classification (NOC) defined as personal actions to prevent, eliminate, or reduce the behaviors associated with sexually transmitted disease.

risk control: sun exposure, a nursing outcome from the Nursing Outcomes Classification (NOC) defined as personal actions to prevent or reduce threats to the skin and eyes from sun exposure.

risk control: tobacco use, a nursing outcome from the Nursing Outcomes Classification (NOC) defined as personal actions to prevent tobacco use.

risk control: unintended pregnancy, a nursing outcome from the Nursing Outcomes Classification (NOC) defined as personal actions to reduce the possibility of unintended pregnancy.

risk control: visual impairment, a nursing outcome from the Nursing Outcomes Classification (NOC) defined as personal actions to prevent, eliminate, or reduce threats to visual function.

risk detection, a nursing outcome from the Nursing Outcomes Classification (NOC) defined as personal actions taken to identify personal health threats.

risk factor [Fr, *risque*, hazard; L, *factor*, maker], a factor that causes a person or a group of people to be particularly susceptible to an unwanted, unpleasant, or unhealthful event such as immunosuppression, which increases the incidence and severity of infection.

risk identification, a nursing intervention from the Nursing Interventions Classification (NIC) defined as analysis of potential risk factors, determination of health risks, and prioritization of risk reduction strategies for an individual or group.

risk identification: childbearing family, a nursing intervention from the Nursing Interventions Classification (NIC) defined as identification of an individual or family likely to experience difficulties in parenting, and prioritization of strategies to prevent parenting problems.

risk identification: genetic, a nursing intervention from the Nursing Interventions Classification (NIC) defined as identification and analysis of potential genetic risk factors in an individual, family, or group.

R

risk management, a function of administration of a hospital or other health facility directed toward identification, evaluation, and correction of potential risks that could lead to injury to patients, staff members, or visitors.

risorius /risôr'ē-əs/ [L, *ridere,* to laugh], one of the 12 muscles of the mouth. A fibromuscular fibrous band, it acts to retract the angle of the mouth, as in a smile.

Risser cast /ris'ər/ [Joseph C. Risser, American surgeon, 1892–1942], an orthopedic device for encasing the entire trunk of the body, extending over the cervical area to the chin. In rare cases, it extends over the hips to the knees. It is used to immobilize the trunk in the treatment of scoliosis and in the preoperative or postoperative correction or maintenance of correction of scoliosis.

RIST, abbreviation for **radioimmunosorbent test.**

risus caninus /rī'səs/ [L, *risus,* laughter, *caninus,* doglike], a grinning facial distortion caused by tension in the occipitofrontalis and other facial muscles as a result of tetanus.

risus sardonicus /särdon'ikəs/ [L, laughter; Gk, *sardonius,* mocking], a wry masklike grin caused by spasm of the facial muscles, as seen in tetanus.

Ritalin, a trademark for a central nervous system stimulant (methylphenidate hydrochloride).

Ritgen maneuver, an obstetric procedure used to control delivery of the fetal head. It involves applying upward pressure from the coccygeal region to extend the head during actual delivery.

ritodrine hydrochloride /rit'ədrēn/, a uterine relaxant prescribed in pregnancy management to stop the uterus from contracting in preterm labor.

ritonavir, a protease inhibitor. It is prescribed in the treatment of AIDS, as part of a multidrug regimen including at least three antiretroviral drugs.

Ritter's disease [Gottfried Ritter von Rittershain, German physician, 1820–1883], a rare, staphylococcal infection of newborns that begins with red spots about the mouth and chin, gradually spreading over the entire body, and followed by generalized exfoliation. Vesicles and yellow crusts may also be present. It is usually fatal unless treated with antibiotics.

ritual /rich'ōōwəl/, **1.** a mental health disorder characterized by repetitive sequences of stereotyped daily life routines, such as repeated handwashing that interferes with an individual's level of functioning. **2.** a prescribed order of ceremonial acts or series of acts. **3.** a detailed procedure followed faithfully or regularly.

ritual circumcision, a surgical procedure for removing the prepuce of the male in Jewish communities or the labia minora of the female in Muslim communities as a religious rite. In Jewish families the male circumcision is usually performed on the eighth day after birth.

rituximab, a miscellaneous antineoplastic prescribed to treat non-Hodgkin's lymphoma (CD20-positive, B cell).

rivastigmine /riv'ah-stig'mēn/, a reversible inhibitor of cholinesterase. It is used as an adjunct in the treatment of mild to moderate dementia of the Alzheimer type.

Rivea corymbosa, a twining vine of the botanical family of Convolvulaceae. The seeds contain indole alkaloids, a source of lysergic acid diethylamide, which have an effect of altered perception when ingested in large quantities. These seeds have been used in religious ceremonies of indigenous Latin American cultures since the era of the Aztecs.

Rivinus' notch, tympanic notch /rēvē'nəs/ [Augustus Q. Rivinus, German anatomist, 1652–1723], a defect in the upper tympanic part of the temporal bone, filled by the upper portion of the tympanic membrane.

rivus lacrimalis /rī'vəs/ [L, stream of tears], a channel between the eyelids and the surface of the eye that normally allows a flow of moisture when the eyes are closed.

rizatriptan, a migraine agent used in the acute treatment of migraine.

RK, 1. abbreviation for **radial keratotomy. 2.** abbreviation for **refractive keratotomy.**

R.L.E., abbreviation for *right lower extremity.*

R.L.L., abbreviation for *right lower lobe of lung.*

r-loop, in molecular genetics, a distinctive loop formation seen under an electron microscope. It is composed of a single helical strand of DNA wound with a hybrid strand containing another single strand of DNA with a strand of RNA.

RLQ, abbreviation for *right lower quadrant.*

RMP, 1. abbreviation for **regional medical program. 2.** abbreviation for *right mentoposterior* fetal position.

RMSF, abbreviation for **Rocky Mountain spotted fever.**

RMT, abbreviation for *right mentotransverse* fetal position.

Rn, symbol for the element **radon.**

RN, symbol for **registered nurse.**

RNA, abbreviation for **ribonucleic acid.**

RNA amplification, an in vitro technique used to increase the number of copies of a specific segment of RNA to aid in its detection.

RNA polymerase, an enzyme that catalyzes the assembly of ribonucleoside triphosphates into RNA, with single-stranded DNA serving as the template.

RNase, abbreviation for **ribonuclease.**

RNA splicing, in molecular genetics, the process by which base pairs that interrupt the continuity of genetic information inDNA are removed from the precursors of messenger RNA.

RNA virus, any of a group of viruses whose genome is composed of RNA, including most viruses that infect animal cells. RNA viruses include *arenavirus, coronavirus, orthomyxovirus, picornavirus, rhabdovirus,* and *togavirus.*

RN, C, abbreviation for *registered nurse, certified.*

RN, CNA, abbreviation for *registered nurse, certified in Nursing Administration.*

RN, CNAA, abbreviation for *registered nurse, certified in Nursing Administration, Advanced.*

RN, CS, abbreviation for *registered nurse, certified Specialist.*

RNP, abbreviation for **ribonuclear protein.**

ROA, abbreviation for *right occipitoanterior* fetal position.

Robaxin, a trademark for a skeletal muscle relaxant (methocarbamol).

Robb, Isabel Hampton, a Canadian-born American nursing educator and writer. She was the first to institute a systematic, step-by-step course for nursing students that integrated clinical experience and classwork and the first educator to arrange for the affiliation of her students at other hospitals for specialized training. She was one of the founders of *The American Journal of Nursing* and of the forerunner of the American Nurses Association.

robertsonian translocation /rob′ərtsō′nē·ən/, the exchange of entire chromosome arms, with the break occurring at the centromere, usually between two non-homologous acrocentric chromosomes. It produces one large, metacentric chromosome and one extremely small chromosome. The latter carries little genetic material and may be lost through successive cell divisions.

Roberts' syndrome /rob′ərts/ [John Bingham Roberts, American surgeon, 1852–1924], a hereditary syndrome, transmitted as an autosomal-recessive trait, consisting of imperfect development of the long bones of the limbs and associated with cleft palate and lip and other anomalies.

Robinow's syndrome /rob′inouz/ [Meinhard Robinow, American physician, 1909–1997], dwarfism associated with increased interorbital distance, malaligned teeth, bulging forehead, depressed nasal bridge, and short limbs.

Robinul, a trademark for an anticholinergic (glycopyrrolate).

Robitussin, a trademark for an expectorant (guaifenesin), also available in various fixed-combination preparations with an antihistamine, with a decongestant, or with a cough suppressant.

robotic /rōbot′ik/, pertaining to a robot, a mechanical or electronic device that resembles a human being, operating automatically or by remote control with the ability to perform a variety of complex tasks.

robotic surgery, the performance of operative procedures with the assistance of robotic technology. It allows great precision and is used for remote-control, minimally invasive procedures.

Rocaltrol, a trademark for a regulator of calcium (calcitriol).

Rocephin, a trademark for a cephalosporin antibiotic (ceftriaxone sodium).

Rochalimaea /rosh′əlimē̄′ə/, a genus of bacteria resembling *Rickettsia* but found extracellularly in an arthropod host. The type species, *R. quintana* (now called *Bartonella quintana*), is a cause of trench fever as transmitted by the body louse. A related bacterium *R. henselae* is a cause of bacillary angiomatosis in immunocompromised humans, including those with HIV infection.

rocker knife, a knife with a rounded blade that cuts with a rocking motion, designed for patients who have functional use of one extremity.

rocking bed, a device that rocks a patient from 30 degrees head up to 15 degrees head down several times a minute. The rocking moves the abdominal contents, and the resulting diaphragmatic movement assists ventilation of the lungs.

Rocky Mountain spotted fever (RMSF), a serious tickborne infectious disease occurring throughout the temperate zones of North and South America, caused by *Rickettsia rickettsii.* It is characterized by chills, fever, severe headache, myalgia, mental confusion, and rash. Erythematous macules first appear on wrists and ankles, spreading rapidly over the extremities, trunk, and face and usually on the palms and soles. Hemorrhagic lesions, constipation, and abdominal distension are also common. Early treatment with doxycycline or tetracycline is important, because more than 20% of untreated patients die from shock and renal failure. Immunity follows recovery. Prevention includes the use of insect repellents, the wearing of protective clothing, frequent inspection of the body and careful removal of wood or dog ticks. Ticks should not be crushed, because infection may be acquired through skin abrasions.

rocuronium /ro′ku-ro′ne-um/, a neuromuscular blocking agent, used as an adjunct in general anesthesia to facilitate endotracheal intubation and as a skeletal muscle relaxant during surgery or mechanical ventilation.

rocuronium bromide, a nondepolarizing neuromuscular blocking agent prescribed as an adjunct to general anesthesia in providing skeletal muscle relaxation.

rod [AS, *rodd*], **1.** a straight cylindric structure. **2.** one of the tiny cylindric elements arranged perpendicular to the surface of the retina. Rods contain the chemical rhodopsin, which adapts the eye to detect low-intensity light.

rodenticide poisoning /rōden′tisīd/ [L, *rodere*, to gnaw, *caedere*, to kill, *potio*, drink], a toxic condition caused by the ingestion of a substance intended for the control of rodent populations.

rodent ulcer /rō′dənt/ [L, *rodere*, to gnaw, *ulcus*, ulcer], a slowly developing serpiginous ulceration of a basal cell carcinoma of the skin.

rod-monochromat /rod′ monəkrō′mət/, a person who is totally color-blind or who lacks retinal cone function.

rods and cones [AS, *rodd*; Gk, *konos*], the light-sensitive cells of the retina. The rods, under the visual purple pigment epithelium, are mainly located around the periphery of the retina. The cones receive color stimuli.

roentgen (R) /rent′gən, ren′jən/ [Wilhelm K. Roentgen, German physicist, 1845–1923], the quantity of x-radiation or gamma radiation that creates 1 electrostatic unit of ions in 1 mL of air at 0° C and 760 mm of pressure. In radiotherapy or radiodiagnosis, the roentgen is the unit of the emitted dose.

roentgen fetometry, the use of radiographic techniques to measure the fetus in utero.

Roferon-A, a trademark for a parenteral antineoplastic (interferon alfa 2a).

Rogers, Martha E. [1914–1994], a nurse theorist who developed the Science of Unitary Human Beings, a nursing theory introduced in 1970. The Rogers' theory has strong ties to the general systems theory with elements of a developmental model. It considers four "building blocks": Energy Fields, Universe of Open Systems, Pattern and Organization, and Four Dimensionality.

Rohrer's constants, the constants in an empiric equation for airway resistance. It is expressed as $R = K_1 + K_2V$, where R is resistance, V is instantaneous volumetric flow rate, K_1 is a constant representing gas viscosity and airway geometry, and K_2 is a constant representing gas density and airway geometry.

Rolando's fissure /rōlan′dōz/ [Luigi Rolando, Italian anatomist, 1773–1831; L, *fissura*, cleft], the central sulcus of the cerebrum.

Rolando's fracture [Luigi Rolando], a fracture of the base of the first metacarpal.

Rolando's gelatinous substance, the apical part of the posterior horn of the spinal cord's gray matter. It appears gelatinous because of its lack of myelinated nerve fibers.

role [Fr, stage character], a socially expected behavior pattern associated with an individual's function in various social groups. Roles provide a means for social participation and a way to test identities for consensual validation by significant others.

role blurring, the tendency for professional roles to overlap and become indistinct.

role change, a situation in which status is retained while role expectations change.

role clarification, gaining the knowledge, information, and cues needed to perform a role.

role conflict, the presence of contradictory and often competing role expectations.

role enhancement, a nursing intervention from the Nursing Interventions Classification (NIC) defined as assisting a patient, significant other, and/or family to improve relationships by clarifying and supplementing specific role behaviors.

role model [Fr, *role*, stage character; L, *modus*, small copy], a person who knowingly or unknowingly inspires others to imitate his or her persona. The role model may be a real person, such as a parent, or a symbolic character such as one depicted in movies or television programs.

role overload, a condition in which there is insufficient time in which to carry out all of the expected role functions.

role performance, a nursing outcome from the Nursing Outcomes Classification (NOC) defined as congruence of an individual's role behavior with role expectations.

role playing, a psychotherapeutic technique in which a person acts out a real or simulated situation as a means of understanding intrapsychic conflicts.

role reversal, the act of assuming the role of another person to appreciate how the person feels, perceives, and behaves in relation to self and to others.

role strain, stress associated with expected roles or positions, experienced as frustration. Role ambiguity is a type of role strain that occurs when shared specifications set for an expected role are incomplete or insufficient to tell the involved individual what is desired and how to do it. Role incongruence is role stress that occurs when an individual undergoes role transitions requiring a significant modification in attitudes and values. Role overqualification is a type of role stress that occurs when a role does not require full use of a person's resources.

roll [OFr, *rolle*], intrinsic joint movements on an axis parallel to the articulating surface. The axis can remain stationary or move in a plane parallel to the joint surface.

roller bandage, a long, tightly wound strip of material that may vary in width. It is generally applied as a circular bandage wrapped around an extremity or the trunk.

roller clamp, a device, usually made of plastic, equipped with a small roller that may be rolled counterclockwise to close off primary IV tubing or clockwise to open it. The roller clamp may also be manipulated to increase and decrease the flow of the IV solution.

rolling effleurage, a circular rubbing stroke used in massage to promote circulation and muscle relaxation, especially on the shoulder and buttocks. It is performed with the hand flat, the palm and closely held fingers acting as a unit.

ROM, 1. abbreviation for **range of motion.** 2. abbreviation for **rupture of membranes.** 3. abbreviation for *right otitis media.* 4. abbreviation for *read-only memory.*

Roman chamomile, the dried flowers of *Chamaemelum nobile* (formerly *Anthemis nobilis*), used as a homeopathic preparation and in folk medicine externally as a counterirritant and internally as a carminative.

Romano-Ward syndrome /rō·mä′nō wôrd/ [C. Romano, Italian physician, b. 1923; O.C. Ward, Irish physician, 20th century], an autosomal-dominant form of the long QT syndrome, characterized by syncope and sometimes ventricular fibrillation and sudden death.

Romberg sign /rom′bərg/ [Moritz H. Romberg, German physician, 1795–1873;

L, *signum,* mark], an indication of loss of the sense of position in which the patient loses balance when standing erect, feet together, and eyes closed.

Rondec-DM, a trademark for a fixed-combination drug containing an antihistamine (carbinoxamine maleate), an antitussive (dextromethorphan hydrobromide), and an adrenergic decongestant and bronchodilator (pseudoepHEDrine hydrochloride).

rongeur forceps /rônzhur′, rôNzhœr′/ [Fr, *ronger,* to gnaw; L, *forceps,* pair of tongs], a kind of biting forceps that is strong and heavy, used for cutting bone.

R-on-T phenomenon, a cardiac event in which a ventricular stimulus causes premature depolarization of cells that have not completely repolarized. It may result in ventricular tachycardia or ventricular fibrillation.

rooming-in, in a hospital, a practice that allows mothers and newborn babies to share accommodations, remaining together in the hospital as they would at home rather than being separated.

room temperature [AS, *rum*; L, *temperatura*], the air temperature as measured in a specific part of a room.

root /rōōt, rŏŏt/ [AS, *rot*], the lowest part of an organ or a structure by which something is firmly attached, such as the anatomic root of the tooth, which is covered by cementum.

root canal file, a small, metal hand instrument with tightly spiraled blades, used for cleaning and shaping a pulp (root) canal.

root canal filling, a material placed in the pulp (root) canal of a tooth to seal the space previously occupied by the dental pulp.

root canal filling spreader, in root canal therapy, a tapered metal instrument used to compress gutta percha and sealer filling material against the sides of the canal to make room for additional gutta percha cones and sealer.

root canal therapy, that aspect of endodontics dealing with the treatment of diseases of the dental pulp, consisting of partial (pulpotomy) or complete (pulpectomy) extirpation of the diseased pulp, cleaning and sterilization of the empty root canal, enlarging and shaping of the canal to receive sealing material, and obturation of the canal with a nonirritating hermetic sealing agent.

root curettage, the debridement and planing of the root surface of a tooth with hand instruments and/or ultrasonic scalers to remove accretions and toxins to induce the development of healthy gingival tissues.

R

root furcation, 1. the anatomic area at which the roots of a multirooted tooth divide. 2. abnormal intraradicular resorption of bone in multirooted teeth, resulting from periodontal disease.

rooting reflex, a normal response in newborns when the cheek is touched or stroked along the side of the mouth to turn the head toward the stimulated side and begin to suck.

root of the lung, the structures that pass between the lung and mediastinum and their sleevelike covering of mediastinal pleura.

root resorption of teeth [AS, *rot*; L, *resorbere*, to suck back; AS, *toth*], destruction of the cementum or dentin of tooth roots due to osteoclastic activity. If only the apex of the root is affected, the root may become shortened and blunted. If the middle of the root is affected, the pulp canal will generally be penetrated.

root retention, a technique that removes the crown of a root canal-treated tooth and retains enough of the root and gingival attachment to support a prosthesis.

root submersion, a root retention in which the tooth structure is reduced below the level of the alveolar crest and the soft tissue is allowed to heal over it.

ROP, abbreviation for *right occipitoposterior* fetal position.

ropinirole, an agent prescribed to treat parkinsonism.

ropivacaine, a local anesthetic prescribed to produce peripheral nerve block, caudal anesthesia, central neural block, and vaginal block.

Rorschach test /rôr'shäk, rôr'shokh/ [Hermann Rorschach, Swiss psychiatrist, 1884–1922], a projective personality assessment test that consists of 10 pictures of inkblots, five in black and white, three in black and red, and two multicolored, to which the subject responds by telling, in as many interpretations as is desired, what images and emotions each design evokes. The test is designed to assess the degree to which intellectual and emotional factors are integrated in the subject's perception of the environment.

ROS, abbreviation for **review of systems.**

rosacea /rōzā'shē·ə/ [L, *rosaceus*, rosy], a chronic inflammatory disease seen in adults of all ages. It has two components: erythema and/or acneiform papules and pustules. It is associated with erythema, pustules, and telangiectasia, especially of the nose, forehead, and cheeks and ocular symptoms of conjunctivitis.

rose fever [L, *rosa* + *febris*, fever], a common misnomer for seasonal allergic rhinitis caused by pollen, most frequently of grasses, that are airborne at the time roses are in bloom. Because rose pollen is not dispersed by the wind, roses are not the cause of common spring and summer allergic reactions.

rose hips, a herbal product taken from a plant native to Europe and Asia, now grown widely in North America. This herb is used as a source of vitamin C and as a treatment for colds, fever, and mild infections. Much of vitamin C is, however, reportedly destroyed during the typical drying processes and storage, and there are insufficient reliable data regarding efficacy for any of its uses.

Rosenberg-Chutorian syndrome /rō'zən berg chŌŌtor'ē·ən/ [Roger N. Rosenberg, American physician, 20th century; Abe Milton Chutorian, American physician, b. 1929], a rare X-linked hereditary syndrome characterized by optic atrophy, progressive sensorineural hearing loss, and polyneuropathy.

Rosen method, a bodywork technique based on the premise that there is a connection between chronic muscular tension and suppressed emotions or trauma. The therapist helps the patient to relax the muscular tension and so to bring the underlying repressed memories to the surface and release them.

Rosenthal's disease, a deficiency of blood coagulation factor XI resulting in a systemic blood-clotting defect that may resemble classical hemophilia. Also known as *Rosenthal's syndrome.*

roseola /rōzē'ələ/ [L, *roseus*], any rose-colored rash.

roseola idiopathica, a skin eruption of symmetric reddish patches in a condition not associated with any other well-defined symptoms of disease.

roseola infantum, a benign viral endemic illness of infants and young children, caused by human herpesvirus 6 and possibly by herpesvirus 7. It is characterized by abrupt high sustained or spiking fever, mild pharyngitis, and lymph node enlargement. Febrile seizures may occur. After 4 or 5 days the fever suddenly drops to normal, and a faint, pink, maculopapular rash appears on the neck, trunk, and thighs. The rash may last a few hours to 2 days. There is no specific therapy or vaccine. Acetaminophen is often used to try to control fever.

roseola symptomatica, a rose-colored eruption that occurs at the onset of a well-defined febrile illness.

Roseolovirus /ro'ze·ō'lovi'rus/, a genus of herpesviruses closely related to the genus *Cytomegalovirus.* It contains the single species human herpesvirus 6, which is the causal agent of roseola infantum.

rose spots [L, *rosa*; ME, *spotte*], small erythematous macules occurring on the upper abdomen and anterior thorax and lasting 2 or 3 days, characteristic of typhoid and paratyphoid fevers.

rosette /rōzet′/, **1.** any structure resembling a rose. **2.** a sporulating body of a malarial parasite.

rosette technique, a method of detecting antigens or antibodies on a cell surface using antibody- or antigen-coated particles, which cause erythrocytes to form a rosette pattern.

rosiglitazone, an oral antidiabetic prescribed to treat stable type 2 DM.

rosin /roz′in/, a solid oleo resin produced by steam distillation of balsam from various species of pine trees. After extraction of turpentine in the process, the rosin remains as an amber mass. It is used in plasters and ointments.

rostellum /rostel′əm/ [L, *rostrum,* beak], **1.** the anterior of a tapeworm scolex, commonly featuring hooklike jaws. **2.** tubular mouth parts of some insects.

rostral /ros′trəl/, beak-shaped.

rostrum /ros′trəm/ [L, beak], a beaklike projection, as the rostrum of the sphenoid bone.

rosuvastatin, an antilipemic agent used as an adjunct in primary hypercholesterolemia (types Ia and Ib), mixed dyslipidemia elevated serum triglycerides, and homozygous low-density lipoprotein receptor disorder.

rot [AS, *rotian*], **1.** to decay. **2.** decomposition.

ROT, abbreviation for *right occipitotransverse* fetal position.

rotary nystagmus /rō′tərē/ [L, *rotare,* to rotate; Gk, *nystagmos,* nodding], a form of nystagmus in which the eyeball makes rotary motions around an axis.

RotaTeq, a trademark for rotavirus vaccine live oral.

rotating tourniquet /rō′tāting/ [L, *rotare,* to rotate; Fr, *tourniquet,* garrote], one of four constricting devices used in a rotating order to pool blood in the extremities. The purpose is to relieve congestion in the lungs in the treatment of acute pulmonary edema. Use of the rotating tourniquet has declined with the development of vasodilating drugs and diuretics.

rotation /rōtā′shən/ [L, *rotare*], **1.** the gyration of a bone around its central axis, one of the four basic movements allowed by the various joints of the skeleton. Some bones, such as the humerus, rotate around their own longitudinal

axis. Alternatively, the axis of rotation may not be quite parallel to the long axis of the rotating bone, as in movement of the radius on the ulna during pronation and supination of the hand. **2.** a turning around an axis. **3.** the turning of the fetal head to descend through the pelvis during birth.

rotator /rō′tātər/ [L, *rotare,* to rotate], a muscle that rotates a structure around its axis, as the cervical, thoracic, and lumbar musculi rotatores, which function to extend and rotate the vertebral column toward the opposite side.

rotator cuff, a musculotendinous structure about the capsule of the shoulder joint, formed by the inserting fibers of the supraspinatus, infraspinatus, teres minor, and subscapularis muscles, which blend with the capsule, and provide mobility and strength to the shoulder joint.

rotatores muscles, the deepest muscles of the transversospinales group. These small muscles are present throughout the length of the vertebral column but are best developed in the thoracic region.

rotavirus /rō′təvī′rəs/, a double-stranded RNA virus that appears as a tiny wheel, with a clearly defined outer layer, or rim, and an inner layer of spokes. It is a cause of acute gastroenteritis with diarrhea, particularly in infants.

rotavirus diarrhea, diarrhea caused by a rotavirus, usually seen in children.

rotavirus gastroenteritis, viral gastroenteritis caused by a rotavirus infection, one of the most common causes of diarrhea in the United States. The virus is usually ingested in contaminated food or water. Young children are particularly susceptible and can suffer severe dehydration or even death.

rotavirus vaccine live oral, a live oral vaccine that protects against rotavirus serotypes G1, G2, G3, G4, and P1. It is used to prevent rotavirus gastroenteritis in infants.

Rothmund-Thomson syndrome /rot′mŏŏnd tom′son/ [August von Rothmund, Jr., German physician, 1830–1906; Mathew Sidney Thomson, English dermatologist, 1894–1969], an autosomal-recessive syndrome occurring principally in females, characterized by the presence of reticulated, atrophic, hyperpigmented, telangiectatic cutaneous plaques and often accompanied by juvenile cataracts; saddle nose; congenital bone defects; disturbances in the growth of hair, nails, and teeth; and hypogonadism.

Roth's spots /roth, rōt/ [Moritz Roth, Swiss physician and pathologist, 1839–1914], pale-centered oval hemorrhages on the retina, observed in several disorders but classically seen in bacterial endocarditis.

rotigotine, a drug used to treat idiopathic Parkinson's disease.

Rotokinetic treatment table /rō'tōkinet'ik/, a special bed equipped with an automatic turning device that completely immobilizes patients while rotating them from 90 to 270 degrees around a horizontal axis.

Rotor's syndrome /rō'tərs/, a rare condition of the liver inherited as an autosomal-recessive trait. It is similar to Dubin-Johnson syndrome but can be distinguished by the normal functioning of the gallbladder and lack of liver pigmentation.

rotoscoliosis /rō'təskō'lē·ō'sis/, a condition in which there is both lateral and rotational spinal deviation.

rouleaux /rōōlō'/, *sing.* **rouleau** [Fr, cylinder], red cells in a microscopic roll or "stack-of-coins" formation that may be caused by abnormal proteins, as in multiple myeloma or macroglobulinemia.

round foramen, one of a pair of rounded apertures in the greater wings of the sphenoid bone.

round ligament [L, *rotundus,* round, *ligare,* to bind], **1.** a curved fibrous band that is attached at one end to the fovea of the head of the femur and at the other end to the transverse ligament of the acetabulum. **2.** a fibrous cord extending from the umbilicus to the anterior part of the liver. It is the remnant of the umbilical vein. **3.** in the female, a fibromuscular band that extends from the anterior surface of the uterus through the inguinal canal to the labium majora.

rounds *informal.* a teaching conference or a meeting in which the clinical problems encountered in the practice of nursing, medicine, or other service are discussed.

round window [L, *rotundus;* ONorse, *vindauga*], a round opening in the medial wall of the middle ear leading into the cochlea and covered by a secondary tympanic membrane.

roundworm, any worm of the class Nematoda, including *Ancylostoma duodenale, Ascaris lumbricoides, Enterobius vermicularis,* and *Strongyloides stercoralis.*

Roussy-Lévy disease /rōōsē' lāvē'/ [Gustave Roussy, French pathologist, 1874–1948; Gabrielle Lévy, French neurologist, 1886–1935], an inherited cerebellar ataxia associated with muscle wasting of the extremities, absence of tendon reflexes, and foot deformities.

route of administration /rōōt, rout/ [Fr, *route,* course; L, *administrare,* to serve], of a drug, any one of the body systems in which a drug may be administered, such as intradermally, intrathecally, intramuscularly, intranasally, intravenously, orally, rectally, subcutaneously, sublingually, topically, or vaginally.

Roux-en-Y /rōō' en wī', rōō' än ēgrek'/ [César Roux, Swiss surgeon, 1857–1926], a treatment for morbid obesity consisting of surgical division of the small intestine to form two arms; the jejunum is anastomosed to a gastric pouch and the bypassed duodenum connects the pylorus with an end-to-side anastomosis into the lower jejunum.

Roux-en-Y gastric bypass, a treatment for morbid obesity consisting of surgical division of the small intestine to form two arms. The jejunum is attached to a stoma into a gastric pouch and the bypassed duodenum connects the pylorus with an end-to-side anastomosis into the lower jejunum.

Rovsing's sign /rov'singz/ [Nils T. Rovsing, Danish surgeon, 1862–1927], an indication of acute appendicitis in which pressure on the left lower quadrant of the abdomen causes pain in the right lower quadrant.

Royal College of Physicians (RCP), a professional organization of physicians in the United Kingdom.

Royal College of Physicians and Surgeons of Canada (RCPSC), a national Canadian organization that recognizes and confers membership on certain qualified physicians and surgeons.

Royal College of Surgeons (R.C.S.), a professional organization of surgeons in the United Kingdom.

Roy, Sister Callista [b. 1939], a nursing theorist who introduced the Adaptation Model of Nursing in 1970 as a conceptual framework for nursing curricula, practice, and research. In the Roy model the human is viewed as an adaptive system. Changes occur in the system in response to stimuli. If the change promotes the integrity of the individual, it is an adaptive response. Otherwise it is a maladaptive response.

Rozerem, a trademark for ramelteon.

RPF, abbreviation for **renal plasma flow.**

rpm, abbreviation for *revolutions per minute.*

RPR test, abbreviation for **rapid plasma reagin test,** a screening test for syphilis.

RQ, abbreviation for **respiratory quotient.**

RRA, abbreviation for **registered record administrator.**

R-R interval, the interval from the peak of one QRS complex to the peak of the next as shown on an ECG.

rRNA, abbreviation for **ribosomal RNA.**

RRT, abbreviation for **registered respiratory therapist.**

RSD, abbreviation for **reflex sympathetic dystrophy.**

RSNA, abbreviation for **Radiological Society of North America.**

RSV, RS virus, abbreviations for **respiratory syncytial virus.**

RT, 1. abbreviation for **registered technologist. 2.** abbreviation for **respiratory therapy.**

RTA, abbreviation for **renal tubular acidosis.**

r.t.c., abbreviation for *return to clinic,* noted on the chart, usually followed by a date on which a subsequent appointment has been made for the patient.

Ru, symbol for the element **ruthenium.**

rub [ME, *rubben,* to scrape], the movement of one surface moving over another, thereby producing friction, as when pleural membranes produce friction rub.

rubber-band ligation, a method of treating hemorrhoids by placing a rubber band around the hemorrhoidal part of the blood vessel, causing it to slough off after a period of time.

rubber dam [ME, *rubben,* to scrape; AS, *demman,* to dam up], a thin sheet of synthetic rubber or natural latex rubber used to isolate one or more teeth during a dental procedure.

rubber dam clamps forceps, a type of forceps with beaks designed to engage holes in a rubber dam clamp to facilitate its placement over teeth.

rubbing alcohol [ME, *rubben,* to scrape; Ar, *alkohl,* essence], a disinfectant for skin and instruments. It contains 70% isopropyl alcohol by volume, the remainder consisting of water and denaturants, with or without color or perfume. It may cause dryness of the skin. Rubbing alcohol is for external use only and is flammable.

rubefacient /roo'bəfā'shənt/ [L, *ruber,* red, *facere,* to make], **1.** a substance or agent that increases the reddish coloration of the skin. **2.** increasing the reddish coloration of the skin.

rubefaction /roo'bəfak'shən/ [L, *ruber,* red, *facer,* to make], a redness of the skin produced by a counterirritant.

rubella /roobel'ə/ [L, *rubellus,* somewhat red], a contagious viral disease, with an incubation time of 12 to 23 days and spread by droplet infection, characterized by fever, symptoms of a mild upper respiratory tract infection, lymph node enlargement, arthralgia, and a diffuse fine red maculopapular rash. The symptoms usually last only 2 or 3 days except for arthralgia, which may persist longer or recur. The illness itself is mild and needs no special treatment. One attack confers lifelong immunity. If a woman acquires rubella in the first trimester of pregnancy, fetal anomalies may result, including heart defects, cataracts, deafness, and mental retardation. Live attenuated rubella vaccine is advised for all children to reduce chances of an epidemic and thus to protect pregnant women. The vaccine is not given to women already pregnant, and it is recommended that pregnancy be avoided for 3 months after the administration of rubella vaccine.

rubella and mumps virus vaccine, a suspension containing live attenuated mumps and rubella viruses. It can be prescribed for immunization against rubella, but generally the trivalent mumps-measles-rubella vaccine is administered instead.

rubella antibody test, a blood test performed to detect immunity to rubella, particularly in pregnant women, and to diagnose rubella in infants.

rubella embryopathy, any congenital abnormality in an infant caused by maternal rubella in the early stages of pregnancy.

rubella titer [L, *rubellus,* somewhat red; Fr, *titre,* standard], a serologic test to determine a patient's state of immunity against rubella.

rubella virus, a togavirus that is the causal agent of rubella.

rubella virus vaccine, a suspension containing live attenuated rubella virus. It is prescribed for immunization against rubella.

rubeola antibody test, a blood test to measure measles infection in patients who cannot be diagnosed clinically and to establish and document immunity.

rubeosis /roo'bē·ō'sis/, a red discoloration of the skin.

rubeosis iridis, the formation of abnormal blood vessels on the anterior of the iris. It may be associated with DM, retinal ischemia, and neovascular glaucoma.

ruber /roo'bər/, *(Latin)* red.

rubescent /roobes'ənt/, reddening.

rubidium (Rb) /roobid'ē·əm/ [L, *rubidus,* reddish], a soft metallic element of the alkali metals group. Its atomic number is 37, and its atomic mass is 85.47. Slightly radioactive, it is used in radioisotope scanning.

Rubinstein-Taybi syndrome /roo'binstīn tā'bē/ [Jack Herbert Rubinstein, American pediatrician, b. 1925; Hooshang Taybi, American radiologist, b. 1919], a congenital condition characterized by mental and motor retardation, broad thumbs and great toes, short stature, characteristic facies, including high-arched palate and straight or beaked nose, various eye abnormalities, pulmonary stenosis, keloid

R

formation in surgical scars, large foramen magnum, and abnormalities of the vertebrae and sternum.

Rubin's test [Isador C. Rubin, American gynecologist, 1883–1958], a test performed in the process of evaluating the cause of infertility by assessing the patency of the fallopian tubes. Carbon dioxide gas (CO_2) is introduced into the tubes under pressure through a cannula inserted into the cervix. The CO_2 is passed through from a syringe connected to a manometer at pressures of up to 200 mm Hg. If the tubes are open, the gas enters the abdominal cavity, and the recorded pressure falls below 180 mm Hg.

rubivirus /roo'bēvī'rəs/, a member of the togavirus family, which includes the rubella virus.

rubor /roo'bôr/, redness, especially when accompanying inflammation.

rubratoxin /roo'brətok'sin/, a mycotoxin produced on cereal grains by certain species of penicillin. It can cause hepatotoxicity in cattle.

rubricyte /roo'brisīt/ [L, ruber, red; Gk, kytos, cell], a nucleated red blood cell; the marrow stage in the normal development of an erythrocyte, synonymous with polychromatophilic normoblast.

rudiment /roo'dimənt/ [L, rudimentum, beginning], an organ or tissue that is incompletely developed or nonfunctional.

rudimentary /roo'dimen'tərē/ [L, rudimentum, beginning], pertaining to something either vestigial or embryonic; undeveloped.

Ruffini's corpuscles /roofe'nēz/ [Angelo Ruffini, Italian anatomist, 1864–1929], a variety of oval-shaped, encapsulated nerve endings in the subcutaneous tissue, located principally at the junction of the dermis and the subcutaneous tissue.

ruga /roo'gə/ pl. **rugae** [L, ridge], a ridge or fold, such as the rugae of the stomach, which are large folds in the mucous membrane of that organ.

rugae of vagina [L, ruga, ridge, vagina, sheath], the transverse ridges on the mucous membrane lining the vagina. They allow the vagina to stretch during childbirth.

rugitus /roo'jitəs/ [L, roaring], the rumbling sound of flatus in the intestines.

rugose /roo'gōs/, wrinkled or corrugated.

RUL, abbreviation for *right upper lobe* of lung.

Ruland, Cornelia M., a nursing theorist who, with Shirley M. Moore, developed the Peaceful End of Life Theory, which asserts that nurses are integral to the creation of peaceful end of life care, which includes freedom from suffering, emotional support, closeness to and participation by significant others, and treatment with empathy and respect.

rule, a guide for conduct or action.

rule of bigeminy [L, regula, model, bis, double, geminus, twin], the tendency of a lengthened ventricular cycle to precipitate a premature ventricular complex.

rule of confidentiality, a principle that personal information about others, particularly patients, should not be revealed to persons not authorized to receive such information.

rule of nines, a formula for estimating the percentage of adult body surface covered by burns by assigning 9% to the head and each arm, twice 9% (18%) to each leg and the anterior and posterior trunk, and 1% to the perineum. This is modified in infants and children because of the proportionately larger head size.

rule of outlet, an obstetric standard for determining whether the pelvic outlet will allow the passage of a fetus. It is calculated from the sum of the transverse and posterior sagittal diameters of the outlet, which must equal at least 15 cm.

rule of three, an arterial oxygen tension that is three times the value of the inspired oxygen concentration. It is regarded as an empiric guide to a temporarily acceptable minimal oxygenation or expression of clinical observation and has no scientific basis.

rum, a spirit distilled from fermented products of sugar cane, including molasses. It may contain up to 60% of ethyl alcohol by volume.

ruminant /roo'minənt/ [L, ruminare, to chew again], pertaining to animals that chew their cud and to human infants that may regurgitate and reswallow a meal.

rumination /roo'minā'shən/ [L, ruminare, to chew again], habitual regurgitation of small amounts of undigested food with little force after every feeding, a condition commonly seen in infants. It may be a symptom of overfeeding, of eating too fast, or of swallowing air. It has little or no clinical significance.

runner's high, a feeling of euphoria experienced by some cross-country runners and joggers. The feeling of elation is believed to be associated with the body's production of endorphins during physical stress.

Runyon classification system /run'yən/, a system of identifying mycobacteria on the basis of pigmentation and growth condition of the organisms. It includes group I, yellow-pigment photochromogens; group II, yellow-to-orange-to-red pigment scotochromogens; group III, white-to-tan nonphotochromogens; and group IV, rapid-growing saprophytes.

rupia /roo´pē·ə/, a pustular eruption associated with secondary syphilis. It is characterized by encrusted ulcers resembling shells on darkly pigmented skin.

rupture /rup´chər/ [L, *rumpere,* to break], **1.** a tear or break in the continuity or configuration of an organ or body tissue, including instances when their tissue protrudes through the opening. **2.** to cause a break or tear.

ruptured hymen, a hymen that has been torn as a result of injury, coitus, or surgery.

rupture of membranes (ROM) [L, *rumpere,* to break, *membrana*], the rupture of the amniotic sac, usually at the start of labor. It may be spontaneous or artificial.

rupture of uterus in pregnancy, a tear or break in the uterus because of trauma or other causes, possibly accompanied by displacement of the fetus and amniotic sac into the peritoneal cavity. The patient may experience acute pain because of tissue damage and irritation of the peritoneal tissues. Excessive loss of blood may be marked by hypotension, fluid volume deficit, and altered cardiac output.

RUQ, abbreviation for *right upper quadrant* of the lung.

Rural Clinics Assistance Act /roo´rəl/, an act of the U.S. Congress that permitted the establishment of clinics in certain areas designated rural and underserved and in some inner cities. The clinics are designed to provide primary care through teams of physicians and nurse practitioners.

rush /rush/, **1.** a pleasurable feeling experienced by users of recreational drugs following an injection of amphetamine or heroin. An amphetamine rush is described as an abrupt awakening, as distinguished from the drowsy drifting rush of heroin use. **2.** a strong wave of contractile activity that travels along the small intestine, usually as a result of irritation or distension.

Russell dwarf [Alexander Russell, twentieth-century Scottish physician; AS, *dweorge*], a person affected with Russell's syndrome, a congenital disorder in which short stature is associated with various anomalies of the head, face, and skeleton and with varying degrees of mental retardation.

Russell's bodies [William Russell, Scottish physician, 1852–1940; AS, *bodig,*

body], the mucoprotein inclusions found in globular plasma cells in cancer and inflammations. The bodies contain surface gamma globulins.

Russell's periodontal index [Albert L. Russell, American dentist], a measure of the extent of periodontal disease in an individual that considers the amount of bone loss around the teeth and the degree of gingival inflammation.

Russell's traction [R. Hamilton Russell, Australian surgeon, 1860–1933; L, *trahere,* to pull along], a unilateral or bilateral orthopedic mechanism that combines suspension and traction to immobilize, position, and align the lower extremities in the treatment of fractured femurs, hip and knee contractures, and disease processes of the hip and knee.

Russian bath /rush´ən/, a hot steam bath followed by a cold plunge.

rusts, microbes that are pathogens of plants, particularly cereal grains. They are also important human allergens.

rusty sputum /rus´tē/ [AS, *rust*; L, *sputum,* spittle], sputum that is reddish, indicative of blood or certain bacteria, such as pneumococcal bacteria, in pneumonia.

ruthenium (Ru) /roothē´nē·əm/ [Ruthenia, region of western Ukraine], a hard, brittle, metallic element. Its atomic number is 44, and its atomic mass is 101.07.

rutherfordium (Rf) [Sir Ernest Rutherford, British physicist, 1871–1937], a synthetic transuranic element. Its atomic number is 104, and its atomic mass is 261.

rutin /roo´tin/, a bioflavonoid obtained from buckwheat and used in the treatment of capillary fragility.

Ruvalcaba's syndrome /roo´väl·kä´bäz/ [R.H. Ruvalcaba, American physician, b. 1934], abnormal shortness of the metacarpal and metatarsal bones, hypogenitalism, and retardation of unknown cause present from birth in males. It is characterized by microcephaly, skeletal abnormalities, hypoplastic genitalia, and mental and physical retardation.

RV, abbreviation for **residual volume.**

RVC, abbreviation for *responds to verbal commands.*

R wave, the positive component of the QRS complex on an ECG.

rxn, RXN, symbol for **drug reaction.**

R

S

S, 1. abbreviation for *second* in SI units. 2. abbreviation for **steady state.** 3. abbreviation for the Latin word *sinister,* "left." 4. abbreviation for the Latin word *sine,* "without."

s̄, s, symbol for the Latin *sine,* "without."

S₁, the first heart sound in the cardiac cycle, occurring at the outset of ventricular systole. It is associated with closure of the mitral and tricuspid valves and is synchronous with the apical pulse.

S1, S2,..., symbols for **sacral nerves.**

S₂, the second heart sound in the cardiac cycle. It is associated with closure of the aortic and pulmonic valves at the outset of ventricular diastole.

S₃, the third heart sound in the cardiac cycle. Normally, it is audible only in children and physically active young adults and usually disappears with age. In older people, it is an abnormal finding and usually indicates myocardial failure.

S₄, the fourth heart sound in the cardiac cycle. It occurs late in diastole on contraction of the atria. Rarely heard in normal subjects, it indicates an abnormally increased resistance to ventricular filling.

SA, 1. abbreviation for **sinoatrial.** 2. abbreviation for **surface area.** 3. abbreviation for **surgeon's assistant.**

saber-sheath trachea /sā′bər/, an abnormally shaped trachea caused by COPD. The diameter of the posterior part of the trachea is increased while the lateral dimension is decreased.

saber shin, a sharp, anterior bowing of the tibia caused by hereditary syphilis.

Sabin-Feldman dye test /sā′bin feld′mən/ [Albert B. Sabin, American virologist, 1906–1993; H.A. Feldman, American epidemiologist, b. 1914; AS, *deag*; L, *testum,* crucible], a serologic test for the diagnosis of toxoplasmosis that depends on the presence of specific antibodies that block the uptake of methylene blue dye by the cytoplasm of the *Toxoplasma* organisms.

sac /sak/ [Gk, *sakkos,* sack], a pouch or a baglike organ, such as the abdominal sac of the embryo that develops into the abdominal cavity.

saccade /sakād′, sak′ədā/ [Fr, *saccader,* to jerk], abrupt, rapid small movements of both eyes.

saccadic eye movement /sakad′ik/, an extremely fast voluntary movement of the eyes, allowing them to accurately refix on an object in the visual field.

saccharide /sak′ərīd/, any of a large group of carbohydrates, including all sugars and starches.

saccharin /sak′ərin/ [Gk, *sakcharon,* sugar], 1. a white crystalline synthetic sweetening agent derived from coal tar. Although it is up to 500 times as sweet as sugar, it has no food value. 2. having a sweet taste, especially cloyingly sweet.

saccharometabolism /sak′ərōmətab′əliz′əm/, the functioning of sugar within a living body.

Saccharomyces /sak′ərōmī′sēz/ [Gk, *sakcharon + mykes,* fungus], a genus of yeast fungi that cause such diseases as bronchitis, moniliasis, and pharyngitis.

saccharomycosis /sak′ərōmīkō′sis/ [Gk, *sakcharon + mykes + osis,* condition], infection with yeast fungi, such as the genera *Candida* or *Cryptococcus.*

saccular, pertaining to a pouch or shaped like a sac.

saccular aneurysm, a localized dilation of a small area of an artery, forming a saclike swelling or protrusion.

sacculated /sak′yələtid/ [L, *sacculus,* small bag], a condition of small sacs, pouches, or saclike dilations.

sacculated pleurisy, inflammation of the pleura with exudate encapsulated in several locations by adhesions.

sacculation /sak′yōōlā′shən/ [L, *sacculus*], the quality of being sacculated, or pursed out with little pouches.

saccule /sak′yōōl/ [L, *sacculus*], a small bag or sac, such as the air saccules of the lungs.—**saccular,** *adj.*

sacculus /sak′yōōləs/ *pl.* **sacculi,** a little sac or bag, especially the smaller of the two divisions of the membranous labyrinth of the vestibule, which communicates with the cochlear duct through the ductus reuniens in the inner ear.

SA conduction time, the time required for an impulse to travel from the sinus node to the atrial musculature. It is measured from the sinoatrial (SA) deflection in the SA nodal

ECG to the beginning of the P wave in a bipolar record, or to the beginning of the high right atrial electrogram in a unipolar record.

sacral, pertaining to the sacrum.

sacral bone, a composite bone formed by the fusion during maturation of five sacral vertebrae that were separate at birth. The sacrum forms the back of the pelvis.

sacral canal, an extension of the vertebral canal through the sacrum.

sacral foramen, any one of several openings between the fused segments of the sacral vertebrae in the sacrum through which the sacral nerves pass.

sacral kyphosis, the dorsally convex curve formed by the sacrum when seen from the side.

sacral micturition center, a center in the sacral spinal cord that contributes to control of the bladder and inhibition of tension of the urethral sphincters.

sacral nerves, the five segmental nerves from the sacral part of the spinal cord. The first four emerge through the anterior sacral foramina and the fifth from between the sacral foramen and the coccyx.

sacral node, a node in one of the seven groups of parietal lymph nodes of the abdomen and the pelvis, situated within the sacrum.

sacral plexus, a network of motor and sensory nerves formed by the lumbosacral trunk from the fourth and fifth lumbar and by the first, second, and third sacral nerves. They converge toward the lower part of the greater sciatic foramen and unite to become a large, flattened band, most of which continues into the thigh as the sciatic nerve.

sacral vertebra, one of the five segments of the vertebral column that fuse in the adult to form the sacrum. The ventral border of the first sacral vertebra projects into the pelvis. The bodies of the other sacral vertebrae are smaller than that of the first and are flattened and curved ventrally, forming the convex, anterior surface of the sacrum.

sacrococcygeal /sā'krōkoksij'ē-əl/ [L, *sacer,* sacred; Gk, *kokkyx,* cuckoo's beak], pertaining to the sacrum and coccyx.

sacrococcygeal teratoma, a common tumor of newborns, found in the primitive pit. It may represent part of the blastopore of lower vertebrates.

sacroiliac /sā'krō-il'ē-ak/ [L, *sacer* + *ilium,* flank], pertaining to the part of the skeletal system that includes the sacrum and the ilium bones of the pelvis.

sacroiliac articulation, an immovable joint in the pelvis formed by the articulation of each side of the sacrum with an iliac bone.

sacroiliac joint, the joint formed by the sacrum and ilium where they meet on either side of the lower back. The tight joint allows little motion and is subject to great stress, as the body's weight pushes downward and the legs and pelvis push upward against the joint. The sacroiliac joint must also bear the leverage demands made by the trunk of the body as it turns, twists, pulls, and pushes.

sacroiliac ligament, one of the three ligaments that stabilizes each sacroiliac joint.

sacroiliitis /sā'krōsī'ē-ī'tis/, an inflammation of the sacroiliac joint.

sacrosciatic /sā'krōsī·at'ik/, pertaining to the sacrum and ischium.

sacrosidase /sakro'sidās/, an enzyme used as a substitute to replace the sucrase activity lacking in sucrase-isomaltase deficiency.

sacrospinalis /sak'rōspīnal'is/ [L, *sacer* + *spina,* backbone], the superficial longitudinal muscle mass on either side of the vertebral column. It extends and flexes the vertebral column and the head, draws the ribs downward, and bends the trunk to the side.

sacrospinous ligament, with the sacrotuberous ligament, an important architectural element of the walls of the true pelvis that links each pelvic bone to the sacrum and coccyx and converts two notches on the pelvic bones into foramina on the lateral pelvic walls.

sacrum /sā'krəm, sak'rəm/ [L, *sacer,* sacred], the large, triangular bone at the dorsal part of the pelvis, inserted like a wedge between the two hip bones. The base of the sacrum articulates with the last lumbar vertebra, and its apex articulates with the coccyx.—**sacral,** *adj.*

SAD, abbreviation for **seasonal affective disorder.**

saddle /sad'əl/ [AS, *sadol*], **1.** a support whose shape fits the contour of the object resting on it. **2.** a saddle-shaped structure or part.

saddle block anesthesia [AS, *sadol;* Fr, *bloc;* Gk, *anaisthesia,* lack of feeling], a form of spinal nerve block in which the area of the body that would touch a saddle, were the patient sitting astride one, is anesthetized. It is performed by injecting a local anesthetic into the subarachnoid CSF space while in the sitting position.

saddle embolism, a thrombus that straddles a dividing blood vessel.

saddle joint, a synovial joint in which surfaces of contiguous bones are reciprocally concavoconvex. A saddle joint permits no axial rotation but allows flexion, extension, adduction, and abduction.

saddle nose [AS, *sadol* + *nosu*], a sunken nasal bridge caused by injury or disease and resulting in damage to the nasal septum.

sadism /sā'dizəm, sad'izəm/ [Marquis Donatien A.F. de Sade, French writer, 1740–1814], **1.** abnormal pleasure derived from inflicting physical or psychologic pain or abuse on others; cruelty. **2.** in psychiatry, a psychosexual disorder characterized by the infliction of physical or psychologic pain or humiliation on another person, either a consenting or a nonconsenting partner, to achieve sexual excitement or gratification.— **sadistic,** *adj.*

sadist /sā′dist/, a person who is afflicted with or practices sadism.

sadomasochism /sā′dōmas′əkiz′əm/ [Marquis de Sade; Leopold von Sacher-Masoch, Austrian author, 1836–1895], a personality disorder characterized by traits of sadism and masochism.

sadomasochist /sā′dōmas′əkist/ [Marquis de Sade; Leopold von Sacher-Masoch], a person who practices sadomasochism.

Saethre-Chotzen syndrome /sā′trə kot′zən/ [Haakon Saethre, Norwegian psychiatrist, 20th century; F. Chotzen, German psychiatrist, 20th century], an autosomal-dominant disorder characterized by acrocephalosyndactyly in which the syndactyly is mild and also by hypertelorism, ptosis, and sometimes mental retardation.

safe home environment, a nursing outcome from the Nursing Outcomes Classification (NOC) defined as physical arrangements to minimize environmental factors that might cause physical harm or injury in the home.

safe period, the period during the menstrual cycle when conception is considered least likely to occur. It comprises approximately the 10 days after menstruation begins and the 10 days preceding menstruation.

safe sex, intimate sexual practices between partners who use condoms or other means to prevent the exchange of body fluids that transmit diseases. Although perfect safety is virtually impossible without abstinence, the known risks of communicable diseases, such as HIV, and/or harmful organisms, such as *Pthirus pubis,* transmitted through sexual contact can be reduced by safe sex practices.

safety director /sāf′tē/ [Fr, *sauver,* to save, *directeur,* manager], a member of a hospital staff whose activities are related to safety functions such as fire prevention, environmental safety, and disaster planning activities.

safety glass, a hard, transparent material that resists shattering on impact. It usually is made as a sandwich of two sheets of glass with an intermediate layer of plastic. Safety glass may also be produced as a tempered material that breaks into rounded granules instead of sharp shards.

safety glasses, impact-resistant lenses that protect the eyes from blows or other kinds of injury. Such lenses are usually made by tempering the glass, substituting plastic for glass, or laminating.

safety system /sāf′te sis′tem/, a system designed to minimize hazards caused by human error. In respiratory therapy it is a system of connections designed to help prevent accidental interchanging of incorrect equipment or gases.

safe wandering, a nursing outcome from the Nursing Outcomes Classification (NOC) defined as safe, socially acceptable moving about without apparent purpose in an individual with cognitive impairment.

safflower oil /saf′lou·er/, a liquid fat containing polyunsaturated fatty acids, derived from the seeds of the safflower plant, *Carthamus tinctorius.* It is commonly mixed with other edible vegetable oils.

sagittal /saj′ətəl/ [L, *sagitta,* arrow], in anatomy, pertaining to a suture or an imaginary line extending from the front to the back in the midline of the body or a part of the body, dividing into right and left parts.

sagittal axis, a hypothetical line through the mandibular condyle that serves as an axis for rotation of the mandible.

sagittal fontanel, a soft area located in the sagittal suture, halfway between the anterior and posterior fontanels. It may be found in some normal newborns and also in some with Down syndrome.

sagittal plane, the anteroposterior plane, or the section parallel to the median plane of the body.

sagittal section, an anteroposterior cross section produced by slicing, laterally or through imaging techniques, a body or body part in a vertical plane parallel to the median plane.

sagittal sinus [L, *sagitta,* arrow, *sinus,* hollow], either of two venous sinuses of the dura mater. The superior venous sinus begins near the crista galli and drains backward to empty into a confluence of sinuses near the occipital area. The inferior venous sinus begins in the lower margin of the cerebral falx and follows the superior venous sinus, emptying into the straight sinus.

sagittal suture, the serrated connection between the two parietal bones of the skull, coursing down the midline from the coronal suture to the upper part of the lambdoidal suture.

sago spleen /sā′gō/, a form of amyloid spleen that mainly affects the Malpighian bodies.

SaH, SAH, abbreviation for **subarachnoid hemorrhage.**

SAIN, abbreviation for **Society for Advancement in Nursing.**

Saint John's wort /sānt jonz wort/, any of various species of the genus *Hypericum. H. perforatum* is the medicinal herb that is used as a mild antidepressant, sedative, and anxiolytic. It is also used topically for inflammation of the skin, contusions, myalgia, and first-degree burns.

Saint's triad [Charles F.M. Saint, twentieth-century South African radiologist], a group of three related conditions, cholelithiasis, diverticulosis, and hiatal hernia, occurring together.

Saint Vitus' dance /sānt vī′təs/, a motor nerve disorder characterized by irregular involuntary jerky movements of the limbs and facial muscles. Historically the condition was once confused with symptoms of a dance mania that reportedly was cured by a pilgrimage to the shrine of Saint Vitus.

Sakati-Nyhan syndrome /sä′kātē nī′han/ [Nadia Sakati, American pediatrician, 20th century; William Leo Nyhan, American pediatrician, b. 1926], an autosomal-dominant type of acrocephalopolysyndactyly characterized also by hypoplastic tibias and deformed, displaced fibulas.

SAL, abbreviation for **sterility assurance level.**

salaam convulsion /säläm′/ [L, *convulsio,* cramp], a violent muscle spasm of the sternomastoid muscles marked by head bobbing or bowing.

salicylate /səlis′əlāt/ [Gk, *salix,* willow, *hyle,* matter], any of several widely prescribed drugs derived from salicylic acid. Salicylates exert analgesic, antipyretic, and antiinflammatory actions. The most important is acetylsalicylic acid, or aspirin. Sodium salicylate also has been used systemically, and it exerts similar effects. In addition to aspirin and sodium salicylate, which are used systemically, methyl salicylate is used topically as a counterirritant in ointments and liniments. Another salicylate, salicylic acid, is too irritating to be used systemically and is used topically as a keratolytic agent.

salicylated /səlis′ilā′tid/ [Gk, *salix,* willow, *hyle,* matter], pertaining to a chemical formed as a salt or ester of salicylic acid.

salicylate poisoning, a toxic condition caused by the ingestion of salicylate, most often in aspirin or oil of wintergreen. Intoxication is characterized by rapid breathing, vomiting, headache, irritability, ketosis, hypoglycemia, and, in severe cases, seizures and respiratory failure.

salicylic acid /sal′isil′ik/, a keratolytic agent prescribed in the treatment of hyperkeratotic skin conditions and as an adjunct in fungal infections.

salicylism /sal′isil′izəm/ [Gk, *salix,* willow, *hyle,* matter, *ismos,* practice], a syndrome of salicylate toxicity.

saline /sā′līn/ [L, *sal,* salt], **1.** pertaining to a substance that contains a salt or salts.

2. pertaining to something that is salty or has the characteristics of common table salt.

saline cathartic [L, *sal,* salt; Gk, *katharsis,* cleansing], one of a large group of cathartics administered to achieve a prompt, complete evacuation of the bowel. A watery semifluid evacuation usually occurs within 3 to 4 hours.

saline enema [L, *sal,* salt; Gk, *enienai,* to send in], a solution of salt and water instilled via the rectum. Hypertonic saline enema is used to treat constipation and for evacuation of fecal contents, by inducing peristalsis. A normal saline enema of 1 teaspoonful of salt per 0.5 L of water is instilled slowly and retained as long as possible to combat shock or replace lost fluids when IV fluids are not available.

saline infusion, the therapeutic introduction of a physiologic salt solution into a vein.

saline irrigation, the washing out of a body cavity or wound with a stream of salt solution, usually an isotonic aqueous solution of sodium chloride.

saline solution, a solution containing sodium chloride. Depending on the use, it may be hypotonic, isotonic, or hypertonic with body fluids.

saliva /səlī′və/ [L,spittle], the clear,viscous fluid secreted by the salivary and mucous glands in the mouth. Saliva contains water, mucin,organic salts,and the digestive enzyme ptyalin. It serves to moisten the oral cavity, to initiate the digestion of starches, and to aid in the chewing and swallowing of food.

salivary duct, any one of the ducts through which saliva passes.

salivary fistula, an abnormal communication from a salivary gland or duct to an opening in the mouth or on the skin of the face or neck.

salivary gland, any one of three pairs of glands secreting into the mouth, thus aiding the digestive process. The salivary glands are the parotid, the submandibular, and the sublingual. They are racemose structures consisting of numerous lobes subdivided into smaller lobules connected by dense areolar tissue, vessels, and ducts.

salivary gland cancer, a malignant neoplastic disease of a salivary gland, occurring most frequently in a parotid gland. About 75% of tumors that develop in the salivary glands are benign, characteristically slow-growing painless mobile masses that are cystic or rubbery in consistency. The most common malignant neoplasms are mucoepidermoid, adenoid cystic, solid, and squamous cell carcinomas.

salivary gland nuclear imaging, a nuclear scan of the salivary glands to visualize inflammation, hypofunction, location and character of tumors, and duct obstruction.

S

salivation /sal'iva'shən/, the process of saliva secretion by the salivary glands.

salivatory /sal'ivətôr'ē/ [L, *saliva*, spittle], stimulating the production of saliva.

sallow /sal'ō/ [ME, *salou*, dirty-gray], yellowish-gray in complexion.

salmeterol, a sympathomimetic long-acting bronchodilator. It is prescribed in the maintenance treatment of reversible bronchospasm associated with asthma (including nocturnal asthma) and COPD and to prevent exercise-induced asthma.

Salmonella /sal'mənel'ə/ [Daniel E. Salmon, American pathologist, 1850–1914], a genus of motile gram-negative rod-shaped bacteria that includes species causing typhoid fever, paratyphoid fever, and some forms of gastroenteritis.

Salmonella enteritidis [Daniel E. Salmon; Gk, *enteron,* intestine], a species of *Salmonella* causing food poisoning and gastroenteritis in humans.

Salmonella **enteritis,** bacterial enteritis caused by species of *Salmonella.*

Salmonella **gastroenteritis,** a type of gastroenteritis caused by species of *Salmonella.* Species causing this in humans include *S. choleraesuis* and *S. enteritidis* and usually enter the body in contaminated food. Symptoms include inflammation of the mucosa, nausea, vomiting, abdominal pain, and bloody diarrhea. A more virulent form can occur in immunocompromised patients, sometimes resulting in septicemia.

salmonellosis /sal'mənəlō'sis/ [Daniel E. Salmon; Gk, *osis,* condition], a form of gastroenteritis, caused by ingestion of food contaminated with a species of *Salmonella.* It is characterized by an incubation period of 6 to 48 hours followed by sudden colicky abdominal pain, fever, and bloody, watery diarrhea. Nausea and vomiting are common, and abdominal signs may resemble those of acute appendicitis or cholecystitis. Symptoms usually last from 4 to 7 days, but diarrhea and fever may persist for up to 2 weeks. There is no specific treatment. Adequate cooking, good refrigeration, and careful handwashing may reduce the frequency of outbreaks.

salol camphor, a clear, oily mixture of two parts of camphor and three parts of phenyl salicylate, used as a local antiseptic.

salpingectomy /sal'pinjek'təmē/ [Gk, *salpinx,* tube, *ektomē,* excision], surgical removal of one or both fallopian tubes. It is performed for removal of a cyst or tumor, excision of an abscess, or, if both tubes are removed, as a sterilization procedure or for tubal pregnancy.

salpingemphraxis /salpinj'emfrak'sis/ [Gk, *salpinx,* tube, *emphraxis,* a stoppage], **1.** an obstruction of the eustachian tube of the ear. **2.** an obstruction of a fallopian tube.

salpingitis /sal'pinjī'tis/ [Gk, *salpinx + itis,* inflammation], an inflammation or infection of the fallopian tube.

salpingography /sal'ping·gog'rəfē/, a radiographic examination of the fallopian tube after injection of a radiopaque contrast medium.

salpingo-oophorectomy /-ō'əfôrek'təmē/, the surgical removal of a fallopian tube and an ovary.

salpingo-oophoritis /-ō'əfôrī'tis/ [Gk, *salpinx,* tube, *oophoron,* ovary, *itis,* inflammation], an inflammation of a fallopian tube and associated ovary.

salpingopharyngeal fold, a small vertical fold that descends from the tubal elevation of the nasopharynx and overlies salpingopharyngeus muscle.

salpingostomy /sal'ping·gos'təmē/ [Gk, *salpinx + stoma,* mouth], the formation of an artificial opening in a fallopian tube to restore patency in a tube whose fimbriated opening has been closed by infection or by chronic inflammation or to drain an abscess or a fluid accumulation. A prosthesis may be inserted to maintain the patency of the fallopian tube and to direct the route of the ova to assist fertilization.

salpinx /sal'pingks/ *pl.* **salpinges** [Gk, tube], a tube such as the fallopian or eustachian tube, the salpinx auditiva, or the salpinx uterina.—**salpingian,** *adj.*

salt /sôlt/ [L, *sal*], **1.** a compound formed by the chemical reaction of an acid and a base. Salts are usually composed of a metal cation and a nonmetal anion. **2.** sodium chloride (common table salt). **3.** a substance such as magnesium sulfate (Epsom salt) used as a purgative.

saltation /saltā'shən/ [L, *saltare,* to dance], a mutation causing a significant difference in appearance between parent and offspring or an abrupt variation in the characteristics of a species.—**saltatorial, saltatoric, saltatory** /sal'tətôr'ē/, *adj.*

saltatory conduction /sal'tətôr'ē/ [L, *saltare + conducere,* to lead together], impulse transmission that skips from node to node, providing rapid transmission.

saltatory evolution, the appearance of a sudden change within a species, caused by mutation; the progression of a species by sudden major changes rather than by the gradual accumulation of minor changes. The phenomenon occurs predominantly in plants as a result of polyploidy.

salt cake, anhydrous sodium sulfate; a technical grade of sodium sulfate used in detergents, dyes, soaps, and other industrial products.

salt depletion, the loss of salt from the body through excessive elimination of body fluids by perspiration, diarrhea, vomiting, or urination, without corresponding replacement.

salted plasma /sôl′tid/, a fluid part of blood that has been treated with sodium or magnesium sulfate to prevent coagulation.

salt-losing nephritis, a disorder characterized by abnormal kidney loss of sodium chloride, hyponatremia, azotemia, acidosis, dehydration, and vascular collapse. Causes include kidney tubule damage, endocrine dysfunction, and GI abnormality.

salt-losing nephropathy, intrinsic renal disease causing abnormal urinary sodium loss in persons ingesting normal amounts of sodium chloride, with vomiting, dehydration, and vascular collapse.

saltpeter /sôlt′pē′tər/ [L, *sal*, salt, *petra*, rock], common name for potassium nitrate, KNO_3, used in gunpowder, pickling substances, and medicines.

salt-poor diet [Gk, *diaita*, way of living], a diet providing 500 mg or less of sodium chloride daily. To ensure that the maximum salt intake does not exceed the limit, it is necessary to record the amount of dietary sodium chloride, including amounts contained in patient medications.

salt substitute, a chemical compound for flavoring foods without adding sodium to the diet. Examples are potassium chloride, monopotassium glutamate, and glutamic acid.

salt wasting, inappropriate sodium excretion in the urine (natriuresis) with hyponatremia and hyperkalemia.

Saluron, a trademark for a thiazide diuretic (hydroflumethiazide).

salvage therapy /sal′vij/ [Fr, *sauver*, to save; Gk, *therapeia*, treatment], therapy administered to sites at which previous therapies have failed and the disease has recurred.

samarium (Sm) /səmer′ē·əm/ [Colonel M. von Samarski, nineteenth-century Russian mine official], a metallic rare earth element. Its atomic number is 62, and its atomic mass is 150.35.

samarium Sm 153 lexidronam (Sm 153-EDTMP), samarium 153 complexed with ethylenediaminetetramethylenephosphonic acid, a bone-seeking diphosphonate complex that concentrates in areas of bone turnover. It is used in the palliative treatment of patients with osteoblastic metastatic bone lesions.

SAMHSA, abbreviation for U.S. *Substance Abuse and Mental Health Services Administration.*

sample [L, *exemplum*], in research, a group or part of the whole that can be used to demonstrate characteristics of the whole. Kinds of samples include cluster, convenience, **random,** and stratified.

sanctuary site /sangk′chŏŏ·er′ē/ [L, *sanctus*, sacred, *situs*, location], an area of the body that is poorly penetrated by pharmacologic agents and therefore is a place in which tumor cells or infectious organisms can escape the effects of drug therapy.

Sanctura, a trademark for trospium.

sand bath, the application of warm dry sand or damp sand to the body.

Sandhoff's disease, a variant of Tay-Sachs disease that includes defects in the enzymes hexosaminidase A and B. It is characterized by a progressively more rapid course and is found in the general population, not restricted as is Tay-Sachs disease.

Sandoz Clinical Assessment—Geriatric, an examination of psychologic function that is administered to elderly people to assist in the diagnostic process.

sandwich generation, members of the middle generation who are trying to raise children and help aging parents at the same time.

sandwich technique, a method of identifying antibodies or antibody-synthesizing cells in a tissue preparation. A solution containing a specific antigen is applied to the preparation. If antibodies to the antigen are present in the tissue, they will bind to the antigen. Unbound antigen is washed away, and then a fluorochrome-labeled antibody specific for the antigen is added. The result is a complex of antigen sandwiched between antibodies, which can be detected by fluorescence microscopy.

Sanfilippo's syndrome /san′filip′ōz/ [Sylvester J. Sanfilippo, American pediatrician, 20th century], four heterogeneous, biochemically distinct but clinically indistinguishable forms of mucopolysaccharidosis characterized biochemically by excretion of the mucopolysaccharide heparin sulfate in the urine and clinically by severe, rapid mental deterioration and relatively mild somatic symptoms. Onset is from 2 to 6 years of age; the head is large, height is normal, Hurler-like features are mild, and hirsutism is generalized; death usually occurs before 20 years of age.

sanguine /sang′gwin/ [L, *sanguis*, blood], pertaining to abundant and active blood circulation, ruddy complexion, and an attitude full of vitality and confidence.

sanguineous /sang·gwin′ē·əs/ [L, *sanguis*, blood], pertaining to blood or containing blood, such as full-blooded.

sanguinopurulent /sang′gwinōpyŏŏr′ələnt/, containing blood and pus.

sanies /sā′ni·ēz/, a thin blood-stained purulent discharge from a wound or ulcer.

sanioserous, containing sanies and serum.

sanious /sā′nē·əs/, pertaining to or resembling sanies.

S

sanitarian [L, *sanitas,* health], a health professional who is an expert in the science of public health.

sanitarium /san′iter′ē·əm/ [L, *sanitas,* health], a facility for the treatment of patients suffering from chronic mental or physical diseases, or the recuperation of convalescent patients.

sanitary landfill /san′iterē/ [L, *sanitas,* health; AS, *land* + *fyllan,* to fill], a solid waste disposal site. It is usually a swamp area, ravine, or canyon, where the waste is compacted by heavy machines and covered with earth.

sanitary napkin, a disposable pad of absorbent material, usually worn to absorb menstrual flow.

sanitation /san′itā′shən/ [L,*sanitas,*health], the science of maintaining a healthful, disease-free, and hazard-free environment.

sanitize /san′itīz/ [L, *sanitas,* health], to take action needed to clean the environment or a part of it, removing or reducing pathogenic microorganisms and their habitats.

San Joaquin fever, the primary stage of coccidioidomycosis.

SA node, abbreviation for *sinoatrial node.*

Sanorex, a trademark for an anorexiant (mazindol).

Sansert, a trademark for a vasoconstrictor (methysergide maleate).

Santyl, a trademark for an enzyme (collagenase).

SaO₂, symbol for the percentage of oxygen *saturation of arterial blood.*

saphenous [Gk, *saphenes,* manifest], pertaining to certain anatomic structures in the leg such as arteries, veins, or nerves.

saphenous nerve /səfē′nəs/ [Gk, *saphenes,* manifest; L, *nervus,* nerve], the largest and longest superficial branch of the femoral nerve, supplying the skin of the medial side of the leg and the skin over the patella. Branches below the knee supply the ankle and the medial side of the foot.

saponaceous /sap′ənā′shəs/ [L,*sapo,*soap], pertaining to soap.

saponification /səpon′ifikā′shən/ [L, *sapo,* soap, *facere,* to make], the production of soap.

saponified, pertaining to a substance chemically hydrolyzed into soaps or acid salts and glycerol by heating with an alkali.

saponin /sap′ənin/ [L, *sapo,* soap], a soapy material found in some plants, especially soapwort (bouncing bet) and certain lilies. It is used in demulcent medications to provide a sudsy quality.

saprogen /sap′rəjən/, a microscopic saprophyte.

saprophyte /sap′rəfīt/ [Gk, *sapros,* rotten, *phyton,* plant], an organism that lives on dead organic matter.—**saprophytic,** *adj.*

saquinavir, an antiviral prescribed to treat HIV in combination with zidovudine and zalcitabine.

saralasin, a competitive antagonist of angiotensin. It is administered by IV injection to assess the role of the renin-angiotensin system in the maintenance of BP.

sarcoadenoma /-ad′ənō′mə/ [Gk, *sarx,* flesh, *aden,* gland, *oma,* tumor], a mixed tumor containing both glandular and connective tissue characteristics.

sarcocarcinoma /-kär′sinō′mə/ [Gk, *sarx,* flesh, *karkinos,* crab, *oma,* tumor], a mixed tumor with characteristics of both sarcomas and carcinomas.

sarcoidosis /sär′koidō′sis/ [Gk, *sarx,* flesh, *eidos,* form, *osis,* condition], a chronic disorder of unknown origin characterized by the formation of tubercles of nonnecrotizing epithelioid tissue. Common sites are the lungs, spleen, liver, skin, mucous membranes, and lacrimal and salivary glands, usually with involvement of the lymph glands. The lesions usually disappear over a period of months or years but progress to widespread granulomatous inflammation and fibrosis.

sarcoidosis cordis, a form of sarcoidosis in which granulomatous lesions develop in the myocardium. In severe cases, cardiac failure may result.

sarcolemma /-lem′ə/ [Gk, *sarx,* flesh, *lemma,* sheath], a membrane that covers smooth, striated, and cardiac muscle fibers.

sarcoma /särkō′mə/ *pl.* **sarcomas, sarcomata** [Gk, *sarx* + *oma,* tumor], a malignant neoplasm of the soft tissues arising in fibrous, fatty, muscular, synovial, vascular, or neural tissue, usually first manifested as a painless swelling. The tumor is composed of cells in a connective tissue matrix and may be highly invasive. Small tumors may be managed by local excision and postoperative radiotherapy, but bulky sarcomas of the extremities may require amputation followed by irradiation for local control and combination chemotherapy to eliminate small foci or neoplastic cells.—**sarcomatous,** *adj.*

sarcoma botryoides /bot′rē·oi′dēz/, a tumor derived from primitive striated muscle cells, occurring most frequently in young children and characterized by a painful edematous polypoid grapelike mass in the upper vagina or on the uterine cervix or the neck of the urinary bladder.

sarcomagenesis /särkō′məjen′əsis/ [Gk, *sarx* + *oma* + *genesis,* origin], the process of initiating and promoting the development of a sarcoma.—**sarcomagenetic,** *adj.*

sarcomere /sär′kōmir/ [Gk, *sarx* + *meros,* part], the smallest functional, contractive unit of a myofibril. Sarcomeres occur as repeating units, extending from one Z line to the next along the length of the myofibril.

sarcopenia /-pē′nē-ə/ [Gk, *sarx,* flesh, *penia,* poverty], a loss of skeletal muscle mass that may accompany aging. Studies indicate that the loss of skeletal muscle for the average normally healthy person amounts to about 20% between about 30 and 70 years of age. The late loss may accelerate as aging progresses. The muscle loss is replaced by fat, usually in a subtle way that is not noticed by the individual. Muscle-strengthening and -building exercises can prevent or reverse much of this problem.

sarcoplasm /sär′kōplaz′əm/ [Gk, *sarx,* flesh, *plassein,* to mold], the semifluid cytoplasm of muscle cells.

sarcoplasmic reticulum /-plas′mik/ [Gk, *sarx* + *plassein,* to mold; L, *reticulum,* little net], a network of tubules and sacs in skeletal muscle fibers that plays an important role in muscle contraction and relaxation by releasing and storing calcium ions.

Sarcoptes scabiei /särkop′tēz skā′bē-ī/ [Gk, *sarx* + *koptein,* to cut; L, *scabere,* to scratch], the genus of itch mite that causes scabies.

sarcosine /sär′kōsēn/, an amino acid occurring as an intermediate in the metabolism of choline in the kidney and liver. It is normally not detectable in human blood or urine.

sarcosinemia, an inborn error of metabolism caused by a defect of the enzyme that breaks down sarcosine, resulting in elevated levels of sarcosine in the blood. Clinical manifestations include poor feeding in an infant with failure to thrive and developmental delays; however, no consistent clinical syndrome has been reported.

SARS, abbreviation for **severe acute respiratory syndrome.**

sartorius /särtôr′ē-əs/ [L, *sartor,* tailor], the longest muscle in the body, extending from the pelvis to the calf of the leg. It acts to flex the thigh and rotate it laterally and to flex the leg and rotate it medially.

satellite cells /sat′əlīt/ [L, *satelles,* attendant; *cella,* storeroom], glial cells (astrocytes) that form around damaged nerve cells and lie close to neuron bodies in the CNS.

satellite clinic [L, *satelles,* attendant; Gk, *kline,* bed], a health care facility usually operated under the auspices of a large institution but situated in a location some distance from the larger health center.

satellite virus, a strain of virus unable to replicate except in the presence of helper virus; considered to be deficient in coding for capsid formation.

satiety /sətī′ətē/, a state of being satisfied, as in the feeling of being full after eating.

satiety center, a locus of nerve tissue in the ventromedial nucleus of the hypothalamus that controls the appetite.

saturated /sach′ərā′tid/ [L, *saturare,* to fill], **1.** having absorbed or dissolved the maximum amount of a given substance such as a solution in which no more of the solute can be dissolved. **2.** an organic compound that contains the maximum number of hydrogen atoms so that only single bonds exist in the carbon chain, as in saturated fatty acids.

saturated calomel electrode (SCE), a reference electrode commonly used in polarography and potentiometry.

saturated fatty acid, a fatty acid in which all of the carbon atoms in the hydrocarbon chain are joined by single bonds. They exist mostly as components of fats (triglycerides) or other lipids of animal origin. A diet high in saturated fatty acids may contribute to a high serum cholesterol level and appears to be associated with an increased incidence of coronary heart disease in some populations.

saturated solution, a solution in which the solvent contains the maximum amount of solute it can dissolve at a particular temperature.

saturation /sach′ərā′shən/ [L, *saturare,* to fill], **1.** a condition in which a solution contains as much solute as can remain dissolved. **2.** a measure of the degree to which oxygen is bound to hemoglobin, expressed as a percentage of the possible limit. **3.** a chemical compound in which all the valency bonds have been filled.

saturational cuing /sach′ərā′shənəl/, a treatment strategy for visuoconstructive disorders by presenting controlled verbal instruction on task analysis and sequence and presenting cues on spatial boundaries.

saturation index of hemoglobin [L, *saturare,* to fill, *index,* pointer], a measure of the amount of hemoglobin in a given amount of blood, compared with normal.

saturnine /sat′ərnīn/, pertaining to lead or lead poisoning.

saturnine tremor, a condition of involuntary muscle contractions in the extremities observed in patients with chronic lead poisoning.

satyr ear /sat′ər/, a congenital abnormality in which the helix of the auricle lacks the usual rolled contour and the tubercle is prominent.

satyriasis /sat′irī′əsis/ [Gk, *satyros,* lecherous, *osis,* condition], excessive, pathologic, or uncontrollable sexual desire in the male.

sauna bath /sô′nə/ [Finn, *sauna*; AS, *baeth*], a bath consisting of exposure to hot vapor to induce sweating, followed by rubbing or light beating of the skin.

saw palmetto, an herbal product harvested from the American dwarf palm. This herb is used to treat benign prostatic hypertrophy, and multiple studies

S

have shown that it can improve urinary symptoms.

saxitoxin /sak'sitok'sin/, a powerful neurotoxin found in bivalve mollusks, including mussels, clams, and scallops. It is produced by certain species of dinoflagellates, which are consumed by the mollusks. Saxitoxin may cause a severe food intoxication in humans who eat the contaminated shellfish.

Sayre's jacket /serz/ [Lewis A. Sayre, American surgeon, 1820–1900; ME, *jaket*], a cast applied for support and immobilization in the treatment of certain abnormalities of the spinal column.

Sb, symbol for the element **antimony.**

SBE, **1.** abbreviation for **self-breast examination. 2.** abbreviation for **subacute bacterial endocarditis.**

SBT, abbreviation for **Shorted Blessed Test.**

sc, 1. abbreviation for the Latin *sine correctione*, "without correction." **2.** abbreviation for *subcutaneously*.

Sc, symbol for the element **scandium.**

SCA, abbreviation for **sudden cardiac arrest.**

SCAB, abbreviation for **single-chain antigen-binding protein.**

scabbard trachea /skab'ərd/, a flattening of the trachea caused by lateral compression by swellings or tumors.

scabicide /skab'isīd/ [L, *scabere*, to scratch, *caedere*, to kill], any one of a large group of drugs that destroy the itch mite, *Sarcoptes scabiei*. These drugs are applied topically in a lotion or cream-based preparation. All are potentially toxic and irritating to the skin.

scabies /skā'bēz/ [L, *scabere*, to scratch], a contagious disease caused by *Sarcoptes scabiei*, the human itch mite, characterized by intense itching of the skin and excoriation from scratching. The mite, transmitted by close contact with infected humans or domestic animals, burrows into outer layers of the skin, where the female lays eggs. Two to 4 months after the first infection, sensitization to the mites and their products begins, resulting in a pruritic papular rash most common on the webs of fingers, flexor surfaces of wrists, and thighs. All contacts are treated simultaneously with topical application of permethrin, crotamiton, or another scabicide. Oral antihistamines and salicylates reduce itching. It is also recommended that clothes and bedding be washed in hot water and dried in a hot dryer.

scabietic /skā'bē·et'ik/ [L, *scabere*, to scratch], pertaining to scabies.

scabrities unguium /skabrish'i·ēz/, a very pronounced thickening and distortion of the nails, separating from skin at the base.

scag, *slang.* heroin.

scald /skôld/ [L, *calidus*, hot], a burn caused by exposure of the skin to a hot liquid or vapor.

scale [OFr, *escale*, husk], **1.** a small thin flake of keratinized epithelium. **2.** to remove encrusted material from the surface of a tooth.

scalene /skā'lēn/ [Gk, *skalenos*, uneven], pertaining to one of the scalenous muscles.

scalenus /skālē'nəs/ [Gk, *skalenos*], one of a group of four muscles arising from the cervical vertebrae with insertions on the first or second rib.

scaler /skā'lər/ [OFr, *escale*, husk], a dental hand instrument used in removing calculus from tooth surfaces.

scaling /skāl'ing/ [OFr, *escale*, husk], removal of plaque and calculus from the surface of a tooth by means of a scaler.

scalp [ME], the skin covering the head, not including the face and ears.

scalpel /skal'pəl/ [L, *scalprum*, knife], a small pointed knife with a convex edge. Some scalpels use interchangeable blades for specific surgical procedures such as operating and amputating.

scalp medication, 1. a cream, ointment, lotion, or shampoo used to treat dermatologic conditions of the scalp. **2.** the application of a medication to the scalp.

scalp vein needle, a thin-gauge needle designed for use in the veins of the scalp or other small veins, especially in infants and children.

scandium (Sc) /skan'dē·əm/ [Scandinavia], a grayish metallic element. Its atomic number is 21, and its atomic mass is 44.956.

scanner /skan'ər/ [L, *scandere*, to climb], equipment used for making a digital representation of an original photographic image or printed material.

scanning [L, *scandere*, to climb], a technique for carefully studying an area, organ, or system of the body by recording and displaying an image of the area. A concentration of a radioactive substance that has an affinity for a specific tissue may be administered intravenously to enhance the image.—**scan,** *n., v.*

scanning electron microscope (SEM), an instrument similar to an electron microscope in that a beam of electrons is used to scan the surface of a specimen. The beam is moved in a point-to-point manner over the surface of the specimen. The image produced appears to be three-dimensional and lifelike.

scanning electron microscopy (SEM), the technique using a scanning electron microscope on a specimen.

scanning laser ophthalmoscope (SLO), an instrument for retinal imaging in which light from a low-power laser beam that scans the retina is reflected back to a sensor. The light detected by the sensor is used to create a full-color composite digital image.

scanning speech, abnormal speech characterized by a staccato-like articulation in which the words are clipped and broken because the person pauses between syllables.

scanography /skanog′rəfē/ [L, *scandere,* to climb; Gk, *graphein,* to record], a method of producing a radiograph of an internal body organ or structure by using a series of parallel beams that eliminate size distortion. The technique is applied most in long-bone radiography.

scan path, distinct eye movement patterns.

scapegoating /skāp′gōting/ [ME, *escapen,* to escape, *goat*], the projection of blame, hostility, or suspicion onto one member of a group by other members to avoid self-confrontation.

scaphocephaly /skaf′ōsef′əlē/ [Gk, *skaphe,* skiff, *kephale,* head], a congenital malformation of the skull in which premature closure of the sagittal suture results in restricted lateral growth of the head, giving it an abnormally long narrow appearance with a cephalic index of 75 or less. —**scaphocephalic, scaphocephalous,** *adj.*

scaphoid /skaf′oid/ [Gk, *skaphe,* skiff, *eidos,* form], boat-shaped, such as the scaphoid bone of the wrist.

scaphoid abdomen, an abdomen with a sunken anterior wall.

scaphoid bone [Gk, *skaphe* + *eidos,* form; AS, *ban*], either of two similar proximal boat-shaped bones of the hand and the foot. The scaphoid bone of the hand is slanted at the radial side of the carpus. The scaphoid bone of the foot is located at the medial side of the tarsus between the talus and cuneiform bones.

scaphoid megalourethra, a large diverticulum on one side of the anterior urethra, owing to a defect in the corpus spongiosum.

scapula /skap′yələ/, one of the pair of large flat triangular bones that form the dorsal part of the shoulder girdle.

scapular line /skap′yələr/, an imaginary vertical line drawn through the inferior angle of the scapula.

scapular reflex, a contraction of the rhomboids and approximation of the scapulae when a stimulus is applied to the midline of the back between the scapulae.

scapulary /skap′yəler′ē/, a suspender for holding a body bandage in place.

scapulocostal syndrome /-ōkos′təl/, a condition in which pain radiates from the upper or posterior shoulder area into the neck and back of the head, down the arm, and around the chest. There may also be a tingling in the fingers. The syndrome is associated with a change in the relationship between the shoulder blade and the thorax.

scapulohumeral /-ōhyo͞o′mərəl/ [L, *scapula* + *humerus,* shoulder], pertaining to the area around the scapula and humerus.

scapulohumeral reflex, a normal response to tapping the vertebral border of the scapula, resulting in adduction of the arm.

scapus /skā′pəs/ [Gk, *skapos,* rod], a stem or shaft, such as the scapus penis or hair (pili).

scarf skin, the epidermis, including the cuticle.

scarification /sker′ifikā′shən/ [L, *scarifare,* to scratch open], multiple superficial scratches or incisions in the skin, such as those made for the introduction of a vaccine.

scarify /sker′əfī/ [L, *scarifare*], to make multiple superficial incisions into the skin; to scratch. Vaccination against smallpox is achieved by scarifying the skin under a drop of vaccine.

scarlatiniform /skär′lətē′nifôrm/ [It, *scarlattina*; L, *forma,* form], resembling the rash of **scarlet fever.**

scarlet fever /skär′lit/ [OFr, *escarlate*; L, *febris,* fever], an acute contagious disease of childhood caused by an erythrotoxin-producing strain of group A hemolytic *Streptococcus.* Signs and symptoms appear 1 to 3 days after exposure to the agent, starting with an abrupt high fever, chills, tachycardia, nausea, vomiting, headache, abdominal pain, malaise, and a sore throat. The tonsils become enlarged, reddened, and covered with patchy exudate. The pharynx is red, and edematous. The tongue is coated and white with red, swollen papillae (white strawberry tongue) until the white coat sloughs off, leaving a red strawberry tongue and red punctate lesions on the palate. A rapidly erupting rash, displayed as pinhead-size red lesions, appears 1 to 2 days after the onset of the sore throat, rapidly covering the body except for the face. The rash concentrates in the axial folds, on the neck, and in the groin and lasts 4 to 10 days. The face is flushed on the cheeks, with a circumoral pallor. After a week, desquamation and peeling begin on the palms and soles. Treatment is aimed at eradicating the streptococcal infection through administration of antibiotics. Antipyretics are given for fever, and analgesics are given for sore throat pain.

scarlet rash [OFr, *escarlate* + *rasche,* scurf], any scarlatina or rosy skin eruption that accompanies an infection, such as scarlet fever or German measles.

scarlet red, an azo dye that has been used to impart color to pharmaceutical preparations.

Scarpa's fascia, the thin, membranous deeper layer of fascia in the abdominal wall.

S

scatemia /skətē′mē·ə/ [Gk, *skatos*, feces, *haima*, blood], a toxemic condition caused by absorption of poisonous or harmful substances from the intestinal tract.

scatologic /skatəloj′ik/, pertaining to **scatology.**

scatology /skatol′əjē/ [Gk, *skatos*, dung, *logos*, science], the scientific study of feces.

scattered radiation /skat′ərd/ [ME, *scateren*, to throw away; L, *radiare*, to emit rays], photons that move in a different direction than the incident photons that produced them, after the interaction of those incident photons.

scattergram /skat′ərgram/ [ME, *scateren*; Gk, *gramma*, record], a graph representing the distribution of two variables in a sample population. One variable is plotted on the vertical axis, the second on the horizontal axis. A scattergram demonstrates the degree or tendency with which the variables occur in association with each other.

scattering [ME, *scateren*], a change in the direction of photons caused by the interaction between photons and matter.

scavenger cell /skav′ənjər/ [ME, *scavager*; L, *cella*, storeroom], a phagocytic cell that removes tissue debris and some invading pathogens. It may or may not be mobile.

Sc.D., abbreviation for *Doctor of Science*.

SCE, abbreviation for **saturated calomel electrode.**

SCFA, abbreviation for **short-chain fatty acids.**

Schamroth window test /sham′rôth/, a test for clubbing of the fingers: The patient holds the fingers back to back against each other. There is normally a diamond-shaped space between the nailbeds and nails of the two fingers. If the space is missing, clubbing is present.

Schedule I, a category of drugs not considered legitimate for medical use. Among the substances so classified by the Drug Enforcement Agency are mescaline, lysergic acid diethylamide, heroin, and marijuana. Special licensing procedures must be followed to use Schedule I substances.

Schedule II, a category of drugs considered to have a strong potential for abuse or addiction but that have legitimate medical use. Among the substances so classified by the Drug Enforcement Agency are morphine, cocaine, pentobarbital, oxycodone, alphaprodine, and methadone.

Schedule III, a category of drugs that have less potential for abuse or addiction than Schedule II or I drugs. Among the substances so classified by the Drug Enforcement Agency are glutethimide and various analgesic compounds containing codeine.

Schedule IV, a category of drugs that have less potential for abuse or addiction than those of Schedules I to III. Among the substances so classified by the Drug Enforcement Agency are chloral hydrate, chlordiazepoxide, meprobamate, and oxazepam.

Schedule V, a category of drugs that have a small potential for abuse or addiction. Among the substances so classified by the Drug Enforcement Agency are many commonly prescribed medications that contain small amounts of codeine or diphenoxylate. The specific drugs in Schedule V vary greatly from state to state.

Schedule for Affective Disorders and Schizophrenia, a semistructured interview administered by a professional and designed to yield diagnostic information about current and lifetime incidences of affective disorders and schizophrenia.

Schedule of Drugs [L, *scheda*, sheet of paper; Fr, *drogue*], a classification system that categorizes drugs by their potential for abuse. The schedule is divided into five groups: Schedules I to V. Schedule I substances are not approved for medical use. All substances in Schedules II to V require a written prescription signed by a physician. Substances in Schedule V may or may not require a written prescription signed by a physician, depending on state law. Specific regulations for dispensing these substances vary from state to state and from institution to institution.

Scheie's syndrome /shāz/ [Harold Glendon Scheie, American ophthalmologist, 1909–1990], a relatively mild variant of Hurler's syndrome and a heritable mucopolysaccharide storage disease, characterized by corneal clouding, claw-hand, involvement of the aortic valve, somewhat coarse facies with a broad mouth, genu valgum, and pes cavus. Stature, intelligence, and life span are normal.

schema /skē′mə/, an innate knowledge structure that allows a child to organize in his or her mind ways to behave in his or her environment.

schematic /skēmat′ik/, pertaining to a schema, model, or diagram representing, without absolute precision, a structure, strategy, or system. An anatomic chart is an example.

schematic eye, 1. a simplified and enlarged illustration of the eye, featuring its anatomic details. **2.** a graphic illustration of the normal eye, with data for curvatures, indices of refraction, and distances between optical elements.

Scheuermann's disease /shoi′ərmonz/ [Holger W. Scheuermann, Danish surgeon, 1877–1960], an abnormal skeletal condition characterized by a fixed kyphosis that occurs most frequently in children between 12 and 16 years of age and is characterized by wedge-shaped deformities of one or several vertebrae. The onset is insidious and often associated with a history of unusual physical activity or participation in sports. The most frequent symptom is poor posture with accompanying symptoms of fatigue and pain in the involved area. In adults, persistent pain in the thoracic area may indicate a degenerative alteration secondary to this disease process. If the disease is diagnosed at the onset, the associated posture may be corrected actively and passively. Otherwise, it becomes fixed within a period of 6 to 9 months. The most effective treatment of Scheuermann's disease is immobilization with a plaster cast or with a Milwaukee brace.

Schick test /shik/ [Bela Schick, Austrian-American physician, 1877–1967], a skin test formerly used to determine immunity to diphtheria in which dilute diphtheria toxin is injected intradermally.

Schick test control [Bela Schick; L, *testum,* crucible; Fr, *controle,* check], a preparation used in carrying out the Schick skin test for determining diphtheria immunity.

Schilder's disease /shil'dərz/ [Paul F. Schilder, Austrian neurologist, 1886–1940], a group of progressive severe neurologic diseases beginning in childhood. All are characterized by demyelination of the white matter of the brain, with muscle spasticity, optic neuritis, aphasia, deafness, adrenal insufficiency, and dementia. Many of the signs resemble those of MS.

Schiller's test /shil'ərz/ [Walter Schiller, Austrian pathologist in the United States, 1887–1960], a procedure for indicating areas of abnormal epithelium in the vagina or on the cervix of the uterus as a guide in selecting biopsy sites for cancer detection. A potassium iodide or aqueous iodine solution is painted on the vaginal walls and cervix under direct visualization. Normal epithelium contains glycogen and stains a deep brown. Abnormal epithelium, containing no glycogen, will not stain, and nonstaining sites may then be included in tissue biopsy samples.

Schilling test /shil'ing/ [Robert F. Schilling, American hematologist, b. 1919], a diagnostic test for pernicious anemia in which vitamin B_{12} tagged with radioactive cobalt is administered orally, and GI absorption is measured by determining the radioactivity of urine samples collected over a 24-hour period. This test is rarely used today.

schindylesis /skin'dile͞'sis/ [Gk, splintering], an articulation (synarthrosis) of certain bones of the skull in which a thin plate of one bone enters a cleft formed by the separation of two layers of another bone such as the insertion of the vomer bone into the fissure between the maxillae and the palatine bones.

Schinzel-Giedion syndrome, a rare syndrome, probably of autosomal-recessive inheritance, of hydronephrosis, skeletal abnormalities, flattened midface, hypertrichosis, seizures, and profound growth and developmental retardation.

Schiötz' tonometer /shē-ets'/ [Hjalmar Schiötz, Norwegian ophthalmologist, 1850–1927; Gk, *tonos,* stretching, *metron,* measure], a tonometer used to measure intraocular pressure by observing the depth of indentation of the cornea made by the weighted plunger on the device after a topical anesthetic is applied.

schisandra, a herb that is native to China, Russia, and Korea. This herb is used for GI disorders, for liver protection, and as a tonic, and may have some efficacy.

schistocelia /shis'tasē'lyə/, a congenital fissure in the wall of the abdomen.

schistocoelia /shis'to-se'le-ah/, gastroschisis.

schistocystis /shis'təsis'tis/ [Gk, *schistos,* cleft, *kystis,* bag], a fissure in the bladder.

schistocyte /shis'təsīt/ [Gk, *schistos,* cleft, *kytos,* cell], an erythrocyte cell fragment characteristic of hemolysis or cell fragmentation associated with severe burns, microangiopathic hemolytic anemias, and intravascular coagulation.

Schistosoma /shis'təsō'mə/ [Gk, *schistos,* cleft, *soma,* body], a genus of blood flukes that may cause urinary, GI, or liver disease in humans and that requires fecal contamination of water and freshwater snails as intermediate hosts. *Schistosoma hematobium,* found chiefly in Africa and the Middle East, affects the bladder, ureter, and pelvic organs, causing painful frequent urination and hematuria. *S. japonicum,* found in Japan, the Philippines, and Eastern Asia, causes GI ulcerations and fibrosis of the liver. *S. mansoni,* found in Africa, the Middle East, the Caribbean, and tropical America, causes symptoms similar to those caused by *S. japonicum.*

schistosomiasis /shis'təsōmī'əsis/ [Gk, *schistos* + *soma*; *osis,* condition], a parasitic infection caused by a species of fluke of the genus *Schistosoma.* It is transmitted to humans, the definitive host, by contact with water containing the infective stage of the parasite, the cercaria. A single fluke may live in one part of the body, depositing eggs frequently, for up to 20 years. The eggs are irritating to mucous membrane, causing it to thicken and become papillomatous. Symptoms depend on the part of the body infected. Depending on the species, treatment may be with praziquantel, oxamniquine, or metrifonate.

S

schistosomicide /shis′təsō′məsīd/ [Gk, *schistos* + *soma*; L, *caedere,* to kill], a drug destructive to schistosomes, blood flukes transmitted by snails to human hosts in many parts of Africa, Brazil, and Asia. —**schistosomicidal,** *adj.*

schistothorax /-thôr′aks/, a congenital cleft in the wall of the thorax.

schizencephaly /skiz′ensef′əlē/, an abnormal cleavage or other division of the brain tissues caused by maldevelopment.

schizoaffective disorder /skit′sō-afek′tiv/ [Gk, *schizein,* to split; L, *affectus,* state of mind, *dis,* opposite of, *ordo,* rank], a psychiatric disorder in which either a major depressive or a manic episode develops concurrent with symptoms of schizophrenia and delusion or hallucination occur for a period without significant mood symptoms.

schizogenesis /skit′səjen′əsis/ [Gk, *schizein* + *genesis,* origin], reproduction by fission. —**schizogenetic, schizogenic, schizogenous,** *adj.*

schizogony, a form of asexual reproduction characteristic of certain protozoa, including sporozoa, in which daughter cells are produced by multiple fission of the nucleus of the parasite (**schizont**) followed by segmentation of the cytoplasm to form separate masses around each smaller nucleus.

schizogyria /skit′səjī′rē-ə/, the presence of wedge-shaped cracks in the convolutions of the brain.

schizoid /skit′soid, skiz′oid/ [Gk, *schizein,* to split, *eidos,* form], **1.** characteristic of or resembling schizophrenia; schizophrenic. **2.** a person, not necessarily a schizophrenic, who exhibits the traits of a schizoid personality.

schizoid personality, a functioning but maladjusted person whose behavior is characterized by extreme shyness, oversensitivity, introversion, seclusion, and avoidance of close interpersonal relationships.

schizoid personality disorder, a personality disorder (*DSM-IV*) characterized by a defect in the ability to form interpersonal relationships, as shown by emotional coldness and aloofness, withdrawn and seclusive behavior, and indifference to praise, criticism, and the feelings of others.

schizont /skitsənt/ [Gk, *schizein* + *genein,* to produce], **1.** reproduction by multiple fission. **2.** the multinucleated cell stage during the asexual reproductive phase in the life cycle of a sporozoon such as the malarial parasite *Plasmodium.*—**schizogonic, schizogonous,** *adj.*

schizonticide /skitson′təsīd/ [Gk, *schizein* + *on,* being; L, *caedere,* to kill], a substance that destroys schizonts.—**schizonticidal,** *adj.*

schizophasia /skit′səfā′zhə, skiz′ə-/ [Gk, *schizein* + *phasis,* speech], the disordered, incomprehensible speech characteristic of some forms of schizophrenia.

schizophrenia /skit′səfrē′nē-ə,skiz′ə-/ [Gk, *schizein,* to split, *phren,* mind], any one of a large group of *DSM-IV* psychotic disorders characterized by gross distortion of reality, disturbances of language and communication, withdrawal from social interaction, and disorganization and fragmentation of thought, perception, and emotional reaction. Apathy and confusion; delusions and hallucinations; rambling or stylized patterns of speech, such as evasiveness, incoherence, and echolalia; withdrawn, regressive, and bizarre behavior; and emotional lability often occur. Characteristics vary in type and severity, and onset may be sudden or insidious. Most patients have both positive and negative psychotic symptoms. Positive symptoms include psychosis as evidenced by distortions of thought content (delusions) and/or perceptual distortion (hallucinations); and disorganization evidenced by disorganized speech and behavior. Negative symptoms include restricted emotional expression (flattened affect), poverty of speech (alogia), apathy, decreased ability to experience pleasure (anhedonia), difficulty naming or describing emotions (alexithymia), and a lack of interest in social relationships. No single cause of the disorder is known; genetic, biochemical, psychological, interpersonal, and sociocultural factors are usually involved. Diagnostic criteria established by *DSM-IV* require two or more of the following: delusions, hallucinations, disorganized speech or behavior, catatonia, or negative symptoms for at least a month with evidence of prodromal manifestations or social, occupational, or self-care impairments for at least 6 months. The hospital milieu is helpful for early disease stages to introduce and regulate antipsychotic medications. Crisis care is indicated for high-risk periods for harm (suicide and/or violence). Antipsychotics are used for control of delusions/hallucinations, and sedatives are administered for agitation. Medication compliance is a long-term focus of treatment. Significant social support is needed for most schizophrenic patients and their families. Support includes supportive psychotherapy; psychosocial skill training; vocational rehabilitation; occupational therapy for ADL; and community support services to promote self-care. Individual and family education are needed about the disease process, including psychosis identification, symptoms of relapse, and medications effects and side effects.

schizophrenic /skit′səfren′ik, skiz′ə-/, **1.** pertaining to schizophrenia. **2.** a person with schizophrenia.

schizophreniform disorder /-fren′ifôrm/ [Gk, *schizein* + *phren*; L, *forma,* form], a *DSM-IV* psychiatric disorder exhibiting the same symptoms as schizophrenia but characterized by an acute onset with resolution in 4 weeks to 6 months.

schizophrenogenic /skit′səfren′əjen′ik, skiz′ ə-/ [Gk, *schizein* + *phren* + *genein,* to produce], tending to cause or produce schizophrenia.

schizotypal personality disorder /skit′sōtī′pəl/ [Gk, *schizein* + *typos,* mark; L, *personalis,* of a person, *dis,* opposite of, *ordo,* rank], a *DSM-IV* psychiatric disorder characterized by oddities of thought, perception, speech, and behavior that are not severe enough to meet the clinical criteria for schizophrenia. Symptoms may include magical thinking inconsistent with cultural norms, such as superstitiousness, belief in clairvoyance and telepathy, and bizarre fantasies; ideas of reference; recurrent illusions, such as sensing the presence of a force or person not actually present; social isolation; peculiar speech patterns, including ideas expressed unclearly or words used deviantly; and exaggerated anxiety or hypersensitivity to real or imagined criticism.

schlieren optics /shlir′ən/ [Ger, *schlieren,* ulcers, streaks], a system that observes the refractive index gradient in solutions containing macromolecules.

Schmidt's syndrome /shmits/ [Adolf Schmidt, German physician, 1865–1918], paralysis on one side, affecting the vocal cord, the soft palate, the trapezius muscle, and the sternocleidomastoid muscle.

Schneiderian carcinoma /shnīdir′ē·ən/, an epithelial malignancy of the nasal mucosa and paranasal sinuses.

Schoenhofer, Savina O., a nursing theorist who, with Anne Boykin, wrote *Nursing as Caring: A Model for Transforming Practice,* which postulates that caring is the end, not the means, of nursing.

school nurse practitioner (S.N.P.), a registered nurse who is qualified through satisfactory completion of a nurse practitioner program to serve as a nurse practitioner in a school system.

school phobia [AS, *scol*; Gk, *phobos,* fear], an extreme separation anxiety disorder of children, usually in the elementary grades, characterized by a persistent irrational fear of going to school or being in a schoollike atmosphere. Such children are usually oversensitive, shy, timid, nervous, and emotionally immature and have pervasive feelings of inadequacy. They typically try to cope with their fears by becoming overdependent on others, especially the parents.

Schüffner's dots [Wilhelm A.P. Schüffner, German pathologist, 1867–1949], coarse pink or red granules seen in the RBCs of patients with tertiary malaria. They are signs of *Plasmodium vivax* or *P. ovale* and are absent in blood cells of patients infected with other types of malaria.

Schuller method, a technique for positioning a patient's head in a true lateral position to produce a radiographic image of the mastoid and petrous portions of the temporal bone as well as the temporomandibular joint of the side closest to the image receptor. Both temporomandibular joints are imaged with the mouth open and closed.

Schultz-Charlton phenomenon, a reaction that occurs when scarlet fever antitoxin or scarlet fever convalescent serum is injected into an area of the skin showing a bright red rash. A blanching of the skin at the site of the injection occurs. Serum from scarlet fever patients does not produce this reaction.

Schultze's mechanism, the delivery of a placenta with the fetal surfaces presenting.

Schwann cell /shwon/ [Theodor Schwann, German anatomist, 1810–1882], any of the cells of ectodermal origin that make up the neurilemma.

schwannoma /shwonō′mə/ *pl.* **schwannomas, schwannomata** [Theodor Schwann; Gk, *oma,* tumor], a benign, solitary, encapsulated tumor arising in the neurilemma (Schwann's sheath) of peripheral, cranial, or autonomic nerves.

schwannosis /shwonō′sis/ [Theodor Schwann;Gk,*osis,*condition], a condition of overgrowth of the neurilemma or sheath of Schwann.

Schwartz-Jampel syndrome /shworts jam′ pəl/ [Oscar Schwartz, American pediatrician, b. 1919; Robert Steven Jampel, American ophthalmologist, b. 1926], an autosomal-recessive disorder characterized by myotonic myopathy, dwarfism, abnormal narrowness of the palpebral fissures in the horizontal direction, joint contractures, and flat facies.

Schwartzman-Sanarelli phenomenon /shvorts′man san′ərel′ē/ [Gregory Schwartzman, American physician, b. 1896; Guiseppe Sanarelli, Italian bacteriologist, 1864–1940], a condition induced experimentally in the investigation of the role of coagulation in renal disease. Animals injected twice with a bacterial endotoxin experience massive disseminated intravascular coagulation with blood clots in the vessels of the kidneys.

sciatic /sī·at′ik/ [Gk, *ischiadikos,* hip joint], pertaining to an area near the ischium such as the sciatic nerve or the sciatic vein.

S

sciatica /sī·at´ikə/, an inflammation of the sciatic nerve, usually marked by pain and tenderness along the course of the nerve through the thigh and leg. It may result in a wasting of the muscles of the lower leg over time.

sciatic hernia, a protrusion of tissue through the greater sciatic notch.

sciatic nerve, a long nerve originating in the sacral plexus and extending through the muscles of the thigh, leg, and foot, with numerous branches.

sciatic scoliosis, lateral curvature of the spine caused by an asymmetric spasm of the spinal muscles, often resulting in a list to one side.

SCID, abbreviation for **severe combined immunodeficiency disease.**

SCID mouse, (*severe combined immunodeficiency*) a strain of mice lacking in T and B lymphocytes and immunoglobulins, either from inbreeding with an autosomal-recessive trait or from genetic engineering, used as a model for studies of the immune system.

science /sī´əns/ [L, *scientia,* knowledge], a systematic attempt to establish theories to explain observed phenomena and the knowledge obtained through these efforts. Pure science is concerned with the gathering of information solely for the sake of obtaining new knowledge. Applied science is the practical application of scientific theory and laws.

Science of Unitary Human Beings, a conceptual model and theory of nursing proposed by Martha Rogers in 1970. Its four basic concepts focus on the nature and direction of "unitary human development": (1) human and environmental energy fields, (2) complete and continuous openness of the energy fields, (3) human energy fields perceived as single waves that give identity to a field, and (4) "pandimensionality," a nonlinear domain without spatial or temporal attributes.

scientific method /sī´əntif´ik/, a systematic, ordered approach to the gathering of data and the solving of problems. The basic approach is the statement of the problem followed by the statement of a hypothesis. An experimental method is established to help confirm or negate the hypothesis. The results of the experiment are observed, and conclusions are drawn from observed results. The conclusions may tend to uphold or to refute the hypothesis.

scientific rationale, a reason, based on supporting scientific evidence, that a particular action is chosen.

scimitar sign /sim´ətər/, an arteriographic sign of encroachment on the popliteal or femoral lumen in adventitial cystic disease.

scimitar syndrome, a radiographic artifact caused by a congenital disorder in which the right lower pulmonary vein drains into the inferior vena cava. On a chest radiograph, the abnormal vessel configuration produces a scimitar-shaped shadow.

scintigram /sin´tigram´/ [L, *scintillare,* to sparkle; Gk, *gramma,* record], a recording of the radioactivity emitted by a tracer in an organism or organ system.

scintigraph /sin´tigraf/, a photograph showing the distribution and intensity of radioactivity in various tissues and organs after the administration of a radiopharmaceutical.

scintillating scotoma /sin´tilā´ting/ [L, *scintillatio,* sparkling; Gk *skotos,* dark, *oma,* tumor], an abnormal area of the visual field that is positive and luminous, sometimes becoming hemianopic and appearing in a migraine aura.

scintillation detector /sin´tilā´shən/ [L, *scintillatio,* sparkling], **1.** a device that detects the light emitted by a crystal subjected to ionizing radiation. A photomultiplier tube in the detector converts the light into an electric signal that can be processed further. **2.** a device used to measure the amount of radioactivity in an area of the body.

scintillation scanning, the process resulting in a scintiscan.

scintiscan /sin´tiscan/, a photographic display of the distribution of a radiopharmaceutical within the body.

scirrhous carcinoma /skir´əs/ [Gk, *skirrhos,* hard, *karkinos,* crab, *oma,* tumor], a hard, fibrous, particularly invasive tumor in which the malignant cells occur singly or in small clusters or strands in dense connective tissue.

scissor gait /siz´ər/ [L, *scindere,* to cut; ONorse, *gata,* way], a manner of walking cross-legged, as observed in spastic paraplegia.

scissor legs [L, *scindere,* to cut; ONorse, *leggr*], legs that are crossed because of a disorder of the adductor muscles of the thigh or a deformity of the hip.

scissors [L, *scindere,* to cut], a sharp instrument composed of two opposing cutting blades held together by a central pin on which the blades pivot. The most common dissecting scissors are the straight Mayo, for cutting sutures; the Snowden-Pencer, for deep, delicate tissue; the long curved Mayo, for deep, heavy, or tough tissue; the short curved Metzenbaum, for superficial, delicate tissue; and the long, blunt curved Metzenbaum, for deep, delicate tissue.

SCL, abbreviation for *soft contact lens.*

sclera /sklir´ə/ [Gk, *skleros,* hard], the tough inelastic white opaque membrane covering the posterior five sixths of the eyebulb. It maintains the size and form of the bulb and attaches to muscles that move the bulb. Posteriorly it is pierced by the optic nerve and, with the transparent cornea, makes up the outermost of three tunics covering the eyebulb.

scleredema /sklir´ədē´mə/ [Gk, *skleros* + *oidema,* swelling], an idiopathic skin disease characterized by nonpitting induration beginning on the face or neck and spreading downward over the body, sparing the hands and feet. There also may be tongue swelling, restriction of eye movements, and pericardial, pleural, and peritoneal effusions.

sclerema neonatorum /sklirē´mə/ [Gk, *skleros* + *neos,* new; L, *natus,* birth], a progressive generalized hardening of the skin and subcutaneous tissue of the newborn. It is usually a fatal condition that results from severe cold stress in severely ill premature infants.

scleritis /sklirī´tis/ [Gk, *skleros,* hard, *itis,* inflammation], an inflammation of the sclera.

scleroconjunctival /sklir´ōkon´jungktī´vəl/, pertaining to the sclera and conjunctiva.

sclerocornea /-kôr´nē·ə/, the cornea and sclera of the eye surface considered as a single layer.

sclerodactyly /sklir´ōdak´tilē/ [Gk, *skleros* + *daktylos,* finger], a musculoskeletal deformity affecting the hands of people with scleroderma. The fingers are fixed in a semiflexed position, with subcutaneous calcification and tightened skin to the wrist. The fingertips may be ulcerated.

scleroderma /sklir´ōdur´mə/ [Gk, *skleros* + *derma,* skin], chronic hardening and thickening of the skin caused by new collagen formation, with atrophy of pilosebaceous follicles. Scleroderma is most common in middle-aged women. It may occur in a localized form (morphea) or as a systemic disease (systemic sclerosis). The most common initial complaints are changes in the skin of the face and fingers. Raynaud's phenomenon occurs with a gradual hardening of the skin and swelling of the distal extremities. As the disease progresses, deformity of the joints and pain on movement occur. Skin changes include edema and then pallor; then the skin becomes firm; finally it becomes slightly pigmented and fixed to the underlying tissues. At this stage the skin of the face is taut, shiny, and masklike, and the patient may have difficulty in chewing and swallowing. Patients with mild forms of scleroderma may live to 30 to 50 years of age. Those with cardiac, renal, pulmonary, or intestinal involvement may die at an earlier age. Localized forms of scleroderma may occur; these cases are benign and appear only as small circumscribed patches on the skin. There are no drugs to cure scleroderma; however, corticosteroids, immunosuppressants, antacids, and histamine receptor antagonists may be useful in treating the symptoms of the disease. Salicylates and mild analgesics are given to ease pain in the joints.

scleroderma heart, a heart condition characterized by interstitial myocardial fibrosis and thickening of the small blood vessels in progressive systemic sclerosis.

sclerodermatitis /-dur´mətī´tis/, an inflammation, thickening, and hardening of the skin.

sclerokeratitis /-ker´ətī´tis/, an inflammation of the sclera and cornea.

scleromalacia perforans /sklir´ōmələ´shə/ [Gk, *skleros* + *malakia,* softening; L, *perforare,* to pierce], a condition of the eyes in which devitalization and sloughing of the sclera occur as a complication of rheumatoid arthritis. The pigmented uvea becomes exposed; and glaucoma, cataract formation, and detachment of the retina may result.

sclerose /sklərōz´/ [Gk, *skleros*], to harden or to cause hardening.—**sclerotic,** *adj.*

sclerosing /sklirō´zing/ [Gk, *skleros,* hard], pertaining to the tissue changes or other factors involved in the progress of sclerosis.

sclerosing hemangioma [Gk, *skleros* + *haima,* blood, *angeion,* vessel, *oma,* tumor], a solid cellular tumor-like nodule of the skin or a mass of histiocytes, thought to arise from a hemangioma by the proliferation of endothelial and connective tissue cells.

sclerosing keratitis [Gk, *skleros,* hard, *keras,* horn, *itis,* inflammation], **1.** a form of corneal inflammation in which nodular infiltrates appear near the margin of the cornea in association with a ring of anterior scleritis. **2.** a form of corneal inflammation characterized by an opaque triangle in the deep layers of the cornea, with the base of the triangle near the sclerosing area.

sclerosing phlebitis [Gk, *skleros,* hard, *phleps,* vein, *itis,* inflammation], inflammation of a vein that has become hardened and obstructed.

sclerosing solution [Gk, *skleros*; L, *solvere,* to dissolve], a liquid containing an irritant that causes inflammation and resulting fibrosis of tissues. It may be used in cauterizing ulcers, arresting hemorrhage, and treating hemangiomas.

sclerosis /sklirō´sis/ [Gk, *skleros,* hard], a condition characterized by hardening of tissue resulting from any of several causes, including inflammation, the deposit of mineral salts, and infiltration of connective tissue fibers.—**sclerotic,** *adj.*

sclerotherapy /-ther´əpē/ [Gk, *skleros,* hard, *therapeia,* treatment], the use of sclerosing chemicals to treat varicosities

S

such as hemorrhoids or esophageal varices. The agent produces inflammation and later fibrosis and obliteration of the lumen.

sclerotic /sklirot′ik/ [Gk, *skleros*, hard], pertaining to induration or hardening.

sclerotomal pain distribution /-tō′məl/, the referral of pain from pain-sensitive tissues covering the axial skeleton along a sclerotomal segment.

sclerotome /sklir′ətōm/ [Gk, *skleros* + *temnein*, to cut], in embryology, the part of the segmented mesoderm layer in the early developing embryo that originates from the somites and gives rise to skeletal tissue of the body.

sclerotylosis /-tilō′sis/, an inherited condition of atrophic fibrosis of the skin. There is overgrowth of the nails and horny skin covering the palms of the hands and plantar surfaces of the feet. The disorder may be accompanied by cancer of the GI tract.

SCMC test, a test for cervical factor infertility. Fresh sperm is put both on a slide with cervical mucus and on a slide without mucus, and motility of the two sperm samples is assessed over time. If the sperm shows irregularities of motility through the mucus, there is cervical factor infertility.

scolex /skō′leks/ *pl.* **scoleces** [Gk, worm], the headlike segment or organ of an adult tapeworm that has hooks, grooves, or suckers by which it attaches itself to the wall of the intestine.

scoliometer /skō′lē·om′ətər/ [Gk, *skoliosis*, curvature], a device for measuring the amount of abnormal curvature in the spine.

scoliosis /skō′lē·ō′sis/ [Gk, *skoliosis*, curvature], lateral curvature of the spine, a common abnormality of childhood, especially in females. Causes include congenital malformations of the spine, poliomyelitis, skeletal dysplasias, spastic paralysis, and unequal leg length. Unequal heights of hips or shoulders may be a sign of this condition. Treatment includes braces, casts, exercises, and corrective surgery.

scoliotic pelvis /skō′lē·ot′ik/ [Gk, *skoliosis*, curvature; L, *pelvis*, basin], an effect of scoliosis in which the sacrum bends to one side, distorting the pelvis.

scombroid /skom′broid/ [Gk, *scombros*, mackerel, *eidos*, form], pertaining to fish of the Scombridae and Scomberesocidae families, which include skipjack, mackerel, bonito, and tuna.

scombroid poisoning, toxic effects of eating scombroid types of fish (such as bonito or tuna) that have begun bacterial decomposition after being caught. It is not limited to consumption of fresh fish; the problem also may affect commercially canned tuna. Symptoms, which usually last no more than 24 hours, include nausea, vomiting, diarrhea, epigastric pain, and urticaria.

scopolamine /skōpol′əmēn/ [Giovanni A. Scopoli, Italian naturalist, 1723–1788], an anticholinergic alkaloid obtained from the leaves and seeds of several solanaceous plants. It is a CNS depressant. It is prescribed for prevention of motion sickness and as an antiemetic, a sedative in obstetrics, and a cycloplegic and mydriatic.

scopophilia /skō′pəfil′ē·ə, skop′-/ [Gk, *skopein*, to look, *philein*, to love], **1.** sexual pleasure derived from looking at sexually stimulating scenes or at another person's genitals; voyeurism. **2.** a morbid desire to be seen; exhibitionism.—**scopophiliac, scopophilic, scoptophiliac, scoptophilic,** *adj., n.*

scopophobia /skō′pə-/ [Gk, *skopein* + *phobos*, fear], an anxiety disorder characterized by a morbid fear of being seen or stared at by others. The condition is commonly seen in schizophrenia.

scorbutic gingivitis /skôrbyoō′tik/ [NL, *scorbutus*, scurvy; L, *gingiva*, gum; Gk, *itis*, inflammation], an abnormal condition characterized by inflamed or bleeding gums and caused by vitamin C deficiency.

scorbutic pose, the characteristic posture of a child with scurvy, with thighs and legs semiflexed and hips rotated outward. The child usually lies motionless in a state of pseudoparalysis, avoiding voluntary movements of the extremities because of the pain that accompanies any motion.

scorpion sting /skôr′pē·on/ [Gk, *skorpios*; AS, *stingan*], a painful wound produced by a scorpion, an arachnid with a hollow stinger in its tail. The stings of many species are only slightly toxic, but some, including *Centruroides sculpturatus* (bark scorpion) of the southwestern United States, may inflict fatal injury, especially in small children. Initial pain is followed within several hours by numbness, nausea, muscle spasm, dyspnea, and convulsion.

scotoma /skōtō′mə/ *pl.* **scotomas, scotomata** [Gk, *skotos,* darkness, *oma,* tumor], a defect of vision in a defined area of the visual field in one or both eyes. A common prodromal symptom is a shimmering film appearing as an island in the visual field.

scotopic vision /skōtop′ik/ [Gk, *skotos,* darkness; L, *visio,* seeing], the ability of the eye to adjust for vision in darkness or dim light.

scout film, a preliminary radiographic film or image made before the administration of contrast material.

scrapie /skrā′pē/, the first of the prion diseases to be recognized, occurring in sheep and goats and characterized by severe pruritus, muscular incoordination, and increasing debility, ending in death.

scratch test [ME, *scratten*; L, *testum*, crucible], a skin test for identifying an allergen, performed by placing a small quantity of a solution containing a suspected allergen on a lightly scratched area of the skin. A wheal forming within 15 minutes indicates an allergy to the substance.

screening [ME, *scren*], **1.** a preliminary procedure such as a test or examination to detect the most characteristic sign or signs of a disorder that may require further investigation. **2.** the examination of a large sample of a population to detect a specific disease or disorder such as hypertension.

screen memory [ME, *scren*; L, *memoria*], a consciously tolerable memory that replaces one that is emotionally painful to recall.

screw /skrōō/ [MFr, *escroue*], a solid cylinder with a helical thread on its exterior surface, used to hold two objects together.

screw artery /skrōō/, a coiled blood vessel in either the uterine mucosa or the retinal macula.

screw clamp [OFr, *escroe*, screw; AS, *clam*, fastener], a device, usually made of plastic, equipped with a screw that can be manipulated to close and open the primary IV tubing for regulating the flow of IV solution.

Scribner shunt [Belding S. Scribner, American physician, b. 1921], a type of arteriovenous bypass, used in hemodialysis, consisting of a special tube connection outside the body.

scripting /skrip′ting/, a technique of family therapy involving the development of new family transactional patterns.

scrofula /skrof′yələ/ [L, *scrofa*, brood sow], *archaic*. a form of TB cutis with abscess formation, usually of the cervical lymph nodes.

scroll ear /skrōl/, a distortion of the ear in which the pinna is rolled forward.

scrotal /skrō′təl/, pertaining to the scrotum.

scrotal cancer, an epidermoid malignancy of the scrotum, characterized initially by a small sore that may ulcerate. The lesion occurs most frequently in elderly men who have been exposed to soot, pitch, crude oil, mineral oils, polycyclic hydrocarbons, or arsenic fumes from copper smelting. Treatment involves wide surgical excision of the tumor and resection of inguinal nodes.

scrotal hernia, an inguinal hernia that has descended into the scrotum.

scrotal nuclear imaging, a nuclear imaging scan, usually done on an emergency basis, that is helpful in diagnosing patients with a sudden onset of unilateral testicular swelling and pain. It can differentiate unilateral testicular torsion from other causes of testicular pain.

scrotal part of ductus deferens, the initial part of the ductus deferens, which is within the scrotum.

scrotal raphe, a line of union of the two halves of the scrotum. It is generally more highly pigmented than the surrounding tissue.

scrotal septum, an incomplete wall of connective tissue and smooth muscle that divides the scrotum into two compartments, each containing a testis.

scrotal swelling, the earliest enlargement of embryonic tissue that will become half of the scrotum.

scrotal tongue, a seldomly used term for a nonpathologic condition in which the tongue is deeply furrowed and resembles the surface of the scrotum. See **fissured tongue.**

scrotal ultrasound, an ultrasound test of the scrotum and its contents to diagnose benign and malignant tumors, benign abnormalities such as testicular abscess and orchitis, and extratesticular lesions such as hydrocele, hematocele, and pyocele and to locate cryptorchid testicles.

scrotum /skrō′təm/, the pouch of skin containing the testes and parts of the spermatic cords. It is divided on the surface into two lateral parts by a ridge that continues ventrally to the undersurface of the penis and dorsally along the middle line of the perineum to the anus. The two layers of the scrotum are the skin and the dartos tunic. The skin is brownish and very thin, is usually wrinkled, and has thinly scattered kinky hairs. The dartos tunic is composed of a thin layer of unstriated muscular fibers around the base of the scrotum. The tunic projects an internal septum that divides the pouch into two cavities for the testes. The scrotum is highly vascular and contains no fat.—**scrotal,** *adj.*

scrubbed team members [ME, *scrobben*, to scrub], the surgeons, physicians, nurses, and technicians who are scrubbed for surgical procedures in a sterile environment.

scrub nurse, a registered nurse who assists surgeons during operations.

scrub room, an operative area where surgeons and surgical teams use disposable sterile brushes and bactericidal soaps to wash and scrub their fingernails, hands, and forearms before performing or assisting in surgical operations.

scrub typhus, an acute febrile disease caused by several strains of the species *Orientia tsutsugamushi* and transmitted from infected rodents to humans by mites. The clinical course ranges from mild to severe and is characterized by a necrotic papule or black eschar at the site of the lesion caused by the bite of the small arachnid. Tender, enlarged regional lymph nodes, fever, severe headache, eye pain, muscle aches, and a generalized rash usually occur. In severe cases the myocardium and the CNS may be involved.

scruple /skrōō′pəl/ [L, *scrupulus,* small stone], a measure of weight in the apothecaries' system, equal to 20 grains or 1.296 g.

sculpting /skulp′ting/, a technique of family therapy involving construction of a live family portrait that depicts family alliances and conflicts.

Sculptra, a trademark for poly-L-lactic acid.

Scultetus binder /skəltē′təs/ [Johann Schultes, German surgeon, 1595–1645], a many-tailed binder or bandage with an attached central piece. The tails are overlapped; the last two, tied or pinned, act to secure the others. A Scultetus binder may be opened or removed without moving the bandaged part of the body.

scurvy /skur′vē/ [Scand, *scurfa,* scabby], severe ascorbic acid deficiency. It is characterized by weakness; anemia; edema; spongy gums, often with ulceration and loosening of the teeth; a tendency to mucocutaneous hemorrhages, and induration of the muscles of the legs. Treatment and prophylaxis of the disease consist of administration of ascorbic acid and inclusion of fresh vegetables and fruits in the diet.

SD, 1. abbreviation for **skin dose.** 2. abbreviation for **standard deviation.**

SDAT, abbreviation for **senile dementia-Alzheimer type.**

SDMS, abbreviation for *Society of Diagnostic Medical Sonographers.*

Se, symbol for the element **selenium.**

SE, abbreviation for **spin echo.**

S.E., abbreviation for **standard error.**

sea-blue histiocyte syndrome, a condition of spleen enlargement and mild thrombocytopenia. Histiocytes in the bone marrow contain cytoplasmic granules that stain bright blue.

seaborgium (Sg) /sēbôr′gē·əm/ [Glenn T. Seaborg, American chemist and educator, 1912–1999], a synthetic radioactive element, with a half-life of 0.9 second. Its atomic number is 106, and its atomic mass is 266. It was first synthesized in 1974.

sealant /sē′lənt/, an agent that protects against access from the outside or leakage from the inside.

sealed source [ME, *seel,* mark; Fr, *sourdre,* to spring], a source of radioactivity that is permanently encased in a container or bonding material to prevent leakage. They are used in the implantation of radionuclides for the treatment of various malignant tumors.

sealer cement, a compound used in filling a pulp canal. It is applied as a plastic that fills depressions in the surface of the canal,

solidifies after insertion, and helps close the apex of the root canal.

seasickness, a form of kinesia caused by traveling on an ocean or the sea.

seasonal affective disorder (SAD) /sē′zənəl/, a *DSM-IV* mood disorder associated with the shorter days and longer nights of autumn and winter. Symptoms include lethargy, depression, social withdrawal, and work difficulties. The patients also consume excess amounts of carbohydrates, gaining weight. The symptoms recede in the spring, when days become longer. The condition is associated with the effect of light on melatonin secretion and is treated with light therapy for 5 to 6 hours per day.

seasonal allergic rhinitis, hay fever.

Seattle Foot /sē·at′əl/, a trademark for a stored-energy foot prosthesis that contains a plastic rod called a keel, which extends from the toe to the heel, where it turns upward toward the ankle.

sea urchin granuloma, a type of foreign body granuloma in which nodules of granulation tissue develop in the skin several months after contact with the silicate in the spines of a sea urchin.

sea urchin sting /ur′chin/ [AS, *sae* + *herichon,* hedgehog], an injury inflicted by any of a variety of sea urchins, in which the skin is punctured and, in some species, venom released. A venomous sting is characterized by pain, muscular weakness, numbness around the mouth, and dyspnea. Immediate removal of the spines is necessary and may require the use of a local anesthetic.

seawater bath [AS, *sae* + *waeter*], a bath taken in warm seawater or saline solution.

sebaceous /sibā′shəs/ [L, *sebum,* sweat], pertaining to sebum, the substance secreted by glands of the skin.

sebaceous cyst, a misnomer for an epidermoid cyst or a pilar cyst.

sebaceous epithelioma, a benign yellowish nodular tumor of sebaceous gland epithelium. It usually appears on the neck or face. It may resemble basal cell carcinoma but is composed mainly of baseloid and sebaceous cells.

sebaceous follicle [L, *sebum,* sweat, *folliculus,* small bag], a sebaceous gland that opens into a hair follicle.

sebaceous gland, one of the many small sacculated organs in the dermis. They are located throughout the body in close association with all types of body hair but are especially abundant in the scalp, face, anus, nose, mouth, and external ear. Each gland consists of a single duct that emerges from a cluster of oval alveoli. The ducts from most sebaceous glands open into the hair follicles, but some open onto the skin surface, as in the labia minora and the free margin of the lips. The sebum secreted by the glands oils the hair and the surrounding skin, helps prevent evaporation of sweat, and aids in the retention of body heat.

sebaceous horn, a solid tissue outgrowth from a sebaceous cyst.

seborrhea /seb′ərē′ə/ [L, *sebum*; Gk, *rhoia*, flow], any of several common skin conditions in which an overproduction of sebum results in excessive oiliness with or without scaling.—**seborrheic** /seb′ərē′ik/, *adj.*

seborrhea capitis [L, *sebum*, sweat; Gk, *rhoia*, flow; L, *caput*, the head], seborrhea of the scalp.

seborrheic blepharitis, a form of seborrheic dermatitis in which the eyelids are erythematous and the margins are covered with a granular crust.

seborrheic dermatitis, a common chronic inflammatory skin disease characterized by greasy scales and yellowish crusts. Common sites are the scalp, eyelids, eyebrows, face, external surfaces of the ears, axillae, central chest, breasts, groin, and gluteal folds. Treatment includes selenium sulfide shampoos, topical and oral corticosteroids, topical antibiotics, proper therapy for any underlying systemic disorder, and avoidance of sweating and external irritants.

seborrheic keratosis, a benign, well-circumscribed, slightly raised, tan to black, warty lesion of the skin of the face, neck, chest, or upper back. The macules are loosely covered with a greasy crust that leaves a raw pulpy base when removed. Itching is common. Treatment includes curettage, electrodesiccation, or cryotherapy.

sebum /sē′bəm/ [L, grease], the oily secretion of the sebaceous glands of the skin, composed of keratin, fat, and cellular debris. Combined with sweat, sebum forms a moist oily acidic film that is mildly antibacterial and antifungal and protects the skin against drying.

Seckel's syndrome, a congenital disorder characterized by a proportionate short stature; a proportionately small head with jaw hypoplasia, large eyes, and a beaklike protrusion of the nose; mental retardation; and various other skeletal, cutaneous, and genital defects.

seclusion¹ /siklōō′zhən/ [L, *secludere*, to isolate], in psychiatry, the isolation of a patient in a special room to decrease stimuli that might be causing or exacerbating the patient's emotional distress. The room is free from objects that the patient might use to cause self-harm or to harm others.

seclusion², a nursing intervention from the Nursing Interventions Classification (NIC) defined as solitary containment in a fully protective environment with close

surveillance by nursing staff for purposes of safety or behavior management.

secobarbital sodium /sek′ōbär′bital/, a barbiturate sedative-hypnotic. It is prescribed in the treatment of insomnia and agitation, and as an anticonvulsant and preoperative sedative.

Seconal, a trademark for a sedative-hypnotic (secobarbital sodium).

secondary /sek′ənder′ē/ [L, *secundus*, second], second in importance or in incidence or belonging to the second order of sophistication or development, such as a secondary health care facility or secondary education.

secondary allergen, an agent that induces allergic symptoms in a person through cross-sensitivity with an agent to which the person is hypersensitive.

secondary amputation, amputation performed after suppuration has begun after severe trauma.

secondary analysis, the study of a problem using previously compiled data.

secondary antibody response, a rapid production of antibodies in response to an antigen in an individual who was exposed previously to the same antigen.

secondary apnea, an abnormal condition in which respiration is absent and will not begin again spontaneously. It may result from any event that severely impedes the absorption of oxygen by the bloodstream. Resuscitation is initiated immediately with artificial ventilation.

secondary areola, a second ring appearing around the areola of the breast during pregnancy that is more pigmented than the areola before pregnancy.

secondary biliary cirrhosis, an abnormal hepatic condition characterized by obstruction of the bile duct with or without infection. It involves periportal inflammation with progressive fibrosis, destruction of parenchymal cells, and nodular degeneration.

secondary bronchial buds, outgrowths of the primary bronchial buds, three on the right side and two on the left, which give rise to the lobes of the lungs and further branch to form the tertiary bronchial buds.

secondary care, the provision of a specialized medical service by a physician specialist or a hospital on referral by a primary care physician.

secondary dementia, dementia resulting from another concurrent form of psychosis.

secondary dental caries, dental caries developing in a tooth already affected by the condition. Often a new cavity forms adjacent to or beneath the restorative filling of an old cavity.

secondary dentition, the set of 32 teeth that appears during and after childhood and

S

usually lasts until old age. In each jaw they include four incisors, two canines, four premolars, and six molars. The secondary teeth erupt first in the lower jaw, beginning with the first molars in about the sixth year. The eruption of each secondary tooth in the upper jaw lags only slightly behind that of the corresponding tooth in the lower jaw. The third molars in many people are badly oriented or so deeply buried in bone that they must be surgically removed. In some individuals, one or all four of the third molars may not develop completely.

secondary disease, any disorder of bodily functions that follows or results from an earlier injury or medical episode.

secondary enuresis [L, *secundus,* second; Gk, *enourein,* to urinate], enuresis in an older child who has demonstrated bedtime control for a year or more. It is typically the result of psychologic stress but also may be an early sign of an organic disorder, such as DM.

secondary fissure, a fissure between the uvula and the pyramid of the cerebellum.

secondary gain, an indirect benefit, usually obtained through an illness or debility. Such gains may include monetary and disability benefits, personal attention, or escape from unpleasant situations and responsibilities.

secondary gangrene [L, *secundus,* second; Gk, *gaggraina*], a form of gangrene in which putrefaction follows the primary tissue necrosis, generating malodorous, toxic products.

secondary gestation [L, *secundus,* second, *gestare,* to bear], a pregnancy in which the ovum becomes displaced from its original site of implantation but continues development at a different location.

secondary glandular failure, the deficiency of a hormone secreted by a particular gland or gland atrophy caused by absence of a stimulus from another gland, as when a pituitary disorder results in hypogonadism.

secondary health care, an intermediate level of health care that includes diagnosis and treatment, performed in a hospital having specialized equipment and laboratory facilities.

secondary hemorrhage [L, *secundus,* second; Gk, *haima,* blood, *rhegnynai,* to burst forth], a hemorrhage that develops 24 hours or more after the original injury or surgery. It is often caused by an infection.

secondary hydrocephalus [L, *secundus,* second; Gk, *hydor,* water, *kephale,* head], hydrocephalus that develops after an injury, hemorrhage, or infection, such as syphilis or meningitis.

secondary hyperaldosteronism, excessive production of aldosterone caused by an extra-adrenal disorder such as heart failure, kidney disease, cirrhosis, or hypoproteinemia.

secondary hypertension, elevated BP associated with any of several primary diseases such as renal, pulmonary, endocrine, and vascular diseases.

secondary immunodeficiency, a loss of immunity caused by a disease process or toxic effect of medication, rather than by a failure or defect in T or B lymphocytes.

secondary infection, an infection by a microorganism that follows an initial infection by another kind of organism.

secondary infertility, infertility occurring in patients who have previously conceived.

secondary iritis [L, *secundus,* second; Gk, *iris,* rainbow, *itis,* inflammation], an inflammation of the iris secondary to another disorder, for example, ankylosing spondylitis or ulcerative colitis.

secondary lymphoid organ, a source of effector lymphocytes, such as the spleen, lymph nodes, or tonsils.

secondary nutrient, a substance that acts as a stimulant to activate the flora of the GI tract to synthesize other nutrients.

secondary occlusal traumatism, occlusal stress that affects previously weakened periodontal structures.

secondary oocyte, an oocyte in the period between the first and second maturation division. It is derived from a primary oocyte shortly before ovulation by a division that splits off the first polar body. If fertilized, it divides into an ootid and the second polar body. Otherwise it perishes.

secondary parkinsonism, a disease of the nervous system caused by degeneration of neurons in the corpus striatum that receive dopaminergic input from the substantia nigra. Unlike idiopathic parkinsonism, the disease does not respond to the administration of levodopa.

secondary peritonitis [L, *secundus,* second; Gk, *peri* + *tenein,* to stretch, *itis,* inflammation], inflammation of the peritoneum caused by the spread of infection from neighboring tissue.

secondary pneumonia [L, *secundus,* second; Gk, *pneumon,* lung], pneumonia that develops during the course of another disease such as diphtheria or tularemia.

secondary polycythemia [L, *secundus,* second; Gk, *polys,* many, *kytos,* cell, *haima,* blood], a form of polycythemia that develops as a result of oxygen deprivation from a disorder such as a pulmonary or cardiac disease.

secondary port, a control device for regulating the flow of a primary and a secondary IV solution. It consists of a Y-shaped plastic apparatus that attaches to the primary IV tubing and allows the primary and secondary IV solutions to flow separately or to flow simultaneously.

secondary prevention, a level of preventive medicine that focuses on early diagnosis, use of referral services, and rapid initiation of treatment to stop the progress of disease processes or a handicapping disability.

secondary radiation, radiation that results from the scattering of primary x-rays. Secondary radiation often accounts for fogging of radiographic film.

secondary relationships, relationships with those who provide or accept services or with acquaintances and friends, as distinguished from family members and intimate friends.

secondary sequestrum, a piece of dead bone that partially separates from sound bone during the process of necrosis but may be pushed back into position.

secondary sex characteristic, any of the external physical characteristics of sexual maturity secondary to hormonal stimulation that develop in the maturing individual. These characteristics include adult distribution of hair and development of the penis or breasts and the labia.

secondary shock, a state of physical collapse and prostration caused by numerous traumatic and pathologic conditions. It develops over time after severe tissue damage and may merge with primary shock, accompanied by various signs such as weakness, restlessness, low body temperature, low BP, cold sweat, and reduced urinary output. BP drops progressively in this state, and death may occur within a relatively short time after onset unless appropriate treatment intervenes. Secondary shock is often associated with heat stroke, crushing injuries, MI, poisoning, fulminating infections, burns, and other life-threatening conditions. The pathologic characteristics of this state reflect changes in the capillaries, which become dilated and engorged with blood.

second-degree burn, a burn that affects the epidermis and the dermis, classified as **superficial** or deep, according to the depth of injury. The superficial type involves the epidermis and the papillary dermis and heals without scarring. The deep type extends into the reticular dermis and results in scarring.

second filial generation (F$_2$), the offspring produced by the mating of two members of the F$_1$ generation or, broadly, by the crossing of any two heterozygous strains.

secondhand smoke, tobacco smoke from the burning end of a cigarette, cigar, or pipe that is inhaled by nonsmokers. The American Heart Association estimated in 2001 that secondhand smoke was implicated in the deaths of 37,000 to 40,000 nonsmokers each year from heart disease and lung cancer.

second-look operation, a second operation performed within 24 hours of the first to ensure that the first was sufficient and that no further debridement is needed.

second messenger, a chemical substance inside a cell that carries information farther along the signal pathway from the internal part of a membrane-spanning receptor embedded in the cell membrane.

second opinion [L, *secundus* + *opinari*, to suppose], a patient privilege of requesting an examination and evaluation of a health condition by a second physician to verify or challenge the diagnosis by a first physician.

second-order change, a change that alters the system itself.

second-order kinetics, a chemical reaction in which the rate of the reaction is determined by the concentration of two chemical reactants involved or the square of the concentration of one chemical reactant.

second-set rejection, failure of an organ or tissue graft in a host who is already immune to the histocompatibility antigens of the graft because of a previous graft with the same antigens.

second sight, 1. an improvement in near vision that may develop in aging as a result of increasing refractivity of the lens nucleus related to development of a nuclear sclerotic cataract. 2. an early increase in the index of refraction of the lens, resulting in a decrease in hyperopia and an increase in myopia. 3. clairvoyance, precognition.

second stage of labor [L, *secundus*, second; OFr, *estage*; L, *labor*, work], the period of childbirth from full dilation of the cervix to delivery of the fetus.

secretagogue /sikrē'təgog/, any agent that induces exocrine, endocrine, or paracrine secretion.

secrete, to discharge a substance into a cavity, vessel, or organ or onto the surface of the skin, as by a gland.—**secretion,** *n.*

secretin /sikrē'tin/ [L, *secernere*, to separate], a digestive hormone that is produced by the S cells lining the duodenum and jejunum when protein of partially digested food enters the intestine from the stomach. It stimulates the pancreas to produce a fluid high in salts but low in enzymes.

secretin-cholecystokinin test, a test for pancreatic function. It is a combination of the secretin test and the cholecystokinin test, measuring pancreatic secretion volume and secretion of bicarbonate, amylase, lipase, and trypsin.

secretin test, a test of pancreatic function after stimulation with a hormone, secretin. The test measures the volume and bicarbonate concentration of pancreatic secretions. A lower than normal volume suggests an obstructing malignancy or CF. Reduced

S

bicarbonate and amylase concentration is usually diagnostic of chronic pancreatitis.

secretion /sikrē'shən/ [L, *secernere*, to separate], **1.** the release of chemical substances manufactured by cells of glandular organs. **2.** a substance released or eliminated.—**secrete**, *v.*, **secretory**, *adj.*

secretoinhibitory /sikrē'tō·inhib'itôr'ē/ [L, *secernere*, to separate, *inhibere*, to restrain], pertaining to a function of inhibiting secretion.

secretor /sikrē'tər/, **1.** a person who releases A, B, or AB blood group antigens into saliva, gastric juice, or other exocrine secretions. **2.** the autosomal-dominant allele that determines this trait.

secretor factor, a substance that triggers the release of ABO blood group antigens into exocrine secretions.

secretory, pertaining to or contributing to the function of secretion.

secretory component, a glycopeptide that is attached to IgA. It is necessary for the secretion of IgA into mucosal spaces.

secretory component deficiency, a failure of GI epithelial cells to produce secretory component, a glycopeptide occurring in secretory IgA. It causes a lack of IgA in external secretions such as tears, saliva, and colostrum, although serum IgA is normal.

secretory duct [L, *secernere*], of a gland, a small duct that has a secretory function and joins with an excretory duct.

secretory IgA, a dimer of class A immunoglobulins, the principal agents of mucosal immunity. IgA is the only immunoglobulin isotype that can pass through mucosal membranes to reach the lumen of internal organs.

secretory immune system, the part of the immune system that secretes immunoglobulins, primarily IgA, onto mucosal surfaces.

secretory phase, the phase of the menstrual cycle after the release of an ovum from a mature ovarian follicle. The corpus luteum develops from the ruptured follicle. It secretes progesterone, which stimulates the development of the glands and arteries of the endometrium, causing it to become thick and spongy. In a negative-feedback response to the increased level of progesterone in the blood, the secretion of LH from the pituitary decreases.

section /sek'shən/ [L, *sectio*, a cutting], **1.** a cut surface or slice of tissue. **2.** the act of cutting tissue.

sectional arch wire /sek'shənəl/ [L, *sectio*, a cutting, *arcus*, bow; AS, *wir*], a wire attached to only a few teeth, usually on one side of a dental arch or in the anterior segment of the arch, to cause or guide orthodontic tooth movement.

sectional impression [L, *sectio*, a cutting, *imprimere*, to press into], a dental impression that is made in sections.

sector scan /sek'tər/, an ultrasound scan in which the transducer or ultrasound beam is rotated through an angle, and the center of rotation is near or behind the surface of the transducer.

Sectral, a trademark for a beta-adrenergic blocking agent (acebutolol).

secundigravida /səkund'dəgrav'idə/ [L, *secundus*, second, *gravidus*, pregnancy], a woman who is pregnant for the second time.—**secundigravid,** *adj.*

secundines /səkun'dīnz/ [L, *secundus*], the placenta, umbilical cord, and membranes of afterbirth.

secundipara /sek'əndip'ərə/ [L, *secundus* + *parere*, to bear], a woman who has borne two viable children in separate pregnancies.

security enhancement, a nursing intervention from the Nursing Interventions Classification (NIC) defined as intensifying a patient's sense of physical and psychological safety.

SED, abbreviation for *skin erythema dose*.

sedation /sidā'shən/ [L, *sedatio*, soothing], an induced state of quiet, calmness, or sleep, as by means of a sedative or hypnotic medication.

sedation management, a nursing intervention from the Nursing Interventions Classification (NIC) defined as the administration of sedatives, monitoring of the patient's response, and provision of necessary psychological support during a diagnostic or therapeutic procedure.

sedative /sed'ətiv/ [L, *sedatio*, soothing], **1.** pertaining to a substance, procedure, or measure that has a calming effect. **2.** an agent that decreases functional activity, diminishes irritability, and allays excitement.

sedative bath, the immersion of the body in water for a prolonged period, used especially as a calming procedure for agitated patients.

sedative filling, a temporary filling material, containing agents such as eugenol (also called oil of cloves) to soothe pulpal pain, used to restore missing tooth structure until definitive treatment can be rendered.

sedative-hypnotic, a drug that reversibly depresses the activity of the CNS, used chiefly to induce sleep and to allay anxiety. Sedative-hypnotics are used in the treatment of insomnia, acute convulsive conditions, and anxiety states and in facilitation of the induction of anesthesia.

sedentary /sed'ənter'ē/ [L, *sedentarius*, sitting], pertaining to a condition of inaction, such as work or recreation that can be performed in the sitting posture.

sedentary living [L, *sedentarius*; AS, *lif*], a pattern of daily living that requires a minimum amount of physical effort.

sediment /sed'imənt/ [L, *sedimentum*, settling], a deposit of relatively insoluble material that settles to the bottom of a container of liquid.

sedimentation /sed'iməntā'shən/ [L, *sedimentum*, settling], the deposition of insoluble materials to the bottom of a liquid. The process may be accelerated by centrifugation.

sedimentation rate (SR) [L, *sedimentum* + *ratum*, rate], the settling rate of red blood cells in a vertical column of anticoagulated whole blood. It is used to monitor inflammatory or malignant disease and to aid in the detection and diagnosis of inflammatory diseases.

sed. rate, *informal.* abbreviation for **erythrocyte sedimentation rate.**

segment /seg'mənt/ [L, *segmentum*, piece cut off], a component, or part of a structure, such as a lobe of the liver or part of the intestine.

segmental bronchus /segmen'təl/ [L, *segmentum*, piece cut off], a secondary bronchus branching from a primary bronchus to a tertiary bronchus.

segmental buds, tertiary bronchial buds.

segmental fracture, a bone break in which several large bone fragments separate from the main body of a fractured bone. The ends of the fragments may pierce the skin, as in an open fracture, or may be contained within the skin, as in a closed fracture.

segmental reflex [L, *segmentum* + *reflectere*, to bend back], a reflex that involves a pathway through only a single segment of the spinal cord.

segmental resection, a surgical procedure in which a part of an organ, gland, or other body part is excised, such as a segmental resection of a part of an ovary performed to diminish the gland's hormonal secretion by decreasing the amount of secretory tissue in the gland.

segmental spinal artery, feeder arteries that enter the intervertebral foramina at every level. They arise predominantly from the vertebral and deep cervical arteries in the neck, the posterior intercostal arteries in the thorax, and the lumbar arteries in the abdomen. They give rise to anterior and posterior radicular arteries and segmental medullary arteries.

segmentation /seg'məntā'shən/ [L, *segmentum* + *atio*, process], **1.** the division of an animal body into repeating, similar sections such as somites or metameres. **2.** the division of a zygote into blastomeres; cleavage.

segmentation method, a technique for filling tooth pulp canals in which a preselected gutta-percha cone is cut into segments. The tip segment is sealed into the apex of a root, and the other segments are usually warmed and condensed against the tip with a plugger.

segmentation nucleus, the nucleus that results from the fusion of male and female pronuclei in a fertilized ovum. Its formation is the final stage in fertilization and initiates the first cleavage of the zygote.

segmented hyalinizing vasculitis /segmen'tid/, a chronic relapsing inflammatory condition of the blood vessels of the lower legs associated with nodular or purpuric skin lesions that may become ulcerated and leave scars.

segmented neutrophil, a neutrophil with a segmented nucleus. Segments are connected by thin nuclear membrane filaments.

segregation, the separation of paired alleles during meiosis so that members of each pair of alleles appear in different gametes.

seizure /sē'zhər/ [Fr, *saisir*, to seize], a hyperexcitation of neurons in the brain leading to abnormal electric activity that causes a sudden, violent involuntary series of contractions of a group of muscles. It may be paroxysmal and episodic, as in a seizure disorder, or transient and acute, as after a head concussion. A seizure may be clonic or tonic; focal, unilateral, or bilateral; generalized or partial.

seizure control, a nursing outcome from the Nursing Outcomes Classification (NOC) defined as personal actions to reduce or minimize the occurrence of seizure episodes.

seizure management, a nursing intervention from the Nursing Interventions Classification (NIC) defined as care of a patient during a seizure and the postictal state.

seizure precautions, a nursing intervention from the Nursing Interventions Classification (NIC) defined as prevention or minimization of potential injuries sustained by a patient with a known seizure disorder.

seizure threshold, the amount of stimulus necessary to produce a convulsive seizure. All humans can have seizures if the provocation is sufficient.

selection /silek'shən/ [L, *seligere*, to choose], **1.** the act or product of choosing. **2.** the process by which various factors or mechanisms determine and modify the reproductive ability of individuals with specific genotypes within a population, thus influencing evolutionary change.

selective abstraction /silek'tiv/ [L, *seligere*, to choose], a type of cognitive distortion in which focus on one aspect of an event negates all other aspects.

S

selective angiography, a radiographic procedure that allows selective visualization of the aorta, the major arterial systems, or a particular vessel. It is performed after a few milliliters of a radiopaque contrast medium has been injected through a percutaneous catheter.

selective estrogen receptor modulator (SERM), an agent that activates some estrogen receptors but not others, thereby having estrogen-like effects on target tissues without affecting other tissues that have estrogen receptors.

selective grinding, any modification of the occlusal forms of the teeth to improve occlusion and tooth function, produced by grinding at selected places.

selective IgA deficiency, a familial or acquired disorder characterized by a lack of serum and secretory immunoglobulin A (IgA). The IgA-deficient patient may appear normal or asymptomatic and is diagnosed by demonstration of less than 5 mg/dL of IgA in serum. Patients have an increased risk of respiratory, GI, and urogenital infections.

selective immunoglobulin deficiency, a condition characterized by inadequate levels of one of the major classes of immunoglobulins.

selective inattention, the screening out of unwanted stimuli, particularly the part of a message that the listener does not want to hear.

selective mutism, a mental disorder of childhood characterized by continuous refusal to speak in social situations by a child who is able and willing to speak to selected persons.

selective neuronal necrosis, a widespread destruction of neurons caused by hypoxic or ischemic events. Only a fraction of the neurons in a given region is destroyed, selected apparently at random.

selective serotonin reuptake inhibitor (SSRI), an antidepressant drug that blocks reuptake of serotonin without blocking reuptake of other biogenic amines such as norepinephrine and dopamine. Advantages over tricyclic antidepressant drugs include fewer anticholinergic side effects (dry mouth, blurred vision, urinary retention) and fewer antihistaminic side effects (sedation, weight gain).

selectivity /sil'ektiv'itē/ [L, *seligere*], **1.** the capacity factor ratios of two substances measured under identical chromatographic conditions. **2.** the ratio of isomeric reaction products formed in a reaction where more than one product may be formed.

selectivity coefficient, the degree to which an ion-selective electrode responds to a particular ion with respect to a reference ion.

selenious acid /sĕ-le'ne-us/, monohydrated selenium dioxide, a source of elemental selenium.

selenium (Se) /silē'nē-əm/ [Gk, *selene*, moon], a metalloid element of the sulfur group. Its atomic number is 34, and its atomic mass is 78.96. Selenium occurs as a trace element in foods, and research continues to determine the most effective daily allowances for different age groups. Although selenium deficiency can result in liver problems and degeneration of muscles in some animals, in humans its need has not yet been clearly defined. The bright orange insoluble powder selenium sulfide is used externally in the control of seborrheic dermatitis, dandruff, and other forms of dermatosis. Selenium is also used in the nuclear medicine compound selenomethionine for diagnosing parathyroid tumors, and as a photoconductive layer of xeroradiographic plates.

selenium sulfide, an antidandruff and antiseborrheic medication. It is prescribed for dandruff, seborrheic dermatitis of the scalp, and treatment of tinea versicolor.

self *pl.* **selves** /selvz/ [AS], **1.** the total essence or being of a person; the individual. **2.** those affective, cognitive, and spiritual qualities that distinguish one person from another; individuality. **3.** a person's awareness of his or her own being or identity; consciousness; ego.

self-acceptance [AS, *self*; L, *accipere*, to take], the recognition and acceptance of one's own qualities and limitations.

self-actualization, in humanistic psychology, the fundamental tendency toward the maximum realization and fulfillment of one's human potential.

self-anesthesia, the self-administered inhalation anesthesia in which whiffs of anesthetic gas are inhaled from a handheld breathing device controlled by the patient. This form of anesthesia is most common in England.

self-awareness enhancement, a nursing intervention from the Nursing Interventions Classification (NIC) defined as assisting a patient to explore and understand his/her thoughts, feelings, motivations, and behaviors.

self-breast examination (SBE), a procedure in which a woman examines her breasts and their accessory structures for evidence of change that could indicate a malignant process. The SBE is usually performed 1 week to 10 days after the first day of the menstrual cycle, when the breasts are smallest and cyclic nodularity is least apparent. The techniques are similar to those of the examination of the breast as performed in the health assessment or physical examination.

self-care, 1. the personal and medical care performed by the patient, usually in collaboration with and after instruction by a health professional. 2. the health care by laypeople of their families, their friends, and themselves, including identification and evaluation of symptoms, medication, and treatment. 3. personal care accomplished without technical assistance, such as eating, washing, dressing, using the telephone, and attending to one's own elimination, appearance, and hygiene. The goal of rehabilitation medicine is maximal personal self-care.

self-care of daily living (ADL), a nursing outcome from the Nursing Outcomes Classification (NOC) defined as the ability to perform the most basic physical tasks and personal care activities independently with or without an assistive device.

self-care assistance, a nursing intervention from the Nursing Interventions Classification (NIC) defined as assisting another to perform activities of daily living.

self-care assistance: bathing/hygiene, a nursing intervention from the Nursing Interventions Classification (NIC) defined as assisting patient to perform personal hygiene.

self-care assistance: dressing/grooming, a nursing intervention from the Nursing Interventions Classification (NIC) defined as assisting a patient with clothes and appearance.

self-care assistance: feeding, a nursing intervention from the Nursing Interventions Classification (NIC) defined as assisting a person to eat.

self-care assistance: IADL, a nursing intervention from the Nursing Interventions Classification (NIC) defined as assisting and instructing a person to perform instrumental activities of daily living (IADL) needed to function in the home or community.

self-care assistance: transfer, a nursing intervention from the Nursing Interventions Classification (NIC) defined as assisting a patient with limitation of independent movement to learn to change body location.

self-care assistance: toileting, a nursing intervention from the Nursing Interventions Classification (NIC) defined as assisting another with elimination.

self-care: bathing, a nursing outcome from the Nursing Outcomes Classification (NOC) defined as the ability to cleanse one's own body independently with or without an assistive device.

self-care: dressing, a nursing outcome from the Nursing Outcomes Classification (NOC) defined as the ability to dress oneself independently with or without an assistive device.

self-care: eating, a nursing outcome from the Nursing Outcomes Classification (NOC) defined as the ability to prepare and ingest food and fluid independently with or without an assistive device.

self-care: hygiene, a nursing outcome from the Nursing Outcomes Classification (NOC) defined as the ability to maintain one's own personal cleanliness and kempt appearance independently with or without an assistive device.

self-care: instrumental activities of daily living (IADL), a nursing outcome from the Nursing Outcomes Classification (NOC) defined as the ability to perform activities needed to function in the home or community independently with or without an assistive device.

self-care: nonparenteral medication, a nursing outcome from the Nursing Outcomes Classification (NOC) defined as the ability to administer oral and topical medications to meet therapeutic goals independently with or without an assistive device.

self-care: oral hygiene, a nursing outcome from the Nursing Outcomes Classification (NOC) defined as the ability to care for one's own mouth and teeth independently with or without an assistive device.

self-care: parenteral medication, a nursing outcome from the Nursing Outcomes Classification (NOC) defined as the ability to administer parenteral medications to meet therapeutic goals independently with or without an assistive device.

self-care status, a nursing outcome from the Nursing Outcomes Classification (NOC) defined as the ability to perform basic personal care and instrumental activities of daily living.

self-care theory, a model, central to Dorothea Orem's concept of nursing, used to provide a conceptual framework for nursing care directed to self-care by the client to the greatest degree possible. The model requires an assessment of the client's capability for self-care and need for care.

self-care: toileting, a nursing outcome from the Nursing Outcomes Classification (NOC) is defined as the ability to toilet one's self independently with or without an assistive device.

self-catheterization, a procedure performed by a patient to empty the bladder by inserting a catheter into the urethra. The procedure is recommended for patients who cannot empty the bladder completely but can retain urine for 2 to 4 hours at a time and who have mental cognition, some manual dexterity, and the ability to insert a catheter into the urethra. This is generally a clean rather than a sterile procedure. The patient is instructed to clean the urinary meatus and labia or glans penis with soap and water, to grasp the

self-concept, the composite of ideas, feelings, and attitudes that a person has about his or her own identity, worth, capabilities, and limitations.

self-confrontation, a technique for behavior modification that depends on a patient's recognition of and dissatisfaction with inconsistencies in his or her own values, beliefs, and behaviors, or between his or her own personal system and that of a significant other.

self-conscious, **1.** the state of being aware of oneself as an individual entity that experiences, desires, and acts. **2.** a heightened awareness of oneself and one's actions as reflected by the observations and reactions of others; socially ill at ease.—**self-consciousness,** *n.*

self-curing resin, any resin that can be polymerized by the addition of an activator and a catalyst without the use of external heat; used in dental restorations and repairs.

self-defeating personality disorder, a personality characterized by a type of behavior that inhibits the individual from achieving his or her own desires and goals. It is characterized by involvement in situations that continuously lead to failure, rejection, and loss even when other options for involvement are available.

self-destructive behavior, any behavior, direct or indirect, that if uninterrupted will ultimately lead to the death of the individual.

self-diagnosis, the diagnosis of one's own health problems, usually without direction or assistance from a physician.

self-differentiation, specialization and diversification of a tissue or body part resulting solely from intrinsic factors.

self-direction of care, a nursing outcome from the Nursing Outcomes Classification (NOC) defined as care recipient actions taken to direct others who assist with or perform physical tasks and personal health care.

self-disclosure, the process by which one person lets his or her inner being, thoughts, and emotions be known to another. It is important for psychologic growth in individual and group psychotherapy.

self-efficacy enhancement, a nursing intervention from the Nursing Interventions Classification (NIC) defined as the strengthening of an individual's confidence in his/her ability to perform a health behavior.

self-esteem[1]**,** the degree of worth and competence one attributes to oneself.

self-esteem[2]**,** a nursing outcome from the Nursing Outcomes Classification (NOC) defined as personal judgment of self-worth.

self-esteem enhancement, a nursing intervention from the Nursing Interventions Classification (NIC) defined as assisting a patient to increase his/her personal judgment of self-worth.

self-fulfilling prophecy, a principle that states that a belief in or the expectation of a particular resolution is a factor that contributes to its fulfillment.

self-healing squamous epithelioma, an inherited condition of skin tumors that appear on the head and resolve spontaneously after a few months, leaving deep-pitted scars. The tumors resemble squamous carcinoma or keratoacanthoma.

self-help group, a group of people who meet to improve their health through discussion and special activities. Characteristically, self-help groups are not led by a professional.

self-hypnosis [AS, *self;* Gk, *hypnos,* sleep], the process of putting oneself into a trancelike state by autosuggestion, such as concentration on a single thought or object. Some subjects are more susceptible than others.

self-hypnosis facilitation, a nursing intervention from the Nursing Interventions Classification (NIC) defined as teaching and monitoring the use of a self-initiated hypnotic state for therapeutic benefit.

self-ideal, a perception of how one should behave based on certain personal standards. The standard may be either a carefully constructed image of the kind of person one would like to be or merely a number of aspirations, goals, or values one would like to achieve.

self-image, the total concept, idea, or mental image one has of oneself and of one's role in society; the person one believes oneself to be.

self-insurance, a system whereby hospitals or health professionals may, in lieu of commercial insurance, assume financial responsibility for their liability.

self-limited, of a disease or condition, tending to end without treatment.

self-limited disease [AS, *self;* L, *limes,* boundary, *dis,* not; Fr, *aise,* ease], a disease restricted in duration by its own pattern of characteristics and not by other influences.

self-management approach, a treatment approach in which patients assume responsibility for their behavior, changing their environment, and planning their future.

self-modification assistance, a nursing intervention from the Nursing Interventions Classification (NIC) defined as reinforcement of self-directed change initiated by the patient to achieve personally important goals.

self-monitoring of blood glucose (SMBG), the use of a glucose meter to enable a patient to recognize glycemic variations. Most self-monitoring systems use the chemical reaction between glucose oxidase and glucose as a basis for measurement. Some devices depend on hydrogen peroxide, which is a product of the same reaction.

self-mutilation restraint, a nursing outcome from the Nursing Outcomes Classification (NOC) defined as personal actions to refrain from intentional self-inflicted injury (nonlethal).

self-other, a concept that characterizes people who believe that the source of power is within the self as opposed to those who believe that it is in others.

self-radiolysis, a process in which a compound is damaged by radioactive decay products originating in an atom within the compound.

self-recognition, the ability of the body's immune system to recognize self-identifying antigens on the body's own cells.

self-regulation, a plan for patients to eliminate health risk behaviors. It includes self-monitoring, self-evaluation, and self-reinforcement.

self-reinforcing adaptation, in occupational therapy, a therapeutic technique in which each successful stage of adjustment stimulates the next more complex step.

self-responsibility, a concept of holistic health by which individuals assume responsibility for their own health.

self-responsibility facilitation, a nursing intervention from the Nursing Interventions Classification (NIC) defined as encouraging a patient to assume more responsibility for his/her own behavior.

self-retaining catheter, an indwelling urinary catheter that has a double lumen. One channel allows urine to drain from the bladder into a collecting bag; the other has a balloon at the bladder end and a diaphragm at the other end. Several centimeters of air or sterile water is injected through the diaphragm to fill the balloon in the bladder and hold the catheter in place.

self-stimulation, a system in which patients control their pain by manipulating an electrical source of nerve stimulation.

self-system, the organization of experiences that acts as a protective mechanism against anxiety.

self-theory, a personality theory that uses one's self-concept in integrating the function and organization of the personality.

self-threading pin, a screwlike pin placed into a hole drilled in tooth dentin to improve the retention of a restoration.

self-tolerance, the absence of an immune response directed against a person's own tissue antigens.

self-transcendence, the ability to focus attention on doing something for the sake of others, as opposed to self-actualization,

in which doing something for oneself is an end goal.

sellar diaphragm, a dural partition consisting of a small horizontal shelf of meningeal dura mater that covers the hypophysial fossa in the sella turcica of the sphenoid bone.

sella turcica /sel′ə tur′sikə/ [L, *sella,* seat, *turcica,* Turkish], a transverse depression crossing the midline on the superior surface of the body of the sphenoid bone and containing the pituitary gland.

Selsun, a trademark for an antidandruff and antiseborrheic (selenium sulfide).

Selzentry, a trademark for maraviroc.

SEM, abbreviation for **scanning electron microscope.**

semantics /siman′tiks/ [Gk, *semantikos,* significant], the study of language with special concern for the meanings of words or other symbols.

semen /sē′mən/ [L, seed], the thick, whitish secretion of the male reproductive organs discharged from the urethra during ejaculation. It contains spermatozoa in their nutrient plasma as well as secretions of the prostate, seminal vesicles, and other glands.—**seminal,** *adj.*

semen analysis, a fluid analysis involving the measurement of freshly collected semen for volume, counting the sperm, evaluating sperm motility, and studying sperm morphology. It is one of the most important aspects of the fertility workup.

semiautomatic external defibrillator /sem′ē-ô′təmat′ik/, a portable apparatus used to restart a heart that has stopped. It is programmed to analyze cardiac rhythms automatically and indicate to a health professional when to deliver a defibrillation shock.

semicanal /-kənal′/, **1.** a canal with an opening on one side. **2.** a deep groove on the edge of a bone that accommodates part of an adjoining bone.

semicircular canal /-sur′kyələr/ [L, *semi-,* half, *circulare,* to go around, *canalis,* channel], any of three bony fluid-filled loops in the osseous labyrinth of the internal ear, associated with the sense of balance.

semicircular duct, one of three ducts that make up the membranous labyrinth of the inner ear.

semicomatose /-kō′mətōs/ [L, *semi,* half; Gk, *koma,* deep sleep], pertaining to a condition of stupor from which a patient can be aroused.

semiconductor /-kənduk′tər/, a solid crystalline substance whose electric conductivity is intermediate between that of a conductor and that of an insulator.

semiconscious /-kon′shəs/, an impaired state of consciousness, characterized by obtundation, stupor, or hypersomnia, from which a patient can be aroused only by energetic stimulation.

semiflexion /-flek'shən/, a limb position midway between full flexion and full extension.

semi-Fowler's position /-fou'lərz/ [L, *semi,* half; George R. Fowler, American surgeon, 1848–1906], placement of a patient in an inclined position, with the upper half of the body raised by elevating the head of the bed approximately 30 degrees.

semihorizontal heart /-hôr'əzon'təl/, an electric "position" of the heart that lies between the horizontal and intermediate positions when the QRS axis is 0 degrees.

semilunar fold of the conjunctiva, a fold of membrane that extends laterally from the lacrimal caruncle. It has a concave free border directed to the cornea. In some individuals it contains smooth muscular fibers.

semilunar hiatus, the deep semilunar groove anterior and inferior to the bulla of the ethmoid bone. The anterior ethmoidal cells, the maxillary sinus, and sometimes the frontonasal duct drain through it via the ethmoid infundibulum.

semilunar valve /-lōō'nər/ [L, *semi* + *luna,* moon, *valva,* folding door], **1.** a valve with half-moon–shaped cusps, such as the aortic valve and the pulmonary valve. **2.** any one of the cusps constituting such a valve. **3.** simple cuplike valves found in the venous and lymphatic vessels.

semimembranosus /-mem'brənō'səs/ [L, *semi* + *membrana,* membrane], one of three posterior femoral muscles. The tendon of insertion forms one of the two medial hamstrings. The muscle functions to flex the leg, rotate it medially after flexion, and extend the thigh.

semimembranous /-mem'brənəs/ [L, *semi,* half, *membrana*], pertaining to a muscle or other tissue that is partly membrane or fascia, such as the semimembranous hamstring muscle.

seminal crest, a prominent portion of the urethral crest on which are the opening of the prostatic utricle and, on either side of it, the orifices of the ejaculatory ducts.

seminal duct /sem'inəl/ [L, *semen,* seed, *ducere,* to lead], any duct through which semen passes, such as the vas deferens or the ejaculatory duct.

seminal emission [L, *semen,* seed, *emittere,* to send out], a discharge of semen.

seminal fluid test, any of several tests of semen to detect abnormalities in a male's reproductive system and to determine fertility. Some common factors considered are seminal fluid liquefaction time and spermatic quantity, morphologic characteristics, motility, volume, and pH.

seminal vesicle, either of the paired saclike glandular structures posterolateral to the urinary bladder in the male and functioning as part of the reproductive system. The seminal vesicles produce a fluid that is added to the secretion of the testes and other glands to form the semen.

seminal vesicle cyst, a cyst in the wall of a seminal vesicle. It may be congenital and associated with other urinary tract anomalies or acquired, such as a result of obstruction of the vesicle.

seminal vesiculitis, inflammation of a seminal vesicle.

semination /sem'inā'shən/, the introduction of semen into the female genital tract.

seminiferous /sem'inif'ərəs/ [L, *semen* + *ferre,* to bear], transporting or producing semen, such as the tubules of the testis.

seminiferous cords, the primordia of the seminiferous tubules, derived from the gonadal cords of the testis.

seminiferous tubules [L, *semen,* seed, *ferre,* to bear, *tubulus*], long, threadlike tubes packed in areolar tissue in the lobes of the testes.

seminoma /sem'inō'mə/ *pl.* **seminomas, seminomata** [L, *semen* + *oma,* tumor], a malignant tumor of the testis. It is the most common testicular tumor and is believed to arise from the seminiferous epithelium of the mature or maturing testis.

semiparametric statistics /sem'ēpar'əmet'rik/ [L, *semi,* half; Gk, *para,* to, at, or from the side of, *metron,* measure], statistical methodology that combines both parametric and nonparametric elements. It is used for estimating population parameters when a function is unknown, e.g., the distribution function of a random variable that has not been observed.

semipermeable /-pur'mē·əbəl/ [L, *semi,* half, *permeare,* to pass through], pertaining to a membrane that allows the passage of some molecules but prevents the passage of others.

semipermeable membrane [L, *semi* + *permeare,* to pass through], a membrane that prevents the passage of some substances but allows the passage of others based on differences in the size, charge, or lipid-solubility of the substances.

semiprone /-prōn'/ [L, *semi,* half, *pronus,* leaning forward], lying on one's side, with the thigh on the upper side flexed against the abdomen and the arm on the lower side extended back.

semirecumbent /-rikum'bənt/, in a reclining position.

semispinalis muscles, the most superficial collection of muscle fibers in the transversospinalis group. They are found in the thoracic and cervical regions and attach to the occipital bone at the base of the skull.

semisupine /-səpīn′/, pertaining to a posture that is between a midposition and the supine position.

semisynthetic /-sinthet′ik/ [L, *semi,* half; Gk, *synthesis,* putting together], pertaining to a natural substance that has been partially altered by chemical manipulation.

semitendinosus /sem′iten′dinō′səs/ [L, *semi* + *tendere,* to stretch], one of three posterior femoral muscles of the thigh. It functions to flex the leg, rotate it medially after flexion, and extend the thigh.

semivertical heart /-vur′tikəl/, an electric "position" of the heart that lies between the intermediate and vertical positions when the QRS axis is 60 degrees.

Semprex-D, a trademark for a fixed-combination drug containing an antihistamine and a decongestant (acrivastine with pseudoepHEDrine hydrochloride).

sender [AS, *sendan,* to send], in communication theory, the person by whom a message is encoded and sent.

seneciosis /senes′ē·ō′sis/, a toxic reaction to the ingestion of plants of the genus *Senecio,* which are used to make bush tea. The poison causes liver damage, particularly in malnourished patients. Common *Senecio* species include ragwort and life root, both used in herbal remedies.

senescence /sənes′əns/ [L, *senescere,* to grow old], the state of growing old.

senescent /sənes′ənt/ [L, *senescere,* to grow old], aging or growing old.—**senescence,** *n.*

senescent cell antigen, an antigen that appears on old RBCs that bind IgG autoantibodies. It is also found on lymphocytes, platelets, and neutrophils.

Sengstaken-Blakemore tube [Robert W. Sengstaken, American neurosurgeon, b. 1923; Arthur H. Blakemore, American surgeon, 1897–1970], a thick catheter having a triple lumen and two balloons, used to produce pressure by balloon tamponade to arrest hemorrhaging from esophageal varices. Attached to a tube, one balloon is inflated in the stomach and exerts pressure against the upper orifice. Similarly attached, another longer and narrower balloon exerts pressure on the walls of the esophagus. The third tube is used for withdrawing gastric contents.

senile /sē′nīl/ [L, *senilis,* aged], pertaining to or characteristic of old age or the process of aging.—**senescent,** *adj.,* **senility,** *n.*

senile arteriosclerosis, hardening of the arteries associated with aging.

senile cataract, a kind of cataract, associated with aging, in which an opacity forms in the crystalline lens of the eye.

senile dementia, dementia occurring in older persons, usually over the age of 65.

Because most cases are due to Alzheimer's disease, the term is sometimes used as a synonym for *dementia of the Alzheimer type, late onset.*

senile dementia–Alzheimer type (SDAT), dementia occurring in older persons, usually over the age of 65, resulting from Alzheimer's disease.

senile dental caries, tooth decay occurring in a person of advanced age. It is usually characterized by cavity formation in or around the cementum layer and root surfaces.

senile involution, a pattern of retrograde changes occurring with advancing age and resulting in the progressive shrinking and degeneration of tissues and organs.

senile nanism, dwarfism associated with progeria.

senile tremor [L, *senilis,* aged, *tremor,* shaking], a tremor associated with aging.

senile vaginitis [L, *senilis,* aged, *vagina,* sheath, *itis,* inflammation], a condition of atrophy of the vagina resulting from the postmenopausal loss of estrogen secretion.

senility /sinil′itē/ [L, *senilis,* aged], the general state of reduced mental and physical vigor associated with aging.

senior centers /sē′nyər/, community agencies for older adults. The centers offer nutritional, recreational, educational, health, and legal services.

Senior Companion Program, a service that offers personal assistance and peer support to homebound and chronically ill older people.

senior patient, in the United States, a Medicare beneficiary enrolled in a health maintenance organization.

senna, an herbal product taken from several *Cassia* species, found across the world. It is used as a laxative.

Sennetsu fever /sənet′soo/, a febrile disease occurring in Japan and Malaysia and caused by the bacterium *Ehrlichia sennetsu.* Symptoms include headache, nausea or vomiting, lymphocytosis, and postauricular and posterior lymphadenopathy.

senopia /senō′pē·ə/ [L, *senex,* old man, *opsis,* vision], an improvement in the near vision of the aged caused by the myopia associated with increasing lenticular nuclear sclerosis.

sensate /sen′sāt/, capable of perceiving sensory stimuli.

sensate focus technique, a therapeutic program for the treatment of erectile dysfunction in males.

sensation /sensā′shən/ [L, *sentire,* to feel], **1.** a feeling, impression, or awareness of a body state or condition that results from the stimulation of a sensory receptor site and transmission of the nerve impulse along an afferent fiber to the brain. **2.** a feeling or an awareness of a mental

S

or emotional state, which may or may not result in response to an external stimulus.

sense [L, *sentire*, to feel], **1.** the faculty by which stimuli are perceived and conditions outside and within the body are distinguished and evaluated. The major senses are sight, hearing, smell, taste, touch, and pressure. Other senses include hunger, thirst, pain, temperature, proprioception, and spatial, temporal, and visceral sensations. **2.** the ability to feel; a sensation. **3.** the capacity to understand; normal mental ability. **4.** to perceive through a sense organ. **5.** pertaining to the sense strand of a nucleic acid.

sense strand, the strand of a double-stranded nucleic acid that encodes the product. In DNA it is the strand that encodes the RNA, having thus the same base sequence except changing T for U in the RNA.

sensibility /sen'sibil'itē/, the ability to perceive sensations and impressions, both physical and psychologic.

sensible /sen'sibəl/, **1.** capable of sensation. **2.** possessing reason or judgment. **3.** capable of being perceived.

sensible perspiration [L, *sensibilis*, perceptible], loss of body fluid through the secretory activity of the sweat glands in a quantity sufficient to be observed.

Sensipar, a trademark for cinacalcet.

sensitive /sen'sitiv/ [L, *sentire*, to feel], **1.** able to perceive and transmit a sensation or stimulus. **2.** affected by low concentrations of antimicrobial drugs, said of microorganisms. **3.** abnormally susceptible to a subject, such as a drug or foreign protein.

sensitive volume [L, *sentire* + *volumen*, paper roll], the part of an object from which a magnetic resonance signal is preferentially acquired because of strong magnetic field inhomogeneity elsewhere.

sensitivity /sen'sitiv'itē/ [L, *sentire*], **1.** capacity to feel, transmit, or react to a stimulus. **2.** susceptibility to a substance such as a drug or an antigen. **3.** the lowest level of a substance that can be detected by a laboratory test procedure.—**sensitive, diagnostic sensitivity,** *adj.*

sensitivity test, a laboratory method for testing the effectiveness of antibiotics. It is usually done on organisms known to be potentially resistant to antibiotic therapy in vitro. A report of a "resistant" finding means the antibiotic is not effective in inhibiting the growth of a pathogen, whereas use of an effective antibiotic results in a "sensitive" report.

sensitivity training group, a group that offers members a supportive atmosphere in which to experiment with and alter behavior patterns and interpersonal reactions.

sensitization /sen'sitizā'shən/ [L, *sentire*; Gk, *izein*, to cause], **1.** reaction in which specific antibodies develop in response to an antigen. Allergic reactions result from excess sensitization to a foreign protein. Sensitization can be induced by immunization, in which a pathogen that has been made noninfectious is introduced into the body. **2.** a photodynamic method of destroying microorganisms through the use of substances, such as fluorescent dyes, that absorb light and emit energy at wavelengths destructive to the organisms. **3.** *nontechnical*. anaphylaxis.—**sensitize,** *v.*

sensitized /sen'sitizd/, pertaining to tissues that have been made reactive to antigens.

sensitized vaccine [L, *sentire*, to feel, *vaccinus*, of a cow], a vaccine that is prepared by suspending microorganisms in their own homologous immune serum.

sensor /sen'sər/, an apparatus designed to react to physical stimuli such as temperature, light, or movement.

sensoriglandular /sen'sərēglan'dyələr/, pertaining to the reflexive secretion by glands triggered by sensory stimulation of a nerve.

sensorimotor /sen'sərēmō'tər/ [L, *sentire*, to feel, *moveo*, to move], pertaining to both sensory and motor nerve functions.

sensorimotor phase [L, *sentire* + *moveo*, to move], the developmental phase of childhood, encompassing the period from birth to 2 years of age, according to piagetian psychology.

sensorimotor therapy, therapy designed to enhance the integration of reflex phenomena and the emergence of voluntary motor behaviors concerned with posture and locomotion.

sensorimuscular /-mus'kyələr/, pertaining to contraction of muscles triggered by sensory stimulation.

sensorineural /sen'sərēnŏŏr'əl/ [L, *sentire*, to feel; Gk, *neuron*, nerve], pertaining to sensory nerves.

sensorineural hearing loss, a form of hearing loss in which sound is conducted normally through the external and middle ear but a defect in the inner ear or auditory nerve results in hearing loss.

sensorium /sensôr'ē·əm/, in psychology, the part of the consciousness that includes the special sensory perceptive powers and their central correlation and integration in the brain. A clear sensorium conveys the presence of a reasonably accurate memory together with a correct orientation for time, place, and person.

sensorivasomotor /-vā'zōmō'tər/, pertaining to the contraction or dilation of a blood vessel in response to a sensory stimulus.

sensory /sen'sərē/ [L, *sentire*, to feel], **1.** pertaining to sensation. **2.** pertaining to a part or all of the body's sensory nerve network.

sensory area [L, *sentire,* to feel, *area,* space], the regions of the cerebral cortex that receive impulses from sensory nerves, including thalamic, nucleic, and parietal lobes.

sensory-based language, the use of nonverbal behavior in neurolinguistic communication. Examples are puzzled expressions, scowling, and finger pointing.

sensory deficit, a defect in the function of one or more of the senses.

sensory deprivation [L, *sentire;* ME, *depriven,* to deprive; L, *atio,* process], an involuntary loss of physical awareness caused by detachment from external sensory stimuli. Such deprivation often results in psychologic disorders such as panic, mental confusion, depression, and hallucinations.

sensory end organ [L, *sentire,* to feel; AS, *ende;* Gk, *organon,* instrument], any of the specialized nerve endings devoted to detection of specific environmental stimuli, such as smell, sight, hearing, temperature, or touch.

sensory function, a nursing outcome from the Nursing Outcomes Classification (NOC) defined as the extent to which an individual correctly senses skin stimulation, sounds, proprioception, taste and smell, and visual images.

sensory function: cutaneous, a nursing outcome from the Nursing Outcomes Classification (NOC) defined as the extent to which stimulation of the skin is correctly sensed.

sensory function: hearing, a nursing outcome from the Nursing Outcomes Classification (NOC) defined as the extent to which sounds are correctly sensed.

sensory function: proprioception, a nursing outcome from the Nursing Outcomes Classification (NOC) defined as the extent to which position and movement of the head and body are correctly sensed.

sensory function: taste and smell, a nursing outcome from the Nursing Outcomes Classification (NOC) defined as the extent to which chemicals inhaled or dissolved in saliva are correctly sensed.

sensory function: vision, a nursing outcome from the Nursing Outcomes Classification (NOC) defined as the extent to which visual images are correctly sensed.

sensory integration, the organization of sensory input for use, a perception of the body or environment, an adaptive response, a learning process, or the development of some neural function.

sensory integrative dysfunction, a disorder or irregularity in brain function that makes sensory integration difficult.

sensory integrative therapy, therapy that involves sensory stimulation and adaptive responses to it according to a child's neurologic needs. Treatment usually involves full body movements that provide vestibular, proprioceptive, and tactile stimulation. The goal is to improve the brain's ability to process and organize sensations.

sensory nerve, a nerve consisting of afferent fibers that conduct sensory impulses from the periphery of the body to the brain or spinal cord via the dorsal spinal roots.

sensory neuropathy, neuropathy or polyneuropathy of sensory nerves.

sensory nucleus of trigeminal nerve, a collection of nerve cells in the pons that serves as the main nucleus for reception of tactile fibers of the trigeminal area.

sensory overload, a condition in which an individual receives an excessive or intolerable amount of sensory stimuli. The effects of sensory overload are similar to those of sensory deprivation, including confusion and hallucination.

sensory pathway [L, *sentire,* to feel; AS, *paeth + weg*], the route followed by a sensory nerve impulse from an end organ to a reflex center in the brain or spinal cord.

sensory receptor [L, *sentire,* to feel, *recipere,* to receive], a specialized nerve ending that, when stimulated, initiates an afferent or sensory nerve impulse.

sensory root [L, *sentire,* to feel], the proximal end of a dorsal afferent nerve as it is attached to the spinal cord.

sensory threshold [L, *sentire,* to feel; AS, *therscold*], the point at which increasing stimuli trigger the start of an afferent nerve impulse. Absolute threshold is the lowest point at which response to a stimulus can be perceived.

sensual /sen'shōō·əl/ [L, *sensualis*], pertaining to a great interest in sex, food, or other sense-satisfying topics.

sentient /sen'shənt/ [L, *sentire,* to feel], possessing sensitivity or powers of sensation and perception.

sentinel gland /sen'tinəl/ [Fr, *sentinelle;* L, *glans,* acorn], a node or growth that is associated with the presence of a nearby tumor or ulcer. An example is a supraclavicular node with cancer cells that have metastasized from an undiscovered primary cancer.

sentinel lymph node biopsy, dissection of the first lymph node in the chain of lymph nodes to catch metastatic tumor cells from a primary breast tumor or melanoma.

sentinel node biopsy, biopsy of a sentinel node (the first lymph node to receive lymphatic drainage from a malignant tumor). It is identified as follows: A dye and a radioactive substance are injected into the body, which causes certain nodes to "light up" like a sentinel, indicating that they are the most appropriate ones for examination. They are detected by both the light created by the dye and the radioactive substance that is monitored by a

S

1216

gamma camera. If the sentinel nodes do not contain malignant cells, it is usually not necessary to remove more distal nodes.

Seoul virus /sōl/, a virus of the genus *Hantavirus* that causes mild to moderately severe epidemic hemorrhagic fever in Asia, primarily Korea and Japan. Several species of rats are the natural hosts.

SEP, abbreviation for **somatosensory evoked potential.**

separating spring /sep'ərāting/ [L, *separare,* to separate; AS, *springan,* to jump], a spring placed between the teeth to obtain separation.

separating wire, a brass wire threaded between two teeth having tight contact in an effort to wedge them slightly apart before fitting a band in the application of an orthodontic appliance.

separation agent /sep'ərā'shən/, a reagent used to separate bound and free tracers in radioassay.

separation anxiety [L, *separare,* to separate, *atio,* process], fear and apprehension caused by separation from familiar surroundings and significant people. The syndrome occurs commonly in an infant separated from its mother or mothering figure or approached by a stranger.

separator /sep'ərātər/ [L, *separare,* to separate], **1.** a device for separating one thing from another. **2.** a device or instrument for wedging teeth apart, especially proximal teeth having a tight contact, as for the examination of proximal surfaces, finishing a restoration, or before banding in orthodontic therapy.

s-EPO, abbreviation for *serum erythropoietin.*

sepsis /sep'sis/ [Gk, *sepein,* to become putrid], infection, contamination.—**septic,** *adj.*

septal /sep'təl/ [L, *saeptum,* enclosure], pertaining to a septum.

septal defect [L, *saeptum,* fence, *defectus,* failure], a defect in the wall separating the left and right sides of the heart. Depending on the size and the site of the defect, various amounts of oxygenated and deoxygenated blood mix, causing a decrease in the amount of oxygen carried in the blood to the peripheral tissues.

septate /sep'tāt/, pertaining to a structure divided by a septum.

septic, pertaining to an infection with pyogenic microorganisms.

septic abortion [Gk, *septikos,* putrid], spontaneous or induced termination of a pregnancy in which the mother's life may be threatened because of the invasion of germs into the endometrium, myometrium, and beyond. The woman requires immediate and intensive care, massive antibiotic therapy,

evacuation of the uterus, and often emergency hysterectomy to prevent death from overwhelming infection and septic shock.

septic arthritis, an acute form of arthritis, characterized by bacterial inflammation of a joint caused by the spread of bacteria through the bloodstream from an infection elsewhere in the body or by contamination of a joint during trauma or surgery. The joint is stiff, painful, tender, warm, and swollen. Parenteral antibiotics are given to prevent destruction of the joint and are continued for several weeks after inflammation has resolved.

septicemia /sep'tisē'mē·ə/ [Gk, *septikos* + *haima,* blood], systemic infection in which pathogens are present in the circulating blood, having spread from an infection in any part of the body. Characteristically, septicemia causes fever, chill, hypotension, prostration, pain, headache, nausea, or diarrhea. It is diagnosed by culture of the blood and is vigorously treated with antibiotics.—**septicemic,** *adj.*

septicemic plague /sep'tisē'mik/, a rapidly fatal form of bubonic plague in which septicemia with meningitis occurs before buboes have had time to form.

septic fever, an elevation of body temperature associated with infection by pathogenic microorganisms or in response to a toxin secreted by a microorganism.

septic infarct [Gk, *septikos,* putrid; L, *infarcire,* to stuff], an infected segment of dead tissue.

septic shock, a form of shock that occurs in septicemia when endotoxins or exotoxins are released from certain bacteria in the bloodstream. These toxins cause vasodilation, resulting in a dramatic fall in BP. Fever, tachycardia, increased respiration rate, and confusion or coma also may occur. Occasionally, septic shock may be caused by the presence of fungi or viruses in the blood.

septic sore throat [Gk, *septikos,* putrid; AS, *sar* + *throte*], a severe throat infection, usually caused by a streptococcus strain, resulting in fever and marked exhaustion.

septooptic dysplasia /sep'tō·op'tik displā'zhə/, a congenital syndrome of hypoplasia of the optic disc with other ocular abnormalities, absence of the septum pellucidum, and hypopituitarism leading to growth deficiency.

septoplasty /sep'tōplas'tē/ [L, *saeptum,* septum; Gk, *plassein,* to form], surgical reconstruction of the nasal septum.

septorhinoplasty /sep'tōrī'nəplas'tē/ [L, *saeptum,* fence], the surgical correction of defects in the nasal septum.

septostomy /septos'təmē/, the creation of an opening in a septum by surgery.

Septra, a trademark for the antibacterial co-trimoxazole (a 1:5 mixture of the antibacterials trimethoprim and sulfamethoxazole).

septum /sep'təm/ *pl.* **septa** [L, *saeptum,* enclosure], a partition or wall such as the interatrial septum that separates the atria of the heart.

septuplet /septup'lit/ [L, *septuplum,* group of seven], any one of seven children born of a single pregnancy.

sequela /sikwē'lə/ *pl.* **sequelae** [L, *sequi,* to follow], any abnormal condition that follows and is the result of a disease, treatment, or injury such as scar formation after a laceration.

sequence /sē'kwəns/ [L, *sequi,* to follow], an order of arrangement of objects or events, as the sequence of peptides in a protein molecule.

sequential chemotherapy, chemotherapy in which several agents are administered one at a time rather than concurrently to optimize dosage and increase patient tolerance.

sequential imaging, a diagnostic procedure used to study physiologic processes by means of a series of closely timed images of the rapidly changing distribution of a radioactive tracer within the body.

sequential line imaging, the construction of a magnetic resonance image from successive lines through the object.

sequential plane imaging, the construction of a magnetic resonance image from successive planes through the object.

sequential point imaging, the construction of a magnetic resonance image from successive point positions in the object.

sequester /sikwes'tər/ [L, *sequestare,* to lay aside], to detach, separate, or isolate, such as patient sequestration to prevent the spread of an infection.

sequestered antigens hypothesis, a proposed explanation for autoimmunity that stresses the relationship between antigen exposure, immunogenic cells, and body cells. It maintains that immunologic tolerance depends on a certain degree of contact between immunologic cells and body cells and on a certain degree of antigen exposure.

sequestered edema, edema localized in the tissues surrounding a newly created surgical wound.

sequestration /sē'kwestrā'shən/ [L, *sequestare,* to lay aside], **1.** the isolation of a patient or group of patients. **2.** a method of controlling hemorrhage of the head or trunk by isolating fluid in the arms and legs from the general circulation. **3.** allowing blood from the systemic circulation to perfuse a nonfunctioning part of a lung.

sequestrum /sikwes'trəm/ *pl.* **sequestra** [L, a deposit], a fragment of dead bone that is partially or entirely detached from the surrounding or adjacent healthy bone.

sequestrum forceps, a forceps with small, powerful teeth used for extracting necrotic or sharp fragments of bone from surrounding tissue.

sequoiasis /sikwoi'əsis/ [sequoia (tree); Gk, *osis,* condition], a type of hypersensitivity pneumonitis common among workers in sawmills where redwood is processed. The antigens are the fungus *Pullularia pullulans* and species of the genus *Graphium,* found in moldy redwood sawdust. Characteristics of the acute disease include chills, fever, cough, dyspnea, anorexia, nausea, and vomiting.

Ser, abbreviation for the amino acid **serine.**

Ser-Ap-Es, a trademark for a fixed-combination antihypertensive drug containing a diuretic (hydrochlorothiazide) and antihypertensives (reserpine and hydrALAZINE hydrochloride).

Serax, a trademark for a benzodiazepine (oxazepam).

serendipity /ser'əndip'itē/ [Serendip, author Horace Walpole's mythic land of pleasant surprises], the act of accidental discovery. A number of important medications have been created through serendipity, such as the discovery of antidepressant activity in iproniazid, which was originally developed to treat TB.

Serentil, a trademark for a phenothiazine antipsychotic (mesoridazine).

Serevent, a trademark for a long-acting sympathomimetic bronchodilator (salmeterol).

serial /sir'ē·əl/ [L, *series,* row], pertaining to a succession, arrangement, or order of items.

serial casting, the process of using a sequence of casts to progressively correct a deformity.

serial determination [L, *series,* row, *determinare,* to limit], a laboratory test that is repeated at stated intervals, as in a series of repeated tests for cardiac enzymes in blood samples taken from a patient with suspected MI.

serial dilution, a laboratory technique in which a substance, such as blood serum, is decreased in concentration in a series of proportional amounts.

serial extraction, a program of selective extraction of primary and sometimes secondary teeth over a period of time, with the objective of relieving crowding and of facilitating the eruption of remaining teeth into improved positions.

serial section [L, *series,* in a row + *sectio*], one of a number of consecutive slices of tissue.

S

serial speech, overlearned speech involving a series of words, such as counting or reciting of days of the week.

series /sir'ēs/ *pl.* **series** [L, in a row], a chain of objects or events arranged in a predictable order, such as the series of stages through which a mature blood cell develops.

serine (Ser) /ser'ēn/, a nonessential amino acid found in many proteins in the body. It is synthesized from glycine or threonin and is a precursor of the amino acids purine, cysteine, and others.

SERM, abbreviation for **selective estrogen receptor modulator.**

sermorelin /ser'mo-rel'in/, a synthetic peptide corresponding to a portion of growth hormone–releasing hormone. The acetate salt is used in the treatment of growth hormone deficiency in prepubertal children.

Sernylan, a trademark for a long-discontinued veterinary anesthetic (phencyclidine hydrochloride), now used illicitly as a euphoric called PCP.

seroconversion /-kənvur'zhən/ [L, *serum,* whey, *conversio,* turned about], a change in serologic test results from negative to positive as antibodies develop in reaction to an infection or vaccine.

serodiagnosis /-dī'əgnō'sis/ [L, *serum,* whey; Gk, *dia,* through, *gnosis,* knowledge], the use of serologic tests in the diagnosis of disease.

serofibrinous pericarditis /-fī'brinəs/ [L, *serum,* whey, *fibra,* fibrin; Gk, *peri,* near, *kardia,* heart, *itis,* inflammation], a form of fibrinous pericarditis marked by a serous exudate.

serofibrinous pleurisy, an inflammation of the pleura with a watery effusion and accumulation of fibrin on the pleural membranes.

serogroup /sēr'o-groop/, **1.** a group of bacteria containing a common antigen, sometimes including more than one serotype, species, or genus. This is an unofficial designation, used in the classification of certain genera of bacteria, such as *Leptospira, Salmonella, Shigella,* and *Streptococcus.* **2.** a group of viral species that are closely related antigenically.

seroimmunity /sir'ō-imyōō'nitē/, immunity conferred by administration of an antiserum.

serologic /-loj'ik/ [L, *serum,* whey; Gk, *logos,* science], pertaining to the branch of medicine concerned with the study of blood sera.

serologic diagnosis /siroloj'ik/ [L, *serum,* whey; Gk, *dia,* through, *gnosis,* knowledge], a diagnosis that is made through laboratory examination of antigen-antibody reactions in the serum.

serologic test [L, *serum,* whey, *testum,* crucible], any diagnostic test made with serum.

serologist /sirol'əjist/ [L, *serum;* Gk, *logos,* science], a bacteriologist or medical technologist who prepares or supervises the preparation and testing of sera used to diagnose and treat diseases and to immunize people against infectious diseases.

serology /sirol'əjē/ [L, *serum;* Gk, *logos,* science], the branch of laboratory medicine that studies blood serum for evidence of infection by evaluating antigen-antibody reactions in vitro.—**serologic, serological,** *adj.*

seroma /sirō'mə/, a lump or swelling caused by an accumulation of serum within a tissue or organ.

Seromycin, a trademark for a tuberculostatic (cycloSERINE).

seronegative /-neg'ətiv/ [L, *serum,* whey + *negare,* to deny], a serologic test with negative results.

seropositive /-pos'itiv/ [L, *serum,* whey + *positivus*], a serologic test with positive results.

seroprevalence /-prev'ələns/, the overall occurrence of a disease within a defined population at one time, as measured by blood tests.

seroprophylaxis /-prō'filak'sis/, the administration of a serum to prevent disease.

seropurulent /-pyōōr'ələnt/, containing serum and pus.

seroreversion /sēr'o-rever'zhun/, spontaneous or induced conversion from a seropositive to a seronegative state.

serosa /sirō'sə/ [L, *serum*], any serous membrane, such as the tunica serosa that lines the walls of body cavities and secretes a watery exudate.

serosanguineous /sir'ōsang-gwin'ē-əs/, **1.** of a discharge, thin and red. **2.** composed of serum and blood.

serotonin /ser'ətō'nin, sir'-/ [L, *serum;* Gk, *tonos,* tone], a naturally occurring derivative of tryptophan found in platelets and in cells of the brain and the intestine. It acts as a potent vasoconstrictor and as a neurotransmitter.

serous /sir'əs/ [L, *serum,* whey], pertaining to, resembling, or producing serum.

serous fluid [L, *serum* + *fluere,* to flow], a fluid that has the characteristics of serum.

serous membrane, one of the many thin sheets of tissue that line closed cavities of the body, such as the pleura lining the thoracic cavity and the pericardium lining the sac that encloses the heart. Between the visceral layer of serous membrane covering various organs and the parietal layer lining the cavity containing such organs is a potential space moistened by serous fluid. The fluid reduces the friction of the structures covered by the serous membrane, such as the lungs, which move against the thoracic walls in respiration.

serovaccination /-vak′sinā′shən/, a technique for producing mixed immunity in which a person is first injected with a serum to establish passive immunity and then is vaccinated to produce active immunity.

serpent ulcer /sur′pənt/ [L, *serpens,* snake], an ulceration of the skin that heals in one area while extending to another.

serpin /ser′pin/, any of a superfamily of inhibitors of serine endopeptidase (serine proteinase), found in plasma and tissue. All are similarly structured single-chain glycoproteins, although each one acts specifically on particular endopeptidases. Among their targets are serine proteinases involved in coagulation, complement activation, fibrinolysis, inflammation, and tissue remodeling.

serrate /ser′āt/, having an edge with notches or sawlike teeth.

serrated suture /ser′ātid/, a suture with sawlike edges, such as most of the sagittal suture.

Serratia /serā′shə/ [L, *serra,* saw teeth], a genus of opportunistic motile, gram-negative bacilli from the family Enterobacteriaceae genus Klebsielleae capable of causing infection in humans, including bacteremia, pneumonia, and UTIs. *Serratia* organisms are frequently acquired in hospitals.

serratus anterior /serā′təs/ [L, *serra,* saw teeth], a thin muscle of the chest wall extending from the ribs under the arm to the scapula. It acts to rotate the scapula and raise the shoulder, as in full flexion and abduction of the arm.

serratus posterior, muscles in the intermediate group of back muscles that elevate and depress the ribs.

Sertoli cell /sertō′lē/ [Enrico Sertoli, Italian histologist, 1842–1910; L, *cella,* storeroom], one of the supporting elongated cells of the seminiferous tubules of the testes. It functions to nourish the developing spermatocytes.

Sertolicell–only syndrome [Enrico Sertoli], a form of male sterility in which only Sertoli cells are present in the seminiferous tubules of the testes. Germinal epithelium is absent, resulting in azoospermia.

sertraline /ser′trah-lēn/, a selective serotonin reuptake inhibitor administered orally in the form of hydrochloride salt as an antidepressant and to treat obsessive-compulsive disorder and panic disorder.

serum /sir′əm/ *pl.* **sera** [L, whey], **1.** the fluid portion of blood that remains subsequent to in-vitro clotting. Unlike plasma, serum lacks fibrinogen and several of the coagulation proteins. **2.** any clear watery fluid that has been separated from its more solid elements, such as the exudate from a blister. **3.** a vaccine or toxoid prepared from the serum of a hyperimmune donor for prophylaxis against a particular infection or poison.

serum albumin, a major protein in blood plasma important in maintaining the osmotic pressure of the blood.

serum bank, a facility for the storage of aliquots of blood serum. The samples are used mainly for medical research.

serum carnosinase deficiency, an autosomal-recessive aminoacidopathy of carnosine metabolism, characterized by urinary excretion of carnosine and accumulation of homocarnosine in the CSF. This deficiency may cause myoclonic seizures, severe mental retardation, and spasticity.

serum creatinine level, the concentration of creatinine in the serum, used as a diagnostic sign of renal impairment.

serumfast /sir′əmfast′/, **1.** resistant (as bacteria) to the destructive effects of sera. **2.** having (as a serum) little or no change in antibody titer.

serum globulin [L, *serum,* whey, *globulus,* small globe], one of a group of proteins in blood serum with antibody qualities. The various types of serum globulins, designated α, β, and γ, have different specific properties.

serum neuritis, a neurologic disorder, usually including the cervical nerves or brachial plexus, occurring 2 to 8 days after the injection of a foreign protein.

serum osmolality [L, *serum,* whey; Gk, *ōsmos,* impulse], a measure of the osmotic concentration of blood serum, expressed as the number of osmoles of solute per kilogram of plasma water.

serum protein [L, *serum,* whey; Gk, *proteios,* first rank], any of the proteins in blood serum.

serum shock, a life-threatening reduction in blood volume and BP caused by the injection of an antitoxin or other foreign serum.

serum sickness, an immunologic disorder that may occur 2 to 3 weeks after the administration of an antiserum. It is caused by an antibody reaction to an antigen in the donor serum and is characterized by fever, splenomegaly, swollen lymph nodes, skin rash, and joint pain.

service dog, a dog trained to aid a disabled person with such tasks as opening or closing doors, picking up dropped items, or pulling a wheelchair.

service of process /sur′vis/ [L, *servus,* a slave, *process,* going forth], in law, the delivery of a writ, summons, or complaint to a defendant. Once delivered or left with the party for whom it is intended, it is said to have been served.

S

servomechanism /sur'vōmek'əniz'əm/, a control system in which feedback is used to correct errors in another system. A biologic example is the mechanism that controls the size of the pupil of the eye as the intensity of light changes.

Serzone, a trademark for an antidepressant drug (nefazodone hydrochloride).

sesame oil /ses'əmē/, a liquid fat derived from the seeds of a plant, *Sesamum indicum.* The seeds are demulcent and have a laxative effect. Both seeds and oil are used as food flavorings. The oil is also used in skin lotions, as an emollient.

sesamoid /ses'əmoid/ [Gk, *sesamon,* sesame, *eidos,* form], nodular objects having the shape and size of sesame seeds.

sesamoid bone [Gk, *sesamon,* sesame, *eidos,* form], any one of numerous small round bony masses embedded in certain tendons that may be subjected to compression and tension. The largest sesamoid bone is the patella, which is embedded in the tendon of the quadriceps femoris at the knee.

sessile /ses'əl/ [L, *sessilis,* sitting], **1.** in biology, attached by a base rather than by a stalk or a peduncle, such as a leaf that is attached directly to its stem. **2.** permanently connected.

set, 1. a predisposition to behave in a certain way. **2.** to reduce a fracture by moving the bones back into a normal position.

setaceous /sētā'shəs/, having or resembling bristles.

setback, the surgical treatment of a bilateral cleft of the palate.

seton /sē'ton/, thread, gauze, or other material passed through subcutaneous tissue or a cyst to create a sinus or fistula.

settlement [AS, *setlan,* to put in place], in law, an agreement made between parties to a suit before a judgment is rendered by a court.

setup [AS, *settan,* to set, *up,* on high], **1.** an arrangement of artificial teeth on a trial denture base. **2.** a laboratory procedure in which teeth are removed from a plaster cast and repositioned in wax. It is used as a diagnostic procedure and in creation of a mold for a positioner appliance.

sevelamer /sĕvel'ahmer/, a phosphate binder. The hydrochloride salt is used to reduce serum phosphorus concentrations in hyperphosphatemia associated with end-stage renal disease.

severe acute respiratory syndrome (SARS), an infectious respiratory illness first reported in Asia and characterized by fever, dry cough, and breathing difficulties, often accompanied by headache and body aches. It is believed to be caused by a strain of coronavirus, and severity ranges from mild illness to death. The infection appears to be spread by close contact with infected individuals by inhalation of droplet nuclei containing the organism or by contact with infected body fluids. The incubation period appears to range from 2 to 10 days. Early signs are rapid onset of fever (greater than 38° C, or 100.4° F), headache, chills, rigors, and achiness. Upper respiratory symptoms (e.g., runny nose and sore throat) are unlikely. After a period of 3 to 7 days, lower respiratory symptoms, such as shortness of breath and a dry cough, develop. Nausea, vomiting, and diarrhea are seen in about 25% of cases. In the next 7 days, mild cases show an abatement of symptoms, and about 20% of patients show a progressive respiratory deterioration with severe dyspnea, hypoxemia, and ARDS. More than half of these patients require mechanical ventilation. Patients with progressive deterioration are at high risk of respiratory failure and death. High initial levels of lactate dehydrogenase and absolute neutrophil counts and an age greater than 60 appear to be predictors of severe disease and death. Immediate isolation (droplet, contact, and respiratory) is required for anyone suspected of having SARS. All suspected cases should be reported to the local public health authorities/state health department and CDC. Treatment is largely supportive and includes rest, humidification, hydration, nutritional support, and oxygen. Analgesics are used for pain. Tracheostomy and/or mechanical ventilation may be indicated to improve respiratory function. There are indications that pulsed steroids may shorten course of disease.

severe combined immunodeficiency disease (SCID) /sivēr'/ [L, *servus,* slave], an abnormal condition characterized by the complete absence or marked deficiency of B cells and T cells with the consequent lack of humoral and cell-mediated immunity. The disease occurs as an X-linked recessive disorder affecting only males and as an autosomal-recessive disorder affecting both males and females. It results in a pronounced susceptibility to infection and is usually fatal. Infants with SCID commonly fail to thrive and have a variety of complications such as sepsis, watery diarrhea, persistent pulmonary infections, and common viral infections that are often fatal. Some of the more obvious symptoms after the infant has used most of the maternal immunoglobulin stores are cyanosis, rapid respirations, and normal chest sounds with an abnormal chest radiographic picture. Most infants with SCID die from severe infection within 1 year after birth. The only satisfactory treatment available to correct immunodeficiency is histocompatible bone marrow transplantation, but that may cause a graft-versus-host reaction, thus increasing the risk of infection and fatal consequences.

severity of pitting scale, a common clinical practice in assessment to assign a positive number for the severity of pitting edema in the lower extremities as follows: +1 = a normal foot and leg contour with a barely perceptible pit. +2 = fairly normal lower extremity contours with a moderately deep pit. +3 = obvious foot and leg swelling with a deep pit. +4 = severe foot and leg swelling that distorts the normal contours with a deep pit.

Sevin, a trademark for carbaryl, a widely used carbamate insecticide that causes reversible inhibition of cholinesterase. Although less toxic than parathion, carbaryl, when concentrated, may produce skin irritation and systemic poisoning characterized by nausea, vomiting, cramps, diarrhea, diaphoresis, excessive salivation, dyspnea, weakness, loss of coordination, and slurred speech. Large doses may cause coma and death.

sex [L, *sexus,* sex], **1.** a classification of male or female based on many criteria, among them anatomic and chromosomal characteristics. **2. coitus.**

sex chromatin, a densely staining mass within the nucleus of all nondividing cells of normal mammalian females. It represents the heterochromatin of the inactivated X chromosome.

sex chromosome, a chromosome that determines the sex of an individual. In humans and other mammals, there are two distinct sex chromosomes, designated X and Y, which appear in females as XX and in males as XY.

sex chromosome mosaic, an individual or organism whose cells contain variant chromosomal numbers involving the X or Y chromosomes. Such variations occur in most of the syndromes associated with sex chromosome aberrations, primarily Turner's syndrome, and may be caused by nondisjunction of the chromosomes during the second meiotic division of gametogenesis or by some error in chromosome distribution during cell division of the fertilized ovum.

sex determination [L, *sexus,* sex + *determinare*], the process of identifying the sex of an individual, based on the presence of the XY chromosome combination in the cells of genetic males or Barr bodies in the cells of genetic females or on secondary sexual characteristics and skeletal variations.

sex deviant, a person whose sexual interests differ markedly from what is accepted as the norm.

sex hormone, any of the androgens, estrogens, or related steroid hormones produced mainly by the testes, ovaries, and adrenal cortices.

sex hormone–binding globulin (SHBG), a protein produced by the liver that binds testosterone and estradiol in the plasma. It has a greater affinity for testosterone. The plasma concentration of SHBG is influenced by liver cirrhosis, hyperthyroidism, obesity (in women), malnutrition, and estrogens.

sexidigitate /sek′sidij′itāt/ [L, *sex,* six], having six digits on one or both hands or feet.

sex-influenced, pertaining to an autosomal genetic trait, such as patterned baldness or gout, that is expressed in both homozygotes and heterozygotes in one sex but only homozygotes in the other sex.

sexism /sek′sizəm/, a belief that one sex is superior to the other and that the superior sex has endowments, rights, prerogatives, and status greater than those of the inferior sex. Sexism results in discrimination in all areas of life and acts as a limiting factor in educational, professional, and psychologic development.—**sexist,** *n., adj.*

sexivalent, pertaining to a chemical with a valence of 6.

sex-limited, pertaining to an autosomal genetic trait that is expressed in only one sex, although the alleles for it may be carried by both sexes. Such traits are typically influenced by hormonal or environmental conditions.

sex-linked, pertaining to genes carried on the sex chromosomes, particularly the X chromosome, or to the traits they control.—**sex linkage,** *n.*

sex-linked disorder, any disease or abnormal condition that is determined by the sex chromosomes or by a defective gene on a sex chromosome. Sex-linked disorders may involve a deviation in the number of either the X or Y chromosomes, as occurs in Turner's syndrome and Klinefelter's syndrome. Other sex-linked disorders are transmitted by single-gene defects carried on the X chromosome. X-linked dominant conditions, such as hypophosphatemic vitamin D–resistant rickets, are rare, and males are more seriously affected than females. In inheritance patterns, X-linked dominant conditions are transmitted by affected males to all of their daughters but none of their sons, by affected heterozygous females to one half of their children regardless of sex, and by affected homozygous females to all of their children. More common are X-linked recessive conditions, such as color blindness and hemophilia. Such conditions are always transmitted by females and predominantly affect males because they have only one X chromosome and all of its genes, whether recessive or dominant, are

S

expressed. There are no known clinically significant traits or conditions associated with the genes on the Y chromosome.

sex-linked ichthyosis, a congenital skin disorder characterized by large thick dry scales with dark color covering the neck, scalp, ears, face, trunk, and flexor surfaces of the body, such as the folds of the arms and the backs of the knees. It is transmitted as an X-linked recessive trait. The condition is managed by topical applications of emollients and the use of keratolytic agents to facilitate removal of the scales.

sex ratio, the proportion of male-to-female progeny, a relationship that varies with the stage of life. The distribution at birth is usually 106 boys to 100 girls, but the ratio shifts in adulthood, so that, because men have a lower life expectancy, the proportion of females is greater. The ratio may also vary with the effects of a particular disease or trait.

sex role, the expectations held by society regarding what behavior is appropriate or inappropriate for each sex.

sex surrogate [L, *sexus* + *surrogare,* substitute], in sex therapy, a professional substitute trained to help the patient overcome inhibitions.

sextuplet /seks′tup′lit/ [L, *sex,* six], one of six children born of a single pregnancy.

sexual /sek′sho͞o·əl/, pertaining to sex.

sexual abuse, the sexual mistreatment of another person by fondling, rape, or forced participation in unnatural sex acts or other perverted behavior.

sexual asphyxia, accidental strangulation by ligature that occurs in an attempt to induce mild cerebral hypoxia during sexual activity for the purpose of enhancing orgasmic pleasure.

sexual assault, the forcible perpetration of an act of sexual contact on the body of another person, male or female, without his or her consent. Legal criteria vary among different communities.

sexual assault testing, a series of tests performed on sexual assault victims that includes testing of vaginal secretions of women for sperm and of cervical secretions and/or blood for STDs.

sexual aversion disorder, a persistent or extreme aversion to or avoidance of all or nearly all genital sexual contact with a partner.

sexual counseling, a nursing intervention from the Nursing Interventions Classification (NIC) defined as use of an interactive helping process focusing on the need to make adjustments in sexual practice or to enhance coping with a sexual event/disorder.

sexual disorder, 1. any disorder involving sexual functioning, desire, or performance.

2. *DSM-IV,* any such disorder that is caused at least in part by psychologic factors. Such a disorder characterized by a decrease or other disturbance of sexual desire is called a *sexual dysfunction,* and that characterized by unusual or bizarre sexual fantasies, urges, or practices is called paraphilia.

sexual dwarf, an adult dwarf whose genital organs are normally developed.

sexual dysfunction, a disorder, condition, mental state or disease that interferes with sexual response in a man, woman, or couple.

sexual fantasy, mental images of an erotic nature that can lead to sexual arousal.

sexual functioning, a nursing outcome from the Nursing Outcomes Classification (NOC) defined as integration of physical, socioemotional, and intellectual aspects of sexual expression and performance.

sexual harassment, an aggressive sexually motivated act of physical or verbal violation of a person over whom the aggressor has some power. Sexual harassment in the workplace is illegal because it represents an abridgement of the victim's right to equal opportunity, privacy, and freedom from assault.

sexual health [L, *sexus,* AS, *haelth*], a condition defined by the World Health Organization as freedom from sexual diseases or disorders and a capacity to enjoy and control sexual behavior without fear, shame, or guilt.

sexual history, in a patient record, the part of the patient's personal history concerned with sexual function and dysfunction. It may include the age at onset of sexual intercourse, the kind and frequency of sexual activity, and the satisfaction derived from it. The extent of the history varies with the patient's age and condition and the reason for securing the history, but a short sexual history is recommended as part of every complete physical examination.

sexual hormones, chemical substances produced in the body that cause specific regulatory effects on the activity of reproductive organs.

sexual identity, a nursing outcome from the Nursing Outcomes Classification (NOC) defined as acknowledgement and acceptance of one's own sexual identity.

sexuality /sek′sho͞o·al′ite/, **1.** the sum of the physical, functional, and psychologic attributes that are expressed by one's gender identity and sexual behavior, whether or not related to the sex organs or to procreation. **2.** the genital characteristics that distinguish male from female.

sexually deviant personality /sek′sho͞o·ələ′/, a sexual behavior that differs significantly from what is considered normal for a society.

sexually transmitted disease (STD), a contagious disease usually acquired by sexual intercourse or genital contact. These diseases are among the most common communicable diseases, and the incidence has risen in recent years despite improved methods of diagnosis and treatment. Historically, the five venereal diseases were gonorrhea, syphilis, chancroid, granuloma inguinale, and lymphogranuloma venereum. To these have been added scabies, herpes genitalis and anorectal herpes and warts, pediculosis, trichomoniasis, genital candidiasis, molluscum contagiosum, hepatitis B, human papillomavirus infection, nonspecific urethritis, chlamydial infections, cytomegalovirus, and HIV.

sexually transmitted disease culture, a microscopic examination or blood test used to detect the presence of STDs, such as gonorrhea, chlamydia, genital herpes, syphilis, hepatitis, AIDS, and others. Cervical cultures are usually done for women, and urethral cultures for men; rectal and throat cultures are done for people who have engaged in anal and oral intercourse.

sexual mores, socially acceptable sexual behavior, usually based on fixed morally binding customs governing sexual behaviors that are harmful to others or the group, such as rape, incest, and sexual abuse of children.

sexual orientation, the clear persistent desire of a person for affiliation with one sex rather than the other.

sexual reassignment, a change in the gender identity of a person by legal, surgical, hormonal, or social means.

sexual reflex, in males, a reflex in which tactile or cerebral stimulation results in penile erection, priapism, or ejaculation.

sexual reproduction [L, *sexus,* sex, *re + producere,* to produce], replication of an organism by the formation of gametes. Generally this requires the fusion of male spermatozoa and female ova. Parthenogenesis is an exception.

sexual response cycle, the four phases of biologic sexual response: excitement, plateau, orgasm, and resolution.

sexual selection, the selection of mates based on the attraction of or preference for certain traits, such as coloration or behavior patterns, so that eventually only those particular traits appear in succeeding generations.

sexual tasks, specific skills learned in various phases of development in the life cycle continuum to allow an adult to function normally in the sexual realm.

sexual therapist, a health care professional with specialized knowledge, skill, and competence in assisting individuals who experience sexual difficulties.

sexual therapy, a type of counseling that aids in the resolution of pathologic conditions so that a healthy sexuality can be maintained.

Sézary syndrome /sāzārē/ [A. Sézary, French dermatologist, 1880–1956], a condition of generalized exfoliating erythroderma, lymphadenopathy, and abnormal circulating T cells. The patient experiences pruritus, alopecia, edema, and nail and pigment changes.

Sf, abbreviation for *Svedberg flotation unit.*

sfc, abbreviation for *spinal fluid count.*

SFD, abbreviation for *small for dates.*

Sg, abbreviation for the element **seaborgium.**

SGA, abbreviation for **small for gestational age.**

SGOT, abbreviation for **serum glutamic oxaloacetic transaminase.**

SGPT, abbreviation for **serum glutamic pyruvic transaminase.**

shadow /shad′ō/ [AS, *sceadu*], in psychology, an archetype that represents the unacceptable aspects and components of behavior.

shadowcasting, a technique for enhancing the visualization of a contoured microscopic specimen, in which a chemical film is deposited on it, making it more visible in relief.

shaft, an elongated cylindric object such as a long bone between the epiphyses.

shaken baby syndrome, a condition of whiplash-type injuries, ranging from bruises on the arms and trunk to retinal hemorrhages, rib fractures, coma, or convulsions, as observed in infants and children who have been violently shaken. This form of child abuse often results in intracranial bleeding from tearing of cerebral blood vessels.

shakes /shāks/, a popular term for the rigor, tremors, or shivering that occurs in intermittent fever or after drug withdrawal.

shake test, a qualitative test for fetal lung maturity. It is more rapid than determination of the lecithin/sphingomyelin ratio.

shallow breathing /shal′ō/ [ME, *schalowe,* little depth], a respiration pattern marked by slow, shallow, and generally ineffective inspirations and expirations. It is usually caused by drugs and indicates depression of the medullary respiratory center.

shamanism, a form of healing that incorporates personal healing, transformation, and regeneration through access to a "higher power." Sickness, disease, and illness are indicators that the individual is out of balance and in disharmony within the essential nature. This type of healing has been used for sexual dysfunction, chronic fatigue

S

syndrome, mental health concerns, and obesity and other eating disorders.

shank, 1. the tibia. 2. the part of a device that connects the functional part to a handle.

shaping [AS, *scieppan,* to shape], a procedure used for conditioning a person undergoing behavior therapy to develop new behavioral responses.

shared governance, an organizational framework proposed by Tim Porter-O'Grady that provides for the full use of nursing resources. This system is designed to reflect the professional character of the participants in the nursing organization and to promote certain positive behaviors and practices. The purpose of shared governance is the establishment of a system in which staff participate fully in all activities that have an impact on their work and their ultimate goal of meaningful patient care.

shared paranoid disorder [AS, *searan,* to shear], a psychopathologic condition characterized by identical manifestations of the same mental disorder, usually ideas, in two closely associated or related people.

shared services, administrative, clinical, or other service functions that are common to two or more hospitals or other health care facilities and that are used jointly or cooperatively by them.

Sharpey's fiber [William Sharpey, Scottish anatomist, 1802–1880], any of the many collagenous bundles of fibers of the periodontal ligament that become embedded in the cementum during its formation.

sharps, any needles, scalpels, or other articles that could cause wounds or punctures to personnel handling them.

shaving stroke [AS, *scafan,* to shave, *strican,* to stroke], a phase of the working stroke of a periodontal curet, used for smoothing or planing a tooth or tooth root surface.

SHBG, abbreviation for **sex hormone-binding globulin.**

SHCC, abbreviation for **Statewide Health Coordinating Committee.**

SHEA, abbreviation for *Society for Healthcare Epidemiology of America.*

shear /shir/ [AS, *scearan,* to cut], an applied force or pressure exerted against the surface and layers of the skin as tissues slide in opposite but parallel planes.

shearling /shir'ling/, a sheepskin placed on a bed to help prevent pressure ulcers.

sheath /shēth/ [AS, *scaeth*], a tubular structure that surrounds an organ or any other part of the body, such as the sheath of the rectus abdominis muscle.

sheath of Schwann [Theodor Schwann, German anatomist, 1810–1882; AS, *scaeth*], a neurilemma sheath of nucleated cells enclosing a nerve fiber.

Sheehan's syndrome [Harold L. Sheehan, English pathologist, 1900–1988], a postpartum condition of pituitary necrosis and hypopituitarism after circulatory collapse resulting from uterine hemorrhaging.

sheep cell test [AS, *sceap;* L, *cella,* storeroom, *testum,* crucible], a method that mixes human blood cells with the RBCs of sheep to determine the absence or the deficiency of human T lymphocytes. When mixed with human blood cells, the RBCs of sheep cluster around the human T lymphocytes and form characteristic rosettes. An absence or a decrease in the number of rosettes indicates a deficiency or absence of T cells.

sheet /shēt/ [AS, *scēte*], 1. a rectangular piece of cotton, linen, and so on for a bed covering. 2. any structure resembling such a covering.

sheet bath [AS, *scēte + baeth*], the application of wet sheets to the body, used primarily as an antipyretic procedure.

sheet wadding, stretchable sheets of cotton padding used to cover the skin before a cast is applied. The stretching allows for some extremity edema without the cast becoming too tight.

shelf [AS, *scylf*], a flat, hard anatomic structure that resembles a ridge or platform.

shell [AS, *scell*], 1. a hard outer protective covering that encloses material. 2. a principal energy level occupied by an electron in an atom.

shellfish poisoning [AS, *scell + fisc*], a toxic neurologic condition that results from eating clams, oysters, or mussels that have ingested the toxin-producing protozoa commonly called the "red tide." The characteristic symptoms appear within a few minutes and include nausea, light-headedness, vomiting, and tingling or numbness around the mouth, followed by paralysis of the extremities and, possibly, respiratory paralysis.

shell shock [AS, *scell;* Fr, *choc*], any of a number of mental disorders, ranging from extreme fear to dementia, commonly attributed to the noise and concussion of exploding shells or bombs but actually a traumatic reaction to the stress of combat.

shell teeth, a type of dental dysplasia in which the teeth have large pulp chambers, insufficient coronal dentin, and, usually, no roots.

sheltered workshop [ME, *sheltrun,* body of guards; AS, *werc + sceoppa,* stall], a facility or program, either for outpatients or for residents of an institution, that provides vocational experience and possibly related vocational rehabilitation services in a controlled working environment.

Shiatsu, a Japanese form of acupressure involving finger pressure at specific points on the body, mainly for the purpose of balancing energy in the body.

shield [AS, *scild*], a material for preventing or reducing the passage of charged particles or radiation. A shield may be designated by the radiation it is intended to absorb or by the kind of protection it is intended to give.

shift [AS, *sciftan,* to divide], **1.** in nursing, the particular hours of the day during which a nurse is scheduled to work. Many innovations in staffing practice currently allow variations on the traditional 5-day, 40-hour week. **2.** an abrupt change in an analytic system that continues at the new level.

shift report, a nursing intervention from the Nursing Interventions Classification (NIC) defined as exchanging essential patient care information with other nursing staff at change of shift.

shift to the left, in hematology, a predominance of immature leukocytes, noted in a differential WBC count. It is usually indicative of an infection or inflammation.

shift to the right, in hematology, a preponderance of polymorphonuclear neutrophils having three or more lobes, indicating maturity of the cell. The phenomenon is common in severe liver disease and advanced pernicious anemia and indicates a relative lack of blood-forming activity.

Shigella /shigel'ə/ [Kiyoshi Shiga, Japanese bacteriologist, 1870–1957], a genus of gram-negative pathogenic bacteria that causes gastroenteritis and bacterial dysentery, such as *Shigella dysenteriae.*

Shigella dysenteriae, a species of the bacterial family Enterobacteriaceae that causes a severe form of dysentery in humans. The *dysenteriae* species of *Shigella* is most common in Asia and is particularly virulent.

Shigella **enteritis,** bacterial enteritis caused by the *Shigella* infection of bacillary dysentery.

Shigella **gastroenteritis,** bacterial gastroenteritis caused by the *Shigella* infection of bacillary dysentery.

shigellosis /shig'əlō'sis/ [Kiyoshi Shiga; Gk, *osis,* condition], an acute highly contagious bacterial infection of the bowel characterized by diarrhea, abdominal pain, and fever. It is transmitted by hand-to-mouth contact with the feces of individuals infected with bacteria of a pathogenic species of the genus *Shigella.* Damage is caused by invasion of bacteria and production of the enterotoxin Shiga toxin. The disease occurs in isolated outbreaks in the United States but is endemic in underdeveloped areas of the world. It is especially common and usually most severe in children. The likelihood of encountering or engendering antibiotic-resistant organisms is very high; therefore the preferred treatment for shigellosis is supportive and the major goal is prevention of dehydration. Antimicrobials are given if the disease is severe or if the likelihood of further transmission is great. Antidiarrheal agents should be avoided. Isolation and strict handwashing precautions are instituted. Shigellosis infections must be reported to the public health department.

shim, a thin tapered piece of material used to fill a gap.

shim coils, current-carrying coils that are used in magnetic resonance to improve the magnetic field homogeneity.

shin splints [AS, *scinu,* shin; ME, *splinte*], lower-leg pain caused by strain of the long flexor muscle of the toes during strenuous athletic activity, such as running. Treatment usually involves rest and exercise therapy.

Shirodkar's operation /shir'odkärz/ [N.V. Shirodkar, Indian obstetrician, 1900–1971], a surgical procedure called a cerclage in which the cervical canal is closed by a purse-string suture embedded in the uterine cervix encircling the canal. It is performed to correct an incompetent cervix that has failed to retain previous pregnancies. If labor begins with the suture in place, the suture is removed promptly, or the infant is delivered by cesarean section, before the uterus ruptures.

shivering /shiv'əring/, involuntary contractions of muscles, mainly of the skin, in response to the chilling effect of low temperatures. Shivering may also occur at the onset of a fever when the body's heat balance is disturbed.

shock [Fr, *choc*], an abnormal condition of inadequate blood flow to the body's tissues, with life-threatening cellular dysfunction. The condition is usually associated with inadequate cardiac output, hypotension, oliguria, changes in peripheral blood flow resistance and distribution, and tissue damage. Causal factors include hemorrhage, vomiting, diarrhea, inadequate fluid intake, or excessive fluid loss, resulting in hypovolemia. Hypovolemic shock is the most common. There is decreased blood flow with a resulting reduction in the delivery of oxygen, nutrients, hormones, and electrolytes to the body's tissues and a concomitant decreased removal of metabolic wastes. Pulse and respirations are increased. BP may decline after an initial slight increase. The patient often shows signs of restlessness and anxiety. There also may be weakness, lethargy, pallor, and cool, moist skin. As shock progresses, the body temperature falls, respirations become rapid and shallow, and the pulse pressure narrows as compensatory vasoconstriction causes the diastolic pressure to be elevated or maintained in the face of a falling systolic BP. Urinary output is reduced. Hemorrhage may be apparent or concealed, although other factors such as vomiting or diarrhea may account for the deficiency of body fluids.

S

shock management, a nursing intervention from the Nursing Interventions Classification (NIC) defined as facilitation of the delivery of oxygen and nutrients to systemic tissue with removal of cellular waste products in a patient with severely altered tissue perfusion.

shock management: cardiac, a nursing intervention from the Nursing Interventions Classification (NIC) defined as promotion of adequate tissue perfusion for a patient with severely compromised pumping function of the heart.

shock management: vasogenic, a nursing intervention from the Nursing Interventions Classification (NIC) defined as promotion of adequate tissue perfusion for a patient with severe loss of vascular tone.

shock management: volume, a nursing intervention from the Nursing Interventions Classification (NIC) defined as promotion of adequate tissue perfusion for a patient with severely compromised intravascular volume.

shock prevention, a nursing intervention from the Nursing Interventions Classification (NIC) defined as detecting and treating a patient at risk for impending shock.

shock therapy [Fr, *choc*; Gk, *therapeia*], a psychotherapeutic procedure for treating depression and other severe disorders by producing an epileptiform convulsion in the patient. The shock is induced by delivering an electric current through the brain.

shock trousers, a rarely used pneumatic garment designed to produce pressure on the lower part of the body, thereby preventing the pooling of blood in the legs and abdomen. They were also used in emergencies in the treatment of hemorrhagic shock. Shock trousers are contraindicated in patients with pulmonary edema, cardiogenic shock, increased intracranial pressure, or eviscerations.

short-acting [AS, *sceort*; L, *agere*, to do], pertaining to or characterizing a therapeutic agent, usually a drug, with a brief period of effectiveness, generally beginning soon after the substance or measure is administered.

short-acting insulin, a clear preparation of regular (crystalline zinc) insulin with an immediate (15 to 30 minutes) onset of action that reaches a peak of action in 2 to 4 hours. The duration of action is 6 to 8 hours.

shortage area /shôr'tij/ [AS, *sceort*; L, *acticum*, process], a geographic area, county as a census tract, or area designated by the federal government as being undersupplied with certain kinds of health care services; a shortage area may be eligible for aid under certain federal programs, including the National Health Service Corps or the Rural Clinics Assistance Act.

short-arm cast, an orthopedic cast applied to immobilize the hand or wrist; it incorporates the hand below the wrist. The short-arm cast is used in treating fractures, for maintaining postoperative positioning, and for correcting or maintaining the correction of deformities of the hand and the wrist.

short below-knee (BK) amputation, transtibial amputation in which the division is in the proximal third of the tibia.

short bones, bones that occur in clusters and usually permit movement of the extremities, such as the carpals and tarsals.

short-bowel syndrome [AS, *sceort*; OFr, *boel*; Gk, *syn*, together, *dromos*, course], a loss of intestinal surface for absorption of nutrients caused by the surgical removal of a section of bowel.

short central artery, a branch from the precommunical part of the anterior cerebral artery.

short-chain fatty acids (SCFA), those having a chain length up to roughly 6 carbon atoms long. They are readily absorbed and are metabolized in the liver and muscle tissues, producing energy.

short-course tuberculosis chemotherapy, a 6-month treatment regimen for patients with TB who would otherwise continue to receive medications for at least 18 to 24 months after sputum has a negative finding for tubercle bacilli. The short course requires a combination of four drugs: isoniazid, rifampin, pyrazinamide, and either ethambutol or streptomycin.

Shorted Blessed Test (SBT), a short screening test measuring orientation and memory and designed to assess cognitive impairment. The test can be used to detect early cognitive changes associated with Alzheimer's disease or other disorders characterized by dementia.

short-gut syndrome, 1. any of the malabsorption conditions resulting from massive resection of the small bowel, the degree and kind of malabsorption depending on the site and extent of the resection. It is characterized by diarrhea, steatorrhea, and malnutrition. **2.** a congenital disorder in which an infant's intestine is too short or underdeveloped to allow normal food digestion. The child is maintained on parenteral nutrition until the intestine grows, develops further, or is replaced by surgical transplantation.

shorting [AS, *sceort*], the fraudulent practice of dispensing a quantity of drug less than that called for in the prescription and of charging for the quantity specified in the prescription.

short-leg cast, an orthopedic cast used for immobilizing fractures in the lower extremities from the toes to the knee. The short-leg cast is also used for treating severe sprains and torn soft tissue of the ankle, for maintaining postoperative positioning and immobilization of the foot and the ankle, and for correcting or maintaining the correction of deformities of the foot or the ankle.

short-leg cast with walker, an orthopedic cast with rubber walkers on the bottom. It immobilizes the leg from the toes to the knee and allows the patient to walk.

Short Portable Mental Status Questionnaire, a 10-item questionnaire used to screen older adults for cognitive impairment. It tests orientation, remote and recent memory, practical skills, and mathematic ability.

short stature [AS, *sceort,* short; L, *statura,* man's height], a body height that is less than 70% of the average for a population of the same age, culture, gender, and other peer factors.

short-term memory, memory of recent events.

short-wave diathermy [AS, *sceort* + *wafian*; Gk, *dia* + *therme,* heat], a method of providing heat deep in the body by short-wave electric currents. It is used to treat chronic arthritis, bursitis, sinusitis, and other conditions.

shotgun therapy [AS, *scot*; ME, *gonne*; Gk, *therapeia,* treatment], *informal.* any treatment that has a wide range of effects and that therefore can be expected to correct an abnormal condition, even though the particular cause is unknown.

shoulder [AS, *sculder*], the junction of the clavicle, scapula, and humerus where the arm attaches to the trunk of the body.

shoulder girdle [AS, *sculder* + *gyrdel*], a partial arch at the top of the trunk formed by the scapula and clavicle.

shoulder-hand syndrome, a neuromuscular condition characterized by pain and stiffness in the shoulder and arm, limited joint motion, swelling of the hand, muscle atrophy, and decalcification of the underlying bones.

shoulder joint, the ball-and-socket articulation of the humerus with the scapula. The joint includes eight bursae and five ligaments. It is the most mobile joint in the body.

shoulder presentation [AS, *sculder*; L, *praesentare,* to show], the part of the fetus that occupies the center of the birth canal when the presentation is associated with a transverse or oblique lie.

shoulder spica cast, an orthopedic cast used to immobilize the trunk of the body to the hips, the wrist, and the hand. It incorporates a diagonal shoulder support between the hip and arm parts. The shoulder spica cast is used in the treatment of shoulder dislocations and injuries and in the positioning and immobilization of the shoulder after surgery.

shoulder subluxation, the separation of the humeral head from the glenoid cavity, resulting in strain on the soft tissues surrounding the shoulder joint.

shreds [AS, *screade,* piece cut off], glossy filaments of mucus in the urine, indicating inflammation in the urinary tract.

shunt [ME, *shunten*], **1.** to redirect the flow of a body fluid from one cavity or vessel to another. **2.** a tube or device implanted in the body to redirect a body fluid from one cavity or vessel to another.

shu points /shoo/, acupressure points.

Shy-Drager syndrome /shī drā'gər/ [G. Milton Shy, American neurologist, 1919–1967; Glenn A. Drager, American physician, b. 1917], a rare progressive neurologic disorder of young and middle-aged adults. It is characterized by orthostatic hypotension, bladder and bowel incontinence, atrophy of the iris, anhidrosis, tremor, rigidity, incoordination, ataxia, and muscle wasting.

Si, symbol for the element **silicon.**

SI, abbreviation for *Système International d'Unités,* the French name for the **International System of Units.**

SIADH, abbreviation for **syndrome of inappropriate antidiuretic hormone secretion.**

sialadenitis /sī'ələd'ənī'tis/, inflammation of one or more of the salivary glands.

sialemesis /sī'ələmē'sis/, vomiting of saliva, or vomiting associated with excessive salivation.

sialic acid /si-al'ik/, any *N*-acyl derivative of neuraminic acid. Various ones are found in polysaccharides, glycoproteins, and glycolipids.

sialidase, an enzyme of the hydrolase class that catalyzes the cleavage of glucosidic linkages between a sialic acid residue and a hexose or hexosamine residue at the nonreducing terminal of oligosaccharides in glycoproteins, glycolipids, and proteoglycans.

sialidosis /sī'əlidō'sis/, a neuronal storage disease of children caused by a deficiency of the enzyme sialidase (neuraminidase). The condition is characterized by a cherry-red spot on the macula, progressive myoclonus, and seizures. There are two types. Type 1 patients have normal physical features and beta-galactosidase levels. Type 2 patients also have short stature, bony abnormalities, and beta-galactosidase deficiency.

sialogogue /sī·al'əgog/ [Gk, *sialon,* saliva, *agogos,* leading], anything that stimulates, promotes, or produces the secretion of saliva.

sialogram /sī·al'əgram/ [Gk, *sialon,* saliva, *gramma,* record], a radiographic image of the salivary glands and ducts.

S

sialography /sī·ŏlog′rəfē/ [Gk, *sialon* + *graphein*, to record], the radiographic examination of the salivary glands after injection of a radiopaque contrast medium.—**sialographic,** *adj.*

sialolith /sī·al′əlith/ [Gk, *sialon* + *lithos,* stone], a calculus formed in a salivary gland or duct.

sialolithiasis /-lithī′əsis/, a pathological condition in which one or more calculi, or stones, are formed in a salivary gland.

sialorrhea /sī·al′ərē′ə/ [Gk, *sialon* + *rhoia,* flow], an excessive flow of saliva that may be associated with various conditions, such as acute inflammation of the mouth, mental retardation, mercurialism, pregnancy, teething, alcoholism, or malnutrition.

Siamese twins /sī′əmēz/ [Chang and Eng, conjoined twins born in Siam (now Thailand) in 1811], conjoined, equally developed twin fetuses produced from the same ovum. The severity of the condition ranges from superficial fusion, such as of the umbilical vessels, to that in which the heads or complete torsos are united and several internal organs are shared.

sib [AS, *sibb,* kin], pertaining to a close blood relationship.

Siberian ginseng, a herb harvested from a shrub found throughout the world, primarily in Russia and China. It is used to improve appetite, to improve circulation, and to treat memory loss, hypertension, insomnia, rheumatism, heart ailments, diabetes, and headache. It can be efficacious in some instances.

Siberian tick typhus /sībir′ē·ən/ [Siberia], a mild acute febrile illness seen in north, central, and east Asia, caused by *Rickettsia sibirica,* transmitted by ticks. It is characterized by a diffuse maculopapular rash, headache, conjunctival inflammation, and a small ulcer or eschar at the site of the tick bite. Treatment with chloramphenicol or tetracycline is associated with an excellent prognosis.

sibilant /sib′ilənt/ [L, *sibilare,* to hiss], a hissing sound or one in which the predominant sound is /s/.

sibling /sib′ling/ [AS, *sibb,* kin], **1.** one of two or more children who have both parents in common; a brother or sister. **2.** pertaining to a brother or sister.

sibling support, a nursing intervention from the Nursing Interventions Classification (NIC) defined as assisting a sibling to cope with a brother's or a sister's illness/ chronic condition/disability.

sibship /sib′ship/ [AS *sibb,* kin, *scieppan,* to shape], **1.** the state of being related by blood. **2.** a group of people descended from a common ancestor who are used as a basis for genetic studies. **3.** brothers and sisters considered as a group.

sibutramine, an appetite suppressant used to treat obesity in conjunction with other treatments.

sic [L], "thus."

sicca complex /sik′ə/, abnormal dryness of the mouth, eyes, or other mucous membranes. The condition is seen in patients with Sjögren's syndrome, sarcoidosis, amyloidosis, and deficiencies of vitamins A and C.

sick, experiencing symptoms of physical illness such as nausea, aches and pains, dizziness, weakness, blurred vision, or malaise.

sick building syndrome, a condition characterized by fatigue, headache, dry eyes, and respiratory complaints affecting workers in certain buildings with limited ventilation. The symptoms seem to be caused by a combination of chemical agents in low concentrations rather than a specific irritant.

sick cell syndrome, a condition characterized by idiopathic hyponatremia in patients with either acute or chronic illness.

sick euthyroid syndrome, a nonthyroidal condition characterized by abnormalities in hormone levels and function test findings related to the thyroid gland. The condition occurs in patients with severe systemic disease.

sickle cell [AS, *sicol,* crescent; L, *cella,* storeroom], an abnormal crescent-shaped RBC containing hemoglobin S, characteristic of sickle cell anemia.

sickle cell anemia, a severe, chronic, hemoglobinopathy that occurs in people homozygous for hemoglobin S (Hb S). The abnormal hemoglobin crystallizes and distorts the erythrocytes. Sickle cell anemia is characterized by crises of joint pain, thrombosis, and fever and by chronic anemia, with splenomegaly, lethargy, and weakness.

sickle cell crisis, an acute episodic condition that occurs in children with sickle cell anemia. The crisis may be vasoocclusive, resulting from the aggregation of misshapen erythrocytes, or anemic, resulting from bone marrow aplasia, increased hemolysis, folate deficiency, or splenic sequestration of erythrocytes. Painful vasoocclusive crisis is the most common of the sickle cell crises. The clumps of sickled erythrocytes obstruct blood vessels, resulting in occlusion, ischemia, and infarction of adjacent tissue. Characteristics of this kind of crisis are leukocytosis, acute abdominal pain from visceral hypoxia, painful swelling of the soft tissue of the hands and feet (hand-foot syndrome), and migratory, recurrent, or constant joint pain, often so severe that movement of the joint is limited. Anemic crisis is characterized by a dramatic, rapid drop in hemoglobin levels resulting from various causes. Aplastic crisis resulting in severe anemia occurs because RBC production is diminished by acute viral, bacterial, or fungal infection. Megaloblastic anemia (another form of anemic crisis) results from folic acid deficiency during periods of accelerated erythropoiesis. Hyperhemolytic crisis, characterized by anemia, jaundice, and reticulocytosis, results from glucose-6-phosphate dehydrogenase deficiency or occurs as a reaction to multiple transfusions. Acute sequestration crisis, which occurs in young children 6 months to 5 years of age, results when large quantities of blood suddenly accumulate in the spleen, causing massive splenic enlargement, severe anemia, shock, and, ultimately, death.

sickle cell dactylitis [AS, *sicol;* L, *cella,* storeroom; Gk, *daktylos,* finger, *itis,* inflammation], a painful inflammation of one or more fingers caused by an attack of sickle cell anemia.

sickle cell hepatopathy, the liver damage that accompanies sickle cell disease, owing especially to vascular occlusion and ischemia, sequestration, and cholestasis.

sickle cell test, a blood screening to detect sickle cell disease and sickle cell trait.

sickle cell thalassemia, a double heterozygous anemia in which the genes for sickle cell and for thalassemia are both inherited. A mild and a severe form may be identified, depending on the degree of suppression of beta-chain synthesis by the thalassemia gene. In the mild form, synthesis is only partially suppressed. In the severe form, beta-chain synthesis is completely suppressed, and only hemoglobin S appears in the RBC. The clinical course is generally as severe as in homozygous sickle cell anemia.

sickle cell trait, the heterozygous form of sickle cell anemia, characterized by the presence of both hemoglobin S and hemoglobin A in the RBCs. Anemia and the other signs of sickle cell anemia do not occur. People who have the trait are informed of and counseled about the possibility of having an infant with sickle cell disease if both parents have the trait.

sickling, the development of sickle-shaped RBCs, as in sickle cell anemia.

sick role [AS, *seoc;* Fr, stage character], a behavior pattern in which a person adopts the symptoms of a physical or mental disorder to be cared for, sympathized with, and protected from the demands and stresses of life.

sick sinus syndrome (SSS) [AS, *seoc;* L, *sinus,* hollow], a complex of arrhythmias associated with sinus node dysfunction. The condition may result from a variety of cardiac diseases, ranging from

cardiomyopathies to inflammatory myocardial disease. SSS is characterized by severe sinus bradycardia, either alone, alternating with tachycardia, or accompanied by atrioventricular block. The most common symptoms are lethargy, weakness, light-headedness, dizziness, and syncope. At present the only treatment is the implantation of a permanent pacemaker.

SICU, abbreviation for *surgical intensive care unit.*

SID, abbreviation for **source-to-image-receptor distance.**

side effect [AS, *side;* L, *effectus*], any reaction to or consequence of a medication or therapy. This can be an effect carried beyond the desired limit or a reaction unrelated to the primary object of the therapy. Usually, although not necessarily, a side effect is undesirable.

sideroblastic anemia /sid'ərōblas'tik/ [Gk, *sideros,* iron, *blastos,* germ], a heterogeneous group of chronic normocytic or slightly macrocytic anemias characterized by decreased erythropoiesis. The red blood cells contain a perinuclear ring of iron-stained granules. Sideroblastic anemia is an acquired disorder and the cause is not understood. Treatment may include extract of liver, pyridoxine, folic acid, and blood transfusion.

siderocyte /sid'ərosīt'/ [Gk, *sideros,* iron, *kytos,* cell], an abnormal erythrocyte in which particles of nonhemoglobin iron are visible as siderotic granules.

sideropenia /sid'ərōpē'nē·ə/, an abnormally low level of serum iron.

siderosis /sid'ərō'sis/ [Gk, *sideros + osis,* condition], **1.** a variety of pneumoconiosis caused by the inhalation of iron dust or particles. **2.** the introduction of color in any tissue caused by the presence of excess iron. **3.** an increase in the amount of iron in the blood.

siderotic granules /sid'ərot'ik/, inclusion bodies seen in the red blood cells of splenectomy patients and in cases of abnormal hemoglobin synthesis, sideroblastic anemia and hemolytic anemia. The granules contain iron, which takes a Prussian blue stain.

siderotic splenomegaly, an enlarged spleen associated with fibrosis and an excessive accumulation of iron and calcium. The condition is seen in sickle cell disease and hematochromatosis.

SIDS, abbreviation for **sudden infant death syndrome.**

SIECUS /sē'kəs/, abbreviation for *Sex Information and Education Council of the United States.*

siemens (S) /sē'mens/ [Ernst Werner von Siemens, German electric inventor, 1816–1892], a unit of electric conductance of a body with a resistance of 1 ohm, allowing 1 ampere of current to flow per volt applied.

sievert (**Sv**) /sē′vərt/ [R.M. Sievert, twentieth-century Swedish physicist], a measure of radiation dose. The sievert has the same units as the gray and is equal to the absorbed dose times the quality factor, which compares the health consequences of that type of radiation with those of x-rays.

sig., abbreviation for the Latin *signetur,* "let it be labeled (according to prescription)."

sigh, a deep breath that may be 1.5 times the normal V_t. It plays a role in pulmonary hygiene.

sight /sīt/ [AS, *gesiht*], **1.** the special sense that enables the shape, size, position, and color of objects to be perceived; the faculty of vision. **2.** that which is seen.

sigma /sig′mə/, Σ, σ, and s, the eighteenth letter of the Greek alphabet.

Sigma Theta Tau International /sig′mə thā′tə tou′/, an international honor society for nurses. Registered nurses and student nurses are invited to join based on academic achievement or contributions to nursing.

sigmoid /sig′moid/ [Gk, *sigma,* the letter S, *eidos,* form], **1.** pertaining to an S shape. **2.** the sigmoid colon.

sigmoid colon, the part of the colon that extends from the one descending colon in the pelvis to the juncture of the rectum.

sigmoid cystoplasty, augmentation cystoplasty using an isolated segment of the sigmoid colon for the graft.

sigmoidectomy /sig′moidek′təmē/ [Gk, *sigma* + *eidos* + *ektomē,* excision], excision of the sigmoid flexure of the colon, most commonly performed to remove a malignant tumor.

sigmoiditis /sig′moidī′tis/, an inflammation of the sigmoid colon.

sigmoid mesocolon /mez′ōkō′lən/ [Gk, *sigma* + *eidos* + *mesos,* middle + *kolon*], a fold of peritoneum that connects the sigmoid colon with the pelvic wall.

sigmoid notch, a concavity on the superior surface of the mandibular ramus between the coronoid and condyloid processes.

sigmoidoscope /sigmoi′dəskōp/ [Gk, *sigma* + *eidos* + *skopein,* to look], an instrument used to examine the lumen of the sigmoid colon. It consists of a tube and a light, allowing direct visualization of the mucous membrane lining the colon.

sigmoidoscopy /sig′moidos′kəpē/, the inspection of the rectum and sigmoid colon by the aid of a sigmoidoscope.

sigmoidostomy /sig′moidos′təmē/, the surgical creation of an anus in the pelvic colon.

sigmoid volvulus, a type of colonic volvulus consisting of twisting of an elongated section of sigmoid colon on its mesenteric axis. It is usually seen in the elderly.

sign /sīn/ [L, *signum,* mark], an objective finding as perceived by an examiner, such as a fever, a rash, or the whisper heard over the chest in pleural effusion. Many signs accompany symptoms. For example, erythema and a maculopapular rash are often seen with pruritus.

signal-average   electrocardiogram (**SAECG**), an ECG study, usually peformed on patients with unexplained LOC or suspected dyshythmias, in which hundreds of QRS complexes are collected, filtered, and analyzed to discover the presence or absence of certain abnormalities in the conducting system of the ventricle.

signal molecule /sig′nəl/ [L, *signum,* mark], a hormone, neurotransmitter, or other agent that transfers information from one cell or organ to another. Examples include steroid hormones, insulin, and growth factors.

signal-to-noise ratio (**SNR**), the number used to describe the relative contributions to a detected signal of the true signal and random superimposed signals or "noise."

signature /sig′nəchər/ [L, *signare,* (sig) to mark], in pharmacy, a part of a prescription containing instructions to the patient about dosage and manner and frequency of administration.

significance /signif′ikəns/ [L, *significare,* to signify], **1.** in research, the statistical probability that a given finding may have occurred by chance alone. **2.** the importance of a study in developing a practice or theory, as in nursing practice.

significance level, the probability of incorrectly rejecting the null hypothesis when such a hypothesis is tested.

significant other /signif′ikənt/, a person who is considered by an individual as being special and as having an effect on that individual.

sign language [L, *signum* + *lingua,* tongue], a form of communication often used with and among deaf people consisting of hand and body movements. Many variations exist, including American Sign Language (**ASL**). Other forms of manual communication are Signed English and finger spelling.

silanization /sil′ənizā′shən/, (in chromatography) the chemical process of converting the SiOH moieties of a stationary form to the ester form.

sildenafil, an erectile agent prescribed to treat erectile dysfunction.

silence, **1.** absence of noise. **2.** a state of producing no detectable signs or symptoms.

silent disease /sī′lənt/ [L, *silens* + *dis* + Fr, *aise,* ease], a disease or other disorder that produces no clinically obvious signs or symptoms.

silent ischemia [L, *silere,* to be silent], an asymptomatic form of myocardial ischemia that may damage the heart muscle. Ischemia is most likely to occur during the first 6 hours after a person awakens in the morning. It is triggered by mental arousal in more than 75% of patients.

silent mutation, an alteration in a DNA sequence that does not result in an amino acid change in a polypeptide.

silent myocardial infarction, an interruption in blood flow to the coronary arteries without the usual signs and symptoms of a heart attack. Such infarctions may be associated with diabetes.

silent peritonitis [L, *silere* + Gk, *peri* + *teinein,* to stretch, *itis,* inflammation], a case of peritonitis that develops without clinical signs or symptoms.

silhouette sign /sil′ōō·et′/, a radiographic artifact caused by an infiltrate that obscures the demarcating line between lung segments.

silica (SiO₂) /sil′i·kə/ [L, *silex,* flint], silicon dioxide, an inorganic compound occurring in nature as agate, sand, amethyst, flint, quartz, and other stones. It is one of the major constituents of dental porcelain and a common filler in resin composites. In granular form, it serves as a dental abrasive and polishing agent.

silica gel /sil′ikə/, a coagulated form of hydrated silica, used as an absorbent of gases and a dehydrating agent.

silicate cement /sil′i·kāt/ [L, *silex,* flint + *caementum,* rough stone], a dental cement that is translucent and porcelain-like when set; formerly used for esthetic temporary and semipermanent restorations of anterior teeth.

silicic acid /silis′ik/, hydrated silicon dioxide. It is used in thin-layer and column chromatography.

silicon (Si) /sil′ikon/ [L, *silex,* flint], a nonmetallic element, second to oxygen as the most abundant of the elements in the earth's crust. Its atomic number is 14, and its atomic mass is 28.09. It occurs in nature as silicon dioxide and in silicates. The silicates are used as detergents, corrosion inhibitors, adhesives, and sealants.

silicone /sil′ikon/ [L, *silex,* flint], any of a large group of inert polymers. Silicones are water-repellent and stable at high temperature. They are useful in medicine as adhesives, lubricants, and sealants. They are also used as a substitute for rubber, especially in prosthetic devices.

silicone-gel breast implant, a type of implant used in reconstructive surgery of the breast and made with synthetic polymers. The implants have been associated with adverse effects on the immune system as well as distorted and painful breasts caused by leakage of the silicone into surrounding tissues. However, a number of statistical studies have not established such a cause-and-effect relationship.

silicone-hydrogel lens, a soft contact lens made of a polymer that contains silicone, which is permeable to oxygen, so that large amounts of oxygen are transmitted to the cornea. Such lenses contain less water than traditional soft lenses and so are more resistant to dehydration and less prone to harbor bacteria and protein deposits.

silicone oil, any of various fluid silicone polymers. Some are injected into the vitreous of the eye to serve as a vitreous substitute during or after certain ophthalmologic surgical procedures.

silicone septum, a vascular access device used in IV therapy. It consists of a silicone partition that covers the port chamber housed in the metal or plastic body of an implanted infusion port.

silicophosphate cement /sil′ikōfos′fāt/, a mixture of silicate and zinc phosphate cements, formerly used as temporary filling material and for cementation of orthodontic bands, indirect restorations, and porcelain jacket crowns.

silicosis /sil′ikō′sis/, a lung disorder caused by continued long-term inhalation of the dust of an inorganic compound, silicon dioxide, which is found in sands, quartzes, flints, and many other stones. Silicosis is characterized by the development of nodular fibrosis in the lungs. In advanced cases, severe dyspnea may develop.

silk suture [AS, *seolc*; L, *sutura,* seam], a braided fine suture material, usually used to close incisions, wounds, and cuts in the skin. It is not absorbed by the body and is removed after approximately 7 days.

silo filler's disease /sī′lō/ [Fr, *ensilotage,* ensilage; AS, *fyllan,* to fill], a rare acute respiratory condition seen in agricultural workers who have inhaled nitrogen oxide as they work with fermented fodder in closed, poorly ventilated areas such as silos. Characteristically, symptoms of respiratory distress and pulmonary edema occur several hours after exposure. LOC may occur.

silver (Ag) [AS, *seolfor*], a whitish precious metal occurring mainly as a sulfide. Its atomic number is 47, and its atomic mass is 107.88. It is used extensively as a component of amalgams of dental fillings and in many medications, especially antiseptics and astringents. Silver nitrate is used externally as an antiseptic and astringent, especially in the prevention of ophthalmia neonatorum. Silver picrate, an ionizable salt of silver, is used in the treatment of trichomoniasis and moniliasis of the vagina.

S

silver amalgam [AS, *seolfor*; Gk, *malagma*], an alloy of silver, tin, copper, mercury, and zinc used in dentistry to fill prepared tooth cavities.

silver cone method, a technique for filling tooth pulp canals. It is outdated because the silver corrodes over time, which permits apical fluid leakage and root canal failure. Retreatment of the root canal is necessary.

Silver dwarf [Henry K. Silver, twentieth-century American pediatrician], a person who has Silver's syndrome, a congenital disorder in which short stature is associated with lateral asymmetry; various anomalies of the head, face, and skeleton; and precocious puberty.

Silverman-Anderson score, a system of assessing the degree of respiratory distress.

silver nitrate (AgNO₃), a topical antiseptic. A 1% solution was traditionally prescribed for the prevention of gonococcal ophthalmia in newborns, but povidone-iodine is now usually used because it is less expensive and has a broader spectrum of action. Stronger concentrations can also be used on wet dressings for cauterizing wounds, removal of granulation tissue and warts, and for prophylaxis following burns.

silver salts poisoning, a toxic condition caused by the ingestion of silver nitrate, characterized by discoloration of the lips, vomiting, abdominal pain, dizziness, and convulsions.

silver sulfadiazine, a topical antibiotic prescribed to prevent or treat infection in second- and third-degree burns.

silver-wire arteries, retinal arterioles that appear as white tubes containing a red fluid when viewed through an ophthalmoscope. The condition occurs as replacement fibrosis associated with hypertension continues and the vessel wall obscures the blood column.

simethicone /simeth′ikōn/, an antiflatulent that helps gases to dissolve in liquid by decreasing the surface tension of gas bubbles. It is prescribed to disperse gas pockets in the GI tract.

simian crease /sim′ē-ən/ [L, *simia,* ape; ME, *creste,* crest], a single crease across the palm produced from the fusion of proximal and distal palmar creases, seen in congenital disorders such as Down syndrome.

simian-human immunodeficiency virus, a chimeric, engineered virus with the envelope of HIV and the cytoplasm and nucleus of simian immunodeficiency virus (SIV). It is used in animal models, because it is a better mimic of HIV than SIV is.

simian immunodeficiency virus (SIV), a lentivirus that produces an AIDS-like disease in nonhuman primates. The cytopathologic changes caused by SIV are similar to those caused by HIV. SIV also shares

with HIV a group of genes lacking in other retroviruses, and animals infected with either virus experience a similar decrease in the number of CD4⁺ lymphocytes.

simian virus 40 (SV40), a vacuolating virus isolated from the kidney tissue of rhesus monkeys. SV40 produces malignancy in human and newborn hamster kidney cells and tumors inoculated into newborn hamsters.

Similac preparations, a trademark for a group of commercial modified milk products that are prepared especially for infant feeding. They are made from a nonfat base of cow's milk supplemented with such substances as lactose, coconut and soy oils, and monosaccharides and disaccharides and are fortified with vitamins and minerals. The ratio of the various nutrients, such as iron or one of the other minerals, is altered in the different preparations to accommodate infants with particular nutritional requirements or nutritional problems, such as nephrogenic diabetes insipidus. The formulas are packaged in both powder and liquid forms.

similia similibus curantur, a homeopathic rule that medication able to produce symptoms in a healthy person will also remove similar symptoms occurring as an expression of disease.

simplate bleeding time test, a blood test for determining how quickly platelets form a plug when an incision is made in the skin. Platelet plug formation is the first step in clotting and, if slower than 8 minutes, indicates platelet deficiency or the effect of a drug, such as aspirin.

simple, 1. describing something composed of only one or a minimum number of parts or elements. **2.** not involved or complicated.

simple angioma [L, *simplex,* not mixed], a tumor consisting of a network of small vessels or distended capillaries surrounded by connective tissue.

simple astigmatism [L, *simplex,* not mixed; Gk, *a + stigma,* point], **1.** simple myopic astigmatism in which one principal meridian is in focus on the retina and the other in front of it. **2.** simple hyperopic astigmatism in which one meridian is focused on the retina and the other behind it.

simple cavity, a cavity that involves only one surface of a tooth.

simple diarrhea [L, *simplex,* not mixed; Gk, *dia + rhein,* to flow], a form of diarrhea in which the loose stools contain normal feces.

simple dislocation [L, *simplex,* not mixed, *dis + locare,* to place], displacement of a joint without a penetrating wound.

simple figure-eight roller arm sling, a sling prepared by placing the patient in a supine or sitting position with the affected arm flexed and adjacent to the chest. The open sling fits under the arm and over the chest. The bandage is fixed with a single turn toward the uninjured side around the arm and chest, crossing the elbow above the external epicondyle. The bandage then is drawn forward under the tip of the elbow, after making a second turn that overlaps two thirds of the first. It is then pulled upward along the flexed arm to the base of the neck on the uninjured side. Finally, the bandage is drawn down over the scapula and across the chest and arm, overlapping and continuing in a figure-eight pattern.

simple fracture, an uncomplicated fracture in which the bone does not break the skin. It usually heals readily.

simple glaucoma [L, *simplex,* not mixed; Gk, *glaucoma,* cataract], chronic open-angle glaucoma without complications but with visual field loss and optic atrophy.

simple goiter [L, *simplex,* not mixed, *guttur,* sore throat], a goiter not accompanied by signs or symptoms of hyperthyroidism.

simple mastectomy, a surgical procedure in which a breast is completely removed and the underlying muscles and adjacent lymph nodes are left intact.

simple phobia, an anxiety disorder characterized by a persistent, irrational fear of specific things such as animals, dirt, light, or darkness.

simple protein, a protein that yields amino acids as the only or chief product on hydrolysis. The class includes albumins, globulins, glutelins, alcohol-soluble proteins, albuminoids, histones, and protamines.

simple reflex [L, *simplex,* not mixed, *reflectere,* to bend back], a reflex with a motor nerve component that involves only one muscle.

simple stomatitis [L, *simplex;* Gk, *stoma,* mouth, *itis,* inflammation], a simple inflammation of the mucous membranes of the mouth with redness, swelling, and an excess of mucus.

simple sugar, a monosaccharide such as glucose.

simple tubular gland, one of the many multicellular glands with only one duct and a tube-shaped part, such as various glands within the epithelium of the intestine.

Simplexvirus /sim′pleksvi′rus/, HSV, a genus of herpesviruses that causes herpes simplex. Species pathogenic in humans includes human herpesvirus 1 and human herpesvirus 2.

Sims' position [James M. Sims, American gynecologist, 1813–1883], a position in which the patient lies on the side with the knee and thigh drawn upward toward the chest. The chest and abdomen are allowed to fall forward. Left Sims' is the position

of choice for administering enemas or conducting rectal examinations.

Sims recumbent position, a variant of the Sims position in which the patient lies on the left side in a modified left lateral position. The upper leg is flexed at hip and knees, the lower leg is straight, and the upper arm rests in a flexed position on the bed.

simultanagnosia /sī′multan′agnō′zhə/, a visual disorder in which a person actually perceives only one element of a picture or object at a time and is unable to absorb the whole.

sinciput /sin′siput/ [L, half a head], the anterior or upper part of the skull.

Sinemet, a trademark for a fixed-combination drug containing a peripheral dopa decarboxylase inhibitor (carbidopa) and an antiparkinsonian (levodopa) that can enter the central nervous system.

Sinequan, a trademark for a tricyclic antidepressant (doxepin hydrochloride).

sinew /sin′yo͞o/ [ME, *sinewe*], the tendon of a muscle, such as the thick, flattened tendon attached to the short head of the biceps brachii.

single-blind study [L, *singulus,* one by one; AS, *blind;* L, *studere,* to be busy], an experiment in which the person collecting data knows whether the subject is in the control or experimental group, but subjects do not.

single-cell gel electrophoresis, a type of gel electrophoresis used to detect the genotoxic potential of environmental hazards, such as radiation, heavy metals, and toxic chemicals. Such agents may cause breaks in the nuclear DNA of cells. When such a cell is lysed and exposed to electrophoresis that denatures its DNA, the damaged DNA moves toward the electric field, making a formation like the tail of a comet.

single-chain antigen-binding (SCAB) protein, a polypeptide that joins an antibody's light chain variable region to the antibody heavy chain variable region. SCABs are used as biosensors, in chemical separations, and in the treatment of cancers and heart disease.

single component insulin [L, *singulus* + *componere,* to bring together, *insula,* island], any highly purified insulin with less than 10 ppm of proinsulin.

single-locus probe (SLP), a sequence of labeled DNA or RNA that can be used to identify a region of DNA tandem repeats found in the genome only once. It may be used in resolving cases of disputed parentage.

single-nucleotide polymorphism (SNP), a genetic polymorphism between two genomes that is based on deletion, insertion, or exchange of a single nucleotide.

S

single-parent family, a family consisting of only the mother or the father and one or more dependent children.

single-photon emission computed tomography (SPECT), a variation of CT in which the ray sum is defined by the collimator holes on the gamma-ray detector rotating around the patient. SPECT units usually consist of large crystal gamma cameras mounted on a gantry that permits rotation of the camera around the patient. Multiple detectors are used to reduce the imaging time.

single room occupant (SRO), a single person, usually an elderly individual, who lives alone in a single room of a low-cost hotel or apartment building.

single sweep scan, an ultrasonic scan that is completed in a single sweep of the sensing device across the area being examined.

single system ureterocele, a ureterocele involving the ureter of a collecting system that is not double. It is usually orthotopic, intravesical, and seen in adults.

singleton /sing′gəltən/, an offspring born alone.

singlet state /sing′glət/, a state of an atom or molecule in which all electrons have paired spins.

sinister /sin′istər/ [L], **1.** left, at the left side, at the left hand. **2.** ominous, potentially dangerous; threatening.

sinistral /sinis′trəl/ [L, sinister, left], relating to the left side.

sinoatrial (SA) /sī′nō-ā′trē-əl/ [L sinus, hollow, atrium, hall], pertaining to the sinus node and atrium.

sinoatrial (SA) block [L, sinus, hollow, atrium, hall; Fr, bloc], a conduction disturbance in the heart during which an impulse formed within the sinus node is blocked or delayed from depolarizing the atria. There are two types of SA block. Type I (SA Wenckebach) is characterized on the ECG by group beating, shortening of P-P intervals, and pauses that are less than twice the shortest cycle. Type II SA block is identified on the ECG by absent P waves without shortening P-P intervals. Causes include excessive vagal stimulation, acute infections, and atherosclerosis. SA block also may be an adverse reaction to quinidine or digitalis.

sinoatrial node, a cluster of hundreds of cells located in the right atrial wall of the heart, near the opening of the superior vena cava. It comprises a knot of modified heart muscle that generates impulses that travel swiftly throughout the muscle fibers of both atria, causing them to contract.

sinoatrial valve, the valve at the opening of the sinus venosus into the primordial right atrium.

sinus /sī′nəs/ [L, hollow], a cavity or channel such as a cavity within a bone, a dilated channel for venous blood, or one permitting the escape of purulent material.

sinus arrest, a heart disorder in which there is a cessation of activity in the sinus node. The ventricles may continue to contract under the control of pacemakers in the atrioventricular node or the ventricles.

sinus arrhythmia, an irregular cardiac rhythm in which the heart rate usually increases during inspiration and decreases during expiration. It is common in children and young adults and has no clinical significance except in elderly patients.

sinus bradycardia, beating of the sinus node at a rate below 60 beats/min.

sinus dysrhythmia, an irregular heart rhythm characterized by alternate increases and decreases in the heart rate. It is often associated with the vagal effects of respiration, which causes the heart rate to increase on inspiration and decrease on expiration. Nonrespiratory sinus dysrhythmia can be caused by MS, digitalis, MI, and increased ICP.

sinusitis /sī′nəsī′tis/ [L, sinus; Gk, itis, inflammation], an inflammation of one or more paranasal sinuses. It may be a complication of a URI; dental infection; allergy; change in atmospheric pressure; or a structural defect of the nose. With swelling of nasal mucous membranes, the openings from sinuses to the nose may be obstructed, resulting in an accumulation of sinus secretions, causing pressure, pain, headache, fever, and local tenderness. Complications include cavernous sinus thrombosis and spread of infection to bone, brain, or meninges. Treatment includes steam inhalations, nasal decongestants, analgesics, and, if infection is present, antibiotics.

sinus node, a cluster of hundreds of cells located in the right atrial wall of the heart, near the opening of the superior vena cava. It comprises a knot of modified heart muscle that generates impulses that travel swiftly throughout the muscle fibers of both atria, causing them to contract.

sinus node dysfunction, any disturbance in the normal functioning of the sinus node, such as slow sinus rate or sinoatrial block, that leads to the development of arrhythmias.

sinus of the vena cava, the space in the right atrium posterior to the terminal crest into which empty both vena cava.

sinusoid /sī′nəsoid/ [L, sinus; Gk, eidos, form], an anastomosing blood vessel that is somewhat larger than a capillary and is lined with reticuloendothelial cells.

sinus rhythm, a cardiac rhythm stimulated by the sinus node. A rate of 60 to 100 beats/min is normal.

sinus surgery, surgery to improve drainage or remove diseased sinus membranes. Open surgery includes the Caldwell-Luc procedure to treat chronic maxillary sinusitis, in which the maxillary sinus is entered by an opening under the upper lip above the teeth, and ethmoidectomy, the removal of all or a part of the mucosal lining and bony partitions between the ethmoid sinuses, to treat ethmoid or sphenoidal sinusitis. Endoscopy is used to treat acute maxillary sinusitis. Endoscopy has replaced many procedures performed with an open approach but has risks associated with the anatomic relationship of the sinuses to multiple systems.

sinus tachycardia [L, *sinus,* hollow; Gk, *tachys,* fast, *kardia,* heart], a rapid heartbeat generated by discharge of the sinus node. The rate is generally 100 to 180 beats/min in the adult, greater than 200 beats/min in an infant and 140 to 200 beats/min in a child.

SiO₂, symbol for **silica.**

si op. sit, in prescriptions, abbreviation for the Latin phrase *si opus sit,* "if necessary."

siphonage /sī′fənij/, a process of drawing off fluid from a cavity with a tube using atmospheric pressure.

sirenomelia /sī′rənōmē′lē·ə/ [Gk, *seiren,* mermaid, *melos,* limb], a congenital anomaly in which there is complete fusion of the lower extremities and no feet.

sirenomelus /sī′rənom′ələs/, an infant who has sirenomelia.

siriasis /sirī′əsis/ [Gk, *sieros,* scorching], sunstroke.

sirolimus, an immunosuppressant prescribed after organ transplantation to prevent rejection. Recommended use is in combination with cyclosporine and corticosteroids.

sister, a term used in the United Kingdom and Commonwealth for a nurse, particularly the head nurse in a hospital, a ward, or an OR.

Sister Joseph's nodule [Sister Mary Joseph Dempsy, U.S. surgical assistant, 1856–1929], a malignant intraabdominal neoplasm of gastric, ovarian, colorectal, or pancreatic origin and metastatic to the umbilicus.

Sister Kenny's treatment [Elizabeth Kenny, Australian nurse, 1886–1952], poliomyelitis therapy in which the patient's limbs and back are wrapped in warm, moist woolen cloths and, after the pain subsides, the patient is taught to exercise affected muscles, especially by swimming. Equally important is passive movement of affected limbs with simultaneous stimulation at the site of muscle origins, carried out after hot packs.

Sistrurus /sis-troo′rus/, a genus of small rattlesnakes widely distributed throughout the United States, having symmetric plates covering their heads.

sitagliptin, an oral antidiabetic. It is used alone or in combination with other antidiabetic agents to treat type 2 DM.

site [L, *situs,* location], 1. location. 2. a quantum of space occupied and defined by a cluster of people.

site visit, a visit made by designated officials to evaluate or gather information about a department or institution. A site visit is a step in the accreditation of an institution and in the funding of many major projects.

sitosterol /sītos′tərôl/ [Gk, *sitos,* food, *stereos,* solid; Ar, *alkohl,* essence], a mixture of sterols derived from plants such as wheat germ, used for treating hyperbetalipoproteinemia and hypercholesterolemia that are unresponsive to other dietary measures. Its use is controversial and use in pregnancy is not recommended.

sitotherapy /sī′tōther′əpē/ [Gk, *sitos,* food], a health maintenance system based on food, diet, and nutrition.

sit-to-stand (STS), 1. in the treatment of balance disorders, a movement in which the base of support is transferred from the seat to the feet. The feet begin to accept the weight first by downward pressure through the heels as the pelvis rolls anteriorly. The weight then moves to the front of the feet as the trunk moves forward and the pelvis lifts from the surface. 2. a transfer activity in which a patient moves from sitting to standing.

situational anxiety /sich′ōō·ā′shənəl/ [L, *situs,* location], a state of apprehension, discomfort, and anxiety precipitated by the experience of new or changed situations or events. Situational anxiety requires no treatment; it usually disappears as the person adjusts to the new experience.

situational crisis, in psychiatry, an unexpected crisis that arises suddenly in response to an external event or a conflict concerning a specific circumstance.

situational depression, in psychiatry, an episode of emotional and psychologic depression that occurs in response to a specific set of external conditions or circumstances.

situational loss, the loss of a person, thing, or quality, resulting from alteration of a life situation, including changes related to illness, body image, environment, and death.

situational support, people who are available and can be depended on to help a patient solve problems.

S

situational theory, a leadership theory in which the manager chooses a leadership style to match the particular situation.

situational therapy, in psychiatry, a kind of psychotherapy in which the milieu is part of the treatment program.

situation relating /sich'ōō·ā'shən/, in nursing research, a study design used to explain or predict phenomena in nursing practice in which a relationship is thought to exist among certain practices or characteristics of the population being studied.

situs /sī'təs/ [L, location], the normal position or location of an organ or part of the body.

sitz bath /sits, zits/ [Ger, *Sitz*, seat; AS, *bjth*], a bath in which only the rectal and perineal areas are immersed in water or saline solution. The procedure is used after childbirth and after rectal or perineal surgery to decrease swelling, inflammation, and pain.

SI units [Fr, système international], the international units of physical amounts. Examples of these units are the mass of a kilogram, the length of a meter, and the precise amount of time in a second.

SIV, abbreviation for **simian immunodeficiency virus.**

Sjögren-Larsson syndrome /shō'gren lär'sən/ [Torsten Sjögren, Swedish pediatrician, 1859–1939; T. Larsson, twentieth-century Swedish pediatrician], a congenital condition, inherited as an autosomal-recessive trait, characterized by ichthyosis, mental deficiency, and spastic paralysis.

Sjögren's syndrome [Henrik S.C. Sjögren, Swedish ophthalmologist, 1899–1986], an immunologic disorder characterized by deficient fluid production by the lacrimal, salivary, and other glands, resulting in abnormal dryness of the mouth, eyes, and other mucous membranes. Atrophy of the lacrimal glands can lead to desiccation of the cornea and conjunctiva with damage to the tissues. Atrophy of the salivary glands results in dental disorders and loss of taste and odor sensations. When the lungs are affected, the dryness increases susceptibility to pneumonia and other respiratory infections. Treatment includes applying artificial tears and using soft contact lenses that can be moistened often, sipping fluids frequently to prevent mouth dryness, and avoiding medications that tend to deplete body fluids.

SK, abbreviation for **streptokinase.**

skelalgia [Gk, *skelos*, leg], pain in the leg.

skeletal fixation /skel'ətəl/ [Gk, *skeletos*, dried up; L, *figere*, to fasten], any method of holding together the fragments of a fractured bone by the attaching of wires, screws, plates, or nails.

skeletal fluorosis, skeletal changes caused by long-term ingestion of excessive fluoride. They may include hyperostosis, osteopetrosis, and osteoporosis.

skeletal function, a nursing outcome from the Nursing Outcomes Classification (NOC) defined as the ability of the bones to support the body and facilitate movement.

skeletal survey, the radiographic examination of the skeletal system for possible fractures or tumors.

skeletal system, all of the bones and cartilage of the body that collectively provide the supporting framework for the muscles and organs.

skeletal traction, one of the two basic kinds of traction used in orthopedics for the treatment of fractured bones and the correction of orthopedic abnormalities. Skeletal traction is applied to the affected structure by a metal pin or wire inserted into the structure and attached to traction ropes. Skeletal traction is often used when continuous traction is desired to immobilize, position, and align a fractured bone properly during the healing process.

skeleton /skel'ətən/ [Gk, *skeletos*, dried up], the supporting framework for the body, comprising 206 bones in the adult that protect delicate structures; provide attachments for muscles; allow body movement; serve as major reservoirs of blood; and produce RBCs, platelets, and most WBCs. The skeleton is divided into the axial skeleton, which has 74 bones; the appendicular skeleton, with 126 bones; and the 6 auditory ossicles. The four types of bones composing the skeleton are long bones, short bones, flat bones, and irregular bones. The skeleton changes throughout life as bone formation and bone destruction proceed concurrently.—**skeletal,** *adj.*

Skene's glands /skēnz/ [Alexander J.C. Skene, American gynecologist, 1838–1900], the largest of the glands opening into the urethra of women. They contain ducts that open immediately within the urethral orifice.

skew /skyōō/ [ME, *skewen,* to escape], a deviation from a line or symmetric pattern, such as data in a research study that do not follow the expected statistical curve of distribution because of the unwitting introduction of another variable.

skilled nursing facility (SNF) [ME, *skil,* distinction], an institution or part of an institution that meets criteria for accreditation established by the sections of the Social Security Act that determine the basis for Medicaid and Medicare reimbursement for skilled nursing care. Skilled nursing care includes rehabilitation and various medical and nursing procedures. Written policies and protocols are formulated with appropriate professional consultation.

Skillern's fracture /skil'ərnz/ [Penn G. Skillern, American surgeon, b. 1882], an open fracture of the distal radius associated with a greenstick fracture of the distal ulna.

skill play [ME, *skil* + *plega*, sport], a form of play in which a child persistently repeats an action or activity until it has been mastered, such as throwing or catching a ball.

skills training, the teaching of specific verbal and nonverbal behaviors and the practicing of these behaviors by the patient.

skimmed milk [Dan, *skumme,* scum removal; AS, *meolc*], milk from which the fat has been removed. Most of the vitamin A is removed with the cream, although other nutrients remain.

skimming [Dan, *skumme*], a practice, sometimes used by health programs that receive their income on a prepaid or capitation basis, of seeking to enroll only relatively healthy individuals as a means of increasing profits by decreasing costs.

skimping [Swed, *skrympa*, to shrink], a practice, sometimes used by health programs that receive their income on a prepaid or capitation basis, of delaying or denying services to enrolled members of the program as a means of increasing profits by decreasing costs.

skin [AS, *scinn*], the tough, supple cutaneous membrane that covers the entire surface of the body. It is composed of a thick layer of connective tissue called the dermis and an epidermis made of five layers of cells. Skin color varies according to the amount of melanin in the epidermis. The skin helps to cool the body when the temperature rises by radiating the heat of increased blood flow in expanded blood vessels and by providing a surface for the evaporation of sweat. When the temperature drops, the blood vessels constrict and the production of sweat diminishes. Modified skin continues into various parts of the body, such as mucous membrane, as in the lining of the vagina, the bladder, the lungs, the intestines, the nose, and the mouth.

skin barrier, an artificial layer of skin, usually made of plastic, applied to skin before the application of tape or ostomy drainage bags. It protects the real skin from chronic irritation.

skin button, a plastic and fabric device that covers the drivelines of an artificial heart at their exit point from the skin. Its purpose is to prevent the transmission of pumping pressure to the surrounding tissues.

skin cancer, a cutaneous neoplasm caused by ionizing radiation, certain genetic defects, or chemical carcinogens, including arsenics, petroleum, tar products, and fumes from some molten metals, or by overexposure to the sun or other sources of ultraviolet light. Skin cancers, the most common and most curable malignancies, are also the most frequent secondary lesions in patients with cancer in other sites. The major risk factor is overexposure to sunlight. Other risk factors include a fair complexion, xeroderma pigmentosa, vitiligo, senile and seborrheic keratitis, Bowen's disease, radiation dermatitis, and hereditary basal cell nevus syndrome. The most common skin cancers are basal cell carcinomas and squamous cell carcinomas.

skin care: donor site, a nursing intervention from the Nursing Interventions Classification (NIC) defined as prevention of wound complications and promotion of healing at the donor site.

skin care: graft site, a nursing intervention from the Nursing Interventions Classification (NIC) defined as prevention of wound complications and promotion of graft site healing.

skin care: topical treatments, a nursing intervention from the Nursing Interventions Classification (NIC) defined as application of topical substances or manipulation of devices to promote skin integrity and minimize skin breakdown.

skin dose (SD), the amount of radiation absorbed by the skin.

skin flap [AS, *scinn*; ME, *flappe*], a layer of skin, usually separated by dissection from deeper layers of tissue.

skinfold calipers, an instrument used to measure the breadth of a fold of skin, usually on the posterior aspect of the upper arm or over the lower ribs of the chest.

skinfold thickness [AS, *scinn* + *fealden* + *thicce*], a measure of the amount of subcutaneous fat, obtained by inserting a fold of skin into the jaws of a caliper. The skinfolds are usually measured on the upper arm, thigh, or upper abdomen, and the caliper measurements are later compared with precalibrated standard tables to assess an individual's body fat content indirectly.

skin graft, a part of skin implanted to cover areas where skin has been lost through burns or injury or by surgical removal of diseased tissue. To prevent tissue rejection of permanent grafts, the graft is taken from the patient's own body or from the body of an identical twin. Skin from another person or animal can be used as a temporary cover for large burned areas to decrease fluid loss. Various techniques are used, including pinch, split-thickness, full-thickness, pedicle, and mesh grafts. A successful new graft of any type is well established in about 72 hours and can be expected to survive unless a severe infection or trauma occurs. Before surgery, both the donor and the recipient site must be free of infection, and the recipient site must

S

have a good blood supply. After surgery, stretching or movement of the recipient site is prevented. Strict sterile technique is used for handling dressings, and antibiotics may be given prophylactically to prevent infection. Good nutrition with a high-protein, high-calorie diet is essential.

Skinner box [Burrhus F. Skinner, American psychologist, 1904–1990; L, *buxus,* box-wood], a boxlike laboratory apparatus used in operant conditioning in animals, usually containing a lever or other device that, when pressed, reinforces by either giving a reward such as food or an escape outlet for removing a punishment such as an electric shock.

skin pigment [AS, *scinn*; L, *pigmentum,* paint], any skin coloring caused by melanin deposits. The coloring may be modified by substances in the blood, such as the several blood pigments, bile, or malarial parasites.

skin prep, a procedure for cleansing the skin with an antiseptic before surgery or venipuncture. Skin preps are performed to kill bacteria and pathologic organisms and to reduce the risk of infection. Various skin prep devices are available for this procedure. Such devices are commonly constructed of plastic, filled with a specific antiseptic, and equipped with an applicator. The antiseptic is applied by rubbing the device in a circular motion over the skin. Some of the most common antiseptics contained in skin prep devices are iodine, povidone-iodine, and ethyl alcohol.

skin self-examination (SSE), the practice of studying one's own skin for early signs of premalignant or malignant tumors. A 5-year study by the Sloan-Kettering Cancer Center in New York found that people who examined themselves, looking for moles that change color, shape, or size, were 44% less likely to die of melanoma than those who did not.

skin substitute, a material used to cover wounds and burns where extensive areas of skin are missing, to promote healing. Effective skin substitutes have both dermal analog and epidermal analog layers, and may be synthetic or manufactured from tissue elements.

skin surveillance, a nursing intervention from the Nursing Interventions Classification (NIC) defined as collection and analysis of patient data to maintain skin and mucous membrane integrity.

skin test, a test to determine the reaction of the body to a substance by observing the results of injecting the substance intradermally or of applying it topically to the skin. Skin tests are used to detect allergens, determine immunity, and diagnose disease.

skin traction, one of the two basic kinds of traction used in orthopedics for the treatment of fractured bones and the correction of orthopedic abnormalities. Skin traction applies pull to an affected body structure by straps attached to the skin surrounding the structure. Kinds of skin traction are adhesive skin traction and nonadhesive skin traction.

skin turgor [AS, *scinn*; L, *turgere,* to swell], the resilience of the normal skin when subjected to physical distortion, such as by pinching or pressing. The relative speed with which the skin resumes its normal appearance after stretching or compression is an indicator of skin hydration. Turgor is slower in older people.

skull [ME, *skulle,* shell], the bony structure of the head, consisting of the cranium and the skeleton of the face. The cranium, which contains and protects the brain, consists of 8 bones; the skeleton of the face is composed of 14 bones.

skullcap, a herb that is native to temperate regions of North America. This herb has been used as folk medicine to treat convulsions, hysteria, and nervous tension, and is a common component of remedies for PMS. There is insufficient reliable evidence regarding its effectiveness.

skull shield, a protective plastic plate worn over a cranial defect.

skull x-ray, radiographic imaging of the bones of the skull, the nasal sinuses, and cerebral calcifications. Skull x-rays have largely been replaced by CT scanning of the brain.

SL, abbreviation for **soda lime.**

slander [Fr, *esclandre,* scandal], any words spoken with malice that are untrue and prejudicial to the reputation, professional practice, commercial trade, office, or business of another person.

slant of occlusal plane [ME, *slenten,* to slope], the angle between the extended occlusal plane and the axis-orbital plane.

SLE, abbreviation for **systemic lupus erythematosus.**

sleep[1] [AS, *slaepan,* to sleep], a state marked by reduced consciousness, diminished activity of the skeletal muscles, and depressed metabolism. People normally experience sleep in patterns that follow four observable, progressive stages. During stage 1 the brain waves are of the theta type, followed in stage 2 by the appearance of distinctive sleep spindles; during stages 3 and 4 the theta waves are replaced by delta waves. These four stages represent three fourths of a period of typical sleep and collectively are called *nonrapid eye movement (NREM)* sleep. The remaining time is usually occupied with *rapid eye* *movement (REM)* sleep. The REM sleep periods, lasting from a few minutes to half an hour, alternate with the NREM periods. Dreaming occurs during REM time. Individual sleep patterns normally change throughout life because daily requirements for sleep gradually diminish from as much as 20 hours a day in infancy to as little as 6 hours a day in old age.

sleep², a nursing outcome from the Nursing Outcomes Classification (NOC) defined as natural periodic suspension of consciousness during which the body is restored.

sleep apnea, a sleep disorder characterized by periods in which respiration is absent. The person is momentarily unable to contract respiratory muscles or to maintain airflow through the nose and mouth.

sleep enhancement, a nursing intervention from the Nursing Interventions Classification (NIC) defined as the facilitation of regular sleep-wake cycles.

sleeping pill, 1. *informal.* a prescription sedative taken for insomnia or for postoperative sedation. **2.** an OTC pill, classified pharmaceutically as an aid to sleeping.

sleep studies, an electrodiagnostic test used to diagnose obstructive sleep apnea (OSA). It is performed in a sleep laboratory, where the patient is monitored by ECG, pulse oximetry, EEG, and electromyography.

sleep terror disorder [AS, *slaepan*; L, *terrere*, to frighten], a condition occurring during stage 3 or 4 of nonrapid eye movement sleep. It is characterized by repeated episodes of abrupt awakening, usually with a panicky scream, accompanied by intense anxiety, confusion, agitation, disorientation, unresponsiveness, marked motor movements, and total amnesia concerning the event. The disorder usually occurs in children.

sleep-wake schedule disorder, a form of dyssomnia caused by a conflict between a person's circadian rhythm and the socioeconomic demands of society, such as work and travel schedules.

slice /slīs/ [OFr, *esclice*], in tomography, a cross-sectional plane of the body selected for imaging.

slice sensitivity profile, a curve showing the effect of broadening of the CT slice thickness along the patient axis in helical CT.

slide clamp [AS, *slidan* + *clam*, fastener], a device, usually constructed of plastic, used to regulate the flow of IV solution. The slide clamp has a graduated opening through which the IV tubing passes.

slide tracheoplasty, surgical treatment of tracheal stenosis by dividing the stenosis at the midpoint, incising the segments vertically on opposite anterior and posterior surfaces, and sliding the segments together to create an anastomosis with a widened lumen.

sliding esophageal hiatal hernia, a protrusion of the cardioesophageal junction and stomach through the esophageal hiatus.

sliding filaments [AS, *slidan*; L, *filamentum*, thread], interdigitated thick and thin filaments of a sarcomere. In muscle contraction, they slide past each other so that the sarcomere becomes shorter, although the filament lengths do not change. The action of the sliding filaments contributes to the increased thickness of a muscle in contraction.

sliding hernia, a protrusion of either the cecum or the sigmoid colon into the parietal peritoneum. The protrusion can be either abdominal or esophageal.

sliding hiatal hernia, a protrusion of the upper stomach and cardioesophageal junction through the diaphragm into the posterior mediastinum.

sliding transfer, the movement of a person in a sitting position from one site to another, such as from a bed to a wheelchair, by sliding him or her along a transfer board.

sling [ME, *slingen*, to hurl], a bandage or device used to support an injured part of the body, especially a forearm.

sling restraint, a therapeutic device, usually constructed of felt, used to assist in the immobilization of patients, especially orthopedic patients in traction. The sling is placed over the pelvis to reduce pelvic motion with lower extremity traction or over the abdominal area as countertraction with Dunlop traction.

slip-on blood pump [ME, *slippen*, slippery, *on*], a plastic mesh device with an attached squeeze bulb, rubber tubing, and pressure gauge, used to help administer large amounts of blood quickly.

slipped femoral epiphysis, a failure of the femoral epiphyseal plate, occurring primarily in overweight adolescents as a result of hormonal changes. Clinical features include hip stiffness and pain, with difficulty in walking. There also may be knee pain and external rotation of the affected leg. The condition is treated by orthopedic surgery.

slipping patella [ME, *slippen*; L, *patella*, small dish], a patella that undergoes recurrent dislocation.

slipping rib, a condition in which a loose ligament allows one of the lower five ribs to slip inside or outside an adjacent rib, causing pain or discomfort.

slit diaphragm, a thin membrane that spans the slit pore of the renal glomerulus.

slit lamp [AS, *slitan*; Gk, *lampein*, to shine], an instrument used in ophthalmology for examining the external, surface, and internal segments of the eye. A high-intensity beam of light is projected through a narrow slit, and a cross section of

S

the illuminated part of the eye is examined through a magnifying lens.

slit-lamp microscope, a microscope for ophthalmic examination. It permits the viewer to examine the endothelium of the posterior surface of the cornea in a projected band of light that is shaped like a slit.

slit-scan radiography, a technique for producing radiographs of body structures without length distortion by scanning a fan-shaped beam of x-rays through a narrow-slit collimator. The beam divergence perpendicular to the scan results in some distortion of width.

slit-ventricle syndrome, a condition of chronic headaches and cardiac disorders affecting shunt-dependent patients. Characteristics include small ventricles and slow reflux of the valve mechanism of the shunt.

SLO, abbreviation for **scanning laser ophthalmoscope.**

Slo-Phyllin, a trademark for a bronchodilator (theophylline).

slough /sluf/ [ME, *sluh*, husk], **1.** to shed or cast off dead tissue, such as cells of the endometrium, shed during menstruation. **2.** the tissue that has been shed.

slow channel, a membrane channel that is slow to become activated, such as the calcium channel, which allows calcium ions to diffuse across membranes.

slow diastolic depolarization [AS, *slaw*, dull], the slow loss of membrane polarization that occurs between action potentials in cells of the sinus and atrioventricular nodes.

Slow-K, a trademark for a slow-release tablet of an electrolyte replacement (potassium chloride).

slow pain, an unpleasant sensory experience that travels a multisynaptic route to the brain via slow-conducting, nonmyelinated nerve fibers.

slow pulse [AS, *slaw*, dull; L, *pulsare*, to beat], a pulse rate of less than 60 beats/min. The rate is common among older people, conditioned athletes, and patients receiving beta-blockers.

slow-reacting substance of anaphylaxis (SRS-A), a group of active substances, including histamine and leukotrienes, that are released during an anaphylactic reaction. They cause the smooth muscle contraction and vascular dilation that cause the signs and symptoms of anaphylaxis.

slow-response action potential, a cardiac action potential produced by the influx of calcium ions without the typical and much faster influx of sodium ions. Such an action potential has a slow upstroke, low amplitude, and consequent slow conduction.

slow stroking, a therapeutic massage technique of slow continuous movement of the hands over the paravertebral areas along the spine from the cervical through the lumbar region. Usually a lubricant is applied to the skin, and the index and middle fingers are used to stroke both sides of the spinal column simultaneously.

slow-twitch (ST) fiber, a muscle fiber that develops less tension more slowly than a fast-twitch fiber. The ST fiber is usually fatigue-resistant and has adequate oxygen and enzyme activity.

slow vestibular stimulation, a feeding therapy technique for disabled children, designed to promote parasympathetic loading.

slow virus, a virus, such as lentivirus, that remains dormant in the body after initial infection. Years may elapse before symptoms occur.

SLP, 1. abbreviation for **single-locus probe. 2.** abbreviation for **speech-language pathologist.**

slurred speech /slurd/ [D, *sleuren*, to drag; ME, *speche*], abnormal speech in which words are not enunciated clearly or completely but are run together or partially eliminated. The condition may be caused by weakness of the muscles of articulation, damage to a motor neuron, cerebellar disease, drug use, or carelessness.

slurry /slur'ē/ [ME, *sloor*, mud], a thin suspension of finely divided solids in a liquid.

Sly syndrome /slī/ [William S. Sly, American physician, b. 1932], a mucopolysaccharidosis caused by deficiency of an enzyme important for the degradation of various mucopolysaccharides. It is characterized by excretion of mucopolysaccharides in the urine and by granular inclusions in granulocytes. Onset is between 1 and 2 years of age with mild-to-moderate Hurler-like features including dysostosis multiplex, pigeon breast, organomegaly, cardiac murmurs, short stature, and moderate mental retardation.

Sm, symbol for the element **samarium.**

smack, *slang*. heroin.

small bowel follow-through (SBF) test, an x-ray with contrast dye (usually barium) performed to identify abnormalities in the small bowel. X-ray films done at timed intervals follow the progression of the contrast medium through the small intestine.

small cardiac vein [AS, *smael*], one of the five tributaries of the coronary sinus that drain blood from the myocardium. It conveys blood from the back of the right atrium and the right ventricle.

smallest cardiac vein, one of the tiny vessels that drain deoxygenated blood from the myocardium into the atria. A few of these vessels end in the ventricles.

small for gestational age (SGA) infant, a newborn whose weight and size at birth fall below the tenth percentile of appropriate for gestational age infants, whether delivered at term or earlier or later than term. Factors associated with smallness or retardation of intrauterine growth other than genetic influences include any disorder causing short stature; malnutrition caused by placental insufficiency; and certain infectious agents, including cytomegalovirus, rubella virus, and *Toxoplasma gondii.* Other factors associated with the smallness of an SGA infant include cigarette smoking by the mother during pregnancy, her addiction to alcohol or heroin, and her having received methadone treatment. Asphyxia may be a significant risk for the SGA infant during labor and delivery if the condition is the result of placental insufficiency.

small intestine, the longest part of the digestive tract, extending for about 7 m from the pylorus of the stomach to the ileocecal junction. It is divided into the duodenum, jejunum, and ileum. It functions in digestion and is the major organ of absorption of prepared food.

smallpox /smôl′poks/ [AS, *smael* + *pocc*], a highly contagious and sometimes fatal viral disease characterized by fever, prostration, and a vesicular, pustular rash. It is caused by one of two species of poxvirus, variola minor (alastrim) or variola major, the latter being the severe and most common form of smallpox. Because human beings are the only reservoir for the virus, worldwide vaccination with vaccinia, a related poxvirus, has been effective in eradicating smallpox. The last recorded case in the world was in Somalia in 1977. Smallpox is a potential agent for bioterrorism.

smallpox vaccine, a vaccine prepared from dried smallpox virus. It is currently indicated only for laboratory workers and certain military personnel who could be exposed to pox-viruses, but this recommendation could change with bioterrorism concerns.

smallpox virus, variola virus.

small saphenous vein, a large superficial vein embedded in the subcutaneous fascia of the leg that passes behind the distal end of the fibula and up the back of the leg to penetrate deep fascia and join the popliteal vein posterior to the knee.

small sciatic nerve [AS, *smael*; Gk, *ischiadikos,* of the hip joint; L, *nervus*], the posterior femoral cutaneous nerve, which pierces the fascia and subdivides into filaments, supplying the skin from the level of the greater trochanter to the middle of the thigh.

SMBG, abbreviation for **self-monitoring of blood glucose.**

smear [AS, *smeoru,* grease], a laboratory specimen for microscopic examination prepared by spreading a thin film of tissue or fluid on a glass slide. A dye, stain, reagent, diluent, or lysing agent may be applied to the specimen, depending on the purpose of the examination.

smegma /smeg′mə/ [Gk, soap], a secretion of sebaceous glands, especially the foul-smelling secretion sometimes found under the foreskin of the penis and at the base of the labia minora near the glans clitoris.

smell [ME, *smellen,* to detect odors], **1.** the special sense that allows perception of odors through the stimulation of the olfactory nerves; olfaction. **2.** any odor, pleasant or unpleasant.

smelling salt [ME, *smellen*; AS, *sealt*], aromatized ammonium carbonate to which may be added ammonia. It is used as a stimulant to arouse a person who has fainted.

Smith fracture [Robert W. Smith, Irish surgeon, 1807–1873], a fracture of the wrist involving volar displacement and angulation of a distal bone fragment.

Smith-Lemli-Opitz syndrome /ō′pitz/ [John Marius Opitz, German-born pediatrician in United States, b. 1935], an autosomal-dominant syndrome consisting of hypertelorism and hernias and, in males, hypospadias, cryptorchidism, and bifid scrotum. Cardiac anomalies, laryngotracheal malformations, imperforate anus, renal defects, lung hypoplasia, and downslanted palpebral fissures may also be present.

Smith-Petersen nail [Marius N. Smith-Petersen, American surgeon, 1886–1953; AS, *naegel,* nail], a three-flanged, stainless steel nail used in orthopedic surgery to anchor the neck of the femur to its head in the repair of an intertrochanteric fracture.

smog, a polluting combination of smoke and fog in the atmosphere.

smoke inhalation [AS, *smoca*; L, *in,* within, *halare,* to breathe], the inhalation of noxious fumes or irritating particulate matter that may cause severe pulmonary damage. Respiratory burns are difficult to distinguish from simple smoke inhalation. Chemical pneumonitis, asphyxiation, and physical trauma to the respiratory passages may occur. Characteristics include irritation of the upper respiratory tract, singed nasal hairs, dyspnea, hypoxia, dusty gray sputum, rhonchi, rales, restlessness, anxiety, cough, and hoarseness. Pulmonary edema may develop up to 48 hours after exposure.

smokeless tobacco [AS, *smoca*; Sp, *tabaco*], **1.** chewing tobacco or tobacco powder that allows the stimulating components of tobacco to be absorbed through the digestive tract or through the mucus membrane in the case of snuff. **2.** a transdermal nicotine patch that can be affixed to the upper part of the body to satisfy the person's craving for nicotine.

smoking cessation assistance, a nursing intervention from the Nursing Interventions Classification (NIC) defined as helping another person to stop smoking.

smoking cessation behavior, a nursing outcome from the Nursing Outcomes Classification (NOC) defined as personal actions to eliminate tobacco use.

smooth chorion, the smooth (nonvillous) and membranous part of the chorion.

smooth muscle [AS, *smoth*], one of three kinds of muscle, composed of elongated, spindle-shaped cells in muscles not under voluntary control, such as the smooth muscle of the intestines, stomach, and other viscera. The nucleated cells of smooth muscle are arranged parallel to one another and to the long axis of the muscle they form. Smooth muscle fibers are shorter than striated muscle fibers, have only one nucleus per fiber, and are smooth in appearance.

smooth muscle relaxant, an agent that reduces the tone of smooth muscle, such as a bronchodilator or vasodilator.

smooth pursuit eye movement, the tracking by the eyes of a slowly moving object at a steady coordinated velocity.

smooth surface cavity, a cavity formed by decay that starts on surfaces of teeth without pits, fissures, or enamel faults.

SMR, abbreviation for **submucous resection.**

smudge cell [ME, *sogen*, to soil], a disrupted lymphocyte, sometimes seen during preparation of blood smears.

Sn, symbol for the element **tin.**

S.N., abbreviation for *student nurse*, used in signing nursing notes (in the United States).

S$_N$2, abbreviation for **bimolecular reaction.**

SNA, 1. abbreviation for **State Nurses Association. 2.** abbreviation for *Student Nurses Association.*

snail [AS, *snagel*, slug], an invertebrate of the order Gastropoda, several species of which are intermediate hosts of the blood flukes that cause angiostrongyliasis in humans.

snakebite [AS, *snacan*, to creep + *bitan*], a wound resulting from penetration of the flesh by the fangs or teeth of a snake. Bites by snakes known to be nonvenomous are treated as puncture wounds; those produced by an unidentified or poisonous snake require immediate attention.

snake venom [AS, *snacan*; L, *venenum*], a poison produced in glands of certain snakes and injected through fangs into a victim's flesh. The exact composition of snake venoms varies with different species, but generally they are complex mixtures of neurotoxins, proteolytic enzymes, and phosphatases. About 20 of more than 100 North American species of snakes are venomous. A venomous snakebite is considered a medical emergency.

snapper /snap′er/, any of various carnivorous marine fish of the family Lutjanidae found in tropical waters. They are often eaten by humans but sometimes contain ciguatoxin and can cause ciguatera.

snapping hip [ME, *snappen*; AS, *hype*], a condition in which a tendon slips over the greater trochanter of the femur when the hip is moved, possibly producing a loud, snapping sound.

snare /sner/ [AS, *sneare*, noose], a device designed for holding a wire noose, used in removing small stalklike growths. The operator tightens the wire around the stalk (peduncle), thus removing the growth.

Sneddon's syndrome /sned′ənz/ [Ian Bruce Sneddon, English dermatologist, b. 1915], a rare condition in which cerebral arteriopathy and ischemia are accompanied by diffuse noninflammatory livedo reticularis.

sneeze [AS, *snesen*, to sneeze], a sudden forceful involuntary expulsion of air through the nose and mouth occurring as a result of irritation to the mucous membranes of the upper respiratory tract.

Snellen chart [Hermann Snellen, Dutch ophthalmologist, 1834–1908], one of several charts used in testing visual acuity. Letters, numbers, or symbols are arranged on the chart in decreasing size from top to bottom.

Snellen's reflex [Hermann Snellen], unilateral congestion of the ear on stimulation of the distal end of the divided great auricular nerve.

Snellen test [Hermann Snellen], a test of visual acuity using a Snellen chart. The person being tested stands 20 feet from the chart and reads as many of the symbols as possible, reading each line and proceeding downward from the top. A score is assigned in the form of a ratio, comparing the subject's performance to that of a statistically normal subject's performance. For example, a person who can read at 20 feet what the average person can read at this distance has 20/20 vision, whereas a person who can read at 20 feet what the average person can read at 40 feet has 20/40 vision.

SNF, abbreviation for **skilled nursing facility.**

snore /snôr/, a harsh rough sound of breathing caused by vibration of the uvula and soft palate during sleep.

snout reflex [ME, *snoute*, muzzle], an abnormal sign elicited by tapping the nose, resulting in a marked facial grimace.

snowball sampling, a method of obtaining subjects for a study by soliciting names of potential subjects from those participating in the study.

snow blindness [AS, *snaw* + *blind*], a condition of photophobia, sometimes accompanied by keratitis or conjunctivitis, as a result of overexposure of the eyes to the glare of sun on snow.

SNP, 1. abbreviation for **sodium nitroprusside. 2.** abbreviation for **single-nucleotide polymorphism.**

S.N.P. abbreviation for **school nurse practitioner** or *student nurse practitioner.*

SNP analysis, analysis of single-nucleotide polymorphisms to assess artificially produced genetic modifications or identify different strains of an organism.

SNR, abbreviation for **signal-to-noise ratio.**

snuff, a powder that is inhaled through the nostrils.

snuff dipping, the practice of extracting juices from moist, fine-cut chewing tobacco placed in the mucobuccal fold of the mouth. The practice has been associated with an increased incidence of leukoplakia, tooth and gum diseases, and oral cancer.

snuffles [D, *snuffelen,* to sniff], a nasal discharge in infancy characteristic of congenital syphilis.

soap [L, *sapo*], a salt formed from fatty acids and an alkali. Soap cleanses because molecules of fat are attracted to the fatty part of the anions of soap in a water solution and are pulled off the dirty surface into the water.

SOAP /sōp′, es′ōā′pē′/, in a problem-oriented medical record, abbreviation for *subjective, objective, assessment,* and *plan,* the four parts of a written account of the health problem. In taking and charting the patient history and physical examination, a SOAP statement is made for each syndrome, problem, symptom, or diagnosis.

soapsuds enema (SSE) [L, *sapo*; D, *sudse,* marsh water; Gk, *enienai*], an evacuent enema made of 1 ounce of soft soap dissolved in 2 pints of hot water and administered at a temperature of 100° F (38° C). It acts by irritating the colon and stimulating peristalsis.

SOB, abbreviation for *short of breath.*

socia /sō′shē·ə/, an ectopic or displaced part of an organ, such as an accessory parotid gland.

social /so′shəl/, pertaining to societies or other groups of people.

Social Behavior Assessment Scale /sō′shəl/, a semistructured interview guide that elicits information from significant others regarding a patient's functioning.

social breakdown syndrome [L, *socius,* partner; AS, *brecan* + *dune*],

deterioration of social and interpersonal skills, work habits, and behavior seen in chronically hospitalized psychiatric patients. Symptoms are a result of the effects of long-term hospitalization rather than the primary illness and include excessive passivity, assumption of the chronic sick role, withdrawal, and apathy.

social class, a grouping of people with similar values, interests, income, education, and occupations.

social deviance, behavior that violates social standards, engendering anger, resentment, and a desire for punishment in a significant segment of the society or culture.

social interaction skills, a nursing outcome from the Nursing Outcomes Classification (NOC) defined as personal behaviors that promote effective relationships.

social involvement, a nursing outcome from the Nursing Outcomes Classification (NOC) defined as social interactions with persons, groups, or organizations.

socialization /sō′shəlīzā′shən/, **1.** the process by which an individual learns to live in accordance with the expectations and standards of a group or society, acquiring the beliefs, habits, values, and accepted modes of behavior primarily through imitation, family interaction, and educational systems; the procedure by which society integrates the individual. **2.** in psychoanalysis, the process of adjustment that begins in early childhood by which the individual becomes aware of the need to accommodate inner drives to the demands of external reality.

socialization enhancement, a nursing intervention from the Nursing Interventions Classification (NIC) defined as facilitation of another person's ability to interact with others.

socialized medicine /sō′shəlīzd/, a system for the delivery of health care in which the expense of care is borne by a governmental agency supported by taxation rather than being paid directly by the client on a fee-for-service or contract basis.

social learning theory, a concept that the impulse to behave aggressively is subject to the influence of learning, socialization, and experience.

social margin, the total of all resources (material, personal, and interpersonal) available to assist an individual in coping with stress.

social marketing, a nursing intervention from the Nursing Interventions Classification (NIC) defined as the use of marketing principles to influence the health beliefs, attitudes, and behaviors to benefit a target population.

social medicine, an approach to the prevention and treatment of disease that is based on the study of human heredity, environment, social structures, and cultural values.

social mobility, the process of moving upward or downward in the social hierarchy.

social motivation, an incentive or drive resulting from a sociocultural influence that initiates behavior toward a particular goal.

social network, an interconnected group of cooperating significant others, who may or may not be related, with whom a person interacts.

social network therapy, the gathering together of patient, family, and other social contacts into group sessions for the purpose of problem solving.

social order, the manner in which a society is organized and the rules and standards required to maintain that organization.

social phobia, an anxiety disorder characterized by a compelling desire for the avoidance of and a persistent, irrational fear of situations in which the individual may be exposed to scrutiny by others. Examples of such situations are speaking, eating, or performing in public and using public lavatories or transportation.

social psychiatry, a field of psychiatry based on the study of social, cultural, and ecologic influences on the development and course of mental diseases.

social psychology, the study of the effects of group membership on the behavior, attitudes, and beliefs of the individual.

social readjustment rating scale, a scale of 43 common events associated with some degree of disruption of an individual's life. The scale was developed by the psychologists T.J. Holmes and R. Rahe, who found that a number of serious physical disorders such as MI, peptic ulcer, and infections, as well as a variety of psychiatric disorders, were associated with an accumulation of 200 or more points on the rating scale within a period of 1 year. Most disruptive on one's life, according to the psychologists, was the death of a spouse, an event that warranted 100 points.

social sanctions, the measures used by a society to enforce its rules of acceptable behavior.

Social Security Act, a U.S. federal statute that provides for a national system of old age assistance, survivors' and old age insurance benefits, unemployment insurance and compensation, and other public welfare programs, including Medicare and Medicaid.

social support, a nursing outcome from the Nursing Outcomes Classification (NOC) defined as reliable assistance from others.

social support programs, services both paid and volunteer provided to older persons including visits with older individuals to decrease loneliness and social isolation, telephone contact for older persons

for similar purposes, and programs that provide a daily call with emergency procedures that go into effect if the telephone is not answered.

social theories of aging, concepts of social and psychologic adjustment in older persons. The theories include activity expressed in adoption of new roles and continuity, which includes retention of physical and social activities from the middle years.

social worker, a person with advanced education in dealing with social, emotional, and environmental problems associated with an illness or disability. A medical social worker usually has completed a master's degree program that includes experience in counseling patients and their families in a hospital setting. A **psychiatric social worker** may specialize in counseling individuals and families in dealing with social, emotional, or environmental problems pertaining to mental illness.

society /səsī'ətē/, a nation, community, or broad group of people who establish particular aims, beliefs, or standards of living and conduct.

Society for Advancement in Nursing (SAIN), a group established for advancement of the profession of nursing through higher education.

sociobiology /sō'sē·ō·bī·ol'əjē/ [L, *socius,* companion; Gk, *bios,* life, *logos,* science], the systematic study of biology as a basis for human behavior. Proponents contend that disease, stress, and aggression are natural pressures for maintaining an optimal level of population.

socioeconomic status /sō'sē·ō·ik'ənom'ik/ [L, *socius,* companion, *oeconomicus,* methodical, *status,* state], the position of an individual on a social-economic scale that measures such factors as education, income, type of occupation, place of residence, and in some populations heritage and religion.

sociogenic /-jen'ik/ [L, *socius;* Gk, *genesis,* origin], pertaining to personal or group activities that are motivated by social values and constraints.

sociolinguistics /-ling·gwis'tiks/, the study of the relationship between language and the social context in which it occurs.— **sociolinguistic,** *adj.*

sociology /sō'sē·ol'əjē/ [L, *socius;* Gk, *logos,* science], the study of group behavior within a society.

sociopath, popular term for antisocial personality.

sociopathy /sō'sē·op'əthē/ [L, *socius,* companion; Gk, *pathos,* disease], a personality disorder characterized by a lack of social responsibility and failure to adapt to ethical and social standards of the community.

sock aid, an adaptive device that enables disabled people who cannot reach their feet to don a pair of socks or stockings. One type consists of a dowel with a cuphook on the end.

socket, the part of a prosthesis into which the stump of the remaining limb fits. Most modern prosthetic sockets are made of plastic.

soda [It, *sodo,* solid], a compound of sodium, particularly sodium bicarbonate or sodium carbonate.

soda lime (SL), a mixture of sodium and calcium hydroxides used to absorb exhaled carbon dioxide in an anesthesia rebreathing system. Soda-lime glass beads are used in air-fluidized beds.

sodium (Na) /sṓdē-əm/ [soda; L, *ium*], a soft grayish metal of the alkaline metals group. Its atomic number is 11, and its atomic mass is 22.99. Sodium is one of the most important elements in the body. Sodium ions are involved in acid-base balance, water balance, transmission of nerve impulses, and contraction of muscles. Sodium is the chief electrolyte in interstitial fluid, and its interaction with potassium as the main intracellular electrolyte is critical to survival. A decrease in the sodium concentration of the interstitial fluid immediately decreases osmotic pressure, making it hypotonic to intracellular fluid osmotic pressure. The kidney is the chief regulator of sodium levels in body fluids. Sodium is also important in the transport of sodium and potassium ions through the cytoplasmic membrane.

sodium arsenite poisoning, a toxic condition caused by the ingestion of sodium arsenite, an insecticide and weed killer. The characteristic symptoms of arsenite poisoning are similar to those of arsenic poisoning, as is the treatment.

sodium barbital, the sodium salt of 5,5-diethylbarbituric acid, a hypnotic and sedative drug.

sodium benzoate, an antifungal agent also used in a test of liver function.

sodium bicarbonate, a common salt (baking soda), sodium is the most important cation in the extracellular fluid and bicarbonate is the most import buffer in the body. It is prescribed in the treatment of metabolic acidosis, gastric hyperacidity, and hyperkalemia to alkalinize the urine as part of the treatment for certain poisonings.

sodium channel blocking agent, any of a class of antiarrhythmic agents that prevent ectopic beats by acting on partially inactivated sodium channels to inhibit abnormal depolarizations.

sodium chloride, common table salt, used in various concentrations as a fluid and electrolyte replenisher, isotonic vehicle, irrigating solution, and enema.

sodium citrate, a sodium salt of citric acid, used as an anticoagulant for blood or plasma that is to be fractionated or for blood that is to be stored. It is also administered orally as a urinary alkalizer.

sodium ferric gluconate, a hematinic used especially in treatment of hemodialysis patients with iron deficiency anemia who are also receiving erythropoietin therapy.

sodium fluoride poisoning, a chronic condition of fluorine poisoning that occurs in some communities where the fluorine concentration in the water supply exceeds 1 ppm. Signs of the condition include mottling of tooth enamel and severe osteosclerosis.

sodium hydroxide, NaOH, a strongly alkaline and caustic compound. It is used as an alkalizing agent in pharmaceuticals.

sodium hypochlorite solution, a 5% aqueous solution of NaOCl (common bleach) used as a disinfectant for utensils and surfaces not harmed by its bleaching action.

sodium iodide, an iodine supplement prescribed in the treatment of thyrotoxic crisis and neonatal thyrotoxicosis, and in the management of hyperthyroidism before thyroidectomy.

sodium lactate injection, an electrolyte replenisher that has been prescribed for metabolic acidosis.

sodium nitrite, an antidote for cyanide poisoning. It is also used as a preservative in cured meats and other foods.

sodium nitroprusside (SNP), a vasodilator prescribed primarily in the emergency treatment of hypertensive crises and in heart failure.

sodium perborate, an oxygen-liberating antiseptic ($NaBO_2 \cdot H_2O_2 \cdot 3H_2O$) that may be used in treating necrotizing ulcerative gingivitis and other kinds of gingival inflammation and bleaching pulpless teeth.

sodium phenylbutyrate, an agent used as adjunctive treatment to control the hyperammonemia of pediatric urea cycle enzyme disorders.

sodium phosphate, a saline cathartic prescribed to achieve prompt, thorough evacuation of the bowel and, in lower dosage, for laxative effect.

sodium phosphate P 32, an antineoplastic, antipolycythemic radioactive agent. It is prescribed for treatment of polycythemia vera, for neoplasms, including myelocytic leukemia, and for localizing tumors of the eye.

sodium phosphates, a combination of monobasic and dibasic sodium phosphates used as an electrolyte replenisher.

sodium-potassium pump, a protein that transports sodium and potassium ions across cell membranes against their

S

concentration gradients. Sodium is normally moved from the inside of the cell, where its concentration is low, to the extracellular fluid, where its concentration is much higher. Potassium is moved in the opposite direction.

sodium sulfate, a saline cathartic for chronic constipation caused by peristaltic disorders. It is prescribed to achieve prompt, thorough evacuation of the bowel and, in lower dosage, for laxative effect.

sodium sulfide, the monosulfide salt of sodium, Na₂S, a flammable, highly irritating compound having a variety of industrial uses.

sodomist /sod′əmist/ [Sodom, biblical city in ancient Palestine], a person who practices sodomy.

sodomy /sod′əmē/ [Sodom, biblical city in ancient Palestine], **1.** anal intercourse. **2.** intercourse with an animal. **3.** a vague term for "unnatural" sexual intercourse. **—sodomize,** v.

soft chancre [AS, softe; Fr, canker], a usually painless local genital ulcer that follows an infection by Haemophilus ducreyi. It is accompanied by suppuration of the inguinal lymphatic nodes, or inguinal buboes. Complications may include phimosis, urethral stricture or fistula, and marked tissue destruction.

soft contact lens (SCL) [AS, softe; L, contingere + lens, lentil], a contact lens made of a flexible plastic material that can be shaped more easily to fit the eyeball than a rigid gas-permeable lens and typically provide good initial comfort. Among the disadvantages of soft lenses are that they are more easily damaged, may not provide vision as sharp as alternative methods in certain cases, and must be disinfected periodically because they tend to harbor bacteria. Most contact lens patients are currently being fit into hyperoxygen-permeable silicone-hydrogel soft lenses.

soft data [AS, softe; L, datum, something given], health information that is mainly subjective as provided by the patient and the patient's family.

soft diet, a diet that is soft in texture, low in residue, easily digested, and well tolerated. It provides the essential nutrients in the form of liquids and semisolid foods such as milk, fruit juices, eggs, cheese, custards, tapioca and puddings, strained soups and vegetables, rice, ground beef and lamb, fowl, fish; mashed, boiled, or baked potatoes; wheat, corn, or rice cereals; and breads.

softening of bones /sô′fəning, sof′əning/ [AS, softe + ban], any disease that results in a loss of the mineral content of the bones.

soft fibroma, a fibroma that contains many cells.

soft mechanical diet, a diet containing ground or pureed foods that are easy to chew, often used by people who have dental problems or are edentulous. It can contain any foods allowed on a regular diet, but in an easy to chew and swallow presentation.

soft neurologic sign, a mild or slight neurologic abnormality that is difficult to detect or interpret.

soft palate, the structure composed of mucous membrane, muscular fibers, and mucous glands, suspended from the posterior border of the hard palate forming the roof of the mouth. When the soft palate rises, as in swallowing and in sucking, it separates the nasal cavity and the nasopharynx from the posterior part of the oral cavity and the oral part of the pharynx.

soft radiation, a relatively long wavelength with less penetrating radiation than short wavelength radiation.

soft water [AS, softe + waeter], water that does not contain salts of calcium or magnesium, which precipitate soap solutions.

sol, a colloidal state in which a solid is suspended throughout a liquid, such as a soap or starch in water. The fluidity of cytoplasm depends on its sol/gel balance.

sol., abbreviation for **solution.**

Solanaceae /sō′lənā′si·ē/, a family of plants that includes the genus Solanum, or nightshades, and more than 1800 species, including deadly nightshade (belladonna), henbane, tomatoes, and potatoes.

solanaceous /sō′lənā′shəs/, pertaining to plants of the Solanaceae family or substances derived from them.

solanine /sō′lənēn/, a steroidal alkaloid found in several species of Solanum such as the nightshades and the green spots on potatoes. It causes hemolysis, CNS depression, and often fatal respiratory failure.

Solanum /sōlā′nəm/ [L, nightshade], a large genus of plants of the family Solanaceae. It includes the potato, tomato, eggplant, several of the nightshades, and many poisonous and medicinal species.

solarium /sōler′ē·əm/ [L, terrace exposed to sun], a large, sunny room or area serving as a lounge for ambulatory patients in a hospital.

solar plexus /sō′lər/ [L, sol, sun, plexus, network], a dense network of nerve fibers and ganglia that surrounds the roots of the celiac and superior mesenteric arteries at the level of the first lumbar vertebra. It is one of the great autonomic plexuses of the body in which the nerve fibers of the sympathetic system and the parasympathetic system combine.

solar radiation, the emission and diffusion of actinic rays from the sun.

Overexposure may result in sunburn, keratosis, skin cancer, accelerated aging, or lesions associated with photosensitivity.

solar sneeze reflex [L, *sol*, sun; ME, *snesen;* L, *reflectere*, to bend back], a sneeze that may be caused by exposure to bright sunlight.

solar therapy [L, *sol*, sun; Gk, *therapeia*, treatment], the therapeutic use of sunlight.

solder /sod′ər/ [L, *solidatio*, making solid], **1.** *n*, a fusible metal or alloy used to unite pieces of metals with higher fusion temperatures. **2.** *v*, to fasten together pieces of metal through the use of this material.

sole [L, *solea*, sole of foot], the plantar surface of the foot.

soleus /sō′lē·əs/ [L, *solea*, sole of foot], one of three superficial posterior muscles of the leg. It is a broad flat muscle lying just under the gastrocnemius. The soleus plantar flexes the foot.

Solganal, a trademark for a gold salt antirheumatic (aurothioglucose).

solid /sol′id/ [L, *solidus*], **1.** a dense body, figure, structure, or substance that has length, breadth, and thickness; is not a liquid or a gas; contains no significant cavity or hollowness; and has no breaks or openings on its surface. **2.** describing such a body, figure, structure, or substance.

solifenacin, an anticholinergic used to treat overactive bladder.

Soliris, a trademark for eculizumab.

solitary coin lesion /sol′iter·ē/ [L, *solitarius*, standing alone, *cuneus*, wedge, *laesus*, injury], a nodule identified on a chest radiographic film by clear normal lung tissue surrounding it. It is often malignant.

solitary play, a form of play among a group of children within the same room or area in which each child engages in an independent activity, using toys that are different from the others' and showing no interest in joining in or interfering with the play of others.

soln, abbreviation for **solution.**

solubility /sol′yəbil′itē/ [L, *solubilis*, able to dissolve], **1.** the maximum amount of a solute that can dissolve in a specific solvent under a given temperature and pressure. **2.** the concentration of a solute in a solvent at its saturation point.

soluble amyloid beta protein precursor test, a test for a decrease in levels of beta amyloid in CSF, used in the diagnosis of Alzheimer's disease and other forms of senile dementia.

Solu-Cortef, a trademark for a glucocorticoid (hydrocortisone sodium succinate).

Solu-Medrol, a trademark for a glucocorticoid (methylprednisolone sodium succinate).

solute /sol′yōōt, sō′lōōt/ [L, *solutus*, dissolved], a substance dissolved in a solution.

solution (sol., soln) /səlōō′shən/ [L, *solutus*], a mixture of one or more substances dissolved in another substance. The molecules of each of the substances disperse homogenously and do not change chemically. A solution may be a gas, a liquid, or a solid.

solvent /sol′vənt/ [L, *solvere*, to dissolve], **1.** any liquid in which another substance can be dissolved. **2.** *informal.* an organic liquid such as benzene, carbon tetrachloride, and other volatile petroleum distillates that, when inhaled, can cause intoxication, as well as damage to mucous membranes of the nose and throat and tissues of the kidney, liver, and brain.

soma /sō′mə/ *pl.* **somas, somata** [Gk, body], **1.** the body, as distinguished from the mind or psyche. **2.** the body, excluding germ cells. **3.** the body of a cell.—**somal, somatic** /sōmat′ik/, *adj.*

Soma, a trademark for a skeletal muscle relaxant (carisoprodol).

somatic cell /sōmat′ik/, any of the cells of body tissue that have the diploid number of chromosomes, as distinguished from germ cells, which contain the haploid number.

somatic chromosome, any autosome in a diploid or somatic cell.

somatic delusion, a false notion or belief concerning body image or body function.

somatic effects, effects of radiation, such as cancer, that occur in an exposed individual.

somatic mutation [Gk, *soma*, body; L, *mutare*, to change], a sudden change in the chromosomal material in somatic cell nuclei affecting derived cells but not offspring.

somatic pain, generally well-localized pain that results from the activation of peripheral nociceptors without injury to the peripheral nerve or CNS.

somatic therapy, a form of treatment pertaining to the body that affects one's physiologic functioning.

somatist /sō′mətist/, a psychotherapist or other health professional who believes that every neurosis and psychosis has an organic cause.

somatization /sō′mətīzā′shən/ [Gk, *soma*, body], a process whereby a mental event is expressed in a body disorder or physical symptom. Examples are peptic ulcers and asthma.

somatization disorder [Gk, *soma + izein*, to cause], a psychiatric disorder characterized by recurrent multiple physical complaints and symptoms for which there is no organic cause. It is classified as a somatoform disorder in *DSM-IV*. The symptoms vary according to the individual and the underlying emotional conflict. Some common symptoms are GI dysfunction, paralysis, temporary blindness, cardiopulmonary distress, painful or irregular

S

menstruation, sexual indifference, and pain during intercourse. Hypochondriasis may develop if the condition is untreated.

somatodyspraxia /-disprak′sē·ə/, an impairment in the ability to plan skilled movements that are nonhabitual. Patients may be able to learn specific motor skills with practice but cannot accomplish unfamiliar tasks.

somatoform disorder /sōmat′əfôrm, sō′mətōfôrm′/ [Gk, *soma;* L, *forma,* form], any of a group of disorders, characterized by symptoms suggesting physical illness or disease, for which there are no demonstrable organic causes or physiologic dysfunctions. The symptoms are usually the physical manifestations of some unresolved intrapsychic factor or conflict.

somatogenesis /sō′matəjen′əsis/ [Gk, *soma* + *genein,* to produce], **1.** in embryology, the development of the body from the germ plasm. **2.** the development of a physical disease or of symptoms from an organic pathophysiological cause.—**somatogenetic, somatogenic,** *adj.*

somatomedin-C test, a blood test most commonly used to detect levels of somatomedin-C, also called insulin-like growth factor. Screening for somatomedin-C provides an accurate reflection of the mean plasma concentration of growth hormone.

somatomegaly /sō′matōmeg′əlē/ [Gk, *soma* + *megas,* large], a condition in which the body is abnormally large as a result of an excessive secretion of somatotropin or an inadequate secretion of somatostatin.

somatoplasm /sô′mətōplaz′əm/ [Gk, *soma* + *plasma,* something formed], the nonreproductive protoplasmic material of the body cells, as distinguished from the reproductive material of the germ cells.

somatopleure /sô′mətōplŏŏr′/ [Gk, *soma* + *pleura,* side], the lateral and ventral tissue layer that forms the body wall of the early developing embryo.—**somatopleural,** *adj.*

somatosensory evoked potential (SEP) /-sen′sərē/ [Gk, *soma;* L, *sentire,* to feel], evoked potential elicited by repeated stimulation of the pain and touch systems. It is the least reliable of the evoked potentials studied as monitors of neurologic function during surgery.

somatosensory system, the components of the central and peripheral nervous systems that receive and interpret sensory information from organs in the joints, ligaments, muscles, and skin. This system processes information about the length, degree of stretch, tension, and contraction of muscles; pain; temperature; pressure; and joint position.

somatosplanchnic /-splangk′nik/ [Gk, *soma* + *splanchna,* viscera], pertaining to the trunk of the body and the viscera.

somatostatin /sō′matōstat′in/, a hormone produced in the hypothalamus that inhibits the release of somatotropin (growth hormone) from the anterior pituitary gland. It also is produced in other parts of the body and inhibits the release of certain hormones, including thyrotropin, adrenocorticotropic hormone, glucagon, insulin, and cholecystokinin, and of some enzymes, including pepsin, renin, secretin, and gastrin.

somatotherapy /-ther′əpē/, the treatment of physical disorders, as distinguished from psychotherapy.

somatotropic /-trop′ik/ [Gk, *soma,* body, *trope,* a turn], pertaining to an agent that influences the body or body cells.

somatotype /sō′mətōtīp′/ [Gk, *soma* + *typos,* mark], **1.** body build or physique. **2.** the classification of individuals according to body build based on certain physical characteristics. The primary types are **ectomorph, endomorph,** and **mesomorph.**

somatovisceral reflex /-vis′ərəl/, a reflex in which visceral functions are activated or inhibited by somatic sensory stimulation.

somatrem /sō′mətrem/, a synthetic polypeptide growth hormone produced by recombinant DNA technology. It is prescribed for growth promotion when patients are not growing because of limited endogenous growth hormone secretion. It is also used to limit cachexia in AIDS patients undergoing antiretroviral treatment and as replacement therapy in adults with documented growth hormone deficiency.

Somatuline Depot, a trademark for lanreotide.

Somavert, a trademark for pegvisomant.

somite /sō′mīt/ [Gk, *soma,* body], any of the paired segmented masses of mesodermal tissue that form along the length of the neural tube during the early stage of embryonic development in vertebrates.

somite embryo, an embryo in any stage of development between the formation of the first and last pairs of somites, which in humans occurs in the third and fourth weeks after fertilization of the ovum.

somnambulism /somnam′byəliz′əm/ [L, *somnus,* sleep, *ambulare,* to walk], **1.** a condition occurring during stage 3 or 4 of nonrapid eye movement sleep that is characterized by complex motor activity, usually culminating in leaving the bed and walking about. The person has no recall of the episode on awakening. The episodes usually last from several minutes to half an hour or longer. **2.** a hypnotic state in which the person has full possession of the senses but no recollection of the episode.

somniloquence /somnil′əkwəns/, talking during sleep or under hypnosis.

somnolent /som'nələnt/ [L, *somnolentia,* sleepy], **1.** the condition of being sleepy or drowsy. **2.** tending to cause sleepiness. —**somnolence,** *n.*

somnolent detachment, in psychology, a term introduced by H.S. Sullivan for a type of security operation in which a person falls asleep when confronted by a highly threatening, anxiety-producing experience.

Somogyi effect (phenomenon) [Michael Somogyi, American biochemist, 1883–1971; Gk, *phainomenon*], a DM rebound effect in which an overdose of insulin induces hypoglycemia. This releases hormones that stimulate lipolysis, gluconeogenesis, and glycogenolysis, leading to hyperglycemia and ketosis. Treatment involves gradually lowering the insulin dose to achieve an optimal level.

Sonata /so-nah'tah/, a trademark for a preparation of zaleplon, used to treat insomnia.

sonographer /sōnog'rəfər/, an allied health professional with special training in the use of ultrasound equipment for diagnostic and therapeutic purposes.

sopor /sō'pər/ [L, deep sleep], a sleep that is as deep or sound as the state of stupor.

soporiferous /sop'ərif'ərəs/ [L *sopor,* deep sleep, *ferre,* to bear], tending to cause deep sleep, such as an agent that induces deep sleep.

soporific /sop'ərif'ik/ [L, *sopor,* deep sleep, *facere,* to make], **1.** pertaining to a substance, condition, or procedure that causes sleep. **2.** a soporific drug.

sorafenib, a miscellaneous antineoplastic used to treat advanced and metastatic murine renal cell carcinoma.

sorbent /sôr'bənt/ [L, *sorbere,* to swallow], **1.** an agent that attracts and retains substances by absorption or adsorption. **2.** the property of a substance that allows it to interact with another compound, usually to make it bind.

sorbic acid /sôr'bik/, a compound occurring naturally in berries of the mountain ash. Commercial sorbic acid derived from acetaldehyde is used in fungicides, food preservatives, lubricants, and plasticizers.

Sorbitrate, a trademark for an antianginal (isosorbide dinitrate).

sordes /sôr'dēz/ *pl.* **sordes** [L, *sordere,* to be dirty], dirt or debris, especially the crusts consisting of food, microorganisms, and epithelial cells that accumulate on teeth and lips during a febrile illness or one in which the patient takes nothing by mouth. Sordes gastricae is undigested food and mucus in the stomach.

sore /sôr, sōr/ [AS, *sar*], **1.** a wound, ulcer, or lesion. **2.** tender or painful.

sore throat [AS, *sar + throte*], any inflammation of the larynx, pharynx, or tonsils.

Sorrin's operation, a surgical technique for treating a periodontal abscess, used especially when the marginal gingiva appears healthy and provides no access to the abscess.

s.o.s., abbreviation for the Latin phrase *si opus sit,* "if necessary."

sotalol /so'tah-lol/, a noncardioselective beta-adrenergic blocking agent, used in the treatment of life-threatening ventricular arrhythmias.

souffle /sōō'fəl/ [Fr, breath], a soft murmur heard through a stethoscope. When detected over the uterus in a pregnant woman, it is usually coincident with the maternal pulse and is caused by blood circulating in the large uterine arteries.

soul food [AS, *sawel + foda*], an American cuisine typically associated with African-Americans of the southern United States.

sound [L, *sub,* under, *unde,* wave], an emission detected by an instrument used to locate the opening of a cavity or canal, to test the patency of a canal, to ascertain the depth of a cavity, or to reveal the contents of a canal or cavity.

sound waves, longitudinal waves of mechanical energy that transmit the vibrations interpreted as sound.

Souques's sign /sōōks/ [Alexandre A. Souques, French neurologist, 1860–1944], in patients with a disease of the corpus striatum, the failure of a seated patient to extend the legs when the chair is pushed backward. The legs normally would be extended to prevent overbalancing.

source-to-image-receptor distance (SID) /sôrs, sōrs/ [OFr, *sourse,* origin; L, *imago,* likeness], the distance between the focal spot on the target of an x-ray tube and the image receptor as measured along the beam.

Southern blot test /suth'ərn/, a gene analysis method used in identification of specific DNA fragments and in diagnosis of cancers and hemoglobinopathies.

Sp, sp., spp., abbreviation for **species.**

SPA, abbreviation for **sperm penetration assay.**

space [L, *spatium*], an area, region, or segment of the body such as the complemental spaces in the pleural cavity that are not occupied by lung tissue and the lymph spaces occupied by lymph.

space adaptation syndrome, the ability to accommodate changes in cardiac function, bone mineral changes, and muscle atrophy while in the weightless state of a space traveler.

space maintainer, a fixed or removable appliance for preserving the space created by the premature loss of one or more teeth.

S

space medicine, a branch of medicine concerned with the effects of travel in space, beyond the atmosphere and pull of gravity, including weightlessness, motion sickness, and restricted physical activity.

space obtainer, an appliance for increasing the space between adjoining teeth.

spacer /spās′ər/ [L, *spatium,* space], on a metered dose inhaler, a chamber between the inhaler canister and the patient's mouth where droplets of medication can slow down and evaporate so that there is less direct impact on the oropharynx, with more medication delivered to the lower respiratory tract instead of being lost in the mouth. This is especially helpful for children.

space regainer, a fixed or removable appliance for moving a displaced secondary tooth into its normal position in a dental arch.

sparfloxacin, an antiinfective prescribed to treat community-acquired pneumonia and chronic bronchitis caused by *Klebsiella pneumoniae, Haemophilus influenzae, H. parainfluenzae,* and *Moraxella catarrhalis.*

sparganosis /spär′gənō′sis/ [Gk, *sparganon,* swaddling clothes, *osis,* condition], an infection with larvae of the fish tapeworm of the pseudogenus Sparganum. It is characterized by painful subcutaneous swellings or swelling and destruction of the eye. Treatment includes surgery and local injection of ethyl alcohol to kill the larvae.

Sparine, a trademark for a phenothiazine antipsychotic and antiemetic (promazine hydrochloride).

spasm /spaz′əm/ [Gk, *spasmos*], **1.** an involuntary muscle contraction of sudden onset such as habit spasms, hiccups, stuttering, or a tic. **2.** a convulsion or seizure. **3.** a sudden transient constriction of a blood vessel, bronchus, esophagus, pylorus, ureter, or other hollow organ.

spasmodic asthma /spazmäd′ik/ [Gk, *spasmos* + *asthma,* panting], an airway obstruction caused by spasms of the bronchioles and inflammation of the bronchial mucosa and characterized by paroxysms of wheezing and coughing.

spasmodic dysmenorrhea /spazmod′ik/, difficult menstruation accompanied by painful contractions of the uterus.

spasmodic dysphonia [Gk, *spasmodes,* spasms, *dys,* bad, *phone,* voice], a speech disorder in which phonation is intermittently blocked by spasms of the larynx.

spasmodic stricture [Gk, *spasmodes;* L, *strictura,* compression], a narrowing of a passage in which there is no organic change, merely muscle spasms.

spasmodic tic [Gk, *spasmodes;* Fr, *tic*], any repetitive movement in which

spasmodic muscle group contractions occur at variable intervals.

spasmodic torticollis [Gk, *spasmodes;* L, *tortus,* twisted, *collum,* neck], a condition in which the head is inclined to one side as a result of episodes of spasms of the neck muscles. It is often transient, and examination seldom reveals a physical cause.

spasmogen /spaz′məjən/, any substance that can produce smooth muscle contractions. Examples are histamine, bradykinin, and serotonin.

spastic /spas′tik/ [Gk, *spastikos,* drawing in], pertaining to spasms or other uncontrolled contractions of the skeletal muscles.—**spasticity,** *n.*

spastic aphonia, a condition in which a person is unable to speak because of spasmodic contraction of the abductor muscles of the throat.

spastic bladder, a form of neurogenic bladder caused by a lesion of the spinal cord above the voiding reflex center. It is marked by loss of bladder control and bladder sensation, incontinence, and automatic, interrupted, incomplete voiding. It is most often caused by trauma but may result from a tumor or MS.

spastic constipation [Gk, *spasmos,* spasm; L, *constipare,* to crowd together], a form of constipation associated with neurasthenia and constrictive spasms in part of the intestine. The condition may be a sign of lead poisoning.

spastic diplegia, paralysis of corresponding parts on both sides of the body.

spastic dysarthria, a type of motor speech disorder affecting speech articulation, caused by lesions of the corticobulbar tracts. It affects strength, speed, precision, ROM, and coordination of speech musculature movements.

spastic dysuria, difficulty in urination caused by bladder spasms.

spastic entropion, entropion that arises from excessive contracture of the oricularis oculi muscle.

spastic gait [Gk, *spasmos,* spasm; ONorse, *gata*], a pattern of walking in which the legs are stiff, the feet plantar-flexed, and movements made by circumduction. The steps also may be accompanied by toe dragging.

spastic hemiplegia, paralysis of one side of the body with increased tendon reflexes and uncontrolled contraction occurring in the affected muscles.

spastic ileus [Gk, *spasmos,* spasm, *eilein,* to twist], a form of intestinal obstruction caused by bowel spasms.

spasticity /spastis′itē/ [Gk, *spastikos,* drawing in], a form of muscular hypertonicity with increased resistance to stretch. It usually involves the flexors of the arms and the extensors of the legs. The hypertonicity is often associated with weakness, increased deep reflexes, and diminished superficial reflexes.

spastic paralysis, an abnormal condition characterized by the involuntary contraction of one or more muscles with associated loss of muscular function.

spastic paraplegia [Gk, *spasmos,* spasm, *para* + *plege,* stroke], a form of partial paralysis mainly affecting older people. It is accompanied by irritability and spastic contractions of the leg muscles.

spastic strabismus [Gk, *spasmos* + *strabismos,* squint], squint caused by spasmodic contractions of ocular muscles.

spatial dance /spā'shəl/ [L, *spatium,* space; ME, *dauncen,* to drag along], the body shifts or movements used by individuals as they try to adjust the distance between themselves and other individuals.

spatial relationships, 1. orientation in space; the ability to locate objects in the three-dimensional external world, using visual or tactile recognition, and to make a spatial analysis of the observed information. **2.** the relative locations of staff and equipment in an OR, with particular emphasis on what is sterile, clean, or contaminated.

spatial resolution, the ability of an imaging system to discriminate between two adjacent high-contrast objects.

spatial zones, the areas of personal space in which most people interact. Four basic spatial zones are the intimate zone, in which distance between individuals is less than 18 inches; the personal zone, between 18 inches and 4 feet; the social zone, extending between 4 and 12 feet; and the public zone, beyond 12 feet.

spatula /spach'ə·lə/ [L], **1.** a flat, blunt, usually flexible instrument, used for spreading plasters and for mixing ointments and masses. **2.** a structure having a flat, blunt end.

SPCA, abbreviation for *serum prothrombin conversion accelerator* (factor VII, one of the coagulation factors).

SPE, abbreviation for **sucrose polyester.**

Spearman's rho /spir'mənz rō'/ [Charles E. Spearman, English psychologist, 1863–1945; *rho,* 17th letter in the Greek alphabet], a statistical test for correlation between two rank-ordered scales. It yields a statement of the degree of interdependence of the scores of the two scales.

special care unit /spesh'əl/ [L, *specialis,* individual], a hospital unit with the necessary specialized equipment and personnel for handling critically ill or injured patients, such as neonatal, burn unit, or cardiac care unit.

special gene system, a plasmid, transposon, or other DNA fragment that is able to transfer genetic information from one cell to another.

specialing /spesh'əling/, *informal.* **1.** in psychiatric nursing, the constant attendance of a professional staff member on a disturbed patient to protect the patient from harming the self or others and to observe the patient's behavior. **2.** in nursing, the giving of nursing care to only one person, such as when acting as a private duty nurse or when caring for a patient whose needs are so great that a nurse is required at all times.

specialist /spesh'əlist/, a health care professional who practices a specialty. A specialist usually has advanced clinical training and may have a postgraduate academic degree.

special sense, the sense of sight, smell, taste, touch, or hearing.

specialty /spesh'əltē/ [L, *specialis*], a branch of medicine or nursing in which the professional is specially qualified to practice by having attended an advanced program of study, passed an examination given by an organization of the members of the specialty, or gained experience through extensive practice in the specialty.

specialty care, specialized medical services provided by a physician specialist.

species (Sp) /spē'sēz, spē'shēz/ *pl.* **species (sp., spp.)** [L, form], the category of living things below genus in rank. A species is a genetically distinct group of demes that share a common gene pool and are reproductively isolated from all other such groups.

species immunity, a form of natural immunity shared by all members of a species.

species-specific [L, *specere,* to see, *facere,* to make], **1.** characteristic of a particular species. **2.** having a characteristic effect on, or interaction with, cells, tissues, or membranes of a particular species; said of an antigen, drug, or infective agent.

species-specific antigen, an antigen that is restricted to a single species but occurs in all members of that species.

specific absorption rate (SAR) /spisif'ik/ [L, *species,* form], in hyperthermia treatment, the rate of absorption of heat energy (W) per unit mass of tissue in units of watts per kilogram (W/kg).

specific activity, 1. the radioactivity of a radioisotope per unit mass of the element or compound, expressed in microcuries per millimole or disintegrations per second per milligram. **2.** the relative radioactivity per unit mass, expressed as counts per minute per milligram.

specific disease, a disorder caused by a special pathogenic organism.

S

specific granule, a secondary granule in the cytoplasm of polymorphonuclear leukocytes that contains lysozyme, vitamin B_{12}–binding protein, neutral proteases, and lactoferrin.

specific granule deficiency, an immunodeficiency state associated with pyodermas and abscesses in which neutrophils fail to make specific granules.

specific gravity (sp. gr.), the ratio of the density of a substance to the density of another substance accepted as a standard. The usual standard for liquids and solids is water. Hydrogen is the usual standard for gases.

specific immunoglobulin, a preparation obtained from human plasma that is preselected for its high antibody count against a specific pathogen.

specificity /spes'əfis'itē/ [L, *species*, form, *facere*, to make], the quality of being distinctive.

specificity of association, the uniqueness of a relationship between a causal factor and the occurrence of a disease.

specific rates, statistical rates in which the events in both the numerator and the denominator are restricted to a specific subgroup of a population.

specific ulcer [L, *species* + *facere*, to make, *ilcus*], ulcer associated with a specific disease, as a syphilitic ulcer.

specific viscosity [L, *species* + *facere*, to make, *viscosus*, sticky], the internal friction of a fluid, which may be measured by comparing the rate of flow of the fluid through a tube with the rate of a standard liquid under standard conditions.

specimen /spes'imən/ pl. **specimens** [L, *specere*, to look], a small sample of something, intended to show the nature of the whole, such as a urine specimen.

specimen management, a nursing intervention from the Nursing Interventions Classification (NIC) defined as obtaining, preparing, and preserving a specimen for a laboratory test.

speckled dystrophy of the cornea /spek'əld/, a familial condition characterized by irregular mottling of the cornea by spots that vary in shape and size, some with clear centers and sharp margins.

speckled pattern, an immunofluorescence pattern produced when serum from a patient with a particular connective tissue disease is placed in contact with human epithelial cells and stained with fluorochrome-labeled animal antisera. Fine, coarse, or large speckles are observed in disorders such as lupus erythematosus and rheumatoid arthritis.

SPECT, abbreviation for **single-photon emission computed tomography.**

SPECTamine, a trademark for a lipid-soluble brain-imaging agent (iofetamine hydrochloride ^{123}I).

spectator ions /spek'tātər/, ions that are not involved in a chemical reaction.

Spectazole, a trademark for an antifungal (econazole nitrate).

spectinomycin hydrochloride /spek'tinōmī'sin/, an antibiotic prescribed in the treatment of gonorrhea and certain infections in penicillin-allergic patients.

Spectrocin, a trademark for a fixed-combination topical drug containing antibacterials (neomycin bacitracin and polymyxin B) and a local anesthetic (lidocaine).

spectrometer /spektrom'ətər/ [L, *spectrum*, image; Gk, *metron*, measure], an instrument for measuring wavelengths of rays of a spectrum, the deviation of refracted rays, and the angles between faces of a prism.

spectrometry /spektrom'ətrē/, the process of measuring wavelengths of light and other electromagnetic waves.—**spectrometric,** *adj.*

spectrophotometry /spek'trōfətom'ətrē/, the measurement of color in a solution by determining the amount of light absorbed in the ultraviolet, infrared, or visible spectrum, widely used in clinical chemistry to calculate the concentration of substances in solution.—**spectrophotometric,** *adj.*

spectroscope /spek'trə·skōp/ [L, *spectrum*, spectrum; Gk, *skopein*, to examine], an instrument for developing and analyzing spectra.

spectroscopy /spek·tros'kə·pē/ [L, *spectrum*, spectrum; Gk, *skopein*, to examine], the propagation and analysis of spectra; examination by means of a spectroscope.

spectrum /spek'trəm/ pl. **spectra** [L, image], **1.** a range of phenomena or properties occurring in increasing or decreasing magnitude. Radiant or electromagnetic energy is arranged on the basis of wavelength and frequency. **2.** the range of effectiveness of an antibiotic. A broad-spectrum antibiotic is effective against a wide range of microorganisms.

specular reflection, a reflection from a smooth surface, such as a mirror. In ultrasonography, such reflections are from smooth surfaces such as organ walls.

speculum /spek'yələm/ [L, mirror], a retractor used to separate the walls of a cavity to make examination possible, such as an ear speculum, an eye speculum, a nasal speculum, or a vaginal speculum.

speech [ME, *speche*], **1.** the utterance of articulate vocal sounds that form words of a language to give expression to one's thoughts or ideas. **2.** communication by means of spoken words. **3.** the faculty of language production, which involves the complex coordination of the muscles and nerves of the organs of articulation.

speech abnormalities, abnormal or difficult function of speech.

speech centers [AS, *spaec;* Gk, *kentron*], either of two motor areas involved in speech. Broca's motor speech area is a unilateral area in the posterior part of the inferior frontal gyrus and is usually on the dominant hemisphere. Wernicke's second motor speech area is an area comprising the posterior part of the superior temporal gyrus next to the transverse temporal gyri and the supramarginal and temporal gyri, also on the dominant hemisphere.

speech dysfunction, any defect or abnormality of speech, including aphasia, alexia, stammering, stuttering, aphonia, and slurring. Speech problems may result from any of a variety of causes, among them neurologic injury to the cerebral cortex; muscular paralysis caused by trauma, disease, or cerebrovascular accident; structural abnormality of the organs of speech; emotional or psychologic tension, strain, or depression; hysteria; and severe mental retardation.

speech-language pathologist (SLP), a health professional with graduate education in human communication, its development, and its disorders. A speech-language pathologist specializes in the measurement and evaluation of language abilities, auditory processes, speech production, and swallowing problems; clinical treatment of speech and language disorders; and research methods in the study of communication problems.

speech-language pathology, 1. the study of abnormalities of speech and language. **2.** the diagnosis and treatment of abnormalities of speech and language as practiced by a speech pathologist.

speech reading [ME, *reden,* to explain], a method of oral communication in which one uses the visual clues of the speaker's lip and facial movements, along with residual hearing. Gestures and "body language" also are observed.

speech reception threshold, the minimum intensity in decibels at which a patient can understand 50% of spoken words; used in tests of speech audiometry.

speech synthesizer [AS, *spaec;* Gk, *synthesis,* placing together], an electronic apparatus with a keyboard that produces sounds that imitate the human voice.

speech therapy [AS, *spaec;* Gk, *therapeia,* treatment], the application of treatments and counseling in the prevention or rehabilitation/remediation of speech and language disorders.

speed [AS, *spedan,* to hasten], **1.** the rate of change of position with time. **2.** *slang.* any stimulating drug, such as amphetamine.

3. a reciprocal of the amount of radiation used to produce an image with various components of an x-ray imaging system, such as screens, film, and image intensifiers. A system using little radiation is "fast," whereas one requiring more radiation is "slow." **4.** the amount of exposure of film to light or x-rays needed to produce a desired image.

speed shock, a sudden adverse physiologic reaction to IV medications or drugs that are administered too quickly. Some signs of speed shock are a flushed face, headache, a tight feeling in the chest, irregular pulse, LOC, and cardiac arrest.

sPEEP, abbreviation for **spontaneous PEEP.**

spell of illness [ME, *spel + illr,* bad], a period regarded by Medicare rules as the number of days between the admission of an insured patient to a hospital and the day that marks the end of a period during which the insured has not been an inpatient in a hospital or a skilled nursing facility.

sperm agglutination test, any of various tests for presence of antisperm antibodies as a cause of infertility, based on the ability of large multivalent isotypes, such as IgM or secretory IgA, to cross-link and agglutinate spermatozoa that have such antibodies. Serum or seminal plasma is mixed with a known concentration of sperm. Immunoglobulins in the mixture then begin agglutinating the sperm. After a given period of time at 37° C, the amount of agglutination is assessed.

sperm antibody, a glycoprotein that specifically recognizes the head or tail of a spermatozoon. The antibodies are found often in vasectomized males and infrequently in infertile males.

spermatic cord /spərmat′ik/ [Gk, *sperma,* seed, *chorde,* string], a structure extending from the deep inguinal ring in the abdomen to the testis. Each cord comprises arteries, veins, lymphatics, nerves, and the vas deferens of the testis.

spermatic fistula, an abnormal passage communicating with a testis or a seminal duct.

spermatid /spur′mətid, spərmat′id/ [Gk, *sperma,* seed], a male germ cell that arises from a spermatocyte and becomes a mature spermatozoon in the last phase of spermatogenesis.

spermatocele /spərmat′əsēl, spur′-/ [Gk, *sperma + kele,* tumor], a cystic swelling, either of the epididymis or of the rete testis, that contains spermatozoa. It is usually painless and requires no therapy.

spermatocide /spərmat′əsīd, spur′-/ [Gk, *sperma;* L, *caedere,* to kill], a chemical substance that kills spermatozoa by reducing

S

their surface tension, causing the cell wall to break down by a bactericidal effect or by creation of a highly acidic environment.

spermatocyte /spur′mətōsīt′/ [Gk, *sperma* + *kytos*, cell], a male germ cell that arises from a spermatogonium.

spermatogenesis /spərmat′əjen′əsis, spur′-/ [Gk, *sperma* + *genesis*, origin], the process of development of spermatozoa, consisting of two stages. In the first stage, spermatogonia become spermatocytes, which develop into spermatids. In the second stage, called spermiogenesis, the spermatids become spermatozoa.—**spermatogenic, spermatogenous** /spur′mətoj′ənəs/, *adj.*

spermatogonium /-gō′nē-əm/ *pl.* spermatogonia [Gk, *sperma* + *gone*, generation], a male germ cell that gives rise to a spermatocyte early in spermatogenesis.

spermatopathia /-path′ē-ə/ [Gk, *sperma, seed, pathos, disease*], pertaining to diseased sperm or their associated organs.

spermatozoon /spur′mətəzō′ən, spərmat′-/ *pl.* **spermatozoa** [Gk, *sperma* + *zoon*, animal], a mature male germ cell that develops in the seminiferous tubules of the testes. Resembling a tadpole, it is about 50 μm (¹/₅₀₀ inch) long and has a head with a nucleus, a neck, and a tail that provides propulsion.

sperm bank [Gk, *sperma,* seed; It, *banca,* bench], a facility for storage of semen to be used for artificial insemination.

sperm head, the oval anterior end of a spermatozoon, which contains the male pronucleus and is surrounded by the acrosome.

spermicidal /spur′misī′dəl/, destructive to spermatozoa.

sperm immobilization test, a test for antisperm antibodies as a cause of infertility, based on the loss of ability of spermatozoa with such surface antibodies to move when complement is present (as it normally is in the female reproductive tract). Serum from the patient is incubated with motile sperm and complement is added. After 1 hour the mixture is then checked to calculate the percentage of formerly motile sperm that can no longer move; a 50% reduction in motility is a positive result for presence of antisperm antibodies.

sperm penetration assay (SPA), a test for the ability of spermatozoa to penetrate oocytes in vitro. Hamster oocytes that lack the zona pellucida are exposed to the spermatozoa in question. Such zona-free oocytes can undergo heterologous membrane fusion with the membranes of spermatozoa that have undergone the acrosome reaction. An assessment is then made of the proportion of oocytes that have been successfully penetrated.

sperm swim-up, the migration of spermatozoa into culture medium.

sperm swim-up technique, any of several methods of checking sperm for motility. A semen sample is centrifuged to form pellets, which are then covered with culture medium. The spermatozoa with greatest motility will swim up into the culture medium and be more suitable for use in in vitro fertilization.

sperm washing, the bathing of fresh sperm with a special solution to remove antibodies and other contaminants so that it can be used for in vitro fertilization or some other technique of artificial insemination.

SPF, abbreviation for **sunscreen protective factor index.**

sp. gr., abbreviation for **specific gravity.**

sphacelous /sfas′ələs/, pertaining to something that is necrotic or gangrenous.

S-phase, the phase of the cell cycle in which DNA is synthesized before mitosis.

sphenoethmoid recess /sfē′nō-eth′moid/ [Gk, *sphen,* wedge, *eidos,* form; L, *recedere,* to retreat], a narrow opening in the lateral wall of the nasal cavity bounded above by the cribriform plate of the ethmoid and the body of the sphenoid and below by the superior nasal concha. It opens into the sphenoidal sinus of the skull.

sphenoid /sfē′noid/ [Gk, *sphen,* wedge, *eidos,* form], wedge-shaped.

sphenoidal fissure /sfēnoi′dəl/ [Gk *sphen,* wedge, *eidos,* form], a cleft between the great and small wings of the sphenoid bone.

sphenoidal sinus, one of a pair of cavities in the sphenoid bone of the skull, lined with mucous membrane that is continuous with that of the nasal cavity.

sphenoid bone, the bone at the base of the skull, anterior to the temporal bones and the basilar part of the occipital bone.

sphenoid fontanel, an anterolateral fontanel that is usually not palpable.

sphenoiditis /sfē′noidī′tis/ [Gk, *sphen,* wedge, *eidos,* form, *itis,* inflammation], an inflammation of the sphenoidal sinus.

sphenomandibular ligament /sfē′nōmandi b′yələr/ [Gk, *sphen* + *eidos*; L, *mandere,* to chew], one of a pair of flat, thin ligaments comprising part of the TMJ between the mandible of the jaw and the temporal bone of the skull.

sphenopalatine artery, the largest vessel supplying the nasal cavity; the terminal branch of the maxillary artery in the pterygopalatine fossa.

sphenoparietal suture, the articulation of the sphenoid bone with the parietal bone in the calvaria.

sphenosquamous suture, the articulation of the sphenoid bone with the anterior edge of the temporal bone.

sphere /sfir/, a globe-shaped object, theoretically generated by a circle revolving on a diameter as its axis.

spherocyte /sfir′əsīt/ [Gk, *sphaira,* sphere, *kytos,* cell], an abnormal spheric RBC that contains more than the normal amount of hemoglobin.—**spherocytic,** *adj.*

spherocytic anemia /sfir′əsit′ik/, autosomal-dominant hemolytic anemia characterized by hemolytic anemia caused by the presence of spherical red blood cells. The cells are fragile and tend to hemolyze in the oxygen-poor peripheral circulatory system. Episodic crises of abdominal pain, fever, jaundice, and splenomegaly occur.

spherocytosis /sfir′ōsītō′sis/, the abnormal presence of spherocytes in the blood.

spheroidal /sfir′oidəl/ [Gk, *sphaira,* ball, *eidos,* form], ball-shaped.

spherule /sfer′yo͞ol/ [Gk, *sphaira,* ball], a small ball.

sphincter /sfingk′tər/ [Gk, *sphingein,* to bind], a circular band of muscle fibers that constricts a passage or closes a natural opening in the body, such as external anal sphincter, which closes the anus.

sphincter ani, a double set of circular muscles at the opening of the anus. One, the sphincter ani internus, consists of a thickened inner circular coat of the bowel smooth muscle; the other, the sphincter ani externus, is a flat sheet of striated, voluntary muscle surrounding the anal orifice.

sphincter choledochus /kōled′əkəs/, a smooth muscle sphincter that encircles the lower end of the bile duct and is part of the sphincter of Oddi.

sphincter muscle of pancreatic duct, a sphincter that surrounds the pancreatic duct just above the hepatopancreatic ampulla.

sphincter of Oddi [Ruggero Oddi, Italian physician, 1864–1913], a sheath of muscle fibers surrounding the lower end of the common bile and pancreatic ducts as they cross the wall of the duodenum.

sphincter of Oddi dysfunction, abdominal pain or jaundice with failure of the sphincter of Oddi to function properly. It may occur several years after cholecystectomy or have another unknown cause.

sphincter pupillae, a muscle that contracts the iris, narrowing the diameter of the pupil of the eye. It is composed of circular fibers arranged in a narrow band about 1 mm wide, surrounding the margin of the pupil toward the posterior surface of the iris.

sphincter spasm, spasm of a sphincter muscle, particularly an anal sphincter.

sphingolipid /sfing′gōlip′id/ [Gk, *sphingein,* to bind, *lipos,* fat], a compound that consists of a lipid and a sphingosine. It is found in high concentrations in the brain and other tissues of the nervous system.

sphingomyelin /sfing′gōmī′əlin/ [Gk, *sphingein* + *myelos,* marrow], any of a group of sphingolipids containing phosphorus. It occurs primarily in the tissue of the nervous system.

sphingomyelin lipidosis, any of a group of diseases characterized by an abnormality in the ability of the body to store sphingolipids. Kinds of sphingomyelin lipidosis include **Gaucher's disease, Niemann-Pick disease,** and **Tay-Sachs disease.**

sphingosine /sfing′gōsēn/, a long-chain, unsaturated amino alcohol, a major constituent of sphingolipids, including sphingomyelins.

sphygmogram /sfig′məgram/ [Gk, *sphygmos,* pulse, *gramma,* record], a pulse tracing produced by a sphygmograph. Sphygmographic abnormalities of rate, rhythm, and form may be diagnostically useful in an assessment of cardiovascular function.

sphygmograph /sfig′məgraf/, an instrument that records the force of the arterial pulse on a tracing, the sphygmogram. —**sphygmographic,** *adj.*

sphygmoid /sfig′moid/ [Gk, *sphygmos,* pulse, *eidos,* form], pertaining to or resembling the pulse.

sphygmomanometer /sfig′mōmənom′ətər/ [Gk, *sphygmos* + *manos,* thin, *metron,* measure], an instrument for indirect measurement of BP. It consists of an inflatable cuff that fits around a limb, a bulb for controlling air pressure within the cuff, and a mercury or aneroid manometer. Pressure in the compressed artery is estimated by the column of mercury it balances when the cuff is inflated.

sphygmoplethysmograph /-pləthis′məgraf/ [Gk, *sphygmos,* pulse, *plethysmos,* increase, *graphein,* to record], an instrument for measuring and recording the arterial pulse curve and blood flow in a limb.

spica [L, *spica,* spike or ear of wheat], a figure-eight bandage that, when applied to a joint, resembles the head of a stalk of wheat.

spica bandage /spī′kə/ [L, *spica,* spike of wheat; Fr, *bande,* strip], a figure-eight bandage in which each turn generally overlaps the previous to form a succession of V-like designs. It may be used to give support, to apply pressure, or to hold a dressing in place on the chest, limbs, thighs, or pelvis.

spica cast, an orthopedic cast applied to immobilize part or all of the trunk of the body and part or all of one or more extremities. It is used to treat various fractures, such as of the hip and the femur, and to correct or maintain the correction of hip deformities.

spicule /spik′yo͞ol/ [L, *spiculum,* point], a small sharp body with a needlelike point.

spider angioma [ME, *spithre;* Gk, *angeion,* vessel, *oma,* tumor], a form of

S

telangiectasis characterized by a central elevated red dot the size of a pinhead from which small blood vessels radiate.

spider bite [ME, *spithre;* AS, *bitan;* L, *potio,* drink], a puncture wound produced by the bite of any of nearly 60 species of venomous spiders found in North America. Some are dangerous to humans, including the black widow, *Latrodectus mactans;* the brown recluse, *Loxosceles reclusa;* and species of jumping spiders and tarantulas. Spider venom may contain enzymatic proteins, including peptides that may affect neuromuscular transmission or cardiovascular function.

spider mite, either *Tetranychus molestissimus* or *T. telarius.*

spider telangiectasia [ME, *spithre;* Gk, *telos,* end, *angeion,* vessel, *ektasis,* dilation], a branched group of dilated capillary blood vessels forming a spider-like image on the skin.

spike, a sharp peak in an electronic recording such as an oscillograph.

spikeboard /spīk´bôrd/, a device that enables people with upper extremity disabilities to stabilize foods for meal preparation, typically used by individuals with functional use of only one hand.

spillway [AS, *spillan,* to destroy, *weg,* wagon track], a channel or passageway through which food normally escapes from the occlusal surfaces of the teeth during chewing.

spin [AS, *spinnan,* to draw threads], **1.** the intrinsic angular momentum of an elementary particle or a nucleus of an atom. **2.** intrinsic joint movements about an axis perpendicular to the articular surface.

spina /spī´nə/ *pl.* **spinae** [L, backbone], **1.** the spinal column. **2.** a spine or a thornlike projection such as the bony projection on the anterior border of the ilium, forming the anterior end of the iliac crest.

spina bifida /bif´ədə, bī´fədə/, a congenital neural tube defect in which there is a developmental anomaly in the posterior vertebral arch. It may occur with only a small deformed lamina separated by a midline gap, or it may be associated with the complete absence of laminae surrounding a large area. Spina bifida that does not involve herniation of the meninges or the contents of the spinal canal rarely requires treatment.

spina bifida anterior, incomplete closure along the anterior surface of the vertebral column.

spina bifida cystica, a developmental defect of the CNS in which a hernial cyst containing meninges (meningocele), spinal cord (myelocele), or both (myelomeningocele) protrudes through a congenital cleft in the vertebral column. The protruding sac is encased in a layer of skin or a fine membrane that readily ruptures, causing the leakage of CSF and an increased risk of meningeal infection. The severity of neurologic dysfunction and associated defects depends directly on the degree of nerve involvement.

spina bifida occulta, defective closure of the laminae of the vertebral column in the lumbosacral region without hernial protrusion of the spinal cord or meninges. It is identified externally by a skin depression or dimple, dark tufts of hair, telangiectasis, or soft subcutaneous lipomas at the site. Because the neural tube has closed, there are usually no neurologic impairments associated with the defect. However, any abnormal adhesion of the spinal cord to the area of the malformation may lead to neuromuscular disturbances.

spinal /spī´nəl/ [L, *spina*], **1.** pertaining to a spine, especially the spinal column. **2.** *informal.* spinal anesthesia, such as saddle block or caudal anesthesia.

spinal anesthesia [L, *spina,* backbone; Gk, *anaisthesia,* lack of feeling], a state of lack of sensation in the lower part of the body produced by injection of a local anesthetic drug into the subarachnoid CSF space.

spinal aperture, a large opening formed by the body of a vertebra and its arch.

spinal block [L, *spina,* backbone; OFr, *bloc*], an obstruction of CSF circulation.

spinal canal, the cavity within the vertebral column.

spinal cord, a long, nearly cylindric structure lodged in the vertebral canal and extending from the foramen magnum at the base of the skull to the upper part of the lumbar region. A major component of the CNS, the adult cord is approximately 1 cm in diameter, with an average length of 42 to 45 cm and a weight of 30 g. The cord is an extension of the medulla oblongata of the brain that extends at the level of the first or second lumbar vertebra. The cord conducts sensory and motor impulses to and from the brain and controls many reflexes. Thirty-one pairs of spinal nerves originate from the cord. It has an inner core of gray material consisting mainly of nerve cell bodies. The cord is enclosed by three protective membranes (meninges): the dura mater, arachnoid, and pia mater.

spinal cord compression, an abnormal and often serious condition resulting from pressure on the spinal cord. The symptoms range from temporary numbness of an extremity to permanent quadriplegia, depending on the cause, severity, and location of the pressure. Causes include spinal fracture, vertebral dislocation, tumor, hemorrhage, and edema associated with contusion.

spinal cord injury, any one of the traumatic disruptions of the spinal cord, often associated with extensive musculoskeletal involvement. Common spinal cord injuries are vertebral fractures and dislocations, such as those commonly suffered by individuals involved in car accidents, airplane crashes, or other violent impacts. Such trauma may cause varying degrees of paraplegia and tetraplegia. Injuries to spinal structures below the first thoracic vertebra may produce paraplegia. Injuries to the spine above the first thoracic vertebra may cause tetraplegia. Injuries that completely transect the spinal cord cause permanent loss of motor and sensory functions activated by neurons below the level of the lesions involved. Spinal cord injuries produce a state of spinal shock, characterized by flaccid paralysis and complete loss of skin sensation at the time of injury. Musculoskeletal complications are associated with the neurologic involvement of spinal cord injuries. Treatment of spinal cord injuries varies considerably and involves numerous approaches, such as orthopedic exercises, ambulatory techniques, and special physical and psychologic therapy.

spinal cord tumor, a neoplasm of the spinal cord of which more than 50% are extramedullary, about 25% are intramedullary, and the rest are extradural. Symptoms depend on the location and rate of growth of the tumor. They usually develop slowly and may progress from unilateral paresthesia and a dull ache to lancinating pain; weakness in one or both legs; abnormal deep tendon reflexes; and, in advanced cases, monoplegia, hemiplegia, or paraplegia. Function of the autonomic nervous system is sometimes disturbed, causing areas of dry, cold, bluish-pink skin or profuse sweating of the lower extremities.

spinal curvature, any persistent, abnormal deviation of the vertebral column from its normal position. Kinds of spinal curvature are **kyphoscoliosis, kyphosis, lordosis,** and **scoliosis.**

spinal fusion, the fixation of an unstable segment of the spine. It is accomplished by skeletal traction or immobilization of the patient in a body cast but most frequently by a surgical procedure. Surgical fusion involves the stabilization of a spinal section with a bone graft or synthetic device introduced through a posterior incision in the lumbar region. In the less frequently fused cervical region, the incision may be anterior or posterior.

spinal headache, a severe headache occurring after spinal anesthesia, lumbar puncture, or epidural anesthesia, caused by a leak of CSF from the subarachnoid space and subsequent lowering of ICP. Severe spinal headache may be accompanied by diminished aural and visual acuity.

spinal manipulation, the forced passive flexion, extension, and rotation of vertebral segments, carrying the elements of articulation beyond the usual range of movement to the limit of anatomic range.

spinal meningitis, an inflammation of the membranes of the spinal cord.

spinal motion segment, two adjacent vertebrae and the connecting tissues that bind them together.

spinal nerves, the 31 pairs of nerves without special names that are connected to the spinal cord and numbered according to the level of the vertebral column at which they emerge. There are 8 cervical, 12 thoracic, 5 lumbar, and 5 sacral pairs, and 1 coccygeal pair. The first cervical pair of nerves emerges from the spinal cord in the space between the first cervical vertebra and the occipital bone. The rest of the cervical pairs and all the thoracic pairs emerge horizontally through the intervertebral foramina of their respective vertebrae. The lumbar, sacral, and coccygeal nerve pairs descend from their points of origin at the lower end of the cord before reaching the intervertebral foramina of their respective vertebrae. Each spinal nerve attaches to the spinal cord by an anterior (or ventral) root and a posterior (or dorsal) root. The posterior roots contain sensory neurons and accompany a distended spinal ganglion within the vertebral foramina. The ventral roots contain motor neuron axons. The sacral plexus in the pelvic cavity comprises certain spinal nerve fibers from the lumbar and sacral regions and gives rise to the great sciatic nerve in the back of the thigh.

spinal reflex [L, *spina* + *reflectere*, to bend back], any reflex with a pathway through the spinal cord but not the brain.

spinal segment, a division of the spinal cord containing a bilateral pair of nerve roots.

spinal shock, a form of shock associated with acute injury to the spinal cord. Temporary suppression of reflexes is controlled by segments below the level of injury. The period of shock may last from hours to months.

spinal stenosis, narrowing of the vertebral canal, nerve root canals, or intervertebral foramina of the lumbar spine caused by encroachment of bone on the space; symptoms are caused by compression of the cauda equina and include pain, paresthesias, and neurogenic claudication.

spinal tract, any one of the ascending (sensory) and descending (motor) pathways for sensory or motor nerve impulses that is found in the white matter of the spinal cord. Twenty-one different tracts lie within the dorsal, ventral, and lateral funiculi of the white substance. The four major ascending tracts are the lateral spinothalamic, the

S

ventral spinothalamic, the fasciculi gracilis and cuneatus, and the spinocerebellar. The four major descending tracts are the lateral corticospinal, the ventral corticospinal, the lateral reticulospinal, and the medial reticulospinal. Touch, pressure, proprioception, temperature, and pain are sensory stimuli transmitted via the spinal tracts. Reflex and voluntary motor activity is regulated by motor nerve stimulation from the brain and brainstem to the motor neurons of the spinal cord.

spinal x-ray studies, radiographic studies of the spine to diagnose degenerative arthritic changes, traumatic fractures, tumor metastasis, spondylosis, spondylolisthesis, and spinal alignment abnormalities.

spin density, a measure of the hydrogen concentration in MRI. It is proportional to the number of hydrogen nuclei precessing at the Larmor frequency and contributing to the magnetic resonance signal.

spindle [AS, *spinel*, to spin], **1.** the fusiform-shaped body of achromatin in the cell nucleus during the late prophase and the metaphase of mitosis. **2.** a type of brain wave, consisting of a short series of changes in electric potential with a frequency of 14 per second. **3.** any one of the special receptor organs comprising the neurotendinous and neuromuscular spindles distributed throughout the body. These kinds of spindles serve as special receptor organs that detect the degree of stretch in a muscle or at the junction of a muscle with its tendon and are essential in maintaining muscle tone.

spindle cell, any of various cells that are shaped like spindles, being more or less round in the middle with two ends that are pointed.

spindle cell carcinoma, a rapidly growing neoplasm composed of fusiform squamous cells.

spine, **1.** the vertebral column, or backbone. **2.** descriptive of a spinous process.

spin echo (SE), a magnetic resonance pulse sequence in which echoes are generated by rephasing spins in the transverse plane using radiofrequency pulses or magnetic field gradients.

spine of scapula [L, *spina,* backbone, *scapulae,* shoulder blades], a sharp-edged plate of bone projecting posteriorly backward from the flattened scapula base.

spinnbarkeit /spin′bärkīt, shpin′-/ [Ger, threadability], the clear slippery elastic consistency characteristic of cervical mucus during ovulation. It has the consistency of an uncooked egg white, and it is a valuable sign of the peak fertile period in a woman's menstrual cycle.

spinning top urethra, deformity of the urethra on urination, with narrowing at the urinary meatus and dilation at the proximal

end. It is seen sporadically in conditions such as prolonged inflammation of the urethra and detrusor instability.

spinocerebellar /spī′nōser′əbel′ər/ [L, *spina* + *cerebellum,* small brain], pertaining to the spinal cord and the cerebellum.

spinocerebellar disorder, an inherited disorder characterized by a progressive degeneration of the spinal cord and cerebellum, often involving other parts of the nervous system as well. They can be inherited as dominant or recessive traits. Onset is usually early, during childhood or adolescence. No effective treatment is known.

spinous /spī′nəs/ [L, *spina,* backbone], pertaining to an object that has the shape of a spine or thorn.

spinous process [L, *spina,* backbone + *processus*], a spinelike projection of bony tissue.

spiral bandage /spī′rəl/ [Gk, *speira,* coil; Fr, *bande,* strip], a roller bandage applied spirally around a limb.

spiral fracture [Gk, *speira,* coil], a bone break that is spiral, oblique, or transverse to the bone's long axis.

spiraling /spī′rəling/, the process by which immunodeficiency allows viral replication, which further depresses the immune system, allowing further viral replication, and so on.

spiral reverse bandage, a spiral bandage that is turned and folded back on itself as necessary to make it fit the contour of the body more securely.

spirit /spir′it/ [L, *spiritus,* breath], **1.** any volatile liquid, particularly one that has been distilled. **2.** a volatile substance dissolved in alcohol.

spirit of ammonia [L, *spiritus,* breath; *Ammon,* temple in Libya], a solution of 3% ammonium carbonate in alcohol with flavorings added. It is mixed with water for use as a stimulant and carminative.

spiritual growth facilitation, a nursing intervention from the Nursing Interventions Classification (NIC) defined as facilitation of growth in a patient's capacity to identify, connect with, and call upon the source of meaning, purpose, comfort, strength, and hope in his/her life.

spiritual healing, the use of spiritual practices, such as prayer, for the purpose of effecting a cure of or an improvement in an illness.

spiritual healing and prayer, the offering of prayers to a higher being or authority for the purpose of reducing stress, promoting healing, or arresting disease. Spiritual healing may be practiced by the individual patient, by groups, or by others with or without the patient's knowledge.

spiritual health, a nursing outcome from the Nursing Outcomes Classification (NOC) defined as connectedness with self, others, higher power, all life, nature, and the universe that transcends and empowers the self.

spiritual support, a nursing intervention from the Nursing Interventions Classification (NIC) defined as assisting the patient to feel balance and connection with a greater power.

spiritual therapy [L, *spiritus,* breath; Gk, *therapeia,* treatment], a form of counseling or psychotherapy that involves moral, spiritual, and religious influences on behavior and physical health.

Spiriva, a trademark for tiotropium.

Spirochaetales /spī'rō-ke-ta'lēz/, the spirochetes, an order of bacteria in which some species are free-living and some parasitic. It includes the disease-causing genera *Borrelia, Leptospira,* and *Treponema.*

Spirochaeta pallida /spī'rəkē'tə/ [Gk, *speira,* coil, *chaite,* hair; L, *pallidus,* pale], a species of flexible spiral motile microorganisms that is the causative agent of human syphilis.

spirochete /spī'rəkēt'/ [Gk, *speira,* coil, *chaite,* hair], any bacterium of the genus *Spirochaeta* that is motile and spiral-shaped with flexible filaments. Kinds of spirochetes include the organisms responsible for leptospirosis, relapsing fever, syphilis, and yaws.—**spirochetal,** *adj.*

spirochetemia /spī'rōkətē'mē·ə/ [Gk, *speira* + coil + *haima,* blood], the presence of spirochetal organisms in the blood.

spirogram /spī'rōgram/ [Gk, *speira* + *gramma,* record], a visual record of respiratory movements made by a spirometer, used in the assessment of pulmonary function and capacity.

spirograph /spī'rəgraf/ [Gk, *speira* + *graphein,* to record], a device for recording respiratory movements.—**spirographic,** *adj.*

spirometer /spīrom'ətər/ [Gk, *speira* + *metron,* measure], an instrument that measures and records the volume of inhaled and exhaled air, used to assess pulmonary function.—**spirometric,** *adj.*

spirometry /spīrom'ətrē/, laboratory evaluation of the air capacity of the lungs by means of a spirometer.—**spirometric,** *adj.*

spironolactone /spī'rənəlak'tōn/, a potassium-sparing aldosterone antagonist diuretic. It is prescribed in the treatment of primary hyperaldosteronism, edema of CHF, cirrhosis of the liver accompanied by edema, nephrotic syndrome, essential hypertension, and hypokalemia.

spittle [AS, *spittan,* spew], saliva.

splanchnic /splangk'nik/, pertaining to the internal organs; visceral.

splanchnic engorgement, the excessive filling or pooling of blood within the visceral vasculature after the removal of pressure from the abdomen, as in the excision of a large tumor or birth of a child.

splanchnic nerves [Gk, *splanchna,* viscera + *nervus*], a network of nerves, mainly preganglionic fibers, with filaments innervating the penis and clitoris, as well as the uterus, rectum, and other structures of the abdominal cavity.

splanchnocele /splangk'nōsēl/ [Gk, *splanchna,* viscera, *kele,* hernia], hernial protrusion of any abdominal viscera.

splanchnocoele /splangk'nōsēl/ [Gk, *splanchna,* viscera, *koilos,* hollow], a part of the embryonic body cavity, or coelom, that gives rise to the abdominal, pericardial, and pleural cavities.

splanchnopleure /splangk'nōplŏŏr/ [Gk, *splanchna* + *pleura,* side], a layer of tissue in the early developing embryo, formed by the union of endoderm and splanchnic mesoderm.—**splanchnopleural,** *adj.*

S-plasty /es'plas'tē/, a technique of plastic surgery in which an S-shaped instead of a straight line incision is made to reduce tension and improve healing in areas where the skin is loose.

splay /splā/, **1.** to spread or turn out. **2.** to spread out, as said of the limbs. **3.** to open, as with the end of a tubular structure by making a longitudinal incision. **4.** to dislocate, as said of a bone.

splayfoot [ME, *splaien;* AS, *fot*], a foot that is flat and extremely everted, away from the midline.

spleen [Gk, *splen*], a soft, highly vascular, roughly ovoid organ situated between the stomach and the diaphragm in the left hypochondriac region of the body. It is considered part of the lymphatic system because it contains localized lymphatic nodules. It is dark purple and varies in shape in different individuals. Research indicates it performs various tasks such as defense, hemopoiesis, blood storage, and destruction/recycling of RBCs and platelets. The spleen also produces leukocytes, monocytes, lymphocytes, and plasma cells in response to an infectious agent. If the body suffers severe hemorrhage, the spleen can contract and increase the blood volume from 350 to 550 mL in less than 60 seconds.—**splenic,** *adj.*

spleen scan, a radiographic scan of the spleen after the injection of radioactive RBCs, performed to detect a tumor, damage, or other problem.

Splendore-Hoeppli phenomenon, the deposition of amorphous, eosinophilic, hyaline material around pathogenic organisms, seen in some fungal and parasitic diseases as the result of a local antigen-antibody reaction.

S

splenectomy /splənek′təmē/ [Gk, *splen* + *ektomē,* excision], the surgical removal of the spleen.

splenic flexure /splen′ik/ [Gk, *splen,* spleen; L, *flectere,* to bend], the left flexure of the colon, as it bends at the junction of the transverse and descending segments of the colon, near the spleen.

splenic flexure syndrome [Gk, *splen;* L, *flectere,* to bend], a recurrent pain and abdominal distension in the left upper quadrant of the abdomen caused by a pocket of gas trapped in the large intestine below the spleen, at the flexure of the transverse and descending colon.

splenic puncture, a perforation of the parenchyma of the spleen to obtain pressure data or inject radiopaque material.

splenius capitis /splē′nē-əs/ [Gk, *splenion,* bandage; L, *caput,* head], one of a pair of deep muscles of the neck and back. It acts to rotate, extend, and bend the head.

splenius cervicis, one of a pair of deep muscles of the neck and back. It acts to rotate, bend, and extend the head and neck.

splenohepatomegaly /splē′nōhep′ətōmeg′əlē/ [Gk, *splen,* spleen, *hepar,* liver, *megas,* great], an abnormal simultaneous increase in the sizes of the liver and spleen.

splenomegaly /splē′nōmeg′əlē, splen′-/ [Gk, *splen* + *megas,* large], an abnormal enlargement of the spleen, as is associated with portal hypertension, hemolytic anemia, Niemann-Pick disease, or malaria.

splenorenal bypass, a technique of renal revascularization involving creation of a vascular prosthesis from the splenic artery to replace the occluded renal artery.

splenosis /splēnō′sis/, multiple splenic growths in the peritoneum resulting from splenic rupture or iatrogenic injury.

splint [D, *splinte,* piece of wood], **1.** an orthopedic device for immobilization, restraint, or support of any part of the body. **2.** a device, usually made of hard acrylic and wire, for anchoring the teeth or modifying the bite.

splinter [D, *splinte*], a sharp, pointed piece of bone or other substance.

splinter fracture [D, *splinte*], a comminuted fracture with thin, sharp bone fragments.

splinter hemorrhage, linear bleeding under a fingernail or toenail, resembling a splinter. It is seen after trauma and in bacterial endocarditis.

splinting¹, the process of immobilizing, restraining, or supporting a body part.

splinting², a nursing intervention from the Nursing Interventions Classification (NIC) defined as stabilization, immobilization, and/or protection of an injured body part with a supportive appliance.

split-brain state, a condition resulting from the disconnection of the two cerebral hemispheres. It is produced when the corpus callosum is surgically divided completely or partially as a treatment for epilepsy or in congential absence of corpus callosum. The cognitive effects are identified as a disconnection syndrome.

split gene [D, *splitten,* to split], a gene whose continuity is interrupted.

split Russell traction, an orthopedic mechanism that combines suspension and traction to immobilize, position, and align the lower extremities in the correction of orthopedic deformities and in the treatment of congenital hip dislocation and hip and knee contractures.

split-thickness skin graft, a tissue transplant involving the epidermis and a part of the dermis. This type of graft is the most commonly used method of covering open burn wounds.

splitting, a primitive defense mechanism that when overused represents a developmental arrest. It is a failure to synthesize the positive and negative experiences and ideas one has of oneself, other people, situations, and institutions.

spondylitic [Gk, *sphondylos,* vertebra], pertaining to a person afflicted with spondylitis.

spondylitis /spon′dəlī′tis/ [Gk, *sphondylos,* vertebra, *itis,* inflammation], an inflammation of any of the vertebrae, usually characterized by stiffness and pain. The condition may be the result of traumatic injury to the spine, infection, or rheumatoid disease.

spondyloarthropathy /spon′dilō′ärthrop′əthē/, any of a set of diseases of the joints and spine. Most commonly affected are the lower extremities, sacroiliac joint, and hip. Pain and restricted motion of the hips and lower back are typical complaints. Many patients also experience eye disorders.

spondylolisthesis /spon′dilō′listhē′sis/ [Gk, *sphondylos* + *olisthanein,* to slip], the partial forward dislocation of one vertebra over the one below it, most commonly the fifth lumbar vertebra over the first sacral vertebra.

spondylosis /spon′dilō′sis/ [Gk, *sphondylos* + *osis*], a condition of the spine characterized by fixation or stiffness of a vertebral joint.

spondylous /spon′diləs/ [Gk, *sphondylos,* vertebra], pertaining to a vertebra.

sponge /spunj/ [Gk, *spongia*], **1.** a resilient absorbent mass used to absorb fluids, apply medication, or cleanse. **2.** *informal.* a folded gauze square used in surgery.

sponge bath, the procedure of washing the patient with a damp washcloth or sponge, used when a full bath is not necessary or when lowering of body temperature is required.

spongioblastoma /spun′jē·ōblastŏ′mə/ *pl.* **spongioblastomas, spongioblastomata** [Gk, *spongia* + *blastos*, germ, *oma*, tumor], a neoplasm composed of spongioblasts, embryonic epithelial cells that develop around the neural tube and transform into cells of the supporting connective tissue of nerve cells or cells of lining membranes of the ventricles and the spinal cord canal.

spongioblastoma unipolare, a rare neoplasm composed of parallel spongioblasts. The tumor may occur near the third ventricle, in the pons and brainstem, in basal ganglia, or in the terminal filament of the spinal cord.

spongy /spun′jē/ [Gk, *spoggia*], pertaining to or resembling a sponge.

spontaneous /spontā′nē·əs/ [L, *sponte*, willingly], occurring naturally and without apparent cause, such as spontaneous remission.

spontaneous abortion, a termination of pregnancy before the twentieth week of gestation as a result of abnormalities of the conceptus or maternal environment.

spontaneous delivery, a vaginal birth occurring without the mechanical assistance of obstetric forceps or vacuum aspirator.

spontaneous fracture, a fracture that occurs without trauma, as a result of bone weakness caused by osteoporosis or by a benign or malignant tumor.

spontaneous generation, the theoretic origin of living organisms from inanimate matter; abiogenesis.

spontaneous labor, a labor beginning and progressing without mechanical or pharmacologic stimulation.

spontaneous PEEP (sPEEP), positive airway pressure applied at the end of the exhalation phase during spontaneous breathing.

spontaneous phagocytosis [L, *sponte*, free will; Gk, *phagein*, to eat, *kytos*, cell, *osis*, condition], ingestion of antigenic particles by phagocytes of the reticuloendothelial system.

spontaneous pneumothorax [L, *sponte*, free will; Gk, *pneuma*, air, *thorax*, chest], the presence of air or gas in the pleural space as a result of a rupture of the lung parenchyma and visceral pleura with no demonstrable cause.

spontaneous remission, 1. the reversal of progress of disease without formal treatment. **2.** the disappearance of symptoms of a mentally ill patient without formal treatment.

spontaneous ventilation, normal, unassisted breathing in which the patient creates the pressure gradient through muscular movements that move air into and out of the lungs.

spontaneous version [L, *sponte*, free will, *vertere*, to turn], a change in the lie of a fetus that occurs without manipulation.

spoon nail [AS, *spon* + *naegel*], a nail of the finger or toe that has a thin and concave outer surface.

sporadic /spôrad′ik/ [Gk, *sporaden*, scattered], of a number of events, occurring at scattered, intermittent, and apparently random intervals.

spore [Gk, *sporos*, seed], **1.** a reproductive unit of some genera of fungi or protozoa. **2.** a form assumed by some bacteria that is resistant to heat, drying, and chemicals. Diseases caused by spore-forming bacteria include anthrax, botulism, gas gangrene, and tetanus.

sporicidal /spôr′isi′dəl/ [Gk, *sporos*, seed; L, *caedere*, to kill], spore-killing, as are certain chemicals or other agents.

sporicide /spôr′isīd/ [Gk, *sporos;* L, *caedere*, to kill], any agent effective in destroying spores, such as compounds of chlorine and formaldehyde, and the glutaraldehydes.

sporiferous /spôrif′ərəs/, producing or bearing spores.

spork, a spoonlike food utensil with fork tines designed for people with upper extremity disabilities.

sporoblast /spôr′ōblast′/ [Gk, *sporos* + *blastos*, germ], any cell that gives rise to a sporozoite or spore during the sexual reproductive phase of the life cycle of a sporozoon. It refers specifically to the cells resulting from the multiple fission of the encysted zygote of the malarial parasite *Plasmodium*, from which the sporozoites develop.

sporocyst /spôr′əsist/ [Gk, *sporos* + *kystis*, bag], **1.** any structure containing spores or reproductive cells. **2.** a saclike structure, or oocyst, secreted by the zygote of certain protists before sporozoite formation. **3.** the second larval stage in the life cycle of parasitic flukes.

sporogenesis /spôr′ōjen′əsis/ [Gk, *sporos* + *genesis*, origin], **1.** the formation of spores.—**sporogeny** /spôroj′ənē/, *n.* **2.** reproduction by means of spores. —**sporogenic,** *adj.*

sporogenous /spôroj′ənəs/ [Gk, *sporos* + *genein*, to produce], describing an animal or plant that produces spores or reproduces by way of spores.

sporogony /spôrog′ənē/ [Gk, *sporos* + *genesis*, origin], reproduction by means of spores. It refers specifically to the formation of sporozoites during the sexual stage of the life cycle of a sporozoon, primarily the malarial parasite *Plasmodium*.

sporont /spôr′ont/ [Gk, *sporos* + *on*, being], a mature protozoal parasite in the sexual reproductive stage of its life cycle.

S

sporonticide /spôron′tisīd/ [Gk, *sporos* + *on*; L, *caedere*, to kill], any substance that destroys sporonts, such as chloroquine and other antimalarial drugs.—**sporonticidal,** *adj.*

sporophore /spôr′əfôr/ [Gk, *sporos* + *pherein*, to bear], the part of an organism that produces spores.

sporophyte /spôr′əfīt/ [Gk, *sporos* + *phyton*, plant], the asexual, spore-bearing stage in organisms that reproduce by alternation of generations.

sporotrichosis /spôr′ōtrikō′sis/ [Gk, *sporos* + *thrix*, hair, *osis*, condition], a common chronic fungal infection caused by the species *Sporothrix schenckii*. It is usually characterized by skin ulcers and subcutaneous nodules along lymphatic channels. Treatment may include amphotericin B in severe cases or itraconazole.

Sporotrichum /spôrot′rikəm/ [Gk, *sporos* + *thrix*, hair], a genus of soil-inhabiting fungi formerly thought to cause sporotrichosis.

Sporozoa /spôr′əzō′ə/ [Gk, *sporos* + *zoon*, animal], a class of parasite in the phylum Protozoa that is characterized by the absence of any external organs of locomotion. Included in this class are the genera *Toxoplasma* and *Plasmodium.*

sporozoite /spôr′əzō′īt/ [Gk, *sporos* + *zoon*, animal], any of the cells resulting from the sexual union of spores during the life cycle of a sporozoon.

sport [ME, *disporten*, to amuse], **1.** an individual that differs drastically from its parents or others of its type because of genetic mutation; a mutant. **2.** a genetic mutation.

sports-injury prevention: youth, a nursing intervention from the Nursing Interventions Classification (NIC) defined as reducing the risk of sports-related injury in young athletes.

sports medicine, a branch of medicine that specializes in the prevention and treatment of injuries resulting from training for and participation in athletic events. Most sports injuries involve muscle sprains, strains, and tears, which frequently result from inadequate preliminary "warm-up" exercises. Among the most common sports injuries are shin splints, pulled hamstring muscles, ankle sprain, and tennis elbow.

sporulation /spôr′yəlā′shən/ [Gk, *sporos*; L, *atus*, process], **1.** a type of reproduction that occurs in fungi, algae, and protozoa and involves the formation of spores by the spontaneous division of a cell into four or more daughter cells, each of which contains a part of the original nucleus. **2.** the formation of a refractile body, or resting spore, within certain bacteria that makes the cell resistant to unfavorable environmental conditions.

spot [ME, blot], in psychotherapy, a small quantum of space that becomes the territorial object and extension of point behavior.

spot film, a radiograph made instantly during fluoroscopy. The technique may be used to make a permanent record of a transient effect or to record with definition and detail a small anatomic area.

spotting [ME, *spot*, blot], the appearance of a blood-stained discharge from the vagina between menstrual periods, during pregnancy, or at the beginning of labor.

sprain, a traumatic injury to the tendons, muscles, or ligaments around a joint, characterized by pain, swelling, and discoloration of the skin over the joint. The duration and severity of the symptoms vary with the extent of damage to the tissues. Treatment includes support, rest, and alternating cold and heat.

sprain fracture, a fracture that results from the separation of a tendon or ligament at the point of insertion, associated with the separation of a bone at the same insertion site.

sprain of ankle or foot [AS, *ancleow, fot*], a sudden traction injury to a muscle, ligament, or capsule in the ankle or foot. The injury is not severe enough to cause a rupture of the tissue.

sprain of back [AS, *baec*], a sudden traction injury to muscles and related tissues of the back. The tissues may have undergone traumatic strain without being ruptured.

spreader bar /spred′ər/, a metal bar with curved hoop areas for attaching hooks or pins for traction.

Sprengel's deformity /shpreng′gəlz/ [Otto Gerhard Karl Sprengel, German surgeon, 1852–1915], congenital elevation of the scapula, resulting from failure of descent of the scapula to its normal thoracic position during fetal life.

spring /spring/ [AS, *springan*, to jump], **1.** a piece of resilient metal, such as a hardened coiled steel wire, that will return to its original shape after bending. **2.** a resilient wire attached to a denture or other appliance.

spring forceps [AS, *springan*, to jump], a kind of forceps that includes a spring mechanism. They are tweezer-like and vary in thickness. With teeth, they can grasp delicate tissue. Without teeth, they can hold thick or slippery tissue.

spring lancet, a very small knife with a spring-triggered blade. It may be used for collecting small specimens of blood for laboratory tests.

sprinter's fracture [Swe, *sprinta*, to spurt; L, *fractura*, to break], a break in the anterior superior or anterior inferior spine of the ilium, caused when the bone is forcibly pulled by a violent muscle spasm.

sprue /sprōō/ [D, *sprouw,* kind of tumor], a chronic degenerative disorder resulting from malabsorption of nutrients from the small intestine and characterized by a broad range of symptoms, including diarrhea; weakness; weight loss; poor appetite; pallor; muscle cramps; bone pain; ulceration of the mucous membrane lining the digestive tract; and a smooth, shiny tongue. It occurs in both tropical and nontropical forms.

Sprycel, a trademark for dasatinib.

spur [AS, *spura*], a projection of bone from a body structure or of metal from an appliance.

sputum /spyōō´təm/ [L, spittle], material coughed up from the lungs and expectorated through the mouth. It contains mucus, cellular debris, or microorganisms, and it also may contain blood or pus. The amount, color, and constituents of the sputum are important in the diagnosis of many illnesses.

sputum collection trap, a plastic trap connected to a suction catheter. Sputum specimens can be contained in the trap and sent for analysis.

sputum culture and sensitivity test, a test for pathogenic bacteria in the sputum of patients with respiratory infections.

sputum cytology, a sputum test to determine the presence of a pulmonary system malignancy. A positive test indicates malignancy, but a negative test means only that if a tumor exists, it is not shedding cells.

sputum specimen [L, spittle + *specere,* to look], a sample of material expelled from the respiratory passages taken for laboratory analysis to determine the presence of pathogens.

squama /skwā´mə/ *pl.* **squamae, 1.** a flattened scale from the epidermis. **2.** the thin, expanded part of a bone, especially in the cranial wall.

squamocolumnar junction /skwā´mōkəl um´nər/, a region of transition from stratified squamous epithelium to columnar epithelium in the cervical canal. It is a location where cells are obtained for Papanicolaou's smears.

squamous /skwā´məs/ [L, *squama,* scale], platelike, scaly, or covered with scales.

squamous blepharitis, a kind of nonulcerative blepharitis in which the edge of the eyelid is covered with small white or gray scales.

squamous cell [L, *squama,* scale, *cella,* storeroom], a flat, scalelike epithelial cell.

squamous cell carcinoma, a slow-growing malignant tumor of squamous epithelium, frequently found in the lungs and skin and occurring also in the anus, cervix, larynx, nose, and bladder. The neoplastic cells characteristically resemble prickle cells and form keratin pearls.

squamous epithelium [L, *squama,* scale; Gk, *epi,* above, *thele,* nipple], a sheet of flattened scalelike cells, attached together at the edges.

squamous epithelium simple, squamous epithelium having only one layer, such as in endothelium, mesothelium, and pulmonary alveoli.

squamous epithelium stratified, epithelium, such as that of typical skin, having a basal layer of cuboidal cells and overlying layers of squamous cells.

square centimeter (cm2) /skwer/, a unit of area measurement equivalent to 1 centimeter in length multiplied by 1 centimeter in width where 1 centimeter equals 0.3937 inch or 0.03281 foot.

square window [OFr, *esquarre* + ME, *wind,* air, *owe,* eye], an angle of the wrist between the hypothenar prominence and forearm. It is used as a reference point for estimating the gestational age of a newborn.

squatting position /skwot´ing/ [Fr, *esquatir,* to press down], a posture in which the knees and hips are flexed and the buttocks are lowered to the level of the heels. It is adopted by children with certain heart diseases as they seek relief from exercise distress.

squeeze dynamometer /skwēz/ [AS, *cwesan,* to press tightly; Gk, *dynamis,* force, *metron,* measure], a device for measuring the muscular strength of the grip of the hand.

squeeze-film lubrication, the exudation of fluid from the cartilage of joints, forming a film in the transient area of impending contact.

squinting eye /skwin´ting/ [D, *schuinte,* oblique; AS, *eage*], the abnormal eye in a person with strabismus that is not aligned with the fixating eye.

Sr, symbol for the element **strontium.**

SR, abbreviation for **sedimentation rate.**

sRNA, abbreviation for *soluble ribonucleic acid.*

SRO, abbreviation for **single room occupant.**

SRS-A, abbreviation for **slow-reacting substance of anaphylaxis.**

SRY, symbol for a "maleness" gene found on the sex-determining region of the Y chromosome. The gene is believed to function as a master control switch that can turn off or on other genes involved in sexual development.

ss, abbreviation for **steady state.**

SSE, 1. abbreviation for **skin self-examination. 2.** abbreviation for **soapsuds enema.**

S

SSKI, a trademark for an expectorant (potassium iodide).

SSRI, abbreviation for **selective serotonin reuptake inhibitor.**

SSS, 1. abbreviation for *sterile saline soak.* **2.** abbreviation for **sick sinus syndrome.**

SSSS, abbreviation for **staphylococcal scalded skin syndrome.**

ST, abbreviation for *slow-twitch.*

stab [ME, *stabbe,* piercing wound], a neutrophilic band.

stab culture [ME, *stabbe,* piercing wound; L, *colere,* to cultivate], a culture made by dipping a needle into an inoculum and then into a transparent gelatin or agar medium.

stabilization /stab′ilĭzā′shən/ [L, *stabilis,* firm, *atus,* process], **1.** the physiologic and metabolic process of attaining homeostasis. **2.** the seating of a fixed or removable denture so that it will not tilt or be displaced under pressure. **3.** the control of induced stress loads and the development of measures to counteract such forces so that the movement of the teeth or of a prosthesis does not irritate surrounding tissues.

stabilization exercises, exercises to develop proximal control in symptom (pain)-free positions, such as sitting on a gymnastic ball and extending one knee to maintain balance and control without pain.

stable /stā′bəl/ [L, *stabilis,* firm], remaining unchanged.

stable angina, angina pectoris in which attacks occur with predictable frequency and duration and are precipitated by circumstances such as exercise or emotional stress that increase myocardial oxygen demands.

stable condition, a state of health or disease from which little if any immediate change is expected.

stable element [L, *stabilis,* firm, *elementum*], a nonradioactive element, one not subject to spontaneous nuclear degeneration. Stable elements include calcium, iron, lead, potassium, and sodium.

staccato speech /stəkä′tō/ [It, detached; ME, *speche*], abnormal speech in which the person pauses between words, breaking the rhythm of the phrase or sentence. The condition is sometimes observed in association with MS.

stadium /stā′dē·əm/, *pl.* **stadia** [Gk, *stadion,* racetrack], a significant stage in a fever or illness such as the fastigium of a febrile illness or the prodromal stage of a viral infection.

Stadol, a trademark for an opioid analgesic (butorphanol tartrate).

staff [AS, *staef*], **1.** the people who work toward a common goal and are employed or supervised by someone of higher rank. **2.** a designation by which a staff nurse is distinguished from a nurse manager or other nurse. **3.** (in nursing education) the nonprofessional employees of the institution such as librarians, technicians, secretaries, and clerks. **4.** (in nursing service administration) the units of the organization that provide service to the line, or administratively defined hierarchy.

staff development¹, a process that assists individuals in an agency or organization in attaining new skills and knowledge, gaining increasing levels of competence, and growing professionally. The process may include such programs as orientation, in-service education, and continuing education.

staff development², a nursing intervention from the Nursing Interventions Classification (NIC) defined as developing, maintaining, and monitoring competence of staff.

staffing, the process of assigning people to fill the roles designed for an organizational structure through recruitment, selection, and placement.

staffing pattern, in hospital or nursing administration, the number and types or categories of staff assigned to the particular units and departments of a hospital or other health care facility. Staffing patterns vary with the unit, department, and shift and with the patient acuity levels.

staff of Æsculapius, a staff carried by Æsculapius, the Greek god of medicine. It is used as the traditional symbol of the physician. A single serpent entwines the staff of Æsculapius.

staff supervision, a nursing intervention from the Nursing Interventions Classification (NIC) defined as facilitating the delivery of high-quality patient care by others.

stage [OFr, *estage*], **1.** a platform. **2.** a period or phase.

stages of dying [OFr, *estage,* stage; ME, *dyen,* to lose life], the five emotional and behavioral stages that may occur after a person or family first learns of approaching death. The stages, identified and described by Elisabeth Kübler-Ross, are denial and shock, anger, bargaining, depression, and acceptance. The stages may occur in sequence or they may recur, as the person moves forward and backward—especially among denial, anger, and bargaining. Caring for a dying person requires sensitivity to the signs of each stage.

staging /stā′jing/, the classification of phases, quantity, or periods of a disease or other pathologic process, as in the TMN clinical method of assigning numeric values to various stages of tumor development.

stagnant anoxia /stag′nənt/ [L, *stagnum,* standing water; Gk, *a,* without, *oxys,* sharp, *genein,* to produce], a condition in which there is inadequate blood flow in the capillaries, causing low tissue oxygen tension and reduced oxygen exchange.

stain [OFr, *desteindre,* to dye], **1.** a pigment, dye, or substance used to impart color to microscopic objects or tissues to facilitate their examination and identification. **2.** to apply pigment to a substance or tissue to examine it under a microscope. **3.** an area of discoloration.

stained film fault, a defect in a radiograph or photograph that appears as a streaky discoloration or abnormal opacity. It is usually caused by contaminated or exhausted development solutions, improper rinsing, inadequate washing, or damage to the film emulsion during processing.

stalk /stôk/, an elongated, more or less slender anatomic structure resembling the stem of a plant.

stammering [AS, *stamerian,* to stutter], a speech dysfunction characterized by pauses, hesitations, and faltering utterances. The term is not commonly used in clinical practice in the United States but is frequently used synonymously with **stuttering** in Great Britain.

stamp cusp [ME, *stampen;* L, *cuspis,* point], a tooth cusp that works in a fossa, such as any of the maxillary lingual cusps.

stance phase of gait [L, *stare,* to stand; Gk, *phainein,* to show; ME, *gate,* a way], the phase of the normal gait cycle that begins with the strike of the heel on the ground and ends with the lift of the toe at the beginning of the swing phase of gait.

standard [OFr, *estandart*], **1.** an evaluation that serves as a basis for comparison for evaluating similar phenomena or substances, such as a standard for the preparation of a pharmaceutical substance or a standard for the practice of a profession. **2.** a pharmaceutical preparation or a chemical substance of known quantity, ingredients, and strength that is used to determine the constituents or the strength of another preparation. **3.** of known value, strength, quality, or ingredients. **4.** predetermined criteria used to provide guidance in the operation of a health care facility to ensure high-quality performance by the personnel. **—standardize,** *v.,* **standardization,** *n.*

standard air chamber, a radiation-measuring device used by national and international calibration laboratories to provide exposure calibrations for ion chambers used in the diagnostic or orthovoltage energy range.

standard bicarbonate, the bicarbonate ion concentration of plasma separated anaerobically from whole blood that has been saturated with oxygen and equilibrated at carbon dioxide pressure of 40 torr at 100° F (38° C). It is a measure of the metabolic disturbance of acid-base balance in a sample of blood after the correction of any respiratory disturbance.

standard curve, a graphic plot of tracer binding versus the known concentration of test substances in a set of standards usually prepared by serial dilution or incremental addition.

standard death certificate, a form for a death certificate that is commonly used throughout the United States.

standard deviation (SD), in statistics, a mathematic statement of the dispersion of a set of values or scores from the mean.

standard error (S.E.), in statistics, the variability in scores that can be expected if measurements are made on random samples of the same size from the same universe of populations, phenomena, or observations. The standard error provides a framework within which a determination of the difference between groups may be made.

standard error of the mean, in statistics, an indication of how well the mean of a sample estimates the mean of a population. It is measured by the standard deviation of the means of randomly drawn samples of the same size as the sample in question.

standard gravity (g), the acceleration caused by gravity at mean sea level, 9.80616 meters per second squared.

standard hydrogen electrode, a reference electrode that is assigned a value of 0.00 volt.

standardized death rate, the number of deaths per 1000 people of a specified population during 1 year. This rate is adjusted to prevent distortion by the age composition of the population.

standardized test, any empirically developed examination with established reliability and validity as determined by repeated evaluation of the method and results.

standard of care, a written statement describing the rules, actions, or conditions that direct patient care. Standards of care guide practice and can be used to evaluate performance.

standard precautions, guidelines recommended by the Centers for Disease Control and Prevention for reducing the risk of transmission of blood-borne and other pathogens in hospitals. The standard precautions synthesize the major features of universal precautions (designed to reduce the risk of transmission of blood-borne pathogens) and body substance isolation (designed to reduce the risk of pathogens from moist body substances) and apply them to all patients receiving care in hospitals, regardless of their diagnosis or presumed infection status. Standard precautions apply to (1) blood; (2) all body fluids, secretions, and excretions, *excluding sweat,* regardless of whether they contain blood; (3) nonintact skin; and (4) mucous membranes. The precautions are designed to reduce the risk of transmission of microorganisms from both recognized and unrecognized sources of infection in hospitals.

standard reference gamble, a method of diagnostic testing in which a decision maker is faced with a choice between a certain outcome or intermediate value and a gamble involving a better or worse outcome. The outcomes are assigned arbitrary numeric values of 100 and 0, respectively. All other outcomes can be assigned values relative to the best and worst outcomes.

standards of nursing practice, a set of guidelines for providing high-quality nursing care and criteria for evaluating care. Such guidelines help assure patients that they are receiving high-quality care. The standards are important if a legal dispute arises over the quality of care provided a patient.

standby guardianship, a legal process in the United States that may name an individual to assume specified health care or financial authority for an elderly person who becomes mentally incapacitated.

standing orders [L, *stare,* to stand, *ordo,* rank], a written document containing rules, policies, procedures, regulations, and orders for the conduct of patient care in various stipulated clinical situations. Standing orders usually name the condition and prescribe the action to be taken in caring for the patient, including the dosage and route of administration for a drug or the schedule for the administration of a therapeutic procedure.

stannous fluoride /stan′əs/ [L, *stannum,* tin, *fluere,* to flow], SnF_2, a substance used in prevention of dental caries, applied topically to the teeth.

stanolone /stan′o-lōn/, a semisynthetic form of dihydrotestosterone, which has been used as an androgenic and anabolic steroid.

stanozolol /stanō′zəlol/, an androgenic anabolic steroid prescribed in the treatment of hereditary angioedema.

stapedectomy /stā′pədek′təmē/ [L, *stapes,* stirrup; Gk, *ektomē,* excision], the removal of the stapes of the middle ear and insertion of a graft and prosthesis, performed to restore hearing in cases of otosclerosis. The stapes that has become fixed is replaced with a graft so that vibrations again transmit sound waves through the oval window to the fluid of the inner ear. The stapes is removed and the opening into the inner ear is covered with a graft of body tissue. One end of a small plastic tube or piece of stainless steel wire is attached to the graft; the other end is attached to the two remaining bones of the middle ear.

stapedius /stəpē′dē-əs/, a small muscle on the wall of the tympanic cavity of the middle ear. It acts reflexively in response to loud sounds to reduce excessive vibrations that could injure the internal ear by pulling the head of the stapes posteriorly out of the oval window.

stapes /stā′pēz/ [L, stirrup], one of the three ossicles in the middle ear, resembling a tiny stirrup, that fits into the oval window. It transmits sound vibrations from the incus to the internal ear.

Staphcillin, a trademark for an antibacterial (methicillin sodium).

staphylococcal infection [Gk, *staphyle,* bunch of grapes, *kokkos,* berry; L, *inficere,* to taint], an infection caused by any one of several pathogenic species of *Staphylococcus,* commonly characterized by the formation of abscesses of the skin or other organs. Staphylococcal infections of the skin include carbuncles, folliculitis, furuncles, and hidradenitis suppurativa. Bacteremia is common and may result in endocarditis, meningitis, or osteomyelitis. Acute gastroenteritis may result from an enterotoxin produced by certain species of staphylococci in contaminated food. Treatment usually includes bed rest, analgesics, and an antimicrobial drug that is resistant to penicillinase, an enzyme secreted by many species of *Staphylococcus.* Surgical drainage, especially of deep abscesses, is often necessary.

staphylococcal pneumonia [Gk, *staphyle* + *kokkos* + *pneumon,* lung], pneumonia caused by a staphylococcus infection.

staphylococcal scalded skin syndrome (SSSS), an infection or mucous membrane colonization with toxin-producing *Staphylococcus aureus.* It is characterized by epidermal erythema, peeling, and necrosis, which give the skin a scalded appearance. This disorder primarily affects infants 1 to 3 months of age and children, but it may also affect adults. Treatment of SSSS commonly includes the administration of systemic antibiotics to prevent secondary infections and the replacement of body fluids to maintain fluid and electrolyte balance.

staphylococcemia /-koksē′mē-ə/, **1.** the presence of staphylococci in the blood. **2.** septicemia caused by staphylococci.

Staphylococcus /staf′ilōkok′əs/ *pl.* **staphylococci** [Gk, *staphyle* + *kokkos,* berry], a genus of nonmotile spheric gram-positive bacteria. Some species are normally found on the skin and in the throat. Certain species cause severe purulent infections or produce an enterotoxin, which may cause nausea, vomiting, and diarrhea. Life-threatening staphylococcal infections may arise within hospitals.—**staphylococcal,** *adj.*

Staphylococcus aureus [Gk, *staphyle* + *kokkos;* L, *aurum,* gold], a species of *Staphylococcus* that produces a golden pigment with some color variations and is commonly found on the skin or nose of healthy people. It is also responsible for a number of pyogenic infections, such as boils, carbuncles, and abscesses. *Staphyloccus aureus* infections have become increasingly more difficult to treat due to the development of resistance to penicillin-related antibiotics. These bacteria are called methicillin-resistant *Staphylococcus aureus* or MSRAs.

staphylokinase /staf′ilōki′nās/, an enzyme, produced by certain strains of staphylococci, that catalyzes the conversion of plasminogen to plasmin in various animal hosts of the microorganism.

staphyloma /staf′ilō′mə/, a bulging of eye contents through a thin region of the cornea or sclera.

staple /stā′pəl/, a piece of stainless steel wire used to close certain surgical wounds.

stapling [ME, *stapel*, stake], a method of fastening tissues together at the end of surgery by using a U-shaped piece of wire as a suture. The ends of the wire are bent toward the center to close the staple.

starch [AS, *stearc*, strong], a polysaccharide composed of long chains of glucose subunits. It is the principal molecule used for the storage of energy in plants.

Stargardt's macular degeneration, an autosomal-recessive type of macular degeneration usually occurring at 6 to 20 years of age and marked by abnormal pigmentation and other changes in the macular area with rapid loss of visual acuity.

Starling's law of the heart, a general rule that the energy of contraction of the heart is a function of the length of the fibers composing the myocardial walls just before contraction.

Starr-Edwards prosthesis [Albert Starr, American physician, b. 1926; M.L. Edwards, American physician, b. 1906; Gk, *prosthesis,* attachment], an artificial cardiac valve. A caged-ball form of device, it obstructs the valve opening and prevents the backward flow of blood.

start hesitation, a characteristic of parkinsonism in which the patient has difficulty initiating walking movements, as if the feet were stuck to the floor.

startle reflex /stär′təl/ [ME, *stertlen*, to rush; Gk, *syn,* together, *dromos,* course], a reflex response to a sudden unexpected stimulus. The reaction may be accompanied by physiologic effects including increased heartbeat and respiration, closing of the eyes, and flexion of trunk muscles. The reaction is rapid, pervasive, and uncontrollable, regardless of the unexpected stimulus, which may be as simple as a touch.

start point [ME, *sterte;* L, *punctum,* prick], the initial nucleotide transcribed from a DNA template in the formation of messenger RNA.

starvation /stärvā′shən/ [ME, *sterven,* to die], **1.** a condition resulting from the lack of essential nutrients over a long period (several days) and characterized by multiple physiologic and metabolic dysfunctions. **2.** the act or state of starving or being starved.

stasibasiphobia /stas′ibas′ifo′bē·ə/, a mental health condition in which a person is convinced that walking or standing is physically impossible. The person may also express a morbid distrust of his or her ability to stand or walk.

stasis /stā′sis, stas′is/ [Gk, standing], **1.** a disorder in which the normal flow of a fluid through a vessel of the body is slowed or halted. **2.** stillness.

stasis dermatitis, a common result of venous insufficiency of the legs, beginning with ankle edema and progressing to tan pigmentation, patchy erythema, petechiae, and induration. Ultimately there may be atrophy and fibrosis of the skin and subcutaneous tissue, with ulcerations that are slow to heal. The involved skin is easily irritated or sensitized to topical medications. The underlying venous insufficiency must be treated. The dermatitis is often treated by bed rest, Burow's solution for oozing lesions, antibiotics for infection, and corticosteroids for reduction of inflammation.

stasis syndrome, overgrowth of bacteria in the small intestine resulting from a variety of conditions causing stasis, particularly disturbances to intestinal motility or decreased acid secretion but also structural abnormalities such as diverticula, fistulae between the colon and upper bowel, or chronic obstruction; it is characterized by malabsorption of vitamin B_{12}, steatorrhea, and anemia.

stasis ulcer, a necrotic craterlike lesion of the skin of the lower leg caused by chronic venous congestion, is often associated with stasis dermatitis and varicose veins. Healing is slow, and care to prevent irritation and infection is essential. Bed rest, elevation, and pressure bandages are usually ordered, and antibiotics if needed for infection.

stat., abbreviation for the Latin word *statim,* "immediately."

state /stāt/ [L, *status,* condition], the circumstances or qualities that characterize a person, thing, or way of being at a particular time.

State Board Test Pool Examination (SBTPE), revised and retitled in 1982 as the NCLEX-RN, an examination prepared by the National Council of State Boards of Nursing for testing the competency of a person to perform safely as a newly licensed registered nurse. Each jurisdiction within the United States and its territories regulates entry into the practice of nursing; each requires the candidate to pass the examination. The content of the examination is planned to test the candidate's knowledge of the nursing process as applied to the broad areas of nursing practice, including maternal and child health, medical and surgical nursing, and psychiatric nursing.

State Nurses Association (SNA), an association of nurses at the state level. The various State Nurses Associations are constituent units of the American Nurses Association.

Statewide Health Coordinating Committee (SHCC), a component of the U.S. national network of Health Systems Agencies.

static /stat'ik/ [Gk, *statikos,* causing to stand], without motion, at rest, in equilibrium.

static cardiac work, the energy transfer that occurs during the development and maintenance of ventricular pressure immediately before the opening of the aortic and pulmonary valves.

static electricity film fault, a defect in a radiograph or a developed photographic film, which appears as lightninglike streaks. It is caused by overly rapid opening of the film packet or transfer of static electricity from the user to the film.

static equilibrium, the ability of an individual to adjust to displacements of his or her center of gravity while maintaining a constant base of support.

static imaging, 1. a diagnostic procedure for visualizing an internal organ or body compartment. A radioactive substance is administered to a patient, and an image or set of images is made of the fixed or slowly changing distribution of the radioactivity. 2. any diagnostic image that is fixed or frozen in time.

static labyrinth, the vestibule of the inner ear. It contains two communicating chambers, the saccule and the utricle, and elicits tonic reflexes on postural muscles in response to changes in head and body positions.

static pressure [Gk, *statikos,* causing to stand; L, *premere,* to press], a condition of equalized BP throughout the body when the heartbeat is stopped. A nonmoving fluid exerts a uniform pressure in all directions.

static reflex [Gk, *statikos,* causing to stand; L, *reflectere,* to bend back], a reflex that helps one maintain normal posture and muscle tone when the body is at rest.

static retinoscopy, a type in which the patient fixes the gaze on an unmoving target at a long distance to relax accommodation.

static scoliosis [Gk, *statikos,* causing to stand, *skoliosis,* curvature], a form of scoliosis resulting from a difference in the length of the legs.

static tremor, irregular involuntary muscle contractions that occur when a patient makes an effort to hold the trunk or limbs in certain positions.

station /stā'shən/ [L, *stare,* to stand], the level of the biparietal plane of the fetal head relative to the level of the ischial spines of the maternal pelvis. An imaginary plane at the level of the spines is designated "zero station." Higher and lower stations are numbered at intervals of 1 cm and labeled as minus above and plus below.

stationary grid /stā'shənər'ē/ [L, *stare;* ME, *gridere,* gridiron], an x-ray grid that does not move or oscillate during the exposure of a radiographic film.

stationary lingual arch, an orthodontic arch wire that is designed to fit the lingual surface of the teeth and soldered to the associated anchor bands.

statistic /stetis'tik/ [L, *status,* condition], a number that describes a property of a set of data or other numbers.

statistical model of patient evaluation, a system based on gross quantitative measurements of similar cases used to determine payment for services.

statistical significance [L, *status,* condition, *significare,* to signify], an interpretation of statistical data that indicates that an occurrence was probably the result of a causative factor and not simply a chance result.

statistics /stətis'tiks/, a mathematic science concerned with measuring, classifying, and analyzing objective information.

status /stā'təs, stat'əs/ [L, condition], 1. a specified state or condition such as emotional status. 2. an unremitting state or condition such as status asthmaticus.

status asthmaticus, an acute, severe, and prolonged asthma attack. It is caused by critically diminished airway diameter resulting from ongoing bronchospasm, edema, and mucus plugging. Hypoxia, cyanosis, and unconsciousness may follow, and the attack may be fatal.

status epilepticus, a medical emergency characterized by continuous seizures lasting more than 30 minutes without interruptions. Status epilepticus can be precipitated by the sudden withdrawal of anticonvulsant drugs, inadequate body levels of glucose, a brain tumor, a head injury, a high fever, or poisoning. Therapy includes IV administration of anticonvulsant drugs, nutrients, and electrolytes.

status marmoratus, the presence in full-term infants of basal nucleus lesions resulting from acute total asphyxia. The lesions have a marbled appearance caused by neuronal loss and an overgrowth of myelin in the putamen, caudate, and thalamus.

statute of limitations /stach′ōōt/ [L, *statuere,* to set up, *limes,* boundary], in law, a statute that sets a limit of time during which a suit may be brought or criminal charges may be made.

statutory rape /stach′ətôr′ē/ [L, *statuere,* to place, *rapere,* to seize], in law, sexual intercourse with a female below the age of consent, which varies from state to state.

stavudine, a synthetic thymidine nucleoside analog. It is prescribed in combination with other drugs for the treatment of adults with advanced HIV infection, generally in those who are intolerant of other approved therapies.

STD, abbreviation for **sexually transmitted disease.**

steady state (s, ss) /sted′ē/ [AS, *stedefast,* firm in its place; L, *status,* condition], a basic physiologic concept implying that the various forces and processes of life are in a state of homeostasis.

steam sterilization [ME, *steme,* vapor; L, *sterilis,* barren], the destruction of all forms of microbial life on an object by exposing the object to moist heat for 15 minutes at 121° F (49.44° C) under high pressure.

steapsin, pancreatic expase.

Stearns' alcoholic amentia /sturnz/ [A. Warren Stearns, American physician, 1885–1959; Ar, *alkohl,* essence; L, *ab,* from, *mens,* mind], a form of insanity brought on by alcohol, characterized by an emotional disturbance of a less severe nature than that of DT but of longer duration and with greater mental clouding and amnesia.

stearrhea [Gk, *stear,* fat, *rhoia,* flow], excessive secretion of fat.

stearyl alcohol, a solid substance, prepared by the catalytic hydrogenation of stearic acid, used in various ointments.

steatorrhea /stē′ətərē′ə/ [Gk, *stear,* fat, *rhoia,* flow], greater than normal amounts of fat in the feces, characterized by frothy foul-smelling fecal matter that floats, as in celiac disease, some malabsorption syndromes, and any condition in which fats are poorly absorbed by the small intestine.

steering wheel injury, a traumatic injury most commonly to the anterior chest wall caused by forward propulsion of the body

of an automobile driver into the steering wheel during a collision. Injuries include broken ribs and sternum, cardiac and pulmonary damage, and tearing of major blood vessels.

Steinmann pin /stīn′mən/ [Fritz Steinmann, Swiss surgeon, 1872–1932; AS, *pinn*], a wide-diameter pin used for heavy skeletal traction, as in the tibia or femur.

Stelazine, a trademark for a phenothiazine antipsychotic agent (trifluoperazine).

stellate /stel′it, -āt/ [L, *stella,* star], star-shaped or arranged in the pattern of a star.

stellate fracture, a fracture in which there are numerous fissures radiating from the central point of impact or injury throughout surrounding bone tissue.

stellate ganglion [L, *stella,* star; Gk, *gagglion,* knot], a large irregular ganglion on the lowest part of the cervical sympathetic trunk fused with the first thoracic ganglion. Its branches communicate with the seventh and eighth cervical nerves.

stem cell [AS, *stemm,* tree, trunk; L, *cella,* storeroom], a formative cell; a cell whose daughter cells may give rise to other cell types. A pluripotential stem cell is one that has the potential to develop into several different types of mature cells, including lymphocytes, granulocytes, thrombocytes, and erythrocytes.

stem cell leukemia, a neoplasm of blood-forming organs in which the predominant malignant cell is too immature to classify. The acute disease has a rapid, relentless course.

stenosis /stinō′sis/ [Gk, *stenos,* narrow, *osis,* condition], an abnormal condition characterized by the constriction or narrowing of an opening or passageway in a body structure. The term is commonly used to describe heart valve and vessel abnormalities as well as narrowing of joint spaces, as in cervical stenosis.—**stenotic,** *adj.*

stenotic [Gk, *stenos,* narrow], pertaining to a structure that is narrowed or strictured.

stent [Charles R. Stent, nineteenth-century English dentist], **1.** a compound used in making dental impressions and medical molds. **2.** a mold or device made of stent, used in anchoring skin grafts. **3.** a rod or threadlike device for supporting tubular structures during surgical anastomosis or for holding arteries open during angioplasty.

step-care therapy, a therapeutic program that begins with a simple, conservative type of treatment but may advance to more complex stages as needed to achieve control of a disease or disorder.

steppage gait /step′ij/ [AS, *staepe;* ONorse, *gata,* way], a gait in which

S

the legs are raised abnormally high, as in patients with footdrop.

stepwedge /step'wej/, an aluminum device that, when exposed to x-rays, displays a range of exposure intensities on a radiograph. These exposure "steps" are analyzed to determine the speed characteristics of the radiographic film.

Sterapred, a trademark for a glucocorticoid (predniSONE).

stereognosis /stir'ē·ŏg·nō'sis/ [Gk, *stereos,* solid, *gnosis,* knowledge], **1.** the faculty of perceiving and understanding the form and nature of objects by the sense of touch. **2.** perception by the sense of the solidity of objects.—**stereognostic,** *adj.*

stereognostic perception /stir'ē·ŏg·nos'tik/ [Gk, *stereos,* solid, *gnosis,* knowledge], the ability to recognize objects by the sense of touch.

stereoisomer /stir'ē·ō·ī'səmər/ [Gk, *stereos,* solid, *isos,* equal, *meros,* part], one of two or more chemical compounds that contain the same atoms linked in the same way but organized differently in space. For example, one may be the nonsuperimposable mirror image of the other.

stereoisomeric specificity /-ī'səmer'ik/ [Gk, *stereos* + *isos,* equal, *meros,* part], specificity of an enzyme for one enantiomer of a racemic mix.

stereoophthalmoscope /stir'ē·ō·ŏf·thal'mə·skōp/, an ophthalmoscope fitted with two eyepieces so that the examiner can view the three-dimensional interior of the eye.

stereopsis, binocular perception of depth or three-dimensional space.

stereoradiography /-ra'dē·og'rəfē/ [Gk, *stereos;* L, *radiare,* to emit rays; Gk, *graphein,* to record], a technique for producing radiographs that give a three-dimensional view of an internal body structure by combining two separate x-ray films, each made from a slightly different angle without movement of the body part being x-rayed.

stereoscopic microscope /-skop'ik/ [Gk, *stereos* + *skopein,* to look], a microscope that produces three-dimensional images through the use of double eyepieces and double objectives.

stereoscopic radiograph, a composite of two radiographs made through stereoradiography.

stereotactic mammography, a radiographic procedure using three-dimensional breast imaging to perform a needle breast biopsy. The three-dimensional imaging assists in locating the lesion and placement of the needle.

stereotactic radiosurgery, stereotaxic surgery in which lesions are produced by ionizing radiation.

stereotactic surgery, any of several techniques for the production of sharply circumscribed lesions in specific tiny areas of pathologic tissue in deep-seated structures of the CNS. The site to be worked on is localized with three-dimensional coordinates. Methods of producing lesions include heat, cold, x-rays, and ultrasound.

stereotaxic instrument /-tak'sik/, an apparatus that fits on the head and helps locate structures in the brain by means of coordinates.

stereotaxic neuroradiography [Gk, *stereos* + *taxis,* arrangement, *neuron,* nerve; L, *radiare,* to emit rays; Gk, *graphein,* to record], a radiographic procedure commonly performed during neurosurgery to guide the insertion of a needle into a specific area of the brain.

stereotype /stir'ē·ə·tīp/ [Gk, *stereos* + *typos,* mark], a generalization about a form of behavior, an individual, or a group.

stereotypic behavior /stir'ē·ō·tip'ik/, a pattern of body movements that has autistic and symbolic meaning for an individual.

stereotypy /ster'ē·ə·tī'pē/ [Gk, *stereos* + *typos,* mark], the persistent inappropriate mechanical repetition of actions, body postures, or speech patterns, usually occurring with a lack of variation in thought processes or ideas.—**stereotypical,** *adj.*

sterile /ster'il/ [L, *sterilis,* barren], **1.** free of living microorganisms. **2.** barren; unable to produce children because of a physical abnormality. **3.** aseptic.—**sterility,** *n.*

sterile field, 1. a specified area that is considered free of microorganisms. **2.** an area immediately around a patient that has been prepared for a surgical procedure. The sterile field includes the scrubbed team members, who are properly attired, and all furniture and fixtures in the area.

sterile meningitis [L, *sterilis,* barren; Gk, *meninx,* membrane, *itis,* inflammation], a form of nonbacterial meningitis, usually involving a viral infection but may also be drug-induced, in which there is a primarily lymphocytic response in the CSF.

sterile water for inhalation, water for injection, sterilized, and containing no antimicrobial agents, except when used in devices in which it is liable to contamination over a period of time (e.g., humidifiers), or other added substances. It is for inhalation therapy only, not for parenteral administration.

sterile water for irrigation, water for injection that is sterilized and contains no antimicrobial agents or other added substances. It is used for irrigation but not for parenteral administration.

sterility /stəril′itē/ [L, *sterilis,* barren], a condition of being unable to conceive or reproduce the species.

sterility assurance level (SAL), the probability that a process makes something sterile. An SAL of 10^{-6} is the recommended probability of survival for organisms on a sterilized device. This level means that there is less than or equal to one chance in a million that an item remains contaminated or nonsterile.

sterilization /ster′ilīzā′shən/ [L, *sterilis*; Gk, *izein,* to cause], **1.** a process or act that renders a person unable to produce children. **2.** a technique for destroying microorganisms or inanimate objects, using heat, water, chemicals, or gases. —**sterilize,** *v.*

sterilize /ster′ilīz/ [L, *sterilis,* barren], **1.** to make powerless to reproduce (infertile), such as by surgery. **2.** to destroy all living organisms and viruses in a material.

sternal /stur′nəl/ [Gk, *sternon,* chest], pertaining to the sternum.

sternal node [Gk, *sternon,* chest; L, *nodus,* knot], a node in one of the three groups of thoracic parietal lymph nodes.

sternal puncture [Gk, *sternon,* chest; L, *punctura*], a diagnostic procedure in which a needle is inserted into the marrow of the sternum to remove bone marrow samples for diagnosis.

Sternheimer-Malbin stain /sturn′hīmər mal′bin/, a crystal violet and safranin stain used in urinalyses to provide additional contrast for certain casts and cells.

sternoclavicular /stur′nōklavik′yələr/ [Gk, *sternon,* chest; L, *clavicula,* little key], pertaining to the sternum and clavicle.

sternoclavicular articulation [Gk, *sternon;* L, *clavicula,* little key], the double gliding joint between the sternum and the clavicle.

sternocleidomastoid /-klī′dōmas′toid/ [Gk, *sternon,* chest, *kleis,* key, *mastos,* breast, *eidos,* form], a muscle of the neck that is attached to the mastoid process of the temporal bone and superior nuchal line and by separate heads to the sternum and clavicle. They function together to flex the head.

sternocostal articulation /-kos′təl/ [Gk, *sternon;* L, *costa,* rib], the gliding articulation of the cartilage of each true rib and the sternum, except the articulation of the first rib, in which the cartilage is directly united with the sternum to form a synchondrosis.

sternohyoideus /stur′nōhī·oi′dē·əs/ [Gk, *sternon* + *hyoeides,* upsilon, U-shaped], one of the four infrahyoid muscles. It acts to depress the hyoid bone.

sternopericardial ligaments, ligaments that attach the fibrous pericardium to the posterior surface of the sternum and help to retain the heart in its position in the thoracic cavity.

sternothyroideus /stur′nōthīroi′de·əs/ [Gk, *sternon* + *thyreos,* shield, *eidos,* form], one of the four infrahyoid muscles. It acts to depress the thyroid cartilage.

sternum /stur′nəm/ [Gk, *sternon*], the elongated flattened bone forming the middle part of the thorax. It supports the clavicles, articulates directly with the first seven pairs of ribs, and comprises the manubrium, the gladiolus (body), and the xiphoid process.

steroid /stir′oid/ [Gk, *stereos* + *eidos,* form], any of a large number of hormonal substances with a similar basic chemical structure, produced mainly in the adrenal cortex and gonads.

steroid acne [Gk, *stereos,* solid; L, *oleum,* oil; Gk, *eidos,* form, *akme,* point], a form of acne caused by the use of corticosteroids.

steroid cell antibody, an IgG glycoprotein that interacts with antigens in the cytoplasm of gonadal or adrenal cells that produce steroids.

steroid hormone [Gk, *stereos,* solid; L, *oleum,* oil; Gk, *eidos,* form, *hormaein,* to set in motion], any of the ductless gland secretions that contain the basic steroid nucleus in their chemical formulae. The natural steroid hormones include androgens, estrogens, and adrenal cortex secretions.

steroid hormone therapy [Gk, *stereos;* L, *oleum,* oil; Gk, *eidos,* form, *hormaein,* to set in motion, *therapeia,* treatment], treatment with any of the steroid hormones, such as the use of estrogen to reduce symptoms of postmenopausal disorders.

steroidogenesis /stiroi′dōjen′əsis/, the biologic synthesis of steroid hormones.

sterol /stir′ôl/ [Gk, *stereos;* Ar, *alkohl,* essence], a large subgroup of steroids containing a hydroxyl group at position 3 and a branched aliphatic side chain of eight or more carbon atoms at position 17. Kinds of sterols include cholesterol and ergosterol.

stertorous /stur′tərəs/ [L, *stertere,* to snore], **1.** pertaining to a respiratory effort that is strenuous or struggling. **2.** having a snoring sound.

stethomimetic /steth′ōmimet′ik/, pertaining to any condition causing or associated with a reduction of chest volume below its normal value.

stethoscope /steth′əskōp/ [Gk, *stethos,* chest, *skopein,* to look], an instrument consisting of two earpieces connected by

S

means of flexible tubing to a diaphragm, which is placed against the skin of the patient's chest or back to hear heart and lung sounds. It is also used to hear bowel sounds.

Stevens-Johnson syndrome [Albert M. Stevens, American pediatrician, 1884-1945; F.C. Johnson, American physician, 1894-1934], a serious, sometimes fatal inflammatory disease affecting children and young adults. It is characterized by the acute onset of fever, bullae on the skin, and ulcers on the mucous membranes of the lips, eyes, mouth, nasal passage, and genitalia. Other complications are pneumonia, pain in the joints, prostration, and perforation of the cornea. It may be an allergic reaction to certain drugs; or it may follow pregnancy, herpesvirus I, or other infection. Treatment includes bed rest, antibiotics for pneumonia, glucocorticoids, analgesics, mouthwashes, and sedatives.

Stewart, Isabel Maitland, a Canadian-born American nursing educator and writer. She was instrumental in upgrading the nursing curriculum and in directing educational policies and became an important figure in international nursing affairs.

STH, abbreviation for **somatotropic hormone.**

sthenic fever /sthen'ik/ [Gk, *sthenos,* power; L, *febris,* fever], high body temperature associated with thirst, dry skin, and often delirium.

stibogluconate sodium /stib'ōglⁿoo'kə nāt/, an antileishmanial. It is a drug of choice for the visceral form of leishmaniasis and has some effect on other forms.

Stickler's syndrome /stik'lərz/ [Gunnar B. Stickler, American physician, 20th century], an autosomal-dominant disorder consisting of myopia progressing to retinal detachment and blindness, and premature degenerative changes in the joints. Sensorineural hearing loss may also occur.

Stieda's fracture /stē'dəz/ [Alfred Stieda, German surgeon, 1869-1945], a break in the internal condyle of the femur.

stiff [OE, *stif*], characterized by rigidity or muscular inflexibility.

stiff joint [OE, *stif*; L, *jungere,* to join], a rigid or inflexible joint, as may be caused by tight connective tissue or by arthritis or other rheumatic disorders.

stiff-man syndrome, a condition of unknown cause characterized by progressive fluctuating rigidity of axial and limb muscles in the absence of signs of cerebral and spinal cord disease but with continuous electromyographic activity.

stigma /stig'mə/ *pl.* **stigmas, stigmata** [Gk, brand], **1.** a moral or physical blemish. **2.** a mental or physical characteristic that serves to identify a disease or condition.

stigmatism /stig'mətiz'əm/ [Gk, *stigma,* brand], **1.** normal visual accommodation and refraction whereby light rays fall onto the retina. **2.** a condition of abnormal skin markings.

stillbirth [AS, *stille,* ME, *burth*], **1.** the birth of a fetus that died before or during delivery. **2.** a fetus, born dead, who weighs more than 500 g and would usually have been expected to live.

stillborn [AS, *stille* + *boren*], **1.** an infant who is born dead. **2.** pertaining to an infant who is born dead.

stimulant /stim'yələnt/ [L, *stimulare,* to incite], any agent that increases the rate of activity of a body system.

stimulant cathartic, a cathartic that acts by promoting the motility of the bowel, especially the longitudinal peristalsis of the colon. The class of stimulant cathartics includes cascara and senna.

stimulate /stim'yəlāt/ [L, *stimulare,* to incite], to excite, as in the process of increasing a vigorous functional activity.

stimulating bath, a bath taken in water that contains an aromatic substance, an astringent, or a tonic.

stimulation /stim'yəlā'shən/ [L, *stimulare,* to incite], the condition of being stimulated.

stimulus /stim'yələs/ *pl.* **stimuli** [L, *stimulare,* to incite], anything that excites or incites an organism or part to function, become active, or respond. —**stimulate,** *v.*

stimulus control, a strategy for self-modification that depends on manipulating the causes of behavior to increase goals or behaviors desired by a patient while decreasing those that are undesired.

stimulus duration, the length of time a stimulus must be applied for the resulting nerve impulse to produce excitation in the receptor tissue.

stimulus generalization, a type of conditioning in which the reaction to one stimulus is reinforced to allow transfer of the reaction to other occurrences.

sting [AS, *stingan*], an injury caused by a sharp, painful penetration of the skin, often accompanied by exposure to an irritating chemical or the venom of an insect or other animal. Kinds of stings include bee, jellyfish, scorpion, sea urchin, and shellfish stings.

stingray /sting'rā/ [AS, *stingan*; L, *raia,* ray-fish], a flat, long-tailed fish bearing barbed spines on its back that are connected to sacs of venom. Spasm of the skeletal muscles, severe local pain, seizures, and dyspnea may occur if the skin is broken by the spines.

stippling [D, *stippen*, to prick], **1.** the appearance of colored dots in some cells when stained. Red stippling in blood cells stained with eosin hematoxylin is a sign of malaria. Blue stippling in RBCs stained with Wright's stain can be a sign of lead poisoning. **2.** the appearance of the retina, as if dotted with light and dark points.

stitch [ME, *stiche*], **1.** a suture. **2.** a sudden sharp pain.

stitch abscess [ME, *stiche*; L, *abscedere*, to go away], an abscess that develops around a suture.

stitch granuloma, a foreign-body granuloma occurring around a buried nonabsorbable suture.

St. John's wort, a herb that is native to Europe and Asia, also now grown in the United States. This herb is used as an antidepressant and antiviral. It has demonstrated efficacy against mild depression and certain other mood disturbances, but does not have demonstrable antiviral efficacy.

St. Louis encephalitis /sănt lo͞o'is/ [St. Louis, Missouri; Gk, *enkephalon,* brain, *itis,* inflammation], a flavivirus infection of the brain transmitted from birds to humans by the bite of an infected mosquito. It occurs most commonly in the central and southern parts of the United States and is characterized by headache, malaise, fever, stiff neck, delirium, and convulsions. Convalescence may be prolonged, and death may result. No antivirus agent or vaccine is available; treatment is supportive.

stochastic effects, effects produced at random without a threshold dose level, the probability of their occurrence being proportional to the dose and their severity being independent of it. In radiation safety, the main stochastic effects are carcinogenesis and genetic mutation.

stock vaccine, an immunizing agent made from a stock microbial strain.

stoma /stō'mə/ *pl.* **stomas, stomata** [Gk, mouth], **1.** a pore, orifice, or opening on a surface. **2.** an artificial opening of an internal organ on the surface of the body, created surgically, such as for a colostomy. **3.** a new opening created surgically between two body structures, such as for a gastroenterostomy.

stomach /stum'ək/ [Gk, *stomakhos,* gullet], the food reservoir and first major site of digestion, located just under the diaphragm and divided into a body and a pylorus. It receives partially processed food and drink funneled from the mouth through the esophagus and gradually feeds liquefied food (chyme) into the small intestine. It is lined with a mucous coat, a submucous coat, a muscular coat, and a serous coat, all richly supplied with blood vessels and nerves and contains fundic, cardiac, and pyloric gastric glands.

stomachache [Gk, *stomakhos,* gullet; ME, *aken,* pain], pain in the stomach area.

stomach drops, a medication that promotes gastric activity.

stomach pump, a pump for withdrawing the contents of the stomach through a tube passed through the mouth or nose into the stomach.

stomach tube, a tube used to introduce nutrients into the stomach, remove fluids and ingested poisons, or decompress the stomach.

stomach wall, the layered structure that makes up the stomach, consisting of a serous coat, a muscular coat, a mucous membrane, and other tissue layers in between.

stomal /stō'məl/ [Gk, mouth], pertaining to one or more stomata or mouthlike openings.

stomal peptic ulcer, a marginal peptic ulcer.

stomatitis /stō'mətī'tis/ [Gk, *stoma* + *itis,* inflammation], any inflammatory condition of the mouth. It may result from infection by bacteria, viruses, or fungi; from exposure to certain chemicals or drugs from vitamin deficiency; or from a systemic inflammatory disease.

stomatitis parasitica [Gk, *stoma,* mouth, *itis,* inflammation, *parasitos,* guest], an inflammation of the mucous membranes of the mouth by a yeast fungus, *Candida albicans,* typically expressed by a white coating on the tongue. It may affect infants or immunosuppressed people with HIV or appear as an outgrowth secondary to antibiotic therapy.

stomatocyte /sto'mah-to-sīt/, an abnormal red blood cell in which a slit or mouthlike area replaces the normal central zone of pallor, often due to edema.

stomatocytosis /sto'mah-to-si-to'sis/, the presence of stomatocytes in the blood, as seen in liver disease and Rh-null syndrome, a rare congenital hemolytic anemia.

stomatognathic system /stō'mətōnath'ik/ [Gk, *stoma* + *gnathos,* jaw + *systema*], the combination of organs, structures, and nerves involved in speech and reception, mastication, and deglutition of food. This system is composed of the teeth, the jaws, the masticatory muscles, the tongue, the lips, surrounding tissues, and the nerves that control these structures.

stomatology /stō'mətol'əjē/ [Gk, *stoma* + *logos,* science], the study of the morphologic characteristics, structure, function, and diseases of the oral cavity.—**stomatologist,** *n.,* **stomatologic,** *adj.*

stomion /stŏ′mē·on/ [Gk, *stoma*], the median point of the oral slit when the mouth is closed.

stomodeum /stom′ədē′əm/ *pl.* **stomodeums, stomodea** [Gk, *stoma* + *odaios*, a way], a depression in the ectoderm located in the foregut of the developing embryo that forms the mouth.—**stomadaeum, stomadeum, stomodaeum,** *adj.*

stone disease, urolithiasis that may have complications when obstructive uropathy or infection develops.

stone retrieval basket, a tiny apparatus consisting of several wires that can be advanced through an endoscope into a body cavity or tube, manipulated to trap a calculus or other object, and withdrawn.

stool culture, a test to determine whether a patient has a bacterial or viral infection of the bowel or parasites.

stool for occult blood test (stool for OB), a stool test performed as part of every routine physical examination to detect the presence of occult blood (OB) in the GI tract. Presence of OB in the stool may indicate benign and malignant GI tumors, ulcers, inflammatory bowel disease, arteriovenous malformation, diverticulosis, and hematobilia.

stop [AS, *stoppian,* to stop], a consonantal speech sound produced by closing off the oral cavity and then releasing with a burst of air, such as an initial /p/.

stopcock, a valve or turning plug that controls the flow of fluid from a container through a tube.

stop needle [AS, *stoppian,* to stop + *naedel*], a needle with a shoulder flange that prevents it from penetrating beyond a certain distance.

storage disease, a metabolic disorder in which certain cells accumulate excessive amounts of lipids, proteins, or other substances.

storage pool, the area of a platelet organelle such as a dense body or an alpha granule where specific chemical constituents are stored.

storage pool disease, inadequate number or contents of platelet delta-granules causing mucocutaneous bleeding. Storage pool disease is usually hereditary and related to oculocutaneous albinism syndromes such as Hermansky-Pudlak syndrome, Chediak-Higashi syndrome, and Wiskott-Aldrich syndrome.

stored-energy foot, a lower-limb prosthesis designed to imitate the springlike action of a natural foot and leg. A device in the prosthesis stores energy when weight is put on the prosthesis. When the weight is shifted to the other leg, the stored energy is released, returning the prosthesis to its original shape.

storm fermentation [OE, *sturm, storm;* L, *fermentum,* leaven], the rapid gaseous clotting of milk caused by *Clostridium perfringens.*

Stoxil, a trademark for an antiviral (idoxuridine).

STP, *slang.* **1.** a psychedelic agent, dimethoxy-4-methylamphetamine. **2.** an abbreviation for *serenity, tranquillity, and peace.*

STPD conditions of a volume of gas, standard temperature, standard pressure, dry; the conditions of a volume of gas at 0° C and 760 torr that contains no water vapor (dry). It should contain a calculable number of moles of a particular gas.

Str., abbreviation for *Streptococcus.*

strabismal /strabiz′məl/ [Gk, *strabismos,* squint], pertaining to the condition of strabismus.

strabismus /strəbiz′məs/ [Gk, *strabismos,* squint], an abnormal ocular condition in which the visual axes of the eyes are not directed at the same point. Paralytic strabismus results from the inability of the ocular muscles to move the eye because of neurologic deficit or muscular dysfunction. The muscle that is dysfunctional may be identified by watching as the patient attempts to move the eyes to each of the cardinal positions of gaze. Nonparalytic strabismus is a defect in the position of the two eyes in relation to each other. The condition may be inherited. The person cannot use the two eyes together but has to fixate with one or the other. The eye that looks straight at a given time is the fixing eye. Some people have alternating strabismus, using one eye and then the other; some have monocular strabismus, which affects only one eye. Visual acuity diminishes with diminished use of an eye, and suppression amblyopia may develop.—**strabismal, strabismic,** *adj.*

straddle injury, injury to the distal urethra by falling astride a blunt object, such as bicycle handlebars or the top of a fence or railing.

straight chiropractic, the practice of chiropractic in strict accordance with the principles of its founder, D.D. Palmer, without additions made by later practitioners. The original definition of subluxation as a vertebral displacement is adhered to, and chiropractic is considered to be nontherapeutic, its purpose being solely to contribute to health by the correction of vertebral subluxations.

straight-leg-raising (SLR) test, a physical examination technique to determine abnormality of the sciatic nerve or tightness of the hamstrings. The presence of sciatica is confirmed by sciatic nerve pain radiating down the limb when the supine person attempts to raise the straightened limb.

straight line blood set /strāt/ [ME, *streght*], a common device, composed of plastic components, for delivering blood infusions. It includes plastic tubing, a clamp, a drip chamber, and a filter.

straight sinus [ME, *streght;* L, *sinus,* hollow], one of the six posterior-superior venous channels of the dura mater, draining blood from the brain into the internal jugular vein. It has no valves and is located at the junction of the falx cerebri with the tentorium cerebelli.

straight wire fixed orthodontic appliance, a fixed orthodontic appliance used for correcting and improving malocclusion. Its design and placement of arch wire brackets and tubes are intended to limit the need for arch wire adjustments.

strain [ME, *streinen*], 1. to exert physical force in a manner that may result in injury, usually muscular. 2. to separate solids or particles from a liquid with a filter or sieve. 3. damage, usually muscular, that results from excessive physical effort. 4. a taxon that is a subgroup of a species. 5. an emotional state reflecting mental pressure or fatigue.

straitjacket /strāt'jakit/ [OFr, *estreit,* strict, *jaquette,* short coat], a coatlike garment of canvas with long sleeves that can be tied behind the wearer's back to prevent arm movement. It is used for restraining violent or uncontrollable people.

strangle /strang'gəl/ [L, *strangulare,* to choke], to cause an interruption of breathing by compressing or constricting the trachea.—**strangulated,** *adj.*

strangulated /strang'gyəlā'tid/ [L, *strangulare,* to choke], pertaining to a constriction or compression of the trachea or other upper airway structure that interrupts the normal flow of air.

strangulated hemorrhoid [L, *strangulare,* to choke; Gk, *haimorrhoise,* vein that discharges blood], a prolapsed hemorrhoid that has become trapped by the anal sphincter, causing the blood supply to become occluded by the sphincter's constricting action.

strangulated hernia [L, *strangulare,* to choke, *hernia,* rupture], a hernia in which the blood vessels have become constricted by the neck of the hernial sac, resulting in ischemia and possible gangrene if blood circulation is not quickly restored.

strangulation /strang'gyəlā'shən/ [L, *strangulare,* to choke], the constriction of a tubular structure of the body such as the trachea, a segment of bowel, or the blood vessels of a limb that prevents function or impedes circulation.

strap [AS, *stropp*], 1. a band, such as that made of adhesive plaster, that is used to hold dressings in place or to attach one thing to another. 2. to bind securely.

strapping, the application of overlapping strips of adhesive tape to an extremity or body area to exert pressure and hold a structure in place, performed in the treatment of strains, sprains, dislocations, and certain fractures.

stratified /strat'ifīd/ [L, *stratum* + *facere,* to make], arranged in layers.

stratified clot, a semisolid mass of coagulated blood that forms in layers within an aneurysm.

stratified epithelium [L, *stratum* + *facere;* Gk, *epi,* above, *thele,* nipple], closely packed sheets of epithelial cells arranged in layers over the external surface of the body and lining most of the hollow structures. The layers may include stratified squamous, stratified columnar, or stratified columnar ciliated types of cells.

stratiform fibrocartilage /strat'ifôrm/ [L, *stratum,* layer, *forma,* form, *fibra,* fiber, *cartilago,* cartilage], a structure made of fibrocartilage that forms a thin coating of osseous grooves through which tendons of certain muscles glide.

stratum /strā'təm, strat'əm/ *pl.* **strata** [L, layer], a uniformly thick sheet or layer, usually associated with other layers, such as the stratum basale of the epidermis.

stratum basale, 1. The deepest of the five layers of the epidermis, composed of cuboidal-shaped cells. This layer provides new cells by mitotic cell division. 2. the deepest layers of the uterine decidua, containing uterine gland terminals.

stratum corneum, the horny, outermost layer of the skin, composed of dead flat cells converted to keratin that continually flakes away. The stratum corneum is thick on the palms of the hands and the soles of the feet but relatively thin over most areas.

stratum granulosum, one of the layers of the epidermis, situated just below the stratum corneum except in the thick skin of the palms of the hands and the soles of the feet, where it lies just under the stratum lucidum.

stratum lucidum, one of the layers of the epidermis, situated just beneath the stratum corneum and present only in the thick skin of the palms of the hands and the soles of the feet.

stratum spinosum, one of the layers of the epidermis, composed of several layers of polygonal cells. It lies on top of the stratum basale and beneath the stratum granulosum and contains tiny fibrils within its cellular cytoplasm.

stratum spongiosum, one of the three layers of the endometrium of the uterus, containing tortuous, dilated uterine glands and a small amount of interglandular tissue.

S

strawberry gallbladder /strô′berē/ [AS, *streawberig*; ME, *gal*, gall; AS, *blaedre*], a tiny yellow gallbladder spotted with deposits on the red mucous membrane, characteristic of cholesterolosis.

strawberry tongue, a strawberry-like coloration of the inflamed tongue papillae. It is a clinical sign of scarlet fever and is also seen in Kawasaki's disease.

stray light [OFr, *estraier*, to wander; AS, *leoht*, illumination], radiant energy that reaches a photodetector and that consists of wavelengths other than those defined by the filter or monochromator.

streak [AS, *strican*, to stroke], a line or a stripe, such as the primitive streak at the caudal end of the embryonic disk.

street virus, a natural infectious agent such as rabies that may be transmitted from a domestic animal or obtained in the wild, outside the laboratory.

strength [AS, *strengou*], the ability of a muscle or a person to produce or resist a physical force.

strength of association, the degree of relationship between a causal factor and the occurrence of a disease, usually expressed in terms of a relative risk ratio.

strength training, a method of improving muscular strength by gradually increasing the ability to resist force through the use of free weights, machines, or the person's own body weight. Strength training sessions are designed to impose increasingly greater resistance, which in turn stimulates development of muscle strength to meet the added demand.

streptavidin /strep′təvī′din/, a biotin-binding protein isolated from streptomyces and used to identify antigens; a widely used reagent for immunoassays.

strep throat [*Streptococcus;* AS, *throte*], *informal.* an infection of the oral pharynx and tonsils caused by a hemolytic species of *Streptococcus,* usually belonging to group A. The infection is characterized by sore throat, chills, fever, swollen lymph nodes in the neck, and sometimes nausea and vomiting. The symptoms usually begin abruptly a few days after exposure to the organism in airborne droplets or after direct contact with an infected person. The throat is diffusely red, and the tonsils often are covered with a yellow or white exudate. Treatment usually includes intramuscular injection of penicillin G benzanthine or the administration of penicillin for 10 days.

Streptobacillus moniliformis [Gk, *streptos,* curved; L, *bacillum,* small rod, *monile,* necklace, *forma,* form], a species of necklace-shaped gram negative, non-motile bacteria that can cause rat-bite fever in humans.

streptococcal, pertaining to any of the species of *Streptococcus.*

streptococcal angina [Gk, *streptos* + *kokkos,* berry; L, *angina,* quinsy], a condition in which feelings of choking, suffocation, and pain result from a streptococcal infection.

streptococcal infection, an infection caused by pathogenic bacteria of one of several species of the genus *Streptococcus* or their toxins. The infections occur in many forms, including cellulitis, endocarditis, erysipelas, impetigo, meningitis, pneumonia, scarlet fever, tonsillitis, and UTI.

streptococcemia/-koksē′mē-ə/ [Gk,*streptos,* curved, *kokkos,* berry], a condition of the presence of streptococci bacteria in the blood.

streptococcus beta-hemolytic, Group A, a strain of streptococcus, group A in the Lancefield classification, that causes necrotizing fasciitis toxic shock syndrome.

streptococcus beta-hemolytic, Group B, a strain of streptococcus that causes human infections such as neonatal sepsis, endocarditis, and septic arthritis.

Streptococcus pneumoniae [Gk, *streptos,* curved, *kokkos,* berry, *pneumon,* lung], any of 70 antigenic types of pneumococcal bacteria that cause pneumonia and other diseases in humans. Most are community acquired, but immunizations are available for 23 strains.

Streptococcus pyogenes [Gk, *streptos,* curved, *kokkos,* berry, *pyon,* pus, *genein,* to produce], a species of *Streptococcus* with many strains that are pathogenic to humans, including the β-hemolytics in Lancefield group A. It causes suppurative diseases such as scarlet fever and strep throat.

Streptococcus (Str.) /strep′təkok′əs/ [Gk, *streptos* + *kokkos,* berry], a genus of nonmotile gram-positive cocci classified by serologic types (Lancefield groups A through T), by hemolytic action (α, β, γ) when grown on blood agar, and by reaction to bacterial viruses (phage types 1 to 86). Many species cause disease in humans.

Streptococcus viridans [Gk, *streptos,* curved, *kokkos,* berry], a poorly defined species of *Streptococcus* similar to *S. pyogenes* strains. It produces alpha-hemolysis in cultures and is a common cause of subacute bacterial endocarditis and other infections in humans such as gingivitis.

streptokinase (sk) /strep′təkī′nās/ [Gk, *streptos* + *kinesis,* motion + *ase,* enzyme], a fibrinolytic activator that enhances the conversion of plasminogen to the fibrinolytic enzyme plasmin. It is used in the treatment of certain cases of pulmonary and coronary embolism.

streptokinase-streptodornase /-strep′tōdôr′nās/, two enzymes derived from a strain of

Streptococcus hemolyticus. It is prescribed for debridement of purulent exudates, clotted blood, radiation necrosis, or fibrinous deposits resulting from trauma or infection.

streptolysin /streptol'isis/ [Gk, *streptos* + *lysein,* to loosen], a filterable substance, produced by streptococci, that liberates hemoglobin from RBCs.

streptomycin sulfate /strep'təmī'sin/, an aminoglycoside antibiotic. It is prescribed in the treatment of TB, endocarditis, and certain other infections.

streptozocin /strep'təzō'sin/, an antineoplastic used in the treatment of neoplasms, including metastatic islet cell tumors of the pancreas. It is an antibiotic substance from *Streptomyces acromogenes.*

stress [OFr, *estrecier,* to tighten], any emotional, physical, social, economic, or other factor that requires a response or change. Stress can be positive or negative. Ongoing chronic stress can result in physical illness. Stress may also be applied therapeutically to promote change, such as implosive therapy for phobic patients. The nature and degree of stress observed in a patient are frequently evaluated by the nurse as part of the ongoing holistic nursing assessment.

stress-adaptation theory, a concept that stress depletes the reserve capacity of individuals, thereby increasing their vulnerability to health problems.

stress amenorrhea [OFr, *estrecier;* Gk, *a* + *men,* month, *rhoia,* to flow], a cessation in menstruation caused by a physical change or mental stress.

stress-bearing area, the portion of the natural oral structures that is available to support a denture.

stress behavior, a change from a person's normal behavior in response to a stressor.

stress echocardiography, ECHO done while the patient is under stress, such as during exercise.

stress fracture, a fracture, often in one or more of the metatarsal bones, caused by repeated, prolonged, or abnormal stress.

stress inoculation, a procedure useful in helping patients control anxiety by substituting positive coping statements for statements that bring about anxiety.

stress kinesic, a type of behavioral characteristic of personal conversation, such as the use of body shifts or movements, that marks the flow of speech and generally coincides with linguistic stress patterns.

stress level, a nursing outcome from the Nursing Outcomes Classification (NOC) defined as the severity of manifested physical or mental tension resulting from factors that alter an existing equilibrium.

stress management, methods of controlling factors that require a response or change within a person by identifying the stressors, eliminating negative stressors, and developing effective coping mechanisms. Examples include progressive muscular relaxation, guided imagery, biofeedback, and breathing techniques.

stressor /stres'ər/ [OFr, *estrecier,* to tighten], anything that causes wear and tear on the body's physical or mental resources.

stress radiography, the radiographic examination of a body area for soft tissue tears or ruptures. The lesions may appear as abnormal gaps between joint surfaces.

stress reaction, an acute maladaptive emotional response to an actual or perceived stressor.

stress test, a test that measures the function of a system of the body when subjected to carefully controlled amounts of physiologic stress, usually exercise but sometimes specific drugs. The data produced allow the examiner to evaluate the condition of the system being tested. Cardiopulmonary function, respiratory function, and intrauterine fetal placental function are tested with stress tests.

stress theory of aging, a stochastic theory of aging that hypothesizes that aging and death result from the effects of environmental stressors that cause wear and tear on cells and disrupt their function. The generation of free radicals during oxidative cell processes is sometimes cited as a specific stressor that disrupts DNA and protein function and so causes aging.

stress ulcer, a gastric or duodenal ulcer that develops in previously unaffected individuals subjected to severe stress, such as a severe burn.

stretching of contractures [AS, *streccan;* L, *contractura,* drawing together], any of several procedures for release of muscle and other structures that have been shortened because of paralysis, spasm, disuse, or fibrosis. The procedures include stretching exercises, tissue grafts, scar tissue removal, tendon transfer, and incision of a joint capsule.

stretch pressure, a rehabilitation technique in which the thumb, fingertips, or palm of the hand is used to stretch a target muscle, followed by briefly maintained pressure.

stretch receptor [AS, *streccan;* L, *recipere,* to receive], specialized sensory nerve endings in muscle spindles or tendons that are stimulated by stretching movements.

stretch reflex [AS, *streccan;* L, *reflectere,* to bend back], a reflex muscle contraction after it is stretched as a result of stimulation of proprioceptors in the muscle.

stretch release, a rehabilitation technique in which the fingertips are placed over the

S

belly of a large muscle and then spread apart in an effort to stretch the skin and underlying muscle. The stretch is done firmly enough to deform the soft tissue temporarily, stimulating cutaneous and muscle efferents and producing facilitation of the underlying muscle.

stria /strī′ə/ *pl.* **striae** [L, furrow], a streak or a linear scar that often results from rapidly developing tension in the skin, such as seen on the abdomen after pregnancy.

striae gravidarum, irregular depressions with red to purple coloration that appear in the skin of the abdomen, thighs, and buttocks of pregnant women.

striatal /strī-ā′təl, strī′ətəl/ [L, *striatus,* striped], pertaining to the corpus striatum.

striatal toe, hyperextension of the great toe.

striated /strī′āted/ [L, *striatus,* striped], identifying something that is striped, is marked by parallel lines, or has structural lines.

striated muscle /strī′ātid/ [L, *striatus,* striped, *musculus,* muscle], any muscle, including all of the skeletal muscles, in which the fibers are divided by bands of cross-striations (stripes) as a result of overlapping of thick and thin myofilaments. Contractions in such muscles are voluntary. The heart, a striated involuntary muscle, is an exception.

stria terminalis, a slender, compact fiber bundle that functions as a limbic pathway running from the amygdaloid complex to the hypothalamus and septum.

stricture /strik′chər/ [L, *stringere,* to tighten], an abnormal temporary or permanent narrowing of the lumen of a hollow organ such as the esophagus, pylorus of the stomach, ureter, or urethra. It is caused by inflammation, external pressure, or scarring.

strict vegetarian [L, *stringere* + *vegetare,* to grow, *arius,* believer], a vegetarian whose diet excludes the use of all foods of animal origin. All foods consumed are plant-based. Such diets, unless adequately planned, may be inadequate in many essential nutrients, particularly vitamin B_{12}.

stridor /strī′dôr/ [L, harsh sound], an abnormal, high-pitched, musical sound caused by an obstruction in the trachea or larynx. It is usually heard during inspiration. Stridor may indicate several neoplastic or inflammatory conditions, including glottic edema, asthma, diphtheria, laryngospasm, and papilloma.

strike [AS, *strican,* to advance swiftly], an action taken collectively by the employees of a company or institution in which they stop reporting for work in an effort to cause the employer to accede to certain demands.

string, a cord, usually made of fiber, configured in a long thin line.

string carcinoma [AS, *strenge,* cord; Gk, *karkinos,* cancer, *oma,* tumor], a malignancy of the large intestine, usually the ascending or transverse colon. On radiologic visualization, it causes the intestine to appear to be tied in segments like a string of large beads.

stringiness /string′inəs/, an abnormal tissue texture caused by fine or stringlike myofascial structures.

string sign, a narrow pyloric canal with congenital pyloric stenosis, or a narrowed bowel segment with regional ileitis. Use of a radiopaque contrast medium causes the narrowed lumen to appear as a thin string on radiographs.

striocerebellar tremor /strī′ōser′əbel′ər/, a combination of static, active, and intentional voluntary muscle contractions with both striatal and cerebellar components. It is associated with hereditary ataxia and diffuse degeneration of the CNS.

strip membranes [Ger, *strippe,* strap; L, *membrana,* thin skin], in obstetrics, a procedure in which an examiner, with the fingers, frees the membranes of the amniotic sac from the wall of the lower segment of the uterus in the small area around the cervical os. It is done to stimulate labor, but because infection or hemorrhage may result, it is not recommended.

stripping, 1. *nontechnical.* a surgical procedure for the removal of the long and short saphenous veins of the legs. 2. the mechanical removal of a very small amount of enamel from the mesial or distal surfaces of teeth to alleviate crowding.

stroke prone profile [AS, *strac*], a predictive index using a complex of risk factors that indicate susceptibility of a person to CVA. The factors include advanced age, hypertension, a history of TIAs, cigarette smoking, heart disorders, associated embolism, family history of CVA, use of oral contraceptives, DM, physical inactivity, and obesity, hypercholesteremia, and hyperlipidemia.

stroke volume, the amount of blood ejected by a ventricle during contraction.

stroke volume index, stroke volume divided by the body surface area.

stroking /strō′king/, running the entire hand over large parts of the body to relax the muscles reflexively and eliminate muscle spasm, improve circulation, or produce a parasympathetic response.

stroma /strō′mə/ *pl.* **stromas, stromata** [Gk, covering], the supporting tissue or the matrix of an organ, as distinguished from its parenchyma.—**stromatic,** *adj.*

Strongyloides /stron'jiloi'dēz/ [Gk, *strongylos,* round, *eidos,* form], a genus of parasitic intestinal nematode. One species, *S. stercoralis,* causes strongyloidiasis, a potentially life-threatening infection under certain circumstances.

strongyloidiasis /stron'jəloidī'əsis/, infection of the small intestine by the roundworm *Strongyloides stercoralis.* It is acquired when larvae from the soil penetrate intact skin, incidentally causing a pruritic rash. The larvae pass to the lungs via the bloodstream, sometimes causing pneumonia. They then migrate up the air passages to the pharynx, are swallowed, and develop into adult worms in the small intestine. Bloody diarrhea and intestinal malabsorption may result. Treatment often includes administration of thiabendazole, ivermectin, and albendazole, in established infections. Early infection is treated with inhaled beta-agonists, antihelminthic therapy works poorly against the larval stage. Proper sanitary methods for the disposal of excrement can eliminate the disease. Wearing shoes prevents contagion from contaminated soil.

strontium (Sr) /stron'sh(ē)əm/ [Strontian, Scotland], a metallic element. Its atomic number is 38, and its atomic mass is 87.62. Chemically similar to calcium, it is found in bone tissue. Isotopes of strontium are used in radioisotope scanning procedures of bone. In addition to four naturally occurring isotopes (^{88}Sr, ^{87}Sr, ^{86}Sr, and ^{84}Sr), 12 artificial strontium isotopes are produced by nuclear reactions. Strontium 90, the longest-lived, is the most dangerous constituent of fallout from atomic bomb tests. It can replace some of the calcium in food, become concentrated in teeth and bones, and continue to emit electrons that can cause death in the host. Strontium 90 becomes concentrated in cow's milk.

Stroop test [John Ridley Stroop PhD., 1897–1973], a test of cognitive ability assessing the ability to direct attention to a task.

structural /struk'chərəl/ [L, *structura,* arrangement], pertaining to the arrangement or pattern of component parts of an object or organism.

structural chemistry [L, *structura,* arrangement], the science dealing with the molecular structure of chemical substances.

structural gene, a gene that specifies the amino acid sequence of a polypeptide.

structural integration, a technique of deep massage intended to help in the realignment of the body by altering the length and tone of myofascial tissues. The basis of the practice is the belief that misalignment of myofascial tissues may have a detrimental effect on a person's energy level, self-image, muscular efficiency, perceptions, and general health.

structural model, a model of family therapy that views the family as an open system and identifies subsystems within the family that carry out specific family functions.

structure /struk'chər/ [L, *structura*], a part of the body, such as the heart, a bone, a gland, a cell, or a limb.

structure-activity relationship (SAR), the relationship between the chemical structure of a drug and its activity.

structured learning therapy /struk'chərd/, a rehabilitation technique used with schizophrenic patients.

Strümpell-Marie disease /strim'pəl märē'/ [Ernst A. von Strümpell, German neurologist, 1853–1925; Pierre Marie, French neurologist, 1853–1940; L, *dis;* Fr, *aise,* ease], ankylosing spondylitis.

strychnine /strik'nin, strik'nīn/ [Gr, *strychnos,* nightshade], a white crystalline alkaloid obtained from the leaves of the *Strychnos nux-vomica* plant. It is extremely toxic to the CNS.

strychnine poisoning [Gk, *strychnos;* L, *potio,* a drink], toxic effects of ingesting strychnine, a CNS stimulant. Symptoms include restlessness and hyperacuity of hearing and vision. Minor stimuli may produce convulsions, but there may be complete muscle relaxation between convulsions. One classic sign of strychnine poisoning is an arched back (opisthotonos).

Stryker wedge frame, a trademark for an orthopedic bed that allows the patient to be rotated as required to either the full supine or the full prone position. It is used in the immobilization of patients with unstable spines, postoperative management of multilevel spinal fusions, and management of severe burn patients.

STS, abbreviation for **sit-to-stand.**

S-T segment, an isoelectric line after the QRS complex on the ECG. It represents phase 2 of the cardiac action potential. Elevation or depression of the S-T segment is the hallmark of myocardial ischemia or injury and coronary artery disease.

Stuartnatal Plus, a trademark for a fixed-combination oral prenatal drug containing vitamins and minerals.

student health status, a nursing outcome from the Nursing Outcomes Classification (NOC) defined as the physical, cognitive, emotional, and social status of a school-age child.

Studer neobladder, a low-pressure type of orthotopic ileal neobladder with ureters

S

attached to the proximal "chimney" of the neobladder.

stump [ME, *stumpe*], the part of a limb that remains after amputation. Also called **residual limb.**

stump hallucination, the sensation of the continued presence of an amputated limb.

stump pain, pain arising in the stump in a person with an amputated limb. It originates from damaged nerves near the site of the amputation.

stunned myocardium, a condition of impaired myocardial contractile function, cellular biochemical characteristics, and microvasculature function in the absence of gross myocardial necrosis. It can last for minutes to days and is caused by ischemia that is either brief or occurs in the area immediately outside an infarct zone.

stupefacient /st(y)o͞o'pəfā'shənt/ [L, *stupere*, to stun, *facere*, to make], an opioid or other agent that has the effect of making a person stuporous.

stupor /st(y)o͞o'pər/ [L, *stupere*, to stun], a state of unresponsiveness in which a person seems unaware of the surroundings. The condition occurs in neurologic and psychiatric disorders.

Sturge-Weber syndrome /sturj web'ər/ [William A. Sturge, English physician, 1850–1919; Frederick P. Weber, English physician, 1863–1962], a congenital neurocutaneous disease marked by a port wine–colored capillary hemangioma over a sensory dermatome of a branch of the trigeminal nerve. The cerebral cortex may atrophy, and generalized or focal seizures, angioma of the choroid, secondary glaucoma, optic atrophy, and new cutaneous hemangiomas may develop.

stuttering [D, *stotteren*], a speech dysfunction usually characterized by excessive abnormal hesitations, blocks, part-word and whole-word repetitions, and audible or silent prolongation of sounds. The cause of stuttering is unknown. Hesitancy and lack of fluency in speech are typical characteristics of normal speech and language development during the preschool years; the child may become conscious of speaking difficulties associated with acquisition and a fear of speaking may develop. Early prevention and evaluation are recommended.

sty [ME, *styanye*, eyelid tumor], a purulent infection of a meibomian or sebaceous gland of the eyelid, often caused by a staphylococcal organism.

stylet /stī'lət, stīlet'/ [It, *stiletto*, dagger], a thin metal probe for inserting into or passing through a needle, tube, or catheter to clean the hollow bore or for inserting into a soft, flexible catheter to make it stiff as the catheter is placed in a vein or passed through an orifice of the body.

styloglossus, a muscle that retracts the tongue and pulls the back of the tongue superiorly. It is innervated by the hypoglossal nerves.

stylohyoideus /stī'lōhī·oi'dē·əs/ [Gk, *stylos*, pillar, *hyoeides*, U-shaped], one of four suprahyoid muscles, lying anterior and superior to the posterior belly of the digastricus. It serves to draw the hyoid bone up and back.

stylohyoid ligament /stī'lōhī'oid/, the ligament attached to the tip of the styloid process of the temporal bone and to the lesser cornu of the hyoid bone.

styloid /stī'loid/ [Gk, *stylos*, pillar, *eidos*, form], long and tapered, like a pen or stylus.

styloid process [Gk, *stylos* + *eidos*; L, *processus*], any of several projections of bone tissue, particularly a projection on the temporal bone.

stylomandibular ligament /stī'lōmandib'yələr/ [Gk, *stylos;* L, *mandere*, to chew, *ligare*, to bind], one of a pair of specialized bands of cervical fascia, forming an accessory part of the temporomandibular joint. It extends from the styloid process of the temporal bone to the ramus of the mandible between the masseter and pterygoideus muscles and separates the parotid gland from the submandibular gland.

stylus /stī'ləs/, **1.** a fine probe. **2.** a wire inserted into a catheter to stiffen it. **3.** a device that imprints electric activity and wave patterns on ECG, EEG, or similar graphic recordings.

styptic /stip'tik/ [Gk, *styptikos,* astringent], **1.** a substance used as an astringent, often to control bleeding. A chemical styptic induces coagulation of blood. A cotton pledget used as a compress to control bleeding is a mechanical styptic. **2.** acting as an astringent or agent to control bleeding.

subacromial /sub'əkrō'mē·əl/ [L, *sub,* beneath; Gk, *akron,* extremity, *omos,* shoulder], pertaining to the area below the acromion.

subacromial bursa [L, *sub,* under; Gk, *akron,* extremity, *omos,* shoulder, *byrsa,* wineskin], the bursa separating the acromion and deltoid muscle from the insertion of the supraspinatus muscle and the greater tubercle of the humerus.

subacute /-əkyo͞ot'/ [L, *sub + acutus,* sharp], **1.** less than acute. **2.** pertaining to a disease or other abnormal condition present in a person who appears to be clinically well.

subacute bacterial endocarditis (SBE), a chronic bacterial infection of the valves of the heart. It is characterized by a slow, quiet onset with fever, heart murmur, splenomegaly, and development of clumps of abnormal tissue, called vegetations, around an intracardiac prosthesis or on the cusps of a valve. Various species of *Streptococcus* or *Staphylococcus* are commonly the cause of SBE. Dental procedures are associated with infection by *Streptococcus viridans,* surgical procedures with *Streptococcus faecalis,* and self-infection (especially by drug abusers) with *Staphylococcus aureus.*

subacute care, 1. a level of treatment that is between chronic and acute. 2. treatment of a disease that is of moderate severity or duration.

subacute glomerulonephritis, an uncommon noninfectious disease of the glomerulus of the kidney characterized by proteinuria, hematuria, decreased production of urine, and edema. Of unknown cause, the disease may progress rapidly, and renal failure may occur. Kidney transplantation and dialysis are the only treatments available.

subacute infection [L, *sub,* beneath, *acutus,* sharp, *inficere,* to stain], a disease condition that is not chronic and that runs a rapid and severe, but less than acute, course.

subacute inflammation, a reactive sign of inflammation with a gradual onset, later increasing to a chronic or severe runs a type of reaction.

subacute myelooptic neuropathy (SMON), a condition of muscular pain and weakness, usually below the T12 vertebra; painful dysesthesia of the limbs; and, in some cases, optic atrophy.

subacute sclerosing panencephalitis, a rare progressive neurological disorder occurring with primary measles infection in children 2 years of age or younger. It has a latency period of 2 to 10 years. It is characterized by diffuse inflammation of brain tissue, personality change, seizures, ataxia myoclonus, visual disturbances, dementia, fever, and death. No effective therapy is known, however some antiviral drugs can slow the progression of the disease. A combination of oral Isoprinosine and interferon alfa injected into ventricles of the brain appears to be the most effective treatment.

subaortic /-ā-ôr′tik/ [L, *sub;* Gk, *aerein,* to raise], pertaining to the area of the body below the aorta.

subaortic stenosis [L, *sub,* beneath; Gk, *aerein,* to raise, *stenos,* narrow, *osis,* condition], a narrowing of the left ventricle outflow tract below the aortic valve.

subapical /-ap′ikəl/, below the peak or apex.

subaponeurotic /-ap′ōnŏŏrot′ik/ [L, *sub,* beneath; Gk, *apo,* from, *neuron,* nerve; L, *tendo*], beneath an aponeurosis.

subarachnoid /sub′ərak′noid/ [L, *sub;* Gk, *arachne,* spider, *eidos,* form], pertaining to the area under the arachnoid membrane and above the pia mater.

subarachnoid cistern, any one of many small subarachnoid spaces that serve as reservoirs for CSF.

subarachnoid hemorrhage (SaH, SAH), an intracranial hemorrhage into the CSF-filled space between the arachnoid and pial membranes on the surface of the brain. The hemorrhage may extend into the brain if the force of the bleeding from the broken vessel is sudden and severe. The cause may be trauma, rupture of an aneurysm, or an arteriovenous anomaly. The first symptom of a subarachnoid hemorrhage is a sudden extremely severe headache that begins in one localized area and then spreads, becoming dull and throbbing. Other characteristics can include dizziness, rigidity of the neck, pupillary inequality, vomiting, seizures, drowsiness, sweating and chills, stupor, and LOC. A brief period of unconsciousness immediately after the rupture is common; severe hemorrhage may result in continued unconsciousness, coma, and death. Delirium and confusion often persist through the first weeks of recovery, and permanent brain damage is common.

subarachnoid hemorrhage precautions, a nursing intervention from the Nursing Interventions Classification (NIC) defined as the reduction of internal and external stimuli or stressors to minimize the risk of rebleeding prior to surgery or an endovascular procedure to secure a ruptured aneurysm.

subarachnoid space, the space between the arachnoid and the pia mater membranes. It contains CSF.

subatomic /-ətom′ik/ [L, *sub,* beneath; Gk, *atomos,* indivisible], pertaining to the particles and phenomena that are within an atom.

subaxillary /-ak′siler·ē/ [L, *sub,* beneath, *axilla,* wing], pertaining to the area beneath the axilla.

subcapital fracture /-kap′itəl/ [L, *sub* + *caput,* head], a fracture located just below the head of a bone that pivots in a ball-and-socket joint, such as the femur.

subcapsular /-kap′s(y)ələr/ [L, *sub,* beneath, *capsula,* little box], pertaining to the area below a capsule.

subcapsular cataract [L, *sub* + *capsula,* little box], a condition marked by opacity or cloudiness beneath the anterior or posterior capsule of the lens of the eye.

subcapsular hematoma, one in the subcapsular space of the kidney. It may be caused by a tumor, trauma, vasculitis, renal infarction, or other disease process.

S

subcapsular space, the potential space between the renal parenchyma and the renal capsules.

subclavian /səbklā′vē-ən/ [L, *sub* + *clavicula,* little key], situated under the clavicle, such as the subclavian vein.

subclavian artery, one of a pair of arteries passing under the clavicle that vary in origin, course, and the height to which they rise in the neck but have six similar main branches supplying the vertebral column, spinal cord, ear, and brain.

subclavian catheter, a central venous catheter inserted through the subclavian vein.

subclavian steal syndrome, a vascular syndrome caused by an occlusion in the subclavian artery proximal to the origin of the vertebral artery. It results in a reversal of the normal BP gradient in the vertebral artery and decreased blood flow distal to the occlusion. It is characterized by episodes of flaccid paralysis of the arm, pain in the mastoid and occipital areas, and a diminished or absent radial pulse on the involved side.

subclavian trunk, one of the two lymphatic vessels, right and left, that drain the right upper limb and the superficial regions of the thoracic and upper abdominal wall.

subclavian vein, the continuation of the axillary vein in the upper body, extending from the lateral border of the first rib to the sternal end of the clavicle, where it joins the internal jugular vein to form the brachiocephalic vein.

subclavius /səbklā′vē-əs/ [L, *sub* + *clavicula*], a short muscle of the chest wall that acts to draw the shoulder down and forward.

subclinical /-klin′ikəl/ [L, *sub;* Gk, *kline,* bed], pertaining to a disease or abnormal condition so mild that it produces no symptoms.

subclinical deficiency, in orthomolecular medicine, deficiency of a nutrient sufficient to affect health but not severe enough to cause classic deficiency symptoms.

subcollateral gyrus /-kəlat′ərəl/ [L, *sub* + *con* + *lateralis;* Gk, *gyros,* turn], a convolution below the collateral fissure or sulcus of the cerebrum.

subconscious /-kon′shəs/ [L, *sub* + *conscire,* to be aware], a lay or popular term for unconscious, or partially conscious. —**subconsciousness,** *n.*

subconscious memory, a thought, sensation, or feeling that is not immediately available for recall to the conscious mind.

subcostales, muscles that span multiple ribs, extending from the internal surfaces of one rib to the internal surface of the second or third rib below. They parallel the course of the internal intercostal muscles and extend from the angle of the ribs to more medial positions on the ribs below.

subcostal nerve, the spinal nerve T12, which supplies skin and muscle of the abdominal wall.

subcrepitant rale, a fine moist rale heard over liquid in the smaller tubes.

subculture /sub′kulchər/ [L, *sub* + *colere,* to cultivate], an ethnic, regional, economic, or social group with characteristic patterns of behavior and ideals that distinguish it from the rest of a culture or society.

subcutaneous /sub′kyŌŌtā′nē·əs/ [L, *sub* + *cutis,* skin], beneath the skin.

subcutaneous adipose tissue [L, *sub,* beneath, *cutis,* skin, *adeps,* fat; OFr, *tissu*], fat deposits beneath the skin.

subcutaneous emphysema, the presence of air or gas in the subcutaneous tissues. The air or gas may originate in the rupture of an airway or alveolus and migrate through the subpleural spaces to the mediastinum and neck. The face, neck, and chest may become swollen. Skin tissues can be painful and may produce a crackling or popping sound as air moves under them. The patient may experience dyspnea and appear cyanotic if the air leak is severe. Treatment may require an incision to release the trapped air.

subcutaneous fascia, a continuous layer of connective tissue over the entire body between the skin and the deep fascial investment of the specialized structures of the body, such as the muscles. It comprises an outer normally fatty layer and an inner thin elastic layer.

subcutaneous injection, the introduction of a hypodermic needle into the subcutaneous tissue beneath the skin, usually on the upper arm, thigh, or abdomen. Heparin, insulin, and emetine are injected in this way. If subcutaneous injections are repeated, each is performed at least 5 cm from the previous site.

subcutaneous mastectomy, a surgical procedure in which all of the breast tissue of one or both breasts is removed, leaving the skin, areola, and nipple intact. The adjacent lymph nodes, pectoralis major, and pectoralis minor are not removed. It may be performed on women who are at great risk of development of breast cancer.

subcutaneous nodule, a small, solid mass, or node beneath the skin that can be detected by touch.

subcutaneous tunnel, a tunnel under the skin between the exit site of an atrial catheter and the entrance into the vein.

subcutaneous wound [L, *sub,* beneath, *cutis,* skin; AS, *wund*], an injury to internal organs, such as by crushing or another violent force, without a break in the surface of the skin.

subcuticular suture /-kyo͞otik′yələr/ [L, *sub,* beneath, *cutis,* skin + *sutura*], a continuous suture placed to draw together the tissues immediately beneath the skin. It may be either absorbable or nonabsorbable, requiring later removal.

subdermal /-der′məl/ [L, *sub;* Gr, *derma,* skin], beneath the dermis.

subdural /-d(y)o͞o′rəl/ [L, *sub + durus,* hard], pertaining to the area under the dura mater and above the arachnoid membrane.

subdural hematoma, an accumulation of blood in the subdural space, usually caused by an injury or fall. It can be acute with rapid bleeding or subacute with accumulation of blood over a longer period of time.

subdural hemorrhage, cerebral hemorrhage into the subdural space, often caused by trauma with resulting damage to the middle meningeal artery.

subdural hygroma, a collection of fluid between the dura mater and arachnoid layers, resulting from a spinal fluid leak through a rupture in the arachnoid tissue.

subdural puncture, a perforation of the space between the dura mater and arachnoid membrane to insert a needle for the injection of diagnostic or therapeutic medications or for aspiration of blood or other fluid.

subdural space [L, *sub,* beneath, *dura, mater,* hard mother, *spatium*], the potential space between the dura mater and the arachnoid membrane.

subendocardial infarction /-en′dōkär′dē-əl/, an MI that involves the innermost layer and in some cases parts of the middle layer of the myocardium but does not extend to the epicardium.

subepicardium /sub′ep-kahr′de-um/, subepicardial layer.

subepidermal /-ep′idur′məl/ [L, *sub,* beneath; Gk, *epi,* above, *derma,* skin], beneath the epidermis.

subepithelial hematoma of renal pelvis, a hematoma from bleeding in the subepithelial tissue of the renal pelvis, usually the result of a coagulopathy, such as in hemophilia, thrombocytopenia, or anticoagulant therapy.

subfertility /sub′fer-til′-te/, diminished reproductive capacity.

subgingival curettage, the debridement of an ulcerated epithelial attachment and subjacent gingival corium to eliminate inflammation and to shrink and restore gingival tissue.

subglottic /-glot′ik/, beneath the glottis.

subiculum /səbik′yələm/, a part of the hippocampal formation consisting of the transition zone between the parahippocampal gyrus and Ammon's horn.

subintimal /-in′timəl/ [L, *sub + intimus,* innermost], pertaining to the area beneath the intima or membrane lining a blood vessel, usually a large artery.

subject contrast, the difference in x-ray beam intensities across the beam area after emerging from the part being radiographed.

subjective /-jek′tiv/ [L, *subjectus,* subject], **1.** pertaining to the essential nature of an object as perceived in the mind rather than to a thing in itself. **2.** existing only in the mind. **3.** that which arises within or is perceived by the individual, as contrasted with something that is modified by external circumstances or something that may be evaluated by objective standards. **4.** pertaining to a person who places excessive importance on his own moods, attitudes, or opinions; egocentric.

subjective data collection, the process in which data relating to a problem are elicited from a patient or a patient's family. The interviewer encourages a full description of the onset, the course, and the character of the problem and any factors that aggravate or ameliorate it.

Subjective Global Assessment, a method of rating a patient's nutritional status, with subjective observations being given values on an ordinal scale. Factors assessed include weight change, appetite or anorexia, subcutaneous tissue and muscle, and GI symptoms.

subjective sensation, a feeling or impression that is not associated with or does not directly result from any external stimulus.

subjective symptoms [L, *subjectus,* subject; Gk, *symptoma*], symptoms that are observed only by the patient and that cannot be objectively confirmed.

subjective vertigo, an inappropriate sensation of bodily movement.

subjects /sub′jekts/, participants, people, animals, or events selected for a study to examine a particular variable or condition.

sublethal allele [L, *sub + letum,* death; Gk, *genein,* to produce], an allele whose presence causes abnormalities or impairs the functioning of an organism but does not cause its death.

sublethal dose /-lē′thəl/ [L, *sub,* beneath, *letum,* death; Gk, *dosis,* giving], a dose of a potentially lethal substance that is not large enough to cause death.

sublimate /sub′limāt/ [L, *sublimare,* to lift up], to refine or divert instinctual impulses and energy from an immediate goal to one that can be expressed in a social, moral, or aesthetic manner acceptable to the person and the society.

S

sublimation /-limā′shən/ [L, *sublimare*],
1. an unconscious defense mechanism by which an unacceptable instinctive drive is diverted to and expressed through a personally approved, socially accepted means.
2. in psychoanalysis, the process of diverting certain components of the sex drive to a socially acceptable, nonsexual goal.
3. change in a physical state from the solid phase directly to the gas phase.

Sublimaze, a trademark for an opioid analgesic (fentanyl).

subliminal /-lim′inəl/ [L, *sub* + *limen*, threshold], taking place below the threshold of sensory perception or outside the range of conscious awareness.

subliminal self [L, *sub*, beneath, *limen*, threshold; AS, *self*], a level of mental activity at which an individual under normal waking conditions may function without consciousness.

sublingual /səbling′gwəl/ [L, *sub* + *lingua*, tongue], pertaining to the area beneath the tongue.

sublingual administration of a medication, the administration of a drug, usually in tablet form, by placing it beneath the tongue until the tablet dissolves. Administering drugs such as nitroglycerin by this route avoids the extensive first-pass metabolism of nitroglycerin that occurs in the liver.

sublingual caruncle [L, *sub*, beneath, *lingua*, tongue, *caruncula*, small piece of flesh], a small fleshy growth under the tongue.

sublingual fold, an elongate fold of mucosa raised by the superior margin of the sublingual gland. It extends from the posterolateral aspect of the floor of the oral cavity to the sublingual papilla beside the base of the frenulum of the tongue at the midline anteriorly.

sublingual gland, one of a pair of small salivary glands situated under the mucous membrane of the floor of the mouth, beneath the tongue. A narrow, almond-shaped structure, it secretes mucus produced by its alveoli.

subluxation complex /-luksā′shən/, a theoretic chiropractic model of motion-segment dysfunction that incorporates the complex interaction of pathologic changes in nervous, muscular, ligamentous, vascular, and connective tissues.

subluxation syndrome, an aggregate of signs and symptoms in chiropractic medicine that relate to pathophysiologic characteristics or dysfunction of spinal and pelvic motion segments or to peripheral joints.

submandibular /-məndib′yələr/ [L, *sub* + *mandible*], pertaining to the area beneath the mandible, or lower jaw.

submandibular duct [L, *sub* + *mandere*, to chew], a duct through which a submandibular gland secretes saliva.

submandibular gland, one of a pair of round walnut-sized salivary glands in the submandibular triangle. The gland secretes both mucus and a thinner serous fluid, which aid the digestive process.

submarginal /sub·mär′ji·nəl/ [L, *sub*, beneath, *margo*, margin], situated inferior to or beneath a margin.

submaxillary /-mak′siler′ē/ [L, *sub* + *maxilla*], pertaining to the area below the maxilla, or upper jaw.

submeatal /-mē·ā′təl/ [L, *sub*, beneath, *meatus*, passage], pertaining to tissues beneath a meatus, such as the mastoid air cells under the acoustic meatus or the hard palate beneath the nasal meatus.

submental /-men′təl/ [L, *sub*+*mentum*, chin], pertaining to the area beneath the chin.

submentovertex /-men′tō′vur′teks/ [L, *sub* + *mentum*, chin, *vertex*, peak], pertaining to a radiographic projection of the skull in which x-rays enter just behind the chin and exit at the top of the head.

submetacentric /sub′metəsen′trik/ [L, *sub*; Gk, *meta*, besides, *kentron*, center], pertaining to a chromosome in which the centromere is located approximately equidistant between the center and one end so that the arms of the chromosomes are not equal in length.

submucous /-m(y)ōō′kəs/, pertaining to a location beneath a mucous membrane.

submucous plexus, one of the two interconnected nerve plexuses of the enteric nervous system.

submucous resection (SMR) [L, *sub* + *mucus* + *re* + *secare*, to cut], a surgical procedure for correcting a deviated nasal septum, leaving the mucous membrane of the septum intact.

subnormal temperature /-nôr′məl/, temperature below the normal body level of 98.6° F (37° C).

suboccipital muscles, a small group of deep muscles in the upper cervical region at the base of the occipital bone. They function to move the head.

suboccipitobregmatic /-aksip′itō′bregmat′ik/ [L, *sub* + *occiput*, back of the head; Gk, *bregma*, front of the head], pertaining to the smallest anteroposterior diameter of an infant's head when the neck is well flexed during labor.

subperiosteal fracture /sub′perē·os′tē·əl/ [L, *sub*; Gk, *peri*, around, *osteon*, bone], a fracture in a bone beneath the periosteum that does not disrupt the periosteum.

subphrenic /-fren′ik/ [L, *sub*; Gk, *phren*, diaphragm], pertaining to the area under the diaphragm.

subphrenic abscess [L, *sub,* beneath; Gk, *phren,* diaphragm; L, *abscedere,* to go away], an abscess that develops on or near the undersurface of the diaphragm, usually as a result of peritonitis or from another visceral site.

subpoena /-pē′nə/ [L, *sub* + *poena,* penalty], in law, a document from a court commanding that a person appear at a certain time and place to testify on a specific matter.

subpoena duces tecum, in law, a subpoena commanding a person to take books, papers, records, or other items to the court.

subpopliteal recess, the smaller of two expansions in the synovial membrane of the knee that lies between the lateral meniscus and the tendon of the popliteus muscle and provides a low-friction surface for the movement of tendons associated with the joint.

subscapular artery, the largest branch of the axillary artery and the major blood supply to the posterior wall of the axilla.

subscapularis /-skap′yələr′is/ [L, *sub,* beneath, *scapulae,* shoulder blades], the muscle arising from the subscapular fossa with insertion in the humerus. It functions to rotate the arm medially.

subscapular nerves, branches of the brachial plexus that innervate the subscapularis muscle. The inferior subscapular nerve also innervates the teres major muscles.

subscriber, in managed care, an individual, agency, or employer that has contracted for services under a health plan.

subserous fascia /-sir′əs/ [L, *sub* + *serum,* whey, *fascia,* band], one of three kinds of fascia, lying between the internal layer of deep fascia and the serous membranes lining the body cavities. It is thin in some areas, such as between the pleura and the chest wall, and thick in other areas, where it forms a pad of adipose tissue.

subsistence /-sis′təns/ [L, *subsistere,* to stand still], the state of being sustained or remaining alive with a minimum of life essentials.

subspecialty /-spesh′əltē/ [L, *sub* + *specialis,* individual], in nursing, a nurse's particular highly specialized professional field of practice, such as dialysis, oncology, neurology, or newborn intensive care nursing.

subspinale /sub′spīnā′lē/, the deepest midline point on the maxilla on the concavity between the anterior nasal spine and the prosthion.

substance /sub′stəns/ [L, *substantia,* essence], 1. any drug, chemical, or biologic entity. 2. any material capable of being self-administered or abused because of its physiologic or psychologic effects.

substance abuse, the overindulgence in and dependence on a stimulant, depressant, or other chemical substance, leading to effects that are detrimental to the individual's physical or mental health or the welfare of others.

Substance Abuse and Mental Health Services Administration (SAMHSA), an agency of the United States Department of Health and Human Services with the function of disseminating accurate and up-to-date information about and providing leadership in the prevention and treatment of addictive and mental disorders.

substance abuse testing, a screening of the urine or blood, or another kind of test, to identify drug use or drug overdose or poisoning from substances such as lead and carbon monoxide.

substance addiction consequences, a nursing outcome from the Nursing Outcomes Classification (NOC) defined as the severity of change in health status and social functioning due to substance addiction.

substance dependence, a maladaptive pattern of substance abuse, leading to clinically significant impairment or distress as manifested by three or more episodes within a 12-month period of tolerance, withdrawal, and use of larger amounts or, over a longer period, a persistent desire or unsuccessful effort to control substance abuse, or investment of a great deal of time in activities necessary to obtain the substance.

substance P, a polypeptide neurotransmitter that stimulates vasodilation and contraction of intestinal and other smooth muscles. It also plays a part in salivary secretion, diuresis, natriuresis, and pain sensation.

substance use prevention, a nursing intervention from the Nursing Interventions Classification (NIC) defined as prevention of an alcoholic or drug-use lifestyle.

substance use treatment, a nursing intervention from the Nursing Interventions Classification (NIC) defined as supportive care of patient/family members with physical and psychosocial problems associated with the use of alcohol or drugs.

substance use treatment: alcohol withdrawal, a nursing intervention from the Nursing Interventions Classification (NIC) defined as care of the patient experiencing sudden cessation of alcohol consumption.

substance use treatment: drug withdrawal, a nursing intervention from the Nursing Interventions Classification (NIC) defined as care of a patient experiencing drug detoxification.

S

substance use treatment: overdose, a nursing intervention from the Nursing Interventions Classification (NIC) defined as monitoring, treatment, and emotional support of a patient who has ingested prescription or over-the-counter drugs beyond the therapeutic range.

substance withdrawal severity, a nursing outcome from the Nursing Outcomes Classification (NOC) defined as the severity of physical and psychological signs or symptoms caused by withdrawal from addictive drugs, toxic chemicals, tobacco, or alcohol.

substandard /-stan'dərd/ [L, *sub,* beneath; OFr, *estandart*], below the predetermined model or measure.

substantia alba /-stan'shə/ [L, *substantia,* essence, *albus,* white], the part of the CNS that is enclosed in myelin sheaths. The myelin contributes a white coloring to otherwise gray nerve tissue.

substantia innominata, nerve tissue immediately inferior to the anterior perforated substance and anterior to the globus pallidus and ansa leticularis.

substantia nigra [L, *substantia,* essence, *niger,* black], a dark band of gray matter lying between the tegmentum of the midbrain and the crus cerebri.

substantive epidemiology /sub'stəntiv/ [L, *substantia;* Gk, *epi,* upon, *demos,* people, *logos,* science], the body of knowledge derived from epidemiologic studies, including for each disease the natural history of the disorder, patterns of occurrence, and risk factors for development of the disorder.

substantivity /-stəntiv'itē/, the property of continuing therapeutic action despite removal of the vehicle, such as applied to certain shampoos.

substernal /-stur'nəl/ [L, *sub;* Gk, *sternon,* chest], pertaining to the area beneath the sternum.

substernal goiter [L, *sub;* Gk, *sternon,* chest; L, *guttur,* throat], a nonbacterial inflammation of the lower thyroid isthmus, often preceded by a viral infection causing fever, tenderness, and enlargement of the thyroid gland. Symptoms may last 2 to 4 months and are usually resolved by corticosteroids.

substitution /-stit(y)oo'shən/, a mental defense mechanism, operating unconsciously, by which an unattainable or unacceptable goal, emotion, or object is replaced by one that is more attainable or acceptable.

substitutive therapy /sub'stit(y)oo'tiv/ [L, *substituere,* to put in place of; Gk, *therapeia,* treatment], a treatment that affects a condition incompatible with or antagonistic to the condition being treated.

substrate /sub'strāt/ [L, *sub* + *stratum,* layer], a chemical acted on and changed by an enzyme in a chemical reaction.

substrate depletion phase, a period during an enzyme assay when the concentration of substrate is falling and the assay is not following zero-order kinetics.

substratum /-strā'təm/ [L, *sub* + *stratum,* layer], any underlying layer; a foundation.

subsystem /sub'sistəm/, a smaller component of a large system composed of individuals or dyads, formed by generation, gender, interest, or function.

subtalar joint, the joint between the large posterior calcaneal facet on the inferior surface of the talus and the corresponding posterior talar facet on the superior surface of the calcaneus. It allows gliding and rotation, which are involved in inversion and eversion of the foot.

subtask work, a part of the whole task in a rehabilitation program but distinguished by changes in speed or direction.

subthalamic nucleus, a biconvex mass of gray matter on the medial side of the junction of the internal capsule and the crus cerebri. Its chief connections are with the globus pallidus.

subthalamus /-thal'əməs/ [L, *sub;* Gk, *thalamos,* chamber], a part of the diencephalon that serves as a correlation center for optic and vestibular impulses relayed to the globus pallidus.—**subthalamic,** *adj.*

subtle /sut'əl/ [L, *subtilis*], **1.** having a low intensity. **2.** not severe and having no serious sequelae, such as a mild infection or inflammation.

subtotal /sub'tōtəl/ [L, *sub,* beneath, *totus,* whole], less than complete.

subtotal hysterectomy [L, *sub* + *totus;* Gk, *hystera,* womb, *extome,* excision], the surgical removal of the body of the uterus without removing the cervix.

subtrochanteric osteotomy /-trō'kənter'ik/ [L, *sub;* Gk, *trochanter,* runner, *osteon,* bone, *temnein,* to cut], a surgical procedure that divides the shaft of the femur below the lesser trochanter to correct ankylosis of the hip joint.

subungual /səbung'gwəl/ [L, *sub* + *unguis,* nail], beneath a fingernail or toenail.

subungual hematoma, a collection of blood beneath a nail that usually results from trauma.

subunit vaccine /sub'yoonit/, a viral immunizing agent that has been treated to remove traces of viral nucleic acid, so that only protein subunits remain. The subunits have less risk of causing adverse reactions.

subventricular zone /-ventrik'yələr/, an area located between the ventricular and intermediate zones in the fetal forebrain, in which neurons of the cerebrum are generated.

subzonal insemination (SUZI), an older technique of micromanipulation used in cases of male factor infertility in which spermatozoa are inserted beneath the perivitelline space after breaching of the zona pellucida by mechanical or chemical means.

subzygomatic, below the zygomatic bone.

succinic acid (HOOC(CH₂)₂COOH) /suksin′ik/, a dicarboxylic acid found in certain hydatid cysts and in lichens, amber, and fossils.

succinylcholine chloride /suk′sinilkō′lēn/, a depolarizing neuromuscular blocker that is a skeletal muscle relaxant. It is prescribed to provide an adjunct to anesthesia, to reduce muscle contractions during surgery or mechanical ventilation, and to facilitate endotracheal intubation.

succus /suk′əs/ *pl.* **succi** [L, juice], a juice or fluid, usually one secreted by an organ, such as succus prostaticus of the prostate.

succussion splash /səkush′ən/ [L, *succutere,* to shake up; ME, *plasche,* puddle], the sound elicited by shaking the body of a person who has free fluid and air or gas in a hollow organ or body cavity. This sound may be present over a normal stomach but also may be heard with hydropneumothorax, large hiatal hernia, or intestinal or pyloric obstruction.

suck [L, *sugere,* to suck], **1.** to draw a liquid or semiliquid into the mouth by creating a partial vacuum through motions of the lips and tongue. **2.** to hold on the tongue and dissolve by the movements of the mouth and action of the saliva. **3.** to draw fluid into the mouth, specifically to draw milk from the breast or nursing bottle.

sucking blisters, the pale soft pads on the upper and lower lips of a baby that look like blisters but are not. They seem to augment the seal of the lips around the nipple or breast. Some babies who have sucked on their own fingers, hands, or arms before birth are born with them.

sucking reflex, involuntary sucking movements of the circumoral area in newborns in response to stimulation. The reflex continues throughout infancy and often occurs without stimulation, such as during sleep.

suckle [L, *sugere*], **1.** to provide nourishment, specifically to breastfeed. **2.** to take in nourishment, especially by feeding from the breast.

suckling, an infant that has not been weaned.

suck-swallow reflex, rhythmic sucking and swallowing movements in an infant when a finger or nipple is placed in the mouth.

Sucostrin, a trademark for a depolarizing neuromuscular-blocker agent (succinylcholine).

sucrose /soo′krōs/ [Fr, *sucre,* sugar], a disaccharide sugar derived from sugar cane, sugar beets, and sorghum and made up of one molecule of glucose and one of fructose joined together in a glycosidic linkage.

sucrose polyester (SPE), a synthetic nonabsorbable fat that, when added to the diet, reduces plasma cholesterol levels by increasing the excretion of cholesterol in the feces.

suction /suk′shən/ [L, *sugere,* to suck], the aspiration of a gas or fluid by reducing air pressure over its surface, usually by mechanical means.

suction biopsy [L, *sugere,* to suck; Gk, *bios,* life, *opsis,* view], a procedure for obtaining tissue or fluid samples from lymph nodes or a deep lesion by using suction and a trochar or cannula.

suction curettage, a method of curettage in which a specimen of the endometrium or the products of conception are removed by aspiration.

Sudafed, a trademark for an adrenergic vasoconstrictor used as a decongestant (pseudoephedrine hydrochloride).

sudden cardiac arrest (SCA), an abrupt, complete loss of heart function that results in loss of blood circulation within the body. An episode of sudden cardiac arrest may be preceded by arrhythmias including ventricular tachycardia or fibrillation. It is not caused by the blockage of coronary arteries. Sudden cardiac arrest is reversible in most patients if it is treated within minutes.

sudden death [ME, *sodain,* to come up; AS, *death*], death that occurs unexpectedly and from 1 to 24 hours after the onset of symptoms, with or without known preexisting conditions.

sudden infant death syndrome (SIDS) [ME, *sodain,* to come up; L, *infans,* unable to speak; AS, *death;* Gk, *syn,* together, *dromos,* course], the unexpected and sudden death of an apparently normal and healthy infant that occurs during sleep, with no physical or autopsic evidence of disease. It is the most common cause of death in children under 1 year of age, with an incidence rate of 1 in every 300 to 350 live births. In the last few years, death scene investigations have been helpful in identifying an unsafe sleep environment as a contributing factor in SIDS cases and it is now recognized that many of these infant deaths are due to asphyxiation and suffocation. In 1992 a report by the American Academy of Pediatrics Task Force on Infant Positioning and SIDS recommended that infants be laid down for

S

sleep in a nonprone position; and in 1994 a "Back to Sleep" campaign was jointly initiated by the American Academy of Pediatrics (AAP) and the National Institute of Child Health and Human Development. Over the next five years, the rate of prone sleep positioning and the rate of SIDS both decreased. Since 2001, the rate has been relatively constant. It is known that the risk of SIDS increases after the first month of life and peaks at 2 to 4 months of age. Infants should be placed for sleep supine as a preventive measure.

sudor /soo'dôr/ [L, sweat], perspiration.

sudoriferous duct /soo'dərif'ərəs/ [L, *sudor*, sweat, *facere*, to make], a duct leading from a sweat gland to the surface of the skin.

sudoriferous gland, one of about two million tiny structures within the dermis that produce sweat. Most of these glands are eccrine glands, producing sweat that carries away sodium chloride, the waste products urea and lactic acid, and the breakdown products from garlic, spices, and other substances. Apocrine sweat glands associated with the coarse hair of the armpits and the pubic region are larger and secrete fluid that is much thicker than that secreted by the eccrine glands. Each sudoriferous gland consists of a single tube with a deeply coiled body and a superficial duct.

sudorific /soo'dərif'ik/ [L, *sudor*, sweat, *facere*, to make], **1.** pertaining to a substance or condition, such as heat or emotional tension, that promotes sweating. **2.** a sudorific agent. Sweat glands are stimulated by cholinergic drugs.

Sufenta, a trademark for an opioid analgesic used in balanced anesthesia (sufentanil citrate).

sufentanil /soo-fen'tah-nil/, an opioid analgesic. The citrate salt is used as an anesthetic or anesthesia adjunct. It is also used for the treatment of obstetric pain.

sufentanil citrate /sufen'tənil/, an analgesic and anesthetic. It is administered intravenously as an adjunct to general anesthesia, and can be used in higher amounts together with 100% oxygen as a primary anesthetic.

suffering severity, a nursing outcome from the Nursing Outcomes Classification (NOC) defined as the severity of anguish associated with a distressing symptom, injury, or loss that has potential long-term effects.

suffocation /suf'əkā'shən/ [L, *suffocare*, to choke], an interruption in breathing with oxygen deprivation, usually caused by an obstruction in the airways. The condition may be accidental or intentional or may result from disease or inadequate levels of respirable gases in the atmosphere.

suffocative goiter /suf'əkā'tiv/ [L, *suffocare*, to choke, *guttur*, throat], an enlargement of the thyroid gland that causes a sensation of suffocation when pressed.

sugar /shoog'ər/ [Gk, *sakcharon*], any of several water-soluble simple carbohydrates. The principal categories of sugars are monosaccharides, disaccharides, and polysaccharides. A monosaccharide is a single sugar such as glucose, fructose, or galactose. A disaccharide is a double sugar such as sucrose (table sugar) or lactose. A polysaccharide is a sugar made up of repeating units of glucose such as cellulose, starch, and glycogen.

sugar alcohol, an alcohol produced by the reduction of an aldehyde or ketone of a sugar.

sugar cataract, a visual disorder associated with diabetes in which sorbitol collects within the lens, causing an osmotic gradient of fluid in the lens. This condition leads to a disruption of the lens matrix and loss of transparency.

suggestibility /səjes'tibil'itē/, pertaining to a person's susceptibility to having his or her ideas or actions influenced or altered by others.

suggestion /səjes'chən/ [L, *suggerere*, to propose], **1.** the process by which one thought or idea leads to another, as in the association of ideas. **2.** the use of persuasion, exhortation, or another technique to implant an idea, thought, attitude, or belief in the mind of another as a means of influencing or altering behavior or states of mind. **3.** an idea, belief, or attitude implanted in the mind of another.

suicidal /soo'isī'dəl/ [L, *sui*, of oneself, *caedere*, to kill], of, relating to, or tending toward self-destruction.

suicide /soo'isīd/ [L, *sui*, of oneself, *caedere*, to kill], **1.** the intentional taking of one's own life. **2.** *informal.* the ruin or destruction of one's own interests. **3.** a person who commits or attempts self-destruction.

suicide gesture, in psychiatric nursing, an apparent attempt by a patient to cause self-injury without lethal consequences and generally without actual intent to commit suicide.

suicide prevention, a nursing intervention from the Nursing Interventions Classification (NIC) defined as reducing the risk for self-inflicted harm with intent to end life.

suicide prevention center, a crisis-intervention facility dealing primarily with people preoccupied with suicidal thoughts. Such facilities are usually operated by professional social workers with special training in counseling possible suicide victims in person or by telephone.

suicide self-restraint, a nursing outcome from the Nursing Outcomes Classification (NOC) defined as personal actions to refrain from gestures and attempts at killing oneself.

suicidology /sōō′isĭdol′əjē/ [L, *sui* + *caedere;* Gk, *logos,* science], the study of the prevention and causes of suicide. —**suicidologist,** *n.*

Sular, a trademark for a calcium channel blocker (nisoldipine).

sulconazole /sul-kon′ah-zōl/, a broad-spectrum topical antifungal agent. The nitrate salt is used in treatment of athlete's foot, ringworm, and *Candida* infections.

sulculus /sul′kyələs/ [L, *sulcus*], a small sulcus.

sulcus /sul′kəs/ *pl.* **sulci** [L, furrow], a shallow depression, or furrow on the surface of an organ, such as cerebral sulcus, that separates the convolutions of the cerebral hemisphere.—**sulcate,** *adj.*

sulfacetamide /sul′fəset′əmīd/, a topical antibacterial. It is most commonly prescribed for the prophylaxis of infection after injury to the cornea and in the treatment of bacterial conjunctivitis and bacterial infections of the skin.

Sulfacet-R, a trademark for a fixed-combination topical antiacne medication containing a keratolytic (sulfur), an antibacterial (sulfacetamide sodium), and a physical barrier (zinc oxide).

sulfADIAZINE /sul′fədī′əzēn/, a sulfonamide antibacterial prescribed in the treatment of infection, particularly of the urinary tract, and in rheumatic fever prophylaxis.

sulfadoxine /sul′fah-dok′sēn/, a long-acting sulfonamide used in combination with pyrimethamine in the prophylaxis and treatment of malaria caused by chloroquine-resistant strains of *Plasmodium falciparum.*

sulfa drugs /sul′fə/, a group of bacteriostatic agents that inhibit the biosynthesis of folic acid.

sulfamethoxazole /sul′fəmethok′səzōl/, a sulfonamide antibacterial. It is prescribed in the treatment of otitis media, prostatitis, epididimytis, bronchitis, and certain UTIs.

sulfamethoxazole and trimethoprim /trī′meth′əprim/, a fixed-combination antibacterial. It is prescribed in the treatment of UTIs, otitis media, chronic bronchitis, traveler's diarrhea, and other infections caused by susceptible strains of bacteria and for *Pneumocystis jirovecii* pneumonitis prophylaxis.

Sulfamylon, a trademark for a topical antiseptic (mafenide acetate).

sulfanilamide /sul′fah-nil′ah-mīd/, a potent antibacterial compound. Although replaced as a systemic agent by more effective and less toxic derivatives, and by antibiotics, it is still used vaginally in the treatment of vulvovaginal candidiasis.

sulfanilic acid /sul′fənil′ik/, a red-tinged white crystalline compound used in the synthesis of sulfonamides and as a reagent in tests for phenol, fecal matter in water, albumin, aldehydes, and glucose.

sulfapyridine /sul′fah-pir′idēn/, a sulfonamide administered orally in treatment of dermatitis herpetiformis.

sulfasalazine /sul′fəsəlaz′ēn/, a sulfonamide, and aminosalicylic acid derivative. It is prescribed in the treatment of mild to moderate ulcerative colitis and as adjunctive therapy in severe cases. It is also used to treat juvenile- and adult-onset forms of rheumatoid arthritis, and has investigational uses for other autoimmune diseases such as ankylosing spondylitis and Crohn's disease.

sulfatase /sul′fətās/, any of a group of enzymes that catalyze the cleavage of inorganic sulfate from sulfate esters to form alcohols.

sulfate (SO_4^{2-}) /sul′fāt/, an anion of sulfuric acid. Natural sulfate compounds such as sodium sulfate, calcium sulfate, and potassium sulfate are plentiful in the body.

sulfatide lipidosis /sul′fətīd/, an inherited lipid metabolism disorder of childhood caused by a deficiency of cerebroside sulfatase enzyme. It results in an accumulation of metachromatic lipids in tissues of the CNS, kidney, spleen, and other organs, leading to dementia, paralysis, and death by 10 years of age.

sulfhemoglobin /sulfhem′əglō′bin/, a trace form of hemoglobin that contains an irreversibly bound sulfur molecule that prevents normal oxygen binding.

sulfhemoglobinemia /-ē′mē·ə/, the presence of abnormal sulfur-containing hemoglobin circulating in the blood.

sulfinpyrazone /sul′finpir′əzōn/, a uricosuric prescribed in the treatment of chronic gout and intermittent gouty arthritis.

sulfiSOXAZOLE /sul′fisok′səzōl/, a sulfonamide antibiotic prescribed in the treatment of conjunctivitis and UTIs, including vaginitis, cystitis, and pyelonephritis.

sulfiting agents /sul′fīting/, food preservatives composed of potassium or sodium bisulfite or potassium metabisulfite. Sulfiting agents are used in the processing of beer, wine, baked goods, soup mixes, and some imported seafoods and by restaurants to impart a "fresh" appearance to salad fruits and vegetables. The chemicals can cause a severe allergic reaction in people who are hypersensitive to sulfites. The reactions are marked by flushing, faintness, hives, headache, GI distress, breathing difficulty, and, in extreme cases, LOC and death.

sulfobromophthalein /sul'fəbrō'məfthal'ēn, -ē-in/, a substance used in its disodium salt form for evaluating the function of the liver.

sulfobromophthalein test, a liver function test in which sulfobromophthalein sodium is introduced into the circulatory system and a blood sample is withdrawn 30 or 45 minutes later. The parenchymal cells remove almost all of the dye within this time if they are functioning normally. The rate of removal is influenced by the blood flow through the portal circulation, the functioning capacity of the liver cells, and the patency of the biliary tract.

sulfonamide /səlfon'əmīd/, originally one of a large group of synthetic bacteriostatic drugs that are effective in treating infections caused by many gram-negative and gram-positive microorganisms. They are bacteriostatic rather than bactericidal. They are used in treating many UTIs.

sulfonates /sul'fənāts/, a class of anticholinesterase compounds used as insecticides.

sulfonylurea /sul'fənilyŏŏr'ē-ə/, an oral antidiabetic agent that stimulates the pancreatic production of insulin.

sulfosalicylic acid /sul'fōsalisil'ik/, a white or faintly pink crystalline substance that is highly water soluble and is used as a reagent in tests for albumin and as an intermediate compound in the manufacture of dyes and surfactants.

Sulfoxyl, a trademark for a fixed-combination topical antiacne medication containing two keratolytics (benzoyl peroxide and sulfur). Benzoyl peroxide directly inhibits the growth of acne bacteria.

sulfur (S) /sul'fər/ [L], a nonmetallic polyvalent tasteless, odorless chemical element that occurs abundantly in yellow crystalline form or in masses, especially in volcanic areas. Its atomic number is 16, and its atomic mass is 32.07. Sulfur has been used in the treatment of gout, rheumatism, and bronchitis and as a mild laxative. The sulfonamides, or sulfa drugs, are used in the treatment of various bacterial infections.

sulfur dioxide, a colorless, nonflammable gas used as an antioxidant in pharmaceutical preparations. It is also an important air pollutant, irritating the eyes and respiratory tract.

sulfuric acid (H₂SO₄), a clear, colorless, oily highly corrosive liquid that generates great heat when mixed with water. An extremely toxic substance, sulfuric acid causes severe skin burns, blindness on contact with the eyes, serious lung damage if the vapors are inhaled, and death if it is ingested.

sulfurous acid (H₂SO₃) /sul'fərəs/, a weak inorganic acid formed by dissolving sulfur dioxide in water, used as a chemical reducing and bleaching agent. It has been used in medicine in skin lotions and nasal and throat sprays. Sulfites formed by the acid may be included in antiseptics, antifermentatives, and antizymotics.

sulindac /sulin'dak/, a nonsteroidal antiinflammatory agent prescribed in the treatment of osteoarthritis, rheumatoid arthritis, and ankylosing spondylitis.

Sultrin Triple Sulfa, a trademark for a fixed-combination vaginal drug containing antibacterials (sulfathiazole, sulfacetamide, and sulfabenzamide).

sumac [Ar, *summaq*], any of a number of species of trees and shrubs in the Anacardiaceae family, including the *Rhus* species, which have poisonous properties.

summary judgment [L, *summa,* total, *jus,* law, *dicere,* to state], in law, a judgment requested by any party to a civil action to end the action when it is believed that there is no genuine issue or material fact in dispute.

summation [L, *summa,* total], **1.** an accumulative effect or action; a total aggregate; totality. **2.** in neurology, the concentration of a neurotransmitter at a synapse, either by increasing the frequency of nerve impulses in each fiber (temporal summation) or by increasing the number of fibers stimulated (spatial summation), so that the threshold of the postsynaptic neuron is overcome and an impulse is transmitted.

summation gallop, a gallop rhythm in which the third and fourth heart sounds are superimposed, appearing as one loud sound; it may occur in some patients with tachycardia but is usually associated with cardiac disease.

summons /sum'əns/ [OFr, *somondre,* to remind secretly], in law, a document issued by a clerk of the court on the filing of a complaint. A sheriff, marshal, or other appointed person serves the summons, notifying a person that an action has been begun against him or her.

sump drain, a drainage device consisting of two tubes, one to allow fluid to be drained from a cavity and the other to allow air to enter the cavity to replace the fluid. It may be attached to a suction apparatus.

Sumycin, a trademark for an antibiotic (tetracycline hydrochloride).

sunburn, a skin injury characterized by redness, tenderness, and possible blistering that results from exposure to actinic radiation from the sun.

sundowning /sun'douning/ [AS, *sunne* + *ofdune,* off the hill], a condition in which persons with cognitive impairment and elderly people tend to become confused or disoriented at the end of the day. With less light, they lose visual cues that help them to compensate for their sensory impairments.

sunitinib, a miscellaneous antineoplastic. It is used to treat advanced renal carcinoma and GI stromal tumors after disease progression or intolerance to imatinib.

sunrise syndrome, a condition of unstable cognitive ability on arising in the morning.

sunscreen protective factor index (SPF), a system of evaluating the effectiveness of various formulations for protecting the skin from actinic rays of the sun. A sun protective factor of 15 means that the sunscreen provides 15 times the protection of unprotected skin. Among the most highly rated sunscreen lotions are nonopaque combinations of paraaminobenzoic acid ester and benzophenone, parol 1789 with incoxide and titanium dioxide.

sun-setting sign, a characteristic of hydrocephalus in which an infant's eyes appear to look only downward, with the sclera prominent over the iris.

sunstroke [AS, *sunne* + *strac*, stroke], a morbid condition caused by overexposure to the sun and characterized by a high temperature and altered LOC.

superantigen, one of a family of related substances including staphylococcal and streptococcal exotoxins that can short-circuit the normal sequence of events leading to activation of helper T cells. Superantigens initiate an uncontrolled proliferation of T cells but do not require processing and presentation by macrophages. The result is either an acute and potentially life-threatening disease such as toxic shock syndrome or a chronic inflammatory process such as rheumatic fever.

supercoat, a protective layer of gelatin to provide protection from scratches and pressure damage of radiographic film. Also called **abrasion layer** or **overcoat.**

supercoiling, the underwinding or overwinding of a DNA helix.

superego /ē′gō/ [L, *super,* over, *ego,* I], in psychoanalysis, that part of the psyche, functioning mostly in the unconscious, that develops when the standards of the parents and of society are incorporated into the ego. The superego has two parts, the conscience and the ego ideal.

superfecundation /sōō′pərfekəndā′shən/ [L, *super* + *fecundare,* to be fruitful], the impregnation of two or more ova released during the same ovulation by spermatozoa from the successive coital acts.

superfetation /-fētā′shən/ [L, *super* + *fetus,* pregnancy], the fertilization of a second ovum after the onset of pregnancy, resulting in the simultaneous development of two fetuses of different degrees of maturity within the uterus.

superficial /-fish′əl/ [L, *superficies,* surface], **1.** pertaining to the surface. **2.** not grave or dangerous.

superficial abscess [L, *superficialis* + *abscedere,* to go away], an abscess that develops above the fascia layer.

superficial fading infantile hemangioma, a superficial temporary salmon-colored patch in the center of the forehead, face, or occiput of many newborns.

superficial implantation, in embryology, the partial embedding of the blastocyst within the uterine wall so that it and later the chorionic sac protrude into the uterine cavity.

superficial inguinal node, a node in one of the two groups of inguinal lymph glands in the upper femoral triangle of the thigh.

superficial nephron, one whose proximal convoluted tubule is in the outer part of the renal cortex and whose loop of Henle goes only a short way into the renal medulla.

superficial penile fascia, the loose external layer of fascial tissue of the penis.

superficial reflex, any neural reflex initiated by stimulation of the skin.

superficial sensation, the awareness or perception of feelings in the superficial layers of the skin in response to touch, pressure, temperature, and pain.

superficial spreading melanoma, the most common melanoma that grows outward, spreading over the surface of the affected organ or tissue. It occurs most commonly on the lower legs of women and the torso of men. The lesion is raised and palpable, unevenly pigmented, and irregularly shaped and has an unclear border.

superficial temporal artery, an artery at each side of the head that can be easily felt in front of the ear and is often used for taking the pulse. It is the smaller of the two terminal branches of the external carotid.

superficial transverse perineal muscles, a pair of flat, band-shaped muscles that stabilize the perineal body.

superficial vein, one of the many veins between the subcutaneous fascia just under the skin.

superinfection /-infek′shən/ [L, *super* + *inficere,* to stain], an infection occurring during antimicrobial treatment for another infection.

superior /səpir′ē·ər/ [L, higher], situated above or oriented toward a higher place, as the head is superior to the torso.

superior aperture of minor pelvis, an opening bounded by the crest and pecten of the pubic bones, the arch-shaped lines of the ilia, and the anterior margin of the base of the sacrum.

superior aperture of thorax, an elliptic opening at the summit of the thorax bounded by the first thoracic vertebra, the first ribs, and the upper margin of the sternum.

superior carotid triangle [L, *superior,* higher; Gk, *karos,* heavy sleep; L, *triangulus*], a triangle bounded by the sternocleidomastoid muscle, in front, by the omohyoid muscle below, and by the stylohyoid and digastric muscles above.

superior cervical ganglion, a very large ganglion in the area of the first and second cervical vertebrae that marks the superior extent of the trunk of the sympathetic nervous system.

superior conjunctival fornix, the space in the fold of the conjunctiva created by the reflection of the conjunctiva covering the eyeball and the lining of the upper lid.

superior costotransverse ligament, one of five ligaments associated with each costotransverse joint, except that of the first rib. It passes from the neck of each rib to the transverse process of the vertebra immediately above.

superior gastric node, a node in one of two sets of gastric lymph glands, accompanying the left gastric artery.

superior genial tubercle, the upper part of a small bony projection located on the internal surface of the mandible, near the lower end of the midline and above the anterior end of the mylohyoid line. It serves for attachment of the genioglossus muscle.

superior gluteal nerve, a nerve formed by branches of the sacral plexus that supplies muscles in the gluteal region.

superior kidney, the renal segment located most superiorly.

superior mediastinum, the upper part of the mediastinum in the middle of the thorax, containing the trachea, esophagus, aortic arch, and origins of the sternohyoideus and the sternothyroideus.

superior mesenteric artery, a visceral branch of the abdominal aorta, arising inferior to the celiac artery, dividing into five branches, and supplying most of the small intestine and parts of the colon.

superior mesenteric node, a node in one of the three groups of visceral lymph nodes that serve the viscera of the abdomen and the pelvis.

superior mesenteric vein, a tributary of the portal vein that drains the blood from the small intestine, the cecum, and the ascending and transverse colons.

superior olivary nucleus [L, *supurus + oliva + nucleus,* nut kernel], a collection of nerve cells appearing as a clump of gray

matter in the pons. It assists in the localization of sound by comparing the time difference between sounds received by the left and right ears.

superior orbital fissure, an elongated cleft between the small and great wings of the sphenoid bone, which transmits cranial nerves III, IV, and VI and the first division of cranial nerve V and the ophthalmic vein.

superior rectal plexus, the submucosal portion of the rectal venous plexus, above the pectinate line.

superior right lateral flexure of rectum, the second bend in the rectum, where it deviates laterally to the right.

superior sagittal sinus, one of the six venous channels in the posterior of the dura mater, draining blood from the brain into the internal jugular vein.

superior subscapular nerve /səbskap′yələr/, one of a pair of small nerves on opposite sides of the body that arise from the posterior cord of the brachial plexus. It supplies the superior part of the subscapularis.

superior tarsal muscle, a collection of smooth muscle fibers in companion with the levator palpebrae superioris passing from the inferior surface of the lavatory to the upper edge of the superior tarsus. Loss of function of either the levator palpebrae superioris or the superior tarsal muscle results in a ptosis of the upper eyelid.

superior temporal gyrus, a rounded elevation on the lateral surface of either temporal lobe of the brain.

superior thoracic artery, a small artery that originates from the anterior surface of the first part of the axillary artery and supplies the upper regions of the medial and anterior axillary walls.

superior thyroid artery, one of a pair of arteries in the neck, usually arising from the external carotid artery, that supplies the thyroid gland and several muscles in the head.

superior ulnar collateral artery, a long slender division of the brachial artery, arising just distal to the middle of the arm, descending to the elbow, and anastomosing with the posterior ulnar recurrent and inferior ulnar collateral arteries.

superior vena cava, the second largest vein of the body, returning deoxygenated blood from the upper half of the body to the right atrium.

superior vena cava syndrome, a condition of edema and engorgement of the veins of the upper body caused by obstruction of the superior vena cava by thrombi or primary pulmonary tumors. Signs and symptoms include a nonproductive cough, breathing difficulty, cyanosis, CNS disorders, and edema of the conjunctiva, trachea, and esophagus.

superior vesical artery, an artery that originates from the root of the umbilical artery and supplies the superior aspect of the bladder and distal parts of the ureter. In men, it may also give rise to an artery that supplies the ductus deferens.

supernatant /-nā′tənt/ [L, *super* + *natare,* to swim], **1.** situated above or on top of something. **2.** the clear upper liquid part of a mixture (a liquid and a solid) after it has been centrifuged.

supernormal excitability /-nôr′məl/, the ability of the myocardium to respond at the end of phase 3 of the cardiac action potential to a stimulus that would be ineffective at other times.

supernormal period, a period of supernormal excitability of the myocardium.

supernumerary nipples /-nōō′mərer′ē/ [L, *super* + *numerus,* number; ME, *neb,* beak], an excessive number of nipples, which are usually not associated with underlying glandular tissue. They may vary in size from small pink dots to that of normal nipples.

supernumerary tooth [L, *super,* above, *numerus,* number; AS, *toth*], any tooth in addition to the normal 32 teeth in secondary dentition or the 20 teeth in deciduous dentition.

superoxide /-ok′sīd/, a common reactive form of oxygen that is formed when molecular oxygen gains a single electron. Superoxide radicals can attack susceptible biologic targets, including lipids, proteins, and nucleic acids.

superoxide dismutase (SOD), an enzyme composed of metal-containing proteins that converts superoxide radicals into less toxic agents. It is the main enzymatic mechanism for clearing superoxide radicals from the body.

supersaturate /-sach′ərāt/ [L, *super,* above, *saturare,* to fill], a solution that contains solute at a concentration greater than the solubility at a given temperature.

supertwins, multiple births of more than two infants. Children of multiple births are more prone to premature birth and are likely to suffer from congenital defects.

supervised fast /sōō′pərvīzd/, a hypoglycemic diagnostic procedure in which glucose levels are measured every 4 to 6 hours in a fasting person until they fall below 50 mg/dL. The fasting person is closely observed, and glucose values are rapidly determined and reported by the laboratory.

supervision /-vizh′ən/, in psychology, a process whereby a therapist is helped to become a more effective clinician through the direction of a supervisor who provides theoretic knowledge and therapeutic techniques.

supervisor /sōō′pərvī′zər/ [L, *super* + *videre,* to see], in hospital or public health nursing, the midlevel management position between the chief nurse executive and nurse managers of a division or of several units. The supervisor's responsibilities are primarily administrative, although they may also provide clinical leadership for the nurses working in a group of units, wards, or divisions.

supervitaminosis /-vī′təminō′sis/ [L, *super,* above, *vita* + *amine;* Gk, *osis,* condition], a condition of ingesting an excessive amount of vitamins in the forms of supplements.

supination /sōō′pinā′shən/ [L, *supinus,* lying on the back], **1.** one of the kinds of rotation allowed by certain skeletal joints, such as the elbow and the wrist joints, which permit the palm of the hand to turn up. **2.** assumption of a supine position, one of lying on the back, face up.—**supinate,** *v.*

supinator longus reflex /sōō′pinā′tər/ [L, *reflectere,* to bend back], a contraction of the brachioradialis muscle, causing flexion at the elbow joint on tapping the point of insertion of the supinator longus muscle at the lower end of the radius.

supine /səpīn′, sōō′pīn/ [L, *supinus*], **1.** position of the arms or body in which the palms of the hands face upward. **2.** lying horizontally on the back.

supine hypotension, a fall in BP that occurs when a pregnant woman is lying on her back. It is caused by impaired venous return that results from pressure of the gravid uterus on the vena cava.

supine position, the position of a person lying on the back.

supplemental inheritance /sup′ləmen′təl/ [L, *supplere,* to complete, *in,* in, *hereditare,* hereditary], the acquisition or expression of a genetic trait or condition through the presence of two independent pairs of nonallelic genes that interact in such a way that one gene supplements the action of the other.

supplementary gene /sup′ləmen′tərē/ [L, *supplere;* Gk, *genein,* to produce], one of two pairs of nonallelic genes that interact in such a way that one pair needs the presence of the other to be expressed, whereas the second pair can produce an effect independently of the first.

supply management, a nursing intervention from the Nursing Interventions Classification (NIC) defined as ensuring acquisition and maintenance of appropriate items for providing patient care.

support /səpôrt′/ [L, *supportare,* to bring up], **1.** to sustain, hold up, or maintain in a desired position or condition, as in physically supporting the abdominal muscles with a scultetus binder or emotionally supporting a client under stress. **2.** the assistance given to this end, such as physical support, emotional support, or life support.

support group[1], **1.** an organization that serves as a link in the network for family caregivers and patients, such as those who are homebound, mentally ill, elderly, or suicidal or who have a specific disorder. The group helps families and patients find a balance of responsibility. **2.** an organization for people who share a common problem.

support group[2], a nursing intervention from the Nursing Interventions Classification (NIC) defined as use of a group environment to provide emotional support and health-related information for members.

supporting area [L, *supportare + area,* space], any of the areas of maxillary or mandibular edentulous ridges that are considered best suited to bear the forces of chewing with functioning dentures.

supporting cells, cells that serve to provide support and protection and perhaps contribute to the nutrition of principal or other cells of certain organs; such cells are found in the labyrinth of the inner ear, organ of Corti, olfactory epithelium, taste buds, and seminiferous tubules.

supportive psychotherapy /səpôr'tiv/, a form of psychotherapy that concentrates on creating an effective means of communication with an emotionally disturbed person rather than on trying to produce psychologic insight into the underlying conflicts.

support system enhancement, a nursing intervention from the Nursing Interventions Classification (NIC) defined as facilitation of support to patient by family, friends, and community.

suppository /səpoz'ətôr'ē/ [L, *sub,* under, *ponere,* to place], an easily melted medicated mass for insertion into the rectum, urethra, or vagina. Theobroma oil, glycerinated gelatin, and high-molecular-weight polyethylene glycols are common vehicles for drugs in suppositories. Drugs administered by rectal suppository are absorbed systemically, and this route is especially useful in babies, in uncooperative patients, and in cases of vomiting or certain digestive disorders.

suppressant /səpres'ənt/ [L, *supprimere,* to press down], an agent that suppresses or diminishes a physical or mental activity.

suppressed menstruation /səprest'/ [L, *supprimere,* to press down + *menstruare*], a failure of menstruation to occur when expected, as in amenorrhea, or menstruation that is suppressed, as with Gn Rit agonists.

suppression /səpresh'ən/ [L, *supprimere*], in psychoanalysis, the conscious inhibition of or effort to conceal unacceptable or painful thoughts, desires, impulses, feelings, or acts.

suppression amblyopia, a partial loss of vision, usually in one eye, caused by cortical suppression of central vision to prevent diplopia. It occurs commonly in strabismus in the eye that deviates and does not fixate.

suppressor gene /səpres'ər/, a gene that is able to reverse the effect of a specific kind of mutation in other genes.

suppressor mutation, a mutation that partially or completely restores a function lost by a primary mutation occurring at a different locus.

suppurate /sup'yərāt/ [L, *suppurare,* to form pus], to produce purulent matter. —**suppuration,** *n.,* **suppurative,** *adj.*

suppuration /sup'yərā'shən/ [L, *suppurare,* to form pus], the production and exudation of pus.

suppurative /sup'yərā'tiv/ [L, *suppurare,* to form pus], pus-forming.

suppurative arthritis, inflammation of a joint with exudation of pus into the joint fluid.

suppurative fever [L, *suppurare,* to form pus, *febris,* fever], a fever accompanied by pus formation.

suppurative pancreatitis [L, *suppurare,* to form pus; Gk, *pan,* all, *kreas,* flesh, *itis,* inflammation], a form of pancreatic inflammation accompanied by the appearance of small abscesses.

suppurative phlebitis [L, *suppurare,* to form pus; Gk, *phleps,* vein, *itis,* inflammation], a vein inflammation that results from septicemia or a nearby pyogenic infection.

supracallosus gyrus /soo'prəkələo'ses/ [L, *supra,* above, *callosus,* hard; Gk, *gyros,* turn], the gray matter covering the corpus callosum of the brain.

supracervical hysterectomy /-sur'vikəl/ [L, *supra,* above, *cervix,* neck; Gk, *hystera,* womb, *ektomē,* excision], a subtotal hysterectomy in which the body of the uterus is removed, leaving the cervix.

supraclavicular /-kləvik'yələr/ [L, *supra,* above, *clavicula,* little key], pertaining to the area above the clavicle, or collar bone.

supraclavicular artery, a branch of the thyrocervical trunk that supplies the muscles on the dorsal surface of the scapula.

supraclavicular nerve, one of a pair of cutaneous branches of the cervical plexus, arising from the third and fourth cervical nerves, mostly from the fourth nerve.

supraclavicular triangle [L, *supra,* above, *clavicula,* little key + *triangulus*], the lower and anterior areas of the neck, bounded by the omohyoid muscle above, the sternocleidomastoid muscle in front, and the clavicle below. The first rib is in the base of the triangle.

supracondylar /-kon'dilər/ [L, *supra,* above; Gk, *kondylos,* knuckle], pertaining to an area above a condyle.

supracondylar fracture [L, *supra;* Gk, *kondylos,* knuckle], a fracture involving the area between the condyles of the humerus or the femur.

supraglenoid tubercle, the site of attachment on the scapula of the biceps brachii muscle.

suprahyoid muscles, a group of four muscles that attach the hyoid bone to the skull.

suprahyoid pharyngotomy, external pharyngotomy in which the suprahyoid muscles are divided and the epiglottic vallecula is entered by following the hyoepiglottic ligament.

suprainfection /-infek'shən/ [L, *supra* + *inficere,* to stain], a secondary infection usually caused by an opportunistic pathogen, such as a fungal infection after the antibiotic treatment of another infection.

supramentale /sōō'prəmentä'lē/ [L, *supra,* above, *mentum,* chin], in radiographic cephalometry, the most posterior midline point in the concavity between the infradentale and pogonion, determined on the lateral head film.

supranasal /sōō'prənä'zəl/ [L, *supra,* above + *nasus,* nose], superior to the nose.

supranuclear gaze disturbance /-nōō'klē·ər/, an inability to direct the eyes to the side contralateral to a lesion in the frontal lobe. If the frontal lobe lesions are bilateral, the patient can maintain fixation and follow visual targets but cannot shift the gaze in any direction in the absence of a target.

supraoptic nucleus /-op'tik/ [L, *supra,* above; Gk, *optikos;* L, *nucleus,* nut kernel], a hypothalamic nucleus that lies above the optic chiasma, with fibers extending to the posterior lobe of the pituitary.

supraorbital /sōō'prə·or'bitəl/ [L, *supra,* above, *orbita,* wheel track], superior to the orbit.

supraorbital artery, a branch of the ophthalmic artery that supplies the scalp.

suprapatellar /-pətel'ər/ [L, *supra,* above, *patella,* small dish], pertaining to a location above the patella.

suprapatellar bursa, an expansion of the synovial membrane of the knee that is a continuation of the articular cavity superiorly between the distal end of the shaft of the femur and the quadriceps femoris muscle and tendon. It provides a low-friction surface for the movement of knee tendons.

suprapelvic /sōō'prə·pel'vik/ [L, *supra,* above + *pelvis,* basin], above the pelvis.

suprapubic /-p(y)ōō'bik/ [L, *supra* + *pubes,* signs of maturity], pertaining to a location above the symphysis pubis.

suprapubic aspiration of urine, a procedure for draining the bladder by inserting a sterile needle through the skin above the pubic arch and into the bladder.

suprapubic catheter [L, *supra* + *pubis* + Gk, *katheter,* a thing lowered into], a urinary bladder catheter inserted through the skin about 1 inch above the symphysis pubis. It is used for closed drainage and may be left in place for a time, sutured to the abdominal skin.

suprarenal /-rē'nəl/ [L, *supra* + *ren,* kidney], pertaining to a location above the kidney.

suprascapular foramen, the route between the base of the neck and the posterior scapular region, formed by the suprascapular notch of the scapula and the superior transverse scapular ligament.

suprascapular ligament /-skap'yələr/ [L, *supra,* above, *scapula,* shoulder blade, *ligare,* to bind], a ligament that extends from the base of the coracoid process to the medial end of the suprascapular notch.

suprascapular nerve [L, *supra* + *scapulae,* shoulder blades], one of a pair of branches from the cords of the brachial plexus. It supplies the shoulder joint, scapula, and associated muscles.

suprasellar /-sel'ər/, above the sella turcica.

supraspinal /-spī'nəl/ [L, *supra,* above, *spina,* backbone], pertaining to an area above the spine.

supraspinal ligament [L, *supra* + *spina,* backbone], the ligament that connects the apices of the spinous processes from the seventh cervical vertebra to the sacrum.

supraspinatus /sōō'prə·spī'nä'tus/ [L, *supra,* above + *spina,* spine], a muscle originating in the supraspinous fossa and inserting in the greater tubercle of the humerus. It functions to abduct the humerus.

supraspinatus syndrome /-spīnä'təs/, pain and tenderness involving the supraspinatus tendon of the arm, restricting abduction of the shoulder.

supraspinous fossa /-spī'nəs/ [L, *supra,* above, *spina,* backbone, *fossa,* ditch], a depressed area on the dorsal surface of the scapula, above the spine.

suprasternal /-stur'nəl/, pertaining to a location above the sternum, adjacent to the neck.

supratentorial /-tentôr'ē·əl/ [L, *supra,* above, *tentorium,* tent], pertaining to a location above a tentorium.

S

supratrochlear artery, one of the two terminal branches of the ophthalmic nerve, with the dorsal nasal artery.

supravaginal hysterectomy /-vaj'inəl/ [L, *supra*, above, *vagina*, sheath; Gk, *hystera*, womb, *ektomē*, excision], a subtotal hysterectomy in which the body of the uterus is removed but the cervix remains.

supraventricular crest, the muscular ridge on the interior dorsal wall of the right ventricle of the heart.

supraventricular tachycardia (SVT) /-ventrik'yələr/ [L, *supra + ventriculus*, little belly], any cardiac rhythm with a rate exceeding 100 beats/min that originates above the branching part of the atrioventricular bundle, that is, in the sinus node, atria, or atrioventricular (AV) junction.

supraversion /soo'prə·ver'zhən/ [L, *supra*, above + *vertere*, to turn], malocclusion in which a tooth or other maxillary or mandibular structure extends farther away from the alveolus than normal, the occluding surfaces of the teeth extending beyond the normal occlusal line.

suprofen /səprō'fən/, an oral nonsteroidal antiinflammatory analgesic used in the treatment of mild-to-moderate pain and primary dysmenorrhea.

sural nerve, a nerve that originates high in the leg between the two heads of the gastrocnemius muscle and supplies skin on the lower posterolateral surface of the leg and the lateral side of the foot and little toe.

sural region /soo'rəl/ [L, *sura*, calf of the leg], the calf of the leg. It is formed by the bellies of the gastrocnemius and soleus muscles.

suramin sodium /soo'rəmin/, an antitrypanosomal and an antifilarial available from the Centers for Disease Control and Prevention. It is used primarily for treatment and prophylaxis of African trypanosomiasis and onchocerciasis.

surcharge, (in the United States) an additional fee charged to health plan enrollees for benefits not provided in the health plan contract.

surface anatomy /sur'fəs/ [L, *superficies*, surface], the study of the structural relationships of the external features of the body to the internal organs and parts.

surface area (SA), the total area exposed to the outside environment. The surface area of an object increases with the square of its linear dimensions. Volume increases as the cube of the object's linear dimensions.

surface biopsy, the removal of living tissue for microscopic examination by scraping the surface of a lesion.

surface tension, the tendency of a liquid to minimize the area of its surface by contracting. This property causes liquids to rise in a capillary tube, affects the exchange of gases in the pulmonary alveoli, and alters the ability of various liquids to wet another surface.

surface therapy, a form of radiotherapy administered by placing one or more radioactive sources on or near an area of body surface.

surface thermometer, a device that detects and indicates the surface temperature of any part of the body.

surfactant /sərfak'tənt/ [L, *superficies*], **1.** an agent such as soap or detergent dissolved in water to reduce its surface tension or the tension at the interface between the water and another liquid. **2.** certain lipoproteins that reduce the surface tension of pulmonary fluids, allowing the exchange of gases in the alveoli of the lungs and contributing to the elasticity of pulmonary tissue.

Surfak, a trademark for a stool softener (docusate calcium).

surfer's nodules [ME, *suffe*, rush; L, *nodus*, knot], nodules on the skin of the knees, ankles, feet, or toes of a surfer caused by repeated contact of the skin with an abrasive, sandy surfboard.

surgeon /sur'jən/, a physician who treats injuries, deformities, and diseases by operative methods.

surgeon general, in the United States, the chief medical officer of the Army, Navy, Air Force, and Public Health Service. In other countries the title may indicate any physician with the rank of general.

surgeon's assistant (SA) /sur'jənz/ [Gk, *cheirourgos*, surgeon; L, *assistere*, to cause to stand], a medical professional trained to assist during surgery and in the preoperative and postoperative periods under the supervision of a licensed physician qualified to practice surgery.

surgery /sur'jərē/ [Gk, *cheirourgia*], the branch of medicine concerned with diseases and trauma requiring operative procedures. —**surgical,** *adj.*

surgical /sur'jikəl/ [Gk, *cheirourgia*], pertaining to the treatment of disease by manipulative and operative methods.

surgical anatomy, in applied anatomy, the study of the structure and morphologic characteristics of the tissues and organs of the body as they relate to surgery.

surgical assistance, a nursing intervention from the Nursing Interventions Classification (NIC) defined as assisting the surgeon/dentist with operative procedures and care of the surgical patient.

surgical assistant, as defined by the American College of Surgeons (ACS), the surgical assistant, under the direct supervision of the surgeon, provides aid in exposure, hemostasis and other technical functions that will help the surgeon to perform a safe operation with optimal results for the patient.

surgical fever [Gk, *cheirourgia*; L, *febris*], a fever that develops after surgery.

surgical hospital, a hospital specializing in surgical procedures.

surgical ligature, the exposure of an unerupted tooth by placing a metal ligature around its cervix. It is done to produce traction on the unerupted tooth and force it through the gingival tissues.

surgical menopause [Gk, *cheirourgia*; L, *men,* month; Gk, *pauein,* to cease], the creation of a menopausal state by surgical removal of the ovaries.

surgical neck of humerus [Gk, *cheirourgia*; AS, *hnecca*; L, *humerus,* shoulder], the shaft of the humerus distal to the tuberosities. It is a region particularly vulnerable to fracture and surgical correction.

surgical pathology, the study of disease by the analysis of tissue specimens obtained during surgery. The surgical pathologist often examines specimens during surgery to determine how the operation should be modified or completed.

surgical precautions, a nursing intervention from the Nursing Interventions Classification (NIC) defined as minimizing the potential for iatrogenic injury to the patient related to a surgical procedure.

surgical preparation, a nursing intervention from the Nursing Interventions Classification (NIC) defined as providing care to a patient immediately prior to surgery and verification of required procedures/tests and documentation in the clinical record.

surgical scrub, 1. a bactericidal soap or solution used by surgeons and surgical nurses before performing or assisting in surgery. 2. the act of washing the fingernails, hands, and forearms with a bactericidal soap or solution in a prescribed manner for a specific period before a surgical procedure.

surgical sectioning, an oral surgery procedure for dividing a tooth to facilitate its removal.

surgical shock [Gk, *cheirourgia*; Fr, *choc*], a condition of shock that may occur during or after surgery, with signs of profound hypotension, decreased urine, increased heart rate, restlessness, and cyanosis of the extremities. Hemoglobin for blood volume may be low, or patient may be bleeding or have a severe infection.

surgical suite, a group of one or more ORs and adjunct facilities, such as a sterile storage area, scrub room, and recovery room.

surgical technology, an allied health profession that focuses on providing an optimal surgical environment for the patient through the performance of sterile and nonsterile roles.

Surmontil, a trademark for an antidepressant (trimipramine maleate).

surrogate /sur′əgāt/ [L, *surrogare,* to substitute], 1. a substitute; a person or thing that replaces another. 2. a person who represents and acts as a parent, taking the place of the father or mother. 3. in psychoanalysis, a substitute parental figure, a symbolic image or representation of another, as may occur in a dream.

surrogate parenting, a form of artificial insemination in which a fertile woman agrees to be impregnated by a sperm donor and to carry the child to term, at which time the offspring is surrendered to another. The surrogate mother usually receives a fee for bearing the child.

sursumversion /sur′sumver′zhən/ [L. *sursum,* upward, *vertere,* to turn], binocular conjugate upward rotation of both eyes.

surveillance¹ /sərvā′ləns/ [Fr, *surveiller,* to watch over], 1. supervision or observation of a patient or a health condition. 2. a detailed examination or investigation for the accurate collection of data to record changes in the character of a population as at a particular time or, in a prospective or longitudinal surveillance, over a period of time.

surveillance², a nursing intervention from the Nursing Interventions Classification (NIC) defined as purposeful and ongoing acquisition, interpretation, and synthesis of patient data for clinical decision making.

surveillance: community, a nursing intervention from the Nursing Interventions Classification (NIC) defined as purposeful and ongoing acquisition, interpretation, and synthesis of data for decision making in the community.

surveillance: late pregnancy, a nursing intervention from the Nursing Interventions Classification (NIC) defined as purposeful and ongoing acquisition, interpretation, and synthesis of maternal-fetal data for treatment, observation, or admission.

surveillance: remote electronic, a nursing intervention from the Nursing Interventions Classification (NIC) defined as purposeful and ongoing acquisition of patient data via electronic modalities (telephone, video, conferencing, e-mail) from distant locations, as well as interpretation and synthesis of patient data for clinical decision making with individuals or populations.

surveillance: safety, a nursing intervention from the Nursing Interventions

S

Classification (NIC) defined as purposeful and ongoing collection and analysis of information about the patient and the environment for use in promoting and maintaining patient safety.

surveyed height of contour /sərvād′/ [OFr, *surveir,* to survey; AS, *heah,* high; It, *contornare,* to surround], a line, scribed or marked on a plaster cast of the teeth by the use of a dental surveyor, that designates the greatest convexity relative to a selected path of denture placement and removal, as well as the placement of removable partial denture retention clasps.

surveyor, a dental instrument composed of a vertical post mounted to a flat metal base, a horizontal arm connected to the vertical post, followed by a vertical stylus which encases a piece of pencil lead. The second portion is a table to which a plaster cast of the teeth is clamped, so that a surveyed height of contour can be established.

survival curve /sərvī′vəl/ [Fr, *survivre,* to survive; L, *curvus,* bent], a plot of the number or percentage of organisms surviving for a given period as a function of radiation dose.

survivor guilt /sərvī′vər/ [OFr, *survivre;* ME, *gilt,* sin], feelings of guilt for surviving a tragedy in which others died. In some cases, the person may believe the tragedy occurred because he or she did something bad; in others, the person may feel guilty for not taking proper steps to avert the tragedy.

susceptibility /səsep′tibil′itē/ [L, *suscipere,* to undertake], the condition of being vulnerable to a disease or disorder.

susceptible /səsep′tibəl/ [L, *suscipere,* to undertake], being predisposed, liable, or sensitive to the effects of an infectious disease, allergen, or other pathogenic agent; lacking immunity or resistance.

suspension /səspen′shən/ [L, *suspendere,* to hang], **1.** a liquid in which small particles of a solid are dispersed, but not dissolved, and in which the dispersal is maintained by stirring or shaking the mixture. **2.** a treatment, used primarily in spinal disorders, consisting of suspending the patient by the chin and shoulders. **3.** a temporary cessation of pain or of a vital process.

suspension sling, a sling usually made of muslin or lightweight canvas and used primarily to provide support, such as against the gravitational pull on an injured arm.

suspensory ligament /səspen′sərē/ [L, *suspendere,* to hang, *ligare,* to bind], any of a number of ligaments that help support an organ or body structure, such as the suspensory ligaments inside the eye that hold the lens in tension.

sustenance /sus′tənəns/ [L, *sustenare,* to sustain], **1.** the act or process of supporting or maintaining life or health. **2.** the food or nutrients essential for maintaining life.

sustenance support, a nursing intervention from the Nursing Interventions Classification (NIC) defined as helping an individual/family in need to locate food, clothing, or shelter.

sustentacular /sus′tentak′yōōlər/ [L, *sustentare,* to support], pertaining to a support or serving to support.

sustentaculum tali, a process of the calcaneus that supports the talus.

susto /sōōs′tō/, a culture-bound syndrome found in Central American populations. It is related to stress engendered by a self-perceived failure to fulfill gender-role expectations.

Sutent, a trademark for sunitinib.

Sutton's disease /sut′ənz/ [Richard Lightburn Sutton, American dermatologist, 1878–1952], a recurrent disease of the mucous membranes of unknown cause characterized by deep crater-like ulcers with inflamed borders that leave scars after healing. It usually involves the mucosa of the lips, cheeks, tongue, palate, and anterior tonsillar pillars, but the pharynx, larynx, and genitalia may also be affected.

sutura /sōōchōō′rə/ *pl.* **suturae** [L, *suture*], an immovable fibrous joint in which certain bones of the skull are connected by a thin layer of fibrous tissue.

sutura dentata, an immovable fibrous joint that is one kind of true suture in which toothlike processes interlock along the margins of connecting bones of the skull.

sutura limbosa, an immovable fibrous joint that is one kind of true suture in which beveled and serrated edges of certain connecting bones of the skull such as the parietal and temporal bones overlap and interlock.

sutura plana, a fibrous joint that is one kind of false suture in which rough contiguous edges of certain bones of the skull such as the maxillae form a connection.

sutura serrata, an immovable fibrous joint that is one kind of true suture in which connecting bones interlock along serrated edges that resemble fine-toothed saws.

sutura squamosa, an immovable fibrous joint that is one kind of false suture in which overlapping beveled edges unite certain bones of the skull, such as the temporal and parietal bone.

suture /sōō′chər/ [L, *sutura*], **1.** a border or a joint, such as between the bones of the cranium. 2. to stitch together cut or torn edges of tissue with suture material. 3. a surgical stitch taken to repair an incision, tear, or wound. 4. material used for surgical stitches, such as absorbable or nonabsorbable silk, catgut, wire, or synthetic material.

suturing, a nursing intervention from the Nursing Interventions Classification (NIC) defined as approximating edges of a wound using sterile suture material and a needle.

Sv, abbreviation for **sievert.**

SV40, abbreviation for **simian virus 40.**

SvO₂, symbol for the percentage of oxygen saturation of mixed venous blood.

SVR, abbreviation for **systemic vascular resistance.**

SVT, abbreviation for **supraventricular tachycardia.**

swab /swob/ [D, *swabber,* ship's drudge], a stick or clamp holding absorbent gauze or cotton, used for washing, cleansing, or drying a body surface; for collecting a specimen for laboratory examination; or for applying a topical medication.

swaddling /swod'ling/ [OE, *swethel,* swaddling band], **1.** long narrow bands of cloth once used to wrap a newborn. **2.** a method of wrapping a newborn, especially a premature or at risk newborn, that provides maximal comfort and containment.

swage /swāj/ [OFr, *souage*], **1.** to shape metal by hammering or by adapting it to a die. **2.** to fuse suture material to a needle, especially an eyeless needle. **3.** a tool or form, often one of a pair, for shaping metal by pressure.

swallow apnea, absence of respiration during the phase of swallowing when the bolus is passing through the oropharyngeal region.

swallowing /swol'ō·ing/ [AS, *swelgan*], the process that usually involves movement of food from the mouth to the stomach via the esophagus. Coordination of muscles is needed from the tongue to the esophageal sphincter.

swallowing examination, an x-ray with contrast dye (usually barium) that is performed to pinpoint problems that exist in a patient who is unable to swallow.

swallowing reflex [AS, *swelgan;* L, *reflectere,* to bend back], a sequence of reflexes that begins when a bolus of food is manipulated by the tongue and other oral cavity muscles to the palate or the pharynx.

swallowing status, a nursing outcome from the Nursing Outcomes Classification (NOC) defined as safe passage of fluids and/or solids from the mouth to the stomach.

swallowing status: esophageal phase, a nursing outcome from the Nursing Outcomes Classification (NOC) defined as safe passage of fluids and/or solids from the pharynx to the stomach.

swallowing status: oral phase, a nursing outcome from the Nursing Outcomes Classification (NOC) defined as preparation, containment, and posterior movement of fluids and/or solids in the mouth.

swallowing status: pharyngeal phase, a nursing outcome from the Nursing Outcomes Classification (NOC) defined as safe passage of fluids and/or solids from the mouth to the esophagus.

swallowing therapy, a nursing intervention from the Nursing Interventions Classification (NIC) defined as facilitating swallowing and preventing complications of impaired swallowing.

Swan-Ganz catheter /swän ganz/ [Harold J.C. Swan, American physician, b. 1922; William Ganz, American cardiologist, b. 1919; Gk, *katheter,* something lowered], a long thin cardiac catheter with a tiny balloon at the tip. It is used to determine left ventricular function by measuring pulmonary capillary wedge pressure.

swan neck deformity /swän/ [D, *zwaan;* AS, *hnecca,* neck; L, *deformis,* misshapen], **1.** an abnormal condition of the finger characterized by flexion of the distal interphalangeal joint and hyperextension of the proximal interphalangeal joint. The condition is seen most often in rheumatoid arthritis. **2.** a structural abnormality of the kidney tubules associated with rickets. The kidney tubule connecting the glomerulus with the convoluted part of the tubule is narrowed into a configuration referred to as "swan neck."

Swanson, Kristen M., a nursing theorist whose Theory of Caring asserts that nursing care is nurturing delivered as a set of interrelated processes that evolve from the nurse's own convictions and knowledge and his or her interaction with the patient. The theory is based on Swanson's Caring Model, which names as the components of caring five basic processes—knowing, being with, doing for, enabling, and maintaining belief (faith in and esteem for the patient).

S wave, the negative component after the R wave in each QRS complex on an ECG.

sway, to rock, teeter, wobble, or swing back and forth.

sweat bath, a bath given to induce sweating.

sweat electrolytes test, a fluid analysis of sweat to indicate whether a patient has CF.

sweat gland abscess, an abscess in a sweat gland, such as in hidradenitis suppurativa.

S

sweat test, a method for evaluating sodium and chloride excretion from the sweat glands, often the first test performed in the diagnosis of CF. The sweat glands are stimulated with a drug such as pilocarpine, and the perspiration produced is analyzed. The eccrine glands of patients with CF produce sodium and chloride concentrations that are three to six times normal.

Swedish massage /swē′dish/ [Fr, *masser*], the most commonly used form of classical Western massage, generally performed in the direction of the heart, sometimes with active or passive movement of the joints. It is used especially for relaxation, relief of muscular tension, and improvement of circulation and ROM.

sweep tapping, a proprioceptive-tactile treatment technique in which the clinician uses a light-touch sweep pattern over the back of the fingers of one of the hands. The stimulus is applied quickly over a dermatomal area, helping the patient to contract the muscle.

Sweet localization method, a radiographic technique for locating a foreign body in the eye by making two radiographic films of the eye while the patient's head is immobilized. A small metal ball and a cone are placed at precise distances from the center of the cornea as register marks while lateral and perpendicular radiographic views of the eye are made. A three-dimensional view of the eye is constructed from the two films, and, guided by the positions of the ball and cone, the location of the foreign body in the eye is plotted from the intersection of lines through the ball and cone.

Sweet's syndrome /swēts/ [Robert Douglas Sweet, English dermatologist, 20th century], a condition usually seen on the upper body of middle-aged women, characterized by one or more large, rapidly extending, erythematous, tender or painful plaques, accompanied by fever and dense infiltration of neutrophils in the upper and middle dermis.

swimmer's ear [AS, *swimman*, to swim + *eare*], *informal.* otitis externa resulting from infection transmitted in the water of a swimming pool.

swimmer's itch, an allergic dermatitis caused by sensitivity to non-human schistosome cercarias that die under the skin, leading to erythema, urticaria, and a papular rash lasting 1 or 2 days. Treatment usually includes oral antihistamines and antipruritic lotions.

swimming reflex, a primitive fetal activity, marked by well-coordinated movements, that is exhibited when the infant's face is placed in water. It normally disappears at 6 months of age.

swineherd's disease, leptospirosis, manifested as a benign meningitis, caused by serovariants of *Leptospira interrogans.* It affects people who work with swine or pork or come in contact with the urine of animal or human carriers.

swing phase of gait [AS, *swingan;* Gk, *phasis,* appearance; ME, *gata,* a way], the phase of the normal gait cycle during which the foot is off the ground. The swing phase follows the stance phase and is divided into the initial swing, the midswing, and the terminal swing stages.

switch site, a point on a chromosome where gene segments unite during segment rearrangement, as in the production of immunoglobulins.

swoon [OE, *geswogen,* unconscious], a fainting spell.

sycosis barbae /sikō′sis/ [Gk, *sycon,* fig, *osis,* condition; L, *barba,* beard], an inflammation of hair follicles of skin that has been shaved. Treatment includes light and infrequent shaving, topical and systemic antibiotics, and daily plucking of infected hairs.

Sydenham's chorea /sīd′ənhamz/ [Thomas Sydenham, English physician, 1624–1689; Gk, *choreia,* dance], a form of chorea associated with rheumatic fever, usually occurring during childhood. The cause is unknown but is thought be a streptococcal infection that initiates an autoimmune mechanism. The choreic movements increase over the first 2 weeks, reach a plateau, and then diminish.

sylvatic plague /silvat′ik/ [L, *sylva,* forest, *plaga,* stroke], an endemic disease of wild rodents caused by *Yersinia pestis* and transmitted to humans by the bite of an infected flea.

sylvian aqueduct /sil′vē·ən/ [Franciscus Sylvius, Dutch anatomist, 1614–1672, L, *aquaductus,* canal], a narrow canal from the third to the fourth ventricle of the midbrain.

sylvian fissure [Franciscus Sylvius; L, *fissura,* cleft], the lateral sulcus of the cerebral hemisphere.

symbiosis /sim′bē·ō′sis/ [Gk, *syn,* together, *bios,* life], **1.** a mode of living characterized by a close association between organisms of different species. **2.** a state in which two people are emotionally dependent on each other. **3.** a pathologic inability of a child to separate from its mother emotionally and sometimes physically.— **symbiotic,** *adj.*

symbiotic /sim′bē·ot′ik/ [Gk, *syn,* together, *bios,* life], characterized by or concerned with symbiosis or living together.

symbiotic phase, in Mahler's system of preoedipal development, the stage between l and 5 months when the infant participates in a "symbiotic orbit" with the mother.

symbol /sim'bəl/ [Gk, *symbolon,* sign], **1.** an image, object, action, or other stimulus that represents something else by reason of conscious association, convention, or another relationship. **2.** an object, mode of behavior, or feeling that disguises a repressed emotional conflict through an unconscious association rather than through an objective relationship, as in dreams and anxiety.

symbolism /sim'bəlizəm/, **1.** the representation or evocation of one idea, action, or object by the use of another, as in systems of writing, poetic language, or dream metaphor. **2.** in psychiatry, an unconscious mental mechanism characteristic of all human thinking in which a mental image stands for but disguises some other object, person, or thought.

Symlin, a trademark for pramlintide.

symmelia /simē'lyə/ [Gk, *syn,* together, *melos,* limb], a developmental anomaly characterized by apparent fusion of the lower limbs. There may be three feet **(tripodial symmelia),** two feet **(dipodial symmelia),** one foot **(monopodial symmelia),** or no feet **(apodal symmelia** or **sirenomelia).**

symmelus /sim'ələs/, a malformed fetus characterized by symmelia.

Symmetrel, a trademark for an antiviral and antiparkinsonian (amantadine hydrochloride).

symmetric /simet'rik/ [Gk, *syn + metron,* measure], (of the body or parts of the body) pertaining to equality in size or shape; very similar in relative placement or arrangement about an axis.—**symmetry,** *n.*

symmetric orientation, in neonatal care, midline positioning of the head with similar alignment of the trunk and extremities. The orientation helps promote even development of tone and function in both sides of the body.

symmetric tonic neck reflex, a normal response in infants to assume the crawl position by extending the arms and bending the knees when the head and neck are extended.

symmetry /sim'ətrē/ [Gk, *syn,* together, *metron,* measure], in anatomy, the correspondence of parts on opposite sides of the body, or equality of parts on both sides of a dividing line.

sympathectomize /sim'pəthek'təmiz/ [Gk, *sympathein,* to feel with, *ektomē,* excision], to interrupt the conduction of nerve impulses along part of the sympathetic trunk by surgery or drugs.

sympathectomy /sim'pəthek'təmē/ [Gk, *sympathein,* to feel with, *ektomē,*

excision], a surgical interruption of part of the sympathetic nerve pathways to relieve chronic pain or to promote vasodilation in vascular diseases, such as arteriosclerosis, claudication, Buerger's disease, and Raynaud's phenomenon. The sheath around an artery carries the sympathetic nerve fibers that control constriction of the vessel. Removal of the sheath causes the vessel to relax and expand and allows more blood to pass through it. The operation also may be done with a vascular graft, to increase the blood flow through the graft area.

sympathetic /sim'pəthet'ik/ [Gk, *sympathein,* to feel with], **1.** displaying of compassion for another's grief. **2.** pertaining to a division of the autonomic nervous system.

sympathetic ganglion [Gk, *sympathein,* to feel with, *gagglion,* knot], a collection of multipolar nerve cells along the course of the sympathetic trunk. Nearly two dozen of the ganglia serve as "cell stations" on efferent pathways between the cervical and sacral parts of the sympathetic trunk.

sympathetic imbalance [Gk, *sympathein,* to feel with; L, *in + balance*], pertaining to vagotony, or vagus nerve tension, and hyperexcitability of the parasympathetic nervous system, as opposed to the sympathetic nervous system.

sympathetic irritation [Gk, *sympathein,* to feel with; L, *irritare,* to tease], inflammation of one organ after inflammation of a related organ, such as when trauma to an eye is followed by similar symptoms in the uninjured eye.

sympathetic nerve [Gk, *sympathein,* to feel with; L, *nervus*], any nerve of the sympathetic branch of the autonomic nervous system.

sympathetic ophthalmia, a granulomatous inflammation of the uveal tract of both eyes occurring after an injury to the uveal tract of one eye. Corticosteroids may be helpful in treatment, but surgical enucleation of the originally injured eye may be necessary to preserve vision in the uninjured eye.

sympathetic pain, distress that occurs in the hemiplegic shoulder as a result of muscle imbalance, with a loss of joint range. It results from loss of active and passive motion, loss of ability to bear weight, and long-standing subluxation without support.

sympathetic symptom [Gk, *sympathein,* to feel with, *symptoma,* that which occurs], a symptom occurring in one body area when the causative lesion is actually in another area.

sympathetic trunk, one of a pair of chains of ganglia extending along the side

S

of the vertebral column from the base of the skull to the coccyx. Each trunk is part of the sympathetic nervous system and consists of a series of ganglia connected by various types of fibers. Each sympathetic trunk distributes branches with postganglionic fibers to the autonomic plexuses, the cranial nerves, the individual organs, the nerves accompanying arteries, and the spinal nerves.

sympathizing eye /sim′pəthī′zing/, in sympathetic ophthalmia, the fellow eye that becomes inflamed by lymphatic or blood-borne metastasis of the causative antigen or microorganism.

sympathomimetic /sim′pəthō′mimet′ik/ [Gk, *sympathein* + *mimesis,* imitation], denoting a pharmacologic agent that mimics the effects of stimulation of organs and structures by the sympathetic nervous system. It functions by occupying adrenergic receptor sites and acting as an agonist or by increasing the release of the neurotransmitter norepinephrine at postganglionic nerve endings. Various sympathomimetic agents are used as decongestants of nasal and ocular mucosa, such as bronchodilators in the treatment of asthma and vasopressors and cardiac stimulants in the treatment of acute hypotension and shock.

sympathomimetic amine, amines that mimic the actions of the sympathetic nervous system. The group includes the catecholamines and drugs that mimic their actions.

sympathomimetic bronchodilator, a medication that reduces bronchial muscle spasm through action that mimics the sympathetic nervous system in producing smooth muscle relaxation. It is commonly a beta$_2$-receptor agonist agent.

sympathy /sim′pəthē/ [Gk, *sympathein*], **1.** an expressed interest or concern regarding the problems, emotions, or states of mind of another. **2.** the relation that exists between the mind and body, causing the one to be affected by the other. **3.** mental contagion or the influence exerted by one individual or group on another and the effects produced, such as the spread of panic, uncontrollable laughter, or yawning. **4.** the physiologic or pathologic relationship between two organs, systems, or parts of the body. —**sympathize,** *v.*

symphalangia /sim′fəlan′jē·ə/ [Gk, *syn,* together, *phalanx,* finger], **1.** a condition, usually inherited, characterized by ankylosis of the fingers or toes. **2.** a congenital anomaly in which webbing of the fingers or toes occurs in varying degrees.

symphocephalus /sim′fōsef′ələs/ [Gk, *symphes,* growing together, *kephale,* head], twin fetuses joined at the head.

symphyseal angle /simfiz′ē·əl/ [Gk, *symphysis,* growing together; L, *angulus,* corner], the angle of the chin, which may be classified as protruding, straight, or receding.

symphysic teratism /simfiz′ik/, a congenital anomaly in which there is a fusion of normally separated parts or organs, such as a horseshoe kidney, or in which parts close prematurely, such as the skull bones in craniostenosis.

symphysis /sim′fəsis/ *pl.* **symphyses** [Gk, growing together], **1.** a line of union, especially a cartilaginous joint in which adjacent bony surfaces are firmly united by fibrocartilage. **2.** *informal.* symphysis pubis.—**symphysic,** *adj.*

symphysis menti, 1. the junction between the two halves of the mandible. **2.** the prominence of the chin.

sympodia /simpō′dē·ə/ [Gk, *syn,* together, *pous,* foot], a congenital developmental anomaly characterized by fusion of the lower extremities.

symptom /simp′təm/ [Gk, *symptoma,* that which happens], a subjective indication of a disease or a change in condition as perceived by the patient. Many symptoms are accompanied by objective signs such as pruritus, which is often reported with erythema and a maculopapular eruption on the skin. Some symptoms may be objectively confirmed, such as numbness of a body part, which may be confirmed by absence of response to a pin prick. Primary symptoms are symptoms that are intrinsically associated with a disease. Secondary symptoms are a consequence of illness and disease.

symptomatic /simp′təmat′ik/ [Gk, *symptoma,* that which happens], having characteristics of a symptom or indications of a specific disease.

symptomatic esophageal peristalsis, a condition in which peristaltic progression in the body of the esophagus is normal but contractions in the distal esophagus are increased in amplitude and duration.

symptomatic impotence [Gk, *symptoma,* that which happens; L, *in + potentia,* power], impotence that is the result of poor health or the use of medications.

symptomatic nanism, dwarfism associated with defects in bone growth, tooth formation, and sexual development.

symptomatic neuralgia [Gk, *symptoma,* that which happens, *neuron,* nerve, *algos,* pain], nerve pain that is secondary to a disease condition.

symptomatic torticollis [Gk, *symptoma;* L, *tortus,* twisted, *collum,* neck], stiff neck caused by a disease in the neck, such as rheumatoid torticollis or myogenic torticollis.

symptomatology /simp′təmətol′əjē/ [Gk, *symptoma* + *logos*, science], the science of symptoms of disease in general or of the symptoms of a specific disease.

symptom-bearer, in psychology, a family member frequently seen as the patient who is functioning poorly because family dynamics interferes with functioning at a higher level.

symptom control, a nursing outcome from the Nursing Outcomes Classification (NOC) defined as personal actions to minimize perceived adverse changes in physical and emotional functioning.

symptom severity, a nursing outcome from the Nursing Outcomes Classification (NOC) defined as the severity of perceived adverse changes in physical, emotional, and social functioning.

symptom severity: perimenopause, a nursing outcome from the Nursing Outcomes Classification (NOC) defined as the severity of symptoms caused by declining hormonal levels.

symptom severity: premenstrual syndrome (PMS), a nursing outcome from the Nursing Outcomes Classification (NOC) defined as the severity of symptoms caused by cyclic hormonal fluctuations.

symptothermal method of family planning /simp′təthur′məl/ [Gk, *symptoma* + *therme,* heat], a natural method of family planning that incorporates the ovulation and basal body temperature methods of family planning.

sympus /sim′pəs/ [Gk, *syn,* together, *pous,* foot], a malformed fetus in which the lower extremities are completely fused or rotated and the pelvis and genitalia are defective.

sympus dipus /dē′pəs/, a malformed fetus in which the lower extremities are fused and both feet are formed.

sympus monopus /mon′əpəs/, a malformed fetus in which the lower extremities are fused and one foot is formed.

synactive model of infant behavior /sinak′tiv/, a major theoretic framework for establishing physiologic stability as the foundation for the organization of motor, behavioral state, and attentive/interactive behaviors in neonates.

synadelphus /sin′ədel′fəs/ *pl.* **synadelphi** [Gk, *syn* + *adelphos,* brother], a conjoined twin with a single head and trunk and eight limbs.

Synalar, a trademark for a glucocorticoid (fluocinolone acetonide).

synapse /sin′aps, sinaps′/ [Gk, *synaptein,* to join], **1.** the region surrounding the point of contact between two neurons or between a neuron and an effector organ, across which nerve impulses are transmitted through the action of a neurotransmitter. Synapses are polarized so that nerve impulses normally travel in only one direction; they are also subject to fatigue, oxygen deficiency, anesthetics, and other chemical agents. **2.** to form a synapse or connection between neurons. **3.** in genetics, to form a synaptic fusion between homologous chromosomes during meiosis.—**synaptic,** *adj.*

synapsis /sinap′sis/ *pl.* **synapses,** the pairing of homologous chromosomes during early meiotic prophase in gametogenesis to form double or bivalent chromosomes.

synaptic /sinap′tik/ [Gk, *synaptein,* to join], pertaining to or resembling a synapse.

synaptic cleft, the microscopic extracellular space at the synapse that separates the membrane of the terminal nerve endings of a presynaptic neuron and the membrane of a postsynaptic cell.

synaptic junction, the membranes of both the presynaptic neuron and the postsynaptic receptor cell together with the synaptic cleft.

synaptic transmission, the passage of a neural impulse across a synapse from one nerve fiber to another by means of a neurotransmitter.

synaptogenesis /sinap′tōjen′əsis/, the formation of synapses between neurons. In humans it begins early in gestation but occurs most rapidly from 2 months before birth to 2 years after birth.

synaptosome /sinap′təsōm/, a presynaptic nerve terminal that has been separated from the rest of the neuron and isolated from homogenates of brain tissue. It appears as a membrane-bound structure containing synaptic vesicles.

synarthrosis, any of several immovable articulations.

syncephalus /sinsef′ələs/ [Gk, *syn* + *kephale,* head], a conjoined twin having a single head and two bodies.

synchilia /singkē′lyə/ [Gk, *syn* + *cheilos,* lip], a congenital anomaly in which there is complete or partial fusion of the lips; atresia of the mouth.

synchondrosis /sing′kondrō′sis/ *pl.* **synchondroses** [Gk, *syn* + *chondros,* cartilage], a cartilaginous joint creating a union between two immovable bones such as the synchondroses of the cranium, the pubic symphysis, the sternum, and the manubrium.

synchorial /singkôr′ē·əl/ [Gk, *syn* + *chorion,* skin], pertaining to multiple fetuses that share a common placenta, as in monozygosity.

synchronized intermittent mandatory ventilation (SIMV) /sing′krənīzd/, periodic

S

assisted mechanical ventilation synchronized with the patient's breathing. Spontaneous breathing by the patient occurs between the assisted mechanical breaths, which occur at preset intervals. The ventilator will provide a mechanical breath if the patient fails to do so within the set interval.

synchronous /sing'krənəs/, occurring at the same time.

synclitism /sing'klitiz'əm/ [Gk, *syn* + *klinein*, to lean], **1.** in obstetrics, a condition in which the sagittal suture of the fetal head is in line with the transverse diameter of the inlet, equidistant from the maternal symphysis pubis and sacrum. **2.** in hematology, the normal condition in which the nucleus and the cytoplasm of the blood cells mature simultaneously and at the same rate.

syncope /sing'kəpē/ [Gk, *synkoptein*, to cut short], a brief lapse in consciousness caused by transient cerebral hypoxia. It may be caused by many different factors, including emotional stress, vagal stimulation, vascular pooling in the legs, diaphoresis, and a sudden change in environmental temperature or body position.

syncretic thinking /singkret'ik/ [Gk, *synkretismos*, combined beliefs; AS, *thencan*, to think], a stage in the development of the cognitive thought processes of the child. During this phase, thought is based purely on what is perceived and experienced. The child is incapable of reasoning beyond the observable or of making deductions or generalizations.—**syncresis**, *n.*

syncytial /sinsish'əl/, pertaining to a syncytium.

syncytial virus, a virus that induces the formation of syncytia, particularly in cell cultures.

syncytiotrophoblast /sinsish'ē-ōtrof'əblast'/ [Gk, *syn* + *kytos*, cell, *trophe*, nutrition, *blastos*, germ], the outer syncytial layer of the trophoblast of an early mammalian embryo. It erodes the uterine wall during implantation and gives rise to the villi of the placenta.—**syncytiotrophoblastic**, *adj.*

syncytium /sinsit'ē-əm/ *pl.* **syncytia** [Gk, *syn* + *kytos*, cell], a group of cells in which the cytoplasm of one cell is continuous with that of adjoining cells, resulting in a multinucleate unit.—**syncytial**, *adj.*

syndactylus /sindak'tiləs/, a person with webbed fingers or toes.

syndactyly /sindak'təlē/ [Gk, *syn* + *daktylos*, finger], a congenital anomaly characterized by the fusion of the fingers or toes.—**syndactyl, syndactylous**, *adj.*

syndemosis, a joint in which two adjacent bones are linked by a ligament, such as the linking of the radius and ulna by an interosseus membrane.

syndesis /sin'dəsis/ [Gk, *syn*, together, *dein*, to bind], surgical fixation of a joint.

syndesmophyte /sindez'məfīt/, a bony growth attached to a ligament. It is found between adjacent vertebrae in ankylosing spondylitis.

syndesmosis /sin'desmō'sis/ *pl.* **syndesmoses** [Gk, *syndesmos*, ligament], a fibrous union in which two bones are connected by interosseous ligaments, such as the anterior and the posterior ligaments in the radioulnar and tibiofibular articulations.

syndrome /sin'drəm/ [Gk, *syn*, together, *dromos*, course], a complex of signs and symptoms resulting from a common cause or appearing in combination to present a clinical picture of a disease or inherited abnormality.

syndrome of inappropriate antidiuretic hormone secretion (SIADH), an abnormal condition characterized by the excessive release of antidiuretic hormone (ADH) that alters the body's fluid and electrolytic balances. It develops in association with diseases that affect the osmoreceptors of the hypothalamus and results in various malfunctions, such as the inability to produce and secrete dilute urine, water retention, increased extracellular fluid volume, and hyponatremia. Common signs and symptoms of SIADH are weight gain despite anorexia, vomiting, nausea, muscle weakness, and irritability. Confirming diagnosis is based on urine osmolality that exceeds 150 mOsm/kg of water and serum osmolality of less than 280 mOsm/kg of water.

syndrome X, a condition characterized by hypertension with obesity, type 2 DM, hypertriglyceridemia, increased peripheral insulin resistance, hyperinsulinemia, and elevated catecholamine levels.

synechia /sinek'ē-ə/ *pl.* **synechiae** [Gk, continuity], an adhesion, especially of the iris to the cornea or lens of the eye. It may develop from glaucoma, cataracts, uveitis, or keratitis or as a complication of surgery or trauma to the eye. Synechiae may prevent or impede flow of aqueous fluid between the anterior and posterior chambers of the eye, resulting in angle closure glaucoma.

synechiotomy /sinek'ē-ot'əmē/ [Gk, *synechia*, continuity, *temnein*, to cut], the surgical division of an adhesion.

syneresis /siner'əsis/ [Gk, *syn* + *hairein*, to draw], the drawing together or coagulation of particles of a gel with separation from the medium in which the particles were suspended, such as occurs in blood clot retraction.

synergist /sin'ərjist/ [Gk, *syn* + *ergein*, to work], an organ, agent, or substance that augments the activity of another organ, agent, or substance.

synergistic /sin′ərjis′tik/ [Gk, *syn,* together, *ergein,* to work], pertaining to the acting or working together of a number of components, as when groups of muscles function in a coordinated manner.

synergistic agent, a substance that augments or adds to the activity of another substance or agent.

synergistic muscles, groups of muscles that contract together to accomplish the same body movement.

synergy /sin′ərje/ [Gk, *syn + ergein,* to work], **1.** the process in which two organs, substances, or agents work simultaneously to enhance the function and effect of one another. **2.** the coordinated action of a set of muscles that work together to produce a specific movement. **3.** a combined action of different parts of the autonomic nervous system, as in the sympathetic and parasympathetic innervation of secreting cells of the salivary glands. **4.** the interaction of two or more drugs to produce a certain effect.

synesthesia /sin′esthē′zhə/, a phenomenon in which sensations of two or more modalities accompany one another, as when a visual sensation is experienced when a particular sound is heard.

syngeneic /sin′jənē′ik/ [Gk, *syn + genesis,* origin], **1.** denoting an individual or cell that has the same genotype as another individual or cell. **2.** denoting tissues that are antigenically similar.

synkinesis /sin′kinē′sis/ [Gk, *syn,* together, *kinesis,* movement], an involuntary movement by one part of the body when an intentional movement is made by another part. In imitative synkinesis, movement may be detected in paralyzed muscles when normal muscles are moved, and vice versa.

synopsis /sinop′sis/ [Gk, *syn,* together, *opsis,* vision], a brief review, condensation, summary, or abridgment.

synostosis /sin′ostō′sis/ [Gk, *syn,* together, *osteon,* bone], the joining of two bones by the ossification of connecting tissues. It occurs normally in the fusion of cranial bones to form the skull.

synostotic joint /sin′ostot′ik/ [Gk, *syn + osteon,* bone], a joint in which bones are connected to bones and there is no movement between them, as in the bones of the adult sacrum or skull.

synotia /sīnō′shə/ [Gk, *syn + ous,* ear], a congenital malformation characterized by the union or approximation of the ears in front of the neck, often accompanied by the absence or defective development of the lower jaw.

synotus /sīnō′təs/, a fetus with synotia.

synovectomy /sin′ōvek′təmē/ [Gk, *syn;* L, *ovum,* egg; Gk, *ektomē,* excision], the removal of a synovial membrane of a joint.

synovia /sinō′vē·ə/, a clear, viscous fluid, resembling the white of an egg, secreted by synovial membranes and acting as a lubricant for many joints, bursae, and tendons. It contains mucin, albumin, fat, and mineral salts.

synovial /sinō′vē·əl/, pertaining to, consisting of, or secreting synovia, the lubricating fluid of the joints, bursae, and tendon sheaths.

synovial bursa, one of the many closed sacs filled with synovial fluid in the connective tissue between muscles, tendons, ligaments, and bones.

synovial chondroma, a rare cartilaginous growth in the connective tissue below the synovial membrane of the joints, tendon sheaths, or bursa.

synovial crypt, a pouch in the synovial membrane of a joint.

synovial joint, a freely movable joint in which contiguous bony surfaces are covered by articular cartilage and connected by a fibrous connective tissue capsule lined with synovial membrane.

synovial membrane, the thin layer of tissue lining the articular capsule surrounding a freely movable joint. The synovial membrane is loosely attached to the external fibrous capsule. It secretes into the joint a thick fluid that normally lubricates the joint but that may accumulate in painful amounts when the joint is injured.

synovialoma /s-no′ve-ah-lo′mah/, a synovial tumor, involving a tendon sheath or joint.

synovial sac, a herniation of a synovial membrane beyond the confines of a joint.

synovial sarcoma, a malignant tumor composed of synovioblasts that begins as a soft swelling and often metastasizes through the bloodstream to the lung before it is discovered.

synovial sheath, any one of the membranous sacs enclosing a tendon of a muscle and facilitating the gliding of a tendon through a fibrous or a bony tunnel, such as that under the flexor retinaculum of the wrist.

synovial tendon sheath, one of the many membranous channels or tubes enclosing various tendons that glide through fibrous and bony tunnels in the body, such as those under the flexor retinaculum of the wrist. One layer of the synovial sheath lines the tunnel, and the other covers the tendon. The sheath secretes synovial fluid, which lubricates the tendon.

synovitis /sin′əvī′tis/, an inflammatory condition of the synovial membrane of

S

a joint as the result of an aseptic wound or a traumatic injury, such as a sprain or severe strain. The knee is most commonly affected. Fluid accumulates around the capsule; the joint is swollen, tender, and painful; and motion is restricted.

synovium /sinō'vē·əm/, a synovial membrane.

syntactic aphasia /sintak'tik/ [Gk, *syn,* together, *taxis,* arrangement, *a, phasis,* not speech], an inability to arrange words in a logical sequence, with the result that what is spoken is not understood.

syntax /sin'taks/ [Gk, *syn* + *taxis,* arrangement], a property of language involving structural cues for the arrangement of words as elements in a phrase, clause, or sentence.

syntaxic mode /sintaks'ik/, the ability to perceive whole, logical, coherent pictures as they occur in reality, according to the H.S. Sullivan theory of psychology.

synteny /sin'tənē/ [Gk, *syn* + *taina,* ribbon], in genetics, the presence on the same chromosome of two or more genes that may or may not be transmitted as a linkage group but that appear to be able to undergo independent assortment during meiosis.

synthermal /sinthur'məl/, possessing the same temperature.

synthesis /sin'thəsis/ [Gk, *synthenai,* to put together], a level of cognitive learning in which the individual puts together the elements of previous learning levels to create a unified whole.

synthesize /sin'thəsīz/ [Gk, *synthesis,* putting together], to form by building, as in forming complex chemical compounds such as proteins from simpler units of amino acids.

synthetic /sinthet'ik/, pertaining to a substance that is produced by an artificial rather than a natural process or material.

synthetic chemistry, the science dealing with the formation of more complex chemical compounds from simpler substances.

synthetic human growth hormone, a synthetic form of somatotropin produced by recombinant DNA techniques from a strain of *Escherichia coli* bacteria. The polypeptide hormone consists of 191 amino acid residues in a sequence identical to that of natural human growth hormone.

synthetic insulin [Gk, *synthesis,* putting together; L, *insula,* island], a form of insulin synthesized in a non–disease-producing strain of *Escherichia coli* bacteria or in yeast cells that has been genetically altered by the addition of the human gene for insulin production.

synthetic vaccines, prophylactic immunization substances prepared by artificial

techniques, such as through peptide synthesis or cloning of DNA.

Synthroid, a trademark for a thyroid hormone (levothyroxine sodium).

Syntocinon, a trademark for an oxytocic (oxytocin).

syntrophism /sin'trəfiz'əm/, **1.** mutual dependence for food or other resources. **2.** a condition in which two strains of bacteria can grow together in a mixed culture in a medium that would not support either alone. Each strain produces a nutrient required by the other.

syntropy /sin'trəpē/ [Gk, *syn,* together, *trepein,* to turn], a tendency for two diseases to merge into one.

syphilis /sif'ilis/ [from the name of a literary figure (1530) who was thus infected (literally, L, lover of swine)], an STD caused by the spirochete *Treponema pallidum,* characterized by distinct stages of effects over a period of years. The first stage *(primary syphilis)* is marked by the appearance of a small painless red pustule on the skin or mucous membrane between 10 and 90 days after exposure. The lesion may appear anywhere on the body where contact with a lesion on an infected person has occurred, but it is seen most often in the anogenital region. It quickly erodes, forming a painless, bloodless ulcer, called a *chancre,* exuding a fluid that swarms with spirochetes. The chancre may not be noticed by the patient, and many people may become infected. It heals spontaneously within 10 to 40 days, often creating the mistaken impression that it was not a serious symptom. The second stage *(secondary syphilis)* occurs about 2 months later, after the spirochetes have multiplied and spread throughout the body. This stage is characterized by general malaise, anorexia, nausea, fever, headache, alopecia, bone and joint pain, and the appearance of a morbilliform rash that does not itch, flat white sores in the mouth and throat, or condylomata lata papules on the moist areas of the skin. The disease remains highly contagious at this stage and can be spread by kissing. The symptoms usually continue for from 3 weeks to 3 months but may recur over a period of 2 years. The third stage **(tertiary syphilis)** may not develop for 3 to 15 or more years. It is characterized by the appearance of soft rubbery tumors, called *gummas,* that ulcerate and heal by scarring. Gummas may develop anywhere on the surface of the body and in the eye, liver, lungs, stomach, or reproductive organs. Tertiary syphilis may be painless, unnoticed except for gummas, or it may be accompanied by deep, burrowing pain. The ulceration of the gummas may result in punched-out areas of the palate, nasal septum, or larynx. Various tissues and structures of the body, including the CNS, myocardium, and valves of the heart, may be damaged or destroyed, leading to mental or physical disability and premature death. Congenital syphilis resulting from prenatal infection may result in the birth of a deformed or blind infant or stillborn child. In some cases, the infant appears to be well until, at several weeks of age, snuffles, sometimes with a blood-stained or mucopurulent discharge, and skin lesions, particularly on the palms and soles or in the genital region, are observed. Such children also may have visual or hearing defects, and progeria and poor health may develop. Patients with primary or secondary syphilis are usually given benzathine, penicillin G benzathine, or an equivalent in a single dose of 2.4 million units intramuscularly. Larger doses of penicillin, 7.2 million units total, are administered in 3 doses 1 week apart for tertiary syphilis. Infants and small children with congenital syphilis are usually given 50,000 units/kg intramuscularly. Treatment of an infected mother with penicillin during the first 4 months of pregnancy usually prevents the development of congenital syphilis in the fetus. Treating the mother with antibiotics later in the pregnancy usually eliminates the infection but may not protect the fetus. Active, serologically documented cases of syphilis must, by law, be reported to local departments of health throughout the United States.

syphilitic, pertaining to, resembling, or infected with syphilis.

syphilitic aortitis, inflammation of the aorta occurring in tertiary syphilis. It is characterized by diffuse dilation with gray, wheal-like plaques containing calcium on the inside and scars and wrinkles on the outside of the aorta. The middle layer of the aortic wall is usually infiltrated with plasma cells and contains fragments of damaged elastic tissue and many newly formed blood vessels. There may be damage to the cardiac valves, narrowing of the mouths of the coronary arteries, and formation of thrombi. Cerebral embolism may result. Signs of syphilitic aortitis are substernal pain, dyspnea, bounding pulse, and high systolic BP.

syphilitic dementia [L, *de* + *mens,* mind], a form of dementia resulting from a syphilis infection. Specific symptoms may vary from memory impairment to personality changes and are severe enough to interfere with social and occupational activities.

syphilitic endocarditis [L, *endon,* within, *kardia,* heart, *itis,* inflammation], a thickening and stretching of the cusps of the aortic valve, with aortic valve incompetence, caused by a syphilis infection of the aorta.

syphilitic fever [L, *febris*], pyrexia that is caused by a syphilis infection.

syphilitic periarteritis, an inflammatory condition of the outer coat of one or more arteries occurring in tertiary syphilis and characterized by soft gummatous perivascular lesions infiltrated with lymphocytes and plasma cells.

syphilitic retinopathy [L, *rete,* net; Gk, *pathos,* disease], an invasion of the retina and optic nerve by a spreading syphilis infection. Primary retinal lesions are associated with the blood vessels, and the choroid layer is often affected first. There may be occlusion of the retinal vessels.

syr., abbreviation for the Latin *syrupus,* "syrup."

syringe /sərinj′, sir′inj/ [Gk, *syrinx,* tube], a device for withdrawing, injecting, or instilling fluids. A syringe for the injection of medication usually consists of a calibrated glass or plastic cylindric barrel having a close-fitting plunger at one end and a small opening at the other to which the head of a hollow-bore needle is fitted. A syringe for irrigating a wound or body cavity or for extracting mucus or another body fluid from an orifice or body cavity is usually larger than the kind used for injection. It often has a rubber bulb at one end and a blunt, soft-tipped flexible tube with an opening at the other end.

syringectomy /sir′injek′təmē/ [Gk, *syrinx,* tube, *ektomē,* excision], a surgical procedure for excising the walls of a fistula.

syringobulbia /siring′gōbul′bē·ə/ [Gk, *syrinx,* tube; L, *bulbus,* swollen root], syringomyelia in which the cavity extends to involve the medulla oblongata.

syringoencephalomyelia /siring′gō·ensef′ə lōmī·ē′lyə/, a progressive disorder characterized by cavitation of the spinal cord. It may occur anywhere from the medulla oblongata to the thoracic segments but usually appears in cervical segments.

syringoma *pl.* **syringomas, syringomata** /sir′ing·gō′mə/, a benign tumor derived from an eccrine sweat gland. It appears as a small smooth papule the color of the underlying skin, often on the upper body of a postpubertal woman. Some are typically multiple, often appearing on the lower eyelids.

syringomeningocele /-məning′gōsēl′/ [Gk, *syrinx,* tube, *meninx,* membrane, *kele,* hernia], a meningocele that is connected to the central canal of the spinal cord.

syringomyelia /-mī·ē′lyə/ [Gk, *syrinx,* tube, *myelos,* marrow], a chronic

S

progressive disease of the spinal cord, marked by elongated central fluid-containing cavities, surrounded by gliosis or a proliferation of neurologic tissue. Although present at birth, onset is insidious and manifestations are often not seen until individuals are in their 20s or 30s. These symptoms are often ambiguous and mimic a host of other diseases. The cervical spine is most commonly affected and manifests as weakness, atrophy, and sensory loss in the shoulders, arms, and hands, including loss of pain and temperature sensation and sweating on the face. Upper extremity reflexes are diminished or absent while weakness, altered gait, spasticity and hyperreflexia may be noted in the lower extremities. Brainstem involvement may cause dysphagia, ptosis, miosis, or diplopia. GI symptoms include nausea, vomiting, weight loss, and abdominal spasms. Respiratory disturbances may manifest during sleep. Joint arthropathy and trophic skin changes may eventually develop. Course of the disease is variable and may result in slow, long-term incapacitation. Disease progress may slow or stop at any time. Diagnosis is made through MRI. Bony abnormalities at the base of the skull and C1-C2 spine and scoliosis may be seen on x-ray. The primary intervention is a cervical decompression laminectomy at C1-C2 spine with repair or removal of bony abnormalities, with possible myelotomy or shunt placement. While surgical intervention halts disease progression, it seldom leads to significant improvement in current neurologic manifestations.

syringomyelocele /siring'gōmī'əlōsēl'/ [Gk, *syrinx* + *myelos*, marrow, *kele*, hernia], a hernial protrusion of the spinal cord through a congenital defect in the vertebral column. The CSF within the central cavities of the cord is greatly increased so that the cord tissue forms a thin-walled sac that lies close to the membrane of the cavity.

syrup of ipecac /sir'əp/, an emetic preparation of ipecac fluid extract, glycerin, and syrup used to treat certain types of poisonings and drug overdoses. It is no longer routinely used.

system /sis'təm/ [Gk, *systema*], a collection or assemblage of parts that, unified, make a whole. Physiologic systems such as the cardiovascular or reproductive system are made up of structures specifically able to engage in processes that are essential to a vital function in the body.

systematic /sis'təmat'ik/ [Gk, *systema*], pertaining to a system.

systematic error [Gk, *systema*; L, *errare*, to wander], a nonrandom statistical error that affects the mean of a population of data and defines the bias between the means of two populations.

systematic heating, the elevation of the temperature of the whole body.

systematic tabulation, in research, mechanical or manual techniques for recording and classifying data for statistical analysis.

systemic /sistem'ik/ [Gk, *systema*], pertaining to the whole body rather than to a localized area or regional part of the body.

systemic circulation [Gk, *systema*; L, *circulare*, to go around], the general blood circulation of the body, not including the lungs.

systemic desensitization, a technique used in behavior therapy for eliminating maladaptive anxiety associated with phobias. The procedure involves the construction by the person of a hierarchy of anxiety-producing stimuli and the general presentation of these stimuli until they no longer elicit the initial response of fear.

systemic heart, side of the heart, which moves oxygenated blood through the systemic circulation.

systemic immunoblastic proliferation, a condition of immature lymphocyte production resulting in rash, breathing difficulty, enlarged spleen, lymphadenopathy, and increased incidence of immunoblastic lymphoma.

systemic infection [Gk, *systema*; L, *inficere*, to stain], an infection in which the pathogen is distributed throughout the body rather than concentrated in one area.

systemic lesion [Gk, *systema*; L, *laesio*, attack], a pathologic disturbance that involves a system of tissues with a common function.

systemic lupus erythematosus (SLE), a chronic inflammatory disease affecting many systems of the body. It is an example of a collagen disease. The pathophysiologic characteristics of the disease include severe vasculitis, renal involvement, and lesions of the skin and nervous system. The initial manifestation is often arthritis. An erythematous rash ("butterfly rash") over the nose and malar eminences, weakness, fatigue, and weight loss also are frequently seen early in the disease. Photosensitivity, fever, skin lesions on the neck, and alopecia where the skin lesions extend beyond the hairline may occur. The skin lesions may spread to the mucous membranes and other tissues of the body. They do not ulcerate but cause degeneration of the affected tissues. Depending on the organs involved, the patient also may have glomerulonephritis, pleuritis, pericarditis, peritonitis, neuritis, or anemia. Renal failure and severe neurologic abnormalities are among the most serious manifestations of the disease. The primary cause of the disease has not been determined; viral infection or dysfunction of the immune system has been suggested. Diagnosis of SLE is made by subjective and objective findings based on physical examination and laboratory findings. In many cases SLE may be controlled with corticosteroid medication administered systemically. Care and treatment vary with the severity and nature of the disease and the body systems that are affected. Fatigue and stress are prevented, and all body surfaces are protected from direct sunlight. As in any disease marked by chronic remission and exacerbation of many distressing symptoms, the patient may require extensive emotional and psychologic support.

systemic mycosis [Gks, *systema* + *mykes, osis,* condition], a fungal infection that involves more than one body system or area.

systemic onset juvenile rheumatoid arthritis, Still's disease.

systemic oxygen consumption, the amount of oxygen consumed by the body per minute.

systemic remedy, a medicinal substance that is given orally, parenterally, or rectally to be absorbed into the circulation for treatment of a health problem. Medication administered systemically may have various local effects, but the intent is to treat the whole body.

systemic sclerosis, a form of scleroderma characterized by formation of thickened collagenous fibrous tissue, thickening of the skin, and adhesion of the skin to underlying tissues. The disease, which may be preceded by Raynaud's phenomenon, progresses to involve the tissues of the heart, lungs, muscles, genitourinary tract, and kidneys.

systemic toxin clearance: dialysis, a nursing outcome from the Nursing Outcomes Classification (NOC) defined as clearance of toxins from the body with peritoneal dialysis or hemodialysis.

systemic vascular resistance (SVR), the resistance the left ventricle must overcome to pump blood through the systemic circulation. As peripheral blood vessels constrict, the SVR increases.

systemic vein, one of a number of veins that drain deoxygenated blood from most of the body. Systemic veins arise in tiny plexuses that receive blood from capillaries and converge into trunks that increase in size as they pass toward the heart. They are larger and more numerous than the arteries, have thinner walls, and collapse when they are empty.

systemic venous hypertension, elevation of the venous pressure, usually detected by inspection of the jugular veins and most often caused by disease of the right heart or pericardium.

system of care /sis′təm/, a framework within which health care is provided, comprising health care professionals; recipients, consumers, or patients; energy resources or dynamics; organizational and political contexts or frameworks; and processes or procedures.

system overload, an inability to cope with messages and expectations from a number of sources within a given time limit.

systems theory, a holistic medical concept in which the human patient is viewed as an integrated complex of open systems rather than as semiindependent parts.

systole /sis′tələ/ [Gk, *systole,* contraction], the contraction of the heart, driving blood into the aorta and pulmonary arteries. The occurrence of systole is indicated by the first heart sound heard on auscultation, by the palpable apex beat, and by the peripheral pulse.—**systolic,** *adj.*

systolic, pertaining to or resulting from a heart contraction.

systolic click [Gk, *systole,* contraction; Fr, *cliqueter,* to click], a sharp, clicking sound heard in midsystole or late systole and believed to originate from the abnormal motion of the mitral valve. The most frequent cause of systolic clicks is prolapse of a mitral valve leaflet.

systolic dysfunction, a loss of cardiac muscle with volume overload and decreased contractility.

systolic ejection period, the amount of time the ventricles spend in systole per minute.

systolic gradient, the difference between the pressure in the left atrium and that in the left ventricle during systole.

systolic murmur, a cardiac murmur occurring during systole. Systolic murmurs include ejection murmurs, often heard in pregnant women or in people with anemia, thyrotoxicosis, or aortic or pulmonary stenosis; pansystolic murmurs, heard in people with incompetence of the mitral or tricuspid valve; and late systolic murmurs, also caused by mitral valve incompetence and, less commonly, by tricuspid regurgitation.

systolic pressure, the BP measured during the period of ventricular contraction (systole). In BP readings, it is the higher of the two measurements.

S

T

T, symbol for **absolute temperature.**

t, symbol for **time.**

T, 1. symbol for **temperature.** 2. abbreviation for **tumor.**

T₁/₂, symbol for the half-life of a radioactive isotope.

T1, T2, ..., symbols for **thoracic nerves.**

T₃, symbol for **triiodothyronine.**

T₄, symbol for **thyroxine.**

T-4 cell, a thymus-derived lymphocyte of the body's immune system that activates the humoral immune system (B cells) and destroys or neutralizes cells or substances identified as "nonself." T-4 cells secrete a substance, interleukin-2, that stimulates the activity of natural killer cells, gamma interferon, and suppressor T-8 cells. HIV commonly targets T-4 cells, with the result that the body's immune defenses are severely damaged and opportunistic infections are allowed to flourish.

Ta, symbol for the element **tantalum.**

TA, abbreviation for **transactional analysis.**

tabes /tā′bēz/ [L, *tabes,* wasting], a gradual, progressive wasting of the body in any chronic disease.

tabes dorsalis [L, *tabes,* wasting, *dorsum,* the back], an abnormal condition characterized by the slow degeneration of all or part of the body and the progressive loss of deep tendon reflexes, caused by syphilis. This disease involves the spinal cord and destroys the large joints of affected limbs in some individuals. A wide-base ataxic gait is usually present. It is often accompanied by incontinence, impotence, and severe flashing pains in the abdomen and extremities.

tabetic crisis /tābet′ik/ [L, *tabes,* wasting; Gk, *krisis,* turning point], an exacerbation of pain in tabes dorsalis because of syphilis.

tabetic gait [L, *tabes,* wasting; ONorse, *gata,* a way], a high-stepping gait associated with tabes dorsalis.

tabetic neuritis [L, *tabes,* wasting; Gk, *neuron,* nerve, *itis,* inflammation], a form of neuritis that accompanies a syphilitic infection or tabes dorsalis, involving the dorsal posterior column spinal pathways.

table [L, *tabula*], 1. any structure with a flat surface. 2. a chart showing columns of data.

tablespoon (Tbs, tbsp), a household spoon that may be used to measure a dose of liquid medicine, equivalent to about 4 fluid drams or ½ fluid ounce or 15 mL.

tablet /tab′lit/ [Fr, *tablette,* lozenge], a small, solid dosage form of a medication. It may be of almost any size, shape, weight, and color. Most tablets are intended to be swallowed whole; but some may be dissolved in the mouth, chewed, or dissolved in liquid before swallowing; and some may be placed in a body cavity.

taboo /təboo′/, something that is forbidden by a society as unacceptable or improper.

taboparesis /tā′bōpərē′sis/ [L, *tabes,* wasting; Gk, *paralyein,* to be palsied], a form of paralysis associated with psychosis in patients with untreated syphilis.

tabula rasa /tā′boolä rä′sä, tab′yəle rä′sə/, a term used to describe a child's mind at birth as a receptive "blank slate."

tache /täsh/ [Fr], a spot, stain, blot, or mark.

tache noire /täsh nô·är′/ [Fr, black spot], a local button-like ulcer with a black center that marks the point of infection in certain rickettsial diseases such as African tick typhus and scrub typhus.

tachistoscope /təkis′təskōp/ [Gk, *tachistos,* rapid, *skopein,* to view], a device used to increase the speed of visual perception by displaying visual stimuli only extremely briefly.

tachometer /təkom′ətər/, a device for measuring speed, such as the rate of blood flow in a vessel.

tachyarrhythmia /tak′ē·ərith′mē·ə/ [Gk, *tachys,* fast, *a* + *rhythmos,* rhythm], an abnormally rapid heartbeat accompanied by an irregular rhythm.

tachycardia /tak′ēkärdē·ə/ [Gk, *tachys,* fast, *kardia,* heart], a condition in which the heart contracts at a rate greater than 100 beats/min. It may occur normally in response to fever, exercise, or nervous excitement. Pathologic tachycardia accompanies anoxia such as that caused by anemia, CHF, hemorrhage, or shock. Tachycardia acts to increase the amount of oxygen delivered to the cells of the body by increasing the rate at which blood circulates through the vessels.—**tachycardiac,** *adj.*

tachycardia-bradycardia syndrome, a disorder characterized by a heart rate that alternates between being abnormally low (less than 60 beats/min) and abnormally high (greater than 100 beats/min).

tachycardiac /-kär′dē·ak/ [Gk, *tachys,* fast, *kardia,* heart], pertaining to or affected by tachycardia.

tachyphagia /-fā′jē·ə/, rapid or hasty eating.

tachyphylaxis /tak′ēfəlak′sis/ [Gk, *tachys* + *phylax,* guard], **1.** in pharmacology, a phenomenon in which the repeated administration of some drugs results in a rapidly appearing and marked decrease in effectiveness. **2.** in immunology, a rapidly developing immunity to a toxin because of previous exposure, such as from previous injection of small amounts of the toxin.

tachypnea /tak′ēpnē′ə/ [Gk, *tachys* + *pnoia,* breathing], an abnormally rapid rate of breathing (more than 20 breaths per minute in adults) such as seen with hyperpyrexia.

tack, the degree of stickiness of an adhesive required to affix a therapeutic foreign substance such as a transdermal delivery device to the skin.

tacrolimus, an immunosuppressive drug that modified biologic response. It is prescribed to suppress the immune system after transplantation of the liver or other organs, and can be applied topically for the treatment of dermatitis unresponsive to other medications.

TAC solution, a solution of tetracaine, epinephrine, and cocaine, used as a local anesthetic in the emergency treatment of uncomplicated lacerations.

tactile /tak′təl/ [L, *tactus,* touch], pertaining to the sense of touch.

tactile amnesia [L, *tactus;* Gk, *amnesia,* forgetfulness], a loss of the ability to determine the shape of objects through the sense of touch.

tactile anesthesia, the absence or lack of the sense of touch in the fingers, possibly resulting from injury or disease. This condition may cause the patient to incur severe burns, serious cuts, contusions, or abrasions.

tactile defensiveness, a sensory integrative dysfunction characterized by tactile sensations that cause excessive emotional reactions, hyperactivity, or other behavior problems.

tactile discrimination [L, *tactus* + *discrimen,* division], the ability to discriminate among objects by the sense of touch.

tactile fremitus, a tremulous vibration of the chest wall during speaking that is palpable on physical examination. Fremitus may be decreased or absent when vibrations from the larynx to the chest surface are impeded by COPD, obstruction,

pleural effusion, or pneumothorax, and increased in pneumonia.

tactile hair [L, *tactus;* AS, *haer*], a hair shaft that is sensitive to the sensation of touch.

tactile hallucination [L, *tactus* + *alucinare,* to wander in mind], a subjective experience of touch in the absence of tactile stimulation.

tactile hyperesthesia [L, *tactus;* Gk, *hyper,* excessive, *aesthesis,* sensitivity], an abnormal increase in the sense of touch.

tactile image, a mental concept of an object as perceived through the sense of touch.

tactile localization [L, *tactus* + *locus,* place], the ability to identify, without looking, the exact point on the body where a tactile stimulus is applied. The localization test is applied in sensory evaluation tests.

tactile sensation [L, *tactus* + *sentire,* to feel], the sensation of touch.

tactile system [L, *tactus;* Gk, *systema*], the part of the nervous system that is concerned with the sense of touch.

tadalafil, an impotence agent used to treat erectile dysfunction.

Taenia /tē′nē·ə/ [Gk, *tainia,* ribbon], a genus of large parasitic intestinal flatworms of the family Taeniidae, class Cestoda. Taeniae are among the most common parasites infecting humans include *T. saginata,* the beef tapeworm, and *T. solium,* the pork tapeworm.

Taenia saginata, a species of tapeworm that inhabits the tissues of cattle during its larval stage and infects the intestines of humans in its adult form.

taeniasis /tēnī′əsis/ [Gk, *tainia* + *osis,* condition], an infection with a tapeworm of the genus *Taenia.* Transmission is through ingestion of undercooked pork containing cysticercus or food contaminated with pig feces containing eggs.

Taenia solium, a species of tapeworm that most commonly inhabits the tissues of pigs during its larval stage and infects the intestine of humans in its adult form.

TAF, abbreviation for **tumor angiogenesis factor.**

tag, a small piece of epidermal and dermal fibrovascular tissue attached by one margin or a pedicle to a main structure.

TAG, abbreviation for *3,4,6-tri-O-acetyl-D-glucal.*

Tagamet, a trademark for a histamine H_2 receptor antagonist (cimetidine).

tai chi, a technique that uses slow, purposeful, motor-physical movements of the body for the purpose of control to increase outer body mass strength and achieve a more balanced physiologic and psychologic state. Tai chi has positive effects on the respiratory, cardiovascular, and cerebral functions in both children and older

T

adults, including reducing the incidence of falls in older people.

tail, the caudal extremity of an organ or body, such as an axillary tail of a mammary gland.

tail fold [AS, *taegel* + *fealdan*, to fold], a curved ridge formed at the caudal end of the early developing embryo. It gives rise to the hindgut in humans.

tail of Spence, the upper outer tail of breast tissue that extends into the axilla.

tail of spermatozoon, the flagellum of a spermatozoon.

Takayasu's arteritis /tä'kəyä'sooz/ [Mikito Takayasu, Japanese surgeon, 1860–1938], an inflammation of the aorta, its major branches, and the pulmonary artery. It is characterized by progressive occlusion of the innominate, left subclavian, and left common carotid arteries above their origins in the aortic arch. Signs of the disorder are absence of a pulse in both arms and in the carotid arteries, transient paraplegia, transient blindness, and atrophy of facial muscles.

take, a popular term for a satisfactory response, as of a vaccination or tissue graft.

talc /talk/ [Ar, *talq*], a native, hydrous magnesium silicate, sometimes containing a small proportion of aluminum silicate, used as a dusting powder and adsorbent in clarifying liquids.

talcosis /talko'sis/, a silicosis-like respiratory disorder caused by inhalation of magnesium silicate dust.

talipes /tal'ipēz/ [L, *talus*, ankle, *pes*, foot], a deformity of the foot and ankle, usually congenital, in which the foot is twisted and relatively fixed in an abnormal position.

talipes valgus, a foot that is flat and extremely everted, away from the midline.

talipes varus, a deformity of the foot in which the heel is turned inward from the midline of the leg.

tallow /tal'ō/, **1.** a hard fat obtained from the bodies of ruminant animals such as cattle and sheep and used in soaps and lubricants. **2.** a vegetable fat obtained from plants, such as the wax myrtle.

talocalcaneonavicular joint, a complex joint in which the head of the talus articulates with the calcaneus and plantar calcaneonavicular ligament below and the navicular in front. It allows gliding and rotation movements, which are involved with inversion and eversion of the foot. It also participates in pronation and supination.

talofibular /tā'lōfib'yələr/, pertaining to the talus and fibula.

talonavicular /tā'lōnəvik'yələr/ [L, *talon*, bird claw, *naviculus*, scaphoid], pertaining to the talus and the navicular bones.

talus /tā'ləs/ *pl.* **tali** [L, ankle], the second largest tarsal bone. It supports the

tibia, rests on the calcaneus, and articulates with the malleoli and navicular bones.

Talwin, a trademark for a mu antagonist/kappa agonist opioid analgesic (pentazocine).

Tambocor, a trademark for an oral antiarrhythmic drug (flecainide acetate).

tambour /tam'boor/, a cylindric drumlike device connected to an air tube and stylus, used to record sphygmographic or other physiologic data.

Tamm-Horsfall protein (THP) [Igor Tamm, American virologist, b. 1922; Frank L. Horsfall, American virologist, 1906–1971], a mucoprotein found in the matrix of renal tubular casts. THP is secreted in the loop of Henle.

tamoxifen /təmok'səfin/, a nonsteroidal antiestrogen used in the palliative treatment of advanced breast cancer in premenopausal and postmenopausal women whose tumors are estrogen-dependent. Tamoxifen has also been used to reduce the incidence of breast cancer in women with a high risk for developing it, and for treating gynecomastia, precocious puberty, and other instances of estrogen excess.

tampon /tam'pon/ [Fr, plug], a pack of cotton, a sponge, or other material for checking bleeding or absorbing secretions in cavities or canals or for holding displaced organs in position.

tamponade /tam'pənād'/ [Fr, *tamponner*, to plug up], stoppage of the blood flow to an organ or a part of the body by pressure or by the compression of a part by an accumulation of fluid, such as in cardiac tamponade.

tamsulosin, a selective adrenergic agent prescribed to treat symptoms of benign prostatic hyperplasia.

tandem mass spectrometry (MS/MS), a two-step technique used to analyze a sample for a predetermined set of substances, either by using a separate mass spectroscope for each step or by performing the steps sequentially using the same spectroscope. It is used in screening newborns for multiple metabolic disorders from a single blood sample.

tandem repeat, appearance of two or more identical segments close to each other within a strand of DNA.

tangentiality /tanjen'chē·al'itē/ [L, *tangere*, to touch], expressions or responses characterized by a tendency to digress from an original topic of conversation. Tangentiality can destroy or seriously hamper the ability of people to communicate effectively. It is frequently seen in schizophrenia.

tangible elements /tan'jibəl/ [L, *tangere* + *elementum*, first principle], objects that can be seen or touched as distinguished from emotions, knowledge, or abstractions.

Tangier disease /tanjir'/ [Tangier Island, Virginia], a rare genetic disorder resulting in a deficiency of high-density lipoproteins, characterized by low blood cholesterol and an abnormal orange or yellow discoloration of the tonsils and pharynx. There also may be enlarged lymph nodes, liver, and spleen; muscle atrophy; and peripheral neuropathy. No specific treatment is known.

tangle /tang'gəl/, a dense mass of interlacing of fibers, sometimes appearing as a loose knot, such as intraneural fibrillary tangle.

taniae coli, three narrow bands of longitudinal muscles in the walls of the large intestine, which are primarily observed in the cecum and colon and less visible in the rectum.

tannic acid /tan'ik/ [Celt, *tann,* oak; L, *acidus,* sour], a substance obtained from the bark and fruit of various trees and shrubs, particularly the nutgalls of oak trees. The acid is used as an astringent and protein precipitant.

tanning [Fr, *tanner,* to tan], a process in which the pigmentation of the skin deepens as a result of exposure to ultraviolet light. Skin cells containing melanin darken immediately.

tantalum (Ta) /tan'tələm/ [Gk, *Tantalus,* mythic king of Phrygia], a silvery metallic element. Its atomic number is 73; its atomic mass is 180.95. Relatively inert chemically, tantalum is used in prosthetic devices such as skull plates and wire sutures.

tantrum /tan'trəm/, a sudden outburst or violent display of rage, frustration, and bad temper, usually occurring in a maladjusted child and certain emotionally disturbed people.

TAO, a trademark for an antibacterial (troleandomycin).

tap [ME, *tappen*], **1.** to strike sharply, as in percussion or testing of reflexes. **2.** to draw off fluid through a small opening.

tape [AS, *taeppe*], strips of material, usually with adhesive, used to secure bandages.

tape-compression folliculitis, inflammation of the hair follicles caused by tape dressings placed over foam or cotton-ball pads under a graduated compression stocking. The condition is more likely to occur in patients with hairy legs, who may perspire during the summer months.

tapering arch /tā'pəring/ [AS, *tapor,* slender, *arcus,* bow], a dental arch that converges from the molars to the central incisors to such a degree that lines passing through the central grooves of the molars and premolars intersect within 1 inch (2.5 cm) anterior to the central incisors.

tapetoretinopathy /tape͞ toret'inop'əthē/, a hereditary visual disorder characterized by degeneration of the sensory retina and pigmentary epithelium. It occurs in pigmentary retinopathy and other eye diseases.

tapetum, 1. a carpet-like layer or covering of tissue. **2.** a thin sheet of fibers covering parts of the brain and continuous with the corpus callosum. **3.** the reflective part of the choroid coat of the eye in many mammals.

tapeworm /tāp'wurm/ [AS, *taeppe* + *wyrm*], a parasitic intestinal worm belonging to the class Cestoda. Tapeworms live as larvae in one or more vertebrate intermediate hosts and grow to adulthood in the intestine of humans. In the human alimentary canal, the worm develops into an adult with an attaching head, or scolex, and numerous hermaphroditic segments, or proglottids, each of which is capable of producing eggs.

tapeworm infection, an intestinal infection by one of several species of parasitic worms, caused by eating raw or undercooked meat infested with tapeworm, its larvae, or food contaminated with feces containing tapeworm eggs. Symptoms of intestinal infection with adult worms are usually mild or absent, but diarrhea, epigastric pain, and weight loss may occur. Diagnosis is made when eggs or parts of the adult worm are passed in the stool. Treatment is with praziquantel and albendazole. Sanitary disposal of fecal material from affected patients is necessary to prevent the passage of larvae or eggs to other humans or other hosts.

tapioca /tap'ē·ō'kə/, tiny starchy balls (pearls) or flakes made from the dried paste of grated cassava root, *Janipha manihot.* It is used as a thickener in a variety of easily digested food items, particularly cereals, soups, and puddings.

tapotement /täpôtmäN'/ [Fr, *tapoter,* to pat], a type of massage in which the body is tapped in a rhythmic manner with the tips of the fingers or the sides of the hands, using short, rapid, repetitive movements.

Taq polymerase /tak/, an enzyme found in the bacillus *Thermus aquaticus,* which lives in hot springs. It is heat resistant and thus can endure the high temperatures of the polymerase chain reaction.

tar /tär/ [AS, *teoru*], a dark, viscid organic mixture produced by the distillation of coal, wood, or vegetable matter. Some forms of tar are used to treat eczema and other skin disorders.

tarantula /təran'chələ/, a popular name for any of a number of species of large, hairy spiders. Although potentially poisonous, most are relatively harmless to humans.

Tarceva, a trademark for erlotinib.

tardive /tär'div/ [L, *tardus,* late], describing a disease in which a period of time passes between exposure and the first symptoms.

T

tardive dyskinesia [L, *tardus,* late; Gk, *dys,* difficult, *kinesis,* movement], an abnormal condition characterized by involuntary repetitive movements of the muscles of the face, limbs, and trunk. This disorder most commonly affects older people who have been treated for extended periods with antipsychotics but can be caused by antidopaminergic medication.

tardy peroneal nerve palsy [L, *tardus;* Gk, *perone,* brooch; L, *nervus;* Gk, *paralyein,* to be palsied], a type of mononeuropathy in which the peroneal nerve is excessively compressed where it crosses the head of the fibula. Such compression may occur when an individual falls asleep with the legs crossed.

tardy ulnar nerve palsy, an abnormal condition characterized by atrophy of the first dorsal interosseous muscle and difficulty in performing fine manipulations. It may be caused by injury of the ulnar nerve at the elbow. Signs and symptoms of this disorder may include numbness of the small finger, of the contiguous half of the proximal and middle phalanges of the ring finger, and of the ulnar border of the hand. Treatment concentrates on the prevention of further injury to the ulnar nerve.

target /tär′git/ [OFr, *targuete,* small shield], **1.** any object area subjected to bombardment by radioactive particles or another form of diagnostic or therapeutic radiation. **2.** a device used to contain stable materials and subsequent radioactive materials during bombardment by high-energy nuclei from a cyclotron or other particle accelerator. **3.** the part of the anode struck by electrons in an x-ray tube.

target cell, **1.** an abnormal RBC characterized by a densely stained center surrounded by a pale, unstained ring circled by a dark, irregular band. Target cells occur in the blood after splenectomy, in anemia, in hemoglobin C disease, and in thalassemia. **2.** any cell having a specific receptor that reacts with a specific hormone, antigen, antibody, antibiotic, sensitized T cell, or other substance.

target organ, **1.** an organ intended to receive a therapeutic dose of irradiation. **2.** an organ intended to receive the greatest concentration of a diagnostic radioactive tracer. **3.** an organ most affected by a specific hormone.

target symptoms, symptoms of an illness that are most likely to respond to a specific treatment.

tarsal /tär′səl/ [Gk, *tarsos,* flat surface], **1.** pertaining to the tarsus, or ankle bone. **2.** relating to the supporting plate of the eyelid.

tarsal arches [Gk, *tarsos,* flat surface; L, *arcus,* rainbow], the superior and inferior branches of the palpebral artery supplying the eyelid.

tarsal bone, any one of seven bones making up the tarsus of the foot, consisting of the talus, calcaneus, cuboid, navicular, and the three cuneiforms.

tarsalgia /tärsal′jə/, foot pain, usually involving fallen arches.

tarsal gland, any one of numerous modified sebaceous glands on the inner surfaces of the eyelids.

tarsal tunnel syndrome, a kind of mononeuropathy characterized by pain and numbness in the sole of the foot. It may be caused by fractures of the ankle that compress the posterior tibial nerve. It may be corrected by appropriate orthopedic therapy or surgery.

tarsometatarsal /tär′sōmet′ətär′səl/ [Gk, *tarsos,* flat surface, *meta,* beyond, *tarsos*], pertaining to the metatarsal bones and the tarsus of the foot.

tarsorrhaphy /tärsôr′əfē/, a surgical procedure for uniting the upper and lower eyelids. It usually is performed in procedures to protect the cornea and may involve only the lateral parts of the eyelids.

tarsus /tär′səs/ *pl.* **tarsi** [Gk, *tarsos,* flat surface], **1.** the flat area of articulation between the foot and the leg or the edge of the eyelid. **2.** any one of the fibrous plates of cartilage that form the eyelids. One tarsal plate shapes and gives solidarity to the edge of each eyelid.

tart, abbreviation for the *tartrate carboxylate anion.*

tartar /tär′tär/ [Fr, *tartre*], any of several compounds containing tartrate, the salt of tartaric acid.

tartaric acid $HOOC(CH_2O)_2COOH$ /tärter′ik/, a colorless or white powder found in various plants and prepared commercially from maleic anhydride and hydrogen peroxide. It is used in baking powder, certain beverages, and tartar emetic.

tartrate /tä′trāt/, **1.** a dianion of tartaric acid. **2.** any salt or ester of tartaric acid.

Tarui's disease /tah′roo̅·ē/, a form of glycogen storage disease in which abnormally large amounts of glycogen are deposited in the skeletal muscle. The disorder is characterized by hemolysis and cramping on exercise but no rise in blood lactate. Biopsy of the affected organ reveals the absence of the enzyme phosphofructokinase.

Tasigna, a trademark for nilotinib.

task functions, behaviors that focus or direct activities toward movements involving work or labor.

task group, a group in which structured verbal or nonverbal exercises are used to help a person gain emotional, physical, and other personal awareness.

task-oriented behavior, actions involving a person's cognitive abilities in an attempt to solve problems, resolve conflicts, and gratify the person's needs to reduce or avoid distress.

taste [ME, *tasten*], the sense of perceiving different flavors in soluble substances that contact the tongue and trigger nerve impulses to special taste centers in the cortex and thalamus of the brain. The four basic traditional tastes are sweet, salty, sour, and bitter. The front of the tongue is most sensitive to salty and sweet substances; the sides of the tongue are most sensitive to sour substances; and the back of the tongue is most sensitive to bitter substances. The middle of the tongue produces virtually no taste sensation.

taste bud, any one of many peripheral taste organs distributed over the tongue and the roof of the mouth. Each taste bud rests in a spheric pocket, which extends through the epithelium. Gustatory cells and supporting cells form each bud, which has a surface opening and an opening in the basement membrane.

taste papilla [OFr, *taster*; L, *papilla*, nipple], small nipple-like elevations on the tongue. They contain the taste buds.

TAT, abbreviation for **tetanus antitoxin.**

tattoo /tatōō′/ [Tahitian, *tatau*, marks], a permanent coloration of the skin by the introduction of foreign pigment. A tattoo may be created deliberately or may accidentally occur when a bit of graphite from a broken pencil point is embedded in the skin.—**tattoo,** *v.*

tau /tou, tō/, T, τ, the nineteenth letter of the Greek alphabet.

tau protein, a microtubule-associated protein that forms insoluble and hyperphosphorylated aggregates in Alzheimer's disease.

taurine /tôr′in/, a derivative of the amino acid cysteine. It is present in bile in combination with cholic acid. It is used in the synthesis of bile salts.

taurodontism /tô′rōdon′tizəm/ [L, *taurus,* bull; Gk, *odous,* tooth], a variation in tooth form characterized by prism-shaped molars with large pulp spaces, resulting from branching of the root only in the middle (mesotaurodontism), or in the apical third or not at all (hypertaurodontism).

Taussig-Bing syndrome /tô′sig bing/ [Helen B. Taussig, American pediatrician, 1898–1986; Richard J. Bing, American cardiologist, b. 1909], a developmental anomaly of the heart, characterized by transposition of the aorta and pulmonary artery. It is accompanied by a subpulmonary ventricular septal defect and ventricular hypertrophy.

tautomer /tô′təmər/, structural isomers that differ only in the position of a hydrogen atom, or proton. Because tautomers can be rapidly interconverted by proton transfer in aqueous solutions, they are usually in equilibrium with one another.

Tavist, a trademark for an antihistamine (clemastine).

taxis /tak′sis/, **1.** movement away from or toward a stimulus. **2.** the reduction of a hernia. **3.** a dislocation of a hernia by means of manipulation.

Taxol, a trademark for an anticancer drug (paclitaxel).

taxonomic /tak′sənom′ik/ [Gk, *taxis,* arrangement, *nomos,* law], pertaining to the orderly classification of organisms into appropriate groups, or taxa, on the basis of interrelationships, with the use of suitable names.

taxonomy /takson′əmē/ [Gk, *taxis,* arrangement, *nomos,* rule], a system for classifying organisms according to their natural relationships based on such common factors as embryology, structure, or physiologic chemistry.—**taxonomic,** *adj.*

Taylor brace [Charles F. Taylor, American surgeon, 1827–1899], a padded steel brace used to support the spine.

Taylor, Effie J. [1874–1970], a Canadian-born American nurse who was graduated from Johns Hopkins School of Nursing and served as a nurse in World War I. She succeeded Annie Goodrich as the dean of Yale University School of Nursing 1934 and served as president of the International Council of Nurses during World War II.

Tay-Sachs disease /tā saks/ [Warren Tay, English ophthalmologist, 1843–1927; Bernard Sachs, American neurologist, 1858–1944], an inherited, neurodegenerative disorder of lipid metabolism caused by a deficiency of the enzyme hexosaminidase A, which results in the accumulation of sphingolipids in the brain. The condition, which is transmitted as an autosomal-recessive trait, occurs predominantly in families of Eastern European Jewish origin, specifically the Ashkenazic Jews. It is characterized by progressive mental and physical retardation and early death. The disease can be diagnosed in utero through amniocentesis.

tazarotene /tah-zar′o-tēn/, a retinoid prodrug used topically in treatment of acne vulgaris and psoriasis.

Tazicef, a trademark for a cephalosporin antibiotic (ceftazidime).

tazobactam /taz′o-bak′tam/, a beta-lactamase inhibitor having antibacterial actions and uses similar to those of sulbactam.

Tb, symbol for the element **terbium.**

TB, 1. abbreviation for **tuberculosis. 2.** abbreviation for *tubercle bacillus.*

T bandage, a bandage in the shape of the letter T. It is used for the perineum and sometimes for the head.

T

TBI, 1. abbreviation for *total body irradiation*. **2.** abbreviation for *traumatic brain injury*.

T-box, a DNA-binding domain shared by a highly conserved family of genes (T-box genes) that act as transcription factors involved in the regulation of various developmental processes.

T-box genes, a highly conserved family of transcription factors having a common DNA-binding sequence (the T-box), which are important in the regulation of a wide variety of developmental processes in animals.

TBP, 1. abbreviation for **bithionol**. **2.** abbreviation for *total bypass*.

Tbs, abbreviation for **tablespoon**.

TBSA, abbreviation for *total body surface area*.

tbsp, abbreviation for **tablespoon**.

TBT, abbreviation for **tracheobronchial tree**.

TBW, abbreviation for **total body water**.

Tc, symbol for the element **technetium**.

TC, abbreviation for **therapeutic community**.

TCA, abbreviation for **tricyclic antidepressant**.

T cell, a lymphocyte that participates in cellular immunity, including cell-to-cell communication. The major T-cell categories are T-helper and T-suppressor cytotoxic cells.

T-cell antigen receptor, a protein present on T cells that combines with antigens to produce discrete immunologic components.

T-cell lymphomas, a heterogenous group of lymphoid tumors representing malignant transformation of the T lymphocytes. Some types of tumors formerly included in this group have been found to be mixtures of T cells and B-cell precursors.

T-cell–mediated hypersensitivity reaction, type IV hypersensitivity reaction.

TCV, abbreviation for **total cell volume**.

Td, abbreviation for **tetanus and diphtheria toxoids**.

TD, 1. abbreviation for **toxic dose**. **2.** abbreviation for *doubling time*.

TDD, abbreviation for **transdermal drug delivery**.

tDNA, abbreviation for **transfer DNA**.

t.d.s., abbreviation for Latin phrase *ter die sumendum,* (to be taken) "three times a day."

Te, symbol for the element **tellurium**.

tea [Chin, *ch'a*], **1.** a beverage prepared from the leaves and leaf buds of an evergreen shrub, *Thea sinensis*. A member of the camellia family, the plant is grown mainly in Asia. Its pharmacologically active components include caffeine, theobromine, theophylline, and tannin. **2.** maté tea, a caffeine beverage prepared from the leaves of *Ilex paraguayensis,* a shrub grown in South America.

teaching: disease process, a nursing intervention from the Nursing Interventions Classification (NIC) defined as assisting the patient to understand information related to a specific disease process.

teaching: foot care, a nursing intervention from the Nursing Interventions Classification (NIC) defined as preparing a patient at risk and/or significant other to provide preventive foot care.

teaching: group, a nursing intervention from the Nursing Interventions Classification (NIC) defined as development, implementation, and evaluation of a patient teaching program for a group of individuals experiencing the same health condition.

teaching hospital [AS, *taecan,* to show how], a hospital associated with a university that has accredited programs in various specialties of medical practice.

teaching: individual, a nursing intervention from the Nursing Interventions Classification (NIC) defined as a planning, implementation, and evaluation of a teaching program designed to address a patient's particular needs.

teaching: infant nutrition 0-3 months, a nursing intervention from the Nursing Interventions Classification (NIC) defined as instruction on nutrition and feeding practices through the first three months of life.

teaching: infant nutrition 4-6 months, a nursing intervention from the Nursing Interventions Classification (NIC) defined as instruction on nutrition and feeding practices from the fourth month through the sixth month of life.

teaching: infant nutrition 7-9 months, a nursing intervention from the Nursing Interventions Classification (NIC) defined as instruction on nutrition and feeding practices from the seventh month through the ninth month of life.

teaching: infant nutrition 10-12 months, a nursing intervention from the Nursing Interventions Classification (NIC) defined as instruction on nutrition and feeding practices from the tenth month through the twelfth month of life.

teaching: infant safety 0-3 months, nursing intervention from the Nursing Interventions Classification (NIC) defined as instruction on safety through the first three months of life.

teaching: infant safety 4-6 months, a nursing intervention from the Nursing Interventions Classification (NIC) defined as instruction on safety from the fourth month through the sixth month of life.

teaching: infant safety 7-9 months, a nursing intervention from the Nursing Interventions Classification (NIC) defined as instruction on safety from the seventh month through the ninth month of life.

teaching: infant safety 10-12 months, a nursing intervention from the Nursing Interventions Classification (NIC) defined as instruction on safety from the tenth month through the twelfth month of life.

teaching: infant stimulation 0-4 months, a nursing intervention from the Nursing Interventions Classification (NIC) defined as teaching parents and caregivers to provide developmentally appropriate sensory activities to promote development and movement through the first four months of life.

teaching: infant stimulation 5-8 months, a nursing intervention from the Nursing Interventions Classification (NIC) defined as teaching parents and caregivers to provide developmentally appropriate sensory activities to promote development and movement from the fifth month through the eighth month of life.

teaching: infant stimulation 9-12 months, a nursing intervention from the Nursing Interventions Classification (NIC) defined as teaching parents and caregivers to provide developmentally appropriate sensory activities to promote development and movement from the ninth month through the twelfth month of life.

teaching: preoperative, a nursing intervention from the Nursing Interventions Classification (NIC) defined as assisting a patient to understand and mentally prepare for surgery and the postoperative recovery period.

teaching: prescribed activity/exercise, a nursing intervention from the Nursing Interventions Classification (NIC) defined as preparing a patient to achieve and/or maintain a prescribed level of activity.

teaching: prescribed diet, a nursing intervention from the Nursing Interventions Classification (NIC) defined as preparing a patient to correctly follow a prescribed diet.

teaching: prescribed medication, a nursing intervention from the Nursing Interventions Classification (NIC) defined as preparing a patient to safely take prescribed medications and monitor for their effects.

teaching: procedure/treatment, a nursing intervention from the Nursing Interventions Classification (NIC) defined as preparing a patient to understand and mentally prepare for a prescribed procedure or treatment.

teaching: psychomotor skill, a nursing intervention from the Nursing Interventions Classification (NIC) defined as preparing a patient to perform a psychomotor skill.

teaching rounds, informal conferences held regularly, often at the beginning of the day. Specific problems in the care of current patients, as well as case presentation of patients with specific diseases, are discussed.

teaching: safe sex, a nursing intervention from the Nursing Interventions Classification (NIC) defined as providing instruction concerning sexual protection during sexual activity.

teaching: sexuality, a nursing intervention from the Nursing Interventions Classification (NIC) defined as assisting individuals to understand physical and psychosocial dimensions of sexual growth and development.

teaching: toddler nutrition, a nursing intervention from the Nursing Interventions Classification (NIC) defined as instruction on nutrition and feeding practices during the second and third years of life.

teaching: toddler nutrition 13-18 months, a nursing intervention from the Nursing Interventions Classification (NIC) defined as instruction on nutrition and feeding practices from the thirteenth month through the eighteenth month of life.

teaching: toddler nutrition 19-24 months, a nursing intervention from the Nursing Interventions Classification (NIC) defined as instruction on nutrition and feeding practices from the nineteenth month through the twenty-fourth month of life.

teaching: toddler nutrition 25-36 months, a nursing intervention from the Nursing Interventions Classification (NIC) defined as instruction on nutrition and feeding practices from the twenty-fifth month through the thirty-sixth month of life.

teaching: toddler safety 13-18 months, a nursing intervention from the Nursing Interventions Classification (NIC) defined as instruction on safety from the thirteenth month through the eighteenth month of life.

teaching: toddler safety 19-24 months, a nursing intervention from the Nursing Interventions Classification (NIC) defined as instruction on safety from the nineteenth month through the twenty-fourth month of life.

teaching: toddler safety 25-36 months, a nursing intervention from the Nursing Interventions Classification (NIC) defined as instruction on safety from the twenty-fifth through the thirty-sixth month of life.

teaching: toilet training, a nursing intervention from the Nursing Interventions Classification (NIC) defined as instruction on determining the child's readiness and strategies to assist the child to learn independent toileting skills.

team nursing [AS, *team,* family; L, *nutrix,* nurse], a decentralized system in which the care of a patient is distributed among the members of a group working in

T

coordinated effort. The charge nurse delegates authority to a team leader who must be a professional nurse. The team leader assigns tasks, schedules care, and instructs team members in details of care.

team practice, professional practice by a group of professionals that may include physicians, nurses, and others such as a social worker, nutritionist, or physical therapist who manage the care of a specified number of patients as a coordinated group, usually in an outpatient setting.

tear /ter/ [ME, *teren,* to rend], to rip, rend, or pull apart by force.

teardrop fracture /tir'drop/ [AS, *tear* + *dropa*; L, *fractura,* break], an avulsion fracture of one of the short bones such as a vertebra, causing a tear-shaped disruption of bone tissue.

tear duct /tir/ [AS, *tear*; L, *ducere,* to lead], any duct that carries tears, including the lacrimal ducts, nasolacrimal ducts, and excretory ducts of the lacrimal glands.

tear gas /tēr/, a gas that produces severe lacrimation by irritating the conjunctivae.

tearing /tir'ing/, watering of the eye usually caused by excessive tear production such as by strong emotion, infection, or mechanic irritation by a foreign body. If the normal amount of fluid tears is produced but not drained into the lacrimal punctum at the nasal border of the eye, tear overflow will occur.

tears /tirz/ [ME, *tere*], a watery saline or alkaline fluid secreted by the lacrimal glands that, along with secretions from the meibomian glands and goblet cells and glands of Zeii, moisten the conjunctiva and cornea.

tears of the perineum /ters/ [ME, *teren*; Gk, *perineos*], a rending of the tissues between the vulva and anus caused by overstretching of the vagina during child delivery.

teaspoon (tsp), a small spoon that may be used to measure a dose of a liquid medication, equal to about 1 fluid dram or 5 mL.

tea tree oil, an herbal product taken from a species of myrtle tree native to coastal Australia. This herb is used topically for acne and fungal infections and has proven efficacy. It has also been added to warm bath water and inhaled for treatment of cough and lower respiratory disorders, but there are no reliable data regarding its efficacy in this instance.

tebutate, a contraction for *tertiary butyl acetate*.

technetium (Tc) [Gk, *technectos,* artificial], a radioactive, metallic element. Its atomic number is 43, and its atomic mass is 99. Isotopes of technetium are used in radioisotope scanning procedures of internal organs such as the liver and spleen.

technetium-99m, the radionuclide most commonly used to image the body in nuclear medicine scans. It is preferred because of its short half-life and because the emitted photon has an appropriate energy for normal imaging techniques.

technical [Gk, *technikos,* skillful], pertaining to a procedure or its results that require special techniques, skills, expertise, or knowledge.

technician /teknish'ən/ [Gk, *technikos,* skillful], a person with special training and experience in some form of technical procedures, usually those involving mechanical adjustments such as maintaining and operating radiologic equipment.

technique /teknēk'/ [Gk, *technikos,* skillful], the method and details followed in performing a procedure such as those used in conducting a laboratory test, a physical examination, a psychiatric interview, a surgical operation, or any process requiring certain skills or an ordered sequence of actions.

technologist /teknol'əjist/ [Gk, *techne,* art, *logos,* science], a person who studies the application of processes for making natural resources beneficial for humans. A medical technologist may work under the supervision of a physician in general clinical laboratory procedures.

technology /teknol'əjē/ [Gk, *techne,* art, *logos,* study], **1.** the application of science or the scientific method to commercial or industrial objectives. **2.** the knowledge and use of science applied to the conversion of natural resources for the benefit of humans.

technology management, a nursing intervention from the Nursing Interventions Classification (NIC) defined as use of technical equipment and devices to monitor patient condition or sustain life.

tectonic /tekton'ik/, **1.** pertaining to variations in structure in the cornea or other parts of the eye. **2.** pertaining to plastic surgery or tissue transplants.

tectorial /tektôr'ē-əl/, pertaining to a rooflike structure or cover.

tectorium /tektôr'ē-əm/, a body structure that serves as an overlying structure or roof.

TED, abbreviation for *threshold erythema dose*.

teether /tē'ther/, an object such as a plastic or rubber teething ring on which an infant can bite or chew during the teething process.

teething /tē'thing/ [AS, *toth*], the physiologic process of the eruption of the deciduous teeth through the gums. It normally begins around the sixth month of life and occurs periodically until the complete set of 20 teeth has appeared at about 30 to 36 months. Discomfort and inflammation result from the pressure exerted against the periodontal tissue as the crown of the tooth breaks through the membranes. General signs of teething include excessive drooling, biting on hard objects, irritability, difficulty in sleeping, and refusal of food.—**teethe,** *v.*

Teflon, a trademark for a substance (polytetrafluoroethylene) used for the construction of surgical implants in restorative surgery and the coating of surgical blades.

tegaserod, a 5-HT$_4$ receptor partial agonist used to treat irritable bowel syndrome where the primary bowel symptom is constipation.

tegmen /teg'mən/, a covering, such as the bone that covers the tympanic cavity.

tegmental /tegmen'təl/ [L, *tegmentum,* cover], of or relating to an integument.

Tegretol, a trademark for an analgesic and anticonvulsant (carbamazepine).

TEIB, abbreviation for *triethylene-immunobenzoquinone.*

teicoplanin /ti-ko-pla'nin/, a glycopeptide antibiotic produced by the bacterium *Actinoplanes teichomyceticus.* It is used as a less toxic alternative to vancomycin in the treatment of moderate to severe infections caused by gram-positive bacteria when other antibiotics cannot be used.

Tekturna, a trademark for aliskiren.

telangiectasia /təlan'jē-ektā'zhə/ [Gk, *telos,* end, *angeion,* vessel, *ektasis,* swelling], permanent dilation of groups of superficial capillaries and venules. Common causes are actinic damage, atrophy-producing dermatoses, rosacea, elevated estrogen levels, and collagen vascular diseases.

telangiectasia lymphatica [Gk, *telos,* end, *angeion,* vessel, *ektasis,* swelling; L, *lympha,* water], a congenital or acquired condition of obstructed dilated lymphatic vessels, resulting in lymphangiomas.

telangiectatic angioma /təlan'jē-ektat'ik/, a tumor composed of dilated blood vessels.

telangiectatic epulis, a benign red tumor of the gingiva, containing prominent blood vessels. Low-grade or chronic irritation is a risk factor.

telangiectatic glioma, a tumor composed of glial cells and a network of blood vessels, which give the mass a vivid pink appearance.

telangiectatic nevus, a common skin condition of neonates, characterized by flat, deep-pink localized areas of capillary dilation that occur predominantly on the back of the neck, lower occiput, upper eyelids, upper lip, and bridge of the nose. The areas disappear permanently by about 2 years of age.

telangiectatic sarcoma, a malignant tumor of mesodermal cells with an unusually rich vascular network.

telbivudine, an antiretroviral used in the treatment of hepatitis B.

telediagnosis /tel'ədī'əgnō'sis/ [Gk, *tele,* far off, *dia,* through, *gnosis,* knowledge], a process whereby a disease diagnosis, or prognosis, is made by the electronic transmission of data between distant medical facilities.

telehealth, the use of telecommunication technologies to provide health care services and access to medical and surgical information for training and educating health care professionals and consumers, to increase awareness and educate the public about health-related issues, and to facilitate medical research across distances.

telekinesis /tel'əkinē'sis/ [Gk, *tele,* far off, *kinesis,* movement], a concept of parapsychology that one can control external events such as the movement of a solid object by the powers of the mind.

telemedicine, the use of telecommunication equipment and information technology to provide clinical care to individuals at distant sites and the transmission of medical and surgical information and images needed to provide that care.

telemetry /telem'ətrē/ [Gk, *tele,* far off, *metron,* measure], the electronic transmission of data between distant points, such as the transmission of cardiac monitoring data.

telencephalization /tel'ensef'əlizā'shən/, a stage in fetal development in which the forebrain begins to assume control over nervous system functions previously directed by more primitive neural centers.

telencephalon /tel'ensef'əlon/ [Gk, *telos,* end, *egekephalos,* brain], the paired brain vesicles or endbrain from which the cerebral hemispheres are derived.

teleology /tel'ē-ol'əjē/ [Gk, *telos,* end, *logos,* science], **1.** the study of ultimate purpose or design in natural phenomena. **2.** a theory that everything is directed toward some final purpose.

telepathist /təlep'əthist/, **1.** a person who believes in telepathy. **2.** a person who claims to have telepathic powers.

telepathy /təlep'əthē/ [Gk, *tele,* far off, *pathos,* feeling], the alleged communication of thought from one person to another by means other than the physical senses. —**telepathic,** *adj.,* **telepathize,** *v.*

telephone consultation, a nursing intervention from the Nursing Interventions Classification (NIC) defined as eliciting a patient's concerns, listening, and providing support, information, or teaching in response to the patient's stated concerns, over the telephone.

telephone counseling, a strategy system to provide support by telephone for patients or family caregivers who are homebound. The system may offer safety provisions and social contacts for frail older persons or the visually impaired as well as suicide-prevention counseling.

telephone follow-up, a nursing intervention from the Nursing Interventions Classification (NIC) defined as providing results of testing or evaluating patient's response and determining potential for problems as a result of previous treatment, examination, or testing, over the telephone.

teleradiology /tel′ə-rā′dē·ol′əjē/, radiology done through remote transmission and viewing of images.

telereceptive /tel′ərəsep′tiv/, pertaining to the exteroceptors of hearing, sight, and smell that detect stimuli distant from the body.

teletherapy /tel′əther′əpē/ [Gk, *tele* + *therapeia*, treatment], radiation therapy administered by a machine that is positioned at some distance from the patient. Typically a teletherapy unit can rotate around a patient, thus allowing the use of multiple beams that intersect at the tumor and lowering the dose to surrounding normal tissue.

telithromycin, an antiinfective used to treat acute bacterial exacerbation of chronic bronchitis caused by *Streptococcus pneumoniae, Haemophilus influenzae,* and *Moraxella catarrhalis;* acute bacterial sinusitis caused by *S. pneumoniae, H. influenzae, M. catarrhalis,* and *Staphylococcus aureus;* and community-acquired pneumonia.

telluric /telōō′rik/ [L, *tellus,* earth], pertaining to the soil and its possible pathogenic influence.

tellurium (Te) /telōō′rē·əm/ [L, *tellus,* earth], an element exhibiting metallic and nonmetallic chemical properties. Its atomic number is 52, and its atomic mass is 127.60. Inhaling vapors of tellurium results in a garlicky breath.

telmisartan, an antihypertensive prescribed to treat hypertension, either alone or in combination with other drugs.

telocentric /tel′əsen′trik/ [Gk, *telos,* end, *kentron,* center], pertaining to a chromosome in which the centromere is located at the end so that the chromosome appears as a straight filament.

telomerase /təlō′mərās/, a DNA polymerase involved in the formation of telomeres and the maintenance of telomere sequences during replication.

telomere /tel′ōmēr/, either of the ends of a chromosome, which possess special properties, among them a polarity that prevents their reunion with any fragment after a chromosome has been broken.

telophase /tel′əfāz/ [Gk, *telos* + *phasis,* appearance], the final of the four stages of nuclear division in mitosis and in each of the two divisions in meiosis in which the newly

produced daughter chromosomes assemble at the poles of the spindle and become long and slender, the nuclear membrane forms around them, the nucleolus reappears, and the cytoplasm begins to divide.

Temaril, a trademark for an antihistamine (trimeprazine tartrate).

temazepam /temaz′əpam/, a benzodiazepine hypnotic agent prescribed for the relief of transient and intermittent insomnia.

Temovate, a trademark for a topical corticosteroid (clobetasol propionate).

temozolomide, a miscellaneous antineoplastic agent prescribed to treat anaplastic astrocytoma with relapse.

temper [L, *temperare,* to moderate], **1.** to moderate or soften the effects. **2.** a state of mind regarding calmness or anger.

temperament /temp′(ə)rəmənt/ [L, *temperamentum,* mixture in proper proportions], the features of a persona that reflect an individual's emotional disposition or the way he or she behaves, feels, and thinks.

temperance /tem′pərəns/, behavior that emphasizes moderation and self-restraint, particularly in the use of alcohol.

temperate phage /tem′pərət/ [L, *temperare,* to moderate; Gk, *phagein,* to eat], a bacteriophage whose genome is incorporated into the host bacterium. It persists through many cell divisions of the bacterium without destroying the host.

temperature (T) /tem′pə(rə)chər/ [L, *temperatura*], **1.** a relative measure of sensible heat or cold. **2.** in physiology, a measure of sensible heat associated with the metabolism of the human body, normally maintained at a constant level of 98.6° F (37° C). **3.** *informal.* a fever.

temperature of infant [L, *temperatura* + *infans,* infant], the neonatal temperature, which normally ranges from 97.7° to 99.5° F (36.5° to 37.5° C). It is unstable because of immature physiologic mechanisms.

temperature regulation, a nursing intervention from the Nursing Interventions Classification (NIC) defined as attaining and/or maintaining body temperature within a normal range.

temperature regulation: intraoperative, a nursing intervention from the Nursing Interventions Classification (NIC) defined as attaining and/or maintaining desired intraoperative body temperature.

temperature scale, a scale for expressing degree of heat, based on absolute zero as a reference point, or with a certain value arbitrarily assigned to such temperatures as the freezing point and boiling point of water.

template /tem′plət/ [L, *templum,* section], the strand of DNA that acts as a model for the synthesis of messenger RNA.

temporal /tem'pərəl/ [L, *tempus,* time, *tempora,* the temples], **1.** pertaining to a limited time. **2.** relating to the temple of the skull. **3.** pertaining to the temporal bone of the skull.

temporal arteritis [L, *temporalis,* temporary, *arteria,* airpipe, *itis,* inflammation], a progressive inflammatory disorder of cranial blood vessels, principally the temporal artery. Symptoms are intractable headache, difficulty in chewing, weakness, rheumatic pains, and loss of vision if the central retinal artery becomes occluded.

temporal artery, any one of three arteries on each side of the head: the superficial temporal artery, the middle temporal artery, and the deep temporal artery.

temporal bone, one of a pair of large bones forming part of the lower cranium and containing various cavities and recesses associated with the ear such as the tympanic cavity and the auditory tube.

temporal bone fracture, a break in the temporal bone of the skull, sometimes characterized by bleeding from the ear. Diminished hearing, facial paralysis, or infection of the tympanic cavity leading to meningitis may occur.

temporal fascia, a tough fan-shaped aponeurosis overlying the temporalis muscle and attached by its outer margin to the superior temporal line and by its inferior margin to the zygomatic arch.

temporal fossa, a narrow fan-shaped space that covers the lateral surface of the skull. It contains the temporalis muscle and the zygomaticotemporal branches of the maxillary nerve.

temporal gyrus, any of three convolutions, inferior, middle, or superior, on the lateral surface of the temporal lobe of the brain.

temporalis /tem'pəral'is/, one of the four muscles of mastication. It is a broad radiating muscle that acts to close the jaws and retract the mandible.

temporal lobe, the lateral region of the cerebrum, below the lateral fissure. Within the temporal lobe of the brain is the center for smell and some association areas for memory and learning.

temporal lobe epilepsy, seizures that arise from the temporal lobe, often associated with mesial sclerosis. Patients may have an aura before these kinds of seizures.

temporal process, the posterior blunt process of the zygomatic bone that articulates with the zygomatic process of the temporal bone to form the zygomatic arch.

temporal subtraction, the subtraction of two or more digitized x-ray images that were acquired at different times. The subtraction process eliminates information in the image that was static.

temporary pacemaker /tem'pərerē/ [L, *temporalis,* temporary, *passus,* step; ME, *maken*], an electronic pacemaker used as an interim treatment when the heart rate is excessively low. It consists of either a pulse generator and battery attached outside the patient's body and connected to a transvenous electrode in the right ventricle, or conductive pads placed on the chest and connected to an external pulse generator by cables.

temporary removable splint [L, *temporalis,* temporary, *remover*; D, *splint*], any of a variety of dental appliances, including occlusal splints, used when limited stability of the teeth is required. It may be placed on or removed from teeth at will.

temporary stopping [L, *temporalis*; AS, *stoppian,* to stop up], a mixture of guttapercha, zinc oxide, white wax, and coloring, used for temporarily sealing dressings in tooth cavities.

temporomandibular /tem'pərō'mandib'yə lər/ [L, *tempora,* the temples, *mandere,* to chew], pertaining to the articulation between the temporal bone and the condyle of the mandible.

temporomandibular joint (TMJ) [L, *tempora + mandere,* to chew, *jungere,* to join], one of a pair of joints connecting the mandible of the jaw to the temporal bone of the skull. It is a combined hinge and gliding joint, formed by the anterior parts of the mandibular fossae of the temporal bone, the articular tubercles, the condyles of the mandible, and five ligaments.

temporomandibular joint capsule, a fibrous protective sheath enclosing the TMJ of the lower jaw.

temporomandibular joint (TMJ) disorder, dysfunction of the TMJ, marked by a clicking or grinding sensation in the joint and often by pain in or about the ears, tinnitus, tiredness, slight soreness of the jaw muscles on waking, and stiffness of the jaw or actual trismus.

temporomandibular joint (TMJ) pain dysfunction syndrome, an abnormal condition characterized by facial pain and by mandibular dysfunction, apparently caused by a defective or dislocated TMJ. Some common indications of this syndrome are clicking of the joint when the jaws move, limitation of jaw movement, subluxation, and temporomandibular dislocation.

temporomandibular ligament [L, *temporalis + mandere,* to chew, *ligare,* to bind], an oblique band of connective tissue that extends downward and backward from the zygomatic process to the neck of the mandible.

temporomaxillary /-mak'siler'ē/, pertaining to the area of the temporal and maxillary bones.

temporooccipital /-oksip'itəl/, pertaining to the area of the temporal and occipital bones.

temporoparietalis /-pərī'ətal'is/[L, *temporalis + paries,* wall], one of a pair of broad, thin muscles of the scalp, divided into three parts, which fan out over the temporal fascia and insert into the galea aponeurotica. The three parts include an anterior temporal part, a superior parietal part, and a triangular part in between. On both sides it acts in combination with the occipitofrontalis to wrinkle the forehead, widen the eyes, and raise the ears.

temsirolimus, a biologic response modifier used to treat renal cell carcinoma.

TEN, abbreviation for **toxic epidermal necrolysis.**

tenacious /tenā'shəs/ [L, *tenax,* holding fast], pertaining to secretions that are sticky or adhesive or otherwise tend to hold together, such as mucus and sputum.

tenacity /tenas'itē/ [L, *tenax,* holding fast], the ability to be persistent or remain attached.

tenaculum /tənak'yələm/ *pl.* **tenacula** [L, holder], a clip or clamp with long handles used to grasp, immobilize, and hold an organ or a piece of tissue.

tenalgia /tenal'jə/, pain referred to a tendon.

tender, responding with a sensation of pain to pressure or touch that would not normally cause discomfort.

tendinitis /ten'dənī'tis/ [L, *tendere,* to stretch; Gk, *itis,* inflammation], inflammation of a tendon, usually resulting from strain.

tendinous, pertaining to or resembling a tendon.

tendinous arch, a linear thickening in the fascia covering the obturator internus muscle that is part of the attachment of the levator ani muscles to the pelvic wall.

tendinous cords, the strands of tendon that anchor the cusps of the mitral and tricuspid valves to the papillary muscles of the ventricles of the heart, preventing prolapse of the valves into the atria during ventricular contraction.

tendo /ten'dō/, a tendon such as the tendo calcaneus, the Achilles tendon.

tendon /ten'dən/ [Gk, *tenon*], any one of many white, glistening bands of dense fibrous connective tissue that attach muscle to bone. Tendons are extremely strong, flexible, and inelastic and occur in various lengths and thicknesses.—**tendinous,** *adj.*

tendon graft, a free graft of tendon used to replace a damaged tendon segment.

tenecteplase /te-nek'te-plās/, a modified form of human tissue plasminogen activator produced by recombinant DNA technology, used as a thrombolytic agent in the treatment of MI.

tenesmic /tənez'mik/ [Gk, *tenedere,* to stretch], pertaining to or resembling tenesmus.

tenesmus /tənez'məs/ [Gk, *tendere,* to stretch], persistent, ineffectual spasms of the rectum or bladder, or ineffectual straining to evacuate the bowel or bladder. —**tenesmic,** *adj.*

tenia /tē'nē-ə/, **1.** any anatomic bandlike structure such as a band of muscle fibers. **2.** a bandage or tape.

teniasis /tēnī'əsis/, an infection of intestinal tapeworms of the genus *Taenia.*

tenodesis splint /tənod'əsis, ten'ōdē'sis/, the fixation of a tendon, sometimes performed by suturing one of its ends to a different point.

tenofovir, an antiretroviral agent used to treat HIV-1 infection with other antiretrovirals.

tenofovir disoproxil fumarate, a prodrug of tenofovir, used in the treatment of HIV-1 infection.

Tenon's capsule, a thin membranous socket that envelops the eyeball from the optic nerve to the ciliary region and allows it to move freely.

tenophony /tenof'ənē/, a heart murmur associated with a defect in the chordae tendineae.

Tenormin, a trademark for a beta blocker (atenolol).

tenosynovitis /ten'ōsin'əvī'tis/ [Gk, *tenon,* tendon, *syn,* together; L, *ovum,* egg; Gk, *itis, inflammation*], inflammation of a tendon sheath caused by calcium deposits, repeated strain or trauma, high levels of blood cholesterol, rheumatoid arthritis, gout, or gonorrhea.

tenotomy /tenot'əmē/ [Gk, *tenon,* tendon, *temnein,* to cut], the total or partial severing of a tendon, performed to correct a muscle imbalance such as in the correction of strabismus of the eye.

TENS, abbreviation for **transcutaneous electrical nerve stimulation.**

Tensilon, a trademark for an anticholinesterase drug (edrophonium).

Tensilon test, a diagnostic technique for verifying the signs of myasthenia gravis by testing the power of skeletal muscles before and after injection of edrophonium hydrochloride.

tensiometer /ten'sē-om'ətər/ [L, *tendere,* to stretch; Gk, *metron,* measure], a device for measuring the surface tension of a liquid.

tension /ten'shən/ [L, *tendere,* to stretch], **1.** the act of pulling or straining until taut. **2.** the condition of being taut, tense, or under pressure. **3.** a state or condition resulting from the psychologic and physiologic reaction to a stressful situation. It is characterized physically by a general increase in muscle tonus, heart rate, respiration rate, and alertness and psychologically by feelings of strain, uneasiness, irritability, and anxiety.

tension headache, a pain that affects the head as the result of overwork or emotional strain and involves tension in the muscles of the neck, face, and shoulder.

tension lines, cleavage lines.

tension pneumothorax [L, *tendere,* to stretch; Gk, *pneuma,* air + *thorax*], the presence of air in the pleural space when pleural pressure exceeds alveolar pressure, caused by a rupture through the chest wall or lung parenchyma associated with the valvular opening. Air passes through the valve during coughing but cannot escape on exhalation. Unrelieved pneumothorax can lead to respiratory arrest.

tensor /ten′sər/ [L, *tendere,* to stretch], any one of the muscles of the body that tenses a structure, such as the tensor fasciae latae of the thigh.

tensor fasciae latae, one of the 10 muscles of the gluteal region, arising from the outer lip of the iliac crest, the anterior superior iliac spine, and the deep fascia lata. It functions to flex the thigh and rotate it slightly medially.

tensor tympani /ten′sər tim′pə·nē/, a muscle originating in the cartilaginous portion of the auditory tube and inserting in the manubrium of the malleus; it functions to tense the tympanic membrane in response to loud noises.

tensor veli palatini, a muscle of the soft palate that is composed of a vertical muscular part and a more horizontal fibrous part that forms the palatine aponeurosis. It tenses the soft palate so that the other muscles attached to the palate can work more effectively, and it opens the pharyngotympanic tube when the palate moves during yawning and swallowing.

tent [ME, *tente*], **1.** a transparent cover, usually of plastic, supported over the upper part of a patient by a frame. Used in the treatment of respiratory conditions, it provides a controlled environment into which steam, oxygen, vaporized medication, or droplets of cool water may be sprayed, such as an oxygen tent. **2.** a cone made of various materials inserted into a cavity or orifice of the body to dilate its opening, such as a laminaria tent. **3.** a pack placed in a wound to hold it open to ensure that healing progresses from the base of the wound upward to the skin.

tentative /ten′tətiv/ [L, *tentare,* to touch], not final or definite, such as an experimental finding that has not been validated.

tenth-value layer (TVL) [ME, *tenpe*; L, *valere,* to be worth; AS, *lecgan,* to

lie], the thickness of material required to attenuate a beam of radiation to one tenth of its original intensity.

tenting of skin /ten′ting/, a slow return of the skin to its normal position after being pinched, a sign of either dehydration or aging, or both.

tentorial herniation /tentôr′ē·əl/ [L, *tentorium,* tent, *hernia,* rupture], the protrusion of brain tissue into the tentorial notch, caused by increased ICP resulting from edema, hemorrhage, or a tumor. Characteristic signs are severe headache, fever, flushing, sweating, abnormal pupillary reflex, drowsiness, hypotension, and LOC.

tentorial notch [L, *tentorium,* tent; OFr, *enochier*], an area occupied by the midbrain and enclosed by the free border of the tentorium cerebelli and the sphenoid bone.

tentorium /tentôr′ē·əm/ *pl.* **tentoria** [L, tent], any part of the body that resembles a tent, such as the tentorium of the hypophysis that covers the hypophyseal fossa.

Tenuate, a trademark for an anorexiant (diethylpropion hydrochloride).

tenure /ten′yər/ [L, *tenere,* to hold], **1.** in a university, a faculty appointment with few limits on the number of years it may be held. **2.** a permanent appointment usually awarded to a person who has advanced to the rank of associate professor and who demonstrates scholarship, community service, and teaching excellence in a specific field of study.

tepid, moderately warm to the touch.

teprotide /tep′rōtīd/, a bradykinin-potentiating peptide.

teramorphous [Gk, *teras,* monster, *morphe,* form], of the nature of or characteristic of a teratic embryo.

teras /ter′əs/ *pl.* **terata** [Gk, monster], a severely deformed fetus.—**teratic,** *adj.*

teratic embryo, a fetus that is grossly malformed and usually nonviable.

teratism /ter′ətiz′əm/, any congenital or developmental anomaly that is produced by inherited or environmental factors or a combination of the two; any condition in which a severely malformed fetus is produced.

teratoblastoma /ter′ətō·blastō′mə/, a teratoma in which not all germ layers are present.

teratogen /ter′ətəjen′/ [Gk, *teras* + *genein,* to produce], any substance, agent, or process that interferes with normal prenatal development, causing the formation of one or more developmental abnormalities in the fetus. The period of highest vulnerability in the developing embryo is from about the third through the twelfth week of gestation, when differentiation of the major organs and systems occurs.—**teratogenic,** *adj.*

teratogenesis /ter'ətōjen'əsis/, the development of physical defects in the embryo. —**teratogenetic,** *adj.*

teratogenous /ter'ətoj'ənəs/ [Gk, *teras,* monster, *genein,* to produce], developed from fetal membranes.

teratoid /ter'ətoid/ [Gk, *teras + eidos,* form], pertaining to malformed physical development; grossly misplaced, misshapen parts.

teratologist /ter'ətol'əjist/, one who specializes in the causes and effects of congenital anomalies and developmental abnormalities.

teratology /-tol'əgē/ [Gk, *teras + logos,* science], the study of the causes and effects of congenital malformations and developmental abnormalities.—**teratologic,** *adj.*

teratoma /ter'ətō'mə/ *pl.* **teratomas, teratomata,** a tumor composed of different kinds of tissue, none of which normally occur together or at the site of the tumor. Teratomas are most common in the ovaries or testes.

terazosin /ter'əzō'sin/, a drug approved for the treatment of benign prostatic hypertrophy. It is also used alone or in combination for the treatment of hypertension.

terbium (Tb) /tur'bē-əm/ [Ytterby, Sweden], a rare earth metallic element. Its atomic number is 65, and its atomic mass is 158.294.

terbutaline sulfate /terbyōō'təlēn/, a beta₂-adrenergic stimulant. It is prescribed as a bronchodilator in the treatment of asthma, bronchitis, and emphysema and as a uterine relaxant to treat premature labor.

teres /tir'ēz, ter'ēz/ *pl.* **teretes** [L, rounded], a long cylindric muscle such as the teres minor or the teres major.

teres major, a thick flat muscle of the shoulder. It functions to adduct, extend, and rotate the arm medially.

teres minor, a cylindric, elongated muscle of the shoulder. It functions to rotate the arm laterally, weakly adduct the arm, and draw the humerus toward the glenoid fossa of the scapula, strengthening the shoulder joint.

teriparatide, a parathyroid hormone used to treat postmenopausal women with osteoporosis and men with primary hypogonadal osteoporosis at high risk for fracture.

term [L, *terminus,* limit], **1.** a specified period of time. **2.** the normal gestation period.

terminal /tur'minəl/ [L, *terminus,* boundary], of a structure or process, near or approaching its end, such as a terminal bronchiole or a terminal disease.—**terminate,** *v.,* **termination,** *n.*

terminal arteriole [L, *terminus,* boundary, *arteriola,* little artery], an arteriole that divides into capillaries.

terminal cancer [L, *terminalis + cancer,* crab], an advanced stage of a malignant neoplastic disease with death as the inevitable prognosis.

terminal crest, a vertical crest on the interior wall of the right atrium that separates the sinus of the vena cava from the rest of the right atrium.

terminal drop, a rapid decline in cognitive function and coping ability that occurs 1 to 5 years before death.

terminal illness [L, *terminalis;* ON, *illr,* bad], an advanced stage of a disease with an unfavorable prognosis and no known cure.

terminal insomnia, a chronic sleep disturbance occurring at the end of a sleep period. It may be indicative of an underlying depressive disorder and treated with an antidepressant.

terminal nerve, a small nerve originating in the vomeronasal epithelium, projecting to the cerebral hemisphere in the region of the olfactory trigone. It is classified by most anatomists as part of the olfactory nerve. It communicates in the nasal cavity with the ophthalmic division of the trigeminal nerve.

terminal part of ileum, the part just before the ileum meets the cecum at the ileal orifice and ileal papilla.

terminal saccular period, the period of prenatal lung development lasting, in different parts of the lungs, from the twenty-sixth week or later until near term. Walls of the air spaces become thinner and the spaces divide into alveolar saccules with adjacent capillaries; type I and type II alveolar cells begin functioning, and surfactant is secreted.

terminal sacs, thin-walled dilations that develop at the ends of the respiratory bronchioles during fetal development. Their appearance marks the point at which limited respiration becomes possible.

terminal stance, one of the five stages in the stance phase of a walking gait, directly associated with the continuation of single limb support or the period during which the body moves forward on the supporting foot.

terminal sulcus of the right atrium, a shallow channel on the external surface of the right atrium between the superior and inferior vena cava.

terminal sulcus of the tongue, a V-shaped depression on the oral and pharyngeal surfaces of the tongue that forms the inferior margin of the fauces between the oral and pharyngeal cavities.

termination codon /tur'minā'shən/, a three-nucleotide sequence (UAA, UAG, or UGA) in RNA that specifies the end of the sequence of amino acids in a polypeptide.

termination phase, the last stage of a therapeutic relationship when attained goals are evaluated and outcomes achieved.

termination sequence, in molecular genetics, a DNA segment at the end of a unit that is transcribed to messenger RNA from the DNA template.

term infant [L, *terminus,* limit], any neonate, regardless of birth weight, born after the end of the thirty-seventh and before the beginning of the forty-third week of gestation.

terminus /tur′minəs/ [L, the end], a boundary or limit.

terpin /tur′pin/, **1.** a diterpene alcohol derived from turpentine oil. **2.** an expectorant ingredient produced through the action of nitric and sulfuric acids on pine oil.

terpin hydrate and codeine elixir, a preparation of the expectorant terpin hydrate, with sweet orange peel tincture, benzaldehyde, glycerin, alcohol, syrup, water, and the antitussive opiate codeine.

Terra-Cortril, a trademark for a topical fixed-combination drug containing a glucocorticoid (hydrocortisone) and an antibiotic (oxytetracycline).

Terramycin, a trademark for an antibiotic (oxytetracycline).

territorial /ter′ətôr′ē-əl/ [L, *territorium,* district], a type of body movement that aids in communication. A territorial will frame an interaction and define an individual's "territory."

territoriality /ter′itôr′ē·al′itē/, an emotional attachment to and defense of certain areas related to one's existence.

tertian /tur′shən/ [L, *tertius,* third], occurring every 48 hours, including the first day of occurrence, such as vivax or tertian malaria, in which fever occurs every third day.

tertian malaria, a form of malaria caused by the protozoan *Plasmodium vivax* or *P. ovale,* characterized by febrile paroxysms that occur every 48 hours. Both types are treated with chloroquine.

tertiary /tur′shē·er′ē, tursh′ərē/ [L, *tertius,* third], **1.** third in frequency or order of use. **2.** belonging to the third level of sophistication of development, such as a tertiary health care facility.

tertiary bronchial buds, outgrowths of the secondary bronchial buds that become the bronchopulmonary segments of the mature lung.

tertiary health care, a specialized, highly technical level of health care that includes diagnosis and treatment of disease and disability. Specialized ICUs, advanced diagnostic support services, and highly specialized personnel are usually characteristic of tertiary health care.

tertiary prevention, a level of preventive medicine that deals with the rehabilitation and return of a patient to a status of maximum usefulness with a minimum risk of recurrence of a physical or mental disorder.

tertiary syphilis [L, *tertius,* third], the most advanced stage of syphilis, resulting in infections of the cardiovascular and neurologic systems and marked by destructive lesions involving many tissues and organs. Late-stage syphilis is symptomatic but not contagious.

tesla /tes′lə/ [Nikola Tesla, American engineer, 1856–1943], a unit of magnetic flux density, defined by the International System of Units as 1 weber per square meter, the equivalent of 1 volt/second per square meter, or 10,000 gauss.

Teslac, a trademark for an antineoplastic (testolactone).

Tessalon, a trademark for a local anesthetic agent **(benzonatate).**

test [L, *testum,* crucible], **1.** an examination or trial intended to establish a principle or determine a value. **2.** a chemical reaction or reagent that has clinical significance. **3.** to detect, identify, or conduct a trial.

testa /tes′tə/ [L, a shell], **1.** an eggshell. **2.** powdered oyster shells used in antacids. **3.** the outer coat of a seed.

Testacealobosia /tes′təsē′lōbā′zhə/, a subclass of ameboid protozoa in which the cells are enclosed in chitinous or a complex membrane envelope, vest, or shell. It includes both marine and freshwater forms.

testamentary capacity /tes′təmen′tərē/, a person's competency to make a will, including the requirement that he or she be aware that a will is being made, of the nature and extent of the property covered by the will, and of the identities of the beneficiaries.

testcross [L, *testum + crux,* cross], **1.** a cross between a dominant and a recessive phenotype to determine either the degree of genetic linkage or whether the dominant phenotype is a result of a homozygous or a heterozygous genotype. **2.** a subject undergoing such a test.

testes, the male gonad, one of two, that produce sperm and testosterone.

testes determining factor (TDF) /tes′tēz/, a gene on the Y chromosome that is believed to determine male sexual development.

test for acetone in urine, a part of routine urinalysis. Normal findings are negative, since acetone and other ketones are not normally present in urine. Exceptions include such cases as poorly controlled diabetic patients, alcoholics, and people who may be fasting or on special high-protein diets.

T

test for lacrimation, a test for possible dry eye and/or keratoconjunctivitis sicca conducted by placing a 35-mm-long piece of filter paper in the lower fornix of the conjunctiva for 5 minutes. Failure of tears to wet as much as 10 mm of the strip indicates inadequate tear production.

testicular /testik′yələr/ [L, *testiculus,* testicle], pertaining to the testicle.

testicular artery, one of a pair of long, slender branches of the abdominal aorta, arising inferior to the renal arteries and supplying the testis.

testicular cancer, a malignant neoplastic disease of the testis occurring most frequently in men between 15 and 35 years of age. Patients with early testicular cancer are often asymptomatic, and metastases may be present in lymph nodes, the lungs, and the liver before the primary lesion is palpable. In the later stages there may be pulmonary symptoms, ureteral obstruction, gynecomastia, and an abdominal mass. Diagnostic measures include transillumination of the scrotum, excretory urography, lymphangiography, and a urine or serum test to evaluate circulating levels of tumor markers. Testis cancers are often curable. Early detection by testicular self-examination enhances chances of cure.

testicular hormone, any androgenic steroid hormone secreted by the Leydig cells in the interstitial tissues of the male gonads. The principal hormone secreted by the cells is testosterone.

testicular microlithiasis, the presence of tiny calcifications in the seminiferous tubules. In some cases it precedes development of a tumor.

testicular self-examination (TSE), a procedure recommended by the National Institutes of Health for detecting tumors or other abnormalities in the male testes. The TSE is conducted in four simple steps, starting by standing in front of a mirror and looking for any swelling on the skin of the scrotum. Next, each testicle is examined with both hands, placing the fingers under the testicle while the thumbs are placed on top. The testicle is then rolled gently between the thumbs and fingers. In the next step the epididymis, a normal cordlike structure on the top and back of each testicle, should be found. A small pea-sized lump is felt for on the front or side of a testicle. TSE should be performed once a month, usually after a warm bath or shower.

testicular sperm extraction (TESE), for men with obstructive azoospermia, extraction of spermatozoa directly from the testis through the skin.

testicular vein, one of a pair of veins emerging from convoluted venous plexuses, forming the greater mass of the spermatic cords.

testimony /tes′timō′nē/ [L, *testimonium,* evidence], the statement of a witness, usually made orally and given under oath, such as at a court trial.

testis /tes′tis/ *pl.* **testes** /tes′tēz/, one of the pair of male gonads that produce sperm and testosterone. The adult testes are suspended in the scrotum by the spermatic cords. Each testis is a laterally compressed oval body about 4 cm long and 2.5 cm wide that weighs about 12 g. The convoluted epididymis lying on the posterior border of the testis contains a tightly coiled tube that is about 20 feet long and connects with the vas deferens through which spermatozoa pass during ejaculation. Each testis consists of several hundred conical lobules containing the tiny coiled seminiferous tubules, each about 75 mm long, in which spermatozoa develop.—**testicular,** *adj.*

test method, a method chosen for experimental testing or study by means of method evaluation.

test of patency of tear duct, a procedure in which drops of a weak sugar solution are placed in the eye. If the patient then detects a sweet taste, the tear duct is assumed open.

testolactone /tes′təlak′tōn/, an antineoplastic androgen analog. It is prescribed as palliative treatment of advanced postmenopausal breast cancer and in premenopausal women whose ovarian function has been terminated.

testosterone /testos′tərōn/, a naturally occurring androgenic hormone prescribed for androgen deficiency, for female breast cancer, and for stimulation of growth, weight gain, and RBC production.

testosterone cypionate, a long-acting form of testosterone.

testosterone enanthate, a long-acting form of testosterone.

testosterone propionate, an androgen given intramuscularly.

testosterone test, a blood test that detects levels of circulating testosterone in men and women. It may be used to evaluate ambiguous sex characteristics, precocious puberty, virilizing syndromes in the female, and infertility in the male.

test tube, a thin glass container with one open end and one closed end. It is used in many common laboratory procedures.

test tube baby, a popular term for an infant conceived through in vitro fertilization, using an ovum removed from the mother. After fertilization the zygote is transplanted to the mother's uterus to develop normally.

TET, 1. abbreviation for *treadmill exercise test*. **2.** abbreviation for **tubal embryo transfer**.

tetanic contraction [Gk, *tetanos*, extreme tension; L, *contractio*, drawing together], a condition of continuous contraction in a voluntary muscle caused by a steady stream of efferent nerve impulses.

tetanus /tet′ənəs/ [Gk, *tetanos*, extreme tension], an acute, potentially fatal infection of the CNS caused by an exotoxin, tetanospasmin, elaborated by the anaerobic bacillus, *Clostridium tetani*. The bacillus is a common resident of the superficial layers of the soil and a normal inhabitant of the intestinal tracts of cows and horses. The toxin is a neurotoxin and one of the most lethal poisons known. *C. tetani* infects only wounds that contain dead tissue. The bacillus may enter the body through a puncture wound, abrasion, laceration, or burn; via the uterus into the bloodstream in septic abortion or postpartum sepsis; or through the stump of the umbilical cord of the newborn. The infection occurs in two clinical forms: one with an abrupt onset, high mortality, and a short incubation period (3 to 21 days); the other with less severe symptoms, a lower mortality, and a longer incubation period (4 to 5 weeks). Wounds of the face, head, and neck are the ones most likely to result in fatal infection. The disease is characterized by irritability, headache, fever, and painful spasms of the muscles resulting in lockjaw, risus sardonicus, opisthotonos, and laryngeal spasm; eventually every muscle of the body is in tonic spasm. The motor nerves transmit the impulses from the infected CNS to the muscles. There is no lesion; even at autopsy no organic lesion is seen and the CSF is clear and normal. Prompt and thorough cleansing and debridement of the wound are essential for prophylaxis. A booster shot of tetanus toxoid is given to previously immunized people; tetanus immune globulin and a series of three injections of tetanus toxoid are given to those not immunized. People who are known to have been adequately immunized within 5 years do not usually require immunization.

tetanus and diphtheria toxoids (Td), an active immunizing agent containing detoxified tetanus and diphtheria toxoids that slowly produce an antigenic response to the diseases. It is used for prophlaxis when treating wounds and is the preferred method for immunization against tetanus and diphtheria in adults and children over 7 years of age. Younger children should be treated with diphtheria, pertussis, and tetanus trivalent vaccine.

tetanus antitoxin (TAT), a tetanus immune serum that neutralizes exotoxins in tetanus infection. It is prescribed for short-term immunization against tetanus after possible exposure to the organism and in tetanus treatment.

tetanus immune globulin (TIG), an injectable solution prepared from the globulin of an immune human. It is effective and much safer than tetanus antitoxin. It is prescribed for short-term immunization against tetanus after possible exposure to the organism and for tetanus treatment.

tetanus toxin, the potent exotoxin produced by *Clostridium tetani*, consisting of two components, one a neurotoxin *(tetanospasmin)* and the other a hemolysin *(tetanolysin)*.

tetanus toxoid, an active immunizing agent prepared from detoxified tetanus toxin that produces an antigenic response in the body, conferring permanent immunity to tetanus infection. It is prescribed for primary active immunization against tetanus, generally in combination with diphtheria and pertussis vaccines.

tetany /tet′ənē/ [Gk, *tetanos*, extreme tension], a condition characterized by cramps, convulsions, twitching of the muscles, and sharp flexion of the wrist and ankle joints. These symptoms are sometimes accompanied by attacks of stridor. Tetany is a manifestation of an abnormality in calcium metabolism, which can occur in association with vitamin D deficiency, hypoparathyroidism, alkalosis, or the ingestion of alkaline salts.

tetrabasic /tet′rəbā′sik/, **1.** describing a compound that has four acidic hydrogen atoms replaced by metal ions. **2.** an alcohol containing four hydroxyl groups.

tetracaine hydrochloride, a local anesthetic used for spinal nerve blockage and topical anesthesia.

tetrachloroethane /-klôr′ō·eth′ān/, a potentially toxic solvent with a sweet, chloroform-like odor. It is used to dissolve fats, waxes, oils, and resins and in the manufacture of paints, varnishes, and rust removers. Symptoms of overexposure include nausea, vomiting, abdominal pain, finger tremors, skin disorders, and liver damage.

tetracycline hydrochloride, an antibiotic prescribed in the treatment of bacterial infections.

tetrad /tet′rad/ [Gk, *tetra*, four], a group of four chromatids of a synapsed pair of homologous chromosomes during the first meiotic prophase of gametogenesis. **—tetradic,** *adj*.

tetradactyly /-dak′tilē/ [Gk, *tetra* + *dactylos*], the presence of only four fingers on each hand or four toes on each foot (quadridigitate).

T

tetraethyl lead /tet′rə·eth′il led/, a potentially toxic, anti-knock gasoline additive. Effects of overexposure include insomnia, lassitude, anxiety, nausea, tremor, pallor, hypothermia, anorexia, and psychosis.

tetrahydrobiopterin /′tet′rəhī′drōbī′op′tər in/, a compound related to folic acid, which functions as a coenzyme in the reactions hydroxylating phenylalanine, tryptophan, and tyrosine by carrying electrons to oxygen. Defects in its biosynthesis or regeneration affect all three hydroxylation reactions, interfere with production of the corresponding neurotransmitter precursors, and result in malignant hyperphenylalaninemia.

tetrahydrocannabinol (THC) /-hi′drōk ənab′inol/, the active principle, occurring as two psychotomimetic isomers, in the hemp plant *Cannabis sativa*, used in the preparation of marijuana, hashish, bhang, and ganja. THC increases pulse rate and has variable effects on BP. It causes conjunctival reddening and a feeling of euphoria. The drug affects memory, cognition, and the sensorium; decreases motor coordination; and increases appetite. Nonintoxicating doses of THC are used experimentally in the treatment of glaucoma and to relieve nausea and increase the appetite in patients receiving cancer chemotherapy.

tetrahydrozoline hydrochloride /-hīdroz′ əlēn/, an adrenergic vasoconstrictor. It is prescribed for the treatment of nasal and nasopharyngeal congestion and as an ophthalmic vasoconstrictor.

tetralogy /tetrol′əjē/ [Gk, *tetra,* four, *logos,* word], any group of four writings, symptoms, or other related factors.

tetralogy of Fallot /falō′/ [Gk, *tetra,* four, *logos,* word; Etienne-Louis A. Fallot, French physician, 1850–1911], a congenital cardiac anomaly that consists of four defects: pulmonary stenosis, ventricular septal defect, malposition of the aorta so that it arises from the septal defect or the right ventricle, and right ventricular hypertrophy. The primary symptoms in the infant are cyanosis, hypoxia, difficulty in feeding, failure to gain weight, and poor development. Treatment consists mainly of supportive measures and palliative surgical procedures until the child is old enough to tolerate total corrective surgery.

tetramer /tet′rəmer/ [Gk, *tetra* + *meros,* part], something that is composed of four parts, such as a protein composed of four polypeptide subunits.

tetraodon poisoning, a reaction caused by a toxin in puffer fish and marine sunfish. It may result in myalgia, paresthesia, and other neuromuscular disorders. Death may result from respiratory paralysis.

tetraparesis /tet′rə·pərē′sis/ [Gk, *tetra,* four, *paresis,* relaxation], muscular weakness affecting all four extremities.

tetrapeptide /-pep′tīd/, a compound formed by four amino acids united by peptide links.

tetraplegia, paralysis of the arms, legs, and trunk of the body below the level of an associated injury to the spinal cord. This disorder is usually caused by spinal cord injury, especially in the area of the fifth to the seventh vertebrae. Automobile accidents and sporting mishaps are common causes. Signs and symptoms commonly include flaccidity of the arms and the legs and the loss of power and sensation below the level of the injury. Cardiovascular complications also may develop from any injury that damages the spinal cord above the fifth cervical vertebra. A major cause of death from such injury is respiratory failure. Other symptoms may include low body temperature, bradycardia, impaired peristalsis, and autonomic dysreflexia. Diagnosis is based on a complete physical and neurologic examination with radiographic pictures of the head, chest, and abdomen to rule out underlying injuries. Spinal x-ray examinations and CT scores and MRI are usually done to evaluate the extent of the injury.

tetraploid **(4n)** /tet′rəploid/ [Gk, *tetraploos,* fourfold, *eidos,* form], **1.** an individual, organism, strain, or cell that has four complete sets of chromosomes, quadruple the haploid number characteristic of the species. **2.** pertaining to such an individual, organism, strain, or cell.—**tetraploidy,** *n.*

tetraploidy /tet′rəploi′dē/, the state or condition of having four complete sets of chromosomes.

tetrasaccharide /-sak′ərīd/, a sugar containing four molecules of monosaccharide.

tetrascelus /tetras′ēləs/, a fetal anomaly with four legs.

tetravalent /-vā′lənt/, pertaining to a chemical with a valency of four.

tetrodotoxism /tet′rō-dō-tok′sizm/, the most severe form of fish poisoning, caused by ingestion of inadequately prepared fish that contain tetrodotoxin. Within minutes, symptoms of malaise, dizziness, and tingling about the mouth appear, which may be followed by ataxia, convulsions, respiratory paralysis, and death.

TF, abbreviation for **transfer factor.**

TFIIE, a general transcription factor involved in complementary DNA encoding. TFIIE consists of two subunits, TFIIE-alpha and TFIIE-beta.

T fracture /tē frak′chər/, an intercondylar fracture in which the fracture lines are T-shaped.

TGC, abbreviation for **time gain compensation.**

TGF, abbreviation for **transforming growth factor.**

TGs, abbreviation for **triglycerides test.**

Th, symbol for the element **thorium.**

THA, abbreviation for **total hip arthroplasty.**

thalamic /thalam′ik/ [Gk, *thalamos,* chamber], pertaining to the thalamus.

thalamic peduncle [Gk, *thalamos,* chamber; L, *pes,* foot], a group of fibers linking the thalamus with the hypothalamus.

thalamic syndrome [Gk, *thalamos* + *syn,* together, *dromos,* course], a vascular disorder involving the ventral and posterolateral nuclei of the thalamus and related nerve fibers. It causes disturbances of sensation and partial or complete paralysis of one side of the body. A major effect is an increased threshold to all stimuli on the opposite side of the body so that any stimuli may cause an exaggerated response.

thalamotomy /thal′əmot′əmē/, the surgical production of lesions within the nuclei of the thalamus, generally performed to treat diseases of the basal ganglia.

thalamus /thal′əməs/ *pl.* **thalami** [Gk, *thalamos,* chamber], one of a pair of large oval nervous structures made of gray matter and forming most of the lateral walls of the third ventricle of the brain and part of the diencephalon. It relays sensory information, excluding smell, to the cerebral cortex. It is composed mainly of gray substance and translates impulses from appropriate receptors into crude sensations of pain, temperature, and touch. It also participates in associating sensory impulses with pleasant and unpleasant feelings, in the arousal mechanisms of the body, and in the mechanisms that produce complex reflex movements.—**thalamic,** *adj.*

thalassemia /thal′əsē′mē·ə/ [Gk, *thalassa,* sea, *a* + *haima,* without blood], production and hemolytic anemia characterized by microcytic, hypochromic red blood cells. Thalassemia is caused by inherited deficiency of alpha- or beta-globin synthesis.

thalassotherapy /thalas′ōther′əpē/ [Gk, *thalassa,* sea], a treatment system based on sea bathing and exposure to sea air.

thalidomide /thalid′əmīd/, a sedative-hypnotic sometimes prescribed for the treatment of leprosy. It is never given to women who are or who might become pregnant.

thallium (Tl) /thal′ē·əm/ [Gk, *thallos,* green line], a soft, bluish-white metallic element that exhibits some nonmetallic chemical properties. Its atomic number is 81, and its atomic mass is 204.38. Many of its compounds are highly toxic.

thallium poisoning, a toxic condition caused by the ingestion or absorption through the skin of thallium salts, especially thallium sulfate. Characteristic of the condition are abdominal pain, vomiting, bloody diarrhea, tremor, delirium, and alopecia.

thanatology /than′ətol′əjē/ [Gk, *thanatos,* death, *logos,* science], the study of death and dying.—**thanatologist,** *n.*

thanatomania /than′ətōmā′nē·ə/ [Gk, *thanatos,* death, *mania,* frenzy], an obsession with death, dying, or suicide.

thanatophoric dwarf /than′ətōfôr′ik/ [Gk, *thanatos* + *phoros,* bearer; AS, *dweorge*], an infant with severe micromelia, the limbs usually extending straight out from the trunk, an extremely narrow chest, and flattened vertebral bodies with wide intervertebral spaces.

Thanatos /than′ətəs/ [Gk, death], a freudian term for the death instinct.

THC, abbreviation for **tetrahydrocannabinol.**

theater /thē′ətər/, **1.** an OR or suite of rooms. **2.** a large room used for lectures and demonstrations.

thebesian foramen /thəbē′zē·ən, tābā′zē·ən/ [Adam C. Thebesius, German physician, 1686–1732], any of the openings of the vena cordis minima into the right atrium.

thebesian vein [Adam C. Thebesius], any of the smallest cardiac veins.

theca /thē′kə/ *pl.* **thecae,** a sheath or capsule such as the theca cordis or pericardium.

theca cells, theca-lutein cells, lutein cells derived from the theca interna.

theca cell tumor [Gk, *theke,* sheath; L, *cella,* storeroom; *tumor,* swelling], an uncommon benign fibroid tumor of the ovary, composed of theca cells and usually containing granulosa (follicular) cells.

thecal /thē′kəl/ [Gk, *theke,* sheath], pertaining to a theca or sheath.

thecoma, a tumor derived from ovarian mesenchyme, consisting of spindle-shaped cells that may contain fat droplets. It is sometimes associated with excessive estrogen production and precocious sexual development in prepubertal girls.

Theden's bandage /tā′dənz/ [Johann C.A. Theden, German surgeon, 1714–1797], a roller bandage applied below the injury and continued upward over a compress, used to stop bleeding.

thelarche /thilär′kē/ [Gk, *thele,* nipple, *archaios,* beginning], the beginning of female pubertal breast development normally occurring between 9 and 13 years of age. Premature thelarche is precocious breast development in a female without other evidence of sexual maturation.

thenar /thē′när/ [Gk, palm of the hand], pertaining to any structure in relation to the ball of the thumb.

thenar eminence [Gk, *thenar*, palm of the hand; L, *eminentia*, projection], a raised fleshy area on the palm of the hand near the base of the thumb.

theobroma oil /thē′ōbrō′mə/, a liquid fat derived from seeds of *Theobroma cacao*, the cocoa plant. It contains a number of fatty acids used in suppositories, ointments, and lubricants.

theobromine /thē′əbrō′min/, a substance (methylxanthine) that is related chemically to caffeine and theophylline but differs from them by the number and distribution of methyl groups. Theobromine occurs naturally in cocoa, cola nuts, and tea. It acts as a diuretic, vasodilator, cardiac stimulant, and smooth muscle relaxant.

Theolair, a trademark for a bronchodilator (theophylline).

theophylline /thē′əfil′ēn/ [L, *thea*, tea; Gk, *phyllon*, leaf], a bronchodilator. It can be prescribed for oral administration to relax the smooth muscle of the bronchial passages in the treatment of bronchospasm in bronchial asthma, bronchitis, and emphysema. Its use has tapered sharply due to the availability of safer and more effective asthma medications that can be administered by inhalation.

theorem /thē′ərəm/ [Gk, *theorein*, to look at], 1. a proposition to be proved by a chain of reasoning and analysis. 2. a rule expressed by symbols or formulae.

theoretic effectiveness /thē′əret′ik/ [Gk, *theorein*; L, *efficere*, to do], of a contraceptive method, the effectiveness of a medication, device, or method in preventing pregnancy if used consistently and exactly as intended, without error.

theoretic plate number (N), a number defining the efficiency of a chromatographic column.

theories of aging, theories proposed to explain aging and death of cells and organisms. They are generally divided into two major groupings. The first group consists of programmed causes, with timed functional changes, and is generally based on genetic theories. The second group, called stochastic theories, consists of theories based on random events occurring over time and includes free radical generation, gradual wear and tear, mutation over time, and differences in metabolic rate.

theory /thē′ərē/ [Gk, *theorein*, to look at], an abstract statement formulated to predict, explain, or describe the relationships among concepts, constructs, or events. Theory is developed and tested by observation and research, using factual data.

theotherapy /thē′ōther′əpē/ [Gk, *theos*, god, *therapeia*, treatment], a therapeutic approach to the prevention, diagnosis, and treatment of disease and dysfunction based on religious or spiritual beliefs.

therapeutic /ther′əpyōō′tik/ [Gk, *therapeuein*, to treat], 1. beneficial. 2. pertaining to a treatment.

therapeutic abortion, 1. a termination of early pregnancy deemed necessary by a physician. 2. informal. any legal induced abortion.

therapeutic communication, a process in which the nurse consciously influences a client or helps the client to a better understanding through verbal or nonverbal communication. Therapeutic communication involves the use of specific strategies that encourage the patient to express feelings and ideas and that convey acceptance and respect.

therapeutic community (TC), in mental health, a treatment facility in which the entire milieu is part of the treatment. The physical environment, the other clients, the staff, and the policies of the facility influence the function of the individual in the ADL in the community.

therapeutic dose [Gk, *therapeia*, treatment, *dosis*, giving], the dose that may be required to produce a desired effect.

therapeutic drug monitoring test (TDM), a blood test that entails taking measurements of blood drug levels to determine effective drug dosages and to prevent toxicity. It is also used to identify noncompliant patients.

therapeutic equivalent, a drug that has essentially the same effect in the treatment of a disease or condition as one or more other drugs.

therapeutic exercise, any exercise planned and performed to attain a specific physical benefit, such as maintenance of the ROM, strengthening of weakened muscles, increased joint flexibility, or improved cardiovascular and respiratory function.

therapeutic gain, the ratio of the biologic effect of a therapy on a tumor compared with the effect on surrounding normal tissue.

therapeutic index (TI), the difference between the minimum therapeutic and minimum toxic concentrations of a drug.

therapeutic play, a nursing intervention from the Nursing Interventions Classification (NIC) defined as purposeful and directive use of toys or other materials to assist children in communicating their perception and knowledge of their world and to help in gaining mastery of their environment.

therapeutic pneumothorax [Gk, *therapeia*, treatment, *pneuma*, air, *thorax*], the intentional introduction of air into the pleural space, causing partial collapse of a lung. It was used in the 1940s for treatment of certain cases of TB.

therapeutic radiopharmaceutical, a radioactive drug administered to a patient to deliver radiation to body tissues internally. Examples are iodine-131, which is used to ablate thyroid tissue in hyperthyroid patients and strontium-90, which is implanted in a sealed source for the treatment of malignancies.

therapeutic recreation, an allied health group, staffed by people with expertise in organizing and supervising recreational activities designed to accelerate recovery from mental or physical disorders.

therapeutic recreation specialist, a person who assists patients in their recovery or rehabilitation after physical or emotional illness or disability by planning and supervising recreation programs.

therapeutics /ther′əpyoo′tiks/ [Gk, *therapeia,* treatment], a branch of health care that is concerned with the treatment of disease, seeking to relieve symptoms or produce a cure.

therapeutic temperature, in hyperthermia treatment, temperatures between 107° and 113° F (42° and 45° C).

therapeutic touch (TT)[1], a healing method based on the premise that the body possesses an energy field that can be affected by the focused intention of the healer, using a consciously directed exchange of energy between practitioner and patient. The practitioner uses the hands as a focus to assess the patient's energy field, to release areas where the free flow of energy is blocked, and to balance the patient's energy by transferring energy from a universal life energy force to the patient.

therapeutic touch[2], a nursing intervention from the Nursing Interventions Classification (NIC) defined as attuning to the universal healing field, seeking to act as an instrument for healing influence, and using the natural sensitivity of the hands to gently focus and direct the intervention process.

therapist /ther′əpist/, a person with special skills, obtained through education and experience, in one or more areas of health care.

therapy /ther′əpē/ [Gk, *therapeia,* treatment], the treatment of any disease or a pathologic condition.

therapy group, a nursing intervention from the Nursing Interventions Classification (NIC) defined as application of psychotherapeutic techniques to a group, including the utilization of interactions between members of the group.

thermal /thur′məl/ [Gk, *thermē,* heat], pertaining to the production, application, or maintenance of heat.

thermal biofeedback, the monitoring of skin temperature as an index of blood flow changes due to the dilatation and constriction of blood vessels. Feedback is displayed to the patient on a video monitor, accompanied by an audible signal. It is used for stress management and in the treatment of Raynaud's disease, hypertension, and migraine.

thermal burn, tissue injury, usually of the skin, caused by exposure to extreme heat.

thermal field size, the area over which therapeutic heating is likely to be produced.

thermalgesia /thur′məljē′zhə/ [Gk, *thermē,* heat, *algos,* pain], pain caused by exposure to high temperatures.

thermalgia /thurmal′jə/, a sensation of intense burning pain sometimes experienced following nerve injuries.

thermal radiation [Gk, *thermē,* heat; L, *radiare,* to shine], the emission of energy in the form of heat.

thermic sense /thur′mik/ [Gk, *thermē,* heat; L, *sentire,* to feel], the network of sense organs and connecting pathways that allow an appreciation of temperature changes.

thermionic emission /ther′mī·on′ik/, the emission of electrons and ions by incandescent bodies.

thermistor /thərmis′tər/ [Gk, *thermē;* L, *resistere,* to withstand], a kind of thermometer for measuring minute changes in temperature.

thermocautery /thur′mōkô′tərē/ [Gk, *thermē + kauterion,* branding iron], the use of a needle or snare heated by direct flame, a heated hydrocarbon vapor, or an electric current in the destruction of tissue.

thermochemistry /-kem′istrē/ [Gk, *thermē,* heat, *chemia,* alchemy], a branch of chemistry that is concerned with the heat changes involved in chemical reactions.

thermocoagulation /-kō·ag′yəlā′shən/ [Gk, *thermē,* heat; L, *coagulare*], the use of high-frequency electric currents to destroy tissue through heat coagulation.

thermocouple /thur′məkup′əl/ [Gk, *thermē;* Fr, *couple,* pair], a temperature-measuring device that relies on the production of a temperature-dependent voltage at the junction of two dissimilar metals.

thermodilution /-dilyoo′zhən/, a method of cardiac output determination. A bolus of solution of known volume and temperature is injected into the right atrium, and the resultant change in blood temperature is detected by a thermistor previously placed in the pulmonary artery with a catheter.

thermodynamics /-dīnam′iks/ [Gk, *thermē,* heat, *dynamis,* power], the science of the interconversion of heat and work.

thermogenesis /thur′mōjen′əsis/ [Gk, *thermē + genesis,* origin], production of heat, especially by the cells of the body. —**thermogenetic,** *adj.*

T

thermograph /thur'məgraf/ [Gk, *thermē* + *graphein*, to record], **1.** a photographic record of the amount of heat radiated from the surface of the body, revealing "hot spots" of potential tumors or other disorders. **2.** a device consisting of a thermometer, inked stylus, and chart for continuous recording of the ambient temperature.

thermography /thərmog'rəfē/, a technique for sensing and recording on film hot and cold areas of the body by means of an infrared detector that reacts to blood flow. —**thermographic**, *adj.*

thermointegrator /thur'mō·in'təgrā'tər/, an instrument used to create a thermal model of an environment, measuring the warmth and coldness as it might be experienced by a living organism in that environment.

thermokeratoplasty /-ker'ətōplas'tē/, a procedure to correct myopia by applying heat to flatten the cornea. The heat shrinks the collagen in the substantia propria layer of the cornea.

thermolabile /thur'məlā'bəl/ [Gk, *thermē*; L, *labilis*, slipping], easily destroyed or altered by heat.

thermoluminescent dosimetry /-lōō'mines'ənt/ [Gk, *thermē*; L, *lumen*, light; Gk, *dosis*, something given, *metron*, measure], a method of measuring the ionizing radiation to which a person is exposed by means of a device that contains a radiation-sensitive crystalline material.

thermomassage /-məsäzh'/, a physical therapy technique that combines heat and massage.

thermometer /thermom'ətər/ [Gk, *thermē* + *metron*, measure], an instrument for measuring temperature. Originally, it consisted of a sealed glass tube marked in degrees of Celsius or Fahrenheit and containing liquid such as mercury or alcohol. The liquid rises or falls as it expands or contracts according to changes in temperature.

thermoneutral environment /-nōō'trəl/ [Gk, *thermē*; L, *neutralis*, neutral; ME, *environ*, around], **1.** an environment that keeps body temperature at an optimum point at which the least amount of oxygen is consumed for metabolism. **2.** an environment that enables a neonate to maintain a body temperature of 97.7° F (36.5° C) with a minimal requirement of energy and oxygen.

thermonuclear /-nōō'klē·ər/ [Gk, *thermē*, heat; L, *nucleus*, nut kernel], pertaining to a reaction in which isotopes of hydrogen (protium, deuterium, or tritium) can be fused at temperatures of nearly 100,000,000° C into heavier nuclei of helium atoms. The process is the source of energy of the sun and is used in the explosion of thermonuclear weapons.

thermopenetration /-pen'ətrā'shən/ [Gk, *thermē*; L, *penetrale*, passing through], the use of diathermic techniques to produce warmth within the body tissues for therapeutic purposes.

thermophilic /-fil'ik/ [Gk, *thermē*, heat, *philein*, to love], pertaining to organisms that thrive in very hot environments (for example, up to 80° C for some bacteria that live in hot springs).

thermophore /thur'məfôr/, a procedure in which heat is applied locally to a body part.

thermoplastic /ther'mō·plas'tik/ [Gk, *thermē*, heat, *plassein*, to mold], softening under heat and capable of being molded into shape with pressure, and then hardening on cooling without undergoing chemical change.

thermoradiotherapy /-rā'dē·ōther'əpē/, a therapeutic process that applies ionizing radiation to any part of the body in which the temperature has been raised by artificial means.

thermoreceptor /-risep'tər/ [Gk, *thermē*, heat; L, *recipere*, to receive], nerve endings that are sensitive to heat or a rise in body temperature.

thermoregulation¹ /-reg'yəlā'shən/ [Gk, *thermē*; L, *regula*, rule], the control of heat production and heat loss, specifically the maintenance of body temperature through physiologic mechanisms activated by the hypothalamus.

thermoregulation², a nursing outcome from the Nursing Outcomes Classification (NOC) defined as balance among heat production, heat gain, and heat loss.

thermoregulation: newborn, a nursing outcome from the Nursing Outcomes Classification (NOC) defined as balance among heat production, heat gain, and heat loss during the first 28 days of life.

thermoregulatory center /-reg'yəlatôr'ē/ [Gk, *thermē*, heat; L, *regula*, rule; Gk, *kentron*, center], one of several centers located in the hypothalamus concerned mainly with the regulation of heat production, heat inhibition, and heat conservation to maintain a normal body temperature.

thermoresistance /-rizis'təns/, an ability to tolerate heat, as in certain thermophilic bacteria.

thermosetting /-set'ing/ [Gk, *thermē*, heat; AS, *settan*, to set], of resins, becoming hard or solid when heat is applied and remaining that way on being cooled; the change is not reversible.

thermostable /-stā'bəl/, unaffected by or resistant to change by an increase in temperature.

thermostasis /-stā'sis/, maintenance of a stable body temperature, as in mammals and birds.

thermostat /thur′məstat/ [Gk, *thermē* + *statos,* standing], a device for the automatic control of a heating or cooling system.—**thermostatic,** *adj.*

thermotaxis /-tak′sis/ [Gk, *thermē* + *taxis,* arrangement], **1.** the normal adjustment and regulation of body temperature. **2.** the movement of an organism in response to heat, either toward the stimulus (positive thermotaxis) or away from the stimulus (negative thermotaxis).

thermotherapeutic penetration /-ther′əp yōō′tik/, the depth to which heating to therapeutic temperatures is likely to extend.

thermotherapy /-ther′əpē/ [Gk, *thermē* + *therapeia,* treatment], the treatment of disease by the application of heat. Thermotherapy may be administered as dry heat with heat lamps, diathermy machines, electric pads, or hot water bottles or as moist heat with warm compresses or immersion in warm water.—**thermotherapeutic,** *adj.*

thermotropism, moving toward a source of heat.

theta /thē′tə, thā′tə/, Θ, θ, the eighth letter of the Greek alphabet.

theta wave [Gk, *theta,* eighth letter of Greek alphabet; AS, *wafian*], one of the several types of brain waves, characterized by a relatively low frequency of 4 to 7 Hz and a low amplitude of 10 μV. Theta waves are the "drowsy waves" of the temporal lobes of the brain.

thiabendazole /thī′əben′dəzōl/, an anthelmintic with antiinflammatory, antipyretic, and analgesic effects. It can be prescribed in the treatment of a range of worm infestations, including hookworms, roundworms, and pinworms, and until recently was the drug of choice for threadworms. Other drugs have fewer adverse effects.

thiaminase /thī·am′inās/, an enzyme present in raw fish that destroys thiamine. A diet containing a substantial amount of raw fish could result in a thiamin deficiency because of the enzyme.

thiamine /thī′əmin/ [Gk, *theion,* containing sulfur, *amine,* ammonia], a water-soluble, crystalline compound of the B vitamin complex, essential for normal metabolism and health of the cardiovascular and nervous systems. Thiamine plays a key role in the metabolic breakdown of glucose to yield energy in body tissues. It is not stored in the body and must be supplied daily. A deficiency of thiamine affects chiefly the nervous system, the circulation, and the GI tract. Symptoms include irritability, emotional disturbances, loss of appetite, multiple neuritis, increased pulse rate, dyspnea, reduced intestinal motility, and heart irregularities. Severe deficiency causes beriberi.

thiazide diuretics, a group of diuretics in the thiazide family. They decrease reabsorption of sodium by the kidney and thereby increase loss of water and sodium. They also increase urinary secretion of chloride, potassium, and to some extent bicarbonate ions. These are the most frequently prescribed diuretics because they are moderately potent and have relatively few side effects.

thiazine-eosinate stain, any of a group of neutral stains used in hematology and histology that combine an eosin dye, usually eosin Y, as the anionic component and one or more thiazine dyes as the cationic component.

thiemia /thī·ē′mē·ə/ [Gk, *theion,* sulfur, *haima,* blood], an excess of sulfur in the blood.

thiethylperazine /thī′eth′ilper′əzēn/, a phenothiazine antiemetic prescribed to control nausea and vomiting.

thiethylperazine malate, the malate salt of thiethylperazine, having the same actions and uses as the base.

thiethylperazine maleate, the maleate salt of thiethylperazine, having the same actions and uses as the base.

thigh [AS, *theoh*], the section of the lower limb between the hip and the knee.

thinking [AS, *thencan,* to think], **1.** the cognitive process of forming mental images or concepts. **2.** the process of cognitive problem solving through the sorting, organizing, and classification of facts.

thin-layer chromatography (TLC), a method of separating two or more chemical compounds in a solution through their differential migrations across a thin layer of adsorbent spread over a glass or plastic plate.

thioamide derivative /thī′ō·am′īd/, one of a group of antithyroid drugs prescribed in the treatment of hyperthyroidism. They act by inhibiting the synthesis of thyroid hormone.

thiobarbituric acid /thī′obahr′bitu′rik/, a compound that differs from barbituric acid only by the presence of a sulfur atom instead of an oxygen atom at the number 2 carbon. It is the parent compound of a class of drugs, the thiobarbiturates.

thioctic acid /thī·ok′tik/, a pyruvate oxidation factor found in liver and yeast, used in bacterial culture media.

thioester /-es′tər/, an important group of biologic chemicals formed by the hydrosulfides (or mercaptans or thiols) and carboxylic acids and identified by a bond between the acyl carbonyl carbon and the thiol sulfur.

thioethanolamine acetyltransferase /-eth′ənol′əmin/, an enzyme that catalyzes the transfer of acetyl groups from acetyl CoA to the sulfur atom of thioethanolamine, producing CoA and S-acetylthioethanolamine.

thioflavine T /-flā′vin/, a yellow dye used as a fluorochrome in histopathology.

thioguanine /-gwä′nēn/, a purine analog, an antineoplastic that acts as an antimetabolite. It is prescribed in the treatment of a variety of malignant neoplastic diseases, especially acute and chronic myelogenous leukemias.

thiopental sodium /-pen′təl/, a widely used, potent, and ultrashort-acting barbiturate used as a general anesthetic induction agent. It has no analgesic properties and therefore must be supplemented by analgesics.

thioridazine hydrochloride /-rid′əzēn/, a phenothiazine antipsychotic. It is prescribed in the treatment of schizophrenia when patients failed to respond to other therapies and in the management of nonpsychotic behavioral disturbances, senility, alcohol withdrawal, and organic brain disease.

thiotepa /-tep′ə/, an antineoplastic alkylating agent prescribed in the treatment of malignant neoplastic diseases, including adenocarcinoma of the breast and ovary, and urinary bladder carcinomas.

thiothixene /-thī′ksēn/, a thioxanthene antipsychotic prescribed in the treatment of acute agitation and mild-to-severe psychotic disorders.

thiouracil /-yŏŏr′əsil/ [Gk, *theion,* sulfur, *ouron,* urine], a chemical compound derived from thiourea that inhibits the formation of thyroxine in the thyroid gland and is used to treat hyperthyroidism.

thioxanthene derivative /-ksan′thēn/, any one of a group of antipsychotic drugs, each of which is similar to the phenothiazines in indication, action, and adverse effects.

third-degree burn, a burn that destroys both the epidermis and the dermis, often also involving the subcutaneous tissue.

third-party reimbursement, reimbursement for services rendered to a person in which an entity other than the receiver of the service is responsible for the payment.

third stage of labor, the expulsion of the placenta, membranes, and a small amount of blood and amniotic fluid, occurring within 5 to 30 minutes after delivery of the fetus.

third ventricle [Gk, *triotus,* below second rank; L, *ventriculus,* little belly], a cavity of the brain bounded on each side by a thalamus and the hypothalamus. It communicates anteriorly with the lateral ventricles and posteriorly with the aqueduct of the midbrain.

third ventriculostomy /ventrik′yəlos′t əmē/ [L, *tertius,* three, *ventriculus,* little belly; Gk, *stoma,* mouth], a surgical procedure for draining CSF into the cisterna

chiasmatis of the subarachnoid space to correct an obstructive type of hydrocephalus, usually in the newborn. It involves an opening on the anterior wall of the floor of the third ventricle into the interpeduncular cistern.

thirst /thurst/ [AS, *Thurst*], a perceived desire for water or other fluid. The sensation of thirst is usually referred to the mouth and throat.

Thiry-Vella fistula /thī′rē vel′ə/ [Ludwig Thiry, Austrian physiologist, 1817–1897; Luis Vella, Italian physiologist, 1825–1886], an artificial passage from the abdominal surface of an experimental animal to an isolated intestinal loop, created surgically for the study of intestinal secretions.

thixotropy /thiksot′rəpē/ [Gk, *this,* touch, *terpin,* to turn], a property of certain gels or colloids that become less viscous when shaken or agitated but revert to their original viscosity after standing.

Thomas' splint [Hugh O. Thomas, English surgeon, 1834–1891], **1.** a rigid splint constructed of steel bars that are curved to fit the involved limb and are held in place by a cast or a rigid bandage. **2.** a rigid metal splint that extends from a ring at the hip to beyond the foot.

thoracentesis /thôr′əsentē′sis/ [Gk, *thorax* + *centesis,* puncture], the surgical perforation of the chest wall and pleural space with a needle to aspirate fluid for diagnostic or therapeutic purposes or to remove a specimen for biopsy.

thoracic, pertaining to the thorax.

thoracic aorta [Gk, *thorax,* chest, *aerein,* to raise], the large upper part of the ascending arch and descending aorta, starting at the lower border of the fourth thoracic vertebra, dividing into seven branches, and supplying many parts of the body such as the heart, ribs, chest muscles, and stomach.

thoracic cage [Gk, *thorax,* chest; L, *cavus,* hollow], the bony framework that surrounds the organs and soft tissues of the chest. It consists of 12 thoracic vertebrae, 12 pairs of ribs, and the sternum.

thoracic cavity [Gk, *thorax,* chest; L, *cavum,* cavity], the cavity enclosed by the ribs, the thoracic part of the vertebral column, the sternum, the diaphragm, and associated muscles.

thoracic constriction of esophagus, a narrowing of the thoracic esophagus where it is compressed by the aortic arch and the left main bronchus.

thoracic duct, the common trunk of all the lymphatic vessels in the body, except those on the right side of the head, the neck, and the thorax; the right upper limb; the right lung; the right side of the heart; and the diaphragmatic surface of the liver.

thoracic fistula, an abnormal opening in the chest wall that ends blindly or communicates with the thoracic cavity.

thoracic kyphosis, the dorsally convex curve formed by the thoracic spinal column when seen from the side.

thoracic medicine, the branch of medicine concerned with the diagnosis and treatment of disorders of the structures and organs of the chest, especially the lungs.

thoracic nerves, the 12 pairs of spinal nerves emerging from the spinal cord at the level of the thorax, including 11 intercostal nerves and one subcostal nerve. They are distributed mainly to the walls of the thorax and the abdomen.

thoracic outlet syndrome, an abnormal condition and a type of mononeuropathy characterized by paresthesia. It may be caused by a nerve root compression by a cervical disk.

thoracic parietal node, one of the lymph glands in the thorax, associated with various lymphatic vessels and divided into sternal nodes, intercostal nodes, and diaphragmatic nodes.

thoracic spine, that part of the spine comprising the thoracic vertebrae.

thoracic surgery [Gk, *thorax,* chest, *cheirourgia,* surgery], the branch of medicine that deals with disease and injuries of the thoracic area by manipulative and operative methods.

thoracic vertebra, one of the 12 bony segments of the spinal column of the upper back designated T1 to T12. T1 is just below the seventh cervical vertebra (C7), and T12 is just above the first lumbar vertebra (L1). The thoracic part of the spine is flexible and has a concave ventral curvature. The thoracic vertebrae are unique in having small lateral facets for articulation with the ribs.

thoracic visceral node, a node in the three groups of lymph nodes connected to the part of the lymphatic system that serves certain structures within the thorax such as the liver, sternum, thymus, pericardium, esophagus, trachea, lungs, diaphragm, and bronchi.

thoracic wall, the musculoskeletal wall of the thorax, consisting of the 12 thoracic vertebrae, the ribs, and the sternum, as well as the intercostal muscles, the subcostales, and the transversus thoracis.

thoracoacromial artery, a short artery originating from the anterior surface of the second part of the axillary artery. It divides into four branches: the pectoral, deltoid, clavicular, and acromial.

thoracodorsal nerve /thôr′əkōdôr′səl/ [Gk, *thorax;* L, *dorsum,* back], the middle subscapular nerve, a branch of the brachial plexus, usually arising between the two subscapular nerves. It courses along the posterior wall of the axilla and terminates in branches that supply the latissimus dorsi.

thoracodynia /-din′ē-ə/ [Gk, *thorax,* chest, *odyne,* pain], chest pain.

thoracolumbar fascia /thôr′əkōlum′bər/, a noncontractile structure that functions in a manner similar to a ligament in the lumbar area. It extends from the iliac crest and sacrum to the thoracic cage and envelops the paravertebral musculature.

thoracolumbar junction, the part of the vertebral column from the eleventh thoracic vertebra to the first lumbar vertebra. The spinal curvature changes from kyphosis to lordosis and the orientation of the facet joints changes from coronal to sagittal.

thoracolumbosacral orthosis (TLSO) /thôr′əkōlum′bō sā′krəl/ [Gk, *thorax,* chest; L, *lumbus,* loin, *sacrum,* sacred], a spinal orthosis that goes over the lumbar, sacral, and thoracic regions and thus limits movement of the thoracic and lumbar spine.

thoracopathy /thôr′əkop′əthē/, any disorder involving the thorax or the organs it contains.

thoracoplasty /thôr′əkoplas′tē/, the surgical reduction in the size of abnormal spaces in the thoracic cavity, such as may result from a collapsed lung.

thoracoscopy, an endoscopic procedure used to directly visualize the pleura, lungs, and mediastinum and to obtain tissue for testing. It is also helpful in staging and dissection of lung cancers.

thoracostomy /thôr′əkos′təmē/ [Gk, *thorax + stoma,* mouth], an incision made into the chest wall to provide an opening for the purpose of drainage.

thoracostomy tube, a catheter inserted through the chest wall to drain fluid from the pleural space.

thoracotomy /thôr′əkot′əmē/ [Gk, *thorax + temnein,* to cut], a surgical opening into the thoracic cavity.

Thoraeus filters /thôrē′əs/, a combination of metals, usually tin, copper, and aluminum, used to modify the quality of orthovoltage x-ray beams and thus improve their penetrating ability.

thorax /thôr′aks/ *pl.* **thoraxes, thoraces** [Gk, chest], the upper part of the trunk or cage of bone and cartilage containing the principal organs of respiration and circulation and covering part of the abdominal organs. It is formed ventrally by the sternum and costal cartilages and dorsally by the 12 thoracic vertebrae and the dorsal parts of the 12 ribs.

Thorazine, a trademark for a phenothiazine antiemetic and tranquilizer (chlorproMAZINE).

thorium (Th) /thôr′ē·əm/ [ONorse, *Thor*, god of thunder], a heavy grayish radioactive metallic element. Its atomic number is 90, and its atomic mass is 232.04. Thorium is used in nuclear medicine and in radiation therapy.

thought broadcasting /thôt/ [AS, *thot*], a symptom of psychosis in which the patient believes that his or her thoughts are "broadcast" beyond the head so that other people can hear them.

thought insertion, a belief by some mentally ill patients that thoughts of other people can be inserted into their own minds.

THP, abbreviation for **Tamm-Horsfall protein.**

Thr, abbreviation for **threonine.**

thready pulse /thred′ē/ [AS, *thraed*; L, *pulsare*, to beat], an abnormal pulse that is weak, somewhat difficult to palpate, and often fairly rapid. The artery does not feel full, and the rate may be difficult to count.

threatened abortion /thret′ənd/ [AS, *threat*, coercion; L, *ab*, away from, *oriri*, to be born], a condition in pregnancy before the twentieth week of gestation characterized by uterine bleeding and cramping sufficient to suggest that miscarriage may result. It is generally managed with rest and observation.

3n, abbreviation for **triploid.**

three-point gait [Gk, *treis*; L, *pungere*, to prick; ONorse, *gata*, way], a pattern of crutch-walking in which the crutches and affected leg are advanced together, alternating with the unaffected leg.

threonine (Thr), an essential amino acid needed for proper growth in infants and maintenance of nitrogen balance in adults.

threshold /thresh′ōld/ [AS, *therscold*], the point at which a stimulus is great enough to produce an effect.

threshold dose [AS, *therscold*; Gk, *dosis*, giving], **1.** a measure of a dose of radiation exposure defined in terms of conditions needed to produce a visible erythema in a given proportion of people exposed. **2.** the minimum dose of a drug needed to produce a measurable response. Administration of drugs at dosages or intervals that do not maintain concentration about the threshold level wastes the medication, and, in cases such as antibiotic treatment or cancer chemotherapy, can have additional adverse consequences due to the selective growth of cancer cells or microorganisms that are more resistant to the medication.

threshold limit values, the maximum concentration of a chemical to which workers can be exposed for a fixed period, such as 8 hours per day, without developing a physical impairment.

threshold of consciousness [AS, *therscold*; L, *conscire*, to be aware], the lowest limit of perception of a stimulus.

threshold stimulus [AS, *therscold*; L, *stimulare*, to incite], a stimulus that is just sufficient to produce a response.

thrill [AS, *thyrlian*, to pierce], a fine vibration, felt by an examiner's hand on a patient's body over the site of an aneurysm or on the precordium, resulting from turmoil in the flow of blood and indicating the presence of an organic murmur of grade 4 or greater intensity.

thrix /thriks/ [Gk], hair.

throat and nose cultures, a microscopic examination used to isolate and identify pathogens such as streptococci, meningococci, gonococci, *Bordetella pertussis*, and *Corynebacterium diphtheriae*. Identification of streptococci is particularly important in a throat culture because rheumatic heart disease or glomerulonephritis may follow a streptococcal pharyngitis.

throb [ME, *throbben*, to beat intensely], a deep, pulsating kind of discomfort or pain. —**throbbing,** *adj., n.*

thrombasthenia /throm′basthē′nē·ə/ [Gk, *thrombos*, lump, *a + sthenos*, not strength], a rare hemorrhagic disease characterized by a defect in platelet-mediated hemostasis caused by an abnormality in the membrane surface of the platelet. The platelets do not aggregate, a clot does not form, and hemorrhage ensues. Transfusion with platelets is effective in controlling the hemorrhage.

thrombectomy /thrombek′təmē/ [Gk, *thrombos + ektomē*, excision], the removal of a thrombus from a blood vessel, performed as emergency surgery to restore circulation to the affected part.

thrombin /throm′bin/, the key enzyme produced during coagulation by activation of prothrombin. Thrombin converts fibrinogen to fibrin, activates factors V, VIII, XI, and XIII, and causes platelet aggregation.

thromboangiitis /throm′bō·an′jē·ī′tis/, an inflammation of the blood vessels associated with thrombosis and accompanied by destruction of the intima.

thromboangiitis obliterans [Gk, *thrombos + angeion*, vessel, *itis*, inflammation; L, *obliterare*, to cancel], an occlusive vascular condition, usually of a leg or a foot, in which the small and medium-sized arteries become inflamed and thrombotic. Early signs of the condition are burning, numbness, and tingling of the foot or leg distal to the lesion. Phlebitis and gangrene may develop as the disease progresses. Pulsation in the limb below the damaged blood vessels is often absent. The goal of therapy is to avoid all factors that decrease the blood supply to the extremity and to use all means possible to increase the supply. Amputation may be necessary if the condition progresses to gangrene with chronic infection and extensive tissue destruction.

thromboarteritis /throm′bō·är′tərī′tis/, arterial inflammation with thrombus formation.

thrombocyst /throm′bəsist/, a membranous sac enclosing a thrombus.

thrombocytopathy /throm′bōsītop′əthē/ [Gk, *thrombos* + *kytos,* cell, *pathos,* disease], any disorder of the blood coagulation mechanism caused by an abnormality or dysfunction of platelets. —**thrombocytopathic,** *adj.*

thrombocytopenia /throm′bōsī′təpē′nē·ə/ [Gk, *thrombos* + *kytos* + *penia,* poverty], a platelet count below the lower limit of the reference interval, usually 150,000/uL. It may be the consequence of decreased production disorders such as acute leukemia, an idiosyncratic drug response, or increased consumption, such as immune thrombocytopenic purpura. Thrombocytopenia is the most common cause of mucocutaneous (systemic) bleeding.

thrombocytopenia–absent radius syndrome, an autosomal-recessive syndrome consisting of thrombocytopenia associated with absence or hypoplasia of the radius and sometimes congenital heart disease and renal anomalies.

thrombocytosis /throm′bōsītō′sis/ [Gk, *thrombos* + *kytos* + *osis,* condition], an abnormal increase in the number of platelets in the blood. Benign thrombocytosis, or secondary thrombocytosis, is asymptomatic. Essential thrombocythemia is characterized by episodes of spontaneous bleeding alternating with thrombotic episodes.

thromboembolism /-em′bəliz′əm/ [Gk, *thrombos* + *embolos,* plug], a condition in which a blood vessel is obstructed by a clot (thrombus) carried in the bloodstream from its site of formation. The area supplied by an obstructed artery may tingle and become cold, numb, and cyanotic. A thromboembolus in the lungs causes a sudden, sharp thoracic or upper abdominal pain, dyspnea, cough, fever, anxiety, and hemoptysis. Obstruction of the pulmonary artery or one of its main branches may be fatal. Treatment includes quiet bed rest, warm wet packs, and anticoagulants to prevent the formation of additional thrombi. Embolectomy may be indicated, especially if the aorta or common iliac artery is obstructed.

thromboendarterectomy /-en′därtərek′təmē/, removal of thrombus and atherosclerotic inner lining from an obstructed artery.

thrombogenesis /-jen′əsis/, formation of a thrombus or blood clot.

thrombogenic /-jen′ik/ [Gk, *thrombos* + *genein,* to produce], pertaining to a thrombus or a factor that causes a thrombus.

thromboid /throm′boid/, **1.** clotlike. **2.** resembling a thrombus.

thrombolysis /thrombol′isis/, the dissolution of a thrombus.

thrombolytic /-lit′ik/ [Gk, *thrombos* + *lysis,* a loosening], pertaining to a drug or other agent that dissolves thrombi.

thrombolytic therapy (TT), administration of a thrombolytic agent such as tissue plasminogen activator, urokinase, or streptokinase to dissolve an arterial clot, such as a clot in a coronary artery in a patient with an acute MI. TT is also used to dissolve clots (thrombus) in venous access devices.

thrombolytic therapy management, a nursing intervention from the Nursing Interventions Classification (NIC) defined as collection and analysis of patient data to expedite safe, appropriate provision of an agent that dissolves a thrombus.

thrombopathy /thrombop′əthē/, a condition in which a clotting ability is deficient for reasons other than thrombocytopenia.

thrombophlebitis /-fləbī′tis/ [Gk,*thrombos*+ *phleps,* vein, *itis,* inflammation], inflammation of a vein accompanied by the formation of a clot. It occurs most commonly as the result of trauma to the vessel wall; hypercoagulability of the blood; infection; chemical irritation; postoperative venous stasis; prolonged sitting, standing, or immobilization; or a long period of IV catheterization. Thrombophlebitis of a superficial vein is generally evident; the vessel feels hard and thready or cordlike and is extremely sensitive to pressure; the surrounding area may be erythematous and warm to the touch, and the entire limb may be pale, cold, and swollen. Deep vein thrombophlebitis is characterized by aching or cramping pain, especially in the calf, when the patient walks or dorsiflexes the foot (Homans' sign).

thrombophlebitis purulenta, inflammation of a vein associated with the formation of a soft, purulent thrombus that infiltrates the wall of the vessel.

thromboplastic /-plas′tik/, **1.** causing clot formation. **2.** pertaining to the role of thromboplastin in forming a clot.

thromboplastin, a complex substance that initiates the clotting process by converting prothrombin to thrombin in the presence of calcium ions.

thrombosed /throm′bōst/, **1.** clotted. **2.** pertaining to a blood vessel in which a thrombus has formed.

thrombosis/thrombō′sis/, *pl.* **thromboses,** an abnormal condition in which a clot (thrombus) develops within a blood vessel.—**thrombotic,** *adj.*

thrombosis indicator test, a blood test to support a diagnosis of disseminated intravascular coagulation and to indicate the effectiveness of anticoagulation therapy

thrombotic microangiopathy, the formation of thrombi in the arterioles and capillaries, as occurs in thrombotic thrombocytopenic purpura and hemolytic uremia syndrome.

thrombotic thrombocytopenic purpura (TTP) [Gk, *thrombos,* lump + *thrombos* + *kytos,* cell, *penia,* poverty; L, *purpura,* purple], a disorder characterized by thrombocytopenia, hemolytic anemia, and neurologic abnormalities. It is accompanied by a generalized purpura with the deposition of microthrombi within the capillaries and smaller arterioles. Therapy includes corticosteroids, splenectomy, and therapeutic plasma exchange.

thromboxane, any of several compounds synthesized by platelets and other cells that cause platelet aggregation and vasoconstriction.

thromboxane-A synthase, an enzyme that catalyzes the conversion in platelets of prostaglandin G_2 to thromboxane A_2. A deficiency of the enzyme causes a defect in the release of platelets.

thromboxane A_2 (TXA$_2$) /thrombok′sān/, biologically active compound derived from prostaglandin G_2. It increases in concentration after injury to blood vessels and stimulates the primary hemostatic response and irreversible platelet aggregation.

thromboxane B_2 (TXB$_2$), a stable metabolite of thromboxane A_2 that has an effect on polymorphonuclear cells and may possess chemotactic activity. It is released during anaphylaxis in laboratory animals.

thrombus /throm′bəs/ *pl.* **thrombi** [Gk, *thrombos,* lump], an aggregation of platelets, fibrin, and red blood cells that attaches to the interior wall of a vein or artery, sometimes occluding the lumen of the vessel.

through-and-through drainage /throo̅/ [ME, *thurgh*; AS, *drachen,* tear drop], a method of irrigating a body organ by inserting two tubes, one to introduce the fluid and another to drain the fluid that accumulates within the organ.

through transmission, a type of ultrasound imaging in which the sound field is transmitted through a specimen and the transmitted energy is picked up on a far surface by a receiving transducer.

thrush [Dan, *troeske,* dryness], candidiasis of the tissues of the mouth. The condition is characterized by the appearance of creamy white patches of exudate on an inflamed tongue or buccal mucosa. It is usually a benign condition in

normal children but may be a sign of HIV infection.

thulium (Tm) /thoo̅′lē·əm/ [L, *Thule,* northern island], a rare earth metallic element. Its atomic number is 69, and its atomic mass is 168.93. Thulium that has been irradiated in a nuclear reactor gives off gamma radiation.

thumb /thum/ [AS, *thuma*], the first and shortest digit on the radial side of the hand, classified by some anatomists as one of the fingers because its metacarpal bone ossifies in the same manner as those of the phalanges. Other anatomists classify the thumb separately, noting that it has a much different articulation with the metacarpal bone (a saddle joint) and is composed of one metacarpal bone and only two phalanges.

thumb forceps, a surgical instrument used to grasp soft tissue, especially while suturing.

thumb sign [AS, *thuma*; L, *signum*], the flexing of the terminal phalanx of the thumb against the flexed index finger, as in holding a piece of paper. It is observed in patients who are unable to adduct the thumb because of an ulnar lesion.

thumbsucking, the habit of sucking the thumb for oral gratification. It is normal in infants and young children as a pleasure-seeking or comforting device, especially when the child is hungry or tired. The habit reaches its peak when the child is between 18 and 20 months of age and usually disappears as the child develops and matures.

thumps, 1. hiccups. 2. spasmodic contractions of the diaphragm.

thyme /tīm, thim/ [Gk, *thymon*], the dried leaves and flowering tops of an herb, *Thymus vulgaris,* which produces a pungent mintlike aroma. It is the source of a volatile oil, tannin, and gum but is used mainly as a flavoring agent.

thymectomy /thīmek′təmē/ [Gk, *thymus*], the surgical removal of the thymus.

thymic /thī′mik/, pertaining to the thymus gland.

thymidine (dThd) /thī′mədēn/, one of the four major nucleosides in DNA. It is formed by the condensation of thymine with deoxyribose.

thymidine kinase, an enzyme of the transferase class that catalyzes a phosphorylation reaction of pyrimidine salvage and phosphorylation of drugs, such as acyclovir and ganciclovir, into a form that will be active against viruses.

thymine, a major pyrimidine base in animal cells, usually occurring condensed with deoxyribose to form the nucleoside deoxythymidine, a component of DNA.

thymol /thī′mol/, a synthetic or natural thyme oil, used as an antibacterial and antifungal, that is an ingredient in some OTC preparations for the treatment of hemorrhoids, acne, and tinea pedis.

thymoma /thīmō′mə/ *pl*. **thymomas, thymomata** [Gk, *thymos,* thyme, flowers, *oma,* tumor], a usually benign tumor of the thymus gland that may be associated with myasthenia gravis or an immune deficiency disorder.

thymosin /thī′məsin/, **1.** a naturally occurring immunologic hormone secreted by the thymus gland. It is present in greatest amounts in young children and decreases in amount throughout life. **2.** an investigational drug derived from bovine thymus extracts and prescribed as an immunomodulator in experimental treatments for certain diseases such as SLE or rheumatoid arthritis.

thymus /thī′məs/ *pl*. **thymuses, thymi** [Gk, *thymos,* thyme, flowers], a single unpaired lymphoid organ that is located in the mediastinum, extending superiorly into the neck to the lower edge of the thyroid gland and inferiorly as far as the fourth costal cartilage. The gland consists of two lateral lobes closely bound by connective tissue, which also encloses the entire organ in a capsule. The thymus is the primary central gland of the lymphatic system. The endocrine activity of the thymus is believed to depend on the hormone thymosin, which is composed of biologically active peptides critical to the maturation and the development of the immune system. The T cells of the cell-mediated immune response develop in this gland before migrating to the lymph nodes and spleen.

thymus-dependent antigen, an antigen that requires the interaction between T and B cells to initiate antibody production.

thymus-independent antigen, an antigen that induces antibody (IgM) production without direct cooperation from T cells.

Thyrar, a trademark for thyroid hormone.

thyroaplasia /thī′rō·aplā′zhə/, variations in any of several defects in the thyroid gland and deficiencies of its secretions.

thyroarytenoid muscles, two broad, flat muscles lateral to the fibroelastic membrane of the larynx and the laryngeal entricles and saccules. Each muscle runs from a vertical line of origin on the lower half of the thyroid angle and adjacent external surface of the cricothyroid ligament to the anterolateral surface of the arytenoid cartilage. They act as sphincters to the laryngeal vestibule and also narrow the laryngeal inlet.

thyrocervical trunk /-sur′vikəl/ [Gk, *thyreos,* shield, *eidos,* form; L, *cervix,* neck + *truncus*], one of a pair of short thick arterial branches arising from the first part of the subclavian arteries close to the medial border of the scalenus anterior and supplying numerous muscles and bones in the head, neck, and back.

thyrocricotomy /-krīkot′əmē/ [Gk, *thyreos,* shield, *eidos,* form, *krikos,* ring, *temnein,* to cut], a tracheotomy procedure in which the cricovocal membrane is divided.

thyrogenic /-jen′ik/ [Gk, *thyreos,* shield, *eidos,* form, *genein,* to produce], pertaining to an origin in the thyroid gland.

thyroglobulin test, a blood test used primarily to detect well-differentiated thyroid cancers.

thyroglossal /-glos′əl/, pertaining to an embryonic duct connecting the thyroid gland and the tongue.

thyrohyoid membrane, a tough fibroelastic ligament that spans between the superior margin of the thyroid cartilage below and hyoid bone above. It is attached to the superior margin of the thyroid laminae and adjacent anterior margins of the superior horns and ascends medial to the greater horns and posterior to the body of the hyoid bone to attach to the superior margins of these structures.

thyroid acropathy /thī′roid/ [Gk, *thyreos,* shield, *eidos,* form, *akron,* extremity, *pathos,* disease], swelling of subcutaneous tissue of the extremities and clubbing of the digits, occurring rarely in patients with thyroid disease and usually associated with pretibial myxedema or exophthalmos.

thyroid cancer, a neoplasm of the thyroid gland, usually characterized by slow growth and a slower and more prolonged clinical course than that of other malignancies. The first sign of cancer may be an increased size of the thyroid gland, a palpable nodule, hoarseness, dysphagia, dyspnea, or pain on pressure. More than half of thyroid malignancies are papillary carcinomas, about one third are follicular carcinomas, and the rest consist of rapidly growing invasive anaplastic carcinomas; medullary carcinomas that secrete calcitonin; and metastatic lesions from primary tumors in the breast, kidneys, or lungs. Total or subtotal thyroidectomy with excision of involved lymph nodes is usually recommended.

thyroid cartilage, the largest cartilage of the larynx, consisting of two laminae fused together at an acute angle in the midline of the anterior neck to form the Adam's apple.

thyroid crisis [Gk, *thyreos,* shield, *eidos,* form, *krisis,* turning point], a sudden exacerbation of symptoms of thyrotoxicosis characterized by fever, sweating, tachycardia, extreme nervous excitability, and pulmonary edema. It usually occurs in a patient whose thyrotoxicosis treatment is inadequate, and the paroxysm is triggered by a stressful infection or injury. If untreated, the crisis is often fatal.

thyroid dermoid cyst, a tumor derived from embryonal tissues that is believed to have developed in the thyroid gland or in the thyrolingual duct.

thyroid dermopathy, pretibial myxedema.

thyroidectomized /thī'roidek'təmīzd/ [Gk, *thyreos,* shield, *eidos,* form, *ektomē,* excision], pertaining to a patient or condition in which the thyroid gland has been removed.

thyroidectomy /thī'roidek'təmē/ [Gk, *thyreos + eidos,* form, *ektomē,* excision], the surgical removal of the thyroid gland. It is performed for colloid goiter, tumors, or hyperthyroidism that does not respond to iodine therapy and antithyroid drugs. All but 5% to 10% of the gland is removed. Regrowth usually begins shortly after surgery, and thyroid function may return to normal. For cancer of the thyroid, the entire gland is removed, followed by iodine-131 remnant ablation.

thyroid function test, any of several laboratory tests performed to evaluate the function of the thyroid gland. Thyroid function tests include protein-bound iodine, butanol-extractable iodine, T_3, T_4, free thyroxine index, thyroxin-binding globulin, TSH, long-acting thyroid stimulator, radioactive iodine uptake, and radioactive iodine excretion.

thyroid gland [Gk, *thyreos,* shield, *eidos,* form], a highly vascular organ at the front of the neck, consisting of bilateral lobes connected in the middle by a narrow isthmus. The majority of the thyroid gland secretes the hormone thyroxin, and other clusters of cells produce the hormone calcitonin. The thyroid gland is essential to normal body growth in infancy and childhood, and its removal greatly reduces the oxidative processes of the body, producing a lower metabolic rate characteristic of hypothyroidism. The thyroid gland is activated by the pituitary thyrotrophic hormone and requires iodine to elaborate thyroxine.

thyroid hormone, an iodine-containing compound secreted by the thyroid gland, predominantly as thyroxine (T_4) and, in smaller amounts but four times more potent, as triiodothyronine (T_3). These hormones increase the rate of metabolism; affect body temperature; regulate protein, fat, and carbohydrate catabolism in all cells; maintain growth hormone secretion, skeletal maturation, and the cardiac rate, force, and output; promote CNS development; stimulate the synthesis of many enzymes; and are necessary for muscle tone and vigor. Production of thyroid hormones is excessive in Graves' disease and toxic nodular goiter (Plummer's disease), diminished in myxedema, and absent in

cretinism. Pharmaceutical preparations of thyroid hormones extracted from animal glands and the synthetic compounds levothyroxine sodium and liothyronine sodium are used as replacement therapy in patients with hypothyroidism.

thyroiditis /thī'roidī'tis/, inflammation of the thyroid gland. Acute thyroiditis caused by staphylococcal, streptococcal, or other infections is characterized by suppuration and abscess formation and may progress to subacute diffuse disease of the gland. Subacute thyroiditis is marked by fever, weakness, sore throat, and a painfully enlarged gland containing granulomas composed of colloid masses surrounded by giant cells and mononuclear cells. Other forms of thyroiditis are chronic lymphocytic thyroiditis (Hashimoto's disease), Riedel's struma, and radiation thyroiditis.

thyroid notch, **1.** (superior) a separation above the anterior border of the thyroid cartilage. **2.** (inferior) a depression in the middle of the lower border of the thyroid cartilage.

thyroid scanning, a radionuclear scan that determines the size, shape, position, and physiologic function of the thyroid gland. It is useful in patients with neck or substernal masses, thyroid nodules, hyperthyroidism, metastatic tumors without a known primary site, and well-differentiated forms of thyroid cancer.

thyroid-stimulating hormone (TSH), a substance secreted by the anterior lobe of the pituitary gland that controls the release of thyroid hormone and is necessary for the growth and function of the thyroid gland. The secretion of TSH is regulated by thyrotropin-releasing hormone, elaborated in the median eminence of the hypothalamus and circulating-thyroid hormone levels.

thyroid-stimulating hormone test (TSH test), a thyroid function test in which TSH is administered intramuscularly and the thyroid gland is monitored over time with scintiscanning or radioimmunoassays for a response or areas of decreased responsiveness. It is also used to monitor exogenous thyroid replacement.

thyroid-stimulating immunoglobulins test, a blood test to diagnose Graves' disease.

thyroid storm, a crisis of uncontrolled thyrotoxicosis caused by the release into the bloodstream of increased amounts of thyroid hormone. Thyroid storm may occur spontaneously or be precipitated by infection, stress, or a thyroidectomy performed on a patient who is inadequately prepared with antithyroid drugs. Characteristic signs are fever that may reach 106° F, a rapid pulse, acute respiratory distress, apprehension, restlessness, irritability, and prostration. The patient may become delirious, lapse into a coma, and die of heart failure.

thyroid ultrasound, an ultrasound examination of the thyroid gland, used to distinguish cystic from solid thyroid nodules, to determine the efficacy of treatment of a thyroid mass, and to study the thyroid gland of pregnant patients.

Thyrolar, a trademark for a thyroid hormone (liotrix).

thyroliberin /thī′rōlib′ərin/, a tripeptide hormone produced by the hypothalamus that stimulates the anterior pituitary gland to release thyrotropin.

thyromegaly /-meg′əlē/ [Gk, *thyreos,* shield, *eidos,* form, *megas,* large], enlargement of the thyroid gland.

thyrotoxic myopathy /-tok′sik/, a condition in thyrotoxicosis consisting of severe weakness in the limb and trunk muscles, including those used in speech and swallowing.

thyrotoxin /-tok′sin/, a theoretic cytotoxin of the thyroid gland, assumed to be a cause of the signs and symptoms of thyrotoxicosis.

thyrotrophic /-trof′ik/ [Gk, *thyreos,* shield, *eidos,* form, *trophe,* nutrition], influencing the thyroid gland, such as the TSH.

thyrotropin alfa, a recombinant form of human thyrotropin. It binds to thyrotropin receptors and stimulates the steps in thyroid hormone synthesis. It is used as a diagnostic adjunct in serum thyroglobulin testing, with or without radioiodine scanning, in follow-up of patients with well-differentiated thyroid cancer.

thyrotropin alpha /-trō′pin/, a TSH made with recombinant DNA technology, it increases the uptake of radioactive iodine in the thyroid and the secretion of thyroxine by the thyroid. It is prescribed in diagnostic tests and to enhance uptake of 131I in the treatment of thyroid cancer.

thyrotropin-releasing hormone (TRH), a substance produced in the hypothalamus that stimulates the release of TSH from the anterior lobe of the pituitary gland.

thyrotropin-releasing hormone stimulation test, a thyroid function test that assesses release of thyrotropin by the pituitary gland. A bolus of thyrotropin-releasing hormone is administered, and serum concentrations of thyrotropin are assessed at intervals. If serum levels do not increase within 30 to 40 minutes, the pituitary thyrotrophs are dysfunctional.

thyroxine (T₄) /thīrok′sēn/, a hormone of the thyroid gland, derived from tyrosine and deiodinated in the periphery to T_3

(triiodothyronine) that stimulates metabolic rate.

thyroxine-binding globulin (TBG), a plasma protein that binds with and transports thyroxine in the blood.

thyroxine-binding globulin test, a blood test used to detect levels of TBG, the major thyroid hormone protein carrier. Elevated TBGs may indicate porphyria or infectious hepatitis, among other conditions, while decreased TBGs may signify various causes of hypoproteinemia (nephrotic syndrome, GI malabsorption, malnutrition).

Ti, symbol for the element **titanium.**

TI, 1. time to inversion; the time interval between the initial 180-degree pulse and the subsequent 90-degree radiofrequency pulse in an inversion recovery pulse sequence. 2. abbreviation for **therapeutic index.**

TIA, abbreviation for **transient ischemic attack.**

tiagabine, an anticonvulsant prescribed as an adjunct treatment for partial seizures.

tibia /tib′ē-ə/ [L, shin bone], the second longest bone of the skeleton, located at the medial side of the leg. It articulates with the fibula laterally, the talus distally, and the femur proximally, forming part of the knee joint.

tibial /tib′ē-əl/ [L, *tibia,* shin bone], pertaining to the largest long bone of the lower leg.

tibialis anterior /tib′ē-ā′lis/ [L, *tibia + anticus,* in front], one of the anterior crural muscles of the leg, situated on the lateral side of the tibia. It dorsiflexes and supinates the foot.

tibial torsion [L, *tibia + torquere,* to twist], a lateral or a medial twisting rotation of the tibia on its longitudinal axis.

tibia valga [L, *tibia,* shin bone, *valgus,* bowlegged], a bowed tibia with the convex surface toward the outside of the leg.

Ticar, a trademark for an antibiotic (ticarcillin).

ticarcillin /tik′ärsil′in/, an extended-spectrum penicillin antibiotic. It is prescribed in the treatment of bacterial septicemia, as well as skin, soft tissue, and respiratory infections caused by both gram-negative and gram-positive organisms, including some strain of *Pseudomonas.*

tic douloureux /tik do͞olo͞oro͞o′/ [Fr, painful spasm], a brief extremely painful attack of trigeminal neuralgia. It is unilateral and limited to the distribution of the trigeminal (fifth cranial) nerve.

tick bite [ME, *tike*; AS, *bitan,* to bite], a puncture wound produced by the toothed beak of a blood-sucking tick, a small, tough-skinned arachnid. Ticks transmit several diseases to humans, and a few species carry a neurotoxin in their saliva that

T

may cause ascending paralysis beginning in the legs. Nervousness, loss of appetite, tingling, and headache, followed by muscle pain and in extreme cases respiratory failure may occur. Symptoms often disappear when the attached tick is carefully removed with forceps.

tick-borne rickettsiosis [ME, *tike* + *beren*; *Rickettsia*; Gk, *osis*, condition], any disease transmitted by Ixodid ticks carrying the *Rickettsia* pathogens, microorganisms smaller than bacteria but larger than viruses. A common infectious species

tick fever, any of various infectious diseases transmitted by the bite of a tick. The causative parasite may be a rickettsia, as in Rocky Mountain spotted fever; a bacterium, such as *Babesia* or *Borrelia;* or a virus, such as that of Colorado tick fever.

tickling, a gentle stimulation of the skin surface that produces pleasurable reflexes.

tick paralysis, a rare progressive reversible disorder caused by several species of ticks that release a neurotoxin that causes weakness, incoordination, and paralysis. The tick must feed on the host for several days before the symptoms appear, and removal of the tick leads to rapid recovery.

ticlopidine /tiklo′pidēn/, a platelet inhibitor used as the hydrochloride salt in the prevention of stroke syndrome.

t.i.d., in prescriptions, abbreviation for the Latin phrase *ter in die* /dē′ā/, "three times a day."

tidal /tī′dəl/ [AS, *tid,* time], pertaining to an alternating process, such as a rise-and-fall, ebb-and-flow, or periodic lapse of time.

tidal volume (TV, V$_t$) [AS, *tid,* time; L, *volumen,* paper roll], the amount of air inhaled and exhaled during normal ventilation. Inspiratory reserve volume, expiratory reserve volume, and tidal volume make up vital capacity.

tide [AS, *tid*], a variation, increase, or decrease, in the concentration of a particular component of body fluids, such as acid tide, fat tide.—**tidal,** *adj.*

tidemark, a transitional zone, appearing as a wavy line, that marks the junction between calcified and uncalcified cartilage.

Tietze's syndrome /tēt′sēz/ [Alexander Tietze, German surgeon, 1864–1927], **1.** a disorder characterized by nonsuppurative swellings of one or more costal cartilages that may accompany chronic respiratory infections. It causes pain that may radiate to the neck, shoulder, or arm, mimicking the pain of coronary artery disease. If the pain is severe, infiltration with procaine and hydrocortisone may provide relief. **2.** albinism, except for normal eye pigment,

accompanied by deaf mutism and hypoplasia of the eyebrows.

TIG, abbreviation for **tetanus immune globulin.**

Tigan, a trademark for an antiemetic (trimethobenzamide hydrochloride).

tigecycline, a broad-spectrum antiinfective used to treat complicated skin and skin structure infections caused by *Escherichia coli, Enterococcus faecalis* (vancomycin-susceptible only), *Staphylococcus aureus, Streptococcus agalactiae, S. anginosus* group, *S. pyogenes,* and *Bacteroides fragilis,* and complicated intraabdominal infections caused by *Citrobacter freundii, Enterobacter cloacae, E. coli, Klebsiella oxytoca, K. pneumoniae, E. faecalis* (vancomycin-susceptible only), *S. aureus* (methicillin-susceptible only), *S. anginosus* group, *B. fragilis, B. thetaiotaomicron, B. uniformis, B. vulgatus, Clostridium perfringens,* and *Peptostreptococcus micros.*

tight junction /tīt/ [ME, *thight,* strong; L, *jungere,* to join], the zonula occludens of the junctional complex between cells in which the plasma membranes of adjacent cells are in direct contact and where there is no intercellular space.

tilt table [AS, *tealt,* unsteady; L, *tabula,* board], an examining table that allows a patient to be raised to an approximate 60-degree angle during study of the response of the patient's circulatory system to gravitational forces. A tilt table is also used to assist recovery from orthostatic hypotension after prolonged immobility.

tiludronate, a parathyroid agent (calcium regulator) prescribed to treat Paget's disease.

timbre /tim′bər/ [Fr], **1.** a characteristic sound quality of a voice or musical instrument, as determined by the harmonics of the sound. **2.** a second metallic sound heard in aortic dilation.

time (t) [AS, *tima*], **1.** a measure of duration. **2.** an interval separating two points in a continuum between the past and future.

time constant, a mathematic term of fixed value used in expressing the rate of change of some variable, such as airflow in the airways, as a function of time.

timed collection, the collection of a specimen such as a urine or stool sample for a specific period of time.

timed cycling, the delivery of gas under positive pressure during inspiration until an adjustable, preselected time interval has elapsed.

time delay, a period between the application of an input and the beginning of the response.

timed vital capacity, a diagnostic test of certain lung disorders determined by the percentage of predicted vital capacity that adults can expire forcefully for at least 3 seconds after a maximal inspiration.

time gain compensation (TGC), increasing amplification of echoes from increasing tissue depths. It is used in ultrasound to correct for increased attenuation of sound with tissue depth.

time trigger, a trigger for initiating assisted ventilation, consisting of a mechanism that measures frequency of respirations and starts assisted ventilation when the respiratory frequency is at a given point.

timolol maleate /tim′əlōl/, a beta-adrenergic receptor blocking agent. It is administered orally for the treatment of angina and hypertension, to reduce post-MI mortality and as migraine prophylaxis. An ophthalmic preparation is used for treating glaucoma, especially chronic open-angle glaucoma.

Timoptic, a trademark for a beta-adrenergic receptor blocking agent (timolol maleate).

tin (Sn) [AS], a whitish metallic element. Its atomic number is 50; its atomic mass is 118.69. Tin(IV) oxide is used in dentistry as a polishing agent for teeth and in some restorative procedures.

Tinactin, a trademark for an antifungal (tolnaftate).

tincture, a plant extract made by soaking herbs in a liquid (such as water, alcohol, vinegar, or glycerine) for a specified length of time, and then straining and discarding the plant material. The remaining liquid is used therapeutically.

tincture (tinct.) /tingk′chər/, a substance in a solution that is dissolved in alcohol.

tincture of iodine [L, *tinctura*; Gk, *ioeides*, violet], a mixture of sodium iodide in an alcohol-water solution used as a skin disinfectant. The term is no longer in official use.

Tindamax, a trademark for tinidazole.

T-independent antigen, an antigen that can trigger B lymphocytes to produce antibodies without the participation of T lymphocytes.

tine, a sharp projecting point, as a prong of a fork.

tinea /tin′ē-ə/ [L, worm], a group of fungal skin diseases caused by dermatophytes of several kinds. The condition is characterized by itching, scaling, and sometimes painful lesions.

tinea capitis, a superficial fungal infection of the scalp, most common in children. Symptoms include severe itching and scaling of the scalp. Treatment with oral antifungal agents, as well as appropriate antibiotics, is necessary. Oral steroids may be necessary to prevent scarring and hair loss.

tinea corporis, a superficial fungal infection of the nonhairy skin of the body, most prevalent in hot, humid climates and usually caused by species of *Trichophyton* or *Microsporum*. Topical fungicides such as miconazole are used for moderate cases; severe infection calls for griseofulvin.

tinea cruris /krŏŏ′ris/, a superficial fungal infection of the groin caused by species of *Trichophyton* or *Epidermophyton floccosum*. It is most common in the tropics and among males. Topical antifungals such as miconazole and clotrimazole are often prescribed. Griseofulvin is used only for severe resistant cases.

tinea nigra, an uncommon superficial fungal infection, caused by *Malassezia furfur* or *werneckii*, characterized by dark lesions on the skin of the hands or occasionally other areas.

tinea pedis, a chronic superficial fungal infection of the foot, especially of the skin between the toes and on the soles. It is common worldwide and is most commonly caused by *Trichophyton rubrum*, *T. mentagrophytes*, and *Epidermophyton floccosum*. Griseofulvin is the most effective treatment, but miconazole and tolnaftate are also used. Drying the feet well after bathing and applying powder between the toes help prevent it.

tinea unguium /un′gwē-əm/, a superficial fungal infection of the nails caused by various species of *Trichophyton* and occasionally by *Candida albicans*. It is more common on the toes than the fingers and can cause complete crumbling and destruction of the nails. Itraconazole and terbinafine are the drugs of choice, but they must be continued until the nail has regrown completely.

tinea versicolor, a fungal infection of the skin caused by *Malassezia furfur* and characterized by finely desquamating, pale tan patches on the upper trunk and upper arms that may itch and do not tan. In dark-skinned people the lesions may be depigmented. The fungus fluoresces under Wood's light and may be easily identified in scrapings viewed under a microscope. Topical and oral antifungal agents may be used as well as repeated applications of selenium sulfide.

Tinel's sign /tinelz′/ [Jules Tinel, French neurosurgeon, 1879–1952], an indication of irritability of a nerve, resulting in a distal tingling sensation on percussion of a damaged nerve. The sign is often present in carpal tunnel syndrome.

tine test /tīn/ [ME, *tind*, rake tooth; L, *testum*, crucible], a widely used tuberculin skin test in which a small disposable disk with multiple tines bearing tuberculin antigen is used to puncture the skin. Induration around the puncture site indicates previous exposure or active disease, requiring further testing.

tingling [ME, *tinklen*, to tinkle], a prickly sensation in the skin or a body part, accompanied by diminished sensitivity to stimulation of the sensory nerves.

tinidazole, an antiprotozoal used to treat amebiasis, giardiasis, and trichomoniasis.

tinnitus /tinī′təs/ [L, *tinnire*, to tinkle], a subjective noise sensation, often described as ringing, heard in one or both ears.

tint, a shade or gradation of a color, usually a pale or less saturated version of the basic shade.

tinted denture base, a denture base that has a color close to that of natural oral tissue.

TINU syndrome, a rare syndrome of tubulointerstitial nephritis and uveitis, often with immunologic alterations.

tinzaparin /tin-zap′ə-rin/, a low-molecular-weight heparin obtained by depolymerization of heparin from porcine intestinal mucosa by using a bacterial enzyme. It acts as an anticoagulant and antithrombotic and is used as an adjunct to warfarin in the treatment of deep venous thrombosis with or without pulmonary embolism.

tiotropium, an anticholinergic and bronchodilator. It is used for long-term treatment of COPD and for once-daily maintenance of bronchospasm associated with COPD, including chronic bronchitis and emphysema.

tip, 1. the end of a pointed object. **2.** an attachment fitted to the end of something else. **3.** a point.

tipped uterus /tipt/ [ME, *tipen*, upset; L, *uterus*, womb], a uterus that is displaced from its normal position.

tip pinch, a grasp in which the tip of the thumb is pressed against any or each of the tips of the other fingers.

tipping, a tooth movement in which the angle of the tooth's long axis is changed.

tipranavir, an antiretroviral that is used in combination with other antiretrovirals to treat HIV.

TIPS, abbreviation for **transjugular intrahepatic portosystemic shunt.**

tip seal, the closure of an ampule accomplished by melting a bead of glass at the neck of the ampule.

tirofiban, an antiplatelet agent prescribed to treat acute coronary syndrome.

tisane /tizän′, tizän′/, a tealike infusion or light drink of a vegetable herb consumed for a claimed medicinal effect.

tissue /tish′o͞o/ [Fr, *tissu,* fabric], a collection of similar cells acting together to perform a particular function.

tissue bank, a facility for storing and maintaining a collection of tissues for future use in transplants.

tissue-base relationship, the relationship of the bottom of a removable dental prosthesis to underlying structures.

tissue committee, a group that evaluates all surgery performed in a hospital or other health care facility.

tissue culture [OFr, *tissu*; L, *colere*, to cultivate], the maintenance of growth in vitro, under artificial conditions, of tissue or organ specimens.

tissue dose, the amount of radiation absorbed by tissue in the region of interest, expressed in rad.

tissue fixation, a process in which a tissue specimen is placed in a fluid that preserves the cells as nearly as possible in their natural state.

tissue fixative, a fluid that preserves cells in their natural state so that they may be identified and examined.

tissue integrity: skin and mucous membranes, a nursing outcome from the Nursing Outcomes Classification (NOC) defined as structural intactness and normal physiological function of skin and mucous membranes.

tissue macrophage [OFr, *tissu*; Gk, *makros,* large, *phagein,* to eat], a large, mobile, highly phagocytic cell derived from monocytes. These cells become mobile when stimulated by inflammation and migrate to the affected area.

tissue perfusion: abdominal organs, a nursing outcome from the Nursing Outcomes Classification (NOC) defined as adequacy of blood flow through the small vessels of the abdominal viscera to maintain organ function.

tissue perfusion: cardiac, a nursing outcome from the Nursing Outcomes Classification (NOC) defined as adequacy of blood flow through the coronary vasculature to maintain heart function.

tissue perfusion: cellular, a nursing outcome from the Nursing Outcomes Classification (NOC) defined as adequacy of blood flow through the vasculature to maintain function at the cellular level.

tissue perfusion: cerebral, a nursing outcome from the Nursing Outcomes Classification (NOC) defined as extent to which blood flows through the cerebral vasculature to maintain brain function.

tissue perfusion: peripheral, a nursing outcome from the Nursing Outcomes Classification (NOC) defined as adequacy of blood flow through the small vessels of the extremities to maintain tissue function.

tissue perfusion: pulmonary, a nursing outcome from the Nursing Outcomes Classification (NOC) defined as adequacy of blood flow through intact pulmonary vasculature to perfuse alveoli/capillary units.

tissue plasminogen activator (TPA), a clot-dissolving substance produced naturally by cells in the walls of blood vessels. It is also manufactured synthetically by genetic engineering techniques. TPA activates plasminogen to dissolve clots and has been used therapeutically to open occluded coronary arteries as well as cerebral arteries.

tissue response, any reaction or change in living cellular tissue when it is acted on by disease, toxin, or other external stimulus.

tissue review, a review of the surgery performed in a hospital or other health care facility. The evaluation is usually made on the basis of the extent of agreement of the preoperative, postoperative, and pathologic diagnoses and on the relevance and acceptability of the diagnostic procedures.

tissue typing, a systematized series of tests to evaluate the intraspecies compatibility of tissues from a donor and a recipient before transplantation.

titanium (Ti) /tītā′nē·əm/ [Gk, *Titan*, mythic giant], a grayish brittle metallic element. Its atomic number is 22, and its atomic mass is 47.88. An alloy of titanium is used in the manufacture of orthopedic prostheses. Titanium dioxide is the active ingredient in a number of topical ointments and lotions.

titer /tī′tər/ [Fr, *titre*, to make a standard], **1.** the normality of a solution or substance, determined by titration to find the equivalence of two reactants. **2.** the extent to which an antibody can be diluted before losing its power to react with a specific antigen. **3.** the highest dilution of a serum that causes clumping of bacteria or other visible reaction.

titillation /tit′ilā′shən/ [L, *titillare,* to tickle], **1.** tickling. **2.** arousal of the senses.

Title [L, *titulus,* title], a section of the Social Security Act that provides for the establishment, funding, and regulation of a service to a specific segment of the population. Examples include Title XIX, which includes medical coverage under Medicaid.

titration /tītrā′shən/, a method of estimating the amount of solute in a solution. The solution is added in small, measured quantities to a known volume of a standard solution until a reaction occurs, as indicated by a change in color or pH or the liberation of a chemical product.

titubation /tich′əbā′shən/ [L, *titubare,* to stagger], unsteady posture characterized by a staggering or stumbling gait and a swaying head or trunk while sitting. It may be a manifestation of cerebellar disease.

TIVA, abbreviation for **total intravenous anesthesia.**

tizanidine, a skeletal muscle relaxant and alpha$_2$-adrenergic agonist prescribed in the acute/intermittent management of increased muscle tone associated with spasticity.

Tl, symbol for the element **thallium.**

TLC, 1. abbreviation for **total lung capacity. 2.** abbreviation for **thin-layer chromatography. 3.** *informal.* abbreviation for *tender loving care.*

TLI, abbreviation for **total lymphoid irradiation.**

TLR, abbreviation for **tonic labyrinthine reflex.**

TLSO, abbreviation for **thoracolumbo-sacral orthosis.**

Tm, symbol for the element **thulium.**

TM, abbreviation for **transcendental meditation.**

TMJ, abbreviation for **temporomandibular joint.**

TMP-SMX, abbreviation for *trimethoprim-sulfamethoxazole.*

TNF, abbreviation for **tumor necrosis factor.**

TNM, a system for staging malignant neoplastic disease.

t.n.t.c., abbreviation for *too numerous to count,* usually applied to organisms or cells viewed on a slide under a microscope.

t.o., abbreviation for *telephone order.*

toadstool, popular name for any of various poisonous mushrooms.

toadstool poisoning /tōd′stoōl/ [AS, *tadige* + *stol*; L, *potio,* drink], a toxic condition caused by ingestion of certain varieties of poisonous mushrooms.

to-and-fro murmur, a friction sound or murmur heard with both systole and diastole.

tobacco /təbak′ō/ [Sp, *tabaco*], a plant whose leaves are dried and used for smoking and chewing, and in snuff.

tobacco withdrawal syndrome, a change in mood or performance associated with the cessation of or reduction in exposure to nicotine. Symptoms may range from lack of concentration to anxiety and temper outbursts.

TOBEC, abbreviation for **total-body electrical conductivity.**

tobramycin sulfate /tō′brəmī′sin/, an aminoglycoside antibiotic prescribed in the treatment of external ocular infection, septicemia, and lower respiratory tract and CNS infections caused by gram-negative bacilli, including *Pseudomonas*.

Tobruk plaster /tō′broōk/, a plaster cast splint with tapes for skin traction coming through openings in the plaster and connected with a Thomas′ splint. It covers and immobilizes the leg from foot to groin.

tocainide /to-ka′nīd/, an agent used as the hydrochloride salt in treatment of ventricular arrhythmias.

tocainide hydrochloride /tōkā′nīd/, an oral lidocaine-type antiarrhythmic. It is prescribed for the suppression of symptomatic ventricular arrhythmias and has unlabeled use for treating trigeminal neuralgia.

tocodynamometer /tō′kōdī′nəmom′ətər/ [Gk, *tokos,* birth, *dynamis,* force, *metron,* measure], an electronic device for monitoring and recording uterine contractions in labor. It consists of a pressure transducer that is applied to the fundus of the uterus by means of a belt, which is connected to a machine that records the duration of the contractions and the interval between them on graph paper.

tocolytic drug /-lit′ik/, any drug used to suppress premature labor.

tocopherolquinone (TQ) /tōkof′ərōlkwī′nōn/, an oxidized form of tocopherol, or vitamin E.

tocotransducer /-transd(y)oo̅′sər/ [Gk, *tokos:* L, *trans,* through, *ducer,* to lead], an electronic device used to measure uterine contractions.

toddler [ME, *toteren,* to walk unsteadily], a child between 12 and 36 months of age. During this period of development the child acquires a sense of autonomy and independence through the mastery of various specialized tasks such as control of body functions, refinement of motor and language skills, and acquisition of socially acceptable behavior, especially toleration of delayed gratification and acceptance of separation from the mother or parents.

toddlerhood /tod′lərhŏŏd′/, the state or condition of being a toddler.

Todd's paralysis [Robert Bentley Todd, English physician, 1809–1860; Gk, *paralyein,* to be palsied], weakness, usually on one side of the body, after a seizure, usually lasting a few minutes, hours, or, occasionally, several days.

toe, any one of the digits of the feet.

toe clonus [AS, *tá;* Gk, *klonos*], an increased reflex activity in the large toe caused by a sudden extension of the first phalanx.

toe drop [AS, *tá* + *dropa*], a condition in which the toes droop and cannot be lifted because of paralysis of the tibial muscles.

toenail [AS, *ta* + *naegel*], one of the heavy ungual structures covering the terminal phalanges of the toes.

Tofranil, a trademark for a tricyclic antidepressant (imipramine hydrochloride).

toilet training, the process of teaching a child to control the functions of the bladder and bowel. Training often begins around 24 months of age, when voluntary control of the anal and urethral sphincters is achieved by most children. Nighttime bladder control may not be achieved until the child is 4 or 5 years of age or older.

token economy [AS, *tacen,* to show; Gk, *oikonomia,* household management], a technique of reinforcement used in behavior therapy in the management of a group of people, such as in hospitals, institutions, or classrooms. Individuals are rewarded for specific activities or behavior with tokens that they can exchange for desired objects or privileges.

TOLAZamide /tolaz′əmīd/, an oral sulfonylurea antidiabetic agent prescribed in the treatment of stable or type 2 DM and for some patients sensitive to other types of sulfonylureas or who have failed to respond to other similar drugs.

tolazoline hydrochloride /tolaz′əlēn/, an alpha adrenergic receptor blocker prescribed in the treatment of persistent pulmonary hypertension of the newborn and in peripheral vascular disease.

TOLBUTamide /tolboo̅′təmīd/, an oral sulfonylurea antidiabetic agent prescribed in the treatment of stable type 2 DM uncontrolled by diet alone and for some patients changing from insulin to oral therapy.

tolcapone, an antiparkinsonian agent.

Tolectin, a trademark for a nonsteroidal antiinflammatory agent (tolmetin sodium).

tolerance /tol′ərəns/ [L, *tolerare,* to endure], a phenomenon by which the body becomes increasingly resistant to a drug or other substance through continued exposure to the substance.

tolerance test, **1.** an investigation of the ability of the body to metabolize a drug or nutrient, as in a glucose tolerance test. **2.** a physical activity drill administered to evaluate the efficiency of blood circulation or of another body system.

Tolinase, a trademark for an antidiabetic agent TOLAZamide).

tolmetin sodium /tol′mətin/, a nonsteroidal antiinflammatory agent prescribed primarily in the treatment of rheumatoid arthritis, juvenile rheumatoid arthritis, and osteoarthritis.

tolnaftate /tolnaf′tāt/, an antifungal prescribed in the treatment of superficial fungus infections of the skin, including tinea pedis, tinea cruris, and tinea versicolor.

Tolosa-Hunt syndrome /tō·lō′sä hunt/ [Eduardo S. Tolosa, Spanish neurosurgeon, 20th century; William Edward Hunt, American neurosurgeon, b. 1921], unilateral ophthalmoplegia associated with pain behind the orbit and in the area supplied by the first division of the trigeminal nerve; it is thought to result from nonspecific inflammation and granulation tissue in the superior orbital fissure or cavernous sinus.

tolterodine, a muscarinic receptor antagonist prescribed to treat overactive bladder (frequency and urgency). It controls bladder incontinence by controlling contractions.

toluene ($C_6H_5CH_3$) /tol′yoo̅·ēn/, an aromatic colorless flammable liquid produced from coal tar, petroleum, or Peruvian tolu balsam. It is used in dyes, explosives, gums, and lacquers and in the manufacture of drugs and the extraction of organic chemicals from plants.

tomogram /tō′məgram/ [Gk, *tome*, section, *gramma*, record], a radiograph produced by tomography.

tomograph /tō′məgraf′/ [Gk, *tome*, section, *graphein*, to record], a radiographic apparatus that makes an image of layers of body tissues at various depths.

tomographic DSA /-graf′ik/, the visualization of blood vessels in the body in three dimensions.

tomography /təmog′rəfē/ [Gk, *tome* + *graphein*, to record], **1.** sectional imaging. **2.** a radiographic technique in which the tube and film are moved synchronously during exposure, producing a blurred radiograph in which objects within the focal plane are seen more clearly than objects outside the focal plane. **3.** a radiographic technique that produces a film representing a detailed cross section of tissue at a predetermined depth. It is a valuable diagnostic tool for the discovery and identification of space-occupying lesions.

tone deafness [Gk, *tonos*, stretching; AS, *deaf*], an inability to detect the pitch or changing pitch of a musical note or a voice change.

tongue /tung/ [AS, *tunge*], the principal organ of the sense of taste that also assists in the mastication and deglutition of food. It is located in the floor of the mouth within the curve of the mandible. Its root is connected to the hyoid bone posteriorly. It is also connected to the epiglottis, soft palate, and pharynx. The use of the tongue as an organ of speech is not anatomic but a secondary acquired characteristic.

tongue-thrust swallow, an immature form of swallowing in which the tongue is projected forward instead of retracted during the act of swallowing. It may result in forward displacement of the maxilla with consequent malocclusion of the teeth.

tonic /ton′ik/, pertaining to a type of afferent or sensory nerve receptor that responds to length changes placed on the noncontractile part of a muscle spindle. It may be triggered by a mechanical external force such as positioning or by an internal stretch caused by intrafusal muscle contraction.

tonic bite, reflexive, sustained jaw closure, accompanied by increased abnormal tone in the jaw muscles, in response to stimulation of the teeth or gums. It is difficult to release, and its force can damage the teeth or an object placed in the mouth.

tonic-clonic seizure, an epileptic seizure characterized by a generalized involuntary muscular contraction and cessation of respiration followed by tonic and clonic spasms of the muscles. Breathing resumes with noisy respirations. The teeth may be clenched, the tongue bitten, and control of the bladder or bowel lost. As this phase of the seizure passes, the person may fall asleep or experience confusion. Usually the person has no recall of the seizure on awakening. A sensory warning, or aura, can precede each tonic-clonic seizure. Anticonvulsant medications are usually prescribed as prophylaxis.

tonic convulsion [Gk, *tonos*, stretching; L, *convulsio*, cramp], a prolonged generalized contraction of the skeletal muscles.

tonicity /tōnis′itē/ [Gk, *tonikos*, stretching], the quality of possessing tone, or tonus.

tonic labyrinthine reflex (TLR) [Gk, *tonikos* + *labyrinthos*, maze; L, *reflectere*, to bend back], a normal postural reflex in animals, abnormally accentuated in decerebrate humans, characterized by extension of all four limbs when the head is positioned in space at an angle above the horizontal in quadripeds or in the neutral erect position in humans.

tonic neck reflex, a normal response in newborns to extend the arm and leg on the side of the body to which the head is quickly turned while the infant is supine and to flex the limbs of the opposite side. The reflex prevents the infant from rolling over until adequate neurologic and motor development occurs and normally disappears by 3 to 4 months of age.

tonic spasm [Gk, *tonos*, stretching + *spasmos*], a sustained contraction of a muscle.

tonitrophobia /tonit′rōfō′bē·ə/, an abnormal fear of thunder.

Tonocard, a trademark for a lidocaine-type oral antiarrhythmic drug (tocainide hydrochloride).

tonoclonic /ton′əklon′ik/ [Gk, *tonos*, stretching, *klonos*, tumult], pertaining to muscular spasms that are tonic and then clonic.

tonofibril /ton′əfī′bril/ [Gk, *tonos*, stretching, *fibrilla*, small fiber], a bundle of fine filaments found in the cytoplasm of epithelial cells. The individual strands, or **tonofilaments,** spread throughout the cytoplasm and extend into the intercellular bridge to converge at the desmosome.

tonofilament /ton′ōfil′əmənt/ [Gk, *tonos*, stretching], a proteinaceous fiber found in epithelial cells. Bundles of tonofilaments form a tonofibril, which has a supporting function.

tonograph /ton′əgraf/, an apparatus that makes a record of tension measurements.

tonography /tōnog′rəfē/, **1.** the measurement over time of intraocular pressure with graphic documentation. **2.** the measurement of tension.

tonometer /tōnom'ətər/ [Gk, *tonos* + *metron*, measure], an instrument used in measuring tension or pressure, especially intraocular pressure.

tonometry /tōnom'ətrē/, the measuring of intraocular pressure by determining the resistance of the eyeball to indentation by an applied force. Applanation tonometry at the slit lamp is considered most accurate and works by recording the pressure needed to indent or flatten the corneal surface.

tonoscillograph /ton'əsil'əgraf/, an apparatus that records arterial and capillary pressures with a corresponding pulse tracing.

tonsil /ton'səl/ [L, *tonsilla*], a small rounded mass of tissue, especially lymphoid tissue such as that composing the palatine tonsils in the oropharynx.

tonsillar /ton'silər/ [L, *tonsilla*], pertaining to the palatine tonsil.

tonsillar crypt [L, *tonsilla*; Gk, *kryptos,* hidden], a small tubular invagination on the surface of a palatine or pharyngeal tonsil.

tonsillar herniation [L, *tonsilla* + *hernia,* rupture], the herniation of tonsils of the cerebellum through the foramen magnum of the skull. It may occur as a result of ICP from an injury or tumor.

tonsillectomy /ton'silek'təmē/ [L, *tonsilla*; Gk, *ektomē*, excision], the surgical excision of the palatine tonsils, performed to prevent recurrent tonsillitis.

tonsillitis /-ī'tis/, an infection or inflammation of a tonsil. Acute tonsillitis, frequently caused by *Streptococcus* infection, is characterized by severe sore throat, fever, headache, malaise, difficulty in swallowing, earache, and enlarged tender lymph nodes in the neck. Treatment includes systemic antibiotics, analgesics, and warm irrigations of the throat. Tonsillectomy is sometimes performed for recurrent tonsillitis or tonsillar abscess.

tonsilloadenoidectomy /ton'silō·ad'ənoid ek'təmē/ [L, *tonsilla*; Gk, *aden*, gland, *eidos*, form, *ektomē*, excision], the surgical removal of tonsil and adenoid tissues.

tonus /tō'nəs/ [Gk, *tonos*, stretching], **1.** the normal state of balanced tension in the body tissues, especially the muscles. Partial contraction or alternate contraction and relaxation of neighboring fibers of a group of muscles hold the organ or the part of the body in a neutral functional position without fatigue. **2.** the state of the body tissues' being strong and fit.

tooth *pl.* **teeth** [AS, *toth*], any one of numerous dental structures that develop in the jaws. Each tooth consists of a crown, which projects above the gum; two to four roots embedded in the alveolus; and a neck, which stretches between the crown and the root. Each tooth also contains a cavity filled with pulp, richly supplied with blood vessels and nerves that enter the cavity through a small aperture at the base of each root. The solid part of the tooth consists of dentin, enamel, and a thin layer of bone on the surface of the root. Two sets of teeth appear at different periods of life: the 20 deciduous teeth appear during infancy, the 32 secondary teeth during childhood and early adulthood.

tooth abscess [AS, *toth*; L, *abscedere*, to go away], a collection of pus on a tooth, usually close to the root and often the result of an untreated cavity. If untreated, the pressure of the abscess may destroy the alveolar bone and adjoining soft tissues.

toothache /tōō'thāk/ [AS, *toth* + *aeca*], pain in a tooth, usually caused by pulpal infection or damage.

tooth alignment, the arrangement of the teeth in relation to their supporting bone or alveolar process, adjacent teeth, and opposing dentition.

tooth bleaching, the process of removing stains or color from teeth by applying chemicals such as hydrogen peroxide.

tooth-borne, describing a dental prosthesis or part of a prosthesis that depends entirely on abutment teeth for support.

tooth-borne base, a denture base restoring an edentulous area that has abutment teeth at each end for support.

toothbrush, an implement of various designs, with bristles fixed to a head at the end of a handle, used for cleaning the teeth and cleaning and massaging the gingival tissues.

tooth eruption, the final stage of odontogenesis, in which a tooth breaks out from its crypt through surrounding tissue.

tooth form, the identifying curves, lines, angles, and contours of a tooth that differentiate it from other teeth.

tooth fulcrum, the axis of movement of a tooth subjected to lateral forces. It is considered to be at the middle third of the part of the tooth root embedded in the alveolus.

tooth germ, a primitive cell in the embryo that is the precursor of a tooth.

tooth inclination, the angle of slope of a tooth or teeth from the vertical plane. Inclinations may be mesial, distal, lingual, buccal, or labial.

tooth rotation [AS, *toth*; L, *rotare*, to rotate], **1.** the turning of a tooth around its longitudinal axis. **2.** the process by which a tooth is turned.

tooth size discrepancy, lack of harmony of size of individual or groups of teeth when related to those within the same arch or the opposing arch.

TOP, abbreviation for *t*emporal, *o*ccipital, and *p*arietal regions of the skull.

tophaceous /tōfā′shəs/, pertaining to the presence of chalky accumulations of uric acid crystals (tophi).

tophaceous gout [L, *tufa*, porous rock], a form of purine metabolism disorder characterized by formation of chalky deposits of sodium biurate under the skin and in the joints. If untreated, the deposits may eventually destroy the involved joints.

tophus /tō′fəs/ *pl.* **tophi** [L, *tufa*, porous rock], a calculus containing sodium urate that develops in fibrous tissue around joints, typically in patients with gout. —**tophaceous,** *adj.*

topical /top′ikəl/ [Gk, *topos,* place], **1.** pertaining to the surface of a part of the body. **2.** pertaining to a drug or treatment applied topically.

topical anesthesia, surface analgesia produced by application of an anesthetic in the form of a solution, gel, or ointment directly to the skin, mucous membrane, or cornea. The most common ingredients include benzocaine, dibucaine, lidocaine, hexylcaine, and tetracaine.

Topicort, a trademark for a topical glucocorticoid (desoximetasone).

topiramate, a miscellaneous anticonvulsant prescribed to treat partial seizures, with or without generalization in adults.

topognosis /top′ognō′sis/ [Gk, *topos* + *gnosis,* recognition], the ability to recognize tactile stimuli.

topogometer /top′ōgom′ətər/ [Gk, *topos,* place, *gonia,* angle, *metron,* measure], a movable fixation target attached to an instrument for measuring the radius of curvature of the cornea. It is used in fitting contact lenses of correct curvature.

topographic /top′əgraf′ik/, in psychiatry, pertaining to a freudian conceptualization of the layers of human consciousness.

topographic anatomy [Gk, *topos,* place, *graphein,* to record, *ana* + *temnein,* to cut], the study of a specific region of a body structure such as a lower leg, including all of the systems in the part and their relationship to each other.

topographic disorientation, a psychiatric disorder based on Freud's topographic model of the mental apparatus, consisting of conscious, preconscious, and unconscious systems for interpreting perceptions of the outside world and internal perceptions.

topography /təpog′refē/ [Gk, *topos,* place, *graphein,* to record], the anatomic description of a body part in terms of the region in which it is located.

topoisomerase /to′pō-ī′sä-mər-ās/, an enzyme involved in mobilization and replication of DNA during cell division.

topoisomerase inhibitors, a class of antineoplastic agents that interfere with the arrangement of DNA in cells.

topology /təpol′əjē/, **1.** orientation of the presenting part of a fetus. **2.** the study of special regions of anatomy. **3.** the science of properties of geometric configuration.

topotecan, an antineoplastic hormone prescribed to treat metastatic carcinoma of the ovary after failure of traditional chemotherapy.

TOPV, abbreviation for *trivalent oral polio vaccine.*

TORCH /tôrch/, abbreviation for *t*oxoplasmosis, *o*ther, *r*ubella virus, *c*ytomegalovirus, and *h*erpes simplex viruses, a group of agents that can infect the fetus or the newborn, causing a constellation of morbid effects called the TORCH syndrome.

TORCH syndrome, infection of the fetus or newborn by one of the TORCH agents. The outcome of a pregnancy complicated by a TORCH agent may be abortion, stillbirth, intrauterine growth retardation, or premature delivery. At delivery and during the first days after birth, an infant infected with any one of the organisms may demonstrate various clinical manifestations such as fever, lethargy, poor feeding, petechiae on the skin, purpura, and pneumonia, hepatosplenomegaly, jaundice, hemolytic and other anemias, encephalitis, microcephaly, hydrocephalus, intracranial calcifications, hearing deficits, chorioretinitis, and microphthalmia. Each of the agents is associated with several other abnormal clinical findings involving abnormal immune response, cataracts, glaucoma, vesicles, ulcers, and congenital cardiac defects. Before pregnancy women may be tested for susceptibility to the rubella virus and inoculated against it if not immune. There are currently no vaccines that confer immunity to the other TORCH agents, but the mother may be serologically tested for antibody levels to them. The congenital effects of TORCH syndrome are not amenable to change or to amelioration by any known treatment.

TORCH test, a series of tests for diseases that exert recognized detrimental effects on the fetus (tests include *t*oxoplasmosis, *o*ther [including syphilis], *r*ubella, *c*ytomegalovirus, and *h*erpes simplex), such as precipitating abortion or premature labor.

Torecan, a trademark for a phenothiazine antiemetic (thiethylperazine maleate).

toremifene, an antineoplastic prescribed to treat advanced breast carcinoma that is not responsive to other therapy in estrogen–receptor–positive patients (usually postmenopausal).

Torisel, a trademark for temsirolimus.

T

Tornalate, a trademark for an orally inhaled bronchodilator (bitolterol mesylate).

torose /tôr'ōs/ [L, *torosus,* bulging], knoblike, knobby, or bulging.

torpor /tôr'pər/, **1.** a state of mental or physical inactivity. **2.** an absence or slowness of response to a stimulus.

torque /tôrk/ [L, *torquere,* to twist], **1.** a twisting force produced by contraction of the medial femoral muscles that tend to rotate the thigh medially. **2.** in dentistry, a force applied to a tooth to rotate it on a mesiodistal or buccolingual axis. **3.** a rotary force applied to a denture base.

torr /tôr/ [Evangelista Torricelli, Italian physicist, 1608–1647], a unit of pressure equal to 1333.22 dynes/cm², or 1.33322 millibars. One torr is the pressure required to support a column of mercury 1 mm high when the mercury is of standard density and subjected to standard acceleration.

torsades de pointes /tôrsäd' de pô·aNt', tôr'säd də point/ [Fr, *torsader,* to twist together, *pointes,* tips], a type of ventricular tachycardia with a spiral-like appearance ("twisting of the points") and complexes that at first look positive and then negative on an ECG. It is precipitated by a long Q-T interval, which often is induced by drugs (quinidine, procainamide, or disopyramide), but which may be the result of hypokalemia or profound bradycardia.

torsemide /tor'se-mīd/, a loop diuretic related to sulfonylurea, used in treatment of edema and hypertension.

torsiometer /tôr'sē·om'ətər/, a device for measuring the amount of torsion of an eye around its anteroposterior axis.

torsion /tôr'shən/ [L, *torquere,* to twist], **1.** the process of twisting in a positive (clockwise) or negative (counterclockwise) direction. **2.** the state of being turned. **3.** in dentistry, the twisting of a tooth on its long axis.

torsion angle, the angle between the axes of any two different portions of long bones, such as between the head and neck of the femur and its long axis.

torsion fracture, a spiral fracture, usually caused by a torsion injury.

torsion of the testis, the axial rotation of the spermatic cord that cuts off the blood supply to the testicle, epididymis, and other structures. Complete ischemia for 6 hours may result in gangrene of the testis. Partial loss of circulation may result in atrophy. Surgical correction is required in most cases.

torso /tôr'sō/ [L, *thyrsus,* stem], the body excluding the limbs.

tort [L, *tortus,* twisted], in law, a civil wrong, other than a breach of contract. Torts include negligence, false imprisonment, assault, and battery. The elements of a tort are: a legal duty owed by the defendant to the plaintiff, a breach of duty, and damage from the breach of duty.—**tortious,** *adj.*

torticollis /tôr'tikol'is/ [L, *tortus,* twisted, *collum,* neck], an abnormal condition in which the head is inclined to one side as a result of the contraction of muscles on that side of the neck. Treatment may include surgery, heat, support, or immobilization, depending on the cause and severity of the condition.

tortipelvis /-pel'vis/ [L, *tortus,* twisted, *pelvis,* basin], a form of muscular dystonia resulting in a distortion of the pelvis or the spine and hips.

tortuous /tôr'chōō·əs/ [L, *tortus,* twisted], having or making twists and turns.

Torulopsis, a genus of Fungi Imperfecti of the family Cryptococcaceae; it is closely related to *Candida.* Some species are normal inhabitants of the skin, respiratory tract, GI tract, and urogenital region but may also cause opportunistic infections.

Torulopsis glabrata, a species of fungus that is part of the normal flora of the human mouth, gut, and urinary tract but that in weak or immunocompromised patients may cause opportunistic infections such as meningitis, pneumonia, cystitis, and fungemia.

torulopsosis /tôr'yəlopsō'sis, tôr'yŏŏlop'sosis/ [L, *torulus,* small swelling; Gk, *opsis,* appearance, *osis,* condition], an infection with the yeast *Torulopsis glabrata,* a normal inhabitant of the oropharynx, GI tract, and skin. *T. glabrata* causes disease in severely debilitated patients, in those with impaired immune function, or sometimes in patients having prolonged urinary catheterization. Systemic infection is usually treated with amphotericin B.

torus levatorius, a broad fold or elevation in the nasopharynx that appears to emerge from just under the opening of the pharyngotympanic tube, continues medially onto the upper surface of the soft palate, and overlies the levator veli palatini muscle.

torus tubarius, an elevation of the rim of the pharyngotympanic tube where it projects into the nasopharynx.

total allergy syndrome, a condition of hypersensitivity to a wide range of substances, including pesticides, insecticides, pharmaceutics, certain metals, and chemicals used in the manufacture of plastics and epoxy resins.

total anomalous venous return [L, *totus,* whole; Gk, *anomalos,* uneven; L, *vena,* vein; ME, *retournen,* to turn back], a rare congenital cardiac anomaly in which the pulmonary veins attach to the right atrium or to various veins draining into the right atrium rather than to the left atrium. Clinical manifestations include cyanosis, pulmonary congestion, and heart failure. Corrective surgery is indicated, usually after one year of age.

total body electric conductivity (TOBEC), a method of measuring body composition by the differences in electric conductivity of fat, bone, and muscle. It is used in clinical studies of weight control in which physicians want to determine if weight loss is caused by fat, water, or other tissues.

total body radiation, radiation that exposes the entire body and, theoretically, all cells in the body.

total body water (TBW), all the water within the body, including intracellular and extracellular water plus the water in the GI and urinary tracts.

total cell volume (TCV), a measure of the adequacy of urea clearance of a hemodialyzer, calculated as the volume of saline necessary to fill its blood compartment.

total cleavage, mitotic division of a fertilized ovum into blastomeres.

total communication, the combined use of oral language and manual communication by a person with hearing loss.

total elbow arthroplasty, arthroplasty of both sides of the elbow joint, with humeral and ulnar components.

total hip arthroplasty (THA), arthroplasty of both sides of the hip joint, with acetabular and femoral components.

total hip replacement, a surgical procedure to correct a hip joint damaged by degenerative disease, often arthritis. The head of the femur and the acetabulum are replaced with metal components. The acetabulum is plastic-coated to avoid metal-to-metal articulating surfaces.

total intravenous anesthesia (TIVA), anesthesia using only IV agents without the use of inhalational agents. TIVA avoids unwanted effects of inhalational agents and the need for complex apparatus. Drugs used are generally of short duration of action and half-life to reduce the risks associated with accumulation.

total iron, the total iron concentration in the blood. The serum reference interval is 50 to 150 mg/dL.

total joint replacement, a surgical procedure for the treatment of severe arthritis and other disorders in which the normal articulating surfaces of a joint are replaced by metal and plastic prostheses.

total lung capacity (TLC), the volume of gas in the lungs at the end of a maximum inspiration. It equals the vital capacity plus the residual capacity.

total lymphoid irradiation (TLI), a method of inducing a strong immunosuppressive effect in patients undergoing bone marrow transplants, treatment of certain lymphomas, or other therapies requiring immunosuppression. TLI involves exposing all lymph nodes, the thymus, and spleen to a total of 2000 rad in 100-rad doses from a linear accelerator before graft implantation.

total macroglobulins, the heavy serum macroglobulins that are elevated in various diseases such as cancer and infections.

total parenteral nutrition (TPN), the administration of a nutritionally adequate hypertonic solution consisting of glucose, protein hydrolysates, minerals, and vitamins through an indwelling catheter into the superior vena cava or other main vein. The procedure is used in prolonged coma, severe uncontrolled malabsorption, extensive burns, GI fistulas, and other conditions in which feeding by mouth cannot provide adequate amounts of the essential nutrients.

total parenteral nutrition (TPN) administration, a nursing intervention from the Nursing Interventions Classification (NIC) defined as preparation and delivery of nutrients intravenously and monitoring of patient responsiveness.

total peripheral resistance, the overall resistance to blood flow through the systemic blood vessels.

total quality management (TQM), an approach to the improvement of the provision of services based on the premise that the overwhelming majority of quality failures are the result of flaws in processes and that quality can be improved by controlling these processes. TQM involves creation of an organizational structure for identifying and improving processes, the use of databased statistical analysis to study processes, and the empowerment of employees to take responsibility for their own tasks in a way that encourages both continuous learning and personal responsibility.

total renal blood flow (TRBF), the total volume of blood that flows into the renal arteries. The average TRBF in a normal adult is 1200 mL per minute.

total thyroxine (T₄) test, a blood test that directly measures the total amount of T_4 present in the patient's blood, with abnormal values indicating either hyperthyroid or hypothyroid states. This test is also used to monitor replacement suppressive therapy.

totem /tōʹtəm/, an animal, plant, force of nature, or inanimate object that represents the tribal ancestor of a clan. It also serves as a tutelary spirit and protector and may communicate through oracles.

totipotency /tō'tipō'tənsē/, the ability of a cell, particularly a zygote, to differentiate into any of a number of specialized cells and thus form a new organism or regenerate a body part.

totipotential cell, an embryonic cell that is capable of developing into any variety of body cells.

touch¹ /tuch/ [Fr, *toucher*, to touch], **1.** the ability to feel objects and to distinguish their various characteristics; the tactile sense. **2.** the ability to perceive pressure when it is exerted on the skin or mucosa of the body. **3.** to palpate or examine with the hand such as the digital examination of the abdomen, rectum, or vagina.

touch², a nursing intervention from the Nursing Interventions Classification (NIC) defined as providing comfort and communication through purposeful tactile contact.

touch deprivation, a lack of tactile stimulation, especially in early infancy. If continued for a sufficient length of time, it may lead to serious developmental and emotional disturbances such as stunted growth, personality disorders, and social regression.

touch receptors [Fr, *toucher*; L, *recipere*, to receive], specialized sensory nerve endings that are sensitive to tactile stimuli.

tourniquet /tur'nikit, tŏŏr'-/ [Fr, turnstile], a device used in controlling hemorrhage, consisting of a wide constricting band applied to the limb close to the site of bleeding. The use of a tourniquet is a drastic measure and is to be used only if the hemorrhage is life-threatening and if other safer measures have proved ineffective.

tourniquet infusion method, a technique of intraarterial regional chemotherapy used in the treatment of osteogenic sarcoma. The technique uses one or two external tourniquets, depending on the location of the tumor, that slow or interrupt the blood flow to a limb temporarily while an anticancer drug such as adriamycin is infused into the area. The method results in a greatly increased concentratin of the drug at the tumor site.

tourniquet test, a test of capillary fragility in which a BP cuff is applied for 5 minutes to a person's arm and inflated to a pressure halfway between the diastolic and systolic BP. The number of petechiae within a circumscribed area of the skin may be counted.

Townes method, a technique for producing radiographic images of the occipital bone, foramen magnum, and dorsum sellae. The patient is supine or facing the x-ray tube with the chin depressed so that the orbitomeatal line is perpendicular. The x-ray beam is angled 30 degrees toward the patient's feet and enters the frontal

bone above the nasal bones and exits the occipital bone.

Toxascaris leonina /toksas'kəris/, a species of nematode found mainly in domestic animals, commonly known as roundworms. It differs from related species in that it spends its entire developmental cycle in the digestive tract, rather than migrating through the lungs.

toxemia /toksē'mē·ə/ [Gk, *toxikon*, poison, *haima*, blood], the presence of bacterial toxins in the bloodstream.— **toxemic,** *adj.*

toxic /tok'sik/ [Gk, *toxikon*], **1.** pertaining to a poison. **2.** pertaining to a severe and progressive disease or condition.

toxic albuminuria [Gk, *toxikon,* poison; L, *albus,* white; Gk, *ouron,* urine], a condition of serum albumin in the urine caused by the presence of toxic substances in the body.

toxic alcohols, poisonous alcohols that can damage the heart, kidneys, and nervous system. Severe poisoning is caused only by ingestion and is marked by progressive stages of CNS depression, acidosis, and renal failure.

toxic amblyopia, partial loss of vision because of retrobulbar neuritis, resulting from poisoning with quinine, lead, wood alcohol, nicotine, arsenic, or certain other poisons.

toxicant /tok'sikənt/, any poisonous agent.

toxic delirium [Gk, *toxikon,* poison; L, *delirare,* to rave], a symptom of disordered mental status as a result of poisoning.

toxic dementia, dementia resulting from excessive use of or exposure to a poisonous substance.

toxic dilation of colon [Gk, *toxikon*; L, *dilatare,* to widen; Gk, *kolon*], a condition of transverse colon dilation as a complication of amebic colitis, ulcerative colitis, or other bowel disease. Symptoms may include cramping, fever, rapid heartbeat, and mental confusion.

toxic dose (TD), in toxicology, the amount of a substance that may be expected to produce a toxic effect.

toxic encephalitis [Gk, *toxikon,* poison, *enkephalos,* brain, *itis,* inflammation], encephalitis caused by heavy metal poisoning. It is characterized by convulsions and cerebral edema.

toxic epidermal necrolysis (TEN), a rare skin disease, characterized by epidermal erythema, superficial necrosis, and skin erosions. This condition, which affects mainly adults, makes the skin appear scalded, often leaving scars. The cause is unknown, but it may result from toxic or hypersensitive reactions, an immune response, or severe physiological stress. Treatment commonly involves the administration of IV fluids to replace body fluids and maintain electrolyte balance. Frequent laboratory analyses are necessary to monitor hematocrit and hemoglobin, serum proteins, electrolytes, and blood gases.

toxic erythema [Gk, *toxikon,* poison, *erythema,* redness], an inexact term sometimes applied to reddish skin eruptions of undetermined origin.

toxic goiter, an enlargement of the thyroid gland associated with exophthalmia and systemic disease.

toxic headache, headache caused by systemic poisoning or associated with illness.

toxic hepatitis, hepatitis produced by a hepatotoxin, such as *Amanita phalloides* toxin, carbon tetrachloride, or any of various drugs.

toxic hepatopathy, liver disease produced by a hepatotoxin such as *Amanita phalloides* toxin, carbon tetrachloride, white phosphorus, or any of various drugs. It can range in severity from subclinical abnormalities to jaundice to fulminant liver failure.

toxicity /toksis'itē/ [Gk, *toxikon*], **1.** the degree to which something is poisonous. **2.** a condition that results from exposure to a toxin or to toxic amounts of a substance that does not cause adverse effects in smaller amounts.

toxic nephropathy, kidney damage caused by the effects of a nephrotoxin. The most common symptoms are dysfunction and then necrosis of the proximal tubules, sometimes progressing to renal failure.

toxic neuritis [Gk, *toxikon,* poison, *neuron,* nerve, *itis,* inflammation], a painful nerve inflammation caused by a metallic, bacterial, or other poison.

toxic nodular goiter, an enlarged thyroid gland characterized by numerous discrete nodules and hypersecretion of thyroid hormones. Typical signs of thyrotoxicosis such as nervousness, tremor, weakness, fatigue, weight loss, and irritability are usually present, but exophthalmia is rare. Anorexia is more common than hyperphagia, and cardiac arrhythmia or CHF may be a predominant manifestation.

Toxicodendron /tok'sikōden'dron/, a genus of plants that includes poison ivy, poison oak, and poison sumac. The toxic agent in the plants is a nonvolatile oil, toxicodendrol.

toxicokinetics /tok'sikō'kinet'iks/, the passage through the body of a toxic agent or its metabolites, usually in an action similar to that of pharmacokinetics.

toxicologist /tok'sikol'əjist/, a specialist in poisons, their effects, and antidotes.

toxicology /-ol'əjē/, the scientific study of poisons, their detection, their effects, and methods of treatment for conditions they produce.—**toxicologic,** *adj.*

toxicology screening, a blood or urine test that detects the most commonly abused nonprescription drugs.

toxic or drug-induced hepatitis, hepatitis resulting from a chemical, parasitic, or metabolic poison.

toxicosis /tok'sikō'sis/ [Gk, *toxikon,* poison, *osis,* condition], a disease condition caused by the absorption of metabolic or bacterial poisons.

toxic psychosis, psychosis that results from the poisonous effects of chemicals or drugs, including those produced by the body itself.

toxic shock syndrome (TSS), a severe acute disease caused by infection with strains of *Staphylococcus aureus,* phage group I, that produces a unique toxin, enterotoxin F. It is most common in menstruating women using high-absorbency tampons but has been seen in newborns, children, and men. The onset of the syndrome is characterized by sudden high fever, headache, sore throat with swelling of the mucous membranes, diarrhea, nausea, and erythroderma. Acute renal failure, abnormal liver function, confusion, and refractory hypotension usually follow, and death may occur. Aggressive volume expansion by the administration of large amounts of IV fluids, assisted ventilation, and administration of vasopressors may be necessary in treating severe TSS.

toxic substance [Gk, *toxikon,* poison; L, *substantia,* essence], any poison.

toxidrome /tok'sidrōm/, a specific syndromelike group of symptoms associated with exposure to a given poison.

toxin /tok'sin/, a poison, usually one produced by or occurring in a plant or microorganism.

toxin-antitoxin [Gk, *toxikon,* poison, *anti,* against + *toxikon*], a mixture of toxin and antitoxin.

toxinology /tok'sinol'əjē/, the study of poisons, with particular emphasis on relatively unstable proteinaceous substances.

Toxocara /tok'sōker'ə/, a genus of ascarid nematodes. *T. canis* affects mainly dogs. *T. mystax* affects cats but may also infect humans, particularly children, causing intestinal and respiratory symptoms and damage to the spleen and liver.

toxocariasis /tok'sōkərī'əsis/ [Gk, *toxo,* bow, *kara,* head, *osis,* condition], infection with the larvae of *Toxocara canis,* the common roundworm of dogs, and with *T. cati,* of cats. Human ingestion of viable eggs, commonly found in soil, leads to the spread of tiny larvae throughout the body, resulting in respiratory symptoms, enlarged liver, skin rashes, eosinophilia, and delayed ocular lesions. Two major forms of the infection exist. Ocular larval migrans (OLM), which can cause an eye disease resulting in blindness, occurs when the worm enters the eye. Visceral larval migrans (VLM) is heavy or repeated infection which causes swelling of organs or the CNS. Symptoms of this form are caused by movement of the worms and are manifested as fever, asthma, or pneumonia. Severe forms are rare, VLM is treated with antiparasitic drugs and anti-inflammatories, OLM is more difficult to treat and usually involves preventing progression of eye damage. Regular worming of pets helps prevent infection.

toxoid /tok'soid/ [Gk, *toxikon,* poison, *eidos,* form], a toxin that has been treated with chemicals or heat to decrease its toxic effect but that retains its antigenic power. It is given to produce immunity by stimulating the creation of antibodies.

toxophore /tok'səfôr/, the part of a toxic molecule that is responsible for the poisonous effect.

Toxoplasma /tok'sōplaz'mə/ [Gk, *toxikon* + *plasma,* something formed], a genus of protozoa with only one known species, *Toxoplasma gondii,* an intracellular parasite of cats and other hosts that causes toxoplasmosis in humans.

toxoplasmosis /tok'sōplazmō'sis/ [Gk, *toxikon* + *plasma* + *osis,* condition], a common infection with the protozoan intracellular parasite *Toxoplasma gondii.* The congenital form is characterized by liver and brain involvement with cerebral calcification, convulsions, blindness, microcephaly or hydrocephaly, and mental retardation. The acquired form is characterized by rash, lymphadenopathy, fever, malaise, CNS disorders, myocarditis, and pneumonitis.

toxoplasmosis antibody titer, a blood test performed on pregnant women to detect toxoplasmosis infection.

Toynbee maneuver /toin'bē/ [Joseph Toynbee, English otologist, 1815–1866], pinching the nostrils and swallowing. If the auditory tube is patent, the tympanic membrane will retract medially.

Toynbee test /toin'bē/ [Joseph Toynbee], performance of the Toynbee maneuver and monitoring of pressure changes in the middle ear. Subsequent middle ear negative pressure or negative pressure followed by ambient pressure usually indicates normal function of the auditory tube.

TPA, abbreviation for **tissue plasminogen activator.**

TPHA, a blood test performed on pregnant women to detect toxoplasmosis infection,

TPN, abbreviation for **total parenteral nutrition.**

TPR, abbreviation for *temperature, pulse, respiration.*

TQ, symbol for **tocopherolquinone.**

TQM, abbreviation for **total quality management.**

TR, 1. abbreviation for *repetition time.* 2. abbreviation for **tricuspid regurgitation.**

trabecula carnea /trəbek'yələ/ *pl.* **trabeculae carneae** [L, little beam, *carneus,* flesh], any one of the irregular bands and bundles of muscle projecting from the inner surfaces near the apex of the ventricles of the heart.

trabeculae, in ophthalmology, the part of the eye in front of the canal of Schlemm and within the angle created by the iris and cornea, responsible for aqueous drainage.

trabecular pattern /trəbek'yələr/ [L, little beam], an irregular meshwork of stress and stress-related struts within a cancellous bone.

trabeculated bladder, a noncompliant, hypotonic bladder resulting from hypertrophy of the muscular coat, usually caused by obstruction of the urethra.

trabeculectomy, creation of a fistula between the anterior chamber of the eye and the subconjunctival space by surgical removal of a portion of the trabecular meshwork, performed to facilitate drainage of the aqueous humor in glaucoma.

trabeculoplasty /trabek'yəlōplas'tē/, a plastic surgery procedure used in the treatment of open-angle glaucoma. An argon laser beam is used to blanch the trabecular network of the eye, thereby permitting drainage of the excess fluid that is causing increased pressure within the eyeball.

trabeculotomy /-ot'əmē/, a surgical opening in an orbital trabecula to increase the outflow of aqueous humor.

trace element [L, *trahere,* to draw, *elementum,* first principle], an element essential to nutrition or physiologic processes, found in such minute quantities that analysis yields a presence of only trace amounts.

trace gas, any gas that represents an extremely small or insignificant portion of a mixture of gases.

tracer [L, *trahere,* to draw], 1. a radioactive isotope that is used in diagnostic x-ray techniques to allow a biologic process to be seen. After introduction into the body, the tracer binds with a specific substance and is followed with a scanner or fluoroscope as it passes through various organs or systems. 2. a mechanical device that graphically records the outline or movements of an object or part of the body. 3. a dissecting instrument that is used to isolate vessels and nerves.— **trace,** *v.*

tracer depot method, a technique used to determine local blood flow through skin or muscle, based on the rate at which a radioactive tracer deposited in a tissue is removed by diffusion into the capillaries and washed out by the local blood supply.

trachea /trāʹkē·ə/ [Gk, *tracheia,* rough artery], a nearly cylindric tube in the neck, composed of C-shaped cartilage and membrane, that extends from the larynx at the level of the sixth cervical vertebra to the fifth thoracic vertebra, where it divides into two bronchi. The trachea conveys air to the lungs.—**tracheal,** *adj.*

tracheal /trāʹkē·əl/ [Gk, *tracheia,* rough artery], pertaining to the trachea.

tracheal breath sound, a normal breath sound heard in auscultation of the trachea. Inspiration and expiration are equally loud; the expiratory sound is heard during the greater part of expiration, whereas the inspiratory sound stops abruptly at the height of inspiration.

tracheal gas insufflation, continuous insufflation of a low flow of fresh gas to the distal endotracheal tube, believed capable of flushing out the anatomic dead space and thus reducing $PaCO_2$.

tracheal tugging [Gk, *tracheia,* rough artery; ME, *toggen*], an effect of an aortic aneurysm in which the trachea is pulled downward with each heart contraction.

tracheitis /trāʹkē·īʹtis/, any inflammatory condition of the trachea. It may be acute or chronic, resulting from infection, allergy, or physical irritation.

tracheobronchial /trāʹkē·ōbrongʹkē·əl/, pertaining to the trachea and bronchi.

tracheobronchial tree (TBT) /-brongʹkē·əl/ [Gk, *tracheia* + *bronchos,* windpipe], an anatomic complex that includes the trachea, bronchi, and bronchial tubes. It conveys air to and from the lungs.

tracheobronchitis /-brongkīʹtis/, inflammation of the trachea and bronchi, a common symptom of pulmonary infection.

tracheobronchomegaly /-brongʹkōmegʹəlē/, an abnormally large upper airway, in which the trachea may be as wide as the spinal column.

tracheoesophageal fistula /-ē·səfäʹjē·əl/ [Gk, *tracheia* + *oisophagos,* gullet], a congenital malformation in which there is an abnormal tubelike passage between the trachea and the esophagus.

tracheoesophageal folds, longitudinal folds in the embryonic respiratory diverticulum that fuse to form the tracheoesophageal septum.

tracheoesophageal puncture (TEP), a one-way synthetic valve placed in a surgically created tracheoesophageal fistula to restore speech after laryngectomy.

tracheoesophageal shunt, surgical formation of a passageway between the trachea and the esophagus that enables a laryngectomee to speak. The operation results in an ability to produce esophageal speech with normal respiration as a source of air and without the need to belch to produce voice sounds.

tracheolaryngeal /-lerinʹjē·əl/, pertaining to the trachea and larynx.

tracheomalacia /-ōmələʹshə/, an eroding of the trachea, usually caused by excessive pressure from a cuffed endotracheal tube.

tracheopharyngeal /-ferinʹjē·əl/, pertaining to the trachea and pharynx.

tracheoplasty /-plasʹtē/, plastic surgery of the trachea.

tracheostenosis /-stənōʹsis/, constriction of the lumen of the trachea.

tracheostomy /trāʹkē·osʹtəmē/ [Gk, *tracheia* + *stoma,* mouth], an opening through the neck into the trachea through which an indwelling tube may be inserted. The tube is suctioned as needed to keep it free from tracheobronchial secretions. The patient is reassured that the tube is open and that air can pass through it. Complications of tracheostomy include pneumothorax, respiratory insufficiency, and obstruction of the tracheostomy tube or its displacement from the lumen of the trachea, pulmonary infection, atelectasis, tracheoesophageal fistula, hemorrhage, and mediastinal emphysema. If the procedure was done as an emergency, the tracheostomy is closed after normal breathing is restored. If the tracheostomy is permanent, such as with a laryngectomy, the patient is taught self-care.

tracheostomy care [Gk, *tracheia,* rough artery, *stoma,* mouth], care of the tracheostomy patient, consisting of maintenance of a patent airway, adequate humidification, aseptic wound care, and sterile tracheal aspiration. Complications can include injury to the vocal cords, gastric distension and regurgitation, occlusion of the endotracheal tube, and an increased risk of infection.

tracheotomy /trāʹkē·otʹəmē/ [Gk, *tracheia* + *temnein,* to cut], an incision made into the trachea through the neck below the larynx, performed to gain access to the airway below a blockage with a foreign body, tumor, or edema of the glottis. The opening may be made as an emergency measure at an accident site, at a hospitalized patient's bedside, or in the OR. If the blockage persists, a tracheostomy tube is inserted; if not, the incision is closed after normal respirations are established.

tracheotomy tube [Gk, *tracheia,* rough artery, *temnein,* to cut; L, *tubus*], a curved hollow tube of rubber, metal, or plastic surgically inserted in the trachea to relieve a breathing obstruction.

trachoma /trəkō′mə/ [Gk, roughness], a chronic infectious disease of the eye caused by the bacterium *Chlamydia trachomatis*. It is characterized initially by inflammation, pain, photophobia, and lacrimation. If untreated, follicles form on the upper eyelids, forming scarring that causes trichiasis and corneal sequelae, eventually causing blindness. Tetracycline, erythromycin, and azithromycin usually provide effective treatment. Scarred eyelids may be surgically repaired.

tracing [L, *trahere,* to draw], a graphic record of a physical event, such as an ECG tracing made by pens on a moving sheet of paper while recording the electric impulses of heart muscle contractions.

tract [L, *tractus,* trail], **1.** an elongated group of tissues and organs that function together as a pathway, such as the digestive tract or the respiratory tract. **2.** in neurology, the neuronal axons that are grouped together to form a pathway; a serial arrangement that serves a common function.

traction /trak′shən/ [L, *trahere,* to draw], **1.** in orthopedics, the process of putting a limb, bone, or group of muscles under tension by means of weights and pulleys to align or immobilize the part to reduce muscle spasm or to relieve pressure on it. **2.** the process of pulling a part of the body along, through, or out of its socket or cavity, such as axis traction with obstetric forceps in delivering an infant.

traction, 90-90, an orthopedic mechanism, used especially in pediatrics, that combines skeletal traction and suspension with a short-leg cast or a splint to immobilize and position the lower extremity in the treatment of a displaced fractured femur.

traction frame, an orthopedic apparatus that supports the pulleys, ropes, and weights by which traction is applied to various parts of the body or by which various parts of the body are suspended. The main components of a traction frame are metal uprights that attach to the bed and support an overhead metal bar.

traction/immobilization care, a nursing intervention from the Nursing Interventions Classification (NIC) defined as management of a patient who has traction and/ or a stabilizing device to immobilize and stabilize a body part.

traction response, the body's reaction to traction applied to the spine. Alterations of certain signs and symptoms of a musculoskeletal disorder may be revealed by traction tests.

trademark, a word, symbol, or device assigned to a product by its manufacturer, registered or not registered, as a part of its identity.

traditional Chinese medicine (TCM), the diverse body of medical theory and practice that has evolved in China, comprising four branches: acupuncture and moxibustion, herbal medicine, qi gong, and tui na. The body and mind are considered together as a dynamic system subject to cycles of change and affected by the environment, and emphasis is on supporting the body's self-healing ability. Fundamental to TCM are the yin yang principle and the concept of basic substances that pervade the body: qi, jing (essence), and shen (spirit), collectively known as the three treasures, and the blood (a fluid and material manifestation of qi) and body fluids (which moisten and lubricate the body). Disease arises from a disturbance of qi within the body, the particular pathologic process depending on the location of the disturbance. A single biomedical disease may be associated with a large number of TCM diagnoses, and one TCM diagnosis may encompass a number of biomedical diseases. Diagnosis is by visual assessment, listening and smelling, questioning, and palpation. Once a diagnosis is established, therapy aims at restoring the body's homeostasis by treating the root cause of the disease.

tragacanth /trag′əkanth/, a white tasteless vegetable gum derived from a shrub, *Astragalus gummifer,* and related species. It is used as a suspending agent in pharmaceutic preparations, particularly powders and tinctures.

tragal /trā′gəl/ [Gk, *tragos,* goat], pertaining to the tragus.

Trager approach, service mark for a bodywork technique whose purpose is to train patients to develop awareness of movement patterns that relieve pain and promote relaxation.

tragion /traj′ēən/ [Gk, *tragos,* goat], a cephalometric landmark located at the superior margin of the tragus of the ear.

tragus /trā′gəs/ *pl.* **tragi** [Gk, *tragos,* goat], a small tonguelike projection of the auricular cartilage of the ear, anterior to the external meatus.

traineeship /trānē′ship/ [L, *trahere,* to draw; AS, *scieppan,* to shape], a grant of money allocated to an individual for advanced study in a given field.

training effect, a rehabilitation effect for heart patients that can be measured by changes in cardiac function.

training grant, a grant of money or other resources to provide training in a particular field.

train-of-four, a test for measuring the level of neuromuscular blockade. Four consecutive stimuli are delivered along the path of a nerve and the response of the muscle is measured in order to evaluate stimuli that are blocked versus those that are delivered. Four equal muscle contractions will result if there is no neuromuscular blockade.

trait [Fr, trace], **1.** a characteristic mode of behavior or any mannerism or physical feature that distinguishes one individual or culture from another. **2.** any characteristic quality or condition that is genetically determined and inherited as part of a specific phenotype.

TRALI, abbreviation for **transfusion-related acute lung injury.**

tramadol, a central analgesic is used to manage moderate-to-severe pain.

TRAM flap, an autogenous myocutaneous flap that uses transverse rectus abdominal muscle (TRAM) to carry lower abdominal skin and fat to the breast for reconstruction.

trance [L, *transire,* to pass across], **1.** a sleeplike state characterized by the complete or partial suspension of consciousness and loss or diminution of motor activity. **2.** a dazed or bewildered condition; stupor. **3.** a state of detachment from one's immediate surroundings, such as in deep concentration or daydreaming.

Trandate, a trademark for an antihypertensive drug (labetalol hydrochloride).

trandolapril, an antihypertensive prescribed to treat hypertension, heart failure, and post-MI/left ventricular dysfunction.

tranexamic acid /tran′eksam′ik/, an agent that combats fibrinolysis by competitively inhibiting activation of plasminogen. It is used in prophylaxis and treatment of hemorrhage associated with excessive fibrinolysis, such as that after oral surgery in patients with hemophilia.

tranquilizer /trang′kwili′zər/ [L, *tranquillus,* calm], a drug prescribed to calm anxious or agitated people, ideally without decreasing their consciousness. Major tranquilizers (now known as antipsychotic drugs) are generally used in the treatment of psychoses. Minor tranquilizers (now known as antianxiety drugs or sedative-hypnotics) are usually prescribed for the treatment of anxiety, irritability, tension, or psychoneurosis. Tranquilizers tend to induce drowsiness and have the potential for causing physical and psychologic dependence.

transabdominal /-abdom′inəl/ [L, *trans,* across, *abdomen,* belly], pertaining to a procedure through the abdominal wall.

transactional analysis (TA) /-ak′shənəl/ [L, *transigere,* to drive through; Gk, *analyein,* to loosen], a form of psychodynamic psychotherapy developed by Eric Berne, based on a role theory that three different coherent organized egos exist throughout life simultaneously in every person, representing the child, the adult, and the parent. Interactions between people are transactions, originating from a person in one of the ego states, and received by another person who may be in a complementary or a crossed ego state.

transaminase, an enzyme that catalyzes the transfer of an amino group from an alpha-amino acid to an alpha-keto acid, with pyridoxal phosphate and pyridoxamine phosphate acting as coenzymes.

transamination[1] /-am′inā′shən/, the reaction between an amino acid and an alpha-keto acid in which the enzyme transaminase induces transfer of the amino group to the alpha-keto acid.

transanimation[2] the resuscitation effort to induce a newborn to breathe.

transaortic /-ā-ôr′tik/ [L, *trans,* across; Gk, *aerein,* to raise], through the aorta.

transcellular transport, transport of molecules through the cells of an epithelial cell layer.

transcellular water /-sel′yələr/ [L, *trans + cella,* storeroom], the part of extracellular water that is enclosed by an epithelial membrane and whose volume and composition are determined by the cellular activity of that membrane.

transcendence /transen′dəns/ [L, *trans + scandere,* to climb], the rising above one's previously perceived limits or restrictions.

transcendental meditation (TM), a psychophysiologic exercise designed to lower levels of tension and anxiety and increase tolerance of frustration. TM has been described as a state of consciousness that does not require any physical or mental control. During meditation, the person enters a hypometabolic state in which there is reduced activity of the adrenergic component of the autonomic nervous system.

transcervical fracture /transur′vikəl/ [L, *trans,* across, *cervix,* neck + *fractura*], a fracture through the neck of the femur.

transcondylar fracture /transkon′dilər/ [L, *trans;* Gk, *kondylos,* condyle], a fracture that occurs transverse and distal to the epicondyles of any one of the long bones.

trans configuration /-kənfig′yərā′shən/ [L, *trans + configurare,* to form from], **1.** an arrangement in which the dominant allele of one pair of genes and the recessive allele of another pair are on the same chromosome. **2.** an arrangement in which at least one mutant gene and one wild-type gene of a pair of pseudoalleles

T

are present on each chromosome of a homologous pair. **3.** in chemistry, a form of isomerism in which two substituent groups occur on opposite sides of a structure such as a ring or a double bond.

transcortical /transkor´tikəl/ [L, *trans,* across + *cortex,* bark], connecting two different parts of the cerebral cortex; also, dependent on disease of the tracts connecting different parts of the cerebral cortex.

transcortin /-kôr´tin/, a diglobulin protein that binds a majority of cortisol in the plasma.

transcranial Doppler ultrasonography, a form of Doppler ultrasonography in which pulses of ultrasound are directed at vascular formations in the base of the skull, allowing measurements of blood flow velocity in the major basal intracranial arteries on a realtime basis.

transcriptase /transkrip´tās/, an enzyme that induces transcription.

transcription /transkrip´shən/ [L, *trans* + *scribere,* to write], the process by which messenger RNA is formed from a DNA template.

transcription factor, a specific protein required for the initiation of transcription by an RNA polymerase.

transcultural nursing /-kul´chərəl/ [L, *trans* + *colere,* to cultivate, *nutrix,* nurse], a field of nursing, founded by Madeleine Leininger, in which the nurse transcends ethnocentricity and practices nursing in other cultural environments.

transcutaneous /-k(y)o͞otā´nē·əs/ [L, *trans* + *cutis,* skin], pertaining to a procedure that is performed through the skin.

transcutaneous electrical nerve stimulation (TENS)[1]**,** a method of pain control by the application of electric impulses to nerve endings. This is done through electrodes that are placed on the skin and attached to a stimulator by flexible wires. The electric impulses generated are similar to those of the body, but different enough to block transmission of pain signals to the brain.

transcutaneous electrical nerve stimulation (TENS)[2]**,** a nursing intervention from the Nursing Interventions Classification (NIC) defined as stimulation of skin and underlying tissues with controlled, low-voltage electric vibration via electrodes.

transcutaneous oxygen/carbon dioxide monitoring, a method of measuring the oxygen or carbon dioxide in the blood by attaching electrodes to the skin. Oxygen is commonly measured through an oximeter, which contains heating coils to raise the skin temperature and increase blood flow at the surface. Transcutaneous carbon dioxide electrodes are similar to blood gas electrodes.

transdermal drug delivery (TDD) /-dur´məl/ [L, *trans;* Gk, *derma,* skin], a method of applying a drug to unbroken skin. The drug is absorbed continuously through the skin and enters the systemic system.

transdermal scopolamine, a method of administration of the motion sickness drug scopolamine by application of a skin patch containing the medication.

transducer /-d(y)o͞o´sər/ [L, *trans* + *ducere,* to lead], a hand-held device that sends and receives ultrasound signals.

transductant /-duk´tənt/, a cell that has acquired a new character by the transfer of genetic material.

transduction /-duk´shən/, a method of genetic recombination by which DNA is transferred from one cell to another by a viral vector.

transect /transekt´/ [L, *trans* + *secare,* to cut], to sever or cut across, as in preparing a cross section of tissue.

transesophageal echocardiography (TEE), an endoscopic/ultrasound test that provides ultrasonic imaging of the heart from a retrocardiac vantage point, thus preventing the interposed subcutaneous tissue, bony thorax, and lungs from interfering with the ultrasound. It is performed to better visualize the mitral valve or atrial septum, to differentiate intracardiac from extracardiac masses and tumors, to diagnose thoracic aortic dissection, to detect valvular vegetation as seen with endocarditis, to determine cardiac sources of arterial embolism, to detect coronary artery disease, and to monitor high-risk patients for ischemia intraoperatively.

***trans*-fatty acids,** stereoisomers of the naturally occurring *cis*-fatty acids, found in margarines and shortenings as artifacts after hydrogenation. A connection has been found between consumption of large amounts of *trans*-fatty acids and increased low-density lipoprotein levels and, thus, increased risk for coronary heart disease.

transfection /-fek´shən/ [L, *trans* + *inficere,* to taint], the process by which a bacterial cell is infected with purified DNA or RNA isolated from a virus after a specific pretreatment. Acute transfection is short-term infection.—**transfect,** *v.*

transfemoral amputation, amputation of the lower leg between the knee and the hip.

transfer[1]**,** to move a person or object from one site to another.

transfer[2]**,** a nursing intervention from the Nursing Interventions Classification (NIC) defined as moving a patient with limitation of independent movement.

transfer agreement /trans'fur/ [L, *transferre*, to carry over, *ad*, toward, *gratus*, pleasure], a written hospital agreement between two health care institutions for the transfer of patients from one to another and the orderly exchange of pertinent clinical information on the patients transferred.

transferase /trans'fərās/ [L, *transferre*; Fr, *diastase*, enzyme], any of a group of enzymes that catalyzes the transfer of a chemical group or radical, such as the phosphate, methyl, amine, or keto groups, from one molecule to another.

transfer DNA (tDNA), DNA transferred from its original source and present in transformed cells.

transference /-fur'əns/ [L, *transferre*], 1. the shifting of symptoms from one part of the body to another, as occurs in conversion disorder. 2. in psychiatry, an unconscious defense mechanism whereby feelings and attitudes originally associated with important people and events in one's early life are attributed to others in current interpersonal situations including psychotherapy.

transference love, in psychoanalytic therapy, a projection of libidinal drives expressed by the patient for the psychoanalyst who has "unconsciously" come to represent a person from the patient's past.

transfer factor (TF), a leukocyte extract that transfers delayed hypersensitivity from one person to another. It has been studied for its possible use in the treatment of chronic mucocutaneous candidiasis and Wiskott-Aldrich syndrome and as a means of transferring antitumor immunity to patients with various types of cancer.

transfer performance, a nursing outcome from the Nursing Outcomes Classification (NOC) defined as the ability to change body locations independently with or without an assistive device.

transferrin /transfer'in/, a plasma protein that is essential in the transport of iron from the intestine into the bloodstream, making it available to the normoblasts in the bone marrow.

transferring /-fur'ing/ [L, *trans*, across, *ferre*, to bring], relocating a person in need from one location to another.

transferrin saturation, percentage of iron binding by the major plasma iron transport protein, measured in the blood to detect iron excess or deficiency.

transfer RNA (tRNA), a kind of RNA that carries an anticodon (three nucleotide bases) and a specific amino acid. The identity of the amino acid is determined by the sequence of nucleotides in the anticodon. Each anticodon is complementary to a specific codon in the messenger RNA. The tRNAs (with their amino acids attached) translate the sequence of codons in messenger RNA into a sequence of amino acids in a polypeptide.

transfixation /-fiksā'shən/, a surgical procedure in which, in an amputation, the soft tissues are cut through from one side to the other, close to the bone. The muscles are then divided from within outward.

transformation /-fôrmā'shən/ [L, *transformare*, to change shape], the integration of exogenous genes into chromosomes in a form that is recognized by the replicative and transcriptional apparatus of the host cell.

transformer /-fôr'mər/ [L, *transformare*, to change shape], an electrical apparatus that changes alternating current of one voltage into a different voltage of the same frequency.

transforming growth factor (TGF), a group of proteins produced by the cells of a tumor that, when inoculated into a normal cell culture, causes a disorderly increase in the number of cells in the culture.

transfusion /-f(y)ōō'zhən/ [L, *trans* + *fundere*, to pour], the introduction into the bloodstream of whole blood or blood components such as plasma, platelets, or packed RBCs. Whole blood may be infused into the recipient directly from a donor matched for the ABO blood group and antigenic subgroups, but more frequently the donor's blood is collected and stored by a blood bank.—**transfuse,** *v.*

transfusion reaction, any adverse event following a blood transfusion, attributed to the transfusion. The most common reactions are allergic, manifested by hives and urticaria, and febrile nonhemolytic, shown by chills and fever. More serious reactions are hemolytic, due to an antibody in the recipient to an antigen on the donor's red cells, anaphylactic, bacterial contamination of the donor unit, transfusion-related acute lung injury (TRALI), and transfusion-associated circulatory overload (TACO). Delayed reactions may include delayed hemolytic, disease transmission, alloimmunization to red cell or HLA antigens, posttransfusion purpura, and transfusion-associated graft-versus-host-disease. Fever is the most common transfusion reaction; urticaria is a relatively common allergic response. A hemolytic reaction from red cell incompatibility is serious and must be diagnosed and treated promptly. Symptoms develop shortly after beginning the transfusion and include a throbbing headache, sudden deep severe lumbar pain, precordial pain, dyspnea, and restlessness. Objective signs include ruddy facial flushing followed by cyanosis and distended neck veins,

T

rapid, thready pulse, diaphoresis, and cold, clammy skin. When a hemolytic reaction is suspected, the transfusion is promptly terminated, and the infusion line kept open with a normal solution of IV fluid. Immediate treatment may include IV mannitol and a solution of 5% dextrose in water to maintain urine flow of more than 100 mL per hour.

transfusion-related acute lung injury (TRALI), a syndrome seen in persons receiving transfusions, characterized by pulmonary edema, dyspnea, hypoxemia, hypotension, and fever. It is thought to be a reaction to antibodies or other components of the donor blood product. Patients need oxygen support. In some cases the syndrome can be fatal.

transgene /trans′jēn/, a gene that has been transferred from one genome into another.—**transgenic,** *adj.*

transient /tran′shənt, tran′zē·ənt/ [L, *transire,* to go through], pertaining to a condition that is temporary, such as TIA.

transient global amnesia (TGA) [L, *transire,* to go through, *globus,* ball; Gk, *amnesia,* forgetfulness], a temporary short-term memory loss followed by full recovery. The disorder tends to affect middle-aged adults and may be attributed to cerebral ischemia. It is usually not accompanied by other mental deficiencies.

transient ischemic attack (TIA), an episode of cerebrovascular insufficiency, usually associated with partial occlusion of a cerebral artery by an atherosclerotic plaque or an embolus. The symptoms vary with the site and degree of occlusion. Disturbance of normal vision in one or both eyes, dizziness, weakness, dysphasia, numbness, or unconsciousness may occur. The attack usually lasts a few minutes. In rare cases symptoms continue for several hours.

transient lower esophageal sphincter relaxation, relaxation of the lower esophageal sphincter in response to gastric distension, lasting for 10 to 30 seconds and resulting in gastroesophageal reflux.

transient monocular blindness, an episode of total or partial loss of vision in one eye, caused by ischemia of the eye and lasting several minutes or longer.

transient myeloproliferative disorder, usually transient leukocytosis associated with Down syndrome and generally diagnosed in the first few weeks of life, often with hepatosplenomegaly, pericardial and pleural effusions, hepatic disease, and a pustular rash. Although spontaneous remission occurs in most cases, some affected infants develop a myelodysplastic syndrome or acute leukemia.

transient myopia [L, *transire,* to go through; Gk, *myops,* nearsighted], a temporary change in visual accommodation secondary to trauma, high blood sugar level, sulfanilamide therapy, and other conditions.

transillumination /-iloo′minā′shən/ [L, *trans,* through, *illuminare,* to light up], **1.** the passage of light through a solid or liquid substance. **2.** the passage of light through body tissues for the purpose of examining a structure interposed between the observer and the light source.

transition /tranzish′ən/ [L, *transire,* to go through], the last phase of the first stage of labor, sometimes indicated by cervical dilation of 8 to 10 cm.

transitional /tranzish′ənəl/ [L, *transire,* to go through], between a previous and a succeeding state, or in a state of becoming something else.

transitional cell carcinoma, a malignant, usually papillary tumor derived from transitional stratified epithelium, occurring most frequently in the bladder, ureter, urethra, or renal pelvis. The majority of tumors in the collecting system of the kidney are of this kind.

transitional epithelium, a form of stratified epithelium found characteristically in the mucous membrane of the ureter and bladder; in the contracted condition it consists of many cell layers, whereas in the stretched condition usually only two layers can be distinguished.

transitional object, an object used by a child to provide comfort and security while he or she is away from a secure base, such as mother or home.

transitory mania /tran′sitôr′ē/ [L, *transire,* to go through; Gk, *mania,* madness], a mood disorder characterized by the sudden onset of manic reactions that are of short duration, usually lasting from 1 hour to a few days.

transjugular intrahepatic portosystemic shunt (TIPS) /tranzjug′yoo̅ōlər/, percutaneous creation of a shunt between the hepatic and portal veins within the liver followed by placement of an expandable stent in the tract created, performed by a transjugular route under radiologic guidance. It is done to treat bleeding esophageal varices.

translation /-lā′shən/ [L, *translatio,* handing over], the process in which the genetic information carried by nucleotides in messenger RNA directs the amino acid sequence in the synthesis of a specific polypeptide.

translocation /-lōkā′shən/ [L, *trans* + *locus,* place], the rearrangement of DNA within a chromosome or the transfer of a segment of one chromosome to a nonhomologous one. Such shifting of genetic material can result in serious disorders, such as Down syndrome or chronic granulocytic leukemia.

translucent /-lōo'sənt/ [L, *trans*, across, *lucens*, shining], pertaining to a medium through which light can pass in a diffused manner so that a field is illuminated but objects cannot be seen distinctly.

transmethylation /-meth'ilā'shən/, the transfer of a methyl group from one compound to another.

transmigration /-mīgrā'shən/ [L, *trans* + *migrare*, to migrate], a movement from one side to another, from inside to outside, or from outside to inside.

transmissible /-mis'ibəl/ [L, *transmittere*, to transmit], capable of being passed from one person or place to another, as in the transmission of a disease.

transmissible spongiform encephalopathy, a group of fatal neurodegenerative diseases that are unique in having either infectious or genetic causes. A homozygous prion protein genotype predisposes individuals to susceptibility to the diseases.

transmission /-mish'ən/ [L, *transmittere*, to transmit], the transfer or conveyance of a thing or condition, such as a neural impulse, an infectious or genetic disease, or a hereditary trait, from one person or place to another.—**transmissible**, *adj.*

transmission-based precautions, safeguards designed for patients documented or suspected to be infected with highly transmissible or epidemiologically important pathogens for which additional precautions beyond standard precautions are needed to interrupt transmission in hospitals. There are three types of transmission-based precautions: airborne precautions, droplet precautions, and contact precautions.

transmission scanning electron microscope, an instrument that transmits a highly magnified, well-resolved, three-dimensional image on a television screen, thus combining the advantages of the electron and the scanning electron microscopes.

transmission scanning electron microscopy (TSEM), a technique using a transmission scanning electron microscope in which the atomic number of the part of the sample being scanned is determined and used to modulate a beam of electrons in a cathode-ray tube and in the beam scanning the sample.

transmitted light [L, *transmittere*, to transmit; AS, *leoht*], light that has been transmitted through a transparent medium.

transmucosal /trans'mu·ko'səl/, entering through, or across, a mucous membrane, as

the administration of a drug via the cavity between the cheek and gum.

transmural /-m(y)ŏor'əl/ [L, *trans* + *murus*, wall], pertaining to the entire thickness of the wall of an organ such as a transmural MI, or through any wall such as the body or cyst of a hollow structure.

transmural infarction, death of myocardial tissue that extends from the endocardium to the epicardium as a result of a MI.

transmutation /-m(y)ŏotā'shən/ [L, *transmutare*, to change], **1.** a mutation that causes a significant species change during evolution. **2.** the conversion of one chemical element into another by radioactive bombardment.

transovarial transmission /-ōver'ē·əl/ [L, *trans* + *ovum*, egg], the transfer of pathogens to succeeding generations through invasion of the ovary and infection of the eggs.

transparent /-per'ənt/ [L, *trans*, across, *parere*, to appear], pertaining to a clear medium that allows for the transmission of light so that objects on the other side are distinguishable.

transparent septum, a triangular double membrane situated in the median plane and separating the anterior horns of the lateral ventricles of the brain.

transpeptidase /-pep'tidās/, an enzyme that catalyzes the transfer of an amino group from one peptide chain to another.

transpeptidation /-pep'tidā'shən/, the transfer of an amino acid from one peptide chain to another.

transplacental /tranz'pləsen'təl/ [L, *trans* + *placenta*, flat cake], across or through the placenta, specifically in reference to the exchange of nutrients, waste products, and other material between the developing fetus and the mother.

transplant /-plant, transplant'/ [L, *transplantare*], **1.** to transfer an organ or tissue from one person to another or from one body part to another to replace a diseased structure, restore function, or change appearance. Skin and kidneys are the most frequently transplanted structures. Preferred donors are identical twins or people having the same blood type and immunologic characteristics. **2.** any tissue or organ that is transplanted. **3.** pertaining to a tissue or organ that is transplanted, a recipient of a donated tissue or organ, or a phenomenon associated with the procedure.

transplantation /-plantā'shən/ [L, *transplantare*, to transplant], the transfer of tissue from one site to another or from one person or organism to another.

transplantation endometriosis [L, *transplantare*, to transplant; Gk, *endon*, within, *metra*, womb, *osis*,

condition], endometrial tissue that is accidentally transplanted to the incision wound during pelvic surgery.

transport /-pôrt/ [L, *trans,* across, *portare,* carry], the movement or transference of biochemical substances from one site to another. Active transport involves an expenditure of energy, whereas passive transport allows movement down a gradient without an energy expenditure.

transport: interfacility, a nursing intervention from the Nursing Interventions Classification (NIC) defined as moving a patient from one facility to another.

transport: intrafacility, a nursing intervention from the Nursing Interventions Classification (NIC) defined as moving a patient from one area of a facility to another.

transport maximum, the highest rate in milligrams per minute at which the renal tubules can transfer a substance either from the tubular luminal fluid to the interstitial fluid or from the interstitial fluid to the tubular luminal fluid, beyond which it may be excreted in the urine. In kidney function tests, it is expressed as T_m with inferior letters representing the substance used in the test, such as T_{mPAH} (transport maximum for *p*-aminohippuric acid).

transposase /-pəzās/, an enzyme involved in the movement of a DNA fragment from one site in the genome to another.

transposition /-pəsish'ən/ [L, *transponere*], **1.** an abnormality occurring during embryonic development in which a body part normally on the left is found on the right or vice versa. **2.** the shifting of genetic material from one chromosome to another at some point in the reproductive process, often resulting in a congenital anomaly.—**transpose,** *v.*

transposition of the great vessels, a congenital cardiac anomaly in which the pulmonary artery arises from the left ventricle and the aorta from the right ventricle and there is no communication between the systemic and pulmonary circulations. Life is impossible with this anomaly unless there are associated cardiac defects, such as a septal defect or a patent ductus arteriosus, that enable the mixing of oxygenated and unoxygenated blood. The primary symptoms are cyanosis and hypoxia, especially in infants with small septal defects, although cardiomegaly is usually evident a few weeks after birth. Signs of CHF develop rapidly, especially in infants with large ventricular septal defects. Surgical correction of the defect is postponed, if possible, until after 6 months of age, when the infant can better tolerate the procedure.

transposon /-pō'sən/ [L, *transponere* + on], a segment of DNA that can move from one place to another in a cell's genome or between a bacterial cell and a plasmid or virus.

transpulmonary pressure /-pul'mənər·ē/, the difference between intraalveolar and intrapleural pressure, or the pressure acting across the lung from the pleural space to the alveoli.

transsection /-ek'shən/ [L, *trans,* across + *sectio*], a cross section of a biologic specimen or a cut across the long axis.

transseptal fiber /-ep'təl/ [L, *trans* + *saeptum,* wall], any of the many filamentous tissues of the gingival system that extend mesially from the supraalveolar cementum of one tooth, through the interdental-attached gingiva above the septum of the alveolar bone, to the distal cementum of an adjacent tooth.

transsexual /-ek'chŏŏ·əl/, a person whose gender identity is the opposite of his or her biologic sex.

transsexualism /-iz'əm/, a condition in which a person has an intense desire to change one's biologic sex and live as a member of the opposite sex. It is considered a psychiatric disorder if the condition continues for more than 2 years.

transtentorial herniation /-tentôr'ē·əl/ [L, *trans* + *tentorium,* tent, *hernia,* rupture], a bulge of brain tissue out of the cranium through the tentorial notch, caused by increased ICP.

transthoracic /-thôras'ik/, across or passing through the thorax.

transthoracic impedence, resistance to transmission of electric current represented by the skin, fat, muscle, and lung tissues in a patient's chest.

transthoracic pacemaker /-thôras'ik/ [L, *trans,* across; Gk, *thorax,* chest; L, *passus,* step; ME, *maken*], a permanent pacemaker with the pulse generator located in the abdominal wall and the pacing wires attached directly to the epicardium.

transtibial amputation, an amputation of the lower leg between the ankle and knee.

transtracheal oxygen /-trā'kē·əl/ [L, *trans,* across; Gk, *tracheia,* rough artery, *oxys,* sharp, *genein,* to produce], the administration of oxygen via a low-flow catheter inserted directly into the trachea.

transtrochanteric osteotomy /-trō'kənter'ik/ [L, *trans,* across; Gk, *trochanter,* runner, *osteon* + *temnein,* to cut], a surgical division of the upper end of the femur through the area of the trochanters.

transubstantiation /-əbstan'chē·ā'shən/, the replacement or substitution of one kind of tissue for another.

transudate /-yədāt/ [L, *trans* + *sudare,* to sweat], a thin and watery fluid passed through a membrane or squeezed through a tissue or into the space between the cells of a tissue.

transudation /-yədā'shən/, 1. the passage of a substance through a membrane as a result of a difference in hydrostatic pressure. 2. the passage of a fluid through a membrane with nearly all the solutes of the fluid remaining in solution or suspension.

transudative ascites /-yōō'dətiv/, an abnormal accumulation in the peritoneal cavity of a fluid that characteristically contains scant amounts of protein and cells.

transuranic element, any of the elements with atomic numbers above that of uranium (whose atomic number is 92).

transurethral laser-induced prostatectomy (TULIP), a type of noncontact laser prostatectomy.

transurethral resection (TUR) /-yōōrē'thrəl/ [L, *trans;* Gk, *ourethra,* urethra; L, *re,* again, *secare,* to cut], the surgical removal of a structure performed through the urethra.

transurethral resection of the prostate (TURP), resection of the prostate by means of a cystoscope passed through the urethra.

transvaginal /-vaj'inəl/ [L, *trans,* across + *vagina,* sheath], performed through the vagina.

transverse /-vurs'/ [L, *transversus,* oblique], at right angles to the long axis of any common part, such as the planes that cut the long axis of the body into upper and lower parts and are at right angles to the sagittal and frontal planes.

transverse cervical nerve, a branch of the cervical plexus that provides cutaneous innervation to the neck.

transverse colon, the segment of the colon that extends from the end of the ascending colon at the hepatic flexure on the right side across the midabdomen to the beginning of the descending colon at the splenic flexure on the left side.

transverse colon volvulus, a rare type of colonic volvulus involving the transverse colon.

transverse fissure, a fissure dividing the dorsal surface of the diencephalon and the ventral surface of the cerebral hemisphere.

transverse foramen [L, *transversus* + *foramen,* hole], an opening through the transverse process of a cervical vertebra.

transverse fracture, a fracture that occurs at right angles to the longitudinal axis of the bone involved.

transverse lie, abnormal presentation of a fetus in which the long axis of the baby's body is across the long axis of the mother's body.

transverse ligament of the atlas, a thick, strong ligament stretched across the ring of the atlas, holding the dens against the anterior arch.

transverse magnetization, the magnetization vector oriented in a plane perpendicular to the main external magnetic field in magnetic resonance.

transverse mesocolon /mez'ōkō'lən/, a broad fold of the peritoneum connecting the transverse colon to the dorsal wall of the abdomen. It is continuous with the greater omentum along the ventral surface of the transverse colon and contains between its layers the vessels that supply the transverse colon.

transverse myelitis [L, *transversus;* Gk, *myelos,* marrow, *itis,* inflammation], an acute attack of spinal cord inflammation involving both sides of the cord.

transverse palatine suture, the line of junction between the processes of the maxilla and the horizontal parts of the palatine bones that form the hard palate.

transverse pericardial sinus, a passage between the superior and posterior reflections of the serous pericardium. It lies posteriorly to the ascending aorta and the pulmonary trunk, anteriorly to the superior vena cava, and superiorly to the left atrium.

transverse plane, any one of the planes cutting across the body perpendicular to the sagittal and frontal planes, dividing the body into superior and inferior parts.

transverse presentation [L, *transversus* + *praesentare,* to show], a presentation of the fetal body in an oblique or transverse position across the birth canal.

transverse process, a process of the vertebra that extends posterolaterally from the junction of the pedicle and lamina on each side and is the site for articulation with the ribs in the thoracic region.

transverse rectal folds, semilunar transverse folds in the rectum that support the weight of feces.

transverse septum, a thick plate of mesodermal tissue that occupies the space between the thoracic cavity and yolk stalk in the early embryo. It gives rise to the central tendon of the diaphragm.

transverse sinus, one of a pair of large venous channels in the posterior superior group of sinuses serving the dura mater.

transverse tarsal joint, the joint formed by the talocalcaneonavicular and calcaneocuboid joints together.

transversospinales muscles, a group of muscles deep to the erector spinae that consist of the semispinalis, multifidus, and rotatores muscles. When these muscles contract bilaterally, they extend the vertebral column. However, when muscles on only one side contract, they pull the spinous processes toward the transverse processes on that side, causing the trunk to turn or rotate in the opposite direction.

transversus abdominis /-vur'səs/, one of a pair of transverse abdominal muscles that are the anterolateral muscles of the abdomen, lying immediately under the internal abdominal oblique. It serves to constrict the abdomen and, by compressing the contents, to assist in micturition, defecation, emesis, parturition, and forced expiration.

transversus thoracis muscles, muscles found on the deep surface of the anterior thoracic wall that lie deep to the internal thoracic vessels and secure these vessels to the wall.

transvesical prostatectomy, prostatectomy through an incision of the urinary bladder.

transvestism /-ves'tizəm/, a tendency to achieve psychic and sexual relief by dressing in the clothing of the opposite sex.

Tranxene, a trademark for a benzodiazepine sedative-hypnotic (clorazepate dipotassium).

tranylcypromine sulfate /tran'əlsip'rə mēn/, a monoamine oxidase inhibitor that acts as an antidepressant. It is prescribed in the treatment of severe reactive or endogenous mental depression without melancholia, and has an unlabeled use for the treatment of post-traumatic stress disorder.

trapeze bar /trapēz'/, a triangular metal apparatus above a bed, used to help the patient move and support weight during transfer or position change.

trapezium /trəpē'zē-əm/ pl. **trapezia, trapeziums** [Gk, *trapezion,* small table], a carpal bone in the distal row of carpal bones. The trapezium articulates with the scaphoid proximally, the first metacarpal distally, and the trapezoideum and the second metacarpal medially.

trapezius /trəpē'zē-əs/ [Gk, *trapezion,* small table], a large, flat triangular muscle of the shoulder and upper back. It acts to rotate the scapula upward; adduct, raise, or lower the shoulder; and retract the shoulder.

trapezoid /trap'əzoid/ [Gk, *trapezion,* small table, *eidos,* form], having the shape of a trapeze, an irregular four-sided figure with one set of parallel sides.

trapezoidal arch /trap'əzoidəl/ [Gk, *trapezion + eidos,* form; L, *arcus,* bow], a dental arch that has slightly less convergence than that of a tapering arch.

trapezoid bone [Gk, *trapezion + eidos; AS, ban*], the smallest carpal bone, located in the distal row of carpal bones between the trapezium and the capitate.

trastuzumab, a miscellaneous antineoplastic prescribed in the treatment of metastatic breast cancer with the overexpression of HER2.

Trasylol /tras'ilol/, a trademark for a preparation of aprotinin, an antihemorrhagic agent.

trauma /trou'mə, trô'mə/ [Gk, wound], **1.** physical injury caused by violent or disruptive action or by the introduction into the body of a toxic substance. **2.** psychic injury resulting from a severe emotional shock.—**traumatic,** *adj.,* **traumatize,** *v.*

trauma center, a service providing emergency and specialized intensive care to critically ill and injured patients.

trauma registry, a repository of data on the incidence, diagnosis, and treatment of acute trauma victims treated by emergency service personnel.

trauma therapy: child, a nursing intervention from the Nursing Interventions Classification (NIC) defined as use of an interactive helping process to resolve a trauma experienced by a child.

traumatic /trômat'ik/ [Gk, *trauma,* wound], pertaining to an injury, usually a serious and unexpected injury.

traumatic abscess, a pus collection that develops in tissue that has been damaged by a wound or injury.

traumatic anesthesia [Gk, *trauma + anaisthesia,* lack of feeling], a total lack of normal sensation in a part of the body, resulting from injury, destruction of nerves, or interruption of nerve pathways.

traumatic delirium, delirium after severe head injury, characterized by alertness and consciousness, with disorientation, confabulation, and amnesia apparent.

traumatic dislocation [Gk, *trauma,* wound; L, *dis + locare*], a dislocation caused by an injury.

traumatic epilepsy [Gk, *trauma,* wound, *epilepsia,* seizure], a form of motor or sensory seizures caused by a brain injury.

traumatic fever, an elevation in body temperature secondary to mechanical trauma, particularly a crushing injury. The increased body temperature may help provide resistance to subsequent infection, and increased local wound temperature may accelerate local healing.

traumatic gangrene [Gk, *trauma,* wound + *gaggraina*], gangrene that follows a severe injury resulting in damage to blood vessels.

traumatic herpes [Gk, *trauma,* wound, *herpein,* to creep], herpes that develops at the site of an injury.

traumatic meningitis [Gk, *trauma,* wound, *meninx,* membrane, *itis,* inflammation], meningitis that develops as a result of injury to the skull or spinal column.

traumatic myelitis [Gk, *trauma,* wound, *myelos,* marrow, *itis,* inflammation], a spinal cord inflammation resulting from an injury.

traumatic myositis, an inflammation of the muscles resulting from a wound or other trauma.

traumatic neuritis [Gk, *trauma,* wound, *neuron,* nerve, *itis,* inflammation], inflammation of a nerve, resulting from an injury.

traumatic neuroma, a mass of nerve elements and fibrous tissue produced by the proliferation of Schwann cells and fibroblasts after severe injury to a nerve.

traumatic occlusion, repeated excessive force in closure of the teeth that injures the teeth, the periodontal tissues, the residual ridge, or other oral structures. The closure extends beyond the reparative ability of the attachment apparatus (cementum, periodontal ligaments, and alveolar bone).

traumatic proctitis, rectal irritation caused by a foreign body in the rectum.

traumatic psychosis [Gk, *trauma,* wound, *psyche,* mind, *osis,* condition], a psychiatric disorder that results from injury to the head, with symptoms usually indicating brain trauma. It is differentiated from psychic trauma in which personality damage can be traced to an unpleasant experience such as sexual assault.

traumatic rhabdomyolysis, skeletal muscle destruction after a crush injury. During reperfusion of the damaged tissue after crushing pressure has been relieved, myoglobin, potassium, and phosphorus are released into the circulation, causing symptoms of renal failure, hypovolemic shock, and hyperkalemia.

traumatic shock [Gk, *trauma,* wound; Fr, *choc*], the emotional or psychologic state after trauma that may produce abnormal behavior. The most common types are hypovolemic shock from blood loss and neurogenic shock, caused by a disruption of the integrity of the spinal cord.

traumatic thrombosis [Gk, *trauma,* wound, *thrombos,* lump, *osis,* condition], intravascular coagulation of a vein or other blood vessel after injury or irritation. The condition may develop as an adverse effect of an IV injection that damages the wall of a vein.

traumatology /trô′mətol′əjē/ [Gk, *trauma* + *logos,* science], **1.** the study of wounds and injuries. **2.** a surgical specialty dealing with the treatment of wounds, injuries, and resulting disabilities.—**traumatologic,** *adj.*

traumatopathy /trô′mətop′əthē/ [Gk, *trauma* + *pathos,* disease], a pathological condition resulting from a wound or injury.—**traumatopathic,** *adj.*

traumatophilia /trô′mətōfil′ē·ə/ [Gk, *trauma* + *philein,* to love], a psychological state in which the individual derives unconscious pleasure from injuries and surgical operations.—**traumatophiliac,** *n.,* **traumatophilic,** *adj.*

traumatopnea /trô′mətop′nē·ə/ [Gk, *trauma* + *pnein,* to breathe], partial asphyxia with collapse of the patient, caused by a penetrating thoracic wound permitting air to enter the pleural space and compress the lungs.

traumatopyra /trô′mətōpī′rə/ [Gk, *trauma* + *pyr,* fire], an elevated temperature resulting from a wound or injury.

traumatotherapy /-ther′əpē/ [Gk, *trauma* + *therapeia,* treatment], the medical, surgical, and psychological treatment of wounds, injuries, and disabilities resulting from trauma.—**traumatotherapeutic,** *adj.*

traumatropism /trômat′rəpiz′əm/ [Gk, *trauma* + *trepein,* to turn], the tendency of damaged tissue to attract microorganisms and promote their growth, frequently causing infections after injuries, especially burns.

travail /trəvāl′/ [OFr, *travaillier,* to work], **1.** physical or mental exertion, especially when distressful. **2.** in obstetrics, the effort of labor and childbirth.

Travelbee, Joyce, a nursing theorist who developed the Human-to-Human Relationship Model and theory, presented in her book *Interpersonal Aspects of Nursing* (1966, 1971). Travelbee based the assumptions of her theory on the concepts of logotherapy. Travelbee believed nursing is accomplished through human-to-human relationships that begin with the original encounter and then progress through stages of emerging identities, developing feelings of empathy, and later of sympathy.

traveler's diarrhea [OFr, *travailler,* to work; Gk, *dia,* through, *rhein,* to flow], any of several diarrheal disorders commonly seen in people visiting regions of the world other than their own. They may be caused by bacterial, viral, or parasitic infections. Symptoms last for a few days and include abdominal cramps, nausea, vomiting, slight fever, and watery stools. Relapse is rare. Treatment depends on identification of the cause and includes rehydration with beverages containing electrolytes. Preventive measures include using pure or boiled water and beverages for drinking and brushing the teeth and eating only fruits and vegetables with a skin or peel that can be removed and discarded before consumption.

travel medicine, the subspecialty of tropical medicine consisting of the diagnosis and treatment or prevention of diseases of travelers.

traverse /travurs'/, **1.** to travel or pass across, over, or through. **2.** a single, complete movement of the x-ray tube around the object being scanned in CT.

travoprost /trav'ō-prōst/, a synthetic prostaglandin analog used in the treatment of elevated intraocular pressure in patients with open-angle glaucoma or ocular hypertension.

tray agglutination test, a type of sperm agglutination test in which small amounts of sperm and serum are mixed on a microscopic tray for examination.

trazodone /traz-ə-dōn/, an antidepressant. The hydrochloride salt is used to treat major depressive episodes with or without prominent anxiety.

TRBF, abbreviation for **total renal blood flow.**

Treacher Collins syndrome [Edward Treacher Collins, English ophthalmologist, 1862–1919], an inherited disorder, characterized by mandibulofacial dysostosis.

treatment [Fr, *traitement*], **1.** the care and management of a patient to combat, ameliorate, or prevent a disease, disorder, or injury. **2.** a method of combating, ameliorating, or preventing a disease, disorder, or injury. Active or curative treatment is designed to cure; palliative treatment is directed to relieve pain and distress; prophylactic treatment focuses on prevention; and causal treatment focuses on the cause of a disorder. Treatment may be pharmacologic, surgical, or supportive.

treatment behavior: illness or injury, a nursing outcome from the Nursing Outcomes Classification (NOC) defined as personal actions to palliate or eliminate pathology.

treatment guardian, a person who is appointed by the court for the purpose of consenting to or refusing medical treatment for a patient.

treatment plan [Fr, *traitement;* L, *planta*], in dentistry, a schedule of procedures and appointments designed to restore, step by step, a patient's oral health. The plan contains the advantages, disadvantages, costs, alternatives, and sequelae of treatment. It must be presented to the patient for approval.

treatment room, a room in a patient care unit, usually in a hospital, in which various treatments or procedures requiring special equipment are performed.

Trecator-SC, a trademark for a tuberculostatic (ethionamide).

Trechona /trikōn'ə/, a genus of spiders, family Dipluridae, the bite of which is toxic and irritating to humans.

tree [AS, *treow*], an anatomic structure with branches that spread out like those of a tree, such as the bronchial tree.

Trematoda /trem'ətō'də/, a class of flatworms, Platyhelminthes, that includes flukes. The adults are external or internal parasites of vertebrates. Intestinal infections in North America are rare except through flukes in foods imported from Asia or the tropics.

trematode /trem'ətōd/ [Gk, *trematodes,* pierced], any species of flatworm of the class Trematoda, some of which are parasitic to humans, infecting the liver, the lungs, and the intestines.

trematodiasis, infection with trematodes (flukes).

trembles /trem'bəls/, a toxic reaction experienced by cattle that have eaten white snakeroot or rayless goldenrod, pasture weeds that contain tremetone, a ketone. The toxic chemical is eliminated in the milk of the cows, causing sickness in humans who drink the milk.

tremor /trem'ər, trē'mər/ [L, shaking], rhythmic, purposeless, quivering movements resulting from the involuntary alternating contraction and relaxation of opposing groups of skeletal muscles occurring in some elderly individuals, certain families, and patients with various neurodegenerative disorders.

tremulous /trem'yələs/ [L, *tremulare,* to tremble], pertaining to tremors, or involuntary muscular contractions.

tremulous pulse [L, *tremulare,* to tremble, *pulsare,* to beat], a feeble, fluttering pulse.

trench fever [OFr, *trenchier,* to cut; L, *febris,* fever], a rare, self-limited infection, caused by *Bartonella,* a rickettsial organism transmitted by body lice, characterized by weakness, fever, rash, and leg pains.

trench foot [OFr, *trenchier,* to cut; AS, *fot*], a condition of moist gangrene of the foot caused by the freezing of wet skin.

Trendelenburg gait /trendel'ənbərg, tren'd(e)lənbŏŏrg/ [Friedrich Trendelenburg, German surgeon, 1844–1924], an abnormal gait associated with a weakness of the gluteus medius. The Trendelenburg gait is characterized by the dropping of the pelvis on the unaffected side of the body at the moment of heelstrike on the affected side.

Trendelenburg position [Friedrich Trendelenburg], a position in which the head is low and the body and legs are on an inclined plane. It is sometimes used in pelvic surgery to displace the abdominal organs upward, out of the pelvis, or to increase the blood flow to the brain in hypotension and shock.

Trendelenburg test [Friedrich Trendelenburg], a simple test for incompetent valves in a person who has varicose veins. The person lies down and elevates the leg to empty the vein, then stands, and the vein is observed as it fills. If the valves are incompetent, the vein fills from above. If the valves are normal, they do not allow backflow of blood, and the vein fills from below.

Trental, a trademark for an oral hemorrheologic drug (pentoxifylline).

trephination /tref′inā′shən/, the surgical excision of a circular piece of bone or other tissue accomplished with a cylindric saw.

trephine /trefīn′, trefēn′/ [Gk, *trypan,* to bore], a circular sawlike instrument used in removing pieces of bone or tissue, usually from the skull.

trepidation /trep′idāshən/ [L, *trepidare,* to tremble], a state of anxiety.

Treponema /trep′ənē′mə/ [Gk, *trepein,* to turn, *nema,* thread], a genus of gram negative spirochetes, including some pathogenic to humans, such as the organisms causing bejel, pinta, syphilis, and yaws.

treponemal antigen test /trep′ənē′məl/, any of various tests detecting specific antitreponemal antibodies in serum in the diagnosis of the *Treponema pallidum* infection of syphilis.

Treponema pallidum, an actively motile, slender spirochetal organism that causes syphilis.

treponematosis /trep′ənē′mətō′sis/ *pl.* **treponematoses** [Gk, *trepein* + *nema* + *osis,* condition], any disease caused by spirochetes of the genus *Treponema.* All these infections are effectively treated with penicillin.

treprostinil, an antiplatelet agent used to treat pulmonary arterial hypertension.

tretinoin /tret′inō′in/, a retinoic acid derivative. It is prescribed in the topical treatment of acne vulgaris and fine wrinkles, and is administered orally for inducing remission in acute promyelocytic leukemia.

Trexan, a trademark for an oral opioid antagonist (naltrexone hydrochloride).

TRF, abbreviation for *thyrotropin-releasing factor.*

TRH, abbreviation for **thyrotropin-releasing hormone.**

TRH stimulation test, TRH test, abbreviation for **thyrotropin-releasing hormone test.**

triacetin /trī·as′ətin/, an antifungal. It is prescribed to suppress the growth of superficial fungus infections of the skin, including athlete's foot.

triad /trī′əd/ [Gk, *trias,* three], a combination of three, such as two parents and a child.

triage /trē·äzh′/ [Fr, *trier,* to sort out], **1.** in military medicine, a classification of casualties of war and other disasters according to the gravity of injuries,

urgency of treatment, and place for treatment. **2.** a process in which a group of patients is sorted according to their need for care. **3.** in disaster medicine, a process in which a large group of patients is sorted so that care can be concentrated on those who are likely to survive.

triage: disaster, a nursing intervention from the Nursing Interventions Classification (NIC) defined as establishing priorities of patient care for urgent treatment while allocating scarce resources.

triage: emergency center, a nursing intervention from the Nursing Interventions Classification (NIC) defined as establishing priorities and initiating treatment for patients in an emergency center.

triage: telephone, a nursing intervention from the Nursing Interventions Classification (NIC) defined as determining the nature and urgency of a problem(s) and providing directions for the level of care required, over the telephone.

trial /trī′əl/, a process of quality testing.

trial forceps [Fr, *trier,* to sort out], an obstetric operation consisting of an attempt to deliver an infant with obstetric forceps. The forceps are applied to the baby's head, and moderate traction is applied. The delivery is continued only if the trial indicates that delivery can be accomplished safely.

trial of labor [Fr, *trier,* to sort out; L, *labor,* work], childbirth in which there is doubt as to whether the head of the fetus will pass through the pelvic brim. The situation must be monitored and assessed carefully to avoid fetal or maternal distress.

triamcinolone /trī′amsin′əlōn/, a corticosteroid. It is prescribed topically as an antiinflammatory agent in the treatment of dermatoses, stomatitis, and lichen planus lesions, is inhaled for the treatment of allergies and asthma, is injected (e.g., into joints) for the treatment of local inflammation, and is taken orally in low doses for treatment of adrenocortical insufficiency and in higher antiinflammatory/immunosuppressive doses for the treatment of systemic diseases such as SLE.

triamterene /trī·am′tərēn/, a potassium-sparing diuretic. It is usually prescribed alone or with another diuretic in the treatment of edema, hypertension, and CHF.

triangle [L, *triangulus,* three-cornered], a predictable emotional process that takes place when there is difficulty in a relationship. The three corners of a triangle can be composed of three people or two people and an object, group, or issue.

triangular bandage /trī·ang′gyələr/, a square of cloth folded or cut into the shape of a triangle. It may be used as a sling, a cover, or a thick pad to control bleeding.

T

triangular bone, the pyramidal carpal bone in the proximal row on the ulnar side of the wrist.

triangularis /trī·ang'gyōōlar'is/ [L], triangular muscle of facial expression.

triangular ligaments, two folds of peritoneum that, with the coronary ligaments, attach the liver to the diaphragm.

Triavil, a trademark for a CNS fixed-combination drug containing a phenothiazine antipsychotic (perphenazine) and a tricyclic antidepressant (amitriptyline hydrochloride).

triazolam /trī·az'əlam/, a benzodiazepine hypnotic agent prescribed in the short-term treatment of insomnia. This drug was withdrawn from the market in the United Kingdom; it continues to be available in the United States.

triazole /trī'ə-zōl, tri-a'zōl/, **1.** an organic compound in which three atoms of the five that make up the ring are nitrogen atoms. **2.** any of a class of antifungal agents that contain this compound.

tribe [L, *tribus*], a taxonomic division of organisms, subordinate to a family and superior to a genus, or subtribe.

tribology /tribol'əjē/ [Gk, *tribo,* to rub, *logos,* science], the study of friction, wear, and lubrication of articulating surfaces.

TRIC /trik/, abbreviation for *trachoma inclusion conjunctivitis* agent, which refers to *Chlamydia trachomatis,* the organism that causes both inclusion conjunctivitis and trachoma.

TRICARE, a health care insurance system for military dependents and members of the military services that covers care not available through the usual U.S. military medical service or public health service facilities.

triceps brachii /trī'seps brak'ē·ī/ [L, three-headed, *brachium,* arm], a large muscle that extends the entire length of the posterior surface of the humerus. It functions to extend the forearm and to adduct the arm.

triceps reflex, a deep tendon reflex elicited by tapping sharply the triceps tendon proximal to the elbow with the forearm in a relaxed position.

triceps skinfold (TSF), the thickness of a fold of skin around the triceps muscle. It is measured primarily to estimate the amount of subcutaneous fat.

triceps surae limp, an abnormal action in the walking or gait cycle, associated with a deficiency in the elevating and propulsive factors on the affected side of the body, especially a deficiency of the triceps surae. Such a deficiency prevents the triceps surae from raising the pelvis and carrying it forward during the walking cycle.

trichiasis /trikī'əsis/ [Gk, *thrix,* hair, *osis,* condition], an abnormal inversion of the eyelashes that irritates the eyeball. It usually follows infection or inflammation.

trichinosis /trik'inō'sis/ [Gk, *thrix* + *osis,* condition], infestation with the parasitic roundworm *Trichinella spiralis,* transmitted by eating raw or undercooked meat containing cysts (pork, bear, or other wild game). Early symptoms of infection include abdominal pain, nausea, fever, and diarrhea; later, muscle pain, tenderness, fatigue, and eosinophilia are observed. Larval penetration of the brain or heart may result in death. Light infections may be asymptomatic. There is no specific treatment. Analgesics, thiabendazole, and corticosteroids may relieve symptoms. Bed rest is recommended to prevent relapse and possible death. After 2 or 3 months, the organisms are completely encysted and cause no further symptoms.

trichlorfon /trī-klôr'fon/, metrifonate.

trichlormethiazide /trī'klôrməthī'əzīd/, a thiazide diuretic prescribed in the treatment of hypertension and edema.

trichloroethylene /trīklôr'ō·eth'ilēn/, a general anesthetic, administered by mask with N_2O, for dentistry, minor surgery, and the first stages of labor. It is not currently used in clinical anesthesia practice in developed countries.

trichoepithelioma /trik'ō·ep'ithē'lē·ō'mə/ *pl.* **trichoepitheliomas, trichoepitheliomata** [Gk, *thrix* + *epi,* above, *thele* nipple, *oma,* tumor], a cutaneous tumor derived from the basal cells of the follicles of fine body hair.

trichoid /trik'oid/, resembling a hair.

trichologia /trik'əlō'jē·ə/ [Gk, *thrix* + *legein,* to pull], an abnormal condition in which a person pulls out his or her own hair, which may be seen in delirium.

trichology /trikol'əjē/, the study of the anatomy, development, and diseases of the hair.

trichomatous /trikom'ətəs/ [Gk, *trichoma,* hairy growth], **1.** pertaining to an introversion of the margin of the eyelid. **2.** pertaining to matted hair or ingrowing hair.

trichomonacide /trik'ōmon'əsīd/ [Gk, *thrix* + *monas,* unit; L, *caedere,* to kill], an agent destructive to *Trichomonas vaginalis,* a parasitic protozoan flagellate that causes a refractory type of vaginitis, cystitis, and urethritis. —**trichomonacidal,** *adj.*

Trichomonas /trik'əmon'əs/, a genus of flagellate protozoa, which includes many species that are parasitic. Some live in the mouth of humans and are found around carious teeth; other species are found in the vagina and urethra of women. They are a cause of trichomoniasis.

Trichomonas tenax, a species of protozoa that is found in the human mouth, particularly in cases of pyorrhea.

Trichomonas vaginalis [Gk, *thrix* + *monas;* L, *vagina,* sheath], a motile protozoan parasite that causes vaginitis with a copious malodorous discharge and pruritus.

trichomoniasis /trik′əmənī′əsis/ [Gk, *thrix* + *monas* + *osis,* condition], a vaginal infection caused by the protozoan *Trichomonas vaginalis.* It is characterized by itching, burning, and frothy, pale yellow to green, malodorous vaginal discharge. In men infection is usually asymptomatic but may be evidenced by a persistent or recurrent urethritis. Infection is transmitted by sexual intercourse, rarely by moist washcloths, or, in newborns, by passage through the birth canal. Treatment is by oral metronidazole and tinidazole. Reinfection is common if sexual partners are not treated simultaneously.

trichopathy /trikop′əthē/ [Gk, *thrix,* hair, *pathos,* disease], any disease condition involving the hair.

trichophagia /trik′ō-fā-j(ē-)ə/, the habit of eating hair, a form of pica.

Trichophyton /trikof′iton/ [Gk, *thrix* + *phyton,* plant], a genus of fungi that infects skin, hair, and nails.

trichosis /trikō′sis/ [Gk, *thrix,* hair, *osis,* condition], any abnormal condition of hair growth, including alopecia, excessive female hair growth, or abnormal hair color.

trichosporosis [Gk, *thrix,* hair, *spora,* seed, *osis,* condition], a fungal disease of the hair shaft caused by *Trichosporon beigelii* that gives the hair a metallic appearance.

trichostrongyliasis /trik′ōstron′jəlī′əsis/ [Gk, *thrix* + *strongylos,* round, *osis,* condition], infestation with *Trichostrongylus,* a genus of nematode worm.

Trichostrongylus /trik′ōstron′jiləs/ [Gk, *thrix* + *strongylos*], a genus of roundworm, some species of which are parasitic to humans, such as *T. orientalis.*

trichotillomania /trik′ōtil′ōmā′nē-ə/ [Gk, *thrix* + *tillein,* to pull, *mania,* madness], an impulse disorder characterized by a desire to pull out one's hair, frequently seen in cases of severe mental retardation and delirium.—**trichomanic, trichotillomanic,** *adj.*

trichromacy /trī-krō′mə-sē/, trichromatic vision.

trichromatic /trī′krō-mat′ik/, **1.** having or pertaining to three different colors. **2.** able to distinguish the three primary colors.

trichromatism /trī-krō′mə-tiz′m/, trichromatic vision.

trichuriasis /trik′yərī′əsis/ [Gk, *thrix* + *oura,* tail, *osis,* condition], infestation with the roundworm *Trichuris trichiura.* The condition is usually asymptomatic, but heavy infestation may cause nausea, abdominal pain, diarrhea, and occasionally anemia and rectal prolapse. It is common in tropical areas with poor sanitation.

Treatment is with mebendazole; prevention includes proper disposal of feces and good personal hygiene.

Trichuris /trikyōōr′is/ [Gk, *thrix* + *oura*], a genus of parasitic roundworms of which the species *T. trichiura* infects the intestinal tract.

Trichuris trichiura, a species of whipworms, commonly found in warm, moist regions of the world. Ingestion of whipworm eggs results in infection in humans; the parasites live mainly in the cecum or large intestine. Heavy infections cause symptoms of abdominal pain and diarrhea; very heavy infections may result in anemia because of intestinal blood loss.

tricitrates /trī-sit′rāts/, a solution of sodium citrate, potassium citrate, and citric acid. It is used as a systemic or urinary alkalizer and neutralizing buffer and for prevention of kidney stones.

triclosan /trī-klō′san/, an antibacterial effective against gram-positive and most gram-negative organisms and exhibiting slight activity against yeasts and fungi. It is used as a detergent in surgical scrubs, soaps, and deodorants.

tricrotic pulse /trīkrot′ik/, an abnormal pulse that has three peaks of elevation on a sphygmogram, representing the pressure wave from the heart in systole followed by two pressure waves in diastole.

tricuspid /trīkus′pid/ [Gk, *treis,* three; L, *cuspis,* point], **1.** pertaining to three points or cusps. **2.** pertaining to the tricuspid valve of the heart. **3.** a tooth with three points or cusps, rare in humans.

tricuspid area [Gk, *treis,* three; L, *cuspis,* point], the region of the chest near the left lower sternum and opposite the fourth and fifth costal cartilages, where sounds of the tricuspid heart valve are best heard by auscultation.

tricuspid atresia, a congenital cardiac anomaly characterized by the absence of the tricuspid valve so that there is no opening between the right atrium and right ventricle. Other cardiac defects such as atrial and ventricular septal defects are usually present, allowing some shunting of blood into the lungs. Clinical manifestations include severe cyanosis, dyspnea, anoxia, and signs of right-sided heart failure. Immediate palliative treatment includes pulmonary artery anastomoses to increase blood flow to the lungs and atrial septostomy if the atrial septal defect is small. Total corrective surgery has been successful in a limited number of older children.

tricuspid insufficiency, incomplete closure of the tricuspid valve, resulting in tricuspid regurgitation.

tricuspid murmur [Gk, *treis,* three; L, *cuspis,* point, *murmur,* humming], one of the heart murmurs caused by a defective tricuspid valve. The tricuspid diastolic and systolic murmurs resemble mitral valve diastolic and systolic murmurs.

tricuspid regurgitation (TR) [Gk, *treis,* three; L, *cuspis,* point, *re + gurgitare,* to flow back again], the backflow of blood from the right ventricle into the right atrium, resulting from imperfect functioning (insufficiency) of the tricuspid valve.

tricuspid stenosis, narrowing or stricture of the tricuspid valve. Clinical characteristics include a diastolic pressure gradient between the right atrium and right ventricle, jugular vein distension, pulmonary congestion, and in severe cases hepatic congestion and splenomegaly.

tricuspid valve, a valve with three main cusps situated between the right atrium and right ventricle of the heart. As the right and left ventricles relax during the diastolic phase of the heartbeat, the tricuspid valve opens, allowing blood to flow into the ventricle. In the systolic phase of the heartbeat, both blood-filled ventricles contract, pumping out their contents, while the tricuspid and mitral valves close to prevent any backflow.

tricyclic antidepressant (TCA), any of a group of antidepressant drugs that contain three fused rings in their chemical structure and that potentiates the action of catecholamines. These drugs rapidly block the reuptake of amine neurotransmitters, but their exact mechanism of their effect is unknown. Besides their use to treat depression, various tricyclic antidepressants are used for other conditions, such as obsessive-compulsive disorder, panic disorder, and neurogenic pain.

tricyclic compound /trīsik′lik/ [Gk, *treis + kyklos,* circle; L, *componere,* to put together], a chemical substance containing three rings in the molecular structure, especially a tricyclic antidepressant drug used in the treatment of reactive or endogenous depression.

Tridesilon, a trademark for a glucocorticoid (desonide).

Tridione, a trademark for an anticonvulsant (trimethadione).

trientene /trī′en-tēn/, a chelating agent used as the hydrochloride salt for chelation of copper in treatment of Wilson's disease.

trientine hydrochloride /trī′en′tēn/, an oral medication for treatment of an inherited defect in copper metabolism (Wilson's disease). It is prescribed for the relief of symptoms of Wilson's disease for people who cannot tolerate penicillamine.

triethanolamine polypeptide oleate-condensate /trī′eth′ənol′əmēn/, a ceruminolytic agent prescribed to reduce excessive earwax, used as a solution in propylene glycol.

trifluoperazine hydrochloride /trī′floo·ō per′əzēn/, a phenothiazine antipsychotic prescribed in the treatment of schizophrenia and other psychotic disorders.

trifluorothymidine /trī′floor′ōthī′mədēn/, an antiviral. It is prescribed in the treatment of keratoconjunctivitis, herpetic keratitis, and other forms of keratitis caused by HSV.

trifocal lens /trīfō′kəl/ [Gk, *treis,* three; L, *focus,* hearth, *lens,* lentil], an eyeglass lens ground with three foci to allow correction of near, intermediate, and far vision.

trifurcation /-furkā′shən/ [Gk, *treis,* three; L, *furca,* fork], pertaining to a vessel or other structure with three branches.

trigeminal /trījem′inəl/ [Gk, *treis,* three; L, *geminus,* twins], pertaining to the three-branch trigeminal (fifth cranial) nerve innervating the face, eyes, nose, mouth, and jaws.

trigeminal nerve [Gk, *treis + geminus,* twin], either of the largest pair of cranial nerves, essential for the act of chewing and general sensibility of the face. The trigeminal nerves have sensory, motor, and intermediate roots and connect to three areas in the brain.

trigeminal neuralgia, a neurologic condition of the trigeminal facial nerve, characterized by paroxysms of flashing, stabbing pain radiating along the course of a branch of the nerve from the angle of the jaw. It is caused by degeneration of the nerve or pressure on it. Any or all of the three branches of the nerve may be affected. The momentary bursts of pain recur in clusters lasting many seconds; paroxysmal episodes of the pains may last for hours.

trigeminal pulse, an abnormal pulse in which every third beat is absent.

trigeminy /trījem′inē/ [Gk, *treis;* L, *geminus,* twin], **1.** a grouping in threes. **2.** a cardiac arrhythmia characterized by the occurrence of three heartbeats in a repeating pattern: two normal beats coupled to an ectopic beat, or two ectopic beats coupled to a normal beat.—**trigeminal,** *adj.*

trigger [D, *trekker,* that which pulls], a substance, object, or agent that initiates or stimulates an action.

triggered activity [D, *trekker,* that which pulls; L, *activus*], rhythmic cardiac activity that results when a series of afterdepolarizations reach the threshold potential.

trigger finger, a phenomenon in which the movement of a finger is halted momentarily in flexion or extension and then continues with a jerk.

trigger point, a point on the body that is particularly sensitive to touch and, when stimulated, becomes the site of a painful neuralgia.

triglyceride /trīglis′ərīd/, a simple fat compound consisting of three molecules of fatty acid (e.g., oleic, palmitic, or stearic) and glycerol. Triglycerides make up most animal and vegetable fats and are the principal lipids in the blood, where they circulate, within lipoproteins.

triglycerides test (TGs), a blood test that detects levels of fats existing within the bloodstream that are transported by very low-density lipoproteins (VLDLs) and chylomicrons. It is done as part of a lipid profile, which also evaluates cholesterol and lipoproteins to assess the risk of coronary and vascular disease.

trigonal muscles, a submucous sheet of smooth muscle at the bladder trigone, continuous with ureteral muscles above and with those of the proximal urethra below.

trigone /trī′gōn/ [Gk, *trigonos,* three-cornered], **1.** a triangular space, especially one at the base of the shoulder. **2.** the first three dominant cusps, considered collectively, of an upper molar.

trigonelline /trig′ōnel′ēn/, an alkaloid derived from various kinds of plant products, including coffee beans, fenugreek, and seeds of *Cannabis sativa,* as well as from sea urchins and jellyfish. Trigonelline is used in the manufacture of poultices and other medicinals.

trigone of the bladder /trīgō′n/, a triangular area of the bladder between the opening of the ureters and the orifice of the urethra.

trigonitis /trī′gənī′tis/, inflammation of the trigone of the bladder, which often accompanies urethritis.

trigonum vesicae, a triangular area of the bladder between the opening of the ureters and the orifice of the urethra.

trihexyphenidyl hydrochloride /trīhex′i fen′idil/, an anticholinergic agent prescribed in the treatment of Parkinson's disease and to control drug-induced extrapyramidal reactions.

trihybrid /trīhī′brid/ [Gk, *treis* + *hybrida,* mixed offspring], pertaining to an individual, organism, or strain that is heterozygous for three specific traits; the offspring of parents differing in three specific gene pairs or that is heterozygous for three particular traits or gene loci being followed.

trihybrid cross, the mating of two individuals, organisms, or strains that have different gene pairs that determine three specific traits or in which three particular characteristics or gene loci are being followed.

trihydric alcohol /trīhid′rik/, an alcohol containing three hydroxyl groups such as glycerin.

triiodothyronine (T₃) /trī′ī·ō′dōthī′rənēn/, a hormone that helps regulate growth and development, helps control metabolism and body temperature, and, by a negative-feedback system, acts to inhibit the secretion of thyrotropin by the pituitary gland. It is the most active thyroid hormone and affects all body processes, including gene expressions. It is a component of various drugs, such as liotrix and liothyronine sodium, used in the treatment of hypothyroidism and simple goiter.

triiodothyronine resin uptake test, a thyroid function test, measuring how many sites on thyroxine-binding globulin are occupied by endogenous triiodothyronine (T₃) and how many sites remain available.

triiodothyronine (T₃) test, a test used to accurately measure thyroid function. It is used primarily to determine hyperthyroidism.

trikates /trī′kāts/, a solution of potassium acetate, potassium bicarbonate, and potassium citrate used as a potassium supplement in the treatment and prevention of hypokalemia.

Trilafon, a trademark for a phenothiazine antipsychotic (perphenazine).

trilaminar blastoderm /trīlam′inər/ [Gk, *treis;* L, *lamina,* plate; Gk, *blastos,* germ, *derma,* skin], the stage of embryonic development in which all three of the primary germ layers, the ectoderm, mesoderm, and entoderm, have formed.

trill [It, *trillare,* to make a ringing sound], a vibratory, quavering, warbling sound, as produced by human voice, birds, insects, or musical instruments.

trilogy of Fallot /tril′əjē, falō′/ [Etienne-Louis A. Fallot, French physician, 1850–1911; Gk, *treis* + *logos,* word], a congenital cardiac anomaly consisting of pulmonary stenosis, interatrial septal defect, and right ventricular hypertrophy.

trimester /trīmes′tər, trī′-/ [L, *trimestris,* three months], one of the three periods of approximately 3 months into which pregnancy is divided. The first trimester includes the time from the first day of the last menstrual period to the end of 12 weeks. The second trimester, closer to 4 months in length than 3, extends from the twelfth to the twenty-eighth week of gestation. The third trimester begins at the twenty-eighth week and extends to the time of delivery.

trimethadione /trī′methədī′ōn/, an anticonvulsant prescribed to prevent absences (petit mal) seizures, particularly seizures that are resistant to other therapies.

T

trimethobenzamide hydrochloride /trī meth′ōben′zəmīd/, an anticholinergic and antiemetic. It is prescribed for the relief of postoperative nausea and vomiting, and nausea and vomiting associated with gastroenteritis.

trimethoprim /trīmeth′əprim/, an antibacterial prescribed in the treatment of infections, particularly of the urinary tract, middle ear, and bronchi.

trimipramine maleate /trimip′rəmēn/, a tricyclic antidepressant prescribed in the treatment of depression.

Trimox, a trademark for an antibiotic (amoxicillin trihydrate).

Trimpex, a trademark for an antibacterial (trimethoprim).

Trinalin, a trademark for a fixed-combination medication containing an antihistamine (azatadine) and a decongestant (pseudoephedrine).

trinucleotide, a combination of three adjacent nucleotide units used to identify a specific amino acid in a genome.

triolein breath test, a breath test for pancreatic function. The fasting patient is administered triolein labeled with either carbon-13 or carbon-14 and levels of labeled carbon dioxide in the exhaled breath are subsequently measured at regular time intervals. Low levels of carbon dioxide indicate inadequate pancreatic lipase, such as with a pancreatic disease or CF.

tripelennamine hydrochloride /trī′pelen′ əmēn/, an antihistamine prescribed in the treatment of rhinitis and hypersensitivity reactions of the skin.

tripe palms, a condition of thickened velvet- or moss-textured palms with a pronounced skin ridge pattern. Tripe palms has been associated with certain malignancies, including lung and stomach cancers and pulmonary carcinomas.

triphasic /trīfā′zik/ [Gk, *treis,* three, *phasis,* appearance], having three phases or stages.

triple-dye treatment, a therapy for burns in which three dyes, 6% gentian violet, 1% brilliant green, and 0.1% acriflavine base, are applied.

triplegia /trīplē′jə/ [Gk, *treis,* three, *plege,* stroke], a condition of paralysis on one side of the body plus paralysis of an arm or leg on the opposite side.

triple-lumen catheter [L, *triplus,* triple, *lumen,* light; Gk, *katheter,* a thing lowered into], any catheter with three separate passages, each of which is marked with the name of a fluid or medication.

triple-lumen drain, a drain consisting of three tubes placed one inside another.

triple point, the combination of temperature and pressure in which a given substance may exist in solid, liquid, and vapor forms all in equilibrium at the same time. Every substance has a theoretic triple point.

triple response, a triad of phenomena that occur in sequence after an intradermal injection of histamine. First, a red spot develops, spreading outward for a few millimeters, reaching its maximal size within 1 minute and then turning bluish. Next, a brighter red flush of color spreads slowly in an irregular flare around the original red spot. Finally, a wheal filled with fluid forms over the original spot.

triple sugar iron reaction, any one of several reactions seen in certain bacterial cultures growing on triple sugar iron agar, a culture medium used to aid in the identification of *Escherichia coli, Proteus, Salmonella, Shigella,* and other pathogenic enteric bacteria.

triple sulfa, a combination of sulfathiazole, sulfacetamide, and sulfabenzamide. It is administered intravaginally in the treatment of bacterial vaginosis caused by *Gardnerella vaginalis.*

triplet /trip′lət/ [L, *triplus*], **1.** any one of three offspring born of the same gestation period during a single pregnancy. **2.** in genetics, the unit of three consecutive bases in one polynucleotide chain of DNA or RNA that codes for a specific amino acid.

triploid (**3n**) /trip′loid/ [L, *triplus* + *eidos*], **1.** an individual, organism, strain, or cell that has three complete sets of chromosomes, triple the haploid number characteristic of the species. **2.** pertaining to such an individual, organism, strain, or cell.—**triploidy,** *n.*

triploidy /trip′loidē/, the state or condition of having three complete sets of chromosomes.

tripod /trī′pod/ [Gk, *treis,* three, *pous,* foot], any object with three legs or three feet.

tripodial symmelia /trīpō′dē·əl/ [Gk, *treis,* three, *pous,* foot, *syn,* together, *melos,* limb], a fetal anomaly characterized by the fusion of the lower extremities and the presence of three feet.

triprolidine /trīprol′idēn/, an antihistamine prescribed in the treatment of hypersensitivity reactions, including rhinitis, skin rash, and pruritus.

tripsis /trip′sis/ [Gk, rubbing], **1.** massage. **2.** the process of reducing the particle size of a substance by grinding it with a mortar and pestle.

triptorelin, a gonadotropin-releasing hormone used to treat advanced prostate cancer.

triradiate cartilage, a secondary ossification center of the hip bone, occurring as a Y-shaped strip in the floor of the acetabulum.

trisaccharide /trīsak′ərīd/ [Gk, *treis,* three, *sakcharon,* sugar], a carbohydrate composed of three monosaccharide units linked together.

trisalicylate /trī′sə·lis′ilāt/, a compound containing three salicylate ions.

trismus /triz′məs/ [Gk, *trismos,* gnashing], a prolonged tonic spasm of the muscles of the jaw.

trisomy /trī′səmē/ [Gk, *treis* + *soma,* body], a chromosomal aberration characterized by the presence of one more than the normal number of chromosomes in a diploid complement; in humans the trisomic cell contains 47 chromosomes and is designated $2n + 1$. —**trisomic,** *adj.*

trisomy 8, a congenital condition associated with the presence of an extra chromosome 8 within the C group. Persons with the condition are slender and of normal height and have a large asymmetric head, prominent forehead, deep-set eyes, low-set prominent ears, and thick lips. There is mild to severe mental and motor retardation, often with delayed and poorly articulated speech. Skeletal anomalies and joint limitation, especially permanent flexion of one or more fingers, may occur. There are unusually deep palmar and plantar creases, which are diagnostically significant. Most trisomy 8 individuals are mosaic.

trisomy 13, a congenital condition caused by the presence of an extra chromosome in the D group, predominantly chromosome 13, although in rare instances chromosome 14 or 15. It is characterized by multiple midline anomalies and CNS defects, including holoprosencephaly, microcephaly, myelomeningocele, microphthalmos, and cleft lip and palate. There is also severe mental retardation; polydactyly; deafness; convulsions; and abnormalities of the heart, viscera, and genitalia. Most infants with the condition are severely affected and do not survive beyond the first 6 months of life.

trisomy 18, a congenital condition caused by the presence of an extra chromosome 18, characterized by severe mental retardation and multiple deformities. Among the most common defects are scaphocephaly or other skull abnormalities; micrognathia; abnormal facies with low-set malformed ears and prominent occiput; cleft lip and palate; clenched fists with overlapping fingers, especially the index over the third finger; clubfeet; and syndactyly. Ventricular septal defect, patent ductus arteriosus, atrial septal defect, and renal anomalies are also common. Survival for more than a few months is rare.

trisomy 22, a congenital condition caused by the presence of an extra chromosome 22 in the G group, characterized by psychomotor retardation and various developmental anomalies. Common defects include microcephaly, micrognathia, hypotonia, hypertelorism, abnormal ears with preauricular tags or fistulas and congenital heart disease. In partial trisomy 22 the extra chromosome is much smaller than the normal pair and causes coloboma of the iris, anal atresia, or both, as well as various other defects.

trisomy syndrome, any condition caused by the addition of an extra member to a normal pair of homologous autosomes or to the sex chromosomes or by the translocation of a part of one chromosome to another. Most trisomies occur as a result of complete or partial nondisjunction of the chromosomes during cell division.

trisplanchnic /trīsplangk′nik/, pertaining to three visceral body cavities: skull, thorax, and abdomen.

trisulfapyrimidines /trīsul′fəpirim′idīnz/, three antibacterials in combination (sulfadiazine, sulfamerazine, and sulfamethazine), rarely prescribed today.

tritium (^{3}H) /trit′ē·əm, trish′əm/ [Gk, *tritos,* third], the radioactive isotope of the hydrogen atom, used as a tracer; a β emitter.

trituration, the process of removing impurities from a substance by grinding it under a solvent in which the impurities are much more soluble than the substance itself.

trivalence /trīvā′ləns/ [Gk, *treis;* L, *valere,* to be worth], an ability of an atom or group of atoms to bond with three monovalent elements in a compound.

trivalent /trīvā′lənt/ [Gk, *treis;* L, *valere,* to be worth], **1.** pertaining to an atom or group of atoms with the capability of bonding with or replacing three monovalent elements. **2.** designating a vaccine that can prevent diseases or conditions.

trivial name, a chemical name that is not derived from a systematic nomenclature system such as the IUPAC nomenclature system. The name may or may not indicate its relationship to molecular structure and its relationship to other chemicals. The name may be accepted as an official nonproprietary designation because of common usage. Examples are caffeine, folic acid, and aspirin.

Tri-Vi-Flor, a trademark for an oral pediatric fixed-combination drug containing sodium fluoride and vitamins A, C, and D.

tRNA, abbreviation for **transfer RNA.**

Trobicin, a trademark for an antibacterial (spectinomycin hydrochloride).

trocar /trō′kär/ [Fr, *trois,* three, *carres,* sides], a sharp, pointed rod that fits inside a tube. It is used to pierce the skin and the wall of a cavity or canal in the body to aspirate fluids, to instill a medication or solution, or to guide the placement of a soft catheter.

T

trochanter /trōkan'tər/ [Gk, runner], one of the two bony projections on the proximal end of the femur that serve as the point of attachment of various muscles.

trochanteric fossa, a fossa on the greater trochanter to which the obturator externus muscle is attached.

trochanter major [Gk, trochanter, runner; L, major, great], a large projection from the proximal end of the shaft of the femur. It is a point of attachment for the gluteus minimus and gluteus medius muscles.

troche /trō'kē/ [Gk, trochos, lozenge], a small oval, round, or oblong tablet containing a medicinal agent incorporated in a flavored, sweetened mucilage or fruit base that dissolves in the mouth, releasing the drug.

trochlea /trok'lē-ə/, a pulley-shaped part or structure.—**trochlear,** adj.

trochlear /trok'lē-ər/ [L, trochlea, pulley], **1.** pertaining to a trochlea or something that is pulley-shaped. **2.** relating to the trochlear (fourth cranial) nerve.

trochlear nerve [L, trochlea, pulley, nervus, nerve], either of the smallest pair of cranial nerves, essential for eye movement and eye muscle sensibility.

trochlear notch of ulna, a large depression in the ulna, formed by the olecranon and coronoid processes, that articulates with the trochlea of the humerus.

trolamine /trol'əmēn/, a contraction for triethanolamine.

troleandomycin /trol'ē·an'dōmī'sin/, a macrolide antibiotic. It is prescribed in the treatment of certain infections, including pneumococcal pneumonia and group A streptococcal infections of the upper respiratory tract. It has orphan drug status for the treatment of corticosteroid-dependent asthma due to its steroid-sparing properties.

Trombiculidae /trom'bikyōō'lidē/, a family of mites, including harvest mites, red bugs, and chiggers. The larvae are parasitic, and the adults are free-living. The mites are disease vectors of typhus, rickettsiae, scrub itch, tsutsugamushi disease, and other infections.

trombiculosis /trombik'yəlō'sis/ [Gk, tromein, to tremble, osis, condition], an infestation with mites of the genus Trombicula, some species of which carry scrub typhus.

Tronothane, a trademark for a local anesthetic (pramoxine hydrochloride).

trophic /trof'ik/ [Gk, trophe, nutrition], pertaining to a nutritive effect on or quality of cellular activity.

trophic action [Gk, trophe, nutrition; L, agere, to do], the stimulation of cell reproduction and enlargement by nurturing and causing growth.

trophic fracture, a fracture resulting from the weakening of bone caused by nutritional disturbances.

trophic hormones, hormones secreted by the anterior lobe of pituitary gland that stimulate target organs.

trophic ulcer, a pressure ulcer caused by external trauma to a part of the body that is in poor condition resulting from disease, vascular insufficiency, or loss of afferent nerve fibers.

trophism /trof'izəm/ [Gk, trophe, nutrition], the influence of nourishment.

trophoblast /trof'əblast'/ [Gk, trophe + blastos, germ], the outermost layer of tissue that forms the wall of the blastocyst of placental mammals in the early stages of embryonic development. It functions in the implantation of the blastocyst in the uterine wall and in supplying nutrients to the embryo.—**trophoblastic,** adj.

trophoblastic cancer /-blas'tik/, a malignant neoplastic disease of the uterus derived from chorionic epithelium, characterized by the production of high levels of HCG. The tumor may be an invasive hydatid mole (chorioadenoma destruens) formed by grossly enlarged vesicular chorionic villi or a malignant uterine choriocarcinoma that arises from nonvillous chorionic epithelium. Initial symptoms are vaginal bleeding and a profuse, foul-smelling discharge; a persistent cough or hemoptysis signals pulmonary involvement. As the disease progresses, there may be frequent hemorrhage, weakness, and emaciation. Hysterectomy is indicated in most cases, but surgery does not eliminate the possibility of a recurrence. Chemotherapy is effective in curing a large percentage of patients with trophoblastic tumors.

trophotropic /trof'ətrop'ik/ [Gk, trophe + trepein, to turn], pertaining to a combination of parasympathetic nervous system activity, somatic muscle relaxation, and cortical beta rhythm synchronization, such as in a resting or sleep state.

trophotropism /trof'ətrop'izəm/, movement toward or away from nutrient sources.

trophozoite /trof'əzō'īt/ [Gk, trophe + zoon, animal], an immature ameboid protozoon. Diseases in which trophozoites may be isolated by bacteriologic studies include amebic dysentery, malaria, and trichomonas vaginitis.

tropical acne /trop'ikəl/, a form of acne that is caused or aggravated by high temperature and humidity. It is characterized by large nodules or pustules on the neck, back, upper arms, and buttocks.

tropical medicine [Gk, tropikos, of the solstice; L, medicina], the branch of medicine concerned with the diagnosis and treatment of diseases commonly occurring in tropic and subtropic regions of the world, generally between 30 degrees north and south of the equator.

tropical sprue, a malabsorption syndrome of unknown cause that is endemic in the tropics and subtropics. It is characterized by abnormalities in the mucosa of the small intestine, resulting in protein malnutrition and multiple nutritional deficiencies, often complicated by severe infection. Symptoms include diarrhea, anorexia, and weight loss. Megaloblastic anemia may result from folic acid and vitamin B_{12} deficiency. Treatment includes administration of antibiotics, particularly tetracycline; folic acid; iron; calcium; and vitamins A, D, K, and B complex; as well as a balanced diet high in protein and normal in fat content.

tropocollagen /trop′əkol′əjən/ [Gk, *trepein,* to turn, *kolla,* glue, *genein,* to produce], fundamental units of collagen fibrils obtained by prolonged extraction of insoluble collagen with dilute acid.

tropomyosin /trop′əmī′əsin/ [Gk, *trepein* + *mys,* muscle], a protein component of sarcomere filaments, which, together with troponin, regulates interactions of actin and myosin in muscle contractions.

troponin /trō′pənin/ [Gk, *trepein,* to turn], a protein in the striated cell ultrastructure that modulates the interaction between actin and myosin molecules.

troponins test, blood tests that measure levels of cardiac troponins (T and I), which are the standard biochemical markers for cardiac disease. This test assists in evaluating patients with suspected acute coronary ischemic syndrome.

trospium, an anticholinergic used to treat overactive bladder.

trough /trôf/ [AS, *trog*], a groove or channel, such as the gingival trough around the neck of a tooth.

Trousseau's sign /trō̅ōsōz′/ [Armand Trousseau, French physician, 1801–1867; L, *signum,* mark], **1.** a test for latent tetany in which carpal spasm is induced by inflating a sphygmomanometer cuff on the upper arm to a pressure exceeding systolic BP for 3 minutes. **2.** a reddened streak, the result of drawing a finger across the skin. It is seen with a variety of nervous system disorders.

Trousseau's syndrome [Armand Trousseau], superficial migratory thrombophlebitis associated with visceral cancer.

trovafloxacin /trō′və-flok′sə-sin/, an antibacterial effective against a broad spectrum of gram-positive and gram-negative organisms. The mesylate salt is used in the treatment of serious infections.

Trp, abbreviation for **tryptophan.**

true birth rate [ME, *treue,* faith + *burthe;* L, *reri,* to calculate], the ratio of total births to the total female population of childbearing age, between 15 and 45 years of age.

true conjugate, a radiographic measurement of the distance from the upper margin of the symphysis pubis to the sacral promontory. It is usually 1.5 to 2 cm less than the diagonal conjugate.

true denticle, a calcified body composed of irregular dentin found in the pulp chamber of a tooth.

true diverticulum [ME, *treue,* faith; L, *diverticulare,* to turn aside], diverticulum that includes all the same tissue layers as the organ from which it originates.

true hermaphroditism [ME, *treue,* faith; Gk, *Hermaphroditos,* son of Hermes and Aphrodite], a condition in which an individual is born with both male and female gonads.

true labor, uterine contractions that result in a change in the cervix and birth of an infant.

true neuroma, any neoplasm composed of nerve tissue.

true oxygen, the calculated concentration as either a percentage or a fraction that, when multiplied by the expiratory minute volume at STPD, gives oxygen uptake.

true suture, an immovable fibrous joint of the skull in which the edges of bones interlock along a series of processes and indentations.

true value, in statistics, a value that is closely approximated by the definitive value and somewhat less closely by the reference value.

true vocal cords [ME, *treue,* faith; L, *vocalis,* of the voice; Gk, *chorde,* string], the vocal folds of the larynx (plicae vocales), as distinguished from the vestibular folds (plicae vestibulares), called false vocal cords.

truncal /trung′kəl/ [L, *truncus*], pertaining to the trunk of the body or to any arterial or nerve trunk.

truncal ataxia, a loss of coordinated muscle movements for maintaining normal posture of the trunk.

truncal obesity, obesity that preferentially affects or is located in the trunk of the body as opposed to the extremities.

truncated /trung′kātid/, **1.** amputated from the trunk. **2.** cut across at right angles to the long axis.

truncus /trung′kəs/ [L, trunk], the main stem of an anatomic part from which branches may arise, such as the sympathetic nerve chain or jugular lymph trunk.

truncus arteriosus [L, trunk; Gk, *arteria,* airpipe], the embryonic arterial trunk that initially opens from both ventricles of the heart and later divides into the aorta and the pulmonary trunk, the two parts separated by the bulbar septum.

T

truncus brachiocephalicus, a branch of the aorta that divides into the right common carotid and right subclavian arteries.

trunk [L, *truncus*], **1.** the main stalk of an anatomic structure with many branches such as an artery or nerve. **2.** the body excluding the head and appendages.

trunk balance, the ability to maintain postural control of the trunk, including the shifting and bearing of weight on each side to free an extremity for a particular function such as reaching and grasping.

Trusopt, a trademark for a carbonic anhydrase inhibitor (dorzolamide hydrochloride).

truss [Fr, *trousser*, to pack up], an apparatus worn to prevent or retard the herniation of the intestines or other organ through an opening in the abdominal wall.

trust [ME, protection], a risk-taking process whereby an individual's situation depends on the future behavior of another person.

truth [AS, *treowo*], a rule or statement that conforms to fact or reality.

truth serum, a common name for any of several sedatives, such as the short-acting barbiturates, that have been administered intravenously in subjects to elicit information that may have been repressed. It has been used successfully in helping to identify amnesia victims.

truth telling, a nursing intervention from the Nursing Interventions Classification (NIC) defined as use of whole truth, partial truth, or decision delay to promote the patient's self-determination and well-being.

trypanocide /tri-pan-ə-sīd/, an agent lethal to trypanosomes.

Trypanosoma /trip′ənōsō′mə/ [Gk, *trypanon*, borer, *soma*, body], a genus of parasitic organisms, several species of which can cause significant diseases in humans. Most *Trypanosoma* organisms live part of their life cycle in insects and are transmitted to humans by insect bites.

trypanosome /trip′ənōsōm′, tripan′-/, any organism of the genus *Trypanosoma*. —**trypanosomal,** *adj.*

trypanosomiasis /trip′ənō′sōmī′əsis/ [Gk, *trypanon* + *soma* + *osis*, condition], an infection by an organism of the *Trypanosoma* genus.

trypsin /trip′sin/ [Gk, *tripsis*, rubbing], a proteolytic digestive enzyme produced by the exocrine pancreas that catalyzes in the small intestine the breakdown of dietary proteins to peptones, peptides, and amino acids.

trypsin, crystallized, a proteolytic enzyme from the pancreas of the ox, *Bos taurus*, that has been used as a debriding agent for open wounds and ulcers.

trypsin inhibitor, one of a group of peptides, present in such varied sources as soybeans, egg white, and human colostrum, that mask or inhibit the active site of the trypsin molecule.

trypsinogen /tripsin′əjən/ [Gk, *tripsis* + *genein*, to produce], the inactive precursor form of trypsin. Trypsinogen is secreted in pancreatic juice and converted to active trypsin through the action of enterokinase in the intestine.

tryptophan (Trp) /trip′təfan/, an amino acid essential for normal growth and nitrogen balance. Tryptophan is the precursor of several important biomolecules, including serotonin and niacin.

TSEM, abbreviation for **transmission scanning electron microscopy.**

tsetse fly /tset′sē, tsē′tsē/ [Afr, *tsetse*; AS, *flyge*], a blood-sucking fly found in regions of Africa. It is an insect of the *Glossina* genus and a secondary host of trypanosomes, which cause African sleeping sickness and other diseases in humans.

TSH, abbreviation for **thyroid-stimulating hormone.**

T-shaped fracture, an intercondylar fracture that has both longitudinal and transverse portions in the form of a T.

TSH assay, thyroid-stimulating hormone test.

TSH test, abbreviation for **thyroid-stimulating hormone test.**

tsp, abbreviation for **teaspoon.**

TSS, abbreviation for **toxic shock syndrome.**

TSTA, abbreviation for *tumor-specific transplantation antigen.*

TT, abbreviation for **thrombolytic therapy.**

t test, a statistical test used to determine whether there are differences between two means or between a target value and a calculated mean.

TTP, abbreviation for **thrombotic thrombocytopenic purpura.**

T tube, **1.** a tubular device in the shape of a T, inserted through the skin into a cavity or a wound, used for drainage. **2.** an apparatus used to connect a source of humidified oxygen to the endotracheal tube so that a spirometer can be attached for the evaluation of tidal volume.

T tube cholangiography, a type of biliary tract radiographic examination in which a water-soluble iodinated contrast medium is injected into the bile duct through an indwelling, T-shaped rubber tube. The tube is inserted in the common bile duct as a routine postoperative procedure to provide drainage.

T tubule system, a system of tubular invaginations along the surface of all striated muscle cell membranes, providing an extension of the membrane into the cells. The system is believed to be part of an extensive endomembrane system involved

1377

in storing calcium ions and in the movement of action potentials into the cells.

T.U., 1. abbreviation for *toxin unit*. **2.** abbreviation for *tuberculin unit*.

tubal abortion /t(y)oō′bəl/ [L, *tubus* + *ab,* away from, *oriri,* to be born], a condition of pregnancy in which an embryo, ectopically implanted, is expelled from the uterine tube into the peritoneal cavity. Tubal abortion is often accompanied by significant internal bleeding, causing acute abdominal and pelvic pain.

tubal air cells, air cells on the floor of the eustachian tube close to the carotid canal.

tubal dermoid cyst, a tumor derived from embryonal tissues that develops in an oviduct.

tubal embryo transfer (TET), 1. a method of ART consisting of retrieval of oocytes from the ovary, followed by their fertilization and culture in the laboratory with placement of the resulting embryos in the fallopian tubes by laparoscopy more than 24 hours after the original retrieval. **2.** laparoscopic transfer of cryopreserved embryos to the fallopian tubes.

tubal factor infertility, female factor infertility caused by an abnormality of the uterine tubes, such as scarring or obstruction following a UTI.

tubal ligation, one of several sterilization procedures in which both fallopian tubes are blocked to prevent conception from occurring.

tubal pregnancy, an ectopic pregnancy in which the conceptus implants in the fallopian tube. Most often the tube, which cannot long contain the growing fetus, ruptures, precipitating an intraperitoneal hemorrhage. If not stopped, the hemorrhaging can lead rapidly to shock and often death.

tube /t(y)oōb/ [L, *tubus*], a hollow, cylindric piece of equipment or structure of the body.

tube care, a nursing intervention from the Nursing Interventions Classification (NIC) defined as management of a patient with an external drainage device exiting the body.

tube care: chest, a nursing intervention from the Nursing Interventions Classification (NIC) defined as management of a patient with an external water-seal drainage device exiting the chest cavity.

tube care: gastrointestinal, a nursing intervention from the Nursing Interventions Classification (NIC) defined as management of a patient with a gastrointestinal tube.

tube care: umbilical line, a nursing intervention from the Nursing Interventions Classification (NIC) defined as management of a newborn with an umbilical catheter.

tube care: urinary, a nursing intervention from the Nursing Interventions

Classification (NIC) defined as management of a patient with urinary drainage equipment.

tube care: ventriculostomy/lumbar drain, a nursing intervention from the Nursing Interventions Classification (NIC) defined as management of a patient with an external cerebrospinal fluid drainage system.

tube feeding, the administration of nutritionally balanced liquefied foods or nutrients through a tube inserted into the esophagus, stomach, duodenum, or jejunum. The conditions for which tube feeding is administered include after mouth or gastric surgery, in severe burns, in paralysis or obstruction of the esophagus, in severe cases of anorexia nervosa, and for unconscious patients or those unable to chew or swallow.

tube feeding care, the nursing care and management of a patient receiving nourishment through a nasogastric tube.

tube gain, the overall electron gain of a photomultiplier tube, calculated as gn, where g is the dynode gain and n is the number of dynodes in the tube. Thus if g is 3 and n is 8, the tube gain is 3^8, or 6561.

tuber /t(y)oō′bər/, a knoblike localized swelling.

tubercle /t(y)oō′bərkəl/ [L, *tuber,* swelling], **1.** a nodule or a small eminence, such as that on a bone. **2.** a nodule, especially an elevation of the skin that is larger than a papule. **3.** a small, rounded nodule produced by infection with *Mycobacterium tuberculosis,* consisting of a gray translucent mass of small spheric cells surrounded by connective tissue.

tubercle of sella turcica, the anterior wall of the sella turcica.

tubercular /t(y)oōbur′kyələr/ [L, *tuber,* swelling], pertaining to or resembling TB.

tuberculid /t(y)oōbur′kyəlid/, recurrent skin or mucous membrane lesions in which the tubercle bacillus is absent. It is the result of sensitivity to mycobacterial antigens in patients with TB.

tuberculin purified protein derivative /toōbur′kyoōlin/, a solution containing a purified protein fraction derived from isolated culture filtrates of strains of *Mycobacterium tuberculosis.* It is used as an aid in the diagnosis of TB, in the Mantoux test, and, for the same purpose in a dried form, in multiple puncture devices.

tuberculin reaction, hardening or blistering as a delayed reaction at the site of a tuberculin test, a positive result.

tuberculin test [L, *tuber + testum,* crucible], a test to determine past or present TB infection based on a positive skin reaction, using one of several methods. A purified protein derivative of tubercle bacilli, called *tuberculin,* is introduced into the skin by scratch, puncture, or intradermal injection. If a raised, red, or hard zone forms surrounding the tuberculin test site, the person is said to be sensitive to tuberculin, and the test is read as positive.

tuberculoma /t(y)ōōbur′kyəlō′mə, tōōbur′kyōōlō′mə/ [L, *tuber;* Gk, *oma,* tumor], a rare tumor-like growth of tuberculous tissue in the CNS, characterized by symptoms of an expanding cerebral, cerebellar, or spinal mass.

tuberculosis (TB) /t(y)ōōbur′kyəlō′sis/ [L, *tuber;* Gk, *osis,* condition], a chronic granulomatous infection caused by an acid-fast bacillus, *Mycobacterium tuberculosis.* It is generally transmitted by the inhalation or ingestion of infected droplets and usually affects the lungs, although infection of multiple organ systems occurs. Listlessness, vague chest pain, pleurisy, anorexia, fever, and weight loss are early symptoms of pulmonary TB. Night sweats, pulmonary hemorrhage, expectoration of purulent sputum, and dyspnea develop as the disease progresses. The lung tissues react to the bacillus by producing protective cells that engulf the disease organism, forming tubercles. Untreated, the tubercles enlarge and merge to form larger tubercles that undergo caseation, eventually sloughing off into the cavities of the lungs. Diagnosis is through biopsy, stain, sputum and gastric cultures, and x-ray studies. The bacillus is generally sensitive to isoniazid, pyrazinamide, paraaminosalicylic acid, streptomycin, rifampin, ethambutol, dihydrostreptomycin, ultraviolet radiation, and heat. A combination of drugs is prescribed, with regular tests of the function of the kidneys, liver, eyes, and ears to discover early signs of drug toxicity. This is particularly important because drug therapy will usually continue for up to 1 year. The disease is not infectious after the bacillus is no longer present in the sputum.

tuberculosis culture, a microbiology culture to diagnose TB. The spread of disease is a possible result of conventional culture techniques, which take 4 to 6 weeks. Newer, more rapid techniques include the BACTEC method, polymerase chain reaction culture methods, and a sputum smear for acid-fast bacillus.

tuberculous /t(y)ōōbur′kyələs/ [L, *tuber*], pertaining to TB.

tuberculous arthritis, a joint inflammation caused by invasion of the joint by TB bacilli that have migrated from a primary infection, usually in the chest.

tuberculous epididymitis, inflammation and swelling of the epididymis caused by infection with *Mycobacterium tuberculosis,* such as from spread of renal tuberculosis.

tuberculous lymphadenitis [L, *tuber* + *lympha,* water; Gk, *aden,* gland, *itis,* inflammation], an inflammation of the lymph glands caused by the presence of *Mycobacterium tuberculosis.*

tuberculous peritonitis [L, *tuber;* Gk, *peri* + *teinein,* to stretch, *itis,* inflammation], an inflammation of the peritoneum that is secondary to a tuberculous infection in the viscera.

tuberculous pneumonia [L, *tuber;* Gk, *pneumon,* lung], a complication of TB in which caseous material is inhaled into the bronchi, leading to bronchopneumonia or lobar pneumonia.

tuberculous prostatitis, a type of granulomatous prostatitis caused by infection with *Mycobacterium tuberculosis.*

tuberculous spondylitis, a rare, grave form of tuberculosis caused by the invasion of *Mycobacterium tuberculosis* into the spinal vertebrae. The intervertebral disks may be destroyed, resulting in the collapse and wedging of affected vertebrae and the shortening and angulation of the spine. The infection characteristically dissects vertebrae anterolaterally and produces abscesses. The pressure of the abscess may cause ischemic paralysis in the subjacent spinal cord, and abscesses in the cervical area may displace or obstruct the trachea and the esophagus.

tuberculum /t(y)ōōbur′kyələm/, a tubercle, nodule, or rounded elevation.

tuberosity /t(y)ōō′bəros′itē/ [L, *tuber*], an elevation or protuberance, especially of a bone.

tuberosity of the tibia, a large oblong elevation at the proximal end of the tibia to which the ligament of the patella attaches.

tuberous carcinoma /t(y)ōō′bərəs/ [L, *tuber;* Gk, *karkinos,* crab, *oma,* tumor], a scirrhous carcinoma of the skin, characterized by nodular projections.

tuberous sclerosis, a familial, neurocutaneous disease characterized by epilepsy, mental deterioration, adenoma sebaceum, nodules and sclerotic patches on the cerebral cortex, retinal tumors, depigmented leaf-shaped macules on the skin, tumors of the heart or kidneys, and cerebral calcifications.

tube-slide agglutination test, a type of sperm agglutination test in which sperm and serum are mixed in a tube and then transferred to a slide for examination.

tuboabdominal gestation /-abdom′inəl/ [L, *tubus* + *abdomen,* belly *gestare,* to bear], an ectopic pregnancy in which the embryo develops while partly in the abdominal cavity and partly in the fallopian tube. The condition usually begins as a tubal pregnancy and extends into the abdomen as development continues.

tubo-ovarian /t(y)o͞o'bō·ōver'ē·ən/ [L, *tubus* + *ovum*, egg], pertaining to the ovary and fallopian tube.

tubo-ovarian abscess [L, *tubus* + *ovum* + *abscedere*, to go away], an abscess involving the ovary and fallopian tube. It is commonly associated with salpingitis.

tubo-ovarian cyst [L, *tubus* + *ovum;* Gk, *kystis,* bag], a cyst that forms by adhesion of the ovary at the fimbriated end of the fallopian tube.

tubo-ovarian gestation [L, *tubus* + *ovum* + *gestare,* to bear], an ectopic pregnancy that develops partly in the fallopian tube and partly in the ovary.

tuboplasty /t(y)o͞o'bōplas'tē/ [L, *tubus,* tube; Gk, *plassein,* to mold], a surgical procedure in which severed or damaged fallopian tubes are repaired in hopes of restoring fertility.

tubular capillary plexus, a vascular network formed by the capillaries around the renal tubules.

tubular necrosis [L, *tubulus,* little tube; Gk, *nekros,* dead, *osis,* condition], the death of cells in the small tubules of the kidneys as a result of disease or injury.

tubule /t(y)o͞o'byo͞ol/ [L, *tubulus*], a small tube, such as one of the collecting tubules in the kidneys, the seminiferous tubules of the testes, or Henle's tubules between the distal and proximal convoluted tubules.—**tubular,** *adj.*

tubulin-binding agents, a group of medications that bind tubulin and arrest cell mitosis; abnormal blood vessels in tumors are particularly sensitive to these agents.

tubuloglomerular feedback, a feedback mechanism in the juxtaglomerular apparatus of the kidney, so that changes in solute concentration at the macula densa link to control of the glomerular filtration rate and help ensure a relatively constant delivery of solutes to the distal tubule.

tuft [Fr, *touffe,* a tuft], an object resembling a tassel, such as a tuft of hair.

tuft fracture [Fr, *touffe,* tuft; L, *fractura,* break], a break in of any one of the distal phalanges.

tug [ME, *toggen,* to pull], a dragging or hauling movement or sensation.

tularemia /to͞o'lərē'mē·ə/ [Tulare, California; Gk, *haima,* blood], an infectious disease of animals caused by the bacillus *Francisella (Pasteurella) tularensis,* which may be transmitted by insect vectors or direct contact. It is characterized in humans by fever, headache, and an ulcerated skin lesion with localized lymph node enlargement or by eye infection, GI ulcerations, or pneumonia, depending on the site of entry and the response of the host. This disease can be fatal if not treated with the appropriate antibiotics. Treatment includes streptomycin, chloramphenicol, and tetracycline. Recovery produces lifelong immunity.

tumescence /t(y)o͞omes'əns/ [L, *tumescere,* to begin to swell], a state of swelling or edema.

tumescent anesthesia, administration of a local infiltration anesthetic (lidocaine) through the use of large volumes of fluid. The technique is applied in liposuction surgery, varicose vein treatment, scalp surgery, dermabrasion, and soft tissue reconstruction.

tumor (T) /t(y)o͞o'mər/ [L], **1.** a swelling or enlargement occurring in inflammatory conditions. **2.** a new growth of tissue characterized by progressive, uncontrolled proliferation of cells. The tumor may be localized or invasive, benign or malignant. A tumor may be named for its location, for its cellular makeup, or for the person who first identified it.

tumor albus, a white swelling occurring in a tuberculous bone or joint.

tumor angiogenesis factor (TAF), a protein that stimulates the formation of blood vessels in tumors.

tumoricidal agent, an agent that is destructive to cancer cells.

tumoricide /t(y)o͞omôr'isīd/, a substance capable of destroying a tumor.—**tumoricidal,** *adj.*

tumorigenesis /t(y)o͞o'mərijen'əsis/, the process of initiating and promoting the development of a tumor.—**tumorigenic,** *adj.*

tumorigenic /-jen'ik/ [L, *tumor,* swelling; Gk, *genein,* to produce], capable of producing tumors.

tumor-induced osteomalacia, oncogenic osteomalacia.

tumor lysis syndrome, an oncologic emergency characterized by a decreased calcium level with elevated phosphate, potassium, and uric acid levels occuring after effective induction chemotherapy of rapidly growing malignant neoplasms; thought to be due to release of intracellular products after cell lysis.

tumor marker, a substance in the body that may be associated with the presence of a cancer.

tumor necrosis factor (TNF), a natural body protein, also produced synthetically, with anticancer effects. The body produces it in response to the presence of toxic substances such as bacterial toxins. Adverse effects are toxic shock and cachexia.

tumor registry, a repository of data on the incidence of cancers and personal characteristics, treatment, and treatment outcomes of patients diagnosed with cancer.

tumor-specific antigen, an antigen produced by a particular type of tumor that

T

does not appear on normal cells of the tissue in which the tumor developed.

tumor suppressor gene, a gene whose function is to limit cell proliferation and loss of whose function leads to cell transformation and tumor growth.

tumor viruses [L, *tumor,* swelling, *virus,* poison], viruses that are capable of directly or indirectly inducing tumor formation. Direct tumor formation may result from inoculation of living cells with tumorigenic viruses. Tumor formation may result from the influence of the virus on normal cells that are transformed into tumor cells.

tumor volume, a part of an organ or tissue that includes both the tumor and adjacent areas of invasion.

tungiasis /tung·gī´əsis/, infestation of the skin with the chigoe *(Tunga penetrans).*

tungsten (W) /tung´stən/ [SW, *tung,* heavy, *sten,* stone; *wolfram,* the German word for tungsten], a metallic element. Its atomic number is 74, and its atomic mass is 183.85. It has the highest melting point of all metals and is used as a target material in x-ray tubes and as filaments in incandescent light bulbs.

tunica /t(y)oo̅´nikə/ [L, tunic], an enveloping coat or covering membrane.

tunica adventitia, the outer layer or coat of an artery or other tubular structure.

tunica albuginea [L, *tunica* + *albus,* white], a tissue covering of white collagenous fibers such as the sclerotic coat of the eyeball and the testes.

tunica intima, the membrane lining an artery.

tunica media, a muscular middle coat of an artery.

tunica vaginalis testis, the serous membrane surrounding the testis and epididymis.

tuning fork /t(y)oo̅´ning/ [Gk, *tonos,* stretching; L, *furca,* fork], a small metal instrument consisting of a stem and two prongs that produces a constant pitch when either prong is struck. It is used by physicians as a screening test of air and bone conduction.

tunnel [OFr, *tonnel,* fowl trap], a canal or passage, such as the carpal tunnel.

tunneled catheter, a central venous catheter left in place for a long period so that scar tissue forms and anchors it in place.

tunnel vision [OFr, *tonnel,* fowl trap; L, *videre,* to see], a defect in sight in which there is a great reduction in the peripheral field of vision, as if looking through a hollow tube or tunnel. The condition occurs in advanced glaucoma.

tunnel wound [OFr, *tonnel;* AS, *wund*], a break in the surface of the body or an organ in which the entry and exit wounds are the same size.

TUR, abbreviation for **transurethral resection.**

turban tumor /tur´bən/ [Turk, *tulbend,* headdress; L, *tumor,* swelling], a benign neoplasm consisting of pink or maroon nodules that may cover the entire scalp, trunk, and extremities.

turbid /tur´bid/ [L, *turbidus,* confused], clouded or obscured, as in solids in suspension in a solution.

turbidimetry /tur´bidim´ətrē/ [L, *turbidus,* confused; Gk, *metron,* measure], measurement of the turbidity (cloudiness) of a solution or suspension in which the amount of transmitted light is quantified with a spectrophotometer or estimated by visual comparison with solutions of known turbidity.

turbidity /tərbid´itē/ [L, *turbidus*], a condition of light scattering in a liquid resulting from the presence of suspended particles.

turbinate /tur´binit/ [L, *turbinum,* topshaped], **1.** pertaining to a scroll shape. **2.** pertaining to the concha nasalis.

turgid /tur´jid/ [L, *turgidus*], swollen, hard, and congested, usually as a result of an accumulation of fluid.—**turgor,** *n.*

turgor /tur´gər/ [L, *turgere,* to be swollen], the expected resiliency of the skin caused by the outward pressure of the cells and interstitial fluid. An evaluation of the skin turgor is an essential part of physical assessment.

turnbuckle cast [AS, *tyrnan;* ME, *bocle,* small shield; ONorse, *kasta*], an orthopedic device used to encase and immobilize the entire trunk, one upper arm to the elbow, and the opposite upper leg to the knee. It is constructed of plaster of paris or fiberglass and incorporates hinges as part of its design in the treatment of scoliosis. The hinges are placed at the level of the apex of the curvature.

Turner's syndrome [Henry H. Turner, American endocrinologist, 1892–1970], a chromosomal anomaly seen in about 1 in 3000 live female births, characterized by the absence of one X chromosome; congenital ovarian failure; genital hypoplasia; cardiovascular anomalies; dwarfism; short metacarpals; "shield chest"; exostosis of tibia; and underdeveloped breasts, uterus, and vagina. Spatial disorientation and moderate degrees of learning disorders are common. Treatment includes genetic counseling, hormone therapy (estrogens, androgens, pituitary growth hormone), and often surgical correction of cardiovascular anomalies and the webbing of the neck skin.

TURP, abbreviation for **transurethral resection of the prostate.**

Tussionex, a trademark for a fixed-combination drug containing an antitussive (hydrocodone) and an antihistamine (phenyltoloxamine citrate).

tussis /tus′is/ [L, *tussis,* cough], a cough or pertussis.

tussive fremitus /tus′iv/ [L, *tussis,* cough, *fremitus,* murmuring], a vibratory cough that can be felt by a hand over the chest of the patient.

TV, abbreviation for **tidal volume,** the amount of air in milliliters per breath.

TVL, abbreviation for **tenth-value layer.**

T wave, the component of the cardiac cycle shown on an ECG as a short, inverted, U-shaped curve after the S-T segment. It represents membrane repolarization phase 3 of the cardiac action potential.

Tweed triangle [Charles Tweed, American dentist, 1895–1970; L, *triangulus,* three-cornered], the triangle formed by the mandibular plane, the Frankfort horizontal plane, and the long axis of the lower central incisor. It is used as a diagnostic aid.

Tween 80 /twēn/, a trademark for a preparation of polysorbate 80, a surfactant.

24-hour clock system, a method of designating time by using the numeric sequence from 00 to 23 for the hours and the numbers 00 to 59 for the minutes in a daily cycle beginning with 0000 (midnight) and ending with 2359 (1 minute before the next midnight).

twilight state [Ger, *Zwielicht,* twilight; L, *status*], an impaired state of consciousness in which the patient may experience visual or auditory hallucinations and responds to them with irrational behavior. The person may be unaware of the surroundings at the time of the experience and have no memory of it later, except perhaps to recall a related dream.

twin [AS, *twinn,* double], either of two offspring born of the same pregnancy and developed from either a single ovum or from two ova that were released from the ovary simultaneously and fertilized at the same time.

twinge /twinj/ [ME, *twengen,* to pinch], a sudden, brief, darting pain.

twinning [AS, *twinn*], **1.** the development of two or more fetuses during the same pregnancy, either spontaneously or through external intervention for experimental purposes in animals. **2.** the duplication of like structures or parts by division.

twin-to-twin transfusion, an intrauterine abnormality of fetal circulation in monozygotic twins, in which blood is shunted directly from one twin to the other.

twin-twin transfusion syndrome, a syndrome caused by twin-to-twin transfusion in which the donor twin develops hypovolemia, hypotension, anemia, microcardia, and growth retardation while the recipient

twin develops hypervolemia, hypertension, polycythemia, cardiomegaly, and CHF. Hydramnios frequently occurs.

twin-wire orthodontic appliance, a fixed orthodontic appliance that typically uses a pair of 0.01-inch (0.25-mm) wires to form the midsection of the arch wire. It is used to correct the crowding of anterior teeth and to expand the dental arch.

twitch [AS, *twiccian*], **1.** the contraction of small muscle units, manifested as a quick, simple, spasmodic contraction of a muscle. **2.** to jerk convulsively.

twitching [AS, *twiccian*], a series of contractions by small muscle units. Twitching that involves large groups of muscle fibers is identified as *fascicular twitching.*

two-point discrimination test, a test of the ability of a person to differentiate touch stimuli at two nearby points on the body at the same time. It is used in studies of possible damage to the parietal regions of the brain.

two-point gait [OE, *twa;* L, *punctus,* pricked; ONorse, *gata,* way], a pattern of crutch-walking in which the right foot and left crutch advance together, followed by the left foot and right crutch.

two-way catheter [AS, *twa* + *weg;* Gk, *katheter,* something lowered], a catheter that has a double lumen, one channel for injection of medication or fluids and the other for removal of fluid or specimens.

TXA₂, abbreviation for **thromboxane A₂.**

TXB₂, abbreviation for **thromboxane B₂.**

Tygacil, a trademark for tigecycline.

tying forceps, a thumb forceps with fine, smooth tips, used for tying sutures in ophthalmologic surgery.

Tykerb, a trademark for lapatinib.

Tylenol, a trademark for an analgesic and antipyretic (acetaminophen).

tylosis /tīlō′sis/, formation of a callus.

tyloxapol /tīlok′səpôl/, an ocular lubricant used to lubricate, clean, and wet artificial eyes to improve wearing comfort. It also has a detergent action that is used to help break up mucus.

tympanectomy /tim′pənek′təmē/ [Gk, *tympanon,* drum, *ektomē,* excision], the surgical removal of the tympanic membrane.

tympanic /timpan′ik/ [Gk, *tympanon,* drum], pertaining to a structure that resonates when struck; drumlike.—**tympanum** /tim′pənəm/ *pl.* **tympana,** *n.*

tympanic antrum, a relatively large, irregular cavity in the superior anterior part of the mastoid process of the temporal bone, communicating with the mastoid air cells and lined by the extension of the mucous membrane of the tympanic cavity.

tympanic cells, tympanic air cells, spaces in the tympanic cavity between the bony projections of the floor or jugular wall that sometimes communicate with the tubal air cells.

tympanic membrane, a thin semitransparent membrane in the middle ear that transmits sound vibrations to the internal ear by means of the auditory ossicles. It is nearly oval in form, with a vertical diameter of about 10 mm, and separates the tympanic cavity from the bottom of the external acoustic meatus.

tympanic membrane thermometer, a device that measures the temperature of the tympanic membrane by detecting infrared radiation from the tissue. Results are obtained within 2 seconds and directly reflect the body's core temperature.

tympanic nerve, a branch of the glossopharyngeal nerve that provides sensory innervation within the middle ear to the mucosa of the cavity, pharyngotympanic tube, and mastoid air cells. It also contributes general visceral efferent fibers, which leave the tympanic plexus in the lesser petrosal nerve.

tympanic reflex, the reflection of a beam of light shining on the eardrum. In a normal ear, a bright, wedge-shaped reflection is seen; its apex is at the end of the malleus, and its base is at the anterior inferior margin of the eardrum.

tympanic resonance [Gk, *tympanon;* L, *resonare,* to sound again], a drumlike or hollow sound heard over a large air space of the body such as the pneumothorax.

tympanic sulcus [Gk, *tympanon,* drum; L, *sulcus,* furrow], a narrow circular groove at the medial end of the osseous part of the external acoustic meatus that holds the tympanic membrane.

tympanic temperature, the body temperature as measured electronically at the tympanic membrane.

tympanogram /timpan'əgram/, a graphic representation of the acoustic impedance and air pressure of the middle ear and mobility of the tympanic membrane, measured as part of the audiologic test battery. Various middle ear pathologies such as otitis media, otosclerosis, or tympanic membrane perforations each yield distinctive tympanograms.

tympanomastoidectomy, mastoidectomy with tympanectomy, done as either closed cavity or open cavity.

tympanoplasty /timpan'əplas'tē/ [Gk, *tympanon + plassein,* to mold], any of several operative procedures on the eardrum or ossicles of the middle ear designed to restore or improve hearing in patients with conductive hearing loss. These operations may be used to repair a perforated eardrum, for otosclerosis, or for dislocation or necrosis of one of the small bones of the middle ear.

tympanosclerosis, a condition characterized by the presence of masses of hard, dense connective tissue around the auditory ossicles in the middle ear.

tympany /tim'pənē/ [Gk, *tympanon,* drum], a loud, high-pitched musical sound percussed over the upper gastric area or a puffed-out cheek.

type 1 diabetes mellitus, an autoimmune disease characterized by inability to metabolize fuels, carbohydrates, protein, and fat because of absolute insulin deficiency. Type 1 diabetes can occur at any age, but its incidence is more common in children. Uncontrolled type 1 diabetes is characterized by excessive thirst, increased urination, increased desire to eat, loss of weight, keta acidosis, diminished strength, and marked irritability. The clinical onset is usually rapid, but approximately one third of patients have a remission within 3 months (honeymoon phase). This stage may continue for days or months, but type 1 diabetes then progresses quickly to a state of total dependence on insulin. Persons with type 1 diabetes can manage their condition with a carbohydratecontrolled meal plan, exercise, and insulin.

type I error, in a test of a statistical hypothesis, the probability of rejecting the null hypothesis when it is true and should be accepted.

type 2 diabetes mellitus, a type of DM characterized by insulin resistance in appropriate hepatic glucose production, and impaired insulin secretion. Onset is usually after 40 years of age but can occur at any age, including during childhood and adolescence. Familial aggregation implies genetic factors and environmental factors, such as obesity and a sedentary lifestyle, superimposed on genetic susceptibility are involved in the onset. The majority (>90%) of persons with type 2 diabetes are obese; in these patients glucose tolerance is often improved by the modest weight loss and increased activity. Persons with type 2 diabetes can manage their disorder with a meal plan, increased activity, oral anti-diabetes agents such as insulin secretagogues, biguanides, alpha glucosidase inhibitors and insulin sensitizers, and insulin.

type II error, in a test of a statistical hypothesis, the probability of accepting the null hypothesis when it is false and should be rejected.

type A personality [Gk, *typos,* mark], a parent ego state characterized by a behavior pattern described by Meyer Friedman and Ray Rosenman as associated with individuals who are highly competitive and work compulsively to meet deadlines. The behavior also is associated with a higher than usual incidence of coronary heart disease.

type B personality, a child ego state characterized by a form of behavior associated by Friedman and Rosenman with people who appear free of hostility and aggression and who lack a compulsion to meet deadlines, are not highly competitive at work and play, and have a lower risk of heart attack.

type E personality, a term introduced by Harriet Braiker to describe professional women who fit neither type A nor type B personality categories, but who have a marked sense of insecurity and strive to convince themselves that they are worthwhile.

typhoid /tī'foid/ [Gk, *typhos,* fever, *eidos,* form], pertaining to or resembling typhus.

typhoid carrier, a person without signs or symptoms of typhoid fever who carries the bacteria that cause the disease and sheds the pathogens in body excretions. The typical typhoid carrier is one who has recovered from an attack of the disease.

typhoid fever [Gk, *typhos,* fever, *eidos,* form; L, *febris,* fever], a bacterial infection usually caused by *Salmonella typhi,* transmitted by contaminated milk, water, or food. It is characterized by headache, delirium, cough, watery diarrhea, rash, and a high fever. The incubation period may be as long as 60 days. Characteristic maculopapular rosy spots are scattered over the skin of the abdomen and chest. Splenomegaly and leukopenia develop first. The disease is serious and may be fatal. Complications include intestinal hemorrhage or perforation and thrombophlebitis. Some people who recover from the disease continue to be carriers and excrete the organism, spreading the disease.

typhoid nodules [Gk, *typhos,* fever; L, *nodulus,* small knot], a liver nodule consisting of a cluster of monocytes and lymphocytes surrounding the typhoid fever pathogen, *Salmonella typhi.*

typhoid pellagra, a form of pellagra in which the symptoms also include continued high temperatures.

typhoid vaccine, a bacterial vaccine prepared from an inactivated dried strain of *Salmonella typhi.* It is prescribed for primary immunization against typhoid fever for adults and children.

typhoid vaccine live oral, a preparation of the attenuated strain *Salmonella typhi* Ty21a.

typhomania /tī'fōmā'nē·ə/, a condition characterized by coma and delirium associated with typhus, typhoid fever, and similar febrile infections.

typhous /tī'fəs/ [Gk, *typhos,* fever], pertaining to typhus fever.

typhus /tī'fəs/ [Gk, *typhos,* fever], any of a group of acute infectious diseases caused by various species of *Rickettsia* and usually transmitted from infected rodents to humans by the bites of lice, fleas, mites, or ticks. These diseases are all characterized by headache, chills, fever, malaise, and a maculopapular rash.

typhus vaccine, any one of three vaccines, each of which is prepared for the different rickettsial organisms that cause epidemic typhus, murine typhus, or Brill-Zinsser disease.

typical /tip'ikəl/ [L, *typicus,* characteristic of a kind], a representative example.

typing [Gk, *typos,* mark], the process of classifying a specimen of blood, tissue, or other substance according to common traits or characteristics.

Tyr, abbreviation for **tyrosine.**

tyramine /tī'rəmēn/ [Gk, *tyros,* cheese, *amine,* ammonia], an amino acid synthesized in the body from the essential amino acid tyrosine. Tyramine stimulates the release of the catecholamines epinephrine and norepinephrine. People taking monoamine oxidase inhibitors should avoid the ingestion of foods and beverages containing tyramine.

tyroma /tīrō'mə/ *pl.* **tyromas, tyromata** [Gk, *tyros* + *oma,* tumor], a new growth or nodule with a caseous or cheesy consistency.

tyromatosis /tī'rōmətō'sis/ [Gk, *tyros* + *oma* + *osis,* condition], a process in which necrotic tissue is broken down and degenerates to a granular, amorphous, caseous mass.

tyrosine (Tyr) /tī'rəsēn/ [Gk, *tyros*], an amino acid synthesized in the body from the essential amino acid phenylalanine. Tyrosine is found in most proteins and is a precursor of melanin and several hormones, including epinephrine and thyroxin.

T

tyrosinemia /tī'rōsinē'mē·ə/ [Gk, *tyros* + *haima,* blood], **1.** a benign, transient condition of the newborn, especially premature infants, in which an excessive amount of the amino acid tyrosine is found in the blood and urine. The disorder is caused by an anomaly in amino acid metabolism, usually delayed development of the enzymes necessary to metabolize tyrosine. It is controlled by dietary measures and vitamin C therapy. **2.** a hereditary disorder involving an inborn error of metabolism of the amino acid tyrosine. The condition is caused by an enzyme deficiency and results in liver failure or hepatic cirrhosis, renal tubular defects that can lead to renal rickets and renal glycosuria, generalized aminoaciduria, and mental retardation. Treatment consists of a diet low in tyrosine and phenylalanine and high in vitamin C.

tyrosinosis /tī'rōsinō'sis/ [Gk, *tyros + osis*, condition], a rare condition resulting from a defect in amino acid metabolism. It is characterized by the excretion of an excessive amount of parahydroxyphenylpyruvic acid, an intermediate product of tyrosine, in the urine. There is no known treatment.

tyrosinurea /tī'rōsinŏŏr'ē·ə/ [Gk, *tyros + ouron,* urine], the presence of tyrosine in the urine.

Tysabri, a trademark for natalizumab.

Tyzeka, a trademark for telbivudine.

Tyzine, a trademark for an alpha-adrenergic drug (tetrahydrozoline hydrochloride).

Tzanck test /tsangk/ [Arnault Tzanck, Russian dermatologist in France, 1886–1954], a microscopic examination of cellular material from skin lesions to help diagnose certain vesicular diseases.

U, **1.** abbreviation for **unit. 2.** symbol for the element **uranium.**

UAO, abbreviation for **upper airway obstruction.**

ubiquinone /yōōbik′winōn/, a naturally occurring organic compound found in the lipid core of mitochondrial membranes. It functions in the electron transport chain as a carrier.

ubiquitin /yōōbik′witin/, a small polypeptide that is involved in histone modification and as a marker for intracellular protein transport and breakdown. It is found in all cells of higher organisms.

Uchida technique, a method of tubal ligation with injection of saline solution beneath the tubal mucosa to separate it from the underlying tube. A portion of mucosa is removed and the mucosa-free tube then retracts to form a stump that is closed with sutures.

UGI, abbreviation for **upper GI.**

UICC, abbreviation for *International Union Against Cancer, Unión internacional contra el cancer, Union internationale contre le cancer, Unio internationalis contra cancrum,* or *Unione internazionale contro il cancro.*

ulcer /ul′sər/ [L, *ulcus,* a sore], a circumscribed, craterlike lesion of the skin or mucous membrane resulting from necrosis that accompanies some inflammatory, infectious, or malignant processes. An ulcer may be shallow, involving only the epidermis, as in pemphigus, or deep, as in a rodent ulcer.—**ulcerate,** *v.,* **ulcerative** /ul′sərā′tiv/, *adj.*

ulceration /ul′sərā′shən/ [L, *ulcus,* a sore], the process of ulcer formation.—**ulcerate,** *v.*

ulcerative blepharitis /ul′sərā′tiv, ul′sərātiv′/ [L, *ulcus + atus,* relating to; Gk, *blepharon,* eyelid, *itis,* inflammation], a form of blepharitis in which a staphylococcal infection of the follicles of the eyelashes and glands of the eyelids results in sticky crusts forming on the lid margins. If the crusts are pulled off, the skin beneath bleeds. Tiny pustules develop in the follicles of the eyelashes and break down to form shallow ulcers.

ulcerative colitis, a chronic, episodic, inflammatory disease of the large intestine and rectum. It is characterized by profuse watery diarrhea containing varying amounts of blood, mucus, and pus. The attacks of diarrhea are accompanied by tenesmus, severe abdominal pain, fever, chills, anemia, and weight loss. Children with the disease may suffer retarded physical growth. Systemic complications include peripheral arthritis, ankylosing spondylitis, kidney and liver disease, and inflammation of the eyes, skin, and mouth. People with severe disease may develop toxic megacolon. There is also an increased risk of cancer of the colon. Diagnosis is based on clinical signs, the results of barium x-ray films of the colon, and colonoscopy with biopsy. Medical treatment with corticosteroids or other antiinflammatory agents may help control the symptoms in some people. Those with severe disease or life-threatening complications may require surgery.

ulcerative inflammation [L, *ulcus + inflammare,* to set afire], the development of an ulcer over an area of inflammation.

ulcerative stomatitis [L, *ulcus;* Gk, *stoma,* mouth, *itis,* inflammation], an infectious disease of the mouth characterized by swollen spongy gums, ulcers, and loose teeth.

ulcerogenic drug /ul′sərōjen′ik/, a drug that produces or exacerbates peptic ulcers, such as aspirin and NSAIDs.

ulceromembranous /ul′sərōmem′brənəs/, describing an ulcer with a membranous exudation.

ulcerous /ul′sərəs/, pertaining to ulcers.

ULD, abbreviation for **upper level discriminator.**

ulegyria /yōō′ləjī′rē·ə/, a cerebral cortex abnormality in which the gyri are narrow and distorted by scars.

ulerythema /yōō′lərithē′mə/, a skin eruption characterized by redness and scarring.

ulna /ul′nə/ [L, elbow], the bone on the medial side of the forearm, lying parallel with the radius. It articulates with the humerus and the radius.

ulnar /ul′nər/ [L, *ulna,* elbow], pertaining to the long medial bone of the forearm.

ulnar artery, a large artery branching from the brachial artery, supplying muscles

1385

in the forearm, wrist, and hand. Arising near the elbow, it passes obliquely in a distal direction to become the superficial palmar arch.

ulnar drift [L, *ulna*, elbow; AS, *drifan*, to drive], a change in the metacarpophalangeal joints because of rheumatoid arthritis and chronic synovitis. The long axes of the fingers make an angle with the long axis of the wrist so that the fingers are deviated to the ulnar side of the hand.

ulnar nerve, one of the terminal branches of the brachial plexus that arises on each side from the medial cord of the plexus. It receives fibers from both cervical and thoracic nerve roots and supplies the muscles and skin on the ulnar side of the forearm and hand.

ulnocarpal /ul′nōkär′pəl/, pertaining to the ulna and carpus or ulnar area of the wrist.

ulnoradial /ul′nōrā′dē·əl/, pertaining to the ulna and radius and the ligaments associated with them.

ulocarcinoma /yōō′lōkär′sinō′mə/ *pl.* **ulocarcinomas, ulocarcinomata** [Gk, *oule*, scar, *karkinos*, crab, *oma*, tumor], any malignant neoplasm of the gums that is classified as a carcinoma.

ulodermatitis /yōō′lōdur′mətī′tis/, dermatitis resulting in the destruction of tissue and scar formation.

uloid /yōō′loid/, resembling scar tissue.

ulterior transactions /ultir′ē·ər/, in transactional analysis, communication that is bilevel. The first level is overt (social), usually of relevant verbal statements. The second level is usually covert (psychologic) and nonverbal and has hidden psychologic meaning.

ultimate strain /ul′timit/, the strain at the point of failure.

ultimate stress, the highest load that can be sustained by a material at the point of failure.

ultrabrachycephalic /ul′trəbrak′ēsəfal′ik/, describing an extremely short, broad skull.

Ultracef, a trademark for a cephalosporin antibiotic (cefadroxil monohydrate).

ultracentrifuge /-sen′trifyōōj/ [L, *ultra*, beyond; Gk, *kentron*, center; L, *fugere*, to flee], a high-speed centrifuge with a rotation rate fast enough to produce sedimentation of protein and viruses, even in blood plasma.

ultradian /-rā′dē·ən/ [L, *ultra* + *dies*, day], pertaining to a biorhythm that occurs in cycles of less than 24 hours.

ultrafilter /-fil′tər/, a semipermeable membrane with pores of a known diameter used to separate colloids and large molecules from water and other small molecules.

ultrafiltrate /-fil′trāt/ [L, *ultra*; Fr, *filtre*, filter], a solution that has passed through a semipermeable membrane with very small pores. It usually contains only low–molecular weight solutes.

ultrafiltration /-filtrā′shən/, a type of filtration, sometimes conducted under pressure, through filters with very small pores, such as those used by an artificial kidney. Ultrafiltration can separate large molecules from smaller molecules in body fluids.

ultra-high-speed handpiece, a device for holding rotary instruments, such as dental burrs, that permits rotational speeds of 100,000 to 450,000 rpm. It is used primarily for the preparation of a tooth or teeth for a restoration.

Ultralente, a trademark for an insulin zinc suspension.

ultraligation /-līgā′shən/, tying or closing off a blood vessel beyond the point where it branches.

ultramicrotome /-mī′krətōm′/, a microtome that cuts very thin slices for examination by electron microscopy.

ultrasonic /ul′trəson′ik/ [L, *ultra*, beyond, *sonus*, sound], pertaining to ultrasound, or sound frequencies so high (greater than 20 kilohertz) that they cannot be perceived by the human ear.

ultrasonic cleaner, a device that transmits high-energy, high-frequency sound waves into a fluid-filled container, used to remove deposits from instruments and appliances.

ultrasonic cleaning, the use of high-frequency vibrations to dislodge deposits from teeth or other objects.

ultrasonic lithotripsy, lithotripsy in which a rigid probe is inserted to the site, and high frequency sound waves disintegrate the calculus.

ultrasonic nebulizer, a humidifier in which an electric current is used to produce high-frequency vibrations in a container of fluid. The vibrations break up the fluid into aerosol particles.

ultrasonics /-son′iks/, the science dealing with sound waves having frequencies above the approximately 20-kHz range of human hearing. It uses a transducer and generates very short pulses of high-frequency sound that are transmitted into the body. Echoes from interfaces within the body are displayed on a cathode ray tube so that images of normal and abnormal structures can be viewed.

ultrasonic scaler, a vibrating crystal-driven high-frequency (18 to 50 kHz) instrument, with a tip for supplying high-frequency vibrations, which produces bubbles that form and collapse, allowing the removal of adherent deposits such as bacteria, biofilm, calculus, and other root surface accretions from the teeth.

ultrasonic wave [L, *ultra,* beyond, *sonus,* sound], a sound wave transmitted at a frequency greater than 20,000 per second, or beyond the normal hearing range of humans.

ultrasonography /-sonog'rəfē/ [L, *ultra* + *sonus,* sound; Gk, *graphein,* to record], the process of imaging deep structures of the body by measuring and recording the reflection of pulsed or continuous high-frequency sound waves.

ultrasonography: limited obstetric, a nursing intervention from the Nursing Interventions Classification (NIC) defined as performance of ultrasound exams to determine ovarian, uterine, or fetal status.

ultrasound /ul'trəsound/ [L, *ultra* + *sonus*], sound waves at the very high frequency of over 20 kHz (vibrations per second). Ultrasound has many medical applications, including fetal monitoring, imaging of internal organs, and, at an extremely high frequency, the cleaning of dental and surgical instruments.—**ultrasonic,** *adj.*

ultrasound dilution technique, a technique for measuring blood flow and access recirculation in hemodialysis patients. Ultrasound sensors are attached to the venous and arterial catheters in their normal positions and blood flow is checked. They are then reversed, the ultrafiltration is turned off, and at a known pumped blood flow rate a bolus of saline is released into the venous catheter to dilute the blood. The velocity of the dilution as it passes through the access apparatus is measured by ultrasonography.

ultrasound imaging, the use of high-frequency sound (several MHz or more) to image internal structures by the differing reflection signals produced when a beam of sound waves is projected into the body and bounces back at interfaces between those structures.

ultrastructure /-struk'chər/, a structure so small that it can be viewed only with an ultramicroscope or electron microscope.

ultraviolet (UV) /-vī'rəlot/ [L, *ultra;* Fr, *violette*], light beyond the range of human vision, at the short end of the spectrum, or that part of the electromagnetic spectrum with wavelengths between about 10 and 400 nm. It occurs naturally in sunlight; it burns and tans the skin and converts precursors in the skin to vitamin D. Ultraviolet lamps are used in the control of infectious airborne bacteria and viruses and in the treatment of psoriasis and other skin conditions.

ultraviolet (UV) lamp, a lamp that emits electromagnetic radiation in a range between 4 and 400 nm, or beyond the violet spectrum of visible light. Equipped with a nickel oxide filter, an ultraviolet lamp radiating at wavelengths around 360 nm can be used to examine hairs infected with certain agents. The pathogens reflect the ultraviolet light with a greenish-yellow fluorescence.

ultraviolet (UV) radiation, a range of electromagnetic waves extending from the violet or short-wavelength end of the visible spectrum to the beginning of the x-ray spectrum. In medicine, ultraviolet radiation is used in the treatment of rickets and certain skin conditions. Milk and some other foods become activated with vitamin D when exposed to this type of energy. Ultraviolet radiation also causes certain substances to fluoresce or phosphoresce, a useful characteristic in such diverse applications as lighting and the identification of minerals.

ultraviolet (UV) rays [L, *ultra,* beyond; OFr, *violette;* L, *radius*], electromagnetic radiations found just beyond the violet edge of the visible spectrum, with wavelengths extending to the beginning of x-rays. The wavelengths range from 390 to 290 nm for near ultraviolet rays to 290 to 20 nm for far ultraviolet wavelengths. Ultraviolet radiation in the region of 260 nm can cause photochemical reactions in deoxyribonucleic molecules, causing mutations and destroying microorganisms, including bacteria and viruses.

ultraviolet (UV) therapy [L, *ultra,* beyond; OFr, *violette;* Gk, *therapeia,* treatment], the therapeutic application to the body of electromagnetic radiation in the ultraviolet region of the spectrum. This therapy is useful in the control of infectious airborne bacteria and viruses and in the treatment of psoriasis and other skin conditions.

umbilical /umbil'ikəl/ [L, *umbilicus,* navel], 1. pertaining to the umbilicus. 2. pertaining to the umbilical cord.

umbilical artery, the first branch of the anterior trunk of the internal iliac artery and the origin of the superior vesical artery. In the fetus, the umbilical artery is large and carries blood from the fetus to the placenta. After birth, the vessel closes distally to the origin of the superior vesical artery and eventually becomes a solid fibrous cord, the medial umbilical ligament.

umbilical artery catheter [L, *umbilicus,* navel; Gk, *arteria,* airpipe, *katheter,* a thing lowered], a catheter inserted into the umbilical artery of a newborn.

umbilical catheterization, a procedure in which a radiopaque catheter is passed through an umbilical artery to provide a newborn with parenteral fluid, to obtain blood samples, or both, or through the

U

umbilical vein for an exchange transfusion or the emergency administration of drugs, fluids, or volume expanders.

umbilical cord, a flexible structure connecting the umbilicus with the placenta in the gravid uterus and giving passage to the umbilical arteries and vein. In the newborn, it is about 2 feet long and ½ inch in diameter.

umbilical fascia, a thickening of the fascia transversalis extending along the median umbilical ligament downward from the umbilicus.

umbilical fissure, a groove on the inferior surface of the liver that holds the ligamentum teres and separates the right and left lobes of the liver.

umbilical fistula, an abnormal passage from the umbilicus to the intestine or more frequently to the remnant of the canal in the median umbilical ligament that connects the fetal bladder with the allantois.

umbilical folds, folds of peritoneum in the urinary bladder covering the embryologic remnants of the urachus and umbilical arteries.

umbilical hernia, a soft, skin-covered protrusion of intestine and omentum through a weakness in the abdominal wall around the umbilicus. It usually closes spontaneously within 1 to 2 years.

umbilical region, the part of the abdomen surrounding the umbilicus, in the middle zone between the right and left lateral regions.

umbilical vasculitis, an inflammation of the umbilical cord and its blood vessels.

umbilical vein, one of three embryonic vessels in the umbilical cord. It functions to return the blood from the placenta and fuses to form a single vein in the umbilical cord.

umbilical vesicle, a pear-shaped structure formed from the yolk sac at about the fourth week of prenatal development that protrudes into the cavity of the chorion and connects to the developing embryo by the yolk stalk at the region of the future midgut.

umbilication /um'bilikā'shən/ [L, *umbilicus,* navel], the process of becoming dimpled or pitted or acquiring a depressed area.

umbilicus /umbilī'kəs, umbil'ikəs/ [L, navel], the point on the abdomen at which the umbilical cord joined the fetal abdomen. In most adults, it is marked by a depression; in some, it is marked by a small protrusion of skin.

umbo [L, knob], a projection on any rounded surface, such as the inner surface of the tympanic membrane where the malleus is attached.

umbrella filter /umbral'ə/, a small, porous, umbrella-shaped device that can be inserted into the vena cava or other blood vessel to trap blood clots.

uncal /ung'kəl/, [L, *uncus,* hook], pertaining to the uncus.

uncal herniation [L, *uncus,* hook, *hernia,* rupture], a condition in which the medial part of the temporal lobe protrudes over the tentorial edge as a result of increased ICP. A dilated pupil on the side of the herniation is a diagnostic sign of the disorder. If uncorrected, the progressive disorder causes pressure on the brainstem after first impinging on the third cranial nerve.

Uncinaria /un'siner'ē·ə/ [L, *uncinus,* hook], a genus of nematode that causes hookworm in dogs, cats, and other carnivores.

uncinate /un'sināt/, having hooks or barbs.

uncipressure /un'sipresh'ər/, pressure with a hook to control a hemorrhage.

uncompensated care /unkom'pənsā'tid/ [ME, *un,* against, not; L, *compendere,* to be equivalent], services provided by a hospital or physician or other health care professional for which no charge is made and for which no payment is expected.

uncompetitive inhibitor /un'kəmpet'itiv/ [ME, *un;* L, *competere,* to compete, *inhibere,* to restrain], an enzymatic inhibitor that appears to bond only to the enzyme-substrate complex and not to free enzyme molecules.

uncomplemented, not united with proteins of the body's immune system and therefore inactive.

unconditioned response /un'kəndish'ənd/ [ME, *un;* L, *conditio,* condition, *respondere,* to reply], a normal, instinctive, unlearned reaction to a stimulus; one that occurs naturally and is not acquired by association and training.

unconjugated monoclonal antibody /unkon'jəgā'tid/, one of a population of antibodies produced from a single clone of B lymphocytes and used for highly selective targeting of tumor cells. The antibodies can destroy malignant cells by direct lysis, by binding to cell receptors, and by mobilization of various killer cells.

unconscious /unkon'shəs/ [ME, *un;* L, *conscire,* to be aware], **1.** unaware of the surrounding environment; insensible; incapable of responding to sensory stimuli. **2.** in psychiatry, the part of the mental function in which thoughts, ideas, emotions, or memories are beyond awareness and rarely subject to ready recall.

unconsciousness /unkon'shəsnəs/, a state of complete or partial unawareness or lack of response to sensory stimuli as a result of hypoxia caused by respiratory insufficiency or shock; from metabolic or chemical brain depressants such as drugs, poisons, ketones, or electrolyte imbalance; or from a form of brain pathologic condition such as trauma, seizures, cerebrovascular accident, brain tumor, or infection. Various degrees of unconsciousness can occur during stupor, fugue, catalepsy, and dream states.

uncus /ung′kəs/ [L, hook], **1.** the hooklike anterior end of the hippocampal gyrus on the temporal lobe of the brain. **2.** a hook-shaped structure.

undecylenic acid /un′desilen′ik/, a topical antifungal agent prescribed in the treatment of athlete's foot and ringworm.

underactive bladder, a condition in which bladder contraction is not of sufficient duration or magnitude to empty the bladder completely.

undercut, 1. the part of a tooth or artificial crown that lies between the height of contour and the gingivae, only if that part has a smaller diameter than the height of the contour. **2.** the contour of a cross-section of a residual ridge that would prevent the placement of a denture or other prosthesis. **3.** the contour of flasking stone that interlocks so as to prevent the separation of parts. **4.** the part of a prepared cavity that creates a mechanical lock or area of retention. It may be desirable in a cavity to be filled with gold foil or amalgam but is undesirable in a cavity prepared for a restoration to be cemented.

underdamping /un′dərdam′ping/ [AS, *under,* beneath, *dampen,* to check], the transmission of all frequency components in electrocardiography without a reduction in amplitude.

underlying assumption /un′dərlī′ing/, a set of rules one holds about oneself, others, and the world. These rules are regarded by the individual as unquestionably true.

undernutrition /-noō′trish′ən/, malnutrition caused by an inadequate food supply or an inability to use the nutrients in food.

underwater exercise /un′dərwô′tər/ [AS, *under* + *woeter*], any physical activity performed in a pool or large tub, such as a Hubbard tank, where the buoyancy of the water facilitates the movement of weak or injured muscles.

underwater seal, a seal formed by water allowed to flow over a tube that exits from the chest cavity of a patient. The water acts as a one-way valve and permits the outflow of air but prevents the ingress of air.

underweight /un′dərwāt′/ [AS, *under* + *wiht*], **1.** a body mass index of less than 18.5. **2.** less than normal in body weight after adjustment for height, body build, and age.

undifferentiated cell /undif′əren′shē·ā′tid/ [AS, *un,* not; L, *differentia,* difference, *cella,* storeroom], a cell that has not yet expressed signs of its future specific type.

undifferentiated family ego mass, an emotional fusion in a family in which all members are similar in emotional expression.

undifferentiated malignant lymphoma [ME, *un;* L, *differe,* to differ, *atus,* process, *malignus,* evil, *lympha,* water; Gk, *oma,* tumor], a lymphoid neoplasm containing stem cells that have large nuclei, a small amount of pale cytoplasm, and ill-defined borders.

undifferentiation /un′difəren′shē·ā′shən/, the lack or absence of normal cell differentiation into an identifiable cell type.— **undifferentiated,** *adj.*

undisplaced fracture /un′displāst, un′displāst′/, a bone break in which cracks in the bone may radiate in several directions but the bone fragments do not separate.

undoing /undoō′ing/ [ME, *un;* AS, *don*], the performance of a specific action that is intended to negate in part a previous action or communication. According to some psychologists, undoing is related to the magical thinking of childhood.

undulant /un′dyələnt/ [L, *unda,* wave], wavelike, such as a vibration, fluctuation, or oscillation.

undulate /un′dyəlit/, to have wavelike fluctuations or oscillations.

undulating pulse /un′dyəlā′ting/, a pulse characterized by a succession of waves without force.

unengaged head /un′engājd′/ [ME, *un;* Fr, *engager,* to involve; AS, *heafod*], the head of a floating fetus.

unequal cleavage /unē′kwəl/ [ME, *un;* L, *aequare,* to make equal; AS, *cleofan,* to split], mitotic division of a fertilized ovum into blastomeres that are larger near the yolky part of the cell (the vegetal pole) and smaller near the nucleus (the animal pole).

unequal pulse [AS, *un,* not; L, *aequare,* to make equal, *pulsare,* to beat], a pulse in which the beats vary in intensity.

unequal twins, two nonjoined fetuses born of the same pregnancy in which only one of the pair is fully formed, with the other showing various degrees of developmental defects.

unfinished business /unfin′isht/, the concerns of a dying patient that require resolution before death can be accepted by the patient.

ung., abbreviation for the Latin word *unguentum,* "unguenta" or "ointment."

ungual /ung′gwəl/, pertaining to the fingernails.

U

unheated serum reagin test, a modification of the VDRL test using unheated serum, used primarily for screening.

uniaxial joint /yoo'ne·ak'se·əl/ [L, *unus,* one, *axis,* axle, *jungere,* to join], a synovial joint in which movement is only in one axis, such as a pivot or hinge joint.

unicaliceal kidney, one with a single papilla, calyx, and collecting system.

UNICEF /yoo'nisef'/, abbreviation for **United Nations International Children's Emergency Fund.**

unicellular reproduction, the formation of a new organism from a female egg that has not been fertilized; parthenogenesis.

unidirectional block /-direk'shənəl/ [L, *unus + dirigere,* to direct; Fr, *bloc*], a pathologic failure of cardiac impulse conduction in one direction while conduction is possible in the opposite direction.

unidisciplinary health care team /-dis'ipliner'ē/, a group of health care workers who are members of the same discipline.

unification model /-kā'shən/ [L, *unus + ficare,* to make whole, *atus,* process, *modulus,* small measure], a theoretic framework based on the close relationship of nursing education and clinical nursing service at the University of Rochester (New York). The faculty of the school of nursing hold joint appointments to the school and the hospital, teaching nursing students and providing clinical leadership in nursing service in the hospital.

uniform /yoo'nifôrm/, **1.** having only one form or shape. **2.** distinctive clothing worn by members of a group.

uniform reporting, the reporting of service and financial data by a hospital in conformance with prescribed standard definitions to permit comparisons with other health facilities.

unilaminar /-lam'inər/, composed of only one layer.

unilateral /-lat'ərəl/ [L, *unus,* one, *latus,* side], involving only one side.

unilateral hypertrophy [L, *unus + latus,* side; Gk, *hyper,* above, *trophe,* nourishment], enlargement of one side or a part of one side of the body.

unilateral long-leg spica cast, an orthopedic cast applied to immobilize one leg and the trunk of the body cranially as far as the nipple line.

unilateral neglect management, a nursing intervention from the Nursing Interventions Classification (NIC) defined as protecting and safely reintegrating the affected part of the body while helping the patient adapt to disturbed perceptual abilities.

unilobular /-lob'yələr/, having only one lobe.

unilocular /-lok'yələr/, having only one locus, chamber, or cell.

uninterrupted suture /unin'tərup'tid/ [AS, *un,* not; L, *interrumpere,* to sever, *sutura*], a continuous suture running forward and backward without interruption.

union /ūn'yən/ [L, *unio*], the process of healing; the renewal of continuity in a broken bone or between the edges of a wound.

uniovular /yoo'nē·ov'yələr/ [L, *unus + ovum,* egg], developing from a single ovum, as in monozygotic twins as contrasted with dizygotic twins.

Unipen, a trademark for an antibiotic (nafcillin sodium).

unipolar /-pō'lər/ [L, *unus,* one + *polus*], pertaining to a nerve cell with only one pole, such as a nerve cell in which the axon and dendrite are fused into a single process a short distance from the cell body.

unipolar depression, a major disorder of mood that is characterized by symptoms of depression only.

unipolar lead [L, *unus + polus,* pole; AS, *laedan,* to lead], **1.** an ECG conductor in which the exploring electrode is placed on the precordium or a limb while the indifferent electrode is in the central terminal. **2.** *informal.* a tracing produced by such a lead on an ECG.

unique radiolytic product /yoonēk'/, a product such as a food substance that has undergone chemical changes as a result of exposure to ionizing radiation.

uniseptate /-sep'tāt/, having only one septum.

unisex /yoo'niseks/ [L, *unus,* one, *sexus,* sex], **1.** concerning only one sex or having reproductive organs of only one sex. **2.** an interchange of sex roles in clothing and hair styles, work assignments, shared restrooms, and activities.

unit (U) /yoo'nit/ [L, *unus*], **1.** a single item. **2.** a quantity designated as a standard of measurement. **3.** an area of a hospital that is staffed and equipped for treatment of patients with a specific condition or other common characteristics.

unitary human conceptual framework /yoo'niter'ē/, a complex theory in nursing that emphasizes the importance of holistic health care and an understanding of the human being in relation to the universal environment.

unit clerk, a person who performs routine clerical and reception tasks in a hospital inpatient care unit.

unit dose, a method of preparing medications in which individual doses of patient medications are prepared by the pharmacy and delivered in individually labeled packets to the patient's unit to be administered by the nurses on an ordered schedule.

unit-dose system, a system of drug distribution in which a portable cart containing a drawer for each patient's medications is prepared by the hospital pharmacy with a 24-hour supply of the medications.

United Nations International Children's Emergency Fund (UNICEF) /yoō'nisef'/, a fund established by the General Assembly of the United Nations in 1946 to aid children in devastated areas of the world. It is funded by contributions from the member nations and acts to prevent disease, including TB, whooping cough, and diphtheria, and provides food and clothing to needy children in more than 50 countries.

United Network for Organ Sharing (UNOS) /yoō'nos/, a national organization for the collection and distribution of body organs that can be used in transplants. Hospitals advise relatives of newly deceased patients about the availability of UNOS service in arranging organ donations.

United States Medical Licensing Examination®, the standardized licensing examination for state licensure of physicians. Developed by the U.S. Federation of State Medical Boards, the examination is based on National Board of Medical Examiners test materials.

United States Pharmacopeia (USP), a compendium recognized officially by the Federal Food, Drug, and Cosmetic Act that contains descriptions, uses, strengths, and standards of purity for selected drugs and for all of their forms of dosage.

United States Public Health Service (USPHS), an agency of the federal government responsible for the control of the arrival from abroad of any people, goods, or substances that may affect the health of U.S. citizens. The agency sets standards for the domestic handling and processing of food and the manufacture of serums, vaccines, cosmetics, and drugs.

unit of blood, a standard measure of approximately 450 to 500 mL of whole blood.

unit of service, any individual, family, aggregate, organization, or community given nursing care.

univalent, referring to a chemical valency of one, or the capacity of one atom of a chemical element to attract one atom of hydrogen or to displace one atom of hydrogen.

univalent reduction, a phenomenon during intracellular metabolism involving oxygen-reduction reactions in which superoxide radicals are produced because

oxygen accepts electrons only one at a time.

Univasc, a trademark for an angiotensin-converting enzyme inhibitor (moexipril).

universal /yoō'nivur'səl/ [L, *universus,* whole world], occurring everywhere and in all things.

universal antidote [L, *universus,* whole world; Gk, *anti,* against, *dotos,* something given], a mixture of 50% activated charcoal, 25% magnesium oxide, and 25% tannic acid, formerly thought to be useful as an antidote for most types of acid, heavy metal, alkaloid, and glycoside poisons. It is now believed that the mixture is no more effective than activated charcoal given with water.

universal cuff, an adaptive device worn on the hand to hold items such as utensils, shaver, or pencil, allowing a patient with a weak grasp to participate more in self-care.

universal donor, type O, Rh-negative red blood cells that may be used for emergency transfusion to any ABO type with minimal risk of incompatibility. Group AB plasma can be transfused to all ABO types.

universalizability principle /yoō'nivur'səlī'zəbil'itē/, a principle that an act is good if everyone should, in similar circumstances, do the same act without exception.

universal precautions, precautions designed to prevent the transmission of blood-borne diseases such as HIV, hepatitis B, and other blood-borne pathogens when first aid or health care is provided. Under universal precautions, blood and certain body fluids of all patients are considered potentially infectious. The precautions include specific recommendations for use of gloves, gowns, masks, and protective eyewear when contact with blood or body secretions containing blood is anticipated.

universal qualifiers, in neurolinguistic programming, the use of terms that give general impressions of limitations, such as *all, common, every, only,* and *never.*

universal recipient [L, *universus* + *recipere,* to receive], a person with blood type AB, who can receive a transfusion of any blood type without agglutination or precipitation effects.

universal tooth coding system, a tooth-numbering system in which the secondary teeth are numbered from 1 (the maxillary right third molar) to 32 (the mandibular right third molar). The deciduous teeth are similarly numbered from 1 to 20, with the numbers preceded by the letter D (for deciduous).

University of Wisconsin solution, a preservation solution used to flush organs before cold storage before transplantation to prevent cold-induced cell injury.

unlicensed assistive personnel, health care workers who are not licensed and who are prepared to provide certain elements of patient care under the supervision of a registered nurse. Unlicensed assistive personnel include patient care technicians, nurses' aides, and certified nursing assistants.

UNLS, abbreviation for *Unified Nursing Language System.*

unmyelinated /unmī′əlinā′tid/ [AS, *un,* not; Gk, *myelos,* marrow], describing a nerve fiber that is not coated with a myelin sheath. An unmyelinated fiber, lacking the whitish sheath, appears as gray matter in the brain.

Unna's paste boot /ōō′nəz/ [Paul G. Unna, German dermatologist, 1850–1929; L, *pasta,* paste; ME, *bote*], a dressing for varicose ulcers formed by applying a layer of a gelatin–glycerin–zinc oxide paste to the leg and then a spiral bandage covered with successive coats of paste to produce a rigid boot.

unoprostone /yōō′no-pros′tōn/, an antiglaucoma agent that decreases elevated intraocular pressure by increasing the outflow of aqueous humor. *Unoprostone isopropyl* is applied topically to the conjunctiva in the treatment of open-angle glaucoma and ocular hypertension.

UNOS /yōō′nos/, abbreviation for **United Network for Organ Sharing.**

unresolved grief /un′rizolvd/, a severe, chronic sorrow reaction in which a person does not complete the resolution stage of the mourning process within a reasonable time.

unroofed coronary sinus, congenital complete or partial absence of the partition dividing the coronary sinus from the left atrium, allowing the shunting of blood from the left atrium through the coronary sinus into the right atrium.

unsaturated /unsach′ərātid/ [ME, *un;* L, *saturare,* to fill], **1.** describing a solution that is capable of dissolving more of the solute; not saturated. **2.** an organic compound in which one or more pairs of carbon atoms are united by double or triple bonds, as in unsaturated fatty acids.

unsaturated alcohol, an alcohol derived from an unsaturated hydrocarbon, such as an alkene or olefin.

unsaturated compound [AS, *un,* not; L, *saturare,* to fill, *componere,* to put together], a chemical compound that contains double or triple bonds.

unsaturated fatty acid, a fatty acid in which some of the carbon atoms in the hydrocarbon chain are joined by double or triple bonds. These bonds are easily split in chemical reactions, and other substances may be joined to the carbon atoms

involved. Monounsaturated fatty acids have only one double or triple bond per molecule. Polyunsaturated fatty acids have more than one double or triple bond per atom. Diets high in polyunsaturated fatty acids and low in saturated fatty acids have been correlated with low serum cholesterol levels in some study populations.

unscrubbed team members /unskrubd′/, the members of a surgical team, including the anesthetist and the circulating nurse, who wear surgical attire but are not gowned or gloved and do not enter the sterile field.

unsocialized aggressive reaction /unso′ shəlīzd/ [ME, *un;* L, *socialis,* companion, *aggressio,* an attack, *re,* again, *agere,* to act], a behavior disorder of childhood characterized by overt and covert hostility, disobedience, physical and verbal aggression, vengefulness, quarrelsome behavior, and destructiveness, often manifested in acts such as lying, stealing, temper tantrums, vandalism, and physical violence against others.

unstable /unstā′bəl/, **1.** in an excited or active state, such as an atom with a nucleus possessing excess energy. **2.** easily broken down or prone to decomposition.

unstable angina [AS, *un,* not, *stabilis,* firm, *angina,* quinsy], thoracic pain that may mark the onset of acute MI. It typically has a sudden onset, sudden worsening, and stuttering recurrence over days and weeks. It carries a more severe short-term prognosis than stable chronic angina.

Unverricht's disease /un′vərikts, ŏŏn′ferishts/ [Heinrich Unverricht, German physician, 1853–1912], an inherited condition characterized by progressive degeneration of gray matter, resulting in myoclonic epilepsy. It appears in patients 8 to 13 years of age and is marked by general neurologic and intellectual decline.

upper airway obstruction (UAO), any abnormal condition of the mouth, nose, or larynx that interferes with breathing when the rest of the respiratory system is functioning normally.

upper esophageal sphincter, the upper 3 to 5 cm of the esophagus, including the cricopharyngeus muscle, which prevents the aspiration of air from the pharynx esophagus.

upper extremity suspension, an orthopedic procedure used in the treatment of fractures and in the correction of orthopedic abnormalities of the upper limbs. The procedure uses traction equipment, including metal frames, ropes, and pulleys, to relieve the weight of the involved upper limb rather than to exert traction.

upper GI (UGI), pertaining to the upper gastrointestinal tract, from the esophagus to and including the duodenum. The term is commonly applied to radiographic or fluoroscopic diagnostic views after ingestion of a barium sulfate solution.

upper GI x-ray study, a series of radiographic films of the upper GI tract, usually with barium sulfate as the contrast medium.

upper level discriminator (ULD), an electronic device used in nuclear medicine to discriminate against all radionuclide pulses whose heights are above a given level.

upper motor neuron paralysis, an injury to or lesion in the brain or spinal cord that causes damage to the cell bodies, axons, or both of the upper motor neurons, which extend from the cerebral centers to the cells in the spinal column. Clinical manifestations include weakness or paralysis, increased muscle tone and spasticity of the muscles involved with little or no atrophy, hyperactive deep tendon reflexes, diminished or absent superficial reflexes, the presence of pathologic reflexes such as Babinski's and Hoffmann's reflexes, and no local twitching of muscle groups.

upper pole ureter, the ureter draining the upper pole of a duplex kidney.

upper respiratory tract (URT), one of the two divisions of the respiratory system. The URT consists of the nose, nasal cavity, ethmoidal air cells, frontal sinuses, sphenoidal sinuses, maxillary sinus, larynx, and trachea. The URT conducts air to and from the lungs and filters, moistens, and warms the air during each inspiration.

UPPP, abbreviation for *uvulopalatopharyngoplasty.*

up-regulation /əp-reg-yə-lā-shən/, increase in expression of a gene. In the narrowest sense, it refers to that in which transcription of a specific mRNA is increased, but is also used more broadly to refer to increase in mRNA levels for a particular gene from any cause.

upsilon /yŏŏp′silon, up′-/, Y, υ, the twentieth letter of the Greek alphabet.

uptake /up′tāk/ [AS, *uptacan*], the drawing up or absorption of a substance.

UR, abbreviation for **utilization review.**

urachal diverticulum, a usually asymptomatic type of vesical diverticulum resulting from a urachus that has closed at the umbilical end but not at the bladder end; seen most often in children, those with prune-belly syndrome, and persons with a bladder outlet obstruction.

urachal sinus, dilation of part of the urachus at the umbilical end, either congenitally or as a result of a urachal cyst that has begun to drain to the surface.

urachus /yŏŏr′əkəs/ [Gk, *ourachos,* urinary tract], in the fetus, an epithelial tube

connecting the apex of the urinary bladder with the umbilicus. It persists throughout life as the median umbilical ligament.

uracil, a pyrimidine base found in RNA that pairs with adenine.

uragogue, an agent that increases production of urine.

uranium (U) /yŏŏrā′nē·əm/ [planet Uranus], a heavy, radioactive metallic element. Its atomic number is 92; its atomic mass is 238.03. Uranium is the heaviest of the natural elements.

uranoschisis /yŏŏ′rənos′kisis/ [Gk, *ouranos,* palate, *schisis,* fissure], cleft palate.

uranostaphyloplasty /-staf′iləplas′tē/ [Gk, *ouranos,* palate, *staphyle,* uvula, *plassein,* to mold], the surgical repair of a cleft palate.

uranostaphyloschisis /yŏŏ′rənōstaf′ilos′kisis/, a fissure that extends from the hard to the soft palate.

urarthritis, inflammation of a joint caused by gout.

urate /yŏŏr′āt/, any salt of uric acid such as sodium urate. Urates are found in urine, blood, and tophi or calcareous deposits in tissues. They also may be deposited as crystals in joints.

uraturia /yŏŏr′ətŏŏr′ē·ə/, the presence of uric acid salts in the urine.

urceiform /ŏŏrsē′ifôrm/, pitcher-shaped.

Ur-defenses /ŏŏr dəfen′səs/, a set of three fundamental beliefs essential for psychologic integrity of the individual, as proposed by Jules Masserman. They are a delusion of invulnerability and immortality, faith in a celestial order, and a wishful fantasy that fellow human beings are potential friends available for mutual service.

urea /yŏŏrē′ə/ [Gk, *ouron,* urine], a normal metabolic waste product from protein metabolism, it is used as a systemic osmotic diuretic and topical emollient. It is prescribed systemically to reduce cerebrospinal and intraocular fluid pressure and is used topically as a keratolytic agent.

urea concentration test, a test of renal efficiency, based on the fact that urea is absorbed rapidly from the stomach into the blood and is excreted unaltered by the kidneys. 15 g of urea is given with 100 mL of fluid, and the urine collected after 2 hours is tested for urea concentration.

urea cycle, a series of enzymatic reactions by which ammonia is detoxified in the liver. In the series of steps for disposing of the ammonia molecule, a waste product of protein metabolism, free enzymatic reactions occur as NH_2 radicals are combined with carbon and oxygen atoms from carbon dioxide to form urea, which is excreted.

U

ureagenesis /yŏŏr′ē·əjen′əsis/, the process by which urea becomes the final waste product of amino acid metabolism and the detoxification of ammonia from the blood.

urea nitrogen appearance, the amount of urea in grams produced by a person's body over a specific period of time. It is calculated as the sum of the urea excreted in the urine plus that found in the blood by calculating BUN. A low figure indicates efficient use of dietary protein. The person's intake of protein must also be known, because a low urea nitrogen appearance is also seen with a low protein diet or malnutrition.

urea nitrogen blood test, a blood test that detects levels of urea nitrogen in the blood, which serve as an index of liver and kidney function and indicate diseases of these organs as well as other conditions that affect their function. More commonly called blood urea nitrogen test.

Ureaplasma urealyticum /-plaz′mə/, a sexually transmitted microorganism that is a common inhabitant of the urogenital systems of men and women in whom infection is asymptomatic. Neonatal death, prematurity, and perinatal morbidity are statistically associated with colonization of the chorionic surface of the placenta by *Ureaplasma urealyticum*. There is no characteristic lesion in the fetus or newborn. Treatment involves oral tetracyclines administered for a period of at least 7 days.

urea rebound, a sudden increase in release of urea into the bloodstream by cells and organs that normally store it, seen in the first 15 minutes to an hour after urea has been removed by dialysis. It is caused by flow-volume dysequilibrium.

urea reduction ratio (URR), the fractional reduction in BUN during a single hemodialysis session, expressed as a percent, measured to assess adequacy of hemodialysis.

urease /yŏŏr′ē·ās/, **1.** an enzyme used in the determination of urea in the blood or urine. **2.** an enzyme that catalyzes the hydrolysis of urea to carbon dioxide and ammonia. **3.** an antitumor enzyme.

Urecholine, a trademark for a cholinergic (bethanechol chloride).

uremia /yŏŏr′ē′mē·ə/ [Gk, *ouron + haima,* blood], the presence of excessive amounts of urea and other nitrogenous waste products in the blood, as occurs in renal failure.—**uremic,** *adj.*

uremic breath, the peculiar odor of the breath in uremic stomatitis.

uremic coma [Gk, *ouron,* urine, *koma,* deep sleep], a stuporous condition resulting from acidosis and the toxic effects of uremia.

uremic convulsion, an episode of involuntary muscle contractions caused by uremia or retention in the blood of substances that would normally be excreted by the kidneys.

uremic frost, a pale frostlike deposit of white crystals on the skin caused by kidney failure and uremia. Urea compounds and other waste products of metabolism that cannot be excreted by the kidneys into the urine are excreted through the small superficial capillaries into the skin, where they collect on the surface.

uremic syndrome, the spectrum of symptoms accompanying uremia.

ureter /yŏŏr′ətər, yŏŏrē′tər/ [Gk, *oureter*], one of a pair of tubes, about 30 cm long, that carries urine from the kidney into the bladder. Each tube is composed of a fibrous, a muscular, and a mucous coat. The ureter enters the bladder through a tunnel that functions as a valve to prevent backflow of urine into the ureter when the bladder contracts. Connecting with the kidneys, the ureters expand into funnel-shaped renal pelves that branch into calyces. Urine is pumped through the ureters by peristaltic waves that occur an average of three times a minute.—**ureteral** /yŏŏrē′terəl/, *adj.*

ureteral duplication, double ureter.

ureteral dysfunction /yŏŏrē′terəl/ [Gk, *oureter + dys,* bad; L, *functio,* performance], a disturbance of the normal peristaltic flow of urine through a ureter, resulting from dysfunction of ureteral motor nerves.

ureteral jet, the pattern of fluid seen when dense urine from the ureter is expelled into the more dilute urine in the bladder; it can be studied to assess function and patency of the bladder.

ureteral orifice, the opening of a ureter into the urinary bladder at one corner of the trigone of the bladder.

ureteral reimplantation, ureteroneocystostomy.

ureteral stent, one inserted into the ureter to maintain patency in stenosis or in healing after trauma or surgery.

uretercystoscope /yŏŏr′ētərsis′təskōp′/ [Gk, *oureter,* ureter, *kystis,* bladder, *skopein,* to view], a cystoscope equipped with ureteric catheters that can be inserted into either ureter.

ureteritis /yŏŏrē′tərī′tis/ [Gk, *oureter + itis*], an inflammatory condition of a ureter caused by infection or by the mechanic irritation of a stone.

ureteroarterial fistula, a rare, life-threatening fistula that communicates between a ureter and a nearby artery, usually seen as a complication of a surgical procedure of the ureter.

ureterocele /yŏōrē′tərōsēl′/ [Gk, *oureter* + *kele*, hernia], a prolapse of the terminal part of the ureter into the bladder. The condition may lead to obstruction of the flow of urine, hydronephrosis, and loss of renal function. Surgical correction is performed to prevent permanent damage to the kidney.

ureterocolonic anastomosis, anastomosis of a ureter to part of the colon, either a detached segment or an in situ segment, so that urine empties into the colon, sometimes as a continent urinary diversion.

ureterography /yŏōrē′tərog′rəfē/ [Gk, *oureter* + *graphein*, to record], the radiologic imaging of a ureter, usually conducted as part of an examination of the urinary tract. The examination may involve injection of a radiopaque medium through a urinary catheter.

ureteropelvic /yŏōrē′tərōpel′vik/, relating to the ureter and renal pelvis.

ureteropelvic junction, the area where the renal pelvis meets the ureter.

ureteroplasty /-plas′tē/ [Gk, *oureter* + *plassein*, to mold], a surgical procedure performed to restructure a ureter, such as when a stricture blocks the normal flow of urine.

ureteropyelonephritis /-pī′əlō′nəfrī′tis/ [Gk, *oureter* + *pyelos*, pelvis, *nephros*, kidney, *itis*, inflammation], an inflammation of the kidney, pelvis, and ureter.

ureterosigmoidostomy /-sig′moidos′təmē/ [Gk, *oureter* + *sigma*, S-shaped, *eidos*, form, *stoma*, mouth], a surgical procedure in which a ureter is implanted in the sigmoid flexure of the intestinal tract.

ureterostomy /-os′təmē/ [Gk, *oureter* + *stoma*, mouth], the surgical creation of a new opening through which a ureter empties onto the surface of the body or into another outlet.

ureterotomy, an incision into a ureter.

ureterovaginal /-vaj′inəl/, pertaining to the ureters and vagina.

ureterovascular hydronephrosis, hydronephrosis caused by crossed vessels next to the kidney that compress or deform the renal pelvis.

urethra /yŏōrē′thrə/ [Gk, *ourethra*], a small tubular structure that drains urine from the bladder. In women, it is about 3 cm long and lies directly behind the symphysis pubis, anterior to the vagina. In men, it is about 20 cm long and begins at the bladder, passes through the center of the prostate gland, goes between two sheets of tissue connecting the pubic bones, and finally passes through the urinary meatus of the penis. In men the urethra is joined by the ejaculatory duct and serves as a passageway for semen during ejaculation, as well as a canal for urine during voiding.

urethral, pertaining to the urethra.

urethral angle, the angle at which the urethra exits the bladder neck.

urethral atresia, imperforation of the urethra.

urethral caruncle [Gk, *ourethra*; L, *caruncula*, small piece of flesh], a small, painful growth in the mucous membrane of the female urethral meatus. It may be a source of bleeding.

urethral crest, a longitudinal midline fold of mucosa that marks the lumen of the urethra in men.

urethral diverticulum, an outpouching of tissue from the urethra into the potential space surrounding the urethra. It occurs predominantly in women and is associated with chronic urologic conditions.

urethral duplication, double urethra.

urethral folds, a pair of folds derived from the cloacal folds. In male embryos they close over the urethral plate and fuse to form the spongy urethra and ventral aspect of the penis. In female embryos they fuse only anterior to the anus and form the labia minora.

urethral hematuria [Gk, *ourethra* + *haima*, blood, *ouron*, urine], blood in the urine as a result of a urethral lesion.

urethral orifice, 1. the external opening of the urethra in the glans penis of a male or the vestibule of a female. 2. internal opening of the urethra at the anterior and inferior angle of the trigone.

urethral sinus, the depression on either side of the urethral crest into which empty the ducts of the prostate.

urethral sphincter, the voluntary muscle at the neck of the bladder that relaxes to allow urination.

urethral swab [Gk, *ourethra*; D, *zwab-ber*], an absorbent pad on a slender rod used to treat lesions or to remove secretions.

urethral syndrome, frequency of urination, urgency, and dysuria with no evidence of infection, obstruction, or other urologic abnormality. There may also be suprapubic pain and difficulty in initiating and maintaining the urine stream.

urethritis/yŏōr′ithrī′tis/, inflammation of the urethra. The condition is characterized by dysuria and is usually the result of an infection in the bladder or kidneys. An antibiotic, a urinary antiseptic, and an analgesic are usually prescribed after the causative organism is identified by bacteriologic culture of a urine specimen.

urethrocele /yŏōrē′thrəsēl/ [Gk, *urethra* + *kele*, hernia], a herniation of the urethra in females. It is characterized by a protrusion of a segment of the urethra and the connective tissue surrounding it into the anterior wall of the vagina. A large urethrocele can cause difficulty in voiding, some degree of incontinence, UTI, and dyspareunia. Surgical repair is the usual treatment.

urethrocutaneous fistula, a cutaneous fistula between the urethra and the skin, such as after repair of hypospadias or exstrophy of the bladder.

urethrocystitis /yŏŏrē´thrōsistī´tis/, inflammation of the urethra and bladder.

urethrocystoscopy /yŏŏrē´thro-sis-tos´kə pe/, cystourethroscopy.

urethrodynia /-din´ē·ə/, pain in the urethra.

urethrography /-g´rəfē/, the radiographic examination of the urethra after the injection of a radiopaque contrast medium into the urethra, usually through a catheter.

urethroplasty /yŏŏrē´thrəplastē´/, a surgical procedure for the repair of a urethra, as in the correction of hypospadias.

urethroscope /-skōp/ [Gk, *ourethra,* urethra, *skopein,* to view], an instrument used to examine the internal surfaces of the urethra.

urethrospasm /-spaz´əm/, a spasm of the musculature of the urethra.

urethrostenosis /-stənō´sis/ [Gk, *ourethra,* urethra, *stenosis,* a narrowing], a stricture of the urethra.

urethrovesical angle, an angle formed by junction of the bladder wall and the urethra.

Urex, a trademark for a urinary tract antibacterial (methenamine hippurate).

urgency /ur´jensē/ [L, *urgere,* to drive on], a feeling of the need to void urine immediately.

URI, abbreviation for **upper respiratory infection.**

uric acid /yŏŏr´ik/, a product of the metabolism of protein that is present in the blood and excreted in the urine.

uricaciduria /yŏŏr´ikas´idŏŏr´ē·ə/ [Gk, *ouron;* L, *acidus,* sour; Gk, *ouron*], an elevated amount of uric acid in the urine, often associated with urinary calculi or gout.

uricosuric drugs /yŏŏr´ikōsŏŏr´ik/ [Gk, *ouron;* L, *acidus,* sour; Gk, *ouron;* Fr, *drogue*], drugs administered to increase the elimination of uric acid.

urinal /yŏŏr´inəl/, an external plastic or metal receptacle for collecting urine.

urinalysis /yŏŏr´inal´isis/ [Gk, *ouron + analysein,* to loosen], a physical, microscopic, or chemical examination of urine. The specimen is physically examined for color, turbidity, and specific gravity. Then it is spun in a centrifuge to allow collection of a small amount of sediment, which is examined microscopically for blood cells, casts, crystals, pus, and bacteria. Chemical analysis may be performed to measure the pH and to identify and measure the levels of ketones, sugar, protein, blood components, and many other substances.

urinary /yŏŏr´iner´ē/, pertaining to urine or the formation of urine.

urinary albumin [Gk, *ouron,* urine; L, *albus,* white], the presence of albumin, a protein, in the urine. Protein is usually not found in the urine because the spaces in the glomerular membrane of the kidney are too small to allow escape of protein molecules. If the membrane is damaged, however, as in some kidney diseases, albumin molecules can leak through into the urine.

urinary bladder [Gk, *ouron;* AS, *blaedre*], the muscular membranous sac in the pelvis that stores urine for discharge through the urethra. It is connected anteriorly with the two ureters and posteriorly with the urethra.

urinary bladder training, a nursing intervention from the Nursing Interventions Classification (NIC) defined as improving bladder function for those with urge incontinence by increasing the bladder's ability to hold urine and the patient's ability to suppress urination.

urinary calculus, a mineral concretion formed in any part of the urinary tract. Calculi may be small enough to be passed with the urine or large enough to obstruct its flow.

urinary casts [Gk, *ouron,* urine; ONorse, *kasta*], cells or particles excreted in the urine having the shape of renal-collecting tubule cells.

urinary catheterization, a nursing intervention from the Nursing Interventions Classification (NIC) defined as insertion of a catheter into the bladder for temporary or permanent drainage of urine.

urinary catheterization: intermittent, a nursing intervention from the Nursing Interventions Classification (NIC) defined as regular periodic use of a catheter to empty the bladder.

urinary continence, a nursing outcome from the Nursing Outcomes Classification (NOC) defined as control of elimination of urine from the bladder.

urinary diversion, surgical creation of an alternate route of flow for urine to replace an absent or diseased portion of the lower urinary tract to preserve renal function.

urinary elimination, a nursing outcome from the Nursing Outcomes Classification (NOC) defined as collection and discharge of urine.

urinary elimination management, a nursing intervention from the Nursing Interventions Classification (NIC) defined as maintenance of an optimum urinary elimination pattern.

urinary flow study, uroflowmetry.

urinary frequency, frequent urination or urgency without an increase in the total daily volume of urine. The condition may result from a bladder or urethral infection, a diminished bladder capacity or other structural abnormalities.

urinary habit training, a nursing intervention from the Nursing Interventions Classification (NIC) defined as establishing a predictable pattern of bladder emptying to prevent incontinence for persons with limited cognitive ability who have urge, stress, or functional incontinence.

urinary hesitancy, a decrease in the force of the stream of urine, often with difficulty in beginning the flow. Hesitancy is usually the result of an obstruction or stricture between the bladder and the external urethral orifice. In men it may indicate an enlargement of the prostate gland; in women it may indicate stenosis of the orifice.

urinary incontinence, inability to control urination, caused by acute or chronic factors. Five classes of chronic incontinence are recognized. Functional incontinence is the result of cerebral clouding and/or physical factors that make it difficult to get to bathroom facilities in time. Overflow incontinence occurs when the urinary tract is obstructed or when the detrusor muscle fails to contract as bladder capacity is reached; spinal cord injury or benign prostatic hypertrophy may be the cause. Stress incontinence is precipitated by coughing, sneezing, or straining; it occurs more often in women and is commonly related to anatomic changes. Urge incontinence is the inability to delay voiding after a sensation of bladder fullness is perceived. Reflex incontinence occurs when there is detrusor hyperreflexia and/or urethral relaxation due to neurologic causes, such as spinal cord injury. Urinary incontinence can have mixed etiologies. Treatment depends on the underlying cause and may include anticipatory toileting, bladder retraining, exercise of perineal muscles, anticholinergic medications, and surgery.

urinary incontinence care, a nursing intervention from the Nursing Interventions Classification (NIC) defined as assistance in promoting continence and maintaining perineal skin integrity.

urinary incontinence care: enuresis, a nursing intervention from the Nursing Interventions Classification (NIC) defined as promotion of urinary continence in children.

urinary meatus, the external opening of the urethra.

urinary output, the total volume of urine excreted daily, normally between 700 and 2000 mL. Various metabolic and renal diseases may increase or decrease urinary output.

urinary overflow, a condition that occurs when a patient's bladder is extremely distended with urine and the patient voids or leaks only a small amount of it. It is usually poorly controlled.

urinary retention care, a nursing intervention from the Nursing Interventions Classification (NIC) defined as assistance in relieving bladder distension.

urinary sediment [Gk, *ouron,* urine; L, *sedimentum,* a settling], solid matter that settles to the bottom of a urine sample that has been allowed to stand for several hours.

urinary space, a narrow chalice-shaped cavity in the renal glomerulus between the visceral layer and the parietal layer of the glomerular capsule, continuous with the lumen of the proximal convoluted tubule.

urinary system assessment, an evaluation of the condition and functioning of the kidneys, ureters, bladder, and urethra and an investigation of concurrent and previous disorders that may be factors in abnormalities in these structures. The patient is asked whether painful urination, frequency or burning on urination, dribbling, a decreased urinary stream, nocturia, stress incontinence, headache, back pain, or increased thirst has occurred. The color, odor, and amount of urine voided and obtained via catheter are determined. The patient's vital signs; any bladder distension; skin condition; neurologic changes; the location, duration, and character of pain; and the presence of bladder spasms are recorded. It is determined whether the patient has hypertension, diabetes, a venereal disease, vaginal or urethral drainage or discharge, or a history that includes cystitis, pyelonephritis, kidney stones, prostatectomy, renal surgery, a kidney transplant, or a venereal infection. The patient's sexual activity; use of coffee, tea, cola beverages, alcohol, perfumed soaps, feminine hygiene sprays, and prescribed and OTC medication; and habit of bathing in a tub or shower are ascertained. A family history of polycystic kidney disease, hypertension, diabetes, or cancer is noted. Laboratory studies include the specific gravity of the patient's urine, casts, protein, red and white cells in the urine, and serum creatinine level. Diagnostic procedures may

U

include cystoscopy, ultrasonic imaging, nuclear imaging, urethroscopy, excretory and IV urography, renal angiography, retrograde studies, ureters, and bladder.

urinary tract, all organs and ducts involved in the secretion and elimination of urine from the body.

urinary tract infection (UTI), an infection of one or more structures in the urinary system. Most UTIs are caused by gram-negative bacteria, most commonly *Escherichia coli* or species of *Klebsiella, Proteus, Pseudomonas,* or *Enterobacter,* although other strains, such as *Staphylococcus* and *Serratia,* are emerging. The condition is more common in women than in men. UTIs may be asymptomatic but are usually characterized by urinary frequency, burning pain with voiding, and, if the infection is severe, visible blood and pus in the urine. Fever and back pain often accompany kidney infections. Diagnosis of the cause and location of the infection is made by microscopic examination and bacteriologic culture of a urine specimen, physical examination of the patient, and, if necessary, various radiologic techniques such as retrograde pyelography or cystoscopy. Treatment includes antibacterial, analgesic, and urinary antiseptic drugs and increased fluid intake up to 3 L/day unless contraindicated. Teaching the patient about increased fluid intake, frequent voiding, and good perineal hygiene is also helpful.

urinary urgency, the sudden, almost uncontrollable, need to urinate.

urinate /yŏŏr′ināt/ [Gk, *ouron,* urine], to excrete urine from the bladder.

urination /yŏŏr′inā′shən/ [Gk, *ouron;* L, *atus,* process], the act of passing urine.

urine /yŏŏr′in/ [Gk *ouron*], the fluid secreted by the kidneys, transported by the ureters, stored in the bladder, and voided through the urethra. Normal urine is clear, straw-colored, and slightly acid; has the odor of urea; and has a specific gravity between 1.003 and 1.035. Its normal constituents include water, urea, sodium chloride, potassium chloride, phosphates, uric acid, organic salts, and the pigment urobilin.—**urinary,** *adj.*

urine culture and sensitivity (C&S), a microscopic study of the urine culture performed to determine the presence of pathogenic bacteria in patients with suspected UTI.

urine flow studies, a noninvasive, uncomplicated urodynamic test that measures the volume of urine expelled from the bladder per second. It is indicated to investigate dysfunctional voiding or suspicious outflow tract obstruction and is done before

and after any procedure designed to modify the function of the urologic outflow tract.

urine glucose test, a qualitative urine test that is usually done as part of a routine urinalysis to screen for the presence of glucose in the urine, which may indicate DM or other causes of glucose intolerance.

urine osmolality, the osmotic pressure of urine, usually greater than the osmolality of serum. The normal values are 500 to 800 mOsm/L after overnight water deprivation.

urine osmolality test, a urine test used in the precise evaluation of the concentrating ability of the kidney. It is also used to monitor fluid and electrolyte imbalance and is valuable in the workup of patients with renal disease, the syndrome of inappropriate antidiuretic hormone (SIADH) secretion, and diabetes insipidus.

urine pH, the hydrogen ion concentration of the urine, or a measure of its acidity or alkalinity. The normal pH value for urine is 4.6 to 8.0.

urine potassium (K^+) test, a 24-hour urine test that detects the urine concentration of potassium, the major cation within cells. Abnormal findings are associated with chronic and acute renal failure, Cushing's syndrome, hyperaldosteronism, alkalosis, diuretic therapy, dehydration, Addison's disease, malnutrition, and malabsorption, among other conditions.

urine sodium (Na^+) test, a 24-hour urine test that evaluates sodium balance in the body by determining the amount of sodium excreted in urine during a 24-hour period. It is useful for evaluating patients with volume depletion, acute renal failure, adrenal disturbances, and acid-base imbalances. It is especially important when the serum sodium concentration is low.

urine specific gravity, a measure of the degree of concentration of a sample of urine. The normal range of urine specific gravity is 1.003 to 1.035, depending on the patient's previous fluid intake, renal perfusion, and renal function.

urinoma /yŏŏr′inō′mə/ *pl.* **urinoma, urinomata,** a cyst filled with urine.

urinometer /yŏŏr′inom′ətər/ [Gk, *ouron* + *metron,* measure], any device for determining the specific gravity of urine.

Urised, a trademark for a urinary fixed-combination drug containing an antibacterial (methenamine), an analgesic (phenyl salicylate), anticholinergics (atropine sulfate and hyoscyamine sulfate), an antifungal (benzoic acid), and an antiseptic (methylene blue).

Urispas, a trademark for a smooth muscle relaxant (flavoxate hydrochloride).

urobilin /yŏŏr′əbī′lin/, a brown pigment formed by the oxidation of urobilinogen, normally found in feces and in small amounts in urine.

urobilinogen /yoŏr′əbĭlĭn′əjən/, a colorless compound formed in the intestine after the breakdown of bilirubin by bacteria.

urobilinuria /yoŏr′ōbĭ′lĭnoŏr′ē·ə/, the presence of excess urobilin in the urine.

urodynamics /-dīnam′iks/ [Gk, *ouron*, urine, *dynamis*, force], the study of the hydrology and mechanics of urinary bladder filling, emptying, and voiding.

uroflowmetry /yoŏr′ōflō′mətrē/, continuous recording of urine flow by means of a device consisting of a cylinder placed on a transducer that weighs the urine entering the cylinder during voiding and plots the flow rate on a time scale.

urofollitropin /-fol′itro′pin/, a preparation of gonadotropins from the urine of postmenopausal women. It contains follicle-stimulating hormone and is used in conjunction with HCG to induce ovulation in the treatment of female infertility and to stimulate multiple oocyte development in ovulatory patients using assisted reproductive technologies.

urogenital /jen′ĭtəl/ [Gk, *ouron;* L, *genitalis*, fruitful], pertaining to the urinary and the reproductive systems.

urogenital hiatus, a U-shaped defect in the muscles in the urogenital triangle that allows the passage of the urethra and vagina.

urogenital peritoneum, the peritoneum lining the urogenital structures in the lower pelvis.

urogenital region, the part of the perineal region that surrounds the external genital organs and the urethral orifice.

urogenital sinus, one of the elongated cavities, formed by the division of the cloaca in early embryonic development, into which open the ureter, mesonephric and paramesonephric ducts, and bladder.

urogenital system, all of the urinary and genital organs and their associated structures, including the kidneys, ureters, bladder, and urethra; the ovaries, fallopian tubes, uterus, clitoris, and vagina (in women); and the testes, seminal vesicles, seminal ducts, prostate, and penis (in men).

urogenital triangle, the triangle in the peritoneum anterior to the imaginary line between the two ischial tuberosities.

urogram /-gram/, an x-ray film of the urinary tract, obtained by urography.

urography /-g′rəfē/ [Gk, *ouron* + *graphein*, to record], the radiographic examination of the urinary system. A radiopaque substance is injected, and radiographs are taken as the substance is passed through or excreted from the part of the system being studied.

urokinase /yoŏr′əkī′nās/, an enzyme produced in the kidney and found in urine that is a potent plasminogen activator of the fibrinolytic system.

urolagnia /yoŏr′əlag′nē·ə/, sexual stimulation gained from acts involving urine, such as watching people urinate or being urinated on.

urolithiasis /yoŏr′ōlithī′əsis/, the presence of calculi in the urinary system.

urologic /-loj′ĭk/ [Gk, *ouron*, urine, *logos*, science], pertaining to the scientific study of the urinary tract.

urologist /yoŏrol′əjist/, a licensed physician who has completed an approved residency program and who specializes in the practice of urology.

urology /yoŏrol′əjē/ [Gk, *ouron* + *logos*, science], the branch of medicine concerned with the study of the anatomy, physiology, disorders, and care of the urinary tract in men and women and of the male genital tract.—**urologic,** *adj.*

urometer /yoŏrom′ətər/ [Gk, *ouron*, urine, *metron*, measure], a type of hydrometer used to measure the specific gravity of a urine sample.

uropathy /yoŏrop′əthē/ [Gk, *ouron* + *pathos*, disease], any disease or abnormal condition of any structure of the urinary tract.—**uropathic,** *adj.*

uroporphyria /yˇoor′ōpôrfir′ē·ə/ [Gk, *ouron* + *porphyros*, purple], a rare genetic disease characterized by excessive secretion of uroporphyrin in the urine, blistering dermatitis, photosensitivity, splenomegaly, and hemolytic anemia. Corticosteroid ointments may be helpful for the skin lesions; splenectomy may be necessary to alleviate the hemolytic anemia. Most patients die from hematologic complications before they reach middle age.

uroporphyrin /yoŏr′ōpôr′firĭn/, a porphyrin normally excreted in the urine in small amounts.

uroporphyrinogen-1-synthase test, a blood test used to detect a deficiency of uroporphyrinogen-1-synthase, associated with porphyria.

uroprotective /pro-tek′tiv/, providing protection of the urinary tract, especially against urotoxicity.

uroradiology /-rā′dē·ol′əjē/, the radiologic study of the urinary tract.

urorectal septum /-rek′təl/ [Gk, *ouron;* L, *rectus*, straight, *saeptum*, wall], a ridge of mesoderm covered with endoderm that in the early developing embryo divides the endodermal cloaca into the urogenital sinus and the rectum.

uroscopy /yoŏros′kəpē/ [Gk, *ouron*, urine, *skopein*, to view], diagnostic examination of urine samples.

U

urostomy /yŏŏros′təmē/, the diversion of urine away from a diseased or defective bladder through a surgically created opening, or stoma, in the skin.

urothelium /yŏŏr″ŏthē′lē·əm/, a layer of transitional epithelium in the wall of the bladder, ureter, and renal pelvis.

urotoxicity /yŏŏr″ŏtoksis′itē/, the toxic quality of the urine.

Uroxatral, a trademark for alfuzosin.

ursodeoxycholic acid /ur′sŏdē·ok′sikol′ik/, a secondary bile salt. It is used in vivo to dissolve cholesterol gallstones.

urticaria /ur′tiker′ē·ə/ [L, *urtica,* nettle], a pruritic skin eruption characterized by transient wheals of varying shapes and sizes with well-defined erythematous margins and pale centers. It is caused by capillary dilation in the dermis that results from the release of vasoactive mediators, or from drugs, food, insect bites, inhalants, emotional stress, exposure to heat or cold, or exercise. Treatment includes antihistamines and removal of the stimulus or allergen.—**urticarial,** *adj.*

urticaria bullosa [L, *urtica,* nettle, *bulla,* bubble], a skin eruption in which the lesions are capped by blisters.

urticaria maculosa [L, *urtica,* nettle, *macule,* spot], a chronic skin eruption in which red lesions form with little or no edema present.

urticaria medicamentosa [L, *urtica,* nettle + *medicina*], a form of skin eruption that follows the use of certain medications, including those containing quinine.

urticaria papulosa [L, *urtica,* nettle, *papula,* pimple], a form of skin eruption affecting mainly children and characterized by reddish macules on which papules develop.

urticaria pigmentosa, an uncommon form of mastocytosis characterized by pigmented skin lesions that usually begin in infancy and become urticarial on mechanical or chemical irritation. Treatment is symptomatic and usually includes antihistamines for relief of itching.

urushiol /ərōō′shē·ôl/, a toxic resin in the sap of certain plants of the genus *Rhus,* such as poison ivy, poison oak, and poison sumac, that produces allergic contact dermatitis in many people.

USAN /yōō′san, yōō′es′ā′en′/, abbreviation for *United States Adopted Names,* an organization that works with pharmaceutical manufacturers to designate names for nonproprietary drugs.

use effectiveness [L, *usus,* make use of, *efficere,* to produce], of a contraceptive method, the actual effectiveness of a medication, device, or method in preventing pregnancy.

use factor, in x-ray shielding design, the fraction of time that an x-ray beam is pointing in any given direction.

useful beam, in radiology, that part of the primary radiation that is permitted to emerge from the tube head assembly of an x-ray machine, as limited by the aperture or port and accessory collimating devices.

useful radiation, the part of direct radiation that is permitted to pass from an x-ray tube housing through the tube head port, aperture, or collimator.

user friendly, presenting operating information or instructions in a form that is familiar and easy to understand.

use test, a procedure used to identify offending allergens in foods, cosmetics, or fabrics by the systematic elimination and addition, one at a time, of specific items associated with the lifestyle of the patient involved.

U-shaped arch, a dental arch in which there is little difference in width between the first premolars and the last molars and in which the curve from canine to canine is abrupt and U-shaped.

Usher's syndrome, an inherited disorder characterized by retinitis pigmentosa and a sensorineural hearing deficit.

USMLE, abbreviation for **United States Medical Licensing Examination**®.

USPHS, abbreviation for **United States Public Health Service.**

USP unit, a dose unit as recommended by the *United States Pharmacopoeia,* the primary legally recognized national drug-standard compendium. Almost all prescription medications are now distributed on a mass basis rather than a unit basis.

USRDS, abbreviation for *United States Renal Data System.*

USR test, abbreviation for **unheated serum reagin test.**

uta /yōō′tə/ [Sp, facial ulcers], a mild cutaneous form of American leishmaniasis, occurring in the Andes of Peru and Argentina, caused by *Leishmania peruana.* The lesions are small and usually occur on the exposed surfaces of the skin, and ordinarily heal spontaneously within 1 year.

ut dict., abbreviation for the Latin phrase *ut dictum,* "as directed."

utend., abbreviation for the Latin phrase *utendus,* "to be used."

uterine /yōō′tərēn/ [L, *uterus,* womb], pertaining to the uterus.

uterine anteflexion [L, *uterus,* womb, *ante,* before, *flectere,* to bend], an abnormal position of the uterus in which the uterine body is bent forward on itself at the juncture of the isthmus of the uterine cervix and the lower uterine segment.

uterine anteversion, a position of the uterus in which the body of the uterus is directed ventrally. Mild degrees of anteversion are of no clinical significance.

uterine appendages, adnexa uteri: the ovaries, fallopian tubes, and associated ligaments.

uterine bleeding [L, *uterus;* ME, *blod*], any loss of blood from the uterus.

uterine bruit, a sound made by the passage of blood through the arteries of the pregnant uterus. The sounds are synchronized with the maternal heart rate.

uterine cancer, any malignancy of the uterus, including the cervix or endometrium.

uterine colic [L, *uterus;* Gk, *kolikos,* pain in the colon], a spasmodic pain originating in the uterus. It is usually caused by dysmenorrhea or extrusion of a fibroid polyp.

uterine fibroid [L, *uterus + fibra,* fiber; Gk, *eidos,* form], a growth of fibrous tissue in the uterus, usually a fibroma, fibromyoma, or leiomyofibroma.

uterine fibroma, a benign encapsulated uterine tumor. It affects about 20% of women over the age of 30. The tumor may develop in the wall of the uterus or be attached to a stalk of tissue originating in the wall. Symptoms may include menstrual disorders and are also likely to be related to the location of the tumor with respect to neighboring organs. They rarely spread or become life-threatening.

uterine glands, simple tubular glands found throughout the thickness and extent of the endometrium. They become enlarged during the premenstrual period.

uterine hemorrhage, bleeding from the uterus. Types of uterine hemorrhage include fetomaternal hemorrhage, in which fetal blood cells leak into the maternal circulation; postmenopausal bleeding; and dysfunctional uterine bleeding.

uterine inertia, abnormal relaxation of the uterus during labor, causing a lack of obstetric progress, or after childbirth, causing uterine hemorrhage.

uterine ischemia, a decreasing or ineffective blood supply to the uterus.

uterine peristalsis, rhythmic movements of the myometrium, seen especially during the follicular phase of the menstrual cycle.

uterine prolapse, the falling, sinking, or sliding of the uterus from its normal location in the body.

uterine retroflexion, a position of the uterus in which its body is bent backward on itself at the isthmus of the cervix and the lower uterine segment. This condition has no clinical significance.

uterine retroversion, a position of the uterus in which the body of the uterus is directed away from the midline, toward the back. Severe retroversion may be accompanied by vague persistent pelvic discomfort and dyspareunia and may prevent the fitting and use of a contraceptive diaphragm.

uterine sinus, one of the small irregular vascular channels in the endometrium of the pregnant uterus.

uterine souffle, a soft, blowing sound made by the blood in the arteries of a pregnant uterus. It is synchronized with the maternal pulse.

uterine sound, a long, flexible sound for exploring the uterus.

uterine subinvolution [L, *uterus + sub,* under, *involere,* to roll up], delayed or absent involution of the uterus during the postpartum period. The causes of subinvolution include retained fragments of placenta, uterine fibromyomas, and infection. Regardless of the cause of the condition, it is characterized by longer and heavier bleeding after childbirth and, on pelvic examination, a larger and softer uterus than would be expected at that time. Treatment includes ergonovine given orally for 2 or 3 days, and, if an infection is present, an antibiotic.

uterine swab [L, *uterus;* D, *zwabber*], an absorbent material on a rod or flattened wire used to obtain specimens or to remove secretions from the uterus.

uterine tetany, a condition characterized by uterine contractions that are extremely prolonged. This condition may be life-threatening to the fetus.

uteroabdominal pregnancy /yōō′tərō′abdom′inəl/ [L, *uterus + abdomen + pregnans*], a twin pregnancy in which one fetus develops in the uterus and the other develops in the abdomen.

utero-ovarian varicocele /yōō′tərō′over′ē·ən/ [L, *uterus + ovum,* egg, *varix,* varicose vein; Gk, *kele,* tumor], a swelling of the veins of the pampiniform plexus of the female pelvis.

uteroplacental sinus /yōō′tərōpləsen′təl/, one of the spaces in the zone of the placenta and the uterine wall where blood is exchanged between the circulations of the fetus and the mother.

uterosacral ligament, a ligament that extends from the cervix to the posterior pelvic wall. It is thought to help stabilize the uterus in the pelvic cavity.

uterosalpingography /yōō′tərōsal′ping·gog′rəfē/ [L, *uterus;* Gk, *salpinx,* tube, *graphein,* to record], a radiographic examination of the uterus and fallopian tubes.

uterotomy /yōō′tərot′əmē/ [L, *uterus;* Gk, *temnein,* to cut], a surgical incision into the uterus.

U

uterovaginal /yōō′tərovaj′inəl/, pertaining to the uterus and vagina.

uterus /yōō′tərəs/ [L, *womb*], the hollow pear-shaped internal female organ of reproduction in which the fertilized ovum is implanted and the fetus develops and from which the decidua of menses flows. The uterus is composed of three layers: the endometrium, the myometrium, and the parametrium. The endometrium lines the uterus and becomes thicker and more vascular in pregnancy and during the second half of the menstrual cycle. The myometrium is the muscular layer of the organ. Its muscle fibers wrap around the uterus obliquely, laterally, and longitudinally. The muscle fibers contract during childbirth to expel the fetus. After childbirth the meshlike network of fibers contracts again, creating a mass of natural ligatures that stops the flow of blood from the large blood vessels supplying the placenta. The parametrium is the outermost layer of the uterus. It is composed of serous connective tissue and extends laterally into the broad ligament. In the adult the organ measures about 7.5 cm long and 5 cm wide at its fundus and weighs approximately 40 g. During pregnancy it is able to grow to many times its usual size, almost entirely by cellular hypertrophy.

uterus bicornis [L, *uterus + bis + cornu*, horn], a uterus that is divided into two parts, usually separate at the upper end and joined at the lower end.

UTI, abbreviation for **urinary tract infection.**

utilitarianism /yōō′tiliter′ē·əniz′əm/ [L, *utilis*, useful, *isma*, practice], a doctrine of ethics that the purpose of all action should be to bring about the greatest happiness for the greatest number of people and that the value of anything is determined by its utility.

utilization review (UR) /yōō′tilizā′shən/ [L, *utilis + atus*, process], an assessment of the appropriateness and economy of an admission to a health care facility or a continued hospitalization.

utricle /yōō′trikəl/ [L, *utriculus*, small bag], the larger of two membranous pouches in the vestibule of the membranous labyrinth of the inner ear. It is an oblong structure that communicates with the semicircular ducts by five openings and receives utricular filaments of the vestibular branch of the vestibulocochlear nerve.

utriculosaccular duct /yōōtrik′yəlōsak′yə lər/ [L, *utriculus + sacculus*, small sack, *ducere*, to lead], a duct connecting the utricle with an endolymphatic duct of the membranous labyrinth.

UV, abbreviation for **ultraviolet.**

uvea /yōō′vē·ə/ [L, *uva*, grape], the vascular, pigmented, middle coat of the eye. —**uveal,** *adj.*

uveal malignant melanoma /yōō′vē·əl məlig′nənt mel′ənō′mə/, the most common type of ocular melanoma, consisting of overgrowth of uveal melanocytes and often preceded by a uveal nevus.

uveitis /yōō′vē·ī′tis/ [L, *uva*; Gk, *itis*], inflammation of the uveal tract of the eye, including the iris, ciliary body, and choroid. It may be characterized by an irregularly shaped pupil, inflammation around the cornea, pus in the anterior chamber, opaque deposits on the cornea, pain, and lacrimation.

uvula /yōō′vyələ/ *pl.* **uvulae** [L, *uva*, grape], the small cone-shaped process suspended in the mouth from the middle of the posterior border of the soft palate, especially the uvula palatina.—**uvular,** *adj.*

uvular /yōō′vyələr/ [L,*uva*, grape], pertaining to the palatine uvula.

uvulectomy /yōō′vyəlek′təmē/ [L, *uva*, grape; Gk, *ektomē*, excision], the surgical removal of the uvula.

uvulitis /yōō′vyəlī′tis/, an inflammation of the uvula. Common causes are allergy and infection.

uvulotomy /yōō′vyəlot′əmē/, the surgical removal of all or part of the uvula.

U wave, a small, rounded wave that follows the T wave on an ECG. Its mechanism is unknown. The U wave becomes taller in hypokalemia and inverted in heart disease. It may signify decreased potassium levels in the blood.

v, 1. abbreviation for **vein.** 2. abbreviation for **venous blood.** 3. in physics, a symbol for the speed of a wave.

V, 1. symbol for the element **vanadium.** 2. symbol for *ventilation capacity of the lung.*

V̇, symbol for *rate of gas flow.*

V_max, the maximum rate of catalysis.

V_t, abbreviation for *tidal volume,* the amount of air in milliliters per breath.

VAC, an anticancer drug combination of vinCRIStine, dactinomycin, and cyclophosphamide.

vaccinal /vak′sinəl/ [L, *vaccinus*], 1. pertaining to vaccinia, to vaccine, or to vaccination. 2. having protective qualities when used by way of inoculation.

vaccination (vacc) /vak′sinā′shən/ [L, *vaccinus,* relating to a cow], any injection of attenuated or killed microorganisms, such as bacteria, viruses, or rickettsia, administered to induce immunity or to reduce the effects of associated infectious diseases. — **vaccinate,** *v.*

vaccine /vaksēn′, vak′sēn, -sin/ [L, *vaccinus*], a suspension of attenuated or killed microorganisms administered intradermally, intramuscularly, orally, or subcutaneously to induce active immunity to infectious disease.

vaccinia /vaksin′ē·ə/ [L, *vaccinus*], an infectious disease of cattle caused by a poxvirus that may be transmitted to humans by direct contact or deliberate inoculation as a vaccine against smallpox. A pustule develops at the site of infection, usually followed by malaise and fever that last for several days. After 2 weeks the pustule becomes a crust that eventually drops off, leaving a scar.

vaccinia immune globulin, a hyperimmune gamma globulin developed for the treatment of skin reactions to immunization against the viral disease vaccinia.

vaccinotherapeutics /vak′sinōther′ə·pyoo′tiks/, a form of therapy that involves injections of bacterial antigens.

VACTERL association, a nonrandom association of congenital anomalies similar to the VATER association but also including cardiac and limb anomalies. The cause is unknown.

vacuole /vak′yoo·ōl/ [L, *vacuus,* empty], 1. a clear or fluid-filled space or cavity within a cell, such as occurs when a droplet of water is ingested by the cytoplasm. 2. a small space in the body enclosed by a membrane, usually containing fat, secretions, or cellular debris. — **vacuolar, vacuolated,** *adj.*

Vacutainer® tube, a brand of tube in which air can be removed to create a vacuum, usually used to draw blood. Vacutainer® is a registered trademark of Becton, Dickinson and Company.

vacuum aspiration /vak′yoo·əm/ [L, *vacuus,* empty, *aspirare,* to breathe upon], a method of removing tissues from the uterus by suction for diagnostic purposes or to remove elements of conception.

Vacuum Assisted Closure (VAC), a trademark for a system that uses the controlled negative pressure of a vacuum to promote healing of certain types of wounds. The edges of the wound are made airtight with foam and a dressing, and a tube is placed in the wound, connecting to a canister that creates a vacuum. Infectious materials and other fluids are then sucked out of the wound.

VAD, abbreviation for **vascular access device.**

vade mecum /vā′dē mē′kəm/ [L, go with me], something carried by a person for constant use.

vagal /vā′gəl/ [L, *vagus,* wandering], pertaining to the vagus nerve.

vagal tone [L, *vagus,* wandering; Gk, *tonos,* stretching], 1. the level of activity in the parasympathetic nervous system. 2. the inhibitory control of the vagus nerve over heart rate and atrioventricular conduction.

vagina /vəji′nə/ [L, sheath], the part of the female genitalia that forms a canal from the orifice through the vestibule to the uterine cervix. It is behind the bladder and in front of the rectum. In the adult woman the anterior wall of the vagina is about 7 cm long, and the posterior wall is about 9 cm long. The muscles of the vagina are innervated by the pudendal nerve and perfused by the vaginal artery.

vaginal atrophy /vaj′ənəl/, a postmenopausal condition of gradually declining tissue activity in the female reproductive tract. It is caused by a cessation of follicular inhibin and estrogen secretion, leading to decreased negative feedback on the release of follicle-stimulating hormone and luteinizing hormone by the anterior pituitary gland. Tissue effects related to estrogen deficiency include atrophy and dystrophy of the vulva and vagina, pruritus vulvae, dyspareunia, cystourethritis, ectropion, and uterovaginal prolapse.

vaginal bleeding, an abnormal condition in which blood is passed from the vagina, other than during the menses. It may be caused by abnormalities of the uterus or cervix, an abnormal pregnancy, endocrine abnormalities, abnormalities of one or both ovaries or one or both fallopian tubes, or an abnormality of the vagina. The following terms are commonly used in describing the approximate amount of vaginal bleeding: *heavy vaginal bleeding,* which is greater than heaviest normal menstrual flow; *moderate vaginal bleeding,* which is equal to heaviest normal menstrual flow; *light vaginal bleeding,* which is less than heaviest normal menstrual flow; *vaginal staining,* a very light flow of blood barely requiring the use of a sanitary napkin or tampon; *vaginal spotting,* the passage vaginally of a few drops of blood; and *bloody show,* an episode of light vaginal bleeding as often occurs in early labor, during labor, and, particularly, at the time of full dilation of the cervix at the end of the first stage of labor.

vaginal cancer, a malignancy of the vagina occurring rarely as a primary neoplasm and more often as a secondary lesion or extension of vulvar, cervical, endometrial, or ovarian cancer. Symptoms of invasive lesions are postmenopausal bleeding, purulent discharge, pain, and dysuria. Ninety percent of vaginal cancers are squamous cell carcinomas; others are clear cell or undifferentiated adenocarcinomas, malignant melanomas, and sarcomas. Depending on the patient's age and condition and the site and extent of the lesion, treatment may be by irradiation or vaginectomy and radical hysterectomy with lymph node dissection. Cryosurgery, topical 5-fluorouracil, and dinitrochlorobenzene may be used, but chemotherapy is not usually effective.

vaginal cornification test, a test for the level of estrogen in a urine sample of a woman. Confirmation is indicated by the appearance of cornified epithelial cells in a vaginal smear of a laboratory animal.

vaginal cyst [L, *vagina,* sheath; Gk, *ksytis,* bag], an abnormal closed sac or pouch in the vaginal tissues.

vaginal delivery, birth of a fetus through the vagina.

vaginal discharge, any discharge from the vagina. A clear or pearly-white discharge occurs normally. The discharge is largely composed of secretions of the endocervical glands. Inflammatory conditions of the vagina and cervix often cause an increase in the discharge, which may then have a foul odor and cause pruritus of the perineum and external genitalia.

vaginal fornix, a recess in the upper part of the vagina caused by the protrusion of the uterine cervix into the vagina.

vaginal hernia, 1. a hernia into the vagina. **2.** a downward protrusion of the cul-de-sac of Douglas between the posterior vaginal wall and the rectum.

vaginal hysterectomy [L, *vagina,* sheath; Gk, *hystera,* womb, *ektomē,* excision], the surgical removal of the uterus through the vagina.

vaginal instillation of medication, the instillation of a medicated cream, suppository, or gel into the vagina, usually to treat a local infection of the vagina or uterine cervix.

vaginal jelly, a contraceptive product containing a spermicide in a jelly medium. It is usually used in conjunction with a contraceptive diaphragm or cervical cap. Some antimicrobial medications are also supplied in the form of a vaginal jelly.

vaginal laparotomy, incision into the abdominal cavity through the vagina.

vaginal lubricant, an ointment or cream used to reduce friction in the vagina.

vaginal mucification test /myo͞o′sifikā′shən/, a test for the presence of progestins in a urine sample of a woman. Confirmation is indicated by the stimulation of mucus production in the vaginal epithelium of a laboratory animal.

vaginal speculum [L, *vagina,* sheath, *speculum,* mirror], a bivalved instrument, with two blades used to hold open the vaginal opening for inspection of the vaginal cavity.

vaginal vault, the enlargement of the internal end of the vagina.

vaginismus /vaj′iniz′məs/ [L, *vagina* + *spasmus,* spasm], a psychophysiologic genital reaction of women, characterized by intense contraction of the perineal and paravaginal musculature, tightly closing the vaginal introitus. It occurs in response to fear of painful intercourse or of pelvic examination. Vaginismus is considered abnormal if it occurs in the absence of genital lesions and if it conflicts with a woman's desire to participate in sexual intercourse or to permit examination, but it may be a normal or physiologic response if painful genital conditions exist or if forcible or premature intromission is anticipated. In some cases the condition is a manifestation of serious mental illness.

vaginitis /vaj′inī′tis/, an inflammation of the vaginal tissues, such as *trichomonas* vaginitis.

vaginography /vaj′inog′rəfē/, the radiographic examination of the vagina after the injection of a radiopaque contrast medium.

vaginolabial hernia /vaj′inōlā′bē-əl/, an inguinal hernia that reaches the tissue of the labium majus.

vaginoperineoplasty /vaj′inōper′inē′əplas′tē/, plastic surgery of the vagina and perineum.

vagosympathetic /vā′gōsim′pəthet′ik/ [L, *vagus*, wandering; Gk, *sympathein*, to feel with], pertaining to the vagus nerve and the cervical part of the sympathetic nervous system.

vagotomy /vāgot′əmē/ [L, *vagus*, wandering, *temnein*, to cut], the cutting of certain branches of the vagus nerve, performed with gastric surgery, to reduce the amount of gastric acid secreted and lessen the chance of recurrence of a gastric ulcer. Because peristalsis will be diminished, a pyloroplasty or an anastomosis of the stomach to the jejunum may be done to ensure proper emptying of the stomach.

vagotonus /vā′gətō′nəs/ [L, *vagus*; Gk, *tonos*, tension], an abnormal increase in parasympathetic activity caused by stimulation of the vagus nerve, especially bradycardia with decreased cardiac output, faintness, and syncope.

vagovagal reflex /vā′gōvā′gəl/ [L, *vagus* + *vagus* + *reflectere*, to bend back], a stimulation of the vagus nerve by reflex in which irritation of the larynx or the trachea results in slowing of the pulse rate.

vagueness /vāg′nəs/, a communication pattern involving the use of global pronouns and loose associations that leads to ambiguity and confusion in communication.

vagus nerve /vā′gəs/ [L, *vagus*, wandering, *nervus*, nerve], either of the longest pair of cranial nerves mainly responsible for parasympathetic control over the heart and many other internal organs, including thoracic and abdominal viscera.

vagus pulse [L, *vagus*, wandering, *pulsare*, to beat], a slow, regular pulse caused by overactivity of the vagus nerve.

Val, abbreviation for **valine.**

valacyclovir /val′a-si′klo-vir/, an ester of acyclovir. The hydrochloride salt is used as an antiviral agent in treatment of genital herpes and herpes zoster in patients who are not immunocompromised.

valdecoxib, a nonsteroidal antiinflammatory used to treat acute and chronic rheumatoid arthritis, osteoarthritis, and primary dysmenorrhea.

valence /vāl′əns/ [L, *valere,* to be strong], **1.** in chemistry, a numeric expression of the capability of an element to combine chemically with atoms of hydrogen or their equivalent. **2.** in immunology, an expression of the number of antigen-binding sites for one molecule of any given antibody or the number of antibody-binding sites for any given antigen.

valence electron, any of the electrons in the highest principal energy level of an atom or ion. They are responsible for the bonding of atoms to form crystals, molecules, and compounds.

valerian, a perennial herb native to Eurasia that is now grown worldwide. This herb is used as a sedative, and is generally considered safe and effective for short-term use.

valeric acid $(CH_3(CH_2)_3COOH)$ /vəler′ik/, an organic acid with a foul odor found in the roots of *Valeriana officinalis*. Commercially prepared, it is used in the production of perfumes, flavors, lubricants, and certain drugs.

valganciclovir /val′gan-si′klo-vir/, a prodrug of ganciclovir, used in treatment of cytomegalovirus infections in immunocompromised patients.

valgus /val′gəs/ [L, bent], describing an abnormal position in which a part of a limb is bent or twisted outward, away from the midline, such as the heel of the foot in talipes valgus (splayfoot).

validation /val′idā′shən/, the reciprocated communication of respect that conveys that the patient's opinions are acknowledged, respected, and heard regardless of whether or not the listener actually agrees with the content.

validation therapy, a nursing intervention from the Nursing Interventions Classification (NIC) defined as use of a method of therapeutic communication with elderly persons with dementia that focuses on emotional rather than factual content.

validity /valid′itē/, in research, the extent to which a test measurement or other device measures what it is intended to measure.

valine (Val) /val′ēn/, an essential amino acid needed for optimal growth in infants and nitrogen equilibrium in adults.

Valisone, a trademark for a glucocorticoid (betamethasone valerate).

Valium, a trademark for a benzodiazepine (diazepam).

vallecula /vəlek′yələ/ [L, little valley], any crevice or depression on the surface of an organ or structure.—**vallecular,** *adj.*

vallecula epiglottica, a furrow between the glossoepiglottic folds of each side of the posterior oropharynx.

vallecular dysphagia /vəlek′yələr/, difficulty or pain on swallowing caused by inflammation of the vallecula epiglottica.

valproate /val-pro′āt/, a salt of valproic acid with anticonvulsant activity similar to that of the acid.

V

valproic acid /valprō′ik/, an anticonvulsant. It is prescribed alone or in combination to treat complex partial seizures, absence seizures occurring alone or in combination with other types of seizures, and is used to treat mania associated with bipolar disorder and for migraines prophylaxis.

valrubicin, an antibiotic antineoplastic prescribed to treat bladder cancer.

Valsalva leak point pressure, the amount of pressure on the bladder by a Valsalva maneuver at which leakage of urine from the urethra occurs. It is a measure of strength of the urethral sphincters.

Valsalva maneuver /valsal′və/ [Antonio M. Valsalva, Italian surgeon, 1666–1723; OFr, *maneuvre,* work done by hand], any forced expiratory effort against a closed airway, such as when an individual holds the breath and tightens the muscles in a concerted, strenuous effort to move a heavy object. Most healthy individuals perform Valsalva maneuvers during normal daily activities without any injurious consequences. However, such efforts are dangerous for many patients with cardiovascular disease, especially if they become dehydrated, increasing the viscosity of their blood and the attendant risk of blood clotting. Patients who may be endangered by performing a Valsalva maneuver are commonly instructed to exhale instead of holding their breath when they move to decrease the risk of cardiovascular trauma.

Valsalva's test [Antonio M. Valsalva; L, *testum,* crucible], a method for testing the patency of the eustachian tubes. With mouth and nose kept tightly closed, the patient makes a forced expiratory effort; if the eustachian tubes are open, air will enter into the middle ear cavities, and the subject will hear a popping sound.

valsartan, an antihypertensive prescribed to treat hypertension, either alone or in combination with other agents.

value /val′yōō/ [L, *valere,* to be strong], a personal belief about the worth of a given idea or behavior.

values clarification[1], a method whereby a person can discover his or her own values by assessing, exploring, and determining what those personal values are and how they affect personal decision making.

values clarification[2], a nursing intervention from the Nursing Interventions Classification (NIC) defined as assisting another to clarify his/her own values to facilitate effective decision making.

value system, the accepted mode of conduct and the set of norms, goals, and values binding any social group.

valve /valv/ [L, *valva,* folding door], a natural structure or artificial device in a passage or vessel that prevents reflux of the fluid contents passing through it.—**valvular,** *adj.*

valve of lymphatics, any one of the tiny semilunar structures in the vessels and trunks of the lymphatic system that helps regulate the flow of lymph and prevents venous blood from entering the system. There are no valves in the capillaries of the system, but there are many in the collecting vessels.

valve of vein, any of the small cusps or folds found in the tunica intima of many veins, serving to prevent backflow of blood.

valvotomy /valvot′əmē/ [L, *valva*; Gk, *temnein,* to cut], the incision into a valve, especially one in the heart, to correct a defect and allow proper opening and closure.

valvula, certain small valves in the body and cusps of the heart valves.

valvular endocarditis, a form of chronic inflammation of the lining membrane of the heart in which the valves are stenotic or incompetent.

valvular heart disease [L, *valva*; AS, *hoert*; L, *dis,* opposite of; Fr, *aise,* ease], an acquired or congenital disorder of a cardiac valve. It is characterized by stenosis and obstructed blood flow and by valvular degeneration and regurgitation of blood. Diseases of aortic and mitral valves are most common and may be caused by congenital defects, bacterial endocarditis, syphilis, or, most frequently, rheumatic fever. Valvular dysfunction results in changes in intracardiac pressure and pulmonary and peripheral circulation. It may lead to cardiac arrhythmia, heart failure, and cardiogenic shock.

valvular regurgitation [L, *valva,* folding door, *re* + *gurgitare,* to flow], a backflow of blood that occurs when the heart contracts but a heart valve fails to close properly.

valvular stenosis, a narrowing or stricture of any of the heart valves, resulting either from a congenital defect or caused by disease.

valvulitis /val′vyəlī′tis/, an inflammation of a valve, especially a cardiac valve. Infected valves degenerate, or their cusps become stiff and calcified, resulting in stenosis and obstructed blood flow.

valvuloplasty /val′vyəlōplas′tē/ [L, *valva,* folding door; Gk, *plassein,* to shape], the use of a balloon-tipped catheter to dilate a cardiac valve.

VAMP /vamp/, abbreviation for a combination drug regimen, used in the treatment of cancer, containing three antineoplastics (vinCRIStine sulfate, methotrexate, and mercaptopurine) and a glucocorticoid (predniSONE).

vanadium (V) /vənā′dē·əm/ [ONorse, *Vanadis,* Freya, goddess of fertility], a grayish metallic element. Its atomic number is 23; its atomic mass is 50.942. Absorption of vanadium compounds results in a condition called vanadiumism, characterized by anemia, conjunctivitis, pneumonitis, and irritation of the respiratory tract.

van Bogaert's disease /van bō′gərts/ [Ludo van Bogaert, Belgian neurophysiologist, b. 1897], a rare familial disorder of lipid metabolism in which the substance cholestanol is deposited in the nervous system, blood, and connective tissue. Individuals with the disease develop progressive ataxia and dementia, premature atherosclerosis, cataracts, and xanthomas of the tendons.

Vanceril, a trademark for a glucocorticoid (beclomethasone dipropionate).

Vancocin Hydrochloride, a trademark for an antibacterial (vancomycin hydrochloride).

vancomycin /van′kōmī′sin/, an antibiotic. It is prescribed in the treatment of infections, particularly staphylococcal infections resistant to other antibiotics and antibiotic-associated pseudomembranous colitis caused by *Clostridium difficile*.

Van Deemter's equation /van dēm′tərz/, an expression of a gas chromatography relationship between the height equivalent to the theoretic plate and linear velocity of the carrier gas.

Van de Graaff generator /van də gräf/ [Robert J. Van de Graaff, American physicist, 1901–1967], a device in which electrically charged particles are sprayed on a moving belt and carried by it to an insulated terminal, where they cause a large electrostatic charge to build up. The generator often is used to inject charged particles into a larger accelerator.

van den Bergh's test /van dən burgs/ [Albert A.H. van den Bergh, Dutch physician, 1869–1943], a test for the presence of bilirubin in the blood serum. Blood is obtained from a patient, and the diluted serum is added to diazo reagent. A blue or violet color indicates the presence of bilirubin.

van der Waals forces /van der wäls, fän/ [Johannes D. van der Waals, Dutch physicist and Nobel laureate, 1837–1923], weak attractive forces between neutral atoms and molecules. They occur because a fluctuating dipole moment in one molecule induces a dipole moment in another. The activity accounts for some deviation from Boyle's law at very low temperatures or very high pressures.

van der Woude's syndrome /van der wō′dəz/, an autosomal-dominant syndrome consisting of cleft lip with or without cleft palate, with cysts of the lower lip.

vanillylmandelic acid (VMA) /vənil′il məndel′ik/, a urinary metabolite of epinephrine and norepinephrine. It may be measured in the urine to determine the levels of these catecholamines. A greater than normal amount of VMA is characteristic of a pheochromocytoma or neuroblastoma.

vanillylmandelic acid and catecholamines test, a 24-hour urine test that is performed primarily to diagnose hypertension secondary to pheochromocytoma. It is also used to detect the presence of neuroblastomas and rare adrenal tumors.

vanishing testis, one that was originally present in the fetus but atrophied in utero because of torsion.

vanishing twin /van′ishing/, a twin embryo or fetus that is aborted during pregnancy.

vanity surgery /van′itē/, plastic surgery performed primarily to make the patient appear more youthful.

Vanoxide, a trademark for a topical fixed-combination drug containing an antibacterial keratolytic (benzoyl peroxide) and an antiinflammatory corticosteroid (hydrocortisone).

Van Rensselaer, Euphenia /van ren′səlir/, an American socialite who entered the first class of the Bellevue Hospital Training School for Nurses in New York. She designed the first nurses' uniform, a blue and white seersucker dress with collar and cuffs, apron, and cap.

Vaponefrin, a trademark for an adrenergic agent (epINEPHrine hydrochloride).

vapor /vā′pər/ *pl.* **vapores, vapors** [L], **1.** an atmospheric dispersion of the gaseous form of a substance that in its normal state is a liquid or solid. **2.** steam, gas, or an exhalation.

vapor bath /vā′pər/, the exposure of the body to vapor, such as steam.

vaporization /vā′pərīzā′shən/ [L, *vapor,* steam], the changing of a liquid or solid (such as dry ice) to a gaseous state.

vaporizer, a device for reducing medicated liquids to a vapor useful for inhalation or application to accessible mucous membranes.

vapor pressure depression, a phenomenon in which the addition of a solute molecule to a solvent will decrease the vapor pressure of the solvent in equilibrium with the liquid phase.

vapor therapy, the therapeutic use of vapors or sprays.

Vaprisol, a trademark for conivaptan.

vardenafil, an impotence agent used to treat erectile dysfunction.

varenicline, a smoking cessation agent. It is used as a smoking deterrent.

variability /ver′ē-əbil′itē/ [L, *variare,* to diversify], the degree of divergence or ability of an object to vary from a given standard or average.

variable /ver′ē-əbəl/, a factor in an experiment or scientific test that tends to vary, or take on different values, while other elements or conditions remain constant.

variable behavior [L, *variare,* to diversify; AS, *bihabban,* to behave], a response, activity, or action that may be modified by individual experience.

variable interval (VI) reinforcement, reinforcement that is offered after varying lapses of time.

variable number of tandem repeats (VNTR), different numbers of tandemly repeated oligonucleotide sequences in the alleles of a gene.

variable ratio (VR) reinforcement, reinforcement that requires variable numbers of responses.

variable region, the part of an immunoglobulin in which the amino acid sequence can differ among molecules of that class of immunoglobulin. The variable region includes the antigen-binding site.

variance /ver'ē-əns/ [L, *variare*], **1.** in statistics, a numeric representation of the dispersion of data around the mean in a given sample. It is represented by the square of the standard deviation and is used principally in performing an analysis of variance. **2.** *nontechnical.* the general range of a group of findings.

variant /ver'ē-ənt/ [L, *variare,* to diversify], an individual or subpopulation that differs from other individuals or subpopulations of its species.

varicella gangrenosa /ver'isel'ə/, a potentially fatal form of varicella (chickenpox) characterized by gangrenous lesions. A fulminating subvariety of the skin disorder may become fatal within a few hours if complicated by hemolytic streptococcus.

varicella virus vaccine live, a preparation of live, attenuated human herpesvirus 3 (varicella-zoster virus) administered subcutaneously for production of immunity to varicella and herpes zoster.

varicella-zoster immune globulin (VZIG) /zos'tər/ [L, *varius,* diverse; Gk, *zoster,* girdle; L, *immunis,* free from, *globulus,* small globe], an immunoglobulin obtained from the blood of uninfected individuals who have high levels of antibodies against varicella-zoster virus. The immunoglobulin can be administered to people exposed to chickenpox to prevent or modify symptoms of the infection.

varicella-zoster virus (VZV) [L, *varius,* diverse; Gk, *zoster,* girdle; L, *virus,* poison], a member of the herpesvirus family, which causes the diseases varicella (chickenpox) with primary infection and herpes zoster (shingles) of the virus reactivator. The virus has been isolated from vesicle fluid in chickenpox, is highly contagious, and may be spread by direct contact or droplets. Dried crusts of skin lesions do not contain active virus particles. Herpes

zoster is produced by reactivation of latent varicella virus, usually several years after the initial infection.

varicelliform /ver'isel'ifôrm/, resembling the rash of chickenpox.

varicocele /ver'əkōsēl'/ [L, *varix,* varicose vein; Gk, *kele,* tumor], a dilation of the pampiniform venous complex of the spermatic cord. The varicocele forms a soft, elastic swelling that can cause pain.

varicose /ver'əkōs/ [L, *varix*], abnormally swollen or dilated.

varicose aneurysm, a blood-filled, saclike projection that connects an artery and one or several veins and that is formed from a localized dilation of the adjoining vessels.

varicose vein, a tortuous, dilated vein with incompetent valves. Causes include congenitally defective valves, thrombophlebitis, pregnancy, and obesity. Varicose veins are common, especially in women, and are usually painless. The saphenous veins of the legs are most often affected. Initially the vein may be palpated but invisible, and the individual may have a feeling of heaviness in the legs that gets worse at night and in hot weather. A dull aching, burning, and cramping also occur after prolonged standing or walking, during menses, when fatigued, and at night. Over time the veins can be seen as dilated, purplish, and ropelike. Venous insufficiency and venous stasis ulcers are the two most common complications. Conservative treatment involves elevation and rest of affected extremity, application of lightweight compression hosiery, and avoidance of prolonged standing. Sclerotherapy may be used for removal of unsightly superficial varicosities. Stripping and ligation may be indicated for chronic venous insufficiency, recurrent thrombophlebitis, and persistent varicosities that are painful or ulcerated and are not responsive to conservative treatment. Long-term management of varicosities is directed at improving circulation and preventing stasis; relieving discomfort; and preventing complications.

varicosis /ver'ikō'sis/ [L, *varix;* Gk, *osis,* condition], a common condition characterized by one or more tortuous, abnormally dilated vessels usually in the legs or the lower trunk. It most often occurs in persons between 30 and 60 years of age. Symptoms include pain and muscle cramps with a feeling of fullness and heaviness in the legs. Dilation of superficial veins is often evident before the condition produces discomfort.

varicosity /ver'ikos'itē/, **1.** an abnormal condition, usually of a vein, characterized by swelling and tortuosity. **2.** a vein in this condition.

variegate /ver′ē·əgāt′/ [L, *varius,* diverse], having characteristics that vary, especially as to color.

variegate porphyria (VP), an uncommon form of hepatic porphyria, characterized by skin lesions and photosensitivity. The condition may be congenital or acquired.

varioloid /ver′ē·əloid′/ [L, *varius;* Gk, *eidos,* form], **1.** resembling smallpox. **2.** a mild form of smallpox in a vaccinated person or one who has previously had the disease.

varix /ver′iks/ *pl.* **varices** [L, varicose vein], a tortuous, dilated vein, artery, or lymphatic vessel.

varnish /vär′nish/, a solution of natural resins and gums or concentrated fluoride used as a protective coating over the surfaces of a dental cavity preparation before restorative material is applied or over a tooth surface after sealing and root planing.

varus /ver′əs/ [L, bent], describing an abnormal position in which a part of a limb is turned inward toward the midline such as the great toe in hallux varus.

vas /vas/ *pl.* **vasa** [L, vessel], any one of the many vessels of the body, especially those that convey blood, lymph, or spermatozoa.

vas afferens, a small arteriole that supplies blood to a renal glomerulus.

vasa vasorum [L, *vas,* vessel], small blood vessels that supply the walls of the arteries and veins.

vascular /vas′kyələr/ [L, *vasculum,* little vessel], pertaining to a blood vessel.

vascular access device (VAD), an indwelling catheter, cannula, or other instrumentation used to obtain venous or arterial access.

vascular death, that caused by vascular pathologic conditions.

vascular endothelial growth factor (VEGF), a peptide factor that stimulates the proliferation of cells of the endothelium of blood vessels. It promotes tissue vascularization and is important in blood vessel formation in tumors.

vascular endothelium, the endothelium that lines the blood vessels.

vascular fasciculus, a fasciculus in the zona externa of the renal medulla.

vascular headache, a classification for certain types of headaches, based on a proposed cause involving abnormal functioning of the blood vessels or vascular system of the brain. Included are migraine, cluster headache, toxic headache, and headache caused by elevated BP.

vascular insufficiency, inadequate peripheral blood flow. Causes include occlusion of vessels by atherosclerotic plaques, thrombi, or emboli; damaged, diseased, or intrinsically weak vascular walls; arteriovenous fistulas; hematologic hypercoagulability; and heavy smoking. Signs of vascular insufficiency include pale, cyanotic, or mottled skin over the affected area; swelling of an extremity; absent or reduced tactile sensation; tingling; diminished sense of temperature; muscle pain, such as intermittent claudication in the calf; and, in advanced disease, ulcers and atrophy of muscles in the involved extremity. Treatment may include a diet low in saturated fats, moderate exercise, sleeping on a firm mattress, avoidance of tobacco products, proper standing or sitting posture, elevation of the involved extremity, use of a vasodilating drug, and, if indicated, repair of an arteriovenous fistula or aneurysm or bypass surgery.

vascularity /vas′kyəler′itē/ [L, *vasculum,* little vessel], the state of blood vessel development and functioning in an organ or tissue.

vascularization /vas′kyələr′īzā′shən/, the process by which body tissue develops proliferating capillaries. It may be natural or induced by surgical techniques.— **vascularize,** *v.*

vascularized graft, a graft in which the blood supply to the grafted tissue is maintained, as with a pedicle flap.

vascular leiomyoma, a neoplasm that has developed from smooth muscle fibers of a blood vessel.

vascular pole of renal corpuscle, the end of the corpuscle and glomerulus where afferent arterioles enter and efferent arterioles exit.

vascular sclerosis [L, *vasculum;* Gk, *skerosis,* hardening], a condition of hyaline degeneration of the blood vessels with hypertrophy of the tunica media and subintimal fibrosis. There also may be a weakening and loss of elasticity in the artery walls.

vascular tumor, an aneurysm.

vascular ultrasound studies, ultrasound studies of the extremities, used to identify vein or artery occlusion.

vasculature /vas′kyəlā′chər/ [L, *vasculum*], the blood vessels in an organ or tissue.

vasculitis /vas′kyəlī′tis/, inflammation of the blood vessels. It may be caused by a systemic disease or an allergic reaction.

vasculogenic impotence /vas′kyələjen′ik/ [L, *vasculum,* little vessel; Gk, *genein,* to produce; L, *in* + *potentia,* power], impotence resulting from an inadequate supply of arterial blood to the penis or venous leakage.

vas deferens /def′ərənz/ *pl.* **vasa deferentia** [L, *vas* + *deferens,* carrying away], the extension of the epididymis of the testis that ascends from the scrotum into the abdominal cavity and joins the seminal vesicle to form the ejaculatory duct.

vasectomy /vasek′təmē/ [L, *vas;* Gk, *ektomē,* excision], a procedure for male sterilization involving the bilateral surgical removal of a part of the vas deferens. Vasectomy is most commonly performed

V

at an outpatient surgery center using local anesthesia.

vasoactive /vā′zō·ak′tiv/ [L, *vas* + *activus*, active], of a drug, tending to cause vasodilation or vasoconstriction.

vasoactive intestinal polypeptide (VIP), a glucagon-secretin hormone found in the pancreas, intestine, and CNS. The hormone stimulates insulin and glucagon release. Gastric secretion, gastric motility, and peripheral vasodilation, as well as hyperglycemia by hepatic glycogenolysis, are inhibited.

vasoconstriction [L, *vas* + *constringere*, to tighten], a decrease in the diameter of a blood vessel. It plays an important role in the control of BP and the distribution of blood throughout the body.—**vasoconstrictive**, *adj.*

vasoconstrictive /-kənstrik′tiv/ [L, *vas*, vessel, *constringere*, to draw tight], able to cause a constriction of blood vessels.

vasoconstrictor /-kənstrik′tər/ [L, *vas* + *constringere*], **1.** pertaining to a process, condition, or substance that causes the constriction of blood vessels. **2.** an agent that promotes vasoconstriction. Cold, fear, stress, and nicotine are common exogenous vasoconstrictors. Internally secreted epinephrine and norepinephrine cause blood vessels to contract by stimulating alpha-adrenergic receptors on the vascular smooth muscle. Alpha-adrenergic sympathomimetic drugs also cause vasoconstriction, and several of these agents are used for this action in maintaining BP during anesthesia and in treating pronounced hypotension resulting from hemorrhage, MI, septicemia, sympathectomy, or drug reactions.

vasodepressor syncope, a sudden loss of consciousness, resulting from cerebral ischemia; secondary to decreased cardiac output, peripheral vasodilation, and bradycardia. The condition may be triggered by pain, fright, or trauma and accompanied by symptoms of nausea, pallor, and perspiration.

vasodilation /-dīlā′shən/ [L, *vas* + *dilatare*], an increase in the diameter of a blood vessel. It is caused by a relaxation of the smooth muscles in the vessel wall.

vasodilator /-dī′lātər/ [L, *vas* + *dilatare*], a nerve or agent that causes dilation of blood vessels by promoting the relaxation of vascular smooth muscle. Chemical vasodilators have been useful in the treatment of acute heart failure in MI, in cases associated with severe mitral regurgitation, and in failure resulting from myocardial disease.

vasoganglion /-gang′glē·on/, a spherical mass of small blood vessels.

vasogenic shock /-jen′ik/ [L, *vas* + *genein*, to produce; Fr, *choc*], shock resulting from peripheral vascular dilation produced by factors such as toxins that directly affect the blood vessels.

vasohypertonic /-hī′pərton′ik/, causing constriction of blood vessels.

vasoinhibitor /-inhib′itər/, an agent that opposes the action of vasomotor nerves, thereby causing arterial dilation and reduced BP.

vasoinhibitory /-inhib′itōr′ē/, inhibiting the activity of vasomotor nerves.

vasomotor /-mō′tər/ [L, *vas* + *movere*, to move], pertaining to the nerves and muscles that control the diameter of the blood vessels. Circularly arranged smooth muscle fibers of arteries and arterioles can contract, causing vasoconstriction, or they can relax, causing vasodilation.

vasomotor center, a collection of cell bodies in the medulla oblongata of the brain that regulates or modulates BP and cardiac function, primarily via the autonomic nervous system.

vasomotor epilepsy, a form of epilepsy characterized by episodes of autonomic dysfunction and extreme contractions of the arteries.

vasomotor paralysis, hypotonia of blood vessels caused by blockage of activity in nerves that stimulate vascular constriction.

vasomotor reflex [L, *vas*, vessel, *movere*, to move, *reflectere*, to bend back], any reflex response of the circulatory system caused by stimulation of vasodilator or vasoconstrictive nerves.

vasomotor rhinitis, chronic rhinitis and nasal obstruction, without allergy or infection, characterized by sneezing, rhinorrhea, nasal obstruction, and vascular engorgement of the mucous membranes of the nose.

vasomotor spasm, an involuntary contraction of the muscles of the small arteries.

vasomotor system, the part of the nervous system that controls the constriction and dilation of the blood vessels.

vasoparesis, a mild form of vasomotor paralysis.

vasospasm, a spasm in a blood vessel.

vasospastic /-spas′tik/, **1.** relating to a spasmodic constriction of a blood vessel. **2.** any agent that produces spasms of the blood vessels.

vasospastic angina, chest pain caused by spasms of the coronary arteries. It has features that differ from those of angina pectoris.

vasostimulation /-stim′yəlā′shən/ [L, *vas*, vessel, *stimulare*, to incite], the promotion of vasomotor activity.

Vasotec, a trademark for an angiotensin-converting enzyme inhibitor (enalapril maleate).

vasovagal reflex, a stimulation of the vagus nerve by reflex in which irritation of the larynx or the trachea results in slowing of the pulse rate.

vasovagal syncope, a sudden LOC resulting from cerebral ischemia, secondary to decreased cardiac output, peripheral vasodilation, and bradycardia and associated with vagal activity. The condition may be triggered by pain, fright, or trauma and is accompanied by symptoms of nausea, pallor, and perspiration.

vasovasostomy /vas′ōvəsos′təmē/ [L, *vas* + *vas*; Gk, *stoma,* mouth], a surgical procedure in which the function of the vas deferens on each side of the testes is restored, having been cut and ligated in a preceding vasectomy. The procedure is performed if a man wants to regain his fertility.

vastus intermedius /vas′təs/ [L, *vastus,* enormous, *inter,* between, *mediare,* to divide], one of the four muscles of the quadriceps femoris group, situated in the center of the thigh. It functions with the other three muscles of the quadriceps to extend the leg.

vastus lateralis, the largest of the four muscles of the quadriceps femoris group, situated on the lateral side of the thigh. It functions to help extend the leg.

vastus medialis, one of the four muscles of the quadriceps femoris group, situated in the medial part of the thigh. It functions in combination with other parts of the quadriceps femoris to extend the leg.

VATER complex, a nonrandom association of congenital anomalies consisting of vertebral defects, imperforate anus, tracheoesophageal fistula, and radial and renal dysplasia.

Vater-Pacini corpuscles /fä′tər päsē′nē/ [Abraham Vater, German anatomist, 1684–1751; Filippo Pacini, Italian anatomist, 1812–1883], kinesioceptors located in joint capsules and ligaments. They are believed to have a protective function of signaling the cerebral cortex when a joint has reached the end position of its range.

Vater's ampulla, a flask-shaped dilation at the end of the common bile duct where the duct joins with the duodenum.

VBP, an anticancer drug combination of vinBLAStine, bleomycin, and cisplatin.

VC, abbreviation for **vital capacity.**

VCO₂, symbol for carbon dioxide output per unit of time.

VCU, abbreviation for **voiding cystourethrography.**

VD, abbreviation for *venereal disease.*

V deflection /diflek′shən/, a deflection on the His bundle electrogram that represents ventricular activation.

VDRL, abbreviation for *Venereal Disease Research Laboratories.*

VDRL test, abbreviation for *Venereal Disease Research Laboratory test,* a serologic flocculation test for syphilis. It is also positive in other treponemal diseases such as yaws.

V̇e, symbol for *expired volume;* V̇E denotes *volume expired in 1 minute.*

Vectibix, a trademark for panitumumab.

vector /vek′tər/ [L, carrier], 1. a quantity having direction and magnitude, usually depicted by a straight arrow. The length of the arrow represents magnitude and the head represents direction. 2. a carrier, especially one that transmits disease. A biologic vector is usually an arthropod in which the infecting organism completes part of its life cycle. A mechanical vector transmits the infecting organism from one host to another but is not essential to the life cycle of the parasite. 3. a retrovirus that has been modified by alteration of its genetic component. Through recombinant DNA techniques, genes that cause harmful effects such as cancer are removed, and genes that mediate synthesis of essential enzymes are added. The vector can then be injected into a patient who suffers from an enzyme deficiency.—**vector,** *v.,* **vectorial,** *adj.*

vectorcardiogram /-kär′dē-əgram′/ [L, *vector,* carrier; Gk, *kardia,* heart, *gramma,* record], a tracing of the direction and magnitude of the heart's electric activity during a cardiac cycle. It is produced by an oscilloscope, which simultaneously records three standard leads.

vectorcardiography /-kär′dē-og′rəfē/ [L, *vector,* carrier; Gk, *kardia,* heart, *graphein,* to record], a method of recording the direction and magnitude of the heart's electric activity.

vecuronium bromide /vek′yərō′nē-əm/, a neuromuscular blocking drug. It is used as an adjunct to general anesthesia, to facilitate endotracheal intubation, and to relax skeletal muscles during surgery or mechanical ventilation.

VEE, abbreviation for *Venezuelan equine encephalitis.*

Veetids, a trademark for an antibacterial (penicillin V potassium).

veganism /veg′əniz′əm/ [L, *vegetare,* to grow, *ismus,* practice], the adherence to a strict vegetarian diet, with the exclusion of all protein of animal origin.

vegetable albumin /vej′(i)təbəl/, albumin protein produced in plants.

vegetal pole /vej′ətəl/ [L, *vegetare* + *polus,* pole], the relatively inactive part of an ovum where the yolk is situated, usually opposite the animal pole.

vegetarian /vej′əter′ē-ən/ [L, *vegetare*], a person who eats only foods of plant origin, including fruits, grains, and nuts. Many vegetarians eat eggs and milk products but avoid all animal flesh.

vegetarianism /vej′əter·ē-əniz′əm/, the theory or practice of eating only foods of plant origin, including fruits, grains, and nuts.

vegetation /vej'ətā'shən/, an abnormal growth of tissue around a valve, composed of fibrin, platelets, and bacteria.

vegetative /vej'ətā'tiv, vej'ətətiv/ [L, *vegetare*], **1.** pertaining to nutrition and growth. **2.** pertaining to the plant kingdom. **3.** denoting involuntary function, as produced by the parasympathetic nervous system. **4.** resting, not active; denoting the stage of the cell cycle in which the cell is not replicating. **5.** leading a secluded, dull existence without social or intellectual activity. **6.** in psychiatry, emotionally withdrawn and passive, as may occur in schizophrenia and depression or in unipolar depression in severe cases.—**vegetate,** *v.*

vegetative endocarditis [L, *vegetare*, to grow; Gk, *endon*, within, *kardia*, heart, *itis*, inflammation], a subacute form of bacterial endocarditis characterized by vegetation on the heart valves. The vegetation may cause ulceration and perforation of the heart valve cusps.

vegetative state, a physical condition in which a previously comatose patient continues to be unable to communicate or respond to stimuli. The eyes may be open, but, because of senile brain disease, cerebral arteriosclerosis, or injury to the cerebral cortex, the patient remains immobile and must be fed and toileted, and all other physical needs attended to.

VEGF, abbreviation for **vascular endothelial growth factor.**

vehicle /vē'ikəl/ [L, *vehiculum*, conveyance], **1.** an inert substance with which a medication is mixed to facilitate measurement and administration or application. **2.** any fluid or structure in the body that passively conveys a stimulus. **3.** any substance, such as food or water, that can serve as a mode of transmission for infectious agents.

vehicle safety promotion, a nursing intervention from the Nursing Interventions Classification (NIC) defined as assisting individuals, families, and communities to increase awareness of measures to reduce unintentional injuries in motorized and nonmotorized vehicles.

veiling glare, loss of contrast due to light scattering within a lens system, as in a fluoroscopic image intensifier.

Veillonella /vā'yənel'ə/ [Adrien Veillon, French bacteriologist, 1864–1931], a genus of gram-negative anaerobic bacteria. The species *Veillonella parvula* is normally present in the alimentary tract, especially in the mouth.

Veillon tube /vāyōn'/, a transparent tube, the ends of which are closed with removable stoppers, one cotton and one rubber. It is used for the laboratory growth of bacteriologic cultures.

vein (v) /vān/ [L, *vena*], any one of the many vessels that convey blood from the capillaries as part of the pulmonary venous system, the systemic venous network, or the portal venous complex. Most of the veins of the body are systemic veins that convey blood from the whole body (except the lungs) to the right atrium of the heart. Each vein is a macroscopic structure enclosed in three layers of different kinds of tissue homologous with the layers of the heart. Veins have thinner coatings and are less elastic than arteries and collapse when cut. They also contain semilunar valves at various intervals.

vein ligation and stripping, a surgical procedure consisting of the ligation of the saphenous vein and its removal from groin to ankle.

vein lumen, the central opening through which blood flows in a vein.

veins of the vertebral column, the veins that drain the blood from the vertebral column, adjacent muscles, and meninges of the spinal cord. These veins form plexuses that are divided into internal and external groups according to their locations inside or outside the vertebral canal.

vein wrapping, the wrapping of an injured nerve with an autologous vein (usually saphenous vein) graft to provide insulation and cushioning following decompression in treatment of entrapment neuropathy.

Velban, a trademark for an antineoplastic (vinBLASTine sulfate).

Velcade, a trademark for bortezomib.

Velcro, a trademark for a type of fastening device with a surface of tiny hooks that adhere to the opposite side, used mainly on fabric products.

velocardiofacial syndrome /vel'ōkär'dē·ō fā'shəl/, an autosomal-dominant syndrome of cardiac defects and characteristic craniofacial abnormalities including cleft palate, jaw abnormalities, and prominent nose. It is often associated with abnormalities of chromosome 22. Learning disabilities occur often; short stature, slender hyperextensible hands and digits, scoliosis, mental retardation, inguinal hernia, auricular abnormalities, and microcephaly occur less frequently.

velocity /vəlos'itē/ [L, *velox*, quick], the rate of change in the position of a body moving in a particular direction. Velocity along a straight line is linear velocity. Angular velocity is that of a body in circular motion.

velocity of growth, the rate of growth or change in growth measurements over a period of time.

velocity of ultrasound, the speed of ultrasound waves in a particular medium. The velocity varies from 331 meters per second (m/sec) in air to 1450 m/sec in fat, 1570 m/sec in blood, and 4080 m/sec in the skull.

velocity spectrum rehabilitation, a rehabilitation program that uses strength training at multiple speeds of movement from slow to fast.

velopharyngeal closure, closure of the nasal airway by the elevation of the posterior and contraction of the posterior and lateral pharyngeal wall. It is needed for vowels and for all consonants except /n/, /m/, and /ng/.

velopharyngeal insufficiency, an abnormal condition resulting from a congenital defect in the structure of the velopharyngeal sphincter. Closure of the oral cavity beneath the nasal passages is not complete. Food may be regurgitated through the nose, and speech is impaired.

Velosef, a trademark for a cephalosporin antibiotic (cephradine).

Velpeau's bandage /velpōz'/ [Alfred A.L.M. Velpeau, French surgeon, 1795–1867], a roller bandage that immobilizes the elbow and shoulder by holding the brachium against the side and the flexed forearm on the chest.

vena cava /vē'nə kā'və/ *pl.* **venae cavae** [L, *vena*, vein, *cavum*, cavity], one of two large veins returning blood from the peripheral circulation to the right atrium of the heart.—**vena caval,** *adj.*

vena caval foramen, an opening in the diaphragm through which the inferior vena cava and vagus nerve pass.

vena comitans *pl.* **venae comitantes,** one of the deep paired veins that accompany the smaller arteries on each side of the artery. The three vessels are wrapped together in one sheath.

veneer /vənir'/ [Fr, *fournir*, to furnish], a layer of tooth-colored material, usually porcelain or acrylic, attached to the surface of a crown or artificial tooth by direct fusion.

venereal /vənir'ē-əl/ [L, *Venus*, goddess of love], pertaining to or caused by sexual intercourse or genital contact.

venereal bubo [L, *Venus*, goddess of love; Gk, *boubon*, groin], a swollen, inflamed lymph gland or node, usually in the groin and sometimes purulent. It is associated with an STD.

venereal urethritis, an inflammation of the male urethra caused by sexually transmitted microorganisms.

venereologist /vənir'ē-ol'əjist/ [L, *Venus*, goddess of love; Gk, *logos*, science], a health professional who specializes in the study of the causes and treatments of venereal diseases.

venereology /-ol'əjē/, the study of the causes and treatments of venereal diseases. —**venereologic,** *adj.*, **venereologist,** *n.*

venerupin poisoning /ven'əroō'pin/, a potentially fatal form of shellfish poisoning that results from ingestion of oysters or clams contaminated with venerupin, a toxin that causes impaired liver functioning, GI distress, and leukocytosis. About one third of the cases are fatal.

Venezuelan hemorrhagic fever, a hemorrhagic fever caused by an arenavirus transmitted to humans by contact with or inhalation of aerosolized excreta of infected rodents. The disease occurs in west central Venezuela, primarily in settlers moving into areas of cleared forest. Initially it is characterized by the gradual onset of fever, malaise, myalgia, and anorexia, followed by prostration, dizziness, headache, back pain, and GI disturbances. Bleeding of the gums is a typical finding, and there may be petechiae on the palate and axillae. Neurologic manifestations such as tremor of tongue and hands, diminished deep tendon reflexes, lethargy, and hyperesthesia often occur. Treatment is supportive, with careful attention to fluid and electrolyte balance.

venipuncture /ven'əpungk'chər/ [L, *vena* + *pungere*, to prick], the transcutaneous puncture of a vein by a sharp rigid stylet or cannula carrying a flexible plastic catheter or by a steel needle attached to a syringe or catheter. It is done to withdraw a specimen of blood, perform a phlebotomy, instill a medication, start an IV infusion, or inject a radiopaque substance for radiologic examination of a part or system of the body. Aseptic technique is required to avoid infection. A quick, skillful insertion is nearly painless for the patient. Specific sequelae to venipuncture vary with the techniques and equipment used.

venoatrial /vē'nō-ā'trē-əl/, pertaining to either vena cava and the right atrium.

venogenic impotence, vasculogenic impotence caused by a disorder in the veins draining the penis, such as a failure to maintain venous occlusion.

venom /ven'əm/ [L, *venenum*, poison], a toxic fluid substance secreted by some snakes, arthropods, and other animals and transmitted by their stings or bites.

venom extract therapy, the administration of antivenin as prophylaxis against the toxic effects of the bite of a specific poisonous snake or spider or other venomous animal.

venom immunotherapy, the reduction of sensitivity to a specific venom by the administration of gradually increasing amounts of that venom.

venomous snake /ven'əməs/, a snake that secretes a poison.

venospasm /vēn'əspaz'əm/ [L, *vena*, vein; Gk, *spasmos*, spasm], a spasmodic constriction of a vein.

venothrombotic /vē'nəthrombot'ik/, producing a venous thrombus.

venotomy /vēnot'əmē/, the surgical opening of a vein.

venous, pertaining to a vein.

venous access device, a catheter designed for continuous access to the venous system. Such devices may be required for long-term parenteral feeding or the administration of IV fluids or medications for a period of several days.

venous access device (VAD) maintenance, a nursing intervention from the Nursing Interventions Classification (NIC) defined as management of the patient with prolonged venous access via tunneled and nontunneled (percutaneous) catheters and implanted ports.

venous blood (v) [L, *vena,* vein; AS, *blod*], dark red deoxygenated blood that has passed from the left ventricle through the systemic circulation en route to the right atrium.

venous blood gas [L, *venosus,* full of veins; AS, *blod*; Gk, *chaos,* gas], the oxygen and carbon dioxide levels in venous blood. Venous blood gas is measured by various methods to assess the adequacy of oxygenation and ventilation and to determine the acid-base status. The oxygen tension of venous blood normally averages 40 mm Hg; the dissolved oxygen content, 0.1% by volume; the total oxygen content, 15.2%; and the oxygen saturation of venous hemoglobin, 75%. The carbon dioxide tension normally averages 46 mm Hg; the dissolved carbon dioxide content, 2.9% by volume; and the total carbon dioxide content, 50%. The normal average pH of venous plasma is 7.37.

venous capillaries [L, *vena,* vein, *capillaris,* hairlike], capillaries that terminate in venules.

venous circulation [L, *vena,* vein, *circulare,* to go around], the movement of blood from the venules, which drain deoxygenated blood from the capillaries, through the veins to the vena cava, and from there through the right atrium and ventricle to the pulmonary circulation of the lungs.

venous cutdown, a small surgical incision made in a vein of a patient who has suffered vascular collapse to permit the introduction of IV fluids or drugs. A cutdown also may be performed for the insertion of a cannula for the withdrawal of blood.

venous foramen, an aperture in the greater wing of the sphenoid bone, through which a small vein passes from the cavernous sinus.

venous hemorrhage, the escape of blood from a vein.

venous hum, a continuous murmur heard on auscultation over the major veins at the base of the neck and around the umbilicus. It is most audible in the neck when the patient is anemic, upright, and looking to the contralateral side.

venous insufficiency, an abnormal circulatory condition characterized by decreased return of venous blood from the legs to the trunk of the body. Edema is usually the first sign of the condition. Treatment usually consists of elevation of the legs, use of elastic hose, and correction of the underlying condition.

venous lake, small benign blue-purple sessile, compressible papules or blebs seen most often on the lips, ears, and face of elderly persons. Histologically, they represent dilated capillaries filled with RBCs and lined with flattened endothelial cells.

venous ligation, the ligation of varicose veins whose valves are ineffective, performed to remove weakened parts of tissues in which thrombi might lodge. During surgery the saphenous vein is ligated at the groin, where it joins the femoral vein. A wire device, called a stripper, is threaded through the lumen of the vein from groin to ankle. The wire and the vein are then pulled from the groin incision.

venous occlusion, the blocking of venous return. It occurs naturally in the penis during an erection or it may be induced artificially in a part, such as in the arm, during venous occlusion plethysmography.

venous plethysmography, a manometric test that measures changes in the volume of an extremity. It is usually performed on a leg to exclude deep-vein thrombosis.

venous pressure, the BP in the veins. It is elevated in CHF, acute or chronic constrictive pericarditis, and venous obstruction caused by a clot or external pressure against a vein. Indications of increased venous pressure are continued distension of veins on the back of the hand when it is raised above the sternal notch and distension of the neck veins when the individual is sitting with the head elevated 30 to 45 degrees.

venous pulse, the pulse of a vein usually palpated over the internal or external jugular veins in the neck. The pulse in the jugular vein is taken to evaluate the pressure of the pulse and the form of the pressure wave.

venous return, the return of blood to the heart via the superior and inferior vena cava and the coronary sinus.

venous sinus, any one of many sinuses that collect blood from the dura mater and drain it into the internal jugular vein. Each sinus is formed by the separation of the two layers of the dura mater.

venous stasis, a disorder in which the normal flow of blood through a vein is slowed or halted.

venous thrombosis, a condition characterized by the presence of a clot in a vein in which the wall of the vessel is not inflamed. Pain, swelling, and inflammation may follow if the vein is significantly occluded.

venous valves, any of the small cusps or folds found in the tunica intima of many veins, serving to prevent backflow of blood.

ventilate /ven'tilāt/ [L, *ventilare*, to fan], **1.** to provide with fresh air. **2.** to provide the alveoli of the lungs with air from the atmosphere and to aerate or oxygenate blood in the pulmonary capillaries. **3.** to open discussion of something, such as one's feelings. —**ventilatory**, *adj.*

ventilation, the process by which gases are moved into and out of the lungs. —**ventilatory,** *adj.*

ventilation assistance, a nursing intervention from the Nursing Interventions Classification (NIC) defined as promotion of an optimal spontaneous breathing pattern that maximizes oxygen and carbon dioxide exchange in the lungs.

ventilation lung scan, a radiographic examination of the lungs, performed while the patient inhales a radioactive gas as a contrast medium and the lungs are scanned to detect nonfunctional or impaired lung areas or other abnormalities.

ventilation-perfusion defect, a disorder in which one or more areas of the lungs receive air but no blood flow or receive blood flow but no air.

ventilation/perfusion (V/Q) ratio, the ratio of pulmonary alveolar ventilation to pulmonary capillary perfusion, both quantities expressed in the same units.

ventilator /ven'tilā'tər/, any of several devices used in respiratory therapy to provide assisted respiration and intensive positive-pressure breathing.

ventilator-associated pneumonia, the most common type of nosocomial pneumonia, a frequently fatal type seen in patients breathing with a ventilator; it is usually caused by aspiration of contaminated secretions or stomach contents.

ventilatory compliance /ven'tilətôr'ē/, the sum of the dynamic compliance of the lung and the compliance of the thoracic cage.

ventilatory rate [L, *ventilare,* to fan, *ratum,* to calculate], the volume of air passing into and out of the lungs per minute.

ventilatory standstill [L, *ventilare,* to fan; AS, *standan* + *stille*], the complete cessation of breathing activity.

venting [Fr, *vent,* breath], in IV therapy, a method for allowing air to enter the vacuum of the IV bottle and displace the IV solution as it flows out. Glass IV bottles are usually equipped with a venting tube attached to the primary IV tubing or to a vent port incorporated with the bottle stopper. Venting is not required with a plastic IV bag, because the bag collapses as the fluid runs out.

Ventolin, a trademark for a bronchodilator (albuterol).

ventral /ven'trəl/ [L, *venter,* belly], pertaining to a position toward the anterior surface of the body; frontward.

ventral horn, the anterior columns of the gray substance of the spinal cord.

ventral recumbent, a prone position.

ventral root [L, *venter,* belly; AS, *rot*], the anterior or motor division of each spinal nerve.

ventricle /ven'trikəl/ [L, *ventriculus,* little belly], a small cavity, such as the right and left ventricles of the heart or one of the cavities filled with CSF in the brain.

ventricles of the brain, the cavities within the brain that are filled with CSF, including the two lateral, the third, and (linked by the aqueduct) the fourth ventricles.

ventricular /ventrik'yələr/ [L, *ventriculus,* little belly], pertaining to a ventricle.

ventricular aneurysm, a localized dilation or saccular protrusion in the wall of a ventricle, occurring most often after an MI. Scar tissue is formed in response to the inflammatory changes of the infarction and weakens the myocardium, allowing its walls to bulge outward when the ventricle contracts.

ventricular bigeminy [L, *ventriculus* + *bis* + *geminus,* twin], a cardiac arrhythmia in which every other beat consists of a premature ventricular beat.

ventricular block [L, *ventriculus;* OFr, *bloc*], an obstruction of the flow of CSF. Causes usually are closure of the foramina of Magendie or Luschka. The condition results in a distension of the brain ventricles because of an increased accumulation of CSF.

ventricular compliance, a property of a heart ventricle in its resting state that determines the relation between the filling of the ventricle and its diastolic pressure.

ventricular dysfunction, an abnormality in the contraction of the ventricles or the motion of the calls.

ventricular ejection [L, *ventriculus* + *ejicere,* to cast out], the forceful expulsion of blood from the ventricles into the aorta and the pulmonary arteries.

ventricular escape [L, *ventriculus;* OFr, *escaper*], the discharge of a normal ventricular pacemaker cell when the sinus or junctional rate of discharge falls below that of the ventricular pacemaker cells.

ventricular extrasystole, a premature beat arising from a ventricle.

ventricular fibrillation (VF), a cardiac arrhythmia marked by rapid depolarizations of the ventricular myocardium. The condition is characterized by a complete lack of organized electric activity, and of ventricular ejection. BP falls to zero, resulting in unconsciousness. Death may occur within 4 minutes. CPR must be initiated immediately, with defibrillation and resuscitative medications given according to ACLS protocol.

ventricular flutter, a condition of very rapid contractions of the ventricles of the heart.

V

ECGs show poorly defined QRS complexes occurring at a rate of 250 beats/min or higher. Cardiac output is severely compromised or absent. The condition is fatal if untreated.

ventricular gallop, an abnormal low-pitched extra heart sound (S₃) heard early in diastole. When it is heard in an older person with heart disease, it indicates myocardial failure.

ventricular gradient, the sum of the areas within the QRS complex and the T wave on the ECG.

ventricular hypertrophy [L, *ventriculus;* Gk, *hyper,* excessive, *trophe,* nourishment], abnormal enlargement of the heart ventricles. It is often caused by hypertension, a valvular disease, or heart failure.

ventricular remodeling, progressive myocardial ventricular dilation, eccentric ventricular hypertrophy, and distortion of left ventricular geometry that persist in the noninfarcted myocardium after an MI has healed. It is associated with impaired functional capacity, CHF, and premature death.

ventricular rhythm [L, *ventriculus;* Gk, *rhythmos*], the recurrent beating of the ventricles, normal or abnormal.

ventricular septal defect (VSD), the most common congenital cardiac anomaly, characterized by one or more abnormal openings in the septum separating the ventricles. The openings permit oxygenated blood to flow from the left to the right ventricle and to recirculate through the pulmonary artery and lungs. Small defects may close spontaneously. Large defects may lead to bacterial endocarditis, lower respiratory tract infections, pulmonary vascular obstructive disease, aortic regurgitation, or CHF.

ventricular standstill, a complete cessation of electric and mechanical activity in the ventricles of the heart.

ventricular systole [L, *ventriculus;* Gk, *systole,* contraction], the contraction of the heart ventricles. It begins with the first heart sound.

ventricular tachycardia, tachycardia of at least three consecutive ventricular complexes with a rate greater than 100 beats/min. It usually originates in a focus distal to the branching of the atrioventricular bundle.

ventriculoatrial shunt /ventrik′yəlō-ā′trē·əl/ [L, *ventriculus* + *atrium,* hall; ME, *shunten*], a surgically created passageway, consisting of plastic tubing and one-way valves, implanted between a cerebral ventricle and the right atrium of the heart to drain excess CSF from the brain in hydrocephalus.

ventriculocisternostomy /-sis′tərnos′təmē/ [L, *ventriculus* + *cisterna,* vessel; Gk, *stoma,* mouth], a surgical procedure performed to treat hydrocephalus. An opening is created that allows CSF to drain through a shunt from the ventricles of the brain into the cisterna magna.

ventriculofallopian tube shunt /-fəlō′pē·ən/, a surgical procedure with limited effectiveness for diverting CSF into the peritoneal cavity. This procedure is used to correct both the obstructive and the communicating types of hydrocephalus.

ventriculogram /ventrik′yəlōgram′/, a radiograph of the cerebral ventricles or the ventricles of the heart.

ventriculography /ventrik′yəlog′rəfē/ [L, *ventriculus;* Gk, *graphein,* to record], **1.** the radiographic examination of a ventricle of the heart after injection of a radiopaque contrast medium. **2.** the radiographic examination of the head after CSF removal from the cerebral ventricles and its replacement by a contrast medium, usually air.

ventriculoperitoneal shunt /-per′itənē′əl/ [L, *ventriculus;* Gk, *peri,* around, *teinein,* to stretch; ME, *shunten*], a surgically created passageway consisting of plastic tubing and one-way valves between a cerebral ventricle and the peritoneum for the draining of excess CSF from the brain in hydrocephalus.

ventriculoperitoneostomy /ventrik′yəlō per′itō′nē·os′təmē/ [L, *ventriculus;* Gk, *peri,* around, *teinein,* to stretch, *stoma,* mouth], a surgical procedure for temporarily diverting CSF in hydrocephalus, usually in the newborn. In this procedure a polyethylene tube is passed from the lateral ventricle subcutaneously down the dorsal spine and is reinserted into the peritoneal cavity, where the diverted fluid is absorbed.

ventriculopleural shunt /-plŏŏr′əl/ [L, *ventriculus;* Gk, *pleura,* rib; ME, *shunten*], a surgical procedure for diverting CSF from engorged ventricles in hydrocephalus, usually in the newborn. In this procedure, CSF is diverted from the lateral ventricle into the pleural cavity.

ventriculoureterostomy /ventrik′yəlō′y ŏŏ rē′təros′təmē/ [L, *ventriculus;* Gk, *oureter,* ureter, *stoma,* mouth], a surgical procedure for directing CSF into the general circulation. It is performed in the treatment of hydrocephalus, usually in the newborn. In this procedure, a polyethylene tube is passed from the lateral ventricle down the dorsal spine subcutaneously to the twelfth rib; the tube is inserted through the paraspinal muscles into a ureter.

ventriculovenous shunt, a surgically created communication between a cerebral ventricle and the internal jugular vein by a plastic tube with an in-line pressure-flow regulator, to permit drainage of CSF for relief of hydrocephalus.

ventrolateral /ven′trōlat′ərəl/, pertaining to the part of the body opposite the back and away from the midline.

ventromedial /ven´trōmē´dē·əl/, pertaining to the part of the body opposite the back and near the midline.

Venturi effect /ventōō´rē/ [Giovanni B. Venturi, Italian physicist, 1746–1822], a modification of Bernoulli's principle, which states that the pressure of a gas is reduced just beyond an obstruction or restriction in the vessel through which the gas is flowing. The effect is a factor in the design of respiratory therapy equipment for mixing medical gases.

Venturi mask, a respiratory therapy face mask designed to allow inspired air to mix with oxygen, which is supplied through a jet at a fixed concentration.

venule /ven´yōōl/ [L, *venula,* small vein], any one of the small blood vessels that gather blood from the capillary plexuses and anastomose to form the veins. —**venular,** *adj.*

VEP, abbreviation for **visual evoked potential.**

VePesid (VP-16), a trademark for an antineoplastic agent (etoposide).

verapamil /verap´əmil/, a calcium channel blocker prescribed for the treatment of vasospastic and exertional angina, supraventricular tachycardia, atrial fibrillation, and atrial flutter.

Veratrum /vərā´trəm/ [L, hellebore], a genus of poisonous herbs of the lily family. The dried rhizomes of the British and American hellebore provide alkaloids that may be used with great caution in herbalism.

verbal language /vur´bəl/ [L, *verbum,* a word, *lingua,* tongue], a culturally organized system of vocal sounds that communicates meaning between individuals.

Verdeso, a trademark for desonide.

Veregen, a trademark for **kunecatechins.**

vergence /vur´jəns/, movement of the eyes in opposite directions (convergence and divergence).

vermicide /vur´misīd/ [L, *vermis,* worm, *caedere,* to kill], an agent that kills worms, particularly those in the intestine.

vermicular /vərmik´yələr/ [L, *vermis,* worm], resembling a worm.

vermicular pulse, a small, rapid pulse that feels like a writhing worm when palpated.

vermiform /vur´mifôrm/ [L, *vermis,* worm, *forma,* form], resembling a worm.

vermiform appendix [L, *vermis + forma,* form, *appendix,* appendage], a wormlike blunt process extending from the cecum. Its length varies from 7 to 15 cm, and its diameter is about 1 cm.

vermifuge /vərmifyōōj´/ [L, *vermis + fugare,* to chase away], an agent that causes the evacuation of intestinal parasitic worms.

vermilion border /vərmil´yən/ [L, *vermillium,* bright red; OFr, *bordure,* frame], the external pinkish-to-red area of the upper and lower lips. It extends from the junction of the lips with the surrounding facial skin on the exterior to the labial mucosa within the mouth.

vermin /vur´min/ [L, *vermis,* worm], any parasitic insect such as a louse or bedbug, regarded as a destructive or disease-carrying pest.

vermis /vur´mis/ *pl.* **vermes** [L], **1.** a worm. **2.** a structure resembling a worm, such as the median lobe of the cerebellum. —**vermiform,** *adj.*

vermis cerebelli /vər´mis ser´əbel´ī/ [L, worm of cerebellum], the narrow median part of the cerebellum, between the two lateral hemispheres; the cranial or superior portion extends from the lingula to the folium vermis, and the inferior or caudal portion from the tuber vermis to the nodulus.

Vermox, a trademark for an anthelmintic (**mebendazole**).

vernal conjunctivitis /vur´nəl/ [L, *vernare,* springlike, *conjunctivus,* connecting; Gk, *itis,* inflammation], a chronic, bilateral inflammation of the conjunctiva, thought to be allergic in origin. The most common symptoms include intense itching and a crusting discharge. Topical corticosteroids may be applied, and desensitization to pollen may be helpful.

vernal keratoconjunctivitis, an ocular inflammatory disease caused by allergic reaction, often occurring in the spring but sometimes year-round. It is characterized by the presence of cobblestone-like bumps on the upper eyelid. There may also be swelling and thickening of the conjunctiva, a mucus discharge, itching, and sensitivity to light.

Verner-Morrison syndrome, a rare syndrome of profuse watery diarrhea, hypokalemia, and achlorhydria, usually associated with excess levels of vasoactive intestinal polypeptide resulting from a tumor (VIPoma) in the pancreas.

Vernet's syndrome /vernāz´/ [Maurice Vernet, French neurologist, 1887–1974], a neurologic disorder caused by injury to the ninth, tenth, and eleventh cranial nerves as they pass through the jugular foramen when leaving the skull. Symptoms include unilateral flaccid paralysis of the palatal, pharyngeal, and intrinsic laryngeal muscles and the sternocleidomastoid and trapezius muscles. The patient also experiences dysphagia, the voice is nasal and hoarse, and there may be some loss of taste sensations.

vernix caseosa /vur´niks kas´ē·ō´sə/ [Gk, resin; L, *caseus,* cheese], a grayish-white cheeselike substance, consisting of sebaceous gland secretions, lanugo, and desquamated epithelial cells, that covers the skin of the fetus and newborn.

verocytotoxin /ver´ōsī´tōtok´sin/, either of two toxins found in certain strains of

Shigella dysenteriae and *Escherichia coli,* causing a type of hemolytic uremic syndrome. Humans are infected by ingesting undercooked meat, unpasteurized milk, and foods contaminated with cattle feces.

verruca /vəroo'kə/ *pl.* **verrucae** [L, *wart*], a benign, viral, warty skin lesion with a rough, papillomatous surface. It is caused by a common contagious papovavirus. Methods of treatment include salicylic acid, cantharidin, electrodesiccation, curette excision, laser excision, and liquid nitrogen.—**verrucose, verrucous,** *adj.*

verruca plana, a small, slightly elevated, smooth, tan or flesh-colored wart, sometimes occurring in large numbers on the face, neck, back of the hands, wrists, and knees, especially in children.

verrucous carcinoma /vəroo'kəs/, a well-differentiated squamous cell neoplasm of soft tissue of the oral cavity, larynx, or genitalia. A slow-growing tumor with displacement of surrounding tissue, rather than invasion or metastasis, occurs.

verrucous dermatitis, any skin rash with wartlike lesions.

verrucous endocarditis [L, *verruca,* wart; Gk, *endon,* within, *kardia,* heart, *itis,* inflammation], a form of heart inflammation characterized by the development of wartlike growths on the heart valves.

Versed, a trademark for a parenteral central nervous system depressant (midazolam hydrochloride).

version /vur'zhən/ [L,*vertere,* to turn], the changing of the fetal position in the uterus, usually done to facilitate delivery.

version and extraction, an obstetric operation in which a fetus presenting head first is turned and delivered feet first. It is performed by reaching deeply into the uterus, grasping the feet and pulling them down, and extracting the infant. The procedure is considered outmoded and hazardous.

vertebra /vur'təbrə/ *pl.* **vertebrae** [L, *joint*], any one of the 33 bones (26 in the adult) of the spinal column, comprising the 7 cervical, 12 thoracic, 5 lumbar, 5 sacral (1 in adult), and 4 coccygeal vertebrae (1 in adult). The vertebrae, with the exception of the first and second cervical vertebrae (atlas and axis), are much alike and are composed of a body, an arch, a spinous process for muscle attachment, and pairs of pedicles and processes.

vertebral /vur'təbrəl/ [L, *vertebra, joint*], pertaining to one or more vertebrae.

vertebral angiography [L, *vertebra;* Gk, *angeion* + *graphein,* to record], the radiographic examination of blood circulation in the spinal area after the injection of radiopaque contrast medium.

vertebral arch [L, *vertebra,* joint, *arcus,* bow], the arch formed on the back of the vertebral body by the pedicles and laminae.

vertebral artery, one of a pair of arteries branching from the subclavian arteries, arising deep in the neck from the cranial and dorsal subclavian surfaces. Each vertebral artery divides into two cervical and five cranial branches, supplying deep neck muscles, the spinal cord and spinal membranes, and the cerebellum.

vertebral-basilar system, an arterial complex in which two vertebral arteries join at the base of the skull to form the basilar artery.

vertebral body, the weight-supporting, solid central part of a vertebra. The pedicles of the arch project from its dorsolateral surfaces.

vertebral canal [L, *vertebra,* joint + *canalis*], the passage formed anterior to the vertebral arches and posterior to the vertebral bodies and occupied by the spinal cord.

vertebral column, the flexible structure that forms the longitudinal axis of the skeleton. In the adult it includes 26 vertebrae arranged in a straight line from the base of the skull to the coccyx. The vertebrae are separated by intervertebral disks. They provide attachment for various muscles such as the iliocostalis thoracis and the longissimus thoracis that give the column strength and flexibility. In adults the five sacral and four coccygeal vertebrae fuse to form the sacrum and the coccyx.

vertebral foramen [L, *vertebra,* joint, *foramen,* a hole], the opening between the neural arch and the body of a vertebra through which the spinal cord passes.

vertebral groove [L, *vertebra,* joint; D, *groove*], a shallow depression on each side of the spinous processes of the vertebrae, occupied by the deep back muscles.

vertebral notch [L, *vertebra,* joint; OFr, *enochier,* notch], either of the concavities on the lower or upper border of a vertebral pedicle.

vertebral rib, one of two lower ribs on either side that are not attached anteriorly.

vertebral subluxation complex, in chiropractic, malfunction of organs or tissue caused by impairment of nerve function that results from restriction of normal motion or from abnormal position of spinal segments.

vertebral-venous system, a group of four interconnected venous networks surrounding the vertebral column.

vertebrate [L, *vertebra,* joint], any animal that possesses a backbone and thus is a member of the subphylum Vertebrata of the phylum Chordata. Vertebrates include fish, amphibians, birds, reptiles, and mammals.

vertebrochondral /vur'təbrōkon'drəl/, pertaining to a vertebra and a costal cartilage.

vertebrocostal /-kos′təl/, pertaining to a vertebra and a rib or a vertebra and a costal cartilage.

vertebrocostal rib, one of the eighth, ninth, and tenth ribs on either side that articulate posteriorly with the vertebrae and have their costal cartilages connected anteriorly by capsular ligaments.

vertebrosternal rib /-stur′nəl/, one of the seven upper ribs on either side that have cartilage articulating directly with the sternum.

verteporfin /ver′tē-por′fin/, a photosensitizing agent that accumulates preferentially in neovasculature, including that in the choroid, such as occurs in age-related macular degeneration, ocular histoplasmosis, or pathologic myopia. The agent is then activated by light of a specific wavelength in the presence of oxygen and causes local damage to the neovascular endothelium followed by vessel occlusion. It is administered intravenously before irradiation of the lesion with light from a compatible laser.

vertex /vur′teks/ [L, summit], **1.** the top of the head; crown. **2.** the apex or highest point of any structure.

vertex presentation, in obstetrics, a fetal presentation in which the vertex of the fetus is the part nearest to the cervical os and can be expected to be born first.

vertical /vur′tikəl/ [L, *vertex,* summit], perpendicular or at a right angle to the plane of the horizon.

vertical angulation [L, *vertex + angulus,* corner], the angle within the vertical plane, relative to a reference in the horizontal or occlusal plane, at which the central x-ray beam is directed during radiography or dental imaging of oral structures.

vertical coordination, a system of community health nurses who serve as links between their level in the organization and those above and below their level and between the agency and the patient.

vertical diplopia [L, *vertex;* Gk, *diploos,* double, *opsis,* vision], a form of double vision in which one image is displaced vertically above the other.

vertically integrated health care, a health delivery system in which the complete spectrum of care, including financial services, is provided within a single organization, such as a health maintenance organization.

vertical nystagmus, a visual abnormality in which the eyes involuntarily move up and down.

vertical resorption, a pattern of bone loss in which the alveolar bone adjacent to an affected tooth is destroyed without simultaneous crestal loss.

vertical strabismus [L, *vertex;* Gk, *strabismos,* squint], a deviation of one eye in a vertical direction from a point of fixation. A common cause is overaction by the inferior oblique muscles or a weakness of the superior oblique muscle, resulting in a quick vertical movement of the eyeball on adduction.

vertical transmission, the transfer of a disease, condition, or trait from one generation to the next, either genetically or congenitally, such as the spread of an infection through breast milk or through the placenta.

vertical vertigo, a sense of instability caused by looking up or down.

verticosubmental /vur′tikō′submen′təl/ [L, *vertex + sub,* below, *mentum,* chin], pertaining to a radiographic projection of the head in which the central ray passes from the vertex of the skull through its base.

vertigo /vur′tigō, vurti′gō/, a sensation of instability, giddiness, loss of equilibrium, or rotation, caused by a disturbance in the semicircular canal of the inner ear or the vestibular nuclei of the brainstem. The sensation that one's body is rotating in space is called subjective vertigo, whereas the sensation that objects are spinning around the body is termed objective vertigo.

very low–density lipoprotein (VLDL), a plasma lipoprotein that is composed chiefly of triglycerides with small amounts of cholesterol, phospholipid, fat-soluble vitamins, and protein. It transports triglycerides primarily from the liver to peripheral sites in the tissues for use or storage.

vesical /ves′ikəl/ [L, *vesica,* bladder], pertaining to a fluid-filled sac, usually the urinary bladder.

vesical calculus, a calculus found in the urinary bladder.

vesical fistula [L, *vesica,* bladder, *fistula,* pipe], an abnormal passage communicating with the urinary bladder.

vesical glands, mucous glands sometimes found in the wall of the urinary bladder, especially in the area of the trigone.

vesical hematuria [L, *vesica,* bladder; Gk, *haima,* blood, *ouron,* urine], the presence of blood in the urine caused by bleeding in the bladder. The urine is bright red.

vesical reflex, the sensation of a need to urinate when the bladder is moderately distended.

vesical sphincter, a circular muscle surrounding the opening of the urinary bladder.

vesicant /ves′ikənt/, a drug capable of causing tissue necrosis when extravasated.

VESIcare, a trademark for solifenacin.

vesicle /ves′ikəl/ [L, *vesicula*], a small bladder or blister, containing clear fluid. **—vesicular,** *adj.*

vesicoabdominal /ves′ikō·abdom′inəl/, pertaining to the urinary bladder and abdominal wall.

vesicoenteric fistula, enterovesical fistula.

vesicoureteral reflux /ves′ikōy‾oorē′tərəl/ [L, *vesica;* Gk, *oureter,* ureter; L, *refluxus,* backflow], an abnormal backflow of urine from the bladder to the ureter, resulting from a congenital defect, obstruction of the outlet of the bladder, or edema or scarring secondary to infection of the lower urinary tract. Reflux increases the hydrostatic pressure in the ureters and kidneys and may cause permanent damage. The condition is characterized by abdominal or flank pain, enuresis, pyuria, hematuria, proteinuria, and bacteriuria accompanied by persistent or recurrent UTIs.

vesicouterine /ves'ikōyōō'tərin, -ēn/ [L, *vesica* + *uterus*, womb], pertaining to the bladder and uterus.

vesicouterine pouch, a shallow pouch that occurs anteriorly between the bladder and uterus.

vesicovaginal /ves'ikōvaj'inəl/, pertaining to the urinary bladder and vagina.

vesicovaginal fistula, a fistula between the bladder and the vagina.

vesicula /vəsik'yələ/ [L], a vesicle or small bladder.

vesicular /vesik'yələr/, pertaining to a blister-like condition.

vesicular appendix, a cystic structure on the fimbriated end of each of the fallopian tubes. It represents a remnant of the mesonephric ducts.

vesicular breath sound (V.S.), a normal sound of rustling or swishing heard with a stethoscope over the lung periphery. It is characteristically higher-pitched during inspiration and fades rapidly during expiration.

vesicular ovarian follicle, graafian follicle.

vesiculitis /vəsik'yəlī'tis/, an inflammation of any vesicle, particularly the seminal vesicles.

vesiculography /vəsik'yəlog'rəfē/, the radiologic examination of the seminal vesicles and adjacent structures, usually after injection of a radiopaque contrast medium into the deferent ducts or, by catheterization, into the ejaculatory ducts.

vesiculotympanitic, both vesicular and tympanitic; said of auscultatory sounds.

vessel /ves'əl/ [L, *vascellum*, small vase], any one of the many tubules throughout the body conveying fluids such as blood and lymph.

vestibular /vestib'yələr/ [L, *vestibulum*, courtyard], pertaining to a vestibule, such as the vestibular part of the mouth, which lies between the cheeks and the teeth.

vestibular apparatus, the inner ear structures that are associated with balance and position sense. They include the vestibule and semicircular canals.

vestibular caecum of cochlear duct, a small blind outpouching at the vestibular end of the cochlear duct.

vestibular fossa, the vaginal vestibule between the vaginal orifice and the fourchette (frenulum of pudendal labia).

vestibular function, the sense of balance.

vestibular gland, any one of four small glands, two on each side of the vaginal orifice. They secrete a lubricating substance.

vestibular nerve [L, *vestibulum*, courtyard + *nervus*], a branch of the eighth cranial nerve associated with the sense of equilibrium. It arises in the vestibular ganglion (Scarpa's ganglion) of the ear.

vestibular neuronitis, a sudden, severe attack of vertigo without symptoms of deafness or tinnitus. It usually affects young or middle-aged adults, is temporary, and follows a URI.

vestibular surface, the surface of a tooth that is directed outward toward the vestibule of the mouth, including the buccal and labial surfaces, and opposite the lingual (or oral) surface.

vestibular toxicity, toxic effects (commonly of drugs) on the vestibule of the ear, resulting in dizziness, vertigo, and loss of balance.

vestibule /ves'tibyōōl/ [L, *vestibulum*, courtyard], a space or cavity that serves as the entrance to a passageway, such as the vestibule of the ear.

vestibule of the aorta, a space within the left ventricle of the heart at the root of the aorta.

vestibule of the ear, the central part of the inner ear, within the osseous labyrinth, involved with the sensation of position and movement.

vestibule of the mouth, the portion of the oral cavity bounded on one side by the teeth and gingivae, or the residual alveolar ridges, and on the other side by the lips (labial vestibule) and cheeks (buccal vestibule).

vestibulocochlear nerve, either of a pair of cranial nerves composed of fibers from the cochlear nerve and the vestibular nerve in the inner ear, conveying impulses of both the sense of hearing and the sense of balance.

vestibulo-ocular reflex /vestib'yəlō·ok'yə lər/, a normal reflex in which eye position compensates for movement of the head. It is induced by excitation of the vestibular apparatus.

vestibuloplasty /vestib'yəlōplas'tē/ [L, *vestibulum*, courtyard; Gk, *plassein*, to shape], plastic surgery of the oral vestibule, particularly modification of the gingival and mucosal tissues to create a deeper or better shaped vestibule usually to aid in the creation of a supporting area.

vestige /ves'tij/ [L, *vestigium*, trace], an imperfectly developed, relatively useless organ or other structure of the body that had a vital function at an earlier stage of life or in a more primitive form of life. —**vestigial**, adj.

veterinarian /vet'əriner'ē·ən/ [L, *veterinarius*, beast of burden], a health professional who specializes in the causes and treatment of diseases and disorders of domestic and wild animals.

veterinary medicine /vet′əriner′ē/, the field of medicine concerned with the health and diseases of animals other than humans.

VF, 1. abbreviation for **ventricular fibrillation.** 2. abbreviation for **visual field.** 3. abbreviation for **vocal fremitus.**

VH, abbreviation for **viral hepatitis.**

VI, abbreviation for *variable interval.*

via /vī′ə, vē′ä/ [L, a way], any passage or course, such as the esophagus or trachea.

viability /vī′əbil′itē/ [L, *vita,* life], the ability to continue living.

viable /vī′əbəl/ [Fr, likely to live], capable of developing, growing, and otherwise sustaining life, such as a normal human fetus at 24 weeks of gestation.—**viability,** *n.*

viable infant, an infant who at birth weighs at least 500 g or is 24 weeks or more of gestational age.

Viagra /vi-ag′rah/, a trademark for a preparation of sildenafil citrate, a treatment for erectile dysfunction.

vial /vī′əl/, a glass container with a metal-enclosed rubber seal.

Vibramycin Monohydrate, a trademark for a tetracycline antibiotic (doxycycline monohydrate).

vibration /vībrā′shən/ [L, *vibrare,* to vibrate], a type of massage administered by quickly tapping with the fingertips or alternating the fingers in a rhythmic manner or by a mechanical device.

vibratory /vī′brətôr′ē/ [L, *vibrare,* to vibrate], causing vibrations or a state of vibration.

vibratory massage, the manipulation of body surfaces with an instrument that produces a rapid tapping sensation.

vibratory sense [L, *vibrare,* to vibrate, *sentire,* to feel], the ability to perceive vibratory sensations. Vibration receptors in the body are found in a variety of locations, from the skin surface to the membranes covering bones.

vibrio /vib′rē-ō/ [L, *vibrare*], any bacterium that is curved and motile, such as those belonging to the genus *Vibrio.* Cholera and several other epidemic forms of gastroenteritis are caused by members of the genus.

Vibrio cholerae, the species of comma-shaped, motile bacillus that is the cause of cholera.

vibrio gastroenteritis, an infectious disease caused by *Vibrio parahaemolyticus* acquired from contaminated seafood. It is characterized by nausea, vomiting, abdominal pain, and diarrhea. Headache, mild fever, and bloody stools also may be present. Spontaneous recovery usually occurs in 2 to 5 days.

Vibrio parahaemolyticus /per′əhē′mōlit′i kəs/, a species of halophic (salt-tolerant) microorganisms of the genus *Vibrio,* found in brackish water. It is the causative agent in food poisoning associated with the ingestion of raw or undercooked shellfish, especially crabs and shrimp. This microorganism is a common cause of gastroenteritis in Japan, aboard cruise ships, and in the eastern and southeastern coastal areas of the United States. Symptoms include watery diarrhea, abdominal cramps, vomiting, headache, chills, and fever. This organism can also cause infection of the skin when an open wound is infected by exposure to seawater. Treatment usually includes bed rest and the oral replacement of fluids. Thorough cooking of seafood prevents the infection.

Vibrio vulnificus, a halophilic (salt-tolerant) species of microorganism whose strains are similar to *V. parahaemolyticus* but differ in that they can ferment lactose. Infection by eating raw seafood causes septicemia, gastroenteritis, and cellulitis, and may be especially severe or even fatal in those with preexisting hepatic disease. Wound infection may occur following exposure to sea water or from injury when handling crabs.

vicarious menstruation /vīker′ē-əs/ [L, *vicarius,* substituted, *menstruare,* to menstruate], discharge of blood from a site other than the uterus at the time when the menstrual flow is normally expected. Such bleeding is usually caused by the increased capillary permeability that occurs during menstruation.

vidarabine /vider′əbēn/, an antiviral agent. It is prescribed as an ophthalmic ointment to treat keratoconjunctivitis and nearby epithelial or superficial keratitis caused by HSV1 or HSV2.

Vidaza, a trademark for azacitidine.

video display terminal (VDT) [L, *videre,* to see, *displicare,* to scatter, *terminus,* end], a cathode-ray tube device with a surface similar to a television screen, used in word processors, computer terminals, and similar equipment. Use of VDTs has been associated with a variety of environmental health complaints, including burning and itching eyes, headaches, and back and arm pain. Published studies indicate the health effects are caused by inadequate or improper office environments, such as unsuitable furniture or light levels, rather than VDT radiation.

videoendoscopy /vid′e-o-en-dos′kah-pe/, endoscopy performed under the guidance of a video camera in the tip of the endoscope.

videolaparoscopy /vid′e-o-lap′ah-ros′kah-pe/, laparoscopic surgery performed under the guidance of a video camera in the tip of the laparoscope.

Videx, a trademark for an antiretroviral acquired immunodeficiency syndrome drug (dideoxyinosine [ddI]).

view /vu/, projection.

vigilambulism /vij'ilam'byəlīz'əm/, a condition in which walking or other motor acts are performed in an unconscious but waking state.

vigilance /vij'iləns/ [L, *vigil,* awake], a state of being attentive or alert.

vigil coma /vij'əl/ [L, *vigil;* Gk, *koma,* deep sleep], a semiconscious state of delirium in which the patient may appear awake, with eyes open and staring, and may make verbal sounds.

vignetting, the peripheral reduction of light intensity in fluoroscopic image intensifiers.

villoma /vilō'mə/ *pl.* **villomas, villomata** [L, *villus,* hair; Gk, *oma,* tumor], a villous neoplasm or papilloma, occurring in the bladder or rectum.

villous adenoma /vil'əs/ [L, *villus,* hair], a slow-growing, soft, spongy, potentially malignant papillary growth of the mucosa of the large intestine.

villous carcinoma, an epithelial tumor with many long velvety papillary outgrowths.

villous chorion, the region of the chorion that bears villi; also known as the shaggy or villous chorion.

villous papilloma, a benign tumor with long, slender processes, usually occurring in the bladder, breast, or a cerebral ventricle.

villus /vil'əs/ *pl.* **villi** [L, shaggy, hair], one of the many tiny projections, barely visible to the naked eye, clustered over the entire mucous surface of the small intestine. Villi are covered with epithelium that diffuses and transports fluids and nutrients. Each villus has a core of delicate areolar and reticular connective tissue supporting the epithelium, various capillaries, and often a single lymphatic lacteal that fills with milky white chyle during the digestion of a fatty meal.—**villous,** *adj.*

vinBLAStine sulfate /vinblas'tēn, -tin/, an antimitotic antineoplastic. It is prescribed in the treatment of many neoplastic diseases such as choriocarcinoma, testicular carcinoma, lung cancer, breast cancer, renal cancer, Hodgkin's disease, and non-Hodgkin's lymphoma.

Vincent's stomatitis [Henri Vincent, French physician, 1862–1950; Gk, *stoma,* mouth, *itis,* inflammation], a painful bacterial infection of the mouth and gums causing ulceration (gingivitis).

vinCRISTine sulfate /vinkris'tēn, -tin/, an antimitotic antineoplastic. It is prescribed in the treatment of many neoplastic diseases such as leukemia, neuroblastoma, lymphomas, and sarcomas. It is often used in combination therapy because its dose-limiting toxicity is different from that of most other cancer chemotherapy drugs.

Vineberg's operation /vīn'bərgs/ [Arthur M. Vineberg, Canadian thoracic surgeon, 1903–1988], a technique in which the internal mammary artery is implanted into the myocardium to improve blood flow to the heart. Common in the 1950s, the procedure has been replaced by others such as saphenous vein grafting.

vinorelbine tartrate, an anticancer mitotic inhibitor prescribed in the treatment of non–small cell lung cancer.

Viokase, a trademark for an enzyme mixture of amylase, lipase, and protease (pancreplipase) derived from hog pancreas.

violence /vī'o-lens/, great force, either physical or emotional, usually exerted to damage or otherwise abuse something or someone.

viosterol /vī'os'tərōl/, synthetic vitamin D_2 in an oil base.

VIP, 1. abbreviation for **vasoactive intestinal polypeptide. 2.** abbreviation for *very important person.* A VIP suite in a hospital is one reserved for such people.

viperine, 1. pertaining to the true vipers. 2. true viper.

VIPoma /vipō'mə/, a type of pancreatic tumor that causes changes in secretion of vasoactive intestinal polypeptide (VIP). VIP causes dilation of blood vessels throughout the body and secretion of fluid and salt in the intestinal tract, resulting in diarrhea.

Vira-A, a trademark for an antiviral (vidarabine).

viral cultures, cultures of the blood, urine, stool, throat, and skin to definitively diagnose viral disease.

viral cystitis, that caused by a viral infection, most often seen in immunocompromised persons infected with BK virus.

viral dysentery /dis'rol/ [L, *virus,* poison; Gk, *dys,* bad, *enteron,* intestine], a form of dysentery caused by a virus and usually characterized by an acute watery diarrhea.

viral gastroenteritis, an inflammation of the intestine caused by a virus. The symptoms usually include abdominal cramps, diarrhea, nausea, and vomiting.

viral hepatitis (VH), a viral inflammatory disease of the liver caused by one of the hepatitis viruses, A, B, C, delta, E, F, G, or H. All have chronic forms except hepatitis A. The disease is transmitted sexually and through blood transfusions and is common among people with behavior risks or HIV infection. Speed of onset and probable course of the illness vary with the kind and strain of virus, but the characteristics of the disease and its treatment are the same.

viral infection, any of the diseases caused by one of approximately 200 viruses pathogenic to humans. Some are the most communicable and dangerous diseases known; some cause mild and transient conditions that pass virtually unnoticed. Viruses are introduced into the body through nonintact skin or mucous membranes or through a transfusion into the bloodstream or transplantation, by droplet infection through the respiratory tract, or by ingestion through the digestive tract into the GI system. After a virus enters the body, it attaches to and enters a cell. The virus directs the cell to produce new virions using chemical building blocks and energy available in the parasitized cell. After a variable period of time, masses of fully grown viruses appear, each able to survive outside the cell until more susceptible cells are found. Techniques used in viral identification and immunization are based on the essential fact that viruses can multiply only inside living cells.

viral keratoconjunctivitis [L, *virus,* poison; Gk, *keras,* horn; L, *conjunctivus,* connecting; Gk, *itis,* inflammation], a combination of inflammation of the cornea and conjunctiva caused by a viral infection.

viral load, measurement of the amount of HIV in the blood expressed as copies per milliliter. Plasma viremia is used to guide treatment decisions and monitor response to treatment.

viral meningitis, meningitis caused by various viruses, such as the coxsackieviruses, mumps virus, and the virus of lymphocytic choriomeningitis, characterized by malaise, fever, headache, nausea, CSF pleocytosis (principally lymphocytic), abdominal pain, stiffness of the neck and back, and a short uncomplicated course.

viral myocarditis, inflammation of the myocardium caused by coxsackievirus.

viral pneumonia, pulmonary infection caused by a virus.

viral therapy, the use of genetically altered viruses to deliver genes to specific sites.

Viramune, a trademark for an antiretroviral nonnucleoside analog (nevirapine).

Virazole, a trademark for an aerosol antiviral drug (ribavirin).

Virchow's node /fir′shōz/ [Rudolf L.K. Virchow, German pathologist, 1821–1902], a firm supraclavicular lymph node, particularly on the left side, that is so enlarged that it is palpable.

Viread, a trademark for an antiretroviral (tenofovir).

viremia /vīrē′mē·ə/ [L, *virus;* Gk, *haima,* blood], the presence of viruses in the blood.

virgin /vur′jən/, **1.** a person who has never had sexual intercourse. **2.** uncontaminated.

virginity /vurjin′itē/, the state of being a virgin.

virile /vir′əl/ [L, *virilis,* masculine], **1.** pertaining to or characteristic of an adult male; masculine; manly. **2.** possessing or exhibiting masculine strength, vigor, force, or energy. **3.** pertaining to the male

sexual functions; capable of procreation.—**virility,** *n.*

virilism /vir′əliz′əm/ [L, *virilis* + *ismus,* practice], **1.** pseudohermaphroditism in a female. **2.** premature development of masculine characteristics in the male.

virilization /vir′əlīzā′shən/ [L, *virilis* + *atus,* process], a process in which secondary male sexual characteristics are acquired by a female, usually as the result of adrenal dysfunction or hormonal medication.

virion /vir′ē·on, vī′rē·on/ [L, *virus,* poison], a single virus particle with a central nucleoid surrounded by a protein coat or capsid. The complete nucleocapsid with a nucleic acid core may constitute a complete virus, such as the adenoviruses and the picornaviruses, or it may be surrounded by an envelope, as in the herpesviruses and the myxoviruses.

virocytes /vī′rəsīts/ [L, *virus;* Gk, *kytos,* cell], lymphocytes altered in appearance and staining that are seen in blood smears from patients with viral diseases.

viroid /vī′roid/, a small infective segment of nucleic acid, usually RNA. It is not translated and is replicated by host cell enzymes. Viroids include segments that are complementary to introns and may bind to intron RNA.

virologist /vīrol′əjist, vir-/, a specialist who studies viruses and diseases caused by viruses.

virology /-l′əjē/ [L, *virus;* Gk, *logos,* science], the study of viruses and viral diseases.—**virologic,** *adj.*

Viroptic, a trademark for an ophthalmic antiviral (trifluridine).

virtual colonoscopy, an imaging technique, used for examination of the colon, in which cross-sectional images acquired by CT or MRI are processed by computer to reconstruct a three-dimensional display of the colonic lumen.

virtual endoscopy, an imaging technique in which cross-sectional images acquired by CT or MRI are processed by computer to reconstruct a three-dimensional display similar to that seen through an endoscope.

virtual reality /vur′chōō·əl/, a system of computer-generated, three-dimensional, imaginary environments with which a person can subjectively interact. Examples include medical research to monitor brain activity in the hippocampus of subjects trying to solve maze problems.

virucidal /vī′rəsī′dəl/, pertaining to the destruction of viruses.

virucide /vī′rəsīd/ [L, *virus* + *caedere,* to kill], any agent that destroys or inactivates a virus.

virulence /vir′yələns/ [L, *virulentus,* poisonous], the power of a microorganism to produce disease.

V

virulent /vir′yələnt/ [L, *virulentus*], pertaining to a very pathogenic or rapidly progressive condition.

virus /vī′rəs/ [L, poison], a minute parasitic microorganism much smaller than a bacterium that, having no independent metabolic activity, may replicate only within a cell of a living plant or animal host. A virus consists of a core of nucleic acid (DNA or RNA) surrounded by a coat of antigenic protein sometimes surrounded by an envelope of lipoprotein. The virus provides the genetic code for replication, and the host cell provides the necessary energy and raw materials. More than 200 viruses have been identified as capable of causing disease in humans.—**viral,** *adj.*

virus shedding, the movement by any route of a virus from an infected host.

virustatic /vī′rəstat′ik/, pertaining to the inhibition of the growth and development of viruses, as distinguished from their destruction.

vis /vis, vēs/ [L, force], energy or power.

Visagraph /vē′zə-graf/, a trademark for a device that records and measures eye movements while the patient is reading.

viscera /vis′ərə/, *sing* **viscus** [L, *viscus*, internal organs], the internal organs enclosed within a body cavity, including the abdominal, thoracic, pelvic, and endocrine organs.

visceral /vis′ərəl/ [L, *viscus,* internal organs], pertaining to the viscera, or internal organs, in the abdominal cavity.

visceral abdominal fascia, the fascia that invests the abdominal viscera.

visceral afferent fibers, the nerve fibers of the visceral nervous system that receive stimuli, carry impulses toward the CNS, and share the sensory ganglia of the cerebrospinal nerves with the somatic sensory fibers. The visceral afferent fibers produce sensations different from those of the somatic afferent fibers. Some of the parts of the body with visceral afferent fibers are the face, scalp, nose, mouth, descending colon, lungs, abdomen, and rectum.

visceral cavity [L, *viscus,* internal organs, *cavum*], **1.** the abdominal cavity containing the viscera. **2.** the cavity of any viscus, such as the stomach.

visceral efferent system [L, *viscus,* internal organs, *effere,* to bear out; Gk, *systema*], the part of the autonomic nervous system that supplies efferent nerve fibers from the CNS to the visceral organs.

visceral inversion, the transposition of the abdominal and thoracic organs to opposite sides of the body.

visceral larva migrans, infestation with parasitic larvae, *Toxocara,* or, occasionally, *Ascaris, Strongyloides,* or other nematodes.

visceral layer of glomerular capsule, the layer of the glomerular capsule overlying the capillaries and composed of podocytes, separated from the parietal layer by the urinary space.

visceral lymph node, a small oval nodular gland that filters lymph circulating in the lymphatic vessels of the thoracic, abdominal, and pelvic viscera.

visceral nervous system, the visceral part of the peripheral nervous system that comprises the whole complex of nerves, fibers, ganglia, and plexuses by which impulses travel from the central nervous system to the viscera and from the viscera to the central nervous system.

visceral obesity, android obesity; so-called from the theory that deep intraabdominal (visceral) fat plays a large role in the associated morbidity and mortality.

visceral pain, pain that results from the activation of nociceptors of the thoracic, pelvic, or abdominal viscera. It is felt as a poorly localized aching or cramping sensation and often referred to cutaneous sites.

visceral pericardium [L, *viscus;* Gk, *peri,* around, *kardia,* heart], the surface of the pericardial membrane that is in direct contact with the heart.

visceral peritoneum, a continuation of the parietal peritoneum reflected at various places over the viscera, forming a complete covering for the stomach, spleen, liver, intestines from the distal duodenum to the upper end of the rectum, uterus, and ovaries; it also partially covers some other abdominal organs. It holds the viscera in position by its folds, including the mesenteries, the omenta, and the ligaments of the liver, spleen, stomach, kidneys, bladder, and uterus.

visceral pleura, the inner layer of pleura that is adjacent to the external lung tissue.

visceral protein status, the amount of protein that is contained in the internal organs.

visceral skeleton [L, *viscus;* Gk, *skeletos,* dried up], the part of the skeleton, including sternum, ribs, pelvis, and vertebrae, that enclose the viscera.

visceral swallow, an immature swallowing pattern of an infant, resembling wavelike contractions of peristalsis.

viscerocranium, the facial skeleton.

visceromotor /vis′ərōmō′tər/, **1.** pertaining to nerve impulses that control visceral smooth muscle. **2.** pertaining to movement of the viscera.

viscerosomatic reaction /vis′ərō′sōmat′ik/ [L, *viscus;* Gk, *soma,* body; L, *re + agere,* to act], a muscular response to stimulation of a nerve-receptor organ in a visceral organ.

viscoelasticity /vis′kō-ē′lastis′itē/, the quality or condition of being both viscous and elastic.

viscosity /viskos'itē/ [L, *viscosus*, sticky], the ability or inability of a fluid solution to flow easily. A solution that has high viscosity is relatively thick and flows slowly because of the adhesive effect of adjacent molecules.

viscous fermentation [L, *viscosus*], the formation of viscous material in milk, urine, or wine by the action of various bacilli.

visibility /vis'əbil'itē/ [L, *visibilitas*, being seen], a condition of being visible under the circumstances of light, distance, and other factors.

visible /viz'ibəl/ [L, *visibilis*, visible], perceptible to the eye.

visible light [L, *visus*, sight; AS, *leoht*], the radiant energy in the electromagnetic spectrum that is visible to the human eye.

visible radiation [L, *visibilis*, vision, *radiare*, to shine], electromagnetic radiation in the wavelengths between infrared and ultraviolet that can be perceived by most normal humans.

visible spectrum [L, *visibilis*, vision, *spectrum*, image], the colors of the spectrum that can be observed by most people, from violet at about 4000 angstrom units (400 nm) through blue, green, yellow, and orange, to red, at about 6500 angstrom units (650 nm).

vision /vizh'ən/ [L, *visus*, vision], the capacity for sight.

vision compensation behavior, a nursing outcome from the Nursing Outcomes Classification (NOC) defined as personal actions to compensate for visual impairment.

vision therapy technician, an allied health professional who evaluates clients and plans and implements vision therapy programs under the supervision of an optometrist.

visit /viz'it/ [L, *visitare*, to see often], 1. a meeting between a practitioner and a client or patient. In the hospital and home the practitioner visits the patient; in the clinic or office the patient visits the practitioner. 2. of a patient, to meet a practitioner to obtain professional services or, of a practitioner, to see a patient or client to render a professional service.

visitation facilitation, a nursing intervention from the Nursing Interventions Classification (NIC) defined as promoting beneficial visits by family and friends.

visiting nurse, a nurse who is responsible for a group of patients in a home setting, usually in a defined geographic area. The nurse makes visits to provide skilled nursing care as prescribed by a physician, particularly for persons unable to leave home for professional care, and to educate patients in matters of self-care.

Visken, a trademark for a beta blocker (pindolol).

Vistaril, a trademark for an antianxiety/antihistamine (hydroxyzine pamoate).

visual /vizh'ōō·əl/ [L, *visus*, vision], pertaining to the sense of sight.

visual accommodation, a process by which the eye adjusts and is able to focus, producing a sharp image at various, changing distances from the object seen. The convexity of the anterior surface of the lens may be increased or decreased by contraction or relaxation of the ciliary muscle.

visual acuity [L, *visus*, vision, *acuitas*, sharpness], 1. a measure of the resolving power of the eye, particularly with its ability to distinguish letters and numbers at a given distance. 2. the sharpness or clearness of vision.

visual agnosia, an inability to recognize objects by sight, although vision is intact.

visual amnesia [L, *visus*, vision; Gk, *amnesia*, forgetfulness], an inability to recognize objects, including written words, previously seen.

visual angle [L, *visus*, vision, *angulus*], the angle between two lines passing from the extremities of an object looked at, through the nodal point of the eye.

visual aphasia [L, *visus*, vision; Gk, *a* + *phasis*, not speech], the inability to understand written language caused by a lesion in the left visual cortex and the connections between the right visual cortex and the left hemisphere.

visual center, the area of the brain concerned with vision.

visual center of the cornea, the point of intersection of the line of sight with the cornea.

visual-evoked potential (VEP), an evoked potential elicited by a repeatedly flashing light or a pattern stimulus. It may be used to confirm optic nerve or visual pathway damage.

visual field (VF), the area of physical space visible to an eye in a given position. The average VF is 65 degrees upward, 75 degrees downward, 60 degrees nasally, and 90 degrees temporally.

visual field defect, one or more spots or defects in the vision that remain constant in position. This fixed defect is usually caused by damage to the retina or visual pathways, such as by retinal detachments, chorioretinitis, traumatic injury, macular degeneration, glaucoma, or a vascular occlusion of the eye or the brain.

visual hallucinations [L, *visus*, vision, *alucinari*], a subjective visual experience in the absence of objective evidence of a corresponding stimulus. Such hallucinations are most likely to be associated with acute organic disorders such as toxic confusional psychoses, delirium, and focal brain diseases and may occur with any stage of schizophrenia.

visualization /vizh'ōō·əlīzā'shən/, an effective means of deepening relaxation

V

and desensitizing a real-life situation that is generally met with stress and tension. The imagery combines positive experiences with actual or perceived negative events or situations in an effort to desensitize the person to the trauma.

visual memory, the ability to create an eidetic image of past visual experiences.

visual-motor coordination, the ability to coordinate vision with the movements or parts of the body.

visual-motor function, the ability to draw or copy forms or to perform constructive tasks.

visual pathway, a pathway over which a visual sensation is transmitted from the retina to the brain. A pathway consists of an optic nerve, the fibers of an optic nerve traveling through the optic chiasm to the lateral geniculate body of the thalamus, and optic radiations terminating in an occipital lobe. Each optic nerve contains fibers from only one retina. The optic chiasm contains fibers from the nasal parts of the retinas of both eyes; these fibers cross to the opposite side of the brain at the optic chiasm.

visual plane, the plane in which the two optic axes lie.

visual response audiometry (VRA), a technique for testing the hearing of older infants and children between the ages of 12 and 30 months. Sounds such as speech and tones are presented through loudspeakers. When the child looks toward the source of the sound, he or she is rewarded by seeing a toy on top of the speaker move or light up.

visual-spatial agnosia, an inability to analyze spatial relationships or to perform simple constructional tasks under visual control.

visuospatial /vizh′oo-ōspā′shəl/, pertaining to the ability to comprehend visual representations and their spatial relationships.

vital /vī′təl/ [L, *vita,* life], pertaining or contributing to life forces.

vital capacity (VC) [L, *vita,* life, *capacitas,* capacity], the maximum volume of air that can be expelled at the normal rate of exhalation after a maximum inspiration, representing the greatest possible breathing capacity. The VC equals the inspiratory reserve volume plus the tidal volume plus the expiratory reserve volume.

vitality test /vītal′itē/, a group of thermal, transillumination, and electrical tests used to evaluate the health of dental pulp.

vital signs¹, the measurements of pulse rate, respiration rate, and body temperature. Although not strictly a vital sign, BP is also customarily included.

vital signs², a nursing outcome from the Nursing Outcomes Classification (NOC) defined as the extent to which temperature, pulse, respiration, and blood pressure are within normal range.

vital signs monitoring, a nursing intervention from the Nursing Interventions Classification (NIC) defined as collection and analysis of cardiovascular, respiratory, and body temperature data to determine and prevent complications.

vital stain [L, *vita,* life; OFr, *desteindre,* to dye], any dye used to impart color to tissues or cells of living organisms.

vital statistics, data relating to births or natality, deaths or mortality, marriages, health, and disease or morbidity.

vital ultraviolet (UV), the ultraviolet wavelengths between 320.0 and 290.0 nm, which are believed to be necessary or helpful for normal growth and health. Ultraviolet radiation at this wavelength converts vitamin D to its first active form.

vitamin /vī′təmin/ [L, *vita + amine,* ammonia], an organic compound essential in small quantities for normal physiologic and metabolic functioning of the body. With few exceptions, vitamins cannot be synthesized by the body and must be obtained from the diet or dietary supplements. No one food contains all the vitamins. Vitamin deficiency diseases produce specific symptoms usually alleviated by the administration of the appropriate vitamin. Vitamins are classified according to their fat or water solubility, their physiologic effects, or their chemical structures; they are designated by alphabetic letters and chemical or other specific names. The fat-soluble vitamins are A, D, E, and K; the B complex and C vitamins are water-soluble.

vitamin A, a fat-soluble, solid terpene alcohol essential for skeletal growth, maintenance of normal mucosal epithelium, reproduction, and visual acuity. It is derived from various carotenoids, mainly beta-carotene, and is present in leafy green vegetables and yellow fruits and vegetables as a precursor and is found preformed in fish liver oils, liver, milk, cheese, butter, and egg yolk. Deficiency leads to atrophy of epithelial tissue resulting in keratomalacia, xerophthalmia, night blindness, and lessened resistance to infection of mucous membranes.

vitamin A₁, one of the two forms of vitamin A that occur in nature. It is a fat-soluble unsaturated alcohol formed by hydrolysis of beta-carotene, one molecule of which yields two molecules of vitamin A₁. Natural sources include fish-liver oils, butterfat, and egg yolk.

vitamin A₂, an alternative form of vitamin A found in the tissues of freshwater fish but not in mammals or saltwater fish. Differences in ultraviolet light absorption spectra are used to distinguish the vitamin A forms.

vitamin B₁₂ test (cyanocobalamin), a blood test that measures levels of vitamin B₁₂, which is necessary for conversion of the inactive form of folate to the active form, a process that is crucial in the formation and function of RBCs. Abnormal levels may indicate leukemia, severe liver dysfunction, myeloproliferative disease, pernicious anemia, malabsorption syndromes, inflammatory bowel disease, and Zollinger-Ellison syndrome, among other conditions.

vitamin B complex, a group of water-soluble vitamins differing from each other structurally and in their biologic effect. All of the B vitamins are found in large quantities in liver and yeast, and they are present separately or in combination in many foods.

vitamin D, a fat-soluble vitamin chemically related to the steroids and essential for the normal formation of bones and teeth and for the absorption of calcium and phosphorus from the GI tract. The vitamin is present in natural foods in small amounts, and requirements are usually met by artificial enrichment of various foods, especially milk and dairy products, and exposure to sunlight. The natural foods containing vitamin D are of animal origin and include saltwater fish, especially salmon, sardines, and herring; organ meats; fish-liver oils; and egg yolk. Deficiency of the vitamin results in rickets in children, osteomalacia, osteoporosis, and osteodystrophy.

vitamin D₃, an antirachitic, white, odorless, crystalline, unsaturated alcohol that is the predominant form of vitamin D of animal origin. It is found in most fish-liver oils, butter, brain, and egg yolk and is formed in the skin, fur, and feathers of animals and birds exposed to sunlight or ultraviolet rays.

vitamin deficiency, a state or condition resulting from the lack of or inability to use one or more vitamins. The symptoms and manifestations of each deficiency vary, depending on the specific function of the vitamin in promoting growth and development and maintaining body health.

vitamin D–resistant rickets, a genetic disease clinically similar to rickets but resistant to treatment with large doses of vitamin D. It is caused by a congenital defect in renal tubular resorption of phosphate and usually occurs in men.

vitamin E, any or all of the group of fat-soluble vitamins that consist of the tocopherols and are essential for normal reproduction, muscle development, resistance of erythrocytes to hemolysis, and various other biochemical functions. It is a fat-soluble antioxidant and acts in maintaining the stability of polyunsaturated fatty acids and other fatlike substances, including vitamin A and hormones of the pituitary, adrenal, and sex glands. The richest dietary sources are wheat germ; soybean, cotton seed, peanut, and corn oils; margarine; whole raw seeds and nuts; soybeans; eggs; butter; liver; sweet potatoes; and the leaves

of many vegetables, such as turnip greens. It is stored in the body for long periods of time, so any deficiency is rare. Deficiency may therefore take from months to years to occur, but results in muscle degeneration, vascular system abnormalities, megaloblastic anemia, hemolytic anemia, infertility, creatinuria, and liver and kidney damage and is associated with the aging process.

vitamin K, a group of fat-soluble vitamins known as quinones that are essential for the synthesis of prothrombin in the liver and of several related proteins involved in the clotting of blood. The vitamin is widely distributed in foods, especially leafy green vegetables, pork liver, yogurt, egg yolk, kelp, alfalfa, fish-liver oils, and blackstrap molasses, and is synthesized by the bacterial flora of the GI tract. It is used to reduce the clotting time in patients with obstructive jaundice and in hemorrhagic states associated with intestinal diseases and diseases of the liver; it is given prophylactically to infants to prevent hemorrhagic disease of the newborn. Deficiency results in hypoprothrombinemia, characterized by poor coagulation of the blood and hemorrhage, and usually occurs from inadequate absorption of the vitamin from the GI tract or the inability to use it in the liver.

vitamin K₁, a yellow, viscous, oil-soluble vitamin, occurring naturally, especially in alfalfa, and produced synthetically. It is used as a prothrombinogenic agent.

vitamin K₂, a pale yellow fat-soluble crystalline vitamin of the vitamin K group that is more unsaturated than vitamin K₁ and slightly less active biologically. It is isolated from putrefied fish meal and synthesized by various bacteria in the GI tract.

vitamin loss [L, *vita*, life, *amine*], reduction in vitamin content of food resulting from the handling and preparation of fresh foods during harvesting, heating, pickling, salting, milling, canning, and other food-processing techniques. Further vitamin losses can occur because of digestive disorders that prevent nutrient absorption and the use of drugs such as isoniazid that are vitamin antagonists.

vitaminology /vī′təminol′əjē/ [L, *vita* + *amine;* Gk, *logos,* science], the study of vitamins, including their structures, modes of action, and function in maintaining body health.

vitamin supplements, any vitamins or provitamins consumed in addition to nutrients in the food eaten.

vitellin /vitel′in/ [L, *vitellus,* yolk], a lipoprotein containing lecithin, found in the yolk of eggs.—**vitelline** /-ēn/ *adj.*

vitelline artery /vitel′in, -ēn/ [L, *vitellus;* Gk, *arteria,* airpipe], any of the embryonic arteries that circulate blood from the primitive aorta of the early developing embryo to the yolk sac.

V

vitelline circulation, the circulation of blood and nutrients between the developing embryo and the yolk sac by way of the vitelline arteries and veins.

vitelline duct, in embryology, the narrow channel connecting the yolk sac with the intestine.

vitelline membrane, the delicate cytoplasmic membrane surrounding the ovum.

vitelline vein, any of the embryonic veins that return blood from the yolk sac to the primitive heart of the early developing embryo.

vitellogenesis /vitel'ōjen'əsis/ [L, *vitellus;* Gk, *genein,* to produce], the formation or production of yolk.—**vitellogenetic,** *adj.*

vitellus, the yolk of an ovum.

vitiligo /vit'ile′gō, -ī′gō/ [L, *vitium,* blemish], a benign acquired skin disease of unknown cause, consisting of irregular patches totally lacking in pigment and often having hyperpigmented borders. The hypopigmented area is caused by loss of melanocytes. Exposed areas of skin are most often affected. Treatment using 8-methoxypsoralen requires extreme care and carefully regulated sun exposure. Some success has been achieved with the use of narrow-band ultraviolet light and topical application of protopic.—**vitiliginous,** *adj.*

vitrectomy /vitrek′təmē/ [L, *vitreus,* glassy; Gk, *ektomē,* excision], a surgical procedure for removing the contents of the vitreous chamber of the eye, which is then replaced by oil, air, or a vitreous substitute.

vitreous /vit′rē·əs/ [L, *vitreus,* glassy], pertaining to the vitreous humor of the eye located in the posterior chamber of the eye.

vitreous cavity [L, *vitreus,* glassy, *cavum,* cavity], the cavity in the eye posterior to the lens that contains the vitreous body and vitreous membrane and is transected by the vestigial remnants of the hyaloid canal.

vitreous degeneration [L, *vitreus,* glassy, *degenerare,* to deviate from kind], a form of hyaline degeneration; the formation of glassy material in the connective tissue of blood vessels and other tissues.

vitreous hemorrhage, a hemorrhage into the vitreous humor of the eye.

vitreous humor, a transparent, semigelatinous substance contained in a thin hyoid membrane filling the cavity behind the crystalline lens of the eye.

vitreous membrane, a membrane that lines the posterior cavity of the eye and surrounds the vitreous body.

vitrification /vit′rifikā′shən/, the conversion of a silicate material by heat and fusion to a glassy substance. Heat converts the material into a viscous liquid, which hardens on cooling.

vitronectin /vit′ro-nek′tin/, a multifunctional adhesive glycoprotein found in serum and various tissues. Its functions include regulation of the coagulation, fibrinolytic, and complement cascades, and it plays a role in hemostasis, wound healing, tissue remodeling, and cancer.

Vivactil, a trademark for a tricyclic antidepressant (protriptyline hydrochloride).

viviparous /vivip′ərəs/ [L, *vivus,* alive, *parere,* to bear], bearing living offspring rather than laying eggs, such as most mammals and some fish and reptiles.

vivisection /viv′əsek′shən/ [L, *vivus,* alive, *secare,* to cut], the performance of surgical operations on living animals, particularly experimental surgery for the purpose of research.

Vivonex, a trademark for a nutritional supplement containing protein, carbohydrate, and fat.

VLDL, abbreviation for **very low-density lipoprotein.**

VMA, abbreviation for **vanillylmandelic acid.**

VNA, abbreviation for *Visiting Nurses Association.*

VNTR, abbreviation for **variable number of tandem repeats.**

VO$_2$, symbol for **oxygen uptake** or consumption.

vocal apparatus /vō′kəl/ [L, *vocalis,* voice, *ad + parare,* to prepare], the larynx, pharynx, and oral and nasal cavities involved in the production of sound.

vocal cord [L, *vocalis,* voice; Gk, *chorde,* string], one of a pair of strong bands of yellow elastic tissue in the larynx enclosed by membranes called vocal folds and attached ventrally to the angle of the thyroid cartilage and dorsally to the vocal process of the arytenoid cartilage.

vocal cord nodule, a small inflammatory or fibrous growth that develops on the vocal cords of people who constantly strain their voices.

vocal cues, a category of nonverbal communication that includes all the noises and sounds that are extra-speech sounds and convey meaning.

vocal folds [L, *vocalis;* AS, *fealdan*], the true vocal cords.

vocal fremitus (VF), the vibration of the chest wall as a person speaks or sings that allows the person's voice to be heard by auscultation of the chest with a stethoscope. Vocal fremitus is decreased in emphysema, pleural effusion, pulmonary edema, and bronchial obstruction, and increased in consolidation as in pneumonia.

vocal paralysis, paralysis of the vocal cords.

vocal register, any of the perceptually distinct regions of vocal quality, each with a characteristic range of pitches, pattern of vocal cord vibration, and tone quality.

vocal resonance [L, *vocalis* + *resonare*, to sound again], **1.** auscultation. **2.** modification of the laryngeal tone as it passes through the pharynx and oral cavity to produce an increase in the intensity and quality of the sound.

vocal tract, the passages from the glottis through the nose and throat that influence the quality of the voice.

Vogt-Koyanagi-Harada syndrome /fōkt kō'yah·nah'ge hah-rah'dah/, a syndrome of uveomeningitis associated with retinochoroidal detachment, temporary or permanent deafness and blindness, and sometimes (usually not permanent) alopecia, vitiligo, and poliosis. The cause is unknown, but it may be an inflammatory autoimmune condition.

Vogt-Spielmeyer disease /fōkt shpēl'mī'er/, the juvenile form of neuronal ceroid-lipofuscinosis, with onset between 5 and 10 years of age. It is characterized by rapid cerebroretinal degeneration, massive loss of brain substance, excessive neuronal storage of lipofuscin, and death within 10 to 15 years.

voice, the acoustic component of speech that is normally produced by vibration of the vocal folds of the larynx.

voiced /voist/ [L, *vox,* voice], said of speech sounds produced with vibration of the vocal cords, such as /b/, /d/, or /z/.

voiceless /vois'ləs/ [L, *vox,* voice; AS, *laes,* less], said of speech sounds produced without vibration of the vocal cords, such as /p/, /t/, or /s/.

voiceprint /vois'print/, a graphic representation of a person's speech pattern electronically recorded. Like a fingerprint, the speech pattern for any individual is distinctive.

voice sounds, auscultatory sounds heard over the lungs or airways when the patient speaks; increased resonance indicates consolidation or an airless lung underlying an effusion. Types include bronchophony, egophony, and pectoriloquy.

void /void/ [ME, *voide,* empty], to empty or evacuate such as urine from the bladder.

voiding cystourethrography (VCU) [ME *voide,* empty; Gk, *kystis,* bag, *ourethra,* urethra, *graphein,* to record], cystourethrography in which radiographs are made before, during, and after voiding.

voiding urethrography [ME, *voide,* empty; Gk, *ourethra* + *graphein,* to record], radiography of the urethra during micturition after the introduction of a radiopaque fluid into the bladder.

vol., abbreviation for **volume.**

vol.%, abbreviation for *volume percent.*

volar /vō'lər/ [L, *vola,* palm, sole], pertaining to the palm of the hand or the sole of the foot.

volatile /vol'ətəl/ [L, *volatilis,* flying], of a liquid, easily vaporized.

volatile solvent, an easily vaporized solvent.

volition /vōlish'ən/ [L, *voluntas,* inclination], **1.** the act, power, or state of willing or choosing. **2.** the conscious impulse to perform or abstain from an act.—**volitional,** *adj.*

volitional /vōlish'ənəl/ [L, *volantas,* inclination], pertaining to the use of one's own will in performing or abstaining from an action.

volitional tremor [L, *volantas,* inclination, *tremor,* shaking], a trembling that begins during voluntary effort, sometimes spreading throughout the body. It may occur in MS and cerebellar disorders.

Volkmann's canal /fōlk'munz/ [Alfred W. Volkmann, German physiologist, 1800–1877], any one of the small blood vessel canals connecting haversian canals in bone tissue.

Volkmann's contracture [Richard von Volkmann, German surgeon, 1830–1889], a serious, persistent flexion contraction of forearm and hand caused by ischemia. A pressure or crushing injury in the region of the elbow usually precedes this condition, and pressure from a cast or tight bandage about the elbow is a common cause. Health care providers must watch for swelling, pallor, coldness, cyanosis, or pain distal to the injury site so that prompt loosening of constriction can restore circulation.

Volkmann's splint [Richard von Volkmann; AS, *splinte,* thin board], a splint that supports and immobilizes the lower leg. A footpiece extends from the foot to the knee on both sides of the splint, allowing ambulation.

volsella forceps /volsel'ə/ [L, *vosella,* tweezers, *forceps,* tongs], a kind of forceps having a small, sharp-pointed hook at the end of each blade.

volt (V) /vōlt/ [Alessandro Volta, Italian physicist, 1745–1827], the unit of electric potential. In an electric circuit, a volt is the force required to send 1 ampere of current through 1 ohm of resistance, or the difference in potential between two points on a conductor carrying a charge of 1 ampere when there is a dissipation of 1 watt between them.

voltage /vō'tij/ [Alessandro Volta], an expression of electromotive force in terms of volts.

voltammetry /voltam'ətərē/, the measurement of an electric current as a function of potential.

voltmeter /vōlt'mētər/, an instrument such as a galvanometer that measures in volts the differences in potential between different points of an electric circuit.

volume (vol.) /vol'yəm, -yōōm/ [L, *volumen,* paper roll], the amount of space occupied by a body, expressed in units of cubic distance.

volume ATPS, abbreviation for *ambient temperature, ambient pressure, saturated*

V

with water vapor conditions of a volume of gas. The conditions exist in a water-sealed spirograph or gasometer when the water temperature equals ambient temperature.

volume BTPS, abbreviation for *b*ody *t*emperature, ambient *p*ressure, *s*aturated with water vapor. These conditions of a volume of gas are used in respiratory physiology to assess lung volume and flow.

volume control fluid chamber, any one of several types of transparent plastic reservoirs with graduated volumetric markings, used to regulate the flow of IV solutions.

volume cycling, the delivery of gas under positive pressure during inspiration until an adjustable, preselected volume has been delivered.

volume imaging, MRI techniques in which MR signals are gathered at once from the whole object volume to be imaged. Many sequential plane imaging techniques can be categorized as volume imaging, at least in principle.

volumetric flow rate /vol′yəmet′rik/, the rate at which a volume of fluid flows past a designated point, usually measured in liters per second.

volumetric glassware, in chemistry, glassware designed and marked to contain or deliver specific volumes of liquid solutions.

volume unit (VU), a unit of a logarithmic scale for expressing the power level of a complex audio frequency electric signal such as that transmitting sound.

volume ventilator, a ventilator that delivers a predetermined volume of gas with each cycle.

voluntary /vol′ənter′ē/ [L, *voluntas,* inclination], referring to an action or thought originated, undertaken, controlled, or accomplished as a result of a person's free will or choice.

voluntary agency, a service agency legally controlled by volunteers rather than by owners or a paid staff.

voluntary hospital system, a nationwide complex of autonomous, self-established, and self-supported private not-for-profit and investor-owned hospitals in the United States.

volunteer /vol′əntir′/ [Fr, *volontaire*], someone who does a task voluntarily and usually without pay.

volutrauma /vol′yoo-trô′mə/, damage to the lung caused by overdistension by a mechanical ventilator set for an excessively high tidal volume. It results in a syndrome similar to adult respiratory distress syndrome.

volvulus /vol′vyələs/ [L, *volvere,* to turn], a twisting of the bowel on itself, causing intestinal obstruction. The condition is frequently the result of a prolapsed segment of mesentery and occurs most often in the ileum, the cecum, or the sigmoid parts of the bowel. If it is not corrected, the obstructed bowel becomes necrotic, and peritonitis and rupture of the bowel occur.

volvulus neonatorum, an intestinal obstruction in a newborn resulting from a twisting of the bowel caused by malrotation or nonfixation of the colon. Typical symptoms include abdominal distension; persistent regurgitation, often accompanied by fecal vomiting; and nonpassage of stools.

vomer /vō′mər/ [L, plowshare], the plow-shaped bone forming the posterior and inferior part of the nasal septum and having two surfaces and four borders.

vomeronasal organ, a structure on each side of the nasal septum believed to be a chemical sensory center for "sixth sense" detection of pheromones.

vomit /vom′it/ [L, *vomere,* to vomit], **1.** to expel the contents of the stomach through the esophagus and out of the mouth. **2.** the material expelled.

vomiting [L, *vomere,* to vomit], the forcible voluntary or involuntary emptying of the stomach contents through the mouth.

vomiting agents, chemicals that induce nausea and vomiting. They are used as aerosols, and exposure is primarily by inhalation, also by ingestion and by skin and eye contact. Their effects progress to difficulty in breathing, nausea, and vomiting. Effects are self-limited, generally disappearing within 2 hours. Death may occur with exposure to high concentrations in confined spaces.

vomiting management, a nursing intervention from the Nursing Interventions Classification (NIC) defined as prevention and alleviation of vomiting.

vomiting of pregnancy, vomiting that occurs during the early months of pregnancy. Factors contributing to the condition include delayed stomach emptying during pregnancy, relaxation of the esophageal sphincter at the opening into the stomach, and relaxation of the diaphragmatic hiatus, which increase the risk of gastric reflux.

vomitus /vom′itəs/ [L, *vomere,* to vomit], pertaining to the material expelled from the stomach during vomiting. Vomitus is sometimes classified by color or other appearances as an indicator of the cause of illness, such as a "coffee-ground" vomitus being a clinical sign of gastric bleeding.

VON, abbreviation for *Victorian Order of Nurses.*

von Gierke's disease /fôn gir′kəz/ [Edgar von Gierke, German pathologist, 1877–1945], a form of glycogen storage disease in which abnormally large amounts of glycogen are deposited in the liver and kidneys. The disorder is characterized by hypoglycemia, metabolic acidosis, dyslipidemia, and hepatomegaly. There is no effective treatment for the disorder. Medical efforts are directed at preventing hypoglycemia and acidosis.

von Hippel–Lindau disease [Eugen von Hippel, German ophthalmologist, 1867–1939; Arvid Lindau, Swedish pathologist, 1892–1958], a hereditary disease characterized by congenital, tumor-like vascular nodules in the retina and hemangioblastomas of the cerebellar hemispheres. Similar spinal cord lesions, cysts of the pancreas, kidneys, and other viscera, seizures, and mental retardation may be present.

von Willebrand disease [Erick A. von Willebrand, Finnish physician, 1870–1949], a congenital, autosomal dominant, mucocutaneous bleeding disorder caused by von Willebrand factor deficiency and subsequent impairment of platelet adhesion to the damaged blood vessel wall.

voracious [L, *vorax*], greedy or gluttonous, with an insatiable appetite.

voriconazole, an antifungal agent used to treat invasive aspergillosis and serious fungal infections.

vortex *pl.* **vortexes, vortices** [L, whirl], a whirlpool effect produced by the whirling of a more or less cylindric mass of fluid (liquid or gas).

vorticose veins, four large veins involved in the venous drainage of the eyeball. They exit through the sclera from each of the posterior quadrants of the eyeball and enter the superior and inferior ophthalmic veins.

voxel /vok'səl/, abbreviation for *vo*lume *el*ement, the three-dimensional version of a pi*xel*.

voyeur /voiyur', vô·äyœr'/ [Fr, *voir,* to see], one whose sexual desire is gratified by the practice of voyeurism.

voyeurism /voi'yəriz'əm, voiyur'izəm/ [Fr, *voyeur*; L, *ismus,* practice], a psychosexual disorder in which a person derives sexual excitement and gratification from looking at the naked bodies and genital organs or observing the sexual acts of others, especially from a secret vantage point.

VP, abbreviation for **variegate porphyria.**

VPF, abbreviation for **vascular permeability factor.**

V/Q, abbreviation for *ventilation/perfusion.*

VR, abbreviation for *variable ratio.*

VRA, abbreviation for **visual response audiometry.**

VRE, abbreviation for *vancomycin-resistant enterococci.*

V.S., 1. abbreviation for **vesicular sound. 2.** abbreviation for *Veterinary Surgeon.* **3.** abbreviation for **vital signs. 4.** abbreviation for *volumetric solution.*

VSD, abbreviation for **ventricular septal defect.**

VU, abbreviation for **volume unit.**

vulgaris /vulger'is/ [L, *vulgus,* common people], common or ordinary.

vulnerable /vul'nərəbəl/ [L, *vulnus,* wound], being in a dangerous position or condition and thereby susceptible to being infected or injured.

vulnerable period, a short period in the cardiac cycle during which activation may result in an ectopic beat. The ventricular vulnerable period corresponds to the apex of the T wave toward its ascending side.

vulvar /vul'vər/, pertaining to the vulva.

vulvar dystrophy, a disorder characterized by skin eruptions of white atrophic pustules, squamous cell hyperplasia, and lichen sclerosis et atrophicus.

vulvectomy /vulvek'təmē/ [L, *vulva,* wrapper; Gk, *ektomē,* excision], the surgical removal of part or all of the tissues of the vulva, performed most frequently in the treatment of malignant or premalignant neoplastic disease.

vulvitis /vulvī'tis/ [L, *vulva,* wrapper; Gk, *itis,* inflammation], an inflammation of the vulva.

vulvocrural /vul'vōkr oo'rəl/ [L, *vulva + crus,* leg], pertaining to the vulva and the thigh.

vulvodynia /vul'vōdin'ē·ə/, chronic pain and discomfort in the female external genitals.

vulvovaginal /vul'vōvaj'inəl/ [L, *vulva + vagina,* sheath], pertaining to the vulva and vagina.

vulvovaginal candidiasis, candidal infection of the vagina, and usually also the vulva, commonly characterized by pruritus, creamy white discharge, vulvar erythema and swelling, and dyspareunia.

vulvovaginitis /vul'vōvaj'inī'tis/, an inflammation of the vulva and vagina or of the vulvovaginal glands.

vv, 1. an abbreviation for *veins.* **2.** an abbreviation for *vice versa.*

v/v, 1. symbol for *volume of dissolved substance per volume of solvent.* **2.** symbol for *volume per volume.*

v/w, symbol for *volume of substance per unit of weight of another component.*

vWF, abbreviation for *von Willebrand's factor.*

VY plasty /vē'wī' plas'tē/, a surgical incision made in a V shape and sutured in a Y shape to lengthen the tissue area.

Vyvanse, a trademark for lisdexamfetamine.

VZIG, abbreviation for **varicella-zoster immune globulin.**

VZV, abbreviation for **varicella-zoster virus.**

V

w, the amount of energy required to ionize a molecule of air, as expressed by w = 33.85 eV/ion pair. This is an important quantity for radiation dosimetry because it allows the extraction of dose from ionization measurements

W, 1. abbreviation of **watt.** 2. symbol for the element **tungsten.**

Waardenburg's syndrome /vär′den bərgz/ [Petrus Johannes Waardenburg, Dutch ophthalmologist, 1886–1979], **1.** an autosomal-dominant disorder characterized by wide bridge of the nose resulting from lateral displacement of the inner canthi and puncta, pigmentary disturbances, including white forelock, heterochromia iridis, white eyelashes, leukoderma, and sometimes cochlear deafness. **2.** an autosomal-dominant disorder characterized by acrocephaly, orbital and facial deformities, and brachydactyly with mild soft tissue syndactyly; cleft palate, congenital glaucoma, cardiac malformation, and contractures of the elbows and knees may also be present.

waddling gait /wod′ling/ [ME, waden, to wade; ONorse, gata, way], a gait characterized by exaggerated lateral trunk movements and hip elevations.

WAGR syndrome, a syndrome of Wilms' tumor, aniridia, genitourinary abnormalities or gonadoblastoma, and mental retardation, resulting from a small interstitial deletion on chromosome 11.

Wagstaffe's fracture /wag′stafs/ [William Wagstaffe, English surgeon, 1834–1910; L, fractura, break], a fracture characterized by separation of the medial malleolus of the tibia.

waiting list, a roll of persons waiting to fill a vacancy, such as a list of candidates waiting for an organ transplant.

wakefulness /wāk′fulnəs/, **1.** an alert state of mind. **2.** sleeplessness or insomnia.

waking imagined analgesia (WIA) [AS, wacian, to awaken; L, imaginari, to picture oneself; Gk, a + algos, without pain], the pain relief experienced by a patient who uses the psychologic technique, usually with the help of an attending nurse or a hospital aide, of concentrating on previous pleasant personal experiences that produced tranquillity. This technique

is often effective in reducing mild to moderate pain.

waking paralysis, paralysis experienced momentarily upon awakening, usually improving within seconds.

Waldeyer's throat ring /wäl′dī·ərz/ [Heinrich W.G. von Waldeyer, German anatomist, 1836–1921; AS, hring], the palatine, pharyngeal, and lingual tonsils that encircle the pharynx.

Wald, Lillian [1867–1940], an American public health nurse, settlement leader, and social reformer who founded the Henry Street Settlement in New York to bring nursing care into the homes of the poor. She was also instrumental in establishing the school nursing system, the federal government's Children's Bureau, and the Nursing Service Division of the Metropolitan Life Insurance Company.

walker /wô′kər/ [AS, wealcan, to roam], **1.** an extremely light, movable apparatus, about waist high, made of metal tubing, used to aid a patient in walking. It has four widely placed, sturdy legs. The patient holds onto the walker and takes a step and then moves the walker forward and takes another step. **2.** A small, rubber or plastic heel attached to the bottom of a walking cast to prevent the cast from slipping on hard surfaces.

Walker-Warburg syndrome /waw′kər vär′bŏŏrg/ [Arthur Earl Walker, American surgeon, b. 1907; Mette Warburg, Danish ophthalmologist, 20th century], a congenital syndrome, usually fatal before the age of 1 year, consisting of hydrocephalus, agyria, various ocular anomalies such as retinal dysplasia, corneal opacity, or microphthalmia, and sometimes encephalocele.

walking belt, a leather or nylon device with handles that fastens around the patient's waist and assists the health care provider with the patient's ambulation.

walking cast [AS, wealcan, to roam; ONorse, kasta], a cast that permits a patient to walk.

walking program, an aerobic exercise regimen of walking 30 to 45 minutes a day 5 or 6 days a week. It may be part of a program to condition the heart or lower BP.

walking reflex, a series of steplike motions of an infant's legs when the infant is held under the arms and with the feet in contact with a surface. The reflex disappears at approximately 4 to 8 weeks of age.

walking rounds [AS, *wealcan*; Fr, *rond*], rounds in which a clinician leads a group of junior clinicians on rounds to visit the patients for whom they are collectively responsible.

walking typhoid [AS, *wealcan*, to roam; Gk, *typhos*, fever, *eidos*, form], an ambulatory subclinical case of typhoid fever. The person may be infected with typhoid but have mild symptoms that do not interfere with the ADL.

walking wounded [AS, *wealcan*, to roam + *wund*], a triage term for an injured person who is ambulatory and has minor injuries.

wall [L, *vallum*, palisade], a limiting structure within the body, such as the wall of the abdominal, thoracic, or pelvic cavities or the wall of a cell.

Wallenberg's syndrome /väl′en bergz/ [Adolf Wallenberg, German physician, 1862–1949], a syndrome resulting usually from occlusion of the vertebral artery, and less often from occlusion of its branch, the posterior inferior cerebellar artery; marked by loss of temperature and pain sensations of the face on the same side as the lesion, contralateral loss of these sensations in the trunk and extremities, and a variety of other neurologic and ocular symptoms, including Horner's syndrome.

wallerian degeneration /waler′ē·ən/ [Augustus V. Waller, English physician, 1816–1870; L, *degenerare*, to degenerate], the fatty degeneration of a nerve fiber after it has been severed from its cell body.

wall stress, the tension within the wall of the left ventricle. It is determined by the pressure in the ventricle, the internal radius of the ventricle, and the thickness of the wall.

wander /won′dər/ [AS, *wandrian*], **1.** to move about purposelessly. **2.** to cause to move back and forth in an exploratory manner.

wandering abscess [AS, *wandrian*; L, *abscedere*, to go away], an abscess that moves through tissue openings to a point some distance from its origin.

wandering atrial pacemaker [AS, *wandrian*; L, *passus*; ME, *maken*], a sinus arrhythmia with an atrial or junctional escape rhythm during the slow phase of the sinus rhythm. Frequently there are atrial fusion beats when impulses from the two pacing sources collide within the atria. An accelerated junctional rhythm that competes with the sinus rhythm is often mislabeled "wandering pacemaker."

Wangensteen apparatus /wang′ənstēn/ [Owen H. Wangensteen, American surgeon, 1898–1981; L, *ad* + *parare,* to prepare], a nasogastroduodenal catheter and suction apparatus used for constant gentle drainage and decompression of the stomach or duodenum.

Wangensteen tube [Owen H. Wangensteen], the catheter part of a Wangensteen apparatus.

ward /wôrd/ [AS, *weard*, guard], **1.** a large room in a hospital for the accommodation of several patients. **2.** a division within a hospital for the care of numerous patients having the same condition, e.g., a maternity ward.

warfarin poisoning /wôr′fərin/ [Wisconsin Alumni Research Foundation + coum*arin*], a toxic condition caused by the ingestion of warfarin accidentally in the form of a rodenticide or by overdose with the substance in its pharmacologic anticoagulant form. The poison accumulates in the body and results in nosebleed, bruising, hematuria, melena, and internal hemorrhage.

warfarin sodium, an oral anticoagulant prescribed for the prophylaxis and treatment of thrombosis, atrial fibrillation, and embolism.

warm-blooded [AS, *wearm* + *blod*], having a relatively high and constant body temperature, such as the temperatures maintained by humans, other mammals, and birds, despite changes in environmental temperatures. Heat is produced in the warm-blooded human body by the catabolism of foods in proportion to the amount of work performed by the tissues in the body. Heat is lost from the body by evaporation, radiation, conduction, and convection. The average temperature of the healthy human is 98.6° F (37° C).

warmup, light calisthenics and stretching exercises intended to increase flexibility, minimize risk of musculoskeletal complications, and gradually increase heart rate before the start of strenuous athletic activity.

washout /wosh′out/ [AS, *wascan,* to wash; ME, *oute*], the elimination or expulsion of one gas or volatile anesthetic agent from the lung alveoli by the administration of another, such as high-flow oxygen.

wasp /wosp/ [L, *vespa*], a thin, narrow-waisted hymenopteran insect with two pairs of membranous wings that are folded lengthwise when at rest like parts of a fan. Many species of wasps can give painful stings that produce severe effects in hypersensitive individuals.

Wassermann blood test /was′ərmən, vos′ərmun/ [August P. von Wassermann, German bacteriologist, 1866–1925], the

W

first standard diagnostic blood test (no longer used) for syphilis based on the complement fixation reaction.

wasted ventilation, the volume of air that ventilates the physiologic dead space in the respiratory system.

waste products [L, *vastare,* to destroy, *producere,* to produce], the products of metabolic activity after oxygen and nutrients have been supplied to a cell. These include mainly carbon dioxide and water, along with sodium chloride and soluble nitrogenous salts, which are excreted in feces, urine, and exhaled air.

wasting [L, *vastare,* to destroy], a process of deterioration marked by weight loss and decreased physical vigor, appetite, and mental activity.

wasting syndrome, a condition characterized by weight loss associated with chronic fever and diarrhea. Over a period of 1 month, the patient may lose 10% of baseline body weight. In cases of HIV infection, the malnutrition of wasting exacerbates the condition.

watchfulness /woch′fəlnes/, continuous supervision provided either openly or unobtrusively as the situation indicates.

water (H_2O) /wô′tər/ [AS, *waeter*], a chemical compound, one molecule of which contains one atom of oxygen and two atoms of hydrogen. Almost three quarters of the earth's surface is covered by water. Essential to life as it exists on this planet, water makes up more than 70% of living things. Pure water freezes at 32° F (0° C) and boils at 212° F (100° C) at 760 mm Hg.

waterbed, a closed rubber bag filled with water and used as a mattress to prevent or treat pressure ulcers by equalizing the patient's weight against the support.

waterborne, carried by water, such as a waterborne epidemic of typhoid fever.

water brash, heartburn with regurgitation into the mouth of fluid that may be sour or almost tasteless.

water for hemodialysis, water for use in hemodialysis, produced by subjecting water meeting the requirements of drinking water regulations to further treatment to reduce chemical and microbiological components. It contains no added antimicrobials and is not intended for injection.

water-hammer pulse, a large-amplitude pulse associated with aortic regurgitation. It is characterized by a full, forcible impulse and immediate collapse, causing a jerking sensation.

Waterhouse-Friderichsen syndrome /wô′tərhous frid′ərik′sən/ [Rupert Waterhouse, English physician, 1873–1958; Carl Friderichsen, Danish physician, 1886–1979], overwhelming cerebrospinal meningitis, most often caused by meningococcal infection, characterized by the sudden onset of fever, cyanosis, petechiae, and collapse from massive, bilateral adrenal hemorrhage. It requires immediate emergency treatment, hospitalization, and intensive care.

watering can perineum, a perineum with numerous fistulas leaking urine owing to abscesses or sometimes strictures of the urethra.

water-in-oil emulsion, one in which water or aqueous solution is the dispersed phase and oil or oleaginous substance is the continuous phase.

water intoxication, an increase in the volume of free water in the body, resulting in dilutional hyponatremia. Clinical manifestations are abdominal cramps, nausea, vomiting, lethargy, and dizziness.

water pollution, the contamination of lakes, rivers, and streams by industrial or community sources of pollutants.

water purification, emergency, methods of purifying unclean water for drinking purposes in emergencies. The three basic techniques include boiling the water and straining it through a cloth, adding 3 drops of tincture (alcoholic solution) of iodine per each quart of the water, and adding 10 drops of 1% chlorine bleach per each quart of water. When purifying chemicals are added, they should be thoroughly mixed with the water, and the mixture allowed to stand for 30 minutes.

watershed infarct /wô′tərshed/, an area of necrosis in the brain caused by an insufficiency of blood where the distributions of cerebral arteries overlap. The condition resembles that of an agricultural field irrigation system, in which the most distant sections may not be irrigated if there is a fall in water pressure.

Waters method, a technique for producing a radiographic image of the facial bones and maxillary sinuses. The patient faces the image receptor (IR) and tilts the forehead away from the IR, with the nose barely touching and the chin resting on surface of the IR. The x-ray beam is perpendicular and passes through the parietal bones and exits at the junction of the patient's nose and upper lip or at the location of the anterior nasal spine.

water-soluble contrast medium, an iodinated contrast medium that is absorbed by the blood and excreted by the kidneys. Among the advantages of a water-soluble contrast medium are that it does not need to be removed after a procedure and it may reduce the length of the procedure.

Watson-Crick helix /wôt′sən krik/ [James Dewey Watson, American geneticist, b.

1928; Francis H. Crick, British biochemist, 1916–2004; Gk, *helix*, coil], a model of the DNA molecule proposed by Watson and Crick as two right-handed polynucleotide chains coiled around the same axis as a double helix. The purine and pyrimidine bases of each strand are on the inside of the double helix and paired according to a Watson-Crick base-pairing rule. Variations in the sequences of the bases determine the genetic information transmitted by the DNA molecule.

Watson, Jean, a nursing theorist who proposed a philosophy and science of caring in 1979 in an effort to reduce the dichotomy between theory and practice. Her Theory of Human Caring reflects an existential phenomenologist's view of psychology and humanities. Caring is a universal social phenomenon that is only effectively practiced interpersonally. According to Watson, caring is a nursing term, and nursing concerns itself with health promotion, restoration, and prevention of illness as opposed to curing. Clients require holistic care that promotes humanism, health, and quality of living.

watt (W) /wot/ [James Watt, Scottish engineer, 1736–1819], the unit of electric power or work in the meter/kilogram/second system of notation. The watt is the product of the voltage and the amperage. One watt of power is dissipated when a current of 1 ampere flows across a difference in potential of 1 volt.

watts per square centimeter (W/cm²), a unit of power density or intensity used in ultrasonography.

wave [AS, *wafian*, to fluctuate], a periodic disturbance in which energy moves through a medium without permanently altering the constituents of the medium.

waveform, 1. the graphic representation of a wave, derived by plotting a characteristic wave against time. 2. the form of an arterial pressure pulse or displacement wave. 3. the representation of a neuromuscular electrical stimulation unit, which is usually a symmetric or asymmetric biphasic pulse with two phases in each pulse. The two phases continually alternate or reverse in direction between positive and negative polarity.

waveform ripple, a temporal variation in the voltage across the x-ray tube.

wavelength, the distance between a given point on one wave cycle and the corresponding point on the next successive wave cycle.

wax, a low-melting-point, high-molecular-weight organic mixture or compound similar to fats and oils but lacking glycerides.

Wb, abbreviation for **weber.**

WBC, abbreviation for *white blood cell.*

wbt, abbreviation for *wet bulb thermometer.*

wc, abbreviation for **wheelchair.**

W chromosome, the sex chromosomes of certain insects, birds, and fish. Females of such animals are heterogametic and have one W and one Z chromosome, whereas males are homogametic and have two Z chromosomes.

W/cm², abbreviation for **watts per square centimeter.**

W/D, 1. abbreviation for *well developed,* often used in the initial identifying statement in a patient record. 2. abbreviation for *withdrawal.*

weakness /wēk'nəs/, a condition of being feeble, fragile, frail, or decrepit or lacking physical strength, energy, or vigor. Causes of weakness include muscle disuse and nerve injury. Partially denervated muscle shows some degree of weakness, whereas completely denervated muscle becomes flaccid. Deep tendon reflexes are diminished or absent, and electromyographic readings are abnormal.

wean [AS, *wenian,* to accustom], 1. to induce a child to give up breastfeeding and accept other food in place of breast milk. 2. to withdraw a person from something on which he is dependent. 3. to remove a patient gradually from dependency on mechanical ventilation.

weanling, a child who has recently been weaned.

weapons of mass destruction (WMD), weapons, such as nuclear or chemical weapons, whose purpose is to kill large numbers of people indiscriminately.

wear-and-tear theory /wer'/, one theory of biologic aging in which structural and functional changes occur during the aging process (e.g., osteoarthritis).

weaver's bottom [AS, *wefan,* to weave, *botm,* undersurface], a form of bursitis affecting the ischial bursae in people whose work requires prolonged sitting in one position.

web, a network of fibers and cells forming a tissue or membrane.

webbed neck /webd/, a congenital thick fold of skin and fascia that stretches from the mastoid process to the clavicle on the lateral aspect of the neck. It occurs in such genetic conditions as Noonan's syndrome and Turner's syndrome.

webbed penis, a penis enclosed by the skin of the scrotum.

webbed toes [AS, *wefan,* to weave, *t*], an abnormality in which the toes are connected by webs of skin.

webbing, skinfolds connecting adjacent structures such as fingers or toes or the neck from the acromion to the mastoid, associated with genetic anomalies.

weber (Wb) /web'ər/ [Wilhelm Edward Weber, German physicist, 1804–1891], a unit of magnetic flux.

W

Weber's sign /web'ərz/ [Hermann D. Weber, English physician, 1823–1918], ipsilateral oculomotor nerve paresis and contralateral paralysis of the face, tongue, and extremities caused by a midbrain lesion.

Weber's tuning fork test, a method of screening auditory acuity. It is especially useful in determining whether a hearing loss in one ear is a conductive or a sensorineural loss. The test is performed by placing the stem of a vibrating tuning fork in the center of the person's forehead, or the midline vertex. The loudness of the sound is equal in both ears if hearing is normal or there is a symmetric hearing loss.

web of causation, an interrelationship of multiple factors that contribute to the occurrence of a disease.

Webril, a trademark for a stretchable cotton material applied over the skin to protect it from plaster irritation.

Wechsler intelligence scales /weks'lər/ [David Wechsler, American psychologist, 1896–1981], a series of standardized tests designed to measure the intelligence at several age levels from preschool through adult by means of questions that examine general information, arrangement of pictures and objects, vocabulary, memory, reasoning, and other abilities.

wedge /wej/ [AS, wecg], **1.** a piece of material thick at one end and tapering to a thin edge at the other end. **2.** to force something into a space of limited size.

wedge fracture /wej/ [AS, wecg, peg; L, fractura, break], a fracture of the vertebral body with anterior compression.

wedge pressure, the BP in the left atrium, determined with a cardiac catheter wedged in the most distal segment of the pulmonary artery.

wedge resection, the surgical excision of part of an organ, such as part of an ovary containing a cyst. The segment excised may be wedge-shaped.

WEE, abbreviation for *western equine encephalitis.*

weeping [AS, wepan, to cry], **1.** crying, lacrimating. **2.** oozing or exuding fluid, such as a sore or rash.

weeping eczema [AS, wepan, to cry; Gk, ekzein, to boil over], an inflammatory form of skin disease marked by a fluid exudate.

weeping lubrication, a form of hydrostatic lubrication in which the interstitial fluid of hydrated articular cartilage flows onto its surface when a load is applied.

Wegener's granulomatosis /wā'gənərz/ [Friedrich Wegener, German pathologist, 1907–1990; L, granulum, little grain; Gk, oma, tumor, osis, condition], an uncommon disease occurring mainly in the fifth decade and characterized by granulomatosis vasculitis of the upper and lower respiratory tract, necrotizing glomerulonephritis, and varying degrees of small-vessel vasculitis. Symptoms may include sinus pain; bloody, purulent nasal discharge; saddle-nose deformity; chest discomfort and cough; weakness; anorexia; weight loss; and skin lesions. Use of cytotoxic drugs, especially cyclophosphamide, has produced long-term remissions in many patients.

Weigert-Meyer rule, in cases of double ureter, the ureter from the upper pole of the kidney usually opens below and medial to the one from the lower pole.

weight (wt) /wāt/ [AS, gewiht], the force exerted on a body by gravitational attraction. As a body moves away from the earth, the weight of the body decreases, but the mass remains constant. Weight is sometimes measured in units of force such as newtons or poundals, but it is usually expressed in pounds or kilograms, as is mass.

weight: body mass, a nursing outcome from the Nursing Outcomes Classification (NOC) defined as the extent to which body weight, muscle, and fat are congruent to height, frame, gender, and age.

weight gain assistance, a nursing intervention from the Nursing Interventions Classification (NIC) defined as facilitating gain of body weight.

weight gain behavior, a nursing outcome from the Nursing Outcomes Classification (NOC) defined as personal actions to gain weight following voluntary or involuntary significant weight loss.

weight holder, a metal T-shaped bar that holds weights for traction.

weightlessness [AS, gewiht; ME, les], a state of absence of apparent weight, as in being beyond the effects of gravitational force in space travel.

weightlifter's headache, a type of headache sometimes experienced by weightlifters and others engaged in resistance forms of exercise. The headache is commonly occipital or upper cervical and comes on suddenly while straining, perhaps as a result of cervical ligament damage.

weightlifting, a resistance form of exercise that involves the lifting of maximum heavy weights in a prescribed manner.

weight loss, a reduction in body weight. The loss may be the result of a change in diet or life-style or a febrile disease. To lose 1 pound a week a person must consume 500 fewer calories daily and/or expend 500 more calories daily through physical activity.

weight loss behavior, a nursing outcome from the Nursing Outcomes Classification (NOC) defined as personal actions to lose weight through diet, exercise, and behavior modification.

weight maintenance behavior, a nursing outcome from the Nursing Outcomes Classification (NOC) defined as personal actions to maintain optimum body weight.

weight management, a nursing intervention from the Nursing Interventions Classification (NIC) defined as facilitating maintenance of optimal body weight and percent body fat.

weight per volume (w/v) solution, the relationship of a solute to a solvent expressed as grams of solute per milliliter of the total solution. An example is 50 g of glucose in 1 L of solution, considered a 5% w/v solution.

weight reduction assistance, a nursing intervention from the Nursing Interventions Classification (NIC) defined as facilitating loss of weight and/or body fat.

weight-reduction diet, a diet used to decrease body weight. It must supply fewer calories than the individual expends each day while supplying all the essential nutrients for maintaining health.

weights and measures, a system of establishing units or parts of quantities of substances, including standards of mass or volume.

weight traction [AS, *gewiht*; L, *trahere*, to draw], traction applied to a limb or part of a limb by means of a suspended weight.

weight training, a type of resistance-training exercise using barbells, dumbbells, or machines to increase muscle strength.

Weill-Marchesani syndrome /vīl märkəsä′nē/ [Georges Weill, French ophthalmologist, 1866–1952; Oswald Marchesani, German ophthalmologist, 1900–1952], a congenital disorder of connective tissue, autosomal dominant or recessive, characterized by brachycephaly, shortened digits, short stature with broad chest and heavy musculature, reduced joint mobility, and a variety of ocular defects.

well baby care [AS, *wyllan,* to wish; ME, *babe*; L, *garrire,* to chatter], periodic health supervision for infants and children to promote optimal physical, emotional, and intellectual growth and development. Such health care measures include routine immunizations to prevent disease, screening procedures for early detection and treatment of illness, and parental guidance and instruction in proper nutrition, accident prevention, and specific care and rearing of the child at various stages of development.

well baby clinic, a clinic that specializes in medical supervision and services for healthy infants.

well-being [AS, *wyllan* + *beon,* to be], achievement of a good and satisfactory existence as defined by the individual.

well-differentiated lymphocytic malignant lymphoma /-dif′ərən′shē·ā′tid/, a lymphoid neoplasm characterized by the predominance of mature lymphocytes.

Wellens' syndrome, the ECG signs of critical proximal left anterior descending coronary artery stenosis in patients with unstable angina.

wellness, a dynamic state of health in which an individual progresses toward a higher level of functioning, achieving an optimum balance between internal and external environments.

Wells' syndrome /welz/ [G.C. Wells, British dermatologist, 20th century], cellulitis with erythema, edema, and often blistering of the skin accompanied by eosinophilia, flame figures, and a mild fever.

welt [OE, *wealtan,* to roll], a raised ridge on the skin, usually caused by a blow, or occurring in dermatographism.

Wenckebach heart block, a form of second-degree atrioventricular block with a progressive beat-to-beat prolongation of the PR interval, finally resulting in a nonconducting P wave.

Werdnig-Hoffmann disease /verd′nig hôf′mun/ [Guido Werdnig, Austrian neurologist, 1844–1919; Johann Hoffmann, German neurologist, 1857–1919], a genetic disorder beginning in infancy or young childhood, characterized by progressive atrophy of the skeletal muscle resulting from degeneration of the cells in the anterior horn of the spinal cord and the motor nuclei in the brainstem. Symptoms include congenital hypotonia; absence of stretch reflexes; flaccid paralysis, especially of the trunk and limbs; lack of sucking ability; fasciculations of the tongue and sometimes of other muscles; and often dysphagia. Treatment is symptomatic, and death generally occurs in early childhood, often from respiratory complications.

Werner's syndrome /wur′nərz, wer′nərz/, an inherited condition of progeria with scleroderma, juvenile cataracts, diabetes mellitus, and hypogonadism.

Wernicke-Korsakoff syndrome, the coexistence of Wernicke's encephalopathy and Korsakoff's syndrome.

Wernicke's aphasia /ver′nikēz/ [Karl Wernicke, German neurologist, 1848–1905], a form of aphasia affecting comprehension of written and spoken words, possibly caused by a lesion in Wernicke's center. The client may articulate normally, but speech is incoherent, with malformed or substitute words and grammatical errors.

Wernicke's center [Karl Wernicke; Gk, *kentron,* center], a sensory speech center

W

located in the posterior temporal gyrus and adjacent angular gyrus in the dominant hemisphere. Wernicke observed in 1874 that patients with brain damage in that area also suffered a loss of speech comprehension.

Wernicke's encephalopathy [Karl Wernicke], an inflammatory, hemorrhagic, degenerative condition of the brain. It is characterized by lesions in several parts of the brain, double vision, opthalmoplegia, involuntary and rapid movements of the eyes, lack of muscular coordination, and decreased mental function, which may be mild or severe. Wernicke's encephalopathy is caused by a thiamine deficiency and is seen in association with chronic alcoholism.

Westcort, a trademark for a glucocorticoid (hydrocortisone valerate).

Westermark's sign [Neil Westermark, German radiologist, b. 1904], on a radiograph of the lung, the absence of blood vessel markings beyond the location of a pulmonary embolism.

Western blot test, a laboratory blood test to detect the presence of antibodies to specific antigens. It is regarded as more precise than ELISA and is sometimes used to check the validity of ELISA tests.

West Nile encephalitis /west nīl/ [West Nile River valley and region in northern Uganda, where the disease was first observed in 1937], a mild, febrile, sporadic disease caused by the West Nile virus, transmitted by *Culex* mosquitoes and occurring chiefly in the summer; infection often does not lead to encephalitis. It may be of sudden onset, and symptoms may include drowsiness, severe frontal headache, maculopapular rash, abdominal pain, loss of appetite, nausea, and generalized lymphadenopathy. Care is supportive; many recover quickly but may experience prolonged malaise.

West Nile virus /west nīl/, a virus of the genus *Flavivirus* that causes West Nile encephalitis. It is transmitted by *Culex* mosquitoes, with wild birds serving as the reservoir, and occurs widely in Africa, Europe, the Middle East, and Asia; it has also been reported in the United States.

West nomogram, a graph used in estimating the body surface area.

West's syndrome, an infantile encephalopathy characterized by spasms, arrest of psychomotor development, and an EEG abnormality of random high-voltage slow waves and spikes from multiple loci.

wet-and-dry-bulb thermometer, an instrument used to measure relative humidity. It consists of a thermometer with a bulb that is wet or moist and one that is kept dry. The relative humidity is calculated from the difference in readings of the thermometers when water evaporates from the wet bulb, decreasing its temperature.

wet dressing [AS, *waet;* Ofr, *dresser,* to arrange], a moist dressing used to relieve symptoms of some skin diseases. As the moisture evaporates, it cools and dries the skin, softens dried sera and sera, and stimulates drainage.

wet nurse, a woman who cares for and breastfeeds another's infant.

wet pack [AS, *waet,* moist; ME, *pakke*], a therapy that involves wrapping the patient in wet sheets with a top covering of a dry blanket, usually to reduce fever.

wet pleurisy [AS, *waet;* Gk, *pleuritis*], pleurisy in which the inflammation has progressed to an effusive state. The escaped fluid has a high specific gravity because of the presence of blood clots and fibrin.

wet tap, accidental puncture of the dura mater while performing extradural anesthesia, so called from the leakage of CSF from the needle hub.

wetting agent, 1. a substance that lowers the surface tension of water to promote wetting. **2.** a detergent such as tyloxapol used as a mucolytic in respiratory therapy.

wet to dry dressing, a wet dressing that is allowed to dry and then is removed. In removal it lightly debrides the wound.

W/F, abbreviation for *white female,* often used in the initial identifying statement in a patient record.

Wharton's jelly /wôr'tənz/ [Thomas Wharton, English anatomist, 1614–1673; L, *gelare,* to congeal], a gelatinous tissue that remains when the embryonic body stalk blends with the yolk sac within the umbilical cord.

wheal /wēl/ [AS, *walu,* pimple], a smooth, slightly elevated area on the skin that is redder or paler than surrounding skin. It is the typical lesion of urticaria.

wheal-and-flare reaction [AS, *walu;* ME, *fleare,* to blaze up; L, *re,* again, *agere,* to act], a skin eruption that may follow injury or injection of an antigen. It is characterized by swelling and redness caused by a release of histamine. The reaction usually occurs in three stages, beginning with the appearance of an erythematous area at the site of injury, followed by development of a flare surrounding the site. Finally a wheal forms at the site as fluid leaks under the skin from surrounding capillaries.

wheat weevil disease, a hypersensitivity pneumonitis caused by allergy to weevil particles found in wheat flour.

wheel, 1. a rigid circular frame designed to revolve about an axis in the center of the disk. **2.** a round cutting or polishing dental instrument.

wheelchair (wc), a mobile chair equipped with large wheels and brakes.

wheelie /wēˈlē/, a wheelchair mobility maneuver in which the front casters are raised and balance is maintained over the large rear wheels. It is used for negotiating steep ramps, steps, curbs, and other rough terrain.

wheeze [AS, *hwesan*, to hiss], **1.** a form of rhonchus, characterized by a high-pitched or low-pitched musical quality. It is caused by a high-velocity flow of air through a narrowed airway and is heard during both inspiration and expiration. It may be caused by bronchospasm, inflammation, or obstruction of the airway by a tumor or foreign body. Wheezes are associated with asthma and chronic bronchitis. Unilateral wheezes are characteristic of bronchogenic carcinoma, foreign bodies, and inflammatory lesions. **2.** to breathe with a wheeze.

whiplash injury [ME, *whippen* + *lasshe*; L, *ijuria*], *informal.* an injury to the cervical vertebrae or their supporting ligaments and muscles marked by pain and stiffness. It usually results from sudden acceleration or deceleration, such as in a rear-end car collision that causes violent back-and-forth movement of the head and neck.

Whipple procedure /hwipˈəl/ [Allen O. Whipple, American surgeon, 1881–1963], radical pancreaticoduodenectomy with removal of the distal third of the stomach, the entire duodenum, and the head of the pancreas, a portion of the jejunum, and the lower half of the common bile duct, with gastrojejunostomy, choledochojejunostomy, and pancreaticojejunostomy.

Whipple's disease [George Hoyt Whipple, American pathologist, 1878–1976], a rare intestinal disease characterized by severe intestinal malabsorption, steatorrhea, anemia, weight loss, arthritis, and arthralgia. People with the disease are severely malnourished and have abdominal pain, chest pain, and a chronic nonproductive cough. Penicillin and tetracycline may alleviate the symptoms.

whirlpool bath /(h)wurl/, the immersion of the body or a part of the body in a tank of warm water agitated by a jet of equally hot water and air, often used to clean infected wounds.

Whitaker test, a pressure-flow study measuring resistance of the ureters to a given flow rate of urine by antegrade pyelography of the renal pelvis and a catheter in the bladder.

white blood cell cast, a hyaline cast that contains WBCs, such as in tubulointerstitial nephritis, pyelonephritis, or glomerulonephritis.

white blood cell (WBC) count and differential count, a two-component blood test that first counts the total number of WBCs (leukocytes) in 1 cubic millimeter of peripheral venous blood and then measures the percentage of each type of leukocyte present in the same specimen (the differential count).

white blood cell scan, a nuclear scan to identify and localize an area of inflammation or infection. The scan is performed 4 to 24 hours after the WBCs are separated from blood drawn from the patient, labeled with technetium or indium, and reinjected.

white cell, *informal.* white blood cell. See also **leukocyte.**

white fibrocartilage [AS, *hwit*; L, *fibra,* fiber, *cartilago*], a mixture of tough, white fibrous tissue and flexible cartilaginous tissue.

white gold, a gold alloy with a high content of palladium or platinum used in dental restorations such as prepared tooth cavities and gold crowns.

white matter, the tissue of the central nervous system and much of the part of the cerebrum, consisting mainly of myelinated nerve fibers, but with some unmyelinated nerve fibers, embedded in a spongy network of neuroglia. It is subdivided in each half of the spinal cord into three funiculi: the anterior, the posterior, and the lateral white column. Each column subdivides into tracts that are closely associated in function.

white noise, a sound in which the intensity is the same at all frequencies within a designated band.

white radiation, a form of radiation that results from the rapid deceleration of high-speed electrons striking a target, as occurs when the electron beam of a tungsten cathode strikes the tungsten or molybdenum target of the anode in an x-ray tube.

white ramus communicans, the communicating nerve branch between sympathetic ganglions and spinal nerves that is largely myelinated and located mainly in the thoracic and upper lumbar region.

white spots film fault, a defect in a radiograph or photograph that appears as scattered white spots throughout the image area.

white thrombus, a clot composed of some combination of blood platelets, fibrin, clotting factors, and WBCs but containing few or no erythrocytes.

white willow bark, a preparation of the bark of various *Salix* species native to central and southern Europe and collectively known as white willow, containing salicin, a precursor of salicylic acid. It is used as an antiinflammatory and antipyretic.

whitlow /(h)witˈlō/ [Scand, *whick,* nail, *flaw,* crack], an inflammation of the end of a finger or toe that results in suppuration.

WHO, abbreviation for **World Health Organization.**

WHO classification of lymphoid neoplasms, a classification of lymphomas,

W

descended from the REAL classification, that divides them into three main categories (B-cell neoplasms, T-cell neoplasms, and Hodgkin's lymphoma) based on morphology, immunophenotype, and genetic abnormalities.

whole blood /hōl/ [AS, *hal* + *blod*], donor blood that is unmodified except for the presence of an anticoagulant. Whole blood is rarely used for transfusion because it is typically separated into red cells, plasma, or other components after collection.

whole-body dose, a measure of radiation exposure, equal to the total amount of ionizing radiation absorbed by the body divided by the body's mass. It is meaningful only for fairly uniform irradiation over the entire body.

whole-body irradiation, ionizing radiation exposure that affects the entire body. Short-term whole-body irradiation can cause injury or death in humans, mainly from damage to the GI tract and the bone marrow. However, such injury occurs only with doses far beyond the diagnostic range, such as with exposure to nuclear weapons. The absorbed dose equivalent limit for whole-body occupational exposure is 5 rem per year. The nonoccupational absorbed dose equivalent limit is 0.5 rem per year.

whole bowel irrigation, a method of treating poisoned patients by flushing large volumes of fluid through the GI tract.

whole milk, cow's milk from which no constituent such as fat has been removed. To be called whole milk, it must contain 3.5% fat, 8.5% nonfat milk solids, and 88% water.

whoop /hoōp, (h)woōp/, a noisy spasm of inspiration that terminates a coughing paroxysm in cases of pertussis. It is caused by a sudden sharp increase in tension on the vocal cords.

whorl /(h)wurl/ [ME, *hwarwy*], a spiral turn, such as one of the turns of the cochlea or of the dermal ridges that form fingerprints.

WIA, abbreviation for **waking imagined analgesia.**

wick humidifier, a respiratory care device in which a piece of paper, sponge, or similar material that absorbs water by capillary action is inserted in the path of the air flow. With the addition of heat, high levels of humidity can be achieved.

Widal's test /vēdäls'/ [Georges F. I. Widal, French physician, 1862–1929], an agglutination test used to aid in the diagnosis of *Salmonella* infections such as typhoid fever. This test measures the level of cold or febrile agglutinins in the blood that causes RBCs to stick together at low or high temperatures. A fourfold increase in titer of agglutinins to O or H antigens is highly suggestive of active infection.

Wiedenbach, Ernestine /wē′dənbak/ [1900–1996], a German-born American nursing educator and writer. She taught maternal and newborn health nursing at Yale School of Nursing, was a leader in family-centered maternity nursing and developed the full range of the art and science of obstetric nursing.

Wiener, Carolyn L., a nursing theorist who, with Marylin J. Dodd, developed the Theory of Illness Trajectory, which involves not only the patient but the family and caregivers. The theory helps elucidate how patients and families tolerate the states of uncertainty caused by the illness and manage the illness.

Wigraine, a trademark for a vasoconstrictor (ergotamine tartrate).

wild-type allele [AS, *wilde,* untamed; Gk, *typos,* mark, *genein,* to produce], a normal or standard form of a gene, as contrasted with a mutant form.

wild-type virus, street virus.

will [AS, *wyllan*], **1.** the mental faculty that enables one consciously to choose or decide on a course of action. **2.** the act or process of exercising the power of choice. **3.** a wish, desire, or deliberate intention. **4.** a disposition or attitude toward another or others. **5.** determination or purpose; willfulness. **6.** in law, an expression or declaration of a person's wishes as to the disposition of property to be performed or take effect after death.

Williams syndrome /wil′yəmz/ [J.C.P. Williams, New Zealand cardiologist, 20th century], supravalvular aortic stenosis, mental retardation, elfin facies, and transient hypercalcemia in infancy.

will to live, a nursing outcome from the Nursing Outcomes Classification (NOC) defined as desire, determination, and effort to survive.

Wilms' tumor /vilms/ [Max Wilms, German surgeon, 1867–1918], a malignant neoplasm of the kidney occurring in young children before the fifth year in 75% of the cases. The most frequent early signs are hypertension, a palpable mass, pain, and hematuria. The tumor, an embryonal adenomyosarcoma, is well encapsulated in the early stage, but it may extend into lymph nodes, the renal vein, or the vena cava and metastasize to the lungs or other sites.

Wilson's disease [Samuel A.K. Wilson, English neurologist, 1878–1937], a rare inherited disorder whereby a decrease in ceruloplasmin causes copper to accumulate slowly in the liver to then be released and taken up in other parts of the body. Hemolysis and hemolytic anemia occur as the copper accumulates in the RBCs. Accumulation in the brain may cause tremors, muscle rigidity, poorly articulated speech, and dementia. Kidney function is diminished; the liver becomes cirrhotic.

Winckel's disease [Franz Von Winckel, German gynecologist, 1837–1911], a fatal disease of the newborn caused by colon bacilli entering the stump of the umbilical cord. It is characterized by hematuria, jaundice, enlarged spleen, collapse, and convulsions.

windburn /wind′burn/ [AS, *wind,* air + *baernan*], a skin disorder caused by exposure to winds.

windchill /wind′chil/, the loss of heat from the body when it is exposed to wind of a given speed at a given temperature and humidity.

windchill factor [AS, *wind,* air, *cele,* cold], the amount of chilling of the body, beyond that resulting from a cold ambient temperature, because of exposure to cool air currents. The windchill factor is expressed in degrees Celsius or Fahrenheit as the effective temperature felt by a person exposed to the weather. Because windchill factors are based on exposure of dry skin to cool air currents, air blowing at the same speed over a wet skin surface would cause additional loss of body heat and a greater windchill.

windchill index, a chart that compares temperatures of the atmosphere with various wind speeds, enabling one to calculate the windchill factor. The comparison is expressed in kilocalories per hour per square meter of skin surface.

winding sheet /wīn′ding/, a shroud for wrapping a dead body.

window [AS, *wind,* air, *owe,* eye], **1.** a surgically created opening in the surface of a structure or an anatomically occurring opening in the surface or between the chambers of a structure. **2.** a specific time period during which a phenomenon can be observed, a reaction monitored, or a procedure initiated.

windowed /win′dōd/, referring to an orthopedic cast that has an opening designed to relieve pressure that may irritate and inflame the skin or to provide access to an incision or a wound.

winegrower's lung /wīn′grō′ərs/, a type of hypersensitivity pneumonitis caused by contact with mold on grapes.

winged scapula /wingd/ [ONorse, *vaengr*; L, *scapula,* shoulderblade], an abnormal prominence of the scapula caused either by projection of posterior angles of the ribs in a flat chest or by paralysis of the serratus anterior muscle.

wink reflex, an automatic closure of the eyelids in response to an appropriate stimulus.

Winstrol, a trademark for an androgen (stanozolol) used as an anabolic agent.

winter cough [AS, *winter* + *cohhetan*], *nontechnical.* a chronic condition characterized by a persistent cough occasioned by cold weather.

wintergreen oil, a volatile oil with a characteristic odor and taste. It is used as a counterirritant in ointments or liniments for muscle pain and also as a flavoring agent.

winter itch, pruritus occurring in cold weather in people who have dry skin, particularly in those who have atopic dermatitis.

wire /wīr/, **1.** a long, slender, flexible structure of metal, used in surgery and dentistry. **2.** to insert such metal strands into a body structure, as into a broken bone to immobilize fragments.

wire suture [AS, *wir*; L, *sutura*], a stainless steel or silver wire used for uniting bone fracture fragments or in dentistry.

wiry pulse /wī′(ə)re/ [AS, *wir*; L, *pulsare,* to beat], an abnormal pulse that is strong but small.

wisdom tooth [AS, *wisdom* + *toth*], a third molar; either of the last teeth on each side of the upper and lower jaw. The wisdom teeth are the last teeth to erupt, often causing considerable pain, dental problems, and the need for extraction.

wish fulfillment [AS, *wiscan,* to wish, *fullfyllan,* to fulfill], **1.** the gratification of a desire. **2.** in psychology, the satisfaction of a desire or the release of emotional tension through such processes as dreams, daydreams, and neurotic symptoms. **3.** in psychoanalysis, one of the primary motivations for dreams in which an unconscious desire or urge is given expression.

wishful thinking [AS, *wiscan* + *thencan,* to think], the interpretation of facts or situations according to one's desires or wishes rather than as they exist in reality, usually used as an unconscious device to avoid painful or unpleasant feelings.

Wiskott-Aldrich syndrome /wis′kot ôl′drich/ [Alfred Wiskott, German pediatrician, 1898–1978; Robert Anderson Aldrich, American pediatrician, 1917–1998], an immunodeficiency disorder inherited as a recessive X-linked trait, characterized by thrombocytopenia; eczema; inadequate T- and B-cell function; and an increased susceptibility to viral, bacterial, and fungal infections and cancer. Treatment includes the prescription of appropriate antibiotics for specific infectious organisms and the administration of transfer factor from activated lymphocytes to increase the resistance to infection and to clear the eczema.

witch doctor, a shamanistic healer whose primary function is to cure the sick members of the community.

witch hazel [AS, *wican,* to bend; Ger, *hasel*], **1.** a shrub, *Hamamelis virginiana,* indigenous to North America, from which an astringent extract is derived. **2.** a solution comprising the extract, alcohol, and water, used as an astringent.

witch's milk, a milklike substance secreted from the breast of the newborn, caused by circulating maternal lactating hormone.

W

withdrawal /withdrô′əl/ [ME, *with* + *drawen,* to take away], a common response to physical danger or severe stress characterized by a state of apathy, lethargy, depression, retreat into oneself, and in grave cases catatonia and stupor.

withdrawal behavior, the physical or psychologic removal of oneself from a stressor.

withdrawal bleeding, the passage of blood from the uterus, associated with the shedding of endometrium that has been stimulated and maintained by hormonal medication. It occurs when the medication is discontinued.

withdrawal method, a contraceptive technique in coitus wherein the penis is withdrawn from the vagina before ejaculation. It is not reliable because small amounts of seminal fluid carrying millions of spermatozoa may be emitted without sensation before full ejaculation.

withdrawal symptoms, the unpleasant, sometimes life-threatening physiologic changes that occur when some drugs are withdrawn after prolonged, regular use. The effects may occur after use of an opioid, antipsychotic, stimulant, sedative-hypnotic, alcohol, corticosteroid, or other substance to which the person has become physiologically or psychologically dependent. Other drug therapy may be used to relieve symptoms of withdrawal. Symptoms can also be managed with a planned schedule of tapering the drug dose over time.

withdrawal syndrome [ME, *with* + *drawen,* to take away; Gk, *syn,* together, *dromos,* course], a physical and mental response after cessation or severe reduction in intake of a substance such as alcohol or opiates that has been used regularly to induce euphoria, intoxication, or relief from pain or distress. The body tissues become dependent on the regular reinforcing effect of the chemical so that interruption of the dosage induces an organic mental state characterized by anxiety, restlessness, insomnia, irritability, impaired attention, and often physical illness.

withdrawn behavior, a condition in which there is a blunting of the emotions and a lack of social responsiveness.

witness, a person who is present and can testify that he or she has personally observed an event, such as the signing of a will or consent form.

W/M, abbreviation for *white male,* often used in the initial identifying statement in a patient record.

WMD, abbreviation for **weapons of mass destruction.**

WOB, abbreviation for **work of breathing.**

wobble /wob′əl/, an eccentric rotation that permits increased resolution of tomographic imaging devices composed of discrete detector systems.

WOCN, an abbreviation for the **Wound, Ostomy and Continence Nurses Society.**

Wolbachia /wol-bak′e-ah/, a genus of bacteria that infect a wide variety of invertebrates, including insects, spiders, crustaceans, and nematodes.

Wolff-Chaikoff effect /wŏŏlf chī′kəf/, the decreased formation and release of thyroid hormone in the presence of an excess of iodine.

wolffian cyst /wôl′fē·ən/ [Kaspar F. Wolff, German anatomist, 1733–1794; Gk, *kystis,* bag], **1.** a cyst of the wolffian duct. **2.** a cyst of a broad ligament of the uterus.

Wolff-Parkinson-White syndrome /wŏŏlf pär′kinsən (h)wīt/ [Louis Wolff, American physician, 1898–1972; John Parkinson, English cardiologist, 1885–1976; Paul Dudley White, American cardiologist, 1886–1973], a disorder of atrioventricular (AV) conduction involving an accessory pathway. This syndrome is often identified by a characteristic delta wave seen on an ECG at the beginning of the QRS complex.

Wolff's law /wôlfs/ [Julius Wolff, German anatomist, 1836–1902], the principle that changes in the form and function of a bone are followed by changes in its internal structure.

Wolf-Herschorn syndrome, a genetic disorder of infants characterized by psychomotor and growth retardation, hypertonicity, seizures, and microcephaly. Other features include craniofacial anomalies, ocular malformations, cleft lip or palate, heart malformations, and scoliosis.

Wolfram syndrome /wool′fram/ [D.J. Wolfram, American physician, 20th century], an autosomal-recessive syndrome, first evident in childhood, consisting of DM, diabetes insipidus, optic atrophy, and neural deafness.

woman, an adult female human.

woman-year [AS, *wifman* + *gear*], in statistics, 1 year in the reproductive life of a sexually active woman; a unit that represents 12 months of exposure to the risk of pregnancy.

wood creosote, that obtained by distilling wood tar, mainly beech *(Fagus sylvatica).* It was formerly used as an expectorant and external antiseptic but is now rarely used in the United States.

Wood's lamp [Robert W. Wood, American physicist, 1868–1955; AS, *glaes*], an illuminating device with a nickel oxide filter that holds back all light except for a few violet rays of the visible spectrum and ultraviolet wavelengths of about 365 nm. It is used extensively to help diagnose fungus infections of the scalp and erythrasma.

wood tick [AS, *wudu*; ME, *tike*], a hard-shelled tick of the Ixodidae family and a natural reservoir of *Rickettsia rickettsii*. One species of wood tick, *Dermacentor andersoni*, is the principal vector in western North America of **Rocky Mountain spotted fever**, transmitted by *R. rickettsii*.

wool fat, a fatty substance obtained from sheep's wool and of which lanolin is a common chemical component.

woolsorter's disease [AS, *wull*; Fr, *sorte*; L, *dis*, opposite of; Fr, *aise*, ease], the pulmonary form of anthrax, so named because it is an occupational hazard to those who handle sheep's wool. Early symptoms mimic those of influenza, but the patient soon develops high fever, respiratory distress, and cyanosis.

word blindness [AS, *word* + *blind*], an inability to understand written language; a form of receptive aphasia caused by lesions in the parietal or parietal-occipital areas of the brain.

word salad, a jumble of words and phrases that lacks logical coherence and meaning, often characteristic of disoriented individuals and persons with schizophrenia.

work hardening, a highly structured, goal-oriented, individualized treatment program designed to maximize a person's ability to return to work, using work (real or simulated) as a treatment modality.

working occlusion [AS, *weorc*; L, *occludere*, to shut], the occlusal contacts of teeth on the side of the jaw toward which the mandible is moved.

working phase, in psychology, the second stage of the therapist-client relationship in which clients explore their experiences. Therapists assist clients in this process by helping them to describe and clarify their experiences, to plan courses of action and try out the plans, and to begin to evaluate the effectiveness of their new behaviors.

working pressure, the recommended pressure, usually about 34 Pa (50 p.s.i.), for oxygen or compressed air leaving a cylinder. It is reduced by a pressure regulator for clinical use in respiratory therapy.

working through, a process by which repressed feelings are released and reintegrated into the personality.

workload, an amount of work to be performed within a specific time period.

work of breathing (WOB), the effort required to inspire air into the lungs. WOB accounts for 5% of total body oxygen consumption in a normal resting state but can increase dramatically during acute illness.

work of worrying, a coping strategy in which inner preparation through worrying increases the level of tolerance for subsequent threats.

workout, 1. a test of ability and endurance. 2. a physical exercise session.

work simplification, the use of special equipment, ergonomics, functional planning, and behavior modification to reduce the physical and psychologic stresses of home maintenance for disabled people or their family members.

work therapy [AS, *weorc*; Gk, *therapeia*, treatment], a therapeutic approach in which the client performs a useful activity or learns an occupation, as in occupational therapy.

work tolerance, the kind and amount of work that a physically or mentally ill person can or should perform.

work-up, the process of performing a complete patient evaluation, including history, physical examination, laboratory tests, and x-ray or other diagnostic procedures to acquire an accurate database on which a diagnosis and treatment plan may be established.

World Health Organization (WHO), an intergovernmental organization within the United Nations system whose purpose is to aid in the attainment of the highest possible level of health by all people. Programs include education for current health issues, proper food supply and nutrition, safe water and sanitation, maternal and child health, immunization against major infectious diseases, and prevention and control of diseases. WHO is coordinating global strategies to control and prevent AIDS.

worm /wurm/ [AS, *wyrm*], any of the soft-bodied, elongated invertebrates of the phyla Annelida, Nemathelminthes, or Platyhelminthes.

wormian bone /vôr'mē·ən/ [Olaus Worm, Danish anatomist, 1588–1654; AS, *ban*], any of several tiny smooth bones, usually found at the serrated borders of the sutures between the cranial bones.

worthlessness /wurth′ləsnəs/, a component of low self-esteem, characterized by feelings of uselessness and inability to contribute meaningfully to the well-being of others or to one's environment.

wound /wo͞ond/ [AS, *wund*], **1.** any physical injury involving a break in the skin, usually caused by an act or accident rather than by a disease, such as a chest wound, gunshot wound, or puncture wound. **2.** to cause an injury, especially one that breaks the skin.

wound care, a nursing intervention from the Nursing Interventions Classification (NIC) defined as prevention of wound complications and promotion of wound healing.

wound care: burns, a nursing intervention from the Nursing Interventions Classification (NIC) defined as prevention of wound complications due to burns and facilitation of wound healing.

wound care: closed drainage, a nursing intervention from the Nursing Interventions

W

Classification (NIC) defined as maintenance of a pressure drainage system at the wound site.

wound clip, a heavy metal clip used to approximate the edges of a skin incision.

wound culture and sensitivity (C&S), a microscopic examination done to determine the presence of pathogens in patients with suspected wound infections.

wound healing, a process to restore to a state of soundness any injury that results in an interruption in the continuity of external surfaces of the body.

wound healing: primary intention, a nursing outcome from the Nursing Outcomes Classification (NOC) is defined as the extent to which cells and tissues have regenerated after intentional closure.

wound healing: secondary intention, a nursing outcome from the Nursing Outcomes Classification (NOC) defined as the extent of regeneration of cells and tissues in an open wound.

wound irrigation[1], the rinsing of a wound or the cavity formed by a wound using a medicated solution, water, or saline, or antimicrobial liquid preparation.

wound irrigation[2], a nursing intervention from the Nursing Interventions Classification (NIC) defined as flushing of an open wound to cleanse and remove debris and excessive drainage.

Wound, Ostomy and Continence Nurses (WOCN) Society, an organization of nurses who manage conditions such as stomas, draining wounds, fistulas, vascular ulcers, pressure ulcers, neuropathic wounds, urinary incontinence, fecal incontinence, and functional disorders of the bowel and bladder.

Wright-Giemsa stain, modified stain using a combination of Wright's stain and Giemsa's stain in order to detect parasites, fungi, viral inclusion bodies, and other organisms in blood smears.

Wright's stain /rīts/ [James H. Wright, American pathologist, 1869–1928; Fr, *teindre,* to dye], a stain containing methylene blue and eosin that is used to color blood specimens for microscopic examination, such as for CBC and particularly for malarial parasites.

wrinkle test /ring′kəl/ [AS, *gewrinclian,* to wind; L, *testum,* crucible], a test for nerve function in the hand by observing the presence of skin wrinkles after the hand has been placed in warm water for 20 to 30 minutes. Denervated skin does not wrinkle.

wrist, the carpus, made up of eight bones arranged in two rows. The proximal row consists of the scaphoid, lunate, triangular, and pisiform. The distal row consists of the greater multiangular, lesser multiangular, capitate, and hamate.

wrist clonus reflex /rist/, a sustained clonic muscle spasm caused by the sudden hyperextension of the wrist joint.

wristdrop [AS, *wrist* + *dropa*], a condition caused by paralysis of the extensor muscles of the hand and fingers or by injury of the radial nerve, resulting in inability to flex the wrist.

wrist ganglion, a cystic enlargement of a tendon sheath on the back of the wrist.

writer's cramp [AS, *writan,* to write, *crammian,* to fill], a painful, involuntary contraction of the muscles of the hand in a person attempting to write. It often occurs after long periods of writing.

wrongful birth /rông′fəl/ [OE, *wrang,* twisted; ME, *burth*], a belief that a birth could have been avoided if the parents had been properly advised by a physician that a pregnancy could occur or that a fetus would be deformed.

wrongful death statute [AS, *wrang* + *death*; L, *statuere,* to place], in law, a statute existing in all states that provides that the death of a person can give rise to a cause of legal action brought by the person's beneficiaries in a civil suit against the person whose willful or negligent acts caused the death.

wrongful life action, in law, a civil suit usually brought against a physician or health facility on the basis of negligence that resulted in the wrongful birth or life of an infant. The parents of the unwanted child seek to obtain payment from the defendant for the medical expenses of pregnancy and delivery, for pain and suffering, and for the education and upbringing of the child.

wt, abbreviation for **weight.**

Wuchereria /voo̅′kə·rē′ē·ə/ [Otto Wucherer, German physician, 1820–1873], a genus of filarial worms found in warm, humid climates. *Wuchereria bancrofti,* transmitted by mosquitoes, is the cause of elephantiasis.

w/v, abbreviation for *weight per volume.*

w/w, abbreviation for *weight per weight.*

Wyburn-Mason's syndrome /wī′bərn·mā′sənz/ [Roger Wyburn-Mason, British physician, 20th century], arteriovenous aneurysms on one or both sides of the brain, with ocular anomalies, especially in the retina, facial nevi, and sometimes mental retardation.

Wycillin, a trademark for an antibacterial (penicillin G procaine).

Wydase, a trademark for an enzyme (hyaluronidase).

Wymox, a trademark for an antibiotic (amoxicillin).

Wytensin, a trademark for an antihypertensive agent (guanabenz).

Xanax, a trademark for a benzodiazepine antianxiety agent (alprazolam).

xanthan gum solution, a solution of xanthan gum, methylparaben, and propylparaben in purified water. It is used as a suspending, stabilizing, emulsifying, and thickening agent.

xanthelasma /zan'thəlaz'mə/ [Gk, *xanthos,* yellow, *elasma,* plate], a planar xanthoma involving the eyelid(s).

xanthelasmatosis/zan'thəlaz'mətō'sis/ [Gk, *xanthos,* yellow, *elasma,* plate, *osis,* condition], a disseminated, generalized form of planar xanthoma frequently associated with reticuloendothelial disorders, especially multiple myeloma.

xanthene /zan'thēn/ [Gk, *xanthos,* yellow], a crystalline organic compound in which two benzene rings are fused to a central pyran ring. The pyran oxygen bridges the two benzene rings. It is a parent chemical structure of many medicinal elements.

xanthine /zan'thīn/ [Gk, *xanthos,* yellow], a nitrogenous by product of the metabolism of nucleoproteins. It is normally found in the muscles, liver, spleen, pancreas, and urine.—**xanthic,** *adj.*

xanthine base [Gk, *xanthos,* yellow], a purine compound occurring in plants and animals as a metabolite of adenine and guanine. It is the parent structure of the methyl xanthine alkaloids that include caffeine in coffee, theophylline in tea, and theobromine in cocoa.

xanthine derivative, any one of the closely related alkaloids caffeine, theobromine, and theophylline. They are variously ingested as components in beverages such as coffee, tea, cocoa, and cola drinks. The xanthine derivatives or methylxanthines have pharmacologic properties that stimulate the central nervous system, produce diuresis, and relax smooth muscles. The ability of the xanthine derivatives to relax smooth muscle is used in certain treatments of asthma. Consumption of xanthine beverages may cause various problems, including restlessness and inability to sleep, GI irritation, and excessive myocardial stimulation characterized by premature systole and tachycardia.

xanthinuria /zan'thinyŏŏr'ē·ə/ [Gk, *xanthos* + *ouron,* urine], **1.** the presence of excessive quantities of xanthine in the urine. **2.** a rare disorder of purine metabolism, resulting in the excretion of large amounts of xanthine in the urine because of the absence of an enzyme, xanthine oxidase, that is necessary in xanthine metabolism.

xanthism /zan'thizəm/, a genetic pigment anomaly characterized by yellow or yellowish-red hair, coppered skin, and reddish-brown irises.

xanthochromia /zan'thəkrō'mē·ə/, a pale yellow or straw-colored discoloration of CSF. It is caused by the presence of hemoglobin breakdown products, indicating that the CSF has contained blood in the recent past.

xanthochromic /zan'thəkrō'mik/ [Gk, *xanthos* + *chroma,* color], having a yellowish color, such as CSF that contains blood or bile.

xanthoderma /zan'thədur'mə/, skin that has a yellow coloration, as in jaundice.

xanthogranuloma /zan'thəgran'yəlō'mə/, *pl.* **xanthogranulomas, xanthogranulomata** [Gk, *xanthos;* L, *granulum,* little grain; Gk, *oma,* tumor], a tumor or nodule of granulation tissue containing lipid deposits.

xanthogranulomatous cholecystitis, a type of chronic cholecystitis characterized by proliferative fibrosis and infiltration by lipid-laden macrophages. It is often accompanied by obstruction from gallstones.

xanthoma /zanthō'mə/ *pl.* **xanthomas, xanthomata** [Gk, *xanthos* + *oma,* tumor], a benign fatty fibrous yellowish plaque, nodule, or tumor that develops in the subcutaneous layer of skin, often around tendons.

xanthoma disseminatum, a benign chronic condition in which small orange or brown papules and nodules develop on many body surfaces, especially on the mucous membrane of the oropharynx, larynx, and bronchi and in skin folds and fissures.

xanthoma palpebrarum, a soft yellow spot or plaque usually occurring in groups on the eyelids.

xanthomasarcoma /zan'thōməsärkō'mə/, *pl.* **xanthomasarcomas, xanthomasarcomata** [Gk, *xanthos* + *oma* + *sarx,* flesh, *oma,* tumor], a giant cell sarcoma of the tendon sheaths and aponeuroses that contains xanthoma cells.

X

xanthoma striatum palmare, a yellow or orange flat plaque or slightly raised nodule occurring in groups on the palms of the hands.

xanthoma tendinosum, a yellow or orange elevated or flat round papule or nodule occurring in clusters on tendons, especially the extensor tendons of the hands and feet, of individuals with hereditary lipid storage disease.

xanthomatosis /zan'thōmətō'sis/ [Gk, *xanthos + oma + osis,* condition], an abnormal condition in which there are deposits of yellowish fatty material in the skin, internal organs, and reticuloendothelial system.

xanthomatosis bulbi, a fatty degeneration of the cornea.

xanthoma tuberosum, a yellow or orange flat or elevated round papule occurring in clusters on the skin of joints, especially the elbows and knees, usually in people who have a hereditary lipid storage disease.

Xanthomonas /zan'thəmon'əs/, a genus of gram-negative rod-shaped aerobic bacteria that produces a yellow pigment.

Xanthomonas maltophilia, a species of *Xanthomonas* bacteria commonly found in water, milk, and frozen food and in the upper respiratory tract, blood, and urine of humans. It is an opportunistic cause of infections in hospitalized and immunocompromised patients. This organism has been re-classified as *Stenotrophomonas maltophila.*

xanthopsia /zanthop'sē·ə/ [Gk, *xanthos + opsis,* sight], an abnormal visual condition in which everything appears to have a yellow hue. It is sometimes associated with jaundice or digitalis toxicity.

xanthosis /zanthō'sis/ [Gk, *xanthos + osis,* condition], 1. a yellowish discoloration sometimes seen in degenerating tissues of malignant diseases. 2. a reversible yellow discoloration of the skin most commonly caused by the ingestion of large amounts of yellow or orange vegetables containing carotene pigment.

xanthosis of retina, a generalized yellow discoloration of the posterior pole of the fundus, sometimes found in diabetic retinopathy.

xanthurenic acid /zan'thŏŏrē'nik/, a metabolite of tryptophan that occurs in normal urine and in elevated levels in patients with vitamin B_6 deficiency.

xanthurenic aciduria, a genetic disorder of tryptophan metabolism characterized by a deficiency of the kynureninase liver enzyme. It is also seen in vitamin B deficiency.

X chromosome, a sex chromosome that in humans and many other animals is present in both sexes, appearing singly in the cells of normal males and in duplicate in the cells of normal females. The chromosome is present in all of the female gametes and one half of the male gametes, is much larger than the Y chromosome, and has many sex-linked genes associated with clinically significant disorders such as hemophilia, Duchenne's muscular dystrophy, and Hunter's syndrome.

Xe, symbol for the element **xenon.**

xenoantibody, an antibody produced in one species to an antigen derived from a different species.

xenoantigen /zē'nō·an'təjən/, an antigen that occurs in organisms of more than one species.

xenobiotic /-bī·ot'ik/ [Gk, *xenos,* strange, *bios,* life], a chemical compound foreign to a given biological system. With respect to animals and humans, xenobiotics include drugs, drug metabolites, and environmental compounds, such as pollutants, that are not produced by the body.

xenodiagnosis /-dī·agnō'sis/, a method of diagnosing a vector-transmitted infection such as Chagas' disease, in which a laboratory-reared, pathogen-free insect is allowed to suck blood from a patient. The intestinal contents of the insect are then examined for the presence of the pathogen.

xenogeneic /-jənē'ik/ [Gk, *xenos + genein,* to produce], 1. denoting individuals or cell types of different species and different genotypes. 2. denoting tissues from different species that are therefore antigenically dissimilar.

xenogenesis /zen'əjen'əsis/, 1. alternation of traits in successive generations; heterogenesis. 2. the theoretic production of offspring that are totally different from both of the parents.—**xenogenetic, xenogenic,** *adj.*

xenograft /zen'əgraft'/ [Gk, *xenos + graphion,* stylus], tissue from another species used as a temporary graft in certain cases, as in treating a severely burned patient when sufficient tissue from the patient or from a tissue bank is not available.

xenology /zēnol'əjē/ [Gk, *xenos,* stranger, *logos,* science], the study of parasites.

xenoma /zēnō'mə/, a tumor that develops on tissue infected with certain parasites.

xenon (Xe) /zen'on, zē'non/ [Gk, *xenos,* strange], a nonreactive gaseous nonmetallic element. Its atomic number is 54; its atomic mass is 131.30.

xenon-133 [Gk, *xenos,* strange], a radioactive isotope of zenon gas, used in radiographic studies of the lung.

xenoparasite /-per'əsīt/, an ectoparasite that has become pathogenic as a result of weakened resistance of the host.

xenophobia /-fō'bē·ə/ [Gk, *xenos + phobos,* fear], an anxiety disorder characterized by a pervasive, irrational fear or uneasiness in the presence of strangers, especially foreigners, or in new surroundings.

Xenopsylla /zen′ōsil′ə/, a genus of parasitic fleas responsible for the transmission of bubonic plague, murine typhus, and other infections. Many of more than 30 species of *Xenopsylla* are vectors of pathogens, including *X. cheopis,* a rat flea found worldwide. It is a vector of *Yersinia pestis,* the bacterial source of murine typhus, as well as of the plague.

xenotype /zen′ətīp/, molecular variation based on differences in structure and antigenic specificity, such as immunoglobulin from different species.

xeroderma pigmentosum (XP), a rare, inherited skin disease characterized by extreme sensitivity to ultraviolet light, exposure to which results in freckles, telangiectases, keratoses, papillomas, carcinoma, and possibly, melanoma. Keratitis and tumors developing on the eyelids and cornea may result in blindness.

xerogram /zir′əgram/ [Gk, *xeros* + *gramma,* record], an x-ray image produced by xeroradiography.

xeromammogram /-mam′əgram/, a type of breast radiograph produced by xeroradiography.

xeromammography /-mamog′rəfē/, the use of xerographic methods to produce radiographic images of the breasts.

xerophthalmia /zir′ofthal′mē·ə/ [Gk, *xeros* + *ophthalmos,* eye], a condition of dry and lusterless corneas and conjunctival areas, usually the result of vitamin A deficiency and associated with night blindness.

xeroradiography /-rā′dē·og′rəfē/ [Gk, *xeros;* L, *radiare,* to emit rays; Gk, *graphein,* to record], a diagnostic x-ray technique in which images are produced electrically rather than chemically, permitting lower exposure times and radiation energies than those of ordinary x-rays. The latent image is made visible with a powder toner similar to that used in a copying machine. Xeroradiography is used primarily for mammography.

xerostomia /zir′əstō′mē·ə/ [Gk, *xeros* + *stoma,* mouth], dryness of the mouth caused by cessation of normal salivary secretion. The condition is a symptom of various diseases such as diabetes, acute infections, hysteria, and Sjögren's syndrome and can be caused by paralysis of facial nerves. It may also result from radiation treatments for cancers of the face, head, or neck.

xerotic keratitis /zirot′ik/ [Gk, *xeros,* dry, *keras,* horn, *itis,* inflammation], an inflammation of the cornea resulting from dryness of the conjunctiva. Underlying causes may be malnutrition, a deficiency of vitamin A, or autoimmune diseases.

xi /zī, sī/, Ξ, ξ, the fourteenth letter of the Greek alphabet.

Xifaxan, a trademark for rifaximin.

xiphisternal articulation /zif′istur′nəl/ [Gk, *xiphos,* sword, *sternon,* chest; L, *articulare,* to divide into joints], the cartilaginous connection between the xiphoid process and the body of the sternum.

xiphodynia /zī′fōdin′ē·ə/, a pain in the xiphoid process.

xiphoid /zif′oid/ [Gk, *xiphos,* sword, *eidos,* form], shaped like a sword; the xiphoid process of the sternum.

xiphoid process /zif′oid/ [Gk, *xiphos* + *eidos,* form; L, *processus,* going forth], the smallest of three parts of the sternum, articulating with the inferior end of the body of the sternum above and laterally with the seventh rib.

xiphopagus /zīfop′əgəs/, conjoined twins united at the xiphoid process of the sternum.

X-linked /eks lingkt/, pertaining to genes or to the characteristics or conditions they transmit that are carried on the X chromosome.—**X linkage,** *n.*

X-linked bulbospinal neuropathy, a hereditary disorder of the spinal cord and medulla oblongata in males, with associated endocrine features, including azoospermia, gynecomastia, glucose intolerance, and feminized skin changes.

X-linked disorder, a disease or disorder associated with genetic abnormalities on the X chromosomes. Examples are the muscular dystrophies and hemophilias.

X-linked–dominant inheritance, a pattern of inheritance in which the transmission of a dominant allele on the X chromosome causes a characteristic to be manifested. X-linked dominant inheritance closely resembles autosomal-dominant inheritance.

X-linked gene, a gene carried on the X chromosome. The corresponding trait, whether dominant or recessive, is always expressed in males, who have only one X chromosome.

X-linked inheritance, a pattern of inheritance in which the transmission of traits varies according to the sex of the person, because the genes on the X chromosome have no counterparts on the Y chromosome. The inheritance pattern may be recessive or dominant. The trait determined by a gene on the X chromosome is always expressed in males.

X-linked lymphoproliferative syndrome, a rare X-linked immunodeficiency in which there is a normal response to childhood infection but infection with Epstein-Barr virus produces a fatal lymphoproliferative disorder. Most patients die of acute infection.

X

X-linked–recessive inheritance, a pattern of inheritance in which transmission of a recessive allele on the X chromosome results in a carrier state in females and characteristics of an abormal condition in males. Unaffected male siblings do not carry the trait. Sons of affected males are unaffected, and daughters of affected males are carriers.

XO, the designation of a cell in which or individual in whom only one sex chromosome is present; the second chromosome is missing so that each cell is monosomic and contains a total of 45 chromosomes.

Xolair, a trademark for omalizumab.

XP, abbreviation for **xeroderma pigmentosum.**

x-ray, 1. electromagnetic radiation with wavelengths between about 0.005 and 10 nm. X-rays are produced when electrons traveling at high speed strike certain materials, particularly heavy metals such as tungsten. They can penetrate most substances and are used to investigate the integrity of certain structures, to therapeutically destroy diseased tissue, and to make radiographic images for diagnostic purposes, as in radiography and fluoroscopy. Discrete x-rays are those with precisely fixed energies that are characteristic of differences between electron-binding energies of a particular element. **2.** a radiograph made by projecting x-rays through organs or structures of the body onto a photographic film. Structures that are relatively radiopaque, such as bones and cavities filled with a radiopaque contrast medium, cast a shadow on the film. **3.** to make a radiograph.—**x-ray,** *adj.*

x-ray dermatitis, a skin inflammation caused by exposure to x-rays. Excessive exposure to x-rays can lead to skin cancer.

x-ray fluoroscopy, real-time imaging using an x-ray source that projects through the patient onto a fluorescent screen or image intensifier. Image-intensified fluoroscopy has replaced conventional fluoroscopy in current practice.

x-ray microscope, a microscope that produces images using x-rays and records them on fine-grain film or projects them as enlargements.

x-ray pelvimetry, a radiographic examination used to determine the dimensions of the bony pelvis of a pregnant woman and, if possible, the biparietal diameter of her baby's head. It is performed when doubt exists as to whether the head can pass safely through the pelvis in labor.

x-ray tube, a large vacuum tube containing a tungsten filament cathode and an anode that often is a tungsten disk. When heated to incandescence, the cathode emits a cloud of electrons that produce x-rays when they strike the surface of the anode at high speed. The anode is designed to deflect the x-rays toward an object to be radiographed.

x-tra density /ek′strə/, an image on an x-ray film caused by the presence of a foreign object such as a bullet or surgical clip in the patient's body.

XX /ekseks′/, the designation for the normal sex chromosome complement in the human female.

XXX syndrome /trip′əleks/, a human sex chromosomal aberration characterized by the presence of three X chromosomes and two Barr bodies instead of the normal XX complement, so that somatic cells contain a total of 47 chromosomes; trisomy X. Individuals with the anomaly show no significant clinical manifestations, although there is usually some degree of mental retardation.

XXX, XXXX, XXXXX /thrē·eks′, fôr·eks′, fīv·eks′/, the designations for abnormal sex chromosome complements in the human female in which there are, respectively, four or five instead of the normal two X chromosomes so that each somatic cell contains a total of 48 or 49 chromosomes.

XXXY, XXXXY, XXYY /thrē′ekswī, fôr′ekswī, dob′əleks-dob′əlwī/, the designations for abnormal sex chromosome complements in the human male in which there are more than the normal one X and one Y chromosome, resulting in a total of 48, 49, or more chromosomes in each somatic cell. The aberration is a variant of Klinefelter's syndrome. In general, the more X chromosomes there are, the greater the number of congenital defects and the severity of mental retardation in the affected individual.

XY /ekswī′/, the designation for the normal sex chromosome complement in the human male.

xylitol /zī′litôl/, a five-carbon sugar alcohol derived from xylose and as sweet as sucrose; used as a noncariogenic sweetener and also as a sugar substitute in diabetic diets.

Xylocaine, a trademark for a local anesthetic (lidocaine).

xylometazoline hydrochloride /zī′lōmetaz′əlēn/, an alpha-adrenergic vasoconstrictor. It is prescribed as an intranasal medication for the treatment of congestion due to colds, hay fever, sinusitis, and other upper respiratory allergies.

xylose /zī′lōs/, an aldopentose sugar produced by hydrolyzing straw and corn cobs. It is incompletely absorbed when taken by mouth and is used in diagnostic studies of the digestive tract.

xylose absorption test, a laboratory test for intestinal absorption of the monosaccharide D-xylose. Absorption of D-xylose occurs readily in the normal intestine but is diminished in malabsorption patients.

xysma /zis'mə/, membranous shreds sometimes found in the feces of patients with diarrhea.

XYY syndrome /eks'dobəlwī'/, the phenotypic manifestation of an extra Y chromosome, which tends to have a positive effect on height and may have a negative effect on mental and psychologic development. However, the anomaly also occurs in normal males.

Xyzal, a trademark for levocetirizine.

Y, symbol for the element **yttrium.**

YAC, abbreviation for **yeast artificial chromosome.**

YAG, abbreviation for *yttrium aluminum garnet,* a crystal used in some types of lasers.

Yallow, Rosalyn Sussman [U.S. medical physicist, b. 1921], co-winner with Roger Guillemin and Andrew Schally of the 1977 Nobel prize for medicine or physiology for her work in endocrinology and development of the radioimmunoassay technique.

yang, a polarized aspect of Qi that is active or positive energy.

Yangtze edema /yang'sē/, a name used in China to describe a localized pruritic and erythematous subcutaneous induration caused by *Gnathostoma spinigerum* larvae in gnathostomiasis.

Yankauer suction catheter, a rigid hollow tube with a curve at the distal end to facilitate the removal of thick pharyngeal secretions during oral pharyngeal suctioning.

yarrow, a herb native to Europe and Asia, now grown in North America. It is used to decrease bleeding, to improve circulation, and to treat GI disorders, hypertension, and thrombi. Chemical analysis supports the possibility of benefical effects, but there are insufficient reliable data from human studies to assess its efficacy.

yaw /yô/ [Carib, *VaVa*], a lesion of the syphilis-like tropical disease of yaws. The initial lesion or primary sore is identified as the mother yaw.

yawn /yôn/ [AS, *geonian*], an involuntary act of opening the mouth wide and taking a deep breath. It tends to occur when a person is bored, drowsy, or depressed and may be accompanied by upper body movements or the act of stretching to aid chest expansion.

yaws /yôs/ [Afr, *yaw,* raspberry,], a chronic nonvenereal infection caused by the spirochete *Treponema pallidum* subspecies *pertenue,* transmitted by direct contact. Yaws has been classified into four stages.a chronic nonvenereal infection caused by the spirochete *Treponema pallidum* subsp. *pertenue,* transmitted by direct contact. It is characterized by chronic, ulcerating sores anywhere on the body but usually on the legs, with eventual tissue and bone destruction, leading to crippling if untreated. It is a disease of unsanitary tropical living conditions and may be effectively treated with penicillin G. All serologic tests for syphilis may be positive in yaws. The infection may afford protection against syphilis.

Yb, symbol for the element **ytterbium.**

Y-cartilage, a Y-shaped band of connective tissue that extends through the acetabulum to join the ilium, ischium, and pubis.

Y chromosome, a sex chromosome that in humans and many other animals is present only in the male, appearing singly in the normal male. It is present in one half of the male gametes and none of the female gametes, is much smaller than the X chromosome, and has genes associated with triggering the development and differentiation of male characteristics.

years of potential life lost (YPLL), an evaluation of the economic, social, and other consequences of premature death in a population from injury or disease as compared to the potential productivity of the deceased if they had lived normal lifespans.

yeast /yēst/ [AS, *gist*], any unicellular, usually oval, nucleated fungus that reproduces by budding. *Candida albicans* is a kind of pathogenic yeast.

yeast artificial chromosome (YAC), a yeast chromosome used in recombinant DNA procedures. It can carry large segments of foreign DNA.

yellow fever, an acute arbovirus infection transmitted by mosquitoes. It is characterized by headache, fever, jaundice, vomiting, and bleeding. There is no specific treatment. Recovery is followed by lifelong immunity. Immunization for travelers to endemic areas is advised.

yellow fever vaccine, a vaccine produced from live, attenuated yellow fever virus grown in chick embryos. It is prescribed for immunization against yellow fever.

yellow jacket venom, a toxin injected by the stings of wasps and hornets. It can induce potentially fatal anaphylactic shock.

yellow marrow, bone marrow in which the fat cells predominate in the meshes of the reticular network.

yellow nail syndrome, a condition in which there is complete or almost complete cessation of nail growth and loss of cuticle. Nails become thickened, convex, opaque, and pale yellow to yellowish green. The condition is associated with pulmonary disorders and lymphedema.

yerba maté, a herbal product taken from an evergreen tree belonging to the holly family that is native to parts of South America. It is used as a diuretic and depurative.

Yersinia /yersin′ē·ə/ [Alexandre E.J. Yersin, French bacteriologist, 1862–1943], a genus of nonmotile ovoid or rod-shaped gram-negative bacteria of the *Enterobacteriaceae* family.

Yersinia **arthritis** [Alexandre E.J. Yersin], a polyarticular inflammation occurring a few days to 1 month after the onset of infection caused by *Yersinia enterocolitica* or *Y. pseudotuberculosis* and usually persisting longer than 1 month. Knees, ankles, toes, fingers, and wrists are most often affected. The clinical presentation may mimic juvenile rheumatoid arthritis, rheumatic fever, or Reiter's syndrome. Treatment is with antibiotics.

Yersinia **enterocolitica,** a ubiquitous species isolated from mammals, birds, and frogs, and from material contaminated by feces. It is transmitted by infected food and water and by person-to-person contact and causes yersiniosis in humans.

Yersinia **pestis** [Alexandre E.J. Yersin; L, *pestis,* plague], a small gram-negative bacterium that causes plague. The primary host is the rat, but other small rodents also harbor the organism.

Yersinia **pseudotuberculosis,** a species found in the intestinal tract of birds, rodents, and other animals; it causes mesenteric adenitis and pseudo-TB in humans who have contact with infected food or animals.

yersiniosis /yərsin′ē·ō′sis/, infection with bacteria of the genus *Yersinia,* especially *Y. enterocolitica,* which causes symptoms such as acute gastroenteritis and mesenteric adenitis in children and arthritis, septicemia, and erythema nodosum in adults.

Y fracture, a Y-shaped fracture of the tissue between condyles.

yield, **1.** an amount or quantity produced in return for an effort or investment. **2.** the energy released by a nuclear reaction.

yin, a polarized aspect of Qi that is passive or negative energy.

yin-yang, a Chinese philosophy that each entity is one but contains two equal and opposite forces. The forces of yang include maleness, the sun, and heat; the forces of yin include femaleness, darkness, and cold. Many holistic care practices are rooted in the belief that there must be a balance between yin and yang forces for health and that illness is the result of imbalance.

yin-yang principle, in Chinese philosophy, the concept of polar complements

existing in dynamic equilibrium and always present simultaneously. In traditional Chinese medicine, a disturbance of the proper balance of yin and yang causes disease, and the goal is to maintain or to restore this balance.

Y-linked /wī′lingkt/, pertaining to genes or to the characteristics or conditions they transmit that are carried on the Y chromosome. **— Y linkage,** *n.*

Yodoxin, a trademark for an antiamebic (diiodohydroxyquin).

yoga, a discipline that focuses on the body's musculature, posture, breathing mechanisms, and consciousness. The goal of yoga is attainment of physical and mental well-being.

yogurt /yō′gərt/ [Turk, *yoghurt*], a slightly acid, semisolid, curdled milk preparation made from either whole or skimmed cow's milk and milk solids by fermentation with organisms from the genus *Lactobacillus.* It is rich in B complex vitamins and a good source of protein. It also provides a medium in the GI tract that retards the growth of harmful bacteria and aids in mineral absorption.

yohimbe, an herbal product taken from the bark of a tree that is native to areas of West Africa. This herb is used to treat male organic impotence due to prostate problems and has proven efficacy when used under medical supervision.

yohimbe bark, a preparation of the bark of *Pausinystalia yohimbe,* used for the same indications as yohimbine hydrochloride. It has also been used traditionally as an aphrodisiac and for skin diseases and obesity.

yoke /yōk/ [L, *jungere,* to join], a connector used to link small cylinders of medical gases, such as portable oxygen tanks, to respiratory equipment.

yolk /yōk, yelk/ [AS, *geolca*], a material rich in fats and proteins that is contained in an ovum and that supplies nourishment to the developing embryo. In humans and most other mammals, yolk is absent or greatly diffused through the ovum because mammalian embryos absorb nutrients directly from the mother through the placenta.

yolk sac, a structure that develops in the inner cell mass of the embryo and expands into a vesicle with a thick part that becomes the primitive gut and a thin part that grows into the cavity of the chorion. After supplying the nourishment for the embryo, the yolk sac usually disappears during the seventh week of pregnancy.

yolk stalk, the narrow duct connecting the yolk sac with the midgut of the embryo during the early stages of prenatal development.

Y

young and middle adult, the stages of life from 22 to 65 years of age.

Young-Helmholtz theory of color vision [Thomas Young, English physician, 1773–1829; Hermann L.F. von Helmholtz, German physician, physicist, and physiologist, 1821–1894], the concept that all color sensations are mediated by three types of retinal receptors, which correspond to three primary colors: red, green, and blue-violet. By their individual and combined activities, the receptors produce the perception of all visible hues.

young-old, a term used to denote a person who is between 55 and 75 years of age.

Young prostatic retractor [Hugh Young, American urologist, 1870–1945], a short straight surgical instrument with blades operated by a knob, for use in open perineal prostatectomy. The device can be inserted through the prostatic urethra and by direct traction used to draw down the prostate gland into the operative field.

Young's operation [Hugh Young, American urologist, 1870–1945], **1.** the surgical construction of a new urethra to repair a structural defect of the penis. **2.** perineal prostatectomy.

Y-plasty /wī′plas′tē/, a method of surgical revision of a scar, using a Y-shaped incision to reduce scar contractures.

YPLL, abbreviation for **years of potential life lost.**

Y-set, a device composed of plastic components, used for delivering IV fluids through a primary IV line connected to a combination drip chamber filter section from which two separate plastic tubes lead to fluid sources. The Y-set also includes three clamps, one for the primary IV line and one for each of the two separate tubes. It is often used to transfuse blood cells for any type of blood administration that must be diluted with saline solution to decrease their viscosity.

ytterbium (Yb) /itur′bē·əm/ [Ytterby, Sweden], a rare earth metallic element. Its atomic number is 70; its atomic mass is 173.04.

yttrium (Y) /it′rē·əm/ [Ytterby, Sweden], a scaly, grayish metallic element. Its atomic number is 39; its atomic mass is 88.905. Radioactive isotopes of yttrium have been used in cancer therapy.

yttrium 90Y ibritumomab tiuxetan, a chelate of ^{90}yttrium and the immunoconjugate ibritumomab tiuxetan, used in the treatment of non-Hodgkin's lymphoma.

zafirlukast, a bronchodilator used for prophylaxis and chronic treatment of asthma in children and adults.

Zakrzewski, Marie /săˈman, tsăˈmon/ /zakshefˈskē/, a Polish-German-American midwife who studied medicine in Berlin and in 1872 organized the first successful American school of nursing at the New England Hospital for Women and Children.

zalcitabine, an antiretroviral nucleoside reverse transcriptase inhibitor analog prescribed in combination with other drugs for the treatment of HIV infections. The sale and distribution of zalcitabine were discontinued in 2006.

zaleplon, a sedative-hypnotic used to treat insomnia.

zanamivir, an antiviral prescribed to treat type A and B influenza in patients who have had symptoms for no more than 2 days.

Zarontin, a trademark for an anticonvulsant (**ethosuximide**).

Zaroxolyn, trademark for a diuretic and antihypertensive (**metolazone**).

Zavesca, a trademark for **miglustat.**

Z chromosome, the sex chromosomes of certain insects, birds, and fish. Females of such animals are heterogametic and have one W and one Z chromosome, whereas males are homogametic and have two Z chromosomes.

ZDV, abbreviation for **zidovudine.**

Zeeman effect /sēˈman, tsāˈmon/ [Pieter Zeeman, Dutch physicist and Nobel Laureate, 1865–1945], a splitting of lines in an emission spectrum into three or more symmetrically placed lines when the radiation source is in a magnetic field.

ZEEP, abbreviation for **zero-end expiratory pressure.**

Zeitgeist /tsītˈgīst/ [Ger], literally, the spirit of the time, a climate of opinion, a convention of thought, or implicit assumptions.

Zemuron, a trademark for a nondepolarizing neuromuscular blocking agent (rocuronium bromide).

Zenapax /zeˈnə-paks/, a trademark for a preparation of daclizumab, an immunosuppressant used after kidney transplantation.

Zenker's diverticulum /tsengˈkerz/ [Friedrich A. Zenker, German pathologist, 1825–1898; L, *diverticulare,* to turn aside], a circumscribed herniation of the mucous membrane of the pharynx as it joins the esophagus. Food may become trapped in the diverticulum and can be aspirated. In most cases the herniation is small, causes no dysfunction, is not diagnosed, and requires no treatment.

zeolites, hydrated silicates of aluminum used in ion exchange water softeners. Synthetic zeolites are used as porous molecular containers for reagents and drugs.

Zephiran Chloride, a trademark for a disinfectant (benzalkonium chloride).

zeranol /zerˈənol/, an estrogenic substance used to fatten livestock. Consumption of beef from zeranol-treated cattle has been associated with precocious puberty in some boys and girls.

Zerit, a trademark for a synthetic thymidine nucleoside analog (stavudine).

zero /zirˈō/ [Ar, *sifr,* cipher], **1.** a symbol for nothing. **2.** the point on most scales from which measurements begin. **3.** absolute zero on the Kelvin scale (0 K), the temperature at which there is no molecular movement, corresponding to −273.15° C or −459.67° F.

zero balance, a state in which the amount of water or an electrolyte excreted from the body is exactly equal to that ingested.

zero dose, the absence of added ligand.

zero-end expiratory pressure (ZEEP) [Ar, *zefiro;* ME, *ende*], pressure in the airways that has returned to ambient or atmospheric pressure at the end of exhalation.

zero fluid balance, a state in which the amount of fluid intake is equal to the amount of fluid output.

zero gravity, a physical state of weightlessness in space or during flight when the centrifugal thrust on a body in a parabolic glide exactly counteracts the force of gravity.

zero-order kinetics, a state at which the rate of an enzyme reaction is independent of the concentration of the substrate.

zero population growth (ZPG), a situation in which there is no population increase during a given year because the total of live births is equal to the total of deaths.

zero-to-three infant stimulation groups, groups that provide therapeutic services for children from birth to 3 years of age, an age group not yet eligible for public school placement.

zero V/Q, an intrapulmonary shunt that allows blood to pass through the lungs

Z

without entering alveolar capillaries, causing hypoxemia.

Zestril, a trademark for an angiotensin-converting enzyme inhibitor and antihypertensive (lisinopril).

zeta /zē′tə, zā′tə/, Z, ζ, the sixth letter of the Greek alphabet.

zetacrit /zā′tə-krit/, the packed-cell volume produced by the zeta sedimentation ratio procedure.

Zetafuge /-fūj/, a trademark for a specially designed centrifuge used in determination of the zeta sedimentation ratio.

zeta potential [Gk, zeta, sixth letter of the Greek alphabet; L, potentia, power], the potential produced by the effective charge of a macromolecule, usually measured at the boundary between what is moving in a solution with the macromolecule and the rest of the solution.

Zetar, a trademark for a topical antieczematic containing coal tar.

zeugmatography /zoog′mətog′rəfē/ [Gk, zeugnynai, to join, graphein, to record], another name for MRI suggesting the role of the gradient magnetic field in joining the radiofrequency magnetic field to a desired local spatial region through nuclear magnetic resonance.

zidovudine (ZDV) /zīdov′ədēn/, a pyrimidine nucleoside analog active against HIV. Its function is to inhibit the reverse transcriptase enzyme of HIV. It is used in combination with other antiretroviral medications in the management of patients with HIV infection who have some evidence of impaired immunity. It also may be used for prophylaxis after exposure to HIV.

Ziehl-Neelsen test /zēl nēl′sən/ [Franz Ziehl, German bacteriologist, 1857–1926; Friedrich K.A. Neelsen, German pathologist, 1854–1894], one of the most widely used methods of acid-fast staining, commonly used in the microscopic examination of a smear of sputum suspected of containing *Mycobacterium tuberculosis*.

Zieve's syndrome [Leslie Zieve, American physician, 1915–2000], a mild spherocytic anemia with transient jaundice and hyperlipidemia found in patients with acute alcoholism and liver cirrhosis.

ZIFT, abbreviation for **zygote intrafallopian transfer.**

ZIG, abbreviation for **zoster immune globulin.**

zileuton, a bronchodilator and leukotriene pathway inhibitor prescribed to treat allergic rhinitis and asthma.

Zimmermann reaction /zim′ərman, tsim′ərmon/ [Wilhelm Zimmermann, German physician, b. 1910], a chromogen reaction previously used for detecting androgens with the 17-keto configuration.

It involves a reaction between an alkaline solution of meta-dinitrobenzene and an active methylene group.

Zinacef, a trademark for a cephalosporin antibiotic (cefuroxime sodium).

zinc (Zn) /zingk/ [Ger, Zink], a bluish-white crystalline metal commonly associated with lead ores. Its atomic number is 30; its atomic mass is 65.38. It is an essential nutrient in the body and is used in numerous pharmaceuticals such as zinc acetate, zinc oxide, zinc permanganate, and zinc stearate. Zinc acetate is used as an emetic, a styptic, and an astringent. Zinc oxide is used internally as an antispasmodic and as a protective in ointments. Zinc permanganate is used as an astringent and in the treatment of urethritis. Zinc stearate is used as a water-repellent protective agent in the treatment of acne, eczema, and other skin diseases.

zinc deficiency, a condition resulting from insufficient amounts of zinc in the diet. It is characterized by abnormal fatigue, decreased alertness, a decrease in taste and odor sensitivity, poor appetite, retarded growth, delayed sexual maturity, prolonged healing of wounds, and susceptibility to infection and injury.

zinc finger, a loop of a transcription factor that is stabilized by a zinc ion coordinated with histidine nitrogen atoms or cysteine sulfur atoms at critical junctures in a protein. Zinc finger formation is an important step in the cloning and sequencing of human general transcription factors.

zinc gelatin, a topical protectant for varicosities and other lesions of the lower limbs.

zinc ointment [Ger, Zink; OFr, oignement], a preparation of 20% zinc oxide in mineral oil or a white petrolatum semisolid base, used as a local surface treatment for various skin disorders.

zinc oxide and eugenol (ZOE), a dental cement composed primarily of zinc salts, eugenol, and rosin, used chiefly in temporary tooth fillings. It has low relative strength and abrasion resistance, but its nearly neutral pH causes minimal irritation to dental pulp. It is intended as a sedative dressing until pain subsides and a more permanent filling can be inserted.

zinc phosphate dental cement, a material for coating or attaching dental inlays, crowns, bridges, and orthodontic appliances and for some temporary restorations of teeth.

zinc salt poisoning, a toxic condition caused by the ingestion or inhalation of a zinc salt. Symptoms of ingestion include a burning sensation of the mouth and throat, vomiting, diarrhea, abdominal and chest pain, and in severe cases shock and coma.

zinc sulfate, an ophthalmic astringent given in drops for nasal congestion or irritation of the eye, applied topically in deodorants, and given orally in tablets to promote healing and as a dietary supplement.

Zinecard, a trademark for a cardioprotective agent against cardiac toxicity induced by doxorubicin **(dexrazoxane).**

ZIP, abbreviation for *zoster immune plasma*.

ziprasidone /zipra'sidōn/, an antipsychotic agent used to treat schizophrenia.

zirconium granuloma, an inflammatory lesion, usually occurring in the axilla as a reaction to zirconium salts in antiperspirants.

Zithromax, a trademark for an antibiotic **(azithromycin).**

Z line, a narrow, darkly staining crossstriation that bisects the I band of skeletal muscles. The distance between Z lines is the length of the sarcomere.

Zn, symbol for the element **zinc.**

zoacanthosis /zō'akanthō'sis/, a dermatitis caused by retention in the skin of foreign bodies such as insect stingers, animal hairs, or bristles.

zoanthropy /zō·an'thrəpē/ [Gk, *zoon,* animal, *anthropos,* human], the delusion that one has assumed the form and characteristics of an animal.—**zoanthropic,** *adj.*

ZOE, abbreviation for **zinc oxide and eugenol.**

zoledronic acid /zō'le-dron'ik/, a bisphosphonate inhibitor of osteoclastic bone resorption, used for the treatment of hypercalcemia of malignancy.

Zollinger-Ellison syndrome /zol'injər el'isən/ [Robert M. Zollinger, American surgeon, 1903–1992; Edwin H. Ellison, American physician, 1918–1970], a condition characterized by severe peptic ulceration, gastric hypersecretion, elevated serum gastrin, and gastrinoma of the pancreas or the duodenum.

zolmitriptan, a migraine agent prescribed in the acute treatment of migraine with or without aura.

Zoloft /zo'loft/, a trademark for preparations of sertraline hydrochloride, an antidepressant, antiobsessional, and antipanic agent.

zolpidem /zōlpi'dem/, a nonbenzodiazepine sedative and hypnotic. The tartrate salt is used in the short-term treatment of insomnia.

zona /zō'nə/ *pl.* **zonae** [Gk, *zone,* belt], a zone, or girdlelike segment of a rounded or spheric structure.

zona fasciculata, the middle part of the adrenal cortex, which is the site of production of glucocorticoids and sex hormones.

zona glomerulosa, the outer part of the adrenal cortex, where mineralocorticoids are produced.

zona pellucida /pəloo'sidə/, the thick, transparent, noncellular membrane that encloses a mammalian ovum. It is secreted by the maturing oocyte during its development in the ovary and is retained until near the time of implantation.

zona radiata, a zona pellucida that has a striated appearance caused by radiating canals within the membrane.

zona reticularis, the innermost part of the adrenal cortex, which borders on the adrenal medulla part of the gland. It acts in consort with the zona fasciculata in producing various sex hormones and glucocorticoids.

zonate /zō'nāt/, having ringed layers with differing colors or textures.

zone [Gk, belt], an area with specific boundaries and characteristics, such as the epigastric, mesogastric, and hypogastric zones of the abdomen or the breasts, lips, or genitals.

zone of equivalence, a region of an antibody-antigen reaction in which concentrations of both reactants are equal.

zonesthesia /zō'nesthē'zhə/ [Gk, *zone* + *aisthesis,* feeling], a painful sensation of constriction, as of a bandage bound too tightly, especially experienced around the waist or abdomen.

zone therapy, the treatment of a disorder by mechanical stimulation and counterirritation of a body area in the same longitudinal zone as the affected organ or region.

zonifugal /zōnif'yəgəl/ [Gk, *zone,* belt; L, *fugere,* to flee], moving from within a zone or area outward.

zonisamide /zō-nis'ə-mīd/, an anticonvulsant agent used to treat epilepsy. It is an adjunctive therapy of partial seizures.

zonography /zōnog'rəfē/ [Gk, *zone* + *graphein,* to record], an x-ray imaging technique used to produce films of body sections similar to those made by tomography.

zonula /zōn'yələ/ *pl.* **zonulae** [Gk, *zone,* belt], a small zone or band.

zonula adherens [L, *zone,* belt, *adhaerere,* to stick], a continuous zone running around the outer surface of a cell in which there is an intercellular space of about 15 to 20 nm width. A component of the junctional complex between cells, the zone contains dense filamentous material.

zonula occludens [L, *zona,* belt, *occludere,* to close up], a component of the junctional complex between cells in which there is no intercellular space and the plasma membranes of adjacent cells are in direct contact.

zonule of Zinn, a ligament composed of straight fibrils radiating from the ciliary body of the eye to the crystalline lens, holding the lens in place and relaxing by the contraction of the ciliary muscle. Relaxation of the ligament allows the lens to become more convex.

zoobiology /-bī·ol'əjē/ [Gk, *zoon,* animal, *bios,* life, *logos,* science], the biology of animals.

zoochemistry /-kem'istrē/ [Gk, *zoon,* animal, *chemeia,* alchemy], the biochemistry of animals.

Z

zoogenous /zō·oj′ənəs/ [Gk, *zoon,* animal, *genein,* to produce], acquired from or originating in animals.

zoograft /zō′əgraft/ [Gk, *zoon + graphion,* stylus], tissue of an animal transplanted to a human, such as a heart valve from a pig to replace a damaged heart valve in a human.

zoologist /zō·ol′əjist/ [Gk, *zoon,* animal, *logos,* science], a person concerned with the scientific study of animals.

zoology /zō·ol′əjē/, the study of animal life.

zoom /zo͞om/, a system of camera lenses that allows an object to remain in focus when the camera approaches or recedes or when the object is viewed close-up or at a distance.

zoomania /zō·əmā′nē·ə/ [Gk, *zoon, mania,* madness], a psychopathologic state characterized by an excessive fondness for and pre-occupation with animals. —**zoomaniac,** *n.*

Zoon balanitis, a benign erythroplasia of the inner surface of the prepuce or the glans penis, characterized histologically by plasma cell infiltration of the dermis, and clinically by a moist, erythematous lesion.

zoonosis /zō·on′əsis, zō′ənō′sis/ [Gk, *zoon + nosis,* disease], a disease of animals that is transmissible to humans from its primary animal host.

zooparasite /zō·oper′əsīt/ [Gk, *zoon + parasitos,* guest], any parasitic animal organism.—**zooparasitic,** *adj.*

zoopathology /-pəthol′əjē/, the study of the diseases of animals.

zoophilia /zō·əfil′ē·ə/ [Gk, *zoon + philein,* to love], **1.** an abnormal fondness for animals. **2.** in psychiatry, a psychosexual disorder in which sexual excitement and gratification are derived from the fondling of animals or from the fantasy or act of engaging in sexual activity with animals. —**zoophile,** *n.,* **zoophilic, zoophilous,** *adj.*

zoophobia /-fō′bē·ə/ [Gk, *zoon + phobos,* fear], an anxiety disorder characterized by a persistent, irrational fear of animals, particularly dogs, snakes, insects, and mice.

zoopsia /zō·op′sē·ə/ [Gk, *zoon + opsis,* vision], a visual hallucination of animals or insects, often occurring in DT.

zootoxin /zō′ətok′sin/ [Gk, *zoon + toxikon,* poison], a poisonous substance from an animal, such as the venom of snakes, spiders, and scorpions.—**zootoxic,** *adj.*

zoster auricularis /zos′tər/, an acute earache with herpetic blebs on the eardrum and external auditory meatus.

zosteriform /zoster′ifôrm/ [Gk, *zoster,* girdle; L, *forma,* form], resembling the pocks seen in herpes zoster infection.

zoster immune globulin (ZIG) [Gk, *zoster;* L, *immunis,* freedom, *globulus,* small sphere], a passive immunizing agent currently in limited experimental use for preventing or attenuating herpes zoster virus infection in immunosuppressed individuals who are at great risk of severe herpes zoster virus infection.

zoster ophthalmicus [Gk, *zoster,* girdle, *ophthalmos,* eye], a herpes infection of the eye and the first division of the trigeminal nerve. The infection frequently involves the cornea. There may be lid edema, ciliary and conjunctival involvement, and pain. Keratitis may be severe. Scarring and glaucoma are common sequelae.

Zovirax, a trademark for an antiviral (acyclovir).

ZPG, abbreviation for **zero population growth.**

Z-plasty /zē′plas′tē/, a method of surgical revision of a scar or closure of a wound using a Z-shaped incision to reduce contractures of the adjacent skin.

Zr, symbol for the element **zirconium.**

z-test, a statistic test using normalized data (*z* values) to compare differences in proportions between sets of data or between individual members of different sets of data.

Z-track, a technique for injecting irritating preparations into muscle without tracking residual medication through sensitive tissues.

Zuckerkandl fascia, the posterior part of the renal fascia.

Zung Self-Rating Depression Scale, a "self-report test" of 20 descriptors of depression on which clients rate themselves on a four-point scale ranging from "a little of the time" to "most of the time." The scale is useful in determining the depth or intensity of a client's depression.

z-value, a normalized value created from a member of a set of data by expressing it in terms of standard deviations from the mean, using the equation

$$z = \frac{x - \bar{x}}{\sigma}$$

where *x* is an item of data, is the mean of the data, and σ is the standard deviation. The mean and standard deviation of the set of such *z* values are 0 and 1, respectively.

zwieback /zwī′bak, zwē′-/ [Ger, *zwie,* twice, *backen,* to bake], a sweetened bread that is enriched with eggs and baked, then sliced and toasted until dry and crisp. It is used as a snack food for children, especially teething infants, or an early food given during convalescence.

zwitterion /tsvit′ərī′ən/, a molecule that has regions of both negative and positive charge. Amino acids such as glycine are almost always present as zwitterions when in neutral solutions.

zygogenesis /zī′gōjen′əsis/ [Gk, *zygon,* yoke, *genesis,* origin], **1.** the formation of a zygote. **2.** reproduction by the union of gametes.—**zygogenetic, zygogenic,** *adj.*

zygoma /zīgō′mə, zig-/ *pl.* **zygomas** [Gk, *zygon,* yoke], **1.** a long slender zygomatic process of the temporal bone, arising from the lower part of the squamous part of the temporal bone, passing forward to join the zygomatic bone, and forming part of the zygomatic arch. **2.** the zygomatic bone that forms the prominence of the cheek.

zygomatic /-mat′ik/ [Gk, *zygon,* yoke], pertaining to the zygoma, or malar bone of the face.

zygomatic arch [Gk, *zygon;* L, *arcus,* bow], an arch formed by the temporal process of the zygomatic bone with the zygomatic process of the temporal bone. The tendon of the temporal muscle passes beneath it.

zygomatic bone [Gk, *zygon;* AS, *ban*], one of the pair of bones that forms the prominence of the cheek, the lower part of the orbit of the eye, and parts of the temporal and infratemporal fossae.

zygomatic nerve, a nerve originating from the maxillary nerve that divides into two branches that supply skin over the temple and skin adjacent to the zygomatic bone.

zygomaticofacial /zī′gōmat′ikōfā′shəl/, pertaining to the facial surface of the zygomatic bone.

zygomatic process [Gk, *zygon;* L, *processus*], **1.** a projection of the frontal bone forming the lateral boundary of the superciliary arch. **2.** a process of the maxilla. **3.** a process of the temporal bone.

zygomatic reflex [Gk, *zygon;* L, *reflectere,* to bend back], movement of the lower jaw toward the percussed side when the zygoma is tapped lightly but sharply.

zygomaticus major /zī′gōmat′ikəs/, one of the 12 muscles of the mouth. It acts to draw the angle of the mouth up and back to smile or laugh.

zygomaticus minor, one of the 12 muscles of the mouth. It acts to deepen the nasolabial furrow in a sad facial expression.

Zygomycetes /zī′gō-mī-sē′tēz/, a class of saprobic and parasitic fungi of the phylum Zygomycota. Important pathogenic organisms are in the orders Entomophthorales and Mucorales.

zygomycosis /zī′gōmīkō′sis/ [Gk, *zygon + mykes,* fungus], an acute, often fulminant, and sometimes fatal fungal infection caused by a class of phycomycetal water molds the *Zygomycetes,* orders *Mucorales* and *Entomophthorales.* It occurs primarily in patients with chronic debilitating diseases, especially uncontrolled DM. Characteristically it begins with fever, pain, and discharge in the nose and paranasal sinuses that progresses to invade the eye and lower respiratory tract. The fungus may enter blood vessels and spread to the brain and other organs. Transmission is usually by inhalation.

zygonema /zī′gənē′mə/ [Gk, *zygon + nema,* thread], the synaptic chromosome formation that occurs in the zygotene stage of the first meiotic prophase of gametogenesis.—**zygonematic,** *adj.*

zygopodium /zī′gōpō′dē·əm/, the part of an embryonic limb consisting of the radius and ulna or the tibia and fibula.

zygopophysial joints, the synovial joints between superior and inferior articular processes on adjacent vertebrae. A thin articular capsule attached to the margins of the articular facets encloses each joint.

zygosis /zīgō′sis/, a form of sexual reproduction in unicellular organisms, consisting of the union of the two cells and fusion of their nuclei.—**zygotic** /zīgot′ik/, *adj.*

zygosity /zīgos′itē/, the characteristics or conditions of a zygote. The form occurs primarily as a suffix denoting genetic makeup, referring specifically to whether the paired alleles determining a particular trait are identical (homozygosity) or different (heterozygosity) or to the condition in twins of having developed from the fertilization of one ovum (monozygosity) or two (dizygosity).

zygospore /zī′gōspôr′/ [Gk, *zygon + sporos,* seed], the spore resulting from the conjugation of two isogamates, as in certain fungi and algae.

zygote /zī′gōt/ [Gk, *zygon,* yoke], the combined cell produced by the union of a sperm pronucleus and an egg pronucleus at the completion of fertilization until the first cleavage.

zygote intrafallopian transfer (ZIFT), retrieval of oocytes from the ovary, followed by their fertilization and culture in the laboratory and placement of the resulting zygotes in the fallopian tubes by laparoscopy 24 hours after oocyte retrieval; used as a means of establishing pregnancy in treatment of infertility.

zygotene /zī′gətēn/ [Gk, *zygon + tainia,* band], the second stage in the first meiotic prophase of gametogenesis, in which synapsis of homologous chromosomes occurs.

Zyloprim, a trademark for a xanthine oxidase inhibitor (allopurinol).

zymogen granules /zī′məjən/ [Gk, *zyme,* ferment, *genein,* to produce; L, *granulum,* little grain], granules found in some secretory exocrine cells. They contain the precursors of enzymes that become active after the granules leave the cell.

zymoprotein /-prō′tēn/ [Gk, *zyme,* ferment, *proteios,* first rank], **1.** a yeast protein. **2.** any protein that functions as an enzyme.

zymorphic /zīmôr′fik/ [Gk, *zyme,* ferment, *morphe,* form], pertaining to fermentation properties.

Z.Z.'Z.", symbol for increasing strength or intensity of contraction.

APPENDIX 1

English-Spanish Translation Guide

English	Spanish
Anatomy	
abdomen	el abdomen/la barriga/la panza
ankle	el tobillo
anus	el ano
appendix	el apéndice
arm	el brazo
back	la espalda
lower back	la parte baja de la espalda
bladder	la vejiga
blood	la sangre
body	el cuerpo
bone	el hueso
bowels	los intestinos, las entrañas, las tripas
brain	el cerebro
breasts	el pecho, los senos
buttocks	las nalgas, las posaderas, las sentaderas
calf	la pantorrilla, el chamorro
chest	el pecho
coccyx	el cóccix
collarbone	los huesos del cuello
ear (inner)	el oído interno
ear (outer)	la oreja
eardrum	el tímpano
ears	las orejas
elbow	el codo
eye	el ojo
face	la cara
fallopian tube	el tubo de falopio
finger	el dedo
foot	el pie
genitals	los genitales
hair (of the head)	el pelo, el cabello
hand	la mano
head	la cabeza
heart	el corazón
heart valve	la válvula del corazón
hip	la cadera
hormone	la hormona
intestines	los intestinos, las tripas
jaw	la quijada
joint	la coyuntura, la articulación
kidney	el riñón
knee	la rodilla
leg	la pierna
ligament	el ligamento
lip	el labio
liver	el hígado
lung	el pulmón
mouth	la boca
muscle	el músculo
neck	el cuello
nerve	el nervio
nose	la naríz
ovary	el ovario

pelvis	la cadera, la pelvis
penis	el pene, el miembro
pulse	el pulso
pupil	la niña del ojo, la pupila
rib	la costilla
saliva	la saliva
shoulder	el hombro
sinus	el seno nasal
skin	la piel
skin (of the face)	el cutis
skull	el cráneo
spine	el espinazo, la columna vertebral
stomach	el estómago, la panza, la barriga
tendon	el tendón
thigh	el muslo
toe	el dedo del pie
tongue	la lengua
tonsils	las angínas, las amígdalas
tooth, molar	el diente, la muela
trachea	la tráquea
urine	la orina
uterus	el útero, la matríz
vagina	la vagina
vein	la vena
wrist	la muñeca

Common Medical Problems

abortion	el aborto
abscess	el absceso
appendicitis	la apendicitis
arthritis	la artritis
asthma	el asma
backache	el dolor de espalda
blindness	la ceguera
bronchitis	la bronquitis
bruise	moretón, magulladura
burn (1st, 2nd, or 3rd degree)	la quemadura (de primer, segundo, o tercer grado)
cancer	el cáncer
chickenpox	la varicela
chills	los escalofrios
cold	el catarro, el resfriado, la gripe
constipation	la constipación, el estreñimiento
convulsion	la convulsión
cough	la tos
cramps	los calambres
cut	cortada, cortadura
deafness	la sordera
diabetes	la diabetes
diarrhea	la diarrea
dizziness	el vértigo, el mareo
epilepsy	la epilepsia
fainting spell	el desmayo
fatigue	la fatiga
fever	la fiebre
flu	la influenza, la gripe
food poisoning	el envenenamiento por comestibles
fracture	la fractura
gallstone	el cálculo biliar, piedra biliar
gastric ulcer	la úlcera gástrica
hallucination	la alucinación
handicap	el impedimento

headache	el dolor de cabeza
heart attack	el ataque al corazón
heartbeat	el latido-el palpito
heart disease	la enfermedad del corazón
heart murmur	el soplo del corazón
hemorrhage	la hemorragia
hemorrhoids	la almorranas, hemorroides
hernia	la hernia
herpes	el herpes
high blood pressure	la presión de la sangre alta
hives	la urticaria, el salpullido
illness	la enfermedad
immunization	la inmunización
infection	la infección
inflammation	la inflamación, la vacuna
injury	la herida, el daño
itch	la picazón-la comezón
laryngitis	la laringitis
lice	los piojos
malaria	la malaria
malignant	maligno(a)
malnutrition	la desnutrició n
measles	el sarampión
meningitis	la meningitis
menopause	la menopausia
miscarriage	un malparto, un aborto, una pérdida
mononucleosis	la mononucleosis infecciosa
multiple sclerosis	la esclerosis múltiple
mumps	las paperas
muscular dystrophy	la distrofía muscular
mute	mudo(a)
obese	obeso(a), gordo(a)
obstruction	la obstrucción
overdose	la sobredosis
overweight	el sobrepeso
pain	el dolor
palsy, cerebral	la parálisis cerebral
paralysis	la parálisis
Parkinson's disease	la enfermedad de Parkinson
pneumonia	la pulmonía
poison ivy/oak	la hiedra venenosa
polio	la poliomelitis/el polio
rabies	la rabia
rash	la roncha, el salpullido, la erupción
redness	enrojecimiento o inflamación
relapse	la recaída
scar	la cicatriz
shock	el choque
sore	la llaga
spasm	el espasmo
spider bite	la picadura de araña
sprain	la torcedura
stomachache	el dolor de estómago
sunstroke	la insolación
swelling	la hinchazón
tetanus	el tétano(s)
tonsillitis	amigdalitis
toothache	el dolor de muela
trauma	el trauma
tuberculosis	la tuberculosis
tumor	el tumor
unconsciousness	inconsciente, sin consciencia

venereal disease	la enfermedad venérea
virus	el virus
vomit	el vómito, los vómitos
weakness	la debilidad
welt	roncha, verdugón
whiplash	concusión de la espina cervical, lastimado del cuello

General Hospital Equipment and Supplies

bandage	la venda, el vendaje
bathtub	la tina
bed	la cama, la bañera
bedpan	la chata, el pato
blanket	cobija, la frisa, la manta
call bell	el timbre
catheter	el catéter, la sonda
crutches	las muletas
operating table	la mesa de operaciones
pillow	la almohada
shower	la ducha
soap	el jabón
stethoscope	el estetoscopio
stretcher	la camilla
syringe	la jeringa
thermometer	el termometro
toilet	el excusado
tongue depressor	el pisalengua
toothbrush	el cepillo de dientes
walker	el apoyador para caminar, el andador
wheelchair	la silla de ruedas

Medications and Related Supplies

alcohol	alcohol
amphetamine	anfetamina
antibiotic	antibiótico
application	aplicación
artifical limb	el miembro artificial
aspirin (for children)	aspirina (para niños)
Bandage	la curita
barbiturate	barbitúrico
birth control pill	la píldora anticonceptiva
booster shot	la inyección secundaria
brace	el braguero
calcium	calcio
capsule	cápsula
cocaine	cocaína
codeine	codeína
cold pack	la compresa fría
compress (hot)	la compresa (caliente)
condom	goma, condón
contact lens	lentes de contacto
contraceptive pills	pastillas anticonceptivas
cotton	algodón
cough syrup	jarabe para la tos
diuretic	diurético
dose	dosis
douche	la ducha, lavado vaginal
dressing	vendaje
dropper	el gotero
drops	gotas
enema	enema
gauze	gasa

glucose	glucosa
hearing aid	el aparato para la sordera, el aparato auricular
heroin	heroína
ice	hielo
ice pack	la bolsa de hielo
insulin	insulina
intrauterine device (IUD)	el dispositivio intrauterino
laxative	laxante, purgante, purga
lotion	loción
narcotic	narcótico
needle	aguja
Novocain	novocaína
ointment	ungüento
pacemaker	el marcapaso
penicillin	penicilina
pill	píldora, pastilla
prosthesis	miembro artificial (prótesis)
sedative	sedante, calmante
sling	el cabestrillo
smelling salts	sales aromáticas
splint	la tablilla
support	el apoyo
suppository	supositorio
syrup of ipecac	jarabe de ipecacuana para provocar vómitos
vitamin	vitamina

Medication Instructions

right	derecho(a)
left	izquierdo(a)
tablespoonful	cucharada
teaspoonful	cucharadita
one-half teaspoonful	media cucharadita
BID	dos veces al día
TID	tres veces al día
QID	cuatro veces al día
every hour	cada hora
each day, daily	cada día, diariamente
every other day	cada otro día
until gone	hasta terminar (acabar)
Let it dissolve in your mouth.	Que se le disuelva en la boca.
as needed for pain	cuando la necesite para el dolor
symptoms	síntomas
insert	inserte
when you get up in the morning	al levantarse
apply	aplique
one-half hour after meals	media hora antes de comidas
now (stat)	ahora (ahora mismo)
before bedtime	antes de acostarse a dormir
before you exercise	antes de hacer ejercicios
chew	mastique
mix	mezcle
dissolved in	disuelto en
Shake well.	Agite bien.
as directed	de acuerdo con las instrucciones
by mouth	por la boca
rub	frote
gargle	haga gargaras
soak	remoje, empape

Tests and Procedures

allergy test	prueba para alergias
analysis	análisis
blood count	recuento (conteo) globular (de sangre)
blood transfusion	la transfusion de sangre
cardiogram	cardiograma
checkup, medical	reconocimiento (chequeo) médico
culture (throat)	cultivo de la garganta
electrocardiogram	electrocardiograma
electroencephalogram	electroencefalograma
enema	la enema
eye test	examen de la vista (de los ojos)
injection	la inyección
laboratory	laboratorio
massage	el masaje
pregnancy test	prueba de embarazo
specimen	muestra (espécimen)
traction	la traccion
urinalysis	análisis de orina
vaccination	la vacuna
x-rays	radiografias (rayos equis)

Assessment (General)

I am_____.	Soy _____.
I would like to examine you now. Please take off your clothes, except for your underwear (and bra), and put on this gown.	Quisiera examinarlo(a) ahora. Por favor, quítese laropa menos la ropa interior (y el sostén) y póngase este camisón o bata.
I am going to take your temperature now. Open your mouth.	Le voy a tomar la temperatura ahora. Abra la boca.
I am going to take your blood pressure now.	Le voy a tomar la presión ahora.
Your blood pressure is low.	Su presión de la sangre es baja.
Your blood pressure is too high.	Su presión de la sangre es demasiado alta.
Here is a prescription to reduce your blood pressure.	Aquí tiene una receta de medicina para bajar la presión de la sangre.
You must follow a diet to lose weight.	Debe seguir una dieta para perder peso.
I am going to start an IV.	Le voy a empezar un suero.
Bend your elbow.	Doble el codo.
Make a fist.	Haga un puño.
I am going to give you an injection.	Le voy a poner una inyección.
Breathe normally.	Respire normalmente.
Cough.	Tosa.
Squeeze my hand.	Apriete mi mano.
You have a slight fever.	Ud. tiene un poco de fiebre.
Hold your leg up.	Levante la pierna.
Stand up and walk.	Parese y camine.
Straighten your leg.	Enderece la pierna.
Bend your knee.	Doble la rodilla.
Push/pull.	Empuje/jale.
Up/down.	Arriba/abajo.
In/out.	Adentro/afuera.
Slow/fast.	Despacio/aprisa.
Rest.	Descanse.
Kneel.	Arrodíllese.
Do you use equipment (canes, crutches, braces)?	¿Usa equipo (bastones, muletals, abrazad eras)?
Do you use a wheelchair?	¿Usa usted una silla de ruedas?
Do you drive a car?	¿Maneja usted un carro?

Can you climb stairs?	¿Puede usted subir las escaleras?
Have you noted any significant weight gain or loss? What is your usual weight?	¿Ha notado pérdida o aumento de peso? ¿Cuál es su peso usual?
How is your appetite?	¿Qué tal su apetito?

Cardiology

Have you ever had chest pain? Where?	¿Ha tenido alguna vez dolor de pecho? ¿Dónde?
Do you notice any irregularity of heart-beat or any palpitations?	¿Nota cualquier latido o palpitación irregular?
Do you get short of breath? When?	¿Tiene falta de aire? Cuándo?
Do you take medicine for your heart? How often?	¿Toma medicina para el corazón? ¿Con qué frecuencia?
Do you know if you have high blood pressure?	¿Sabe usted si tiene la presión de la sangre alta?
Is there a history of hypertension in your family?	¿Hay historia de hipertensión o presión de la sangre alta en su familia?
You have had a heart attack.	Ha tenido un ataque al corazón.
Be sure to tell us if you have chest pains or if you feel anything unusual.	Debe avisarnos si tiene dolores de pecho o si siente algo anormal.

Diabetes

You have diabetes.	Usted tiene diabetes.
Your doctor will regulate your dosage.	Su médico le indicará su dosis de medicina.

Ears, Nose, and Throat

Do you have any hearing problems?	¿Tiene Ud. problemas de oir?
Do you use a hearing aid?	¿Usa Ud. un audífono?
Do your ears ring?	¿Siente un tintineo o silbido en los oídos?
Do you have allergies?	¿Tiene alergias?
Do you have a cold?	¿Tiene usted un resfriado/resfrío/gripe?
Do you have sore throats frequently?	¿Le duele la garganta con frecuencia?
Have you ever had strep throat?	¿Ha tenido alguna vez (infección de lagarganta)?
I want to take a throat culture. Open your mouth. This will not hurt.	Quiero hacer un cultivo de la garganta. Abra la boca. Esto no le va a doler.

Endocrinology

Have you ever had problems with your thyroid?	¿Ha tenido alguna vez problemas con la tiroide?

Gastrointestinal

What foods disagree with you?	¿Qué alimentos le caen mal?
Do you get heartburn?	¿Suele tener ardor en el pecho?
Do you have indigestion often?	¿Tiene indigestión con frecuencia?
Are you going to vomit?	¿Va a vomitar (arrojar)?
Do you have blood in your vomit?	¿Tiene usted vómitos con sangre?

Headache

Do you have headaches?	¿Tiene Ud. dolores de cabeza (jaquecas)?
Do you have migraines?	¿Tiene Ud. migrañas (jaquecas)?
What causes the headaches?	¿Qué le causa los dolores de cabeza?
Are there any changes in your vision?	¿Hay algunos cambios en su vista?

Neurology

Have you ever had a head injury?	¿Ha tenido alguna vez una lesión en la cabeza?
Have you ever had a sports injury?/ motorcycle accident?	¿Ha tenido alguna vez una lesión debido a un deporte o accidente en su motocicleta?

Do you have convulsions?	¿Tiene convulsiones?
Do you see double?	¿Ve usted doble?
Do you have tingling sensations?	¿Tiene hormigueos?
Do you have numbness in your hands, arms, or feet?	¿Siente entumecidos las manos, los brazos, o los pies?
Have you ever lost consciousness? For how long?	¿Perdió alguna vez el sentido? ¿Por cuánto tiempo?
How frequently does this happen?	¿Con qué frecuencia ocurre esto?
Is this hot or cold?	¿Está frío o caliente esto?
Am I sticking you with the point or the head of the pin?	¿Le estoy pinchando con la cabeza delalfiler?

Obstetrics and Gynecology

(Women) How old were you when your periods started? How many days between periods?	¿Cuántos años tenía cuando tuvo la primera regla/periodo menstrual? ¿Cuántos días entre las reglas/periodo menstrual?
How often do you get your periods?	¿Cada cuándo le viene la regla/periodo menstrual?
When was your last menstrual period?	¿Cuándo fue su última regla/periodo menstrual?
When was your last Pap smear?	¿Cuándo fue su última prueba de Papanicolado?
Would you like information on birth control methods?	¿Quiere usted. información sobre los métodos del control de la natalidad? (los métodos anticonceptivos)?
Do you have an IUD in place?	¿Le han puesto un aparato intrauterino anticonceptivo?
How many children do you have?	¿Cuántos hijos tiene?
Have you ever been pregnant?	¿Ha estado embarazada/encinta?
Has your water broken? When?	¿Se le rompió la bolsa de agua(s)? ¿Cuándo?
When did your pains begin?	¿Cuándo le comenzaron los dolores?
How many minutes apart are they now?	¿Cuántos minutos pasan entre uno y otro dolor?
Do you have a lot of pain?	¿Tiene usted mucho dolor?
Open your mouth and breathe. Do not push.	Abra la boca y respire por la boca. No empuje.
Every time the pain comes, push.	Cuando le venga el dolor, empuje.
It is not possible for your baby to be born vaginally; we are going to do a cesarean section.	No es posible que su bebé nazca por la vagina; pore so vamos a hacerle una cesárea.

Ophthalmology

Have you had pain in your eyes?	¿Ha tenido dolor en los ojos?
Do you wear glasses?	¿Usa usted anteojos/gafas/lentes/espejuelos?
Were you exposed to anything that could have injured your eye?	¿Fue expuesto a cualquier cosa que pudiera haberle dañado el ojo?
Do your eyes water much?	¿Le lagrimean mucho los ojos?
I am going to put drops in your eyes in order to examine them. This medicine may burn at first.	Le voy a poner gotas en los ojos para examinarlos. Esta medicina puede arderle al principio.
Please look into this apparatus.	Favor de mirar dentro de este aparato.

Orthopedics

You have broken (a bone).	Usted se ha quebrado/roto (un hueso).
You have dislocated (a joint).	Usted se ha dislocado (una coyuntura).
You have pulled (a muscle).	Usted se ha lastimado (un músculo).
You have sprained (a muscle)/(a ligament).	Usted se ha torcido (un músculo)/(unligamento).
You will need a cast.	Necesita un yeso.

Do you feel pain when you stand?	¿Siente dolor al pararse?
Do you feel pain when you bend?	¿Siente dolor al doblarse?
We need to take some x-rays.	Necesitamos tomarle unos rayos X.
You must wear a sling whenever you are out of bed.	Usted debe llevar un cabestrillo cuando no este en la cama.

Pain

What were you doing when the pain started?	¿Qué hacía usted cuando le comenzó el dolor?
Where is the pain exactly?	¿Dónde le duele, exactamente?
How severe is the pain? Mild, moderate, sharp, or severe?	¿Qué tan fuerte es el dolor? ¿Ligero, moderado, agudo, severo?
Have you ever had this pain before?	¿Ha tenido este dolor antes? ¿Ha sido siempre así?
Does it hurt when I press here? How did the accident happen?	¿Le duele cuando le aprieto aquí? ¿Cómo sucedió el accidente?
How did this happen? How long ago?	¿Cómo sucedío esto? ¿Cuanto tiempo hace?

Pulmonary/Respiratory

Do you smoke? How many packs a day?	¿Fuma usted? ¿Cuántos paquentes al día?
How long have you been coughing?	¿Desde cúando tiene tos?
Does it hurt when you cough?	¿Al toser, siente dolor
Do you cough up phlegm?	¿Al toser, escupe usted flema(s)?
Do you cough up blood?	¿Al toser, escupe usted sangre?
Do you wheeze?	¿Le silba a usted el pecho?
Have you ever had asthma?	¿Ha tenido asma alguna vez?
Have you ever had:	¿Ha tenido alguna vez:
tuberculosis?	tuberculosis?
pneumonia?	pulmonía?
emphysema?	enfisema?
bronchitis?	bronquitis?
Breathe deeply.	Aspire profundamente. (Respire profundo.)

Spanish adapted from Lister S, Wilber CJ: *Medical Spanish: the instant survival guide*, ed 4, London, 2004, Butterworth. Reviewed by Dr. Frances Munet-Vilaro RN, PhD.

APPENDIX 2

American Sign Language and Manual Communication

The Alphabet

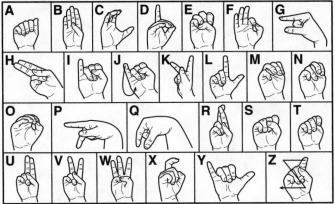

American Sign Language and Manual Communication

The Alphabet

Numbers

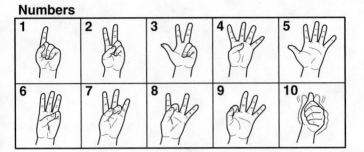

Numbers

MMR	Maternal mortality rate; measles-mumps-rubella	**PID**	Pelvic inflammatory disease
MRI	Magnetic resonance imaging	**PKU**	Phenylketonuria
MS	Multiple sclerosis	**PM**	Postmortem; evening
VA	Motor vehicle accident	**PMH**	Past medical history
N/A	Not applicable	**PMI**	of maximal impulse
Na	Sodium	**PMN**	Polymorphonuclear neutrophil leukocytes (polys)
NaCl	Sodium chloride		
NANDA	North American Nursing Diagnosis Association	**PMS**	Premenstrual syndrome
		PND	Paroxysmal nocturnal dyspnea
N & V; N/V	Nausea and vomiting		
NG; ng	Nasogastric	**PO; p.o.**	Orally (per os)
NICU	Neonatal intensive care unit	**PPD**	Purified protein derivative (TB test)
NIDDM	Noninsulin-dependent diabetes mellitus	**PRN; p.r.n.**	As required (pro re nata)
		pro time	Prothrombin time
NKA	No known allergies	**PSA**	Prostate-specific antigen
NPO; n.p.o.	Nothing by mouth (non per os)	**pt**	Pint
		PT	Prothrombin time; physical therapy
NS	Normal saline		
NSAID	Nonsteroidal antiinflammatory drug	**PTT**	Partial thromboplastin time
		PVC	Premature ventricular contraction
NSR	Normal sinus rhythm		
O_2	Oxygen	**R**	Respiration; right; Rickettsia; roentgen
OB	Obstetrics		
OBS	Organic brain syndrome	**RBC, rbc**	Red blood cell; red blood count
OD	Optical density; overdose; right eye (oculus dexter)		
		RDA	Recommended daily/dietary allowance
OOB	Out of bed		
OR	Operating room	**RDS**	Respiratory distress syndrome
ORIF	Open reduction and internal fixation		
		Rh	Rhesus factor; rhodium
OS	Left eye (oculus sinister)	**RLE**	Right lower extremity
OT	Occupational therapy	**RLL**	Right lower lobe
OTC	Over-the-counter	**RLQ**	Right lower quadrant
OU	Each eye (oculus uterque)	**RML**	middle lobe of lung
oz	Ounce	**RNA**	Ribonucleic acid
p̄	After	**R/O**	Rule out
P-A; PA; P/A	Posterior-anterior	**ROM**	Range of motion
PALS	Pediatric advanced life support	**ROS**	Review of systems
		RR	Recovery room; respiratory rate
Para I, II, etc.	Unipara, bipara, tripara, etc.		
		RT	Radiation therapy; reading test; respiratory therapy
PAT	Paroxysmal atrial tachycardia		
		R/T	Related to
PCA	Patient-controlled analgesia	**RUE**	Right upper extremity
		RUL	Right upper lobe
PCWP	Pulmonary capillary wedge pressure	**RUQ**	Right upper quadrant
		s̄	Without
PDA	Patient ductus arteriosus	**S-A; SA; S/A**	Sinoatrial
PE	Physical examination	**Sed rate**	Sedimentation rate
PEEP	Positive-end expiratory pressure	**SGOT**	Serum glutamic oxaloacetic transaminase
PEFR	Peak expiratory flow rate	**SGPT**	Serum glutamic pyruvic transaminase
PERRLA	Pupils equal, regular, react to light and accommodation		
		SI	Système International
		SIDS	Sudden infant death syndrome
PET	Positron emission tomography		
		SLE	Systemic lupus erythematosus
PICC	Percutaneously inserted central catheter		
		SNF	Skilled nursing facility
		SOB	Shortness of breath